1995/96	1996/97	1997/98	1998/99	1999/2000	**2000/01**		Para No.
—	—	—	—	10%	**10%**	Starting rate	3
—	—	—	—	£1,500	**£1,520**	Starting rate limit	3
20%	20%	20%	20%	20%	**20%**	Lower rate	3, 5
£3,200	£3,900	£4,100	£4,300	—	—	Lower rate limit (taxable income)	3, 5
25%	24%	23%	23%	23%	**22%**	Basic rate	3, 5
£21,100	£21,600	£22,000	£22,800	£26,500	**£26,880**	Basic rate band (taxable income)	3, 5
£24,300	£25,500	£26,100	£27,100	£28,000	**£28,400**	Basic rate limit (taxable income)	3, 5
40%	40%	40%	40%	40%	**40%**	Higher rate	3, 5
—	—	—	—	10%	**10%**	Schedule F ordinary rate	9
—	—	—	—	32.5%	**32.5%**	Schedule F upper rate	9
—	—	—	—	—	—	Wife's Earned Income Relief Maximum	23
						PERSONAL ALLOWANCES	
£3,525	£3,765	£4,045	£4,195	£4,335	**£4,385**	Single/Personal	14, 21
£1,720	£1,790	£1,830	£1,900	£1,970	—	Married/Married couple's	15, 22
							14, 15, 24
£4,630	£4,910	£5,220	£5,410	£5,720	**£5,790**	Age—Single/Personal (65 or over)	
£4,800	£5,090	£5,400	£5,600	£5,980	**£6,050**	—Single/Personal (75 or over)	
£2,995	£3,115	£3,185	£3,305	£5,125	**£5,185**	—Married/Married couple's (65 or over)	
£3,035	£3,155	£3,225	£3,345	£5,195	**£5,255**	—Married/Married couple's (75 or over)	
£14,600	£15,200	£15,600	£16,200	£16,800	**£17,000**	—Income limit	
£1,720	£1,790	£1,830	£1,900	£1,970	**£2,000**	Widow's bereavement (death before 6.4.00)	16
£1,720	£1,790	£1,830	£1,900	£1,970	—	Addition re child if claimant single or claimant's wife ill	17
£1,200	£1,250	£1,280	£1,330	£1,380	**£1,400**	Blind Persons	19
						CLASS 4 NIC	
7.3%	6%	6%	6%	6%	**7%**	—rate	
£6,640–£22,880	£6,860–£23,660	£7,010–£24,180	£7,310–£25,220	£7,530–£26,000	**£4,385–£27,820**	—band	
						DISCRETIONARY TRUST INCOME	
—	—	—	—	—	—	Additional rate	
35%	34%	34%	34%	34%	**34%**	Flat rate	
—	—	—	—	25%	**25%**	Schedule F trust rate	

Tolley's Income Tax 2000–01

85th Edition

by Glyn Saunders MA
David Smailes FCA
Gina Antczak FCA ATII
from an original text by
Eric L Harvey FCA

Tolley Publishing

Published by Tolley
2 Addiscombe Road
Croydon CR9 5AF England
020-8686 9141

Typeset by Interactive Sciences Ltd, Gloucester

Printed and bound in Great Britain by The Bath Press, Bath

ISBN 0 75450 836–6

About This Book

This is the 85th edition of Tolley's Income Tax. It includes the income tax provisions of the Finance Act 2000, relevant case law, statements by the Revenue and other official bodies, and further important information concerning income tax, up to 1 July 2000. A summary of the contents of the 2000 Act is included in chapter 94.

Income and corporation tax law was consolidated in the Income and Corporation Taxes Act 1988, capital allowances legislation in the Capital Allowances Act 1990 and legislation relating to corporation tax on capital gains in the Taxation of Chargeable Gains Act 1992. A summary of the approach adopted to the citation of consolidated statutory references is included overleaf.

This work includes the income tax law and practice for at least six years (i.e. for 1994/95 onwards and sometimes earlier) and so provides comprehensive information for claims, late assessments etc. There is a twelve-year summary of rates and allowances inside the front cover. The inside back cover contains a table of the main tax rates for 2000/01 and a table of the main taxable social security benefits. An index and tables of leading cases and statutes provide quick reference to the subject and to the legislation.

Comments on this annual publication and suggestions for improvements are always welcomed.

TOLLEY PUBLISHING

Consolidation of Tax Enactments

With effect generally for 1988/89 and subsequent years of assessment (and for companies' accounting periods ending after 5 April 1988), the *Taxes Acts* provisions relating to income tax and corporation tax are consolidated in the *Income and Corporation Taxes Act 1988* (*ICTA 1988*). The consolidation does not affect the application of the provisions concerned, but references to provisions which ceased to have effect before 6 April 1988 are omitted, as is the commencement date of the consolidated provisions (unless still relevant to application of the current provisions).

Tolley's Income Tax 2000/01, continues, as in previous years, to set out the position for the six years before 2000/01, i.e. for 1994/95 to 1999/2000, but occasional references are still required to earlier years. In strictness, the legislation applicable to years before 1988/89 is that in force prior to the consolidation referred to above, and the Revenue (while acknowledging that 'on previous consolidation, inspectors, Commissioners and taxpayers alike got used to the new references in dealing with previous periods'), have indicated that claims etc. for those years should refer to the statute then applicable.

Accordingly, the approach which has been adopted to statutory references in this issue is as follows:

(i) Remaining references to the previous consolidation Act are in the form '*ICTA 1970, s XXX*' or '*ICTA 1970, XX Sch*'. Where there has been no change in the legislation in the last six years, no statutory reference other than that for *ICTA 1988* is quoted.

(ii) Where the legislation has changed during the last six years, the earlier provisions continue to be described in the text, and the appropriate earlier statutory reference is quoted. Legislation current during that six years but now repealed is similarly dealt with. Where any part of the current legislation was introduced during that six years, the commencement date is quoted, but the statutory reference for that date is generally omitted.

(iii) In any case where a claim or election for a year before 1988/89 may be involved, the appropriate earlier statutory reference is quoted. The earlier reference is also given in certain cases where the reference may have achieved a particular familiarity, e.g. in the case of *sections 154(2)*, *189* or *460* of *ICTA 1970*.

(iv) Where a full pre-consolidation statutory reference is required, this may be obtained from Tolley's Income Tax 1987/88 or an appropriate earlier edition.

(v) The Table of Statutes in this edition includes all references to earlier legislation appearing in the text (as above).

A similar approach has been adopted on the consolidation of the enactments relating to capital allowances in the *Capital Allowances Act 1990*, which took effect generally for chargeable periods ending after 5 April 1990, and to those relating to corporation tax on capital gains in the *Taxation of Chargeable Gains Act 1992*, which took effect generally for chargeable periods beginning after 5 April 1992.

Contents

The following subjects are in the same alphabetical order in this section.
A detailed index and tables of cases and statutes are at the end of the section.

PAGE

i Twelve-Year Summary of Rates and Allowances—1989/90 to 2000/01
v About This Book
vi Consolidation of Tax Enactments
x Abbreviations and References

CHAPTER

1 Allowances and Tax Rates—Applicable to individuals
2 —Examples
3 Anti-Avoidance
4 Appeals
5 Assessments

6 Back Duty
7 Bankruptcy
8 Banks
9 Building Societies

10 Capital Allowances
11 Capital Gains Tax
12 Cash Basis
13 Certificates of Deposit
14 Certificates of Tax Deposit
15 Charities
16 Children
17 Claims
18 Clubs and Societies
19 Compensation for loss of Employment (and Damages)
20 Connected Persons
21 Construction Industry Tax Scheme

22 Deceased Estates
23 Deduction of Tax at Source
24 Diplomatic, etc. Immunity—Individuals and Organisations
25 Double Tax Relief

26 Enterprise Investment Scheme (and BES)
27 European Community Legislation
28 Excess Liability
29 Exempt Income
30 Exempt Organisations

31 Friendly Societies
32 Funding Bonds

Contents

33 Government Stocks

34 Herd Basis

35 Inland Revenue: Administration
36 Inland Revenue: Confidentiality of Information
37 Inland Revenue Explanatory Pamphlets Etc.
38 Inland Revenue Extra-Statutory Concessions
39 Inland Revenue Press Releases
40 Inland Revenue Statements of Practice
41 Interest on Overpaid Tax
42 Interest and Surcharges on Unpaid Tax
43 Interest Payable
44 Interest Receivable

45 Life Assurance Policies
46 Losses

47 Married Persons
48 Medical Insurance
49 Mineral Royalties
50 Mutual Trading

51 Non-Residents and other Overseas Matters

52 Offshore Funds

53 Partnerships
54 Patents
55 Pay As You Earn
56 Payment of Tax
57 Payment of Tax—Table of Due Dates
58 Penalties
59 Pensions
60 Personal Pension Schemes (and Stakeholder Pensions)
61 Personal Service Companies Etc.
62 Post-Cessation Etc. Receipts and Expenditure (Trades, professions and vocations)

63 Remittance Basis
64 Residence, Ordinary Residence and Domicile
65 Retirement Annuities
66 Retirement Schemes for employees
67 Returns

68 Schedule A—Property Income
69 Schedule B
70 Schedule C—Paying and Collecting Agents
71 Schedule D, Cases I and II—Profits of Trades, Professions Etc.
72 Schedule D, Case III—Interest Receivable Etc.
73 Schedule D, Cases IV and V—Overseas Income
74 Schedule D, Case VI—Miscellaneous Income
75 Schedule E—Emoluments
76 Schedule F—Dividends Etc.
77 Scientific Research Associations

78 Self-Assessment
79 Self-Assessment—Key Dates
80 Self-Employed Persons
81 Settlements
82 Share Incentives and Options
83 Social Security
84 Statutory Bodies
85 Stock Dividends

86 Time Limits—Fixed Dates
87 Time Limits—Miscellaneous
88 Trade Unions

89 Underwriters
90 Unit Trusts

91 Venture Capital Trusts
92 Vocational Training Relief

93 Woodlands

94 Finance Act 2000—Summary of Provisions

95 Table of Leading Cases

96 Table of Statutes

97 Index

Abbreviations and References

ABBREVIATIONS

ACT	=	Advance Corporation Tax.
CAA	=	Capital Allowances Act.
CA	=	Court of Appeal.
CCA	=	Court of Criminal Appeal.
CCAB	=	Consultative Committee of Accountancy Bodies.
CES	=	Court of Exchequer (Scotland).
Cf.	=	compare.
CGT	=	Capital Gains Tax.
CGTA 1979	=	Capital Gains Tax Act 1979.
CIR	=	Commissioners of Inland Revenue ('the Board').
Ch D	=	Chancery Division.
CJEC	=	Court of Justice of the European Communities.
CS	=	Scottish Court of Session.
DSS	=	Department of Social Security.
EC	=	European Communities.
EEC	=	European Economic Community.
EU	=	European Union.
Ex D	=	Exchequer Division (now absorbed into Chancery Division).
FA	=	Finance Act.
FII	=	Franked Investment Income.
HC	=	High Court.
HC(I)	=	High Court of Ireland.
HL	=	House of Lords.
ICAEW	=	Institute of Chartered Accountants in England and Wales.
ICTA	=	Income and Corporation Taxes Act.
IHT	=	Inheritance Tax.
IHTA 1984	=	Inheritance Tax Act 1984.
IR	=	Inland Revenue.
KB	=	King's Bench Division.
LIFFE	=	London International Financial Futures Exchange.
NI	=	Northern Ireland.
PC	=	Privy Council.
PDA	=	Probate, Divorce and Admiralty Division. (Now Family Division).
QB	=	Queen's Bench Division.
RI	=	Republic of Ireland (Eire).
s	=	Section.
SC(I)	=	Irish Supreme Court.
Sch	=	Schedule.
SI	=	Statutory Instrument.
SP	=	Inland Revenue Statement of Practice.
Sp C	=	Special Commissioners.
SR&O	=	Statutory Rules and Orders.
SSAP	=	Statement of Standard Accounting Practice.
TCGA 1992	=	Taxation of Chargeable Gains Act 1992.
TMA 1970	=	Taxes Management Act 1970.
VAT	=	Value Added Tax.
VATA 1994	=	Value Added Tax Act 1994.

Abbreviations and References

REFERENCES

AER	=	All England Law Reports (Butterworths, Halsbury House, 35 Chancery Lane, London WC2A 1EL).
ATC	=	Annotated Tax Cases (Gee & Co. (Publishers) Ltd., South Quay Plaza, 183 Marsh Wall, London E14 9FS).
ITC	=	Irish Tax Cases (Government Publications, 1 and 3 G.P.O. Arcade, Dublin 1).
LTR	=	Law Times Reports.
SC	=	Special Commissioners.
SLR	=	Scottish Law Reporter.
SLT	=	Scots Law Times.
SSCD	=	Simon's Tax Cases Special Commissioners' Decisions (Butterworths, as above).
STC	=	Simon's Tax Cases (Butterworths, as above).
STI	=	Simon's Tax Intelligence (Butterworths, as above).
TC	=	Official Tax Cases (H.M. Stationery Office, P.O. Box 276, SW8 5DT).
TLR	=	Times Law Reports.
TR	=	Taxation Reports (Gee & Co., as above).

The first number in the citation refers to the volume, and the second to the page, so that [1995] 1 AER 15 means that the report is to be found on page fifteen of the first volume of the All England Law Reports for 1995. Where no volume number is given, only one volume was produced in that year. Some series have continuous volume numbers.

Where legal decisions are very recent and in the lower courts, it must be remembered that they may be reversed on appeal. But references to the official Tax Cases ('*TC*') may generally be taken as final.

In English cases, Scottish and N. Irish decisions (unless there is a difference of law between the countries) are generally followed but are not binding, and Republic of Ireland decisions are considered (and vice-versa).

Acts of Parliament, Cmnd. Papers, 'Hansard' Parliamentary Reports and Statutory Instruments (SI) formerly Statutory Rules and Orders (SR & O)) are obtainable from H.M. Stationery Office (bookshop at 49, High Holborn, WC1V 6HB; orders to P.O. Box 276, London SW8 5DT). Telephone orders should be made to 020-7873 9090. **Hansard** references are to daily issues and do not always correspond to the columns in the bound editions. **N.B.** Statements in the House, while useful as indicating the intention of enactments, have no legal authority if the Courts subsequently interpret the wording of the Act differently, but see 4.7 APPEALS for circumstances in which evidence of parliamentary intent may be considered by the Courts.

BOOKS

Inland Revenue explanatory books and pamphlets may be obtained (free) from any local Inspector of Taxes. See list in Chapter 37.

Inland Revenue Press Releases and Statements of Practice are obtainable individually from Inland Revenue Information Centre, SW Wing, Bush House, Strand, London WC2B 4RD (tel. 020–7438 6420/5), and are published on the Revenue's website (http:/www.inlandrevenue.gov.uk/news/press.htm).

Retention of Tolley's. Subscribers should preserve each year's edition of 'Tolley's' because the necessity of including considerable new material each year involves the omission of some older and less important matter.

Abbreviations and References

Tolley's Corporation Tax 2000/01 is the companion publication to Tolley's Income Tax and sets out the application of the taxing statutes to the income and capital gains of companies up to and including the 2000 Finance Act. £59.95.

Tolley's Capital Gains Tax 2000/01 is a detailed guide to the statutes and case law up to and including the 2000 Finance Act. In the same alphabetical format as Tolley's Income Tax and Tolley's Corporation Tax. £59.95.

Tolley's Inheritance Tax 2000/01 is a detailed guide to the statutes and case law up to and including the 2000 Finance Act. £59.95.

Tolley's Value Added Tax 2000/01 is a comprehensive guide to value added tax, covering legislation, Customs & Excise notices and leaflets and all other relevant information. It is published in two editions, up to March 2000 and up to and including the 2000 Finance Act. £85.00 (includes both editions).

Tolley's Tax Computations 2000/01 contains copious worked examples covering income tax, corporation tax, capital gains tax, inheritance tax and value added tax. £54.95.

Tolley's Tax Cases 2000 contains over 2,500 summaries of cases up to 1 January 2000 relevant to current legislation. £54.95.

Tolley's Practical Tax is an eight-page, fortnightly newsletter containing news, articles and items of practical use to all involved with UK tax. By subscription only.

1 Allowances and Tax Rates—Applicable to individuals

1.1 This chapter provides a general introduction to UK income tax. All rates and allowances for the fiscal year 1994/95 onwards are included in order to provide comprehensive information for claims etc. (and where a rate in force for 1994/95 commenced in an earlier year, that earlier year is shown). Changes are shown for and from the year in which they commenced with current rates etc. in **bold type**. A separate **twelve-year summary** of rates and allowances appears inside the front cover.

Headings in this chapter are:

1.2 Fiscal year
1.3 Rates of tax 2000/01
1.4 Earlier history
1.5 Rates of tax 1999/2000 to 1994/95
1.6 Total income
1.7 Earned income
1.8 Investment income
1.9 Dividends and other savings income
1.10 Deductions in computing total income
1.11 Claims
1.12 Non-residents
1.13 Indexation of personal reliefs
1.14 Personal allowance
1.15 Married couple's allowance
1.16 Widow's bereavement allowance
1.17 Additional relief in respect of children
1.18 Children's tax credit
1.19 Blind persons
1.20 Other reliefs

Allowances etc. obsolete 1990/91 onwards

1.21 Single person's allowance
1.22 Married man's allowance
1.23 Wife's earned income relief
1.24 Age allowance

1.2 The **Fiscal Year** (or 'year of assessment' or 'tax year') runs from **6 April to 5 April** (e.g. the fiscal year 2000/01 is from 6 April 2000 to 5 April 2001 inclusive). **Total Income** (see 1.6 below) less **Personal Allowances** (see 1.14 to 1.19 below) equals **Taxable Income**.

1.3 **RATES OF TAX — 2000/01** [*ICTA 1988, s 1(2); SI 2000 No 806; FA 2000, s 31*]

	Rate	On Taxable Income	Cumulative tax
Starting Rate	10%	0–£1,520	£152
Basic Rate	22%	£1,521–£28,400	£6,065.60
Higher Rate	40%	Over £28,400	

The figure of £1,520 is known as the starting rate limit and the figure of £28,400 as the basic rate limit. [*ICTA 1988, s 1(2A)(3); FA 1999, s 22(2)(3)*].

Where income tax at the basic rate has been deducted from income, and that income is chargeable (in whole or part) at the starting rate (before 1999/2000, at the lower rate), repayment of the excess tax deducted may be claimed. [*ICTA 1988, s 1(6A); FA 1992, s 9(8); FA 1999, s 22(6)*].

Since 1996/97, a lower rate of **20%** has been applied to savings income to the extent that such income does not exceed the basic rate limit (treating it as the highest part of an individual's income). For 1999/2000 onwards, the starting rate applies instead to such income to the extent that it falls within the starting rate band. See 1.9 below. Before 1999/2000 the lower rate also applied to income chargeable under Schedule F (i.e. UK company dividends etc. together with related tax credits), or income of the same nature received from non-UK resident companies, but see 1.9 below as regards the special rates applicable to such income from 6 April 1999. [*ICTA 1988, ss 1A, 207A; FA 1993, s 77; FA 1996, s 73, Sch 41 Pt V(1); FA 1999, s 22(7); FA 2000, s 32*].

1.4 Allowances and Tax Rates—Applicable to individuals

See 81.5 SETTLEMENTS as regards rate applicable to certain trust income. See 1.13 below as to indexation of tax bands.

Scottish variable rate. With effect for 2000/01 and subsequent years of assessment, the Scottish Parliament has the power to increase or reduce the basic rate of income tax in any year of assessment by up to three percentage points (in half-point steps). The rate so varied will apply to the income of Scottish taxpayers other than income from savings or distributions to which the lower or Schedule F rate applies (see 1.9 below). An individual is treated as a Scottish taxpayer in relation to any year of assessment if he is treated as UK resident for income tax purposes (see 64 RESIDENCE, ORDINARY RESIDENCE AND DOMICILE) and either:

(*a*) he spends at least as much time during the year in Scotland as elsewhere in the UK;

(*b*) he is a member of Parliament for a Scottish constituency, a member of the European Parliament for Scotland or a member of the Scottish Parliament; or

(*c*) his principal UK residence is located in Scotland for at least as much of the tax year as it is not located in Scotland and he spends at least part of the tax year in that Scottish residence.

[*Scotland Act 1998, Pt IV*].

See also Revenue Press Release 23 February 1998 for a Government technical paper commenting on the tax varying power of the Scottish Parliament, and setting out the Government's policy intentions where that power interacts with other parts of the tax system.

1.4 **EARLIER HISTORY**

For 1973/74 onwards, a unified income tax system replaced the previous dual structure of income tax and surtax on the incomes of individuals. A single graduated tax, comprising a basic rate and higher rates, became applicable to all income, whether earned or unearned, and an investment income surcharge commenced as an additional flat rate charge on investment incomes exceeding certain limits. [*FA 1971, ss 32–39, Schs 6, 7; FA 1972, ss 65, 66*]. Earned income relief as such was abolished. [*FA 1971, s 32(2)*]. For 1978/79 and 1979/80 a lower rate applied to the first slice of taxable income. [*FA 1978, s 14; FA 1980, s 18(2)*]. The investment income surcharge was abolished for 1984/85 onwards. [*FA 1984, Sch 7 para 1*].

For rates of tax for 1999/2000 to 1994/95, see 1.5 below.

1.5 **RATES OF TAX—1999/2000 TO 1994/95**

Lower, basic and higher rate for 1999/2000 [*ICTA 1988, s 1(2); SI 1999 No 597; FA 1999, ss 22(1), 23*]

	Rate	On Taxable Income	Cumulative tax
Starting Rate	10%	0–£1,500	£150
Basic Rate	23%	£1,501–£28,000	£6,245
Higher Rate	40%	Over £28,000	

Lower, basic and higher rate for 1998/99 [*ICTA 1988, s 1(2); SI 1998 No 755; FA 1998, s 25*]

	Rate	On Taxable Income	Cumulative tax
Lower Rate	20%	0–£4,300	£860
Basic Rate	23%	£4,301–£27,100	£6,104
Higher Rate	40%	Over £27,100	

Lower, basic and higher rate for 1997/98 [*ICTA 1988, s 1(2); SI 1996 No 2952; FA 1997, s 54(1)(2)*]

	Rate	On Taxable Income	Cumulative tax
Lower Rate	20%	0–£4,100	£820
Basic Rate	23%	£4,101–£26,100	£5,880
Higher Rate	40%	Over £26,100	

Lower, basic and higher rate for 1996/97 [*ICTA 1988, s 1(2); FA 1996, s 72*]

	Rate	On Taxable Income	Cumulative tax
Lower Rate	20%	0–£3,900	£780
Basic Rate	24%	£3,901–£25,500	£5,964
Higher Rate	40%	Over £25,500	

Lower, basic and higher rate for 1995/96 [*ICTA 1988, s 1(2); FA 1995, s 35; SI 1994 No 3012*]

	Rate	On Taxable Income	Cumulative tax
Lower Rate	20%	0–£3,200	£640
Basic Rate	25%	£3,201–£24,300	£5,915
Higher Rate	40%	Over £24 ,300	

Lower, basic and higher rate for 1994/95 [*ICTA 1988, s 1(2); FA 1994, s 75*]

	Rate	On Taxable Income	Cumulative tax
Lower Rate	20%	0–£3,000	£600
Basic Rate	25%	£3,001–£23,700	£5,775
Higher Rate	40%	Over £23,700	

1.6 **TOTAL INCOME**

of an individual is the sum of income from all sources, calculated in accordance with tax legislation, after all allowable deductions from each source of income have been made, less certain charges etc. (see 1.10 below). [*ICTA 1988, s 835*]. See also 28 EXCESS LIABILITY.

See Revenue Relief Manual, Re 50 *et seq.*.

Exemptions. See list under 29 EXEMPT INCOME.

Simon's Direct Tax Service. See **E1.401** *et seq.*.

1.7 **EARNED INCOME**

is income arising to an individual from:

(i) any office or employment of profit, or property attached thereto. [*ICTA 1988, s 833(4)*]. (See *Recknell Ch D 1952, 33 TC 201*). Includes maternity pay (see 55.33 PAY AS YOU EARN);

(ii) the *personal* carrying on of a trade, profession or vocation (including certain POST-CESSATION RECEIPTS (62) chargeable under *ICTA 1988, s 103* or *s 104* [*ICTA 1988, s 107*] and, from 6 April 1993, Lloyd's underwriting profits [*FA 1993, s 180*], see 89.3 UNDERWRITERS). [*ICTA 1988, s 833(4)*]. This does not include: a sleeping partnership; trustees carrying on business for minors, etc. (*Shiels' Trustees CS 1914, 6 TC 583*) (except, in practice, where a trustee carrying on such a business is himself a beneficiary—see also *Dale HL 1953, 34 TC 468*, and *White v Franklin CA 1965, 42 TC 283*); interest received by solicitor on bank deposits made out of clients' funds in his hands (*Brown v CIR HL 1964, 42 TC 42; Northend v White Ch D 1975, 50 TC 121*);

(iii) deferred pay, pensions, etc., given in respect of past services (whether of the individual or individual's spouse or parent, or any deceased person, and regardless of whether or not the individual contributed to the pension, etc.), including Civil List pensions, voluntary pensions under *ICTA 1988, s 58(2)* or *s 133* (see 59.1 PENSIONS) and chargeable payments on retirement or removal from office (see 19.4 COMPENSATION FOR LOSS OF EMPLOYMENT). Also, annuities under PERSONAL PENSION SCHEMES (60) or RETIREMENT ANNUITIES (65) so far as attributable to contributions on which relief has been given. Also partnership retirement annuities as specified in *ICTA 1988, s 628* (see 53.5 PARTNERSHIPS). [*ICTA 1988, s 833(4)(5); FA 1988, Sch 3 para 21*];

(iv) social security benefits (other than specified exemptions, see 83 SOCIAL SECURITY). [*ICTA 1988, ss 150, 151, 617, 833(5)(c)*];

(v) annuities for giving up (after attaining age of 55) uncommercial agricultural land, see under 71.77 SCHEDULE D, CASES I AND II. [*ICTA 1988, s 833(5)(d)*];

(vi) inventor's income from patents [*ICTA 1988, s 529*] (see under 54 PATENTS);

(vii) distribution of assets of body corporate carrying on mutual business to certain recipients [*ICTA 1988, s 491(5)*], see Tolley's Corporation Tax under Mutual Companies;

(viii) sale of earnings for capital sum [*ICTA 1988, s 775(2)*], see 3.10 ANTI-AVOIDANCE;

(ix) know-how sale by non-trading vendor who devised it [*ICTA 1988, s 531(6)*], see 71.67 SCHEDULE D, CASES I AND II;

(x) furnished holiday lettings [*ICTA 1988, s 503*], see 68.9 SCHEDULE A; and

(xi) certain share option charges under *ICTA 1988, ss 138, 185* (see 82.4, 82.5, 82.39, 82.40 SHARE INCENTIVES AND OPTIONS).

1.8 **INVESTMENT (OR UNEARNED) INCOME**

is the income *other than earned income* included in the total income. It includes the following.

(i) **Annual payments** either made otherwise than by an individual, or made in pursuance of an 'existing obligation' (but see below re 1995/96 onwards). This includes **annuities** (except that the capital portion of a purchased life annuity or annuity certain is exempt from tax, and certain retirement annuities are treated as earned income, see 1.7(iii) above) and, to the extent outlined below, **maintenance payments** (alimony) under a Court Order or enforceable agreement. Such income may be received after deduction of income tax at the basic rate (but most maintenance payments made after 5 April 1989 (see 47.10 MARRIED PERSONS) are made without deduction of tax as are certain annual payments made under tax avoidance schemes (see 3.19 ANTI-AVOIDANCE)). The gross amount of annual payments is assessable on the recipient but a credit is given for tax deducted (which means that if tax at the basic rate is deducted *and* the recipient is only liable to basic rate tax, there is no further liability).

An annual payment made by an individual, or by a Scottish partnership in which at least one partner is an individual, and (for 1999/2000 and earlier years) not made in pursuance of an 'existing obligation', does not form part of the taxable income of the person to whom it is made or of any other person, but excluded are payments of interest, payments due before 6 April 2000 under charitable covenants, payments made for *bona fide* commercial reasons in connection with the payer's trade, profession or vocation and payments within 3.19 ANTI-AVOIDANCE. For 1995/96 and subsequent years, this rule also applies to payments treated as income of the payer under *ICTA 1988, ss 660A, 660B* (see 81.13–81.18 SETTLEMENTS) *even if* made under an 'existing obligation', which means, for example, that a payment due and made after 5 April 1995 under a pre-15 March 1988 non-charitable deed of covenant will not count as the income of the recipient for tax purposes.

An '*existing obligation*' means a binding obligation under

(*a*) a Court Order made, whether or not in the UK, before 15 March 1988, or applied for before 16 March 1988 and made before the end of June 1988, or

(*b*) a deed executed, or written agreement made, before 15 March 1988 and received by an inspector of taxes before the end of June 1988, or

(*c*) an oral agreement made before 15 March 1988, written particulars of which were received by an inspector before the end of June 1988, or

(*d*) a Court Order or written agreement made after 14 March 1988 or a maintenance assessment under the Child Support Act 1991 (or NI equivalent) which replaces, varies or supplements an order or agreement within these provisions, but only if

  (i) the obligation is for a person to make periodical payments of maintenance (excluding instalments of a lump sum) to or for the benefit of his or her divorced or separated spouse, or to any person under 21 for his own benefit, maintenance or education, or to any person for the benefit etc. of a person under 21, and

  (ii) the previous order etc. was for the benefit etc. of the same person.

A payment to or for the benefit of a person who attained the age of 21 before the due date of the payment but after 5 April 1994 which is made in pursuance of an obligation within (*a*), (*b*) or (*c*) above is deemed *not* to have been made in pursuance of an existing obligation (and after 5 April 1995, payments within (*b*) and (*c*) above to those aged 18 and over are disregarded — see 47.10 MARRIED PERSONS). This treatment is extended to payments made after 5 April 1996, in pursuance of an obligation within (*a*) above, to or for the benefit of a child who attained the age of 21 before 6 April 1994.

Payments due between a husband and wife at a time when they are living together are, notwithstanding (*a*)–(*d*) above, effectively regarded as being other than in pursuance of an existing obligation.

[*ICTA 1988, s 347A; FA 1988, s 36, Sch 3 para 32; F(No 2)A 1992, s 62(2); FA 1994, s 79(2); FA 1995, Sch 17 para 4(1); FA 1996, s 149; FA 1999, Sch 20 Pt III(6); FA 2000, s 41(2)(9); SI 1992 No 2642*].

Maintenance payments received under existing obligations and falling due before 6 April 2000 are taxable only to the extent of the aggregate amount of such payments received from the same person which formed part of the recipient's taxable income (before the above-mentioned deduction) for 1988/89; such payments will usually be receivable without deduction of tax at source (but see 47.10 MARRIED PERSONS for exceptions). In addition, where the payments are received from a divorced or separated spouse, the recipient may claim a maximum deduction equal to the married couple's allowance (see 1.15 below). No deduction may be made in respect of payments due at a time when the beneficiary has remarried. Payments received from a divorced or separated spouse include payments received by a third party for the benefit of the person concerned and payments received by that person for the maintenance of a child of the family, being a person under 21 who is a child of both parties to the marriage or has been treated by them both as a child of their family, but excluding a child who has been boarded out with them by a public authority or voluntary organisation.

Maintenance payments falling due **after 5 April 2000**, whether or not under an existing obligation, do not form part of the recipient's income for tax purposes.

[*FA 1988, ss 37, 38, 40, Sch 3 para 33; FA 1994, Sch 26 Pt V(1); FA 1999, s 36(7)(8), Sch 20 Pt III(6)*].

See also 47.10 MARRIED PERSONS.

Simon's Direct Tax Service. See B5.3.

(ii) **Dividends etc. and other savings income**. See 1.9 below for the special provisions applicable to such income.

Simon's Direct Tax Service. See B5.222.

(iii) **Property income** assessed under SCHEDULE A (68) and SCHEDULE D, CASE VI (74) other than from furnished holiday lettings (see 68.9).

1.9 DIVIDENDS AND OTHER SAVINGS INCOME

Dividends etc.. In addition to receiving the cash amount of a UK dividend or other qualifying distribution, a UK resident receives a 'tax credit' of a proportion of the dividend etc. received. For payments made before 6 April 1999, this is found by the formula

$$\frac{I}{100 - I}$$

where I is the lower rate of income tax, expressed as a percentage, for the year of assessment. Thus the tax credit is one-quarter of the dividend etc.. No tax credit is available in respect of 'foreign income dividends' within *ICTA 1988, Pt VI, Ch VA* (see Tolley's Corporation Tax under Foreign Income Dividends) or certain other payments treated as if they were foreign income dividends (see 3.21 ANTI-AVOIDANCE). Foreign income dividends are, in any event, abolished after 5 April 1999.

From 6 April 1999, the tax credit is a fixed proportion (the 'tax credit fraction') of the dividend etc.. This is initially set at one-ninth.

The income assessable on the UK resident is the sum of the dividend etc. and the attached tax credit, with the tax credit being available against the liability.

For 1998/99 and earlier years, income from UK dividends etc. which would otherwise be chargeable at the basic rate is instead chargeable at the lower rate, so that the liability thereon is fully satisfied by the tax credit. The tax credit may generally be repaid if the allowances are not exhausted by other income, and if dividend etc. income exceeds the basic rate limit, it is taxed at the higher rate (with a tax credit at the lower rate). For this purpose, the dividend etc. income is (together, for 1996/97 onwards, with other savings income) treated as the top slice of income (see below).

For 1999/2000 onwards, following the change referred to above in the rate of tax credit, special rates of tax apply to income from dividends etc. (but not to other types of savings income, see below). Where the income falls within the basic rate limit (treating dividend etc. income as the top slice of income), the rate is the 'Schedule F ordinary rate', initially set at 10%, so that the liability is met by the tax credit. To the extent that the income exceeds the basic rate limit, the rate is the 'Schedule F upper rate', initially set at 32.5% (equivalent to a further liability of 25% of the amount of the dividend etc., which is the same as that applicable before 6 April 1999). Also from 6 April 1999, the provisions for payment of the tax credit (e.g. where there are unused personal allowances) are abolished, and tax credits may only be set against liability in respect of qualifying distributions brought into charge. See, however, 29.10, 29.21 EXEMPT INCOME for a five-year extension of tax credit payments in certain cases.

The Schedule F ordinary rate or, before 6 April 1999, the lower rate applies equally to non-qualifying UK company distributions and (unless taxable on the remittance basis under *ICTA 1988, s 65(5)(b)*, see 73.5 SCHEDULE D, CASES IV AND V) income consisting of foreign dividends etc. chargeable under Schedule D, Case V, which do not, however, carry a tax credit.

[*ICTA 1988, ss 1A, 1B, 14(3), 207A, 231, 231A; FA 1993, ss 77, 78(1)(3); FA 1996, s 73, Sch 41 Pt V(1); F(No 2)A 1997, ss 30, 31*].

The definition of 'excess liability' throughout the *Taxes Acts* is amended to take account of the above provisions. See also 81.5 SETTLEMENTS as regards income of discretionary trusts and 71.82 SCHEDULE D, CASES I AND II as regards dealers in securities.

No tax credit. A UK resident (other than a company) who is not entitled to a tax credit on a distribution is treated as having paid Schedule F ordinary rate tax (before 6 April 1999, lower rate tax) on the distribution. Any Schedule F upper rate tax (before 6 April 1999, higher rate tax) is reduced by the tax so treated as paid. The income is not available to cover tax on charges (see 1.10 below) and the notional tax deducted is not repayable. Where non-entitlement to a tax credit in respect of a qualifying distribution arises from the recipient being non-UK resident (and not a company) or, before 6 April 1999, from the distribution being a 'foreign income dividend' (see above), the distribution is for these purposes grossed up at the Schedule F ordinary rate of tax (before 6 April 1999, the lower rate of tax). [*ICTA 1988, ss 233(1)(1A), 246C, 246D; F(No 2)A 1992, s 19(4); FA 1993, Sch 6 para 2; FA 1994, Sch 16 para 1; FA 1996, s 122(3)–(5), Sch 6 paras 5, 28, Sch 27 para 2, Sch 41 Pt V(1); F(No 2)A 1997, s 31, Sch 4 para 6, Sch 6 para 3*]. See also 81.5 SETTLEMENTS as regards income of discretionary trusts.

Certain payments (and other items normally treated as distributions) made by a company for the redemption, repayment or purchase of its own shares are not treated as distributions [*ICTA 1988, s 219*] and consequently have no tax credit and are not treated as income (but see 71.82 SCHEDULE D CASES I AND II as regards dealers in securities). See Tolley's Corporation Tax regarding purchase by a company of its own shares.

A non-resident individual who claims personal allowances (see 51.11 NON-RESIDENTS AND OTHER OVERSEAS MATTERS) is entitled to a tax credit in respect of any qualifying distribution as if he were resident in the UK. [*ICTA 1988, s 232*].

Tax credits set off or repaid which ought not to have been set off or repaid may be assessed, the tax due on such an assessment being payable (subject to the normal appeal procedures) within 14 days after the issue of the notice of assessment. [*ICTA 1988, s 252*].

For foreign dividends paid through agents, see SCHEDULE C (70)

See Simon's Direct Tax Service D1.401.

Savings income (including interest). For 1996/97 and subsequent years, 'savings income' is chargeable to income tax at the lower rate (provided in the case of an individual that it is not chargeable at the starting rate or the higher rate — see below). This applies to 'savings income' received by any person other than a discretionary trust (see 81.5 SETTLEMENTS) or unauthorised unit trust (see 90.2 UNIT TRUSTS). The starting rate of income tax applies to savings income for 1999/2000 onwards to the extent that it falls within the starting rate band (treating savings income as the second top slice of income below dividends etc. — see below). Where tax is deductible at source (see below) from 'savings income', then (regardless of the recipient's status) the deduction is at the lower rate. See Revenue Press Release 9 November 1999 as regards tax repayments due for 1999/2000 where liability is at the starting rate and the taxpayer is not within self-assessment. Where, exceptionally, basic rate tax has been deducted at source, repayment of the excess tax deducted can be claimed. For these purposes, '*savings income*' comprises:

(*a*) any income chargeable under SCHEDULE D, CASE III (72), *except for* annuities and other annual payments that are not interest (see 1.8(i) above and 23.10 DEDUCTION OF TAX AT SOURCE) and rents etc. under *ICTA 1988, s 119* and (for 1996/97 only) *s 120* (re mines, quarries and electric wayleaves, see 23.14 DEDUCTION OF TAX AT SOURCE); *however*, purchased life annuities (see 23.11(*c*) DEDUCTION OF TAX AT SOURCE, and including those excluded under 23.11(*c*)(i))are *not* excluded and the lower rate thus applies;

(*b*) foreign income chargeable under SCHEDULE D, CASES IV AND V (73) and equivalent to income within (*a*) above but arising from securities or other possessions outside the UK, *except for* income so chargeable on the remittance basis (see 73.5 SCHEDULE D, CASES IV AND V) and payments made out of a foreign estate of a deceased person and chargeable under Case IV (see 22.3 DECEASED ESTATES); and

(*c*) (for 1998/99 and subsequent years) amounts chargeable under the accrued income scheme, other than certain charges on trustees (see 74.6 *et seq.* SCHEDULE D, CASE VI).

Until 5 April 1999, it additionally includes UK company distributions and '*equivalent foreign income*' (i.e. foreign company distributions chargeable under SCHEDULE D, CASES IV AND V (73) which would be chargeable under SCHEDULE F (76) if the paying company were UK-resident (subject to the same exceptions as apply under (*b*) above)). See above as regards dividends and other such distributions after 5 April 1999 and generally.

Savings income is chargeable at the higher rate to the extent that it falls within an individual's higher rate band. If the income has suffered lower rate tax at source, excess liability is payable at the difference between the higher and lower rates. For the purpose of determining this extent, savings income is, until 5 April 1999, treated as the top slice of income, but before taking into account income chargeable under *ICTA 1988, s 148* (payments and benefits on loss of office, see 19.5 COMPENSATION FOR LOSS OF EMPLOYMENT) or *ICTA 1988, s 547(1)(a)* (life assurance gains, see 45.13 LIFE ASSURANCE POLICIES). From 6 April 1999, when dividends and other distributions (and equivalent foreign income) cease to be treated as savings income (see above), they are treated as the top slice in priority to savings income.

Before 1996/97, similar provisions applied, but only to dividend income (see above).

[*ICTA 1988, ss 1A, 4(1A); FA 1996, s 73; FA 1997, Sch 18 Pt VI(2); F(No2)A 1997, s 31; FA 1998, s 100; FA 1999, s 22(7); FA 2000, s 32*].

For whether solicitors' client account interest is savings income, see 44.2 INTEREST RECEIVABLE.

Interest is receivable under deduction of tax at source where it is annual interest paid *by* a company (including a partnership of which a company is a member), *by* a local authority, or *to* a person whose usual place of abode is outside the UK [*ICTA 1988, s 349(2)(3)*], including interest on company debentures and other securities. Bank and building society interest is excluded, but deduction of tax is imposed under separate provisions. See 8.2 BANKS and 9.3 BUILDING SOCIETIES for further details and for exceptions. Otherwise, interest is generally receivable gross. See 29.13 EXEMPT INCOME for interest on 'TESSAs' and other tax-exempt interest, and see also 33 GOVERNMENT STOCKS.

Simon's Direct Tax Service. See B5.222.

1.10 DEDUCTIONS IN COMPUTING TOTAL INCOME

The following are deductible to the extent indicated in arriving at total income (see 1.6 above).

(i) **Charges on income**, i.e. sums paid under legal obligation and which may or must be paid under deduction of tax (see 23.2, 23.3 DEDUCTION OF TAX AT SOURCE). These consist of annuities and patent royalties and (subject to the wide exclusions referred to below) annual payments. [*ICTA 1988, s 348(1)(2)(a), s 349(1)*].

Annual payments. There is a general exclusion from relief against total income, subject to the exceptions referred to below. See 1.8(i) above for details of annual payments and 23 DEDUCTION OF TAX AT SOURCE (and 47.10 MARRIED PERSONS as regards maintenance payments) for the circumstances in which income tax at the basic or lower rate should be deducted. The payer, having deducted tax at source, will be assessed to that tax to the extent, if any, that it exceeds the tax he has borne on his income. [*ICTA 1988, s 350(1)(1A); FA 1996, Sch 6 paras 8, 28*]. *If he fails to deduct tax*, he obtains no relief for the payment. [*ICTA 1988, s 276; FA 1994, Sch 8 para 11*]. Certain payments under deeds of covenant and under maintenance agreements between parent and child are ineffective for the purposes of excess liability (i.e. excess of higher rate(s) of income tax over basic rate) (see 81.29 SETTLEMENTS), and no deduction is made from total income for excess liability purposes in those cases, nor for certain annual payments made under tax avoidance schemes (see 3.19 ANTI-AVOIDANCE).

An annual payment made by an individual, or by a Scottish partnership in which at least one partner is an individual, and falling due after 14 March 1988 is excluded from relief as a charge on the income of the person making it. Exceptions are

(*a*) payments under 'existing obligations' (see 1.8(i) above, and also below as regards maintenance payments),

(*b*) payments of interest (but see (ii) below),

(*c*) payments due before 6 April 2000 under charitable covenants,

(*d*) payments made for *bona fide* commercial reasons in connection with the payer's trade, profession or vocation, and

(*e*) payments within *ICTA 1988, s 125* (see 3.19 ANTI-AVOIDANCE).

As regards (*a*) above, for 1995/96 and subsequent years a payment treated as income of the payer under *ICTA 1988, ss 660A, 660B* (see 81.13–81.18 SETTLEMENTS) is not a charge on the income of the payer even if made under an 'existing obligation', which would apply for example to a payment due and made after 5 April 1995 under a pre-15 March 1988 non-charitable deed of covenant.

[*ICTA 1988, s 347A(1)(2); FA 1988, s 36(1)(3); FA 1995, Sch 17 para 4(1); FA 1999, Sch 20 Pt III(6); FA 2000, s 41(2)(9)*].

See 47.10 MARRIED PERSONS for special rules regarding maintenance payments, in particular the reduced relief for payments within (*a*) above for 1994/95 to 1999/2000 inclusive and the general abolition of such relief for 2000/01 onwards (from which time such payments attract a limited relief and then only if they are qualifying maintenance payments).

(ii) **Interest payable** by the taxpayer insofar as it is allowable for tax purposes and has not been allowed as a deduction in computing profits. Higher rate relief is denied in certain cases. For 1999/2000 and earlier years, most mortgage interest is relieved either by deduction at source under MIRAS or by way of a reduction in tax payable; such interest is *not* deductible in arriving at total income. Mortgage interest relief is abolished after 5 April 2000. See 43.3 INTEREST PAYABLE.

(iii) **Qualifying donations** to charities before 6 April 2000 (see 15.16 CHARITIES). (See 15.12 CHARITIES as regards relief for qualifying donations made after 5 April 2000.) [*FA 1990, s 25(6) as originally enacted*].

(iv) **Losses** relieved under *ICTA 1988, ss 380, 381* (see 46.3, 46.13 LOSSES). [*ICTA 1988, ss 380(1), 381(2)*].

(v) (Before 6 April 1999) costs of a **qualifying course of vocational training** (see 92 VOCATIONAL TRAINING RELIEF). [*FA 1991, s 32(2); FA 1999, s 59*].

(vi) **Post-cessation expenditure** (see 62.4 POST-CESSATION RECEIPTS AND EXPENDITURE). [*ICTA 1988, s 109A(1); FA 1995, s 90*].

(vii) (From 6 April 1995) **post-employment deductions** (see 75.23 SCHEDULE E). [*FA 1995, s 92(1)*].

(viii) **Class 4 National Insurance contributions.** For 1995/96 and earlier years, a claim may be made to deduct 50% of such contributions an individual is liable to pay (as finally determined) in respect of the year of assessment. [*ICTA 1988, s 617(5); FA 1996, s 147*]. See 83.7 SOCIAL SECURITY.

Deductions as above are, subject to any express provisions to the contrary, treated as reducing income of different descriptions in the order which will result in the greatest reduction in tax liability. [*ICTA 1988, s 835(4)*].

See Revenue Relief Manual Re 73, 100 *et seq.*.

Simon's Direct Tax Service. See **E1.501** *et seq.*.

See also 28 EXCESS LIABILITY.

1.11 CLAIMS

Allowances unclaimed or not deducted from assessments (and relief for unused tax credits on dividends or tax suffered by deduction at source) may be claimed within five years after 31 January following the tax year for which the claim is made (for 1995/96 and earlier years, six years after the end of that tax year). [*TMA 1970, s 43; FA 1994, ss 196, 199(2)(a), Sch 19 para 14*]. See 17 CLAIMS. But relief is given only in respect of tax actually borne by the claimant, i.e., no relief on income the tax on which he is entitled to charge at the basic rate against, or deduct from any payment to, any other person. [*ICTA 1988, ss 256(3)(c)(ii), 276; FA 1994, s 77(1), Sch 8 para 11*]. Allowances depend upon 'the facts as they exist at the time' and cannot afterwards be withdrawn (or fresh assessments made) by reason of facts 'which arose after the year of assessment' (*Dodworth v Dale KB 1936, 20 TC 285*).

See 7 BANKRUPTCY for claims by bankrupts.

1.12 NON-RESIDENTS

pay income tax at the full rates on chargeable income, with none of the following reliefs except those available to Commonwealth subjects etc. (see 51.11 NON-RESIDENTS AND OTHER

OVERSEAS MATTERS) and under certain DOUBLE TAX RELIEF (25) agreements. See, however, 64.5 RESIDENCE, ORDINARY RESIDENCE AND DOMICILE as regards year permanent residence begins or ends.

1.13 INDEXATION OF PERSONAL RELIEFS AND TAX THRESHOLDS

Unless Parliament otherwise determines, the starting rate band, the basic rate band, the higher rate bands (where applicable) and certain personal reliefs are increased by the same percentage as the percentage increase (if any) in the retail price index (or any substitute index) for the September preceding the year of assessment over that for the previous September. The resultant figure in the case of tax bands (other than the starting rate band) and income limits is rounded up to the nearest £100 and in the case of the starting rate band and the personal reliefs to the nearest £10. The personal reliefs affected are the personal allowance, the married couple's allowance, the blind person's allowance and, from 2002/03, the children's tax credit (see 1.18 below).

The new figures are specified in a statutory instrument by HM Treasury before the year of assessment, but (for 1999/2000 and subsequent years) no change is required in PAY AS YOU EARN (55) deductions or repayments before 18 May in the year of assessment. [*ICTA 1988, ss 1(4)(5A)(6), 257C; FA 1988, s 33, Sch 3 para 5; FA 1993, s 107; FA 1997, s 56(2)(3); FA 1998, s 27(2); FA 1999, ss 22(4), 25, 30(3)*].

1.14 PERSONAL ALLOWANCE [*ICTA 1988, s 257; FA 1988, s 33; SI 1992 No 622; FA 1993, s 52; FA 1994, s 76; SI 1994 No 3012; FA 1995, s 36; SI 1995 No 3031; FA 1996, ss 74, 134, Sch 20 para 13; SI 1996 No 2952; FA 1997, s 55; SI 1998 Nos 755, 2704; FA 1999, s 24; SI 1999 Nos 597, 3038; SI 2000 No 806*]

The personal allowance is available to all claimants (subject to the rules relating to non-UK residents, see 51.11 NON-RESIDENTS AND OTHER OVERSEAS MATTERS).

From 1992/93	£3,445
For 1995/96	£3,525
For 1996/97	£3,765
For 1997/98	£4,045
For 1998/99	£4,195
For 1999/2000	£4,335
For 2000/01	**£4,385**

Where the claimant is at any time in the year of assessment aged 65 (or aged 75) or over, or would have been but for his or her death in that year, a higher allowance is available. Where total income exceeds an income limit, that higher allowance is reduced by one half of the excess until the allowance is the same as the ordinary personal allowance. The income level at which the higher allowance ceases is shown in the right hand column below.

	Personal allowance		Income	Maximum income	
	65 to 74	75 or over	limit	65 to 74	75 or over
From 1992/93	£4,200	£4,370	£14,200	£15,710	£16,050
For 1995/96	£4,630	£4,800	£14,600	£16,810	£17,150
For 1996/97	£4,910	£5,090	£15,200	£17,490	£17,850
For 1997/98	£5,220	£5,400	£15,600	£17,950	£18,310
For 1998/99	£5,410	£5,600	£16,200	£18,630	£19,010
For 1999/2000	£5,720	£5,980	£16,800	£19,570	£20,090
For 2000/01	**£5,790**	**£6,050**	**£17,000**	**£19,810**	**£20,330**

Subject to any express provisions to the contrary, deductions to be made from a person's total income, including the personal allowance, are to be treated as reducing income of different descriptions in the order which will result in the greatest reduction of his income tax liability. [*ICTA 1988, s 835(4)*].

See 1.13 above as to indexation.

See 47.5 MARRIED PERSONS as regards certain transitional reliefs.

See 1.21 below for the single person's allowance which applied before 1990/91.

1.15 **MARRIED COUPLE'S ALLOWANCE** [*ICTA 1988, ss 256, 257A; FA 1988, s 33; FA 1991, s 22; FA 1992, s 10(3); FA 1993, s 52; FA 1994, ss 77(1)(2)(6)–(10), 78, Sch 8 para 1; SI 1995 No 3031; FA 1996, s 134, Sch 20 para 14; SI 1996 No 2952; FA 1998, s 27(1); SI 1998 No 755; SI 1999 No 597; FA 1999, ss 31, 32, 35; SI 2000 No 806*]

The married couple's allowance is **abolished** for 2000/01 and subsequent years of assessment *except* in the case of couples one of whom was born before 6 April 1935, for which see further below. Subject to this, the allowance is available (subject to the rules relating to non-UK residents, see 51.11 NON-RESIDENTS AND OTHER OVERSEAS MATTERS) to a claimant who is, at any time in the year of assessment, a married man whose wife is living with him (see 47.7 MARRIED PERSONS). For polygamous marriages under Moslem law, see *Nabi v Heaton CA 1983, 57 TC 292*, in which, at the Revenue's request, the taxpayer's appeal from the Ch D decision against him was allowed by consent.

From	1990/91	£1,720
For	1996/97	£1,790
For	1997/98	£1,830
For	1998/99	£1,900
For	**1999/2000**	**£1,970**

Tax relief for the married couple's allowance is given at a reduced rate, 20% for 1994/95, 15% for 1995/96 to 1998/99 inclusive, and 10% thereafter. The allowance is no longer given as a deduction from total income, but is given instead by means of a reduction in the claimant's income tax liability. The reduction is the smaller of the specified percentage (i.e. 10% for 1999/2000) of the allowance and what would otherwise be the claimant's total income tax liability. For this purpose, 'total income tax liability' is before deducting any double tax relief and excludes any basic rate tax deducted at source from charges on income or other payments (and is before giving credit for tax suffered at source on the claimant's income and tax credits on dividends). Other reductions in income tax liability are made before that for married couple's allowance.

No more than one allowance may be claimed for any year of assessment, and where marriage takes place during the year of assessment (and the husband had not previously in that year been entitled to the married couple's allowance), the allowance is reduced by one-twelfth for each fiscal month (i.e. ending on 5 May, 5 June, etc.) of the year ending before the date of the marriage.

A man marrying in a year of assessment and otherwise entitled to the additional personal allowance in respect of children (see 1.17 below) may elect that the marriage be disregarded for the purposes of both that allowance and the married couple's allowance. [*ICTA 1988, s 261; FA 1988, Sch 3 para 6; FA 1999, s 33*].

Where death takes place during the year of assessment, the full allowance is available for that year. The allowance is not reduced if the husband remarries during the year in which his wife dies.

See 1.13 above as to indexation.

See 47.2, 47.5 MARRIED PERSONS as regards transfer of allowances and certain transitional reliefs.

See 1.22 below for the married man's allowance which applied before 1990/91.

Spouse reaching age 65 before 6 April 2000. As indicated above, following the general abolition of the married couple's allowance for 2000/01 and subsequent years of assessment, it continues to be available where either spouse was born before 6 April 1935. In such cases (and also for years prior to 2000/01), where the claimant or his wife is at any time in the year of assessment aged 65 (or aged 75) or over, or would have been but for his or her death in that year, a higher allowance is available (but with relief restricted, and calculated, as above). Where the claimant's total income exceeds an income limit, that higher allowance is reduced by one half of the excess (less any reduction made in the claimant's personal allowance age increase, see 1.14 above) until the allowance is the same as the ordinary married couple's allowance. As a consequence of the abolition of the ordinary married couple's allowance for 2000/01 and subsequent years of assessment, the minimum figure for 1999/2000 and subsequent years is based on the ordinary 1999/2000 figure of £1,970, indexed for future years in the normal way (see 1.13 above). For 2000/01, it is £2,000. The maximum income level at which the higher allowance ceases is shown in the right hand column below.

	Married couple's allowance		Income limit	Maximum income	
	65 to 74	75 or over		65 to 74	75 or over
For 1994/95	£2,665	£2,705	£14,200	£17,600	£18,020
For 1995/96	£2,995	£3,035	£14,600	£19,360	£19,780
For 1996/97	£3,115	£3,155	£15,200	£20,140	£20,580
For 1997/98	£3,185	£3,225	£15,600	£20,660	£21,100
For 1998/99	£3,305	£3,345	£16,200	£21,440	£21,900
For 1999/2000	£5,125	£5,195	£16,800	£25,880	£26,540
For 2000/01	**£5,185**	**£5,255**	**£17,000**	**£26,180**	**£26,840**

The figures in the right hand column may vary where entitlement to the higher allowance is by virtue of the wife's age rather than the husband's, or where the wife is 75 or over.

For 2001/02 and subsequent years, a man entitled to claim the married couple's allowance cannot claim the children's tax credit (see 1.18 below). At any time when a woman is married to and living with such a man, she is regarded as having no child resident with her. She can thus only claim the children's tax credit for a year of assessment if there is a time during the year when she is *not* married to and living with him. Any person may, however, elect (by notice to the Revenue) to disclaim the married couple's allowance for any year of assessment, and where such an election is in force the person is treated as not entitled to claim it for that year (so that entitlement to the children's tax credit may arise).

1.16 **WIDOW'S BEREAVEMENT ALLOWANCE** [*ICTA 1988, ss 256, 262; FA 1988, Sch 3 para 7; F(No 2)A 1992, Sch 5 para 7; FA 1994, s 77(1)(5)(8)(9), Sch 8 para 9; FA 1998, s 27(1); FA 1999, ss 34, 35; SI 2000 No 806*]

These provisions cease to have effect in relation to deaths after 5 April 2000.

Where a married man whose wife is living with him dies, his widow is entitled to an allowance for the year of his death, and for the following year provided she does not remarry before the beginning of that year, of an amount equal to the married couple's allowance (see 1.15 above) for the year, in addition to any other available reliefs. The allowance is still due if the couple stopped living together before the husband's death, provided that they separated in the year of death and are still married at the time of his death. (Revenue Independent Taxation Handbook, In 523, 524).

From	1990/91	£1,720
For	1996/97	£1,790
For	1997/98	£1,830
For	1998/99	£1,900
For	1999/2000	£1,970
For	**2000/01**	**£2,000**

Where an allowance is due for 2000/01 (in respect of a death in 1999/2000), the amount is the minimum amount of married couple's allowance available in that year for couples at least one of whom was born before 6 April 1935 (see 1.15 above).

Tax relief for the allowance is given at a reduced rate, 20% for 1994/95, 15% for 1995/96 to 1998/99 inclusive, and 10% for 1999/2000 and 2000/01, and is given by means of a reduction in the widow's income tax liability. The reduction is the smaller of the specified percentage (i.e. 10% for 1999/2000) of the allowance and what would otherwise be the widow's total income tax liability. For this purpose, 'total income tax liability' is as defined in 1.15 above, except that it is before any reduction on account of married couple's allowance (see below).

Where a widow is entitled for the year of her husband's death both to the bereavement allowance and (as a result of an election (see 47.2 MARRIED PERSONS)) to the whole or part of the married couple's allowance, the married couple's allowance is given by way of reduction in the late husband's income tax liability of the year of death, to the extent that there is sufficient liability to cover it. The widow is entitled to a reduction by reference to any excess allowance.

These provisions cease to have effect in relation to deaths after 5 April 2000.

1.17 **ADDITIONAL RELIEF IN RESPECT OF CHILDREN** [*ICTA 1988, ss 256, 259–261A; FA 1988, ss 30, 35, Sch 3 paras 5, 6; F(No 2)A 1992, Sch 5 paras 5, 6; FA 1994, s 77(1)(3)(4)(8)(9), Sch 8 paras 6–8; FA 1996, s 134, Sch 20 paras 17, 18; FA 1998, ss 26, 27(1); FA 1999, s 33*]

This relief is abolished for 2000/01 and subsequent years.

A relief equal in amount to the married couple's allowance (see 1.15 above) is claimable by

(i) any woman who is not throughout the year of assessment married and living with her husband,

(ii) a man who is neither married and living with his wife for the whole or part of a year of assessment nor entitled to the transitional personal reliefs available to certain separated couples (see 47.5(*c*) MARRIED PERSONS), and

(iii) a man (for 1996/97 and subsequent years, an individual) who, for the whole or part of a year of assessment, is married, the spouse being totally incapacitated (physically or mentally) throughout the year (for which see Revenue Independent Taxation Handbook, In 594),

who has a 'qualifying child' resident with him/her for the whole or part of the year.

From	1990/91	£1,720
For	1996/97	£1,790
For	1997/98	£1,830
For	1998/99	£1,900
For	**1999/2000**	**£1,970**

Relief under (i) and (ii) above is not available for the year of separation, for which special provisions apply (see below), for 1993/94 and subsequent years.

The relief is given at a reduced rate, 20% for 1994/95, 15% for 1995/96 to 1998/99 inclusive, and 10% for 1999/2000, and is given by means of a reduction in the claimant's income tax liability. The reduction is the smaller of the specified percentage (i.e. 10% for 1999/2000) of the additional relief and what would otherwise be the claimant's total income tax liability. For this purpose, 'total income tax liability' is as defined in 1.15 above, except that it is before any reduction on account of married couple's allowance and/or widow's bereavement allowance.

A claimant is entitled to only one relief for a year of assessment no matter how many 'qualifying children' are resident with him/her during the year. A woman is not entitled to relief under (i) above for a year of assessment during any part of which she is married and living with her husband unless the 'qualifying child' is resident with her during a part of the year when she is not married and living with her husband.

A man marrying in a year of assessment may claim that his marriage be disregarded for the purposes of both this relief and the married couple's allowance (see 1.15 above).

Where an unmarried couple live together as husband and wife at any time in the year of assessment, and they would both otherwise be entitled to claim the additional relief, then neither of them will be entitled to the relief in respect of any child other than the youngest of the children for whom either of them could otherwise claim relief, i.e. relief to the couple is restricted to one allowance.

A '*qualifying child*' must be born in, or under sixteen at the commencement of, the year of assessment or over sixteen and receiving full-time instruction at a university, college, school or other educational establishment or undergoing full-time training by an employer (for not less than two years) for a trade, profession or vocation (for 1995/96 and earlier years, the employer may be required to furnish particulars of such training). A child who enrols on a two year YTS training programme normally satisfies this latter condition. See generally Revenue Independent Taxation Handbook, In 653–655. The child must be resident with the claimant for the whole or part of the year, and must be a 'child of the claimant' or, if not, must be under eighteen and maintained for the whole or part of the year at the claimant's expense. 'Custody' of child is not required.

The Revenue consider that, to be 'resident with' the claimant, a child must have his or her home with the claimant. While it is possible for a child to have more than one home, it is not accepted that any short visit, e.g. for a holiday, makes the place so visited a home. (Revenue Tax Bulletin November 1992 p 44, and see Revenue Independent Taxation Handbook, In 640).

'*Child of the claimant*' includes a stepchild, an illegitimate child whose parents have married each other after his birth and a child adopted under the age of eighteen.

Age of child. A child is 'over sixteen' or 'over eighteen' at the beginning of a year of assessment if its sixteenth or eighteenth birthday falls either on the first day of that year (i.e. 6 April) or during the previous year.

Apportionment of the relief may be made between two or more persons as may be agreed between them or, failing agreement, in proportion to the length of the periods the child resided with them respectively during the year. Failing agreement, the apportionment is to be made by the appellate General Commissioners for the division in which one of the claimants resides (or Special Commissioners if none of the claimants resides in the United Kingdom). Each claimant is entitled to make oral or written representations.

The Board may direct that a claim to relief which requires apportionment be dealt with by the Commissioners. Where an individual is apportioned amounts in respect of two or more children, his total relief is limited to the lesser of the sum of those amounts and the full relief available for one child. An individual is not entitled to relief in respect of the same child as another person if he alone is entitled to relief in respect of another child.

Year of separation. The additional relief is available in the year of assessment of 'separation' to a spouse with whom a qualifying child resides during the year but after the separation, but not where it is already available to that spouse under (iii) above. The amount of the relief is reduced by any married couple's allowance available to the spouse (see 1.15 above, 47.2 MARRIED PERSONS), unless that allowance has been transferred to that spouse because the other spouse's income was insufficient fully to utilise the allowance (see 47.2 MARRIED PERSONS). Only one relief is available to a spouse, regardless of the number of qualifying children resident with the spouse. The relief is given at a reduced rate, and by means of an income tax reduction, as above.

Where another person is entitled to the additional relief in respect of the same child, whether under this or under the general provision, the total relief (which may not exceed the married couple's allowance) is apportioned between them (subject to the same procedural rules as apply in relation to the general provision above). '*Separation*' for these purposes means separation under a Court order or deed of separation or in circumstances that it is likely to be permanent.

This relief is abolished for 2000/01 and subsequent years.

1.18 **CHILDREN'S TAX CREDIT** [*ICTA 1988, s 257AA, Sch 13B; FA 1999, ss 30, 35, Sch 3; FA 2000, ss 34, 39(9)*]

For **2001/02** and subsequent years of assessment, an income tax reduction (a '*children's tax credit*') is available by reference to the following amount to a claimant with whom a 'qualifying child' is resident during the whole or part of the year.

From	**2001/02**	**£4,420**

The amount is, however, reduced by £2 for every £3 of the claimant's income in respect of which income tax is chargeable at the higher rate or Schedule F upper rate (see 1.3, 1.9 above) for the year. See also 1.15 above as regards interaction with married couple's allowance for couples at least one of whom was born before 6 April 1935.

The income tax reduction is the smaller of 10% of the available amount and what would otherwise be the claimant's total income tax liability. For this purpose 'total income tax liability' is before deducting any double tax relief and excludes any basic rate tax deducted at source from charges on income or other payments (and is before giving credit for tax suffered at source on the claimant's income and tax credits on dividends). The reduction is made before that for the married couple's allowance (where still applicable, see 1.15 above).

A '*qualifying child*' is a child under 16 who either is a child of the claimant (including an illegitimate child or stepchild) or is maintained by, and at the expense of, the claimant for any part of a year of assessment.

Child living with more than one adult: married and unmarried couples. Special provision is made for cases where, at any time in a year of assessment, a child (the '*relevant child*') is a qualifying child in relation to both of a husband and wife living together or a man and a woman living together as husband and wife. These are referred to below as the 'partners', and as the 'higher-earning' or 'lower-earning' partner by reference to total income for the year. If both partners have the same total income, they may elect for one of them to be treated as the lower-earning partner, and if they do not make an election neither of them is entitled to the children's tax credit for the year. The lower-earning partner is not entitled to the children's tax credit in respect of the relevant child, except that if neither partner is liable to higher rate or Schedule F upper rate tax on any part of his or her income, then, if the lower earning partner so claims, the amount by reference to which the credit is given is divided equally between the partners. Alternatively, the partners may elect, by notice to the Revenue, for the whole of the amount to be allocated to the lower earning partner. Such an election may be for one year or for a number of consecutive years and must be made before the start of the year (or first year) for which it is to have effect on the basis of assumptions about the partners' incomes for that year. It may be made on such assumptions during the year (or first year) for which it is to have effect provided that:

(*a*) it is made during the first 30 days of that year following written notification having been given to the Revenue before the start of the year of the intention to make the election; or

(*b*) the partners marry in that year; or

(*c*) the partners start to live together as man and wife during that year; or

(*d*) a relevant child becomes resident with the partners in that year, no relevant child having previously been resident with them during that year; or

(*e*) it is assumed that the lower-earning partner in that year will have been the higher-earning partner in the previous year.

The election may be withdrawn by the making of another election superseding the first or by notice to the Revenue by either partner. In the latter case, the withdrawal has effect for the year of assessment in which the notice is given and for subsequent years. An election for one year in any event does not have effect for the next year or for subsequent years where the lower-earning partner in the second year was the higher-earning partner in the first.

Where a partner whose children's tax credit exceeds his or her total income tax liability for a year of assessment gives notice to the Revenue, the other partner will be entitled to the excess amount by reference to which the credit is available, in addition (where relevant) to any existing entitlement. The notice must be given on or before the fifth anniversary of the 31 January next following the end of the year of assessment, in such form as the Board may determine, and is irrevocable.

Child living with more than one adult: other cases. Special provision is also made for cases where a child is a qualifying child in relation to two or more persons (the 'taxpayers') with whom he is resident at the same or different times during a year of assessment and the above provisions for married and unmarried couples do not apply. The amount by reference to which the credit is given is divided amongst all such people who make a claim either as agreed between all the taxpayers concerned or, in default of agreement, as determined by the General Commissioners for a division in which one of the taxpayers resides (as the Revenue directs), or, if all the taxpayers are non-resident, by the Special Commissioners. The case is heard in the same manner as an appeal, with any of the taxpayers being entitled to appear and be heard or to make written representations. A taxpayer may aggregate amounts allotted under this provision in respect of a number of children, but not so as to total more than the full amount available in respect of a single child.

Combined cases. Where, in any year of assessment, a child is a relevant child for the purposes of the provisions relating to married and unmarried couples (as above) and either

(i) he is a relevant child in relation to more than one pair of partners, or

(ii) the provisions for other cases described above would apply to him for that year but for the fact of his being a relevant child under the married and unmarried couples provisions,

the provisions for other cases described above are first applied, treating each pair of partners under the married and unmarried couples rules as a single person to whom the amount to be allotted is determined, and the married and unmarried couples provisions then apply to each pair of partners by reference to the amount so allotted to them.

Changes of circumstances. Where a 'relevant event' takes place in a year of assessment in relation to a child, and either the child is, immediately before the event, a qualifying child in relation to both parties to the event, or as a result of the event the child becomes, or stops being, a qualifying child in relation to any person, then all the above provisions apply in relation to the child's residence as if each of the following were a separate year of assessment:

(A) the period ending with the day before the first (or only) such event;

(B) the period starting with the day of the last (or only) such event; and

(C) any period starting with the day of one such event and ending with the day before the next.

The amount by reference to which the credit is given is apportioned to such periods at the rate of 1/365th for each day in a period. A person's income is, however, taken as his or her income for the whole year and not just for the period concerned. A '*relevant event*' is the marriage of a man and a woman, or their starting to live together as husband and wife, or a husband and wife ceasing to live together, or a man and woman who have been living together as husband and wife (without being married) ceasing to do so.

Claims. Initial claim forms will be sent in Summer 2000 to those PAYE taxpayers receiving either married couple's allowance or additional personal allowance (see 1.15, 1.17 above) in 1999/2000. (Revenue Tax Bulletin December 1999 p 707).

1.19 **BLIND PERSONS** [*ICTA 1988, s 265; FA 1988, Sch 3 para 8; FA 1994, s 82; FA 1996, ss 75, 134, Sch 20 para 19; FA 1997, s 56; SI 1998 No 755; SI 1999 No 597; SI 2000 No 806*]

From	1994/95	£1,200
For	1996/97	£1,250
For	1997/98	£1,280
For	1998/99	£1,330
For	1999/2000	£1,380
For	**2000/01**	**£1,400**

Allowance as above may be claimed if a person is, throughout the whole or part of the year, registered as blind under *National Assistance Act 1948, s 29* (or Scottish or NI equivalent).

By concession, a person becoming entitled to the blind person's allowance by being registered during the year will (subject to the normal time limit for claims) also be given the allowance for the previous year if, at the end of that year, the evidence on which the registration was based (e.g. the ophthalmologist's certificate) had already been obtained. (Revenue Pamphlet IR 1, A86).

For transfer of allowances between spouses, see 47.2 MARRIED PERSONS.

See 1.14 above re *ICTA 1988, s 835(4)* (order of set-off), which applies equally to blind person's allowance.

1.20 For Life Assurance Relief, see 45.1 *et seq.* LIFE ASSURANCE POLICIES. For relief for medical insurance premiums, see 48 MEDICAL INSURANCE. For Mortgage Interest Relief, see 23.13 DEDUCTION OF TAX AT SOURCE and 43.6 *et seq.* INTEREST PAYABLE. For Retirement Annuity Relief and relief for Personal Pension Contributions, see 65 RETIREMENT ANNUITIES and 60 PERSONAL PENSION SCHEMES.

THE ALLOWANCES BELOW ARE OBSOLETE FOR 1990/91 AND LATER YEARS

1.21 **SINGLE PERSON'S ALLOWANCE** [*ICTA 1988, s 257(1)(b); ICTA 1970, s 8(1)(b) as amended; FA 1988, ss 25(1)(b), 33; SI 1989 No 467*]

(to an unmarried, separated or divorced person or widow(er))

For	1988/89	£2,605
For	1989/90	£2,785

Where election was made for separate taxation of wife's earned income, the single allowance was given to both the husband and wife *instead* of the married allowance (see 1.22 below) being given to the husband and wife's earned income relief (see 1.23 below) being granted on wife's earnings.

The allowance is **abolished** for 1990/91 and later years. See now 1.14 above.

1.22 **MARRIED MAN'S ALLOWANCE** [*ICTA 1988, s 257(1)(a); ICTA 1970, s 8(1)(a) as amended; FA 1988, ss 25(1)(a), 33; SI 1989 No 467*]

(to a married man whose wife (not including common law wife, see *Rignell v Andrews Ch D 1990, 63 TC 312*) was living with him (see 47.7 MARRIED PERSONS) or was wholly maintained by him, see *Holmes v Mitchell Ch D 1990, 63 TC 718*). No married allowance if husband made maintenance etc. payments to his separated wife under Court Order or enforceable agreement which could be deducted from his income for tax purposes (see 47.10 MARRIED PERSONS).

For	1988/89	£4,095
For	1989/90	£4,375

Where marriage took place during the year of assessment (and the husband had not previously in that year been entitled to married allowance), the married allowance was reduced by one-twelfth of excess over single allowance for each fiscal month (i.e. ending 5 May, 5 June etc.) which ended before date of marriage. Thus, reduction per month was one-twelfth of £1,490 for 1988/89 and one-twelfth of £1,590 for 1989/90. [*ICTA 1988, s 257(8)*].

A man marrying in a year of assessment entitled to allowances under *ICTA 1988, s 259* (see 1.17 above) could, for that year, disclaim the higher married allowance and be treated as not married for the purpose of such allowances. [*ICTA 1988, s 261; ICTA 1970, s 15*].

Where a wife's income was, as was normally the case, treated as that of her husband, any excess of the married allowance over the husband's income could, in effect, be set against the wife's income in addition to any wife's earned income relief (see 1.23 below).

The allowance is **abolished** for 1990/91 and later years. See now 1.15 above.

1.23 **WIFE'S EARNED INCOME RELIEF** [*ICTA 1988, s 257(6)(7); ICTA 1970, s 8(2) as amended; FA 1988, ss 25(1)(b), 33; SI 1989 No 467*]

Granted in respect of wife's own earned income, including social security retirement pension from her own contributions, unemployment benefit, and invalid care allowance paid to wife (but excluding any other social security benefits and any pension in respect of *husband's past services*). The relief was not available for the tax year in which the marriage occurred (unless on 6 April). Amount of relief as below, regardless of taxpayer's or wife's age.

For	1988/89	Amount of wife's earnings	maximum relief £2,605
For	1989/90	Amount of wife's earnings	maximum relief £2,785

Wife's earned income included a bona fide salary, paid to her as such, for genuine services rendered in her husband's business, and also her share of profit if actually in partnership with him. In *Thompson v Bruce KB 1927, 11 TC 607* held no allowance for alleged salary where not charged in accounts and no other evidence of payment. Also includes maternity pay [*ICTA 1988, ss 150(b), 833(5)(c)*], see 55.33 PAY AS YOU EARN.

The relief is **abolished** for 1990/91 and later years. See now 1.14 above.

1.24 **AGE ALLOWANCE** [*ICTA 1988, s 257(2)–(6); ICTA 1970, s 8(1)(1A)(1B) as amended; FA 1988, ss 25(1)(c)–(g), 33; SI 1989 No 467; FA 1989, s 31*]

Where a person, or his wife, was aged 65 or more in a year of claim and had total income not exceeding the limit as below, an age allowance was given (instead of the ordinary single or married allowances in 1.21 and 1.22 above) as follows.

					Maximum income	
		Single	Married	Income limit	Single	Married
For	1988/89	£3,180	£5,035	£10,600	£11,463	£12,010
For	1989/90	£3,400	£5,385	£11,400	£12,630	£13,420

A higher rate of age allowance was given where a person, or his wife, was aged 75 or more (80 for 1988/89). The rates were as follows.

					Maximum income	
		Single	Married	Income limit	Single	Married
For	1988/89	£3,310	£5,205	£10,600	£11,658	£12,265
For	1989/90	£3,540	£5,565	£11,400	£12,910	£13,780

Where the total income exceeded the limit, the allowance was reduced by one-half of the excess (two-thirds for 1988/89 and earlier years) until the allowance was the same as the ordinary single or married allowance. The income level at which the allowance ceased to be effective is shown in the two right-hand columns above.

Note that any building society or bank interest received under deduction of composite rate tax was grossed up at basic rate and included in total income.

There was no age allowance where election was made for separate taxation of wife's earned income, and it did not apply to increase the amount of wife's earned income relief (see 1.23 above). Where marriage took place during the year of assessment (and the husband had not previously in that year been entitled to a married allowance), the married allowance (i.e. for 1989/90 £5,385 (or £5,565) less any reduction for income over £11,400) was reduced by one-twelfth of the excess over the single allowance (i.e. £3,400 (or £3,540) less any reduction or £2,785 if husband under 65) for each fiscal month (i.e. ending 5 May, 5 June etc.) which ended before the date of marriage. If taxpayer died in year of assessment in which he would have been 65 (or 75/80) or more, he was treated as having been of that age in that year.

The allowance is **abolished** for 1990/91 and later years. See now 1.14, 1.15 above.

2 Allowances and Tax Rates—Examples

The following examples illustrate the method of calculating tax payable **for 2000/01**. References in brackets are to items above (under 1 ALLOWANCES AND TAX RATES).

2.1 A **single person** aged under 65 receives earned income of £15,000, net building society interest of £352 and national savings bank ordinary account interest of £152.

		£	£
(1.7)	Earned income		15,000
(1.9)	Building society interest received	352	
	Tax deducted	88	
		—	440
	National savings bank ordinary account interest (£152 less £70 exempt)		82
(1.6)	Total income		15,522
(1.14)	*Deduct* Personal allowance		4,385
	Taxable income		£11,137
(1.3)	Tax liability (non-savings income):		
	£1,520 at 10%		152.00
	£9,095 at 22%		2,000.90
(1.9)	(savings income):		
	£522 at 20%		104.40
			£2,257.30
	Deduct BSI tax deducted		88.00
	Tax payable		£2,169.30

2.2 **Repayment claim.** A single person aged under 65 years receives earned income of £2,700 (no Schedule E tax having been deducted at source), plus bank deposit interest of £1,600 (net of £400 tax deducted at source).

		£
(1.7)	Earned income	2,700
(1.9)	Bank deposit interest (£1,600 + £400)	2,000
(1.6)	Total income	4,700
(1.14)	*Deduct* Personal allowance	4,385
	Taxable income	£315
(1.9)	Tax liability: £315 at 10% (starting rate)	31.50
	Deduct Tax deducted at source	400.00
	Income tax repayable	£368.50

2.3 Allowances and Tax Rates—Examples

2.3 **Dividend taxation.** A **married man** has income from self-employment assessable in 2000/01 of £26,000. He also receives UK dividends in that year of £8,100 (with tax credit attached £900). Both he and his wife were under 65 at 5 April 2000.

		£	£
(1.7)	Earned income	26,000	
(1.9)	Dividends (incl. tax credit)	9,000	
(1.6)	Total income	35,000	
(1.14, 1.15)	*Deduct* Personal allowance	4,385	
	Taxable income	30,615	
(1.3)	Tax liability on non-dividend income:		
	£1,520 at 10% (starting rate)		152.00
	£20,095 at 22%		4,420.90
(1.9)	Tax liability on dividends: (£28,400 – £21,615 =)		
	£6,785 at 10% (Schedule F ordinary rate)		678.50
	£2,215 at 32.5% (Schedule F upper rate)		719.87
			5,971.27
	Deduct Tax credit on dividends		900.00
	Income tax payable		£5,071.27

2.4 **Age increase in personal/married couple's allowance.** A married man aged 78 has a total income of £21,100 (which does not include any dividend or savings income).

		£	£
(1.6)	Total income	21,100	21,100
(1.14) (1.15)	Income limit	17,000	
	Excess	4,100	
(1.14)	Personal allowance (75 and over)	6,050	
	Less reduction for excess ($\frac{1}{2}$ × 4,100)	2,050	
		4,000	
	Since this is below the basic personal allowance of £4,385, the reduction is limited to £1,665 and the full £4,385 is allowable		4,385
	Taxable income		£16,715

		£	£
(1.3)	Tax liability: £1,520 at 10%		152.00
	£15,195 at 22%		3,342.90
			3,494.90
(1.15)	*Deduct* Married couple's allowance £4,870 (see below) at 10%		487.00
	Tax payable		£3,007.90
(1.15)	Married couple's allowance (75 and over)		5,255
	Less reduction for excess	2,050	
	less reduction in personal allowance	1,665	385
			£4,870

2.5 **Transfer of married couple's allowance.** A married man aged 68 has a total income of £7,200. His wife, aged under 65, has a total income of £10,000. She elects to receive one-half of the minimum married couple's allowance. Neither spouse has any savings or dividend income.

Husband		£
(1.6)	Total income	7,200
(1.14)	Personal allowance	5,790
	Taxable income	£1,410
(1.3)	Tax liability: £1,410 at 10%	141.00
(1.15)	*Deduct* Married couple's allowance (£5,185 – $\frac{1}{2}$ × £2,000) = £4,185 £4,185 at 10% = £418.50 but restricted to	141.00
	Tax payable	Nil
Wife		
(1.6)	Total income	10,000
(1.14)	Personal allowance	4,385
	Taxable income	£5,615
(1.3)	Tax liability: £1,520 at 10%	152.00
	£4,095 at 22%	900.90
		1,052.90
(1.15)	*Deduct* Married couple's allowance (under election) £1,000 at 10%	100.00
	Tax payable (subject to below)	£952.90

The unused balance of the husband's married couple's allowance is (£418.50 – £141) × $\frac{100}{10}$ = £2,775. On a claim, this may be transferred to the wife, who will then be entitled to a further income tax reduction of £277.50 (£2,775 at 10%), reducing tax payable to £675.40.

2.6 **Charitable donations.** Z, a married man in his thirties, has income and makes payments in the year to 5 April 2001 as follows.

	£
Earnings	39,000
Building society interest (inclusive of tax deducted at source)	8,000
	47,000
Deeds of covenant to charities	net 3,120
	£43,880

In October 2000, Z makes a settlement of £20,000 on his parents which produces income of £365 (received gross on a National Savings Bank investment account) in 2000/01. The capital is to revert to him on the death of the last surviving parent.

On 31 March 2001, Z makes a single gift to charity of £312.

Z's income tax liability for the year 2000/01 is

	£		£
Tax at lower and basic rates			
Total income note (*a*)	47,365		
Deduct Personal allowance	(4,385)		
	£42,980		
Tax at 10% on £1,520 (lower rate band)			152.00
Tax at 22% on £33,095			7,280.90
Tax at 20% on £8,365			1,673.00
Deduct Tax retained at basic rate on donations £4,400 at 22% note (*b*)			(968.00)
			8,137.90
Tax at the higher rate		£	
Basic rate tax band		26,880	
Extension re charitable donations note (*b*)		4,400	
		31,280	
£1,520 at Nil (10% – 10%)		—	
31,280 at Nil (22% – 22%)		—	
1,815 at 18% (40% – 22%)		326.70	
8,365 at 20% (40% – 20%)		1,673.00	
£42,980			1,999.70
Total tax borne			£10,137.60

The position could be more simply laid out as follows.

	£
Total income	47,365
Deduct Personal allowance	4,385
Taxable income	£42,980
Tax at 10% on £1,520	152.00
Tax at 22% on £31,280	6,881.60
Tax at 40% on £10,180	4,072.00
	£11,105.60

The figure of £11,105.60 will be reduced by tax paid under PAYE and by tax of £1,600 deducted at source from savings income, with the balance payable by self-assessment. As Z has retained tax of £968 on payments, he has effectively suffered tax of £10,137.60 (£11,105.60 – £968) for the year.

Notes

(*a*) Income arising from certain settlements of income only is treated as income of the settlor (see 81.17 SETTLEMENTS). Thus, £365 is added to Z's total income.

(*b*) The single donation to charity is treated as paid under deduction of basic rate tax from the grossed-up amount (£400) (see 15.12 CHARITIES). The gross equivalent of covenanted payments, similarly treated, is £4,000 (£3,120 × $\frac{100}{78}$).

3 Anti-Avoidance

Cross-references. See CAPITAL ALLOWANCES at 10.9, 10.22 and 10.38(iii) for sales between connected persons and 10.35 re certain leasing arrangements; 25 DOUBLE TAX RELIEF for amounts taxed abroad; 43.2(ii) INTEREST PAYABLE for certain interest; 45.5 LIFE ASSURANCE POLICIES for withdrawal of life assurance relief; 46.1 LOSSES for restrictions relating to the use of losses in a trade, profession or vocation; 46.9(*c*) LOSSES for restrictions on the use of losses arising from first-year allowances to leasing partnerships or under certain other arrangements; 52 OFFSHORE FUNDS; 53.14 PARTNERSHIPS in relation to certain company partnership arrangements; 68.27 and 68.28 SCHEDULE A for certain transactions in short leases; 74.6 *et seq.* SCHEDULE D, CASE VI for accrued income scheme; 81.13 to 81.30 SETTLEMENTS for provisions treating income of settlements as income of settlor.

Other sources. See Tolley's Anti-Avoidance Provisions.

3.1 **For the general approach of the Courts** to transactions entered into solely to avoid or reduce tax liability, leading cases are *Duke of Westminster v CIR HL 1935, 19 TC 490; W T Ramsay Ltd v CIR, Eilbeck v Rawling HL 1981, 54 TC 101; CIR v Burmah Oil Co Ltd HL 1981, 54 TC 200 and Furniss v Dawson (and related appeals) HL 1984, 55 TC 324. See also Cairns v MacDiarmid CA 1982, 56 TC 556; Ingram v CIR Ch D, [1985] STC 835; Craven v White and related appeals HL 1988, 62 TC 1; Shepherd v Lyntress Ltd Ch D 1989, 62 TC 495; Moodie v CIR and Sinnett HL 1993, 65 TC 610; Hatton v CIR Ch D, [1992] STC 140; Ensign Tankers (Leasing) Ltd v Stokes HL 1992, 64 TC 617; Countess Fitzwilliam and Others v CIR and related appeals HL, [1993] STC 502; Pigott v Staines Investment Co Ltd Ch D 1995, 68 TC 342;* and *CIR v McGuckian HL 1997, 69 TC 1.*

The classical interpretation of the constraints upon the Courts in deciding cases involving tax avoidance schemes is summed up in Lord Tomlin's statement in the *Duke of Westminster* case that '. . . every man is entitled if he can to order his affairs so that the tax attaching . . . is less than it otherwise would be.' The case concerned annual payments made under covenant by a taxpayer to his domestic employees, which were in substance, but not in form, remuneration. The judgment was thus concerned with the tax consequences of a single transaction, but in *Ramsay*, and subsequently in *Furniss v Dawson*, the Courts have set bounds to the ambit within which this principle can be applied in relation to modern sophisticated and increasingly artificial arrangements to avoid tax. *Ramsay* concerned a complex 'circular' avoidance scheme at the end of which the financial position of the parties was little changed, but it was claimed that a large CGT loss had been created. It was held that where a preconceived series of transactions is entered into to avoid tax, and with the clear intention to proceed through all stages to completion once set in motion, the *Duke of Westminster* principle does not compel a consideration of the individual transactions and of the fiscal consequences of such transactions taken in isolation.

The HL opinions in *Furniss v Dawson* are of outstanding importance, and establish, inter alia, that the *Ramsay* principle is not confined to 'circular' devices, and that if a series of transactions is 'preordained', a particular transaction within the series, accepted as genuine, may nevertheless be ignored if it was entered into solely for fiscal reasons and without any commercial purpose other than tax avoidance, even if the series of transactions as a whole has a legitimate commercial purpose.

However, in *Craven v White* the House of Lords indicated that for the *Ramsay* principle to apply all the transactions in a series have to be pre-ordained with such a degree of certainty that, at the time of the earlier transactions, there is no practical likelihood that the transactions would not take place. It is not sufficient that the ultimate transaction is simply of a kind that was envisaged at the time of the earlier transactions.

The inheritance tax case *Fitzwilliam v CIR* appears to further restrict the application of the *Ramsay* principle, in that the HL found for the taxpayer in a case in which all their

Lordships agreed that, once the scheme was embarked upon, there was no real possibility that the later transactions would not be proceeded with. There is, however, some suggestion that a decisive factor was that the first step in the transactions took place before the rest of the scheme had been formulated.

See ICAEW Guidance Note TR 588 'Furniss v Dawson' for guidance on the Revenue approach to the application of the principles outlined above.

Simon's Direct Tax Service. See **A1.316, A1.317**.

Anti-avoidance legislation is intended to counteract transactions designed to avoid taxation, but *bona fide* transactions may sometimes be caught also. The provisions relating to individuals (some of which may also relate to companies) are detailed below and as further indicated in the cross-references above. For provisions relating only to companies, see Tolley's Corporation Tax, and see Tolley's Capital Gains Tax for CGT provisions.

3.2 Cancellation of tax advantages from certain transactions in securities. [*ICTA 1988, ss 703–709*].
3.3 Sale of securities with arrangement to repurchase. [*ICTA 1988, s 729*].
3.4 Sale of right to annuities, dividends or interest. [*ICTA 1988, s 730*].
3.5 Treatment of price differential on sale and repurchase of securities. [*ICTA 1988, ss 730A, 730B*].
3.6 Income received on securities held for one month or less. [*ICTA 1988, ss 731–735*].
3.7 'Manufactured' dividends or interest after sale 'cum div'. [*ICTA 1988, s 737*].
3.8 Transfer of assets abroad. [*ICTA 1988, ss 739–746*].
3.9 Trading transactions at other than market price. [*ICTA 1988, s 770*].
3.10 Capital sums received in lieu of earnings. [*ICTA 1988, ss 775, 777, 778*].
3.11 Transactions in land. [*ICTA 1988, ss 776–778*].
3.12 Land sold and leased back. [*ICTA 1988, s 779*].
3.13 Land sold and leased back. [*ICTA 1988, s 780*].
3.14 Leases of assets other than land. [*ICTA 1988, ss 781, 783, 784*].
3.15 Leases of assets (other than land) previously owned for trade, etc., by taxpayer. [*ICTA 1988, s 782*].
3.16 Loan transactions. [*ICTA 1988, s 786*].
3.17 Persons exempt from tax (restrictions regarding pre-acquisition dividends, etc., received on 10% holdings). [*ICTA 1988, ss 235, 236*].
3.18 Persons exempt from tax (restriction regarding certain bonus issues). [*ICTA 1988, s 237*].
3.19 Annual payments for non-taxable consideration. [*ICTA 1988, s 125*].
3.20 Dealings in commodity futures. [*ICTA 1988, s 399*].
3.21 Companies buying their own shares and other special dividends. [*FA 1997, s 69, Sch 7*].
3.22 Futures and options. [*ICTA 1988, s 127A, Sch 5AA*].
3.23 Arrangements to pass on value of tax credit. [*F(No 2)A 1997, s 28*].

3.2 CANCELLATION OF TAX ADVANTAGES FROM CERTAIN TRANSACTIONS IN SECURITIES [*ICTA 1988, ss 703–709*]

Where, in consequence of transaction(s) in securities (including interests in companies not limited by shares, and such transaction(s) coupled with liquidation of a company), *combined with* any of the relevant circumstances mentioned below, a person is able to obtain a tax advantage, the Board of Inland Revenue may make adjustments counteracting that advantage (having first given notice of their intention to do so), unless the person concerned is able to show that the transactions were made (1) for *bona fide* commercial reasons or in the ordinary course of investment management, and (2) without tax advantages being their main object, or one of their main objects. [*ICTA 1988, s 703*]. For 'transactions in securities' see *CIR v Joiner HL 1975, 50 TC 449* and *Laird Group plc v CIR, [2000] SSCD 75* (a tribunal case, see (v) below), and for '*bona fide* commercial reasons' see *Laird Group* and *CIR v Brebner HL 1967, 43 TC 705*, *Clark v CIR Ch D 1978, 52 TC 482* and *Marwood Homes Ltd v CIR (Sp C 106), [1997] SSCD 37*. In *Lewis (as a trustee of the Redrow Staff Pension Scheme) v CIR (Sp C 218), [1999] SSCD 349*, a distribution by way of purchase of its own shares by a company from the trustees of its pension scheme, pursuant to legislation requiring the trustees to reduce their holding, was held to be a transaction carried out by the trustees both for *bona fide* commercial reasons and in the ordinary course of investment management.

The relevant circumstances are those where a person:

A in connection with (i) the distribution, transfer or realisation of a company's profits, income, reserves or other assets, or (ii) a sale or purchase of securities followed by the purchase or sale of the same or other securities, *receives an abnormal amount* (see definition below) *by way of dividend* (or other qualifying distribution, see *ICTA 1988, s 14(2)*) which is taken into account for purposes of (*a*) tax exemption or (*b*) setting-off losses against profits or income or (*c*) group relief (see *ICTA 1988, s 402*) or (*d*) (before 6 April 1999) calculating a company's advance corporation tax liability, or (*e*) (before 2 July 1997) the application of a surplus of franked investment income under *ICTA 1988, s 242* or *s 243*, or (*f*) payments within *ICTA 1988, s 348* or *s 349(1)*, or (*g*) setting against income of interest paid, or (*h*) the application of franked investment income in relation to 'shadow ACT' computations (see Tolley's Corporation Tax under Advance Corporation Tax), or

B in connection with A(i) and (ii) above, *becomes entitled to a deduction from profits because of a decrease in value of securities* held, formerly held, or sold which arises from payment of a dividend thereon or from any other dealing with a company's assets (or where another company obtains the benefit of such a deduction by way of group relief), or

C in consequence of a transaction whereby (see *CIR v Garvin HL 1981, 55 TC 24* and *Bird v CIR HL 1988, 61 TC 238*, and contrast *Emery v CIR Ch D 1980, 54 TC 607*) another person has received or subsequently receives an abnormal amount (see definition below) by way of dividend, or has become, or subsequently becomes, entitled to a deduction, as in B above, *receives a consideration not taxable as income* (apart from the present provisions) representing the value of a company's trading stock, future receipts, or assets which are, or would otherwise have been, available for distribution (see *CIR v Brown CA 1971, 47 TC 217*) as dividend, and which, in the case of a company incorporated abroad, do not represent a return of capital to subscribers, or

D in connection with the distribution of the profits, income, reserves or other assets of a company (including any body corporate) under the control of *five or fewer persons*, or whose shares are not listed and dealt in on the Stock Exchange (but excluding in either case any company under control of one or more companies to which D does not apply), *receives a consideration not taxable as income* as in C above, or

E in connection with (i) the transfer of the assets of a company to which D above applies, to another such company, or (ii) a transaction in securities in which two or more such companies are concerned, receives, in the form of *share capital or securities* of such a company, any non-taxable consideration representing the value of distributable assets of such a company. (Adjustments under this heading may be made immediately if the consideration consists of securities or redeemable share capital, but in the case of non-redeemable share capital *not unless*, and until, *that capital is repaid* (including repayments in liquidation).)

As regards D above, there are provisions effective from 29 April 1996 for the additional exclusion of companies whose shares are dealt in on the Unlisted Securities Market, until the closure of that Market.

[*ICTA 1988, s 704; FA 1996, s 175; F(No 2)A 1997, Sch 8 Pt II(4); FA 1998, Sch 3 para 33; SI 1999 No 358, reg 23*].

C, D and E above are in practice unlikely to apply unless the company in question has (or has recently had) distributable reserves. (Revenue Inspector's Manual, IM 4516–4518).

See Revenue Tax Bulletin November 1992 p 37 for the Revenue view on the application of these provisions in relation to payments of intra-group dividends outside any group income election.

For **other cases** under C and D above, see *CIR v Cleary HL 1967, 44 TC 399; Anysz v CIR Ch D 1977, 53 TC 601; Williams v CIR HL 1980, 54 TC 257; CIR v Wiggins Ch D 1978, 53 TC 639.* In determining 'under the control' in D, the relevant date is the date of the dividend (*CIR v Garvin* above).

An abnormal amount by way of dividend etc. is one which substantially exceeds either

(*a*) a normal return on the consideration provided for the shares, with market value at time of acquisition used if less than consideration or if no consideration provided, and, in determining 'normal return', regard will be had to length of time the shares were held and other distributions received in respect of them, or

(*b*) the proportion of the dividend arising during ownership (where the dividend is at a fixed rate and the recipient sells, disposes of, or acquires an option to sell, the securities within six months of purchase). [*ICTA 1988, s 709(4)–(6)*].

'Dividend' includes interest and any other qualifying distribution. The amount of a qualifying distribution includes the related tax credit for these purposes (*CIR v Universities Superannuation Scheme Ltd Ch D 1996, 70 TC 193*).

Tax advantage means any relief or repayment (or increases thereof) or avoidance or reduction of a charge or assessment to tax, whether effected by receipts accruing as non-taxable or by deductions from profits or gains. For distributions made on or after 8 October 1996, it is made clear that this includes a tax credit, or (before 6 April 1999) the payment of an amount in respect of a tax credit. [*ICTA 1988, s 709(1)(2A); FA 1997, s 73; F(No 2)A 1997, Sch 4 para 19*].

For 'tax advantage' see *CIR v Cleary HL 1967, 44 TC 399* (tax advantage obtained where taxpayers' company purchased shares from them) and contrast *CIR v Kleinwort, Benson Ltd Ch D 1968, 45 TC 369* (no tax advantage where merchant bank purchased debentures with interest in arrear shortly before redemption). The decision in *Sheppard and another (Trustees of the Woodland Trust) v CIR (No 2) Ch D 1993, 65 TC 724* that no tax advantage could arise where relief was obtained by virtue of charitable exemption was doubted in *CIR v Universities Superannuation Scheme Ltd Ch D 1996, 70 TC 193*, in which the opposite conclusion was reached. Prior to the hearing of the latter case, the Revenue had, in any event, indicated that they would continue to proceed under *ICTA 1988, s 703* on the footing that tax-exempt bodies obtain a tax advantage whenever they receive abnormal dividends, since they considered that there would have been good grounds for challenging the earlier decision had it not been for a defect in the assessment under appeal. This continues to be the Revenue approach. (Revenue Tax Bulletin August 1993 p 90, April 1998 p 537, October 1998 pp 590–592). For the quantum of the tax advantage, see *Bird v CIR HL 1988, 61 TC 238.* On the question of whether a tax advantage was a 'main object' of a transaction, see *Marwood Homes Ltd v CIR (Sp C 106), [1997] SSCD 37.* See also *Laird Group plc v CIR, [2000] SSCD 75* (a tribunal case, see (v) below).

3.2 Anti-Avoidance

Procedure.

(i) The Board must notify person (or personal representatives if deceased [*ICTA 1988, s 703(11)*]) that they have reason to believe *section 703* may apply to him in respect of transaction(s) specified in notification. [*ICTA 1988, s 703(9)*]. See *Balen v CIR CA 1978, 52 TC 406*. No assessment may be made later than six years after the chargeable period to which the tax advantage relates. [*ICTA 1988, s 703(12)*].

(ii) Person notified may make, within 30 days, statutory declaration that in his opinion *section 703* does not apply and state supporting facts and circumstances. [*ICTA 1988, s 703(9)*]. For acceptance of late statutory declarations, see Revenue Tax Bulletin April 1999 p 656.

(iii) The Board must then either take no further action or send declaration together with certificate that they see reason to take further action (and any counter-statement they wish to submit) to tribunal (appointed by Lord Chancellor) which will decide either (*a*) there is no prima facie case for proceeding further (against this the Crown cannot appeal) or (*b*) there is such a case. [*ICTA 1988, s 703(10)*]. The taxpayer is not entitled to see the Board's counter-statement nor to be heard by the tribunal (*Wiseman v Borneman HL 1969, 45 TC 540*). See also *Howard v Borneman HL 1975, 50 TC 322* and *Balen v CIR CA 1978, 52 TC 406*.

(iv) If tribunal decides there is a case, or *if no statutory declaration is made by taxpayer*, the Board will make adjustments to counteract the specified tax advantages and notify the taxpayer. [*ICTA 1988, s 703(3)*].

(v) Taxpayer may, within 30 days, appeal to Special Commissioners against adjustments. After appeal has been heard and determined either side may, by notice within 30 days to the Special Commissioners, require the appeal to be re-heard by the tribunal, with usual rights of further appeal by case stated in the High Court. As regards re-hearing applications, see *Marwood Homes Ltd v CIR, [1998] SSCD 53* (for the tribunal decision in which see *[1999] SSCD 44*). [*ICTA 1988, ss 705–705B; SI 1994 No 1813; FA 1998, Sch 3 para 34*].

(vi) The Board have power to require of any person information (within 28 days of written notice) relevant to transaction(s) which it appears to the Board may give rise to a liability on that person under these provisions. [*ICTA 1988, s 708*]. For the way in which the Board should exercise these powers, see *R v CIR (ex p. Preston) HL 1985, 59 TC 1*.

(vii) The application of these provisions is outside self-assessment, so that returns should be made without having regard to a possible charge (although taxpayers may wish to draw the inspector's attention to any correspondence with the Section 703 Compliance Unit (see below) in connection with any particular transaction). Enquiries into the possible application of these provisions will accordingly be carried out independently of any enquiry into the self-assessment return (see 78.11 SELF-ASSESSMENT). (Revenue Tax Bulletin April 2000 pp 742, 743).

Distributions, etc.. For 1998/99 and earlier years, there are provisions whereby income tax paid by a person under D or E above may be treated by a company as advance corporation tax. Advance corporation tax is abolished after 5 April 1999. [*ICTA 1988, s 703(4)–(6); FA 1993, Sch 6 para 12; FA 1998, Sch 3 para 32(3)(5)*]. With effect for assessments made after 5 April 1999, the income tax payable by a person under D or E above is limited to that which would arise in respect of a qualifying distribution of an amount equal to the consideration referred to in D or E above (as appropriate) received on the same day as that consideration. [*ICTA 1988, s 703(3A); FA 1998, Sch 3 para 32(2)(4)*].

Clearance. Taxpayer may take the initiative by submitting to the Board particulars of any transaction effected or contemplated; the Board may, within 30 days of receipt, call for further information (to be supplied within 30 days). Subject to this, they must notify their decision within 30 days of receipt of the particulars or further information, and if they are satisfied that no liability arises the matter is concluded as regards that transaction by itself, provided that all facts and material particulars have been fully and accurately disclosed. [*ICTA 1988, s 707*]. The Revenue is not obliged to give reasons for refusal of clearance but where the applicant has given full reasons for his transactions the main grounds for refusing clearance will be indicated. A refusal to give clearance indicates that counteraction would be taken if the transaction were completed. (Revenue Pamphlet IR 131, SP 3/80, 26 March 1980).

Applications for clearance should be directed to Inland Revenue, Section 703 Compliance Unit (SIS2), Room 522, 22 Kingsway, London WC2B 6NR. Where application is made in a single letter for clearance under *ICTA 1988, s 707* and under *ICTA 1988, s 215* (demergers) and/or *ICTA 1988, s 225* (company purchase of own shares), an additional copy or copies of the letter should be enclosed. Where application is also made for capital gains tax clearances, a copy of the letter should in addition be sent to Inland Revenue, Capital and Valuation Division (CGT), Sapphire House, 550 Streetsbrook Road, Solihull, West Midlands B91 1QU.

Simon's Direct Tax Service. See **B3.701** *et seq.*.

3.3 SALE OF SECURITIES WITH ARRANGEMENT TO REPURCHASE — INCOME ASSESSABLE ON SELLER [*ICTA 1988, s 729*]

Where the owner of any securities sells them under an agreement (or option subsequently exercised) to buy them back (or 'similar securities' as defined) so that a dividend or interest thereon is paid to another person, that interest is treated for all tax purposes as his; if the transaction is carried out with a dealer, it is similarly ignored in the latter's accounts. This does not apply to Eurobonds (see 3.6(*a*) below) or to stock issued by a foreign government in a currency other than sterling, where both vendor and purchaser are dealers in securities, nor to income to which 3.16(ii) below applies. The Board have power to obtain information.

'Securities' are defined to exclude securities within the accrued income scheme (see 74.6 *et seq.* SCHEDULE D, CASE VI).

These provisions are **abolished** where the agreement is made on or after 6 November 1996 (the day appointed for the bringing into effect of *ICTA 1988, s 737A* (see 3.7 below) in relation to overseas securities). [*FA 1996, s 159(1); SI 1996 No 2646*].

Simon's Direct Tax Service. See **B3.725**.

3.4 SALE OF RIGHT TO ANNUITIES, DIVIDENDS OR INTEREST—INCOME ASSESSABLE ON SELLER [*ICTA 1988, s 730; FA 1996, Sch 7 para 23*]

Where the owner of securities sells or transfers the right to the interest, dividends, annuities etc. therefrom *but not to the securities themselves*, such interest etc. (or the proceeds, when sold or realised in such a way that tax is deductible by virtue of *ICTA 1988, s 18(3B)* (see 72.2 SCHEDULE D, CASE III) (for 1995/96 and earlier years, and for accounting periods ending before 1 April 1996, under SCHEDULE C (70) or *ICTA 1988, s 123(3)*) is treated for tax purposes as income of that owner (or of the beneficiary entitled to the income) and no other person, for the fiscal year in which the right to receive the interest was sold. If the interest etc. on the securities is paid gross, an assessment under Schedule D, Case VI is made on the owner unless he shows that the proceeds of any sale etc. have been taxed as above. If tax would have been chargeable on the remittance basis on the interest etc. under Schedule D,

Cases IV or V, the Case VI assessment is correspondingly limited to the amounts remitted. The Board have power to obtain information.

This section applies chiefly to coupons sold through agents abroad not liable to deduct tax (Hansard 27 June 1938 col 1575), but it may have a wider application.

Simon's Direct Tax Service. See **B3.726.**

3.5 **TREATMENT OF PRICE DIFFERENTIAL ON SALE AND REPURCHASE OF SECURITIES** [*ICTA 1988, ss 730A, 730B; FA 1995, s 80*]

Subject to the exception mentioned below, where a person (the 'original owner') has transferred securities to another person (the 'interim holder') under an agreement to sell them entered into on or after 1 May 1995, and the original owner or a CONNECTED PERSON (20) is required to buy them back under, or in consequence of the exercise of an option acquired under, the same or a 'related' agreement at a different price, the difference between the sale and repurchase price is treated for income and corporation tax purposes as a payment of interest which:

(*a*) where the repurchase price is greater than the sale price, is made by the repurchaser on a deemed loan from the interim holder of an amount equal to the sale price; and

(*b*) otherwise is made by the interim holder on a deemed loan from the repurchaser of an amount equal to the repurchase price.

In either case, the deemed interest is treated for income and corporation tax purposes as becoming due when the repurchase price becomes due and, accordingly, as paid when that price is paid. For income and corporation tax purposes (other than those of the current provisions and *ICTA 1988, ss 737A, 737C* (see 3.7 below)), and for the purposes of *TCGA 1992* (unless *TCGA 1992, s 263A*, see below, applies), the repurchase price is treated as reduced by the amount of the deemed interest where (*a*) above applies or as increased by that amount where (*b*) above applies. For the purposes of *ICTA 1988, s 209(2)(d)(da)* (interest treated as a distribution, see Tolley's Corporation Tax under Distributions) any deemed interest payment under (*a*) above is deemed to be interest in respect of securities issued by the repurchaser and held by the interim holder.

The repurchase price, in a case where *ICTA 1988, s 737A* (see 3.7 below) applies (or would apply were it in force in relation to the securities in question) is that price which is or would be applicable by virtue of *ICTA 1988, s 737(3)(b), (9)* or *(11)(c)*. For corporation tax purposes, for accounting periods ending after 31 March 1996, deemed interest under these provisions is treated as payable under a loan relationship, in respect of which the debits and credits to be brought into account are trading or non-trading according to the extent to which the repurchase is in the course of activities forming an integral part of the company's trade. See Tolley's Corporation Tax under Loan Relationships. Previously, deemed interest was treated (if it would not otherwise be so) as yearly interest for the purpose of relief under *ICTA 1988, s 338* as a charge on income (see Tolley's Corporation Tax under Profit Computations). For other purposes, the Revenue generally accept that the deemed interest is short interest, except where it is clear that the transaction was entered into as a substitute for long term finance, and in particular where it is clear finance was arranged in this way specifically to avoid deduction of tax at source. (Revenue Tax Bulletin December 1995 p 266).

The exception referred to above disapplies these provisions (unless regulations under *ICTA 1988, s 737E*, see 3.7 below, otherwise provide) if the agreement(s) in question are non-arm's length agreements, or if all the benefits or risks arising from fluctuations in the market value of the securities accrue to, or fall on, the interim holder.

The Treasury has power to make regulations providing for an amount of deemed interest under these provisions to fall within the exemptions for pension business of insurance companies, for exempt approved pension schemes or superannuation funds or certain other such schemes, or for funds held for personal pension schemes or retirement annuity contracts. See *SI 1995 No 3036* (as amended) as regards payments after 1 January 1996.

See also *SI 1998 No 3177, regs 16, 17* as regards securities which, prior to their repurchase, are converted from currencies of States which have adopted the euro into euros.

[*ICTA 1988, s 730A; FA 1995, s 80(1)(5); FA 1996, Sch 14 para 37*].

Where the above provisions apply (or would apply were the sale and repurchase price different), the acquisition and disposal by the interim holder, and (except where the repurchaser is or may be different from the original owner) the disposal and acquisition (as repurchaser) by the original owner, are disregarded for capital gains tax purposes. This does not, however, apply:

(A) where the repurchase price falls to be computed by reference to provisions of *ICTA 1988, s 737C* (see 3.7 below) which are not in force in relation to the securities when the repurchase price becomes due; or

(B) if the agreement(s) in question are non-arm's length agreements, or if all the benefits or risks arising from fluctuations in the market value of the securities accrue to, or fall on, the interim holder; or

(C) in relation to any disposal or acquisition of qualifying corporate bonds (see Tolley's Capital Gains Tax under Qualifying Corporate Bonds) where the securities disposed of by the original owner, or those acquired by him or another person as repurchaser, are not such bonds.

See also *SI 1998 No 3177, regs 14–18* as regards conversions of securities from currencies of States which have adopted the euro into euros.

[*TCGA 1992, s 263A; FA 1995, s 80(4)(5)*].

Interpretation. For the above purposes, the following apply.

(i) Agreements are 'related' if entered into in pursuance of the same arrangement.

(ii) References to buying back securities include buying back similar securities, and 'repurchase' is construed accordingly. Securities are 'similar' if they give entitlement to the same rights against the same persons as to capital, interest and dividends, and to the same enforcement remedies. Where securities are converted from the currency of a State which has adopted the euro into euros (a '*euroconversion*'), the new securities are treated as 'similar' (see *SI 1998 No 3177, regs 3, 14*).

(iii) 'Securities' has the same meaning as in *ICTA 1988, s 737A* (see 3.7 below).

[*ICTA 1988, s 730B; FA 1995, s 80(1)*].

The Treasury has broad powers to make regulations providing for the above provisions to apply with modifications (including exceptions and omissions) in relation to cases involving any arrangement for the sale and repurchase of securities where the obligation to repurchase is not performed, or the repurchase option not exercised, or where provision is made by or under any agreement:

(*a*) for different or additional securities to be treated as, or included with, securities which, for the purposes of the repurchase, are to represent securities transferred in pursuance of the original sale; or

(*b*) for any securities to be treated as not included with securities which, for repurchase purposes, are to represent securities transferred in pursuance of the original sale; or (*c*) for the sale or repurchase price to be determined or varied wholly or partly by reference to fluctuations, in the period from the making of the agreement for the original sale, in the value of securities transferred in pursuance of that sale, or in the value of securities treated as representing those securities, or for any person to be required, where there are such fluctuations, to make any payment in the course of that period and before the repurchase price becomes due.

Regulations may also make such modifications in relation to cases where corresponding arrangements are made by an agreement, or by related agreements, in relation to securities which are to be redeemed in the period after their sale, those arrangements being such that the vendor (or a person connected with him), instead of being required to repurchase the securities or acquiring an option to do so, is granted rights in respect of the benefits that will accrue from their redemption. They may also provide for modifications in relation to cases involving any arrangement for the sale and repurchase of securities in relation to which there is an agreement which would not have been entered into by persons dealing at arm's length.

[*ICTA 1988, s 737E; FA 1995, s 83(1)*].

Although of wider general application, these provisions were introduced as part of a package of measures designed to facilitate an open market in the sale and repurchase of gilt-edged securities ('gilt repos'). See also 3.7 below, 33.3 GOVERNMENT STOCKS, 71.82 SCHEDULE D, CASES I AND II and Tolley's Corporation Tax under Income Tax in Relation to a Company.

Simon's Direct Tax Service. See **A7.1205.**

3.6 **INCOME RECEIVED ON SECURITIES HELD FOR ONE MONTH OR LESS — or held for more than one month but not more than six months** *and either* purchase or sale was not at current market price *or* agreement regarding sale was made at, or before, purchase (see *ICTA 1988, s 731(3); FA 1996, Sch 20 para 36*). [*ICTA 1988, ss 731–735*].

Effects as regards various classes of recipient are as in (*a*) to (*d*) below.

In calculating period of one or six months, sale under prior option is regarded as a sale at option date [*ICTA 1988, s 731(4)*], and a sale of 'similar securities' is taken into account. [*ICTA 1988, s 731(5)(10)*]. A purchase or sale effected as a direct result of the exercise of a 'qualifying option' (broadly, a traded or financial option within *TCGA 1992, s 144(8)*) is treated as being at current market price (and so excluded from these provisions) if the first buyer acquired, or became subject to, the option on arm's length terms. [*ICTA 1988, s 731(4A)–(4C); FA 1991, s 55*]. The '*appropriate amount*' is the pre-acquisition portion of the dividend, interest etc. calculated from last 'ex-div' day. [*ICTA 1988, s 735(3); FA 1996, Sch 38 para 9*]. See *ICTA 1988, s 735(4)* (as amended) if no last 'ex-div' day. In the case of (*a*) below, the portion taken is of net interest after deduction of tax and the amounts of actual dividends. In the case of (*b*), (*c*) and (*d*) below, it is the gross amount of interest and the amounts of dividends plus related tax credits. In all cases, special rules apply in relation to foreign income dividends within *ICTA 1988, Pt VI, Ch VA* (prior to their abolition after 5 April 1999). [*ICTA 1988, s 731(9)–(9B), s 735(1)(2); FA 1994, Sch 16 para 17; F(No 2)A 1997, Sch 6 para 14*].

These provisions do not apply where the purchaser is required by the purchase agreement to make to the vendor, before his re-sale of the securities, a payment representative of the interest, or where the purchaser is treated by *ICTA 1988, s 737A(5)* (see 3.7 below) as being required to make a payment representative of a dividend on them, where the payment is required, or treated as required, to be made on or after 1 May 1995. [*ICTA 1988, s 731(2A); FA 1995, s 81*].

As regards income payable on or after 19 March 1997, where there is a 'repo agreement' in relation to any securities, neither their purchase or repurchase, nor their sale or sale back, is taken into account under these provisions. The securities purchased by the original owner from the person to whom securities were sold under the agreement (the '*interim holder*') are instead treated under these provisions as the same securities, and as purchased at the same time, as his original holding. This does not, however, apply if the agreement(s) under which the arrangements are made are on non-arm's length terms, or if the interim holder bears any of the benefits or risks of market value fluctuations before the securities are repurchased. There is a '*repo agreement*' if the original owner sells the securities in pursuance of an agreement, and under the same or a related agreement either:

(i) is required to buy back the securities; or

(ii) will be required to buy them back on the exercise by the interim holder of an option under the agreement; or

(iii) is entitled to receive from the interim holder an amount equal to any redemption proceeds.

See *ICTA 1988, s 730B* (under 3.5 above) for 'related agreements', 'securities' and the extended meaning of 'buying back' securities.

[*FA 1997, s 77*].

(*a*) **Share dealers.** The net 'appropriate amount' of the interest etc. is treated for all tax purposes as a reduction of the purchase price, unless already caught by *ICTA 1988, s 729* (see 3.3 above). This treatment does not apply to overseas securities if *ICTA 1988, s 732(4)* complied with.

Except as below, this provision does not apply to:

(i) a market maker in securities of the kind concerned, selling the securities in the ordinary course of business; or

(ii) in circumstances prescribed by Treasury regulations, either a recognised clearing house so prescribed or a member of a recognised investment exchange so prescribed, where the securities are sold after a date so prescribed in the ordinary course of business. *SI 1992 No 568* prescribes such circumstances in relation to The London Clearing House Ltd, and members of The London International Financial Futures Exchange (Administration and Management) trading in equity options on The London International Financial Futures and Options Exchange; or

(iii) a 'Eurobond' dealer; or

(iv) securities which are rights in a unit trust scheme (see 90.1 UNIT TRUSTS) where the subsequent sale is carried out in the ordinary course of business by the manager of the scheme.

For the purposes of (iii) above, a '*Eurobond*' is a security (A) which is neither preference stock nor preference share capital, (B) which is issued in bearer form, (C) which carries a right to interest at a fixed rate or at a rate bearing a fixed relationship to a standard published base rate, (D) which carries no right to any other form of benefit whether in nature of interest, participation in profits or otherwise (although it may carry a right to convert into a security of another description or to subscribe for further securities, of any description), and (E) the interest on which is payable without deduction of income tax or similar foreign tax.

Where the interest receivable by the first buyer is payable after 1 July 1997, (i)–(iv) above are replaced by a general exclusion where that interest falls to be taken into account in computing the first buyer's Schedule D, Case I or II profits (see 71.82 SCHEDULE D, CASES I AND II).

[*ICTA 1988, s 732; FA 1990, s 53; FA 1991, s 56; FA 1996, Sch 41 Pt V(21); F(No 2)A 1997, s 26*].

Special exemptions apply in certain circumstances for dealers on the Tradepoint exchange. [*SI 1995 No 2050*].

See *ICTA 1988, s 731(7)(8)* regarding change in ownership, or commencement, of trade.

The Board may make regulations by statutory instrument, effective from a day to be appointed therein, imposing conditions for the exclusion of market makers to apply, and making appropriate provision in regard to recognised investment exchanges other than the Stock Exchange. [*ICTA 1988, s 738(1)*].

(*b*) **Person entitled to exemption from tax.** Exemption does not extend to the gross 'appropriate amount' of the interest etc. and any annual payment out of the interest etc. is treated as not paid out of taxed income. [*ICTA 1988, s 733*].

(*c*) **Traders other than share dealers** (whether company or not). The gross 'appropriate amount' of the interest etc. and tax thereon is ignored in calculating loss repayment claim under *ICTA 1988, s 380* or *s 381*. [*ICTA 1988, s 734(1)* and see 46.3 LOSSES].

(*d*) **Companies other than share dealers.** The gross 'appropriate amount' and tax thereon is ignored for tax purposes except that net equivalent is treated as capital distribution in calculation of chargeable gain. [*ICTA 1988, s 734(2)*].

'Securities' are defined to exclude those within the accrued income scheme (see 74.6 *et seq.* SCHEDULE D, CASE VI). [*ICTA 1988, s 731(9)*].

Simon's Direct Tax Service. See **B3.727** *et seq.*.

3.7 'MANUFACTURED' DIVIDENDS OR INTEREST

The provisions of *ICTA 1988, s 736A, Sch 23A* (introduced by *FA 1991, s 58, Sch 13*) have effect in relation to certain cases (see (*a*)–(*e*) below) where, under a contract or other arrangement for the transfer of shares or securities, a person is required to pay to the other party an amount representing a dividend or payment of interest thereon.

Where these provisions apply, the intention is that both payer and recipient of the amount in question should be in the same position, for tax purposes, as if the payment had in fact been a dividend or payment of interest. See *Schedule 23A paras 2–6* (as amended) for the detailed mechanism by which this is achieved in each case. See also *FA 1998, s 102* (introducing, *inter alia*, *ICTA 1988, ss 231AA, 231AB*) for the denial of tax credits in certain cases involving stock lending or repurchase agreements, and for provisions to secure the position following the abolition of advance corporation tax from 6 April 1999.

The circumstances in which these provisions apply are as follows.

(*a*) *Manufactured dividends on UK equities.* This applies where one of the parties to a transfer of UK equities is required to pay the other an amount (a '*manufactured dividend*') representative of a dividend thereon. Special provisions apply in relation to foreign income dividends within *ICTA 1988, Pt VI, Ch VA* (until their abolition after 5 April 1999).

(*b*) *Manufactured interest on UK securities.* This applies where one of the parties to a transfer of UK securities is required to pay the other an amount ('*manufactured interest*') representative of a periodical payment of interest thereon. (See Tolley's

Corporation Tax under Loan Relationships special cases for the corporation tax treatment of manufactured interest.)

(*c*) *Manufactured overseas dividends.* This applies where one of the parties to a transfer of overseas securities (including, before 1 April 2001, quoted Eurobonds held in a recognised clearing system, see 23.3 DEDUCTION OF TAX AT SOURCE) is required to pay the other an amount (a '*manufactured overseas dividend*') representative of an overseas dividend thereon.

(*d*) *Dividends and interest passing through the market.* This applies to payments made before 1 July 1997 where one of the parties to a transfer of securities, who is entitled to a dividend or periodical payment of interest either as registered holder of the securities or, directly or indirectly, from a person from whom he acquired them or to whom he transferred them, is required to pay the other an amount (a '*manufactured payment*') representative of that dividend or interest.

(*e*) *Unapproved manufactured payments.* This applies in relation to any manufactured payment made before 1 July 1997, where a person makes a payment which is:

(i) a manufactured dividend (or, before 28 May 1996, a manufactured overseas dividend or interest payment) (see (*a*)–(*c*) above) in connection with a stock lending arrangement which is excluded from the provisions of *ICTA 1988, s 129* (see 71.82 SCHEDULE D, CASES I AND II) by Treasury regulations under that *section* (see *SI 1993 No 2003*); or

(ii) any other manufactured dividend (or, before 28 May 1996, manufactured interest payment), otherwise than in connection with a stock lending arrangement within *ICTA 1988, s 129* (see 71.82 SCHEDULE D, CASES I AND II), in respect of UK securities or equities, where the person making the payment is neither a market maker in relation to securities or equities of the kind in question nor, in circumstances prescribed in 'dividend manufacturing regulations' (see below), a recognised clearing house or a member of a recognised investment exchange (within *Financial Services Act 1986*) as so prescribed.

See now below as regards stock lending arrangements generally.

As regards (*c*) above, the Board may arrange for manufactured overseas dividends to be paid without deduction of tax in certain cases where a double taxation agreement is in force with the territory in which the recipient of the dividend (not being UK resident) is resident. See *SI 1993 No 1957* as amended by *SI 1995 No 1551* and *SI 1996 No 2654*.

There are provisions to counteract any artificial allocation of a payment between the manufactured dividend or interest and the associated stock lending fee.

The Treasury may make 'dividend manufacturing regulations' for the purposes of these provisions which may, *inter alia*, change the definition of an 'unapproved manufactured payment' in (*e*) above (see *SI 1996 No 1226*, revoked from 1 July 1997 by *SI 1997 No 987*) and extend the circumstances in which (*a*)–(*c*) above may apply. See *SI 1993 No 2004* (amended by *SI 1995 No 1324*, *SI 1996 Nos 1229, 2643* and *SI 1997 Nos 987, 988, 2706*) and *SI 1996 No 1826* (amended by *SI 1996 No 2642*). See also *SI 1992 Nos 569, 2074* and *SI 1995 No 2052* (as amended), which were revoked from 1 July 1997 by *SI 1997 No 987*. [*ICTA 1988, s 736A, Sch 23A; FA 1991, s 58, Sch 13 para 1; FA 1993, Sch 6 para 19; FA 1994, s 123(2)–(5)(7), s 124; FA 1995, s 82; FA 1996, s 159(4)–(9), Sch 14 para 52; FA 1997, Sch 10 paras 4, 7(2), 10–13, 16(1); F(No 2)A 1997 s 24(13), Sch 6 para 17; FA 2000, Sch 40 Pt II(17); SI 1992 No 173; SI 1992 No 1346; SI 1993 No 933; SI 1997 No 991*].

A payment which is representative of a qualifying distribution consisting of a payment by a company on the redemption, repayment or purchase of its own shares, or on the purchase of rights to acquire its own shares, is treated as if it were representative of a dividend on the shares concerned. [*FA 1997, Sch 7 para 7(3)*].

The Treasury has power to make regulations providing for any manufactured payment within *Schedule 23A* to be treated as falling within the exemptions for pension business of insurance companies, for exempt approved pension schemes or superannuation funds or certain other such schemes, or for funds held for personal pension schemes or retirement annuity contracts. [*ICTA 1988, s 737D; FA 1995, s 83(1)*]. See *SI 1995 No 3036* (as amended) as regards payments after 1 January 1996.

Special regulations apply to transactions on the Tradepoint exchange. [*SI 1995 No 2052*].

Stock lending arrangements. In relation to, and to transfers under, arrangements made on or after 1 July 1997, following the repeal of the special provisions for approved arrangements (see 71.82 SCHEDULE D, CASES I AND II), special rules apply to stock lending arrangements. Where, under such an arrangement, interest (including dividends) on stock transferred is paid to a person other than the lender, with no provision for the lender to receive a payment representative of that interest, *Schedule 23A* (and regulations thereunder) apply as if the borrower were required to make, and did make, such a payment on the date the interest it represents is paid. [*ICTA 1988, s 736B; FA 1997, Sch 10 paras 3, 7(1); SI 1997 Nos 987, 991, 992, 993; SI 1999 No 621*]. See also (*e*) above.

See generally Revenue Inspector's Manual, IM 4345 *et seq.*.

Treatment of tax deducted. The following provisions are repealed in relation to any payment of a manufactured dividend or manufactured interest made on or after 1 July 1997. [*FA 1997, Sch 10 paras 8, 16(1); SI 1997 Nos 987, 991*]. See now (*a*) and (*b*) above. Prior to repeal, *ICTA 1988, s 737* had effect, subject to *ICTA 1988, Sch 23A* (above), where one party to the transfer of shares or securities (not being a UK resident company) was required to pay to the other an amount representing a dividend (or other qualifying distribution) or a periodical payment of interest thereon. *ICTA 1988, s 350(1), Sch 16* (see 23.3 DEDUCTION OF TAX AT SOURCE) apply as if such a payment were an annual payment made, after deduction of tax, other than out of profits or gains brought into charge to income tax. Where the payment was such that, in relation to a recipient chargeable to income tax, it would be chargeable under Schedule F (i.e. as a dividend), the deduction of tax is deemed to have been made at the lower rate of income tax. The charge under *section 350(1)* on the dividend manufacturer is then at the lower rate, rather than at the basic rate. After 5 April 1996, as a consequence of the introduction of a lower rate charge on 'savings income' (see 1.9 ALLOWANCES AND TAX RATES), deduction at the lower rate is extended to all payments within these provisions.

Excluded from the operation of *section 737* as above are:

(i) interest or a dividend (not being a qualifying distribution) payable gross;

(ii) a payment which, under stock exchange rules, is required to be equivalent to the gross interest or dividend (not being a qualifying distribution);

(iii) a 'manufactured overseas dividend' (see (*c*) above);

(iv) a payment made by a non-UK resident other than in the course of a trade carried on in the UK through a branch or agency or by a member of a recognised investment exchange prescribed in the regulations; and

(v) a manufactured dividend representing a foreign income dividend within *ICTA 1988, Pt VI, Ch VA.*

As regards (iv) above, if the payment is received by a UK resident (or a non-resident who receives it for the purposes of a trade carried on through a UK branch or agency), he is assessable and chargeable with the amount of income tax which the payer would have been required to account for and pay had he been UK resident. (For 1995/96 and earlier years, and for accounting periods ending before 1 April 1996, this applied only to UK resident recipients, and did not apply where the recipient showed that the payer was entitled to payment of the dividend, etc. either as registered holder of the shares or securities, or directly or indirectly from a person from whom he acquired, or to whom he transferred, the shares or securities, and who was entitled to the dividend, etc. as registered holder of the shares or securities.)

Also excluded, from 2 January 1996, is interest on gilt-edged securities (as defined under *TCGA 1992*), except that the Treasury has broad powers to make regulations bringing such interest within *section 737* with such modifications as may be specified.

No income or corporation tax relief is available, where *section 737* applies (other than to manufactured interest within *FA 1996, s 97*), for any amount required to be deducted from the payment on account of income tax.

'Dividend manufacturing regulations' (see above) may modify the above provisions in any case where a payment is made by a non-UK resident carrying on a trade in the UK through a branch or agency or by a member of a recognised investment exchange prescribed in the regulations. See *SI 1992 Nos 569, 2074*.

[*ICTA 1988, s 737; FA 1991, s 58, Sch 13 para 3; FA 1993, Sch 6 para 14; FA 1994, Sch 16 para 18; FA 1995, s 82; FA 1996, s 159(2)(9), Sch 6 para 18, Sch 14 para 38, Sch 41 Pt V(21); SI 1992 No 173; SI 1992 No 1346; SI 1993 No 933; SI 1995 No 2933*].

In relation to payments made before the date(s) from which *section 737* is amended as above, where one party to a contract for the sale of shares or securities is required to pay to the other an amount representing a dividend (or other qualifying distribution) or a periodical payment of interest thereon, *ICTA 1988, s 350(1), Sch 16* (see 23.3 DEDUCTION OF TAX AT SOURCE) apply as if such a payment were an annual payment made, after deduction of tax, other than out of profits or gains brought into charge to income tax. This does not apply where:

(i) the payer is entitled to the interest, etc. either as the registered holder of the shares or securities or from a person from whom he purchased them;

(ii) the payment is of interest or of a dividend which is not a qualifying distribution and is payable gross (but this does not apply to certain building society interest);

(iii) the payment is, under stock exchange rules, required to be equivalent to the gross interest or dividend (not being a qualifying distribution);

(iv) payments are made by certain market makers dealing in the shares or securities concerned in the ordinary course of business; or

(v) the payment is made by a non-UK resident and the sale concerned was effected through a broker.

As regards (i) above, where the payer is UK resident and purchased the shares or securities (other than through a broker) from a non-UK resident, the condition is that the payer must either be entitled to the interest, etc. as the registered holder of the securities or show that he acquired the shares or securities, directly or indirectly, from a person who was so entitled.

As regards (v) above, however, unless the broker shows that the payer was entitled to the interest, etc. as the registered holder of the shares or securities, or that he acquired the shares or securities directly or indirectly from a person so entitled, *ICTA 1988, s 350(1)* applies as if the payment through the broker were an annual payment by the broker made, after deduction of tax, other than out of profits or gains brought into charge to income tax.

[*ICTA 1988, s 737 prior to amendment as above*].

The Revenue have appropriate information [*ICTA 1988, s 737(8)*] and regulatory [*ICTA 1988, s 738*] powers.

The charge under these provisions takes precedence over that under the accrued income scheme, see 74.32 SCHEDULE D, CASE VI.

Sale and repurchase of securities. *ICTA 1988, s 737* (prior to its repeal) and *Sch 23A* (above) and the dividend manufacturing regulations thereunder apply where, on or after an appointed day (see below), a person (the 'transferor') agrees to sell any 'securities', and under the same agreement (or under another agreement under the same arrangement) he (or a person connected with him (within *ICTA 1988, s 839*)) is required to buy back the same or 'similar' securities, or acquires an option (which he subsequently exercises) to buy them back, and the following conditions are fulfilled:

(*a*) as a result of the transaction, a dividend on the securities is receivable by a person other than the transferor;

(*b*) the agreement(s) do not contain a requirement for an amount representative of the dividend to be paid to the transferor on or before the date the repurchase price becomes due; and

(*c*) it is reasonable to assume that the repurchase price took into account the fact that the dividend was receivable by a person other than the transferor.

They apply as if the person from whom the securities are repurchased (or from whom the transferor has the right to repurchase them) were required under the arrangements for transfer of the securities to pay the transferor an amount representative of the dividend mentioned in (*a*) above, and a payment were accordingly made by that person to the transferor on the date the repurchase price of the securities becomes due. For the corporation tax treatment of such deemed payments, see Tolley's Corporation Tax under Loan Relationships (special cases).

'*Securities*' means UK equities and securities and overseas securities (as under *ICTA 1988, Sch 23A para 1(1)*), and securities are '*similar*' if they carry the same entitlement as to capital and interest (or dividends) and the same enforcement remedies. Where securities are converted from the currency of a State which has adopted the euro into euros (a '*euroconversion*'), the new securities are treated as 'similar' (see *SI 1998 No 3177, regs 3, 14*). References in *ICTA 1988, s 737A* to dividends are, in the case of UK securities, to periodical payments of interest, and in the case of overseas securities, to overseas dividends (as under *ICTA 1988, Sch 23A para 1(1)*).

The 'appointed day' is such day as the Treasury may by order appoint for this purpose. In relation to UK equities and UK securities, it is 1 May 1995. In relation to overseas securities, it is 6 November 1996.

There are special provisions (in *ICTA 1988, s 737C*) for determining the amount of the deemed manufactured dividend or interest for these purposes, and for a corresponding adjustment to be made for tax purposes to the repurchase price of the securities.

See also *SI 1998 No 3177, reg 17* as regards securities which, prior to their repurchase, are converted from currencies of States which have adopted the euro into euros.

[*ICTA 1988, ss 737A, 737B, 737C; FA 1994, s 122; FA 1996, s 159(1)(3), Sch 6 paras 19, 28; FA 1997, Sch 10 para 11(2), Sch 18 Pt VI(10); SI 1995 No 1007; SI 1996 No 2645*].

The Treasury has broad powers to make regulations providing for *ICTA 1988, ss 737A–737C* to apply with modifications (including exceptions and omissions) in relation to cases involving any arrangement for the sale and repurchase of securities where the obligation to repurchase is not performed, or the repurchase option not exercised, or where provision is made by or under any agreement:

(*a*) for different or additional securities to be treated as, or included with, securities which, for the purposes of the repurchase, are to represent securities transferred in pursuance of the original sale; or

(*b*) for any securities to be treated as not included with securities which, for repurchase purposes, are to represent securities transferred in pursuance of the original sale; or

(*c*) for the sale or repurchase price to be determined or varied wholly or partly by reference to fluctuations, in the period from the making of the agreement for the original sale, in the value of securities transferred in pursuance of that sale, or in the value of securities treated as representing those securities, or for any person to be required, where there are such fluctuations, to make any payment in the course of that period and before the repurchase price becomes due.

Regulations may also make modifications in relation to cases where corresponding arrangements are made by an agreement, or by related agreements, in relation to securities which are to be redeemed in the period after their sale, those arrangements being such that the vendor (or a person connected with him), instead of being required to repurchase the securities or acquiring an option to do so, is granted rights in respect of the benefits that will accrue from their redemption.

See *SI 1995 No 3220* as regards such modification in cases where securities are redeemed rather than being repurchased, and where other securities are substituted for those originally transferred.

[*ICTA 1988, s 737E; FA 1995, s 83(1)*].

See also 3.6 above and, as regards application of accrued income scheme to such securities, 74.23 SCHEDULE D, CASE VI.

Simon's Direct Tax Service. See **B3.738–B3.743.**

3.8 **TRANSFER OF ASSETS ABROAD — income payable to person abroad assessable on UK resident in certain circumstances.** [*ICTA 1988, ss 739–746*]

Liability of transferor. Where, as a result of a transfer of assets, either alone or in conjunction with any associated operations (see below), income becomes payable to non-residents, or to persons not domiciled in the UK, then the following provisions apply.

(*a*) If, by virtue of the transfer, either alone or in conjunction with associated operations (see *Vestey v CIR HL 1979, 54 TC 503* overruling *Congreve v CIR HL 1948, 30 TC 163*; and also *CIR v Pratt and Others Ch D 1982, 57 TC 1*), the transferor, being an individual ordinarily resident in the UK, has power to enjoy, forthwith or in the future, any income of a non-resident or non-domiciled person which would be taxable if it were the income of the resident individual received in the UK, that income is deemed, for all tax purposes, to be the income of that individual.

(*b*) If such a resident individual receives, or is entitled to, any capital sum by way of loan, etc. (see *Lee KB 1941, 24 TC 207*), or other non-income payment not for full consideration, which is in any way connected with the transfer, etc., the income which, by virtue of the transfer, etc., has become payable to the non-resident or non-domiciled person is deemed for all tax purposes to be income of the resident. A sum which a third person receives, or is entitled to receive, at the individual's direction or by assignment of the right to receive it, is treated as such a capital sum. There is no deemed income for a year of assessment in respect of a loan to the individual which has been wholly repaid before the beginning of that year.

These provisions do not apply if the Board are satisfied (subject to review by the Special Commissioners) that avoidance of tax was not a main purpose of the transfer or associated operations, or that they were *bona fide* commercial transactions not designed for the avoidance of tax. [*ICTA 1988, ss 739, 741*]. For successful appeals against Revenue refusals of relief, see *Beneficiary v CIR (Sp C 190), [1999] SSCD 134* (in which the grounds were that a transfer involved tax mitigation rather than tax avoidance) and *Carvill v CIR (Sp C 233), [2000] SSCD 143* (in which the Special Commissioner accepted that the transfer had been for *bona fide* commercial purposes).

In the case of *CIR v Willoughby HL 1997, 70 TC 57*, the Revenue's refusal of exemption under *section 741* in relation to 'personal portfolio bonds' (the holder of which has a degree of control of the management of the underlying investments but no proprietary interest therein) was overturned on appeal. For the treatment of cases affected by this decision, see Revenue Press Release 18 December 1997. Broadly, except where such bonds have been used as part of wider tax avoidance schemes, *section 739* will not be applied to income arising on them. Open cases affected by the decision (including the residence aspect of the decision referred to in (I) below), and those in which an assessment became final on or after 16 December 1994 (when the Court of Appeal found in favour of the appellant), will be settled in accordance with the House of Lords' decision. In personal portfolio bond cases which became final before 16 December 1994, the Revenue will consider applications made to them for repayment of tax with repayment supplement. Such applications should be sent to Overseas Life Assurance Group, Special Compliance Office, Barkley House, PO Box 20, Castle Meadow Road, Nottingham NG2 1BA. In all personal portfolio bond cases affected by the House of Lords' decision, repayments will, where appropriate, be restricted, or assessments made, to take account of chargeable event liabilities (see 45.13 *et seq.* LIFE ASSURANCE POLICIES) arising within normal time limits as at 18 December 1997.

For income arising after 25 November 1996 (regardless of when the transfer of assets took place), it is made clear by *FA 1997, s 81* that these provisions apply:

(I) regardless of whether or not the individual with power to enjoy the income was ordinarily resident in the UK when the transfer of assets took place. This reverses the decision in *CIR v Willoughby HL 1997, 70 TC 57* on this point (and see above for cases affected by that decision), and is stated by the Revenue to confirm their long-standing practice;

(II) where the purpose of the transfer is the avoidance of any form of direct taxation, and not just income tax (again apparently confirming long-standing Revenue practice).

For 1996/97 onwards, where a non-UK resident or domiciled person realises a profit from the discount on a relevant discounted security (see 72.2 SCHEDULE D, CASE III), it is treated for these purposes as income of that person. [*FA 1996, Sch 13 para 12*].

For the above purposes an individual is deemed to have power to enjoy income of a non-resident or non-domiciled person if

(i) the income is so dealt with by *any* person so as to benefit the individual at some point of time, whether as income or not, or

(ii) the income increases the value to the individual of assets held by him or for his benefit, or

(iii) the individual receives, or is entitled to receive, at any time any benefit provided out of the income, or out of money available by the effect of associated operations on that income or assets representing it, directly or indirectly, or

(iv) the individual may obtain beneficial enjoyment of the income in the event of the exercise of one or more powers, by whomsoever exercisable and whether with or without the consent of any other person, or

(v) the individual is able to control application of the income,

regard being had to the substantial effect of the transfer and associated operations and bringing into account all resultant benefits to the individual whether or not he has rights in law or equity to those benefits. [*ICTA 1988, s 742(2)(3)*].

Companies incorporated abroad, or regarded under double taxation arrangements as resident outside the UK, are, for this purpose, always to be treated as resident abroad, even if technically resident in UK. [*ICTA 1988, s 742(8); FA 1990, s 66*].

Reference to an individual includes the individual's wife or husband. [*ICTA 1988, s 742(9)(a)*].

For *premiums on leases etc.* in the case of persons resident in the Republic of Ireland but not in UK, see *ICTA 1988, s 746*.

Income falling under the above headings is not chargeable at the basic (or lower) rate to the extent that it has borne such tax by deduction. From 6 April 1999, this applies equally to Schedule F ordinary rate tax. The charge is under SCHEDULE D, CASE VI (74), except that, from 6 April 1999, dividends and certain similar classes of income are brought within the normal provisions relating to income chargeable under SCHEDULE F (76). A non-domiciled individual is only chargeable on any income *deemed* to be his if he would have been chargeable if it had in fact been his income. All deductions and reliefs to be given to the individual assessed as if he had actually received the income. If it is received subsequently, not again assessed. [*ICTA 1988, s 743; FA 1996, Sch 6 paras 20, 28; F(No 2)A 1997, Sch 4 para 20*]. Appeals are to Special Commissioners. [*TMA 1970, s 31(3)(b)*].

The Board have power to demand from any person, under penalty, particulars of transactions where he acted for others (even if he considers no liability arises), and of what part he took in them. [*ICTA 1988, s 745; FA 1989, Sch 12 para 17; FA 1995, Sch 17 para 18; FA 1996, Sch 37 para 2*]. These powers limited in the case of *solicitors* (but not accountants or others), and *bankers* are not obliged to furnish particulars of any *ordinary* banking transactions carried out in the *ordinary* course of a banking business. 'Bank' for this purpose is defined by *ICTA 1988, s 840A* (see 8.1 BANKS). See *Royal Bank of Canada Ch D 1971, 47 TC 565*, where held particulars required were not ordinary banking transactions and *Clinch v CIR QB 1973, 49 TC 52* for powers of Revenue.

See *Philippi v CIR CA 1971, 47 TC 75* for burden on taxpayer to prove that avoidance was not a purpose.

'*Associated operation*'. See *ICTA 1988, s 742(1)* and *Corbett's Exors CA 1943, 25 TC 305; Bambridge HL 1955, 36 TC 313* and *Fynn CD 1957, 37 TC 629*.

For general principles see the above cases and *Cottingham's Exors CA 1938, 22 TC 344; Beatty cases KB 1940, 23 TC 574; Lord Howard de Walden CA 1941, 25 TC 121; Aykroyd KB 1942, 24 TC 515; Latilla HL 1943, 25 TC 107; Sassoon CA 1943, 25 TC 154; Vestey's Exors HL 1949, 31 TC 1; Ramsden Ch D 1957, 37 TC 619; Chetwode v CIR HL 1977, 51 TC 647; Vestey (Nos 1 & 2) HL 1979, 54 TC 503; CIR v Schroder Ch D 1983, 57 TC 94; CIR v Brackett Ch D 1986, 60 TC 134, 639; CIR v Botnar CA, [1999] STC 711.*

Liability of non-transferor. Where, as a result of a transfer of assets, either alone or in conjunction with associated operations (see above), income becomes payable to a non-resident, or to a person not domiciled in the UK, *and* an individual ordinarily resident in the UK who is not liable as the transferor under *ICTA 1988, s 739* (see above) receives a benefit provided out of those assets, then the following provisions apply to benefits received and relevant income arising after 9 March 1981 irrespective of when the transfer or associated operations took place. They do not, however, apply if the Board are satisfied (subject to review by the Special Commissioners) that avoidance of tax was not a main purpose of the transfer or associated operations, or that they were *bona fide* commercial transactions not designed for the avoidance of tax (and see above). [*ICTA 1988, ss 740(1), 741*].

For 1996/97 onwards, where a non-UK resident or domiciled person realises a profit from the discount on a relevant discounted security (see 72.2 SCHEDULE D, CASE III), it is treated for these purposes as income of that person. [*FA 1996, Sch 13 para 12*].

The value of the benefit, up to the amount of relevant income of years of assessment up to and including the year in which received, is treated as income of the resident individual for all tax purposes for that year and charged under Schedule D, Case VI. Any excess of benefit is carried forward against relevant income of subsequent years and taxed accordingly. [*ICTA 1988, s 740(2)(4)*].

'*Relevant income*' of a year of assessment is any income arising in that year to a non-resident or non-domiciled person and which by virtue of the transfer or associated operations mentioned above can directly or indirectly be used for providing a benefit for the resident individual or enabling a benefit to be provided for him. [*ICTA 1988, s 740(3)*].

An individual domiciled outside the UK is not taxable on a benefit not received in the UK in respect of any 'relevant income' on which, if he had received it, he would not, because of his domicile, have been taxable. *ICTA 1988, s 65(6)–(9)* (income applied outside UK treated in certain cases as received in UK, see 63.4 REMITTANCE BASIS) applies as if the benefit were income arising from possessions outside the UK. [*ICTA 1988, s 740(5)*].

Where a benefit otherwise giving rise to a charge under these provisions is in whole or part a capital payment subject to certain capital gains tax charges, it is to that extent treated as having already been treated as income under these provisions. [*ICTA 1988, s 740(6); TCGA 1992, Sch 10 para 14; FA 2000, Sch 26 para 6*].

The provisions of *ICTA 1988, ss 742(8)–(10), 745* apply, see above.

Exclusion of double charge. No income can be charged more than once under the above provisions and where there is a choice as to persons to be assessed the Board may allocate income as appears just and reasonable. The Board's decision is appealable to the Special Commissioners. Income is treated as having been charged to tax

(A) in full, where charged under *ICTA 1988, s 739* as income;

(B) to the extent of the value of any benefit charged under (iii) above, and

(C) to the amount of relevant income taken into account in charging any benefit under *ICTA 1988, s 740*. [*ICTA 1988, s 744*].

Trustees and personal representatives. In relation to benefits received on or after 15 June 1989, relevant income for *section 740* purposes (see above) includes income arising to trustees or personal representatives before 6 April 1989, notwithstanding that one or more of the trustees or personal representatives was not resident outside the UK, unless they have been charged to tax in respect of that income. [*FA 1989, s 111(8)*].

Accrued income on certain securities. See 74.32 SCHEDULE D, CASE VI as regards deemed income arising on transfer of certain securities.

Controlled foreign companies. See also Tolley's Corporation Tax under Controlled Foreign Companies as regards *ICTA 1988, ss 739, 740* relief in certain cases where a charge is made in respect of profits of such companies.

Revenue interpretation. For an article giving the Revenue interpretation of a number of aspects of these provisions, see Revenue Tax Bulletin April 1999 pp 651, 652.

Simon's Direct Tax Service. See **E1.721** *et seq.*.

3.9 **TRANSFER PRICING**

For 1998/99 and earlier years of assessment, where either the buyer or the seller (being a 'body of persons' or a partnership) is controlled by the other party to the contract, or both are such bodies controlled by the same person(s), any sale (including letting and hiring of property, grant or transfer of rights or licences, or giving of business facilities) at a price other than market price at the time of completion or, if earlier, of giving possession may (if the Board of Inland Revenue so direct) be adjusted by the Revenue as follows.

(i) If the price is **below** market price, the latter is substituted in computing the *seller's* profits unless the buyer, being a UK resident trader, is entitled to deduct the price paid in computing his own profits.

(ii) If the price is **above** market price, the latter is substituted in computing the *buyer's* profits unless the seller, being a UK resident trader, would have to bring in, as a trade receipt, the price received. [*ICTA 1988, s 770*].

The extension of these provisions to the 'giving of business facilities' is capable of bringing the making of interest-free loans within their scope (*Ametalco UK v CIR; Ametalco Ltd v CIR (Sp C 94), [1996] SSCD 399*).

'*Control*', for this purpose, means power of a person (including nominees and certain connected persons, and their nominees), by shareholding or voting power (whether direct or through another company) or under articles of association, to secure that the company's affairs are conducted according to that person's wishes. It includes, for partnerships, the right to a share of more than one-half of the firm's assets or profits. For whether control at company meeting is necessary, see *Irving v Tesco Stores Holdings Ltd Ch D 1982, 58 TC 1*. As to trustee holdings, see *CIR v Lithgows CS 1960, 39 TC 270*. [*ICTA 1988, ss 773(2)(3), 840*].

The Board may serve notices specifying the information required (with penalties for non-compliance) on a *company* if it or an associated company was party to a relevant transaction. If one party to a transaction which may be within *ICTA 1988, s 770* is a non-resident 51% subsidiary of a UK parent, notice may be served on the parent for access to the books, etc. of the subsidiary (subject to appeal to Special Commissioners). An inspector may in certain circumstances and with the Board's authority enter premises to examine books, etc.

Where a direction is given, all necessary adjustments are made, by assessment, repayment or otherwise, to give effect to it. [*ICTA 1988, s 770(3)*]. This applies equally to adjustment of open assessments (*Glaxo Group Ltd and Others v CIR CA 1996, 68 TC 166*). Appeals involving questions arising from directions are to that extent to be referred to and determined by the Special Commissioners. [*ICTA 1988, s 772(8)*].

Nothing in *section 770* is to affect the operation of any provisions of *CAA 1990*. [*ICTA 1988, s 773(1)*].

In 1995 and 1996, the OECD published its report 'Transfer Pricing Guidelines for Multinational Enterprises and Tax Administrations' and supplementary material, containing guidelines on the general principles to be applied in determining transfer prices for tax purposes. These can be purchased from HMSO outlets. An article in the Revenue Tax Bulletin October 1996 pp 345–349 sets out the Revenue's position on those guidelines and also provides some practical guidance on the operation of the Mutual Agreement Procedure contained in UK double taxation conventions.

An Inland Revenue leaflet 'The Transfer Pricing of Multinational Enterprises' is also available from the Board, drawing attention to the UK provisions and to the Board's powers.

For 1999/2000 and subsequent years of assessment, and subject to transitional arrangements (see below), *sections 770–773* are replaced by a new *ICTA 1988, s 770A, Sch*

28AA. [*FA 1998, s 108(1)(2)(5), Sch 16*]. *Schedule 28AA* is to be construed so as best to secure consistency between the effect given to the basic rules of the *Schedule* (under *paragraph 1*, see below) and the principles of the OECD model tax convention and transfer pricing guidelines. [*ICTA 1988, Sch 28AA para 2*]. The guidelines are currently published by the OECD as 'Transfer Pricing Guidelines for Multinational Enterprises and Tax Administrations', and can be purchased from HMSO outlets. An article in the Revenue Tax Bulletin October 1996 pp 345–349 sets out the Revenue's views on those guidelines and provides practical guidance on the operation of the mutual agreement procedure contained in UK double taxation conventions. See also the Revenue leaflet 'The Transfer Pricing of Multinational Enterprises'.

Schedule 28AA applies where provision (the '*actual provision*') has been made or imposed as between two persons (the '*affected persons*') by means of a transaction or series of transactions, and at the time the provision was made or imposed either

- (I) one of the affected persons was directly or indirectly participating in the management, control or capital of the other, or
- (II) there was a person or persons who was or were directly or indirectly participating in the management, control or capital of each of the affected persons.

Except as below, if the actual provision differs from the provision which would have been made at arm's length as between independent enterprises (or if no provision would have been so made) and confers a 'potential advantage' in relation to UK taxation on one of the affected persons or (whether or not the same advantage) on each of them, the profits and losses (and certain items treated as losses) of the potentially advantaged person, or of each of them, are computed for tax purposes as if the arm's length provision had been made or imposed (or, as the case may be, no provision made) instead of the actual provision.

A 'transaction' for these purposes includes schemes or arrangements of any kind, understandings and mutual practices (whether or not legally enforceable), and a 'series' of transactions includes a number of transactions entered into in pursuance of, or in relation to, the same scheme or arrangement. A series of transactions is not prevented from being regarded as the means by which provision has been made or imposed between two persons by reason only that there is no transaction in the series to which both those persons are parties, or one or more transactions to which neither of them is a party, or that the parties to any scheme or arrangement in pursuance of which the transactions are entered into do not include one or both of them.

A person is for these purposes treated as directly participating in the management, control or capital of another person at a particular time if and only if, at that time, the other person is a body corporate or partnership which that person controls (within *ICTA 1988, s 840*, see 20.8 CONNECTED PERSONS). Similarly indirect participation requires that the person (the '*potential participant*') either would be taken to be participating directly if certain rights and powers (see *ICTA 1988, Sch 28AA para 4(3)–(6)(10)–(12)*), including future rights and powers, were attributed to him, or is one of a number of 'major participants' in the other person's enterprise. A person is a '*major participant*' in another person's enterprise when the other person is a body corporate or partnership, and he is one of two persons who control (as above) the other person, each of whom has at least 40% of the holdings, etc. giving that control (again after attribution of certain rights and powers as above).

The actual provision confers a '*potential advantage*' on a person in relation to UK taxation where its effect, compared to that of the corresponding arm's length provision, would be a reduction in chargeable profits or increase in losses (or conversion of profits into losses) of that person for any chargeable period. Where, however, the following conditions are satisfied in relation to each of the persons as between whom an actual provision was made, no such potential advantage is conferred on either of them (except in the case of 'ring-fenced trades', see below):

(*aa*) they are within the charge to income or corporation tax in respect of profits arising from the activities in relation to which the actual provision was made or imposed (and not exempt in respect of all or any part of the income or profits from those activities), and where it is an income tax charge which applies, they are UK-resident for all chargeable periods for which it so applies;

(*bb*) they neither have an entitlement to a foreign tax credit in any chargeable period in relation to profits from such activities, nor would have any such entitlement if there were any such profits or if they exceeded a certain amount;

(*cc*) the amounts taken into account in computing profits or losses from such activities for any chargeable period in relation to which (*aa*) above is satisfied do not include any income from which a deduction is made for foreign tax (where no credit is allowable); and

(*dd*) (in the case of a person who is an insurance company within *ICTA 1988, s 431*) the profits from such activities in respect of which the company is within the charge to corporation tax do not include any in the computation of which acquisition expenses have been brought into account under *FA 1989, s 86* or in relation to which a lower rate of tax is fixed by *FA 1989, s 88* or *s 88A* (see Tolley's Corporation Tax under Life Insurance Companies).

[*ICTA 1988, Sch 28AA paras 1–5, 14*].

Elimination of double counting. Where a potential advantage is conferred (as above) on only one of the affected persons (the '*advantaged person*'), and the other person (the '*disadvantaged person*') is within (*aa*) above (or would be if any exemption from tax were disregarded), then (except as below) the disadvantaged person may claim application of the arm's length provision rather than the actual provision (over-riding any applicable time limits for the necessary adjustments). Such a claim may only be made if the arm's length provision has similarly been applied in the case of the advantaged person (in his return or following a determination, see below), and the computations in the case of each of them on that basis must be consistent. The claim must be made within two years of the making of the return or the giving of the notice taking account of the determination, as the case may be, and a claim based on a return which is subsequently the subject of such a notice may be amended within two years of the giving of the notice. (These time limits may be extended in certain cases where the Board fails to give proper notice to disadvantaged persons, see below.)

Where such a claim is made, it is assumed, as respects any foreign tax credit which has been or may be given to the disadvantaged person, that that foreign tax does not include tax which would not be or have become payable if the arm's length provision had also been substituted for the purposes of that tax, and that the profits from the activities in relation to which the actual provision was made or imposed and in respect of which the tax credit relief arises are reduced to the same extent as they are treated as reduced by virtue of the claim.

Where the application of the arm's length provision in a computation following such a claim involves a reduction in the amount of any income, and that income also falls to be treated as reduced under *ICTA 1988, s 811(1)* by an amount of foreign tax (where credit relief is not available), the former reduction is treated as made before the latter, and the deductible foreign tax excludes that paid on so much of the income as is represented by the amount of the former reduction.

Any adjustment to double tax reliefs as above may be given effect by set-off against any relief or repayment arising from the claim, and may be made without regard to any time limit on assessments or amendments.

[*ICTA 1988, Sch 28AA paras 6, 7*].

Capital allowances and capital gains. These provisions do not affect the computation of capital allowances or balancing charges under *CAA 1990*, or of capital gains or allowable losses under *TCGA 1992*, and do not require any income or losses to be treated as on capital rather than revenue account. [*ICTA 1988, Sch 28AA para 13*].

Determinations requiring the sanction of the Board. A determination of an amount falling to be brought into account under these provisions, other than in certain cases where an agreement has been reached between the Board and the person concerned (see *FA 1998, s 110(5)–(7)*), requires the Board's sanction. Where such a determination is made for the purpose of giving a closure notice, giving a notice amending a partnership assessment or making a discovery assessment, and the notice of the closure, amendment or discovery assessment is given to any person without the determination, so far as taken into account in the notice or assessment, having been approved by the Board, or without a copy of the Board's approval having been served on that person at or before the time the notice was given, the closure or amendment notice or discovery assessment is deemed to have been given or made (and in the case of an assessment notified) as if the determination had not been taken into account. The approval must apply specifically to the case in question and the amount determined, but may otherwise be given (either before or after the making of the determination) in any such form or manner as the Board may determine. An appeal relating to a determination approved by the Board may not question the Board's approval except to the extent that the grounds for questioning the approval are the same as the grounds for questioning the determination itself. [*FA 1998, s 110*]. For the requirement that the Revenue give notice of determinations to persons who it appears to them may be 'disadvantaged persons' (as above) by reference to the subject-matter of the determination, see *FA 1998, s 111*.

Appeals. An appeal against an amendment of a return, the refusal of a claim or a discovery assessment or determination involving the application of *Schedule 28AA* lies to the Special Commissioners. Where the appeal relates to any provision as between two persons each within (*aa*) above, each person is entitled to appear before and be heard by the Special Commissioners, or to make written representations to them, and the Commissioners must determine that aspect of the appeal separately from any other, that separate determination being treated as made in an appeal to which each of those persons was a party. [*ICTA 1988, Sch 28AA para 12*].

Miscellaneous. Amounts brought into account in respect of exchange gains and losses and financial instruments adjustments (see Tolley's Corporation Tax under those chapters) are not subject to application of an arm's length provision as above, but this does not affect the application of *Schedule 28AA* for the purposes of *FA 1993, ss 136, 136A* in the case of certain loan interest (see Tolley's Corporation Tax under Exchange Gains and Losses). [*ICTA 1988, Sch 28AA para 8*]. There are also special provisions relating to transactions involving oil and gas [*ICTA 1988, Sch 28AA paras 9, 10*] and to 'ring-fenced' oil and gas exploration activities. [*ICTA 1988, Sch 28AA para 11*].

The provisions apply to unit trust schemes (see 90.1 UNIT TRUSTS) as if they were bodies corporate, with appropriate modification. [*ICTA 1988, Sch 28AA para 14(5)*].

Transitional provisions. Schedule 28AA does not apply in the case of any potentially disadvantaged person as respects the consequences, at any time before 17 March 2001, of the difference between an actual and an arm's length provision if:

(1) the actual provision is made or imposed under contractual arrangements entered into by that person before 17 March 1998;

(2) the control requirement in (I) or (II) above (as the case may be) is satisfied in the case of the actual provision and that person only by his indirect participation as a major participant in the other person's enterprise (see above);

(3) that person's rights and obligations under the actual provision have not been varied or continued by a transaction entered into after 17 March 1998 and before that time; and

(4) that person is not, and has not been, a party to any transaction by virtue of which he could, in the period between 17 March 1998 and that time, have secured the variation or termination of those rights and obligations.

[*FA 1998, s 108(6)*].

The Revenue International Division, Room 311, Melbourne House, Aldwych, London WC2B 4LL may be approached for pre-transaction guidance on the likely tax treatment in particular cases when financial arrangements are in the process of being put in place. See Revenue Tax Bulletin October 1998 pp 579–582 for guidance on the record-keeping required for self-assessment under the above provisions and on the application of the provisions to financial transactions and arrangements; December 1998 pp 603–605 for guidance on penalties under those provisions; and April 2000 pp 740–742 for the practical implications of the new regime for non-UK resident landlords.

Advance pricing agreements. A taxpayer may apply to the Board for an agreement, on a prospective basis, on the resolution of complex transfer pricing issues relating to any one or more of the following matters which fall, or might fall, to be determined.

(*a*) The attribution of income to a branch or agency through which the taxpayer has been carrying on, or is proposing to carry on, a trade in the UK.

(*b*) The attribution of income to any permanent establishment of the taxpayer (wherever situated) through which he has been carrying on, or is proposing to carry on, any business.

(*c*) The extent to which income which has arisen or which may arise to the taxpayer is to be taken for any purpose to be income arising outside the UK.

(*d*) The treatment for tax purposes of any provision operating between the taxpayer and any 'associate' of his. Persons are '*associates*' for this purpose if (as in (I) and (II) above in relation to *Schedule 28AA*) one directly or indirectly participates, at the time of the making or imposition of the provision, in the management, control or capital of the other, or the same person or persons so participate in the management, control or capital of each of them (with further special provision in relation to sales of oil).

(*e*) The treatment for tax purposes of any provision operating between a 'ring fence trade' carried on by the taxpayer and any other activities the taxpayer carries on. A '*ring fence trade*' for this purpose is a trade which is treated as a separate trade under *ICTA 1988, s 492(1)* (oil extraction activities, see Tolley's Corporation Tax under Oil Companies), or would be so treated if a different trade were also carried on.

The application must set out the taxpayer's understanding of what would, in his case, be the effect, in the absence of any agreement, of the provisions in relation to which clarification is sought, and in what respects clarification is required. He must also propose how the clarification might be effected in a manner consistent with that understanding.

Where the Board and the taxpayer have entered into such an agreement (an 'advance pricing agreement' or 'APA') in relation to a chargeable period, then (except as below) any questions relating to those matters are, to the extent provided for in the APA, to be determined in accordance with the APA rather than by reference to the legislative provisions which would otherwise have applied. However, where the relevant matter falls within (*d*) or (*e*) above and not within (*a*), (*b*) or (*c*) above, the only legislative provisions which can be displaced are those contained in *Schedule 28AA* (as above). Where an APA relating to a chargeable period beginning or ending before the date of the APA provides for the manner in which consequent adjustments are to be made, those adjustments are to be made in the manner provided for in the APA.

An APA does not, however, have effect in relation to the determination of any question which relates to:

(i) a time after that from which an officer of the Board has revoked the APA in accordance with its terms; or

(ii) a time after or in relation to which any provision of the APA has not been complied with, where the APA was conditional upon compliance with that provision; or

(iii) any matter as respects which any other essential conditions have not been, or are no longer, satisfied.

The APA must contain a declaration that it is made for the purposes of *FA 1999, s 85*. It may be made on or after 27 July 1999 and may apply in relation to any chargeable period ending on or after that date (and this may include periods ending before the date of the APA). It is for the Board to ensure that the APA is modified so as to be consistent with any double taxation arrangements.

Where the APA makes provision for its modification or revocation by the Board, this may take effect from such time (including a time before the modification or revocation) as the Board may determine.

Any party to an APA must provide the Board with all such reports and other information as he may be required to provide under the APA or by virtue of any request made by an officer of the Board in accordance with its terms.

An APA is deemed never to have been made where, before it was made, the taxpayer fraudulently or negligently provided the Board with false or misleading information in relation to the application for the APA or in connection with its preparation, and the Board notifies the taxpayer that the APA is nullified by reason of the misrepresentation. A penalty not exceeding £10,000 may apply for so giving such false or misleading information.

[*FA 1999, ss 85, 86*].

Effect of APA on third parties. Where an APA has effect in relation to any provision between the taxpayer and another person, then in applying the 'double counting' rules (see above) of *Schedule 28AA* to the other person, the arrangements set out in the APA similarly apply in determining any question as to

(A) whether the taxpayer is a person on whom a potential advantage in relation to UK taxation is conferred by the actual provision, or

(B) what constitutes the arm's length provision in relation to the actual provision.

This is subject to any APA made between the Board and the other person. The notice requirements of *FA 1998, s 111* are correspondingly amended.

[*FA 1999, s 87*].

For a detailed explanation of how APAs are administered, see Revenue Pamphlet IR 131, SP 3/99, 31 August 1999. The contact address for APA applications and other information is Andrew Hickman, Business Tax Group (APA), Inland Revenue, International Division, Victory House, 30–34 Kingsway, London WC2B 6ES (tel. 020–7438 6916; fax 020–7438 7629) or, where oil taxation is involved, Janice Cross, Deputy Director (APAs), Inland Revenue, Oil Taxation Office, Melbourne House, Aldwych, London WC2B 4LL (tel. 020–7438 7579; fax 020–7438 6910). See also Revenue Tax Bulletin October 1999 pp 697, 698 for a note on the scope of agreements, and for procedural guidance relating to bilateral agreements in the light of the Revenue's experiences and observations in concluding agreements with treaty partners under double tax treaty mutual agreement procedures.

Arbitration Convention. The Convention (*90/463/EEC*) on the elimination of double taxation in connection with the adjustment of profits of associated enterprises requires Member States to adopt certain procedures and to follow the opinion of an advisory commission in certain cases of dispute relating to transfer pricing adjustments. The Convention came into force on 1 January 1995 and will continue in force until December 2004, with automatic five-year extensions thereafter unless the signatory States decide otherwise (see Revenue Tax Bulletin August 1998 pp 575, 576). *ICTA 1988, s 815B* makes provision for domestic legislation and agreements to be over-ridden where necessary under the Convention, and *ICTA 1988, s 816(2A)* and *FA 1989, s 182A* provide the necessary information powers and confidentiality requirements in relation to disclosures of information to an advisory commission. [*F(No 2)A 1992, s 51*]. See Revenue Tax Bulletin October 1997 pp 465–467 for guidance on Arbitration Convention procedures. Enquiries about the application of the Convention may be made to Andrew Hickman, Inland Revenue, International Division, Victory House, 30–34 Kingsway, London WC2B 6ES (tel. 020–7438 6916, fax. 020–7438 7629) or, in relation to sales of oil, etc., to Janice Cross, Oil Taxation Office, Melbourne House, Aldwych, London WC2B 4LL (tel. 020–7438 7579, fax. 020–7438 6910).

Simon's Direct Tax Service. See **B3.927**.

3.10 **CAPITAL SUMS RECEIVED IN LIEU OF EARNINGS** [*ICTA 1988, ss 775, 777, 778*]

Where

(i) transactions or arrangements are made (having as their *main* object, or one of their main objects, the avoidance or reduction of income tax) which enable some other person to enjoy profits, gains, income, copyrights, licences or rights, etc., deriving, directly or indirectly, from occupational activities, past or present, which an individual (whether resident in the UK or not [*ICTA 1988, s 775(9)*]) carries on wholly or partly in the UK, and

(ii) in connection therewith, or in consequences thereof, that individual obtains, for himself or for some other person, *a capital amount* (i.e. any amount not otherwise includible in any computation of income for tax purposes [*ICTA 1988, s 777(13)*])

any such amount is (subject to certain exceptions, as below) to be treated as *earned income* of that individual, assessable under Schedule D, Case VI, arising when the capital sum is receivable (or, if it consists of property or a right, when it is sold or realised [*ICTA 1988, s 775(7)*]). [*ICTA 1988, s 775(1)–(3), (8)*].

Exemptions. Capital amounts from the disposal of

(*a*) shares in a company, so far as their value is attributable to the value of the company's business as a going concern, or

(*b*) assets (including goodwill) of a profession or vocation, or a share in a professional or vocational partnership, so far as their value is attributable to the value of the profession, etc., as a going concern.

But the above exemptions do not apply to any part of the capital amount which represents any part of the going-concern value of the business, profession, etc., as above, materially deriving from prospective income, etc., from the individual's activities in the occupation, whether as partner or employee, for which he has not received full consideration (disregarding all capital amounts). [*ICTA 1988, s 775(4)–(6)*].

Where the person charged to tax is not the one for whom the capital amount was obtained (see (ii) above) he may recover from the latter person any part of that tax which he pays (for which purpose the Revenue will supply, on request, a certificate of income in respect of which tax has been paid). [*ICTA 1988, s 777(8)*].

The various provisions applicable to *ICTA 1988, s 776*, which are listed in 3.11 below under 'General', also apply for purposes of this section.

Simon's Direct Tax Service. See **E1.702** *et seq.*.

3.11 **TRANSACTIONS IN LAND** [*ICTA 1988, ss 776–778*]

The following provisions apply to all persons, whether UK residents or not, if all or any part of the land in question is in the UK. [*ICTA 1988, s 776(14)*].

Where

(*a*) land (or any property deriving its value from land) is acquired with the sole or main object of realising a gain from disposing of it, or

(*b*) land is held as trading stock, or

(*c*) land is developed with the sole or main object of realising a gain from disposing of it when developed,

any capital gain from disposal of the land or any part of it (i.e. any amount not otherwise includible in any computation of income for tax purposes [*ICTA 1988, s 777(13)*]) which is realised (for himself or for any other person) by the person acquiring, holding or developing it (or by any connected person, as defined by *ICTA 1988, s 839* (see 20 CONNECTED PERSONS), or a person party to, or concerned in, any arrangement or scheme to realise the gain indirectly or by a series of transactions) is, subject as below, treated for all tax purposes as income of the person realising the gain (or the person who transmitted to him, directly or indirectly, the opportunity of making that gain [*ICTA 1988, s 776(8)*]) assessable, under Schedule D, Case VI, for the chargeable period in which the gain is realised. [*ICTA 1988, s 776(1)–(3)*]. See *Yuill v Wilson HL 1980, 52 TC 674* and its sequel *Yuill v Fletcher CA 1984, 58 TC 145; Winterton v Edwards Ch D 1979, 52 TC 655*; and *Sugarwhite v Budd CA 1988, 60 TC 679. Bona fide* transactions, not entered into with tax avoidance in view, may be caught by the legislation—see *Page v Lowther and Another CA 1983, 57 TC 199.*

'*Land*' includes buildings, and any estate or interest in land or buildings. [*ICTA 1988, s 776(13)(a)*].

'*Property deriving its value from land*' includes any shareholding in a company, partnership interest, or interest in settled property, deriving its value, directly or indirectly, from land, and any option, consent or embargo affecting the disposition of land. [*ICTA 1988, s 776(13)(b)*]. See, however, 'Exemptions' below.

Land is '*disposed of*' for the above purposes if, by any one or more transactions or by any arrangement or scheme (whether concerning the land or any property deriving its value therefrom), the property in, or control over, the land is effectively disposed of. [*ICTA 1988, s 776(4)*]. Any number of transactions may be treated as a single arrangement or scheme if they have, or there is evidence of, a common purpose. [*ICTA 1988, s 776(5)(b)*]. See also under 'General' below.

For the date of the capital gain where instalments involved, see *Yuill v Fletcher CA 1984, 58 TC 145.*

Exemptions.

(i) An individual's gain made from the *sale, etc., of his residence* exempted from capital gains tax under *TCGA 1992, s 222* or which would be so exempt but for *TCGA 1992, s 224(3)* (acquired for purpose of making a gain). [*ICTA 1988, s 776(9)*].

(ii) A gain on the sale of *shares in a company holding land as trading stock* (or a company owning, directly or indirectly, 90% of the ordinary share capital of such a company) *provided that* the company disposes of the land by normal trade and makes all possible profit from it, and the share sale is not part of an arrangement or scheme to realise a land gain indirectly. [*ICTA 1988, s 776(10)* and see *Chilcott v CIR Ch D 1981, 55 TC 446*].

(iii) (If the liability arises solely under (c) above.) Any part of the gain fairly attributable to a period *before the intention was made* to develop the land. [*ICTA 1988, s 776(7)*].

Gains are to be computed 'as is just and reasonable in the circumstances', allowance being given only for expenses attributable to the land disposed of, and the following may be taken into account.

(A) If a leasehold interest is disposed of out of a freehold, the Sch D, Case I treatment in such a case of a person dealing in land (see 71.77 SCHEDULE D, CASES I AND II).

(B) Any adjustments under *ICTA 1988, s 99(2)(3)* for tax on lease premiums. [*ICTA 1988, s 776(6)*].

Where the computation of a gain in respect of the development of land (as under (*c*) above) is made on the footing that the land or property was appropriated as trading stock, that land, etc., is also to be treated for purposes of capital gains tax (under *TCGA 1992, s 161*) as having been transferred to stock. [*ICTA 1988, s 777(11)*].

Where, under *ICTA 1988, s 775* or *s 776*, tax is assessed on, and paid by, a person other than the one who actually realised the gain, the person paying the tax may recover it from the other party (for which purpose the Revenue will, on request, supply a certificate of income in respect of which tax has been paid). [*ICTA 1988, s 777(8)*].

Clearance. The person who made or would make the gain may (if he considers that (*a*) or (*c*) above may apply), submit to his Inspector of Taxes particulars of any completed or proposed transactions. If he does so the inspector must, within 30 days of receiving those particulars, notify the taxpayer whether or not he is satisfied that liability under this section does not arise. If the inspector is so satisfied no assessment can thereafter be made on that gain, provided that all material facts and considerations have been fully and accurately disclosed. [*ICTA 1988, s 776(11)*].

General. See *ICTA 1988, s 777(2)(3)* for provisions to prevent avoidance by the use of indirect means to transfer any property or right, or enhance or diminish its value, e.g., by sales at less, or more, than full consideration, assigning share capital or rights in a company or partnership or an interest in settled property, disposal on the winding-up of any company, partnership or trust, etc. For ascertaining whether, and to what extent, the value of any property or right is derived from any other property or right, value may be traced through any number of companies, partnerships and trusts, at each stage attributing property held by the company, partnership or trust to its shareholders, etc., 'in such manner as is appropriate to the circumstances'. [*ICTA 1988, s 777(5)*]. Where the person liable is non-resident, the Board may direct that any part of an amount taxable under these provisions on that person be paid under deduction of tax as if made other than out of taxable income. [*ICTA 1988, s 777(9)*].

For the above purposes the Revenue may require, under penalty, any person to supply them with any particulars thought necessary, including particulars of

(I) transactions, etc., in which he acts, or acted, on behalf of others, and

(II) transactions, etc., which in the opinion of the Revenue should be investigated, and

(III) what part, if any, he has taken, or is taking, in specified transactions, etc. (Under this heading a *solicitor* who has merely acted as professional adviser is not compelled to do more than state that he acted and give his client's name and address.) [*ICTA 1988, s 778*].

The transactions of which particulars are required need not be identified transactions (*Essex v CIR CA 1980, 53 TC 720*).

Simon's Direct Tax Service. See **B3.636.**

3.12 **LAND SOLD AND LEASED BACK — TAX DEDUCTIONS FOR RENT ARE LIMITED TO COMMERCIAL RENT** [*ICTA 1988, s 779; FA 1995, Sch 6 para 27*]

Where, after 14 April 1964, land (or any interest or estate in land) is transferred from one person to another (by sale, lease, surrender or forfeiture of lease, etc.) and

(*a*) under a lease of the land, or any part of it, granted then or subsequently by the transferee to the transferor, or

(*b*) as a result of a transaction or transactions affecting the land or interest,

the transferor, or any person associated with him, becomes liable to pay any lease rent (including any premium treated as rent — see 68.28 SCHEDULE A), or rent charge on, or connected with, the land which would be allowable

(i) as a deduction from trading profits, or

(ii) in computing profits or losses under Case VI, or

(iii) as a management expense under *ICTA 1988, s 75* or *s 76*, or

(iv) against Schedule E emoluments, under *ICTA 1988, s 198(1)*, or

(v) as a deduction in computing profits from woodlands, or

(vi) in computing profits under Schedule A,

the allowance for tax purposes in respect of that rent or other payment (apart from any portion which properly relates to services, tenant's rates, or the use of assets other than land) is limited to the commercial rent of the land to which it relates for the period for which the payment is made. In the case of a lease, '*commercial rent*' means the open-market rent, at the time the actual lease was created, under a lease whose duration and repair terms are the same as under the actual lease but stipulating a rent payable at uniform intervals at a uniform rate, or progressively increasing proportionately to any increases provided by the actual lease. For other transactions, it is the open market rent which would be payable under a tenant's repairing lease (as defined by *ICTA 1988, s 779(12)*) for the period over which payments are to be made, or 200 years if they are for a longer period or are perpetual.

Any part of a payment which is disallowed under the above provisions may be carried forward as an addition to the next subsequent payment, and so on. All payments for the same period are amalgamated, including apportioned parts of periods which overlap. A payment for a period falling, wholly or partly, beyond one year from the date of payment is treated as being for the year commencing with the date on which it is paid. [*ICTA 1988, s 779(5)–(7)*].

'Associated persons'.

A. Husband and wife, their relatives and spouses,

B. the trustee of a settlement and the settlor or any person associated with him,

C. a person and any body, or bodies of persons (including partnerships) which he, or any persons associated with him, or he and any persons associated with him, controls (as under *ICTA 1988, s 840*, see 20.8 CONNECTED PERSONS and note that, in the case of a partnership, control means the right to more than a half share in assets or income),

D. any bodies of persons associated with the same person under C above,

E. joint owners of the land, etc. the subject of disposal, including their associates,

F. the transferor and any other transferor acting in concert, or reciprocally, with him, and their associates,

G. any two or more companies participating in the reconstruction, or amalgamation, of a company or companies. [*ICTA 1988, s 779(11), s 783(10); FA 1995, Sch 17 para 19*].

Simon's Direct Tax Service. See **B3.647.**

3.13 **LAND SOLD AND LEASED BACK — PROPORTION OF CAPITAL SUM RECEIVED IS TO BE TAXED AS INCOME IN CERTAIN CIRCUMSTANCES** [*ICTA 1988, s 780; FA 1988, s 75*]

As regards arrangements as in *ICTA 1988, s 779* (see 3.12 above), made after 21 June 1971, where the lease when sold has no more than 50 years still to run and the period for which the premises are leased back is 15 years or less, the increased rent payable, so far as it does not exceed a commercial rent (see 3.12 above), is allowable as a deduction from profits, but of the consideration received by the lessee for giving up the original lease (or undertaking to pay an increased rent) a proportion equivalent to one-fifteenth of that consideration multiplied by the number of years by which the term of the lease-back falls short of 16 years will be treated as assessable income, not capital. Appropriate adjustment to be made where the lease-back is of part only of the property previously leased. For the above purposes the term of the new lease is deemed to end on any date whereafter the rent payable is reduced, or, if the lessor or lessee has power to determine the lease or the lessee has power to vary its terms, on the earliest date on which the lease can be so determined or varied.

Simon's Direct Tax Service. See **B3.648.**

3.14 **LEASES OF ASSETS OTHER THAN LAND — CAPITAL SUM RECEIVED BY PERSON WHO PAYS LEASE RENTALS IS TAXABLE —**

to the extent of tax allowances on such lease rentals. [*ICTA 1988, ss 781, 783, 784*]

Where any payment under a lease, created after 14 April 1964, of any asset not falling under *ICTA 1988, s 779* (see 3.12 above) or *s 782* (see 3.15 below), is allowable

(i) as a deduction from trading profits, or

(ii) in computing profits or losses under Schedule D, Case VI, or in respect of woodlands, or

(iii) as a management expense under *ICTA 1988, ss 75, 76* or

(iv) against Schedule E emoluments,

then if at any time the person making the payment has obtained, or obtains, a capital sum (i.e. any money, or money's worth, not chargeable as profits, etc., of a trade, profession, or from woodlands nor chargeable under Case VI) in respect of the lessee's interest in the lease (including by surrender to the lessor, assignment, subleasing, or receipt under insurance — and see *ICTA 1988, s 783*), or any person associated with the payer has obtained a capital sum for an interest in the asset, the recipient of that capital sum is assessed, under Case VI, for the year in which the capital sum was obtained, on a figure equal to the amount of the payment under the lease which is allowable for tax purposes as above (or the effectively allowable part of it, where the whole or part of the period in which the payment would normally be allowed is not a basis period for assessment), subject to the overriding limitation that the amount(s) so charged shall not exceed the capital sum received (or, where the lease is a hire-purchase agreement, that sum less the recipient's capital expenditure on the asset — see *ICTA 1988, s 784*).

Apportionments are made in the case of recipients who are partners or persons with a joint interest in the asset. 'Associated persons' are as listed in A to E of 3.12 (relating to *ICTA 1988, s 779*) above. [*ICTA 1988, s 783(10)*]. Assessments to give effect to the above provisions may be made up to five years after 31 January following the tax year in which the allowable payment was made (for 1995/96 and earlier years, six years after the end of that tax year) or, for corporation tax purposes, six years after the end of the accounting period in which it was made. [*ICTA 1988, s 781(8); FA 1996, s 135, Sch 21 para 21*].

Simon's Direct Tax Service. See **B3.661–B3.665.**

3.15 **LEASES OF ASSETS (OTHER THAN LAND) PREVIOUSLY OWNED FOR TRADE ETC. BY TAXPAYER —**

deductions for lease rentals are limited to commercial rent. [*ICTA 1988, s 782*]

Any payment under a lease, created after 14 April 1964, of any asset (other than land or an interest in land) which at any time prior to the lease was used for the purpose of the lessee's trade (or any other trade carried on by him) and was then owned by the person carrying on the trade in which it was used is limited, in computing profits or losses of the lessee's trade, to the commercial rent of the asset for the period covered by the payment, i.e. a rent representing a reasonable return, by uniform instalments at uniform intervals over the remainder of the asset's anticipated normal working life (as under *ICTA 1988, s 782(6)*), on its market value at the time the lease was created. *ICTA 1988, s 782(3)–(5)* contains similar provisions (disallowed payments carried forward etc.) to *ICTA 1988, s 780(4)–(6)* — see 3.12 above.

Simon's Direct Tax Service. See **B3.664.**

3.16 **LOAN TRANSACTIONS** [*ICTA 1988, s 786*]

Where, with reference to lending money or giving credit (or varying the terms of a loan or credit):

(i) a transaction provides for the payment of an *annuity or other annual payment* — that payment is treated as if it were of annual interest. [*ICTA 1988, s 786(3)*];

(ii) a transaction provides for the sale or transfer of any securities or other income-producing property and for the transferor's subsequent acquisition of, or of an option on, the same or any other property from the transferee — an amount equal to any income from the property transferred arising before repayment of the loan etc. is treated as income of the former owner, assessable under Schedule D, Case VI. This provision is **abolished** where the initial agreement for sale or transfer is made on or after an appointed day (which will be the day appointed for the bringing into effect of *ICTA 1988, s 737A* (see 3.7 above) in relation to overseas securities). [*ICTA 1988, s 786(4); FA 1996, s 159(1)*];

(iii) any person *assigns, surrenders, waives or forgoes* income on property (without a sale or transfer of the property) — that person is assessable under Schedule D, Case VI, on a sum equal to the income assigned, surrendered, waived etc. [*ICTA 1988, s 786(5)*];

(iv) if credit is given for the purchase price of property and during the subsistence of the debt, the purchaser's rights to income from the property are suspended or restricted

— he is treated for the purpose of (iii) above as if he had made a surrender of that income. [*ICTA 1988, s 786(6)*].

Transactions with CONNECTED PERSONS (20) are included.

Simon's Direct Tax Service. See **E1.555.**

3.17 **PERSONS EXEMPT FROM TAX —**

restriction regarding pre-acquisition dividends etc. received on 10% holdings. [*ICTA 1988, ss 235, 236; FA 1993, s 78(6), Sch 6 para 3; FA 1997, s 70; F(No 2)A 1997, Sch 4 para 7*]

An exempt person will not be able to recover a tax credit in respect of any part of a distribution made before 6 April 1999 related to profits (as defined — see *ICTA 1988, s 236 as amended*) arising before acquisition of the shares if the shares held (together with any associated holding) are 10% or more of that class. The income will not then be exempt from tax and will become liable to tax, or, as the case may be, additional tax at the difference between the lower rate and the rate applicable to trusts (see 81.5 SETTLEMENTS) in force when the distribution is made and will not be available for purposes of *ICTA 1988, s 348* and *s 349(1)*, nor may interest paid within *ICTA 1988, s 353* be set against it. These provisions do not apply to certain payments treated as qualifying distributions (see 3.18 below). See *CIR v Sheppard and another (Trustees of the Woodland Trust) (No 2) Ch D 1993, 65 TC 724* for attribution of profits to a distribution where waiver resulted in whole distribution being received although only 60% of shares held.

These provisions are **repealed** for distributions made **on or after 6 April 1999.**

Simon's Direct Tax Service. See **B3.734.**

3.18 **PERSONS EXEMPT FROM TAX —**

restriction regarding certain bonus issues. [ICTA 1988, s 237; FA 1993, Sch 6 para 3; FA 1994, Sch 9 para 2; F(No 2)A 1997, Sch 4 para 7]

Where, before 6 April 1999, 'bonus issues' are treated as a distribution by virtue of *ICTA 1988, s 209(3), s 210,* or *s 211*, a recipient entitled to exemption from tax or the setting-off of losses against income shall have such bonus issue and related tax credit ignored in the repayment or loss calculation and be liable to tax as in 3.17 above on such bonus issue unless it represents a normal return, as defined. Such 'bonus issues' are not available for purposes of *ICTA 1988, s 348* and *s 349(1)*, nor may interest paid and otherwise deductible under *ICTA 1988, s 353* be set against them.

These provisions are **repealed** for distributions made **on or after 6 April 1999.**

Simon's Direct Tax Service. See **B3.735.**

3.19 **ANNUAL PAYMENTS FOR NON-TAXABLE CONSIDERATION** [*ICTA 1988, s 125; FA 1989, s 109(2); FA 1995, Sch 17 para 2, Sch 29 Pt VIII(8)*]

Any payment (whenever the liability to make it was incurred, but subject to exceptions as below) of an annuity or other annual payment charged with tax under SCHEDULE D, CASE III (72), not being interest, and made for a consideration which is *not wholly* included in the income for tax purposes of the person making the annual payment, shall be paid without deduction of tax and not allowed as a deduction from, or a charge on, his income for the purposes of income tax and corporation tax. Certain admission rights in return for annual payments to charities are disregarded for this purpose (see 15.17(*b*) CHARITIES).

Exceptions to the above provisions are any payments (i) which, for 1994/95 and earlier years, are income of the recipient within *ICTA 1988, s 674A(1)(a)(c)* or *s 683(1)(a)(c)* or *(6)* (to a former partner or his dependants under a partnership agreement or under a maintenance agreement or in consideration for the acquisition of a business) or, for 1995/96 onwards, which fall within 81.17(i) or (ii) SETTLEMENTS, or (ii) to an individual for surrendering, assigning or releasing an interest in settled property to a person having a subsequent interest or (iii) of any annuity granted in the ordinary course of a business of granting annuities or (iv) any annuity charged on an interest in settled property and granted before 30 March 1977 by an individual to a company whose business was wholly or mainly in acquiring such interests or which was carrying on life assurance business in the UK. For Scotland, reference to settled property refers to property held in trust. For position prior to these provisions see *CIR v Plummer HL 1979, 54 TC 1*, and *Moodie v CIR and Sinnett HL 1993, 65 TC 610*, in which the decision in *Plummer* on similar facts was reversed on *Ramsay* principles (see 3.1 above).

A payment to which these provisions apply is excluded from the *FA 1988* provisions as to the non-deductibility and exemption from tax of certain annual payments falling due after 14 March 1988 (see 1.8(i) and 1.10(i) ALLOWANCES AND TAX RATES).

Simon's Direct Tax Service. See **E1.503.**

3.20 **DEALING IN COMMODITY FUTURES — withdrawal of loss relief.** [*ICTA 1988, s 399; FA 1997, s 80(4)*]

Where there was a trade of dealing in commodity futures carried on in partnership in which one or more partners was a company and there were arrangements made or scheme effected (whether by the partnership agreement or otherwise) after 5 April 1976 so that the sole or main benefit expected from the partnership was tax relief under *ICTA 1988, s 380* (trading losses set-off against general income of an individual) or *ICTA 1988, s 393(2)* (trading losses set-off against total profits of a company) or *ICTA 1988, s 381* (losses in early years of a trade set-off against general income of an individual in earlier years), such relief will not be given. Where relief has been given, it will be withdrawn by an assessment under Schedule D, Case VI.

ICTA 1988, s 399 does not apply to a loss arising from a transaction to which *ICTA 1988, Sch 5AA* applies (see 3.22 below).

Simon's Direct Tax Service. See **D2.408.**

3.21 **COMPANIES BUYING THEIR OWN SHARES AND OTHER SPECIAL DIVIDENDS** [*FA 1997, s 69, Sch 7; F(No 2)A 1997 ss 24(14), 25, 36(3), Sch 6 para 21, Sch 8 Pt II (8)(9)(11)(12)*]

The special treatment described below applies to qualifying distributions, made after 7 October 1996 and **before 6 April 1999** by UK-resident companies, which fall within either or both of the following.

(*a*) Payments made on the redemption, repayment or purchase by the company of its own shares, or on the purchase of rights to acquire its own shares (see Tolley's Corporation Tax under Purchase by a Company of its Own Shares).

(*b*) Distributions in relation to which there are any kind of arrangements by virtue of which one or more of the 'specified matters' is or was to any extent made in any way referable to, or to the carrying out of, a transaction in securities (within *ICTA 1988, s 703*, see 3.2 above). This does not apply where that transaction was completed before 8 October 1996 unless some or all of the arrangements were made on or after that date. The '*specified matters*' are whether the distribution is made, the time it is made, its form and its amount.

Subject to the exceptions and modifications referred to below, such distributions are treated as foreign income dividends ('FIDs', see 1.9 ALLOWANCES AND TAX RATES and Tolley's

Corporation Tax under Foreign Income Dividends) with effect from 8 October 1996, over-riding the election for such treatment under *ICTA 1988, s 246A*. The dividend certificate must state that the distribution is a FID by virtue of these provisions.

Distributions treated as income of trustees. Where a distribution within (*a*) above is or has been made to trustees (other than trustees of a unit trust scheme within *ICTA 1988, s 469* (see 90.2 UNIT TRUSTS)), or passed on to them through personal representatives, the 'relevant part' (and a corresponding part of the deemed FID) is treated as income within *ICTA 1988, s 686* to which the 34% discretionary trust rate accordingly applies (see 81.5 SETTLEMENTS). This has effect from 1997/98, and is deemed to have had effect for 1996/97, but only for distributions made on or after 5 December 1996. The '*relevant part*' of the distribution is so much (if any) as does not fall to be treated as income of the settlor and is not income either

(i) within *ICTA 1988, s 686(2)(a)* (i.e. income to be accumulated or which is payable at the trustees' or any other person's discretion), or

(ii) arising under a trust established for charitable purposes only, or

(iii) from investments or deposits or other property held for pension purposes (as under *ICTA 1988, s 686(2)(c)*).

There are consequential changes to *section 686* to ensure that income defrayed to meet trust management expenses is taxable only at the basic or lower rate of tax, as appropriate.

See SETTLEMENTS at 81.5 and generally.

Exceptions. The following distributions are excluded from the application of these provisions in the circumstances described.

(1) *Stock options.* A distribution is not within (*b*) above solely because it is made in consequence of an election in respect of a stock dividend option (see 85.1 STOCK DIVIDENDS).

(2) *Fixed rate preference share dividends.* A dividend on a fixed rate preference share (as defined) is not within (*b*) above by reason only that a specified matter is made referable to the issue terms.

(3) *Pre-sale distributions.* An 'excepted pre-sale distribution' is not within (*b*) above if the only transactions in securities to which any of the specified matters are referable are 'relevant transactions'.

A distribution is an '*excepted pre-sale distribution*' if, on or within 14 days of the making of the distribution, there is a '*major change in the ownership*' of the distributing company, i.e. if a single person acquires a holding of, or two or more persons between them acquire holdings together amounting to, 75% or more of its ordinary share capital. A '*relevant transaction*' is any transaction in securities by which any such holding is acquired. In comparing a person's holdings at any two dates, he is to be treated at the later date as having acquired whatever he did not hold at the earlier date, irrespective of intervening acquisitions and disposals. It is beneficial ownership which is considered, and comparisons are made in percentage terms throughout. Acquisitions of shares on death are left out of account, as is any gift which was unsolicited and made without regard to these provisions. Where the existence of extraordinary rights or powers renders ownership of the ordinary share capital an inappropriate test of change of ownership, holdings of all kinds, or of any particular kind, of share capital, voting power or any other special kind of power may be taken into account instead.

(4) *Manufactured dividends.* Payment of an amount consisting of a manufactured dividend (within *ICTA 1988, Sch 23A*, see 3.7 above) is generally excluded from the

operation of these provisions. However, where that amount is representative of a distribution to which these provisions apply, the payment is deemed to be such a distribution, except insofar as *Schedule 23A* makes different provision in relation to the payment. Where the distribution of which that amount is representative is within (*a*) above, the payment is treated for the purposes of *Schedule 23A* as representative of a dividend on the shares concerned in the redemption, etc..

(5) *Dividends within groups of companies.* See Tolley's Corporation Tax under Groups of Companies as regards exclusion from these provisions of certain distributions subject (before 6 April 1999) to a group income election under *ICTA 1988, s 247.*

Dealers in securities. For the special treatment of distributions within these provisions received by dealers in securities before 2 July 1997, see 71.82 SCHEDULE D, CASES I AND II.

Authorised unit trusts. For the treatment of distributions within these provisions in the distribution accounts of authorised unit trusts, see 90.1 UNIT TRUSTS.

For the Revenue's views on the scope of these provisions, with a number of illustrative examples, see Revenue Tax Bulletin June 1997 pp 429–434.

These provisions are repealed for distributions made after 5 April 1999.

Simon's Direct Tax Service. See **D1.110A.**

3.22 **FUTURES AND OPTIONS —**

transactions with guaranteed returns. [ICTA 1988, s 127A, Sch 5AA; FA 1997, s 80, Sch 11; FA 1998, s 99]

The special provisions described below apply to a 'disposal of futures or options' if it is one of two or more 'related' transactions, and it is reasonable to assume that a main purpose of the transactions, taken together, is or was to produce a 'guaranteed return', either from the disposal itself or together with another such disposal or disposals. The likely effect of the transactions, and/or the circumstances in which they, or any of them, is or are entered into, are taken into account for this purpose.

A disposal is a *'disposal of futures or options'* if it consists in a disposal of one or more 'futures' or 'options' or of any combination thereof. A *'future'* is any outstanding rights and obligations under a commodity or financial futures contract, and an *'option'* is one listed on a recognised stock or futures exchange or otherwise relating to currency, shares, stock, securities, an interest rate or rights under a commodity or financial futures contract. The existence or timing of a disposal is determined in accordance with *TCGA 1992, ss 143(5)(6), 144, 144A* (see Tolley's Capital Gains Tax under Disposal) and other relevant provisions of that *Act*, modified as necessary for this purpose, on the assumption that all futures are assets. However, a disposal consisting in the grant of an option, which precedes at least one 'related' transaction which is a disposal other than the grant of an option, is deemed for these purposes to be made at the time of (or of the first) such subsequent disposal (except insofar as the provisions of *TCGA 1992* referred to above require the grant of an option and the transaction entered into to fulfil obligations under the option to be treated as a single transaction, and determine the time at which that single transaction is treated as entered into).

Transactions are *'related'* for these purposes if they are entered into in pursuance of a scheme or arrangements (including understandings of any kind, whether or not legally enforceable). This may include transactions with different parties, or with parties different from the parties to the scheme or arrangements. It also includes any case in which it would be reasonable to assume, from the likely effect of the transactions and/or the circumstances in which they, or any of them, is or are entered into, that neither or none of them would have been entered into independently of the other(s).

A '*guaranteed return*' is produced wherever risks from fluctuations in the subject matter to which the futures or options (or their value) are referable are so eliminated or reduced as to produce a return equating, in substance, to interest and not significantly attributable (otherwise than incidentally) to any such fluctuations. This includes any case where a main reason for the choice of subject matter is that it appears that there is no (or only an insignificant) risk that it will fluctuate. The return from one or more disposals is for these purposes that represented by the total net profits or gains (or all but an insignificant part of those profits or gains), aggregating where appropriate profits or gains of persons who are 'associated' (as specially defined) in relation to the disposals.

Profits or gains realised **after 4 March 1997** from a transaction to which these provisions apply (whether capital or not) are treated as income of the person by whom they are realised, chargeable under SCHEDULE D, CASE VI (74) for the chargeable period in which the disposal takes place. There are exclusions for profits or gains within the financial instruments provisions of *FA 1994, Pt IV, Ch II* (see Tolley's Corporation Tax under Financial Instruments) or arising to an authorised unit trust within *ICTA 1988, s 468* (see 90.1 UNIT TRUSTS), and for so much of any profits or gains as is chargeable under Case I or Case V of Schedule D on the person to whom they arise. A loss sustained after 4 March 1997 is similarly a Case VI loss within *ICTA 1988, s 392* or *s 396* for the chargeable period of the disposal. The profits or gains (or losses) are not otherwise brought into account for tax purposes (other than as receipts for a Case I computation for life insurance companies under *FA 1989, s 83*, see Tolley's Corporation Tax under Life Insurance Companies).

With effect for transactions taking place on or after 6 February 1998, the charge is extended to cases where there are related transactions one of which is or would be the creation or acquisition of a future or option, and another of which is or would be the running of the future to delivery or the exercise of the option, and the latter transaction is not treated under the current provisions as a disposal of a future or option. (Transactions are related for this purpose if they would be but for *TCGA 1992, s 144(2)* or *(3)*, which in certain cases treat the grant or exercise of an option and the transaction in fulfilment of the obligations under the option as a single transaction, see Tolley's Capital Gains Tax under Disposal.) The current provisions then apply to the parties to the future or option as if there was a disposal of the future or option under the arrangements for the related transactions immediately before the future runs to delivery or, as the case may be, the option is exercised. The disposal is treated, in the case of a person whose rights and entitlements under the future or option have a market value at that time, as at that value, or in the case of any other person as made for nil consideration with costs equivalent to those required at arm's length to obtain release of his obligations and liabilities under the future or option. There are special provisions preventing double charge or relief under the current provisions and capital gains tax (or corporation tax on chargeable gains), for which see *ICTA 1988, Sch 5AA para 4A(5)–(10)*.

Trusts. Where profits or gains are treated as income arising to trustees under these provisions, *ICTA 1988, s 686* (rate applicable to trusts, see 81.5 SETTLEMENTS) applies to so much of that income as is not treated as income of the settlor. The exclusion of income within *section 686(2)(c)* (income arising under charitable trusts or from property held for certain retirement benefit or personal pension schemes) applies equally for this purpose.

Transfer of assets abroad. Any profit or gain realised by a person resident or domiciled outside the UK from a transaction within these provisions is treated as income becoming payable to that person under *ICTA 1988, ss 739, 740* (see 3.8 above) in determining whether a UK ordinarily resident individual has an income tax liability in respect of the profit or gain.

Insurance companies. For the purposes of *ICTA 1988, s 432A* (see Tolley's Corporation Tax under Life Insurance Companies), income and losses under these provisions are generally treated as gains or losses accruing on the disposal of an asset.

Simon's Direct Tax Service. See **B7.204**.

3.23 **ARRANGEMENTS TO PASS ON VALUE OF TAX CREDIT** [*F(No 2)A 1997, s 28*]

Special provisions apply where:

(*a*) a person ('A') is entitled to a tax credit in respect of a qualifying distribution made after 1 July 1997;

(*b*) arrangements (as widely defined) subsist such that another person ('B') obtains, whether directly or indirectly, a payment representing any of the value of the tax credit;

(*c*) the arrangements (whether or not made directly between A and B) were entered into for an 'unallowable purpose'; and

(*d*) had B been entitled to and received the distribution when it was made, he would not have been entitled to payment of the tax credit and, if a company, could not have used the income consisting of the distribution to frank a distribution made in the same accounting period (after using any actual franked investment income).

They apply equally where an amount representing any of the value of the tax credit is applied at the direction of, or otherwise in favour of, some other person, as if that other person had obtained a payment representing that value.

Where these provisions apply:

(i) no claim may be made for payment of the tax credit or for set-off against tax on other income;

(ii) the income consisting of the distribution is not regarded as franked investment income; and

(iii) no transitional charity relief payment (see 15.6 CHARITIES) may be claimed.

This does not, however, apply to the extent that the tax advantage otherwise obtained under the arrangements is cancelled or reduced by any other provision. 'Tax advantage' for this purpose is as under *ICTA 1988, s 709* (see 3.2 ANTI-AVOIDANCE), but also includes the obtaining of a payment representing any of the value of a tax credit where, had the person obtaining the payment been entitled to and received the distribution when it was made, he would not have been entitled to payment of the tax credit and, if a company, could not have used the income consisting of the distribution to frank a distribution made in the same accounting period (after using any actual franked investment income).

Arrangements are entered into for an '*unallowable purpose*' if any person is a party to the arrangements for purposes which include a purpose other than a business or commercial purpose (which includes the efficient management of investments). The purpose of obtaining a tax advantage for any person is not a business or commercial purpose unless it is not a main purpose of entering into the arrangements.

Simon's Direct Tax Service. See **D1.101A**.

4 Appeals

(See also Revenue Pamphlet IR 37.)

Cross-references. See 6.8 BACK DUTY for investigatory powers of Revenue; 17.9 CLAIMS for appeals in respect of claims; 52.7 OFFSHORE FUNDS; 56.2 PAYMENT OF TAX for payment of tax pending appeal; 58.5, 58.6 and 58.7 PENALTIES for appeals relating to penalties and 64.8 RESIDENCE, ORDINARY RESIDENCE AND DOMICILE. See also 78 SELF-ASSESSMENT.

Simon's Direct Tax Service. See A3.5, A3.7.

4.1 RIGHT OF APPEAL

The majority of appeals are against assessments, the right of appeal being conferred by *TMA 1970, s 31* but, with unimportant exceptions, the taxpayer may appeal against any formal decision by an inspector or the Board. In particular a decision on CLAIMS (17) may be appealed [*TMA 1970, s 42*] as may coding under PAY AS YOU EARN (55). [*SI 1993 No 774, reg 11*]. Further, certain matters are dealt with as appeals, e.g. disputes as to the transfer price of trading stock on a discontinuance (see 71.83 SCHEDULE D, CASES I AND II).

Unless otherwise stated or required by the context, the following paragraphs apply to all appeals and matters treated as appeals, and not only to appeals against assessments.

An appeal once made cannot be withdrawn (*R v Special Commrs (ex p Elmhirst) CA 1935, 20 TC 381*) but see 4.4 below for the withdrawal of appeals by agreement and 4.7 below regarding appeals to the High Court.

As regards 1996/97 and subsequent years, see also 78.31 SELF-ASSESSMENT.

4.2 TIME LIMIT FOR APPEALS ETC.

An appeal *against an assessment* must be made within 30 days of the date of issue of the notice of assessment and state the grounds of appeal, but grounds not stated may be advanced at any hearing of the appeal if the Commissioners allow. [*TMA 1970, s 31(1), (5); F(No 2)A 1975, s 67(1)*]. An appeal against a decision on a claim must be made within 30 days of receipt of written notice of the decision except for certain overseas matters (see 64.8 RESIDENCE, ORDINARY RESIDENCE AND DOMICILE). There is no time limit for appeals against PAYE codings.

A **late appeal** may be accepted by the inspector if there is reasonable excuse for the delay and if he does not accept it he must refer the application to the Commissioners for their decision. [*TMA 1970, s 49*]. If they refuse, their decision is not subject to appeal by way of stated case (*R v Special Commrs (ex p Magill) QB (NI) 1979, 53 TC 135*), but is subject to judicial review (see *R v Hastings and Bexhill General Commrs and CIR (ex p Goodacre) QB 1994, 67 TC 126*, in which a refusal was quashed and the matter remitted to a different body of Commissioners).

As regards 1996/97 and subsequent years, see also 78.31 SELF-ASSESSMENT.

4.3 JURISDICTION OF COMMISSIONERS

As regards 1996/97 and subsequent years, see also 78.33 SELF-ASSESSMENT.

An appeal is made to the General or Special Commissioners. Notice of the appeal is given in writing to the appropriate inspector or officer of the Board. If not settled by agreement (4.4 below) it is heard by the Commissioners. Appeals relating to most personal allowances and certain other reliefs are heard only by the General Commissioners. [*TMA 1970, s 42, Sch 2*]. Appeals against assessments made by the Board and assessments made under *ICTA*

1988, s 350 (see 23.3 DEDUCTION OF TAX AT SOURCE), against any decision of the Board and relating to double taxation relief by agreement and a number of technical matters, mainly overseas matters or regarding financial bodies, are heard only by the Special Commissioners. [*TMA 1970, s 31(3) as amended, s 42, Sch 2*]. Subject to this, the appeal is to the General Commissioners, unless the taxpayer elects for the Special Commissioners, either when the appeal is made or separately but within the time limit for making the appeal. Such an election is, however, disregarded if the appellant and the inspector so agree in writing before the appeal is determined, or if before the appeal is determined the inspector refers the election to the General Commissioners (after notifying the appellant) and they so direct. They must give such a direction unless satisfied that the appellant has arguments to present or evidence to adduce on the merits of the appeal. Such a direction may be revoked at any time before determination of the appeal if that condition is subsequently satisfied. The decision to give or revoke a direction is final. [*TMA 1970, s 31(5A)–(5E), s 46(1), Sch 2 paras 1A–1E; FA 1984, s 127, Sch 22 para 3; SI 1984 No 1836*]. In deciding when to list an appeal for hearing, inspectors treat appeals to the Special Commissioners in exactly the same way as those to the General Commissioners. The taxpayer's agreement (or, failing that, the General Commissioners' direction) that an election for hearing by the Special Commissioners be disregarded will only be sought when a decision is needed to arrange the listing of the appeal for hearing, and then only where the inspector is satisfied that it is a delay appeal and not a contentious one. (Revenue Press Release 26 February 1990).

Appeals to the General Commissioners may, if the parties so apply and the Commissioners consent, be transferred to the Special Commissioners (and vice versa) despite the expiry of the time limit for election as above or the making of such an election. [*TMA 1970, s 44(3)*]. In addition, the General Commissioners may arrange that an appeal brought before them be transferred to the Special Commissioners, with the Special Commissioners' consent, if, after considering any representations made to them by the parties to the appeal, the General Commissioners consider that, because of the complexity of, or likely time required to hear, the appeal, it should be so transferred. [*TMA 1970, s 44(3A); FA 1984, s 127, Sch 22 para 5; SI 1984 No 1836*].

Where an appeal against an assessment to tax on chargeable gains is on a question of the value of any land, or of a lease of land, then the question is determined on a reference to the Lands Tribunal. [*TMA 1970, s 47*].

Where the General Commissioners have jurisdiction, rules for prescribing the appropriate Division are in *TMA 1970, Sch 3* as amended, although the parties may come to an agreement that the proceedings be brought before any body of General Commissioners specified in the agreement. [*TMA 1970, s 44(1)(2); FA 1988, s 133(2)*]. The Board may, however, direct that specified proceedings be brought before the General Commissioners for a specified division, provided that the inspector notifies the other party of the effect of that direction, unless

(i) the other party objects to the direction within 30 days of the service of the inspector's notice, or, in the case of an appeal, has elected for a hearing in the place where he ordinarily resides (see below), or

(ii) the proceedings are subject to the special rules applicable where more than one taxpayer may be a party to the proceedings.

Any such direction may be superseded by an agreement between the parties (as above). [*TMA 1970, s 44(1A)(1B); FA 1988, s 133(1)(3)*]. A list has been published of the division of General Commissioners with which the Board will, under these provisions, generally seek to link those tax offices dealing with substantial groups of companies and trusts. (Revenue Press Release 19 December 1988).

For appeals against *assessments* the broad effect of *TMA 1970, Sch 3* is to designate the Division in which the appellant's trade etc. is carried on. If he has no trade etc., an employee may elect for the Division in which he ordinarily resides (or, in practice, any other Division he nominates), otherwise it is the Division in which he is employed (or, at the inspector's election, the Division in which the assessment was made). The election for Division of residence etc. must strictly be made by written notice not later than the notice of appeal, but the Revenue will in practice accede to a request by an employee subsequent to the appeal being made but before it is set down for hearing (and notwithstanding an election by the inspector as above) for the hearing to be in the Division in which he resides or in any other Division the employee nominates. See Revenue Tax Bulletin May 1993 p 70 and February 1997 p 387. If the taxpayer has no trade etc. or employment, the Division of residence applies, which also applies to appeals relating to personal allowances irrespective of the place of any trade etc. or employment. Corporation tax appeals are heard in the Division in which the company carries on its trade or where its head office is situated. These rules are, however, directory and not mandatory (*CIR v Adams CA 1971, 48 TC 67; Murphy v Elders Ch D 1973, 49 TC 135*) and a decision of the Commissioners cannot be invalidated for want of jurisdiction if there was no objection to jurisdiction before the decision. [*TMA 1970, s 44(4)*]. See also *R v Kingston & Elmbridge Commrs QB 1972, 48 TC 75; R v St Pancras Commrs QB 1973, 50 TC 365; Parikh v Birmingham North Commrs CA, [1976] STC 365.*

The Special Commissioners go on circuit to the chief provincial towns, but appeals to them may generally by arrangement be heard in London, which is usually more convenient if it is intended to engage counsel.

The Lord Chancellor has powers, by regulation, to provide for the transfer of appeals between the General and Special Commissioners or between General Commissioners for different divisions, and for varying the number of General or Special Commissioners required or permitted to hear appeals. Different provision may be made for different cases and different circumstances. [*TMA 1970, s 46A; F(No 2)A 1992, Sch 16 para 3*]. See now *SI 1994 Nos 1811–1813* and 4.6 below.

4.4 SETTLEMENT OF APPEALS BY AGREEMENT

Where agreement, written or otherwise, has been reached at any time between the Revenue and the appellant or agent on his behalf on any appeal to General or Special Commissioners, against any assessment or decision under appeal, the assessment or decision as upheld, varied, discharged or cancelled by that agreement, is treated as if it had been determined on appeal, provided that (*a*) taxpayer may withdraw from the agreement by giving written notice within 30 days of making it, (*b*) verbal agreements reached are of no effect unless confirmed in writing by either side (the date of such confirmation then being the effective date of 'determination'). [*TMA 1970, s 54*]. The agreement must specify the figure for assessment or a precise formula for ascertaining it (*Delbourgo v Field CA 1978, 52 TC 225*). The inspector has no power unilaterally to 'vacate' an assessment (*Baylis v Gregory CA, [1987] STC 297*). An agreement as to partial set-off of a loss in a year of assessment does not bind the parties as to the amount of the loss carried forward and available in subsequent years (*Tod v South Essex Motors (Basildon) Ltd Ch D 1987, 60 TC 598*). For the extent to which further assessments or error or mistake relief claims are permissible if an appeal has been determined by agreement, see 5.3 ASSESSMENTS.

The issue of an amended notice of assessment by the inspector does not of itself constitute an agreement under *TMA 1970, s 54* (*Schuldenfrei v Hilton CA, [1999] STC 821*). For the general requirements for an agreement, see *Cash & Carry v Inspector (Sp C 148), [1998] SSCD 46.*

An agreement under *TMA 1970, s 54* does not prevent an assessment being revised to correct an error, where the effect of the error was that the common intention of the parties was not recorded by the agreement (*R v HMIT ex p Bass Holdings Ltd QB 1992, 65 TC*

495). An agreement based on a mutual mistake of fact was thereby vitiated, so that the taxpayer could proceed with his appeal (*Fox v Rothwell (Sp C 50), [1995] SSCD 336*).

A taxpayer cannot withdraw an appeal made to Commissioners (see 4.1 above) but if, having appealed, he, or his agent acting in that appeal, gives the inspector oral or written notice of his desire not to proceed, then, unless the inspector gives written notice of objection within 30 days thereof, the appeal is treated as if settled by agreement, as above, at the date of the taxpayer's notification. [*TMA 1970, s 54(4)*].

4.5 THE HANDLING OF TAXPAYERS' APPEALS

Appeal meetings must be notified to the appellant and the inspector (or other Revenue party) (see 4.6 below). In practice the inspector normally gives details of appeals ready for hearing to the clerk who, after consulting the inspector and, in important appeals, the taxpayer or his agent as appropriate, makes the necessary arrangements, notifies the inspector and issues notices of the hearing to the appellant. In some Divisions he may, by arrangement, also notify the appellant's agent.

4.6 APPEALS HEARD BY COMMISSIONERS

The Lord Chancellor has wide regulatory powers in relation to the practice and procedure to be followed in connection with appeals, including the power to make different provision for different cases and different circumstances. [*TMA 1970, ss 56B–56D; F(No 2)A 1992, Sch 16 para 4; FA 1994, s 254*]. With effect from 1 September 1994, regulations are brought in governing the jurisdiction of the General Commissioners and the procedure for proceedings before them. [*SI 1994 No 1812*]. Similar regulations apply in relation to the Special Commissioners [*SI 1994 No 1811*], and *SI 1994 No 1813* makes consequential and complementary amendments to other enactments.

In relation to the General Commissioners, these regulations do not apply to any proceedings set down (or first set down) for hearing by notice given before 1 September 1994 if any party to those proceedings so elects (by notice to the Clerk to the Commissioners) prior to commencement of the hearing (or to the recommencement of adjourned proceedings which were commenced before 1 September 1994). They also do not apply to any proceedings under *TMA 1970, s 100C* (see 58.6 PENALTIES) in respect of which a summons was issued prior to 1 September 1994 to the defendant to appear before them at a time and place stated in the summons. Where these regulations *do* apply to proceedings set down (or first set down) for hearing by notice given before 1 September 1994, anything done in relation to those proceedings before that date which, if the proceedings had commenced on or after that date, could have been done pursuant to these regulations, is to have effect as if done pursuant to these regulations. [*SI 1994 No 1812, reg 1*].

In relation to the Special Commissioners, these regulations do not apply to any proceedings set down for hearing by notice given before 1 September 1994, or in respect of which a summons was issued before that date. [*SI 1994 No 1811, reg 1*].

Where these regulations do not apply, the jurisdictional and procedural rules were broadly similar, the most significant difference being the absence of the powers of the Special Commissioners to hear cases in public, to publish their decisions and to award costs in certain cases. For details of the earlier rules, see Tolley's Income Tax 1994/95 or earlier edition.

The remainder of this section deals with the rules applicable from 1 September 1994, and with the general and case law which is of continuing application.

(*a*) **General Commissioners.**

Constitution of Tribunal. Two or more, but not more than five, General Commissioners for a division may hear any proceedings. [*SI 1994 No 1812, reg 2*]. They will themselves decide which one of them will preside at the hearing. Where possible at least three will sit, and, with the consent of all the parties, proceedings may be continued by one or more of them. [*SI 1994 No 1812, reg 11*]. For the effect of personal business connection between a Commissioner and a party to proceedings, see *R v Holyhead Commrs (ex p Roberts) QB 1982, 56 TC 127.*

The Clerk to the Commissioners, who is frequently a local solicitor, normally attends the meeting to take minutes and to advise them as required, but a meeting without a Clerk would not be invalid (*Venn v Franks CA 1958, 38 TC 175*).

Preparation for hearing. *Listing and notice of hearing.* Except in relation to proceedings under *TMA 1970, s 100C* (see 58.6 PENALTIES), any party to the proceedings may serve notice on the Clerk to the Commissioners that he wishes a date for the hearing to be fixed, on receipt of which the Clerk must send notice to each party of the place, date and time of the hearing. Unless the parties otherwise agree, or the Commissioners otherwise direct, the date must not be earlier than 28 days after the date of the Clerk's notice. [*SI 1994 No 1812, reg 3*].

Witnesses. A General Commissioner, on the application of any party to the proceedings, may issue a witness summons (in Scotland, a witness citation) requiring any person in the UK either to attend the hearing of those proceedings to give evidence or to produce any relevant document in his possession, custody or power. The party applying for issue of the summons is responsible for its service (for which see *reg 4(3)*), and attendance may not be required within seven days of service unless the witness informs the Clerk that he accepts shorter notice. That party must also agree to meet the witness' reasonable travelling expenses. The witness may apply, by notice served on the Clerk, for the Commissioners to set aside the summons (in whole or part), on which application the party on whose application the summons was issued is entitled to be heard.

Except in Scotland, a witness so summoned to give evidence may only be cross-examined by the party on whose application the summons was issued if the Commissioners decide that the witness is a hostile witness and give leave.

A witness cannot be compelled to give evidence or produce documents which he could not be compelled to give or produce in an action in a court of law. An auditor or tax adviser (within *TMA 1970, s 20B(10)*) cannot be compelled to produce any document which he would not be obliged to deliver or make available by notice under *TMA 1970, s 20(3)* or *(8A)* (having regard to *TMA 1970, s 20B(9)–(13)*), and copies of, or of parts of, documents may similarly be produced in certain cases (see 6.8 BACK DUTY).

In the event of failure by a witness to attend in obedience to the summons, or refusal to be sworn or to affirm, or refusal to answer any lawful question or to produce a document he is required to produce by the summons, the Commissioners may summarily determine a penalty not exceeding £1,000, to be treated as tax charged by an assessment and due and payable.

[*SI 1994 No 1812, reg 4*].

Joint hearings. The Commissioners have powers to direct that two or more proceedings, in one or more divisions, with common issues be heard at the same time or consecutively within one division, either of their own motion or on an application by any of the parties to any of those proceedings. All the parties must be notified, and are entitled to be heard before such a direction is given. On the giving of a direction, the Clerk must send notice of its date and terms to all parties. [*SI 1994 No 1812, reg 6*]. The Commissioners have an inherent power to deal with two or more appeals simultaneously where the appellants' affairs are so intermingled as to be incapable of separation, and where they are satisfied that it would result in no injustice to either party (*Johnson v Walden; King v Walden CA 1996, 68 TC 387*).

Postponements and adjournments. The Commissioners may postpone or adjourn the hearing of any proceedings, the Clerk being responsible for notifying all parties of the place, date and time of the postponed or adjourned hearing (unless announced before an adjournment in the presence of all parties). Where a hearing is adjourned for the obtaining of further information or evidence, the Commissioners may direct the parties regarding the disclosure of such information or evidence prior to resumption. [*SI 1994 No 1812, reg 8*]. In *Packe v Johnson Ch D 1991, 63 TC 507*, a determination was quashed because of the Commissioners' refusal to consider all relevant information in deciding to refuse an adjournment at a second hearing.

Other matters in preparation for hearing. There are also regulations dealing with the agreement of documents [*SI 1994 No 1812, reg 5*], the joinder of additional parties to the proceedings [*SI 1994 No 1812, reg 7*] and the admission of expert evidence [*SI 1994 No 1812, reg 9*].

Hearing and determination of proceedings. Hearings are in private, except that certain persons with official responsibilities may be present, and may remain present during, but not take part in, the Commissioners' deliberations. With the consent of the parties, the Commissioners may permit any other person to attend the hearing. [*SI 1994 No 1812, reg 13*].

Power to obtain information. The Commissioners may, at any time before final determination of the proceedings, serve on any party to the proceedings (other than the Revenue) notice requiring that party, within a specified time,

(i) to deliver such particulars as may be required to determine any issue of the proceedings, and

(ii) to make available for inspection by the Commissioners or by an officer of the Board such specified or described books, accounts, etc. in his possession or power as may, in their opinion, contain information relevant to the proceedings.

For unsuccessful challenges relating to the issue of notices under these and the similar powers previously contained in *TMA 1970, s 51*, see *Johnson v Blackpool General Commrs and CIR CA 1997, 70 TC 1*, *Eke v Knight CA 1977, 51 TC 121* and *Khan v Newport General Commrs and CIR Ch D 1994, 70 TC 239.*

The Commissioners may summarily determine a penalty (to be treated as tax charged in an assessment and due and payable) of up to £300 for failure to comply with such a notice, plus up to £60 per day for continuing failure after such a penalty is determined. Any officer of the Board (and the Commissioners in the case of (ii)) may, at all reasonable times, take copies of, or extracts from, any such particulars, books, etc.. [*SI 1994 No 1812, reg 10*].

Representation at hearing. A party to the proceedings may be represented by any person, except that the Commissioners may, if satisfied that there are good and sufficient reasons for doing so, refuse to permit a party to be represented by a particular person, not being a legally qualified person or a member of an incorporated society of accountants. In practice, most bodies of Commissioners permit the taxpayer to be represented by any person who they are satisfied is competent to present the appellant's case. The Revenue may be represented by a barrister, advocate, solicitor or any officer of the Board. [*SI 1994 No 1812, reg 12*].

The Revenue representative is normally an inspector. The secretary or 'other proper officer' represents a company (the liquidator if in liquidation). [*TMA 1970, s 108*].

Failure to attend hearing. Where a party fails to attend or be represented at a hearing of which he has been duly notified, the Commissioners may postpone or adjourn a hearing or (unless satisfied that there is good and sufficient reason for such failure, and after considering any written or other representations) hear and determine the proceedings. [*SI 1994 No 1812, reg 14*]. Determinations in the absence of the taxpayer or his agent have been upheld where notice of the meeting was received by the appellant (*R v Tavistock Commrs (ex p Adams) QB 1969, 46 TC 154; R v Special Commr (ex p Moschi) CA, [1981] STC 465* and see *Fletcher & Fletcher v Harvey CA 1990, 63 TC 539*), but Commissioners were held to have acted unreasonably in refusing to re-open proceedings when taxpayer's agent was temporarily absent when the appeal was called (*R & D McKerron Ltd v CIR CS 1979, 52 TC 28*). Where the taxpayer was absent through illness, a determination was quashed because the Commissioners, in refusing an adjournment, had failed to consider whether injustice would thereby arise to the taxpayer (*R v Sevenoaks Commrs (ex p Thorne) QB 1989, 62 TC 341* and see *Rose v Humbles CA 1971, 48 TC 103*). See also *R v O'Brien (ex p Lissner) QB, 1984 STI 710* where the determination was quashed then the appellant had been informed by the inspector that the hearing was to be adjourned.

Procedure and evidence at hearing. The Commissioners have wide discretion as to the manner in which the proceedings are conducted, and should seek to avoid inappropriate formality. They may require any witness to give evidence on oath or affirmation, and may admit evidence which would be inadmissible in a court of law (and see *Taylor v Cox (Sp C 163), [1998] SSCD 179* for the acceptance of computer-generated documents in evidence). Evidence may be given orally or, if they so direct, by affidavit or statement recorded in a document (and they may, on their own motion or on the application of any party, at any stage require the personal attendance as a witness of the maker of such a statement or affidavit or the person who recorded the statement). They may take account of the nature and source of any evidence, and the manner in which it is given, in assessing its truth and weight. The parties may be heard in any order, but are entitled to give evidence, to call witnesses, to question witnesses (including other parties who give evidence), and to address the Commissioners both on the evidence and on the subject matter of the proceedings. [*SI 1994 No 1812, reg 15*]. A party to the proceedings cannot insist on being examined on oath (*R v Special Commrs (in re Fletcher) CA 1894, 3 TC 289*). False evidence under oath would be perjury under criminal law (*R v Hood Barrs CA [1943] 1 AER 665*). A taxpayer was held to be bound by an affidavit he had made in other proceedings (*Wicker v Fraser Ch D 1982, 55 TC 641*). A remission to Commissioners to hear evidence directed at the credit of a witness was refused in *Potts v CIR Ch D 1982, 56 TC 25*. Rules of the Supreme Court under which evidence can be obtained from a witness abroad cannot be used in proceedings before the Commissioners (*In re Leiserach CA 1963, 42 TC 1*). As to hearsay evidence under *Civil Evidence Act 1968*, see *Forth Investments Ltd Ch D 1976, 50 TC 617* and *Khan v Edwards Ch D 1977, 53 TC 597*.

The inspector is entitled to ask the Commissioners to exercise their powers to increase an assessment, and to adduce evidence in support of his application (*Glaxo Group Ltd and others v CIR CA 1996, 68 TC 166*).

The Commissioners are under no obligation to adjourn an appeal for the production of further evidence (*Hamilton v CIR CS 1930, 16 TC 28; Noble v Wilkinson Ch D*

1958, 38 TC 135), and were held not to have erred in law in determining assessments in the absence abroad of the taxpayer (*Hawkins v Fuller Ch D 1982, 56 TC 49*).

The taxpayer has no general right to conduct his appeal in writing without attending the hearing (*Banin v Mackinlay CA 1984, 58 TC 398*), although written pleadings may, at the Commissioners' discretion, be taken into account (*Caldicott v Varty Ch D 1976, 51 TC 403*).

In reaching their decision, the Commissioners may not take into account matters appropriate for application for judicial review (*Aspin v Estill CA 1987, 60 TC 549*). They do not generally have the power to review on appeal the exercise of a discretion conferred on the Revenue by statute (see *Slater v Richardson & Bottoms Ltd Ch D 1979, 53 TC 155; Kelsall v Investment Chartwork Ltd Ch D 1993, 65 TC 750*) (although in certain cases such power of review is itself statutory; see e.g. *SI 1993 No 743, reg 10(4)*, which in effect reversed the decision in *Richardson & Bottoms Ltd* above).

For the extent to which Commissioners may use their local knowledge, see *Forest Side Properties (Chingford) Ltd v Pearce CA 1961, 39 TC 665.*

Onus of proof. The onus is on the appellant to displace an assessment (but see 6.2 BACK DUTY for onus on Crown to prove fraud or wilful default to support extended time limit assessments). See *Brady v Group Lotus Car Companies plc CA 1987, 60 TC 359* where onus of proof remained with taxpayer where amount of normal time limit assessment indicated contention of fraud. The general principle emerges in appeals against estimated assessments in 'delay cases' (see 4.5 above) which are the bulk of appeals heard by the General Commissioners. For examples of cases in which the Commissioners have confirmed estimated assessments in the absence of evidence that they were excessive, see *T Haythornthwaite & Sons Ltd v Kelly CA 1927, 11 TC 657; Stoneleigh Products Ltd v Dodd CA 1948, 30 TC 1; Rosette Franks (King St) Ltd v Dick Ch D 1955, 36 TC 100; Pierson v Belcher Ch D 1959, 38 TC 387.* In a number of cases, the Courts have supported the Commissioners' action in rejecting unsatisfactory accounts (e.g. *Cain v Schofield Ch D 1953, 34 TC 362; Moll v CIR CS 1955, 36 TC 384; Cutmore v Leach Ch D 1981, 55 TC 602; Coy v Kime Ch D 1986, 59 TC 447*) or calling for certified accounts (e.g. *Stephenson v Waller KB 1927, 13 TC 318; Hunt & Co v Joly KB 1928, 14 TC 165; Wall v Cooper CA 1929, 14 TC 552*). In *Anderson v CIR CS 1933, 18 TC 320*, the case was remitted where there was no evidence to support the figure arrived at by the Commissioners (which was between the accounts figure and the estimated figure assessed), but contrast *Bookey v Edwards Ch D 1981, 55 TC 486*. The Commissioners are entitled to look at each year separately, accepting the appellant's figures for some years but not all (*Donnelly v Platten CA (NI) 1980, [1981] STC 504*). Similarly, the onus is on the taxpayer to substantiate his claims to relief (see *Eke v Knight CA 1977, 51 TC 121; Talib v Waterson Ch D, [1980] STC 563*).

For the standard of proof required in evidence, see *Les Croupiers Casino Club v Pattinson CA 1987, 60 TC 196.*

The Commissioners' decision. The Revenue representative must not be present while the Commissioners are deliberating their decision unless the other party or parties (or their representative(s)) are also present (*R v Brixton Commrs KB 1912, 6 TC 195*). The Commissioners' determination was quashed where the Clerk had discussed the case with Revenue representatives between hearing and announcement of determination (*R v Wokingham Commrs (ex p Heron) QB, 1984 STI 710*).

If it appears to the Commissioners that the appellant has been over- or under-charged by any assessment under appeal, they must reduce or increase that assessment accordingly, but otherwise the assessment stands good. A determination of income assessable determines the appeal; if the Commissioners alter the assessment, they are not obliged to determine the revised tax payable. [*TMA 1970, s 50(6)–(8); SI 1994 No 1813*]. Only the assessment by which the taxpayer was overcharged may be reduced under *TMA 1970, s 50(6)*. Any decision is by a majority of the Commissioners hearing the proceedings, with the presiding Commissioner having a casting vote where necessary. The final determination may be announced orally at the end of the hearing or may be reserved. In either case, the Clerk to the Commissioners must send to each party a notice (including in most cases details of the procedure for appeals from the General Commissioners) setting out the determination, and unless the determination was given at the hearing, the date of such notice is the date of the determination. [*SI 1994 No 1812, reg 16; SI 1999 No 3293, reg 3*]. Where the Clerk announced the decision wrongly, it was held that the correct decision stood good (*R v Morleston & Litchurch Commrs KB 1951, 32 TC 335*) (and see below under *Miscellaneous: Irregularities*).

Where Commissioners determined appeals in principle and held a further hearing to adjust assessments, their action in refusing to admit further evidence for the taxpayer at the later hearing was upheld (*R v St Marylebone Commrs (ex p Hay) CA 1983, 57 TC 59*). They are entitled, however, to alter their decision in principle at a later hearing (*Larner v Warrington Ch D 1985, 58 TC 557*). See also *Gibson v Stroud Commrs Ch D 1989, 61 TC 645*.

A decision of the Commissioners is not legally binding on them or any other Commissioners in any other proceedings, even on appeal by the same taxpayer against a similar assessment for another year (*CIR v Sneath CA 1932, 17 TC 149* and cf. *Edwards v 'Old Bushmills' Distillery HL 1926, 10 TC 285; Abdul Caffoor Trustees PC 1961, 40 ATC 93*).

Review of the Commissioners' final determination. A decision of the Commissioners is generally final and conclusive [*TMA 1970, s 46(2)*], but the Commissioners may review and set aside or vary their final determination on the application of any party or of their own motion where they are satisfied that either

(1) it was wrongly made as a result of administrative error, or

(2) a party entitled to be heard failed to appear or be represented for good and sufficient reason, or

(3) relevant information had been supplied to the Clerk or to the appropriate inspector or other Revenue officer prior to the hearing but was not received by the Commissioners until after the hearing.

A written application for such a review must be made to the Commissioners not later than 14 days after the date of the notice of the determination (or by such later time as the Commissioners may allow), stating the grounds in full. Where the Commissioners propose of their own motion to review a determination, they must serve notice on the parties not later than 14 days after the date of the notice of the determination.

The parties are entitled to be heard on any such review or proposed review. If practicable, the review is to be determined by the Commissioners who decided the case, and if they set aside the determination, they may substitute a different determination or order a rehearing before the same or different Commissioners. A decision to vary or substitute a final determination is to be notified in the same way as the original determination (see above).

[*SI 1994 No 1812, reg 17*].

See 4.8 below as regards application for judicial review where the Commissioners have acted unfairly or improperly.

Special procedure. *Proceedings relating to tax on chargeable gains.* Where material, the market value of an asset or the apportionment of an amount or value is, if so required by any party, to be recorded in the final determination. They may be proved in any proceedings relating to tax on chargeable gains by a certificate signed by the Clerk to the Commissioners (in certain cases the clerk or registrar of another tribunal), or by the inspector where the appeal was settled by agreement, stating the material particulars. [*SI 1994 No 1812, reg 18; SI 1999 No 3293, reg 4*].

Reference to other tribunals. Certain questions relating to the value of land or of an interest in land may be referred to the appropriate Lands Tribunal, and similarly in relation to unquoted shares to the Special Commissioners (see *TMA 1970, s 46B*). The instant proceedings may be determined without awaiting the outcome of such referral. [*SI 1994 No 1812, reg 19; SI 1999 No 3293, reg 5*].

Miscellaneous. *Irregularities.* Any irregularity resulting from failure to comply with regulations or with any Commissioners' direction given before a final determination is reached, shall not, of itself, render the proceedings void, and before reaching that determination the Commissioners may, and if they consider that any person has been prejudiced by the irregularity must, give such direction as they think just to cure or waive any irregularity which comes to their attention. Clerical errors in any document recording a direction or decision of the Commissioners may be corrected by any of the Commissioners concerned (or by the Clerk if all the Commissioners have died or ceased to be Commissioners) by certificate under his hand. [*SI 1994 No 1812, reg 24*].

Notices must be in writing unless the Commissioners authorise them to be given orally. [*SI 1994 No 1812, reg 25*].

Service of any notice or document (other than a witness summons, see above) may be by post, by (legible) facsimile transmission etc. or by delivery at the proper address. [*SI 1994 No 1812, reg 26(1)*]. The persons and addresses to whom and which a document may be sent or delivered are set out in *SI 1994 No 1812, reg 26(2)(3)*, and the provisions for substituted or waived service in certain cases in *SI 1994 No 1812, reg 27*.

Penalties. Any appeal against summary penalties determined under regulations as above lies to the High Court (in Scotland, the Court of Session). [*TMA 1970, s 53; SI 1994 No 1813*].

Guidance notes on Appeals to the General Commissioners (TAXGUIDE 4/00) were published in June 2000 by the Tax Faculty of the ICAEW.

(*b*) **Special Commissioners**

The provisions applicable to the General Commissioners (see (*a*) above) apply equally to the Special Commissioners, with the following variations.

Constitution of Tribunal. Any one, two or three of the Special Commissioners may hear any proceedings. If two or three Commissioners are sitting, the Presiding Special Commissioner, or, if he is not sitting, the Commissioner nominated by him, shall preside at the hearing. With the consent of all parties, proceedings may be continued by any one or two of the Commissioners unless the Presiding Special Commissioner otherwise directs. [*SI 1994 No 1811, regs 2, 13*].

Preparation for hearing. *Listing and notice of hearing.* Before notifying the parties of the place, date and time of a hearing, the Clerk to the Commissioners must satisfy himself that the Special Commissioners have jurisdiction over the proceedings and that he has sufficient particulars for determination. The Presiding Special Commissioner may direct that such notifications are not to be sent. [*SI 1994 No 1811, reg 3*].

General power to give directions. The Commissioner(s) have wide direction-giving powers, on the application of any of the parties to proceedings or of their own motion. Applications by the parties (otherwise than during the hearing) must be in writing to the Clerk, and if not made with the consent of all the parties, must be served by the Clerk on any affected party, who may object. [*SI 1994 No 1811, reg 4*].

Witnesses. The maximum penalty which the Commissioner(s) may summarily determine for failure to attend or refusal to be sworn or affirm, to answer any lawful question or to produce documents as required is £10,000. [*SI 1994 No 1811, regs 5, 24(2)*].

Preliminary hearing. Where it appears to a Special Commissioner that any proceedings would be facilitated by holding a preliminary hearing, he may, on the application of a party or of his own motion, give directions for such a hearing to be held. The Clerk to the Special Commissioners must give to all the parties 14 days notice (or such shorter time as the parties agree or the Commissioner sees fit to impose) of the time and place of the hearing. On a preliminary hearing, the Commissioner has wide direction-giving powers, and may, if the parties so agree, determine the proceedings without any further hearing. [*SI 1994 No 1811, reg 9*]. See below as regards powers of Commissioner to obtain information on preliminary hearing of any proceedings. For a refusal by a Special Commissioner to determine a preliminary point of law, see *Investment Trust v CIR (Sp C 173), [1998] SSCD 287.*

Hearing and determination of proceedings. *Hearings in public or private.* Hearings before the Special Commissioner(s) are in public, unless any party applies by notice to the Clerk for the hearing (or any part) to be in private. A Revenue application for a private hearing requires in addition a direction by a Special Commissioner. The rules for attendance at a private hearing follow those before the General Commissioners (as above). [*SI 1994 No 1811, reg 15*].

Power to obtain information. The powers of General Commissioners to obtain information apply to both a preliminary hearing before a Special Commissioner and to the hearing of the proceedings, except that the specific penalty provisions for failure to comply with a notice do not apply (although the general penalty for failure to comply with Commissioner's direction, see below, *does* apply). [*SI 1994 No 1811, regs 10, 24(1)*].

The Commissioners' decision. The recording of the Commissioner(s)' decision must contain a statement of the facts found and the reasons for the determination. After reserving the final determination, the Commissioner(s) may give a written decision in principle on one or more of the issues arising, and adjourn the making of the final determination until after that decision has been issued and any further questions arising from it have been agreed by the parties or decided by the Commissioner(s) after hearing the parties. A decision in principle must contain a statement of the facts and the reasons for the decision, and these need not be repeated in the document recording the final determination. [*SI 1994 No 1811, reg 18; SI 1999 No 3292, reg 4*].

Review of the Commissioners' decision in principle may proceed in the same way as a review of a final determination. [*SI 1994 No 1811, reg 19*].

Publication of decisions in principle or final determinations. The Presiding Special Commissioner may arrange for the publication of such reports of decisions in principle and final determinations as he considers appropriate. If the proceedings (or any part) were held in private, he must ensure that the report is in a form which, so far as possible, prevents the identification of any person whose affairs are dealt with. [*SI 1994 No 1811, reg 20*]. An application for non-publication of a decision on the grounds of inadequate anonymity, or for publication of a short summary only, was refused by the Presiding Special Commissioner in *Y Co Ltd v CIR (Sp C 69), [1996] SSCD 147*. The policy on anonymisation was quoted as: 'In cases where anonymisation is required, the Presiding Special Commissioner will seek to achieve this in co-operation with the parties. If a decision or determination cannot be anonymised to the complete satisfaction of the party requiring it, the Presiding Special Commissioner's policy is to report it in as anonymised a form as he, in consultation with the Special Commissioner[s] deciding the case, considers to be appropriate. To this there is one exception, which is that no report will be published where the decision cannot be effectively anonymised and to report it would defeat the ends of justice, e.g. where particulars of a secret process would otherwise have to be disclosed or in cases where minors were involved. The Presiding Special Commissioner will consider cases falling outside this exception on their merits.' A substantial number of cases (averaging some 50 per year from early 1995) is now reported, and these are referred to in the text of this publication where relevant. The Special Commissioners expect to have their attention drawn in appropriate cases to any of their previous published decisions which is relevant, unless superseded by a higher court decision. The Revenue consider that, whilst not creating any binding legal precedent, these decisions may be relevant in other cases, particularly if not appealed against, but that it would be inappropriate to enter into any discussion of a case which is, or may be, the subject of appeal to the High Court. (Revenue Tax Bulletin October 1995 pp 258, 259).

Orders for costs. The Commissioner(s) may make an order awaiting costs (in Scotland expenses) of, or incidental to, the hearing of any proceedings against any party who has, in their opinion, acted wholly unreasonably in connection with the hearing, but not without giving that party the opportunity of making representations against the award. The award may be of all or part of the costs of the other party or parties, such costs to be taxed in the county court (in Scotland the sheriff court) if not agreed. In Northern Ireland, the Commissioners may determine the costs. [*SI 1994 No 1811, reg 21*]. For cases in which costs were awarded, see *Scott and another (trading as Farthings Steak House) v McDonald (Sp C 91), [1996] SSCD 381* (on taxpayer application) and *Phillips v Burrows (Sp C 229A), [2000] SSCD 112* (on Revenue application), and for cases in which costs were refused, see *Salt v Young (Sp C 205), [1999] SSCD 249* (on Revenue application) and *Carter v Hunt (Sp C 220), [2000] SSCD 17* and *Self-assessed v Inspector of Taxes (No 2)(Sp C 224), [2000] SSCD 47* (on taxpayer application). Only in 'a very rare case' would the Court interfere with the Commissioners' decision as regards costs (see *Gamble v Rowe Ch D 1998, 71 TC 190*, where a refusal of costs was upheld).

Penalty for failure to comply with Commissioner(s)' direction. The Commissioner(s) may summarily determine a penalty of up to £10,000 for any such failure, to be treated as if it were tax charged in an assessment and due and payable. [*SI 1994 No 1811, reg 24(1)(3)*].

An **explanatory booklet** 'Appeals and Other Proceedings before the Special Commissioners' (October 1994) dealing with procedural and other points is available free of charge from the Clerk to the Special Commissioners, 15/29 Bedford Avenue, London WC1B 3AS (tel. 0207–631 4242).

Simon's Direct Tax Service. See A3.5.

4.7 **APPEALS TO THE HIGH COURT**

Prior to the determination of an appeal by the Commissioners, the Court may be prepared to consider an application seeking a determination as to whether the Revenue may make use of certain 'tax-altering' provisions in relation to the assessments under appeal (*Balen v CIR Ch D 1976, 52 TC 406; Beecham Group plc v CIR Ch D 1992, 65 TC 219*). In general, 'there is an absolute exclusion of the High Court's jurisdiction only when the proceedings seek relief which is more or less co-extensive with adjudicating on an existing open assessment . . . the more closely the High Court proceedings approximate to that in their substantial effect, the more ready the High Court will be, as a matter of discretion, to decline jurisdiction.' (*Glaxo Group Ltd and others v CIR Ch D 1995, 68 TC 166*).

Case stated procedure — General Commissioners. Within 30 days of the date of final determination of an appeal (or of the variation or substitution of such a determination, see above), any party dissatisfied with the determination as being erroneous in point of law (for which see e.g. *Billows v Robinson CA 1991, 64 TC 17*) may serve notice on the Clerk requiring the Commissioners to state and sign a case for the opinion of the High Court (in Scotland the Court of Session, in Northern Ireland the Court of Appeal (NI)), setting forth the facts and final determination of the Commissioners. See *Grainger v Singer KB 1927, 11 TC 704* as regards receipt of the case. The 30 day time limit for requesting a case does not apply to the payment of the fee (*Anson v Hill CA 1968, 47 ATC 143*). The Commissioners may serve notice on the person who required the stated case requiring him, within 28 days, to identify the question of law on which he requires the case to be stated. They may refuse to state a case until such notice is complied with, or if they are not satisfied that a question of law is involved, or if the requisite fee (see below) has not been paid. A requirement for a case to be stated becomes invalid if the determination to which it relates is set aside or varied. [*SI 1994 No 1812, regs 20, 23; SI 1999 No 3293, reg 6*].

A fee of £25 is payable to the Clerk by the person requiring the case before he is entitled to have it stated. [*TMA 1970, s 56(3); SI 1994 No 1813*]. A single case may have effect as regards each of a number of appeals heard together (*Getty Oil Co v Steele and related appeals Ch D 1990, 63 TC 376*).

If the taxpayer dies, his personal representatives stand in his shoes (*Smith v Williams KB 1921, 8 TC 321*).

Although the case stated procedure envisages the determination of the proceedings before the Commissioners, where an appeal has been decided in principle but there may be considerable delay in reaching figures for the formal determination, the Court will accept a case stated in principle (see e.g. *Rank Xerox Ltd v Lane HL 1979, 53 TC 185*).

The case stated procedure is not open to a successful party to an appeal (*Sharpey-Schafer v Venn Ch D 1955, 34 ATC 141*), but where another party requires a case, the successful party may invite the Commissioners to include in the case an additional question relating to another ground on which the Commissioners had found against it (*Gordon v CIR CS 1991, 64 TC 173*). In the case of a partnership, the procedure is available to any one of the partners, with or without the consent of the others (*Sutherland & Partners v Barnes & Gustar CA 1994, 66 TC 663*).

Consideration of draft case. Within 56 days of receipt of a notice requiring a stated case (or of the Commissioners being satisfied as to the question of law involved), the Clerk must send a draft of the case to all the parties. Written representations thereon may be made to the Clerk by any party within 56 days after the draft case is sent out, with copies to all the other parties, and within a further 28 days further representations may similarly be made in response. Any party to whom copies of representations are not sent may apply to the Clerk for a copy. The validity of a case after it has been stated and signed (see below), and of any subsequent proceedings, is not affected by a failure to meet these time limits or by a failure to send copies of representations to all parties. [*SI 1994 No 1812, reg 21*].

An application for the taxpayer's name to be withheld was refused (*In re H Ch D 1964, 42 TC 14*) as was an application for the deletion of a passage possibly damaging the taxpayer (*Treharne v Guinness Exports Ltd Ch D 1967, 44 TC 161*). An application for judicial review on the ground that the case did not cover all matters in dispute was refused in *R v Special Commrs (ex p Napier) CA 1988, 61 TC 206*. In *Danquah v CIR Ch D 1990, 63 TC 526*, an application for the statement of a further case was refused where the case did not set out all the questions raised by the taxpayer in the originating motion by which he had sought an order directing the Commissioners to state a case. The proper course was for the taxpayer to apply for remission of the case for amendment under *TMA 1970, s 56(7)*. See also *Consolidated Goldfields plc v CIR Ch D 1990, 63 TC 333* (dealt with further below) in which a request to remit a case to the Commissioners for further findings of fact was refused.

Preparation and submission of final case. As soon as may be after the final date for representations (see above and see *McKinney v Hagans Caravans (Manufacturing) Ltd CA(NI) 1997, 69 TC 526*), the Commissioners, after taking into account any representations, must state and sign the case. In the event of the death of a Commissioner, or of his ceasing to be a Commissioner, the case is to be signed by the remaining Commissioner(s) or, if there are none, by the Clerk. The case is then sent by the Clerk to the person who required it to be stated, and the other parties notified accordingly.

In England, Wales and Scotland, the party requiring the case must transmit it to the High Court (in Scotland, the Court of Session) within 30 days of receiving it, and at or before the time he does so must notify each of the other parties that the case has been stated on his application and send them a copy of the case. The fact that the same case may have been transmitted timeously by another party, where there are cross-appeals, does not relieve the appellant of the requirement to transmit the case timeously if his appeal is to be heard (*Petch v Gurney CA 1994, 66 TC 743*). The 30 day time limit (under the similar earlier provisions of *TMA 1970, s 56(4)*) is mandatory (*Valleybright Ltd (in liquidation) v Richardson Ch D 1984, 58 TC 290; Petch v Gurney CA 1994, 66 TC 743*), and may run from the date the case is received by the taxpayer's authorised agent (*Brassington v Guthrie Ch D 1991, 64 TC 435*). The notification (and copy) to the other parties is required only to give 'adequate notice' of the appeal and not to be 'too long delayed' (*Hughes v Viner Ch D 1985, 58 TC 437*). In Northern Ireland, slightly different rules apply (and see *CIR v McGuckian CA (NI) 1994, 69 TC 1*).

[*SI 1994 No 1812, regs 22, 23*].

The High Court (or Court of Session or Court of Appeal (NI)) hears and determines any question(s) of law arising on the case, and may reverse, affirm or amend the determination of the Commissioners, or may remit the matter to the Commissioners with the opinion of the Court thereon, or may make such other order as seems to it fit. In certain circumstances, this may include the power to uphold an assessment as if it had been made under a section other than that under which it was in fact made (*CIR v McGuckian CA (NI) 1994, 69 TC 1*). The Court may also cause the case to be sent back for amendment (see further below). An appeal from the decision of the High Court lies (in England and Wales) to the Court of Appeal and thence (with leave) to the House of Lords. In certain cases, 'leap-frog' appeals direct from the High Court to the House of Lords may be permitted under *Administration of Justice Act 1969, s 12* (see e.g. *Fitzleet Estates Ltd v Cherry HL 1977, 51 TC 708*). In the case of an appeal against a decision on an appeal against an assessment, tax must be paid in accordance with the Commissioners' decision. Following the decision on appeal, any tax overpaid is refunded with such interest as the Court may allow, and any amount undercharged is due and payable 30 days after the inspector issues a notice of the amount due. [*TMA 1970, s 56(6)–(9)*].

Once set down for hearing, a case cannot be declared a nullity (*Way v Underdown CA 1974, 49 TC 215*) or struck out under *Order 18, rule 19 of the Rules of the Supreme Court* (*Petch v Gurney CA, [1994] STC 689*), but the appellant may withdraw (*Hood Barrs v CIR (No 3) CA 1960, 39 TC 209*, but see *Bradshaw v Blunden (No 2) Ch D 1960, 39 TC 73*). Where the appellant was the inspector and the taxpayer did not wish to proceed, the Court refused to make an order on terms agreed between the parties (*Slaney v Kean Ch D 1969, 45 TC 415*).

The Court may, however, return a case for amendment. [*TMA 1970, s 56(7)*]. In *Consolidated Goldfields plc v CIR Ch D 1990, 63 TC 333*, the taxpayer company's request that the High Court remit a case to the Commissioners for further findings of fact was refused. Although the remedy was properly sought, it would only be granted if it could be shown that the desired findings were (*a*) material to some tenable argument, (*b*) reasonably open on the evidence adduced, and (*c*) not inconsistent with the findings already made. See also *Carvill v CIR Ch D 1996, 70 TC 126*. However, in *Fitzpatrick v CIR CS 1990, [1991] STC 34*, a case was remitted where the facts found proved or admitted, and the contentions of the parties, were not clearly set out, despite the taxpayer's request for various amendments and insertions to the case, and in *Whittles v Uniholdings Ltd Ch D 1993, 68 TC 528*, remission was appropriate in view of the widely differing interpretations which the parties sought to place on the Commissioners' decision (and the case was remitted a second time (see *[1993] STC 767*) to resolve misunderstandings as to the nature of a concession made by the Crown at the original hearing and apparent inconsistencies in the Commissioners' findings of fact). See also *Bradley v London Electric plc Ch D, [1996] STC 231*. If a case is remitted, the taxpayer has the right to attend any further hearing by the Commissioners (*Lack v Doggett CA 1970, 46 TC 497*) but the Commissioners may not, in the absence of special circumstances, admit further evidence (*Archer-Shee v Baker CA 1928, 15 TC 1; Watson v Samson Bros Ch D 1959, 38 TC 346; Bradshaw v Blunden (No 2) Ch D 1960, 39 TC 73*), but see *Brady v Group Lotus Car Companies plc CA 1987, 60 TC 359* where the Court directed the Commissioners to admit further evidence where new facts had come to light suggesting the taxpayers had deliberately misled the Commissioners. Errors of fact in the case may be amended by agreement of the parties prior to hearing of the case (*Moore v Austin Ch D 1985, 59 TC 110*). See *Jeffries v Stevens Ch D 1982, 56 TC 134* as regards delay between statement of case and motion for remission.

A new question of law may be raised in the Courts on giving due notice to the other parties (*Muir v CIR CA 1966, 43 TC 367*) but the Courts will neither admit evidence not in the stated case (*Watson v Samson Bros Ch D 1959, 38 TC 346; Cannon Industries Ltd v Edwards Ch D 1965, 42 TC 625; Frowd v Whalley Ch D 1965, 42 TC 599*, and see *R v Great Yarmouth Commrs (ex p Amis) QB 1960, 39 TC 143*) nor consider contentions evidence in support of which was not produced before the Commissioners (*Denekamp v Pearce Ch D 1998, 71 TC 213*).

Following the decision in *Pepper v Hart HL 1992, 65 TC 421* (see 75.13 SCHEDULE E), the Courts are prepared to consider the parliamentary history of legislation, or the official reports of debates in Hansard, where all of the following conditions are met.

(*a*) Legislation is ambiguous or obscure, or leads to an absurdity.

(*b*) The material relied upon consists of one or more statements by a Minister or other promoter of the Bill together if necessary with such other parliamentary material as is necessary to understand such statements and their effect.

(*c*) The statements relied upon are clear.

For the requirements preliminary to reference to extracts from Hansard in any hearings, see Supreme Court Practice Direction issued 20 December 1994 (*1995 STI 98*).

Many Court decisions turn on whether the Commissioners' decision was one of fact supported by the evidence, and hence final. The Court will not disturb a finding of fact if there was reasonable evidence for it, notwithstanding that the evidence might support a different conclusion of fact. The leading case is *Edwards v Bairstow & Harrison HL 1955, 36 TC 207*, in which the issue was whether there had been an adventure in the nature of trade. The Commissioners' decision was reversed on the ground that the *only* reasonable conclusion from the evidence was that there had been such an adventure. For a discussion of the application of this principle, see *Milnes v J Beam Group Ltd Ch D 1975, 50 TC 675*.

A Court decision is a binding precedent for itself or an inferior Court except that the House of Lords, while treating its former decisions as normally binding, may depart from a previous decision should it appear right to do so. For this see *Fitzleet Estates Ltd v Cherry HL 1977, 51 TC 708*. Scottish decisions are not binding on the High Court but are normally followed. Decisions of the Privy Council and of the Irish Courts turning on comparable legislation are treated with respect. A Court decision does not affect other assessments already final and conclusive (see 5.5 ASSESSMENTS) but may be followed, if relevant, in the determination of any open appeals against assessments and in assessments made subsequently irrespective of the years of assessment or taxpayers concerned (*Re Waring decd Ch D, [1948] 1 AER 257; Gwyther v Boslymon Quarries Ltd KB 1950, 29 ATC 1; Bolands Ltd v CIR SC(I) 1925, 4 ATC 526*). Further, a Court decision does not estop the Crown from proceeding on a different basis for other years (*Hood Barrs v CIR (No 3) CA 1960, 39 TC 209*). A general change of practice consequent on a Court decision may affect error or mistake relief (see 17.10 CLAIMS) or retrospective Schedule E assessments under *ICTA 1988, s 206* (see 75.1(3) SCHEDULE E).

For joinder of CIR in non-tax disputes, see *In re Vandervell's Trusts HL 1970, 46 TC 341*.

Special Commissioners. In the case of an appeal to the Special Commissioners, if the appellant or the Revenue is dissatisfied in point of law with a decision (whether in principle or on final determination) or with a decision varying or substituting such a decision, appeal may (except in certain Lands Tribunal cases) be made to the High Court. Under *Order 55* of the Supreme Court Practice, the appeal must be lodged in the High Court within 28 days from the date on which notice of the decision is given. Further appeal may be made to the Court of Appeal and thence (with leave) to the House of Lords. A 'leap-frog' appeal to the Court of Appeal may be made if all the parties agree, the Commissioners certify that a point of law is involved relating wholly or mainly to the construction of an enactment which was fully argued and considered before them, and the leave of the Court of Appeal has been obtained. In Scotland appeals are to the Court of Session, in Northern Ireland to the Court of Appeal (NI), and thence in either case to the House of Lords. When a decision against which an appeal has been made is set aside or varied (see above), the appeal is treated as withdrawn.

In the case of an appeal against a decision on an appeal against an assessment, tax must be paid in accordance with the Commissioners' decision. Following the decision on appeal, any tax overpaid is refunded with such interest as the Court may allow, and any amount undercharged is due and payable 30 days after the inspector issues a notice of the amount due. [*TMA 1970, ss 56A, 58; SI 1994 No 1813; SI 1999 No 3294*].

For the general statutory provisions and case law applicable equally to Special Commissioners, see above in relation to General Commissioners.

Simon's Direct Tax Service. See A3.7.

4.8 JUDICIAL REVIEW (PREROGATIVE ORDERS)

A taxpayer who is dissatisfied with the exercise of administrative powers may in certain circumstances (e.g. where the Revenue has exceeded or abused its powers or acted contrary to the rules of natural justice, or where the Appeal Commissioners have acted unfairly or improperly) seek a remedy in one of the prerogative orders of mandamus, prohibition or certiorari. This is now done by way of application for judicial review under *Supreme Court Act 1981, s 31* and *Order 53 of the Rules of the Supreme Court*. As regards time limit on such applications, see *R v CIR (ex p Allen) QB 1997, 69 TC 442*.

The issue on an application for leave to apply for judicial review is whether there is an arguable case (*R v CIR (ex p Howmet Corporation and another) QB, [1994] STC 413*). The procedure is generally used where no other, adequate, remedy, such as a right of appeal, is available. See *R v Special Commrs (ex p Stipplechoice Ltd) (No 1) CA 1985, 59 TC 396*, *R v HMIT (ex p Kissane and Another) QB, [1986] STC 152*, *R v Sevenoaks Commrs (ex p Thorne) QB 1989, 62 TC 341*, *R v Hastings and Bexhill General Commrs and CIR (ex p Goodacre) QB 1994, 67 TC 126* and *R v CIR (ex p Ulster Bank Ltd) CA 1997, 69 TC 211*.

There is a very long line of cases in which the courts have consistently refused applications where a matter should have been pursued through the ordinary channels as described above. See, for example, *R v Special Commrs (ex p Morey) CA 1972, 49 TC 71; R v Special Commrs (ex p Emery) QB 1980, 53 TC 555; R v Walton General Commrs (ex p Wilson) CA, [1983] STC 464; R v Special Commrs (ex p Esslemont) CA, 1984 STI 312; R v Brentford Commrs (ex p Chan) QB 1985, 57 TC 651; R v CIR (ex p Caglar) QB 1995, 67 TC 335.* See also, however, *R v HMIT and Others (ex p Lansing Bagnall Ltd) CA 1986, 61 TC 112* for a successful application where the inspector issued a notice under a discretionary power on the footing that there was a mandatory obligation to do so, and *R v Ward, R v Special Commr (ex p Stipplechoice Ltd) (No 3) QB 1988, 61 TC 391*, where insufficient notice was given of revision of an accounting period under *ICTA 1988, s 12(8)* prior to appeal hearing.

In *R v CIR (ex p J Rothschild Holdings) CA 1987, 61 TC 178*, the Revenue were required to produce internal documents of a general character relating to their practice in applying a statutory provision, but in *R v CIR (ex p Taylor) CA 1988, 62 TC 562* discovery of internal Revenue correspondence was refused as there was no material indication that it had any bearing on the question of whether the decision taken by the inspector could be challenged. In *R v CIR (ex p Unilever plc) CA 1996, 68 TC 205*, an application for judicial review for a Revenue decision to refuse a late loss relief claim was successful. The Revenue's refusal was 'so unreasonable as to be, in public law terms, irrational' in view of an administrative procedure established with the company over many years of raising assessments on estimates of net taxable profits, adjusted when the final accounts became available without regard to the loss claim time limit. A confirmation by the local inspector that capital allowances were available in relation to an enterprise zone property trust scheme was not binding where the promoters were aware that clearance applications were required to be made to a specialist department, and failed to disclose that the scheme involved 'artificial provisions' (*R v CIR (ex p Matrix-Securities Ltd) HL 1994, 66 TC 587*). As regards informal advice by the Revenue generally, they were not bound by anything less than a clear, unambiguous and unqualified representation (*R v CIR (ex p MFK Underwriting Agencies Ltd) QB 1989, 62 TC 607*), and in *R v CIR (ex p Bishopp and another) QB, [1999] STC 531*, an application for judicial review of informal advice given by the Revenue in relation to a proposed transaction was refused. See generally 35.6 INLAND REVENUE: ADMINISTRATION. See also *R v CIR (ex p Camacq Corporation) CA 1989, 62 TC 651*, where a Revenue decision to revoke its authorisation to pay a dividend gross was upheld, and *R v CIR (ex p S G Warburg & Co Ltd) QB 1994, 68 TC 300*, where a decision not to apply a published practice was upheld.

See 6.8 BACK DUTY as regards challenges to the validity of notices under *TMA 1970, s 20*.

The first step is to obtain leave to apply for judicial review from the High Court. Application for leave is made ex parte to a single judge who will usually determine the application without a hearing. The Court will not grant leave unless the applicant has a sufficient interest in the matter to which the application relates. See *CIR v National Federation of Self-employed and Small Businesses Ltd HL 1981, 55 TC 133* for what is meant by 'sufficient interest' and for discussion of availability of judicial review generally, and cf. *R v A-G (ex p ICI plc) CA 1986, 60 TC 1.*

Time limit. Applications must be made **within three months** of the date when the grounds for application arose. The Court has discretion to extend this time limit where there is good reason, but is generally very reluctant to do so. See e.g. *R v HMIT (ex p Brumfield and Others) QB 1988, 61 TC 589*. Grant of leave to apply for review does not amount to a ruling that application was made in good time (*R v Tavistock Commrs (ex p Worth) QB 1985, 59 TC 116*).

Simon's Direct Tax Service. See **A3.9.**

4.9 **COSTS**

Costs may be awarded by the Courts in the usual way. In suitable cases, e.g. 'test cases', the Revenue may undertake to pay the taxpayer's costs. There is no general provision for the award of costs of appearing before Commissioners, but see 4.6 above as regards award of costs of Special Commissioners' hearings against parties acting 'wholly unreasonably'. Costs awarded by the Courts may include expenses connected with the drafting of the Stated Case (*Manchester Corporation v Sugden CA 1903, 4 TC 595*). Costs of a discontinued application for judicial review were refused where the Revenue was not informed of the application (*R v CIR ex p Opman International UK QB 1985, 59 TC 352*). Law costs of appeals not allowable for tax purposes (*Allen v Farquharson KB 1932, 17 TC 59; Rushden Heel* and *Smith's Potato* cases *HL 1948, 30 TC 298 & 267*, and see *Spofforth KB 1945, 26 TC 310*).

5 Assessments

Cross-references. See 71.3 SCHEDULE D, CASES I AND II for bases of assessments on business profits. As regards particular assessments see also 6 BACK DUTY; 28.1 EXCESS LIABILITY; 53 PARTNERSHIPS; 75 SCHEDULE E and 55 PAY AS YOU EARN for assessments on employment income; 81 SETTLEMENTS for assessment on trust income.

Simon's Direct Tax Service A3.2.

Self-assessment. The provisions described in this chapter relate in the main to periods before those for which SELF-ASSESSMENT (78) applies, i.e. before 1996/97 (1997/98 in the case of partnerships whose business commenced before 6 April 1994). They continue to apply (so far as relevant) for corporation tax purposes until corporate self-assessment is introduced (i.e. for accounting periods ending on or after a day to be set, but which will not be before early 1999). However, many aspects of the self-assessment provisions are couched in similar terms to those previously applicable, so that the case law may continue to be of relevance.

5.1 ASSESSMENTS

Assessments to tax are made by inspectors, or their delegates [*TMA 1970, s 113(1A)(1B)*] and notices of assessment are served, which must also state the date issued and the time limit for making APPEALS (4). [*TMA 1970, s 29(1)(2)(5); F(No 2)A 1975, s 44(5)*]. Assessments may, where income is charged for a year of assessment on the amount arising in that year, be raised during the year, subject to later adjustment. [*TMA 1970, s 29(1)(c); FA 1988, s 119*]. The assessment must include a statement of the tax actually payable (*Hallamshire Industrial Finance Trust Ltd v CIR Ch D 1978, 53 TC 631*). A taxpayer may request the inspector (on form 64–8) to provide a copy of any assessment to an agent. An assessment becomes binding if not appealed against within 30 days of the date of issue. [*TMA 1970, s 31; F(No 2)A 1975, s 67(1)*]. The inspector's power of assessment is not limited to persons or sources of income within the area of his tax office (*R v Tavistock Commrs (ex p Adams) CA 1971, 48 TC 56*). See 4.3 APPEALS for jurisdiction of Commissioners on appeal.

In the absence of a satisfactory return the inspector may make an assessment to the best of his judgment. [*TMA 1970, s 29(1)(b)*]. As to this, see *Van Boeckel v C & E Commrs QB 1980, [1981] STC 290*, relating to the comparable VAT provision of *FA 1972, s 31(1)*, *Blackpool Marton Rotary Club v Martin CA 1989, 62 TC 686* and *Phillimore v Heaton Ch D 1989, 61 TC 584*.

An assessment defective in form or containing errors may be validated by *TMA 1970, s 114(1)* if the person and income assessed are apparent, e.g. where the person assessed was later found to have received the income as trustee (*Martin v CIR CS 1938, 22 TC 330*). See also *Fleming v London Produce Co Ltd Ch D 1968, 44 TC 582, Hart v Briscoe Ch D 1977, 52 TC 53* and *Vickerman v Mason's Personal Representatives Ch D 1984, 58 TC 39*. But where the assessment was under Schedule D, Case VII it was held that *section 114(1)* could not be used to treat the assessment as under Case I (*Bath & West Counties Property Trust Ltd v Thomas Ch D 1977, 52 TC 20*, although for special reasons, including the Crown option between Cases, the Court used its powers under *TMA 1970, s 56(6)* to alter the assessment, for which see also *CIR v McGuckian CA(NI), [1994] STC 888*) or to validate an assessment where wrong year of assessment had been entered through a copying error (*Baylis v Gregory CA, [1987] STC 297*).

Income under Schedules A or D is assessable on the person receiving or entitled to it. [*ICTA 1988, ss 21(1), 59(1)*]. Trustees, guardians, etc. are assessable in respect of income of incapacitated persons including minors (see 16.3 CHILDREN) and there are provisions for charging non-residents through agents, etc. (see 51.4 NON-RESIDENTS AND OTHER OVERSEAS

MATTERS) but these provisions do not preclude the non-resident himself being assessed if he can be reached (*CIR v Huni KB 1923, 8 TC 466; Whitney v CIR HL 1925, 10 TC 88*).

An assessment once made cannot be 'vacated' (*Baylis v Gregory*, above).

5.2 **CHOICE BY REVENUE**

In making assessments, the Revenue has an option, where more than one Case of Schedule D is applicable, to elect to tax under the Case which is most advantageous to it (*Liverpool London and Globe Insurance Co v Bennett HL 1913, 6 TC 327*). This case related to unremitted foreign interest, which could not then be assessed under Case IV, but the Revenue successfully contended that it formed part of the taxpayer's '*trading profits*' assessable under Case I (and cf. *Butler v Mortgage Co of Egypt CA 1928, 13 TC 803*).

But there is no such power of selection between the Schedules. 'A subject matter of taxation properly assessed . . . under one Schedule, cannot be brought into assessment under another Schedule' (Lord Dunedin and Lord Tomlin in *Salisbury House Estate v Fry HL 1930, 15 TC 266*). And see *Sywell Aerodrome Ltd v Croft KB 1941, 24 TC 126; Mitchell & Edon v Ross HL 1961, 40 TC 11.*

5.3 **FURTHER ASSESSMENTS ON 'DISCOVERY'**

If an inspector or the Board 'discover' that income has not been assessed or has been under-assessed or that excessive relief has been given, a further assessment can be made. [*TMA 1970, s 29(3)(4)*]. The existence of an assessment under appeal capable of being increased and determined in the correct amount does not preclude the making of a further assessment and the consequent determination of both the original assessment and the further assessment (*Duchy Maternity Ltd v Hodgson Ch D 1985, 59 TC 85*). Discovery has been given a very wide meaning by the Courts. There is a discovery by the inspector if he comes to the honest conclusion that there has been under-assessment (*R v Kensington Commrs (ex p Aramayo) HL 1915, 6 TC 279, 613; R v St Giles, etc. Commrs (ex p Hooper) KB 1915, 7 TC 59*; but see *Scott and another (trading as Farthings Steak House) v McDonald (Sp C 91), [1996] SSCD 381* for a case in which the Special Commissioner found that there had been no honest *bona fide* discovery by the inspector). It has been established in a number of cases that *a change of opinion* or rectification of an error by the Revenue, including an arithmetical error in calculating the tax, without the ascertainment of any new facts amounts to discovery and this is so notwithstanding that the former opinion had been notified to the taxpayer (*Brodie's Trustees v CIR KB 1933, 17 TC 432; Williams v Grundy Trustees KB 1933, 18 TC 271; British Sugar Mfrs Ltd v Harris CA 1937, 21 TC 528; CIR v Mackinlay's Trustees CS 1938, 22 TC 305; Steel Barrel Co Ltd v Osborne (No 2) CA 1948, 30 TC 73; Commercial Structures Ltd v Briggs CA 1948, 30 TC 477; Jones v Mason Investments Ch D 1966, 43 TC 570; Vickerman v Mason's Personal Representatives Ch D 1984, 58 TC 39*). (See 56.6 PAYMENT OF TAX for remission of tax in cases of official error.) A further assessment may be made on incomplete information supplied on behalf of the taxpayer (*McLuskey's Executrix v CIR CS 1955, 36 TC 163*) and successive further assessments are permissible (*Cansick v Hochstrasser Ch D 1961, 40 TC 151*). See also *Beatty v CIR Ch D 1953, 35 TC 30; Multipar Syndicate Ltd v Devitt KB 1945, 26 TC 359.* A Court decision does not estop the Crown from proceeding on a different basis for other years (*Hood Barrs v CIR (No 3) CA 1960, 39 TC 209*).

If in the determination of an appeal *including a determination by agreement under TMA 1970, s 54* (see 4.4 APPEALS) a matter has been adjudicated or agreed, the Revenue cannot re-open the matter by making a further assessment (*Cenlon Finance Co Ltd v Ellwood HL 1962, 40 TC 176*). However, the matter must have been dealt with specifically (*Kidston v Aspinall Ch D 1963, 41 TC 371; Young v Duthie Ch D 1969, 45 TC 624; Skinner v Berry Head Lands*

Ltd Ch D 1970, 46 TC 377; Parkin v Cattell CA 1971, 48 TC 462) or clearly have been raised by implication, so that an inspector of average experience must have appreciated it was being made (*Olin Energy Systems Ltd v Scorer HL 1985, 58 TC 592*). A further assessment is not precluded where an appeal was settled by an agreement based on trading profits which were incorrectly stated (*Gray v Matheson Ch D 1993, 65 TC 577*). For a case in which assessments raised under *ICTA 1988, s 770* (transfer pricing, see 4.4 ANTI-AVOIDANCE) were discharged, the relevant licensing agreements having been submitted to the inspector prior to a *section 54* agreement, see *Newidgets Manufacturing Ltd v Jones (Sp C 197), [1999] SSCD 193.*

Similar considerations apply in determining whether an agreement under *TMA 1970, s 54* prevents a taxpayer making an error or mistake relief claim under *TMA 1970, s 33* (see 17.9 CLAIMS) (and see *Grafton Ltd v CIR (Sp C 172), [1998] SSCD 278*).

The Revenue have issued a Statement of Practice setting out their view of the application in practice of the case law outlined above. The following are listed as specific circumstances in which there are clearly no grounds for *not* making discovery assessments:

(*a*) profits or income have not earlier been charged to tax because of any form of fraudulent or negligent conduct;

(*b*) the inspector has been misled or misinformed in any way about the particular matter at issue;

(*c*) there is an arithmetical error in a computation which had not been spotted at the time agreement was reached, and which can be corrected by the making of an in date discovery assessment;

(*d*) an error is made in accounts and computations which it cannot reasonably be alleged was correct or intended, e.g. the double deduction from taxable profits of a particular item (say group relief).

The Statement of Practice also makes it clear that, by concession, the principles determining the making of a further assessment following settlement of an appeal by agreement will also be applied where agreement is reached prior to the issue of an assessment. Also by concession, whether or not there has been an appeal, a discovery assessment will not be made where, although the matter in question may not have been the subject of a specific agreement within the case law principles outlined above, the inspector's decision was based on full and accurate disclosure and was a tenable view, so that the taxpayer could reasonably have believed the inspector's decision to be correct. (Revenue Pamphlet IR 131, SP 8/91, 26 July 1991).

See 17.11 CLAIMS as regards the making of claims, etc. relevant to further assessments.

See 78.15 SELF-ASSESSMENT as regards 'discovery' assessments for 1996/97 and subsequent years.

Simon's Direct Tax Service. See A3.231–A3.233.

5.4 DOUBLE ASSESSMENT

'The taxing acts . . . nowhere authorise the Crown to take Income Tax twice over in respect of same source for same period of time' (Lord Sumner in *English Sewing Cotton Co HL 1923, 8 TC* at *513*). An *alternative* income tax assessment may, however, be raised in respect of transactions already the subject of a final CGT assessment (*Bye v Coren CA 1986, 60 TC 116*), and where more than one of a number of alternative assessments become final and conclusive, the Crown may institute collection proceedings in respect of any one (but not more than one) of them (*CIR v Wilkinson CA 1992, 65 TC 28*). For alternative assessments generally, see *Lord Advocate v McKenna CS, [1989] STC 485.*

Where there has been double assessment for the same cause and for the same chargeable period a claim may be made to the Board (with right of appeal to the Commissioners having jurisdiction to hear appeals against the assessment, or the later of the assessments, to which the appeal relates) for the overcharge to be vacated. [*TMA 1970, s 32*]. See 17.10 CLAIMS for Error or Mistake relief.

5.5 **FINALITY OF ASSESSMENTS**

An assessment cannot be altered after the notice has been served except in accordance with the express provisions of the *Taxes Acts*. [*TMA 1970, s 29(6)*]. As regards the figure for the income assessed, the principal provisions are as those for APPEALS (4.4). Other examples are certain of the bases of assessment provisions, e.g. *ICTA 1988, s 62(10)*, enabling an assessment to be reduced in the opening years of a business. Where over-assessment results from an *error or mistake* in a return, see 17.10 CLAIMS. An assessment as determined on appeal or not appealed against is final and conclusive.

5.6 **SOCIAL SECURITY CONTRIBUTIONS**

Class 4 contributions (which are levied on profits etc.) are shown separately on notices of assessment under Schedule D. See 83.7 SOCIAL SECURITY.

5.7 **TIME LIMITS**

An assessment or additional assessment cannot be made later than six years from the end of the tax year to which it relates (or accounting period in the case of a company) [*TMA 1970, s 34*] except in cases of fraudulent or negligent conduct (for 1982/83 and earlier years, cases of fraud, wilful default or neglect) [*TMA 1970, ss 36–41; FA 1989, s 149*, see 6.4 BACK DUTY] or where there is specific statutory provision for later assessment (including, for, broadly, 1997/98 and earlier years, Sch E assessments on delayed remuneration, see *TMA 1970, s 35; FA 1998, Sch 27 Pt III(9)* and 75.1 SCHEDULE E). But assessments on personal representatives in respect of deceased's income before death must be made within three years after end of tax year in which death occurred. [*TMA 1970, s 40(1)*]. See also 6.5 BACK DUTY regarding deceased persons.

For 1996/97 and later years, the general time limit is five years after 31 January following the tax year and the time limit where the taxpayer is deceased is three years after 31 January following the tax year of death (see 78.30 SELF-ASSESSMENT).

An assessment is made on the date on which the inspector authorised to make it signs a certificate in the appropriate assessments volume that he made certain assessments including the assessment in question (*Honig v Sarsfield CA 1986, 59 TC 337*).

5.8 **TOLERANCE LIMIT OF ASSESSMENT**

Where pensioners and single women under 65 have no income apart from the standard Social Security pension, and such pension exceeds the single person's allowance, no direct assessment will be made on the excess if the tax payable is £75 or less. This tolerance is to minimise work which is cost ineffective. But if an assessment has to be made in any event (for instance because the taxpayer has asked for it to check his tax position) any underpayment is collected in the normal way even if it is less than the assessing tolerance (Revenue Pamphlet IR 131, A12). See 56.7 PAYMENT OF TAX for tolerances on repayment of tax.

5.9 **BASES OF ASSESSMENT**

The summary on the following page is subject to the detailed explanations in the other sections of this book under the headings shown in the first column, and particularly, as regards Schedule D, to adjustments in cases of **change of accounting period** (adjustment of preceding year's assessment), **new business** (adjustment of first, second and third years' assessments), **new source of income** (adjustment of first, second and (sometimes) third years' assessments), **discontinuance of business** (adjustment of last three years' assessments), **cessation of certain sources of income or death** (adjustment of last two years' assessments), **losses in trading or farming, change of ownership of business** (adjustment of last three and next three years' assessments). The Finance Act 1994 introduces a **current year basis of assessment for Schedule D** with effect as noted in the summary below.

The adjustments regarding new and discontinued sources of income apply to **each item of untaxed income**, such as changes in War Loan holdings, purchase or sale of foreign stocks and shares etc., etc. Thus in many cases of income of this kind, adjustments will be required every year, and it will be necessary to prepare the annual return forms and check assessments carefully. This is of no application where the current year basis of assessment (see above) is in force.

Where overseas items are concerned, the REMITTANCE BASIS (63) applies in certain circumstances. In some other circumstances percentage deductions may be made in arriving at assessable income, see 64.2 RESIDENCE, ORDINARY RESIDENCE AND DOMICILE.

Assessments on companies are on an actual basis. See Tolley's Corporation Tax. For full details of capital gains tax, see Tolley's Capital Gains Tax.

Assessed under	Source	Basis on which Assessed
Schedule A	Rents receivable from lands, houses, buildings etc.	Rents or receipts arising in the tax year.
B	The *occupation* of Woodlands managed on a commercial basis for profit, where no election made for assessment under Sch D. Abolished after 5 April 1988.	One-third gross annual value.
C	Government and public authority Stocks etc.	Actual interest etc. paid.
Sch D, Case I	Trades etc.	Usually on profits based on annual account ending in preceding tax year.*
" " II	Professions and vocations.	Usually on profits based on annual account ending in preceding tax year.*
" " III	War Loan and other Government Stocks, Deposit Interest, Treasury Bills, Discounts etc. not taxed at source.	Usually on amount arising in preceding tax year.**

5.9 Assessments

Assessed under			Source	Basis on which Assessed
"	"	IV	Overseas securities.	Usually on amount arising in preceding tax year.**
"	"	V	Overseas possessions.	
"	"	VI	Sundry profits not included above, such as guaranteeing a loan, underwriting etc. (where not a *trade* etc. assessable under Case I) and previously furnished lettings (see 68.1 SCHEDULE A).	Usually on actual profits for tax year.
Schedule E			Offices and Employments, Pensions etc. other than foreign pensions.	Total income from the particular employment etc., for current tax year.
Schedule F			From 6 April 1973. Dividends and certain other distributions, plus tax credits, from companies resident in the UK.	Actual dividends etc. payable in tax year.
Capital Gains Tax			Chargeable gains.	Actual gains for tax year.

* For 1994/95 and subsequent years (subject to opening years rules) as regards trades, professions and vocations commenced after 5 April 1994 and for 1996/97 for those commenced on or before that date (subject to transitional provisions), usually on profits based on annual account ending in current tax year.

** For 1994/95 and subsequent years as regards income from a source first arising after 5 April 1994 and otherwise for 1996/97 and subsequent years (subject to transitional provisions), usually on amount arising in current tax year.

6 Back Duty

Cross-reference. See 71.28 SCHEDULE D, CASES I AND II for in-depth examination of business accounts.

Simon's Direct Tax Service A3.15, A3.16.

Self-assessment. Many of the provisions described in this chapter relate to periods before those for which SELF-ASSESSMENT (78) applies, i.e. before 1996/97 (1997/98 in the case of partnerships whose business commenced before 6 April 1994). They continue to apply (so far as relevant) for corporation tax purposes until corporate self-assessment is introduced (i.e. for accounting periods ending on or after a day to be set, but which will not be before early 1999). However, many aspects of the self-assessment provisions are couched in similar terms to those previously applicable, so that the case law may continue to be of relevance.

6.1 BACK DUTY CLAIMS

Such claims are made by the Inland Revenue where they consider tax has been lost by a taxpayer's fraudulent or negligent conduct (or by his fraud or wilful default or by his neglect). In such cases, the normal time limits for assessment are extended (see 6.4 below), interest is chargeable on the understated tax (see 6.6 below) and PENALTIES (58) are incurred which the Board may mitigate.

The Revenue have published a Code of Practice (No 2, available from local tax offices) setting out their standards for the way in which investigations are conducted and the rights and responsibilities of taxpayers. Codes of Practice 8 and 9, dealing with Special Compliance Office Investigations in cases other than suspected serious fraud and cases of such fraud respectively, were published in January 1995 and are available from the Special Compliance Office, Angel Court, 199 Borough High Street, London SE1 1HZ. Code 11, dealing with enquiries into self-assessment income tax returns by local tax offices, was published in July 1996, and will be issued at the start of every such enquiry (except that in certain simple cases a short, single-page version will be issued).

For the validity of tax amnesties see *CIR v National Federation of Self-employed and Small Businesses Ltd HL 1981, 55 TC 133.*

6.2 FRAUD OR WILFUL DEFAULT

See 6.4 below as regards the replacement of 'fraud, wilful default or neglect' assessments by 'fraudulent or negligent conduct' assessments. The later expression is not defined, and the following cases may be of continued assistance in this respect.

Unexplained capital increases or admitted omissions may be held evidence of fraud or wilful default (*Amis v Colls Ch D 1960, 39 TC 148; Woodrow v Whalley Ch D 1964, 42 TC 249; Hudson v Humbles Ch D 1965, 42 TC 380; Hillenbrand CS 1966, 42 TC 617; Young v Duthie Ch D 1969, 45 TC 624; James v Pope Ch D 1972, 48 TC 142*; and cf. *Brimelow v Price Ch D 1965, 49 TC 41*). Taxpayer's deliberate exclusion of wife's income when making return held wilful default (*Brown v CIR Ch D 1965, 42 TC 583*) but not where husband unaware of wife's omissions (*Wellington v Reynolds Ch D 1962, 40 TC 209*). Wilful default may be by agent (*Clixby v Pountney Ch D 1967, 44 TC 515; Pleasants v Atkinson Ch D 1987, 60 TC 228*). Where Commissioners found fraud on the basis of the inspector's evidence at a hearing which the taxpayer or his agent did not attend, the case was remitted to be heard by different Commissioners (*Ottley v Morris Ch D 1978, 52 TC 375*).

The onus of proving fraud or wilful default is on the Crown (see e.g. *Hurley v Taylor CA 1998, 71 TC 268*), but the onus is on the taxpayer to prove the assessments are excessive (*Johnson v Scott CA 1978, 52 TC 383; Jonas v Bamford Ch D 1973, 51 TC 1; Nicholson v*

Morris CA 1977, 51 TC 95 and cf. *Barney v Pybus Ch D 1957, 37 TC 106* and *R v Spec Commrs (ex p Martin) CA 1971, 48 TC 1*). Acceptance of an inadequate estimated assessment may amount to wilful default (*Nuttall v Barrett Ch D 1992, 64 TC 548*). Once the unreliability of one year's accounts has been demonstrated, the Commissioners are entitled to make their own estimate for other years (*Brittain v Gibbs Ch D 1986, 59 TC 374*). For the standard of proof required, see *Les Croupiers Casino Club v Pattinson CA 1987, 60 TC 196*. For finding required of Commissioners, see *Rea v Highnam Ch D 1990, 63 TC 287*.

6.3 NEGLECT

See 6.4 below as regards the replacement of 'fraud, wilful default or neglect' assessments by 'fraudulent or negligent conduct' assessments.

Neglect means negligence or a failure to give any notice, make any return or to produce or furnish any document or other information required by or under the *Taxes Acts*. [*TMA 1970, s 118 as enacted*]. See the note at 67.1 RETURNS as regards reasonable excuse for failure to make returns.

6.4 EXTENDED TIME LIMITS

Note. See also 78.30 SELF-ASSESSMENT as regards assessments for 1996/97 and subsequent years.

Except where specifically provided, the normal time limit for assessments is 6 years after the tax year concerned. [*TMA 1970, s 34*]. In certain cases, however, extended limits apply to assessments for the purpose of making good a loss of tax.

Assessments made after 26 July 1989 relating to 1983/84 and subsequent years (or to accounting periods ending after 31 March 1983). Where the loss of tax arises due to the *fraudulent or negligent conduct* of a person (or of a person acting on his behalf), an assessment may be made at any time not later than 20 years after the end of the chargeable period to which it relates. Partners of a person responsible for fraudulent or negligent conduct may similarly be assessed for such years in respect of additional partnership profits. If the person assessed so requires, the assessment may give effect to reliefs or allowances to which he would have been entitled had he made the necessary claims within the relevant time limits (excluding certain elections for the transfer inter-spouse of the married couple's allowance). [*TMA 1970, s 36; FA 1989, s 149; F(No 2)A 1992, Sch 5 para 9(2)*]. For a case in which appeals against assessments raised out of the normal time limit were allowed on the grounds that, on the balance of probabilities, the Revenue had not proved fraudulent or negligent conduct, see *Rochester (UK) Ltd and another v Pickin (Sp C 160), [1998] SSCD 138*. In the case of personal representatives of offenders, such assessments in respect of deceased's income before death must be made within three years after the tax year in which he died. [*TMA 1970, s 40(2)*]. See 5.7 ASSESSMENTS as regards the date an assessment is made.

Assessments made before 27 July 1989 or relating to 1982/83 and earlier years (or to accounting periods ending before 1 April 1983). Where an assessment for any year (a 'normal year') has been made within six years thereafter for the purpose of making good tax lost by a taxpayer's *fraud, wilful default or neglect*, assessments for any of the six years prior to that 'normal year', for recovering tax lost by his neglect, may, by leave of a General or Special Commissioner, be made at any time up to the end of the tax year following that in which tax under the assessment for the normal year is finally determined. [*TMA 1970, s 118(4), s 37(3), s 41(1)*]. In the case of personal representatives of offenders, such assessments in respect of deceased's income before death must be made within three years after the tax year of death. [*TMA 1970, s 40(2)*]. Granting of leave by a Commissioner does not involve a hearing, and taxpayer is not entitled to appear or be heard (*Day v Williams CA 1969, 46 TC 59; Pearlberg v Varty HL 1972, 48 TC 14* and *Nicholson v Morris CA 1977, 51 TC 95*). The Revenue are only required to provide the Commissioner with such information as will allow him to make a judgement as to whether there are reasonable grounds for believing that there has, or may have, been a loss of tax due to the taxpayer's fraud, wilful default or neglect, and are not obliged to make full and frank disclosure of all facts known to them (*Re McGuckian CA(NI), [2000] STC 65*). For jurisdiction of Commissioners see *CIR v Adams CA 1971, 48 TC 67; Murphy v Elders Ch D 1973, 49 TC 135* and cf. *F Lack Ltd v Doggett CA 1970, 46 TC 524*. See also *R v Spec Commrs (ex p Morey) CA 1972, 49 TC 71* (use of prerogative orders disapproved) but contrast *R v Spec Commrs (ex p Stipplechoice Ltd) (No 1) CA 1985, 59 TC 396* where judicial review was granted in the absence of any other adequate remedy (and see *R v Spec Commrs (ex p Stipplechoice Ltd) (No 2) QB 1986, 59 TC 396* for the decision against the taxpayer on that review). The decision in *O'Mullan v Walmsley QB (NI) 1965, 42 TC 573* that such assessments are invalid unless the assessment for the 'normal year' was expressly stated to be for making good tax lost by fraud, default or neglect was not followed in *Thurgood v Slarke Ch D 1971, 47 TC 130*. 'What matters is not the purpose of the assessor but of the assessment.' See also *R v Spec Commrs (ex p Rogers) CA 1972, 48 TC 46; Knight v CIR CA 1974, 49 TC 179* and *R v Holborn Commrs (ex p Rind) QB 1974, 49 TC 656*.

If the person to be assessed so requires, the assessment may give effect to reliefs or allowances to which he would have been entitled had the necessary claims been made within the relevant time limits. [*TMA 1970, s 37(8)*].

Once an assessment (under *TMA 1970, s 37(3), s 41(1)*, or, being one of a number of assessments not more than six years apart, under *TMA 1970, s 36*, above) has been made more than six years after the end of a tax year (an 'earlier year') an assessment for any year up to six years before that earlier year may be made for recovering tax lost by taxpayer's neglect, but only by leave of the General or Special Commissioners on their being satisfied (on a Revenue application, at which taxpayer may appear and be heard) that reasonable grounds exist for believing that tax for that year has been so lost.

Applications to Commissioners for this purpose may be made up to the end of the tax year following final determination of liability under the assessment for the 'earlier year'. This provision applies separately to income tax and capital gains tax. [*TMA 1970, s 37*].

Adaptation of these provisions to partnerships is provided by *TMA 1970, s 38*.

Married couples. Where total income of 1990/91 or any subsequent year is increased as a result of fraudulent or negligent conduct assessments, this does not affect the validity of any blind person's allowance or certain other allowances transferred from husband to wife which are determined by reference to total income or given as a reduction in total income tax liability. The husband's allowances are correspondingly reduced. [*TMA 1970, s 37A; FA 1988, Sch 3 para 30; FA 1989, s 149(4); F(No 2)A 1992, Sch 5 para 9(3); FA 1994, Sch 8 para 13*].

6.5 **Deceased persons.** Assessments on deceased's income or capital gains arising or accruing before death must be made within three years after the tax year in which he dies. [*TMA 1970, s 40(1)*]. Assessments for any of the six years of assessment preceding that of death, for the purpose of making good tax lost by deceased's fraudulent or negligent conduct, may also be made within the same time limit, but not later. [*TMA 1970, s 40(2); FA 1989, s 149(4)*]. See 78.30 SELF-ASSESSMENT as regards 1996/97 and later years. If the deceased was in *partnership* valid assessments on the partnership may be made outside that limit, but will be enforceable only against the surviving partners (*Harrison v Willis CA 1965, 43 TC 61*). See 5.7 ASSESSMENTS as regards the date an assessment is made.

6.6 INTEREST ON UNDERPAID TAX

Note. The provisions described below do not apply where the new self-assessment interest provisions of *TMA 1970, s 86* have effect (see 42.1 INTEREST AND SURCHARGES ON UNPAID TAX). [*FA 1996, Sch 18 paras 4, 17(3)(4)*].

Where an assessment is made for making good tax lost through

(*a*) a 'failure' to give a notice, make a return, or provide a document or other information, or

(*b*) an error in any information or return, etc. supplied

after 26 July 1989, the tax attributable to that failure or error is chargeable with interest, if an inspector or the board so determines. 'failure' includes failure to do something at a particular time or within a particular period; and the exclusion in *TMA 1970, s 118(2)* (see 67.1 RETURNS) does not apply. [*TMA 1970, s 88(1)(7); FA 1989, ss 159, 160(1)*].

A determination under these provisions can be made at any time within six years of the end of the chargeable period for which the tax is charged, or within three years of the final determination of the amount of that tax. Notice of the determination must specify

(i) the date of issue,

(ii) the amount of tax carrying interest, and the assessment by which it was charged,

(iii) the date when, for *TMA 1970, s 88* purposes, it ought to have been paid, and

(iv) the time within which an appeal against the determination may be made.

The general APPEALS (4) provisions apply, except for *TMA 1970, s 50(6)–(8)* (see 4.6(*c*)(*e*) APPEALS). On appeal, the Commissioners can set aside or confirm the determination, or alter it in respect of the amount of tax or the date. For collection purposes, an interest certificate may be supplied by the inspector, or other officer of the Board, and the collector. [*TMA 1970, ss 70(3), 88A; FA 1989, s 160(2)(3)*].

Where an assessment is made for making good tax lost by fraud, wilful default or neglect (see 6.2, 6.4 above) which occurred **before 27 July 1989**, the tax attributable to that fraud, etc. is chargeable with interest. [*TMA 1970, s 88(1)*]. The amount of interest is certified by the General or Special Commissioners under *TMA 1970, s 70(3)*, following an application by the Revenue at which the taxpayer is entitled to appear and be heard (*Nicholson v Morris CA 1977, 51 TC 95*). There is no appeal by way of case stated (*R v Holborn Commissioners (ex p Rind) QB 1974, 49 TC 656*). For the limited extent to which regard should be had to events after the making of an assessment in determining whether *TMA 1970, s 88* applies, see *Billingham v Myers CA 1996, 68 TC 512.*

Tax carrying interest under TMA 1970, s 88 does not also carry interest under *TMA 1970, s 86* (see 42.2 INTEREST AND SURCHARGES ON UNPAID TAX). It is payable gross (and not deductible for tax purposes) from the date when the tax ought to have been paid (but without the alternative of 30 days after the date of issue of the notice of assessment, see 56.1 PAYMENT OF TAX) to the date of actual payment. The Board have power to mitigate interest payable and to stay or compound any recovery proceedings. [*TMA 1970, ss 88–90; FA 1989, s 161*]. See also 58 PENALTIES and 67.2 RETURNS, and note that the provisions of *TMA 1970, s 88* are applied to underpaid Class 4 national insurance contributions by *Social Security Contributions and Benefits Act 1992, Sch 2 para 6* (see also *Social Security (Consequential Provisions) Act 1992, Sch 4 paras 1, 8, 9*).

Rates of interest are generally as for interest on unpaid tax, i.e. as follows.

3%p.a.	for periods up to 18 April 1967
4%p.a.	from 19 April 1967 to 30 June 1974
9%p.a.	from 1 July 1974 to 31 December 1979
12%p.a.	from 1 January 1980 to 30 November 1982
8%p.a.	from 1 December 1982 to 30 April 1985
11%p.a.	from 1 May 1985 to 5 August 1986
8.5%p.a.	from 6 August 1986 to 5 November 1986
9.5%p.a.	from 6 November 1986 to 5 April 1987
9%p.a.	from 6 April 1987 to 5 June 1987
8.25%p.a.	from 6 June 1987 to 5 September 1987
9%p.a.	from 6 September 1987 to 5 December 1987
8.25%p.a.	from 6 December 1987 to 5 May 1988
7.75%p.a.	from 6 May 1988 to 5 August 1988
9.75%p.a.	from 6 August 1988 to 5 October 1988
10.75%p.a.	from 6 October 1988 to 5 January 1989
11.5%p.a.	from 6 January 1989 to 5 July 1989
12.25%p.a.	from 6 July 1989 to 5 November 1989
13%p.a.	from 6 November 1989 to 5 November 1990
12.25%p.a.	from 6 November 1990 to 5 March 1991
11.5%p.a.	from 6 March 1991 to 5 May 1991
10.75%p.a.	from 6 May 1991 to 5 July 1991
10%p.a.	from 6 July 1991 to 5 October 1991
9.25%p.a.	from 6 October 1991 to 5 November 1992
7.75%p.a.	from 6 November 1992 to 5 December 1992
7%p.a.	from 6 December 1992 to 5 March 1993
6.25%p.a.	from 6 March 1993 to 5 January 1994
5.5%p.a.	from 6 January 1994 to 5 October 1994
6.25%p.a.	from 6 October 1994 to 5 March 1995
7%p.a.	from 6 March 1995 to 5 February 1996
6.25%p.a.	from 6 February 1996 to 30 January 1997
8.5%p.a.	from 31 January to 5 August 1997
9.5% p.a.	from 6 August 1997 to 5 January 1999
8.5% p.a.	from 6 January 1999 to 5 March 1999
7.5% p.a.	from 6 March 1999 to 5 February 2000
8.5% p.a.	**from 6 February 2000 to**

Interest factor tables for use as ready reckoners in calculating interest on overdue tax are published by the Revenue and updated as rates change (although not after 5 April 1999). For computational simplicity, these treat the change from 6.25% p.a. to 8.5% p.a. on 31 January 1997 as applying only from 6 February 1997. (Revenue Press Release 11 March 1999).

6.7 UNDERSTATED PROFITS ETC.

The measure of understated profits, etc., is calculated from the available data, but if this is unsatisfactory, on the increase of capital from year to year, with adjustments for cost of living, etc. See for this, cases mentioned at 6.2 and 6.4 above and *Deacon v Roper Ch D 1952, 33 TC 66; Horowitz v Farrand Ch D 1952, 33 TC 221; Moschi v Kelly CA 1952, 33 TC 442; Kilburn v Bedford Ch D 1955, 36 TC 262; Roberts v McGregor Ch D 1959, 38 TC 610; Chuwen v Sabine Ch D 1959, 39 TC 1; Erddig Motors Ltd v McGregor Ch D 1961, 40 TC 95; Hellier v O'Hare Ch D 1964, 42 TC 155; Hurley v Young Ch D 1966, 45 ATC 316; Hope v Damerel Ch D 1969, 48 ATC 461; Driver v CIR CS 1977, 52 TC 153; Kovak v Morris CA 1985, 58 TC 493* and cf. *Rose v Humbles CA 1971, 48 TC 103*. For a case in which similar principles were applied in determining directors' true remuneration, see *Billows v Robinson Ch D 1989, 64 TC 17.*

Inspectors will not automatically insist on annual capital statements (see above) where understated profits can be measured satisfactorily in other ways, such as by use of expected rates of gross trading profits. (Revenue Press Release 1 August 1977).

A certificate of full disclosure may be required by the Revenue from a taxpayer during a back duty enquiry stating that complete disclosure has been made of, *inter alia*, all: banking, savings and loan accounts, deposit receipts, Building Society and Co-operative Society accounts; investments including Savings Certificates and Premium Bonds and loans (whether interest bearing or not); other assets, including cash and life assurance policies, which taxpayer and his wife now possess, or have possessed, or in which they have or have had any interest or power to operate or control during a stated period; gifts in any form, by taxpayer or wife to children or to other persons during stated period; sources of income and all income derived therefrom and of all facts bearing on liability to income tax, capital gains tax and other duties for the stated period. Great care must be exercised before signing such a certificate since subsequent discovery of an omission could lead to heavy penalties.

Independent taxation. Inspectors will respect the right of confidentiality between husband and wife under independent taxation in all cases, including investigation cases. However, the underlying interdependence remains and inspectors, in investigating one spouse, may need information from or concerning the other. Although inspectors will make every effort to avoid unwarranted disclosure and the gratuitous passing of information, it remains open to them to take such action as is necessary to enable them to perform their duties. In effect, married persons are in the same position with regard to confidentiality as are single persons.

Husbands remain liable for tax, etc. on the wife's income or gains for years prior to the introduction of independent taxation. The inspector will, however, normally agree to the wife settling any such liability personally. (ICAEW Memorandum TR 778, 8 January 1990).

6.8 **INVESTIGATORY POWERS**

FA 1989, ss 142–148 amended *TMA 1970, ss 20–20D* to extend the Revenue's powers to obtain the production of accounts, books and other information. The revised powers are described below.

For these purposes, '*document*' means anything in which information of any description is recorded, but does not include personal records or journalistic material (within *Police and Criminal Evidence Act 1984, ss 12, 13*) (and those exclusions apply also to particulars contained in such records or material). The documents concerned are those in the possession or power of the person receiving the notice. Photographic, etc. facsimiles may be supplied provided the originals are produced if called for, and documents relating to any pending tax appeal need not be delivered. There are special provisions relating to computer records (see *FA 1988, s 127*). Documents in a person's 'possession or power' are those actually in existence at the time the notice is given, and not any which would have to be brought into existence in order to satisfy the notice.

(*a*) Where an **inspector** is of the reasonable opinion that documents contain, or may contain, information relevant to any tax liability of a person he may (with the Board's authority and the consent of a General or Special Commissioner (who is excluded from subsequent appeal proceedings)) by notice in writing require that person to deliver such documents to him (but only after that person has been given reasonable opportunity to produce them). Applications to a Commissioner for consent to issue a notice are held *ex parte* (see *Applicant v Inspector of Taxes (Sp C 189), [1999] SSCD 128*). For challenges to the validity of notices, see *R v CIR (ex p T C Coombs & Co) HL 1991, 64 TC 124; R v CIR (ex p Taylor) CA 1988, 62 TC 562; (No 2) CA 1990, 62 TC 578*; also *Kempton v Special Commrs and CIR Ch D 1992, 66 TC*

249, where the validity of the notice was confirmed although the only evidence on which the inspector relied related to omissions from the returns of a fellow director of the taxpayer concerned, and *R v Macdonald and CIR (ex p Hutchinson & Co Ltd and others) QB 1998, 71 TC 1*, in which the notice was quashed in view of the failure of the Revenue either to put before the Commissioner a letter setting out the taxpayer's substantive response to precursor notices (which had failed for technical reasons), or to address the issues raised by the taxpayer in their summary of reasons (see below) for applying for consent to the notice. In *R v CIR (ex p Banque Internationale à Luxembourg SA) QB, 2000 STI 919*, an application based *inter alia* on the protections afforded by the European Convention on Human Rights was refused.

(*b*) An **inspector** may similarly by notice in writing require a person to furnish him with such particulars as he may reasonably require as being relevant to any tax liability of that person (again after reasonable opportunity has been given for their production).

(*c*) An **inspector** may similarly by notice in writing require any other person (including the Director of Savings) to deliver to him (or, if the person so elects, make available for inspection by a named officer of the Board) documents relevant to any tax liability of a taxpayer. A copy of the notice must be sent to the taxpayer concerned unless, in a case involving suspected fraud, a General or Special Commissioner directs otherwise. Production of documents originating more than six years before the notice cannot be required (unless the Commissioner who gave consent to the notice specifically allows it on being satisfied there is reasonable ground for believing loss of tax through fraud).

For general limitations on these powers, see *R v O'Kane and Clarke (ex p Northern Bank Ltd) and related application QB 1996, 69 TC 187*, and for a review of the procedural and other requirements, see *R v CIR (ex p Ulster Bank Ltd) CA 1997, 69 TC 211*, in which *ex p Northern Bank Ltd* was in part disapproved.

A notice cannot require the production by a statutory auditor of his audit papers, nor by a tax adviser of communications with a client (or with any other tax adviser of his client) relating to advice about the client's tax affairs. This exemption does not, however, apply to explanatory documents concerning any other documents prepared with the client for, or for delivery to, the Revenue, unless the Revenue already has access to the information contained therein in some other document. Similarly, where a notice does not identify the taxpayer to which it relates (see below), the exemption does not apply to any document giving the name or address of any taxpayer to whom the notice relates (or of a person acting on their behalf) unless the Revenue already has access to the information contained therein. Where the exemption is so disapplied, either the document must be delivered or made available to the Revenue or a copy of the relevant parts must be supplied (which parts must be available if required for inspection). The Revenue's application of these provisions in practice is set out in a Statement of Practice (Revenue Pamphlet IR 131, SP 5/90, 11 April 1990). In particular, it is made clear that accountants' working papers will be called for only where voluntary access has not been obtained and it is considered absolutely necessary in order to determine whether a client's accounts or returns are complete and correct. Requests for access may on occasion extend to the whole or a particular part of the working papers, rather than just to information explaining specific entries, and the Revenue will usually be prepared to visit the accountants' or clients' premises to examine the papers and to take copies or extracts. These restrictions on the use of its powers by the Revenue do not apply in the circumstances described under (*d*) below.

'*Taxpayer*' includes an individual who has died (but any notice must be given within six years of the death) and a company which has ceased to exist.

A notice may, subject to conditions, be given which does not specify the taxpayer to whom it relates, with the specific consent of a Special Commissioner, and subject to appeal (within 30 days) by the person on whom it is served on the ground that it would be onerous for him to comply with it. For an unsuccessful application for judicial review of the issue of such a notice, see *R v CIR (ex p Ulster Bank Ltd) QB, [2000] STC 537.*

(*d*) An inspector may similarly by notice in writing (with the Board's authority and the consent of a Circuit judge in England and Wales, a sheriff in Scotland or a County Court judge in NI) require a tax accountant (i.e. a person who assists another in the preparation of returns, etc. for tax purposes) who has been convicted of a tax offence or incurred a penalty under *TMA 1970, s 99* (see 58.3 PENALTIES) (in relation to which no appeal is pending) to deliver documents relevant to any tax liability of any of his clients. The notice must be issued within twelve months of the final determination of the conviction or penalty award.

(*e*) The **Board** may require, by notice in writing, a person to deliver or furnish, to a named officer of theirs, documents or information as specified in (*a*) and (*b*) above. Notices will not, however, be given under this power unless there are reasonable grounds for believing that that person may have failed, or may fail, to comply with any provision of the *Taxes Acts,* and that any such failure is likely to have led, or to lead, to serious prejudice to the proper assessment or collection of tax.

Where notice under (*a*), (*b*) or (*c*) above is given after 3 May 1994, the taxpayer concerned must be provided with a written summary of the inspector's reasons for applying for consent to the giving of the notice (unless, in the case of (*c*), a Commissioner has directed that the taxpayer need not be sent a copy of the notice itself). Such a summary may exclude information which might identify an informant, or which the Commissioner is satisfied might prejudice the assessment or collection of tax, although a summary written so as not to compromise these requirements should nevertheless be provided. However, in a case within (*c*) above, the courts refused to quash such a notice where no written summary had been provided to the taxpayers whose liabilities were under investigation (*R v CIR (ex p Continental Shipping Ltd and Atsiganos SA) QB 1996, 68 TC 665*).

For guidance on the question of whether documents and records are the property of the client or of the accountant, see ICAEW Memorandum TR 781, 23 February 1990.

The notice must specify or describe the documents or particulars required, the time limit for production (generally not less than 30 days) and, except as above, the name of the taxpayer or client, as appropriate; and the person to whom they are delivered may take copies. There are severe penalties for the falsification, concealment, disposal or destruction of a document which is the subject of a notice or formal request (see (*a*) above), unless strict conditions and time limits are observed.

[*TMA 1970, ss 20–20BB, s 20D; FA 1989, ss 142–145, s 148, s 168(2); FA 1990, s 93; FA 1994, s 255; Civil Evidence Act 1995, Sch 1 para 6*]. For failure to comply with a notice, see 58.4 PENALTIES.

Notices (other than those under (*d*) above and those which relate to an unnamed taxpayer) may relate to tax liabilities in EU member States other than the UK [*FA 1990, s 125(1)(2)(6)*] or in any other territory with which the UK has entered into arrangements providing for the obtaining of information. [*FA 2000, s 146(3)(4)*].

For an article setting out the Revenue's view on the question of claims to legal or professional privilege in relation to requests for information under these provisions (other than where tax evasion or tax fraud is suspected), see Revenue Tax Bulletin April 2000 pp 743–746.

Order for delivery of documents in serious tax fraud cases. Under *TMA 1970, s 20BA, Sch 1AA*, introduced by *FA 2000, s 149, Sch 39*, the Board may apply to the appropriate judicial authority (a Circuit judge in England and Wales, a sheriff in Scotland or a County Court judge in NI) for an order requiring any person who appears to have in his possession or power documents specified or described in the order to deliver them to an officer of the Board within ten working days after the day of service of the notice, or such longer or shorter period as may be specified in the order. The judicial authority must be satisfied, on information on oath given by an authorised officer of the Board, that there is reasonable ground for suspecting that an offence involving serious tax fraud has been or is about to be committed, and that the documents may be required as evidence in proceedings in respect of the offence. In Scotland, a single sheriff may make orders in respect of persons anywhere in Scotland as long as one of the orders relates to a person residing or having a place of business at an address in the sheriff's own sheriffdom. Orders may not be made in relation to items subject to legal privilege (as defined) unless they are held with the intention of furthering a criminal purpose. Failure to comply with an order is treated as contempt of court, and there are severe penalties for falsification of documents.

Schedule 1AA lays down detailed requirements in relation to such applications, and these may be supplemented by regulations. In particular, a person is entitled to notice of intention to apply for such an order, and to appear and be heard at the application, unless the judicial authority is satisfied that this would seriously prejudice investigation of the offence. Until the application has been dismissed or abandoned, or an order made and complied with, any person given such notice must not conceal, destroy, alter or dispose of any document to which the order sought relates, or disclose information etc. likely to prejudice the investigation, except with the leave of the judicial authority or the written permission of the Board. Professional legal advisers may, however, disclose such information etc. in giving legal advice to a client or in connection with legal proceedings, provided that it is not disclosed with a view to furthering a criminal purpose. Failure to comply with these requirements is treated as failure to comply with an order under these provisions. The procedural rules where documents are delivered in accordance with an order are as under *TMA 1970, s 20CC(3)–(9)* (see 6.9 below). Draft regulations under *Schedule 1AA* were published on 19 June 2000.

Simon's Direct Tax Service. See **A3.150** *et seq.*.

6.9 **Search and seizure.** Where there is reasonable suspicion of serious tax fraud, and there are reasonable grounds for believing that use of the procedure under *TMA 1970, s 20BA* (see 6.8 above) might seriously prejudice the investigation, the Board may apply to a Circuit judge, etc. (as in 6.8(*d*) above) for a warrant to enter premises within 14 days to search and to seize any things which may be relevant as evidence. There are detailed procedural rules governing searches and the removal of documents, etc. [*TMA 1970, ss 20C, 20CC, 20D; FA 1989, ss 146, 147; FA 2000, s 150*]. The warrant need not specify the suspected fraud or the documents, etc., searched for (*Rossminster Ltd HL 1979, 52 TC 160*). For the proper procedure in seeking and obtaining judicial review of a decision to grant such a warrant, and interim injunctions, see *R v CIR (ex p Kingston Smith (a firm)) QB 1996, 70 TC 264*. For the validity of warrants, see *R v CIR (ex p Tamosius & Partners) QB, [1999] STC 107*.

6.10 **Barristers, advocates or solicitors.** A notice under 6.8(*a*), (*b*), (*c*) or (*d*) above to a barrister, advocate or solicitor can be issued only by the Board (although that power may be delegated, see *R v CIR (ex p Davis Frankel & Mead) QB, [2000] STC 595*) and he cannot (without his client's consent) be required to deliver under 6.8(*c*) and (*d*) above documents protected by professional privilege. [*TMA 1970, s 20B(3)(8)*]. As regards the search and seizure powers in 6.9 above, there is similarly an exclusion for documents protected by professional privilege or, from 28 July 2000, 'legal privilege' as more widely defined (but excluding items held with the intention of furthering a criminal purpose) [*TMA 1970, s 20C(4); FA 1989, s 146(4); FA 2000, s 150(4)*], and see also 6.8 above as regards similar protection in relation to an order under *TMA 1970, s 20BA* in cases involving serious tax fraud. See *R v CIR (ex p Goldberg) QB 1988, 61 TC 403* as regards nature of documents subject to privilege, but note that the decision in that case was doubted in *Dubai Bank Ltd v Galadari CA, [1989] 3 WLR 1044*, a non-tax case. In relation to search and seizure under 6.9 above, it was held in *R v CIR (ex p Tamosius & Partners) QB, [1999] STC 1077* that the presence of independent counsel to determine the issue of privilege was 'to be encouraged', although it would not prevent action by the courts if counsel was wrong.

For an article setting out the Revenue's view on the question of claims to legal or professional privilege in relation to requests for information under these provisions (other than where tax evasion or tax fraud is suspected), see Revenue Tax Bulletin April 2000 pp 743–746.

6.11 OFFERS BY TAXPAYER

Where back duty arises, the taxpayer may offer a sum in full settlement of liability for tax, interest and penalties. The practice of the Board of Inland Revenue in cases of tax fraud is as follows.

(i) The Board may accept a money settlement instead of instituting criminal proceedings in respect of fraud alleged to have been committed by a taxpayer.

(ii) They can give no undertaking that they will accept a money settlement and refrain from instituting criminal proceedings even if the case is one in which the taxpayer has made full confession and has given full facilities for investigation of the facts. They reserve to themselves full discretion in all cases as to the course they pursue.

(iii) But in considering whether to accept a money settlement or to institute criminal proceedings, it is their practice to be influenced by the fact that the taxpayer has made a full confession and has given full facilities for investigation into his affairs and for examination of such books, papers, documents or information as the Board may consider necessary.

(Revenue Press Release 18 October 1990).

See *CIR v Nuttall CA 1989, 63 TC 148* for confirmation of power to enter into such agreements. Amounts due under such an agreement which are unpaid may be pursued by an action for a debt, but the Crown does not rank as a preferential creditor in respect of the sums due (*Nuttall* above; *CIR v Woollen CA 1992, 65 TC 229*). See *R v CIR (ex p Mead and Cook) QB 1992, 65 TC 1* as regards Revenue discretion to seek monetary settlements or institute criminal proceedings. See *R v CIR (ex p Allen) QB 1997, 69 TC 442* for an unsuccessful application for judicial review of a Revenue decision to take criminal proceedings.

The Crown Prosecution Service ('CPS') is not precluded from instituting criminal proceedings in circumstances where the Revenue has accepted a monetary settlement. (*R v W and another CA, [1998] STC 550*). The Attorney-General made it clear, however, in a Parliamentary Written Answer, that proceedings brought by the CPS will ordinarily encompass charges relating to tax evasion only in circumstances where that is incidental to allegations of non-fiscal criminal conduct. A 'Convention between Prosecuting Authorities to provide arrangements for ensuring effective co-ordination of decision making and handling in related cases which are the responsibility of different authorities' was established on 11 February 1998 (for which see the Attorney General's Press Release of that date). See Hansard Vol 310, No 155 at Cols 230, 231 and Revenue Tax Bulletin June 1998 pp 544, 545.

See generally Revenue Pamphlet IR 73 as regards negotiation of settlements.

Relief for retirement annuity premiums and personal pension contributions. Where an offer as above is made and accepted by the Board in settlement of liabilities which include tax on relevant earnings assessable for a year which ended more than six years earlier, unused retirement annuity and personal pension relief (see 65.5 RETIREMENT ANNUITIES and 60.6 PERSONAL PENSION SCHEMES) which would have arisen if an assessment had been made on such earnings may be set against premiums or contributions paid within six months of acceptance of the offer on election by the taxpayer, within the same six months, for such relief to be given. Relief is, however, only available to the extent that the premiums or contributions exceed the maximum applying for the year of assessment in which they are paid, although the normal time limits apply in relation to the payment of premiums up to that maximum. See now, however, 60.6 PERSONAL PENSION SCHEMES for the prohibition on carry forward of relief for personal pension contributions after 5 April 2001. This practice also applies where assessments have been made and appealed against but the appeals have not been formally determined, if the tax for the years concerned is included in the settlement. (Revenue Pamphlet IR 131, SP 9/91, 31 July 1991, replacing SP 9/80, which dealt only with retirement annuities).

Simon's Direct Tax Service. See **A3.1645**.

6.12 OFFENCE OF FRAUDULENT EVASION OF INCOME TAX

A person who is knowingly concerned in the fraudulent evasion of income tax (by him or any other person) is liable, on summary conviction, to imprisonment for up to six months and/or a fine not exceeding the statutory maximum (£5,000), or on conviction on indictment, to imprisonment for up to seven years and/or an unlimited fine. This applies to things done or omitted after 31 December 2000. [*FA 2000, s 144*].

7 Bankruptcy

Simon's Direct Tax Service A3.1107.

7.1 Income received by trustee during bankruptcy is not income of bankrupt for purposes of claiming personal allowances, etc. (*Fleming CS 1928, 14 TC 78*). Trustee is assessable on such income including profits of bankrupt's business continued by him notwithstanding requirement to hand over to creditors (*Armitage v Moore QB 1900, 4 TC 199*). And see *Hibbert v Fysh CA 1962, 40 TC 305* (bankrupt assessable on remuneration retainable by him). The trustee continues generally to act following the death (undischarged) of the bankrupt as if he or she were still alive.

For the Revenue approach to dealing with personal insolvency under SELF-ASSESSMENT (78), see Revenue Tax Bulletin April 1998 pp 530, 531.

See 56.5 PAYMENT OF TAX for Crown Priority and 58.9 PENALTIES for penalties awarded against a bankrupt. See also Tolley's Capital Gains Tax under Settlements.

8 Banks

8.1 For the tax treatment of banks themselves, and for certain exemptions, see Tolley's Corporation Tax (under Banks).

Interest payable in UK to a UK bank, and interest paid by a UK bank, are both payable gross (see 23.3(ii) DEDUCTION OF TAX AT SOURCE) except as detailed in 8.2 below, but payments by individuals to banks of certain home mortgage interest are made after deduction of tax, see 23.13 DEDUCTION OF TAX AT SOURCE. For savings bank interest etc., see 29.13 EXEMPT INCOME.

In general, the term 'bank' is defined by reference to the carrying on of a *bona fide* banking business, but for certain purposes it is specially defined as:

(*a*) the Bank of England;

(*b*) an institution authorised under the *Banking Act 1987*;

(*c*) a European authorised institution (within the *Banking Co-ordination (Second Council Directive) Regulations 1992*) in relation to the establishment of a branch of which the requirements of *Sch 2 para 1* of those regulations have been complied with; or

(*d*) an international organisation of which the UK is a member and which is designated as a bank for the particular purpose by Treasury order (e.g. the European Investment Bank, see *SI 1996 No 1179*).

See 3.8 ANTI-AVOIDANCE, 15.10 CHARITIES, 23.3(ii) DEDUCTION OF TAX AT SOURCE, 67.4 RETURNS. [*ICTA 1988, s 840A; FA 1996, Sch 37 para 1(1)*].

Returns. Banks must make returns of interest paid to depositors, see 67.4 RETURNS.

8.2 **DEDUCTION OF TAX FROM INTEREST** [*ICTA 1988, ss 480A–482; FA 1990, Sch 5 paras 7–12; SI 1990 No 2232; FA 1991, ss 75, 82; SI 1992 Nos 12–15; F(No 2)A 1992, Sch 8 para 4; SI 1992 No 3234; FA 1993, ss 59, 183(2); SI 1994 No 295; FA 1995, s 86; SI 1995 No 1370; FA 2000, s 111(3)(6)*]

Any 'deposit-taker' paying or crediting interest on a 'relevant deposit' must deduct therefrom a sum representing income tax thereon (at the lower rate (before 1996/97, the basic rate) for the year of assessment in which the payment is made), unless the conditions for gross payment contained in *The Income Tax (Deposit-takers) (Interest Payments) Regulations 1990* (*SI 1990 No 2232*) (see below) are met. Income tax chargeable under SCHEDULE D, CASE III (72) on such interest is computed on the full amount of the interest arising in the year. *ICTA 1988, s 349* (see 23.3 DEDUCTION OF TAX AT SOURCE) does not apply to such payments.

The deposit-taker must treat all deposits as relevant deposits unless satisfied to the contrary, but if so satisfied may treat a deposit as not being a relevant deposit until he comes into possession of information reasonably indicative that the deposit is, or may be, a relevant deposit.

For these purposes '*deposit-taker*' means the Bank of England, any institution authorised under the *Banking Act 1987* (or municipal bank within that *Act*), the Post Office, any local authority and any other deposit-taker prescribed by Treasury order. A 'European deposit-taker' within *SI 1992 No 3218, reg 82(3)* is included (see *SI 1992 No 3234*). A '*relevant deposit*' (subject to the exclusions below) is a deposit where either:

(*a*) the person beneficially entitled to any interest is an individual (or the persons so entitled are all individuals), or is a Scottish partnership all the partners of which are individuals; or (*b*) the person entitled to the interest receives it as the personal representative of a deceased individual (but note particularly the ordinary residence requirement at (xii) below); or

(*c*) (from 6 April 1996) the interest arises to the trustees of a discretionary or accumulation trust (as under *ICTA 1988, s 686*, see 81.5 SETTLEMENTS). This does not apply to deposits made before 6 April 1995 unless the deposit-taker has, since that date but before the making of the payment, been notified by the Board or the trustees that the interest is income of such a trust (and the Board has wide information powers in relation to such notices). The form of notification by the trustees is laid down by *SI 1995 No 1370*, under which payments may continue to be made gross for up to 30 days after receipt of notice (whether by the trustees or by the Revenue) where deduction within that period has not become reasonably practicable. Notification may be cancelled by the Revenue where appropriate. There are transitional provisions treating the source as ceasing where a payment on a deposit made before 6 April 1996 is brought within the scheme before 6 April 1998.

Excluded are:

(i) deposits in respect of which a CERTIFICATE OF DEPOSIT (13) has been issued for £50,000 or more (or foreign equivalent at the time the deposit is made) and which are repayable within five years;

(ii) non-transferable deposits of £50,000 or more (or foreign equivalent at the time the deposit is made) repayable at the end of a specified period of not more than five years;

(iii) a '*qualifying deposit right*', i.e. a right to receive an amount in pursuance of a deposit of money under an arrangement under which no certificate of deposit has been issued, although the person entitled to the right could call for the issue of such a certificate, which otherwise meets the conditions in (i) above;

(iv) debentures (as defined in *Companies Act 1985, s 744*);

(v) loans made *by* a deposit-taker in the ordinary course of his business;

(vi) debts on securities listed on a recognised stock exchange;

(vii) deposits in a '*general client account deposit*', i.e. a client account, other than an account for specific clients, if the depositor is required by law to make payments representing interest to any of the clients whose money it contains;

(viii) Lloyd's UNDERWRITERS (89) premiums trust funds;

(ix) deposits by Stock Exchange money brokers (recognised by the Bank of England) in the course of business as such a broker;

(x) deposits held at non-UK branches of UK resident deposit-takers;

(xi) deposits with non-UK resident deposit-takers held other than in UK branches; and

(xii) deposits in respect of which the 'appropriate person' has declared in writing to the deposit-taker that:

(1) where (*a*) above applies, the individual (or all of the individuals) concerned is (are), at the time of the declaration, not ordinarily resident in the UK; or

(2) where (*b*) above applies, the deceased, at the time of his death, was not ordinarily resident in the UK; or

(3) where (*c*) above applies, at the time of the declaration the trustees are not UK resident and do not have any reasonable grounds for believing that any of the

beneficiaries (as defined for this purpose) is a UK ordinarily resident individual or a UK resident company.

The '*appropriate person*' is any person beneficially entitled to the interest, or entitled to receive it in his capacity as a personal representative or trustee, or to whom it is payable. The declaration must be in such form, and contain such information, as is required by the Board, and must include an undertaking to notify the deposit-taker should any individual concerned become ordinarily resident in the UK, or the trustees or any company concerned become resident in the UK, or any UK ordinarily resident individual or UK-resident company become a beneficiary of the trust to which the declaration relates. The Revenue have powers to review all declarations received by a deposit-taker. For declarations made before 6 April 2001, a certificate by the deposit-taker is required in cases where the declaration of non-ordinary residence does not include the depositor's permanent address, but from that date the address must be included in any such declaration. Declarations in similar terms made to a building society which converts to company status (see 9.3, 9.6 BUILDING SOCIETIES) are, by concession, treated as having been made to the successor company. (Revenue Pamphlet IR 1, A69).

The deposit-taker has to treat all deposits as relevant deposits unless satisfied to the contrary, but if so satisfied can treat a deposit as not being a relevant deposit until he comes into possession of information reasonably indicative that the deposit is, or might be, a relevant deposit.

The Treasury and the Board are given wide powers to alter the legislation by statutory instrument, in particular in relation to the declaration required at (xii) above.

In the case of depositors who make the appropriate declaration for their deposit to be excluded from being a relevant deposit (see (xii) above) to a deposit-taker other than a bank, the normal deduction rules under *ICTA 1988, s 349(2)* are disapplied by *section 349(3)(h)* (introduced by *FA 1993, s 59*) as they are disapplied in the case of banks by *section 349(3)(a)* (and see Revenue Press Release 21 January 1993).

The collection procedure of *ICTA 1988, Sch 16* applies, *mutatis mutandis*, to such payments whether or not the deposit-taker is UK-resident.

For repayment claims on behalf of persons incapable of managing their own affairs, see Revenue Tax Bulletin April 1996 p 301.

The Inland Revenue Financial Intermediaries and Claims Office may be contacted for technical advice in relation to the basic rate tax scheme on 0151–472 6156.

Gross payment may be made where the person beneficially entitled to the interest is UK ordinarily resident (see 64.6 RESIDENCE, ORDINARY RESIDENCE AND DOMICILE) and has supplied the appropriate certificate to the deposit-taker to the effect that he is unlikely to be liable to income tax for the year of assessment in which the payment is made or credited (taking into account for this purpose all interest arising in the year of assessment concerned which would, in the absence of such a certificate, be received under deduction of lower or basic rate tax). The certificate must be in prescribed form and must contain the name, permanent address, date of birth and (where applicable) national insurance number of the person beneficially entitled to the interest, and the name (and if necessary branch) of the deposit-taker and account number. It must also contain an undertaking to notify the deposit-taker if the person beneficially entitled to the payment becomes liable to income tax for the year in which the payment is made or credited. Revenue Explanatory Leaflet IR 110 outlines the conditions for certification (which are described in detail below) and contains the appropriate Form R85(1990) on which application may be made (and of which further copies may be obtained from banks, building societies, post offices and tax offices). Leaflet

IR 111 explains the procedure for reclaiming tax deducted where no Form R85(1990) is in effect, and contains the appropriate claim Form R95(1991).

Such a certificate may only be given by:

(i) a depositor aged 16 or over at the beginning of the year of assessment in which the payment is made or credited, or who attains age 16 during that year, who is beneficially entitled to the payment; or

(ii) the parent or guardian of a person beneficially entitled to the payment who is under 16 at the beginning of that year; or

(iii) a person authorised by power of attorney to administer the financial affairs of the person beneficially entitled to the payment; or

(iv) the parent, guardian, spouse, son or daughter of a mentally handicapped person, or any person appointed by a court to manage the affairs of a mentally handicapped person; or

(v) a person appointed by the Secretary of State to receive benefits on behalf of a person who is for the time being unable to act.

A certificate may not be given where the payment is treated as income of a parent of the person beneficially entitled to the payment, or where the Board has issued a notice in relation to the account concerned requiring deduction of tax (see below).

The certificate must be supplied before the end of the year of assessment in which the payment is made or credited, or, in the case of a certificate given by a person who will attain 16 years of age during a year of assessment, before the end of that year.

A person who gives such a certificate fraudulently or negligently, or fails to comply with any undertaking contained in the certificate, is liable under *TMA 1970, s 99A* (introduced by *FA 1991, s 82*) to a penalty up to £3,000.

Tax deducted from payments in a year prior to receipt of a certificate relating to that year may be refunded, and a like amount recovered by the deposit-taker from the Board, provided that a certificate of deduction of tax (see 23.7 DEDUCTION OF TAX AT SOURCE) has not been furnished to the depositor prior to receipt of the gross payment certificate.

In Revenue Press Release 13 August 1992, the Revenue position as regards incorrect certification for gross payment was explained. In asking those who had registered to reconsider their position (and, if appropriate, to ask for their registration with the bank or building society to be cancelled), the Revenue made clear that where, as a result of their audited sample, cases of incorrect registration were identified, gross payment would cease and tax (and possibly interest and penalties) would be imposed in respect of any interest already received. No interest and penalties would be applied in cases of simple misunderstanding of the position, and a penalty would be considered only where false or fraudulent declarations had knowingly been made on the registration form (or there had been a deliberate failure to cancel the registration).

A certificate ceases to be valid:

(*a*) where the deposit-taker is notified (as above) that the person beneficially entitled to the payment is liable to income tax for the year in which the payment is made;

(*b*) where it was given by a parent or guardian, at the end of the year of assessment in which the person beneficially entitled to the payment attains 16 years of age;

(*c*) where it was given by a person who attained 16 years of age during the year of assessment in which a payment was made or credited, but who was not the holder of the account to which the certificate relates, and that person fails to become the holder before the first payment is made or credited after the end of that year of assessment;

(*d*) where the deposit-taker is notified that the person by or on whose behalf the certificate was given has died; and

(*e*) where the Board, having reason to believe that a person beneficially entitled to a payment of interest has become liable to income tax, give notice requiring the deposit-taker to deduct tax from payments of interest made, more than 30 days after the issue of the notice (or from earlier payments, if practicable), to or for the benefit of that person on a specified account held by or on behalf of that person.

A notice under (*e*) above must be copied to the person to whom it refers, and a further certificate in respect of the account referred to in the notice may not be given by or on behalf of that person (unless the notice is subsequently cancelled, see below).

A notice under (*e*) above may be cancelled (and the deposit-taker and person referred to in the notice so informed) if the Board are satisfied that the person referred to in the notice was not at the date of the notice, and has not since become, liable to income tax, or is no longer so liable.

Certificates of non-liability given by a building society which converts to company status are, by concession, treated as having been given to the successor company. (Revenue Pamphlet IR 1, A69).

Joint accounts. The position as regards certification by each of joint holders of an account is considered separately. Payments are apportioned equally to each joint holder, and tax deducted in respect of that part of a payment to which certification does not apply. The deposit-taker may, however, deduct tax from the whole of payments in respect of joint accounts where certification does not apply to all the joint holders, after giving notice to the Board of its intention to do so (which notice the deposit-taker may subsequently cancel).

Information. The Board may by notice require any deposit-taker (within not less than 14 days) to furnish them with such information (including books, records etc.) as they require, in particular

(I) for verification of payments made without deduction of tax and of the validity of certification for gross payment, and

(II) for verification of the amount of tax deducted from payments of interest (but this does not include copies of books, records etc. from which the depositor can be ascertained).

Copies of the deposit-taker's books, records etc. must be made available when required by the Board. Certificates for gross payment must be retained for at least two years after they expire.

Subject to *FA 1989, s 182(5)* (see 36.4 INLAND REVENUE: CONFIDENTIALITY OF INFORMATION), information obtained under these provisions may not be used other than for the purposes of the provisions or for the ascertainment of the tax liability of the deposit-taker or of the person beneficially entitled to interest paid without deduction of tax to whom the information relates.

The Board may also make regulations providing for the exclusion from its information powers of accounts held by non-UK ordinary residents or non-UK resident trustees.

For Revenue audit powers and further information powers, see *SI 1992 Nos 12, 15.*

The Revenue have published a Code of Practice (No 4) setting out their standards for the carrying out of inspections of tax deduction schemes operated by financial intermediaries.

Simon's Direct Tax Service. See **D4.1101** *et seq.*.

9 Building Societies

9.1 For years up to and including 1985/86, a Building Society normally entered into special arrangements with the Revenue. For the years 1986/87 to 1990/91 inclusive, this system was replaced by regulations (see *SI 1986 No 482 as amended*) made by statutory instrument by the Board, although the revised system operated on broadly similar lines to the previous arrangements. [*ICTA 1988, s 476*].

For 1991/92 and subsequent years, building societies deduct lower or basic rate tax from interest payments unless a certificate is supplied to the effect that the recipient is unlikely to be liable to income tax for the year. [*ICTA 1988, s 477A; FA 1990, s 30, Sch 5*]. Regulations provide for the detailed implementation of the scheme (see *The Income Tax (Building Societies) (Dividends and Interest) Regulations 1990, SI 1990 No 2231*).

For these purposes, a building society is one within the meaning of the *Building Societies Act 1986*. [*ICTA 1988, s 832(1)*].

9.2 **Returns.** Building societies are required to make returns of dividends and interest paid to investors. [*TMA 1970, s 17; SI 1986 No 482; FA 1990, s 92; SI 1990 No 2231; F(No 2)A 1992, s 29*]. See 67.4 RETURNS.

9.3 **INTEREST AND DIVIDENDS PAID TO INVESTORS** [*ICTA 1988, ss 477A, 482A; TMA 1970, s 99A; FA 1990, Sch 5 paras 4, 10; FA 2000, s 111(4)(6), s 145(10)(11); SI 1990 No 2231; FA 1991, ss 52, 75, 82, Sch 11; SI 1992 Nos 10, 11, 2915; SI 1994 No 296; SI 1995 No 1184; SI 1996 No 223*]

Except in the case of certain marketable securities (see below), building societies are required under regulations (*SI 1990 No 2231*) made under *ICTA 1988, s 477A* to deduct a sum representing income tax (at the lower rate (before 1996/97, the basic rate) for the year of assessment in which the payment is made) thereon from all payments or credits of dividends or interest in respect of shares in, deposits with or loans to the society, unless gross payment is authorised under the conditions described below. The deduction requirements of *ICTA 1988, s 349* (see 23.3 DEDUCTION OF TAX AT SOURCE) do not apply to such payments. Whether or not gross payment applies, such interest etc. is chargeable under SCHEDULE D, CASE III (72) on the current year basis.

For repayment claims on behalf of persons incapable of managing their own affairs, see Revenue Tax Bulletin April 1996 p 301.

The Inland Revenue Financial Intermediaries and Claims Office may be contacted for technical advice in relation to the tax deduction scheme on 0151–472 6156.

Gross payment. Interest and dividends are payable without deduction of tax where, at the time of payment, they fall into one of the following categories.

(*a*) A payment to an individual not ordinarily resident in the UK who is beneficially entitled to the payment, or jointly so entitled with other such individuals.

(*b*) A payment to trustees of a trust in the income of which no person has an interest apart from individuals not ordinarily resident in the UK.

(*c*) A payment to personal representatives in respect of an investment (or another investment representing an investment) forming part of the estate of a deceased person who was not ordinarily resident in the UK at the time of his death.

(*d*) A payment to a charity exempt under *ICTA 1988, s 505(1)(c)*.

(*e*) A payment to a pension fund approved under *ICTA 1988, s 592(1)* or whose application for approval is under consideration.

(*f*) A payment of interest on a bank loan.

(*g*) A payment under a CERTIFICATE OF DEPOSIT (13) issued after 5 April 1983 under which the society is obliged within five years of issue to pay £50,000 or more (exclusive of interest); or on a non-transferable sterling deposit of £50,000 or more for a fixed period of less than five years (which, for deposits made after 5 April 1991, must prohibit partial withdrawals or additions). Such certificates of deposit and other non-transferable deposits may be denominated in a foreign currency, the equivalent £50,000 limit being determined at the time of the deposit.

(*h*) A payment on a deposit by a subsidiary of a building society with its parent society (where an election for gross payment is in force).

(*i*) A payment for the purposes of an approved personal pension scheme (see 60.2 PERSONAL PENSION SCHEMES).

(*j*) A payment in respect of a general client deposit account (see 8.2(vii) BANKS).

(*k*) A payment to a local authority within *ICTA 1988, s 842A*.

(*l*) A payment into a Lloyd's UNDERWRITERS (89) premiums trust fund.

(*m*) All payments to companies (defined to include all bodies corporate and unincorporated associations other than partnerships and local authority associations), health service bodies (within *ICTA 1988, s 519A*) and trustees of unit trust schemes (within *Financial Services Act 1986, s 75(8)*).

(*n*) A payment in respect of a 'qualifying deposit right' (as defined below).

(*o*) A payment in respect of an investment held at a non-UK branch.

(*p*) (From 3 May 1995) a deemed interest payment under *ICTA 1988, s 730A(2)* (price differential on sale and repurchase of securities, see 3.5 ANTI-AVOIDANCE).

(*q*) (From 6 April 1996) a payment to trustees of a discretionary or accumulation trust (within *ICTA 1988, s 686*, see 81.5 SETTLEMENTS) where the trustees are non-UK resident and all beneficiaries (as widely defined) are either non-UK ordinarily resident individuals (or Scottish partnerships comprising such individuals) or non-UK resident companies.

Gross payment also applies where the person beneficially entitled to the interest is UK ordinarily resident (see 64.6 RESIDENCE, ORDINARY RESIDENCE AND DOMICILE) and has supplied the appropriate certificate to the society to the effect that he is unlikely to be liable to income tax for the year of assessment in which the payment is made or credited (taking into account for this purpose all interest arising in the year of assessment concerned which would, in the absence of such a certificate, be received under deduction of lower or basic rate tax). The conditions for certification, and related Revenue information powers, are similar to those described at 8.2 BANKS in relation to gross payment to non-ordinary residents.

Scottish partnerships consisting only of individuals not ordinarily resident in the UK are within the requirements at (*a*) and (*b*) above. A payment within (*a*)–(*f*) or (*l*) above may not be made gross unless the society has a written declaration in a prescribed form from the investor certifying that the relevant conditions are met. This requirement also applies to most companies and to unit trust scheme trustees.

Interest payments completely exempt from income tax (e.g. under TESSAs or SAYE schemes or personal equity plans (see 29.13, 29.21 EXEMPT INCOME)), are also paid gross. See also below as regards interest on 'quoted Eurobonds'.

Where payments are made gross, liability arises on the recipient under Case III of Schedule D. The commencement and cessation provisions which applied before 1996/97 (see 72.4

SCHEDULE D, CASE III) applied where a building society investment ceased to be or became a 'relevant investment', i.e. one where dividends or interest payable in respect of it were sums in respect of which the society was required to account for and pay an amount representing income tax.

Marketable securities. Dividends or interest paid in respect of shares or securities (other than 'qualifying certificates of deposit' or a 'qualifying deposit right') listed, or capable of being listed, on a recognised stock exchange when the dividend, etc. became payable are not within the regulations under *ICTA 1988, s 477A* referred to above, but are subject to deduction of tax under *ICTA 1988, s 349* unless the securities are within the 'quoted Eurobonds' exclusion (see 23.3(ii) DEDUCTION OF TAX AT SOURCE). 'Permanent interest bearing shares' (see Tolley's Corporation Tax under Building Societies) issued by a society are within these provisions.

A '*qualifying certificate of deposit*' is a CERTIFICATE OF DEPOSIT (13) for £50,000 or more (exclusive of interest) (or foreign equivalent at the time of the deposit) repayable within five years. A '*qualifying deposit right*' is a right to receive an amount in pursuance of a deposit of money under an arrangement under which no certificate of deposit has been issued, although the person entitled to the right could call for the issue of such a certificate, which otherwise meets the same conditions as a qualifying certificate of deposit. [*ICTA 1988, s 349(3A)(3B)(4), s 477A(1A); FA 1991, Sch 11 paras 1, 2; F(No 2)A 1992, Sch 8 paras 2, 3*].

Code of Practice. The Revenue have published a Code of Practice (No 4) setting out their standards for the carrying out of inspections of tax deduction schemes operated by financial intermediaries.

Simon's Direct Tax Service. See **D4.727–D4.730.**

9.4 INTEREST PAYABLE TO BUILDING SOCIETIES

Payments to a building society in respect of advances normally comprise capital repayment plus interest. The interest portion will, for interest paid before 6 April 2000, generally be 'relevant loan interest' which will be paid under deduction of tax by most borrowers (see 23.13 DEDUCTION OF TAX AT SOURCE). Otherwise, no tax is deductible from such payments but the payer is given tax relief (subject to certain restrictions, see 43.5 *et seq.* INTEREST PAYABLE) on the interest portion each year (either by adjustments in PAYE coding or by discharge or repayment).

Where building society interest is paid in connection with a trade, profession or vocation and the payer's income is not sufficient for relief to be given in full, any unrelieved balance may be carried forward against subsequent profits as under *ICTA 1988, s 385*, or used in a terminal loss claim under *ICTA 1988, s 388*. [*ICTA 1988, s 390*]. See under 46 LOSSES.

9.5 TAX LIABILITY OF A BUILDING SOCIETY ITSELF

See Tolley's Corporation Tax (under Building Societies).

9.6 TRANSFER OF BUILDING SOCIETY BUSINESS TO COMPANY

The acquisition by members of shares on such a transfer is granted certain reliefs from capital gains tax and from treatment as a distribution. [*FA 1988, s 145, Sch 12; TCGA 1992, ss 216, 217*]. See Tolley's Corporation Tax under Building Societies.

Declarations made as to the ordinary residence of depositors and certificates of non-liability given to societies (see 9.3 above) are treated as having been made or given to the successor company. (Revenue Pamphlet IR 1, A69).

Simon's Direct Tax Service. See **D4.771–D4.773.**

10 Capital Allowances

Simon's Direct Tax Service B2.

10.1 Capital allowances (balancing charges) are a deduction from (addition to) the profits etc. of trades, professions, employments, vocations, offices and occupation of woodlands assessed under Schedule D, in arriving at the taxable amount. The amount of depreciation charged in the accounts of a business is not so allowed. For *income tax* purposes, for 1996/97 and earlier years as regards trades etc. commenced before 6 April 1994, most capital allowances are *deducted from the assessment* and not treated as expenses in the accounts. [*CAA 1990, s 140 as originally enacted*]. For income tax purposes, for 1994/95 and subsequent years as regards trades etc. commenced after 5 April 1994 and for 1997/98 and subsequent years as regards trades etc. commenced on or before that date, and for corporation tax purposes, capital allowances (or balancing charges) are treated as trading expenses (or receipts) of the period of account (see 10.2(vi) below), or for corporation tax the accounting period, to which they relate. [*CAA 1990, ss 140, 144; FA 1994, s 211*]. See also 10.2(vi) and (vii) below. See Tolley's Corporation Tax for matters with special relevance to companies.

Capital allowances are granted in respect of certain types of expenditure detailed in 10.3 to 10.52 below.

Headings in this chapter are as follows.

10.2 Matters of general application
10.3 Agricultural buildings and works
10.5 Cemeteries and Crematoria
10.7 Dredging
10.9 Dwelling-houses let on assured tenancies
10.10 **Industrial buildings**
10.11 — Qualifying buildings
10.12 — Qualifying expenditure
10.13 — Initial allowances
10.14 — Writing-down allowances
10.15 — Balancing allowances and charges
10.17 — Making of allowances and charges
10.18 — Hotels
10.19 — Enterprise zones
10.21 — Small workshops
10.22 — General matters
10.23 Know-how
10.24 **Machinery and plant**
10.25 — Eligible expenditure
10.27 — First-year allowances
10.28 — Writing-down allowances
10.30 — Balancing allowances and charges
10.32 — Making of allowances and charges
10.34 — Entitlement to allowances for fixtures
10.35 — Leasing of machinery and plant
10.37 — Old scheme before 27 October 1970
10.38 — General matters
10.39 **Mines, oil wells**
10.40 — Qualifying expenditure
10.41 — Limitations on qualifying expenditure
10.42 — Writing-down allowances
10.43 — Disposal receipts
10.44 — Balancing allowances and charges
10.45 — Making of allowances and charges
10.46 — Machinery and plant allowances
10.47 — Transitional provisions
10.49 — 'Old scheme' before 1 April 1986
10.50 Patent rights
10.52 Scientific research/research and development

10.2 **MATTERS OF GENERAL APPLICATION**

(i) **Composite sales** may be apportioned by Commissioners despite separate prices attributed in sale agreement. [*CAA 1990, ss 150, 151*]. See *Fitton v Gilders & Heaton Ch D 1955, 36 TC 233,* and *Wood v Provan CA 1968, 44 TC 701.*

(ii) **Subsidies.** All expenditure met, or to be met, directly or indirectly by the Crown or by any government or public or local authority (except through Regional Development Grants or NI equivalent (for which see *SI 1995 No 611, SI 1997 No 660, SI 1999 No 719* and predecessor orders)) is treated as not having been incurred by any person, so that no capital allowance is due in respect of it. For the scope of 'public authority', see *McKinney v Hagans Caravans (Manufacturing) Ltd CA(NI) 1997, 69 TC 526.*

A contribution by any other person is generally ignored, unless the contributor could himself obtain a capital allowance in respect of it under *CAA 1990, s 154* (see below), or obtain a deduction against trading profits, in which case the recipient's expenditure is reduced by the amount of the contribution in determining his capital allowances. [*ICTA 1988, s 91(9), s 532(1); CAA 1990, s 153*]. Where a contribution is towards expenditure on dredging (10.7 below), however, the person incurring the expenditure will receive full allowances only if the contributions are made for the purposes of that person's trade. [*CAA 1990, s 134(8)*]. Certain contributions by pools promoters towards football ground improvements are disregarded despite being an allowable deduction in the pools promoter's trade (see 71.85 SCHEDULE D, CASES I AND II). [*FA 1990, s 126*]. Scientific research capital allowances (10.52 below) are not available where expenditure is met by a contribution by any other person. [*CAA 1990, s 153(1)(4)*].

Repaid grants. Where a grant which has been deducted from expenditure qualifying for capital allowances (as above) is later repaid (in whole or part), the repayment will, by concession, be treated as expenditure qualifying for capital allowances. Where allowances were restricted in respect of a contribution from a person (other than the Crown or a public body) who himself obtained either a capital allowance under *CAA 1990, s 154* or a trading deduction for his contribution (as above), this treatment is dependent upon the repayment falling to be taxed on the recipient through a balancing charge or as a trading receipt. (Revenue Pamphlet IR 1, B49).

Contributors towards capital expenditure on an asset may receive allowances where the contribution is for the purposes of the contributor's (or his tenant's) trade, profession or vocation, and where the expenditure would, apart from the contribution, have attracted capital allowances, as if the asset were at all material times used for trade purposes (so that balancing adjustments do not apply to such contributions). The allowances are such as would have been made if the contribution had been expended on the provision for the contributor's trade of a similar asset. On a transfer of the trade, or part thereof, the allowances (or part) are passed to the transferee.

No allowances are available to the contributor, however, where the person incurring the expenditure and the contributor are CONNECTED PERSONS (20).

These provisions do not apply to mineral depletion allowances (10.49(*a*) below), cemeteries and crematoria (10.5 below), scientific research allowances (10.52 below) or dredging (10.7 below), although contributions towards dredging are treated as expenditure by the contributor on that dredging. [*CAA 1990, ss 134(8), 154, 155; ICTA 1988, s 532*].

(iii) **Time expenditure incurred.** Capital expenditure (other than that constituted by an 'additional VAT liability' — see (v) below) is generally treated, for capital allowance purposes, as incurred on the date on which the obligation to pay becomes unconditional, whether or not payment is in whole or part required to be made by some later date, *except that* it is treated as incurred on a later date in the following circumstances.

(*a*) Where any part of the expenditure is required to be paid on or by a date more than four months after the date determined as above, it is treated as incurred on that later date.

(*b*) Where an obligation to pay becomes unconditional earlier than in accordance with normal commercial usage, with the sole or main benefit expected being that, under these provisions, the expenditure would be treated as incurred in an earlier chargeable or basis period, it is instead treated as incurred on the date on or before which it is required to be paid.

(*c*) Where any other provision requires expenditure to be treated as incurred on a later date than that laid down by these provisions (including (*a*) and (*b*) above), the expenditure is treated as incurred on that later date.

[*CAA 1990, s 159(2)(3)(5)–(8); FA 1991, Sch 14 para 14; FA 1994, Sch 26 Pt V(24); FA 1997, Sch 15 paras 7, 9*].

Where, as a result of an event such as the issuing of a certificate, an obligation to pay becomes unconditional before one month has elapsed after the start of a chargeable or basis period, but the asset concerned has become the property of, or is otherwise attributed under the contract to, the person having the obligation at or before the end of the immediately preceding chargeable or basis period, the obligation is treated as becoming unconditional immediately before the end of that earlier period. [*CAA 1990, s 159(4); FA 1994, Sch 26 Pt V(24)*].

(iv) **Exclusion of double allowances.** Where an allowance is made to a person under one of the codes of allowances listed below, he cannot obtain an allowance under another of those codes, in respect of either the same expenditure or expenditure in respect of an asset to which the first-mentioned allowance relates, nor can such expenditure qualify for machinery and plant allowances (see 10.28 below). Similarly, neither an amount of capital expenditure qualifying for machinery and plant allowances nor an asset to which it relates can qualify for any of the allowances listed. The allowances in question are

(*a*) industrial buildings allowances (10.10–10.23 below);

(*b*) allowances for expenditure on dredging (10.7 below);

(*c*) agricultural buildings allowances (10.3 below);

(*d*) scientific research allowances (10.52 below);

(*e*) allowances for mines and oil wells (10.39–10.46 below);

(*f*) allowances for dwelling-houses let on assured tenancies (10.9 below).

[*CAA 1990, s 147; FA 1993, Sch 13 para 13*].

For chargeable periods ending on or after 24 July 1996 (but not in relation to expenditure incurred before that date), there are special provisions preventing double allowances in relation to machinery or plant treated as fixtures (see 10.34 below). [*CAA 1990, s 147(2A)–(2D); FA 1997, Sch 16 para 7*].

These provisions do not prevent the purchaser of an asset from claiming allowances on a different basis from the vendor, where alternative bases of claim are permissible. (Revenue Capital Allowances Manual, CA 1060).

(v) **VAT capital goods scheme.** Under the VAT capital goods scheme, the input tax originally claimed on the acquisition of certain capital assets is subject to amendment within a specified period of adjustment in accordance with any increase or decrease in the extent to which the asset is used in making taxable, as opposed to exempt, supplies for VAT purposes. The items covered by the scheme are limited to land and buildings (or parts of buildings) worth £250,000 or more and computers (and items of computer equipment) worth £50,000 or more. See Tolley's Value Added Tax under Capital Goods for a full description of the scheme.

Special capital allowances provisions apply where a VAT adjustment is made under the capital goods scheme. [*FA 1991, s 59, Sch 14*]. These affect allowances for industrial buildings, machinery and plant and scientific research, and the provisions specific to each are described in the appropriate sections of this chapter. General definitions and provisions are described below.

'*Additional VAT liability*' and '*additional VAT rebate*' in relation to any capital expenditure mean, respectively, an amount which a person becomes liable to pay or an amount which he becomes entitled to deduct by way of adjustment under any 'VAT capital items legislation' (as defined) in respect of input tax on an asset on the construction or provision of which the expenditure was wholly or partly incurred. Generally (but see below), such a liability or rebate is to be regarded as incurred or made on the last day of the 'relevant VAT interval'. The '*relevant VAT interval*' is that one of the periods of which, under the VAT capital items legislation, the applicable VAT period of adjustment consists, in which occurred the increase or decrease in use giving rise to the additional VAT liability or rebate.

For the purpose *only* of determining the chargeable period for which a capital allowance or balancing charge may be made in respect of it (or for which it is to be brought into account in connection with the making of such allowances or charges), an additional VAT liability or rebate is to be regarded as incurred or made at a time (referred to below as the relevant time) determined as follows:

(*a*) where a VAT return (in which the liability or rebate is accounted for) is made to Customs and Excise, the relevant time is a time within the chargeable period or its basis period which includes the last day of the period covered by that return;

(*b*) if, before the making of a return as in (*a*) above, Customs and Excise assess the liability or rebate as due or repayable, the relevant time is the day on which the assessment is made;

(*c*) if the trade (or profession, vocation, employment etc. — see 10.24 below) is permanently discontinued (or treated as such for tax purposes) before the liability or rebate has been accounted for in a VAT return and before the making of an assessment as in (*b*) above, the relevant time is the last day of the chargeable period related to the discontinuance.

Where an allowance or charge falls to be determined by reference to a proportion only of the expenditure incurred or a proportion only of what that allowance or charge would otherwise have been, any allowance or charge in respect of an additional VAT liability or rebate in respect of that expenditure is similarly apportioned.

[*CAA 1990, s 159A; FA 1991, Sch 14 para 14; FA 1994, Sch 26 Pt V(24)*].

Simon's Direct Tax Service. See **B2.103, B2.104.**

(vi) **Periods of account/chargeable periods.** For 1994/95 and subsequent years as regards trades, etc. commenced after 5 April 1994 and for 1997/98 and subsequent years as regards trades, etc. commenced on or before that date, capital allowances given in taxing the trade, etc. are, for income tax purposes, given by reference to 'periods of account' (see 10.1 above). Previously, they were calculated by reference to the basis period for the year of assessment for which they were made. A '*period of account*' means a period for which accounts are made up, except that where such a period exceeds 18 months, it is deemed to be split into two or more periods of account, beginning on, or on an anniversary of, the date on which the actual period begins. Where, exceptionally, there is an interval between two periods of account, it is deemed to form part of the first such period, and where two periods of account overlap, the common period is deemed to form part of the first such period only. For non-traders, a period of account is a year of assessment. [*CAA 1990, ss 140, 160; FA 1994, ss 211, 212(1)*]. Consequentially, references in the capital allowances provisions to the basis period for a chargeable period are repealed, and such references in this chapter should be construed accordingly. [*FA 1994, s 211(2), s 213(1), s 214(5), Sch 26 Pt V (24)*].

Any reference in the capital allowances provisions to a chargeable period is, for income tax purposes, a reference to a period of account, except that for 1996/97 and earlier years as regards trades, etc. commenced before 6 April 1994, it is a reference to a year of assessment. For corporation tax purposes, a chargeable period is an accounting period. [*CAA 1990, s 161(2); FA 1994, ss 211(2), 212(2)*].

(vii) **Transitional rule on changeover to new system.** 10.1 above mentions the change to the system for dealing with capital allowances for income tax purposes, i.e. a change from treating an allowance as a deduction from the Schedule D, Case I or II assessment to treating it as a trading expense. For trades, etc. commenced before 6 April 1994 and continuing beyond 5 April 1997, any capital allowances claimed for 1996/97 and earlier years but unrelieved (due to an insufficiency of profits) are treated as trading expenses for the first period of account (see (vi) above) ending after 5 April 1997. [*FA 1994, Sch 20 para 9*].

(viii) **Finance leasing.** See 71.68 SCHEDULE D, CASES I AND II as regards restrictions on capital allowances where certain finance leasing arrangements are involved. See also 10.28, 10.38(iii)(vi) below.

10.3 **AGRICULTURAL BUILDINGS AND WORKS**

After 31 March 1986, a new code of capital allowances applies to qualifying expenditure on agricultural buildings and works, replacing the provisions in *CAA 1968, ss 68, 69,* subject to transitional provisions (see below). [*CAA 1990, ss 122–133*].

Qualifying buildings, etc.. Writing-down and (in certain cases) initial allowances (see below) are given in respect of capital expenditure incurred on the construction, reconstruction, alteration or improvement of farmhouses (but see below), farm or forestry buildings, cottages, fences or other works (such as drainage and sewerage works, water and electricity installations or land reclamation) for the purposes of husbandry or forestry. [*CAA 1990, ss 123, 124(1), 124A, 131; FA 1993, Sch 12 paras 2, 3*]. See below as regards ending of forestry allowances. '*Husbandry*' includes any method of intensive rearing of livestock or fish on a commercial basis for the production of food for human consumption [*CAA 1990, s 133(1)*] and, normally, the use of land for the growing of bulbs (Tolley's Practical Tax 1986 p 23). Cottages occupied by retired farm workers and buildings constructed to provide welfare facilities for employees may qualify for allowances, as may farm shops to the extent that they sell produce of the farm. (Revenue Capital Allowances Manual, CA 4533, 4534).

Qualifying expenditure. Allowances are available where a person has a 'major interest' in any agricultural or forestry land (but see below) and incurs capital expenditure as set out above for the purposes of husbandry or forestry on that land, excluding any proportion of such costs relating to the land itself. The asset does not have to be on the land in question, e.g. a farmworker's cottage in a nearby village might qualify. (Revenue Capital Allowances Manual, CA 4504). '*Agricultural land*' is land, buildings etc. in the UK occupied wholly or mainly for the purposes of husbandry (as above), and '*forestry land*' is woodlands in the UK (and buildings occupied with, and for the purposes of, those woodlands) which are the subject of an election for taxation under Schedule D (see 93 WOODLANDS — the election ceased to be available after 14 March 1988, subject to transitional provisions). A '*major interest*' in land means the fee simple estate in the land or an agreement to acquire that interest (or Scottish equivalent) or a lease. A creditor who has conveyed or assigned an interest in land by way of security will still be treated as entitled to the interest provided that he has a related right of redemption. [*CAA 1990, ss 123, 125, 131, 133(1)(4)(6)(7)*]. On **farmhouses** a maximum of only one-third of expenditure may be taken into account for allowances and, in general, expenditure on other assets only partly used for agricultural, etc. purposes is only eligible in such proportion as is just. Partial use may include occupation by a part-time farm worker. (Revenue Capital Allowances Manual, CA 4532). [*CAA 1990, s 124(1)(2), s 124A(4); FA 1993, Sch 12 paras 2, 3*]. For the meaning of 'farmhouse', see *Lindsay v CIR CS 1953, 34 TC 289; CIR v Whiteford & Sons CS 1962, 40 TC 379*; *Korner v CIR HL 1969, 45 TC 287* and Revenue Capital Allowances Manual, CA 4530 (including the circumstances in which it may be accepted that a farm has two farmhouses). For what constitutes capital expenditure on the construction of a farmhouse or other agricultural building, see Revenue Capital Allowances Manual, CA 4515, 4516.

Buildings, etc. bought unused. Similar provisions apply as in the case of industrial buildings (see 10.12 below). [*CAA 1990, ss 127, 127A; FA 1993, Sch 12, paras 5, 6*].

Market gardening, whether of plants and flowers or for the production of food, is treated in the same way as farming for allowance purposes, and a house which is the centre of such operations is treated as a farmhouse (see above). (Revenue Capital Allowances Manual, CA 4509).

Forestry land. Allowances (under the current or old code (see below)) in respect of forestry land or use cease for chargeable periods beginning after 19 June 1989. Allowances for 1989/90 or for company accounting periods straddling that date are apportioned on a time basis to the part ending on that date and to the other part, those apportioned to the other part not being made.

Where an election for Schedule D treatment of forestry income (see 93.2 WOODLANDS) is in force for a chargeable period beginning before 6 April 1993, allowances continue to be available notwithstanding the above. Where the period concerned is a company accounting period ending after 5 April 1993, allowances given otherwise than in taxing a trade are time-apportioned, those falling in the part of the period after that date not being made. Allowances given in taxing a trade are similarly denied by virtue of the transitional provisions referred to at 93.3 WOODLANDS. Initial allowances under *CAA 1990, s 124A* (see below) are not available in respect of expenditure incurred for the purposes of forestry. [*CAA 1990, s 131; FA 1993, Sch 12 para 9*].

Initial allowances. An initial allowance is available in respect of qualifying expenditure incurred under a contract entered into in the twelve-month period **1 November 1992 to 31 October 1993 inclusive** or for the purpose of securing compliance with obligations incurred under a contract entered into during that period, but not for expenditure incurred under a contract entered into for the purpose of securing compliance with obligations under a contract entered into before 1 November 1992. The qualifying building must come to be used for the purposes of husbandry before 1 January 1995, and, if this condition is not satisfied or if the building first comes to be used for purposes other than husbandry, any initial allowance given will be withdrawn. The initial allowance is **20%** of the expenditure incurred, and is given for the chargeable period related to the incurring of the expenditure. For income tax purposes and, as regards company accounting periods ended after 30 September 1993, for corporation tax purposes, either a smaller initial allowance may be claimed or the initial allowance not claimed at all; for earlier accounting periods, a company may disclaim the initial allowance in whole or in part by giving written notice to the inspector within two years after the end of the accounting period concerned. [*CAA 1990, s 124A(1)–(3), (5)–(7); FA 1993, Sch 12 para 3*].

Writing-down allowances are made at **4% p.a.** during a period of 25 years beginning on the first day of the chargeable period (see 10.2(vi) above) relating to the incurring of the expenditure, so as to give aggregate allowances (including any initial allowance) up to the amount of that expenditure. If, by virtue of a transfer of the relevant interest (see below), the total allowances during the writing-down period would be less than the amount of the expenditure, then the difference is made up in the chargeable period in which the writing-down period ends. If the buildings, etc. in fact come to be first used other than for the purposes of husbandry or forestry, no writing-down allowance can be made in respect of the related expenditure and any allowance previously given is withdrawn. A writing-down allowance is given for the same chargeable period as an initial allowance under *CAA 1990, s 124A* (see above) in respect of the same expenditure, but only if the building etc. comes to be used for the purposes of husbandry before the end of that chargeable period. [*CAA 1990, s 123, s 124(2), s 124B, s 126(6); FA 1993, Sch 12 paras 3, 4(3)*]. If the conditions are met when the expenditure is incurred and the first use is for the purposes of husbandry, allowances continue throughout the writing-down period without regard to any change of use of the building in later years. (Revenue Capital Allowances Manual, CA 4566).

Transfer of relevant interest. Where a person entitled to allowances in respect of capital expenditure as above ceases to own the 'relevant interest' in the land (or part) concerned giving rise to that entitlement, and another person acquires that interest, the right to the writing-down allowances (or part) is transferred to the new owner of the interest (proportionate allowances being given where the transfer falls during a chargeable or basis period of either the former or the new owner). The right to an initial allowance is not transferred to the new owner (subject to the provisions referred to above for buildings etc. bought unused). [*CAA 1990, s 126(1)–(3); FA 1993, Sch 12 para 4(1)(2); FA 1994, Sch 26 Pt V(24)*].

The '*relevant interest*' is the major interest in the land to which the person who incurred the expenditure was entitled when he incurred it (the interest in reversion to all others where two or more major interests in the land were held). A major interest remains the relevant interest where a lease, etc. is created to which the interest is subject, and, where a lease which is a relevant interest is surrendered or reverts, the interest into which it merges becomes the relevant interest (unless a new lease takes effect on the extinguishment). [*CAA 1990, s 125(2)–(4), s 126(4)*]. If a new lease is granted to the former lessee, the new lease is treated as a continuation of the old lease. If it is granted to a person other than the former lessee, the relevant interest is treated as acquired by the new lessee if he makes a payment to the former lessee for the assets representing the expenditure in question. In any other case, the landlord under the former lease is treated as acquiring the relevant interest. [*CAA 1990, s 126(5)*].

Balancing events. A '*balancing event*' occurs when the relevant interest in land is acquired by another person (see above) or when the building, etc. on construction of which the expenditure was incurred is demolished, destroyed, or otherwise ceases to exist as such, *provided that* a written election to that effect is made. The election must be made (i) for income tax for 1996/97 onwards (subject to (ii) below), within twelve months after 31 January following the tax year in which ends the chargeable period related to the occurrence of the balancing event, (ii) for income tax for 1996/97 only as regards trades etc. commenced before 6 April 1994 and as respects events in the basis period for that year, on or before 31 January 1999, and (iii) for income tax for earlier years and for corporation tax, within two years after the end of such chargeable period. The election must be made jointly in the case of acquisition of the relevant interest, but otherwise by the former owner only. An election may not be made by a person outside the charge to UK tax, nor if the sole or main benefit of an acquisition was the obtaining of an allowance (but ignoring *CAA 1990, s 157*, see below). [*CAA 1990, s 129; FA 1993, Sch 12 para 8; FA 1994, Sch 26 Pt V(24); FA 1996, s 135, Sch 21 para 33*].

Where a balancing event occurs in a chargeable or basis period for which an allowance would otherwise have been available, no such allowance is made, but a balancing adjustment arises for that period on or to the person entitled to the relevant interest immediately before the balancing event. If the residue of expenditure immediately before the balancing event (i.e. after deducting any allowances previously given) exceeds any sale, compensation, etc. receipts, a balancing allowance equal to that excess is made. If any sale, compensation, etc. receipts exceed that residue, a balancing charge is made equal to the excess (but limited to the allowances previously given to the person on whom the charge arises). Allowances made to a husband before 6 April 1990 in respect of his wife's relevant interest are treated as having been made to the wife for these purposes on a balancing event on or after that date. [*CAA 1990, s 128; FA 1993, Sch 12 para 7; FA 1994, Sch 26 Pt V(24)*].

Where a balancing event occurs on the transfer of the relevant interest, the writing-down allowances available to the new owner consist of the residue of expenditure (see above) immediately before the balancing event, plus any balancing charge or less any balancing allowance consequent on that event, spread over the period from the balancing event to the end of the original 25 year writing-down period. [*CAA 1990, s 129(3); FA 1994, Sch 26 Pt V(24)*].

Making of allowances and charges. An initial, writing-down or balancing adjustment for a chargeable period is given or made in taxing a trade. If no trade is carried on in that chargeable period, then, for 1995/96 and subsequent years for income tax purposes and on or after 1 April 1998 for corporation tax purposes, allowances and charges are treated as expenses and receipts of a Schedule A business (see 68.4 SCHEDULE A) or, where the taxpayer is not, in fact, carrying on such a business, of a deemed Schedule A business. Previously, allowances were given by discharge or repayment of tax, primarily against agricultural or (where applicable, see above) forestry income and income which is the subject of a balancing charge. A balancing charge was made under Schedule D, Case VI for income tax or treated as agricultural etc. income of a company. [*CAA 1990, s 132; FA 1995, Sch 6 para 35; FA 1998, s 38, Sch 5 para 59*]. Allowances are given in taxing a trade in accordance with *CAA 1990, s 140* in the same way as for industrial buildings allowances to traders (see 10.17 below). See also 10.2(vi) and (vii) above.

Double allowances. See 10.2(iv) above.

There are **connected person** and **anti-avoidance provisions** in respect of certain balancing events, similar to those applicable to industrial buildings allowances (see 10.22(i) below). [*CAA 1990, ss 130, 133(8)(9), 157, 158(5)*].

Transitional provisions. The former provisions of *CAA 1968, ss 68, 69* continue to apply to expenditure incurred before 1 April 1987 under a contract entered into before 14 March 1984 by the person incurring the expenditure. [*CAA 1990, ss 122, 133(3)*].

'Old scheme' for expenditure incurred before 1 April 1986. Writing-down allowances are (and initial allowances, in certain cases, were) given by way of discharge or repayment of tax (and not in taxing a trade), primarily against assessments on agricultural or forestry income. Any balance of allowances due for a year of assessment may be carried forward without time limit against future such income, or may (on a claim within two years of the end of the year of assessment) be set against other income of the year of assessment or of the following year. [*CAA 1968, ss 68(1)(2)(3), 71*]. See above as regards ending of forestry allowances.

An *initial allowance of 20%* of expenditure incurred (after 11 April 1978) could be claimed for the year of assessment following the year to 31 March (or such other date as was agreed with the inspector) in which the expenditure was incurred. An individual was able to claim a specified reduced amount. [*CAA 1968, s 68(1)(3A)(6); FA 1978, s 39*].

10.4 Capital Allowances

For expenditure for which an initial allowance was available as above (and for pre-12 April 1978 expenditure), a *writing-down allowance of 10%* may be claimed annually for the year of assessment for which the initial allowance was available and subsequent years, until the initial and writing-down allowances exhaust the expenditure. If the conditions are met when the expenditure is incurred, allowances continue throughout the writing-down period without regard to any change of use of the building in later years, and even if it is destroyed. (Revenue Capital Allowances Manual, CA 4656). In the case of sales, transfers of property, change of tenants, etc., the transferee takes over the writing-down allowances for the remainder of the writing-down period, the allowance for the year of sale, etc. being apportioned. [*CAA 1968, s 68(1)(4)(5); CAA 1990, s 122*]. See also *Sargaison v Roberts Ch D 1969, 45 TC 612.*

Simon's Direct Tax Service. See **B2.5.**

10.4 *Example*

Farmer Jones prepares accounts annually to 31 December and has incurred the following expenditure

		£
12.1.91	Extension to farmhouse	12,000
3.6.92	Construction of cattle court	15,000
26.4.93	Erection of barn	10,000
15.10.00	Replacement barn for that acquired on 26.4.93 which was destroyed by fire in September 2000. The insurance proceeds totalled £5,200	20,000

The agricultural buildings allowances are as follows.

Date of expenditure	Cost	Residue brought forward	Allowances Initial 20%	Allowances WDA 4%	Residue carried forward
	£	£	£	£	£
1992/93 (basis period — year to 31.12.91)					
12.1.91	4,000			160	3,840
1993/94 (basis period — year to 31.12.92)					
12.1.91	4,000	3,840		160	3,680
3.6.92	15,000			600	14,400
	£19,000	£3,840		£760	£18,080
1994/95 (basis period — year to 31.12.93)					
12.1.91	4,000	3,680		160	3,520
3.6.92	15,000	14,400		600	13,800
26.4.93	10,000		2,000	400*	7,600
	£29,000	£18,080	£2,000	£1,160	£24,920

Date of expenditure	Cost	Residue brought forward	Allowances: Initial 20%	Allowances: WDA 4%	Residue carried forward
	£	£	£	£	£
1995/96 (basis period — year to 31.12.94)					
12.1.91	4,000	3,520		160	3,360
3.6.92	15,000	13,800		600	13,200
26.4.93	10,000	7,600		400	7,200
	£29,000	£24,920		£1,160	£23,760
1996/97 (basis period — two years to 31.12.96)					
12.1.91	4,000	3,360		160	3,200
3.6.92	15,000	13,200		600	12,600
26.4.93	10,000	7,200		400	6,800
	£29,000	£23,760		£1,160	£22,600
1997/98 (period of account — year to 31.12.97)					
12.1.91	4,000	3,200		160	3,040
3.6.92	15,000	12,600		600	12,000
26.4.93	10,000	6,800		400	6,400
	£29,000	£22,600		£1,160	£21,440
1998/99 (period of account — year to 31.12.98)					
12.1.91	4,000	3,040		160	2,880
3.6.92	15,000	12,000		600	11,400
26.4.93	10,000	6,400		400	6,000
	£29,000	£21,440		£1,160	£20,280
1999/2000 (period of account — year to 31.12.99)					
12.1.91	4,000	2,880		160	2,720
3.6.92	15,000	11,400		600	10,800
26.4.93	10,000	6,000		400	5,600
	£29,000	£20,280		£1,160	£19,120

Date of expenditure	Cost	Residue brought forward	Allowances Initial 20%	WDA 4%	Residue carried forward
	£	£	£	£	£
2000/01 (period of account — year to 31.12.00)					
(i) No election for a balancing adjustment					
12.1.91	4,000	2,720		160	2,560
3.6.92	15,000	10,800		600	10,200
26.4.93	10,000	5,600		400	5,200
15.10.00	20,000			800	19,200
	£49,000	£19,120		£1,960	£37,160
(ii) Election for a balancing adjustment					
12.1.91	4,000	2,720		160	2,560
3.6.92	15,000	10,800		600	10,200
15.10.00	20,000			800	19,200
	£39,000	£13,520		£1,560	£31,960

Balancing allowance

	£	
Proceeds	5,200	
Written-down value	5,600	
Balancing allowance		£400

* In order to qualify for a writing-down allowance in addition to an initial allowance in 1994/95, the original barn must have been brought into use before 6 April 1995.

10.5 **CEMETERIES AND CREMATORIA** [*ICTA 1988, s 91*]

Cemeteries. In computing profits of a trade consisting of or including the carrying on of a cemetery, a deduction as a trading expense of any period is allowed for

(i) *cost of land* (including cost of levelling, draining or making suitable) *sold for interments,* or in relation to which *interment rights are sold,* in that period, and

(ii) a *proportion* (based on ratio of number of grave spaces sold in the period to that number plus those still available) of the *residual capital expenditure* at the end of the period. *Capital expenditure* for this purpose is expenditure on any building or structure (excluding dwelling houses) and underlying or surplus land, likely to have little or no value when the cemetery is full. (Certain expenditure before the 1954/55 basis period is excluded.) The *residue* is the balance of such expenditure after deducting amounts previously allowed under this section and any sale or insurance etc. receipts in respect of assets (the subject of such expenditure) sold or destroyed.

Changes of ownership of the trade (whether otherwise treated as a discontinuance or not) are ignored — allowances continue as they would to the original trader. [*ICTA 1988, s 91(5)*].

For the treatment of lump sums for grave maintenance, etc., see Revenue Inspector's Manual, IM 2061–2063.

Crematoria attract similar allowances, substituting memorial garden plots for cemetery land, grave-spaces or interments. [*ICTA 1988, s 91(7)*]. See also *Bourne v Norwich Crematorium Ch D 1967, 44 TC 164.*

For the treatment of expenditure and receipts in connection with the provision of niches and memorials, see Revenue Inspector's Manual, IM 2071, 2072.

Simon's Direct Tax Service. See **B3.1131, B3.1132.**

10.6 *Example*

GE, who operates a funeral service, owns a cemetery for which accounts to 31 December are prepared. The accounts to 31.12.00 reveal the following

(i)	Cost of land representing 110 grave spaces sold in period	£3,400
(ii)	Number of grave spaces remaining	275
(iii)	Residual capital expenditure on buildings and other land unsuitable for interments	£18,250

The allowances available are £

(*a*) Item (i) 3,400

(*b*) $\dfrac{110}{110 + 275} \times £18{,}250$ 5,214

£8,614

Note

(*a*) £8,614 will be allowed as a deduction in computing GE's Schedule D, Case I profits for the accounting period ending on 31 December 2000.

10.7 DREDGING [*CAA 1990, ss 134, 135*]

Writing-down, balancing and, in certain cases, initial allowances (see below) may be claimed for capital expenditure on **dredging** incurred for the purposes of a *qualifying trade* (provided that neither industrial buildings allowances (see 10.10 below) nor machinery and plant allowances (see 10.24 below) are available in respect of the same expenditure).

'*Dredging*' must be done in the interests of navigation, and either

(i) the qualifying trade must consist of the maintenance or improvement of navigation of a harbour, estuary or waterway, or

(ii) the dredging must be for the benefit of vessels coming to, leaving or using docks or other premises used in the qualifying trade.

It includes removal, by any means, of any part of, or projections from, any sea or inland water bed (whether then above water or not), and the widening of any inland waterway.

A '*qualifying trade*' is one either within (i) above or within the industrial buildings allowance definitions at 10.11(*a*)–(*c*) below. Expenditure only partly for a qualifying trade is apportioned as may be just, and for this purpose, where part only of a trade qualifies, the qualifying and non-qualifying parts are treated as separate trades.

Initial allowances are given for the year of assessment in whose basis period (see 71.3 SCHEDULE D, CASES I AND II) the expenditure is incurred at the following rates.

From 6 April 1956 — 10%
From 15 April 1958 — 15% (5% where certain investment allowances were payable between 8 April 1959 and 16 January 1966).

[*CAA 1968, s 67(1)(a)(8), Sch 1*].

Initial allowances are **abolished** for expenditure incurred **after 31 March 1986,** unless incurred before 1 April 1987 under a contract entered into before 14 March 1984 by the person incurring the expenditure. [*FA 1985, s 61*].

Expenditure incurred for a trade before it is carried on, or in connection with a dock etc. before it is occupied for a qualifying trade, attracts allowances as if the trade was carried on, or the dock etc. occupied, when the expenditure was incurred. The initial allowance is then given for the first year of assessment in whose basis period both the trade is carried on and the dock etc. occupied. [*CAA 1968, s 67(7); CAA 1990, s 134(7)*].

Writing-down allowances are given to the person for the time being carrying on the trade, at a rate fixed by the date expenditure was incurred, during a writing-down period of 25 years (50 years for expenditure incurred before 6 November 1962) beginning with the period for which the initial allowance is available (as above), or until initial and writing-down allowances exhaust the expenditure. The rates are as follows.

Before 6 November 1962 — 2% p.a.
From 6 November 1962 — 4% p.a.

The writing-down allowances are first given in the period for which initial allowances are (or would have been) given. In any year of assessment for only part of which a person is chargeable to income tax in respect of the trade, the annual writing-down allowance is apportioned on a time basis, but this is of no application where allowances fall to be treated as trading expenses (see 10.1 above). [*CAA 1990, s 134(1), s 135(2), s 146; FA 1994, s 211(2), s 213(9), Sch 26 Pt V(24)*].

A **balancing allowance** is given for the year of assessment of *permanent discontinuance* of the trade, equal to expenditure incurred less initial and writing-down allowances given, to the person last carrying on the trade. The allowance includes expenditure incurred before 6 April 1956, but in relation to such expenditure, all possible allowances (other than initial allowances) are deemed to have been given in respect of 1955/56 and earlier years as if the provisions introduced by *FA 1956* had always been in force. [*CAA 1990, s 134(2)(3)*].

Permanent discontinuance includes sale of the business (unless it is a sale between CONNECTED PERSONS (20), or without change of control, or one the sole or main benefit of which appears to be a capital allowance advantage, see *CAA 1990, s 157*), but not deemed discontinuance under *ICTA 1988, s 113* (change in person(s) carrying on trade) or certain corporation tax provisions. [*CAA 1990, s 134(4)*].

Excess allowances. Where the allowances for a year of assessment exceed the assessment for the year, the balance may be carried forward without time limit while the trade continues. Alternatively, allowances may create or enhance a trade loss. See 46 LOSSES generally. [*CAA 1990, s 140 as originally enacted*]. This is of no application where allowances fall to be treated as trading expenses (see 10.1 above).

Simon's Direct Tax Service. See **B2.8.**

10.8 *Example*

D is the proprietor of an estuary maintenance business preparing accounts to 30 June. Expenditure qualifying for dredging allowances is incurred as follows.

	£
Year ended 30.6.99	4,000
Year ended 30.6.00	5,000

On 2 January 2001, D sells the business to an unconnected third party.

The allowances available are

Date of expenditure	Cost	Residue brought forward	Allowances WDA 4%	Residue carried forward
	£	£	£	£
1999/2000 (year ended 30.6.99)				
1999	4,000	—	160	3,840
2000/01				
Year ended 30.6.00				
1999	4,000	3,840	160	3,680
2000	5,000	—	200	4,800
			£360	
Six months ending 2.1.01				
1999	4,000	3,680	($\frac{6}{12}$) 80	3,600
2000	5,000	4,800	($\frac{6}{12}$) 100	4,700
			180	£8,300
Balancing allowance			8,300	
			£8,480	
Total allowances 2000/01 (360 + 8,480)			£8,840	

10.9 **DWELLING-HOUSES LET ON ASSURED TENANCIES** [*CAA 1990, ss 84–97*]

Legislation was introduced by *FA 1982* to give capital allowances on expenditure incurred by an *'approved body'* (i.e. a body specified by the Secretary of State under *Housing Act 1980, s 56(4)*), on the construction of buildings consisting of, or including, dwelling-houses let on assured and certain other tenancies, after 9 March 1982 and before 1 April 1987 (subsequently extended until **31 March 1992**). [*CAA 1990, ss 84(1), 96(3)*]. The provisions were substantially modified following repeal of the relevant sections of the *Housing Act 1980* by the *Housing Act 1988*.

A *qualifying dwelling-house* is a dwelling-house let on a tenancy being an assured tenancy within *Housing Act 1980, s 56* (or, not being an assured shorthold tenancy, within *Housing Act 1988*) and continues to qualify at any time when

(i) it is subject to a regulated tenancy or a housing association tenancy (as defined in the *Rent Act 1977*), and

(ii) the landlord under the tenancy either is or has been an approved body.

[*CAA 1990, s 86(1)(2)(4), s 97(1)*].

A dwelling-house does not qualify

(*a*) unless the landlord is a company (applicable to expenditure contracted and incurred after 4 May 1983, or where a person other than a company becomes entitled to the 'relevant interest' after that date) and either is entitled to the relevant interest in the dwelling-house or is the person who incurred the capital expenditure on the construction of the building containing it; or

(*b*) if the landlord is a housing association approved under *ICTA 1988, s 488* (co-operative housing association) or is a self-build society under the *Housing Associations Act 1985*; or

(*c*) if the landlord and tenant, or a company of which the tenant is a director, are CONNECTED PERSONS (20); or

(*d*) if the landlord is a close company and the tenant is a participator, or associate of a participator, in that company; or

(*e*) if the tenancy is part of a reciprocal arrangement between the landlords or owners of different dwelling-houses designed to counter the restrictions in (*c*) or (*d*) above. [*CAA 1990, s 86*].

Capital expenditure appropriate to a dwelling-house is limited to £60,000 if it is in Greater London and £40,000 elsewhere, and is:

(A) where the building consists of a single qualifying dwelling-house, the whole of the expenditure on its construction;

(B) where the dwelling-house forms part of a building, (i) the proportion of capital expenditure attributable to that dwelling-house, and (ii) such proportion of the capital expenditure on any common parts of the building as is just and reasonable, but not exceeding one-tenth of the amount in (i). [*CAA 1990, s 96(1)(2)*].

The acquisition of, or of rights in or over, any land is not included in expenditure incurred on the cost of construction of a building for these purposes. [*CAA 1990, s 97(2)*].

Any capital expenditure incurred on repairs is treated as if incurred on the construction for the first time of that part of the building. [*CAA 1990, s 93(1)*].

Buildings bought unused. The provisions in *CAA 1990, s 91* are similar to those in *CAA 1990, s 10*, for which see 10.12, 10.13 below.

Subsidies. See 10.2(ii) above.

After the coming into force of the *Housing Act 1988, Pt I*, any assured tenancy (other than an assured shorthold tenancy) for the purposes of that *Act* is treated as an assured tenancy within the *Housing Act 1980, s 56*, but only in relation to capital expenditure incurred on the building either

(I) before 15 March 1988 (or under a contract entered into before that date) by a company which was on that date an approved body (see above) or by the vendor to such a company of the relevant interest in the building sold before use, or

(II) by a company as in (I) which, before 15 March 1988, bought or contracted to buy the relevant interest in the building. [*CAA 1990, s 84(2)(3)*].

Initial allowances were, and **writing-down allowances** are, given in a similar manner, at similar rates and under similar conditions as for industrial buildings, for which see 10.13,

10.14 below. [*FA 1982, Sch 12 para 1; FA 1984, s 58, Sch 12 para 3; CAA 1990, ss 85, 87(7)(8); FA 1994, s 213(7), Sch 26 Pt V(24)*]. Initial allowances available only by reason of *Housing Act 1980, s 56B* (as enacted by *Housing and Planning Act 1986*), and to which effect could not otherwise be given, could, on a claim before 1 April 1988, be given effect. [*F(No 2)A 1987, s 72(2)*].

References to 'temporary disuse' [*CAA 1990, s 89(2)*], 'residue of expenditure' [*CAA 1990, s 90*], and 'relevant interest' should be taken as they apply for industrial buildings allowances, but it should be noted that the creation of a subsidiary interest (e.g. leasehold out of freehold) does not transfer the relevant interest. [*CAA 1990, s 95*].

Balancing allowances and charges are made in a similar manner and under similar conditions as for industrial buildings in *CAA 1990, s 4* (see 10.15 below). [*CAA 1990, ss 87, 88; FA 1994, Sch 26 Pt V(24)*].

Where *cessation of qualifying use occurs* otherwise than by sale or transfer of the relevant interest, that interest is treated as having been sold at the time of cessation at the open market price. [*CAA 1990, s 89(1)*].

Making of allowances and charges. Allowances and charges are made in a similar way as they apply to lessors and licensors of industrial buildings, for which see 10.17 below. [*CAA 1990, ss 92, 140–145; FA 1995, Sch 6 para 34; FA 1998, s 38, Sch 5 para 58*].

Holding over by lessee etc. Where the relevant interest in relation to the capital expenditure incurred on the construction of a building is an interest under a lease, the following provisions apply. The lease will be treated as continuing where (i) with the consent of the lessor, a lessee remains in possession of any building after his lease ends and without a new lease being granted, (ii) where a lease ends and a new lease is granted to the same lessee under an option available in the first lease, and (iii) where a lease ends and another lease is granted to a different lessee who pays a sum to the first lessee (i.e. the transaction is treated as an assignment). However, where a lease ends and the lessor pays any sum to the lessee in respect of the building, the transaction is treated as if the lease had come to an end by reason of its surrender in consideration of the payment. [*CAA 1990, s 94*].

Double allowances. See 10.2(iv) above.

Connected persons and other anti-avoidance provisions. The provisions of *CAA 1990, ss 157, 158* apply to certain sales as they apply to sales of industrial buildings (see 10.22 below) but an election is only available if both the seller and the buyer are, at the time of the sale (or, for sales after 14 January 1989, were at any earlier time), approved bodies. Due to a drafting error, the original provisions allowed such an election only if that condition was *not* fulfilled, and an election made before 1 April 1983 on that basis remains valid. [*F(No 2)A 1983, s 6(2)*]. Any transfer of relevant interest which is not a sale will be treated as a sale other than at market price under these provisions but there is no balancing allowance or charge if the dwelling-house is treated as having been sold for a sum equal to the residue of expenditure before the sale. [*CAA 1990, ss 87(5), 88(4)*].

Simon's Direct Tax Service. See **B2.9**.

10.10 INDUSTRIAL BUILDINGS

Allowances are given in respect of certain capital expenditure (see 10.12 below) on industrial buildings or structures (see 10.11 below), and are available to traders and to lessors and licensors of industrial buildings for use by traders. The main elements of the scheme of allowances are dealt with as follows

10.11 Capital Allowances (Industrial Buildings)

10.11 Qualifying buildings
10.12 Qualifying expenditure
10.13 Initial allowances
10.14 Writing-down allowances
10.15 Balancing allowances and charges
10.17 Making of allowances and charges
10.18 Hotels
10.19 Enterprise zones
10.21 Small workshops
10.22 General matters

Simon's Direct Tax Service. See **B2.2.**

10.11 **Qualifying buildings.** An 'industrial building or structure' is a building etc., or part of a building etc., in use either

(*a*) for the purposes of a trade, or part of a trade (which must be a self-contained part, see Revenue Capital Allowances Manual, CA 1310, 1311), consisting of

- (i) the manufacture or processing of goods or materials, or
- (ii) after 9 March 1982, the maintaining or repairing of goods or materials (but not goods etc. employed by the person carrying out the repair or maintenance in any trade or undertaking unless that trade etc. itself qualifies the building as an industrial building etc.), or
- (iii) the storage of (*a*) raw materials for manufacture, (*b*) goods to be processed, (*c*) goods manufactured or processed but not yet delivered to any purchaser, or (*d*) goods on arrival in the UK from a place outside the UK, or
- (iv) the working of mines, oil wells, etc. or foreign plantations, or
- (v) agricultural operations on land not occupied by the trader, or
- (vi) catching fish or shellfish; or

(*b*) for the purposes of

- (i) a trade, or part of a trade, carried on in a mill, factory or other similar premises, or
- (ii) a transport, dock, inland navigation, water, sewerage, electricity, hydraulic power, bridge or tunnel undertaking, or
- (iii) in relation to any chargeable or basis period ending after 5 April 1991, a toll road undertaking or, for expenditure incurred after 5 April 1995, a 'highway undertaking' (see below); or

(*c*) for the welfare of workers employed in a trade or undertaking within (*a*) or (*b*) above; or

(*d*) as a sports pavilion for the welfare of workers employed in any trade; or

(*e*) as a qualifying hotel (see 10.18 below).

As regards (*a*) above, following the decision in *Bestway (Holdings) Ltd v Luff Ch D 1998, 70 TC 512*, the Revenue have changed their view in two respects.

(A) Previously they had considered that, provided it was self-contained, anything done in the course of a trade was part of a trade for this purpose (see Revenue Capital Allowances Manual, CA 1310, 1311). Their revised view is that, whilst the activities in question do not need to be self-contained, they must be a significant, separate and identifiable part of the trade carried on.

(B) They previously considered the main test under (*a*)(iii) above to be whether the further conditions as to use of the goods or materials stored were satisfied. They have now adopted the Court's preliminary test that the determining factor in deciding whether a building is used for storage is the purpose for which the goods or materials are kept or held — it is used for storage only if the purpose of keeping them there is their storage as an end in itself and not some other purpose.

This change of view is most likely to be significant in wholesale trades where it has previously been accepted that there was a qualifying part trade of storage of goods or materials to be used in the manufacture of other goods or materials or subjected to a process. For allowances to continue to be available, the storage must be conducted as a purpose and end in itself, not just as a necessary and transitory incident of the conduct of the wholesale business. Where claims have previously been accepted under the earlier view, the revised view should be applied to claims for chargeable periods ending after 31 December 1999. (Revenue Tax Bulletin December 1999 pp 710, 711).

A building the whole of which is in use partly for qualifying and partly for non-qualifying purposes may qualify for allowances in full provided that the qualifying use is at least 10% of the total use. (Revenue Capital Allowances Manual, CA 1328). See also *Saxone Lilley & Skinner (Holdings) Ltd* below.

Excluded from the definition of 'industrial buildings or structure' are buildings etc. in use as, or as part of, dwelling-houses, retail shops, showrooms, offices or hotels (but see 10.18 below as regards expenditure on hotels after 11 April 1978), or on buildings etc. for purposes ancillary thereto, except that (1) where only part of a building, representing 25% (10% for expenditure incurred before 16 March 1983 or deemed so incurred under *CAA 1990, s 10(1)(2)*, see 10.12 below) or less of the total cost, falls within these exclusions, the whole building continues to qualify, and (2) buildings etc. constructed for occupation by, or welfare of, employees in mines, oil wells, etc. or foreign plantations, and likely to have little or no value on the ending of the working of the mine etc. or of the foreign concession, also qualify. Note that when alterations, extensions etc. or changes in use result in the 25% limit in (1) being exceeded, no amendment is made to allowances for basis periods before that of the change, and allowances continue to be available in respect of that part of the building etc. not excluded. Similarly, where the 25% condition commences to be met, allowances are available for the whole of the building etc. only for the basis period of the change and subsequent basis periods. See Revenue Capital Allowances Manual at CA 1344 for what is an 'office' for these purposes, and at CA 1350–1354 for purposes 'ancillary' to those of a retail shop. In *Girobank plc v Clarke CA 1998, 70 TC 387*, a bank document and data processing centre was held not to be an office. In *Sarsfield v Dixons Group plc CA 1998, 71 TC 121*, a warehouse used by a group distribution company for receiving, storing and delivering goods purchased by the group for sale from its shops was held to be used for purposes ancillary to those of the group's retail shops.

Buildings etc. *outside the UK* can only qualify if the trade for which they are in use is assessable under Schedule D, Case I or Case V. A building etc. used by more than one licensee of the same person only qualifies if each of the licensees uses the building, or his part of it, for the purposes of a trade as above under licences granted after 9 March 1982. [*CAA 1990, ss 14, 18; FA 1991, s 60(4)(10); FA 1993, s 113(6); FA 1995, ss 99(5), 101*].

A '*highway undertaking*' (see (*b*)(iii) above) means so much of any undertaking relating to the design, building, financing and operation of roads as is carried on for the purposes of, or in connection with, the exploitation of 'highway concessions'. A '*highway concession*', in relation to a road, means any right, in respect of public use of the road, to receive sums from the Government, or, in the case of a toll road, the right to charge tolls. [*CAA 1990, s 21(5AA); FA 1995, s 99(7)*].

(*c*) above is regarded by the Revenue as including canteens, day nurseries, garages, hard tennis courts, hostels and indoor sports halls. It does not, however, include buildings excluded as above from being industrial buildings or structures (e.g. a grocery shop with extended hours for the convenience of workers, or holiday accommodation). Also as regards (*c*) above, the workers for whose welfare a building is provided must be workers engaged directly in the productive, manufacturing or processing side of the business, rather than office staff or management, although the whole of a building provided for staff generally may qualify provided use by production workers is not negligible. Similarly use by outsiders as well as workers does not exclude the building from relief. (Revenue Capital Allowances Manual, CA 1304–1307).

For cases in which industrial buildings allowances were **refused** see *Dale v Johnson Bros KB(NI) 1951, 32 TC 487* (warehouse — contrast the non-tax case *Crusabridge Investments Ltd v Casings International Ltd Ch D 1979, 54 TC 246*); *CIR v National Coal Board HL 1957, 37 TC 264* (colliery houses capable of alternative use); *Bourne v Norwich Crematorium Ch D 1967, 44 TC 164* (furnace chamber, etc.); *Abbott Laboratories Ltd v Carmody Ch D 1968, 44 TC 569* (separate administrative block); *Buckingham v Securitas Properties Ltd Ch D 1979, 53 TC 292* (building used for wage packeting); *Vibroplant Ltd v Holland CA 1981, 54 TC 658* (depots of plant hire contractor, but now see (*a*)(ii) above); *Copol Clothing Co Ltd v Hindmarch CA 1983, 57 TC 575* (inland storage of goods imported in containers); *Carr v Sayer Ch D 1992, 65 TC 15* (quarantine kennels, claimed under (*a*)(iii)(*d*) above); *Girobank plc v Clarke CA 1998, 70 TC 387* (bank document and data processing centre); *Bestway (Holdings) Ltd v Luff Ch D 1998, 70 TC 512* (cash-and-carry wholesale warehouse); and *Sarsfield v Dixons Group plc CA 1998, 71 TC 121* (warehouse used by retail group distribution company for receiving, storing and delivering goods).

For cases where allowances were **granted**, see *CIR v Lambhill Ironworks Ltd CS 1950, 31 TC 393* (drawing office); *Kilmarnock Equitable Co-operative Society Ltd v CIR CS 1966, 42 TC 675* (coal packing not ancillary to retail shop); *Saxone Lilley & Skinner (Holdings) Ltd v CIR HL 1967, 44 TC 122* (warehouse for shoes both bought and manufactured).

Temporary disuse. A building etc. which falls temporarily out of use after a period in which it qualified as an 'industrial building or structure' is treated as continuing to so qualify during disuse. [*CAA 1990, s 15*]. All disuse other than that preceding demolition or dereliction is in practice regarded as temporary.

10.12 **Qualifying expenditure** is the cost of construction of the building etc. including the cost of preparing, cutting, tunnelling or levelling land, but excluding expenditure on the land itself or on rights therein. [*CAA 1990, ss 1(1), 21(1)*]. A just apportionment is required to exclude unallowable expenditure (and see *Bostock v Totham Ch D 1997, 69 TC 356* as regards the basis of such apportionment). [*CAA 1990, s 21(3)*]. Anything with four walls and a roof is a building for these purposes, provided that it is of a reasonably substantial size. Anything smaller may be a structure. A structure is something which has been artificially erected or constructed, and which is distinct from the surrounding earth, e.g. roads, paved car parks or tennis courts, tunnels, culverts, bridges, walls and fences. (Revenue Capital Allowances Manual, CA 1040, 1041). The fees of professionals involved in the design and construction of a building etc. (e.g. architects, quantity surveyors and engineers) are also included. (Revenue Capital Allowances Manual, CA 1035). Expenditure on repairs which is, exceptionally, disallowable in computing profits is treated as the cost of constructing that part of the building [*CAA 1990, s 12*], and the cost of preparing etc. land as a site for the installation of machinery or plant is, if no relief would otherwise be available under industrial buildings or machinery and plant allowances, treated as attracting allowances as if the machinery or plant were a building. [*CAA 1990, s 13*]. Where, for the purpose of erecting a new building on the same site, costs are incurred in demolishing an existing building, and the costs cannot be taken into account in calculating a balancing adjustment (see 10.15 below) on the demolished building (e.g. because more than 25 (or 50) years has elapsed since the building was first used), the demolition costs may be treated as expenditure on construction of the new building. (Revenue Capital Allowances Manual, CA 1034, 1244).

Roads on an industrial trading estate will be treated as industrial buildings or structures. [*CAA 1990, s 18(8)*]. See 10.25 below for certain expenditure on existing buildings treated as being on machinery or plant.

The following are considered by the Revenue to be excluded from being qualifying expenditure: expenditure on obtaining planning permission (although if a builder's costs are inclusive of such expenditure, no apportionment will be made); capitalised interest; public enquiry costs; land drainage and reclamation and landscaping; and legal expenses. (Revenue Capital Allowances Manual, CA 1036, 1039, 1042).

Abortive expenditure. Expenditure (including professional fees) incurred on the construction of a building which never becomes an industrial building, etc. (e.g. because it is never completed) cannot be qualifying expenditure. (Revenue Capital Allowances Manual, CA 1035, 1051).

Buildings bought unused. If the 'relevant interest' (see 10.14 below) in a building etc. is sold before it is used, the purchaser (the last purchaser if more than one before the building is used) is treated as having incurred on its construction, at the time the purchase price becomes payable, the lesser of the actual cost of construction and the net purchase price of the interest (excluding any part attributable to the land, see Revenue Capital Allowances Manual, CA 1119). 'Use' means use for any purpose, but does not include occupation by a tenant for fitting out prior to use. (Revenue Capital Allowances Manual, CA 1110). Where the original expenditure was incurred by a builder as part of his trade of constructing such buildings with a view to sale, the purchaser's deemed construction cost is the net purchase price paid by him or, if there have been previous sales unused, the lesser of the net purchase price paid by him and the net price paid to the builder on the first sale. (Note that this latter provision does not apply for agricultural buildings allowances purposes, for which the provisions are otherwise similar.) [*CAA 1990, s 10(1)–(3)*]. Except where the purchase price is specially defined by virtue of an election under *CAA 1990, s 11* (see 10.14 below), the net purchase price of the interest includes acquisition costs, i.e. legal fees, surveyors' fees and stamp duty. (Revenue Capital Allowances Manual, CA 1118).

The initial allowance under *CAA 1990, s 2A* (see 10.13 below) can be claimed by the purchaser (or last purchaser) of an unused building regardless of the date of sale providing some or all the actual construction expenditure falls within those provisions, i.e. it is incurred in, broadly, the year ending 31 October 1993. It can also be claimed where the actual construction expenditure was incurred by a builder (as above) *at any time* before 1 November 1993, the sale occurs between 1 November 1992 and 31 October 1993 inclusive and the vendor has been entitled to the relevant interest since before 1 November 1992. Such construction expenditure is deemed for these purposes to fall within *section 2A*. In both circumstances, it remains a condition that the building comes to be used before 1 January 1995 (see 10.13 below). Where only part of the actual construction expenditure is within *section 2A*, the purchaser's deemed construction cost is computed as above and then divided into a *section 2A* element qualifying for the initial allowance and a residual element qualifying only for writing-down allowances. The *section 2A* element is the proportion of the deemed expenditure that corresponds to the proportion of actual construction expenditure that is within *section 2A*. [*CAA 1990, s 10(3A), s 10C(1)–(10); FA 1993, s 113(3)(4)*].

Appropriation from trading stock. A building appropriated by a builder from trading stock to capital account (with a corresponding market value credit to profit and loss) and let as an industrial building, etc. is eligible for writing-down allowances based on the construction cost (rather than on the transfer value). Initial allowances are not available in these circumstances. (Revenue Capital Allowances Manual, CA 1212).

Arrangements affecting the value of purchased interest. Where certain 'arrangements' have been entered into relating to, or with respect to, any interest in or right over a building, etc., special rules apply for determining any amount which is to be taken to be:

(*a*) for the purposes of *CAA 1990, ss 10–10C* (buildings bought unused or, after use, from original builder or, in certain cases, within two years after first use (see above and 10.19 below)), the sum paid on the sale of the relevant interest, and

(*b*) for the purposes of *CAA 1990, ss 1–8* (allowances and charges generally, see above and 10.13–10.19 below), the amount of any sale, etc. moneys payable, where a person is deemed under any of *CAA 1990, ss 10–10C* to have incurred expenditure on the construction of the building, etc. of an amount equal to the price paid on a sale of the relevant interest.

The '*arrangements*' in question are those

(i) entered into at or before the 'specified time',

(ii) having the effect at that time of enhancing the value of the relevant interest in the building, etc., and

(iii) containing any provision having an artificial effect on pricing,

and as regards (iii) above, arrangements are treated as containing such a provision to the extent that they go beyond what, at the time they were entered into, it was reasonable to regard as required by the prevailing market conditions in similar arm's length transactions. For examples of the sort of arrangements considered by the Revenue to be most likely to be used, see Revenue Capital Allowances Manual, CA 1487.

The '*specified time*' is the time of the fixing of the sale price:

(A) in relation to the determination of an amount within (*a*) above, for the sale in question; and

(B) in relation to the determination of an amount within (*b*) above, for the sale by reference to which the amount of the deemed expenditure fell to be determined under any of *CAA 1990, ss 10–10C*.

Where these provisions apply, the amount falling to be determined is reduced to the extent that, on a just apportionment, the sale price or the amount of the sale, etc. moneys is more than it would have been if the arrangements had not contained the provision in (iii) above.

These provisions apply to determinations after 28 November 1994, unless the 'specified time' (see above) would be the time of the fixing of a sale price which either became payable before 29 November 1994 or, being an amount becoming payable before 6 April 1995, was fixed by a contract entered into before 29 November 1994. [*CAA 1990, s 10D; FA 1995, s 100*].

10.13 **Initial allowances.** In general, initial allowances were **abolished** for expenditure incurred after 31 March 1986, or after 31 March 1987 in the case of expenditure incurred after 13 March 1984 under a contract entered into before 14 March 1984 by the person incurring the expenditure. [*FA 1984, Sch 12 para 1*]. However, they continue to be available

(*a*) at a rate of 100% for certain expenditure in enterprise zones (see 10.19 below), and

(*b*) at a rate of 20% for certain expenditure incurred in, broadly, the year ending 31 October 1993 (see further below),

and to any additional VAT liability (see 10.2(v) above) in respect of such expenditure.

[*CAA 1990, ss 1(1), 2A; FA 1991, Sch 14 para 2*]. The general rules governing availability of initial allowances are described below.

Initial allowances were temporarily reintroduced by *FA 1993* and are available in respect of qualifying expenditure (see 10.12 above) incurred under a contract entered into in the twelve-month period **1 November 1992 to 31 October 1993 inclusive** or for the purpose of securing compliance with obligations incurred under a contract entered into during that period, but not for expenditure incurred under a contract entered into for the purpose of securing compliance with obligations under a contract entered into before 1 November 1992. See also below for the rules generally governing availability of initial allowances, which apply equally to these provisions. The qualifying building must come to be used before 1 January 1995, and, if this condition is not satisfied, any initial allowance given will be withdrawn. The initial allowance is **20%** of the expenditure incurred. These provisions do not apply where initial allowances would otherwise be available, i.e. under (*a*) or (*b*) above. They do apply to qualifying hotels (see 10.18 below), and also in respect of any 'additional VAT liability' (see 10.2(v) above) incurred in respect of expenditure falling within these provisions. [*CAA 1990, s 2A; FA 1993, s 113(1)*].

Initial allowances are available to a person incurring qualifying expenditure (see 10.12 above) on a building etc. which is to be in use as an 'industrial building or structure' (see 10.11 above) for a trade carried on by that person or by his lessee or, for licences granted after 9 March 1982, by his licensee. [*CAA 1968, s 1(1)(1A); FA 1982, s 74; CAA 1990, s 1(1)(4)*]. See also 10.12 above as regards buildings bought unused. An initial allowance is given for the chargeable period related to the incurring of the expenditure. [*CAA 1990, s 1(1)*]. Expenditure for the purposes of a trade incurred by a person about to carry it on is treated as if incurred on the day the trade is actually commenced, but this applies only for the purpose of determining the chargeable period for which the allowance may be made (and not, for example, to determine the availability or otherwise of an initial allowance under *CAA 1990, s 2A* — see above). [*CAA 1968, s 1(6); CAA 1990, s 1(10)*]. See also 10.12 above as regards buildings bought unused and 10.2(iii) above generally as to the time at which expenditure is treated as being incurred.

The *rate* of allowance depends on the date on which the expenditure was actually incurred [*FA 1980, s 75(5); FA 1981, s 73(3); FA 1984, Sch 12 para 1; CAA 1990, s 6(5), s 19(6)*], except that in the case of expenditure deemed under *CAA 1968, s 5(1)* to have been incurred on the construction of a building bought unused (see 10.12 above) (and disregarding the 20% allowance introduced by *FA 1993* (see above)),

(i) the reduced rates of allowance for expenditure incurred after 13 March 1984 apply as if the expenditure was incurred at the latest time any expenditure was in fact incurred on its construction [*FA 1984, Sch 12 para 1*], and

(ii) otherwise, where such expenditure is deemed to have been incurred after 10 March 1981, the deemed date governs the rate of allowance [*FA 1981, s 73(3)*].

The rates of initial allowance (other than that introduced by *FA 1993* — see above) are

After 5 April 1944	— 10%
After 5 April 1952	— Nil
After 14 April 1953	— 10%
After 6 April 1954	— Nil
After 17 February 1956	— 10%
After 14 April 1958	— 15%
After 7 April 1959	— 5%
After 16 January 1966	— 15%
After 5 April 1970	— 30% (40% if building in development or intermediate area or N. Ireland)

After 21 March 1972 — 40%
After 12 November 1974 — 50% (20% on hotels and 100% in enterprise zones and on certain small workshops, from later dates, see 10.18, 10.19 and 10.21 below)
After 10 March 1981 — 75% (— as above —)
After 13 March 1984 — 50% (— as above, omitting reference to workshops from 27 March 1985 —)
After 31 March 1985 — 25% (— as above —)

Initial allowances may be claimed in whole or part by individuals and partnerships and, for accounting periods ended after 30 September 1993, by companies. For earlier accounting periods, companies may disclaim all or part of such allowances by notice in writing within two years of the end of the accounting period. [*FA 1981, s 73(2); CAA 1990, s 1(5); FA 1990, Sch 17 para 2*].

Initial allowances are withdrawn if, when the building etc. comes to be used, it is not an 'industrial building or structure'. [*CAA 1968, s 1(5); CAA 1990, s 1(6)*].

10.14 **Writing-down allowances** are available where a qualifying building (see 10.11 above) is in use as such (or in temporary disuse following such use, see 10.11 above) at the end of a chargeable period (formerly basis period — see 10.2(vi) above). They are available to the person entitled to an interest which is the 'relevant interest' in the building at the end of that period. For this purpose, an entitlement to a highway concession (see 10.11 above) in respect of a road constitutes an interest in the road. A writing-down allowance can be given for the same chargeable period as an initial allowance (see 10.13 above) in respect of the same expenditure. Allowances may be claimed in whole or part (see Revenue Capital Allowances Manual, CA 1211).

For expenditure incurred between 6 April 1946 and 5 November 1962 inclusive, the rate of allowance is 2% p.a.

For expenditure incurred **after 5 November 1962**, the rate of allowance is **4% p.a.** (but see 10.19, 10.21 below as regards 25% annual allowances in certain cases).

The allowances are calculated on the qualifying expenditure (see 10.12 above) incurred, and continue until the 'residue of expenditure' is nil. The annual writing-down allowance is available in full where the expenditure is incurred during the basis period, but is proportionately reduced or increased where the chargeable period is less or more than twelve months. [*CAA 1990, s 3(1)(2)(4)(5); FA 1991, s 60(3); FA 1994, s 213(2), Sch 26 Pt V(24); FA 1995, s 99(2)*]. For lessors of industrial buildings, however, the basis period is the year of assessment itself, so that the full allowance is available regardless of the date of commencement of letting in the year. [*CAA 1990, s 160(5); FA 1994, s 212(1)*].

Where an 'additional VAT liability' (see 10.2(v) above) is incurred in respect of any qualifying expenditure, the amount of the liability qualifies for writing-down allowances as if it were additional capital expenditure incurred on the construction in question; the 'residue of expenditure' is increased by that amount at the time the liability is incurred. For chargeable or basis periods ending after the time the liability is incurred, writing-down allowances are given of the proportion of the residue of expenditure immediately after that time which the length of the chargeable period bears to the length of the period from the date of the incurring of the liability to the 25th anniversary of the first use of the building for any purpose. Similar provisions apply where an 'additional VAT rebate' (see 10.2(v) above) is made, the residue being reduced by the amount thereof (but see 10.15 below where the rebate exceeds the residue). [*CAA 1990, s 3(2A)–(2C), s 8(12A); FA 1991, Sch 14 paras 3, 5(2); FA 1994, Sch 26 Pt V(24)*].

If the 'relevant interest' in a building is sold, and the sale is an event which may give rise to a balancing adjustment under *CAA 1990, s 4(1)* (see 10.15 below), subsequent writing-down allowances are given to the purchaser and are calculated on the 'residue of expenditure' immediately after the sale, spread over the period from the date of sale to the 25th anniversary of the first use of the building for any purpose (50th anniversary for expenditure incurred before 6 November 1962). [*CAA 1990, s 3(3); FA 1994, Sch 26 Pt V(24)*].

For a sale *before 18 December 1980* (or pursuant to a contract made before that date) at a time when the building etc. was not in use as an 'industrial building or structure', so that no balancing adjustment arose (see 10.15 below), writing-down allowances to the purchaser (for subsequent basis periods at the end of which the building etc. has reverted to use as an 'industrial building or structure') continue at the rate after the most recent sale while in use as an 'industrial building or structure' or, if there has been no such sale, the full 4% (or 2%) rate. [*CAA 1968, s 2; FA 1981, s 74*].

'*Residue of expenditure*' is original capital expenditure

minus all industrial buildings and scientific research allowances (see 10.52 below) granted, including balancing allowances, and

minus 'notional writing-down allowances' for periods, following first use of the building for any purpose and including, where appropriate, periods before 1946/47, at the end of which the building etc. was not in use as an 'industrial building or structure', and

plus any balancing charges made, and

plus or *minus* any 'additional VAT liability' or 'additional VAT rebate' (see 10.2(v) above) incurred or made in respect of that expenditure.

Where the Crown is entitled to the relevant interest for a period immediately before a sale etc., allowances and charges which could have been made if the building had been in use by a non-corporate trader entitled to that interest for that period are taken into account for this purpose. This treatment applies also to prior entitlement by any person not within the charge to UK tax.

Where a balancing charge arises on the excess of allowances given over adjusted net cost following a sale after non-qualifying use (see 10.15 below), the residue after the sale is restricted to the net sale proceeds. [*CAA 1990, s 3(2A)(b), s 8; FA 1991, Sch 14 paras 3(1), 5; FA 1994, s 213(3), Sch 26 Pt V(24)*].

'*Notional allowances*' are calculated on the original qualifying expenditure or, if the building etc. has subsequently been sold in circumstances such that a balancing adjustment might have arisen under *CAA 1990, s 4(1)* (see 10.15 below), at the appropriate rate following that sale. [*CAA 1990, s 8(7)*].

'*Relevant interest*' is, in relation to any expenditure incurred on the construction of the building or structure, the interest (freehold or leasehold) in that building etc. to which the person who incurred the expenditure was entitled when he incurred it. Where a person incurs expenditure on a road in respect of which he is entitled to a highway concession (see 10.11 above) and does not otherwise have an interest in the road, the highway concession is the relevant interest in relation to that expenditure. The creation of a subsidiary interest (e.g. leasehold out of freehold) does not transfer the relevant interest. [*CAA 1990, s 20; FA 1991, s 60(5); FA 1995, s 99(6)* and *Woods v R M Mallen (Eng) Ltd Ch D 1969, 45 TC 619*].

But where a long lease is granted out of a 'relevant interest' the lessor and the lessee may jointly elect for allowances to apply to the leasehold interest. The grant of the lease is then regarded as a sale to the lessee, the capital sum as the purchase price, and the lessee's interest as replacing all the lessor's relevant interest. The election is not available if lessor and lessee are 'connected persons' (unless the lessor has statutory functions) or if the sole or main benefit which may be expected to accrue to the lessor is a balancing allowance (see

10.15 below). The election must be in writing to the inspector within two years after the date on which the lease takes effect. [*CAA 1990, s 11*].

Buildings bought after use. Where a person carrying on a trade, consisting wholly or partly of the construction of buildings or structures with a view to their sale, incurs expenditure on such a construction and after the building has been used, he sells the relevant interest in the course of the trade, the purchaser is entitled to allowances as if the original expenditure had been capital expenditure and all appropriate writing-down allowances and balancing allowances or charges (see 10.15 below) had been made to or on the vendor. Normally, the effect will be that the purchaser obtains allowances on the lesser of the net purchase price and the cost of construction. This provision applies in any case where the purchase price becomes payable after 26 July 1989. [*CAA 1990, s 10(4)(5)*]. Previously, a similar rule operated by extra-statutory concession. (Revenue Pamphlet IR 1, B20).

10.15 **Balancing allowances and charges.** A balancing allowance or charge may arise when a building etc. is sold, destroyed or permanently put out of use, or when the 'relevant interest' (see 10.14 above) is lost on termination of a lease or foreign concession, or when a highway concession (see 10.11 above) is brought to or comes to an end (see also below), *provided that* that event occurs within 25 years (50 years for expenditure incurred before 6 November 1962) of the building's first being used. On a sale etc. **after 17 December 1980** (unless pursuant to a contract made on or before that date) of a building etc. which has been an industrial building or structure (or used for scientific research (from 6 April 2000, research and development), see 10.52 below) throughout the 'relevant period', the balancing adjustment is calculated as follows. If the 'residue of expenditure' (see 10.14 above) immediately before the sale etc. exceeds the proceeds of any sale, insurance, salvage or compensation, the difference is allowed as a balancing allowance; if it is less, the difference is the subject of a balancing charge. [*CAA 1990, s 4(1)–(4); FA 1995, s 99(3)*]. Where the building etc. has at any time in the 'relevant period' been neither an 'industrial building or structure' nor in use for scientific research (or research and development), a balancing charge will be made to recover all allowances given where the proceeds of sale, insurance, salvage or compensation equal or exceed the 'capital expenditure'. Where these proceeds are nil or less than the 'capital expenditure', a balancing allowance will be given (or a balancing charge made) on the excess of the 'adjusted net cost' of the building etc. over the allowances given (or *vice versa*). For this purpose, the allowances given include all industrial buildings, scientific research (or research and development), and mills, factories or exceptional depreciation allowances, and any balancing charge raised may not exceed the total of such allowances, less any balancing charges previously made. Allowances made to a husband before 6 April 1990 in respect of his wife's relevant interest are treated as having been made to the wife for this purpose on a balancing event on or after that date.

'*Relevant period*' means the period beginning at the time when the building was first used for any purpose and ending with the event giving rise to the balancing adjustment, unless there have been previous sales, when the relevant period begins on the day following the last sale.

'*Capital expenditure*' means the expenditure incurred on the construction of the building (less any balancing charge made in respect of an 'additional VAT rebate' — see below) or, in the case of a 'second-hand' building, the residue of expenditure (see 10.14 above) at the beginning of the relevant period, together (in either case) with the net cost of demolition (as under *CAA 1990, s 8(12)*, see below) if appropriate.

'*Adjusted net cost*' means the amount by which capital expenditure exceeds the proceeds, reduced in the proportion that the period of qualifying use bears to the relevant period.

[*CAA 1990, s 4(5)–(12); FA 1991, Sch 14 para 4(4)(5); FA 1994, Sch 26 Pt V(24); FA 2000, Sch 19 para 8*].

Successive sales etc. during non-use as industrial building. Where there are two or more sales etc. in a period during which a building etc. is not an 'industrial building or structure', a balancing adjustment arises only on the first such sale etc. [*CAA 1990, s 4(2); FA 1991, Sch 14 para 4(2)*].

Additional VAT rebate. Where an 'additional VAT rebate' (see 10.2(v) above) is made in respect of qualifying expenditure, and this exceeds the residue of expenditure (see 10.14 above), a balancing charge, equal to the excess, will be made. [*CAA 1990, s 4(1)(e)(2A); FA 1991, Sch 14 para 4(1)(3)*].

In the case of a *highway concession* (see above), no balancing adjustment arises (and writing-down allowances continue) where, on the coming to an end of the concession, the period for which it was granted is extended, i.e. the person entitled to it is granted a renewal of the concession in respect of the whole or part of a road, or he or a CONNECTED PERSON (20) is granted a new concession in respect of the same road (or part of it or a road of which it is part). Where the extension relates to part only of a road, a 'just and reasonable' apportionment is made to determine the expenditure in respect of which a balancing adjustment arises. [*CAA 1990, s 4(2AA)(2AB); FA 1995, s 99(4)*].

On a sale etc. **before 18 December 1980** (or pursuant to a contract made before that date), a balancing adjustment arose only when the building etc. was in use as an 'industrial building or structure' at the time of the sale etc. Any balancing adjustment which did arise was calculated as follows. If the 'residue of expenditure' (see 10.14 above) immediately before the sale etc. exceeded the proceeds of any sale, insurance, salvage or compensation, the difference was allowed as a balancing allowance; if it was less, the difference was the subject of a balancing charge, subject to two restrictions:

(*a*) the charge may not exceed the total of industrial buildings, scientific research, and mills, factories or exceptional depreciation allowances given; and

(*b*) where during any part of the 'relevant period' (see below) the building etc. has not attracted writing-down or scientific research allowances, the charge is reduced to the proportion which the parts of the 'relevant period' which were included in basis periods for which such allowances were given bears to the whole of the 'relevant period'. For this purpose the *'relevant period'* is the period from first use of the building to date of the sale etc. or, if that date is not the last day of a basis period, the most recent day before the sale etc. which was the last day of a basis period.

A restriction similar to that in (*b*) above could be placed on balancing allowances on election by the vendor. [*CAA 1968, s 3 as originally enacted*].

Demolition. The net cost (after crediting sales of materials and scrap) of demolition borne by the person concerned is added to 'residue of expenditure' for balancing allowance and balancing charge calculations. [*CAA 1990, s 8(12)*]. Where this is not possible (e.g. because more than 25 (or 50) years has elapsed since the building was first used), and if the holder of the relevant interest demolishes the building for the purpose of erecting a new building on the same site, the demolition costs may be treated as expenditure by the holder on construction of the new building. (Revenue Capital Allowances Manual, CA 1034, 1244).

See also 10.22(i) below as regards certain transactions between connected persons and other anti-avoidance provisions.

10.16 *Examples*

Initial and writing-down allowances and balancing adjustments

Prior to commencing business on 1 June 1993, P incurred the following expenditure.

10.16 Capital Allowances (Industrial Buildings)

	£
10.1.93 Plot of land	50,000
20.2.93 Clearing and levelling site	20,000
20.4.93 Construction of factory	500,000
	£570,000

The factory was brought into use for a qualifying purpose on commencement of trade, remained in such use until 1 May 2000, when it was sold to Y for £550,000, being £480,000 for the factory and £70,000 for the land. P drew up accounts annually to 31 May, and did not elect for the second and third years of assessment to be taxed on an actual basis. Y draws up accounts to 30 April, having commenced trading on 1 May 2000, and uses the factory for a qualifying purpose.

The allowances available to P are as follows.

Year of assessment			Residue of expenditure
			£
1993/94	Qualifying expenditure		520,000
	Initial allowance	20% of £520,000	(104,000)
	Writing-down allowance	4% of £520,000	(20,800)
			395,200
1994/95, 1995/96, 1996/97, 1997/98, 1998/99, 1999/2000	Writing-down allowance for 6 years	4% of £520,000 × 6	(124,800)
			270,400
2000/01	Sale proceeds		(480,000)
	Balancing charge		£209,600

The allowances available to Y are as follows.

Date of first use	1.6.93
Date of purchase by Y	1.5.00
Number of years remaining	18 years 1 month
Residue of expenditure	£480,000

Y is therefore entitled to writing-down allowances of £26,544 p.a. until total allowances reach £480,000. His first writing-down allowance will be given for the period of account 1.5.00 to 30.4.01.

Notes

(*a*) Writing-down allowances are first due in 1993/94, being P's first chargeable period, but are *not* restricted to the length of the basis period (which runs from 1 June 1993 to 5 April 1994) (see 10.14 above).

(*b*) No allowances are due on the cost of the land (see 10.12 above).

Non-qualifying purposes and balancing adjustments

A, B and C entered into partnership in 1974 and prepare accounts annually to 31 March. The partnership incurred £40,000 of capital expenditure in 1984 (and after 13 March 1984) on the construction of a building which was brought into use as an industrial building on 1 April 1985. After three years of use for a qualifying industrial purpose, it was used for three years, from 1 April 1988 to 31 March 1991, for non-qualifying purposes after which the original qualifying activity was resumed until the building was destroyed by fire.

The fire occurred on 1 October 2000 with an insurance recovery of (i) £50,000 (ii) £35,000. The partnership's industrial buildings allowance position for the period of account 1 April 2000 to 31 March 2001 will be as follows.

Year ended 31 March 2001: Balancing charge

(i) *Proceeds exceed cost*		
Actual allowances given	note (*a*)	£37,600
Balancing charge		£37,600

		£
(ii) *Proceeds less than cost*		
Net cost (£40,000 – £35,000)		5,000
Reduction $\frac{3y}{15y\ 6m}$	note (*b*)	(968)
Adjusted net cost		4,032
Allowances given	note (*a*)	37,600
Excess		£33,568
Balancing charge		£33,568

Notes

(*a*) Allowances given in previous years are

	£
Initial allowance £40,000 × 50%	20,000
Writing-down allowances £40,000 × 4% × 11	17,600
	£37,600

Writing-down allowances would not have been given for the three years 1989/90 to 1991/92 as the building was not an industrial building at the end of the basis period for each of those years (see 10.14 above).

(*b*) In example (ii), the net cost is reduced by the proportion which the period of non-qualifying use bears to the total period from first use to date of balancing event (see 10.15 above).

10.17 **Making of allowances and charges.** Allowances to traders are given as a deduction in taxing the trade (but see below), and must be claimed in the annual return [*CAA 1990,* *s 140(3); FA 1994, s 211*] or, more commonly in practice, in computations accompanying accounts in support of a return. A highway undertaking (see 10.11 above) is treated as a trade. [*CAA 1990, s 21(5A), s 140(6), s 140(11) as originally enacted; FA 1991, s 60(6)(8); FA 1994, s 211; FA 1995, s 99(8)*]. See 17.10 CLAIMS as regards error or mistake relief claims following omission. For 1996/97 and earlier years as regards trades commenced before 6 April 1994, allowances are calculated by reference to events in the basis period for the year of assessment of claim (see 71.3 SCHEDULE D, CASES I AND II), except that

(*a*) where basis periods overlap, expenditure in the common period is treated as incurred only in the earlier period,

(*b*) expenditure in an interval between two basis periods is treated as incurred in the later period unless it is the period of permanent discontinuance of the trade, in which case it is treated as incurred in the earlier period.

[*CAA 1990, s 160 as originally enacted*].

If the deduction exceeds the assessment for the year, the balance may be carried forward to following years, until exhausted, while the trade continues. [*CAA 1990, s 140(4) as originally enacted*]. Alternatively, allowances may create or enhance a trade loss, see 46 LOSSES generally and 46.9(*e*) LOSSES for restrictions on use of allowances.

Balancing allowances to, and charges on, traders are made in the same way, the latter normally by separate assessment.

For 1994/95 and subsequent years as regards trades commenced after 5 April 1994 and for 1997/98 and subsequent years as regards trades commenced on or before that date, allowances and charges to traders are treated as trading expenses and receipts [*CAA 1990, s 140; FA 1994, s 211*] and are calculated by reference to events in periods of account (see 10.2(vi) above). See 10.2(vii) above as regards transitional relief for unused allowances carried forward under *CAA 1990, s 140(4) as originally enacted* (see above).

Where an allowance or charge falls to be made in a period during which a building is temporarily out of use but deemed still to be an industrial building (see 10.11 above) and, since it was last used as such, the trade in question has ceased (or, where the relevant interest was subject to a lease, or the building used under licence, the lease or licence has come to an end), such allowances and charges are dealt with in the same way as those falling to be made to or on lessors (see below). Where, after 28 April 1996, a balancing charge falls to be made on any person following such a period of temporary disuse, and the most recent use was as an industrial building, etc. for the purposes of a trade carried on by that person which has since ceased, the same deductions can be made from the charge as can be made under *ICTA 1988, s 105* from a post-cessation receipt (see 62.1 POST-CESSATION ETC. RECEIPTS AND EXPENDITURE) (without prejudice to the deduction of any amounts allowable against the balancing charge under other provisions); similar reliefs were previously available by concession (Revenue Pamphlet IR 1, B19). [*CAA 1990, s 15(2)(2A)(3), s 15ZA, s 15A; FA 1996, Sch 39 para 1(2)(4); FA 1998, s 38, Sch 5 paras 48–50, Sch 27 Pt III(4)*].

Lessors (and licensors) of industrial buildings etc. may claim allowances for a year of assessment under the normal claims procedure (see 17 CLAIMS). For 1995/96 and subsequent years for income tax purposes and on or after 1 April 1998 for corporation tax purposes, allowances and balancing charges are treated as expenses and receipts of a Schedule A business (see 68.4 SCHEDULE A) or, where the lessor is not, in fact, carrying on such a business, of a deemed Schedule A business. Previously, allowances were given by discharge or repayment of tax, primarily against income from (or balancing charges on) leased industrial buildings etc. Any balance of allowances so given may be carried forward and set against such income and charges without time limit, or, for income tax, may alternatively be claimed against other income of the same or the following year of assessment. Such a claim had to be made within two years of the end of the year of assessment for which relief is claimed. An election may, in practice, be withdrawn within the time limit for making it, provided that the corresponding liability has not been settled and agreed. Late elections may be accepted where an in-date indication of an intention to elect has in effect been accepted by the inspector. (Revenue Capital Allowances Manual, CA 156, 157). Balancing charges were raised under Schedule D, Case VI for income tax and treated as Schedule A income for corporation tax. [*CAA 1990, ss 9, 141; FA 1994, Sch 26 Pt V(24); FA 1995, Sch 6 para 29; FA 1997, Sch 18 Pt VI (11); FA 1998, s 38, Sch 5 para 47*]. (For corporation tax relief against profits generally, see Tolley's Corporation Tax under Capital Allowances.)

Tenancies. Where, after 26 March 1980, capital expenditure is incurred on a qualifying building (see 10.11 above) and its first use is by a tenant-occupier for the purposes of a trade, the initial allowance is given for the period in which the expenditure is incurred, even if the tenancy commences on a later date. Expenditure before 27 March 1980 qualified for the allowances when the tenancy began or is treated as incurred on that date if the tenancy had not then begun. [*CAA 1968, s 1(4); FA 1980, s 76; CAA 1990, ss 1(1), 161(2)*].

Double allowances. See 10.2(iv) above.

For allowances to companies generally, see Tolley's Corporation Tax.

10.18 **Hotels.** Expenditure incurred after 11 April 1978 and before 1 April 1986, or before 1 April 1987 under a contract entered into before 14 March 1984 by the person incurring the expenditure, on construction or extension of a qualifying hotel attracts an initial allowance of 20% and **writing-down allowances** of **4% p.a.**. The **20%** initial allowance under *CAA 1990, s 2A* for expenditure incurred in, broadly, the year ending 31 October 1993 (see 10.13 above) applies equally to qualifying hotels. Subsequent expenditure attracts the writing-down allowance only. For this purpose, expenditure incurred before a trade commenced was not treated under *CAA 1968, s 1(6)* as incurred after the date it was in fact incurred, and expenditure on a building bought unused was treated as having been incurred at the latest time any expenditure was in fact incurred on its construction. Certain expenditure on fire safety and thermal insulation may be treated as on machinery and plant, see 10.25 below.

A '*qualifying hotel*' must: (i) have accommodation in building(s) of a permanent nature; (ii) be open for at least four months during April–October; (iii) have at least ten letting bedrooms, i.e. private bedrooms for letting to the public generally and not normally in same occupation for more than a month; (iv) offer sleeping accommodation consisting wholly or mainly of letting bedrooms and (v) its services must normally include providing breakfast and evening meals, making beds and cleaning rooms. The provision of breakfast and dinner must be offered as a normal event in the carrying on of the hotel business and must not be exceptional or available only on request. (Revenue Pamphlet IR 131, SP 9/87, 22 September 1987). Buildings provided for the welfare of employees are regarded as part of a qualifying hotel but not accommodation for an individual (including a partner) or his household carrying on the hotel, unless under 25% of the total cost (10% for expenditure incurred or deemed incurred before 16 March 1983).

Qualification under the above conditions is by reference to the twelve months ending with the last day of the taxpayer's chargeable or basis period or, if the hotel's trade commences (or fully qualifies) during such period, the twelve months from the commencing or qualifying date. Qualification ceases when the trade ceases. An hotel in temporary disuse (see 10.11 above) ceases to qualify two years after the end of the basis period in which it fell out of use. An hotel outside the UK may qualify provided that the profits, etc. are assessable under Schedule D, Case I.

Balancing adjustments arise on the first sale etc. falling within *CAA 1990, s 4* (see 10.15 above) (whether or not the hotel is at the time a 'qualifying hotel') or, if the hotel ceases to qualify and there is no such sale etc. within two years of the end of the chargeable period (formerly basis period — see 10.2(vi) above) in which it ceases to qualify, at the end of that two years, when the hotel is treated as having been sold at open market value. [*FA 1978, s 38, Sch 6; FA 1985, s 66; CAA 1990, ss 7, 19; FA 1990, Sch 13 para 1; FA 1994, Sch 26 Pt V(24)*].

10.19 **Enterprise zones.** An 'enterprise zone' is an area designated as such by the Secretary of State (or Department of the Environment for Northern Ireland). [*CAA 1990, s 21(4)*]. Areas designated are as follows.

Zones whose ten-year life expires after 31 March 2000

Ashfield, see East Midlands (No 7)
Barnsley, see Dearne Valley
Bassetlaw, see East Midlands (No 4)
Dearne Valley (Nos 1 to 6) (from 3 November 1995, *SI 1995 No 2624*)
Derbyshire (NE), see East Midlands (Nos 1 to 3)
Doncaster, see Dearne Valley
Easington, see East Durham
East Durham (Nos 1 to 6) (from 29 November 1995, *SI 1995 No 2812*)
East Midlands (Nos 1 to 3) (from 3 November 1995, *SI 1995 No 2625*)
East Midlands (No 4) (from 16 November 1995, *SI 1995 No 2738*)
East Midlands (No 7) (from 21 November 1995, *SI 1995 No 2758*)
Holmewood, see East Midlands (Nos 1 to 3)
Lanarkshire (Hamilton) (from 1 February 1993, *SI 1993 No 23*)
Lanarkshire (Monklands) (from 1 February 1993, *SI 1993 No 25*)
Lanarkshire (Motherwell) (from 1 February 1993, *SI 1993 No 24*)
Rotherham, see Dearne Valley
Sunderland (Castletown and Doxford Park) (from 27 April 1990, *SI 1990 No 794*)
Sunderland (Hylton Riverside and Southwick) (from 27 April 1990, *SI 1990 No 795*)
Tyne Riverside (North Tyneside) (No 1) (from 19 February 1996, *SI 1996 No 106*)
Tyne Riverside (North Tyneside) (No 2) (from 26 August 1996, *SI 1996 No 1981*)
Tyne Riverside (North Tyneside and South Tyneside) (from 21 October 1996, *SI 1996 No 2435*)

Zones whose ten-year life expired before 1 April 2000

Allerdale, see Workington (Allerdale)
Arbroath, see Tayside (Arbroath)
Belfast (from 21 October 1981, *SR 1981 No 309*)
Clydebank (from 3 August 1981, *SI 1981 No 975*)
Corby (from 22 June 1981, *SI 1981 No 764*)
Delyn (from 21 July 1983, *SI 1983 No 896*)
Dudley (Round Oak) (from 3 October 1984, *SI 1984 No 1403*)
Dudley (not Round Oak) (from 10 July 1981, *SI 1981 No 852*)
Dundee, see Tayside (Dundee)
Flixborough, see Glanford (Flixborough)
Gateshead (from 25 August 1981, *SI 1981 No 1070*)
Glanford (Flixborough) (from 13 April 1984, *SI 1984 No 347*)
Glasgow (from 18 August 1981, *SI 1981 No 1069*)

Hartlepool (from 23 October 1981, *SI 1981 No 1378*)
Inverclyde (from 3 March 1989, *SI 1989 No 145*)
Invergordon (from 7 October 1983, *SI 1983 No 1359*)
Isle of Dogs (from 26 April 1982, *SI 1982 No 462*)
Kent (NW) (zones 1 to 5 only) (from 31 October 1983, *SI 1983 No 1452*)
Kent (NW) (zones 6 and 7 only) (from 10 October 1986, *SI 1986 No 1557*)
Lancashire (NE) (from 7 December 1983, *SI 1983 No 1639*)
Liverpool (Speke) (from 25 August 1981, *SI 1981 No 1072*)
London, see Isle of Dogs
Londonderry (from 13 September 1983, *SR 1983 No 226*)
Lower Swansea Valley (from 11 June 1981, *SI 1981 No 757*)
Lower Swansea Valley (No 2) (from 6 March 1985, *SI 1985 No 137*)
Middlesbrough (Britannia) (from 8 November 1983, *SI 1983 No 1473*)
Milford Haven Waterway (North Shore) (from 24 April 1984, *SI 1984 No 443*)
Milford Haven Waterway (South Shore) (from 24 April 1984, *SI 1984 No 444*)
Newcastle (from 25 August 1981, *SI 1981 No 1071*)
Rotherham (from 16 August 1983, *SI 1983 No 1007*)
Salford Docks (from 12 August 1981, *SI 1981 No 1024*)
Scunthorpe (Normanby Ridge and Queensway) (from 23 September 1983, *SI 1983 No 1304*)
Speke, see Liverpool (Speke)
Swansea, see Lower Swansea Valley and Lower Swansea Valley (No 2)
Tayside (Arbroath) (from 9 January 1984, *SI 1983 No 1816*)
Tayside (Dundee) (from 9 January 1984, *SI 1983 No 1817*)
Telford (from 13 January 1984, *SI 1983 No 1852*)
Trafford Park (from 12 August 1981, *SI 1981 No 1025*)
Wakefield (Dale Lane and Kingsley) (from 23 September 1983, *SI 1983 No 1305*)
Wakefield (Langthwaite Grange) (from 31 July 1981, *SI 1981 No 950*)
Wellingborough (from 26 July 1983, *SI 1983 No 907*)
Workington (Allerdale) (from 4 October 1983, *SI 1983 No 1331*)

Advantageous provisions apply to expenditure on the construction of an industrial building or structure, a qualifying hotel or a commercial building or structure, which is incurred (or contract entered into) within ten years of the inclusion of the site in an enterprise zone. Expenditure incurred more than 20 years after a site was first included in an enterprise zone does not attract enterprise zone allowances, regardless of when the contract for the expenditure was entered into. [*CAA 1990, ss 1(1)(2), 17A; FA 1990, Sch 13 para 1; F(No 2)A 1992, Sch 13 para 10*].

'*Qualifying hotel*' has the same meaning as in *CAA 1990, s 19*, see 10.18 above. (Note that any hotel not qualifying under this heading will qualify as a commercial building.)

'*Commercial building or structure*' means a building or structure, other than an industrial building or a qualifying hotel, which is used for the purposes of a trade, profession or vocation or as an office for any purpose, but does not include any building in use as, or as part of, a dwelling house. [*CAA 1990, s 21(5)*].

The allowances given are as follows.

An initial allowance of 100% is given but an individual or partnership or, for accounting periods ended after 30 September 1993, a company need not claim the full amount; for earlier accounting periods, a company may disclaim all or part of the initial allowance by notice in writing to the inspector within two years after the relevant accounting period. If any part of the initial allowance is not claimed then **writing-down allowances at 25% p.a.** of cost on the straight line basis will apply to the unclaimed balance. [*CAA 1990, ss 1, 6; FA 1990, Sch 17 para 2*].

For the above purposes, the following special rules apply.

(i) *Date expenditure incurred. CAA 1990, s 1(10)* (pre-trading expenditure treated as incurred on first day of trading, see 10.13 above) does not apply in determining whether expenditure attracts enterprise zone allowances (i.e. whether it is incurred at a time when the building etc. is in an enterprise zone).

As regards buildings bought unused, where the purchase price becomes payable after 15 December 1991, the normal rules under *CAA 1990, s 10* apply (see 10.12 above), except that:

(*a*) where some or all of the actual construction expenditure is incurred (or incurred under a contract entered into) within ten years of the inclusion of the site in an enterprise zone, a corresponding proportion of the purchaser's deemed expenditure is treated as giving rise to entitlement to enterprise zone allowances, notwithstanding that it may be deemed to have been incurred outside that ten-year period;

(*b*) where (*a*) does not apply, the purchaser's deemed expenditure is treated as not giving rise to entitlement to enterprise zone allowances, notwithstanding that it may be deemed to have been incurred during the ten-year period.

Where some of the actual construction expenditure falls within (*a*) above and some or all of the balance would qualify for a 20% initial allowance by virtue of the provisions in 10.12 above, the above provisions and those in 10.12 above interact. The purchaser can thus obtain a 100% enterprise zone initial allowance on part of his deemed expenditure and the 20% initial allowance on another part or, where appropriate, on the balance.

Where the purchase price of a building bought unused became payable before 16 December 1991, *CAA 1990, s 10(1)* does not apply, and the Revenue accept this as allowing the purchaser to treat his expenditure as having been incurred (or incurred under a contract entered into) on the date(s) the actual construction expenditure was incurred (or contract entered into). (Revenue Press Release 16 December 1991). [*CAA 1990, ss 10A, 10C(11); F(No 2)A 1992, Sch 13 paras 2–7, para 14; FA 1993, s 113(4)*].

(ii) *Buildings purchased within two years of first use.* Where some or all of the construction expenditure on a building first used after 15 December 1991 is incurred (or incurred under a contract entered into) within ten years of the inclusion of the site in an enterprise zone, and the 'relevant interest' (see 10.14 above) is sold during the two years (but see below) following the first use of the building (whether or not there have been any sales while the building was unused), then on that sale (or the first such sale) the normal balancing allowance or charge rules apply to the vendor (see 10.15 above), but the purchaser is deemed to have incurred expenditure on purchase of a building bought unused (see 10.12 and (i) above). A proportion of the deemed expenditure corresponding to the proportion of the actual construction expenditure which was incurred within ten years of the inclusion of the site in the enterprise zone is treated as giving rise to entitlement to enterprise zone allowances, notwithstanding that it may be deemed to have been incurred outside the ten-year period. The balance of the deemed expenditure does not attract enterprise zone allowances. If the purchase is directly from a person who constructed the building in the course of a trade of constructing such buildings for sale, the part of the purchaser's deemed expenditure which does *not* attract enterprise zone allowances is calculated by reference to the actual expenditure of the vendor if that is less than the price actually paid by the purchaser. [*CAA 1990, s 10B; F(No 2)A 1992, Sch 13 paras 8, 9, 15*]. The two year period is extended to 31 August 1994 where it would otherwise end within the period beginning 13 January 1994 and ending 31 August 1994, and the relevant interest is sold within that period and outside the two year period. [*FA 1994, s 121*].

(iii) *Machinery and plant* which is to be an integral part of a building will not be subject to the restriction of first-year allowances to lessors under *CAA 1990, s 22(4)* (see 10.35(*a*) below) (and see now below).

(iv) *Balancing charge on realisation of capital value.* Where capital expenditure on construction of a building etc. in an enterprise zone has been incurred (or is deemed to have been incurred) under a contract entered into after 12 January 1994 (or which becomes unconditional after 25 February 1994), and 'capital value' is received in respect of the building etc., a balancing charge (but not a balancing allowance) may arise. This applies generally where the payment is made (or an agreement to make it made) seven years or less after the date of the agreement relating to the expenditure (or the date on which that agreement became unconditional). Where, however, there are certain guaranteed exit arrangements, it applies throughout the normal balancing adjustment period (i.e. 25 years from first use, see 10.15 above).

'Capital value' is realised when a sum is paid which is attributable to an interest in land to which the relevant interest in the building etc. in question is or will be subject, e.g. where a lease is granted out of the relevant interest, unless *CAA 1990, s 11* (see 10.14 above) applies to the grant of that interest. There are detailed provisions as to the form and amount of the capital value, and as to its attribution to the grant of the interest. See Revenue Capital Allowances Manual, CA 1440 *et seq.*.

[*CAA 1990, s 4(1)(dd)(9A), s 4A; FA 1994, s 120*].

(v) *Partially completed buildings.* For the Revenue interpretation of the allowances available where a partially completed building is acquired in an enterprise zone, see Revenue Tax Bulletin June 1998 p 553.

(vi) It should be noted that where a building etc. in an enterprise zone is sold and the purchaser is *not* treated as having incurred expenditure on its construction, the residue of expenditure (if any) is allowed over the balance of the period of 25 years from first use of the building etc., and not at the 25% writing-down rate (see Revenue Capital Allowances Manual, CA 1427).

An 'additional VAT liability' (see 10.2(v) above) incurred in respect of qualifying expenditure, within ten years of the inclusion of the site in the enterprise zone, is itself qualifying expenditure for the chargeable period related to the incurring of the liability. [*CAA 1990, s 1(1A); FA 1991, Sch 14 para 1*]. Where a 100% initial allowance was not claimed on the expenditure to which the additional VAT liability relates, a 100% allowance may nevertheless generally be claimed for the additional VAT liability. If less than the full 100% allowance is claimed for the additional VAT liability, writing-down allowances for the whole of the expenditure on the building, etc. in question will be recomputed as under 10.14 above, resulting in a substantial reduction in the rate of annual allowance. See Revenue Capital Allowances Manual, CA 1216.

For balancing adjustments after non-qualifying use, see 10.15 above. For transfers between connected persons, etc., see 10.22(i) below.

For the special treatment for tax purposes of investors in enterprise zone property trusts, see *SI 1988 No 267* and *SI 1992 No 571* (and see Revenue Inspector's Manual, IM 4213 *et seq.*).

Machinery or plant. Expenditure on machinery or plant, or on thermal insulation treated as machinery or plant under *CAA 1990, s 67*, which is to be an integral part of an industrial or commercial building in an enterprise zone may be treated as part of the expenditure on construction of the building, and so attract the 100% initial allowance (see 10.2(iv) above). A claim for expenditure on machinery or plant, etc. to be so treated does not prevent a subsequent purchaser of the building from claiming machinery and plant allowances on that expenditure and industrial buildings allowances on the fabric of the building. (Revenue Capital Allowances Manual, CA 1060).

10.20 *Examples*

(i)

In 1998, J, a builder, incurs expenditure of £400,000 on the construction of a building in a designated enterprise zone. The whole of the expenditure was incurred (or contracted for) within ten years of the site's first being included in the zone. In January 1999, he sells the building unused to K for £600,000 (excluding land). In February 1999, K lets the building to a trader who immediately brings it into use as a supermarket. K claims a reduced initial allowance of £50,000. In March 2001, he sells the building to L for £750,000 (excluding land).

K's allowances are as follows.

		£	Residue of expenditure £
1998/99	Qualifying expenditure		600,000
	Initial allowance (maximum 100%)	50,000	
	Writing-down allowance 25% of £600,000	150,000	
	Total IBA due	200,000	(200,000)
1999/2000	Writing-down allowance	150,000	(150,000)
			250,000
2000/01	Writing-down allowance	—	—
	Sale proceeds		(750,000)
			£500,000
	Balancing charge (restricted to allowances given)		£350,000

Notes

(*a*) K's qualifying expenditure would normally be the lesser of cost of construction and the net price paid by him for the building. However, on purchase from a builder, whose profit on sale is taxable as a trading profit, his qualifying expenditure is equal to the net price paid for the relevant interest (excluding the land). See 10.12, 10.19(i) above.

(*b*) K's allowances and balancing charges are treated as expenses and receipts of a Schedule A business. See 10.17 above. K could have claimed a 100% initial allowance in 1998/99 if he had so wished.

(*c*) Providing the building continues to be used for a qualifying purpose, L can claim writing-down allowances over the remainder of the 25-year writing-down period. His qualifying expenditure is restricted to £600,000, i.e. the residue of expenditure (£250,000) plus the balancing charge on K. See 10.14 above.

(*d*) In this example, the first sale after the building was first used took place just over two years after the date of first use. If the sale had taken place within two years after first use, the balancing charge on K would have been computed in the same manner, but L could have claimed an initial allowance and 25% writing-down allowances as if he had bought the building unused. His qualifying expenditure would again have been restricted to £600,000, being the lesser of the price paid by him for the relevant interest in the building and that paid on the original purchase by K from the builder. See 10.19(ii) above.

(ii)

The facts are as in (i) above, except that, of the £400,000 construction expenditure actually incurred, only £360,000 is incurred (or contracted for) within ten years of the site's first being included in an enterprise zone, and the first sale occurred after the expiry of that ten-year period.

K's qualifying expenditure of £600,000 (arrived at as in (i) above) is divided into an enterprise zone element and a non-enterprise zone element.

The enterprise zone element is $£600{,}000 \times \frac{360{,}000}{400{,}000} = \underline{£540{,}000}$

The non–enterprise zone element is £600,000 – £540,000 = $\underline{£60{,}000}$

The non-enterprise zone element does not qualify for enterprise zone allowances. See 10.19(i) above. (It could have qualified for normal IBAs if the building had been an industrial building.)

K's allowances are as follows.

			Residue of expenditure
		£	£
1998/99	Qualifying expenditure (enterprise zone element)		540,000
	Initial allowance (maximum 100%)	50,000	
	Writing-down allowance (25% of £540,000)	135,000	
		185,000	(185,000)
1999/2000	Writing-down allowance	135,000	(135,000)
			220,000
2000/01	Writing-down allowance	—	—
	Sale proceeds $£750{,}000 \times \frac{540{,}000}{600{,}000}$		(675,000)
			£455,000
	Balancing charge (restricted to allowances given)		£320,000

L's qualifying expenditure is £540,000, i.e. the residue of £220,000 plus the balancing charge of £320,000 on K.

Note

(*a*) The apportionment of sale proceeds in 2000/01 is considered to be a 'just apportionment' as required by *CAA 1990, s 21(3)*.

10.21 **Small and very small workshops.** Expenditure incurred after 26 March 1980 and before 27 March 1985 on the construction of an industrial building (or permanently separated part of a larger building, intended and suitable for separate occupation, but common facilities are excepted) of, before 27 March 1983, 2,500 square feet or less, and, after 26 March 1983 and before 27 March 1985, 1,250 square feet or less of gross internal floor space (including ancillary works) qualified for an initial allowance of 100% with similar rights to reduce or disclaim this and receive writing-down allowances of 25% as described in 10.19 above. Similarly the provisions stated at (i), (iii) in 10.19 above applied also to small workshops. [*FA 1980, s 75, Sch 13 Pt I; FA 1982, s 73*]. (Revenue Pamphlet IR 131, SP 6/80, 9 July 1980). For balancing adjustments after non-qualifying use, see 10.15 above. For transfers between connected persons, etc., see 10.22(i) below.

See Revenue Pamphlet IR 131, SP 4/80, 26 March 1980 for the application of these provisions where individual units in a larger development did not exceed 2,500 square feet.

The limit of 1,250 square feet could be exceeded in certain cases where existing buildings were converted into separate units. [*FA 1983, s 31*].

10.22 **General matters.**

(i) *Connected persons and other anti-avoidance provisions.* Special provisions apply to sales of industrial buildings etc. where

(*a*) the sale results in no change of control, or

(*b*) the sole or main benefit apparently arising is the obtaining of an industrial buildings allowance.

For transfers after 10 March 1981 (unless contracted for on or before that date), (*a*) also covers sales between CONNECTED PERSONS (20), and transfers other than by way of sale, and (*b*) includes cases where the anticipated benefit is a reduction in a charge or the *increase* of an allowance. Normally, where these provisions apply, market value is substituted for purchase price (if different). However, for transactions within (*a*) but not (*b*), the parties may elect for the substitution of the residue of expenditure (see 10.14 above) if this is lower than market value, and for any subsequent balancing charge on the buyer to be calculated by reference to allowances given to both buyer and seller. Such an election is *not* available if the circumstances are such that an allowance or charge which otherwise would or might fall, in consequence of the sale, to be made to or on *any* of the parties to the sale cannot fall to be made. The election must be made within two years after the sale. The election also covers qualifying hotels and commercial buildings etc. in enterprise zones. For sales of industrial buildings etc. before 16 March 1993 (or under a pre-16 March 1993 contract or a contract entered into for the purpose of securing compliance with obligations under a pre-16 March 1993 contract) the circumstances in which an election was not available were that either party was non-UK resident and that an allowance or charge could not be made to or on *that* party in consequence of the sale. [*CAA 1990, ss 21(6)(7), 157, 158; FA 1993, s 117(2)(4)(5); FA 1994, s 119(1)*].

Balancing allowances (see 10.15 above) are restricted on sales after 13 June 1972 where the relevant interest (see 10.14 above) in an industrial building etc. is sold subject to a subordinate interest (e.g. in a sale and lease-back) and either

(1) the seller, the purchaser of the interest, and the grantee of the subordinate interest (or any two of them) are CONNECTED PERSONS (20), or

(2) the sole or main benefit appears to be the obtaining of an industrial buildings allowance.

In such cases the net sale proceeds are increased, in determining any balancing allowance, by

(A) where less than a commercial rent is payable under the subordinate interest, the difference between actual sale proceeds and open market value had a commercial rent been payable, and

(B) the amount of any premium receivable for the grant of the subordinate interest and not chargeable under *ICTA 1988, s 34* (see 68.27 SCHEDULE A),

but not by more than is required to eliminate any balancing allowance. The residue of expenditure (see 10.14 above) following the sale is, however, calculated as if the balancing allowance had been made without the application of these provisions. [*CAA 1990, s 5*].

(ii) *Double allowances.* See 10.2(iv) above.

(iii) *Partnerships* are entitled to industrial buildings allowances in respect of qualifying expenditure (see 10.12 above) on industrial buildings or structures (see 10.11 above).

On a change of partnership, if the trade is treated as continuing, unexhausted allowances are carried forward, and subsequent balancing adjustments (see 10.15 above) made as if the new partnership had carried on the trade before the change. Allowances continue to be calculated as though there had been no change, being apportioned between the old and the new partnerships for the year of assessment of the change. If however the trade is treated as ceasing, only continuing partners may carry forward their share of unexhausted allowances, as a loss to set against their future profit shares. [*CAA 1990, s 152(3)*]. See also (iv) below as regards allowances on successions to trades.

(iv) *Successions.* Where a trade changes hands (other than in certain partnership changes (see (iii) above)) unexhausted allowances may not be carried forward to the new owner. Unless the change is not treated as a permanent cessation (see 53.6 PARTNERSHIPS), any asset transferred, without being sold, to the new owner for continuing use in the trade is treated as sold at open market value on the date of change, although no initial allowance is available to the new owner. [*CAA 1990, s 152(1)(2)*].

10.23 'KNOW-HOW' [*ICTA 1988, s 530*]

Expenditure on acquiring 'know-how' for use in a trade (expenditure before commencement of the trade being treated as incurred on commencement) attracts **writing-down** and **balancing allowances** (as below), insofar as it is not otherwise deductible for income or corporation tax purposes. [*ICTA 1988, s 530(1)(7)*]. For expenditure incurred after 31 March 1986, a balancing charge may arise (see below). For receipts arising from sales of know-how, see generally 71.67 SCHEDULE D, CASES I AND II.

'*Know-how*' means any industrial information and techniques of assistance in (*a*) manufacturing or processing goods or materials, (*b*) working, or searching, etc. for, mineral deposits, or (*c*) agricultural, forestry or fishing operations. [*ICTA 1988, s 533(7)*]. For expenditure on offshore divers' training courses treated as on know-how, see Revenue Capital Allowances Manual, CA 6034.

Expenditure incurred before 1 April 1986

A *writing-down allowance* of one-sixth per annum of the expenditure incurred is available during the six years beginning with the chargeable period in whose basis period the expenditure was incurred. A *balancing allowance* is given of the expenditure unallowed on the trade ceasing during that six years. [*ICTA 1988, s 530(6)(8)*].

Expenditure incurred after 31 March 1986

For any chargeable period for which a trader has 'qualifying expenditure' exceeding any 'disposal value' to be brought into account, a *writing-down allowance* is made of 25% of the excess (proportionately reduced or increased where the period is less or more than one year, or if the trade has been carried on for part only of a chargeable period) except that a *balancing allowance* of the whole of the excess is made if the chargeable period is that of permanent discontinuance of the trade. If qualifying expenditure is less than the disposal value to be brought into account, a *balancing charge* is made on the trader in the amount of the difference.

'*Qualifying expenditure*' of a chargeable period is the aggregate of any capital expenditure on know-how incurred before the end of the chargeable period or its basis period which has not, in whole or part, previously formed part of qualifying expenditure, and any unallowed balance of expenditure brought forward from the previous chargeable period.

The *disposal value* to be brought into account for any chargeable period is the net proceeds of any sale in that period or its basis period (including any consideration for a restrictive covenant connected with the disposal) of know-how on which the trader incurred expenditure for use in a trade carried on by him.

[*ICTA 1988, s 530(2)–(5), s 531(8); FA 1994, s 214(6), Sch 26 Pt V(24)*].

Excess allowances may be used as under Dredging (10.7 above).

Simon's Direct Tax Service. See B2.615 *et seq.*.

10.24 MACHINERY AND PLANT

Allowances are available in respect of certain capital expenditure on machinery and plant etc. (see 10.25 below) to the person incurring the expenditure, where the machinery or plant etc. is provided

(i) for the purposes of a trade carried on by him, or

(ii) for letting (insofar as not included in (i) above) other than for use in a dwelling-house or flat.

[*CAA 1990, ss 22(1), 24(1), 61(1)*].

For this purpose, provision for the purposes of a profession or vocation, or the occupation of woodlands assessable under Schedule D, or necessarily for use in the performance of the duties of an office or employment, or for use in estate management or the management of investment companies etc., satisfies the requirement for provision for the purposes of a trade. [*CAA 1990, s 27*]. See 75.43 SCHEDULE E for special provisions relating to private cars and cycles used partly for the purposes of an office or employment. Plant provided by a vicar so as to give visual sermons was held not to comply with the requirement that it be provided necessarily for use in the performance of his duties (*White v Higginbottom Ch D 1982, 57 TC 283*). Expenditure on assets used for providing business entertainment (other than for certain overseas customers) is excluded [*ICTA 1988, s 577(1)(c)*], as is certain expenditure incurred by members of the House of Commons, the Scottish Parliament or the Wales or Northern Ireland Assemblies in or in connection with the provision or use of residential or overnight accommodation. [*CAA 1990, s 74; FA 1999, Sch 5 para 2(3)*].

For 2000/01 and subsequent years (for corporation tax, for accounting periods ending after 20 March 2000), trades (and activities treated as trading) only partly within the charge to income tax or corporation tax are treated as consisting of separate trades in respect of those activities which are within the charge and those which are not. The machinery and plant provisions apply only in respect of the former activities, the latter being treated as if they did not constitute a trade (or deemed trade). This exclusion does not, however, affect the application of *CAA 1990, ss 39–50* (leased assets, see 10.35 below), *CAA 1990, s 64A* (oil profit-sharing contracts) or *CAA 1990, ss 75–78* (sale and leaseback transactions and successions, see 10.38(iii)(xi) below), which are of application to non-UK trading activities. [*CAA 1990, s 83(2A); FA 2000, s 75(1)(6)*]. See 10.28(C) below as regards as regards writing-down allowances in cases involving partial use for non-trading purposes.

Allowances in respect of leased assets are available to the lessor and not the lessee, irrespective of the accounting treatment adopted. (Revenue Press Release 27 October 1986). See, however, 10.34 below as regards fixtures which become part of land or buildings. For a case in which leasing arrangements did not amount to a trade, see *Gold Fields Mining and Industrial Ltd v GKN (United Kingdom) plc Ch D, [1996] STC 173.*

Unless otherwise specified, the provisions described below apply to expenditure incurred after 26 October 1970. See 10.37 below as regards expenditure incurred on or before that date and certain other expenditure subject to the earlier provisions.

The main elements of the scheme of allowances are dealt with as follows.

10.25 Eligible expenditure

10.26 Restrictions on eligible expenditure

10.27 First-year allowances

10.28 Writing-down allowances

10.30 Balancing allowances and charges

10.32 Making of allowances and charges

10.34 Entitlement to allowances for fixtures

10.35 Leasing

10.37 Expenditure incurred before 27 October 1970

10.38 General matters

Simon's Direct Tax Service. See B2.3.

10.25 **Eligible expenditure.** The capital expenditure eligible for allowances includes that on alteration of existing buildings incidental to the installation of machinery or plant for trade purposes [*CAA 1990, s 66*] and on demolition of machinery etc. which it replaces. [*CAA 1990, s 62*]. Costs of moving plant from one site to another and re-erecting it, so far as not deductible in computing profits, qualify for allowances. (Revenue Capital Allowances Manual, CA 1544). Capital expenditure on animals and other living creatures kept for the purposes of farming or any other trade, or on shares in such animals, etc., is excluded. [*CAA 1990, s 82(2); FA 2000, s 76*].

'Capital expenditure' excludes any sums allowed as deductions or brought in as receipts in computing the claimant's profits and any sums payable under deduction of tax. [*CAA 1990, s 159(1)(1A); FA 1997, Sch 15 paras 7, 9; FA 1998, s 38, Sch 5 para 60, Sch 27 Pt III(4)*].

Whether the machinery or plant is new or secondhand is generally irrelevant (but see 10.38(iii) below as regards certain sales between connected persons etc.).

Meaning of machinery or plant: leading cases. Machinery and *plant* are not statutorily defined. *Machinery* is accordingly given its ordinary meaning, but *plant* has been considered in many cases. It includes apparatus kept for permanent employment in the trade, but a line is drawn between that which performs a function in the business operations (which may be plant) and that which provides the place or setting in which these operations are performed (which is not). See *Cole Bros Ltd v Phillips HL 1982, 55 TC 188* (electric wiring and fittings in department store held not to be plant) and *St. John's School v Ward CA 1974, 49 TC 524* (prefabricated school buildings held not to be plant) and contrast *CIR v Barclay, Curle & Co Ltd HL 1969, 45 TC 221* (dry docks, including cost of excavation, held to be plant) and *CIR v Scottish & Newcastle Breweries Ltd HL 1982, 55 TC 252* (lighting and decor of licensed premises held to be plant). If an item used for carrying on a business does not form part of the premises and is not stock-in-trade, then it is plant (*Wimpy International Ltd v Warland CA 1988, 61 TC 51*).

Permanent employment demands some degree of durability, see *Hinton v Maden & Ireland Ltd HL 1959, 38 TC 391* (shoe manufacturer's knives and lasts, average life three years, held to be plant). In practice, a life of two years or more is sufficient, and this applies equally as regards animals functioning as apparatus with which a trade is carried on (see Revenue Capital Allowances Manual, CA 1540, 1571).

Held to rank as plant. Movable office partitions (*Jarrold v John Good & Sons Ltd CA 1962, 40 TC 681*); mezzanine platforms installed in a warehouse (but not ancillary lighting) (*Hunt v Henry Quick Ltd Ch D 1992, 65 TC 108*); swimming pools for use on caravan site (*Cooke v Beach Station Caravans Ltd Ch D 1974, 49 TC 514*); grain silos (*Schofield v R & H Hall Ltd CA(NI) 1974, 49 TC 538*); barrister's books (*Munby v Furlong CA 1977, 50 TC 491*); Building Society window screens (*Leeds Permanent Building Society v Proctor Ch D 1982, 56 TC 293*); light fittings (*Wimpy International Ltd v Warland CA 1988, 61 TC 51*).

In relation to certain 'qualifying films' (broadly, British or European films, see 71.58 SCHEDULE D, CASES I AND II), a *film production* business producing and retaining a master print of a film with an anticipated life of two years or more may elect to treat the cost as capital expenditure on plant. See *Ensign Tankers (Leasing) Ltd v Stokes HL 1992, 64 TC 617* for relief to investor in film production partnership. Otherwise, see now 71.58 SCHEDULE D, CASES I AND II for relief of production costs treated as revenue expenditure and for special relief for preliminary expenditure.

Held not to be plant. Stallions (*Earl of Derby v Aylmer KB 1915, 6 TC 665*); wallpaper pattern books (*Rose & Co Ltd v Campbell Ch D 1967, 44 TC 500*); canopy over petrol-filling station (*Dixon v Fitch's Garage Ltd Ch D 1975, 50 TC 509*); ship used as floating restaurant (*Benson v Yard Arm Club Ltd CA 1979, 53 TC 67*); false ceilings (*Hampton v Fortes Autogrill Ltd Ch D 1979, 53 TC 691*); a football stand (*Brown v Burnley Football Co Ltd Ch D 1980, 53 TC 357*); an inflatable tennis court cover (*Thomas v Reynolds Ch D 1987, 59 TC 502*); shop fronts, wall and floor coverings, suspended floors, ceilings and stairs, etc. (*Wimpy International Ltd v Warland, Associated Restaurants Ltd v Warland CA 1988, 61 TC 51*); permanent quarantine kennels (allowances having been granted for movable kennels) (*Carr v Sayer Ch D 1992, 65 TC 15*); lighting ancillary to mezzanine platform installation qualifying as plant (*Hunt v Henry Quick Ltd Ch D 1992, 65 TC 108*); a planteria (a form of glasshouse, see also below) (*Gray v Seymours Garden Centre (Horticulture) CA 1995, 67 TC 401*); access site and wash hall containing car wash equipment (*Attwood v Anduff Car Wash Ltd CA 1997, 69 TC 575*); housing for underground electricity sub-station (*Bradley v London Electricity plc Ch D 1996, 70 TC 155*); golf putting greens (*Family Golf Centres Ltd v Thorne (Sp C 150), [1998] SSCD 106*).

In *McVeigh v Arthur Sanderson & Sons Ltd Ch D 1968, 45 TC 273,* held that cost of blocks etc. of a wallpaper manufacturer (admitted to be plant) should include something for the designs but the designs, following *Daphne v Shaw KB 1926, 11 TC 256,* were not plant. (*Daphne v Shaw* has since been overruled by *Munby v Furlong* above.)

Interest etc. on money borrowed to finance purchases of plant and charged to capital, held not eligible for capital allowances (*Ben-Odeco Ltd v Powlson HL 1978, 52 TC 459* and cf *Van Arkadie v Sterling Coated Materials Ltd Ch D 1982, 56 TC 479*). It is understood that the Revenue consider this exclusion to apply also to architects' fees and preliminary expenses on plant included in building works. (Tolley's Practical Tax 1983 p 28.)

Cable television. The cost of provision and installation of ducting in connection with construction of cable television networks is regarded as expenditure on machinery or plant. (Revenue Press Release 15 March 1984).

Glasshouses are likely to be accepted as plant only where, during construction, sophisticated environmental control systems are permanently installed, incorporating e.g. a computer system controlling heating, temperature and humidity control, automatic ventilation systems and automatic thermal or shade screens. (Revenue Tax Bulletin November 1992 p 46, June 1998 p 552). See for example *Gray v Seymours Garden Centre (Horticulture) CA, [1995] STC 706*, where a 'planteria' was held to be premises. See also 10.26 below and, as regards whether glasshouses are 'long-life assets', 10.28(G) below.

See generally Revenue Capital Allowances Manual, CA 1510–1999.

Certain expenditure on buildings is treated for capital allowance purposes as being on machinery and plant (unless a deduction could be obtained otherwise).

(i) *Fire safety expenditure* incurred in a trade in taking steps specified in a notice under *Fire Precautions Act 1971, s 5(4)* (or which might have been so specified but were in fact specified in a letter or other document from the fire authority on application for a fire certificate under that *Act*) and similarly for expenditure incurred in order to avoid restriction of use of premises by an order under *section 10* of that *Act*. [*CAA 1990, s 69*]. Applies by Order to hotels and boarding houses (*SI 1972 No 238*) and to premises of factories, offices, shops and railways with minimum of 10 employees (*SI 1976 No 2009*). *Lessors of such premises* may claim allowances on contributions towards tenants' qualifying expenditure (under *CAA 1990, s 154*) or own similar direct expenditure. All these provisions also apply by concession to NI. (Revenue Pamphlet IR 1, B16.)

(ii) *Thermal insulation of existing industrial building.* If the expenditure is by a person letting the building (otherwise than in course of trade), then,

(*a*) for 1995/96 and 1996/97 for income tax purposes, the allowances are given as expenses of a Schedule A business (see 68.4 SCHEDULE A), the letting being deemed to be in connection with such a business whether or not such a business is, in fact, carried on. (For 1997/98 and subsequent years, the Schedule A business is in any event treated as a trade for these purposes, see 68.7(*a*) SCHEDULE A.); and

(*b*) for 1994/95 and earlier years for income tax purposes, the allowances are primarily against income (I) from any industrial building taxed under Schedule A, or (II) arising from a balancing charge on an industrial building.

For corporation tax purposes, the treatment was as in (*b*) above before 1 April 1998, from which date all machinery and plant used in a Schedule A business is treated, by virtue of *CAA 1990, s 28A*, as used in a trade.

[*ICTA 1988, s 32(1B)(1C); CAA 1990, s 67; FA 1994, Sch 26 Pt V(24); FA 1995, Sch 6 paras 8(3), 32; FA 1997, Sch 15 paras 1, 5, Sch 18 Pt VI(11); FA 1998, s 38, Sch 5 para 56, Sch 27 Pt III(4)*].

(iii) *Sports ground expenditure* incurred by a trade to comply with a safety certificate issued or to be issued under the *Safety of Sports Grounds Act 1975* or certified by local authority as falling within requirements if such certificates had been applied for. Also, expenditure incurred after 31 December 1988 by a trade in respect of a 'regulated stand' (as defined by the *Fire Safety and Safety of Places of Sport Act 1987*) to comply with a safety certificate (as defined by that *Act*) issued for the stand or to take steps specified by the local authority as being necessary under the terms, or proposed terms, of such a safety certificate issued, or to be issued, by it. [*CAA 1990, s 70*]. See also 10.2(ii) above as regards certain contributions to expenditure.

(iv) *Quarantine premises.* Expenditure incurred before 16 March 1988 (or before 1 April 1989 under a contract entered into before 16 March 1988) by a trader to alter or replace authorised quarantine premises (as defined under the *Diseases of Animals Act 1950*) to comply with legal requirements. [*FA 1980, s 71; FA 1985, Sch 14 para 15; FA 1988, s 94*].

On any disposal the disposal value (see 10.30 below) of (i)–(iv) above is taken as nil.

(v) *Hotels and restaurants.* The Revenue regard as eligible for capital allowances expenditure on *apparatus* to provide electric light or power, hot water, central heating, ventilation or air conditioning, alarm and sprinkler systems. Also on cost of hot water pipes, baths, wash basins etc. Also expenditure on alterations to *existing* buildings which is incidental to the installation of plant and machinery. (CCAB Statement, 9 August 1977.) See now *Cole Bros Ltd v Phillips HL 1982, 55 TC 188* and *CIR v Scottish & Newcastle Breweries Ltd HL 1982, 55 TC 252.*

See below for provisions restricting allowances for certain expenditure on buildings and structures.

Expenditure on security assets. Expenditure incurred after 5 April 1989, by an individual, or partnership of individuals, carrying on a trade, profession or vocation, in connection with the provision for or use by the individual, or any of them, of a security asset (being an asset which improves personal security), is treated as if it were capital expenditure on machinery or plant qualifying for writing-down allowances (see 10.28 below). On any disposal the disposal value (see 10.30 below) is taken as nil. These provisions do not apply where the expenditure is otherwise eligible, either by means of writing-down allowances or as a Schedule D, Case I or II deduction, for tax relief. They apply only where certain conditions, very similar to those described in 71.81 SCHEDULE D, CASES I AND II, are satisfied, both as regards the provision or use of the asset and the type of asset that may qualify. An appropriate proportion of the expenditure may qualify in cases where the asset is intended to be used only partly to improve personal physical security. [*CAA 1990, ss 71, 72*]. See also 75.35 SCHEDULE E.

Computer software. Where capital expenditure is incurred after 9 March 1992 on the acquisition of computer software for trade purposes, the software, if it would not otherwise be machinery or plant, is treated as such for capital allowance purposes. Similarly where capital expenditure is incurred after that date in acquiring for trade purposes a right to use or otherwise deal with computer software, both the right and the software are treated as machinery or plant provided for trade purposes and (so long as entitlement to the right continues) as belonging to the person incurring the expenditure.

Where, after 9 March 1992, a right is granted to another person to use or deal with the whole or part of software or rights which are treated as machinery or plant, and the consideration for the grant consists of (or would if it were in money consist of) a capital sum, a disposal value (see 10.28 below) has to be brought into account (unless the software or rights have previously begun to be used wholly or partly for non-trade purposes, or the trade for which they were used has been permanently discontinued). The amount of the disposal value to be brought into account is the net consideration in money received for the grant, plus any insurance moneys or other capital compensation received in respect of the software by reason of any event affecting that consideration, except that open market value is substituted where

(*a*) the consideration for the grant was not, or not wholly, in money, or

(*b*) no consideration, or money consideration less than open market value, was given for the grant.

(*b*) does not, however, apply where there is a Schedule E charge in respect of the grant of the right, or where the person to whom the right is granted can obtain machinery or plant or scientific research allowances for his expenditure.

Where a disposal value falls to be calculated in relation to software or rights over which a right has previously been granted as above, that disposal value is increased by the disposal value taken into account in relation to that grant in determining whether it is to be limited by reference to the capital expenditure incurred (see 10.28 below). [*CAA 1990, s 24(6A), s 26(1)(ea)(eb)(ec)(2AA), s 67A; F(No 2)A 1992, s 68; FA 1994, Sch 26 Pt V(24)*].

See also 71.72 SCHEDULE D, CASES I AND II.

Enterprise zones. Expenditure on machinery or plant which is to be an integral part of an industrial or commercial building in an enterprise zone may qualify for 100% industrial buildings allowance. See 10.19 above.

Notification of expenditure. For 1997/98 and earlier years (or for company accounting periods ending before 1 April 1998), a claim for first-year allowances or writing-down allowances in respect of expenditure on machinery or plant cannot be made unless notice of the expenditure is given to the Revenue, in such form as may be required by the Board (see below). The time limit within which notice must be given is (i) for income tax for 1996/97 onwards (subject to (ii) below), twelve months after 31 January following the tax year in which ends the chargeable period concerned, (ii) for income tax for 1996/97 only as regards trades etc. commenced before 6 April 1994, the period up to and including 31 January 1999, and (iii) for income tax for earlier years and for corporation tax (where, in both cases, the chargeable period ended on or after 30 November 1993), within two years after the end of the chargeable period concerned. For chargeable periods ending before 30 November 1993, the notice condition is met if (i) the expenditure was included in a tax computation given to the inspector before that date, or (ii) notice of the expenditure is given to the inspector, in such form as may be required by the Board (see below), not later than *three* years after the end of the relevant chargeable period (or, if that period ends after 30 November 1990, before 3 May 1994 if later).

The period within which the notice or computation is required may be extended in any particular case at the Board's discretion, but this will not be done routinely. The criteria for acceptance of a late notification are as follows.

(1) There must be good reason, arising out of circumstances beyond the taxpayer's and agent's control, why notification could not be given timeously.

(2) In the case of a large construction project extending over several years and involving expenditure on a variety of assets, including machinery and plant, it may be impossible to complete final allocation of the expenditure between different classes of asset timeously. In such cases, refinement of the allocation will be accepted after the time limit has passed provided that reasonable estimates have been made within the time limit and there is no undue delay in finalising the details.

(3) The application for extension, and notification of the expenditure involved, must be made within a reasonable period (normally no more than three months) after the expiry of the circumstances giving rise to late notification.

(4) The following will *not* constitute acceptable reasons for late notification.

(*a*) Oversight or negligence on the part of the taxpayer or agent.

(*b*) Delay for any reason except where (1) above applies.

(*c*) The taxpayer's absence or illness, unless it arose at a critical time preventing timeous notification, there was good reason for notification not being given before the absence or illness, (in the case of absence) there was a good reason why the taxpayer was unavailable, and there was no one else who could have given timeous notification on the taxpayer's behalf.

(Revenue Pamphlet IR 131, SP 6/94, 4 August 1994).

Where the time limit has not been met for a particular chargeable period, the expenditure concerned may still form part of the qualifying expenditure for a subsequent period where the time limit for that period has not expired and the machinery or plant still belongs to the claimant at some time in that period or (where relevant) its basis period. A failure to meet the deadline cannot be rectified by an error or mistake claim (see 17.10 CLAIMS).

Form of notification. No form of notification is specified. Generally, it will be sufficient if the expenditure is included in a tax computation. It will, however, be advisable to give enough information to identify the asset concerned, as well as the amount of the expenditure, without listing each and every item where large numbers of similar assets are purchased. Where revenue expenditure in a profit computation is subsequently recategorised as machinery or plant expenditure, the original computation will be regarded as notice of the expenditure for these purposes. Inclusion of the expenditure in a document prepared primarily for non-tax purposes (e.g. annual accounts or valuation reports) will not be sufficient. Where, exceptionally, tax computations are not available in time to meet the deadline, the inspector may be notified separately in writing before it expires, such notification to include as a minimum the aggregate amount of the expenditure on which a claim may be made. (Revenue Pamphlet IR 131, SP 6/94, 4 August 1994; Revenue Press Release 17 December 1993). Under self-assessment, there is no requirement to send in a capital allowances computation and no separate provision in the return to notify expenditure. The Revenue therefore accept that a capital allowance claim incorporated in a self-assessment return (or amended return) gives satisfactory notification of the expenditure included in the underlying computation, provided that the return is made within the notification time limit (as above). (Revenue Tax Bulletin June 1998 p 551).

These notification provisions are **abolished** for 1998/99 onwards and for company accounting periods ending after 31 March 1998.

[*FA 1994, s 118, Sch 26 Pt V(24); FA 1996, s 135, Sch 21 para 48; FA 2000, s 73*].

10.26 **Restrictions on eligible expenditure.** For expenditure incurred after 29 November 1993 (subject to transitional provisions, see below), *CAA 1990, Sch AA1* is introduced by *FA 1994, s 117* to exclude certain expenditure from the definition of machinery and plant for capital allowance purposes. Assets which have been held to be plant under specific court decisions will continue to qualify for machinery and plant allowances, and assets not covered by the *FA 1994* provisions remain subject to prevailing case law on plant. (Revenue Press Release 17 December 1993).

Transitional provisions. Expenditure is not affected by the *FA 1994* provisions where it is incurred before 6 April 1996 in pursuance of a contract entered into either before 30 November 1993 or for the purposes of securing compliance with obligations under a contract entered into before that date. [*FA 1994, s 117(2)*].

Expenditure on buildings which does not qualify for allowances. Expenditure on the construction or acquisition of a building will not qualify for machinery and plant allowances where it is incurred after 29 November 1993 (subject to the above transitional provisions). For these purposes the expression 'building' includes:

(*a*) any assets forming an integral part of the building;

(*b*) any assets which do not form an integral part of the building because they are movable or for some other reason, but are nevertheless of a kind which are normally incorporated into buildings; and

(*c*) any of the following:

(i) walls, floors, ceilings, doors, gates, shutters, windows and stairs;

(ii) mains services, and systems, of water, electricity and gas;

(iii) waste disposal systems;

(iv) sewerage and drainage systems;

(v) shafts or other structures in which lifts, hoists, escalators and moving walkways are installed; and

(vi) fire safety systems.

'Electrical systems' include lighting systems.

[*CAA 1990, Sch AA1 para 1(1)(2)(4), para 5(1); FA 1994, s 117(1)*].

Expenditure on buildings not excluded from qualifying for allowances. Expenditure incurred on the construction or acquisition of any assets listed in (1) to (20) below, of which (1) to (16) are included in the expression 'building', is not excluded from qualifying for machinery and plant allowances.

(1) Electrical, cold water, gas and sewerage systems provided mainly to meet the particular requirements of the trade, or provided mainly to serve particular machinery or plant used for the purposes of the trade.

(2) Space or water heating systems; powered systems of ventilation, air cooling or air purification; and any ceiling or floor comprised in such systems.

(3) Manufacturing or processing equipment; storage equipment, including cold rooms; display equipment; and counters, checkouts and similar equipment.

(4) Cookers, washing machines, dishwashers, refrigerators and similar equipment; washbasins, sinks, baths, showers, sanitary ware and similar equipment; and furniture and furnishings.

(5) Lifts, hoists, escalators and moving walkways.

(6) Sound insulation provided mainly to meet the particular requirements of the trade.

(7) Computer, telecommunication and surveillance systems (including their wiring or other links).

(8) Refrigeration or cooling equipment.

(9) Sprinkler equipment and other equipment for extinguishing or containing fire; fire alarm systems.

(10) Burglar alarm systems.

(11) Strong rooms in bank or building society premises; safes.

(12) Partition walls, where moveable and intended to be moved in the course of the trade.

(13) Decorative assets provided for the enjoyment of the public in the hotel, restaurant or similar trades.

(14) Advertising hoardings; and signs, displays and similar assets.

(15) Swimming pools (including diving boards, slides and structures on which such boards or slides are mounted).

(16) Any machinery (including devices for providing motive power) not within any other item in (1) to (15) above.

(17) Any cold store.

(18) Any building provided for testing aircraft engines run within the building.

(19) Any caravan provided mainly for holiday lettings. (By concession, the wide definition of 'caravan' in *Caravan Sites and Control of Development Act 1960, s 29(1)* is used for this purpose in relation to caravans on holiday caravan sites, see Revenue Pamphlet IR 1, B50.)

(20) Any moveable building intended to be moved in the course of the trade.

An asset does not fall within (1) to (16) above if its principal purpose is to insulate or enclose the interior of the building or to provide an interior wall, a floor or a ceiling which (in each case) is intended to remain permanently in place.

'Electrical systems' include lighting systems.

[*CAA 1990, Sch AA1 para 1(3)(4), para 5(1); FA 1994, s 117(2)*].

Expenditure on structures not qualifying for allowances. 'Structure' means a fixed structure of any kind, other than a building. [*CAA 1990, Sch AA1 para 5(1)(a); FA 1994, s 117(1)*]. A structure is 'any substantial man-made asset' (see Revenue Press Release 17 December 1993).

Expenditure on the construction or acquisition of a structure or other assets listed in (A) to (G) below, or on any works involving the alteration of land, will not qualify for machinery and plant allowances where it is incurred after 29 November 1993 (subject to the above transitional provisions).

(A) Any tunnel, bridge, viaduct, aqueduct, embankment or cutting.

(B) Any way or hard standing, such as a pavement, road, railway or tramway, a park for vehicles or containers, or an airstrip or runway.

(C) Any inland navigation, including a canal or basin or a navigable river.

(D) Any dam, reservoir or barrage (including any sluices, gates, generators and other equipment associated with it).

(E) Any dock (and see below).

(F) Any dike, sea wall, weir or drainage ditch.

(G) Any structure not in (A) to (F) above, with the exception of an industrial structure (other than a building) that is or is to be an industrial building or structure within the meaning of *CAA 1990, s 18* (see 10.11 above), which is slightly amended for this purpose.

As regards (E) above, 'dock' includes any harbour, wharf, pier, marina or jetty, and any other structure in or at which vessels may be kept or merchandise or passengers may be shipped or unshipped.

[*CAA 1990, Sch AA1 para 2(1)(2)(4), para 5(1); FA 1994, s 117(1)*].

Expenditure on structures not excluded from qualifying for allowances. Expenditure incurred on assets listed in (I) to (XII) below or on the construction or acquisition of any asset of a description within any of the items in (1) to (16) above is not excluded from qualifying for machinery and plant allowances.

(I) Dry docks.

(II) Any jetty or similar structure provided mainly to carry machinery or plant.

(III) Pipelines, or underground ducts or tunnels with a primary purpose of carrying electricity cables.

(IV) Towers provided to support floodlights.

(V) Any reservoir incorporated into a water treatment works or any service reservoir of treated water for supply within any housing estate or other particular locality.

(VI) Silos provided for temporary storage or on the construction or acquisition of storage tanks.

(VII) Slurry pits or silage clamps.

(VIII) Fish tanks or fish ponds.

(IX) Rails, sleepers and ballast for a railway or tramway.

(X) Structures and other assets for providing the setting for any ride at an amusement park or exhibition.

(XI) Fixed zoo cages.

(XII) Expenditure on the alteration of land for the purpose only of installing machinery or plant.

[*CAA 1990, Sch AA1 para 2(3)(4); FA 1994, s 117(1)*].

Interests in land. Expenditure on the construction or acquisition of machinery or plant does not include expenditure on the acquisition of any interest in land incurred after 29 November 1993 (subject to the above transitional provisions), but this restriction does not apply to any asset which is so installed or otherwise fixed in or to any description of land as to become, in law, part of that land. The definition of 'land' in the *Interpretation Act 1978, Sch 1* is accordingly amended for these purposes to omit the words 'buildings and other structures', but otherwise 'interest in land' for these purposes has the same meaning as that for fixtures under leases in *CAA 1990, s 51* (see 10.34 below). [*CAA 1990, Sch AA1 paras 3, 5; FA 1994, s 117(1)*].

General exemptions. Expenditure falling within *CAA 1990, ss 67, 67A, 68, 69, 70, 71* (relating to thermal insulation, computer software, films, tapes and discs, fire safety, safety of sports grounds and security assets, see 10.25 above) is not affected by the above provisions. [*CAA 1990, Sch AA1 para 4; FA 1994, s 117(1)*].

Glasshouses. Nothing in the above provisions affects the question of whether expenditure on the construction or acquisition of any glasshouse for growing plants is expenditure on the provision of machinery or plant, where the glasshouse is designed so that the required environment (that is air, heat, light, irrigation and temperature) is controlled automatically by devices incorporated into its structure. [*CAA 1990, Sch AA1 para 5(2); FA 1994, s 117(1)*]. See, however, 10.25 above for the Revenue approach to allowances for such expenditure, and 10.28(G) below as regards whether glasshouses are 'long-life assets'.

10.27 **First-year allowances** were generally available (and see further below as regards their reinstatement in certain cases) for the basis period (see 10.32 below) in which expenditure on machinery and plant (see 10.25 above) was incurred, provided that the machinery etc. belonged to the claimant at some time during that period (but see 10.38(vii) below as regards certain expenditure by a lessee), and that that period was not also the period of permanent discontinuance of the trade. [*CAA 1990 s 22(1); FA 1971, s 41(1)*]. 'Belongs' has its ordinary meaning and normally entails a right of disposition over the thing possessed. See also *Bolton v International Drilling Co Ltd Ch D 1982, 56 TC 449*, *Ensign Tankers (Leasing) Ltd v Stokes HL 1992, 64 TC 617* and *Melluish v BMI (No 3) Ltd HL 1995, 68 TC 1*. However, following the decision in *Stokes v Costain Property Investments Ltd CA 1984, 57 TC 688*, specific provisions were introduced to determine entitlement to allowances for machinery or plant which are fixtures (see 10.34 below). For a case in which allowances in respect of leased machinery were refused because the leasing arrangements did not amount to a trade, see *Gold Fields Mining and Industrial Ltd v GKN (United Kingdom) plc Ch D, [1996] STC 173*. For ownership of certain assets transferred under oil production sharing contracts to the government or representative of the production territory, see *CAA 1990, s 64A* (introduced by *FA 2000, s 81*).

Expenditure incurred for the purposes of, and prior to the commencement of, a trade is treated as incurred on the first day of trading, except that this does not apply to impose the reduced rates of first-year allowance applicable after 13 March 1984, or for the purposes of the provisions described at 10.34 below as regards entitlement to allowances. [*CAA 1990, s 83(2); FA 1971, s 50(4); FA 1984, Sch 12 para 2(4); FA 1985, s 59(7)*]. Instalment payments under contract are 'incurred' as they fall due. See 10.2(iii) generally as regards the date on which expenditure is treated as having been incurred.

The **rates** of allowance are

After 26 October 1970	— 60%	*After* 13 March 1984	— 75%
After 19 July 1971	— 80%	*After* 31 March 1985	— 50%
After 21 March 1972	— 100%		

Abolition. Universal first-year allowances were generally **abolished** for expenditure **after 31 March 1986**, although they continued at the 100% rate for expenditure incurred before 1 April 1987 under a contract entered into before 14 March 1984 either by the person incurring the expenditure or by another person (the 'lessee') who had arranged to lease the machinery or plant from the person incurring the expenditure (the 'lessor'), where the lessor had either taken over the lessee's obligations under the contract or entered into a new contract discharging those obligations (payments under such a new contract being treated as under the original contract for these purposes). [*FA 1971, s 42; FA 1972, s 67; FA 1984, s 58, Sch 12 para 2*]. They continue to be available at the 100% rate, however, for any 'additional VAT liability' (see 10.2(v) above) incurred in respect of such expenditure at a time when the machinery or plant is provided for the purposes of the trade (the allowance being given for the chargeable period related to the incurring of the liability). [*CAA 1990, ss 22, 23; FA 1991, Sch 14 para 6; FA 1994, Sch 26 Pt V(24)*]. See also 10.35 below as regards rented television sets.

Reinstatement of first-year allowances for small and medium-sized businesses. First-year allowances are reinstated for expenditure incurred **after 1 July 1997** (and for any 'additional VAT liability', see 10.2(v) above, incurred, at whatever time, in respect of such expenditure) by a 'small or medium-sized enterprise' (see below), subject to the general conditions of *CAA 1990, s 22(1)* (see above and below) being satisfied. The rate is **50%** for expenditure incurred **before 2 July 1998** (**12%** in the case of long-life assets, see 10.28(G) below) and **40%** for expenditure incurred **after 1 July 1998** (but long-life assets are excluded).

For such expenditure on the provision of machinery or plant primarily for use in **Northern Ireland**, the rate is increased to **100%** for expenditure incurred **after 11 May 1998 and before 12 May 2002** (and for any additional VAT liability in respect thereof). Excluded, however, is expenditure on long-life assets, on aircraft or hovercraft or on goods vehicles for use in a trade consisting primarily of the conveyance of goods, and unauthorised expenditure on machinery or plant for use primarily in agriculture, fishing or fish farming or in any transportation, storage, preparation, processing or packaging activities carried out in bringing any agricultural produce, fish or fish product to market. Expenditure is unauthorised for this purpose unless it is authorised by the Department of Agriculture for Northern Ireland, and provision is made for the necessary exchange of information between the Revenue and that Department. Expenditure is also excluded where, when it is incurred, the person incurring it intends the machinery or plant to be used partly outside NI, and there are arrangements (of which the transaction under which the expenditure is incurred forms part) from which the main benefit, or one of the main benefits, which could reasonably be expected is the obtaining of a first-year allowance (or greater first-year allowance) in respect of so much of the expenditure as is attributable (on a just and reasonable basis) to the intended use outside NI. There are also provisions for the withdrawal of first-year allowances if, within two years of the expenditure being incurred (five years where the expenditure concerned exceeds £3.5 million), and at a time when the machinery or plant belongs to the person who incurred it (or a connected person), the primary use to which it is put is a use outside NI, or it is held for use otherwise than primarily in NI. Any person whose return is rendered incorrect by such a change of use must (subject to penalty) amend the return within three months of becoming aware that it has become incorrect. Claims for the 100% allowance could not be made before 27 July 1999, the day appointed for the purpose by the Treasury, but may then relate to times before that day, and all such claims made within twelve months of the appointed day are valid notwithstanding other time limits. Claims could, however, be made on a provisional basis in advance of the appointed day (see Revenue Press Release 12 May 1998).

For expenditure on **information and communications technology** incurred by a 'small enterprise' (as distinct from a 'small and medium-sized enterprise' as referred to above), the rate is similarly increased to **100%** for expenditure incurred **after 31 March 2000 and before 1 April 2003** (and for any additional VAT liability in respect thereof). Qualifying '*information and communications technology*' is divided into three classes: computers and associated equipment (but excluding computerised control or management systems or other systems that are part of a larger system whose principal function is not processing or storing information); other qualifying equipment (i.e. WAP and third generation mobile telephones and data network reception and transmission devices for use with television sets, and similar devices capable of receiving and transmitting information from and to data networks); and software (i.e. the right to use or otherwise deal with software for the purposes of equipment within the first two classes). The class of 'other qualifying equipment' may be further defined or added to by Treasury order.

CAA 1990, s 83(2) (pre-trading expenditure, see above) is disregarded in determining, for the purposes of the reinstatement of first-year allowances, the date on which expenditure is incurred. The reinstated allowances are not available for assets which would be long-life assets apart from the transitional provisions of *CAA 1990, s 38H* (see 10.28(G) below) or which are within the exclusions from long-life asset treatment by virtue of being motor cars, ships or railway assets (see 10.28(G)(ii)–(iv)). There is also an exclusion where the machinery or plant was provided in connection with a change in the nature or conduct of a trade or business carried on by a person other than the person incurring the expenditure on its provision, and the obtaining of a first-year allowance was the main benefit, or one of the main benefits, which could reasonably be expected to arise from the making of the change.

[*CAA 1990, s 22(1)(1AA)(3C)–(3G)(6B)–(6E), s 22B, s 22C; F(No 2)A 1997, s 42; FA 1998, ss 83, 84; FA 1999, ss 77, 78; FA 2000, ss 70, 71; SI 1999 No 2119*].

'*Small or medium-sized enterprise*' is defined for this purpose by reference to the *Companies Act 1985, s 247* (or NI equivalent) definition of 'small or medium-sized company'. Broadly, the requirement is that two of the following three conditions are fulfilled: that the turnover not exceed £11.2 million; that the assets not exceed £5.6 million; and that there be not more than 250 employees. The enterprise must qualify as small or medium-sized in either the year in which the expenditure was incurred or the previous year. In the case of a company which is a member of a group of companies, the requirements apply to the group as a whole. For expenditure incurred after 11 May 1998 (but not for the purposes of the allowances available for expenditure incurred before 2 July 1998, or for the purposes of the allowances available for expenditure incurred in the following year where the contract was entered into before 12 May 1998), the group which has to be considered in this context includes any international group of which the company is a member. [*CAA 1990, s 22A; F(No 2)A 1997, s 43; FA 1998, s 85(2)(3)(10)(11); FA 2000, s 70(2)*]. '*Small enterprise*' is similarly defined, but by reference to the *Companies Act 1985* definition of 'small company', i.e. where two of the following three conditions are fulfilled: that the turnover does not exceed £2.8 million; that the assets are not more than £1.4 million; and that there be not more than 50 employees. [*CAA 1990, s 22AA; FA 2000, s 72*].

First-year allowances were previously reinstated at a rate of **40%** in respect of expenditure incurred **after 31 October 1992 and before 1 November 1993** (and any 'additional VAT liability' (see 10.2(v) above) incurred, at whatever time, in respect of such expenditure), subject to the general conditions of *CAA 1990, s 22(1)* (see above and below) being satisfied. *CAA 1990, s 83(2)* (pre-trading expenditure — see above) is disregarded in determining for this purpose the date on which expenditure is incurred. [*CAA 1990, s 22(1)(3B); FA 1993, s 115(1)(2)*].

Exclusions. First-year allowances are **not** given on the following:

(i) **Cars** and road vehicles, unless they are

(*a*) of a type constructed primarily for carrying goods, or

(*b*) of a type unsuitable for use, and not commonly used, as private vehicles, or

(*c*) provided wholly or mainly for a trade of hire to, or carriage of, members of the public (i.e. not where hiring etc. is limited to a certain class of customers, such as business connections or group companies).

As regards (*b*) above, see Schedule E benefits case of *Gurney v Richards Ch D, [1989] STC 682* (fire brigade car equipped with flashing light held within excluded class), decided on similarly worded legislation (see 75.15 SCHEDULE E). See also *Bourne v Auto School of Motoring Ch D 1964, 42 TC 217* (driving school cars) and *Roberts v Granada TV Rental Ltd Ch D 1970, 46 TC 295* (mini-vans, etc.).

(*c*) above applies only if the vehicle was either not normally on hire etc. to the same person (or a person connected with him, see 20 CONNECTED PERSONS) for a period of thirty or more consecutive days or for ninety or more days in any twelve month period; or was provided to a person who himself satisfied those conditions in using it wholly or mainly for a trade of hire etc. to members of the public (e.g. a taxi driver). These restrictions do not, however, apply to vehicles supplied for the use of persons receiving a social security mobility allowance, disability living allowance or war pensioners' mobility supplement and certain other like payments. [*CAA 1990, ss 22(4)(b), 36; FA 1971, s 43; F(No 2)A 1979, s 14; FA 1984, s 61; SI 1984 No 2060; SI 1991 No 2874*].

See above as regards the somewhat wider exclusion in relation to expenditure incurred after 2 July 1997.

(ii) Assets involved in certain partnership changes and other successions (see 10.38(viii), (xi) below). [*CAA 1990, ss 77, 78; FA 1971, Sch 8 paras 13, 15(3)*].

(iii) Assets acquired in sales between connected persons (as under *ICTA 1988, s 839*, see 20 CONNECTED PERSONS), or in sale and lease-back transactions, or in transactions the sole or main benefit of which would be the obtaining of capital allowances. [*CAA 1990, s 75; FA 1971, Sch 8 paras 3, 4; FA 1972, s 68*]. See also 10.38(iii) below.

(iv) Assets attracting investment grants which, although withdrawn after 26 October 1970, continued to apply to certain prior contracts. Ships, however, were granted first-year allowances on expenditure less investment grant. [*FA 1971, Sch 8 para 1*].

(v) (With respect to chargeable periods whose basis periods ended before 1 April 1985), assets disposed of without having been brought into use for trade purposes (any allowances previously given being withdrawn). [*FA 1971, s 41(2); FA 1985, s 55(2)*]. Such assets are to be regarded as never having qualified for allowances (*Burman v Westminster Press Ltd Ch D 1987, 60 TC 418*).

(vi) Certain assets used for leasing (see 10.35 below).

Partial use for non-trade purposes results in first-year allowances being scaled down as is just and reasonable. [*CAA 1990, s 79; FA 1971, Sch 8 para 5; FA 1985, Sch 14 para 2*]. See 10.28(C) below as regards writing-down allowances in such cases.

Claims. A claim may be made for all or any part of the allowances available. [*CAA 1990, s 22(7); FA 1990, Sch 17 para 3*].

This provision does not, however, apply to **ships**, for which the trader may by notice in writing require the postponement of the whole allowance to a later period or periods or, in the case of a company for an accounting period ended before 1 October 1993, disclaim it, or may require the allowance to be reduced, in which case he may also require that reduced allowance to be postponed. The time limit within which notice must be given is (i) for income tax for 1996/97 onwards (subject to (ii) below), twelve months after 31 January following the tax year in which ends the chargeable period for which the allowance is due, (ii) for income tax for 1996/97 only as regards trades etc. commenced before 6 April 1994, twelve months after 31 January following the chargeable period, and (iii) for income tax for earlier years and for corporation tax, two years after the end of the chargeable period. With respect to expenditure incurred before 1 April 1985, these provisions applied only to expenditure on new ships. Also, in respect of expenditure incurred before 14 March 1984, a claim in respect of a new ship could only require the postponement of all or part of the allowance, and postponed allowances could not be claimed in a later period if 10.35(*g*) below applied. Where a previous owner of a ship was denied first-year allowances through disposing of the ship without its having been brought into use for trade purposes, his ownership was ignored in determining whether the ship was 'new'. [*CAA 1990, s 30; FA 1971, Sch 8 para 8; FA 1980, Sch 12 para 1(2); FA 1984, s 59; FA 1985, s 58(1); FA 1989, Sch 13 para 15; FA 1990, Sch 17 para 7; FA 1993, Sch 13 para 3; FA 1996, s 135, Sch 21 para 27*]. See 10.28(B) below as regards writing-down allowances for ships.

10.28 **Writing-down allowances** are available for any chargeable period (see 10.2(vi) above) other than that of permanent discontinuance to any person who has incurred expenditure on machinery etc. (see 10.25 above) which belongs or has belonged to him (but see 10.38(vii) below as regards certain expenditure by a lessee) (and which, in relation to chargeable periods whose basis periods end before 1 April 1985, is or has been in use for trade or leasing purposes). [*CAA 1990, s 24(1); FA 1971, s 44(1); FA 1985, s 55(2)*]. See 10.27 above and 10.34 below for meaning of 'belongs'. See 10.38(iii) below as regards restrictions under connected persons and other anti-avoidance provisions.

The allowance is **25% p.a.** (proportionately reduced or increased where the chargeable period is less or more than one year, or if the trade has been carried on for part only of a chargeable period) of the excess of 'qualifying expenditure' over 'disposal value' for that period. [*CAA 1990, s 24(2); FA 1994, s 213(4)*].

Qualifying expenditure of a chargeable period whose basis period ends after 31 March 1985 is the sum of:

(i) the residue of qualifying expenditure brought forward from the preceding chargeable period;

(ii) the balance, after deducting any first-year allowance (see 10.27 above) given, of any expenditure which has not formed part of the qualifying expenditure for any previous chargeable period, and which does not qualify for a first-year allowance (ignoring any failure to claim or any disclaimer) for the chargeable period in question;

(iii) the balance, after deducting the first-year allowance, of any expenditure in respect of which a first-year allowance is made where a 'disposal value' (see below) falls to be brought in, in respect of the machinery or plant on which the expenditure was incurred, in the chargeable period in question; and

(iv) net cost during the basis period for the chargeable period under review of demolition of machinery and plant not replaced by the trader.

[*CAA 1990, ss 25(1)(5)(6), 62; FA 1990, Sch 17 para 6; FA 1994, Sch 26 Pt V(24)*].

Where an 'additional VAT liability' (see 10.2(v) above) is incurred in respect of expenditure qualifying for writing-down allowances, at a time when the machinery or plant in question is provided for the purposes of the trade, it is itself expenditure (on the machinery or plant in question) qualifying for writing-down allowances. [*CAA 1990, s 24(1A); FA 1991, Sch 14 para 7(1)*].

For a chargeable period whose basis period ended before 1 April 1985, expenditure on machinery or plant is only brought into qualifying expenditure if the machinery or plant was or had been in use for trade purposes in or before the basis period for the chargeable period in question. Also, (iii) above does not apply, but there is instead an addition to qualifying expenditure of the cost less 'disposal value' of any machinery or plant sold in the basis period for the chargeable period under review without having been brought into use for trade purposes. [*FA 1971, s 44(4), Sch 8 paras 4, 14; FA 1985, Sch 14 paras 3(2), 5*].

As regards (i) above, expenditure which was not qualifying expenditure for a previous chargeable period cannot be qualifying expenditure for a subsequent chargeable period unless the machinery or plant on which it was incurred belongs to the person who incurred the expenditure at some time in the subsequent period. [*FA 1994, s 118(6); FA 2000, s 73*].

As regards (ii) above, expenditure incurred by a trader after 13 March 1984 which qualifies for a first-year allowance in a chargeable period is *not* excluded from being qualifying expenditure of that period where either

(1) the trader, not having claimed the first-year allowance, so elects (for chargeable periods ended before 1 October 1993, this applied only to traders other than companies), or

(2) the trader (being a company) disclaimed the first-year allowance for an accounting period ended before 1 October 1993, or

(3) part of the first-year allowance was disclaimed or a reduced allowance required to be given (see 10.27 above),

in which case the fraction of the total expenditure corresponding to the proportion of the available first-year allowances not taken may be included in qualifying expenditure. The time limit for the election in (1) above is (i) for income tax for 1996/97 onwards (subject to (ii) below), twelve months after 31 January following the tax year in which the chargeable period ends, (ii) for income tax for 1996/97 only as regards trades etc. commenced before 6 April 1994, twelve months after 31 January following the chargeable period, and (iii) for income tax for earlier years and for corporation tax, two years after the end of the chargeable period. [*CAA 1990, s 25(2)(3)(4)(9); FA 1990, Sch 17 para 6; FA 1996, s 135, Sch 21 para 26*].

Finance lessors. For expenditure incurred after 1 July 1997 (or in the following twelve months under a contract entered into on or before that date), only a proportion of capital expenditure during a chargeable period on the provision of machinery or plant for leasing under a 'finance lease' (see 10.38(iii) below) may be brought in as qualifying expenditure for that period. The proportion is the same as the proportion of the chargeable period which falls after the time the expenditure was incurred, so that e.g. only one-quarter is brought in where expenditure is incurred three months before the end of a twelve-month period. This does not apply where a disposal value is brought in in respect of the machinery or plant in the same period. The balance of the expenditure may be brought in in the following chargeable period or periods. [*CAA 1990, s 25(5A)–(5C); F(No 2)A 1997, s 44*]. See Revenue Tax Bulletin June 1998 pp 539–544 for a general article on how these and associated capital allowance restrictions are intended to operate. In particular the following apply in relation to the current provisions.

(*a*) As a transitional measure, up to the end of 2001, lessors may agree with the local inspector to adopt a mean expenditure date for weekly or monthly batches of small items, or some other form of simplified calculation giving broadly the correct result. Thereafter, any basis adopted must ensure that no more than the correct amount is included in qualifying expenditure, e.g. by using the end rather than the mean date for batched items.

(*b*) Where the limit on allowances for cars costing over £12,000 applies (see (A) below), it operates after the restriction under these provisions.

(*c*) Where the machinery or plant is a fixture let under an equipment lease and does not belong to the lessor at any time during the chargeable period in which the expenditure is incurred, because the lessee has not commenced trading (see 10.34(*b*) below), no allowances are due for that period. The restriction thus does not apply, and the expenditure is brought in in full in the period in which the fixture first belongs to the lessor (i.e. in which the lessee starts to trade). If the lessee starts to trade during the period in which the expenditure is incurred, the expenditure is apportioned from the date the expenditure is incurred, and not from the date the lessee starts to trade.

See also 10.38(iii)(vi) below, 71.68 SCHEDULE D, CASES I AND II as regards finance lease allowance restrictions.

Disposal value for a chargeable period whose basis period ends after 31 March 1985 is that calculated for any machinery or plant provided for trade purposes which belongs to the trader at some time in the basis period, and in respect of which, in that basis period, one of the following events occurs, being the first such event to occur.

(i) The machinery or plant ceases to belong to the trader.

(ii) He loses possession of it, and it is reasonable to assume the loss is permanent.

(iii) It ceases to exist as such.

(iv) It begins to be used wholly or partly other than for trade purposes (but see (B) below).

(v) The trade is, or is treated as, permanently discontinued.

For a chargeable period whose basis period ended before 1 April 1985, disposal value is brought in for any machinery or plant which, after being in use for trade purposes, ceased to belong to the trader, or ceased permanently to be used for trade purposes, in the basis period.

The amount to be brought into account depends upon the nature of the event.

(*a*) On a sale, it is the net sale proceeds plus any insurance or capital compensation received by reason of any event which affected the sale price (but see (*b*) below).

(*b*) On a sale at less than market value, market value is substituted for the actual sale price, unless the buyer can claim machinery and plant or scientific research allowances for his expenditure, or is charged to tax under Schedule E in respect of the sale.

(*c*) On demolition or destruction, it is the net amount received for the remains plus any insurance or capital compensation receipts.

(*d*) On permanent loss, it is any insurance or capital compensation receipts.

(*e*) On permanent discontinuance of the trade preceding an event in (*a*)–(*d*) above, it is the value under (*a*)–(*d*) as appropriate.

(*f*) On any other event, it is open market value (except that no disposal value is brought in when machinery etc. was given away resulting in a charge on the recipient under Schedule E).

Where an 'additional VAT rebate' (see 10.2(v) above) is made in respect of expenditure qualifying for allowances, a disposal value equal to the amount of that rebate must be brought into account for the chargeable period related to the making of the rebate.

The disposal value may not, however, exceed the cost (reduced by any 'additional VAT rebates' (see above), and if the event is itself the making of an additional VAT rebate, by any other disposal value previously brought into account) (but see 10.38(iii) below as regards certain transactions between connected persons). [*CAA 1990, s 24(6)–(8), s 26; FA 1971, s 44(5)(6); FA 1985, Sch 14 para 3(3); FA 1991, Sch 14 paras 7(2), 8; FA 1994, Sch 26 Pt V(24)*].

The exemptions under (*b*) and (*f*) above where there is a charge to tax under Schedule E apply where there would be such a charge but for the exemptions from a charge under *ICTA 1988, s 148* (see 19.5, 19.6 COMPENSATION FOR LOSS OF EMPLOYMENT (AND DAMAGES)). (Tolley's Practical Tax 1984 p 114).

Claims. A claim may be made for all, none, or any part of the allowances available. [*CAA 1990, s 24(3)(4); FA 1990, Sch 17 para 5*].

Items not included in 'pool' of qualifying expenditure are

(A) *Motor cars costing over £12,000* acquired for purposes of a trade (other than vehicles constructed primarily for carrying goods, unsuitable as private vehicles, or provided for a trade of public hire or conveyance, see 10.27(i) above). The car is treated as being acquired for the purposes of a *separate and distinct trade* commencing immediately after the beginning of the basis period related to the incurring of the expenditure and ending when the car begins to be used for purposes other than those of the actual trade. Writing-down allowances are calculated on this basis but are limited to a *maximum of £3,000 a year* (proportionately reduced or increased for chargeable periods of less or more than a year). The allowances, or charges, are made to, or on, the actual trade.

For expenditure incurred or treated as incurred before 11 March 1992 or under a contract entered into before that date, the figures are £8,000 and £2,000 respectively.

Where a car of which the *retail price when new* exceeded £12,000 is *hired* for business purposes, the hire charge is treated for tax purposes as reduced in the proportion which £12,000 plus one-half of the excess bears to that original price. If the price paid for the car by the lessor when new is known, it can be used as the retail price when new, but otherwise the manufacturer's list price, net of any discount generally available but inclusive of extras and VAT, should be used. (Revenue Tax Bulletin April 2000 p 746). For hire expenditure under a contract entered into before 11 March 1992, the figure is £8,000 in each case. The restriction does not apply if the car is within the exceptions listed at (*a*)–(*c*) under 10.27(i) above. The restriction also does not apply to any separate maintenance charge explicitly specified in the contract (see Tolley's Practical Tax 1986 p 63). Any subsequent rental rebate (or other release within *ICTA 1988, s 94*, see 71.44 SCHEDULE D, CASES I AND II) is reduced for tax purposes in the same proportion as the hire charge restriction. (This applies where the rebate etc. is made on or after 29 April 1996, but similar relief was previously available by extra-statutory concession (see Revenue Pamphlet IR 1, B28).) [*CAA 1990, ss 34–36; F(No 2)A 1992, s 71; FA 1994, s 213(5)(6); FA 1996, Sch 39 para 1(3)(4)*]. As regards hire purchase agreements under which there is an option to purchase for a sum not more than one per cent of the retail price when new, the finance charge element, which strictly falls within the definition of a hire charge, is excluded from this restriction. [*CAA 1990, s 35(3)(4); FA 1991, s 61*].

Motor cars costing £12,000 (£8,000) or less must, for 1999/2000 and earlier years, be included in the separate 'pool' mentioned in 10.35(*a*) below. The separate pool is abolished for, broadly, 2000/01 onwards. [*CAA 1990, s 41(1)(c); FA 2000, s 74*].

(B) *Ships.* Where a trader incurs expenditure on a ship for trade purposes (not for a deemed trade of letting, see (E) below), the ship is treated for writing-down allowances as if provided for a notional separate 'single ship trade'. Allowances and charges which would be made in the single ship trade are made for the same period in the actual trade. For expenditure incurred after 26 July 1989, these provisions do not apply where the ship is provided for leasing or otherwise for letting on charter, unless it appears that the ship will be used in the 'requisite period' only for a 'qualifying purpose' (as defined in 10.35(*d*) below), and do not apply where the overseas leasing provisions in 10.35 below apply.

The single ship trade is treated as being permanently discontinued at the time when the ship begins to be used wholly or partly for non-trade purposes. If, before that time, it starts to be used in the 'requisite period' other than for a 'qualifying purpose' (as defined in 10.35(*c*)(*d*) below), the trade is treated as ceasing when it starts to be so used. Where, as a result, a disposal value falls to be brought in, no balancing adjustment is made in the single ship trade, but a corresponding adjustment is made in the actual trade by an addition to qualifying expenditure or the bringing in of a disposal value. If the ship ceases to belong to the trader without having been brought into use for the trade, the single ship trade is again treated as being permanently discontinued, but in addition writing-down allowances previously given or postponed are withdrawn and the corresponding amount added to the qualifying expenditure of the actual trade.

A trader may elect for any of the following.

(i) Postponement, in whole or part, of allowances to a later period.

(ii) That the separate trade provisions shall not apply, the balance of qualifying expenditure being added to the actual trade.

(iii) That any part of the expenditure be transferred to the pool of the actual trade.

The time limit within which notice of any of the above must be given is (i) for income tax for 1996/97 onwards (subject to (ii) below), twelve months after 31 January following the tax year in which ends the chargeable period concerned, (ii) for income tax for 1996/97 only as regards trades etc. commenced before 6 April 1994, twelve months after 31 January following the chargeable period, and (iii) for income tax for earlier years and for corporation tax, two years after the end of the chargeable period. Where, as a result of (ii) above, there is deemed to be a permanent discontinuance of the single ship trade, no balancing adjustment is made in respect of that trade, but an addition to or subtraction from the qualifying expenditure of the actual trade is made.

[*CAA 1990, ss 31–33; FA 1990, Sch 17 para 8; FA 1994, Sch 26 Pt V(24); FA 1996, s 135, Sch 21 paras 28, 29; FA 1998, Sch 5 para 52*].

See also 10.30 below as regards balancing charges on disposals of ships.

(C) *Partial use for other purposes.* Where machinery or plant is acquired for trade purposes but will also be used for other purposes, a first-year allowance, where available, can be given but is scaled down as is just and reasonable. Writing-down allowances, etc., similarly scaled down, will be calculated primarily as if the machinery were acquired for a separate 'notional' trade starting at the commencement of the basis period in which it is acquired for the purposes of the actual trade and being permanently discontinued when the machinery starts to be used wholly for purposes other than those of the actual trade (and see further below). If an asset in use wholly for trade purposes begins to be used partly for other purposes, it is treated as permanently ceasing to be used for the purposes of the (actual) trade at the beginning of the period of the change in use, so that its open market value (see (*f*) above), or cost if lower, is deducted from qualifying expenditure and is treated as the acquisition cost in the 'notional' trade. [*CAA 1990, s 79; FA 1990, Sch 17 para 14; FA 1994, Sch 26 Pt V(24)*].

Where, after 20 March 2000, circumstances change such that the non-trade use proportion increases during a period of account, and the open market value of the machinery or plant at the end of the period exceeds the qualifying expenditure for the period by more than £1 million, then if no disposal value would otherwise be brought into account for the period, the notional trade is treated as permanently discontinued immediately before the end of the period, and the disposal value so brought into account in the notional trade is treated as qualifying expenditure of the immediately following period in a new notional trade. [*CAA 1990, s 79A; FA 2000, s 75(2)(6)*].

See 10.24 above for the application of these provisions to cases where trading activities are in part not within the charge to UK tax.

See also *Kempster v McKenzie Ch D 1952, 33 TC 193* and *G H Chambers (Northiam Farms) Ltd v Watmough Ch D 1956, 36 TC 711* and Revenue Capital Allowances Manual, CA 2422, 2423 as regards further adjustment for any element of personal choice.

(D) Where *contributions are received* as reimbursement of day-to-day depreciation. [*CAA 1990, s 80*]. See 10.38(xii) below.

(E) *Machinery etc., on lease.* A person incurring expenditure on machinery, etc., which he lets otherwise than in the course of a trade, and not for use in a dwelling-house, is treated as if he had incurred that expenditure in a *separate trade* beginning at the commencement of the first letting and not ending until letting permanently ceases. [*CAA 1990, s 61; FA 1994, Sch 26 Pt V(24); FA 1998, s 38, Sch 5 para 55, Sch 27 Pt III(4)*]. See 10.35 below as regards restrictions in making allowances and 10.38(vii) below as regards machinery, etc. a lessee is required to provide under his lease.

(F) *Short-life assets.* Allowances for expenditure incurred by a trader on such an asset are calculated as if the asset was acquired for a separate notional trade, which is permanently discontinued when the asset starts to be used wholly or partly for purposes other than those of the actual trade. The allowances are given, and charges made, for the corresponding chargeable period in the actual trade. If, following a permanent discontinuance of the notional trade on which a balancing allowance arose (see 10.30 below), an 'additional VAT liability' (see 10.2(v) above) is incurred in respect of the asset, a further balancing allowance of that amount is given for the chargeable period related to the incurring of the liability.

The Revenue accept that it may not be practicable for individual computations to be maintained for every short-life asset, especially where they are held in very large numbers. Statement of Practice SP 1/86 sets out examples of acceptable bases of computation where the inspector is satisfied that the actual life in the business of a distinct class of assets with broadly similar average lives, before being sold or scrapped, is likely to be less than five years.

The trader may elect in writing for any machinery or plant (except as below) to be a *short-life asset*. The election is irrevocable and the time limit within which it must be made is (i) for income tax for 1996/97 onwards (subject to (ii) below), twelve months after 31 January following the tax year in which ends the chargeable period in which the expenditure (or earliest expenditure) is incurred, (ii) for income tax for 1996/97 only as regards trades etc. commenced before 6 April 1994, as regards expenditure incurred in the basis period for that year, the period up to and including 31 January 1999, and (iii) for income tax for earlier years and for corporation tax, two years after the end of the chargeable period or (for income tax only) its basis period.

In general, inspectors will require sufficient information in support of an election to minimise the possibility of any difference of view at a later date (e.g. on a disposal) about what was and was not covered by the election, and to ensure that assets are not in any of the excluded categories (see below). Where separate identification of short-life assets acquired in a chargeable period is either impossible or impracticable, e.g. similar small or relatively inexpensive assets held in very large numbers, perhaps in different locations, then the information required in support of the election may be provided by reference to batches of acquisitions. (Revenue Pamphlet IR 131, SP 1/86, 15 January 1986).

The following can *not* be short-life assets.

(i) A ship.

(ii) A motor car (see 10.27(i) above).

(iii) An asset leased other than in the course of a trade.

(iv) An asset used partly for non-trade purposes.

(v) An asset the subject of a 'wear and tear' subsidy.

(vi) An asset received by way of gift or whose previous use by the trader did not attract capital allowances (see 10.38(v)(ix) below).

(vii) Machinery or plant provided for leasing unless likely to be used in the 'requisite period' only for a 'qualifying purpose' (as defined in 10.35(*c*)(*d*) below), excluding in any case vehicles within 10.35(AA) below.

(viii) A leased asset within *CAA 1990, s 43* (see 10.35(*f*) below).

(ix) A rented television set within the transitional provisions in 10.35 below.

(x) An asset leased outside the UK within 10.35 below.

(xi) An asset expenditure on which is within the long-life asset provisions (see (G) below).

As regards (vii) above, if, before the notional trade is otherwise treated as permanently discontinued, the asset starts to be used in the 'requisite period' other than for a 'qualifying purpose', the notional trade is treated as ceasing when it starts to be so used. No balancing adjustment is made in the actual trade, but the qualifying expenditure in the notional trade at the start of the period is added to qualifying expenditure for the actual trade (or, if it is 'old expenditure' (see 10.35 below), added to the special pool in 10.35(*a*) below).

If a disposal value does not fall to be brought into account (other than by virtue of the grant of certain computer software rights (see 10.25 above) or an 'additional VAT rebate' (see above)) on the notional trade for a chargeable period ending no later than four years after the end of the chargeable period related to the incurring of the expenditure (or earliest expenditure), then in the first chargeable period ending thereafter (or in its basis period) the notional trade is treated as being permanently discontinued. No balancing adjustment is made, but the trader's qualifying expenditure for that period in his actual trade is increased by the balance of qualifying expenditure in the notional trade.

Also if, before the notional trade is treated as permanently discontinued, the asset is disposed of to a connected person within *ICTA 1988, s 839* (see 20 CONNECTED PERSONS), the asset is treated as continuing to be subject to an election made under these provisions at the time the original election was made. If the trader and the connected person so elect (not more than two years after the end of the chargeable period in which, or in the basis period for which, the disposal occurred), the disposal is treated as at a price equal to the notional trade qualifying expenditure of the period of the disposal, and *CAA 1990, s 75* (see 10.38(iii) below) does not apply. If no election is made, the normal connected person rules apply (see 10.38(iii) below), but the bar on substituting market value for a lesser sale price where the buyer is entitled to capital allowances (see (*b*) above) is lifted. [*CAA 1990, ss 37, 38; FA 1991, Sch 14 para 9; F(No 2)A 1992, s 68(7); FA 1993, Sch 13 para 4; FA 1994, Sch 26 Pt V(24); FA 1996, s 135, Sch 21 para 30; FA 1997, Sch 14 para 3*].

(G) *Long-life assets.* There are special provisions for chargeable periods ending on or after 26 November 1996 relating to certain expenditure on 'long-life assets'. These do not apply to expenditure incurred before 26 November 1996, or to expenditure incurred before 1 January 2001 under a contract entered into before 26 November 1996 (except that the later start date does not apply to any increased expenditure resulting from a variation of the contract on or after 26 November 1996). Writing-down allowances and balancing adjustments for such expenditure are calculated as if the asset was acquired for a separate notional trade, for whose purposes it is used so long as and to the extent that it is used for the purposes of the actual trade, and which is treated as permanently discontinued only if the actual trade is (or is treated as) permanently discontinued. All assets within these provisions are dealt with in the same notional trade, unless the asset is already dealt with in a separate notional trade under *CAA 1990, s 31* (single ship trade, see (B) above), *s 61* (leasing, see (E) above), *s 79* (part non-trade use, see (C) above) or *s 80* (wear and tear subsidies, see 10.38(xii) below). If an allowance so determined is not claimed or a reduced claim is made, the computation in the notional trade is correspondingly adjusted.

Writing-down allowances in the notional trade (or in the notional trade under *CAA 1990, ss 31, 61, 79* or *80* where the asset in question falls within one of those provisions) are at an annual rate of **6%** (instead of 25% or, in the case of certain leased assets (see 10.35 below), 10%). Where capital allowances have been claimed for expenditure within these provisions, any expenditure on the same asset for which allowances are subsequently claimed, unless it is within the excluded categories described below, is also treated as being within these provisions if it would not otherwise be so. This over-rides the exclusion of expenditure within the cash limit referred to below.

Where a disposal value less than the 'notional written-down value' would otherwise fall to be brought into account in respect of expenditure on machinery or plant which has attracted restricted allowances as above, an adjustment may be required. Where the event giving rise to the disposal value is part of a scheme or arrangement a main object of which is the obtaining or increasing of allowances or deductions, or the reduction or elimination of charges, under these provisions, the 'notional written-down value' is substituted for the disposal value. The '*notional written-down value*' is the disposal value which would result in no balancing adjustment being required, assuming that no other expenditure were taken into account in determining the qualifying expenditure, that the expenditure was not excluded from these provisions by reason of being within the lower limit referred to below, and that all allowances had been made in full.

Subject as below, a '*long-life asset*' is machinery or plant which it is reasonable to expect will have a useful economic life of at least 25 years (or where such was a reasonable expectation when it was new). The useful economic life is taken as the period from first use until it ceases to be, or to be likely to be, used as a fixed asset of a business. Where part only of expenditure on an asset falls within these provisions (see below), that part and the remainder are each treated as expenditure on a separate item of machinery or plant, any necessary apportionment being made on a just and reasonable basis. As an introduction to a detailed discussion of what constitutes a long-life asset (including twelve examples), the Revenue have stated that they 'will generally accept the accounting treatment as determining whether an asset is long-life provided it is not clearly unreasonable'. (Revenue Tax Bulletin August 1997 pp 445–450). For whether glasshouses (for which see generally 10.25, 10.26 above) are long-life assets, see Revenue Tax Bulletin June 1998 p 552. For aircraft, see Revenue Tax Bulletin June 1999 pp 671, 672 and April 2000 pp 739, 740.

The following can *not* be long-life assets.

(i) Fixtures (see 10.34 below) in, or machinery or plant provided for use in, a building used wholly or mainly as a dwelling-house, showroom, hotel, office or retail shop or similar retail premises, or for purposes ancillary to such use.

(ii) Motor cars (see 10.27(i) above) or vehicles excluded from being such under 10.27(i)(*c*).

(iii) (In relation to expenditure incurred before 1 January 2011) ships of a seagoing kind, other than oil/gas rigs etc. and ships of a kind used or chartered primarily for sport or recreation (which does not encompass passenger ships or cruise liners).

(iv) (In relation to expenditure incurred before 1 January 2011) 'railway assets' used only for a 'railway business' (as defined).

Lower limit. There is a limit below which these provisions do not apply for expenditure in a chargeable period throughout which an individual taxpayer (or, in the case of a partnership of individuals, at least half of such individuals) devote(s) substantially the whole of his (their) time to the carrying on of the trade or profession for the purposes of which the expenditure was incurred. The provisions do not generally apply for such a chargeable period unless the total of such expenditure in the period which is or otherwise would be within the provisions exceeds £100,000 (or *pro rata* for periods of other than twelve months), disregarding certain expenditure which is not subject to the limit (see below). All expenditure under a contract is for this purpose treated as incurred in the first chargeable period in which any expenditure under the contract is incurred. Expenditure is excluded from the operation of the above limit where it is either:

(*a*) on a share in machinery or plant; or

(*b*) a contribution treated as machinery or plant expenditure under *CAA 1990, s 154* (see 10.2(ii) above); or

(*c*) on machinery or plant for leasing (whether or not in the course of a trade).

For corporation tax purposes, a £100,000 limit similarly applies (without the requirements as to full-time working in the trade) to expenditure by companies, except that the limit is, where relevant, divided by one plus the number of associated companies (as under *ICTA 1988, s 13*, see Tolley's Corporation Tax under Small Companies Rate).

Secondhand assets. A secondhand asset is excluded from these provisions where the previous owner has properly claimed allowances for expenditure on its provision, and that expenditure did not fall within these provisions, but would have done so if either:

(1) expenditure before the commencement dates referred to above was not prevented from being within these provisions; or

(2) the exclusion of secondhand assets did not apply; or

(3) these (or any successor) provisions applied for chargeable periods ending before 26 November 1996.

A provisional claim to 25% allowances may be made by a purchaser before the vendor has made the appropriate return, provided that reasonable steps have been taken to establish that entitlement will arise, and that the appropriate revisions will be made, and assessments accepted, if entitlement does not in the event arise. (Revenue Tax Bulletin August 1997 p 450).

Short life assets. Expenditure to which these provisions apply is excluded from the short life asset provisions (see (F) above).

[*CAA 1990, ss 38A–38H; FA 1997, Sch 14*].

For an article explaining how the Revenue interpret and plan to operate these provisions, see Revenue Tax Bulletin August 1997 pp 445–450.

10.29 *Examples*

(A) Short-life assets

A runs a small business. He prepares trading accounts to 30 September each year, and buys and sells machines as follows.

	Cost	Date of acquisition	Disposal proceeds	Date of disposal
Machine X	£20,000	30.4.97	£10,000	1.12.98
Machine Y	£25,000	1.9.97	£4,000	1.12.01

A elects under *CAA 1990, s 37* for both machines to be treated as short-life assets. His pool of qualifying expenditure brought forward at the beginning of period of account 1.10.96–30.9.97 is £80,000.

A's capital allowances are as follows.

	Pool	Machine X	Machine Y	Allowances
	£	£	£	£
Period of account 1.10.96–30.9.97				
WDV b/f	80,000			
Additions		20,000	25,000	
FYA 50%			(12,500)	12,500
WDA 25%	(20,000)	(5,000)	—	25,000
	60,000	15,000	12,500	£37,500
Period of account 1.10.97–30.9.98				
WDA 25%	(15,000)	(3,750)	(3,125)	£21,875
	45,000	11,250	9,375	
Period of account 1.10.98–30.9.99				
Disposal		(10,000)		
Balancing allowance		£1,250		1,250
WDA 25%	(11,250)		(2,344)	13,594
				£14,844
	33,750		7,031	
Period of account 1.10.99–30.9.00				
WDA 25%	(8,437)		(1,758)	£10,195
	25,313		5,273	
Period of account 1.10.00–30.9.01				
WDA 25%	(6,328)		(1,318)	£7,646
	18,985		3,955	
Period of account 1.10.01–30.9.02				
Transfer to pool	3,955		(3,955)	
	22,940		—	
Disposal	(4,000)			
	18,940			
WDA 25%	(4,735)			£4,735
WDV c/f	£14,205			

Note

The chargeable period related to the incurring of the expenditure on both machines in this example is the period of account 1.10.96–30.9.97. The fourth anniversary of the end of that chargeable period is 30.9.01. The balance of expenditure on Machine Y is thus transferred to the pool in the period of account 1.10.01–30.9.02, this being the first chargeable period ending after 30.9.01.

(B) Long-life assets

B prepares trading accounts to 31 December. In the year to 31 December 1999, he has built new factory premises for use in his trade, which include a building mainly in use as offices (on which 20% of the cost of the premises is expended). Industrial buildings allowances are available on the construction expenditure. The machinery and plant pool written-down value at 1 January 1999 is £800,000, and the disposal value brought in in respect of machinery and plant on his previous premises is £720,000. Machines installed in the new factory cost £920,000. His business is *not* classified as small or medium-sized, so that first-year allowances are not available.

He also claims machinery and plant allowances for expenditure of £520,000 incurred on fixtures integral to the new premises, which are agreed to have an expected life in excess of 25 years. Of this expenditure, it is agreed £120,000 should be apportioned to the offices.

On 1 May 2000 he incurs additional expenditure on upgrading the fixtures of £19,000, none of it relating to office fixtures.

On 1 October 2001 he moves to new premises, disposing of the old premises for a consideration including £425,000 relating to the integral fixtures (of which £95,000 relates to the office fixtures) and £510,000 relating to other machinery and plant.

Machinery and plant in the new premises costs £960,000, none of which relates to integral fixtures (which are included in the industrial buildings allowances claim for the new premises).

The machinery and plant allowances computations for relevant periods are as follows.

	Pool	Notional trade	Total allowances
	£	£	
Year ending 31.12.99			
WDV b/f	800,000	—	
Additions (see note (*a*))	1,040,000	400,000	
Disposals	(720,000)	—	
	1,120,000	400,000	
WDA	280,000	24,000	£304,000
WDV c/f	840,000	376,000	
Year ending 31.12.00			
Additions (see note (*b*))	—	19,000	
	840,000	395,000	
WDA	210,000	23,700	£233,700
WDV c/f	630,000	371,300	

	Pool	Notional trade	Total allowances
	£	£	
	b/f 630,000	b/f 371,300	
Year ending 31.12.01			
Additions (see note (*c*))	960,000	—	
Disposals	(605,000)	(330,000)	
	985,000	41,300	
WDA (see notes)	246,250	2,478	£248,728
WDV c/f	£738,750	£38,822	

Notes

(*a*) Expenditure on fixtures provided for use in offices is excluded from being on long-life assets (regardless of whether the office building itself attracts industrial buildings allowances because it represents not more than 25% of the overall cost of premises otherwise qualifying).

(*b*) Additional expenditure on long-life assets is within the provisions even if within the annual *de minimis* limit.

(*c*) The separate notional trade is treated as ceasing only on permanent discontinuance of the actual trade. Allowances therefore continue to be given at 6% p.a. on the residue of expenditure on long-life assets despite their having been disposed of.

10.30 **Balancing allowances and charges.** A balancing charge will be made in any chargeable period (including that of permanent discontinuance of the trade (or notional trade)) in which disposal value exceeds qualifying expenditure (see 10.28 above), and will be equal to the excess. [*CAA 1990, s 24(2)(5)*].

A balancing allowance will arise, only in the period of permanent discontinuance of the trade (or notional trade), of the whole of any excess for the period of qualifying expenditure over disposal value (see 10.28 above). [*CAA 1990, s 24(2)(b)*].

Where machinery etc. has been *partly used for non-trade purposes*, and is thus treated as in use for a separate notional trade (see 10.28(C) above), any balancing adjustment is reviewed on a just and reasonable basis in the light of allowances given and non-trade use. [*CAA 1990, s 79(5); FA 1994, Sch 26 Pt V(24)*].

Deferment of balancing charges on ships. With effect for chargeable periods or basis periods ending after 20 April 1994, balancing charges on ships may be deferred and set against subsequent expenditure on ships for a maximum of six years from the date of disposal. A claim for deferment of the whole or part of a balancing charge may be made by a trader where an event within 10.28(i)–(iii) above (events giving rise to disposal value) occurs after 20 April 1994 with respect to a 'qualifying ship' (the old ship). A '*qualifying ship*' is, broadly, a ship of a sea-going kind of 100 gross registered tons or more, excluding ships of a kind used or chartered primarily for sport or recreation (but passenger ships and cruise liners are not so excluded) and oil/gas rigs etc.. The provisions also apply to ships of less than 100 tons in cases where the old ship is totally lost or is damaged beyond worthwhile repair. A ship brought into use in the trade on or after 20 July 1994 must within three months of first use (unless disposed of during those three months) be registered in the UK, the Channel Islands, Isle of Man, a colony (as to which see Revenue Tax Bulletin April 1995 p 208, June 1998 p 553), a European Union State or a European Economic Area State and must continue to be so until at least three years from first use or, if earlier, until disposed of to an unconnected person. The old ship must not be one that falls to be excluded from the main pool of qualifying expenditure under the provisions for leased assets (see 10.28(E) above and 10.35(*a*) below), assets used only partly for the trade (see 10.28(C) above) or assets attracting a subsidy towards wear and tear (see 10.38(xii) below).

The balancing charge on the old ship is in effect calculated as if allowances had been granted, and the charge arises, in a separate single ship trade, with appropriate assumptions where that is not the case (see *CAA 1990, s 33B; FA 1995, s 94*).

Deferment is achieved by increasing qualifying expenditure by the amount deferred, thus reducing the excess of disposal value over qualifying expenditure. The *maximum deferment* is the *lowest* of (i) the amount treated as brought into account in respect of the old ship under *section 33B* (see above), (ii) the amount to be expended on new shipping (see below), so far as not already set against an earlier balancing charge, in the six years starting with the date of disposal of the old ship, (iii) the total balancing charge for the chargeable period in question (excluding charges on certain assets held outside the main pool of qualifying expenditure, and (iv) the amount needed to reduce the trading profit to nil (disregarding losses brought forward), no deferment being possible if no such profit has been made. Where current year basis does not yet apply, capital allowances (other than any brought forward) and balancing charges are treated as trading expenses and receipts of the basis period in determining the profit or loss for the purpose of (iv) above. If the amount actually expended within (ii) above turns out to be less than the amount deferred, the amount of the deficiency is reinstated as a balancing charge for the chargeable period to which the claim relates.

Where an amount is expended on new shipping within the six-year period allowed and is identified by the trader or, in default, determined by the inspector as to be attributed to any part of an amount deferred, an amount equal to the amount so matched is brought into account as a disposal value of the single ship trade (see 10.28(B) above) for the chargeable period in which (or in the basis period for which) the expenditure is incurred, thus reducing the amount on which writing-down allowances may be claimed. No amount of expenditure can be attributed to a deferment if there is earlier expenditure on new shipping within the said six-year period which has not been attributed to that or earlier deferments. An attribution may be varied by the trader by notice to the inspector within a specified time (see *CAA 1990, s 33F(3)* and *FA 1995, s 98(6)(b)*).

For the purposes of these provisions, an amount is expended on new shipping if it is capital expenditure, incurred by the claimant wholly and exclusively for the purposes of the trade, on a ship (the new ship) which will be a qualifying ship (see above) for at least three years from first use or, if earlier, until disposed of to an unconnected person. Expenditure is treated as incurred by the claimant if it is incurred by a successor to his trade following a partnership change (see 53.6 PARTNERSHIPS) or company reconstruction (see Tolley's Corporation Tax) in consequence of which the trade was not treated as discontinued. Expenditure incurred on a ship which has belonged to either the trader or a connected person within the previous six years or which is incurred mainly for tax avoidance reasons does not qualify. The new ship must be one to which the 'single ship trade' provisions at 10.28(B) above apply. If an election is made to disapply those provisions or transfer expenditure to the main pool (see 10.28(B)(ii)(iii) above), the expenditure in question is deemed never to have been expenditure on new shipping (but must nevertheless be taken into account in matching expenditure with deferments, so that either election prevents further matching of amounts already deferred). Expenditure does not qualify if the overseas leasing provisions at 10.35 below come to apply to the new ship.

For income tax purposes, where current year basis applies, the claim for deferment must be made within twelve months after 31 January following the year of assessment in which the chargeable period of deferment ends. Where current year basis does not yet apply, the claim must be made within two years after the end of that chargeable period. For corporation tax purposes, the provisions relating to capital allowances claims apply also to claims for deferment. Where a claim for deferment is found to be erroneous as a result of subsequent circumstances, the trader must, within three months of the end of the chargeable period in which those circumstances first arise, notify the inspector accordingly (failure to do so incurring a penalty under *TMA 1970, s 98*). A claim could not be made before 31 May 1996; the period for making a claim is extended, where it would otherwise end earlier, until 31 May 1997.

Where the disposal giving rise to the balancing charge occurs **on or after 29 April 1996**, there is provision for the balancing charge to be set against expenditure on new shipping by another member of the same *group of companies* as the shipowner (within *ICTA 1988, Pt X, Ch IV*, see Tolley's Corporation Tax under Groups of Companies). Such expenditure is, however, excluded where the ship ceases to belong to the fellow group member without being brought into use for trade purposes, or where, within three years of being so brought into use, a disposal value falls to be brought in in respect of the ship (although these exclusions do not apply in the case of total loss of, or commercially irreparable damage to, the ship). Expenditure is similarly excluded where the group relationship between the two companies ceases after the expenditure is incurred and within three years after the commencement of trade use (again disregarding events after the total loss etc. of the ship). Claims, assessments and adjustments relating to this extended relief could not be made before 31 January 1997, but may relate to times before that day, and all such claims, etc. made within twelve months of that day are valid notwithstanding any other time limits.

[*CAA 1990, ss 33A–33F; FA 1995, ss 94–98; FA 1996, Sch 35; SI 1996 No 1323; SI 1997 No 133*].

10.31 *Example*

Writing-down allowances, motor cars, partial non-business use, acquisitions from connected persons and balancing adjustments

A is in business as a builder and demolition contractor. His business qualifies as a small business for the purposes of first-year allowances. He makes up his accounts to 5 April. The accounts for the year to 5 April 2001 reveal the following additions and disposals.

	£
Additions	
Plant	
Dumper Truck	5,000
Excavator	32,000
Bulldozer	20,000
	£57,000
Fittings	
Office furniture	£2,000
Motor Vehicles	
Land Rover	6,000
Van	5,000
Car 1 (used by A)	12,200
Car 2 (no private use)	2,000
	£25,200

Disposals	Cost	Proceeds
	£	£
Excavator	32,000	30,000
Digger loader	15,000	4,000
Car (Audi)	5,200	4,200
Fittings	3,500	500
	£55,700	£38,700

The dumper truck was bought second-hand from Q, brother of A, but had not been used in a trade. The truck had originally cost Q £6,000, but its market value at sale was only £2,000.

The excavator was sold without having been brought into use.

The bulldozer and car 2 were both purchased from P, father of A and had originally cost P £25,000 and £3,500 respectively. Both assets had been used for trading purposes. In both cases the price paid by A was less than the market value.

The Audi sold and the new car 1 are both used for private motoring by A. Private use has always been 30%.

The written-down values at 5 April 2000 of the general machinery and plant pool and the Audi are £7,500 and £3,900 respectively.

The capital allowances for period of account year to 5 April 2001 are

	Expenditure qualifying for FYAs 40%	Pool 25%	Car pool 25%	Motor vehicles Audi	Motor vehicles Car 1	Total allowances
	£	£	£	£	£	£
WDV b/f		7,500		3,900		
Additions						
Excavator (note (*a*))	32,000					
Dumper truck (notes (*b*)(*c*))		2,000				
Bulldozer (notes (*b*)(*d*))		20,000				
Furniture	2,000					
Land Rover and van	11,000					
Cars			2,000		12,200	
	45,000					
FYA (40%)	(18,000)					18,000
Transfer to pool (£32,000 less 40% (note (*a*))	(19,200)	19,200				
	7,800					
Disposals						
Excavator		(30,000)				
Digger		(4,000)				
Fittings		(500)				
Audi				(4,200)		
		c/f 14,200	c/f 2,000	(£300)	c/f 12,200	

	Expenditure qualifying for FYAs 40%	Pool 25%	Car pool 25%	Motor vehicles Audi	Motor vehicles Car 1	Total allowances
	£	£	£	£	£	£
		b/f 14,200	b/f 2,000		b/f 12,200	
WDA (25%)		(3,550)	(500)			4,050
WDA (restricted)					(3,000)	3,000
Private use restriction (Car 1)						(900)
Transfer to pool	(£7,800)	7,800				
WDV c/f		£18,450	£1,500		£9,200	
Total allowances						£24,150
Balancing charge (Audi) £300 less 30% private use						(£210)

Notes

(*a*) First-year and writing-down allowances are available even though an item of machinery or plant is disposed of without being brought into use, always provided that the expenditure was incurred wholly and exclusively for trade purposes and the appropriate notification is made. See 10.27, 10.28 above. Where a disposal value falls to be brought into account for the same period of account as that in which a first-year allowance is made in respect of that item of expenditure, the expenditure is not precluded from being qualifying expenditure of that period. See 10.27 above.

(*b*) No first-year allowance is available in respect of an item of machinery or plant purchased from a connected person. See 10.27(iii) above.

(*c*) Qualifying expenditure on the dumper truck is restricted to the lowest of

(i) open market value;

(ii) capital expenditure incurred by the vendor (or, if lower, by a person connected with him);

(iii) capital expenditure incurred by the purchaser.

See 10.38(iii) below.

(*d*) Qualifying expenditure on the bulldozer is the lesser of A's actual expenditure and the disposal value brought into account in the vendor's computations (see 10.38(iii) below). (The vendor's disposal value would have been open market value but for the fact that the purchaser is himself entitled to claim capital allowances on the acquisition (see 10.28 above).) A's qualifying expenditure is thus equal to his actual expenditure. The same applies to the purchase of Car 2.

(*e*) Car 1, by virtue of its costing over £12,000, is not pooled (see 10.28(A) above). Car 2 is separately pooled (see 10.35(*a*) below), it being assumed that the abolition of the new pool is deferred to 2001/02 by election. See note (*d*) above as regards the amount of qualifying expenditure to be brought into account in respect of Car 2. The Audi was not pooled as it was used partly for non-trade purposes (see 10.28(C) above).

(*f*) The writing-down allowance on Car 1 is restricted to £3,000 before adjustment for private use (see 10.28(A) above).

10.32 **Making of allowances and charges.** For 1994/95 and subsequent years as regards trades commenced after 5 April 1994 and for 1997/98 and subsequent years as regards trades commenced on or before that date, allowances to **traders** are treated as trading expenses [*CAA 1990, s 140; FA 1994, s 211*] and are calculated by reference to events in periods of account (see 10.2(vi) above). See 10.2(vii) above as regards transitional relief for unused allowances carried forward under *CAA 1990, s 140(4)* as originally enacted (see below).

Allowances must be claimed in the annual return [*CAA 1990, s 140(3); FA 1994, s 211*] (In practice and before self-assessment they were more commonly claimed in computations accompanying accounts in support of a return.) This applies equally to companies for accounting periods ending after 30 September 1993. [*CAA 1990, s 145A, Sch A1; FA 1990, s 102, Sch 16*]. See Tolley's Corporation Tax. See 17.10 CLAIMS as regards error or mistake relief claims following omission.

For 1996/97 and earlier years as regards trades commenced before 6 April 1994, allowances due to traders (other than companies) were given as a deduction in taxing the trade and not as a deduction in arriving at the profits of the trade. [*CAA 1990, ss 73, 140(1)(2) as originally enacted*]. Allowances were calculated by reference to events in the basis period for the year of assessment of claim (see 71.3 SCHEDULE D, CASES I AND II), except that

(*a*) where basis periods overlap, expenditure in the common period is treated as incurred only in the earlier period, and

(*b*) expenditure in an interval between two basis periods is treated as incurred in the later period unless it is the period of permanent discontinuance of the trade, in which case it is treated as incurred in the earlier. [*CAA 1990, s 160 as originally enacted*].

Any excess of allowances over profits for a year of assessment could be carried forward without time limit against future profits of the trade. [*CAA 1990, s 140(4) as originally enacted*]. Alternatively, allowances could create or augment a trade loss, see 46 LOSSES generally and 46.9(*c*)(*d*)(*e*) for restrictions on use of allowances.

Allowances due to individual or partnership **non-trading lessors** are given on a claim for a year of assessment by way of discharge or repayment of tax, primarily against income from letting machinery or plant. Any excess of allowances over such income for a year of assessment may be carried forward without time limit against future such income. For 1996/97 and earlier years, allowances on expenditure incurred before 27 March 1980 (or under a contract entered into before that date where the machinery etc. was brought into use before 28 March 1982) could, on election within twelve months after 31 January following the tax year for which relief was given (for 1995/96 and earlier years, two years after the end of that tax year), be set against the lessor's other income of the year of assessment or of the following year, provided that the machinery etc. was at some time in the year of assessment used for the purposes of a trade carried on by the lessee. An election could, in practice, be withdrawn within the time limit for making it, provided that the corresponding liability had not been settled and agreed. Late elections may be accepted where an in-date indication of an intention to elect had in effect been accepted by the inspector. (Revenue Capital Allowances Manual, CA 156, 157). For corporation tax purposes, allowances are given by discharge or repayment, primarily against letting income, and charges are treated as income from the letting. [*CAA 1990, s 73(2)(4), s 141; FA 1971, s 48; FA 1980, s 70(3); FA 1995, Sch 6 para 33; FA 1996, s 135, Sch 21 para 34; FA 1997, Sch 18 Pt VI(11); FA 1998, s 38, Sch 5 para 57, Sch 27 Pt III(4)*]. See also below re Schedule A businesses.

Balancing charges are assessed on traders and (under Schedule D, Case VI) on non-trading lessors, again by reference to events in the appropriate basis period (or year of assessment). For 1994/95 and subsequent years as regards trades commenced after 5 April 1994 and for 1997/98 and subsequent years as regards trades commenced on or before that date, charges on traders are treated as trading receipts and are calculated by reference to events in periods of account (see 10.2(vi) above). A charge arising on the disposal etc. of machinery or plant purchased (or treated as purchased) before 27 October 1970 (see 10.37 below) may be postponed by deducting from it the cost of machinery etc. bought in replacement, other than machinery etc. either used partly for non-trade purposes, or the subject of wear and tear subsidies (see 10.38(xii) below), or motor cars costing over £12,000. [*CAA 1990, ss 24(5), 73, 140; CAA 1968, s 40; FA 1971, Sch 8 para 17; FA 1994, s 211, Sch 26 Pt V(24); FA 1995, Sch 6 para 33*].

Schedule A business. With effect for 1995/96 and 1996/97 (subject to transitional provisions), the above provisions concerning allowances to and charges on non-trading lessors do not apply for income tax purposes where the letting of machinery or plant is connected with the carrying on of a Schedule A business (see 68.3, 68.4 SCHEDULE A). In such a case, allowances/charges are made in taxing the business and treated as expenses/ receipts of the business. For corporation tax accounting periods ending after 31 March 1997, allowances made by virtue of *CAA 1990, s 28A* are given, by discharge or repayment of tax, primarily against Schedule A income, and charges treated accordingly (see also 68.15(v) SCHEDULE A). For 1997/98 and subsequent years, for income tax purposes, the Schedule A business is in any event treated as a trade for these purposes, see 68.7(*a*) SCHEDULE A, and this treatment is extended to corporation tax from 1 April 1998. [*ICTA 1988, s 32(1B); CAA 1990, s 73(1A); FA 1995, Sch 6 para 8(3); FA 1997, Sch 15 paras 1, 6; FA 1998, s 38, Sch 5 para 57, Sch 27 Pt III(4)*].

10.33 *Examples*

Basis periods under preceding year basis

S commenced business on 1 May 1991 preparing accounts annually to 30 April. The following expenditure was incurred.

	Plant	Motor Car
	£	£
Period 1.5.91 – 5.4.92	10,000	4,000 (no private use)
Period 6.4.92 – 30.4.92	2,000	
Period 1.5.92 – 31.10.92	3,500	
Period 1.11.92 – 30.4.93	4,000	
Period 1.5.93 – 31.10.93	1,500	
Period 1.11.93 – 30.4.94	4,500	

An item of plant was sold for £500 (original cost £1,000) on 27.4.92.

Profits will be assessed as follows

1991/92 Period 1.5.91 – 5.4.92 (actual)
1992/93 Year ended 30.4.92 (first 12 months)
1993/94 Year ended 30.4.92 (preceding year)
1994/95 Year ended 30.4.93 (preceding year)
1995/96 Year ended 30.4.94 (preceding year)

10.33 Capital Allowances (Machinery and Plant)

The capital allowances are

	Qualifying for FYAs	Pool	Pool for cars	Total
	£	£	£	£
1991/92 (basis period 1.5.91 – 5.4.92)				
Plant		10,000		
Motor car			4,000	
		10,000	4,000	
Allowances				
WDA 25% × $\frac{11}{12}$		(2,292)	(917)	£3,209
WDV at 5.4.92		7,708	3,083	
1992/93 (basis period 6.4.92 – 30.4.92)				
Plant		2,000		
Disposals		(500)		
		9,208	3,083	
Allowances				
WDA 25%		(2,302)	(771)	£3,073
WDV at 5.4.93		6,906	2,312	
1993/94 (no basis period)				
Allowances				
WDA 25%		(1,727)	(578)	£2,305
WDV at 5.4.94		5,179	1,734	
1994/95 (basis period 1.5.92 – 30.4.93)				
Plant	4,000	3,500		
	4,000	8,679	1,734	
Allowances				
FYA 40%	(1,600)			1,600
WDA 25%		(2,170)	(434)	2,604
	2,400	6,509	1,300	
Transfer to pool	(2,400)	2,400		
WDV at 5.4.95		8,909	1,300	
Total allowances 1994/95				£4,204

	Qualifying for FYAs	Pool	Pool for cars	Total
	£	£	£	£
1995/96 (basis period 1.5.93 – 30.4.94)				
Plant	1,500	4,500		
	1,500	13,409	1,300	
Allowances				
FYA 40%	(600)			600
WDA 25%		(3,352)	(325)	3,677
	900	10,057	975	
Transfer to pool	(900)	900		
WDV at 5.4.96		£10,957	£975	
Total allowances 1995/96				£4,277

Notes

(*a*) The period 1.5.91 – 5.4.92 falls into the profits basis periods for 1991/92, 1992/93 and 1993/94. It will therefore form the capital allowances basis period for the first year, 1991/92.

(*b*) The period 6.4.92 – 30.4.92 falls into the profits basis periods for both 1992/93 and 1993/94. Again, for capital allowances, the overlap will fall into the earlier year, 1992/93.

(*c*) In 1991/92, $\frac{11}{12}$ of a full year's writing-down allowance will be given because the business was in operation for only eleven months of that period (see 10.28 above). If a first-year allowance had been available, it would not have fallen to be restricted in this way.

Changeover from preceding year to current year basis of assessment.

Transitional year. Interval between basis periods

S continues to trade beyond the turn of the century. He has the following expenditure on machinery and plant in the three years to 30 April 1997.

	Plant	Motor Car
	£	£
Year ended 30 April 1995	3,043	
Year ended 30 April 1996	2,300	4,800
Year ended 30 April 1997	6,400	

The new car was a replacement for the old, which was traded in at a value of £775. There continued to be no private use of either car. An item of plant was sold for £300 in the year to 30 April 1995.

10.33 Capital Allowances (Machinery and Plant)

The capital allowances for the years 1996/97 and 1997/98 are as follows.

		Pool	Pool for cars	Total allowances
		£	£	£
1996/97	(basis period 1.5.94 – 30.4.96)			
	WDV at 6.4.96	10,957	975	
	Additions	5,343	4,800	
	Disposals	(300)	(775)	
		16,000	5,000	
	Allowances			
	WDA 25%	(4,000)	(1,250)	5,250
	WDV c/f	12,000	3,750	
	Total allowances 1996/97			£5,250
Period of account 1.5.96 – 30.4.97 (1997/98)				
	Additions	6,400		
		18,400	3,750	
	Allowances			
	WDA 25%	(4,600)	(938)	£5,538
	WDV c/f	£13,800	£2,812	

Notes

(*a*) The capital allowances basis period for 1996/97 is the period on the profits of which income tax falls to be computed (*CAA 1990, s 160(2) as originally enacted*), which in this case is the two years to 30 April 1996 under the transitional rules (see 71.20 SCHEDULE D, CASES I AND II).

(*b*) The capital allowances of £5,250 for 1996/97 are deductible from the averaged profit for that year (see 71.20 SCHEDULE D, CASES I AND II) in arriving at the taxable profit. The capital allowances are not themselves subject to averaging.

(*c*) For 1997/98 and subsequent years (for businesses commenced before 6 April 1994), capital allowances are given by reference to periods of account (see 10.2(vi) above and the examples below). The allowances of £5,538 for the year to 30 April 1997 are deductible as a trading expense in arriving at the taxable profit for that year. The profit thus arrived at is taxable in 1997/98 on a current year basis, with overlap relief accruing for that part of the profit (*before* capital allowances) which arose before 6 April 1997 (see 71.22 SCHEDULE D, CASES I AND II).

Periods of account

James commences business on 1 October 1998 preparing accounts initially to 30 September. He changes his accounting date in 2000, preparing accounts for the 15 months to 31 December 2000. The following capital expenditure is incurred.

	Plant	Motor Car
	£	£
Year ended 30 September 1999	12,000	4,000 (no private use)
Period ended 31 December 2000	7,500	
Year ended 31 December 2001	4,000	

An item of plant was sold for £500 (original cost £1,000) on 25 September 2000. James' business is a small business for the purposes of first-year allowances.

Profits *before* capital allowances but otherwise as adjusted for tax purposes are as follows.

	£
Year ended 30 September 1999	18,000
Period ended 31 December 2000	25,000
Year ended 31 December 2001	24,000

The capital allowances are

	Qualifying for FYAs	Pool	Pool for cars (n.b. see note (*c*))	Total
	£	£	£	£
Year ended 30.9.99				
Qualifying expenditure	12,000		4,000	
FYA 40%	(4,800)			4,800
WDA 25%			(1,000)	1,000
	7,200			
Transfer to pool	(7,200)	7,200		
WDV at 30.9.99		7,200	3,000	
Total allowances				£5,800
15 months ended 31.12.00				
Additions	7,500			
Disposals		(500)		
		6,700		
FYA 40%	(3,000)			3,000
WDA 25% × $\frac{15}{12}$		(2,094)	(938)	3,032
	4,500	4,606		
Transfer to pool	(4,500)	4,500		
WDV at 31.12 00		c/f 9,106	c/f 2,062	
Total allowances				£6,032

	Qualifying for FYAs	Pool	Pool for cars (n.b. see note (*c*))	Total
	£	£	£	£
		b/f 9,106	b/f 2,062	
Year ended 31.12.01				
Additions	4,000			
FYA 40%	(1,600)			1,600
WDA 25%		(2,277)	(516)	2,793
	2,400	6,829		
Transfer to pool	(2,400)	2,400		
WDV at 31.12.01		9,229	1,546	
Total allowances				£4,393

Taxable profits for the accounting periods concerned are

	Before CAs	CAs	After CAs
	£	£	£
Year ended 30 September 1999	18,000	5,800	12,200
Period ended 31 December 2000	25,000	6,032	18,968
Year ended 31 December 2001	24,000	4,393	19,607

Taxable profits for the first four years of assessment of the business are

	£	£
1998/99 (1.10.98–5.4.99) (£12,200 × $\frac{6}{12}$)		6,100
1999/2000 (y/e 30.9.99)		12,200
2000/01 (1.10.99–31.12.00)	18,968	
Deduct Overlap relief £6,100 × $\frac{3}{6}$	3,050	
		15,918
2001/02 (y/e 31.12.01)		19,607

Notes

(*a*) For businesses commencing after 5 April 1994, capital allowances are calculated by reference to periods of account and are treated as trading expenses (see 10.1, 10.2(vi) above).

(*b*) Where a period of account exceeds 12 months, writing-down allowances are proportionately increased (see 10.28 above).

(*c*) The separate car pool is incorrectly shown as continuing after 5 April 2000 (see 10.35(*a*) below). This will be corrected in future editions.

Period of account exceeding 18 months

Bianca commenced business on 1 October 1998 preparing accounts initially to 30 June. She changes her accounting date in 2000/01, preparing accounts for the 21 months to 31 March 2001. The business qualifies as a small business for the purposes of first-year allowances. The following capital expenditure is incurred.

	Plant	Motor Car
	£	£
Period ended 30 June 1999	24,000	16,000 (no private use)
Period ended 31 March 2001	10,000	
Year ended 31 March 2002	2,150	

Of the £10,000 of expenditure incurred in the 21-month accounting period to 31 March 2001, £3,000 was incurred in the 12 months to 30 June 2000 and £7,000 in the nine months to 31 March 2001.

An item of plant is sold for £675 (original cost £1,000) on 3 November 2000.

Profits *before* capital allowances but otherwise as adjusted for tax purposes are as follows.

	£
Period ended 30 June 1999	30,000
Period ended 31 March 2001	75,000
Year ended 31 March 2002	50,000

The capital allowances are

	Qualifying for FYAs	Pool	Pool for cars	Total
	£	£	£	£
9 months ended 30.6.99				
Qualifying expenditure	24,000		16,000	
FYA 40%	(9,600)			9,600
WDA £3,000 × $\frac{9}{12}$			(2,250)	2,250
	14,400			
	(14,400)	14,400		
WDV at 30.6.99		14,400	13,750	
Total allowances				£11,850
12 months ended 30.6.00				
Additions	3,000			
FYA 40%	(1,200)			1,200
WDA 25%		(3,600)		3,600
WDA £3,000			(3,000)	3,000
	1,800	10,800		
Transfer to pool	(1,800)	1,800		
WDV at 30.6.00		c/f 12,600	c/f 10,750	
Total allowances				£7,800

	Qualifying for FYAs	Pool	Pool for cars	Total
	£	£	£	£
		b/f 12,600	b/f 10,750	
9 months ended 31.3.01				
Additions	7,000			
Disposals		(675)		
		11,925		
FYA 40%	(2,800)			2,800
WDA 25% × $\frac{9}{12}$		(2,236)	(2,016)	4,252
	4,200	9,689		
Transfer to pool	(4,200)	4,200		
WDV at 31.3.01		13,889	8,734	
Total allowances				£7,052
Year ended 31.3.02				
Additions	2,150			
FYA 40%	(860)			860
WDA 25%		(3,472)	(2,184)	5,656
	1,290	10,417		
Transfer to pool	(1,290)	1,290		
WDV at 31.3.02		11,707	6,550	
Total allowances				£6,516

Taxable profits for the accounting periods concerned are

	Before CAs	CAs	After CAs
	£	£	£
Period ended 30 June 1999	30,000	11,850	18,150
Period ended 31 March 2001	75,000	(7,800 + 7,052)	60,148
Year ended 31 March 2002	50,000	6,516	43,484

Taxable profits for the first four years of assessment of the business are

	£	£
1998/99 (1.10.98 – 5.4.99) (£18,150 × $\frac{6}{9}$)		12,100
1999/2000 (1.10.98 – 30.9.99):		
1.10.98 – 30.6.99	18,150	
1.7.99 – 30.9.99 (£60,148 × $\frac{3}{21}$)	8,593	
		26,743
2000/01 (1.10.99 – 31.3.01) (£60,148 × $\frac{18}{21}$)	51,555	
Deduct Overlap relief	(12,100)	
		39,455
2001/02 (y/e 31.3.02)		43,484

Notes

(*a*) Where a period of account for capital allowances purposes would otherwise exceed 18 months, it is broken down into shorter periods, the first beginning on the first day of the actual period and each subsequent period beginning on an anniversary of the first day of the actual period. No period can therefore exceed 12 months. See 10.2(vi) above.

(*b*) The capital allowances computed for the notional periods of account referred to in (*a*) above are deductible in aggregate in arriving at the adjusted profit for the actual accounting period.

(*c*) An accounting period exceeding 18 months cannot normally result in an immediate change of basis period. However, the conditions of *ICTA 1988, s 62A* do not have to be satisfied if the change of accounting period occurs in the second or third year of assessment of a new business, as in this example. See 71.15 SCHEDULE D, CASES I AND II.

10.34 **Entitlement to allowances for fixtures.** For expenditure incurred after 11 July 1984 (but excluding, for chargeable periods ending after 23 July 1996, expenditure under a contract entered into on or before that date, or pursuant to an obligation in a lease, or agreement for a lease, entered into on or before that date), there are special provisions to determine entitlement to allowances on fixtures which, by law, become part of the building or land on which they are installed or otherwise fixed, including any boiler or water-filled radiator installed as part of a space or water heating system. A dispute may arise as to whether fixtures have, in law, become part of a building or land. Where two or more persons' tax liabilities are affected by the outcome of such a dispute, the question is determined *for tax purposes* by the Special Commissioners, before whom all those persons are entitled to appear and be heard or to make written representations. [*CAA 1990, s 51(1)–(2A)(7); FA 1997, Sch 16 para 2(5)(6); FA 2000, s 78*].

In *J C Decaux (UK) Ltd v Francis (Sp C 84), [1996] SSCD 281*, automatic public conveniences and other street furniture such as bus shelters were held to be fixtures forming part of the land (and see (*a*) below).

These provisions determine to whom fixtures belong for allowance purposes in each of the various circumstances described at (*a*)–(*g*) below, and deny allowances to any other person in respect of those fixtures (except to a person contributing towards the capital expenditure, see 10.2(ii) above). Where fixtures are accordingly treated as ceasing to belong to a person at any time without being permanently severed from the land, and the interest as a result of which they were previously treated as belonging to him continues in existence (or would do so but for being merged in another interest), the fixtures are treated as being sold at that time for capital allowance purposes. The *deemed sale price* (subject as below) of the fixtures is

(1) on a sale of the qualifying interest at open market value or higher, or where the purchaser's expenditure can be taken into account for capital allowance purposes, that part of the sale price which falls (or would, if there were an entitlement, fall) to be treated for capital allowance purposes as on the provision of the fixtures;

(2) on the grant of a lease out of the qualifying interest, so much of the consideration for the lease as falls to be treated for capital allowance purposes as expenditure by the lessee on the provision of the fixtures;

(3) if neither (1) nor (2) applies, the amount which, if that interest were sold in the open market at that time, would be treated for capital allowance purposes as expenditure by the purchaser on provision of the fixtures (ignoring the event giving rise to the deemed sale).

[*CAA 1990, s 51(1)(8), s 59(1)–(6)*].

Although the rules apply strictly on an asset-by-asset basis, the Revenue in practice accept that they may be applied to groups of assets provided that this does not distort the tax computation. (Revenue Tax Bulletin June 1998 p 552).

For chargeable periods ending after 23 July 1996, and where the event concerned occurs after that date, fixtures are treated as disposed of at their 'notional written-down value' (if greater than would otherwise be the case) where the event giving rise to the bringing in of a disposal value is part of a scheme or arrangement having tax avoidance (whether by increased allowances or reduced charges) as a main object. The '*notional written-down value*' is the disposal value which would give rise to no balancing adjustment, disregarding all other qualifying expenditure and assuming full allowances to have been granted. [*CAA 1990, s 59A; FA 1997, Sch 16 para 5*].

A special election is available for chargeable periods ending on or after 19 March 1996 where the disposal value of fixtures falls to be determined under (1) or (2) above at a time on or after that date. Subject as below and to *CAA 1990, ss 56C, 56D* (see (*h*) below) and *s 59A* (above), the purchaser and former owner may jointly elect to fix the amount so determined at a figure not exceeding either the capital expenditure treated as incurred on the fixtures by the former owner or the actual sale price (or capital sum). The remainder (if any) of the sale price (or capital sum) is attributed to the other property included in the sale. The notice of election must be given to the Board within two years after the interest is acquired or the lease granted, and is irrevocable. A copy must also accompany the return of the persons making the election. The notice must contain prescribed information and must quantify the amount fixed by the election, although if subsequent circumstances reduce the maximum below that fixed, the election is treated as being for that reduced maximum amount. There are provisions for the determination of questions relating to such elections by appeal Commissioners. Where any person becomes aware that a return of his has become incorrect because of such an election (or because of subsequent circumstances affecting the election), the necessary amendments to the return must be notified to an officer of the Board within three months of his becoming so aware (or by 19 June 1997 if later), subject to penalties for failure. [*CAA 1990, s 51(6A), s 59B, s 59C; FA 1997, Sch 16 para 2(4)(7), para 6, para 9; FA 1999, Sch 11 para 6*]. In practice, the Revenue normally accept an election covering a group of fixtures, or all the fixtures in a single property, but not one covering fixtures in different properties (e.g. where a portfolio of properties is sold). (Revenue Tax Bulletin June 1998 p 552).

There are also special rules for determining the disposal value to be brought in where the qualifying interest expires, where the trade ceases, and where the fixtures start to be used for non-trade purposes. [*CAA 1990, s 59(7)–(9)*].

The expenditure by the new owner of the fixtures which attracts capital allowances is restricted to any disposal value brought in on the former owner. This does not apply where the fixtures cease to belong to the former owner on or after 24 July 1996, and where they so ceased before that date continue *not* to apply where the former owner's expenditure was under a contract entered into on or before 11 July 1984 (or pursuant to an obligation in a lease, or agreement for a lease, entered into on or before that date), notwithstanding the repeal of the general transitional saving provision for chargeable periods ending on or after 24 July 1996 (see above). [*CAA 1990, s 59(10)(11); FA 1997, Sch 16 para 2(8), Sch 18 Pt VI(12)*].

For these purposes an '*interest in land*' is

(i) the fee simple estate in the land;

(ii) in Scotland, the estate or interest of the proprietor of the *dominium utile* (in the case of property other than feudal property, the owner);

(iii) any leasehold estate in, or in Scotland lease of, the land;

(iv) an easement or servitude;

(v) a licence to occupy land;

and any agreement to acquire an interest as at (i)–(iv) above. Where an interest is conveyed or assigned by way of security subject to a right of redemption, the interest is treated as continuing to belong to the person having the redemption right. [*CAA 1990, s 51(3)(4)*]. As regards (v) above, for the Revenue view of when a licence to occupy land exists for these purposes, see Revenue Tax Bulletin June 2000 p 761.

(*a*) *Expenditure incurred by holder of interest in land.* Where a person having an interest in land incurs capital expenditure on fixtures which become part of that land, for the purposes of a trade (or, before 1 April 1998, for leasing purposes), then, subject to (*b*)–(*f*) below, the fixtures are treated as belonging to that person. If there are two or more such persons, with different interests, the only interest to be taken into account for this purpose is

(i) an easement or servitude, or any agreement to acquire same;

(ii) if (i) does not apply to any of those interests, a licence to occupy the land;

(iii) if neither (i) nor (ii) applies to any of those interests, that interest which is not directly or indirectly in reversion on any other of those interests in the land (in Scotland, that of whichever of those persons has, or last had, the right of use of the land).

[*CAA 1990, s 52; FA 1998, s 38, Sch 5 para 53*].

In *J C Decaux (UK) Ltd v Francis (Sp C 84), [1996] SSCD 281*, suppliers to local authorities of automatic public conveniences and other street furniture such as bus shelters, which were held to be fixtures forming part of the land, were held not to have an interest in the land.

(*b*) *Expenditure incurred by equipment lessor.* Where an equipment lessor incurs capital expenditure on machinery or plant for leasing, and an agreement is entered into for lease of the machinery or plant as fixtures, otherwise than as part of the land to which they are attached, to another person for the purposes of a trade carried on or to be carried on by him (or, before 1 April 1998, for leasing), an election may be available to the lessor and lessee. Provided that

(i) the use under the agreement is not in a dwelling-house,

(ii) the lessee is within the charge to UK tax on profits from the trade for use in which the equipment is leased (or, before 1 April 1998, from the leasing on of the equipment), and

(iii) (except as below) if the expenditure had been incurred by the lessee, he would, under (*a*) above, have been entitled to allowances in respect of that expenditure as being expenditure on the fixtures,

they may jointly elect in writing for the fixtures to be treated, from the time the expenditure is incurred, as belonging to the lessor and not the lessee. Where, however, the lessee's trade is not being carried on at the time of the agreement, the election takes effect from the later of the time the expenditure is incurred and the time the trade begins to be carried on. Also, where the following conditions are satisfied, (ii) and (iii) above, and the requirement that the fixtures are leased for the purposes of the lessee's trade, do not apply:

(1) the machinery or plant becomes a fixture by being fixed to land which is neither a building nor part of a building;

(2) the lessee has an interest in that land when he takes possession of the machinery or plant under the agreement;

(3) under the terms of the agreement the lessor is entitled, at the end of the lease period, to sever the machinery or plant from the land to which it is then fixed, whereon it will belong to the lessor;

(4) the nature of the machinery or plant and the way it is fixed to the land are such that its use does not, to any material extent, prevent its being used, after severance, for the same purposes on different premises; and

(5) the agreement is such as falls under normal accountancy practice to be treated, in the accounts of UK incorporated equipment lessors, as an operating lease.

For 2000/01 and subsequent years (for corporation tax, for accounting periods ending after 20 March 2000), the requirement at (ii) above is repealed, having been superseded by the requirement that non-UK activities of a trade be treated as a separate trade not generally treated as constituting a trade (or deemed trade) for the purposes of machinery and plant capital allowances (see 10.24 above). This general requirement is accordingly *not* disapplied where (1)–(5) above are satisfied.

For chargeable periods ending before 19 March 1997, and in relation to agreements entered into before that day, the election is not available where the lessee's trade was not being carried on at the time of the agreement, and the waiver of certain requirements (as above) where conditions (1)–(5) above are satisfied does not apply. For chargeable periods ending before 24 July 1996, and for expenditure incurred by the lessor before that date, conditions (i) and (ii) above do not apply, and (iii) above is replaced by a requirement that, if the expenditure had been incurred by the lessee, the equipment would, under (*a*) above, have been treated as belonging to him (for which see *Melluish v BMI (No 3) Ltd HL 1995, 68 TC 1*).

The time limit for the election is (i) for income tax for 1996/97 onwards (subject to (ii) below), within twelve months after 31 January following the tax year in which ends the lessor's chargeable period in which the expenditure is incurred, (ii) for income tax for 1996/97 only as regards trades etc. commenced before 6 April 1994, on or before 31 January 1999, and (iii) for income tax for earlier years and for corporation tax, within two years after the end of the lessor's chargeable period in which, or in the basis period for which, the expenditure was incurred. No election is available if lessor and lessee are CONNECTED PERSONS (20).

Where expenditure is incurred on or after 28 July 2000 and before 1 January 2008 on machinery or plant consisting of a boiler, heat exchanger, radiator or heating control installed in a building as part of a space or water heating system, and the agreement for the lease is approved under the Affordable Warmth programme by the Secretary of State (or the responsible Scottish, Welsh or NI body), these provisions have effect without any requirement for the equipment to be leased for the purposes of a trade carried on by the equipment lessee and without (i)–(iii) above having to be satisfied. If the approval is withdrawn, it is treated as never having had effect, and all necessary consequential adjustments must be made. The taxpayer must notify the inspector, within three months of his becoming aware that a return of his has become incorrect by reason of the withdrawal of approval, of the amendments to the return required in consequence of the withdrawal, subject to penalties for failure.

See also (*g*) below.

Such an agreement as is described above, or a lease entered into pursuant to such an agreement, is referred to below as an *'equipment lease'*. [*CAA 1990, s 53; FA 1996, s 135, Sch 21 para 31; FA 1997, Sch 16 para 3; FA 1998, s 38, Sch 5 para 54, Sch 27 Pt III(4); FA 2000, s 75(5)(6), s 79*].

(*c*) *Expenditure included in consideration for acquisition of existing interest in land.* Where a person acquires a pre-existing interest in land to which fixtures are attached, for a consideration in part treated for capital allowance purposes as being expenditure on provision of the fixtures, and (for chargeable periods ending before 24 July 1996, or where the acquisition was before that date) either no person had previously been entitled to allowances on the fixtures, or any person previously so entitled is or has been required to bring in a disposal value (other than by virtue of an 'additional VAT rebate' — see 10.2(v) above) in respect of them, then the fixtures are treated as belonging to the person acquiring the interest. This applies equally where the fixtures in question were previously let under an 'equipment lease' (see (*b*) above) and, in connection with the acquisition, the purchaser pays a capital sum to discharge the lessee's obligations under that lease. [*CAA 1990, s 54; FA 1991, Sch 14 para 10; FA 1997, Sch 16 paras 2, 4, 5*]. See now (*h*) below.

(*d*) *Expenditure incurred by incoming lessee: election to transfer right to allowances.* Where a person with an interest in land to which fixtures are attached grants a lease (or enters into an agreement for a lease) and, apart from (*f*) below, he would (or if chargeable to tax would) be entitled, for the chargeable period relating to the grant of the lease (or the agreement), to capital allowances in respect of the fixtures, and the consideration given by the lessee falls in part to be treated for capital allowance purposes as expenditure on the provision of the fixtures, an election may be available to the lessor and lessee. They may jointly elect (in writing within two years of the date on which the lease or agreement takes effect) that, from the grant of the lease (or the agreement), the fixtures are treated as belonging to the lessee and not to the lessor. No election is, however, available if lessor and lessee are CONNECTED PERSONS (20), or (where the lease was granted before 24 July 1996) if it appears that the sole or main benefit to the lessor from the grant of the lease (or the agreement) and the election would be enhanced capital allowances or a reduced balancing charge (and see now *CAA 1990, s 59A*, above). [*CAA 1990, ss 52, 55, 57(5); FA 1997, Sch 18 Pt VI (12)*].

(*e*) *Expenditure incurred by incoming lessee: lessor not entitled to allowances.* Where

- (i) (*d*) above does not apply because the lessor is not entitled to capital allowances in respect of the fixtures,
- (ii) at the time of grant of the lease (or the agreement) no person has previously become so entitled,
- (iii) before that time the fixtures have not been used for trade purposes by the lessor or a person connected with him (see 20 CONNECTED PERSONS), and
- (iv) the consideration given by the lessee includes a capital sum falling to be treated wholly or partly as expenditure on the provision of the fixtures,

the fixtures are treated as belonging to the lessee. For chargeable periods ending after 23 July 1996, and where the lease was granted after that date, (ii) above does not apply (but see now (*h*) below). [*CAA 1990, ss 52, 56; FA 1997, Sch 16 paras 3, 4, 6*].

(*f*) *Cases where fixture is to be treated as ceasing to belong to a particular person.* Where a person to whom fixtures are treated as belonging under (*a*), (*c*), (*d*) or (*e*) above ceases for any reason to have the interest giving rise to that treatment, the fixtures are at that time treated as ceasing to belong to him for capital allowance purposes. An agreement to acquire an interest and the interest subsequently acquired under the agreement are treated for this purpose as the same interest. Similarly, an interest into which the interest in question is merged, or an interest consisting of a new lease or licence following termination of a previous lease or licence which was the interest in question, is treated as the same interest as the interest in question. If the interest in question is a lease, and the lessee remains in possession with the lessor's consent following its termination without a new lease, the interest is treated as continuing as long as the possession continues.

Where, under these provisions, fixtures are treated as ceasing to belong to a person on termination of a lease or licence, they are treated as commencing to belong to the lessor or licensor immediately before the termination.

Where fixtures treated under these provisions as belonging to a person are severed from the land to which they are attached, they are treated as ceasing to belong to that person, unless they in fact belong to him. [*CAA 1990, s 57*].

(*g*) *Special provisions as to equipment lessors.* Where an election is made under (*b*) above, and either

(i) the lessor assigns his rights under the equipment lease; or

(ii) the lessee's financial obligations under the lease are discharged,

then the fixtures are treated as ceasing to belong to the lessor by reason of a sale by him.

If (i) above applies, then, from the time of the assignment, the fixtures are treated as belonging to the assignee for capital allowance purposes, and the consideration for the assignment treated as consideration for the fixtures. If the assignee makes any further assignment, he is treated under this provision as if he were the original lessor.

If (ii) above applies and a capital sum is paid in consideration of the discharge, that sum is treated as consideration for the fixtures, and the fixtures are treated from the time of the payment as belonging to the lessee (or to any other person in whom his obligations under the lease have become vested). [*CAA 1990, s 58*].

(*h*) *Fixtures in respect of which more than one person gets an allowance.* For chargeable periods ending after 23 July 1996, where (*c*) or (*e*) above would otherwise apply, they are treated as not applying (and as never having applied) where the following conditions are satisfied:

(i) an interest in any land in which the whole or part of the land to which the fixtures are attached is comprised is held by any person immediately after the '*relevant time*' (i.e. in relation to (*c*) above, the time when the purchaser acquires his interest in the land to which the fixtures are attached, or, in relation to (*e*) above, the time of the grant of the lease, but in either case disregarding events before 24 July 1996);

(ii) that interest is not the one acquired by the purchaser (in relation to (*c*) above) or by the lessee (in relation to (*e*) above);

(iii) the fixtures fall to be treated (other than under *CAA 1990, s 154* (contributions to expenditure), see 10.2(ii) above) as having belonged to the person with that interest, in consequence of his having incurred expenditure on its provision, immediately before the relevant time; and

(iv) that person is entitled to, and claims, an allowance in respect of that expenditure.

Where any person becomes aware that a return of his has become incorrect because of the operation of this provision, the necessary amendments to the return must be notified to an officer of the Board within three months of his becoming so aware (or by 19 June 1997 if later), subject to penalties for failure.

[*CAA 1990, ss 51(6A), 56A; FA 1997, Sch 16 para 2(4)(7), para 4, para 9*].

Where, for chargeable periods ending after 23 July 1996:

(A) fixtures are treated under these provisions as belonging to any person in consequence of his incurring capital expenditure on their provision;

(B) the fixtures fall or have fallen (other than under *CAA 1990, s 154* (contributions to expenditure, see 10.2(ii) above)) to be treated as having belonged at a 'relevant earlier time' to a person (who may be the same as the person within (A) above) in consequence of his incurring expenditure other than that within (A) above, and that person, having claimed an allowance for that expenditure, must bring in a disposal value for the fixtures by reason of an event occurring after 23 July 1996,

so much (if any) of the expenditure referred to in (A) above as exceeds the 'maximum allowable amount' is disregarded under these provisions or, as the case may be, is taken to be expenditure which should never have been taken into account.

A '*relevant earlier time*' is a time before that taken under these provisions to be the earliest time when the fixtures belonged to the person referred to in (A) above in consequence of the expenditure referred to therein. A time is, however, disregarded if, subsequently but before that earliest time, the machinery or plant was sold other than as a fixture to an unconnected person (see 20 CONNECTED PERSONS).

The '*maximum allowable amount*' is the sum of the disposal value referred to in (B) above and so much (if any) of the expenditure referred to in (A) above as is deemed under *CAA 1990, s 66* (installation costs, see 10.25 above) to be on provision of the fixtures. Where (B) above is satisfied in relation to more than one event, only the most recent event is taken into account for this purpose.

Where any person becomes aware that a return of his has become incorrect because of the operation of this provision, the necessary amendments to the return must be notified to an officer of the Board within three months of his becoming so aware (or by 19 June 1997 if later), subject to penalties for failure.

[*CAA 1990, ss 51(6A), 56B; FA 1997, Sch 16 para 2(4)(7), para 4, para 9*].

Where, for chargeable periods ending after 23 July 1996:

(1) a person has claimed industrial buildings allowances for expenditure partly on the provision of machinery or plant, and transfers the relevant interest in the building, etc. concerned; and

(2) the transferee, or any other person to whom the machinery or plant is subsequently treated under these provisions as belonging, claims machinery and plant allowances for expenditure incurred thereon at a time after 23 July 1996 when it is a fixture in the building, etc.,

the claim may not exceed the '*relevant amount*', i.e. the proportion of the consideration for the transfer referred to in (1) above attributable to the fixture. It is assumed for this purpose that the transfer was a sale for an amount equal to the residue of expenditure (see 10.14 above) immediately after the transfer.

A similar restriction applies where scientific research or research and development allowances have previously been claimed.

[*CAA 1990, ss 56C, 56D; FA 1997, Sch 16 para 4; FA 2000, Sch 19 para 8*].

See generally Revenue Capital Allowances Manual, CA 2510–2664.

Finance leasing. See 71.68 SCHEDULE D, CASES I AND II as regards restrictions on capital allowances where certain finance leasing arrangements are involved. See also 10.28 above, 10.38(iii)(vi) below.

10.35 **Leasing of machinery and plant.** Legislation regarding capital allowances on machinery and plant provided for leasing was first introduced in 1980 and was mainly concerned with restricting the availability of first-year allowances. Further legislation introduced in 1982 restricted, and in some cases prohibited, writing-down allowances on machinery and plant leased to non-UK resident lessees in certain circumstances. Following the phasing out of first-year allowances, much of the original legislation was no longer appropriate and the leasing provisions were widely amended by the *Finance Act 1986* but so as to broadly retain those relating to overseas leasing. For the purposes of applying the 1986 changes expenditure incurred after 31 March 1986 (with the exceptions below) was designated 'new expenditure'. The current provisions are contained in *CAA 1990, ss 39–50.*

For the purposes of these provisions, a 'lease' includes a sub-lease, with 'lessor' and 'lessee' being construed accordingly, and 'leasing' is regarded as including the letting of any asset on hire or of a ship on charter (and see *Barclays Mercantile Industrial Finance Ltd v Melluish Ch D 1990, 63 TC 95* at (*d*) below). [*CAA 1990, s 50(1)(2)*].

'*New expenditure*' means expenditure incurred after 31 March 1986 on machinery and plant other than certain cars costing £12,000 or less (see (*a*) below), provided that it is not 'old expenditure'. '*Old expenditure*' means the following.

(A) Certain expenditure for which a first-year allowance (other than an allowance for a small or medium-sized enterprise under *CAA 1990, s 22(3B)–(3E)*) would (apart from the leasing restrictions) be available (see 10.27 above).

(B) Certain expenditure incurred before 1 June 1986 on 'television sets' (to which separate provisions applied — see below).

(C) Certain expenditure on acquisition of an asset by a person connected with (see 20 CONNECTED PERSONS), or succeeding to a trade carried on by, the person who originally incurred expenditure on its acquisition before 1 April 1986.

[*CAA 1990, s 50(3); FA 1993, Sch 13 para 11(1); F(No 2)A 1997, s 42(6); FA 1998, s 85(4); FA 2000, s 71(2)*].

Assets leased outside the UK. The provisions described below apply to both 'new' and 'old expenditure' on the provision of machinery or plant which at any time in the 'requisite period' is leased to a person who

(1) is not resident in the UK, and

(2) does not use the machinery etc. exclusively for earning profits chargeable to UK tax, being either profits from a trade carried on in the UK or from exploration or exploitation activities carried on in the UK or its territorial sea.

Where there is a chain of leases, the Revenue now consider that the provisions apply where any lessee in the chain falls within (1) and (2) above. Their view had previously been that only the end lessee need be considered, and they will act in accordance with their earlier view for leasing arrangements entered into before 19 April 1999, or within three months after that date where the principal terms had been agreed in writing before that date (e.g. in an agreed term-sheet or accepted offer letter) and had not materially altered in the intervening period. (Revenue Tax Bulletin April 1999 p 654).

For the purpose of (2) above, profits chargeable to UK tax do not include profits in respect of which the trader etc. is entitled to tax relief under a double taxation agreement. This does not apply in the case of leases entered into before 16 March 1993 for which, in addition, the use of the machinery etc. does not have to be *exclusively* for the purposes stated. The provisions do not apply where the leasing is either 'short-term leasing' (see (*e*) below) or, as regards 'new expenditure' only, the leasing of a ship, aircraft or transport container used for a 'qualifying purpose' by virtue of *CAA 1990, s 39(6)–(9)* (see (*d*) below). [*CAA 1990, s 42(1)(8), s 50(3A); FA 1993, s 116(2)–(4)*]. The provisions apply to expenditure incurred on or after 10 March 1982. There was an exclusion for expenditure consisting of payments made under a contract entered into before that date or, under certain conditions relating to arrangements in existence at that date, before 1 April 1984, provided in either case that the machinery was brought into use before 1 April 1985. [*FA 1982, s 70(10)(12)*].

The provisions referred to above are as follows.

(*a*) *Restriction of writing-down allowances and separate pooling.* Writing-down allowances on machinery or plant within these provisions are restricted to **10% p.a.** (instead of the normal 25% p.a.). This does not, however, displace the 6% rate applicable to certain long-life assets (see 10.28(G) above). [*CAA 1990, s 42(2); FA 1997, Sch 14 para 5*]. For this purpose, the machinery etc. is treated as being provided for a separate notional trade, i.e. it is separately pooled. The notional trade is regarded as permanently discontinued when all items in the separate pool begin to be used wholly or partly for purposes other than those of the actual trade (or are disposed of, lost or cease to exist). A lessor need not claim the full amount of writing-down allowances. When machinery and plant in the separate pool is disposed of to a CONNECTED PERSON (20) (otherwise than on an occasion when the trade is treated as continuing) the 'disposal value' is its open market value or, if lower, its original cost, and the person acquiring it may claim allowances on the same value. [*CAA 1990, s 41(1)–(3)(5); FA 1990, Sch 17 para 9*].

The above separate pooling provisions do not apply to cars costing over £12,000, assets used partially for non-trade purposes, long-life assets and assets for which contributions are received towards wear and tear, all of which remain outside the main pool of qualifying expenditure in any case (see 10.28(A)(C)(G) above, 10.38(xii) below). The restriction on writing-down allowances *does* so apply (except to long-life assets, see above). *Cars costing £12,000 or less* (£8,000 for expenditure incurred or treated as incurred before 11 March 1992), and which are not leased so as to be otherwise within these provisions, had previously also to be included in a separate pool under *section 41* but *not* the same pool as that used for leased assets. [*CAA 1990, s 41(1)(c)(4)(6), s 42(2); FA 1997, Sch 14 para 4*]. The car pool also included any 'old expenditure' on machinery and plant provided for leasing which was precluded by *CAA 1990, s 22(4)(c)* from qualifying for a first-year allowance (or would have been if a first-year allowance had not already been precluded by *CAA 1990, s 75* (sales between connected persons etc.)). [*CAA 1990, s 41(1)(b)*]. This separate 'car and old expenditure' pool is, however, abolished for 2000/01 onwards (for corporation tax, for accounting periods ending after 31 March 2000), subject to an election for the cessation to be delayed by one year in relation to any particular notional trade. Any balance of qualifying expenditure over disposal value(s) brought into account in the immediately preceding accounting period of the notional trade is treated as qualifying expenditure brought forward to the following period in the actual trade. [*FA 2000, s 74*].

(*b*) *Prohibition of allowances.* No writing-down or balancing allowances are available in respect of expenditure to which the overseas leasing provisions apply if the machinery etc. is used other than for a 'qualifying purpose' (see (*d*) below) and

(i) there is more than one year between consecutive payments due under the lease, or

(ii) any payments other than periodical payments are due under the lease or under any collateral agreement, or

(iii) any payment expressed monthly under the lease or any collateral agreement is not the same as any other such payment, but disregarding variations due to changes in rates of tax, capital allowances, interest which is linked with rates applicable to inter-bank loans or changes in premiums for insurances of any kind by a person not connected with the lessor or lessee, or

(iv) either the lease is for a period exceeding thirteen years or there is any provision for its extension or renewal or for the grant of a new lease so that the leasing period could exceed thirteen years, or

(v) at any time, the lessor or CONNECTED PERSON (20) could be entitled to receive from the lessee or any other person a payment (not insurance moneys) of an amount determined before expiry of the lease and referable to the value of the machinery etc. at or after that expiry (whether or not the payment relates to a disposal of the machinery etc.).

[*CAA 1990, s 42(3)*].

Where allowances (including any first-year allowance) have been made (and not fully withdrawn under the excess relief provisions in (*g*) below) but by reason of any event in the 'requisite period' (see (*c*) below) are found to be prohibited as above (assuming, where relevant, first-year allowances to be so prohibited), the net allowances are clawed back by means of a balancing charge. For this purpose only, the allowances made on an item of 'new expenditure' are determined as if that were the only item, i.e. as if it had not been pooled with any other item of machinery etc. Where an item was acquired from a CONNECTED PERSON (20), or as a part of a series of transactions with connected persons, allowances made to those persons are also taken into account in computing the balancing charge, with any actual consideration on a connected persons transaction being ignored and with the amount of such allowances being adjusted as is 'just and reasonable in the circumstances' where balancing allowances/charges have already been made in respect of the item in question. This does not apply in the case of transactions between connected persons on which the trade was treated as continuing under *ICTA 1988, s 113(2)* or *s 114(1)* (partnership changes treated as a continuation) or *ICTA 1988, s 343(2)* (company reconstruction without change of ownership) or *CAA 1990, s 77(1)* (succession to trade before 30 July 1988 between connected persons). [*CAA 1990, s 42(3)–(9); FA 1993, Sch 13 para 6; F(No 2)A 1997, s 42(6); FA 1998, s 85(4); FA 2000, s 71(2)*].

(*c*) '*Requisite period*'. The '*requisite period*', for 'new expenditure' and for 'old expenditure' falling within the overseas leasing provisions and not used for a 'qualifying purpose' (see (*d*) below), is the period of ten years after the asset is first brought into use by the person who incurred the expenditure, but ends earlier if the asset ceases to belong to that person (but ignoring a disposal to a CONNECTED PERSON (20) or on a partnership change which is treated as a continuation under *ICTA 1988, s 113(2)* or disregarded under *ICTA 1988, s 114(1)*). For other 'old expenditure', the '*requisite period*' is one of four years, with the same rule as above for earlier disposals. For leases entered into before 16 March 1993, what would otherwise have been a ten-year maximum requisite period was reduced to a maximum of four years if the machinery etc. was used for a 'qualifying purpose' (see (*d*) below); for later leases, this applies only in defining the '*requisite period*' for the purposes of the provisions for writing-down allowances on ships (see 10.28(B) above) and the short-life asset provisions (see 10.28(F) above). [*CAA 1990, s 40(4)(5); FA 1993, s 116(1)*].

(*d*) '*Qualifying purpose*'. Machinery or plant on which a person (the buyer) has incurred expenditure is used for a '*qualifying purpose*' at any time if, at that time:

(i) it is used by a lessee for the purposes of a trade (other than leasing), the buyer's expenditure was 'new expenditure' and had the lessee bought the machinery etc. himself at that time, and incurred 'new expenditure' in doing so, it would have fallen to be wholly or partly included in his qualifying expenditure for writing-down allowances; or

(ii) it is used by a lessee for the purposes of a trade (other than leasing), the buyer's expenditure was 'old expenditure' and had the lessee bought the machinery etc. himself at that time, and incurred capital expenditure in doing so, he would have been entitled to a first-year allowance (disregarding the withdrawal of such allowances after 31 March 1986 (see 10.27 above) and ignoring double allowances provisions (see 10.38(iv) below)); or

(iii) the buyer uses it for 'short-term leasing' (see (*e*) below); or

(iv) the lessee uses it for 'short-term leasing' and is either UK resident or so uses it in the course of a trade carried on in the UK; or

(v) the buyer uses it for the purposes of a trade other than leasing.

For the purposes of (iii) and (v) above, where during the 'requisite period' (see (*c*) above) an asset is disposed of to a connected person, or on a partnership change treated as a continuation under *ICTA 1988, s 113(2)* or disregarded under *ICTA 1988, s 114(1)*, the new owner is treated as the 'buyer'. [*CAA 1990, s 39(1)–(5)(10); FA 1993, Sch 13 para 5(1)*].

As regards (i) and (ii) above, the use by the lessee must be *wholly* for the purposes of a trade otherwise than for leasing, but the word 'leasing' is to be construed in accordance with the narrow test applicable to leases of land, so that distribution agreements entered into by film lessee companies were not leases for these purposes but arrangements entered into in the ordinary course of the lessees' businesses (*Barclays Mercantile Industrial Finance Ltd v Melluish Ch D 1990, 63 TC 95*).

Without prejudice to (i)–(v) above, a ship is also used for a '*qualifying purpose*' at any time when it is let on charter in the course of a trade of operating ships if the lessor is resident, or carries on his trade, in the UK and is responsible as principal (or appoints another person to be responsible in his stead) for navigating and managing the ship and for defraying substantially all its expenses except those directly incidental to a particular voyage or charter period. The same applies with necessary modifications in relation to aircraft. However, neither ship nor aircraft chartering qualifies if the main object, or one of them, of the chartering (or of a series of transactions of which the chartering was one) was the obtaining by any person of a first-year allowance or, for 'new expenditure' only, an unrestricted writing-down allowance. A transport container is also used for a '*qualifying purpose*' at any time when it is leased in the course of a trade carried on in the UK or by a UK resident if either the trade is one of operating ships or aircraft and the container is at other times used by the trader in connection with such operation, or the container is leased under a succession of leases to different persons who, or most of whom, are not connected with each other. [*CAA 1990, s 39(6)–(9); FA 1993, Sch 13 para 5(2)*].

(*e*) '*Short-term leasing*' means leasing an item of machinery or plant in such a manner

(i) that (A) the number of consecutive days for which it is leased to the same person will normally be less than 30 and (B) the total number of days to the same person in any period of 12 months will normally be less than 90, or

(ii) that (A) the number of consecutive days for which it is leased to the same person will not normally exceed 365 and (B) the aggregate of the periods for which it is leased to lessees not falling within (*d*)(i)(ii) above will not exceed 2 years in the 'requisite period' (see (*c*) above) or, where the requisite period exceeds 4 years, in any period of 4 consecutive years falling within the 'requisite period'.

For the above purposes, persons who are connected with each other (see CONNECTED PERSONS (20)) will be treated as the same person and where machinery or plant is leased from a pool of items of similar description and not separately identifiable, all the items in the pool may be treated as used for short-term leasing if substantially the whole of the items in the pool are so used. [*CAA 1990, s 40(1)–(3)*].

(*f*) *Joint lessees.* Where machinery or plant on which 'new expenditure' has been incurred

(i) is leased (otherwise than by 'permitted leasing' — see below) to two or more persons jointly, and

(ii) at least one of the joint lessees is a person within (1) and (2) above,

the normal 25% writing-down allowance, and where applicable first-year allowances as reinstated for small or medium-sized enterprises, is due only to the extent that it appears that the profits of the trade or trades (other than leasing) in which the item is used during the 'requisite period' (see (*c*) above), or the period of the lease if shorter, will be chargeable to income tax or corporation tax. The part of the expenditure so qualifying for normal allowances is treated as if it were expenditure on a separate item of machinery etc. with the remaining part treated as expenditure within the overseas leasing provisions, with such apportionments as are necessary. [*CAA 1990, s 43; FA 1993, Sch 14 para 7; FA 1997, Sch 14 para 6; F(No 2)A 1997, s 42(8); FA 1998, s 85(7); FA 2000, s 71(3)*]. Excess relief is recoverable under (*g*) below if at any time in the requisite period while the item is so leased, no lessee uses it for the purposes of such a trade or if, at the end of the requisite period, it appears that the actual extent of such trade use was less than anticipated. In the latter case the amount of excess relief recoverable is in proportion to the reduction in use and any disposal value subsequently brought into account is apportioned to the extent of such trade use as determined at the end of the requisite period. [*CAA 1990, s 44; FA 1993, Sch 13 para 8*]. Broadly similar provisions apply in relation to both first-year and writing-down allowances on 'old expenditure'. [*CAA 1990, s 45*].

'*Permitted leasing*' means 'short-term leasing' (see (*e*) above) or the leasing of a ship, aircraft or transport container which is used for a 'qualifying purpose' by virtue of *CAA 1990, s 39(6)–(9)* (see (*d*) above). [*CAA 1990, s 50(3)*].

(*g*) *Recovery of excess relief.* Where 'new expenditure' has qualified for the normal 25% writing-down allowance (or for first-year allowances) and the machinery or plant is at any time in the 'requisite period' (see (*c*) above) used for the purpose of leasing to a non-resident within (1) and (2) above, otherwise than by 'permitted leasing' (see (*f*) above), any 'excess relief' is recovered. This is achieved by means of a balancing charge of an amount equal to the excess relief, to be made on the person to whom the item then belongs, for the chargeable period in which, or in the basis period for which, the change of use occurs. The item is removed from the general pool of qualifying expenditure by means of a disposal value equal to the item's written-down value for capital allowances purposes. The sum of the excess relief and the disposal value is then regarded as qualifying expenditure for the next chargeable period in the separate notional trade for assets leased overseas (see (*a*) above). The '*excess relief*' is the excess, if any, of the allowances made, up to and including the chargeable period in question, over the maximum writing-down allowances that could have been made if the expenditure had been within (*a*) or (*b*) above from the outset. The allowances made are determined for this purpose as if the item in question were the only item, i.e. as if it had not been pooled with any other item of machinery etc.

Where the person on whom the balancing charge falls to be made acquired the item in question from a CONNECTED PERSON (20), or as part of a series of transactions with connected persons, normal writing-down allowances and any first-year allowance made to those persons are taken into account in computing the excess relief, with any actual consideration on a connected persons transaction being ignored and with the amount of excess relief being adjusted as is 'just and reasonable in the circumstances' where balancing allowances/charges have already been made in respect of the item in question. This does not apply in the case of transactions between connected persons on which the trade was treated as continuing under *ICTA 1988, s 113(2)* or *s 114(1)* (partnership changes treated as a continuation) or *ICTA 1988, s 343(2)* (company reconstruction without change of ownership) or *CAA 1990, s 77* (succession to trade between connected persons). Where relief has been obtained by means of a balancing allowance instead of claiming (or by disclaimer of) a normal writing-down allowance or first-year allowance, excess relief is recovered under these provisions suitably modified.

In the case of ships, any allowance deferred (see 10.27, 10.28(B) above) may not be made for any chargeable period in or after which the change of use occurs, but is instead treated as qualifying expenditure for the next chargeable period in the separate notional trade.

[*CAA 1990, s 46; FA 1990, Sch 17 para 10; FA 1993, Sch 13 para 9; FA 1994, Sch 26 Pt V(24); FA 1997, Sch 14 para 7; F(No 2)A 1997, s 42(6); FA 1998, s 85(5); FA 2000, s 71(3)*].

Broadly similar recovery rules apply to both first-year and writing-down allowances on 'old expenditure'. As regards first-year allowances, these rules apply when any non-qualifying use of the leased assets occurs during the requisite period. [*CAA 1990, s 47; FA 1990, Sch 17 para 11; FA 1994, Sch 26 Pt V(24)*].

(*h*) *Information* (e.g. names of lessees) must be provided to the Revenue under *CAA 1990, s 48* where 'new expenditure' on machinery or plant has qualified for a normal 25% writing-down allowance and/or reinstated first-year allowances for small or medium-sized enterprises and the item is leased (other than by 'permitted leasing' — see (*f*) above), at any time in the 'requisite period' (see (*c*) above), to a non-resident within (1) and (2) above, or to joint lessees at least one of whom is such a person. The time limit for providing the information is three months after the end of the chargeable period or basis period in which the item is first so leased, extended to 30 days after the informant came to know that the item was being so leased (if he could not reasonably have been expected to know earlier). [*CAA 1990, s 48(2)–(7), s 50(3); FA 1993, Sch 13 para 10; FA 1994, Sch 26 Pt V(24); FA 1997, Sch 14 para 8; F(No 2)A 1997, s 42(6); FA 1998, s 85(5); FA 2000, s 71(3)*]. Broadly similar information provisions apply under *CAA 1990, s 49* in respect of 'old expenditure'.

Where 'new expenditure' has not yet qualified for a normal writing-down allowance and the item is used for permitted leasing to a non-resident within (1) and (2) above, a claim for a writing-down allowance thereon must be accompanied by a certificate describing the permitted leasing. This also applies to reinstated first-year allowances for small or medium-sized enterprises. [*CAA 1990, s 48(1)(7), s 50(3); FA 1990, Sch 17 para 12; FA 1993, Sch 13 para 10; FA 1997, Sch 14 para 8; F(No 2)A 1997, s 42(6); FA 1998, s 85(5); FA 2000, s 71(3)*].

Restriction of first-year allowances. 'New expenditure' is not automatically precluded from qualifying for the temporary 40% first-year allowance under *CAA 1990, s 22(3B)* for expenditure incurred after 31 October 1992 and before 1 November 1993 (see 10.27 above), but *is* so precluded if:

(I) it appears that the expenditure would fall within the provisions for assets leased outside the UK (see above); or

(II) the expenditure is incurred after 13 April 1993 and each of the following conditions is satisfied:

(*a*) a first-year allowance would have been precluded under the provisions below if the expenditure had been 'old expenditure'; and

(*b*) the person to whom the machinery etc. is to be, or is, leased, or a person connected with him, used the machinery etc. for any purpose at any time before its provision for leasing.

[*CAA 1990, s 22(6A); FA 1993, s 115(3)*].

As regards first-year allowances for small or medium-sized enterprises for certain expenditure incurred after 1 July 1997 (see 10.27 above), these are **not** available where the machinery or plant is provided for leasing. [*CAA 1990, s 22(6B)(d); F(No 2)A 1997, s 42(5); FA 1998, s 85(1); FA 2000, s 71(2)*].

As regards 'old expenditure', machinery or plant provided for leasing does not qualify for a first-year allowance unless it appears that it will be used *only* for a 'qualifying purpose' (see (*d*) above) during the 'requisite period' (see (*c*) above). This exclusion does not apply to the provision of

(AA) vehicles wholly or mainly for use by persons in receipt of certain social security mobility allowances/supplements and disability living allowances, or

(BB) machinery or plant which is to be an integral part of a building qualifying for enterprise zone allowances (see 10.19 above), or

(CC) machinery or plant fixed to a building or land of which the person incurring the expenditure is the lessor, where a transfer of his interest in the building etc. would operate to transfer his interest in the machinery etc.

[*CAA 1990, s 22(4)(c)(5)(6)(11)*].

For 'old expenditure' only, *information* must be provided to the Revenue under *CAA 1990, s 23.*

See (*f*) above for the position where machinery or plant is leased under certain circumstances to joint lessees. See (*g*) above for recovery of excess relief, including first-year allowances.

Temporary provisions for 'foreign to foreign' leasing. The first-year allowance was restricted to 25%, and separate pooling applied, for expenditure incurred after 23 October 1979 and before 1 June 1980 if the machinery or plant was at any time in the requisite period being leased under a finance lease (as defined) to a non-UK resident who did not use it for the purposes of a trade carried on in the UK or for exploration or exploitation activities in a designated area of the continental shelf. [*FA 1980, s 72(4), Sch 12 Pt I*].

Transitional provisions for television or viewdata etc. sets. First-year allowances were not precluded for expenditure on a television set or viewdata receiver (as defined) or teletext receiver (as defined) where the expenditure was incurred *and* delivery made to the person incurring it during a transitional period starting on 1 June 1980 and ending on 31 May 1984 for a television set and 31 May 1986 for a teletext or viewdata receiver. For expenditure incurred after 9 March 1982, the provisions were extended to cover teletext and viewdata adaptors. If sets were used other than for a 'qualifying purpose' (see (*d*) above) (for example, if they were used for leasing to a private individual) within the 'requisite period' (see (*c*) above), first-year allowances, normally 100%, were reduced to 75% and 50% respectively for sets delivered (to the person incurring the expenditure) in the penultimate year and final year of the transitional period, and separate pooling applied. The general reductions in first-year allowances for expenditure incurred after 13 March 1984 (see 10.27 above) did not apply to such expenditure. [*FA 1980, s 72(5), Sch 12 Pt II; FA 1982, s 77; FA 1983, s 33*].

Finance leasing. See 71.68 SCHEDULE D, CASES I AND II as regards restrictions on capital allowances where certain finance leasing arrangements are involved. See also 10.28 above, 10.38(iii)(vi) below.

10.36 *Examples*

Separate pooling

L has a leasing business preparing accounts annually to 31 May. In the year to 31 May 1999, his expenditure included the following.

		£
(i)	Machine 1, leased to M Ltd, a UK resident company for the purposes of its trade	20,000
(ii)	Machine 2, leased to N, a UK resident individual, for private use	8,000
(iii)	Machine 3, leased to P, a non-UK resident, for his overseas trade	16,000
(iv)	Fixtures and fittings for use in L's business	2,000
(v)	Motor car used by L entirely for business	6,000

At 1 June 1998, there is a written-down value of £40,000 brought forward in L's machinery and plant pool.

The leasing in (iii) above is neither 'short-term leasing' (see 10.35(*e*) above) nor the leasing of a ship, aircraft or transport container to be used for a 'qualifying purpose' (see 10.35(*d*) above).

L's capital allowances for 1999/2000, assuming no capital expenditure for the year to 31 May 1999 other than as listed above, are as follows.

	Main Pool	Car Pool	Pool for overseas leasing	Total allowances
	£	£	£	£
WDV b/f	40,000			
Additions	30,000	6,000	16,000	
WDA 25%	(17,500)	(1,500)		19,000
WDA 10%			(1,600)	1,600
WDV c/f	£52,500	£4,500	£14,400	
Total allowances				£20,600

Notes

(*a*) Machines 1 and 2 go into the general pool for machinery and plant, as do the fixtures and fittings. Machine 3 goes into a separate pool by virtue of its falling within *CAA 1990, s 42* (assets leased outside the UK). The car also goes into a separate pool. See 10.35(*a*) above.

(*b*) The writing-down allowance for Machine 3 is restricted to 10%.

Recovery of excess relief

M, who has a 30 September accounting date, incurred expenditure of £16,000 in March 1998 on a machine leased to Q Ltd, a company trading in the UK. In May 2001, Q Ltd terminated the lease and M then leased the machine, with effect from June 2001, to P Ltd, a company resident in Panama, for the purposes of its trade there. The leasing was not 'permitted leasing'.

A balancing charge arises in 2001/02 (period of account year to 30.9.01) as follows.

Actual allowances

		Total allowances
	£	£
Expenditure (year ended 30.9.98)	16,000	
WDA 25% for 1999/2000	4,000	4,000
	12,000	
WDA 25% for 2000/01	3,000	3,000
	9,000	
WDA 25% for 2001/02	2,250	2,250
Residue of expenditure	£6,750	
	Total allowances claimed	£9,250

Notional allowances

		Total allowances
	£	£
Expenditure (year ended 30.9.98)	16,000	
WDA 10% for 1999/2000 note (*a*)	1,600	1,600
	14,400	
WDA 10% for 2000/01	1,440	1,440
	12,960	
WDA 10% for 2001/02	1,296	1,296
	£11,664	
	Notional allowances	£4,336

Balancing charge, equal to the excess of actual allowances over notional allowances, for 2000/01 note (*b*)	£4,914

M will then be deemed to have incurred qualifying expenditure of £11,664 (equal to the residue of expenditure plus the balancing charge) for the year ending 30.9.02, i.e. the chargeable period following that in the period of account for which the change of use arose, and will then be entitled to writing-down allowances of 10% for that and subsequent chargeable periods. The expenditure will constitute, or form part of, a separate pool.

Notes

(*a*) Notional writing-down allowances are restricted to 10% notwithstanding the fact that the machine was used for a qualifying purpose up to May 2001. It is leased to a person within 10.35(1) and (2) above at some time in the requisite period.

(*b*) In practice, the machine would originally have been included in the general pool for machinery and plant. For the purpose of calculating the balancing charge, it is assumed to have been the only item of machinery and plant qualifying for writing-down allowances. In 2001/02, a disposal value equal to the residue of expenditure (£6,750) must be deducted from the pool.

10.37 **'Old scheme' before 27 October 1970.** A different system of reliefs and charges (the 'old scheme') applies to expenditure before 27 October 1970 and to certain later expenditure (see below). A summary is given below, see Tolley's Income Tax 1981/82 or earlier editions for more detailed coverage. Most machinery etc. subject to old scheme was, however, brought into the 'pool' of qualifying expenditure under the current scheme (see 10.28 above) following the *FA 1976* provisions (see below).

(*a*) *Expenditure after 26 October 1970 to which old scheme applies* is that on machinery etc.

(i) purchased from a connected person (within *ICTA 1988, s 839*, see 20 CONNECTED PERSONS) who incurred his expenditure before 27 October 1970; or

(ii) purchased from a person who incurred his expenditure before 27 October 1970, where the sole or main benefit from the transaction(s) appears to be the obtaining of relief under the current scheme; or

(iii) first brought into use by the purchaser after 26 October 1970, where the later expenditure consists of hire purchase instalments; or

(iv) purchased in a sale and lease-back transaction from a person who incurred his expenditure before 27 October 1970; or

(v) which belonged (or was treated as belonging) to the purchaser at any time before 27 October 1970.

(iv) and (v) apply only to expenditure incurred after 13 June 1972.

[*FA 1971, s 40(2)(3); FA 1972, s 68(1)*].

(*b*) *FA 1976 'pooling' provisions.* Commencing with the first basis period (first accounting period for a company) ending after 5 April 1976, any balance of unallowed expenditure incurred up to 26 October 1970 is to be added to the 'pool' of unallowed expenditure incurred after that date (see 10.28 above) except for

(i) ships;

(ii) cars where writing-down allowances are restricted (see (*c*)(iii) below);

(iii) items with partial use for other purpose (see 10.28(C) above);

(iv) items leased (see (*c*)(iv) below);

(v) items on which subsidies are received for wear and tear (see 10.38(xii) below);

(vi) items on which the alternative method of calculating writing-down allowances has been used (see (*c*)(ii) below);

(vii) items on hire purchase contracts which are uncompleted at beginning of the first basis (or accounting) period mentioned above;

(viii) items where an election is made (within two years from end of first period affected) for these provisions not to apply. The election is irrevocable.

The writing-down allowance (for (ii) to (vii) above) will be at 25% and ships (at (i) above) will continue to receive free depreciation. [*CAA 1990, s 82(1); FA 1976, s 39, Sch 15*].

(*c*) *System of allowances.*

(i) An *initial allowance* of (from 15 April 1958) 30% (10% where an investment allowance was also available) was made. [*CAA 1968, s 18, Sch 1 para 1*].

(ii) *Writing-down allowances* were granted for a basis period at the end of which machinery etc. was in use for the trade etc. Various rates applied, and a 'normal' (written-down value) method, an 'alternative' (straight-line) method and a 'special' (mines, oil wells etc.) method were available. New ships could be depreciated freely. [*CAA 1968, ss 19–31, Sch 4*].

(iii) *Cars* did not attract initial allowances (except with restrictions similar to those in 10.27(i) above). The maximum writing-down allowance was £500. [*CAA 1968, ss 18(3), 32, Sch 2*].

(iv) *Lessees of plant* were entitled to writing-down allowances only on a 'just and reasonable' proportion of capital expenditure incurred, provided that they were responsible for its maintenance and bore the cost of wear and tear. [*CAA 1968, s 43*]. Special provisions applied to lessees of ships. [*CAA 1968, s 43(2)*]. *Lessors of plant* could claim a capital allowance of the wear and tear borne by them in any basis period. [*CAA 1968, s 42*].

(v) *Hire purchase.* Initial allowances were given on the capital portion of each instalment, writing-down allowances on the capital portion of the full price for any basis period at the end of which the machinery etc. was in use for trade etc. purposes. [*CAA 1968, ss 18(7), 19(1), 20(1)*].

(*d*) *Balancing allowance or charge* arises when machinery etc. (not transferred to 'pool' under *FA 1976* provisions, see (*b*) above) ceases to belong to the trader, or permanently ceases to be used for the trade, or when the trade is permanently discontinued. [*CAA 1968, s 33(1)*].

The amount of the allowance or charge is the difference between (A) the sum of all sale, insurance, salvage or compensation proceeds, and (B) the 'expenditure still unallowed', i.e. the original cost less all initial, annual, scientific research and exceptional depreciation allowances already made on the plant (including previous balancing allowances). [*CAA 1968, ss 33, 41, 86*]. But where demolition of plant etc. gives rise, or might give rise, to a balancing allowance or charge, the net cost of demolition (after crediting sales of materials or scrap) is added to the 'expenditure unallowed' as above. [*CAA 1968, s 36*]. A balancing charge cannot exceed the total of allowances previously given [*CAA 1968, s 33(5)*] and may be postponed by deducting from it cost of plant bought in replacement, but allowances in respect of that plant are then calculated on the reduced amount. [*CAA 1968, s 40; FA 1971, Sch 8 para 17*].

Machinery etc. is to be treated as if sold at open-market price if

(i) it is given away, or sold at less than market price, or

(ii) it ceases to be used for a trade by being transferred to other use, or is retained by the transferor on a transfer of a trade not treated as a discontinuance, or

(iii) on permanent discontinuance of the trade it is retained or given away, or sold at less than market price. [*CAA 1968, s 34*].

But these provisions do not apply if the gift or sale at less than market price is already caught by *CAA 1968, s 78* (sales between controlled bodies) or by *ICTA 1970, s 196, FA 1976, Pt III* or *ICTA 1988, Pt V, Ch II* ('benefits in kind', see 75.11 *et seq.* SCHEDULE E), or is, in certain circumstances, between partners. [*CAA 1968, ss 34, 44, 79(2)*]. Also, former and subsequent owners may jointly elect to continue calculations on written-down value, but in that case any subsequent balancing adjustments will be calculated by reference to original cost. [*CAA 1968, s 35*].

10.38 Machinery and plant—General matters.

(i) *Abortive expenditure.* When a person is entitled to the benefit of a contract under which he incurs capital expenditure on the provision of machinery or plant for trade purposes, and he shall or may become the owner of the machinery or plant on performance of the contract, the machinery or plant is treated as belonging to him. [*CAA 1990, s 60(1)(a)*]. Capital allowances are accordingly available for the expenditure as it is incurred, and if the person ceases to be entitled to the benefit of the contract without becoming the owner of the machinery or plant, the provisions described at (vi) below crystallise a deemed disposal of the machinery or plant. [*CAA 1990, s 60(2)*]. These provisions do not apply to 'fixtures' within *CAA 1990, ss 51 et seq.* (see 10.34 above). [*CAA 1990, s 60A; FA 2000, s 80*].

(ii) *Car leasing* (see 10.27(i) above). Where a car is sold to the lessee or his nominee or connected person at less than the open market value at the end of the leasing contract, or some other variation of the traditional kind of contract, the Revenue will consider what adjustment may be necessary to the tax liabilities of the taxpayers affected. The adjustments may be to treat the car as stock-in-trade of the lessor rather than an asset qualifying for capital allowances, or substituting the open market value for the sale proceeds, or disallowing the lessee's rental payments as not being wholly and exclusively for the trade, or taxing any benefit obtained by the person connected with the lessee who acquires the car (Revenue Press Release 26 July 1978). See special legislation re leasing in 10.35 above and re motor cars costing over £12,000 in 10.28(A) above.

(iii) *Connected persons and other anti-avoidance measures.* See 10.27(iii) above as regards first-year allowance restrictions, and 10.37(*a*) above as regards certain expenditure to which current scheme does not apply. See 20 CONNECTED PERSONS for a definition of that term.

(*a*) For disposals of machinery etc. acquired as a result of transaction(s) between connected persons, the disposal value (see 10.28 above) may not exceed the greatest cost incurred on it by any of the participants in the transaction(s) (after deducting any 'additional VAT rebates', see 10.2(v) above, made to the participant). [*CAA 1990, s 26(3)(4); FA 1991, Sch 14 para 8(3)*].

(*b*) Where machinery etc. is purchased from a connected person, or in a sale and lease-back transaction, or in transaction(s) from which the sole or main benefit appears to be the obtaining of an allowance under the current provisions, no first-year allowances are given, and writing-down allowances and balancing adjustments ignore any excess of the expenditure (including any 'additional VAT liability' incurred in respect thereof — see 10.2(v) above) incurred over the disposal value to be brought into account on the seller. Where no disposal value is so brought into account (e.g. where the seller is non-UK resident), allowances are given on the smallest of

(1) open market value on acquisition,

(2) the purchaser's expenditure, and

(3) the capital expenditure, if any, incurred by the seller or any person connected with him,

with modifications to allow for 'additional VAT liabilities' and 'rebates' — see 10.2(v) above.

These restrictions do not apply to the supply of unused machinery etc. in the ordinary course of trade. Also, for chargeable periods ending before 12 May 1998, where the machinery etc. has not before the sale been used in a trade carried on by the seller or any person connected with him, first-year allowances *are* given, on the smallest of (1), (2) and (3) above.

These provisions apply to contracts for future delivery and hire purchase contract assignments as they apply to direct sales. [*CAA 1990, ss 75, 76; FA 1991, Sch 14 para 11; FA 1998, s 85(8)(9)*]. The 'sole or main benefit' restriction referred to above does not generally apply to straightforward finance leasing transactions (*Barclays Mercantile Industrial Finance Ltd v Melluish Ch D 1990, 63 TC 95*). However, with effect for expenditure incurred on or after 2 July 1997 (unless incurred in the following twelve months under a contract entered into before that date), the above rules are amended to further restrict allowances where machinery or plant is leased under a 'finance lease'. The general rules are applied in such cases, where the machinery or plant is used for non-trading activities, as if those activities were trading activities. Also, in the case of sale and leaseback transactions, the amount on which allowances are given is restricted to a notional written-down value for the seller, and allowances are denied altogether to the finance lessor where the lessor has substantially divested himself of any risk that the lessee will default. A '*finance lease*' is any arrangements for machinery or plant to be leased or made available such that, if the lessor (and all persons connected (within *ICTA 1988, s 839*) with the lessor) were UK-incorporated companies, the arrangements (or arrangements in which they are comprised) would fall, in accordance with normal accountancy practice, to be treated in the accounts of one or more of those companies (including any consolidated group accounts) as a finance lease or as a loan. [*CAA 1990, ss 76(7), 76A, 82A; F(No 2)A 1997, ss 46, 47*].

With effect from 28 July 2000, in the case of sale and leaseback type transactions within the above provisions, a joint (irrevocable) election may be made by the seller (or assignor) and the lessor (within two years of the sale, etc.) provided that

(A) the seller (or assignor) incurred capital expenditure on acquiring the machinery or plant unused (and not second-hand) and not under a transaction itself within the above provisions,

(B) the sale, etc. takes place not more than four months after the machinery or plant is first brought into use for any purpose, and

(C) the seller (or assignor) has not claimed capital allowances for the expenditure or included it in a pool of qualifying expenditure.

The effect of the election is that no allowances are made to the seller (or assignor) in respect of the expenditure, and for the capital allowances which are accordingly available to the lessor in respect of the machinery or plant to be given by reference to the lesser of the amounts in (2) and (3) above, i.e. disregarding the current market value at the time of the sale, etc. (and, in the case of finance leases, the notional written-down value for the seller).

[*CAA 1990, s 76B; FA 2000, s 77*].

See Revenue Tax Bulletin June 1998 pp 539-544 for a general article on how these and associated capital allowance restrictions are intended to operate. In particular the article considers sale and leaseback by novation or new contract, or on defeased terms, and assets with long build times. See also 10.28 above, 10.38(vi) below and 71.68 SCHEDULE D, CASES I AND II as regards finance lease allowance restrictions.

See (xi) below as regards successions to trades between connected persons.

(iv) *Double allowances.* See 10.2(iv) above.

(v) A *gift of machinery etc.*, brought into use after 26 July 1989 for the purposes of the donee's trade, entitles the donee to writing-down allowances, as if he had purchased it from the donor, from the basis period in which he first so uses it. Allowances will, subject to (iii) above, be calculated on open market value at the time when brought into use. [*CAA 1990, s 81(1)–(3)*]. Previously, it was necessary for the gift to have resulted in open market value being brought into account on the donor as disposal value, although in practice, allowances were generally also available where the plant was not used for trade purposes by the donor. [*CAA 1990, s 81(4)*]. Where the gift is brought into use between 1 November 1992 and 31 October 1993 inclusive, the donee's deemed expenditure qualifies for the 40% first-year allowance introduced by *FA 1993* (see 10.27 above). [*CAA 1990, s 81(1A); FA 1993, Sch 13 para 12(1)*].

(vi) *Hire purchase.* If machinery etc. is acquired under a hire purchase agreement, it is treated as belonging to the person who will become the owner on performance of the contract. When it is brought into trade use, the full outstanding capital cost (i.e. excluding the hire or interest element) attracts capital allowances immediately. Any such capital payments made *before* the machinery etc. is brought into use attract allowances as they fall due. If the contract is not completed, and the trader does not in fact become the owner, the machinery etc. is treated as ceasing to belong to him when he loses the benefit of the contract. He must then bring in as its disposal value (see 10.28 above) any consideration, compensation etc. he may receive, plus, if the machinery etc. has been brought into trade use, the capital element of all instalments not paid, subject to an overall limit of the full cost of the machinery etc. under the contract. [*CAA 1990, s 60*]. See 10.28(A) above as regards hire purchase agreements relating to certain motor cars.

CAA 1990, s 60 does not apply to expenditure incurred on 'fixtures' within *CAA 1990, s 51 et seq.* (see 10.34 above), and if (at a time on or after 28 July 2000) machinery or plant which has been treated under *section 60* as belonging to a person becomes such a fixture, it is treated as ceasing to belong to that person at that time (unless it is treated as belonging to him under *section 51 et seq.*). [*CAA 1990, s 60A; FA 2000, s 80*].

With effect for chargeable periods ending on or after 2 July 1997, *CAA 1990, s 60* similarly does not apply (except in relation to deemed ownership of the asset concerned) to expenditure incurred after 1 July 1997 (unless it is incurred in the following twelve months under a contract entered into on or before that date) on the provision of machinery or plant for leasing under a 'finance lease' (see 10.38(iii) above). [*CAA 1990, s 60(2A); F(No 2)A 1997, s 45*]. See Revenue Tax Bulletin June 1998 pp 539–544 for a general article on how these and associated capital allowance restrictions are intended to operate. In particular it is noted that the commencement rules for the current provisions apply before the deeming rule in *CA 1990, s 60*, so that where the asset is brought into trade use by the lessor in a chargeable period ending on or after 2 July 1997, the deeming rule only applies to expenditure actually incurred before that date (or in the following twelve months under an existing contract). See also 10.28, 10.38(iii) above and 71.68 SCHEDULE D, CASES I AND II as regards finance lease allowance restrictions.

(vii) A *lessee required to provide machinery etc.* under the terms of his lease, and using it for trade purposes, is treated as if he owned it, but after termination of the lease, any disposal value (see 10.28 above) on disposal etc. is brought into account on the *lessor*, not the lessee. This does not, however, apply where the machinery, etc. becomes, by law, part of the building in which it is installed or attached (see 10.34 above) under a lease entered into after 11 July 1984 unless pursuant to an agreement made on or before that date. [*CAA 1990, s 61(4)*].

(viii) *Partnerships* are entitled to allowances on assets used for the partnership trade, and either owned by the partnership or owned by a partner and not let to the partnership.

On a *change of partnership*, if the trade is treated as continuing, unexhausted allowances are carried forward and subsequent balancing adjustments (see 10.30 above) made as if the new partnership had carried on the trade before the change. Allowances continue to be calculated as though there had been no change, being apportioned between the old and the new partnership for the year of assessment of the change. If however the trade is treated as ceasing, only continuing partners may carry forward their share of unexhausted allowances, as a loss to set against their future profit shares (but see 10.1 above as regards changes for 1994/95 onwards for trades etc. commenced after 5 April 1994 and for 1997/98 onwards as regards trades etc. commenced on or before that date). [*CAA 1990, ss 65, 78(3)(4)*].

See also (xi) below as regards allowances on successions to trades.

(ix) *Previous use outside trade.* Where a trader brings into use for the trade machinery etc. which he previously owned for purposes not entitling him to machinery and plant allowances in respect of the trade, allowances (excluding first-year allowances except as below) are calculated as if the trader had, on bringing it into use for the trade, incurred expenditure on its acquisition of its open market value on a sale at that time. (Actual cost, if less, is substituted for open market value where the machinery, etc. is brought into trade use after 20 March 2000. The actual cost for this purpose is reduced to the extent that it would have been reduced under *CAA 1990, ss 75–76A* (see (iii) above) had it been expenditure on machinery or plant for use in the trade.) This treatment does not apply to machinery etc. previously used only for the purposes specified in 10.49(*b*) and (*c*) below which applied before 1 April 1986 in relation to mines, oil wells, etc. In such a case, the full cost is treated as expenditure incurred when the machinery is brought into trade use. Where the machinery etc. is brought into use between 1 November 1992 and 31 October 1993 inclusive, the trader's deemed expenditure qualifies for the 40% first-year allowance introduced by *FA 1993* (see 10.27 above). First-year allowances are not, however, available where machinery etc. is transferred from one trade to another carried on by the same person and is brought into use in the second trade after 13 April 1993. [*FA 1971, Sch 8 para 7; FA 1985, Sch 14 para 8; CAA 1990, s 81; FA 1993, Sch 13 para 12; FA 2000, s 75(3)(6)*].

(x) *Renewals basis* is generally available as an alternative to capital allowances as above. A deduction is allowed in computing profits of the cost of a replacement item less the proceeds of sale (or scrap value) of the item replaced. Where, however, the replacement item is an improvement on that replaced, the deduction is restricted to the cost of replacing like with like. See *Caledonian Railway Co v Banks CES 1880, 1 TC 487; Eastmans Ltd v Shaw HL 1928, 14 TC 218; Hyam v CIR CS 1929, 14 TC 479.*

Cost of renewals of trade implements, utensils etc. allowed as a deduction under *ICTA 1988, s 74(1)(d)*, but cf. *Hinton v Maden & Ireland Ltd HL 1959, 38 TC 391* and also see *Peter Merchant Ltd v Stedeford CA 1948, 30 TC 496* (provision for future renewals not allowable). Replacement of parts is allowed under general principles so far as identity of machinery etc. is retained. For further details of 'renewals basis' and change from renewals basis to normal capital allowances, see Revenue Pamphlet IR 1, B1.

See generally Revenue Inspector's Manual, IM 996–1000e.

(xi) *Successions.* Where a trade changes hands (other than in certain partnership changes (see (viii) above)) unexhausted allowances may not be carried forward to the new owner. Unless the change is not treated as a permanent cessation (see 53.6 PARTNERSHIPS), any asset transferred, without being sold, to the new owner for continuing use in the trade is treated as sold at open market value on the date of change, although no first-year allowance (where otherwise applicable) is available to the new owner.

If a beneficiary succeeds to a trade under a deceased proprietor's will or intestacy, he may elect for written-down value to be substituted (if less) for the open market value. [*CAA 1990, s 78; FA 1990, Sch 13 para 3*].

Where the old and new owners are 'connected' with each other, each is within the charge to UK tax on profits of the trade, and the successor is not a dual resident investing company (see *ICTA 1988, s 404*), they may elect, within two years of the date of change, for any machinery or plant continuing to be used in the trade to be treated as transferred at a price giving rise to no balancing allowance or charge, and for allowances to be given to the successor disregarding the change of ownership. For this purpose, persons are '*connected*' if

(*a*) they are CONNECTED PERSONS (20) within *ICTA 1988, s 839*, or

(*b*) one of them is a partnership in which the other has the right to a share of assets or income, or both are partnerships in both of which some other person has the right to such a share, or

(*c*) one of them is a body corporate over which the other has control (within *ICTA 1988, s 840*), or both are bodies corporate, or one a body corporate and one a partnership, over both of which some other person has control.

An election in relation to a succession occurring after 26 July 1989 will preclude the application of *CAA 1990, s 38G* (long-life assets, see 10.28(G) above), *CAA 1990, s 78* (see above) and the similar provisions in *CAA 1990, s 41* (see 10.35(*a*) above).

In relation to successions occurring before 29 July 1988, such an election (with similar effect) can only be made where the old and new owners are CONNECTED PERSONS (20) within *ICTA 1988, s 839*, but the requirement that both are within the charge to UK tax is omitted, and the restriction on dual resident investing companies did not apply before 1 April 1987. No time limit is specified for such an election. [*CAA 1990, s 77; FA 1997, Sch 14 para 9*].

(xii) *Wear and tear allowances.* Where any sums, not otherwise taxable on the recipient, are payable to him, directly or indirectly, by any other person in respect of, or to take account of, the wear and tear of plant or machinery used in the recipient's trade, no capital allowances are available for that plant or machinery. Where the sums only partially offset that wear and tear, a first-year allowance, where available, can be given, but scaled down as is just and reasonable. Writing-down allowances are calculated as if the machinery were used solely for a separate 'notional' trade and only a just proportion allowed against the actual trade. Balancing adjustments are similarly debarred or restricted. [*CAA 1990, s 80; FA 1990, Sch 17 para 15*]. See 10.2(ii) above as regards certain other subsidies.

10.39 **MINES, OIL WELLS**

The original capital allowances for mines, oil wells, etc. contained in *CAA 1968, ss 51–66, Schs 5, 6* (the '*old code*', see 10.49 below) are repealed **after 31 March 1986** and a new code introduced for expenditure incurred in a 'trade of mineral extraction' after that date, subject to transitional provisions (see 10.47 below) which may apply to certain expenditure incurred before 1 April 1987. [*CAA 1990, Pt IV*]. For these purposes, any accounting or basis period beginning on or before 31 March 1986 and ending after that date is split into two such periods, the first ending on that date and the second commencing on 1 April 1986. [*FA 1986, s 55(3)(4)*].

A '*trade of mineral extraction*' is a trade consisting of or including the working of a source of '*mineral deposits*', i.e. such deposits of a wasting nature including any natural deposits or geothermal energy capable of being lifted or extracted from the earth. [*CAA 1990, s 121(1)(2)*].

The main elements of the new code are dealt with as follows.

10.40 Qualifying expenditure
10.41 Limitations on qualifying expenditure
10.42 Writing-down allowances
10.43 Disposal receipts
10.44 Balancing allowances and charges
10.45 Making of allowances and charges
10.46 Machinery and plant allowances
10.47 Transitional provisions
10.49 'Old scheme' before 1 April 1986

Simon's Direct Tax Service. See **B2.4**.

10.40 **Qualifying expenditure.** The new code applies to '*qualifying expenditure*', i.e. expenditure on

(*a*) '*mineral exploration and access*' (i.e. searching for or discovering and testing the mineral deposits of any source, or winning access to any such deposits),

(*b*) acquisition of a '*mineral asset*' (i.e. any mineral deposits or land comprising mineral deposits, or any interest in or right over such deposits or land),

(*c*) construction of any works, in connection with the working of a source of mineral deposits, which are likely to become of little or no value when the source ceases to be worked, and

(*d*) construction of works which are likely to become valueless when a foreign concession under which a source of mineral deposits is worked comes to an end.

Included in (*a*) above is abortive expenditure on seeking planning permission for the undertaking of mineral exploration and access or the working of mineral deposits. Expenditure on the acquisition of, or of rights in or over, mineral deposits or the site of a source of such deposits falls into (*b*) rather than (*a*) above. [*CAA 1990, ss 105(1)(7), 121(1)*].

Qualifying expenditure also includes certain contributions, for the purposes of a trade of mineral extraction carried on outside the UK, to the cost of accommodation outside the UK for employees engaged in working a source, and related public and welfare services and facilities, provided that the buildings etc. are likely to be of little or no value when the source ceases to be worked, that the expenditure does not result in the acquisition of an asset, and that relief is not due under any other provision of the *Tax Acts*. Net expenditure incurred on the 'restoration' of a mining site within three years of the cessation of the trade is also qualifying expenditure, treated as incurred on the last day of trading, unless relieved elsewhere. [*CAA 1990, ss 108, 109*].

The following are, however, *not* qualifying expenditure.

(i) Expenditure on, or treated as being on, machinery or plant (except certain pre-trading expenditure, see below).

(ii) Expenditure on acquisition of, or of rights in or over, the site of works as in (*c*) or (*d*) above.

(iii) Expenditure on works constructed wholly or mainly for processing the raw products, unless the process is designed to prepare the raw products for use as such.

(iv) Expenditure on buildings and structures for occupation by or welfare of workers.

(v) Expenditure on construction of any part of a building or structure for use as an office where such expenditure exceeds one-tenth of the capital expenditure on the whole building.

[*CAA 1990, s 105(4)(5)*].

Time expenditure incurred. The normal rules (see 10.2(iii) above) apply, and, additionally, *pre-trading expenditure* is generally treated as incurred on the first day of trading, although expenditure within (*a*) above may not thereby become qualifying expenditure. Certain net expenditure on machinery or plant sold, demolished, destroyed or abandoned before commencement of a trade of mineral extraction is treated as qualifying expenditure incurred on the first day of the mineral extraction trade. Certain other expenditure on mineral exploration and access incurred before commencement of a trade of mineral extraction is treated as incurred on the first day of that trade (i.e. where another trade was previously carried on). [*CAA 1990, ss 105(2), 106, 107, 120(1)(2)*].

10.41 **Limitations on qualifying expenditure.** Where expenditure includes the acquisition of an interest in land, an amount equal to the 'undeveloped market value' of the land is excluded. '*Undeveloped market value*' is the open market value of the land at the time of acquisition ignoring the mineral deposits and assuming that development of the land (other than that already begun or for which planning permission has already been granted by a general development order) is, and will remain, unlawful. Where the undeveloped market value includes the value of buildings which are subsequently demolished or otherwise permanently cease to be used, their value, excluding the land, less the amount of any capital allowances received in respect of them, is treated as qualifying expenditure incurred at the time of cessation of use. The special provisions regarding the time of acquisition of land (see 10.40 above) do not apply for these purposes. [*CAA 1990, s 110*].

Where a deduction has been allowed under *ICTA 1988, s 87* in respect of a premium under a lease (see 68.28 SCHEDULE A), the qualifying expenditure allowable in respect of acquisition of the interest in land to which the premium relates is correspondingly reduced. [*CAA 1990, s 111*].

Qualifying expenditure is also restricted where the asset is acquired from another person, and either that person or an earlier previous owner incurred expenditure on it in connection with a trade of mineral extraction. Broadly, the amount qualifying is limited to the amount of expenditure incurred by the most recent previous owner who used it in connection with a trade of mineral extraction, net of any allowances made to or on that person. Where the asset is a mineral asset in the UK, no restriction applies

(*a*) if the asset was acquired under a contract for sale made before 16 July 1985 from a person who incurred expenditure on it in connection with a trade of mineral extraction, or

(*b*) if no previous owner after 31 March 1986 has incurred expenditure on it in connection with a trade of mineral extraction.

Where an asset representing expenditure on mineral exploration or access is acquired from a person who incurred that expenditure without carrying on a trade of mineral extraction, qualifying expenditure is restricted to the expenditure incurred by the seller.

A similar restriction applies where assets are transferred between companies under common control, unless an election is made under *CAA 1990, s 158* for the transfer to be treated as made at tax written-down value.

If the expenditure includes the cost of an oil licence, the qualifying expenditure is limited to the amount of the original licence fee paid.

In any case where the expenditure is incurred both in mineral exploration and access and in the acquisition of a mineral asset, the qualifying amount in respect of the former is limited to the amount incurred by the previous trader in that respect. In relation to claims made after 25 November 1996, expenditure which has already been allowed as a deduction to the previous trader is not treated as expenditure on mineral exploration and access for this purpose.

[*CAA 1990, ss 113–118; FA 1997, s 66*].

10.42 **Writing-down allowances.** After 31 March 1986 the following allowances are given in respect of qualifying expenditure incurred in connection with a trade of mineral extraction in a chargeable or basis period, or treated as so incurred, net of any disposal receipts (see 10.43 below).

Acquisition of a mineral asset (see 10.40(*b*) above) and certain pre-trading expenditure	**10% p.a.**
Other qualifying expenditure	**25% p.a.**

Allowances for subsequent chargeable periods are calculated by applying the same percentages to the balance of expenditure after adjustment for disposal receipts and allowances and charges given or made for earlier periods. [*CAA 1990, s 98; FA 1994, s 213(8)*].

10.43 **Disposal receipts.** When an asset, in respect of the acquisition of which a person has incurred qualifying expenditure, permanently ceases to be used in a trade of mineral extraction carried on by him (by disposal or otherwise), the disposal value calculated as under *CAA 1990, s 26* (see 10.28 above) must be brought into account. A mineral asset is treated as ceasing to be so used at any time when it begins to be used in a way which constitutes development which is neither development for the purposes of a trade of mineral extraction carried on by him nor *'existing permitted development'*, i.e. development lawfully carried out prior to the acquisition or for which planning permission is granted by a general development order (or foreign equivalent). Where the qualifying expenditure has been restricted in accordance with the rules regarding acquisition of an interest in land (see

10.41 above) the disposal value is correspondingly restricted. Any capital receipt is similarly brought into account to the extent that it is attributable to qualifying expenditure. [*CAA 1990, ss 99, 112; FA 1994, Sch 26 Pt V(24)*].

10.44 **Balancing allowances and charges.** A balancing charge arises in any chargeable period in which, or in whose basis period, the sum of disposal receipts (see 10.43 above) for that and earlier periods and the net allowances made for earlier periods in respect of any qualifying expenditure exceeds the expenditure. The charge is on the lesser of that excess and the net allowances made for earlier periods.

A balancing allowance arises for any chargeable period in which any of the following circumstances apply.

(*a*) On permanent discontinuance of the trade.

(*b*) On permanent cessation of the working of certain mineral deposits. If two or more mineral assets derive from a single asset, the adjustment will not arise until the deposits comprised in all the assets concerned cease to be worked.

(*c*) Where neither (*a*) nor (*b*) applies, but a disposal receipt falls to be brought into account as in 10.43 above.

(*d*) In respect of certain pre-trading expenditure where the machinery or plant is sold, etc., or the mineral exploration and access has ceased, before commencement of the trade of mineral extraction.

(*e*) Where a person incurs expenditure on mineral exploration and access in respect of search, exploration or inquiry and does not then or subsequently commence a related trade of mineral extraction.

(*f*) Where qualifying expenditure has been incurred consisting of a contribution to the cost of temporary overseas employee accommodation and related public and welfare services and facilities, and the buildings or works permanently cease to be used in connection with a trade of mineral extraction.

(*g*) Where assets are lost, cease to exist as such, or begin to be used for another purpose outside the trade of mineral extraction.

The amount of the balancing allowance is the excess of the qualifying expenditure over the sum of disposal receipts of that and earlier periods and the net allowances made for earlier periods.

The excess of any demolition costs over monies received for the remains of an asset representing qualifying expenditure is added to that expenditure for the purposes of balancing adjustments and is not then treated as expenditure incurred on any replacement asset. [*CAA 1990, ss 100–103; FA 1994, Sch 26 Pt V(24)*].

10.45 **Making of allowances and charges.** All allowances and charges under these provisions are made in taxing the trade of mineral extraction. [*CAA 1990, s 104*]. The miscellaneous and general provisions of *CAA 1990* generally apply to allowances under the new code, which are in most cases treated in the same way as other capital allowances for the purposes of other provisions in the *Tax Acts*.

10.46 **Machinery and plant allowances.** Machinery and plant is normally excluded from relief under the current provisions, but certain pre-trading expenditure may qualify (see 10.40

above). [*CAA 1990, ss 105(4), 106*]. The normal machinery and plant rules (see 10.24 *et seq.* above) apply to machinery and plant provided for the purposes of mineral exploration and access, subject to the necessary minor modifications. Where such expenditure is incurred prior to the date of commencement of the trade of mineral extraction, it is treated as sold immediately before that date and as re-acquired on that date. The capital expenditure on re-acquisition is deemed to be the actual expenditure previously incurred. [*CAA 1990, s 63*].

10.47 **Transitional provisions.** An irrevocable election could be made for initial allowances under the old code to continue to apply to expenditure incurred, by a person carrying on a trade of mineral extraction, in the year ending 31 March 1987 under a contract entered into by that person before 16 July 1985 in respect of which, but for the new code of allowances, an initial allowance would have been available under *CAA 1968, s 56*. The old code of allowances then continue to apply until 31 March 1987.

The election had to be made in writing within two years after the end of the chargeable or basis period in which the expenditure (or the first part of the expenditure after 31 March 1986) was incurred. Where an election was made, the new code applies after 31 March 1987 instead of 31 March 1986. [*FA 1986, Sch 14 para 2*].

Where expenditure had not been fully relieved under the provisions of *CAA 1968, ss 57, 60* and *61,* the balance is treated for allowance purposes under the new code as incurred on the '*relevant day*' (i.e. the day from which the new code applies to the expenditure in question). Where such expenditure had been fully relieved but the asset or assets so acquired continue in use after the relevant day, the expenditure is treated as having been incurred on the relevant day, with allowances equal to the expenditure having been made under the new code, for the purposes of subsequent balancing adjustments. [*FA 1986, Sch 14 para 4; CAA 1990, s 119(3)*].

Expenditure on mineral exploration and access, or on acquisition of mineral assets, or on construction of certain works, which did not qualify for allowances under the old code because either the trade, or output from the source, had not commenced, or for some other reason, is treated as incurred on 1 April 1986 and relieved as appropriate under the new code.

Special rules apply where the old code expenditure on a mineral asset included the acquisition of an interest in land, allowing the value of that interest to remain within the relievable expenditure where some relief had already been given under the old code, but bringing that value into account when calculating subsequent balancing adjustments. [*FA 1986, Sch 14 paras 5–7; CAA 1990, s 119(2)(3)*].

In making balancing adjustments where old code expenditure has been brought under the new code, allowances given under the old code will be taken into account together with those given under the new code. [*CAA 1990, s 119(4)(5)*].

10.48 *Example*

X has for some years operated a mining business with two mineral sources, G and S. Accounts are prepared to 30 September. On 31 December 2000 the mineral deposits and mineworks at G are sold at market value to Z for £80,000 and £175,000 respectively. A new source, P, is purchased on 30 April 2001 for £170,000 (including land with an undeveloped market value of £70,000) and the following expenditure incurred before the end of the accounting period ended 30 September 2001.

	£
Machinery and plant	40,000
Construction of administration office	25,000
Construction of mining works which are likely to have little value when mining ceases	50,000
Staff hostel	35,000
Winning access to the deposits	150,000
	£300,000

During the year to 30 September 2001, X incurred expenditure of £20,000 in seeking planning permission to mine a further plot of land, Source Q. Permission was refused.

Residue of expenditure brought forward (based on accounts to 30 September 2000)		£
Mineral exploration and access	– Source G	170,000
	– Source S	200,000
Mineral assets	– Source G	95,250
	– Source S	72,000

The mineral extraction allowances due for the year ending 30.9.01 are as follows.

Source G	£	£
Mineral exploration and access		
WDV b/f	170,000	
Proceeds	175,000	
Balancing charge	£5,000	(5,000)
Mineral assets		
WDV b/f	95,250	
Proceeds	80,000	
Balancing allowance	£15,250	15,250
Source S		
Mineral exploration and access		
WDV b/f	200,000	
WDA 25%	(50,000)	50,000
WDV c/f	£150,000	
Mineral assets		
WDV b/f	72,000	
WDA 10%	(7,200)	7,200
WDV c/f	£64,800	

Source P	£	£
Mineral exploration and access		
Expenditure	150,000	
WDA 25%	(37,500)	37,500
WDA c/f	£112,500	
Mineral assets		
Expenditure	100,000	
WDV 10%	(10,000)	10,000
WDV c/f	£90,000	
Mining works		
Expenditure	50,000	
WDA 25%	(12,500)	12,500
WDV c/f	£37,500	
Source Q		
Mineral exploration and access		
Expenditure	20,000	
WDA 25%	(5,000)	5,000
WDV c/f	£15,000	
Total allowances (net of charges)		£132,450

Notes

(*a*) Allowances are not due on either the office or staff hostel although the hostel may qualify for industrial buildings allowances (see 10.11 above). Machinery and plant qualify for machinery and plant allowances (see 10.24 above) rather than for mineral extraction allowances (see 10.46 above).

(*b*) Abortive expenditure on seeking planning permission is qualifying expenditure as if it were expenditure on mineral exploration and access (see 10.40 above).

(*c*) The undeveloped market value of land is excluded from qualifying expenditure and from disposal receipts (see 10.41, 10.43 above).

10.49 **'Old scheme' before 1 April 1986.** For capital allowances on plant and machinery used in mines, etc., see above and *CAA 1968, s 23,* for special method applicable to expenditure up to 26 October 1970. Allowances were also given for capital expenditure on the following.

(*a*) [1963/64 onwards]. Acquiring UK mineral deposits, land comprising them or rights over such land [*CAA 1968, s 60*].

Writing-down allowances were given as follows–

First 10 years of working source.........½ 'royalty value' of output in the chargeable period or its basis period.

Next 10 years (i.e. up to 20)...............¼th 'royalty value' of output in the chargeable period or its basis period.

Thereafter...$\frac{1}{10}$th 'royalty value' of output in the chargeable period or its basis period.

'*Royalty value*' means amount of reasonable royalties on output in chargeable or basis period that would be payable if the source had been acquired under lease, expiring after that output produced, less any royalties actually payable. [*CAA 1968, s 60(11)*].

Total writing-down allowances including those deemed to have been made before 1963/64, plus capital receipts not to exceed amount of capital outlay. Where a source ceased to be worked, a balancing charge, or allowance, limited to the part appropriate to years after 1962/63, was made on the difference between the cost of acquiring the source (less its residual market value, etc.) and the total of allowances.

(*b*) Searching for, discovering, testing or winning access to deposits [*CAA 1968, s 51(2)(a)*] including plant, etc., so used (but not if initial or annual allowances had at any time previously been made in respect of that plant). [*CAA 1968, s 52*].

Capital allowances for such plant were given only on the diminution in its value attributable to its use in searching for, discovering, etc., the deposits. [*CAA 1968, Sch 5 paras 1, 2*]. See *CAA 1968, s 59* for restriction if purchase was not from mining concern etc. Outlay by mining etc. concerns on searching for, discovering, etc., deposits which were abandoned without the source being worked was allowed as a revenue expense as were unsuccessful planning applications for permission to explore and successful applications where the exploration itself was unsuccessful. [*CAA 1968, s 62;* Revenue Pamphlet IR 131, SP 4/78, 6 November 1978].

(*c*) Construction of works likely to be of little or no value when the source was no longer worked, or when a foreign concession under which the source was worked came to an end. [*CAA 1968, ss 51(2)(b), 56*].

(*d*) Cost of acquiring mineral deposits abroad (or rights over them) [*CAA 1968, s 53*], or of acquiring land abroad in connection with working a mine, etc., under a foreign concession, if likely to be valueless, at the end of the concession, to the person then working it. [*CAA 1968, s 54*]. But not including plant, industrial buildings etc. Where land etc. purchased from UK resident, allowances restricted to his cost. [*CAA 1968, Sch 5 paras 3–5*].

(*e*) (Overseas mines, etc., only.) Capital sums contributed, after 5 April 1952, towards the cost of the buildings, services and works ancillary thereto occupied by or giving welfare facilities for employees or their dependants, if those buildings, etc., were likely to be of little or no value when working of the source ceased. But no allowance for expenditure resulting in the *acquisition of a capital asset* by the person making it or if other allowances due. Allowance of one-tenth of the expenditure was given in each of 10 years, commencing with the year in the basis period for which the contribution was made (for corporation tax, beginning with the chargeable period in which the expenditure was incurred). [*CAA 1968, s 61*].

There were provisions for continuation to successor for balance of the relevant years. [*CAA 1968, s 61(3)(4)*].

Allowable expenditure under the above headings did not include the following.

(i) Cost of the site or the deposits (except as under (*a*) or (*d*) above).

(ii) Machinery or plant (other than under (*b*) or (*e*) above).

(iii) Processing works, other than for preparing the raw material.

(iv) Buildings for workers' occupation or welfare, except for (*e*) above.

(v) Buildings (or parts thereof, if exceeding $\frac{1}{10}$th) used as offices. [*CAA 1968, s 51(3)(4)*].

(A) **Initial Allowances.** (*Applicable only to expenditure under (c) above.*)

Rate of allowance. 40% on expenditure incurred after 14 April 1953. (The 40% rate was reduced to 20% where expenditure (before 17 January 1966) also qualified for investment allowance.) [*CAA 1968, s 56, Sch 1 para 1(2)(c)*].

The rate was increased to 100% (or such lesser amount as the taxpayer specified) on expenditure incurred after 26 October 1970 on the construction of works in a *development area* or in N. Ireland. [*FA 1971, s 52*].

(B) **Writing-down allowances** (other than under (*a*) and (*e*) above). Calculated each year as a fraction of *'residue of expenditure'* (cost less previous allowances, other than investment allowances and less capital receipts not resulting in balancing allowance or charge) corresponding to the ratio that *output in chargeable period or 'basis period'* bore to the sum of that output plus *'potential future output'*. Minimum allowance one-twentieth, but in respect of expenditure incurred after 3 April 1963, and before 17 January 1966, on constructing works in, or providing plant, etc., for use in, a former *'development district'* the taxpayer could himself specify the fraction to be applied. Except in this latter case, adjustments including revision of allowances for final six years, claimable when source ceased to be worked or concession came to an end. [*CAA 1968, s 57*].

(C) **Balancing allowances or charges** (with modifications in the case of sources worked before 6 April 1952) were made if assets included above were sold to a buyer who continued to work the whole or part of the source. [*CAA 1968, s 58*]. 'Residue of expenditure', included net cost (after crediting sales of materials and scrap) of demolition falling on the person concerned. [*CAA 1968, s 55*]. Such buyer received writing-down allowances on lesser of purchase price or 'residue of expenditure' immediately after sale. [*CAA 1968, s 58(7)*]. For expenditure incurred prior to commencement of trading, and for treatment of assets, as above, acquired from a person who had not worked the source, see *CAA 1968, s 59*.

Except for (*a*) above, there were provisions for the substitution of open market value for sale consideration on certain **'sole or main benefit'** transactions, **sales without change of control** and **sales between connected persons** subject in the latter cases to an election for residue of expenditure to be substituted instead. [*CAA 1968, s 78, Sch 7 paras 1, 4*].

Allowances were **given in taxing the trade**, in the same way as machinery and plant allowances are given to traders (see 10.32 above).

10.50 PATENT RIGHTS

Writing-down allowances are available, and **balancing adjustments** made, in respect of capital expenditure on

(*a*) purchase of patent rights (i.e. the right to do or authorise the doing of anything which would, apart from that right, be a patent infringement), or

(*b*) obtaining a right to acquire future patent rights,

provided that either the allowance falls to be made in taxing the purchaser's trade or any income receivable in respect of the rights would be liable to tax. Expenditure incurred by a person for the purposes of a trade he is about to carry on is treated as incurred on the first day of trading, provided that the rights are still held at that time. [*ICTA 1988, ss 520–523, s 528; FA 1994, Sch 26 Pt V(24)*].

Expenditure incurred after 31 March 1986

For any chargeable period (see 10.2(vi) above) for which a person has 'qualifying expenditure' exceeding any 'disposal value' to be brought in, a writing-down allowance of 25% of the excess (proportionately reduced or increased if the period is less or more than one year or the allowance falls to be made in taxing a trade carried on for only part of a chargeable period) is made, except that a *balancing allowance* of the whole of the excess is made where:

(*a*) the chargeable period is that of permanent discontinuance of the trade in taxing which the allowance falls to be made; or

(*b*) (*a*) above does not apply but during the period the last of the patent rights, expenditure on which has been taken into account in determining qualifying expenditure and which have not been wholly disposed of, comes to an end without any such rights being revived.

For any chargeable period for which a person's qualifying expenditure is less than the disposal value to be brought in, a *balancing charge* is made on him on the amount of the difference. [*ICTA 1988, s 520(1)(4)–(6); FA 1994, s 214(4)*].

'Qualifying expenditure' for a chargeable period is the aggregate of any capital expenditure on patent rights incurred before the end of the chargeable period or its basis period which has not, in whole or part, previously formed part of qualifying expenditure, and any unallowed balance brought forward from the previous chargeable period. [*ICTA 1988, s 521(1); FA 1994, Sch 26 Pt V(24)*].

A *disposal value* falls to be brought in for a chargeable period in which, or in the basis period for which, a person sells the whole or part of any patent rights on the purchase of which he has incurred capital expenditure. The value to be brought in is the net sale proceeds, except that:

(1) the sale proceeds to be brought in shall not exceed the capital expenditure incurred on purchase of the rights; and

(2) where the rights were acquired as a result of a transaction between CONNECTED PERSONS (20) (or a series of such transactions), (1) above shall have effect as if it referred to the highest capital expenditure incurred on the purchase of those rights by any of those connected persons. [*ICTA 1988, s 521(2)–(4); FA 1994, Sch 26 Pt V(24)*].

Connected persons and anti-avoidance. Where a person incurs capital expenditure after 26 July 1989 on the purchase of rights either from a connected person (see 20 CONNECTED PERSONS), or so that it appears that the sole or main benefit from the sale and any other transactions would have been the obtaining of an allowance under these provisions, the amount of that expenditure taken into account in determining any writing-down allowance or balancing allowance or charge to or on the purchaser may not exceed an amount determined as follows:

(I) where a disposal value (see above) falls to be brought into account, an amount equal to that value;

(II) where no disposal value falls to be brought into account, but the seller receives a capital sum chargeable under Schedule D, Case VI (see 54.5 PATENTS), an amount equal to that sum;

(III) in any other case, an amount equal to the smallest of

(i) open market value of the rights;

(ii) the amount of capital expenditure, if any, incurred by the seller on acquiring the rights;

(iii) the amount of capital expenditure, if any, incurred by any person connected with the seller on acquiring the rights.

[*ICTA 1988, s 521(5)–(7); FA 1989, Sch 13 para 27*]. Previously, the restriction was by reference to the disposal value only. See also (2) above.

Expenditure incurred before 1 April 1986

This expenditure is allowable in full, by equal annual instalments (or pro rata for shorter periods), over the shortest of

(i) seventeen years,

(ii) the period of the rights purchased, and

(iii) if the rights purchased begin a year or more after the date from which the patent became effective, and are not for a specified period, seventeen years less the number of complete years from the patent becoming effective to the rights being purchased (minimum writing-down period one year),

beginning with the year of assessment in whose basis period the expenditure is incurred. [*ICTA 1988, s 522(3)–(5)*].

Balancing adjustments arise where, before the end of the writing-down period (see above), any of the following events occur.

(A) The rights come to an end without subsequently being revived.

(B) The rights (or remaining rights) are sold, the net proceeds of sale being

(i) less than the unallowed expenditure, or

(ii) greater than the unallowed expenditure.

(C) Part of the rights is sold, the net proceeds of sale being greater than the unallowed expenditure.

Where (A) or (B)(i) apply, a *balancing allowance* is given on the unallowed expenditure (less net sale proceeds, if any) provided that writing-down allowances have been given in respect of the rights (or would have been given but for the sale etc.).

Where (B)(ii) or (C) apply, a *balancing charge* is made on the excess of net sale proceeds over unallowed expenditure (but limited to allowances granted in respect of the rights).

Where part of the rights is sold but (C) does not apply, writing-down allowances for the year of assessment in whose basis period the sale takes place and subsequent years are recalculated after deducting net sale proceeds from the unallowed expenditure before the period of the sale.

Balancing allowances and charges are given or made for the year of assessment in whose basis period the related event occurs, and no writing-down allowance is made for that year. [*ICTA 1988, s 523*].

Connected persons and anti-avoidance. There are provisions for the substitution of open market value for sale consideration on certain 'sole or main benefit' transactions, sales without change of control and sales between connected persons, subject in the latter cases to an election for unallowed expenditure to be substituted instead. [*CAA 1990, ss 157, 158; ICTA 1988, s 532*]. However, where the inventor is the seller, no such election is available unless he sells to own controlled company at less than market value, in which case allowances and charges (and, if the purchaser agrees, capital gains tax) may be based on actual price paid (Revenue Pamphlet IR 1, B17).

Making of allowances and charges. *Traders*, using patent rights for purposes of a trade chargeable under Schedule D, Case I, may claim allowances and suffer charges in taxing the trade. Excess allowances may be used as under Dredging (10.7 above); this is of no application where allowances fall to be treated as trading expenses (see 10.1 above).

Non-traders may only set allowances against income from patents, excess allowances being carried forward without time limit. Balancing charges are assessed under Schedule D, Case VI. [*ICTA 1988, s 528; FA 1994, Sch 26 Pt V(24)*].

Trading partnerships and successions are treated in the same way as for industrial buildings allowances (see 10.22(iii)(iv)).

See 54 PATENTS for treatment of patent royalties and capital sums received, and 71.73 SCHEDULE D, CASES I AND II for trading income and expenses re patents.

Simon's Direct Tax Service. See **B2.602** *et seq.*.

10.51 *Example*

P, who prepares accounts to 31 December, acquires three new patent rights for trading purposes.

	Date	Term	Cost
Patent 1	20.2.86	20 years	£6,800
Patent 2	19.4.99	15 years	£4,500
Patent 3	5.10.00	5 years	£8,000

On 1.10.00 P sold his rights under patent 1 for £5,000 and on 1.12.00 he sold part of the rights under patent 2 for £2,000.

The allowances for each patent are

Patent 1	£
Expenditure	6,800
1987/88 (basis period — y/e 31.12.86)	
WDA $\frac{1}{17}$ × £6,800	(400)
	6,400
1988/89 to 1999/2000	
WDA $\frac{1}{17}$ × £6,800 × 12 years	(4,800)
	1,600
2000/01 (period of account — y/e 31.12.00)	
Disposal proceeds	(5,000)
Balancing charge	£3,400

Patents 2 and 3	Pool	WDA
1999/2000 (period of account — year to 31.12.99)		
	£	£
Expenditure (patent 2)	4,500	
WDA 25%	(1,125)	£1,125
	3,375	
2000/01 (period of account — year to 31.12.00)		
Expenditure (patent 3)	8,000	
Disposal proceeds (patent 2)	(2,000)	
	9,375	
WDA 25%	(2,344)	£2,344
WDV c/f	£7,031	

10.52 **SCIENTIFIC RESEARCH/RESEARCH AND DEVELOPMENT** [*CAA 1990, ss 137–139; FA 2000, s 68, Sch 19*]

Capital expenditure incurred by a trader on (for 1999/2000 and earlier years) 'scientific research', or (for 2000/01 and subsequent years) 'research and development', related to the trade, and undertaken directly or on his behalf (i.e. by an agent or other person in a similar contractual relationship, see *Gaspet Ltd v Elliss CA 1987, 60 TC 91*), attracts a **100% allowance.** A just apportionment may be made of expenditure which partly qualifies. The allowance is also available where the expenditure is incurred before commencement of the trade. An 'additional VAT liability' (see 10.2(v) above) incurred, in respect of qualifying expenditure, before the asset ceases to belong to the trader is itself qualifying expenditure.

For 1996/97 and earlier years as regards trades commenced before 6 April 1994, the allowance may be deducted in taxing the trade for the year of assessment in whose basis period the expenditure is incurred, except that

(i) where basis periods overlap, expenditure in the common period is treated as incurred only in the earlier period,

(ii) expenditure in an interval between two basis periods is treated as incurred in the later period, unless it is the period of permanent discontinuance of the trade, in which case it is treated as incurred in the earlier period, and

(iii) expenditure incurred before commencement of the trade gives rise to an allowance for the year of assessment in which the trade is commenced.

For 1994/95 and subsequent years as regards trades commenced after 5 April 1994 and for 1997/98 and subsequent years as regards trades commenced on or before that date, the allowance is deducted as a trading expense of the chargeable period (see 10.2(vi) above) in which the expenditure is incurred (or, in the case of pre-trading expenditure, the chargeable period beginning with commencement of trade).

No allowances are available in respect of expenditure on the acquisition of, or of rights in or over, *land* except insofar as, on a just apportionment, the expenditure is referable to such acquisition of a building or other structure already constructed on the land, or of machinery or plant which forms part of such a building, etc..

Expenditure on provision of a *dwelling* does not qualify for allowances, except that where not more than one quarter of the expenditure (disregarding any 'additional VAT liability' or 'rebate' — see 10.2(v) above) on a building consisting partly of a dwelling and partly of a building used for scientific research is justly apportionable to the dwelling, the whole of the expenditure may be the subject of allowance.

[*CAA 1990, ss 137, 140(1)(2)(5); FA 1985, s 63(7); FA 1991, Sch 14 para 12; FA 1994, ss 211, 213(10); FA 2000, Sch 19 para 8*].

'*Scientific research*' is defined as activities in the fields of natural or applied science for the extension of knowledge. [*CAA 1990, s 139(1)*]. Any question of whether, and to what extent, any activities constitute scientific research, or any asset is used for scientific research, is ultimately referred to the Secretary of State for a final decision. [*CAA 1990, s 139(3)*]. For the Revenue approach to such questions, see Revenue Capital Allowances Manual, CA 5000–5011. For a case in which allowances were refused on the grounds that the research was not related to the trade of publishing *inter alia* the findings of the research, see *Salt v Golding (Sp C 81), [1996] SSCD 269.*

'*Research and development*' means activities treated as such under normal UK company accounting practice, subject to any Treasury regulations excluding or adding any activities within the definition. It includes oil and gas exploration and appraisal (within *ICTA 1988, s 837B*). Any dispute as to what constitutes research and development is subject to the normal appeal procedures. [*ICTA 1988, s 837A; FA 2000, Sch 19 paras 1, 10*].

For special provisions relating to oil licences, see *CAA 1990, ss 138A, 138B.*

A **balancing adjustment** arises when an asset representing allowable scientific research or research and development expenditure ceases to belong to the trader. The 'disposal value' of the asset, up to a maximum of the amount of the expenditure (less any 'additional VAT rebate' falling to be treated as a trading receipt — see below), is normally treated as a trading receipt accruing at the time of the event giving rise to the adjustment or, if earlier, immediately before permanent discontinuance of the trade. A deduction may similarly be given for net demolition costs in respect of assets destroyed. (For 1997/98 and earlier years, where the event giving rise to the adjustment took place before the chargeable period for which an allowance in respect of the expenditure was due (disregarding any allowance due in respect of an 'additional VAT liability' — see above), an allowance was instead made of the excess (if any) of the expenditure over the disposal value and was allowed in taxing the trade for the chargeable period of that event.) The amount of the '*disposal value*' depends on the nature of the event giving rise to the adjustment:

(1) if the asset is sold at open market value or higher, it is the sale proceeds;

(2) if the asset is destroyed, it is the sum of any compensation received and any receipts for the remains of the asset *less* any demolition costs;

(3) in any other event, it is the open market value.

In the event of a sale, the asset ceases to belong to a person at the earlier of the time of completion and the time when possession is given.

An 'additional VAT rebate' (see 10.2(v) above) made in respect of allowable scientific research or research and development expenditure before the asset in question ceases to belong to the trader is treated as a trading receipt accruing for the chargeable period related to the making of the rebate or, if earlier, immediately before permanent discontinuance of the trade.

[*CAA 1990, s 138(1)–(5)(8), s 139(4); FA 1991, Sch 14 para 13: FA 2000, Sch 19 para 8*].

Double allowances, etc.. See 10.2(iv) above. No balancing charge is made on a sale giving rise to an industrial building or machinery and plant balancing charge (see 10.15, 10.30 above), and balancing allowances are similarly restricted for chargeable or basis periods ending before 27 July 1989. [*CAA 1990, s 138(6)(7); FA 1994, Sch 26 Pt V(24)*].

Excess allowances may be used as under dredging (see 10.7 above).

Connected persons and other anti-avoidance provisions apply to substitute open market value for sale consideration on certain 'sole or main benefit' transactions, sales without change of control and sales between connected persons. For most sales, the election referred to at 10.22(i) above is available, with the result that an asset representing expenditure for which the 100% allowance has been made will be treated as transferred for nil consideration. [*CAA 1990, ss 157, 158; FA 1993, s 117(3)–(5); FA 1994, s 119(1)*].

For expenditure of a revenue nature, see 71.80 SCHEDULE D, CASES I AND II.

Simon's Direct Tax Service. See **B2.7**.

10.53 *Example*

C is in business manufacturing and selling cosmetics, and he prepares accounts annually to 30 June. For the purposes of this trade, he built a new laboratory adjacent to his existing premises, incurring the following expenditure.

		£
April 1997	Laboratory building	50,000
June 1997	Technical equipment	3,000
March 1998	Technical equipment	4,000
July 1998	Plant	2,500
August 1999	Extension to existing premises comprising 50% further laboratory area and 50% sales offices.	30,000

In July 1998 a small fire destroyed an item of equipment originally costing £2,000 in June 1997; insurance recoveries totalled £3,000. In March 1999, the plant costing £2,500 was sold for £1,800.

The allowances due are as follows.

	£
1997/98 (period of account year ended 30.6.97)	
Laboratory building	50,000
Technical equipment	3,000
	£53,000
1998/99 (period of account year ended 30.6.98)	
Technical equipment	4,000
	£4,000
1999/2000 (period of account year ended 30.6.99)	
Net expenditure on plant sold (note (*a*))	700
Balancing adjustment on equipment destroyed (note (*b*))	(2,000)
	(£1,300)
2000/01 (period of account year ended 30.6.00)	
Extension	£15,000

Note

(*a*) As the plant was sold in the period of account in which the expenditure was incurred, the balancing charge of £1,800 may be set against the expenditure of £2,500, resulting in a net deduction of £700.

(*b*) The destruction of the equipment in the year to 30 June 1999 results in a balancing adjustment limited to the allowance originally given. The deemed trading receipt accrues in the period of account in which the event occurred.

11 Capital Gains Tax

For full details of CGT provisions, see Tolley's Capital Gains Tax. For date due see 56.1(*e*) PAYMENT OF TAX. See also 78.19 SELF-ASSESSMENT.

11.1 CAPITAL GAINS TAX (CGT)

The legislation applying to individuals and companies was consolidated by the *Taxation of Chargeable Gains Act 1992* (*TCGA 1992*) and references to that Act are given throughout this book where appropriate. For full details see Tolley's Capital Gains Tax.

11.2 EXCLUSION OF AMOUNTS OTHERWISE TAXED

Gains for CGT purposes are calculated exclusive of receipts chargeable to income tax or corporation tax (except items giving rise to balancing charges for CAPITAL ALLOWANCES (10) purposes). However, the capitalised value of a rentcharge, ground annual, feu duty or other series of income receipts can be taken into account for CGT purposes. [*TCGA 1992, s 37*].

11.3 RATE OF CGT

For 1999/2000 and subsequent years, the rate of CGT applicable to an individual is equivalent to the lower rate of income tax or, where the individual is liable at the higher rate or Schedule F upper rate on any part of his income, the higher rate. Where there is no higher rate or Schedule F upper rate income tax liability, but the amount chargeable to CGT exceeds the unused part of the basic rate band, the CGT rate on the excess is equivalent to the higher rate of income tax. For this purpose, the basic rate band is the whole of the amount up to the basic rate limit. For 1999/2000, the starting rate of income tax does not apply to CGT; for 2000/01 onwards, it so applies to the extent that taxable gains, if treated as though they were the top slice of income, would fall within the starting rate band. See 1.3 ALLOWANCES AND TAX RATES for the lower rate, the higher rate, the basic rate limit and the starting rate, and 1.9 ALLOWANCES AND TAX RATES as regards the Schedule F upper rate.

For 1998/99 and earlier years, the rate of CGT was equivalent to the basic rate of income tax or, where the individual was liable at the higher rate on any part of his income, the higher rate. Similar provisions applied as above where the amount chargeable to CGT exceeded the unused part of the basic rate band. In addition, where part or all of the lower rate band was unused, a corresponding part of the chargeable gains was chargeable at a rate equivalent to the lower rate (instead of the basic rate) of income tax.

In determining for the above purposes whether income is liable at the higher or Schedule F upper rate of income tax, and the unused part of the basic rate band, account is taken of various provisions of the *Income Tax Acts* requiring additions to or deductions from total income.

For 1998/99 onwards, the rate of CGT applicable to gains accruing to the trustees of a settlement or the personal representatives of a deceased person is equivalent to the 'rate applicable to trusts' (see 81.5 SETTLEMENTS). Before 1998/99, this applied only to gains accruing to trustees of accumulation and discretionary settlements.

[*TCGA 1992, ss 4–6; F(No 2)A 1992, s 23; FA 1994, Sch 26 Pt V; FA 1995, Sch 29 Pt VIII(8); F(No 2)A 1997, Sch 4 paras 24, 25; FA 1998, s 120, Sch 27 Pt III(29); FA 1999, s 26; FA 2000, s 37*].

For 1993/94 to 1998/99 inclusive, special computational provisions apply for a year of assessment for which all or part of an individual's lower rate band is utilised by dividend income (or, for 1996/97 onwards, 'savings income' — see 1.9 ALLOWANCES AND TAX RATES) and he has chargeable gains. The effect is to allocate to the gains that part of the lower rate band which is so utilised, with the individual's basic rate limit being reduced by the amount so allocated (and the gains chargeable at the higher rate being correspondingly reduced or eliminated where relevant). [*TCGA 1992, s 4(3A)(3B); FA 1993, Sch 6 para 22; FA 1996, Sch 6 paras 27, 28; FA 1999, s 26(4), Sch 20 Pt III(1)*].

Simon's Direct Tax Service. See **C1.107**.

11.4 SET-OFF OF INCOME TAX RELIEFS AGAINST CAPITAL GAINS

See 46.5 LOSSES for set-off of trading losses against capital gains. See 62.4 POST-CESSATION ETC. RECEIPTS AND EXPENDITURE for relief for certain post-cessation expenditure, and 75.23 SCHEDULE E for relief for certain post-employment expenditure.

12 Cash Basis

General note. See 12.2 below as regards **withdrawal** of cash basis.

Simon's Direct Tax Service B4.202.

12.1 **Periods of account beginning before 7 April 1999.** Business profits should be computed on an earnings basis (see 71.1 SCHEDULE D, CASES I AND II) but in practice the cash basis (where profits measured by excess of cash receipts over cash outlay, ignoring debtors and creditors, accruals, unbilled or uncompleted work) or some other recognisable basis short of a full earnings basis, is accepted for individuals or partnerships carrying on professions or vocations (*not trades*) if desired and provided the profits computed on the new basis will not, taking one year with another, differ materially from the profits computed on the earnings basis. The Revenue do, however, insist on the earnings basis for the first three accounting years of a new profession including one treated as new on a partnership change (see 53.6 PARTNERSHIPS) and, on the change to a cash etc. basis, require a written undertaking that bills for services rendered for work done will be issued at regular and frequent intervals. See *Walker v O'Connor (Sp C 74), 1996 STI 709* for a case in which the cash basis was held not to be permissible in opening years.

The change must be a complete one. For example, receipts after the change for work done before the change must be brought into account on the cash basis notwithstanding that they have already been brought into the earnings basis (*Morrison CS 1932, 17 TC 325*) and similarly expenses accrued due but unpaid which were debited in the accounts on the earnings basis may again be charged in the subsequent accounts on the cash basis when they are paid. Receipts after a cessation or change of basis which would otherwise escape assessment are assessable as post-cessation receipts etc. (see 62 POST-CESSATION ETC. RECEIPTS AND EXPENDITURE). *Note.* There is no relief for this 'double charge' on any later charge to post-cessation receipts.

A change from the cash basis to the earnings basis will be accepted but not a subsequent claim to revert to a cash basis. (Revenue Pamphlet IR 131, A27). The above does not apply to barristers, see below.

See *Rankine v CIR CS 1952, 32 TC 520*, for limitation of Revenue's rights of revision on change-over of basis and *Wetton, Page & Co v Attwooll Ch D 1962, 40 TC 619*, for Revenue's rights to insist on earnings basis notwithstanding use of cash basis in other years. See also *McCash & Hunter v CIR CS 1955, 36 TC 170* (outgoing partner's share of receipts when cash basis applies).

Barristers are normally assessed on a cash basis but may elect to change to the earnings basis (or adopt that basis from commencement of practice). The earnings basis need not include work in progress. A change to the earnings basis or cessation of practice will attract a charge on POST-CESSATION ETC. RECEIPTS AND EXPENDITURE (62). (Revenue Pamphlet IR 131, A3).

See further Revenue Inspector's Manual IM 1201 *et seq.*.

12.2 **Position from 7 April 1999.** For periods of account beginning **on or after 7 April 1999** (subject only to the exemption referred to below for certain barristers and advocates), there is a statutory requirement for Schedule D, Case I and II profits to be computed on an accounting basis giving a 'true and fair view' (subject to any adjustment under specific legislation), for which see generally 71.40 SCHEDULE D, CASES I AND II. Broadly, this requires profits to be computed on the earnings basis, so that the cash basis (as above) may no longer be employed for tax purposes. Periods of account beginning before 7 April 1999 and still current on 7 April 2000 are treated for this purpose as having ended on 6 April 1999, with a new period having begun on 7 April 1999 (which is thus subject to these provisions). A period of account for these purposes is any period for which accounts are drawn up. [*FA 1998, ss 42, 45*].

Barristers and advocates are exempt from these requirements for periods of account ending not more than seven years after they first hold themselves out as available for fee-earning work. They may instead compute their profits either on the cash basis (as above) or by reference to fees earned whose amount has been agreed or in respect of which a fee note has been delivered, provided that a basis so adopted is applied consistently. If an accounting basis complying with *FA 1998, s 42* (as above) is adopted for a period of account, then that *section* applies for all subsequent periods of account. [*FA 1998, s 43*].

Change of accounting basis on which profits computed for tax purposes. For any change after 5 April 1999, from one period of account to the next, from an accounting basis according with law and practice applicable immediately before the change to one according with law and practice applicable immediately after the change, an adjustment is required as follows for tax purposes (replacing the provisions of *ICTA 1988, s 104(4)*, see 62.2 POST-CESSATION ETC. RECEIPTS AND EXPENDITURE, and any rule of law as to the adjustments required in those circumstances).

A *positive* adjustment is treated as income arising on the first day of the first period of account after the change (subject to the spreading provisions described below), chargeable under SCHEDULE D, CASE VI (74). For loss relief purposes it is treated as profits of the trade, etc. for the chargeable period for which it is charged to tax, and in the case of an individual for whom the income from the trade etc. is 'relevant earnings' (see 60.8 PERSONAL PENSION SCHEMES, 65.7 RETIREMENT ANNUITIES) or earned income within *ICTA 1988, s 833(4)(c)* (see 1.7(ii) ALLOWANCES AND TAX RATES) it is similarly relevant earnings or earned income. A *negative* adjustment is treated as an expense of the trade, etc. for the first period after the change.

The amount of the adjustment is calculated in three steps.

(*a*) The taxable receipts and allowable expenses of periods before the change are determined on the old and new bases, and the net understatement of profits (or overstatement of losses) on the old basis compared with the new basis determined (a negative figure resulting if there is a net overstatement of profits or understatement of losses).

(*b*) This figure is then adjusted for any difference between the closing stock or work in progress for the last period of account before the change and the opening stock or work in progress for the first period of account after the change.

(*c*) If the change of accounting basis is to comply with *FA 1998, s 42* (as above), a further adjustment may be made in respect of any change of accounting basis before 6 April 1999. This will reflect any receipts or expenses brought into account in more than one period of account or not brought into account in any period of account, and any difference between the closing stock or work in progress for the last period of account before the change and the opening stock or work in progress for the first period of account after the change.

No further deduction is allowed in any period of account for amounts deducted in arriving in the figures at (*a*) or (*b*) above as representing an overstatement of profit. Similarly amounts may not be deducted in arriving in the figure at (*c*) above as representing an overstatement of profit if previously brought into account, and amounts which are deducted in arriving at the figure in (*c*) above may not be deducted again on a subsequent change of accounting basis.

For these purposes only items brought into account in the same trade, etc., and in accordance with the law and practice then applicable, are considered. Deemed discontinuances under *ICTA 1988, s 113(1)* (see 71.25 SCHEDULE D, CASES I AND II) or *ICTA 1988, s 337(1)* (company beginning or ceasing to carry on a trade) prevent a trade, etc. being the same trade, etc. for this purpose.

Where an individual has been entitled to compute the profits of his profession or vocation (but *not* a trade) on a basis which does not meet the requirements of *FA 1998, s 42*, and the change of accounting basis is to comply with that *section*, either on its coming into effect or on the exemption for barristers and advocates coming to an end or ceasing to apply, any adjustment charge (as above) is (subject to the election described below) spread over ten years. In the year of assessment in which it would otherwise be chargeable in full and in each of the next eight years of assessment, the amount brought into charge is the lesser of one-tenth of the full amount of the adjustment charge and one-tenth of the Schedule D, Case II profits of the profession or vocation for the year of assessment (disregarding capital allowances and balancing charges). The balance of the adjustment charge is brought in in the following year of assessment. If the profession or vocation is (or is treated as) permanently discontinued before the whole of the adjustment charge has been charged to tax, the restriction of payments by reference to Schedule D, Case II profits ceases to apply. The individual may elect (by notice in writing to the Revenue before 31 January following a year of assessment) for the part of the adjustment charge treated as income of the year of assessment to be increased to a specified amount (up to the balance not previously brought into charge). Following such an election, the payments in later years are reduced as if the original amount of the adjustment charge had been reduced by the additional amount treated as arising in the year for which the election was made (subject to any further election). See Revenue Tax Bulletin February 1999 pp 625, 626 for a short article on the working of the 'catching-up' charge.

In the case of trades, professions or vocations carried on in *partnership*, the adjustment is calculated as if the partnership were an individual (or, for corporation tax purposes, a company) resident in the UK. Each partner's share is determined according to the profit-sharing arrangements for the twelve months immediately before the date of the change of accounting basis or, if the ten-year spreading provisions (as above) apply, the twelve months immediately preceding that date or the anniversary of that date falling in the year of assessment of charge. An election for accelerated payment in any year of assessment (as above) must be made by all persons who were partners in the twelve months immediately preceding the anniversary of the date of change in that year. If there is a discontinuance (or deemed discontinuance) before the whole of the adjustment charge has been charged to tax, each partner's share of any amount chargeable on or after the discontinuance is determined according to the profit-sharing arrangements

(i) if the discontinuance occurs on the date of change of accounting basis, for the twelve months ending immediately before that date,

(ii) if it occurs after that date but before the first anniversary thereof, for the period between that date and the date of discontinuance,

(iii) if it occurs after the first anniversary of the date of change, for the period between the immediately preceding anniversary and the date of discontinuance,

and any election after the discontinuance for accelerated payment (as above) must be made by each former partner separately.

In the case of the death of an individual otherwise liable to payments of an adjustment charge spread over ten years (as above), the *personal representative* assumes the outstanding liabilities and may make any election for accelerated payment (as above).

[*FA 1998, s 44, Sch 6*].

As regards valuation of professional work in progress, see 71.83 SCHEDULE D, CASES I AND II.

13 Certificates of Deposit

Simon's Direct Tax Service B3.736.

13.1 A certificate of deposit is any document relating to money, in any currency, which has been deposited with the issuer or some other person, being a document which recognises an obligation to pay a stated amount to bearer or to order, with or without interest, and being a document by the delivery of which, with or without endorsement, the right to receive that stated amount, with or without interest, is transferable. [*ICTA 1988, s 56(5)*]. It does not include bearer bonds. (CCAB Memorandum June 1973).

13.2 Profits or gains (other than in respect of interest) on certificates of deposit acquired after 6 March 1973 will be taxable under Schedule D, Case VI (if not taxable as a trading receipt). A loss on a certificate of deposit can be offset against interest assessable in respect of it. These provisions do not apply to exempt pension funds and charities. [*ICTA 1988, s 56(1)(a)(2)(3), s 398*].

13.3 Where, in a transaction in which no certificate of deposit or security (as defined by *TCGA 1992, s 132*) is issued, but an amount becomes payable with interest (by a bank, similar institution or person regularly engaging in similar transactions), then if the right to receive the amount or interest is disposed of or exercised, any profit (or loss) will be treated as in 13.2 above. [*ICTA 1988, s 56(1)(b)*]. Where a right to receive an amount (with or without interest) in pursuance of a deposit of money comes into existence without a certificate of deposit, but the person entitled to the right could call for the issue of such a certificate, a profit (or loss) on disposal of the right before the issue of such a certificate is similarly treated as in 13.2 above. [*ICTA 1988, s 56A; F(No 2)A 1992, Sch 8 para 1*].

13.4 13.1–13.3 above do not apply for corporation tax purposes for accounting periods ending after 31 March 1996 (subject to transitional provisions). [*ICTA 1988, s 56(4A)(4B); FA 1996, Sch 14 para 6*]. See now Tolley's Corporation Tax under Loan Relationships.

14 Certificates of Tax Deposit

Simon's Direct Tax Service A3.1327–A3.1329.

14.1 A taxpayer (including partnerships, companies and personal representatives) may make deposits, evidenced by Certificates of Tax Deposit, with Collectors of Taxes for the subsequent payment of tax generally (other than PAYE and tax deducted from payments to construction sub-contractors and corporation tax — see further below). If a deposit is tendered in respect of any liability, that liability will be treated as paid on the later of the certificate date and the normal due date for that liability (see 57 PAYMENT OF TAX). The minimum initial deposit is £2,000 with minimum additions of £500. Deposits of £100,000 or over must be made by direct remittance to the Bank of England.

Series 7 Certificates are not available for purchase for use against corporation tax liabilities.

Interest, which is payable gross but taxable, will accrue for a maximum of six years from the date of deposit to the date of payment of tax or, if earlier, the 'deemed due date' for payment of the liability against which the deposit (plus accrued interest) is set. The '*deemed due date*' is generally the normal due date for payment of the tax under the relevant legislation, and does not change if for any reason an assessment is made late or the liability is not payable until later (e.g. following settlement of an appeal). A deposit may be withdrawn for cash at any time but will then receive a reduced rate of interest. Where a certificate is used in settlement of a tax liability, interest at the higher rate up to the normal due date may be less than interest at the encashment rate up to the reckonable date. In such circumstances the taxpayer may instruct the Collector to calculate interest on the latter basis. (ICAEW Technical Release TAX 13/93, 30 June 1993). The rates of interest, published by the Treasury, and calculated by reference to the rate on comparable investment with the Government, vary with the size and period of the deposit, and the rate payable on a deposit is adjusted to the current rate on each anniversary of the deposit.

Deposits are not transferable except to personal representatives of a deceased person or by a company for tax payable by other members of a group of companies. It is understood that certificates held in the name of a partnership may, with written authorisation from all the partners, be used in settlement of partners' individual liabilities. (Tolley's Practical Tax 1993 p 183).

Rates of interest are given at 14.2, 14.3 and 14.4 below. Information on current rates may be obtained from the Reuters Monitor Service, Page Index TREG and TREH, from any Collector of Taxes, or from Inland Revenue Financial Accounts Office on Worthing (01903) 700222 ext 2064/5.

14.2 The rates of interest on date of deposit or anniversary on Series 6 and Series 7 Certificates for deposits of under £100,000 (and, before 16 November 1992, for other deposits withdrawn for cash) are (from 1 January 1994 to 1 July 2000)

	Used to pay tax	Withdrawals for cash
1 January 1994–8 February 1994	$1\frac{3}{4}$%	1%
9 February 1994–12 September 1994	$1\frac{1}{2}$%	$\frac{3}{4}$%
13 September 1994–7 December 1994	2%	1%
8 December 1994–2 February 1995	$2\frac{1}{2}$%	$1\frac{1}{4}$%
3 February 1995–13 December 1995	3%	$1\frac{1}{2}$%

	Used to pay tax	Withdrawals for cash
14 December 1995–18 January 1996	$2\frac{1}{2}$%	$1\frac{1}{4}$%
19 January 1996–10 March 1996	$2\frac{3}{4}$%	$1\frac{1}{2}$%
11 March 1996–6 June 1996	$2\frac{1}{2}$%	$1\frac{1}{4}$%
7 June 1996–30 October 1996	$2\frac{1}{4}$%	$1\frac{1}{4}$%
31 October 1996–6 May 1997	$1\frac{1}{4}$%	$1\frac{1}{4}$%
7 May 1997–8 June 1997	$2\frac{3}{4}$%	$1\frac{1}{2}$%
9 June 1997–10 July 1997	3%	$1\frac{1}{2}$%
11 July 1997–7 August 1997	$3\frac{1}{4}$%	$1\frac{3}{4}$%
8 August 1997–6 November 1997	$4\frac{1}{2}$%	$2\frac{1}{4}$%
7 November 1997–8 October 1998	4%	2%
9 October 1998–5 November 1998	$3\frac{3}{4}$%	2%
6 November 1998–7 January 1999	$3\frac{1}{4}$%	$1\frac{3}{4}$%
8 January 1999–4 February 1999	$2\frac{1}{2}$%	$1\frac{1}{4}$%
5 February 1999–10 June 1999	$1\frac{3}{4}$%	1%
11 June 1999–8 September 1999	$1\frac{1}{2}$%	$\frac{3}{4}$%
9 September 1999–3 November 1999	$1\frac{3}{4}$%	1%
4 November 1999–13 January 2000	2%	1%
14 January 2000–10 February 2000	$2\frac{1}{4}$%	$1\frac{1}{4}$%
11 February 2000 onwards	$2\frac{1}{2}$%	$1\frac{1}{4}$%

14.3 The rates of interest on date of deposit or anniversary on Series 6 or Series 7 Certificates for deposits of £100,000 or more used to meet a scheduled liability are (from 1 January 1994 to 1 July 2000)

	Period of deposit in months				
	Under 1	1 but under 3	3 but under 6	6 but under 9	9 but under 12
1 January 1994–12 September 1994	$1\frac{1}{2}$%	4%	$3\frac{3}{4}$%	$3\frac{3}{4}$%	$3\frac{1}{2}$%
13 September 1994–7 December 1994	2%	$4\frac{3}{4}$%	$4\frac{3}{4}$%	5%	$5\frac{1}{2}$%
8 December 1994–2 February 1995	$2\frac{1}{2}$%	$5\frac{1}{4}$%	$5\frac{1}{2}$%	$5\frac{3}{4}$%	6%
3 February 1995–13 December 1995	3%	$5\frac{3}{4}$%	$5\frac{3}{4}$%	6%	$6\frac{1}{4}$%
14 December 1995–18 January 1996	$2\frac{1}{2}$%	$5\frac{1}{2}$%	5%	5%	$4\frac{3}{4}$%
19 January 1996–10 March 1996	$2\frac{3}{4}$%	$5\frac{1}{4}$%	$4\frac{3}{4}$%	$4\frac{3}{4}$%	$4\frac{1}{2}$%
11 March 1996–6 June 1996	$2\frac{1}{2}$%	5%	$4\frac{3}{4}$%	$4\frac{3}{4}$%	$4\frac{1}{2}$%
7 June 1996–30 October 1996	$2\frac{1}{4}$%	$4\frac{3}{4}$%	$4\frac{3}{4}$%	$4\frac{3}{4}$%	$4\frac{3}{4}$%
31 October 1996–6 May 1997	$2\frac{1}{2}$%	$5\frac{1}{4}$%	5%	5%	5%
7 May 1997–8 June 1997	$2\frac{3}{4}$%	$5\frac{1}{2}$%	$5\frac{1}{4}$%	$5\frac{1}{2}$%	$5\frac{1}{4}$%
9 June 1997–10 July 1997	3%	$5\frac{1}{2}$%	$5\frac{1}{2}$%	$5\frac{1}{2}$%	$5\frac{1}{2}$%
11 July 1997–7 August 1997	$3\frac{1}{4}$%	6%	$5\frac{3}{4}$%	$5\frac{3}{4}$%	6%
8 August 1997–6 November 1997	$4\frac{1}{2}$%	6%	6%	6%	$5\frac{3}{4}$%
7 November 1997–4 June 1998	4%	$6\frac{1}{2}$%	$6\frac{1}{2}$%	$6\frac{1}{4}$%	$6\frac{1}{4}$%
5 June 1998–8 October 1998	4%	$6\frac{1}{2}$%	$6\frac{1}{4}$%	$6\frac{1}{4}$%	6%
9 October 1998–5 November 1998	$3\frac{3}{4}$%	$6\frac{1}{4}$%	$5\frac{3}{4}$%	$5\frac{1}{2}$%	$5\frac{1}{4}$%
6 November 1998–10 December 1998	$3\frac{1}{4}$%	$5\frac{3}{4}$%	$5\frac{1}{4}$%	5%	$4\frac{3}{4}$%
11 December 1998–7 January 1999	3%	$5\frac{1}{4}$%	$4\frac{3}{4}$%	$4\frac{1}{2}$%	$4\frac{1}{4}$%
8 January 1999–4 February 1999	$2\frac{1}{2}$%	5%	$4\frac{1}{2}$%	4%	4%
5 February 1999–8 April 1999	$1\frac{3}{4}$%	$4\frac{1}{2}$%	4%	$3\frac{3}{4}$%	$3\frac{3}{4}$%
9 April 1999–10 June 1999	$1\frac{3}{4}$%	$4\frac{1}{4}$%	4%	$3\frac{3}{4}$%	$3\frac{3}{4}$%
11 June 1999–8 September 1999	$1\frac{1}{2}$%	4%	4%	4%	4%
9 September 1999–3 November 1999	$1\frac{3}{4}$%	$4\frac{1}{2}$%	$4\frac{1}{2}$%	$4\frac{1}{2}$%	$4\frac{1}{2}$%

14.4 Certificates of Tax Deposit

	Period of deposit in months				
	Under 1	1 but under 3	3 but under 6	6 but under 9	9 but under 12
4 November 1999–13 January 2000	2%	5%	$4\frac{3}{4}\%$	$4\frac{3}{4}\%$	$4\frac{3}{4}\%$
14 January 2000–10 February 2000	$2\frac{1}{4}\%$	5%	5%	5%	$5\frac{1}{4}\%$
11 February 2000 onwards	$2\frac{1}{2}\%$	$5\frac{1}{4}\%$	5%	$5\frac{1}{4}\%$	$5\frac{1}{4}\%$

14.4 The rates of interest on date of deposit or anniversary on Series 6 or Series 7 Certificates for deposits of £100,000 or more withdrawn for cash are (from 1 January 1994 to 1 July 2000)

	Period of deposit in months				
	Under 1	1 but under 3	3 but under 6	6 but under 9	9 but under 12
1 January 1994–8 February 1994	1%	$2\frac{1}{4}\%$	2%	2%	$1\frac{3}{4}\%$
9 February 1994–12 September 1994	$\frac{3}{4}\%$	2%	2%	$1\frac{3}{4}\%$	$1\frac{3}{4}\%$
13 September 1994–7 December 1994	1%	$2\frac{1}{2}\%$	$2\frac{1}{2}\%$	$2\frac{1}{2}\%$	$2\frac{3}{4}\%$
8 December 1994–2 February 1995	$1\frac{1}{4}\%$	$2\frac{3}{4}\%$	$2\frac{3}{4}\%$	3%	3%
3 February 1995–13 December 1995	$1\frac{1}{2}\%$	3%	3%	3%	$3\frac{1}{4}\%$
14 December 1995–18 January 1996	$1\frac{1}{4}\%$	$2\frac{3}{4}\%$	$2\frac{1}{2}\%$	$2\frac{1}{2}\%$	$2\frac{1}{2}\%$
19 January 1996–10 March 1996	$1\frac{1}{2}\%$	$2\frac{3}{4}\%$	$2\frac{1}{2}\%$	$2\frac{1}{2}\%$	$2\frac{1}{4}\%$
11 March 1996–6 June 1996	$1\frac{1}{4}\%$	$2\frac{1}{2}\%$	$2\frac{1}{2}\%$	$2\frac{1}{2}\%$	$2\frac{1}{4}\%$
7 June 1996–30 October 1996	$1\frac{1}{4}\%$	$2\frac{1}{2}\%$	$2\frac{1}{2}\%$	$2\frac{1}{2}\%$	$2\frac{1}{2}\%$
31 October 1996–6 May 1997	$1\frac{1}{4}\%$	$2\frac{3}{4}\%$	$2\frac{1}{2}\%$	$2\frac{1}{2}\%$	$2\frac{1}{2}\%$
7 May 1997–10 July 1997	$1\frac{1}{2}\%$	$2\frac{3}{4}\%$	$2\frac{3}{4}\%$	$2\frac{3}{4}\%$	$2\frac{3}{4}\%$
11 July 1997–7 August 1997	$1\frac{3}{4}\%$	3%	3%	3%	3%
8 August 1997–6 November 1997	$2\frac{1}{4}\%$	3%	3%	3%	3%
7 November 1997–4 June 1998	2%	$3\frac{1}{4}\%$	$3\frac{1}{4}\%$	$3\frac{1}{4}\%$	$3\frac{1}{4}\%$
5 June 1998–8 October 1998	2%	$3\frac{1}{4}\%$	$3\frac{1}{4}\%$	$3\frac{1}{4}\%$	3%
9October 1998–5 November 1998	2%	$3\frac{1}{4}\%$	3%	$2\frac{3}{4}\%$	$2\frac{3}{4}\%$
6 November 1998–10 December 1998	$1\frac{3}{4}\%$	3%	$2\frac{3}{4}\%$	$2\frac{1}{2}\%$	$2\frac{1}{2}\%$
11 December 1998–7 January 1999	$1\frac{1}{2}\%$	$2\frac{3}{4}\%$	$2\frac{1}{2}\%$	$2\frac{1}{4}\%$	$2\frac{1}{4}\%$
8 January 1999–4 February 1999	$1\frac{1}{4}\%$	$2\frac{1}{2}\%$	$2\frac{1}{4}\%$	2%	2%
5 February 1999–10 June 1999	1%	$2\frac{1}{4}\%$	2%	2%	2%
11 June 1999–8 September 1999	$\frac{3}{4}\%$	2%	2%	2%	2%
9 September 1999–3 November 1999	1%	$2\frac{1}{4}\%$	$2\frac{1}{4}\%$	$2\frac{1}{4}\%$	$2\frac{1}{4}\%$
4 November 1999–13 January 2000	1%	$2\frac{1}{2}\%$	$2\frac{1}{2}\%$	$2\frac{1}{2}\%$	$2\frac{1}{2}\%$
14 January 2000–10 February 2000	$1\frac{1}{4}\%$	$2\frac{1}{2}\%$	$2\frac{1}{2}\%$	$2\frac{1}{2}\%$	$2\frac{3}{4}\%$
11 February 2000 onwards	$1\frac{1}{4}\%$	$2\frac{3}{4}\%$	$2\frac{1}{2}\%$	$2\frac{3}{4}\%$	$2\frac{3}{4}\%$

15 Charities

(See also Revenue Pamphlets IR 64 and IR 65, 'Giving to Charity: How businesses/individuals can get tax relief', IR 75, 'Tax Reliefs for Charities' and IR 113, 'Gift Aid — A Guide for Donors and Charities', all of which are due to be updated following *FA 2000*.)

Cross-references. See 13.2 CERTIFICATES OF DEPOSIT for exemption of gains; 30 EXEMPT ORGANISATIONS for other exempt organisations; 71.54 SCHEDULE D, CASES I AND II for employees seconded to charities.

Simon's Direct Tax Service C4.5.

Other sources. See Tolley's Charities Manual.

15.1 CHARITY, CHARITABLE PURPOSES — GENERAL PRINCIPLES

'Charity' means any body of persons or trust established for charitable purposes only. [*ICTA 1988, s 506(1)*]. The meaning of charity is also governed by general law. Under the *Recreational Charities Act 1958, s 1* the provision, in the interest of social welfare, of facilities for recreation or other leisure time occupation, is deemed to be charitable (subject to the principle that, unless the trust is for the relief of poverty (*Dingle v Turner HL 1972, 1 AER 878*), a trust or institution to be charitable must be for the public benefit). Charities may be registered under the *Charities Act 1993*. The CIR as an interested party may appeal to the High Court against a decision of the Charity Commissioners and *Charities Act 1993, s 10* provides for the exchange of information between the Charity Commissioners and the CIR.

Subject to the above, what is a charity rests largely on judicial interpretation. A leading case is *Special Commrs v Pemsel HL 1891, 3 TC 53* in which Lord Macnaghten laid down that 'charity' should be given its technical meaning under English law and comprises 'four principal divisions; trusts for the relief of poverty, trusts for the advancement of education, trusts for the advancement of religion and trusts beneficial to the community and not falling under any of the preceding heads. The trusts last referred to are not the less charitable . . . because incidentally they affect the rich as well as the poor'. In the same case it was held that in relation to tax the English definition should be applied to Scottish cases (and cf. *Jackson's Trustees v Lord Advocate CS 1926, 10 TC 460* and *CIR v Glasgow Police Athletic Assn HL 1953, 34 TC 76*). The concept of 'charity' may change with changes in social values (cf. *CIR v Trustees of Football Association Youth Trust HL 1980, 54 TC 413*).

The charity reliefs are not available to overseas charities (*Gull KB 1937, 21 TC 374; Dreyfus Foundation Inc v CIR HL 1955, 36 TC 126*).

Where land given for educational and certain other charitable purposes ceases to be used for such purposes and, under the *Reverter of Sites Act 1987*, is held by the trustees on a trust for sale for the benefit of the revertee, then unless the revertee is known to be a charity, there is a deemed disposal and reacquisition for capital gains purposes, which may give rise to a chargeable gain. Any income arising from the property will be liable to income tax, and a chargeable gain may also arise on a subsequent sale of the land. By concession, where the revertee is subsequently identified as a charity or disclaims all entitlement to the property (or where certain orders are made by the Charity Commissioners or the Secretary of State), provided that charitable status is re-established within six years of the date on which the land ceased to be held on the original charitable trust, any capital gains tax paid as above in the interim period will be discharged or repaid (with repayment supplement where appropriate) as will any income tax (provided that the income charged was used for charitable purposes). Partial relief will be given where the above conditions are only satisfied in respect of part of the property concerned. A request by the trustees for postponement of the tax payable will be accepted by the Revenue where the revertee has not been identified and this concession may apply. (Revenue Pamphlet IR 1, D47).

The *Charitable Trusts (Validation) Act 1954* provides for validating as charitable a pre-1953 trust if its property was in fact applied for charitable purposes only, notwithstanding that the trust also authorised its application for non-charitable purposes (cf. *Vernon & Sons Ltd Employees Fund v CIR Ch D 1956, 36 TC 484; Buxton v Public Trustees Ch D 1962, 41 TC 235*).

A donation by one charity to another has been applied for charitable purposes even though merely added to the funds of the other charity (*Helen Slater Charitable Trust Ltd CA 1981, 55 TC 230*).

The application of income to the making of loans at interest to the subsidiaries from whom the income was derived was held to be for charitable purposes in *Nightingale Ltd v Price (Sp C 66), [1996] SSCD 116.*

As regards the time at which charitable purposes arise, see *Guild and Others (as Trustees of the William Muir (Bond 9) Ltd Employees' Share Scheme) v CIR CS 1993, 66 TC 1* (trustees of share scheme required to repay loans out of proceeds of distribution and to apply balance to charitable purposes; held not to apply proceeds of distribution for charitable purposes).

For general restrictions on reliefs, see 15.10 below.

The Revenue have issued a booklet 'Guidelines on the Tax Treatment of Disaster Funds' (obtainable free of charge from Customer Services Manager, Financial Intermediaries and Claims Office, St John's House, Merton Road, Bootle, Merseyside L69 9BB (tel. 0151–472 6106) or FICO (Scotland), Trinity Park House, South Trinity Road, Edinburgh EH5 3SD (tel. 0131–551 8127)) to help people organising disaster appeal funds to decide what form their fund should take and to deal with any tax implications. See generally Revenue publication 'Fund-Raising for Charity' (15.7 below), which also in particular replaces paras 27 and 28 of this booklet.

A leaflet 'Setting up a Charity in Scotland' is also available free of charge from Inland Revenue FICO (Scotland), who may be contacted for enquiries on whether a body is charitable.

A 'Charity Fund-raising Pack' is available free of charge from Customer Services Manager, FICO, St John's House, Merton Road, Bootle, Merseyside L69 9BB (tel. 0151–472 6106) or FICO (Scotland) (as above). It contains three booklets: 'Trading by Charities' (an Inland Revenue booklet); 'VAT — Charities' (Customs and Excise); and 'Charities and Fund-raising: A Summary' (Charity Commissioners). The Charity Commissioners for England and Wales have also published more comprehensive advice for charity trustees in 'Charities and Fund-raising' (CC20), available from any of their offices, including St Alban's House, 57–60 Haymarket, London SW1Y 4QX. Detailed guidance on the use of professional fund-raisers and commercial participation is available in the Home Office publication 'Charitable Fund-raising: Professional and Commercial Involvement' (ISBN 0 11 341133 2, £5.50 from HMSO, tel. 0207–873 9090).

The Revenue have published a Code of Practice (No 5) setting out their standards for the carrying out of inspections of charities' records.

Simon's Direct Tax Service. See **C4.505**.

15.2 CHARITY, CHARITABLE PURPOSES — EXAMPLES

Relevant cases are summarised below under appropriate headings.

(*a*) **Almshouse.** Inmates need not be destitute (*Mary Clark Home Trustees v Anderson KB 1904, 5 TC 48*).

(*b*) **Arts.** A musical festival association and the Royal Choral Society have been held to be charitable (*Glasgow Musical Festival Assn CS 1926, 11 TC 154; Royal Choral Socy v CIR CA 1943, 25 TC 263*) but not companies formed to produce plays in association with the Arts Council (*Tennent Plays Ltd v CIR CA 1948, 30 TC 107*) or with the aim of furthering the theatre and dramatic taste (*Associated Artists Ltd v CIR Ch D 1956, 36 TC 499*).

(*c*) **Benevolent funds, etc.** for the relief of widows and orphans of members held charitable (*Society for the Relief of Widows and Orphans of Medical Men KB 1926, 11 TC 1; Baptist Union, etc. Ltd v CIR KB (NI) 1945, 26 TC 335*) but not a death benefit fund (*Royal Naval etc. Officers' Assn Ch D 1955, 36 TC 187*) nor a fund set up to promote the formation of mutual provident associations (*Nuffield Foundation v CIR; Nuffield Provident Guarantee Fund v CIR KB 1946, 28 TC 479*).

(*d*) **Education.** A trust for the advancement of education does not require an element of poverty to be charitable (*R v Special Commrs (ex p University College of N. Wales) CA 1909, 5 TC 408*). The technical college of a trade association was held to be charitable (*Scottish Woollen Technical College v CIR CS 1926, 11 TC 139*) as was the Students' Union of a medical college (*London Hospital Medical College Ch D 1976, 51 TC 365*) and a trust to promote sports in schools, etc. (*CIR v Trustees of Football Association Youth Trust HL 1980, 54 TC 413*). See also *Educational Grants Assn Ltd CA 1967, 44 TC 93; Abdul Caffoor Trustees v Ceylon Income Tax Commr PC 1961, 40 ATC 93*. For 'public school' see (*h*) below.

(*e*) **Hospital.** A Friendly Society's convalescent home was exempted (*Royal Antediluvian Order of Buffaloes v Owens KB 1927, 13 TC 176*).

(*f*) **Political and similar objects** (including the reform of the law) are not charitable purposes. Objects held not to be charitable include the reform of the law on vivisection (*National Anti-Vivisection Socy HL 1947, 28 TC 311*) and temperance (*Temperance Council etc. of England KB 1926, 10 TC 748*), simplified spelling (*Hunter 'C' Trustees v CIR KB 1929, 14 TC 427*), fostering Anglo-Swedish relations (*Anglo-Swedish Socy v CIR KB 1931, 16 TC 34*), Jewish resettlement (*Keren Kayemeth Le Jisroel Ltd v CIR HL 1932, 17 TC 27*) and a memorial fund for Bonar Law (*Bonar Law Memorial Trust v CIR KB 1933, 17 TC 508*).

(*g*) **Professional associations etc.** Professional associations are generally not admitted to be established for charitable purposes; they benefit their members, any wider public advantage being incidental (*R v Special Commrs (ex p Headmasters' Conference) KB 1925, 10 TC 73; General Medical Council v CIR CA 1928, 13 TC 819; Geologists' Assn v CIR CA 1928, 14 TC 271; Midland Counties Institution of Engineers v CIR KB 1928, 14 TC 285; General Nursing Council for Scotland v CIR CS 1929, 14 TC 645; Master Mariners (Honourable Company of) v CIR KB 1932, 17 TC 298*). But contrast *Institution of Civil Engineers v CIR CA 1931, 16 TC 158*, where the Institution was held to be charitable, any benefit to members being incidental. Members' clubs and social clubs are not charitable (*Scottish Flying Club v CIR CS 1935, 20 TC 1; Sir H J Williams's Trustees v CIR HL 1947, 27 TC 409*). An agricultural society for the general promotion of agriculture was held charitable (*CIR v Yorkshire Agricultural Socy CA 1927, 13 TC 58*) but not a statutory Pig Marketing Board (*Pig Marketing Board (Northern Ireland) v CIR KB (NI) 1945, 26 TC 319*) nor a society to promote foxhound breeding (*Peterborough Royal Foxhound Show Socy v CIR KB 1936, 20 TC 249*) (but it was given relief under a predecessor to *ICTA 1988, s 510* on its annual show — see 30.1 EXEMPT ORGANISATIONS).

(*h*) **Public school.** A school may be for the public benefit and qualify for the relief notwithstanding that it derives substantial receipts from fees (*Blake v Mayor etc. of London CA 1887, 2 TC 209; Ereaut v Girls' Public Day School Trust Ltd HL 1930,*

15 TC 529, and contrast *Birkenhead School Ltd v Dring KB 1926, 11 TC 273*). A Quaker school exclusively for children of members of the Society of Friends was refused relief (*Ackworth School v Betts KB 1915, 6 TC 642*) but a Roman Catholic school which admitted non-Catholic pupils qualified for relief (*Cardinal Vaughan Memorial School Trustees v Ryall KB 1920, 7 TC 611*).

(*i*) **Religion.** Charitable relief was refused for trusts to advance the 'religious, moral, social and recreative life' of Presbyterians in Londonderry (*Londonderry Presbyterian Church House Trustees v CIR CA(NI) 1946, 27 TC 431*), for the promotion and aiding of 'Roman Catholicism' in a particular district (*Ellis v CIR CA 1949, 31 TC 178*) and for the 'religious, educational and other parochial requirements' of the Roman Catholic inhabitants of a parish (*Cookstown Roman Catholic Church Trustees v CIR QB (NI) 1953, 34 TC 350*). In each case, the objects included non-charitable elements which prevented the whole being charitable. Relief was also refused to the Oxford Group (*Oxford Group v CIR CA 1949, 31 TC 221*).

(*j*) **Miscellaneous.** A nursing home (*Peebleshire Nursing Assn CS 1926, 11 TC 335*) and a holiday home (*Roberts Marine Mansions Trustees CA 1927, 11 TC 425*) providing services for members etc. at reduced fees held to be charitable, as was a non-profit-making company for publishing law reports (*Incorpd. Council of Law Reporting v A-G CA 1971, 47 TC 321*). Relief refused to a trust to maintain an historic building because it also had a non-charitable object (*Trades House of Glasgow v CIR CS 1969, 46 TC 178*) and to a Society established mainly with philanthropic objects which, in the event, were not achieved (*Hugh's Settlement Ltd v CIR KB 1938, 22 TC 281*). The inclusion of an object 'to promote the development of industry, commerce and enterprise' and ancillary objects prevented the objects as a whole of a Training and Enterprise Council from being charitable (*Oldham TEC v CIR Ch D 1996, 69 TC 231*).

15.3 SPECIFIC EXEMPTIONS AND RELIEFS FROM TAX

Apart from the exemptions at 15.4–15.9 below, charities are subject to tax on investment and rental income and gains and on profits from trades carried on in order to raise funds. The Schedule D exemptions at 15.4, 15.5 and 15.7 below are not general exemptions and hence do not extend to trades not falling within 15.7 below or to Case VI income generally (cf. *Grove v Young Men's Christian Association KB 1903*, *4 TC 613* and *Rotunda Hospital, Dublin v Coman HL 1920*, *7 TC 517*).

The exemptions are subject to the restrictions at 15.10 below.

Claims can be made, generally within the time limit at 17.4 CLAIMS, to Inland Revenue, FICO (Trusts and Charities), St John's House, Merton Road, Bootle, Merseyside L69 9BB or, in Scotland, FICO (Scotland), Trinity Park House, South Trinity Road, Edinburgh EH5 3SD. [*ICTA 1988, s 505(1)*]. The Board have powers to require the production of books, documents etc. relevant to any claim for exemption under *ICTA 1988, s 505(1), s 507* (see 30.3, 30.9, 30.14, 30.20 EXEMPT ORGANISATIONS) or *s 508* (see 77.1 SCIENTIFIC RESEARCH ASSOCIATIONS) leading to the repayment of income tax or the payment of tax credits. [*F(No 2)A 1992, s 28*].

Simon's Direct Tax Service. See **C4.518** *et seq.*.

15.4 **Rents — Schedules A and D.** Profits or gains in respect of rents or other receipts from an estate, interest or right in or over any land (whether in the UK or elsewhere) vested in any person for charitable purposes are exempt to the extent they are applied to charitable purposes only. [*ICTA 1988, s 505(1)(a); FA 1996, s 146(2)(5)*]. For 1995/96 and earlier years (and company accounting periods ended on or before 31 March 1996), the exemption did not strictly apply to rents etc. from land outside the UK, but such rents were exempt by concession. (Revenue Pamphlet IR 1, B9). Also, the legislation specifically referred to 'lands . . . belonging to a hospital, public school or almshouse, or vested in trustees for charitable purposes'. The special relief to hospitals etc. could often be covered by the relief to trusts for charitable purposes (cf. *Scottish Woollen Technical College v CIR CS 1926, 11 TC 139*) and was in any case of reduced importance since the abolition by *FA 1963* of the Schedule A charge on owner-occupied property.

15.5 **Interest and distributions.** Income of a charity, or applicable for charitable purposes under an Act of Parliament, charter, decree, deed of trust or will, is exempt so far as applied to charitable purposes and consisting of **Schedule C** income (see below), **Schedule D, Case III** income (or equivalent overseas income within **Schedule D, Case IV or V**), **Schedule D, Case V** income consisting of distributions which would be within Schedule F if the paying company were UK resident or distributions within **Schedule F**.

For 1995/96 and earlier years (and company accounting periods ended on or before 31 March 1996), the Schedule D exemption strictly applied only to yearly interest and annual payments but was extended by concession to bank interest whether yearly or not, to gross building society interest and dividends, to profits on discounting transactions within Schedule D, Case III and to overseas income not strictly exempt (Revenue Pamphlet IR 1, B9 — superseded by *FA 1996, s 146*).

Where under a will, a business was bequeathed to trustees to carry it on and pay the net profits to a charity, the amounts so paid were held to be annual payments (*R v Special Commrs (ex p Shaftesbury Homes) CA 1922, 8 TC 367*). In *Lawrence v CIR KB 1940, 23 TC 333* copyright royalties were held to be annual payments. For annual payments generally, see 23.10 DEDUCTION OF TAX AT SOURCE.

Schedule C income of trustees which is applicable towards repairs of any cathedral, college, church, chapel etc., is also exempt so far as applied to those purposes only. For 1996/97 and subsequent years, the charge (and corresponding exemptions) under Schedule C is transferred to Schedule D. [*ICTA 1988, s 505(1)(c)(d); FA 1996, s 146(3)(5), Sch 7 para 19*].

For restrictions to the exemption in the case of certain distributions made before 6 April 1999, see 3.17, 3.18 ANTI-AVOIDANCE.

15.6 **Dividend tax credits.** Before 6 April 1993, the tax credit attached to a qualifying distribution was at the basic rate of income tax (i.e. 25% of the gross amount of the distribution, which is equivalent to one-third of the actual amount of the distribution). [*ICTA 1988, s 231(1)*]. From 6 April 1993 to 5 April 1999, the tax credit is at the lower rate of income tax (i.e. 20% of the gross amount of the distribution, equivalent to 25% of the actual amount of the distribution). [*FA 1993, s 78(1)(3)*]. From 6 April 1999, it is further reduced to 10% of the gross amount of the distribution, i.e. one-ninth of the actual amount of the distribution. Also from 6 April 1999, however, the tax credit attached to a qualifying distribution ceases to be repayable to exempt bodies, including charities. [*F(No 2)A 1997, s 30*]. For the compensatory transitional reliefs following each of these changes, see below. For restrictions on the recovery of tax credits in the case of certain distributions made before 6 April 1999, see 3.17, 3.18 ANTI-AVOIDANCE.

Transitional relief following reduction in rate of tax credit from 6 April 1993. As a transitional relief for charities (and for other bodies similarly treated under *ICTA 1988, s 507* (see 30.3, 30.9, 30.14, 30.20 EXEMPT ORGANISATIONS) or *s 508* (see 77.1 SCIENTIFIC RESEARCH ASSOCIATIONS)), a compensatory payment may be claimed by the charity etc. in respect of qualifying distributions received from UK companies between 6 April 1993 and 5 April 1997 inclusive, and in respect of which the charity etc. is entitled to payment of the attached tax credit. The payment is in addition to payment of the tax credit itself, and is treated for the purposes of *ICTA 1988, s 252* (see Tolley's Corporation Tax under Advance Corporation Tax) as if it were a payment of tax credit.

The claim must be made within two years after the end of the chargeable period in which the distribution is made. Where (and to the extent that) the claim is accepted, the charity etc. will be entitled to be paid by the Board, out of money provided by Parliament, a proportion of the amount or value of the distribution as follows:

(*a*) one-fifteenth for a distribution made in 1993/94;

(*b*) one-twentieth for a distribution made in 1994/95;

(*c*) one-thirtieth for a distribution made in 1995/96;

(*d*) one-sixtieth for a distribution made in 1996/97.

Any entitlement to a payment under these provisions is subject to a power of the Board to determine, whether before or after the payment is made, and having regard to *ICTA 1988, s 236, s 237* and *s 703* (see 3.17, 3.18 and 3.2 *et seq.* ANTI-AVOIDANCE respectively), that the charity etc. is to be treated as not entitled to the payment or to a part of it. An appeal may be made against any such decision by written notice to the Board within 30 days of receipt of written notification of the decision, the appeal being to the Special Commissioners.

[*FA 1993, s 80*].

Claims for payments under these transitional arrangements should be made on a special claim form R68 (TR), to be completed in addition to the usual form (R68) claiming payment of tax credits on dividends.

Transitional relief following abolition of repayment of tax credits from 6 April 1999. As a transitional relief for charities (and for other bodies similarly treated under *ICTA 1988, s 507* (see 30.3, 30.9, 30.14, 30.20 EXEMPT ORGANISATIONS) or *s 508* (see 77.1 SCIENTIFIC RESEARCH ASSOCIATIONS)), a compensatory payment may be claimed by the charity etc. in respect of qualifying distributions received from UK companies between 6 April 1999 and 5 April 2004 inclusive, provided that the charity is entitled to exemption from tax in respect of the distribution. The payment is treated for the purposes of *ICTA 1988, s 252* (see Tolley's Corporation Tax under Advance Corporation Tax) as if it were a payment of tax credit.

The claim must be made within two years after the end of the chargeable period in which the distribution is made. Where (and to the extent that) the claim is accepted, the charity etc. will be entitled to be paid by the Board, out of money provided by Parliament, a proportion of the amount or value of the distribution as follows:

(*a*) 21% for a distribution made in 1999/2000;

(*b*) 17% for a distribution made in 2000/01;

(*c*) 13% for a distribution made in 2001/02;

(*d*) 8% for a distribution made in 2002/03;

(*e*) 4% for a distribution made in 2003/04.

Any entitlement to a payment under these provisions is subject to a power of the Board to determine, whether before or after the payment is made, and having regard to *ICTA 1988, s 703* (see 3.2 *et seq.* ANTI-AVOIDANCE), that the charity etc. is to be treated as not entitled to the payment or to a part of it. An appeal may be made against any such decision by written notice to the Board within 30 days of receipt of written notification of the decision, the appeal being to the Special Commissioners. For the purposes of *section 703 et seq.*, the payment is treated as repayment of tax. *F(No 2)A 1997, Sch 5* similarly removes or restricts the right to payments under these provisions where anti-avoidance provisions in *ICTA 1988, ss 235–237* (see 3.17, 3.18 ANTI-AVOIDANCE) would have applied before 6 April 1999 to deny repayment of tax credits.

[*F(No 2)A 1997, s 35, Sch 5*].

15.7 **Trading profits — Schedule D.** Profits of trades carried on (in the UK or elsewhere) by, and applied solely for the purposes of, charities are exempted if either

(*a*) the trade is exercised in the course of carrying out a primary purpose of the charity; or

(*b*) the work is mainly carried on by its beneficiaries.

[*ICTA 1988, s 505(1)(e); FA 1996, s 146(4)(5)*].

See also the specific exemptions at (i)–(iv) below.

For 1995/96 and earlier years (and company accounting periods ending before 1 April 1996), the extension of the exemption to overseas trades applied only by concession. (Revenue Pamphlet IR 1, B9). For trades held to fall within the exemption, see *Glasgow Musical Festival Assn CS 1926, 11 TC 154*; *Royal Choral Society v CIR CA 1943, 25 TC 263* and *Dean Leigh Temperance Canteen Trustees v CIR Ch D 1958, 38 TC 315*. For regular trading within Case I see *British Legion, Peterhead Branch v CIR CS 1953, 35 TC 509*. (In practice, the Revenue may in such cases allow a reasonable deduction for services etc. provided free.) For annual shows of agricultural societies, see 30.1 EXEMPT ORGANISATIONS.

A 'Charity Fund-raising Pack' is available from the Financial Intermediaries and Claims Office (see 15.1 above for details), which includes a Revenue publication 'Trading by Charities' (available separately) giving advice on the tax treatment of particular types of trade commonly carried on by charities. This incorporates the guidance given in the earlier Revenue booklet 'Fund-Raising for Charity'. It includes guidance as to the type of fund-raising activities originally covered by ESC C4 (see (ii) below) and the conditions the activities must satisfy, the kind of profits covered by the concession and the consequences if an event is not covered by it, and offers a telephone helpline which charities may call for further advice.

(i) **Exemption for small trades.** For 2000/01 onwards and for accounting periods of charity companies beginning on or after 1 April 2000, a tax exemption applies, on a claim made to the Board, to profits and other income which is chargeable to tax under Schedule D, Case I or Case VI and is not otherwise exempted from tax, provided the income is applied solely for the purposes of the charity and either

(*a*) the gross income (potentially within this exemption and before deducting expenses) for the chargeable period, i.e. the tax year or company accounting period, does not exceed the 'requisite limit'; or

(*b*) the charity had, at the beginning of the chargeable period, a reasonable expectation that its gross income (as above) would not exceed that limit.

The '*requisite limit*' is the greater of

(1) £5,000, and

(2) the lesser of £50,000 and 25% of the charity's total incoming resources for the chargeable period.

Both the above monetary limits are proportionately reduced for chargeable periods of less than twelve months.

The extension of the exemption to SCHEDULE D, CASE VI (74) income is intended to cover miscellaneous fund-raising activities not within Case I. Certain specified tax charges under Case VI are excluded.

[*FA 2000, s 46*].

The Revenue's interim guidance is that they will consider any evidence to satisfy the reasonable expectation test in (*b*) above. Such evidence may include minutes of meetings at which the expectations were discussed, copies of cash-flow forecasts and business plans prepared for these meetings and copies of the previous year's accounts.

(ii) **Small-scale fund-raising events.** Before 1 April 2000, profits from events such as bazaars, jumble sales, gymkhanas, carnivals etc., arranged by voluntary organisations or charities, held for, and promoted as being held for, the purpose of raising funds for charity, are not taxed if

(*a*) the organisation or charity is not regularly carrying on these trading activities,

(*b*) it is not competing with other traders, and

(*c*) the profits are transferred to charities or otherwise applied for charitable purposes.

After 31 March 2000, the exemption is extended to cover up to 15 of each type of event in any one location in any financial year of the charity etc. and includes events accessed electronically. Small events, e.g. jumble sales or coffee mornings, do not count toward the limit to the extent that the gross takings therefrom do not exceed £1,000 in any week. The limit of 15 is increased or reduced proportionately for financial years of more or less than 12 months.

The extended exemption brings the definition of a qualifying event in line with the corresponding VAT exemption for fund-raising events, for which see the corresponding chapter of Tolley's Value Added Tax. Any event meeting the criteria for the VAT exemption will automatically qualify for the income tax exemption if the condition at (*c*) above is satisfied.

(Revenue Pamphlet IR 1, C4 revised by Revenue Press Release 31 March 2000).

(iii) **Lotteries.** For 1995/96 and subsequent years, lottery profits applied solely to the charity's purposes are exempt, provided that the lottery is promoted and conducted in accordance with *Lotteries and Amusements Act 1976, s 3* or *s 5* (or NI equivalent). [*ICTA 1988, s 505(1)(f); FA 1995, s 138*]. Similar relief for earlier periods is given on a concessional basis. (Revenue Press Release 11 July 1994).

(iv) **Underwriting commissions** are taxable, whether chargeable under Schedule D, Case I (as trading income) or Case VI. Where, however, a charity was granted exemption from tax on commissions chargeable under Case VI for 1995/96 or earlier years, such treatment was not disturbed. From 6 April 1996, all such exemption ceased. See Revenue Tax Bulletin December 1995 p 265.

15.8 **Capital Gains.** Charities are exempt from capital gains tax on gains applicable, and applied, for charitable purposes. [*TCGA 1992, s 256(1)*]. But this exemption does not apply to gains arising where property which ceases to be subject to charitable trusts is then deemed to have been sold, and immediately re-acquired, at market value. Any CGT on such gains may be assessed within three years after the year of assessment in which the cessation occurs. [*TCGA 1992, s 256(2)*]. For payments made after 9 August 1998 (and for earlier payments in cases where the tax liability remains open), the exemption applies to liability under *TCGA 1992, s 87* in respect of capital payments received from offshore trusts. (Revenue Tax Bulletin August 1998 pp 573, 574). See also 44.5, 44.6 INTEREST RECEIVABLE for exemption from charge in respect of deep discount securities and 52.8 OFFSHORE FUNDS as regards certain offshore gains.

15.9 **Miscellaneous.** Charities are exempt from tax on offshore income gains — see 52.8 OFFSHORE FUNDS.

Charitable unit trust schemes are excluded from the normal income tax treatment of unauthorised unit trusts, and are thus able to pass on their income to participating charities without deducting tax. [*SI 1988 No 267; SI 1994 No 1479*].

15.10 **Restrictions on exemptions.** A restriction of the exemptions in 15.3 above applies in any chargeable period in which a charity

(*a*) has 'relevant income and gains' of £10,000 or more (but see below) which exceed the amount of its 'qualifying expenditure', and

(*b*) incurs, or is treated as incurring, 'non-qualifying expenditure'.

Where (*a*) and (*b*) above apply, exemption under *ICTA 1988, s 505(1)* and *TCGA 1992, s 256* is not available for so much of the excess at (*a*) as does not exceed the 'non-qualifying expenditure' incurred in that period. Where the exemption is not so available, the charity may, by notice in writing, specify which items of its 'relevant income and gains' are wholly or partly to be attributed to the amount concerned (covenanted payments to the charity, see 15.17 below, being treated as a single item where due from individuals before 6 April 2000 or from companies before 1 April 2000). If, within 30 days of a request to do so, the charity does not give such notice, the Board determines the attribution. [*ICTA 1988, s 505(3)(6); FA 1995, Sch 17 para 7; FA 2000, s 41(5)(9)*].

The £10,000 *de minimis* limit in (*a*) above is proportionately reduced where a chargeable period is less than twelve months, and does not apply where two or more charities acting in concert are engaged in transactions aimed at tax avoidance and where the Board, by notice in writing, so direct. An appeal, as against a decision on a claim, may be made against such a notice. [*ICTA 1988, s 505(4)(7)(8)*].

'*Relevant income and gains*' means the aggregate of

(i) income which, apart from *ICTA 1988, s 505(1)*, would not be exempt from tax, together with any income which is taxable notwithstanding *section 505(1)*, and

(ii) gains which, apart from *TCGA 1992, s 256*, would be chargeable gains, together with any gains which are chargeable gains notwithstanding *section 256*. [*ICTA 1988, s 505(5)*].

'*Non-qualifying expenditure*' is expenditure other than 'qualifying expenditure'. If the charity invests any funds in an investment which is not a 'qualifying investment', or makes a loan (not as an investment) which is not a 'qualifying loan', the amount invested or lent is treated as non-qualifying expenditure. Where the investment or loan is realised or repaid in whole or in part in the chargeable period in which it was made, any further investment or lending of the sum realised or repaid in that period is, to the extent that it does not exceed the sum originally invested or lent, ignored in arriving at non-qualifying expenditure of the period.

Where the aggregate of the qualifying and non-qualifying expenditure incurred in a chargeable period (the '*primary period*') exceeds the relevant income and gains of that period, so much of the excess as does not exceed the non-qualifying expenditure constitutes '*unapplied non-qualifying expenditure*'. Except to the extent (if any) that it represents the expenditure of 'non-taxable sums' received in the primary period, the unapplied non-qualifying expenditure may be treated as non-qualifying expenditure of a chargeable period ending not more than six years before the end of the primary period. '*Non-taxable sums*' are donations, legacies and other sums of a similar nature which, apart from *ICTA 1988, s 505(1)* and *TCGA 1992, s 256*, are not within the charge to tax.

Where an amount of unapplied non-qualifying expenditure (the '*excess expenditure*') falls to be treated as non-qualifying expenditure of earlier periods, it is attributed only to those periods in which, apart from the attribution in question but taking account of any previous attribution, the relevant income and gains exceed the aggregate of the qualifying and non-qualifying expenditure in that period; and such attribution is not to be greater than the excess. Attributions are made to later periods in priority to earlier periods. Any excess expenditure which cannot be attributed to an earlier period is ignored altogether for attribution purposes. Adjustments by way of further assessments, etc. are made in consequence of an attribution to an earlier period. [*ICTA 1988, s 506(1)(4)–(6), Sch 20 Pt III*].

'*Qualifying expenditure*' is expenditure incurred for charitable purposes only. A payment made (or to be made) to a body situated outside the UK is not qualifying expenditure unless the charity concerned has taken all reasonable steps to ensure that the payment will be applied for charitable purposes. Expenditure incurred in a particular period may be treated as incurred in another period if it is properly chargeable against income of that other period and is referable to commitments (contractual or otherwise) entered into before or during that other period. [*ICTA 1988, s 506(1)–(3)*].

'*Qualifying investments*' are the following.

(A) Investments within *Trustee Investments Act 1961, Sch 1 Pts I, II (para 13 (mortgages, etc.) excepted) and III.*

(B) Investments in a common investment fund established under *Charities Act 1960, s 22* (or NI equivalent) or *Charities Act 1993, s 24* or similar funds under other enactments.

(C) Investments in a common deposit fund established under *Charities Act 1960, s 22A* or *Charities Act 1993, s 25* or similar funds under other enactments (from 1 September 1992).

(D) Any interest in land other than a mortgage, etc.

(E) Shares or securities of a company listed on a recognised stock exchange (within *ICTA 1988, s 841*) or dealt in on the Unlisted Securities Market.

(F) Units in unit trusts within *Financial Services Act 1986*.

(G) Deposits with a recognised bank or licensed institution (but see below) in respect of which interest is payable at a commercial rate, but excluding a deposit made as part of an arrangement whereby the bank, etc. makes a loan to a third party.

(H) CERTIFICATES OF DEPOSIT (13) within *ICTA 1988, s 56(5)*.

(I) Loans or other investments as to which the Board are satisfied, on a claim, that the loans or other investments are made for the benefit of the charity and not for the avoidance of tax (whether by the charity or by a third party). Loans secured by mortgage, etc. over land are eligible.

Deposits within (G) above (and money placed within (3) below) on or after 29 April 1996 must be with a bank within *ICTA 1988, s 840A* (see 8.1 BANKS) rather than with a recognised bank or licensed institution.

'*Qualifying loans*'. A loan which is not made by way of investment is a qualifying loan if it is one of the following.

(1) A loan made to another charity for charitable purposes only.

(2) A loan to a beneficiary of the charity which is made in the course of carrying out the purposes of the charity.

(3) Money placed on a current account with a recognised bank or licensed institution (as in (G) above) otherwise than under arrangements as in (G) above.

(4) A loan, not within (1) to (3) above, as to which the Board are satisfied, on a claim, that the loan is made for the benefit of the charity and not for the avoidance of tax (whether by the charity or by a third party).

[*ICTA 1988, Sch 20 Pts I, II; Charities Act 1992, Sch 6 para 17; SI 1992 No 1900; FA 1996, Sch 37 paras 2, 5, 10, Sch 38 para 6*].

Payments between charities. Any payment received by one charity from another, other than in return for full consideration, which would otherwise not be chargeable to tax (and which is not of a description within any of the relieving provisions of *ICTA 1988, s 505(1)*, see 15.4–15.7 above), is chargeable to tax under Schedule D, Case III, but is eligible for relief under *ICTA 1988, s 505(1)(c)* (see 15.5 above) as if it were an annual payment. [*ICTA 1988, s 505(2)*].

Simon's Direct Tax Service. See **C4.527**.

15.11 **GIFT AID DONATIONS BY INDIVIDUALS**

Gifts of money made by individuals to charities which are 'qualifying donations' (see 15.13 below) attract tax relief under the Gift Aid scheme described below. Significant changes were made to the scheme with effect from 6 April 2000, including the removal of the £250 minimum limit on qualifying donations and the inclusion in Gift Aid of payments under deed of covenant. For the Gift Aid scheme as it applies to company donors, see the corresponding chapter of Tolley's Corporation Tax.

For the purposes of these provisions, '*charity*' has the meaning in 15.1 above but also includes the bodies listed in *ICTA 1988, s 507* (see 30.3, 30.9, 30.14, 30.20 EXEMPT ORGANISATIONS). [*FA 1990, s 25(12)(a)*].

15.12 **Donations after 5 April 2000.** The provisions described below apply to gifts made after 5 April 2000 other than by deed of covenant, and also to covenanted payments (see 15.17 below) *due* after that date. [*FA 2000, s 39(10)*]. An amount due after 5 April 2000 under a pre-existing deed of covenant providing for payment of a fixed gross amount is determined as if basic rate tax continued to be deductible at source, even though this is not, in fact, the case (see 15.17 below). [*FA 2000, s 41(8)*].

The donor. Where a 'qualifying donation' to charity is made by an individual ('*the donor*') in a tax year, then, for that year, he is treated for the purposes of income tax (and capital gains tax) as if

(*a*) the gift had been made after deduction of income tax at the basic rate; and

(*b*) the basic rate limit (see 1.3 ALLOWANCES AND TAX RATES) were increased by an amount equal to the 'grossed up amount of the gift', i.e. the amount which, after deducting income tax at the basic rate for the tax year in which the gift is made, leaves the amount of the gift.

The donor obtains higher rate relief, where applicable, by virtue of (*b*) above. For this purpose, higher rate relief means relief for the excess of tax at the higher rate over tax at the basic rate for which relief is effectively given at source by virtue of (*a*) above. The increase in the basic rate limit does not apply for the purposes of computing top-slicing relief as in 45.13 LIFE ASSURANCE POLICIES.

To the extent, if any, necessary to ensure that he is charged to an amount of income tax and capital gains tax equal to the tax treated under (*a*) above as deducted from the gift, the donor is *not* entitled to personal reliefs. These include both reliefs given by deduction from total income (e.g. the personal allowance) and reliefs given as a tax reduction, but the restriction does not adversely affect the donor's ability to transfer unused children's tax credit to a partner as in 1.18 ALLOWANCES AND TAX RATES, or unused married couple's allowance to a spouse as in 47.2 MARRIED PERSONS. Where the tax treated as deducted nevertheless exceeds what would otherwise be his income tax and capital gains tax liability for the year, the donor is liable to income tax at the basic rate on so much of the gift as is necessary to recover an amount of tax equal to the excess. However, in determining *for this purpose* what would otherwise be his liability, the following charges and credits are disregarded:

(*a*) any basic rate tax charged by virtue of *ICTA 1988, ss 3, 348* or *ss 349, 350* (tax due by the maker of annual payments — see 23 DEDUCTION OF TAX AT SOURCE);

(*b*) any notional tax treated as having been paid under *ICTA 1988, s 233(1)(a)* (taxation of certain recipients of distributions — see 1.9 ALLOWANCES AND TAX RATES), *ICTA 1988, s 249(4)(a)* (see 85.1 STOCK DIVIDENDS), or *ICTA 1988, s 547(5)(a)* (gains on LIFE ASSURANCE POLICIES (45.13));

(*c*) any personal reliefs, or relief for maintenance payments, falling to be given by way of an income tax reduction (see 1.15, 1.16, 1.18 ALLOWANCES AND TAX RATES, 47.10 MARRIED PERSONS);

(*d*) any DOUBLE TAX RELIEF (25) (whether given under a double tax agreement or unilaterally);

(*e*) any set-off of tax deducted, or treated as deducted, from income *other than*

(i) tax treated as deducted from income by virtue of *ICTA 1988, s 421(1)(a)* (taxation of borrower when loan released etc. — see 28.3 EXCESS LIABILITY), or

(ii) tax treated as deducted from a relevant amount within the meaning of *ICTA 1988, s 699A* (untaxed sums comprised in the income of an estate — see 22.3 DECEASED ESTATES) except to the extent that the relevant amount is or would be paid in respect of a distribution chargeable to income tax under Schedule F; and

(*f*) any set-off of tax credits on dividends (see 1.9 ALLOWANCES AND TAX RATES).

For the purposes of applying the income limit for age-related personal allowance and married couple's allowance (see 1.14, 1.15 ALLOWANCES AND TAX RATES), the donor's total income is reduced by the aggregate grossed up amount of his qualifying donations for the tax year.

[*FA 1990, s 25(1)(6)(a)(c), (8)–(9A)(12)(d); FA 2000, s 39(6)*].

See the examples at 15.15 below.

The charity. The receipt by a charity of a qualifying donation is treated as the receipt, under deduction of basic rate tax for the tax year in which the gift is made, of an annual payment equal to the grossed up amount of the gift. [*FA 1990, s 25(10)*]. The charity can reclaim the basic rate tax from the Revenue.

15.13 *Qualifying donations.* A '*qualifying donation*' is a gift to a charity by the donor which meets the following conditions:

(*a*) it takes the form of a payment of a sum of money;

(*b*) it is not subject to a condition as to repayment;

(*c*) it is not deductible under the payroll deduction scheme — see 15.18 below);

(*d*) neither the donor nor any person connected with him (see 20 CONNECTED PERSONS) receives any benefit, in consequence of making it, in excess of specified limits (see 15.14 below);

(*e*) it is not conditional on or associated with, or part of an arrangement involving, the acquisition of property by the charity, otherwise than by way of gift, from the donor or a person connected with him;

(*f*) either

(i) at the time it is made the donor is UK-resident or performs duties which by virtue of *ICTA 1988, s 132(4)(a)* (Crown employees serving overseas — see 75.2 SCHEDULE E) are treated as being performed in the UK, or

(ii) the grossed up amount of the gift (see 15.12(*b*) above) would, if in fact made, be payable out of profits or gains brought into charge to income tax or capital gains tax; and

(*g*) the donor gives the charity an 'appropriate declaration' in relation to it.

An '*appropriate declaration*' for the purposes of (*g*) above is a declaration which is given in the form and manner prescribed by regulations made by the Board. Draft regulations were published by the Revenue on 21 February 2000 which included provision for declarations to be made orally, in writing, by fax or via the internet. Payments under a pre-6 April 2000 deed of covenant need not be covered by a declaration.

[*FA 1990, s 25(1)–(3A)(11); FA 2000, s 39(1)–(4)*].

As regards (*d*) above, the benefit does not have to be received from the charity to be taken into account (see *St Dunstan's v Major (Sp C 127), [1997] SSCD 212*, in which the saving of inheritance tax by personal representatives as a result of the variation of a will to provide for a donation which would otherwise qualify under these provisions constituted a benefit).

The release of a loan not for consideration and not under seal cannot amount to a gift of money (see *Battle Baptist Church v CIR and Woodham (Sp C 23), [1995] SSCD 176*).

15.14 *Limits on donor benefits.* Where the donor or a person connected with him (see 20 CONNECTED PERSONS) receives a benefit or benefits in consequence of making the gift, the gift will not be a qualifying donation if either:

(*a*) the aggregate value of the benefits received exceeds

(i) where the gift is £100 or less, 25% of the amount of the gift;

(ii) where the gift is greater than £100 but not more than £1,000, £25;

(iii) where the gift is greater than £1,000, 2.5% of the amount of the gift; or

(*b*) the aggregate of the value of the benefits received in relation to the gift and the value of any benefits received in relation to any qualifying donations previously made to the charity by the donor in the same tax year exceeds £250.

Where a benefit:

(1) consists of the right to receive benefits at intervals over a period of less than twelve months;

(2) relates to a period of less than twelve months; or

(3) is one of a series of benefits received at intervals in consequence of making a series of gifts at intervals of less than twelve months,

the value of the benefit and the amount of the gift are 'annualised' for the purposes of (*a*) above. Where a one-off benefit is received in consequence of making a gift which is one of a series of gifts made at intervals of less than twelve months, the amount of the gift (but not the value of the benefit) is likewise annualised. For these purposes a gift or benefit is '*annualised*' by multiplying the amount or value by 365 and dividing the result by the number of days in the period of less than twelve months or the average number of days in the intervals of less than twelve months as appropriate.

In applying the above limits, the benefit of a right of free or reduced-price admission for the donor or a member of his family

(A) to view property, the preservation of which for the public benefit is the sole or main purpose of the charity; or

(B) to observe wildlife, the conservation of which for the public benefit is the sole or main purpose of the charity;

is disregarded provided that the opportunity to make gifts which attract such a right is available to members of the public.

[*FA 1990, s 25(2)(e), (4)–(5G)(11); FA 2000, s 39(1)(3)(5)*].

15.15 *Examples*

Higher rate taxpayer. Ronan, a single man under 65, has total income of £35,000 for 2000/01 (which for simplicity can be taken to consist entirely of earned income). During that year, he makes various single donations and covenanted payments to charity, all of them qualifying donations, amounting in total to £585.

	£
Total income	35,000
Less Personal Allowance	4,385
Taxable Income	£30,615
Tax Liability	
1,520 @ 10%	152.00
27,630 @ 22%	6,078.60
29,150	
1,465 @ 40%	586.00
£30,615	
	£6,816.60

Note

The basic rate limit of £28,400 is increased by the grossed up amount of the qualifying donations (£585 × 100/78 = £750) and becomes £29,150. Ronan thereby saves tax of £135 (£750 × 18% (40% – 22%)). The charities will reclaim basic rate tax of £165 (£750 × 22%) and will thus receive £750 in all. The net cost to Ronan is £450 (£585 – £135), a saving of 40%. (The tax relief can, in fact, exceed 40% where the effect of extending the basic rate limit is that an additional amount of savings/dividend income falls within the basic rate band and is taxed at 20%/10% instead of at 40%/32.5%.)

Low income taxpayer. Rod, a single person of 66, has a State pension of £3,600 and dividends of £2,520 (with tax credits of £280) for 2000/01. He makes a qualifying donation of £390 to charity.

		£
Pension		3,600
Dividends plus tax credits		2,800
Total income		6,400
Less Personal Allowance	5,790	
Restricted by (note (*a*))	490	5,300
Taxable Income		£1,100
Tax Liability		
£1,100 @ 10% (starting rate)		110.00
Deduct tax credits on dividends (note (*b*))		110.00
		Nil

Notes

(*a*) The personal allowance is restricted by such amount as is necessary to leave tax of £110.00 in charge, this being the amount of basic rate tax deemed to have been deducted at source from the qualifying donation (£390 × 22/78 = £110). Although the donor's liability is, in fact, reduced to nil by dividend tax credits, no further charge arises in respect of the donation (as such credits are among the items to be disregarded for this purpose — see 15.12 above).

(*b*) Although dividend tax credits of £280 are available, the deduction is limited to the amount necessary to reduce the liability to nil (as, for 1999/2000 onwards, dividend tax credits are not repayable — see 1.9 ALLOWANCES AND TAX RATES).

15.16 **Donations before 6 April 2000.** Where a 'qualifying donation' to charity is made by an individual before 6 April 2000, it is treated as if it were a covenanted payment (see 15.17 below) made at the same time as the gift, i.e. as if it were a payment of the corresponding grossed up amount paid under deduction of basic rate tax. Higher rate relief is available where appropriate in respect of the grossed up amount. Where the covenanted payment, had it been made, would not, or not wholly, have been payable out of income taxed at the basic (or higher) rate, the basic rate tax deemed to have been deducted (or the difference between that tax and tax at the lower or starting rate) or a corresponding proportion thereof, is chargeable on the donor.

ICTA 1988, ss 348 et seq. (annual payments — see 23.1 *et seq.* DEDUCTION OF TAX AT SOURCE) do not apply to such deemed payments. The charity may, however, claim repayment of tax deemed to have been deducted (as in 15.17(*a*) below).

A gift is a '*qualifying donation*' if it satisfies the conditions at 15.13(*a*)(*b*)(*c*) and (*e*) above, plus each of the following conditions:

(*a*) its amount is at least £250;

(*b*) it is not, in fact, a covenanted payment to charity;

(*c*) either of the following applies:

(i) neither the donor nor a person connected with him (see 20 CONNECTED PERSONS) receives a benefit in consequence of the gift, or

(ii) the aggregate value of all such benefits so received in consequence of the gift does not exceed one-fortieth of the amount of the gift, and the total value of such benefits so received in respect of the gift and any other gifts made by the donor to the charity earlier in the tax year does not exceed £250;

(*d*) the donor is UK resident at the time of the gift; and

(*e*) the donor gives the charity a certificate in prescribed form (i.e. Form R190(SD)) in relation to the gift, to the effect that the gift satisfies all the necessary conditions, and that the tax deemed to have been deducted has been or will be accounted for, either directly or by payment out of taxed income. (After 5 April 1999, charities no longer have to submit forms R190(SD) in support of a repayment claim, but need to retain the forms for inspection by FICO at any time.)

[*FA 1990, s 25; FA 1991, s 71(5)(6); FA 1993, s 67(2)(4); FA 1995, s 74, Sch 17 para 26*].

See 15.21 below for Millennium Gift Aid.

Simon's Direct Tax Service. See **E1.504**.

15.17 **COVENANTED PAYMENTS DUE BEFORE 6 APRIL 2000**

The separate tax relief below for payments to a charity made under a deed of covenant by an individual is withdrawn for payments *falling due* after 5 April 2000, as is the entitlement under *ICTA 1988, s 348(3)* and the requirement under *ICTA 1988, s 349(1)* to deduct tax at source. [*ICTA 1988, s 348(3), s 349(1); FA 2000, s 41(3)(4)(9)*]. Such payments are no longer charges on income (see 1.10 ALLOWANCES AND TAX RATES), but instead are dealt with under the Gift Aid regime (see 15.11–15.14 above). Where a covenanted payment falling due before 6 April 2000 is made on or after that date, the rules below continue to apply (with tax deductible at the basic rate in force when the covenanted payment fell due, rather than when it is made).

A '*covenanted payment to charity*' is a payment under a covenant in favour of a body of persons or trust established for charitable purposes only (including any of the bodies mentioned in *ICTA 1988, s 507* — see 30.3, 30.9, 30.14, 30.20 EXEMPT ORGANISATIONS) and under which the annual payments become payable for a period which can exceed three years. The covenant must not be for a consideration in money or money's worth and can only be terminable within the three-year period with the consent of the charity. [*ICTA 1988, s 347A(7)(8); FA 1995, Sch 17 para 4(2); FA 2000, s 41(2)(9)*].

(*a*) **'Tax-free' subscriptions to charities.** If made by deed of covenant legally binding the taxpayer to pay for a period capable of exceeding three years such a sum as, after deduction of tax at the basic rate, will leave a stated amount, the charity benefits by treating that *gross* sum as its income and claiming refund of the difference as tax deducted from it. In practice, some covenants provide for payment of a fixed gross amount, in which case similar consequences ensue but the net payment to be made by the donor varies with changes in the basic rate of tax. An expiring deed must be renewed immediately if the arrangement is desired to continue; relief to charity has been refused on payments made between the expiry of the old deed and the coming into operation of the new. See 81.24 SETTLEMENTS as regards continuation of relief for payments under certain revocable covenants where the power of revocation could have, but has not, been exercised (and see Revenue Press Release 24 March 1993 for guidance on the use of revocable covenants). See 81.22 and 81.29 SETTLEMENTS regarding additional tax relief for higher rate taxpayers and effectiveness of deed of covenant generally. The provisions covered at 81.22, 81.24 and 81.29 have no application for 1995/96 and later years. See 15.16 above as regards certain donations treated as made under covenant. See *Racal Group Services Ltd v Ashmore CA 1995 68 TC 86* for an unsuccessful attempt retrospectively to amend a deed to achieve the intended effect for tax purposes.

(*b*) Covenanted payments must be **pure income** in the hands of the charity and not a payment by the covenantor for goods, services or benefits to him (see 23.10 DEDUCTION OF TAX AT SOURCE and *Campbell & Anor v CIR HL 1968, 45 TC 427;*

National Book League CA 1957, 37 TC 455; Taw & Torridge Festival Socy Ltd v CIR Ch D 1959, 38 TC 603). In relation to charities (and certain bodies treated as charities) for the preservation of property or the conservation of wildlife, certain admission rights in return for payments to the charity are ignored for this purpose. [*FA 1989, s 59; FA 2000, s 41(7)(9)*]. Generally, in the case of ordinary small subscriptions, benefits available to subscribers up to 25% of the subscription are ignored. (Revenue Press Release 20 March 1990).

(*c*) The long-standing practice of the Revenue, to accept **retrospective validation** of payments made earlier in the tax year in which the deed was made, ceased for covenants made after 30 July 1990. This followed the decision in *Morley-Clarke v Jones CA 1985, 59 TC 567*, see 47.10 MARRIED PERSONS. (Revenue Pamphlet IR 131, SP 4/90, 20 March 1990).

(*d*) The insertion of **escape clauses** in a deed which enable the covenantor of his own volition to terminate the covenant without the consent of the charity concerned (e.g. where payments cease on the covenantor voluntarily ceasing to work for his current employer) may invalidate the covenant for tax purposes. Covenants which had been accepted by the Revenue as valid, and on which repayments of tax had been made, but which were invalid as a result of escape clauses, were treated as effective until they expired. (Revenue Pamphlet IR 131, SP 4/90, 20 March 1990).

(*e*) For **claims** relating to deeds of covenant, from 6 April 1999, individuals are no longer required to complete form R185(Covenant) and companies are not required to complete form R185(AP). (The deeds themselves are now used by FICO for audit purposes.) All claims by a charity are made on a new single sheet form R68 accompanied by a schedule or schedules of income included in the claim (although previously approved computerised schedules could continue to be used until 5 April 2000). Previously, for deeds of covenant by individuals, forms R185(Covenant) were required for the first-year claims and, for covenants by companies, forms R185(AP) were required for all payments. The new single sheet form R68 replaced a four-page form requiring similar details. Proper records must be kept in support of claims, and should be retained for up to six years after the expiry of the covenants. (Revenue Press Release 7 May 1992). See generally the Charity Tax Pack obtainable from Inland Revenue, FICO (Trusts and Charities), St John's House, Merton Road, Bootle, Merseyside L69 9BB.

(*f*) To minimise any delay in making **repayments** of tax to charities, the Revenue will, in general, provisionally repay tax apparently suffered by deduction before the full verification procedure has been completed, but they reserve the right to make enquiries into the claim at a later date, which may result in a payment back to the Revenue. (Revenue Pamphlet IR 131, SP 3/87, 26 March 1987).

(*g*) **Claims for repayment** must be made within five years after 31 January following the tax year in which the payment is due (for 1996/97 onwards, previously within six years from the date on which the payment is due). A claim for repayment of tax deducted from covenanted donations was refused where the claim was made more than six years after the end of the years of assessment within which the payments were due, although the payments had in fact been made within the six years preceding the date of claim (*CIR v Crawley Ch D 1986, 59 TC 728*).

A Revenue leaflet 'Deeds of Covenant — Guidance for Charities' is available free of charge from Customer Services Manager, Financial Intermediaries and Claims Office, St John's House, Merton Road, Bootle, Merseyside L69 9BB (tel. 0151-472 6043) to help charities to get their arrangements right for tax purposes. It includes simple forms of covenant for individual donors which charities can use if they wish. See also Revenue Tax Bulletin October 1998 pp 597, 598 for additional commentary on the validity of covenants.

15.18 **PAYROLL DEDUCTION SCHEME**

An employee may make charitable donations of any amount in any year of assessment (for 2000/01 onwards, previously limited to £1,200 per tax year for 1996/97 onwards and £900 for 1994/95 and 1995/96) by deduction from wages or salaries subject to PAYE (55). Tax relief will be allowed as if the amounts so deducted were allowable expenses, provided that

(*a*) the scheme is of a kind approved by the Board,

(*b*) the employer is authorised by the employee to deduct from pay donations requested to be paid to a charity or charities,

(*c*) the deductions constitute gifts by the employee (and, for 1999/2000 and earlier years only, are not payments under deeds of covenant), and

(*d*) the employer pays the donations to an approved agent, who pays them to a charity (or charities), or the employer pays them directly to a charity (or charities) approved by the Board as an agent for the purpose of paying sums to other charities.

For these purposes, '*charity*' is as defined in 15.1 above, but, as regards payroll deductions made for 2000/01 onwards, also includes the bodies listed in *ICTA 1988, s 507* (see 30.3, 30.9, 30.14, 30.20 EXEMPT ORGANISATIONS).

Administrative regulations may be made by statutory instrument regarding such matters as

(i) the grant or withdrawal of approval by the Board of schemes and agents, and appeals to the Special Commissioners against the Board's decision,

(ii) the requirements of terms of schemes and qualifications of agents,

(iii) the production of documents and records by a participating employer or agent within a specified time, and

(iv) production of other information to the Revenue.

The first such regulations are contained in *The Charitable Deductions (Approved Schemes) Regulations 1986* (*SI 1986 No 2211*) as amended.

Penalties apply for failure to comply with (iii) and (iv) above under *TMA 1970, s 98*.

A Prospectus 'Charities — Payroll Giving Schemes' was published by the Revenue in June 1986 giving details of the tax relief proposals.

Lists of approved agency charities have been issued by the Revenue, and will be added to from time to time. (Revenue Press Releases 11 March 1987, 11 May 1987, 16 July 1987, 5 October 1987).

As regards payroll deductions made after 5 April 2000 and before 6 April 2003, the agent, or agency charity, will pay to the nominated charity a supplement equal to 10% of the payroll deduction. The supplement is funded or reimbursed by the Revenue and must be paid by the agent etc. within a period to be prescribed by Treasury regulations. No claim for funding or reimbursement will be accepted after 5 April 2004. Regulations may require agents etc. to notify the Revenue of any failure to comply and the reasons therefor, and to keep appropriate records; they may also provide for the recovery of funds incorrectly provided or reimbursed to agents etc..

[*ICTA 1988, s 202; FA 1993, s 68; FA 1996, s 109; FA 2000, s 38*].

Administrative costs. Voluntary contributions made by an employer to assist a charitable agency with its costs in managing a payroll giving scheme on the employer's behalf are deductible in computing the profits of a trade, profession or vocation, or as management expenses of an investment company. [*ICTA 1988, s 86A; FA 1993, s 69*].

Simon's Direct Tax Service. See E4.948.

15.19 **GIFTS IN KIND TO CHARITIES**

With effect **from 27 July 1999**, relief is available to persons (including companies) carrying on a trade, profession or vocation who give certain articles to charities within *ICTA 1988, s 506* (see 15.1 above) or to bodies treated as such under *ICTA 1988, s 507(1)* (see 30.3, 30.9, 30.14, 30.20 EXEMPT ORGANISATIONS). The gift must consist of either:

(*a*) articles manufactured, or of a type sold, in the course of the donor's trade; or

(*b*) machinery or plant (see 10.25 CAPITAL ALLOWANCES) used in the donor's trade, profession or vocation.

Where the donor is eligible for the relief, no amount is required to be brought into account for tax purposes in respect of the donated article either as a trading receipt or (for capital allowance purposes) as a disposal value. However, if the donor or any connected person (see 20 CONNECTED PERSONS) receives any benefit in any way attributable to the gift, the donor is chargeable on an amount equal to the value of that benefit, for the chargeable period in which it is received, under either Schedule D, Case I or II or, if he is not chargeable to tax under either of those Cases for that period, under Schedule D, Case VI.

[*ICTA 1988, s 83A; FA 1999, s 55*].

See 15.21 below for the earlier, more limited relief for gifts for third world health or education.

15.20 **GIFTS OF SHARES AND SECURITIES TO CHARITIES**

Income tax relief is available on a non-arm's length disposal after 5 April 2000, by an individual to a 'charity', of the whole of the beneficial interest in a 'qualifying investment'. This is in addition to the pre-existing capital gains tax relief for assets generally, for which see the corresponding chapter of Tolley's Capital Gains Tax. '*Charity*' has the meaning in 15.1 above, but also includes the bodies listed in *ICTA 1988, s 507* (see 30.3, 30.9, 30.14, 30.20 EXEMPT ORGANISATIONS). A '*qualifying investment*' is any of the following:

(*a*) shares or securities listed or dealt in on a recognised stock exchange (within *ICTA 1988, s 841*);

(*b*) units in an authorised unit trust (within *ICTA 1988, s 468*);

(*c*) shares in an open-ended investment company (within *ICTA 1988, s 468* as modified for the purpose); and

(*d*) an interest in an OFFSHORE FUND (52.3).

On a claim to that effect (within the time allowed at 17.4 CLAIMS), the market value of the investment at the time of the disposal, or the excess of that value over any consideration given for the disposal, is deductible in computing the donor's total income for the tax year of disposal. See below as regards adjustments for incidental costs and consequential benefits. The deduction is disregarded for the purposes of computing top-slicing relief in respect of gains on LIFE ASSURANCE POLICIES (45.13). Where the claim is made, no relief is available under 15.19 above or any other provision in respect of the same disposal.

The market value of the investment is determined as for capital gains tax purposes, with an interest in an offshore fund being valued in a similar way for this purpose as units in a unit trust.

In computing the amount deductible, any consideration receivable at a future time, contingently or otherwise, is brought fully into account as it is for capital gains tax purposes (see Tolley's Capital Gains Tax under Disposal).

The amount deductible is increased by any incidental costs of disposal (construed as for capital gains tax purposes) incurred by the person making it. Where consideration is received for the disposal, this increase is limited to the excess, if any, of the deemed consideration for capital gains tax purposes (disposal deemed to be at no gain/no loss) over the actual consideration.

The amount deductible is reduced by the value of any benefits received, in consequence of the disposal, by the person making it or a person connected with him (within 20 CONNECTED PERSONS).

The cost of the asset to the charity for capital gains tax purposes is reduced by the amount deductible as above, or, if it is less than that amount, is reduced to nil.

[*ICTA 1988, s 587B; FA 2000, s 43*].

A similar relief is available to companies (see the corresponding chapter of Tolley's Corporation Tax).

15.21 **GIFTS FOR RELIEF OVERSEAS**

Two reliefs were introduced for a limited period for gifts to charities aimed at either the relief of poverty or the advancement of education.

Gifts of money ('Millennium Gift Aid'). Relief is available for gifts made by individuals in the period beginning on 31 July 1998 and ending on 31 December 2000 (though see below) to charities which have given the required notification to the Revenue, where it may reasonably be expected that the sum given will be applied for, or in connection with, one or more of the following.

(*a*) The relief of poverty in one or more countries or territories designated for the purpose.

(*b*) The advancement of education in one or more countries or territories designated for the purpose.

(*c*) (In relation to gifts made after 5 April 1999) the relief of poverty in the case of persons from any country or territory designated for the purpose who are refugees or who have suffered displacement as a result of organised intimidation or oppression or of war or other armed conflict.

The countries or territories are in each case designated by Treasury order (or are of a description specified in such an order). As regards (*a*) and (*b*) above, see *SI 1998 No 1868* and Revenue Press Release 31 July 1998 — some 80 of the world's poorest countries are designated for this purpose. As regards (*c*) above, see *SI 1999 No 2118*, which designates refugees and displaced persons from Kosovo for this purpose.

The 'qualifying donations' provisions of *FA 1990, s 25* (see 15.16 above) apply to such gifts, but with a minimum gift of £100 (rather than £250). Gifts of less than £100 may be aggregated for this purpose and treated as a single gift made at the time of the last of the gifts so aggregated, provided that:

(i) no gift of £250 or more, and not more than one gift of £100 or more, is so aggregated;

(ii) the condition as regards consequential benefits (see 15.16(iii) above) would be satisfied by reference to that single gift; and

(iii) the donor gives a certificate that each gift qualifies (or would but for the £100 minimum qualify), that (ii) above is satisfied, and that he or she has paid or suffered sufficient income tax to cover basic rate tax on the grossed-up amount of the aggregated gift.

Where gifts so aggregated include gifts made in different years of assessment, the single gift is treated as having suffered tax at the basic rate for the year in which the first of the gifts so aggregated was made.

These provisions are made largely redundant for donations after 5 April 2000 by the removal of the minimum limit for donations generally (see 15.11 above). However, these provisions can still be used to aggregate a gift made after 5 April 2000 (and on or before 31 December 2000) with one made in an earlier tax year, thus enabling the earlier gift to qualify for relief where it was less than £100 and the charity to reclaim tax at the higher basic rate prevailing at the time of the earlier gift. Amendments are made to link these provisions with the revised conditions at 15.13 above for qualifying donations generally. Where two or more gifts are treated as a single gift made after 5 April 2000, relief is given as in 15.12 above.

[*FA 1998, s 48; FA 1999, ss 56, 57; FA 2000, s 42*].

Gifts in kind. Relief is available for gifts made in the period beginning on 31 July 1998 and **ending on 26 July 1999** (the relief being replaced after that date by the wider relief described at 15.19 above) to persons (including companies) carrying on a trade, profession or vocation who give certain articles to charities for use, either for medical purposes (including medical research and health promotion) or by an educational establishment, in a country or territory designated for the purpose by Treasury order (or of a description specified in such an order). See *SI 1998 No 1868* and Revenue Press Release 31 July 1998 — some 80 of the world's poorest countries are designated for this purpose.

The gift must consist of either:

(*a*) articles manufactured, or of a type sold, in the course of the donor's trade; or

(*b*) machinery or plant (see 10.25 CAPITAL ALLOWANCES) used in the donor's trade, profession or vocation.

Where the donor claims the relief, no amount is required to be brought into account for tax purposes in respect of the donated article either as a trading receipt or (for capital allowance purposes) as a disposal value. However, if the donor or any connected person (see 20 CONNECTED PERSONS) receives any benefit in any way attributable to the gift, the donor is chargeable on an amount equal to the value of that benefit, for the chargeable period in which it is received, under either Schedule D, Case I or II or, if he is not chargeable to tax under either of those Cases for that period, under Schedule D, Case VI.

A claim must be made (for income tax purposes) by 31 January in the next year of assessment but one following the year in the basis period for which the gift was made (e.g. by 31 January 2001 for a gift made in a period of account ending 31 December 1998) or (for corporation tax purposes) within two years of the end of the accounting period in which the gift was made. It must specify the article given and the charity to which it was given.

[*FA 1998, s 47; FA 1999, s 55(2)(3)*].

See now 15.19 above for the wider relief which replaces this provision from 27 July 1999.

16 Children

16.1 Child allowances were phased out from 1977/78 onwards by the introduction of the non-taxable child benefit. The remaining allowance is the additional personal allowance in respect of children (see 1.17 ALLOWANCES AND TAX RATES), which is abolished from 6 April 2000. A new children's tax credit (see 1.18 ALLOWANCES AND TAX RATES) is introduced from 6 April 2001.

16.2 All the income of a child is assessable on him (subject to below) and he has full entitlement to personal allowances and reliefs. In most cases only the personal allowance (see 1.14 ALLOWANCES AND TAX RATES) will be claimable.

16.3 Returns and claims may be made by a child in respect of income within his control but otherwise these are the responsibility of his parent, guardian, tutor or any trustee [*TMA 1970, ss 72, 118*] who is also liable for payment of any tax in default of payment by the child, with right of recovery. [*TMA 1970, s 73*]. Where assessment should primarily be made on the guardian, tutor or trustee, an assessment in the name of the child is not precluded (*R v Newmarket Commrs (ex p Huxley) CA 1916, 7 TC 49*).

16.4 If a parent makes a settlement in favour of his child, then the income arising thereon is treated (subject to certain exceptions) as that of the parent and not of the child for tax purposes. The definition of 'settlement' for this purpose is wide enough to cover gifts e.g. of money, or shares. See 81.18, 81.21 SETTLEMENTS. See also the other provisions in 81.13 to 81.30 SETTLEMENTS whereby income of a settlement can be treated as that of the settlor for tax purposes.

16.5 Any reference to a child in the *Tax Acts*, is to be construed as including reference to an adopted child. [*ICTA 1988, s 832(5)*].

16.6 **Contingency claims in respect of income up to 5 April 1969** in relation to certain settlements, see 81.12 SETTLEMENTS.

17 Claims

Cross-references. See ALLOWANCES AND TAX RATES AT 1.11 onwards for claims to personal allowances and reliefs; 25 DOUBLE TAX RELIEF for claims under DTR agreements etc.; 43 INTEREST PAYABLE for relief for interest paid; 51.11 NON-RESIDENTS AND OTHER OVERSEAS MATTERS for reliefs claimable by non-residents; 53.6 PARTNERSHIPS where change of partners or proprietors; 64.7 RESIDENCE, ORDINARY RESIDENCE AND DOMICILE for residence, etc. claims; 81 SETTLEMENTS for claims by beneficiaries and contingent trust claims.

17.1 CLAIMS AND ELECTIONS UNDER SELF-ASSESSMENT

Claims and elections may be made to the local Inspector of Taxes (or to the Board of Inland Revenue in certain specified cases) whenever the *Taxes Acts* provide for relief to be given or other thing to be done.

A new formal procedure applies for 1996/97 and subsequent years (i.e. under self-assessment) as regards the making of claims and elections. A claim for a relief, allowance or tax repayment (other than one to be given effect by a PAYE coding adjustment — see also 17.3 below) must be for an amount quantified at the time of the claim. Where notice has been given by the Revenue requiring the delivery of a return (see 78.5, 78.8 SELF-ASSESSMENT), a claim, etc. (other than one to be given effect by a PAYE coding adjustment) can only be made at any time by inclusion in such a return (or by virtue of an amendment to a return) *unless it could not be so included* either at that time or subsequently. In the case of a partnership business, a claim or election under any of numerous provisions specified in *TMA 1970, s 42(7)* must be made by a partner nominated by the partnership if it cannot be included in a partnership return (or amendment thereto). See 17.3 below for provisions applying where a claim etc. is made otherwise than by inclusion in a return.

Where a claimant discovers an error or mistake has been made in a claim (whether or not made in a return), he may make a supplementary claim within the time allowed for making the original claim.

[*TMA 1970, s 42; FA 1994, ss 196, 199(2)(a), Sch 19 para 13; FA 1995, s 107(1)–(3)(7)(9); FA 1996, ss 128(1), 130; FA 1998, Sch 27 Pt III(4)*].

See 17.5 below as regards the making of income tax claims by telephone or other method not in writing.

Simon's Direct Tax Service. See E1.830–E1.833.

17.2 **Claims for relief involving two or more years.** The provisions described below are introduced to facilitate the administration under self-assessment of claims, elections etc. which affect more than one tax year. They generally deem the claim to be that of the later year (with consequent effect on the dates from which interest on unpaid and overpaid tax will run) and have effect where the year to which the claim relates, or is so deemed to relate, is 1996/97 or a subsequent year of assessment.

Relief for losses and other payments. A claim, under whatever provision, for a loss incurred or payment made (for example, a personal pension contribution) in one year of assessment to be carried back to an earlier year need not be made in a return, is treated as a claim for the year of loss or payment (the later year), must be for an amount equal to what would otherwise have been the tax saving for the earlier year (after taking into account any associated claims, see below, to which effect has already been given) and is given effect *in relation to the later year* by repayment, set-off etc. or by treating the said amount for the purposes of 78.19 SELF-ASSESSMENT as a tax payment made on account. See Revenue Tax Bulletin April 1996 p 299 for the practical effect.

These provisions were deferred for the purposes of retirement annuity/personal pension payments until 1997/98, so that such payments made in 1996/97 and carried back to 1995/96 will continue to be given effect in the 1995/96 assessment. The Revenue have also confirmed that under the new provisions a carry-back claim (whether in the return for the year of payment or not) will be given immediate effect provided that the tax return for the earlier year has been made and the tax calculated. Relief is given in terms of tax by set-off or repayment, and, provided that the claim (and payment) is made before 31 January in the year of payment, may be by set-off against outstanding liabilities for the earlier year. Relief will be given by repayment where there are no outstanding liabilities and none which will arise within 35 days of the date the claim is processed. INTEREST ON OVERPAID TAX (41) can, however, run only from 31 January following the year of payment. (Revenue Tax Bulletin December 1996 pp 361–365, June 1997 p 443).

See 78.17 SELF-ASSESSMENT as regards special treatment of retirement annuity/personal pension payments for the purposes of interim payments on account for 1996/97 only.

Where a member of a pre-6 April 1994 partnership carries back a loss or pension contribution from 1997/98 to 1996/97, then, although in accordance with the above provisions the relief is quantified by reference to his share of the 1996/97 composite partnership assessment, the relief, and any repayment, is due to him personally and not to the partnership. (Revenue Tax Bulletin August 1997 pp 451, 452).

Averaging of farming or market gardening profits. Where a farmer or market gardener makes a claim under *ICTA 1988, s 96* to average the profits of two consecutive years of assessment (see 71.57(*a*) SCHEDULE D, CASES I AND II), the claim is treated as a claim for the later of those years. To the extent that the claim would otherwise have affected the profits of the earlier of those years, it must be for an amount equal to the tax that would consequently have become payable or repayable for that earlier year (after taking into account any associated claims, see below, to which effect has already been given) and is given effect *in relation to the later year* by increasing the tax payable or treating the said amount for the purposes of 78.19 SELF-ASSESSMENT as a tax payment made on account, whichever is appropriate. Where the later year is included in a subsequent averaging claim, i.e. it is then averaged with the following year, the application of these provisions to the first claim is ignored in computing the effect of the subsequent claim.

Where, having made an averaging claim, a person then makes, amends or revokes any other claim for relief for either of the two years affected, which would be out of time but for the provisions of *section 96*, the claim, amendment or revocation is treated as relating to the later of the two years. To the extent that it relates to income for the earlier year, the amount claimed (or, as appropriate, the increase or reduction therein) must be equal to the tax that would consequently have become payable or repayable for that earlier year (after taking into account any associated claims, see below, to which effect has already been given) and is given effect *in relation to the later year* by increasing the tax payable or treating the said amount for the purposes of 78.19 SELF-ASSESSMENT as a tax payment made on account, whichever is appropriate.

For articles on these rules and on the completion of the relevant tax returns, see Revenue Tax Bulletin February 1997 pp 392–394 and August 1998 p 575.

Election for post-cessation receipts to be treated as if received on date of discontinuance. Where a person elects under *ICTA 1988, s 108* (see 62.1 POST-CESSATION ETC. RECEIPTS AND EXPENDITURE) for a post-cessation receipt to be treated as if received on the date of cessation of trade rather than in the year of receipt (the later year), the election is treated as a claim for the later year, must be for an amount equal to what would otherwise have been the additional tax payable for the year of assessment (the earlier year) in which the sum is treated as received (after taking into account any associated claims, see below, to which effect has already been given) and is given effect *in relation to the later year* by increasing the tax payable for that year.

Backward spreading of lump sums for copyright etc. Where a claim is made under *ICTA 1988, s 534, s 537A* or *s 538* to spread back lump sum receipts for copyrights etc. over more than one year of assessment (see 71.51 SCHEDULE D, CASES I AND II), the claim is treated as a claim for the year of assessment into whose basis period the lump sum would have fallen had the claim not been made (the payment year). To the extent that the claim would otherwise have affected the profits of an earlier year of assessment, it must be for an amount equal to the additional tax that would consequently have become payable for that earlier year (after taking into account any associated claims, see below, to which effect has already been given) and is given effect *in relation to the payment year* by increasing the tax payable for that year.

For the purposes of all the above provisions, two claims, elections etc. (including, where appropriate, amendments and revocations) by the same person are *'associated'* in so far as the same year of assessment is the earlier year in relation to both.

[*TMA 1970, s 42(11A), Sch 1B; FA 1996, s 128(2), Sch 17*].

Simon's Direct Tax Service. See **A3.609**.

17.3 **Claims etc. not included in returns.** Subject to any specific provision requiring a claim or election to be made to the Board, a claim or election made otherwise than in a return (see 17.1 above) must be made to an officer of the Board. The claim etc. must include a declaration by the claimant that all particulars are correctly stated to the best of his information or belief. No claim requiring a tax repayment can be made unless the claimant has documentary proof that the tax has been paid or deducted. The claim must be made in a form determined by the Board and may require, *inter alia*, a statement of the amount of tax to be discharged or repaid and (except as below) supporting information and documentation. In the case of a claim by or on behalf of a person who is not resident (or who claims to be not resident or not ordinarily resident or not domiciled) in the UK, the Revenue may require a statement or declaration in support of the claim to be made by affidavit.

For UK-resident individuals, the requirement to send vouchers – certificates of tax credit and UK tax deducted – with repayment claims made outside the self-assessment return no longer applies (and contrary instructions on 1997/98 claim forms may be disregarded). (Revenue Tax Bulletin December 1997 p 491).

A person who may wish to make a claim must keep all such records as may be requisite for the purpose and must preserve them until such time as the Revenue may no longer enquire into the claim (see below) or such enquiries are treated as completed. There is a maximum penalty of £3,000 for non-compliance in relation to any claim *actually made*. Similar provisions and exceptions apply as in 78.10 SELF-ASSESSMENT as to the preservation of copies of documents instead of originals and the exception from penalty for non-compliance in relation to dividend vouchers, interest certificates etc..

Provisions similar to those in 78.7 SELF-ASSESSMENT (amendments of self-assessments) apply to enable a claimant (within twelve months of the claim) or officer of the Board (within nine months of the claim) to amend a claim, etc. The Revenue have power of enquiry into a claim etc. (or amendment thereof) similar to that in 78.11 SELF-ASSESSMENT (enquiries into returns). Notice of intention to enquire must be given by the first anniversary of 31 January following the year of assessment (or where the claim relates to a period other than a year of assessment the first anniversary of the end of that period) or, if later, the quarter day (meaning 31 January, 30 April etc.) next following the first anniversary of the date of claim etc.. In the event of such an enquiry, they have power to call for documents similar to that in 78.12 SELF-ASSESSMENT. Where an enquiry is in progress, an officer of the Board may give provisional effect to the claim etc. (or amendment thereof) to such extent as he thinks fit. Provisions similar to those in 78.13 SELF-ASSESSMENT apply as regards amendments of claims upon completion of an enquiry. The Revenue must give effect to such an amendment, by assessment if necessary, within 30 days after it is made. An appeal may be made against a Revenue amendment to a claim following an enquiry, written notice of appeal to be given normally within 30 days after the amendment is made (extended to three months where certain specified issues concerning residence are involved). If an amendment is varied on appeal, the Revenue have a further 30 days to give effect to the variation. Where a claim etc. does not give rise to a discharge or repayment of tax (for example, a claim to carry forward trading losses), there are provisions as to disallowance of such claims on enquiry similar to those in 78.13 SELF-ASSESSMENT in respect of claims, etc. included in returns, with appeal procedures similar to those above.

Appeals against amendments to claims are normally made to the General Commissioners. Where the claim was made to the Board or under certain specified provisions, appeal is to the Special Commissioners, and in other cases, there are rules, similar to those in 4.3 APPEALS, enabling the taxpayer to elect to bring the appeal before the Special Commissioners. If the taxpayer also has an appeal pending concerning an assessment and the appeals relate to the same income, both appeals must be to the same body of Commissioners.

[*TMA 1970, s 42(11), Sch 1A; FA 1994, ss 196, 199(2)(a), Sch 19 paras 13, 35; FA 1995, s 107(10)(11), Sch 20; FA 1996, s 124(4), s 130(6)–(8), Sch 19 paras 8–10, Sch 22 para 9; FA 1998, Sch 19 para 42*].

See 17.5 below as regards the making of income tax claims by telephone or other method not in writing and also the use of photocopied blank claim forms.

Claims given effect by PAYE coding adjustment. Claims for a tax year may be made during that year, and thus before a tax return is issued, and given effect by adjustment to a PAYE code (see 55.4 PAY AS YOU EARN), for example a claim to married couple's allowance. Such in-year claims may subsequently be reflected in a tax return. Where no such return is issued, the claim will become final under the above provisions by the first anniversary of 31 January following the tax year, i.e. the final date for the Revenue to give notice of intention to enquire. Except in cases of 'discovery' (see 78.15 SELF-ASSESSMENT), the Revenue will in practice apply the same deadline to claims rolled forward from one year to the next and automatically included in code numbers and to those included on the basis of preliminary information given by the taxpayer before the start of the tax year. (Revenue Tax Bulletin October 1996 pp 350, 351).

Simon's Direct Tax Service. See **A3.608**.

17.4 **General time limit for claims.** *Unless otherwise prescribed*, a claim relating to 1996/97 or a subsequent year with respect to income tax (or capital gains tax) must be made within five years after 31 January following the year of assessment to which it relates. [*TMA 1970, s 43(1); FA 1994, ss 196, 199(2)(a), Sch 19 para 14*]. (See 17.8 below for the position as regards earlier years and as regards corporation tax.)

17.5 **GENERAL**

Claims are personal matters and (except in the case of trustees for persons under disability etc.) can be made only by the person entitled to the relief (cf. *Fulford v Hyslop Ch D 1929, 8 ATC 588*). For claims to personal allowances etc. by persons receiving tax-free annuities, see 23.17 DEDUCTION OF TAX AT SOURCE. See 67.2 RETURNS for signing of claims by attorney.

Where an official form is provided for use in making a claim or election not included in a return, it is permissible to fill out a photocopy of the blank form, provided that, where double sided copying is not available, all the pages (including any notes) are present and attached in the correct order. Although such copying is in strictness a breach of HMSO copyright, this will only be pursued if forms are copied on a large scale for commercial gain. (Revenue Pamphlet IR 131, SP 5/87, 15 June 1987). See also 67.2 RETURNS.

Telephone claims etc.. The Board have powers to accept income tax claims by telephone (or by any other method not in writing), where a written claim would otherwise be required, for which purpose they must publish general directions as regards the circumstances in which, and conditions subject to which, such claims will be accepted. The time for making the claim and the contents may not be altered by the directions. No directions may be given in relation to claims by an individual as trustee, partner or personal representative, to CAPITAL ALLOWANCES (10) claims or to claims under *TMA 1970, Sch 1B* (see 17.2 above). Directions may similarly be given as regards the making of elections, the giving of notice, the amendment or withdrawal of claims, elections and notices and the amendment of returns. [*FA 1998, s 118*]. All tax offices now offer certain telephone services, as described in Revenue Pamphlet IR 1, SP 2/98, 24 August 1998, with which was published a corresponding direction. These include acceptance of claims to personal allowances and flat rate expenses and notification of benefit changes, in addition to general guidance and assistance. An experimental Call Centre offering more extensive services is available to employees and pensioners whose tax affairs are dealt with in Scotland. Details of the services available through the Call Centre are set out in Revenue Pamphlet IR 131, SP 8/98, 18 December 1998, with which again a corresponding direction was published. If the experiment is successful the Revenue will consider expanding the use of such Centres.

17.6 TAX REPAYMENT CLAIMS

For an example of claims for repayment of tax, see 2.2 ALLOWANCES AND TAX RATES —EXAMPLES. Forms for making repayment claims can be obtained from the local Inspector of Taxes (whose address in case of difficulty can be obtained from the Secretary, Inland Revenue, Somerset House, London WC2R 1LB) or by completing Form R95(D). A non-resident should apply to the Inland Revenue, Financial Intermediaries and Claims Office, Foreign Division, 1st Floor, St John's House, Merton Road, Bootle, Merseyside L69 9BB.

It became the practice to dispense in some cases with claim forms, provided the annual return form (see 67.2 RETURNS) is correctly filled up and sufficient tax deduction vouchers at the appropriate rate (lower or basic) are sent to the inspector to cover the amount reclaimable for that year. For UK-resident individuals, the requirement to send vouchers – certificates of tax credit and UK tax deducted – with repayment claims made outside the self-assessment return no longer applies (and contrary instructions on 1997/98 claim forms may be disregarded). (Revenue Tax Bulletin December 1997 p 491).

Where an individual's income for 1998/99 and earlier years is comprised of UK dividends (which have related tax credits) and other income taxed by deduction, there is no need to wait until the end of the tax year. The claim can be sent in as soon as sufficient income has been received to cover both the allowances claimed and any 'charges' on the income (see 1.10 ALLOWANCES AND TAX RATES). Alternatively, interim claims may be made for part allowances. However, repayments are only made during the tax year where the total involved exceeds £50. Claims for lesser amounts will not be processed until either the amount exceeds £50 or, if earlier, the end of the tax year. (Revenue Press Release 29 March 1989). Tax credits cease in any event to be payable after 5 April 1999 (see 1.9 ALLOWANCES AND TAX RATES).

Late claims. Where an over-payment of tax has arisen because of official error, and there is no doubt or dispute as to the facts, claims to repayment of tax are accepted outside the statutory time limits. (Revenue Pamphlet IR 1, B41).

17.7 ADDITIONAL ALLOWANCES

The inspector should be notified promptly of additional allowances so that relief can be given in the current PAYE coding or other assessments.

17.8 TIME LIMITS FOR CLAIMS

See 86 TIME LIMITS—FIXED DATES and 87 TIME LIMITS—MISCELLANEOUS for details. **Unless otherwise prescribed, a claim for 1995/96 or an earlier year must be made within six years** of the end of the tax year ('year of assessment') to which it relates (or the end of the accounting period, in the case of a company). [*TMA 1970, s 43(1)*]. Such claims for the tax year 1991/92 must accordingly be made by 5 April 1998. See, however, 86.1(*d*)(i) TIME LIMITS—FIXED DATES as regards claims following late assessment. See also 15.17(*g*) CHARITIES as regards claims in relation to late payments under covenant. See also 17.11 below.

See 17.4 above as regards 1996/97 and later years (i.e. under self-assessment). The six-year limit remains unchanged for corporation tax purposes.

Simon's Direct Tax Service. See **A3.620** *et seq.*.

17.9 APPEALS IN RESPECT OF CLAIMS

1995/96 and earlier years. An unfavourable decision by the inspector, or Board, on a claim, may be appealed against in writing within 30 days of receipt of written notice of the decision or within three months on matters affecting non-residents relating to (*a*) personal reliefs or (*b*) residence, ordinary residence or domicile or (*c*) exemption of pension funds for overseas employees. Appeals from decision of the inspector are to the General Commissioners or (at taxpayer's option) to the Special Commissioners, and those from decision of the Board to the Special Commissioners. [*TMA 1970, Sch 2; FA 1996, Sch 22 para 6, Sch 41 Pt V(12)*]. See under 4 APPEALS for this and for appeals to the High Court.

See 17.3 above and 78.31, 78.33 SELF-ASSESSMENT as regards 1996/97 and subsequent years.

17.10 ERROR OR MISTAKE RELIEF [*TMA 1970, s 33*]

1995/96 and earlier years. Relief may be claimed in writing, within six years after the end of the year of assessment in which the assessment was made, against any over-assessment due to an error or mistake (including an omission) in any return or statement. The relief is given because the return etc. was wrong and hence does not apply where the assessment is not on the basis of the return. No relief is allowed if the return or statement was made in accordance with the basis or practice generally prevailing at the time, or if the relevant circumstances of the case render relief inequitable.

The relief, which is given by repayment, is determined by the Board with appeal from them to the Special Commissioners and from them, but only on a point of law arising in connection with the computation of the income or gains, to the High Court. (See *Rose Smith & Co Ltd v CIR KB 1933, 17 TC 586*; *Carrimore Six Wheelers Ltd CA 1944, 26 TC 301* and *CA 1947, 28 TC 422*; *Arranmore Investment Co Ltd v CIR CA(NI) 1973, 48 TC 623*; *Eagerpath Ltd v Edwards Ch D, [1999] STC 771.*)

1996/97 and later years (self-assessment). The error or mistake relief provisions continue to apply for 1996/97 and subsequent years. They apply by reference to an overcharge to tax under a self-assessment as well as under any other assessment. The time limit for claiming error or mistake relief, in the case of an income tax or capital gains tax assessment, is five years after 31 January following the year of assessment to which the return in question relates. No relief is available in respect of an error or mistake in a claim which is included in a return (but see 17.1 above as regards supplementary claims). [*TMA 1970, s 33; FA 1994, ss 196, 199(2)(a), Sch 19 para 8*].

Error or mistake relief is extended to cover an error or mistake in a partnership statement (see 78.9 SELF-ASSESSMENT) by reason of which the partners allege that their self-assessments were excessive. The claim to relief must be made by one of the partners within five years after the filing date for the partnership return (see 78.8 SELF-ASSESSMENT). Where the claim results in an amendment to the partnership statement, the Board will, by notice, make any necessary amendments to the self-assessments of all persons who were partners at any time in the period covered by the partnership statement. [*TMA 1970, s 33A; FA 1994, ss 196, 199(2)(a), Sch 19 para 9; FA 1996, Sch 22 para 5*].

For relief for double assessment, see 5.4 ASSESSMENTS. For re-opening of accounts in respect of 'late' receipts and payments, see 71.28 SCHEDULE D, CASES I AND II. For alteration of past claims on farming and market gardening profits, see 71.57 SCHEDULE D, CASES I AND II.

See generally Revenue Inspector's Manual, IM 3750–3756.

Simon's Direct Tax Service. See **A3.10**.

17.11 FURTHER ASSESSMENTS

In the case of a discovery leading to an assessment under *TMA 1970, s 29* (see 78.15 SELF-ASSESSMENT (before self-assessment, *TMA 1970, s 29(3)* — see 5.3 ASSESSMENTS) which is made after 26 July 1989, and is not for making good a loss of tax attributable to fraudulent or negligent conduct (see 6.4 BACK DUTY),

(*a*) any 'relevant' claim, election, application or notice which could have been made or given within the normal time limits may be made or given within one year of the end of the chargeable period in which the assessment is made, and

(*b*) any 'relevant' claim, etc. previously made or given, except an irrevocable one, can, with the consent of the person(s) by whom it was made or given (or their personal representatives), be revoked or varied in the manner in which it was made or given.

Certain elections for the transfer inter-spouse of the married couple's allowance are excluded from this treatment.

A claim, etc. is '*relevant*' to an assessment for a chargeable period if

(i) it relates to, or to an event occurring in, the chargeable period, and

(ii) it, or its revocation or variation, reduces, or could reduce,

  (A) the increased tax liability resulting from the assessment, or

  (B) any other liability of the person for that chargeable period or a later one ending not more than one year after the end of the period in which the assessment is made.

The normal APPEALS (4) provisions apply, with any necessary modifications.

If the making, etc. of a claim, etc. (as above) would alter another person's tax liability, the consent of that person (or his personal representatives) is needed. If such alteration is an increase, the other person cannot make, etc. a claim, etc. under the foregoing provisions.

If the reduction, whether resulting from one or more than one claim, etc., would exceed the additional tax assessed, relief is not available for the excess. If the reduction, so limited, involves more than one period, or more than one person, the inspector will specify by notice in writing how it is to be apportioned; but within 30 days of the notice (or last notice if more than one person is involved) being given, the person, or persons jointly, can specify the apportionment by notice in writing to the inspector. [*TMA 1970, ss 43A, 43B; FA 1989, s 150; F(No 2)A 1992, Sch 5 para 9(4); FA 1993, Sch 14 para 2; FA 1994, ss 196, 199, Sch 19 para 15*].

18 Clubs and Societies

18.1 A club or society is liable to corporation tax on its taxable income and capital gains which includes interest received and profits from trading activities with non-members (see under 50 MUTUAL TRADING). See *CIR v Worthing Rugby Football Club Trustees CA 1987, 60 TC 482* and *Blackpool Marton Rotary Club v Martin Ch D 1988, 62 TC 686* and, for non-proprietary members' golf clubs, Revenue Tax Bulletin August 1994 p 156. See also 18.5 below. For a case in which the Special Commissioner declined to make a distinction between profits arising from ordinary members and those arising from associate members, see *Westbourne Supporters of Glentoran Club v Brennan (Sp C 22), [1995] SSCD 137.* Generally, see Revenue explanatory pamphlet IR 46 'Clubs, Societies and Voluntary Associations'.

See also Revenue Tax Bulletin October 1998 p 600 for the Revenue approach to such bodies with trivial liabilities.

18.2 **Holiday clubs and thrift funds** formed annually are not legally entitled to relief, but where income is received which has not been subjected to composite rate tax, tax assessed on income paid or applied to members is restricted to the tax charge which would have arisen had the members received the income directly. (Revenue Pamphlet IR 1, C3). The concession is withdrawn with effect from April 2001. See Revenue Press Release 3 March 2000.

18.3 **Loan and Money Societies.** Society may account for income tax at average rate (calculated by reference to the average rate which would be applicable if investors were charged directly) on dividends etc. grossed up at that average rate, after taking into account contributions from members to meet management expenses. The grossed-up amount is deductible in computing corporation tax liability of society. (Revenue Pamphlet IR 1, C2). The concessional treatment is withdrawn with effect from April 2001. See Revenue Press Release 3 March 2000.

18.4 **Lotteries etc..** See 71.30 SCHEDULE D, CASES I AND II.

18.5 **Members' sports clubs.** For the Revenue's views on the circumstances in which a members' sports club's commercial activities can give rise to taxable trading profits (or to allowable trading losses), see Revenue Tax Bulletin December 1997 pp 488–490.

VAT repayments. See Revenue Tax Bulletin April 1995 p 209.

18.6 **Transfer fees.** See 71.72 SCHEDULE D, CASES I AND II as regards transfer fees paid by football and other sports clubs.

19 Compensation for Loss of Employment (and Damages)

Cross-references. See 59.4 PENSIONS for war service payments etc.; 71.48 SCHEDULE D, CASES I AND II ('Compensation, Damages etc. — Receipts') and 71.47 ('Compensation, Damages etc. — Payments') for treatment in relation to trading profits and 71.54 for allowability of payments to employees; 75.32 SCHEDULE E for Redundancy Payments, 75.34 for Restrictive Covenants, 75.41 for certain payments to MPs etc. and 75.45 for wages in lieu of notice.

Simon's Direct Tax Service E4.8.

19.1 The following paragraphs apply to lump sums paid on termination of an office or employment and, at 19.7 below, to the reduction of an award for damages by reference to the tax liability.

19.2 SUMS RECEIVABLE ON TERMINATION OF OFFICE OR EMPLOYMENT — SUMMARY

In determining the correct treatment for tax purposes of a sum receivable by a director or employee on termination of his office or employment, it is first necessary to see whether it is taxable under the general rules of SCHEDULE E (75). See 19.3 below for an outline of the principles to be applied. If it is within the general rules, it is taxable in full under PAYE (55) at the time of the payment.

If it is not within the general rules of Schedule E, such a sum will generally be taxable under that Schedule by the special legislation in *ICTA 1988, s 148*. See 19.4, 19.5 below for the application of *section 148*, and 19.6 below for exemptions.

19.3 COMPENSATION FOR LOSS ETC. OF OFFICE OR EMPLOYMENT — GENERAL TAX LAW

The following principles apply in determining whether a sum received in compensation for loss, etc. of office or employment is taxable under the general rules of SCHEDULE E (75). See 19.4 *et seq.* below as regards such payments not within these rules.

Any payment made to a director or employee by way of reward for services, past, present or future, is within the general charge. It was considered by the Revenue that this could include any termination payment received under the terms of a contract of service, or where there was an expectation of receiving such a payment firm enough to allow the payment to be viewed as part of the reward for services (see e.g. Revenue Pamphlet IR 131, SP 1/81, 10 March 1981). In *Mairs v Haughey HL 1993, 66 TC 273*, however, it was held that a non-statutory redundancy payment would not be within the general Schedule E charge, being compensation for the employee's not being able to receive emoluments from the employment rather than emoluments from the employment itself. (The case concerned a payment for the waiver of a contingent right to such a payment, which was to be accorded the same tax treatment.) Following the decision in *Mairs v Haughey*, SP 1/81 was replaced by Revenue Statement of Practice SP 1/94. This acknowledges that lump sum payments under a non-statutory redundancy scheme are liable to income tax only under *ICTA 1988, s 148*, provided that they are genuinely made solely on account of redundancy as defined in *Employment Rights Act 1996, s 139*, whether the scheme is a standing scheme forming part of the conditions of service or an *ad hoc* scheme devised to meet a particular situation. SP 1/94 indicates, however, that the Revenue is concerned to distinguish payments which are in reality terminal bonuses or other reward for services, which are fully taxable under the general Schedule E rules, and that in view of the often complex arrangements for redundancy, and the need to consider each scheme on its own facts, employers may submit proposed schemes (together with any explanatory letter to be sent to employees) to the inspector for advance clearance. (Revenue Pamphlet IR 131, SP 1/94, 17 February 1994 as revised).

The following decided cases reflect the different approaches the courts have adopted in relation to such compensation. Proper compensation for loss of office is usually exempt (see *Clayton v Lavender Ch D 1965, 42 TC 607*) except where payable under service agreement (see *Dale v De Soissons CA 1950, 32 TC 118*) or under rights conferred by company's articles (*Henry v Foster CA 1932, 16 TC 605*). But an agreed sum payable for waiving such rights was held not assessable (*Hunter v Dewhurst HL 1932, 16 TC 605*), as also a payment in lieu of agreed pension (*Wales v Tilley HL 1943, 25 TC 136*). Payment in settlement of claim re breach of service contract also exempt (*Du Cros v Ryall KB 1935, 19 TC 444*), but cf. *Carter v Wadman CA 1946, 28 TC 41*. Voluntary payments on retirement held to be personal testimonials and not assessable (*Cowan v Seymour CA 1919, 7 TC 372; Mulvey v Coffey HC(I) 2 ITC 239*). A transfer fee paid by his old club to a professional footballer held to be assessable under general Schedule E rules and not as a termination payment (*Shilton v Wilmshurst HL 1991, 64 TC 78*).

Sums paid on cessation of office in lieu of future income were held not to be assessable in *Duff v Barlow KB 1941, 23 TC 633; Carter v Wadman CA 1946, 28 TC 41; Henley v Murray CA 1950, 31 TC 351;* and *Clayton v Lavender Ch D 1965, 42 TC 607. Hofman v Wadman KB 1946, 27 TC 192*, in which the decision was against the taxpayer, was not followed in *Clayton v Lavender*. But the following items paid during continuance of office were held liable: agreed sum paid to director to remain in office (*Prendergast v Cameron HL 1940, 23 TC 122*); for surrender of rights to fees or commission (*Leeland v Boarland KB 1945, 27 TC 71; Wilson v Daniels KB 1943, 25 TC 473; Bolam v Muller KB 1947, 28 TC 471* and *McGregor v Randall Ch D 1984, 58 TC 110*); and for accepting lower fees (*Wales v Tilley HL 1943, 25 TC 136*). See also *Williams v Simmonds Ch D 1981, 55 TC 17*. Payments under *Employment Rights Act 1996*, or NI equivalent, are exempt from tax [*ICTA 1988, s 579*] but must be included for the purposes of *ICTA 1988, s 148* (in practice, similar treatment is given to non-statutory redundancy payments under certain conditions), see 19.5 below. A proposed supplementary redundancy payment which, following a change in circumstances, was made to all employees whether or not made redundant, was held to be assessable under the general Schedule E rules where made to employees not made redundant (*Allan v CIR; Cullen v CIR CS 1994, 66 TC 681*).

See 75.45 SCHEDULE E for the Revenue view of payments in lieu of notice.

Sum paid as compensation for loss of benefit under an abandoned refuse salvage scheme held assessable (*Holland v Geoghegan Ch D 1972, 48 TC 482*).

See 3.10 ANTI-AVOIDANCE regarding capital sums received in lieu of earnings. [*ICTA 1988, s 775*].

See generally Revenue Schedule E Manual, SE 2620 *et seq.*.

19.4 COMPENSATION FOR LOSS OF OFFICE AND OTHER TERMINAL PAYMENTS — SPECIAL LEGISLATION

The general legal position in 19.3 above is modified by special legislation as explained in 19.5, 19.6 below. A payment taxable under any other provisions is not within this special legislation, but *a compensation payment which does not fall within the special legislation nevertheless remains subject to the general law.*

For the interaction of these provisions and *Gourley* principles (see 19.7 below) see *Stewart v Glentaggart Ltd CS 1963, 42 ATC 318; Bold v Brough QB, [1963] 3 AER 849* and *Parsons v BNM Laboratories Ltd CA, [1963] 2 AER 658*.

19.5 **TERMINAL PAYMENTS WITHIN ICTA 1988, s 148 CHARGE**

Payments and other benefits 'received' **after 5 April 1998** in connection with the termination of a person's office or employment (or with any change in the duties thereof or emoluments therefrom), and not otherwise chargeable to tax (see also 19.4 above), are chargeable to tax under *ICTA 1988, s 148* if *and to the extent that* they amount in aggregate to more than **£30,000**. The charge is under Schedule E for the year of assessment in which the payment or benefit is received. For these purposes, a cash benefit is treated as '*received*' when payment is made (including any payment on account) or when the recipient becomes entitled to require such payment. A non-cash benefit is treated as '*received*' when it is used or enjoyed. Where a payment or benefit, or the right to receive it, was brought into charge before 1998/99, it is not charged a second time on its receipt after 5 April 1998. See 19.6 below for exceptions from the charge under *section 148*.

A benefit includes anything which, disregarding any exemption, would be an emolument of the office or employment (or would be charged to tax as such) if were received for performance of the duties thereof. However, a right to receive payments or benefits is not itself regarded as a benefit. The charge applies regardless of who provides the payment or benefit and whether or not it is provided in pursuance of a legal obligation.

[*ICTA 1988, s 148; FA 1998, s 58(1)(4)*].

The charge under *section 148* applies to payments and other benefits received directly or indirectly in consideration or in consequence of, or otherwise in connection with, the termination (or change) by the employee himself, by a spouse, other relative or other dependant of his or by his personal representatives, or provided on his behalf or to his order. The charge is on the employee or, in the event of his death, on his personal representatives. For the reporting requirements in relation to taxable termination payments, see 55.9 PAY AS YOU EARN.

Non-cash benefits. The amount taxable, in the case of a non-cash benefit, is its cash equivalent normally as determined in accordance with *ICTA 1988, s 596B* (see 66.9 RETIREMENT SCHEMES) which applies the Schedule E rules for taxing benefits-in-kind received by employees earning £8,500 p.a. or more and directors (see 75.13–75.20 SCHEDULE E) and an appropriately modified version of the living accommodation rules at 75.29 SCHEDULE E. If, however, a greater figure would apply if the benefit were a Schedule E, Case I emolument chargeable under *ICTA 1988, s 19(1)*, this is taken instead; this is intended to bring into charge any appreciation in the value of an asset since its acquisition by the employer or other person providing the benefit (Treasury Explanatory Notes to Finance (No 2) Bill 1998). Where the cash equivalent of a beneficial loan (see 75.17 SCHEDULE E) is charged under *section 148* for any tax year, the taxpayer is treated as having paid interest for that year of an amount equal to that brought into charge (but not to the extent that the amount otherwise chargeable is covered by the £30,000 threshold); general principles then apply to determine whether such notional interest is allowable for tax purposes (see 43 INTEREST PAYABLE).

Application of £30,000 threshold. The £30,000 threshold is utilised against payments and benefits received in earlier tax years before those of later years. In any one tax year, the threshold (or so much of it as remains unutilised in earlier years) is set firstly against any cash benefits as they are received and any balance is set against the aggregate of non-cash benefits for the year. The threshold applies to the aggregate of payments and benefits provided in respect of the same person in respect of the same employment or of different employments with the same employer or 'associated' employers (as defined in *ICTA 1988, Sch 11 para 8*) or successors.

[*ICTA 1988, Sch 11 paras 1, 2, 7, 8, 12–16; FA 1998, s 58(2)(4), Sch 9 Pt I*].

See Revenue Tax Bulletin October 1998 pp 582–587 for an article (with numerous examples) describing the changes brought about by the above provisions.

Similar rules applied to payments and other benefits 'received' (as above) before 6 April 1998, with the fundamental difference that all chargeable amounts were treated as received on the date of termination (or change) (or, in the case of a payment in commutation of annual or other periodical payments, the date the commutation was effected) and were thus taxable for the year of assessment in which that date fell. There was no statutory rule for valuing non-cash benefits. Any person making a payment within *section 148* in any tax year had to notify the inspector in writing within 30 days after the end of that year. [*ICTA 1988, ss 148, 188(4)(5)(7)*]. Continuing benefits (e.g. the use of a car or a beneficial loan) included in a termination settlement were taxable under *section 148* on the value of the right to receive the future benefits. See *George v Ward (Sp C 30), [1995] SSCD 230* (value of provision of car for limited period following termination held within *section 148*, but by reference to period actually made available rather than for longer period for which original termination agreement provided). For 1996/97 and 1997/98 only, pending new legislation, the Revenue were prepared to accept, as an alternative to the strict application of *section 148*, the adoption by the taxpayer of an alternative basis whereby the benefits are taxed as they are received or enjoyed (but not so as to alter the year for which they are taxable). The annual benefit is to be calculated as required by *ICTA 1988, s 596B* (see above). The self-assessment return for the year of termination should include the benefit so calculated for that year; the Revenue will thereafter make separate assessments for that year in respect of the benefits enjoyed or received in subsequent years. Where, however, the taxpayer can demonstrate that the total benefits assessed on this basis exceed those assessable on the strict basis, the excess will not be collected. For details of how these arrangements are applied in practice, see Revenue Tax Bulletin June 1997 pp 427–429.

Section 148 is an independent Schedule E charging provision, not confined to the rules of the Cases under *ICTA 1988, s 19(1)* (see 75.1 SCHEDULE E) (*Nichols v Gibson CA 1996, 68 TC 611*).

A statutory redundancy payment is included for the purpose of *section 148*. [*ICTA 1988, s 580(3)*]. For the position as regards a payment under a non-statutory redundancy scheme, see 19.3 above.

Where, as part of an arrangement relating to the termination of an employment, both parties agree that the employer will make a special contribution into an approved retirement benefit scheme on behalf of the employee the Revenue will not charge under *section 148* provided the benefits are within the limits provided by the scheme. A similar exemption will apply to the purchase of an annuity for the employee so long as the transaction is approved under *ICTA 1988, Pt XIV*. See 66.4 RETIREMENT SCHEMES. (Revenue Pamphlet IR 131, SP 2/81, 10 March 1981).

For MPs see *ICTA 1988, s 190*, and for European MPs, 75.41 SCHEDULE E.

Expenses incurred by taxpayer in obtaining an award for unfair dismissal or securing fresh employment held not deductible (*Warnett v Jones Ch D 1979, 53 TC 283*).

See 75.23 for exemption from *section 148* for payment made or benefit provided to reimburse the employee for cost of indemnity insurance or certain liabilities relating to the employment.

As to whether *compensation to auditor* and others falls within *section 148*, see 75.24 SCHEDULE E.

Simon's Direct Tax Service. See **E4.805**.

19.6 EXCEPTIONS AND RELIEFS FROM ICTA 1988, s 148 CHARGE

(i) Payments and other benefits where termination arises from death, injury or disability of the holder of the office. [*ICTA 1988, s 188(1)(a), Sch 11 para 3; FA 1998, Sch 9 para 3, Sch 27 Pt III(9)*]. 'Disability' covers not only a condition resulting from a sudden affliction but also continuing incapacity to perform the duties of an office or employment arising out of the culmination of a process of deterioration of physical or mental health caused by chronic illness. (Revenue Pamphlet IR 131, SP 10/81, 3 November 1981). See e.g. *Horner v Hasted Ch D, [1995] STC 766* (relief refused). (See, however, 66.12 RETIREMENT SCHEMES as regards certain *ex gratia* payments under unapproved arrangements which may be chargeable under *ICTA 1988, s 596A*.)

(ii) Benefits provided before 1 December 1993, or on or after that date under retirement benefit schemes entered into before that date and not varied on or after that date, for the provision of which the holder has been charged under *ICTA 1970, s 220* or *ICTA 1988, s 595*. [*ICTA 1988, s 188(1)(c); FA 1994, s 108(7)(8)*]. (See also now 66.9 RETIREMENT SCHEMES.)

(iii) Payments and other benefits under schemes described in *ICTA 1970, s 221(1)(2) or ICTA 1988, s 596(1)* (see 66 RETIREMENT SCHEMES), but payments for loss of office, or loss or diminution of earnings, are exempted only if the loss etc. is due to ill-health or the payment is properly a benefit earned by past service. [*ICTA 1988, s 188(1)(d)(2), Sch 11 para 4; FA 1998, Sch 9 Pt I, Sch 27 Pt III(9)*].

(iv) Certain payments and other benefits (including commutation of annual sums) provided to *HM Forces*. [*ICTA 1988, s 188(1)(e), Sch 11 para 5; FA 1998, Sch 9 Pt I, Sch 27 Pt III(9)*].

(v) Benefit from Commonwealth overseas government superannuation schemes, or compensation for loss of career etc., due to constitutional changes there, paid to a former public servant of that territory (for certain definitions see *Overseas Development and Cooperation Act 1980*). [*ICTA 1988, s 188(1)(f), Sch 11 para 6; FA 1998, Sch 9 Pt I, Sch 27 Pt III(9)*].

(vi) Payments and other benefits where certain foreign service (as defined) is included. Depending on length of foreign service in relation to total service, payments etc. may be wholly exempt or the amount otherwise chargeable may be proportionately reduced. [*ICTA 1988, s 188(3), Sch 11 paras 9–11; FA 1998, Sch 9 Pt I, Sch 27 Pt III(9)*].

(vii) A special contribution by an employer into an approved retirement benefit scheme or an approved personal pension scheme (or purchase of an approved annuity from a Life Office) to provide benefits for the employee as part of an arrangement relating to the termination of an employment. (Revenue Pamphlet IR 131, SP 2/81, 10 March 1981).

(viii) Legal costs. Where an employee takes action to recover compensation for loss of office etc., any legal costs recovered from the employer are strictly chargeable under *section 148*, without any deduction for the costs incurred. By concession, tax will not be charged on such recovered costs where either:

(*a*) the dispute is settled without recourse to the courts, and the costs are paid direct to the employee's solicitor under the settlement agreement, in full or partial discharge of the solicitor's bill of costs incurred by the employee only in connection with the termination of the employment; or

(*b*) the dispute goes to court, and the costs are paid in accordance with a court order (including where they are paid direct to the employee).

Other professional costs, such as accountancy fees, are not covered by this concession, but it does cover legal costs incurred by the employee's solicitor in consulting other professionals for the specific claim or in paying the expenses of expert professional witnesses. (Revenue Pamphlet IR 1, A81; Revenue Tax Bulletin October 1994 p 170).

Simon's Direct Tax Service. See **E4.806, E4.807**.

19.7 **DAMAGES — REDUCTION FOR TAX**

Tax liability is taken into account in fixing *damages* for injury, see *British Transport Commission v Gourley HL 1955, 34 ATC 305*. For application of *Gourley* principle see *West Suffolk CC v W Rought Ltd HL 1956, 35 ATC 315* and contrast *Stoke-on-Trent City Council v Wood Mitchell & Co Ltd CA 1978, [1979] STC 197* (compulsory purchase of land); *Lyndale Fashion Mfrs v Rich CA 1972, [1973] STC 32* (tax on damages calculated as if top slice of income after expenses deducted); *In re Houghton Main Colliery Ch D 1956, 23 ATC 320* (lump sum payable re pensions); *Stewart v Glentaggart CS 1963, 42 ATC 318; Parsons v BNM Labs CA 1963, 42 ATC 200* (damages for wrongful dismissal); *McGhie & Sons v BTC QB 1962, 41 ATC 144* (prohibition from mining under railway — cf. 71.48(*c*) SCHEDULE D, CASES I AND II); and *John v James Ch D, [1986] STC 352* (no deduction for tax paid by defendant on sums wrongfully retained or for tax plaintiff would have been liable for on these sums or on compound interest award). But cf. *Spencer v Macmillan's Trustees CS 1958, 37 ATC 388* (breach of contract). A PAYE refund was deducted in *Hartley v Sandholme QB, [1974] STC 434*. In a case involving taxable damages paid to a large group of Lloyd's Names, it was held that the fact that certain of the Names would receive a tax benefit, due to the differential tax rates applicable to the damages and the corresponding loss reliefs, did not require a departure from the general principle that no account is to be taken of taxation where both damages and lost profits are taxable (*Deeny and others v Gooda Walker Ltd HL 1996, 68 TC 458*).

As regards whether interest on awarded damages should take account of the extent to which the damages are taxable, see *Deeny and others v Gooda Walker Ltd (in liquidation) and others (No 4) QB, [1995] STC 696.*

Simon's Direct Tax Service. See **E4.821** *et seq.*.

20 Connected Persons

[*ICTA 1988, s 839 as amended*]

Simon's Direct Tax Service. See **C2.110.**

20.1 For many tax purposes, certain persons are treated as being so closely involved with each other that they must either be viewed as the same person or that transactions between them must be treated differently from transactions 'at arm's length'. These 'connected persons' are defined for tax purposes as below.

20.2 **An individual** is connected with his spouse or with relatives (including their spouses) of his or his spouse. It appears that a widow or widower is no longer a spouse (*Vestey's Exors and Vestey v CIR HL 1949, 31 TC 1*). Spouses divorced by decree nisi remain connected persons until the decree is made absolute (*Aspden v Hildesley Ch D 1981, 55 TC 609*). See definition of relative in 20.8 below.

20.3 **A trustee of a settlement,** in his capacity as such, is connected with

(*a*) the settlor (if an individual) (see 20.8 below), and

(*b*) any person connected with the settlor (if within (*a*)), and

(*c*) a body corporate connected with the settlement (see 20.8 below).

20.4 **A partner** is connected with the person with whom he is in partnership and with the spouse or relative of that person except in connection with acquisitions and disposals of partnership assets made pursuant to bona fide commercial arrangements.

20.5 **A company is connected with another company if**

(*a*) the same person controls both, or

(*b*) one is controlled by a person who has control of the other in conjunction with persons connected with him, or

(*c*) a person controls one company and persons connected with him control the other, or

(*d*) the same group of persons controls both, or

(*e*) the companies are controlled by separate groups which can be regarded as the same by interchanging connected persons.

20.6 **A company is connected with another person who** (either alone or with persons connected with him) **has control of it**. It is understood that the Revenue will accept that a partnership and a company under common control are connected in relation to the treatment for capital allowances of assets transferred on a succession (Tolley's Practical Tax 1981 p 142).

20.7 **Persons acting together to secure or exercise control of a company** are treated in relation to that company as connected with each other and with any other person acting on the direction of any of them to secure or exercise such control. For the meaning of 'acting together to secure or exercise control', see *Steele v EVC International NV (formerly European Vinyls Corp (Holdings) BV) CA 1996, 69 TC 88*. Control may be 'exercised' passively. See *Floor v Davis HL 1979, 52 TC 609.*

20.8 '*Company*' includes any body corporate, unincorporated association or unit trust scheme (within *ICTA 1988, s 469*). It does not include a partnership.

'*Control*' is as defined by *ICTA 1988, s 416* (see Tolley's Corporation Tax under Close Companies) but see below as regards *ICTA 1988, s 840* definition.

'*Relative*' means brother, sister, ancestor or lineal descendant.

'*Settlement*' includes any disposition, trust, covenant, agreement, arrangement or, for 1995/96 onwards, transfer of assets. [*ICTA 1988, s 681(4) (repealed); ICTA 1988, s 660G(1); FA 1995, Sch 17 para 1*]. See also 81.16 SETTLEMENTS.

'*Settlor*' is any person by whom the settlement was made or who has directly or indirectly (or by a reciprocal arrangement) provided, or undertaken to provide, funds for the settlement. [*ICTA 1988, s 681(4) (repealed); ICTA 1988, s 660G(1)(2); FA 1995, Sch 17 para 1*].

'*A body corporate connected with the settlement*' is a close company (or one which would be close if resident in the UK) the participators in which include the trustees of the settlement, or a company of which such a close company etc. has control. 'Control' is as defined in *ICTA 1988, s 840*, i.e. the power of a person by shareholding or voting power (whether directly or through another company), or under Articles of Association or other regulating document, to secure that the company's affairs are conducted according to his wishes. [*ICTA 1988, s 681(5) (repealed); ICTA 1988, s 682A(2), s 839(3A); FA 1995, Sch 17 paras 11, 20*].

21 Construction Industry Tax Scheme

See also Revenue Pamphlets IR 14/15(CIS), IR 40(CIS), IR 109, IR 116(CIS), IR 117(CIS), IR 148, IR 157 and IR 164(CIS).

Simon's Direct Tax Service E5.5.

21.1 SCHEME APPLICABLE FROM 1 AUGUST 1999

With effect for payments made **on or after 1 August 1999**, the scheme for deduction of tax from payments to construction sub-contractors who do not have a tax certificate entitling them to gross payment, and the arrangements and conditions for the issue of such certificates, are substantially revised. The revised scheme is described at 21.2 *et seq.* below. It is intended that, under the revised scheme, most sub-contractors will *not* hold tax certificates, but will hold registration cards (see 21.3 below) and receive payments after deduction on account of tax. The main changes from the scheme as it applied before 1 August 1999 (see 21.8 below) are as follows.

(*a*) The 23% deduction is replaced by a deduction of a percentage determined by the Treasury by order, which may not exceed the basic rate (and is set at 18% for 2000/01).

(*b*) A minimum anticipated annual turnover (prescribed by regulation and, in the case of firms or companies, broadly geared to the number of individuals who are partners or directors) is a precondition for the issue of a tax certificate.

(*c*) The limited certificates for school leavers and where a bank guarantee is in force are withdrawn.

(*d*) A general exemption from deduction is provided where conditions to be prescribed are met in relation to a payment under any contract and to the person making the payment.

(*e*) All public offices and departments of the Crown, and such statutory bodies as are designated in regulations, are normally to be treated as contractors for the purposes of the deduction scheme. However, for these and the other public bodies treated as contractors, an exemption based on the average annual construction expenditure test already used for businesses is introduced. Government departments treated as contractors will be subject to the same obligations, sanctions and Revenue powers of enforcement as other contractors.

(*f*) The average annual expenditure on construction operations which renders the person incurring the expenditure a contractor for the purposes of the deduction scheme is increased from £250,000 to £1,000,000.

(*g*) The conditions for a tax certificate for an individual partner in a firm are generally aligned with those for sole traders, insofar as they relate to the circumstances of the individual. The individual conditions relating to the length of time the business has been carried on are removed.

(*h*) The fine (maximum £5,000) on summary conviction for certain fraudulent attempts to obtain or misuse a tax certificate is replaced by a penalty up to £3,000.

Exemption certificates covering periods beginning before and ending after 31 July 1999 cease to have effect after that date.

Registration cards. As referred to above, in conjunction with the revised deduction scheme, a mandatory registration card system is introduced for sub-contractors not holding a tax certificate. See 21.2, 21.3 below. In outline, the registration card system is as follows.

(i) The card carries the sub-contractor's name and photograph, the tax reference and the national insurance number.

(ii) Contractors are required to check cards before making payments under deduction.

(iii) The cards are available on request to anyone working, or intending to work, in the construction industry.

(iv) A penalty of up to £3,000 applies for failure by a contractor to take the necessary steps to require the production of registration cards and to check their validity, or to make accurate returns in relation to registration card payments (unless there were reasonable grounds for accepting the validity of a card and all reasonable steps were taken to ensure the correctness of the return).

Transitional arrangements. For the period 1 August 1999 to 5 September 1999, arrangements were made for the issue by tax offices of temporary Tax Payment Cards (forms CIS65) which enabled contractors to make payments under deduction of tax in certain cases where the sub-contractor had not applied for a registration card or certificate in time for the scheme commencement or, exceptionally, had applied for but not received it. Additionally, up to 5 November 1999, contractors were able to accept registration card, temporary tax payment card or certificate details where the document was photocopied onto the sub-contractor's original headed paper, and where contractors still believed they would be unable to pay their workers and/or complete the appropriate vouchers, they could apply for a dispensation. Payments after 5 November 1999 can only be made where the full new scheme conditions are complied with. (Revenue Press Releases 7 July 1999, 15 July 1999).

Scheme review. A joint working group, comprising officials from the Revenue and the Department of the Environment, Transport and the Regions and construction industry representatives, has been set up to review the new construction industry scheme. Individual representations, which the group will take into account, may be made to Philip Hogan, Construction Industry Scheme Review, Compliance Division, Inland Revenue, 22 Kingsway, London WC2B 6NR (e-mail: philip.hogan@ir.gsi.gov.uk).

21.2 **Payments from which tax must be deducted.** Where a 'contractor' carrying on a business which includes 'construction operations' makes any payment (except as below) to, or to the nominee of, a 'sub-contractor' under a contract relating to 'construction operations' in the UK or on offshore installations within UK territorial waters, then, unless the recipient meets the conditions for gross payment (see 21.4 below), the payer must deduct, and pay over to the Revenue, a specified percentage of so much of the payment (excluding any VAT and CITB levy) as does not represent the cost of materials. Before making any such payment, the contractor must ensure that the sub-contractor produces a valid registration card (see 21.3 below), and must satisfy himself that the person producing it is the person to whom it was issued (or an authorised user of a company card, being a director or secretary of the company), unless he has done so on a previous occasion and has no reason to doubt that it remains valid for the person who produced it. Possession of a registration card by a sub-contractor does not, however, relieve the contractor of the responsibility to establish whether the sub-contractor is employed or self-employed (see 21.7 below). A penalty not exceeding £3,000 may apply for failure by a contractor to carry out these checks. These provisions do not apply to payments under a contract of employment, payments chargeable under Schedule E by virtue of *ICTA 1988, s 134* (workers supplied by agencies — see 75.46 SCHEDULE E), or payments excluded by regulations. The percentage deduction rate is determined by the Treasury by order, and may not exceed the basic rate of income tax. [*ICTA 1988, s 559(1)–(4A), s 560(1),* *s 561(1), s 566(2B), s 567(1)(b); FA 1995, s 139, Sch 27 para 1; FA 1996, s 178(1); FA 1998, s 55(2)(3); SI 1993 No 743, reg 7F; SI 1998 Nos 2620, 2622, reg 8; SI 2000 No 922*].

The specified rate of deduction is reduced from 23% to 18% with effect from 6 April 2000. [*SI 2000 No 921*].

It is understood that the 'cost of materials' which may be excluded in determining the amount subject to deduction may include a reasonable commercial charge for plant supplied by the sub-contractor for the period of the contract. Where a sub-contractor does not supply evidence of the cost to him of materials, the contractor should make a fair estimate of the actual cost. See Revenue Pamphlet IR 14/15(CIS), paras 3.3, 3.4.

A '*sub-contractor*' is a party to a contract relating to 'construction operations' who is under a duty to carry out, or to furnish his own, or others', labour in the carrying out of, such operations, or otherwise answerable to the contractor for the carrying out of such operations by others. See generally Revenue Pamphlet IR 14/15(CIS), paras 2.8–2.11.

A '*contractor*' is:

(*a*) any person carrying on a business which includes 'construction operations';

(*b*) any person carrying on a business at any time if his average annual expenditure on construction operations in the three years up to the end of his last period of account exceeded £1,000,000 or, where the business was not being carried on at the beginning of that three-year period, if his total expenditure on such operations up to the end of that last period of account exceeded £3,000,000. A person who is a contractor under this provision will continue within that definition until he satisfies the Board that his expenditure on construction operations has been below £1,000,000 in each of three successive years beginning in or after that period of account. For the purposes of these expenditure limits, where a trade is transferred from one company to another and *ICTA 1988, s 343* (no change of ownership) applies, the transferor's expenditure will be treated as the transferee's, with apportionment by the Board (subject to appeal) when only part of the trade is transferred; and

(*c*) any public office or department of the Crown; any local authority; any development corporation or new town commission; the Commission for the New Towns; the Housing Corporation; the Secretary of State for Wales (in relation to a contract made under *Housing Associations Act 1985, s 89*); any housing association or trust; Scottish Homes; the Northern Ireland Housing Executive; any NHS trust (or NI equivalent); and the Corporate Officers of the Houses of Parliament. Apart from the Secretary of State for Wales, such offices, departments and bodies are, however, defined as contractors only at a time when their average annual expenditure on 'construction operations' in the three-year period to 31 March immediately preceding that time exceeded £1,000,000, but once so included they continue to be so until expenditure on 'construction operations' has been below £1,000,000 in each of three successive years after the end of the three-year period.

The definition includes a person who is himself a sub-contractor in relation to construction operations, e.g. a gang-leader.

[*ICTA 1988, s 559(1), s 560(2)–(5); FA 1995, Sch 27 para 2; FA 1998, Sch 8 para 2(2)–(4); Government of Wales Act 1998, Sch 16 para 58; SI 1993 No 743, reg 3A, Sch A1; SI 1998 No 2622, regs 4, 37; SI 1999 No 2159, reg 9*].

Where payments by any of the bodies, etc. which are contractors by virtue of (*b*) or (*c*) above are made under a contract in respect of which the total contract payments (excluding materials) do not exceed (and are not likely to exceed) £1,000, and the body, etc. is approved by the inspector for the purpose, the payments are excluded from the application of these provisions. [*SI 1993 No 743, reg 20B; SI 1998 No 2622, reg 13*].

Private householders having work done on their own premises are *not* contractors for these purposes. See generally Revenue Pamphlet IR 14/15(CIS), paras 2.3–2.7.

'*Construction operations*' are widely defined to cover installing heating, lighting, drainage, etc. systems, internal cleaning of buildings in the course of their construction, alteration or repair, and internal or external painting, as well as constructing, altering, repairing or demolishing buildings, walls, roadworks, etc., but to *exclude* drilling for oil or gas, mining operations, the professional work of architects, surveyors, etc., the installation, etc. of sculptures, murals, and other artistic works, signwriting, advertisements, seating, blinds, shutters, security and public address systems, computer or telecommunications wiring through pre-existing ducts and the manufacture of components for heating, lighting, drainage, etc. systems. The Treasury may add to these categories by order made by statutory instrument. [*ICTA 1988, s 567*]. Carpet fitting is outside the scope of the scheme. (Revenue Pamphlet IR 131, SP 12/81, 20 November 1981). For detailed guidance on the scope of 'construction operations', see Appendix B to Revenue Pamphlet IR 14/15(CIS).

A signed *tax payment voucher* (form CIS25) must be given by the contractor to the sub-contractor within 14 days of the end of a tax month in respect of all payments made under deduction of tax as above during the month. The contractor must also within 14 days of the end of each tax month either send the top copies of all forms CIS25 to the Inland Revenue (where three-part forms CIS25(I) or (M) have been used) or transmit specified particulars to them electronically (where single-part forms CIS25(E) have been used). [*SI 1993 No 743, reg 7; SI 1998 No 2622, reg 7*].

See generally Revenue Pamphlets IR 14/15(CIS), chapter 3 and IR 164(CIS) 'Advice to sub-contractors going onto deduction'. As regards disputes about, or corrections to, deductions, see IR 14/15(CIS), paras 7.3–7.5.

21.3 **Registration cards** (see 21.2 above) are issued or replaced by an inspector or other person nominated by the Board. An inspector may require their surrender or cancel them. They must be produced for inspection, or surrendered, when required by any authorised officer of the Board. A refusal to issue or replace a registration card, or its cancellation, is subject to the normal right of appeal, although it is expected that cards will be available on request to anyone intending to commence work, or working, within the construction industry. They need only complete a form, supply a photograph and attend an identity check (see Revenue Pamphlet IR 14/15(CIS), para 1.6).

Cards (form CIS4(P)) other than temporary cards carry the sub-contractor's name, photograph and signature, the national insurance number (or, exceptionally, a 'system identifier'), and a distinctive reference number assigned to the card. They may also include a name under which the business is carried on. They have no expiry date. In the case of a partner in a firm, they must include the name of the firm for which the partner is acting. Company cards issued to a director or secretary of the company authorised to use the card must similarly include the name of the company for whom the director or secretary is acting. If a business name is included on a partner's or company card, it must be the same for all partners or directors and secretaries. Temporary registration cards (form CIS4(T)), which carry a date of expiry instead of the national insurance number, may be issued with a maximum validity of three months.

[*ICTA 1988, s 566(2A); FA 1996, s 178; SI 1993 No 743, regs 7A–7E, Sch 1; SI 1998 No 2622, regs 8, 38*].

See 21.7 below as regards penalties relating to registration card failures.

21.4 **Sub-contractors' tax certificates.** Where a tax certificate (form CIS5 or CIS6) has been issued to a sub-contractor and is in force when a payment is made, and the various regulatory requirements as regards production and validation, etc. of the certificate (see below) are complied with, the deduction requirements under 21.2 above do not apply. Possession of a tax certificate by a sub-contractor does not, however, relieve the contractor of the responsibility to establish whether the sub-contractor is employed or self-employed (see 21.7 below). Certificates form CIS5, which do not have to be produced to contractors (see alternative verification procedure described below) and which obviate the requirement to supply gross payment vouchers to contractors (see below), may only be issued when the inspector considers that a form CIS6 certificate would be inappropriate in all the circumstances. The Inland Revenue have indicated that a CIS5 certificate will only be issued to a company which either

(*a*) is a plc or a subsidiary of a plc, or

(*b*) has a turnover of at least £3 million, or has taken over and will continue an established concern with such a turnover which was previously owned by a director or directors of the company and which met certain other conditions as to previous compliance, or

(*c*) is a subsidiary or associate of an established company holding a CIS5 (or predecessor 714C) certificate (and which would still qualify for a CIS 5 certificate), or

(*d*) shows that operating with a CIS6 certificate would cause substantial difficulties.

As regards (*d*), evidence would have to be produced either of an administrative need, i.e. that using CIS6 certificates would involve either a high volume of vouchers – normally 300 or more per year but 150 or more per year may suffice in certain cases – or an excessive amount of time spent travelling specifically to present a certificate – at least 200 hours over a three-year period or 100 hours in any one of those years, or of a commercial need, i.e. where the applicant's trade is largely based on, or potentially involves, work for contractors who give work only to CIS5 certificate holders. (Revenue Tax Bulletin April 1999 pp 635, 636).

For more detailed guidance on the issue of CIS5 certificates, see Revenue Subcontractors in the Construction Industry Manual.

Verification. Before a gross payment can be made, and subject to the alternative verification procedure described below for CIS5 certificate holders, the sub-contractor must produce the certificate to the contractor, who must satisfy himself by inspecting the certificate that the sub-contractor is the user of the certificate (or authorised to produce it on behalf of a company which is the user). Where the user receives the payment as a nominee, the person nominating the user must also produce his certificate for validation. Further inspections of the certificate are not required for so long as the contractor has no reason to doubt that it is still valid.

There is an alternative verification procedure where the user of a CIS5 certificate (not being a nominee) has notified the inspector of particulars of the company bank account into which payments, which must be under a written contract between the company and the contractor, are to be made. The user may produce to the contractor a 'certification document' signed by the secretary or a director of the company, and provided that the contractor has no reason to doubt that the information shown on the document is correct (and the payment date falls within the period of validity of the certificate referred to in the document), he may make payments gross. The certification document must certify that the company is the user of a valid company tax certificate form CIS5. It must specify the name, address (of the registered office) and registration number of the user, the distinctive number, expiry date (and, if any, commencement date) of the certificate, and details of the nominated bank account. It may also include the user's business name. To allay any doubt concerning the certification document, the contractor may, within 14 days of receipt of the document, apply to the inspector for confirmation that a valid certificate has been issued to the company and that the information on the certification document agrees with the inspector's records.

[*SI 1993 No 743, regs 33, 34; SI 1998 No 2622, reg 25*].

Payments. Payments to a holder of certificate form CIS5 should only be made by cheque or credit transfer, and *never* by cash (see Revenue Pamphlet IR 14/15(CIS), paras 5.12, 5.13).

Completion of vouchers. A sub-contractor with a certificate form CIS6 must, within 14 days after the end of each income tax month, give two signed copies of a gross payment voucher (form CIS24) containing specified particulars to the contractor in respect of all contract payments received gross in the month (or, if the contractor so requests, for each such payment). The contractor must complete the form with his distinctive reference number and deliver the appropriate copy to the sub-contractor. Where vouchers are not supplied, or are incorrectly completed, by the sub-contractor, and further payments are due, the contractor should reconsider the validity of the certificate. Duplicates should be requested of vouchers claimed to have been lost in the post. If a proper voucher is not supplied despite the contractor taking reasonable steps to obtain one, he should report the matter to the Revenue.

Where a sub-contractor has a certificate form CIS5, the contractor must complete a construction gross payment voucher (form CIS23(M) or CIS23(I)) containing specified particulars in respect of all gross payments in any income tax month (or transmit the specified particulars to the Inland Revenue electronically). Within 14 days after the end of each income tax month the contractor must forward to the Inland Revenue all forms CIS24, CIS23(M) or CIS23(I) given to or obtained or completed by him in the month. [*SI 1993 No 743, regs 35, 37A, 38, 39; SI 1998 No 2622, regs 26, 29–31*].

Issue of a certificate. Application for a tax certificate is made on form CIS2 or CIS3 as appropriate, and at least one month should be allowed for the application to be approved. Ten working days should be allowed after notification of approval for issue of the certificate.

For a tax certificate to be issued, the Revenue must be satisfied that the sub-contractor is carrying on a business in the UK consisting of or including the carrying out of construction operations (see 21.2 above), or the furnishing (or arranging for the furnishing) of labour for such operations, with proper premises, equipment, stock and other facilities. There must be a bank account through which the business is substantially conducted and proper records must be kept, and the applicant must also satisfy the 'turnover test' described at 21.5 below. Certificates are normally valid for either three years or one year, depending on the basis on which the turnover test is satisfied (see 21.5 below), although the initial issue of certificates under the new scheme will adjust the three-year period by up to six months to achieve an even rate of expiry of certificates. Certificates issued to partners in a firm or to a company at different times will have a common expiry date. The Board has wide powers to cancel certificates and require their surrender (and see 21.7 below).

An *individual applicant* (whether or not a partner in a firm) must have complied timeously with all tax and national insurance obligations (including supplying accounts and other information relating to any business of the applicant to the inspector on request) in respect of periods ending within the three years preceding the date of application (the '*qualifying period*'). There must be reason to expect that future such obligations will be complied with, and provided that this expectation is not rendered open to doubt, 'minor and technical failings' in relation to past obligations may be disregarded at the Board's discretion (but see *T & C Hill (Haulage) v Gleig (Sp C 227), [2000] SSCD 64* for a case in which refusal of a certificate was upheld on the grounds of late submission of returns and payment of tax liabilities after the due date). See Revenue Pamphlet IR 40(CIS), Appendix 2 for the Revenue interpretation of 'minor and technical failings'. Where the applicant claims not to have been subject to an obligation for these purposes, he must satisfy the Board of that fact by evidence prescribed by regulation, and where he claims to have been non-resident, he must also satisfy the Board by such evidence that any comparable foreign obligations have been met (see *SI 1993 No 743, regs 22–23B; SI 1998 No 2622, regs 15–17*). Any company of which the individual had control (within *ICTA 1988, s 416(2)–(6)*) during the qualifying period must also satisfy those conditions in respect of any accounting period ending within the qualifying period at a time when the applicant had such control.

A *company applicant* (whether or not a partner in a firm) must have a similarly satisfactory record of past and prospective compliance with all its taxation and national insurance and certain Companies Act obligations. In *Gorge Fabrications Ltd v Wilson (Sp C 214), [1999] SSCD 293*, the Special Commissioner upheld an inspector's refusal of a certificate to a company which had, within the three year period in question, entered into a voluntary arrangement with its creditors resulting in 75% of its outstanding corporation tax liabilities (amounting to £2,927) remaining unpaid (its PAYE/NIC liabilities of over £30,000 having been treated as preferential and met in full). The Board may also, in certain cases where there is a limited history of construction operations, or where there has been a change of control, issue a direction under *ICTA 1988, s 561(6)* that the directors (and, if the company is close, the beneficial shareholders) must satisfy any or all of the conditions imposed on individual applicants (see above). Where the introduction of a new shareholder into a close private company results in a change of control, the company must notify the inspector of the new shareholder within 30 days (see *SI 1993 No 743, reg 42*).

Each of the *partners in a firm* (applying as such), in addition to meeting the requirements for individual or company applicants (as above), as appropriate, must also satisfy the requirements as to the meeting of tax obligations (and requests by the inspector) in relation to the firm's business.

[*ICTA 1988, ss 561, 562, 564, 565; FA 1995, Sch 27 paras 3–7; SI 1993 No 743, regs 25, 26; SI 1998 No 2622, regs 19, 20; SI 1999 No 2156*].

Changes in a business. Where an individual or firm incorporates, or a partnership becomes a sole trader, the new business will require a new certificate. However, if the business is essentially the same, the new business may apply immediately on the basis of the three-year test (applied in the light of the particular circumstances of the case), rather than having to wait six months to apply on the basis of the six-month test. Changes in the number of partners in a firm or directors/shareholders in a company, without any change in the business, do not require the turnover test to be re-applied before the certificate falls to be renewed, unless the inspector suspects manipulation of the threshold provisions. New partners/directors can apply for additional certificates. (Revenue Pamphlet IR 40(CIS) p 6).

Old scheme certificates. Certificates issued under the scheme applicable before 1 August 1999 cease to have effect after 31 July 1999 regardless of the expiry date shown on the certificate. [*SI 1998 No 2620, reg 4*].

Simon's Direct Tax Service. See **E5.525** *et seq.*.

21.5 **Turnover test.** *Individuals (other than in relation to applications as partners in firms).* The turnover test requires the applicant to satisfy the Board that, during the period of validity of the certificate, the aggregate annual amount of 'relevant payments' received is likely to be not less than the 'individual turnover threshold' of £30,000. (It should, however, be noted that Revenue Pamphlet IR 40(CIS) states: 'If you are using the six month test, you should show the actual amount you received in the period. Where you are using a three year test on the basis of accounts, we would not expect you to adjust figures for gross construction turnover and materials for debtors or creditors to arrive at the net "payments received" in the three years. Just use the figures earned, as shown in your accounts.')

'*Relevant payments*' are all payments, net of the cost of materials, under contracts relating to, or to the work of individuals participating in the carrying out of, construction operations (see 21.2 above), whether or not within the scheme (i.e. including work for private householders, etc.).

To satisfy the Board, either a six-month test or a three-year test must be satisfied (and depending on which test is satisfied, the certificate will generally be valid for one year or three years (subject to variation on the initial issue, see 21.4 above) respectively). The six-month test is not available where the applicant has been a sub-contractor for a continuous period of four years up to the date of application and three successive one-year certificates have been issued to him.

The six-month test requires the production of evidence (i.e. tax payment vouchers and gross payment vouchers and documentary evidence of relevant payments and of the direct cost of materials) that relevant payments (i.e. turnover) during a consecutive period of up to six tax months in the year preceding the date of application amounted to at least 70% of the individual turnover threshold (i.e. currently £21,000).

The three-year test requires the production of such evidence that relevant payments (i.e. turnover) in a consecutive period of three years in the four years preceding the date of application averaged at least 90% of the average of the individual turnover thresholds for those three years (i.e. currently £27,000) and were at least equal to that threshold in two of the three years. Accounts will also generally be required.

Companies. The turnover test requires a company applicant to satisfy the Board that either

(i) the annual receipts test is satisfied, or

(ii) all the company's shareholders are themselves companies limited by shares with current valid certificates.

The annual receipts test requires that, during the period of validity of the certificate, the aggregate annual amount of 'relevant payments' (as above) received is likely to be not less than the smaller of

(*a*) the individual turnover threshold (currently £30,000), as above, multiplied by the number of 'relevant persons' in relation to the company, and

(*b*) a specified amount (currently £200,000).

A person is a '*relevant person*' in relation to a company if he is a director of the company or (where the company is a close company) a beneficial owner of shares in the company. To satisfy the Board as regards (*a*) above, the six-month or three-year tests described above in relation to individual applicants are applied, but by reference to the '*multiple company turnover threshold*', i.e. (subject to special rules where a business is transferred by an individual or firm to a company as a going concern) the individual turnover threshold multiplied by the number of relevant persons. For the six-month test, the number of relevant persons is the maximum number at any time in the six-month (or shorter) period concerned. For the three-year test it is the maximum number at any time in the relevant year, except that for applications before 1 August 2001, by concession, the maximum number at any point during the last six months of the three-year period may be substituted for each of the three years if this will assist the sub-contractor to meet the test. (Revenue Pamphlet IR 1, B52). As regards (*b*) above (the '*alternative company turnover threshold*'), the three-year test is applied, but by reference to the £200,000 annual limit.

Individuals applying as partners in firms. The turnover test requires the partners in the firm to satisfy the Board that, during the period of validity of the certificate, the aggregate annual amount of 'relevant payments' (as above) received is likely to be not less than the smaller of

(A) the sum of the individual turnover threshold (as above) multiplied by the number of individual partners and, for each corporate partner (other than a company within (ii) above), the turnover threshold which would have applied if the company had itself applied for a certificate (as above), and

(B) a specified amount (currently £200,000).

To satisfy the Board as regards (A) above, the six-month or three-year tests described above in relation to individual applicants are applied, but by reference to the '*multiple partnership turnover threshold*', i.e. the individual turnover threshold multiplied by the sum of the number of individual partners and the number of relevant persons which would have been taken into account under (*a*) above in relation to company partners. For the six-month test, the number of partners is the maximum number at any time in the six-month (or shorter) period concerned. For the three-year test it is the maximum number at any time in the relevant year, except that for applications before 1 August 2001, by concession, the maximum number at any point during the last six months of the three-year period may be substituted for each of the three years if this will assist the subcontractor to meet the test. (Revenue Pamphlet IR 1, B52). As regards (B) above (the '*alternative partnership turnover threshold*'), the three-year test is applied, but by reference to the £200,000 annual limit.

[*ICTA 1988, s 562(2A)(2B), s 564(2A)–(2C), s 565(2A)–(2D); FA 1995, Sch 27 paras 4, 6, 7; FA 1998, Sch 8 paras 3–5; FA 1999, s 53; SI 1993 No 743, regs 21A–21E; SI 1998 No 2622, reg 14; SI 1999 No 2159, regs 4–6*].

See generally Revenue Tax Bulletin December 1998 pp 615–617 and, as regards how the test is applied where the applicant's business changes (e.g. where a partnership becomes a sole trader or *vice versa* or a sole trader or partnership becomes a company, or where sole traders or partnerships merge to form a new partnership), June 1999 pp 667, 668.

Simon's Direct Tax Service. See E5.513 *et seq.*.

21.6 **Renewal of certificates.** Applications for renewal of a certificate may be made at any time within six months before the date of expiry. The conditions are exactly the same as for the initial issue. [*SI 1993 No 743, reg 27*].

21.7 **Administration.** Detailed administrative arrangements for the operation of the scheme are contained in *The Income Tax (Sub-contractors in the Construction Industry) Regulations 1993* (*SI 1993 No 743*) as amended by the *(Amendment) Regulations 1998* (*SI 1998 No 2622*) and *1999* (*SI 1999 No 825*). The arrangements for accounting for deductions and for interest on unpaid or overpaid tax (see *SI 1993 No 743, regs 8–19; SI 1998 No 2622, regs 9, 10; SI 1999 No 825, reg 2; SI 2000 No 1151*) broadly follow those for PAYE (see 55.8 PAY AS YOU EARN and Revenue Pamphlet IR 14/15(CIS), chapter 6), and there are detailed provisions governing the form and use of sub-contractor's tax certificates (see *SI 1993 No 743, reg 24, 1 Sch; SI 1998 No 2622, regs 18, 38; SI 1999 No 2159, reg 10*) and the requirements for contractors' end of year returns of all payments to sub-contractors (see *SI 1993 No 743, reg 40A; SI 1998 No 2622, reg 33*). See also below under *Failure to deduct and under-deduction*. The Inland Revenue have powers to inspect records of contractors and sub-contractors (see *SI 1993 No 743, reg 41; SI 1998 No 2622, reg 34; SI 1999 No 2159, reg 8*). Further regulations may be made by statutory instrument. [*ICTA 1988, s 566; FA 1995, Sch 27 para 9; FA 1998, Sch 8 para 6*]. See Revenue Pamphlet IR 109 as regards negotiation of settlements. The Revenue have published a Code of Practice (No 3, available from local tax offices) setting out their standards for the way in which inspections of contractors' records are conducted and the rights and responsibilities of taxpayers.

Contractors are able to submit some of the vouchers information using electronic data interchange ('EDI'). [*SI 1993 No 743, reg 7(4)(b), reg 37A(2)(b), reg 40A(9)(b), reg 44A;*

SI 1998 No 2622, regs 7(4)(5), 29, 33, 35]. Full details should have been sent to all known contractors and sub-contractors by the end of 1998. For an outline of how EDI may be used, see Revenue Press Release 1 September 1998.

Multiple contractors. There are provisions allowing a contractor to elect to be treated as a different contractor for each of any specified groups of sub-contractors. [*SI 1993 No 743, reg 4*].

Appeals. There is a right of appeal (to the Commissioners, within 30 days) against the refusal or cancellation of a sub-contractor's tax certificate, and the Commissioners have the jurisdiction to review the exercise of any discretionary powers by the Board. [*ICTA 1988, s 561(9)*]. See also below under *Failure to deduct and under-deduction* and *Assessment*.

Cancellation. A certificate may at any time be cancelled by the Board, and its surrender demanded, if it was issued on false information, or has been misused by the holder, or if the holder no longer meets the requirements for the issue of a certificate or if, in the case of a company, there has been a change of control (within *ICTA 1988, s 840*) and the information required concerning that change has not been furnished. [*ICTA 1988, s 561(8)*].

Employment status. Where a worker in the construction industry is recategorised as an employee, the Revenue adopt a practical approach to the year of change. The liability for the year is calculated as if there was a Schedule D cessation, but with no prior year adjustments, and a Schedule E commencement on the date of the change. Schedule D profits of the year of cessation are generally taken either as those actually arising in the year or as the appropriate proportion of the profits from the end of the previous year's basis period to cessation, but any basis giving a reasonable result may be accepted. A due proportion of a full year's capital allowances is given for the final year, with no disposal value being brought in. See Taxation Vol 138, No 3596 p 643, 6 March 1997 for this and other aspects.

Possession of a registration card (see 21.3 above) or tax certificate (see 21.4 above) by a sub-contractor does not relieve the contractor of the responsibility to establish whether the sub-contractor is employed or self-employed. A telephone helpline (0345–335588) is available for contractors and workers needing general assistance in determining whether workers are employed or self-employed.

See generally Revenue Pamphlets IR 56 and IR 148 and Revenue Tax Bulletin April 1997 pp 405–413.

Penalties. For fraudulent attempts to obtain or misuse a certificate, penalties of up to £3,000 may be exacted. [*ICTA 1988, s 561(10)(11); FA 1995, Sch 27 para 3*]. A maximum penalty of £3,000 similarly applies for failure to comply with obligations in relation to registration cards (see 21.2 above). [*ICTA 1988, s 566(2B)–(2F); FA 1996, s 178*]. Penalties under *TMA 1970, s 98A* apply in cases of failure to make required end-of-year returns. [*SI 1993 No 743, reg 40A(16); SI 1998 No 2622, reg 33*]. See also 58.7 PENALTIES as regards negotiated settlements.

Deduction of tax. If exemption is not obtained, but a registration card is produced, the sub-contractor will receive payments under deduction of tax as under 21.2 above, and will receive from the contractor(s) form(s) CIS25 vouching the tax deducted (see 21.2 above). He will be treated for tax purposes as having received the full amount, the tax deducted and vouched on forms CIS25 being treated as a payment in respect of his income or corporation tax liability on the profits of the trade in the year of assessment or accounting period in which the deduction was made. In the case of an individual, any excess is treated as a payment on account of his Class 4 contributions under the *Social Security Acts*. [*ICTA 1988, s 559(4)–(5A); FA 1995, s 139(1); FA 1998, Sch 8 para 2(1)*]. To the extent that any liability for a year of assessment is met by tax deducted in that year, no interest charge will arise in e.g. a case of failure to notify liability.

Provisional repayments to individuals (or partners in firms) of tax vouched on forms CIS25 may, on application to the inspector, be made before the end of the tax year to which they relate. They may not be made after the end of the tax year. All earlier year income tax and Class 4 national insurance liabilities of the business must have been paid, and repayment is restricted to the excess of the deductions over the sum of the liability to income tax and Class 4 national insurance for the year on profits or gains of the business and on any income arising during the year up to the date of application from which tax has not been deducted (in either case whether or not yet due and payable) and any other sums due and payable from the applicant, including sums he has himself deducted as a contractor. A claim, accompanied by all the forms CIS25 relevant to the claim, is required on form CIS40 (obtainable from local tax offices), or form CIS41 in the case of a partner. In the case of a claim by a partner, the form must be signed by all individual partners and by the secretary or a director of all corporate partners. [*SI 1993 No 743, reg 20A; SI 1998 No 2622, reg 12*].

Failure to deduct and under-deduction. If the contractor fails to deduct the tax, he is nevertheless liable for the tax which should have been deducted (see *Ladkarn Ltd v McIntosh Ch D 1982, 56 TC 616*). However, where the Collector is satisfied that the contractor took reasonable care, and that the failure was due to an error made in good faith or to a genuine belief that the payment was not subject to deduction, the Collector may waive the liability. An appeal may be made (within 30 days) against a decision not so to waive liability. Liability in respect of such failure may also be waived at the contractor's request where the inspector is satisfied that the sub-contractor to whom the payment was made either was not chargeable to tax thereon or has made the appropriate return and paid the tax and any Class 4 contributions. [*SI 1993 No 743, reg 10*].

See Revenue Pamphlet IR 109 as regards negotiation of settlements.

Assessment. If the inspector considers it necessary to do so in all the circumstances, he may raise an assessment on the contractor in any amount which, to the best of his judgement, the contractor is liable to pay under the scheme regulations. The assessment is treated in the same way as an income tax assessment for assessment, appeal and recovery purposes. Tax is due and payable 14 days after the date of the assessment. [*SI 1993 No 743, reg 14*]. As regards interest on tax unpaid or overpaid on such assessments, similar provisions apply as in 55.8 PAY AS YOU EARN. [*SI 1993 No 743, regs 16–18*].

21.8 SCHEME APPLICABLE BEFORE 1 AUGUST 1999

For detailed coverage of the scheme applicable before 1 August 1999, see the 1998/99 or earlier editions of this work. For a summary of the main changes on introduction of the new scheme from 1 August 1999, see 21.1 above. The provisions under the earlier scheme which are more likely to be of continuing relevance (e.g. in relation to failure to deduct, recovery of amounts deducted, assessments on contractors and penalties) are similar to those applicable under the new scheme (see 21.7 above), except that a maximum penalty of £3,000 for fraudulent attempts to obtain or misuse a certificate replaces the maximum fine of £5,000 under the old scheme.

Certificates issued under the old scheme cease to have effect after 31 July 1999 regardless of the expiry date shown on the certificate. [*SI 1998 No 2620, reg 4*].

22 Deceased Estates

Cross-references. See 28.6 EXCESS LIABILITY, 42.9 INTEREST AND SURCHARGES ON UNPAID TAX and 43.6 and 43.23 INTEREST PAYABLE.

Simon's Direct Tax Service C4.1.

22.1 Personal representatives of a deceased person (being either executors appointed under the will or administrators if there was no will) are assessable for all tax due from the deceased to the date of his death. [*ICTA 1988, s 60(8), s 62(9), s 63(3) as originally enacted; ICTA 1988, s 60(4); TMA 1970, s 74; FA 1994, s 200*]. Personal allowances may be claimed in full for the year of death.

Income may be assessed and charged on and in the name of any one or more of the personal representatives to whom it arises (in the case of income consisting of life assurance policy gains arising after 5 April 1998, on any one or more of the personal representatives in the year of assessment in which the gains arise) or on any subsequent personal representatives of the deceased. [*FA 1989, s 151; FA 1998, Sch 14 paras 6, 7*].

See 71.9 SCHEDULE D, CASES I AND II for discontinuance of a business on death and 71.36 for trading (or not) by the executors. See 6.4 and 6.5 BACK DUTY for time limits for assessments. See Tolley's Capital Gains Tax for capital gains tax position on death.

22.2 Personal representatives are also liable to income tax at the basic or lower rate (as appropriate) on estate income which they receive subsequent to the death. Dividends falling due after death are treated as the income of the estate, and not of the deceased, for all tax purposes, including exemption claims, although they accrued before the death (*Reid's Trustees v CIR CS 1929, 14 TC 512; CIR v Henderson's Exors CS 1931, 16 TC 282*), and the same principle applies in respect of interest payments, including bank and building society interest, falling due after the date of death. An exception (for deaths before 6 April 1996) is interest falling within the accrued income scheme (see 74.15 SCHEDULE D, CASE VI). The accrued annuity to the date of death of an annuitant is income of his estate and not his income (*Bryan v Cassin KB 1942, 24 TC 468*) and similarly as to the accrued income of which he was life-tenant (*Wood v Owen KB 1940, 23 TC 541; Stewart's Exors v CIR Ch D 1952, 33 TC 184*).

22.3 **Income from deceased estates during administration.** [*ICTA 1988, ss 695–702*]. Residuary income of an estate comprises aggregate income therefrom *less* interest and annual payments charged thereon, sums payable out of residue under law of intestacy, admissible expenses of administration and any income from assets vesting during or on completion of administration. [*ICTA 1988, ss 697(1), 701(6)*]. An annual payment falling due after 14 March 1988 and made by personal representatives in satisfaction of a liability of the deceased is treated as if made by an individual for the purpose of applying the provisions of *FA 1988, s 36* excluding such payments from being a charge on income (see 1.10(i) ALLOWANCES AND TAX RATES). [*ICTA 1988, s 347A(3); FA 1988, s 36(1)*].

Limited interests (e.g. life tenants). Sums paid (including assets transferred, debts released etc.) to a beneficiary *during administration* are treated as his income for the tax year of payment. Any amount which remains payable in respect of the limited interest *on completion of administration* after 5 April 1995 is deemed to have been paid to the beneficiary as income for the tax year in which the administration period ends or, if that interest has ceased earlier (because of the beneficiary's death), as income for the tax year in which the interest ceased. Where the administration period ended before 6 April 1995, the beneficiary's income for each tax year covered by the administration period was revised, by additional assessment or repayment of tax, to the proportion allocated to that year on a time basis of the income deemed to have *accrued* from day to day throughout the administration period. [*ICTA 1988, s 695(2)(3), s 700, s 701(12); FA 1995, Sch 18 para 2*]. **Absolute interests.** Sums paid (including assets transferred, debts released etc.) to a beneficiary *during administration* and after 5 April 1995 are treated as his income for the tax year of payment except to the extent that aggregate payments of income for that and earlier years (including any made before 6 April 1995) exceed the beneficiary's aggregate entitlement to the residuary income of the estate for that and earlier years. If *on completion of administration* after 5 April 1995 the aggregate income entitlement exceeds the aggregate payments of income, the excess is deemed to have been paid to the beneficiary immediately before the end of the administration period. Payments to a beneficiary before 6 April 1995 were treated as his income for the tax year to which they related (not necessarily the year of payment). On completion of administration before 6 April 1995, the beneficiary's income for each tax year covered by the administration was revised to his actual ascertained share of the estate residuary income *arising* in that year. [*ICTA 1988, s 696(3)–(3B)(5), s 700, s 701(12); FA 1995, Sch 18 para 3*].

In each case payments out of a UK estate are 'grossed-up' at the basic, lower or (from 6 April 1999) Schedule F ordinary rate, as appropriate (see 1.9 ALLOWANCES AND RATES), for the year of assessment of receipt, and treated as received under deduction of such tax. For this purpose, payments are assumed to be made out of the beneficiary's share of income bearing tax at the basic rate before they are made out of his share of income bearing tax at the lower rate or (from 6 April 1999) at the Schedule F ordinary rate, and (from 6 April 1999) at the lower rate before the Schedule F ordinary rate. Payments out of a foreign estate are directly assessed, without grossing, under Schedule D, Case IV (although, for 1995/96 onwards, certain sums ('*relevant amounts*') treated as having suffered tax at source, e.g. life assurance gains and UK stock dividends, *are* grossed up at the basic, lower or (from 6 April 1999) Schedule F ordinary rate of tax as appropriate, no repayment of which may be made, and this applies also from 2 July 1997 to distributions within *ICTA 1988, s 233(1)* in respect of which the recipient is not entitled to a tax credit, and from 6 April 1999 to any distribution chargeable under SCHEDULE F (76) (see 1.9 ALLOWANCES AND TAX RATES)). [*ICTA 1988, s 246D(1)–(3A), s 695(4), s 696(3)–(6), s 699A, s 701(3A); FA 1993, Sch 6 para 11; FA 1994, Sch 16 para 1; FA 1995, s 76(1)(4); FA 1996, Sch 6 para 5; F(No 2)A 1997, ss 21, 23, Sch 6 paras 3, 12*]. Income bearing tax at the lower rate or the Schedule F ordinary rate is treated in the hands of the recipient as chargeable under *ICTA 1988, s 1A* at whichever of those rates applies (see 1.9 ALLOWANCES AND RATES), except that income paid indirectly through a trustee and taxable under *ICTA 1988, s 698(3)* on the ultimate recipient is instead so treated in the hands of the trustee (unless it is within *ICTA 1988, s 686*, see 81.5 SETTLEMENTS). [*ICTA 1988, s 698A; FA 1993, Sch 6 para 11(2); FA 1996, Sch 6 para 17; F(No 2)A 1997, s 33(1)(11)*].

In computing estate residuary income for 1995/96 onwards in the case of an absolute interest, any excess of allowable deductions over income for any year is carried forward and treated as an allowable deduction of the following year. [*ICTA 1988, s 697(1A); FA 1995, Sch 18 para 4(1)(3)*]. Previously, by concession, such an excess was allowed in computing the net residuary income of the preceding or succeeding years for higher rate tax. (Revenue Pamphlet IR 1, A13). If the total benefits received by a beneficiary with an absolute interest on completion of administration after 5 April 1995 are less than the amount taken to be his residuary income, the deficiency is applied in reducing the said amount, firstly for the tax year in which the administration ends, then for the previous year and so on. Previously, such a deficiency was applied in reducing proportionately the income for each tax year covered by the administration period. [*ICTA 1988, s 697(2); FA 1995, Sch 18 para 4(2)(3)*].

Assessments may be made or adjusted and relief may be claimed by virtue of these provisions within, for 1996/97 and later years, three years after 31 January following the year of assessment in which administration was completed (for earlier years, three years following the end of that year of assessment). [*ICTA 1988, s 700(3); FA 1996, s 135, Sch 21 para 20*].

By concession, a residuary legatee, or legatee with a limited interest, who is not resident or not ordinarily resident in the UK, may claim to have his tax liability on income from the estate adjusted to what it would be if such income had arisen to him directly from the respective sources of residuary income. For 1999/2000 and later years, the relief or exemption must be claimed within five years and ten months of the end of the year of assessment in which the beneficiary is deemed to have received the income, and is dependent upon the personal representatives having made all required estate returns, paid all tax and any interest, surcharge and penalties, and keeping available for inspection any relevant tax certificates and copies of the estate accounts for all years of the administration period showing details of all sources of estate income and payments to beneficiaries. No tax will be repayable in respect of income which, if received by a UK-resident beneficiary, would be a 'relevant amount' (as above) within *ICTA 1988, s 699A*. For 1998/99 and earlier years, relief or exemption must be claimed not later than three years after the end of the year of assessment in which the administration of the estate is completed, or within six years of the end of the year of assessment in which the estate income arose, whichever is the later. (Revenue Pamphlet IR 1, A14; Revenue Press Release 1 April 1999). However, where the legatee is resident in a country with which the UK has a double taxation agreement, and the 'Other Income' Article in that agreement gives sole taxing rights in respect of such income to that country, the above concession does not apply, and the tax paid by the personal representatives will be repaid to the legatee, subject to the conditions in the Article being met. (Revenue Pamphlet IR 131, SP 3/86, 2 April 1986).

The treatment of rights held by personal representatives in relation to other deceased estates, and of successive interests in the residue of an estate, are dealt with in *ICTA 1988, s 698(1)–(2); FA 1995, Sch 18 para 5*. Discretionary payments out of the income of the residue of an estate, whether made directly by the personal representatives or through a trustee etc., are income of the recipient when paid. [*ICTA 1988, s 698(3)*]. This applies whether the payments are out of income as it arises, or out of income arising to the personal representatives in earlier years and retained pending exercise of the discretion. See Revenue Pamphlet IR 131, SP 4/93, 16 March 1993, under which claims and supplementary claims on this basis are invited for 1986/87 onwards.

For Revenue information powers, see *ICTA 1988, s 700(4)*. A personal representative has a duty to supply a beneficiary on request with a statement of income and tax borne for a year of assessment. [*ICTA 1988, s 700(5)(6); FA 1995, Sch 18 para 6*].

For relief from overlapping of inheritance tax and excess liability on accrued income, see 28.6 EXCESS LIABILITY.

Simon's Direct Tax Service. See **C4.115** *et seq.*.

22.4 *Examples*

Limited interest

Mrs D died on 5 January 1999 leaving her whole estate with a life interest to her husband and then the capital to her children on his death. The administration of the estate is completed on 7 February 2001. Mr D receives payments on account of income of £1,200 on 30 September 1999, £2,500 on 31 December 2000, £1,050 on 7 February 2001 and £326 on 31 May 2001.

The actual income and deductible expenses of the estate were as follows.

	1998/99 (from 6.1.99)	1999/2000	2000/01 (to 7.2.2001)
	£	£	£
Interest received (net)	750	2,400	2,000
Other income (gross)	400	600	200
Basic rate tax thereon	(92)	(138)	(44)
Expenses	(150)	(450)	(400)
Net income available for distribution	£908	£2,412	£1,756

D's income from the estate for tax purposes is calculated as follows.

	1998/99	1999/2000		2000/01	
		Basic rate income	*Lower rate income*	*Basic rate income*	*Lower rate income*
	£	£	£	£	£
Net income	Nil	770*	430*	156**	3,720**
Basic rate tax		(230)		(44)	
Lower rate tax			(108)		(930)
Gross income	Nil	£1,000	£538	£200	£4,650

* The payments to the beneficiary in each year must be allocated between (i) income bearing tax at the basic rate and (ii) income bearing tax at the lower rate, (i) taking priority over (ii). Total basic rate income for 1998/99 and 1999/2000 is £770 (£400 + £600 – £92 – £138), so £770 of the £1,200 payment in 1999/2000 is deemed to have been made out of basic rate income.

** Total basic rate income for the three tax years is £926 (£400 + £600 + £200 – £92 – £138 – £44) of which £770 was paid out in 1999/2000 leaving £156 of the 2000/01 payments to be allocated to basic rate income. The balance of the 2000/01 payments (£2,500 + £1,050 + £326 – £156 = £3,720) is deemed to have been made out of lower rate income.

Note

(*a*) The £326 paid in May 2001 is deemed to have been paid in 2000/01, being the tax year in which the administration period ends.

Absolute interest

C died on 5 July 1998 leaving his estate of £400,000 divisible equally between his three children. The income arising and administration expenses paid in the administration period which ends on 25 January 2001 are as follows.

	Period to 5.4.99		Year to 5.4.00		Period to 25.1.01	
	£	£	£	£	£	£
Interest income (net)		15,000		8,850		3,000
Administration expenses chargeable to income		(1,500)		(750)		(300)
		c/f 13,500		c/f 8,100		c/f 2,700

	Period to 5.4.99		Year to 5.4.00		Period to 25.1.01	
	£	£	£	£	£	£
		b/f 13,500		b/f 8,100		b/f 2,700
Other income (gross)	10,000		3,200		1,000	
Basic rate tax thereon payable by executors	(2,300)		(736)		(220)	
		7,700		2,464		780
Net income distributed		£21,200		£10,564		£3,480
Each child's share		£7,067		£3,521		£1,160

Dates and amounts of payments to *each* child are as follows.

	Payment	Allocated to tax years (see 22.3 above)
	£	
30.4.99	5,000	1999/2000
16.10.99	3,000	1999/2000
21.6.00	2,000	2000/01
22.1.01	1,000	2000/01
30.7.01	748	2000/01

The children's income for tax purposes is as follows.

	1998/99	1999/2000	2000/01
Each child's share of basic rate income	Nil	3,388*	260
Basic rate tax	Nil	1,012	73
Gross basic rate income	Nil	£4,400	£333

* $£(7,700 + 2,464) \times \frac{1}{3} = £3,388$

	1998/99	1999/2000	2000/01
Each child's share of lower rate income	Nil	4,612	3,488
Lower rate tax	Nil	1,153	872
Gross lower rate income	Nil	£5,765	£4,360

Notes

(*a*) Each beneficiary would receive tax certificates (Forms R185E) showing the gross amount of his entitlement and the tax paid by the executors. Where the estate has income bearing tax at the lower rate (i.e. savings income), or, from 6 April 1999, dividend income bearing tax at the Schedule F ordinary rate, the tax certificate should show such income separately from income which has borne tax at the basic rate.

(*b*) In the hands of a beneficiary, estate income which has borne tax at the lower rate or, from 6 April 1999, at the Schedule F ordinary rate is treated as income within *ICTA 1988, s 1A*. Therefore, the beneficiary will have a further liability only to the extent that the income exceeds the basic rate limit. Where the income is subject to lower rate tax, the beneficiary will be able to reclaim tax at only 20% to the extent that the income is covered by personal reliefs.

(*c*) Payments to a beneficiary of an estate are deemed to be made out of his share of income bearing tax at the basic rate in priority to his share of income bearing tax at the lower rate. Therefore, administration expenses chargeable to income are effectively relieved primarily against lower rate income.

(*d*) The beneficiaries' shares of basic rate income are grossed up at the rate for the year to which they are allocated, rather than by reference to the tax accounted for by the personal representatives.

22.5 **Residence of personal representatives.** See 64.5 RESIDENCE, ORDINARY RESIDENCE AND DOMICILE for special provisions where personal representatives are partly UK resident and partly non-UK resident.

22.6 Otherwise the tax position in respect of deceased estates is similar to that of settlements (or trusts as they are often called) and reference should be made to the following items under 81 SETTLEMENTS which contain details of tax cases relating to both deceased estates and settlements.

81.3 Assessments on trust income.
81.7 Personal position of trustee.
81.8 Income of beneficiaries.
81.9 Annuities etc. out of capital.
81.10 Foreign trust income.
81.11 Claims by trustees and beneficiaries.

23 Deduction of Tax at Source

Cross-references. See 3.19 ANTI-AVOIDANCE re annual payments for non-taxable consideration; 8 BANKS and 9 BUILDING SOCIETIES for interest; 15.17 CHARITIES regarding deeds of covenant; 21 CONSTRUCTION INDUSTRY TAX SCHEME; 25.6 DOUBLE TAX RELIEF for reduced rate of deduction on payments abroad; 25.5(*a*) DOUBLE TAX RELIEF for alimony payable by non-resident; 32 FUNDING BONDS; 33.3 GOVERNMENT STOCKS for certain payments gross; 43 INTEREST PAYABLE; 44 INTEREST RECEIVABLE; 48 MEDICAL INSURANCE; 49 MINERAL ROYALTIES; 51.8 NON-RESIDENTS AND OTHER OVERSEAS MATTERS for non-resident entertainers and sportsmen; 55 PAY AS YOU EARN; 60.1 PERSONAL PENSION SCHEMES for personal pension scheme contributions; 65.1 RETIREMENT ANNUITIES for retirement annuity premiums; 66.5 RETIREMENT SCHEMES for additional voluntary contributions and for refunds of pension and superannuation contributions; 75.34 SCHEDULE E for payments for restrictive covenants; 81.5 SETTLEMENTS for distributions from discretionary and accumulation trusts; 89 UNDERWRITERS for transfers to special reserves; 92 VOCATIONAL TRAINING RELIEF for vocational training costs.

Simon's Direct Tax Service A3.4.

23.1 Income tax (at the basic or lower rate, whichever is applicable) *may* legally be deducted by the payer from certain annuities and other annual payments and certain royalties, which are paid out of taxed income, within the terms of *ICTA 1988, s 348* (see 23.2 below) and *must* be deducted from the payments listed in 23.3 below. Tax may also be deducted from certain mortgage loan interest, see 23.13 below. See Revenue Tax Bulletin February 1996 pp 277–280 for a list showing the rate at which tax should be deducted from various types of payment made after 5 April 1996 and for commentary on the various deduction arrangements.

The **payer** thus obtains tax relief other than at the higher rate in respect of such payments. He may also be able to deduct the payments as charges on income in arriving at his EXCESS LIABILITY (28). For **companies** the payments may rank as charges on income for corporation tax, see Tolley's Corporation Tax under Profit Computations.

The **recipient** has, because of the deduction of tax, suffered income tax at the basic or lower rate (whichever is applicable) on the income. If he is not liable, or not wholly liable, on such income at that rate, he can recover from the Revenue any excess tax suffered so far as not adjusted in direct assessments on him. On the other hand, if his total income is high enough, further liability will arise on him at the higher rate of income tax. See 1.9 ALLOWANCES AND TAX RATES for the circumstances in which the recipient is liable at the lower rate (as opposed to the basic rate) on savings income for 1996/97 and later years.

A payment made under deduction of tax is income (equal to the grossed-up equivalent) of the year of assessment by reference to the basic or lower rate of tax for which tax is deducted from the payment, without regard to the period of accrual (and see *CIR v Crawley Ch D 1986, 59 TC 728*). [*ICTA 1988, s 835(6); FA 1996, Sch 6 paras 24, 28*].

For the deduction of tax from VAT-inclusive amounts, see Revenue Inspector's Manual, IM 3900.

Headings in this chapter are as follows.

23.2	Circumstances where payer *may* deduct tax	23.5	Rate of tax deductible
		23.6	Alterations in basic rate
23.3	Circumstances where payer *must* deduct tax	23.7	Certificate of tax deducted
		23.8	Omission to deduct tax
23.4	Deduction of tax under foreign agreements or by non-residents	23.9	Alimony, maintenance, separation allowances, etc.

23.1 Deduction of Tax at Source

23.10 Annual payments, etc.
23.11 Annuities
23.12 Dividends and interest
23.13 Mortgage interest (MIRAS)
23.14 Rents etc. under *ICTA 1988, s 119* and *s 120*
23.15 Royalties
23.16 Tax-free arrangements
23.17 Tax-free annuities etc.
23.18 Voluntary allowances

23.2 **CIRCUMSTANCES WHERE PAYER MAY DEDUCT TAX** [*ICTA 1988, s 348*]

The permissible tax deduction, as 23.1 above, applies to

(*a*) any annuity or other annual payment charged with tax under SCHEDULE D, CASE III (72), not being interest (but see 1.8(i) ALLOWANCES AND TAX RATES for certain annual payments excluded from the charge to tax, 23.9 below re alimony, maintenance, separation allowances, etc., 23.13 below for certain relevant loan interest, and also see 3.19 ANTI-AVOIDANCE re annual payments made for non-taxable consideration and 81.5 SETTLEMENTS re payments out of discretionary trusts),

(*b*) (i) any royalty or other sum paid in respect of the user of a patent, and

(ii) (before 6 April 1997) electric line wayleaves [*ICTA 1988, s 120; FA 1997, Sch 18 Pt VI(2)*] and (before 1 May 1995) mining rents and royalties [*ICTA 1988, s 119; FA 1995, s 145*] (see 23.14 below),

provided that the payment is wholly out of profits or gains brought into charge to income tax. (N.B. As the profits of UK companies are not charged to income tax, *ICTA 1988, s 348* does not apply to them and payments by them will be within *ICTA 1988, s 349* — see 23.3 below.)

The payer is entitled to deduct tax and it will be detrimental to himself if he fails to do so. See 23.8 below regarding omission to deduct tax.

The tax deductible is at the basic rate for the year in which the payment became due, irrespective of the date of actual payment. Where the payment would constitute 'savings income' (see 1.9 ALLOWANCES AND TAX RATES) of the recipient (whatever his status), deduction is at the lower rate instead for 1996/97 and subsequent years (although the only type of payment within *section 348* to which this should apply is a purchased life annuity). [*ICTA 1988, s 4; FA 1996, s 73(2)–(4), Sch 6 paras 2, 28*]. (Cf. *Re Sebright Ch D 1944, 23 TC 190.*) It is accordingly income of the recipient of the year when due — an important point if the recipient wishes to claim repayment of the tax deducted (*CIR v Crawley Ch D 1986, 59 TC 728*).

See 15.17 CHARITIES as regards covenanted donations.

Simon's Direct Tax Service. See **A3.403**.

23.3 **CIRCUMSTANCES WHERE PAYER MUST DEDUCT TAX** *[ICTA 1988, ss 349, 350]*

Income tax *must* be deducted from the following.

(i) Payments specified in 23.2(*a*) and (*b*) above which are not payable, or not wholly payable, out of profits or gains brought into charge to income tax. [*ICTA 1988, s 349(1); FA 1995, Sch 29 Pt VIII(22); FA 1997, Sch 18 Pt VI(2)*]. See 74.2 SCHEDULE D, CASE VI as regards certain payments to theatrical 'angels'.

The payer must deduct tax from such payments, and must inform the Revenue, who will make an assessment to collect that tax. Appeals against that assessment are to the Special Commissioners. [*TMA 1970, s 31(3)*]. Payments by UK companies are within *section 349(1)* but the tax is accounted for under *ICTA 1988, Sch 16*, see Tolley's Corporation Tax.

The obligation to deduct is upon 'the person by or through whom' the payment is made and see *Rye & Eyre v CIR HL 1935, 19 TC 164; Aeolian Co Ltd v CIR KB 1936, 20 TC 547* and *Howells v CIR KB 1939, 22 TC 501*. But liability under *section 350* does not arise until the annual payment is actually 'paid'.

Tax is deductible at the basic rate in force at the time of payment. Where the payment would constitute 'savings income' (see 1.9 ALLOWANCES AND TAX RATES) of the recipient (whatever his status), deduction is at the lower rate instead for 1996/97 and subsequent years (but the same comment applies as in 23.2 above as regards application). [*ICTA 1988, s 4; FA 1996, s 73(2)–(4), Sch 6 paras 2, 28*].

Where a payment from which tax should have been deducted is made in full, there is no right to recover the under-deduction by deduction from later payments (*Tenbry Investments Ltd v Peugeot Talbot Motor Co Ltd Ch D, [1992] STC 791*).

If a payment is made by an individual in a later year than the year when due and it could have been made out of taxed income in that due year, an allowance will be made in any assessment to collect the tax for the tax which could have been deducted if the payment had been made when due. A similar allowance may be made in the case of a trust or other non-trading institution (not within the charge to corporation tax) in cases of hardship. (Revenue Pamphlet IR 1, A16 as revised).

The profits or gains to be taken into account are those assessed (or received less tax) for the year of assessment in which the payment was made. Hence, except where the concession A16 applies, accumulated income of previous years cannot be taken into account (*Luipaard's Vlei Estate v CIR CA 1930, 15 TC 573*) and, for a trader, the Case I assessment for the year after deducting any losses forward and capital allowances is taken into account irrespective of the actual profits of the year (*A-G v Metropolitan Water Board CA 1927, 13 TC 294; Trinidad Petroleum Development Co Ltd v CIR CA 1936, 21 TC 1*). For the individual, *section 349(1)* will normally be applicable only if his annual payments, etc. exceed his aggregate income of the year (cf. *CIR v Plummer HL 1979, 54 TC 1*). However, trustees may be liable under *section 350* where annual payments etc. are made out of capital of the trust fund irrespective of the trust income, see 81.9 SETTLEMENTS.

Loss Relief. Where payments are made under deduction of tax but the payer has no income assessable to income tax the tax deducted will be collected by assessment under *section 350*. But if this position arises by reason of a loss sustained in a trade, etc. in the year, or brought forward, a sole trader or partnership may treat amounts so assessed as if they were trading losses under *ICTA 1988, s 385* and carry them forward for computing profits of the same business for the following years, except where they fall into the list given under 46.17(*a*) LOSSES. [*ICTA 1988, s 387*].

(ii) Yearly interest of money chargeable to tax under Case III of Schedule D (disregarding the modifications made for corporation tax purposes, see 72.1 SCHEDULE D, CASE III), but only if paid

(*a*) by a company or local authority (otherwise than in a fiduciary or representative capacity), or

(*b*) by or for a partnership of which a company is a member, or

(*c*) to a person whose usual place of abode is outside the UK. [*ICTA 1988, s 349(2); FA 1996, Sch 14 para 18*].

As regards (*c*) above, tax need not be deducted from payments of interest to the UK branch of a non-resident company trading in the UK through that branch, where the branch profits are liable to corporation tax under *ICTA 1988, s 11* and not exempted under a double tax treaty. (Revenue Tax Bulletin August 1993 p 87).

Where interest received by a company is charged to tax as a trading receipt (see Tolley's Corporation Tax under Loan Relationships), this does not affect the requirement for deduction of tax by the payer (see Revenue Tax Bulletin August 1999 pp 685, 686).

Interest under the *Late Payment of Commercial Debts (Interest) Act 1998* (or under a contractual right but for which that *Act* would have applied) is *not* 'yearly interest'. (Revenue Tax Bulletin August 1999 pp 686, 687).

For advances made on or after 29 April 1996, interest payable on an advance from a bank (within *ICTA 1988, s 840A*, see 8.1 BANKS) within the charge to corporation tax in respect of it, and interest paid by such a bank in the ordinary course of its business, is excluded. Previously, the exclusion applied to interest payable in the UK on an advance from a bank carrying on a *bona fide* banking business in the UK (see *Hafton Properties Ltd v McHugh Ch D 1986, 59 TC 420*) or paid by such a bank in the ordinary course of such a business (for which see Revenue Pamphlet IR 131, SP 4/96, 13 May 1996, revising SP 12/91, 9 October 1991). There are transitional provisions preserving relief as regards interest payable or paid on or after 29 April 1996 on an advance made before that day. National Savings Bank interest is always paid without deduction of tax. [*ICTA 1988, s 349(3)(a)(b)(3AA)(3AB); FA 1996, Sch 37 Pt II; FA 1997, s 78*]. See, however, 23.13 below as regards 'relevant loan interest' and 8.2 BANKS as regards special deduction schemes. See 8.2 BANKS also for exclusion from *section 349(2)* of certain interest payments by bodies other than banks where those payments are not within the special deduction scheme. [*ICTA 1988, s 349(3)(h); FA 1993, s 59*].

As regards payments by building societies, only interest and dividends paid after 24 July 1991 on certain 'marketable securities' is within *section 349*. [*ICTA 1988, s 349(2)(3A); FA 1991, Sch 11 para 1*]. See BUILDING SOCIETIES (9) generally and at 9.3 in particular. Interest paid to a society is payable gross unless it is 'relevant loan interest', see 23.13 below. [*ICTA 1988, s 369(1); FA 1994, s 81(3)*].

'*UK public revenue dividends*' (i.e. any income from securities which is paid out of the UK or NI public revenue, but excluding interest on local authority stock (see (*a*) above)) are, from 1 April 2001, payable under deduction of tax, subject to any provision to the contrary in the *Taxes Acts* (and see in particular 33.3 GOVERNMENT STOCKS for the general exemption of gilt-edged securities). The Board has wide powers to make regulations governing the accounting arrangements and modifying *ICTA 1988, ss 349, 350* in their application to UK public revenue dividends. [*ICTA 1988, ss 349(3C)(4), 350A; FA 2000, s 112(2)–(5)*]. For the deduction of tax from UK public revenue dividends by paying agents before 1 April 2001, see *ICTA 1988, ss 118A–118K* and regulations thereunder.

Interest paid on '*quoted Eurobonds*' (i.e. listed securities issued by a company and carrying a right to interest) is excluded from the above provisions for deduction of tax from interest from 1 April 2001. For payments made before that date, the exclusion applies only where the security is in bearer form and

(I) the payment is made by or through a person who is not in the UK; or

(II) where (I) above does not apply, either

- (i) the bond is held in a 'recognised clearing system' (as designated by the Board), or
- (ii) the beneficial owner of the bond is non-UK resident and is beneficially entitled to the interest.

The Board has regulatory powers to disapply (II) above unless certain declarations confirming eligibility are received by the payer or the Board has issued the appropriate notice (for regulations made under which see *SI 1996 No 1779*). Before 29 April 1996, different requirements applied in relation to (II) above. [*ICTA 1988, ss 124, 841A; FA 1996, Sch 7 para 26, Sch 29 para 4, Sch 38 para 6, Sch 41 Pt V(19); FA 2000, s 111(2)(6), Sch 40 Pt II(17)*]. See also Revenue Press Release 1 August 1984 as regards designation as a 'recognised clearing system', and *FA 1989, s 116* (repealed by *FA 1996, Sch 41 Pt V(3)*) as regards certain payments of interest to Netherlands Antilles subsidiaries which were treated as being within *section 124*.

Tax is deductible at the lower rate (for 1995/96 and earlier years, the basic rate) in force for the tax year in which payment is made. [*ICTA 1988, s 4; FA 1996, s 73(2)–(4), Sch 6 paras 2, 28*].

For the procedure under which companies pay income tax so deducted to the Revenue, see *ICTA 1988, Sch 16* and Tolley's Corporation Tax.

(iii) The following, as under (i) above, except that they cannot qualify for the loss relief described.

(*a*) Rents paid to non-residents chargeable under Schedule A or Schedule D, Case VI. [*ICTA 1988, ss 42A, 43; FA 1995, s 40(3); SI 1995 No 2902*]. Special provisions apply from 6 April 1996. See 68.24 SCHEDULE A.

(*b*) Sale of British patent rights by a non-resident. [*ICTA 1988, s 524*]. See 54 PATENTS.

(*c*) Copyright royalties, public lending right payments and design royalties payable to a non-resident. [*ICTA 1988, ss 536, 537, 537B; FA 1995, s 115(10)*]. See 23.15 below and 51.10 NON-RESIDENTS AND OTHER OVERSEAS MATTERS.

(iv) (For 1995/96 and earlier years) income charged under SCHEDULE C (70). [*ICTA 1988, s 44, Sch 3; FA 1996, Sch 7 paras 7, 27*].

(v) (Before 1 April 2001) UK public revenue and foreign dividends etc. paid in UK through an agent (and see now (ii) above and 23.12 below).

See 15.17 CHARITIES as regards covenanted donations.

Simon's Direct Tax Service. See A3.404.

23.4 DEDUCTION OF TAX UNDER FOREIGN AGREEMENTS, OR BY NON-RESIDENTS

UK tax legislation cannot alter rights not within the jurisdiction of UK courts. See *Keiner v Keiner QB 1952, 34 TC 346* (tax not deductible from alimony under American agreement paid by UK resident ex-husband to non-resident ex-wife); *Bingham v CIR Ch D 1955, 36 TC 254* (maintenance payments under foreign Court Order not deductible in arriving at total income as tax not deductible); *Westminster Bank v National Bank of Greece HL 1970, 46 TC 472* (interest on foreign bonds paid in London by guarantor held within Case IV and tax not deductible). But where under a UK contract a non-resident paid interest to another non-resident and the payer died, held his executors (resident in UK) must deduct tax from interest they paid (*CIR v Broome's Exors KB 1935, 19 TC 667*). And where 'free of tax' alimony was payable under UK agreements, etc., payments by the ex-husband no longer resident in the UK were held to have been paid subject to deduction of tax, the onus being on the Crown to collect the tax if the payments were within *section 349* (*Stokes v Bennett Ch D 1953, 34 TC 337*). See also *CIR v Ferguson HL 1969, 46 TC 1*.

23.5 **RATE OF TAX DEDUCTIBLE**

For *ICTA 1988, s 348* purposes, the basic (or lower) rate when payment becomes **due** applies, see 23.2 above.

For *ICTA 1988, s 349* purposes, the basic (or lower) rate when payment is **made** applies, see 23.3(i) and (ii) above.

In other words, the tax deductible is at the basic (or lower) rate in force for the year in which the payment is due if paid out of taxed profits or gains or, in any other case, the rate for the year in which the payment is made.

For 1995/96 and earlier years, tax is deductible at the basic rate. This continues for 1996/97 and later years except where the payment would constitute 'savings income' (including interest) (see 1.9 ALLOWANCES AND TAX RATES) of the recipient (whatever his status), in which case tax is deductible at the lower rate. [*ICTA 1988, s 4; FA 1996, s 73(2)–(4), Sch 6 paras 2, 28*].

23.6 **ALTERATIONS IN TAX RATE**

Where deductions are made by reference to a tax rate greater or less than the rate subsequently fixed for the tax year:

(*a*) **under-deductions** in respect of any half-yearly or quarterly payments of interest, dividends or other annual payments, other than company dividends and other distributions, are charged under Schedule D, Case III (for 1995/96 and earlier years, under Schedule D, Case VI). [*ICTA 1988, s 821(1); FA 1996, Sch 6 paras 22, 28*];

(*b*) **under-deductions** in respect of any rent, interest, annuity or other annual payment, any copyright royalties or public lending right payments paid to non-residents and patent royalties (and, where previously applicable, mining rents etc. under *ICTA 1988, s 119* and *s 120*) may be deducted from future payments or, if none, recovered from the payee. [*ICTA 1988, s 821(2)(3); FA 1997, Sch 18 Pt VI(2)*]. See *Nesta v Wyatt KB 1940, 19 ATC 541*;

(*c*) **over-deductions** of tax under *section 349* or from interest on government securities can generally be recovered from the Revenue provided that the tax has been accounted for and no adjustment made between the parties. See *Provisional Collection of Taxes Act 1968, s 2*; and

(*d*) **over-deductions** of tax by a 'body corporate' on interest (not being a distribution) on its securities may be adjusted in the next payment but any repayments must be made no later than a year from the passing of the Act imposing the tax, and enure to the benefit of the person entitled at date of adjustment or repayment. [*ICTA 1988, s 822; FA 1996, Sch 6 paras 23, 28*].

23.7 **CERTIFICATE OF TAX DEDUCTED**

A certificate of tax deducted under *ICTA 1988, ss 339, 348, 349, 480A* or *687* (re payments under discretionary trusts), or under regulations made under *ICTA 1988, s 477A* (*SI 1990 No 2231*, see 9.3 BUILDING SOCIETIES) must be given by payer upon written request by recipient. [*ICTA 1988, s 352; FA 1990, Sch 5 para 11*].

23.8 **OMISSION TO DEDUCT TAX**

(*a*) The provisions for the deduction of tax do not preclude assessment of the recipient if tax is not deducted (*Glamorgan County Quarter Sessions v Wilson KB 1910, 5 TC*

537; Renfrew Town Council v CIR CS 1934, 19 TC 13; Grosvenor Place Estates Ltd v Roberts CA 1960, 39 TC 433). These cases were decided when the legislation (cf. *subsection (1)(a)* (as originally enacted) of *ICTA 1970, s 52* (the predecessor to *ICTA 1988, s 348*)) precluded assessment on the recipient if the payment was out of taxed income. This provision was abolished for 1973/74 onwards by *FA 1971, Sch 14 Pt II*. However where in a case within *ICTA 1988, s 348* (23.2 above) tax is not deducted, the Crown nevertheless effectively collects from the payer the tax he failed to deduct [*ICTA 1988, s 3, s 256(3)(c)(ii), s 276(1)(1A); FA 1994, s 77(1), Sch 8 para 11*] and does not need to have recourse to the recipient.

(*b*) Tax not deducted at the time of payment cannot generally be recovered afterwards. For this see *Shrewsbury v Shrewsbury CA 1907, 23 TLR 224; Re Hatch Ch D 1919, 1 Ch 351; Ord v Ord KB 1923, 39 TLR 437; Taylor v Taylor CA 1937, 16 ATC 218; Brine v Brine KB 1943, 22 ATC 177; Hemsworth v Hemsworth KB 1946, 25 ATC 466; Tenbry Investments Ltd v Peugeot Talbot Motor Co Ltd Ch D, [1992] STC 791*. But where trustees omitted to deduct tax from annuities through an honest error of fact, not an error of law, they were authorised to recoup the tax from future payments (*Re Musgrave, Machell v Parry Ch D, [1916] 2 Ch 417*). See also *Turvey v Dentons (1923) Ltd QB 1952, 31 ATC 470*. Only net amount of alimony available to satisfy contra account (*Butler v Butler CA 1961, 40 ATC 19*). See also *Fletcher v Young CS 1936, 15 ATC 531; Hollis v Wingfield CA 1940, 19 ATC 98*.

(*c*) The Courts may rectify documents shown not to embody the intentions of the parties. For cases where rectification sought in relation to deduction of tax see *Burroughes v Abbott Ch D 1921, 38 TLR 167; Jervis v Howle & Talke Colliery Co Ltd Ch D 1936, 15 ATC 529; Fredensen v Rothschild Ch D 1941, 20 ATC 1; Van der Linde v Van der Linde Ch D 1947, 26 ATC 348; Whiteside v Whiteside CA 1949, 28 ATC 479*.

(*d*) Where a person having the right to do so does not deduct tax under *ICTA 1988, s 348* from annual payments such as maintenance payments to another person under a Court Order or other legally binding agreement, concessionary relief is available equal to the amount of any repayment which would have been due to the recipient had the right to deduct tax been properly exercised. (Revenue Pamphlet IR 1, A52). The concession is of limited application after 5 April 1989. See also 47.10 MARRIED PERSONS.

(*e*) A penalty of £50 is incurred by refusal to allow the deduction of tax, and any 'agreement' not to deduct is void to that extent. [*TMA 1970, s 106*]. See 23.17 below for 'free of tax' payments.

23.9 ALIMONY, MAINTENANCE, SEPARATION ALLOWANCES, ETC.

falling due before 6 April 1989, and chargeable to tax under SCHEDULE D, CASE III (72), were subject to deduction of tax under *ICTA 1988, ss 348, 349(1)* in the normal way, whether they arose under a Court Order or under an agreement (including a parol agreement — see *Peter's Exors v CIR CA 1941, 24 TC 45*). If paid (i) under an overseas agreement or Court Order or (ii) by a non-resident, see 23.4 above. For 'free of tax' payments see 23.16 and 23.17(*d*) below.

Payments falling due in the year 1989/90 and subsequently must normally be made *without* deduction of tax. [*FA 1988, s 38(7)*]. Exceptions were payments made before 6 April 1996 to, or for the maintenance of, a child aged 21 or over where made under a Court Order or payments made before 6 April 1995 to or for a child aged 18 or over where made under an agreement, *where such payments were made under an 'existing obligation'* (see 1.8(i) ALLOWANCES AND TAX RATES). Such payments were subject to deduction of tax under *ICTA 1988, ss 348, 349(1)*.

23.10 **ANNUAL PAYMENTS, ETC.**

The broad rule is that annual payments are recurrent payments which, in the hands of the recipient, are 'pure income profit' and not e.g. elements in the computation of the profits of the recipient. Leading cases are *Earl Howe v CIR CA 1919, 7 TC 289* (insurance premiums under covenant not annual payments) and *CIR v Epping Forest Conservators HL 1953, 34 TC 293* (yearly contributions to meet the deficiencies of a charity held to be annual payments). Payments for the use of chattels not annual payments (*In re Hanbury, decd CA 1939, 38 TC 588*). See also *CIR v Whitworth Park Coal Co Ltd HL 1959, 38 TC 531*. Payments to a County Council under deed of covenant in consideration of the Council's paying special school fees of the covenantor's handicapped child held not annual payments (*Essex County Council v Ellam CA 1989, 61 TC 615*). The profits of a business bequeathed to a charity were held to be annual payments (*R v Special Commrs (ex p Shaftesbury Homes) CA 1922, 8 TC 367*). For covenanted subscriptions see *CIR v National Book League CA 1957, 37 TC 455* and *Taw & Torridge Festival Society Ltd v CIR Ch D 1959, 38 TC 603* (but see also 15.17(*b*) CHARITIES). Covenanted payments to a charity as part of arrangements under which it acquired the business of the payer not annual payments (*Campbell v CIR HL 1968, 45 TC 427*). Payments by a film company of a share of certain receipts as part of arrangements for cancellation of a contract were annual payments (*Asher v London Film Productions Ltd CA 1943, 22 ATC 432*) as were payments under a guarantee of the dividends of a company (*Aeolian Co Ltd v CIR KB 1936, 20 TC 547; Moss Empires Ltd v CIR HL 1937, 21 TC 264*). But not payments by the principal subscribers to a newsfilm service to make good its operating deficit (*British Commonwealth International Newsfilm Agency Ltd v Mahany HL 1962, 40 TC 550*).

Instalments of the purchase price of a mine held not annual payments (*Foley v Fletcher 1858, 7 WR 141*) nor instalment repayments of a debt (*Dott v Brown CA 1936, 15 ATC 147*). Where the Secretary of State for India acquired a railway in consideration of annuities for 48 years, tax held to be deductible only from the interest element actuarially ascertained (*Scoble v Secretary of State for India HL 1903, 4 TC 478, 618* and cf. the two *East India Rly.* cases at *21 TLR 606* and *40 TLR 241*). Similarly where shares were sold for payments over 125 years, the actuarially ascertained interest element in the payments was held to be income in the hands of the recipient for surtax (*Vestey v CIR Ch D 1961, 40 TC 112*). See also *Goole Corporation v Aire, etc. Trustees KB 1942, 21 ATC 156* (tax held deductible from interest element in yearly payments to local authority to meet street repairs). In *CIR v Church Commissioners HL 1976, 50 TC 516* rent charges paid as the consideration for property were held wholly income and not (as contended for Crown) partly income and partly capital. The HL judgments are an important review of the possibility of dissecting periodical payments in return for valuable consideration between income and capital and *Vestey v CIR* above, although not overruled, was called 'the high water of dissection cases' (Lord Wilberforce) and some of the reasoning in it was not approved. See also *Chadwick v Pearl Life Insce KB 1905, 21 TLR 456*. For reimbursement of expenditure calculated by reference to an interest factor, see *Re Euro Hotel (Belgravia) Ltd Ch D 1975, 51 TC 293* and *Chevron Petroleum (UK) Ltd v BP Petroleum Development Ltd Ch D 1981, 57 TC 137*.

Payments in satisfaction of the transfer of a business, etc., and based on profits held not to be annual payments in *CIR v Ramsay CA 1935, 20 TC 79* and *CIR v Ledgard KB 1937, 21 TC 129* but contrast *CIR v Hogarth CS 1940, 23 TC 491*. Payments of a percentage of receipts over 40 years for the use of a secret process held to be annual payments (*Delage v Nugget Polish Co Ltd KB 1905, 21 TLR 454*) as were quarterly payments for the use of a firm's name etc. (*Mackintosh v CIR KB 1928, 14 TC 15*). See also *CIR v 36/49 Holdings Ltd CA 1943, 25 TC 173*. Where a business was bequeathed for life and the trustees were directed to carry a percentage of the profits to reserve, the amounts set aside were held to be annual payments (*Stocker v CIR KB 1919, 7 TC 304*).

In *Watkins v CIR KB 1939, 22 TC 696*, payments by a husband for the maintenance of his wife (of unsound mind) were held not to be annual payments. See 23.9 above for alimony payments. Payments to trustees as 'remuneration' are annual payments (*Baxendale v Murphy KB 1924, 9 TC 76; Hearn v Morgan KB 1945, 26 TC 478*) but not Schedule E remuneration (*Jaworski v Institution of Polish Engineers CA 1950, 29 ATC 385*).

For amounts taxable under *ICTA 1988, s 775* or *s 776* (see 3.10 and 3.11 ANTI-AVOIDANCE), if the person entitled is resident abroad the Revenue may direct that they be treated as annual payments subject to deduction of tax under *ICTA 1988, s 349(1)*. [*ICTA 1988, s 777(9)*]. Such a direction may, however, only be made once there is entitlement to the consideration, i.e. on execution of a contract (*Pardoe v Entergy Power Development Corp Ch D, [2000] STC 286*).

For annual payments under certain life assurance policies (e.g. Guaranteed Income Bonds) not treated as such for tax purposes, see 45.15(*h*) LIFE INSURANCE POLICIES.

See also 3.19 ANTI-AVOIDANCE where certain annual payments are made for non-taxable consideration.

23.11 ANNUITIES

(*a*) **General.** In the absence of provisions to the contrary annuities are (i) within SCHEDULE D, CASE III (72) unless payable under foreign contracts etc. (when they are foreign possessions within SCHEDULE D, CASE IV (73), (ii) subject to deduction of tax under *ICTA 1988, ss 348, 349(1)* and (iii) this is so notwithstanding that the annuity may have been granted for valuable and sufficient consideration. Hence, (iv) an annuity cannot be dissected between the capital, if any, in consideration of the annuity and an 'interest element'. For a full discussion of this, see the HL opinions in *CIR v Church Commissioners HL 1976, 50 TC 516*. See also 23.10 above. For tax-free annuities see 23.17 below.

Statutory exceptions to this general rule are below.

(*b*) **Annuities for non-taxable consideration.** See 3.19 ANTI-AVOIDANCE.

(*c*) **Purchased life annuities.** The capital element in such annuities, whenever purchased, is **not treated as income** (except where, for other tax purposes, a lump sum payment has to be taken into account in computing profits or losses). This applies to any *life annuity* (i.e., one payable for a period ending with, or ascertainable only by reference to, the end of a life—notwithstanding that it may also end at a fixed term, or on the happening of a contingency, during the life or may extend beyond the end of the life) *purchased for money or money's worth* from a person whose business is to grant life annuities — but **not including any annuity**

(i) treated, for other tax purposes, as being partly payment or repayment of a capital sum, or

(ii) bought with sums ranking for relief under provisions for retirement annuities (see 65 RETIREMENT ANNUITIES) or as life assurance premiums, etc. under *ICTA 1988, ss 266, 273* (see 45.1 *et seq.* LIFE ASSURANCE POLICIES), or

(iii) purchased under direction in a will, or in substitution for an annuity charged on income of settled property, or

(iv) purchased under any sponsored superannuation scheme (see *ICTA 1988, s 624* and 66 RETIREMENT SCHEMES), or retirement annuity scheme (see 65 RETIREMENT ANNUITIES), or in recognition of services, past or present, in any employment, or

(v) purchased under or for the purposes of a retirement benefits scheme approved under *ICTA 1988, s 591* (discretionary approval, see 66.4 RETIREMENT

SCHEMES) or in pursuance of any obligation imposed, or offer or invitation made, under or in connection with any such scheme, or

(vi) payable under approved personal pension arrangements (see 60 PERSONAL PENSION SCHEMES), or

(vii) purchased, for purposes connected with giving effect to any pension-sharing order or provision under *Welfare Reform and Pensions Act 1999, s 24(1)*, for consideration which derives: from an approved retirement benefits scheme within *ICTA 1988, s 596(1)* (see 66.1 RETIREMENT SCHEMES); from sums satisfying the conditions for relief under *ICTA 1988, s 619* (retirement annuity premiums, see 65.1 RETIREMENT ANNUITIES); from schemes or arrangements within (iv) or (vi) above; or from the surrender or partial surrender of an annuity within (v) above or this subparagraph, or of a contract for such an annuity.

[*ICTA 1988, ss 656(1), 657, 659D; FA 1999, s 80, Sch 10 paras 16, 17*].

Subject as below, the *capital element* is constant throughout and is, normally, that part of an annuity payment which bears to the full amount the same proportion as the purchase price of the annuity bears to the actuarial value of the total annuity payments, based on mortality tables but excluding any element of discounting, and calculated as at the date the first payment begins to accrue. For prescribed mortality tables see *SI 1956 No 1230* as amended by *SI 1991 No 2808*, and *Rose v Trigg Ch D 1963, 41 TC 365.*

Where the term but not the amount of the annuity does not depend solely on the duration of a life or lives, the calculation of the capital element is varied as may be just, and where the purchase price covers more than a pure annuity, that price is similarly apportioned.

But where the *amount* of any annuity payment depends on a contingency other than the duration of a life or lives the exempt capital element will not be calculated as above but will be arrived at by spreading the purchase price of the annuity rateably over its expected term (as at the date the first annuity payment begins to accrue) and allocating to each annuity payment a part corresponding to the length of the period for which the annuity payment is made. [*ICTA 1988, s 656; FA 1991, s 76*]. If the capital element exceeds the annuity payment, the excess may be carried forward for allowance in determining the capital element in the next payment or payments. (See Revenue Pamphlet IR 1, A46).

Sellers of annuities are notified of annuities affected by *ICTA 1988, s 656(1)–(4)* and of the capital element in them: until then they continue to deduct tax and account for it, where appropriate, as before. Any tax over- or under-deducted from payments made before the notification is repaid to or charged on the payee, subject to time limits. [*ICTA 1988, s 656(5)(6)*, and *IT (Purchased Life Annuities) Regulations 1956* (*SI 1956 No 1230*), and *Amendment Regulations 1960* (*SI 1960 No 2308*) and *1990* (*SI 1990 No 626*)].

For 1996/97 and subsequent years, the income element of a purchased life annuity is chargeable to income tax at the lower rate (to the extent that it does not fall within an individual's higher rate band) and tax is deductible at source at the lower rate (see 1.9 ALLOWANCES AND TAX RATES).

As to tax on sale, surrender, etc., of rights under a life annuity contract see 45.15 LIFE ASSURANCE POLICIES and *ICTA 1988, ss 542, 543.*

Other life, or terminable, annuities are taxed under *ICTA 1988, s 348.*

(*d*) **Annuities out of approved superannuation funds.** See 66.5(*d*) RETIREMENT SCHEMES.

(*e*) **'Capital and income'** policies are those where in the event of death within a selected period, a lump sum and an annuity for the rest of the period is paid. The annuity may (conditionally) be treated as instalments of capital, not subject to tax deduction. Some companies arrange for return of part of *capital* over a number of years, followed by an ordinary annuity subject to tax deduction. But if assigned or settled for benefit of a third party see 81.9 SETTLEMENTS.

(*f*) For **children's education policies** see *Perrin v Dickson CA 1929, 14 TC 608* in which the yearly payments were held to be a return of the premiums with interest, only the interest being taxable. The decision was questioned in *Sothern-Smith v Clancy CA 1940, 24 TC 1.* Purchased life annuities are now regulated, see (*c*) above.

(*g*) For **guaranteed income bonds** and similar life policies, see 45.15(*h*) LIFE INSURANCE POLICIES.

23.12 DIVIDENDS AND INTEREST

Banks, etc.. See 8 BANKS.

British companies etc.. See 1.9 ALLOWANCES AND TAX RATES.

Building societies. See 9 BUILDING SOCIETIES.

Government stock. See 33 GOVERNMENT STOCKS, 70 SCHEDULE C.

Local authority and statutory corporation stock. Tax is deductible under *ICTA 1988, s 349(2)* (see 23.3(ii) above) but not if borrowing is in foreign currency (or, for securities issued before 6 April 1982, in the currency of a territory outside the scheduled territories) and Treasury so direct. Interest is then exempt from income tax (but not corporation tax) if the beneficial owner is not resident in UK. [*ICTA 1988, ss 349(2), 581*].

Foreign dividends (including foreign Government or public revenue dividends) are, before 1 April 2001, generally subject to deduction of tax at, from 6 April 1999 (see *FA 2000, s 33*) the Schedule F ordinary rate of tax (see 1.9 ALLOWANCES AND RATES) (previously, the lower rate of tax) under the paying and collecting agents arrangements under *ICTA 1988, ss 118A–118K* and associated regulations. For an article on the scope of these arrangements, see Revenue Tax Bulletin August 1996 p 329. There are reliefs *inter alia* for payments to non-UK residents, or to non-UK resident trustees of certain discretionary or accumulation trusts for non-UK resident beneficiaries, for certain payments held in 'recognised clearing systems' (see 23.3(ii) above), for dividends payable by non-UK resident companies to UK companies holding 10% or more of the voting power in the paying company, and for various payments constituting exempt income in the hands of the recipient. From 1 April 2001 these provisions are abolished by *FA 2000, s 111(1)(6)*, but see 23.3(ii) DEDUCTION OF TAX AT SOURCE as regards the deduction regime introduced in their place in relation to UK public revenue dividends. As regards the other sources, to which deduction no longer applies, enhanced information powers are available to the Revenue (see 67.4 RETURNS).

For 1995/96 and earlier years (and for company accounting periods ending before 1 April 1996), similar provisions applied by the inclusion of such payments within SCHEDULE C (70).

23.13 MORTGAGE INTEREST ('MIRAS')

Mortgage interest on home loans may be paid after deduction of tax if the interest is 'relevant loan interest' paid by a 'qualifying borrower' to a 'qualifying lender'. This scheme is commonly known as MIRAS: Mortgage Interest Relief At Source.

Where the loan is within (*a*)(ii) below (loans to purchase life annuities), tax is deducted at the basic rate for the year in which the payment becomes due up to 1999/2000, the rate being fixed at **23%** thereafter. Where it is within (*a*)(i) or (iii) below, the deduction is at 20% for interest due in 1994/95, at 15% for interest due in 1995/96, 1996/7 and 1997/98, and at 10% for interest due after 5 April 1998, relief **ceasing altogether** for interest paid on such loans after (as a general rule) 5 April 2000 (see below and 43.3 INTEREST PAYABLE). No further tax relief is available, but nor is tax relief clawed back if the borrower has insufficient liability to cover it.

Payments of 'relevant loan interest' are not deductible in computing total income. Interest payments do not attract relief from income tax at the higher rate(s) (but see below as regards certain bridging loans).

It is understood that relief under MIRAS may be claimed retrospectively where interest under a mortgage meeting all the qualifying conditions for inclusion in the scheme was paid outside MIRAS, and relief for the interest thereby lost (e.g. where there was no taxable income). (Tolley's Practical Tax 1993 p 120).

Qualifying lenders are able to recover from the Government the tax deducted from interest payments received. Where the lender was not entitled to such a payment, the Board may assess and recover such overpayments and obtain interest and penalties where appropriate.

Relevant loan interest is not deductible from profits etc. under Schedule D, Case I or II or VI. [*ICTA 1988, ss 74(1)(o), 369; FA 1991, s 27(2); F(No 2)A 1992, s 19(3)(5); FA 1993, s 58, Sch 6 para 1; FA 1994, s 81(3)–(7), Sch 9 para 1; FA 1996, Sch 18 paras 6, 17(1)–(4)(8); F(No 2)A 1997 s 15(2)(3); FA 1999, s 38, Sch 4 para 4; FA 2000, s 83(3)(4)*]. Form Miras 5, a certificate of interest paid, is available on demand from the lender, although building societies normally notify the tax office direct.

For a general explanation of the scheme, see Revenue Pamphlet IR 63 'Mortgage interest relief at source'.

'Relevant loan interest' is interest which is paid and payable in the UK to a 'qualifying lender', where

(*a*) it is interest

(i) paid before, generally, 6 April 2000 (see below) on loans for purchase of land, caravan or houseboat *in the UK* which, when the interest is paid, is used 'wholly or to a substantial extent' (see below) as the only or main residence of the borrower under *ICTA 1988, ss 354(1), 355* (as altered for this purpose), see 43.6 INTEREST PAYABLE, or where the borrower resides in job-related accommodation within *ICTA 1988, s 356*, see 43.16 INTEREST PAYABLE; or

(ii) on pre-9 March 1999 loans to a borrower aged 65 or over to purchase life annuities secured on land *in the UK* under *ICTA 1988, s 365*, see 43.24 INTEREST PAYABLE; or

(iii) paid before, generally, 6 April 2000 (see below) on an option mortgage in respect of which an option notice was in force on 31 March 1983 and to which the conditions in (*a*)(i) above apply (with minor modifications), and

(*b*) apart from the current provisions, the whole of the interest in (*a*)(i) or (*a*)(ii) above (ignoring the tax relief limit — see 43.10 INTEREST PAYABLE) would be eligible for relief under *ICTA 1988, s 353* (see 43.3 INTEREST PAYABLE) or would be deductible from profits etc. under Schedule D, Case I or II or VI.

As regards (*a*)(i) and (iii) above, interest on such loans ceases to be relevant loan interest following the withdrawal of relief for such interest with effect, generally, for payments made after 5 April 2000 (and see 43.3 INTEREST PAYABLE).

The election referred to in 43.3 INTEREST PAYABLE (where interest is dually eligible for relief) also has effect for determining whether interest falls within (*a*)(i) above.

[*ICTA 1988, s 370; FA 1988, s 42(3)(c); FA 1994, Sch 9 para 10; FA 1995, Sch 29 Pt VIII(2); FA 1999, s 39, Sch 4 para 5*].

The Revenue normally regard the condition in (*a*)(i) above as satisfied if at least two-thirds of the property is used as the borrower's main residence. (Revenue Tax Bulletin August 1995 p 230). In practice, where no part of the home is used exclusively for business purposes, there will be only incidental business use. (MIRAS 30 (1996 Amendments) para 4.13). See *R v Inspector of Taxes (ex p. Kelly) CA 1991, 64 TC 343* for disallowance of interest on mixed purpose loans.

Interest on home improvement loans and on loans for the purchase of property to be used, wholly or substantially, as the only or main residence of the borrower's dependent relative or separated or former spouse is within (*a*)(i) above if it would be eligible for tax relief (see 43.6 *et seq.* INTEREST PAYABLE), that is, broadly speaking, if the loan was made, or deemed to be made, before 6 April 1988, and if within (*b*) above.

If non-qualifying expenditure is added to otherwise qualifying loans, the loans must be taken out of MIRAS. In practice, however, lenders may treat as qualifying expenditure sums advanced:

(1) by miscellaneous debits to the borrower's account by virtue of the mortgage deed or rules, e.g. buildings insurance premiums, legal costs in the event of arrears, or realisation expenses;

(2) to pay premiums due on indemnity insurance, mortgage protection and guarantee policies, or loan protection policies (including limited costs of incidental sickness and redundancy cover); or

(3) to pay costs of mortgage deed preparation, stamp duty, valuation and survey fees, and legal costs.

(MIRAS 30 (1995) para 10.22).

Certain administration fees charged to loan account are similarly disregarded, up to £300 in the first year and £150 p.a. thereafter. (MIRAS 30 (1995) para 10.23).

Where unauthorised arrears of interest are capitalised, the loan should strictly be excluded from the MIRAS scheme as being of a mixed quality. In practice, such action will only be taken where, when the loan is recalculated, the capitalised interest exceeds the greater of 12 months' arrears and £1,000, and no satisfactory arrangements have been made to reduce the arrears. Even then, in certain cases of hardship, no action will be taken. (MIRAS 30 (1995) paras 10.4, 10.5). See also 43.10 INTEREST PAYABLE as regards extension of the tax relief limit by up to £1,000 where interest is capitalised.

Interest on a *home improvement loan* (i.e. a loan applied wholly in improving or developing land or buildings or in paying off another similar loan), if otherwise eligible (see 43.6 *et seq.* INTEREST PAYABLE), is *not* relevant loan interest unless

(i) it is paid to a building society or a local authority or the NI Housing Executive, or

(ii) the qualifying lender has given notice to the Board that he is prepared to have such loans, made after such date as specified in the notice, brought within the tax deduction scheme, or

(iii) it is interest to which (*a*)(iii) above applies. [*ICTA 1988, s 372; FA 1999, Sch 4 para 6*].

Loans over the tax relief limit. (See 43.10 INTEREST PAYABLE.) Interest on such loans is not relevant loan interest unless all the loans to be taken into account are by the same qualifying lender, and only interest on loans up to the limit is then relevant loan interest. For loans made before 6 April 1987, there is an additional requirement that the lender has given notice to the Board that he is prepared to have such loans brought within the tax deduction scheme. [*ICTA 1988, s 373(1)–(5); FA 1988, s 42(3)(d); FA 1999, Sch 4 para 7*]. See also 43.10 INTEREST PAYABLE as regards extension of the limit by up to £1,000 where interest is capitalised.

Joint borrowers. Interest on a loan which is to joint borrowers who are not husband and wife (i.e. living together and not separated) is not relevant loan interest unless each of the borrowers is a qualifying borrower and in relation to each of them, considered separately, the whole of that interest is relevant loan interest. [*ICTA 1988, s 373(6)(7); FA 1999, Sch 4 para 7*].

'Penalty' interest charged on the early redemption of a loan within MIRAS is not relevant loan interest (although this does not apply to interest charged for the whole of the month in which redemption occurs). Similarly a penalty charged for changing the terms of a loan, including a penalty for changing from a fixed to a variable rate, is not relevant loan interest. However, a replacement loan need not be regarded as mixed purpose merely because, in part, it replaces such a charge. (MIRAS 30 (1995) para 10.46).

Option to deduct interest under Schedule A. Where a qualifying borrower carries on or proposes to carry on a Schedule A business (see 68.4 SCHEDULE A) and gives notice to the Board that relevant interest on a loan is to be deducted in computing profits, interest paid on that loan after the date specified in the notice is to be paid outside MIRAS. The notice is irrevocable and must be given within 22 months after the end of the tax year in which the specified date falls. The Board must notify the lender, and there are provisions whereby any tax deducted by the borrower after the specified date can be reclaimed by the Revenue and reimbursed to the lender. The loan remains outside MIRAS until the Board gives notice to both borrower and lender that it is to be brought back within the scheme, which they will do only when the Schedule A business is permanently discontinued or the proposal to carry it on is finally abandoned. [*ICTA 1988, s 375A; FA 1995, Sch 6 para 18; FA 1999, Sch 4 para 10*].

Property used for both residential and business purposes. See 43.2 INTEREST PAYABLE for Revenue Concession applicable where part of a borrower's main residence is used for business (including a Schedule A business) purposes. The concession applies equally to a loan within MIRAS. (Revenue Pamphlet IR 1, A89). This is, however, subject to the property being used 'wholly or to a substantial extent' as the borrower's residence (see (*a*)(i) above). Where this condition is satisfied, *all* the interest qualifies for relief through MIRAS (subject to the £30,000 maximum). Where the part of the loan attributed to residential use under Concession A89 is less than £30,000, all or part of the interest attributed to the business use will have been relieved through MIRAS. The business deduction is reduced accordingly (see Revenue Tax Bulletin August 1995 pp 230–232 for worked examples).

A 'qualifying borrower' is an individual who pays 'relevant loan interest'. In relation to interest paid at a time when an individual (or spouse, if not permanently separated) holds an office or employment the emoluments from which would otherwise be chargeable to tax under Case I, II or III of Schedule E, the individual is **not** a qualifying borrower if he or she has some special exemption or immunity (e.g. diplomatic) from such charge. [*ICTA*

1988, s 376(1)–(3)]. The exclusion of European Union employees from the scheme by virtue of their Schedule E exemption does not conflict with Community law (*Tither v CIR CJEC, [1990] STC 416*). Interest paid for and on behalf of a borrower may be treated as though paid by the borrower. (MIRAS 30 (1995) paras 10.43–10.45). Where a borrower dies, the loan should be removed from MIRAS immediately the lender is advised of the death by the personal representatives, except in the case of the death of a joint married borrower where the surviving borrower continues to use the property as the only or main residence. (MIRAS Central Unit Guidance Letter 31 May 1989).

A 'qualifying lender' is any of the following: a building society; a local authority; the Bank of England; the Post Office; an insurance company authorised to carry on long-term business (e.g. life assurance) in the UK; a company successor to a trustee savings bank; a registered or incorporated friendly society or branch; a development corporation; the Commission for the New Towns; the Housing Corporation; Housing for Wales (or the Secretary of State if the loan is made by him under *Housing Associations Act 1985, s 79*); the Northern Ireland Housing Executive; the Scottish Special Housing Association; the Development Board for Rural Wales; the Church of England Pensions Board; and an existing lender under the mortgage option scheme.

The Board may also register as a qualifying lender any of the following bodies: a recognised bank or licensed deposit-taking institution; an insurance company authorised to carry on general insurance business in the UK; a 90% subsidiary of any such bank, institution or company; and any other body whose activities and objects it considers qualify the body for inclusion. The registration may apply generally or only in relation to a particular description of loan, and applies from a specified date, and the terms of registration may be varied by the Board. Registration may be cancelled where it appears to the Board that an application for registration by the lender concerned would be refused. At least 30 days notice is required to be given of variation or cancellation. There is a right of appeal (within 30 days) to the Special Commissioners against a refusal, variation or cancellation of registration. Applications for registration should be made to Inland Revenue, FICO (Financial Intermediaries Technical), St John's House, Merton Road, Bootle, Merseyside L69 9BB, stating the grounds on which the applicant qualifies and giving their full legal title or registered name.

An updated Register of Qualifying Lenders was published on 16 July 1998 and is available for inspection at Tax Enquiry Centres, or may be purchased (price £1 post free) from Inland Revenue, Reference Library, Room 28, New Wing, Somerset House, Strand, London WC2R 1LB or by personal callers at the Inland Revenue Information Centre, SW Wing, Bush House, Strand, London WC2B 4RD.

[*ICTA 1988, s 376(4)–(6), s 376A; Housing Act 1988, Sch 17 para 115; F(No 2)A 1992, Sch 9 para 3; FA 1994, s 142; Government of Wales Act 1998, Sch 16 para 55; FA 1999, Sch 4 para 11*].

Administration of the tax deduction scheme. The scheme does not apply to any relevant loan interest unless

(*a*) the borrower, or each joint borrower, has given notice to the lender in the prescribed form certifying (i) that he is a qualifying borrower and (ii) that the interest is relevant loan interest and (iii) such other matters as may be prescribed; or

(*b*) the Board have notified the lender and the borrower that the interest may be paid under deduction of tax; or

(*c*) the interest is on a loan which was, on 31 March 1983, an option mortgage loan; or

(*d*) the loan was made before the commencement date (see above), and is of a description specified by regulations made by the Board.

Where any of the above requirements are met, tax may be deducted from the interest: on and after the date of the notice in (*a*); on and after the date specified in the Board's notification in (*b*), and where that date is retrospective the Board may repay the amount which was under-deducted from interim interest paid (together with INTEREST ON OVERPAID TAX (41)), subject to recovery powers for amounts wrongly repaid; on and after the commencement date (see above) for (*c*) and (*d*). [*ICTA 1988, ss 374, 375(8)(8A); FA 1995, s 112(4); FA 1999, s 41, Sch 4 paras 8, 9*].

Where the relevant loan interest is payable to a building society or other specified qualifying lender under a loan agreement requiring combined payments (i.e. a number of regular payments which are part repayment of capital and part payment of interest) on a loan made before 1 April 1983, the qualifying lender may give notice to the qualifying borrower that each net payment (i.e. each payment from the interest element of which tax has to be deducted) will be of the same amount (unless there is a change in the deductible rate of income tax or in the rate of interest charged by the borrower) and that payments will be determined so as to secure that the period of the loan remains unchanged. The borrower may, however, give counter-notice that each net payment must be of the same amount (again subject to deductible tax rate or interest rate changes) and that the amount of each combined payment must not exceed what would have been the amount of the first combined payment, less tax, after the giving of notice by the lender, apart from these provisions. If such notice is given the borrower may, whenever he chooses, make additional capital repayments so as to secure repayment of the loan within a period not shorter than that originally agreed. Subsequent variations may be made by agreement. [*ICTA 1988, s 377; FA 1994, s 81(8); FA 1999, Sch 4 para 12*].

Where, on or after 1 May 1995, tax is deducted from interest which has never been relevant loan interest or which is paid otherwise than by a qualifying borrower, the interest is treated as such providing either condition (*a*) or condition (*b*) above is fulfilled. The tax deducted is, however, recoverable from the borrower by assessment. Interest is chargeable under *TMA 1970, s 86* (see 42.1 INTEREST AND SURCHARGES ON UNPAID TAX) (and previously under *TMA 1970, s 88* (see 6.6 BACK DUTY) by reference to a due date of 1 December following the tax year in which the deduction was made). Where the borrower fraudulently or negligently makes a false statement or representation, he will be liable to a penalty not exceeding the amount of tax consequently deducted. [*ICTA 1988, s 374A; FA 1995, s 112(1)(5); FA 1996, Sch 18 paras 7, 17(5)(6)*].

Except as below, if at any time interest ceases to be relevant loan interest or a person paying relevant loan interest ceases to be a qualifying borrower, the borrower must notify the lender, and where tax has been deducted from a payment made between that time and the notification the payment is treated as relevant loan interest, but any excess relief or deduction above proper entitlement is recoverable from the borrower by assessment, with potential interest and, for deductions made on or after 1 May 1995, penalties. If a qualifying lender has reason to believe that interest is no longer relevant loan interest or a borrower is no longer a qualifying borrower, he must inform the Board. Failure to do so incurs penalties.

Form Miras 3, available from the lender, enables the borrower to claim tax relief where a qualifying loan is excluded from MIRAS.

Where it appears to the Board that any qualifying condition under the scheme is not, or may not be, fulfilled, they must give notice to the lender and the borrower and the tax deduction scheme will not apply to the relevant loan interest due between dates specified in the notice and any subsequent notice.

These provisions do *not*, however, apply where interest ceases to be relevant loan interest by virtue of the general cessation of mortgage interest relief (see above and 43.3 INTEREST PAYABLE).

[*ICTA 1988, s 375(1)–(7)(8B); FA 1994, Sch 9 para 11; FA 1995, s 112(2)(3)(5); FA 1996, Sch 18 paras 8, 17(1); FA 1999, Sch 4 para 9*].

Where interest is treated as relevant loan interest only by virtue of *ICTA 1988, s 375(2)*, it may nevertheless be deductible against total income or for Schedule D, Case I or II purposes if it would be so deductible under general principles. [*ICTA 1988, s 74(1)(o), s 369(3); FA 1994, s 81(4), Sch 9 para 1*].

The Treasury may make regulations to apply the above provisions to housing associations and self-build societies which borrow from qualifying lenders and the Board may make regulations regarding the administration of the scheme, its application to personal representatives and trustees, the inspection of records, appeals and generally. [*ICTA 1988, s 378; FA 1999, Sch 4 para 13*]. The first such regulations made by the Board deal mainly with the bringing of loans into the scheme; with 'limited loans' (broadly those over the interest relief limit — see 43.10 INTEREST PAYABLE); with variations of amounts due under existing loans brought within the scheme; with the reimbursement of lenders for tax deducted by borrowers; and with information and penalty powers and appeal procedures. [*The Income Tax (Interest Relief) Regulations 1982 (SI 1982 No 1236) as amended*]. The *(No 2) Regulations 1983* (*SI 1983 No 311*) supplement the principal regulations, and the *(No 3) Regulations 1985* (*SI 1985 No 1252*) amend the procedures for bringing limited loans into the scheme. The (*Housing Associations*) *Regulations 1988* (*SI 1988 No 1347*) and (*Amendment*) *Regulations 1995* (*SI 1995 No 1212*) and *1996* (*SI 1996 No 2616*) deal with housing associations and self-build societies.

Interest paid by a housing association or self-build society is not relevant loan interest if

(A) it is interest on a home improvement loan made on or after 6 April 1988 (and not deemed to have been made before that date), or

(B) by virtue of *FA 1988, s 44* (loans for residence of dependent relative, etc.) it would not be relevant loan interest if paid by a member of the association or society.

(See 43.6 *et seq.* INTEREST PAYABLE.)

[*FA 1988, ss 43(3), 44(6); FA 1999, Sch 20 Pt III(7)*].

An explanatory lenders booklet (MIRAS 30) is available to existing MIRAS lenders and those thinking about coming into the scheme.

The Revenue have published a Code of Practice (No 4) setting out their standards for the carrying out of inspections of tax relief at source schemes operated by financial intermediaries.

The Inland Revenue Financial Intermediaries and Claims Office may be contacted in relation to MIRAS on 0151–472 6160 to 6167 as regards repayments or 0151–472 6155 for technical advice.

Simon's Direct Tax Service. See **A3.430–A3.435**.

23.14 RENTS ETC. UNDER ICTA 1988, s 119 AND s 120

Under *ICTA 1988, s 119*, where rent (as defined) was payable before 1 May 1995 for any 'easement' (as defined) 'used, occupied or enjoyed' in connection with any of the 'concerns' specified in *ICTA 1988, s 55(2)*, tax was deductible as for patent royalties, see 23.15(*b*) below. See *New Sharlston Collieries CA 1936, 21 TC 69; Hope CS 1937, 21 TC 116* and *Fitzwilliam's Collieries Co v Phillips HL 1943, 25 TC 430*. Payments made on or after that date are made gross. [*FA 1995, s 145*]. If the rent is paid in produce of the concern the recipient is charged, on its value, under Schedule D, Case III. [*ICTA 1988, s 119(2)*].

Section 119(2) held to cover value of coals received free (*Baillie CS 1936, 20 TC 187*) and payments under short-term agreements for the extraction of, respectively (*a*) all sand and gravel, and (*b*) all coal, on certain lands (*Stratford v Mole & Lea KB 1941, 24 TC 20* and *Old Silkstone Collieries Ltd v Marsh KB 1941, 24 TC 20*. Cf. *Craigenlow Quarries Ltd CS 1951, 32 TC 326*). But not payments for extracting fluorspar from old lead mining dumps (*Rogers v Longsdon Ch D 1966, 43 TC 231*) or shingle from foreshore (*Duke of Fife's Trustees v Geo. Wimpey CS 1943, 22 ATC 275*) because there was no 'concern'. For cases involving sales of slag etc. but not rents etc. within *section 119*, see 71.71 SCHEDULE D, CASES I AND II.

The provisions of *ICTA 1988, s 122* (see 49 MINERAL ROYALTIES) altering the taxation treatment of recipients of mineral royalties and rents did not displace the payer's obligation (before 1 May 1995) to deduct income tax at the basic rate when paying those royalties, etc. [*ICTA 1988, s 122(1)*].

Deduction at source as above continued to apply until 5 April 1997 to rents for easements in connection with electric telegraph or telephone wires or cables (including poles, pylons, related apparatus and transformers) except, by payer's election, to sums of £2.50 p.a. or under (which are then assessable on recipient under Schedule D, Case III) but if any such rent was paid under deduction of tax by a person carrying on a radio relay service the payment was nevertheless deductible in calculating profits for Schedule D, Case I but for purposes of *ICTA 1988, ss 348, 349* deemed not to be payable out of taxed profits. [*ICTA 1988, s 120; FA 1997, s 60*].

Other property rentals, including ground rents, are payable in full and assessable on recipient, see 68 SCHEDULE A.

23.15 **ROYALTIES**

(*a*) **Copyright royalties, public lending right payments** and **design royalties** paid to non-residents are taxed by deduction under *ICTA 1988, s 349(1)*. [*ICTA 1988, ss 536, 537, 537B; FA 1995, s 115(10)*]. This does not apply to professional authors (Hansard 10 November 1969, Vol 791, Col 31). Payer is assessable, even if he has not deducted the tax (*Rye & Eyre v CIR HL 1935, 19 TC 164*). See 51.10 NON-RESIDENTS AND OTHER OVERSEAS MATTERS.

(*b*) **Patent royalties** are payable under deduction of tax. [*ICTA 1988, s 348(2), s 349(1)(b)*]. Instalments of fixed amount for five-year use of patent held capital (*Desoutter Bros Ltd KB 1936, 15 ATC 49*). A lump sum payment on signing a ten-year agreement held capital but ten fixed yearly payments royalties (*CIR v British Salmson Aero Engines Ltd CA 1938, 22 TC 29*). Awards by a Royal Commission for use of inventions and patents in 1914–1918 war held patent royalties (*Constantinesco v Rex HL 1927, 11 TC 730; Mills v Jones HL 1929, 14 TC 769*). See also *Jones v CIR KB 1919, 7 TC 310; Wild v Ionides KB 1925, 9 TC 392; International Combustion Ltd v CIR KB 1932, 16 TC 532* and cf. *Rank Xerox Ltd v Lane HL 1979, 53 TC 185*.

For the treatment of capital sums for the acquisition or from the sale of patents, see 54 PATENTS.

(*c*) **Mining royalties,** see 23.14 above.

23.16 **TAX-FREE ARRANGEMENTS**

An agreement which provides for an annual payment without deduction of tax is void [*TMA 1970, s 106(2)*] but a provision to pay interest at a stated rate after deduction of tax is treated as requiring payment at the gross rate. [*ICTA 1988, s 818(2)*]. An agreement to make payments 'free of tax' is not avoided by *TMA 1970, s 106(2)* (*CIR v Ferguson HL 1969, 46 TC 1*). See 23.17 below for tax-free annuities.

23.17 **TAX-FREE ANNUITIES ETC.**

(*a*) **General**. A direction under a will or settlement for an annuity to be paid 'free of tax' (or similar wording) is a direction to pay an annuity of such an amount which after deduction of the tax will produce the specified figure (cf. *CIR v Ferguson HL 1969, 46 TC 1*). This is a matter, however, in which it is important the wording used should express clearly and unambiguously what is intended. The large number of court cases referred to below have arisen mostly because of the imprecision of the relevant wording.

The wording was held *not* to confer freedom from tax in *Abadam v Abadam 1864, 10 LT 53* ('payable without any deduction whatsoever'); *Shrewsbury v Shrewsbury Ch D 1906, 22 TLR 598* ('clear of all deductions'); *In re Loveless Ch D 1918, 34 TLR 356* ('clear'); *In re Well's Will Trusts Ch D 1940, 19 ATC 158* ('clear of all deductions'); *In re Best's Marriage Settlement Ch D 1941, 20 ATC 235* ('such a sum as shall after deductions'); *CIR v Watson CS 1942, 25 TC 25* (annuity payable out of 'whole free residue' of income); *In re Hooper Ch D 1944, 1 AER 227* ('free of all duty . . . and . . . free of all deductions whatsoever'); *In re Wright Ch D 1952, 31 ATC 433* ('net'). The wording was held to confer freedom from tax in *In re Buckle 1894, 1 Ch 286* ('free of legacy duty and every other deduction' under a codicil to a will in which originally 'clear of all deductions whatsoever, except income tax'); *In re Shrewsbury Estate Acts CA 1923, 40 TLR 16* ('clear of all deductions whatsoever for taxes or otherwise'). *In re Hooper* above was not followed in *In re Cowlishaw Ch D 1939, 18 ATC 377* where the wording was similar, but in a later case (*In re Best's Marriage Settlement* above) *Cowlishaw* was described as special to its context.

(*b*) **Surtax/excess liability.** All the decisions below relate to super-tax or surtax but it would seem that, suitably adapted, they are equally applicable to excess liability (see 28.1 EXCESS LIABILITY). Here it is relevant that an annuity is investment income.

An annuity of a sum such 'as after deduction of the income tax' would give the prescribed amount was held not to be free of super-tax (*In re Bates Ch D 1924, 4 ATC 518*). However an annuity 'free of income tax' was held to be free of surtax on the ground that surtax was an additional income tax and there was no indication in the will to restrict the wording to 'income tax as known for many years'. The previous decision was distinguished as there the wording referred to 'deduction' and surtax was not deductible at source (*In re Reckitt CA 1932, 11 ATC 429*; followed in *Prentice's Trustees CS 1934, 13 ATC 612*). A direction to pay an annuity free of super-tax was held to cover surtax (*In re Hulton Ch D 1930, 9 ATC 570*).

The surtax is normally taken as the part of the annuitant's total surtax proportionate to the ratio of the annuity grossed at the standard rate to the annuitant's total income (*In re Bowring 1918, 34 TLR 575*; followed in *In re Doxat 1920, 125 LT 60* and other cases). In *Baird's Trustees CS 1933, 12 ATC 407* the surtax was calculated on the basis that the annuity was the annuitant's only income, but this decision was distinguished in *Richmond's Trustees 1935 CS, 14 ATC 489* and *In re Bowring* was followed. See also *In re Horlick's Settlement CA 1938, 17 ATC 549.*

The surtax/excess liability borne on behalf of the annuitant by the trust fund is itself, grossed-up, income in his hands (*Meeking v CIR KB 1920, 7 TC 603; Lord Michelham's Trustees v CIR CA 1930, 15 TC 737.* See also *Shrewsbury & Talbot v CIR KB 1936, 20 TC 538* and compare *CIR v Duncanson KB 1949, 31 TC 257*). The practice is to treat the liability so borne for year 1 as an addition for grossing-up purposes to the annuity for year 2.

(*c*) **Tax repayments of annuitants.** In a tax-free annuity the question arises whether the benefit conferred on the annuitant should be limited to the tax actually suffered by him after taking into account his allowances etc.

Where the annuity under a will was 'free of income tax' it was held that the annuitant must hand to the trustees a part of the tax repaid to her on account of her reliefs, in proportion to the ratio of the net annuity to her net income after tax (*In re Pettit, Le Fevre v Pettit Ch D 1922, 38 TLR 787*). But where the annuity was expressed to be of such an amount as after deduction of the tax at the current rate would give the prescribed sum it was held, distinguishing *In re Pettit*, that the annuitant was entitled to retain any tax repaid to him (*In re Jones Ch D 1933, 12 ATC 595*). For cases in which these two decisions were considered and applied as appropriate to the precise wording of the provision of the annuity, see *Richmond's Trustees CS 1935, 14 ATC 489; In re Maclennan CA 1939, 18 ATC 121; In re Eves Ch D 1939, 18 ATC 401; Rowan's Trustees CS 1939, 18 ATC 378; In re Jubb Ch D 1941, 20 ATC 297; In re Tatham Ch D 1944, 23 ATC 283; In re Williams Ch D 1945, 24 ATC 199; In re Bates's Will Trusts Ch D 1945, 24 ATC 300; In re Arno CA 1946, 25 ATC 412. Tatham* and *Arno* give useful reviews of the subject as does *CIR v Cook HL 1945, 26 TC 489* (in which it was held that the Revenue must repay the tax on the grossed-up amount of a tax-free annuity notwithstanding that the annuitant would not be liable to tax if the annuity was not grossed-up and that the whole of the repayment would be handed over to the trustees). The annuitant must, if required by the trustees, exercise his right to repayment (*In re Kingcombe Ch D 1936, 15 ATC 37*). If the annuitant is a married woman *In re Pettit* applies to tax repayable to the husband but, if necessary, she must apply for separate assessment (*In re Batley CA 1952, 31 ATC 410*). It applies to loss relief (*In re Lyons CA 1951, 30 ATC 377*). For the effect of an *In re Pettit* refund on the annuitant's total income for surtax see *CIR v Duncanson KB 1949, 31 TC 257.*

(*d*) **Tax-free alimony etc. payments.** The *In re Pettit* rule (see (*c*) above) does not apply to tax-free Court Orders and in *CIR v Ferguson HL 1969, 46 TC 1*, Lord Diplock explicitly refrained from deciding whether it applied to a separation agreement. Whether a free of tax Court Order would confer freedom from surtax/ excess liability does not seem to have arisen. Subject to the foregoing (*a*), (*b*) and (*c*) above apply, where appropriate, to tax-free alimony payments, etc.

For tax-free alimony payments by non-residents, see *Ferguson* above and *Stokes v Bennett Ch D 1953, 34 TC 337.*

(*e*) For **overseas taxes** under tax-free annuities, see *Re Frazer Ch D 1941, 20 ATC 73* and compare *Havelock v Grant KB 1946, 27 TC 363.*

23.18 VOLUNTARY ALLOWANCES

Not assessable on recipient (unless a misnomer for payments for services). But *voluntary pensions* by employers are assessable on recipient under Schedule E and tax is deductible by employers (see 55 PAY AS YOU EARN and 59.4 PENSIONS). See 23.9 above regarding alimony and separation allowances.

24 Diplomatic, etc. Immunity—Individuals and Organisations

Simon's Direct Tax Service D4.334, E5.401.

24.1 *Diplomatic Agents* (i.e. heads of mission or members of diplomatic staff) of foreign states (recognised by HM Government, see *Caglar v Billingham (Sp C 70), [1996] SSCD 150*) are exempt from tax except on income or capital gains arising from *private* investments or immovable property in the UK under *Diplomatic Privileges Act 1964*. Similar exemption is given to *Agents-General* and their staffs [*ICTA 1988, s 320; TCGA 1992, s 11*] (and see Revenue Pamphlet IR 1, A39 as regards certain Hong Kong officials). *Consuls* and *official agents* of foreign States in UK (not British subjects or citizens of Eire and not trading) are exempt on income from their official employment [*ICTA 1988, s 321*] and are also, subject to Order in Council, exempt under SCHEDULE D, CASES IV AND V (72) (and, for 1995/96 and earlier years, treated as non-resident under *ICTA 1988, s 48* and *s 123(4)* as regards foreign dividends), provided they are permanent employees or were not ordinarily resident in UK immediately prior to that employment. [*ICTA 1988, s 322; FA 1990, Sch 14 para 4; FA 1996, Sch 7 para 15*]. See also *Consular Relations Act 1968*.

International organisations (e.g. the United Nations (*SI 1974 No 1261*)), their representatives, officers, members of committees, persons or missions etc. may be specified by Order in Council as exempt from certain taxes under *International Organisations Act 1968*. Also other bodies under the *European Communities Act 1972* (e.g. the North Atlantic Salmon Conservation Organisation (*SI 1985 No 1773*)) and certain financial bodies under the *Bretton Woods Agreements Act 1945* (e.g. the International Monetary Fund (*SI 1946 No 36*)). Also exemption from income tax is given to the remuneration of the Commissioners of the European Communities and their staffs under *Art. 13 of Chap. V of the Protocol on the Privileges and Immunities of the European Communities*. See *Hurd v Jones CJEC, [1986] STC 127* as regards exemption of certain payments out of Community funds, although see now *SI 1990 No 237*. See also *Tither v CIR CJEC, [1990] STC 416*, where exclusion of EU official from MIRAS scheme upheld. The Treasury may also designate any of the international organisations of which the UK is a member for the purpose of exemption from various requirements for the deduction of tax from payments made in the UK (see e.g. *SI 1997 No 168*). [*ICTA 1988, s 582A; FA 1991, s 118; FA 1996, Sch 7 para 22, Sch 29 para 6*].

See 64 RESIDENCE, ORDINARY RESIDENCE AND DOMICILE for definition of resident etc.

25 Double Tax Relief

[*ICTA 1988, ss 788–816*]

(See also Revenue Pamphlet IR 6.)

Cross-reference. See generally 51 NON-RESIDENTS AND OTHER OVERSEAS MATTERS.

Simon's Direct Tax Service. See Binder 9 International.

Other sources. See Tolley's Double Taxation Relief.

25.1 Where the same income is liable to be taxed in both the UK and another country, relief may be available

(*a*) under the specific terms of a double tax agreement between the UK and that other country — see 25.2 below [*ICTA 1988, s 788*];

(*b*) under special arrangements with Eire — see 25.3 below; or

(*c*) under the unilateral double tax relief provisions contained in UK tax legislation — see 25.4 below. [*ICTA 1988, s 790*].

25.2 **DOUBLE TAX AGREEMENTS** [*ICTA 1988, ss 788, 789*]

A list is given below of the bilateral agreements made by the UK which are currently operative. For details of agreements, see Simon's Direct Tax Service F4. Representations on points interested parties would like to see addressed in negotiating particular treaties, or on other matters relating to the treaty negotiation programme or the treaty network, should be addressed to Mrs Jas Sahni, Inland Revenue, International Division, 2nd Floor, Victory House, 30–34 Kingsway, London WC2B 6ES.

Under these agreements certain classes of income derived from those countries by UK residents are given complete exemption from income taxes in the country from which they arise and reciprocal exemption from UK income tax or corporation tax is given to similar income derived from the UK by residents of those countries. Exemption may also be granted in respect of capital gains taxes, as provided for by *TCGA 1992, s 277*, and in respect of corporation tax on capital gains.

Other classes of income or gain derived from those countries are not exempted, or only partially exempted, by the agreements and in these cases relief from UK income tax, etc., is generally given in the agreement (but to UK residents only [*ICTA 1988, s 794*]) in the form of a credit, calculated by reference to the foreign tax suffered, which is set against and reduces the UK tax chargeable on the doubly-taxed income or gain. [*ICTA 1988, s 793*]. See example in 25.8 below.

As regards the concept of 'permanent establishment' on which taxation rights are based under most treaties, the Revenue take the view that a website, or a server on which e-commerce is conducted through a website, is not of itself a permanent establishment. (Revenue Press Release 11 April 2000).

Double tax agreements normally contain a 'mutual agreement procedure' enabling a taxpayer who considers that the action of a tax authority has resulted, or will result, in taxation not in accordance with the agreement to present his case to the competent authority in his state of residence. The UK competent authority is the Inland Revenue, and the address to which all relevant facts and contentions should be sent is International Division, Melbourne House, Aldwych, London WC2B 4LL. For the presentation of such cases, and for giving effect to solutions and agreements reached under such procedures, see *ICTA 1988, s 815AA* introduced by *FA 2000, Sch 30 para 28.*

In *R v CIR (ex p. Commerzbank AG) QB 1991, 68 TC 252,* INTEREST ON OVERPAID TAX (41) was held not to fall within the scope of double tax agreements, although on a reference to the European Court of Justice (see *68 TC 264*), the Court upheld the view that, in the case of companies resident in EC Member States, such discrimination against non-UK resident companies was prevented by the relevant Articles of the Treaty of Rome. See also 41.2 INTEREST ON OVERPAID TAX as regards treatment of EC resident individuals following this decision, and Revenue Double Taxation Relief Manual, DT 1950 *et seq.* for Revenue approach to non-discrimination claims generally.

For the scope of 'dividends' attracting treaty relief, see *Memec plc v CIR CA 1998, 71 TC 77* (in which receipts under a silent partnership agreement were held not to attract relief), and see Revenue Tax Bulletin February 1999 p 627 for an article on the classification of foreign entities for UK tax purposes. The general abolition of the repayment of tax credits after 5 April 1999 does not affect the entitlement of a non-UK resident to payment in respect of a tax credit under double tax agreements (although it should be noted that in practice, with the reduction after that date to one-ninth in the rate of tax credit, such repayments will be very limited). [*F(No 2)A 1997, s 30(9)(10)*]. Similarly, the tax credit payment restrictions applicable to pension funds in relation to distributions made after 1 July 1997 do not apply to non-residents' entitlements under such arrangements. [*ICTA 1988, s 231A(6)(b); F(No 2)A 1997, s 19(2), Sch 8 Pt II(9)*].

Special relationships: interest. Agreements under *ICTA 1988, s 788* making provision in relation to interest may also have a provision dealing with cases where, owing to a special relationship, the amount of interest paid exceeds the amount which would have been paid in the absence of that relationship, and requiring the interest provision to be applied only to that lower amount. Any such special relationship provision has to be construed:

(*a*) as requiring account to be taken of all factors, including whether, in the absence of the relationship, the loan would have been made at all, or would have been in a different amount, or a different rate of interest and other terms would have been agreed. This does not apply, however, where the special relationship provision expressly requires regard to be had to the debt on which the interest is paid in determining the excess interest, and accordingly expressly limits the factors to be taken into account, and in the case of a loan by one company to another, the fact that it is not part of the lending company's business to make loans generally is disregarded; and

(*b*) as requiring the taxpayer either to show that no special relationship exists or to show the amount of interest which would have been paid in the absence of that relationship.

[*ICTA 1988, s 808A; F(No 2)A 1992, s 52*].

Special relationships: royalties. Agreements may make similar provision in relation to royalties. Where they are payable on or after 28 July 2000, any royalties special relationship provision, unless it expressly requires regard to be had to the use, right or information for which royalties are paid in determining the excess royalties, has to be construed as requiring account to be taken of all factors. These include:

(A) in the absence of the relationship, whether the royalty agreement would have been made at all, or the rate or amount of royalties and other terms which would have been agreed; and

(B) if the asset in respect of which the royalties are paid (or any asset which it represents or from which it is derived) had previously been in the beneficial ownership of

 (i) the person liable to pay the royalties,

(ii) a person who has at any time carried on a business which, when the royalties fall due, is carried on in whole or part by the person liable to pay the royalties, or

(iii) a person who is or has been an 'associate', as specially defined, of a person within (i) or (ii),

amounts paid under the transaction(s) which resulted in the asset falling into its present beneficial ownership, the amounts which would have been so paid in the absence of the special relationship, and the question as to whether the transaction(s) would have taken place at all in the absence of that relationship.

The taxpayer must also show either that no special relationship exists, or the amount of royalties which would have been paid in the absence of the relationship, and if he cannot show that (B) above does not apply, he must show that the transaction(s) mentioned therein would have taken place in the absence of a special relationship, and the amounts which would then have been paid under those transaction(s).

[*Sec 808B; FA 2000, Sch 30 para 25*].

Under many double tax agreements, **employees working in the UK**, who are resident in the overseas country but not resident in the UK, and who are not physically present in the UK for more than 183 days in the year of assessment, are exempt from UK tax on earnings paid by or on behalf of a non-UK resident employer. For this purpose, fractions of days are counted. (CCAB Memorandum TR 508, 9 June 1983). This exemption does not usually apply to public entertainers (and see now 51.4(*b*) NON-RESIDENTS AND OTHER OVERSEAS MATTERS), nor, under certain agreements, does it extend to employees working on the UK continental shelf (see Revenue Press Release 3 March 1989). For employees commencing a work assignment in the UK after 1 July 1995, and in all cases for 1996/97 onwards, claims will be refused where the cost of an employee's remuneration is borne by a UK resident company acting as the 'economic employer'. This would apply where, for example, the employee is seconded to the UK company, which obtains the benefit and bears the risks in relation to work undertaken by the employee, and to which the non-resident employer recharges the remuneration costs. It would also apply where the non-resident employer carries on a business of hiring out staff to other companies. (Revenue Tax Bulletin June 1995 p 220). In the absence of a formal contract of employment, the Revenue would not consider a UK company to be the employer of a short term business visitor who is in the UK for less than 60 days in a tax year, provided that that period does not form part of a more substantial period when the taxpayer is in the UK. (Revenue Tax Bulletin October 1996 p 358).

The specific provisions of the particular agreement concerned must be examined carefully. For relevant Court decisions, see Tolley's Tax Cases.

Where double tax relief applies no deduction for foreign tax is allowed in assessing the foreign income or gain [*ICTA 1988, ss 795(2), 811(2)*] but if a taxpayer elects not to take credit allowable by an agreement, any foreign tax paid on that income in the place where it arises is *deductible* from the income for purposes of UK assessment, *except* that it is not so deductible where the UK assessment is on the basis of *remittances* to the UK. [*ICTA 1988, ss 805, 811*]. See 25.5(*b*)(iii) below. Where tax on overseas income is not relieved, or is only partly relieved, under an agreement, unilateral relief (see 25.4 below) will normally apply.

The following provisions supersede those of *ICTA 1988, s 790* (Unilateral Relief) to the extent, and as from the operative dates, specified in the various reciprocal agreements currently operative with the countries and territories that follow (*SI* numbers in round brackets).

Antigua and Barbuda (1947/2865; 1968/1096), **Argentina** (1997/1777) from 6 April 1998 (UK) and 1 January 1998 (Argentina), **Australia** (1968/305; 1980/707), **Austria** (1970/1947; 1979/117; 1994/768), **Azerbaijan** (1995/762) from 6 April 1996 (UK) and 1 January 1996 (Azerbaijan),

Bangladesh (1980/708), **Barbados** (1970/952; 1973/2096), **Belarus** (1995/2706) (and see note below), **Belgium** (1987/2053), **Belize** (1947/2866; 1968/573; 1973/2097), **Bolivia** (1995/2707) from 6 April 1996 (UK) and 1 January 1996 (Bolivia), **Bosnia-Hercegovina** (see note below), **Botswana** (1978/183), **British Honduras** (see Belize), **Brunei** (1950/1977; 1968/306; 1973/2098), **Bulgaria** (1987/2054), **Burma** (see Myanmar),

Canada (1980/709; 1980/780; 1980/1528; 1985/1996; 1987/2071; 1996/1782), **China** (1981/1119; 1984/1826; 1996/3164) (and see note below), **Croatia** (see note below), **Cyprus** (1975/425; 1980/1529), **Czech Republic** (see note below),

Denmark (1980/1960; 1991/2877; 1996/3165),

Eire (see 25.3 below), **Egypt** (1980/1091), **Estonia** (1994/3207) from 6 April 1995 (UK) and 1 January 1995 (Estonia),

Falkland Islands (1997/2985) from 6 April 1997 (UK) and 1 January 1997 (Falkland Islands), **Faroe Islands** (1961/579; 1971/717; 1975/2190) until 6 April 1997, **Fiji** (1976/1342), **Finland** (1970/153; 1980/710; 1985/1997; 1991/2878; 1996/3166), **France** (1968/1869; 1973/1328; 1987/466; 1987/2055),

Gambia (1980/1963), **Germany** (1967/25; 1971/874), **Ghana** (1993/1800, and see note below) from 6 April 1995 (UK) and 1 January 1995 (Ghana), **Greece** (1954/142), **Grenada** (1949/361; 1968/1867), **Guernsey** (1952/1215; 1994/3209), **Guyana** (1992/3207),

Hungary (1978/1056),

Iceland (1991/2879), **India** (1981/1120; 1993/1801), **Indonesia** (1994/769) from 6 April 1995 (UK) and 1 January 1995 (Indonesia), **Isle of Man** (1955/1205; 1991/2880; 1994/3208), **Israel** (1963/616; 1971/391), **Italy** (1990/2590), **Ivory Coast** (1987/169),

Jamaica (1973/1329), **Japan** (1970/1948; 1980/1530), **Jersey** (1952/1216; 1994/3210),

Kazakhstan (1994/3211; 1998/2567), **Kenya** (1977/1299), **Kiribati and Tuvalu** (1950/750; 1968/309; 1974/1271), **Korea (South)** (1996/3168) (new treaty applies from 6 April 1997 (UK) and 1 January 1997 (Korea)),

Latvia (1996/3167) from 6 April 1997 (UK) and 1 January 1997 (Latvia), **Lesotho** (1997/2986) from 6 April 1998 (UK) and 1 April 1998 (Lesotho), **Luxembourg** (1968/1100; 1980/567; 1984/364),

Macedonia (see note below), **Malawi** (1956/619; 1964/1401; 1968/1101; 1979/302), **Malaysia** (1973/1330; 1987/2056; 1997/2987) (new treaty applies from 6 April 1999 (UK) and 1 January 1999 and 1 January 2000 (Malaysia)), **Malta** (1995/763) (new treaty applies from 6 April 1996 (UK) and 1 January 1996 (Malta)), **Mauritius** (1981/1121; 1987/467), **Mexico** (1994/3212) from 6 April 1994, **Mongolia** (1996/2598) from 6 April 1997 (UK) and 1 January 1997 (Mongolia), **Montserrat** (1947/2869; 1968/576), **Morocco** (1991/2881), **Myanmar** (1952/751),

Namibia (1962/2352; 1967/1490), **Netherlands** (1967/1063; 1980/1961; 1983/1902; 1990/2152), **New Zealand** (1984/365), **Nigeria** (1987/2057), **Norway** (1985/1998),

Oman (1998/2568) from 6 April 1996 (UK) and 1 January 1996 (Oman),

Pakistan (1987/2058), **Papua New Guinea** (1991/2882), **Philippines** (1978/184), **Poland** (1978/282), **Portugal** (1969/599),

Romania (1977/57), **Russia** (1994/3213) from 6 April 1998 (UK) and 1 January 1998 (Russia)(and see note below),

St. Christopher (St. Kitts) and Nevis (1947/2872), **Sierra Leone** (1947/2873; 1968/1104), **Singapore** (1997/2988) from 6 April 1998 (UK) and 1 January 1999 (Singapore), **Slovak Republic** (see note below), **Slovenia** (see note below), **Solomon Islands** (1950/748; 1968/574; 1974/1270), **South Africa** (1969/864), **South West Africa** (see Namibia), **Spain** (1976/1919; 1995/765), **Sri Lanka** (1980/713), **Sudan** (1977/1719), **Swaziland** (1969/380), **Sweden** (1961/619; 1984/366), **Switzerland** (1978/1408; 1982/714; 1994/3215),

Thailand (1981/1546), **Trinidad and Tobago** (1983/1903), **Tunisia** (1984/133), **Turkey** (1988/932),

Uganda (1993/1802), **Ukraine** (1993/1803) (see note below), **U.S.A.** (1946/1331; 1955/499; 1961/985; 1980/568; 1980/779; 1994/1418; 1996/1781), **U.S.S.R.** (see note below), **Uzbekistan** (1994/770) from 6 April 1995 (UK) and 1 January 1995 (Uzbekistan) (and see note below),

Venezuela (1996/2599) from 6 April 1997 (UK) and 1 January 1997 (Venezuela), **Vietnam** (1994/3216) from 6 April 1995 (UK) and various dates (Vietnam),

Yugoslavia (see note below),

Zambia (1972/1721; 1981/1816), **Zimbabwe** (1982/1842).

Shipping & Air Transport only—Algeria (Air Transport only) (1984/362), Argentina (but see now above), Belarus (but see now above), Brazil (1968/572), Cameroon (Air Transport only) (1982/1841), China (Air Transport only) (1981/1119), Ethiopia (Air Transport only) (1977/1297), Hong Kong (Air Transport only) (1998/2566) from 6 April 1998 (UK) and 1 April 1998 (Hong Kong), Iran (Air Transport only) (1960/2419), Jordan (1979/300), Kuwait (Air Transport only) (1984/1825), Lebanon (1964/278), Russia (but see now above), Saudi Arabia (Air Transport only) (1994/767) from 3 October 1994, Venezuela (but see now above), U.S.S.R. (see note below), Ukraine (but see now above), Uzbekistan (but see now above), Zaire (1977/1298).

(*Notes. China.* The Convention published as *SI 1984 No 1826* does not apply to the Hong Kong Special Administrative Region which came into existence on 1 July 1997. (Revenue Tax Bulletin October 1996 p 357). See above as regards Air Transport agreement.

Czechoslovakia. The Convention published as *SI 1991 No 2876*, which took effect from 6 April 1992 (UK) and 1 January 1992 (Czechoslovakia), is treated as remaining in force between the UK and, respectively, the Czech Republic and the Slovak Republic. (Revenue Pamphlet IR 131, SP 5/93, 19 March 1993).

Ghana. The Convention published as *SI 1978 No 785* was subsequently found never to have been ratified in Ghana and consequently never to have had effect. The Arrangement published as *SR&O 1947 No 2868* with the Gold Coast accordingly continued in effect, and was reapplied from 6 April 1991 until such time as the new Convention (*SI 1993 No 1800*) came into effect. (Revenue Press Release 31 January 1991).

U.S.S.R. The Convention published as *SI 1986 No 224* (which also continued in force the air transport agreement published as *SI 1974 No 1269*) is to be regarded as having been in force between the UK and Uzbekistan and the Russian Federation, and as continuing in force in Belarus, until the coming into force of, respectively, *SI 1994 No 770*, *SI 1994 No 3213* and *SI 1995 No 2706*. As regards the other former Soviet Republics, the UK will continue to apply the provisions of that Convention on the basis that it is still in force until such time as new arrangements take effect with particular countries. (Revenue Tax Bulletin June 1998 p 559).

Yugoslavia. The Convention published as *SI 1981 No 1815* is treated as remaining in force between the UK and, respectively, Croatia, Slovenia, Macedonia, and the Federal Republic of Yugoslavia. The position as regards the remainder of former Yugoslavia remains to be established. (Revenue Tax Bulletin June 1998 p 559).)

25.3 **EIRE** [*ICTA 1988, s 68; FA 1994, s 207(5); SI 1976 Nos 2151, 2152; SI 1995 No 764; SI 1998 No 3151*]

A Convention and Protocol 1976 (as subsequently amended) replace previous provisions between UK and Eire (the Republic of Ireland (RI)). Shipping and air transport profits, certain trading profits not arising through a permanent establishment, interest, royalties, pensions (other than Government pensions and salaries which are normally taxed by the paying Government only) are taxed in the country of residence. Salaries, wages and other similar remuneration (including directors) is taxed in the country where earned unless the employer is non-resident and the employee is present for not more than 183 days in the fiscal year and is not paid by a permanent establishment.

The Revenue take the view that a website, or a server on which e-commerce is conducted through a website, is not of itself a permanent establishment. (Revenue Press Release 11 April 2000).

Where income is taxable in both countries, relief is given in the country of residence for the tax payable in the country of origin.

The recipient of a dividend from a company resident in the other country is entitled to the related tax credit (except where the recipient is a company which controls, alone or with associates, 10% or more of the voting power of the paying company). Income tax up to 15% of aggregate of dividend and tax credit may be charged in country of source (but not on charity or superannuation scheme exempt in other country).

Capital gains on immovable property (and assets of a permanent establishment or fixed base) are taxed in country where situate, and gains on other property in the taxpayer's country of residence with credit given in the other country if also taxed there.

A further Convention relates to inheritance tax (previously capital transfer tax) (UK) and capital acquisitions tax (RI). Relief attaches to the property subject to the charge and is given by each country allowing a credit against its own tax if the property is situated in the other country.

25.4 **UNILATERAL RELIEF BY UK** [*ICTA 1988, ss 790, 794*]

Taxes, other than those for which credit is available under the bilateral double tax agreements in 25.2 above, payable under the law of any territory outside the UK (and see 25.3 above for Eire) and computed by reference to income or gain *arising in that territory* are allowed (to the extent defined below) as a credit against UK income tax or corporation tax paid on that income or gain by UK residents. Relief is only available against UK tax chargeable under the same Schedule and Case as that under which the foreign income on which the foreign tax was borne is chargeable (*George Wimpey International Ltd v Rolfe Ch D 1989, 62 TC 597*). Where appropriate an apportionment must be made to determine what part of income may be regarded as 'arising in' the overseas territory, and in making that apportionment it is the principles of UK tax law which are to be applied (see *Yates v GCA International Ltd and cross-appeal Ch D 1991, 64 TC 37* and Revenue Pamphlet IR 131, SP 7/91, 26 July 1991). The machinery and limits (with modifications as below) are substantially the same as those under which the bilateral agreements operate and the credit given is, basically, such as would be allowable were a double taxation agreement in force with the territory concerned. [*ICTA 1988, s 790(1)–(4), s 794*]. See example in 25.8 below.

With effect from 21 March 2000, it is made clear that unilateral relief will not be allowed where credit could be claimed under a double tax agreement under 25.2 above, or in cases or circumstances in which such an agreement made on or after that date specifically prohibits relief. [*ICTA 1988, s 793A(2)(3); FA 2000, Sch 30 para 5*].

The modifications are:

(*a*) The foreign taxes must be charged on income or profits and correspond to income tax or corporation tax in the UK, but may include similar taxes payable under the law of a province, state or part of a country, or a municipality or other local body. [*ICTA 1988, s 790(12)*]. See *Yates v GCA International Ltd and cross-appeal Ch D 1991, 64 TC 37* where a tax imposed on gross receipts less a fixed 10% deduction was held to correspond to UK income tax or corporation tax. Following that decision, the Revenue amended their practice. (Revenue Pamphlet IR 131, SP 7/91, 26 July 1991). For claims made on or after 13 February 1991, and earlier claims unsettled at that date, foreign taxes will be examined to determine whether, in their own legislative context, they serve the same function as UK income and corporation taxes in relation to business profits, and are thus eligible for unilateral relief. As regards those overseas taxes which the Inland Revenue considers admissible (or inadmissible) for relief, these are listed by country in the Revenue Double Taxation Relief Manual, which is available for inspection at Tax Enquiry Centres, at D2100 *et seq.*. See also Revenue Inspector's Manual, IM 1121, and Revenue Tax Bulletin August 1995 p 244 and October 1996 p 358 as regards recent re-classification of certain South African, Algerian, Argentinian, Brazilian and Peruvian taxes. Current information may be obtained on 020–7438 6643.

(*b*) The restriction to tax on '*income or gain arising in the territory*' does not apply in the case of the Channel Islands or the Isle of Man, and credit is given for CI or IOM tax if the claimant is resident for the particular year of assessment or accounting period either in the UK or the Channel Islands, or IOM as the case may be. [*ICTA 1988, s 790(5)(a), s 794(2)(a)*].

(*c*) Income from personal or professional services performed in a territory is deemed to arise in that territory, and credit for overseas tax on income from employments, etc. (where duties wholly or mainly performed in the overseas territory) is given against income tax under Schedule E on that income if the claimant is resident for the year of assessment either in UK or in the overseas territory. [*ICTA 1988, s 790(4), s 794(2)(b)*].

(*d*) Where an overseas company carries on a banking business through a UK branch or agency and suffers foreign tax on interest on a foreign loan made through that branch etc., double tax relief is available as if the UK branch were a UK bank. Tax payable in a country where the overseas company is taxable by reason of its domicile, residence or place of management is excluded. [*ICTA 1988, s 794(2)(c)*]. For accounting periods ending after 20 March 2000, this is replaced by a wider relief available on similar terms to all non-UK resident persons (whether companies or individuals) with UK branches or agencies. [*ICTA 1988, s 794(2)(bb); FA 2000, Sch 30 para 4(4)–(6)(14)*].

Foreign tax levied by reference to the value of assets employed to produce income chargeable to UK tax may, in practice, be allowed as a business expense under normal Schedule D, Case I rules. (Revenue International Tax Handbook, ITH 602).

Simon's Direct Tax Service. See **F1.145** *et seq.*.

25.5 **SPECIFIC MATTERS**

(*a*) **Alimony.** Where alimony payments etc. under UK Court Order or agreement (technically a UK source) are made by an overseas resident, concessional relief by way of credit is allowed where (i) the payments are made out of the overseas income of the payer and subject to tax there, (ii) UK income tax if deducted from the payments is duly accounted for, and (iii) the payee is resident in the UK and effectively bears the overseas tax. (Revenue Pamphlet IR 1, A12).

(*b*) (i) **Amounts assessable in UK on the remittance basis.** Where double tax credit for foreign tax is allowable in respect of it, any income which is assessable on the basis of *remittance* is treated, for UK assessment purposes, as increased by the *foreign tax* on that income (but ignoring any notional tax under (*h*) below). [*ICTA 1988, s 795(1)(3)*].

(ii) **Amounts assessable in UK on the arising basis.** Where income or gain is assessable to income tax or corporation tax on the basis of the full amount arising (not on remittance as in (i) above), and double tax credit is allowable in respect of foreign tax suffered on it, *no deduction* may be made for foreign tax on that, or any other, income or gain.

If the income is a dividend, credit is given for foreign taxes deducted from the dividend plus (either if provided for under the specific terms of a double tax agreement *or* if covered by unilateral relief under *ICTA 1988, s 790(6)*, which only applies to UK recipient companies with 10% holdings, etc., in the overseas company) 'underlying tax', being overseas taxes paid on the profits of the paying company (but ignoring any notional tax under (*h*) below). If credit for underlying tax is available, then the dividend is grossed-up by such tax for UK assessment purposes. [*ICTA 1988, s 795(2)*]. See further details in Tolley's Corporation Tax.

(iii) **If the taxpayer does not take any credit** by way of either bilateral or unilateral relief, or if no UK double tax credit is otherwise allowable in respect of foreign income, any foreign tax paid on that income in the place where it arises is deductible from the income for purposes of UK assessment, *except* where the UK assessment is on the basis of *remittances* to the UK. Where foreign tax for which such a deduction has been given is subsequently adjusted after 20 March 2000, similar provisions to those which apply by virtue of *ICTA 1988, s 806(3)–(6)* in the case of foreign tax credits (see 25.5(*e*) below) apply as regards the requirement to notify the Revenue of the adjustment and extended time limit for assessments, etc.. [*ICTA 1988, ss 805, 811; FA 2000, Sch 30 para 27*].

(*c*) **Business Profits.** Where a UK resident pays tax in an overseas country on *business profits* arising there, that tax is allowed as a business expense if no double tax credit is allowable against UK tax on those profits, or the right to credit is forgone.

(*d*) **Capital Gains.** Relief for foreign taxes on *capital gains* is given against, and is limited to, the amount of UK capital gains tax on those gains. [*TCGA 1992, s 277*]. Capital gains accruing to companies are subject to corporation tax, and relief is available accordingly.

(*da*) **Utilisation of unused relief.** The provisions which, from 31 March 2001, permit companies to pool certain dividends for the purposes of relief of eligible unrelieved tax, and also allow a limited carry back or carry forward or sideways of unused relief (see Tolley's Corporation Tax under Double Tax Relief) apply *mutatis mutandis* to unrelieved foreign tax in respect of any dividend income arising after 30 March 2001 to a UK branch or agency of a non-UK resident person. Such relief must be claimed (specifying the amount to which each of the available options is to apply) within six years of the end of the chargeable period in which the unrelieved foreign tax arose (or, if later, within one year of the end of the chargeable period in which the foreign tax in question is paid). [*ICTA 1988, s 806K; FA 2000, Sch 30 para 22*].

(*e*) **Claims** for credit under double tax arrangements must be made within, for 1996/97 and later years, five years after 31 January following the tax year in which the income or gain falls to be charged to tax (for earlier years, six years after the end of that tax year) or, for corporation tax purposes, six years after the end of the accounting period concerned. After 20 March 2000, claims may be made (if later) up to (for income tax) 31 January following the tax year in which the foreign tax is paid or (for corporation tax) one year after the end of the accounting period in which the foreign tax is paid. [*ICTA 1988, s 806(1); FA 1996, s 135, Sch 21 para 23; FA 2000, Sch 30 para 20*]. Claims in respect of overlap profits (see (*j*) below) must be made within, for 1996/97 and later years, five years after 31 January following the latest tax year for which relief is due (for earlier years and also as regards claims in respect of opening years (see (*j*) below), six years after the latest such tax year). [*ICTA 1988, s 804(7); FA 1996, s 135, Sch 21 para 22*].

Written notice must be given to the Revenue where any credit allowed for foreign tax has become excessive by reason of an adjustment of the amount of any foreign tax payable (except in the case of Lloyd's UNDERWRITERS (89) where the consequences of such an adjustment are dealt with under regulations). This applies to adjustments made on or after 17 March 1998, and the notice must be given within one year after the making of the adjustment. The maximum penalty for failure to comply is the amount by which the credit was rendered excessive by the adjustment. The time limit for assessments etc. to be revised following such an adjustment is extended to six years after the adjustment is finalised. [*ICTA 1988, s 806(2)–(6); FA 1998, s 107*]. For the Revenue view of what constitutes an 'adjustment', and when an adjustment is made, see Revenue Tax Bulletin June 1999 p 673.

Claims for relief other than by way of credit must made to the Board. [*ICTA 1988, s 788(6)*]. For appeals, see 64.8 RESIDENCE, ORDINARY RESIDENCE AND DOMICILE. Pending final agreement a provisional allowance can usually be obtained on application to the inspector.

(*f*) **Exchange rate.** Foreign tax is normally converted into sterling at the rate of exchange obtaining on the date it became payable. (Revenue Double Taxation Relief Manual, DT 845). Where part of foreign tax repaid and sterling was devalued in the period between payment and repayment, held relief due on net tax in foreign currency at the old rate (*Greig v Ashton Ch D 1956, 36 TC 581*).

(*g*) **Limit on Relief.** Where income is chargeable to *UK income tax*, credit for foreign tax suffered on that income is set against the income tax chargeable in respect of the doubly-taxed income. [*ICTA 1988, ss 790(4), 793*]. But the relief is limited to the *difference* between the income tax (before double tax relief, but after any other income tax reduction) which would be borne by the claimant

(i) if he were charged on his *total income* (computed as in (*b*) above), and

(ii) if he were charged on that income *excluding* the income in respect of which the credit is to be allowed. [*ICTA 1988, s 796; FA 1994, Sch 8 para 12*].

In no case may total double tax credits exceed the total income tax payable by the claimant for the year of assessment (less any income tax he is entitled to charge against any other person and any tax deemed to have been deducted at source from a charitable donation made after 5 April 2000 under the Gift Aid scheme). [*ICTA 1988, s 796(3); FA 1990, s 25(6)(b); FA 2000, s 39(6)(10)*].

For claims made after 20 March 2000, it is in addition provided that relief is limited to that which would be allowed if all reasonable steps had been taken, including all relevant claims, elections, etc., under the law of the territory concerned or under double tax arrangements with that territory, to minimise the foreign tax payable.

Guidance is to be published on what the Revenue considers taxpayers can and cannot reasonably be expected to do, but the former is likely to include appeals against excessive assessments, claims for reliefs generally known to be available, and selection of any option which produces a lower tax liability, and the latter is likely to include claims to reliefs whose availability is uncertain, and where disproportionate expenditure would be required to pursue a claim, substituting carry-forward claims for carry-back claims and *vice versa*, and attempting to exercise influence the taxpayer does not have on the underlying tax paid by a subsidiary. [*ICTA 1988, s 795A; FA 2000, Sch 30 para 6*].

(*h*) **Lloyd's UNDERWRITERS (89).** For special arrangements for double tax relief for underwriters, in particular under SELF-ASSESSMENT (78), see *SI 1997 No 405*.

(*i*) **Notional Tax.** Under *ICTA 1988, s 788(5)* it may be provided that any tax which would have been payable in a foreign country but for a relief under the law of that territory given with a view to promoting industrial, commercial, scientific, educational or other development therein is nevertheless treated for purposes of credit against UK tax as if it had been paid. For example, credit is given for tax given up by Singapore under Singapore *Economic Expansion Incentives (Relief from Income Tax) Act 1967* (Revenue Press Release 9 May 1969) and by Malaysia under *sections 21, 22, 26* of *Malaysian Investment Incentives Act 1968* (Revenue Press Release 5 March 1970). For restrictions on relief available to companies in respect of such notional tax, see Tolley's Corporation Tax under Double Tax Relief.

(*j*) **Opening and Closing Years** [*ICTA 1988, s 804 as originally enacted*]. The following provisions apply for 1995/96 and earlier years as regards trades, professions and vocations commenced, and other sources of income first arising, before 6 April 1994 (see also (*n*) below). Credit for foreign tax paid in respect of income arising in the first three years of assessment on a new source of income (including, for Cases I & II of Schedule D, any period overlapping the end of those three years if the profits of that period affect the assessment for a later year) is allowed against UK income tax chargeable for any year in respect of that income, notwithstanding that credit for that foreign tax has already been allowed in an earlier year.

There are overriding provisions limiting the credit allowable for any year by reference to the total of credit due for all the relevant years above, and for cases where the number of UK periods of assessment exceeds the number of foreign periods. Also provision for recovery, by Case VI assessment, of excessive credit arising from operation of the ceased source rules so far as any income fails thereunder to enter into any basis period for assessment.

Overlap profits [*ICTA 1988, s 804; FA 1994, s 217; FA 1996, s 135, Sch 21 para 22*]. For 1994/95 and subsequent years as regards trades, etc. commenced after 5 April 1994 and for 1996/97 and subsequent years as regards those commenced on or before that date, provisions similar to those above apply by reference to 'overlap profits' (see 71.19 SCHEDULE D, CASES I AND II) arising in taxing a trade, etc. Recovery of excess credit applies where, and to the extent that, relief is given for overlap profits either on cessation of the trade or on a change of accounting date resulting in a basis period of longer than twelve months. Recovery is achieved by reducing the credit otherwise available for the year of relief and, if there is still an excess, by assessment under Case VI.

See also (*n*) below.

(*k*) **Partnerships.** It was held in the case of *Padmore v CIR CA 1989, 62 TC 352* that, where profits of a non-UK resident partnership were exempt under the relevant double tax treaty, the profit share of a UK resident partner was thereby also exempt.

This decision was, however, reversed by subsequent legislation with retrospective effect, see 53.15 PARTNERSHIPS.

(*ka*) **Prevention of double relief.** For claims made after 20 March 2000, credit may not be given for foreign tax for which relief is available in the territory in which it would otherwise be payable, either under the law of that territory in consequence of any double tax agreement or in cases or circumstances in which such an agreement made on or after that date specifically prohibits relief. [*ICTA 1988, s 793A(1); FA 2000, Sch 30 para 5*].

(*l*) **Royalties and 'know-how' payments.** Notwithstanding that credit for overseas tax is ordinarily given only against income which arises (or is deemed to arise) in the overseas territory concerned, the Revenue treatment as regards this class of income is as follows.

Income payments made by an overseas resident to a UK trader for the use, in that overseas territory, of any *copyright, patent, design, secret process or formula, trade mark, etc.*, may be treated, for credit purposes (whether under double tax agreements or by way of unilateral relief) as income arising outside the UK — *except* so far as they represent consideration for services (other than merely incidental) rendered in the UK by the recipient to the payer (Revenue Pamphlet IR 1, B8).

For the treatment of sales of 'know-how' etc., see 71.67 SCHEDULE D, CASES I AND II.

(*m*) **Transfer pricing.** Under Convention *90/463/EEC*, Member States are required to adopt certain procedures, and to follow the opinion of an advisory commission, in transfer pricing disputes. *ICTA 1988, s 815B* makes provision for domestic legislation and double tax agreements to be overridden where necessary under the Convention (which came into force on 1 January 1995). [*F(No 2)A 1992, s 51*]. See 3.9 ANTI-AVOIDANCE.

(*n*) **Transitional provisions on changeover from preceding year to current year basis of assessment.** Special provisions apply as regards trades, professions and vocations commenced before 6 April 1994 and sources of income within Schedule D, Cases IV and V first arising before that date, where the trade, etc. or other source continues (uninterrupted) beyond 6 April 1997.

(1) Where the assessment for 1996/97 is itself computed under the transitional rules in 71.20 SCHEDULE D, CASES I AND II or 73.9 SCHEDULE D, CASES IV AND V (such that a percentage of the profits/income of an extended basis period is charged to tax), any credit for foreign tax is similarly computed.

(2) Where credit has been given for foreign tax in respect of the opening years of assessment under *ICTA 1988, s 804 as originally enacted* (see (*j*) above) and the trade or other source later ceases, recovery of any excess credit is made by assessment under Case VI. The excess credit is calculated as if no income had escaped tax under the transitional rules mentioned in (1) above and as if (1) above had itself not applied.

(3) Where the trade, etc. ceases in 1997/98 or 1998/99 and either of the directions in 71.24 SCHEDULE D, CASES I AND II is given, or the source of Case IV or V income ceases before 6 April 1998, (1) and (2) above do not apply and *ICTA 1988, s 804* has effect as originally enacted (see (*j*) above).

(4) In applying the transitional rules mentioned in (1) above, any double tax relief to be given by deduction under *ICTA 1988, s 811* because no credit is allowable (see (*b*)(iii) above) is given *before* applying the appropriate percentage.

[*FA 1994, Sch 20 paras 10–14; FA 1995, s 122(4)(5)*].

25.6 **PAYMENTS ABROAD BY UK RESIDENTS**

Interest, etc.. Under *SI 1970 No 488* (as amended) a UK resident paying to a resident of a country with which the UK has a double tax agreement income which under that agreement is wholly or partially relieved (other than a dividend or other distribution by a company) may be required, by notice from the Board of Inland Revenue, to make such payments without deducting UK income tax, or under deduction of tax at, or not exceeding, a specified rate. Applications for such relief from deduction should be sent to Inland Revenue, FICO (International), Fitzroy House, PO Box 46, Nottingham NG2 1BD. Where a notice is given, the payer, if otherwise chargeable with, or liable to account for, tax on such payments (under *ICTA 1988, s 349*, etc., see 23.3 DEDUCTION OF TAX AT SOURCE) is exempted from that liability if the notice requires him to pay the income gross, and in other cases need account for tax only at the rate specified. The payer may, nevertheless, treat the gross amount of the payment as a loss for relief purposes, while if the payment is made by a company it is treated for purposes of *ICTA 1988, s 338(4)* as if tax has been deducted from it and accounted for under *ICTA 1988, s 349*. Where the payer would have been entitled (under *ICTA 1988, s 348*) to retain the tax deducted (as having made the payment out of income subjected to income tax) he is given, against the income tax otherwise payable by him for that year, an allowance equal to the additional tax which, but for the notice, he would have been entitled to deduct from the payment.

For Revenue practice in relation to claims for payment of interest to non-residents without deduction of tax, and in particular where payments are made in full in advance of the issue (or refusal) of a gross payment notice, see Revenue Tax Bulletin August 1994 p 153.

For review of applications for relief from deduction where loans are re-denominated from one currency to another (e.g. to or from the euro), see Revenue Tax Bulletin February 1999 pp 631, 632.

Provisional relief. From 1 September 1999, a Provisional Treaty Relief scheme is introduced for two types of loan, the one-to-one company loan (provided that there is no common shareholding or ownership) and the syndicated loan, where there is a syndicate manager. This allows the UK borrower to apply for immediate authority to make payments incorporating the treaty relief, pending FICO's decision on the issue of a formal notice. It is a condition of the scheme that the recipient's application for relief (certified by the overseas tax authority) is received by FICO within three months of the provisional authority, and if that condition is not met, or the relief is found not to be due, FICO will look to the payer for the tax that should have been deducted (and any interest thereon). In the case of a syndicated loan, the requirement is for a composite application for relief (which does not need overseas tax authority certification) which must be made by the syndicate manager within three months of the provisional authority. Application for provisional relief is made on form PTRPAY1 (in the case of one-to-one loans) or form PTRSM1 (in the case of syndicated loans), which may be obtained from Complex Claims Group (Provisional Treaty Relief Scheme), FICO, Fitz Roy House, PO Box 46, Nottingham NG2 1BD (tel. 0115-974 1904, fax. 0115-974 1918). Explanatory 'Guidelines' may be obtained from the same address. For a summary of the scheme, see Revenue Tax Bulletin June 1999 pp 668–670.

Dividends. Under *SI 1973 No 317*, the Revenue may make arrangements with a UK resident company whereby it may pay to a non-resident shareholder that part of the tax credit relating to a dividend to which he is entitled under the terms of a double tax agreement. See Tolley's Corporation Tax (under Double Tax Relief). All such arrangements cease on 6 April 1999. [*SI 1999 No 1927*]. See generally Revenue Tax Bulletin February 1999 pp 626, 627.

25.7 **COMPANIES**

Companies enjoy the benefit of the foregoing double tax reliefs and they can in certain circumstances claim relief for underlying taxes in respect of overseas dividends receivable by them (being the overseas taxes borne by the paying company on its profits). See 25.5(*b*)(ii) above and Tolley's Corporation Tax (under Double Tax Relief).

25.8 **EXAMPLE OF RELIEF BY CREDIT**

A single man has, for 2000/01, UK earnings of £16,000 and foreign income from property of £2,000 on which foreign tax of £400 has been paid. He is entitled to the personal allowance of £4,385.

(*a*) *Tax on total income*

Earnings	16,000	
Income from property	2,000 (foreign tax £400)	
	18,000	
Personal allowance	4,385	
Taxable income	£13,615	
Tax on £13,615 @ 10/22%		£2,812.90

(*b*) *Tax on total income less foreign income*

Earnings	16,000	
Personal allowance	4,385	
Taxable income	£11,615	
Tax on £11,615 @ 10/22%		£2,372.90

The difference in tax between (*a*) and (*b*) is £440. The foreign tax is less than this and full credit of £400 is available against the UK tax payable. If the foreign tax was £600, the credit would be limited to £440 and the balance of £160 would be unrelieved.

26 Enterprise Investment Scheme (and BES)

(See also Revenue Pamphlets IR137 and (as regards the BES) IR51 and IR85.)

26.1 The Enterprise Investment Scheme ('EIS') was introduced by *FA 1994, s 137, Sch 15* in respect of shares issued on or after 1 January 1994. It 'revives' the earlier legislation governing the Business Expansion Scheme ('BES'), which was withdrawn by *F(No 2)A 1992* for shares issued after 31 December 1993, but with substantial amendment. The EIS is described at 26.2 *et seq.* below. The BES is dealt with at 26.18 *et seq.* below.

Revenue practices and concessions which apply to the BES are, where relevant, carried forward to the EIS.

The EIS is dealt with in this chapter under the following headings.

26.2 Conditions for relief
26.3 — qualifying individual
26.4 — eligible shares
26.5 — qualifying company
26.6 — qualifying business activity
26.7 — qualifying trade
26.8 Form of relief
26.9 — example
26.10 Limits on relief
26.11 Claims for relief
26.12 Restriction or withdrawal of relief
26.13 — examples
26.14 Subsidiary companies
26.15 Married persons
26.16 EIS company becoming wholly-owned subsidiary of new holding company
26.17 Miscellaneous

See generally Revenue Inspector's Manual, IM 6925–7044.

Simon's Direct Tax Service. See E3.1.

26.2 **CONDITIONS FOR RELIEF**

A 'qualifying individual' is eligible for relief under the EIS if

(*a*) 'eligible shares' in a 'qualifying company' for which he has subscribed (wholly in cash as regards shares issued after 5 April 1998) are issued to him fully paid up (without taking account of any undertaking to pay cash to the company at a future date),

(*b*) those shares (and, for issues after 5 April 1998, all other shares comprised in the same issue) are issued to raise money (i.e. cash, see *Thompson v Hart Ch D, [2000] STC 381*) for the purpose of a 'qualifying business activity', and

(*c*) the money so raised (or all but an insignificant amount of it) is employed wholly for that purpose by the end of the twelve months following the issue or, if the only 'qualifying business activity' falls within 26.6(*a*) below, and if later, by the end of the twelve months starting when the company (or subsidiary) began to carry on the 'qualifying trade'.

With effect from 27 November 1996, there is an additional condition that the 'active company' must, throughout the 'relevant period' (as defined in 26.6 below), either:

(i) be within 26.5(*a*) below; or

(ii) be such a company as would be within (i) if its purposes were disregarded to the extent that they consist

(A) in holding shares in or securities of, or making loans to, any of the company's subsidiaries, or

(B) in holding and managing property used by the company or any of its subsidiaries either for research and development (as defined) from which a 'qualifying trade' (see 26.7 below) to be carried on by any of them is intended to be derived, or for the purposes of a 'qualifying trade' or trades carried on by any of them, or

(C) in making loans to the parent company; or

(iii) be a '90% subsidiary' of the 'qualifying company' which either

(A) apart from purposes capable of having no significant effect (other than on incidental matters) on the extent of its activities, exists wholly for the purpose of carrying on activities consisting in holding and managing property used by the company or any of its subsidiaries either for research and development (as defined) from which a qualifying trade to be carried on by any of them is intended to be derived, or for the purposes of a qualifying trade or trades carried on by any of them, or

(B) has no corporation tax profits and no part of its business consists in the making of investments.

The '*active company*' is the 'qualifying company' unless the 'qualifying business activity' consists in a subsidiary of the 'qualifying company' carrying on or preparing to carry on a 'qualifying trade', research and development or oil exploration (see below), in which case it is that subsidiary. Due to a defect in *Finance Act 1998*, it was sufficient as regards shares issued after 5 April 1998 and before 6 April 1999 for the active subsidiary to be a 75% subsidiary of the qualifying company. As regards shares issued after 5 April 1999, reverting to the rules for those issued before 6 April 1998, it must be a '90% subsidiary'.

For these purposes, a '*90% subsidiary*' is a subsidiary that would satisfy the conditions given at 26.14(*a*) below if references to 90% were substituted for references to 75% and, as regards shares issued after 5 April 1998, the let-out for *bona fide* commercial disposals of interests in the subsidiary were disregarded.

Although a winding-up or dissolution in the relevant period generally prevents a company meeting the above conditions, they are deemed met if the winding-up or dissolution is for *bona fide* commercial reasons and not part of a scheme a main purpose of which is tax avoidance, with the additional proviso before 21 March 2000 that any net assets are distributed to members (or dealt with as *bona vacantia*) before the end of the relevant period or (if later) the end of three years from the commencement of winding-up. After 20 March 2000 (both in relation to shares issued after that date and to pre-existing shares to which EIS income tax relief or capital gains tax deferral relief remains attributable), a company does not cease to meet the above conditions by reason of anything done as a consequence of its being in administration or receivership (both as defined by *ICTA 1988, s 312(2A)*), provided everything so done and the making of the relevant order are for *bona fide* commercial (and not tax avoidance) reasons.

[*ICTA 1988, s 289(1)–(1D)(3)(9), s 312(1); FA 1994, Sch 15 para 2; FA 1997, Sch 8 paras 1, 2; FA 1998, s 74, Sch 13 para 1(1)(2)(5); FA 1999, s 71; FA 2000, Sch 17 paras 9(2), 12, 15*].

(*b*) above will not be satisfied where money is raised to acquire shares in a company carrying on a qualifying trade unless the intention is to hive up the trade without any avoidable delay. (Revenue Inspector's Manual, IM 6972a). As regards (*c*) above, cash whose retention can reasonably be regarded as necessary or advisable for financing current trade requirements is regarded as employed for trade purposes provided it is readily available for use in that way. Money raised to meet the expenses of the share issue is ignored. (Revenue Inspector's Manual, IM 6974).

Relief is denied unless the shares are subscribed for and issued for *bona fide* commercial purposes and not as part of a scheme or arrangement a main purpose of which is the avoidance of tax. [*ICTA 1988, s 289(6); FA 1994, Sch 15 para 2; FA 1998, s 74, Sch 13 para 1(3)*].

Relief is available where eligible shares are held on a bare trust for two or more beneficiaries as if each beneficiary had subscribed as an individual for all of those shares, and as if the amount subscribed by each was the total subscribed divided by the number of beneficiaries. [*ICTA 1988, s 311(2); FA 1994, Sch 15 para 26(a)*].

Relief is also available where shares are subscribed for by a nominee for the individual claiming relief, including the managers of an investment fund approved by the Board for this purpose (an '*approved fund*'). With regard to an approved fund closed for the acceptance of further investments, the provisions of *ICTA 1988, ss 289A, 289B* (dealing with the form and attribution of relief, see 26.8 below) apply as if the eligible shares were issued at the time at which the fund was closed, provided that the amount subscribed on behalf of the individual for eligible shares issued within six months after the closure of the fund is not less than 90% of the individual's investment in the fund. [*ICTA 1988, s 311(1)(2A)(2B); FA 1988, s 53; FA 1994, Sch 15 para 26(b)*]. The Revenue have published guidelines setting out the principal criteria used in deciding whether to approve an investment fund for this purpose, and covering the procedures to be followed in applying for approval. They are available free of charge from Brian Lodde, Inland Revenue, Company Tax Division, Room M22, West Wing, Somerset House, London WC2R 1LB.

For the manner in which the scheme operates where a company wishes to raise money by a single issue of shares either partly for preparing to carry on a trade and partly for the subsequent carrying on of that trade, or for more than one qualifying business activity (e.g. for a trade carried on by one subsidiary and for research and development carried on by another), see Revenue Tax Bulletin April 1996 pp 305, 306.

For the date on which shares are issued, see *National Westminster Bank plc v CIR; Barclays Bank plc v CIR HL 1994, 67 TC 1.*

26.3 A '*qualifying individual*' is an individual who subscribes for the 'eligible shares' on his own behalf and who (except as below) is not at any time in the 'designated period' — see below (as regards shares issued before 6 April 1998, at any time in the 'relevant period' — see below) 'connected with' the issuing company (i.e. provided that there is no such connection at any time in that period, see *Wild v Cannavan CA 1997, 70 TC 554*). He is '*connected with*' the issuing company) if he is either:

(*a*) an employee, partner, or director of, or an employee or director of a partner of, the issuing company or any 'subsidiary'; or

(*b*) an individual who directly or indirectly possesses or is entitled to acquire (whether he is so entitled at a future date or will at a future date be so entitled)

   (i) more than 30% of the voting power, the issued ordinary share capital, or the loan capital and issued share capital of the issuing company or any 'subsidiary' (loan capital including any debt incurred by the company for money borrowed, for capital assets acquired, for any right to income created in its favour, or for insufficient consideration, but excluding a debt incurred for overdrawing a bank account in the ordinary course of the bank's business), or

   (ii) such rights as would entitle him to more than 30% of the assets of the issuing company or any 'subsidiary' available for distribution to the company's equity holders (as under *ICTA 1988, Sch 18 paras 1, 3* — see Tolley's Corporation Tax under Groups of Companies); or (*c*) an individual who has control (as defined by *ICTA 1988, s 840*, see 20.8 CONNECTED PERSONS) of the issuing company or any 'subsidiary'; or

(*d*) an individual who subscribes for shares in the issuing company as part of an arrangement providing for another person to subscribe for shares in another company with which, were that other company an issuing company, the individual (or any other individual party to the arrangement) would be connected as above,

and rights or powers of 'associates' (within *ICTA 1988, s 417(3)(4)* but excluding a brother or sister) are taken into account in determining what he is entitled to acquire for the purposes of (*b*) above (see *Cook v Billings Ch D, [1999] STC 661* on the similar wording under the earlier BES provisions, see 26.20 below).

As regards (*b*)(i) above, an individual is not connected with the company by virtue only of the fact that he or an associate is a shareholder if at that time the company has issued no shares other than subscriber shares and has neither commenced business nor made preparations for doing so. This applies by statute in relation to shares issued after 5 April 1998, but a similar exclusion, aimed at the investor who acquires one of two subscriber shares in a company from company formation agents, previously applied by concession (Revenue Pamphlet IR 1, A76).

A '*subsidiary*' for these purposes is a company more than 50% of whose ordinary share capital is at any time in the 'relevant period' owned by the issuing company, regardless of whether or not that condition is fulfilled while the individual falls within (*a*)–(*d*) above in respect of it.

As regards (*a*) above, directorships are taken into account only where the individual or an associate (or a partnership of which either of them is a member) receives or is entitled to receive, during the 'designated period' — see below (as regards shares issued before 6 April 1998, during the 'relevant period'), a payment (whether directly or indirectly or to his order or for his benefit) from the issuing company or a 'related person' other than by way of

(i) payment or reimbursement of allowable expenditure under Schedule E,

(ii) interest at no more than a commercial rate on money lent,

(iii) dividends, etc. representing no more than a normal return on investment,

(iv) payment for supply of goods at no more than market value,

(v) rent at no more than a reasonable and commercial rent for property occupied, or

(vi) any reasonable and necessary remuneration for services rendered (other than secretarial or managerial services, or those rendered by the payer) which is chargeable under Schedule D, Case I or II,

and a '*related person*' is any company of which the individual or an associate is a director and which is a subsidiary of the issuing company, or a partner of the issuing company or a subsidiary, 'subsidiary' for this purpose requiring ownership of more than 50% of ordinary share capital at some time in the 'relevant period'.

For these purposes, in the case of a person who is both a director and an employee of a company, references to him in his capacity as a director include him in his capacity as an employee, but otherwise he is not treated as an employee.

The '*designated period*' for these purposes is

(1) (for shares issued after 5 April 2000) the period beginning two years before the issue of the shares and ending immediately before the third anniversary of the issue date or, if later and where relevant, the third anniversary of the date of commencement of the intended trade referred to in 26.6(*a*) below; or

(2) (for shares issued before 6 April 2000) the seven-year period beginning two years before the issue of the shares.

The '*relevant period*' for these purposes is the period beginning with the incorporation of the company or, if later, two years before the date of issue of the shares and ending

(I) (for shares issued after 5 April 2000) immediately before the third anniversary of the issue date or, if later and where relevant, the third anniversary of the date of commencement of the intended trade referred to in 26.6(*a*) below; or

(II) (for shares issued before 6 April 2000) five years after the issue date.

An individual who is connected with the issuing company may nevertheless qualify for relief if he is so connected only by reason of his (or his associate's) being a director of (or of a partner of) the issuing company or any subsidiary receiving, or entitled to receive, remuneration (including any benefit or facility) as such, provided that:

(A) the remuneration (leaving out any within (vi) above) is reasonable remuneration for services rendered to the company as a director;

(B) he subscribed for eligible shares in the company at a time when he had never been either

(i) connected with the issuing company, or

(ii) involved (as sole trader, employee, partner or director) in carrying on its (or its subsidiary's) trade, business, profession or vocation (or any part thereof) (in relation to shares issued before 6 April 1998, an employee of a person who had previously carried on the issuing company's trade etc. or part thereof),

and where those conditions are satisfied in relation to an issue of eligible shares, subsequent issues are treated as fulfilling (B) where they would not otherwise do so, provided that they are made within three years (for shares issued before 6 April 2000, five years) of the date of the last issue which did fulfil (B). Where relevant, and in relation only to shares issued after 5 April 2000, the said three-year period is replaced by a longer period beginning with the date of the last such issue and ending with the date of commencement of the intended trade referred to in 26.6(*a*) below.

Parallel trades. For shares issued **before 29 November 1994**, relief may be denied if, on the date of issue of the shares (or, if later, the date on which the company commences trading) the individual is both one of a group of persons who either control the company (within *ICTA 1988, s 416*) or together own more than a half share (determined as under *ICTA 1988, s 344(1)(a)(b)(2)(3)*) in the trade carried on by the company, and also, individually or as one of a group, so controls another company or has such an interest in another trade, business, profession or vocation. Where the trade (or a substantial part of it) carried on by the issuing company is concerned with the same or similar types of property or provides the same or similar services or facilities, and serves substantially the same outlets or markets, as the other trade etc. or the trade etc. carried on by the other company, the individual will not qualify for relief in respect of any shares in the issuing company. Rights and powers of associates are taken into account, as are trades etc. carried on by companies more than 50% of whose ordinary share capital is, at the relevant date (as above), owned by the company concerned.

[*ICTA 1988, ss 291, 291A, 291B, 292, 312(1)(1A)(a); FA 1994, Sch 15 paras 5, 6; FA 1995, s 66(2); FA 1998, s 74, Sch 13 paras 6–8, 23, Sch 27 Pt III(14); FA 2000, Sch 17 paras 2, 3, 6(2)–(4)*].

Simon's Direct Tax Service. See **E3.106** *et seq.*.

26.4 '*Eligible shares*' are new ordinary shares which, throughout the three years beginning with the date of issue (five years for shares issued before 6 April 2000), carry no present or future preferential right to dividends or to assets on a winding-up and no present or future right (for shares issued before 6 April 1998, present or future preferential right) to redemption. If, for shares issued after 5 April 2000, the company satisfied the qualifying business activity requirement by virtue of 26.6(*a*) below and the trade had not yet commenced on the issue date, these conditions must be satisfied throughout the period from date of issue to immediately before the third anniversary of commencement. [*ICTA 1988, ss 289(7), 312(1); FA 1994, Sch 15 para 2; FA 1998, s 74, Sch 13 para 1(4), Sch 27 Pt III(14); FA 2000, Sch 17 paras 1, 6(3), 8*].

26.5 A '*qualifying company*' may be resident in the UK or elsewhere. It must, throughout the 'relevant period' (see 26.6 below), be 'unquoted' and either

(*a*) exist wholly for the purpose of carrying on one or more 'qualifying trades' (see 26.7 below) (disregarding purposes incapable of having any significant effect on the extent of the company's activities), or

(*b*) be the 'parent company of a trading group'.

Before 27 November 1996, condition (*b*) above required the business of the company to consist of holding shares in or securities of, or making loans to, 'qualifying subsidiaries' (see 26.14 below), with or without the carrying on of one or more qualifying trades. Under similar BES provisions to those applicable before 27 November 1996, a company falling within (*a*) for part of the relevant period and within (*b*) for the remainder was regarded as meeting the condition throughout the period. (ICAEW Technical Memorandum TR831, 19 April 1991).

A company is '*unquoted*' if none of its shares, etc. are listed on a recognised stock exchange or on a foreign exchange designated for the purpose, or dealt in on the Unlisted Securities Market (now closed) or outside the UK by such means as may be designated for the purpose. Securities on the Alternative Investment Market ('AIM') are treated as unquoted for these purposes. (Revenue Press Release 20 February 1995). If it is unquoted at the time of the share issue, it does not cease to be unquoted in relation to those shares solely because they are listed on an exchange which becomes a recognised stock exchange or is designated by an order made after the date of the issue (see Revenue Inspector's Manual, IM 6986).

The '*parent company of a trading group*' is a company all of whose subsidiaries are 'qualifying subsidiaries' (see 26.14 below) provided that, in relation to the business consisting of the activities, taken together, of the company and its subsidiaries, neither the business nor a substantial part of it consists in either or both of

(I) excluded activities within 26.7(*a*)–(*m*) below (with the same exceptions from (*e*) as are set out in the following text in 26.7), and

(II) non-trading activities (not including, as regards shares issued after 5 April 1998, research and development (as defined) and oil exploration).

Activities are for this purpose disregarded to the extent that they consist (*a*) in holding shares in or securities of, or making loans to, any of the company's subsidiaries, or (*b*) in holding and managing property used by the company or any of its subsidiaries either for research and development (as defined) from which a 'qualifying trade' (see 26.7 below) to be carried on by any of them is intended to be derived, or for the purposes of a 'qualifying trade' or trades carried on by any of them. They are similarly disregarded to the extent that they consist in making loans to the company or, in the case of a subsidiary whose main purpose is the carrying on of 'qualifying trade(s)' and whose other purposes are incapable of significantly affecting the extent of its activities (other than in relation to incidental matters), in activities not in pursuance of its main purpose.

Although a winding-up or dissolution in the relevant period generally prevents a company meeting the above conditions, they are deemed met if the winding-up or dissolution is for *bona fide* commercial reasons and not part of a scheme a main purpose of which is tax avoidance, with the additional proviso before 21 March 2000 that any net assets are distributed to members (or dealt with as *bona vacantia*) before the end of the relevant period or (if later) the end of three years from the commencement of winding-up. After 20 March 2000 (both in relation to shares issued after that date and to pre-existing shares to which EIS income tax relief or capital gains tax deferral relief remains attributable), a company does not cease to meet the above conditions by reason of anything done as a consequence of its being in administration or receivership (both as defined by *ICTA 1988, s 312(2A)*), provided everything so done and the making of the relevant order are for *bona fide* commercial (and not tax avoidance) reasons.

The company must not at any time in the relevant period either

(i) (in relation to shares issued before 6 April 1998) have share capital which includes any issued shares not fully paid up (or which would not be fully paid up if any undertaking to pay cash to the company at a future date were disregarded), or

(ii) (subject to 26.16 below) control another company other than a qualifying subsidiary (see 26.14 below), 'control' being construed in accordance with *ICTA 1988, s 416(2)–(6)* and being considered with or without connected persons within *ICTA 1988, s 839*, or

(iii) (subject to 26.16 below) be a 51% subsidiary of another company or otherwise under the control of another company, 'control' being construed in accordance with *ICTA 1988, s 840* (after 20 March 2000, previously in accordance with *ICTA 1988, s 416(2)–(6)*) and again being considered with or without connected persons, or

(iv) be capable of falling within (ii) or (iii) by virtue of any arrangements (as very broadly defined).

Gross assets test. In relation to shares issued after 5 April 1998, the value of the company's gross assets must not exceed £15 million immediately before the issue of EIS shares and must not exceed £16 million immediately afterwards. If the company has 'qualifying subsidiaries' (see 26.14 below), the test applies by reference to the aggregate gross assets of the company and all such subsidiaries (disregarding certain assets held by any such company which correspond to liabilities of another). The general approach of the Revenue to the gross assets test is that the value of a company's gross assets is the sum of the value of all of the balance sheet assets. Where accounts are actually drawn up to a date immediately before or after the issue, the balance sheet values are taken provided that they reflect usual accounting standards and the company's normal accounting practice, consistently applied. Where accounts are not drawn up to such a date, such values will be taken from the most recent balance sheet, updated as precisely as practicable on the basis of all the relevant information available to the company. Values so arrived at may need to be reviewed in the light of information contained in the accounts for the period in which the issue was made, and, if they were not available at the time of the issue, those for the preceding period, when they become available. The company's assets immediately before the issue do not include any advance payment received in respect of the issue. Where shares are issued partly paid, the right to the balance is an asset, and, notwithstanding the above, will be taken into account in valuing the assets immediately after the issue regardless of whether it is shown in the balance sheet. (Revenue Pamphlet IR 131, SP 5/98, 30 November 1998).

The Treasury may, by statutory instrument, amend any of the above provisions in relation to shares issued after 16 March 1998.

[*ICTA 1988, ss 293, 298(4), 312(1)–(1E)(2A); FA 1994, Sch 15 para 7; FA 1997, Sch 8 paras 1, 4; FA 1998, ss 70(2)(4), 74, Sch 13 paras 9, 23, Sch 27 Pt III(14); FA 2000, Sch 17 paras 9(1)(4), 10–12, 14, 15*].

Land and buildings. Subject to an exemption for small issues (see below), there is an additional exclusion if, at any time during the relevant period **and before 29 November 1994**, the value of the company's 'interests in land' (or, where lower, the value of those interests immediately after the issue of the shares, adjusted as below) exceeds half the value of all its assets (or such other fraction as the Treasury may substitute by statutory instrument). The value of those interests is for this purpose the aggregate of the market values of each such interest less debts secured thereon (including by floating charges), unsecured debts not falling due within twelve months and any amount paid up in respect of shares carrying a present or future preferential right to the company's assets on a winding-up. The value of the company's assets as a whole is similarly the aggregate market value less the company's debts and liabilities (including any amount paid up in respect of shares carrying a present or future preferential right to the company's assets on a winding-up, but excluding any other share capital, share premium account or reserves). Any question, on appeal, of the value of an interest in land is determined by the appropriate Lands Tribunal.

An 'interest in land' is valued on the assumption that there is no source of mineral deposits in the land exploitable other than by opencast mining or quarrying, and ignoring any oil exploration borehole.

Where the company is a member of a partnership, the value of any 'interest in land' held by the partnership is apportioned as on a dissolution of the partnership.

A qualifying company and its subsidiaries are treated as one company for these purposes, but ignoring any debts and liabilities between such companies.

'*Interest in land*' is widely defined to include rights related to land, and rights to obtain an interest etc. from another which depend on that other's ability to grant the interest etc., but excludes the interest of a creditor secured by any mortgage or charge over land. Valuation of such an interest excludes any plant or machinery which is, in law, part of the land etc..

The adjustments referred to above to the value of the company's interests in land held immediately after the issue of the shares are:

(A) the addition of the cost(s) (i.e. consideration given, ignoring any discount for postponement of right to receive it) of any subsequent acquisitions of interests in land, and of any enhancement expenditure relating to interests in land; and

(B) the deduction of any consideration for the disposal of, or grant of any interest out of, any interest in land, or derived from the ownership of interests in land (but excluding rent).

The value of an interest falls to be adjusted where the interest is under a lease at rent exceeding a full market rent. Contingent liabilities are disregarded unless and until the Board is satisfied that they have become enforceable and have been (or are being) enforced, whereon the necessary adjustments are made.

These restrictions do not apply where the total raised by the issue in question and any other issue in the previous twelve months does not exceed £50,000 and where that limit is exceeded, they apply only to the excess. The figure of £50,000 is reduced where, at any time in the relevant period, the company (or a subsidiary) carries on a trade in partnership, or in a joint venture, with another company.

Any restriction of relief under these provisions is apportioned amongst the qualifying individuals subscribing for otherwise eligible shares in proportion to their subscriptions, subject to determination on appeal by the General (or, in certain cases, the Special) Commissioners.

These restrictions ceased to apply with effect from 29 November 1994.

[*TMA 1970, s 47B; ICTA 1988, s 293(8A)(8B), ss 294–296, s 312(1A); FA 1988, s 52; FA 1994, Sch 15 paras 8, 9; FA 1995, s 66(3)*].

Advance provisional approval. A company may submit its proposals for using the EIS to the inspector who normally deals with its tax affairs. If satisfied as to the purposes for which the money raised will be used, the company's status as a qualifying company and the eligibility of the shares to be issued under the proposals, the inspector may grant advance provisional approval, of which investors may be informed, although in the end the question of whether the company qualifies for the scheme is one of fact which cannot be determined in advance. (Revenue Pamphlet IR 137, page 30).

Simon's Direct Tax Service. See **E3.115** *et seq.*.

26.6 Any of the following is a '*qualifying business activity*' in relation to the issuing company, provided that, at any time in the 'relevant period' when it is carried on, it is carried on 'wholly or mainly in the UK'.

(*a*) The issuing company or any subsidiary (within *ICTA 1988, s 308*, see 26.14 below) carrying on a 'qualifying trade' which it is carrying on on the date of issue of the shares, or preparing to carry on such a trade which, on the date of issue of the shares, it intends to carry on 'wholly or mainly in the UK' and which it begins to carry on within two years after that date.

(*b*) The issuing company or any subsidiary carrying on either 'research and development' or oil exploration which it is carrying on on the date of issue of the shares, or which it begins to carry on immediately afterwards, and from which it is intended will be derived a 'qualifying trade' which the company or a subsidiary will carry on 'wholly or mainly in the UK'.

As regards (*a*) above, 'preparing' to carry on a trade refers to the setting up of the trade, and not e.g. to market research aimed at discovering whether it would be worthwhile starting a trade, or to preparatory research and development or exploration. (Revenue Inspector's Manual, IM 6973).

As regards (*b*) above, in relation to oil exploration, there are further conditions relating to exploration and appraisal or development licences. In relation to shares issued after 5 April 2000, '*research and development*' has the meaning given by *ICTA 1988, s 837A* (see 10.52 CAPITAL ALLOWANCES). Previously, it meant any activity intended to result in a patentable invention (within *Patents Act 1977*) or in a computer program.

The '*relevant period*' for these purposes is the period beginning with the date of issue of the shares and ending either three years after that date or, where (*a*) above applies and the company (or subsidiary) was not carrying on the 'qualifying trade' on that date, three years after the date on which it begins to carry on the trade.

[*ICTA 1988, s 289(2)(4)(5)(8), s 312(1)(1A)(b); FA 1994, Sch 15 para 2; FA 2000, Sch 17 paras 6(4), 15*].

In considering whether a trade is carried on '*wholly or mainly in the UK*', the totality of the trade activities is taken into account. Regard will be had, for example, to where capital assets are held, where any purchasing, processing, manufacturing and selling is done, and to where the employees customarily carry out their duties. No one of these factors is itself likely to be decisive in any particular case. Accordingly a company may carry on some such activities outside the UK and yet satisfy the requirement, provided that the major part of them, that is over one-half of the aggregate of these activities, takes place within the UK. Thus relief is not excluded solely because a company's products or services are exported, or because its raw materials are imported, or because its raw materials or products are stored abroad, or because its marketing facilities are supplied from abroad. Similar principles apply in considering the trade(s) carried on by a company and its qualifying subsidiaries.

In the particular case of a ship chartering trade, the test is satisfied if all charters are entered into in the UK and the provision of crews and management of the ships while under charter take place mainly in the UK. If these conditions are not met, the test may still be satisfied depending on all the relevant facts and circumstances.

(Revenue Pamphlet IR 131, SP 7/98, 30 November 1998, replacing SP 2/94, 9 May 1994, as revised).

For the manner in which the scheme operates where a company wishes to raise money by a single issue of shares for more than one qualifying business activity (e.g. for a trade carried on by one subsidiary and for research and development carried on by another), see Revenue Tax Bulletin April 1996 pp 305, 306.

Simon's Direct Tax Service. See E3.125 *et seq.*.

26.7 To be a '*qualifying trade*' a trade may not, at any time in the 'relevant period' (as defined in 26.6 above), consist to a substantial extent of, or of a combination of:

(*a*) dealing in land, commodities or futures, or in shares, securities or other financial instruments; or

(*b*) dealing in goods otherwise than in an ordinary trade of wholesale or retail distribution (see below); or

(*c*) banking, insurance or any other financial activities; or

(*d*) oil extraction activities (but without prejudice to relief in respect of oil exploration (see 26.6(*b*) above) for which the activities would otherwise qualify); or

(*e*) leasing or letting or receiving royalties or licence fees; or

(*f*) providing legal or accountancy services; or

(*g*) 'property development';

(*h*) farming or market gardening;

(*j*) holding, managing or occupying woodlands, any other forestry activities or timber production;

(*k*) operating or managing hotels or comparable establishments (including guest houses, hostels and other establishments whose main purpose is to offer overnight accommodation with or without catering) or property used as such;

(*l*) operating or managing nursing homes or residential care homes (both as defined) or property used as such;

(*m*) providing services or facilities for any trade, profession or vocation concerned in (*a*) to (*l*) and carried on by another person (other than a parent company), where one person has a 'controlling interest' in both trades.

Exclusions (*g*)–(*l*) (and the reference to those in exclusion (*m*)) apply in relation to shares issued **after 16 March 1998**. Exclusions (*k*) and (*l*) apply only if the person carrying on the activity in question has an estate or interest (e.g. a lease) in the property concerned or occupies that property.

Adventures and concerns in the nature of trade, and trades not carried on commercially and with a view to the realisation of profits, are also generally excluded.

The Revenue regard as 'substantial' for the above purposes a part of a trade which consists of 20% or more of total activities, judged by any reasonable measure (normally turnover or capital employed). (Revenue Inspector's Manual, IM 6997). (*a*) above does not exclude the activities of a builder whose method of trading is to buy land on which building work is to be done and sell it on completion of that work. It does exclude cases where steps taken to make land more saleable include e.g. the refurbishment of existing buildings on the land. (Revenue Inspector's Manual, IM 6998).

As regards (*b*) above, a trade of wholesale or retail distribution is a trade consisting of the offer of goods for sale either to persons for resale (or processing and resale) (which resale must be to members of the general public) by them ('*wholesale*') or to the general public ('*retail*'), and a trade is not an ordinary wholesale or retail trade if it consists to a substantial extent of dealing in goods collected or held as an investment (or of that and any other activity within (*a*)–(*m*) above), and a substantial proportion of such goods is held for a significantly longer period than might reasonably be expected for a vendor trying to dispose of them at market value. Whether such trades are 'ordinary' is to be judged having regard to the following features, those under (A) supporting the categorisation as 'ordinary', those under (B) being indicative to the contrary.

(A) (i) The breaking of bulk.

(ii) The purchase and sale of goods in different markets.

(iii) The employment of staff and incurring of trade expenses other than the cost of goods or of remuneration of persons connected (within *ICTA 1988, s 839*) with company carrying on such a trade.

(B) (i) The purchase or sale of goods from or to persons connected (within *ICTA 1988, s 839*) with the trader.

(ii) The matching of purchases with sales.

(iii) The holding of goods for longer than might normally be expected.

(iv) The carrying on of the trade at a place not commonly used for wholesale or retail trading.

(v) The absence of physical possession of the goods by the trader.

As regards the application of (*e*) above in relation to shares issued after 5 April 2000, a trade is not excluded from being a qualifying trade solely because at some time in the relevant period it consists to a substantial extent in the receiving of royalties or licence fees substantially attributable (in terms of value) to the exploitation of 'relevant intangible assets'. An intangible asset is an asset falling to be treated as such under normal UK company accounting practice. A '*relevant intangible asset*' is an asset the whole or greater part of which (in terms of value) has been created by the company carrying on the trade or by a company which throughout the creation of the asset was the 'parent company' of that company or a qualifying subsidiary (within 26.14 below) of that parent company. A '*parent company*' is for these purposes a company with one or more 51% subsidiaries which is not itself a 51% subsidiary. Where the asset is 'intellectual property', it is treated as created by a company only if the right to exploit it vests in that company (alone or with others). The term '*intellectual property*' incorporates patents, trade marks, copyrights, design rights etc. and foreign equivalents.

As regards the application of (*e*) above in relation to shares issued before 6 April 2000, a company engaged throughout the relevant period in the production of original master films, tapes or discs is not excluded from the scheme by reason only of its receipt by way of trade of royalties or licence fees, provided that all royalties and licence fees received by it in the relevant period are in respect of films etc. produced by it in that relevant period or in respect of by-products arising therefrom. The company may also be engaged in the distribution of films produced by it in the relevant period. Similarly royalties and licence fees attributable to research and development which a company carrying on a trade has engaged in throughout the relevant period do not prevent the trade being a qualifying trade.

Also as regards (*e*) above, a trade will not be excluded by reason only of its consisting of letting ships, other than oil rigs or pleasure craft (as defined), on charter, provided that

(i) the company beneficially owns all the ships it so lets,

(ii) every ship beneficially owned by the company is UK-registered,

(iii) throughout the relevant period, the company is solely responsible for arranging the marketing of the services of its ships, and

(iv) in relation to every letting on charter, certain conditions as to length and terms of charter, and the arm's length character of the transaction, are fulfilled,

and if any of (i)–(iv) above is not fulfilled in relation to certain lettings, only those lettings are taken into account in determining whether a substantial part of the trade consists of activities within (*a*)–(*m*) above.

In relation to (*e*) above, the Revenue has given its views on the scope of the exclusions in its Tax Bulletin, although these may be superseded in relation to shares issued after 5 April 2000. The leasing and letting exclusion covers all cases where (subject to reasonable conditions imposed by the trader) the customer is free to use the property as his own. Where this is not so – e.g. the hire of chauffeur-driven cars, or storage of articles by the trader in warehouses or safes – the exclusion does not apply. Royalties and licence fees are received where property rights are exploited by the company granting permission to another to make use of the property. In the case of royalties, the exclusion applies regardless of whether the company itself brought that property into existence (although see above as regards film and research and development royalties and licence fees). In the case of licence fees, the grant of the right to use the property is often incidental to the supply of services, and the exclusion does not apply in such cases. Similarly where, although there is no direct provision of services, continuous work is required to keep the property in a fit state for use, the question to be considered is whether such work is or is not greater than the work involved in obtaining the fees. The Revenue thus consider that receipts from an actively supervised gymnasium, with trainers in attendance to advise on personal fitness programmes and the use of equipment, are not licence fees, whereas receipts from letting out tennis courts to the general public by the hour are licence fees. The description of what is in effect a season ticket for the use of property as a membership fee (e.g. in the case of some sports clubs) does not affect the status of the payments. (Revenue Tax Bulletin August 1995 pp 240, 241).

'*Property development*' in (*g*) above means the development of land by a company, which has (or has had at any time) an 'interest in the land' (as defined), with the sole or main object of realising a gain from the disposal of an interest in the developed land.

As regards (*m*) above, a person has a '*controlling interest*' in a trade carried on by a company if he controls (within *ICTA 1988, s 416*) the company; or if the company is close and he or an 'associate' is a director of the company and the owner of, or able to control, more than 30% of its ordinary share capital; or if at least half of its ordinary share capital is directly or indirectly owned by him. In any other case it is obtained by his being entitled to at least half of the assets used for, or income arising from, the trade. In either case, the rights and powers of a person's 'associates' are attributed to him. '*Associate*' is as under *ICTA 1988, s 417(3)(4)*, but excluding brothers and sisters.

The Treasury may, by statutory instrument, amend any of the above conditions.

[*ICTA 1988, ss 297, 298; FA 1994, Sch 15 paras 10, 11; FA 1997, Sch 8 para 5; FA 1998, Sch 12 paras 1, 2, 5(1), Sch 13 paras 10, 11; FA 2000, Sch 17 para 13*].

Simon's Direct Tax Service. See E3.126 *et seq.*.

26.8 FORM OF RELIEF

Relief is (except as below) given for the year of assessment in which the shares were issued, by a reduction in what would otherwise be the individual's income tax liability by the lesser of

(*a*) tax at the lower rate (currently 20%) for the year on the amount (or aggregate amounts) subscribed for eligible shares in respect of which he is eligible for relief, and

(*b*) an amount sufficient to reduce that liability to nil.

In determining what would otherwise be the individual's income tax liability for the year for these purposes, no account is taken of:

(i) any income tax reduction in respect of personal reliefs (see 1.15, 1.16, 1.17 ALLOWANCES AND TAX RATES) or qualifying maintenance payments (see 47.10 MARRIED PERSONS);

(ii) any income tax reduction in respect of interest relief (see 43.5 INTEREST PAYABLE);

(iii) any income tax reduction in respect of medical insurance (see 48.1 MEDICAL INSURANCE);

(iv) any reduction of liability to tax by way of DOUBLE TAX RELIEF (25);

(v) any basic rate tax on income the tax on which the individual is entitled to charge against any other person or to deduct, retain or satisfy out of any payment; or

(vi) any basic rate tax deemed to be deducted at source from a charitable donation made after 5 April 2000 under the Gift Aid scheme (see 15.12 CHARITIES).

Where shares in respect of which the individual is eligible for relief are issued before 6 October in a year of assessment, he may claim relief as if up to one half of the shares had been issued in the preceding year of assessment, subject to an overall limit of £25,000 (£15,000 as regards shares actually issued before 6 April 1998) on the amount of subscriptions which may be so treated. See 17.2 CLAIMS for general provisions regarding claims for payments made in one year of assessment to be carried back to an earlier year.

[*ICTA 1988, s 289A(1)–(5); FA 1990, s 25(6)(b)(7); FA 1994, Sch 15 para 2; FA 1998, s 74, Sch 13 para 2; FA 2000, s 39(6)(10)*].

Relief for loss on disposal. ICTA 1988, s 574 (see 46.18 LOSSES), which grants income tax relief for certain losses on shares in unquoted trading companies, applies on the disposal by an individual of shares to which relief is attributable (see below) as it applies to shares in 'qualifying trading companies' under that *section. ICTA 1988, ss 575(1)(3), 576(1)–(3)* are similarly applied for this purpose (though *section 576(1)* was not so applied for disposals before 6 April 1998). [*ICTA 1988, s 305A; FA 1994, Sch 15 para 20; FA 1998, Sch 13 para 18*].

Attribution of relief to shares. Subject to any reduction or withdrawal of relief (see 26.12 *et seq.* below), where an individual's income tax liability is reduced for a year of assessment as above by reason of an issue or issues of shares made (or treated as made) in that year, the income tax reduction is attributed to that issue or those issues (being apportioned in the latter case according to the amount subscribed for each issue). Issues of shares of the same class by a company to an individual on the same day are treated as a single issue for this purpose. A proportionate amount of the reduction attributed to an issue is attributed to each share in the issue (and adjusted correspondingly for any subsequent bonus issue of shares of the same class and carrying the same rights).

An issue to an individual part of which is treated as having been made in the preceding year (as above) is treated as two separate issues, one made on a day in the previous year, for the purposes of the above and other specified provisions.

Where relief attributable to an issue of shares falls to be withdrawn or reduced, the relief attributable to each of the shares in question is reduced to nil (if relief is withdrawn) or proportionately reduced (where relief is reduced).

[*ICTA 1988, s 289B; FA 1994, Sch 15 para 2; FA 1998, s 74, Sch 13 para 3*].

On a *reorganisation of share capital* falling within *TCGA 1992, s 126(2)(a)* (i.e. where shares or debentures are allotted in proportion to an existing holding), the relief attributable to shares is reduced where both the amount subscribed for the shares and their market value immediately before the reorganisation exceed their market value immediately after the reorganisation. The reduction is in the same proportion as the lower of those two excesses bears to the amount subscribed for the shares. A similar reduction applies where, at any time in the 'relevant period' (see 26.3 above), rights on such a reorganisation are disposed of, and the reduction would have applied had the rights not been disposed of but the allotment made by virtue of the rights. **No reduction applies**, however, where the reorganisation occurred, or the rights were disposed of, **after 28 November 1994**. [*ICTA 1988, s 305; FA 1994, Sch 15 para 19; FA 1995, s 66(4)*].

For the purposes of INTEREST ON OVERPAID TAX (41), any repayment of tax is treated as being in respect of tax payable in the year of assessment in which the shares are issued or, if later, the year in which the issuing company (or subsidiary) completed its first four months' trading (or, where relevant, ceased trading). [*ICTA 1988, s 289A(9); FA 1994, Sch 15 para 2*]. For 1996/97 and subsequent years, see 17.2 CLAIMS.

Simon's Direct Tax Service. See **E3.140** *et seq.*.

26.9 *Examples*

Mr Jones is a married man with a salary of £32,000 per annum and no other income. Both he and his wife were born after 5 April 1935. In 2000/01 he subscribes for ordinary shares in two unquoted companies issuing shares under the enterprise investment scheme (EIS).

A Ltd was formed by some people in Mr Jones' neighbourhood to publish a local newspaper. 200,000 ordinary £1 shares were issued at par in August 2000 and the company started trading in September 2000. Mr Jones subscribed for 16,000 of the shares. Mr Jones becomes a director of A Ltd in September 2000, receiving director's fees of £5,000 per annum (£2,500 in 2000/01), a level of remuneration which is considered reasonable for services rendered by him to the company in his capacity as a director.

B Ltd, which is controlled by an old friend of Mr Jones, has acquired the rights to manufacture in the UK a new type of industrial cleaning solvent and requires additional finance. Mr Jones subscribed for 8,000 ordinary £1 shares at a premium of £1.50 per share in October 2000. The issue increases the company's issued share capital to 25,000 ordinary £1 shares.

Mr Jones will obtain tax relief in 2000/01 as follows.

Amount eligible for relief

	£
A Ltd notes (*a*) and (*b*)	16,000
B Ltd note (*c*)	Nil
Total (being less than the maximum of £150,000)	£16,000

	£
Salary	32,000
Director's remuneration (A Ltd)	2,500
Total income	34,500
Deduct Personal allowance	4,385
Taxable income	£30,115

Tax payable:	
1,520 @ 10%	152.00
26,880 @ 22%	5,913.60
1,715 @ 40%	686.00
	6,751.60
Deduct EIS relief £16,000 @ 20%	3,200.00
Net tax liability	£3,551.60

Notes

(*a*) Mr Jones is entitled to relief on the full amount of his investment in A Ltd regardless of the amount of relief claimed by other investors.

(*b*) The fact that Mr Jones becomes a paid director of A Ltd *after* an issue to him of eligible shares does not prevent his qualifying for relief in respect of those shares providing his remuneration as a director is reasonable and he is not otherwise connected with the company (see 26.3 above).

(*c*) Mr Jones is not entitled to relief against his income for his investment of £20,000 in B Ltd. As a result of the share issue he owns more than 30% of the issued ordinary share capital (8,000 out of 25,000 shares) and is therefore regarded as connected with the company and denied relief. See 26.3 above.

In 2001/02 Mr Jones subscribes for shares in three more unquoted companies trading in the UK and issuing shares under the EIS.

C Ltd is a local company engaged in the manufacture of car components. It issues a further 300,000 ordinary £1 shares at £1.80 per share in June 2001 and Mr Jones subscribes for 7,500 shares costing £13,500, increasing his stake in the company to 2%. He had originally held 13,500 shares, acquired by purchase at arm's length in May 1999 for £16,200.

D Ltd has been trading as a hotel and restaurant company for several years and requires an injection of capital to finance a new restaurant. Mr Jones and three other unconnected individuals each subscribe for 18,750 ordinary £1 shares at par in November 2001. The balance of 120,000 shares are held by Mr Jones' sister and niece.

E Ltd is an electronics company controlled by two cousins of Mr Jones. The company is seeking £1.5 million extra capital to enable it to expand and take advantage of new computer technology and raises it via the EIS. Mr Jones subscribes for 127,500 ordinary £1 shares at par in December 2001.

Mr Jones's salary is increased to £50,000 for 2001/02.

If he makes the optimum claims Mr Jones will obtain tax relief as follows

2000/01

C Ltd note (*a*) £6,750 @ 20% =	£1,350

2001/02

Amount eligible for relief

	£
C Ltd (£13,500 – £6,750 carried back)	6,750
D Ltd	18,750
E Ltd	127,500
Total	£153,000
But amount eligible for relief restricted to subscriptions of	£150,000

Relief given (assuming 2001/02 rates and allowances unchanged from 2000/01

	£
Salary	50,000
Director's remuneration	5,000
Total income	55,000
Deduct Personal allowance	4,385
Taxable income	£50,615
Tax payable:	
1,520 @ 10%	152.00
26,880 @ 22%	5,913.60
22,215 @ 40%	8,886.00
	14,951.60
Deduct EIS relief:	
£150,000 @ 20% = £30,000, but restricted to	14,951.60
Net tax liability	Nil

Attribution of relief to shares note (*b*)

	£
C Ltd shares $\frac{6{,}750}{153{,}000} \times £14{,}952$	660
D Ltd shares $\frac{18{,}750}{153{,}000} \times £14{,}952$	1,832
E Ltd shares $\frac{127{,}500}{153{,}000} \times £14{,}952$	12,460
	£14,952

Notes

(*a*) Since the C Ltd shares were issued before 6 October 2001, Mr Jones may elect to carry back up to half the amount subscribed, subject to an overriding maximum of £25,000, to the preceding tax year. The relief will be given in addition to that previously claimed for 2000/01 (see the example above). If Mr Jones had previously claimed relief on say £148,000 in 2000/01 the amount carried back would be restricted to £2,000 as relief in any one year may not be given on subscriptions of more than the annual maximum for that year. See 26.8 above and 26.10 below.

(*b*) Relief is restricted in this example by (i) the £150,000 maximum (see 26.10 below) and (ii) an insufficiency in Mr Jones' tax liability. The relief attributable to each issue of shares (which will be relevant in the event of a disposal of the shares or withdrawal of relief—see 26.12 below) is found by apportioning the income tax reduction by reference to the amounts subscribed for each issue. (For this purpose, half of the C Ltd shares are regarded as having been separately issued in the previous year.) The relief so attributed to each issue is then apportioned equally between all the shares comprised in that issue. See 26.8 above.

26.10 LIMITS ON RELIEF

(See 26.15 below as regards relief for married persons.)

Except in the case of investments through 'approved funds' (see 26.2 above), relief is restricted to investments of £500 or more in any one company in any year of assessment.

There is in all cases an upper limit of £150,000 (£100,000 as regards shares issued before 6 April 1998) on the amount in respect of which an individual may obtain relief in a year of assessment (regardless of whether the shares were issued in that year or in the following year). For 1993/94, however, the limit under the BES of £40,000 applied to the aggregate of relief under both schemes.

[*ICTA 1988, s 290, 311(3); FA 1988, s 53; FA 1994, Sch 15 para 3; FA 1998, s 74, Sch 13 para 4*].

As regards shares issued before 6 April 1998, there was also a restriction on the total amount of eligible shares which could be issued by a company within a specified period (see below) and attract relief. Where the money raised in such a period exceeded £1,000,000 the excess did not qualify for relief. The period specified was the longer of (*a*) six months ending with the date of issue of the shares, and

(*b*) the period from the preceding 6 April to the date of issue.

Amounts raised which did not attract relief because the subscriber was not a qualifying individual (see 26.3 above), or had exceeded his personal limit or invested under the permitted minimum (see above), or because of an earlier application of these provisions, were not taken into account for the purposes of this restriction.

The limit was increased to £5,000,000 in the case of certain shipping concerns. This applied:

(i) in the case of a qualifying company within 26.5(*a*) above, where the qualifying trade(s) carried on by the company consisted wholly or substantially wholly of operating or letting of charter ships other than oil rigs or pleasure craft, subject to conditions similar to those which apply to lettings of such ships in respect of there being a qualifying trade (see 26.7 above);

(ii) in the case of a qualifying company within 26.5(*b*) above, where each subsidiary was a 'shipping company' and if, apart from purposes capable of having no significant effect (other than on incidental matters) on the extent of its activities, the company existed wholly for either or any combination of the following purposes.

(A) The carrying on of activities consisting (*a*) in holding shares in or securities of, or making loans to, any of the company's subsidiaries, or (*b*) in holding and managing property used by the company or any of its subsidiaries either for research and development from which a qualifying trade to be carried on by any of them is intended to be derived, or for the purposes of a qualifying trade or trades carried on by any of them.

(B) The carrying on of a qualifying trade or trades within (i) above.

A subsidiary is a '*shipping company*' for this purpose if it satisfies the conditions imposed on the qualifying company under (ii) above, or would satisfy them if the permissible activities under (ii)(A) included the making of loans to the qualifying company, or if it has no corporation tax profits and no part of its business consists in the making of investments.

Before 27 November 1996, (ii) above was replaced by a requirement for qualifying companies within 26.5(*b*) above that the qualifying trade required to be carried on by the company and/or its subsidiaries was within (i) above.

For the purposes of the above limits, amounts raised under the BES scheme were also taken into account.

Where, at any time in the 'relevant period' (see 26.6 above), the company issuing the shares (or a subsidiary) carried on any trade or part in partnership, or as a joint venture, with a company or companies (with or without other persons), the limit of £1,000,000 or £5,000,000 (as above) was divided by the total number of companies (but counting the issuing company and its subsidiaries as a single company) which were members of the partnership or parties to the joint venture.

Where these provisions restricted the amount of relief available to two or more individuals, the total relief available was apportioned amongst them according to the respective amounts subscribed for shares giving rise to the restriction and which would otherwise be eligible for relief.

[*ICTA 1988, s 290A; FA 1988, s 51(1); FA 1994, Sch 15 para 4; FA 1997, Sch 8 paras 1, 3; FA 1998, s 74, Sch 13 para 5, Sch 27 Pt III(14)*].

26.11 CLAIMS FOR RELIEF

A claim for relief in respect of eligible shares issued by a qualifying company in a year of assessment cannot be allowed until the trade (or research and development or oil exploration) has been carried on for four months, but may otherwise be given at any time when it appears that the relief conditions may be satisfied. Where, for *bona fide* commercial reasons and not as part of a scheme or arrangement a main purpose of which was tax avoidance, a company carries on a trade for less than four months by reason of its being wound up or dissolved or (for shares issued after 20 March 2000) by reason of anything done as a consequence of its being in administration or receivership, a claim may be allowed after the trade so ceases. [*ICTA 1988, s 289A(6)–(8A); FA 1994, Sch 15 para 2; FA 2000, Sch 17 paras 9(3), 12*].

A claim for relief must be made not earlier than the end of the four-month period referred to above, and, for 1995/96 and earlier years, not later than twelve months after an inspector authorises (on Form EIS 2) the issue of a certificate (Form EIS 3) by the company. For 1996/97 and later years, the claim must be made not later than the fifth anniversary of 31 January following the year of assessment for which relief is claimed. The claimant must have received the said certificate before making the claim, and for shares issued before 6 April 1996 the certificate had to accompany the claim. The certificate must state that the conditions for relief, except insofar as they fall to be satisfied by the individual, are satisfied in relation to the eligible shares in question. A certificate may not be issued without the inspector's authority; where a notice under *ICTA 1988, s 310(2)* (see 26.17 below), or a notice of certain chargeable events under the EIS capital gains deferral provisions mentioned at 26.17 below, has been given to the inspector, an authority given before receipt of the notice, and not renewed thereafter, has no effect. For appeal purposes, the inspector's refusal to authorise a certificate is treated as the refusal of a claim by the company.

Before issuing such a certificate, the company must supply to the inspector a statement (Form EIS 1) that those conditions were fulfilled from the beginning of the 'relevant period' (see 26.6 above), and that statement must contain such information as the Board may reasonably require, and a declaration that it is correct to the best of the company's knowledge and belief. The statement must be furnished to the inspector within two years after the end of the year of assessment in which the shares in question were issued (or, if the four-month period referred to above ends in the following year, within two years after the end of that four-month period).

If a certificate or statement is made fraudulently or negligently, or a certificate was issued despite being prohibited (as above), the company is liable to a fine of up to £3,000.

Special provisions (see *ICTA 1988, s 311(4)–(6)*) apply in relation to the issue of certificates where shares are held through an approved fund (see 26.2 above).

No application for postponement of tax pending appeal can be made on the ground that relief is due under these provisions unless a claim has been duly submitted.

For the purposes of INTEREST ON UNPAID TAX (41), tax charged by an assessment is regarded as due and payable notwithstanding that relief is subsequently given on a claim under these provisions, but is regarded as paid on the date on which a claim is made resulting in relief being granted, unless it was either in fact paid earlier or not due and payable until later. Interest is not refunded in respect of any subsequent discharge or repayment of tax giving effect to relief under these provisions.

[*ICTA 1988, ss 306, 311(4)–(6); FA 1994, Sch 15 para 21; FA 1996, ss 134, 135, Sch 20 paras 22, 23, Sch 21 para 7; FA 1998, s 74, Sch 13 para 19, Sch 27 Pt III(14)*].

26.12 RESTRICTION OR WITHDRAWAL OF RELIEF

The following provisions apply to restrict or withdraw relief in certain circumstances. References to a reduction of relief include its reduction to nil, and references to the withdrawal of relief in respect of any shares are to the withdrawal of the relief attributable to those shares (see 26.8 above). Where no relief has yet been given, a reduction applies to reduce the amount which apart from the provision in question would be the relief, and a withdrawal means ceasing to be eligible for relief in respect of the shares in question. [*ICTA 1988, s 312(4); FA 1994, Sch 15 para 27*].

Where an event giving rise to complete withdrawal of relief occurs at the same time as a disposal at a loss, the disposal is regarded as occurring first, so that relief may be only partially withdrawn (as below). (Revenue Inspectors' Manual, IM 7024).

Disposal of shares. Where eligible shares to which relief is attributable (see 26.8 above) are disposed of (or an option granted the exercise of which would bind the grantor to sell them) before the end of the 'relevant period' (see 26.3 above):

(*a*) if the disposal is at arm's length, relief attributable to those shares (see 26.8 above) is withdrawn or, if that relief exceeds an amount equal to lower rate tax (for the year in which the relief was given) on the disposal consideration, reduced by that amount;

(*b*) otherwise, the relief is withdrawn.

Where the relief attributable to the shares was less than the lower rate of tax for the year of issue on the amount subscribed for the issue, the amount referred to in (*a*) above is correspondingly reduced. For this purpose, shares are treated as having been issued in an earlier year where relief was carried back as in 26.8 above.

A share exchange is treated as a disposal for these purposes (Revenue Assessment Procedures Manual, AP 4977), unless it occurs after 5 April 1998 and is within *ICTA 1988, s 304A* — see 26.16 below).

For the above purposes, disposals are identified with shares of the same class issued earlier before shares issued later (i.e. first in/first out (FIFO)). For disposals after 5 April 1998, where shares within two or more of the categories listed below were acquired on the same day, any of those shares disposed of (applying the FIFO basis) are treated as disposed of in the order in which they are listed, as follows:

(i) shares to which neither EIS income tax relief nor EIS capital gains deferral relief (see 26.17 below) is attributable;

(ii) shares to which deferral relief, but not income tax relief, is attributable;

(iii) shares to which income tax relief, but not deferral relief, is attributable;

(iv) shares to which both of those reliefs are attributable.

Any shares within (iii) or (iv) above which are treated as issued on an earlier day by virtue of the carry-back provisions at 26.8 above are to be treated as disposed of before any other shares within the same category. Shares transferred between spouses living together are treated as if they were acquired by the transferee spouse on the day they were issued (see also 26.15 below). Shares comprised in a 'new holding' following a reorganisation to which *TCGA 1992, s 127* applies (see Tolley's Capital Gains Tax under Shares and Securities) are treated as having been acquired when the original shares were acquired.

Relief is also withdrawn where, during the relevant period, an option is granted to the individual, the exercise of which would bind the grantor to purchase shares. There are provisions for identifying the shares to which an option granted after 5 April 1998 relates, where these form part of a larger holding.

[*ICTA 1988, ss 299, 312(4B); FA 1994, Sch 15 para 12; FA 1998, s 74, Sch 13 paras 12, 23(5), Sch 27 Pt III(14)*].

See Simon's Direct Tax Service E3.146.

Loan linked investments. Relief is denied where

(*a*) a loan is made to the individual subscribing for shares or to an 'associate' (see 26.3 above) by any person at any time in the 'relevant period' (see 26.3 above), and

(*b*) the loan would not have been made, or would not have been made on the same terms, if he had not subscribed, or had not been proposing to subscribe, for the shares.

The granting of credit to, or the assignment of a debt due from, the individual or associate is counted as a loan for these purposes.

[*ICTA 1988, s 299A; FA 1993, s 111(1); FA 1994, Sch 15 para 13*].

For this restriction to apply, the test is whether the lender makes the loan on terms which are connected with the fact that the borrower (or an associate) is subscribing for eligible shares. The prime concern is why the lender made the loan rather than why the borrower applied for it. Relief would not be disallowed, for example, in the case of a bank loan if the bank would have made a loan on the same terms to a similar borrower for a different purpose. But if, for example, a loan is made specifically on a security consisting of or including the eligible shares (other than as part of a broad range of assets to which the lender has recourse), relief would be denied. Relevant features of the loan terms would be the qualifying conditions to be satisfied by the borrower, any incentives or benefits offered to the borrower, the time allowed for repayment, the amount of repayments and interest charged, the timing of interest payments, and the nature of the security. (Revenue Pamphlet IR 131, SP 6/98, 30 November 1998, replacing SP 3/94, 9 May 1994, as revised).

See Simon's Direct Tax Service E3.149.

Pre-arranged exits. In relation to shares issued after 1 July 1997, relief is denied if arrangements (as very broadly defined) under which the shares are issued to an individual (or arrangements preceding the issue but relating to it)

(*a*) provide for the eventual disposal by the investor of the shares in question or other shares or securities of the company; or

(*b*) provide for the eventual cessation of a trade of the company or of a person connected with it; or

(*c*) provide for the eventual disposal of all, or a substantial part of, the assets of the company or of a person connected with it; or

(*d*) provide (by means of any insurance, indemnity, guarantee or otherwise) complete or partial protection for investors against the normal risks attaching to EIS investment (but excluding arrangements which merely protect the company and/or its subsidiaries against normal trading risks).

Arrangements with a view to the company becoming a wholly-owned subsidiary of a new holding company within the terms of *ICTA 1988, s 304A* (see 26.16 below) are excluded from (*a*) above. Arrangements applicable only on an unanticipated winding-up of the company for commercial reasons are excluded from (*b*) and (*c*) above.

[*ICTA 1988, ss 299B, 312(1); FA 1998, s 71(1)(5); FA 2000, Sch 17 para 14, Sch 40 Pt II(5)*].

See Simon's Direct Tax Service E3.141.

Value received from company. Where an individual subscribes for eligible shares in a company, and during the designated period as in 26.3 above (as regards shares issued before

6 April 1998, during the 'relevant period' as in 26.3 above and whether before or after the issue), 'receives value' from the company, any relief attributable to those shares (see 26.8 above) and not previously reduced in respect of the 'value received' is withdrawn or, if that relief exceeds an amount equal to lower rate tax (for the year in which the relief was given) on the 'value received', reduced by that amount. That amount is correspondingly reduced where the relief attributable to the shares was less than the lower rate of tax for the year of issue on the amount subscribed for the issue.

As regards shares issued on or after 6 April 1998, the above applies equally to 'value received' from a person who is connected (within *ICTA 1988, s 839* — see 20 CONNECTED PERSONS) with the issuing company at any time in the relevant period (whether or not at the time value is received). As regards shares issued before that date, it applied to 'value received' from a company which is a 51% subsidiary of the issuing company (i.e. a company more than 50% of whose ordinary share capital it owns) at any time in the relevant period (whether before or after the value is received).

An individual '*receives value*' from a company if it:

(*a*) repays, redeems or repurchases any part of his holding of its share capital or securities, or makes any payment to him for giving up rights on its cancellation or extinguishment; or

(*b*) repays any debt to him other than one incurred by the company on or after the date on which he subscribed for the shares which are the subject of relief and otherwise than in consideration of the extinguishment of a debt incurred before that date; or

(*c*) pays him for the cancellation of any debt owed to him other than an '*ordinary trade debt*' (i.e. one incurred for normal trade supply of goods or services on normal trade credit terms (not in any event exceeding six months)) or one in respect of a payment falling within 26.3(i) or (vi) above; or

(*d*) releases or waives any liability of his to the company (which it is deemed to have done if discharge of the liability is twelve months or more overdue) or discharges or undertakes to discharge any liability of his to a third person; or

(*e*) makes a loan or advance to him (defined as including the deferring by him of any debt either to the company (other than an 'ordinary trade debt' (as above)) or to a third person but assigned to the company) which has not been repaid in full before the issue of the shares; or

(*f*) provides a benefit or facility for him; or

(*g*) transfers an asset to him for no consideration or for consideration less than market value, or acquires an asset from him for consideration exceeding market value; or

(*h*) makes any other payment to him except one either falling within 26.3(i)–(vi) above or in discharge of an 'ordinary trade debt' (as above); or

(*i*) is wound up or dissolved in circumstances such that the company does not thereby cease to be a 'qualifying company' (see 26.5 above), and he thereby receives any payment or asset in respect of ordinary shares held by him.

However, an individual does *not* receive value from a company by reason only of the payment to him (or to an associate) of reasonable remuneration (including any benefit or facility) for services as a company director, and for this purpose, if the individual is also an employee of the company, references to him in his capacity as a director include him in his capacity as an employee.

The amount of value received by the individual is that paid to or receivable by him from the company; or the amount of his liability extinguished or discharged; or the difference between the market value of the asset and the consideration (if any) given for it; or the net cost to the company of providing the benefit. In the case of value received within (*a*), (*b*) or (*c*) above, the market value of the shares, securities or debt in question is substituted if greater than the amount receivable.

Additionally, the individual '*receives value*' from the company if any person connected with the company (within 26.3 above) purchases any shares or securities of the company from him, or pays him for giving up any right in relation to such shares or securities. The value received is the amount receivable or, if greater, the market value of the shares, etc..

All payments or transfers, direct or indirect, to, or to the order of, or for the benefit of, an individual or 'associate' (see 26.3 above) are brought within these provisions, as are payments, etc. made by any person connected with the company (within *ICTA 1988, s 839*).

Where relief is withdrawn or reduced by reason of a disposal (see above) after 5 April 1998, the individual is not treated as receiving value in respect of the disposal.

As regards value received after 5 April 1998, an individual who acquired eligible shares by means of an inter-spouse transfer within 26.15 below is treated for the above purposes as having subscribed for the shares.

[*ICTA 1988, ss 300, 301, 312(1); FA 1994, Sch 15 paras 14, 15; FA 1998, s 74, Sch 13 paras 13, 14; FA 2000, Sch 17 paras 4, 8*].

See Simon's Direct Tax Service E3.147.

Value received other than by claimant. Relief is also restricted or withdrawn where an individual has obtained relief attributable (see 26.8 above) to eligible shares in a company, and at any time during the designated period as in 26.3 above, the company or any '51% subsidiary of the company repays, redeems or repurchases any of its share capital belonging to a member other than

(i) the individual or

(ii) another individual whose relief is thereby withdrawn or reduced (as above) or who thereby suffers a qualifying chargeable event under the capital gains deferral provisions mentioned at 26.17 below, or

(iii) a company whose investment relief under the Corporate Venturing Scheme (see Tolley's Corporation Tax) is thereby withdrawn or reduced,

or makes any payment to any such member for giving up rights on the cancellation or extinguishment of any of the share capital of the company or subsidiary. The relief is withdrawn or, if it exceeds an amount equal to lower rate tax (for the year in which the relief was given) on the sum receivable by the member, reduced by that amount. That amount is correspondingly reduced where the relief attributable to the shares was less than the lower rate of tax for the year of issue on the amount subscribed for the issue. That amount is also apportioned between individuals (by reference to amounts subscribed) where the receipt of value causes a withdrawal or reduction of more than one individual's relief. Where the receipt of value falls into the designated period for more than one issue of eligible shares, the value received is similarly apportioned between issues.

A '*51% subsidiary*' of a company is one of which the company owns more than 50% of the ordinary share capital at any time in the relevant period (defined as in 26.3 above), whether or not at the time of the receipt of value.

Slightly different provisions applied in relation to shares issued before 6 April 1998. In particular, the old provisions applied by reference to value received in the relevant period (defined as in 26.3 above) rather than the above-mentioned designated period and any apportionment between individuals was by reference to relief otherwise available rather than amounts subscribed. Also, the old provisions applied by reference to the nominal value of the share capital concerned if this was greater than the sum receivable by the member.

This restriction of relief does not apply to the redemption, within twelve months of issue, of any share capital of nominal value equal to the authorised minimum issued to comply with *Companies Act 1985, s 117* (or NI equivalent) where the company subsequently issues eligible shares.

Where in the designated period — as above (as regards shares issued before 6 April 1998, the relevant period — as above), a member of the issuing company receives, or is or may become entitled to receive, any 'value' from the company or a 51% subsidiary (as above), then in applying the 30% test under 26.3(*b*)(i) above at any subsequent time, the following amounts are treated as reduced:

(*a*) the amount of the company's ordinary share capital;

(*b*) the amount of that capital which, under 26.3(*b*) above, the individual directly or indirectly possesses or is entitled to acquire; and

(*c*) the amount at (*a*) not included in (*b*).

The reduction in (*b*) and (*c*) above is in each case the same proportion of the total amount as the value received by the member(s) entitled to the shares comprising the amount bears to the sum subscribed for those shares. The reduced amount at (*a*) is the sum of those at (*b*) and (*c*).

A member receives or is entitled to receive '*value*' where any payments, etc. are made to him which, if made to an individual, would fall within (*d*)–(*h*) above, excluding those within (*h*) made for full consideration. The amount of value received is as described above in relation to such payments, etc..

The capital '*relevant*' to a provision is those shares whose proportion of the total issued ordinary share capital is in each case compared with the appropriate percentage of that capital.

[*ICTA 1988, s 303; FA 1994, Sch 15 para 17; FA 1998, s 74, Sch 13 para 15; FA 2000, Sch 16 para 2(2), Sch 17 paras 5, 8*].

Where, by virtue of a provision comparable to *ICTA 1988, s 303* above, a repayment, redemption etc. of share capital causes a withdrawal or reduction of investment relief given to one or more companies, in respect of the full amount repaid etc., under the Corporate Venturing Scheme ('CVS') (see Tolley's Corporation Tax), there is provision to ensure that no withdrawal or reduction is made under *section 303*. A withdrawal etc. of CVS investment relief is also disregarded for the purposes of *section 303* if the amount repaid etc. exceeds the amount in respect of which the relief was given by no more than £1,000. These exemptions are subject to the absence of any 'repayment arrangements' (as defined) throughout the one year ending with the date of issue of the shares to which the CVS investment relief is attributable. Where the above-mentioned excess (if any) is greater than the *de minimis* limit or the exemptions are prevented from applying, the amount of that excess is taken as the sum receivable by the member for the purposes of *section 303*.

Under the comparable CVS provision mentioned above, a repayment etc. of an insignificant amount (judged by reference to the greater of the market value of the shares to which it relates and the amount received by the member in question, and to the market value of the remaining share capital) is disregarded. A repayment etc. disregarded under that provision is also disregarded for the purposes of *ICTA 1988, s 303*.

[*ICTA 1988, s 303A; FA 2000, Sch 16 para 2(3)*].

See Simon's Direct Tax Service E3.148.

Replacement capital. Relief attributable (see 26.8 above) to any shares in a company held by an individual is withdrawn if, at any time in the 'relevant period' (see 26.3 above), the company (or any subsidiary, as specially defined for this purpose) begins to carry on as its trade, business, profession or vocation (or part) a trade, etc. (or part) previously carried on at any time in that period otherwise than by the company or a subsidiary, or acquires the whole or the greater part of the assets used for a trade, etc. previously so carried on, and the individual is a person who, or one of the group of persons who together, either

(*a*) owned more than a half share (ownership and, if appropriate, respective shares being determined as under *ICTA 1988, s 344(1)(a)(b)(2)(3)* (see Tolley's Corporation Tax under Losses) at any such time in the trade etc. previously carried on, and also own or owned at any such time such a share in the trade etc. carried on by the company, or

(*b*) control (within *ICTA 1988, s 416*), or at any such time have controlled, the company, and also, at any such time, controlled another company which previously carried on the trade, etc..

For these purposes, interests, etc. of 'associates' (see 26.3 above) are taken into account. There are special rules relating to shares held by certain directors of, or of a partner of, the issuing company or any subsidiary.

Relief is also withdrawn if the company, at any time in the relevant period, comes to acquire all the issued share capital of another company, and where the individual is a person who, or one of a group of persons who together, control or have, at any such time, controlled the company and who also, at any such time, controlled the other company.

[*ICTA 1988, s 302; FA 1994, Sch 15 para 16*].

See Simon's Direct Tax Service E3.151.

Assessments for withdrawing or reducing relief are made under Schedule D, Case VI for the year of assessment for which the relief was given. Relief may not be withdrawn on the grounds that the company is not a qualifying company (see 26.5 above), that the requirements as to the purpose of the issue or the application of the proceeds are not fulfilled (see 26.2(*b*)(*c*) above) or that the requirements of 26.2(i)–(iii) above are not met, unless either the company has given notice under *ICTA 1988, s 310* (see 26.17 below) (or the equivalent capital gains deferral provisions) or the inspector has given notice to the company of his opinion that relief was not due (against which notice the company may appeal as though it were refusal of a claim by the company). Such notice by the inspector may not be given, nor any assessment withdrawing relief be made, more than six years after the end of the year of assessment in which the period mentioned in 26.2(*c*) above ends or, if later, the event giving rise to withdrawal occurs, but this restriction is without prejudice to the extension of time limits in cases of fraudulent or negligent conduct (see 6.4 BACK DUTY). The determination of a comparable appeal under the capital gains deferral provisions mentioned at 26.17 below is conclusive for the purposes of an appeal under these provisions. No assessment may be made by reason of any event occurring after the death of the person to whom the shares were issued.

Where a person has made an arm's length disposal of all the eligible shares issued to him by a company in respect of which relief has been given, no assessment may be made in respect of those shares by reason of any subsequent event unless he is at the time of that event 'connected with' the company (as under 26.3 above). As regards shares issued before 6 April 1998, this rule operated by reference to disposals of all the *ordinary* shares.

The reckonable date for the purposes of 42.2 INTEREST AND SURCHARGES ON UNPAID TAX (or, where the self-assessment interest provisions have effect, the relevant date — see 42.1 INTEREST AND SURCHARGES ON UNPAID TAX) is the date on which the event took place which gave rise to the withdrawal of relief, *except that*:

(a) where relief is withdrawn under the general anti-avoidance provision of *ICTA 1988, s 289(6)* (see 26.2 above) or by virtue of the pre-arranged exit provisions of *ICTA 1988, s 299B* (see above), it is the date on which relief was granted or, if relief was given under PAYE, 5 April in the year of assessment in which relief was given;

(b) where relief is withdrawn due to failure to meet the condition at 26.2(*c*) above, it is the date on which relief was granted; and

(c) where relief is withdrawn as a result of the grant of an option the exercise of which would bind the grantor to purchase the shares (see above), it is the date of grant of the option.

[*ICTA 1988, s 307; FA 1989, s 149(4); FA 1993, s 111(3); FA 1994, Sch 15 para 22; FA 1996, Sch 18 paras 5, 17(3); FA 1998, s 71(2)(5), s 74, Sch 13 para 20*].

See Simon's Direct Tax Service E3.152.

26.13 *Examples*

In June 2002, Mr Jones, the investor in 26.9 above, sells 18,000 ordinary £1 shares in C Ltd (see 26.9 above), in an arm's length transaction, for £45,000.

The position is as follows.

Income tax

2000/01	£
Relief attributable to 3,750 shares treated as issued in 2000/01:	
3,750 shares at £1.80 per share = £6,750 @ 20%	1,350
Consideration received $\left(\frac{3,750}{18,000} \times £45,000\right)$ = 9,375 @ 20%	1,875
Excess of lower rate tax on consideration over relief	£525
Relief withdrawn—Schedule D, Case VI assessment	£1,350

2001/02	£
Relief attributable to 750 shares	
750/3,750 × £660	132
Consideration received	
$\left(\frac{750}{18,000} \times £45,000\right)$ = £1,875 × 132/(1,350 @ 20%) = £917 @ 20%	183
Excess of lower rate tax on adjusted consideration over relief	£51
Relief withdrawn—Schedule D, Case VI assessment	£132

Capital gains tax

2002/03	£	£
Disposal proceeds (18,000 shares)		45,000
Cost: 13,500 shares acquired May 1999	16,200	
4,500 shares acquired June 2001	8,100	24,300
Chargeable gain (subject to taper relief)		£20,700

Notes

(*a*) For both income tax and capital gains tax purposes, a disposal is matched with acquisitions on a first in/first out basis (see 26.12 above and Tolley's Capital Gains Tax). Thus, the 18,000 shares sold in June 2002 are matched with 13,500 shares purchased in May 1999 and with 4,500 of the 7,500 EIS shares subscribed for in June 2001. For these purposes, 3,750 of the 7,500 EIS shares are treated as having been issued in 2000/01 (by virtue of Mr Jones' carry-back claim — see 26.9 above). Therefore, those shares are treated as disposed of in priority to those on which relief was given in 2001/02.

(*b*) EIS relief is withdrawn if shares are disposed of before the end of the requisite three-year period (five years for shares issued before 6 April 2000). In this example, relief attributable to the shares sold is fully withdrawn as consideration received, reduced as illustrated, exceeds the relief attributable. See the example below for where the reverse applies. The consideration is reduced where the relief attributable (A) is less than tax at the lower rate on the amount subscribed (B), and is so reduced by applying the fraction A/B. See 26.12 above.

(*c*) Relief is withdrawn by means of a Schedule D, Case VI assessment for the year(s) in which relief was given (see 26.12 above).

(*d*) The capital gain on the disposal is fully chargeable as the shares are not held for the requisite three-year period (see Tolley's Capital Gains Tax).

In December 2002 Mr Jones disposes of his 18,750 ordinary £1 shares in D Ltd (see 26.9 above), in an arm's length transaction, for £15,000.

The position is as follows.

Income tax

2001/02	£
Relief attributable to shares sold	1,832
Consideration received $£15{,}000 \times \dfrac{1{,}832}{£18{,}750 \times 20\%} = £7{,}328$ @ 20%	1,466
Excess of relief over lower rate relief on adjusted consideration	£366
Relief withdrawn—Schedule D, Case VI assessment	£1,466

Capital gains tax

2002/03

	£	£
Disposal proceeds (December 2002)		15,000
Cost (November 2001)	18,750	
Less Relief attributable to shares:		
£1,832 – £1,466	366	
		18,384
Allowable loss		£3,384

Notes

(*a*) The EIS relief withdrawn is limited to the consideration received, reduced as illustrated, at the lower rate of tax for the year for which relief was given. If the disposal had been made otherwise than by way of a bargain made at arm's length, the full relief would have been withdrawn. See 26.12 above.

(*b*) An allowable loss may arise for capital gains tax purposes on a disposal of EIS shares, whether or not the disposal occurs within the requisite three-year period. In computing such a loss, the allowable cost is reduced by EIS relief attributable to the shares (and not withdrawn). See Tolley's Capital Gains Tax.

(*c*) A loss, as computed for capital gains tax purposes, may be relieved against income on a claim under *ICTA 1988, s 574* (losses on unquoted shares — see 46.18 LOSSES).

26.14 SUBSIDIARY COMPANIES

The existence of certain subsidiaries in the 'relevant period' (see 26.6 above) does not prevent the parent being a qualifying company (see 26.5 above). The conditions imposed on any such subsidiary are:

(*a*) (i) the qualifying company, or another of its subsidiaries, must possess at least 75% (as regards shares issued before 6 April 1998, 90%) of both the issued share capital and the voting power, and be beneficially entitled to at least 75% (as regards shares issued before 6 April 1998, 90%) of the assets available for distribution to equity holders on a winding-up etc. (see *ICTA 1988, Sch 18 paras 1, 3*) and of the profits available for distribution to equity holders,

(ii) no other person may have control (within *ICTA 1988, s 840*, see 20.8 CONNECTED PERSONS) of the subsidiary, and

(iii) no arrangements (as very broadly defined) may exist whereby (i) or (ii) could cease to be satisfied; and

(*b*) (before 27 November 1997) that it must either exist wholly, or substantially wholly, for the purpose of carrying on one or more qualifying trades (see 26.7 above), or be a 'property managing' or 'dormant' subsidiary.

The condition at (*a*) above must continue to be satisfied until the end of the relevant period, except that the winding-up or dissolution, during that period, of the subsidiary or of the qualifying company does not prevent those conditions being satisfied, provided that the winding-up etc. meets the conditions applied in relation to qualifying companies (see 26.5 above). The conditions are also not regarded as ceasing to be satisfied by reason only of the disposal of the interest in the subsidiary within the relevant period if it can be shown to be for *bona fide* commercial reasons and not part of a tax avoidance scheme.

A '*property managing*' subsidiary is one which exists wholly (or substantially wholly) for the purpose of holding and managing property used by the qualifying company, or a subsidiary, for the purposes of a qualifying trade or trades carried on by the qualifying company or a subsidiary, or for the purposes of research and development from which such a qualifying trade is intended to be derived.

A '*dormant*' subsidiary is one with no corporation tax profits, and no part of whose business consists in the making of investments.

[*ICTA 1988, ss 308, 312(1); FA 1994, Sch 15 paras 23, 24; FA 1997, Sch 8 paras 1, 6; FA 1998, s 74, Sch 13 para 21; FA 2000, Sch 17 para 14*].

See also now 26.2(iii) above for permitted subsidiaries.

Simon's Direct Tax Service. See E3.117.

26.15 MARRIED PERSONS

The provisions for withdrawal of relief on the disposal of shares in respect of which relief has been given (see 26.12 above) do not apply to transfers between spouses living together. On any subsequent disposal or other event, the spouse to whom the shares were so transferred is treated as if he or she were the person who subscribed for the shares, and as if his or her liability to income tax had been reduced in respect of those shares by the same amount, and for the same year of assessment, as applied on the subscription by the transferor spouse. Any assessment for reducing or withdrawing relief is made on the transferee spouse. As regards inter-spouse transfers after 5 April 1998, the identification rules for disposals at 26.12 above apply to determine the extent (if any) to which shares to which relief is attributable are comprised in the transfer. [*ICTA 1988, s 304; FA 1994, Sch 15 para 18; FA 1998, Sch 13 para 16*].

26.16 EIS COMPANY BECOMING WHOLLY-OWNED SUBSIDIARY OF NEW HOLDING COMPANY

Where a company (Company A) has issued eligible shares (the old shares) under the enterprise investment scheme (a certificate having been issued on Form EIS 3 — see 26.11 above) and, by means of an exchange of shares, all of its shares are acquired by a company (Company B) in which the only previously issued shares are subscriber shares, then, subject to the further conditions below being satisfied, the exchange is not regarded as involving a disposal of the old shares (and a consequent withdrawal of relief) and an acquisition of the Company B shares (the new shares). EIS relief attributable to the old shares is regarded as attributable instead to the new shares for which they are exchanged. For EIS purposes generally, the new shares stand in the shoes of the old shares, e.g. as if they had been subscribed for and issued at the time the old shares were subscribed for and issued and as if anything done by or in relation to Company A had been done by or in relation to Company B.

The further conditions are as follows.

(*a*) The new shares must be issued after 5 April 1998.

(*b*) The consideration for the old shares must consist entirely of the issue of the new shares.

(*c*) The consideration for old shares of each description must consist entirely of new shares of the 'corresponding description'.

(*d*) New shares of each description must be issued to holders of old shares of the 'corresponding description' in respect of and in proportion to their holdings.

(*e*) Before the issue of the new shares, on the written application of either Company A or Company B, the Board must have notified to that company their satisfaction that the exchange

(i) is for *bona fide* commercial reasons; and

(ii) does not form part of a scheme or arrangements designed to avoid liability to corporation tax or capital gains tax.

The Board may, within 30 days of an application, request further particulars, which must then be supplied within 30 days of the request (or such longer period as they may allow in any particular case).

For the purposes of (*c*) and (*d*) above, old and new shares are of a '*corresponding description*' if, assuming they were shares in the same company, they would be of the same class and carry the same rights.

References above to 'shares' (other than those to 'eligible shares' or 'subscriber shares') include references to 'securities'

An exchange within these provisions does not breach the conditions at 26.5(ii)–(iv) above (definition of 'qualifying company').

[*ICTA 1988, s 304A; TCGA 1992, s 138(2); FA 1998, Sch 13 para 17*].

Simon's Direct Tax Service. See E3.121.

26.17 **MISCELLANEOUS**

Capital gains tax. In determining the gain or loss on a disposal of shares to which any income tax relief is attributable (see 26.8 above):

(*a*) if a loss would otherwise arise, the consideration the individual is treated as having given for the shares is treated as reduced by the amount of the relief;

(*b*) if the disposal is after the end of the 'relevant period' (see 26.3 above) and a gain would otherwise arise, the gain is not a chargeable gain (although this does not prevent a loss arising in these circumstances from being an allowable loss). Where the reduction in liability in respect of the issue of the shares was less than the amount corresponding to lower rate income tax on the amount subscribed for the shares (other than because there is insufficient income tax liability to make full use of the relief), there is a corresponding reduction in the amount of the gain which is not chargeable.

Where a gain (or part of a gain) on a disposal is not a chargeable gain under (*b*) above, but the income tax relief on the shares disposed of is reduced on account of value received from the company by the claimant or by other persons (see 26.12 above) before the disposal but after 28 November 1994, then a corresponding proportion of the gain is brought back into charge.

The identification rules of *ICTA 1988, s 299* (see 26.12 above) apply for the above purposes.

See further *TCGA 1992, ss 150A, 150B* as amended and introduced by *FA 1994, Sch 15 paras 28–34* and *FA 1995, Sch 13 paras 1–3*, and as further amended by *FA 1998, Sch 13 paras 24, 25, Sch 27 Pt III(14)*. For full coverage, see the corresponding chapter of Tolley's Capital Gains Tax.

Capital gains deferral relief. General reinvestment relief was available for reinvestment into qualifying shares acquired before 6 April 1998 but such relief for reinvestment into shares on which EIS income tax relief was claimed was prohibited by *TCGA 1992, s 164MA*. However, a specific relief was introduced by *FA 1995, s 67, Sch 13 para 4(3)* whereby any chargeable gain accruing after 28 November 1994 could be deferred to the extent that it could be matched with an investment in EIS shares to which income tax relief was attributable (see 26.8 above).

In relation to EIS shares issued after 5 April 1998, significant changes were made to the deferral relief provisions. In particular, it is no longer a requirement that the shares qualify for income tax relief nor that the individual be unconnected with the company. However, the company itself must be a qualifying company (as in 26.5 above) and certain other EIS income tax relief conditions are adopted. The provisions are also extended to trustees. These changes are intended to compensate for the abolition of general reinvestment relief. There is no limit on the amount of the gain that can be deferred under the new provisions (previously the income tax relief annual maximum at 26.10 above would have applied), but the gross assets test at 26.5 above does limit the amount that may be invested in any one EIS company (or group).

Deferral relief applies where

(*a*) a chargeable gain would otherwise accrue to an individual

 (i) on the disposal by him of any asset; or

 (ii) on the occurrence of a chargeable event under these provisions or the provisions governing reinvestment into VCT shares (see 91.14 VENTURE CAPITAL TRUSTS); or

 (iii) (as regards shares issued after 5 April 1998) to give effect to a withdrawal of general reinvestment relief;

(*b*) the individual makes a 'qualifying investment'; and

(*c*) the individual is UK resident or ordinarily resident both when the chargeable gain accrues to him and when he makes the qualifying investment, and is not, at the time he makes the investment, regarded as resident outside the UK for the purposes of any double taxation arrangements the effect of which would be that he would not be liable to tax on a gain arising on a disposal, immediately after their acquisition, of the shares comprising the qualifying investment, disregarding any exemption available under *TCGA 1992, s 150A* (see above).

Subject to the further conditions referred to above, a '*qualifying investment*' is a subscription *wholly in cash* for eligible shares (broadly, *new* ordinary, non-preferential, shares) in a qualifying EIS company which are issued within the one year immediately preceding or the three years immediately following the time the chargeable gain in question accrues. These time limits may be extended by the Board in individual cases. If the shares are issued *before* the gain accrues, they must still be held at the time it accrues. The deferred gain is brought back into charge on the occurrence of (and at the time of) any one of a number of specified chargeable events, in particular the disposal (at any time) of the shares in question.

[*TCGA 1992, s 150C, Sch 5B; FA 1995, Sch 13 para 4; FA 1998, s 74, Sch 13 paras 26–36, Sch 27 Pt III(14); FA 1999, s 73, Sch 8; FA 2000, Sch 17 para 7*].

For full coverage, see the corresponding chapter of Tolley's Capital Gains Tax.

See Simon's Direct Tax Service C3.10.

Information. Certain events leading to withdrawal or reduction of income tax relief must be notified to the inspector, generally within 60 days, by either the individual who received the relief, the issuing company, or any person connected with the issuing company having knowledge of the matter. The inspector may require such a notice and other relevant information where he has reason to believe it should have been made. The penalty provisions of *TMA 1970, s 98* apply for failure to comply.

The inspector also has broad powers to require information in other cases where relief may be withdrawn, restricted or not due. The requirements of secrecy do not prevent his disclosing to a company that relief has been given or claimed on certain of its shares. [*ICTA 1988, s 310; FA 1993, s 111(2); FA 1994, Sch 15 para 25; FA 1998, s 71(3)–(5), s 74, Sch 13 para 22, Sch 27 Pt III(14)*].

See Simon's Direct Tax Service E3.155.

26.18 **BUSINESS EXPANSION SCHEME**

As indicated at 26.1 above, the predecessor to the Enterprise Investment Scheme, the Business Expansion Scheme ('BES') ceased to apply to shares issued after 31 December 1993, although the BES legislation has been 'revived' to apply to the EIS. In view of the numerous amendments, the provisions applicable to the BES are described fully at 26.19 *et seq.* below. Statutory references are to the provisions before amendment by *FA 1994, Sch 15.*

The BES is dealt with in this chapter under the following headings.

26.19	Conditions for relief	26.27	Restriction or withdrawal of relief
26.20	— qualifying individual	26.28	Subsidiary companies
26.21	— qualifying company	26.29	Married persons
26.22	— eligible shares	26.30	BES company becoming wholly-owned subsidiary of new holding company
26.23	— qualifying trade	26.31	Miscellaneous
26.24	Method of giving relief		
26.25	Limits on relief		
26.26	Claims for relief		

See generally Revenue Inspector's Manual, IM 6500–6922.

Simon's Direct Tax Service. See E3.2.

26.19 **Conditions for relief.** A 'qualifying individual' who subscribes for 'eligible shares' in a 'qualifying company' issued after 5 April 1983 and before 1 January 1994 may claim income tax relief on his investment, provided that the purpose of the issue is to raise money (i.e. cash, see *Thompson v Hart Ch D, [2000] STC 381*) for a 'qualifying trade' carried on by the company (or by certain subsidiaries of the company, see 26.28 below) or which it intends to carry on and in fact commences within two years of the issue. For shares issued after 5 April 1985 and before 1 January 1994, the money may alternatively (or in addition) be raised for 'research and development', to be carried on by the company (or, for shares issued after 18 March 1986 and before 1 January 1994, by a subsidiary of the company), from which the 'qualifying trade' is intended to be derived, and which is being carried on at or immediately after the time of issue of the shares. [*ICTA 1988, s 289(1)(a)–(c)(8)(a)(ii), s 308; F(No 2)A 1992, s 38*].

For the date on which shares are issued, see *National Westminster Bank plc v CIR; Barclays Bank plc v CIR HL 1994, 67 TC 1.*

See 26.27, 26.31 below for denial of relief in certain cases.

'*Research and development*' means any activity intended to result in a patentable invention or computer program. [*ICTA 1988, s 312(1)*].

For shares issued after 25 July 1986 and before 1 January 1994, the relief is extended to the raising of money for oil exploration from which a 'qualifying trade' is intended to be derived and which is being carried on by the company (or by a subsidiary) at or immediately after the time of issue of the shares. The exploration must be carried out solely within the area to which an exploration licence granted to the company (or to a subsidiary) applies, and that licence must be held throughout the three years from the date of issue of the shares. Neither the company nor any subsidiary may, at the time of issue of the shares, hold an appraisal or development licence relating to the same area, but where such a licence is granted in the three years following the issue of the shares, that licence and the exploration licence are treated as a single exploration licence for the purposes of these provisions. Also, for these purposes only, a trade consisting to any substantial extent of oil extraction activities may be a 'qualifying trade' notwithstanding the exclusion of such trades from the general provisions (see 26.23(*d*) below). [*ICTA 1988, s 289(1)(d)(2)(3), s 297(9); F(No 2)A 1992, s 38*].

For shares issued after 28 July 1988 and before 1 January 1994, the relief is further extended to the raising of money by a company which, or a subsidiary of which, carries on, or intends to carry on, '*qualifying activities*', i.e. activities consisting of or connected with the provision and maintenance of certain dwelling-houses let, or to be let, by the company on 'qualifying tenancies', provided that those activities are conducted, throughout the '*relevant period*' (i.e. the period of four years from date of issue of the shares), on a commercial basis with a view to profit. All dwelling-houses are included except:

(*a*) those with a 'market value' exceeding £85,000 (£125,000 in Greater London) (both figures variable by Treasury Order);

(*b*) those unfit for human habitation or sub-standard (within *Housing Act 1985, ss 604, 508* or Scottish or NI equivalent);

(*c*) those already let, i.e.

- (i) where, before the '*relevant date*' (i.e. the date on which the company or a subsidiary first acquired an interest in the house or the related land), the company or any of its subsidiaries had made arrangements for letting the whole or part of the house in question, or
- (ii) where at that date the whole or part of the house in question was let, or
- (iii) where after that date the whole or any part of the house in question has been let other than on a 'qualifying tenancy';

(*d*) those already qualifying for relief, i.e. a dwelling-house within these provisions in which an interest has been owned by another company (or subsidiary) at any time since that company issued shares qualifying for relief under these provisions; or

(*e*) those qualifying for writing-down allowances under *CAA 1990, s 85* (see 10.9 CAPITAL ALLOWANCES).

For shares issued after 9 March 1992, (*c*) above is modified so as not to exclude certain prior lettings (or prior arrangements for lettings) to persons who had previously been 'owner-occupiers' (as defined) of the dwelling-houses concerned.

Companies or subsidiaries which are registered housing associations are excluded from the above provisions.

'*Market value*' for the purpose of (*a*) above is the expected open market sale price of the dwelling-house at the time of issue of the shares (or, if later, at the date when the company or a subsidiary first acquired an interest in the property), but on the assumptions that it was then in the same state as at the date of the valuation and that the sale was with vacant possession and was on specified terms as to title (see *FA 1988, Sch 4 para 13(4)*). For valuations before 20 March 1990, an additional assumption had to be made that the locality in which the property is situated was then in the same state as at the date of the valuation as regards occupation and use of other premises in the locality, transport services and other local facilities and amenities.

A '*qualifying tenancy*' is a tenancy which is, for the purposes of the *Housing Act 1988* (or Scottish or NI equivalent), an assured tenancy other than an assured shorthold tenancy (in Scotland, an assured tenancy other than a short assured tenancy, in NI, a tenancy complying with prescribed requirements and conditions), except that neither a tenancy granted for a premium within *TCGA 1992, Sch 8*, nor a tenancy of a dwelling-house in relation to which an option to purchase has been granted to the tenant or an 'associate' (see 26.20(iii) below) of his, can be a qualifying tenancy. [*FA 1988, s 50, Sch 4; FA 1990, s 73; F(No 2)A 1992, s 40*].

Relief is allowed only when the company (or subsidiary) has carried on the trade, research and development, exploration or activities for four months. If, before the trade has been carried on for four months, the company (or subsidiary) is dissolved or wound up for *bona fide* commercial reasons, and not as part of a scheme the main purpose (or one such purpose) of which was tax avoidance, relief will nevertheless be available (except in the case of a company carrying on 'qualifying activities', see above). [*ICTA 1988, s 289(8)(13); FA 1988, Sch 4 para 2*].

Relief is available where eligible shares issued after 18 March 1986 are held on a bare trust for two or more beneficiaries as if each beneficiary had subscribed as an individual for all of those shares, and as if the amount subscribed by each was the total subscribed divided by the number of beneficiaries. [*ICTA 1988, s 311(2)*].

Relief is also available where shares are subscribed for by a nominee for the individual claiming relief, including the managers of an investment fund approved by the Board for this purpose (an '*approved fund*'). With regard to an approved fund closing after 15 March 1988 (i.e. when no further investments in it are to be accepted after that date) relief is given to an individual (see 26.24, 26.25 below), and certain provisions relating to married couples (see 26.29 below) applied, as if the eligible shares were issued at the time at which the fund was closed, provided that the amount subscribed on behalf of the individual for eligible shares issued within six months of closure of the fund is not less than 90% of the individual's investment in that fund. [*ICTA 1988, s 311(1)(2A)(2B)(3); FA 1988, s 53*]. Detailed guidance on the criteria and related matters for approval of such funds are available from Inland Revenue, Company Tax Division (Business Expansion Scheme), Room 109, New Wing, Somerset House, London WC2R 1LB.

26.20 A '*qualifying individual*' must be resident and ordinarily resident in the UK at the time of the issue, must subscribe for the shares on his own behalf, and must not, at any time in the 'relevant period', be 'connected with' the issuing company (or a subsidiary of that company) (i.e. provided that there is no such connection at any time in that period, see *Wild v Cannavan CA 1997, 70 TC 554*). He is so '*connected with*' any company

(i) of which he is an employee, partner or director, or of a partner of which he is an employee or director, except that as a director he is only 'connected with' a company from which he (or a partnership of which he is a member) receives or is entitled to receive, during the five years following the issue, a payment other than by way of

(*a*) payment or reimbursement of allowable expenditure under Schedule E,

(*b*) interest at a commercial rate on money lent,

(*c*) dividends, etc. representing a normal return on investment,

(*d*) payment for supply of goods at no more than market value, or

(*e*) any reasonable and necessary remuneration for services rendered (other than secretarial or managerial services, or those rendered by the company itself) which is chargeable under Schedule D, Case I or II;

(ii) (in relation to 'qualifying activities', see 26.19 above) if he occupies, or is a tenant of, a dwelling-house in which the company has an interest superior to any he holds;

(iii) of which an associate (as defined by *ICTA 1988, s 417(3)(4)* but excluding a brother or sister) meets any of the conditions at (i) or (ii) above;

(iv) if he directly or indirectly possesses or is entitled to acquire

(*a*) more than 30% of its voting power, its issued ordinary share capital, or its loan capital and issued share capital together (loan capital including any debt incurred by the company for money borrowed, for capital assets acquired, for any right to income created in its favour, or for insufficient consideration, but excluding a debt incurred by overdrawing a bank account in the ordinary course of the bank's business), or

(*b*) rights entitling him to more than 30% of its assets available for distribution to the company's equity holders (as defined at *ICTA 1988, Sch 18 paras 1, 3* — see Tolley's Corporation Tax under Groups of Companies); or

(v) of which he has control (as defined by *ICTA 1988, s 840*, see 20.8 CONNECTED PERSONS);

and in applying (iv) and (v), rights and powers of his associates are not attributed to him (see *Cook v Billings and others Ch D, [1999] STC 661*).

An investor who acquires one of two subscriber shares in a company from company formation agents will, by concession, not be regarded as being connected with the company by virtue of (iv)(*a*) above solely because, until further shares are issued, he holds 50% of the company's issued share capital, provided that the company enters into no other transactions in the meanwhile. (Revenue Pamphlet IR 1, A76).

For shares issued after 5 April 1986, an individual treated under *ICTA 1988, s 132(4)(a)* as performing the duties of his employment in the UK (see 75.2(i) SCHEDULE E) is treated for this purpose as resident and ordinarily resident in the UK.

A '*subsidiary company*' is included within (i) to (v) above if it is a subsidiary during the relevant period, whether or not it becomes a subsidiary before, during or after the year of assessment in respect of which the individual claims relief and whether or not it is a subsidiary during the time that the circumstances in (i) to (v) above exist.

'*Relevant period*' in this context means the period from the date of incorporation of the company (or, if later, two years before the shares were issued) to five years after the issue of the shares.

Relief is denied where reciprocal arrangements are made aimed at circumventing this provision.

Parallel trades. Relief may be denied in respect of shares in a company issued after 18 March 1986 where, on the date of issue of the shares (or, if later, the date on which the company commences trading), the individual subscribing for the shares is both one of a group of persons who either control the company (within *ICTA 1988, s 416*) or together own more than a half share (determined as under *ICTA 1988, s 344(1)(a)(b), (2), (3)*) in the trade, business, profession or vocation carried on by the company and also, individually or as one of a group, has such an interest in another company. Where a substantial part of the trade, etc. carried on by the issuing company or by a subsidiary is concerned with the same or similar types of property or provides the same or similar services or facilities, and serves substantially the same outlets or markets, as the other company's trade, etc., no relief is available in respect of the shares subscribed for. Rights and powers of associates (see 26.20(iii) above) are taken into account.

This restriction does not apply in respect of a company carrying on 'qualifying activities' (see 26.19 above).

See 26.21 below for similar restrictions applying for shares issued before 19 March 1986.

[*ICTA 1988, s 289(12), s 291, s 309(5); FA 1988, Sch 4 paras 4, 5*].

26.21 A '*qualifying company*' must be incorporated in the UK. It must throughout the 'relevant period' be unquoted, be resident only in the UK, and must either

(*a*) exist (or exist mainly) either to carry on one or more 'qualifying trades' 'wholly or mainly in the UK' or to carry on 'qualifying activities' (see 26.19 above), or

(*b*) consist of holding shares or securities of, or making loans to, 'qualifying subsidiaries' (see 26.28 below), with or without either the carrying on of one or more 'qualifying trades' 'wholly or mainly in the UK' or the carrying on of 'qualifying activities'.

A company falling within (*a*) for part of the 'relevant period' and within (*b*) for the remainder is regarded as meeting this condition throughout the 'relevant period'. (ICAEW Technical Memorandum TR 831, 19 April 1991).

For shares issued after 18 March 1986, the qualifying trade(s) carried on by the company and its qualifying subsidiaries must, as a whole, be carried out 'wholly or mainly in the UK'. Although a winding-up or dissolution in the 'relevant period' generally prevents a company meeting these conditions, they are deemed met if the winding-up or dissolution is for *bona fide* commercial reasons and not part of a scheme the main purpose (or one such purpose) of which is tax avoidance, *provided that* any net assets are distributed to its members (or dealt with as *bona vacantia*) before the end of the 'relevant period' or (if later) the end of three years from the commencement of winding-up.

'*Relevant period*' in this context means the period from the date of issue of the shares to three years after that date or, if later, three years after the 'qualifying trade' was commenced following issue of the shares. The alternative later date does not apply to shares issued wholly or partly for research and development (see 26.19 above). The period is four years from the date of issue in relation to a company carrying on 'qualifying activities' (see 26.19 above).

In considering whether a trade is carried on '*wholly or mainly in the UK*', the totality of the trade activities is taken into account. Although no one factor is likely to be decisive, such things as the locations at which capital assets are held, and where purchasing, processing, manufacturing and selling is done, and the places where employees customarily carry out their duties will, for example, be relevant. A company may carry on some such activities outside the UK and yet satisfy the requirement that the major part, that is to say more than one-half, of the trade activities as a whole takes place in the UK. Thus relief is not excluded solely because some or all of a company's products or services are exported, or because its raw materials are imported, and the warehousing of raw materials, the storage of products pending sale or the availability of marketing facilities outside the UK would similarly not be sufficient by themselves to deny relief. Similar principles apply in considering the trade(s) carried on by a company and its qualifying subsidiaries.

In the particular case of a ship chartering trade, the test is satisfied if all charters are entered into in the UK and the provision of crews and management of the ships while under charter take place mainly in the UK. If these conditions are not met, the test may still be satisfied depending on all the relevant facts and circumstances. (Revenue Pamphlet IR 131, SP 4/87, 23 April 1987). The 'crew provision and management' test replaces an earlier 'port of call' test, but where relief was given under that earlier test, it will not be withdrawn if the revised test is not satisfied. (Revenue Pamphlet IR 131, SP 7/86, 12 September 1986; Revenue Press Release 23 April 1987).

A company is '*unquoted*' if none of its shares, stocks or debentures is listed on the Stock Exchange or dealt in on the Unlisted Securities Market.

The company must also not at any time in the relevant period either

(i) have share capital which includes any issued shares not fully paid-up; or

(ii) control another company (other than a 'qualifying' subsidiary, see 26.28 below, and subject to 26.30 below), or be controlled by another company (control being as defined by *ICTA 1988, s 416*, and being considered with or without connected persons under *ICTA 1988, s 839* (see 20 CONNECTED PERSONS)); or

(iii) be a 51% subsidiary of another company or itself have a 51% subsidiary (other than a 'qualifying' subsidiary, see 26.28 below, and subject to 26.30 below); or

(iv) be capable of falling within (ii) or (iii) by virtue of any arrangements.

Parallel trades. For shares issued before 19 March 1986, there was an additional exclusion if an individual who, after 5 April 1983, had acquired a 'controlling interest' in the company's trade, or the trade of any subsidiary of the company, also had or had had such an interest in another trade concerned with similar goods or services, or serving a similar market, at any time in the period from two years before to three years after the later of the date of issue of the shares and the date the company or subsidiary commenced the trade. This restriction did not apply where the *same* trade was previously carried on by the person with the 'controlling interest' as was subsequently carried on by the 'qualifying company'. (Tolley's Practical Tax 1985 p 31).

In the case of a trade carried on by a company, a person has a '*controlling interest*' if he controls (within the definition of *ICTA 1988, s 416*) the company; or if the company is close and he is a director of the company and the owner of, or able to control, more than 30% of its ordinary share capital; or if at least half of its ordinary share capital is directly or indirectly owned by him or by an 'associate' of his. In any other case it is obtained by his being entitled to at least half of the assets used for, or income arising from, the trade. In either case, the rights and powers of any person's 'associates' are attributed to the person. '*Associate*' is as defined at 26.20(iii) above.

Simplified provisions apply in relation to shares issued after 18 March 1986 by disqualification from relief of certain individuals (see 26.20 above).

Land and buildings. For shares issued after 18 March 1986 other than by a company carrying on 'qualifying activities' (see 26.19 above), subject to an exemption for small issues, there is an additional exclusion if, at any time during the relevant period **and before 29 November 1994**, the value of the company's 'interests in land' (or, where lower, the value of those interests immediately after the issue of the shares, adjusted as below) exceeds half the value of all its assets (or such other fraction as the Treasury may substitute by statutory instrument). The value of those interests is for this purpose the aggregate of the market values of each such interest less debts secured thereon (including floating charges), unsecured debts not falling due within twelve months and any amount paid up in respect of shares carrying a present or future preferential right to the company's assets on its winding-up. The value of the company's assets as a whole is similarly the aggregate market value less the company's debts and liabilities (including any amount paid up in respect of shares carrying a present or future preferential right to the company's assets on its winding-up, but excluding any other share capital, share premium account or reserves). Any question, on appeal, of the value of an interest in land is determined by the appropriate Lands Tribunal.

An 'interest in land' is valued on the assumption that there is no source of mineral deposits in the land exploitable other than by opencast mining or quarrying. Where the company is a member of a partnership, the value of any 'interest in land' held by the partnership is apportioned as on a dissolution of the partnership. A qualifying company and its subsidiaries are treated as one company for these purposes, but ignoring any debts and liabilities as between such companies.

'*Interest in land*' is widely defined to include rights related to land, and rights to obtain an interest, etc. from another which depend on that other's ability to grant the interest, etc., but excludes the interest of a creditor secured by any mortgage or charge over land. Valuation (after 28 July 1988) of such an interest excludes any plant or machinery which is, in law, part of the land, etc.

The adjustments (referred to above) to the value of the company's interests in land held immediately after the issue of the shares are:

(1) the addition of the cost(s) (i.e. consideration given, ignoring any discount for postponement of right to receive it) of any subsequent acquisitions of interests in land, and of any enhancement expenditure relating to interests in land; and

(2) the deduction of any consideration for the disposal of, or grant of any interest out of, any interest in land, or derived from the ownership of interests in land (but excluding rent).

The value of an interest falls to be adjusted where the interest is under a lease at rent exceeding a full market rent. Contingent liabilities are disregarded unless and until the Board is satisfied that they have become enforceable and have been (or are being) enforced, whereon the necessary adjustments are made.

These restrictions do not apply where the total raised by the issue in question and any other issue in the previous twelve months (but not before 19 March 1986) does not exceed £50,000, and where it does exceed £50,000 they apply only to the excess. The figure of £50,000 is reduced where, at any time in the relevant period, the company (or a subsidiary) carries on a trade in partnership, or in a joint venture, with another company.

Any restriction of relief under these provisions is apportioned amongst the qualifying individuals subscribing for otherwise eligible shares in proportion to their subscriptions, subject to determination on appeal by the General (or, in certain cases, the Special) Commissioners.

These restrictions ceased to apply with effect from 29 November 1994.

[*ICTA 1988, s 289(12), ss 293–296, s 298(1)(2), s 312(1)(2); TMA 1970, s 47B; FA 1988, s 52, Sch 4 paras 2(4), 6, 7; FA 1995, s 68(2); FA 1998, Sch 13 para 38*].

26.22 '*Eligible shares*' means new ordinary shares which, for five years after issue, carry no present or future preferential rights to dividends or assets (on a winding-up) or to be redeemed. [*ICTA 1988, s 289(4)*].

26.23 A '*qualifying trade*' may not at any time in the 'relevant period' (as defined in 26.21 above) consist to any 'substantial' extent of, or (for shares issued after 18 March 1986) of a combination of

(*a*) dealing in commodities, shares, securities, land or futures; or

(*b*) dealing in goods otherwise than in an ordinary trade of wholesale or retail distribution (see below); or

(*c*) banking, insurance or any other financial activities; or

(*d*) in relation to shares issued after 25 July 1986, oil extraction activities (but without prejudice to relief in respect of oil exploration (see 26.19 above) for which the activities would otherwise qualify); or (*e*) leasing or letting or receiving royalties or licence fees; or

(*f*) providing legal or accountancy services; or

(*g*) providing services and facilities for any trade, profession or vocation concerned in (*a*) to (*f*) and carried on by another person (other than a parent company), where one person has a 'controlling interest' (see 26.21 above) in both trades; or

(*h*) in relation to shares issued after 13 March 1984 and before 19 March 1986, farming; or

(*j*) in relation to shares issued after 19 March 1985 and before 19 March 1986, 'property development', i.e. development of land by a company which has, or has had, an interest in it (as defined, including certain rights to acquire land but excluding ordinary interests of creditors), with the sole or main object of realising a gain on its disposal.

Adventures and concerns in the nature of trade, and trades not carried on commercially and with an expectation of profits, are also generally excluded.

It is understood that the Revenue regard as '*substantial*' a part of a trade which consists of 20% or more of total turnover. (Tolley's Practical Tax 1987 p 162).

As regards (*a*) above, it is not intended to exclude from relief what is mainly a building trade, despite the technical position that what the builder sells is the land with the buildings on it. (Tolley's Practical Tax 1984 p 206). (See, however, (*j*) above, itself replaced after 18 March 1986 by the 'land and buildings' provisions described at 26.21 above.)

As regards (*b*) above, a trade of wholesale or retail distribution is a trade consisting of the offer of goods for sale either to persons for resale (or processing and resale) (which resale must, for shares issued after 18 March 1986, be to members of the general public) by them ('wholesale') or to the general public ('retail') and, for shares issued after 18 March 1986, a trade is not an ordinary wholesale or retail trade if it consists to a substantial extent of dealing in goods collected or held as an investment (or of that and any other activity within (*a*)–(*j*) above), and a substantial proportion of such goods is held for a significantly longer period than might reasonably be expected to dispose of them at market value. Whether such trades are 'ordinary' is to be judged having regard to the following features, those under (A) supporting the categorisation as 'ordinary', those under (B) being indicative to the contrary.

(A) (i) The breaking of bulk.

(ii) The purchase and sale of goods in different markets.

(iii) The employment of staff and incurring of trade expenses other than the cost of goods or of remuneration of persons connected (see 20 CONNECTED PERSONS) with a company carrying on such a trade.

(B) (i) The purchase or sale of goods from persons connected (as in (A)(iii) above) with the trader.

(ii) The matching of purchases with sales.

(iii) The holding of goods for longer than might normally be expected.

(iv) The carrying on of the trade at a place not commonly used for wholesale or retail trading.

(v) The absence of physical possession of the goods by the trader.

As regards (*e*) above, with effect from 26 July 1984 a company engaged in the production of original master films, tapes or discs is not excluded from the scheme by reason only of its receipts by way of trade of royalties or licence fees in respect of films, etc. produced by it or in respect of by-products arising therefrom. In relation to shares issued after 16 March 1987, the company may also be engaged in the distribution of films produced by it in the relevant period, but the royalties or licence fees must relate to films, etc. produced by it in that period.

Similarly, after 19 March 1985 royalties and licence fees attributable to research and development (see 26.19 above) which a company carrying on a trade has engaged in throughout the relevant period do not prevent the trade being a qualifying trade.

Also as regards (*e*) above, for shares issued after 18 March 1986, a trade will not be excluded by reason only of its consisting of letting ships, other than oil rigs or pleasure craft (as defined), on charter, provided that

- (i) the company beneficially owns all ships it so lets,
- (ii) every ship beneficially owned by the company is UK registered,
- (iii) throughout the relevant period (as defined in 26.21 above) the company is solely responsible for arranging the marketing of the services of its ships, and
- (iv) in relation to every letting on charter, certain conditions as to length and terms of charter, and the arm's length character of the transaction, are fulfilled.

If any of the conditions at (i)–(iv) above is not fulfilled in relation to certain lettings, only those lettings are taken into account in determining whether a substantial part of the trade consists of activities within (*a*)–(*j*) above.

The Treasury may, by statutory instrument, amend any of the above conditions.

[*ICTA 1988, ss 289(12), 297, 298*].

26.24 **Method of giving relief.** Relief is given on the amount subscribed (subject to certain limits, see 26.25 below) as a deduction, in the year of assessment of the share issue (but see below), from total income after any other deductions including personal allowances. It does not affect the computation of total income for the purposes of age allowance or dependent relative income limits, life assurance premium limit, and top-slicing relief on life policy etc. gains (or, where previously available, on lease premiums, termination payments and stock relief clawbacks). [*ICTA 1988, s 289(5)(14)*].

In relation to shares issued after 5 April 1987, relief in respect of shares issued before 6 October in a year of assessment may be claimed partly for the year of assessment of the share issue and partly for the preceding year. The deduction for the preceding year may not exceed one half of the total relief in respect of the shares, and the total of relief carried back to the preceding year may not exceed £5,000 in any year of assessment. [*ICTA 1988, s 289(6)(7)*]. See 26.19 above as regards time of issue of certain shares subscribed for through approved funds.

For repayment supplement purposes (see 41 INTEREST ON OVERPAID TAX) any repayment of tax is treated as being in respect of tax payable in the year of assessment in which the shares are issued or, if later, the year in which the issuing company completed its first four months' trading (see 26.19 above). [*ICTA 1988, s 289(15)*].

For treatment of married persons, see 26.29 below.

26.25 **Limits on relief.** (See 26.29 below as regards relief for married persons.)

Except in the case of investments through 'approved funds' (see 26.19 above), relief is restricted to investments of £500 or more in any one company in a year of assessment. In all cases, there is an upper limit of £40,000 on the relief which may be given to an individual for a year of assessment. [*ICTA 1988, ss 290, 311(3)*]. For 1993/94, the £40,000 limit applies to the aggregate of relief under both the BES and the EIS (see 26.1 *et seq.* above). [*FA 1994, Sch 15 para 3(3)*].

For shares issued after 15 March 1988, there is also a restriction on the total amount of eligible shares which may be issued by a company within a specified period (see below) and attract relief. Where the money raised in such a period exceeds £750,000 (£500,000 before 1 May 1990), the excess does not qualify for relief. The period specified is the longer of

(*a*) six months ending with the date of issue of the shares, and

(*b*) the period from the preceding 6 April to the date of issue.

As regards (*a*) above, shares issued before 16 March 1988 are taken into account for these purposes. There are, however, transitional provisions where shares are issued after 15 March 1988 but before 6 April 1988 in pursuance of a prospectus published or written offer made before 15 March 1988, increasing the permitted maximum to £1,000,000 in relation to the shares so issued.

Amounts raised which do not attract relief because the subscriber was not a qualifying individual (see 26.20 above), or had exceeded his personal limit or invested under the permitted minimum (see above), or because of an earlier application of these provisions, are not taken into account for the purposes of this restriction.

The limit is increased to £5,000,000 where the only qualifying trade(s) carried on by the issuing company (or by its subsidiaries) consist wholly or substantially wholly of operating or letting on charter ships other than oil rigs or pleasure craft, subject to similar conditions as apply to lettings of such ships in respect of their being a qualifying trade (see 26.23 above). The limit is also increased to £5,000,000 in the case of a company carrying on 'qualifying activities' (see 26.19 above), i.e. broadly the letting of assured tenancy housing.

The £750,000 (£500,000) and £5,000,000 permitted maxima may be varied by Treasury order.

Where, at any time within the 'relevant period' (see 26.21 above), the company issuing the shares (or a subsidiary) carries on any trade or qualifying activities (or part thereof) in partnership, or as a joint venture, with a company (with or without other persons), the appropriate permitted maximum (as above) is divided by the total number of companies (but counting the issuing company and its subsidiaries as one company) which are members of the partnership or parties to the joint venture.

Where these provisions restrict the amount of relief available to two or more individuals, the total relief available is apportioned between them according to the respective amounts subscribed for shares giving rise to the restriction. [*ICTA 1988, s 290A; FA 1988, s 51, Sch 4 para 3; SI 1990 No 862*].

26.26 **Claims for relief.** A claim for relief in respect of any shares issued by a company in a year of assessment must be made not earlier than the date on which relief becomes allowable (see 26.19 above), and must be made within two years of the end of that year of assessment (or, if later, within two years of the end of the initial period of trading giving rise to eligibility for relief, see 26.19 above). It must be accompanied by a certificate (Revenue Form BES 3) issued by the company stating that the conditions for relief, in respect of the company and the trade or activities, are satisfied in relation to these shares. Before issuing such a certificate, the company must supply to the inspector a statement that those conditions were fulfilled from the beginning of the relevant period (as defined in 26.20 or 26.21 above as appropriate), and such statement must contain such information as the Board may reasonably require and be in such form as the Board may direct (i.e. Revenue Form BES 1 (New)), and must contain a declaration that it is correct to the best of the company's knowledge and belief. It is the Revenue's view (see Revenue Tax Bulletin August 1992 p 31) that Form BES 1 (New) can be submitted immediately after issuing the shares, even though the money raised has not yet been used, provided that the qualifying trade or activities have actually been carried on for the requisite four month period. A certificate may not be issued without the inspector's authority, nor where a notice under *ICTA 1988, s 310(2)* (see 26.31 below) has been given to the inspector. For appeal purposes, the inspector's refusal to authorise a certificate is treated as the refusal of a claim by the company. If such a certificate or statement is made fraudulently or negligently, or should not have been made (see above), the company is liable to a fine of up to £3,000 (before 27 July 1989, £250 or £500 in the case of fraud). The provisions are suitably modified where relief is claimed on shares held by an 'approved fund' (see 26.19 above).

No application for postponement of tax pending appeal on the ground that relief under the current provisions is due can be made unless a claim has been duly submitted.

For the purpose of calculating interest on overdue tax (see 42 INTEREST AND SURCHARGES ON UNPAID TAX), tax charged by an assessment is regarded as due and payable notwithstanding that relief is subsequently given on a claim under these provisions, but is regarded as paid on the date on which a claim is made which results in relief being granted, unless it was either in fact paid earlier or not due and payable until later. Interest is not refunded in consequence of any subsequent discharge or repayment of tax giving effect to relief under these provisions. [*ICTA 1988, s 306; FA 1988, Sch 4 para 10; FA 1989, s 170(3)(6)*].

26.27 **Restriction or withdrawal of relief.** Relief allowed in the 'relevant period' (as defined at 26.20 or 26.21 above as appropriate) may be withdrawn if on any subsequent event it appears that the claimant was not entitled to relief. [*ICTA 1988, s 289(10)*].

Where an event giving rise to complete withdrawal of relief occurs at the same time as a disposal at a loss, the disposal is regarded as occurring first, so that relief may be only partially withdrawn (as below). (Revenue Inspector's Manual, IM 6600).

Loan linked investments. For claims made after 15 March 1993, relief is denied in respect of shares issued after 15 March 1993 where

(*a*) a loan is made to the individual subscribing for the shares or to an 'associate' (within *ICTA 1988, s 417(3)(4)* but excluding a brother or sister) by any person at any time in the relevant period (as defined in 26.20 above), and

(*b*) the loan would not have been made, or would not have been made on the same terms, if he had not subscribed, or had not been proposing to subscribe, for the shares.

The granting of credit to, or the assignment of a debt due from, the individual or an associate of his is counted as a loan for these purposes.

[*ICTA 1988, s 299A; FA 1993, s 111*].

For the date on which shares are issued, see *National Westminster Bank plc v CIR; Barclays Bank plc v CIR HL 1994, 67 TC 1.*

For this restriction to apply, the test is whether the lender makes the loan on terms which are connected with the fact that the borrower (or an associate) is subscribing for eligible shares. The prime concern is why the lender made the loan rather than why the borrower applied for it. Relief would not be disallowed, for example, in the case of a bank loan if the bank would have made a loan on the same terms to a similar borrower for a different purpose. But if, for example, a loan is made specifically on a security consisting of or including the eligible shares (other than as part of a broad range of assets to which the lender has recourse), relief would be denied. Relevant features of the loan terms would be the qualifying conditions to be satisfied by the borrower, any incentives or benefits offered to the borrower, the time allowed for repayment, the amount of repayments and interest charged, the timing of interest payments, and the nature of the security. (Revenue Pamphlet IR 131, SP 6/98, 30 November 1998, replacing SP 3/94, 9 May 1994, as revised).

Disposal of shares. Where an individual disposes of shares, on the purchase of which relief was obtained, before the end of the 'relevant period' (as defined in 26.20 above), then

(*a*) if the disposal is not at arm's length, all relief is withdrawn;

(*b*) otherwise, relief is withdrawn to the extent of the amount or value of consideration received.

Relief is also withdrawn in respect of options granted after 18 March 1986, the exercise of which would bind the grantor to purchase any shares (a 'put' option), where the option is granted during the relevant period (as above) to the individual who subscribed for the shares.

Sales out of, and options over, a holding of ordinary shares of any class in a company on only part of which relief has been obtained are treated as relating to shares on which relief has been obtained rather than others, and to those on which relief has been obtained under the original provisions rather than those on which relief has been obtained under the current provisions. Subject to this, disposals are identified with shares of the same class issued earlier before shares issued later (i.e. first in/first out (FIFO)). Shares are treated as being of the same class only if they would be so treated if dealt with on the Stock Exchange. For disposals after 5 April 1998, where shares in respect of which relief has been given (and not withdrawn) and shares in respect of which no relief has been given (or relief has been withdrawn) were acquired on the same day, any of those shares disposed of (applying the FIFO basis) are treated as relating to the latter in priority to the former. Shares transferred between spouses living together are treated as if they were acquired by the transferee spouse on the day they were issued (see also 26.29 below). Shares comprised in a 'new holding' following a reorganisation to which *TCGA 1992, s 127* applies (see Tolley's Capital Gains Tax under Shares and Securities) are treated as having been acquired when the original shares were acquired.

For these purposes, in relation to options granted after 18 March 1986, the grant of an option the exercise of which would bind the grantor to sell the shares (a 'call' option) is treated as a disposal of the shares. The grant of such an option to the proprietor of the company will not result in withdrawal of relief provided that full market value will be received on exercise of the option. (Revenue Press Release 18 March 1986).

Where, on a capital reorganisation, new shares or debentures are allotted (without payment) in proportion to a holding of shares which have attracted relief, and are treated for capital gains tax as being the same asset, the disposal of the new shares or debentures is treated as a disposal of shares which have attracted relief.

[*ICTA 1988, s 299; FA 1998, Sch 13 para 39*].

Value received from company. Subject to the above, entitlement to relief in respect of shares issued by a company is reduced by the amount of any 'value received' from the company (including any company which, during the 'relevant period', is a subsidiary of that company, whether it becomes a subsidiary before or after the individual receives any value from it) during the 'relevant period' (as defined in 26.20 above). Value received is disregarded for these purposes to the extent that it has already resulted in a reduction of relief.

An individual '*receives value*' from a company if it:

(i) repays, redeems or repurchases any part of his holding of its share capital or securities, or makes any payment to him for the cancellation of rights; or

(ii) repays any debt to him other than one incurred by the company on or after the date on which he subscribed for the shares which are the subject of relief and otherwise than in consideration of the extinguishment of a debt incurred before that date; or

(iii) pays him for the cancellation of any debt owed to him other than an '*ordinary trade debt*' – i.e. one incurred for normal trade supply of goods or services on normal trade credit terms (not in any event exceeding six months) – or one in respect of a payment falling within 26.20(i)(*a*) or (*e*) above; or

(iv) releases or waives any liability of his to the company (which it is deemed to have done if discharge of the liability is twelve months or more overdue) or discharges or undertakes to discharge any liability of his to a third person; or

(v) makes a loan or advance to him (defined as including the incurring by him of any debt either to the company (other than an 'ordinary trade debt' — see (iii) above) or to a third person but assigned to the company) which, in relation to shares issued after 18 March 1986, has not been repaid in full before the issue of the shares; or

(vi) provides a benefit or facility for him; or

(vii) transfers an asset to him for no consideration or for consideration less than market value, or acquires an asset from him for consideration exceeding market value; or

(viii) makes any other payment to him except one either falling within 26.20(i)(*a*)–(*e*) above or in discharge of an 'ordinary trade debt' (see (iii) above); or

(ix) is wound up or dissolved in circumstances such that the company does not thereby cease to be a 'qualifying company' (see 26.21 above), and he thereby receives any payment or asset in respect of ordinary shares held by him.

The amount of value received by the individual is that paid to or receivable by him from the company; or the amount of his liability extinguished or discharged; or the difference between the market value of the asset and the consideration (if any) given for it; or the net cost to the company of providing the benefit. In the case of value received within (i), (ii) or (iii) above, the market value of the shares, securities or debt in question is substituted if greater than the amount receivable.

Additionally, the individual 'receives value' from the company if any person 'connected with' the company (see 26.20 above) purchases any shares or securities of the company from him, or pays him for giving up any right in relation to such shares or securities. The value received is the amount receivable, or, if greater, the market value of the shares, etc.

All payments or transfers, direct or indirect, to, or to the order of, or for the benefit of, an individual or an 'associate' (as defined at 26.20(iii) above) of his are brought within these provisions, as are payments, etc. made by any person connected with the company.

Any reduction in relief is apportioned between eligible shares as appears just and reasonable to the inspector or, on appeal, the Commissioners. For shares issued before 19 March 1986, however, relief is, where appropriate, withdrawn or withheld in respect of shares issued earlier before shares issued later. [*ICTA 1988, ss 300, 301, 309(8)*].

Value received other than by claimant. Relief is also reduced where, in the 'relevant period' (as defined in 26.20 above), the issuing company (including a subsidiary at any time during the relevant period) repays, redeems or repurchases any of its share capital belonging to any member other than (i) the individual, or (ii) another individual whose relief is thereby withdrawn or reduced (see above). The reduction is the amount receivable by the member or, if greater, the nominal value of the share capital in question (with relief being restricted in proportion to the relief otherwise available where two or more individuals are involved). Under the current provisions, this restriction of relief does not apply in relation to the redemption on a date fixed before 15 March 1983 of any share capital, nor in relation to the redemption, within twelve months of issue, of any shares issued after 5 April 1983 to comply with *Companies Act 1985, s 117* or NI equivalent (public company not to do business unless certain requirements as to share capital complied with). The rules for identification of shares to which a reduction of relief applies are as described above in relation to value received from the company.

Where, in the 'relevant period', a member of the issuing company receives, or is entitled to receive, any 'value' from the company, then in applying the percentage limits referred to at 26.20(iv) above, the following amounts are treated as reduced:

(i) the amount of the company's issued ordinary share capital;

(ii) the amount of that capital 'relevant' to the provisions in question; and

(iii) the amount at (i) not included in (ii).

The reduction in (ii) and (iii) is in each case the same proportion of the total amount as the 'value' received by the member(s) entitled to the shares comprising the amount bears to the sum subscribed for those shares. The reduced amount at (i) is the sum of those at (ii) and (iii).

The capital '*relevant*' to a provision is those shares whose proportion of the total issued ordinary share capital is in each case compared with the appropriate percentage of that capital.

A member receives '*value*' from the company where any payments, etc. are made to him which, if made to an individual, would fall within (iv) to (viii) inclusive above, excluding those within (viii) made for full consideration. The amount of value received is as defined above. [*ICTA 1988, ss 303, 309(4)(8)*].

Replacement capital. An individual is not entitled to relief in respect of shares issued by a company where, at any time in the relevant period (as defined in 26.20 above), the company (or a subsidiary) either begins to carry on a business (or part) previously carried on at any such time otherwise than by the company or a subsidiary, or acquires the whole or greater part of the assets used for a business so carried on, and the individual is a person who, or one of the group of persons who together, either

(i) owned more than a half share (ownership and, if appropriate, respective shares being determined as under *ICTA 1988, s 344(1)(a)(b)(2)(3)* (see Tolley's Corporation Tax under Losses)) at any such time in the business previously carried on, and also own or owned at any such time such a share in the business carried on by the company, or

(ii) control, or at any such time have controlled, the company, and also, at any such time, controlled another company which previously carried on the trade.

For these purposes, the interests, rights and powers of a person's associates (as defined by *ICTA 1988, s 417(3)(4)* but excluding a brother or sister) are attributed to that person.

An individual is similarly not entitled to relief in respect of shares in a company which, at any time in the relevant period, comes to acquire all the issued share capital of another company, and where the individual is the person who, or one of the persons who together, control or have, at any such time, controlled the company and who also, at any such time, controlled the other company. [*ICTA 1988, s 302; FA 1988, Sch 4 para 9*].

Assessments for withdrawing relief are made under Schedule D, Case VI for the year of assessment for which relief was given, and will rank as earned income if the relief withdrawn was out of earned income (CCAB Memorandum TR 511, 31 August 1983). Where relief in respect of an issue has been claimed for each of two years of assessment (see 26.24 above), relief is withdrawn in respect of the earlier year in priority to the later year. If the event giving rise to the withdrawal occurred after the date of claim, assessments may be made at any time within six years after the end of the year of assessment in which the event occurs, without prejudice to the extension of the time limits in cases of fraudulent or negligent conduct (see 6.4 BACK DUTY). No assessment may be made by reason of any event occurring after the death of the person to whom the shares were issued.

Where a person has made an arm's length disposal of all the ordinary shares issued to him by a company in respect of which relief has been given, no assessment may be made in respect of those shares by reason of any subsequent event unless he is at the time of that event 'connected with' the company (as defined in 26.20 above).

The reckonable date for the purpose of 42.2 INTEREST AND SURCHARGES ON UNPAID TAX (or, where the self-assessment interest provisions apply, the relevant date — see 42.1 INTEREST AND SURCHARGES ON UNPAID TAX) is the date on which the event took place which gave rise to the withdrawal of relief, *except that* where relief is withdrawn under the anti-avoidance provisions (see 26.31 below), it is the date on which relief was granted unless the relief was given under PAYE, in which case it is 5 April in the year of assessment in which relief was so given. [*ICTA 1988, s 307; FA 1989, s 149(4); FA 1993, s 111(3); FA 1996, Sch 18 paras 5, 17(3)*].

26.28 **Subsidiary companies.** The existence of certain subsidiaries does not prevent the parent being a 'qualifying company' (see 26.21 above), and a 'qualifying trade' (see 26.23 above) or 'qualifying activities' (see 26.19 above) being carried on by the subsidiary may enable shares issued by the parent to attract relief under the current provisions. The necessary modifications to those provisions apply where such a subsidiary company exists. [*ICTA 1988, ss 308, 309; FA 1988, Sch 4 paras 11, 12*].

In relation to shares issued after 18 March 1986, the conditions imposed on any such subsidiary are that it (or each of them) must exist wholly (or substantially so) for the purpose of carrying on one or more qualifying trades, or be a 'property managing' or 'dormant' subsidiary, and that, until the end of the relevant period (as defined in 26.21 above):

(*a*) the qualifying company, or another of its subsidiaries,

  (i) possesses at least 90% of both the issued share capital and voting power,

  (ii) is beneficially entitled to at least 90% of the assets available for distribution to equity holders on a winding-up, etc. (as to which see *ICTA 1988, Sch 18 paras 1, 3*),

  (iii) is beneficially entitled to at least 90% of the profits of the subsidiary available for distribution to equity holders (as above);

(*b*) no other person has control (as defined by *ICTA 1988, s 840*, see 20.8 CONNECTED PERSONS) of the subsidiary; and

(*c*) no arrangements exist whereby (*a*) or (*b*) above could cease to be satisfied.

In the case of a company or subsidiary carrying on 'qualifying activities' (i.e. the provision and maintenance of private rented housing, see 26.19 above), the conditions are that the subsidiary (or each of them) must either

(A) be a 'dormant' subsidiary or exist wholly (or substantially so) for the purpose of carrying on substantially only 'qualifying activities', or

(B) exist wholly (or substantially so) for the purposes of holding and/or managing a single block of flats more than half of which are let by the qualifying company or any of its subsidiaries in the course of 'qualifying activities',

and, until the end of the relevant period (as defined in 26.21 above), (*a*)–(*c*) above must be satisfied (in the case of subsidiaries within (B) above, substituting 51% for 90% in each case).

A '*property managing*' subsidiary is one which exists wholly (or substantially so) for the purpose of holding and managing property used by the qualifying company, or a subsidiary, for the purposes of a qualifying trade or trades carried on by the qualifying company or a subsidiary, or for the purposes of research and development from which such a qualifying trade is intended to be derived.

A '*dormant*' subsidiary is one with no corporation tax profits, and no part of whose business consists in the making of investments.

The winding-up or dissolution, in the relevant period, of the subsidiary or of the qualifying company does not prevent the above conditions being satisfied, provided that the winding-up, etc. meets the conditions applied in relation to qualifying companies (see 26.21 above). Those conditions are also not regarded as ceasing to be satisfied by reason only of the disposal of the interest in the subsidiary within the relevant period if it can be shown to be for *bona fide* commercial reasons and not part of a tax avoidance scheme. [*ICTA 1988, s 308; FA 1988, Sch 4 para 11; F(No 2)A 1992, s 39*].

For shares issued before 19 March 1986, the conditions imposed until the end of the relevant period on any subsidiary are that

(i) the 'qualifying company' possesses all the issued share capital and voting power,

(ii) no other person has control (as defined by *ICTA 1988, s 840*, see 20.8 CONNECTED PERSONS), and

(iii) no arrangements exist whereby (i) and (ii) could cease to be satisfied,

and that it was incorporated in the UK and itself satisfies all the conditions for being a 'qualifying company' as regards residence and purpose and is an unquoted company and not wholly or partly a holding company (see 26.21 above). The winding-up or dissolution, in the relevant period, of the subsidiary or of the qualifying company does not prevent the above conditions being met, provided that the winding-up etc. meets the conditions applied in relation to qualifying companies (see 26.21 above). [*ICTA 1988, s 308(6)*].

26.29 **Married persons.** Full reliefs are given separately to husbands and wives, whether or not they are living together. Relief is not withdrawn (see 26.27 above) on inter-spouse transfers while they are living together. On any later disposal to a third person of shares previously the subject of an inter-spouse transfer *inter vivos*, however, the normal provisions for withdrawal apply, the assessment being made on the transferor in relation to the later disposal.

Where relief was given for 1989/90 or earlier in respect of shares issued to a married man or woman who was living with his/her spouse at the time of issue, and it falls to be withdrawn by virtue of a disposal of the shares by the spouse who subscribed for them, the assessment withdrawing relief is made on the spouse making the disposal by reference to the reduction of tax flowing from the relief, regardless of the allocation of the relief for the year for which it was given.

As regards inter-spouse transfers after 5 April 1998, the identification rules for disposals at 26.27 above apply to determine the extent (if any) to which shares on which relief has been given (and not withdrawn) are comprised in the transfer.

[*ICTA 1988, s 304(5)(6); FA 1988, Sch 3 para 12; FA 1998, Sch 13 para 40*].

See 26.19 above as regards the deemed time of issue of shares subscribed for through approved funds.

26.30 **BES company becoming wholly-owned subsidiary of new holding company.** Like provisions to those at 26.16 above (Enterprise Investment Scheme), but with appropriate modifications, apply to enable a BES company to become, by means of an exchange of shares, a wholly-owned subsidiary of a new holding company. Subject to all the conditions being satisfied, the exchange is not treated as a disposal and acquisition (and thus does not give rise to a withdrawal of relief) and BES relief given (and not withdrawn) in respect of the old shares is treated as if it had been so given in respect of the new shares for which they are exchanged. The provisions apply where the new shares are issued after 5 April 1998. [*ICTA 1988, s 304A; FA 1998, Sch 13 para 41*].

26.31 **Miscellaneous.** *Anti-avoidance.* Relief otherwise due to an individual is denied where shares are issued other than for *bona fide* commercial reasons or as part of a scheme the main purpose (or one such purpose) of which was tax avoidance. [*ICTA 1988, s 289(11)*].

Capital gains tax considerations. In relation to shares issued after 18 March 1986, in respect of which relief has been given and not withdrawn, any gain or loss on a disposal of the shares as a result of which relief is not withdrawn is not a chargeable gain or allowable loss for capital gains tax purposes. This applies on a subsequent disposal to a third party where shares in respect of which relief has been given have previously been transferred on a no gain/no loss basis between spouses, but where either *TCGA 1992, s 135* or *s 136* would otherwise apply on a share exchange, etc., it will only apply if relief is withdrawn (except, after 28 November 1994, where the new holding is, broadly, in a company which has issued BES shares or, after 5 April 1998, where the exchange is within 26.30 above).

In relation to shares issued before 19 March 1986, on a disposal, other than between spouses, of shares in respect of which relief has been given and not withdrawn, the allowable expenditure for capital gains tax purposes is determined without regard to that relief, except that where the expenditure exceeds the consideration (i.e. a loss), the expenditure is reduced by the lesser of (*a*) the amount of that relief and (*b*) the excess. Indexation allowance (until it ceases to be available from April 1998) is similarly based on the reduced cost (*Quinn v Cooper Ch D 1998, 71 TC 44*). Where *TCGA 1992, s 135* or *s 136* would otherwise have applied in relation to an exchange of such shares after 5 April 1988 and before 1 January 1990, an election could be made (before 6 April 1991) for the *section* not to apply (unless the relief is withdrawn). This resulted from a consolidation error in *ICTA 1988* which was subsequently corrected with retrospective effect apart from the availability of this election.

Identification of securities for these purposes is as under 26.27 above.

Where only part of a holding of ordinary shares has attracted relief, and there has been a reorganisation of share capital within *TCGA 1992, s 126*, the new holding of shares is treated as two new holdings, one identified with shares attracting relief, the other with the remainder of the shares originally held. In relation to reorganisations after 18 March 1986, a new holding is treated as if it consists of the shares in respect of which relief has been given, both for the purposes of capital gains tax relief and for the rules regarding disposal of shares (see 26.27 above). On certain reorganisations involving allotment of shares for payment, however, *TCGA 1992, ss 127–130* do not apply, and the reorganisation is treated as a disposal in the usual way, and relief may be reduced (with a corresponding adjustment to the capital gains tax base cost).

[*ICTA 1988, s 305; FA 1990, Sch 14 paras 17, 19; TCGA 1992, ss 39(3), 150; FA 1995, ss 68(3), 69; FA 1996, s 134, Sch 20 para 54; FA 1998, Sch 13 para 42, Sch 27 Pt III(14)*].

For detailed coverage, see the corresponding chapter of Tolley's Capital Gains Tax.

Information. Certain events leading to withdrawal of relief must be notified to the inspector, generally within 60 days, by either the individual who received the relief, the issuing company, or any person connected with that company having knowledge of the matter. The inspector may require such a notice and other relevant information where he has reason to believe it should have been made. The penalty provisions of *TMA 1970, s 98* apply for failure to comply.

The inspector also has broad powers to require information in other cases where relief may be withdrawn, restricted, or not due. The requirements of secrecy do not prevent his obtaining such information as he requires. [*ICTA 1988, s 310; FA 1993, s 111(2)*].

27 European Community Legislation

27.1 Statements of the European Council and European Commission are graded under the *EC Treaty* as follows.

(*a*) **Regulations** are binding in their entirety and have general effect in all Member States. They are directly applicable in the legal systems of Member States and do not have to be implemented by national legislation.

(*b*) **Directives** are binding as to result and their general effect is specific to named Member States. The form and methods of compliance are left to individual Member States, which are normally given a specific period in which to implement the necessary legislation.

(*c*) **Decisions** are binding in their entirety and are specific to a Member State, commercial enterprise or private individual. They take effect on notification to the addressee.

(*d*) **Recommendations and opinions** are not binding and are directed to specific subjects on which the Council's or Commission's advice has been sought.

27.2 European Community law is effective in the UK by virtue of *European Communities Act 1972, s 2*, and the European Court of Justice has held that 'wherever the provisions of a Directive appear . . . to be unconditional and sufficiently precise, those provisions may . . . be relied upon as against any national provision which is incompatible with the Directive insofar as the provisions define rights which individuals are able to assert against the State' (*Becker v Finanzamt Munster-Innenstadt [1982] 1 CMLR 499*). Judgments in the European Court of Justice also have supremacy over domestic decisions, even if the proceedings commenced in another Member State.

27.3 In contrast to the extensive application of EU legislation in the VAT sphere, direct taxes are currently subject to only the following three specific measures.

(*a*) *Council Regulation 2137/85* (25 July 1985) concerning European Economic Interest Groupings.

(*b*) *Directive 90/434/EEC* (23 July 1990) concerning mergers, divisions, transfers of assets and exchanges of shares concerning companies of different Member States.

(*c*) *Directive 90/435/EEC* (23 July 1990) concerning distributions of profits to parent companies.

As regards (*a*), see the related UK legislation at 53.19 PARTNERSHIPS. As regards (*b*), the UK legislation is dealt with in Tolley's Corporation Tax under Capital Gains, and a minor consequential amendment at 82.41 SHARE INCENTIVES AND OPTIONS. As regards (*c*), a minor amendment is dealt with at 23.12 DEDUCTION OF TAX AT SOURCE. The Revenue Consultative Document on EC Direct Tax Measures published in December 1991 sets out the manner in which (*b*) and (*c*) are considered to be implemented by these legislative changes.

For a case on the application of *Directive 90/434/EEC*, see *Leur-Bloem v Inspecteur der Belastingdienst/Ondernemingen Amsterdam 2 (Case C-28/95) ECJ, [1997] STC 1205.*

In addition to the above, *Convention 90/436/EEC* (23 July 1990), concerning arbitration in double taxation disputes arising from transfer pricing adjustments, came into force on 1 January 1995. See 3.9 ANTI-AVOIDANCE, 25.5(*m*) DOUBLE TAX RELIEF and 36.2(*o*), 36.4 INLAND REVENUE: CONFIDENTIALITY OF INFORMATION.

27.4 Three further *Directives* have been proposed, concerning interest and royalty payments between parent and subsidiary companies, relief for losses of branches or subsidiaries in other Member States, and carry-over of losses of undertakings. The first has now been withdrawn, and there is currently little prospect of progress on adoption of the other two.

28 Excess Liability

Cross-references. See 1.3 ALLOWANCES AND TAX RATES for current unified tax rates (lower, basic and higher) and 1.4 for a description of the changeover to unified income tax in 1973/74.

28.1 **'Excess Liability'** means the excess of income tax liability over what it would be if all taxable income were charged at the basic rate (or, as appropriate, starting rate, lower rate or Schedule F ordinary rate) to the exclusion of the higher rate or Schedule F upper rate. (See 1.9 ALLOWANCES AND TAX RATES as regards Schedule F ordinary and upper rates, applicable for 1999/2000 onwards.) Although it is only so defined for certain specific purposes of the *Taxes Acts*, it is used for convenience in this chapter to refer to all such liabilities.

Returns, assessments and appeals. There is no provision for a return of total income for the purposes of excess liability. The ordinary annual return (see 67.2 RETURNS) will enable the total income and the relevant deductions – see 28.2(*a*) below – to be ascertained. The normal provisions for ASSESSMENTS (5) and APPEALS (4) apply to excess liability as they do to basic rate liability. Where the income is received untaxed, any appropriate excess liability is included with liabilities at other rates in the assessment on the income or, as regards Schedule E income, dealt with under PAY AS YOU EARN (55). The excess rate liability on other income is separately assessed. [*ICTA 1988, s 5(4); FA 1994, Sch 26 Pt V(23); FA 1996, Sch 6 paras 3, 28*]. For due dates of payment and related matters, see 56.1 PAYMENT OF TAX. See also 78.17 to 78.20 SELF-ASSESSMENT.

Relationship to surtax. Excess liability replaced surtax which, similarly, was charged by reference to the total income of individuals. Court decisions on appeals against assessments to surtax (or its predecessor, super-tax) apply to excess liability where the relevant legislation is now applicable to it, and the majority of cases referred to below (and in other parts of this work to which reference is made) do in fact involve surtax etc. appeals.

28.2 INCOME CHARGEABLE TO EXCESS LIABILITY—GENERAL

(*a*) Excess liability is charged by reference to the total income of an individual and any investment income included in it. [*ICTA 1988, s 1(2)*]. Total income is the aggregate income from all sources. [*ICTA 1988, s 835(1)*]. 'Charges on income' (28.4 below), personal allowances given by deduction [*ICTA 1988, s 256; FA 1994, s 77(1)*], any interest payments eligible for relief by deduction and any other such reliefs, e.g. allowable LOSSES (46), are deducted to give the amount on which the excess liability is calculated.

The personal allowances are deducted after any other deductions and will not reduce the investment income surcharge payable for years of assessment before 1984/85 unless they exceed in aggregate the earned income plus the investment income covered by the nil rate. Subject to this and to any express provisions to the contrary (e.g. those providing for the order in which losses are to be allowed), the deductions are treated as reducing income of different descriptions in the order which results in the greatest tax reduction. [*ICTA 1988, s 835(3)–(5); FA 1971, s 34(4)*]. Hence for years before 1984/85 if there is any investment income surcharge liability, charges on income or interest will normally be deducted against investment income first.

For what is investment income see 1.8 ALLOWANCES AND TAX RATES.

For 2000/01 onwards, qualifying donations to charity under Gift Aid are not a charge on income, but are relieved, in computing excess liability, by extending the basic rate band (see 15.12 CHARITIES).

(*b*) There are various provisions under which amounts not within the normal charging rules of the Schedules and Cases are nevertheless to be treated as income of a person, or income of one person is to be deemed income of another. This legislation includes the following.

(i) Much of the ANTI-AVOIDANCE (3) legislation.

(ii) The settlements legislation in *ICTA 1988, ss 660–689*. See 81.13 *et seq.* SETTLEMENTS.

For other provisions relating specifically to excess liability, see 28.3 below.

(*c*) **Assessments** which have become *final and conclusive* for income tax are also final and conclusive in estimating total income. [*ICTA 1988, s 835(7)*].

(*d*) **Dividends, interest, annual payments, etc. receivable.** Income received under deduction of tax is income of the year by reference to which the rate of tax is determined, irrespective of the period over which it accrued, and similarly for dividends within Schedule F. [*ICTA 1988, s 835(6)(a); FA 1996, Sch 6 paras 24, 28*]. Where securities are sold through the Stock Exchange, the interest or dividend for the period spanning the date of sale is income of the vendor or purchaser according to whether they were sold ex- or cum-dividend etc. irrespective of the period of accrual (cf. *Wigmore v Summerson KB 1925, 9 TC 577* and *CIR v Oakley KB 1925, 9 TC 582*). But see 28.3(*c*) below as regards certain sales cum-dividend etc. and 74.6 *et seq.* SCHEDULE D, CASE VI as regards the accrued income scheme. Where the transfer of shares bequeathed under a will was delayed, dividends paid before the transfers were held to be income of the legatee (*CIR v Hawley KB 1927, 13 TC 327*). But where the controlling shareholder of a company set up a scheme under which the employees were contingently entitled to shares he owned, the dividends were held to be his pending the contingency (*CIR v Parsons CA 1928, 13 TC 700*). See also *Spence v CIR CS 1941, 24 TC 311* where dividends on shares sold and later recovered because of fraudulent misrepresentation by the purchaser were held to be income of the vendor.

Income due is not assessable before it is received (*Lambe v CIR KB 1933, 18 TC 212*, mortgage interest due but not received from company in hands of receiver not assessable) and this is so even though the non-receipt is because right to the income has not been exercised (*Dewar v CIR CA 1935, 19 TC 561; Woodhouse v CIR KB 1936, 20 TC 673*). But where a shareholder refused to accept dividends tendered to her, surtax assessments including the dividends were upheld (*Dreyfus v CIR Ch D 1963, 41 TC 441*). See also *St Lucia Usines v Colonial Treasurer PC 1924, 4 ATC 112*.

Interest receivable on National Savings Certificates and on Tax Reserve Certificates is exempt. Special treatment applies to certain interest from Building Societies (see 28.3(*a*) below), and to interest from National Savings Banks (see 29.13(iv) EXEMPT INCOME).

(*e*) **Partnership income.** A partner's share of the partnership profits (arrived at as in 53.5 PARTNERSHIPS), is part of his total income, any higher rate liability on the share being included in the partnership assessment (where relevant — see 53.3 PARTNERSHIPS). Where the ownership of partnership profits was subject to a future contingency and they were meanwhile carried to suspense, it was held that the profits could not meanwhile be assessed to super-tax (*Franklin v CIR KB 1930, 15 TC 464*). Similarly, amounts payable under a partnership agreement to the widow of a deceased partner, but not paid, were held not to be income of the widow (*Lebus's Exors CA 1946, 27 TC 136*). In *Dreyfus v CIR CA 1929, 14 TC 560*, it was held that the taxpayer's share of the profit of a French 'société en nom collectif' was not part of his total income.

(*f*) **Settlements.** Where the legislation at (*b*)(iii) above does not apply, the income of a beneficiary under a settlement or trust (including a will trust) falls to be determined under general principles. For this see SETTLEMENTS at 81.8 and also at 81.10 for foreign trust income, 81.5 for discretionary and accumulation trusts, 81.9 for annuities and other annual payments and 23.17 DEDUCTION OF TAX AT SOURCE for 'free of tax' annuities. For income from deceased estates during administration see 22.3 DECEASED ESTATES.

(*g*) **Other matters.** A balancing charge is part of total income (*CIR v Lloyds Bank (Scott's Exors) Ch D 1963, 41 TC 294*). For income assigned for certain purpose see *CIR v Paterson CA 1924, 9 TC 163* and *Perkins' Exors v CIR KB 1928, 13 TC 851* (in which the income was held to be income of the assignor) and compare *Wolverton v CIR HL 1931, 16 TC 467*. For case where the ownership of income was in dispute, see *Shenley v CIR KB 1945, 27 TC 85*.

In *Vestey v CIR Ch D 1961, 40 TC 112* the taxpayer sold shares of an estimated value of £2m for £5.5m payable in equal instalments over 125 years. He was held to be assessable to surtax on the interest element in the instalments, calculated on actuarial lines. (Some of the reasoning in this decision was not approved by the HL in *CIR v Church Commissioners HL 1976, 50 TC 516*.)

28.3 INCOME CHARGEABLE TO EXCESS LIABILITY—PARTICULAR PROVISIONS

(*a*) The following are treated as income not liable to basic rate (or lower or Schedule F ordinary rate, see below) income tax but (after grossing-up at that rate) are subject to excess liability.

(i) Close company loans to a participator or associate of a participator which are written off or released are grossed up at the Schedule F ordinary rate of income tax (before 6 April 1999, the lower rate) and taxed as if they were dividends (see 1.9 ALLOWANCES AND TAX RATES), with no entitlement to repayment of the notional tax credit. [*ICTA 1988, s 421; FA 1993, s 77(4); FA 1996, s 122(6), Sch 6 paras 9, 28; F(No 2)A 1997, Sch 4 para 11*].

(ii) Restrictive covenant payments in respect of pre-9 June 1988 undertakings, in connection with an office or employment. [*ICTA 1988, s 313*]. See 75.34 SCHEDULE E.

(*b*) **Gains on 'non-qualifying' insurance policies, etc.** are subject to excess liability, with top-slicing relief. See 45.13 LIFE ASSURANCE POLICIES.

28.4 CHARGES ON INCOME

(*a*) **General.** The term 'charges on income' is derived from *TMA 1970, s 8(8)* (as originally enacted). The deduction, subject to (*b*) below, is for annuities or other annual payments (other than interest), patent royalties (and, previously, certain mining, etc. rents and royalties) payable under DEDUCTION OF TAX AT SOURCE (23) out of the income. [*ICTA 1988, s 3; FA 1995, Sch 29 Pt VIII(22); FA 1997, Sch 18 Pt VI(2)*]. In *Bingham v CIR Ch D 1955, 36 TC 254* a deduction was refused for alimony payable under a foreign Court Order as the payer was not empowered to deduct tax at source (cf. *Keiner v Keiner QB 1952, 34 TC 346*). Tax is deductible only if the payment is 'pure income profit' in the hands of the recipient and not e.g. an element entering into the computation of his business receipts. Hence a deduction was refused for insurance premiums payable under covenant on policies lodged as part of a mortgage security (*Earl Howe v CIR CA 1919, 7 TC 289*).

Where an interest in a business is transferred in consideration for periodical payments based on subsequent profits, whether the payments are 'annual payments' rests on the facts. See *Ramsay CA 1935, 20 TC 79* and *Ledgard KB 1937, 21 TC 129* in which a deduction was refused and contrast *Hogarth CS 1940, 23 TC 491*. Whether a payment is an 'annual payment' may arise in a number of contexts other than in arriving at total income. See 23.10 DEDUCTION OF TAX AT SOURCE for other cases.

(*b*) **Statutory modifications** of the general rule include the following.

(i) The settlements legislation, in particular, for 1994/95 and earlier years, *ICTA 1988, ss 660–662*, under which income under certain dispositions is treated as income of the settlor, *ICTA 1988, ss 663–671*, dealing similarly with settlements on children and certain revocable settlements, and *ICTA 1988, ss 683, 684*, which broadly prohibit the deduction for excess liability of annual payments by a settlor other than for certain specified purposes. See 81.22–81.24, 81.29 SETTLEMENTS. These provisions are replaced for 1995/96 and later years by those at 81.13–81.18 SETTLEMENTS under which certain income of a settlement may fall to be treated for all tax purposes as that of the settlor.

See 81.22, 81.29 SETTLEMENTS for the definition of, and special treatment accorded to, covenanted payments to charity before 1995/96.

(ii) Annual payments made for a non-taxable consideration and not involving a settlement within the legislation (*CIR v Plummer HL 1979, 54 TC 1*) are payable in full and are not deductible for excess liability purposes. [*ICTA 1988, s 125*]. See 3.19 ANTI-AVOIDANCE.

(iii) Payments due after 14 March 1988 under non-charitable covenants, unless, for 1994/95 and earlier years, made under an 'existing obligation' (see 1.8(i) ALLOWANCES AND TAX RATES, and see also 47.10 MARRIED PERSONS) are not, in any case, charges on income. [*ICTA 1988, s 347A; FA 1988, s 36; FA 1995, Sch 17 para 4(1); FA 1999, Sch 20 Pt III(6)*]. See 15.17 CHARITIES and (iv) below as regards charitable covenants.

(iv) Payments falling due after 5 April 2000 under charitable deeds of covenant are not charges on income (see 15.17 CHARITIES) but are instead dealt with under the Gift Aid regime (see 15.12 CHARITIES).

(*c*) **Timing and method of deduction.** Charges are deducted for the year which determines the rate of tax deductible, see 23.5 DEDUCTION OF TAX AT SOURCE. [*ICTA 1988, s 835(6)(b)*]. For the order of allowance against different types of income see 28.2(*a*) above.

28.5 INTEREST PAYABLE

Interest payable does not rank as a 'charge on income' within 28.4 above for income tax purposes, but may be allowable either as a deduction in computing business profits or as a deduction in arriving at total income or as a reduction in income tax liability. For this see 43 INTEREST PAYABLE. For the corporation tax position, see Tolley's Corporation Tax under Profit Computations.

28.6 OVERLAP BETWEEN EXCESS LIABILITY AND INHERITANCE TAX ON A DEATH

Where, on a death, income accrued at the death is treated both as capital of the estate for inheritance tax purposes and as residuary income of the estate in the hands of a beneficiary having an absolute interest in the residue, in arriving at the excess liability of the beneficiary the residuary income is reduced by the grossed-up amount of the inheritance tax attributable to the excess of the accrued income over any liabilities taken into account in both valuing the estate and arriving at the residuary income. [*ICTA 1988, s 699; FA 1993, Sch 6 para 6; FA 1996, Sch 6 paras 13, 28; F(No 2)A 1997, Sch 4 para 17; FA 1999, s 22(9)*].

28.7 OVERSEAS MATTERS

There are no special provisions regarding the excess liability treatment of non-residents or overseas income and accordingly the normal rules apply unless modified by double tax agreements. Subject to any such relevant agreement a non-resident will be within the charge to excess liability as regards his UK income (see *Brooke v CIR CA 1917, 7 TC 261*) and is assessable in his own name if he can be served with a notice of assessment (cf. *CIR v Huni KB 1923, 8 TC 466; Whitney v CIR HL 1925, 10 TC 88*).

For the treatment of personal allowances, see 51.11 NON-RESIDENTS AND OTHER OVERSEAS MATTERS.

29 Exempt Income

Cross-references. See 1 ALLOWANCES AND TAX RATES for the various personal allowances against income and 1.8(i) for certain annual payments not treated as taxable income; 17.6 CLAIMS for repayment of tax suffered; 23.11(*c*) DEDUCTION OF TAX AT SOURCE for exemption of capital portion of purchased life annuities; 30 EXEMPT ORGANISATIONS; 64.2 RESIDENCE, ORDINARY RESIDENCE AND DOMICILE for certain percentage deductions; 59.4 PENSIONS; 74.4 SCHEDULE D, CASE VI for relief for furnished room lettings; 81.30 SETTLEMENTS — re maintenance funds for historic buildings; 89 UNDERWRITERS for transfers to special reserve funds.

The following income is exempt from income tax and any tax suffered may be reclaimed.

29.1 **Adoption allowances** paid under the *Adoption Allowance Regulations 1991* (or Scottish equivalent) which would otherwise be regarded as annual payments within SCHEDULE D, CASE III (72) are not taxable. (Revenue Pamphlet IR 1, A40).

29.2 **Compensation for loss of employment etc. up to £30,000.** See 19.4 COMPENSATION FOR LOSS OF EMPLOYMENT for details of exemptions and reliefs for these and other terminal payments at the end of an employment.

29.3 **Compensation for mis-sold pensions products (and interest thereon). Personal pensions etc..** Exemption from both income tax and capital gains tax is conferred on the receipt at any time of a capital sum (which may include a sum otherwise chargeable to income tax) by way of compensation for loss, or likely loss, caused by certain 'bad investment advice' concerning personal pensions etc. '*Bad investment advice*' is investment advice (as defined by *Financial Services Act 1986, Sch 1 para 15*) in respect of which an action has been or may be brought against the adviser for negligence, breach of contract or fiduciary obligation or by reason of a contravention actionable under *Financial Services Act 1986, s 62.* The exemption applies where a person (whether or not the person suffering loss), acting on such advice at least some of which was given after 28 April 1988 and before 1 July 1994 (at which date new regulatory safeguards came into force), either

(*a*) joined a personal pension scheme or took out a retirement annuity contract (see 60 PERSONAL PENSION SCHEMES, 65 RETIREMENT ANNUITIES) whilst eligible, or reasonably likely to become eligible, to join an occupational pension scheme (i.e. an approved retirement benefits scheme, relevant statutory scheme or pre-6 April 1980 approved superannuation scheme — see 66.1, 66.13 RETIREMENT SCHEMES FOR EMPLOYEES); or

(*b*) left, or ceased to pay into, an occupational pension scheme and instead joined a personal pension scheme or took out a retirement annuity contract; or

(*c*) transferred to a personal pension scheme his accrued rights under an occupational pension scheme; or

(*d*) left an occupational pension scheme and instead entered into arrangements for securing relevant benefits (see 66.1 RETIREMENT SCHEMES FOR EMPLOYEES) by means of an annuity contract with an insurance company.

Interest on the whole or part of a capital sum within the above exemption is itself exempt from income tax to the extent that it covers a period ending on or before the earliest date on which the amount of the capital sum is first determined, whether by agreement or by a court, tribunal, commissioner, arbitrator or appointee.

[*FA 1996, s 148*].

Freestanding additional voluntary contribution schemes ('FSAVCSs'). Where liability would otherwise arise, the following payments will not be chargeable to income tax (although this will not apply to annuities or other annual payments arising from the compensation), and their receipt will not be treated as the disposal of an asset for capital gains tax purposes.

(i) The payment of a capital sum by way of compensation determined in accordance with the Financial Services Authority guidance for the performance of the review required by the Authority of specified categories of FSAVCSs sold between 28 April 1988 and 15 August 1999 inclusive, and made as a result of the review.

(ii) The payment of interest on the whole or part of the sum within (i) for a period ending on or before the earliest date on which the capital sum was determined.

(Revenue Press Release 28 February 2000).

29.4 **Damages and compensation for personal injury.** Income tax relief is available where an agreement is made settling a claim or action for damages for personal injury (as widely defined) under which the damages are to consist wholly or partly of periodical payments, or where a court order incorporates such terms. This applies equally in relation to interim court order payments and voluntary payments on account. Periodical payments received **on or after 29 April 1996** (irrespective of when the agreement or order was made or took effect) are not regarded as income for income tax purposes, and are paid without deduction of tax under *ICTA 1988, s 348(1)(b)* or *s 349(1)* (see 23.2, 23.3 DEDUCTION OF TAX AT SOURCE). This applies as regards the person ('A') entitled to the damages under the agreement or order, and also

(*a*) any person receiving the payments on behalf of A; and

(*b*) any trustee receiving the payments on trust for A's benefit under a trust under which A is (during his lifetime) the sole beneficiary,

and sums paid on to (or for the benefit of) A by a person within (*b*) above are not regarded as A's income for income tax purposes.

Any or all of the periodical payments may (if the agreement etc., or a subsequent agreement, so provides) be under one or more annuities purchased or provided for (or for the benefit of) A by the person otherwise liable for the payments.

The above provisions apply equally to annuity payments under a compensation award under the Criminal Injuries Compensation Scheme. The Treasury may also apply them (with any necessary modifications) to any other scheme or arrangement making similar provision.

[*ICTA 1988, ss 329AA, 329AB; FA 1996, s 150, Sch 26*].

For payments received **before 29 April 1996 and after 1 May 1995,** broadly similar provisions apply. Where a person received a sum as, or on behalf of, the annuitant under an annuity purchased for him pursuant to a 'qualifying agreement' (whenever made), that sum is not regarded as income for income tax purposes, and is paid without deduction of tax under *ICTA 1988, s 349(1)* (see 23.3 DEDUCTION OF TAX AT SOURCE). Similar relief applies to annuities pursuant to qualifying awards under the Criminal Injuries Compensation Scheme.

An agreement is a '*qualifying agreement*' if it is made settling a claim or action for personal injury (including any disease and any physical or mental impairment), and if the damages under the agreement are to consist wholly or partly of periodical payments, to be received by the person entitled to them as the annuitant under one or more annuities purchased for him by either the person against whom the claim or action was brought or his insurer. Claims or actions under the *Fatal Accidents Act 1976* or NI equivalent are included. Payments under the annuity or annuities must correspond in amount and timing to the periodical payments under the agreement. The periodical payments may be for the life of the claimant, for a specified period or of a specified number or minimum number, or include payments of more than one of those descriptions. The amounts of the periodical payments (which need not be at a uniform rate or intervals) may be specified in the agreement, with or without provision for increases, or may be adjustable in a specified manner to preserve their real value, or may be partly so specified and partly so adjustable.

Where an agreement would be a qualifying agreement but for the fact that the substitution of the annuity payments for the periodical payments is under a later agreement and from a future date, the later agreement is a '*qualifying agreement*'. Similarly, where the person liable to make the periodical payments (or his insurer) purchases an annuity or annuities, which is or are assigned to the claimant under a later agreement, that later agreement is the '*qualifying agreement*'. The requirements described above as to payments under the annuity or annuities and the periodical payments apply to such qualifying agreements with the necessary modifications.

[*ICTA 1988, ss 329A, 329B, 329C; FA 1995, s 142; Criminal Injuries Compensation Act 1995, s 8*].

29.5 **Foreign service allowance** to a person in the service of the Crown representing compensation for the extra cost of living abroad. [*ICTA 1988, s 319*].

29.6 **Gallantry awards.** Annuities and additional pensions paid by virtue of holding the award to holders of the Victoria Cross or the George Cross are exempt, as are additional pensions paid to holders of the Military Cross, the Distinguished Flying Cross, the Distinguished Conduct Medal, the Conspicuous Gallantry Medal, the Distinguished Service Medal, the Military Medal or the Distinguished Flying Medal and annuities paid to holders of the Albert Medal or the Edward Medal. [*ICTA 1988, s 317*].

29.7 **German and Austrian annuities and pensions for victims of Nazi persecution** under German or Austrian law are not treated as income for any income tax purpose. [*ICTA 1988, s 330*].

29.8 **Guaranteed income bonds, etc..** See 45.15(*h*) LIFE INSURANCE POLICIES as regards annuities and annual payments under certain life insurance policies which are excluded from treatment as such.

29.9 **Housing grants.** Except where the expense recouped is deductible from profits, amounts received, under any relevant Act, towards expenses incurred, by the recipient or another, in providing, maintaining or improving residential accommodation are not assessable. [*ICTA 1988, s 578*].

29.10 **Individual savings accounts. From 6 April 1999,** individuals aged 18 or over who are resident and ordinarily resident in the UK are able to subscribe up to £5,000 in each tax year (£7,000 in 1999/2000 and 2000/01) to an individual savings account set up in accordance with regulations. The account may contain three components: cash (including National Savings); life insurance; and stocks and shares. Of the annual subscription, no more than £1,000 (£3,000 in 1999/2000 and 2000/01) may go into cash and £1,000 into life insurance. The restrictions on the scope of investments in stocks and shares are generally more relaxed than those applicable to personal equity plans (see 29.21 below). Shares acquired under approved profit-sharing or SAYE share option schemes (see 82.9,

82.38 SHARE INCENTIVES AND OPTIONS) may be transferred in at market value (with no capital gains tax liability) within the annual subscription limits, but public offer and demutualisation issues may not be transferred in. Life insurance products have to be of the single premium type (i.e. there must be no obligation to keep up premium payments in order to obtain policy benefits), although policies with recurrent single premiums or regular monthly premiums are acceptable. There is no minimum subscription, no lifetime limit and no loss of relief on withdrawals. It is guaranteed that the arrangements will continue for at least ten years.

Personal equity plans (see 29.21 below) held at 5 April 1999 may continue to be held without affecting the ability to invest in an individual savings account. Similarly investments in TESSAs started before 6 April 1999 will not affect individual savings account investments, and the capital (but *not* the accrued interest) in a maturing TESSA may be transferred to an individual savings account in addition to the normal investment limits.

There is an exemption from income tax and capital gains tax on the investments, and for the first five years for which the accounts are available (i.e. until 5 April 2004), *FA 1998, s 76* disapplies the rule introduced by *F(No 2)A 1997, s 30* preventing payment of the tax credit attached to UK dividends (see 1.9 ALLOWANCES AND TAX RATES), so that the 10% tax credit is payable (and regulations make similar provision in respect of non-resident holders of accounts — see below). (*FA 1998, s 76* also makes similar provision in relation to holders of personal equity plans, see 29.21 below.) Similar provision made in relation to insurance company and friendly society investments referable to individual savings account business.

The necessary regulation-making powers are provided in general by amendment to the personal equity plan regulations [*FA 1998, s 75*], and in relation to life insurance investments and FRIENDLY SOCIETIES (31) by *FA 1998, s 77*. Accounts, which must be administered by managers, may be offered by financial institutions or by independent providers. Managers will be able to offer accounts either accepting overall subscriptions (which must be able to accept the annual maximum, and so *must* offer a stocks and shares component and *may* offer either or both of the other two components) or accepting one of the three components (within the applicable annual maximum, including a £3,000 maximum in relation to a stocks and shares account).

The Individual Savings Account Regulations 1998 (*SI 1998 No 1870* as amended) provide for the setting up by Revenue-approved accounts managers of plans in the form of an account (an ISA) under which individuals may make certain investments, for the conditions under which they may invest and under which the accounts are to operate, for relief from tax in respect of account investments, and for general administration. The regulations, which are summarised below, generally take effect on 6 April 1999, although earlier applications can be made to subscribe to an account for 1999/2000 or to obtain approval as an account manager.

General. An application to subscribe to an ISA may be made by an individual who is 18 or over and who is resident and ordinarily resident in the UK (or is a non-UK resident Crown employee performing duties treated under *ICTA 1988, s 132(4)(a)* (see 75.2 SCHEDULE E) as performed in the UK). Joint accounts are not permitted. An investor who subsequently fails to meet the residence requirement may retain the account and the right to tax exemptions thereunder but can make no further subscriptions to the account until he again comes to meet that requirement. In Scotland, a *curator bonis* appointed in respect of an individual qualifying as above but incapable of managing his affairs may subscribe to an ISA in his capacity as such without affecting his right to subscribe in any other capacity.

An ISA is made up of *one or more* of the following: a stocks and shares component, a cash component and an insurance component (see below re qualifying investments for each of these components). It must be designated from the outset as a maxi-account, mini-account or TESSA only account, such designation continuing to have effect for any year in which the investor makes a subscription to the account.

A *maxi-account* must comprise a stocks and shares component (*with or without* other components). The maximum subscription per tax year is £5,000 (£7,000 for 1999/2000 and 2000/01only) of which a maximum of £1,000 (£3,000 for 1999/2000 and 2000/01) may be allocated to a cash component and £1,000 to an insurance component. In any tax year in which an investor subscribes to a maxi-account he cannot subscribe to any other ISA apart from a TESSA only account.

A *mini-account* must consist of a single specified component. The maximum subscription (per tax year) is £3,000 if that component is stocks and shares, £1,000 if it is insurance and £1,000 (£3,000 for 1999/2000 and 2000/01 only) if it is cash. In any tax year in which an investor subscribes to a mini-account, he cannot subscribe to another mini-account consisting of the same component or to a maxi-account.

A *TESSA only account* is an account consisting of a cash component only and limited to capital (*not* accumulated interest) transferred from a TESSA (see 29.13(iii) below) within six months following its maturity after 5 April 1999 (or after 5 January 1999 where no follow-up TESSA is opened). Such transfers are not subject to any annual subscription limit, and may also be made to a maxi-account or to a cash component mini-account without counting towards the annual subscription limits for such accounts. Continuing subscriptions after 5 April 1999 to a TESSA or follow-up TESSA do not affect an individual's ISA annual subscription limits.

Subscriptions to an ISA must be made in cash (and must be allocated irrevocably to the agreed component or single component) except that shares acquired by the investor under a savings-related (SAYE) share option scheme (see 82.38 SHARE INCENTIVES AND OPTIONS) or appropriated to him under an approved profit sharing scheme (see 82.9 SHARE INCENTIVES AND OPTIONS) may be transferred to a stocks and shares component. Such transfers count towards the annual subscription limits, by reference to the market value of the shares at the date of transfer. No chargeable gain or allowable loss arises on the transfer. A transfer of SAYE scheme shares must be made within 90 days after the exercise of the option. A transfer of shares appropriated under a profit sharing scheme must be made within 90 days after the earlier of the release date (see 82.10 SHARE INCENTIVES AND OPTIONS) and the date on which the investor instructed the scheme trustees to transfer ownership of the shares to him.

ISA investments cannot be purchased otherwise than out of cash held by the account manager and allocated to the particular component concerned, and cannot be purchased from the investor or the investor's spouse.

The title to ISA investments (other than cash deposits, national savings products and certain insurance policies) is vested in the account manager (or his nominee) either alone or jointly with the investor, though all ISA investments are in the beneficial ownership of the investor. The investor may elect to receive annual reports and accounts etc. in respect of ISA investments and/or to attend and vote at shareholders' etc. meetings.

The statements and declarations to be made when applying to subscribe to an ISA are specified. The maximum penalty for an incorrect statement or declaration is the amount (if any) of income tax and/or capital gains tax underpaid as a result. Assessments to withdraw tax relief or otherwise recover tax underpaid may be made (under SCHEDULE D, CASE VI (74)) in the case of income tax) on the account manager or investor. The Revenue have power to require information from, and to inspect records of, account managers and investors.

Tax exemptions. Except as stated below, no income tax or capital gains tax is chargeable on the account manager or the investor in respect of interest, dividends, distributions or gains on ISA investments. Capital losses are not allowable. As stated in the introduction above, tax credits on UK dividends paid before 6 April 2004 are repayable (via the account manager). An investor who ceases to be UK-resident is treated as continuing to be so resident as regards his entitlement to repayment of tax credits.

Interest on a cash deposit held within a stocks and shares component or insurance component is, however, taxable at the lower rate of income tax, such tax to be accounted for by the account manager (by set-off against tax repayments or otherwise). There is no further liability; the interest does not form part of the investor's total income and the tax paid cannot be repaid to the investor.

Life assurance gains on policies held within an insurance component are not subject to income tax (and a deficiency on termination is not deductible from the investor's total income). If it comes to the account manager's notice that such a policy is invalid, i.e. its terms and conditions do not provide (or no longer provide) that it be held only as a qualifying insurance component investment, a chargeable event then occurs, with any gain taxable under SCHEDULE D, CASE VI (74). If the policy has already terminated, the chargeable event is deemed to have occurred at the end of the final policy year (see 45.15(*a*) LIFE ASSURANCE POLICIES). Any previous chargeable event which actually occurred in relation to the policy is similarly taxed, by reference to the time it occurred. Basic rate income tax is payable by the account manager (with the Revenue also having power to assess the investor). Any higher rate tax due is payable by the investor by assessment within five years after 31 January following the year of assessment in which the chargeable event occurred or was deemed to occur. Top-slicing relief (see 45.13 LIFE ASSURANCE POLICIES) is available in the same way as for non-ISA-related chargeable events.

Exempt income and gains do not have to be reported in the investor's personal tax return.

Further capital gains matters. A transfer of ISA investments by an account manager to an investor is deemed to be made at market value, with no capital gain or allowable loss arising. An investor is treated as holding shares or securities in an ISA in a capacity other than that in which he holds any other shares etc. of the same class in the same company, so that share identification rules (see Tolley's Capital Gains Tax under Shares and Securities — Identification Rules) are applied separately to ISA investments (and separately as between different ISAs held by the same investor). The normal share reorganisation rules are disapplied in respect of ISA investments in the event of a reorganisation of share capital involving an allotment for payment, e.g. a rights issue. Shares transferred to an ISA in the limited circumstances described above are deemed for these purposes to have been ISA investments from, in the case of SAYE option scheme shares, their acquisition by the investor and, in the case of profit sharing scheme shares, the earlier of the release date (see 82.10 SHARE INCENTIVES AND OPTIONS) and the date on which the investor instructed the scheme trustees to transfer ownership of the shares to him. Where the investor held shares eligible for transfer to an ISA and other shares of the same class but not so eligible, disposals are generally identified primarily with the latter, thus preserving to the greatest possible extent the eligibility of the remaining shares.

Qualifying investments

Stocks and shares component. Qualifying investments for a stocks and shares component are as follows.

(*a*) Shares issued by a company (other than an investment trust, but see (*e*) below) wherever incorporated, and officially listed on a recognised stock exchange. There are rules to allow the official listing condition to be treated as satisfied in the case of shares issued under a public offer and due to be listed.

(*b*) Securities (i.e. secured or unsecured loan stock and similar) issued by a company wherever incorporated, and with a minimum residual term of five years from the date when first held under the ISA. Either the securities must be officially listed on a recognised stock exchange or the shares in the issuing company or its 75% holding company must be so listed. In the case of securities of an investment trust, the trust must satisfy the two qualifying conditions at (*e*) below.

(*c*) Gilt-edged securities and gilt strips with at least five years to run to maturity from the date when first held under the ISA.

(*d*) Securities issued by or on behalf of a government of a European Economic Area State (comprising the EU plus Norway, Iceland and Liechtenstein and excluding for this purpose the UK), and strips of such securities, with at least five years to run to maturity from the date when first held under the ISA.

(*e*) Shares in a qualifying investment trust listed in the Official List of the Stock Exchange. Broadly, in order to qualify, an investment trust must have no 'eligible rental income' (within *ICTA 1988, s 508A* — see Tolley's Corporation Tax under Unit and Investment Trusts) *and* not more than 50% in value of its investments can be securities otherwise within any of (*b*)–(*d*) above but having less than five years to run to maturity from the date when first acquired by the trust.

(*f*) Units in

- a securities fund (broadly an authorised unit trust or part of an umbrella scheme — see 90.1 UNIT TRUSTS), or
- a warrant fund (broadly a type of authorised unit trust investing in warrants or part of an umbrella scheme of that category),

or shares in

- a securities company (broadly an open-ended investment company (OEIC) or part of an umbrella company), or
- a warrant company (broadly a type of OEIC investing in warrants or part of an umbrella company of that category),

or units in, or shares of,

- a relevant UCITS (an Undertaking for Collective Investment in Transferable Securities situated in and authorised by an EU Member State other than the UK, or part of such an undertaking equivalent to part of an umbrella scheme or umbrella company),

where the fund, company or UCITS satisfies the equivalent of the 50% condition in (*e*) above.

(*g*) Units in a fund of funds (as defined), subject to the condition that not more than 50% in value of its investments can be investments which would otherwise be within (*f*) above but do not themselves satisfy the 50% condition therein mentioned.

(*h*) Shares acquired by the investor under a SAYE share option scheme or appropriated to him under an approved profit sharing scheme which are transferred into the ISA as mentioned under 'General' above.

(*j*) Cash held on deposit pending investment in any of the above.

The term '*company*' does not for the above purposes include an OEIC, a UCITS or an industrial and provident society (or 51% subsidiary thereof).

Cash component. Qualifying investments for a cash component are as follows.

(i) Cash deposited in a deposit account with a building society, an institution authorised under *Banking Act 1987* or certain European institutions entitled to accept deposits in the UK.

(ii) Cash deposited in a building society share account.

(iii) Units in a money market fund (as defined).

(iv) Units in a fund of funds (as defined) which permits investment only in units in money market funds.

(v) Designated national savings products.

A deposit or share account within (i) or (ii) above is not a qualifying investment if is 'connected' with any other account held within those categories (whether or not by the investor). For this purpose, accounts are '*connected*' if either was opened with reference to the other or with a view to enabling the other to be opened, or facilitating the opening of the other, on particular terms *and* the terms on which the cash component account was opened would have been significantly less favourable to the investor if the other had not been opened. The Revenue will accept that an account is not a connected account if it is a 'feeder' account opened to enable investors to fund future deposits into an ISA, provided that the interest on the feeder account is in line with the interest paid on the account manager's other savings accounts (see Revenue Guidance Notes for ISA Managers).

Insurance component. Qualifying investments for an insurance component are policies of life insurance satisfying specified conditions and cash held on deposit pending investment in such policies. The insurance must be on the life of the ISA investor only and its terms and conditions must provide:

(A) that the policy may only be owned or held as a qualifying investment for an ISA insurance component;

(B) that, if found to be in breach of (A) above, it shall automatically terminate (and see also above under 'Tax exemptions');

(C) for an express prohibition of any transfer to the investor of the policy or the rights conferred thereby or any share or interest therein (other than cash proceeds on termination or partial surrender); and

(D) that the policy etc. cannot be assigned other than by transfer of title between approved ISA managers or by its vesting in the investor's personal representatives.

The policy must constitute long-term insurance business (as defined) and must not be a contract to pay a life annuity, a personal portfolio bond (see 45.13 LIFE ASSURANCE POLICIES) or a contract constituting pension business (as defined). There must be no contractual obligation to pay any premium other than the first (so regular premium policies are excluded). 'Connected' policies are excluded in much the same way as connected accounts are excluded from a cash component (see above). The making of loans by, or by arrangement with, the insurer to, or at the direction of, the ISA investor is prohibited.

Account managers. The regulations cover qualification as an account manager, Revenue approval and withdrawal thereof, appointment of UK tax representatives of non-UK account managers, account managers ceasing to act or to qualify, claims for tax relief and agreement of liabilities, annual returns of income and of information, annual and interim tax repayment claims, record-keeping, and information to be provided to investors. Subject to conditions, an ISA (or part thereof) may at the investor's request be transferred from one Revenue-approved account manager to another.

[*SI 1998 No 1870; SI 1998 No 3174; SI 2000 No 809*].

Separate regulations modify existing tax legislation so far as it concerns individual savings account business of insurance companies. [*SI 1998 No 1871; SI 1998 No 3174*].

Closure and death. Subject to the ISA terms and conditions, an investor may close an ISA at any time without affecting tax exemptions up to the date of closure. Where an investor dies, income and gains in respect of ISA investments which arise after the date of death but before the date of closure are not exempt.

See generally Revenue Booklet ISA 1 'The Answers on ISAs'.

Simon's Direct Tax Service. See E3.7.

29.11 Income from **international organisations** may be exempt under specific provisions, see 24 DIPLOMATIC IMMUNITY.

29.12 Annual payments under certain **insurance policies**. Where an individual's insurance policy provides income benefits which may be payable for more than one year, those benefits constitute annual payments within SCHEDULE D, CASE III (72). In practice, tax was not collected where insurance benefits were provided in times of sickness, disability or unemployment to meet existing specified obligations such as loan repayments. (Revenue Press Release REV 6, 28 November 1995). Also, by concession, sickness benefits which compensate for lost earnings were generally exempt for the first twelve months. (Revenue Pamphlet IR 1, A83). See 71.64 SCHEDULE D, CASES I AND II, 75.37 SCHEDULE E.

Annual payments falling to be made after 5 April 1996 under certain policies are exempt from income tax under new statutory provisions (and see also below as regards earlier payments). The exemption, described below, will most commonly apply to mortgage payment protection insurance, permanent health insurance, creditor insurance (to meet existing commitments, possibly including domestic utility bills, in event of accident, sickness, disability or unemployment) and certain kinds of long-term care insurance (but only where the policy is taken out before the need for care becomes apparent). (Revenue Press Release REV 6, 28 November 1995).

The exemption is generally restricted to payments that would otherwise be taxed under Schedule D, Case III or, in the case of equivalent non-UK policies, Schedule D, Case V. Payments to be taken into account in computing business profits are thus excluded. However, where an employer takes out a group policy to meet the cost of employees' sick pay and the policy would otherwise qualify under these provisions, the proportion of any payment attributable (on just and reasonable apportionment) to employees' contributions to premiums is exempt from Schedule E. The exemption does not apply if any premiums under the policy (disregarding in the case of the Schedule E exemption an employer's share of premiums) have to any extent qualified for tax relief, either as a deduction from total income or in computing income from any source (e.g. business profits).

For an annual payment to qualify for the exemption:

(*a*) it must be made under a policy (or part of a policy) providing insurance against a 'qualifying risk';

(*b*) the provisions of the policy which insure against that risk must be 'self-contained';

(*c*) the policy must make no provision for payments relating to that risk other than for a period throughout which the 'relevant conditions of payment' are satisfied; and

(*d*) the provisions of the policy relating to that risk must always have been such that the insurer runs a genuine risk of loss (i.e. proceeds payable must be capable of exceeding premiums received plus an investment return on those premiums).

A '*qualifying risk*' is either a risk of physical or mental illness, disability, infirmity or defect (including a risk of an existing condition deteriorating) or a risk of loss of employment (including loss of self-employment). The persons at risk may include the insured, his spouse and, for policies connected with the meeting of liabilities under an identified transaction, a person jointly liable with the insured or his spouse.

The '*relevant conditions of payment*' are satisfied for as long as the illness etc. or unemployment continues (including in the case of illness etc. any related period of convalescence or rehabilitation) or for as long as the income of the insured etc. (apart from benefits under the policy) is less, in circumstances so insured against, than it otherwise would be. If any such period ends as a result of the death of the insured etc., it is extended to any period immediately following (so that benefits paid to the deceased's spouse or estate are brought within the exemption).

The requirement for the relevant provisions of the policy to be '*self-contained*' is an anti-avoidance measure. The provisions of a policy covering different kinds of benefits are self-contained unless the terms of the policy (possibly including the fixing of the amount of premiums), or the way in which they are given effect, in relation to the qualifying risk would have been significantly different if the policy insured only against the qualifying risk (except where the only difference is that certain benefits are applied for reducing other benefits under the policy). A broadly similar rule applies where there are multiple policies. In each case, regard must be had to all the persons for whose benefit insurance is provided against the qualifying risk.

There are provisions enabling benefits relating to illness etc. to qualify for the exemption if paid under an individual policy derived from and superseding an employer's group policy where an employee has left the employment as a consequence of the occurrence insured against.

The exemption also applies to annual payments falling due before 6 April 1996, whether or not made before that date, provided that the only or main purpose of the policy was to secure that the insured would be able to meet liabilities arising from identified transactions (actual or proposed, and including credit arrangements and services to residential premises) none of which could be entered into after any of the circumstances insured against arose, and that the policy provided for the right to annual payments to cease when all liabilities in question were discharged.

For a simplified explanation of the exemption, see Revenue Pamphlet IR 153.

[*ICTA 1988, ss 580A, 580B; FA 1996, s 143*].

Benefits which are wholly exempt are paid without deduction of tax. Where they are partially exempt (e.g. in the case of a company policy to which the employee contributes) or the policy holder's income, including the maximum benefits payable, is below taxable income limits, the insurer may pay benefits gross on receipt of an appropriate declaration from the recipient (on form R91). (Revenue Tax Bulletin December 1996 p 377).

29.13 **Interest** —

(i) on damages for personal injuries or death [*ICTA 1988, s 329*] including similar interest awarded by a foreign court if also exempt from tax in that country (Revenue Pamphlet IR 1, A30);

(ii) on certain UK government stocks held by non-residents (see 33.2 GOVERNMENT STOCKS) and certain borrowings in foreign currency by local authorities and certain STATUTORY BODIES (84) (see 23.12 DEDUCTION OF TAX AT SOURCE);

(iii) on **tax-exempt special savings accounts ('TESSAs')**. Bonuses are also exempt. An account is a 'TESSA' if the following conditions (and any others specified by regulation by the Board) are satisfied when the account is opened.

(*a*) It must be opened by an individual aged 18 or more **before 6 April 1999**.

(*b*) It must be with a building society or an institution authorised under *Banking Act 1987*; it must not be a joint account and must not be held on behalf of another person; it must be identified as a TESSA, and the account-holder must not simultaneously hold another TESSA; and it must not be 'connected with' any other account. An account is '*connected with*' another if either was opened with reference to the other, or with a view to enabling or facilitating the opening of the other on particular terms, and the terms on which either was opened would have been significantly less favourable to the holder if the other had not been opened. In relation to TESSAs opened after 1 January 1996, accounts may be held with certain European authorised institutions entitled to accept deposits in the UK (which must, however, appoint UK tax representatives or make similar arrangements for discharging their duties under the scheme). By concession, accounts opened on or before that date may be transferred to such institutions after that date. (Revenue Pamphlet IR 1, A92).

(*c*) There must not be a notice in force given by the Board to the society or institution prohibiting it from operating new TESSAs.

(*d*) It must be transferable from one society or institution to another which is entitled to, and does, operate TESSAs, on terms agreed between the account-holder and any society or institution concerned.

As regards the requirement at (*b*) above that the account must not be held on behalf of another person, in Scotland, by concession, a *curator bonis* may open a TESSA on behalf of an incapacitated person aged 18 or more, whose name must, however, be shown on the application form. Any details given in returns etc. by the bank or building society holding the account must be those of the incapacitated person and not those of the *curator bonis*. (Revenue Pamphlet IR 1, A79).

A society or institution intending to operate or to cease to operate TESSAs must comply with notification requirements. The Board have powers (subject to appeal) to prohibit a society or institution from operating TESSAs. An application by an individual for a TESSA must contain information specified by regulation, and a statement that false statements in connection with the application may result in penalties or prosecution. On a transfer within (*d*) above, the transferor must supply the transferee with details of the account as specified by regulation.

An account continues to be a TESSA for five years from its being opened (or until the earlier death of the account-holder), or until any of the conditions set out above ceases to be satisfied or any of the following events occurs.

(I) The deposit of more than £3,000 in the first twelve months the account is open, of more than £1,800 in any succeeding twelve-month period, or of more than £9,000 in total.

(II) A withdrawal reducing the balance on the account below the aggregate of earlier deposits and lower or basic rate income tax (whichever is applicable) on any interest or bonus previously paid on the account. The rate applicable is the lower rate, except as regards interest etc. paid or credited before 6 April 1996 where it is the basic rate (being in each case the rate in force for the tax year in which the interest etc. was paid or credited).

(III) The assignment of any rights of the account-holder in respect of the account or the use of such rights as security for a loan.

When an account ceases to be a TESSA (other than on the expiry of the five-year period from its opening or the death of the account-holder), the *Income Tax Acts* have effect as if, immediately after it so ceased, the account were credited with an amount of interest equal to the interest and bonuses payable during the period it was a TESSA.

The Board have the necessary regulatory powers to require information, both aggregate and individual, and the maintenance and inspection of records, and to impose certain requirements as to UK tax representation on European authorised institutions. Penalties apply in relation to notices under those powers.

Follow-up TESSAs. Where a TESSA reaches the end of its five year life (without having ceased to be tax-exempt) and the total amount deposited was over £3,000, the holder may, within the following six months, open another 'follow-up' TESSA in which the maximum deposit in the first twelve months is the total amount deposited in the earlier TESSA (excluding any accumulated interest in that account). An account is not connected with another account (see (*b*) above) merely because it is a follow-up account.

[*ICTA 1988, ss 326A–326D; FA 1990, s 28; TCGA 1992, s 271(4); FA 1995, ss 62, 63; FA 1996, Sch 6 para 7; FA 1998, s 78; SI 1990 No 2361; SI 1995 Nos 1929, 3236, 3239; SI 1996 No 844*].

The Inland Revenue Financial Intermediaries and Claims Office may be contacted for technical advice in relation to TESSAs on 0151–472 6157.

See generally Revenue Pamphlet IR 114.

See 29.10 above as regards the introduction in 1999 of the individual savings account. The regulations governing such accounts permit the transfer in of the capital from maturing TESSAs (but *not* the accumulated interest) without affecting the amount which can be subscribed to an individual savings account, and TESSA subscriptions similarly do not affect the individual savings account limits;

(iv) to the extent of the first £70 for each individual of **National Savings Bank** interest on deposits other than investment deposits. [*ICTA 1988, s 325*];

(v) on **Government Savings Certificates.** See 33.6 GOVERNMENT STOCKS;

(vi) on **Save As You Earn** (SAYE) certified contractual savings schemes (bonuses under such schemes also being exempt), provided (for schemes certified after 30 November 1994 and for contracts entered into after that date under earlier schemes) that they are linked to share option schemes (see 82.38 SHARE INCENTIVE AND OPTIONS). SAYE schemes may be offered by a wide range of providers, including (for schemes established after 1 May 1995) certain European authorised institutions. Treasury authorisation is required for the operation of such schemes. [*ICTA 1988, s 326, Sch 15A; FA 1990, s 29, Sch 14 para 5; FA 1995, s 65, Sch 12; SI 1995 No 1778*];

(vii) on overpaid inheritance tax. [*IHTA 1984, ss 233(3), 235(2)*];

(viii) on certain repayments, see 41 INTEREST ON OVERPAID TAX;

(ix) being loan interest paid by its members to a credit union. [*ICTA 1988, s 487; FA 1996, Sch 14 para 31*];

(x) on refunds of amounts over-repaid by borrowers in respect of **student loans** made under specified statutory provisions. [*ICTA 1988, s 331A; FA 1999, s 60*];

(xi) (by concession) consisting of compensation payments paid on bank accounts owned by Holocaust victims. (Revenue Press Release 8 May 2000).

Certain income (see 28.3(*a*) EXCESS LIABILITY) is exempt from basic or lower rate income tax only.

29.14 **Long service awards** to employees, within limitations set out in 75.26 SCHEDULE E.

29.15 **Luncheon vouchers** if the conditions shown in 75.30 SCHEDULE E are complied with.

29.16 **Members of Parliaments or Assemblies.** The following payments made pursuant to a House of Commons resolution are disregarded as income for tax purposes:

(i) accommodation allowances paid for additional overnight expenses incurred in performing parliamentary duties (and see 75.29 SCHEDULE E); and

(ii) reimbursed costs relating to travel between the UK and any European Union institution in Brussels, Luxembourg or Strasbourg or (from 1 April 1999) the national parliament of another member State. (See generally 75.43 SCHEDULE E.)

[*ICTA 1988, s 200; FA 1993, s 124; FA 1999, s 51*].

Additionally, for 1996/97 and subsequent years, ministers and certain other office-holders in the UK Government, the Scottish Parliament or the Wales or Northern Ireland Assemblies are exempt from tax under SCHEDULE E (75) in respect of the provision of transport or subsistence to them or their families or households by or on behalf of the Crown, or the re-imbursement of expenditure on such provision. 'Transport' for this purpose includes any car (with or without a driver) and any other benefit in connection with such a car (including fuel). 'Subsistence' includes food, drink and temporary accommodation. The exemption does *not* extend to the provision of mobile telephones for 1998/99 and earlier years (see 75.16 SCHEDULE E), but see now 75.13(xxiii) SCHEDULE E as regards the general exemption of such provision thereafter. [*ICTA 1988, s 200AA; FA 1996, s 108; FA 1999, s 44(5)(6), Sch 5 para 3*].

Payments to members of the Scottish Parliament or the Wales or Northern Ireland Assemblies in respect of necessary overnight expenses or EU travel expenses are similarly disregarded for income tax purposes. The former are additional expenses necessarily incurred for the purpose of performing duties as a member in staying away from home overnight, either where the body of which he is a member sits or in the area he represents, and the latter are the cost of, and any additional expenses incurred in, travelling between the UK and any EU institution in Brussels, Luxembourg or Strasbourg or the national parliament of another member State. [*ICTA 1988, s 200ZA; FA 1999, Sch 5 para 2(1)*].

29.17 **Miners'** free coal or cash in lieu thereof is exempt by concession. (Revenue Pamphlet IR 1, A6).

29.18 **Non-residents** are exempt from tax on income and capital gains from: certain GOVERNMENT STOCKS (33); securities of the Inter-American Development Bank [*ICTA 1988, s 583*]; securities of the OECD Support Fund [*OECD Support Fund Act 1975, s 4*] and certain other international organisations designated by statutory instrument [*ICTA 1988, s 324*], including the Asian Development Bank (*SI 1984 No 1215*), the African Development Bank (*SI 1984 No 1634*), the European Bank for Reconstruction and Development (*SI 1991 No 1202*) and any of the European Communities or the European Investment Bank (*SI 1985 No 1172*); and from certain pensions, see 59.4 PENSIONS. See also 25.2 DOUBLE TAX RELIEF.

29.19 Certain **overseas income** is exempt from UK tax under specific DOUBLE TAX RELIEF (25) agreements. If not so exempt, double tax relief may nevertheless be claimable. In some circumstances, overseas income is only assessable on the REMITTANCE BASIS (63). See also 51 NON-RESIDENTS AND OTHER OVERSEAS MATTERS.

29.20 Certain **pensions** are exempt, see 59.4 PENSIONS.

29.21 **Personal equity plans.** A 'qualifying individual' may subscribe a specified maximum to a personal equity plan to which no-one else may subscribe. Revised regulations came into force on 6 April 1989 (the *1989 Regulations*) (subsequently amended) modifying the original provisions (the *1986 Regulations*). **No further subscriptions are permitted to personal equity plans after 5 April 1999.** Plans held on that date may continue to be held outside the individual savings account regime which commenced on 6 April 1999 (see 29.10 above). Reliefs available in respect of plan investments are aligned with those available in individual savings accounts. In particular, *FA 1998, s 76* permits the payment of a 10% tax credit on UK dividends until 5 April 2004. The value of plan investments does not affect the amount which may be subscribed to an individual savings account.

A '*qualifying individual*' must be 18 years of age or over, and either resident and ordinarily resident in the UK or a non-resident Crown employee serving overseas whose duties are treated as performed in the UK (see 75.2(i) SCHEDULE E). Subscriptions may be made to only one general plan and one 'single company plan' (see below) in any tax year. From 6 April 1996, a *curator bonis* appointed in Scotland for a qualifying individual suffering from incapacity may subscribe to a plan in his capacity as such, regardless of any subscription he may make in another capacity.

Under the *1989 Regulations*, a maximum of £6,000 may be invested through a 'plan manager' in a personal equity plan in any tax year. For so long as the various conditions continue to be met, dividends and interest on securities are tax-free (and the plan manager may reclaim the related tax credits including, from 21 August 1998, those relating to investors who have subsequently ceased to be UK residents). There is no capital gains tax liability (nor is there relief for losses) on the sale of an investment under the plan.

Up to £3,000 per tax year may be invested in a 'single company plan' (often known as a 'corporate PEP') in addition to any investment in a general plan as described above. A '*single company plan*' allows investment only in shares of one designated company, and an additional condition imposed is that substantially the whole of the cash subscribed to the plan, or from realisation of plan shares, must be reinvested in plan shares within 42 days, or transferred (with interest) to the investor within 14 days thereafter.

Regulations impose certain requirements as to UK tax representation on European authorised institutions and certain other European plan managers.

Conditions applicable to both 'general' and 'single company' plans. All transactions involving plan investments must be carried out at open market prices, and investments may not be purchased from the plan investor or spouse. Subscription to a plan must be by payment of cash to the plan manager for investment by him, except that

(*a*) qualifying shares allotted under public offers, and

(*b*) (in relation to single company plans, see below) certain shares acquired under employee share schemes,

may be transferred into plans. As regards (*a*) above, the shares must be transferred to the plan within 42 days of allotment, and their cost included within the overall investment limit. This applies also to shares in a building society issued on conversion to plc status and (from 20 March 1997) to shares in a mutual insurer transferring its business to a company limited by shares (so that no part of the annual limit is used in the case of free shares on building society conversion or on demutualisation). The fact that a new issue may take the form of separate offers on slightly different terms (e.g. to employees or customers of the issuing company) does not prevent the shares being eligible for transfer into a plan. (Revenue Press Releases 6 October 1989, 17 October 1990).

With effect from 23 May 1996, shares acquired in a public offer may not be transferred into a PEP where:

(1) the allocation of shares to the investor is connected with the allocation of other classes of shares or securities in the company (or rights to them) or of shares or securities (or rights to them) in another company; and

(2) the shares are offered on terms which are significantly more favourable than if they had not been so connected.

Cash held in a plan must be within the overall limit, must be held in sterling and must be invested in a designated account with a deposit-taker or building society (see 8 BANKS, 9 BUILDING SOCIETIES). Interest is paid gross and will be exempt from tax altogether, so long as it is eventually invested in plan shares, securities or unit trusts. (Revenue Press Release 17 October 1990). If interest etc. exceeding £180 in a year is paid by the plan manager to or for the plan investor in respect of cash held within a plan, the plan manager must account for a sum representing lower rate (before 1996/97 basic rate) tax on all such interest payments in the year; the interest payments are for all purposes treated as interest taxable under SCHEDULE D, CASE III (72) in the year in which they arise, the lower or basic rate liability on which is satisfied as above.

General plans. The investments which may be purchased, made or held under a general plan after 5 July 1995 are:

(i) ordinary shares in UK-incorporated companies (other than investment trusts or open-ended investment companies) listed on a recognised stock exchange in an EU Member State or dealt in (prior to its abolition) on the Unlisted Securities Market (but not the Alternative Investment Market, see Revenue Press Release 20 February 1995);

(ii) '*qualifying EC shares*' (i.e. shares issued by a company incorporated in a Member State other than the UK and listed on a recognised stock exchange in a Member State), provided that they form part of the authorised share capital of the company, carry no fixed, guaranteed or secured redemption rights or preferential rights to dividends or to company property in a liquidation, and are neither shares carrying no right to a profit share other than fixed dividends nor shares carrying no right to fixed dividends but carrying a right of conversion into shares which do carry such a right. The company must not be an open-ended investment company within *Financial Services Act 1986, s 75(8)*, and must not derive the principal part of its income from shareholdings each of which represents 10% or less of the voting power in the company concerned;

(iii) shares other than ordinary shares, issued by a company incorporated in a Member State and listed on a recognised stock exchange in a Member State, not being shares in an investment trust, an open-ended investment company or an authorised credit institution (as defined, and including the European equivalent);

(iv) securities (i.e. any loan stock or similar security, whether secured or unsecured) issued by a company incorporated in the UK, not being securities of an investment trust, an open-ended investment company or an authorised credit institution (as defined), provided that:

(*a*) at the date of issue and throughout the period of the loan they either carry a right to interest at a fixed percentage rate (or a series of consecutive such rates) or carry no right to interest;

(*b*) they are denominated in sterling;

(*c*) judged at the date when first held under the plan, the terms of issue do not require the loan to be repaid or the security to be re-purchased or redeemed, or allow the holder to so require except in circumstances unlikely to occur, within five years;

(*d*) the securities are not deep gain securities within *FA 1989, Sch 11* and do not fall to be treated as such by virtue of *FA 1989, Sch 11 paras 21(2), 22(2), 22A(2)* or *22B(3)* (see 44.7 INTEREST RECEIVABLE); and

(*e*) at least one of the following conditions is satisfied:

(I) the ordinary shares in the issuing company are listed on a recognised stock exchange in a Member State;

(II) the securities are so listed; or

(III) the issuing company is a 75% subsidiary (within *ICTA 1988, s 838*) of a company whose ordinary shares are so listed;

(v) units in an authorised unit trust (as specially defined and excluding certain pension schemes with restricted investment powers ('feeder funds') and schemes which may invest wholly in warrants ('warrant funds')), provided that at least 50% in value of the investments held by the trust are either

(I) ordinary shares in UK-incorporated companies (other than investment trusts),

(II) qualifying EC shares and shares within (iii) above (or shares which would be such shares if quoted on a recognised stock exchange in a Member State),

(III) securities which would be within (iv) above if the condition in (iv)(*c*) required the judgement to be made when they were first acquired by the unit trust, and disregarding the condition in (iv)(*e*),

(IV) shares in (and securities meeting the conditions in (iv)(*a*)–(*d*) above of) an investment trust 50% of the value of the investments of which are within (I) or (II) above, or would be within (III) above if the date in question were that on which the securities were first acquired by the investment trust, and

(V) (from 8 August 1997) shares in open-ended investment companies (subject to conditions similar to those applicable under (IV) above) and certain investments in umbrella schemes or companies.

(vi) units in a fund of funds (i.e. a unit trust scheme investing in authorised unit trusts or open-ended investment companies) where at least 50% of the investments held meet conditions similar to those applicable under (v) above;

(vii) (from 8 August 1997) shares in an open-ended investment company subject to conditions similar to those applicable to authorised unit trust units (see (v) above);

(viii) (from 8 August 1997) units or shares in certain umbrella schemes or companies otherwise meeting the conditions in (v) or (vii) above;

(ix) shares in (and securities meeting the conditions in (iv)(*a*)–(*d*) above of) an investment trust (including a 'split-level' trust, see Revenue Press Release 3 May 1989) 50% of the value of the investments of which meet conditions similar to those applicable under (v) above;

(x) subject to an overall limit of one-quarter of the maximum subscription (less any amounts payable for qualifying investment trust shares allotted under public offers, see (*a*) above, and transferred to the plan), investments not within (v)–(ix) above which meet the following conditions:

(A) in the case of units in authorised unit trusts or umbrella schemes, 50% of the investments held by the trust are either ordinary shares in UK-incorporated companies (other than investment trusts or open-ended investment companies) or 'other quoted shares' (i.e. shares listed on a recognised stock exchange which satisfy the conditions applicable to qualifying EC shares under (ii) above), or shares in investment trusts, open-ended investment companies or umbrella schemes or companies at least 50% of whose investments are such ordinary or other quoted shares;

(B) in the case of funds of funds, at least 50% of the investments held by the constituent unit trusts are ordinary shares in UK-incorporated companies (other than investment trusts or open-ended investment companies) or other quoted shares (as in (A) above);

(C) in the case of investment trusts, at least 50% of the investments held by the trust are either ordinary shares in UK-incorporated companies (other than investment trusts or open-ended investment companies) or other quoted shares (as in (A) above), or units or shares in authorised unit trusts, open-ended investment companies or umbrella schemes or companies 50% of the value of whose investments are such ordinary or other quoted shares; and

(D) in the case of open-ended investment companies or umbrella companies, at least 50% of the investments held by the company are either ordinary shares in UK-incorporated companies (other than investment trusts or open-ended investment companies) or other quoted shares (as in (A) above), or units or shares in authorised unit trusts, open-ended investment companies or umbrella schemes or companies 50% of the value of whose investments are such ordinary or other quoted shares; and

(xi) cash.

An occasional inadvertent fall below the 50% levels referred to in (v)–(x) above will generally be disregarded, see Revenue Press Release 3 May 1989.

Cash received by the plan manager from dividends, disposals etc. may be reinvested in any qualifying investments within (i)–(ix) above, and in unit trusts, funds of funds, open-ended investment companies and investment trusts *not* within (v)–(ix) above provided that the market value of such investments does not immediately thereafter exceed one-quarter of the market value of all plan investments.

Certain investments held on 5 April 1990 which failed to meet the test for qualification ('non-qualifying investments') may continue to be held under a plan, provided that

(*a*) the total of such investments made during 1989/90 and held at that date did not exceed £2,400, and

(*b*) apart from the reinvestment of proceeds of sale of non-qualifying investments, the amount invested in non-qualifying investments in 1990/91 did not exceed £900, and

(*c*) after 5 April 1991, the total amount invested in authorised unit trusts, funds of funds and investment trusts does not exceed one-quarter of the subscription limit.

Single company plans. The investments which may be purchased, made or held under a single company plan are:

(i) where the company designated for the purposes of the plan is a UK company (other than an investment trust or venture capital trust) quoted on a recognised stock exchange or dealt in on the Unlisted Securities Market, ordinary shares in the company, and ordinary shares or 'qualifying EC shares' 'representing' those shares;

(ii) provided that the designated company is not an open-ended investment company within *Financial Services Act 1986, s 75(8)*, and does not derive the principal part of its income from shareholdings each of which represents 15% or less by value of its investments, 'qualifying EC shares' issued by the company, and 'qualifying EC shares' or ordinary shares within (i) above 'representing' those shares;

(iii) investments in units comprising ordinary shares or 'qualifying EC shares' in the designated company (restricted as in (i) or (ii) above respectively) which are 'paired' with ordinary shares or 'qualifying EC shares' in another company meeting the condition in (i) or (ii) above respectively; or

(iv) cash.

In addition, the plan investor may subscribe to a plan by transferring to the plan manager shares in the designated company which were appropriated to the plan investor under an approved profit-sharing scheme or acquired by exercise of options under a SAYE share option scheme (see 82.9, 82.38 SHARE INCENTIVES AND OPTIONS). Shares acquired under SAYE schemes must be transferred in within 90 days of exercise of the option, those appropriated under profit-sharing schemes within 90 days of the earlier of the date the plan investor directed the trustees of the scheme to transfer the shares to him and the 'release date' in relation to the shares (see 82.9 SHARE INCENTIVES AND OPTIONS). The sum of the market value of shares so transferred to a plan and of the cost of any new issue shares so transferred (see general conditions above) must, together with any cash subscribed, be within the overall subscription limit for the single company plan.

'*Qualifying EC shares*' are shares issued by a company incorporated in a Member State other than the UK and officially listed on a recognised stock exchange in a Member State. Shares '*represent*' other shares when there is a company reorganisation under which, for capital gains tax purposes, they are (or would but for being plan investments be) equated with the other shares. Shares in two companies are '*paired*' where it is provided in their governing instruments that no share in either company may be acquired otherwise than as part of a unit comprising one share in each company, such units being offered for sale at the same time and at the same price or, where sales are in more than one country, at a broadly equivalent price.

Cash received by the plan manager from dividends, disposals etc. may be reinvested in other shares within (i)–(iii) above. Where the cash arises in respect of shares transferred in from a profit-sharing or SAYE share option scheme (see above), it may be re-invested in similar shares even where they are not otherwise qualifying investments.

Pre-1990 plans. Plans under the *1986 Regulations* operated by reference to calendar years rather than tax years. There was an overall limit of £3,000 (£2,400 before 22 April 1988) per year of which the greater of £540 (£420 before 22 April 1988) and one-quarter of the plan subscription could be invested in investment trusts and authorised unit trusts.

[*ICTA 1988, ss 333, 333A; TCGA 1992, s 151; FA 1991, s 70; FA 1993, s 85; FA 1995, s 64; SI 1986 No 1948; SI 1989 No 469; SI 1990 No 678; SI 1991 Nos 733, 2774; SI 1992 No 623; SI 1993 No 756; SI 1995 Nos 1539, 3287; SI 1996 Nos 846, 1355; SI 1997 Nos 511, 1716; SI 1998 No 1869*].

General. A list of registered plan managers may be obtained by sending a self-addressed A4 size envelope to (or calling at) Inland Revenue Information Centre, SW Wing, Bush House, Strand, London WC2B 4RD. The list is updated quarterly. An information pack on personal equity plans aimed at plan managers is available from the Inland Revenue Library, Mid-Basement, Somerset House, price £3.50.

The Inland Revenue Financial Intermediaries and Claims Office may be contacted in relation to personal equity plans on 0151–472 6110 as regards repayments or 0151–472 6157 for technical advice.

See generally Revenue Pamphlet IR 89.

See 29.10 above as regards the introduction in 1999 of the new individual savings account 'building upon the experience of TESSAs [see 29.12(iii) above] and PEPs'.

Simon's Direct Tax Service. See E3.3.

29.22 **Profit-related pay** under a registered scheme is wholly or partly exempt within certain limits. See 75.31 SCHEDULE E.

29.23 **Redundancy payments** under *Employment Rights Act 1996* (or NI equivalent). [*ICTA 1988, s 579*]. See also 75.32 SCHEDULE E.

29.24 **Repayment supplement** in respect of income tax or capital gains tax repayments (see 41 INTEREST ON OVERPAID TAX) or VAT repayments (under *VATA 1994, s 79*, see Tolley's Value Added Tax under Payment of Tax) is disregarded for income tax purposes. (*Note.* Interest payable on certain VAT repayments under *VATA 1994, s 80* is *not* exempt.) [*ICTA 1988, ss 824(8), 827(2)*].

29.25 Certain lump sums under PERSONAL PENSION SCHEMES (60), RETIREMENT ANNUITIES (65) and RETIREMENT SCHEMES (66).

29.26 **Sandwich courses.** Where an employee is released by employer to take a full-time educational course at a university, technical college or similar institution open to the public at large, payments for periods of attendance may be treated as exempt from income tax. Conditions are (i) that the course lasts at least one academic year, with an average of at least 20 weeks per year of full-time attendance, and (ii) that the rate of payment does not exceed the greater of (*a*) £7,000 p.a. (£5,500 before 6 April 1992, £5,000 before 6 April 1989) and (*b*) the rate of payment an individual in similar personal circumstances would have received as a grant from one of the public awarding bodies on a scale fixed by the Secretary of State for Education and Science (e.g. a Research Council Studentship). For this purpose, university fees etc. paid or reimbursed by employer are ignored. Where the rate of payment exceeds the limit, the full payments are taxable, but where a rate of payment is increased during a course, only subsequent payments are taxable, and periods where payments are thus taxable nonetheless count towards the requisite periods of attendance. (Revenue Pamphlet IR 131, SP 4/86, 8 August 1986; Revenue Press Releases 12 April 1989, 18 November 1992). See 92 VOCATIONAL TRAINING RELIEF as regards certain training courses.

29.27 **Scholarship** income and bursaries. [*ICTA 1988, s 331*]. In *Clayton v Gothorp Ch D 1971, 47 TC 168*, discharge of loan made by employer for training course held not scholarship income but was emoluments. See 29.26 above and 75.20 SCHEDULE E for where scholarship awarded by employer of parent etc. Covenanted 'parental contributions' under *Education Act 1962* not an educational endowment (*Gibbs v Randall Ch D 1980, 53 TC 513*).

29.28 Certain **Social Security** benefits (see 83 SOCIAL SECURITY) and corresponding foreign benefits (Revenue Pamphlet IR 1, A24) and payments under Jobmatch programme (Revenue Pamphlet IR 1, A97). Disabled Person's Vehicle Maintenance Grants under

National Health Service Act 1977, Sch 2 para 2 or corresponding Scottish or NI Act. [*ICTA 1988, s 327*]. Also Sickness and Disablement Benefits from Approved and Friendly Societies to the extent specified in Revenue Pamphlet IR 1, A26.

29.29 For 1995/96 and earlier years, discounts on **Treasury securities** issued after 6 March 1973 are exempt from tax under Schedule D, Case III [*ICTA 1988, s 126; FA 1996, Sch 41 Pt V(3)*] without this exemption resulting in a charge under Schedule D, Case VI. They are still chargeable to tax if they constitute trading profits. This exemption does not apply to Treasury Bills, to 'deep discount securities' issued by public bodies or 'deep gain securities' (see 44.5, 44.7 INTEREST RECEIVABLE), or to certain gilt-edged securities which are treated as deep discount or deep gain securities. [*FA 1989, s 95; FA 1996, Sch 41 Pt V(3)*]. See now 72.2 SCHEDULE D, CASE III (and Tolley's Corporation Tax under Loan Relationships as regards accounting periods ending after 31 March 1996).

29.30 **Wages in lieu of notice** in some instances. See 75.45 SCHEDULE E.

29.31 **War Gratuities, Bounties or Gratuities** to men and women voluntarily re-enlisting; training bounties to reservists; mess and ration allowances, training expenses, allowances and efficiency bounties to members of reserve and auxiliary forces [*ICTA 1988, s 316*] but Civil Defence Corps bounties are not exempt because these are paid by local authorities and therefore not 'out of the public revenue' (*Lush v Coles Ch D 1967, 44 TC 169*).

29.32 **War widows etc.**. Pensions payable in respect of death due to (*a*) service in the armed forces, including before 3 September 1939 or (*b*) wartime service in the merchant navy or (*c*) war injuries, and similar pensions payable by foreign governments, are exempt from tax. The exemption also applies to the amount of any other pension which replaces an exempt pension withheld or abated. [*ICTA 1988, s 318*].

29.33 **Wound and disability pensions** to HM Forces. [*ICTA 1988, s 315*]. See 59.4(ii) PENSIONS.

30 Exempt Organisations

Exemption is given to the organisations etc. below to the extent indicated.

30.1 **Agricultural societies** established to promote 'the interests of agriculture, horticulture, livestock breeding or forestry' are exempt from tax on profits or gains 'from any exhibition or show held for the purposes of the society ... if applied solely to the purposes of the society'. [*ICTA 1988, s 510*]. See *Peterborough Royal Foxhound Show Society v CIR KB 1936, 20 TC 249; Glasgow Ornithological Assn CS 1938, 21 TC 445*. An agricultural society may also qualify for charitable relief, see 15.2(*g*) CHARITIES.

30.2 Non-resident central **banks** as specified by Order in Council are exempt from tax on certain classes of income [*ICTA 1988, s 516*] and the issue departments of the Reserve Bank of India and the State Bank of Pakistan are exempt from all taxes. [*ICTA 1988, s 517; TCGA 1992, s 271(8)*].

30.3 **The British Museum and Natural History Museum** may claim exemption as if they were charities. [*ICTA 1988, s 507; TCGA 1992, s 271(6)(a); FA 1989, s 60; Museums and Galleries Act 1992, Sch 8 para 1(8)(9)*].

30.4 **Charities** are generally exempt but see full details under 15 CHARITIES.

30.5 CLUBS AND SOCIETIES (18). There is restriction of liability in a few special circumstances.

30.6 **The Crown** is not generally within the taxing Acts; see *ICTA 1988, s 49(2)* and *s 829(2)*. See *ICTA 1988, s 829* as amended by *FA 1993, s 122* as to assessment, deduction and payment of tax by Crown public offices and departments.

30.7 Under DIPLOMATIC IMMUNITY ETC. (24), there are certain exemptions.

30.8 FRIENDLY SOCIETIES (31) have certain exemptions.

30.9 **Historic Buildings and Monuments Commission for England** may claim exemption as if it were a charity. [*ICTA 1988, s 507; TCGA 1992, s 271(7)*].

30.10 **Housing Associations** and approved self-build societies have certain exemptions. [*ICTA 1988, ss 488, 489*]. See Tolley's Corporation Tax.

30.11 **International Maritime Satellite Organisation.** An overseas signatory is exempt in respect of any receipt from the Organisation. [*ICTA 1988, s 515; TCGA 1992, s 271(5)*].

30.12 **Local authorities,** local authority associations and health service boards, as defined by *ICTA 1988, ss 842A, 519(3), 519A* respectively as amended, are exempt. [*ICTA 1988, ss 519, 519A as amended; TCGA 1992, s 271(3)*].

30.13 MUTUAL TRADING (50). There are some special tax provisions.

30.14 **National Heritage Memorial Fund** may claim exemption as if it were a charity. [*ICTA 1988, s 507; TCGA 1992, s 271(7)*].

30.15 SCIENTIFIC RESEARCH ASSOCIATIONS (77) are generally exempt.

30.16 Some STATUTORY BODIES (84) receive a measure of exemption.

30.17 Approved **Superannuation Funds, personal pension schemes** etc. are exempt from tax on investment income and on chargeable gains arising on investments the income of which is exempt from tax. See 60 PERSONAL PENSION SCHEMES, 65 RETIREMENT ANNUITIES and 66 RETIREMENT SCHEMES. Income from, or from transactions relating to, futures and options contracts is within the exemption. See further 71.32 SCHEDULE D, CASES I AND II.

30.18 TRADE UNIONS (88), including employers' associations and Police Federations, which are registered are exempt on provident benefit income under certain conditions.

30.19 Authorised UNIT TRUSTS (90), investment trusts and VENTURE CAPITAL TRUSTS (91) are exempt from corporation tax on their chargeable gains. [*TCGA 1992, s 100(1); FA 1995, s 72(2)*].

30.20 The **United Kingdom Ecolabelling Board** may claim exemption as if it were a charity (see 15 CHARITIES). [*ICTA 1988, s 507(1)(e); SI 1992 No 2383, reg 2*].

30.21 **Visiting forces** and associated civilians from designated countries. [*ICTA 1988, s 323; FA 1990, Sch 14 para 4*]. See *SI 1961 No 580*, *SI 1964 No 924* and *SI 1998 Nos 1513, 1514*.

31 Friendly Societies

Simon's Direct Tax Service D4.601 *et seq.*.

31.1 **Friendly societies** are within the charge to corporation tax on income and capital gains. There are, however, exemptions from tax for:

(i) unregistered societies with incomes not exceeding £160 p.a.; and

(ii) registered or incorporated societies, in respect of 'tax exempt life or endowment business'.

[*ICTA 1988, ss 459, 460(1)(2); F(No 2)A 1992, Sch 9 paras 4, 5*].

Incorporated societies, following enactment of the *Friendly Societies Act 1992*, attract the same exemptions etc. as registered societies, and there are provisions to ensure that no tax charges arise on the incorporation of a registered society under that *Act*. [*F(No 2)A 1992, Sch 9; ICTA 1988, ss 461A–461C, s 465A; TCGA 1992, ss 217A–217C*].

Following the general abolition, from 6 April 1999, of tax credit payments, and their temporary reinstatement in relation to individual savings account investments (see 29.10 EXEMPT INCOME), they are similarly reinstated in relation to distributions to friendly societies in respect of tax exempt business until 5 April 2004. [*FA 1998, s 90*].

'*Tax exempt life or endowment business*' is broadly life or endowment business consisting of the granting of annuities of annual amounts not exceeding £156, or of the assurance of gross sums under contracts under which the total premiums payable in any twelve-month period do not exceed a maximum figure as follows:

for contracts made after 30 April 1995	£270
for contracts made after 24 July 1991 and before 1 May 1995	£200
for contracts made after 31 August 1990 and before 25 July 1991	£150
for contracts made after 31 August 1987 and before 1 September 1990	£100

For contracts made after 13 March 1984 and before 1 September 1987, the limit on the assurance of gross sums was by reference to the amount of the gross sum assured, and was set at £750. For contracts made before 14 March 1984, the limit was £500, and that on the granting of annuities £104. Where the premium under a contract made after 31 August 1987 and before 1 May 1995 is increased by a variation after 24 July 1991 and before 1 August 1992 or after 30 April 1995 and before 1 April 1996, the contract is to be treated for these purposes as having been made at the time of the variation. In determining these limits, no account is taken of any bonus or addition declared upon an assurance or accruing thereon by reference to an increase in the value of any investments, or of any bonus or addition declared upon an annuity. In relation to premium limits, so much of any premium as relates to exceptional risks of death is disregarded, as is 10% of premiums payable more frequently than annually. [*ICTA 1988, s 460(2)(c)(d)(3)–(6); FA 1990, s 49(1)(2); FA 1991, Sch 9 para 1; F(No 2)A 1992, Sch 9 para 5; FA 1995, Sch 10 para 1*]. For detailed requirements for exemption, see Tolley's Corporation Tax under Friendly Societies.

31.2 **Individual limit.** The total amount of business which a person may have outstanding with registered or incorporated friendly societies is limited:

(i) to an annuity or annuities totalling not more than £156 p.a. (£416 p.a. where all the contracts were made before 14 March 1984); and

(ii) to a gross sum assured under a contract or contracts under which the total premiums payable in any twelve-month period do not exceed any of the following limits:

for all contracts	£270
for contracts made after 24 July 1991 and before 1 May 1995	£200
for contracts made after 31 August 1990 and before 25 July 1991	£150
for contracts made before 1 September 1990	£100

unless all the contracts were made before 1 September 1987. For these purposes, a premium under an annuity contract made before 1 June 1984 by a 'new society' (see 31.3 below) is brought into account as if the contract were for the assurance of a gross sum. For contracts made before 1 September 1987, a limit was imposed by reference to the gross sum(s) assured, the limit being £750 (£2,000 if all the contracts were made before 14 March 1984). Where the premium under a contract made after 31 August 1987 and before 1 May 1995 is increased by a variation after 24 July 1991 and before 1 August 1992 or after 30 April 1995 and before 1 April 1996, the contract is to be treated for these purposes as having been made at the time of the variation. No account is, however, taken of (*a*) so much of any premium as relates to exceptional death risk, (*b*) 10% of premiums payable more frequently than annually, and (*c*) £10 of the premiums payable in a twelve month period under any contract made before 1 September 1987 by a society which is not a 'new society' (see 31.3 below).

The restrictions on both gross sum and annuity contracts are applied without taking into account any bonus or addition declared upon an assurance or accruing thereon by reference to an increase in the value of any investments. An annuity contract made before 1 June 1984 by a 'new society' is for these purposes treated as providing both the annual sum assured and a gross sum equal to 75% of the premiums which would be payable if the annuity ran its full term or the person died at age 75. [*ICTA 1988, s 464; FA 1990, s 49(3)(4); FA 1991, Sch 9 para 3; F(No 2)A 1992, Sch 9 para 11; FA 1995, Sch 10 para 2*]. If, after 18 March 1985, a person obtains a policy which causes his contracts to exceed the above limits, the policy will not be a 'qualifying policy' (see 31.3 below), but without affecting earlier policies. [*ICTA 1988 Sch 15 para 6*].

31.3 **Qualifying policies** attract income tax relief on the premiums paid (for insurances made before 14 March 1984), and the proceeds are generally free of any income tax charge (see 45.1, 45.13 LIFE ASSURANCE POLICIES). Except as below, all policies issued by friendly societies before 19 March 1985 in the course of tax exempt life or endowment business (see 31.1 above) are qualifying policies. [*ICTA 1970, Sch 1 para 3 as originally enacted*]. A policy issued *or varied* after 18 March 1985 is a qualifying policy only if it satisfies the conditions in *ICTA 1988, Sch 15 paras 3, 4 as amended*. Broadly, these are the same as the conditions imposed under *ICTA 1988, s 462* on policies which a friendly society may issue in the course of its tax exempt life or endowment business (see Tolley's Corporation Tax under Friendly Societies), but in addition the minimum sum assured must be at least 75% of the total premiums payable, and contracts made before 25 July 1991 with a 'new society' must be with a person over the age of 18. [*ICTA 1988, Sch 15 para 3(1); FA 1991, Sch 9 para 4*]. For the detailed application of the 75% test, see *ICTA 1988, Sch 15 para 3(5)–(11).*

Certain policies issued under contracts made before 20 March 1991, and expressed at the outset not to be made in the course of tax-exempt life or endowment business, were subsequently determined to have been within the statutory definition of that business. A similar situation arose in relation to certain contracts for qualifying policies assumed, at the outset of the contract, not to be made in the course of tax-exempt life or endowment business (without being expressed either to be or not to be so). Where the society so elected, profits attributable to such contracts are treated as not being within the exemption. [*ICTA 1988, s 462A; FA 1991, Sch 9 para 2*]. However, such an election does not affect the tax position of the member holding the policy. By concession, the member will be taxed on the basis of the original assumption he will have been given that no charge to tax would arise on the surrender or maturity of the policy. (Revenue Press Release 12 June 1991). See Tolley's Corporation Tax under Friendly Societies for details of the society's election.

A '*new society*' is a society which either was registered after 3 May 1966 or was registered in the three months before that date but did not carry on any life or endowment business during that period (or a successor incorporated society). [*ICTA 1988, s 466(2); F(No 2)A 1992, Sch 9 para 14(5)*].

If any rights under a health insurance policy (within *Friendly Societies Act 1974, Sch 1 para 1*) issued by a new society (see above) are wholly or partly surrendered after 18 March 1985, the policy ceases to be a qualifying policy. [*ICTA 1988, Sch 15 para 4(3)(b)*].

31.4 **Non-qualifying policies.** A gain on a chargeable event in respect of a policy which is not a qualifying policy (see 31.3 above), or in respect of certain life annuity contracts, may give rise to a charge to income tax (see 45.13 LIFE ASSURANCE POLICIES). If such a gain arises on a policy issued in the course of a society's tax exempt life or endowment business (see 31.1 above), it is chargeable to basic and higher rates of income tax, with no deemed payment of basic rate liability, and with 'top-slicing relief' (see 45.13 LIFE ASSURANCE POLICIES) applying only to the higher rate tax. [*ICTA 1988, ss 540, 542, 550; FA 1987, s 30(8)*].

31.5 **Qualifying distributions.** If a society registered after 31 May 1973, with certain exceptions, or one registered before that date if the registrar so directs, makes a payment to a member (in excess of his contributions and not in the course of life or endowment business), this is a qualifying distribution for income and corporation tax purposes (see Tolley's Corporation Tax under Distributions). [*ICTA 1988, s 461(2)(3)*].

31.6 See 3.17 ANTI-AVOIDANCE for restriction of tax recovery regarding pre-acquisition dividends, etc. on 10% holdings, and 3.18 regarding certain bonus issues.

32 Funding Bonds

Simon's Direct Tax Service A3.425.

32.1 **Funding Bonds etc.** issued in respect of interest by any Government, public authority or institution, or company are treated as income equal to bonds' value when issued; but their eventual redemption is not treated as a payment of the interest. 'Bonds' includes 'stocks, shares, securities or certificates of indebtedness'. Persons by or through whom the bonds are issued and who, if the amount treated as income had been an actual payment of interest, would have been required to deduct tax therefrom, must retain a proportionate amount of these bonds equal to tax at the lower rate (for 1995/96 and earlier years, the basic rate) on their value, and are accountable to the Revenue accordingly, with the right to tender the bonds in payment. Where retention is impracticable they may be relieved of liability on their furnishing a list of recipients, who are then assessed direct under Schedule D, Case VI. [*ICTA 1988, s 582; FA 1996, s 134, Sch 6 para 14, Sch 20 para 32*].

33 Government Stocks

Cross-references. See 3 ANTI-AVOIDANCE for dividend-stripping and bond-washing transactions; 14 CERTIFICATES OF TAX DEPOSIT; 23 DEDUCTION OF TAX AT SOURCE; 70 SCHEDULE C for the position of paying and collecting agents.

Simon's Direct Tax Service A7.11.

33.1 GENERAL TAX PROVISIONS

The provisions of *FA 1996, ss 80–105, Schs 8–15* introduced a new taxation regime for corporation tax purposes for gilt-edged and other securities. Broadly, for accounting periods ending after 31 March 1996, all interest and profits or losses in respect of securities is brought in on revenue account, either on an accruals or on a mark-to-market basis. This regime **does not apply for income tax**. However, **for 1996/97 and subsequent years** for income tax purposes, a new simplified regime (see 72.2 SCHEDULE D, CASE III) is introduced for dealing with discounts on securities, replacing the existing deep discount, deep gain and qualifying convertible securities provisions (see 44.5, 44.7, 44.8 INTEREST RECEIVABLE) and taking precedence over the accrued income scheme (see 74.6 *et seq.* SCHEDULE D, CASE VI). There continues to be a capital gains tax exemption for gilt-edged and most other securities.

For 1996/97 and subsequent years (and for company accounting periods ending after 31 March 1996), Government and foreign securities are chargeable under Schedule D, Case III, IV or V as appropriate, and, until 31 March 2001, are subject to the paying and collecting agents arrangements under *ICTA 1988, ss 118A–118K* and associated regulations. For an article on the scope of these arrangements, see Revenue Tax Bulletin August 1996 p 329. Previously (but generally to similar effect) they were chargeable under SCHEDULE C (70). From 1 April 2001, these arrangements are abolished. [*FA 2000, s 111(1)(6)*]. See 33.3 below and, as regards continuing deduction arrangements for UK public revenue dividends (other than gilt-edged securities), 23.3(ii) DEDUCTION OF TAX AT SOURCE.

33.2 INTEREST—TAX EXEMPTION FOR NON-RESIDENTS

The Treasury has powers to issue securities ('FOTRA securities') on terms that the profits or gains arising from the securities are exempt from tax provided that they are beneficially owned by persons not ordinarily resident in the UK (see RESIDENCE, ORDINARY RESIDENCE AND DOMICILE (64)). From 6 April 1998, however, *FA 1998, s 161* provides for all gilt-edged securities issued before that date without that status to be treated as if they were FOTRA securities (except 3.5% War Loan, which is in effect treated in the same way as FOTRA securities under its terms of issue). Before that date, the list of FOTRA securities was as follows.

9 % Conversion 2000	$6\frac{3}{4}$% Treasury 2004
9 % Conversion 2011	7 % Treasury 2001
$9\frac{1}{2}$% Conversion 2001*	7 % Treasury 2002
$9\frac{3}{4}$% Conversion 2003*	$7\frac{1}{4}$% Treasury 2007
$2\frac{1}{2}$% Treasury Index-linked 2024	$7\frac{1}{2}$% Treasury 2006
$4\frac{1}{8}$% Treasury Index-linked 2030	$7\frac{3}{4}$% Treasury 2006
$4\frac{3}{8}$% Treasury Index-linked 2004	$7\frac{3}{4}$% Treasury 2012/15
$5\frac{1}{2}$% Treasury 2008/12	8 % Treasury 2000
6 % Treasury 1999	8 % Treasury 2003
$6\frac{1}{4}$% Treasury 2010	8 % Treasury 2002/06

8 % Treasury 2013	$8\frac{3}{4}$% Treasury 2017
8 % Treasury 2015	9 % Treasury 2008
8 % Treasury 2021	9 % Treasury 2012
$8\frac{1}{2}$% Treasury 2000*	$9\frac{1}{2}$% Treasury 1999
$8\frac{1}{2}$% Treasury 2005	$3\frac{1}{2}$% War Loan
$8\frac{1}{2}$% Treasury 2007	Floating rate Treasury 1999

Further and current information relating to exempt stocks may be obtained from Gilt-Edged and Money Markets Division, Bank of England, Threadneedle Street, London EC2R 8AH (tel. 0207–601 4540). A restricted market operates in those stocks marked with an asterisk because of the small amounts still in issue.

Provided that any conditions imposed are complied with, nothing in the *Tax Acts* overrides such exemption, although this does not confer any exemption from charge where income is treated under anti-avoidance provisions as income of a UK resident, etc. (see 81.17, 81.18 SETTLEMENTS, 3.8 ANTI-AVOIDANCE). See *FA 1996, s 154, Sch 28*. For 1995/96 and earlier years (and for company accounting periods ending before 1 April 1996), *ICTA 1988, s 47* (which is repealed by *FA 1996, Sch 28 para 1*) applied to broadly similar effect.

If interest forms part of the profits of a UK trade, exemption does not generally apply (depending on the Treasury conditions of issue) (see *Owen v Sassoon Ch D 1950, 32 TC 101*).

See 51.9 NON-RESIDENTS AND OTHER OVERSEAS MATTERS for the special position of *non-resident banks, insurance companies and dealers in securities* carrying on business in the UK.

For the exemption of non-residents from income tax on interest on local authority securities expressed in a foreign currency, see 23.12 DEDUCTION OF TAX AT SOURCE.

33.3 INTEREST — DEDUCTION OF TAX

From 6 April 1998, interest on gilt-edged securities (excluding, for payments made before 1 April 2001, those held in bearer form) is paid without deduction of tax [*ICTA 1988, s 50(A1); F(No 2)A 1997, s 37(2)(8); FA 2000, s 112(1)*], although the option of deduction continues to be available (see *F(No 2)A 1997, s 37* generally and below and, from 1 April 2001, 23.3(ii) DEDUCTION OF TAX AT SOURCE). See Revenue Tax Bulletin February 1998 pp 511, 512 for an article explaining the effect of the changes on gilt holders.

Before 6 April 1998, interest on gilt-edged securities was generally payable under deduction of tax, but the Treasury could direct that interest on certain securities should be paid gross [*ICTA 1988, ss 50(1), 51AA; FA 1996, s 155*], although the recipient could nevertheless apply to the Bank of England for income tax to be deducted. Gross payment applied to all existing strippable Government stocks from 7 June 1997, and to all subsequent strippable issues. Interest on 3.5% War Loan, on registered stocks and bonds on the National Savings Stock Register and stocks held through any Savings Bank was also paid gross.

The procedure whereby paying agents deduct and account for tax is laid down in *ICTA 1988, ss 118A-118K* (introduced by *FA 1996, s 156, Sch 29* and as subsequently amended) and regulations thereunder (see *SI 1996 No 1780*, *SI 1997 No 2705*, *SI 1999 No 823*), although these provisions are repealed from 1 April 2001 (and see now 23.3(ii) DEDUCTION OF TAX AT SOURCE). CHARITIES (15) generally receive payments gross on presentation to the paying agent of evidence of charitable status. For an article on the scope of these procedural rules, see Revenue Tax Bulletin August 1996 p 329.

Also until 5 April 1998, the Treasury had powers to make regulations for gross payment of interest on gilt-edged securities held by corporate bodies and in certain other circumstances under specified arrangements, and, until 5 April 1999, for periodic accounting for tax on such interest (which is, however, abolished for interest falling due on or after 1 April 1999). (These powers relate to the 'gilt repos' market introduced on 2 January 1996.) See *SI 1995 No 2934*, *SI 1996 No 21* (as amended). See also *SI 1995 Nos 3223, 3224, 3225* (as amended) and *SI 1999 Nos 623, 624*. [*ICTA 1988, ss 51A, 51B; FA 1995, ss 77, 78; FA 1996, Sch 6 para 4; F(No 2)A 1997, s 37(5)(8); FA 1998, s 37(1); SI 1995 No 2932; SI 1999 No 619*]. See Tolley's Corporation Tax under Income Tax in Relation to a Company.

33.4 **DISCOUNT ON TREASURY SECURITIES**

For 1995/96 and earlier years (and for company accounting periods ending before 1 April 1996), discount on Treasury securities issued after 6 March 1973 is exempt from tax under Schedule D, Case III without this giving rise to a charge under Schedule D, Case VI [*ICTA 1988, s 126; FA 1996, Sch 41 Pt V(3)*] but is still chargeable to tax if it constitutes trading profits. This exemption does not apply to Treasury Bills, to 'deep discount securities' issued by public bodies or 'deep gain securities' (see 44.5, 44.7 INTEREST RECEIVABLE), or to certain gilt-edged securities which are treated as deep discount or deep gain securities. [*FA 1989, s 95; FA 1996, Sch 41 Pt V(3)*]. See now 72.2 SCHEDULE D, CASE III and Tolley's Corporation Tax under Loan Relationships.

33.5 **PREMIUM SAVINGS BONDS**

Prizes are free of both income tax and capital gains tax.

33.6 **SAVINGS CERTIFICATES**

All income arising from savings certificates (as defined) (and including index-linked) and tax reserve certificates is exempt from tax except that arising from

(i) savings certificates purchased by or on behalf of a person in excess of the amount authorised under the regulations of the particular issue, or

(ii) Ulster savings certificates, unless the holder is resident and ordinarily resident in NI when the certificates are repaid or he was so resident and ordinarily resident when he purchased them. [*ICTA 1988, s 46*]. By concession, where repayment is made after the death of the holder, who was resident and ordinarily resident in NI when he purchased them, the exemption is allowed. (Revenue Pamphlet IR 1, A34).

34 Herd Basis

See generally Revenue Inspector's Manual, IM 2300–2318b.

Simon's Direct Tax Service B3.515 *et seq.*.

34.1 Animals and other living creatures kept for the purposes of farming or similar trades (e.g. animal or fish breeding) are generally treated as trading stock (see 71.83 SCHEDULE D, CASES I AND II) unless an election is made under *ICTA 1988, s 97, Sch 5* for the 'herd basis' to apply. [*ICTA 1988, s 97, Sch 5 paras 1, 9(1)(2)*]. Animals etc. are exempt from capital gains tax as wasting assets within *TCGA 1992, s 45*.

34.2 **Availability of election for herd basis.** An election for the herd basis may apply to animals etc., whether kept singly or as part of a production herd or flock etc., which are kept wholly or mainly for the sale of products of living animals or of their young, and to shares in such animals etc.. [*ICTA 1988, Sch 5 para 1(2), para 8(1)(5), para 9(2)(4); FA 2000, s 76(2)(3)*]. An election must apply to all herds consisting of animals of the same species (irrespective of breed), kept for production of products of the same kind, which are kept by the farmer making the election, including herds which he ceased to keep before, or first keeps after, the making of the election. [*ICTA 1988, Sch 5 paras 2(1), 8(6)*].

34.3 An election for the herd basis **may not apply** to animals kept wholly or mainly for farm work or for public exhibition or racing or other competitive purposes. [*ICTA 1988, Sch 5 paras 7, 9(5)*]. Immature animals are not treated as part of a herd for these purposes unless the land on which the herd is kept is such that the replacement of animals which die or cease to form part of the herd can only be by animals bred and reared on that land (e.g. acclimatised hill sheep), and then only to the extent that they are necessarily bred and maintained in the herd for the purposes of replacement. Female animals become mature when they produce their first young (and laying birds when they first lay). [*ICTA 1988, Sch 5 para 8(2)–(4), para 9(3)*].

34.4 The **election must be made** in writing, specifying the class of herd to which it applies. As respects 1996/97 and subsequent years, the election must be made not later than:

(*a*) for individual farmers, twelve months after 31 January following the qualifying year of assessment, i.e. the first tax year (excluding that in which the trade commences) in the basis period for which a production herd of the class specified was first kept by the individual; and

(*b*) for partnerships, twelve months after 31 January following the year of assessment in which ends the qualifying period of account, i.e. the first period of account during the whole or part of which a production herd of the class specified was first kept by the partnership.

For corporation tax purposes, as respects accounting periods ending on or after the appointed day for the introduction of self-assessment for companies (see Tolley's Corporation Tax under Assessments and Appeals), the time limit is two years after the end of the qualifying accounting period, i.e. the first accounting period during the whole or part of which a production herd of the class specified was first kept by the company.

[*ICTA 1988, Sch 5 para 2(2)(3)(6); FA 1994, ss 196, 199(2), Sch 19 para 43(1)(3)*].

See, however, 34.8 below as regards compulsory slaughter.

The election is irrevocable and has effect for, respectively, the qualifying year of assessment, period of account or accounting period (see above) and subsequently. For individuals, the election also has effect for the tax year in which the trade commenced if that year immediately precedes the qualifying year of assessment. [*ICTA 1988, Sch 5 para 2(4)–(6); FA 1994, Sch 19 para 43(2)(3)*].

Previously, the election had to be made within two years after the end of either

(i) the first period of account for which an account was made up for farming, or

(ii) the first year of assessment or company accounting period for which farming profits were chargeable under Schedule D, Case I (or loss relief given under *ICTA 1988, s 380, s 393(2)* or *s 393A(1)*) and in which (or, where applicable, in the basis period for which) a production herd of the class specified in the election was kept,

and had effect from the first year of assessment or company accounting period affected by it. [*ICTA 1988, Sch 5 para 2(2)–(4), para 8(7)*].

Where there is a change in the persons carrying on a trade, then whether or not there is a continuation election (see 53.6 PARTNERSHIPS), a further election is required if the herd basis is to continue to apply. (Revenue Tax Bulletin May 1992 p 20, June 1997 p 442).

See 34.5 below as regards renewal of right of election where there is a five-year gap in keeping a herd of a particular class.

34.5 **Consequences of election.** Where a herd basis election is in force, the animals in the herd are in effect treated as capital assets. The initial cost of the herd and of additions to the herd is not deductible as a trading expense, and its value is not brought into account. A profit or loss on the sale within a twelve-month period (without replacement, see 34.6 below) of the whole or a substantial (i.e. normally 20% or more) part of the herd is similarly not brought into account. Where, however, within five years of such a sale, another herd of the same class is (or begins to be) acquired (or replacement animals are or begin to be acquired), the normal replacement provisions (see 34.6 below) apply, the proceeds of the sale being treated as received at the time of the corresponding acquisition(s). However, the sale, for reasons beyond the farmer's control, of animals subsequently replaced by animals of inferior quality may not give rise to a greater trading receipt than the amount allowed as a deduction in respect of the replacement animals. [*ICTA 1988, Sch 5 para 3(1)(2)(8)(9)*].

Where a farmer ceases to keep any herd of a particular class for a period of at least five years, he is thereafter treated as if he had never previously kept a herd of that class. [*ICTA 1988, Sch 5 para 4*].

The addition to a herd of an animal previously treated as trading stock, otherwise than by way of replacement (see 34.6 below), gives rise to a trading receipt equal to the cost of acquiring or breeding it and rearing it to maturity. [*ICTA 1988, Sch 5 para 3(3)*]. In practice, if the animal is included in stock at market value (being lower than cost), that figure will similarly be substituted as the trading receipt on appropriation to the herd.

The sale without replacement (see 34.6 below) of an animal from a herd gives rise to a trading profit or loss, calculated by reference to the cost of acquiring or breeding it (or its market value if acquired other than for valuable consideration) and of rearing it to maturity. [*ICTA 1988, Sch 5 para 3(10)*].

34.6 **Replacement animals.** The replacement of an animal dying or ceasing to be a member of a herd gives rise to a trading receipt of any proceeds of sale of the animal replaced, and a trading deduction of the cost of the replacement animal (so far as not otherwise allowable under Schedule D, Case I) but limited to the cost of an animal of similar quality to that replaced. Where the animal replaced was compulsorily slaughtered, and the replacement animal is of inferior quality, the trading receipt is restricted to the amount of the corresponding deduction. [*ICTA 1988, Sch 5 para 3(4)–(6)*]. See 34.5 above as regards animals not replaced. Whether a particular animal brought into the herd replaces an animal disposed of for these purposes is a question of fact, requiring a direct connection between the disposal and the later addition rather than a simple restoration of numbers. As a practical matter, inspectors will accept that replacement treatment is appropriate where animals are brought into the herd within twelve months of the corresponding disposal. Where disposal and replacement are in different accounting periods, the overall profit or loss may either be brought in in the first period and any necessary adjustment made in the second, or the profit or loss arising in the first period may be held over to the second period. Where the interval is more than twelve months, there is unlikely to be sufficient evidence to support the necessary connection where the new animal is bought in. Where animals are home bred, however, a longer interval may be reasonable where e.g. there is insufficient young stock to replace unexpected disposals. (Revenue Tax Bulletin October 1994 p 169, February 1997 p 396).

Where the whole herd is replaced, this is treated as the replacement of a number of animals, being the smaller of the number in the old herd and in the new. [*ICTA 1988, Sch 5 para 3(7)*]. Where the new herd is the larger, the net increase will be treated as additions to the herd. Where the new herd is the smaller, but not substantially so (i.e. the provisions described in 34.5 above in relation to a substantial reduction do not apply), the net reduction in the number of animals is treated as giving rise to a corresponding sale without replacement (see 34.5 above). [*ICTA 1988, Sch 5 para 3(11)*].

34.7 **Insurance, compensation, etc..** Any reference to sale proceeds in the foregoing provisions includes a reference, in the case of the death or destruction of an animal, to insurance or compensation moneys received and to proceeds of carcass sales. [*ICTA 1988, Sch 5 para 3(12)*].

34.8 **Compulsory slaughter.** Where compensation is received for the whole, or a substantial part (i.e. normally 20% or more), of a herd compulsorily slaughtered by order under animal diseases laws, the farmer may, notwithstanding the time limits in 34.4 above, elect for the herd basis to apply. As respects 1996/97 and subsequent years, the election must be made not later than:

(*a*) for individual farmers, twelve months after 31 January following the qualifying year of assessment, i.e. the first year of assessment in the basis period for which the compensation falls (or would otherwise fall) to be taken into account as a trading receipt; and

(*b*) for partnerships, twelve months after 31 January following the year of assessment in which ends the qualifying period of account, i.e. the first period of account in which the compensation falls (or would otherwise fall) to be taken into account as a trading receipt.

For corporation tax purposes, as respects accounting periods ending on or after the appointed day for the introduction of self-assessment for companies (see Tolley's Corporation Tax under Assessments and Appeals), the time limit is two years after the end of the qualifying accounting period, i.e. the first accounting period in which the compensation falls (or would otherwise fall) to be taken into account as a trading receipt. The election has effect for, respectively, the qualifying year of assessment, period of account or accounting period and subsequently.

Previously, the election was for the herd basis to apply for the year of assessment for which the compensation receivable was (or would otherwise have been) assessable and all subsequent years. Notice of election had to be given within two years of the end of that year, except that where that year was the second year of assessment of a new business, notice of election could (for income tax only) be given not later than the giving of any notice under *ICTA 1988, s 62(2)* for the current year basis of assessment to apply (see 71.4 SCHEDULE D, CASES I AND II). Where the compensation was relevant to a loss relief claim under *ICTA 1988, s 380* for an earlier year, the election applied also for such an earlier year.

[*ICTA 1988, Sch 5 para 6; FA 1994, ss 196, 199(2), Sch 19 para 43(4)*].

Compensation paid under the BSE Suspects Scheme and the BSE Selective Cull (where the animal was born after 14 October 1990) is for compulsory slaughter, and for these purposes includes Selective Cull 'top-up' payments. Payments under the Calf Processing Scheme, the Over Thirty Month Scheme and the BSE Selective Cull where the animal was born before 15 October 1990 are *not* for compulsory slaughter. See Revenue Tax Bulletin February 1997 pp 396, 397 for this and for the application of these provisions to BSE compensation generally. Where the herd basis does not apply, see 71.57(*b*) SCHEDULE D, CASES I AND II.

34.9 **Anti-avoidance.** There are provisions for the prevention of avoidance of tax in the case of a transfer between connected persons or where the sole or main benefit relates to its effect on a herd basis election. [*ICTA 1988, Sch 5 para 5*].

34.10 **Information, etc..** Where an election has effect, returns may be required as to the animals, and products thereof, kept by any person affected by the election. Repayments etc. may be made as required to give effect to the election. [*ICTA 1988, Sch 5 paras 10, 11*].

34.11 *Example*

A farmer acquires a dairy herd and elects for the herd basis to apply. The movements in the herd and the tax treatment are as follows.

Year 1	*No*	*Value*
		£
Mature		
Bought @ £150	70	10,500
Bought in calf @ £180		
(Market value of calf £35)	5	900
Immature		
Bought @ £75	15	1,125

Herd Account	£
70 Friesians	10,500
5 Friesians in calf (5 × £(180 – 35))	725
75 Closing balance	£11,225

Trading Account	£
5 Calves (5 × £35)	175
15 Immature Friesians	1,125
Debit to profit and loss account	£1,300

Year 2		No	Value £
Mature			
Bought @ £185		15	2,775
Sold @ £200	note (*a*)	10	2,000
Died		3	—
Immature			
Born		52	—
Matured @ 60% of market value of £200	note (*a*)	12	1,440

Herd Account

			£	£
75		Opening balance		11,225
		Increase in herd		
	15	Purchases	2,775	
	12	Transferred from trading stock	1,440	
	27		4,215	
	(13)	Replacement cost £4,215 × $\frac{13}{27}$	2,029	
14		Non-replacement animals cost		2,186
89		Closing balance		£13,411

Trading Account

	£
Sale of 10 mature cows replaced	(2,000)
Transfer to herd — 14 animals	(2,186)
Cost of 13 mature cows purchased to replace those sold/deceased ($\frac{13}{15}$ × £2,775)	2,405
Net credit to profit and loss account note (*b*)	£(1,781)

Year 3		No	Value £
Mature			
Jerseys bought @ £250		70	17,500
Friesians slaughtered @ £175 (market value £185)		52	9,100
Immature			
Friesians born		20	—
Matured			
Friesians @ 60% of market value of £190	note (*a*)	15	1,710

Herd Account

			£	£
89	Opening balance			13,411
	Increase in herd			
18	Jerseys			4,500
	52 Improvement Jerseys @	250		
	less Market value of Friesians	185		
	52 @	65		3,380
	Transfer from trading stock			
15	Friesians			1,710
122	Closing balance			£23,001

Trading Account

		£
Compensation		(9,100)
Transfer to herd		(1,710)
Purchase of replacements	note (*c*) (52 × £185)	9,620
Net credit to profit and loss account		£(1,190)

Year 4

The farmer ceases dairy farming and sells his whole herd.

	No	*Value* £
Mature		
Jerseys sold @ £320	70	22,400
Friesians sold @ £200	52	10,400
Immature		
Friesians sold @ £100	65	6,500

Herd Account

			£
Opening balance			23,001
52	Friesians		
70	Jerseys		
(122)	Sales		(32,800)
—	Profit on sale	note (*d*)	£(9,799)

Trading Account

	£
Sale of 65 immature Friesians	(6,500)
Credit to profit and loss account	£(6,500)

Notes

(*a*) The use of 60% of market value was originally by agreement between the National Farmers' Union and the Revenue (see now Revenue Business Economic Note 19:

Farming — Stock Valuation for Income Tax purposes, at paragraph 7.2). Alternatively, the actual cost of breeding or purchase and rearing could be used.

(*b*) As the cost of rearing the 12 cows to maturity will already have been debited to the profit and loss account, no additional entry is required to reflect that cost. Due to the fact that the animals were in opening stock at valuation and will not be in closing stock, the trading account will in effect be debited with that valuation.

(*c*) The cost of the replacements is restricted to the cost of replacing like with like.

(*d*) Provided these animals are not replaced by a herd of the same class within five years the proceeds will be tax-free (see 34.5 above).

35 Inland Revenue: Administration

35.1 The levying and collection of income tax, surtax and capital gains tax is administered by the **Commissioners of Inland Revenue** (normally referred to as the Board), Somerset House, London WC2R 1LB. [*TMA 1970, s 1(1)*].

Under them are local **inspectors of taxes**, permanent civil servants with an expert knowledge of tax law, who are responsible for making most assessments, and dealing with claims and allowances, and *to whom all enquiries should be addressed*.

The Inland Revenue maintains an internet site (http://www.inlandrevenue.gov.uk/home.htm) which provides access to detailed information on many aspects of the Revenue's activities, including publications, press releases and contact points.

35.2 **Collectors of Taxes** are also permanent civil servants and their duties for the most part relate only to the collection of tax. [*TMA 1970, ss 60–70*].

35.3 **Commissioners.** Appeals against assessments or amendments of self-assessments are heard by

(*a*) the General Commissioners (local persons appointed on a voluntary basis by the Lord Chancellor or, in Scotland, by the Secretary of State) [*TMA 1970, s 2; FA 1975, s 57; FA 1988, s 134(1)*], or

(*b*) the Special Commissioners (full-time civil servants, being barristers, advocates or solicitors etc. of at least ten years' standing, appointed for this purpose) [*TMA 1970, s 4; FA 1984, s 127, Sch 22 para 1; Courts and Legal Services Act 1990, Sch 10 para 30*].

The Lord Chancellor has powers, by regulation, to change the names by which the General and Special Commissioners are to be referred to. [*F(No 2)A 1992, s 75*].

See 4.3, 4.6 APPEALS as regards jurisdiction of Commissioners and the conduct of appeals before them.

35.4 **'Care and management' powers.** For the validity of amnesties by the Board, see *CIR v National Federation of Self-Employed and Small Businesses Ltd HL 1981, 55 TC 133.* INLAND REVENUE EXTRA-STATUTORY CONCESSIONS (38) have been the subject of frequent judicial criticism (see Lord Edward Davies' opinion in *Vestey v CIR (No 1) HL 1979, 54 TC 503* for a review of this) but their validity has never been directly challenged in the Courts. In *R v HMIT (ex p Fulford-Dobson) QB 1987, 60 TC 168*, a claim that the Revenue had acted unfairly in refusing a concession where tax avoidance was involved was rejected, but the taxpayer's right to seek judicial review of a Revenue decision to refuse the benefit of a concession was confirmed in *R v HMIT (ex p Brumfield and Others) QB 1988, 61 TC 589.* A decision by the Revenue to revoke its authorisation to pay a dividend gross was upheld in *R v CIR (ex p Camacq Corporation) CA 1989, 62 TC 651.* For a general discussion of the Board's care and management powers and an example of a ruling by the Court that the Board had exercised a discretionary power reasonably, see *R v CIR (ex p Preston) HL 1985, 59 TC 1.* Where a discretionary power is given to the Revenue, it is an error in law to proceed on the footing that the power is mandatory (*R v HMIT and Others (ex p Lansing Bagnall Ltd) CA 1986, 61 TC 112*). See also *R v CIR (ex p J Rothschild Holdings) CA 1987, 61 TC 178*, where the Revenue were required to produce internal documents of a general character relating to their practice in applying a statutory provision.

The Revenue policy of selective prosecution for criminal offences in connection with tax evasion does not render a decision in a particular case unlawful or *ultra vires*, provided that the case is considered on its merits fairly and dispassionately to see whether the criteria for prosecution were satisfied, and that the decision to prosecute is then taken in good faith for the purpose of collecting taxes and not for some ulterior, extraneous or improper purpose (*R v CIR (ex p Mead and Cook) QB 1992, 65 TC 1*). See *R v CIR (ex p Allen) QB 1997, 69 TC 442* for an unsuccessful application for judicial review of a Revenue decision to take criminal proceedings.

The social security authorities are authorised to disclose information held by them to the Commissioners of Inland Revenue, or persons providing certain services to the Commissioners, for investigative purposes or in relation to national insurance contributions. [*FA 1997, s 110; Social Security Administration Act 1992, s 121F; Social Security Contributions (Transfer of Functions, etc.) Act 1999, Sch 6 para 1; Tax Credits Act 1999, Sch 5 para 7; SI 1997 No 1603*].

35.5 **Equitable liability.** For the circumstances in which the Revenue may accept a reduced sum in respect of certain assessed liabilities, see 56.9 PAYMENT OF TAX.

35.6 **Inland Revenue rulings.** For the extent to which taxpayers may rely on guidance given by the Revenue, see the letter from the Deputy Chairman to the various professional bodies following the decision in *R v CIR (ex p Matrix-Securities Ltd) HL 1994, 66 TC 587.* A code of practice in this area is to be published.

Following responses to consultation, plans for a system of pre-transaction rulings are not to be proceeded with for the time being, although the possibility of a selective scheme for product rulings is to be explored. These would relate to arrangements where the characteristics of participating taxpayers would not affect the ruling, such as financial instruments or savings plans marketed by insurance companies. There would be a charge for such rulings. A system of post-transaction rulings (without charge), to be given after the transaction has occurred but before the taxpayer makes his tax return, was introduced during 1997. See Code of Practice 10 (as revised April 1998) for the procedures in obtaining such rulings.

35.7 **Taxpayer's Charter.** The Board of Inland Revenue and HM Customs and Excise have jointly produced a Taxpayer's Charter setting out the principles they try to meet in their dealings with taxpayers, the standards they believe the taxpayer has a right to expect, and what people can do if they wish to appeal or complain. Copies are available from local tax or collection offices and from local VAT offices.

A series of codes of practice, setting out the standards of service people can expect in relation to specific aspects of the Revenue's work, is published to support the Taxpayer's Charter. Each code states the standards which the Revenue sets itself and the rights of taxpayers in particular situations. The first three, covering mistakes by the Revenue (see 35.8 below), the conduct of tax investigations (see 6.1 BACK DUTY) and the conduct of inspections of employers' PAYE records (see 55.1 PAYE) were first published in February 1993, and are available from local tax offices. Codes 4 and 5, relating to financial intermediaries and charities (see 15.1 CHARITIES) respectively, were first published in July 1993, copies being sent to the institutions concerned, and are available from FICO, St John's House, Merton Road, Bootle, Merseyside L69 9BB. Codes 6 and 7, on collection of tax generally and collection from employers and construction industry contractors, were first published in November 1994 and are available from local tax offices. Codes 8 and 9, on Special Compliance Office Investigations in cases other than suspected serious fraud and cases of such fraud respectively, were first published in January 1995 and are available from the Special Compliance Office, Angel Court, 199 Borough High Street, London SE1 1HZ. Code 10, on the provision by the Revenue of information and advice, was first published in

June 1995 and is available from local tax offices. Code 11, dealing with enquiries into self-assessment income tax returns by local tax offices, was first published in July 1996, superseding Code 2 as regards such returns. It will be issued at the start of every such enquiry (except that in certain simple cases a short, single-page version will be issued). Code 14 (there currently being no Codes 12 or 13), dealing with enquiries into self-assessment company tax returns, was first published in July 1999, superseding Code 2 as regards such returns. It will be given to the company concerned at the start of every enquiry (except that where a simple enquiry is expected to be settled by a brief exchange of correspondence and not to involve penalties, a single-page version of the Code will be issued instead).

35.8 **Revenue error.** Code of Practice 1 (see 35.7 above), 'Mistakes by the Inland Revenue' (revised March 1996), gives general advice on the circumstances in which compensation may be claimed from the Revenue as a consequence of Revenue error. (The Code also refers to waivers of tax under Extra-statutory Concession A19, see 56.6 PAYMENT OF TAX.) These fall into three categories.

(*a*) *Delays in replying to letters or other enquiries*, where, without good reason, there is a delay totalling six months or more (over and above the 28 days within which replies should normally be given).

(*b*) *Serious error*, e.g. the adoption of a wholly unreasonable view of the law, or the pursuit of enquiries into obviously trivial matters, or a simple or trivial mistake which the Revenue should have known could lead to far more serious consequences.

(*c*) *Persistent error*, even though not serious, e.g. where a mistake is continued after it has been pointed out, or the same type of mistake keeps being made, or there are a lot of unconnected mistakes within a year or in connection with a period of assessment.

In cases within (*a*), interest on overdue tax will be waived, and repayment supplement paid, for the period of the delay, and reasonable costs resulting from the delay reimbursed. Where (*b*) or (*c*) applies, the Revenue will reimburse reasonable loss or expense incurred directly because of the error, including professional and personal expenses and lost earnings, and incidental expenses such as postal and telephone charges. In exceptional circumstances, consolatory payments may also be made.

Repayment claims resulting from mistakes by the Revenue or any other Government department will be accepted up to 20 years after the year affected by the mistake.

35.9 **Revenue Adjudicator.** A taxpayer who is not satisfied with the Revenue response to a complaint has the option of putting the case to an independent Adjudicator for the Inland Revenue. The Adjudicator's office opened on 1 May 1993, and will consider complaints about the Revenue's handling of a taxpayer's affairs, e.g. excessive delays, errors, discourtesy or the exercise of Revenue discretion, where the events complained of occurred after 5 April 1993. Matters subject to existing rights of appeal are excluded.

The Adjudicator will also investigate complaints about Customs and Excise.

The address is Adjudicator's Office for the Inland Revenue and Customs and Excise, 3rd Floor, Haymarket House, 28 Haymarket, London SW1Y 4SP (tel. 0207-930 2292). A leaflet 'How to complain about the Inland Revenue' is obtainable from that office in a number of different languages.

Complaints normally go to the Adjudicator only after they have been considered by the Controller of the relevant Revenue office, and where the taxpayer is still not satisfied with the response received. The alternatives of pursuing the complaint to the Revenue's Head Office, to an MP, or (through an MP) to the Ombudsman continue to be available. The Adjudicator reviews all the facts, considers whether the complaint is justified, and, if so, makes recommendations as to what should be done. The Revenue will normally accept the recommendations 'unless there are very exceptional circumstances'.

The Adjudicator publishes an annual report to the Board.

(Revenue Press Release 17 February 1993).

Leave to apply for judicial review of the rejection by the Adjudicator of a complaint concerning the use of information from unidentified informants was refused in *R v Revenue Adjudicator's Office (ex p Drummond) QB 1996, 70 TC 235.*

35.10 **Open Government.** Under the Government's 'Code of Practice on Access to Government Information', the Revenue (in common with other Government departments) is to make information about its policies and decisions more widely available. Revenue Pamphlet IR 141 ('Open Government') sets out the information to be made available, and how it may be obtained, and the basis on which a fee may be charged in certain circumstances to offset the cost of providing the information. Copies of the Code of Practice may be obtained by writing to Open Government, Room 417b, Office of Public Service and Science, 70 Whitehall, London SW1A 2AS (tel. 0345 223242). The Revenue has also published its own Code of Practice on the provision of information and advice (see 35.7 above).

As part of the Revenue's response to this process, most internal Revenue guidance manuals are now available for purchase (subject to the withholding of certain material under the exemptions in the Code of Practice).

35.11 **Employers' helpline.** A joint employers' telephone helpline has been set up on 0345 143 143 by the Inland Revenue, Contributions Agency and Customs & Excise for general enquiries about PAYE, national insurance and value added tax registration. The service is available from 0830 to 1700 on working days. Calls will be charged at local rates. See also 21.7 CONSTRUCTION INDUSTRY TAX SCHEME.

There is also a helpline for **new employers** on 0845–607 0143 (0800 to 2000 weekdays, 1000 to 1600 weekends), where the employer may register for PAYE, order an information pack on the operation of payroll tax and national insurance, and obtain help and information on payroll queries. Arrangements may also be made for access to business support teams and workshops providing further assistance.

35.12 **Use of electronic communications.** The Commissioners of Inland Revenue (and Customs and Excise) are given broad powers to make regulations, by statutory instrument, to facilitate two-way electronic communication in the delivery of information, e.g. tax returns (and see 67.3 RETURNS for existing legislation), and the making of tax payments. The regulations may allow or require the use of intermediaries such as Internet service providers. They will have effect notwithstanding any existing legislation requiring delivery or payment in a manner which would otherwise preclude the use of electronic communications or intermediaries. [*FA 1999, ss 132, 133*]. The intention is to develop a range of electronic services which taxpayers can use as an alternative to paper if they so wish. One of the first services to be offered will be to allow unrepresented taxpayers to file their self-assessment tax returns via the Internet, and this is expected to be in place in 2000/01. (Joint Revenue and Customs & Excise News Release CW 1, 9 March 1999).

See *The Income Tax (Electronic Communications) Regulations 2000* (*SI 2000 No 945*), which make provision for electronic communications in relation to delivery of returns and other information under *TMA 1970, ss 8, 9* or *9A* (see 78.5–78.7, 78.11 SELF-ASSESSMENT) and payments or repayments in connection with the operation of those *sections.*

Incentives for electronic communications. Regulations may be made by statutory instrument by the Commissioners of Inland Revenue in relation to matters under their care and management (and by the Commissioners of Customs and Excise in relation to theirs) for the provision of incentives to use electronic communications. These may include discounts (or payments or repayments), or additional time for compliance or payment, or more convenient intervals for the delivery of information or the making of payments. Anything received by way of incentive is not regarded as income for tax purposes. The regulations may make provision as to the conditions of entitlement to incentives and for their withdrawal (which may be authorised to be made by direction), and may provide for penalties up to £1,000 for failure to comply with any specified provision. They may make different provision for different cases, and may make such incidental, supplemental, consequential or transitional provision as the Commissioners think fit. [*FA 2000, s 143, Sch 38*].

See 67.3 RETURNS for initial proposed incentives for making certain returns over the internet.

35.13 **INTERNATIONAL EXCHANGES OF INFORMATION**

ICTA 1988, s 815C (introduced by *FA 2000, s 146*) enables agreements with other governments for the exchange of information necessary for the purposes of income tax, corporation tax and capital gains tax (and corresponding taxes in the territory of the counterparty) to have effect. The Revenue may not, however, disclose information under any such arrangements unless they are satisfied that the counterparty is bound by, or has undertaken to observe, rules of confidentiality at least as strict as those applying in the UK. The power under *TMA 1970, s 20(1)–(8)(8C)–(9)* (see 6.8 BACK DUTY) to call for information relevant to income tax, corporation tax or capital gains tax liabilities is accordingly extended to liabilities to the corresponding taxes in a counterparty territory.

Similar provisions in relation to inheritance tax apply under *IHTA 1984, s 220A* introduced by *FA 2000, s 147*.

36 Inland Revenue: Confidentiality of Information

36.1 The Revenue consider that the confidentiality of information maintained by their Department 'is essential to their traditional approach to their task and is deeply embedded in their practice'. (*Royal Commission on Standards of Conduct in Public Life 1976, para 111*). All officers of the Inland Revenue, together with General and Special Commissioners, are required to make declarations that information received in the course of duty will not be disclosed except for the purposes of such duty or for the purposes of the prosecution of revenue offences or as may be required by law. [*TMA 1970, s 6, Sch 1*]. As to production in Court proceedings of documents in the possession of the Revenue, see *Brown's Trustees v Hay CS 1897, 3 TC 598; In re Joseph Hargreaves Ltd CA 1900, 4 TC 173; Shaw v Kay CS 1904, 5 TC 74; Soul v Irving CA 1963, 41 TC 517; H v H HC 1980, 52 TC 454*. For the overriding of confidentiality by the public interest in the administration of justice, see *Lonrho plc v Fayed and Others (No 4) CA 1993, 66 TC 220.*

Following the transfer of the functions of the Contributions Agency to the Inland Revenue, appropriate provision is made for the internal distribution of information. [*Social Security Contributions (Transfer of Functions, etc.) Act 1999, s 7*].

36.2 The Inland Revenue are authorised to disclose information to the following.

(*a*) **Charity Commissioners for England and Wales.** There are wide powers under which information may be exchanged between the Charity Commissioners and the Commissioners of Inland Revenue, in particular enabling the Revenue to disclose details of institutions which they consider to have been carrying on non-charitable activities or applying funds for non-charitable purposes. [*Charities Act 1993, s 10*].

(*b*) **Business Statistics Office of the Department of Industry** or to the **Department of Employment.** The Revenue are authorised to disclose, for the purposes of statistical surveys, the names and addresses of employers and employees and the number of persons employed by individual concerns. [*FA 1969, s 58; F(No 2)A 1987, s 69; SI 1990 No 1840*].

(*c*) **Tax authorities of other countries.** The Revenue are authorised to disclose information where it is necessary to do so for the operation of double taxation agreements [*ICTA 1988, s 816; TCGA 1992, s 277(4); IHTA 1984, s 158(5)*] and agreements may provide for such exchange, particularly in relation to prevention of fiscal evasion. [*ICTA 1988, s 788(2)*]. Disclosure may also be made to the tax authorities of other Member States of the EC which observe similar confidentiality and use only for tax purposes [*FA 1978, s 77; FA 1990, s 125(5)(6)*], and similar rules apply in relation to any information exchange arrangements under *ICTA 1988, s 815C* or *IHTA 1984, s 220A* (see 35.13 INLAND REVENUE: ADMINISTRATION). [*ICTA 1988, s 816(2ZA); IHTA 1984, s 220A(4)(5); FA 2000, ss 146(2), 147(1)*]. See also the 'working arrangement' between USA and UK in Revenue Press Release 2 March 1978.

(*d*) **Customs and Excise.** The Revenue and Customs and Excise are authorised to disclose information to each other for the purpose of their respective duties. [*FA 1972, s 127*].

(*e*) **Occupational Pensions Board.** The Revenue are authorised to disclose information about pension schemes. [*Social Security Act 1973, s 89(2)*].

(*f*) **Social Security Departments.** Information held by the Revenue relating to national insurance contributions, statutory sick pay or statutory maternity pay may, and must if an authorised social security officer so requires, be supplied to the social security authorities for use in relation to social security, child support or war pensions. Other information may similarly be supplied to those authorities in relation to the prevention, detection, investigation or prosecution of social security offences or in checking social security information. [*Social Security Administration Act 1992, ss 121E, 122; Social Security Administration (Fraud) Act 1997, s 1; Social Security Contributions (Transfer of Functions, etc.) Act 1999, Sch 6 paras 1, 2*]. The Revenue will also supply the names and addresses of absent parents and, where appropriate, their employers, in cases where they are liable under the *Social Security Acts* to maintain lone parent families receiving income support. (Revenue Press Release 9 May 1990). (See 35.4 INLAND REVENUE: ADMINISTRATION for supply of information *by* social security authorities.) From 5 October 1999, the Board may, and must if an authorised social security officer so requires, supply to the social security authorities information held for the purposes of functions relating to working families' tax credit and disabled person's tax credit (for which see 83.6 SOCIAL SECURITY) for use by those authorities for the purposes of functions relating to social security benefits, child support or war pensions. [*Tax Credits Act 1999, Sch 5 para 2*].

(*g*) **Assistance to police investigation into suspected murder or treason.** [*Royal Commission on Standards of Conduct in Public Life 1976, para 93*].

(*h*) **Non-UK resident entertainers and sportsmen.** In connection with the deduction of tax from certain payments to such persons, the Board may disclose relevant matters to any person who appears to the Board to have an interest. [*ICTA 1988, s 558(4)*].

(*i*) **Land Registry.** Particulars of land and charges. [*Land Registration Act 1925, s 129*].

(*j*) **Department of Environment.** Information regarding option mortgages and qualification of housing associations for certain grants. [*FA 1982, s 26, Sch 7 para 12; Housing Associations Act 1985, s 62*].

(*k*) **Parliamentary Commissioner for Administration.** Information required for the purposes of his investigations. [*Parliamentary Commissioner Act 1967, s 8*].

(*l*) **National Audit Office.** Information required for the purposes of the Office's examinations. [*National Audit Act 1983, s 8*].

(*m*) **Data Protection.** Any information necessary for the discharge of the Registrar's or Tribunal's functions. [*Data Protection Act 1984, s 17*].

(*n*) **Secretary of State for Scotland and Scottish Housing Association.** Information regarding status of housing associations and refusals of charitable exemption. [*Tenants' Rights etc. (Scotland) Act 1980, s 1*].

(*o*) An **advisory commission** set up under the Convention (*90/463/EEC*) on the elimination of double taxation in connection with the adjustment of profits of associated enterprises (see 3.9 ANTI-AVOIDANCE). [*ICTA 1988, s 816(2A); F(No 2)A 1992, s 51(2)*].

(*p*) As regards information held for the purposes of functions relating to working families' tax credit and disabled person's tax credit (for which see 83.6 SOCIAL SECURITY), a **local authority** (or authorised delegate) for use in the administration of housing benefit or council tax benefit. Information must also be provided in the opposite direction if the Board so require but only for use for purposes relating to the aforementioned tax credits. [*Tax Credits Act 1999, Sch 5 paras 4, 5*].

(*q*) The **Health and Safety Executive**, the **Government Actuary's Department**, the **Office for National Statistics** or the **Occupational Pensions Regulatory Authority** in relation to national insurance contributions, statutory sick pay or statutory maternity pay. [*Social Security Administration Act 1992, s 122AA; Social Security Contributions (Transfer of Functions, etc.) Act 1999, Sch 6 para 3*].

(*r*) **Minimum wage legislation.** Any information obtained by an officer of the Board acting under *National Minimum Wage Act 1998, s 13(1)(b)* may be used for the purpose of any of the functions of the Board. The Secretary of State may similarly supply to the Board any information supplied to him under *section 16(2)* of that *Act*. [*FA 2000, s 148*].

36.3 From 5 October 1999, consequent upon the introduction of working families' tax credit and disabled person's tax credit (for which see 83.6 SOCIAL SECURITY), the Board may pool the information they hold for the purposes of their functions relating to those tax credits and to tax, national insurance contributions, statutory sick pay, statutory maternity pay and certain functions under *Pension Schemes Act 1993* (and corresponding NI legislation). There is also provision for the exchange of information held for the purposes of functions relating to the aforementioned tax credits between the Board and persons providing services to the Board, for use in the exercise of those functions. [*Tax Credits Act 1999, Sch 5 para 1*].

36.4 It is a criminal offence for a person to disclose information held by him in the exercise of tax functions about any matter relevant to tax in the case of an identifiable person. This applies equally as regards national insurance contributions, statutory sick pay, statutory maternity pay, working families' tax credit and disabled person's tax credit. The above do not apply if (or if he believes) he has lawful authority or the information has lawfully been made available to the public, or if the person to whom the matter relates has consented. [*FA 1989, s 182; FA 1995, Sch 29 Pt VIII(16); Government of Wales Act 1998, Sch 12 para 31; Social Security Contributions (Transfer of Functions, etc.) Act 1999, Sch 6 para 9; Tax Credits Act 1999, s 12; SI 1999 No 527*]. Similar provisions apply to members of an advisory commission set up under the Convention on transfer pricing arbitration (see 3.9 ANTI-AVOIDANCE). [*FA 1989, s 182A; F(No 2)A 1992, s 51(3)*].

37 Inland Revenue Explanatory Pamphlets Etc.

Simon's Direct Tax Service H5.

The Board publish explanatory pamphlets (with supplements from time to time) on Inland Revenue taxes, a catalogue of which is available. These are listed below, with the date of the latest edition in brackets, and are obtainable free of charge from any office of HM Inspector of Taxes, unless otherwise stated. Many of them (including those for which a charge is made) are available on the Inland Revenue's Internet site (see 35.1 INLAND REVENUE: ADMINISTRATION). As regards Inland Revenue internal guidance manuals, see 35.10 INLAND REVENUE: ADMINISTRATION.

IR 1 Extra-Statutory Concessions as at 31 August 1999 (January 2000).

IR 6 Double Taxation Relief for Companies (March 1994).

IR 12 Practice notes on the approval of occupational pension schemes. (Loose-leaf publication available only by subscription to the Pension Schemes Office mailing list (fee for year ended 31 March 1999 £20) through S R Communications Plc, Unit 9, Deptford Trading Estate, Blackhorse Road, London SE99 7TR (0207 463-8167)).

IR 14/15(CIS) Construction Industry Scheme (December 1998).

IR 16 Share Acquisitions by Directors and Employees — Explanatory Notes (March 1997).

IR 20 Residents and Non-residents — Liability to Tax in the United Kingdom (December 1999).

IR 33 Income Tax and School Leavers (May 2000).

IR 34 Income Tax — PAYE (January 1996).

IR 37 Appeals against Tax (April 1999).

IR 40(CIS) Construction Industry Scheme: Conditions for Getting a Sub-contractor's Tax Certificate (December 1998).

IR 41 Income Tax and Job Seekers (April 2000).

IR 45 Income Tax, Capital Gains Tax and Inheritance Tax: What Happens when Someone Dies (September 1997).

IR 46 Income Tax and Corporation Tax: Clubs, Societies and Voluntary Associations (January 2000).

IR 56 Employed or Self-employed? (April 1999).

IR 60 Income Tax and Students (June 1997).

IR 64 Giving to Charity: How Businesses can get Tax Relief (November 1993).

IR 65 Giving to Charity: How Individuals can get Tax Relief (November 1993).

IR 67 Capital Taxation and the National Heritage (December 1986 with insert). (Obtainable from Inland Revenue Library, Room 28, New Wing, Somerset House, Strand, London WC2R 1LB (tel. 0207-438 6648)). Price £5.20.

IR 68 Accrued Income Scheme (December 1990).

IR 69 Expenses: Form P11D — How to Save Yourself Work (April 1999).

IR 72 Inland Revenue Investigations: The Examination of Business Accounts (May 1995).

IR 73 Inland Revenue Investigations: How Settlements are Negotiated (January 1994).

IR 76 Personal Pension Schemes: Guidance Notes (1999). (Obtainable from Pension Schemes Office, Yorke House, PO Box 62, Castle Meadow Road, Nottingham NG2 1BG (tel. 0115-974 1670)).

IR 78 Personal Pensions (December 1991).

IR 87 Letting and Your Home (December 1999).

IR 88 Capital Tax Relief for National Heritage Property — How to Make a Claim (August 1989). (Obtainable as IHT 2 below).

IR 89 Personal Equity Plans (October 1998).

IR 90 Tax Allowances and Reliefs (December 1999).

IR 93 Separation, Divorce and Maintenance Payments (March 1997).

IR 95 Approved Profit Sharing Schemes — An Outline for Employees (June 1996).

IR 96 Approved Profit Sharing Schemes — Explanatory Notes (June 1996). (Obtainable from Inland Revenue Visitors' Information Centre, Ground Floor, SW Wing, Bush House, Strand, London WC2B 4RD).

IR 97 Approved SAYE Share Option Schemes — An Outline for Employees (June 1996).

IR 98 Approved SAYE Share Option Schemes — Explanatory Notes (June 1996). (Obtainable as IR 96 above).

IR 101 Approved Company Share Option Plans — An Outline for Employees (June 1996).

IR 102 Company Share Options — Explanatory Notes (June 1996). (Obtainable as IR 96 above).

IR 109 Employer Compliance Reviews and Negotiations (March 2000).

IR 110 A Guide for People with Savings (February 2000).

IR 114 TESSA: Tax-free Interest for Taxpayers (October 1998).

IR 115 Tax and Childcare (October 1992).

IR 116(CIS) Guide for Subcontractors with Tax Certificates (April 1999).

IR 117(CIS) A Subcontractor's Guide to the Deduction Scheme (April 1999).

IR 119 Tax Relief for Vocational Training (September 1999).

IR 120 You and the Inland Revenue (April 1999). (Special versions of this leaflet are available relating to the Special Compliance Office, the Financial Intermediaries and Claims Office, the Pension Schemes Office, the Enforcement Office and the Capital Taxes Office. The first is available from Angel Court, 199 Borough High Street, London SE1 1HZ (tel. 0207-234 3708), the second from St John's House, Merton Road, Bootle, Merseyside L69 9BB (tel. 0151-472 6106), the third from Yorke House, PO Box 62, Castle Meadow Road, Nottingham NG2 1BG (tel. 0115-974 1670), the fourth from Durrington Bridge House, Barrington Road, Worthing, West Sussex BN12 4SE and the fifth from Ferrers House, PO Box 38, Castle Meadow Road, Nottingham

	NG2 1BB (tel. 0115-974 2400) and other Capital Taxes Offices in Edinburgh and Belfast. The leaflet is available in a range of languages and in Braille, large print and audio tape formats.)
IR 121	Income Tax and Pensioners (January 2000).
IR 122	Volunteer Drivers (June 2000).
IR 125	Using Your Own Car for Work (June 1999).
IR 126	Corporation Tax Pay and File — A General Guide (July 1995).
IR 129	Occupational Pension Schemes — An Introduction (June 1995).
IR 131	Statements of Practice as at 31 August 1999 (January 2000).
IR 134	Income Tax and Relocation Packages (October 1997).
IR 136	Income Tax and Company Vans — A Guide for Employees and Employers (March 1994).
IR 137	The Enterprise Investment Scheme (July 1999).
IR 138	Living or Retiring Abroad? (October 1995).
IR 139	Income from Abroad? (October 1995).
IR 140	Non-resident Landlords, their Agents and Tenants (April 1999).
IR 141	Open Government (March 2000).
IR 143	Income Tax and Redundancy (May 2000).
IR 144	Income Tax and Incapacity Benefit (February 1995).
IR 145	Low Interest Loans Provided by Employers: A Guide for Employees (January 1997).
IR 148	Construction Industry: Are your Workers Employed or Self-employed? (April 1999).
IR 150	Taxation of Rents — A Guide to Property Income (March 2000).
IR 152	Trusts — An Introduction (September 1996).
IR 153	Tax Exemption for Sickness or Unemployment Insurance Payments (February 1997).
IR 155	PAYE Settlement Agreements (April 2000).
IR 156	Our Heritage — Your Right to See Exempt Works of Art (December 1996).
IR 160	Inland Revenue Enquiries under Self-Assessment (April 1999).
IR 161	Tax Relief for Employees' Business Travel (January 1998).
IR 162	A Better Approach to Local Office Enquiry Work under Self-Assessment (April 1999).
IR 163	Millennium Gift Aid (September 1998).
IR 166	The Euro (December 1998).
IR 167	Charter for Inland Revenue Taxpayers (April 1999).
IR 168	How Tax Credit Settlements are Negotiated (March 2000).
IR 169	Venture Capital Trusts (February 2000).

IR 170	Blind Person's Allowance (December 1999)
IR 171	Income Tax: A Guide for People with Children (December 1999).
IR 172	Income Tax and Company Cars (February 2000).
IR 173	Tax Credits — A Summary for Employers (Working Families' Tax Credit and Disabled Person's Tax Credit)(December 1999).
IR 175	Supplying Services through a Limited Company or Partnership (April 2000).
CGT 1	Capital Gains Tax — An Introduction (April 1999).
IHT 2	Inheritance Tax on Lifetime Gifts (September 1998). (Obtainable from Capital Taxes Office, Ferrers House, PO Box 38, Castle Meadow Road, Nottingham NG2 1BB (tel. 0115-974 2400) and other Capital Taxes Offices in Edinburgh and Belfast).
IHT 3	Inheritance Tax — An Introduction (April 1999).
IHT 8	Alterations to an Inheritance following a Death (May 1995). (Obtainable as IHT 2 above).
IHT 11	Inheritance Tax — Payment of Inheritance Tax from National Savings (August 1998). (Obtainable as IHT 2 above).
IHT 13	Inheritance Tax and Penalties (February 1996). (Obtainable as IHT 2 above).
IHT 14	Inheritance Tax — The Personal Representatives' Responsibilities (February 2000). (Obtainable as IHT 2 above).
IHT 15	Inheritance Tax — How to Calculate the Liability (August 1996). (Obtainable as IHT 2 above).
IHT 16	Inheritance Tax — Settled Property (March 2000). (Obtainable as IHT 2 above).
IHT 17	Inheritance Tax — Businesses, Farms and Woodlands (August 1996). (Obtainable as IHT 2 above).
IHT 18	Inheritance Tax — Foreign Aspects (August 1996). (Obtainable as IHT 2 above).
480	Expenses and Benefits — A Tax Guide (January 2000).
490	Employee Travel — A Tax and NICs Guide for Employers (January 1998)
CIS FACT 5	The New Construction Industry Scheme — A Handy Guide (October 1998).
CWG 1	Employer's Quick Guide to PAYE and NICs (January 2000).
CWG 2	Employer's Further Guide to PAYE and NICs (January 2000).
NE 1	First Steps as a New Employer (April 1999).
NE 3	New and Small Employers — Support with your Payroll (June 2000).
SAT 1	The New Current Year Basis of Assessment, explaining how the new system will replace the existing rules of assessment for the self-employed (July 1995). Also available on disk. (Obtainable from Inland Revenue Library, Room 28, New Wing, Somerset House, Strand, London WC2R 1LB). Price £7.50.
SAT 2	Self-Assessment — The Legal Framework, explaining how the rules on the assessment and collection of income and capital gains taxes will change (July 1995). Also available on disk. (Obtainable as SAT 1 above). Price £5.00.

37 Inland Revenue Explanatory Pamphlets Etc.

SAT 3	Self-Assessment — What it will mean for Employers (July 1995). (Obtainable from Inland Revenue Enquiry Centre, Ground Floor, SW Wing, Bush House, Strand, London WC2B 4RD (tel. 0207-438 7772)). Free.
SA/BK3	Self-Assessment — A Guide to Keeping Records for the Self-Employed (June 1995).
SA/BK4	Self-Assessment — A General Guide to Keeping Records (December 1997).
SA/BK6	Self-Assessment — Penalties for Late Tax Returns (October 1997).
SA/BK7	Self-Assessment — Surcharges for Late Payment of Tax (October 1997).
SA/BK8	Self-Assessment — Your Guide (October 1997).
AO 1	How to Complain about the Inland Revenue (February 2000). (Also available in a range of languages, code RAO).
CB(1)	Setting up a Charity in Scotland (February 1993). (Obtainable from FICO (Scotland), Trinity Park House, South Trinity Road, Edinburgh EH5 3SD (tel. 0131-551 8127). Also obtainable in Gaelic (December 1995)).
CS 2	Trading by Charities — Guidelines on the Tax Treatment of Trades Carried on by Charities (September 1998). (Obtainable from Customer Services Manager, FICO, St John's House, Merton Road, Bootle, Merseyside L69 9BB (tel. 0151-472 6106)).
CWL 1	Starting Your Own Business? (May 2000).
CWL 2	National Insurance Contributions for Self-Employed People. Class 2 and Class 4 (May 2000).
Inst 1	A Modern System for Corporation Tax Payments — A Guide to Quarterly Instalment Payments (November 1998).
ISA 1	The Answers on ISAs (March 1999).
PSO 1	Occupational Pension Schemes — A Guide for Members of Tax-Approved Schemes (April 1995). (Obtainable as IR 76 above).
SVD 1	Shares Valuation Division — An Introduction (May 1999).
—	The euro — Tax and national insurance options for UK businesses from 1 January 1999 (January 1999).
—	List of bodies approved by the Inland Revenue under *ICTA 1988, s 201* (subscriptions to professional bodies). (Obtainable from Inland Revenue Library, 28 New Wing, Somerset House, Strand, London WC2R 1LB). Price £5.00.
—	Register of Qualifying Lenders under the MIRAS scheme. (Obtainable from Inland Revenue Library, 28 New Wing, Somerset House, Strand, London WC2R 1LB). Price £1.00.
—	Explanatory notes on the provisions of *ICTA 1988, Pt XVII, Ch IV* (Controlled Foreign Companies). (Obtainable from Inland Revenue Library, 28 New Wing, Somerset House, Strand, London WC2R 1LB). Price £10.00.

— Working families tax credit and Disabled person's tax credit. (December 1998). (Obtainable from Inland Revenue Enquiry Centre, SW Wing, Bush House, Strand, London WC2B 4RD). Free.

— Capital gains tax reform — the 1998 Finance Act. (Copies were issued free to those on the Inland Revenue's database of agents. Further copies obtainable price £5 (post free) from Inland Revenue Library, 28 New Wing, Somerset House, Strand, London WC2R 1LB).

— Charities — Payroll Giving Schemes, explaining how the proposals for tax relief are expected to work. (Obtainable from Customer Services Manager, FICO, St John's House, Merton Road, Bootle, Merseyside L69 9BB (tel. 0151-472 6106)). Free.

— Guidelines on the tax treatment of disaster funds, giving guidelines on the organisation of disaster appeal funds. (Obtainable from Customer Services Manager, FICO, St John's House, Merton Road, Bootle, Merseyside L69 9BB (tel. 0151-472 6106)). Free.

— Fund-raising for charity, giving guidance on the operation of Extra-statutory Concession C4 (see 15.7 CHARITIES). (Obtainable from Customer Services Manager, FICO, St John's House, Merton Road, Bootle, Merseyside L69 9BB (tel. no. 0151-472 6106)). Free.

— The tax treatment of top-up pension schemes. (Obtainable from Inland Revenue Library, 28 New Wing, Somerset House, Strand, London WC2R 1LB). Price £1.50.

— Business economic notes. See 71.28 SCHEDULE D, CASES I AND II.

— Codes of Practice. See 35.7 INLAND REVENUE: ADMINISTRATION.

'Appeals and Other Proceedings before the Special Commissioners' (October 1994), dealing with procedural and other points, is available free of charge from the Clerk to the Special Commissioners, 15/29 Bedford Avenue, London WC1B 3AS (tel. 0207-631 4242).

The Board also issue Concessions, Press Releases and Statements of Practice, summaries of, and references to which, are included in the following three chapters and elsewhere under the appropriate chapter heading. A Revenue Tax Bulletin is also published bi-monthly (annual subscription £22), relevant items from which are referred to in the appropriate chapter.

38 Inland Revenue Extra-Statutory Concessions

Simon's Direct Tax Service H4.

The following is a summary of the concessions published in the Revenue Pamphlet IR 1 (2000) (or in earlier editions where still relevant) or subsequently announced, insofar as they relate to subjects dealt with in this book. It should be borne in mind that in a particular case there may be special circumstances which will require to be taken into account in considering the application of a concession. A concession will not be given in any case where an attempt is made to use it for tax avoidance (and see *R v HMIT (ex p Fulford-Dobson) QB 1987, 60 TC 168*). See also 35.4 INLAND REVENUE: ADMINISTRATION.

A. APPLICABLE TO INDIVIDUALS

A1 **Flat rate allowances for cost of tools and special clothing** may be claimed. See 75.25 SCHEDULE E.

A2 **Meal vouchers.** Certain vouchers are exempt from income tax. See 75.30 SCHEDULE E.

A4 **Directors' travelling expenses.** Certain expenses paid by employers are not assessable. See 75.13(ix), 75.43 SCHEDULE E.

A5 **Expenses allowances and benefits in kind.**

(*a*) Removal expenses paid by employer in certain circumstances are not assessable. See 75.13(x) SCHEDULE E.

(*b*) Bridging loans provided by employer in certain circumstances are not assessable. See 75.13(x), 75.17 SCHEDULE E.

Withdrawn after 5 April 1993, subject to transitional arrangements.

A6 **Miners: free coal and allowances in lieu** are exempt from income tax.

A7 **Business (or other source of income) passing to spouse on death of trader.** Discontinuance provisions are not enforced. (Withdrawn following the introduction of a current year basis of assessment.) See 71.9 SCHEDULE D, CASES I AND II, 72.4 SCHEDULE D, CASE III.

A8 **Loss relief for capital allowances unused on the cessation of a business.** Capital allowances brought forward are used to reduce the profits of the final year. (Obsolete for 1997/98 onwards.) See 46.7 LOSSES.

A9 **Doctors' and dentists' superannuation contributions** under the NHS are allowable as deductions under Schedule D but alternatives apply where premiums for retirement annuities are also paid. See 66.11 RETIREMENT SCHEMES.

A10 **Overseas pension schemes.** Income tax is not charged on certain lump sums on termination of employment overseas. See 59.4(vi) PENSIONS.

A11 **Residence in the UK: year of commencement or cessation of residence.** Liability to tax is computed by reference to the period of residence in that year. See 64.5 RESIDENCE, ORDINARY RESIDENCE AND DOMICILE.

A12 **Double taxation relief: alimony etc. under UK court order or agreement: payer resident abroad.** Relief by way of credit is allowed in certain circumstances. See 25.5(*a*) DOUBLE TAX RELIEF.

A13 **Administration of estates: deficiencies of income allowed against income of another year.** (Obsolete for 1995/96 onwards.) See 22.3 DECEASED ESTATES.

A14 **Deceased person's estate: residuary income received during the administration period.** A legatee resident abroad may have his tax liability on estate income adjusted as if the income had arisen to him directly. See 22.3 DECEASED ESTATES.

A16 **Annual payments (other than interest) paid out of income not brought into charge to income tax.** If payment is made in a year later than when due, and it could have been made out of taxed income in that due year, an allowance will be made (when collecting under *ICTA 1988, s 350*) for the tax which the payer would have been entitled to deduct (under *ICTA 1988, s 348*) and retain if the payment had been made at the due date. See 23.3(i) DEDUCTION OF TAX AT SOURCE.

A17 **Death of taxpayer before due date for payment of tax.** Interest on tax overdue may not begin to run until after probate or letters of administration are obtained. See 42.9 INTEREST AND SURCHARGES ON UNPAID TAX.

A19 **Arrears of tax arising through official error.** Relief is given. See 56.6 PAYMENT OF TAX for current details.

A21 **Schedule A: deferred repairs: property passing from husband to wife (or vice versa) on death.** Expenditure on maintenance or repairs attributable to ownership of the deceased spouse is allowable to the surviving spouse. (Withdrawn with effect from 6 April 1995.) See 68.15 SCHEDULE A.

A22 **Long service awards** are exempt from tax within limitations. See 75.26 SCHEDULE E.

A24 **Foreign social security benefits.** Payments by foreign governments to UK residents which correspond to UK benefits exempt under *ICTA 1988, s 617(1)(2)* will also be exempt from tax. See 29.28 EXEMPT INCOME, 83.4 SOCIAL SECURITY.

A25 **Crown Servants engaged overseas** may be exempted from UK tax. See 75.2(i) SCHEDULE E.

A26 **Sick benefits.** The practice as regards assessment is explained. Superseded by new concession from 6 April 1994. See 75.37 SCHEDULE E.

A27 **Mortgage interest relief: temporary absences from mortgaged property.** Absences of up to one year, or longer if occasioned by employment, are ignored in determining if a property is an only or main residence. See 43.6, 43.15 INTEREST PAYABLE.

A29 **Farming and market gardening: relief for fluctuating profits.** For this purpose, 'farming' includes the intensive rearing of livestock or fish on a commercial basis for the production of food for human consumption. See 71.57 SCHEDULE D, CASES I AND II.

A30 **Interest on damages for personal injuries (foreign court awards)** will be exempt from income tax if also exempt in the country in which award made. See 29.13(i) EXEMPT INCOME.

A31 **Life assurance premium relief by deduction: pre-marriage policies: premium relief after divorce** continues where one party pays on life of the other. See 45.4(*f*) LIFE ASSURANCE POLICIES.

A32 **Tax relief for life assurance premiums: position of certain pension schemes which are unapproved after 5 April 1980.** Relief is continued. See 45.10(ii) LIFE ASSURANCE POLICIES.

A33 **Lump sum retirement benefits: changes after 5 April 1980.** Previous tax exemption is continued under certain conditions. See 66.12 RETIREMENT SCHEMES.

A34 **Ulster savings certificates: certificates encashed after death of registered holder.** Accumulated interest is exempt from income tax if the deceased was resident and domiciled in NI at time of purchase. See 33.6 GOVERNMENT STOCKS.

A35 **Mortgage interest relief: year of marriage.** Relief continues where one spouse vacates own mortgaged house to live in mortgaged house of other spouse. Superseded by *FA 1993, s 57.* See 43.12 INTEREST PAYABLE.

A37 **Tax treatment of directors' fees received by partnerships and other companies.** Under certain conditions, such fees may be included in the Schedule D assessment of the partnership, see 75.24 SCHEDULE E, or in the corporation tax assessment of the other company, see 75.1(1) SCHEDULE E.

A38 **Retirement annuity relief: death and disability benefits.** An individual in a scheme providing a pension only on death or disability will not be treated as being in pensionable employment. See 65.7 RETIREMENT ANNUITIES.

A39 **Exemption for Hong Kong officials.** Relief under *ICTA 1988, s 320* (see 24.1 DIPLOMATIC IMMUNITY) is extended to salaries of certain Hong Kong officials working in the UK. Obsolete.

A40 **Adoption allowances,** under approved schemes, are not taxable. See 29.1 EXEMPT INCOME.

A41 **Qualifying life assurance policies: statutory conditions** may be relaxed in certain circumstances. See 45.12(*h*) LIFE ASSURANCE POLICIES.

A42 **Chargeable events: loans to policyholders** may not be treated as partial surrenders in certain circumstances. (Obsolete.) See 45.15(*f*) LIFE ASSURANCE POLICIES.

A43 **Interest relief: investment in partnerships and close companies** may continue to attract relief where the partnership is incorporated or the close company's shares reorganised. See 43.19–43.22 INTEREST PAYABLE.

A44 **Education allowances under Overseas Service Aid Scheme,** payable to officers in the public service of certain overseas territories, which the UK government has undertaken to exempt from income tax, are so exempted. See 75.2(i) SCHEDULE E.

A45 **Life assurance policies: variation of term assured policies.** A term assurance policy for a term of ten years or less will not be disqualified under *ICTA 1988, Sch 15 paras 17(2)(b), 18* because of a reduction in the rate of premium to less than half as a result of a similar reduction in the sum assured or an extension of the term (resulting in a total term still not exceeding ten years). See 45.12(*d*) LIFE ASSURANCE POLICIES.

A46 **Variable purchased life annuities: carry forward of excess of capital element.** Any excess of the capital element over the annuity payment may be carried forward for allowance in determining the capital element in future payments. See 23.11(*c*) DEDUCTION OF TAX AT SOURCE.

A47 **House purchase loans made by life offices to staffs of insurance associations** may be treated in the same way as loans by a life office to a full-time employee. See 45.15(*f*) LIFE ASSURANCE POLICIES.

A49 **Widow's pension paid to widow of Singapore nationality, resident in the UK, whose husband was a UK national employed as a Public Officer by the Government of Singapore** is included in the exemption provided by *ICTA 1988, s 616(1)*. See 59.2 PENSIONS.

A51 **Repayment supplement: life assurance premium relief.** The repayment supplement provisions (see 41.2 INTEREST ON OVERPAID TAX) apply also to repayments of excessive clawback under *ICTA 1988, ss 268, 269* (see 45.5 LIFE ASSURANCE POLICIES) and to relief by repayment under *ICTA 1988, Sch 14 para 6(1)* where relief is not obtained by deduction (see 45.1 LIFE ASSURANCE POLICIES).

A52 **Maintenance payments: concessionary relief.** Where a person fails to deduct tax under *ICTA 1988, s 348* from annual payments made under a Court Order or other legally binding agreement, relief may concessionally be granted equal to the amount of repayment which would have been due to the recipient had the right to deduct tax been properly exercised. Obsolete. See 23.8 DEDUCTION OF TAX AT SOURCE, 47.10 MARRIED PERSONS.

A55 **Arrears of foreign pensions,** or increases thereof, granted retrospectively may, where they are chargeable on the arising basis under Schedule D, Case V and it is advantageous to the taxpayer, be taxed as if the arrears arose in the years to which they relate, rather than being assessed in one sum as they arise. See 59.2 PENSIONS.

A56 **Benefits in kind: tax treatment of accommodation provided by employers.** The rules are modified in relation to Scotland. See 75.29 SCHEDULE E.

A57 **Suggestion schemes.** Awards to employees under such schemes are not charged to tax provided that certain conditions are satisfied. See 75.26 SCHEDULE E.

A58 **Travelling and subsistence allowance when public transport disrupted.** Such allowances, or the provision of facilities by the employer, are not charged to tax. See 75.13(v), 75.43 SCHEDULE E.

A59 **Home to work travel of severely disabled employees.** Provision of transport facilities or financial assistance is not charged to tax. (Revised by Revenue Press Release 28 June 2000.) See 75.13(vi), 75.15, 75.43 SCHEDULE E.

A60 **Agricultural workers' board and lodging** will, subject to conditions, not be charged to tax even where a higher wage in lieu could be taken. See 75.7 SCHEDULE E.

A61 **Clergymen's heating and lighting etc. expenses.** Certain sums paid or reimbursed are not charged to tax. See 75.9 SCHEDULE E.

A62 **Pensions to employees disabled at work.** The excess over the normal ill health retirement pension is not charged to tax. See 59.4(iii) PENSIONS.

A63 **External training courses — expenses borne by employer.** Certain such expenses do not give rise to a charge to tax on the employee. (Obsolete for 1997/98 onwards.) See 75.42 SCHEDULE E.

A64 **External training courses — expenses borne by an employee** may be allowed as a deduction. (Withdrawn from 1 September 2000 by Revenue Press Release 25 July 2000.) See 75.42 SCHEDULE E.

A65 **Workers on offshore oil and gas rigs or platforms — free transfers from or to mainland.** No charge to tax arises in respect of such transfers or certain mainland accommodation and subsistence. See 75.13(viii), 75.43 SCHEDULE E.

A66 **Employees' late night journeys from work to home.** Where the cost of occasional journeys is borne by the employer, the employee will not, subject to various conditions, be charged to tax on the benefit he receives. See 75.13(vii), 75.43 SCHEDULE E.

A68 **Payments out of a discretionary trust which are emoluments taxable under Schedule E.** Trustees may reclaim tax on certain payments to beneficiaries. See 81.5 SETTLEMENTS.

A69 **Composite rate tax: non-resident depositors.** Certain declarations made to a society are treated as having been made to a successor company. See 8.2 BANKS, 9.6 BUILDING SOCIETIES.

A70 **Small gifts to employees by third parties and staff Christmas parties** may be exempted from income tax. See 75.13(xvi), 75.26 SCHEDULE E.

A71 **Company cars for family members.** In relation to the car scale charge: (*a*) a double charge is prevented where cars are supplied to members of the same family by the same employer; and (*b*) the charge is apportioned where use is shared. See 75.15 SCHEDULE E.

A72 **Pension schemes and accident insurance policies.** The exemption from the benefits charge for provision of death or retirement benefits is extended to all family and household beneficiaries. See 75.13(iii) SCHEDULE E.

A73 **Lloyd's underwriters: repayment of tax withheld where there is an overall loss.** Tax deducted by the managing agent may be repaid to the Name. Obsolete. See 89.5 UNDERWRITERS.

A74 **Meals and light refreshments provided for employees** may escape charge to tax as a benefit. (Revised by Revenue Press Release 19 November 1999.) See 75.13(iv) SCHEDULE E.

A76 **Business expansion scheme and enterprise investment scheme subscriber shares.** Relief will not be denied to subscribers for such shares because they may, for a short period, hold in excess of 30% of the issued share capital. (This concession is superseded by *FA 1998, Sch 13 para 8(1)* as regards EIS shares issued after 5 April 1998.) See 26.3, 26.20 ENTERPRISE INVESTMENT SCHEME (AND BES).

A77 **Motor mileage allowances paid to volunteer drivers.** Only part of the mileage profit will be taxed for periods before 1995/96. See 74.2 SCHEDULE D, CASE VI.

A78 **Residence in the UK: accompanying spouse.** A concessional treatment is introduced for the determination of the residence and ordinary residence status of spouses accompanying individuals in full-time employment abroad. See 64.5, 64.6 RESIDENCE, ORDINARY RESIDENCE AND DOMICILE.

A79 **Tax exempt special savings accounts (TESSAs).** A *curator bonis* in Scotland may open a TESSA on behalf of an incapacitated person. Obsolete. See 29.13 EXEMPT INCOME.

A80 **Blanket partnership continuation elections.** Elections covering all future partnership changes (until withdrawn) may be accepted in the case of certain large partnerships. Obsolete. See 53.6 PARTNERSHIPS.

A81 **Termination payments and legal costs.** Certain legal costs recovered from the employer will not be charged under *ICTA 1988, s 148*. See 19.6(viii) COMPENSATION FOR LOSS OF EMPLOYMENT (AND DAMAGES).

A82 **Repayment supplement to individuals resident in EC Member States** will be paid in certain cases following the decision in the *Commerzbank AG* case. See 41.2 INTEREST ON OVERPAID TAX.

A83 **Benefits under permanent health insurance policies.** Benefits under self-funded policies may be exempt for the first twelve months. (Supersedes Concession A26 above.) See 71.64 SCHEDULE D, CASES I AND II, 75.37 SCHEDULE E. Obsolete — see now the statutory provisions at 29.12 EXEMPT INCOME.

A84 **Allowances paid to Detached National Experts** on secondment to the European Commission are exempt from income tax. See 75.2(i) SCHEDULE E.

A85 **Transfers of assets by employees and directors to employers and others.** Certain employer's transaction costs will not be charged as a benefit. See 75.13(xxi) SCHEDULE E.

A86 **Blind person's tax allowance.** The allowance will be granted for the year before registration where the evidence on which registration was based was available at the end of that year. See 1.19 ALLOWANCES AND TAX RATES.

A87 **Loss relief on accounts basis.** The long-standing practice of allowing loss relief under *ICTA 1988, s 380* on the accounts basis rather than the strict fiscal year basis is confirmed. Obsolete. See 46.10 LOSSES.

A88 **Cessation adjustment where loss relief has been allowed on accounts basis.** Relief will be given for certain losses otherwise falling not to attract relief. Obsolete. See 46.10 LOSSES.

A89 **Mortgage interest relief — property used for residential and business purposes.** Interest relief may be obtained both under *ICTA 1988, s 353* and as a deduction in computing profits and losses. See 23.13 DEDUCTION OF TAX AT SOURCE, 43.2 INTEREST PAYABLE.

A90 **Jobmatch pilot scheme.** Payments and training vouchers provided under the scheme are exempt from income tax. Obsolete. See generally 83.4 SOCIAL SECURITY.

A91 **Living accommodation provided by reason of employment.** A charge will not be raised under *ICTA 1988, s 146* where the *ICTA 1988, s 145* charge was based on the full market rent, and the combined charge under those *sections* will be restricted where the accommodation is provided to more than one director or employee. See 75.29 SCHEDULE E.

A92 **TESSAs — European authorised institutions.** Accounts opened before 2 January 1996 may be transferred to such institutions on or after that date. Obsolete. See 29.13(iii) EXEMPT INCOME.

A93 **Payments from offshore trusts to minor unmarried child of settlor: claim by settlor for credit of tax paid by trustees** against his liability to tax on income distributed to or for the benefit of the child will be allowed. See 81.5 SETTLEMENTS.

A94 **Profits and losses of theatre backers (angels)** may in certain cases be treated as within Schedule D, Case VI, and the requirement for deduction of tax from certain payments is waived. See 74.2 SCHEDULE D, CASE VI.

A95 **Small lump sum retirement benefits schemes.** Relief for employee contributions to personal pension schemes or retirement annuity contracts may not be withdrawn where certain lump sum retirement benefits accrue in respect of the same employment. See 60.8 PERSONAL PENSION SCHEMES, 65.7 RETIREMENT ANNUITIES.

A96 **Old life insurance policies — insurer stopping collection of premiums.** Such a change will, in certain circumstances, not be treated as an alteration of the policy for tax purposes. See 45.13 LIFE ASSURANCE POLICIES.

A97 **Jobmatch programme.** Income tax is not charged on payments under the Jobmatch programme or in respect of training vouchers received under its terms. See 29.28 EXEMPT INCOME, 83.4 SOCIAL SECURITY.

A98 **Cessation adjustments under self-assessment transitional rules.** Interest otherwise arising due to cessation adjustments at the direction of the inspector during the transitional period will not generally be charged. See 42.1 INTEREST AND SURCHARGES ON UNPAID TAX.

The following concessions await publication in IR 1.

A99 **Tax treatment of compensation for mis-sold freestanding additional voluntary contribution schemes.** Certain compensation payments are exempted from tax. (Revenue Press Release 28 February 2000). See 29.3 EXEMPT INCOME.

Tax exemption for compensation paid on bank accounts owned by Holocaust victims. Uprating payments to restore the purchasing power of amounts held in such accounts is exempt from income tax and death duties. (Revenue Press Release 8 May 2000). See 29.13(xi) EXEMPT INCOME.

B. CONCESSIONS APPLICABLE TO INDIVIDUALS AND COMPANIES

B1 **Machinery and plant: changes from 'renewals' to 'capital allowances' basis.** Capital allowances may be claimed provided all items of the same class are changed to new basis. See 10.38(ix) CAPITAL ALLOWANCES.

B4 **Maintenance and repairs of property obviated by alterations etc.: Schedule A assessments.** The estimated cost of the repairs etc. may be allowed. See 68.15 SCHEDULE A.

B5 **Maintenance expenses of owner-occupied farms not carried on on a commercial basis** may be claimed under *ICTA 1988, s 33*. See 71.57 SCHEDULE D, CASES I AND II.

B7 **Benevolent gifts by traders** are allowable in certain circumstances. See 71.84 SCHEDULE D, CASES I AND II.

B8 **Double tax relief: income consisting of royalties and 'know-how' payments** arising to a UK resident from abroad. See 25.5(*l*) DOUBLE TAX RELIEF.

B9 **Bank interest, etc. received by charities** is exempt. Now superseded by *FA 1996, s 146*. See 15.5, 15.7 CHARITIES.

B10 **Income of contemplative religious communities or of their members,** having a common fund and not being charities, is partly regarded as income of each monk or nun up to £2,730 each for 1993/94 (£2,669 for 1992/93; £2,619 for 1991/92; £2,518 for 1990/91; £2,327 for 1989/90; £2,142 for 1988/89; £1,986 for 1987/88). For 1995/96 and subsequent years, the allowable figure is set at the basic personal allowance for the year (see 1.14 ALLOWANCES AND TAX RATES). Where the aggregate of 'allowable figures' exceeds income of the community, the excess may be set against chargeable gains of that or (in the case of an excess arising in a year up to and including 1994/95) a subsequent year.

B11 **Compensation for compulsory slaughter of farm animals** may be treated as profits spread over the following three years. See 71.57 SCHEDULE D, CASES I AND II.

B13 **Untaxed interest paid to non-residents.** No action is taken to recover the tax unless an agent is chargeable or a set-off is available against a tax claim. (Now superseded by *FA 1995, s 128*.) See 51.3 NON-RESIDENTS AND OTHER OVERSEAS MATTERS.

B16 **Fire safety: capital expenditure incurred on certain trade premises (a) in Northern Ireland, and (b) by lessors.** (*a*) Provisions relating to fire safety expenditure in the UK are extended to NI, and (*b*) relief is allowed where lessor incurs the expenditure himself, if similar expenditure by the tenant would have qualified for relief. See 10.25(i) CAPITAL ALLOWANCES.

B17 **Capital allowances: sale of invented patent to an associate.** Where an inventor sells a patent to his own controlled company at less than open market value, the actual sale price is taken for assessment and capital allowances, and (subject to the purchaser's agreement) for capital gains tax. Obsolete. See 10.50 CAPITAL ALLOWANCES.

B18 **Payments out of discretionary trusts.** Beneficiaries may claim certain reliefs as if they had received the income out of which the payment was made directly. See 81.5 SETTLEMENTS.

B19 **Capital allowances for buildings: balancing charge after cessation of trade.** The assessment under Schedule D, Case VI may be offset by trading losses and unused capital allowances. Superseded by *CAA 1990, s 15A* and subsequently *s 15ZA(3)*. See 10.17 CAPITAL ALLOWANCES.

B20 **Capital allowances for buildings: sales by property developers of buildings which have been let.** Writing-down allowances are made to the purchaser even though the developer's expenditure on construction has been on revenue account. Now superseded by *CAA 1990, s 10(4)(5)*. See 10.14 CAPITAL ALLOWANCES.

B25 **Schedule D, Case V losses.** Relief is extended in certain cases. (Obsolete for 1998/99 onwards.) See 73.4 SCHEDULE D, CASES IV AND V.

B27 **Approved employee share schemes: jointly owned companies.** A scheme operated by a jointly owned company may nevertheless be granted approval. See 82.2 SHARE INCENTIVES AND OPTIONS.

B28 **Leased cars costing over £12,000: rebate of hire charges** will be treated as non-taxable in the same proportion as the hire charges were themselves disallowed under *CAA 1990, s 35(2)*. Now superseded by *CAA 1990, s 35(2A)*. See 10.28(A) CAPITAL ALLOWANCES.

B29 **Treatment of income from caravan sites where there is both trading and associated letting income.** In such circumstances the receipts from caravan pitch site income and from letting caravans may be treated as receipts of the trading activities. See 68.4 SCHEDULE A, 74.4 SCHEDULE D, CASE VI.

B30 **Income from property in Scotland: property managed as one estate.** The tax treatment will continue to be by reference to 1978 gross rateable values where appropriate. See 68.7(*e*) SCHEDULE A—PROPERTY INCOME.

B31 **Capital allowances: plant or machinery which is a fixture in a business building situated within an enterprise zone** may attract 100% initial allowances. Now superseded by *FA 1989, Sch 13 para 28*. See 10.19 CAPITAL ALLOWANCES.

B35 **Borrowing and lending of securities: gilt lending to redemption.** Certain transactions are treated as being within *ICTA 1988, s 129*. Obsolete. See 71.82 SCHEDULE D, CASES I AND II.

B36 **Borrowing and lending of securities: replacement loans.** Certain transactions are treated as being within *ICTA 1988, s 129*. Obsolete. See 71.82 SCHEDULE D, CASES I AND II.

B37 **The herd basis: shares in animals.** The herd basis may be applied to a share in an animal in the same way as if the share were a whole animal. Now superseded by *FA 2000, s 76*. See 34.2 HERD BASIS.

B38 **Tax concessions on overseas debts.** Relief may be available where they form part of profits assessable under Schedule D, Case I or Case II. See 71.92 SCHEDULE D, CASES I AND II.

B39 **Contributions to overseas pension schemes.** Employer contributions otherwise denied relief are allowed in certain circumstances. Now superseded by *FA 1989, s 76(6A)–(6C)*. See 66.10 RETIREMENT SCHEMES.

B40 **UK investment managers acting for non-resident clients.** The exemptions of *TMA 1970, ss 78(2), 82* are extended in certain cases. See 51.4(*b*) NON-RESIDENTS AND OTHER OVERSEAS MATTERS.

B41 **Claims to repayment of tax.** Where an over-payment of tax has arisen because of official error, and there is no doubt or dispute as to the facts, claims to repayment of tax are accepted outside the statutory time limit (generally six years from the end of the tax year concerned). See 17.6 CLAIMS.

B42 **'Free gifts' and insurance contracts.** Certain incentive gifts offered in connection with the issue of insurance policies are disregarded. See 45.6 LIFE ASSURANCE POLICIES.

B43 **Alterations to old pension funds.** Certain minor rule amendments may be made without loss of exemption. See 66.13 RETIREMENT SCHEMES.

B44 **Profit-related pay: extraordinary items.** Existing treatment of certain items in the statutory profit and loss account is preserved following the replacement of SSAP6 by FRS3. See generally 75.31(K) SCHEDULE E.

B45 **Automatic penalties for late company and employers' and contractors' end-of-year returns.** A temporary short period of grace is allowed for submission of annual returns following the introduction of automatic penalties. Obsolete. See 58.4 PENALTIES.

B46 **Automatic penalties for late company and employers' and contractors' end-of-year returns.** A short period of grace is allowed for submission of annual returns. See 58.4 PENALTIES.

B47 **Furnished lettings of dwelling houses — wear and tear of furniture.** As an alternative to the renewals basis, an allowance of 10% of rent may be claimed. (Replaces Statement of Practice A19.) See 68.8 SCHEDULE A, 74.4 SCHEDULE D, CASE VI.

B48 **A deduction for an employer's national insurance Class 1A contributions when computing profits for tax purposes.** Such a deduction may be given in the same way as for secondary Class 1 contributions. Now superseded by *FA 1997, s 65*. See 71.54 SCHEDULE D, CASES I AND II.

B49 **CAA 1990, s 153 — repaid grants.** Capital allowances will be given for repayments of grants which were deducted from expenditure qualifying for capital allowances. See 10.2(ii) CAPITAL ALLOWANCES.

B50 **Capital allowances for caravans on holiday caravan sites.** An extended definition of 'caravan' applies for this purpose. See 10.26(19) CAPITAL ALLOWANCES.

B52 **Subcontractors in the construction industry: the multiple turnover tests.** Until 1 August 2001, the number of partners or directors taken into account in determining the three-year turnover threshold may be taken as the maximum number at any time in the last six months of the three-year period, rather than at any time in the whole period, where this is more favourable. See 21.5 CONSTRUCTION INDUSTRY TAX SCHEME.

The following concession awaits publication in IR 1.

B53 **Non-UK resident individuals and companies and chargeable event gains on life policies, life annuities and capital redemption policies.** (i) The treatment, in the case of non-residents, of life assurance gains is brought more into line with that of other forms of income. (ii) The reporting requirements in relation to non-resident policy holders are relaxed. (iii) The transitional reliefs for holders of personal portfolio bonds issued before 17 March 1998 are extended. (Revenue Press Release 23 November 1999). See 45.13 LIFE ASSURANCE POLICIES.

C. CONCESSIONS APPLICABLE TO COMPANIES ETC.

C1 **Credit for underlying tax: dividends from trade investments in overseas companies.** (*a*) A few UK double tax agreements provide relief for underlying tax on income from ordinary portfolio investments and where these are in force, credit is also given for underlying taxes along a chain of shareholdings (see 25.5(*b*) DOUBLE TAX RELIEF). (*b*) Insurance companies in receipt of dividends from overseas companies, in which there is at least 10% control of voting power or the dividend is referable to insurance business of the UK company, are given credit for underlying taxes along a chain of shareholdings. See Tolley's Corporation Tax.

C2 **Loan and money societies.** There is restricted liability to tax on dividends and interest to members. Withdrawn from April 2001. See 18.3 CLUBS AND SOCIETIES.

C3 **Holiday clubs and thrift funds.** There is restricted liability to tax on profits or interest to members. Withdrawn from April 2001. See 18.2 CLUBS AND SOCIETIES.

C4 **Trading activities for charitable purposes.** Profits are not taxed under certain conditions. See 15.7(ii) CHARITIES.

C30 **Authorised unit trusts and open-ended investment companies — waivers of distributions.** Distribution treatment is disapplied in the case of certain *de minimis* waivers of distributions (or accumulations). See 90.1 UNIT TRUSTS.

C31 **Scientific research associations.** Tax exemptions will temporarily continue under the previous practice following a change in the DTI guidance on the qualification requirements. See 77.1 SCIENTIFIC RESEARCH ASSOCIATIONS.

D. CONCESSIONS RELATING TO CAPITAL GAINS

D27 **Earn-outs.** The capital gains concession concerning the application of *TCGA 1992, s 135* to takeovers including an earn-out element is extended to trading profits of financial concerns. (Superseded by *FA 1997, s 89*.) See 71.82 SCHEDULE D, CASES I AND II.

D46 **Relief against income for capital losses on the disposal of unquoted shares in a trading company.** Relief will be allowed in certain cases where a company without assets is dissolved and either no distribution is made during winding-up, or no final distribution is made. Superseded by statutory provision for events treated as disposals after 5 April 2000. See 46.18 LOSSES.

D47 **Temporary loss of charitable status due to reverter of school and other sites.** Liabilities which may arise in the period before charitable status is re-established will be discharged or repaid. See 15.1 CHARITIES.

39 Inland Revenue Press Releases

The following is a summary in date order of Press Releases referred to in this Part (other than those containing Statements of Practice, as to which see 40 INLAND REVENUE STATEMENTS OF PRACTICE). Certain pre-18 July 1978 Press Releases were reissued as Statements of Practice on 18 June 1979 (see 40 INLAND REVENUE STATEMENTS OF PRACTICE).

Copies of any individual Press Release may be obtained from Inland Revenue Information Centre, SW Wing, Bush House, Strand, London WC2B 4RD (tel. 0207-438 6420/6425/7772). A charge (currently £100) is made for Press Releases (including Extra-Statutory Concessions and Statements of Practice) mailed weekly throughout a calendar year. To receive Press Releases, application can be made to Tolley, 2 Addiscombe Road, Croydon, Surrey CR9 5AF (tel. 0208-686 9141). A separate application is needed to subscribe to the Revenue's Tax Bulletin for an annual charge of £22, which should be made to Inland Revenue, Finance Division, Barrington Road, Worthing, West Sussex BN12 4XH.

9.5.69 **Double tax agreement with Singapore: matching of incentive reliefs.** Credit is given against UK tax for tax given up by Singapore to pioneer industries. See 25.5(*i*) DOUBLE TAX RELIEF.

5.3.70 **Double tax agreement with Malaysia: matching of incentive reliefs.** Credit is given against UK tax for tax given up by Malaysia to pioneer industries. See 25.5(*i*) DOUBLE TAX RELIEF.

2.3.78 **Double taxation: exchange of information with the USA.** Notes on the 'working arrangement' with the US Internal Revenue Service. See 36.2(*c*) INLAND REVENUE: CONFIDENTIALITY OF INFORMATION.

26.7.78 **Car leasing schemes.** Where a car is sold to the lessee etc. at less than the open market value at the end of the contract, the Revenue will consider what adjustments may be necessary to the tax liabilities affected. See 10.38(ii) CAPITAL ALLOWANCES.

26.7.79 **Administrative simplification to help pensioners.** The Revenue are notified by the Department of Health and Social Security of the amounts of retirement and widows pensions. See 83.3 SOCIAL SECURITY.

16.6.80 **Life assurance premium relief: ICTA 1988, Sch 15 para 14: disqualification of certain life policies.** Guidance is given as to the application of this legislation. See 45.11 LIFE ASSURANCE POLICIES.

26.1.81 **Transfer pricing of multinational enterprises: notes for guidance.** See 3.9 ANTI-AVOIDANCE.

4.2.81 **Life assurance premiums paid to the UK branch of an overseas life office.** Relief is available. See 45.4(*c*) LIFE ASSURANCE POLICIES.

13.2.81 **Travelling and subsistence allowances paid to site-based staff employees in the construction and allied industries.** Revenue practice is explained and extended. See 75.43 SCHEDULE E.

25.6.81 **Sick pay.** The taxation of sick pay under *ICTA 1988, s 149* will not apply to sums received under sick pay policies to the extent that premiums are paid by employees for their own benefit. See 75.37 SCHEDULE E.

25.6.82 **Deep discounted and indexed stock.** The Revenue's views on the taxation of rolled-up interest are stated. See 44.9 INTEREST RECEIVABLE.

25.1.83 **Deferred listing of delay appeals.** See 4.5 APPEALS.

30.3.83 **'Freelance' workers in the film and allied industries.** Revised treatment of such workers operates from 6 April 1983. See 75.24 SCHEDULE E.

13.3.84 **Net of tax pay.** Special forms and tax tables are available to employers. See 75.40 SCHEDULE E.

15.3.84 **Cable television: capital allowances** are available on ducting. See 10.25 CAPITAL ALLOWANCES.

17.5.84 **Furnished holiday lettings and caravans.** The application of *ICTA 1988, s 503* to caravan lettings is clarified. See 68.4, 68.9 SCHEDULE A, 74.4 SCHEDULE D, CASE VI.

31.7.84 **Offshore funds: applications for certification as a distributing fund.** The procedure is explained. See 52.7 OFFSHORE FUNDS.

1.8.84 **ICTA 1988, s 124: interest on quoted Eurobonds.** The requirements for designation as a 'recognised clearing system' are outlined. See 23.3 DEDUCTION OF TAX AT SOURCE.

2.11.84 **Incentive awards and prizes for employees: taxed award schemes.** See 75.40 SCHEDULE E.

23.7.85 **Extra-statutory concession: benefits in kind: the tax treatment of accommodation provided for employees.** Annual value is in practice taken as gross rateable value. See 68.7(*e*) SCHEDULE A.

18.3.86 **Business Expansion Scheme.** The grant of certain options will not result in withdrawal of relief. See 26.27 ENTERPRISE INVESTMENT SCHEME (AND BES).

15.4.86 **Voluntary lifeboatmen: tax treatment of call-out fees.** See 55.45 PAYE.

27.10.86 **Capital allowances: changes in accounting practice for plant and machinery under lease or subject to hire purchase.** The tax treatment is unaffected. See 10.24 CAPITAL ALLOWANCES.

11.3.87 **Payroll giving scheme for charities: approval of agency charities.** A list of approved agency charities is published, and will be added to from time to time. See 15.18 CHARITIES.

11.5.87 **Payroll giving schemes for charities: approval of agency charities.** Additions are made to the list published on 11 March 1987. See 15.18 CHARITIES.

16.7.87 **Payroll giving schemes for charities: approval of agency charities.** Additions are made to the lists previously published. See 15.18 CHARITIES.

5.10.87 **Payroll giving scheme for charities: approval of agency charities.** Additions are made to the lists previously published. See 15.18 CHARITIES.

22.12.87 **Inland Revenue further guidance on profit-related pay.** See 75.31 SCHEDULE E.

39 Inland Revenue Press Releases

22.1.88 **Life assurance: variation of qualifying policies.** After 24 February 1988, the Revenue will not certify, as qualifying policies, any new life assurance policies which allow for variations such that, under contract law, a new policy would be created. See 45.12 LIFE ASSURANCE POLICIES.

1.2.88 **Annual return form for profit-related pay.** The form of return to be used is published. See 75.31 SCHEDULE E.

4.2.88 **Occupational pensions: publication of Inland Revenue model rules and guidance notes for simplified occupational pension schemes.** See 66.4 RETIREMENT SCHEMES.

15.3.88 **Alimony, maintenance, etc.: retrospective Court Orders.** Revenue Statement of Practice SP 6/81 will not apply to Court Orders made or varied after 30 June 1988. See 47.10 MARRIED PERSONS.

15.3.88 **Reduction of basic rate of income tax.** The consequences are outlined, including the adjustments to be made where tax is deducted from certain payments. See 23.6 DEDUCTION OF TAX AT SOURCE.

14.4.88 **Unapproved employee share schemes.** A charge will not normally arise under *FA 1988, s 78* in respect of 'equity ratchets'. See 82.5(*a*) SHARE INCENTIVES AND OPTIONS.

2.9.88 **New tax unit for agricultural gangmasters.** See 71.57(*c*) SCHEDULE D, CASES I AND II.

19.12.88 **Tax appeals and other proceedings: place of hearing by General Commissioners.** See 4.3 APPEALS.

3.2.89 **Profit-related pay simplified.** A number of modifications are introduced either prior to enactment or by concession. See 75.31 SCHEDULE E.

3.3.89 **Double taxation: taxation of certain non-residents working on the UK continental shelf.** See 25.2 DOUBLE TAX RELIEF.

14.3.89 **Measures based on recommendations of the Keith Committee.** Transitional provisions apply to penalties for late submission of PAYE, etc. returns. See 58.4 PENALTIES.

29.3.89 **Cutting the cost of handling claims for repayment of income tax.** From 6 April 1989, repayments under £50 will not be made during the tax year to which the claim relates. See 17.6 CLAIMS, 56.7 PAYMENT OF TAX.

12.4.89 **Scholarship and apprenticeship schemes for employees.** The exempt limit under Revenue Statement of Practice SP 4/86 is increased to £5,500 p.a.. See 29.26 EXEMPT INCOME.

3.5.89 **Personal equity plans: relaxations to 75% test.** See 29.21 EXEMPT INCOME.

19.7.89 **Tax relief for medical insurance.** The permissible benefits are outlined. See 48.6 MEDICAL INSURANCE.

28.7.89 **FA 1989: the new simpler system of assessment for earnings.** Notes on the operation of PAYE. See 55.1 PAY AS YOU EARN, 75.1 SCHEDULE E.

1.8.89 **Setting Revenue rates of interest** for repayment supplement, overdue tax, and official rate purposes. The rates are in future to be set automatically by reference to a formula based on certain bank base lending rates. See 41 INTEREST ON OVERPAID TAX, 42 INTEREST AND SURCHARGES ON UNPAID TAX.

6.10.89 **Personal equity plans: new issue shares** on slightly different terms from those offered to the general public will not thereby be excluded from transfer into a plan. See 29.21 EXEMPT INCOME.

7.11.89 **Simpler accounts for small businesses.** From April 1990, businesses with a turnover under £10,000, and landlords with gross rental income under £10,000, may submit simplified three-line accounts. See 68.6 SCHEDULE A.

10.11.89 **Abolition of domestic rates and introduction of community charge.** The tax consequences are outlined. See 68.15 SCHEDULE A, 71.54, 71.78 SCHEDULE D, CASES I AND II, 75.7, 75.9, 75.10, 75.29 SCHEDULE E.

18.1.90 **Incentives for employees: improvements to the taxed award scheme.** Schemes may cover higher rate as well as basic rate liabilities. See 75.40 SCHEDULE E.

26.2.90 **Elections for an appeal to be heard by the Special Commissioners.** The circumstances in which an inspector will seek to have such an appeal heard by the General Commissioners are explained. See 4.3 APPEALS.

20.3.90 **New tax reliefs to encourage charitable giving.** Certain benefits available to subscribers to charitable organisations are ignored for the purposes of relief for covenanted payments. See 15.17(*b*) CHARITIES.

19.4.90 **Benefits in kind: valuation of living accommodation provided for employees in England and Wales.** The consequences of the ending of the domestic rates system are outlined. See 75.29 SCHEDULE E.

9.5.90 **Tracing of absent parents: Inland Revenue assistance to DSS.** The Revenue will supply to the DSS information relating to such parents where they are liable to maintain lone-parent families on income support. See 36.2(*f*) INLAND REVENUE: CONFIDENTIALITY OF INFORMATION.

17.10.90 **Changes to personal equity plans.** Pending the issue of revised regulations, certain changes to the rules for qualifying investments are applied by concession. The treatment of interest following abolition of composite rate tax is outlined. See 29.21 EXEMPT INCOME.

18.10.90 **Co-operation in investigations — 'Hansard leaflet'.** The Board's practice in relation to acceptance of money settlements is explained. See 6.11 BACK DUTY.

22.11.90 **Benefits in kind — employer-provided living accommodation.** Revenue practice is revised where employees are provided with more than one property. See 75.29 SCHEDULE E.

12.12.90 **PAYE — 'K' codes.** A new code, prefix 'K', is to be introduced from 6 April 1993 in cases where non-PAYE emoluments exceed allowances. See 55.4 PAY AS YOU EARN.

31.1.91 **Double taxation: Ghana.** The 1977 Convention was never formally ratified in Ghana, and has therefore never had effect in place of the 1947 Arrangement. See 25.2 DOUBLE TAX RELIEF.

39 Inland Revenue Press Releases

19.3.91 **Quarterly payments for small employers** of PAYE and NIC are to be introduced from 6 April 1991. See 55.8 PAY AS YOU EARN.

5.4.91 **Benefits in kind: loans provided by employers.** A new basis of determining the official rate of interest is introduced from 6 April 1991. See 75.17 SCHEDULE E.

11.4.91 **Finance lease rental payments.** A new statement of practice (SP 3/91) is issued, and some aspects of finance leases clarified. See 71.68 SCHEDULE D, CASES I AND II.

12.6.91 **Finance Bill: friendly societies — tax-exempt policies.** An extra-statutory concession applies in relation to certain wrongly classified policies. See 31.3 FRIENDLY SOCIETIES.

24.10.91 **PAYE 'K' codes.** Some amendments are made to arrangements for the proposed new code following consultation. See 55.4 PAY AS YOU EARN.

1.11.91 **Simpler accounts for small businesses: increase in the numbers who can benefit.** The limit for the submission of three-line accounts is increased to £15,000 from 6 April 1992. See 68.6, 68.19 SCHEDULE A.

16.12.91 **Enterprise zone capital allowances.** By concession, certain amounts payable before 16 December 1991 for the purchase of unused buildings are treated as incurred on the date the construction expenditure was incurred. See 10.19 CAPITAL ALLOWANCES.

10.2.92 **Claims to repayment of tax.** Late claims arising as a result of official error are admitted by extra-statutory concession. See 17.6 CLAIMS, 56.6 PAYMENT OF TAX.

7.5.92 **Charitable giving.** The requirements for repayment claims relating to deeds of covenant are revised. See 15.17(*e*) CHARITIES.

13.8.92 **Tax on savings — getting it right.** The Revenue's attitude to cases of incorrect registration for gross payment of interest is explained. See 8.2 BANKS.

12.11.92 **Enhanced capital allowances for machinery, plant and buildings.** First-year and initial allowances are reintroduced generally for a limited period. See 10.3, 10.13, 10.18, 10.27 CAPITAL ALLOWANCES.

18.11.92 **Scholarship and apprenticeship schemes at universities and technical colleges.** Revenue Statement of Practice SP 4/86 is amended and reprinted with an increased exemption limit. See 29.26 EXEMPT INCOME.

21.12.92 **Enhanced capital allowances for machinery, plant and buildings.** The temporary reinstatement of initial allowances for agricultural and industrial buildings (see Revenue Press Release 12 November 1992 above) is also to apply to buildings purchased unused from traders in buildings. See 10.3, 10.13 CAPITAL ALLOWANCES.

21.1.93 **Deposit interest: amendment to tax deduction at source rules.** Deduction will not be required from interest paid by deposit-takers other than banks to certain non-ordinarily resident individuals. See 8.2 BANKS.

21.1.93 **Taxation of in-house benefits in kind.** The Revenue explain how they intend to deal with such benefits following the decision in *Pepper v Hart*. See 75.13 SCHEDULE E.

17.2.93 **Remission of tax in cases where information has not been used within a reasonable time.** The income limits for remission are increased. See 56.6 PAYMENT OF TAX.

16.3.93 **Council tax: income tax and corporation tax implications.** See 68.15 SCHEDULE A, 71.54, 71.78 SCHEDULE D, CASES I AND II, 75.7, 75.10(*a*), 75.29 SCHEDULE E.

24.3.93 **Charitable giving: covenants.** Guidance is given concerning revocable covenants. See 15.17(*a*) CHARITIES.

1.4.93 **Payments to the Inland Revenue by electronic funds transfer** are treated as received one working day before value is received by the Revenue. See 56.1 PAYMENT OF TAX.

14.4.93 **New statutory exemption for relocation packages.** Aspects of the operation of the provisions introduced by *FA 1993*, and of the phasing out of the previous extra-statutory concessions, are explained. See 75.33 SCHEDULE E.

19.5.93 **Interest and penalties on employers' and contractors' deductions.** Deadlines of 19 June 1993 and 19 May 1994 are set for submission without penalty of 1992/93 and 1993/94 returns respectively. See 58.4 PENALTIES.

23.7.93 **Tax repayments to EC resident companies.** Claims to repayment supplement may be made following the *Commerzbank AG* decision. See 41.2 INTEREST ON OVERPAID TAX.

17.12.93 **Capital allowances for machinery and plant.** The *FA 1994* provisions restricting the availability of allowances, and requiring notification of expenditure, are explained. See 10.25, 10.26 CAPITAL ALLOWANCES.

2.2.94 **Tax treatment of interest paid by Government departments.** Following the decision in *Esso Petroleum Co Ltd v MOD*, no steps will be taken to seek out, nor make further payments to, the recipients of payments of interest other than on securities before the date of the decision. See 70.1 SCHEDULE C.

31.3.94 **Self-assessment — transition to current year basis: anti-avoidance provisions** to counter movements between accounts after 31 March 1994 are to be introduced. See 72.4 SCHEDULE D, CASE III.

11.7.94 **Charities: tax treatment of lotteries.** Provisions exempting certain lottery income for 1995/96 onwards were introduced in the 1995 Finance Bill. Exemption for earlier years continues to be granted on a concessional basis. See 15.7(iii) CHARITIES.

21.7.94 **Company cars — cash alternatives.** The legislation introduced in the 1995 Finance Bill is aimed at preventing avoidance of national insurance contributions by the offer of cash alternatives to company car provision. See 75.15 SCHEDULE E.

8.9.94 **Individuals coming to the UK to take up employment — administrative measures.** Procedures following arrival in the UK are explained. See 64.5 RESIDENCE, ORDINARY RESIDENCE AND DOMICILE.

29.11.94 **Self-assessment.** Deduction of tax from payments to non-resident landlords will not be required where the tax is included in payments on account made under self-assessment arrangements. See 68.24 SCHEDULE A.

29.11.94 **Taxation of income from property and self-assessment.** The renewals basis or wear and tear allowances will continue to be available for furnished lettings under the new Schedule A regime introduced by *FA 1995*. See 68.8 SCHEDULE A.

39 Inland Revenue Press Releases

29.11.94 **Self-assessment: transition to current year basis — anti-avoidance provisions.** Guidance on the Revenue interpretation of certain expressions used in the legislation is contained in the commentary published with the draft legislation. See 71.20 SCHEDULE D, CASES I AND II.

29.11.94 **Investment managers.** Extra-statutory concession B40 may continue to apply until 5 April 2005 in certain cases which fall outside the *FA 1995* provisions limiting the chargeable income of non-residents. See 51.1 NON-RESIDENTS AND OTHER OVERSEAS MATTERS.

4.1.95 **Trusts and settlements — simplification of income tax 'benefit to settlor' rules.** See 81.13 *et seq.* SETTLEMENTS.

10.2.95 **Schedule A transitional proposals.** Guidance notes on the introduction of the *FA 1995* provisions. See 68.22 SCHEDULE A.

17.2.95 **Finance Bill 1995, Clause 114, 23 Schedule: investment managers.** See 51.6 NON-RESIDENTS AND OTHER OVERSEAS MATTERS.

20.2.95 **The Stock Exchange alternative investment market (AIM) — tax reliefs for investment in companies joining AIM.** Shares in such companies are treated as unquoted for tax purposes. See 26.5 ENTERPRISE INVESTMENT SCHEME, 29.21(i) EXEMPT INCOME, 46.18 LOSSES, 91.3 VENTURE CAPITAL TRUSTS.

31.3.95 **Personal equity plans.** Draft regulations permitting investment in certain corporate bonds are published. See 29.21 EXEMPT INCOME.

16.5.95 **Personal incidental expenses — guidance for employers** on the practical application of the *FA 1995* provisions. See 75.43 SCHEDULE E.

14.7.95 **Profit-related pay — interest and penalties** may apply for late and incorrect returns for 1994/95 and subsequent years. See 75.31 SCHEDULE E.

17.7.95 **Withdrawal of tax relief for approved executive share option schemes.** It was announced that all income tax reliefs under such schemes were to be withdrawn from 17 July 1995, but see now Revenue Press Release 27 July 1995 (below). See 82.39 SHARE INCENTIVES AND OPTIONS.

27.7.95 **Approved executive share option schemes.** Income tax reliefs under such schemes are withdrawn for options granted on or after 17 July (subject to transitional provisions) (replacing Revenue Press Release 17 July 1995 (above)). See 82.39 SHARE INCENTIVES AND OPTIONS.

14.9.95 **Venture capital trusts.** Inadvertent breaches of the 70% 'qualifying holdings' limit will not generally result in withdrawal of approval. See 91.2 VENTURE CAPITAL TRUSTS.

19.10.95 **Insurance commissions rebated to ordinary policyholders will not be taxed.** Statement of Practice SP 5/95 is to be revised. See 71.64 SCHEDULE D, CASES I AND II.

28.11.95 **Tax exemption for sickness or unemployment insurance payments (REV 6).** Certain benefits meeting specified existing obligations are in practice tax free. See 29.12 EXEMPT INCOME, 71.64 SCHEDULE D, CASES I AND II, 75.37 SCHEDULE E.

28.11.95 **Taxation of car and mileage allowances (REV 32).** FPCS rates may be used in calculating taxable profits and allowable deductions in respect of business use of an employee's private car. See 75.43 SCHEDULE E.

21.3.96 **Carry-back of personal pension contributions made in 1996/97.** Contributions carried back to 1995/96 will be taken into account in determining the interim payment required for 1996/97. See 78.17 SELF-ASSESSMENT.

1.4.96 **Interest and repayment interest — effective date of payment of tax and NICs.** See 56.1 PAYMENT OF TAX.

4.4.96 **Self-assessment — early settlement of a deceased taxpayer's tax affairs or those of a trust or estate following cessation.** Returns will, on request, be issued before the end of the tax year, and early written confirmation given if there is to be no enquiry into the return. See 78.5, 78.11 SELF-ASSESSMENT.

29.4.96 **Bovine spongiform encephalopathy (BSE) and farm stock taking valuations.** The Revenue approach is clarified, and special arrangements instituted in the short term. See 71.57 SCHEDULE D, CASES I AND II.

30.4.96 **Tax treatment of premiums and benefits under locum and fixed practice expenses insurance policies.** The Revenue now consider premiums under such policies allowable, and benefits taxable. See 71.64 SCHEDULE D, CASES I AND II.

31.5.96 **Disclosure and discovery under self-assessment.** A Revenue paper discusses disclosure requirements, with particular reference to the possibility of a discovery assessment. See 78.5, 78.15 SELF-ASSESSMENT.

14.6.96 **Employers' and contractors' end-of-year returns.** Penalties for late 1995/96 returns may be subject to mitigation. See 58.4 PENALTIES.

29.7.96 **Self-assessment — provision of information from taxpayer statements of account to authorised agents.** See 79.1 SELF-ASSESSMENT—KEY DATES.

3.9.96 **Self-assessment — Inland Revenue unveil new tax returns for next year.** See 78.1 SELF-ASSESSMENT.

27.1.97 **Self-assessment: payments on account for 1996/97 — calculation of interest following late issue of statements on account.** Interest will in certain cases run from 30 days after the issue of notification of the amount due. See 78.22 SELF-ASSESSMENT.

4.2.97 **Self-assessment — valuations for capital gains tax.** The Revenue will, on request, check asset valuations. See 78.5 SELF-ASSESSMENT.

4.2.97 **Old life insurance policies: insurer stopping collection of premiums — new extra-statutory concession.** Such a change will, in certain circumstances, not be treated as an alteration of the policy for tax purposes. See 45.13 LIFE ASSURANCE POLICIES.

12.12.97 **Self-assessment — provision of information from taxpayer statements of account to authorised agents.** See 78.17 SELF-ASSESSMENT.

18.12.97 **Taxation of offshore personal portfolio bonds and residence of transferors of assets.** The Revenue explain how they propose to deal with the taxation of transfers of assets following the House of Lords' decision in *CIR v Willoughby.* See 3.8 ANTI-AVOIDANCE.

39 Inland Revenue Press Releases

3.2.98 **Self-assessment deadline**. The circumstances in which a penalty for late delivery of a return may be waived are outlined. See 78.26 SELF-ASSESSMENT.

23.2.98 **Ministers clarify scope of Scottish Parliament's tax varying power.** See 1.3 ALLOWANCES AND TAX RATES.

17.3.98 **Taxation of life insurance policy holders.** The annual charge on personal portfolio bonds will not commence before 6 April 1999. See 45.13 LIFE ASSURANCE POLICIES.

25.3.98 **Tax treatment of expenditure on films.** A revised Statement of Practice replaces those previously applicable with effect from 25 March 1998 (subject to transitional arrangements). See 71.58 SCHEDULE D, CASES I AND II.

31.3.98 **Inland Revenue launch 'faster working' scheme for their self-assessment enquiries.** See 78.11 SELF-ASSESSMENT.

12.5.98 **Increased capital allowances for small and medium-sized businesses in Northern Ireland**. Provisional claims to 100% first-year allowances may be made in advance of the appointed day for claims to be validly made. See 10.27 CAPITAL ALLOWANCES.

16.7.98 **Personal portfolio bonds — publication of draft regulations.** See 45.13 LIFE ASSURANCE POLICIES.

31.7.98 **Eighty countries eligible for millennium Gift Aid announced.** See 15.21 CHARITIES.

4.8.98 **Pension schemes and self-assessment for 1997/98 and 1998/99.** Tax returns will be sent to 20% of pension scheme trustees for 1997/98, and to all such trustees for 1998/99. See 78.4 SELF-ASSESSMENT.

1.9.98 **The construction industry scheme trading electronically.** An outline is given of how electronic data interchange will be used. See 21.7 CONSTRUCTION INDUSTRY TAX SCHEME.

23.10.98 **Construction industry tax scheme: type of certificate issued to limited companies.** Guidance is given on the conditions for issue of the CIS5 (previously 714C) rather than the CIS6 (previously 714P) certificate under the new scheme. See generally 21.4 CONSTRUCTION INDUSTRY TAX SCHEME.

20.1.99 **Interest factor tables** for interest on overpaid and unpaid tax are published by the Revenue. See 6.6 BACK DUTY, 41.2 INTEREST ON OVERPAID TAX, 42.2 INTEREST AND SURCHARGES ON UNPAID TAX.

5.3.99 **Employees to get help with uniform cleaning costs.** Fire service and healthcare workers are entitled to flat rate allowances. See 75.25 SCHEDULE E.

9.3.99 **Help for green transport — revised Concession A66 (IR 5).** Revenue extra-statutory concession A66 (employees' late night travel home) is extended to provision of transport home following a breakdown of car-sharing arrangements, and tax-free allowances introduced for cyclists. See 75.43 SCHEDULE E.

9.3.99 **New choice for taxpayers — returns via the Internet.** The planned extension of the use of electronic communication is outlined. (Joint Press Release with Customs and Excise.) See 35.12 INLAND REVENUE: ADMINISTRATION.

11.3.99 **Interest factor tables** for interest on overpaid and unpaid tax are published by the Revenue. See 6.6 BACK DUTY, 41.2 INTEREST ON OVERPAID TAX, 42.2 INTEREST AND SURCHARGES ON UNPAID TAX.

1.4.99 **Trusts and estates in administration: revised extra-statutory concessions.** Revenue Concessions A14, A93, B18 and D40 are revised. See 22.3 DECEASED ESTATES, 81.5 SETTLEMENTS.

28.5.99 **New deal for the unemployed.** Certain payments made in 1997/98 and 1998/99 are to be treated as tax-free. See 83.4 SOCIAL SECURITY.

7.7.99 **Construction industry tax scheme.** Special arrangements are made for the first few weeks of the new scheme. See 21.1 CONSTRUCTION INDUSTRY TAX SCHEME.

15.7.99 **Construction industry tax scheme — transitional arrangements.** Further arrangements are made for the period to 5 November 1999. See 21.1 CONSTRUCTION INDUSTRY TAX SCHEME.

20.7.99 **Tax provisions move closer to accounting practice.** The Revenue accept certain decisions moving the tax treatment of provisions closer to accounting practice. See 71.40, 71.49, 71.78, 71.79(*b*), 71.83 SCHEDULE D, CASES I AND II.

23.9.99 **Personal services provided through intermediaries.** The Revenue publish details of new rules to be included in *FA 2000* to 'tackle tax avoidance' using service companies and similar intermediaries such as partnerships. See 61.1, 61.12 PERSONAL SERVICE COMPANIES ETC..

9.11.99 **Rate of tax on savings income and chargeable gains.** The starting rate is to be applied to savings income with retrospective effect from 6 April 1999. See 1.9 ALLOWANCES AND TAX RATES.

9.11.99 **Personal allowance and WFTC uprating.** The 2000/01 levels for the various components of Working Families' and Disabled Person's Tax Credits are announced. See 83.6 SOCIAL SECURITY.

19.11.99 **Reform of Class 1A national insurance to include exemption of tax and NICs charges on some employee benefits.** Certain minor benefits are exempted and concession A74 extended. See 75.13(iv)(xxvii) SCHEDULE E.

23.11.99 **Cuts in red tape for life insurance companies.** New concessions are introduced. See 45.13 LIFE ASSURANCE POLICIES.

14.12.99 **Authorised mileage rate for cars, pedal cycles and motorcycles.** The FPCS rates and pedal cycle rate are unchanged for 2000/01, and a fixed motor cycle rate introduced from 6 April 2000. See 75.43 SCHEDULE E.

25.1.00 **Deregulatory change setting official rate of interest on beneficial loans in advance.** See 75.17 SCHEDULE E.

7.2.00 **Personal services provided through intermediaries — guidance.** The Revenue publish detailed guidance to assist in deciding whether a worker would have been an employee if engaged by a client directly rather than through an intermediary such as a service company or partnership. They give specific advice on 'standard contracts' said to be common to service company workers in the information technology industry engaged through agencies. See 61.4 PERSONAL SERVICE COMPANIES ETC..

39 Inland Revenue Press Releases

16.2.00 **Discounts to boost use of the internet.** Tax discounts for submitting returns via the internet and paying the tax due electronically are introduced for one year. See 55.9 PAYE, 67.3 RETURNS, 78.1 SELF-ASSESSMENT.

28.2.00 **Tax treatment of compensation for mis-sold freestanding additional voluntary contribution schemes.** By concession, certain compensation payments are exempted from tax. See 29.3 EXEMPT INCOME.

3.3.00 **New Revenue Pamphlet IR 1 published.** Concessions C2 and C3 are withdrawn from April 2001. See 18.2, 18.3 CLUBS AND SOCIETIES.

21.3.00 (BN1D) **Extra discount for employers paying tax credits.** Following Press Release 16 February 2000 above, a further £50 discount will be available where employers pay working families' or disabled person's tax credits. See 55.9 PAYE, 67.3 RETURNS.

11.4.00 **Electronic commerce — tax status of websites and servers.** The Revenue take the view that a website, or a server on which e-commerce is conducted through a website, is not of itself a permanent establishment. See 25.2, 25.3 DOUBLE TAX RELIEF.

8.5.00 **Tax exemption for compensation paid on bank accounts owned by Holocaust victims.** By concession, uprating payments to restore the purchasing power of amounts held in such accounts is exempt from income tax and death duties. See 29.13(xi) EXEMPT INCOME.

28.6.00 **More help for disabled workers: revised extra-statutory concession A59.** See 75.13(vi), 75.15, 75.43 SCHEDULE E.

25.7.00 **Ending of vocational training relief and of extra-statutory concession A64** from 1 September 2000. See 75.42 SCHEDULE E, 92.1 VOCATIONAL TRAINING RELIEF.

40 Inland Revenue Statements of Practice

Simon's Direct Tax Service H3.

The following is a summary of those Statements of Practice published in Revenue Pamphlet IR 131 (2000), or subsequently announced, which are referred to in this book.

Statements are divided into those originally published before 18 July 1978 (which are given a reference letter (according to the subject matter) and consecutive number, e.g. A34) and later Statements (which are numbered consecutively in each year, e.g. SP 6/94).

Certain Statements marked in IR 131 as obsolete continue to be referred to in the text (having been relevant within the last six years), and the original source is quoted in such cases, as it is where the Statement awaits inclusion in IR 131.

Copies of individual SP-denominated Statements are available free of charge from Inland Revenue Information Centre, SW Wing, Bush House, Strand, London WC2B 4RD (large SAE to accompany postal applications) (tel. 0207-438 6420/6425/7772).

As regards Inland Revenue internal guidance manuals, see 35.10 INLAND REVENUE: ADMINISTRATION.

A3 **Barristers: the cash basis.** Although normally assessed on a cash basis, barristers may elect to change to the earnings basis. (Obsolete from 2000/01 onwards.) See 12.1 CASH BASIS.

A4 **Partnerships: change in membership.** Where a continuation election is made it may be revoked within the original time limit for making the election. Obsolete. See 53.6 PARTNERSHIPS.

A6 **Schedule E: VAT.** For PAYE purposes, VAT is excluded from payments for services supplied by a person holding an office in the course of carrying on a trade, profession or vocation. See 55.44 PAY AS YOU EARN.

A7 **Benefits in kind and VAT.** Expenses and other benefits chargeable on an employee include VAT, if any. See 55.9 PAY AS YOU EARN, 75.13 SCHEDULE E.

A8 **Stock dividends.** The interpretation of *ICTA 1988, s 251(2)* is clarified. See 85.1 STOCK DIVIDENDS.

A9 **Schedule E assessments (1995/96 and earlier): repayment supplement.** Attribution of repayments etc. between years. See 41.2 INTEREST ON OVERPAID TAX.

A10 **Airline pilots.** Revenue practice re duties deemed to be performed in the UK. See 75.2 SCHEDULE E.

A12 **Assessing tolerance.** Where the only income is the standard Social Security pension which exceeds the single person's allowance, no direct assessment is made if the tax payable is £75 or less. Obsolete. See 5.8 ASSESSMENTS and 75.1(2) SCHEDULE E.

A13 **Completion of return forms by attorneys.** In cases of illness, infirmity or old age of the taxpayer, the Revenue will accept the signature of an attorney who has full knowledge of the taxpayer's affairs. See 67.2 RETURNS.

A16 **Living expenses abroad: Schedule D, Cases I and II.** A UK resident living abroad for the purposes of his trade etc. will have his personal living expenses allowed. See 71.90 SCHEDULE D, CASES I AND II.

40 Inland Revenue Statements of Practice

A19 **Furnished lettings: wear and tear allowance.** Revenue practice when giving wear and tear allowances is stated. (Re-classified as concession, see 38.B47 INLAND REVENUE EXTRA-STATUTORY CONCESSIONS.) See 68.8 SCHEDULE A, 74.4 SCHEDULE D, CASE VI.

A27 **Accounts on a cash basis.** (Obsolete from 2000/01 onwards.) See 12.1 CASH BASIS.

A30 **Settlements: benefit to settlor's future spouse.** An explanation is given of the concept 'possible future spouse'. See 81.25 SETTLEMENTS.

A32 **Goods taken by traders for personal consumption.** The Revenue's practice in applying *Sharkey v Wernher* is stated. See 71.83 SCHEDULE D, CASES I AND II.

A33 **Relief for interest payments: loans applied in acquiring an interest in a partnership.** Salaried partners in a professional firm may claim relief in certain circumstances. See 43.22 INTEREST PAYABLE.

A34 **Relief for interest payments: loans for purchase or improvement of land.**

(*a*) Husband and wife living together are given relief for interest paid by either even if the property is owned wholly or partly by the other.

(*b*) A person who inherits property subject to a mortgage is entitled to tax relief for mortgage interest if, and only if, the person from whom he inherited the property was so entitled.

See 43.12 INTEREST PAYABLE.

B1 **Treatment of VAT.** Guidance on the general principles applied in dealing with VAT in tax computations. See 71.93 SCHEDULE D, CASES I AND II.

B6 **Goods sold subject to reservation of title.** Such goods should normally be treated as purchases in the buyer's accounts and sales in the supplier's accounts provided that both parties agree. See 71.83 SCHEDULE D, CASES I AND II.

C1 **Lotteries and football pools.** Where part of the cost of a ticket is to be donated to a club, etc., that part is, in certain circumstances, not treated as a trading receipt. See 71.30 SCHEDULE D, CASES I AND II.

SP 3/78 **Close companies: income tax relief for interest on loans applied in acquiring an interest in a close company.** Relief continues after company ceases to be close. See 43.19 INTEREST PAYABLE.

SP 4/78 **Mining companies: expenditure on planning permission applications.** The cost of unsuccessful applications etc. will be allowed. Obsolete. See 10.49(*b*) CAPITAL ALLOWANCES.

SP 3/79 **Payment of life assurance premiums on which commission is payable to the policyholder.** (Superseded by SP 5/95 below.) See 71.64 SCHEDULE D, CASES I AND II.

SP 4/79 **Life assurance premium relief — children's policies.** This is relaxed by SP 11/79 below. See 45.4(*g*) LIFE ASSURANCE POLICIES.

SP 7/79 **Benefits in kind: cheap loans — advances for expenses** to an employee will not be a taxable benefit provided certain conditions are met. See 75.17 SCHEDULE E.

SP 8/79 **Compensation for acquisition of property under compulsory powers.** Re-imbursement of revenue costs are trading receipts. See 71.48(*d*) SCHEDULE D, CASES I AND II.

SP 11/79 **Life assurance premium relief — children's policies.** Relief will be given in certain circumstances on premiums on policies taken out by children under twelve. See 45.4(*g*) LIFE ASSURANCE POLICIES.

SP 3/80 **ICTA 1988, s 707: Cancellation of tax advantages from certain transactions in securities: procedure for clearance in advance.** The procedure is explained. See 3.2 ANTI-AVOIDANCE.

SP 4/80 **Industrial buildings allowance: industrial workshops constructed for separate letting to small businesses.** A global basis will be used for giving allowances. See 10.21 CAPITAL ALLOWANCES.

SP 6/80 **Small workshops allowance.** Clarifies eligibility for the allowance. Obsloete. See 10.21 CAPITAL ALLOWANCES.

SP 9/80 **Investigation settlements: retirement annuity relief.** Entitlement to relief where an investigation is settled by voluntary offer. See 6.11 BACK DUTY. Now replaced by SP 9/91, see below.

SP 10/80 **Mortgage interest relief: year of marriage.** Relief may be granted on more than one property. See 43.12 INTEREST PAYABLE.

SP 11/80 **Liability on gains arising on life and capital redemption policies and life annuities.** Non-residents will not be charged in certain circumstances. (Superseded by Revenue Concession B53.) See 45.13 LIFE ASSURANCE POLICIES.

SP 15/80 **Maintenance payments: payment of school fees.** Relief may be given to a parent paying fees direct to a school as part of a Court Order. See 47.10 MARRIED PERSONS.

SP 16/80 **Lorry drivers: relief for expenditure on meals** where there is a full-time travelling appointment. Also refers to subsistence etc. allowances when working temporarily away from home. See 75.43 SCHEDULE E.

SP 1/81 **Non-statutory redundancy payments** will be liable only under *ICTA 1988, s 148* in certain circumstances. Superseded by SP 1/94 below. See 19.3 COMPENSATION FOR LOSS OF EMPLOYMENT.

SP 2/81 **Contributions to retirement benefit schemes on termination of employment.** Such payments by the employer on behalf of an employee will not be chargeable under *ICTA 1988, s 148*. See 19.5, 19.6(vii) COMPENSATION FOR LOSS OF EMPLOYMENT.

SP 5/81 **Expenditure on farm drainage.** The net cost of restoring drainage is allowable as revenue expenditure. See 71.57(*b*) SCHEDULE D, CASES I AND II.

SP 6/81 **Maintenance payments under Court Orders: retrospective dating.** Payments before the date of the Order can be taken into account for tax purposes under certain circumstances. The practice ceases for Orders made or varied after 30 June 1988. See 47.10 MARRIED PERSONS.

40 Inland Revenue Statements of Practice

SP 10/81 **Payments on account of disability resulting in cessation of employment.** The interpretation of 'disability' in *ICTA 1988, Sch 11 para 3* (formerly in *ICTA 1988, s 188(1)(a)*) is extended. See 19.6(i) COMPENSATION FOR LOSS OF EMPLOYMENT.

SP 11/81 **Additional redundancy payments.** Allowance under *ICTA 1988, s 90* will also apply to a partial discontinuance of a trade. See 71.54 SCHEDULE D, CASES I AND II.

SP 12/81 **Construction industry tax deduction scheme: carpet fitting** is considered to be outside the scope of the scheme. See 21.2 CONSTRUCTION INDUSTRY TAX SCHEME.

SP 1/82 **Interaction of income tax and inheritance tax on assets put into settlement.** Income of a settlement will not be treated as income of the settlor solely because the trustees have power to pay, or do pay, inheritance tax on assets put into the settlement by the settlor. See 81.16(*e*) SETTLEMENTS.

SP 5/83 **Use of Schedules in making personal tax returns.** The Revenue requirements are detailed. Obsolete. See 67.2 RETURNS.

SP 1/84 **Trade unions: provident benefits: legal and administrative expenses.** See 88.1 TRADE UNIONS.

SP 5/84 **Employees resident but not ordinarily resident in the UK: liability under Schedule E, Cases II and III.** Revenue practice on apportionment of emoluments between UK and non-UK duties of an employment is explained. See 75.2 SCHEDULE E.

SP 6/84 **Non-resident lessors: FA 1973, s 38.** The conditions under which profits of such lessors of mobile drilling rigs, etc. are exempt from tax are outlined. See 51.13 NON-RESIDENTS AND OTHER OVERSEAS MATTERS.

SP 4/85 **Income tax: relief for interest on loans used to buy land occupied for partnership business purposes.** Relief may be available where interest is paid by the partnership, and a similar practice may apply to controlling directors' loans to purchase land occupied by the company. (Obsolete.) See 43.3 INTEREST PAYABLE.

SP 6/85 **Income tax: incentive awards: calculation of the amount assessable.** The basis on which expenses are included is outlined. See 75.44(*a*) SCHEDULE E.

SP 1/86 **Capital allowances: machinery and plant: short-life assets.** Guidance is given on some practical aspects of the arrangements in *CAA 1990, ss 37, 38*. See 10.28(F) CAPITAL ALLOWANCES.

SP 2/86 **Offshore funds.** Various aspects of the legislation are clarified. See 52.3, 52.4, 52.5 OFFSHORE FUNDS.

SP 3/86 **Income tax: payments to a non-resident from UK discretionary trusts or UK estates during the administration period: double taxation relief.** A change of practice replaces extra-statutory concessions A14 and B18 in certain cases. See 22.3 DECEASED ESTATES, 81.5 SETTLEMENTS.

SP 4/86 **Scholarship and apprenticeship schemes for employees.** Certain payments to employees attending full-time educational courses are exempt from income tax. See 29.26 EXEMPT INCOME.

SP 7/86 **Business Expansion Scheme: overseas activities.** The requirement that trade(s) be carried on 'wholly or mainly in the UK' is clarified. See 26.21 ENTERPRISE INVESTMENT SCHEME (AND BES). Now superseded by SP4/87, see below.

SP 9/86 **Income tax: partnership mergers and demergers.** The application of the succession rules is explained. See 53.8 PARTNERSHIPS.

SP 1/87 **Exchange rate fluctuations.** The Revenue practice following the *Marine Midland* decision is explained. See 71.56 SCHEDULE D, CASES I AND II.

SP 3/87 **Repayment of tax to charities on covenanted and other income.** See 15.17(*f*) CHARITIES.

SP 4/87 **Business Expansion Scheme: ship chartering and overseas activities.** SP 7/86 (see above) is revised. See 26.21 ENTERPRISE INVESTMENT SCHEME (AND BES).

SP 5/87 **Tax returns: the use of substitute forms.** The conditions for acceptance of facsimile and photocopied returns and other forms are set out. See 17.5 CLAIMS, 67.2 RETURNS.

SP 9/87 **Capital allowances: hotels: FA 1978, s 38.** The Revenue interpretation of the provision of breakfast and evening meals by a qualifying hotel is set out. See 10.18 CAPITAL ALLOWANCES.

SP 2/88 **Civil tax penalties and criminal prosecution cases.** The Revenue practice as regards pursuit of such penalties is set out. See 58.10 PENALTIES.

SP 6/89 **Delay in rendering tax returns: interest on overdue tax: TMA 1970, s 88.** SP 3/88 above is revised to remove the 'reasonable excuse' waiver. See 67.2 RETURNS.

SP 8/89 (Revised) **Independent taxation: mortgage interest relief time limit for married couples' allocation of interest elections.** The normal application of Revenue discretion to extend the time limits is explained. See 43.12 INTEREST PAYABLE.

SP 3/90 **Stocks and long-term contracts.** The Revenue practice as regards bases of valuation and changes therein is explained. See 71.83 SCHEDULE D, CASES I AND II.

SP 4/90 **Charitable covenants.** Revised practices in relation to retrospective validation and escape clauses are explained. See 15.17(*c*)(*d*) CHARITIES.

SP 5/90 **Accountants' working papers.** The Revenue's approach to the use of its information powers in relation to accountants' working papers is explained. See 6.8 BACK DUTY.

SP 2/91 **Residence in the UK: visits extended because of exceptional circumstances.** Extra days spent in the UK may be ignored for certain purposes. See 64.5 RESIDENCE, ORDINARY RESIDENCE AND DOMICILE.

SP 3/91 **Finance lease rental payments.** The practice in relation to deduction of rental payments is explained. See 71.68 SCHEDULE D, CASES I AND II.

SP 4/91 **Tax returns.** The principles followed by the Revenue in designing tax returns and determining the information required in them are explained. Obsolete. See 67.1 RETURNS.

SP 7/91 **Double taxation: business profits: unilateral relief.** The practice as regards admission of foreign taxes for unilateral relief is revised. See 25.4 DOUBLE TAX RELIEF.

40 Inland Revenue Statements of Practice

SP 8/91 **Discovery assessments.** The Revenue practice as regards the making of further assessments following 'discovery' is explained. See 5.3 ASSESSMENTS.

SP 9/91 **Investigation settlements: retirement annuities and personal pension relief.** Special premium relief is given where an investigation is settled by voluntary offer. See 6.11 BACK DUTY.

SP 12/91 **Income tax: 'in the ordinary course' of banking business.** The Revenue interpretation of this expression is explained. (Replaced by SP 4/96 below.) See 23.3 DEDUCTION OF TAX AT SOURCE.

SP 13/91 **Ex gratia awards made on termination of an office or employment by retirement or death.** A revised practice, and extended system of approval, applies after 31 October 1991. See 66.12 RETIREMENT SCHEMES.

SP 14/91 **Tax treatment of transactions in financial futures and options.** The circumstances in which such transactions will be considered to constitute trading are outlined. See 71.32 SCHEDULE D. CASES I AND II.

SP 15/91 **Treatment of investment managers and their overseas clients.** The Revenue view of the application of *TMA 1970, s 78* is explained. See 51.4(*b*) NON-RESIDENTS AND OTHER OVERSEAS MATTERS.

SP 16/91 **Accountancy expenses arising out of accounts investigations.** Revenue practice on the allowance of such expenses is explained. See 71.69 SCHEDULE D, CASES I AND II.

SP 17/91 **Residence in the UK: when ordinary residence is regarded as commencing where the period to be spent here is less than three years.** See 64.6 RESIDENCE, ORDINARY RESIDENCE AND DOMICILE.

SP 1/92 **Directors' and employees' emoluments: extension of time limits for relief on transition to receipts basis of assessment.** Revenue practice is explained. Obsolete. See 75.1 SCHEDULE E.

SP 6/92 **Accident insurance policies: chargeable events and gains on policies of life insurance.** Certain accident insurance policies will no longer be considered policies of life insurance for these purposes. See 45.13 LIFE ASSURANCE POLICIES.

SP 7/92 **Profit-related pay — use of pool determination formulae** will not normally meet the scheme registration requirements after 2 August 1992. See 75.31 SCHEDULE E.

SP 9/92 **Partnerships: circumstances in which late elections will be accepted.** (Obsolete for 1997/98 onwards.) See 53.6 PARTNERSHIPS.

SP 1/93 **Tax treatment of expenditure on films and certain similar assets.** Guidance on procedural points relating to relief for film production and preliminary expenditure. (Incorporates updated guidance from SP 2/83 and SP 2/85. See now SP 1/98 below.) See 71.58 SCHEDULE D, CASES I AND II.

SP 4/93 **Deceased persons' estates: discretionary interests in residue.** Payments out of income of the residue are treated as income of the recipient for the year of payment, whether out of income as it arises or out of income arising in earlier years. See 22.3 DECEASED ESTATES.

SP 5/93 **UK/Czechoslovakia double taxation Convention.** The Convention is regarded as applying to the Czech and Slovak Republics. See 25.2 DOUBLE TAX RELIEF.

SP 15/93 **Business tax computations rounded to nearest £1,000** will be accepted from certain large businesses. See 71.28 SCHEDULE D, CASES I AND II.

SP 1/94 **Non-statutory redundancy payments.** Revenue practice following the decision in *Mairs v Haughey* is explained. Supersedes SP 1/81 above. See 19.3 COMPENSATION FOR LOSS OF EMPLOYMENT.

SP 2/94 **Enterprise investment scheme and venture capital trust scheme — location of activity.** The requirement that trade(s) be carried on 'wholly or mainly in the UK' is clarified. Replaced by SP 7/98 below. See 26.6 ENTERPRISE INVESTMENT SCHEME (AND BES), 91.3(*b*) VENTURE CAPITAL TRUSTS.

SP 3/94 **Business expansion scheme, enterprise investment scheme, capital gains tax reinvestment relief and venture capital trust scheme — loans to investors.** The requirements for denial of relief on loan-linked investments are explained. Replaced by SP 6/98 below. See 26.12, 26.27 ENTERPRISE INVESTMENT SCHEME (AND BES), 91.5 VENTURE CAPITAL TRUSTS.

SP 4/94 **Enhanced stock dividends received by trustees of interest in possession trusts.** The Revenue view on the tax treatment of such dividends is explained. See 85.6 STOCK DIVIDENDS.

SP 6/94 **Capital allowances — notification of expenditure on machinery and plant made outside the normal time limit.** The general criteria are explained. See 10.25 CAPITAL ALLOWANCES.

SP 5/95 **Taxation of receipts of insurance and personal pension scheme commissions.** The Revenue view of the taxation consequences of a number of different arrangements is set out. (Supersedes SP 3/79 above, and now superseded by SP 4/97 below.) See 71.64 SCHEDULE D, CASES I AND II.

SP 6/95 **Legal entitlement and administrative practice** in relation to repayments of tax is revised (superseding SP 1/80 above). See 56.7 PAYMENT OF TAX.

SP 7/95 **Venture capital trusts — value of gross assets.** The Revenue's general approach to the valuation of gross assets in determining whether a holding is a 'qualifying holding' is explained. (Replaced by SP 5/98 below.) See 91.3(*e*) VENTURE CAPITAL TRUSTS.

SP 8/95 **Venture capital trusts — default terms in loan agreements.** Certain event of default clauses will not disqualify a loan from being a security for the purposes of approval. See 91.2 VENTURE CAPITAL TRUSTS.

SP 1/96 **Notification of chargeability to income tax and capital gains tax for tax years 1995/96 onwards.** Employees are relieved in certain circumstances of the obligation to notify chargeability in respect of benefits, etc.. See 78.4 SELF-ASSESSMENT.

SP 2/96 **Pooled cars: incidental private use.** The Revenue interpretation of the requirement that private use of pooled vehicles be 'merely incidental' to business use is explained. See 75.15(*v*) SCHEDULE E.

SP 3/96 **ICTA 1988, s 313 — termination payments made in settlement of employment claims.** The circumstances in which a charge will not arise are clarified. See 75.34 SCHEDULE E.

SP 4/96 **Income tax — interest paid in the ordinary course of a bank's business.** The Revenue interpretation of this requirement is explained (revising SP 12/91 above). See 23.3 DEDUCTION OF TAX AT SOURCE.

SP 5/96 **PAYE settlement agreements.** The detailed operation of the scheme is explained. See generally 55.12 PAY AS YOU EARN.

SP 1/97 **The electronic lodgement service.** The Revenue operation and detailed requirements of the scheme are explained. See 67.3 RETURNS.

SP 4/97 **Taxation of commission, cashbacks and discounts.** The Revenue's views are outlined. See 71.46 SCHEDULE D, CASES I AND II.

SP 1/98 **Tax treatment of expenditure on films.** SP 1/93 (and the earlier SP 2/83 and SP 2/85) are revised and replaced. See 71.58 SCHEDULE D, CASES I AND II.

SP 2/98 **Business by telephone.** Details are given of the services available by telephone from tax offices. See 17.5 CLAIMS.

SP 5/98 **Venture capital trusts and the enterprise investment scheme — value of 'gross assets'.** The Revenue's general approach to the valuation of gross assets is explained. Replaces SP 7/95 above. See 26.5 ENTERPRISE INVESTMENT SCHEME (AND BES), 91.3(*e*) VENTURE CAPITAL TRUSTS.

SP 6/98 **Enterprise investment scheme, venture capital trusts, capital gains tax reinvestment relief and business expansion scheme — loans to investors.** The requirements for denial of relief on loan-linked investments are explained. Replaces SP 3/94 above. See 26.12, 26.27 ENTERPRISE INVESTMENT SCHEME (AND BES), 91.5 VENTURE CAPITAL TRUSTS.

SP 7/98 **Enterprise investment scheme, venture capital trusts and capital gains tax reinvestment relief — location of activity.** The requirement that trade(s) be carried on 'wholly or mainly in the UK' is clarified. Replaces SP 2/94 above. See 26.6 ENTERPRISE INVESTMENT SCHEME (AND BES), 91.3(*b*) VENTURE CAPITAL TRUSTS.

SP 8/98 **Business by telephone — East Kilbride call centre.** Details are given of the expanded services available by telephone from the call centre on an experimental basis. See 17.5 CLAIMS.

SP 1/99 **Self-assessment enquiries — TMA 1970, ss 9A, 12AC.** Where an enquiry remains open for agreement of a capital gains tax valuation, the Revenue will not take advantage of this fact to raise further enquiries which could otherwise not be made. See 78.11 SELF-ASSESSMENT.

SP 3/99 **Advance pricing agreements (APAs).** The detailed administration of the scheme of APAs relating to transfer pricing issues is explained. See 3.9 ANTI-AVOIDANCE.

41 Interest on Overpaid Tax

[*ICTA 1988, s 824; FA 1988, Sch 13 para 7; FA 1989, ss 110(5), 114(4), 158(2), 178, 179; FA 1994, ss 196, 199(2)(a), Sch 19 para 41; FA 1997, s 92; FA 1999, s 41; SI 1978 No 1117; SI 1979 No 1687; SI 1982 No 1587; SI 1985 No 563; SI 1986 Nos 1181, 1832; SI 1987 Nos 513, 898, 1492, 1988; SI 1988 Nos 756, 1278, 1621, 2185; SI 1989 Nos 1000, 1297; SI 1993 No 753; SI 1996 No 3187; SI 1997 Nos 2707, 2708*]

Cross-reference. See also 55.8 PAY AS YOU EARN.

Simon's Direct Tax Service A3.616.

41.1 1996/97 ONWARDS (SELF-ASSESSMENT)

Under self-assessment for 1996/97 and subsequent years (1997/98 and subsequent years as regards partnership businesses commenced before 6 April 1994), a repayment by the Revenue of income tax (including tax credits) paid by or on behalf of an individual, a partnership, a trust or the personal representatives of a deceased person carries interest at the rate(s) listed below. The amount by which the repayment is so increased is known as a **repayment supplement**. The interest runs from the 'relevant time' until the date on which the order for the repayment is issued by the Revenue. Repayment supplement is added in similar fashion to any repayment of a penalty imposed under any provision of *TMA 1970* (see 58 PENALTIES and 78.25–78.29 SELF-ASSESSMENT) or of a surcharge imposed under *TMA 1970, s 59C* (see 42.4 INTEREST AND SURCHARGES ON UNPAID TAX) and to any payment under *ICTA 1988, s 375(8)* equal to the amount a borrower was entitled to deduct from mortgage interest payments (see 23.13 DEDUCTION OF TAX AT SOURCE). Repayment supplement does not count as a person's income for any tax purpose. The '*relevant time*' is,

(*a*) as regards interim payments (see 78.17 SELF-ASSESSMENT) and other payments of income tax not deducted at source, the date of the payment,

(*b*) as regards income tax deducted at source, 31 January following the year of assessment for which the tax is deducted,

(*c*) as regards a penalty or surcharge, the date on which the penalty or surcharge was paid, and

(*d*) as regards a payment under *ICTA 1988, s 375(8)*, 31 January next following the year of assessment in which the mortgage interest was paid *unless* the interest was paid before 6 April 1996, in which case it is 5 April next following that year.

Income tax is deducted at source for a year of assessment for these purposes if it is so deducted (or treated as deducted) from any income, or treated as paid on any income, in respect of that year, or if it is a tax credit in respect of that year (but excluding tax deducted under PAYE (55) in respect of previous years). Repayments in respect of income tax for a year of assessment are attributed first to the final payment (see 78.19 SELF-ASSESSMENT) of income tax for that year, secondly in two equal parts to the interim payments for that year, and finally to income tax deducted at source for that year. Where a payment was made in instalments, any repayment is attributed to later instalments before earlier ones.

Rates of interest are:

4% p.a.	from 31 January 1997 to 5 August 1997
4.75% p.a.	from 6 August 1997 to 5 January 1999
4% p.a.	from 6 January 1999 to 5 March 1999
3% p.a.	from 6 March 1999 to 5 February 2000
4% p.a.	**from 6 February 2000 to**

It will be noted that rates are considerably lower than those by reference to which interest is charged on late paid tax (see 42.1 INTEREST AND SURCHARGES ON UNPAID TAX). The rates are adjusted automatically by reference to changes in the average of base lending rates of certain clearing banks, and are announced by Revenue Press Release. For details of the relationship to base rates, see *SI 1989 No 1297, reg 3AB* as inserted from 31 January 1997 by *SI 1996 No 3187.*

It is understood that a denominator of 365 is used in calculations of repayment interest regardless of whether or not a leap year is involved.

In contrast to the position prior to 1996/97 (see 41.2 below), there is no requirement that the taxpayer be resident in the UK or EC.

Repayments relating to claims under *ITA 1952, s 228* (income accumulated under trusts, see 81.12 SETTLEMENTS) are treated as repayments of tax paid for the year of assessment in which the contingency happened. The above provisions do not apply to repayments of post-war credits or amounts paid by order of a court having power to allow interest (for which see 56.2 PAYMENT OF TAX).

Although interest on tax paid otherwise than at source runs from the date the tax was paid, even if this falls before the due date, the Revenue state that they will not pay repayment supplement on any amount deliberately overpaid (Revenue Press Release 12 November 1996). This is intended to deter taxpayers from using the Revenue as a source of tax-free interest. Where a payment of tax is not set against any liability and repayment is not claimed, the payment remains on record until the next liability arises, but no repayment supplement will be given. (Revenue Tax Bulletin June 1999 p 674). As regards the date on which payment is treated as made, see 56.1 PAYMENT OF TAX and 78.24 SELF-ASSESSMENT. Repayment supplement is not paid in respect of out of date claims, since the amount repaid is regarded as an *ex gratia* payment made without acceptance of any legal liability (Revenue Claims Manual, RM 5104).

Repayment supplement applies also to Class 4 national insurance contributions (see 83.7 SOCIAL SECURITY) and to tax paid by employers under PAYE (see 55.8 PAY AS YOU EARN).

41.2 **1995/96 AND EARLIER YEARS**

The provisions described below apply where the tax repayable relates to 1995/96 and earlier years (and to 1996/97 in the case of tax repayable to a partnership commenced before 6 April 1994).

A repayment (or set-off) to an individual by the Revenue of income tax (including tax credits and tax deducted under PAYE), surtax, capital gains tax or the special charge under *FA 1968, Pt IV*, repaid more than twelve months after the year of assessment to which it relates, carries tax-free interest ('a repayment supplement'), which will not be a person's income for any tax purpose, provided that the individual was resident in the UK for that year of assessment. A payment under *ICTA 1988, s 375(8)* equal to the amount a borrower was entitled to deduct from mortgage interest payments (see 23.13 DEDUCTION OF TAX AT SOURCE) is treated for this purpose as a repayment of tax for the year of assessment in which the interest was paid. Repayment supplement applies also to Class 4 national insurance contributions (see 83.7 SOCIAL SECURITY).

The **rates of interest** are adjusted automatically by reference to changes in the average of base lending rates of certain clearing banks, and are announced in Revenue Press Releases. (Revenue Press Release 1 August 1989). The relationship to base rates was revised from 31 January 1997 (see *SI 1996 No 3187*). The rates are as follows.

6% p.a.	before 6 April 1974
9% p.a.	from 6 April 1974 to 5 January 1980
12% p.a.	from 6 January 1980 to 5 December 1982
8% p.a.	from 6 December 1982 to 5 May 1985
11% p.a.	from 6 May 1985 to 5 August 1986
8.5% p.a.	from 6 August 1986 to 5 November 1986
9.5% p.a.	from 6 November 1986 to 5 April 1987
9% p.a.	from 6 April 1987 to 5 June 1987
8.25% p.a.	from 6 June 1987 to 5 September 1987
9% p.a.	from 6 September 1987 to 5 December 1987
8.25% p.a.	from 6 December 1987 to 5 May 1988
7.75% p.a.	from 6 May 1988 to 5 August 1988
9.75% p.a.	from 6 August 1988 to 5 October 1988
10.75% p.a.	from 6 October 1988 to 5 January 1989
11.5% p.a.	from 6 January 1989 to 5 July 1989
12.25% p.a.	from 6 July 1989 to 5 November 1989
13% p.a.	from 6 November 1989 to 5 November 1990
12.25% p.a.	from 6 November 1990 to 5 March 1991
11.5% p.a.	from 6 March 1991 to 5 May 1991
10.75% p.a.	from 6 May 1991 to 5 July 1991
10% p.a.	from 6 July 1991 to 5 October 1991
9.25% p.a.	from 6 October 1991 to 5 November 1992
7.75% p.a.	from 6 November 1992 to 5 December 1992
7% p.a.	from 6 December 1992 to 5 March 1993
6.25% p.a.	from 6 March 1993 to 5 January 1994
5.50% p.a.	from 6 January 1994 to 5 October 1994
6.25% p.a.	from 6 October 1994 to 5 March 1995
7% p.a.	from 6 March 1995 to 5 February 1996
6.25% p.a.	from 6 February 1996 to 30 January 1997
4% p.a.	from 31 January 1997 to 5 August 1997
4.75% p.a.	from 6 August 1997 to 5 January 1999
4% p.a.	from 6 January 1999 to 5 March 1999
3% p.a.	from 6 March 1999 to 5 February 2000
4% p.a.	**from 6 February 2000 to**

Interest factor tables for use as ready reckoners in calculating repayment supplement are published by the Revenue and updated as rates change (although not after 5 April 1999). For computational simplicity, these treat the change from 6.25% p.a. to 4% p.a. on 31 January 1997 as applying only from 6 February 1997. (Revenue Press Release 11 March 1999).

It is understood that a denominator of 365 is used in calculations of repayment interest regardless of whether or not a leap year is involved.

The interest will run to the end of the tax month (i.e. sixth day of one calendar month to fifth day of following month) in which the repayment order is issued and will commence as follows.

Tax originally paid	*Interest commences*
More than 12 months after year of assessment	From end of year of assessment in which tax was paid
In any other case	From end of 12 months following year of assessment

Where a repayment relates to tax paid in two or more years of assessment, it shall be treated, as far as possible, as representing later rather than earlier years.

Repayments relating to claims under *ITA 1952, s 228* (income accumulated under trusts, see 81.12 SETTLEMENTS) are treated as repayment of tax paid for the year of assessment in which the contingency happened.

Repayment supplement is not paid in respect of out of date claims, since the amount repaid is regarded as an *ex gratia* payment made without acceptance of any legal liability. (Revenue Claims Manual, RM 5104).

Schedule E tax deducted under PAYE will be attributed to the year of assessment in which deducted, and repayments will be attributed to particular years according to regulations made by the Board. See Revenue Pamphlet IR 131, A9 and *SI 1975 No 1283*.

The above provisions also apply to partnerships, trusts and deceased estates, but not to repayments of post-war credits or amounts paid by order of a court having power to allow interest (for which see 56.2 PAYMENT OF TAX). They are extended to repayments of excessive clawback of life assurance premium relief, and to relief by repayment for such premiums where relief is not obtained by deduction (see 45.5, 45.1 LIFE ASSURANCE POLICIES). (Revenue Pamphlet IR 1, A51).

In *R v CIR (ex p. Commerzbank AG) QB 1991, 68 TC 252*, repayment supplement was held not to fall within the scope of double tax agreements, although on a reference to the European Court of Justice (see *68 TC 264*), the Court upheld the view that, in the case of companies resident in EC Member States, such discrimination against non-UK resident companies was prevented by the relevant Articles of the Treaty of Rome. For repayment supplement payable to non-UK EC resident companies following this decision, see Revenue Press Release 23 July 1993. By concession, repayment supplement is also added to tax repayments to non-UK EC resident individuals on the same basis as applies to UK resident individuals. The concession also applies to repayments of income tax to individuals since 12 July 1987, and equally to partnerships, trustees and personal representatives. Claims should be sent to Inland Revenue, FICO, Fitz Roy House, PO Box 46, Nottingham NG2 1BD or Claims (International), St John's House, Merton Road, Bootle, Merseyside L69 9BB (to the latter address in the case of claims relating to repayments made by other offices). (Revenue Pamphlet IR 1, A82 as revised).

See also 55.8 PAY AS YOU EARN.

41.3 UNAUTHORISED DEMANDS FOR TAX

There is a general right to interest under *Supreme Court Act 1981, s 35A* in a case where a taxpayer submits to such an unauthorised demand, provided that the payment is not made voluntarily to close a transaction (*Woolwich Equitable Building Society v CIR HL 1992, 65 TC 265*). (*Note.* The substantive decision against the Revenue which gave rise to the repayment was subsequently upheld in the HL. See *R v CIR (ex p. Woolwich Equitable Building Society) HL 1990, 63 TC 589*.)

41.4 REVENUE ERROR

The Revenue have published a Code of Practice (No 1, available from local tax offices) setting out the circumstances in which they will consider paying a repayment supplement on money owed to the taxpayer for any period during which there has been undue delay on the part of the Revenue. See 35.8 INLAND REVENUE: ADMINISTRATION.

41.5 OVER-REPAYMENTS

Where a repayment supplement has been overpaid it may be recovered by an assessment under Schedule D, Case VI. See 56.8 PAYMENT OF TAX and 78.34 SELF-ASSESSMENT.

42 Interest and Surcharges on Unpaid Tax

Cross-references. See also 55.8 PAY AS YOU EARN.

Simon's Direct Tax Service A3.1320 *et seq.*.

42.1 1996/97 ONWARDS (SELF-ASSESSMENT) AND ASSESSMENTS RAISED AFTER 5 APRIL 1998

The provisions of *TMA 1970, s 86*, as amended for self-assessment and described below, apply in respect of income tax (and capital gains tax) for 1996/97 and subsequent years (1997/98 and subsequent years as regards partnership businesses commenced before 6 April 1994), i.e. under self-assessment, **and also** for 1995/96 and earlier years where the tax is charged by an assessment first raised after 5 April 1998. [*FA 1995, s 110(2)*]. Where these provisions have effect, *TMA 1970, s 88* (interest on tax recovered to make good loss of tax due to taxpayer's fault — see 6.6 BACK DUTY) does not have effect. [*FA 1996, Sch 18 paras 4, 17(3)(4)*]. Tax paid more than 28 days after the due date is also subject to a surcharge, with an additional surcharge where payment is more than six months late (see 42.4 below).

Interest is charged by the Revenue on late payments of income tax, whether they be interim payments or a balancing payment (see 78.17, 78.19 SELF-ASSESSMENT) or tax payable under an assessment made by the Revenue or as a result of a Revenue amendment to a self-assessment following an enquiry (see 78.13 SELF-ASSESSMENT). Interest accrues from the 'relevant date' (even if a non-business day) to the date of payment. For the two interim payments under 78.17 SELF-ASSESSMENT, the '*relevant dates*' are the due dates, i.e. 31 January in the year of assessment and the following 31 July. In any other case, the '*relevant date*' is 31 January following the year of assessment (with the one statutory exception that where the due date of a final payment is deferred until three months after notice is given to deliver a return — see 78.19 SELF-ASSESSMENT — the relevant date is identically deferred). Where the due date for payment is later than the relevant date, either under the circumstances in 78.20 SELF-ASSESSMENT or because a successful application is made to postpone tax on a pre-1996/97 assessment (see 56.2 PAYMENT OF TAX), this does *not* alter the relevant date for interest purposes.

There are provisions to remit interest charged on interim payments to the extent that an income tax repayment is found to be due for the year. There are also provisions covering the situation where a taxpayer makes a claim to dispense with or reduce his interim payments (see 78.17 SELF-ASSESSMENT) and the total income tax liability for the year is found to be such that interim payments should have been made or should have been greater. Interest is chargeable as if each interim payment due had been equal to half the current year's liability or half the previous year's liability, whichever is less.

[*TMA 1970, s 86; FA 1995, s 110; FA 1996, s 131, Sch 18 paras 3, 17(1)(2)*].

In practice, where a self-assessment return is submitted by 30 September for calculation by the Revenue of the tax due (see 78.6 SELF-ASSESSMENT), the relevant date is deferred until 30 days after notification of the liability to the taxpayer if this occurs later than 31 December following the tax year (Revenue Self-Assessment Manual — Interest, penalties and surcharge section — para 1.2.1), and see 42.9 below re executors.

As regards the date on which payment of tax is treated as made, see 56.1 PAYMENT OF TAX and 78.24 SELF-ASSESSMENT.

Rates of interest are:

8.5% p.a. from 31 January 1997 to 5 August 1997
9.5% p.a. from 6 August 1997 to 5 January 1999
8.5% p.a. from 6 January 1999 to 5 March 1999
7.5% p.a. from 6 March 1999 to 5 February 2000
8.5% p.a. from 6 February 2000 to

See 42.2 below for earlier rates, which will still apply under these provisions where an assessment for 1994/95 or an earlier year is raised after 5 April 1998.

Interest charges are calculated automatically and, however small, will appear on taxpayer statements of account under self-assessment. There is no *de minimis* limit for charging interest. It will be noted that the above rates are greater than those by reference to which interest is paid by the Revenue (see 41.1 INTEREST ON OVERPAID TAX). The rates are adjusted automatically by reference to changes in the average of base lending rates of certain clearing banks, and are announced by Revenue Press Release. For the relationship to base rates, see *SI 1989 No 1297, reg 3* as substituted from 31 January 1997 by *SI 1996 No 3187*.

It is understood that a denominator of 366 is used in calculations of such interest regardless of whether or not a leap year is involved.

Interest is also chargeable on late payment of surcharges (see 42.4 below) and penalties (see 78.25 SELF-ASSESSMENT). [*TMA 1970, ss 59C(6), 103A; SI 1989 No 1297, reg 3; SI 1998 Nos 310, 311*].

Interest is payable gross and recoverable (as if it were tax charged and due and payable under the assessment to which it relates) as a Crown debt; it is not deductible from profits or income [*TMA 1970, ss 69, 90*] and is refundable to the extent that tax concerned is subsequently discharged (and any repayment may be treated as a discharge for this purpose). [*TMA 1970, s 91; FA 1996, Sch 18 para 4(2), para 17(3)(4)*].

Transitional cessation adjustments. Where a business which commenced before 6 April 1994 ceases trading in 1997/98 or 1998/99, the inspector may direct that the 1995/96 and 1996/97 assessments (in the case of a cessation in 1998/99, only the 1996/97 assessment) be revised to the actual profits arising in the year(s) of assessment (see 71.24 SCHEDULE D, CASES I AND II). By concession, where an interest charge under *TMA 1970, s 86* would otherwise arise as a result of the adjustments required following such a direction, including increased payments on account required for 1996/97 and/or 1997/98, such interest will not normally be sought. The concession does not apply to interest arising in relation to any of those years for any other reason. (Revenue Pamphlet IR 1, A98).

Interest is also charged on Class 4 national insurance contributions (see 83.7 SOCIAL SECURITY) and to tax paid by employers under PAYE (see 55.8 PAY AS YOU EARN).

Simon's Direct Tax Service. See **E1.825**.

42.2 **ASSESSMENTS FOR 1995/96 AND EARLIER YEARS RAISED BEFORE 6 APRIL 1998**

The provisions of *TMA 1970, s 86* described below, and in 42.3, apply where the tax payable relates to **1995/96 and earlier years** (and to 1996/97 in the case of tax payable by a partnership commenced, or deemed to commence, before 6 April 1994). However, they do *not* apply where an assessment for 1995/96 or earlier is made on or after 6 April 1998.

For notices of assessment for Schedules A, C, D and E and to excess liability on taxed investment income, if tax is not paid on the date it becomes due and payable (see 56.1 PAYMENT OF TAX), interest is chargeable from that date (even if it is a non-business day) on *each assessment*. [*TMA 1970, s 86(1)(2)(5)(6) as amended; SI 1993 No 753*].

Interest under *section 86* applies also to Class 4 national insurance contributions (see 83.7 SOCIAL SECURITY).

Rates of interest are adjusted automatically by reference to changes in the average of base lending rates of certain clearing banks, and are announced in Revenue Press Releases. (Revenue Press Release 1 August 1989). The relationship to base rates was revised from 31 January 1997 (see *SI 1996 No 3187*). The rates are as follows.

6%p.a.	from 19 April 1969 to 30 June 1974
9%p.a.	from 1 July 1974 to 31 December 1979
12%p.a.	from 1 January 1980 to 30 November 1982
8% p.a.	from 1 December 1982 to 30 April 1985
11% p.a.	from 1 May 1985 to 5 August 1986
8.5% p.a.	from 6 August 1986 to 5 November 1986
9.5% p.a.	from 6 November 1986 to 5 April 1987
9% p.a.	from 6 April 1987 to 5 June 1987
8.25% p.a.	from 6 June 1987 to 5 September 1987
9% p.a.	from 6 September 1987 to 5 December 1987
8.25% p.a.	from 6 December 1987 to 5 May 1988
7.75% p.a.	from 6 May 1988 to 5 August 1988
9.75% p.a.	from 6 August 1988 to 5 October 1988
10.75% p.a.	from 6 October 1988 to 5 January 1989
11.5% p.a.	from 6 January 1989 to 5 July 1989
12.25% p.a.	from 6 July 1989 to 5 November 1989
13% p.a.	from 6 November 1989 to 5 November 1990
12.25% p.a.	from 6 November 1990 to 5 March 1991
11.5% p.a.	from 6 March 1991 to 5 May 1991
10.75% p.a.	from 6 May 1991 to 5 July 1991
10% p.a.	from 6 July 1991 to 5 October 1991
9.25% p.a.	from 6 October 1991 to 5 November 1992
7.75% p.a.	from 6 November 1992 to 5 December 1992
7% p.a.	from 6 December 1992 to 5 March 1993
6.25% p.a.	from 6 March 1993 to 5 January 1994
5.5% p.a.	from 6 January 1994 to 5 October 1994
6.25% p.a.	from 6 October 1994 to 5 March 1995
7% p.a.	from 6 March 1995 to 5 February 1996
6.25% p.a.	from 6 February 1996 to 30 January 1997
8.5% p.a.	from 31 January 1997 to 5 August 1997
9.5% p.a.	from 6 August 1997 to 5 January 1999
8.5% p.a.	from 6 January 1999 to 5 March 1999
7.5% p.a.	from 6 March 1999 to 5 February 2000
8.5% p.a.	**from 6 February 2000 to**

[*FA 1989, ss 178, 179; SI 1974 No 966; SI 1979 No 1687; SI 1982 No 1587; SI 1985 No 563; SI 1986 Nos 1181, 1832; SI 1987 Nos 513, 898, 1492, 1988; SI 1988 Nos 756, 1278, 1621, 2185; SI 1989 Nos 1000, 1297; SI 1996 No 3187; SI 1997 Nos 2707, 2708*].

Interest factor tables for use as ready reckoners in calculating interest on overdue tax are published by the Revenue and updated as rates change (although not after 5 April 1999). For computational simplicity, these treat the change from 6.25% p.a. to 8.5% p.a. on 31 January 1997 as applying only from 6 February 1997. (Revenue Press Release 11 March 1999).

It is understood that a denominator of 366 is used in calculations of such interest regardless of whether or not a leap year is involved.

See under 56.1 PAYMENT OF TAX for the date on which tax is treated as having been paid, and under 56.3 PAYMENT OF TAX for collection.

The provisions of *TMA 1970, ss 69, 90, 91* apply as they do under 42.1 above.

42.3 **ASSESSMENTS (OR AMENDMENTS) AGAINST WHICH APPEAL IS MADE**

On application by the taxpayer, in relation to an appeal against an assessment (other than a self-assessment), or against an amendment of a self-assessment, the inspector may agree (or the Commissioners may determine) that part of the tax charged which may be postponed (see 56.2 PAYMENT OF TAX). Any tax which is *not postponed* then becomes due and payable as if it were charged by an assessment or amendment notice of which was issued on the date of the determination or agreement and against which there had been no appeal. On the determination of the substantive appeal, any *postponed tax* or *extra tax* becomes due and payable as if it were tax charged by an assessment or amendment notice of which was issued on the date on which the inspector issues to the appellant a notice a notice of the total amount payable in accordance with the determination, and against which there had been no appeal. [*TMA 1970, s 55(3)(6)(9); FA 1989, s 156(2); FA 1994, ss 196, 199, Sch 19 para 18(2)*].

For assessments raised before 6 April 1998 for 1995/96 and/or earlier years, interest on postponed and non-postponed tax and, for notices of assessment issued after 30 July 1982, on an increased liability following settlement of the appeal, then runs from a 'reckonable date' which is the date on which the tax becomes due and payable (see 56.2 PAYMENT OF TAX) *unless* that date is later than the date given by the following Table, in which case the reckonable date is the later of the date given by the Table and the date on which the tax under the assessment would have been due and payable had there been no appeal against it (any additional tax being treated as if it had been charged by the original assessment) (see 56.1 PAYMENT OF TAX). The Table referred to above is as follows.

Description of tax	*Latest date*
Income tax under Schedules A or D	1 July following the end of the year of assessment.
Higher rate tax and investment income surcharge on income taxed at source (other than under PAYE)	for tax in respect of 1980/81 and later years, 1 June following the December after the end of the year for which assessed (for tax in respect of years before 1980/81, 1 January following the end of the year for which assessed).
Capital gains tax	for tax in respect of 1980/81 and later years, 1 June following the December after the end of the year for which assessed (for tax in respect of years before 1980/81, 1 January following the end of the year for which assessed).

See under 70 SCHEDULE C for related provisions. [*TMA 1970, s 86; FA 1989, s 156(1)*]. For Schedule E assessments, the reckonable date is strictly 14 days after the first application by the Collector for payment, but it is understood that, in the event of an appeal, the due date is recalculated to 14 days after the issue of a fresh demand note.

Example

Mr X has a business assessable under Schedule D, Case I. On 25 November 1995 he receives an estimated assessment for 1995/96 showing a tax liability of £21,000. He appeals on 20 December and also applies for postponement of tax of £5,000 which is agreed by the inspector on 14 January 1996. He pays the first instalment of tax £8,000 (one-half) on 1 March 1996 and the second instalment on 1 July 1996. The appeal is determined by the Commissioners on 31 July 1996 and on 5 August 1996 the inspector issues notice of the total tax payable of £23,000 (an increase of £2,000). Mr X pays the amount outstanding, £7,000, on 30 September 1996.

The dates of consequence are as follows

(i)	Due dates of payment had there been no appeal	One-half on 1 January 1996 One-half on 1 July 1996
(ii)	Revised due dates of payment of non-disputed sum (£16,000) and dates from which interest will run	One-half (£8,000) on 13 February 1996 (30 days after agreement) One–half (£8,000) on 1 July 1996
(iii)	Due date of determined balance —£7,000	4 September 1996 (30 days after notice of tax payable)
(iv)	Date from which interest will run on determined balance	1 July 1996 (the 'reckonable date')

Note. The due date of the first non-disputed payment of £8,000 is also postponed (from 1 January to 13 February 1996). Although the tax in dispute is not payable until 4 September 1996, interest will run (on both the tax postponed and the increase) from the previous 1 July until paid. The total interest payable is thus

$$8{,}000 \times \frac{17}{366} \times 6.25\% = \quad 23.22$$

$$7{,}000 \times \frac{91}{365} \times 6.25\% = \quad 109.08$$

$$£132.30$$

Interest on tax becoming due after determination of an appeal by the Courts. Any outstanding tax charged in accordance with the Commissioners' decision must be paid before an appeal can be heard by the High Court, and if on the determination of the appeal further tax is found to be chargeable, it becomes due and payable thirty days from the date on which the inspector issues to the taxpayer a notice of the total amount payable. [*TMA 1970, s 56(9) as amended*]. For assessments raised before 6 April 1998 for 1995/96 and/or earlier years, interest under *TMA 1970, s 86* runs from the later of the Table date (see above) and the date on which the tax would have become due and payable if charged by the original assessment (without an appeal being made). [*TMA 1970, s 86 (3A); FA 1989, s 156(1)*]. If a taxpayer in NI exercised his right to appeal to the county court instead of to the Commissioners, the same rule applies if a case is stated for the opinion of the Court of Appeal in NI. [*TMA 1970, s 59(6) as amended*]. See now 4.3 APPEALS as regards NI appeals.

42.4 SURCHARGES ON UNPAID TAX

The provisions described below apply **for 1996/97 and subsequent years** and **also apply** in respect of assessments for 1995/96 and/or earlier years which are raised after 5 April 1998. [*FA 1995, s 109(2)*].

Where income tax (or capital gains tax) has become payable, whether under a self-assessment in accordance with *TMA 1970, s 59B* (see 78.19 SELF-ASSESSMENT) or an assessment raised by the Revenue or as a result of a Revenue amendment to a self-assessment following an enquiry (see 78.13 SELF-ASSESSMENT), and any of the tax remains unpaid more than 28 days after the due date, the taxpayer is liable to a surcharge of 5% of the unpaid tax. A further 5% surcharge is levied on any tax still unpaid more than six months after the due date. The due date is normally 31 January following the year of assessment, but see 78.19, 78.20 SELF-ASSESSMENT for exceptions. As regards a pre-1996/97 assessment first raised after 5 April 1998, the due date is 30 days after the issue of the notice of assessment, though this is deferred to the extent that any tax is postponed on appeal (see 56.1, 56.2 PAYMENT OF TAX).

Interest (at the rate in 42.1 above) will accrue on an unpaid surcharge with effect from the expiry of 30 days beginning with the date of the notice imposing the surcharge. An appeal may be made, within that same 30-day period, against the imposition of a surcharge as if it were an assessment to tax. The Commissioners may, on appeal, set aside the surcharge if it appears to them that, *throughout* the period from the due date until payment, the taxpayer had a reasonable excuse for not paying the tax. Inability to pay the tax, i.e. due to insufficient funds, is not to be regarded as a reasonable excuse. For the Revenue's general approach to what constitutes a 'reasonable excuse' for late payment, see Revenue Tax Bulletin April 1998 pp 527–529. Common examples which the Revenue might regard as reasonable are where a cheque is lost in the post or by the Revenue (although evidence may be required to show that every effort was made to pay by the due date); where a cheque is dishonoured solely through bank error (and payment made immediately after the taxpayer learned of the bank's action); serious illness of the taxpayer or a close relative or domestic partner which began shortly before the due date; or the death of a close relative or domestic partner at or around the due date. Examples of excuses *not* considered reasonable by the Revenue are the fact that the return had not been submitted; pressure of work; failure by a tax agent; not knowing how much to pay; or the absence of a reminder that the tax is due. It is, however, stressed that these are the Revenue's views, and that it is for the Commissioners to adjudicate where the taxpayer takes a different view. Although, as stated above, the 'reasonable excuse' must strictly continue throughout the period of default in payment, in practice the Revenue normally allow a further 14 days for payment to be made after the excuse has ceased (for which see also Revenue booklet SA/BK7).

See also *Steeden v Carver (Sp C 212), [1999] SSCD 283*, in which reliance on the Revenue's advice as to the practical extension of a deadline, unequivocally given, was held to be 'as reasonable an excuse as could be found'.

There are provisions to prevent a double charge where tax has been taken into account in determining the tax-geared penalties of *TMA 1970, s 7* (see 78.4 SELF-ASSESSMENT), *s 93(5)* (tax-geared penalty for failure to make return for income tax and capital gains tax; see 78.26 SELF-ASSESSMENT), *s 95* (incorrect return etc. for income tax or capital gains tax; see 58.3 PENALTIES, 78.28 SELF-ASSESSMENT) and *s 95A* (incorrect return etc. for partnerships; see 78.28 SELF-ASSESSMENT). Any such tax will not be subject to a surcharge. The Board have discretion to mitigate, or to stay or compound proceedings for recovery of, a surcharge and may also, after judgment, entirely remit the surcharge.

[*TMA 1970, s 59C; FA 1994, ss 194, 199(2)(a); FA 1995, s 109*].

No surcharge will be imposed where a taxpayer has entered into a 'Time to Pay' arrangement (see 56.3 PAYMENT OF TAX), provided that the payment proposals are received by the Revenue before the relevant surcharge date, they lead to an acceptable agreement to settle the full liability for the self-assessment year, and the terms of the arrangement are adhered to, such that it is not cancelled. (Revenue Self-Assessment Manual — Payments section — para 7.2.48).

See generally Revenue booklet SA/BK7.

42.5 COMPANIES

Special provisions apply to advance corporation tax (prior to its abolition from 6 April 1999) and to income tax deducted from payments made by a company. See Tolley's Corporation Tax.

42.6 EXCHANGE RESTRICTIONS

Where foreign income cannot be remitted to UK due to government action in the country of origin, and tax thereon is held over by agreement with the Board, interest ceases to run from the date when the Board were first in possession of relevant facts — *no interest* if that date within three months after tax due. Interest recommences from the date of any subsequent demand, but this *latter* interest remitted if payment made within three months of demand. [*TMA 1970, s 92*]. See 51.14 NON-RESIDENTS AND OTHER OVERSEAS MATTERS.

42.7 REVENUE ERROR

The Revenue have published a Code of Practice (No 1, available from local tax offices) setting out the circumstances in which they will consider waiving a charge to interest on unpaid tax where there has been undue delay on the part of the Revenue. See 35.8 INLAND REVENUE: ADMINISTRATION.

42.8 TAX LOST THROUGH FAULT OF TAXPAYER

Where an assessment is made for making good tax lost through taxpayer failure or error (previously, by fraud, wilful default or neglect of the taxpayer), the tax is chargeable with interest under *TMA 1970, s 88* and not under *TMA 1970, s 86*, at 42.2 above, from the date when the tax ought originally to have been paid. See 6.6 BACK DUTY. This no longer applies where the self-assessment interest provisions of *TMA 1970, s 86* have effect (see 42.1 above).

42.9 EXECUTORS

Executors unable to pay tax before obtaining probate may have concessional treatment so that interest on tax falling due after the date of death runs from 30 days after the date on which probate or letters of administration are obtained. (Revenue Pamphlet IR 1, A17).

42.10 VALUE ADDED TAX, INSURANCE PREMIUM TAX, LANDFILL TAX AND CLIMATE CHANGE LEVY

Interest on overdue or under-declared VAT, insurance premium tax, landfill tax or climate change levy is not allowed as a deduction for income or corporation tax purposes. [*ICTA 1988, s 827(1)(1B)(1C)(1D); FA 1994, Sch 7 para 31; FA 1996, Sch 5 para 40; FA 2000, Sch 7 para 4*].

43 Interest Payable

Cross-references. See 3.16 ANTI-AVOIDANCE; 8 BANKS; 9 BUILDING SOCIETIES; 23 DEDUCTION OF TAX AT SOURCE; 28.5 EXCESS LIABILITY for interest on loans to pay insurance premiums; 32 FUNDING BONDS for interest paid by issue of bonds; 42 INTEREST ON UNPAID TAX; 70 SCHEDULE C regarding paying and collecting agents for government stocks etc..

Simon's Direct Tax Service E1.530 *et seq.*.

Note. See Tolley's Corporation Tax under Loan Relationships for the special provisions applicable for accounting periods ending after 31 March 1996 to all profits and losses in respect of company 'loan relationships'.

The headings in this chapter are as follows.

43.1	Deduction of tax from interest payments
43.2	Business interest payable
43.3	Relief for interest paid — general
43.4	— example
43.5	Relief for interest paid — restricted categories of loan — general provisions
43.6	Loans for purchasing property as only or main residence
43.7	— temporary relief following cessation of residence
43.8	— home improvement loans
43.9	— dependent relatives, former or separated spouses
43.10	— limit on amount of loan eligible for relief
43.11	— example
43.12	— married couples
43.13	— substitution of security
43.14	— example
43.15	Loans for purchasing property let at a commercial rent
43.16	Loans for purchasing property where borrower in job-related living accommodation
43.17	Loans for purchasing property — general matters
43.18	Loans for purchasing machinery or plant
43.19	Loans for purchasing interest in close company
43.20	Loans for purchasing interest in co-operative
43.21	Loans for purchasing interest in employee-controlled company
43.22	Loans for purchasing interest in partnership
43.23	Loans to pay inheritance tax
43.24	Loans for purchasing life annuity
43.25	Exclusion of double relief

43.1 DEDUCTION OF TAX FROM INTEREST PAYMENTS

In general, tax is deductible from annual interest paid by companies but not by individuals (except on certain home mortgage loans, etc.), but see details under 23.3(ii) and 23.13 DEDUCTION OF TAX AT SOURCE. See also 8.2 BANKS and 9.3 BUILDING SOCIETIES.

43.2 BUSINESS INTEREST PAYABLE

Interest incurred wholly and exclusively for business purposes is an allowable deduction from profits assessable under Schedule D, Case I or II (including interest on money borrowed for use as capital in the business, see *ICTA 1988, s 74(1)(f)*). [*ICTA 1988, s 74(1)(m), s 817(1)(b)*]. Interest incurred wholly and exclusively for the purposes of a Schedule A business (for 1995/96 onwards, subject to transitional provisions) is similarly an allowable deduction from the profits of that business (see 68.3, 68.5 SCHEDULE A). [*ICTA*

1988, s 21(3); FA 1995, s 39]. For disallowance of interest where capital account overdrawn, see *Silk v Fletcher (Sp C 201), [1999] SSCD 220.*

Exceptions are as follows.

(i) **Interest payable to non-residents** is deductible only so far as it is payable at a reasonable commercial rate [*ICTA 1988, s 74(1)(n)*] and either

 (*a*) is paid under deduction of tax in accordance with *ICTA 1988, s 349*, see 23.3(ii) DEDUCTION OF TAX AT SOURCE (in which case the gross amount of the interest is deductible from profits, see *ICTA 1988, s 82(5)*), or

 (*b*) is contractually payable abroad (and is in fact so paid) by a UK resident sole trader or partnership either on a liability incurred for purposes of the foreign activities of the trade, etc., or in a currency other than sterling (for securities issued before 6 April 1982, in the currency of a territory outside the scheduled territories). But deduction of interest in these circumstances is not permitted if the recipient is a partner in the trade, or both payer and recipient are under common control.

 [*ICTA 1988, s 82; FA 1995, Sch 6 para 13; FA 1998, Sch 27 Pt III(4)*].

(ii) **Anti-avoidance.** Where interest is paid, no relief will be allowed, if, at any time, a scheme has been effected or arrangements made such that the sole or main benefit expected to accrue was a reduction in tax liability by means of the relief. [*ICTA 1988, s 787*]. See also *Cairns v MacDiarmid CA 1982, 56 TC 556* and *Lancaster v CIR (Sp C 232), [2000] SSCD 138.*

(iii) **'Relevant loan interest'**, see 23.13 DEDUCTION OF TAX AT SOURCE.

The restrictions in 43.3 *et seq.* below do not apply to interest deductible in computing business profits, but if interest so deductible is also allowable within those restrictions, relief may instead be claimable under *ICTA 1988, s 353*. See 43.3 below as to this. Where interest wholly and exclusively for business purposes is dealt with under *section 353* but not wholly relieved because of insufficiency of income, the unrelieved interest can be treated as a trading loss. [*ICTA 1988, s 390*]. See 46.17(*b*) LOSSES.

Where part of a borrower's main residence is used exclusively for business purposes, then by concession, for 1995/96 onwards (but reflecting pre-existing practice), a loan to buy the property may be treated as proportionately divided into two separate loans, mortgage interest relief (see 43.3 below) and relief for interest as a business (including a Schedule A business) deduction being available respectively. Where the exclusive business use occurs only sometimes (but for a significant amount of time), the concession still applies but with duration of use also taken into account in apportioning the loan. (Revenue Pamphlet IR 1, A89). See 23.13 DEDUCTION OF TAX AT SOURCE for the MIRAS (mortgage interest relief by deduction at source) position, and see Revenue Tax Bulletin August 1995 pp 229–232 for worked examples. Mortgage interest relief ceases, however, to be available after 5 April 2000.

Schedule D, Case VI. Where profits are assessable under Schedule D, Case VI, it is understood that in practice interest incurred wholly and exclusively for the purposes of earning those profits (e.g. on money borrowed to purchase properties let furnished) is an allowable deduction.

43.3 RELIEF FOR INTEREST PAID—GENERAL

Subject to the provisions in this and the following paragraphs, relief for interest may be given *for income tax purposes* for the year of assessment in which paid. For interest paid by companies within the charge to corporation tax, see Tolley's Corporation Tax. For the exclusion of double relief where the interest ranks as business interest, see 43.25 below.

43.3 Interest Payable

Subject to the restrictions in this paragraph and in 43.5 et seq. below, relief is given on interest paid. [*ICTA 1988, s 353(1); FA 1994, s 81(1)*]. The following should, however, be noted.

(i) **Interest on loan for property bought by partner for partnership use.** Before the 1995 Finance Act changes to the taxation of income from property (see 68.2 *et seq.* SCHEDULE A), there was doubt concerning the correct treatment of interest paid by a partnership, and charged in its accounts, on a loan (other than an overdraft) taken out by an individual partner to purchase land (including buildings etc.) occupied rent-free by the partnership and used for business purposes. In practice, the payment was treated as rent for the use of the land, and thus as eligible to be an allowable expense in computing partnership profits. The rental income in the individual partner's hands was then regarded as covered by the interest for which he was liable, assuming the interest would qualify for relief under 43.15 below. No deduction was allowed in computing partnership profits where no rent or interest was paid by the partnership. (Revenue Pamphlet IR 131, SP 4/85, 5 February 1985).

Following the 1995 Finance Act changes, SP 4/85 is considered obsolete. It is considered that relief as a trading expense for interest payable by the partnership on the individual's behalf would be available in the normal way. The individual's Schedule A business computation would include the interest payments made by the company on his behalf, but these would be offset by a deduction for the interest payable by the individual (which would be allowable regardless of the interest payments having been met by the partnership). The Schedule A business profit would therefore generally be nil. (Revenue Tax Bulletin June 1997 pp 437, 438).

Refusal of application of the benefit of SP 4/85 was approved (in judicial review proceedings) where a bank loan to a partnership was made in conjunction with an interest-free loan by the partnership to an individual partner to enable him to purchase land for partnership use (*R v HMIT (ex p Brumfield and Others) QB 1988, 61 TC 589*).

(ii) **Interest on loan for property bought by controlling director for company use.** The Statement of Practice referred to at (i) above also dealt with occupation by a company for business purposes of land, etc. owned by a controlling director, where the company paid the interest on a loan (other than an overdraft) taken out by the director to purchase the land. In practice, if the interest was treated as emoluments of the director, relief as an allowable expense was generally available to the company. Where the company instead paid rent, this was an allowable expense to the company, and the director could set his interest payments against the rent received under *ICTA 1988, s 355(1)(b)*. Where the company paid neither rent nor interest, no deduction would be allowed to the company for the interest paid by the director. (Revenue Pamphlet IR 131, SP 4/85, 5 February 1985).

It is now considered that relief as a trading expense for interest payable by the company on the director's behalf would be available in the normal way, and that the payments would not normally constitute either emoluments or a benefit of the director. The director's Schedule A business computation would include the interest payments made by the company on the director's behalf, but these would be offset by a deduction for the interest payable by the director (which would be allowable regardless of the interest payments having been met by the company). The Schedule A business profit would therefore generally be nil. (Revenue Tax Bulletin June 1997 pp 437, 438).

(iii) **Hire purchase charges** (the excess of the hire purchase payments over the cash price) are not interest and therefore not within this relief. (Some hire purchase agreements may specify that the whole balance of the rental after the initial payment is payable within seven days but will leave the hirer the option of paying that balance over a defined period on interest terms. At the date the option is exercised a loan is created and the interest on that loan is true interest under *section 353* and will qualify for relief if other relevant conditions are satisfied, e.g. on a residential caravan.)

No relief is given to the extent that the interest exceeds a reasonable commercial rate. [*ICTA 1988, s 353(3)(b)*].

Where interest is business interest (see 43.2 above), see 43.25 below for the exclusion of double relief, 43.2 above where property used for both residential and business purposes and 46.17 LOSSES for the treatment of unrelieved interest as a trading loss.

No relief is given if the interest is within the anti-avoidance provisions of *ICTA 1988, s 787*, see 43.2(ii) above.

Note. Where interest is 'relevant loan interest' (see 23.13 DEDUCTION OF TAX AT SOURCE) the provisions under *section 353* (above) do not apply. [*ICTA 1988, s 353(2)*].

Rate of relief and method of giving relief. Interest on certain types of loan is relieved by way of a deduction in computing total income, and thus attracts relief at marginal rates. The categories of loan in question are those for the purpose of

(A) purchasing property let at a commercial rent (not generally applicable after 1994/95 — see 43.15 below), the deduction being available only against letting income,

(B) purchasing machinery or plant (see 43.18 below),

(C) purchasing an interest in, or, where appropriate, making a loan or advance to, a close company, co-operative, an employee-controlled company or a partnership (see 43.19 to 43.22 below), or

(D) paying inheritance tax (see 43.23 below).

However, interest on the categories of loan within (I)–(III) below is relieved by way of a reduction in income tax liability and does not reduce total income. Interest within (I) or (II) below attracts relief at 20% for 1994/95, at 15% for 1995/96, 1996/97 and 1997/98, and at **10% for 1998/99 and 1999/2000**, relief being **abolished thereafter** (the applicable rate being determined by reference to the year of actual payment, regardless of when payment was due). The abolition of relief also applies to payments made before 6 April 2000 (but after 8 March 1999) either under a scheme or arrangement etc. made after 8 March 1999 for a tax-avoidance purpose or of interest not due until after 5 April 2000. For when a scheme etc. is made for a tax-avoidance purpose, see *FA 1999, s 38(5)(6)*. Interest within (III) below continues to attract relief at the basic rate of tax in force for the year of payment up to 1999/2000, relief being fixed at **23%** thereafter. The loans in question are those for the purchase of

(I) the borrower's only or main residence (see 43.6 to 43.12, and also 43.17, below),

(II) a residence intended to become the borrower's only or main residence, where the borrower lives in job-related accommodation (see 43.16 below), or

(III) a life annuity, where the loan is secured on land (see 43.24 below).

The reduction in liability is the smaller of the applicable percentage (as above) of the amount of interest eligible for relief and what would otherwise be the borrower's total income tax liability. For this purpose, 'total income tax liability' is as defined in 1.15 ALLOWANCES AND TAX RATES, except that it is before any reductions on account of personal reliefs and maintenance payments (where such items are also relieved by way of reduction in income tax liability — see 1.15 to 1.17 ALLOWANCES AND TAX RATES and 47.10 MARRIED PERSONS).

Where, for any tax year, an amount of interest is eligible for relief partly as a deduction and partly as a reduction in liability (for example, because the loan is a mixed loan or there is a change in the use of a property), it is apportioned by reference to the proportions of the amount borrowed (not the amount still outstanding) applied for different purposes and, where relevant, the different uses to which property is put from time to time.

Where particular interest payments would be eligible for relief both under (A) above and under (I) or (II) above, they will be treated as eligible under (A) above (so that relief is given by deduction) unless the borrower elects to the contrary. Such an election must take effect from the commencement of dual eligibility or from the beginning of a later tax year, remains in force until withdrawn with effect from the beginning of a tax year, and applies to all such interest payments made while it has effect. An election or withdrawal must be made by written notice, specifying the effective date, before the end of the tax year following that in which the effective date falls. See Revenue Tax Bulletin December 1994 p 173 for general commentary on the election. The provisions dealing with such dual eligibility are not relevant, and are repealed, following the repeal of the provisions at 43.15 below (interest on loans to purchase let property). For 1995/96 to 1999/2000 inclusive, a borrower who is eligible for mortgage interest relief in respect of a let property may choose each year whether to claim such relief (restricted to the applicable percentage on a maximum of £30,000) or to deduct the interest in computing the profits of the Schedule A business. As regards inclusion of the loan within MIRAS (mortgage interest relief by deduction at source), see 23.13 DEDUCTION OF TAX AT SOURCE.

[*ICTA 1988, s 353(1A)–(1H); FA 1994, s 81(2); FA 1995, s 42(2), Sch 29 Pt VIII(2); F(No 2)A 1997, s 15(1)(3); FA 1999, s 38, Sch 4 para 1; FA 2000, s 83(2)(4)*].

43.4 *Example*

Scott is a married man with the following details for 1999/2000: Schedule D, Case II £16,585, bank deposit interest (net) £640, dividend income (net) £900, investment made under enterprise investment scheme (EIS) £500, interest paid gross on a £40,000 endowment mortgage taken out some years ago for purchase of main residence £3,000, payment under charitable deed of covenant (net) £77. Scott's wife has no income.

Scott's tax liability for 1999/2000 is computed as follows.

	£
Schedule D, Case II	16,585
Bank deposit interest (gross)	800
Dividends plus tax credits	1,000
	18,385
Deduct Charges (covenanted donation) (gross)	100
Total income	18,285
Deduct Personal allowance	4,335
Taxable income	£13,950
Tax payable;	
1,500 @ 10% (starting rate)	150.00
10,650 @ 23%	2,449.50
800 @ 20%	160.00
1,000 @ 10% (Schedule F ordinary rate)	100.00
13,950	2,859.50

	£
Deduct EIS relief £500 @ 20%	100.00
	2,759.50
Deduct Mortgage interest relief: $£3,000 \times \frac{30,000}{40,000} = 2,250$ @ 10%	225.00
	2,534.50
Deduct Married couple's allowance: £1,970 @ 10%	197.00
	2,337.50
Add Basic rate tax retained on covenanted donation	23.00
Total tax liability	2,360.50
Deduct Tax suffered at source on bank deposit interest	(160.00)
Tax credits on dividends	(100.00)
Net tax liability	£2,100.50

43.5 RELIEF FOR INTEREST PAID — RESTRICTED CATEGORIES OF LOAN — GENERAL PROVISIONS

Tax relief for interest paid on private borrowings will only be granted if the loan falls within any of the categories below (and even then will not be given on overdrafts, credit card or similar arrangements). [*ICTA 1988, s 353(1)(3)(a)*].

Relief is not granted unless the loan proceeds are so applied within a reasonable time, nor if the loan proceeds are used for some other purpose first. The giving of credit can be treated as a loan. Proportionate relief is granted where part only of a debt fulfils the required conditions. [*ICTA 1988, s 367(2)–(4)*].

Relief is available on similar terms on loans replacing either prior eligible loans under 43.6, 43.15 or 43.16 below, or loans which would have been eligible but for their inclusion in the MIRAS deduction scheme (see 23.13 DEDUCTION OF TAX AT SOURCE), subject to the abolition of such reliefs after 5 April 2000. [*ICTA 1988, s 354(1)(c); FA 1999, Sch 4 para 2*]. See *Lawson v Brooks Ch D 1991, 64 TC 462* for denial of relief for loan replacing overdraft relating to expenditure otherwise eligible for relief.

For loans to persons other than building societies or local authorities, claims to relief must be supported by a statement by the lender of the date and amount of the debt, the name and address of the debtor and the interest paid in the year of assessment. [*ICTA 1988, s 366*]. See generally Revenue Tax Bulletin April 1995 p 210.

Higher rate relief. Interest payments on a loan for the purchase of

(*a*) the borrower's only or main residence (see 43.6 *et seq.* below), or

(*b*) a residence intended to become the borrower's only or main residence, where the borrower lives in job-related accommodation (see 43.16 below), or

(*c*) a life annuity, where the loan is secured on land (see 43.24 below),

for which relief is available do not attract relief from income tax at the higher rate(s). See 23.13 DEDUCTION OF TAX AT SOURCE for the application of this restriction in relation to loans within the MIRAS scheme. See 43.7 below for relief for certain bridging loans. [*ICTA*

1988, s 353(4)(5); FA 1991, s 27(1); F(No 2)A 1992, s 19(3); FA 1993, Sch 6 para 1; FA 1994, Sch 9 para 3].

See 43.3 above for further reductions, applying for 1994/95 to 1999/2000 inclusive, in the rate of tax relief for interest within (*a*) and (*b*) above, and for the abolition of such relief from 6 April 2000.

43.6 **LOANS FOR PURCHASING PROPERTY AS ONLY OR MAIN RESIDENCE**

Relief is given for interest paid **before** (generally) **6 April 2000** (see 43.3 above) on a loan for the purchase of land by a person owning an estate or interest in the property, where the property is at the time the interest is paid used as the **only or main residence of the borrower.** Where that condition is not satisfied, relief is granted if the interest is paid less than twelve months after the loan and the property is so used within that twelve months. The Inland Revenue have power to extend such periods if it appears reasonable for them to do so. [*ICTA 1988, s 354(1)(a), s 355(1)(a)(2)(3); FA 1999, Sch 4 para 2*]. For what is the main residence, see *Frost v Feltham Ch D 1980, 55 TC 10*. See generally Simon's Direct Tax Service E1.535 *et seq.*.

See 43.5 above for denial of higher rate relief (but see 43.7 below as regards certain bridging loans). See 43.3 above for the restriction of tax relief to 20% for 1994/95, 15% for 1995/96, 1996/97 and 1997/98 and 10% for 1998/99 and 1999/2000, and for the method of giving such relief.

Concessionally, temporary absences of up to one year are left out of account in determining whether a property is used as the owner's only or main residence for purposes of allowing mortgage interest relief. Up to four years are allowed if a person's employment requires him to move from a property occupied before his departure as his only or main residence for a period not expected to exceed four years and there is reasonable expectation of his return to the property. Where an individual has moved his home abroad by reason of his employment as a Crown servant (within *ICTA 1988, s 132(4)(a)*, see 75.2(i) SCHEDULE E), the concession applies without the four year time limit. The concession will also apply if a person acquires an interest in property, (e.g. by exchange of contracts) but is prevented from occupying it as his home by his move, or if a property is purchased and occupied for at least three months during a period of leave from an overseas tour of duty. The four year period will re-apply if the property is reoccupied for at least three months. If the property is let during the owner's absence, the benefit of the concession may be claimed, where appropriate, if this is more favourable than claiming a deduction in computing the Schedule A business profits (or, before 6 April 1995, relief against the lettings income) (see 43.15 below). (Revenue Pamphlet IR 1, A27).

Interest on an overdraft on the security of the deed of a residence is not allowable (*Walcot-Bather v Golding Ch D 1979, 52 TC 649*).

Additional interest charges. 'Penalty' interest charged on the early redemption of a loan within MIRAS does not qualify for relief (although this does not apply to interest charged for the whole of the month in which redemption occurs). Similarly a penalty charged for changing the terms of a loan, including a penalty for changing from a fixed to a variable rate, does not qualify for relief. However, a replacement loan need not be regarded as mixed purpose merely because, in part, it replaces such a charge. (MIRAS 30 (1995), para 10.46).

Administration fees. An allowance in respect of such fees reasonably incurred in arranging or servicing a qualifying loan will be regarded as qualifying expenditure up to £300 in respect of the first year of a loan, and up to £150 p.a. thereafter. (MIRAS 30 (1995) para 10.23).

Deceased persons. Interest paid by personal representatives of a deceased person, or by trustees of a settlement made by his will, is eligible for relief if the deceased used the property as his only or main residence at his death (or he resided in job-related living accommodation and the property was used by him as a residence or where he intended to use it in due course as his only or main residence) and, at the time the interest is paid, the property is used as the only or main residence of the widow or widower or, for interest paid before 6 April 1988, a dependent relative (or the widow or widower resides in job-related living accommodation and the property is used by such a relative or is intended to be used as the only or main residence). Interest paid after 5 April 1988 at a time when the property is used as the only or main residence of a dependent relative qualifies for relief only if the deceased died before 6 April 1988 *and* the property was so used by the dependent relative before that date. [*ICTA 1988, s 358; FA 1988, s 44(4); FA 1999, Sch 4 para 2*]. Interest paid by a person who has inherited property subject to a mortgage is allowable only if it was allowable when paid by the person from whom he inherited. See Revenue Pamphlet IR 131, A34.

House exchanges. Where houses are exchanged, so long as any loan on the old property is redeemed and a new loan on the new property taken out, the new loan (including any further loan to meet the difference in value) qualifies for relief in the normal way. (MIRAS 30 (1995) para 10.25).

Simon's Direct Tax Service. See **E1.535A**.

43.7 **Temporary relief following cessation of residence.** Relief under 43.6 above generally requires that, at the time the interest is paid, the land etc. is used as the only or main residence of the payer. Where the land etc. ceases at any time to be used as the only or main residence, and the borrower's intention at that time is to take steps within the following twelve months with a view to its disposal, that condition will be treated as satisfied until the end of those twelve months or, if earlier, until the borrower abandons his intention to dispose of the land etc. The Board may direct that the period of twelve months be extended in any particular case if it appears reasonable to do so.

Relief for interest on another loan used by the borrower for the purchase of a new property is eligible for relief to the extent it would be if no interest were payable on the loan on the former residence (in particular in relation to the qualifying limit, see 43.10 below).

[*ICTA 1988, s 355(1A)(1B); FA 1993, s 57; FA 1994, Sch 9 para 12; FA 1999, Sch 4 para 2*].

See also 75.17 SCHEDULE E for bridging loans from employers and reimbursement of interest paid.

43.8 **Home improvement loans.** Interest paid on 'home improvement loans' is also eligible for relief until 5 April 2000, subject to the general requirements described above and below, if paid on a loan made before 6 April 1988. A loan made after 5 April 1988 is deemed to have been made before 6 April 1988 if it is proved by written evidence that it is made in pursuance of an offer made by the lender before that date, such offer being either in writing or evidenced by a note or memorandum made by the lender before that date. A '*home improvement loan*' means a loan to defray money applied in improving or developing land or buildings on land, otherwise than by the erection of a new building (which is not part of an existing residence) on land which immediately before the improvement or development began had no building on it. The definition is extended to include a loan replacing, directly or indirectly, such a loan (so that a replacement loan taken after 5 April 1988 does not attract relief). [*ICTA 1988, s 354(1)(b), s 355(1)(a)(2A)–(2C); FA 1988, s 43(1); FA 1999, Sch 4 para 2*]. Where interest on such a loan continues to qualify for relief for 1994/95 to 1999/2000 inclusive, it does so at the reduced rate applicable for loans used to purchase the borrower's only or main residence, relief being given by way of reduction in tax liability (see 43.3 above).

43.9 **Dependent relatives, former or separated spouses.** Interest paid on loans made before 6 April 1988 (subject to the further condition below) is also eligible for relief until 5 April 2000 where the property is, at the time the interest is paid (or within a twelve month, or longer, period as described above), used as the only or main residence of

(i) a dependent relative (incapacitated by old age or infirmity from maintaining himself, or the widowed, separated or divorced mother) of the borrower or his spouse, the residence being provided rent-free and without other consideration, or

(ii) a separated (under Court Order, deed of separation or in circumstances likely to be permanent) or former spouse.

The further condition is that interest paid on the loan at a 'relevant time' was eligible for relief *only* because the property concerned was used as the only or main residence of *the same* dependent relative or former or separated spouse. '*Relevant time*' means either the last time when interest was paid on the loan before 6 April 1988 or, if no such interest was paid before that date, any time within twelve months (or such longer period as the Board may allow in the circumstances of a particular case) after the date on which the loan was made, except that the latter time does not apply if, at any time after the loan was made and before the property comes to be used as the only or main residence of the dependent relative, etc., the property is used for any other purpose. A loan made after 5 April 1988 is deemed to have been made before 6 April 1988 in certain circumstances, these being identical to those described above for home improvement loans. [*ICTA 1988, s 355(1)(a); FA 1988, s 44(1)–(3)(5); FA 1999, Sch 4 para 2*]. Where interest on such a loan continues to qualify for relief for 1994/95 to 1999/2000 inclusive, it does so at the reduced rate applicable for loans used to purchase the borrower's only or main residence, relief being given by way of reduction in tax liability (see 43.3 above).

43.10 **Limit on amount of loan eligible for relief.** For payments made after 31 July 1988 of '*qualifying interest*' (i.e. interest eligible for relief under 43.6–43.9 above or 43.16 below), the 'qualifying maximum' amount of loan on which interest may attract relief (currently £30,000) generally applies per residence (the '*residence basis*') rather than (as previously) per person. [*ICTA 1988, ss 356C(1), 356D(1), 367(5); FA 1988, s 41; FA 1989, s 46; FA 1990, s 71; FA 1991, s 26; FA 1992, s 10(4); FA 1993, s 55; FA 1994, s 80, Sch 9 para 7; FA 1996, s 76; FA 1997, s 57; F(No 2)A 1997, s 16; FA 1999, s 37, Sch 4 para 2*]. The residence basis does not, however, apply to a payment of qualifying interest if

(*a*) the payment is under a loan made before 1 August 1988,

(*b*) qualifying interest was payable in relation to the residence for 1 August 1988 by someone other than the person making the payment or his spouse,

(*c*) qualifying interest is payable in respect of the residence throughout the period from 1 August 1988 to the date of payment by the person making the payment or by his spouse, and

(*d*) someone other than the person making the payment or his spouse owns an estate, interest or property in the residence throughout the period in (*c*) above, and, at any time during that period, at least one such person is a person by whom qualifying interest is payable in respect of the residence at some time within the period.

A loan made after 31 July 1988 is treated as if made before 1 August 1988 if it is proved by written evidence both that it was made in pursuance of an offer made before that date and either made in writing or evidenced by a note or memorandum made by the lender before that date, and that it was used to defray money applied in pursuance of a binding contract entered into before that date. In relation to such loans, for the purpose of (*b*)–(*d*) above, the date on which interest first becomes payable (or the latest of such days where more than one loan is involved) is substituted for 1 August 1988. Where these exceptions to the residence basis apply to payments of qualifying interest under one loan, they also apply to such payments made under other loans if made by the same person or by his spouse in respect of the same residence in the same 'period'. The qualifying maximum in respect of a loan excepted as above is restricted to the lesser of £30,000 and the amount on which interest was payable immediately before 1 August 1988 or, if later, the first day for which interest is payable. Payments of interest which is qualifying interest due only to the residence in question being the only or main residence of a dependent relative or former or separated spouse of the person making the payment (but see 43.9 above for the restricted circumstances in which such interest is eligible for relief) are also excepted from the residence basis. Where payments of qualifying interest would otherwise be excepted from the residence basis, the persons liable to pay such interest may jointly elect that the residence basis should apply to all qualifying interest paid by any person in relation to the residence, such election being irrevocable. For 1996/97 to 1999/2000 inclusive, the election must be made within twelve months after 31 January following the year of assessment in which falls the first 'period' for which it is made. Previously, an election first had effect for the period *in which* it was made.

References above to a spouse do not include, except where stated, a separated spouse.

[*ICTA 1988, ss 356C, 357(1A)–(1C); FA 1988, s 42(1)(2); FA 1996, s 135, Sch 21 para 9; FA 1999, Sch 4 para 2*].

Where the residence basis does apply to a payment of qualifying interest, and all the interest payable for any 'period' in relation to a 'residence' is payable by one person, relief is available in full to the extent that the amount on which it is payable does not exceed the qualifying maximum. Where the interest payable for any 'period' in relation to a 'residence' is payable by more than one person, relief is available to each payer only to the extent that the amount on which the interest is payable by him does not exceed the 'sharer's limit' for the 'period' in his case. Prior loans on which interest is similarly eligible for relief operate to reduce the relief available in any event, and joint loans are for these purposes divided equally between the parties to the loan in determining the amount on which each pays interest. [*ICTA 1988, s 356A(1)(2), s 356D(6)–(8); FA 1999, Sch 4 para 2*].

'*Residence*' for these purposes means a building or part thereof occupied or intended to be occupied as a separate residence, or a caravan or house-boat. A building or part of a building designed for permanent use as a single residence is treated as a single residence even if it is temporarily divided into two or more parts which are, or are to be, occupied as separate residences.

A '*period*', in relation to any person, begins with any of the following:

(i) a day which is the first day for which qualifying interest is payable by any person in respect of the residence in question (notwithstanding that such interest may previously have been payable in respect of the residence);

(ii) a day immediately following a day on which any other person ceased to be liable for qualifying interest (notwithstanding that such interest continues to be payable in respect of the residence);

(iii) the beginning of a year of assessment,

and ends with the day immediately preceding the next day within (i)–(iii) above or, if sooner, with the last day for which the person concerned is liable to pay qualifying interest.

[*ICTA 1988, s 356D(2)(3); FA 1988, s 42(1); FA 1999, Sch 4 para 2*].

The '*sharer's limit*' for any period is the amount arrived at by dividing the qualifying maximum for the year of assessment in which the period falls by the number of persons liable to pay qualifying interest for the period in respect of the residence. (Interest treated as falling within 43.15 below by virtue of the dual eligibility provisions in 43.3 above was treated as qualifying interest for the purpose of determining the number of persons so liable.) If, however, any person's limit then exceeds the amount on which he actually pays interest and another person's limit falls short of the amount on which he pays interest, the limits are adjusted accordingly, any excess being eliminated and any shortfall thereby reduced. Where two or more persons have shortfalls, the total excess is apportioned between them on a pro rata basis. [*ICTA 1988, s 356A(2)–(8), s 356D(4); FA 1988, s 42(1); FA 1994, Sch 9 para 6; FA 1995, Sch 29 Pt VIII(2); FA 1999, Sch 4 para 2*]. See 43.12 below for special provisions relating to married couples.

In determining whether the amount on which interest is payable exceeds the qualifying maximum or any sharer's limit, no account is taken of any interest which has been added to the capital and which does not exceed £1,000. [*ICTA 1988, s 356D(10), s 357(6); FA 1988, s 42(1); FA 1999, Sch 4 para 2*].

43.11 *Examples*

On 1 April 1999, Mr Romeo and Miss Juliet took out a joint mortgage for £65,000 for the purchase of a London flat to be used as their main residence. Gross interest paid in 1999/2000 amounts to £4,850.

Interest relief for 1999/2000

Mr Romeo

Amount on which interest is payable	£32,500
Sharer's limit — £30,000 (qualifying maximum) ÷ 2 =	£15,000
Interest paid	£2,425
Relief restricted to £2,425 × $\frac{15,000}{32,500}$ =	£1,119

Miss Juliet

Identical calculation—relief restricted to	£1,119

Adjustment of sharer's limits

Three friends, A, B and C, decide to pool their resources and buy a house to be shared as their main residence. Each contributes his own savings and obtains a mortgage to fund the balance of his one-third share of the purchase price. The mortgages are all taken out in May 1999 and the amounts thereof, and interest paid thereon for 1999/2000, are as follows.

	Mortgage	Interest payable (gross)
	£	£
A	7,000	560
B	14,000	1,120
C	16,000	1,280

Each has a sharer's limit of £10,000 (£30,000 ÷ 3). As A's limit exceeds the amount on which he pays interest, the excess is divided between B and C, each of whose limits falls short of the amount on which he pays interest. B and C have shortfalls of £4,000 and £6,000 respectively, a total shortfall of £10,000, so A's excess of £3,000 is divided between them as follows.

B— $\frac{4}{10}$ × £3,000 = £1,200 (revised sharer's limit £11,200)

C— $\frac{6}{10}$ × £3,000 = £1,800 (revised sharer's limit £11,800)

A's sharer's limit is reduced to £7,000.

Interest relief for 1999/2000 is then calculated as follows.

A— $\frac{7,000}{7,000}$ × £560 = £560

B— $\frac{11,200}{14,000}$ × £1,120 = £896

C— $\frac{11,800}{16,000}$ × £1,280 = £944

43.12 **Married couples.** Special provisions apply in relation to married couples who are not separated under Court Order or deed of separation or in circumstances such that the separation is likely to be permanent.

Application of qualifying maximum. A husband and wife who are not separated may jointly elect that, for the year in question (or for a period within that year), qualifying interest payable by either or both of them be allocated between them in whatever proportions they choose, and that either of their sharer's limits (see 43.10 above) be increased by any amount specified (with a corresponding reduction in the other's limit). The election must be made in prescribed form (i.e. form 15 (1990)) within twelve months after 31 January following the first year of assessment for which it is to apply, and, once made, continues to have effect for subsequent years until withdrawn. A notice of withdrawal may be given by either husband or wife in prescribed form (i.e. form 15–1 (1990)) within twelve months after 31 January following the first year of assessment for which it is to apply, and has effect for subsequent years (without prejudice to the right to make a fresh election). For 1995/96 and earlier years, election or withdrawal had to be made within twelve months of the end of the year of assessment concerned. All such time limits may be extended by the Revenue, having regard to the circumstances in any particular case. This discretion will normally be exercised where the lateness was due to sickness, absence abroad or serious personal difficulties, or to the unavailability (through no fault of the taxpayers or their advisors) of information essential to the decision to make or withdraw the election (Revenue Pamphlet IR 131, SP 8/89, 1 February 1990).

Where a married couple who are not separated have two residences, so that the husband pays interest on one, being his main or intended main residence, and the wife similarly pays interest on the other, the residence that was purchased first is to be regarded as the couple's only or main residence, the other residence being treated as the only or main residence of neither of them.

[*ICTA 1988, ss 356B, 367(1); FA 1988, s 42(1), Sch 3 para 14; FA 1995, s 42(2); FA 1996, s 135, Sch 21 para 8; FA 1999, Sch 4 para 2*].

See generally Revenue Pamphlet IR 86.

Year of marriage. If one spouse goes to live in the other spouse's home which is being purchased under a mortgage and sells his or her own property, the interest for the period the property is vacant will be allowed, concessionally, in addition to the interest on the loan for the new matrimonial home, provided that the property is sold within twelve months from the date it is vacated (Revenue Pamphlet IR 1, A35).

Where two people, each buying a main residence before marriage with the aid of a loan, buy a joint residence and sell their existing properties, the bridging loan provisions (see 43.7 above) will be regarded as applying to all three properties, whether or not the relevant property continues to be used as the owner's only or main residence (Revenue Pamphlet IR 131, SP 10/80, 24 September 1980).

See also 43.7 above as regards more general relief from 16 March 1993.

43.13 **Substitution of security.** Interest relief as under 43.6 above is extended in certain cases where a person purchases an estate or interest in land etc. (the '*new estate*') after 15 March 1993, and a 'security substitution arrangement' takes effect after that date in connection with the purchase.

A '*security substitution arrangement*' is an arrangement under which:

(*a*) the new estate becomes security for an existing loan or loans, and another estate etc. ceases to be security for the loan(s);

(*b*) the other estate etc. was not absorbed into, or given up to obtain, the new estate;

(*c*) immediately before the arrangement took effect, interest on the loan(s) was eligible for relief under 43.6 above or 43.16 below (job-related accommodation); and

(*d*) had the loan(s) been applied in purchasing the new estate, interest would have been so eligible for relief.

Where there is more than one loan and one or more of them would not satisfy (*c*) above, these provisions are applied only in relation to such of the loans as do fall within (*c*) above.

Where the above conditions are met, then as regards interest paid on the loan after the time the new estate became security for the loan, the loan is treated for the purposes of 43.6 above as if:

(i) it had been made at that time; and

(ii) the amount then outstanding (insofar as it did not exceed the 'relevant amount') had been used at that time to purchase the new estate,

and similarly where two or more loans are the subject of such arrangements.

The '*relevant amount*' is generally an amount equal to the purchase price of the new estate. The definition varies, however, where there is a loan (referred to below for convenience as an 'additional loan') eligible for relief under 43.6 above or 43.16 below, and actually used to any extent to purchase the new estate at or before the time the security substitution took place, or treated under an earlier security substitution arrangement as if before that time it had been so used. In those circumstances, the '*relevant amount*' is the difference between the purchase price of the new estate and the amount of the additional loan(s).

These provisions do not apply where the amount of any additional loan(s) (as above) equals the purchase price of the new estate. Where an additional loan is or was only partly used (or treated as used) in purchasing the new estate, it is only taken into account for the above purposes to the extent that it is or was or was treated as so used.

The exclusion from relief under 43.6 above of interest within the MIRAS scheme (see 23.13 DEDUCTION OF TAX AT SOURCE) does not affect the determination of eligibility for the purposes of these provisions.

[*ICTA 1988, ss 357A, 357C(1)–(3); FA 1993, s 56; FA 1994, Sch 9 para 7; FA 1995, s 42(2); FA 1999, Sch 4 para 2*].

Treatment of loans following security substitution. Where, after the above provision has applied to treat a loan as having been used to defray the purchase cost of a new estate, a new loan is actually used to any extent for that purpose and would otherwise be eligible for relief under 43.6 above or 43.16 below, such relief is restricted. As regards interest paid on the new loan after the time it is so used (the '*material time*'), any part so used is eligible for relief only to the extent that it does not exceed the 'applicable amount', and relief for a number of such loans is similarly restricted in the aggregate. The '*applicable amount*' is the difference between the purchase price of the new estate and any earlier eligible loans or part loans in respect of the purchase (including those eligible by virtue of an earlier application of these provisions). [*ICTA 1988, s 357B; FA 1993, s 56; FA 1994, Sch 9 para 7; FA 1995, s 42(2); FA 1999, Sch 4 para 2*].

Joint purchases. Where the purchase is a joint purchase, and any of the money applied in the purchase is not attributable to all the joint purchasers, these provisions apply to the share of the new estate, and the attributable part of the purchase cost, of each of the purchasers to whom it is attributable. [*ICTA 1988, s 357C(4)–(6); FA 1993, s 56; FA 1999, Sch 4 para 2*].

43.14 *Example*

James has outstanding the following loans (all with the same lender).

	£
House purchase (main residence)	80,000
Home improvement loan 1 (made before 6 April 1988)	20,000
Home improvement loan 2 (made in 1991)	3,000

In October 1999, James arranges to sell his home for £90,000 and to buy a new home for £95,000. The lender agrees to substitute the new property as security for the three existing loans and to make a further advance of £5,000 to cover the difference between the proceeds of the old property and the cost of the new. The new arrangements all take effect from 6 October 1999.

Interest rates charged by the lender throughout 1999/2000 are 7.5% on both the original house purchase loan and the new advance and 10% on both home improvement loans.

The interest qualifying for tax relief for 1999/2000 is calculated as follows.

6.4.99–5.10.99 (six months)

	£
$£80,000 \times 7.5\% \times \frac{6}{12}$	3,000
$£20,000 \times 10\% \times \frac{6}{12}$	1,000
Total interest on qualifying loans	£4,000
Allowable interest $= £4,000 \times \dfrac{30,000}{100,000} =$	£1,200

6.10.99–5.4.2000 (six months)

The existing loans, restricted as below but disregarding home improvement loan 2 which is a non-qualifying loan, are regarded as having been made on 6.10.99 for the purchase of the new property.

The existing loans qualifying for relief are restricted to the lesser of

(i) the amount of the qualifying loans outstanding (i.e. £100,000), and

(ii) the purchase price of the new property (£95,000) *less* the loan actually used in purchasing the new property (£5,000) (i.e. £90,000).

The total loans outstanding (disregarding home improvement loan 2) are £105,000. Of this amount, £90,000 qualifies as above and the new advance of £5,000 qualifies under normal principles. Therefore, £95,000 of the total loans is a qualifying loan and the balance of £10,000 is not.

Allowable interest is calculated as follows.

						£
85,000	$\times 7.5\% \times \frac{6}{12}$	=	3,188	$\times \frac{95}{105}$	=	2,884
20,000	$\times 10\% \times \frac{6}{12}$	=	1,000	$\times \frac{95}{105}$	=	905
£105,000	total interest		£4,188	qualifying interest		£3,789

Allowable interest = $£3,789 \times \frac{30,000}{95,000} =$ £1,197

Total allowable interest 1999/2000 £(1,200 + 1,197) £2,397

43.15 **LOANS FOR PURCHASING PROPERTY LET AT A COMMERCIAL RENT**

Relief is given for interest paid **before 6 April 1995** (see below) on a loan for the purchase of land by a person owning an estate or interest in the property where the property is, in any period of 52 weeks comprising the time at which the interest is payable and falling wholly or partly within the year of assessment, **let at a commercial rent** for more than 26 weeks and, when not so let, either available for letting at such a rent *or* used as in 43.6 above *or* prevented from being so available or used by construction or repair work. [*ICTA 1988, s 355(1)(b); FA 1995, s 42(1)*]. Interest is also eligible under this paragraph on loans applied in improving or developing land. Interest falling within *section 355(1)(b)* is allowable only against income from letting that or any other land, but unallowed interest may be carried forward against such income (while the land in respect of which the interest is paid continues to be eligible) of the following and subsequent years of assessment (but see below). [*ICTA 1988, s 355(4); FA 1994, Sch 9 para 4; FA 1995, Sch 29 Pt VIII(2)*].

If an individual lets his property at a commercial rent whilst he is away, the benefit of the concession re temporary absences in 43.6 above may be claimed, where appropriate, if this is more favourable than a claim for relief against letting income. (Revenue Pamphlet IR 1, A27). If the loan is within the MIRAS scheme, this should not prevent relief being obtained against the letting income, where appropriate, provided that an adjustment is made for the MIRAS relief. (Taxation Vol 125, No 3269 p 707, 20 September 1990). See 43.3 above for the election available for 1994/95 onwards where interest is eligible both under these provisions and under those in 43.6 above.

Interest may generally be relieved under these provisions against rent paid by a partnership to a partner, or by a company to a controlling director, in respect of land owned by the partner or director occupied for business purposes by the partnership or company. See 43.3(i)(ii) above where the interest is in these circumstances paid by the partnership or company direct.

Repeal of above provisions. The provisions of *ICTA 1988, s 355(1)(b)* and *s 355(4)* are repealed with effect in relation to interest paid on or after 6 April 1995. With effect for **1995/96 and subsequent years**, interest incurred wholly and exclusively for the purposes of a Schedule A business (see 68.4 SCHEDULE A) is an allowable deduction as an expense in arriving at the profits of that business. Extra-statutory Concession A27 (referred to above) continues to apply if the benefit of the concession is more favourable than a deduction in arriving at the Schedule A business profits. A borrower who is eligible for mortgage interest relief, before its abolition from 6 April 2000, in respect of a let property may choose each year whether to claim such relief (restricted to the applicable percentage on a maximum of £30,000) or to deduct the interest in computing the Schedule A business profits. As regards inclusion of the loan within MIRAS (mortgage interest relief by deduction at source), see 23.13 DEDUCTION OF TAX AT SOURCE.

For 1995/96 only,

(*a*) if under transitional provisions a source of property income ceasing in that year falls to be taxed otherwise than in accordance with the new Schedule A rules (see 68.3 SCHEDULE A and, in the case of property outside the UK, 73.4 SCHEDULE D, CASES IV AND V), and

(*b*) the source includes any land etc. satisfying the condition of *section 355(1)(b)* (see above).

interest paid before the time of cessation continues to be deductible under the above provisions. Unrelieved interest brought forward from 1994/95 and earlier years may also be relieved in 1995/96 against income from a source within (*a*) above. [*FA 1995, s 42(3)–(5)*]. Otherwise, such unrelieved interest is relievable in 1995/96 and subsequent years as a Schedule A loss (see 68.13(C) SCHEDULE A). See also 68.22 SCHEDULE A for Revenue policy where some interest would otherwise be unrelieved on the transition from relief on a payments basis to relief on an accruals basis.

Simon's Direct Tax Service. See **E1.535B, E1.535C.**

43.16 LOANS FOR PURCHASING PROPERTY WHERE BORROWER IN JOB-RELATED LIVING ACCOMMODATION

Relief is given for interest paid before (generally) 6 April 2000 (see 43.3 above) on a loan for the purchase of land by a person owning an estate or interest in the property who is in **job-related living accommodation** at the time the interest is paid, provided that:

(i) the property is used by him as a residence, or is so used within twelve months of the loan if the interest is paid within that time; or

(ii) the property is intended to be used in due course as his only or main residence.

Relief can relate to only one property in the case of any one borrower.

See 43.5 above as regards denial of higher rate relief. See 43.3 above for the restriction of tax relief to 20% for 1994/95, 15% for 1995/96, 1996/97 and 1997/98 and 10% for 1998/99 and 1999/2000, and for the method of giving such relief.

As regards 'home improvement loans', rules identical to those described in 43.6 above apply, as they do to restrict the amount of loans eligible for relief by reference to a qualifying maximum.

'*Job-related living accommodation*' is living accommodation which is provided to a person or spouse either:

(A) by reason of employment where (*a*) it is necessary for the proper performance of his duties for the employee to reside in the accommodation, or (*b*) the employment is such that it is customary for employees to be provided with accommodation for the better performance of their duties, or (*c*) there is a special threat to the employee's security, and he resides in the accommodation as part of special security arrangements in force; or

(B) under an arm's length contract requiring him or his spouse to carry on a trade, profession or vocation on premises or other land provided (under a tenancy or otherwise) by another person and to live on the premises or on other premises provided by that other person.

Neither (A)(*a*) nor (A)(*b*) above applies to accommodation provided to a director by a company, or associated company, unless he has no material interest (5% with or without associates) in the company of which he is a director *and either* he is a full-time working director *or* the company is non-profit making (i.e. it does not carry on a trade, nor is its main function the holding of investments or other property) *or* the company is a charity. (B) above does not apply if the accommodation is provided, wholly or in part, by a company in which the borrower or spouse has a material interest (as above), or by any person(s) with whom the borrower or spouse is in partnership. [*ICTA 1988, s 356; FA 1988, s 43(2); FA 1994, Sch 9 para 5; FA 1995, s 42(2); FA 1999, Sch 4 para 2*].

It is understood that certain accommodation occupied by Ministry of Defence employees who extend their overseas tour beyond four years may be regarded as job-related for these purposes (Tolley's Practical Tax 1986 p 167).

Simon's Direct Tax Service. See **E1.546**.

43.17 **LOANS FOR PURCHASING PROPERTY — GENERAL MATTERS**

In relation to the reliefs described at 43.6–43.16 above, land includes buildings, caravans and house-boats in UK or Eire (but not elsewhere, see *Ockendon v Mackley Ch D 1982, 56 TC 1*). [*ICTA 1988, s 354(1); FA 1999, Sch 4 para 2*]. Loans replacing a prior eligible loan are themselves eligible. [*ICTA 1988, s 354(1)(c); FA 1999, Sch 4 para 2*]. See, however, 43.8 above as regards replacement home improvement loans. '*Improving or developing*' includes capital expenditure on making-up, sewering, lighting etc., adjoining or service roads. Also making good dilapidations in existence at the time of the purchase, but not other maintenance or repairs (but see below). [*ICTA 1988, s 354(2); FA 1995, Sch 29 Pt VIII(1); FA 1999, Sch 4 para 2*]. If the interest in land is a rentcharge etc. or an interest as chargee or mortgagee, the interest payable is not eligible (this has no effect for, broadly, 1995/96 and subsequent years). [*ICTA 1988, s 354(4); FA 1995, Sch 29 Pt VIII(2); FA 1999, Sch 4 para 2*]. A tenant occupier who is in the process of purchasing property with money advanced by the landlord on loan is treated as the owner of that property in relation to any interest paid on the loan before the property actually passes to him. [*ICTA 1988, s 354(7); FA 1999, Sch 4 para 2*]. There are provisions preventing avoidance by sales between husband and wife, or connected persons etc. [*ICTA 1988, s 355(5); FA 1999, Sch 4 para 2*].

The further provisions in *ICTA 1988, s 367(2)–(4)* (see 43.5 above) apply to all loans within 43.6–43.23.

The Revenue have indicated that the following are considered to be '*improvements*' for these purposes.

Home extensions/Loft conversions
Insulation of roofs/walls
Connection to main drainage
Landscaping gardens
Major reconstruction, e.g. conversion to flats
Rebuilding a facade
Inserting or renewing damp-proof course
Extensive repointing,
Installing kitchen or bedroom units fixed to and part of the building
Installation of bathrooms, showers, etc.
Recovering/Reconstructing a roof
Construction of swimming pools, saunas, etc.
Underpinning
Renewing electrical installations
Dry rot, wet rot or timber treatment

pebble-dashing, texture-coating or stone-cladding
Erecting garages, garden sheds, greenhouses or fences
Double glazing/Replacement of windows and doors
Central or solar heating installations (excluding portable and night storage radiators not fixed to a permanent spar outlet)
Extensive replacement of guttering
Installation of fire or burglar alarms
Fire precaution works
Laying driveways, patios or paths
Permanent installation of water softening equipment
Replacement of one form of central heating with another (e.g. moving from oil to gas)

(Taxation Vol 114, No 2988 p 483, 30 March 1985).

Caravans acquired under a hire purchase agreement may concessionally attract relief subject to certain conditions. The local inspector should be consulted as to the current position.

Loan replacing *bank overdraft*. Where an eligible property is acquired by means of an overdraft which is within twelve months replaced by a loan, the Board will concessionally allow relief for the loan interest (up to 5 April 2000) if it can be demonstrated that the overdraft was used solely for the property acquisition (Revenue Pamphlet IR 11, para 33). (*Note.* Although IR 11 is no longer available, it is understood that this concession still applies, see Tolley's Practical Tax 1990 p 15.) See *Lawson v Brooks Ch D 1991, 64 TC 462* for denial of relief for loan replacing overdraft where the overdraft was not a 'temporary accommodation'.

43.18 LOANS FOR PURCHASING MACHINERY OR PLANT

Relief is given for interest paid on a loan for the purchase of machinery or plant

(*a*) for use in the trade, etc., of a partnership of which the individual is a member and which is entitled to capital allowances on that machinery under *CAA 1990, s 65*, or

(*b*) for the purposes of an *office or employment* he holds, and in respect of which he is entitled to capital allowances under *CAA 1990, Pt II* (or would be so entitled but for some contribution made by his employer) (and see 75.43 SCHEDULE E for special provisions relating to use of private car or cycle for such purposes).

Relief is not so granted on interest payable more than three years after the end of the year of assessment in which the debt was incurred, and is applied to a proportionate part of the interest where use is in part other than in (*a*) or (*b*) above. [*ICTA 1988, s 359*].

Simon's Direct Tax Service. See **E1.533.**

43.19 LOANS FOR PURCHASING INTEREST IN CLOSE COMPANY

Relief is given for interest paid on a loan (or replacement loan) for the purchase of ordinary shares in, or making a loan to, a close company, provided that the borrower is an individual either (i) with, together with certain associates, a 'material interest' (broadly more than 5% of ordinary share capital at the date of payment of the interest) in the close company or (ii) when the interest is paid, the individual holds any ordinary shares of the close company and (between purchase or loan and relevant interest payment) he has worked for the greater part of his time in the actual management or conduct of the business of that close company or an associated company. As regards this last condition, the facts of each particular case have to be considered, but individuals will normally be regarded as meeting the requirement if they are directors or have significant managerial or technical responsibilities. They must, however, be involved in the overall running and policy-making of the company as a whole—responsibility for just a particular area is not sufficient. (Revenue Tax Bulletin

November 1993 p 102). See also Revenue Inspector's Manual IM 3804. If the company exists wholly or mainly to hold investments or property, the individual must not reside in property of the company unless he has worked for the greater part of his time in the actual management or conduct of that company or an associated company. [*ICTA 1988, ss 360, 360A(1), 363(4); FA 1989, s 48*]. The associates whose interests are taken into account in applying the 'material interest' test for loans made after 5 April 1987 do not include the trustees of profit sharing schemes under *FA 1978* (see 82.9, 82.10 SHARE INCENTIVES AND OPTIONS), and for loans made after 26 July 1989 do not generally include the trustees of an employee benefit trust (as defined), as a beneficiary of which the borrower has an interest in shares or obligations of the company, unless the 5% ordinary share capital test would be satisfied without their inclusion (for which purpose certain payments received from the trust are treated as giving rise to beneficial ownership of ordinary share capital). Certain other variations in the general definition of 'associate' in *section 360A(2)* apply to loans made before 14 November 1986. [*ICTA 1988, s 360(4), s 360A(2)–(7), Sch 9 para 39; FA 1989, s 48*].

Relief is denied in relation to shares in respect of which a claim is made to relief under the enterprise investment scheme or the business expansion scheme (see 26 ENTERPRISE INVESTMENT SCHEME (AND BES)) or, in relation to shares acquired after 5 April 1998, for deferral of a chargeable gain on reinvestment in an enterprise investment scheme investment, by the person acquiring them or their spouse. [*ICTA 1988, s 360(3A); FA 1989, s 47; FA 1998, s 79*].

The close company (see Tolley's Corporation Tax) must, both at the time the shares are acquired (or the loan made) and throughout the accounting period in which the interest is paid, comply with *ICTA 1988, s 13A(2)* (as introduced by *FA 1989, s 105*) and thus satisfy the conditions for not being a close investment-holding company (see Tolley's Corporation Tax under Close Companies). [*FA 1989, Sch 12 para 12*]. The Revenue's practice in the case of investment in a start-up trading company is to allow relief so long as trading commences within a reasonable time after the investment is made, provided that the company remains close when trading starts. (ICAEW Technical Release TAX 15/92, 23 October 1992).

Where shares were subscribed for in a 'shell' company to enable it to acquire a business, but the business had not been acquired at the time of the subscription, it could fairly be said that the company existed for the purpose of carrying on that business, so that interest on a loan for the purchase of the shares qualified for relief under these provisions (*Lord v Tustain Ch D 1993, 65 TC 761*).

If relief is claimed on a loan to a close company, the money must be used within a reasonable time for the purposes of its business (or that of an associated close company as defined above). [*ICTA 1988, s 360(1)(b), s 367(2)*]. Capital recoveries by the individual (by sale or repayment of ordinary shares, repayment by the company of its loan, or the assignment of the debt due from it etc.) are treated as a reduction of the loan with corresponding reduction of the interest allowable. [*ICTA 1988, s 363(1)–(3)*]. The interest will continue to be allowed if the company ceases to be close after the application of the loan monies (Revenue Pamphlet IR 131, SP 3/78, 19 October 1978). Conversely, it is understood that relief will be given where a loan is used to purchase shares in an 'open' company which by that acquisition becomes a close company (Tolley's Practical Tax 1981 p 99).

Interest paid by the guarantor of a bank loan to a close company is not within the relief (*Hendy v Hadley Ch D 1980, 53 TC 353*).

Interest on a loan applied to the purchase of a close company's convertible loan stock can qualify for relief under these provisions. Relief will, however, cease from the date on which the loan stock is converted to ordinary share capital, since this constitutes a capital recovery (see above). (Revenue Tax Bulletin February 1992 p 13).

Relief on a loan qualifying as above will not be discontinued where shares in the close company are exchanged for, or replaced by, shares in another close company, or by shares in a co-operative (see 43.20 below), or by shares in an employee-controlled company (see 43.21 below), provided that relief would have been available if the loan had been a new loan taken out to invest in the new entity. The usual restriction applies where any capital recovered from the close company is not used to repay the loan. (Revenue Pamphlet IR 1, A43).

Simon's Direct Tax Service. See **E1.547.**

43.20 LOANS FOR PURCHASING INTEREST IN CO-OPERATIVE

Relief is given for interest paid on a loan (or replacement loan) for the purchase of a share or shares in, or making a loan to, a co-operative. Such relief only applies to interest on a loan made after 10 March 1981 and the individual must (between purchase or loan and the relevant interest payment) have worked for the greater part of his time as an employee of the co-operative, or of a subsidiary of that body, which continues to be a co-operative when the interest is paid. A loan to a co-operative must be used wholly and exclusively for the purposes of the business of that body or of a subsidiary. Capital recoveries by the individual (by sale or replacement of the shares, repayment by the co-operative of its loan, or the assignment of the debt due from it etc.) are treated as a reduction of the loan with corresponding reduction of the interest allowable.

'*Co-operative*' (and 'subsidiary') means a common ownership enterprise or a co-operative enterprise as defined in the *Industrial Common Ownership Act 1976, s 2*. [*ICTA 1988, s 361(1)(2), s 363*].

Relief on a loan qualifying as above will not be discontinued where shares in the co-operative are exchanged for, or replaced by, shares in another co-operative, or by shares in a close company (see 43.19 above), or by shares in an employee-controlled company (see 43.21 below), provided that relief would have been available if the loan had been a new loan taken out to invest in the new entity. The usual restriction applies where any capital recovered from the co-operative is not used to repay the loan. (Revenue Pamphlet IR 1, A43).

Simon's Direct Tax Service. See **E1.548.**

43.21 LOANS FOR PURCHASING INTEREST IN EMPLOYEE-CONTROLLED COMPANY

Relief is given for interest paid on a loan (or replacement loan) for the purchase of any part of the ordinary share capital of an employee-controlled company by an individual, provided that:

(*a*) the company is, from the date of purchase of the shares to that of payment of the interest, resident only in the UK, unlisted on the Stock Exchange, and either a trading company (i.e. its business consists wholly or mainly of the carrying on of trade(s)) or the holding company of a trading group (i.e. the business of its 75% subsidiaries, taken together, consists wholly or mainly of carrying on trade(s));

(*b*) the shares are acquired before, or not later than twelve months after, the company becomes an 'employee-controlled company';

(*c*) the company is an 'employee-controlled company' throughout a period of at least nine months in the year of assessment in which the interest is paid, unless it is the year in which it first becomes an employee-controlled company;

(*d*) the individual (or spouse, but see further below) is a full-time employee of the company (i.e. works for the greater part of his time as an employee or director of the company or of a 51% subsidiary) from the date of application of the loan proceeds to the date of payment of the interest (or, if the interest is paid after cessation of the employment, the later of the date of cessation and twelve months before the interest payment date i.e. interest is eligible for relief for twelve months after full-time employment ceases);

(*e*) the individual has, from the date of application of the loan proceeds to the interest payment date, not recovered any capital from the company other than amounts treated as reducing the loan (see below).

Capital recoveries by the individual (by sale or replacement of the shares, repayment of the loan, etc.) are treated as reducing the loan and, correspondingly, the interest allowable.

A company is an '*employee-controlled company*' if more than 50% of both the issued share capital and the voting power is beneficially owned by full-time employees (see (*d*) above) (or spouses, but see below) of the company, but ignoring the excess over 10% of any holding of a person (and spouse, but see below) which exceeds 10% of either issued share capital or voting power. Where an individual and spouse are *both* full-time employees, this 10% test is applied to each separately ignoring the other's holding.

As regards (*d*) above and the definition of employee-controlled company, for interest paid after 5 April 1990 (unless the loan was used before that date as required for relief under these provisions) neither the employment of a spouse nor the shares held by a spouse are taken into account in determining whether the conditions for relief for interest paid on such loans are met. Replacement loans made after that date attract interest relief only if the loan replaced was applied after that date or would have attracted relief if it had been applied after that date. [*ICTA 1988, s 361(3)–(8), s 363; FA 1988, Sch 3 para 15*].

Relief on a loan qualifying as above will not be discontinued where shares in the employee-controlled company are exchanged for, or replaced by, shares in another such company, or by shares in a close company (see 43.19 above), or by shares in a co-operative (see 43.20 above), provided that relief would have been available if the loan had been a new loan taken out to invest in the new entity. The usual restriction applies where any capital recovered from the company is not used to repay the loan. (Revenue Pamphlet IR 1, A43).

Simon's Direct Tax Service. See **E1.549.**

43.22 LOANS FOR PURCHASING INTEREST IN PARTNERSHIP

Relief is given for interest on a loan (or replacement loan) for the purchase of a share of, or making an advance to, a partnership to an individual who (throughout the period between application of the proceeds of the loan and payment of relevant interest) has been a member of the partnership otherwise than as a limited partner. If relief is claimed on a loan to the partnership, the money must be used for the purposes of its trade, profession or vocation. [*ICTA 1988, s 362*]. Salaried partners in a professional firm who are allowed independence of action in handling the affairs of clients and so to act that they will be indistinguishable from general partners in their relations with clients, can claim relief. (See Revenue Pamphlet IR 131, A33.)

For a case in which relief was denied where 'the true net result of the circular transaction [involving a series of payments between spouses] was that no money was contributed or advanced to the partnership which it did not already have', see *Lancaster v CIR (Sp C 232), [2000] SSCD 138.*

Capital recoveries by the individual (from sale of his partnership interest, repayment of capital or loan etc.) are treated as a reduction of the loan with corresponding reduction of the interest allowable. [*ICTA 1988, s 363*].

Relief on a loan qualifying as above will not be discontinued where the partnership is incorporated into a close company (see 43.19 above), a co-operative (see 43.20 above) or an employee-controlled company (see 43.21 above), or there is a partnership reconstruction involving a merger or demerger, provided that relief would have been available if the loan had been a new loan taken out to invest in the new entity. The usual restriction applies where any capital recovered from the partnership is not used to repay the loan. (Revenue Pamphlet IR 1, A43).

Anti-avoidance measures on changeover to current year basis of assessment. Where

(*a*) the transitional rules at 71.20 SCHEDULE D, CASES I AND II apply to determine the basis period for 1996/97 for a partnership business commenced before 6 April 1994 (other than where, exceptionally, the 1996/97 assessment is on an actual basis), and

(*b*) a claim for interest relief is made by a partner under the above provisions in respect of a loan made after 31 March 1994 to defray money contributed or advanced to a partnership (but *not* to purchase an interest in the partnership),

there is a restriction on the amount of interest eligible for relief on any of the loan proceeds contributed or advanced to the partnership otherwise than wholly or mainly for *bona fide* commercial reasons (which does not include the obtaining of a tax advantage) or wholly or mainly for a purpose other than the reduction of the partnership's borrowings for a period falling wholly or partly within the transitional period (see 71.20 SCHEDULE D, CASES I AND II). Relief for interest paid in respect of the transitional period on that part of the loan proceeds is restricted to the appropriate percentage (as defined in 71.20 SCHEDULE D, CASES I AND II) of that interest. This does not apply if the aggregate amount of that interest is less than £15,000. These provisions apply to interest on a replacement loan as they would have applied in respect of the original loan. The discovery provisions of *TMA 1970, ss 29, 30B* apply with the same modifications and related time limits as in 71.20 SCHEDULE D, CASES I AND II. [*FA 1995, s 123, Sch 22 paras 2, 11, 21(2); SI 1997 No 1158*].

Further anti-avoidance provisions apply where a claim for interest relief under the above provisions is made by a partner for 1997/98 in respect of a loan made after 31 March 1994 and there is a transitional overlap profit (see 71.22 SCHEDULE D, CASES I AND II) on the changeover to the current year basis. Subject to a *de minimis* limit of £7,500 for application of these provisions, that partner's transitional overlap profit (as reduced where applicable by the anti-avoidance provisions at 71.22) is reduced by the amount of interest paid in respect of the transitional overlap period (see 71.22 SCHEDULE D, CASES I AND II) on any part of the loan proceeds which was contributed or advanced by him to the partnership otherwise than wholly or mainly for *bona fide* commercial reasons or wholly or mainly for a purpose other than the reduction of partnership borrowings for a period falling wholly or partly within the transitional overlap period. Similar notice provisions and time limits apply as in 71.22 as to the amendment of a self-assessment to give effect to the foregoing. [*FA 1995, Sch 22 paras 5, 12; SI 1997 No 1158*].

Simon's Direct Tax Service. See **E1.550.**

43.23 LOANS TO PAY INHERITANCE TAX

Relief is given for interest on a loan (or replacement loan) to personal representatives to pay inheritance tax or estate duty before a grant of representation or confirmation (payable on delivery of the affidavit etc.), or interest thereon, on personalty of which the deceased was competent to dispose at his death (and which passes to the personal representatives as such, or would if it were situate in UK). The interest must be paid in respect of the period of one year from the making of the loan. Unrelieved interest in a year of assessment can be carried to previous year(s) of assessment and then, if still unrelieved, to succeeding years of assessment. [*ICTA 1988, s 364*].

Simon's Direct Tax Service. See **E1.552.**

43.24 **LOANS FOR PURCHASING LIFE ANNUITY**

Relief is given for interest on a loan for the purchase of a life annuity by a borrower aged 65 or over under a scheme in which 90% or more of the proceeds of the loan are applied to the purchase by the borrower of an annuity ending with his death (or the last death of two or more annuitants aged 65 or over which include the borrower). The loan must be secured on land in the UK or Eire in which the borrower or one of the annuitants owns an estate or interest. Interest is not eligible unless payable by the borrower or one of the annuitants.

The loan must have been made before 9 March 1999, or in pursuance of an offer made by the lender before that date (and either written or evidenced by a note or memorandum made by the lender before that date). However, replacement loans made on or after 27 July 1999 qualify for relief if the old loan did so, and this applies where only part of the new loan is applied in paying off the old loan, provided that at least 90% of the balance of the new loan not applied in paying off the old loan is applied to the purchase of an annuity ending with the life of the person to whom the loan is made (or of the survivor of two or more persons including that person).

See 43.5 above as regards denial of higher rate relief. See 43.3 above for the method of giving relief.

As regards loans made from 27 March 1974 onwards (*a*) the borrower or each of the annuitants must use the land as his only or main residence when the interest is paid or (in relation to interest payments on or after 27 July 1999) have so used it immediately before 9 March 1999, and (*b*) relief is granted on loans up to £30,000 only, with apportionment where payable by two or more annuitants. In relation to interest paid after 15 March 1993 and before 27 July 1999, where the condition at (*a*) ceased at any time to be satisfied, and it was intended to take steps, within the twelve months following cessation of use as the only or main residence, with a view to disposal of the land, the condition is treated as satisfied until the end of those twelve months or, if earlier, until the intention to dispose of the land is abandoned. The twelve month period could be extended at the Board's discretion in any particular case (irrespective of whether the period began before 16 March 1993). In relation to interest paid on or after 27 July 1999, a similar provision allows the condition at (*a*) to be treated as satisfied where it ceased to be satisfied at a time within the twelve months ending with 8 March 1999 and it was then intended to take steps to dispose of the land within the following twelve months.

[*ICTA 1988, ss 357(1), 365; F(No 2)A 1983, s 3; FA 1984, s 22; FA 1985, s 37; FA 1986, s 20; FA 1987, s 25; FA 1988, s 41; FA 1989, s 46; FA 1990, s 71; FA 1991, s 26; FA 1992, s 10(4); FA 1993, ss 55, 57(3)(5); FA 1994, s 80; FA 1996, s 76; FA 1997, s 57; F(No 2)A 1997, s 16; FA 1999, ss 37, 39, 40; FA 2000, s 83(1)(4)*].

Simon's Direct Tax Service. See **E1.553.**

43.25 **EXCLUSION OF DOUBLE RELIEF**

Provisions for exclusion of double relief or relief by different methods are in *ICTA 1988, s 368*. The general rule is that any interest relieved under *ICTA 1988, s 353* is not deductible for any other purpose. If a payment of interest on a debt has been allowed under 43.2 above in computing the profits of a period, no relief can be given under *ICTA 1988, s 353* on that payment and on any interest on the same debt in any years of assessment for which the period is the basis period (see 71.4 SCHEDULE D, CASES I AND II onwards). Conversely, if a payment of interest has been relieved under *section 353*, that payment cannot be deducted in computing profits for any year of assessment and any payment of interest on the same debt cannot be deducted in computing the profits for assessment for the year in which *section 353* relief was given. For these purposes, all business overdrafts are treated as one debt. [*ICTA 1988, s 368; FA 1994, Sch 9 para 9; FA 1995, Sch 6 para 17*]. Also, if any interest is eligible for deduction of tax at source as 'relevant loan interest' (see 23.13 DEDUCTION OF TAX AT SOURCE), then relief under *section 353* will not apply. [*ICTA 1988, s 353(2)*]. See 43.2 above for concession where property used for both residential and business purposes.

44 Interest Receivable

Note. See Tolley's Corporation Tax under Loan Relationships for the special provisions applicable for accounting periods ending after 31 March 1996 to all profits and losses in respect of company 'loan relationships'.

44.1 Interest is receivable gross unless tax is deductible under *ICTA 1988, s 349* (see 23.3(ii) DEDUCTION OF TAX AT SOURCE) or under paying and collecting agent arrangements (see SCHEDULE C (70)) or unless received from a building society (see 9.3 BUILDING SOCIETIES) or from a bank (see 8.2 BANKS) without a gross payment certificate being in force.

44.2 The recipient of interest is assessable thereon under SCHEDULE D, CASE III (72), or under SCHEDULE D, CASES IV AND V (73) if the interest is from abroad, which see at 72.4 and 73.9 respectively as regards basis of assessment, and in particular for adjustments for opening and closing years. See 71.66 SCHEDULE D, CASES I AND II for the assessment of interest received in the course of a business.

See 1.8(iii) ALLOWANCES AND TAX RATES as regards taxation of 'savings income'.

Interest received under deduction of tax (see 44.1 above) is income of the year of assessment in which the payment falls due, without regard to the period of accrual.

Solicitors' client accounts. Designated client account interest passed on to the client by a solicitor is within SCHEDULE D, CASE III (72) and hence potentially 'savings income' (see 1.8(iii) ALLOWANCES AND TAX RATES). Payments made to clients in respect of money held in undesignated client accounts are similarly treated from 6 April 1998. Before that date, they are treated as within SCHEDULE D, CASE VI (74), and hence cannot be 'savings income'. (Revenue Tax Bulletin February 1998 pp 512, 513).

44.3 A list of certain types of interest which are exempt from tax is shown in 29.13 EXEMPT INCOME.

44.4 See 3 ANTI-AVOIDANCE for transactions regarding the transfer of interest etc., and see 74.6 *et seq.* SCHEDULE D, CASE VI as regards the accrued income scheme.

44.5 DEEP DISCOUNT SECURITIES

For **1995/96 and earlier** years, and for accounting periods ending **before 1 April 1996**, the discount element on 'deep discount securities' is brought into charge to income tax or corporation tax (rather than to capital gains tax or corporation tax on chargeable gains) on 'disposal' or redemption. [*ICTA 1988, s 57, Sch 4*]. The provisions are replaced, **for 1996/97 onwards**, by the income tax provisions of *FA 1996, Sch 13* (see 72.2 SCHEDULE D, CASE III), and, for accounting periods ending **after 31 March 1996**, by the corporation tax provisions of *FA 1996, Pt IV, Ch II* (see Tolley's Corporation Tax under Loan Relationships).

A '*deep discount security*' is a redeemable security issued by a company after 13 March 1984 at a discount exceeding either 15% of the amount payable on redemption overall or $\frac{1}{2}$% per annum to the earliest possible redemption date. Shares, index-linked securities and securities within *ICTA 1988, s 209(2)(c)* (see Tolley's Corporation Tax under Distributions) are excluded. Also excluded are securities issued after 31 July 1990 by a company which are convertible into share capital in a company (whether or not the issuing company), securities issued after that date where the terms of issue provide more than one date for redemption at the option of the holder, and securities which were qualifying convertible securities (see 44.8 below) at the time of issue. The amount payable on redemption excludes any amount payable by way of interest.

In relation to a security issued in a currency other than sterling, the level of discount is tested in the currency of issue. (Revenue Tax Bulletin November 1993 p 100). For securities issued with a period to maturity of less than a year, the $\frac{1}{2}$% p.a. test is applied pro rata to the length of the period. (Revenue Tax Bulletin November 1993 p 101).

A redeemable security issued by a '*public body*' (i.e. a government or public or local authority, not being a company, in the UK or elsewhere) at a deep discount (as above) is also a '*deep discount security*' unless it is

(*a*) an index-linked security, or

(*b*) a 'gilt-edged security' (as defined for capital gains tax purposes) issued before 14 March 1989 (or under the same prospectus as a gilt-edged security issued before that date) or issued, other than on the original issue, under a prospectus under which no securities were issued before that date, where all the securities on the original issue are gilt-edged securities and not deep discount securities, or

(*c*) not a gilt-edged security, and was issued under the same prospectus as any other security issued previously which is not a deep discount security.

As regards (*b*) and (*c*) above, certain securities which would, apart from those provisions, be deep discount securities are generally treated as such where at some time the aggregate nominal value of securities issued under the same prospectus which would (apart from (*b*) or (*c*) above) be deep discount securities exceeds that of those which would not, and the deemed treatment applies to events occurring after that time as if the securities in question had been issued and acquired as such.

Where securities issued by a company before 14 March 1984 are exchanged, on or after that date, for new securities which would otherwise be deep discount securities, the new securities are *not* deep discount securities if

(1) the original securities would not have been deep discount securities if issued after 13 March 1984;

(2) the earliest redemption date of the new securities is not later than that for the original securities; and

(3) the amount payable on redemption of the new securities does not exceed that on the original securities.

[*ICTA 1988, Sch 4 paras 1, 19–21; FA 1989, Sch 10 paras 2, 7; FA 1990, s 59, Sch 10 para 26*].

A '*disposal*' of a deep discount security is as defined for capital gains tax purposes (see Tolley's Capital Gains Tax under Disposals), but also includes the occasion of a conversion or exchange of securities within *TCGA 1992, s 132* or *s 135(3)*, and a deemed disposal immediately before the death of the holder. However, unless the security converted or exchanged is a 'chargeable security' within the coupon-stripping provisions (see 44.6 below), conversion or exchange, for no consideration other than the new securities, into securities which are also deep discount securities, and for which the earliest redemption date is no later than that for the original securities, is not a disposal for these purposes. In this case the 'accrued income' is carried forward to the new holding of securities. The conversion or exchange of a 'chargeable security' is always a disposal for these purposes. [*ICTA 1988, Sch 4 para 7*].

The **charge** to income or corporation tax is on the 'accrued income' attributable to the period from acquisition to disposal, and is under Schedule D, Case III or Case IV. The REMITTANCE BASIS (63) applies to a Case IV charge on a non-UK domiciled person or on a non-UK ordinarily resident British or Irish subject, by reference to sums remitted in the year of assessment of charge. Otherwise, the charge is on the amount arising from disposals in the year of assessment. See, however, 44.6 below as regards the charge on certain securities issued to exploit this delayed charge.

The '*accrued income*' is the aggregate of 'income elements' of each 'income period' (or part) in the period of ownership.

'*Income element*' for an 'income period' is the amount obtained by the formula

$$\frac{A \times B}{100} - C$$

where

A is the issue price plus 'income elements' of all previous 'income periods'.

B is the 'yield to maturity', i.e. the annual percentage appreciation rate (compounded at the end of each 'income period') required for the issue price to grow to the redemption value at the earliest possible redemption date, after allowing for any interest payments.

C is the interest (if any) attributable to the 'income period'.

'*Income period*' is the period to which any interest is attributable, or, if no interest is payable, the year to anniversary of issue of the security, or shorter period from such an anniversary or the date of issue to the earliest redemption date. Where a period of ownership includes part of an 'income period', the income element is apportioned on a straight line basis.

The company issuing the security (and a public body issuing such a security after 31 July 1989) is required to state on the bond certificate the amount of the income element for each income period in the security's life. Redemption proceeds are payable gross, without deduction of tax under *ICTA 1988, ss 348–350* or *s 123.*

[*ICTA 1988, Sch 4 paras 1, 4, 13; FA 1989, Sch 10 para 6*].

On **early redemption** (or **winding-up** of an issuing company), the accrued income attributable to the period of ownership ending on the redemption (or on a payment being made in respect of the security in the winding-up) is the amount paid on the redemption (or winding-up) *less* either (i) the issue price, or (ii) if the security was not acquired by the holder on its issue, the sum of the issue price and the accrued income from its issue to the holder's acquisition of it. [*ICTA 1988, Sch 4 paras 11, 11A; FA 1989, Sch 10 paras 4, 5*]. See, however, 44.6 below as regards certain securities issued by companies subject to charge on accrued income at the end of each income period during the period of ownership.

For **capital gains tax** purposes (or for the purposes of corporation tax on chargeable gains):

(i) consideration for the disposal is reduced by the amount of the accrued income during the period of ownership (and any excess of that accrued income over actual consideration is treated as enhancement expenditure immediately before the disposal);

(ii) on a conversion or exchange of securities (see above) any sum payable to the beneficial owner in addition to the new holding is treated in the same way as the consideration at (i) above;

(iii) on a 'no gain-no loss' disposal, the deemed consideration is increased by the accrued income arising during the disponer's period of ownership; and

(iv) capital gains tax identification rules are applied.

[*TCGA 1992, s 118*]

Exemptions. No charge arises under these provisions where

(A) the amount otherwise chargeable is applicable and applied for charitable purposes, or

(B) either

  (i) immediately before the disposal the security was held for the purposes of an exempt approved retirement benefits scheme (see 66.4 RETIREMENT SCHEMES), or

  (ii) the disposal was a stock lending transfer within *ICTA 1988, s 129(3)* (see 71.82 SCHEDULE D, CASES I AND II).

[*ICTA 1988, Sch 4 paras 14, 15, 16; FA 1989, Sch 10 para 7*].

Miscellaneous points.

(*a*) *Time of disposal.* Where a transaction in deep discount securities is under a contract, it takes place at the time the contract is made, or, if the contract is conditional, at the time at which the condition is satisfied. [*ICTA 1988, Sch 4 para 8*].

(*b*) *Letters of allotment.* A security comprised in any letter of allotment or similar instrument is treated as issued unless the right to the security is provisional and has still to be accepted. [*ICTA 1988, Sch 4 para 1(3)*].

(*c*) *Issuing company deduction.* For the deduction of the discount in the issuing company's computation, see Tolley's Corporation Tax under Profit Computations. Broadly, the company is allowed a deduction in each accounting period of the income elements in income periods ending in the accounting period. [*ICTA 1988, Sch 4 para 5*].

(*d*) *Identification of securities* disposed of follows the capital gains tax rules in *TCGA 1992, s 108* (see Tolley's Capital Gains Tax under Shares and Securities — Identification Rules). [*ICTA 1988, Sch 4 para 12*].

(*e*) *Trustees* on whom a charge arises under these provisions on a disposal are chargeable at the rate applicable to trusts (see 81.5 SETTLEMENTS) for the year of the disposal, except to the extent that they are trustees of a non-authorised unit trust (see 90.1 UNIT AND INVESTMENT TRUSTS) of which the amount charged is treated as income. [*ICTA 1988, Sch 4 para 17; FA 1989, Sch 10 para 7; FA 1993, Sch 6 para 18*].

(*f*) UNDERWRITERS (89). For the underwriting year 1993 and earlier years, an underwriter is treated as absolutely entitled as against the trustees to securities forming part of his premiums trust fund (within *ICTA 1988, s 457; FA 1993, s 184(1)*). Securities held in premiums trust funds are to be regarded as disposed of by the trustees at market value on 31 December and as reacquired by them at market value on 1 January (commencing with 31 December 1989 and 1 January 1990) provided that they actually form part of the fund at the end of 31 December or the beginning of 1 January, as appropriate. For this purpose, stock lending transactions (see 71.82 SCHEDULE D, CASES I AND II) may be required to be disregarded, so that securities transferred are treated as still forming part of the fund. Where taxable income arises under these provisions in respect of securities forming part of a premiums trust fund, it is taxable in accordance with the rules in *ICTA 1988, s 450(1)* (see 89.4 UNDERWRITERS) rather than for the year of assessment in which the disposal occurs. The deemed disposal and reacquisition apply equally for capital gains tax purposes. For the underwriting year 1994 and subsequent years, the deep discount security provisions have no application to premiums trust funds. For 1992/93 and subsequent years, they also have no application to new-style special reserve funds under *FA 1993* (see 89.7(*b*) UNDERWRITERS). They continue to apply with respect to ancillary trust funds (see 89.3 UNDERWRITERS). For the purposes of the application of the provisions to ancillary trust funds and old-style special reserve funds, the underwriter is treated as absolutely entitled as against the trustees to securities forming part of the fund. There is no deemed disposal on death in respect of securities forming part of any of the above-mentioned funds. [*ICTA 1988, Sch 4 para 18; TCGA 1992, s 118(5)(6); FA 1989, s 96(2), Sch 10 para 7; FA 1993, s 176(3)(b), s 183(5)(6), Sch 23 Pt III(12)*].

(*g*) *New issues.* Where

(i) securities of a particular kind are issued (being the original issue of securities of that kind),

(ii) new securities of the same kind are issued subsequently, and after 18 March 1991,

(iii) a sum (the 'extra return') is payable by the issuer in respect of each new security, to reflect the fact that interest is accruing on the old securities and calculated accordingly, and

(iv) the issue price of each new security includes an element (separately identified or not) representing payment for the extra return,

then, for the purposes of the deep discount security provisions, the issue price of each new security is deemed to exclude the extra return referred to at (iii) above. [*ICTA 1988, Sch 4 para 11B; FA 1991, Sch 12 paras 3, 5*].

(*h*) *Interest etc. on debts between associated companies or to associates of banks.* Certain debts owed by non-UK resident companies (or certain third parties) to UK resident 'associated' companies (within *ICTA 1988, s 416*), or by any company to a UK resident company associated with a company carrying on a UK banking business, are classed as 'qualifying debts'. Where the debt on a deep discount security is a qualifying debt, it is treated as transferred for the purposes of the above provisions on becoming or ceasing to be a qualifying debt, at the end of each accounting period, and on the provisions in question coming into force. [*FA 1993, ss 61, 62, 64, 66; FA 1995, ss 88, 89*]. See Tolley's Corporation Tax under Profit Computations for the detailed provisions.

These provisions are **abolished** for **1996/97 onwards** and (subject to transitional provisions) for accounting periods ending **after 31 March 1996.** [*FA 1996, Sch 14 para 50, Sch 15 para 19, Sch 41 Pt V(3)*]. See now 72.2 SCHEDULE D, CASE III and see Tolley's Corporation Tax under Loan Relationships.

Simon's Direct Tax Service. See **B5.410–B5.414**.

44.6 **'Coupon-stripping'.** For 1995/96 and earlier years and for accounting periods ending before 1 April 1996, a special basis of charge applies to deep discount securities (see 44.5 above) issued by a company after 18 March 1985 which are '*chargeable securities*', i.e. where they were issued in any of the following circumstances.

(*a*) (i) Immediately before the issue, the issuing company held (i.e. had a beneficial interest in) 'relevant securities' representing at least 75% of the market value of all its assets; or

(ii) the terms of issue were determined by reference to (without necessarily reflecting) the terms of issue of 'relevant securities' which the issuing company was holding or intended to acquire.

(*b*) (i) The criteria in (*a*) would apply if 'relevant securities' included 'UK corporate bonds'; and

(ii) the criteria in (*a*) would have applied if such bonds had been deep discount securities when acquired.

(*c*) Neither (*a*) nor (*b*) above applies, and at any time during the first income period of securities of the particular kind (i.e. which are, or would be, dealt in on a stock exchange as being of the same kind), the company's assets include 'relevant securities' representing at least 75% of the market value of all its assets.

(*d*) The security was issued on a conversion or exchange falling within *TCGA 1992, ss 132, 135(3), 136(1)* (see Tolley's Capital Gains Tax under Shares and Securities) and the original securities were within (*a*) or (*b*) above or this provision, or were within (*c*) above where the condition therein had been fulfilled in their case by the time of the conversion or exchange.

The company must state on the bond certificate of any security within (*a*), (*b*) or (*d*) above that tax is chargeable under these provisions.

'*Relevant securities*' means securities within the accrued income provisions of *ICTA 1988, s 710 et seq.* (see 74.6 *et seq.* SCHEDULE D, CASE VI) but excluding '*UK corporate bonds*', i.e. sterling securities issued by a UK resident company (and not convertible into or redeemable in any other currency) the debt on which represents (and has always represented) a normal commercial loan (as defined in *ICTA 1988, Sch 18 para 1(5)* — see Tolley's Corporation Tax under Groups of Companies).

Where a person acquires a chargeable security, there is a **charge** under Schedule D, Case III or Case IV (as appropriate) *on the current year basis* at the end of each 'income period' (see 44.5 above) falling wholly or partly within the period of ownership. The charge is on an amount equal to the 'income element' (see 44.5 above) for the income period (or the part thereof falling within the period of ownership).

On a **disposal** or deemed disposal (see 44.5 above) of the chargeable security, the total amount charged under these provisions is deducted from the income otherwise chargeable under 44.5 above (without, however, affecting the Capital Gains Tax position). Similarly, the total amount charged under these provisions is deducted from the accrued income in arriving at the charge on early redemption or on winding-up.

CHARITIES (15) are exempt from any charge under these provisions on any amount applicable and applied for charitable purposes.

[*ICTA 1988, Sch 4 paras 2, 3, 4(1), 11(2), 14; TCGA 1992, s 118*].

See 44.5 above as regards abolition and replacement of these provisions.

Simon's Direct Tax Service. See **B5.415**.

44.7 DEEP GAIN SECURITIES

For **1995/96 and earlier** years, and for accounting periods ending **before 1 April 1996**, where there is a 'transfer' of a 'deep gain security' for an amount exceeding the acquisition cost, an amount equal to the difference (net of any acquisition or transfer costs) is treated as income of the transferor, chargeable to tax under Schedule D, Case III or IV, arising in the year of assessment of the transfer and assessable on the current year basis. '*Transfer*' is defined but specifically excludes the conversion of a security into share capital in a company. The amount obtained for the transfer includes any amount to which the transferor is entitled, whether or not he actually obtains that amount. A similar charge arises where a 'deep gain security' is redeemed. [*FA 1989, Sch 11 paras 4, 5, 6; FA 1990, Sch 10 para 27(2)*]. The provisions are replaced, **for 1996/97 onwards**, by the income tax provisions of *FA 1996, Sch 13* (see 72.2 SCHEDULE D, CASE III), and, for accounting periods ending **after 31 March 1996**, by the corporation tax provisions of *FA 1996, Pt IV, Ch II* (see Tolley's Corporation Tax under Loan Relationships).

Trustees on whom a charge arises under these provisions are chargeable at the rate applicable to trusts (see 81.5 SETTLEMENTS) for the year of the disposal, except to the extent that they are trustees of a non-authorised unit trust (see 90.1 UNIT AND INVESTMENT TRUSTS) of which the amount charged is treated as income. [*FA 1989, Sch 11 para 11; FA 1993, Sch 6 para 20*].

On the death of the person entitled to a 'deep gain security', there is a deemed market value transfer to his personal representatives immediately before his death, and the personal representatives are similarly treated as transferring a security at market value on a transfer of the security to a legatee (as widely defined). Transfers between CONNECTED PERSONS (20), whenever made, are similarly treated as at market value, as are any transfers other than for money's worth or other than at arm's length. Foreign currency transactions and costs are translated into sterling on the day of the transfer (or redemption) or acquisition by reference to the London closing rate of exchange for that day. [*FA 1989, Sch 11 paras 7, 8, 9, 12*].

A '*deep gain security*' is a redeemable security which meets the following conditions.

(*a*) At the time of issue (and assuming redemption) the amount payable on redemption (or on any one of a number of possible occasions of redemption) might constitute a 'deep gain'. For this purpose, 'redemption' does not include:

(i) any redemption which may be made before maturity only at the option of the issuer;

(ii) for securities issued before 13 November 1991, any redemption which may be made before maturity otherwise than by exercise by the holder of the security of an option exercisable only on the effluxion of time or the happening of an event which (judged at the time of the security's issue) is certain or likely to occur;

(iii) for securities issued after 12 November 1991, any redemption which may be made before maturity otherwise than at the option of the holder of the security, and as regards which (judged at the time of the security's issue) the event occasioning redemption

(A) is such that, if it occurred and there was no provision for redemption, the interests of the holder of the security at the time of the occurrence might be adversely affected,

(B) is neither certain nor likely to occur, and

(C) is not one of a number of events occasioning or allowing redemption before maturity at least one of which is certain or likely to occur,

and provided that the obtaining of a tax advantage by any person is not the main benefit or one of the main benefits expected to accrue from the provision for redemption.

(A) above is fulfilled if it is fulfilled by reference to any one potential holder, whether or not it is fulfilled by reference to other potential holders. In determining whether (B) or (C) is fulfilled in a case where the security is one which, under the terms of issue, can be converted into or exchanged for a security of a different kind, neither condition is treated as fulfilled unless it is fulfilled having regard only to circumstances in which (judged at the time of issue of the security) the right to convert or exchange cannot be, or is unlikely to be, exercised;

(iv) for securities issued after 12 November 1991, any redemption which may be made before maturity at the option of the holder of the security and as regards which (judged at the time of the security's issue) the conditions in (iii) above are fulfilled in relation to the event allowing the option to be exercised.

Where, however, a security which would be a deep gain security but for (iii) or (iv) above is redeemed before maturity, it is treated, as regards the redemption, as if it were, and had been acquired as, a deep gain security, where either:

(1) it was, immediately before redemption, held by a person connected with the issuer (within *ICTA 1988, s 839*, see 20 CONNECTED PERSONS); or

(2) it was transferred in the period of one year before the redemption by a person so connected with the issuer.

(*b*) The security is neither a deep discount security (see 44.5 above); nor a company share; nor a 'qualifying indexed security' (and see *Investor v Inspector of Taxes (Sp C 171), [1998] SSCD 244*, where a claim for exclusion was denied); nor a 'convertible security'; nor is it a gilt-edged security (as defined for capital gains tax purposes) which either

(i) was issued before 14 March 1989, or under the same prospectus as any gilt-edged security issued before that date, or

(ii) was issued, other than on the original issue, under a prospectus under which no securities were issued before 14 March 1989, where all the securities on the original issue are gilt-edged securities and not deep gain securities;

nor is it a security, other than a gilt-edged security, which was issued under the same prospectus as any other security issued earlier which is not a deep gain security.

As regards (ii) above and the paragraph which follows it, certain securities which would, apart from those provisions, be deep gain securities are generally treated as such where at some time the aggregate nominal value of securities issued under the same prospectus which would (apart from (ii) above and the paragraph following it) be deep gain securities exceeds that of those which would not, and the deemed treatment applies to events occurring after that time as if the securities in question had been acquired as such.

An amount payable on redemption constitutes a '*deep gain*' if the issue price is less than that amount (excluding any amount payable by way of interest) by more than 15% of that amount (excluding interest) or one-half per cent per annum of that amount (excluding interest) for each complete year between issue and redemption. [*FA 1989, Sch 11 paras 1, 19A, 20, 21, 21A; FA 1990, s 57; F(No 2)A 1992, Sch 7 paras 2, 4, 5*].

A '*qualifying indexed security*' is a security which, under the terms of issue (including those on which it may be offered by an agent or underwriter), satisfies the following conditions.

(i) The amount payable on redemption (excluding interest) must be precisely determined by the retail prices index (or foreign currency local equivalent), although the adjustment may lag behind the period in question by up to eight months. Securities quoted on a recognised stock exchange at the time of issue or, for securities issued after 8 June 1989, within one month thereafter (or on 8 June 1989 if issued on or before that date) may alternatively satisfy this condition where the amount payable on redemption is linked to a quoted share prices index. In relation to securities issued before 9 June 1989, this condition is not prevented from being satisfied by a guaranteed minimum amount being payable on redemption provided that either

(*a*) the minimum amount does not constitute a deep gain (as above), or

(*b*) the minimum amount arises only in 'qualifying circumstances'.

Also, this condition is not prevented from being satisfied by a guaranteed minimum amount equal to a specified percentage (being no greater than 10) of the issue price being payable on redemption or, for securities issued after 8 June 1989, where the amount to be paid on redemption in any of the circumstances in (*b*) above is to be not more than the issue price.

(ii) There must be no provision for redemption in, or conversion into, a different currency.

(iii) Indexed interest (the indexation of which must meet conditions similar to those in (i) above) must be payable at least annually at not less than a reasonable commercial rate.

(iv) The issue must have a stated life of not less than five years from the date of issue, and within that five year period the holder must not be able to require the purchase or repurchase of the security, or its conversion or redemption (in the latter case other than in 'qualifying circumstances').

See *Investor v Inspector of Taxes (Sp C 171), [1998] SSCD 244* for a case in which the requirement at (i) above was held not to be met. The Revenue consider that, as regards (i) above, the share prices index used must relate to the exchange on which the security is quoted, and that as regards (iii) above, the index in question must be applied directly to the interest payable, i.e. without any formula restriction and not e.g. in inverse proportion to index movements. (Revenue Tax Bulletin February 1995 p 196).

The following are '*qualifying circumstances*'.

(I) There is a fundamental change, detrimental to the interests of the holder of the security, in the rules of index in question.

(II) The index ceases to be published without comparable replacement.

(III) For securities issued before 13 November 1991, any circumstances except those in which the holder of the security exercises an option exercisable only on the effluxion of time or the happening of an event which (judged at the time of issue) is certain or likely to occur.

(IV) For securities issued after 12 November 1991, any circumstances for redemption which may be made before maturity otherwise than at the option of the holder of the security and as regards which the conditions set out at (*a*)(iii) above are fulfilled.

(V) For securities issued after 12 November 1991, any circumstances for redemption which may be made before maturity at the option of the holder of the security and as regards which the conditions set out at (*a*)(iv) above are fulfilled.

Where the issuer and the holder agree (after 13 March 1989) to vary the terms under which it is held, and, had the terms as so varied applied on issue, the security would be a deep gain security, it is treated as having been acquired as such from the date of the agreement.

The Treasury has power by regulations to modify any of the above conditions. [*FA 1989, Sch 11 paras 2, 22, 23; FA 1990, s 58; F(No 2)A 1992, Sch 7 para 3*].

A '*convertible security*' is a security issued by a company before 9 June 1989 under the terms of which it can be converted into or exchanged for share capital (by whatever name called) in that or any other company, and in relation to which the following condition is satisfied at some time in the period of one month following the day of issue. The condition is that either

(A) the security was quoted on a recognised stock exchange, or

(B) share capital in the company into whose shares the security may be converted or exchanged (but not necessarily those shares themselves) was so quoted, or

(C) both (A) and (B) are satisfied (though not necessarily at the same time). [*FA 1989, Sch 11 para 3*].

Convertible securities: special rules. A security which at the time of issue is a 'qualifying convertible security' (see 44.8 below) but would otherwise be a deep gain security is treated as not being a deep gain security. If, however, it ceases to be a qualifying convertible security, then, as regards any subsequent event in relation to it, including a transfer or acquisition, it is treated as if it were a deep gain security and had been acquired as such (whenever it was acquired). Where a security which would otherwise have been a deep discount security (see 44.5 above) ceases to be a qualifying convertible security, it is similarly treated, as regards subsequent events, as if it were, and had been acquired as, a deep gain security. [*FA 1989, Sch 11 paras 22A, 22B; FA 1990, Sch 10 para 27*].

Exemptions apply as for deep discount securities (see 44.5 above). [*FA 1989, Sch 11 paras 14, 15, 16*].

Miscellaneous points.

(1) *Accrued income scheme.* A transfer within these provisions is excluded from charge under the accrued income scheme (see 74.6 *et seq.* SCHEDULE D, CASE VI). [*FA 1989, Sch 11 para 17*].

(2) *Deduction of tax* under *ICTA 1988, s 123, ss 348–350* (see 23 DEDUCTION OF TAX AT SOURCE) does not apply to the proceeds of redemption of a deep gain security. [*FA 1989, Sch 11 para 18*].

(3) *Foreign domiciliaries* (and Commonwealth and Irish citizens not ordinarily resident in the UK) chargeable under Schedule D, Case IV are assessed on the remittance basis. [*FA 1989, Sch 11 para 13*].

(4) *Identification of securities* follows the capital gains tax rules of *TCGA 1992, s 108*. [*FA 1989, Sch 11 para 19*].

(5) *Underwriters.* Special provisions apply to disposals of securities forming part of the trust funds of Lloyd's UNDERWRITERS (89). These are broadly similar to those relating to deep discount securities (see 44.5 above). [*FA 1989, Sch 11 para 10; FA 1993, s 176(3)(c), s 183(5)(6), Sch 23 Pt III(12)*].

(6) *New issues.* In the circumstances set out in 44.5(*g*) above, the issue price, for the purposes of the deep gain security provisions, is adjusted as there mentioned. [*FA 1989, Sch 11 para 3A; FA 1991, Sch 12 paras 4, 5*].

(7) *Securities without a particular redemption date.* In the case of such securities, all the provisions of *FA 1989, Sch 11* which refer to 'redemption before maturity', 'redeemed before maturity' or 'redemption which may be made before maturity' are to be read as if the words 'before maturity' were omitted. [*FA 1989, Sch 11 para 22C; F(No 2)A 1992, Sch 7 para 6*].

(8) *Interest etc. on debts between associated companies or to associates of banks.* Certain debts owed by non-UK resident companies (or certain third parties) to UK resident 'associated' companies (within *ICTA 1988, s 416*), or by any company to a UK resident company associated with a company carrying on a UK banking business, are classed as 'qualifying debts'. Where the debt on a deep gain security is a qualifying debt, it is treated as transferred at market value for the purposes of the above provisions on becoming or ceasing to be a qualifying debt, at the end of each accounting period, and on the provisions in question coming into force. [*FA 1993, ss 61, 62, 65; FA 1995, ss 88, 89*]. See Tolley's Corporation Tax under Profit Computations for the detailed provisions.

These provisions are **abolished** (subject to transitional provisions) for **1996/97 onwards** and for accounting periods ending **after 31 March 1996.** [*FA 1996, Sch 14 para 57, Sch 15 para 20, Sch 41 Pt V(3)*]. See now 72.2 SCHEDULE D, CASE III and see also Tolley's Corporation Tax under Loan Relationships. The **transitional provisions** for income tax purposes apply where a person (the 'relevant person') held a qualifying indexed security on 5 April 1996 (31 March 1996 in the case of certain authorised unit trust holdings) and did not dispose of it on that date, and does not otherwise fall to be treated for capital gains tax purposes as having disposed of it on that date, and a 'relevant event' occurs. A '*relevant event*' occurs on the first occasion after that date when the relevant person (or a spouse to whom the security has been transferred within *TCGA 1992, s 58*) is treated for capital gains tax purposes as disposing of the security (or of any asset falling to be treated as the same as the security) other than on an inter-spouse transfer. In those circumstances, the chargeable gain or allowable loss which would have accrued to the relevant person on a disposal at market value on 5 April 1996 (or 31 March 1996) is brought into account as accruing to the person making the disposal constituting the relevant event, in the year of assessment in which that event occurs. If a qualifying indexed security held both on and immediately after 5 April 1996 (or 31 March 1996) is a 'relevant discounted security' within *FA 1996, Sch 13* (see 72.2 SCHEDULE D, CASE III), its acquisition on or before that date is treated for the purposes of that *Schedule* as having been at its market value on that date. [*FA 1996, Sch 15 paras 27–29*].

Simon's Direct Tax Service. See **B5.420–B5.423**.

44.8 **QUALIFYING CONVERTIBLE SECURITIES**

For **1995/96 and earlier** years, and for accounting periods ending **before 1 April 1996**, securities issued after 8 June 1989 which are convertible into the ordinary share capital of the issuing company, give the investor an option to put the security back to the issuer and meet certain qualifying conditions ('*qualifying convertible securities*') are excluded from the rules for deep gain securities (see 44.7 above). A person disposing of such a security by putting it back to the issuer or transferring it before the expiry of a put option is, however, chargeable to income tax or corporation tax on the income components accruing while he has held it. [*FA 1990, s 56, Sch 10*]. The provisions are replaced, **for 1996/97 onwards**, by the income tax provisions of *FA 1996, Sch 13* (see 72.2 SCHEDULE D, CASE III), and, for accounting periods ending **after 31 March 1996**, by the corporation tax provisions of *FA 1996, Pt IV, Ch II* (see Tolley's Corporation Tax under Loan Relationships).

A security issued by a company after 8 June 1989 is a '*qualifying convertible security*' at the time of its issue if it meets each of the following conditions.

(*a*) It is not a share, is redeemable and its issue does not fall, wholly or partly, to be treated, by virtue of *ICTA 1988, s 209(2)(c)*, as, or as part of, a company distribution (see Tolley's Corporation Tax under Distributions).

(*b*) It is quoted on a recognised stock exchange or is so quoted within one month after the issue date.

(*c*) Under the terms of the issue

- (i) the security can be converted into ordinary share capital (as defined by *FA 1990, Sch 10 para 11(5)*) in the issuing company,
- (ii) it carries either no right to interest or a right to interest at a fixed (not variable) rate determined at the time of issue, and
- (iii) any amount payable, either on redemption (at any time) or by way of interest, is payable in the currency in which the issue price is denominated.

(*d*) At the time of issue, the security is subject to one (and one only) 'qualifying provision for redemption'.

(*e*) The yield to redemption (as defined by *FA 1990, Sch 10 para 9*) for the 'relevant redemption period' represents no more than a reasonable commercial return. The '*relevant redemption period*' is the 'redemption period' which ends with the day on which the occasion for redemption under the 'qualifying provision for redemption' falls.

(*f*) The security is either a deep discount security (see 44.5 above) or a deep gain security (see 44.7 above), but only because of the 'qualifying provision for redemption'. *ICTA 1988, Sch 4 para 21* and *FA 1989, Sch 11 para 22B(1)*, which prevent a qualifying convertible security from being a deep discount or deep gain security, are to be disregarded for this purpose.

(*g*) The obtaining of a tax advantage within *ICTA 1988, s 709(1)* (see 3.2 ANTI-AVOIDANCE) by any person is not the main benefit, or one of the main benefits, that might be expected to accrue from issuing the security.

(*h*) Where the security carries a right to interest, the first (or only) interest payment day must fall either one year or six months after the day of issue, and subsequent interest payment days (if any) must continue to fall at yearly or six-monthly intervals respectively.

Having satisfied the above conditions at the time of issue, a security continues to be a qualifying convertible security unless at any time

(i) it becomes subject to a new qualifying provision for redemption and the conditions in *FA 1990, Sch 10 para 4(3)* are not satisfied, or

(ii) any of the prohibited events listed below occurs in relation to the security,

in which case the security ceases to be a qualifying convertible security at the time in question. Any of the following is a prohibited event.

(A) The security ceases to be quoted on a recognised stock exchange.

(B) It becomes subject to a provision under which either of the conditions at (*c*)(ii) or (iii) above will no longer be satisfied.

(C) It becomes subject to a provision which would be a 'qualifying provision for redemption' but for the fact that the conditions at (II) and (III) below are not fully satisfied.

(D) There is a time when more than 10% of the securities issued, under the prospectus under which the security concerned was issued, are held by companies which are at that time linked companies within the meaning of *FA 1988, Sch 11 para 4* (see Tolley's Corporation Tax under Capital Gains).

[*FA 1990, Sch 10 paras 2–5, 9, 11*].

A '*qualifying provision for redemption*', in relation to a security, is a provision which

(I) provides for redemption before maturity only at the option of the person holding the security for the time being,

(II) provides for such redemption on one occasion only, which must occur on the last day of an 'income period', and

(III) is such that the amount payable on the exercise of the option is fixed (not variable), is determined at the time the security becomes subject to the provision and constitutes a 'deep gain'.

[*FA 1990, Sch 10 para 1*].

The amount payable on redemption on exercise of the option under a provision for redemption constitutes a '*deep gain*' if the issue price is less than that amount (excluding any amount payable by way of interest) by more than 15% of that amount (excluding interest) or one-half per cent per annum of that amount (excluding interest) for each complete year between day of issue and the occasion for redemption under the provision concerned. Where, however, the security became subject to one or more qualifying provisions for redemption before becoming subject to the provision concerned, the above applies with the substitution of 'base amount' for 'issue price' and of 'base day' for 'day of issue'. The '*base amount*' is the amount payable on redemption on exercise of the option provided for by the previous qualifying provision for redemption or, if there was more than one, the one to which the security last became subject. The '*base day*' is the day on which the occasion for redemption falls under that previous, or last, qualifying provision for redemption. [*FA 1990, Sch 10 paras 6, 11(2)*].

An '*income period*' is the inclusive period from day of issue to the first (or only) interest payment day or any period from one interest payment day to the next. Where the security carries no right to interest, an income period is any period of one year ending with an anniversary of the day of issue. [*FA 1990, Sch 10 para 7*].

A '*redemption period*' is the inclusive period from the day of issue to the day on which falls the first (or only) occasion for redemption under a qualifying provision for redemption, or any period beginning with a day after that on which one such occasion falls and ending with the day on which the next such occasion falls. [*FA 1990, Sch 10 para 8*].

A **chargeable event** occurs where there is either a 'transfer' or a redemption (in exercise of the option under a qualifying provision for redemption) of a security which at that time is a qualifying convertible security and, in the case of a transfer, is subject to at least one qualifying provision for redemption under which the occasion for redemption has not arrived. ('*Transfer*' is defined but specifically excludes a transfer made on the conversion of a security into ordinary share capital of a company.) The 'chargeable amount' is treated as income of the person making the transfer or exercising the option, chargeable to tax under Schedule D, Case III or IV, arising in the year of assessment in which the chargeable event occurs and assessable on a current year basis. [*FA 1990, Sch 10 paras 10, 12*].

The '*chargeable amount*' is the lesser of the amount obtained on transfer or redemption (excluding interest), by the person making the transfer or entitled to the security immediately before redemption, and the 'total income element'. Except in cases where transfers are deemed to be at market value, i.e. on death, transfers between connected persons etc. or deemed transfers by trustees of Lloyd's premium trust funds, any amount which a person is entitled to obtain, but does not obtain, on transfer or redemption is treated for this purpose as having been obtained. [*FA 1990, Sch 10 para 13*].

The '*total income element*' is the sum of the 'income elements' for each income period (if any) the whole of which, and the 'partial income elements' for each income period (if any) part of which, consists of or falls within the ownership period, i.e. the period from date of acquisition to date of chargeable event. The '*income element*' for an income period is the amount obtained by the formula

$$\frac{A \times B}{100} - C$$

where

A is the issue price plus income elements of all previous income periods.

B is the figure included in the percentage representing the yield to redemption for the redemption period which consists of the income period or in which the income period falls.

C is the amount of interest (if any) payable for the income period.

The '*partial income element*' for an income period is the income element for that period apportioned in accordance with the number of days in that income period which consist of or fall within the ownership period. [*FA 1990, Sch 10 paras 14, 15*].

Exemptions apply as for deep discount securities (see 44.5 above). [*FA 1990, Sch 10 paras 21–23*].

Miscellaneous points.

(1) Provisions broadly similar to those for deep gain securities (see 44.7 above) apply as regards *death*, transfers to *legatees*, transfers between CONNECTED PERSONS (20) etc. and transfers by *trustees*. [*FA 1990, Sch 10 paras 16, 17, 19; FA 1993, Sch 6 para 21*].

(2) Special provisions apply to securities forming part of the trust funds of Lloyd's UNDERWRITERS (89). These are broadly similar to those relating to deep discount securities (see 44.5 above). [*FA 1990, Sch 10 para 18; FA 1993, s 176(3)(d), s 183(5)(6), Sch 23 Pt III(12)*].

(3) Provisions identical to those described at (3) and (4) in 44.7 above, as regards *foreign domiciliaries etc.* and *identification of securities*, apply in respect of qualifying convertible securities. [*FA 1990, Sch 10 paras 20, 24*].

(4) *Issuing company deduction*. Where a qualifying convertible security is redeemed in circumstances such that a chargeable event occurs, the excess of the amount paid on redemption (excluding interest) over the issue price may be deducted in the issuing company's computation for the account period of redemption. See also Tolley's Corporation Tax under Profit Computations. [*FA 1990, Sch 10 para 25*].

These provisions are **abolished** for **1996/97 onwards** and (subject to transitional provisions) for accounting periods ending **after 31 March 1996**. [*FA 1996, Sch 14 para 58, Sch 15 para 21, Sch 41 Pt V(3)*]. See now 72.2 SCHEDULE D, CASE III and see Tolley's Corporation Tax under Loan Relationships.

Simon's Direct Tax Service. See **B5.425–B5.429**.

44.9 **Deep discounted and indexed stock.** In as far as it is not within the specific legislation at 44.5 *et seq.* above, the Revenue consider that the discount on deep discounted stock (i.e. stock issued at a price well below par value and with a low interest rate) represents the reward for the use of the money over the period of the loan and as such will be treated, when it is paid on redemption, as chargeable to tax as rolled-up interest in the lender's hands and allowable against the borrower's profits for corporation tax purposes (whether or not there have been intermediate transactions during the life of the stock).

Corporate stock issued on an indexed basis and bearing a reasonable commercial rate of interest will generally be treated as follows:

(*a*) if the indexation constitutes a capital uplift of the principal on redemption to take account of no more than the fall in real value because of inflation, the lender (other than a bank or financial concern) will be liable only to capital gains tax on the uplift and the borrowing company will have no deduction against its profits.

(*b*) if the indexation applies to the interest element and additional sums of interest are rolled-up to be paid with the capital on redemption, the indexed and the rolled-up interest, when paid, will be given the same treatment as non-indexed interest.

(Revenue Press Release 25 June 1982).

Following the repeal of the provisions described at 44.5–44.8 above, and their replacement, for 1996/97 onwards, by the income tax provisions of *FA 1996, Sch 13* (see 72.2 SCHEDULE D, CASE III), and, for accounting periods ending after 31 March 1996, by the corporation tax provisions of *FA 1996, Pt IV, Ch II* (see Tolley's Corporation Tax under Loan Relationships), these considerations no longer apply.

45 Life Assurance Policies

The headings in this chapter are as follows.

45.1	Life assurance premium relief	45.10	— exemptions
45.2	— limits on amount of admissible premiums	45.11	— disqualification of certain life policies
45.3	— admissible premiums	45.12	— notes
45.4	— notes	45.13	Life assurance gains
45.5	Withdrawal of life assurance premium relief	45.14	— example
45.6	Qualifying policies	45.15	— partial surrenders etc.
45.7	— policies payable only on death within a specified period	45.16	— example
		45.17	Offshore policies
45.8	— endowment policies	45.18	— substitution of policies
45.9	— whole-life policies	45.19	— tax on chargeable events

45.1 LIFE ASSURANCE PREMIUM RELIEF

Relief for premiums paid on qualifying life assurance policies (see 45.3 below) ceases to be available for insurances made after 13 March 1984, other than certain deferred annuity contracts (see 45.3(i) below), certain part payments to friendly societies (see 45.3(ii) below) and certain industrial assurance policies (see 45.12(*b*) below). See 60.2 PERSONAL PENSION SCHEMES, 65.2 RETIREMENT ANNUITIES as regards certain types of life assurance contract for persons not in pensionable employment which continue to attract full relief against income. Relief ceases for a contract made before 14 March 1984 if the policy is terminated or varied (including the exercise of an option to change the terms of the policy) so as to increase the benefits secured or extend the term of the insurance (disregarding increased benefits in consideration of the cessation of house to house collection of premiums). [*ICTA 1988, s 266(3)(c), Sch 14 para 8(3)–(8); FA 1996, s 167(5)(6)*].

As regards whether contracts of insurance purporting to be made prior to midnight on 13 March 1984 in relation to a wide range of differing circumstances had in fact been completed at that time, see *Legal & General Assurance Society Ltd v CIR; Legal & General (Unit Assurance) Ltd v CIR (Sp C 96), [1996] SSCD 419*. The Revenue have an immediate enforceable right to recover amounts deducted from premiums under *The Income Tax (Life Assurance Premium Relief) Regulations 1978 (SI 1978 No 1159), reg 10(6)*, without issuing assessments under *TMA 1970* (*United Friendly Insurance plc v CIR Ch D 1998, 70 TC 627*).

Tax relief where applicable is generally given to UK residents (except children under 12), whether they have taxable income or not, by deduction from admissible premiums (see 45.3 below) up to certain limits (see 45.2 below). The deduction is $12\frac{1}{2}$% (but see 45.3(ii) below where relief is by reduction of total income). The deductions will normally be calculated by the life offices etc. (who will recover from the Board) without a specific claim being required. The Board may make regulations by statutory instrument to implement this scheme of 'premium relief by deduction'. [*ICTA 1988, s 266(4)(5), Sch 14 para 7; FA 1988, s 29; FA 1996, Sch 18 para 11(3)(4), para 17(1)–(4)(8)*]. Under the scheme relief will normally be allowed without the intervention of a tax office and PAYE taxpayers do not require a coding allowance for premiums.

The Inland Revenue Financial Intermediaries and Claims Office may be contacted in relation to life assurance premium relief on 0151–472 6169 as regards repayments or 0151–472 6152 for technical advice.

Simon's Direct Tax Service. See **E2.10**.

45.2 **Limits on amounts of admissible premiums.** Relief is not given on premiums to the extent that they exceed

(*a*) **£1,500 or one-sixth of total income,** whichever is the greater. [*ICTA 1988, s 274(1)*]. See also 45.4(*j*) below for married persons and 1.6 ALLOWANCES AND TAX RATES for definition of total income.

(*b*) **£100** for policies not securing a capital sum at death. [*ICTA 1988, s 274(2)*].

The restrictions in (*a*) and (*b*) are not to take into account any additional 'war insurance premiums'. [*ICTA 1988, s 274(4); FA 1996, s 134, Sch 20 para 20*]. Where the limits seem likely to be exceeded by the deductions, the Board may require some premiums to be paid in full. Any over- or under-deductions in a year will be adjusted by assessment or claim to repayment. [*ICTA 1988, Sch 14 paras 4–6; FA 1996, Sch 18 para 11(2), para 17(5)(7)*].

45.3 **Admissible premiums.** Subject to the cessation of relief for policies made after 13 March 1984 (see 45.1 above), admissible premiums are as follows.

(i) **Life assurance premiums** (and payments under **contracts for deferred annuities** (but see 45.4(*b*) below and note limit at 45.2(*b*) above)) paid by an individual in respect of policies (or deferred annuities) on either the individual's own life or that of his spouse. The insurance or contract must be made by the individual. Policies effected after 19 March 1968 must be 'qualifying policies', see 45.6 below. [*ICTA 1988, s 266(1)–(3)*]. See 60 PERSONAL PENSION SCHEMES, 65 RETIREMENT ANNUITIES for the special provisions relating to annuities under such arrangements.

(ii) Proportion of members' contributions to trade unions allocated to superannuation benefits in addition to any portion allocated to funeral benefits or life assurance.

Relief is given by deducting one-half of the portion from total income. A similar deduction applies to a part payment to a registered or incorporated friendly society in respect of an eligible insurance or contract (excluding certain sickness, etc. insurances or contracts made after 31 August 1996). The deduction applies also to payments to an organisation of persons in police service provided the allocated portion is £20 or more per annum. [*ICTA 1988, s 266(6)(7)(13); F(No 2)A 1992, Sch 9 para 2; FA 1996, s 171(3)(4)*].

(iii) Statutory deductions from salary for deferred pension to widow or widower or provision for children after claimant's death, including similar compulsory deductions under any contract of employment — the relief for such deductions being given at the full basic rate. [*ICTA 1988, s 273; FA 1988, Sch 3 para 10*].

Employers' contributions under retirement schemes not approved by the Revenue may be relieved in some circumstances as if they were life assurance premiums paid by the employee, see 66.2 RETIREMENT SCHEMES.

45.4 **Notes.**

(*a*) Policies as under 45.3(i) above are only eligible for relief if they secure capital sum at *death* whether or not in conjunction with any other benefit e.g. disability benefit or option to receive an annuity.

(*b*) No allowance during period of deferment on '*deferred policies*'. [*ICTA 1988, s 266(3)(a)(d)*].

But neither (*a*) nor (*b*) applies to policies (i) in connection with *bona fide* employees' pension schemes as defined or for the benefit of persons engaged in any particular trade, profession, vocation or business, or (ii) taken out by teachers in secondary schools (as so called in 1918) pending setting up of a pension scheme. [*ICTA 1988, s 266(11)*].

(*c*) The insurance contract must be made with either (i) insurance company legally established in UK, *or lawfully carrying on business in UK*, (ii) underwriters, (iii) registered or incorporated friendly society, (iv) (deferred annuities) National Debt Commissioners. [*ICTA 1988, s 266(2)(a)(13); F(No 2)A 1992, Sch 9 para 2*]. *Note.* Included under (i) is a policy issued and managed overseas but where the premium is paid to the UK branch of the insurance company (Revenue Press Release 4 February 1981).

(*d*) Premiums allowed only so far as *paid* i.e. not covered by advances (*Hunter v A-G HL 1904, 5 TC 13*), nor repayment of advances (*R v Special Commissioners (ex parte Horner) KB 1932, 17 TC 362*). A premium paid otherwise than in the year in which it becomes due and payable is treated as paid in that year. [*ICTA 1988, s 266(4)*].

Non-residents must pay their premiums in full but will be given relief as appropriate under *ICTA 1988, s 278* (see 51.11 NON-RESIDENTS AND OTHER OVERSEAS MATTERS). Premiums to foreign life assurance companies etc. will be payable in full without relief but see Note in (*c*) above. A member of the armed forces or the wife or husband of such a member is treated as resident in the UK. [*ICTA 1988, s 266(8)(9), Sch 14 para 6; FA 1988, Sch 3 para 9; FA 1996, Sch 18 para 11(2), para 17(5)(7)*].

(*e*) No allowance for joint insurance on two directors' lives (*Wilson v Simpson KB 1926, 10 TC 753*).

(*f*) *Accident and Sickness Policies.* Relief allowed only on proportion of premium relative to death benefit.

(*g*) *Children's Policies.* Premiums allowable if paid by parent for (i) life endowment on his own life, maturing when school fees begin, or when child may go into business, etc., or (ii) for securing series of payments on specified dates if parent dies earlier. But no relief to parent where policy is on life of *child* unless it is an industrial assurance policy or policy issued by a registered or incorporated friendly society on the life of a child or grandchild and the annual premiums do not exceed £64. [*ICTA 1988, Sch 14 paras 2, 3; F(No 2)A 1992, Sch 9 para 18*].

Policy by child on own life. The Board are of the opinion that no relief is in strictness due on premiums on a policy taken out by a child under age twelve, but are prepared to allow relief as follows. An industrial branch policy or friendly society policy as above will receive relief. Where an ordinary branch policy is taken out on the life of a child and is assigned to him or he possesses or acquires the whole interest in the policy, relief on premiums paid by him may be allowed (provided the other conditions are satisfied) where the policy was taken out (*a*) after the child had attained age twelve; (*b*) before 1 March 1979 and before the child attained age twelve; or (*c*) on or after 1 March 1979 before the child attained age twelve and he has attained that age. (Revenue Pamphlet IR 131, SP 11/79, 1 November 1979 relaxing SP 4/79, 28 February 1979.)

(*h*) *Borrowings* (at intervals) against life policies may be treated as taxable income. Payments by way of loan under a contract or arrangement, made after 6 April 1949, providing (i) for such payments to be made at intervals during a period dependent on human life, (ii) that the loans, being secured on a life policy, are *not repayable* until the capital benefit accrues payable, and that (iii) the capital benefit *increases* with the length of the period (otherwise than by reason of the insured's right to share in profits of the insurer) are taxable as annual payments under Schedule D, Case III, or Case V, if made to a resident under a foreign contract, as income from a foreign possession under *ICTA 1988, s 65(1)*. The section does not apply if the Board are satisfied that it is not one of the objects of the contract, etc., to secure for recipient the equivalent of an annuity equal to the periodic loan payments. [*ICTA 1988, s 554*]. But see 45.15(*f*) below.

(*j*) *Married persons.* Premiums paid by one spouse on the life of the other (in addition to relief on premiums paid on his or her own life) will be eligible for relief to the paying spouse even after divorce, unless the divorce was before 6 April 1979. [*ICTA 1988, Sch 14 para 1(1)*]. This treatment is extended to premiums paid by a divorced person on policies taken out prior to the marriage (Revenue Pamphlet IR 1, A31).

The premium relief limits in 45.2 above apply separately and in full to each spouse.

(*k*) See 45.6 and 45.13 below regarding Qualifying and Non-Qualifying Policies respectively, effected after 19 March 1968.

45.5 **WITHDRAWAL OF LIFE ASSURANCE PREMIUM RELIEF**

(i) **Clawback of relief on early surrender etc. within four years**

There was a 'clawback' of the tax relief given on premiums payable on a qualifying policy (see 45.6 below) issued in respect of an insurance made after 26 March 1974 and before 14 March 1984 (when relief ceased to be available) where within four years

(*a*) the policy was wholly or partly surrendered (including certain loans, see 45.15(*f*) below), or

(*b*) there was a sum payable on the policy (other than on death) by way of participation in profits, or

(*c*) the policy was wholly or partly made paid-up.

The body which issued the policy had to pay the clawback to the Revenue out of the sum falling due at the following rate for 1988/89 and earlier years.

Time of surrender etc.	*Clawback of total premiums payable to date*	*Clawback limit*
In year 1 or 2	$\frac{3}{6}$ths of 30% i.e. 15%	Surrender value less 85% of total premiums payable to date
In year 3	$\frac{2}{6}$ths of 30% i.e. 10%	Surrender value less 90% of total premiums payable to date
In year 4	$\frac{1}{6}$th of 30% i.e. 5%	Surrender value less 95% of total premiums payable to date

For partial surrenders etc. the clawback limit could not exceed the value withdrawn or the surrender value if the policy was made paid-up and account was taken of any earlier clawbacks on the same policy. If the annual premium on a policy was increased by more than 25% over the first annual premium (or the annual premium at 26 March 1974 where a policy was issued before that date), the additional premiums and rights obtained were treated as relating to a new policy.

The above provisions did not apply to policies issued in connection with sponsored superannuation schemes or certain approved retirement benefit schemes or if the event under (*a*) or (*c*) arose because of the winding-up of the issuing body. [*ICTA 1988, s 268*]. For replacement of one policy by another, see 45.12(*d*) below.

(ii) **Clawback of relief on surrender etc. after four years**

If in the fifth or any later year from the making of an insurance either (*a*) or (*b*) (other than on death or maturity) in (i) above occurs and either event has occurred before, a clawback will be made of 12% (15% for 1988/89 and earlier years of assessment) on the lower of the premiums payable in that year and the sum payable by reason of the event.

If two or more events occur in the same year the total clawback is limited to the appropriate percentage (as above) of the premiums payable in that year. Account is taken of any clawback also due under *section 268* (above) on a policy treated as new because of an increase in premiums, see (i) above.

The above provisions apply to qualifying policies made after 26 March 1974 but not to industrial assurance policies. [*ICTA 1988, s 269*].

(iii) **Reduction in relief where clawback occurs**

Where there has been a clawback under (i) or (ii) above, the tax relief on the relevant premiums is reduced by the same amount and the increased liability arising from the loss of the tax relief is set against the clawback suffered (earlier years first), with any excess clawback reclaimable by the taxpayer within six years after the end of the year of assessment in which the event happens.

The relevant premiums are, for (i) above, the total premiums payable under the policy up to the event giving rise to the clawback and, for (ii) above, the premiums payable in the year in which the event happens. [*ICTA 1988, s 270*].

(iv) Provisions apply for the collection etc. of the clawback by the Revenue from the life office and for the taxpayer to be given, within 30 days by the life office, a statement of the clawback amount and how calculated. [*ICTA 1988, s 272*].

Simon's Direct Tax Service. See **E2.1051** *et seq.*.

45.6 **QUALIFYING POLICIES**

A policy effected after 19 March 1968 qualifies for life assurance relief only if it provides no 'benefits' other than a capital sum (see 45.12(*a*) below for definition) payable only on death (or on death or earlier disability) or survival for specified term and it also fulfils the conditions set out in 45.7–45.9 below, subject to the exemptions in 45.10 below. [*ICTA 1988, s 266(3)(b), Sch 15 Pt I*].

By concession, free gifts offered as incentives in connection with life insurance policies are disregarded in determining whether a policy is a qualifying policy (and in computing any gain arising in respect of a non-qualifying policy, see 45.13 below), provided that the aggregate cost to the insurer of all gifts in connection with a policy (or a 'cluster' of policies) does not exceed £30. The concession applies in relation to all liabilities unsettled at 7 December 1993. (Revenue Pamphlet IR 1, B42).

See 45.17 below for conditions relating to 'new non-resident policies' issued in respect of an insurance made after 17 November 1983 by a company not resident in the UK.

Note. From 1 April 1976, the certification of new qualifying policies (other than friendly society policies) was transferred from the issuing body to the Revenue (with right of appeal if certificate refused). Certification of policies issued before 1 April 1976 but varied on or after that date remained the responsibility of the life office. [*ICTA 1988, Sch 15 Pt II*]. Certification of policies is to be **abolished** altogether from a day to be appointed for the purpose by the Board, except for certification in relation to a time before that day, and subject to the rights of appeal in relation to refusals. A certificate issued under the old rules continues to be conclusive evidence that a policy is a qualifying policy. [*FA 1995, s 55(1)–(3); FA 1996, s 162(1)*].

Simon's Direct Tax Service. See E2.1032.

45.7 **Policies payable only on death** (or earlier disability) **within a specified period** ('Term Assurance').

(*a*) If the period *does not exceed ten years*, any surrender value must not exceed the return of premiums paid. [*ICTA 1988, Sch 15 para 1(4)*].

(*b*) If the specified term *exceeds ten years*, premiums must be payable at yearly, or shorter intervals, during at least ten years or three-quarters of the term, whichever is less, or until the assured's earlier death (or disability), and those payable in any one year, excluding any loading for exceptional mortality risk, must not exceed

(i) twice the amount of the premiums payable in any other year, nor

(ii) one-eighth of the total premiums which would be payable if the policy ran for the full term (or, if appropriate, the sooner of ten years or three-quarters of the term). [*ICTA 1988, Sch 15 para 1(3)(8)*].

(*c*) For policies issued on or after 1 April 1976, if the specified term ends after the age of 75 years and the policy provides for any payment on the whole or partial surrender of the policy, the capital sum payable on death must not be less than 75% of the total premiums payable if death occurred at 75 years of age. In the case of a policy payable on one of two lives, the age of the older is taken if the sum is payable on the death of the first, and the age of the younger is taken if payment arises on the death of the survivor. If limited to death after 16 (or some lower age) the benefit on earlier death must not exceed the return of premiums paid. [*ICTA 1988, Sch 15 para 1(5)*].

In calculating total premiums, there will be ignored any weighting due to premiums being payable at lesser than annual intervals (generally taken to be 10% if the reduction is not specified) and in calculating the capital sum, the smallest amount is used if more than one is payable. [*ICTA 1988, Sch 15 para 1(6)(9); FA 1996, s 167(7)*].

Short-term assurances. A policy will not be a qualifying policy under 45.6 above if the capital sum is payable only if death or disability occurs less than one year after making the insurance. [*ICTA 1988, Sch 15 para 10*].

45.8 **Endowment policies.** Term must be for at least ten years, or until the assured's earlier death (or disability). The policy must not provide for any capital benefit to be paid (other than on whole or part surrender of the policy or bonus additions to it or on disability) during its continuance, but it must guarantee on death (or death after 16 or some lower specified age) a sum at least equal to 75% of the total premiums (less any weighting due to premiums being paid at lesser than annual intervals, generally taken to be 10% if the reduction is not specified) which would be payable if the policy ran full term. For a policy effected on or after 1 April 1976 by a person over 55 years of age, the 75% requirement is reduced by 2% for each year the age exceeds 55. If limited to death after 16 (or some lower age) the benefit on earlier death must not exceed the return of premiums paid.

Premiums must be payable annually, or at shorter intervals, for a period of not less than ten years or until death, etc. Limitations (i) and (ii) under 45.7(*b*) above apply, but with exclusion of wording in brackets at end of (ii). For a policy payable on one of two lives, the rules under 45.7(*c*) above apply. [*ICTA 1988, Sch 15 para 2; FA 1996, s 167(7)*].

45.9 **Whole-life policies.** Premiums must be payable annually, or at shorter intervals, until the assured's death (or his earlier disability, if so provided) or for a specified period of at least ten years should he live longer than that period. Premium limitations (i) and (ii) under

45.7(*b*) above apply except that the total premiums under (ii) are those for the first ten years or for the specified period, as above, if longer. The provisions under 45.7(*c*) above also apply. [*ICTA 1988, Sch 15 para 1(2)*].

45.10 **Exemptions.** The above restrictions do not apply to the following.

(i) Policies solely for the payment on an individual's death (or disability) of a sum substantially equal to the then balance of a mortgage (repayable by annual, or shorter, instalments) on his residence or business premises. [*ICTA 1988, s 266(10)(a)*].

(ii) Policies under a sponsored superannuation scheme (as defined by *ICTA 1988, s 624*), if at least half the cost of the scheme is borne by the employer. [*ICTA 1970, s 19(4)(b)*]. This provision was repealed on 6 April 1980 [*FA 1971, Sch 14 Pt I*] but is continued, for policies issued before that date, by extra-statutory concession (Revenue Pamphlet IR 1, A32).

(iii) Policies issued in connection with approved occupational pension scheme under *ICTA 1988, s 590 et seq.* [*ICTA 1988, s 266(10)(b)*].

Although the above policies are not qualifying policies, relief under 45.1 to 45.4 above is available on premiums paid (subject to the general restrictions) and they are not subject to the charge on life assurance gains (see 45.13 and 45.15 below).

(iv) Certain policies issued by a friendly society in the course of its tax-exempt life business are qualifying policies. See 31.3 FRIENDLY SOCIETIES.

45.11 **Disqualification of certain life policies.** A policy (issued in the UK or elsewhere) effected in the course of long-term business is not a 'qualifying policy' if it is 'connected with' another policy the terms of which provide benefits greater than would reasonably be expected if any policy 'connected with' it were disregarded.

A policy is 'connected with' another policy if

(*a*) they are at any time simultaneously in force, and

(*b*) either of them is issued with reference to the other, or with a view to enabling or facilitating the other to be issued on particular terms. (See Revenue Press Release 16 June 1980 for guidelines.)

This applies to policies issued in respect of insurances made after 25 March 1980 and to an insurance made on or before that date which is connected with one made after it, but not in relation to premiums paid before that date on the earlier policy.

In relation to policies issued in respect of insurances made after 22 August 1983, the above restriction applies where either of the policies concerned provides such excessive benefits as are mentioned above. With respect to payments made after 22 August 1983, this extension of the restriction also applies to insurances made before that date if further premiums exceeding £5 p.a. are made after that date.

A revised definition of 'long-term insurance business' applied before 23 August 1983.

A person issuing a policy which by virtue of the above is not a qualifying policy (or a policy which causes another policy to cease to be a qualifying policy) is required to give written notice of the fact to the Board within three months of issue. The Board may require any person who appears to them to be concerned in the issue of such a policy (but not a solicitor who only gave advice) to provide them with such information as they think necessary, and as that person has or can reasonably obtain, for the purposes of this provision within a specified time of not less than 30 days. The penalty provisions of *TMA 1970, s 98* apply. [*ICTA 1988, Sch 15 para 14*].

45.12 **Notes.**

(*a*) '*Capital sum*' includes a series of capital sums, or a sum varying with the circumstances. Bonus additions, an option to take an annuity, a payment on whole or part surrender, or a waiver of premiums in the event of disability *do not constitute 'benefits'*. [*ICTA 1988, Sch 15 para 1(7)(9)*].

(*b*) For *Industrial assurance* policies and *Family Income and Mortgage Protection* policies, see *ICTA 1988, Sch 15 paras 7–9*. After 1 April 1976, industrial insurance policies are generally regarded as qualifying policies although not within the appropriate conditions. In addition, industrial assurance policies issued in respect of insurances made after 13 March 1984 continue to attract premium relief (see 45.1 above) as if issued on or before that date provided that

(i) the proposal form was completed on or before that date,

(ii) the policy was prepared for issue before 1 April 1984, and

(iii) before 1 April 1984 the policy was permanently recorded in the issuer's books in accordance with its normal business practice. [*ICTA 1988, Sch 14 para 8(3)*].

Industrial assurance ceases to be a distinct form of business for tax purposes for accounting periods beginning after 31 December 1995. However, the special treatment afforded to industrial assurance policies will continue to be given to policies issued by any company on or after a day to be appointed for the purpose by the Board, where the company had previously issued qualifying policies in the course of industrial assurance business and was, on 28 November 1995, offering such policies of the same type as those offered on or after the appointed day. [*ICTA 1988, Sch 15 para 8A; FA 1996, s 167(1)(8)*].

(*c*) A variation after 19 March 1968 to a policy taken out before that date so as to increase benefits or extend term ranks as a new policy. [*ICTA 1988, Sch 14 para 8(1)(2)*]. See, however, 45.13 below as regards cessation of premium collection on certain old policies which is not regarded as a variation.

(*d*) Where, after 24 March 1982, a qualifying policy is replaced by another qualifying policy as a result of a variation in the life or lives assured (e.g. on marriage or divorce), both policies are treated for the following purposes as a single qualifying policy made at the time of the earlier policy provided that (*a*) any sum becoming payable in connection with the earlier policy is retained by the insurer and applied towards any premium on the later policy and (*b*) no consideration (apart from the benefits under the new policy) is received by any person in connection with the ending of the earlier policy. Any sum applied as in (*a*) is treated neither as a premium for premium clawback purposes (see 45.5 above) nor for the purposes of life assurance gain computations (see 45.13 below) nor as a capital sum received for the latter purposes. The replacement policy is also treated as made at the same time as the original policy for relief purposes (see 45.1 above) provided that the benefits conferred by the replacement policy are substantially equivalent to those under the original policy. [*ICTA 1988, Sch 14 para 8(6), Sch 15 para 20*]. For the effect of other substitutions for and variations to policies generally, see *ICTA 1988, Sch 15 paras 17–20* and note concession in Revenue Pamphlet IR 1, A45.

(*e*) A body issuing a policy which is certified by the Board as being a qualifying policy (or which is in the appropriate standard form) must, within three months of receipt of a written request by the policyholder, supply a certificate to that effect. Such a certificate must similarly be supplied where a policy is varied in a significant respect, but continues to be a qualifying policy (although certain variations to pre-20 March 1968 policies are ignored for this purpose). [*ICTA 1988, Sch 15 para 22*]. This requirement will **cease to apply** following the abolition of certification (see 45.6 above). [*FA 1995, s 55(4); FA 1996, s 162(1)*].

(*f*) Any option to vary a policy issued before 1 April 1976 is disregarded until it is exercised and the policy is then subject to the new qualifying conditions. A policy issued after 1 April 1976 with an option to vary the terms or to have another policy issued in substitution for it is only a qualifying policy if all the specified conditions would continue to be satisfied after the exercise of the option. [*ICTA 1988, Sch 15 para 19*].

(*g*) As a result of legal advice received, the Revenue have not, since 24 February 1988, certified as a qualifying policy any new life assurance policy which may be converted or fundamentally restructured in such a way as to constitute, under contract law, a rescission of the original contract and the creation of a new one, e.g. the conversion of a whole life policy to an endowment policy or vice versa. Such conversions, etc. may arise by means of an agreement between the policyholder and the insurer or by the exercising of an option contained in the terms of the policy. Previously, such alterations were regarded as variations of the existing contract which did not, therefore, prejudice the qualifying status of the policy. Policies certified and sold before 25 February 1988 will not lose their qualifying status even if subsequently converted or restructured. (Revenue Press Release 22 January 1988). Certification is to be abolished (see 45.6 above).

(*h*) The Revenue may concessionally disregard certain minor infringements of the conditions for recognition as a qualifying policy relating to:

- (i) policies back-dated by not more than three months, which may for certain purposes be treated as if the assurance was made on the earlier date;
- (ii) reductions in first year premiums which do not result in any value being credited to the policyholder;
- (iii) trivial non-recurring infringements of arithmetical tests; and
- (iv) policies which could have been certified as qualifying but which were not so certified when the assurance was made.

(Revenue Pamphlet IR 1, A41).

45.13 LIFE ASSURANCE GAINS

If a life policy effected after 19 March 1968 is not a qualifying policy (see 45.6 above), then

(*a*) no life assurance relief is granted on the premiums [*ICTA 1988, s 266(3)(b)*] (cf. 45.5 above re qualifying policies), and

(*b*) on the happening of a 'chargeable event' within *ICTA 1988, s 540*, a 'gain' is treated as arising, there is a charge to income tax at the excess of the higher rate over the basic rate on the 'gain' [*ICTA 1988, ss 539 et seq.*] (and see (A) below as regards a charge on certain qualifying policies). The gain is for all other purposes treated as an addition to total income.

Certain types of policy are excluded from these provisions (see *ICTA 1988, s 539(2) as amended*).

For the duty of insurers to inform the inspector of chargeable events, see *ICTA 1988, s 552* and *SI 1997 No 265*. In relation to non-resident policy holders, see the concession announced in Revenue Press Release 23 November 1999. For the requirement for most overseas insurers (as widely defined) to nominate a UK tax representative responsible for providing such information, see *ICTA 1988, ss 552A, 552B* (introduced by *FA 1998, s 87* with effect from 6 April 1999) and regulations thereunder (see *SI 1999 No 881*).

See 45.19 below for 'new non-resident policies' which are not qualifying policies.

A charge under (*b*) above does not arise if a new policy is issued on exercise of an option under a maturing policy and the proceeds of the maturing policy are fully applied to pay premium(s) under the new policy, *unless* the new policy is issued to a person who was an infant when the maturing policy was issued, and the maturing policy secured a capital sum within a month of his attaining age 25, or on the policy anniversary following his attaining that age. [*ICTA 1988, s 540(2)*].

The 'gain' (taxable as in (*b*) above) is the excess, over premiums paid, of

(i) the surrender value of the policy *immediately prior to the death* plus any 'relevant capital payments' received previously (e.g. by surrender of bonus rights, etc.), or

(ii) any sum received on the *maturity* of the policy, or for the *surrender*, or *assignment* for value, of rights under it (plus any prior 'relevant capital payments'). [*ICTA 1988, s 541*]. But see 45.12(*d*) above for replacement of a policy.

A *'relevant capital payment'* is any capital sum (not attributable to disability) paid or conferred before the chargeable event. See also 45.15(*h*) below.

See 45.6 above as regards certain 'free gifts' given as incentives in relation to the issue of a policy, which are disregarded for these purposes.

See Revenue Pamphlet IR 131, SP 6/92, 3 July 1992 as regards certain accident insurance policies providing cover against dying as a result of an accident, which, from the date of issue of the Statement, are not regarded as life insurance policies for these purposes. The Statement of Practice applies mainly to group policies, under which a gain might otherwise arise on payment of a death benefit as a result of earlier payments under the policy.

See 45.15 below for computation of the gain realised on partial surrenders etc.

If the gain arises to a trust, the settlor is liable as under (*b*) above. [*ICTA 1988, s 547(1)(a)*]. There is special provision from 6 April 1998 (but excluding certain cases where a settlor had died before 17 March 1998) where, immediately before the chargeable event, the settlor was dead, non-resident or (in the case of a company or 'foreign institution' (as defined)) had come to an end, or the policy was held as security for a debt owed by the trustees. There is similarly special provision from that date where a policy is beneficially owned by, or held as security for a debt owed by, a foreign institution. [*ICTA 1988, s 547(1)(d)(e)(5AA)(9)–(13); FA 1998, Sch 14 paras 1, 7*]. For the right to recover tax paid from trustees, see *ICTA 1988, s 551* (individuals) or (for companies from 6 April 1998) *s 551A* (introduced by *FA 1998, Sch 14 para 3*).

For the method of charging gains where two or more persons have an interest in a policy, see *ICTA 1988, s 547(3)* or (for chargeable events on or after 6 April 1998) *s 547A* (introduced by *FA 1998, Sch 14 para 2*).

For the charge under *FA 1989, s 90, Sch 9* on gains arising on policies held by companies, see Tolley's Corporation Tax under Profit Computations.

There is an exemption for gains arising on retirement annuities approved under *ICTA 1988, s 621* and occupational pension schemes approved under *ICTA 1988, s 590 et seq.* See 65 RETIREMENT ANNUITIES, 66 RETIREMENT SCHEMES.

A charge on the gain, as under (*b*) above, also arises (if the policy was taken out after 19 March 1968 or varied, so as to increase benefits or extend term, after that date) on

(A) a qualifying policy if, within the lesser of ten years from inception or three-quarters of its term, it is surrendered or assigned for value, in whole or in part. Also, if it is converted to a paid-up policy within that period and any of the events as in (i) or (ii) above occur. [*ICTA 1988, s 540(1)(b)*]. See 45.15 below.

(B) life annuity contracts (including those issued in connection with 'Guaranteed Income Bonds'). The charge is on the total amount received up to and including surrender or assignment (excluding the proportion of any annual receipts already taxed as income) less premium etc. paid. [*ICTA 1988, ss 542, 543*]. For contracts made after 26 March 1974, any gains will be chargeable at the basic rate under Schedule D, Case VI. This is in addition to the charge at the higher rates under the provisions above, and does not apply to gains on certain policies issued by non-UK resident companies within the charge to tax in a territory within the European Economic Area. [*ICTA 1988, s 547(6)(6A); FA 1995, s 56(1)*]. Capital sums payable on death under contracts made after 9 December 1974 are treated as a surrender of the contract. [*ICTA 1988, s 542(2)*]. See also 45.15 below.

(C) a capital redemption policy (under which a premium is paid for a return or returns on a specified date or dates in the future). The charge is on the total amounts received up to and including maturity, surrender or assignment (excluding the proportion of any annual receipts already taxed as income) less premium etc. paid. [*ICTA 1988, s 545*]. Also applicable to companies. See also 45.15(*g*) below.

Gains on certain policies issued by FRIENDLY SOCIETIES (31) may also be taxable at the basic rate. [*ICTA 1988, s 547(7)*].

Cessation of premium collection on old policies. Where an insurer decides to cease collecting premiums on certain types of policy held for a specified period, and any change to the benefits is limited to a deduction of no more than the premiums forgone, this will, by concession, not be treated as an alteration to the policy for these purposes (and for the purposes of 45.12(*c*) above). This is dependent upon the change not itself being a chargeable event, the policy being at least 20 years old at the time of the change, and there being no option under the policy (whether or not previously exercised) for reduction of the premiums to a nominal amount in connection with a right to make partial surrenders after the date of the reduction. (Revenue Pamphlet IR 1, A96).

'Assignment' for the above purposes does not include an assignment between *spouses living together* or by way of *security for debt*. [*ICTA 1988, s 540(4)*]. There are exemptions from the general charge under (*b*) above, and from the charge under (A) and (B) above, for *assignees* (for money or money's worth) in respect of policies or life annuity contracts issued or made before 26 June 1982 and assigned before that date, who will normally be liable to capital gains tax on their gains. But the original beneficial owner of a policy or contract which *has been re-assigned to him* is not exempt from the income tax charge on subsequent gains. Also, the exemption is denied where a policy or contract was assigned for money or money's worth before 26 June 1982 and, after 23 August 1982, either

(i) the policy is reassigned for money or money's worth (other than between spouses or as security for a debt or on the discharge of a debt so secured), or

(ii) further capital is injected, or

(iii) loans are taken against security of the policy, etc., except that (iii) does not apply

(*a*) unless the policy, etc. was issued in respect of an insurance or contract made after 26 March 1974, and the sum is lent to, or at the direction of, the individual who, at the time of the loan, owns the rights conferred by the policy, etc., or

(*b*) if the policy is a qualifying policy (see 45.6 above), and either a commercial rate of interest is payable on the sum lent, or it is lent to a full-time employee of the issuing body to assist in the purchase or improvement of his only or main residence.

[*ICTA 1988, ss 540(3), 542(3), 544*].

Gains arising from partial surrenders prior to an assignment by gift are chargeable on the donor. [*ICTA 1988, s 541(4)*].

'Top-slicing relief'. An individual may claim that the additional tax payable by him as a result of (*b*) above shall be calculated as follows. Divide the gain by the number of *complete* years the policy has run (i) since the previous chargeable event (see 45.15(*b*) below) or (ii) since the start of the policy if there is no previous chargeable event, or on final termination of the policy. Calculate additional tax in the relevant year (of maturity etc.) payable on the gain as so divided treated as if it were the top slice of the taxpayer's income (but allowing a credit for tax at the basic rate and, where applicable, starting rate (before 1999/2000, lower rate) on that amount). Multiply the tax so calculated by the number of complete years the policy has run (as in (i) or (ii)). This gives the total liability on the full gain. This procedure will normally have the effect that the total gain is taxed at lower rates than if it was simply all brought in as additional income of one year. [*ICTA 1988, s 550; F(No 2)A 1992, s 19(2); FA 1999, s 22(8)*]. For this purpose the charge to basic rate income tax on gains under life annuity contracts (see (B) above) and friendly society policies (see above) will be ignored. [*ICTA 1988, s 547(6)(c)(7)*].

Non-residents. By concession, individuals and companies which are non-UK resident throughout (respectively) a year of assessment or an accounting period beginning after 5 April 1999 are not liable to UK tax on gains on chargeable events occurring at any time during such a year, unless, in the case of a company, the policy or contract is held as property used or held by a UK branch or agency of the company. Certain benefits and gains treated as income are not affected by this concession. (Revenue Press Release 23 November 1999). For earlier years of assessment and accounting periods, non-residents are not charged to tax if the proceeds of the policy or contract were not payable in the UK and the policy or contract was made outside the UK by either an overseas branch of a resident insurance company or by a non-resident insurance company. (Revenue Pamphlet IR 131, SP 11/80, 9 October 1980).

Personal portfolio bonds. The Treasury has wide powers by regulation to impose a yearly charge in relation to 'personal portfolio bonds', in addition to any other charge under the life assurance gains provisions. Subject to any additional conditions imposed by regulation, a '*personal portfolio bond*' is a life assurance policy, life annuity contract or capital redemption policy under whose terms:

(i) some or all of the benefits are determined by reference to the value of, or income from, any description of property (whether or not specified in the policy or contract), or fluctuations in, or in an index of, the value of such property; and

(ii) some or all of the property, or such an index, may be selected by or on behalf of the holder (or any of two or more holders) of the policy or contract and/or CONNECTED PERSONS (20).

There may be an exclusion where the only property or index which may be selected is of a description prescribed by regulation.

The annual charge will be on a deemed gain of 15% of the sum of the total premiums paid up to the end of each policy year and the total of deemed gains of earlier years. A deemed gain will also arise when the policy terminates or any other chargeable event occurs. The additional charge will not be imposed in respect of any policy year ending before 6 April 1999. (Revenue Press Release 17 March 1998).

[*ICTA 1988, s 553C; FA 1998, s 89*].

For the regulations, see *SI 1999 No 1029*. See also Revenue Press Release 23 November 1999 for concessional extension of the transitional relief under those regulations for policies taken out before 17 March 1998.

Guidance Notes for Insurers and Practitioners, setting out the Revenue's interpretation of the personal portfolio bond legislation and the way they apply the law in practice, are published by the Revenue on their website (see 35.1 INLAND REVENUE: ADMINISTRATION). Enquiries about the legislation or the Guidance Notes should be addressed to Personal Portfolio Bond Group, Financial Institutions Division, Room S21 West Wing, Somerset House, Strand, London WC2R 1LB (tel. 020–7438 7343/7595).

Simon's Direct Tax Service. See E3.5.

45.14 *Example*

A single policyholder realises, in 2000/01, a gain of £2,600 on a non-qualifying policy which she surrenders after $2\frac{1}{2}$ years. Her other income for 2000/01 comprises earned income of £27,700 and dividends plus tax credits amounting to £3,895.

The tax chargeable on the gain is calculated as follows.

	Normal basis		Top-slicing relief claim
	£		£
Policy gain	2,600		1,300
Earnings	27,700		27,700
Dividends	3,895		3,895
	34,195		32,895
Personal allowance	4,385		4,385
	£29,810		£28,510
Tax applicable to policy gain			
Higher rate			
	£		£
£1,410 at 40%	564.00		—
£110 at 40%	—		44.00
	564.00		44.00
Deduct			
Basic rate			
£1,410 at 22%	310.20		—
£110 at 22%	—		24.20
			£19.80
Appropriate multiple 2 × £19.80			£39.60
Tax chargeable lower of	£253.80	and	£39.60

Tax payable is therefore as follows.

1,520 @ 10% (starting rate)	152.00
21,795 @ 22%	4,794.90
3,895 @ 10% (Schedule F ordinary rate)	389.50
1,190 @ 22%	261.80
28,400	
1,410 @ 40%	564.00
£29,810	
	c/f 6,162.20

	Normal basis	Top-slicing relief claim
	£	£
		b/f 6,162.20
Deduct: Tax credits on dividends (£3,895 @ 10%)	389.50	
Basic rate of tax on policy gain (£2,600 @ 22%)	572.00	
Top-slicing relief (£253.80 – £39.60)	214.20	1,175.70
Tax liability (subject to PAYE deductions)		£4,986.50

45.15 **Partial surrenders etc..** The following provisions apply in relation to the charging of income tax at the excess of the higher rates over the basic rate, plus the investment income surcharge (if applicable), on gains realised on the *partial surrender* (or *partial assignment* for money's worth) of life policies, capital redemption policies and annuity contracts.

(*a*) **'Policy year'** is any twelve months reckoning from the commencement of the policy etc. and subsequent anniversaries. If the final policy year ends in the same year of assessment as the termination of the policy etc. by death, maturity or total surrender, the two periods shall be treated as the final year. [*ICTA 1988, s 546(4)*].

(*b*) **'Chargeable event'.** Partial surrenders and assignments in any policy year may give rise to a taxable chargeable event at the end of that year. A chargeable event occurs where the 'reckonable aggregate value' (see below) exceeds the 'allowable aggregate amount' (see below).

On termination of a policy (by death, maturity, total surrender or assignment) all gains arising from previous chargeable events are deducted from the overall gain on that policy. A deficiency arising on termination is deductible from total income, but only for the purposes of ascertaining EXCESS LIABILITY (28), insofar as it does not exceed the total gains on previous chargeable events. [*ICTA 1988, ss 540–543, s 545, s 549*].

(*c*) **'Reckonable aggregate value'** is the total value of all surrenders and assignments of the policy since its commencement (but excluding any policy year prior to the first such year falling wholly after 13 March 1975), less the total of such values which have been brought into account in earlier chargeable events. [*ICTA 1988, s 546(1)(2)*].

(*d*) **'Allowable aggregate amount'** is the total of annual fractions of one-twentieth (with a maximum of 20 twentieths) of the premiums, and lump sums, paid since the policy commenced (but excluding the fractions relating to policy years prior to the first such year falling wholly after 13 March 1975), less the total of such fractions which have been brought into account in earlier chargeable events. [*ICTA 1988, s 546(1)(3)*].

(*e*) **Bonuses.** Surrender (or automatic payment) of a bonus is treated as a surrender of rights with consequent calculation under (*b*) above. [*ICTA 1988, s 539(4)*].

(*f*) **Loans** by the body issuing the policy will be treated as surrenders (with consequent calculation under 45.5 (clawback) or (*b*) above (chargeable event)) on policies made after 26 March 1974, except where lent on qualifying policies at a commercial rate of interest or (for loans made before 6 April 2000) to assist in the purchase or improvement of an only or main residence of a full-time employee of the issuing body or of an insurance association serving the insurance market (see Revenue

Pamphlet IR 1, A47). Any repayment of the loan will be treated as a premium when the calculation of any gain is made for the final year. [*ICTA 1988, s 548; FA 1999, Sch 4 paras 16, 18(3)*]. By concession, a loan-back option exercised in connection with a concurrent retirement annuity contract with the same insurer may not be treated as a surrender. (Revenue Pamphlet IR 1, A42). There is no tax charge on a loan to an elderly person in connection with a life annuity contract to the extent that the interest is eligible for relief under *ICTA 1988, s 365* (see 43.24 INTEREST PAYABLE). [*ICTA 1988, s 548(3)(b)*].

(*g*) **Capital redemption policies.** Where the sums payable are chargeable as annual payments under Schedule D, no further charge to tax will arise under the above provisions. [*ICTA 1988, s 545(1)(a)*].

(*h*) **Payments under certain life policies (commonly 'Guaranteed Income Bonds').** Special provisions apply to any contract of insurance within *Insurance Companies Act 1982, Sch 1 Class I* or *III* which is neither an annuity contract nor a contract effected in the course of the insurer's pension business (within *ICTA 1988, s 431B* or appropriate earlier enactment). Such policies are often in the form of so-called Guaranteed Income Bonds. A '*relevant excepted benefit*' is so much of any payment by the insurer under such a policy as:

(*a*) falls (apart from the current provisions) to be treated as interest or an annual payment;

(*b*) is not payable under provisions of the policy which, taken alone, would constitute a different sort of policy (for which see below); and

(*c*) does not represent interest for late payment on any other part of the payment or on the whole or part of any other payment by the insurer under the policy.

As regards (*b*) above, a contract is a 'different sort of policy' if it falls within any other *Class* of *Insurance Companies Act 1982, Sch 1* or within *Schedule 2* to that *Act* (and would in most cases relate to sickness benefits). (*c*) above refers to any interest on the whole or part of a payment for a period beginning on or after the date of the event or contingency giving rise to the payment.

For all tax purposes (and with full retrospective effect):

(i) a relevant excepted benefit is treated as being neither interest nor an annual payment, and as being a 'relevant capital payment' within *ICTA 1988, s 541* (or earlier enactment) (see 45.13 above); and

(ii) on payment of a relevant excepted benefit, there is treated as having been a surrender of a part of the rights conferred by the policy in question or, in the case of the final payment, of all the remaining rights, the value of the rights (or part) surrendered being equal to the amount of the payment.

[*FA 1997, s 79*].

(*i*) **'Top-slicing relief'** applies as under 45.13 above.

45.16 *Example*

Jade took out a policy on 4 February 1993 for a single premium of £15,000. The contract permits periodical withdrawals.

(i) Jade draws £750 p.a. on 4 February in each subsequent year.

There is no taxable gain because at the end of each policy year the 'reckonable aggregate value' (RAV) does not exceed the 'allowable aggregate amount' (AAA).

		£
At 3.2.97 withdrawals have been		2,250 (RAV)
Deduct 4 × $\frac{1}{20}$ of the sums paid in		3,000 (AAA)
		No gain

(ii) On 20.7.97 Jade withdrew an additional £3,500.

		£
At 3.2.98 withdrawals have been		6,500 (RAV)
Deduct 5 × $\frac{1}{20}$ of the sums paid in		3,750 (AAA)
Chargeable 1997/98		£2,750

(iii) Jade made no annual withdrawal on 4.2.98 but on 4.2.99 made a withdrawal of £1,000.

In the year 1999/2000 the position is

	£	£
At 3.2.00 withdrawals have been		7,500
Deduct Withdrawals at last charge		6,500
		1,000(RAV)
Deduct 7 × $\frac{1}{20}$ of the sums paid in	5,250	
less amount deducted at last charge	3,750	
		1,500(AAA)
		No gain

(iv) Jade surrendered the policy on 1.7.00 for £13,250, having made a further £1,000 withdrawal on 4.2.00.

In the year 2000/01, the position is

	£	£
Proceeds on surrender		13,250
Previous withdrawals		8,500
		21,750
Deduct: Premium paid	15,000	
Gains previously charged	2,750	
		17,750
Chargeable 2000/01		£4,000

Notes

(*a*) The gain on final surrender of the policy is calculated under *ICTA 1988, s 541* (see 45.13 above).

(*b*) The gains in (ii) and (iv) above are subject to top-slicing relief (see 45.13 above).

45.17 OFFSHORE POLICIES

Conditions. A policy issued in respect of an insurance made after 17 November 1983 by a company resident outside the UK (a '*new non-resident policy*') will not be a qualifying policy under *ICTA 1988, Sch 15 Pt II* (see 45.6 above) until either (*a*) the premiums are payable to, and are business receipts of, a UK branch of the issuing company and the company is lawfully carrying on life assurance business in the UK; or

(*b*) the policy holder is a UK resident and a portion of the issuing company's income from the investments of its life assurance fund is charged to corporation tax by virtue of *ICTA 1988, s 445*.

[*ICTA 1988, Sch 15 para 24; FA 1995, s 55(5)*].

Policies issued under insurances made before 18 November 1983 are not affected by the above unless they are varied after 17 November 1983 so as to increase the benefits secured or to extend the term of the insurance, in which event they are treated as issued after 17 November 1983. A variation includes the exercise of an option. [*ICTA 1988, Sch 15 para 27; FA 1995, s 55(7)*].

As regards chargeable events on or after 17 March 1998 in relation to policies issued in respect of insurances made (or varied to increase the benefits or extend the term) on or after that date, special provisions apply to life assurance policies with non-UK residents. If, immediately before the happening of the event, they are not 'new non-resident policies' (as above), they are treated as such, and they are in any event not treated as qualifying policies. The gains are thus chargeable at the basic as well as the higher rate of tax (and the exclusion from the basic rate charge of policies issued by the UK branch of an overseas company does not apply). Similarly, for contracts made after the coming into force of the first regulations under *ICTA 1988, s 458A* (applying life assurance provisions generally to capital redemption business — see Tolley's Corporation Tax), a capital redemption policy with a non-UK resident which, immediately before a chargeable event, is not a 'new offshore capital redemption policy' (see 45.19 below) is treated as such in relation to that event. [*ICTA 1988, ss 553A, 553B; FA 1998, s 88*].

Simon's Direct Tax Service. See **E2.1048**.

45.18 **Substitution of policies.** Where one policy is substituted for another and the old policy was a 'new non-resident policy' but the new policy is not, the rules in *ICTA 1988, Sch 15 paras 17–20* (see 45.12(*d*) above) are modified as follows.

(*a*) If the old policy and any related policy (any preceding policy in a chain of substituted policies) would have been, or, where certification was required, would have been capable of being, a qualifying policy were it not for the 'new non-resident policy' rules, then it is assumed to have been a qualifying policy for the purposes of *ICTA 1988, Sch 15 para 17(2)*.

(*b*) If the new policy would otherwise be, or, where certification is still required, be capable of being, a qualifying policy, it will nevertheless not qualify unless the circumstances are those specified in *ICTA 1988, Sch 15 para 17(3)* (regarding residence, benefits, the issuing company etc.).

(*c*) The company issuing the new policy must certify that the old policy for which it is substituted was issued by a company outside the UK with whom they have arrangements for issuing substitute policies to persons coming to the UK.

The modification in (*c*) above also applied where the old policy was a qualifying policy issued on or before 17 November 1983 which would have been a non-qualifying 'new non-resident policy' if issued after that date while the new policy is issued after that date and is not a 'new non-resident policy'.

If the new policy confers an option to have another policy substituted for it or to have any of its terms changed and thereby falls within *ICTA 1988, Sch 15 para 19(3)* it is to be treated for the purposes of that sub-paragraph as having been issued in respect of an insurance made on the same day as the old policy. [*ICTA 1988, Sch 15 paras 25, 26; FA 1995, s 55(6)*].

45.19 **Tax on chargeable events.** The income tax charge on gains from non-qualifying new non-resident policies is under Schedule D, Case VI and includes basic rate tax as well as the normal charge at higher rates (see 45.13 above). This also applies to '*new offshore capital redemption policies*', i.e. capital redemption policies issued in respect of contracts made after 22 February 1984 by non-UK resident companies. It does not apply to gains on new non-resident policies if the conditions in (*a*) or (*b*) in 45.17 above are fulfilled at all times between the date of issue and the date of the gain, or to gains on certain policies issued by non-UK resident companies within the charge to tax in a territory within the European Economic Area. [*ICTA 1988, s 553(6)(6A)(7)(10); FA 1995, s 56(2); FA 1996, s 168(5)*].

Except as below, the gain which would be chargeable is reduced by multiplying it by the fraction of which the denominator is the number of days for which the policy (and any preceding related policy) has run before the chargeable event and the numerator is the number of those days when the policy holder was a UK resident. No reduction is, however, made where, at any time during the life of the policy, it was held either

(*a*) by a trustee resident outside the UK, or by two or more trustees any of whom was so resident, *unless* the policy was issued in respect of an insurance made on or before 19 March 1985 *and* it was on that date held by a trustee resident outside the UK or by two or more trustees any of whom was so resident, or

(*b*) (from 6 April 1998) by a '*foreign institution*' (i.e. a company or other institution of non-UK residence or domicile) *unless* the policy was issued in respect of an insurance made on or before 16 March 1998 *and* it was on that date held by a foreign institution.

The gain thus reduced is chargeable to tax in full under Schedule D, Case VI (see above) but any top-slicing relief due under *ICTA 1988, s 550* (see 45.13 above) is computed by reference to higher (and additional) rate tax only. [*ICTA 1988, s 553(3)–(6); FA 1998, Sch 14 paras 4, 7*].

The denominator in the 'appropriate fraction' in the top-slicing relief calculation is altered for these purposes to the number of complete years the policy has run before the chargeable event less any complete years in which the policy holder was not resident in the UK. [*ICTA 1988, s 553(8)*].

Where there is a substitution of policies within 45.18 above and the new policy is a qualifying policy there is no chargeable event on the surrender of rights under the old policy and the new policy is treated as having been issued in respect of an insurance made on the same day as the old policy. [*ICTA 1988, s 553(1)*].

If at any time a previously qualifying 'new non-resident policy' ceases to fulfil the conditions of either (*a*) or (*b*) in 45.17 above it is brought within the chargeable events legislation of *ICTA 1988, s 539 et seq.* from that time onwards. [*ICTA 1988, s 553(2); FA 1995, s 55(8)*].

The provisions of *ICTA 1988, s 550(5)* regarding the operation of top-slicing relief when there is more than one chargeable event do not apply to 'new non-resident policies' or to 'new offshore capital redemption policies'. [*ICTA 1988, s 553(9)*].

46 Losses

Cross-references. See 19 COMPENSATION FOR LOSS OF EMPLOYMENT; 51.12 NON-RESIDENTS AND OTHER OVERSEAS MATTERS for trade carried on and controlled abroad; 53 PARTNERSHIPS; 68.13 SCHEDULE A; 71.44 SCHEDULE D, CASES I AND II for loss of loans; 73.3 SCHEDULE D, CASES IV AND V for deficiencies on overseas lettings; 74 SCHEDULE D, CASE VI.

Simon's Direct Tax Service E1.6.

46.1 Restrictions on the use of losses apply to companies where control changes [*ICTA 1988, ss 768, 769*] for which see Tolley's Corporation Tax. Also in relation to certain company partnership arrangements [*ICTA 1988, s 116*], see 53.14 PARTNERSHIPS. Loss relief cannot be claimed in respect of the special type of bonus issue described in *ICTA 1988, s 237* (prior to its repeal from 6 April 1999, see 3.18 ANTI-AVOIDANCE) nor for certain partnerships dealing in commodity futures (see 3.20 ANTI-AVOIDANCE). See also under 3 ANTI-AVOIDANCE generally for restrictions regarding certain transactions in securities etc.. See Tolley's Capital Gains Tax for capital losses. See 46.9 below for other restrictions.

Headings in this chapter are as follows.

46.2	Trading etc. losses	46.11	— example
46.3	Set-off of trading losses etc. against other income	46.12	Losses carried forward
		46.13	Losses in early years of a trade
46.4	— example	46.14	— example
46.5	Set-off of trading losses etc. against capital gains	46.15	Terminal losses
		46.16	— example
46.6	— example	46.17	Treatment of annual payments and interest as losses
46.7	Treatment of capital allowances		
46.8	— example	46.18	Losses on shares in unquoted trading companies
46.9	Restrictions on above reliefs		
46.10	Notes	46.19	— example

46.2 TRADING ETC. LOSSES

Trading, etc. losses are generally computed according to the same rules as apply in computing profits. [*FA 1998, s 46(2)*]. Relief may be obtained for trading losses

(*a*) by **Set-off** against other income in same year of assessment (and succeeding year if trade etc. still carried on, or preceding year where post-Finance Act 1994 provisions apply). See 46.3 to 46.10 below.

(*b*) by **Carry-forward** against subsequent profits of the same trade. See 46.12 below.

(*c*) by carry-back of **Losses in early years of a trade.** See 46.13 below.

(*d*) by carry-back of a **Terminal Loss.** See 46.15 below.

No part of any loss relieved under (*a*) or (*c*) above for a year of assessment is available for relief in subsequent years. [*ICTA 1988, s 382(3) as originally enacted*].

Where a loss can be relieved under more than one head and it is sufficiently large, the taxpayer can select the order in which the different heads are to be applied, but the whole of the income or profits available for relief under one head must be relieved before passing to the next (*Butt v Haxby Ch D 1982, 56 TC 547*).

For certain pre-trading expenses treated as a trading loss, see 71.76 SCHEDULE D, CASES I AND II. For other reliefs claimable by companies, see Tolley's Corporation Tax (under Losses).

Relief against income may be obtained for losses on shares in unquoted trading companies. See 46.18 below.

See 17.2 CLAIMS for further provisions regarding claims for a loss incurred in one year of assessment to be carried back to an earlier year.

46.3 **SET-OFF OF TRADING LOSSES ETC. AGAINST OTHER INCOME** [*ICTA 1988, s 380*]

Pre-Finance Act 1994. The following provisions apply **in respect of losses sustained in 1995/96 and earlier years in trades, etc. commenced before 6 April 1994. They do not apply to trades, etc. commenced on or after that date**. Subject as below, on a claim being made within two years of the end of any year of assessment, a taxpayer may elect to set against income of that year (i) **any loss he sustained in that year** in a trade, profession, employment or vocation carried on by him either solely or in partnership, or from woodlands assessed under Schedule D [*ICTA 1988, s 380(4)*], and (ii) **any loss so sustained in the last preceding year** (so far as not already relieved, and provided the taxpayer still carries on the trade, etc.), and discharge or repayment of tax may be claimed accordingly. Where relief is claimed for a year under (ii) above, it is given in priority to relief under (i) above in respect of a loss sustained in that year. [*ICTA 1988, s 380(1)(2)*]. The order of priority of relief for a loss for which claims are made under both (i) and (ii) above is determined according to the order in which claims are made or, if they are made at the same time, as specified by the claimant. (Revenue Tax Bulletin May 1992 p 20).

For late claims see 46.10(*c*) below.

'*Losses*' means losses computed in the same way as trading profits are computed under Schedule D, Case I or II. [*ICTA 1988, s 382(4)*]. This refers to computation of the amount of the loss, and not to the basis period by reference to which a loss is to be computed (*Gascoine v Wharton Ch D 1996, 69 TC 147*). In practice, claims for losses of an accounting year ending in the year of assessment are generally accepted (see 46.10(*a*) below).

Post-Finance Act 1994. The following provisions apply **in respect of losses sustained in 1994/95 and subsequent years in trades, etc. commenced after 5 April 1994** and **in respect of losses sustained in 1996/97 and subsequent years in trades, etc. commenced on or before that date**. [*FA 1994, s 209(7)(9); FA 1995, s 118*]. Where in a year of assessment a person sustains a loss in a trade, profession, vocation or employment, carried on solely or in partnership, he may make a claim, within, for 1996/97 and later years, twelve months after 31 January following that year of assessment (for earlier years, two years after the end of that year), for relief against income (i) of the year in which the loss is incurred, or (ii) of the year preceding that in which the loss is incurred. Where, against income of the same year, claims are made both under (i) in respect of that year's loss and under (ii) in respect of the following year's loss, (i) takes precedence. [*ICTA 1988, s 380(1)(2); FA 1994, s 209(1), Sch 20 para 8*]. See above for the order of priority where both claims are made for the same loss.

For late claims see 46.10(*c*) below.

'*Losses*' means losses computed in the same way **and in respect of the same basis period** as profits are computed under Schedule D, Case I or II (see 71.11 to 71.19 SCHEDULE D, CASES I AND II for basis period rules). Where, as a result of basis periods overlapping, an amount of loss would otherwise fall to be included in the computations for two successive years of assessment, it is not to be so included for the second of those years. As regards trades, etc. commenced before 6 April 1994, this definition applies for 1997/98 and subsequent years ('losses' being defined as above for earlier years). [*ICTA 1988, s 382(3)(4); FA 1994, s 209(3)(8); FA 1995, s 118*].

Transition from pre- to post-Finance Act 1994 provisions. During the transitional period, relief under *section 380* may be claimed for the same year under both the old rules (e.g. under *section 380(1)*) and the new rules (e.g. under *section 380(1)(b)*). Since there is no statutory order of priority in these circumstances, reliefs are given in the order which saves most tax. In practice, the taxpayer may choose the order in which reliefs are given. (Revenue Tax Bulletin December 1994 p 184).

Simon's Direct Tax Service. See **E1.602, E1.604**.

46.4 *Examples*

Business commenced before 6 April 1994 — transition to current year basis

Y, a single man, has been carrying on a trade for some years and prepares accounts to 31 December each year. His results as adjusted for tax for the four years to 31 December 1997 are as follows.

	Trading profit/(loss)		Other income
	£		£
31.12.94	10,000	1995/96	5,000
31.12.95	(20,000)	1996/97	9,000
31.12.96	(6,000)	1997/98	6,000
31.12.97	12,000		

Y claims relief under *ICTA 1988, s 380(1)* and *(2)* (as originally enacted) for the 1995/96 loss, and under *ICTA 1988, s 380(1)(a)* (as amended) for the 1996/97 loss. The assessments for the relevant years are then as follows.

1995/96	£	£
Trading income (year ended 31.12.94)		10,000
Other income		5,000
Total income		15,000
Deduct Loss 1995/96 (*section 380(1)*)		15,000
		—
1996/97		
Trading income (note (*a*))		—
Other income		9,000
		9,000
Deduct Loss 1995/96 (balance) (*section 380(2)*)	5,000	
Loss 1996/97 (*section 380(1)(a)*)	4,000	9,000
		—

1997/98	£	£
Trading income		12,000
Deduct Loss 1996/97 (balance b/f) (*section 385*)		2,000
		10,000
Other income		6,000
Assessable 1997/98		£16,000

Utilisation of losses

1995/96		
Loss available		20,000
Deduct Utilised 1995/96	15,000	
1996/97	5,000	20,000
1996/97		
Loss available		6,000
Deduct Utilised 1996/97	4,000	
1997/98	2,000	6,000

Alternatively, L could claim relief for the 1995/96 loss only under *ICTA 1988, s 380(2)* (as originally enacted), and for the 1996/97 loss under *subsection (b)* of *ICTA 1988, s 380(1)* (as amended). The assessments for the relevant years would then be as follows.

1995/96	£
Trading income (year ended 31.12.94)	10,000
Other income	5,000
Total income	15,000
Deduct Loss 1996/97 (*section 380(1)(b)*)	6,000
Assessable 1995/96	£9,000
1996/97	
Trading income (note (*a*))	—
Other income	9,000
	9,000
Deduct Loss 1995/96 (*section 380(2)*)	9,000
	—
1997/98	
Trading income	12,000
Deduct Loss 1995/96 (balance b/f)(*section 385*)	11,000
	1,000
Other income	6,000
Assessable 1997/98	£7,000

Utilisation of losses

1995/96		£
Loss available		20,000
Deduct Utilised 1996/97	9,000	
1997/98	11,000	20,000
1996/97		
Loss available		6,000
Deduct Utilised 1995/96		6,000

This could enable L to use his personal allowances and lower rate band in both 1995/96 and 1997/98, rather than only in 1997/98.

Note

(*a*) Under the current year basis transitional provisions (see 71.20 SCHEDULE D, CASES I AND II), the 1996/97 trading income assessment is based on the profits of the two years to 31.12.96. Since a loss was incurred in both those years, the assessment is nil.

Business commenced after 5 April 1994

L, a single woman, commences to trade on 1 July 1996, preparing accounts to 30 June, and has the following results (as adjusted for tax purposes and after capital allowances) for the first four years.

	Profit/(loss)
	£
Year ended 30 June 1997	9,000
Year ended 30 June 1998	3,000
Year ended 30 June 1999	(1,000)
Year ended 30 June 2000	(7,000)

L has other income of £6,000 for 1999/2000 and £6,500 for 2000/01, having had no other income in the earlier years.

The taxable profits for the first four tax years of the business are as follows.

	£
1996/97 (1.7.96–5.4.97) (£9,000 × $\frac{9}{12}$)	6,750*
1997/98 (y/e 30.6.97)	9,000
1998/99 (y/e 30.6.98)	3,000
1999/2000 (y/e 30.6.99)	Nil
2000/01 (y/e 30.6.00)	Nil

* Overlap relief accruing – £6,750.

L claims relief under *ICTA 1988, s 380(1)(a)* (set-off against income of the same year) for the 1999/2000 loss (£1,000). She also claims relief under *ICTA 1988, s 380(1)(b)* (set-off against income of the preceding year) for the 2000/01 loss (£7,000), with a further claim being made under *ICTA 1988, s 380(1)(a)* for the balance of that loss.

The tax position for 1999/2000 and 2000/01 is as follows.

	£
1999/2000	
Total income before loss relief	6,000
Deduct Claim under *section 380(1)(a)* note (*a*)	1,000
	5,000
Deduct Claim under *section 380(1)(b)*	5,000
Revised total income	Nil

	£
2000/01	
Total income before loss relief	6,500
Deduct Claim under *section 380(1)(a)* (balance)	2,000
Revised total income	4,500
Deduct Personal allowance	4,385
Taxable income	£115

Loss utilisation

	£
1999/2000	
Loss available under *section 380(1)(a)*	1,000
Deduct Utilised in 1999/2000	1,000
Loss available under *section 380(1)(b)*	7,000
Deduct Utilised in 1999/2000	5,000
Loss available for relief in 2000/01 under *section 380(1)(a)*	£2,000
2000/01	
Balance of loss available under *section 380(1)(a)*	2,000
Deduct Utilised in 2000/01	2,000

Note

(*a*) Where losses of two different years are set against the income of one tax year, then, regardless of the order of claims, relief for the current year's loss is given in priority to that for the following year's loss (see 46.3 above). This is beneficial to the taxpayer in this example as it leaves £2,000 of the 2000/01 loss to be relieved in that year.

Losses in early years — business commenced after 5 April 1994

Q commenced trading on 1 February 1998 and prepared accounts to 31 December. He made a trading loss of £20,900 in the 11 months to 31 December 1998 and profits of £18,000 and £16,000 in the years to 31 December 1999 and 2000 respectively. He has substantial other income for 1997/98 and 1998/99 and makes claims under *ICTA 1988, s 380* for both years.

Taxable profits/(allowable losses) are as follows.

	£	£
1997/98 (1.2.98–5.4.98) (£20,900) × $\frac{2}{11}$		(3,800)
1998/99 (1.2.98–31.1.99)		
1.2.98–31.12.98	(20,900)	
Less already allocated to 1997/98	3,800	
	(17,100)	
1.1.99–31.1.99 £18,000 × $\frac{1}{12}$	1,500	
		(15,600)
1999/2000 (y/e 31.12.99)		18,000
(Overlap relief accruing—£1,500)		
2000/01 (y/e 31.12.00)		16,000

Notes

(*a*) Losses available for relief for 1997/98 and 1998/99 are £3,800 and £15,600 respectively. If both years' losses are carried forward under *ICTA 1988, s 385* instead of being set against other income (under either *ICTA 1988, s 380* or *s 381*), the aggregate loss of £19,400 will extinguish the 1999/2000 profit and reduce the 2000/01 profit by £1,400. Note that although the actual loss was £20,900, there is no further amount available for carry-forward: the difference of £1,500 has been used in aggregation in 1998/99.

(*b*) The net profit for the first three accounting periods is £13,100 (£18,000 + £16,000 – £20,900). The net taxable profit for the first four tax years is £14,600 (£18,000 + £16,000 – £3,800 – £15,600). The difference of £1,500 represents the overlap relief accrued (see 71.19 SCHEDULE D, CASES I AND II). Note that the overlap profit of £1,500 is by reference to an overlap period of *three* months, i.e. 1.2.98 to 5.4.98 (two months — overlap profit nil) and 1.1.99 to 31.1.99 (one month — overlap profit £1,500).

46.5 **SET-OFF OF TRADING LOSSES ETC. AGAINST CAPITAL GAINS** [*FA 1991, s 72*]

Where losses arise and a person makes a claim under *ICTA 1988, s 380* as in 46.3 above, a further claim may be made in the same notice of claim for the determination of the '*relevant amount*', which is so much of the trading loss as

(*a*) cannot be set off against the claimant's income for the year of claim, and

(*b*) has not already been relieved for any other year.

A separate claim for relief under *FA 1991, s 72* will be accepted where (i) relief under *ICTA 1988, s 380* had previously been claimed and a claim under *FA 1991, s 72* could have been made, (ii) a separate claim under *FA 1991, s 72* is made within the time limits for the original *section 380* claim, (iii) after the *section 380* relief there is a balance of unrelieved trading losses, and (iv) all other conditions for *FA 1991, s 72* relief are satisfied. (Revenue Tax Bulletin August 1993 p 87). A claim under *FA 1991, s 72* may be made even though there is no income for the year of claim to justify making a claim under *section 380* alone. (Revenue Inspector's Manual, IM 3517).

The claim is not deemed to be determined until the relevant amount for the year can no longer be varied, whether by the Commissioners on appeal or on the order of any court.

The relevant amount, as finally determined, is to be treated for the purposes of capital gains tax as an allowable loss accruing to the claimant in the year up to the '*maximum amount*', i.e. the amount on which the claimant would be chargeable to capital gains tax for the year, disregarding the effect of this provision and of the capital gains tax annual exemption. In computing the maximum amount, no account is taken of any event occurring after the determination of the relevant amount and in consequence of which the maximum amount might otherwise be reduced by virtue of any capital gains tax legislation. Thus if, as a result of a subsequent reduction in the chargeable gains against which the maximum amount is set, the maximum amount exceeds those chargeable gains, the excess is carried forward as an allowable capital loss.

Losses claimed under this provision are relieved in priority to allowable capital losses brought forward.

No amount treated as an allowable loss under this provision may be deducted from chargeable gains accruing in a year of assessment which begins after the claimant has ceased to carry on the trade in which the loss was sustained.

Relief under this provision is treated in the same way as relief under *section 380* as regards prevention of double relief (see 46.2 above, 46.12 below) and set-off of capital allowances (see 46.7 below). [*FA 1991, s 72; FA 1994, Sch 26 Pt V(24)*].

Simon's Direct Tax Service. See **E1.603**.

46.6 *Example*

M has carried on a trade for some years, preparing accounts to 30 June each year. For the year ended 30 June 2000 he makes a trading loss of £17,000. His assessable profit for 1999/2000 is £5,000, and his other income for both 1999/2000 and 2000/01 amounts to £2,000. He makes a capital gain of £12,200 and a capital loss of £1,000 for 2000/01 and has capital losses brought forward of £5,800. The gain is after indexation allowance to April 1998 and qualifies for a 25% deduction for taper relief. M makes claims for loss relief, against income of 1999/2000 and income and gains of 2000/01, under *ICTA 1988, s 380(1)(b), s 380(1)(a)* and *FA 1991, s 72* respectively.

Calculation of 'relevant amount'

	£
Trading loss—year ended 30.6.00	17,000
Relieved against other income for 2000/01 (*section 380(1)(a)*)	(2,000)
Relieved against income for 1999/2000 (*section 380(1)(b)*)	(7,000)
Relevant amount	£8,000

Calculation of 'maximum amount'

	£
Gains for 2000/01	12,200
Deduct Losses for 2000/01	(1,000)
Unrelieved losses brought forward	(5,800)
	5,400
Deduct Taper relief — £5,400 @ 25%	1,350
Maximum amount	£4,050

Relief under *FA 1991, s 72*

	£	£
Gains for the year		12,200
Losses for the year	1,000	
Relief under *FA 1991, s 72*	4,050	
		5,050
Gain (covered by annual exemption)		£7,150
Capital losses brought forward and carried forward		£5,800

Loss memorandum

	£
Trading loss	17,000
Claimed under *section 380(1)(a)*	(2,000)
Claimed under *section 380(1)(b)*	(7,000)
Claimed under *FA 1991, s 72*	(4,050)
Unutilised loss	£3,950

Note

In this example, £50 of the capital gains tax annual exemption of £7,200 is wasted, but the brought forward capital losses are preserved for carry-forward against gains of future years. If M had *not* made the claim under *FA 1991, s 72*, his net gains for the year of £11,200 would have been reduced to the annual exempt amount by deducting £4,000 of the losses brought forward. (Taper relief would be irrelevant as the untapered net gains would be exempt in any case.) A further £1,800 of capital losses would remain available for carry-forward against future gains and a further £4,050 of trading losses would have been available for carry-forward against future trading profits. So the effect of the claim is to preserve capital losses at the expense of trading losses.

46.7 **TREATMENT OF CAPITAL ALLOWANCES**

For 1996/97 and earlier years as regards businesses commenced before 6 April 1994 (see below for later years and as regards businesses commenced on or after that date), a loss for *ICTA 1988, s 380* purposes may be **increased**, or **created**, by treating as a deduction in computing the trading results for that year any **capital allowances** due for the *year of assessment for which the year of loss is the basis year* (so far as they exceed balancing charges for that year of assessment, as reduced by any capital allowances brought forward from earlier years which would, without those balancing charges, be ineffective in that year). [*ICTA 1988, s 383; FA 1994, s 214(1)(b)*]. For this purpose the basis year for any year of assessment is the tax year which coincides with, or contains the end of, the relevant basis period as defined for capital allowances by *CAA 1990, s 160*, but where, under this definition, a year of assessment would be the basis year for itself and also another year of assessment it is to be the basis year for the former year only. [*ICTA 1988, s 383(5)(a)*].

But where the capital allowances to be taken into account are (*a*) those for the year of claim itself, being its own basis year, or (*b*) where *section 380(2)* (*as originally enacted*) is invoked (see 46.3 (ii) above), those for the preceding year, the allowances claimable are limited, under (*a*), to the amount of such allowances non-effective in the year of claim, or, under (*b*), to the amount non-effective in both that and the preceding year. [*ICTA 1988, s 383(3)*].

Capital allowances due for a year of assessment do not include such allowances brought forward from earlier years, but, for the purpose of offsetting profits, allowances for an earlier year are to be applied in priority to allowances for a later year. [*ICTA 1988, s 383(5)(b)(d)*].

On a cessation of business it is concessional practice, where this treatment would otherwise result in a loss of relief, to treat capital allowances brought forward as a *reduction* of the profits of the final year (instead of an offset against the assessment) (Revenue Pamphlet IR 1, A8).

Except as regards partners in cases of actual or notional discontinuance, or where a terminal loss claim is made under *ICTA 1988, s 388* (see 46.15 below), any capital allowances for a given year which are used as above for relief under *section 380* are, to that extent, treated as having been effectively allowed for all tax purposes.

Where a partner makes a *section 380* claim which includes capital allowances, the written consent is required of all persons (or their personal representatives) engaged in carrying on the trade from the end of the year of loss to the making of the claim, except if the loss occurred before an event treated as a discontinuance of the trade, no consent is required from any person so engaged in the trade only since the discontinuance. [*ICTA 1988, s 383(9)(10)*].

Order of use. Where a loss increased or created under the above provisions is not wholly used, the actual loss sustained, if any, is used first, then any capital allowances. [*ICTA 1988, s 383(6)*].

For 1994/95 and subsequent years as regards businesses commenced after 5 April 1994 and for 1997/98 and subsequent years as regards businesses commenced on or before that date, capital allowances are treated as trading expenses of periods of account (see 10.1, 10.2(vi) CAPITAL ALLOWANCES). They are thus automatically included in the amount of any trading loss (as adjusted for tax purposes).

Transitional position. Where, in a continuing business, there is a loss in the accounts for the year ending in 1995/96 (i.e. the year of loss is 1995/96), that year is not the basis period for 1996/97 (or any other year of assessment) under the current year basis transitional rules (see 71.20 SCHEDULE D, CASES I AND II), so that no capital allowances are strictly available to augment a loss claim for 1995/96. The Revenue will, however, not refuse a claim under *ICTA 1988, s 383* for 1995/96 provided that the allowances claimed are those which would have been available if the preceding year basis had continued to apply for 1996/97, and that the claim includes an undertaking that any allowances so relieved will be deducted from those available for claim in 1996/97, including any to be given effect by set-off against any balancing charges arising in that year. Where the allowances so claimed for 1995/96 exceed those available for 1996/97, the excess is recovered as a balancing charge for 1996/97. (Revenue Tax Bulletin February 1996 pp 286–289).

Simon's Direct Tax Service. See **E1.605**.

46.8 *Example*

A carries on a trade for which accounts are prepared to 31 December each year. The results for the two years ended 31 December 1994 are as follows.

Year to	Sch D, Case I profit
31.12.93	£25,000
31.12.94	£4,500
	Capital Allowances
1994/95	£10,000
1995/96	£6,100

The assessment for 1994/95 would be as follows.

	£
Case I profit — year ended 31.12.93	25,000
Deduct Capital allowances	10,000
Adjusted Case I profit	15,000
Deduct Claim under *section 380(1)*	1,600
Taxable income	£13,400

Utilisation of losses under *section 380(1)*

Loss available for 1994/95
1995/96 assessment

	£
Case I profit — year ended 31.12.94	4,500
Deduct Capital allowances (part)	4,500
	—
Available for claim under *section 380(1)*	
Capital allowances (balance)	£1,600

For the years ended 31 December 1995 and 31 December 1996, a Schedule D, Case I loss of £10,000 and profit of £15,000 arise respectively, and the capital allowance computation (all relating to plant and machinery) for 1996/97 is as follows.

	£
WDV b/f	36,000
Additions (year to 31.12.95)	4,000
(year to 31.12.96)	8,000
Disposals (year to 31.12.95)	(6,000)
(year to 31.12.96)	(18,000)
	24,000
Writing down allowance	6,000
WDV c/f	£18,000

The allowances which may be claimed in augmentation of the £10,000 loss for 1995/96 are those which would have been available if the preceding year basis had continued to apply for 1996/97, i.e. those which would have been available for a basis period year ended 31 December 1995, as follows.

	£
WDV b/f	36,000
Additions	4,000
Disposals	(6,000)
	£34,000
Writing down allowance	£8,500

The loss available for 1995/96 is thus (10,000 + £8,500 =) £18,500.

The capital allowances available for 1996/97 (£6,000 as above) are reduced by the allowance brought forward for relief in 1995/96 (£8,500), so that a balancing charge of £2,500 arises in 1996/97.

Note

(*a*) It is not obligatory to include capital allowances in a *section 380* claim, or, as in this example, to create a loss by taking capital allowances into account. If A's income had been lower, he might have wasted personal reliefs by claiming the loss relief of £1,600.

46.9 **RESTRICTIONS ON ABOVE RELIEFS**

(*a*) **Non-commercial basis** [*ICTA 1988, s 384; FA 1994, s 214(1)(c), s 216(3)(d); FA 1996, s 134, Sch 20 para 25*]. As regards losses (and capital allowances) which would normally form the basis of relief as above, **relief under** *ICTA 1988, s 380* **will not be given unless,** for the year of assessment concerned (or by the end of it, if the trading method was changed during that year), the trade, profession or vocation was carried on

(i) on a commercial basis, and

(ii) with a view to realisation of profit in that trade, etc., or any larger undertaking of which it forms part.

The test is a subjective one — see *Walls v Livesey (Sp C 4), [1995] SSCD 12* on similar wording in *ICTA 1988, s 504(2)(a)*. In *Wannell v Rothwell Ch D 1996, 68 TC 719* an individual's speculative dealing in stocks and shares and commodity futures was held to be trading but not on a commercial basis. See also *Brown v Richardson (Sp C 129), [1997] SSCD 233*, and the Revenue Tax Bulletin article (October 1997 pp 472, 473) commenting on that decision, and *Delian Enterprises v Ellis (Sp C 186), [1999] SSCD 103.*

A trade is treated as complying with the requirement at (ii) above if at the relevant time it was being carried on so as to afford a reasonable expectation of profit.

For the Revenue approach generally, see Revenue Inspector's Manual, IM 3375–3379.

(The above restrictions do not apply to losses incurred in the exercise of functions conferred by or under any enactment, including a local or private Act.)

(*b*) **Farming and market gardening** [*ICTA 1988, s 397; FA 1994, s 214(3); FA 1996, s 134, Sch 20 para 27*]. Except as below, **relief will not be given under** *ICTA 1988, s 380* above for any loss (or any related capital allowances under *ICTA 1988, s 383* above) incurred in a trade of farming or market gardening if losses from that trade, computed under the normal Schedule D, Case I rules but ignoring capital allowances, were also incurred in each of the five years preceding the year of assessment. Similarly, if such a trade is carried on by a company a loss incurred in any accounting period may not be set off against total profits (under *ICTA 1988, s 393(2)* or *s 393A(1)*, see Tolley's Corporation Tax) if there would still be a loss if capital allowances were ignored and there was a loss (similarly computed) in each of the chargeable periods wholly or partly comprised in the five years preceding that accounting period.

Disallowance under *ICTA 1988, s 397* **does not apply** if:

(i) the farming, etc., is part of, and ancillary to, a larger trading undertaking, or

(ii) the farming, etc., activities in the year are carried on in a way which might reasonably be expected to produce profits in the future and the activities in the preceding five years could not reasonably have been expected to become profitable until after the year under review. [*ICTA 1988, s 397(3)(4)*].

See 71.57(*d*) SCHEDULE D, CASES I AND II for relief for repairs etc. on owner-occupied farms.

The Revenue concessionally extend the five-year time limits above to eleven years from commencement in the case of a thoroughbred horse blood stock breeder, provided that the business is potentially profitable. (Revenue Inspector's Manual, IM 2350g).

(*c*) **Leasing by individuals.** [*ICTA 1988, s 384(6)–(8); FA 1994, s 214(2)*]. Where an individual (alone or in partnership) incurs expenditure on machinery or plant for leasing in the course of a trade, any capital allowances are not to be included (either under *ICTA 1988, s 383* above or otherwise) in calculating loss relief under *section 380* above unless the individual carries on the trade for a continuous period of at least six months in, or beginning or ending in, the year of loss (i.e. the tax year in which the loss is sustained) and he devotes substantially the whole of his time to the trade throughout the year of loss or, if the trade begins or ceases (or both) in that year, for a continuous period of at least six months beginning or ending in that year. This prohibition also applies if the asset is not leased but payments in the nature of royalties or licence fees are to accrue from rights granted in connection with it. Any relief given will be withdrawn by assessment under Schedule D, Case VI. The foregoing provisions are without prejudice to *CAA 1990, s 142* (see 46.9(*d*) and (*e*) below). For capital allowances on assets not leased in the course of a trade, see 10.28(D) CAPITAL ALLOWANCES.

First-year allowances —

(*d*) **Leasing partnerships.** [*CAA 1990, s 142(1)(4)*]. Where expenditure is incurred on machinery or plant for leasing in the course of a trade carried on, or to be carried on, by a partnership including a company and an individual (with or without other partners), any loss arising from a first-year allowance (where available — see 10.27 CAPITAL ALLOWANCES) on that expenditure will not be allowed as set-off against the general income of the individual under *section 380*. For this purpose, letting a ship on charter will be regarded as leasing.

(*e*) **First-year allowances—arrangements.** [*CAA 1990, s 142(2)*]. Where an individual incurs expenditure giving rise to a first-year allowance (see (*d*) above), no relief will be given to him for that allowance under *section 380* if, under an arrangement or scheme, a tax saving was expected as the sole or main benefit of the expenditure and (i) he was in partnership then or later, or (ii) he transferred the trade etc., or the relevant asset, to a connected person, or (iii) he transferred the asset to any person at lower than the open market price.

Any relief given will be withdrawn under (*d*) or (*e*) above by assessment under Schedule D, Case VI. [*CAA 1990, s 142(3)*].

Simon's Direct Tax Service. See **E1.606**.

46.10 **NOTES** [*ICTA 1988, s 380*]

(*a*) **Apportionments in arriving at amount of loss.** *The following comments apply as regards losses sustained in 1996/97 and earlier years in trades, etc. commenced before 6 April 1994.* Relief claimed under *section 380* is in strictness available for the loss which arose in the year of assessment, but by long-standing concessionary practice (confirmed by Revenue Pamphlet IR 1, A87), relief is allowed for the loss of the year to the normal accounting date in the tax year (i.e. the 'accounts basis'). This does not, however, apply:

(i) to the first three years of assessment of a new business (or in the fourth year where the third year's assessment was adjusted under *ICTA 1988, s 62*, see 71.4 SCHEDULE D, CASES I AND II);

(ii) to any year of assessment immediately following a year for which relief under either *section 380* or *section 381* (see 46.13 below) has been allowed on the strict basis of the loss of the year to 5 April;

(iii) in the year of assessment of cessation; or

(iv) to a loss made by a partner in a year during which a partnership change has taken place for which a continuation election has been made under *ICTA 1988, s 113(2)* (see 53.6 PARTNERSHIPS) and relief under *ICTA 1988, s 381* (see 46.13 below) could be claimed by any partner for that year.

These exclusions are by reference to the year of assessment in which the loss was sustained, not that for which relief is claimed. Where an exclusion applies, or where the claimant does not wish the concessionary practice to be applied, the loss must be calculated on the strict basis. Where losses are apportioned on the strict basis, profits must be similarly apportioned in determining the loss (if any) available for relief. Any balance of loss unutilised is available for carry forward (see 46.12 below).

Example

A long-established business has the following agreed results.

Year ended 30 September 1991	Profit	£25,000
Year ended 30 September 1992	Profit	£20,000
Year ended 30 September 1993	Loss	£50,000
Year ended 30 September 1994	Profit	£30,000

If relief is claimed under *section 380* on the strict fiscal year basis, the loss sustained in 1992/93 is (£25,000 – £10,000 =) £15,000, which may be set against the £25,000 assessable on the preceding year basis for 1992/93. The loss sustained in 1993/94 is (£25,000 – £15,000 =) £10,000, which may be set against the £20,000 assessable on the preceding year basis for 1993/94. The balance of losses unrelieved (£25,000) may be carried forward and set against the 1995/96 assessment of £30,000.

If relief is instead claimed on the accounts year basis, the entire loss of £50,000 is available for 1993/94 against the £20,000 trading profits assessable for that year (and against any other 1993/94 and, if so claimed, 1994/95 income). Any unrelieved balance is then set against the 1995/96 assessment of £30,000.

Cessation adjustment. Where a business ceases in 1996/97 or earlier (or in 1997/98 where the Revenue have given a direction under *FA 1994, Sch 20 para 3(2)* (see 71.24 SCHEDULE D, CASES I AND II) that the pre-*FA 1994* provisions shall continue to apply) and relief is claimed under *section 380* for the loss of the year of assessment of cessation, then if *section 380* relief has been allowed for the penultimate year on the accounts basis, the loss incurred in that year after the accounting date will not be relieved. In these circumstances, whether or not terminal loss relief is claimed under *ICTA 1988, s 388* (see 46.15 below), concessionary *section 380* relief is available. The following amounts will be calculated in terms of tax for those consecutive years before that of cessation for which relief has been allowed under *section 380* on the accounts basis.

(A) The relief allowed for those years (up to a maximum of six).

(B) The relief which would have been given for the same years if the losses had been computed on the strict basis.

(C) If terminal loss relief has been allowed, the amount (if any) which would no longer be due following the computation at (B).

A repayment will then be made for the year of cessation of the lesser of

(1) the excess of (B) over ((A) + (C)), and

(2) tax at the claimant's marginal rate for the year of cessation on the part of the penultimate year's loss arising after the accounting date and not the subject of terminal loss relief.

A claim for the additional concessional relief arising from the recomputation should be made at the same time as the *section 380* claim for the year of cessation.

Where the recomputation at (B) creates a loss for the year preceding the first of the consecutive years for which claims were made, a late claim under *section 380* will be accepted for the loss of that year unless it is more than six years before the year of cessation. The claim should be made within 30 days of the date on which effect is given to the *section 380* claim for the year of cessation (as above).

(Revenue Pamphlet IR 1, A88; Revenue Tax Bulletin June 1995 p 223).

Example

B ceases trading on 30 September 1996 and has the following agreed results for the last few years.

Year ended 30 September 1996	Loss	£9,000
Year ended 30 September 1995	Loss	£10,000
Year ended 30 September 1994	Loss	£12,000
Year ended 30 September 1993	Loss	£4,000
Year ended 30 September 1992	Profit	£3,000

B has other sources of income and claims relief under *section 380(1)* for each year's loss (including the final year) against other income of that year. No terminal loss relief is claimed. Losses are calculated on the accounts year basis apart from that for 1996/97 which has to be computed on the strict fiscal year basis. B's marginal tax rate for all relevant years (both before and after giving loss relief) is 40%. Relief is available under the above concession as follows.

(A) Relief allowed for consecutive years before year of cessation (in terms of tax)

		£
1995/96	£10,000 @ 40%	4,000
1994/95	£12,000 @ 40%	4,800
1993/94	£4,000 @ 40%	1,600
		£10,400

(B) Relief recalculated for those years on strict basis (in terms of tax)

		£
1995/96	£(5,000 + 4,500) @ 40%	3,800
1994/95	£(6,000 + 5,000) @ 40%	4,400
1993/94	£(2,000 + 6,000) @ 40%	3,200
		£11,400

The Revenue will repay the lesser of

(1) excess of (B) over (A) =	£1,000
(2) £4,500 (1.10.95 to 5.4.96) @ 40%	£1,800

They will therefore repay £1,000. In addition, they will accept a late *section 380* claim in respect of a loss calculated on the strict basis for 1992/93: £(2,000 – 1,500) = £500 @ 40% = £200 repayable.

For losses sustained in 1994/95 and subsequent years in trades, etc. commenced after 5 April 1994 and those sustained in 1997/98 and subsequent years in trades, etc. commenced on or before that date, the loss for a year of assessment is taken to be that of the basis period for that year, which will normally be the account ending within that year (see 71.11 to 71.19 SCHEDULE D, CASES I AND II for basis period rules).

(*b*) **Effects of a claim.** The effect in particular cases of using *section 380* as regards personal allowances, higher rate income tax, etc. should be carefully considered. See 1 ALLOWANCES AND TAX RATES. The cancellation of the Schedule D assessment may result in a *ICTA 1988, s 350* assessment on any annuities etc. paid less tax (see 1.10 ALLOWANCES AND TAX RATES). The section may advantageously be used when a business is declining and may cease, or the rate of tax is likely to fall; or when a partner or sole owner dies or retires.

(*c*) **Late claims.** Although there is no provision for the acceptance of late claims under *section 380* (or *section 381*), such relief may be granted as would have been due if a timeous claim had been made where the taxpayer or agent either:

(i) was misled by some relevant and uncorrected Revenue error; or

(ii) made an informal claim within the time limit which he or she reasonably believed to be an acceptable claim, and the need to formalise the claim was not pointed out by the Revenue within the time limit; or

(iii) was effectively prevented from making a timeous claim for reasons beyond his or her control,

and provided that the late claim is made within a reasonable period (not normally more than three months) after the expiry of the excuse. As regards (*c*) above, acceptable reasons do *not* normally include: delays in preparing the accounts (unless for reasons beyond the taxpayer's or agent's control); delays in the Revenue's agreeing the accounts (although valid claims may be made before the accounts are either submitted or agreed, provided that the loss is clearly identified); misunderstandings and failures to communicate between taxpayer and agent; oversight or neglect by current or previous agents; ignorance of the statutory time limits; or deliberate delays because it was unclear at the expiry of the time limit whether the claim was advantageous. (Revenue Tax Bulletin December 1994 p 183). See further Revenue Inspector's Manual, IM 3358, 3359. See also IM 3360 as regards withdrawal of claims.

(*d*) **No double allowance.** Losses claimed under *section 380* (to the extent they are allowed) cannot be also carried forward against future years' assessments under *ICTA 1988, s 385*, see below.

46.11 *Example*

Losses in transitional period on changeover to current year basis

K carries on a business which commenced before 6 April 1994 and continues beyond 5 April 1999. He has no other source of income. He prepares accounts to 31 August and has the following results (as adjusted for tax purposes, but before capital allowances) for the four years to 31 August 1997.

	Profit/(loss)
	£
Year ended 31 August 1994	13,000
Year ended 31 August 1995	20,000
Year ended 31 August 1996	(14,000)
Year ended 31 August 1997	5,300

Capital allowances are as follows.

	£
1995/96	2,000
1996/97	1,000
Year ended 31 August 1997	500

The taxable profits before taking account of loss reliefs are as follows

	£	£
1995/96 (y/e 31.8.94)	13,000	
Less capital allowances	2,000	
		11,000
1996/97 (y/e 31.8.95)	20,000	
(y/e 31.8.96)	Nil	
	£20,000	
$£20,000 \times \frac{12}{24}$	10,000	
Less capital allowances	1,000	
		9,000
1997/98 (y/e 31.8.97) (net of capital allowances)		4,800*

* Transitional overlap relief accrued (1.9.96–5.4.97): $£5,300 \times \frac{7}{12} = £3,092$.

The loss of £14,000 for the year ended 31 August 1996 may be treated under normal Revenue practice (see 46.10(*a*) above) as a loss for 1996/97. K wishes to obtain loss relief against the earliest possible income. *The tax position after taking into account the appropriate loss relief claims is as follows*

	£
1995/96 Total income before loss relief	11,000
Deduct Claim under *section 380(1)(b)*	11,000
Revised total income	Nil
1996/97 Total income before loss relief	9,000
Deduct Claim under *section 380(1)(a)*	3,000
Revised total income	£6,000

The position for 1997/98 is not affected.

Loss utilisation

	£
Loss for 1996/97	14,000
Used in 1995/96 under *section 380(1)(b)*	(11,000)
Used in 1996/97 under *section 380(1)(a)*	(3,000)

Notes

(*a*) A loss in one part of the transitional period on changeover to current year basis (see 71.20 SCHEDULE D, CASES I AND II) is treated as nil for the purpose of averaging a profit in that period to arrive at the taxable profit for 1996/97. The profit is still averaged over the full length of the transitional period.

(*b*) If the results for years ended 31 August 1995 and 1996 had been reversed, so that the loss were treated as a loss for 1995/96, the tax position before loss reliefs would have been the same. Loss relief could then have been claimed under *ICTA 1988, s 380(1)(2) as originally enacted* to achieve the same position as above.

46.12 **LOSSES CARRIED FORWARD** [*ICTA 1988, s 385; FA 1994, s 209(4)(5)(8), s 216(3)(e); FA 1995, s 118*]

Any balance of trading, etc. **loss not used as above** (or otherwise under the Act) may be carried forward without time limit as a set-off against the first following profits (or, if insufficient, the next, and so on) of the same business by the same owner. See *Bispham v Eardiston Farming Co Ch D 1962, 40 TC 322* as to effect of *ICTA 1988, s 53* (all farming by a person treated as one trade) on the carry forward of farming losses.

(*a*) **Annual payments and interest.** See 46.17 below.

(*b*) **Certain investment income.** Where full relief under *ICTA 1988, s 385* cannot be given for any year because of the insufficiency of the Schedule D profits, these may be increased for the purpose by adding to them taxed interest and dividends on investments arising in that year which, had they not been taxed, would have formed part of the trading receipts. In that event repayment of tax may be due. [*ICTA 1988, s 385(4)*]. See 71.66 SCHEDULE D, CASES I AND II. See also *ICTA 1988, s 458(2)* for special provisions relating to capital redemption business.

(*c*) **Private businesses converted into companies** [*ICTA 1988, s 386; FA 1994, s 216(3)(f)*]. Any unrelieved balance of loss from pre-conversion years may be made use of by individuals so transferring their business mainly for shares allotted to themselves or their nominees, as follows.

For any year *throughout which* they retain the beneficial ownership of the shares and the company carries on the business, the loss may be used as a set-off (under *ICTA 1988, s 385*) against any income derived from the company. The set-off must be used first against direct assessments (e.g. on director's fees, etc.) but any balance may be used to reclaim tax on dividends, etc. from the company. In practice, relief should not be refused so long as shares representing at least 80% of the consideration received for the business are retained. (Revenue Inspector's Manual, IM 3552).

(*d*) **Partners.** In the case of partnerships, each partner's proportion of the loss belongs to him individually, and to the extent to which he does not use it in claims under *ICTA 1988, s 380* (see 46.3 above) it is carried forward and set against his individual statutory proportion of the subsequent year's assessments (even if there is a notional discontinuance [*ICTA 1988, s 385(5) as originally enacted*]). Consequently, when a partner dies or retires, his share of any unexhausted loss claims lapses. For 1994/95 and subsequent years as regards partnership trades, etc. commenced, or treated as commenced, after 5 April 1994 and for 1997/98 and subsequent years as regards those commenced on or before that date, each individual partner's share of a profit or loss is treated as derived from a trade carried on by him alone (see 53.3 PARTNERSHIPS), and loss reliefs, including that under *ICTA 1988, s 385*, are given accordingly.

(*e*) **Carry forward of loss in first accounts.** A loss used to offset a profit in arriving at the opening years' assessments for businesses commenced before 6 April 1994 (see

71.4 SCHEDULE D, CASES I AND II) has been relieved and hence is not available for carry forward. Where so used twice, twice the amount is treated as relieved (*Scott Adamson CS 1932, 17 TC 679; Westward Television v Hart CA 1968, 45 TC 1*). As regards the opening years' assessments for businesses commenced after 5 April 1994 (see 71.12 SCHEDULE D, CASES I AND II), *ICTA 1988, s 382(3)(4)* apply (see 46.3 above) to prevent an amount of loss being taken into account twice where basis periods overlap. [*ICTA 1988, s 385(1); FA 1994, s 209(4)*].

(*f*) **Use of loss against subsequent profits.** A loss carried forward must be set against the first subsequent profits, although the latter might otherwise have been completely offset by personal allowances, etc., for that year.

(*g*) **Time limits for claims.** Claims relating to the amount of losses must be made within, for 1996/97 and subsequent years, five years after 31 January following the tax year in which they arose (for earlier years, six years after the end of that tax year). For 1994/95 and subsequent years as regards businesses commenced after 5 April 1994 and for 1997/98 and subsequent years as regards businesses commenced on or before that date, the loss is then relieved automatically with no further claim being necessary. Previously, a further claim for relief for losses carried forward had to be made within six years of the end of tax year for which relief is claimed. [*ICTA 1988, s 385(8); TMA 1970, s 43; FA 1994, s 196, s 199(2)(a), s 209(5), Sch 19 para 14*]. For a case turning on the failure to establish the year(s) in which losses from an abortive business venture arose, see *Richardson v Jenkins Ch D 1995, 67 TC 246.*

(*h*) **Change of ownership of a company.** Restrictions on the carry forward of losses are contained in *ICTA 1988, ss 768, 769*. See Tolley's Corporation Tax.

(*i*) **Balancing charge on an industrial building after cessation of trade.** Trading losses may be set off against the charge arising in these circumstances. See 10.17 CAPITAL ALLOWANCES.

(*j*) **Change of residence.** Where, on a sole trader becoming or ceasing to be UK resident, the trade is deemed to be permanently discontinued and a new one commenced, losses of the 'old' trade may be carried forward under *ICTA 1988, s 385* and set against profits of the 'new' trade. See 71.27 SCHEDULE D, CASES I AND II (and see 53.15 PARTNERSHIPS for a similar rule as regards an individual trading in partnership).

Simon's Direct Tax Service. See **E1.610** *et seq.*.

46.13 **LOSSES IN EARLY YEARS OF A TRADE** [*ICTA 1988, ss 381, 382(3)(4); FA 1994, ss 209(2)(3)(7)–(9), 216(3)(c); FA 1995, s 118; FA 1996, ss 134, 135, Sch 20 para 24, Sch 21 para 10*]

If an individual (including a partner) sustains a loss in a trade, profession or vocation in any of the first four years of assessment from commencement of trading, he may claim relief for that loss against his other income of the preceding three years, earlier years first. The trade (or if part of a larger undertaking, the whole undertaking) must have been carried on during the period of loss on a commercial basis with a reasonable expectation of profits during that period or within a reasonable time thereafter (an objective test — see *Walls v Livesey (Sp C 4), [1995] SSCD 12*). There is no relief where the trade was previously carried on by the spouse earlier than the three years of assessment preceding the loss. Any change in a partnership is disregarded for an individual who is engaged in the trade immediately before and after that change.

Simon's Direct Tax Service. See **E1.621**.

Notes.

(*a*) **Claims** must be in writing within, for 1996/97 and later years, twelve months after 31 January following the year of assessment in which the loss occurred (for earlier years, two years after the end of that year of assessment). For late claims, see 46.10(*c*) above.

(*b*) **Computation of losses** is as for *ICTA 1988, s 380* purposes (see 46.3 above) and, to the extent they are allowed, such losses cannot be claimed under any other relieving provision.

(*c*) **Capital allowances and stock relief** may be included in the loss in similar manner as described in 46.7 above and are subject to the restrictions in 46.9(*c*)(*d*)(*e*) above.

(*d*) **Overseas trades.** Individuals (including partners) carrying on trade abroad may claim relief.

(*e*) **Woodlands.** A claim under this section does not apply to woodlands brought within Schedule D by an election under *ICTA 1970, s 111* or *FA 1988, Sch 6 para 4* (see 93.2, 93.3 WOODLANDS).

(*f*) See also 71.76 SCHEDULE D, CASES I AND II as regards **pre-trading expenditure**.

46.14 *Example*

F, a single person, commences to trade on 1 December 1997, preparing accounts to 30 November. The first four years of trading produce losses of £12,000, £9,000, £2,000 and £1,000 respectively, these figures being as adjusted for tax purposes and after taking account of capital allowances. For each of the four years of assessment 1994/95 to 1997/98, F had other income of £8,000.

The losses for tax purposes are as follows.

	£	£
1997/98 (1.12.97–5.4.98) (£12,000 × $\frac{4}{12}$)		4,000
1998/99 (y/e 30.11.98)	12,000	
Less already allocated to 1997/98	4,000	
		8,000
1999/2000 (y/e 30.11.99)		9,000
2000/01 (y/e 30.11.00)		2,000
2001/02 (y/e 30.11.01) note (*b*)		1,000

Loss relief under *ICTA 1988, s 381* is available as follows.

	1997/98	1998/99	1999/2000	2000/01
	£	£	£	£
Losses available	4,000	8,000	9,000	2,000
Set against total income				
1994/95	4,000	—	—	—
1995/96	—	8,000	—	—
1996/97	—	—	8,000	—
1997/98	—	—	1,000	2,000
	£4,000	£8,000	£9,000	£2,000

Revised total income is thus £4,000 for 1994/95, nil for 1995/96 and 1996/97 and £5,000 for 1997/98.

Notes

(*a*) Losses are computed by reference to the same basis periods as profits. Where any part of a loss would otherwise fall to be included in the computations for two successive tax years (as is the case for 1997/98 and 1998/99 in this example), that part is excluded from the computation for the second of those years.

(*b*) The loss for the year ended 30 November 2001 in this example is not available for relief under *ICTA 1988, s 381* as it does not fall into the first four *tax years* of the business (even though it is incurred in the first four years of trading). It is of course available for relief under *ICTA 1988, s 380* (depending on other income for 2000/01 and 2001/02) or for carry-forward under *ICTA 1988, s 385*.

46.15 **TERMINAL LOSSES** [*ICTA 1988, s 388; FA 1994, s 209(6)(7), s 214(1)(d); FA 1995, s 118*]

On the permanent discontinuance of any trade, profession or vocation (or the occupation of woodlands assessed under Schedule D), losses sustained in the twelve months before the date of discontinuance, so far as not otherwise relieved, may be carried back and set off against profits of the trade, etc., charged to income tax under Schedule D (plus, in the case of a trade, interest or dividends arising which, had they not been taxed otherwise, would have been chargeable under Schedule D, Case I as trading profits) for the three years of assessment prior to that in which the discontinuance occurs, relief being given first for the latest of those years, and so on. For 1994/95 and subsequent years as regards businesses commenced after 5 April 1994 and for 1996/97 and subsequent years as regards businesses commenced on or before that date, the eligible profits are those for the tax year in which the discontinuance occurs and the three tax years preceding it. Losses for this purpose include unrelieved capital allowances for the twelve months before discontinuance, but excluding any such allowances brought forward from earlier years. For 1994/95 and subsequent years as regards businesses commenced after 5 April 1994 and for 1997/98 and subsequent years as regards businesses commenced on or before that date, capital allowances are automatically included in a trading loss (see 46.7 above) and are thus no longer considered separately. [*ICTA 1988, s 388(6)(7), s 389(5)–(7); FA 1994, s 214(1)(d)(e)*].

(*a*) So far as profits of any year were applied in making any payment from which tax was deducted but not accounted for because the payment was made out of taxed profits [*ICTA 1988, s 348*], those profits must, for relief purposes, be treated as reduced by the amount so applied. In such cases, losses available against prior years are reduced by a similar amount unless the payment is one which, had it not been paid out of taxed profits, could have been assessed under *ICTA 1988, s 350* and treated as a loss under *ICTA 1988, s 387*.

(*b*) Losses for this purpose must be computed on the same basis as profits under Schedule D, Cases I and II, and, insofar as they are relieved as terminal losses, cannot also be claimed under any other relieving provision.

(*c*) On a partnership change treated as a permanent discontinuance (under *ICTA 1988, s 113*, see 53.6 PARTNERSHIPS) a retiring partner may claim his terminal loss against his share of partnership profits for the three preceding years as above (even if they include a period before a previous discontinuance), but no claim under this section may be made by a continuing partner. For 1994/95 and subsequent years as regards partnership trades, etc. commenced, or treated as commenced, after 5 April 1994 and for 1997/98 and subsequent years as regards those commenced on or before that date, each individual partner's share of a profit or loss is treated as derived from a trade carried on by him alone (see 53.3 PARTNERSHIPS), and terminal loss relief is available accordingly to an outgoing partner. All individual partners may claim terminal loss relief on a discontinuance or deemed discontinuance of the actual partnership trade, but the latter will occur only where there is no continuing partner (see 53.6 PARTNERSHIPS). [*ICTA 1988, s 389(3)–(5); FA 1994, s 214(1)(e), s 216(3)(g)(4)*]. For company partners see *ICTA 1988, s 114(3)(c)* and 53.14 PARTNERSHIPS.

(*d*) Where the trade discontinued is, or includes, the working of a mine, oil well, etc., special provisions obviate dual claims under this section and *CAA 1990, s 17(1)*. [*ICTA 1988, s 389(2)*].

Simon's Direct Tax Service. See **E1.622.**

46.16 *Examples*

(A)

A carries on a trade and prepares accounts to 31 December each year. A ceases to trade on 30 September 1996 and the results for the four years and nine months to date of cessation are as follows.

Period	Trading profit/(loss)
	£
31.12.92	3,500
31.12.93	5,000
31.12.94	600
31.12.95	(1,200)
30.9.96	(1,500)

Year of assessment	Capital allowances	Non-trade annual payments
	£	£
1993/94	1,800	300
1994/95	1,500	300
1995/96	1,800	—
1996/97	1,600	—

The terminal loss available is as follows.

			£
1996/97 $\frac{6}{9} \times$ £1,500			1,000
Capital allowances			1,600
1995/96 $\frac{3}{9} \times$ £1,500		500	
$\frac{3}{12} \times$ £1,200		300	800
Capital allowances			
$\frac{6}{12} \times$ £1,800	note (*a*)		900
			£4,300

The assessments for these years are as follows.

Year	Assessment		*Section 388* relief	Revised
		£	£	
1993/94	Profits	3,500		
	Capital allowances	1,800		
		£1,700	800	£900
1994/95	Profits	5,000		
	Capital allowances	1,500		
		£3,500	3,200	£300
1995/96	Profits	600		
	Capital allowances	600		
		—		Nil
1996/97		Nil		Nil
			£4,000	(see below)

		£
Terminal loss as above		4,300
Less: Utilised in 1994/95		3,200
		1,100
Less: Deduction for non-trade charges	note (*b*)	300
		800
Less: Utilised in 1993/94		800
		Nil

Notes

(*a*) The capital allowances of £900 for 1995/96 which are included in the terminal loss do not have to be restricted as only £600 of the total of £1,800 is set against the 1995/96 assessment. If £1,000 had been required to offset the 1995/96 assessment the 1995/96 capital allowances included in the terminal loss would have been restricted to £800.

(*b*) The profits available for set-off against *ICTA 1988, s 388* loss relief are reduced by the annual payments which were paid out of income subject to tax. As they were non-trade charges, the terminal loss available against income of prior years is similarly reduced. See 46.15(*a*) above.

(*c*) A could obtain more relief if he made a claim under *ICTA 1988, s 380(1)* for 1994/95 and then made a reduced claim for *ICTA 1988, s 388* terminal loss relief as follows

	£
Section 380 relief 1994/95	
Profit for the year ended 31.12.94	600
Capital allowances (1995/96)	1,800
	£1,200

The terminal loss available would then be

	£
As calculated above	4,300
Deduct 1995/96 Capital allowances relieved under *section 380*	900
	£3,400

The position would then be

Year	Assessments	*Section 380* relief	*Section 388* relief	Revised
	£	£	£	£
1993/94	1,700		1,100	600
1994/95	3,500	1,200	2,000	300
1995/96	Nil			Nil
1996/97	Nil			Nil
		£1,200	£3,100	(see below)

	£
Terminal loss as above	3,400
Less: Utilised in 1994/95	2,000
	1,400
Less: Deduction for non-trade charges	300
	1,100
Less: Utilised in 1993/94	1,100
Balance	Nil

(B)

B, a trader with a 30 September year end, ceases to trade on 30 June 2000. Tax-adjusted results for his last two accounting periods are as follows.

	Trading Profit/(loss)
Year ended 30 September 1999	£28,000
Nine months to 30 June 2000	(£9,000)

The terminal loss available is as follows.

	£	£
2000/01 (6.4.00 to 30.6.00)		
£9,000 × $\frac{3}{9}$		3,000
1999/2000 (1.7.99 to 5.4.00)		
1.10.99 to 5.4.00 £9,000 × $\frac{6}{9}$	6,000	
1.7.99 to 30.9.99 (£28,000) × $\frac{3}{12}$	(7,000)	
	(1,000)	Nil
Terminal loss		£3,000

Note

In determining the part of a terminal loss arising in a part of the final twelve months (the terminal loss period) that falls into any one year of assessment, a profit made in that period must be netted off against a loss in that period. In this example, no net loss is incurred in that part of the terminal loss period falling in 1999/2000. However, the two different years of assessment are looked at separately, so that the 'net profit' of £1,000 falling within 1999/2000 does not have to be netted off against the 2000/01 loss and is instead treated as nil. The £6,000 losses which cannot form part of the terminal loss claim may be relieved under *ICTA 1988, s 380* (see 46.3 above), and in practice, where other income is sufficient, the whole of the £9,000 would in many cases be claimed under *ICTA 1988, s 380.*

46.17 TREATMENT OF ANNUAL PAYMENTS AND INTEREST AS LOSSES

(*a*) **Assessments under ICTA 1988, s 350** in respect of annual payments, royalties, etc. not paid out of taxed income (see 23.3 DEDUCTION OF TAX AT SOURCE) may be treated as losses and carried forward under *ICTA 1988, ss 385, 386* or allowed as terminal losses under *ICTA 1988, s 388* [*ICTA 1988, ss 387, 389(1); FA 1997, Sch 18 Pt VI(2)(10)*]. Further, where such payments are made to residents of a country with which a DOUBLE TAX RELIEF (25) agreement is in force and are thereby exempt from UK tax, so that no assessment under *ICTA 1988, s 350* is made in respect of them, the amounts thereof can nevertheless be similarly carried forward (*SI 1970 No 488*). But these provisions do not apply to *section 350* assessments arising from—

(i) payments not made wholly and exclusively for the purposes of the trade etc.,

(ii) payments charged to capital, or not ultimately borne by the person assessed,

(iii) yearly interest paid under deduction of tax under *ICTA 1988, s 349(2)* (see 23.3(ii) DEDUCTION OF TAX AT SOURCE),

(iv) (before 6 April 1996) certain rental payments to non-residents (see 68.24 SCHEDULE A),

(v) copyright royalties and design royalty and public lending right payments paid to non-residents (see *ICTA 1988, ss 536–537B*),

(vi) sales of patent rights by non-residents (see *ICTA 1988, s 524* and 54 PATENTS),

(vii) (before 6 April 1997) rents for cable wayleaves etc., paid by radio relay services (see *ICTA 1988, s 120(4)* and 23.14 DEDUCTION OF TAX AT SOURCE),

(viii) interest payments to purchaser re sales of securities falling under *ICTA 1988, s 737* (prior to repeal, see 3.7 ANTI-AVOIDANCE).

(*b*) *Interest payments.* Where relief is claimed under *ICTA 1988, s 353* (see 43.3 INTEREST PAYABLE) in respect of interest paid wholly and exclusively for the purposes of a trade etc. and full effect cannot be given to such relief due to an insufficiency of income, the amount unallowed may be carried forward as a loss under *ICTA 1988, s 385* or treated as a terminal loss under *ICTA 1988, s 388*. [*ICTA 1988, s 390*].

46.18 **LOSSES ON SHARES IN UNLISTED TRADING COMPANIES** [*ICTA 1988, ss 574–576; FA 1988, Sch 14 Pt VIII; FA 1989, Sch 12 para 14; FA 1994, s 210, Sch 20 para 8; FA 1995, s 119; FA 1996, Sch 38 para 6; FA 1998, s 80, Sch 27 Pt III(16); FA 2000, s 63(2)–(4), Sch 16 para 3(3)*]

An individual may claim relief from income tax, instead of from capital gains tax, for an allowable loss (as computed for capital gains tax purposes) on a disposal of ordinary shares or stock in a qualifying trading company for which he subscribed and which were issued to him by the company in consideration of money or money's worth, or were transferred to him *inter vivos* by his spouse who had similarly subscribed for them. Where, for shares subscribed for before 10 March 1981, the consideration was deemed equal to the market value under *CGTA 1979, s 19(3)*, the loss allowable on disposal cannot exceed what the loss would have been without applying that subsection. For shares subscribed for after 9 March 1981, market value is not substituted where the consideration is less than market value. [*TCGA 1992, s 17(2)(b)*]. The temporary relief for indexation losses provided for by *FA 1994, s 93, Sch 12* applies to losses claimed under these provisions [*FA 1994, Sch 12 paras 3(3), 6, 7*] (and see Tolley's Capital Gains Tax under Indexation).

Relief is available only if

(i) the disposal is at arm's length for full consideration, or

(ii) it is by way of a distribution on a winding-up, or

(iii) the value of the shares has become negligible and a claim to that effect made under *TCGA 1992, s 24(2)* (see Tolley's Capital Gains Tax under Losses), or

(iv) a deemed disposal occurs after 5 April 2000 under *TCGA 1992, s 24(1)* (which deems the entire loss, destruction, dissipation or extinction of an asset to be a disposal — see Tolley's Capital Gains Tax under Disposal).

By concession, relating to events before 6 April 2000, relief is not denied, provided that all the other conditions are fulfilled, where the company has no assets and is dissolved, the shareholder has not received a distribution in the course of dissolving or winding up the company (or an anticipated final distribution has not been made), and the shareholder has not made a deemed disposal of the shares under *TCGA 1992, s 24(2)*. (Revenue Pamphlet IR 1, D46). This concession is effectively replaced by (iv) above.

As regards shares issued **after 5 April 1998**, a '*qualifying trading company*' is a company which at all times in the relevant period (i.e. the period ending with the date of disposal of the shares and beginning with the incorporation of the company, or, if later, one year before the date on which the shares were issued) has been an 'unquoted' company (as defined for the purposes of the Enterprise Investment Scheme (EIS) — see 26.5 ENTERPRISE INVESTMENT SCHEME (AND BES)) and which

(*a*) either (i) is an 'eligible trading company' (see below) on the date of disposal, or (ii) has ceased to be an eligible trading company within three years before that date and has not since that cessation been an 'excluded company', an investment company or a non-eligible trading company, *and* (*b*) either (i) has been an eligible trading company for a continuous period of at least six years prior to the disposal (or prior to the cessation in (*a*)(ii) above, as the case may be), or (ii) has been an eligible trading company for a shorter continuous period ending with the disposal or cessation and has not previously been an excluded company, an investment company or a non-eligible trading company, *and*

(*c*) has carried on its business wholly or mainly in the UK throughout the relevant period (as defined above).

As regards shares issued **before 6 April 1998**, a '*qualifying trading company*' is a company none of whose shares have at any time in the relevant period (i.e. ending with the date of disposal of the shares and beginning with the incorporation of the company, or, if later, one year before the date on which the shares were subscribed for) been listed on a recognised stock exchange and which

(*aa*) either (i) is a trading company (i.e. a company, other than an excluded company, whose business consists wholly or mainly of the carrying on of a trade or trades, or which is the holding company of a 'trading group') on the date of the disposal or (ii) has ceased to be a trading company within the previous three years and has not since that time been an investment company or an 'excluded company'; and

(*bb*) either (i) has been a trading company for a continuous period of six years ending on the date of disposal of the shares or the time it ceased to be a trading company; or (ii) if shorter, a continuous period ending on that date or that time and had not before the beginning of that period been an excluded company or an investment company; and

(*cc*) it has been resident in the UK since incorporation until the date of disposal.

Securities on the Alternative Investment Market ('AIM') are treated as unlisted for these purposes. (Revenue Press Release 20 February 1995).

An '*eligible trading company*' is a company which is, or would be, a qualifying company for the purposes of the EIS (see 26.5 ENTERPRISE INVESTMENT SCHEME (AND BES). For this purpose, the EIS legislation is applied (by *ICTA 1988, s 576(4A)(4B)*) with appropriate minor modifications; for example, certain references to the relevant period for EIS purposes are replaced with references to the date of disposal or ceasing to be an eligible trading company (whichever is relevant) or whichever is the relevant continuous period (see (*b*) above). This represents a narrowing of the loss relief against income rules as regards shares issued after 5 April 1998 in that the company which issued the shares must satisfy the EIS requirements as to, *inter alia*, qualifying activities, qualifying trades, gross assets and, where applicable, group structure. However, it is *not* a condition that the company issued the shares under the EIS, that the shares be held for a minimum period or that any EIS income tax relief has been, or could have been, claimed in respect of them.

An '*excluded company*' is a company whose trade consists mainly of dealing in land, in commodities or futures or in shares, securities or other financial instruments (as regards shares issued before 6 April 1998 — dealing in shares, securities, land, trades or commodity futures) or is not carried on on a commercial basis with a reasonable expectation of profit, or which is the holding company of a non-trading group, or which is a building society (see 9 BUILDING SOCIETIES) or a registered industrial and provident society within *ICTA 1988, s 486(12)*.

A '*trading group*' is a group (i.e. a company and its 51% subsidiaries) the business of the members of which, taken together, consists wholly or mainly in the carrying on of a trade or trades (disregarding any trade carried on by a subsidiary which is an excluded company or, as regards shares issued before 6 April 1998, which is non-UK resident).

Claims must be in writing within, for 1996/97 and later years, twelve months after 31 January following the year of assessment *in which the loss is incurred* (for 1994/95 and

1995/96, two years after the end of that year of assessment). A loss may be claimed against income.

(I) of the year in which the loss is incurred, or

(II) of the year preceding that in which the loss is incurred.

Where, against income of the same year, claims are made both under (I) in respect of that year's loss and under (II) in respect of the following year's loss, (I) takes precedence. Where both claims are made for the same loss, no order of priority is specified but it is considered that the Revenue would follow the same practice as for loss relief under *ICTA 1988, s 380* (see 46.3 above).

Relief under the above provisions is given in priority to relief under *ICTA 1988, s 380* (see 46.3 above) and *ICTA 1988, s 381* (see 46.13 above) for the same year of assessment. The relief cannot also be allowed for capital gains tax purposes and appropriate adjustments will be made to avoid double relief.

Identification. Where an individual holds shares of the same class only some of which qualify for the above relief because they were subscribed for, and both the subscription shares and the other shares form part of the same holding (i.e. a number of shares of the same class held by one person in one capacity, whether or not pooled for capital gains tax purposes), then in determining the extent (if any) to which a disposal relates to shares subscribed for (qualifying shares), disposals are to be identified with acquisitions on a last in/first out (LIFO) basis.

For disposals after 5 April 1998, there is an exception to the above rule where the holding includes *any* of the following:

(A) Shares in respect of which Business Expansion Scheme (BES) relief has been given and not withdrawn (see 26 ENTERPRISE INVESTMENT SCHEME (AND BES));

(B) Shares to which Enterprise Investment Scheme (EIS) income tax relief is attributable (see 26 ENTERPRISE INVESTMENT SCHEME (AND BES));

(C) Shares to which EIS capital gains deferral relief is attributable (see 26.17 ENTERPRISE INVESTMENT SCHEME (AND BES)).

In such a case, disposals are identified in accordance with the identification rules generally applicable to BES and EIS shares (broadly, first in/first out (FIFO) — see 26.12, 26.27 ENTERPRISE INVESTMENT SCHEME (AND BES)).

Loss relief under these provisions on the disposal of qualifying shares forming part of a larger holding is restricted to the sums that would have been allowable as deductions in computing the loss if the qualifying shares had been acquired and disposed of as a separate holding (see Step 4 in the example at 46.19 below). (Note that even for disposals before 30 November 1993 when indexation allowance could create or increase a loss, the term 'deductions' here did not include indexation allowance — see Revenue Capital Gains Manual, CG 58378.)

Revenue Capital Gains Manual, CG 58377 identifies four steps in the computation of loss relief under these provisions where a share pool does not entirely consist of qualifying shares. Step 1 is to compute the allowable loss for capital gains tax purposes under normal capital gains tax principles and identification rules (see Tolley's Capital Gains Tax under Shares and Securities — Identification Rules). Step 2 is to identify the qualifying and non-qualifying shares included in the disposal (using the special identification rules described above). If it is found that the disposal comprises both, Step 3 is to apportion the loss, on a just and reasonable basis, between qualifying and non-qualifying shares. Step 4 is to compare the loss so attributed to the qualifying shares with the actual allowable expenditure incurred on those shares and to apply, if necessary, the restriction mentioned above.

Note that, for capital gains tax (though not corporation tax) purposes, share pooling is abolished for *acquisitions* after 5 April 1998, although existing pools at 5 April 1998 are retained. The *principal* identification rule for disposals (other than of EIS and BES shares) after that date is a LIFO basis. See Tolley's Capital Gains Tax.

Anti-avoidance. Any claim to relief will bring in the provisions of *TCGA 1992, s 30* (value-shifting to give a tax-free benefit) so that the relief may be adjusted for any benefit conferred whether tax-free or not.

Company reconstructions etc.. Where the shares disposed of represent a new holding identifiable under *TCGA 1992, s 127* with 'old shares' after a reorganisation or reduction of share capital, relief is not available unless it could have been given (on the disposal of the old shares for full consideration) at the reorganisation etc. had this legislation been in force and had the reorganisation been a chargeable occasion producing a loss. Where the reorganisation did not so qualify, but new consideration was given for the new holding, relief is limited to such of that new consideration as is an allowable deduction. Where *TCGA 1992, s 137* operates to make a disposal of shares on a reconstruction etc., no relief is available under the above provisions. '*New consideration*' is money or money's worth but excluding any surrender or alteration to the original shares or rights attached thereto, and the application of assets of the company or distribution declared but not made out of the assets. See Revenue Capital Gains Manual CG58400 *et seq.*.

Application to EIS shares. It is formally provided that the provisions described above apply to a loss on the disposal by an individual of shares to which EIS income tax relief is attributable (see 26 ENTERPRISE INVESTMENT SCHEME (AND BES)). However, the above-mentioned LIFO identification rules do not apply to such disposals (whether made before or on or after 6 April 1998). [*ICTA 1988, s 305A; FA 1994, s 137, Sch 15 para 20; FA 1998, Sch 13 para 18*].

Simon's Direct Tax Service. See **E1.627**.

46.19 *Example*

X is a semi-retired business executive. Over the years he has acquired several shareholdings in unlisted companies and he has suffered the following losses.

(i) 500 shares in A Ltd (a qualifying trading company) which X subscribed for in 1990. Allowable loss for CGT purposes on liquidation in June 1999 — £12,000.

(ii) 500 shares in B Ltd which X subscribed for in 1992 at £10 per share. B Ltd traded as a builder until 1995 when it changed its trade to that of buying and selling land. X received an arm's length offer for the shares of £3 per share in May 1999 which he accepted.

(iii) In 1987, X subscribed for 2,000 shares in C Ltd at £50 per share. In 1992 his aunt gave him a further 1,000 shares. The market value of the shares at that time was £60 per share.

The company has been a qualifying trading company since 1983 but has fallen on hard times recently. A company offered X £20 per share in June 2000. X accepted the offer to the extent of 1,500 shares.

The treatment of these losses in relation to income tax would be as follows.

(i) Loss claim — *ICTA 1988, s 574*, 1999/2000 or 1998/99 — £12,000

(ii) No loss claim under *ICTA 1988, s 574* is possible as company is an 'excluded company' (see 46.18 above).

(iii) *Step 1.* Compute the allowable loss for capital gains tax purposes.

Share pool

	Shares	Qualifying expenditure
		£
1987 subscription	2,000	100,000
1992 acquisition	1,000	60,000
	3,000	160,000
2000 disposal	(1,500)	(80,000)
Pool carried forward	1,500	£80,000

(An indexed pool should also have been maintained but is ignored here for convenience and because indexation allowance cannot increase a loss in any case.)

	£
Disposal consideration 1,500 × £20	30,000
Allowable cost $\frac{1,500}{3,000}$ × £160,000	80,000
Allowable capital loss	£50,000

Step 2. Applying a LIFO basis, identify the qualifying shares (500) and the non-qualifying shares (1,000) comprised in the disposal.

Step 3. Calculate the proportion of the loss attributable to the qualifying shares.

Loss referable to 500 qualifying shares $\frac{500}{1,500}$ × £50,000 £16,667

Step 4. Compare the loss in *Step 3* with the actual cost of the qualifying shares, *viz.*

Cost of 500 qualifying shares $\frac{500}{2,000}$ × £100,000 £25,000

No restriction is necessary as the cost of the qualifying shares exceeds the loss in *Step 3.*

Loss claim — *ICTA 1988, s 574* for 2000/01 or 1999/2000 — £16,667

(The loss not relieved against income (£50,000 – £16,667 = £33,333) remains an allowable loss for capital gains tax purposes.)

Utilisation of losses

X makes all possible claims under *ICTA 1988, s 574* so as to obtain relief against the earliest possible income. He is a single man and has total income, before *section 574* relief, of £7,000 for 1998/99, £11,500 for 1999/2000 and £9,000 for 2000/01.

The *section 574* losses available as above are as follows.

	1999/2000 disposals	2000/01 disposals
	£	£
A Ltd shares	12,000	
C Ltd shares		16,667

Section 574 claims are made as follows.

	£
1998/99	
Total income	7,000
Claim under *section 574(1)(b)*	(7,000)
Revised total income	Nil
1999/2000	
Total income	11,500
Claim under *section 574(1)(a)* note (*b*)	(5,000)
	6,500
Claim under *section 574(1)(b)*	(6,500)
Revised total income	Nil
2000/01	
Total income	9,000
Claim under *section 574(1)(a)*	(9,000)
Revised total income	Nil

Loss utilisation

	£
1999/2000 loss	
Loss available	12,000
Relief claimed for 1998/99 (*section 574(1)(b)*)	(7,000)
Relief claimed for 1999/2000 (*section 574(1)(a)*)	(5,000)

	£
2000/01 loss	
Loss available	16,667
Relief claimed for 1999/2000 (*section 574(1)(b)*)	(6,500)
Relief claimed for 2000/01 (*section 574(1)(a)*)	(9,000)
Unused balance note (*c*)	£1,167

Notes

(*a*) In this example, losses have been set against preceding year's income first, as X wished to obtain relief against earliest possible income, but this need not be the case.

(*b*) Where two years' losses are set against one year's income, the current year's loss is relieved in priority to that of the following year.

(*c*) The unused balance of the 2000/01 loss cannot be relieved under *section 574* due to insufficiency of income and therefore reverts to being a capital loss available to reduce chargeable gains.

47 Married Persons

(See also Revenue Pamphlets IR 80, 83, 90, 91.)

Cross-references. See 1.14, 1.15, 1.21–1.24 ALLOWANCES AND TAX RATES; 2 ALLOWANCES AND TAX RATES—EXAMPLES; 26.15, 26.29 ENTERPRISE INVESTMENT SCHEME (AND BES); 43.12 INTEREST PAYABLE; 53.13 PARTNERSHIPS; 64.5 RESIDENCE, ORDINARY RESIDENCE AND DOMICILE (residence).

Simon's Direct Tax Service E5.1.

The headings in this chapter are as follows.

47.1 Independent taxation
47.2 — personal reliefs
47.3 — example
47.4 — jointly held property
47.5 — transitional reliefs
47.6 — example
47.7 'Living together'
47.8 Decree of nullity
47.9 When the marriage ends
47.10 — alimony, maintenance, separation allowances, etc.
47.11 — examples

47.1 INDEPENDENT TAXATION

For 1990/91 and subsequent years, married persons are treated separately for taxation purposes, subject to transitional provisions (see 47.5 below). The aggregation of income under *ICTA 1988, s 279* for earlier years does not affect the question of the existence or amount of a married woman's income for 1990/91 or subsequent years. [*FA 1988, s 32, Sch 3 para 25*].

47.2 **Personal reliefs.** Husband and wife are each entitled to the personal allowance (see 1.14 ALLOWANCES AND TAX RATES) in their own right. The husband is entitled to the married couple's allowance (see 1.15 ALLOWANCES AND TAX RATES) for a year of assessment at any time during which his wife is living with him. For 2000/01 and subsequent years of assessment, the married couple's allowance is only available where one of the spouses was born before 6 April 1935, so that the allowance will in due course cease to be available at all. [*ICTA 1988, ss 257, 257A; FA 1988, s 33; FA 1994, s 77; FA 1996, s 134, Sch 20 para 14; FA 1999, s 31*].

Transfer of married couple's allowance. A wife may elect to be entitled to claim one-half of the married couple's allowance for any year of assessment (ignoring any age-related increase), the husband's entitlement being correspondingly reduced. Alternatively, they may jointly elect for the wife to be able to claim the full amount of the basic allowance, the husband's entitlement being restricted to any age-related increase, although the husband may then elect to be able to claim back one-half of the basic allowance (the wife's entitlement being correspondingly reduced). A woman may not, however, be entitled to more than one reduction under these provisions in any year of assessment.

For 1999/2000 and subsequent years, as a consequence of the abolition of the married couple's allowance after that year except where one of the spouses was born before 6 April 1935, the transfer is restricted to the minimum amount below which the allowance may not be reduced by reference to the income of the claimant. This is initially set at the amount of the basic allowance for 1999/2000 (i.e. £1,970), and is subject to the normal indexation provisions for subsequent years.

An election under these provisions has to be made in prescribed form (i.e. form 18) before the first year of assessment for which it is to have effect (or within the first 30 days of that year if prior notification of intention to elect has been given to the inspector before the beginning of that year), and has effect until withdrawn or until a different election is made.

If an election is to have effect for the year of assessment of marriage, it may be made during that year, but will only apply for that year to the reduced basic or minimum allowance available. An election may be withdrawn with effect from the year following that in which notice of withdrawal is given.

[*ICTA 1988, s 257BA; F(No 2)A 1992, Sch 5 para 2; FA 1994, Sch 8 para 2; FA 1999, s 32*].

Where a spouse's entitlement to an income tax reduction in respect of the married couple's allowance (including, in the case of the husband, any age-related increase in the basic allowance) exceeds his or her total income tax liability (see 1.15 ALLOWANCES AND TAX RATES), the excess may, if he or she so notifies the inspector, be claimed as a reduction in the other spouse's income tax liability (in addition to any reduction to which he or she is entitled as above). The notification to the inspector must be given in prescribed form and is irrevocable. It must be given within five years after 31 January following the year of assessment to which it is to apply (for 1994/95 and 1995/96, within six years after the end of that year of assessment).

[*ICTA 1988, s 257BB; F(No 2)A 1992, Sch 5 para 2; FA 1994, Sch 8 para 3; FA 1996, s 135, Sch 21 para 4; FA 2000, s 39(8)(10)*].

Transfer of blind person's allowance. Blind person's allowance (see 1.19 ALLOWANCES AND TAX RATES) may be transferred from husband to wife and *vice versa* to the extent that the allowance exceeds the total income of the claimant. For this purpose total income is as reduced by all other deductions other than those in respect of payments for which relief is obtained by deduction of basic rate tax in respect of retirement benefit or personal pension scheme contributions (see 66.5(*a*) RETIREMENT SCHEMES, 60.1 PERSONAL PENSION SCHEMES) or vocational training costs (until abolition of the relief for such costs, see 92.1 VOCATIONAL TRAINING RELIEF). Transfer of the relief must be notified to the inspector in prescribed form within five years after 31 January following the year of assessment to which it is to apply (before 1996/97, within six years after the end of that year of assessment). The notice is irrevocable. [*ICTA 1988, s 265; FA 1988, Sch 3 para 8; FA 1989, s 33(10), s 57(4); FA 1991, s 33(4); F(No 2)A 1992, Sch 5 para 8; FA 1994, Sch 8 para 10, Sch 10 para 3, Sch 26 Pt V; FA 1996, s 135, Sch 21 para 6; FA 1999, Sch 20 Pt III(15)*].

Simon's Direct Tax Service. See **E5.103**.

47.3 *Example*

Transfer of surplus married couple's allowance

Mr Grey is a sole trader and made a profit of £500 in the year to 30 April 1999. Mr Grey has been married for some years, and he and his wife are under 65. He has building society interest of £2,640 (net) for 1999/2000 and his wife has a salary of £15,000 and building society interest of £1,760 (net). Mr and Mrs Grey receive interest of £2,240 (net) in 1999/2000 from a bank deposit account in their joint names. Mr Grey elects under *ICTA 1988, s 257BB(2)* to transfer the unused balance of his married couple's allowance for 1999/2000 to his wife.

The couple's tax position for 1999/2000 is as follows.

	Mr Grey	Mrs Grey
	£	£
Schedule D, Case I	500	—
Schedule E	—	15,000
Building society interest (gross)	3,300	2,200
Bank deposit interest (gross)	1,400	1,400
Total income	c/f 5,200	c/f 18,600

	Mr Grey	Mrs Grey
	£	£
	b/f 5,200	b/f 18,600
Deduct Personal allowance	4,335	4,335
Taxable income	£865	£14,265
Tax payable:		
865/1,500 @ 10%	86.50	150.00
9,165 @ 23%		2,107.95
3,600 @ 20%		720.00
	86.50	2,977.95
Deduct Married couple's allowance		
£1,970 @ 10% = £197, but restricted to	86.50	
Deduct Surplus married couple's allowance £(197 – 86.50)		110.50
Total tax liabilities	Nil	2,867.45
Deduct Tax at source:		
Building society interest	(660.00)	(440.00)
Bank deposit interest	(280.00)	(280.00)
Net tax (repayment)/liability (subject to wife's PAYE deductions)	£(940.00)	£2,147.45

See also 2.5 ALLOWANCES AND TAX RATES—EXAMPLES for an example of transfer of married couple's allowance for 2000/01 onwards where one spouse was born before 6 April 1935.

47.4 **Jointly held property.** Special rules apply for the apportionment between spouses living together of income arising from property held in their joint names. Provided that at least one of them is beneficially entitled to that income, they are treated as beneficially entitled to it in equal shares, except in the following circumstances.

(i) Where the income is earned income or, not being earned income, is assessable in the name of a partnership.

(ii) To the extent that the income is by any other provision of the *Income Tax Acts* treated as the income either of the spouse who is not beneficially entitled to the income, or of a third party.

(iii) Where the husband and wife are not beneficially entitled to the income in equal shares, and they make a declaration of their beneficial interests in the income to which the declaration relates and the property from which that income arises, provided that the beneficial interests of the husband and wife in the property correspond to their beneficial interests in the income.

A declaration under (iii) above has effect in relation to income arising on and after the date of the declaration, and continues to have effect unless and until the beneficial interests of the spouses in either the income or the property cease to accord with the declaration. Notice of a declaration must be given to the inspector, in a prescribed form (i.e. form 17) and manner, within 60 days of the date of the declaration. [*ICTA 1988, ss 282A, 282B; FA 1988, s 34*].

Simon's Direct Tax Service. See **E5.103A**.

47.5 **Transitional reliefs.** Three transitional reliefs are available. They **cease to have effect after 1999/2000**.

(*a*) *Husband with excess allowances.* Where a husband and wife were living together at any time during 1990/91, and for the whole or any part of 1989/90 the wife's income is aggregated with that of the husband for income tax purposes (and no election for separate taxation was in force for 1989/90), the wife is entitled to a deduction from her total income for 1990/91 of an amount equal to the excess of the husband's 1989/90 allowances over the sum of the husband's total income for 1990/91 and the wife's allowances (apart from these transitional provisions) for 1990/91.

Where they were living together for part only of 1989/90, and the aggregation rules do not apply to them for any part of 1989/90, the wife is entitled to a deduction from her total income for 1990/91 of an amount equal to the excess of the husband's allowances (other than wife's earned income relief) for 1989/90 over his total income for 1990/91. The deduction is, however, reduced by the excess, if any, of the allowances to which the wife would be entitled for 1990/91 apart from these provisions over the lesser of

(i) her total income for 1989/90, and

(ii) her allowances for that year other than the additional relief for children, widow's bereavement allowance (see 1.17, 1.16 ALLOWANCES AND TAX RATES) and allowances transferred from her husband.

Transitional relief may also be available for 1991/92 or any subsequent year (the '*year in question*') at any time during which the husband and wife are living together, where they were also living together throughout the immediately preceding year of assessment, and the wife made a deduction from her total income under these transitional provisions for that immediately preceding year (see below). Where that deduction is greater than the excess of the wife's allowances given by deduction for the year in question over those for the immediately preceding year (in both cases apart from transitional relief under these provisions), and the husband's allowances given by deduction for the year in question (other than blind person's allowances (see 1.19 ALLOWANCES AND TAX RATES) and (before 1994/95) married couple's allowance (see 1.15 ALLOWANCES AND TAX RATES)) exceed his total income for that year, the wife is entitled to a deduction for the year in question of the lesser of

(A) the deduction under these transitional relief provisions for the immediately preceding year of assessment *less* any increase in her allowances (*other than* under these transitional relief provisions) for the year in question over those for the immediately preceding year, and

(B) the excess of her husband's allowances for the year in question (other than blind person's and married couple's allowances) over his total income for that year.

In determining for the above purpose the excess of the wife's allowances given by deduction for 1994/95 over those for 1993/94, deductions for 1993/94 in respect of allowances falling to be given by way of reduction in tax liability for 1994/95 are disregarded (so that like is compared with like). (In practice, this is likely to be relevant only as regards married couple's allowance — see 1.15 ALLOWANCES AND TAX RATES.)

In determining whether the wife made a deduction from her total income under these transitional provisions for the immediately preceding year, and the amount thereof, it is assumed that such deduction is made after all other deductions except any in respect of business expansion scheme investments.

Total income for all the purposes of these transitional reliefs is as reduced by all deductions other than those in respect of investments under the business expansion scheme (see 26 ENTERPRISE INVESTMENT SCHEME (AND BES)) and in respect of payments for which relief is obtained by deduction of basic rate tax in respect of retirement benefit or personal pension scheme contributions (66.5(*a*) RETIREMENT SCHEMES, 60.1 PERSONAL PENSION SCHEMES), relevant loan interest (23.13 DEDUCTION OF TAX AT SOURCE), MEDICAL INSURANCE (48) premiums, and vocational training costs (92 VOCATIONAL TRAINING RELIEF). Any separate assessment election for 1989/90 is similarly disregarded in determining the husband's excess allowances for that year. For 1994/95 and subsequent years, payments of relevant loan interest and medical insurance premiums are not relieved by deduction from total income, and are therefore no longer relevant.

Transitional relief under these provisions is available only if notice is given by the husband. The notice must be in writing and in prescribed form (i.e. form 575) to the inspector, and is irrevocable. For 1996/97 and later years, the notice must be given within five years after 31 January following the year of assessment to which it relates. Previously, it had to be given within six years after the end of that year of assessment.

These provisions cease to apply after 1999/2000.

[*ICTA 1988, s 257D; FA 1988, s 33; FA 1989, s 33(10), s 57(4); F(No 2)A 1992, Sch 5 para 3; FA 1994, Sch 8 para 4, Sch 10 para 3, Sch 26 Pt V; FA 1996, s 135, Sch 21 para 5; FA 1999, s 32(2)(4)*].

(*b*) *The elderly.* Where, for 1989/90, a claimant was entitled (disregarding any separate assessment election) to the age allowance determined by reference to his wife's age and not his own (i.e. he was under 65 or under 75, as the case may be, throughout 1989/90), and the amount of that allowance exceeded the aggregate of the personal and married couple's allowances available for 1990/91 apart from these transitional provisions, then for any subsequent year at any time in which he had the same wife living with him, his personal allowance was £3,400 or £3,540, as appropriate (subject to restriction by reference to an income limit in the same way as the normal age increase, see above). The indexation provisions (see above) did *not* apply to these figures. The personal allowance was thus frozen at this figure until such time as the claimant became entitled himself to the increased personal allowance for those aged over 65 (or 75). [*ICTA 1988, s 257E; FA 1988, s 33; FA 1996, s 134, Sch 20 para 15; FA 1999, s 32(2)(4)*]. These provisions are of no practical application for 1996/97 onwards as the normal personal allowance is higher than £3,540 (and has been higher than £3,400 since 1992/93). They are formally repealed after 1999/2000.

(*c*) *Separated couples.* Where, before 6 April 1990, a husband and wife ceased to live together, but they continued to be married to one another and the wife is wholly maintained by the husband, then, subject to conditions as below, they may be treated as continuing to live together for the purposes of entitlement to married couple's allowance and the transitional relief for the elderly (see (*b*) above), although not for the purposes of transfer of excess allowances to the wife (see (*a*) above) or of married couple's allowance (see 47.2 above). This applies to any year of assessment for which the husband is not entitled to make a deduction in respect of maintenance payments in computing his income for tax purposes, provided that, for 1989/90, he was entitled to the married person's allowance, and that, in relation to years of assessment after 1990/91, he has been entitled to the married couple's allowance under this provision in each intervening year.

These provisions cease to apply after 1999/2000.

[*ICTA 1988, s 257F; FA 1988, s 33; F(No 2)A 1992, Sch 5 para 4; FA 1994, Sch 8 para 5; FA 1996, s 134, Sch 20 para 16; FA 1999, s 32(2)(4)*].

Simon's Direct Tax Service. See E2.203, E2.204, E2.302.

47.6 *Example*

Husband with excess allowances: transitional relief

A man married before 6 April 1989 and under 65 has a total income of £1,000 in 1989/90 and 1990/91, £2,500 in 1991/92 and 1992/93, £3,250 in 1993/94 and £3,400 in 1994/95. His wife, also under 65, has earned income of £10,000 in each of those years. Each is entitled only to the normal personal reliefs. The surplus allowances available for transfer to the wife in 1990/91 were as follows.

	£	£
Married couple's allowance		1,720
Less husband's total income for 1990/91	1,000	
less personal allowance	3,005	—
Allowance transferable to wife		1,720
Husband's reliefs for 1989/90 (including wife's earned income relief)		7,160
Less husband's 1990/91 total income	1,000	
wife's 1990/91 reliefs (including transferred married couple's allowance)	4,725	5,725
Transitional relief available to wife		1,435
Total allowances available to wife are thus		
personal allowance		3,005
married couple's allowance transferred		1,720
transitional relief		1,435
		6,160

The surplus allowances available for 1991/92 were as follows.

Married couple's allowance		1,720
Less husband's total income for 1991/92	2,500	
less personal allowance	3,295	—
Allowance transferable to wife		1,720
Wife's transitional relief for 1990/91		1,435
Less wife's 1991/92 allowances (including transferred married couple's allowance but excluding transitional allowance)	5,015	
less 1990/91 allowances (including transferred married couple's allowance but excluding transitional allowance)	4,725	290
		1,145

	£	£
Husband's 1991/92 personal allowance	3,295	
Less 1991/92 total income	2,500	795
Transitional relief available to wife (lesser of £1,145 and £795)		795
Total allowances available to wife are thus		
personal allowance		3,295
married couple's allowance transferred		1,720
transitional relief		795
		5,810
The surplus allowances available for 1992/93 were as follows.		
Married couple's allowance		1,720
Less husband's total income for 1992/93	2,500	
less personal allowance	3,445	—
Allowance transferable to wife		1,720
Wife's transitional relief for 1991/92		795
Less wife's 1992/93 allowances (including transferred married couple's allowance but excluding transitional allowance)	5,165	
less 1991/92 allowances (including transferred married couple's allowance but excluding transitional allowance)	5,015	150
		645
Husband's 1992/93 personal allowance	3,445	
Less 1992/93 total income	2,500	945
Transitional relief available to wife (lesser of £645 and £945)		645
Total allowances available to wife are thus		
personal allowance		3,445
married couple's allowance transferred		1,720
transitional relief		645
		5,810
The surplus allowances available for 1993/94 were as follows.		
Married couple's allowance		1,720
Less husband's total income for 1993/94	3,250	
less personal allowance	3,445	—
Allowance transferable to wife		1,720

	£	£
Wife's transitional relief for 1992/93		645
Less wife's 1993/94 allowances (including transferred married couple's allowance but excluding transitional allowance)	5,165	
less 1992/93 allowances (including transferred married couple's allowance but excluding transitional allowance)	5,165	—
		645
Husband's 1993/94 personal allowance	3,445	
Less 1993/94 total income	3,250	195
Transitional relief available to wife (lesser of £645 and £195)		195
Total allowances available to wife are thus		
personal allowance		3,445
married couple's allowance transferred		1,720
transitional relief		195
		5,360

The surplus allowances available for 1994/95 were as follows.

Wife's transitional relief for 1993/94		195
Less wife's 1994/95 allowances given by deduction (excluding transitional allowance)	3,445	
less 1993/94 allowances (excluding transferred married couple's allowance and transitional allowance)	3,445	—
		195
Husband's 1994/95 personal allowance	3,445	
Less 1994/95 total income	3,400	45
Transitional relief available to wife (lesser of £195 and £45)		45
Total allowances available to wife (by deduction from total income) are thus		
personal allowance		3,445
transitional relief		45
		3,490

In addition, she is entitled to the unused married couple's allowance of £1,720 at 20%, given by way of reduction in her income tax liability.

Note. For 1995/96 and subsequent years, no transitional relief is available as the increase in the wife's personal allowance for 1995/96 of (£3,525 – £3,445 =) £80 exceeds the £45 transitional relief available for 1994/95.

47.7 'LIVING TOGETHER'

A married woman is treated as '*living with her husband*' unless they are

(*a*) separated under a Court Order or separation deed, or

(*b*) in fact separated in circumstances which render permanent separation likely.

[*ICTA 1988, s 282*].

A husband and wife may be separated even though living under the same roof if they have become two households (*Holmes v Mitchell Ch D 1990, 63 TC 718*).

47.8 DECREE OF NULLITY

A decree of nullity does not operate retrospectively to disentitle the husband to the married allowance during the years the parties lived together (*Dodworth v Dale KB 1936, 20 TC 285*).

47.9 WHEN THE MARRIAGE ENDS

A marriage may end by death, by divorce or by separation (which for tax purposes is when the parties cease 'living together', as defined in 47.7 above). Effects are as below.

(*a*) The **husband** is entitled to the full married couple's allowance (see 1.15 ALLOWANCES AND TAX RATES) for the year of assessment in which the marriage ends. If he remarries in the same year, the proportionate reduction in such allowances by reference to the length of the part of the year of assessment before the marriage took place does not apply.

(*b*) The **wife**, in addition to her personal allowance for the year of assessment and, if appropriate, the additional personal allowance for children (see 1.17 ALLOWANCES AND TAX RATES), is entitled to any of the married couple's allowance not used against her husband's income and, if the husband dies, to the widow's bereavement allowance (see 1.16 ALLOWANCES AND TAX RATES). All these allowances may be set against any income of the year or, where relevant, used to reduce the total tax liability for the year.

(*c*) See 71.9 SCHEDULE D, CASES I AND II for concessional continuation treatment of business previously carried on by, or in partnership with, deceased spouse.

(*d*) Interest payable by each former spouse on a property held on a joint tenancy or as tenants in common will be allowable, subject to the usual conditions, but the allowance may be restricted where the amount of the mortgage on which a former spouse pays interest exceeds the value of his/her interest in the property. (CCAB Memorandum TR 500, 10 March 1983).

47.10 **Alimony, maintenance, separation allowances, etc.**. See generally Revenue Pamphlet IR 93 and Simon's Direct Tax Service E5.104 *et seq.*.

Payments of alimony and maintenance falling due **after 14 March 1988** and made other than under an 'existing obligation' (see 1.8(i) ALLOWANCES AND TAX RATES) are not charges on the income of the person making the payment and tax is not deductible at source. Such payments do not form part of the taxable income of the person to whom they are made or of any other person. Where such payments are 'qualifying maintenance payments', the payer obtains relief as below. **For 2000/01 onwards**, relief is restricted to cases where at least one of the former spouses was aged 65 or over on 5 April 2000. Relief is available by reference to the lesser of

(*a*) the aggregate amount of 'qualifying maintenance payments' made by the payer which fall due in that year, and

(*b*) the amount of the married couple's allowance for that year (see 1.15 ALLOWANCES AND TAX RATES) or, from 2000/01 onwards and where still available, the minimum amount of that allowance available for couples at least one of whom was born before 6 April 1935, i.e. the 1999/2000 figure of £1,970 after indexation,

reduced, for 1999/2000 and earlier years, by the aggregate amount of any other maintenance payments attracting relief for that year. Relief is given at a reduced rate, 20% for 1994/95, 15% for 1995/96 to 1998/99 inclusive, and 10% thereafter, by means of a reduction in the payer's income tax liability. The reduction is the smaller of the specified percentage (i.e. 10% for 1999/2000) of the amount established above and what would otherwise be the payer's total income tax liability. For this purpose, 'total income tax liability' is as defined in 1.15 ALLOWANCES AND TAX RATES, except that it is before any reductions on account of personal reliefs (where these are also given by way of reduction in income tax liability — see 1.15 to 1.17 ALLOWANCES AND TAX RATES).

So much of the aggregate of payments under existing obligations which attract tax relief as does not exceed the married couple's allowance is treated as if it were a qualifying maintenance payment made otherwise than under an existing obligation, and thus attracts the above relief subject to the overall limit.

A '*qualifying maintenance payment*' is a periodical payment (other than an instalment of a lump sum) which

(A) is made under a UK (from 1992/93 a European Community, from 1 January 1994 a European Economic Area) Court Order, or under a written agreement the proper law of which is the law of a part of the UK (from 1992/93 a part of the European Community, from 1 January 1994 a part of the European Economic Area), or under a maintenance assessment made under the *Child Support Act 1991* (or NI equivalent),

(B) is made by one party to a marriage (or former marriage) either

(i) to or for the benefit of, and for the maintenance of, the other party, or

(ii) to the other party for the maintenance by that other party of a 'child of the family',

(C) is due at a time when

(i) the two parties are not a married couple living together within *ICTA 1988, s 282(1)* and disregarding *section 282(2)* (see 47.7 above), and

(ii) the party to whom or for whose benefit the payment is made has not remarried, and

(D) does not attract tax relief for the person making the payment, apart from the deduction specified above.

As regards (B) above, for payments falling due after 5 April 2000 there is an additional requirement that at least one of the parties to the marriage (or former marriage) was born before 6 April 1935.

As regards (C)(ii) above, the fact that the subsequent marriage may itself have been dissolved is irrelevant (*Norris v Edgson Ch D, [2000] STC 494*).

The above conditions were not satisfied by a payment made by the taxpayer to a former spouse for the maintenance of their child where the agreement required the payment to be made to the child (*Billingham v John Ch D 1998, 70 TC 380*), nor by payments made by one party to a marriage to pay off the joint mortgage on a house continuing to be occupied by the other (*Otter v Andrews (Sp C 181), [1999] SSCD 67*).

(B) above is treated as satisfied in relation to periodical payments made to or retained by the Secretary of State after 5 April 1993 under a maintenance assessment under the *Child Support Act 1991* (or NI equivalent) by one party to a marriage (whether or not dissolved or annulled) where the other party is, for the purposes of that *Act*, a parent of the child(ren) to whom the assessment relates. Assessments under *section 7* of that *Act* (right of child in Scotland to apply for maintenance assessment) are excluded from this treatment. Payments to the Secretary of State under *Social Security Administration Act 1992, s 106* or *Jobseekers Act 1995, s 23* (or NI equivalent of either) by one party to a marriage (whether or not dissolved or annulled) in respect of income support or an income-based jobseeker's allowance claimed by the other party are similarly treated as satisfying (B) above in relation to payments falling due after 5 April 1993.

A '*child of the family*' is a person under 21 who is either a child of both parties to a marriage or has been treated by them both as a child of their family, but excluding a child who has been boarded out with them by a public authority or voluntary organisation.

[*ICTA 1988, s 347B; FA 1988, ss 36, 38(3A), 40, Sch 3 para 13; F(No 2)A 1992, ss 61, 62(1); FA 1994, s 79(1)(3)–(6)(8); Jobseekers Act 1995, Sch 2 para 15; FA 1998, s 27(1), Sch 27 Pt III(1); FA 1999, s 36(1)–(6)(8), Sch 20 Pt III(6); SI 1992 No 2612*].

Payments under 'existing obligations' (see 1.8(i) ALLOWANCES AND TAX RATES). For years of assessment before 1989/90, and except in the case of **small maintenance payments**, tax was deductible from payments, unless the Order directs them to be made in full, or without deduction of tax, or free of tax, in which cases the payments must be grossed up for all tax purposes. Under Scots law, an appropriately worded minute of agreement between the parties, registered for preservation and execution with the Court of Session, will have the same effect as a Court Order for these purposes (see Tolley's Practical Tax 1983 p 179).

Where an interim Court Order (which cannot apply to payments for a period exceeding three months) is made, it is understood that the Revenue treat payments under the Order as not being annual payments, so that tax could not be deducted or repaid.

Where maintenance payments to a divorced or separated spouse, or to the mother of his illegitimate child, are annual payments from which the spouse or father could deduct tax under *ICTA 1988, s 348*, but were made gross, the Revenue, by concession,

(i) allow to the payer against any tax retained in charge in respect of the maintenance payments a sum equal to the balance of any relief or repayment the recipient could have claimed had tax been deducted, but which cannot be allowed against the recipient's tax liability, and

(ii) regard the payments in the recipient's hands as taxed before receipt, but as not being available for repayment.

Similar concessional relief is available where payments are made direct to a child under a Court Order.

After 5 April 1989, the concession was of relevance only to payments under 'existing obligations' either due before 6 April 1989, or payable under a Court Order in favour of a child of 21 or over or, before 6 April 1995, under an agreement in favour of a child of 18 or over. The concession is of no relevance to payments made after 5 April 1996.

(Revenue Pamphlet IR 1, A52).

See 23.8(*b*) DEDUCTION OF TAX AT SOURCE for recovery of tax not deducted at time of payment and 23.16 for orders 'free of tax' and 25.5(*a*) DOUBLE TAX RELIEF where payer is resident abroad.

Payments satisfying the conditions set out below are to be made without deduction of tax and are not charges on income. For payments due in 1989/90 to 1993/94 inclusive, the payer may, in computing his total income, claim a deduction of the lesser of

(*aa*) the aggregate amount of such payments falling due and made by him in the year of assessment, and

(*bb*) the aggregate amount of payments due in 1988/89 which also satisfied the conditions set out below and for which he was entitled to tax relief for 1988/89.

The Revenue have in the past in practice allowed relief by reference to the full amount paid in 1988/89 notwithstanding that the payer's income was insufficient to allow full relief to be given for the payments. This practice is no longer applied (although claimants already receiving relief on this basis will not be affected by withdrawal of the practice). (Revenue Tax Bulletin February 1995 p 193).

For payments due in *1994/95 to 1999/2000 inclusive*, the deduction is limited to the excess, if any, of the amount established as above over the amount of the married couple's allowance (see 1.15 ALLOWANCES AND TAX RATES). So much of the amount established as above as does *not* exceed the married couple's allowance is treated as if it were a qualifying maintenance payment made otherwise than under an existing obligation, and relief is thus given (subject to an overall limit) at a reduced rate and by way of a reduction in income tax liability rather than by deduction in computing total income (see above).

Payments due in *1989/90 to 1999/2000 inclusive* will form part of the recipient's taxable income and be chargeable under Schedule D, Case III (generally on a current year basis, see 72.4(*a*) SCHEDULE D, CASE III), or Case V if arising outside the UK, but only to the extent of the aggregate amount of payments received from the same payer which satisfied the conditions below and which formed part of his taxable income for 1988/89 (disregarding the deduction of up to £1,490 for that year). In addition, where the payments meet the conditions in (B) and (C) above, the recipient may claim, in respect of such payments, a deduction not exceeding an amount equal to the married couple's allowance for the year (see 1.15 ALLOWANCES AND TAX RATES). Where part of the aggregate payments falls to be treated, as regards the payer, as a qualifying maintenance payment (see above), this does *not* affect the tax position of the recipient, who continues to be taxed as if such part were a payment under an existing obligation.

These provisions apply to annual payments falling due in 1989/90 or any subsequent year which

(AA) are made in pursuance of an existing obligation under a Court Order, in the UK or elsewhere, or a written or oral agreement, or (after 5 April 1993) a maintenance assessment under the *Child Support Act 1991* (or NI equivalent),

(BB) are made by an individual either

- (i) to or for the benefit of, and for the maintenance of, his or her spouse or ex-spouse, or
- (ii) to any person under 21 for his own benefit, maintenance or education, or
- (iii) to any person for the benefit, maintenance or education of a person under 21, and

(CC) are, apart from these provisions, within the charge to tax under Schedule D, Case III or Case V and are not, under any provision of *ICTA 1988, Pt XV* (see 81 SETTLEMENTS), regarded as the income of the payer.

Payments due **after 5 April 2000** under existing obligations cease to attract relief under these provisions and do not form part of the recipient's taxable income. If at least one of the parties to the former marriage was aged 65 or over on 5 April 2000 and the payments satisfy the other conditions for qualifying maintenance payments (see above), the payer is entitled to the limited relief still available under *ICTA 1988, s 347B* (see above).

[*FA 1988, s 38; F(No 2)A 1992, s 62(3); FA 1994, s 79(7)(8); FA 1999, s 36(7)(8), Sch 20 Pt III(6); SI 1992 No 2642*].

Before 6 April 1996, payments under a Court Order to, or for the maintenance of, a child aged 21 or over, continued to be made with deduction of tax (where such payments continued to be treated as made under an existing obligation — see 1.8(i) ALLOWANCES AND TAX RATES). Before 6 April 1995, payments under an agreement to, or for the maintenance of, a child aged 18 or over fell within *ICTA 1988, s 683* (see 81.29 SETTLEMENTS), and were thus within (CC) above, and made under deduction of tax. Where such payments are made on or after the said dates, they are disregarded for tax purposes. See also 23.9 DEDUCTION OF TAX AT SOURCE.

Where maintenance payments are made for 1999/2000 and earlier years under existing obligations such that the above rules would apply, the payer may elect that they be treated as maintenance payments other than under existing obligations, so that *ICTA 1988, s 347B* (above) will apply if they are qualifying maintenance payments. The election must cover all such payments falling due in a year of assessment for which it has effect. It must be made in prescribed form (i.e. Form 142) and within, for 1996/97 and later years, twelve months after 31 January following the first year of assessment to which it is to apply (previously, twelve months after the end of that first year), will continue to have effect for subsequent years and is irrevocable. A person making such an election must, within 30 days of the date on which it is made, give notice thereof to every recipient of a payment affected by the election. [*FA 1988, s 39; FA 1996, s 135, Sch 21 para 25; FA 1999, Sch 20 Pt III(6)*].

General matters. Court Orders for alimony generally take into account the income and tax liabilities of both parties.

Maintenance receipts, where taxable, are investment income.

If, under a **Divorce Court Order,** payments are made *to the wife* for the maintenance of children, such income is for tax purposes the wife's and not the children's (see *Stevens v Tirard CA 1939, 23 TC 321; Spencer v Robson KB 1946, 27 TC 198*). Where a Court orders payment direct to the child, the income is that of the child. Under Scots law, where a child is entitled to aliment in his own right but payment is made to the parent with custody *qua tutrix* (or *tutor, curator, curatrix*), the income is that of the child for tax purposes. (*Huggins v Huggins 1981 SLT 179*). In strict law, the retrospective variation of an Order is not effective for tax purposes (*Morley-Clarke v Jones CA 1985, 59 TC 567*). In practice, however, where, before 1 July 1988, an Order, whether original or varying an existing Order, provides for payments for a period prior to the date of that Order, the Revenue will accept that such payments can be taken into account for tax purposes provided (i) the payments do not relate to a period before the date of application for the Order, (ii) the parties agree, and (iii) there has been no undue delay by the parties in pressing the application. (Revenue Pamphlet IR 131, SP 6/81, 8 September 1981). For Orders made or varied after 30 June 1988 which provide for retrospective payments, only payments made on or after the date of the Order count towards the limit on which tax relief is available in any year. Payments made under a legally binding written agreement before the Court Order may of course qualify in their own right. (Revenue Press Release 15 March 1988). Payments made under an agreement voluntarily entered into by a father in favour of his children, for their maintenance following separation, and later confirmed by a Court Order, were not made under that Order and were thus ineffective for tax purposes (*CIR v Craw CS 1985, 59 TC 56*).

Where the Court orders maintenance payments by a former spouse direct to his/her child who is living with the other spouse and an element is included to cover school fees, those fees may be paid direct to the school in *full* out of the *net* amount due under the maintenance order after tax at the basic rate has been deducted (assuming deduction at source to be still applicable) from the total amount payable, including the school fees. The payments will form part of the taxable income of the child, subject to the general rules outlined above. The Order normally includes: 'that part of the Order which reflects the school fees shall be paid to the (headmaster/bursar/school secretary) as agent for the said child and the receipt of that payee shall be sufficient discharge'. The onus will be on the parties themselves to produce evidence, where requested, that the person receiving the school fees has agreed to act as agent for the child and that the contract for the payment of the fees (which is most easily proved if in writing) is between the child (not the spouse making the payments) and the school. (Revenue Pamphlet IR 131, SP 15/80, 14 November 1980 and see Tolley's Practical Tax 1983 p 124). From 6 April 2000, relief is no longer available for payments direct to children (see above).

See also *Sherdley v Sherdley HL, [1987] STC 217*, where the validity of such arrangements was considered and affirmed in a case where an Order was sought against himself by the parent having custody.

47.11 *Examples*

Maintenance payments (1999/2000 and earlier years): Court Orders before 15 March 1988

Mr Smith separated from his wife on 31 October 1987. For 1999/2000 he has assessable Schedule D, Case I profits of £23,000 and building society interest of £4,000 (net). He pays mortgage interest of £2,400 on a home loan of under £30,000 which is outside the MIRAS scheme. Under a Court Order dated 5 March 1988, Mr Smith paid £50 per week maintenance directly to his son, Paul, aged 17 in 1999/2000, who lives with Mrs Smith, and £70 per week maintenance to Mrs Smith. On 1 June 1990, the payments to Mrs Smith were increased by the Court to £100 per week. In 1999/2000, Mrs Smith has earnings of £6,000. Paul Smith has no other income.

1999/2000		
Mr Smith	£	£
Earned income		23,000
Building society interest	4,000	
Add Tax deducted at source	1,000	5,000
		28,000
Deduct: Maintenance payments:		
Wife £70 × 52 note (*a*)	3,640	
Son £50 × 52	2,600	
	6,240	
Less the first £1,970 note (*b*)	1,970	
		(4,270)
Total income		23,730
Deduct Personal allowance		4,335
Taxable income		£19,395

	£	£
Tax payable:		
1,500 @ 10%		150.00
12,895 @ 23%		2,965.85
5,000 @ 20%		1,000.00
		4,115.85
Deduct Mortgage interest relief £2,400 @ 10%		240.00
		3,875.85
Deduct Maintenance £1,970 @ 10% note (*b*)		197.00
Total tax liability		3,678.85
Deduct Tax paid on building society interest		1,000.00
Net tax liability		£2,678.85
Mrs Smith		
Earned income		6,000
Maintenance note (*a*)	3,640	
Deduction note (*a*)	1,970	
		1,670
Total income		7,670
Deduct Personal allowance note (*c*)		4,335
Taxable income		£3,335
Tax payable:		
1,500 @ 10%		150.00
1,835 @ 23%		422.05
		£572.05
Paul Smith		
Maintenance		2,600
Deduct Personal allowance (restricted)		2,600
Taxable income		Nil
Tax payable/repayable		Nil

Notes

(*a*) The tax relief and the amount chargeable on the recipient is limited to the relief obtainable and the amount forming part of the recipient's income for 1988/89. The recipient may then deduct from the amount otherwise chargeable an amount equal to the married couple's allowance for the year, providing the payments are from a divorced or separated spouse. See 47.10 above.

(*b*) For 1999/2000, the first £1,970 of allowable maintenance payments attracts relief at 10%, such relief being given as an income tax reduction (see 47.10 above).

(*c*) Mrs Smith may also be entitled to the additional personal allowance in respect of Paul if all the conditions of *ICTA 1988, s 259* are satisfied (see 1.17 ALLOWANCES AND TAX RATES).

Maintenance payments: Court Orders after 14 March 1988

Mr Green separated from his wife in June 1997 and, under a Court Order dated 15 July 1998, pays maintenance of £300 per month to his ex-wife and £100 per month to his daughter, payments being due on the first of each calendar month commencing 1 August 1998. Mr Green has earned income of £18,000 and dividends of £4,500 for 1999/2000. He re-marries on 6 October 1999.

	£	£
1999/2000		
Mr Green		
Earned income		18,000
Dividends	4,500	
Add Tax credits (£4,500 × $\frac{1}{9}$)	500	5,000
Total income		23,000
Deduct Personal allowance		4,335
Taxable income		£18,665
Tax payable:		
1,500 @ 10% (starting rate)		150.00
12,165 @ 23%		2,797.95
5,000 @ 10% (Schedule F ordinary rate)		500.00
		3,447.95
Deduct Maintenance relief — wife: £3,600 paid, but restricted to £1,970 @ 10%		197.00
		3,250.95
Deduct Married couple's allowance £1,970 × $\frac{6}{12}$ = £985 @ 10%		98.50
Total tax liability		3,152.45
Deduct Tax credits		500.00
Net tax liability (subject to PAYE deductions)		£2,652.45

48 Medical Insurance

(See Revenue Pamphlet IR 103.)

Simon's Direct Tax Service E2.9.

Note. The provisions described in this chapter are repealed by the Finance (No 2) Act 1997. See 48.1 below.

48.1 Subject to the **abolition** of this relief (see below), where a UK resident individual makes a payment in respect of a private medical insurance premium under an 'eligible contract' insuring a UK resident individual or individuals who, or each of whom, is aged 60 or over at the date of the payment (or, where a married couple is insured, at least one of whom is aged 60 or over at that time), he may claim relief (see below) for the payment, provided that he is not entitled to any other relief or deduction in respect of the payment and does not make it out of resources provided by another person for the purpose of enabling it to be made. Crown employees treated as performing their duties in the UK under *ICTA 1988, s 132(4)(a)* (see 75.2(i) SCHEDULE E) are treated as UK resident for these purposes. Where a payment is made under a contract insuring a married couple one of whom is 60 or over, and the said spouse dies, a subsequent payment under the same contract is not disqualified from relief by virtue of the surviving spouse being under 60.

[*FA 1989, s 54(1)–(3C)(9); FA 1994, Sch 10 paras 2, 4*].

Regulations provide for the payment to be made under deduction of basic rate tax, the payee reclaiming the tax deducted from the Revenue, and for relief to be withdrawn, and the related tax accounted for, in prescribed circumstances. The Revenue consider that where a payment *may* be made under deduction of basic rate tax, basic rate relief can *only* be obtained by deduction. The tax deducted from payments is not clawed back where the individual is liable only at the lower rate of income tax or has no, or insufficient, income tax liability. For relief to be given by deduction at source, the individual must provide a notice of entitlement to relief, containing specified information and undertakings, etc., to the person to whom payments are made under the contract. That person must be either a 'qualifying insurer' (see 48.4 below) or a managing agent, either with Lloyd's or for a 'qualifying insurer'. The insurer (or agent) must have no reason to doubt any of the information given by the individual, must have undertaken to observe the requirements of the regulations (and, in the event of failure, must satisfy the Board that he is able and willing to observe them in future), and must have undertaken that, before entering into a further contract, he will give notice to the individual of his obligation to notify the insurer of any relevant changes in his (or the insured's) circumstances. Any refunded payments must not exceed the payment actually made, and any amount recovered from the Board in respect of tax deducted from payments which are refunded must be accounted for to the Board. There are detailed regulations for the recovery from the Board of tax deducted from payments, and for approval of standard forms of contract. [*FA 1989, s 54(4)–(8); FA 1996, s 129; SI 1989 No 2387; SI 1994 Nos 1518, 1527*].

The Inland Revenue Financial Intermediaries and Claims Office may be contacted in relation to private medical insurance on 0151–472 6172 as regards repayments or 0151–472 6157 for technical advice.

These provisions are **abolished** by *F(No 2)A 1997, s 17*. Relief ceases altogether for payments received by the insurer after 5 April 1999. It is not available for payments in respect of premiums under contracts entered into after 1 July 1997, unless either:

(*a*) the contract was entered into (other than by way of renewal of an earlier contract) before 1 August 1997 in pursuance of a written proposal received by or on behalf of the insurer before 2 July 1997, and at least one payment in respect of a premium under the contract was received by the insurer before 1 August 1997; or (*b*) the contract was entered into before 1 August 1997, by way of renewal of an earlier contract the period of insurance under which ended before 2 July 1997, and at least one payment in respect of a premium under the renewal contract was received by the insurer before 1 August 1997.

As regards (*b*) above, a contract is treated as having been entered into by way of renewal of an earlier contract only if the earlier contract was with the same insurer and was an 'eligible contract' when it was entered into, and there was no gap between the periods of insurance under the two contracts.

48.2 A contract is an '*eligible contract*' if, at the date it was entered into, the insurer was a 'qualifying insurer' approved by the Board for these purposes, and the period of insurance does not exceed one year from that date. As regards approval of qualifying insurers, see *SI 1989 No 2387, regs 12–14* as amended by *SI 1994 No 1527, reg 11*. No benefit other than an 'approved benefit' must have been provided by virtue of the contract, and the contract must not be, or have been, 'connected with' another contract.

The contract must, at the time payment is made thereunder, meet the conditions at 48.6(*a*)–(*d*) below. Where a contract confers one or more 'material rights', but the total cost to the insurer of providing benefits in pursuance thereof would not exceed £30 (which amount is variable by Treasury order), this does not preclude eligibility. There is an anti-avoidance provision to prevent the above limit being by-passed by means of certain linked contracts. A '*material right*' is a right which does not otherwise meet the conditions for eligibility and is not a right to a cash benefit.

[*FA 1989, s 55(1)–(6)(11)–(13), s 56; FA 1994, Sch 10 paras 5, 6*].

There is no reason in principle why members of group schemes cannot come within the scope of the relief, provided that the scheme meets the qualifying conditions. (ICAEW Technical Release TAX 17/93, 28 September 1993).

48.3 A contract is '*connected with*' another contract at any time if they are both in force at that time; one was entered into with reference to the other or to enable the other to be entered into on particular terms or to facilitate the other being so entered into; and the terms on which one of the contracts was entered into would have been significantly less favourable to the insured but for the other being entered into. [*FA 1989, s 55(7)*].

48.4 A '*qualifying insurer*' is any insurer lawfully carrying on business in the UK of any of the classes specified in *Insurance Companies Act 1982, Sch 2 Pt I*, or an insurer not carrying on business in the UK but doing so in another EC country (or, from 1 January 1994, a country within the European Economic Area) and meeting certain other conditions as to status and location. [*FA 1989, s 55(8)*].

48.5 A benefit is an '*approved benefit*' if it is provided in pursuance of rights as under 48.6(*a*) below or as specified by regulations under 48.6(*b*) below. One or more benefits otherwise provided (and which are not cash benefits) are also approved benefits if their total cost to the insurer does not exceed £30 (which amount is variable by Treasury order). [*FA 1989, s 55(9)(10)(12)(13); FA 1994, Sch 10 para 5(6)(7)*].

48.6 The conditions a contract must meet are that:

(*a*) it either provides indemnity in respect of all or any of the costs of all or any of the treatments, medical services and other matters prescribed by regulations for these purposes or, in addition to such indemnity, provides cash benefits falling within rules prescribed by such regulations;

(*b*) it confers no other right except as may be specified by regulations;

(*c*) the premium is reasonable; and

(*d*) it satisfies such other requirements as may be specified by regulations.

As regards (*a*) above, the treatments, etc. specified in the regulations are the treatment of the insured consisting of medical or surgical procedures (including diagnosis, drugs and dressings) for the relief of illness or injury, and services for the purposes of or consequent upon such treatment consisting of:

(i) accommodation and other (including nursing) services in a hospital where the insured is a private patient charged for the accommodation or for treatments, etc. (as above);

(ii) home nursing;

(iii) accommodation for up to 14 days' convalescence following discharge from hospital;

(iv) transport by private ambulance (including by air ambulance) accompanied (where medically necessary) by one other person to or from hospital or to or from accommodation provided for convalescence; and

(v) physiotherapy, occupational therapy, speech therapy, chiropody and podiatry, prosthesis and orthopty (including necessary equipment).

The treatment must either

(A) be given to the insured as a private patient in a hospital by or under the supervision of a registered medical or dental practitioner, or

(B) in the case of surgical procedures performed by a registered medical practitioner providing personal medical services for persons in a particular locality, be given to the insured as a private patient of that practitioner,

and physiotherapy services and equipment must be provided to the insured and must be associated with treatment given to the insured by or under the supervision of a registered medical practitioner.

Treatments are excluded if they were not provided free under the *National Health Service Act 1977* (or Scottish or NI equivalent), in the five years preceding the date the contract was entered into, more often than they were provided in the UK other than under that *Act*.

The allowable cash benefit may not exceed £5 for each night in a hospital as a private patient charged for the accommodation.

Other rights within (*b*) above are the right to terminate the contract and receive a refund in respect of the unexpired period of cover, waiver or refund by the insurer of payments for a period during which the insured is receiving treatment covered by the contract, and the right to enter into a further contract at the expiry of the current contract.

[*SI 1994 No 1518*].

Contracts are not permitted to cover charges for 'alternative medicine', dental procedures in a general dental practice, general ophthalmic procedures not carried out in hospital, and medical or surgical procedures (other than GP operations as above) not on an in-, out- or day-patient basis. (Revenue Press Release 19 July 1989).

48.7 Supplementary regulatory powers are provided, and the provisions of the *Taxes Management Act 1970* applied as necessary. [*FA 1989, s 57; FA 1996, s 129, Sch 18 paras 12, 17(1)–(4)(8)*].

49 Mineral Royalties

[*ICTA 1988, s 122; TCGA 1992, ss 201–203*]

Simon's Direct Tax Service. See C2.1111.

49.1 Where a person resident or ordinarily resident in the UK is entitled to receive mineral royalties (i.e. so much of any rents, tolls, royalties or periodical payments as relates to the winning and working of minerals other than water, peat, topsoil, etc.) under a lease, licence or agreement conferring a right to win and work minerals in the UK or under a sale or conveyance of such minerals, only one-half of any such royalties receivable in any year of assessment or accounting period is treated as income for purposes of income tax or corporation tax on profits other than chargeable gains.

Management expenses available for set-off against those royalties, under *ICTA 1988, s 121* or under Schedule A, are similarly reduced by one-half.

Where Betterment Levy (which was abolished after July 1970) was not chargeable on the grant of the lease, or any subsequent renewal, extension or variation of it, the other half of the royalties receivable is treated as a chargeable gain for purposes of capital gains tax (or corporation tax on chargeable gains).

Where, on the last disposition (before 23 July 1970) affecting the lease, Betterment Levy was chargeable under Case B (as defined by *Land Commission Act 1967, Pt III*) the chargeable gain, as above, is limited to a fraction (base value of that disposition/consideration received) of one-half of the royalties received. After 5 April 1988, this limitation applies only if it applied to a chargeable period ending on or before that date. But if such a lease is renewed, extended or varied after 22 July 1970, one-half of any subsequent royalty receipt is treated as a chargeable gain.

Where payments under a mineral lease, etc. relate both to the winning and working of minerals and to other matters, the part to be treated as mineral royalties for these purposes will be calculated under regulations made by the Board. See *SI 1971 No 1035*.

These chargeable gains are assessable in full, without any deduction on account of expenditure incurred.

Income tax was deductible from royalty payments made before 1 May 1995, but if the recipient was not a person chargeable to corporation tax the excess tax so suffered was set against CGT payable as above, any balance thereafter remaining being repaid.

Terminal Losses. If the mineral lease comes to an end while the person entitled to receive the royalties still has an interest in the land, and an allowable loss would then arise to him if he sold his interest for a price equal to its market value, he may claim to be treated for CGT (or corporation tax) purposes as if he had sold, and immediately reacquired, his interest at that price, the resultant loss being allowed, at his election, either (*a*) against CGT etc. for the year in which the lease expires, or (*b*) against chargeable gains, in respect of mineral royalties under the lease, within the previous 15 years.

50 Mutual Trading

Simon's Direct Tax Service B3.236 *et seq.*.

50.1 A person cannot derive a taxable profit from trading with himself except in certain cases of self-supply by a trader of trading stock, see *Sharkey v Wernher HL 1955, 36 TC 275* and 71.83 SCHEDULE D, CASES I AND II. This is extended to a group of persons engaged in mutual activities of a trading nature, if there is an identifiable 'fund' for the common purpose with complete identity between contributors to, and participators in, the fund (the *mutuality principle*). A body not liable as regards transactions with members may nevertheless be liable under Schedule D, Case I on transactions with non-members and is liable in the ordinary way on any investment etc. income. Whether the mutuality principle applies depends on the facts. For mutual insurance see *Styles v New York Life Insce Co HL 1889, 2 TC 460* (an early leading case on the mutuality principle but there are now special provisions for life insurance companies — see Tolley's Corporation Tax); *Jones v South-West Lancs Coal Owners' Assn HL 1927, 11 TC 790; Cornish Mutual Assce Co Ltd HL 1926, 12 TC 841; Municipal Mutual Insce Ltd v Hills HL 1932, 16 TC 430; Faulconbridge v National Employers' Mutual General Insce Assn Ltd Ch D 1952, 33 TC 103.* For other cases see *Liverpool Corn Trade Assn Ltd v Monks KB 1926, 10 TC 442* (trade association providing corn exchange etc. held to be trading and not 'mutual' — but see 71.84 SCHEDULE D, CASES I AND II for special arrangement available for trade associations); *English & Scottish CWS Ltd v Assam Agricultural IT Commr PC 1948, 27 ATC 332* (wholesale co-operative with two members held to be trading and not mutual — there was no 'common fund'). Similarly a members' club is not trading and not liable on its surplus from the provision of its facilities for members (*Eccentric Club Ltd CA 1923, 12 TC 657*) but liable on the surplus attributable to non-members (*Carlisle and Silloth Golf Club v Smith CA 1913, 6 TC 48; NALGO v Watkins KB 1934, 18 TC 499; Doctor's Cave Bathing Beach (Fletcher) v Jamaica IT Commr PC 1971, 50 ATC 368*).

For distribution of assets by a company carrying on mutual business, see Tolley's Corporation Tax.

51 Non-Residents and other Overseas Matters

Cross-references. See 64 RESIDENCE, ORDINARY RESIDENCE AND DOMICILE for the meaning of those terms. See also ANTI-AVOIDANCE AT 3.8 regarding income payable to person abroad assessable on UK resident in certain circumstances; 3.9 for trading transactions with a non-resident under common control; 23 DEDUCTION OF TAX AT SOURCE for certain payments to non-residents; 24 DIPLOMATIC IMMUNITY, including international organisations etc.; 25 DOUBLE TAX RELIEF; 33.2 GOVERNMENT STOCKS for exemption on certain stocks held by non-residents; 47.7 MARRIED PERSONS where one spouse is resident abroad; 53 PARTNERSHIPS; 59 PENSIONS; 63 REMITTANCE BASIS; 70 SCHEDULE C regarding paying and collecting agents; 73 SCHEDULE D, CASES IV AND V under which assessments are raised on income from overseas securities and possessions; 75.3 to 75.6 SCHEDULE E for earnings from work done abroad and expenses.

The Revenue Financial Intermediaries and Claims Office (FICO) publishes an occasional Non-Residents Newsletter aimed at keeping agents who deal with non-residents up to date and informed about current issues that may affect them. The newsletter may be accessed on the Revenue's website (see 35.1 INLAND REVENUE: ADMINISTRATION). The November 1999 issue includes a useful list of telephone numbers on which advice may be sought on general matters or in relation to particular clients.

Headings in this chapter are as follows.

51.1 Limit on income chargeable on non-residents
51.2 — example
51.3 Collection of tax
51.4 Non-residents trading in UK — 1995/96 and earlier years
51.5 Non-residents trading in UK — 1996/97 and subsequent years
51.6 — persons not treated as UK representatives for tax purposes
51.7 — obligations etc. imposed on UK representatives
51.8 Non-resident entertainers and sportsmen
51.9 Non-resident banks, insurance companies and dealers in securities
51.10 Payments of annual sums to non-residents
51.11 Personal allowances for certain non-residents
51.12 Trades etc. carried on and controlled abroad
51.13 United Kingdom
51.14 Unremittable overseas income

51.1 LIMIT ON INCOME CHARGEABLE ON NON-RESIDENTS

For **1996/97 and subsequent years** (and see below as regards 1995/96), the income tax chargeable on the total income of a non-UK resident is not to exceed the aggregate of

(i) the tax which would otherwise be chargeable if 'excluded income' and any personal allowances due (see 51.11 below) were both disregarded, and

(ii) the tax deducted from so much of the 'excluded income' as is subject to deduction of income tax at source (including tax credits and tax treated as deducted at source).

Income is '*excluded income*' if it falls into one of the categories below and is not income in relation to which the non-resident has a UK representative for the purposes of the provisions at 51.5 to 51.7 below (i.e. income from or connected with a trade etc. carried on in the UK through a branch or agency, subject to the exclusions at 51.6). The categories are:

(*a*) income chargeable under SCHEDULE C (70), SCHEDULE D, CASE III (72) or SCHEDULE F (76);

(*b*) income chargeable under Schedule D, Case VI by virtue of *ICTA 1988, s 56* (see 13 CERTIFICATES OF DEPOSIT);

(*c*) certain social security benefits (including state pensions);

(*d*) income not falling within (*a*)–(*c*) above and not being Lloyd's underwriting profits, which arises as mentioned in 51.6(2)(3) below (certain income from trading in the UK through a broker or investment manager); and

(*e*) any income designated for these purposes by Treasury regulations.

These provisions do not apply to limit the income tax chargeable on a settlement if any actual or potential beneficiary, whether his interest is absolute or discretionary, is an individual ordinarily resident in the UK or a UK resident company.

These provisions replace Revenue extra-statutory concessions B13 (which covered income within (*a*), (*b*) and, in practice, (*c*) above — see 51.3 below) and B40 (which covered broadly the same ground as (*d*) above — see 51.4 below). There may 'exceptionally' be arrangements set up before 29 November 1994 which fall outside the statutory provisions and to which ESC B40 will continue to apply until, at the latest, 5 April 2005 (see Revenue Press Release IR 31, 29 November 1994).

These provisions also have limited application for **1995/96** to income from certain transactions carried out through brokers and investment managers and to income within (*c*) above. In order to be excluded income, the income must arise after 5 April 1995 and must not be income in relation to which the non-resident would have a UK representative if the provisions in 51.5 to 51.7 below applied for 1995/96. The provisions apply to income within (*a*) or (*b*) above only if it arises from a transaction

(i) which is carried out on the non-resident's behalf by a person then carrying on the business of a broker or, in the case of an investment transaction (as defined), of providing investment management services,

(ii) which is carried out in the ordinary course of that business, and

(iii) in respect of which the remuneration received by the broker or investment manager was at a rate not less than would have been customary for that class of business.

For the purposes only of applying (*d*) above, the provisions at 51.6 below are treated as applying for 1995/96. Extra-statutory concession B13 continues to apply for 1995/96 to income within (*a*) or (*b*) above which is not covered by the above provisions.

[*FA 1995, s 128*].

See Tolley's Corporation Tax under Residence for corresponding provisions applicable to non-resident companies.

Simon's Direct Tax Service. See **B3.126**.

51.2 *Example*

Hugh and Elizabeth are not resident in the UK throughout 2000/01. They are each entitled to a UK personal allowance under the provisions in 51.11 below. Their tax liabilities on total UK income for 2000/01, disregarding the limit under *FA 1995, s 128*, are as follows.

	Hugh	Elizabeth
	£	£
Net rental income (Schedule A) (received gross)	2,000	5,000
Bank interest (received gross)	4,465	565
Dividends	3,600	—
Tax credits	400	—
Total UK income	c/f 10,465	c/f 5,565

	Hugh	Elizabeth
	£	£
	b/f 10,465	b/f 5,565
Deduct Personal allowance	4,385	4,385
Taxable UK income	£6,080	£1,180

Tax on total UK income:

	£	£
£1,520/1,180 @ 10%	152.00	118.00
£560 @ 20% (lower rate on interest)	112.00	
£4,000 @ 10% (Schedule F ordinary rate)	400.00	
	664.00	118.00
Deduct Tax credits	400.00	
	£264.00	£118.00

But tax is limited under *FA 1995, s 128* as follows.

	£	£
Schedule A	2,000	5,000

(Bank interest and dividends are 'excluded income' — see 51.1 above.)

£1,520/£1,520 @ 10%	152.00	152.00
£480/£3,480 @ 22%	105.60	765.60
	£257.60	£917.60

Hugh's UK income tax liability is therefore restricted to £257.60 (plus £400.00 in tax credits, which cannot be reclaimed). Elizabeth's liability is not reduced under *FA 1995, s 128* and is thus £118.00.

51.3 **COLLECTION OF TAX**

The concession described below is replaced by the provisions at 51.1 above with effect as stated in that paragraph.

Although tax is legally assessable by notice served abroad, there are difficulties in collection. Where untaxed interest is paid to a person who for any year of assessment is regarded as non-resident, no action is taken to recover the tax unless a trustee or an agent or branch having the management and control of the interest is chargeable or a set-off is available against a claim to repayment of tax deducted from other UK income (unless repayment arises due to the other income being exempt from UK tax or treated as such under a double tax agreement). This applies equally to discounts, to profits on disposals of certificates of deposit, to building society dividends paid gross, to amounts representing interest on general client accounts, to 'income elements' chargeable in respect of a deep discount security and to 'deep gains' (see 44.5, 44.7 INTEREST RECEIVABLE). (Revenue Pamphlets IR1, B13 and IR 20 (1993), para 7.8). In practice state pensions are similarly treated (see *Taxation* 24 August 1989, p 632). UK Courts will not enforce the Revenue laws of other countries. See *Govt of India v Taylor HL 1955, 34 ATC 10,* and *US Govt v Brokaw, Shaheen and Seatrain CA 1971, 50 ATC 95.*

51.4 **NON-RESIDENTS TRADING IN UK — 1995/96 AND EARLIER YEARS**

The provisions of *TMA 1970, ss 78–85* described in (*a*)–(*c*) below no longer apply for 1996/97 and subsequent years for income tax and for company accounting periods beginning after 31 March 1996. They are replaced by provisions described at 51.5 to 51.7 below. See also 51.1 above (limitation on income chargeable on non-residents).

See DOUBLE TAX RELIEF (25) agreements generally. Subject to these the general position is as follows.

(*a*) **Assessability of UK profits.** The location of a business depends on from where it is managed and controlled (see 51.12 below) but a non-resident is liable on profits from a business 'exercised within' the UK [*ICTA 1988, s 18(1)(a)(iii)*] and is therefore liable if trading in the UK notwithstanding that the centre of control of his business is abroad (cf. *A-G v Alexander [1874] 10 Ex D 20*).

Where a non-resident carries on a trade partly in and partly outside the UK, the charge to UK tax is limited to the profits from the part of the trade carried on in the UK. The Revenue have reaffirmed that the profits from a part of a trade carried on in the UK are to be measured on the arm's length principle set out in the OECD model tax convention and explained in OECD publications, irrespective of whether a double tax agreement applies. (Revenue Tax Bulletin August 1995 pp 237–239).

The primary factors in deciding whether there is trading in the UK is whether or not the contracts for the sale of goods or performance of services are made in the UK, but each case depends on the facts. For cases illustrating this principle see *Erichsen v Last CA 1881, 1 TC 351, 537; 4 TC 422*, and the cases referred to at (*b*) below.

If profits 'cannot in any case be readily ascertained', the assessment will be made on percentage of turnover, particulars of which agent (see below) is obliged to disclose; if goods made abroad, on selling profits only. (With rights of appeal against percentage to Commissioners and from them to a board of referees to be appointed for this purpose by the Treasury.) [*TMA 1970, ss 80, 81*].

Provisions to prevent avoidance by sales at other than market price, where one of the parties is controlled by the other, are contained in *ICTA 1988, s 770* (see 3.9 ANTI-AVOIDANCE).

(*b*) **UK Agents.** A non-resident trading in the UK will generally do so through a UK agent or branch. Such an agent etc. is personally assessable on all profits arising directly or indirectly through a regular UK agency, branch, etc., whether in receipt of the profits or not but he may retain the tax out of money coming into his hands and be indemnified. Certain providers of investment management services are excluded from the operation of *TMA 1970, s 78(1)*. [*TMA 1970, ss 78, 79, 83, 84; FA 1985, s 50; FA 1991, s 81*]. For whether a lawyer acting for a non-resident company in a single trading transaction was the company's UK agent, see *Willson v Hooker Ch D, [1995] STC 1142*. For the Revenue's view on the effect of UK trading on the exclusion of investment managers from *TMA 1970, s 78*, the meaning of 'investment transactions' in that context, and the relevant factors in determining whether the active management of a portfolio on behalf of a non-resident client constitutes the exercise of a trade in the UK by that client, see Revenue Pamphlet IR 131, SP 15/91, 29 November 1991 and Revenue Tax Bulletin November 1992 p 44.

These provisions do not preclude assessment on the non-resident direct (if he can be served with a notice of assessment) whether or not he has an agent (cf. *Tischler v Apthorpe QB 1885, 2 TC 89*). For cases where a non-resident has been held to be trading in the UK and assessed through an agent, see *Wingate & Co v Webber CES 1897, 3 TC 569* (Glasgow agent of foreign ship-owner); *Watson v Sandie & Hull QB*

1897, 3 TC 611 (commission agent selling in own name); *Thomas Turner (Leicester) Ltd v Rickman QB 1898, 4 TC 25* and *Macpherson & Co v Moore SCS 1912, 6 TC 107* (agent's sales subject to principal's approval and goods consigned to agent for delivery); *Wilcock v Pinto & Co CA 1924, 9 TC 111* and *Belfour v Mace CA 1928, 13 TC 539* (agent's sales subject to approval by principal and goods consigned by principal); *Brackett v Chater Ch D 1986, 60 TC 134* (provision of consultancy services in UK to non-resident company). For cases in which the non-resident, assessed through an agent, was held not to be trading in the UK see *Grainger & Son v Gough HL 1896, 3 TC 311, 462* (commission agent merely transmitted orders for execution by principal); *Smidth & Co v Greenwood HL 1922, 8 TC 193* (contracts executed by principal abroad — *TMA 1970, s 79* is a machinery provision not extending the scope of the charge); *Boston Deep Sea Fishing v Farnham Ch D 1957, 37 TC 505* (no agency).

But under *TMA 1970, s 82,* bona fide brokers or general commission agents, although they may act regularly for a non-resident, are not chargeable on the latter's profits, provided they receive not less than the remuneration customary in that class of business and provided they are not authorised persons carrying on the regular agency of the non-resident. See for this *Gavazzi v Mace KB 1926, 10 TC 698; Tarn v Scanlan HL 1927, 13 TC 91; Rowson v Stephen KB 1929, 14 TC 543; Fleming v London Produce Co Ltd Ch D 1968, 44 TC 582; Firestone Tyre & Rubber Co Ltd v Lewellin HL 1957, 37 TC 111.*

Where an agent is specifically protected from assessment under *TMA 1970, s 78(1)* by the terms of the provisions described above relating to investment managers (*TMA 1970, s 78(2)*) or brokers and general commission agents (*TMA 1970, s 82(1)*), the Revenue, by concession, do not seek to assess the non-resident directly, or the agent under *TMA 1970, s 79* or *ICTA 1988, s 59* (income under Schedule D assessable on the person entitled to it). The concession does not apply to income on which a non-resident's liability is not pursued under extra-statutory concession B 13 (see 51.3 above), or if the employment of the UK agent exceeds the normal use of investment managers, brokers or general commission agents within the appropriate exemption, or if the non-resident has some other UK presence, not within those exemptions, carrying on activities related to the agency transactions. (Revenue Pamphlet IR 1, B40).

For 'double foreigner' transactions, i.e. sales etc. by one non-resident to another, see *TMA 1970, s 82(2)* and *Maclaine & Co v Eccott HL 1926, 10 TC 481* and *W H Muller & Co v Lethem HL 1927, 13 TC 126.*

See also 51.4(*d*) below.

(*c*) **Companies.** For the charge to corporation tax on non-resident companies, see *ICTA 1988, s 11* and Tolley's Corporation Tax. The provisions of *TMA 1970, ss 78–84*, described at (*a*) and (*b*) above, apply with any necessary adaptations to companies. [*TMA 1970, s 85; F(No 2)A 1987, Sch 6 para 7*].

51.5 NON-RESIDENTS TRADING IN UK — 1996/97 AND SUBSEQUENT YEARS

The provisions described below apply where a non-UK resident carries on a trade in the UK through a branch or agency (which means any factorship, agency, receivership, branch or management [*TMA 1970, s 118(1)*]). They establish the obligations and liabilities of UK representatives of such non-residents under self-assessment (and apply equally for corporation tax), and replace *TMA 1970, ss 78–85* (see 51.4 above). The new provisions have effect for 1996/97 and subsequent years for income tax and capital gains tax and for company accounting periods beginning after 31 March 1996. See also 78.38 SELF-ASSESSMENT.

For whether activities of a non-resident person constitute trading in the UK, see Revenue Inspector's Manual, IM 170 *et seq*..

Where a non-resident carries on a trade partly in and partly outside the UK, the charge to UK tax is limited, under general principles, to the profits from the part of the trade carried on in the UK (whether or not through a branch or agency). See also 51.4(*a*) above for assessability of UK profits generally. The Revenue have reaffirmed that the profits from a part of a trade carried on in the UK are to be measured on the arm's length principle set out in the OECD model tax convention and explained in OECD publications, irrespective of whether a double tax agreement applies. (Revenue Tax Bulletin August 1995 pp 237–239).

Meaning of 'UK representative'. For the purposes of 51.7 below and subject to 51.6 below (persons not treated as UK representatives), a branch or agency in the UK through which a non-resident carries on (solely or in partnership) a trade, profession or vocation is his UK representative in relation to the following:

(*a*) such income from the trade etc. as arises, directly or indirectly, through or from the branch or agency;

(*b*) any income from property or rights used by, or held by or for, the branch or agency;

(*c*) capital gains arising in connection with the branch or agency and chargeable under *TCGA 1992, s 10* (see Tolley's Capital Gains Tax); and

(*d*) certain other amounts where the non-resident is an overseas life insurance company.

Where the non-resident ceases to carry on the trade etc. through the branch or agency, it continues to be his UK representative for tax purposes in relation to amounts arising during the period of the agency. A UK representative is a legal entity distinct from the non-resident. Where the branch or agency is a partnership, the partnership is the non-resident's UK representative. If a trade etc. is carried on in the UK by a non-resident in partnership with at least one UK resident partner, the partnership itself is the UK representative in relation to the non-resident's share of UK profits. [*FA 1995, s 126*].

Simon's Direct Tax Service. See **B3.125.**

51.6 **Persons not treated as UK representatives for tax purposes.** The following are not treated as UK representatives for the purposes of 51.7 below.

(1) *Casual Agents.* An agent is not treated as a non-UK resident's UK representative in relation to income etc. arising from so much of any business as relates to transactions carried out through the agent otherwise than in the course of carrying on a regular agency for the non-resident.

(2) *Brokers.* A broker is not treated as a non-resident's UK representative in relation to income etc. arising from so much of any business as relates to transactions carried out through the broker and satisfying all the following conditions:

  (i) the broker was carrying on the business of broker at the time of the transaction;

  (ii) the transaction was carried out in the ordinary course of that business;

  (iii) the remuneration for that transaction was at a rate not less than would have been customary for that class of business; and

  (iv) the broker is not the non-resident's UK representative in relation to income chargeable to tax for the same chargeable period which is not excluded under these provisions.

(3) *Investment managers.* An investment manager is not treated as a non-resident's UK representative in relation to income etc. arising from so much of any business as relates to investment transactions (as defined) carried out through the investment manager and satisfying all the following conditions:

(i) the manager was carrying on the business of providing investment management services at the time of the transaction;

(ii) the transaction was carried out in the ordinary course of that business;

(iii) the manager, when acting on the non-resident's behalf in that transaction, did so in an independent capacity;

(iv) the '20% condition' is satisfied in relation to the transaction (see below);

(v) the remuneration for the investment management services in question was at a rate not less than would have been customary for that class of business; and

(vi) the manager is not the non-resident's UK representative in relation to income chargeable to tax for the same chargeable period which is not excluded under these provisions.

A person is not to be regarded as acting in an independent capacity on behalf of the non-resident (see (iii) above) unless, having regard to its legal, financial and commercial characteristics, the relationship between them is a relationship between persons carrying on independent businesses that deal with each other at arm's length (and see Revenue Press Release 17 February 1995).

The '*20% condition*' (see (iv) above) is that, broadly, the investment manager and persons connected with him may not have a beneficial entitlement to more than 20% of the non-resident's excluded income (see 51.1 above) from transactions carried out by the investment manager on his behalf. The condition must be satisfied throughout a qualifying period which must at least consist of the chargeable period for which the income from the transaction in question is chargeable to tax and which may be no more than five years comprising two or more chargeable periods. Failure to satisfy the condition is disregarded if it was for reasons beyond the control of the manager and persons connected with him and they did not fail to take reasonable mitigating action. If a transaction satisfies the conditions at (i) to (vi) above except for the 20% condition, it is regarded as satisfying *all* conditions to the extent of any income etc. which does *not* represent excluded income to which the manager etc. has or has had a beneficial entitlement. Special rules apply to determine whether or not the 20% condition is satisfied in relation to a transaction carried out for a collective investment scheme (within *Financial Services Act 1986*) in which the non-resident is a participant; broadly, the condition is treated as satisfied by each participant if the scheme (were it taxable as a separate entity) would not be regarded as carrying on a trade in the UK or if it would be so regarded but the 20% rule is satisfied by reference to the scheme's taxable income.

Persons are connected if they are connected within *ICTA 1988, s 839* (see 20 CONNECTED PERSONS).

Exceptionally, a non-resident who does not qualify for the limitation on charge under these investment manager rules may have enjoyed the protection of extra-statutory concession B40 (see 51.4(*b*) above) up to 5 April 1995. Provided that the arrangements concerned were set up before 29 November 1994, concession B40 will continue to apply in these circumstances until 5 April 1996 or, if the arrangements are in respect of a jointly-held fund marketed before 29 November 1994, for the intended life of the fund when marketed (or until 5 April 2005 if earlier). (Revenue Inspector's Manual, IM 226).

(4) *Lloyd's members' agents and managing agents.* A Lloyd's members' agent or syndicate managing agent is not treated as a non-resident Lloyd's underwriter's UK representative in relation to income etc. arising from his Lloyd's business (or, in the case of a managing agent, from the syndicate in question). See 89 UNDERWRITERS generally.

General. Where a person acts as broker or investment manager as part only of a business, that part is deemed to be a separate business for the purposes of (2) and (3) above. A person carries out a transaction on behalf of another where he either undertakes it himself or instructs a third party to do so. Income arising from so much of a business as results from transactions carried out through a branch or agency includes income from property or rights which as a result of the transactions are used by, or held by or for, that branch or agency.

[*FA 1995, s 127*].

51.7 **Obligations etc. imposed on UK representatives.** As regards the taxation of any amounts in relation to which a non-UK resident has a UK representative (see 51.5, 51.6 above), legislation making provision for, or in connection with, the assessment, collection and recovery of income tax, corporation tax and capital gains tax, and interest on tax, has effect as if the obligations and liabilities of the non-resident were *also* obligations and liabilities of the UK representative. The discharge of an obligation or liability by either the non-resident or the UK representative is treated as discharging the corresponding obligation or liability of the other. The non-resident is bound by any acts or omissions of his UK representative. Where an obligation or liability depends on the serving of a notice or other document or the making of a request or demand, it is not treated as having been imposed on the UK representative unless the notice etc. was served on or copied to him or he was notified of the request or demand. A person is not guilty of a criminal offence by virtue of these provisions except where he committed the offence himself or consented to or connived in its commission.

Independent agents. An '*independent agent*' of a non-resident is any person who is the non-resident's UK representative in respect of any agency from the non-resident in which he was acting on the non-resident's behalf in an independent capacity (see 51.6(3) above). The provisions above apply equally to independent agents as to other UK representatives, with the following applying in addition.

As regards his obligations to furnish information (including anything contained in a return, self-assessment, account, statement or report provided to the Revenue), the independent agent is not required to do anything beyond what is practicable by acting to the best of his knowledge and belief after having taken all reasonable steps to obtain the information. In such a case, the non-resident is not discharged from his own obligation to furnish the information, but is also not bound by any error or mistake in the information so furnished by the agent unless it results from the non-resident's own act or omission or one to which he consented or in which he connived. An independent agent is entitled to be indemnified in respect of any liability discharged by him on the non-resident's behalf under these provisions and to retain, out of monies due by him to the non-resident, amounts sufficient to cover any such liability, whether or not already discharged. An independent agent is not liable to any civil penalty or surcharge in respect of any act or omission which is neither his own nor one to which he consented or in which he connived, providing he can show that he could not recover the penalty etc. out of monies due to the non-resident after being indemnified for his other liabilities.

[*FA 1995, Sch 23*].

51.8 NON-RESIDENT ENTERTAINERS AND SPORTSMEN

Any person making a payment or transfer (including by way of loan) for, in respect of, or which in any way derives either directly or indirectly from, the performance of a 'relevant activity' performed in the UK by an entertainer or sportsman (as broadly defined) who is not resident in the UK in the year of assessment in which that activity is performed, is required to deduct and account to the Revenue for an amount representing income tax, at a rate which may not exceed the basic rate of income tax for the year of assessment. In the case of a transfer, the actual worth of what is transferred is treated as being a net amount corresponding to a gross amount from which income tax at the basic rate has been deducted. That gross amount is treated as the value of the transfer and the net value is the cost to the transferor less any contribution made by the entertainer or sportsman.

A '*relevant activity*' is an activity performed in the UK by an entertainer or sportsman in his character as such on or in connection with (including promotion of) a commercial occasion or event (including participation in live or recorded transmissions of any kind) for which he is entitled to receive a payment or transfer or which is designed to promote commercial sales or activity by any means.

Payments or transfers from which tax need not be withheld under these provisions are as follows.

(i) A payment subject to deduction of tax under some other provision of the *Taxes Acts* than *ICTA 1988, s 555(2)* and *The Income Tax (Entertainers and Sportsmen) Regulations 1987* (*SI 1987 No 530*).

(ii) An arm's length payment made to a person resident and ordinarily resident in the UK, who is not connected or associated with the payee, for services ancillary to the performance of a relevant activity.

(iii) Payments representing royalties from the sale of sound recordings.

(iv) Any total amount paid in a tax year by a payer, together with persons connected or associated with him, to a non-UK resident entertainer or sportsman, together with persons connected or associated with him, which does not exceed £1,000.

The *Regulations* provide for arrangements to be made in writing between the payer, the entertainer or sportsman, or other recipient of the payment, and the Board of Inland Revenue for a reduced tax payment representing, as nearly as may be, the actual liability of the entertainer or sportsman, to apply. Such application must be made not later than 30 days before the payment (or transfer) falls to be made and the full basic rate deduction must be made from any payment or transfer made before approval is given by the Board. There are provisions to prevent any payment suffering withholding tax more than once where it passes through an intermediary, and for reductions to apply where there is a double taxation agreement in force. Similarly, there are anti-avoidance provisions to prevent payments or transfers being routed through third parties such as controlled companies and similar entities.

The sum accounted for to the Revenue is treated as paid on account of the income or corporation tax liability of a person other than the person so accounting for it, whether a liability under the *Regulations*, under *ICTA 1988, ss 555 et seq.* or under any other provision of the *Taxes Acts*. The charge under *ICTA 1988, s 555(2)* applies in place of any charge under Schedule E (any amount charged under which shall be treated as an expense of the 'Schedule 11 trade' (see below)), under *ICTA 1988, ss 660–685* (Settlements) or under Schedule D (where the connected payment is a receipt falling to be included in the computation of profits of a company which provides the services of the entertainer or sportsman). A recipient is entitled to claim in writing that a tax payment deducted is excessive and *TMA 1970, s 42* (see 4 APPEALS) applies to such claims.

Computation of liability of entertainer or sportsman. Where a payment or other transfer is made within these provisions, the relevant activity is treated as performed in the course of a trade, profession or vocation (the '*Schedule 11 trade*', so called because these provisions were originally enacted in *FA 1986, Sch 11*) exercised in the UK and thus chargeable to tax under Schedule D, Case I or II (to the extent that it would not otherwise be so treated) unless it is performed in the course of an office or employment.

Payment of tax is due, whether or not it has been withheld from the connected payment or transfer, before, or at the time when, a quarterly return (see below) is made, whether or not an assessment has been made.

Assessment to tax. An assessment may be made, in relation to a tax year or other period, on a current year (not a preceding year) basis and any apportionment, division or aggregation by reference to tax years or other periods may be made as is just and reasonable. The 'Schedule 11 trade' is thus treated separately from the 'world-wide trade' of an entertainer or sportsman, but for the purposes of loss relief under *ICTA 1988, ss 381, 385* they are treated as the same trade, although losses in early years will be relieved only by reference to the date of commencement of the world-wide trade. Terminal loss relief under *ICTA 1988, s 388* will only be given in respect of the Schedule 11 trade if the world-wide trade ceases in the same period.

All other provisions of the *Taxes Acts* as to the time within which an assessment may be made apply to such an assessment as do the provisions for out of time assessments. Tax charged by an assessment is payable within 14 days of the issue of the notice, or by the due date of payment of the tax (see above) if this is earlier. The collection and recovery procedures and the provisions relating to interest on overdue tax in *TMA 1970* apply to such assessments. The penalty provisions of *TMA 1970, s 98* (see 58.4 PENALTIES) also apply.

Returns (including returns of payments for which a nil deduction rate applied) must be made quarterly in respect of the periods to 30 June, 30 September, 31 December and 5 April within 14 days of the end of each period. The Board may require, in writing, within a specified time, certain information regarding payments, payees and relevant activities. The penalty provisions of *TMA 1970* apply to failure to submit returns (see 67.2 RETURNS).

[*ICTA 1988, ss 555–558; SI 1987 No 530*].

Simon's Direct Tax Service. See **E5.8.**

51.9 **NON-RESIDENT BANKS, INSURANCE COMPANIES AND DEALERS IN SECURITIES** carrying on business in the UK.

(i) For 1995/96 and earlier years and for accounting periods ending before 1 April 1996, such bodies are not exempt on income from overseas securities, stocks or shares, by reason of non-residence. [*ICTA 1988, s 474(1); FA 1995, Sch 8 para 25(1); FA 1996, Sch 7 para 18*]. (See *Owen v Sassoon Ch D 1950, 32 TC 101*). See now 72.1 SCHEDULE D, CASE III.

(ii) Where exempt on certain GOVERNMENT STOCKS (33) an amount equal to interest at the average rate for the period under review on all money borrowed for purposes of the business up to the total cost of any such tax-free securities held is disallowed in the computation of profits or losses and excluded from the definition of 'charges on income' for purposes of *ICTA 1988, s 338* (see Tolley's Corporation Tax). Expenses of acquiring, holding or dealing with the tax-free securities and any profits or losses arising therefrom are also excluded from computation. For 1996/97 and subsequent years, and for accounting periods ending after 31 March 1996, this applies only to $3\frac{1}{2}$% War Loan 1952 or later, and the prohibition on relief as a charge on income is replaced by a prohibition on relief as a loan relationship debit. [*ICTA 1988, s 475; FA 1995, Sch 8 para 25(1); FA 1996, Sch 14 para 27, Sch 28 para 3*].

(iii) Where receipts of interest or dividends have been treated as tax-exempt under double taxation arrangements, they are not to be excluded from trading income etc. so as to give rise to losses for set-off against income etc. [*ICTA 1988, s 808*].

(iv) See also Tolley's Corporation Tax.

51.10 **PAYMENTS OF ANNUAL SUMS TO NON-RESIDENTS**

Copyright royalties, public lending right payments and **design royalties** (or 'sums paid periodically') paid *'by or through* any person' in the UK to a person whose usual place of abode is outside the UK are subject to deduction of tax on the net sum (i.e. less commission). [*ICTA 1988, ss 536, 537, 537B; FA 1995, s 115(10)*]. This does not apply to professional authors (Hansard 10 November 1969, Vol 791, Col 31). See Revenue Inspector's Manual, IM 4005 as regards meaning of 'usual place of abode'.

Payment to foreign author for right to sell translation, held to be within *ICTA 1988, s 536* (*Longmans, Green KB 1932, 17 TC 272*). Also that solicitors of the payers remitting royalties to non-residents must deduct tax and account to Revenue (*Rye & Eyre v CIR HL 1935, 19 TC 164*).

The Inland Revenue may call for a return of payments. [*TMA 1970, s 16*]. See 67.6 RETURNS.

51.11 **PERSONAL ALLOWANCES FOR CERTAIN NON-RESIDENTS** [*ICTA 1988, s 278; FA 1988, s 31; FA 1996, ss 134, 145, Sch 20 para 21; FA 1999, Sch 20 Pt III(3)*]

As mentioned under 64.3 RESIDENCE, ORDINARY RESIDENCE AND DOMICILE, a non-resident is liable to UK tax without any deduction for personal allowances etc. except under specific double tax treaties or in cases where the individual concerned is eligible for relief as below. (Foreigners resident here have the same rights to relief as British subjects, and where assessments are made on the ground of *'residence'* here, the taxpayer is entitled to the full allowances. But this does not apply to persons assessed because temporarily employed here, but not technically 'resident'.)

The non-resident individuals eligible for reliefs are as follows.

(i) All Commonwealth citizens and citizens of Republic of Ireland.

(ii) For 1996/97 onwards, all nationals of States within the European Economic Area (EEA), which comprises all EU States plus, as at 28 November 1995, Norway, Iceland and Liechtenstein.

(iii) Persons who are or who have been in service of the Crown.

(iv) Missionaries.

(v) Servants of British Protectorates.

(vi) Residents in the Isle of Man or Channel Islands.

(vii) Persons abroad for health reasons (including health of wife or family) after residence in UK.

(viii) Widows or widowers of Crown Servants.

For the status of Hong Kong residents who were previously British Dependent Territories citizens following the transfer of sovereignty on 30 June 1997, see Revenue Tax Bulletin October 1996 pp 357, 358. It is expected that most will continue to be able to claim allowances under *ICTA 1988, s 278* either as British Nationals (Overseas) or as British Overseas citizens.

All personal reliefs under *ICTA 1988, Pt VII, Ch 1* are available in full to non-resident individuals within (i)–(viii) above, except that no relief is given to a wife under *ICTA 1988, s 257D* (see 47.5 MARRIED PERSONS), prior to its abolition after 5 April 2000, in respect of excess allowances of her husband where the husband is not UK resident.

Claims are made to the Board. Claimants should contact Inland Revenue, FICO (International), St John's House, Merton Road, Bootle, Merseyside, L69 9BB, except that Crown employees or Crown pensioners should contact Inland Revenue, Public Departments (Technical Unit) Foreign Section, Ty-Glas, Llanishen, Cardiff, Wales, CF4 5WN. A right of appeal to the Special Commissioners, within three months of the notice of the Board's decision, is given by *TMA 1970, s 42(3), Sch 2 para 3* or (from 1996/97) *TMA 1970, Sch 1A paras 9(2), 10.*

Simon's Direct Tax Service. See **E6.201, E6.202**.

51.12 TRADES ETC. CARRIED ON AND CONTROLLED ABROAD

A trade, profession or vocation carried on by a UK resident is within Schedule D, Case I or II if carried on wholly or partly in the UK but within Case V if carried on wholly abroad [*ICTA 1988, s 18(1)(a)(ii)(3); FA 1995, Sch 6 para 2*] subject to special rules as regards trades etc. in Eire. [*ICTA 1988, s 68; FA 1994, s 207(5)*]. This is so notwithstanding the wide wording of the Case I charging rule in *ICTA 1988, s 18(3)* (*Colquhoun v Brooks HL 1889, 2 TC 490*). A non-resident is chargeable on trading etc. in the UK (see 51.4 above).

Where a business is 'carried on' for this purpose depends on from where it is managed and controlled, irrespective of where the day-to-day business activities are conducted. See for this *Trustees of Ferguson, decd v Donovan Supreme Court (IFS) 1927, 1 ITC 214* (trustees delegated control of Australian business to Australian company and did not interfere in any way; held not within Case I) and contrast *Ogilvie v Kitton CES 1908, 5 TC 338* (Canadian business managed by Canadians but 'head and brains' in UK where owners resided; Case I applied) and *Spiers v Mackinnon KB 1929, 14 TC 386*. For trades carried on by companies, see 51.9 above, and for trades carried on by partnerships, see 53.15 PARTNERSHIPS.

Where assessments are under Schedule D, Case V (see 73 SCHEDULE D, CASES IV AND V), income is nevertheless computed under the rules applicable to SCHEDULE D, CASES I AND II (71). For 1994/95 and subsequent years as regards businesses commenced after 5 April 1994 and for 1997/98 and subsequent years as regards businesses commenced on or before that date, the basis period rules in 71.11 to 71.19 SCHEDULE D, CASES I AND II apply, as does *ICTA 1988, s 113* (see 53.6 PARTNERSHIPS) (see also 73.9 SCHEDULE D, CASES IV AND V). [*ICTA 1988, s 65(3); FA 1994, s 207(2)(6), s 218*]. Loss relief under *ICTA 1988, ss 380–386* and *s 388* (see 46 LOSSES) is available only against other overseas trading, etc. income, certain foreign emoluments (see 75.6 SCHEDULE E) or foreign pensions or annuities from which a deduction is allowable (see 59.1(iv), 59.2 PENSIONS). [*ICTA 1988, s 391*]. These provisions apply equally to income from Eire. [*ICTA 1970, Sch 12 Pt III; ICTA 1988, s 68*].

The REMITTANCE BASIS (63) applies to persons not domiciled in the UK and to persons who, being Commonwealth or Eire citizens, are not ordinarily resident in the UK. [*ICTA 1988, s 65(4); FA 1996, s 134, Sch 20 para 3*].

Travelling expenses. A deduction may be claimed for expenses incurred in a business carried on abroad (and not assessable on the REMITTANCE BASIS (63)) in travelling between any place in the UK and any place where the business is carried on, either (*a*) for the individual, provided that his absence is wholly and exclusively for the performance of the functions of the business, or

(*b*) where there is absence from the UK for a continuous period of 60 days or more, for the spouse and any children under 18 (at beginning of outward journey) accompanying the individual at the beginning of the period of absence or visiting him during that period, including the return journey, but with a limit of two outward and return journeys per person in any year of assessment.

Where (*a*) above applies, a deduction may also be claimed for expenditure incurred on board and lodging at the overseas location.

Where more than one business is carried on at the overseas location, travelling, etc., expenses are apportioned between them. [*ICTA 1988, s 80*].

Travelling between overseas businesses. Where more than one business is carried on abroad (and at least one is within *section 80*, as above), and absence from the UK is solely for business purposes, a deduction may be claimed for travelling between them. The deduction will normally be given in taxing the trade at the place of destination, but, exceptionally, where this trade is not within *section 80*, as above, it will be given in taxing the trade at the place of departure. Where more than one business is carried on at the place of destination or, exceptionally, at the place of departure, the expenses are apportioned between them. [*ICTA 1988, s 81*].

See 71.27 SCHEDULE D, CASES I AND II for provisions applying where an individual carrying on a business wholly or partly abroad **becomes or ceases to be UK resident**.

Partnerships abroad. See 53.15 PARTNERSHIPS.

51.13 UNITED KINGDOM

The United Kingdom for tax purposes comprises England, Scotland, Wales and Northern Ireland. The Channel Islands and the Isle of Man are not included. Great Britain comprises England, Scotland and Wales only.

Territorial extension of tax area. The territorial sea of the UK is regarded as part of the UK for tax purposes. Emoluments, profits and gains from exploration or exploitation activities in a designated area (under *Continental Shelf Act 1964, s 1(7)*), are treated as arising in the UK. A resident licence holder under *Petroleum (Production) Act 1934* or *Petroleum Act 1998, Pt I* may be held accountable for the liability of a non-resident and may be required by inspector to provide information concerning transactions with other persons and emoluments and other payments made. [*ICTA 1988, s 830; FA 1973, s 38, Sch 15; TCGA 1992, 276; Petroleum Act 1998, Sch 4 para 5*]. As regards liability of non-resident lessors of mobile drilling rigs, vessels or equipment used in conjunction with exploration or exploitation activities, see Revenue Pamphlet IR 131, SP 6/84, 31 July 1984. See 25.2 DOUBLE TAX RELIEF as regards certain UK exemptions *not* extended to continental shelf workers.

51.14 UNREMITTABLE OVERSEAS INCOME

Where the *'income arising'* basis applies, such income which

(i) cannot, despite reasonable endeavour, be remitted to the UK, by reason of laws or executive action of, or the impossibility of obtaining foreign currency in, the territory concerned, and

(ii) the person chargeable has not realised outside that territory for sterling or an unblocked currency may be omitted from assessments. For 1995/96 and earlier years, the taxpayer had to give written notice before the relevant assessments became final. For 1996/97 and later years, the relief must be claimed within twelve months after 31 January following the year of assessment in which the income arises.

When, for 1995/96 and earlier years, the Inland Revenue consider that the above conditions are no longer satisfied, the income becomes assessable (at its value at that date taking into account foreign taxes chargeable on it in the territory concerned), and assessments may be made within six years thereafter. When, for 1996/97 and later years, the conditions cease to be satisfied at any time, the income is treated as arising *at that time* and is taxable accordingly (valued as at that time, taking into account foreign taxes, and, if source of income ceased before that time, charged under SCHEDULE D, CASE VI (74)). Disputes are settled by appeal to the Special Commissioners. [*ICTA 1988, s 584; FA 1996, s 134, Sch 20 para 33*].

Delayed remittances of overseas income. Where income under Schedule D, Cases IV or V or Schedule E, Case III is assessable on the REMITTANCE BASIS (63) the taxpayer may claim that so much of any remittance in the basis year for a year of assessment as consists of income which **arose before that basis year** shall be excluded from that year and treated as income of the basis year(s) for the year(s) of assessment in which it arose, provided that, despite reasonable endeavour, the income could not previously be remitted, by reason of the laws or executive action of, or the impossibility of obtaining foreign currency in, the territory of origin. The claim must be made within, for 1996/97 and later years, five years after 31 January following the tax year of remittance (for earlier years, six years after the end of that tax year). [*ICTA 1988, s 585; FA 1996, ss 134, 135, Sch 20 para 34, Sch 21 para 16*].

Interest does not run on the unpaid tax if Inland Revenue are informed promptly, see details under 42.6 INTEREST AND SURCHARGES ON UNPAID TAX.

See 71.92 SCHEDULE D, CASES I AND II for relief for certain unremittable income forming part of the profits of trades within Case I of Schedule D.

Simon's Direct Tax Service. See E1.326.

52 Offshore Funds

Simon's Direct Tax Service D4.431–D4.436.

52.1 **INTRODUCTION**

After 31 December 1983 'offshore income gains' arising on disposals of certain interests in offshore funds which are considered not to distribute sufficient income are charged to income tax or corporation tax under Schedule D, Case VI rather than to capital gains tax. Broadly, the capital gains tax regime applies to any part of such a gain accruing before 1 January 1984 but the whole of the gain arising thereafter (without indexation) is taxed as income. Special provisions apply to funds operating equalisation arrangements.

See generally Revenue Inspector's Manual, IM 4075–4121.

Disposal of material interests in non-qualifying offshore funds. The offshore fund rules apply to a disposal by any person of an asset:

(*a*) if, at the time of the disposal, the asset constitutes a **'material interest'** in an **'offshore fund'** (see 52.3 below) which is or has at any 'material time' been a **'non-qualifying offshore fund'** (see 52.4 below); or

(*b*) if

(i) at the time of the disposal, the asset constitutes an interest in a UK resident company or in a unit trust scheme within *ICTA 1988, s 469(7)* which has UK resident trustees, and

(ii) at a 'material time' after 31 December 1984 the company or unit trust was a 'non-qualifying offshore fund' and the asset constituted a 'material interest' in that fund. For this purpose the provisions of *CGTA 1979, s 78,* equating original shares with a new holding on reorganisation, apply.

[*ICTA 1988, s 757(1); FA 1984, s 92(1)*].

A '*material time*' is any time after 31 December 1983 or, if later, the earliest date on which any 'relevant consideration' was given for the acquisition of the asset. '*Relevant consideration*' is that given by or on behalf of the person making the disposal or a predecessor in title which would be taken into account in determining any gain or loss on disposal under *TCGA 1992*. [*ICTA 1988, s 757(7); FA 1990, Sch 14 para 10*].

With some modifications, a disposal occurs for offshore fund purposes if there would be a disposal under *TCGA 1992*. Death is an occasion of charge as the deceased is deemed to have made a disposal at market value, immediately before his death, of any asset which was or had at any time been a 'material interest' in a 'non-qualifying offshore fund'. In addition, *TCGA 1992, s 135(3)* will not apply, and there will therefore be a disposal at market value, if an exchange or arrangement is effected under *TCGA 1992, s 135* or *s 136* in such a way that securities etc. in a company, which is or was at a material time a 'non-qualifying offshore fund', are exchanged for assets etc. which do not constitute interests in such a fund. [*ICTA 1988, s 757(2)–(6)*].

52.2 **Offshore funds operating equalisation arrangements.** There are specific provisions to enable funds operating 'equalisation arrangements' to satisfy the 'distribution test' (see 52.5 below) which the nature of such funds might otherwise preclude. As a corollary, provision is also made to ensure that the 'accrued income' paid to outgoing investors as part of their capital payments is treated as income for tax purposes when the fund qualifies as a distributor.

Definition. For these purposes, an offshore fund operates *'equalisation arrangements'* where the first distribution paid to a person acquiring a 'material interest' by way of 'initial purchase' includes a payment which is a return of capital (debited to the fund's 'equalisation account') determined by reference to the income which had accrued to the fund in the period before that person's acquisition. An acquisition is by way of *'initial purchase'* if it is by way of direct purchase from the fund's managers in their capacity as such.

'Accrued income' chargeable to income tax — application of offshore fund rules. A disposal is one to which the offshore fund provisions apply, subject to exception below, if it is a disposal by any person of a 'material interest' in an 'offshore fund' operating equalisation arrangements where

(i) the disposal proceeds are not a trading receipt; and

(ii) the fund *is not*, and *has not been*, at any material time (see above) a 'non-qualifying offshore fund' (see 52.4 below)

(i.e. the provisions apply also to *distributing* funds (see 52.5 below) with equalisation arrangements).

Capital gains tax rules for disposals apply as they do for other offshore fund disposals (see 52.1 above) with some variations. Death is not treated as a disposal in this context. In addition, *TCGA 1992, s 127* (reorganisations etc.) (including that section as applied by *TCGA 1992, s 135* (exchange of securities) or by *TCGA 1992, s 132* (conversion of securities)) does not apply and there is a disposal at market value in such circumstances.

Exception. The offshore fund legislation does *not* apply as indicated above to a disposal where the fund's income for the period preceding the disposal is of such a nature that the part relating to the interest in question is in any event chargeable under Schedule D, Case IV or Case V on the person disposing of the interest (or would be so chargeable if residence/domicile/situation of assets requirements were met).

[*ICTA 1988, s 757(2)(3), s 758; FA 1989, s 81*].

52.3 MATERIAL INTERESTS IN OFFSHORE FUNDS

An **'offshore fund'** is

(*a*) a company resident outside the UK; or

(*b*) a unit trust scheme within *ICTA 1988, s 469(7)* which has non-UK resident trustees; or

(*c*) any other arrangements taking effect under overseas law which create rights in the nature of co-ownership under that law,

in which any person has a 'material interest'. From 29 November 1994, it must also be a 'collective investment scheme' within *Financial Services Act 1986*. [*ICTA 1988, s 759(1)(1A); FA 1995, s 134(1)–(3)(8)*].

A **'material interest'** is one which, when acquired, could reasonably be expected to be realisable (by any means, either in money or in asset form) within seven years for an amount reasonably approximate to its proportionate share of the market value of the fund's assets. For these purposes, an interest in an offshore fund which at any time is worth substantially more than its proportionate share of the fund's underlying assets is not to be regarded as so realisable. [*ICTA 1988, s 759(2)–(4)*]. If shares in a quoted overseas company have habitually been traded at or near net asset value, and an investor in these shares had a reasonable expectation, on acquisition, of a future sale at or near such value, those shares are likely to represent a 'material interest'. (Revenue Pamphlet IR 131, SP 2/86, 7 March 1986).

Exceptions. The following are not material interests.

(i) Interests in respect of loans etc. made in the ordinary course of banking business.

(ii) Rights under insurance policies.

(iii) Shares in a company resident outside the UK where

(*a*) the shares are held by a company and the holding is necessary or desirable for the maintenance and development of a trade carried on by the company, or by an associated company within *ICTA 1988, s 416*; and

(*b*) the shares confer at least 10% of the voting rights and, on winding-up, a right to at least 10% of the assets after discharging all prior liabilities; and

(*c*) the shares are held by not more than ten persons and all confer both voting rights and a right to assets on winding-up; and

(*d*) at the time of acquisition of the shares the company could reasonably expect to realise its interest for market value within seven years only by virtue of (I) an arrangement requiring the company's fellow participators to purchase its shares and/or (II) provisions of either the overseas company's constitution or an agreement between the participators regarding that company's winding-up.

(iv) Interests in companies resident outside the UK at any time when the holder is entitled to have the company wound up and to receive in that event in the same capacity more than 50% of the assets after discharging all prior liabilities.

[*ICTA 1988, s 759(5)–(8)*].

The Revenue have also indicated that normal commercial loans or other debt instruments entitling the lender to no more than a fixed return of principal on redemption, and which are not geared to the underlying asset value of the borrower's business, are not regarded as 'material interests'. (Revenue Pamphlet IR 131, SP 2/86, 7 March 1986).

'Market value' for the purposes of the offshore funds legislation is determined according to capital gains tax rules with necessary modifications of *TCGA 1992, s 272(5)* (market value in relation to rights in unit trust schemes) where appropriate. [*ICTA 1988, s 759(9)*].

52.4 NON-QUALIFYING OFFSHORE FUNDS

An offshore fund is **'non-qualifying'** except during an 'account period' in respect of which it is certified by the Board as a distributing fund pursuing a 'full distribution policy' (see 52.5 below). For these purposes, the first *'account period'* begins when the fund begins to carry on its activities or, if later, on 1 January 1984. An *'account period'* ends on the fund's accounting date or, if earlier, twelve months from the beginning of the period or on the fund's ceasing to carry on its activities. In addition, if the fund is a non-UK resident company, an *'account period'* ends when it becomes UK resident, and if the fund is a unit trust with non-UK resident trustees, it ends when those trustees become UK resident. [*ICTA 1988, s 760(1)(2)(8)–(10); FA 1984, s 95(8)*].

Conditions for certification. Subject to the modifications of conditions for certification in certain cases noted below, an offshore fund is not to be certified as a 'distributing fund' for any account period if, at any time in that period:

(*a*) more than 5% by value of the fund's assets consists of interests in other offshore funds (but see below); or

(*b*) more than 10% by value of the fund's assets consists of interests in a single company. For this purpose

(i) the value of an interest in a single company is determined as at the most recent occasion (in that account period or earlier) on which the fund acquired an interest in that company for money or money's worth. However an occasion is disregarded if it is one on which *TCGA 1992, s 127* (equation of original shares and new holding) applied, including that *section* as applied by later provisions of *TCGA 1992* (reorganisations, conversion of securities etc.), and on which no consideration is given for the interest other than the interest in the original holding,

(ii) an interest is disregarded, except for determining the total value of the fund's assets, if it consists of a current or deposit account provided in the normal course of its banking business by a company whose business it is to provide such account facilities in any currency for members of the public and bodies corporate, and

(iii) Government-owned national or supra-national bodies whose activities are directed not with a view to commercial profits, but to the exercise of a wider social or economic function, are not regarded as companies for this purpose (Revenue Pamphlet IR 131, SP 2/86, 7 March 1986); or

(*c*) the fund's assets include more than 10% of the issued share capital, or any class of it, in any company; or

(*d*) there is more than one class of material interests (see 52.2 above) in the fund and, were each class and the assets represented by it in a separate offshore fund, each such separate fund does not pursue a 'full distribution policy'. For this purpose, interests held solely by persons involved in the management of the fund's assets are disregarded if they carry no right or expectation to participate in profits and no right to anything other than the return of the price paid on winding-up or redemption.

Where, however, the Board are satisfied that an apparent failure to comply with any of (*a*)–(*c*) above occurred inadvertently and was remedied without unreasonable delay, that failure may be disregarded.

[*ICTA 1988, s 760(3)–(7), Sch 27 para 14*].

Modifications of conditions for certification. The conditions for certification in (*a*) to (*d*) above are modified in certain cases.

(A) **Investments in second tier funds.** If offshore funds ('primary funds') would fail to meet the conditions in (*a*) to (*c*) above because of investments in other offshore funds (referred to below as 'second tier funds') which could themselves be certified as qualifying distributing funds (without any modification of the (*a*) to (*c*) conditions), then the primary funds' interests in the second tier funds are left out of account, except for determining the total value of the primary funds' assets, in establishing whether the primary funds are prevented by (*a*) to (*c*) above from being certified as distributing funds. In addition, where the above applies, if at any time in a primary fund's account period that fund's assets include an interest in another offshore fund or in any company and the qualifying second tier fund's assets also include an interest in that other fund or company, then the primary fund's interest is aggregated with its proportionate share of the second tier fund's interest in determining whether the primary fund is within the limits in (*a*) to (*c*) above. Its share of the second tier fund's interest is the proportion which the average value during its account period of its own holding of interests in the second tier fund bears to the average value during the period of all interests in the second tier fund. [*ICTA 1988, s 760(3), Sch 27 paras 6, 7, 9*].

(B) **Investments in trading companies.** Where the assets of an offshore fund include an interest in a company whose business is wholly the carrying on of of trade(s) the limit of 10% of a fund's assets invested in a single company in (*b*) above is increased to 20% and the 10% limit on the proportion of a class of share in any company in (*c*) above is increased to allow holdings of less than 50%. For these purposes companies are excluded if their business consists to any extent of banking or moneylending or of dealing, including dealing by way of futures contracts and traded options, in commodities, currency, securities, debts or other assets of a financial nature. [*ICTA 1988, s 760(3), Sch 27 paras 4(2), 10*]. Dealing in commodities, currency and financial assets incidental to the business of a company will be disregarded in determining whether the company is trading. (Revenue Pamphlet IR 131, SP 2/86, 7 March 1986).

(C) **Wholly-owned subsidiaries.** Where an offshore fund has a wholly-owned subsidiary company, the receipts, expenditure, assets and liabilities of the fund and the subsidiary are aggregated so that the fund and the subsidiary are treated as one for the purposes of determining whether the fund is within the limits in (*a*) to (*d*) above. In the same way, the interest of the fund in the subsidiary and any distributions or other payments between the fund and the subsidiary are left out of account. A wholly-owned subsidiary is one owned either directly and beneficially by the fund, or directly by the trustees of the fund for the benefit of the fund, or, in the case of a fund within 52.3(*c*) above, in some other equivalent manner. Where the subsidiary has only one class of issued share capital, ownership of at least 95% of that capital by the offshore fund constitutes the subsidiary a wholly-owned subsidiary for this purpose, and only a corresponding proportion of the subsidiary's receipts, expenditure, assets and liabilities are then aggregated with those of the offshore fund. [*ICTA 1988, s 760(3), Sch 27 para 11*].

(D) **Subsidiary dealing and management companies.** The investment restriction in (*c*) above does not apply to so much of an offshore fund's assets as consists of share capital of a company which is either

(1) a wholly-owned subsidiary of the fund (as defined in (C) above) whose sole function is dealing in material interests in the offshore fund for management and administrative purposes and which is not entitled to any distribution from the fund; or

(2) a subsidiary management company of the fund whose sole function is to provide the fund, or other funds with an interest in the company, with advisory services or administrative, management and related property holding services on arm's length commercial terms. For the purposes of determining whether a company is a subsidiary management company of a fund, that company and any wholly-owned subsidiary companies it may itself have are regarded as a single entity. [*ICTA 1988, s 760(3), Sch 27 para 12*].

(E) **Disregard of certain investments.** Certain holdings which would otherwise fall within the restriction at (*c*) above are not taken into account for the purposes of that restriction. This applies where no more than 5% of the value of the offshore fund's assets consists of such holdings and of interests in other non-qualifying offshore funds. [*ICTA 1988, s 760(3), Sch 27 para 13*].

52.5 THE DISTRIBUTION TEST

An offshore fund pursues a '**full distribution policy**' with respect to an account period if

(*a*) a distribution is made for that account period or for some other period falling wholly or partly within that period; and (*b*) subject to modifications below, the distribution represents at least 85% of the fund's income and not less than 85% of its 'UK equivalent profits' for that period; and

(*c*) the distribution is made during or within six months after the end of the account period (the six month limit may be extended at the Board's discretion); and

(*d*) the distribution is in a form such that any part of it received in the UK by a UK resident which is not part of the profits of a trade etc. is chargeable under Schedule D, Case IV or Case V.

These conditions may equally be satisfied by any two or more distributions taken together. [*ICTA 1988, Sch 27 para 1(1)*].

The basic conditions in (*a*) to (*d*) above are modified in certain cases (see 52.6 below).

A fund is treated as pursuing a full distribution policy for any account period in which there is no income and no 'UK equivalent profits', or for account periods ending after 28 November 1994 for which gross fund income does not exceed 1% of the average value of fund assets during the period, but it will not be so treated for any account period for which no accounts are prepared. [*ICTA 1988, Sch 27 para 1(2)(3); FA 1995, s 134(4)(9)*].

Non-UK legal restrictions. Where in an account period an offshore fund is subject to non-UK legal restrictions on making distributions by reason of an excess of losses over profits as computed according to the law in question, a deduction is allowed from the fund's income of any amount which cannot be distributed but which would otherwise form part of the fund's income for that account period. [*ICTA 1988, Sch 27 para 1(6)*].

Apportionment of income and distributions between account periods. Where a period for which accounts are made up or for which a distribution is made covers the whole or part of two or more account periods of the fund, the income or distribution is apportioned on a time basis according to the number of days in each period. A distribution made out of specified income but not for a specified period is attributed to the account period in which the income arose. Where no period or income is specified, a distribution is treated as made for the last account period ending before the distribution. If the distribution made, or treated as made, for an account period exceeds the income of that period the excess is reallocated to previous periods, to later periods before earlier ones, until exhausted, unless the distribution was apportioned on a time basis as mentioned above in which case the excess is first reapportioned on a just and reasonable basis to the other account period(s). [*ICTA 1988, Sch 27 para 1(4)(5)*].

'UK equivalent profits' of an offshore fund are the total profits, excluding chargeable gains, on which, after allowing for any deductions available, corporation tax would be chargeable, assuming that

(i) the offshore fund is a UK resident company in the account period in question, but in no other; and

(ii) the account period is an accounting period of that company; and

(iii) any dividends or distributions from a UK resident company are included.

The effects of *FA 1993, ss 125–133* (exchange gains and losses) and *FA 1994, ss 159, 160, Sch 18 para 1* (profits and losses on interest rate and currency contracts) (see Tolley's Corporation Tax under Exchange Gains and Losses and Financial Instruments respectively) are ignored for this purpose, and it is assumed that income tax, rather than corporation tax, rules apply, as they do for unauthorised unit trusts, as regards certain creditor relationships of the fund (see generally Tolley's Corporation Tax under Loan Relationships).

Any UK government securities or securities of foreign states which are exempt from tax (see 33.2 GOVERNMENT STOCKS) must be brought into account in determining the fund's total profits.

Whether a fund is trading will turn on the particular facts, but in general a fund would not normally be regarded as trading in respect of relatively infrequent transactions, or where the intention was merely to hedge specific investments which were not associated with trading activities. (Revenue Pamphlet IR 131, SP 2/86, 7 March 1986).

The deductions referred to above include a deduction equal to that allowed against a fund's income where non-UK legal restrictions prevent distribution (see above) and a deduction equal to any foreign capital tax allowed as a deduction in determining the fund's income for the account period in question.

Interest paid to a non-UK resident is deductible in the same way as if it were paid to a UK resident. UK income tax (whether suffered by deduction or by assessment) is available as a deduction. (Revenue Pamphlet IR 131, SP 2/86, 7 March 1986).

[*ICTA 1988, Sch 27 para 5; FA 1994, s 176(2); FA 1996, Sch 10 para 3*].

52.6 MODIFICATIONS OF DISTRIBUTION TEST

The basic rules of the distribution test in 52.5(*a*) to (*d*) above are modified in various circumstances.

(*a*) **Funds operating equalisation arrangements.** Where an offshore fund operates such arrangements (see 52.2 above) throughout an account period (see 52.4 above), an amount equal to any 'accrued income' which is part of the consideration for certain disposals in that period is treated as a distribution for the purposes of the distribution test. This applies to a disposal

(i) which is a disposal of a material interest in the fund to either the fund or the fund managers in their capacity as such; and

(ii) which is one to which the offshore fund rules apply (whether or not by virtue of their application to disposals from distributing funds with equalisation arrangements — see 52.2 above), or which is one to which the rules would apply if the provisions regarding the non-application of *TCGA 1992, ss 127, 135* applied generally and not only for the purpose of determining whether a disposal from a distributing fund with equalisation arrangements is brought within the rules (see 52.2 above); and

(iii) which is not a disposal within the *exception* at 52.2 above (where the income of the fund is, or would be, chargeable to tax under Schedule D, Case IV or V in any event).

The '*accrued income*' referred to above is that part of the consideration which would be credited to the fund's equalisation account if the interest were resold to another person by way of 'initial purchase' (see 52.2 above) on the same day. However there are provisions to ensure that this accrued income figure is reduced where the interest disposed of was acquired by way of initial purchase (by any person) after the beginning of the account period by reference to which the accrued income is calculated. In addition, where an offshore commodity dealing fund (see also (*c*) below) operates equalisation and there is a disposal within (i) to (iii) above, one half of the accrued income representing commodity profits is left out of account in determining what part of the disposal consideration represents accrued income.

For the purposes of the distribution test, the distribution which the fund is treated as making on a disposal is treated as being paid to the person disposing of his interest, in the income form required by 52.5(*d*) above, out of the income of the fund for the account period of disposal. Where a distribution is made to the managers (in their capacity as such) of a fund operating equalisation arrangements it is disregarded for the purposes of the distribution test except to the extent that it relates to that part of the period for which the distribution is made during which the managers (in that capacity) held that interest. [*ICTA 1988, Sch 27 paras 2, 4(4)*].

(*b*) **Funds with income taxable under Schedule D, Case IV or V on investors.** Where sums forming part of the income of an offshore fund within 52.3(*b*) or (*c*) above are chargeable to tax under Schedule D, Case IV or V on the holders of interests in the fund (or would be so chargeable were the necessary residence etc. rules met), any such sums which are not actually part of a distribution complying with the part of the distribution test in 52.5(*c*) and (*d*) above are treated as distributions which do so comply made out of the income of which they are part and paid to the holders of the interests in question. [*ICTA 1988, Sch 27 para 3*].

(*c*) **Funds with commodity dealing income.** Where an offshore fund's income includes commodity dealing profits, half of those profits are left out of account in determining the fund's income and UK equivalent profits for the purposes of the distribution test in 52.5(*b*) above. '*Commodities*' are defined as tangible assets dealt with on a commodity exchange, excluding currency, securities, debts or other financial assets. '*Dealing*' includes dealing by way of futures contracts and traded options. Where the fund's income includes both commodity dealing profits and other income, its expenditure is apportioned on a just and reasonable basis and the non-commodity dealing business is treated as carried on by a separate company when determining what expenditure, if any, is deductible under *ICTA 1988, s 75* (management expenses of investment companies). See also (*a*) above for position where a commodity dealing fund operates equalisation arrangements. [*ICTA 1988, Sch 27 para 4; FA 1988, Sch 13 para 12*].

(*d*) **Wholly-owned commodity dealing subsidiaries.** In a situation within 52.4(C) above, the fund and the subsidiary dealing company are similarly treated as a single entity for the purposes of the distribution test. [*ICTA 1988, Sch 27 para 11*].

(*e*) **Investments in second tier funds.** In a situation within 52.4(A) above, the UK equivalent profits of the primary fund for the period are increased by its 'share' of the 'excess income' (if any) of the second tier fund in determining whether not less than 85% of the primary fund's UK equivalent profits are distributed. The '*excess income*' of the second tier fund is the amount by which its UK equivalent profits exceeds its distributions. There are provisions for apportioning excess income between periods on a time basis when the account periods of the primary and second tier funds do not coincide. The primary fund's '*share*' of the excess income is the proportion which the average value during its account period of its own holding of interests in the second tier fund bears to the average value of all interests in that fund. [*ICTA 1988, Sch 27 paras 6, 8, 9*].

52.7 CERTIFICATION PROCEDURE

Fund requesting certification. Application for certification as a distributing fund for an account period must be made within six months of the end of that period and should be sent to Inland Revenue Technical Division (Offshore Funds), Room 208, St John's House, Merton Road, Bootle, Merseyside, L69 9BB (tel 0151-922 6363 ext 2100). The application must be accompanied by a copy of the fund's accounts covering or including the account period for which certification is sought (including balance sheet, income and expenditure account, and, where prepared, the report for investors and the statement of source and application of funds), and provision of the following information in relation to the account period in question will assist the Board in its consideration of the application.

(1) The fund's full name.

(2) The account period for which certification is sought.

(3) A copy of any fund prospectus or explanatory memorandum.

(4) Details of any equalisation arrangements in force.

(5) An analysis of the fund's investment portfolio at the last accounting date, unless supplied in the accounts. This should include the percentage value of the fund's assets represented by each investment, and the percentage interest of the fund in each class of share capital of any unquoted company, and should identify any holding in other offshore funds (including whether they are considered to be distributing funds).

(6) A copy of the accounts of any wholly-owned subsidiary of the fund dealing either in commodities or in material interests in the fund.

(7) A copy of the accounts of any subsidiary management company in which the fund has an interest.

(8) A computation of the fund's UK equivalent profits or, failing this, a summary analysis of surpluses on realisation taken directly to the fund reserves.

(9) In respect of each class of share in the fund, the amount and date of each distribution (actual or projected) in respect of the account period, and the aggregate amount of deemed distributions made in respect of the period by way of equalisation.

(Revenue Press Release 31 July 1984).

Where the Board is satisfied that the necessary conditions are met it must certify the fund as a distribution fund for the period in respect of which application was made. The Board must give written notice if, after application, it determines that no certificate should be issued. It must also give notice where it appears that the accounts or other information provided do not make full and accurate disclosure of all relevant matters, in which case any notice of certification previously given is void. The fund may appeal to the Special Commissioners against Board decisions within ninety days. The Special Commissioners have jurisdiction to review any decision of the Board relevant to a ground of the appeal. [*ICTA 1988, Sch 27 paras 15, 16*].

Investor requesting certification. No appeal may be brought against a tax assessment (see 52.8 below) on the grounds that a fund should have been certified as a distributing fund in respect of an account period. However, where a fund does not apply for certification, an investor, who is assessed to tax for which he would not be liable if the fund were certified, may by notice in writing require the Board to take action with a view to determining whether the fund should be so certified.

If more than one request from an investor is received, the Board is taken to have complied with each if it complies with one.

Broadly, the procedure is as follows.

(i) The Board invites the fund to apply for certification. The time limit for application (see above) is then extended, if necessary, to 90 days from the date of the Board's invitation.

(ii) If the fund does not then apply for certification the Board must determine the question as if such application had been made having regard to any accounts or information provided by the investor.

(iii) If, after the Board has determined that the fund should not be certified, other accounts or information are provided which were not previously available, the Board must reconsider their determination.

(iv) The Board must notify the investor who requested the Board to take action of their decision.

(v) The Revenue has wide powers enabling it to disclose to interested parties information regarding Board or Special Commissioner decisions or details of any notice given to a fund regarding a lack of full and accurate disclosure of information (see above).

[*ICTA 1988, Sch 27 paras 17, 18, 20*].

Postponement of tax. There are provisions to enable an investor to apply for tax assessed to be postponed pending the Board's determination of the question of certification. [*ICTA 1988, Sch 27 para 19*].

52.8 CHARGE TO INCOME OR CORPORATION TAX OF OFFSHORE GAIN

Where a disposal to which the offshore fund rules apply (including a disposal of a holding in a distributing fund operating equalisation arrangements — see 52.2 above) gives rise to an 'offshore income gain', then subject to below, that gain is treated for all purposes as income assessable under Schedule D, Case VI arising to the investor at the time of disposal.

For the Revenue practice as regards identification of part disposals out of mixed holdings where a non-qualifying offshore fund has subsequently obtained distributor status, see Revenue Inspector's Manual, IM 4121.

The following provisions have effect in relation to income tax or corporation tax on offshore income gains as they have in relation to capital gains tax (or corporation tax) on chargeable gains.

(*a*) *TCGA 1992, s 2* (persons chargeable).

(*b*) *TCGA 1992, s 10* (gains accruing to non-residents and non-resident companies carrying on a trade in the UK through a branch or agency) except that assets need not be situated in the UK.

(*c*) *TCGA 1992, s 12* (foreign assets of UK resident or ordinarily resident persons with foreign domicile chargeable on remittance basis).

Charitable exemption applies similarly to that for capital gains (see 15.8 CHARITIES).

Where a disposal to which the offshore fund rules apply is one of settled property, any offshore income gain will escape the Schedule D, Case VI charge provided that the general administration of the trust is ordinarily carried on outside the UK and a majority of the trustees are not resident or not ordinarily resident in the UK. [*ICTA 1988, s 761; FA 1990, Sch 14 para 11*].

52.9 COMPUTATION OF OFFSHORE INCOME GAIN

The computation of the gain depends upon whether the disposal is of an interest in a non-qualifying fund (see 52.10 below) or of an interest involving an equalisation element (see 52.11 below).

52.10 **Disposals of interests in non-qualifying funds.** A *'material disposal'* (one to which the offshore fund rules apply otherwise than by virtue of the provisions regarding distributing funds operating equalisation arrangements — see 52.2 above and 52.11 below) gives rise to an *'offshore income gain'* equal to the 'unindexed gain' or, if less, the 'post-1983 gain'.

Subject to the modifications to the CGT rules mentioned in 52.1 above and to exceptions below, the *'unindexed gain'* is the gain calculated under CGT rules without indexation allowance and without regard to any income tax or corporation tax charge arising under the offshore fund rules. The exceptions are as follows.

(*a*) Where there has been indexation on an earlier disposal on a no gain/no loss basis within *TCGA 1992, s 56(2)*, the unindexed gain on the material disposal is computed as if indexation had not been available on the earlier disposal and, subject to that, as if the earlier disposal had produced neither gain nor loss.

(*b*) If the material disposal forms part of a transfer to which *TCGA 1992, s 162* applies (rollover relief on transfer of business), the unindexed gain is computed without any deduction falling to be made under that section in computing a chargeable gain.

(*c*) Any claim for relief under *FA 1980, s 79* (relief for gifts) does not affect the computation of the unindexed gain on the disposal. (See now *TCGA 1992, s 67*.)

(*d*) In the case of an insurance company carrying on life assurance business, where a profit from overseas life assurance business, attributable to a material disposal, is taken into account in the computation under *ICTA 1988, s 441*, the unindexed gain, if any, accruing on disposal is computed as if *TCGA 1992, s 37(1)* did not apply. For accounting periods beginning before 1 January 1992, this applies equally where a profit arising from general annuity business attributable to a material disposal is taken into account (or would be but for the provisions relating to offshore income gains of insurance companies (see 52.12 below)) in the computation under *ICTA 1988, s 436*.

(*e*) Where the computation of the unindexed gain would otherwise produce a loss, the unindexed gain is treated as nil so that no loss can arise on a material disposal.

[*ICTA 1988, Sch 28 paras 1–3, 5; FA 1990, Sch 7 para 7; FA 1991, Sch 7 para 10*].

'Post-1983 gains'. A person making a material disposal who acquired, or is treated as having acquired, his interest in the offshore fund before 1 January 1984, is treated as having disposed of and immediately reacquired his interest at market value on that date. The offshore income gain from 1 January 1984 to the date of disposal is then calculated in the ordinary way. If the person making the material disposal acquired his interest by way of a deemed no gain/no loss disposal (other than those arising by virtue of the indexation provisions of *FA 1982, s 86(5), Sch 13*) any previous owner's acquisition of the interest is treated as his acquisition of it. [*ICTA 1988, Sch 28 para 4*].

52.11 **Disposals involving an equalisation element.** A disposal is a '*disposal involving an equalisation element*' if it is a disposal to which the offshore fund rules apply by virtue of the provisions relating to distributing funds operating equalisation arrangements (see 52.2 above). Such a disposal gives rise to an '*offshore income gain*' of an amount equal, subject to below, to the 'equalisation element' relevant to the asset disposed of. [*ICTA 1988, Sch 28 para 6(1)(3)*].

The 'equalisation element' is the amount which would be credited to the fund's equalisation account in respect of accrued income if, on the date of the disposal, the asset disposed of were acquired by another person by way of 'initial purchase' (see 52.2 above). However, where the person making the disposal acquired the asset in question after the beginning of the account period by reference to which the accrued income is calculated, or at or before the beginning of that period where that period began before and ended after 1

January 1984, there are provisions to ensure that the equalisation element is reduced to exclude any part which accrued prior to either 1 January 1984 or to the investor's period of ownership. Where any of the accrued income represents commodity dealing profits (within 52.6(*c*) above) half of that income is left out of account in determining the equalisation element. [*ICTA 1988, Sch 28 para 6(2)(4)–(6)*].

'Part I gains'. Where the offshore income gain as computed above would exceed the 'Part I gain', the offshore income gain is reduced to the lower figure. If there is no 'Part I gain' there can be no offshore income gain. The '*Part I gain*' is, broadly, the amount which would be the offshore income gain on the disposal if the disposal were a 'material disposal' within 52.10 above (i.e. within *ICTA 1988, Sch 28 Part I*) as modified by certain consequential amendments. [*ICTA 1988, Sch 28 paras 7, 8*].

52.12 MISCELLANEOUS

Offshore income gains accruing to persons resident or domiciled abroad. There are consequential provisions made in connection with gains accruing to certain non-resident investors in offshore funds which modify, for the purposes of the offshore fund legislation, provisions relating to

(*a*) chargeable gains accruing to certain non-resident companies under *TCGA 1992, s 13*;

(*b*) gains of non-resident settlements under *TCGA 1992, ss 80–98*;

(*c*) avoidance of tax by the transfer of assets abroad under *ICTA 1988, ss 739, 740.*

To the extent that an offshore income gain is treated by virtue of (*a*) or (*b*) above as having accrued to any person resident or ordinarily resident in the UK, that gain is not deemed to be the income of any individual under *ICTA 1988, s 739* or *s 740* or any provision of *ICTA 1988, Pt XV* (settlements). [*ICTA 1988, s 762*].

Capital gains tax. There are provisions to prevent a double charge to tax when a disposal gives rise to both an offshore income gain and a chargeable gain for capital gains tax purposes.

Where an offshore income gain arises on a 'material disposal' within 52.10 above, that gain is deducted from the sum which would otherwise constitute the amount or value of the consideration in the calculation of the capital gain arising under *TCGA 1992* (on 'the 1992 Act disposal'), although the offshore gain is not to be taken into account in calculating the fraction under *TCGA 1992, s 42(2)* (part disposal).

Where the 1992 Act disposal forms part of a transfer within *TCGA 1992, s 162* (rollover relief on transfer of business wholly or partly for shares) then, in determining the amount of the deduction from the gain on the old assets, the offshore income gain is deducted from the value of the consideration received in exchange for the business.

Where an exchange of shares or securities constitutes a disposal of an interest in an offshore fund (see 52.1 and 52.2 above), the amount of any offshore income gain to which the disposal gives rise is treated as consideration for the new holding.

Where the offshore fund provisions apply to a disposal of an interest in a fund operating equalisation arrangements (see 52.2 above) and the disposal

(*a*) is not to the fund or to its managers in their capacity as such, and (*b*) gives rise to an offshore income gain in accordance with 52.11 above, and

(*c*) is followed subsequently by a distribution to either the person who made the disposal or to a person connected with him (within *ICTA 1988, s 839*, see 20 CONNECTED PERSONS) and that distribution is referable to the asset disposed of,

then the subsequent distribution (or distributions) is (are) reduced by the amount of the offshore income gain.

[*ICTA 1988, s 763*].

Proposed retrospective legislation. It is proposed to introduce measures in the 1998 Finance Bill, effective for disposals on or after 6 March 1998, removing the exemption from capital gains tax on the disposal of an interest in a trust which has at any time been an offshore trust, and where the interest disposed of originated in a trust which has at any time been an offshore trust. (Revenue Press Release 6 March 1998).

Offshore income gains of insurance companies. Income attributable to offshore income gains, so far as referable to general annuity business, is deducted from the receipts to be taken into account in computing the insurance company's profits from that business. [*ICTA 1988, s 437(2)(a); FA 1990, Sch 6 para 6*].

Offshore income gains of trustees. Any offshore income gains arising to trustees and assessable under Schedule D, Case VI will be charged at the rate applicable to trusts (see 81.5 SETTLEMENTS) for the year in question. [*ICTA 1988, s 764; FA 1993, Sch 6 para 13*]. However such tax paid is available for set-off against the amount assessable on discretionary trustees under *ICTA 1988, s 687(2)(b)* (see 81.5 SETTLEMENTS). [*ICTA 1988, s 687(3)(e)*].

Where trustees hold assets for a person who would be absolutely entitled as against the trustees but for being a minor, any offshore income gains liable to income tax which accrue on the disposal of those assets are deemed to be paid to that person for the purposes of the provisions regarding settlements on children in *ICTA 1988, s 660B* (for 1995/96 onwards — see 81.18 SETTLEMENTS) and, for earlier years, *ICTA 1988, ss 663–670* (see 81.23 SETTLEMENTS). [*ICTA 1988, s 660B(4), s 663(2) (repealed); FA 1995, Sch 17 para 1*].

52.13 *Example*

R, who is resident, ordinarily resident and domiciled in the UK, invests in non-qualifying offshore funds as follows.

(i) **ABC fund**		£
30.11.82	1,000 shares purchased at £10 per share	10,000
1.1.84	Market value per share = £20	20,000
1.4.01	On amalgamation with XYZ fund (an offshore fund which is not and has not been non-qualifying) the 1,000 original shares are exchanged for 2,000 new shares in XYZ which have a value of £15 per share	30,000

(ii) **DEF fund**		£
1.8.83	500 units purchased at £25 per unit	12,500
1.1.84	Market value per unit = £20	10,000
1.2.01	500 units sold for £40 per unit	20,000

R has offshore income gains and capital gains/losses in 2000/01 as follows.

Offshore income gains

Disposal on 1.2.01 of 500 DEF units

	Post-1983 gain	Unindexed gain
	£	£
Disposal proceeds	20,000	20,000
Market value at 1.1.84	10,000	
Cost		12,500
	£10,000	£7,500

As the unindexed gain is less than the post-1983 gain, the offshore income gain chargeable under Schedule D, Case VI is £7,500.

Disposal on 1.4.01 of 1,000 ABC shares

Disposal consideration	30,000	30,000
Market value at 1.1.84	20,000	
Cost		10,000
	£10,000	£20,000

The offshore income gain chargeable under Schedule D, Case VI is the £10,000 post-1983 gain as this is less than the unindexed gain.

Capital gains computation

Disposal on 1.2.01 of 500 DEF units

	£
Disposal proceeds	20,000
Offshore income gain	7,500
	12,500
Cost	12,500
Chargeable gain/allowable loss	Nil

Disposal on 1.4.01 of 1,000 ABC shares

There is no capital gains tax liability as the share exchange is not treated as a disposal for capital gains tax purposes. [*TCGA 1992, s 135*]. See Tolley's Capital Gains Tax.

Note

(*a*) The £10,000 offshore income gain arising on the exchange of ABC shares for XYZ shares will be treated as part of the acquisition cost for capital gains tax purposes on a subsequent disposal of XYZ shares (see 52.12 above).

53 Partnerships

[*ICTA 1988, ss 111–115*]

Cross-reference. See also 61 PERSONAL SERVICE COMPANIES ETC..

Simon's Direct Tax Service C3.2, E5.3.

Other sources. See Tolley's Partnership Taxation.

53.1 An English partnership is not a legal entity in the same way as a company, but a collection of separate persons. In Scotland, a firm is a legal person, see *Partnership Act 1890, s 4(2)*. However, the *Taxes Acts* are in general applied to Scottish partnerships in the same way as they are applicable to the rest of the UK.

For 1996/97 and earlier years as regards partnership trades, etc. commenced before 6 April 1994, the profits of a trade or profession carried on by a partnership are assessed jointly on the partnership (see 53.3 below) and to this extent it is treated for tax purposes as an entity distinct from its members. This does not apply for later years or as regards partnership trades, etc. commenced (or treated as commenced — see 53.6 below) after 5 April 1994; the taxable profits of the trade, etc. are apportioned between the partners, each of whom is then taxed on his own share. See also 78.5, 78.8, 78.9, 78.13, 78.16, 78.27 SELF-ASSESSMENT for provisions regarding partnership returns and general compliance; these apply to all partnerships, whenever trade commenced, but generally do not apply before 1996/97. For a general discussion of the tax treatment of partnerships, see *R v City of London Commrs (ex p Gibbs) HL 1942, 24 TC 221.*

Headings in this chapter are as follows.

53.2	Nature of partnership	53.12	Excess liability
53.3	Assessment and computation of profits	53.13	Wife as partner
53.4	— example	53.14	If a company is a partner
53.5	Apportionment between partners	53.15	Non-resident partners and partnerships controlled abroad
53.6	Changes in partners, etc.	53.16	Partnership retirement annuities
53.7	— example	53.17	Loans for purchasing interest in partnership
53.8	— partnership mergers and demergers	53.18	Capital gains tax on partnerships
53.9	Double succession	53.19	European Economic Interest Groupings
53.10	Losses		
53.11	Effect of partnership changes on losses and capital allowances		

53.2 NATURE OF PARTNERSHIP

Whether a partnership exists and, if so, from what date is a question of fact (*Williamson CS 1928, 14 TC 335; Calder v Allanson KB 1935, 19 TC 293*). The existence of a formal partnership agreement is not conclusive of the existence of a partnership (*Hawker v Compton KB 1922, 8 TC 306; Dickenson v Gross KB 1927, 11 TC 614*). Equally, whether a partnership can ante-date the date of the agreement is a question of fact (*Ayrshire Pullman Services v CIR CS 1929, 14 TC 754; Waddington v O'Callaghan KB 1931, 16 TC 187; Taylor v Chalklin KB 1945, 26 TC 463; Alexander Bulloch & Co v CIR CS 1976, 51 TC 563; Saywell v Pope Ch D 1979, 53 TC 40*).

Joint transactions may amount to a partnership or joint trading for tax purposes—see *Morden Rigg & Eskrigge v Monks CA 1923, 8 TC 450* (joint cotton transactions); *Gardner & Bowring Hardy v CIR CS 1930, 15 TC 602* (temporary joint coal merchanting); *Lindsay Woodward & Hiscox v CIR CS 1932, 18 TC 43* (joint transactions in whisky in violation of USA law); *Geo. Hall & Son v Platt Ch D 1954, 35 TC 440* (joint crop growing). See also *Fenston v Johnstone KB 1940, 23 TC 29.*

The *Limited Partnership Act 1907* allows the formation of limited partnerships, in which the liability of one or more (but not all) of the partners for the firm's debts is limited to a specified amount. See also 53.10 below.

Where a partnership terminated with open forward contracts, subsequently completed, it was held to continue trading notwithstanding that some of the partners had formed a new partnership to carry on a similar business (*Hillerns & Fowler v Murray CA 1932, 17 TC 77*). A doctor who sold his practice, helping the purchaser for a short time on a profit-sharing basis, was held not to be a partner (*Pratt v Strick KB 1932, 17 TC 459*).

A partnership set up for tax avoidance purposes may nevertheless be a true partnership (*Newstead v Frost HL 1980, 53 TC 525*).

A Rotary Club is not a partnership (*Blackpool Marton Rotary Club v Martin Ch D 1988, 62 TC 686*).

See 68.5 SCHEDULE A as regards joint ownership and exploitation of property.

See generally Revenue Inspector's Manual, IM 231–237.

Simon's Direct Tax Service. See **E5.302.**

53.3 ASSESSMENT AND COMPUTATION OF PROFITS

Pre-Finance Act 1994. For 1996/97 and earlier years as regards partnership trades, etc. commenced before 6 April 1994, the profits of a trade or profession carried on by a partnership are assessed in the first place as a whole, exactly as if it were the business of a sole trader. The assessment is computed in accordance with the basis period rules applicable to individuals (see 71.4 to 71.9, and, as regards 1996/97 only, 71.20, 71.24 SCHEDULE D, CASES I AND II by reference to the profits of the whole business. A 'joint assessment' is then made on the firm, and the Crown have the legal right (in default) to demand the whole of the tax from any partner. [*ICTA 1988, s 111 as originally enacted* and see *Stevens v Britten CA 1954, 33 ATC 399* and *Harrison v Willis CA 1965, 43 TC 61* (re deceased partner)]. See 53.12 below for excess liability.

Although 1996/97 is generally the first year of self-assessment, partnerships whose businesses commenced before 6 April 1994 continue to be assessable as separate entities for that year only (see also below). See Revenue Tax Bulletin April 1996 pp 293–298 for an article explaining the relationship between the 1996/97 partnership assessment and the self-assessment returns issued for that year to partnerships and partners, including *inter alia* details of proposed arrangements for allocating allowances, reliefs and rate bands and the effect of appeal and postponement applications against partnership assessments. See Revenue Tax Bulletin August 1997 pp 450–456 for an article answering a number of questions on self-assessment and on the transition to current year basis of assessment as it impacts on partnerships and partners. Points covered include the allocation of personal allowances etc., reliefs carried back from 1997/98 to 1996/97, an error in the Revenue tax calculation guide, returning details of partners' personal expenses, returning accounts information where a sole trader becomes a partnership and *vice versa*, a change of partners on 5 April 1997 with a continuation election, revision to 1996/97 assessment where business ceases before 5 April 1999, returning details of a continuing source of untaxed interest in the event of a pre-6 April 1997 change of partners, overlap relief on untaxed interest, returning details of taxed income, and capital allowances in partnerships involving both individuals and companies. A further article in Revenue Tax Bulletin February 1998 pp 513, 514 considers the Schedule A adjustments required where the accounts basis was used up to 1994/95, the fiscal year basis for 1995/96 and 1996/97, and the current year basis for 1997/98 onwards.

Post-Finance Act 1994. For 1994/95 and subsequent years as regards partnership trades, etc. commenced (or treated as commenced — see 53.6 below) after 5 April 1994 and for 1997/98 and subsequent years as regards partnership trades, etc. commenced on or before that date, the partnership is not generally treated for tax purposes as an entity which is separate and distinct from its members. The profits or losses of the trade, profession or business are computed in like manner as if the partnership were a UK resident individual (for 1994/95 only, as if it were an individual). Each individual's share (see 53.5 below) of the profit or loss (as adjusted for tax purposes) is taxed or relieved as if it derived from a trade, etc. (the deemed trade) carried on by him alone. The deemed trade is treated as commencing at the time the individual becomes a partner, or, if the actual trade, etc. was previously carried on by him alone, at the time the actual trade commenced. Similar rules apply as regards cessations.

The deemed trade is taxed in accordance with the normal basis period rules (see 71.11 to 71.19 SCHEDULE D, CASES I AND II). A change of partnership accounting date results in a change of basis period of a partner's deemed trade only if it would have resulted in a change of basis period of the partnership if the partnership were taxed as a separate entity (see 71.15 SCHEDULE D, CASES I AND II). Where a change of accounting date in the second or third year of assessment of a partner's deemed trade fails to result in a change of basis period (because the necessary conditions are not satisfied), the 'opening years' rules (see 71.12 SCHEDULE D, CASES I AND II) are modified so as to determine the basis period for that year of assessment by reference to the old accounting date.

[*ICTA 1988, s 111(1)–(5)(10)–(13); FA 1994, s 215(1); FA 1995, s 117(1)(a)(2)(4)*].

For partnership trades commenced before 6 April 1994, the transitional rules at 71.20 to 71.24 SCHEDULE D, CASES I AND II apply, although as regards 1996/97 they apply to the partnership as a separate entity.

See 78.2 SELF-ASSESSMENT as regards anti-avoidance measures preventing exploitation of the transitional provisions, and in particular 43.22 INTEREST PAYABLE as regards artificial changes in partnership financing arrangements.

Non-trading income. Where the post-Finance Act 1994 rules apply to a trading or professional partnership to which non-trading income (or a relievable non-trading loss) accrues, each individual partner is taxed on his share, computed by reference to profit sharing ratios for the period of account of the trade etc. In the case of untaxed income (as defined) from one or more sources, the normal basis period rules (see 71.11 to 71.19 SCHEDULE D, CASES I AND II) apply as if each individual's share of the income (or loss) were profits (or losses) of a second deemed trade carried on by him alone. The second deemed trade is treated as commencing at the time the individual becomes a partner and ceasing when he ceases to be a partner, with each source of the income treated as continuing until he ceases to be a partner. The same comments apply as above as regards changes of partnership accounting date. Where overlap relief (see 71.19) in respect of untaxed income falls to be deducted in a year of assessment (because of a change of accounting date or a permanent discontinuance of the second deemed trade) and the deduction exceeds the partner's share of untaxed income for that year, the excess is deductible in computing his income for that year. [*ICTA 1988, s 111(7)–(9)(12)(13); FA 1994, s 215(1); FA 1995, s 117(1)(a)(2)*]. Strictly, in the case of income from property of a partnership commenced before 6 April 1994, the fiscal year basis applies for 1995/96 and 1996/97 (see 68.5

SCHEDULE A). If, however, an accounts basis (whether current or preceding year) was adopted for 1994/95 for Schedule A (or furnished lettings) income, the current year accounts basis may in practice be applied for 1995/96 and 1996/97 (to avoid a switch to the fiscal year basis just for those two years). (Revenue Tax Bulletin August 1995 p 242). See also 68.5 SCHEDULE A. For the treatment of any transitional adjustment needed because of gaps between the basis periods for 1994/95 and 1995/96, see generally 68.22 SCHEDULE A and, for further guidance, Revenue Tax Bulletin February 1996 pp 283–285. These special rules for non-trading untaxed income apply only where the associated trade or profession is carried on *in partnership*, so that, for example, if one partner is left to carry on the partnership business as a sole trader, his second notional trade ceases at that time and untaxed income is subsequently taxed on a fiscal year basis.

General. The assignment by a partner of part of his share in the partnership was ineffective for the purpose of displacing his liability to income tax on that part of his share of partnership profits (*Hadlee and Another v Commissioner of Inland Revenue (NZ) PC, [1993] STC 294*).

See *MacKinlay v Arthur Young McClelland Moores & Co HL 1989, 62 TC 704* as to prohibition on deduction of certain payments made to partners in connection with partnership business.

If a **company** is a partner, see 53.14 below.

Capital gains which arise from the disposal of partnership assets are charged on the partners separately. [*TCGA 1992, s 59; FA 1995, Sch 29 Pt VIII(16)*]. See Tolley's Capital Gains Tax.

Adjustments to profits will include items below.

(i) **Law costs** and stamps re partnership deeds are not normally permissible deductions.

(ii) **Partners'** salaries, domestic and personal expenses, interest credited on capital and any benefit of financial value given to a partner are not permissible deductions for tax purposes, being regarded as part of the taxable profits. See e.g. *PDC Copyprint (South) v George (Sp C 141), [1997] SSCD 326* as regards partners' salaries. But this does not necessarily apply to payments to a partner for goods or services 'altogether disconnected with the partnership business as such' and where the firm's premises are owned by a partner, *bona fide* rent paid to him under legal agreement is a proper deduction for tax purposes (*Heastie v Veitch CA 1933, 18 TC 305*). Contributions towards partners' removal expenses, where partner moved in the interests of the firm, are not deductible (*MacKinlay v Arthur Young McClelland Moores & Co HL 1989, 62 TC 704*).

(iii) **Taxed charges,** payable out of firm's income, are added back in computing the firm's taxable profits, and tax on them has to be accounted for. The Revenue accept the view that a partner's personal taxed investment income is available to cover his share of partnership charges. Should there be an excess of partnership taxed charges over partnership income, an assessment under *ICTA 1988, s 350* would therefore be made only to the extent that each individual partner's share of the excess is not covered by his own private investment income.

See also 71 SCHEDULE D, CASES I AND II for adjustments to profits generally and 75.24 SCHEDULE E for director's fees received by professional partnership.

Simons' Direct Tax Service. See **E5.311** *et seq.*.

53.4 *Example*

Partnership trading and investment income under current year basis

X and Y began to trade in partnership on 1 July 1996, preparing first accounts to 30 September 1997 and sharing profits equally. Z joins the firm as an equal partner on 1 October 1998. Y leaves the firm on 31 March 2000. Accounts are prepared to that date to ascertain Y's entitlement, but the accounting date then reverts to 30 September and the partnership does not give notice to the Revenue of a change of accounting date, so that there is no change of basis period. In addition to trading profits, the partnership had a source of lettings income which ceased in September 1999, and is in receipt of both taxed and untaxed interest, the latter from a source commencing in October 1997. Taxed interest is received on 31 March each year. Revised figures as adjusted for tax purposes are as follows.

	Schedule D, Case I	Schedule A	Schedule D, Case III	Taxed interest (gross)
	£	£	£	£
15 months to 30.9.97	30,000	4,500	—	750
Year to 30.9.98	24,000	5,000	1,000	1,500
Year to 30.9.99	39,000	3,000	600	300
6 months to 31.3.00	19,500	—	225	165
6 months to 30.9.00	14,000	—	140	—

The partners' shares of taxable income from the partnership for the years 1996/97 to 2000/01 inclusive are as follows.

Schedule D, Case 1	X	Y	Z
	£	£	£
1996/97			
1.7.96–5.4.97 (£30,000 × $\frac{9}{15}$)	9,000	9,000	
1997/98			
1.10.96–30.9.97 (£30,000 × $\frac{12}{15}$)	12,000*	12,000*	
* Overlap relief accrued:			
1.10.96–5.4.97 (£30,000 × $\frac{6}{15}$)	6,000	6,000	
1998/99			
Y/e 30.9.98	12,000	12,000	
1.10.98–5.4.99 (£39,000 × $\frac{6}{12}$ × $\frac{1}{3}$)			6,500
1999/2000			
Y/e 30.9.99	13,000	13,000	13,000*
1.10.99–31.3.00		6,500	
		19,500	
Less overlap relief		(6,000)	
		13,500	
* Overlap relief accrued			
1.10.98–5.4.99 (as above)			6,500

Schedule D, Case 1	X	Y	Z
	£	£	£
2000/01			
Y/e 30.9.00			
1.10.99–31.3.00	6,500		6,500
1.4.00–30.9.00	7,000		7,000
	13,500		13,500
Schedule A			
1996/97			
1.7.96–5.4.97 (£4,500 × $\frac{9}{15}$)	1,350	1,350	
1997/98			
1.10.96–30.9.97 (£4,500 × $\frac{12}{15}$)	1,800*	1,800*	
* Overlap relief accrued			
1.10.96–5.4.97 (£4,500 × $\frac{6}{15}$)	900	900	
1998/99			
Y/e 30.9.98	2,500	2,500	
1.10.98–5.4.99 (£3,000 × $\frac{6}{12}$ × $\frac{1}{3}$)			500
1999/2000			
Y/e 30.9.99	1,000	1,000	1,000*
1.10.99–31.3.00		—	
		1,000	
Less overlap relief		(900)	
		100	
* Overlap relief accrued			
1.10.98–5.4.99 (as above)			500
Schedule D, Case III			
1998/99			
Y/e 30.9.98	500	500	
1.10.98–5.4.99 (£600 × $\frac{6}{12}$ × $\frac{1}{3}$)			100
1999/2000			
Y/e 30.9.99	200	200	200*
1.10.99–31.3.00		75	
		275	
* Overlap relief accrued			
1.10.98–5.4.99 (as above)			100

Schedule D, Case 1	X	Y	Z
	£	£	£
2000/01			
Y/e 30.9.00			
1.10.99–31.3.00	75		75
1.4.00–30.9.00	70		70
	145		145
Taxed interest			
1996/97 (received 31.3.97)	375	375	
1997/98 (received 31.3.98)	750	750	
1998/99 (received 31.3.99)	100	100	100
1999/2000 (received 31.3.00)	55	55	55
2000/01	**	—	**

** Each to be based on one-half of interest received 31.3.01.

Note

Taxed investment income is taxed on a fiscal year basis as for an individual, but is apportioned between the partners according to their shares for the accounting period in which the income arises.

53.5 **APPORTIONMENT BETWEEN PARTNERS**

Pre-Finance Act 1994. For 1996/97 and earlier years as regards partnership trades, etc. commenced before 6 April 1994, apportionment of the assessment on the firm is made between the individual partners according to their shares under the partnership agreement *for the year of assessment.*

Where partners have salaries, fluctuating commission or interest on capital, plus certain percentages of the balance of profits, each partner's proportion of the statutory assessment on the firm is his actual salary, commission and interest for the year of assessment, plus his percentage of the balance of the assessment after deducting all these salaries etc. This has been established in cases relating to appeals against super-tax assessments, including *Rutherford v CIR CS 1926, 10 TC 683* and *Lewis v CIR CA 1933, 18 TC 174.*

Each partner is entitled to have all reliefs due to him personally deducted from his share [*ICTA 1988, s 277 as originally enacted*] and the tax payable by the firm is reduced accordingly. If this does not exhaust all his allowances, any balance can be set against other income of his or, if the firm receives untaxed income or rents assessable under Schedule A, any unexhausted balance of allowances due to a partner may be set against his share of these.

Post-Finance Act 1994. For 1994/95 and subsequent years as regards partnership trades, etc. commenced (or treated as commenced — see 53.6 below) after 5 April 1994 and for 1997/98 and subsequent years as regards partnership trades, etc. commenced on or before that date, the taxable profits of the partnership for a period of account are apportioned between the individual members in accordance with their shares under the partnership agreement *for that period.* [*ICTA 1988, s 111(3); FA 1994, s 215(1)(4)(5); FA 1995, s 117].* See 53.3 above as regards non-trading income.

General. The profit share of a partner actively engaged in the business is 'earned income', unlike that of a 'sleeping partner'. (In practice, however, it is treated as 'earned' whenever there is some degree of active participation and regular oversight.)

53.6 CHANGES IN PARTNERS, ETC.

Pre-Finance Act 1994. The following provisions apply for 1996/97 and earlier years as regards partnership trades, etc. commenced before 6 April 1994. Note that a deemed cessation and recommencement after 5 April 1994 (and before 6 April 1997) will immediately bring the 'new' partnership into the post-Finance Act 1994 regime.

In the event of any change in the persons comprising the partnership, the business is automatically treated as having ceased and a new business commenced at the date of change. [*ICTA 1988, s 113(1) as originally enacted*]. This means that the cessation and new business provisions set out in 71.3 SCHEDULE D, CASES I AND II will apply, subject to the special rules referred to below.

But, if *all partners* (or their executors) *before and after the change* (provided always there is one partner common to both periods) jointly so elect by notice to the inspector within two years of the change the continuing basis will apply. [*ICTA 1988, s 113(2) as originally enacted*]. The profit assessable for the year of change is then computed as if there had been no change, and is apportioned 'as may be just' (normally on a time basis) and the apportioned amounts assessed separately on the old and new firms. [*ICTA 1988, s 113(3) as originally enacted*]. Such an election can be made in the case of, e.g.

(*a*) a sole proprietor taking in a partner, or

(*b*) all partners going out except one, or

(*c*) death of a partner,

but not where there is

(i) a complete change of all the persons carrying on the business, or

(ii) dissolution of partnership, each partner taking over part of the business.

A claim outside the two-year limit may be admitted where it is made as soon as is reasonably possible in all the circumstances and where it is late because of either

(A) a relevant and uncorrected Revenue error resulting in the partners or their agent being misled as to whether the requirements of the legislation had been met, or

(B) the unavailability at a crucial time, and for unforeseeable reasons (e.g. serious illness), of a required signatory (or of an agent for such a signatory where no-one else could reasonably be expected to stand in his shoes), or

(C) some other difficulty in obtaining the required signatures, provided that, before the expiry of the time limit, the Revenue had been clearly notified that each signatory had decided to make the election and been given the reasons why the election could not be made in time.

An election will not be admitted where it was made late through oversight or negligence, or because of the temporary refusal of a partner to sign it, or where it was deliberately delayed because its effect on the partners' taxation liabilities was unclear when the time limit expired. (Revenue Pamphlet IR 131, SP 9/92, 23 November 1992). See also Revenue Tax Bulletin February 1993 p 56 for an example of a Revenue decision on a late claim.

Where a partner has genuinely disappeared and all reasonable attempts to trace him or her have been exhausted, an election signed by the remaining partners will be accepted provided that they sign an indemnity. (Revenue Inspector's Manual, IM 253).

Where an election is made it may be revoked provided the notice of revocation is signed by all interested parties and given within the limit of two years for making the election. (Revenue Pamphlet IR 131, A4).

But if a company is a partner, see 53.14(iii) below.

See 71.9 SCHEDULE D, CASES I AND II for concession on death of husband or wife who were in partnership.

Blanket continuation elections. By concession, a 'blanket' continuation election, covering all future partnership changes (until any or all of the partners withdraw from the arrangement), will be accepted where

(I) the firm has at least 50 partners, or at least 20 non-UK resident partners, immediately after the first change under the election,

(II) new partners add their names to the election, and

(III) the Revenue are indemnified by all partners before the first change under the election, and by all subsequent new partners, against any loss of tax arising from a claim by any partner or former partner that the election was invalid so that the cessation basis should have been applied to a particular change or changes.

(Revenue Pamphlet IR 1, A80).

No continuation election. Where an election under *section 113(2)* as above could be, but is not, made in respect of a partnership change (other than a change from sole trader to partnership or vice versa) before 6 April 1994, the commencement rules of assessment (see 71.4 SCHEDULE D, CASES I AND II) are revised. For the year of assessment of the change and the following three years, the new partnership is assessed on the actual profits arising in the year of assessment in question. The new partners may, in addition, elect (within seven years after the end of the fifth year of assessment) for both the fifth and sixth years of assessment to be assessed on the actual profits arising in those years. [*ICTA 1988, s 61(4), s 62(4)(5)*].

Post-Finance Act 1994. For 1994/95 and subsequent years as regards partnership trades, etc. commenced (or treated under the above provisions as commenced) after 5 April 1994 and for 1997/98 and subsequent years as regards partnership trades, etc. commenced on or before that date, a partnership trade, etc. is *not* treated as discontinued and recommenced on a change of partner providing there is at least one continuing partner (which also covers the situation where a sole trader begins to carry on the trade in partnership or a former partner begins to carry it on as a sole trader). The election under *section 113(2)* for the continuing basis is no longer relevant. [*ICTA 1988, s 113; FA 1994, s 215(4)(5), s 216(1)(2)*]. New partners are taxed on their profit share under the opening years provisions at 71.12 SCHEDULE D, CASES I AND II and outgoing partners are taxed on their share under the closing year provisions at 71.17 SCHEDULE D, CASES I AND II (see also 53.3 above).

Simon's Direct Tax Service. See **E5.312.**

53.7 *Examples*

General

P, Q and R have carried on a profession in partnership for a number of years, sharing profits in the ratio 2:2:1. Accounts are made up to 30 June. P leaves the partnership on 30 June 1994 and Q and R share profits 3:2 for the year to 30 June 1995 and equally thereafter. On 30 June 1997, Q leaves the partnership and on 1 July 1997, S becomes a partner. Profits are then shared between R and S in the ratio 2:1.

Results for relevant years up to 30 June 1999 are as follows.

Year ended	Partners' salaries				Adjusted Profit
	P	Q	R	S	
	£	£	£	£	£
30.6.91	9,000	9,000	4,500	—	40,000
30.6.92	12,000	12,000	6,000	—	70,000
30.6.93	4,000	4,000	2,000	—	72,000
30.6.94	18,000	13,000	11,500	—	60,000
30.6.95	—	12,500	12,500	—	80,000
30.6.96	—	12,000	17,000	—	85,000
30.6.97	—	4,000	11,000	—	95,000
30.6.98	—	—	5,000	—	101,000
30.6.99	—	—	2,000	—	110,000

The adjusted profit figures above are after adding back partners' salaries. There are no capital allowances to be taken into account.

The tax position for the years 1992/93 to 1999/2000 is as follows.

(i) if continuation election made on change in partners on 30.6.94

Assessments on partnership of P, Q & R

		£
1992/93 (y/e 30.6.91)		40,000
1993/94 (y/e 30.6.92)		70,000
1994/95 (y/e 30.6.93 × $\frac{3}{12}$)		18,000

Assessments on partnership of Q & R

1994/95 (y/e 30.6.93 × $\frac{9}{12}$)		54,000
1995/96 (y/e 30.6.94)		60,000
1996/97	£	
Y/e 30.6.95	80,000	
Y/e 30.6.96	85,000	
	£165,000	
	£165,000 × $\frac{12}{24}$ =	82,500

Taxable profits of Q, R & S individually from 1997/98

	Q	R	S
	£	£	£
1997/98			
Y/e 30.6.97			
Profits £(95,000 – 11,000 – 4,000)	40,000	40,000	
Salaries	4,000	11,000	
	44,000	51,000	
1.7.97–5.4.98			
£((101,000 – 5,000) × $\frac{1}{3}$ × $\frac{9}{12}$)			24,000
Less transitional overlap relief:			
(1.7.96–5.4.97 — £44,000 × $\frac{9}{12}$)	33,000		
Schedule D, Case II	£11,000	£51,000*	£24,000

	Q	R	S
	£	£	£
* Transitional overlap relief accrued: (1.7.96–5.4.97 — £51,000 × $\frac{9}{12}$)	—	£38,250	—
1998/99			
Y/e 30.6.98			
Profits £(101,000 – 5,000)		64,000	32,000
Salary		5,000	—
Schedule D, Case II		£69,000	£32,000*
* Overlap relief accrued: (1.7.97–5.4.98 as above)			£24,000
1999/2000			
Y/e 30.6.99			
Profits £(110,000 – 2,000)		72,000	36,000
Salary		2,000	—
Schedule D, Case II		£74,000	£36,000

(ii) if no continuation election made on change in partners on 30.6.94

Assessments on partnership of P, Q & R

	Preceding year	Actual		
	£		£	£
1992/93	40,000	$\frac{3}{12}$ × 30.6.92	17,500	
		$\frac{9}{12}$ × 30.6.93	54,000	
				71,500
1993/94	70,000	$\frac{3}{12}$ × 30.6.93	18,000	
		$\frac{9}{12}$ × 30.6.94	45,000	
				63,000
	£110,000			£134,500

Higher figure of the two is £134,500, so assessments on actual.

1994/95	$\frac{3}{12}$ × 30.6.94	£15,000

Taxable profits of Q, R & S individually from 1994/95

	Q	R	S
	£	£	£
1994/95			
1.7.94–5.4.95			
Profits £(80,000 – 25,000) × $\frac{9}{12}$	24,750	16,500	
Salaries × $\frac{9}{12}$	9,375	9,375	
Schedule D, Case II	£34,125	£25,875	

	Q	R	S
	£	£	£
1995/96			
Y/e 30.6.95			
Profits £(80,000 – 25,000)	33,000	22,000	
Salaries	12,500	12,500	
Schedule D, Case II	£45,500*	£34,500*	
* Overlap relief accrued:			
(1.7.94–5.4.95 as above)	£34,125	£25,875	
1996/97			
Y/e 30.6.96			
Profits £(85,000 – 29,000)	28,000	28,000	
Salaries	12,000	17,000	
Schedule D, Case II	£40,000	£45,000	
1997/98			
Y/e 30.6.97			
Profits £(95,000 – 15,000)	40,000	40,000	
Salaries	4,000	11,000	
	44,000	51,000	
1.7.97–5.4.98			
£((101,000 – 5,000) × $\frac{1}{3}$ × $\frac{9}{12}$)			24,000
Less overlap relief (see 1995/96)	34,125		
Schedule D, Case II	£9,875	£51,000	£24,000
1998/99			
Y/e 30.6.98			
Profits £(101,000 – 5,000)		64,000	32,000
Salary		5,000	—
Schedule D, Case II		£69,000	£32,000*
* Overlap relief accrued:			
(1.7.97–5.4.98 as above)			£24,000
1999/2000			
Y/e 30.6.99			
Profits £(110,000 – 2,000)		72,000	36,000
Salary		2,000	—
Schedule D, Case II		£74,000	£36,000

Partnership assessments are allocated between partners as follows.

(iii) if continuation election made (see (i) above)

Partnership of P, Q & R

	P	Q	R	Total
	£	£	£	£
1992/93				
Salaries $\frac{3}{12} \times$ 30.6.92	3,000	3,000	1,500	7,500
$\frac{9}{12} \times$ 30.6.93	3,000	3,000	1,500	7,500
				15,000
Balance 2:2:1	10,000	10,000	5,000	25,000
Division of assessment	£16,000	£16,000	£8,000	£40,000
1993/94				
Salaries $\frac{3}{12} \times$ 30.6.93	1,000	1,000	500	2,500
$\frac{9}{12} \times$ 30.6.94	13,500	9,750	8,625	31,875
				34,375
Balance 2:2:1	14,250	14,250	7,125	35,625
Division of assessment	£28,750	£25,000	£16,250	£70,000
1994/95				
Salaries $\frac{3}{12} \times$ 30.6.94	4,500	3,250	2,875	10,625
Balance 2:2:1	2,950	2,950	1,475	7,375
Division of assessment	£7,450	£6,200	£4,350	£18,000
Partnership of Q & R				
1994/95				
Salaries $\frac{9}{12} \times$ 30.6.95		9,375	9,375	18,750
Balance 3:2		21,150	14,100	35,250
Division of assessment		£30,525	£23,475	£54,000
1995/96				
Salaries $\frac{3}{12} \times$ 30.6.95		3,125	3,125	6,250
Balance to 30.6.95 at 3:2		5,250	3,500	8,750
				15,000
Salaries $\frac{9}{12} \times$ 30.6.96		9,000	12,750	21,750
Balance from 1.7.95 at 1:1		11,625	11,625	23,250
Division of assessment		£29,000	£31,000	£60,000

	P	Q	R	Total
	£	£	£	£
1996/97				
Salaries $\frac{3}{12}$ × 30.6.96		3,000	4,250	7,250
$\frac{9}{12}$ × 30.6.97		3,000	8,250	11,250
				18,500
Balance 1:1		32,000	32,000	64,000
Division of assessment		£38,000	£44,500	£82,500

(iv) if continuation election not made (see (ii) above)

Partnership of P, Q & R

	P	Q	R	Total
	£	£	£	£
1992/93				
Salaries $\frac{3}{12}$ × 30.6.92	3,000	3,000	1,500	7,500
$\frac{9}{12}$ × 30.6.93	3,000	3,000	1,500	7,500
				15,000
Balance 2:2:1	22,600	22,600	11,300	56,500
	£28,600	£28,600	£14,300	£71,500
1993/94				
Salaries $\frac{3}{12}$ × 30.6.93	1,000	1,000	500	2,500
$\frac{9}{12}$ × 30.6.94	13,500	9,750	8,625	31,875
				34,375
Balance 2:2:1	11,450	11,450	5,725	28,625
Division of assessment	£25,950	£22,200	£14,850	£63,000
1994/95				
Salaries $\frac{3}{12}$ × 30.6.94	4,500	3,250	2,875	10,625
Balance 2:2:1	1,750	1,750	875	4,375
Division of assessment	£6,250	£5,000	£3,750	£15,000

A comparison can now be made of taxable profits under the two options under consideration.

(v) If continuation election made in respect of 30.6.94 change

	P	Q	R	S	Total
	£	£	£	£	£
1992/93	16,000	16,000	8,000		40,000 (1)
1993/94	28,750	25,000	16,250		70,000 (1)
1994/95 (PQR)	7,450	6,200	4,350		18,000 (1)
1994/95 (QR)		30,525	23,475		54,000 (1)
1995/96		29,000	31,000		60,000 (1)
1996/97		38,000	44,500		82,500 (1)

	P	Q	R	S	Total
	£	£	£	£	£
1997/98		11,000	51,000	24,000	86,000 (2)
1998/99			69,000	32,000	101,000 (2)
1999/2000			74,000	36,000	110,000 (2)
	£52,200	£155,725	£321,575	£92,000	£621,500
Overlap relief c/f			£38,250	£24,000	£62,250

(1) = Partnership to be assessed in one sum.

(2) = Partners to be taxed individually on their shares.

(vi) If no continuation election made in respect of 30.6.94 change

	P	Q	R	S	Total
	£	£	£	£	£
1992/93	28,600	28,600	14,300		71,500 (1)
1993/94	25,950	22,200	14,850		63,000 (1)
1994/95 (PQR)	6,250	5,000	3,750		15,000 (1)
1994/95 (QR)		34,125	25,875		60,000 (2)
1995/96		45,500	34,500		80,000 (2)
1996/97		40,000	45,000		85,000 (2)
1997/98		9,875	51,000	24,000	84,875 (2)
1998/99			69,000	32,000	101,000 (2)
1999/2000			74,000	36,000	110,000 (2)
	£60,800	£185,300	£332,275	£92,000	£670,375
Overlap relief c/f			£25,875	£24,000	£49,875

(1) = Partnership to be assessed in one sum.

(2) = Partners to be taxed individually on their shares.

Summary

The difference between (v) and (vi) above, after taking overlap relief into account, is £61,250 ((£621,500 – £62,250) – (£670,375 – £49,875)).

With a continuation election, 12 months' profits escape tax, being half the profits for the two-year period to 30.6.96, £82,500. In addition, 9 months' profits (1.7.96 to 5.4.97) attract transitional overlap relief, £71,250. Total drop-out of profits is thus £153,750 (£82,500 + £71,250).

With no continuation election, 21 months' profits escape tax, being profits for the period 1.7.90 to 5.4.92, a total of £92,500.

The difference in profits escaping tax is thus proved to be £61,250 (£153,750 – £92,500).

Transition to current year basis — new partner joining in 1996/97

A and B have traded in partnership since before 6 April 1994, preparing accounts to 30 June and sharing profits equally. C joins the firm on 1 January 1997 with a one-third profit share.

The three partners make a continuation election. Profits as adjusted for tax purposes for relevant years are as follows.

	£
Year to 30.6.94	36,000
Year to 30.6.95	38,000
Year to 30.6.96	42,000
Year to 30.6.97	45,000
Year to 30.6.98	48,000

Assessments will be as follows.

	Total	A	B	C
	£	£	£	£
Partnership assessments				
1995/96 (y/e 30.6.94)	36,000	18,000	18,000	N/A
1996/97 (2 yrs to 30.6.96 × $\frac{1}{2}$ = 40,000)				
6.4.96 to 31.12.96($\frac{3}{4}$)	30,000	15,000	15,000	N/A
1.1.97 to 5.4.97 ($\frac{1}{4}$)	10,000	3,334	3,333	3,333
	40,000	18,334	18,333	3,333
Individual self-assessments				
1997/98				
A and B (y/e 30.6.97)				
1.7.96 to 31.12.96 × $\frac{1}{2}$		11,250	11,250	
1.1.97 to 30.6.97 × $\frac{1}{3}$		7,500	7,500	
		18,750	18,750	
C (1.1.97 to 31.12.97 × $\frac{1}{3}$) see note (*a*) below				
1.1.97 to 30.6.97 × $\frac{1}{3}$				7,500
1.7.97 to 31.12.97 × $\frac{1}{3}$				8,000
				15,500
1998/99				
A and B (y/e 30.6.98 × $\frac{1}{3}$)		16,000	16,000	
C (y/e 30.6.98 × $\frac{1}{3}$)				16,000
Overlap relief				
A and B (Transitional overlap relief)				
1.7.96 to 5.4.97 — $\frac{9}{12}$ × £18,750 each		14,063	14,063	
C				
Transitional overlap relief:				
1.1.97 to 5.4.97 — $\frac{3}{6}$ × £7,500				3,750
Actual overlap relief:				
1.7.97 to 31.12.97				8,000
Total overlap relief (overlap period — 9 months each)		14,063	14,063	11,750

Notes

(*a*) 1997/98 is only C's second tax year of trading and his basis period must be determined in accordance with the opening years rules at 71.12 SCHEDULE D, CASES I AND II. It is thus his first twelve months of trading. This is the case even though the concept of partners' individual basis periods did not apply to C's first year, 1996/97.

(*b*) C's overlap relief is partly transitional and partly the result of a genuine overlap of basis periods. The distinction would be of importance only if the anti-avoidance rules at 71.22 SCHEDULE D, CASES I AND II came into play.

53.8 **Partnership mergers and demergers.** Where two businesses carried on in partnership merge, it is a question of fact whether the new partnership has succeeded to the businesses of the old partnerships, or whether the old businesses have ceased and a new business resulted from the merger which is different in nature from either of the two old businesses. Disparity of size between the old partnerships will not of itself be a significant matter. Clearly the former is more likely to be the case where the two old businesses carried on the same sort of activities, and the latter where they were themselves different in nature. Where the former is the case, *section 113* applies. Under the pre-Finance Act 1994 rules (see 53.6 above), the partners could elect in respect of one or both (or neither) of the old businesses for the continuation basis to apply, with apportionment of the profits of the new partnership where an election is made for only one of the old businesses. Under the post-Finance Act 1994 rules, both businesses are treated as continuing in these circumstances. Where the new partnership does not succeed to the old businesses, *section 113* has no application.

Similar considerations apply where a partnership is divided up and two or more partnerships are formed, in determining whether any of the separate partnerships has succeeded to the business of the original partnership. *section 113* will apply, and a continuation election (where still relevant) be available, only where one of the businesses carried on after the division is so large in relation to the rest as to be recognisably the business previously carried on. If, however, it appears to the Revenue that a demerger has taken place for fiscal reasons, and is more apparent than real, they might wish to argue that the same trade is carried on after the demerger as before (so that, under the pre-Finance Act 1994 rules, a *section 113(2)* election could be made, with the result that the special rules referred to in 53.6 above would apply).

Similar principles apply where sole traders merge into partnership or a partnership business is demerged and carried on by sole traders.

(Revenue Pamphlet IR 131, SP 9/86, 10 December 1986 as revised).

See *C Connelly & Co v Wilbey Ch D 1992, 65 TC 208* for a case in which it was held that neither part of a demerged partnership succeeded to the former partnership trade (and in which legal costs relating to the dissolution were disallowed).

The amalgamation of two sole traders into partnership in *Humphries v Cook KB 1934, 19 TC 121* was held to result in the commencement of a new business and the cessation of both the old businesses, but this is applied sparingly by the Revenue, mainly where the new partnership business is of a different nature from those previously carried on.

For a discussion of the general principles outlined above and their interaction with current year basis of assessment and the transition thereto, see Revenue booklet SAT 1(1995), chapter 8. Under the post-Finance Act 1994 rules in 53.6 above, a continuation basis automatically applies on a *partial* change of ownership of a *continuing* business.

See 62.2 POST-CESSATION ETC. RECEIPTS AND EXPENDITURE for change in the basis of accounting.

Simon's Direct Tax Service. See **E5.313**.

53.9 **DOUBLE SUCCESSION**

Where there has been a change in partners in respect of which election for continuation basis has been given (where relevant — see 53.6 above), and between that change and the end of the second year of assessment following there is either a permanent discontinuance, or a further change treated as such, all the provisions of *ICTA 1988, s 63 as originally enacted* (as to basis of assessment for the final period and for the two years preceding discontinuance) apply to that discontinuance as if the earlier change had not occurred. [*ICTA 1988, s 113(3)(b) as originally enacted*]. A retiring partner who joins in a continuation election should therefore bear in mind that if a further change occurs within two years and a continuation election is not made on that occasion, there may be an increase in his assessable profits under *section 63.*

53.10 **LOSSES**

Partnership losses, as computed for tax purposes, are apportioned between the individual partners in the same way as are profits. The loss of each partner may (*a*) be set off against his other income [*ICTA 1988, s 380*] or (*b*) be carried forward against his share of subsequent profits of the partnership [*ICTA 1988, s 385*], including in certain circumstances where a partnership business is converted into a company [*ICTA 1988, s 386*] or (*c*) be used in a terminal loss claim. [*ICTA 1988, s 388*]. For further details of these loss claims, see under 46 LOSSES.

Similarly, losses made by a partner in other businesses may be set-off against his share of partnership profits under *section 380.*

Where the firm as a whole makes a profit (as computed for tax purposes) but, after the allocation of prior shares to other partners the result is that *an individual partner makes a loss*, the practice is not to allow that partner to claim relief for that loss, either against his other income under *section 380* or by carrying it forward under *section 385*; and that where there is a partnership loss, the aggregate amount available to loss-making partners cannot exceed that loss.

Limited partnerships. In *Reed v Young HL 1986, 59 TC 196*, it was held that the share of the loss of a limited partner (see 53.2 above) for *section 380* purposes was not restricted to the amount of her contribution to the partnership capital. The decision was, however, reversed by legislation. Where an individual 'limited partner' in a partnership sustains a loss or incurs capital expenditure in the partnership trade, or pays interest in connection with it, relief may be restricted. An allowance for capital expenditure which creates or augments a trading loss under *ICTA 1988, s 383(1)* (see 46.7 LOSSES) is for this purpose treated as made for the year of loss, and not for the year of assessment for which the year of loss is the basis year.

A '*limited partner*' is a partner carrying on a trade:

(*a*) as a limited partner in a limited partnership registered under the *Limited Partnerships Act 1907*; or

(*b*) as a general partner in a partnership, but who is not entitled to take part in the management of the trade, and who is entitled to have his liabilities for debts or obligations incurred for trade purposes discharged or reimbursed by some other person, in whole or beyond a certain limit; or

(*c*) who, under the law of any territory outside the UK, is not entitled to take part in the management of the trade, and is not liable beyond a certain limit for debts or obligations incurred for trade purposes.

The restriction applies to any excess of the loss, etc. sustained by, or allowance for expenditure made to, a limited partner in respect of a trade as above for a year of assessment over his 'contribution' to the trade at the end of that year of assessment (or at the time he ceased to carry on the trade if he did so during that year of assessment). That excess may not be relieved under:

(i) *ICTA 1988, s 380* (see 46.3 LOSSES);

(ii) *ICTA 1988, s 381* (see 46.13 LOSSES);

(iii) *CAA 1990, s 141* (see 10.17, 10.32 CAPITAL ALLOWANCES); or

(iv) *ICTA 1988, s 353* (see 43.3 INTEREST PAYABLE),

other than against profits arising from the same trade.

If relief has previously been given under any of the provisions at (i)–(iv) above to the individual for a loss, etc. or allowance in the partnership trade in any year of assessment at any time during which the individual carried on the trade as a limited partner, relief for the loss, etc. or allowance for the year of assessment in question is restricted by the excess of the sum of the loss, etc. or allowance for that year of assessment and earlier amounts so relieved, over the 'contribution'.

The partner's '*contribution*' to the trade at any time is the aggregate of:

(A) capital contributed and not directly or indirectly withdrawn (excluding any the partner is or may be entitled to withdraw at any time he carries on the trade as a limited partner, or which he is or may be entitled to require another person to reimburse to him); and

(B) any profits of the trade to which he is entitled but which he has not received in money or money's worth.

Similar provisions apply to company partners (see Tolley's Corporation Tax under Partnerships).

[*ICTA 1988, s 117*].

See generally Revenue Inspector's Manual, IM 239, 240.

Simon's Direct Tax Service. See **E5.321** *et seq.*.

53.11 EFFECT OF PARTNERSHIP CHANGES ON LOSSES AND CAPITAL ALLOWANCES

(*a*) If, under the provision in 53.6 above, the business is *treated as continuing*,

- (i) continuing partners can bring forward their own shares of past losses under *ICTA 1988, s 380* and *ICTA 1988, s 385* but the shares of losses of outgoing partners lapse, and new partners do not share in any past losses; and
- (ii) unused capital allowances can be brought forward indefinitely.

(*b*) If, under the above provisions or otherwise, the change is *treated as a discontinuance*,

- (i) each continuing partner can bring forward his share of past losses for use under *ICTA 1988, ss 380, 385* (or, should it apply, *ICTA 1988, s 386*). Claims for carry-forward of losses under *ICTA 1988, s 385* only may be increased by adding to the loss capital allowances for the part of the year before the change. [*ICTA 1988, ss 113, 380(3), 385(5), 386(4), all as originally enacted*]. Shares of losses of outgoing partners lapse; and
- (ii) all unused capital allowances (apart from above) lapse entirely.

See 10.22, 10.38(viii) CAPITAL ALLOWANCES.

The above rules apply for 1996/97 and earlier years as regards partnership businesses commenced before 6 April 1994. For 1997/98 and subsequent years as regards such businesses and for 1994/95 and subsequent years as regards partnership businesses commenced, or treated as commenced, after 5 April 1994, these rules cease to be directly relevant. A change of partner will not result in the business being treated as a discontinuance if there is a continuing partner (see 53.6 above). Capital allowances are given as trading expenses of the partnership business (see 10.1 CAPITAL ALLOWANCES), and, therefore, unused allowances are not carried forward as a separate item. Each partner's share of the business is treated separately for loss relief purposes (see 53.3 above). Where a person leaves a partnership, his own share of the business is treated as discontinued (see 53.3 above); he can claim loss reliefs (including terminal loss relief — see 46.15 LOSSES) to the same extent as if he ceased carrying on a business as a sole trader (see generally 46 LOSSES).

53.12 EXCESS LIABILITY

Any EXCESS LIABILITY (28) of the partners on the profits is included in the joint assessment on the firm under *ICTA 1988, s 111* (where applicable — see 53.3 above). See also 28.2(*e*) EXCESS LIABILITY.

53.13 WIFE AS PARTNER

This is treated as a case where a wife has separate earnings, and appropriate additional deductions and personal reliefs can be claimed. It is not necessary to prove actual payment if the fact of her partnership is established. See generally Revenue Inspector's Manual, IM 263.

53.14 IF A COMPANY IS A PARTNER

(i) **Assessments.** Where one of the partners carrying on a trade, profession or business in partnership is a company, the partnership profits are computed as under corporation tax (see Tolley's Corporation Tax) but ignoring distributions, charges on income, capital allowances, pre-trading expenditure (see 71.76 SCHEDULE D, CASES I AND II) and any losses brought forward, and without regard to any change in the partners carrying on the trade. The company is chargeable to corporation tax as if its apportioned share of profits, and of the other items as above, arose from a trade it carried on alone. For 1996/97 and earlier years as regards partnership trades, etc. commenced before 6 April 1994, the profits (computed as above) apportionable to individual partners are assessed to income tax as if they were those of a normal partnership of individuals (see above), capital allowances etc., for the accounting period being treated as for the tax years comprising that period, with apportionment where necessary. But, regardless of any difference between the partners' interests in the year of assessment and those in the basis year, the total assessed on the individual partners for any year of assessment for which those profits form the basis cannot be less than the amount of the total profits of the basis period, reduced by the company's share, as above. For 1994/95 and subsequent years as regards partnership trades, etc. commenced, or treated as commenced, after 5 April 1994 and for 1997/98 and subsequent years as regards those commenced on or before that date, individual partners are charged tax in respect of their profit shares and given relief for losses in the same way as if all the partners were individuals. [*ICTA 1988, ss 111(2), 114, 115(1)–(3); FA 1994, s 215; FA 1995, ss 117, 125(4)*].

(ii) Yearly interest of money chargeable to tax under SCHEDULE D, CASE III (72) (as it applies for income tax purposes) paid by a partnership of which a company is a member must be paid under deduction of income tax at the lower rate (before

1996/97, the basic rate) in force for the year in which the payment is made. [*ICTA 1988, s 349(2)(b)*].

(iii) **On a partnership change** (see 53.6 above) *ICTA 1988, s 113(1)* applies only if an individual begins or ceases to be a partner (and in such a case an election for continuation basis may be made only if there is at least one continuing individual; notice under *ICTA 1988, s 113(2)* requiring signature solely by the individual partners before and after the change). This is of no application for 1994/95 and subsequent years as regards partnership trades, etc. commenced (or treated as commenced) after 5 April 1994 and for 1997/98 and subsequent years as regards those commenced on or before that date. [*ICTA 1988, s 114(3)(b); FA 1991, Sch 15 para 3; FA 1994, s 215(3)–(5); FA 1995, Sch 29 Pt VIII(15)*].

(iv) There are restrictions that apply in certain circumstances (where there are arrangements for transferring relief for losses etc.) on the use (*a*) by a partner company's losses in a partnership against its other income and (*b*) of a partner company's losses outside the partnership against its partnership profits. [*ICTA 1988, s 116*]. See Tolley's Corporation Tax (under Losses). See 3.20 ANTI-AVOIDANCE for withdrawal of losses from a company partnership dealing in commodity futures.

See 71.22 SCHEDULE D, CASES I AND II as regards the calculation of transitional overlap relief for individuals in partnership with a company. See generally Revenue Inspector's Manual, IM 266.

Simon's Direct Tax Service. See **D4.8**.

53.15 NON-RESIDENT PARTNERS AND PARTNERSHIPS CONTROLLED ABROAD

Pre-Finance Act 1995. The following rules apply for 1996/97 and earlier years as regards partnership trades etc. commenced before 6 April 1994 and for 1994/95 only (where applicable) as regards those commenced, or treated as commenced, on or after that date. A partnership doing part of its business in the UK but *controlled and managed from abroad* is assessable to the extent only of its business in the UK. [*ICTA 1988, s 112 as originally enacted* (extended by *ICTA 1988, s 115(5)* to apply for corporation tax purposes where one of the partners is a company)]. But assessment not avoided by two firms, one in the UK and one abroad, trading jointly (*Morden, Rigg & Co v Monks CA 1923, 8 TC 450*). For *control and management*, see 51.12 NON-RESIDENTS AND OTHER OVERSEAS MATTERS. For European Economic Interest Groupings, see 53.19 PARTNERSHIPS.

Where a partnership business is carried on partly abroad and partly in the UK (**or wholly abroad**) and one or more partners are resident in the UK, then:

(*a*) if control lies abroad, liability is under Case I on the whole of the profits made in UK and under Case V on UK residents' share of foreign profits (see *Colquhoun v Brooks HL 1889, 2 TC 490*);

(*b*) if control lies in UK, liability is wholly under Case I on the full profits made in UK *plus* the resident partners' shares of foreign profits arising to them;

(*c*) where a partnership business is controlled and managed abroad but one partner is a company resident in UK, that company may be assessed to corporation tax on its share of profits as if the partnership were itself resident.

A partnership set up abroad for tax avoidance purposes was held to be an overseas partnership in *Newstead v Frost HL 1980, 53 TC 525.*

Post-Finance Act 1995. The following rules apply for 1995/96 and subsequent years as regards partnership trades etc. commenced, or treated as commenced, after 5 April 1994 and for 1997/98 and subsequent years as regards those commenced on or before that date.

Partner non-UK resident. The general assessment and computation rules of *ICTA 1988, s 111* (see 53.3 above) are applied to a non-UK resident member of a trading etc. partnership in such a way as to ensure that he is taxed only on his share of profits earned in the UK (whereas UK resident partners are taxed on their share of worldwide profits). This mirrors and makes explicit the position under the pre-Finance Act 1995 regime. A similar rule applies to a non-resident company partner.

Individual partner's change of residence. Where a partnership trade or profession is carried on wholly or partly outside the UK and an individual partner becomes or ceases to be UK resident, he is treated for income tax purposes as ceasing to be a partner at that time and becoming a partner again immediately afterwards. His share of a loss sustained before the change may nevertheless be carried forward under *ICTA 1988, s 385* and set against his share of profits after the change.

Individual partner resident but not domiciled etc. in the UK. Where a partnership trade etc. is carried on wholly or partly outside the UK and controlled and managed outside the UK, an individual partner who is UK resident, but to whose overseas trading income the REMITTANCE BASIS (63.1) would normally apply, is taxed under Case V on that basis in respect of his share of the partnership profits earned outside the UK. This mirrors and confirms the position under the pre-Finance Act 1995 regime.

[*ICTA 1988, s 112(1)–(1B), s 115(4); FA 1995, s 125(1)(2)(5)*].

Subject to the exception above, UK-resident partners are chargeable under Case I on both UK and foreign profits, regardless of where the partnership is controlled.

General. In the case of *Padmore v CIR CA 1989, 62 TC 352*, it was held that, where profits of a non-UK resident partnership were exempt under the relevant double tax treaty, the profit share of a UK resident partner was thereby also exempt. This decision is, however, reversed by *ICTA 1988, s 112(4)(5)*, to the effect that arrangements under a double tax treaty relieving partnership income or capital gains from UK tax are not to affect any UK tax liability in respect of a UK resident partner's share of such income or gains. Such a partner is similarly entitled to the corresponding share of the tax credit in respect of a UK company qualifying distribution to a share of which he is entitled. Where a partnership includes a company, these provisions apply equally for corporation tax purposes. In the case of a partnership falling within the post-Finance Act 1995 regime (see above), the provisions apply where the partnership either resides outside the UK or carries on any trade etc. the control and management of which is outside the UK (which effectively mirrors the position under the previous regime). [*ICTA 1988, s 112(4)–(6), s 115(5); FA 1995, s 125(3)(5)*]. These changes are deemed always to have had effect. [*F(No 2)A 1987, s 62(2)*].

Simon's Direct Tax Service. See **E5.306.**

53.16 PARTNERSHIP RETIREMENT ANNUITIES

Annual payments for the benefit of a former partner (who has ceased to be a partner on retirement, because of age or ill-health, or on death), or the widow, widower or dependant of a former partner, are treated as earned income up to the limit below and, up to that limit, do not reduce the investment income of the payer.

The payments must be made under (*a*) the partnership agreement, or (*b*) an agreement replacing or supplementing the partnership agreement, or (*c*) an agreement with an individual who acquires the whole or part of the partnership business.

The limit referred to above is 50% of the average of the former partner's share of profits or gains (included in his tax return) in the best three of the last seven years of assessment in which he was required to devote substantially the whole of his time to the partnership (or to any other partnership of which he was a member — in which case the profits or gains of that partnership can be included in the calculations). Profits or gains not assessable to income tax are included in the calculation as if they were so assessable. [*ICTA 1988, s 628; FA 1988, Sch 3 para 19*].

To the extent that they exceed or are outside the above provisions, partnership retirement annuities are investment income in the hands of the recipients.

Indexation. The above limit of profits on which the earned income element of the annuity is calculated can be increased by the same percentage increase as the increase in the retail prices index between the December in the year of assessment in which the former partner left the partnership and the December preceding the year in which the annuity income is assessed. [*ICTA 1988, s 628(4)*]. The first six years of the last seven years of assessment which are the basis for computing the limit (as above) are also to be increased by indexation. The increase for each of these six years is to be by the same percentage increase as the percentage increase in the retail prices index for the month of December in the seventh year over that for the month of December in each of the previous six years. [*ICTA 1988, s 628(3)*].

Incorporation. Where a partnership business is incorporated, or a company takes over a partnership, and the agreement in either case refers to the company assuming responsibility for payment of an annuity to a former partner, then provided that the annuity is commercial in amount, the payment is not prevented by *ICTA 1988, s 338(5)(b)* from being treated by the company as a charge on income. *ICTA 1988, s 125* (annual payments for non-taxable consideration, see 3.19 ANTI-AVOIDANCE) is not in practice considered to apply to such payments in respect of a *bona fide* commercial transaction. (Revenue Tax Bulletin August 1994 p 151).

See also 65 RETIREMENT ANNUITIES and 81.29(v) SETTLEMENTS.

Simon's Direct Tax Service. See C3.225.

53.17 LOANS FOR PURCHASING INTEREST IN PARTNERSHIP

See 43.22 INTEREST PAYABLE as regards relief for interest on a loan to an individual for purchasing a share of or making an advance to a partnership, and for anti-avoidance measures applying in connection with certain such loans on the changeover to the current year basis of assessment.

53.18 CAPITAL GAINS TAX ON PARTNERSHIPS

See Tolley's Capital Gains Tax.

53.19 EUROPEAN ECONOMIC INTEREST GROUPINGS [*FA 1990, s 69, Sch 11*]

A European Economic Interest Grouping ('EEIG') within *EEC Directive No. 2137/85* (which applies to all EEIGs established within the European Economic Area), wherever it is registered, is regarded as acting as the agent of its members. Its activities are regarded as those of its members acting jointly, each member being regarded as having a share of EEIG property, rights and liabilities, and a person is regarded as acquiring or disposing of a share of the EEIG assets not only where there is an acquisition or disposal by the EEIG while he is a member but also where he becomes or ceases to be a member or there is a change in his share of EEIG property.

A member's share in EEIG property, rights or liabilities is that determined under the contract establishing the EEIG or, if there is no provision determining such shares, it will correspond to the profit share to which he is entitled under the provisions of the contract. If the contract makes no such provision, members are regarded as having equal shares.

Where the EEIG carries on a trade or profession, the members are regarded for the purposes of tax on income and gains as carrying on that trade or profession in partnership. The amount on which members are chargeable to income tax in respect of the trade or profession is computed (but not assessed) jointly, and the original provisions of *ICTA 1988, s 112* (see 53.15 above) concerning partnerships controlled abroad are correspondingly amended in the case of EEIGS. [*ICTA 1988, s 510A; FA 1990, Sch 11 paras 1, 5; FA 1995, Sch 29 Pt VIII(16)*].

Contributions to an EEIG from its members are not assessable on the EEIG, and the members are not assessable on distributions from the EEIG (which is equally not obliged to account for ACT thereon). (Revenue EEIGs Manual, EEIG 34).

For the purposes of securing that members of EEIGs are assessed to income tax, corporation tax or capital gains tax, an inspector may, in the case of an EEIG which is registered, or has an establishment registered, in Great Britain or Northern Ireland, by notice require the EEIG to make a return containing such information as the notice may require, accompanied by such accounts and statements as the notice may require, within a specified time. In any other case, he may issue a similar notice to any UK resident member(s) of the EEIG (or if none is so resident, to any member(s)). Notices may differ from one period to another and by reference to the person on whom they are served or the description of EEIG to which they refer. Where a notice is given to an EEIG registered in Great Britain or Northern Ireland (or having an establishment registered there), the EEIG must act through a manager, except that if there is no manager who is an individual, the EEIG must act through an individual designated as a representative of the manager under the *Directive*. The return must in all cases include a declaration that, to the best of the maker's knowledge, it is correct and complete, and where the contract establishing the EEIG requires two or more managers to act jointly for the EEIG to be validly bound, the declaration must be given by the appropriate number of managers. [*TMA 1970, s 12A; FA 1990, Sch 11 para 2; FA 1994, ss 196, 199, Sch 19 para 2*]. See 67.1 RETURNS as regards the form and content of returns.

A penalty not exceeding £300 (and £60 per day for continued failure) may be imposed in the case of failure to comply with a notice under the above provisions. No penalty may be imposed after the failure has been remedied, and if it is proved that there was no income or chargeable gain to be included in the return, the maximum penalty is £100. Fraudulent or negligent delivery of an incorrect return, etc. or of an incorrect declaration may result in a penalty not exceeding £3,000 for each member of the EEIG at the time of delivery. For 1996/97 and subsequent years, the £300 and £60 penalties are multiplied by the number of members of the EEIG (but subject to the overall £100 maximum in the circumstances described above); the daily penalty may only be imposed by the Commissioners (on an application to them by the Revenue) and has effect from the day following notification of imposition. [*TMA 1970, s 98B; FA 1990, Sch 11 para 3; FA 1994, ss 196, 199, Sch 19 para 30*].

The provisions of *TMA 1970, ss 36, 40* for extended time limits for assessments in cases of fraudulent or negligent conduct (see 6.4, 6.5 BACK DUTY) are amended so that any act or omission on the part of the EEIG or a member thereof is deemed to be the act or omission of each member of the EEIG. [*TMA 1970, s 36(4), s 40(3); FA 1990, Sch 11 para 4*].

Simon's Direct Tax Service. See **D4.901–D4.903**.

54 Patents

[*ICTA 1988, ss 524–529*]

Cross-references. See 10.50 CAPITAL ALLOWANCES for allowances on capital expenditure in acquiring patent rights; 23.15(*b*) DEDUCTION OF TAX AT SOURCE for patent royalties; 25.5(*l*) DOUBLE TAX RELIEF for DTR treatment of patent royalties from abroad and 71.73 SCHEDULE D, CASES I AND II for trading receipts and expenses re patents.

Simon's Direct Tax Service B3.841 *et seq.*.

54.1 **Patent rights** means the right to do or authorise the doing of anything which would, but for the right, be an infringement of a patent. [*ICTA 1988, s 533(1)*].

54.2 **Expenses** (otherwise than for the purpose of a trade) of devising inventions, agents' charges, patent office fees, etc. (including fees, expenses, etc. for rejected or abandoned applications) are allowable from income from patents with a right to carry forward indefinitely unallowed balances against future assessable patent income. [*ICTA 1988, s 526*].

54.3 **Patent income** of inventors is treated as earned income. [*ICTA 1988, s 529*].

54.4 **Patent royalties** are always assessable (*Kirke CA 1944, 26 TC 208*). Where royalties are received, less tax, for user of a patent which comprises two or more complete years, the income tax or corporation tax liabilities are reducible, on application, to the total that would have been payable if the royalties had been paid by equal instalments (corresponding to the number of complete years concerned, but not exceeding six years) made at yearly intervals ending with the date of actual receipt. [*ICTA 1988, s 527*].

54.5 **Sales of patent rights** (including receipts for rights for which a patent has not yet been granted [*ICTA 1988, s 533(5)(6)*]) are treated according to the residence of the vendor.

(*a*) **Resident** (*all patents*). Any capital sum received is assessable under Schedule D, Case VI (after deducting capital cost where purchased [*ICTA 1988, s 524(7)–(9)*]), but spread equally over year of receipt and five succeeding years thereafter, or wholly charged in year of receipt if written election made. [*ICTA 1988, s 524(1)(2)*]. See also *Green v Brace Ch D 1960, 39 TC 281*.

(*b*) **Non-Resident** (*UK patents only*). Purchaser must deduct tax at basic rate from purchase money and account to Revenue under *ICTA 1988, s 349(1)* [*ICTA 1988, s 524(3)*]. But this procedure may be modified by DOUBLE TAX RELIEF (25) agreements. The non-resident may, however, (i) claim relief for the cost to him of acquiring the patent, and (ii) elect to have the net sum treated as arising over that and subsequent periods, to a total of six years. [*ICTA 1988, s 524(4)*].

The election in (*a*) above must be made within, for 1996/97 and later years, twelve months after 31 January following the year of assessment in which the sum was received (for earlier years, two years after the end of that year of assessment) or, for corporation tax purposes, two years after the end of the accounting period in which it was received. The election in (*b*) above applies only for income tax, with the same time limits as above. [*ICTA 1988, s 524(2)(2A)(4); FA 1996, s 135, Sch 21 para 15*].

54.6 **On death, winding-up or partnership change**, any charges under *ICTA 1988, s 524* above for subsequent years become assessable, but personal representatives of deceased person, or each partner, may claim (within 30 days of the assessment) that such amount be spread back equally to the years beginning with the year of receipt and ending with the year in which the death or change occurred. [*ICTA 1988, s 525*].

55 Pay As You Earn

[*ICTA 1988, s 203*]

Cross-references. See also 61.12 PERSONAL SERVICE COMPANIES ETC., 78.37 SELF-ASSESSMENT.

Simon's Direct Tax Service E4.9.

Other sources. See Butterworths Schedule E Compliance Manual.

55.1 Pay as you earn (PAYE) is a system of collection of tax from salaries, wages, etc. See under 75 SCHEDULE E for provisions regarding amount assessable, allowable deductions etc. and see 83.3 SOCIAL SECURITY for taxable benefits.

PAYE is subject to regulations which were consolidated in *The Income Tax (Employments) Regulations 1993* (*SI 1993 No 744*). Subsequent amendments are made in *SI 1993 No 2276; SI 1994 Nos 775, 1212; SI 1995 Nos 216, 447, 853, 1284; SI 1996 Nos 804, 980, 1312, 2381, 2554, 2631, 2969; SI 1997 No 214; SI 1998 No 2484; SI 1999 Nos 70, 824, 2155; SI 2000 No 1152*. Regulation-making powers in *ICTA 1988, s 203(10)* (inserted by *FA 1998, s 119*) enable provision to be made for acceptance by the Revenue of the use of electronic means of transmission by employers (and see now *SI 1998 No 2484*).

See also Revenue Pamphlet P7 (Employer's Guide to PAYE) and IR 34 (Income Tax — PAYE), IR 109 (Employer Compliance Reviews and Negotiations) and IR 173 (Tax Credits — A Summary for Employers (Working Families' Tax Credit and Disabled Person's Tax Credit)). See Revenue Press Release 28 July 1989 for guidance on operation of PAYE under the receipts basis of assessment (see 75.1 SCHEDULE E). See also Revenue booklet SAT 3 'Self Assessment: What it will mean for Employers', available free from tax offices.

The Revenue have published a Code of Practice (No 3, available from local tax offices) setting out their standards for the way in which inspections of employers' records are conducted and the rights and responsibilities of taxpayers.

The outline of PAYE is stated below but reference should be made to the Revenue publications noted above.

For PAYE audits and investigations, see Butterworths Schedule E Compliance Manual.

Getting payroll records in order. The Revenue offer a free service to employers to ensure their payroll records are in order, and that errors in employees' personal details and national insurance numbers are identified and corrected before end-of-year returns are required. Employers may also ask for their records to be cross-checked with Revenue records, so that the Revenue may pursue any discrepancies directly with employees and make appropriate amendments. To register for this service, employers should contact Customer Account Services in Kings Lynn (tel. 0155 36 66 866) or Newcastle (tel. 0191 22 56 110).

See also 35.11 INLAND REVENUE: ADMINISTRATION as regards telephone helplines available to employers.

55.2 **All payments of emoluments** assessable under SCHEDULE E (75) are subject to deduction of tax under the PAYE system, including lump sums and late commissions even though they may relate to earlier years. Emoluments are assessable in the year of assessment of receipt (see 75.1 SCHEDULE E). The definition of 'emoluments' is wide enough to include certain deemed Schedule E income arising from share transactions (see 75.19 SCHEDULE E, 82.4, 82.5 SHARE INCENTIVES AND OPTIONS) but does not include payments only part of which is assessable under Schedule E (*CIR v Herd HL 1993, 66 TC 29*). It was held in *Paul Dunstall Organisation Ltd v Hedges (Sp C 179), [1999] SSCD 26* that 'payment' need not be payment in money (but see Taxation Vol 142, No 3692 p 429, 4 February 1999 for an article doubting the correctness of this decision).

Extension of scope. The following items are brought within the scope of PAYE (from 25 May 1994 in the case of (*a*)–(*d*)) by virtue of regulations under *ICTA 1988, ss 203F–203K* (introduced by *FA 1994, ss 127–131*).

(*a*) '*Tradeable assets*', i.e. assets (including any property, subject to specific exclusions) capable of being sold or otherwise realised in specified markets, or in relation to which 'trading arrangements' exist at the time the asset is provided. With effect from 6 April 1998, the provisions are revised to apply to 'readily convertible assets' (as defined rather more widely than 'tradeable assets', see *ICTA 1988, s 203F(2)–(3C)* introduced by *FA 1998, s 65(3)*) on the basis of the best estimate which can reasonably be made of the amount likely to be chargeable. They are also extended from that date to anything enhancing the value of such an asset in which the employee (or a member of his family or household) has an interest. See Revenue Tax Bulletin August 1998 pp 563–573 for a detailed Revenue view of the application of PAYE to 'readily convertible assets'. Transitory provisions applied from 2 July 1997 to 5 April 1998 which widened the definition of 'tradeable assets' to apply to the assignment or transfer of trade debts to employees.

(*b*) 'Non-cash vouchers' (see 75.44(*a*) SCHEDULE E), not excluded by regulation, where, at the time the asset is provided, either the vouchers themselves, or the goods for which they can be exchanged, are capable of being sold or otherwise realised in specified markets, or are vouchers for goods for which 'trading arrangements' exist. From 6 April 1998, these provisions are revised to refer to non-cash vouchers capable of being exchanged for anything which would be a 'readily convertible asset' (see below) or which would themselves be such assets but for the exclusion of non-cash vouchers.

(*c*) 'Credit tokens' (see 75.44(*d*) SCHEDULE E), not excluded by regulation, on each occasion they are used to obtain money, or to obtain goods which, when they are obtained, are capable of being sold or otherwise realised in specified markets, or are goods for which 'trading arrangements' exist. From 6 April 1998, these provisions are revised to refer to the use of such tokens to obtain either money or anything which would be a 'readily convertible asset' (see below).

(*d*) 'Cash vouchers' (see 75.44(*b*) SCHEDULE E), not excluded by regulation, when received by the employee.

(*e*) (From 6 April 1998) a gain within *ICTA 1988, s 135* on the exercise of a share option, an amount chargeable under *ICTA 1988, s 140A* (conditional acquisition of shares) by virtue of the conditionality ceasing or any disposal of the employee's beneficial interest, or a gain within *ICTA 1988, s 140D* (convertible shares) (see respectively 82.3, 82.7, 82.8 SHARE INCENTIVES AND OPTIONS). Broadly, where the shares in respect of which the charge arises are 'readily convertible assets' within (*a*) above (see below), the provisions relating to such assets apply on such an event by reference to the best estimate of the amount chargeable under *ICTA 1988, s 135* etc. in respect of the event in question (taking account, in relation to events after 28 July 2000, of any deduction likely to be available for employer national insurance contributions borne by the employee — see 82.3 SHARE INCENTIVES AND OPTIONS).

(*f*) (From 6 April 1998) a payment in cash or in the form of a 'readily convertible asset' (within (*a*) above and see below) on the assignment or release of a share option, to the extent of the amount likely to be thereby chargeable under *ICTA 1988, s 135* (and see (*e*) above) and regardless of whether or not the underlying shares are themselves 'readily convertible assets'.

As regards (*a*), (*b*) and (*c*) above, '*trading arrangements*' are broadly arrangements, not excluded by regulation, which enable the recipient to obtain an amount not substantially less than the expense incurred in provision of the asset, goods or voucher concerned, including the use of an asset or goods as security for a loan or advance. Regulations exclude from (*a*) and (*e*) above (and from (*f*) above but only to the extent of non-cash payments) shares, or rights over shares, in the employing company (or a company controlling that company) provided (from 27 November 1996) that they are acquired under certain approved schemes, and from (*c*) and (*d*) above the use of cash vouchers and credit tokens to meet, or to obtain cash used to meet, allowable expenditure. [*ICTA 1988, ss 203F–203L; FA 1994, ss 127–131; FA 1998, ss 64–69; FA 2000, s 56(2); SI 1994 No 1212; SI 1996 No 2969; SI 1998 No 1891*].

See 55.4 below as regards accounting for tax in respect of items within (*a*)–(*e*) above. See Revenue Tax Bulletins May 1994 p 212, February 1997 p 385 and April 2000 pp 734, 735 for practical considerations in operating PAYE in these circumstances. For notes on the status of shares as 'readily convertible assets' where there is either a long stop provision or a prohibition on employees selling shares, see Revenue Tax Bulletin April 2000 pp 735, 736.

For the application of the *Ramsay* principle (see 3.1 ANTI-AVOIDANCE) to a PAYE avoidance scheme, see *DTE Financial Services Ltd v Wilson Ch D, [1999] STC 1061.*

Employee non-resident, or non-ordinarily resident, in the UK. Where such an employee works (or is likely to work) both inside and out of the UK in a year of assessment, and some of his income is assessable under Schedule E, Case II (see 75.1 SCHEDULE E) and an as yet unascertainable part may prove not to be assessable, an officer of the Board may, on application by the employer or a person designated by the employer, by notice direct that a proportion of any payment made in the year is to be dealt with as assessable income under PAYE. If no direction is made, the whole of any payment must be so dealt with. The direction may similarly be withdrawn (with at least 30 days notice) by a further notice. These provisions are without prejudice to any income assessment on the employee and to any rights to repayment, or obligations to repay, income tax over- or underpaid. [*ICTA 1988, s 203D; FA 1994, s 126*]. This provision has effect from 3 May 1994, but similar arrangements in force before that date are retrospectively validated by *FA 1994, s 133(3)*.

Assessments. Subject as follows, formal assessments under Schedule E are made each year to equate deductions with true liability and any overpayments are refunded by a payable order usually issued at the same time as the notice of assessment, while underpayments are collected in the next, or the next following, year, by coding adjustments. But see 41 INTEREST ON OVERPAID TAX for attribution of deductions and repayments.

Formal assessments need not be made in cases where both coding and deduction of tax under it are correct, unless taxpayer gives notice within five years after the end of the year of assessment. [*ICTA 1988, s 205*]. But see administrative practice at 56.7 PAYMENT OF TAX.

55.3 **All persons making payments of such emoluments** are required to deduct the appropriate amount of tax from each payment (or repay over-deductions) by reference to PAYE Tax Tables, which are so constructed that, as near as may be, tax deducted from payments to date from previous 5 April corresponds with the correct time proportion to date of the net total tax liability (after allowances and reliefs) of the recipient on those emoluments for the year. [*ICTA 1988, s 203; FA 1988, Sch 3 para 4*]. See *Andrews v King Ch D 1991, 64 TC 332* as regards extended definition of 'employer' and *Booth v Mirror Group Newspapers plc QB, [1992] STC 615* as regards application of the PAYE regulations where emoluments are paid by a third party.

There are provisions to determine whether anything occurring constitutes a payment for PAYE purposes. These equate to the rules in 75.1 SCHEDULE E for determining when emoluments are to be treated as received. [*ICTA 1988, s 203A; FA 1989, s 45*].

The 'total tax' may include adjustments for any previous year and it 'may be assumed' that payments to date bear the same proportion to the total emoluments as that part of the year bears to the whole. [*ICTA 1988, s 203(6)–(8)*]. Employers are also required to deduct national insurance contributions at the same time as PAYE tax is deducted.

Employers may elect to operate separate PAYE schemes for different groups of employees. [*SI 1993 No 744, reg 3*].

Payments by intermediaries. Where a payment of, or on account of, emoluments is made by an 'intermediary' of the employer (i.e. a person acting on behalf, and at the expense, of the employer or a person 'connected' (within *ICTA 1988, s 839*, see 20 CONNECTED PERSONS) with the employer, or trustees holding property for persons including the employer), then unless the intermediary deducts and accounts for tax under PAYE (whether or not the PAYE regulations apply to him), the employer is to be treated from 25 May 1994 as having made the payment (grossed up where the recipient is entitled to the amount after deduction of any income tax). [*ICTA 1988, ss 203B, 203J, 203L; FA 1994, ss 125, 131; SI 1994 No 1212*]. See 55.4 below as regards the regulations required to deal with accounting for tax in respect of such notional payments.

Non-UK employer. Where, during any period, an employee works for a person (the 'relevant person') other than his employer, and any payment of, or on account of, his assessable income for work done in that period is made by the employer (or by an intermediary (see above) of the employer or, from 6 April 1998, of the relevant person) outside the scope of PAYE, the relevant person is treated for PAYE as having made the payment (grossed up where the employee is entitled to the payment after deduction of any income tax). From 6 April 1998 this applies also to any items brought within the scope of PAYE under *ICTA 1988, ss 203F–203I* (see 55.2 above). [*ICTA 1988, s 203C; FA 1994, s 126; FA 1998, s 69*]. This provision and *ICTA 1988, s 203E* (see below) replace *SI 1993 No 744, reg 4* with effect from 3 May 1994, prior to which *reg 4* is retrospectively validated by *FA 1994, s 133*.

Agency workers. Where agency workers are brought within Schedule E under *ICTA 1988, s 134* (see 75.46 SCHEDULE E), the agency and not the client is, from 6 April 1998, treated as the employer for the purposes of *ICTA 1988, ss 203B–203K* (other than *ICTA 1988, s 203E*)(see above and 55.2 above) except in certain cases where payment is made on behalf of, and at the expense of, the client or a connected person (see 20 CONNECTED PERSONS). [*ICTA 1988, s 203L(1A)–(1C); FA 1998, s 69*].

Mobile UK workforce. Where a person (the 'relevant person') has entered, or is likely to enter, into an agreement that employees of another person (the 'contractor') will work for him, but not as his employees, for a period, and it is likely that PAYE will not be deducted or accounted for in accordance with the regulations on payments made by (or on behalf of) the contractor of, or on account of, assessable income of those employees for that period, the Board may by notice to the relevant person direct that he apply PAYE to any payments made by him in respect of work done in that period by such employees of the contractor. So much of the payment as is attributable to the work done by each such employee is treated for this purpose as a payment of assessable income of that employee. The notice must specify the relevant person and the contractor to whom it relates, and may similarly be withdrawn by further notice, and notices must, where reasonably practicable, be copied to the contractor. [*ICTA 1988, s 203E; FA 1994, s 126*]. This provision and *ICTA 1988, s 203C* (see above) replace *SI 1993 No 744, reg 4* with effect from 3 May 1994, prior to which *reg 4* is retrospectively validated by *FA 1994, s 133*.

55.4 **The tax deductions to be made** are those appropriate to the employee's 'code' (calculated by the inspector, and notified to both employer and employee, to take account of personal allowances and reliefs due, certain higher rate liabilities and reliefs, underpayments from earlier years, and emoluments such as benefits in kind from which deductions cannot be made). The code generally represents the total allowances due omitting the final digit. Notice of objection to a code or revised code may be made to the inspector and in default of agreement an appeal can be taken to General Commissioners.

See, respectively, 78.6 SELF-ASSESSMENT and 17.3 CLAIMS for the position for 1996/97 onwards on the coding out of liabilities and on claims for reliefs etc. given effect by adjustments to codes.

Tax offices only notify an employer if there is a change in an employee's code. Until such notification an employer will continue to use the same code from year to year. [*SI 1993 No 744, regs 6, 8, 13*].

Code suffixes H or L are to enable quicker adjustments for change in higher (married or bereaved) or lower (single) allowances, but T will require special notification from the inspector. Suffixes P or V indicate that the full single or married age-related allowance is given, and Y that the over 75 allowances are given.

The taxpayer may require that T is substituted for H, L, P or V. Prefix D indicates higher rates of tax applicable.

Prefix K requires an *addition* to be made in arriving at taxable pay. This enables the correct tax to be deducted in cases where emoluments such as benefits in kind from which deduction cannot be made exceed allowances, but subject to a maximum deduction of 50% of cash pay.

Code BR indicates that tax is to be deducted at the basic rate without any allowances, and code NT indicates that no tax is to be deducted.

Where a notional payment is brought within PAYE by regulations made by virtue of *ICTA 1988, s 203B, ss 203F–203I* or *s 203C* (see 55.2, 55.3 above), the income tax thereon is to be deducted, at a prescribed time, from any actual payment(s) to the employee. Where, due to an insufficiency of actual payments, all or part of the tax cannot be so deducted, the employer (or person treated as such) must account to the Board, within a prescribed time, for any tax he is required, but unable, to deduct. The amount so deducted or accounted for is treated as an amount paid by the employee in respect of his own liability (for a prescribed year). As regards any amount the employer has accounted for (being unable to deduct it from any payments made to the employee), if the employee does not make good the amount to the employer within 30 days of the date on which the employer is treated as making the payment, the employee is treated as receiving emoluments of that amount on that date. [*ICTA 1988, ss 144A, 203J; FA 1994, ss 131, 132; FA 1998, s 69; SI 1994 No 1212; SI 1998 No 1891*]. The regulations, which came into force on 25 May 1994, also provide the rules for accounting for tax on notional payments. For notes on the application of these provisions to share-related benefits, see Revenue Tax Bulletin April 2000 pp 734, 735.

55.5 **Tax Tables** show, in relation to each 'code', the cumulative 'free pay' for each weekly (or monthly) period, which is subtracted from the total gross pay down to that period leaving 'taxable pay' on which is calculated the tax due from (or refundable to) the employee.

Modified systems of deduction may be authorised by the inspector in cases of fixed salaries or wages. [*SI 1993 No 744, reg 20*].

55.6 **Deductions working sheets** (Form P11 (New)) must be kept in each fiscal year by every employer in respect of each employee for recording the employee's pay, tax and related

National Insurance contributions. An employer may use his own forms if approved by the Revenue. [*SI 1993 No 744, reg 38*].

55.7 As to **recovery from employee** of tax under-deducted see *SI 1993 No 744, reg 42(2)(3)* as amended by *SI 1995 No 447*. See also *Bernard & Shaw Ltd v Shaw KB 1951, 30 ATC 187*, and for wilful failure by employer to deduct correct tax, *R v CIR (ex p Chisholm) QB 1981, 54 TC 722, R v CIR (ex p Sims) QB 1987, 60 TC 398* and *R v CIR (ex p Cook) QB 1987, 60 TC 405*. In *R v CIR (ex p McVeigh) QB 1996, 68 TC 121*, accounting entries purporting to deduct tax, where tax not paid over to Revenue, were held not to constitute deduction of tax for these purposes. For tax accounted for by employer in respect of certain notional payments, see 55.4 above.

55.8 **The net tax deducted by the employer and national insurance contributions must be paid to the Collector** within 14 days after the end of each month, except in certain cases where payment may be made quarterly. Quarterly payment applies where employees are on authorised fixed pay arrangements (see 55.5 above) or where the employer has reasonable grounds for believing that the average monthly total to be paid to the Collector in respect of deductions under PAYE (disregarding any deduction therefrom in respect of working families' and disabled person's tax credits) and the CONSTRUCTION INDUSTRY TAX SCHEME (21), national insurance contributions (again disregarding tax credit adjustments) and student loan repayments, less any tax credits the employer is required to pay, will be less than £1,500 in the current year. (Before 2000/01, the limit was £1,000 and the average monthly payment was determined without regard to tax credits or student loan repayments.) [*SI 1993 No 744, regs 40–42; SI 1993 No 2276; SI 1995 No 216; SI 1999 No 824; SI 2000 No 1152*]. A deduction may be made for payments of Statutory Sick and Maternity Pay. If no tax has been paid within that 14 days, or the Collector is not satisfied that any payment made satisfies the employer's liability, the Collector, if he is not aware of the amount the employer is liable to pay, can give notice requiring a return within 14 days showing the amount of that liability. [*SI 1993 No 744, reg 47*]. The inspector has powers to determine the amount of tax payable where it appears to him that tax may have been payable under these regulations but has not been paid. The determination applies as if it were an assessment to tax. [*SI 1993 No 744, reg 49; SI 1995 No 447*].

Interest is charged at the prescribed rate (see 42.2 INTEREST AND SURCHARGES ON UNPAID TAX) on tax unpaid in respect of determinations for 1991/92 and earlier years made after 19 April 1988, from 14 days after the end of the year of assessment to which the determination relates (or from 19 April 1988 if later). [*ICTA 1988, s 203(2)(d); FA 1988, s 128(1); SI 1993 No 744, reg 50*]. In respect of tax payable for 1992/93 and subsequent years, interest is so charged on tax unpaid by 19 April in the tax year following that for which it was payable whether or not it is the subject of a determination. Also in respect of tax payable for 1992/93 and subsequent years, interest on overpaid tax runs at the prescribed rate (see 41.2 INTEREST ON OVERPAID TAX) from (for tax paid for 1996/97 and subsequent years) the 14th day after the end of the year in respect of which the tax was paid (or, if later, from the date of payment of the tax), or (for tax paid for 1995/96 and earlier years) the end of the year after that in respect of which the payment was made (or in the case of a repayment of tax paid more than twelve months after the end of the year for which it was paid, from the end of the year in which the tax was paid). [*ICTA 1988, s 203(2)(dd); FA 1988, s 128(1); FA 1994, ss 196, 199, Sch 19 para 38; SI 1993 No 744, regs 51, 53, 53A; SI 1996 No 1312, regs 9, 10*]. In either case, such interest is paid without deduction of tax and is not taken into account in computing income for tax purposes. [*ICTA 1988, s 203(9); FA 1988, s 128(2)*]. Cheque payments are treated as made on the day of receipt by the collector (and see 56.1 PAYMENT OF TAX).

Interest may also arise in the case of late paid or overpaid Class 1 or 1A national insurance contributions (see *SI 1993 No 821*).

Employer is not entitled to charge Revenue with costs of PAYE collection (*Meredith v Hazell QB 1964, 42 TC 435*). Revenue have power to inspect wages sheets and other records to ensure regulations being observed. [*ICTA 1988, s 203(2)(b); SI 1993 No 744, reg 55*]. Where money is stolen, the employer is liable (*A-G v Antoine KB 1949, 31 TC 213*).

55.9 **After the end of each year the employer must**, in respect of each employee for whom he was required to maintain a deductions working sheet, send to the Inspector, or (in the case of (*a*), and if so required) the Collector of Taxes, the following.

(*a*) Not later than 19 May

(i) an End of Year Return P14 (top and first copy),

(ii) a declaration on form P35 (including a nil return where appropriate).

(*b*) Not later than 6 July

(i) particulars on form P9D of emoluments given to an employee otherwise than in money; payments made on behalf of employee and not repaid; relocation expenses in excess of the tax-free limit (see 75.33 SCHEDULE E); and certain other payments etc. not treated as 'pay',

(ii) for all employees with emoluments at a rate of £8,500 p.a. or more and for all directors (except full-time service directors with no material interest in the company or employed by non-profit making companies or charities [*ICTA 1988, s 167(5)*] earning less than £8,500 p.a.), a return on form P11D showing additionally

(A) payments to employee for expenses,

(B) sums put at employee's disposal and paid away by him,

(C) expenses incurred by employer in connection with providing the employee with services, benefits or facilities falling under *ICTA 1988, ss 154–165* (see 75.11 *et seq.* SCHEDULE E),

but excluding relocation expenses (see (i) above) within the tax-free limit. For the use of substitute forms P11D, see Revenue Tax Bulletin August 1996 p 334.

Supplementary returns (form P38A) must be submitted with form P35 for all employees for whom a deductions working sheet is not required.

[*SI 1993 No 744, regs 43–46; SI 1993 No 2276, reg 8*]. See 58.4 PENALTIES as regards a period of grace for submission of returns under (*a*) above.

A return by the employer is also required by 6 July following the end of the tax year (commencing 6 July 1999) in respect of any employee (or former employee) awarded termination payments and other benefits within *ICTA 1988, s 148* (see 19.5 COMPENSATION FOR LOSS OF EMPLOYMENT (AND DAMAGES)) totalling more than £30,000 in the tax year. [*SI 1993 No 744, reg 46ZA; SI 1999 No 70*].

For the additional requirements for returns for 1996/97 and subsequent years, including information to be supplied to employees, see 78.37 SELF-ASSESSMENT.

Value added tax paid, if any, must be included in above. (Revenue Pamphlet IR 131, A7). See 55.44 below.

See 67.5 RETURNS and 78.37 SELF-ASSESSMENT for employers' returns generally.

Internet filing discount. From April 2001 small businesses filing their PAYE end-of-year returns via the internet and paying any tax due electronically will receive a discount of £50 for one year. A further £50 will be available where there are one or more working families' or disabled person's tax credit cases. (Revenue Press Releases 16 February 2000, 21 March 2000 (BN1D)). See 67.3 RETURNS as regards other electronic filing discounts.

Simon's Direct Tax Service. See **E4.965** *et seq.*.

55.10 Employers must also give each employee annually **a certificate** showing his total taxable emoluments for the year and total tax deducted therefrom, his appropriate code, National Insurance number, and the employer's name and address etc. [*SI 1993 No 744, reg 39*]. This certificate is produced automatically as the third sheet of the End of Year Return, or a substitute form P60 may be used or other document approved by the Revenue.

55.11 For **Penalties** see 58.4 PENALTIES and *TMA 1970, ss 98, 98A*. See also Revenue Pamphlet IR 109.

55.12 **PAYE settlement agreements.** The Revenue and an employer may make a non-statutory agreement, known as an 'annual voluntary settlement', whereby the employer settles by way of lump sum an amount approximating to the tax otherwise payable by his employees on items covered by the settlement, which will be minor, incidental benefits and expenses payments, e.g. reimbursement of telephone expenses, late night taxis home and benefits shared between a number of employees. The employer is then relieved of including such benefits and expenses in the returns at 55.9(*b*) above and the employees do not have to declare them or include them in their total income.

A statutory framework for such arrangements, known as 'PAYE settlement agreements', is established by regulations provided for by *ICTA 1988, s 206A* (introduced by *FA 1996, s 110*) with effect for 1996/97 and subsequent years. See *SI 1996 No 2631* and Revenue Statement of Practice SP 5/96, 15 October 1996 for the detailed rules governing such agreements and the scope of payments and benefits covered. These are described in some detail in an article in the Revenue Tax Bulletin December 1996 pp 365–369. Separate legislation enables national insurance contributions to be comprised in such settlements (and see 71.54 SCHEDULE D, CASES I AND II).

See also Revenue Pamphlet IR 155.

Simon's Direct Tax Service. See **E4.968**.

55.13 **Annual payments.** Tax on certain periodic redundancy and other similar payments by a former employer which are strictly assessable under Schedule D, Case III as annual payments, and payable under deduction of basic rate tax, may, where it is convenient and with the agreement of the parties and the inspector, be dealt with instead under PAYE (Revenue Tax Bulletin February 1995 p 196).

55.14 **Annuities** paid out of superannuation funds approved under *ICTA 1970, s 208* which have not sought approval under subsequent legislation and to which no contributions have been made since 5 April 1980 (see 66.13 RETIREMENT SCHEMES) continue to be charged under Schedule E and subject to PAYE. [*ICTA 1988, s 608*].

55.15 **Benefits in kind** are within PAYE and are usually dealt with by a deduction from the allowances in arriving at the coding (and see *R v Walton Commrs (ex p Wilson) CA, [1983] STC 464*). See 55.4 above as regards prefix K codes issued in certain cases where benefits etc. exceed allowances. See also 55.2 above as regards certain other non-cash emoluments brought within PAYE.

55.16 **Cars provided for private use.** See 75.15(ii) SCHEDULE E for computation of the charge. Quarterly returns are required within 28 days of the end of the quarter on Form P46(car), starting with the quarter to 5 July 1994, showing employees first or no longer provided with a car, or provided with a change of car or an additional car, or already provided with a car but becoming a director or starting to earn at the rate of £8,500 p.a. or more during the quarter. [*SI 1993 No 744, reg 46A; SI 1994 No 775*]. The Form asks in each case for details of the make, model and cubic capacity of the car (and whether it is petrol or diesel), of the list price of the car and accessories, of any capital contribution by the employee, and of the expected annual business mileage band. The pamphlet also explains the procedures for dealing with existing cars at the commencement of the new scheme.

Returns on Form P11D (see 55.9(ii) above) continue to be required.

55.17 **Charitable donations** of any amount (for 200/01 onwards, previously limited to £1,200 in any year of assessment from 1996/97, £900 for 1994/95 and 1995/96) may be an allowable deduction for PAYE purposes. See 15.18 CHARITIES.

55.18 **Crown priority.** The provisions of *Insolvency Act 1986, s 386, Sch 6* apply to PAYE which the bankrupt was liable to deduct from emoluments paid in the twelve months before the date of the bankruptcy order or, if earlier, the date of appointment of an interim receiver. See 56.5 PAYMENT OF TAX.

55.19 **Director's remuneration.** Credit of remuneration voted to a director to an account with the company constitutes 'payment' for PAYE purposes. See generally ICAEW Technical Release TAX 11/93, 9 July 1993, as regards tax implications of payments to directors. [*ICTA 1988, s 203A(1)(c); FA 1989, s 45*]. See 55.3 above and 75.1 SCHEDULE E.

55.20 **Disabled person's tax credit** due to an individual in receipt of emoluments within PAYE is payable by the employer from 6 April 2000, such payment to be funded by the Revenue. [*Tax Credits Act 1999, s 6; SI 1999 No 3219*]. See Revenue Tax Bulletin October 1999 pp 691–693, and see 83.6 SOCIAL SECURITY.

55.21 **Domestic workers and nannies.** See Revenue Pamphlet IR 53 for simplified guidelines on the operation of PAYE by taxpayers likely to be employing domestic workers or nannies for the first time.

55.22 **Employee arriving.** A new employee should produce a form P45 and the employer should start a Deductions Working Sheet from the particulars on that form and send Part 3 to the tax office. If a form P45 (or other code authorisation) is not produced, the employer should complete form P46, ask the employee to sign the appropriate certificate on the back, and send to the tax office. A Deductions Working Sheet must be prepared and tax deducted in accordance with the instructions relating to the certificate signed by the employee. The employee should be given a Coding Claim form P15 to complete and this should be sent to the tax office. [*SI 1993 No 744, regs 25, 28–34 as amended*]. See 55.40 below as regards tax refunds.

55.23 **Employee dying.** On death of employee, the employer must forthwith send all parts of P45 to inspector together with name and address of personal representative, if known. [*SI 1993 No 744, reg 27*].

55.24 **Employee leaving** must be given certificate (form P45) by former employer showing code, pay and tax deductible to date of leaving (split, for 1996/97 onwards, if more than one employment). [*SI 1993 No 744, reg 23; SI 1996 No 804, reg 3*]. This produced to new employer [*SI 1993 No 744, reg 25*] ensures continuity and provides data for commencement of new deduction working sheet.

Payments to employees who have left and which are not included in P45 must have tax deducted at the basic rate. [*SI 1993 No 744, reg 24*].

Employee retiring. At retirement on pension of an employee, the employer must, within 14 days, inform inspector on form P160 and continue operating code on Week 1/Month 1 basis. [*SI 1993 No 744, reg 26(1)(2); SI 1996 No 804, reg 5*].

55.25 **Exemption.** Where the employee has no other employment and rate of payment is less than a weekly or monthly rate equal to $\frac{1}{52}$nd or $\frac{1}{12}$th respectively of the personal allowance, no tax is deductible. If employee has other employment this limit is reduced to £1 per week (£4 per month). [*SI 1993 No 744, reg 28(1)(b)(2)*].

55.26 **Expense payments etc.** must (except as regards pure reimbursement to subordinate employees of specific outlay incurred) be included with pay and taxed with it, unless exempted by notification from the inspector under *ICTA 1988, s 166* (or under the earlier legislation in *ICTA 1970, s 199* or *FA 1976, s 70*).

55.27 **Free of tax payments, awards etc..** For remuneration payable free of tax, taxed incentive awards etc., see 75.40 SCHEDULE E.

55.28 **H.M. Forces.** Members of the reserve and auxiliary forces will generally have basic rate tax deducted from pay. [*SI 1993 No 744, regs 59–70; SI 1997 No 214*].

55.29 **Holiday pay.** Tax is normally deductible from holiday pay, but by arrangement with the employer it may be paid in full, compensating adjustments being made either in the coding, or by a system of credits which spreads the tax on the holiday pay over the whole year. Holiday pay paid to a participant in a holiday stamp scheme by the scheme management company is taxed at the basic rate at the time of payment. [*SI 1993 No 744, reg 73*].

55.30 **Incapacity benefit**, where taxable (see 83.3 SOCIAL SECURITY), is brought within PAYE by *SI 1995 No 853.*

55.31 **Jobseekers allowance** (so far as taxable, see 83.3 SOCIAL SECURITY) is brought within PAYE by *SI 1996 No 2381.*

55.32 **Local councillors' attendance allowances.** The councillor may opt for deduction of basic rate tax from such allowances (net of an appropriate amount in respect of allowable expenditure) rather than deduction by reference to the appropriate code. [*SI 1993 No 744, regs 56–58*].

55.33 **Maternity pay** under **Employment Protection (Consolidation) Act 1978** is assessable under SCHEDULE E (75). The payment qualified for wife's earned income relief (see 1.23 ALLOWANCES AND TAX RATES). [*ICTA 1988, s 150*].

55.34 **Overseas matters.** Where an employee works abroad, see Employer's Guide to PAYE. See *SI 1993 No 744, reg 28(4)(b)(5)* as regards pensions. A non-resident employer must operate PAYE in respect of any emoluments of his employees within Schedule E if he has a 'trading presence' in the UK (*Clark v Oceanic Contractors Incorporated HL 1982, 56 TC 183*). See also *Bootle v Bye; Wilson v Bye (Sp C 61), [1996] SSCD 58*. See also 55.3 above as regards payments by intermediaries.

55.35 **Records.** Wages sheets, deductions working sheets, certificates and other records required to be maintained under the PAYE regulations and not required to be sent to the Revenue must be retained by the employer for not less than three years after the end of the year to which they relate. [*SI 1993 No 744, reg 55(12)*]. There are special provisions relating to inspection of computer records (see *FA 1988, s 127* and *SI 1993 No 744, reg 55(7)*). See Revenue Pamphlets IR 71 and IR 109 as regards inspection of records and negotiation of settlements. See also Revenue Tax Bulletin October 1998 pp 588, 589.

55.36 **Religious Centres.** If a Local Religious Centre does not expect to pay anyone £100 or more in a tax year, no action is required under PAYE. For anyone to whom the Centre does expect to pay £100 or more in a tax year, but who has no other job, records need to be kept for three years of name, address, national insurance number and the amount paid in the tax year. For any such person who has (or may have) another job, the Centre does not need to deduct tax, but should write to TIDO(LRC), Ty Glas, Llanishen, Cardiff CV4 5ZG giving details of name, address and national insurance number and of both the amount paid to the following 5 April and the amount expected to be paid in a full tax year. (Taxation, 16 February 1995, p 462).

55.37 **Seamen** are subject to standard PAYE procedures on wages from employment. Travelling expenses and subsistence allowances paid to seafarers making regular journeys to the same UK port are subject to PAYE. (Hansard 26 February 1981 Vol 999 Col 442).

55.38 **Suffixes to codes.** See 55.4 above.

55.39 **Superannuation contributions** ('net pay arrangement'). Employees' superannuation contributions authorised by the Pension Schemes Office are deducted from gross pay for PAYE purposes, but National Insurance contributions are calculated on gross pay. [*SI 1993 No 744, reg 2*].

55.40 **Tax refunds** by employer to new employee before 6 April 1996 could not exceed £200 unless authorised by inspector. [*SI 1993 No 744, reg 25(6)*; *SI 1996 No 804, reg 4(c)*].

Tax refunds arising during unemployment are made directly by inspector [*SI 1993 No 744, reg 37*] but refunds are withheld from the unemployed who claim taxable state benefit and from strikers until the end of the strike. [*ICTA 1988, s 204*; *SI 1993 No 744, reg 36*]. See 55.43 below.

55.41 **Termination payments.** For the reporting requirements in relation to taxable termination payments, see 55.9 above.

55.42 **Tronc arrangements.** Gratuities and service charge shares under tronc arrangements are emoluments and the tronc-master is regarded as responsible for the tax deductions under PAYE. [*SI 1993 No 744, reg 5; SI 1994 No 775; SI 1996 No 1312, reg 3*]. For a case in which informal arrangements, under which directors of the employing company collected gratuities and divided them between themselves and the employees, were held not to constitute a tronc, see *Figael Ltd v Fox CA 1991, 64 TC 441*.

55.43 **Unemployed persons and strikers receiving taxable social security etc. benefits.** The Department of Employment (the Department of Social Services for NI) maintain a record of the claimant's previous cumulative pay and tax in the tax year and of any taxable benefit paid to him. At the end of the claimant's period of benefit claim (or at the end of the tax year, if earlier) the Department calculate his tax position, make any repayments of tax due to him and notify the details to him and to his inspector of taxes. Detailed procedures apply to the provision of information between all the parties involved. [*SI 1993 No 744, regs 81–93*]. See also 55.40 above and Revenue Pamphlets IR 41, IR 42 and IR 43.

55.44 **Value added tax.** Emoluments paid to a person holding an office in the course of carrying on a trade, profession or vocation and subject to VAT on services supplied by him should exclude the VAT element for PAYE purposes. (Revenue Pamphlet IR 131, A6). See also 55.9 above.

55.45 **Voluntary lifeboatmen** call-out fees, although taxable, are not subject to deduction of tax under PAYE. (Revenue Press Release 15 April 1986).

55.46 **Working families' tax credit** due to an individual in receipt of emoluments within PAYE is payable by the employer from 6 April 2000, such payment to be funded by the Revenue. [*Tax Credits Act 1999, s 6; SI 1999 No 3219*]. See Revenue Tax Bulletin October 1999 pp 691–693, and see 83.6 SOCIAL SECURITY

56 Payment of Tax

Cross-references. See 42 INTEREST ON UNPAID TAX and 55 PAY AS YOU EARN.

(See also Table at 57 PAYMENT OF TAX—DUE DATES.)

Simon's Direct Tax Service A3.13.

Note re self-assessment. For **1997/98 and subsequent years**, under self-assessment, income tax (on all sources of taxable income) for a year of assessment will be payable by means of two interim payments of equal amounts, based normally on the liability for the previous year and due on 31 January in the year of assessment (commencing on 31 January 1997) and the following 31 July, and a final balancing payment due on the following 31 January (on which date any capital gains tax liability will also be due for payment). Taxpayers will have the right to reduce their interim payments if they believe their liability will be less than that for the previous year or to dispense with interim payments if they believe they will have no liability. Interim payments will not in any case be required where substantially all of a taxpayer's liability is covered by deduction of tax at source, including PAYE, or where the amounts otherwise due are below *de minimis* limits to be prescribed by regulations. See 78.17 to 78.20 SELF-ASSESSMENT for details, and for the special arrangements which apply **for 1996/97 only**.

56.1 For **1995/96 and earlier years,** for **individuals and partnerships,** income tax (including higher rate income tax and investment income surcharge where applicable) and capital gains tax is payable as follows.

(*a*) On **profits** of

(i) trades and professions assessed under Schedule D, Cases I and II; or

(ii) foreign businesses assessed under Schedule D, Case V

— as to one-half on 1 January falling within the tax year, and one-half on 1 July following the end of that year or, if later, 30 days after the date of issue of the notice of assessment. For partnerships which commenced before 6 April 1994, these payment dates continue to apply **for 1996/97**. [*ICTA 1988, s 5(2)(3); FA 1994, Sch 26 Pt V(23)*].

(*b*) **On income charged under Schedule E**

(i) where PAYE is applied — by deduction from emoluments as and when paid [*ICTA 1988, s 203*] and

(ii) where the income is assessed — 14 days after the first application by the Collector [*SI 1993 No 744, reg 105(2)*]. For payment by employers of tax deducted, see 55.8 PAY AS YOU EARN.

(*c*) **On other income received gross** — on 1 January falling within the tax year, or 30 days after the date of issue of the notice of assessment, whichever is the later. [*ICTA 1988, s 5(1); FA 1994, Sch 26 Pt V(23)*]. For Schedule A for 1994/95 and earlier years, see 68.20 SCHEDULE A.

(*d*) **On other income received under deduction of basic or lower rate income tax,** or which is treated as having been so received, or to which the 'tax credit' attaches under *ICTA 1988, s 231* — on 1 December following the end of the year for which assessed, or 30 days after the date of issue of the notice of assessment, whichever is the later. [*ICTA 1988, s 5(4); FA 1994, Sch 26 Pt V(23); FA 1996, Sch 6 paras 3, 28*].

(*e*) On **capital gains** — on 1 December following the end of the year for which assessed, or 30 days after the date of issue of the notice of assessment, if later. [*TCGA 1992, s 7; FA 1995, Sch 29 Pt VIII(14)*].

Tax under the **paying and collecting agents** arrangements is payable within 14 days after the end of the month in which the dividend, etc. is paid. [*ICTA 1988, s 118F(2); FA 1996, Sch 29 para 1*]. These arrangements are abolished after 31 March 2001. [*FA 2000, s 111(1)(6)*]. For 1995/96 and earlier years, see 70 SCHEDULE C.

Effective dates of payment. With effect generally from 6 April 1996, these are taken to be as follows.

(1) *Cheques, cash, and postal orders* handed in at the Revenue office or received by post — the day of receipt by the Revenue *unless* received by post following a day on which the office was closed, in which case it is the day (or the first day) on which the office was closed.

(2) *Electronic funds transfer* — one working day immediately before the date the value is received.

(3) *Bank giro or Girobank* — three working days prior to the date of processing by the Revenue.

(Revenue Press Release 1 April 1996).

Previously, effective dates were considered to be as follows.

(i) *Cheques sent through the post* — the date on which an in-date cheque is posted but, because of the impossibility of referring to all postmarks, the practice is to take the third working day before the day on which the Collector received the cheque. First-class official paid envelopes or labels are enclosed with first applications for payment of tax and although there is no requirement for a taxpayer to make payment by first-class post, he has the means to do so without incurring any postal charge.

(ii) *Cash and in-date cheques tendered personally* — the date of the tender.

(iii) *Post-dated cheques* — the date of the cheque.

(iv) *Bank giro credit* — the date stamped on the payslip by the bank's cashier.

(v) *National Giro bank in-payment* — the date stamped on the payslip by the Post Office counter clerk.

(vi) *National Giro bank transfer* — the date of the Inland Revenue's National Giro bank statement on which the item appears.

(Tolley's Practical Tax 1981 p 42).

Where a payment of tax is made by electronic funds transfer, an effective date of payment one working day immediately before the date value is received by the Revenue is allowed. (Revenue Press Release 1 April 1993).

See 78.24 SELF-ASSESSMENT as regards cheques received by the Revenue after 5 April 1996.

56.2 PAYMENT OF TAX PENDING APPEAL

Where the appeal to the Commissioners is against an assessment, the full amount charged will be due and payable as in 56.1 above unless (except for 56.1(*b*)(ii) above — Schedule E) the appellant applies for the Commissioners to determine, in the same way as the appeal, the amount of tax to be postponed. The application must be made in writing to the inspector within thirty days after the date of the issue of the notice of assessment, stating the amount of tax believed to be overcharged, and the grounds for that belief. Application may be made outside the normal thirty day time limit if there is a change in the circumstances of the case giving grounds for belief that the appellant is overcharged. In the Revenue view, this requires a change in the circumstances in which the original decision not to apply for postponement was made, not just a change of mind, e.g. further accounts work indicating a substantially excessive assessment, or further reliefs becoming due. (Notes of CCAB meeting with Revenue on the 1982 Finance Bill, TR 477, 22 June 1982.) Any tax not postponed by the Commissioners shall be due and payable as if charged by an assessment issued at the time of the Commissioners' decision and against which no appeal is pending. If circumstances change, a further application to the Commissioners may be made by either party giving notice to the other. The appellant and an inspector may agree the amount of tax to be postponed and written confirmation of such agreement shall be treated as if the Commissioners had so determined. On determination of the appeal any tax overpaid is repaid; any tax postponed or not previously charged becomes due and payable as if charged under an assessment issued when the inspector issues to the appellant notice of the total amount payable. [*TMA 1970, s 55, s 56(9)(b), s 59(6)(b); F(No 2)A 1975, s 45; FA 1982, s 68; FA 1989, s 156(2); FA 1990, s 104(2)(4)*]. For what is a determination of an appeal for this purpose, see 4.6(*a*) APPEALS. See also 42.3 INTEREST AND SURCHARGES ON UNPAID TAX for interest which might run before the due date of payment of the tax. See 78.31 SELF-ASSESSMENT for the application of these provisions for 1996/97 and subsequent years.

In cases of appeals to the Courts, the tax must be paid first in accordance with the determination of the Commissioners. Tax overpaid consequent on the Court's decision is repaid (with, at the Court's discretion, interest) even though further appeal is possible (see e.g. *T & E Homes Ltd v Robinson CA 1979, 52 TC 567*), and any tax not previously charged is due and payable 30 days after the date of notification of the total amount payable. [*TMA 1970, s 56(9)*].

See also 42.3 INTEREST AND SURCHARGES ON UNPAID TAX.

56.3 **COLLECTION AND GENERALLY**

The Collector may distrain (poind in Scotland). [*TMA 1970, ss 61–64; FA 1989, ss 152–155*]. See also *Herbert Berry Associates Ltd v CIR HL 1977, 52 TC 113*. Where amount due (or any instalment) is less than £1,000, Collector may within six months of due date take summary magistrates' court proceedings. The limit is raised to £2,000 as respects 1996/97 and later years — see 78.35 SELF-ASSESSMENT. The Collector may recover the tax by proceedings in the County Court. [*TMA 1970, ss 65, 66; FA 1984, s 57; SI 1989 No 1300; SI 1991 Nos 724, 1625*]. But for limitations in Scotland and N. Ireland see *TMA 1970, s 65(4), s 66(3)(4), s 67; FA 1976, s 58; FA 1995, s 156*, and for time limits for proceedings see *Mann v Cleaver KB 1930, 15 TC 367* and *Lord Advocate v Butt CS 1992, 64 TC 471*. Unpaid tax (and arrears) may also be recovered (with full costs) as a Crown debt in the High Court. [*TMA 1970, s 68*]. The amount of an assessment which has become final cannot be re-opened in proceedings to collect the tax (*Pearlberg CA 1953, 34 TC 57; CIR v Soul CA 1976, 51 TC 86*), and it is not open to the taxpayer to raise the defence that the Revenue acted *ultra vires* in raising the assessment (*CIR v Aken CA 1990, 63 TC 395*).

See 53.3 PARTNERSHIPS for joint liability of firm. For whether unpaid tax is a business liability for commercial etc. purposes, see *Conway v Wingate CA 1952, 31 ATC 148; Stevens v Britten CA 1954, 33 ATC 399; R v Vaccari CCA 1958, 37 ATC 104; In re Hollebone's Agreement CA 1959, 38 ATC 142*.

'Time to Pay' arrangements. By concession, under a 'time to pay' arrangement, a taxpayer enters into a negotiated agreement with the Revenue, which takes full account of his circumstances (e.g. illness, unemployment, unforeseen short-term business difficulties), and thereby commits to settle his tax liabilities by regular instalments. Clear reasons for allowing settlement over an extended period that runs beyond the due date must be established during negotiations and any such arrangement is normally subject to adequate provision being made to settle future liabilities on time. INTEREST ON UNPAID TAX (42) is chargeable in the normal way on the full amount unpaid at the due date and not just on overdue instalments. However, a surcharge may be avoided where a 'Time to Pay' arrangement is in force (see 78.21 SELF-ASSESSMENT). (Revenue HINT/Self-Assessment Manual, para 7.2.1, Personal Contact Manual, para 4.8).

56.4 COMPANIES

Companies resident in the UK pay corporation tax and are not assessable to income tax on their profits.

They must deduct income tax from payments of yearly interest (see 23.3(ii) DEDUCTION OF TAX AT SOURCE) as well as from other annual payments, and account for such income tax to the Revenue. See Tolley's Corporation Tax.

56.5 CROWN PRIORITY

Crown priority in bankruptcy was abolished with effect from 29 December 1986, except for sums due at the 'relevant date'

(*a*) on account of net tax deductions the bankrupt was liable to make under PAYE (55) from emoluments paid during the twelve months before that date, and

(*b*) in respect of deductions required to be made in the twelve months before that date under the CONSTRUCTION INDUSTRY TAX SCHEME (21).

The '*relevant date*' is the date of the making of the bankruptcy order, or, if an interim receiver was appointed before that date, the date on which he was first appointed after presentation of the bankruptcy petition. [*Insolvency Act 1986, s 386, Sch 6* and corresponding Scottish legislation].

56.6 REMISSION OR REPAYMENT OF TAX IN CASES OF OFFICIAL ERROR

Arrears of tax. Arrears of income or capital gains tax may be waived if they result from the Revenue's failure to make proper and timely use of information supplied by:

(*a*) a taxpayer about his or her own income, gains or personal circumstances;

(*b*) an employer, where the information affects a taxpayer's coding; or

(*c*) the DSS about a taxpayer's retirement, disability or widow's State pension.

The waiver will normally apply only where the taxpayer could reasonably have believed that his or her tax affairs were in order, and either:

(i) was notified of the arrears more than twelve months after the end of the tax year in which the Revenue received the information indicating that more tax was due; or

(ii) was notified of an over-repayment after the end of the tax year following the year in which the repayment was made.

Exceptionally, arrears notified less than twelve months after the end of the relevant tax year may be waived if the Revenue either failed more than once to make proper use of the facts they had been given about one source of income, or allowed the arrears to build up over two whole tax years in succession by failing to make proper and timely use of information they had been given.

(Revenue Pamphlet IR 1, A19).

Where the arrears were notified before 11 March 1996, a similar concession applies under A19, but the proportion of the tax which can be remitted depends on the taxpayer's gross income, as follows.

Taxpayer's gross income	Tax remitted
£	£
0–15,500	All
15,501–18,000	Three-quarters
18,001–22,000	One-half
22,001–26,000	One-quarter
26,001–40,000	One-tenth

The income to be considered is that for the year in which the arrears are to be met, although in practice the preceding year's income is considered. If this produces an anomaly, income of the current year may be estimated. (ICAEW Technical Memorandum TR 627, August 1986).

These scales apply separately to husbands and wives.

The concession is given only where the taxpayer was notified of the arrear after the end of the tax year following that in which it arose, unless the Revenue had made repeated errors in that period or the arrear had built up over two whole years in succession as a direct result of the Revenue's failure to make proper and timely use of the information.

Special consideration will continue to be given to the exceptional case of a taxpayer with large family responsibilities whose income is just above the normal limits for full or partial remission.

Where an **overpayment** of tax has arisen because of official error, and there is no doubt or dispute as to the facts, claims to repayment of tax are accepted outside the statutory time limits. (Revenue Press Release 10 February 1992).

56.7 OVERPAYMENT OF TAX

The Revenue's administrative practice relating to repayments of tax is as below.

(i) Where an assessment has been made and this shows a repayment due to the taxpayer, repayment is invariably made of the full amount.

(ii) Under SELF-ASSESSMENT (78), any amount repayable will be repaid on request.

(iii) Where the end-of-year check applied to Schedule E taxpayers who have not had a tax return for the year in question shows an overpayment of £10 or less, the repayment is not made automatically.

(iv) Where tax assessed has been paid to the Collector in excess of the amount due, and the discrepancy is not noted before the payment has been processed, the excess is not repaid routinely by the computer system unless it is £1 or more, or where clerical intervention is required unless it is £10 or more.

The above tolerances are to minimise work which is highly cost ineffective, they cannot operate to deny a repayment to a taxpayer who has claimed it. (Revenue Pamphlet IR 131, SP 6/95, 31 March 1995 as revised). Provisional repayments will not be made during the tax year to which a claim or claims relate if the tax involved does not exceed £50 in total. (Revenue Press Release 29 March 1989).

See 56.6 above as regards claims in cases of official error. See 5.8 ASSESSMENTS for assessing tolerances on certain state pensions. See also 17.6 CLAIMS as regards repayment procedures.

Allocation of overpayments against underpayments. Where there are underpayments of tax, overpayments will automatically be reallocated against any other tax or Class 4 NICs (or interest thereon) outstanding in respect of the amended assessment unless the amendment is processed before 1 June following the end of the year of assessment and either the amount to be reallocated to the second instalment is £1,000 or more or the tax is not yet due and the taxpayer requests that no reallocation should be made. (Revenue Assessed Taxes Manual, AT 8.701 *et seq.*). For an article on Revenue practice re allocations of overpayments under SELF-ASSESSMENT (78), see Revenue Tax Bulletin June 1999 pp 673, 674.

56.8 OVER-REPAYMENTS OF TAX

For 1995/96 and earlier years, tax over-repaid (by actual payment or set-off) and not assessable in the normal way under *TMA 1970, s 29* (see 5.1 ASSESSMENTS) may be recovered by assessment under Schedule D, Case VI as if it were unpaid tax. Any associated excess repayment supplement may be included in the assessment. The time limit for such assessment is, if necessary, extended to the end of the chargeable period following that in which the repayment was made (without prejudice to the extended time limits which apply in cases of fraudulent or negligent conduct, see 6.4 BACK DUTY). [*TMA 1970, s 30; FA 1982, s 149; FA 1989, s 149(3); FA 1990, s 105*]. See 78.34 SELF-ASSESSMENT as respects over-repayments for 1996/97 and subsequent years.

56.9 EQUITABLE LIABILITY

Where all other possible remedies have been exhausted by the taxpayer, the Revenue may be prepared to consider applying 'equitable liability' where it is clearly demonstrated that a liability assessed is greater than it would have been had the returns and supporting documentation been submitted at the proper time, provided that acceptable evidence is produced of what the correct liability should have been. It will not be sufficient to seek to replace the assessment with the taxpayer's (or accountant's) estimate of the liability. In such cases, the Revenue may be prepared to accept a reduced sum based on the evidence provided, having regard to all the relevant circumstances of the case, and not to pursue its right of recovery of the full amount. Full payment of the reduced sum would be expected.

The application of equitable liability is conditional on the taxpayer's affairs being brought fully up to date, and would be very unlikely to be applied more than once in favour of the same taxpayer.

Under self-assessment, even where, in the absence of a return, the Revenue has determined a taxpayer's liability, the taxpayer has until five years after the statutory filing date (or, if later, one year after the determination) to displace the determination with their own self-assessment (see 78.14 SELF-ASSESSMENT). The point should therefore not often be reached where a determination can no longer be replaced, but where that does occur and the above conditions are fulfilled, equitable liability may be extended to meet this situation.

(Revenue Tax Bulletin August 1995 pp 245, 246).

57 Payment of Tax—Due Dates

57.1 The Table below relates to tax for **1995/96 and earlier years** (and **for 1996/97** for Schedule D on partnerships which commenced before 6 April 1994). See 78.17 to 78.20 SELF-ASSESSMENT for due dates of interim and final payments for 1996/97 and subsequent years.

INDIVIDUALS AND PARTNERSHIPS	BASIC RATE AND HIGHER RATE	INVESTMENT INCOME SURCHARGE (1983/84 and earlier)
SCHEDULE D Cases I & II: Profits from trades and professions. Case V: Foreign business.	One-half on 1 January in tax year. One-half on 1 July following end of tax year.	—
SCHEDULE E Employment, PAYE	Deductible from emoluments as and when paid, or 14 days after first application by the Collector.	—
OTHER INCOME RECEIVED GROSS e.g. Rents, Development Gains.	1 January in tax year.	1 January in tax year.
OTHER INCOME RECEIVED UNDER DEDUCTION OF TAX, i.e. where basic or lower rate tax deducted or deemed to be deducted or if received with tax credits e.g. Dividends.	1 December following end of tax year.	1 December following end of tax year.

NOTES:

A. **If assessments are made later than dates in Table above,** see 56.1 PAYMENT OF TAX for due dates then applicable.

B. **If payments are made later than due dates,** see 42 INTEREST ON UNPAID TAX.

C. **Underwriters.** See 89 UNDERWRITERS.

58 Penalties

Cross-references. See 6 BACK DUTY. See also 67.1 RETURNS as regards reasonable excuse for failure to make returns. See also 78.10, 78.25 to 78.29 SELF-ASSESSMENT, 83.7 SOCIAL SECURITY.

Simon's Direct Tax Service A3.802 *et seq.*.

58.1 NOTIFICATION OF CHARGEABILITY

For **1988/89 to 1994/95** inclusive, a person chargeable to income tax for a year of assessment who has neither delivered a return for that year nor been required under *TMA 1970, s 8* (see 67.2 RETURNS) to do so must, within one year after the end of that year, notify the inspector, in respect of each source of income (except as below), that he is so chargeable. The maximum penalty for failure is the tax liability in respect of income from each undeclared source for that year under assessments made more than twelve months after the end of the year. Partners are liable only in respect of their share of the income concerned. The sources of income which do not have to be so notified are those in respect of which

(*a*) all payments, etc. are dealt with under PAYE (55), or

(*b*) all income has been assessed or taken into account either in determining the chargeable person's liability to tax or under PAYE (55), or

(*c*) the income is chargeable under Schedule F or is other income from which income tax has been, or is treated as having been, deducted (other than under the CONSTRUCTION INDUSTRY TAX SCHEME (21)), provided that the chargeable person is not liable for that year other than at the basic or lower rate, or

(*d*) the chargeable person could not become liable under assessments made more than twelve months after the end of the year.

Before 1988/89, the penalty for failure was £100 (in addition to any interest, etc. payable), and the exceptions referred to above were not specified. [*TMA 1970, s 7; FA 1988, s 120; F(No 2)A 1992, s 19(1)*].

Similar requirements apply in respect of notification of chargeable gains. [*TMA 1970, s 11A; FA 1988, s 122; FA 1995, s 115(3)*].

See 58.7 below as regards mitigation of penalties.

Self-assessment. See 78.4 SELF-ASSESSMENT as regards 1995/96 and subsequent years.

58.2 FAILURE TO RENDER RETURN

For **1995/96 and earlier years,** a person who fails to make a return when required to do so by notice under *TMA 1970, s 8* (individual), *s 9* (partnership), *s 12* (capital gains) or (for 1989/90 and earlier years) *ICTA 1988, s 284(4)* (married person), may become liable to a penalty.

For notices served after 5 April 1989, the maximum penalty is £300. A penalty of up to £60 per day may in addition be incurred if the failure continues after such a penalty has been imposed (but not for any day for which such a daily penalty has already been imposed). Neither penalty may be imposed after the failure has been remedied. If the failure continues beyond the end of the tax year following that in which the notice was served, a further penalty may be imposed not exceeding the amount of tax charged under assessments made after that following year on income or gains which should have been included in the return. If, however, the defaulter proves that there was no income or chargeable gain to be included in the return, the penalty under these provisions may not exceed £100. [*TMA 1970, s 93(1)(2)(5)(7); FA 1988, Sch 3 para 28; FA 1989, s 162*].

For notices served before 6 April 1989, the maximum initial penalty is £50. This penalty (and the daily penalty referred to below) is avoided if the return is rendered before penalty proceedings are commenced. If failure continues beyond the end of the tax year following that in which the notice was served, the amount of tax charged on assessments made after that year on income which should have been included in the return is added, as a penalty, to the £50 maximum, and without prejudice to the normal charge. A further penalty of £10 per day is incurred if failure continues after having been declared by Court or Commissioners before whom penalty proceedings have been commenced. If the defaulter can prove there was no income or chargeable gains to be included in the return, the total penalty cannot exceed £5. [*TMA 1970, s 93(1)(2)(5)(7) as originally enacted*].

In relation to all such notices, tax-based penalties may be reduced in respect of excess PAYE deductions, and partnership assessments are taken into account (other than in relation to partnership returns) only insofar as they relate to income of the defaulter. Assessments may not be taken into account in relation to more than one penalty, but assessments on personal representatives are taken into account following the death of the defaulter. [*TMA 1970, s 93(3)(4)(6)*].

Political objections do not justify failure to make returns (*Turton v Birdforth Commrs Ch D 1970, 49 ATC 346*), nor do objections to the system of taxation (*Walsh v Croydon Commrs Ch D 1987, 60 TC 442*). The submission of a return marked 'to be advised' or some similar phrase does not satisfy the requirements and penalties may be incurred (*Cox v Poole General Commrs Ch D 1987, 60 TC 445*). See generally *Caesar v Inspector of Taxes (Sp C 142), [1998] SSCD 1.*

See 58.7 below as regards mitigation of penalties.

Self-assessment. See 78.26, 78.27 SELF-ASSESSMENT as regards 1996/97 and subsequent years.

58.3 **NEGLIGENCE OR FRAUD**

For negligently or fraudulently making or submitting an incorrect return, accounts, claim for allowance or relief, etc., the maximum penalty is the amount of income tax (including surtax) and capital gains tax underpaid by reason of the incorrectness, for the tax year in which return, etc., delivered, the year after, and any preceding year. For returns, etc. before 27 July 1989, the maximum penalty is £50 plus, in the case of negligence, the amount of the tax so underpaid or, in the case of fraud, twice that amount, and for this purpose, *negligence* includes any innocent error not rectified without unreasonable delay after discovery.

Accounts are deemed to have been submitted by taxpayer unless he proves they were submitted without his consent or connivance. [*TMA 1970, ss 95–97; FA 1989, s 163*].

For position if agent negligent etc., see *Mankowitz v Spec Commrs Ch D 1971, 46 TC 707* and cf. *Clixby v Pountney Ch D 1967, 44 TC 515.* Assisting in or inducing the preparation or delivery of any information, return, accounts or other document known to be incorrect and to be, or to be likely to be, used for any tax purpose carries a maximum penalty of £3,000. Before 27 July 1989, assisting in, or inducing, the making or delivery of a return or accounts known to be incorrect carried a maximum penalty of £500. [*TMA 1970, s 99; FA 1989, s 166*].

See 58.7 below as regards mitigation of penalties.

58.4 **OTHER RETURNS ETC.**

For failure to render any return, certificate, statement or other document required, whether by notice or otherwise, under the provisions listed in the Table in *TMA 1970, s 98*, the maximum penalty is £300, plus £60 for each day the failure continues after that penalty is imposed (but not for any day for which such a daily penalty has already been imposed). For failure, etc. before 27 July 1989, the penalties are £50 and £10 per day respectively, and the daily penalty applies for each day the failure continues after having been declared by the court or Commissioners before whom penalty proceedings were commenced.

The maximum penalty for fraudulently or negligently making an incorrect return, etc. is £3,000 (for failure, etc. before 27 July 1989, £250 in the case of negligence, £500 in the case of fraud).

Penalties for failure to render information etc. required by notice cannot be imposed after the failure is rectified, and daily penalties can similarly not be imposed where the information etc. was required other than by notice. For failure, etc. before 27 July 1989, penalties could not be imposed if the failure had been rectified before proceedings for recovery of the penalty had been commenced. [*TMA 1970, s 98; FA 1989, s 164*].

Special penalties are imposed for failure to make annual returns required under PAYE (see 55.9(*a*) PAY AS YOU EARN) or the construction industry scheme (see 21.7 CONSTRUCTION INDUSTRY TAX SCHEME) by the statutory filing date, i.e. by 19 May following the end of the year of assessment for which the return is required. As regards returns required for 1994/95 and subsequent years, these are a penalty of £100 for each month or part month (up to twelve) during which the failure continues and for each 50 persons (or part where the total is not a multiple of 50) in respect of whom particulars should have been included in the return, and, if the failure continues beyond twelve months, an additional penalty of the amount payable for the year of assessment to which the return relates which remained unpaid at 19 April following that year. If an incorrect return is fraudulently or negligently made, the penalty is the difference between the amount payable under the return and the amount which would have been payable had the return been correct. [*TMA 1970, s 98A; FA 1989, s 165; SI 1993 No 743, reg 40A; SI 1993 No 744, regs 43, 104; SI 1994 No 2508; SI 1998 No 2622, reg 33*]. For 1994/95 returns, a period of grace of 14 days from the statutory filing date was allowed during which the automatic penalties will not be charged. (Revenue Pamphlet IR 1, B45). For subsequent returns, this will apply provided that the return is received on or before the last business day within seven days following the filing date. (Revenue Pamphlet IR 1, B46). For late 1995/96 or 1996/97 returns, where the statutory penalty exceeds the total of the tax and national insurance contributions which should be shown on the return, the penalty will normally be reduced to the amount of those duties (or £100 if greater). A reduced penalty might not apply, for example, where the Revenue believe the return shows an incorrect amount of deductions. (Revenue Press Release 14 June 1996; Revenue Tax Bulletin April 1997 p 422). For returns due for 1989/90 to 1993/94 inclusive, the Revenue are able to take proceedings before the Appeal Commissioners for an initial penalty of up to £1,200 per 50 employees, with penalties for continuing failure of up to £100 per 50 employees per month for up to twelve months. In the first year, no proceedings were taken in relation to returns submitted by 19 August 1990, but this three-month period of grace was successively reduced. (Revenue Press Release 14 March 1989). The final date for submission without penalty for 1992/93 returns was 19 June 1993, that for 1993/94 returns 19 May 1994. (Revenue Press Release 19 May 1993).

See 53.19 PARTNERSHIPS as regards penalties under *TMA 1970, s 98B* in relation to European Economic Interest Groupings.

Failure to allow access to computer records renders a person liable to a £500 penalty. [*FA 1988, s 127*].

For unlawfully possessing or disposing of an exemption certificate relating to a sub-contractor in the construction industry or making false statements relating thereto, the maximum fine is £5,000. [*F(No 2)A 1975, s 70(9)(10); ICTA 1988, s 561(10)–(13)*].

See 58.7 below as regards mitigation of penalties.

58.5 **COMMISSIONERS' PRECEPTS ETC.**

Summary penalties (to be treated as tax assessed and due and payable) may be determined by Commissioners against any party to proceedings before them who fails to comply with a precept, order for inspection etc. (see 4.6 APPEALS). The maximum penalty is £300 in the case of the General Commissioners, £10,000 in the case of the Special Commissioners (and in the case of the General Commissioners, a daily penalty up to £60 may also be imposed for continuing failure). A penalty up to £10,000 may similarly be imposed for failure to comply with any other direction of the Special Commissioners (including in relation to a preliminary hearing). [*SI 1994 No 1811, reg 24(1)(3); SI 1994 No 1812, reg 10(1)(3)(4)*]. If a person on whom a witness summons is served (see 4.6 APPEALS) fails to attend in obedience thereto, or attends but refuses to be sworn or to affirm, or refuses to answer any lawful question, or refuses to produce any document required by the summons, the Commissioners may summarily determine a penalty against that person, to be treated as tax assessed and due and payable. The maximum penalty is £1,000 in the case of the General Commissioners, £10,000 in the case of the Special Commissioners. [*SI 1994 No 1811, reg 24(2)(3); SI 1994 No 1812, reg 4(12)(13)*]. Before 1 September 1994, similar provisions applied under *TMA 1970, ss 51–53*, except that the maximum penalty for failure to comply with precepts etc. was in all cases £300 plus £60 per day (£3,000 in cases of fraudulently or negligently incorrect returns) under *TMA 1970, s 98* (see P6004 above), and the maximum penalty in relation to a witness summons was £50 in all cases.

Appeal against such summary penalties lies to the High Court (or Court of Session). [*TMA 1970, s 53 (as inserted by SI 1994 No 1813)*]. For the procedure on such appeals, see *QT Discount Foodstores Ltd v Warley Commrs Ch D 1981, 57 TC 268* and, for a case in which penalties were quashed because the taxpayer's evidence that he was unable to supply the information in question was not properly tested, *Boulton v Poole Commrs Ch D 1988, 60 TC 718*.

For appeals against penalties for non-compliance with precepts etc. see *Shah v Hampstead Commrs Ch D 1974, 49 TC 651; Chapman v Sheaf Commrs Ch D 1975, 49 TC 689; Toogood v Bristol Commrs Ch D 1976, 51 TC 634* and *[1977] STC 116; Campbell v Rochdale Commrs Ch D 1975, 50 TC 411; B & S Displays Ltd v Special Commrs Ch D 1978, 52 TC 318; Galleri v Wirral Commrs Ch D 1978, [1979] STC 216; Beach v Willesden Commrs Ch D 1981, 55 TC 663; Stoll v High Wycombe Commrs and CIR Ch D 1992, 64 TC 587; Wilson v Leek Commrs and CIR Ch D 1993, 66 TC 537.*

58.6 **PROCEDURE**

Events occurring after 26 July 1989. Except in the case of

(*a*) penalty proceedings instituted before the courts in cases of suspected fraud (see below), or

(*b*) penalties under

(i) *TMA 1970, s 93(1)(a)* (see 58.2 above),

(ii) *TMA 1970, s 94(1)* before the substitution by *F(No 2)A 1987, s 83*,

(iii) *TMA 1970, s 98(1)(i)* (see 58.4 above),

(iv) *TMA 1970, s 98A(2)(a)(i)* (see 58.4 above), or

(v) *TMA 1970, s 98B(2)(a)* (see 58.4 above),

(for which see further below),

an authorised officer of the Board may make a determination imposing any penalty under the *Taxes Acts* of an amount which he considers correct or appropriate. This does not apply to penalties awarded summarily by Commissioners (see 58.5 above).

The notice of determination must state the date of issue and the time within which an appeal can be made. It cannot be altered unless

(i) there is an appeal (see below), or

(ii) an authorised officer discovers that the penalty is or has become insufficient (in which case he may make a further determination), or

(iii) the penalty arises under *TMA 1970, s 94(6)* or *FA 1998, Sch 18 para 18(2)*, and an authorised officer subsequently discovers that the amount of tax is or has become excessive (in which case it is to be revised accordingly).

A penalty under these provisions is due 30 days after the date of issue of the notice of determination, and is treated as tax charged under an assessment and due and payable. A determination which could have been made on a person who has died can be made on his personal representatives, and is then payable out of the estate. [*TMA 1970, ss 100, 100A; FA 1989, s 167; SI 1994 No 1813; FA 1998, Sch 19 para 38*].

Appeals. Subject to the following, the general APPEALS (4) provisions apply to an appeal against a determination as if it were an appeal against an assessment to tax. *TMA 1970, s 50(6)–(8)* (see 4.6(*c*)(*e*) APPEALS) do not, however, apply, and instead, on appeal, the Commissioners can

(A) in the case of a penalty which is required to be of a particular amount, set the determination aside, confirm it, or alter it to the correct amount, and

(B) in any other case, set the determination aside, confirm it if it seems appropriate, or reduce it (including to nil) or increase it as seems appropriate (but not beyond the permitted maximum, as above).

Without prejudice to any right to have a case stated by the General Commissioners for the opinion of the High Court, or to appeal against a Special Commissioners' decision (see 4.7 APPEALS), an appeal lies to the High Court (in Scotland, the Court of Session). [*TMA 1970, s 100B; FA 1989, s 167; SI 1994 No 1813*].

Proceedings before Commissioners. For a penalty within (*b*)(i)–(v) above, an authorised officer may commence proceedings before the General or Special Commissioners. The proceedings are by way of information in writing to the Commissioners, and upon summons issued by them to the defendant (or defender), and are heard and decided in a summary way. An appeal lies to the High Court (or Court of Session) on a question of law or, by the defendant (defender), against the amount. The court can set the determination aside, confirm it if it seems appropriate, or reduce it (including to nil) or increase it as seems appropriate (but not beyond the permitted maximum, as above). The penalty is treated as tax charged in an assessment and due and payable. [*TMA 1970, s 100C; FA 1989, s 167*].

Proceedings before court. If the Board consider that liability arises from fraud by any person, proceedings can be brought in the High Court (or Court of Session). If the court does not find fraud proved, it can nevertheless impose a penalty to which it considers the person liable. [*TMA 1970, s 100D; FA 1989, s 167*].

Events occurring before 27 July 1989. In the case of failure to make returns, etc. (see 58.2 to 58.4 above) inspector may himself commence penalty proceedings before General Commissioners (penalty then limited to £50, except where any further delay); penalties for failure to comply with precepts etc. are awarded by the Commissioners summarily (see 58.5 above). Subject to this, penalty proceedings require an order of CIR and may be commenced before General or Special Commissioners, High Court or Court of Session. On appeal, the court may confirm, reduce or increase any penalty imposed by the Commissioners. Any proceedings which were, or could have been, commenced against a deceased person may be commenced or continued against his personal representatives (any penalty being a debt of the estate). [*TMA 1970, s 100 as originally enacted*].

General matters. Non-receipt of notice of the hearing at which Commissioners awarded penalties cannot be raised by way of appeal to the Court (*Kenny v Wirral Commrs Ch D 1974, 50 TC 405, Campbell v Rochdale Commrs Ch D 1975, 50 TC 411*).

For validity of penalty proceedings while assessments open, see *A-G for Irish Free State v White 1931, 38 TC 666* and *R v Havering Commrs (ex p Knight) CA 1973, 49 TC 161*. For other procedural matters, see *Collins v Croydon Commrs Ch D 1969, 45 TC 566; Bales v Rochford Commrs Ch D 1964, 42 TC 17; Sparks v West Brixton Commrs Ch D, [1977] STC 212; Moschi v Kensington Commrs Ch D 1979, 54 TC 403*; and for other appeals against penalties for failure to make returns, see *Dunk v Havant Commrs Ch D 1976, 51 TC 519; Napier v Farnham Commrs CA, [1978] TR 403; Garnham v Haywards Heath Commrs Ch D 1977, [1978] TR 303.*

For variation, etc. of penalties by the court, see *Dawes v Wallington Commrs Ch D 1964, 42 TC 200; Salmon v Havering Commrs CA 1968, 45 TC 77; Williams v Spec Commrs Ch D 1974, 49 TC 670; Wells v Croydon Commrs Ch D 1968, 47 ATC 356; Taylor v Bethnal Green Commrs Ch D 1976, [1977] STC 44; Stableford v Liverpool Commrs Ch D 1982, [1983] STC 162; Sen v St. Anne, Westminster Commrs Ch D, [1983] STC 415; Willey v CIR and East Dereham Commrs Ch D 1984, 59 TC 640; Jolley v Bolton Commrs Ch D, [1986] STC 414; Lear v Leek Commrs Ch D 1986, 59 TC 247; Delapage Ltd v Highbury Commrs and CIR Ch D 1992, 64 TC 560.*

For the test used by the court in considering whether penalties excessive, see *Brodt v Wells Commrs Ch D 1987, 60 TC 436.* Per Scott LJ, penalties awarded by different bodies of Commissioners 'should, in relation to similar cases, bear some resemblance to one another'.

A mere denial of liability to penalties implies an intention by the taxpayer to set up a case in refutation, and details must be supplied (*CIR v Jackson CA 1960, 39 TC 357*).

Statements made or documents produced by or on behalf of a taxpayer are admissible as evidence in proceedings against him notwithstanding that reliance on CIR's practice in cases of full disclosure may have induced him to make or produce them. [*TMA 1970, s 105; FA 1989, s 168(5)*].

58.7 **MITIGATION OR LIMITATION OF PENALTIES**

CIR may mitigate penalties before or after judgment. [*TMA 1970, s 102; FA 1989, s 168(4)*]. In considering mitigation, credit will be given for co-operation of taxpayer (Revenue Press Release 1 August 1977). A binding agreement by a taxpayer to pay an amount in composition cannot be repudiated afterwards by him or his executors (*A-G v Johnstone KB 1926, 10 TC 758; A-G v Midland Bank Trustee Co KB 1934, 19 TC 136; Richards KB 1950, 33 TC 1*).

For the validity of tax amnesties see *R v CIR (ex p National Federation of Self-employed and Small Businesses Ltd) HL 1981, 55 TC 133.*

For power of Revenue to enter into agreements in full settlement of liabilities in investigation cases, see 6.11 BACK DUTY.

Where **two or more tax-geared penalties** relate to the same liability, the aggregate amount of the penalties is, for 1988/89 and subsequent years of assessment, limited to the greater or greatest penalty applicable. [*TMA 1970, s 97A; FA 1988, s 129*].

See also 67.1 RETURNS as regards 'reasonable excuse' for failure to fulfil obligations.

Negotiated settlements. In the case of tax-based penalties where a maximum penalty of 100% is in strict law exigible, the inspector will start with the figure of 100% and then take the following factors into account in arriving at the penalty element which he will expect to be included in any offer in settlement of liabilities.

(*a*) Disclosure. A reduction of up to 20% (or 30% where there has been full voluntary disclosure), depending on how much information was provided, how soon, and how that contributed to settling the investigation.

(*b*) Co-operation. A reduction of up to 40%, depending upon a comparison of the extent of co-operation given in the investigation with the co-operation which the inspector believes would have been possible.

(*c*) Gravity. A reduction of up to 40%, depending upon the nature of the offence, how long it continued and the amounts involved.

(Revenue Pamphlet IR 73).

Simon's Direct Tax Service. See **A3.813, A3.1645.**

58.8 TIME LIMITS

Events occurring after 26 July 1989. The time within which a penalty can be determined, or proceedings commenced, depends on the penalty, as follows.

(*a*) If the penalty is ascertainable by reference to tax payable, the time is

(i) six years after the penalty was incurred, or

(ii) a later time within three years after the determination of the amount of the tax (except that this alternative does not apply if the tax was payable by a person who has died, it is charged in an assessment made more than six years after the chargeable period for which it is charged (for 1996/97 and subsequent years, six years after 31 January following the chargeable period), and the determination would be made in relation to the personal representatives).

(*b*) If the penalty arises under *TMA 1970, s 99* (see 58.3 above), the time is 20 years after the date when it was incurred.

(*c*) In any other case, the time is six years from the time when the penalty was, or began to be, incurred.

[*TMA 1970, s 103; FA 1989, s 169; FA 1994, ss 196, 199, Sch 19 para 32*].

Events occurring before 27 July 1989. Normally, penalty proceedings may be commenced within six years after the date the penalty was incurred, but in cases of fraud or wilful default this limit is extended to three years after final determination of tax liability, although this does not apply to personal representatives of a deceased defaulter. The time limit is also extended in cases where a penalty is calculated by reference to tax under an assessment for any year (see 58.2 and 58.3 above) made within six years thereafter. Proceedings may be commenced within three years of the final determination of that tax. But where proceedings could not have been commenced but for this extension, tax on assessments under *TMA 1970, s 37, s 39* or *s 40(2)* (see 6.4 and 6.5 BACK DUTY) is left out of account in penalty calculations. [*TMA 1970, s 103 as originally enacted*].

Final determination of tax. Provisional agreement of the amount due subject to the inspector's being satisfied with statements of assets, etc. is not final determination for these purposes (*Carco Accessories Ltd v CIR CS 1985, 59 TC 45*).

58.9 BANKRUPTS

Penalties awarded after a bankruptcy are provable debts, but in practice the Revenue does not proceed for penalties during a bankruptcy where there are other creditors. The trustee may agree to compromise any penalties awarded but the compromise must also be agreed by the bankrupt. (*Re Hurren Ch D 1982, 56 TC 494*).

58.10 **LIABILITY UNDER CRIMINAL LAW**

'False statements to prejudice of Crown and public revenue' are indictable as a criminal offence (*R v Hudson CCA 1956, 36 TC 561*).

Apart from the above, false statements in income tax returns, or for obtaining any allowance, reduction or repayment may involve liability to imprisonment for up to two years, under the *Perjury Act 1911, s 5*, for 'knowingly and wilfully' making materially false statements or returns for tax purposes. Also, in Scotland, summary proceedings may be taken under *TMA 1970, s 107*.

The Revenue practice as regards the seeking of civil penalties where a criminal prosecution has been brought for fraud are set out in Revenue Pamphlet IR 131, SP 2/88, 10 May 1988.

See 6.11 BACK DUTY as regards acceptance of money settlements instead of institution of criminal proceedings. See 35.4 INLAND REVENUE: ADMINISTRATION as regards Revenue powers generally.

Offence of fraudulent evasion of income tax. A person who is knowingly concerned in the fraudulent evasion of income tax (by him or any other person) is liable, on summary conviction, to imprisonment for up to six months and/or a fine not exceeding the statutory maximum (£5,000), or on conviction on indictment, to imprisonment for up to seven years and/or an unlimited fine. This applies to things done or omitted after 31 December 2000. [*FA 2000, s 144*].

58.11 **VALUE ADDED TAX AND EXCISE**

VAT penalties and surcharge are not allowed as a deduction for tax purposes. [*ICTA 1988, s 827(1)*]. See Tolley's Value Added Tax under Penalties. Excise penalties under *FA 1994, ss 8–11* are similarly disallowed. [*ICTA 1988, s 827(1A); FA 1994, s 18(7)*].

58.12 **INSURANCE PREMIUM TAX, LANDFILL TAX AND CLIMATE CHANGE LEVY**

Penalties and interest under the insurance premium tax, landfill tax and climate change levy provisions are not allowed as a deduction for tax purposes. [*ICTA 1988, s 827(1B)(1C)(1D); FA 1994, Sch 7 para 31; FA 1996, Sch 5 para 40; FA 2000, Sch 7 para 4*].

59 Pensions

Cross-references. See also 60 PERSONAL PENSION SCHEMES, 65 RETIREMENT ANNUITIES and 66 RETIREMENT SCHEMES.

59.1 PENSIONS ASSESSABLE UNDER SCHEDULE E

The following pensions are assessable under Schedule E as earned income on the full amount of the pensions arising (even if paid to a non-UK resident except (iv) and subject to 59.3 below).

(i) Retirement and widows' pensions etc. from UK government. [*ICTA 1988, s 617*]. See list at 83.3 SOCIAL SECURITY.

(ii) Pensions payable by the Crown or out of UK public revenue. [*ICTA 1988, s 19(1), para 2*].

(iii) Other pensions — unless paid by or on behalf of a person outside the UK. [*ICTA 1988, s 19(1), para 3*]. But see 59.4 below.

(iv) Pensions payable in the UK to a resident of the UK by an agent of the government of a British dominion or protectorate or country mentioned in *British Nationality Act 1981, Sch 3* in respect of foreign service [*ICTA 1988, s 19(1), para 4*] as increased by exchange, and with no allowance for such deductions as costs of unsuccessful lawsuit against government (*Magraw v Lewis KB 1933, 18 TC 222*). A deduction of one-tenth is allowed. [*ICTA 1988, s 196*].

(v) *Voluntary pensions* or 'annual payments' paid by employers or their successors to retired employees (or their relatives or dependants), notwithstanding that they are paid voluntarily and may be discontinued at any time [*ICTA 1988, s 133*] — except if from non-UK payer, see 59.2(ii) below.

(vi) Pensions in respect of RETIREMENT SCHEMES (66) unless the Inland Revenue direct that Schedule D, Case III shall apply. [*ICTA 1988, s 597*].

(vii) Periodical payments out of the House of Commons Members' Fund. [*ICTA 1988, s 613(3)*].

Disability payments from a company pension fund were assessable under Schedule E as pensions (*Johnson v Holleran Ch D 1988, 61 TC 428; Johnson v Farquhar Ch D 1991, 64 TC 385*).

A pension assessable under Schedule E is not an employment, so that no charge can arise on the provision of benefits in kind (see 75.13 SCHEDULE E) to retired employees. This applies in particular to the provision after retirement of medical insurance under the former employer's group medical scheme, other than in the exceptional case where the expense of providing such insurance represents a specific part of the retired person's pension or a supplementary pension. (Revenue Schedule E Manual, SE 3215).

59.2 PENSIONS ASSESSABLE UNDER SCHEDULE D, CASE V

The following pensions are assessable under Case V, as earned income.

(i) Pensions paid by or on behalf of a person outside UK — unless 59.1(iv) above applies. [*ICTA 1988, s 58(1)*].

(ii) Voluntary pensions in respect of former employment paid by or on behalf of a person outside UK. [*ICTA 1988, s 58(2)*].

The assessment is on 90% of the full amount arising in the current year of assessment (or, for earlier years, the preceding year of assessment (with adjustments in opening and closing years), see 73.9 SCHEDULE D, CASES IV AND V), *unless* the recipient is not domiciled in the UK, or being a British subject or Eire citizen is not ordinarily resident in the UK, in which case the assessment is on the amount remitted to the UK (see 63 REMITTANCE BASIS). [*ICTA 1988, s 65(1)(2)(4)–(9); FA 1974, s 22(2)*]. Arrears or retrospective increases of pensions chargeable on the arising basis may be taxed as if they arose in the years to which they relate. (Revenue Pamphlet IR 1, A55).

Where the UK government assumed responsibility under *Overseas Pensions Act 1973, s 1* for overseas pensions payable immediately before 6 April 1973, payments by them are treated as being from overseas, except as regards statutory increases. [*ICTA 1988, s 616(3)*]. See also Revenue Pamphlet IR 1, A49.

59.3 RELIEFS IN RESPECT OF PENSIONS FROM OR TO OVERSEAS

Relief may be claimable under the specific terms of a double tax treaty with the country concerned or by means of unilateral double tax relief granted in the UK. See 25 DOUBLE TAX RELIEF. Certain double tax reliefs are continued despite the British Government having assumed responsibility for payment. [*ICTA 1988, s 616(3)(4)*].

British and certain other persons resident abroad can claim UK personal allowances, see 51.11 NON-RESIDENTS AND OTHER OVERSEAS MATTERS.

59.4 EXEMPTIONS FROM UK TAX

(i) Voluntary pensions not arising out of past employment or not paid by past employers or their successors. Where a voluntary pension is paid annually out of his own pocket by someone other than the employer (e.g. by one of the directors of a company) it does not fall under 59.1(v) above. But if the lump sum, or the total of periodic payments, exceeds £30,000, the recipient may be assessable on the excess under *ICTA 1988, s 148*, see 19 COMPENSATION FOR LOSS OF EMPLOYMENT (AND DAMAGES).

(ii) **Wound and Disability Pensions of members of Armed Forces** or retired pay of disabled officers (including nurses) and compensation paid to Mercantile Marine, or for injuries under War Compensation Acts. [*ICTA 1988, s 315*]. This exemption covers pensions given for causes attributable to or aggravated by naval, military or air-force service, and additions for that reason to ordinary pensions. But not e.g. pensions to parents for loss of sons. Where a member of Armed Forces invalided by service disability and awarded combined long service and disability pension, the whole pension is exempt because not possible to identify taxable part. (Hansard 29 June 1978 Cols 654/5).

(iii) **Employees disabled at work.** Any pension awarded, on retirement through disability caused by injury on duty or by a work-related illness (or by war wounds), in addition to a retirement pension, or any excess above a normal pension on retirement through ill-health where the excess is attributable to such disablement. (Exemption does not apply to pensions paid out of approved exempt schemes, see 66 RETIREMENT SCHEMES.) (Revenue Pamphlet IR 1, A62).

(iv) Pensions payable to a non-UK resident under the *Pensions (India, Pakistan and Burma) Act 1955*; from the UK fund of a country mentioned in the *British Nationality Act 1981, Sch 3* by virtue of a post-1956 enactment or of a British colony, protectorate etc., or under the Overseas Superannuation Scheme. The exemption does not apply to certain increases under *Pensions (Increase) Acts*. [*ICTA 1988, s 615(1)(2)(a)–(d)(4)*].

(v) Pensions paid to non-UK residents under *Overseas Service Act 1958* (if in respect of foreign service), from Central African Pension Fund or Overseas Service Pension Fund. [*ICTA 1988, s 615(1)(2)(e)–(g)*].

(vi) Lump sum 'relevant benefits' (see 66.1 RETIREMENT SCHEMES) received by an employee (or by his dependants or personal representatives) from

(*a*) a *superannuation fund* within *ICTA 1988, s 615(6)* (see 59.6 below), or

(*b*) an *overseas retirement benefits scheme* or *provident fund* where certain conditions as to the employee's foreign service are met.

As regards (*b*) above, exemption may be total or partial depending on the length of foreign service, and this is determined in the same way as the statutory exemption from charge under *ICTA 1988, s 148* for foreign service payments (see 19.6 COMPENSATION FOR LOSS OF EMPLOYMENT (AND DAMAGES)) (Revenue Pamphlet IR 1, A10).

(vii) For exemptions for pensions to *war widows etc.*, see 29.32 EXEMPT INCOME.

(viii) For exemption of pensions of *victims of Nazi persecution*, see 29.7 EXEMPT INCOME.

59.5 CONTRIBUTIONS TO SECURE PENSIONS

Social Security contributions are not allowed as a deduction for tax purposes unless made by an employer in respect of an employee. [*ICTA 1988, s 617(3)(4); FA 1997, s 65; FA 1999, s 61*]. See 71.54 SCHEDULE D, CASES I AND II and 83 SOCIAL SECURITY.

Superannuation Fund deductions are allowed as set out under 66 RETIREMENT SCHEMES.

Self-employed persons and those not in an occupational scheme can secure relief for contributions as set out under 60 PERSONAL PENSION SCHEMES and 65 RETIREMENT ANNUITIES.

59.6 OVERSEAS PENSIONS FUNDS

Pension Funds for Overseas Employees — Exemption (as for a person not domiciled, resident or ordinarily resident in UK) applies to income (including gains otherwise assessable to capital gains tax) from investments or other property of a fund (*a*) established under irrevocable trusts in connection with a trade carried on wholly or partly overseas (*b*) solely to provide superannuation benefits to overseas employees (incidental duties in UK ignored), and (*c*) recognised by both employer and employees. Annuities to non-residents are payable gross, and trustees are not liable under *ICTA 1988, s 349(1)*. [*ICTA 1988, s 614(5), s 615(3)(6); TCGA 1992, s 271(1)(c); FA 1999, Sch 10 para 11*].

Overseas Superannuation Scheme Fund, and pension funds established in UK by Government of *any colony, protectorate*, etc. — investment or deposit income and capital gains exempt. [*ICTA 1988, s 614(3); TCGA 1992, s 271(1)(c)*].

60 Personal Pension Schemes (and Stakeholder Pensions)

(See the Revenue Guidance Notes on Pension Schemes IR 76.)

Cross-references. See 65 RETIREMENT ANNUITIES and 66 RETIREMENT SCHEMES generally.

Simon's Direct Tax Service E7.4.

General note. The provisions under *ICTA 1988, ss 618–629* for retirement annuity contracts for the self-employed and those in non-pensionable employment were, for new schemes, replaced, after 30 June 1988, by the regime for personal pension schemes under *ICTA 1988, ss 630–655*, designed to encourage employees who wish to do so to opt out of company pension schemes in favour of independent arrangements not linked to any one employment. Retirement annuity schemes contracted before 1 July 1988 continue, however, to be dealt with under the earlier provisions now in *ICTA 1988, ss 618–629* (see 65 RETIREMENT ANNUITIES) and the new personal pension scheme provisions adopt many of the features of those earlier provisions.

Stakeholder pensions. From 6 April 2001, the personal pension scheme provisions are adapted to accommodate the introduction of stakeholder pensions, for which provision is to be made by regulations. These will have to be facilitated by most employers (subject to alternative provision of the opportunity to join a conventional personal pension scheme in certain cases), and will offer a simplified form of scheme with low annual charges, on a contract basis as an alternative to the current trust regime. The major new element is the ability to pay up to £3,600 into a scheme without reference to earnings, but a number of other significant changes are also made, as described below.

Application for approval under the new regime (or amendment of an existing scheme to incorporate the revised provisions) cannot be made before 1 October 2000. [*FA 2000, Sch 13 para 30*]. Schemes approved before 6 April 2001 are deemed to include certain of the new provisions on or after that date (for which see further below). [*FA 2000, Sch 13 para 28*].

The headings in this chapter are as follows.

60.1	Outline of provisions	60.6	Unused relief carried forward
60.2	Contract requirements	60.7	— example
60.3	Limits of relief	60.8	Relevant earnings
60.4	— example	60.9	Mis-sold personal pensions etc.
60.5	Contributions related back		

60.1 OUTLINE OF PROVISIONS

Relief is available in respect of contributions payable by an individual under arrangements made in accordance with a 'personal pension scheme' (see 60.2 below). Before 6 April 2001, eligibility to make contributions to a scheme is determined by the possession of 'relevant earnings' (see 60.8 below). From that date, in consequence of the introduction of stakeholder pensions (contributions to which may, to a limited extent, be made without reference to earnings), a scheme may not be approved if it accepts contributions from a member (or his employer) during a year of assessment unless one of the following applies.

(*a*) The member has actual (i.e. not presumed) net relevant earnings (see 60.8 below) for that year.

(*b*) The member does not have actual net relevant earnings but is, for some part of that year, *not* in 'pensionable employment' (see 60.8 below), and either

(i) at some time in that year the member is UK-resident and ordinarily resident, or

(ii) at some time in that year the member was, or was the spouse of, a person in an employment the duties of which are treated as performed in the UK under *ICTA 1988, s 132(4)(a)* (Crown servants, see 75.2(i) SCHEDULE E), or

(iii) the member was UK-resident and ordinarily resident both at some time in the preceding five years of assessment and when the personal pension arrangements were made.

(*c*) Where neither (*a*) nor (*b*) above applies, and throughout that year the member *is* in 'pensionable employment' (see 60.8 below), and

(i) the member satisfies either (*b*)(i), (*b*)(ii) or (*b*)(iii) above,

(ii) the member is not, and has not been, a 'controlling director' (see 60.8 below) of any company at any time in that year or in the preceding five years of assessment (disregarding years before 2000/01),

(iii) for at least one of the preceding five years of assessment (but excluding years before 2000/01), the aggregate of the member's grossed-up remuneration (i.e. remuneration as defined by Treasury order and increased in accordance with such an order) from each office and each employment held on 5 April in that year does not exceeed the 'remuneration limit' (initially set at £30,000 but variable by Treasury order) for the year in which the contributions are made, and

(iv) the total of the contributions made in that year by the member or his employer, together with any other such contributions made in that year under approved personal pension arrangements made by the member, does not exceed the 'earnings threshold' (see 60.3 below) for that year.

The Treasury may by order provide for persons claiming to be so eligible to make contributions to provide such declarations, certificates or other evidence in support of the claim as the order may require.

There must be provision for repayment of ineligible contributions (which, in the case of a contribution causing the limit in (*c*)(iv) above to be exceeded, requires repayment only of the excess over the earnings threshold and of any subsequent contributions in the year, to enable that condition to be met).

Schemes approved before 6 April 2001 are deemed to include provision prohibiting acceptance of contributions from (or in respect of) members not satisfying any of the above conditions.

[*ICTA 1988, ss 632A, 632B; FA 2000, Sch 13 paras 8, 28(2)(3)(8)*].

For 2000/01 and earlier years, the contributions paid in a year of assessment may, subject to certain limits (see 60.3 below), be deducted from the individual's 'relevant earnings' (see 60.8 below) as assessed for that year. In the case of Schedule E employees, and subject to conditions prescribed by regulations (see *SI 1988 No 1013*), relief is given by deduction of basic rate tax, which may be recovered by the scheme administrator. Relief other than by deduction at source, and higher rate relief in all cases, is given on a claim being made (on form PP120 or in the income tax return) by deduction or set off in an assessment.

For 2001/02 and subsequent years, relief for contributions in any year is given up to a maximum of the greater of the 'earnings threshold' for the year and, where (*c*) above does not apply, the 'maximum amount' for the year (see 60.3 below). Relief for all contributions is given by deduction of basic rate tax (subject to conditions to be prescribed by regulations) recoverable by the administrator. Higher rate relief is, on a claim, given by an addition to the basic rate limit of the amount of contributions in respect of which relief is available for the year.

In addition, any contribution to such a scheme by the employer is not chargeable to tax on the individual under Schedule E. There are provisions for adjustment of relief following alterations in the individual's liability to tax, and for the prevention of double relief.

The Revenue consider that where a payment *may* be made under deduction of basic rate tax, basic rate relief can *only* be obtained by deduction. The tax deducted from valid contributions is not clawed back where the individual is liable only at less than the basic rate of income tax or has no income tax liability. The Inland Revenue Financial Intermediaries and Claims Office may be contacted in relation to personal pensions on 0151–472 6109/6110/6161/6170 as regards repayments, on 0151–472 6171/6172/6173/6364 for general advice, or on 0151–472 6022 for technical advice.

[*ICTA 1988, ss 639, 643(1); FA 2000, Sch 13 paras 15, 28(6)–(8)*].

Income and gains on scheme investments are exempt from income tax and capital gains tax, and there are similar reliefs in relation to authorised unit trusts which are also approved personal pension schemes. [*ICTA 1988, s 643(2); TCGA 1992, s 271(1)(h)(j)*]. See 71.32 SCHEDULE D, CASES I AND II as regards futures and options contracts.

There are special provisions relating to salaries of members of the House of Commons or the Scottish Parliament. [*ICTA 1988, s 654; FA 1999, Sch 5 para 6*].

An annuity payable under such a scheme is treated as earned income of the annuitant to whom it is made payable by the terms of the arrangements. Annuity payments made after 5 April 1995 are dealt with under PAYE, rather than (as previously) being paid under deduction of tax under Schedule D, Case III (see 23.11 DEDUCTION OF TAX AT SOURCE) (unless the Board direct that Schedule D, Case III shall apply until a specified date). [*ICTA 1988, s 643(3)(4), s 648A; FA 1994, s 109*]. Income withdrawals (within 60.2(ii) or (iv) below) are also earned income of the recipient assessable under Schedule E and dealt with under PAYE. [*FA 1995, Sch 11 para 11*]. Payments, etc. from a scheme to or for the benefit of an individual who has made arrangements in accordance with the scheme, but which are not authorised under scheme rules, are chargeable under Schedule E on that individual [*ICTA 1988, s 647*], as are contributions by the employer to such a scheme where the arrangements are not approved (see 60.2 below). [*ICTA 1988, s 648*].

Where a lump sum refund of contributions is paid under 60.2(viii) below in a case where the member's death occurred after he had elected for income withdrawals under 60.2(ii) below, the scheme administrator is charged under Schedule D, Case VI on the gross payment at the rate of 35% (variable by Treasury order). [*ICTA 1988, s 648B; FA 1995, Sch 11 para 12*].

Contributions to personal pension schemes are not deductible in arriving at profits for Class 4 national insurance purposes (see 83.7 SOCIAL SECURITY). [*Social Security Contributions and Benefits Act 1992, Sch 2 para 3(2)(g)*].

Administrators. A charge on the administrator of a scheme is treated as charged on all present and future administrators and is assessable in the name of the administrator, but is not assessable on persons who are no longer administrators. [*ICTA 1988, s 658A; FA 1998, s 98(1)*]. SELF-ASSESSMENT (78) does not apply to charges on administrators. [*TMA 1970, s 9(1A); FA 1998, s 98(2)(3)*]. Where there is no scheme administrator or he cannot be traced, there is provision for notices etc. to be delivered to certain other persons. [*ICTA 1988, s 653A; FA 1998, s 97*].

Information and penalties. The inspector may require information on scheme contributions and refunds, and copies of scheme accounts. There are penalties for giving false information in support of an application for approval (see 60.2 below) or for the purpose of obtaining relief from or repayment of tax under these provisions, or for failure to supply information as above or in relation to regulations regarding deduction of tax from contributions (see above). From 31 July 1998, the Revenue have available extensive regulatory powers to make provision for additional information requirements (displacing those referred to above). [*ICTA 1988, ss 651A, 652, 653; TMA 1970, s 98; FA 1989, s 170(4); FA 1998, s 96, Sch 27 Pt III(21)*].

See generally Revenue Pamphlet IR 78.

Simon's Direct Tax Service. See E7.4.

60.2 **CONTRACT REQUIREMENTS**

For approval under ICTA 1988, s 631 (which, from 6 April 2001, may be conditional), a personal pension scheme must be established by:

(*a*) a person authorised under *Financial Services Act 1986, Pt I, Ch III* to carry on investment business, and who carries on business either of issuing insurance policies or annuity contracts or of managing authorised unit trust schemes (see 90.1 UNIT TRUSTS);

(*b*) a building society (see 9 BUILDING SOCIETIES);

(*c*) a pension company which is an associate of a building society;

(*d*) an institution authorised under *Banking Act 1987* or a subsidiary or holding company (or a subsidiary of the holding company) of such an institution;

(*e*) a recognised bank or licensed institution within *Banking Act 1979*;

(*f*) (from 24 October 1997) an EC insurance company lawfully carrying on long term business, or providing long-term insurance, in the UK, and certain European banking institutions; or

(*g*) such other person as the Treasury may specify by order.

There must be a person responsible for administration of the scheme who is resident in the UK. [*ICTA 1988, ss 631, 632, 638(1); FA 1988, s 54; FA 2000, Sch 13 para 6; SI 1988 No 993; SI 1997 No 2388*].

The scheme may not provide for benefits to an individual participant other than the following.

(i) A life annuity payable to the participant, commencing not earlier than age 50 and not later than age 75 (except as follows) and which, except as detailed at (v) below, must not be capable of assignment or surrender other than for the purpose of giving effect to a pension-sharing order or provision under *Welfare Reform and Pensions Act 1999, s 24(1)*. An annuity may commence earlier than age 50 in the event of the participant becoming physically or mentally incapacitated from carrying on his occupation, or any similar one, or if earlier retirement is customary in his occupation. As regards the latter, the following early retirement ages have been agreed by the Superannuation Funds Office.

30 Downhill skiers.
35 Athletes; badminton players; boxers; cyclists; dancers; footballers; ice hockey players; models; national hunt jockeys; real tennis players; rugby league players; rugby union players; squash players; table tennis players; tennis players; wrestlers.
40 Cricketers; divers (saturation, deep sea and free swimming); golfers; motor-cycle riders (motocross or road racing); motor racing drivers; snooker and billiards players; speedway riders; trapeze artistes.
45 Flat racing jockeys; members of the reserve forces.

These pension ages apply only to arrangements funded by contributions in respect of relevant earnings from the occupation or profession in question. For professional sportsmen, the earnings must arise from activities as such, e.g. tournament earnings and appearance and prize money, and not from sponsorship or coaching (for which separate arrangements may be made). (Revenue Pamphlet IR 76, Appendix 10).

(ii) Where schemes (or amendments) are approved on or after 1 May 1995, income withdrawals, i.e. payments of income other than by way of annuity, during a period of deferral of the purchase of an annuity under (i) above, where the participant so elects. Income withdrawals may not commence before the participant attains the age of 50 (subject to provision for earlier commencement as under (i) above) and must not continue after the participant attains the age of 75. The right to such income withdrawals must not be capable of assignment or surrender other than for the purpose of giving effect to a pension-sharing order or provision under *Welfare Reform and Pensions Act 1999, s 24(1)*. The aggregate income withdrawals in each successive twelve month period starting with the 'pension date' must be between 35% and 100% (inclusive) of the annual amount of the annuity purchasable on the 'relevant reference date'. The '*pension date*' for this purpose is the date on which the member elects to make income withdrawals, and the '*relevant reference date*' is the pension date for the first three years of withdrawals, and thereafter the first day of each successive three year period. The annuity purchasable on any such date is determined by reference to the value on that date, as determined by the scheme administrator, of the accrued rights under the scheme (net of any lump sum payable on that date) and the Government Actuary's annuity rate tables (copies of which may be obtained free of charge from Supplies Section, Pension Schemes Office, Yorke House, PO Box 62, Castle Meadow Road, Nottingham NG2 1BG (tel. 0115–974 1670)). The basis on which those Tables are prepared is prescribed in *The Personal Pension Schemes (Tables of Rates of Annuities) Regulations 1996* (*SI 1996 No 1311*).

For schemes approved on or after 1 October 2000, provision is made for the alignment of different relevant reference dates where income withdrawals are taken from schemes with multi-segmented arrangements. Broadly, reviews of all such arrangements are aligned on the relevant reference date for the arrangement with the earliest pension date (disregarding certain arrangements no longer in operation). Provision is also made from that date allowing reviews after the initial period to be by reference to a particular day in the 60 days before the relevant reference date.

From 6 April 2001, where income withdrawals have been taken, schemes may make provision for different parts of the fund to be used to purchase different annuities (which may commence on different days), with corresponding provision for the review dates for continuing income withdrawal arrangements.

(iii) A life annuity payable after the death of the participant to the surviving spouse or to a dependant, which, except as detailed at (v) below, must not be capable of assignment or surrender other than for the purpose of giving effect to a pension-sharing order or provision under *Welfare Reform and Pensions Act 1999, s 24(1)*. Such an annuity may, however, cease on the marriage of the annuitant or, in the case of an annuity to a surviving spouse, if there ceases to be any dependant under the age of 18 before the surviving spouse attains age 45. An annuity to a dependant under 18 at the time the annuity first becomes payable *must* cease on his attaining age 18 or on the later of his attaining age 18 and ceasing full-time education, unless the dependency was not only because of his being under age 18.

The aggregate of such annuities (or if they vary the initial aggregate) must not exceed the annuity (or highest annuity) payable to the participant under the scheme or, if he died before receiving an annuity under the scheme, the highest annuity that would have been payable under the scheme (ignoring any lump sum commutation, see (vi) below) had it been purchased on the day before his death. Where payments of such an annuity were or would have been affected by the making of any pension-sharing order or provision under *Welfare Reform and Pensions Act 1999, s 24(1)*, those amounts are determined as if the only payments of the annuity to be taken into account were those that have been or would have been so affected.

An annuity to a surviving spouse who is under 60 at the time of the participant's death may be deferred to a time not later than the attainment of that age or, if an annuity is payable for a term certain under (v) below which terminates after attainment of that age, the termination of that annuity.

(iv) Where schemes (or amendments) are approved on or after 1 May 1995, income withdrawals (as under (ii) above) during a period of deferral of the purchase of an annuity under (iii) above, where the person entitled to the annuity so elects. The limitations and conditions on the amount of withdrawals are as under (ii) above, but by reference to the date of death of the participant rather than the date of election for income withdrawals, and without the provisions for alignment of review dates under multi-segmented arrangements. Withdrawals may not be made where an annuity under (iii) above has been deferred until the surviving spouse attains age 60, or after the payments under an annuity purchased under (iii) above by the person concerned would have ceased, or after that person attains the age of 75 or (if earlier) after the participant would have attained that age. The right to such income withdrawals must not be capable of assignment or surrender other than for the purpose of giving effect to a pension-sharing order or provision under *Welfare Reform and Pensions Act 1999, s 24(1)*.

(v) An annuity as at (i) or (iii) above may continue for a term certain not exceeding ten years if the original annuitant dies within that term, and such an annuity may be assigned by will or by the annuitant's personal representatives in distributing his estate. The annuity is regarded as being for a term certain even if it may terminate on the happening, after the original annuitant's death but within that term, of the marriage of the annuitant to whom it becomes payable, or of his attaining age 18, or of the later of his attaining age 18 and ceasing full-time education.

(vi) If the participant so elects, the benefits under the scheme may be partially commuted for a lump sum at the time when the annuity at (i) above is first payable or the time at which he elects to make income withdrawals under (ii) above. The lump sum must not exceed one-quarter of the difference between the total value at that time of the benefits under the scheme and the value at that time of the protected rights under *Social Security Act 1986* (or NI equivalent) (except that where the scheme came into existence before 27 July 1989, the protected rights reduction did not apply as regards arrangements made before that day), and must not be capable of assignment or surrender other than for the purpose of giving effect to a pension-sharing order or provision under *Welfare Reform and Pensions Act 1999, s 24(1)*. In relation to schemes approved before 27 July 1989, the reduction for protected rights was not required, but is nevertheless treated as being included in the rules where the lump sum arrangements are made on or after that date. There was also an overriding limit on the lump sum of £150,000 (variable by Treasury order), but any scheme rule applying a fixed limit (other than in relation to lump sums payable out of transfer payments) is treated as not applying to lump sums payable on or after that date.

(vii) A lump sum may be payable on the death of the participant before age 75.

(viii) If no annuity under (i) or (iii) above has become payable at the time of the participant's death, a lump sum representing a return of contributions with reasonable interest or bonuses (or if contributions are invested in a unit trust scheme, the sale or redemption price of the units) may be payable. Where schemes (or amendments) are approved on or after 1 May 1995, the lump sum may be payable on or after the participant's death, but, where the death occurred after the participant had elected for income withdrawals (within (ii) above), within two years after the death (and see 60.1 above as regards charge to tax on lump sums so payable). Also in relation to such approvals, a refund of contributions is after allowing for any withdrawals within (ii) or (iv) above, no lump sum may be paid to a surviving spouse who has elected for deferral to age 60 under (iii) above, and the prohibition where an annuity has become payable under (iii) above applies only to a lump sum payable to the person who purchased the annuity. Where schemes (or amendments) are approved on or after 29 April 1996, a lump sum may also be payable (without time limit) on the death of a person who has deferred an annuity and taken income withdrawals under (iv) above (the lump sum being required to take account of any annuity purchased under (iii) above in favour of another person).

A scheme may also make provision for insurance against a risk relating to the non-payment of contributions, so that the premiums attract relief (although any contributions paid on a claim do not do so), but this ceases to apply to insurance contracts made after 5 April 2001. Premiums on existing contracts (including those under personal pension arrangements taken out before 6 April 2001 with an option for such insurance, whether or not exercised before that date, and notwithstanding any premium variations on or after that date) will continue to attract relief. Where premiums on a contract taken out after 5 April 2001 accordingly do not attract relief, any contributions paid from claim proceeds will be capable of doing so.

Where a scheme is approved on or after 1 May 1995, it must (except in such cases as may be prescribed by regulations) prohibit the acceptance of further contributions and the making of transfer payments after the date on which an annuity within (i) above is first payable or the participant elects for income withdrawals within (ii) above. In the latter case, minimum contributions within (C) below may continue to be accepted with effect from 6 April 1996. [*SI 1996 No 805*].

An annuity within (i) or (iii) above or a lump sum within (vii) above must be payable by an authorised insurance company, which in the case of (i) and (iii) above may be chosen by the participant or the annuitant. For the definition of 'authorised insurance company', see *ICTA 1988, s 630* and, from 1 May 1995, *ICTA 1988, s 659B, 659C* introduced by *FA 1995, s 59(4)(5), s 60.*

As regards the requirements relating to pension-sharing arrangements (which apply from 1 December 2000) referred to in (i)–(iv) and (vi) above, these apply in relation to approvals from 10 May 2000. For pension-sharing generally, see Pension Schemes Office Update No 62, 28 April 2000.

[*ICTA 1988, s 630, ss 633–637A; FA 1989, Sch 7 paras 2, 11, 12; F(No 2)A 1992, Sch 9 para 17; FA 1995, Sch 11 paras 1–8; FA 1996, s 172; FA 1999, Sch 10 paras 12–14; FA 2000, Sch 13 paras 5, 6, 9–12, 28(4); SI 2000 No 1093*].

A scheme must also satisfy any requirements laid down by the Board as to the making, acceptance and application of transfer payments. [*ICTA 1988, s 638(2)*]. See *The Personal Pension Schemes (Transfer Payments) Regulations 1988* (*SI 1988 No 1014*) and *(Amendment) Regulations 1989* (*SI 1989 No 1115*). These are further amended with effect from 19 March 1997 (*(Amendment) Regulations 1997* (*SI 1997 No 480*)) to permit transfers to free-standing additional voluntary contribution schemes, without losing the right to commute part of the fund at retirement (and see Treasury Press Release 31 January 1997 and Pension Schemes Office Update No 34, 26 September 1997).

Contributions may only be accepted from

(A) the individual participants in the scheme,

(B) their employers, and

(C) in respect of certain minimum contributions (the 'contracted-out' rebate), the Secretary of State.

Contributions within (A) and (B) above by or in respect of a participant, together with those under any other schemes arranged by the participant, must not exceed the 'maximum amount' for the year of assessment or (for 2001/02 onwards), if greater, the earnings threshold for that year (see 60.3 below). Any excess must be repaid to the participant to the extent of his contributions, otherwise to the employer. A scheme must not accept contributions within (C) above in respect of service as a director whose emoluments are excluded from being relevant earnings (see 60.8 below), and such minimum contributions may only be accepted where either the participant is not in pensionable employment at the time the contributions are paid, or the scheme rules prohibit acceptance of contributions from the participant or employer. Schemes must (unless regulations prescribe to the contrary) prohibit the acceptance of contributions, or the making of transfer payments, after the date on which benefits are first taken under (i) or (ii) above (subject, from 6 April 2001, to *ICTA 1988, s 638ZA*, see below, which provides for benefits to be taken separately in respect of different parts of the scheme funds). For 2001/02 onwards, schemes may accept contributions in cash or equivalent (as previously) or in the form of the transfer (at market value) of shares acquired under a savings-related share option scheme, an approved profit-sharing scheme or an employee share ownership plan (see 82.38, 82.9, 82.11 SHARE INCENTIVES AND OPTIONS), provided that the transfer takes place within 90 days of the right to acquire the shares being exercised.

[*ICTA 1988, s 638(3)–(13); FA 1988, s 55(2)(4); FA 1995, Sch 11 para 9; FA 2000, Sch 13 para 13*].

From 6 April 2001, schemes may provide for multiple annuities, and for different annuities to commence on different days, and for deferral elections to be made at different times in relation to different portions of the fund (and for corresponding availability of multiple lump sums, each subject to corresponding limitations). There are detailed provisions for applying the general restrictions on benefits where such multiple arrangements are made, effectively treating each annuity or withdrawal arrangement as deriving from a separate scheme. [*ICTA 1988, s 638ZA; FA 2000, Sch 13 para 14*].

Approval by the Board cannot be effective before 1 July 1988. Regulations provide for provisional approval to be granted. [*ICTA 1988, s 655(4)(5); FA 1988, s 54(2)(c); SI 1987 No 1765; SI 1988 No 1437; FA 1989, Sch 7 para 9*].

The Revenue have available from 31 July 1998 extensive further regulatory powers to prescribe restrictions on approval of personal pension schemes. [*ICTA 1988, s 638A; FA 1998, s 94*].

Withdrawal of approval. If, in the Board's opinion, the facts concerning a personal pension scheme do not warrant the continuance of approval, it may be withdrawn. Approval may similarly be withdrawn in relation to any individual arrangements made under such a scheme. Withdrawal must be by written notice to the scheme administrator (and to the individual if appropriate), and must state the grounds for withdrawal and the date from which it is effective (which must not be before the date when the facts first warranted withdrawal). Approval may be withdrawn from the date on which arrangements were made where, in the Board's opinion, the securing of the provision of benefits under the arrangements was not the sole purpose of the individual in making them. [*ICTA 1988, s 650*]. There is provision for notice of withdrawal to be given to certain other persons where there is no scheme administrator or he cannot be traced. [*ICTA 1988, s 653A; FA 1998, s 97*]. See Pension Schemes Office Update No 33, 26 September 1997, as regards rebated and shared commissions on transfer of funds between investment vehicles.

Where approval of any personal pension arrangements is withdrawn (as above) after 16 March 1998, tax at 40% is charged under Schedule D, Case VI on the value, immediately before approval was withdrawn, of the properly attributable part of the assets held for the purposes of the scheme under which the arrangements were made. The value of assets is their market value, except that rights or interests in respect of money lent directly or indirectly to any person who made or contributed to the arrangements (or CONNECTED PERSONS (20)) are valued at the amount owing (including unpaid interest). The person liable for the tax is the scheme administrator, but there is provision for recourse to the person who made the arrangements in certain cases. Approval of arrangements may be withdrawn for these purposes notwithstanding that approval may simultaneously be withdrawn from the whole scheme. [*ICTA 1988, ss 650(6), 650A; FA 1998, s 95*]. Assets which are the subject of a charge under *ICTA 1988, s 650A* (as above) are treated for capital gains tax purposes as acquired at the time of withdrawal of approval for a consideration equal to the amount on which tax was charged (without there being any deemed disposal at that time). [*TCGA 1992, s 239B; FA 1998, s 95(3)*].

Appeals against refusal or withdrawal of approval (including approval of conversion of a retirement benefits scheme under *ICTA 1988, Sch 23ZA*, see below) must be made to the Board within 30 days of the notice of refusal or withdrawal, and lie to the Special Commissioners. Their decision on an appeal against withdrawal may be to alter the effective date of the withdrawal. [*ICTA 1988, s 651; FA 2000, Sch 13 para 24*].

Refunds of contributions. For the circumstances in which contributions are repaid, and the procedural requirements, see Revenue Guidance Notes IR 76, Pt 18.

Trivial funds. Where a member's fund under a scheme is insufficient to provide an annuity of at least £260 p.a. or the fund does not exceed £2,500, the fund may be repaid to the member (net of expenses) if certain conditions are met (including the member's not being a member of another scheme or in receipt of an annuity from any scheme). The repayment (net of any permissible lump sum payment under the scheme) is chargeable under Schedule E on the member (under *ICTA 1988, s 647* — see 60.1 above). (Revenue Guidance Notes IR 76, para 9.32).

Conversion of certain approved retirement benefits schemes to approved personal pension schemes. From 1 October 2000, the trustees of any retirement benefits scheme (see 66.1 RETIREMENT SCHEMES) which is eligible (broadly, money purchase schemes which could be approved as personal pension schemes under *ICTA 1988, s 631* as above, for which purpose retirement benefits schemes may be treated as consisting of different elements so as to identify those eligible for conversion) may apply to the Board of Inland Revenue for approval of the scheme (or part) as a personal pension scheme instead of as a retirement benefits scheme (or part). If the application is granted, it will apply from a specified date (not earlier than 6 April 2001). For the detailed conditions, see *ICTA 1988, Sch 23ZA.* In particular, in considering approval, the Board may require valuations of benefits and assets to be undertaken in respect of specified individual members and may require any excess assets to be dealt with in a particular way. The Board may also impose conditions as to the contributions which may be made between the date of any such valuation and the date of conversion to a personal pension scheme. [*ICTA 1988, ss 611(3), 631A, Sch 23ZA; FA 2000, Sch 13 paras 4, 7, 27*].

Simon's Direct Tax Service. See **E7.403**.

60.3 LIMITS OF RELIEF

For **2000/01 and earlier years,** a contribution paid by an individual under approved personal pension arrangements may be deducted from or set off against 'relevant earnings' for the year of assessment in which the payment is made. The maximum amount for which relief is available is $17\frac{1}{2}\%$ of 'net relevant earnings' (see 60.8 below), with increased limits for older individuals as indicated in the following table where the individual is in the age range indicated at the beginning of a year of assessment.

36 to 45	20%
46 to 50	25%
51 to 55	30%
56 to 60	35%
61 or more	40%

Any excess of 'net relevant earnings' over an allowable maximum is disregarded. The allowable maximum is the same as the 'permitted maximum' referred to at 66.4 RETIREMENT SCHEMES (i.e. £91,800 for 2000/01). Any employer contribution is deducted from the overall contribution limit, but minimum contributions within 60.2(C) above are ignored for this purpose. Within the overall limit, contributions to secure a lump sum payable on the death of the participant are limited to 5% of 'net relevant earnings'. [*ICTA 1988, ss 639(1), 640, 640A; FA 1989, Sch 7 paras 3, 4; FA 1995, Sch 11 para 10*].

For the deduction of basic rate tax from certain contributions, see 60.1 above.

For **2001/02 and subsequent years**, relief for contributions in any year is given up to a maximum of the greater of the 'earnings threshold' for the year and (except in the case of 'concurrent' schemes within 60.1(*c*) above) the 'maximum amount' for the year (which remains as for 2000/01 and earlier years, see above, including the cap on net relevant earnings). The '*earnings threshold*' is £3,600, subject to variation by the Treasury by order. As previously, any employer contribution is deducted from the overall contribution limit, with minimum contributions within 60.2(C) above being ignored for this purpose. Within the overall limit, contributions to secure a lump sum payable on the death of the participant are restricted:

(*a*) where the life assurance contract was made (or could have been made) before 6 April 2001, to **5%** of net relevant earnings; or

(*b*) where the contract was made on or after that date (and not by exercise of an option available before that date), to **10%** of the aggregate allowable contributions made by employer and employee for that year other than for death benefits.

[*ICTA 1988, ss 630(1)(1A), 639(1), 640, 640A; FA 2000 Sch 13 paras 16, 28(6)–(8)*].

For the deduction of basic rate tax from contributions, see 60.1 above.

Where relief is also available for qualifying retirement annuity premiums in a year of assessment, the relief available for personal pension contributions is correspondingly reduced. [*ICTA 1988, s 655(1)(a); FA 2000, Sch 13 para 25*]. See following Example.

Simon's Direct Tax Service. See **E7.407**.

60.4 *Example*

C is an employee whose date of birth is 30 April 1948 and who does not participate in his employer's occupational pension scheme. His earnings, as computed for Schedule E purposes, for 1999/2000 and 2000/01 are £92,000 and £97,000 respectively. C pays annual retirement annuity premiums of £6,000 under long-standing contracts. For all years up to and including 1998/99, he has paid additional retirement annuity premiums and personal pension scheme contributions so as to take maximum advantage of the relief available to him; he thus has no unused relief.

In August 1999, C makes a contribution of £15,900 (less basic rate tax) to a personal pension scheme. In December 1999, his employer contributes £750 to this scheme.

In the year ended 5 April 2001, C and his employer make contributions of £21,000 (less basic rate tax) and £1,000 respectively to the scheme.

The maximum relief is calculated as follows.

1999/2000

	£	£
Maximum relief for personal pension contributions:		
25% of capped net relevant earnings of £90,600		22,650
Deduct retirement annuity relief claimed	6,000	
employer's contribution	750	6,750
Relief due		15,900
Amount paid		15,900
Unused relief		Nil
		£
Maximum relief for retirement annuity premiums:		
$17\frac{1}{2}$% of net relevant earnings of £92,000		16,100
Amount paid		6,000
		10,100
Less relief claimed for personal pension contributions		15,900
Unused relief		Nil
Total relief due (£15,900 + £6,000)		£21,900

2000/01

	£	£
Maximum relief for personal pension contributions:		
30% of capped net relevant earnings of £91,800		27,540
Deduct retirement annuity relief claimed	6,000	
employer's contribution	1,000	7,000
Relief due		20,540
Amount paid		21,000*
Unused relief		Nil
		£
Maximum relief for retirement annuity premiums:		
20% of net relevant earnings of £97,000		19,400
Amount paid		6,000
		13,400
Less relief claimed for personal pension contributions		20,540
Unused relief		Nil
Total relief due (£20,540 + £6,000)		£26,540

* For 2000/01, there are excess contributions of £460 which do not qualify for relief, and which must be repaid. Such an excess is deemed to relate primarily to contributions made by the individual rather than by his employer (see 60.2 above).

60.5 CONTRIBUTIONS RELATED BACK

For contributions paid **before 6 April 2001**, an individual who makes a qualifying contribution in a year of assessment (whether or not he has relevant earnings for that year) may elect that the contribution (or part) be treated as paid

(*a*) in the last preceding year of assessment, or

(*b*) if he had no net relevant earnings in the last preceding year, in the last preceding year but one.

Form PP43 is available from the inspector for the purpose of making such an election. For contributions paid in 1996/97 and later years, the election must be made on or before 31 January following the year of assessment in which the contribution is paid (for earlier years, on or before 5 July following that year of assessment).

Where such an election is made, the contribution is treated as having been paid in the year elected and not in the year actually paid. See 17.2 CLAIMS as regards how relief for contributions carried back to 1996/97 and subsequent years is given. An election is in practice treated by the Revenue as operative only up to the maximum available for relief for the year specified in the election. If the amount specified in the election becomes excessive as a result of an adjustment to the assessment for the year specified, the unrelievable proportion will fall back into the actual year of payment.

For years before 1997/98, *Lloyd's underwriters* may elect that a qualifying contribution paid in the year may be related back to the third previous year of assessment before the year of payment (i.e. a contribution paid in 1994/95 could be related back to relevant earnings assessed for 1991/92). The earlier year must have unused relief attributable to relevant earnings from Lloyd's underwriting activities. The election must be made before the end of the year of assessment in which the contribution is paid. Where such an election is made the normal provisions for relating back contributions do not apply. The election ceases to be available for 1997/98 and subsequent years, for which the basis of assessment of Lloyd's underwriters is changed (see 89.2 UNDERWRITERS).

[*ICTA 1988, s 641; FA 1993, s 183(3); FA 1994, s 228(2)(4); FA 1996, s 135, Sch 21 para 18; FA 2000, Sch 13 para 17*].

For contributions paid **after 5 April 2001**, a person who pays a contribution on or before 31 January in any year of assessment may, at or before the time the contribution is paid, irrevocably elect for the contribution (or part) to be treated as having been paid in the preceding year of assessment and not in the year in which it was actually paid. [*ICTA 1988, s 641A; FA 2000, Sch 13 para 18*].

Simon's Direct Tax Service. See E7.410.

60.6 UNUSED RELIEF CARRIED FORWARD

For **2000/01 and earlier years**, relief available for a year of assessment which is not used in that year may be carried forward and used to cover that part of a qualifying contribution paid in any of the next six years which exceeds the relief limit (see 60.3 above) for that year. Relief is given in the year in which the contribution is paid although the maximum relief for that year must be used first. Unused relief for earlier years must be used before that for later years. Form PP42 is available from the inspector for claiming such relief.

Where an assessment on an individual's earnings becomes final and conclusive more than six years after the end of the year to which it relates, and as a result there is an amount of unused relief for that year, that amount shall not be available for any of the following six years. However, that relief may be covered by a qualifying contribution paid within six months of the date on which the assessment becomes final and conclusive. Relief is given in the year of assessment in which the contribution is paid but is not allowed unless the maximum contribution allowable for that year (see 60.3 above) is paid. Although the extra contribution representing the unused relief must be paid within the specified six months, the maximum contribution for the year of assessment in which the extra contribution is paid may be paid at any time within the normal time limits for that year. If relief is given for a contribution in this way, it may not be given under the normal carry-forward rule. Relief is given in a similar way where relevant earnings for a year which ended more than six years previously are not formally assessed but are taken into account in an offer in settlement in a back duty case. See 6.11 BACK DUTY.

Where contributions are made under both approved personal pension arrangements and retirement annuity contracts (see 65 RETIREMENT ANNUITIES) in a year of assessment, the unused relief that may be utilised in that year is correspondingly reduced. For the method of calculating the reduction, see *Brock v O'Connor (Sp C 118), [1997] SSCD 157.*

No unused relief for personal pension contributions may be carried forward to 2001/02 or any later year.

[*ICTA 1988, s 642; FA 2000, Sch 13 para 19*].

Simon's Direct Tax Service. See E7.411.

60.7 *Example*

P, who was born in 1975, entered non-pensionable employment in September 1997 and his recent personal pension scheme contribution record, assuming no unused relief before 6 April 1997, is as follows.

Year	Net relevant earnings	Maximum relief due	Amount paid	Unused relief
	£	£	£	£
1997/98	15,000	2,625	2,425	200
1998/99	19,000	3,325	2,200	1,125
1999/2000	22,000	3,850	3,375	475

In 2000/01, P pays a personal pension scheme contribution of £5,000 (less basic rate tax). His net relevant earnings for that year are £24,000.

P has excess contributions for 2000/01 as follows.

Net relevant earnings	£24,000
	£
Maximum relief (£24,000 × 17$\frac{1}{2}$%)	4,200
Contributions made	5,000
Excess contributions	£800

Tax relief on the excess contributions can be obtained in the following way.

In 1999/2000

£475 may be related back to 1999/2000 and relief obtained for that year (see 60.5 above).

In 2000/01

The remainder (£325) is matched on a first in, first out basis with the unused relief brought forward (see 60.6 above).

	£	£
Excess contributions as above		800
Deduct amount related back to 1999/2000		475
		325
Unused relief 1997/98	200	
Unused relief 1998/99	125	325

Thus, full relief is obtained for the £5,000 paid in 2000/01 and P's revised relief record is as follows.

Year	Net relevant earnings	Maximum relief due	Amount relieved	Unused relief	Unused relief c/f
	£	£	£	£	£
1997/98	15,000	2,625	2,425	200	200
1998/99	19,000	3,325	2,200	1,125	1,325
1999/2000	22,000	3,850	3,850	—	1,325
2000/01	24,000	4,200	4,525	(325)	1,000

Notes

(*a*) The balance of the 1998/99 unused relief, i.e. £1,000, cannot be carried forward to 2001/02.

(*b*) As an alternative to carrying back £475 to 1999/2000, P could have utilised an additional £475 of his 1998/99 unused relief and obtained relief in 2000/01 for the whole of the £5,000 paid in that year. The £475 unused relief for 1999/2000 would then be carried forward together with £525 of the 1998/99 relief. A further possibility is to carry back £1,800 to 1999/2000, thus utilising all unused relief in that year and leaving £1,000 unused relief for 2000/01. This would be advantageous if the taxpayer's marginal tax rate were higher in the earlier year.

(*c*) Unused relief in 2001/02 and subsequent years cannot be carried forward.

60.8 RELEVANT EARNINGS

'*Relevant earnings*' of an individual for the purposes of such schemes is chargeable income which is included in one of the following categories.

(*a*) Income from an office or employment which is not 'earnings from pensionable employment', and income from property which is either attached thereto or forms part of the emoluments therefrom.

(*b*) Income chargeable under Schedule D immediately derived from the carrying on, individually or in partnership, of his trade, profession or vocation. This includes enterprise allowances (see 71.85 SCHEDULE D, CASES I AND II) and POST-CESSATION RECEIPTS (62).

(*c*) Income from patent rights treated as earned income under *ICTA 1988, s 529*.

It does not include any amount in respect of which tax is chargeable under Schedule E which arises from acquisitions or disposals of shares or interests in shares, or from rights to acquire shares, or any amount in respect of which tax is chargeable under *ICTA 1988, s 148* (see 19.5 COMPENSATION FOR LOSS OF EMPLOYMENT (AND DAMAGES)), or income of the individual as director of a company whose income is wholly or mainly investment income and which is controlled (within *ICTA 1988, s 840*) by the individual, with or without past or present directors of the company. Nor does it include emoluments of a person who is a 'controlling director' at any time in the year of assessment in question, or who has been one at any time during the period of ten years prior to that year, if at any time in the year of assessment any of the following circumstances apply to him.

(i) He is in receipt of benefits under a 'relevant superannuation scheme' payable in respect of past service with the company.

(ii) He is in receipt of benefits under a personal pension scheme, the scheme has received a transfer payment from a 'relevant superannuation scheme', and the transfer payment was in respect of past service with the company.

(iii) He is in receipt of benefits under a 'relevant superannuation scheme', the benefits are payable in respect of past service with another company, and the emoluments are for a period during which the company of which he is a 'controlling director' has carried on a trade or business previously carried on by the second company, which itself carried on the trade or business at any time during the period of service in respect of which the benefits are payable.

(iv) He is in receipt of benefits under a personal pension scheme, the scheme received a transfer payment from a 'relevant superannuation scheme', the transfer payment was in respect of past service with another company, and the emoluments are for a period during which the company of which he is a 'controlling director' has carried on a trade or business previously carried on by the second company, which itself carried on the trade or business at any time during the period of service in respect of which the transfer payment was made.

For these purposes benefits which would have been received in respect of past service but for the transfer of rights under a pension-sharing order or provision under *Welfare Reform and Pensions Act 1999, s 24(1)* are treated as being received in respect of such service. Benefits received *as* an ex-spouse are, however, excluded. Transfer payments similarly do not include any made for the purpose of giving effect to a pension-sharing order or provision.

A person is a '*controlling director*' if he is a director within *ICTA 1988, s 612(1)* and comes within the meaning of *ICTA 1988, s 417(5)(b)* (which broadly refers to ownership, or direct or indirect control, with or without associates, of 20% or more of ordinary share capital). '*Relevant superannuation scheme*' has the same meaning as in *ICTA 1988, s 645(1)* (see below). References to benefits and transfer payments payable in respect of past service include benefits and transfer payments partly so payable.

In determining 'net relevant earnings' (see below), relevant earnings are determined before deducting capital allowances (other than those deductible in computing profits) but inclusive of any balancing charges.

A married woman's relevant earnings are *not* relevant earnings of her husband for these purposes.

[*ICTA 1988, s 644; FA 1989, Sch 7 para 5, Sch 12 para 16; FA 1999, Sch 10 para 15*].

'*Earnings from pensionable employment*' are earnings from an office or employment in respect of service in which the individual is a participant in a 'relevant superannuation scheme'. Such schemes under which benefits are restricted to an annuity to a surviving spouse or dependant and/or a lump sum on death in service are disregarded for this purpose. See also below as regards concessional relief in the case of certain small lump sum retirement benefits schemes. Where the only benefit paid under a scheme in respect of a period of employment was a refund of contributions (or where no benefit accrued in a non-contributory scheme), earnings from that employment are relevant earnings for the purposes of carry-forward of unused relief (see 60.6 above). (Revenue Guidance Notes IR 76, para 7.12).

A '*relevant superannuation scheme*' is a scheme established by a person other than the individual concerned, an object of which is the provision of retirement benefits, and which is (or, in the case of certain foreign emoluments, corresponds to) a scheme within 66.1(*a*)–(*c*) RETIREMENT SCHEMES. It does not include a scheme converted to a personal pension scheme under *ICTA 1988, Sch 23ZA* (see 60.2 above).

It is irrelevant for this purpose where the duties of the office or employment are performed, and whether or not the individual is chargeable to tax in respect of it.

[*ICTA 1988, s 645; FA 1989, Sch 7 para 6; FA 2000, Sch 13 para 20*].

'*Net relevant earnings*' are relevant earnings, as above, less deductions which would be made therefrom in computing the individual's total income for income tax, being:

(i) deductions which but for *ICTA 1988, s 74(1)(m), (p) or (q)* could be made in computing his profits or gains (i.e. various payments, subject to deduction of tax at source, made for business purposes, but excluding e.g. annuities to former partners, which would be prohibited under *ICTA 1988, s 74(1)(a)*);

(ii) deductions made by virtue of *ICTA 1988, s 198* (allowable expenses), *ICTA 1988, s 201* (professional subscriptions) or *ICTA 1988, s 332(3)* (clergymen's expenses); or

(iii) deductions in respect of losses, or of capital allowances, relating to activities any profits from which would be relevant earnings of the individual.

'Relevant earnings' for this purpose are those earnings before giving effect to any capital allowance not an allowable deduction in arriving at profits, but after taking account of balancing charges.

Other amounts deducted in charging the individual's income to tax (e.g. for earnings from work done abroad, see 75.3 SCHEDULE E, or under the current provisions) do not reduce net relevant earnings.

Where

(A) in any year of assessment 2000/01 or earlier, contributions are relieved against relevant earnings, or

(B) in any year of assessment 2001/02 or later, higher rate relief for contributions is given by an extension of the basic rate limit (see 60.1 above),

and a deduction for a loss or allowance under (iii) above is treated as made to any extent out of income other than relevant earnings, net relevant earnings for the next year are treated as reduced to that extent, any balance being carried forward to the third year, and so on.

In the case of partnership profits, net relevant earnings are the share of partnership income (as computed for tax purposes) after allowable deductions for partnership payments and capital allowances.

[*ICTA 1988, s 646; FA 2000, Sch 13 para 21*].

However, where an individual holds two or more 'associated' employments in a year, at least one of which is pensionable (as above) and one not, the earnings from the non-pensionable employment(s) are taken into account only to the extent that those from the pensionable employment(s) do not exceed the allowable maximum (see 60.3 above). Employments are '*associated*' if one employer controls the other, or both are controlled by a third person, directly or indirectly, at any time in the year. [*ICTA 1988, s 646A; FA 1989, Sch 7 para 8*].

Presumption of same level of net relevant earnings for five years. Where a member of a personal pension scheme provides evidence (as prescribed by regulations made by the Board) of the amounts needed to calculate his net relevant earnings for any year of assessment (the '*basis year*') to the scheme administrator (whether or not he was a member of the scheme in the basis year), it is presumed that those amounts (and hence the net relevant earnings) are the same in each of the five years of assessment following the basis year. The earliest year to which such a presumption may apply is 2001/02. This is subject to such conditions or exceptions as may be prescribed by regulations made by the Board.

Certain particulars furnished under the *Personal Pension Schemes (Relief at Source) Regulations 1988* (*SI 1988 No 1013*), *reg 5* for years before 2001/02 are treated as satisfying the evidence requirement in relation to a basis year for the purposes of the above presumption.

Where such evidence is provided for a later basis year, it supersedes that provided for the earlier basis year. If the actual net relevant earnings are higher in the later year, the supersession has effect for the later basis year and subsequent years of assessment In any other case, it has effect only for years of assessment later than the last of the five years following the earlier basis year. The order in which evidence is presented in relation to different basis years is immaterial for these purposes.

Where the member has no actual (as opposed to presumed) relevant earnings for a year of assessment not earlier than 2001/02 (the '*break year*'), but had actual relevant earnings for the preceding year (the '*cessation year*') and was entitled to make contributions in excess of the earnings threshold (see 60.3 above) in any one or more of the six years of assessment preceding the break year (the '*reference years*'), special rules apply to any of the five years of assessment following the cessation year other than a year or years

(*a*) for which there were actual relevant earnings, or

(*b*) throughout which the member held a pensionable office or employment (as above), or

(*c*) immediately following a year excluded under (*a*) or (*b*).

In applying the presumption (as above) to any such year, the basis year may be any one of the reference years for which the requisite evidence is provided, whether or not there is a gap of more than five years and notwithstanding the supersession rules (as above). If such evidence has been provided for more than one reference year, the member may nominate which is to be the basis year for this purpose, by written notice to the scheme administrator. Years excluded by (*a*)–(*c*) above in relation to one break year are not thereby excluded in relation to a different break year.

[*ICTA 1988, ss 646B–646D; FA 2000, Sch 13 paras 22, 23, 28(8), 29*].

Simon's Direct Tax Service. See E7.409.

Small lump sum retirement benefits schemes. Concessional relief applies where an employee has

(A) paid contributions to a personal pension scheme (or premiums on a retirement annuity contract), or the employer has made such contributions for the employee's benefit, for a year of assessment (see 60.3 above), and

(B) accrued benefits, for the same year and in respect of the same office or employment, under an approved retirement benefits scheme

  (i) under the rules of which the only benefit on retirement (other than from additional voluntary contributions) is a lump sum not exceeding £400 per year of pensionable service, and

  (ii) whose rules provide for no such lump sum to accrue (or for the lump sum to be waived) in respect of any period for which contributions are made to a personal pension scheme or retirement annuity contract.

The tax relief for the personal pension contributions (or retirement annuity premiums) will not be withdrawn provided that

(1) the lump sum benefit entitlement for the period is waived or does not accrue, and

(2) the personal pension scheme (or retirement annuity contract) is not cancelled.

(Revenue Pamphlet IR 1, A95).

60.9 MIS-SOLD PERSONAL PENSIONS ETC.

See 29.3 EXEMPT INCOME for the exemption from income and capital gains tax of compensation awards for mis-sold personal pensions, etc..

The Pension Schemes Office has issued guidance on how such compensation payments should be applied and the consequences for tax purposes. The general recommendation is that compensation should be paid into an appropriate pensions vehicle to secure the benefits lost as a result of the bad advice. Where possible this should result in reinstatement or instatement into an occupational pension scheme. Payments of cash in hand would be appropriate only where the individual concerned has already retired (or died) and catching-up payments are required or, exceptionally, where it is impractical for redress to be achieved by the provision of retirement benefits. Regulations provide for the conditions under which such reinstatements may be achieved and for the disapplication of provisions under which they might otherwise be prevented, e.g. earnings cap provisions. (Pension Schemes Office Updates Nos 21, 22 August 1996 and 26, 24 March 1997). Regulations to ensure that reinstatement may be made on appropriate terms are contained in *The Occupational Pension Schemes (Transitional Provisions) (Amendment) Regulations 1996* (*SI 1996 Nos 3115, 3234*), *The Retirement Benefits Schemes (Continuation of Rights of Members of Approved Schemes) (Amendment) Regulations 1996* (*SI 1996 Nos 3114, 3233*) and *The Retirement Benefits Schemes (Tax Relief on Contributions) (Disapplication of Earnings Cap) (Amendment) Regulations 1996* (*SI 1996 No 3113*), all effective from 1 January 1997.

61 Personal Service Companies Etc.

61.1 **INTRODUCTION**

With effect for 2000/01 and subsequent tax years (and see 61.2 below), provisions are introduced 'to remove opportunities for the avoidance of tax and Class 1 national insurance contributions (NICs) by the use of intermediaries, such as [personal] service companies or partnerships, in circumstances where an individual worker would otherwise be an employee of the client or the income would be income from an office held by the worker' (Annex to Revenue Press Release 23 September 1999). These are based on rules first published as Revenue Budget Press Release IR35 on 9 March 1999 (though significant changes were made subsequently) and thereafter commonly referred to as the 'IR35' proposals.

The rules do not prevent an individual providing his services through an intermediary. Instead, where the individual would otherwise have been categorised under pre-existing case law and practice as an employee in relation to a particular engagement, his income from that engagement is deemed to have been paid to him (if not *actually* paid to him) by the intermediary as remuneration which is within SCHEDULE E (75) and subject to PAY AS YOU EARN (55) and NICs. This applies even if the income is, in fact, paid to the individual in some other way, for example in the form of dividends from a personal service company (but see 61.14 below) or as a share of partnership profits within Schedule D, Case I or II, or is retained within the intermediary. Some allowance is made for deductible expenses (see 61.8, 61.9 below). Although proposed as an attack on avoidance, the provisions apply to any situation within their ambit (see 61.3, 61.5 below) and are not dependent on the taxpayer's motive.

The tax provisions are contained in *FA 2000, s 60, Sch 12* and are described in this chapter. For the NIC position, see *The Social Security Contributions (Intermediaries) Regulations 2000 (SI 2000 No 727)* (or, as regards Northern Ireland, *SI 2000 No 728*), and see Tolley's National Insurance Contributions.

The Revenue have published on a dedicated website — at http://www.inlandrevenue.gov.uk/ir35 — their answers to a number of so-called 'Frequently Asked Questions' (FAQs) on both the tax and NICs aspects of these provisions. A selection of these is reproduced, together with a worked example, in Revenue Tax Bulletin June 2000 pp 751–757. See also Revenue Pamphlet IR 175.

The operation of *ICTA 1988, s 134* (workers supplied by agencies — see 75.46 SCHEDULE E) is not affected by these provisions. [*FA 2000, Sch 12 para 24*]. *Section 134* applies only where the worker engaged through the agency is an individual. If a service company, for example, is engaged by a client via an independent agency, the provisions in this chapter may well apply but will not directly affect the agency.

The remainder of this chapter is set out under the following headings.

61.2 Commencement

61.3 Services provided through an intermediary

61.4 — Whether or not employment?

61.5 Intermediaries to which these provisions apply

61.6 — Supplementary

61.7 The 'Deemed Schedule E payment'

61.8 — Computation of Deemed Schedule E payment

61.9 — Supplementary

61.10 — Example

61.11 Tax treatment of Deemed Schedule E payment
61.12 — PAYE
61.13 — Computation of intermediary's business profits
61.14 Relief where dividends etc. paid by intermediary
61.15 Earlier date of Deemed Schedule E payment in certain cases
61.16 Multiple intermediaries
61.17 Transition
61.18 Deciding employment status — Summary of Revenue Tax Bulletin article

61.2 COMMENCEMENT

The provisions have effect for **2000/01 and subsequent tax years in relation to services performed after 5 April 2000**. Payments and other benefits received on or before that date in respect of services performed after that date are treated for these purposes as received in the tax year 2000/01 and are thus brought within the scope of these provisions. [*FA 2000, Sch 12 para 22*]. As regards non-corporate intermediaries, see also the transitional measure at 61.17 below.

61.3 SERVICES PROVIDED THROUGH AN INTERMEDIARY

The provisions apply in relation to an engagement where the following conditions are all present:

(*a*) an individual (the worker) personally performs, or is under an obligation personally to perform, services for a 'business' carried on by another person (the client);

(*b*) the services are provided not under a contract directly between worker and client but under arrangements involving a third party (the 'intermediary') to which these provisions apply (see 61.5 below); and

(*c*) if the services had been provided under a direct contract as mentioned in (*b*) above, the worker would have fallen to be categorised for income tax purposes as an employee of the client (see 61.4, 61.18 below).

The term '*intermediary*' in (*b*) above can refer to a company or to an individual. It is expressly provided that the term also refers to a partnership or unincorporated body of which the worker is a member. The fact that the worker may hold an office, for example a directorship, with the client does not prevent the provisions from applying.

The term '*business*' in (*a*) above includes any activity carried on by a government or public or local authority (in the UK or elsewhere) or by a body corporate, unincorporated body or partnership. It also implicitly includes a business, but not any other activity, carried on by an individual. For the purposes of these provisions generally, a business means a trade, profession or vocation and also includes a Schedule A business (as in 68.4 SCHEDULE A). Domestic or other services provided to an individual not in business (a householder for example) are outside the scope of the provisions, regardless of the test in (*c*) above.

[*FA 2000, Sch 12 paras 1, 21(1)*].

61.4 **Whether or not employment?** In applying the test at 61.3(*c*) above, i.e. whether or not the worker would have been an employee if engaged directly, the circumstances to be taken into account include the terms on which the services are provided, having regard to the terms of contracts forming part of the arrangements (as in 61.3(*b*) above) under which the services are provided. [*FA 2000, Sch 12 para 1(4)*]. Otherwise, no statutory rules are provided, the test instead being based on pre-existing case law and practice as to the distinction between employment and self-employment — see 75.24 SCHEDULE E, Tolley's National Insurance Contributions under Categorisation and Revenue Pamphlet IR 56. See also Revenue Tax Bulletin February 2000 pp 715–723 for a comprehensive article and practical illustrations devoted to the *FA 2000* provisions. The main text of this article is summarised at the end of this chapter — at 61.18 below. It is the reality of the working relationship that counts, irrespective of whether the parties have chosen to attach a different label to it (*Massey v Crown Life Insurance Co CA 1977, [1978] 2 All ER 576*).

Workers with signed contracts extending beyond 6 April 2000 were able to seek an opinion from the Revenue as to whether or not the contract would fall within the *FA 2000* provisions. The Revenue have also identified a standard contract said to be common to service company workers engaged, through agencies, in the information technology industry. Such a contract requires the worker

(*a*) to work where the client requests, for an agreed number of hours per week, and at an agreed hourly rate;

(*b*) to keep a timesheet for checking by the client;

(*c*) to be subject to the client's control; and

(*d*) not to sub-contract the work to anyone else.

Where a worker is engaged for a month or more on a contract of this type, and cannot demonstrate a recent history of work including engagements which have the characteristics of self-employment, the Revenue will treat the engagement as being within the *FA 2000* provisions. (Note that whilst this may be a convenient rule of thumb, the taxpayer is not precluded from arguing for a different treatment.) Where the contract is for less than a month, the Revenue will consider each case on its merits. (Revenue Press Release 7 February 2000 and Revenue Tax Bulletin February 2000 p 717).

61.5 INTERMEDIARIES TO WHICH THESE PROVISIONS APPLY

The provisions apply only if the intermediary meets the relevant conditions below.

Where the intermediary is a company, the provisions apply in relation to an engagement if either

(*a*) the worker has a 'material interest' (see below) in the intermediary, or

(*b*) the payment or benefit in 61.7(ii) below is received or receivable by the worker directly from the intermediary and can reasonably be taken to represent remuneration for services provided by the worker to the client.

The provisions do not, however, apply if either of the above is satisfied but the intermediary is an associated company (within *ICTA 1988, s 416*) of the client by reason of both the client and itself being under the control of the worker (or of the worker and another person).

For these purposes, the worker has a '*material interest*' in a company if he, and/or certain 'associates' of his (within *FA 2000, Sch 12 para 19* and with the extended meaning of 'husband and wife' at 61.6(*c*) below),

(i) beneficially owns or is able to control (directly or indirectly) more than 5% of the ordinary share capital, or

(ii) possesses, or is entitled to acquire, rights to more than 5% of any distributions that the company may make, or

(iii) (where the company is a close company) possesses, or is entitled to acquire, rights to more than 5% of the assets available for distribution among the participators (within *ICTA 1988, s 417(1)*) in a winding-up or in any other circumstances.

[*FA 2000, Sch 12 paras 3, 21(1)*].

Where the intermediary is a partnership, the provisions apply in relation to payments or benefits received or receivable by the worker as a member of the partnership if

(A) the worker, *alone or with one or more 'relatives'*, is entitled to at least 60% of partnership profits; or

(B) most of the partnership profits derive from provision of services under engagements within 61.3 above to a single client (or to a single client and his 'associates' — within *FA 2000, Sch 12 para 19*); or

(C) the partnership profit sharing arrangements are such that the income of any of the partners is based on the income which that partner generates from engagements within 61.3 above.

'*Relative*' is broadly defined to include a spouse (or cohabitant treated as such — as in 61.6(*c*) below), parent or remoter forebear, child or remoter issue, or brother or sister). Most family partnerships are thus potentially within these rules.

In addition, the provisions apply in relation to payments or benefits received or receivable by the worker directly from the partnership, but in a capacity other than as a member of the partnership, if they can reasonably be taken to represent remuneration for services provided by the worker to the client.

[*FA 2000, Sch 12 paras 4, 21(4)*].

Where (exceptionally) the intermediary is an individual, the provisions apply in relation to a payment or benefit if it is received or receivable by the worker directly from the intermediary and can reasonably be taken to represent remuneration for services provided by the worker to the client. [*FA 2000, Sch 12 para 5*].

Overseas intermediaries. There is no requirement that the intermediary be resident or incorporated in the UK. An offshore service company, for example, can fall within these provisions (and see 61.11 below as regards place of business). See also Revenue FAQs — as in 61.1 above.

61.6 **Supplementary.** For the purposes of the above (and of these provisions generally),

(*a*) whether a person is an '*associate*' of an individual is construed in accordance with *ICTA 1988, s 417(3)(4)* (with the extended meaning of 'husband and wife' at (*c*) below), except that special rules apply to determine whether an individual is an associate of an employee benefit trust of which he is a beneficiary;

(*b*) a payment or benefit receivable from a partnership or unincorporated association includes any such payment or benefit to which a person may be entitled in his capacity as a member of the partnership or association;

(*c*) a payment or benefit provided to a member of an individual's family or household (within *ICTA 1988, s 168(4)* but treating a man and woman cohabiting as a couple as if they were husband and wife) is treated as provided to the individual; and

(*d*) anything done by an 'associate' (as defined) of an intermediary is treated as done by the intermediary.

[*FA 2000, Sch 12 para 19(1)(a), (2)–(6), para 21(2)–(4)*].

61.7 **THE 'DEEMED SCHEDULE E PAYMENT'**

If, as regards any engagement within 61.3 above, in any tax year

(i) the intermediary is within these provisions by virtue of 61.5 above, and

(ii) the worker (or an 'associate' of his) receives, is entitled to receive, or has rights entitling him to receive, from the intermediary (directly or indirectly) a payment or other benefit not chargeable to tax under Schedule E,

the intermediary is deemed to have made to the worker, normally on 5 April in that tax year (though see 61.15 below for exceptions), a payment (a '*deemed Schedule E payment*') the amount of which is computed as in 61.8 below and which is chargeable to tax under Schedule E. Where such payments would be treated as having been made in respect of multiple engagements, a single such payment is deemed to have been made. See 61.12 below as regards the application of PAYE. [*FA 2000, Sch 12 para 2*].

See 61.6 above for the meaning of 'associate' in relation to an individual and other supplementary provisions.

The above provisions are not triggered by a payment subject to deduction of tax under *ICTA 1988, s 555* (payments to non-resident entertainers and sportsmen — see 51.8 NON-RESIDENTS AND OTHER OVERSEAS MATTERS). [*FA 2000, Sch 12 para 6*].

61.8 **Computation of deemed Schedule E payment.** The deemed payment in 61.7 above is computed as follows (and see the supplementary points at 61.9 below).

(1) Take the total of all 'payments and other benefits' (see 61.9 below) received by the intermediary in the tax year in respect of engagements falling within 61.7 above by reference to the worker (the '*relevant engagements*') and reduce it by **5%** (see 61.9 below).

Where a payment received by the intermediary has been subjected to deduction of tax at source under the CONSTRUCTION INDUSTRY TAX SCHEME (21), it is the gross amount before tax that must be brought into account in arriving at this total.

(2) Add in any 'payments and other benefits' (see 61.9 below) received direct by the worker (and see 61.6(*c*) above) in that tax year in respect of the relevant engagements, *from anyone other than the intermediary*, that are not chargeable under Schedule E but would have been if the worker had been employed by the client.

(3) Deduct

(*a*) any expenses met (see below) by the intermediary in that tax year which, if incurred by the worker as an employee of the client, would have been deductible under normal rules — see 75.10 SCHEDULE E,

(*b*) any capital allowances which on that basis could have been claimed by the worker under *CAA 1990, s 27* (see 10.24 CAPITAL ALLOWANCES), and

(*c*) any contributions made to an approved occupational or personal pension scheme by the intermediary in that tax year for the benefit of the worker which, if made by an employer for the benefit of an employee, would not be regarded as the employee's income for tax purposes — see 60 PERSONAL PENSION SCHEMES and 66 RETIREMENT SCHEMES. Exclude any excess contributions made and later repaid.

(4) Deduct

(*a*) any 'payments or other benefits' (see 61.9 below) received in that tax year by the worker from the intermediary and chargeable under Schedule E in his hands (but excluding anything already deducted under (3)(*a*) above), and (*b*) any employer's Class 1 and Class 1A NICs (on salary and benefits-in-kind) payable by the intermediary for that tax year in respect of the worker.

If the result is a negative amount, or is nil, there is no deemed Schedule E payment. In any other case, the deemed Schedule E payment is the amount which, together with employer's NICs thereon, is equal to the result of applying steps (1)–(4) above. In other words, allowance is made at this point for the fact that employer's NICs are chargeable on the deemed payment itself (see Tolley's National Insurance Contributions).

[*FA 2000, Sch 12 paras 7, 8, 21(1)*].

For the purposes of (3)(*a*) above, an intermediary 'meets' an expense on the date it pays the bill (Revenue FAQs — as in 61.1 above).

See the Example at 61.10 below.

61.9 **Supplementary.** For the purposes of computing the deemed Schedule E payment as in 61.8 above, any amounts received by the intermediary that refer to more than one worker, or partly to a worker and partly to other matters, are to be apportioned on a just and reasonable basis. [*FA 2000, Sch 12 para 9*].

For the purposes of 61.8(1), (2) and (4) above, a '*payment or other benefit*' includes anything that would be an emolument of a Schedule E employment or would be chargeable to tax as such. The amount of a payment or cash benefit is taken to be the amount received. The amount of a non-cash benefit is found in the same way as in 19.5 COMPENSATION FOR LOSS OF EMPLOYMENT and will normally be the amount computed under the employee benefit-in-kind rules at 75.13–75.20 SCHEDULE E. A payment or cash benefit is treated as received when payment is actually made (or a payment is made on account). A non-cash benefit is treated as received when it is used or enjoyed. [*FA 2000, Sch 12 para 10*].

The 5% deduction at 61.8(1) above is a standard allowance intended to cover the intermediary's running costs. It is given regardless of the actual occurrence or amount of such running costs, and does not have to be justified or supported by records. The limited deductions at 61.8(3) above, based on actual expenditure, are given in addition to the 5% deduction. The 5% deduction applies purely for the purpose of computing the deemed Schedule E payment under these provisions, and is not deductible in computing the business profits of the intermediary (actual running costs being deductible or not, as the case may be, under normal rules — see 71 SCHEDULE D, CASES I AND II and see also 61.13 below as regards partnerships). See 61.13 below as regards deductibility of the deemed Schedule E payment itself.

61.10 *Example*

Harry is a systems analyst trading through his own personal service company, ABC Ltd, in which he owns 99% of the ordinary shares. During 2000/01, he is engaged at different times by two independent companies, DEF Ltd and GHJ Ltd (the client companies), in each case under a contract between the client company and ABC Ltd. It is accepted that each engagement is in the nature of employment and is within the provisions covered in this chapter. ABC Ltd is paid £40,000 by DEF Ltd and £20,000 by GHJ Ltd for the services provided by Harry.

For 2000/01, Harry draws a salary of £28,000 from ABC Ltd which is taxed under PAYE and on which employer's NICs of, say, £3,400 are due. He is also provided with a company car on which the taxable benefit is £4,000 and on which Class 1A NICs of, say, £500 are due. ABC Ltd makes pension contributions of £3,100 into an approved scheme on Harry's behalf and reimburses motor expenses of £1,500 which, if Harry had been employed directly by the client companies, would have been qualifying travelling expenses within

75.10(*a*) SCHEDULE E. It pays a salary of £4,300 to Harry's wife who acts as company secretary and administrator.

The deemed Schedule E payment is computed, using steps numbered in accordance with 61.8 above, as follows.

		£	£	£
Step (1)	Total amount from relevant engagements			60,000
	Deduct 5%			3,000
				57,000
Step (2)	Not applicable			
Step (3)	*Deduct* (*a*) Schedule E expenses	1,500		
	(*b*) Not applicable	—		
	(*c*) Pension contributions	3,100	4,600	
Step (4)	*Deduct* Salary	28,000		
	Benefits	4,000		
	Employer's Class 1 NICs	3,400		
	Employer's Class 1A NICs	500	35,900	40,500
Total				£16,500

Deemed Schedule E payment £16,500 × $\frac{100}{112.2}$	14,706
Employer's NICs due on deemed payment £14,706 @ 12.2%	1,794
Total as above	£16,500

Note

The salary paid by ABC Ltd to Harry's wife is not deductible in arriving at the deemed Schedule E payment, except to the extent that it, and other expenses of the company, are covered by the 5% deduction at 61.8(1) above. (The salary may of course be deductible under the rules of SCHEDULE D, CASE I (71) in computing ABC Ltd's taxable business profits.)

61.11 TAX TREATMENT OF DEEMED SCHEDULE E PAYMENT

The deemed Schedule E payment is generally treated in the same way as an actual payment of emoluments, as if the worker were employed by the intermediary and as if the relevant engagements (see 61.8(1) above) were undertaken by him in the course of performing the duties of that employment. The PAYE provisions are applied as in 61.12 below. Where

(*a*) the worker is UK-resident,

(*b*) the services in question are provided in the UK, and

(*c*) the client carries on business in the UK,

the intermediary is treated as having a place of business in the UK (and is thus obliged to operate PAYE for example — see 55.34 PAY AS YOU EARN) even if this is not, in fact, the case.

To the extent that, by reason of any combination of

(i) the worker being resident, ordinarily resident or domiciled outside the UK,

(ii) the client being resident or ordinarily resident outside the UK, and

(iii) the services in question being provided outside the UK,

the worker would not be chargeable under Schedule E if employed directly by the client, he is not chargeable in respect of the deemed Schedule E payment. (See 75.2, 75.6 SCHEDULE E for the relevant Schedule E charging provisions.)

In particular, the deemed Schedule E payment counts

(A) to determine whether the worker is a 'higher paid employee' for the purposes of the benefit-in-kind rules (see 75.11 SCHEDULE E);

(B) as emoluments for the purpose of deducting, under *ICTA 1988, s 198*, qualifying travelling expenses and other necessary expenses incurred by the worker (see 75.10(*a*) SCHEDULE E); and

(C) as relevant earnings for personal pension contributions purposes (see 60.8 PERSONAL PENSION SCHEMES).

[*FA 2000, Sch 12 para 11*].

Where the work is carried out outside the UK, and the worker is UK-resident and ordinarily resident, a service company may suffer foreign tax. Where the company's tax liability is insufficient to give full effect to DOUBLE TAX RELIEF (25), the Revenue suggest that the balance of foreign tax may be allowed against UK tax (but not NICs) on the deemed Schedule E payment, but only where it is possible to directly link the work in the overseas country and the deemed payment (Revenue FAQs — as in 61.1 above).

61.12 **PAYE.** By virtue of 61.11 above, the intermediary must account for tax under PAY AS YOU EARN (55) as if the deemed Schedule E payment to the worker were an actual payment of emoluments. Where, as is normally the case, the Schedule E payment is deemed to be made on 5 April in the tax year (see 61.7 above), then, strictly, the total tax, employee's NICs and employer's NICs due in respect of the deemed payment must be paid over to the Revenue on or before 19 April following the tax year (as in 55.8 PAY AS YOU EARN), which may leave insufficient time for the amount of the deemed payment to be computed. In practice, the Revenue will accept a lower, provisional amount on account. They must be notified on Employer's Annual Return Form P35 (due by the following 19 May — see 55.9 PAY AS YOU EARN) that the amount paid is provisional (if this remains the case). The balance due must be paid (and a supplementary P35 submitted) by the following 31 January. Provided that deadline is met, the Revenue will not seek to recover the underpaid tax in the meantime and will not seek PENALTIES (58.4). **Interest on overdue tax** will, however, accrue from 19 April following the tax year as normal (see 55.8 PAY AS YOU EARN). (Revenue FAQs — as in 61.1 above, Revenue Pamphlet IR 175).

Where the intermediary fails to account for PAYE on a deemed Schedule E payment, then, in addition to their powers to recover such tax and impose interest and penalties, the Revenue also have the option of using pre-existing rules (see 55.7 PAY AS YOU EARN) to collect the tax and NICs direct from the worker (Annex to Revenue Press Release 23 September 1999).

See 61.16 below as regards joint and several liability of multiple intermediaries.

61.13 **Computation of intermediary's business profits.** Subject to the special rules below for partnerships, a deemed Schedule E payment (and related employer's NICs) is an allowable expense in computing the business profits (or losses) of the intermediary, for the purposes of SCHEDULE D, CASES I AND II (71), for the period of account in which the payment is treated as made (but for no other period of account). [*FA 2000, Sch 12 para 17*].

Partnerships — special rules. The above applies equally where the intermediary is a partnership except that:

(*a*) the deduction for the deemed Schedule E payment can reduce the partnership profits to nil for tax purposes but it cannot create a trading loss; and

(*b*) the expenses of the partnership in connection with the relevant engagements (see 61.8(1) above) are deductible only to the extent that in any tax year they do not exceed the sum of

(i) the 5% deduction at 61.8(1) above, and

(ii) the amounts that would have been deductible under Schedule E if the worker had been employed directly by the client and had incurred the expenses himself.

[*FA 2000, Sch 12 para 18*].

61.14 RELIEF WHERE DIVIDENDS ETC. PAID BY INTERMEDIARY

A relief from double taxation is available where a **company** intermediary is treated as making a deemed Schedule E payment in any tax year and also pays a dividend (or otherwise makes a distribution) in that or a subsequent tax year. A claim for relief must be made in writing by the intermediary. Relief is given by reducing the dividend (not the deemed Schedule E payment) but only if the Revenue are satisfied that this is necessary to avoid a double charge to tax. The reduction is made, as far as practicable, by setting the amount of the deemed payment against

(*a*) dividends etc. of the same tax year in priority to those of other years;

(*b*) dividends etc. received by the worker before those received by another person; and

(*c*) dividends etc. of earlier years before those of later years.

Where a dividend is reduced, the associated tax credit is correspondingly reduced. See 1.9 ALLOWANCES AND TAX RATES for taxation of dividends and other distributions generally.

[*FA 2000, Sch 12 para 13*].

61.15 EARLIER DATE OF DEEMED SCHEDULE E PAYMENT IN CERTAIN CASES

As stated in 61.7 above, the deemed Schedule E payment is normally treated as made on 5 April in the relevant tax year. If, however, a 'relevant event' occurs in relation to the intermediary in that tax year and before that date, the deemed Schedule E payment is treated as made immediately before that event, or, if there is more than one, immediately before the first of them. The fact that the deemed payment is treated as made before the end of the tax year does not affect the way in which it is computed and the receipts and other matters that are taken into account.

In relation to a **company** intermediary, any of the following is a '*relevant event*':

(*a*) where the worker is a member of the company (which normally means a shareholder), his ceasing to be a member;

(*b*) where the worker holds an office with the company (for example, as a director), his ceasing to hold that office;

(*c*) where the worker is an employee of the company, his ceasing to be an employee.

In relation to a **partnership** intermediary, any of the following is a '*relevant event*':

(i) the dissolution of the partnership or cessation of the partnership trade;

(ii) a partner ceasing to act as such;

(iii) where the worker is an employee of the partnership, his ceasing to be an employee.

Where the intermediary is an **individual** and the worker is employed by him, a '*relevant event*' occurs if the worker ceases to be so employed.

[*FA 2000, Sch 12 para 12*].

61.16 MULTIPLE INTERMEDIARIES

Where, in the case of an engagement within 61.3 above, the arrangements (as in 61.3(*b*) above) involve one or more intermediaries within 61.5 above, then, except as below, these provisions apply separately in relation to each such intermediary.

Where a payment or other benefit has been made or provided, directly or indirectly, by one such intermediary to another in respect of the engagement, the amount taken into account at 61.8(1) or (2) above (computation of deemed Schedule E payment) in relation to any intermediary is to be reduced as necessary so as to avoid double-counting.

All such intermediaries are jointly and severally liable to account for PAYE (55) on a deemed Schedule E payment treated as made by any of them in respect of the engagement in question, or in respect of multiple engagements which include the engagement in question, except that an intermediary is excepted from such liability if has not received any payment or benefit in respect of the engagement(s).

[*FA 2000, Sch 12 paras 14–16*].

61.17 TRANSITION

An **individual or partnership intermediary** carrying on a pre-existing business at 6 April 2000 and treated under these provisions as making one or more deemed Schedule E payments for 2000/01 may elect that the business be deemed to have been permanently discontinued on 5 April 2000 and that a new business be deemed to have commenced on 6 April 2000. The opening years and closing year rules at 71.12, 71.17 SCHEDULE D, CASE I have effect, but for the purpose of enabling trading losses to be carried forward under *ICTA 1988, s 385* (see 46.12 LOSSES) the 'old' and 'new' businesses are treated as the same business. The election must be included in a personal or partnership tax return (as the case may be) delivered on or before its due date (see 78.5, 78.8 SELF-ASSESSMENT). [*FA 2000, Sch 12 para 23*].

The purpose of providing for such an election would appear to be to give an unincorporated business the option of obtaining tax relief for the same tax year as that in which the first deemed Schedule E payment falls to be taxed in the worker's hands. Otherwise, for example, a continuing intermediary business making a deemed payment on 5 April 2001 in relation to income received for its period of account ending on, say, 30 April 2001 would not obtain relief for that payment (as a business expense) until the tax year 2001/02, whereas the payment falls to be taxed under PAYE (and attracts NICs) for 2000/01. However, whether such an election would be of benefit overall can be judged only by taking account of *all* its consequences.

61.18 DECIDING EMPLOYMENT STATUS — SUMMARY OF REVENUE TAX BULLETIN ARTICLE

The following is a summary of the main text of the article in Revenue Tax Bulletin February 2000 pp 716–723 referred to at 61.4 above. The views expressed are those of the Revenue, who emphasise that their role is 'to provide advice and guidance about the employment status resulting from a given set of circumstances, not to impose any particular status. The terms and conditions of any engagement are entirely a matter for the parties involved.' See also 61.4 above as regards the Revenue's identification of a 'standard contract' and their advice thereon (which is included in the said article but not covered again below). See also 75.24 SCHEDULE E, particularly as regards relevant case law.

Whether a worker would have fallen to be treated as an employee of the client if engaged directly by the client rather than though an intermediary depends on a range of factors. However, it is not a mechanical exercise of running through a checklist with a view to adding up, and comparing, the number of factors pointing towards employment and self-employment respectively. The overall effect must be evaluated, which is not necessarily the same as the sum of the individual factors; the factors may not be of equal weight or importance in a given situation and may also vary in importance from one situation to another. See also *Hall v Lorimer CA 1993, 66 TC 349*. The intention of the parties may be conclusive if, but only if, the evidence is otherwise evenly balanced.

It is first necessary to establish the terms and conditions of the engagement, which is usually achieved mainly by considering the contract (whether written, oral or implied — or a mixture of those) between the client and the intermediary. Next, it is necessary to consider any relevant surrounding facts, for example whether the worker has other clients and a business organisation. In this context, other contracts under which the worker's services are supplied by the intermediary may be taken into account, as may any business organisation of the intermediary which is relevant to that supply.

Relevant factors in determining whether a contract is a 'contract for service' (i.e. employment) or a 'contract for services' (self-employment) are listed below.

(*a*) Does the client have the right to exercise **control** over the worker? This may be a right to control what work is done, where or when it is done and/or how it is done. A working relationship involving no control at all is unlikely to be employment. Where the client has the right to determine *how* the work is done or *what* work is carried out, this is, in either case, a strong pointer towards employment.

(*b*) Personal service is an essential element of a contract of employment. If the worker has the freedom to choose whether to do the job himself or hire a **substitute** to do it for him or a helper to provide substantial help, this points towards self-employment.

(*c*) The provision by the worker of significant **equipment** and/or materials which are fundamental to the engagement is a strong pointer towards self-employment. If the client provides the office space (where relevant) and equipment, this points towards employment. Note that in some trades it is not uncommon for *employees* to provide their own small tools.

(*d*) The taking on by the worker of **financial risk**, for example his buying significant assets and materials and/or quoting a fixed price for the job with the consequent risk of bearing the extra costs if it overruns, is a strong pointer towards self-employment.

(*e*) **Basis of payment.** Employees tend to be paid a fixed wage or salary, weekly or monthly, and possibly bonuses or overtime. A self-employed contractor tends to be paid a fixed sum for a particular job. (Piece work or payment by commission can be a feature of both employment and self-employment.)

(*f*) A person who may **profit from sound management**, i.e. his reward for the job varies according to his ability to organise the work effectively and reduce overheads, may well be self-employed. Though not mentioned in the Tax Bulletin text, an obligation to correct unsatisfactory work in the worker's own time and at his own expense suggests self-employment.

(*g*) A person who becomes **'part and parcel' of the client's organisation** may well be an employee.

(*h*) A **right of dismissal** is a common feature of employment. A contract for services, on the other hand, usually ends only when it is completed or is breached.

(*j*) The right to sick pay, holiday pay, pensions, expenses and/or other **employee benefits** points towards employment, though their absence does not necessarily indicate self-employment — especially where the engagement is short-term.

(*k*) **Length of engagement**. A long period working for one engager is typical of employment, but is not conclusive. Where a single engagement is covered by a series of short contracts, it is the length of the engagement that is relevant, and not the length of each contract.

(*l*) It may be appropriate to take into account factors which are personal to the worker and have little to do with the terms of the particular engagement. For example, if a skilled worker works for a number of clients and has a business-like approach to securing his engagements (perhaps involving expenditure on office accommodation, office equipment etc.), this points towards self-employment. Such **personal factors** carry less weight in the case of an unskilled worker, where factors like a high degree of control exercised by the client are more likely to be conclusive of employment.

62 Post-Cessation Etc. Receipts and Expenditure (Trades, professions and vocations)

[*ICTA 1988, ss 103–110; FA 1995, s 90*]

Cross-reference. See 12 CASH BASIS.

Simon's Direct Tax Service B4.221 *et seq.*.

62.1 POST-CESSATION ETC. RECEIPTS

Earnings basis. Where a trade, etc., the profits of which are computed 'by reference to earnings' (as defined by *ICTA 1988, s 110(3)*) is permanently discontinued (or treated as such) all **sums received on or after the discontinuance** (other than those exempted below) arising from the carrying on of the trade, etc., during any period before its discontinuance (including the amount, or arm's length value, of any consideration for a transfer of the right to receive them, and any recoveries or releases of items previously allowed as bad or doubtful debts) which are not otherwise chargeable to tax nor already brought into account for any period before the discontinuance are chargeable under Schedule D, Case VI.

Where the profits are not computed 'by reference to earnings' there is a similar charge on amounts received after the discontinuance which, if the earnings basis had applied, would have been left out of account because the date on which they became due or the date on which the amount was ascertained fell after the discontinuance. [*ICTA 1988, s 103(1)(2)(4); FA 1994, s 144(3)*]. Receipts within the legislation will include, *inter alia*, royalties and similar amounts which under decisions such as *Carson v Cheyney's Exor HL 1958, 38 TC 240*, prior to the legislation, had been held not to be taxable.

The charge is for the year of receipt (or as if received on the date of discontinuance if received by the person who carried on the trade before the discontinuance (or his personal representatives) in a tax year beginning within six years after the discontinuance *and election made* within two years thereafter, or, for 1996/97 and later years, within one year after 31 January following the year of receipt). [*ICTA 1988, s 108; FA 1996, s 128(4)*]. Where an election is made, the charge is still under Case VI of Schedule D, so that the Case I cessation provisions do not apply in relation to it (*Gilmore v Inspector of Taxes (Sp C 206), [1999] SSCD 269*). See 17.2 CLAIMS for the way in which effect is given to this election.

Deductions. Deductions may be made of any expenses or losses (other than arising from the discontinuance) which are not otherwise allowable (and have not been allowed under any other provision) but which would have been allowable to the previous owner if the trade, etc., had not ceased (or, before 6 April 1999, changed its 'conventional' basis, see below) and any unused balance of his CAPITAL ALLOWANCES (10) down to the date of discontinuance (or change). [*ICTA 1988, s 105; FA 1995, s 78(6); FA 1998, Sch 27 Pt III(6)*].

Exemptions.

(i) Sums received by a non-resident (or his agent) for income arising outside the UK,

(ii) a lump sum received by an author's executor, etc., for total or partial assignment of copyright or public lending right in his literary, dramatic, musical or artistic work or of design right in his design,

(iii) sums realised for transfer of closing trading stock or professional work in progress (these are already dealt with by *ICTA 1988, ss 100, 101* see 71.83 SCHEDULE D, CASES I AND II). [*ICTA 1988, s 103(3)*].

Deemed discontinuance. The above provisions also apply on a change of ownership which, under *ICTA 1988, s 113* (see 71.25 SCHEDULE D, CASES I AND II) or *ICTA 1988, s 337(1)* (company beginning or ceasing to carry on a trade), is treated as a permanent discontinuance, but if, on such a change, the right to receive sums as above is transferred from the previous owner to his successor the only liability under these sections is on the latter, who has to include as normal trade receipts, for the periods in which they are received, all such sums arising from the transfer. [*ICTA 1988, s 106(2)*]. Deduction may be made for any debts taken over on the discontinuance which prove bad, so far as not already allowed to the previous owner in computations for periods before the change. [*ICTA 1988, s 89*]. The provisions also apply to an individual leaving a partnership such that his deemed trade is permanently discontinued under the post-Finance Act 1994 provisions in 53.3 PARTNERSHIPS. [*ICTA 1988, s 110(2); FA 1994, s 215(1A); FA 1995, s 117(1)(b)(3)*].

Simon's Direct Tax Service. See **B4.221** *et seq.*.

62.2 **'Conventional' basis.** Where a trade, profession or vocation previously taxed on a 'conventional' basis, i.e. on the CASH BASIS (12) or otherwise than 'by reference to earnings' (see 62.1 above), is permanently discontinued (or treated as such), treatment as above applies to all receipts on or after the discontinuance arising from carrying on the trade etc. so far as their amount or value was not taken into account in computing the profits before the discontinuance. Similarly chargeable is any amount received for work in progress transferred or realised after discontinuance. The charge does not extend to amounts otherwise chargeable (including amounts chargeable under 62.1 above) nor to the sums referred to in exemptions (i) and (ii) in 62.1 above. [*ICTA 1988, s 104(1)–(3)(6)*].

Where, before 6 April 1999, a trade etc. changes from a 'conventional' basis to an earnings basis or to a different 'conventional' basis so that receipts drop out of computation, there is a similar charge on receipts after the change (and before any discontinuance). [*ICTA 1988, s 104(4)(5); FA 1998, Sch 27 Pt III(6)*]. For changes on or after that date, see 12.2 CASH BASIS.

Professional work in progress. Where, in the case of a profession or vocation, there has been a change, before 6 April 1999, from a conventional basis to an earnings basis or a different conventional basis *and* the work in progress at the change has been allowed as a deduction after the change, the amount of that work in progress (if not counterbalanced by a previous credit) will be charged as above under Schedule D, Case VI. [*ICTA 1988, s 104(7); FA 1998, Sch 27 Pt III(6)*]. For changes on or after that date, see 12.2 CASH BASIS.

Relief. In the case of an individual who was carrying on the trade, etc., on 18 March 1968 (profits of the trade, etc., not having been computed on an earnings basis at any time between that date and the discontinuance, or change, as above) any net amount chargeable on him under *section 104* above (but not any amount chargeable under *section 103*), is (subject as below) reduced by 5% for each year, or part year, by which his age at 5 April 1968 exceeded 51, up to a maximum of 75%, if he was then 65 or over. [*ICTA 1988, s 109*]. But the above reduction does not apply to any excess of a partner's share in post-cessation receipts over the amount which would have been apportioned to him had his share been calculated at the same rate as his average participation in partnership profits for the three tax years ending with that in which the discontinuance, or change, took place. [*ICTA 1988, s 109(5)*].

62.3 **Earned income.** Receipts assessable as above are treated as earned income if profits before the discontinuance or change of basis were previously so treated. [*ICTA 1988, s 107*].

62.4 **POST-CESSATION EXPENDITURE**

Relief against total income (and capital gains, see below) is available for certain payments made after 28 November 1994 in connection with a trade etc. which has been permanently discontinued (or treated as such — see 62.1 above) and within seven years after the discontinuance. Relief is given for the year in which the payment is made and unused relief cannot be carried forward (but may qualify as a deduction under *ICTA 1988, s 105* from post-cessation receipts of later years — see 62.1 above). The relief is not available to companies.

Payments qualifying for this relief are those made wholly and exclusively:

(*a*) in remedying defective work done, goods supplied or services rendered or by way of damages (awarded or agreed) in respect of defective work etc.;

(*b*) in meeting legal and professional fees in connection with a claim that work done etc. was defective;

(*c*) in insuring against such a claim or against the incurring of such legal etc. fees; or

(*d*) for the purpose of collecting a debt taken into account in computing profits of the former trade etc..

In addition, where an unpaid debt taken into account in computing profits of the former trade etc. proves to be bad in any part of the year of claim (and the claimant gives notice of that fact in making the claim) or is wholly or partly released as part of a voluntary arrangement or compromise (see 71.44 SCHEDULE D, CASES I AND II), then, to the extent that the former trader is entitled to the benefit of that debt, he is treated as making a payment qualifying for relief under these provisions and equal to the amount lost or released. To the extent that relief is then given under these provisions, any subsequent recovery of the debt is taxed as a post-cessation receipt (see 62.1 above) with no deduction available against it under *section 105*. (Where the claim was for 1994/95 or 1995/96, the Revenue had to be notified of a bad debt before the end of the year of claim.)

Where relief becomes available in respect of a payment within any of (*a*) to (*d*) above, the following are taxed as post-cessation receipts with no deduction available against them under *section 105*: (i) in the case of (*a*) or (*b*), any insurance proceeds, or similar, to allow the payment to be made or to reimburse it, (ii) in the case of (*c*), any refund of the insurance premium, or similar receipt, and (iii) in the case of (*d*), any sum received to meet the costs of collecting the debt. Where the receipt occurs in an earlier tax year than the related payment, it is treated as instead having been received in the year of payment.

Set-off of unpaid expenses against relief. Where a deduction was made in computing profits or losses of the former trade etc. in respect of an expense not actually paid, relief otherwise due and claimed under these provisions is reduced by the amount of any such expenses remaining unpaid at the end of the year to which the claim relates (to the extent that those expenses have not so reduced relief for an earlier year). If an unpaid expense has reduced relief but is subsequently paid, wholly or partly, the amount paid (or, if less, the amount of the reduction) is treated as a payment qualifying for relief under these provisions for the year of payment.

Exclusion of double relief. Relief is not available in respect of an amount for which income tax relief is otherwise available. In determining whether an amount could otherwise be relieved under *section 105* (deduction from post-cessation receipts — see 62.1 above), amounts not available for relief under these provisions are assumed to be relieved under *section 105* in priority to amounts that are so available.

Time limit. The relief must be claimed within two years after the year of assessment in which the payment is made where that year is 1994/95 or 1995/96. For later years, the time limit is twelve months after 31 January following the tax year of payment.

Relief against capital gains. Where a claim is made as above and the claimant's income for the year is insufficient to fully utilise the relief, he may include in his claim an additional claim to have the excess relief treated as an allowable loss for that year for capital gains tax purposes. The allowable loss may not exceed the amount of the claimant's gains for the year *before* deducting any losses brought forward, the capital gains tax annual exemption or any relief available under *FA 1991, s 72* for trading losses (see 46.5 LOSSES); any excess over that amount is *not* available to carry forward against gains of a later year.

[*ICTA 1988, ss 109A, 110; FA 1995, s 90; FA 1996, s 134, Sch 20 para 5*].

See generally Revenue Tax Bulletin October 1995 pp 256, 257.

Simon's Direct Tax Service. See **B4.231** *et seq.*.

62.5 *Example*

Simcock ceased trading in October 1999. In 2000/01 the following events occur in connection with his former trade.

(i) He pays a former customer £9,250 by way of damages for defective work carried out by him in the course of the trade.

(ii) He incurs legal fees of £800 in connection with (i) above.

(iii) He incurs debt collection fees of £200 in connection with trade debts outstanding at cessation and which were taken into account as receipts in computing profits.

(iv) He writes off a trade debt of £500, giving the Revenue notice of his having done so.

(v) He incurs legal fees of £175 in relation to a debt of £1,000 owing by him to a supplier which, although disputed, was taken into account as an expense in computing his trading profits.

(vi) He eventually agrees to pay £500 in full settlement of his liability in respect of the debt in (v) above, paying £250 in March 2001 and the remaining £250 in May 2001.

In 2001/02 he receives £3,000 from his insurers in full settlement of their liability with regard to the expense incurred in (i) above.

For 2000/01, his total income before taking account of the above events is £9,000, and he also has capital gains of £8,400 (with £1,000 capital losses brought forward from 1999/2000).

He makes a claim under *ICTA 1988, s 109A* for 2000/01 and a simultaneous claim under *FA 1995, s 90(4)* to have any excess relief set against capital gains.

Simcock's tax position is as follows.

2000/01

	£	£
Income		
Total income before *section 109A* claim		9,000
Deduct post-cessation expenditure —		
(i)	9,250	
(ii)	800	
(iii)	200	
(iv)	500	
(v)	—	
(vi) *less* expenses unpaid at 5.4.01 (£1,000 – £250)	(750)	
	10,000	
Restricted to total income	(9,000)	(9,000)
Excess relief	£1,000	
Capital gains		
Gains before losses brought forward and annual exemption		8,400
Deduct excess post-cessation expenditure (as above)		1,000
Net gains for the year		7,400
Losses brought forward	1,000	
Used 2000/01	200	200
Losses carried forward	£800	
Net gains (covered by annual exemption)		£7,200

2001/02

He will have taxable post-cessation receipts of £3,000 arising from the insurance recovery. He will be able to offset expenses of £175 under (v) above which, whilst not within *section 109A*, should qualify as a deduction under *section 105* (see 62.1 above). He will also have post-cessation expenditure of £250 in respect of the further payment under (vi) above, the 2000/01 post-cessation expenditure having been restricted by more than that amount.

63 Remittance Basis

Cross-references. See RESIDENCE, ORDINARY RESIDENCE AND DOMICILE at 64.4 for domicile, 64.5 for residence, 64.6 for ordinarily resident; NON-RESIDENTS AND OTHER OVERSEAS MATTERS at 51.12 for trades etc. carried on abroad and 51.14 for unremittable overseas income; see 25.3 DOUBLE TAX RELIEF regarding Eire.

63.1 APPLICATION

The remittance basis (i.e. UK tax assessments are restricted to sums actually remitted to the UK out of such income or gains (grossed up in certain cases where credit for foreign tax is allowable, see 25.5(*b*)(i) DOUBLE TAX RELIEF)) applies to UK residents in respect of overseas income and gains as follows.

(A) **Persons not domiciled in the UK.**

- (i) **Capital gains** from disposal of assets abroad (with no allowance for losses arising abroad).
- (ii) **Emoluments** from an employer not resident in UK or Eire where the duties are performed wholly abroad (see 75.2 SCHEDULE E, Case III(*a*)) but this only applies if the employee is also ordinarily resident in the UK (otherwise see (B) below).
- (iii) **Investment income etc.** from abroad assessable under SCHEDULE D, CASES IV AND V (73). [*ICTA 1988, s 65(4)(5); FA 1994, s 207(3); FA 1996, s 134, Sch 20 para 3*]. But such income from Eire is assessable on the full amount arising, whether remitted or not. [*ICTA 1988, s 68; FA 1994, s 207(5)*].
- (iv) **Pensions** from overseas as described in 59.2 PENSIONS.
- (v) **Trades etc.** controlled abroad, see under 51.12 NON-RESIDENTS AND OTHER OVERSEAS MATTERS. Except trades etc. in Eire. [*ICTA 1988, s 68; FA 1994, s 207(5)*].

(B) **Persons not ordinarily resident in the UK.**

Emoluments in respect of duties performed wholly abroad, see Case III(*b*) in 75.2 SCHEDULE E.

(C) **Persons not ordinarily resident in the UK who are also either British subjects or Eire citizens.**

Investment income etc. — per (A)(iii) above.

Pensions — per (A)(iv) above.

Trades etc. — per (A)(v) above.

Note. Employments are not treated as being abroad for the above purposes if they comprise certain Crown duties or sea or air duties. See 75.2 SCHEDULE E.

63.2 BASIS OF ASSESSMENT

Where assessment is under Schedule D, Cases IV or V (i.e. investment income etc., pensions and trades as under 63.1(A)(iii), (iv) and (v) and (C) above) the remittances to be taken into account are those of the preceding tax year subject to adjustments when a source commences or ceases, or, where the current year basis applies, those of the current year (see 73.9 SCHEDULE D, CASES IV AND V). Otherwise the assessment is on the actual remittances in the tax year (subject to the addition of any foreign tax for which credit is allowable, see 25.5(*b*)(i) DOUBLE TAX RELIEF).

See 25.5(*b*) DOUBLE TAX RELIEF for double tax relief claimable.

Simon's Direct Tax Service. See **E1.323** *et seq.*.

63.3 **REMITTANCES—GENERAL**

A remittance of capital is not taxable as such (unless within the provisions of capital gains tax, see Tolley's Capital Gains Tax) but a taxable remittance may include the proceeds of investments made abroad out of overseas income (*Scottish Provident Institution v Farmer CS 1912, 6 TC 34*). Where the proceeds were of investments made before the taxpayer came to reside in the UK, there was no liability (*Kneen v Martin CA 1934, 19 TC 33*). Similarly a remittance from a foreign bank into which overseas income had been paid may be assessable, dependent on the circumstances. For this see *Walsh v Randall KB 1940, 23 TC 55* (sterling draft on foreign bank in favour of London hospital received by taxpayer before handing to hospital, held to be remittance) and *Thomson v Moyse HL 1960, 39 TC 291* (dollar cheques on US bank sold to Bank of England held to be remitted) and compare *Carter v Sharon KB 1936, 20 TC 229* (drafts on foreign bank posted abroad to taxpayer's daughter for maintenance, held not to be remittance as, under relevant foreign law, gift to daughter completed on posting of draft). See also *Fellowes-Gordon v CIR CS 1935, 19 TC 683*. In *Harmel v Wright Ch D 1973, 49 TC 149* an amount received via two South African companies, ending as a loan from one of them, was held to be a remittance of South African emoluments within Schedule E, Case III. Where, contrary to the customer's instructions, a bank erroneously remitted untaxed overseas income to him, it was held there was no liability (*Duke of Roxburghe's Exors v CIR CS 1936, 20 TC 711*).

63.4 **CONSTRUCTIVE REMITTANCES** [*ICTA 1988, s 65(6)–(9)*]

Income arising abroad to a person *ordinarily resident* in the UK and which he applies abroad towards the satisfaction of

(*a*) a debt (or interest thereon) for money lent him in the UK, or

(*b*) a debt for money lent to him abroad and brought here, or

(*c*) a loan incurred to satisfy such debts,

is treated as received by him in the UK.

Where an ordinarily resident person imports money lent to him abroad the debt for which has at that time already been wholly or partly satisfied, the loan is treated as a remittance at the date of importation to the extent that the debt is satisfied.

Income **hypothecated in any form to the lender** so that the amount of a loan debt, or the time of its repayment, depends directly or indirectly on the amount of property so available to the lender, is treated as having been applied towards satisfaction of the loan. '*Lender*' includes any person for the time being entitled to repayment.

These provisions regarding constructive remittances are contained in Schedule D, Cases IV and V legislation and are applied to emoluments assessable under Schedule E, Case III by *ICTA 1988, s 132(5)* and to capital gains tax by *TCGA 1992, s 12(2)*.

Simon's Direct Tax Service. See **E1.324**.

64 Residence, Ordinary Residence and Domicile

Cross-reference. See 51 NON-RESIDENTS AND OTHER OVERSEAS MATTERS for situations in which the residence, ordinary residence or domicile of an individual may be of relevance for income tax purposes. See generally Revenue Pamphlets IR 20, to which reference is made throughout this chapter, IR 138 and IR 139.

See also 1.3 ALLOWANCES AND TAX RATES as regards Scottish taxpayers to whom the Scottish variable basic rate of income tax may apply from 2000/01 onwards.

Simon's Direct Tax Service E6.

64.1 UK tax liability may depend on a person's **domicile** (the country or state which is his 'natural home', see 64.4 below), on whether or not he is **resident** in the UK for tax purposes in a particular tax year (which is primarily a matter of physical presence, see 64.5 below) or, occasionally, on whether or not he is ordinarily resident in the UK (see 64.6 below). EU law does not prevent a Member State from imposing more onerous fiscal charges on nationals resident in another Member State than those imposed on resident nationals (*Werner v Finanzamt Aachen-Innenstadt (Case C–112/91) CJEC, 1993 STI 376*).

64.2 A person who is **resident** in the UK is liable to UK tax on all his income and gains, whether from UK or overseas sources, subject to limited categories of EXEMPT INCOME (29).

Assessments are limited to remittances to the UK out of the income or gains in the circumstances listed under REMITTANCE BASIS (63).

Deductions are made from the amounts assessable as follows.

Emoluments. Employments wholly abroad where the employee is abroad for a qualifying period (as defined) of 365 days or more — a deduction of 100% is made (i.e. complete exemption). See 75.3 SCHEDULE E.

Overseas pensions. A deduction of 10% may be made, as set out in 59.1(iv) and 59.2 PENSIONS.

64.3 **Non-residents** are liable to UK tax on UK income, including income from property etc. in the UK, income from trades, professions etc. exercised in the UK [*ICTA 1988, s 18(1)(a)(iii)*] and on emoluments from offices or employments for duties performed in the UK (but see 75.6 SCHEDULE E regarding 'foreign emoluments', being emoluments of a non-domiciled person from a foreign employer). [*ICTA 1988, s 19(1)*].

See also 29.18 EXEMPT INCOME and 33.2 GOVERNMENT STOCKS for the special exemption to non-residents in respect of certain government stocks and 23.12 DEDUCTION OF TAX AT SOURCE for a similar relief in respect of the interest or dividends on certain foreign stocks and securities payable in the UK.

The appropriate double tax agreement should be examined for exemptions and for restrictions on the rates of tax to be borne. Otherwise non-residents are chargeable at the full rate and not entitled to personal or other reliefs. Thus a person carrying on a business in the UK but claiming to be non-resident may thereby have his tax allowances reduced or even refused. But see 51.11 NON-RESIDENTS AND OTHER OVERSEAS MATTERS for reliefs available to certain Commonwealth subjects and others.

Non-residents have no liability on overseas income.

64.4 DOMICILE

It may be necessary to determine domicile in relation, *inter alia*, to the assessment of income from foreign possessions and securities (see 73.5 SCHEDULE D, CASES IV AND V), of 'foreign emoluments' (see 75.6 SCHEDULE E) and of certain chargeable gains (see Tolley's Capital Gains Tax).

A person may have only one place of domicile at any given time denoting the country or state considered his permanent home. He acquires a **domicile of origin** at birth (normally that of his father). It may be changed to a **domicile of choice** (to be proved by subsequent conduct). If a domicile of choice is established but later abandoned (by actual action, not by intention or declaration only — see *Faye v CIR* below) reversion to domicile of origin is automatic.

Domicile is a highly technical matter and does not necessarily correspond with either residence or nationality (see *Earl of Iveagh v Revenue Commissioners Supreme Court (IFS) [1930] IR 431*, *Fielden v CIR Ch D 1965, 42 TC 501*, and *CIR v Cohen KB 1937, 21 TC 301*). This last case shows how difficult it is to displace a domicile of origin by a domicile of choice, but contrast *In re Lawton Ch D 1958 37 ATC 216*. A new domicile of choice may be acquired whilst continuing to be resident in the domicile of origin, but only if the residence in the domicile of choice is the 'chief residence' (*Plummer v CIR Ch D 1987, 60 TC 452*). See also *In re Wallach HC 1949, 28 ATC 486*, *Faye v CIR Ch D 1961, 40 TC 103*, *Buswell v CIR CA 1974, 49 TC 334*, *Steiner v CIR CA 1973, 49 TC 13*, *CIR v Bullock CA 1976, 51 TC 522*, *In re Furse decd., Furse v CIR Ch D, [1980] STC 597*, *Re Clore decd. (No 2) Ch D, [1984] STC 609*, *Anderson v CIR (Sp C 147), [1998] SSCD 43* and *Mrs F and S2 (personal representatives of F (dec'd)) v CIR (Sp C 219), [2000] SSCD 1.*

In determining domicile for tax purposes at any time **after 5 April 1996**, no action taken at any time in relation to registration as an 'overseas elector', or in voting as such, is taken into account in determining domicile, unless the person whose liability is being determined (whether or not the person whose domicile is in question) wishes it to be taken into account (in which case the domicile determination applies only for the purpose of ascertaining the liability in question). An '*overseas elector*' is broadly a non-resident British citizen to whom the parliamentary franchise is extended under *Representation of the People Act 1985, s 1* or *s 3*. [*FA 1996, s 200*].

See 64.5 below for administrative procedures for determination of domicile in certain cases.

Married women. Up to 31 December 1973, a woman automatically acquired the domicile of her husband on marriage. From 1 January 1974 onwards, the domicile of a married woman is to be ascertained 'by reference to the same factors as in the case of any other individual capable of having an independent domicile' except that a woman already married on that date will retain her husband's domicile until it is changed by acquisition or revival of another domicile. [*Domicile and Matrimonial Proceedings Act 1973, ss 1, 17(5)*]. But an American woman who married a husband with UK domicile before 1974 will be treated, for determining her domicile, as if the marriage had taken place in 1974. See Article 4(4) of the US/UK Double Tax Agreement. A **widow** retains her late husband's domicile unless she later acquires a domicile of choice (and see *CIR v Duchess of Portland Ch D 1981, 54 TC 648*).

Minors. The domicile of a minor normally follows that of the person on whom he is legally dependent. Under *Domicile and Matrimonial Proceedings Act 1973, s 3* (which does not extend to Scotland), a person first becomes capable of having an independent domicile when he attains 16 or marries under that age. Under *section 4* of that *Act*, where a child's father and mother are alive but living apart, his domicile is that of his mother if he has his home with her and has no home with his father.

Simon's Direct Tax Service. See **E6.3**.

64.5 RESIDENCE

General. There is relatively little statutory guidance on the determination of the 'residence' of an individual, despite its importance in determining the individual's tax liabilities (see 64.1–64.3 above). It has been held by the courts that residence is a question of fact for the Appeal Commissioners to decide on the particular circumstances of each case, and there are a number of important decisions indicative of the courts' views (see below). See also 64.8 below regarding appeals. A person can be resident for a particular tax year in more than one country for tax purposes (or may even be resident in none).

For practical purposes, the Revenue's interpretation as set out in Pamphlet IR 20 and other sources referred to below is, subject to appeal, likely to determine the issue in any particular case.

There are three circumstances in which the residence status of an individual is subject to statutory provisions.

(*a*) An individual in the UK for some temporary purpose only, and not with the intention of establishing his residence here, is UK resident for any year of assessment in which he is physically present in the UK for six months or more in aggregate, and is not resident for any year of assessment in which he is not physically present in the UK for six months or more. In determining whether the individual is in the UK for some temporary purpose only and not with the intention of establishing his residence here one of the considerations is that an individual is regarded as resident if visits to the UK average 91 days or more per tax year, calculated over a maximum of four years (see Revenue Pamphlet IR 20, para 2.10 for method of averaging). (Revenue Pamphlet IR 131, SP 2/91, 19 March 1991). The question is determined without regard to any 'available accommodation' in the UK (see below). [*ICTA 1988, s 336; FA 1993, s 208(1)(4)*]. Strictly, periods of time in terms of hours are relevant in determining a period of presence in the UK (see *Wilkie v CIR Ch D 1951, 32 TC 495*) but in practice six months are regarded as 183 days, ignoring (normally) days of arrival and departure. (Revenue Pamphlet IR 20, para 1.2).

(*b*) A Commonwealth or Eire citizen whose ordinary residence (see 99.6 below) has been in the UK, and who has left the UK for the purpose only of occasional residence abroad, continues to be UK resident. [*ICTA 1988, s 334*]. 'Occasional residence' is not defined, but generally refers to short stays on holiday or business trips (and see *Reed v Clark Ch D 1985, 58 TC 528*).

(*c*) The residence of an individual working full time in a trade, profession or vocation no part of which is carried on in the UK, or in an office or employment all of the duties of which are performed outside the UK (other than any whose performance is merely incidental to the duties abroad), is determined without regard to any place of abode maintained for his use in the UK. [*ICTA 1988, s 335*]. As to whether duties are incidental, see *Robson v Dixon Ch D 1972, 48 TC 527* (airline pilot employed abroad but occasionally landing in UK where family home maintained, held UK duties more than incidental). See also Revenue Pamphlet IR 20, paras 5.7, 5.8. 'Full-time' employment (here and in relation to Revenue concession A11 referred to below), in an ordinary case involving a standard pattern of hours, requires an individual working hours clearly comparable with those in a typical UK working week. See Revenue Pamphlet IR 20, para 2.5 for this and for the Revenue interpretation of the requirement in less straightforward cases.

'Available accommodation' does not depend on ownership but whether any accommodation is in fact maintained for occupation at any time by the individual concerned. A house owned and let out on a lease which denies availability is ignored, as is a renting of less than two years of furnished accommodation (or one year of unfurnished accommodation) during temporary stay. A house owned but left empty of furniture, or only available during a part of the year when the person is not in the UK, or situated too far away from a UK destination visited briefly on business for its use to be practical, may similarly be ignored. (Revenue Pamphlet IR 20 (1996), paras 4.2, 4.3, 4.4).

Case law. Resident in Eire making monthly visits to UK as director of British company (having no UK residence, but a permanent one in Eire) held to be resident and ordinarily resident in UK (*Lysaght v CIR HL 1928, 13 TC 511*) (but cf. *CIR v Combe CS 1932, 17 TC 405*). Officer succeeding to Eire estate, intending to return there permanently but prevented by military duties in UK, held on facts to be resident in both countries (*Lord Inchiquin v CIR CA 1948, 31 TC 125*). In *CIR v Brown KB 1926, 11 TC 292* and *CIR v Zorab KB 1926, 11 TC 289*, however, held that retired Indian civil servants making periodical visits to the UK, but having no business interests here, were not UK resident.

An American holding a lease of a shooting box in Scotland and spending two months there every year (*Cooper v Cadwalader CES 1904, 5 TC 101*), and a merchant usually resident and doing business in Italy but owning house in UK where he resided less than six months (*Lloyd v Sulley CES 1884, 2 TC 37*) were both held to be UK resident.

A Belgian who had at his disposal, for the visits he paid here, a house owned not by him but by a company which he controlled, so that it was in fact available whenever he chose to come, was held to be UK resident (*Loewenstein v De Salis KB 1926, 10 TC 424*). In *Withers v Wynyard KB 1938, 21 TC 724*, however, an actress (after 18 months abroad) performing in UK, and for $3\frac{1}{2}$ months in 1933/34 occupying a leasehold flat (unable to be disposed of and sublet when possible), was held to be non-resident for that year.

Where neither the individual nor spouse physically present in UK during tax year, although children here, the individual was non-resident (*Turnbull v Foster CES 1904, 6 TC 206*). See also *Reed v Clark Ch D 1985, 58 TC 528*, where individual held non-resident for tax year of absence from UK during which continuing trade carried on. If, however, either an individual or spouse, while they are still living together, has established a UK family home, any visit during a tax year, however short, to that home, may render the individual UK resident for that tax year (although cf. *Withers v Wynyard* above).

Revenue practice. Revenue Pamphlet IR 20 (to which paragraph numbers in the following text refer) considers the application of the above tests first generally, then in relation to those leaving the UK, then in relation to those coming to the UK.

General. Some physical presence in the UK during a tax year is normally required for an individual to be regarded as UK resident for that year, and the individual will invariably be so regarded where that physical presence is for six months or more in the year (as in (*a*) above). (para 1.2).

Strictly, residence status applies only by reference to whole tax years. By concession, however, an individual coming to the UK to take up permanent residence or to stay for at least two years, or leaving the UK to live abroad permanently (or for at least three years), is treated as UK resident only from the date of arrival or up to and including the date of departure, tax liabilities which are affected by residence status being calculated on the basis of the period of residence. In either case, the Revenue must be satisfied that the person was not ordinarily resident in the UK (see 64.6 below) prior to arrival or on departure. Similarly, subject to the further conditions as described below in relation to leaving the UK, an individual (and accompanying spouse) going abroad under a contract of employment will be so treated only up to and including the date of departure and from the date of return to the

UK. The provisions limiting the income chargeable on non-residents (see 51.1 NON-RESIDENTS AND OTHER OVERSEAS MATTERS) do not apply to the non-resident part of a split year. This concession previously applied to temporary visitors coming to stay for at least three years, with a shorter period applying only in the case of those coming to the UK to take up employment expected to last at least two years, but the concession has been revised to apply the two year period for all temporary visitors. (paras 1.5–1.7; Revenue Pamphlet IR 1, A11 and A78 (as revised)). See also 73.11, 73.12 SCHEDULE D, CASE VI, 75.3 SCHEDULE E.

Full personal allowances are available for the year permanent residence begins or ends. (para 7.4).

For commentary on aspects of Revenue practice in relation to available accommodation, see ICAEW Technical Release TAX 20/94, 30 November 1994.

Leaving the UK. Short trips abroad, e.g. on holiday or business trips, do not alter the residence status of a person who usually lives in the UK (see (*b*) above). (para 2.1).

An individual (and accompanying spouse) leaving to work abroad 'full-time' (see (*c*) above) under a contract of employment is treated as non-UK resident provided that both the absence from the UK and the employment cover a complete tax year, and that any interim visits to the UK do not amount to either 183 days or more in any tax year or an average of 91 days or more per tax year (averaged over a maximum of four years (see para 2.10 for method of averaging), and ignoring days spent in the UK for exceptional circumstances beyond the person's control, for example own or family illness). Similar conditions apply to an individual leaving to work abroad full-time in a trade, profession or vocation. These conditions are applied separately in relation to the employee and the accompanying spouse, but must be satisfied by the employee for the concession to be available to the accompanying spouse. See also 64.6 below as regards ordinary residence of the accompanying spouse. (paras 2.2–2.6).

An individual leaving the UK permanently is nevertheless treated as continuing to be UK resident if visits to the UK average 91 days or more per tax year (subject to exceptional circumstances, as above). (para 2.7). Some evidence will normally be required in support of a claim to have become non-resident (and non-ordinarily resident, see 64.6 below), e.g. steps taken to acquire a permanent home abroad, and, if UK property is retained, a reason consistent with the stated aim of permanent residence abroad. If such evidence is satisfactory, or, where such evidence is not available, if the absence abroad is for a settled purpose, UK residence (and ordinary residence) will be treated as ceasing on the day after departure from the UK, provided that absence from the UK has covered at least a whole tax year and that interim visits to the UK have not exceeded 182 days in any tax year and have averaged less than 91 days per tax year (as above). If such evidence is lacking, and the absence abroad is not for a settled purpose, UK residence and ordinary residence will be treated as continuing, subject to review if the absence actually extends to three years after departure or if evidence becomes available to show that the absence is permanent (and provided that the 182- and 91-day tests (as above) are satisfied). (paras 2.8, 2.9).

Coming to the UK. UK residence (and ordinary residence, see 64.6 below) will commence on the date of arrival in the UK where an individual whose home has been abroad comes to the UK to live here permanently or intending to stay for three years or more (disregarding holidays or short business trips abroad). (para 3.1). Otherwise, short-term visitors will be treated as resident for a tax year in which they are in the UK for 183 days or more in the year (see (*a*) above), or from the fifth tax year where in the preceding four tax years regular visits have been made to the UK averaging 91 days or more per tax year (subject to exceptional circumstances, as above). If such visits are clearly intended on arrival in the UK, residence will commence with the first of those four years, and if the decision to make such visits is taken before the start of the fifth year, residence will commence with the year in which the decision was taken. (para 3.3). Longer-term visitors are treated as resident throughout any period for which they come to the UK for a purpose (such as employment) that will mean remaining (apart from holidays or short business trips) for at least two years. This will also apply if accommodation is owned or is acquired or taken on a lease of three years or more in the year of arrival. Otherwise (and subject to the usual 183-day rule) such visitors will be treated as resident from the beginning of the tax year in which such accommodation is acquired or leased. (paras 3.7, 3.11).

It is understood that, in practice, an individual arriving in the UK with no fixed intentions regarding residence but who during the visit sets up a permanent residence in the UK is deemed resident and ordinarily resident from the date of arrival, provided that that date and the date of change of plan fall within the same tax year. Back assessments are understood to be made only where the visitor's intentions on arrival were admitted or quite clear.

An individual who comes to the UK not as a short-term visitor but with the intention of remaining in the UK may be regarded as UK resident even if UK visits are within the above limits. Whether an individual is a short-term visitor will depend on e.g. the reason for coming to the UK and the general background to the normal living pattern. An habitual visitor who stays in accommodation owned or available for less than 91 days in each tax year is unlikely to have the intention of remaining in the UK for at least three years and would, if this is so, be treated as a short-term visitor. (Taxation Practitioner October 1994, p 26).

As regards visits for education, see 64.6 below.

Administrative procedures. Individuals who come to the UK to take up employment are asked to complete Form P86 to enable their residence status to be considered. This form also includes a section on domicile so that, in straightforward cases (where, e.g., a person never domiciled in the UK comes here only to work and with the intention of leaving the UK when the employment ceases), the two matters may be dealt with together. In less straightforward cases, Form DOM1 has been introduced to obtain the information necessary to the determination of domicile. On leaving the UK, a shortened Form P85 (Form P85(S)) enables any repayment to be claimed in straightforward cases. Otherwise, Form P85 continues to be used.

As regards individuals who are not regarded as ordinarily resident in the UK on arrival, enquiries as to any change in circumstances now begin only after a complete tax year has elapsed since arrival, although individuals are expected to report any actual changes in their circumstances without delay, whether or not that period has elapsed. (Revenue Press Release 8 September 1994).

Under *self-assessment* from 1996/97 onwards, Forms P85, P85(S), P86 and DOM1 continue in operation, but individuals who regard themselves as not resident, not ordinarily resident or not domiciled in the UK are required to self-certify their status in the self-assessment tax return and to complete the 'NON-RESIDENCE ETC.' supplementary pages to the return. The Revenue no longer provide residence 'rulings' but will give specific advice in limited circumstances. Revenue queries on residence status and domicile aspects may be made as part of an enquiry into the self-assessment return or into an initial claim made outside the return (see 78.11 SELF-ASSESSMENT, 17.3 CLAIMS). See Revenue Tax Bulletin June 1997 pp 425–427.

Residence of trustees and personal representatives. Where at least one of the trustees of a settlement is non-UK resident and at least one is UK resident, then provided that the settlor (including any person providing or undertaking to provide funds directly or indirectly for the settlement) satisfies a further condition (or, if there is more than one settlor, that at least one of them satisfies that condition), the non-UK resident trustee(s) is (are) treated as UK resident for income tax purposes. Otherwise, the UK resident trustee(s) is (are) treated as not resident in the UK and as resident elsewhere for those purposes.

Similar rules apply to determine the residence of personal representatives.

The condition to be met in relation to trustees is that the settlor is resident, ordinarily resident or domiciled in the UK at a 'relevant time'. A '*relevant time*' is the time of the settlor's death in relation to a testamentary disposition or intestacy, otherwise it is the time, or each of the times, when he has provided funds for the settlement. In relation to personal representatives, the condition is that the deceased was resident, ordinarily resident or domiciled in the UK at the time of his death.

See 3.8 ANTI-AVOIDANCE as regards certain circumstances in which the above rules do not apply. [*FA 1989, ss 110, 111*].

Special provision is made for the assessment of trustees and personal representatives to income tax. See 81.3 SETTLEMENTS.

Simon's Direct Tax Service. See **E6.1**.

64.6 ORDINARY RESIDENCE

The term 'ordinary residence' is not defined in the *Taxes Acts*. See below for the case law on its interpretation. Broadly, it denotes greater permanence than the term 'residence' (see 64.5 above), and is equivalent to habitual residence; if an individual is resident year after year, he is ordinarily resident. An individual may be resident in the UK under the six months rule of *ICTA 1988, s 336* (see 64.5(*a*) above) without becoming ordinarily resident. Equally, he may be ordinarily resident without being resident in a particular year, e.g. because he usually lives in the UK but is absent on an extended holiday throughout a tax year. (Revenue Pamphlet IR 20, para 1.3).

An individual will be treated as ordinarily resident in the UK if he visits the UK regularly and either has available accommodation (see 64.5(*c*) above) or his visits average (for which see Revenue Pamphlet IR 20, para 3.6) 91 days or more per tax year (ignoring days spent in the UK for exceptional circumstances beyond his control, for example his own or family illness). Ordinary residence will commence from 6 April in the tax year of first arrival if the intention to make such visits to the UK for at least four tax years is clear on that first visit, or from 6 April in the fifth tax year after four years of such visits (unless the decision to make regular visits was made in an earlier tax year, in which case it applies from 6 April in that earlier year). (Revenue Pamphlet IR 20, paras 3.4, 3.5).

If an individual regarded as ordinarily resident solely because of the availability of accommodation disposes of it and leaves the UK within three years of arrival, he is normally treated as not ordinarily resident for the duration of his stay (assuming this is to his advantage). (Revenue Pamphlet IR 20, para 3.12).

See 64.5 above for administrative procedures in certain cases.

Longer-term visitors — commencement of ordinary residence. If it is clear on arrival in the UK that the intention is to stay for at least three years (disregarding holidays and short business trips abroad), ordinary residence commences on arrival. An individual coming to the UK, but not intending to stay more than three years (and not buying or leasing for three years or more accommodation for use in the UK), is treated as ordinarily resident from the beginning of the tax year following the third anniversary of arrival. If, before the beginning of that tax year, either there is a change in the individuals' intention (i.e. to an intention to stay in the UK for three years or more in all) or accommodation for use in the UK is bought (or leased for three years or more), ordinary residence is treated as commencing at the beginning of the tax year in which either of those events happens (or from the date of arrival in the UK if later). (Revenue Pamphlet IR 131, SP 17/91, 4 December 1991 and Revenue Pamphlet IR 20, paras 3.8–3.11).

Education. A student who comes to the UK for a period of study or education and will be in the UK for less than four years will be treated as not ordinarily resident providing (i) he does not own or buy (or lease for three years or more) accommodation in the UK, and (ii) he will not, following his departure from the UK, be returning regularly for visits averaging 91 days or more (see Revenue Pamphlet IR 20, para 3.6) per tax year. (Revenue Pamphlet IR 20, para 3.13).

Spouse accompanying employee working overseas. Where a person going abroad for full-time employment (see 64.5 above) was accompanied by a spouse who was within the concession (Revenue Pamphlet IR 1, A11) described at 64.5 above, and who retained available accommodation in the UK, the accompanying spouse was treated as not ordinarily resident throughout the period of absence, provided that the absence was three years or more and UK visits averaged less than 91 days per tax year. Where an intended period of absence of three years or more was cut to less than three years because of the unexpected termination of the spouse's employment, the shorter period might qualify provided that it included a complete tax year and UK visits averaged less than 91 days per tax year. (Revenue Pamphlet IR 1, A78 (as revised)).

Cases

In *Reid v CIR SC 1926, 10 TC 673*, British subject held '*ordinarily resident*' here although no fixed residence either here or abroad and regularly absent abroad $8\frac{1}{2}$ months every year. But she had here an address, family ties, banking account and furniture stored.

Levene v CIR HL 1928, 13 TC 486 was decided similarly. (British subject abroad for health reasons since 1918, no fixed residence here since (or abroad till 1925), but having ties with this country and in the 'usual ordering of his life', making habitual visits to UK 20 weeks yearly for definite purposes.) The judgments in this case interpreted the meaning of 'ordinarily resident' by the following phrases: 'habitually resident', 'residence in a place with some degree of continuity', and 'according to the way a man's life is usually ordered'. In *Peel v CIR CS 1927, 13 TC 443*, although appellant had his business and house in Egypt, he was held ordinarily resident here because he also had a house here, and spent an average of 139 days of each year in the UK.

In *Kinloch v CIR KB 1929, 14 TC 736*, a widow living mostly abroad with a son at school here, who had won an appeal in previous years but continued regular annual visits, was held to be resident and ordinarily resident.

In *Elmhirst v CIR KB 1937, 21 TC 381* appellant held on facts to have been ordinarily resident although denying any intention at the time to become so. And see *Miesegaes v CIR CA 1957, 37 TC 493* (minor at school here for five years, spending the occasional vacation with his father in Switzerland, held ordinarily resident). See also cases under 64.5 above.

In *R v Barnet London Borough Council (ex p Nilish Shah) HL 1982, [1983] 1 AER 226* (a non-tax case), the words 'ordinarily resident' were held to mean 'that the person must be habitually and normally resident here, apart from temporary or occasional absence of long or short duration'.

Simon's Direct Tax Service. See **E6.1**.

64.7 VISITS ABROAD AND CLAIMS TO NON-RESIDENCE (AND TO NON-ORDINARY RESIDENCE)

Visits abroad are differentiated as follows.

(*a*) **Absence from UK for full-time work abroad.** An individual working abroad in the circumstances specified in 64.5(*c*) above will normally be regarded as not resident and not ordinarily resident for his period of absence if the period includes at least one complete tax year and if his visits to the UK do not exceed the limits specified in 64.5(*a*) and (*b*) above. (Revenue Pamphlet IR 20, para 2.2).

(*b*) **Absence from UK for other reasons.** Where an individual goes abroad and intends to remain abroad for at least three years, he may claim to be treated as neither resident nor ordinarily resident from the day after departure, provided that he has been absent for at least a whole tax year and visits to the UK have not exceeded 182 days in any tax year or averaged more than 90 days in any tax year (as regards both of which tests see further 64.5 above). Such a claim must be supported by suitable evidence (e.g. acquiring permanent living accommodation abroad and making appropriate arrangements in relation to any property owned in the UK). (Revenue Pamphlet IR 20, paras 2.7, 2.8).

In the absence of such evidence, the same treatment may be claimed where the absence abroad is for a settled purpose, e.g. where there is a fixed object or intention in which the individual is going to be engaged for an extended period of time. Otherwise, UK residence and ordinary residence will be treated as continuing, subject to review if the absence actually extends beyond three years or if evidence becomes available to show that the absence is permanent (and provided that the 182- and 91-day tests (as above) are satisfied). (Revenue Pamphlet IR 20, para 2.9).

In any event, an individual will be regarded as resident in the UK in the circumstances described in 64.5(*a*) above, and as both resident and ordinarily resident in the circumstances described in 64.5(*b*) above. (Revenue Pamphlet IR 20, paras 3.3, 3.4).

See 64.5 above as regards the relevance of available accommodation in the UK for 1992/93 and earlier years.

64.8 APPEALS

Ordinary residence and domicile in relation to Schedule E and CGT are determined by the Board. [*ICTA 1988, s 207*]. Claims to the remittance basis in respect of overseas income on the grounds of ordinary residence or domicile outside the UK (see 73.5 SCHEDULE D, CASES IV AND V), claims to the special reliefs referred to at 64.3 above and certain double tax claims (see 25.5(*e*) DOUBLE TAX RELIEF) are made to the Board. Any appeal from a Board decision is to the Special Commissioners [*TMA 1970, Sch 1A para 10, Sch 2 para 3*] and the normal time limit of 30 days is extended to three months if on a question of residence, ordinary residence or domicile. [*TMA 1970, s 42(3)(b), Sch 1A para 9(2)(b)*]. Other disputes regarding residence are settled by way of appeal against the relevant assessment in the ordinary way.

65 Retirement Annuities

Cross-references. See 60 PERSONAL PENSION SCHEMES (AND STAKEHOLDER PENSIONS). See also 53.16 PARTNERSHIPS for partnership retirement annuities and 66 RETIREMENT SCHEMES generally.

Simon's Direct Tax Service E7.3.

General note. The provisions under *ICTA 1988, ss 618–629* for retirement annuity contracts for the self-employed and those in non-pensionable employment are, for new schemes, replaced, after 30 June 1988, by the regime for personal pension schemes under *ICTA 1988, ss 630–655*, designed to encourage employees who wish to do so to opt out of company pension schemes in favour of independent arrangements not linked to any one employment. See 60 PERSONAL PENSION SCHEMES (AND STAKEHOLDER PENSIONS). Retirement annuity schemes contracted before 1 July 1988 continue, however, to be dealt with under the earlier provisions.

The headings in this chapter are as follows.

65.1 Outline of provisions
65.2 Contract requirements
65.3 Limits of relief
65.4 Premiums related back
65.5 Unused relief carried forward
65.6 Cancellation of retirement annuity contract
65.7 Relevant earnings
65.8 Trust schemes
65.9 Interaction between retirement annuity premiums and personal pension contributions

65.1 OUTLINE OF PROVISIONS

Where an individual pays a 'qualifying premium' in a year of assessment under a contract made before 1 July 1988 and approved by the Board of Inland Revenue under *ICTA 1988, s 620* or *s 621*, the amount of that premium may, subject to certain limits (see 65.3 below), be deducted from his 'relevant earnings' (see 65.7 below) as assessed for that year from a trade, profession, vocation, office or employment. [*ICTA 1988, ss 618(1), 619(1), 620(1); FA 1988, s 54*]. These arrangements do not apply to income from a pensionable office or employment (see 65.7 below). Retirement annuity premiums are not deductible in arriving at profits for Class 4 national insurance purposes (see 83.7 SOCIAL SECURITY). [*Social Security Contributions and Benefits Act 1992, Sch 2 para 3(2)(f)*].

Relief may be granted on a provisional basis in respect of renewal premiums, whether fixed or variable, without proof of payment being required before the due date for payment of tax (although proof of payment is of course required in due course). (Revenue Tax Bulletin May 1992 p 19).

An annuity payable under such a contract (so far as it derives from premiums in respect of which relief was given) is treated as earned income when received by an annuitant to whom it is made payable under the terms of the contract. [*ICTA 1988, s 619(1)*]. It will normally be paid under deduction of tax under Schedule D, Case III (see 23.11 DEDUCTION OF TAX AT SOURCE).

Simon's Direct Tax Service. See E7.3.

65.2 CONTRACT REQUIREMENTS

For approval under ICTA 1988, s 620, the annuity contract must have as its main object the provision for an individual of a life annuity in old age. It must be made by an individual with a person carrying on life annuity business in the UK, and, subject as follows, **must preclude**

(*a*) any payment during the life of the individual other than a life annuity to him commencing not earlier than age 60 and not later than age 75, and

(*b*) any payment after his death other than

(i) a life annuity (not greater than his original annuity) to his surviving spouse, or

(ii) if no annuity becomes payable either to the individual or his spouse, the return of premiums paid, with reasonable interest or bonuses out of profits.

An annuity under *section 620* may, if so provided and if the individual so elects before the annuity first becomes payable, be *partially commuted* for a lump sum not exceeding three times the annual amount of the remaining part of the annuity, but subject to this all annuities must be incapable of total or partial surrender, commutation or assignment.

For approved contracts made after 16 March 1987 (but before 1 July 1988), however, the maximum lump sum which may be paid to the individual is £150,000 (or such other sum as may be specified by Treasury order), regardless of the terms of the contract. Alternatively, the individual and the person(s) to whom premiums are payable were able jointly to elect (before the end of January 1988) for the approval of the contract to be cancelled *ab initio*.

But the Inland Revenue may, conditionally, approve a contract, otherwise satisfying the above, even though it contains one or more of the following provisions:

(i) the individual's life annuity to commence at age earlier than 60 in the event of his becoming incapacitated from carrying on his occupation, or any similar one,

(ii) the individual's life annuity to commence earlier than age 60 if his occupation is one in which retirement before that age is customary (see below),

(iii) a life annuity, after the individual's death, for a dependant other than the surviving spouse,

(iv) an annuity to continue for a term certain (not exceeding 10 years) despite death within that term, and for such an annuity to be capable of assignment by will, or by the annuitant's personal representatives in distributing his estate,

(v) suspension, or termination, of the annuity, in the event of marriage, remarriage, or otherwise,

(vi) the value of the accrued rights to be paid as a premium for another approved annuity contract or personal pension scheme, if required by the individual, widow, widower or dependant having the accrued rights.

[*ICTA 1988, s 618(2)(4), s 620(1)–(4); FA 1988, s 54*].

As regards (ii) above, the following early retirement ages have been agreed by Superannuation Funds Office.

30 Downhill skiers.
35 Athletes; badminton players; boxers; cyclists; dancers; footballers; ice hockey players; models; national hunt jockeys; real tennis players; rugby league players; rugby union players; squash players; table tennis players; tennis players; wrestlers.
40 Cricketers; divers (saturation, deep sea and free swimming); golfers; motorcycle riders (motocross or road racing); motor racing drivers; snooker and billiards players; speedway riders; trapeze artistes.
45 Flat racing jockeys; members of the reserve forces.

50 Croupiers; money broker dealers; newscasters (ITV); offshore riggers; rugby league referees.

55 Air pilots; brass instrumentalists; distant water trawlermen; firemen (part-time); inshore fishermen; moneybroker dealer directors and managers responsible for dealers; nurses, physiotherapists, midwives or health visitors who are females; psychiatrists (who are also maximum part-time specialists employed within the NHS solely in the treatment of the mentally disordered); singers.

These pension ages apply only to arrangements funded by premiums in respect of relevant earnings from the occupation or profession in question. For professional sportsmen, the earnings must arise from activities as such, e.g. tournament earnings and appearance and prize money, and not from sponsorship or coaching (for which separate arrangements may be made).

For approval under ICTA 1988, s 621, (term assurance or family income cover) the contract must be made by an individual with a person carrying on life annuity business in the UK. It must either

(*a*) have as its main object the provision of a life annuity for the surviving spouse or other dependants of the individual, or

(*b*) have as its sole object the provision of a lump sum on the death of the individual before age 75.

Unless the Revenue otherwise allow, a contract within (*a*) must also satisfy the following conditions:

(i) any annuity payable must be incapable of total or partial surrender, commutation or assignment;

(ii) if payable to the individual's surviving spouse or dependant, it must be a life annuity commencing on the individual's death;

(iii) if payable to the individual, it must be a life annuity commencing after the age of 60 and, unless payable as a result of the death of a person to whom an annuity would otherwise have been payable, commencing before the age of 75;

(iv) if, as a result of death, no annuity is payable, the only sums which may be paid under the contract are by way of return of premiums, reasonable interest on premiums or bonuses out of profits.

[*ICTA 1988, s 621(1)–(4)*].

Simon's Direct Tax Service. See **E7.302.**

65.3 LIMITS OF RELIEF

Relief is given only by deduction from relevant earnings, and the amount of qualifying premiums which may be deducted from relevant earnings in any year of assessment is subject to an overall limit which is a percentage of 'net relevant earnings' in that year (see 65.7 below). See 65.5 below for relief carry-forward. [*ICTA 1988, s 619(2)(3)*].

The overall limit is 17½% of net relevant earnings although older individuals are allowed a higher percentage (see below). Premiums paid under *ICTA 1988, s 621* approved contracts may not exceed 5% of net relevant earnings, and are included in the overall limit of 17½%.

Increased limits for older individuals. The overall limits are increased as indicated in the following table where the individual is in the age range indicated at the beginning of a year of assessment.

51 to 55	20%
56 to 60	22½%
61 or more	27½%

[*ICTA 1988, s 626*].

Where relief is also available for personal pension scheme contributions in a year of assessment, the relief available for those contributions is correspondingly reduced. [*ICTA 1988, s 655(1)(a)*]. See Example at 60.4 PERSONAL PENSION SCHEMES (AND STAKEHOLDER PENSIONS).

Simon's Direct Tax Service. See **E7.321**.

65.4 PREMIUMS RELATED BACK

An individual who pays a qualifying premium in a year of assessment (whether or not he has relevant earnings for that year) may elect that the premium (or part of it, see Tolley's Practical Tax 1982 p 132) be treated as paid

(*a*) in the last preceding year of assessment, or

(*b*) if he had no net relevant earnings in the last preceding year, in the last preceding year but one.

For premiums paid in 1996/97 and later years, the election must be made on or before 31 January following the year of assessment in which the premium is paid. For earlier years, the election had to be made before the end of the year of payment although the Revenue normally allowed concessionally an additional three months, i.e. up to and including 5 July following the year of payment.

Where such an election is made, the premium is treated as having been paid in the year elected and not in the year actually paid. [*ICTA 1988, s 619(4); FA 1996, s 135, Sch 21 para 17*]. See 17.2 CLAIMS as regards how relief for premiums carried back to 1996/97 and subsequent years is given. An election is in practice treated by the Revenue as operative only up to the maximum available for relief for the year specified in the election. If the amount specified in the election becomes excessive as a result of an adjustment to the assessment for the year specified, the unrelievable proportion will fall back into the actual year of payment. (Tolley's Practical Tax 1984 p 158).

For years before 1997/98, *Lloyd's underwriters* may elect that a qualifying premium paid in the year may be related back to the third previous year of assessment before the year of payment (i.e. a premium paid in 1994/95 could be related back to relevant earnings assessed for 1991/92). The earlier year must have unused relief attributable to relevant earnings from Lloyd's underwriting activities. The election must be made before the end of the year of assessment in which the premium is paid. Where such an election is made the normal provisions for relating back premiums under *ICTA 1988, s 619(4)* (above) do not apply. The election ceases to be available for 1997/98 and subsequent years, for which the basis of assessment of Lloyd's underwriters is changed (see 89.2 UNDERWRITERS). [*ICTA 1988, s 627; FA 1993, s 183(3); FA 1994, s 228(2)(4)*].

Simon's Direct Tax Service. See **E7.324**.

65.5 UNUSED RELIEF CARRIED FORWARD

Relief available for a year of assessment which is not used in that year may be carried forward and used to cover that part of a qualifying premium paid in any of the next six years which exceeds the relief limit (see 65.3 above) for that year. Relief is given in the year in which the premium is paid although the maximum relief for that year must be used first. Unused relief for earlier years must be used before that for later years.

Where an assessment on an individual's earnings becomes final and conclusive more than six years after the end of the year to which it relates, and as a result there is an amount of unused relief for that year, that amount shall not be available for any of the following six years. However that relief may be covered by a qualifying premium paid within six months of the date on which the assessment becomes final and conclusive. Relief is given in the year of assessment in which the premium is paid but is not allowed unless the maximum premium allowable for that year (see 65.3 above) is paid. Although the extra premium representing the unused relief must be paid within the specified six months, the maximum premium for the year of assessment in which the extra premium is paid may be paid at any time within the normal time limits for that year. If relief is given for a premium in this way, it may not be given under the normal carry-forward rule. [*ICTA 1988, s 625*]. Relief is given in a similar way where relevant earnings for a year which ended more than six years previously are not formally assessed but are taken into account in an offer in settlement in a back duty case. See 6.11 BACK DUTY.

Where contributions are made under approved personal pension arrangements (see 60.1 PERSONAL PENSION SCHEMES (AND STAKEHOLDER PENSIONS)) in a year of assessment, the unused relief that may be utilised in that year is correspondingly reduced. [*ICTA 1988, s 655(1)(b)*]. For the method of calculating the reduction, see *Brock v O'Connor (Sp C 118), [1997] SSCD 157.* See Example at 60.7 PERSONAL PENSION SCHEMES (AND STAKEHOLDER PENSIONS).

Simon's Direct Tax Service. See E7.323.

65.6 CANCELLATION OF CONTRACT

The Pension Schemes Office has indicated that cancellation of a policy under a retirement annuity contract may be agreed to where there has been some fundamental misconception as to the nature of the policy. Where the Life Office accepts that a valid case of misapprehension by the taxpayer has arisen, and is anxious to cancel the policy *ab initio* and refund the premiums paid, the matter would be viewed sympathetically. Such a case may be settled on the basis that there was no valid contract at the outset, so that *ICTA 1988, s 620(2)* would not be breached. It is for the taxpayer to contact the Life Office, who should then approach the Pension Schemes Office. This would not extend to the case where a contract has been in existence for a number of years, and a premium is subsequently paid which for some reason is not fully tax-relieved. (Tolley's Practical Tax 1983 p 157, 1985 p 22).

65.7 RELEVANT EARNINGS

'*Relevant earnings*' of an individual is chargeable income which is included in one of the following categories.

(*a*) Income from an office or employment which is not a 'pensionable office or employment', and income from property which is either attached thereto or which forms part of the emoluments therefrom. This includes amounts assessed as benefits in kind. It also includes any amounts charged in respect of profits on shares acquired under share incentive schemes (see 82.4, 82.5 SHARE INCENTIVES AND OPTIONS), and the excess over the exempt limit of any lump sum termination payment (see 19.5 COMPENSATION FOR LOSS OF EMPLOYMENT (AND DAMAGES)).

(*b*) Income chargeable under Schedule D immediately derived from the carrying on, individually or in partnership, of his trade, profession or vocation. This includes enterprise allowances (see 71.85 SCHEDULE D, CASES I AND II) and POST-CESSATION RECEIPTS (60).

(*c*) Income from patent rights treated as earned income under *ICTA 1988, s 529.*

It does not include remuneration of a controlling director of an investment company. A married woman's relevant earnings are her own and not her husband's for the purpose of determining entitlement to retirement annuity relief. The amount from each such source is the statutory income of the year of assessment (i.e. ignoring any 'conventional' basis of assessment — see Tolley's Practical Tax 1982 p 131) before deducting capital allowances (other than those actually deductible in computing profits) but inclusive of any balancing charges. [*ICTA 1988, s 623(1)(2)(5), s 624(3); FA 1989, Sch 12 para 15*]. See 75.32 SCHEDULE E as regards treatment as relevant earnings of certain payments to redundant steel workers.

A '*pensionable office or employment*' is one to which any sponsored superannuation scheme applies which provides for retirement, etc., and under which any part of the cost is borne otherwise than by the holder of the office etc. (and is not assessable under Schedule E rules on him). See, however, below for concessional relief in the case of certain small lump sum retirement benefits schemes. An office or employment may be 'pensionable' even if the holder performs the duties partly outside the UK or is not chargeable to tax in respect of it. If the holder of such an office, etc., having an option, does not join the scheme, his office is treated, for this purpose, as non-pensionable. [*ICTA 1988, s 623(3)(4), s 624(1)(2)*]. By concession, where an individual is treated as in pensionable employment solely because provision is made under a scheme or arrangement existing on 14 October 1980, fully or partly at the cost of the employer, for a benefit in pension form payable only on death or disability, the employment will be treated as non-pensionable for any tax year in which the individual has not become entitled to benefit as a result of that provision. Relief will be available on a year to year basis for the period of employment or until benefit becomes payable. Employment in the tax year in which such a contingency occurs will be regarded as pensionable and no retirement annuity relief will be available for that year, but relief given for previous years will not be affected. (Revenue Pamphlet IR 1, A38). The Pension Schemes Office has ruled that an office or employment is non-pensionable up to the date on which the employee, etc. first becomes entitled to benefits under a retirement scheme, even if these benefits are calculated by reference to earlier periods of service. (Tolley's Practical Tax 1982 p 131). It is, however, understood that where an employee receives a refund of premiums paid while in pensionable employment, that employment is *not* thereby rendered non-pensionable. (Tolley's Practical Tax 1986 p 135, 1990 p 95). See below, however, as regards personal pension schemes.

'*Net relevant earnings*' are relevant earnings, as above, less deductions which would be made therefrom in computing the individual's total income for income tax, being

(i) deductions which but for *ICTA 1988, s 74(1)(m), (p) or (q)* could be made in computing his profits or gains (i.e. various payments, subject to deduction of tax at source, made for business purposes – excluding e.g. annuities to former partners, which would be prohibited under *ICTA 1988, s 74(1)(a)* – see Tolley's Practical Tax 1983 p 73), or

(ii) deductions in respect of losses, or of capital allowances, relating to activities any profits from which would be relevant earnings of the individual. [*ICTA 1988, s 623(6)*].

Other amounts deducted in charging the individual's income to tax (e.g. for earnings from work done abroad, see 75.3 SCHEDULE E, or under the current provisions) do not reduce net relevant earnings.

Where an individual has relevant earnings but no other income, and he obtains 100% capital allowances on the cost of constructing a small workshop for letting, the capital allowances will not reduce his net relevant earnings for retirement annuity relief purposes (Tolley's Practical Tax 1981 p 59).

If, in any year for which an individual claims relief, a deduction for a loss or allowance under (ii) above is treated as made to any extent out of income other than relevant earnings, his net relevant earnings for the next year are treated as reduced to that extent, any balance being carried forward to the third year, and so on. [*ICTA 1988, s 623(7)*].

In the case of partnership profits, net relevant earnings are the share of partnership income (as computed for tax purposes) after allowable deductions for partnership payments and capital allowances. [*ICTA 1988, s 623(9)*].

Simon's Direct Tax Service. See E7.322.

Small lump sum retirement benefits schemes. Concessional relief applies where an employee has

(*a*) paid premiums to a retirement annuity contract (or the employee or employer had made personal pension scheme contributions) for a year of assessment (see 65.3 above), and

(*b*) accrued benefits, for the same year and in respect of the same office or employment, under an approved retirement benefits scheme

- (i) under the rules of which the only benefit on retirement (other than from additional voluntary contributions) is a lump sum not exceeding £400 per year of pensionable service, and
- (ii) whose rules provide for no such lump sum to accrue (or for the lump sum to be waived) in respect of any period for which premiums are paid to a retirement annuity contract (or personal pension scheme).

The tax relief for the retirement annuity premiums (or personal pension contributions) will not be withdrawn provided that

(1) the lump sum benefit entitlement for the period is waived or does not accrue, and

(2) the retirement annuity contract (or personal pension scheme) is not cancelled.

(Revenue Pamphlet IR 1, A95).

65.8 TRUST SCHEMES

The retirement annuity provisions also apply to contributions under a trust scheme, approved by the Inland Revenue, administered in the UK and established under irrevocable trusts by *a body representing a substantial proportion of the individuals engaged* (in UK, or in England, Scotland, Wales or NI) *in a particular occupation* (or group of occupations), for providing retirement annuities for them, with or without subsidiary benefits for their families or dependants. If the scheme is approved, income from investments or deposits of any fund maintained for the purpose of that fund is exempt from income tax. Gains are similarly exempt from capital gains tax. [*ICTA 1988, s 620(5)(6), s 621(5); TCGA 1992, s 271(1)(d)*]. See 71.32 SCHEDULE D, CASES I AND II as regards futures and options contracts.

Relief ceases to be available under such schemes to a person by whom contributions are first paid after 30 June 1988, even though the scheme may have been established on or before that date. [*ICTA 1988, s 618; FA 1988, s 54*].

65.9 INTERACTION BETWEEN RETIREMENT ANNUITY PREMIUMS AND PERSONAL PENSION CONTRIBUTIONS

Example

Y is self-employed and pays both retirement annuity premiums (RAPs), under a pre-1 July 1988 contract, and contributions to a personal pension scheme (PPCs). He had no unused relief brought forward at 6 April 1990, on which date he was 48 years of age. His net relevant earnings (NRE), RAPs paid and PPCs paid in each of the years 1990/91 to 2000/2001 are as set out below. At no time does Y elect to carry back an RAP or a PPC to a previous year.

	NRE	*Earnings cap*	*PPCs paid*	*RAPs paid*
	£	£	£	£
1990/91	67,000	64,800	1,500	10,000
1991/92	72,000	71,400	7,500	10,000
1992/93	74,000	75,000	8,000	10,000
1993/94	78,000	75,000	12,000	10,000
1994/95	90,000	76,800	15,000	10,000
1995/96	120,000	78,600	14,000	10,000
1996/97	125,000	82,200	16,000	10,000
1997/98	127,500	84,000	16,550	10,000
1998/99	140,000	87,600	20,660	10,000
1999/00	155,000	90,600	21,710	10,000
2000/01	90,000	91,800	21,500	10,000

Y's records of amounts paid and tax relief given will look as follows

Personal pension contributions (PPCs)

		Maximum				
		PPC	*RAPs*	*PPCs*	*Unused relief*	
	NRE	*relief*	*relieved*	*paid*	*For year*	*Cumulative*
	£	£	£	£	£	£
1990/91	64,800	16,200 (1)	(10,000)	(1,500)	4,700	4,700
1991/92	71,400	17,850 (1)	(10,000)	(7,500)	350	5,050
1992/93	74,000	18,500 (1)	(10,000)	(8,000)	500	5,550
1993/94	75,000	22,500 (2)	(10,000)	(12,000)	500	6,050
1994/95	76,800	23,040 (2)	(10,000)	(15,000)	(1,960)	4,090
1995/96	78,600	23,580 (2)	(10,000)	(14,000)	(420)	3,670
1996/97	82,200	24,660 (2)	(10,000)	(16,000)	(1,340)	1,350 (4)
1997/98	84,000	25,200 (2)	(10,000)	(16,550)	(1,350)	Nil
1998/99	87,600	30,660 (3)	(10,000)	(20,660)	Nil	Nil
1999/00	90,600	31,710 (3)	(10,000)	(21,710)	Nil	Nil
2000/01	90,000	31,500 (3)	(10,000)	(21,500)	Nil	Nil

(1) = Relief at 25%

(2) = Relief at 30%

(3) = Relief at 35%

(4) = £3,670 b/f *less* £1,340 relieved in 1996/97 *less* £980 remaining for 1990/91 which cannot be carried forward beyond 1996/97 (although relief for the £980 could have been obtained by an election to treat part of the 1997/98 premium as having been paid in 1996/97). The £1,350 consists of the aggregate unused relief for 1991/92, 1992/93 and 1993/94.

The aggregate for each year of the 'RAPS relieved' and 'PPCs paid' columns above represents the total relief given in each year.

Retirement annuity premiums (RAPs)

	NRE	*Maximum PPC relief*	*RAPs relieved*	*PPCs paid*	*Unused relief For year*	*Unused relief Cumulative*
	£	£	£	£	£	£
1990/91	67,000	11,725 (5)	(10,000)	1,725	(1,500)	225
1991/92	72,000	12,600 (5)	(10,000)	2,600	(7,500)	(225)*
1992/93	74,000	12,950 (5)	(10,000)	2,950	(8,000)	Nil*
1993/94	78,000	15,600 (6)	(10,000)	5,600	(12,000)	Nil*
1994/95	90,000	18,000 (6)	(10,000)	8,000	(15,000)	Nil*
1995/96	120,000	24,000 (6)	(10,000)	14,000	(14,000)	Nil
1996/97	125,000	25,000 (6)	(10,000)	15,000	(16,000)	Nil*
1997/98	127,500	25,500 (6)	(10,000)	15,500	(16,550)	Nil*
1998/99	140,000	31,500 (7)	(10,000)	21,500	(20,660)	840
1999/00	155,000	34,875 (7)	(10,000)	24,875	(21,710)	4,005
2000/01	90,000	20,250 (7)	(10,000)	10,250	(21,500)	Nil

(5) = Relief at 17.5%

(6) = Relief at 20%

(7) = Relief at 22.5%

* Unused relief carried forward cannot be reduced to a negative figure, so is merely reduced to nil.

Notes

(*a*) The maximum relief for PPCs for any year is reduced by any RAPs relieved in that year. One effect of this is that if a combination of RAPs and PPCs is to be relieved in any year, the maximum relief available for that year (excluding unused relief brought forward) is restricted by reference to the earnings cap.

(*b*) In computing unused retirement annuity relief for any year, any PPCs relieved in that year must be deducted.

(*c*) The maximum potential relief for the ten years illustrated (taking the higher of the two maxima for each year) is £270,465. The total relief given is £264,420. Of the difference of £6,045, £980 is unused relief for 1990/91 which is lost under the six-year rule. The balance of £5,065 arises from the operation of the earnings cap for 1995/96 onwards.

(*d*) As regards the method of calculation of unused relief, see *Brock v O'Connor (Sp C 118), [1997] SSCD 157.*

66 Retirement Schemes for Employees

(See also Revenue Pamphlet IR 12 (1991) as amended by later Memoranda and Updates issued by the Inland Revenue Pension Schemes Office at Yorke House, PO Box 62, Castle Meadow Road, Nottingham NG2 1BG. For tax district practice generally, see Revenue Inspector's Manual, IM 8000 *et seq.*.)

Cross-references. See 59 PENSIONS generally and in respect of overseas pension funds; 60 PERSONAL PENSION SCHEMES; and 65 RETIREMENT ANNUITIES.

Simon's Direct Tax Service E7.2.

The headings in this chapter are as follows.

66.1	Whether payments by employer are assessable on employee	66.9	Unapproved retirement benefit schemes
66.2	Life assurance relief	66.10	Deductibility by employer
66.3	Conditions for approval — history	66.11	Other schemes
66.4	Conditions for approval after 5 April 1973	66.12	Lump sum on retirement etc.
66.5	Effects of approval	66.13	Schemes ceasing to be approved at April 1980
66.6	Schemes approved before 27 July 1989	66.14	Mis-sold freestanding additional voluntary contribution schemes
66.7	Schemes approved before 23 July 1987	66.15	Overseas pensions and pension funds
66.8	Pension scheme surpluses	66.16	Social Security Acts

66.1 WHETHER PAYMENTS BY EMPLOYER ARE ASSESSABLE ON EMPLOYEE

Payments by an employer pursuant to a 'retirement benefits scheme' for the provision of 'relevant benefits' for an employee are treated as income of that employee unless

(*a*) the scheme is approved by the Inland Revenue, or

(*b*) the scheme is a 'relevant statutory scheme', or

(*c*) the scheme is set up by a non-UK government for the benefit (or primarily for the benefit) of its employees, or

(*d*) the employee exercises his employment outside the UK so that no tax is chargeable under Cases I or II of SCHEDULE E (75), or

(*e*) the employee receives 'foreign emoluments' (i.e. those of a non-domiciled person working for non-resident employer) and the scheme corresponds to (*a*), (*b*) or (*c*) above.

[*ICTA 1988, s 595(1), s 596(1)(2); FA 1989, Sch 6 para 8*].

See Revenue Explanatory Booklet 'The Tax Treatment of Top-Up Pension Schemes' for the Revenue view of when a charge arises under *section 595(1)*. Where a payment has been the subject of such a charge, the employer should provide the employee with a notice of the charge, which the employee should retain in order to show that benefits arising under the scheme are not chargeable to tax under *ICTA 1988, s 596A* (see 66.9 below).

Where payments have been treated as income of an employee as above, but the employee subsequently proves to the satisfaction of the Board that no payment in respect of the benefits has so far been made and that some event has occurred by reason of which no such payment will be made (in both cases other than as a consequence of a pension-sharing order or provision under *Welfare Reform and Pensions Act 1999, s 24(1)*), the tax paid will be repaid on application within six years of the event in question. Partial repayment may also be given on a just and reasonable basis. [*ICTA 1988, s 596(3)(4); FA 1999, Sch 10 para 5*].

'*Retirement benefits scheme*' is defined as including any scheme, deed or arrangement (even if for single employee and even if the pension is to commence immediately) providing 'relevant benefits'. Approved personal pension schemes providing such benefits (see 60.2 PERSONAL PENSION SCHEMES) and national schemes are not included. [*ICTA 1988, s 611; FA 1999, Sch 10 para 9; FA 2000, Sch 13 para 4*]. Benefits payable to the employee's wife or husband (or widow or widower), children, dependants or personal representatives are included. [*ICTA 1988, s 595(5); FA 1999, Sch 10 para 4*].

'*Relevant benefits*' are any pension, lump sum, gratuity, etc. either (i) on retirement or death, or (ii) by virtue of a pension-sharing order or provision under *Welfare Reform and Pensions Act 1999, s 24(1)*, or (iii) in anticipation of retirement, or (iv) in connection with past service, after retirement or death, or (v) in anticipation of or in connection with any change in the nature of the employee's service, *other than* benefits afforded solely by reason of accidental disablement or death by accident during employment. [*ICTA 1988, s 612(1); FA 1999, Sch 10 para 10*].

A '*relevant statutory scheme*' is a statutory scheme established before 14 March 1989, or established on or after that date and entered in the register maintained by the Board for that purpose, or a parliamentary pension scheme (as defined). [*ICTA 1988, s 611A; FA 1989, Sch 6 para 15; FA 1999, Sch 5 para 5*].

As regards certain lump sum payments on retirement, etc., see 66.12 below.

Employee is widely defined in *ICTA 1988, s 612(1)* and includes a director.

66.2 **LIFE ASSURANCE RELIEF**

Where approval was not obtained, and the payment by the employer is made under such an insurance or contract that life assurance relief (see 45.1 LIFE ASSURANCE POLICIES) would be obtained if made by the individual, then that individual is eligible for life assurance relief thereon. [*ICTA 1988, s 595(1)(b)*].

66.3 **CONDITIONS FOR APPROVAL — HISTORY**

Up to 5 April 1973, schemes for employees generally could be approved under *ICTA 1970, s 208* and a scheme for specific individuals (often referred to as a 'top-hat' scheme) could be approved under *ICTA 1970, s 222.*

After 5 April 1973, new schemes, or existing schemes materially altered, had to comply with new provisions which apply to *all* schemes after 5 April 1980 when *ICTA 1970, s 208, ss 220–225* were repealed. [*FA 1971, Sch 3*]. See 66.13 below.

Schemes existing at 5 April 1973 accordingly had to be amended to comply with the new provisions on or before 5 April 1980, in order for approval to be continued after that date.

66.4 **CONDITIONS FOR APPROVAL AFTER 5 APRIL 1973** [*ICTA 1988, Pt XIV, Ch 1; FA 1988, Sch 3 para 18; FA 1989, Sch 6 paras 3, 4; FA 1991, ss 34–36*]

Subject to provision for discretionary approval (see below), the following conditions apply.

(*a*) The scheme must be established in connection with a trade or undertaking carried on in the UK by a UK resident, and there must be a UK resident who will be responsible for carrying out all statutory duties imposed on the administration of the scheme.

(*b*) The employer must contribute to the scheme and both he and the employees to whom the scheme relates must recognise it, every employee who is, or has a right to be, a member of the scheme being given particulars of all essential features of it which concern him.

(*c*) The sole purpose of the scheme must be to provide employees (or their widows or widowers, children, dependants or personal representatives) with 'relevant benefits' (see 66.1 above)

(i) on, after, or in anticipation of, *retirement at a specified age*, which must be not later than 75 or earlier than 60,

(ii) on, or after, *death*,

(iii) on, or in anticipation of, or in connection with, *a change in the nature* of the employee's service with the employer.

(*d*) Employee's contributions must not be returnable in any circumstances (but see 66.5(*c*) below regarding existing schemes).

(*e*) The employee's pension must not exceed *one-sixtieth* of his final remuneration for each year of service up to a maximum of 40. '*Final remuneration*' is the average annual remuneration of the last three years' service.

(*f*) No pension may be commuted except where the scheme allows an employee to do so. A lump sum so obtained must not exceed *three-eightieths* of the employee's final remuneration for each year of service up to a maximum of 40; i.e. the maximum lump sum is $1\frac{1}{2}$ years' pay. (For schemes approved after 16 March 1987 and before 27 July 1989, and for any person who before 1 June 1989 became a member of a scheme which came into existence before 14 March 1989 but was not approved before 27 July 1989, there is excluded from final remuneration for this purpose any excess over £100,000.)

(*g*) The normal pension payable to the widow or widower of an employee dying after retirement must not exceed *two-thirds of the pension.*

(*h*) Approval may be withdrawn if in the Board's opinion its continuance is not warranted, from a specified date (not earlier than that on which the facts first ceased to warrant approval). An alteration to a scheme invalidates any earlier approval unless the alteration has been approved by the Board, either specifically or in general regulations.

(*i*) Where more than one retirement benefits scheme applies to a particular class or description of employees, approval of any such scheme, so far as it relates to such employees, is considered by reference to all such schemes. The schemes to be considered are specified as schemes approved or seeking approval under these provisions, funds within *ICTA 1988, s 608* (see 66.13 below) and any relevant statutory schemes (see 66.1 above).

With effect from 10 May 2000, the conditions for approval are amended to make provision for pension-sharing arrangements under e.g. *Welfare Reform and Pensions Act 1999, s 24(1)* (or NI equivalent), and generally for the provision of benefits for ex-spouses (or their widows or widowers, children, dependants or personal representatives). Where a scheme member's rights are transferred under such arrangements, they may not be replaced with rights the scheme member would not have been able to acquire had there been no such transfer. Schemes approved before 10 May 2000 which continue to be approved on and after 1 December 2000 (when the pension-sharing rules come into operation) are treated as containing certain of the provisions for automatic approval. This does not apply to simplified defined contribution schemes or in certain cases where the member is a 'moderate earner' (broadly an employee who is not a controlling director and whose earnings at the date the marriage ends do not exceed one-quarter of the 'permitted maximum' (see below) for the year in which it ends), and the provisions are modified in certain other cases. See *The Retirement Benefits Schemes (Sharing of Pensions on Divorce or Annulment) Regulations 2000* (*SI 2000 No 1085*). As regards pension-sharing generally, see Pension Schemes Office Update No 62, 28 April 2000.

[*ICTA 1988, ss 590, 591B, 612(1); FA 1989, Sch 6 para 3(4); FA 1991, ss 34, 36; FA 1999, Sch 10 paras 2, 18(5); SI 2000 No 1093*].

As regards (*a*) above, with effect from 3 May 1994, there are detailed provisions for determining who is the administrator of a scheme, responsible for all the tax affairs of the scheme. Broadly, the administrator of a scheme set up under a trust is the trustee or trustees of the scheme, and the administrator of a scheme not set up under a trust is the sponsor or sponsors of the scheme. In either case a different person or persons (who must be UK resident) may be appointed as administrator by written notice, and such person(s) must be so appointed if none of the trustees or sponsors, as the case may be, is UK resident. Such an appointment made after the establishment of the scheme is an alteration of the scheme requiring Revenue approval. [*ICTA 1988, s 611AA; FA 1994, s 103(1)*]. Previously, the administrator was the person or persons having the management of the scheme. [*ICTA 1988, s 612(1); FA 1994, s 103(2)*]. There are provisions dealing with the position where a scheme has no administrator (e.g. where the trustees or sponsors are non-UK resident and have made no appointment), or no administrator can be traced, or the administrator is in default (considered serious by the Board). In such cases responsibilities and liabilities pass to any UK resident trustee or sponsor who can be traced (where a different administrator has been appointed), or ultimately to the employer (provided that the employer is a contributor to the scheme — failing which, if the scheme is a trust scheme, they pass to the sponsor(s) of the scheme) or the UK branch or agent of a non-UK resident employer. [*ICTA 1988, s 606; FA 1994, s 104; FA 1998, Sch 15 para 5*]. A charge on the administrator of a scheme is treated as charged on all present and future administrators (without prejudice to the exclusion from charge under *ICTA 1988, s 591C* of certain independent trustees, see below) and is assessable in the name of the administrator. It is not assessable on persons who are no longer administrators. SELF-ASSESSMENT (78) does not apply to charges on administrators (or on persons to whom the Revenue has recourse for tax on administrators under *section 606* (see above) or *section 606A* (see below)). [*ICTA 1988, s 658A; TMA 1970, s 9(1A); FA 1998, s 98*].

Further restrictions were introduced by *FA 1989, Sch 6* which apply to schemes approved after 26 July 1989, but, where a scheme came into existence before 14 March 1989, only as regards new members after 31 May 1989.

(i) Where an employee is a member of a scheme by virtue of two or more 'relevant associated employments', or of a scheme which, in relation to the employee, is 'connected with' one or more other approved schemes, new limits on pension and commuted pension are applied by reference to a 'relevant amount' and to the aggregate payable in respect of all such employments or schemes.

(ii) In arriving at an employee's final remuneration for the purposes of (*e*) or (*f*) above, any excess over the 'permitted maximum' for the year in which his participation in the scheme ceases is disregarded. Where this restriction applies, the earlier permitted maximum referred to in (*f*) above is abolished.

Employments are '*relevant associated employments*' for this purpose if an employee has held both or all of them, and become entitled to benefits in respect of both or all of them, during a period during which both or all of the employers were 'associated', and a scheme is '*connected with*' another in relation to an employee if a period of service under both of two 'associated' employers gives rise to entitlement to benefits under one scheme by reference to service with one employer and under the other scheme by reference to service with the other employer. Employers are '*associated*' if one is 'controlled' by the other or both are 'controlled' by a third person. '*Control*' may be direct or indirect and in relation to companies is determined in accordance with *ICTA 1988, s 840* (or, if the company is a close company, *ICTA 1988, s 416*).

The '*relevant amount*' is, in the case of pensions, $\frac{1}{60}$th, and in the case of commuted pension, $\frac{3}{80}$ths of the 'permitted maximum' for the year of assessment in which the benefits become payable, for each year of qualifying service (up to a maximum of 40), with a corresponding allowance for part years. Where there are relevant associated employments, all periods counting for benefit at the time the benefits become payable are taken into account, but periods counting by virtue of more than one such employment are included only once. Where schemes are connected with one another in relation to the employee, all periods counting for benefit for the purposes of all the connected schemes at the time the benefits become payable are taken into account, but periods counting for the purposes of more than one scheme are included only once.

The '*permitted maximum*' is £76,800 for 1994/95, £78,600 for 1995/96, £82,200 for 1996/97, £84,000 for 1997/98, £87,600 for 1998/99, £90,600 for 1999/2000 and £91,800 for 2000/01. It is increased in line with the retail prices index (unless Parliament sets a different figure) but is not reduced if the retail prices index falls.

[*ICTA 1988, s 590(3), ss 590A–590C; FA 1989, Sch 6 para 3(2)(3), para 4; SI 1991 No 734; SI 1992 No 624; FA 1993, ss 106, 107; SI 1993 No 2950; SI 1994 No 3009; SI 1995 No 3034; SI 1996 No 2951; SI 1998 No 758; SI 1999 No 592; SI 2000 No 807*].

Remuneration does not include anything chargeable under Schedule E arising from the acquisition or disposal of shares (or interests in shares) or from rights to acquire shares, nor anything in respect of which tax is chargeable under *ICTA 1988, s 148* (see 19.5 COMPENSATION FOR LOSS OF EMPLOYMENT (AND DAMAGES)). [*ICTA 1988, s 612(1)*].

Discretionary approval. The Board are given discretion, subject to regulations, to approve a scheme not fully complying with the above conditions (e.g. by allowing retirement up to 10 years before the ages prescribed in (*c*)(i) above, or earlier if incapacitated; by providing benefits in excess of the limits in (*e*) above on retirement after less than 40 years' service; by modifying the definition of 'final remuneration'; by providing a pension, and a lump sum up to four times final remuneration, for the widow(er) or dependants of an employee dying in service; by permitting certain increases in pensions in payment; by providing for the commutation in full of trivial pensions (i.e. up to £260 p.a.); by including a trade carried on partly overseas or by a non-resident; or by allowing the return of employees' contributions in certain contingencies) and, in respect of schemes in existence on 6 April 1980, will exercise that discretion to preserve benefits earned, or rights arising out of prior service, before the date of the approval of the scheme under the new code or 5 April 1980, whichever is the earlier, and to preserve any rights to death-in-service benefits existing under the scheme at 26 February 1970. Discretion is also given to approve schemes which allow members to have their benefits secured by means of an annuity contract with an insurance company of their choice, and schemes to which the employer is not a contributor which provide benefits additional to those under the employer's scheme. A condition for discretionary approval is that the employee's contribution must not exceed 15% of remuneration (and see now 66.5(*a*) below). [*ICTA 1988, s 591; FA 1994, s 107; FA 1995, ss 59(2), 60(1); FA 1999, Sch 10 para 3*]. Restrictions relating to the discretionary approval of small self-administered schemes (generally those with less than twelve members) are contained in *The Retirement Benefits Schemes (Restriction on Discretion to Approve) (Small Self-administered Schemes) Regulations 1991* (*SI 1991 No 1614*) (as amended), and those relating to discretionary approval of additional voluntary contribution schemes in *The*

Retirement Benefits Schemes (Restriction on Discretion to Approve) (Additional Voluntary Contributions) Regulations 1993 (*SI 1993 No 3016*) (as amended), from which existing approved schemes were excepted by *The Retirement Benefits Schemes (Restriction on Discretion to Approve) (Excepted Schemes) Regulations 1996* (*SI 1996 No 1582*) and *2000* (*SI 2000 No 1087*) — see also Pension Schemes Office Update No 18, 11 July 1996. See generally Revenue Pamphlet IR 12 (1997) and Pension Schemes Office Updates No 47, 24 July 1998 and No 48, 24 August 1998.

The Revenue have published model rules and guidance notes for simplified occupational pension schemes, satisfying certain specified criteria and aimed primarily at the smaller employer. There are two types of simplified scheme: 'final salary' and 'defined contribution'. The model scheme documents, if used unaltered, will enable schemes to obtain immediate tax approval. Copies may be obtained from the Pension Schemes Office (tel. 0115-974 0000). (Revenue Press Release 4 February 1988; SFO Memorandum No 94 February 1988).

Discretionary approval may be *withdrawn* in the same way as mandatory approval (see (*h*) above). Where regulations place certain restrictions on approval by reference to circumstances other than the provision of benefits, 36 months grace is given before withdrawal of approval after the regulations concerned come into effect. [*ICTA 1988, ss 591A, 591B; FA 1991, ss 35, 36*].

The Board has wide information powers, including prescriptive regulation-making powers, in relation to approved and statutory schemes, and from 3 May 1994 penalties of up to £3,000 may be imposed in cases of fraudulent or negligent false statements or representations. [*ICTA 1988, ss 605, 605A; FA 1994, ss 105, 106; FA 1998, Sch 15 para 4; SI 1995 Nos 3103, 3125*]. See also Pension Schemes Office Updates No 39, 25 February 1998, No 47, 24 July 1998 and No 48, 24 August 1998. For inspection visit procedure, see Pension Schemes Office Update No 32, 26 September 1997.

Changes to increase flexibility of schemes. The Pension Schemes Office have announced changes to the requirements for scheme approval in two areas. These are introduced with effect from 30 June 1999. Trustees of existing schemes may choose whether or not to amend scheme rules to offer these options to members.

(I) *Additional voluntary contributions ('AVCs').* Benefits from AVCs may be allowed to be taken at any time between ages 50 and 75 (and earlier if the member leaves employment due to incapacity), whether or not a person has retired or is drawing the main scheme benefits. (Currently, AVC benefits must be taken at the same time as the main scheme benefits.) Thus they may be able to be taken early (e.g. on a move from full- to part-time employment) or late (to boost income later in retirement).

(II) *Money purchase occupational schemes (including free-standing AVCs).* On retirement, members may have the option to defer purchase of the annuity up to (at latest) age 75 and to make income withdrawals (which are taxable under PAYE) during the deferral period, on terms similar to those already available in relation to personal pension schemes (see 60.2 PERSONAL PENSION SCHEMES).

For details, see Pension Schemes Office Update No 54, 30 June 1999.

Insured loanback arrangements. See Pension Schemes Office Update No 43, 22 April 1998 as regards the actions expected of trustees to avoid loss of approval of wholly insured schemes in cases where loans by the life office to the employer, which are secured on a policy or polices held by the scheme to provide benefits for a controlling director, are subject to foreclosure.

Tax on cessation of approval of certain schemes. A special charge to tax applies where approval of certain schemes is withdrawn on or after 2 November 1994 (under *ICTA 1988, s 591A* or *s 591B*, see above, but other than by a notice given before that day under *section*

591B(1)), unless the scheme is instead approved as a personal pension scheme under *ICTA 1988, Sch 23ZA para 3* (see 60.2 PERSONAL PENSION SCHEMES). This applies to any scheme which either:

(A) immediately before the date of cessation of approval, had less than twelve individual members; or

(B) at any time within the year preceding that date, had a member who has at any time been a 'controlling director' (within *ICTA 1988, s 417(5)(b)*) of a company which has contributed to the scheme; or

(C) (where that date is after 16 March 1998) has, at any time in the three years ending with that date, received, in respect of any person, a transfer value represented in which were contributions made to *any* 'approved pension arrangements', by or in respect of that person, by reference to:

  (i) service by him with a company of which he is or has been a controlling director; or

  (ii) remuneration in respect of any such service; or

  (iii) income chargeable under Schedule D immediately derived from his carrying on or exercising (including in partnership) a trade, profession or vocation.

As regards (C) above, a scheme receives a 'transfer value' when it comes to hold for its own purposes any sum or asset held for the purposes of any other 'approved pension arrangements'. 'Contributions' to such arrangements include any made in accordance with, or for the purposes of, the arrangements, and any premium or other consideration under an annuity contract for which the arrangements provide. '*Approved pension arrangements*' are those approved, or being considered for approval, under the current provisions, personal pension schemes, annuity contracts entered into for the purposes of any such scheme or arrangements, and retirement annuity contracts.

Any person to whom, at any particular time, a benefit under a scheme is being or may be provided in respect of his past or present employment is a member of the scheme at that time for these purposes.

Tax is charged under SCHEDULE D, CASE VI (74) at a rate of 40% on the value, as it stands immediately before the date approval ceases, of the assets held for the purposes of the scheme. The value of such assets is the market value, except that rights or interests in respect of money lent directly or indirectly to certain persons are valued at the amount owing (including unpaid interest). The charge is on the scheme administrator, except that where the scheme administrator is constituted by persons including a person who is an 'approved independent trustee', that person is not liable for the tax. An '*approved independent trustee*' is a person approved by the Board as a trustee of the scheme who is not connected (within *ICTA 1988, s 839*) with either a member or fellow trustee of the scheme or an employer who has contributed to the scheme. There are provisions (for schemes approved on or before 17 March 1998) which, subject to limited exceptions, prevent the removal of such a trustee on or after that date without his being immediately replaced.

Where an employer has become liable under *ICTA 1988, s 606* (see above) to any tax arising under these provisions on a cessation of approval after 16 March 1998, but has failed to pay the tax in full, there are provisions for recourse to scheme members who are or have been controlling directors (or by reference to whom the condition in (C) above was satisfied for the purpose of the tax charged) *pro rata* to their share of the scheme.

For the purposes of taxation of capital gains, assets in respect of which a charge arises as above are treated as having been acquired immediately before the date of cessation of approval for a consideration equal to the amount on which tax is charged under these provisions, without any corresponding deemed disposal.

For the procedures leading to withdrawal of approval, see Revenue Tax Bulletin August 1995 p 233.

[*ICTA 1988, ss 591C, 591D, 606A; FA 1995, s 61; FA 1998, Sch 15 paras 1, 2, 6, 7; FA 2000 Sch 13 para 3*].

See Pension Schemes Office Update No 10, 1 November 1995 (with subsequent changes in Update No 25, 24 March 1997 and No 31, 5 September 1997) or Revenue Tax Bulletin December 1995 p 266 as regards measures to prevent avoidance of a charge under *ICTA 1988, s 591C* by payment of a transfer value to a pension scheme subsequently transferred offshore (and see further 66.9 below). See also Pension Schemes Office Update No 33, 26 September 1997, as regards rebated and shared commissions on transfer of funds between investment vehicles.

An exempt approved scheme is any approved scheme as above which is established under irrevocable trusts, or any other approved scheme which the Board may direct as exempt. [*ICTA 1988, s 592(1)*].

66.5 **EFFECTS OF APPROVAL**

(*a*) **Payments by employer** of ordinary annual contributions to an exempt approved scheme are deductible as an expense for tax purposes in the tax year (or chargeable period) in which paid. A payment by the employer to the scheme discharging the employer's liability under *Social Security Pensions Act 1975, s 58B* or *Pension Schemes Act 1993, s 144* (or NI equivalent) is treated as a contribution to the scheme, and if the trade etc. has ceased before the payment is made, is deductible as if paid on the last day on which the trade etc. was carried on. Contributions other than ordinary annual contributions are also deductible, but the Revenue may require these to be spread. Tax relief is given only for contributions actually paid, and not e.g. for any provision for such contributions. [*ICTA 1988, s 592(4)–(6A)*]. See Revenue Pamphlet IR 12 (1991) para 5.7 *et seq.* and Pension Schemes Office Update No 16, 30 May 1996 for practice on spreading of contributions (broadly over up to four years where special contributions amount to £500,000 or more in a chargeable period (£25,001 or more for chargeable periods ending before 1 June 1996)). A Revenue decision on spreading is not subject to review on appeal (*Kelsall v Investment Chartwork Ltd Ch D 1993, 65 TC 750*). Where employer's business changes hands see *Clarke v Musker Ch D 1956, 37 TC 1.* Legal and other expenses of establishing a scheme and running expenses of revenue nature will be allowed. (Revenue Pamphlet IR 12 (1991) paras 5.9, 5.10). For repayments out of overfunded schemes, see 66.8 below. See Simon's Direct Tax Service E7.231.

Payments by employees of contributions to exempt approved schemes are allowed as an expense in the tax year in which paid, provided that they do not in total exceed 15% (or such higher percentage as the Board may prescribe) of remuneration of that year. Remuneration in excess of the permitted maximum (see 66.4 above) is disregarded for this purpose (although this limitation does not apply in the circumstances prescribed by regulation by the Board for this purpose, see *SI 1990 No 586; SI 1993 No 3221; SI 1996 No 3113*), and where there is more than one employment, the 15% limit must not be exceeded in respect of any one of them. Where contributions are to a scheme to which the employer does not contribute, regulations provide for them to be made under deduction of basic rate tax. The tax deducted from payments is not clawed back where the individual is liable only at less than the basic rate of income tax or has no income tax liability. [*ICTA 1988, s 592(7)(8), s 593; FA 1989, Sch 6 paras 5, 21; SI 1987 No 1749; SI 1990 No 585*]. See Simon's Direct Tax Service E7.232.

It is proposed to amend the relevant regulations to permit additional voluntary contribution fund benefits to be taken at any time between age 50 and age 75, irrespective of actual retirement. (Treasury Press Release 31 January 1997).

(*b*) The exempt approved fund itself is exempt from income tax on income from investments or deposits held for the purposes of the scheme and from liability under capital gains tax on gains from disposals of investments so held. [*ICTA 1988, s 592(2)(3), s 659; TCGA 1992, s 271(1)(g); FA 1996, s 134, Sch 20 para 63*]. Exemption also applies to certain payments received in replacement of lost dividends or interest under stock lending, etc. arrangements (see 71.82 SCHEDULE D, CASES I AND II). See 71.32 SCHEDULE D, CASES I AND II as regards futures and options contracts, and *Clarke v British Telecom Pension Fund Trustees CA, [2000] STC 222* as regards sub-underwriting commissions. See also 66.13 below.

See 90.2 UNIT TRUSTS as regards certain pooled pension funds.

(*c*) **Repayments to employee.** Where contributions are repaid to an employee during his lifetime from an exempt approved scheme or a relevant statutory scheme, the administrator is chargeable at 20% under Schedule D, Case VI on lump sums and contributions repaid, and has no statutory right to deduct tax, but deduction may be made where the rules of the scheme so authorise. The charge does not apply where the employment was carried on outside the UK (i.e. if the employee worked abroad for at least 75% of the period of scheme membership, see Revenue Inspector's Manual, IM 8133). [*ICTA 1988, s 598; SI 1988 No 504; FA 1989, Sch 6 para 10*].

The rate of 20% will also generally apply to any excess of a lump sum paid, in special circumstances, in commutation of an employee's entire pension over the sums specified in *ICTA 1988, s 599.*

Certain other unauthorised payments to employees may be the subject of charge under *ICTA 1988, s 600.*

As regards repayments from overfunded schemes, see 66.8 below.

(*d*) **Pensions payable** are assessable under Schedule E unless Inland Revenue direct that Schedule D, Case III, shall apply. Similarly where scheme funds are used to acquire an annuity for a member, annuity payments after 3 May 1994 are dealt with under PAYE rather than (as previously) being paid under deduction of tax under Schedule D, Case III (although it is understood that in practice the Revenue were previously prepared to agree to PAYE being applied where appropriate). [*ICTA 1988, s 597; FA 1994, s 110*]. Pensions under the unapproved voluntary pension scheme of a foreign company were held to be assessable under Case V (*Bridges v Watterson Ch D 1952, 34 TC 47*).

66.6 SCHEMES APPROVED BEFORE 27 JULY 1989

Approved schemes: general. *FA 1989, Sch 6 Pt II* came into effect on 14 March 1989, and applies in relation to any retirement benefits scheme approved by the Board before 27 July 1989, notwithstanding anything to the contrary in the scheme rules or (in relation to schemes approved before 23 July 1987, see 66.7 below) in *ICTA 1988, Sch 23.* The Board may, however, make regulations disapplying or modifying any of its provisions where appropriate (and certain such disapplications and modifications are contained in *The Retirement Benefits Schemes (Continuation of Rights of Members of Approved Schemes) Regulations 1990* (*SI 1990 No 2101* and *(Amendment) Regulations 1993* (*SI 1993 No 3220*), *1996* (*SI 1996 Nos 3114, 3233*) and *1999* (*SI 1999 No 1963*), which also give the Board power to disapply any of the provisions by direction in any particular case). Also, the administrator of a scheme may, before the end of 1989, elect for it not to apply and for approval of the scheme to cease from the date of approval or, if the scheme came into existence before 14 March 1989, from 1 June 1989 if earlier. [*FA 1989, Sch 6 para 19*]. The revised rules are applied to all members of schemes which came into existence after 13 March 1989, but only as regards employees who became members after 31 May 1989 of schemes which were in existence on 13 March 1989. An employee who became a member of a scheme after 16 March 1987 and before 1 June 1989 may, for these purposes, elect (by written notice in prescribed form to the scheme administrator) to be treated as having become a member of the scheme on 1 June 1989. [*FA 1989, Sch 6 para 29*].

Remuneration. Any excess of '*relevant annual remuneration*' (i.e. the annual remuneration on which scheme benefits are based) over the 'permitted maximum' (see 66.4 above) is disregarded in calculating benefits and any excess of remuneration over that maximum is disregarded for the purposes of any restriction on the aggregate of employee and employer contributions. The maximum allowable employee contribution is restricted as described in 66.5(*a*) above. [*FA 1989, Sch 6 paras 20, 22, 30*].

Accelerated accrual. If the scheme permits commutation of pension for a lump sum, that lump sum may not exceed the greater of $\frac{3}{80}$ths of relevant annual remuneration for each year of service up to a maximum of 40 and the initial pension payable in the first year (assuming the employee survives the year and ignoring the effects of commutation or allocation to provide benefits for survivors) multiplied by 2.25. Where any lump sum is payable otherwise than by way of commutation, it must not exceed $\frac{3}{80}$ths of relevant annual remuneration for each year of service up to a maximum of 40, or, if greater, the number of eightieths of relevant annual remuneration by reference to which the pension payable under the scheme is calculated (up to a maximum of 120). [*FA 1989, Sch 6 paras 23, 24*].

Associated employments and connected schemes. The provisions described in 66.4 above are applied in relation to pensions payable in respect of service in any of 'relevant associated employments' or in 'connected schemes', except that the permitted rate of accrual is $\frac{1}{30}$th of the permitted maximum for each year of qualifying service, with a maximum of 20 years. [*FA 1989, Sch 6 paras 25, 26*].

Augmentation. Where an employee has contributed to an approved voluntary scheme to which the employer did not contribute, to supplement benefits under the main scheme, then in relation to any augmentation of benefits after the employee has ceased to be a member of the scheme, the limits on benefits under the main scheme rules are reduced by any benefits provided by the voluntary scheme. [*FA 1989, Sch 6 para 27*].

Centralised schemes. In relation to such schemes, the references above to the date the scheme came into existence are replaced by a reference to the date the employee commenced participation in the scheme. A '*centralised scheme*' is a retirement benefits scheme established to enable any employer, other than an employer 'associated' with the person by whom the scheme is established, to participate in it as regards his employees. An employer is '*associated*' with a person if one controls the other or both are under the control of a third person (whether directly or indirectly). [*FA 1989, Sch 6 para 28*].

Additional voluntary contributions. *FA 1989, Sch 6 Pt III* applies to schemes approved before 27 July 1989 which make provision for the payment by employees of voluntary contributions (again subject to variation by regulation by the Board) notwithstanding anything to the contrary in the scheme rules.

(*a*) Where the employer does not contribute to the scheme and the provision for voluntary contributions is freestanding, a limit is imposed on benefits, equal to the main scheme limit on such benefits reduced by benefits under that scheme plus any similar benefits under other schemes providing additional benefits. This applies only to benefits provided after 26 July 1989. [*FA 1989, Sch 6 para 32*].

(*b*) The scheme administrator must repay surplus funds to the employee or his personal representatives (deducting therefrom the amount he is required to account for under *ICTA 1988, s 599A*, see 66.8 below), where total benefits exceed the relevant limits. The method of calculating the surplus is to be prescribed by regulations. [*FA 1989, Sch 6 paras 33, 34*].

Simon's Direct Tax Service. See E7.226.

66.7 SCHEMES APPROVED BEFORE 23 JULY 1987

ICTA 1988, Sch 23 (or its predecessor) came into effect on 17 March 1987, and applies in relation to any retirement benefits scheme approved by the Board before 23 July 1987, notwithstanding anything to the contrary in the scheme rules. The Board may, however, make regulations disapplying or modifying any of its provisions where appropriate (and certain such disapplications and modifications are contained in *The Occupational Pension Schemes (Transitional Provisions) Regulations 1988* (*SI 1988 No 1436*) and *(Amendment) Regulations 1993* (*SI 1993 No 3219*) and *1996* (*SI 1996 Nos 3115, 3234*), which also give the Board power to disapply any of these provisions by direction in any particular case). Also, the administrator of a scheme could, before the end of 1987, elect for it not to apply and for approval of the scheme to cease on and after 17 March 1987 (or the date of approval if later). [*ICTA 1988, Sch 23 para 1; FA 1988, s 56*]. See also 66.6 above for further supplementary rule changes which apply notwithstanding the provisions of *Schedule 23*.

Accelerated accrual. Where an employee joins a scheme after 16 March 1987, the maximum rate of accrual of pension is one-thirtieth of '*relevant annual remuneration*' (i.e. the annual remuneration on which scheme benefits are based) for each year up to a maximum of 20. If commutation for a lump sum is allowed, a formula is laid down for determining the maximum lump sum which may be paid. This is in no case less than three-eightieths of relevant annual remuneration for each year of service up to a maximum of 40 (the '*basic rate lump sum*') and is increased by a percentage of the difference between the basic rate lump sum and a maximum rate lump sum as prescribed by the Board by regulation. That percentage derives from the ratio between the full pension under the scheme and the maximum allowable pension (as above), in both cases after deducting a pension of one-sixtieth of average annual remuneration for each year of service up to a maximum of 40. If the scheme provides for a lump sum other than by commutation of pension, similar limits apply, but with a somewhat faster accrual rate. [*ICTA 1988, Sch 23 paras 2–4, 9; SI 1987 No 1513*].

Final remuneration. Where a scheme member retires after 16 March 1987, his relevant annual remuneration is determined with the meaning of 'remuneration' restricted as in 66.4 above. In the case of an employee who at any time in his last ten years of service has been a 'controlling director' of the employer company (broadly a director controlling 20% of its ordinary share capital), relevant annual remuneration is restricted to his highest average annual remuneration for any period of three or more years ending in his last ten years of service. A similar restriction applies to an employee whose relevant annual remuneration, so far as ascertained by reference to years beginning after 5 April 1987, would otherwise exceed £100,000 (or such other figure as is prescribed by Treasury order), but if he retires before 6 April 1991, a higher limit of his 1986/87 remuneration may apply where appropriate. [*ICTA 1988, Sch 23 para 5*].

Lump sums. Where an employee joins a scheme after 16 March 1987, any lump sum calculated by reference to relevant annual remuneration must disregard any excess of that remuneration over £100,000 (or such other figure as may be prescribed by Treasury order). [*ICTA 1988, Sch 23 para 6*].

Additional voluntary contributions. No commutation of a pension for a lump sum is permitted where an employee enters into arrangements to pay such contributions after 7

April 1987, to the extent that the pension is secured by those contributions. Benefits provided before 27 July 1989 from such voluntary contribution schemes acted to reduce any maxima otherwise applicable to benefits under the employer's scheme (and see now 66.6 above). [*ICTA 1988, Sch 23 paras 7, 8; FA 1989, Sch 6 para 17*].

Simon's Direct Tax Service. See E7.227.

66.8 **PENSION SCHEME SURPLUSES**

Payments to employers. A 40% charge may arise on any payment (or transfer of money's worth) out of a scheme which is or has been an exempt approved scheme (see 66.4 above). No charge arises where:

(*a*) the employer is a charity (see 15 CHARITIES) or would otherwise be entitled to exemption in respect of the payment apart from the current provisions; or

(*b*) the payment was made before the scheme was approved; or

(*c*) the payment was made

  (i) in winding up the scheme, provided the winding-up was commenced before 19 March 1986, or

  (ii) following application to the Board before that date for assurance that the payment would not lead to withdrawal of approval; or

(*d*) the payment was of a description prescribed for this purpose by regulation. Under *The Pension Scheme Surpluses (Administration) Regulations 1987* (*SI 1987 No 352*), this exclusion applies to reimbursement of certain expenditure by the employer on behalf of the scheme; commercial loans to, or repayment of loans or interest to, the employer; certain payments in respect of members' obligations to the employer; and reimbursement of a state scheme premium to which *Social Security Pensions Act 1975, s 42* or *s 45* applies.

Where a charge arises, the payment to which it relates is treated neither as income for tax purposes nor as brought into charge to tax.

The amount charged is recoverable by the Board from the employer, and the Treasury is empowered to make regulations (see below) regarding the assessment and collection of the amount recoverable, which is treated for this purpose as an amount of income tax chargeable under Schedule D, Case VI (or, where the employer is a company, an amount of corporation tax). It is not, however, available for any exemption, relief or set-off. *The Pension Scheme Surpluses (Administration) Regulations 1987* (*SI 1987 No 352*) require the scheme administrator to deduct the amount charged in making the payment to the employer, and, within 14 days of making the payment, to make a return to the Board and account for the amount deducted without the making of any assessment. An assessment may be made on the employer under which the tax due is reduced by any amount deducted and accounted for by the administrator, and if the full amount of tax and interest thereon is not paid within 60 days of the date of the notice of assessment, the tax and interest unpaid may be assessed on the administrator in the name of the employer, becoming due and payable within 14 days of the date of the notice of assessment. The administrator may recover any amount so assessed and paid from the employer.

The *Regulations* referred to above also provide for appeals and postponement applications to be made in the normal way against assessments under these provisions, and for interest on unpaid tax so assessed to run from the 15th day after the date of the payment to the employer. The Board may require information from the administrator or employer where there is reason to believe that a surplus payment has been made in respect of which no return, or an incorrect return, has been made. The penalty provisions of *TMA 1970, s 98* (see 58.4 PENALTIES) apply where information is not provided. [*ICTA 1988, ss 601, 602*].

Where scheme assets transferred to an employer in breach of trust were returned to the trustees, the tax paid under *ICTA 1988, s 601* was recoverable from the Revenue (*Hillsdown Holdings plc v CIR Ch D, [1999] STC 561*).

Certain payments out of an exempt approved scheme, to which the above provisions do not apply, are charged to tax on the employer as a trading receipt or, if the scheme did not relate to a trade, under Schedule D, Case VI. [*ICTA 1988, s 601(5)*].

Insured loanback arrangements. See Pension Schemes Office Update No 43, 22 April 1998 as regards the possibility of a charge under the above provisions in the case of wholly insured schemes where loans by the life office to the employer, which are secured on a policy or polices held by the scheme to provide benefits for a controlling director, are subject to foreclosure.

Payments to employees. Where a payment or transfer of money's worth is made to or for an employee or to his personal representatives in pursuance of a duty to return surplus funds held for an exempt approved or relevant statutory scheme (see 66.6 above), the payment is grossed up at 32% (33% before 6 April 2000, 34% before 6 April 1997, 35% before 6 April 1996, variable by Treasury order) and the scheme administrator is charged to tax under Schedule D, Case VI at that rate on the grossed-up amount. Such a payment, etc. made to or for an employee is treated as income of the employee for the year of payment, etc., chargeable under Schedule D, Case VI, received under deduction of basic rate tax from a corresponding gross amount. No repayment of the tax notionally deducted may be made, and the income is chargeable only at rates other than the basic and lower rates. A payment so chargeable is not chargeable under *ICTA 1988, ss 598, 599, 600* (see 66.5(*c*) above) or under certain regulations relating to old schemes. [*ICTA 1988, s 599A; FA 1989, Sch 6 para 12; F(No 2)A 1992, s 19(2); FA 1996, s 122(7); SI 1996 No 830; SI 1997 No 369; SI 2000 No 600*].

Restriction of surpluses. *The Pension Scheme Surpluses (Valuation) Regulations 1987* (*SI 1987 No 412*) (subsequently amended by *SI 1989 No 2290*) apply to all exempt approved schemes. The administrator of the scheme is required to provide, within three months of its being signed, either a written valuation of the scheme assets and liabilities (on the basis prescribed in those *Regulations*) or a certificate in prescribed form stating that such assets do not exceed such liabilities by more than 5%, with the signatory in either case being an actuary within the regulatory prescription. Such a valuation or certificate is required whenever scheme assets and liabilities are valued, and in any event within three and a half years (five years in certain cases) of the previous valuation (or the establishment of the scheme). Where such assets exceed such liabilities by more than 5%, the administrator must, within six months of the date of signature of the valuation or certificate, submit proposals for reducing or eliminating the surplus by any or all of the following means.

(A) Making payments to the employer.

(B) Suspending or reducing (for five years or less) employer's and/or employees' contributions.

(C) Providing new or improved scheme benefits.

(D) Any other way which may be prescribed by regulation.

The proposals must secure that, within a prescribed time, the excess will be reduced to not more than 5% (and where the proposals include any repayments to the employer, the excess must not be reduced *below* 5%). The prescribed time for this purpose is

(i) where (A) applied, six months,

(ii) where (B) applies, a maximum of five years,

(iii) where (C) applies, six months,

(iv) in any other case, such period as is agreed with the Board,

beginning 30 days after the Board has notified its approval of the proposals (or 30 days after the final determination of an appeal). Under (D), a longer period is allowed in certain cases where a scheme has been in existence less than 15 years, or has ceased to admit new members, or has less than 30 members.

If proposals are not submitted within the prescribed time, or are not agreed, or are not carried out, only a fraction of the scheme income and gains attract exemption from the date of the valuation or certificate referred to above until the Board is satisfied that the excess no longer exceeds 5%. The fraction continuing to attract exemption is that obtained by dividing the Board's estimate of scheme liabilities, increased by 5%, by their estimate of scheme assets, both as at the date of the valuation or certificate.

The above provisions are modified in their application to schemes with twelve members or less and insured schemes (i.e. schemes the contributions to which (other than members' voluntary contributions) are invested wholly by way of insurance premiums) which require that contribution levels take account of surpluses. From 28 December 1989, they are similarly modified in their application to schemes approved by reference to limitations on aggregate contributions and lump sum and death benefits, and to insured schemes providing only lump sum death benefits before retirement age.

There are appeal provisions, and penalties apply under *TMA 1970, s 98* for failure to supply a valuation or certificate, or to furnish the Board with certain additional information. [*ICTA 1988, Sch 22*].

Simon's Direct Tax Service. See **E7.248, E7.249.**

66.9 UNAPPROVED RETIREMENT BENEFIT SCHEMES

A charge applies in respect of any payment or benefit in kind provided pursuant to a funded unapproved retirement benefit scheme ('FURBS'), i.e. a scheme not within 66.1(*a*)–(*c*) above. The charge is under Schedule E or, where the recipient is not an individual, under Schedule D, Case VI (in the latter case being a charge on the administrator of the scheme at a special rate of 40% (variable by Treasury order)). There are various exemptions (see below). The charge is made for the year of assessment in which the payment or benefit is received. Except as mentioned below, the amount of the charge is:

(*a*) in the case of a cash benefit, the amount received; or

(*b*) in the case of a non-cash benefit, the cash equivalent of the benefit or, for 1998/99 and subsequent years and if greater, the amount chargeable under the normal Schedule E, Case I rules if the benefit were taxable as an emolument. The cash equivalent of the benefit is determined under the Schedule E rules, see 75.13–75.21, 75.29 SCHEDULE E, modified as appropriate in the case of living accommodation, and, for 1998/99 and subsequent years, where the benefit is a beneficial loan, with relief being available in respect of the notional interest as under those rules (see 75.17 SCHEDULE E).

Where the scheme is entered into after 30 November 1993, or varied after that day with a view to the provision of the benefit, there is an exemption for any pension or annuity to the extent that it is chargeable under *ICTA 1988, s 19(1)* (see 75.1 SCHEDULE E), and for any pension or other benefit chargeable under *ICTA 1988, s 58* (see 59.2 PENSIONS). There is also an exemption for any lump sum provided under the scheme to the employee or certain other persons (which applies to the charge under *ICTA 1988, s 19(1)* or *s 148* (see 19.5 COMPENSATION FOR LOSS OF EMPLOYMENT (AND DAMAGES)) as well as to that under the current provisions) where the employee has been taxed under *ICTA 1988, s 595(1)* (see 66.1 above) in respect of contributions by the employer, except that if any of the income or gains of the scheme out of which the lump sum is provided is not brought into charge to UK tax (where the income or gains were chargeable to tax in the first place — see ICAEW Technical Release TAX 9/94, 7 June 1994), the exemption does not apply, although certain deductions may be made from the lump sum brought into charge in respect of employee contributions and employer contributions charged on the employee under *section 595(1)*. Income and gains are not for this purpose treated as brought into charge to tax merely because a tax charge arose on cessation of approval of the scheme under *ICTA 1988, s 591C* (see 66.4 above). A proportionate deduction is allowed where the lump sum is provided on the part disposal of an asset, and there is an expectation that a further lump sum will be received.

Where the scheme was entered into on or before 30 November 1993 and has not been varied after that day, there is an exemption to the extent that the payment or benefit is chargeable under Case I, II or III of Schedule E (see 75.1 SCHEDULE E), or can be shown to be attributable to the payment of a sum treated as income and charged to tax under *section 595(1)* (see 66.1 above).

[*ICTA 1988, s 591D(6), ss 596A–596C; FA 1989, Sch 6 para 9; FA 1994, s 108(1)–(6); FA 1995, s 61(1); FA 1998, s 93; FA 1999, Sch 10 para 6*].

For a case in which approval was withdrawn from a scheme on transfer of the scheme assets to an unapproved scheme, see *R v CIR (ex p Roux Waterside Inn Ltd) QB 1997, 70 TC 545*. See also 66.4 above.

See 59.4(vi) PENSIONS as regards lump sum benefits from overseas schemes, and generally Revenue Explanatory Booklet 'The Tax Treatment of Top-Up Pension Schemes'.

See generally Revenue Schedule E Manual, SE 2700 *et seq.*.

Simon's Direct Tax Service. See E7.256.

66.10 DEDUCTIBILITY BY EMPLOYER

See 66.5(*a*) above regarding exempt approved schemes. Expenses incurred in, or with a view to, providing benefits pursuant to a non-approved scheme, i.e. a scheme not within 66.1(*a*)–(*c*) above, are not allowed as a SCHEDULE D, CASES I AND II (71) deduction (nor as a management expense under *ICTA 1988, s 75*) unless the benefits are within the charge to income tax on receipt or payments made are treated as income when paid by virtue of *ICTA 1988, s 595(1)* (see 66.1, 66.2, 66.9 above), and those exceptions do not apply unless the sums concerned have actually been expended. These restrictions do not, however, apply to contributions incurred on or after 29 April 1996 to overseas superannuation funds within *ICTA 1988, s 615(6)* (see 59.6 PENSIONS), or to retirement benefits schemes established outside the UK which correspond to schemes within 66.1(*a*)–(*c*) above and under which payments or provisions are made for the benefit either of employees in receipt of foreign emoluments or of employees not resident in the UK whose duties are performed wholly outside the UK or are incidental to duties so performed. (Similar relief was previously available by extra-statutory concession, see Revenue Pamphlet IR 1, B39.) [*FA 1989, s 76; FA 1996, Sch 39 para 2*].

In cases not involving approved funds, a company's initial lump sum to cover past service on the setting up of a contributory pension scheme was disallowed as capital (*Atherton v British Insulated & Helsby Cables Ltd HL 1925, 10 TC 155*) as was a lump sum contribution to an employees' benevolent fund (*Rowntree & Co Ltd v Curtis CA 1924, 8 TC 678*). However, a series of payments to trustees to build up an indeterminate fund for the benefit of employees for whom pension arrangements might prove inadequate was allowable (*Jeffs v Ringtons Ltd Ch D 1985, 58 TC 680*). The cost of an annuity to replace a pension was allowed (*Hancock v General Reversionary & Investment Co Ltd KB 1918, 7 TC 358*) but not the cost of a policy for payment to a company of annuities equal to (allowable) pensions it paid (*Morgan Crucible Co Ltd v CIR KB 1932, 17 TC 311*). A gratuity on retirement was allowed (*Smith v Incorporated Council of Law Reporting KB 1914, 6 TC 477*) as was a lump sum in commutation of (allowable) premiums under a staff assurance scheme (*Green v Cravens Railway Wagon Co Ch D 1951, 32 TC 359*) but not premiums paid by a 'family company' to secure pensions for its directors (*Samuel Dracup & Sons Ltd v Dakin Ch D 1957, 37 TC 377*) nor payments to commute voluntary pensions on the cessation of trading (*Anglo Brewing Co Ltd KB 1925, 12 TC 803*).

A sum transferred from an unapproved fund on reconstruction as approved was allowed, under facts of that case (*Lowe v Peter Walker & R Cain CA 1935, 20 TC 25*).

66.11 OTHER SCHEMES

Doctors and Dentists. For NHS practitioners assessable under Schedule D who pay both superannuation contributions and retirement annuity premiums, the statutory basis of relief is for full relief to be given for retirement annuity premiums based on net relevant earnings (including NHS earnings) within the normal relief limits, with no relief for the superannuation contributions. By concession, relief may instead be allowed in full for the superannuation contributions, with retirement annuity premiums attracting relief on one of the following bases.

(*a*) In respect of non-NHS earnings only (taken as net relevant earnings less superannuation contributions multiplied by $16\frac{2}{3}$), with unused relief brought forward being calculated using the concessionary basis applied for years in which relief has been given.

(*b*) Up to the amount of the largest premium on which relief was allowed for 1969/70, 1970/71 or 1971/72, restricted, if necessary, to keep the total relief (on NHS contributions and retirement annuity premiums) within the appropriate pre-1971/72 limits (with no carry-forward of surplus premiums).

(Revenue Pamphlet IR 1, A9). It is understood that this concession is treated as applying equally to personal pension scheme contributions. See Simon's Direct Tax Service E7.322A.

Members of Parliaments and Assemblies. For tax purposes, salaries of members of the House of Commons are treated as reduced by contributions to House of Commons Members' Fund. [*ICTA 1988, s 613(1)*]. Periodical payments out of the Fund are assessable under Schedule E. [*ICTA 1988, s 613(3)*]. Trustees of the Fund and of other pension funds maintained for the UK or Scottish Parliaments or the Wales or Northern Ireland Assemblies are exempt from income tax on fund income. [*ICTA 1988, s 613(4); FA 1999, Sch 5 para 4*].

Pilot's benefit fund. The Board may approve a fund established under the *Pilotage Act 1983* as if it were a retirement benefits scheme notwithstanding that some of the usual conditions are not satisfied. Contributions will be allowable as an expense under Schedule D and pensions paid out will be earned income. [*ICTA 1988, s 607*].

Relevant statutory scheme established under a public general Act (but not any national scheme). Employees' contributions are allowable deductions from income for purposes of Schedule E, subject to the same limits as under 66.5(*a*) above. [*ICTA 1988, s 594; FA 1989, Sch 6 para 6*]. For contributions repaid to employees see 66.5(*c*) above.

66.12 LUMP SUM ON RETIREMENT ETC.

A lump sum benefit paid to a person, whether on his retirement or otherwise, will not be chargeable to tax under Schedule E if (*a*) it is from a scheme within *ICTA 1970, s 221(1)(2)* or *ICTA 1988, s 596(1)* and is neither an unauthorised payment under the scheme's rules chargeable to tax under *ICTA 1988, s 600*, nor a payment for premature retirement (other than one which would be covered by the exemption at 19.6(iii) COMPENSATION FOR LOSS OF EMPLOYMENT (AND DAMAGES)), or (*b*) it is a lump sum provided before 1 December 1993 (or on or after that date under a scheme entered into before that date and not varied on or after that date) for the provision of which the holder has been charged under *ICTA 1970, s 220* or *ICTA 1988, s 595* (see 66.1 above), or (*c*) it is paid under approved personal pension arrangements under *ICTA 1988, s 631* (see 60 PERSONAL PENSION SCHEMES). This exemption from tax shall be deemed always to have had effect. [*ICTA 1988, s 189; FA 1988, s 57; FA 1994, s 108(7)(8); FA 1998, s 58, Sch 9 para 1*]. See also 59.4(iv)–(vi) PENSIONS and 19.3 and 19.6 COMPENSATION FOR LOSS OF EMPLOYMENT (AND DAMAGES) and, as regards the successor to (*b*) above, 66.9 above.

Lump sums paid from *ICTA 1970, s 208* schemes which have not sought approval under the new code (see 66.3 and 66.4 above and 66.13 below) will by concession continue to enjoy exemption from tax under Schedule E. (Revenue Pamphlet IR 1, A33).

Ex gratia payments. Where *ex gratia* lump sum payments of 'relevant benefits' (see 66.1 above) are made on retirement or death by virtue of any 'arrangement', the Revenue consider that the arrangement constitutes a retirement benefits scheme, and unless that scheme has obtained Revenue approval, the benefits paid will be taxable under *ICTA 1988, s 596A* (see 66.1 above). Where Revenue approval *has* been obtained, the payments will not be chargeable to tax.

The question of what constitutes 'retirement' for these purposes depends on the facts of each particular case. See ICAEW Technical Release TAX 15/92, 23 October 1992 for the Revenue view of a number of borderline hypothetical cases.

'*Arrangement*' for these purposes includes any system, plan, pattern or policy connected with the payment, and this would include e.g. a decision at a meeting to make a payment on an employee's retirement, a decision to make a payment under a delegated authority, or the existence of a common practice for the making of such payments to a particular class of employee. Revenue approval may be given in relation to such non-contractual arrangements provided that:

(i) the payment is the only lump sum relevant benefit potentially payable in respect of the employment (unless the payment is made on retirement and there is a scheme providing death in service benefits); and

(ii) the normal requirements for approval of contractual retirement benefits schemes (e.g. as regards limits on benefits) are met.

Approval in these circumstances should be sought from the Pension Schemes Office, and PAYE applied to any payments made before such approval is received. Approval need *not* be sought for a single payment to a particular employee, provided that it meets the condition at (i) above and that the total of payments in connection with the retirement, etc. (including any from 'associated employers' (see 66.4 above)) does not exceed one-twelfth of the 'permitted maximum' for the year of payment (see 66.4 above).

(Revenue Pamphlet IR 131, SP 13/91, 31 October 1991).

Payments on redundancy or loss of office, or because of death or disability due to accident, are not covered by the above practice. This applies equally to cases of unfair dismissal (see Law Society Press Release 7 October 1992) and to ill-health early retirement (see Revenue Schedule E Manual, SE 2722).

Where exceptionally an *ex gratia* payment is not covered by the above practice, the payment will, unless taxable under the general rules of Schedule E, be taxable under *ICTA 1988, s 148* (subject to the usual exemptions) (see 19.2 *et seq.* COMPENSATION FOR LOSS OF EMPLOYMENT (AND DAMAGES)).

66.13 SCHEMES CEASING TO BE APPROVED AT APRIL 1980

Where a scheme was an approved superannuation scheme under *ICTA 1970, s 208* immediately before 6 April 1980 and has not been approved under the new rules above and no contributions have been paid to it since 5 April 1980, exemption from income tax may be claimed on income from investments or deposits, underwriting commissions and transactions in certificates of deposit (otherwise taxable under Schedule D, Case VI), and from capital gains tax on gains from investments held for the purposes of the scheme. Any annuity paid out of such a scheme will be charged under Schedule E and PAYE applied. [*ICTA 1988, s 608; TCGA 1992, s 271(2); FA 1996, s 134, Sch 20 para 63*]. By concession, certain minor rule amendments may be made to benefits provided under such schemes without the loss of tax exemptions (see Revenue Pamphlet IR 1, B43).

See 71.32 SCHEDULE D, CASES I AND II as regards futures and options contracts.

66.14 MIS-SOLD FREESTANDING ADDITIONAL VOLUNTARY CONTRIBUTION SCHEMES

See 29.3 EXEMPT INCOME as regards concessionary tax exemption of certain compensation payments (and interest thereon) for mis-sold schemes.

66.15 OVERSEAS PENSIONS AND PENSION FUNDS

See under 59 PENSIONS. See also 90.2 UNIT TRUSTS as regards certain pooled funds in which overseas funds participate.

66.16 SOCIAL SECURITY ACTS

Contributions by business employers in respect of employees are allowable for tax purposes, see 83.2 SOCIAL SECURITY.

67 Returns

Cross-reference. See also 78.5–78.9 SELF-ASSESSMENT.

Simon's Direct Tax Service A3.1.

67.1 The Revenue have considerable powers to obtain information and these are generally exercised initially by the requirement to complete and submit various returns, with PENALTIES (58) for non-compliance, omissions or incorrect statements. Explanatory notes are usually issued with the returns.

Following the changes introduced by *FA 1990* in the requirements in relation to the making of returns (see 53.19 PARTNERSHIPS, 67.2, 67.10 below, and 81.3 SETTLEMENTS), the principles followed by the Revenue in designing return forms and in determining the information required in them are explained in Revenue Pamphlet IR 131, SP 4/91, 1 May 1991.

It is generally provided that a person is deemed not to have failed to do anything required to be done where there was a reasonable excuse for the failure and, if the excuse ceased, provided that the failure was remedied without unreasonable delay after the excuse had ceased. Similarly, a person is deemed not to have failed to do anything required to be done within a limited time if he did it within such further time as the Board, or the Commissioners or officer concerned, may have allowed. [*TMA 1970, s 118(2); F(No 2)A 1987, s 94*]. See, however, 6.6 BACK DUTY. In *Creedplan Ltd v Winter (Sp C 54), [1995] SSCD 352*, the Special Commissioner, in confirming a penalty under *TMA 1970, s 94(1)(a)*, considered that 'there is no reasonable excuse . . . for sending in a return which was less than was required' (but cf. *Akarimsons Ltd v Chapman (Sp C 116), [1997] SSCD 140* in which a penalty under *TMA 1970, s 94(1)(b)* was quashed). Similarly, in relation to an interest charge under *TMA 1970, s 88* (see 6.6 BACK DUTY), it was held that reliance on an accountant was not a reasonable excuse in relation to omission of a dividend from a return (*Nunn v Gray (Sp C 123), [1997] SSCD 175*). See, however, *Steeden v Carver (Sp C 212), [1999] SSCD 283*, in which reliance on the Revenue's advice as to the practical extension of a deadline, unequivocally given, was held to be 'as reasonable an excuse as could be found'.

67.2 ANNUAL RETURNS OF INCOME

1995/96 and earlier years

For 1995/96 and earlier years (see 78.5–78.7 SELF-ASSESSMENT for the position thereafter), for the purposes of assessing a person to income tax, an inspector may by notice require that person to provide a return within a time limit specified in the notice and to supply with the return any information, accounts and statements relating to information contained in the return that may be required. The return must include a declaration that, to the best of the knowledge of the person making it, it is complete and correct. The information, accounts and statements required by the notice may differ in relation to different periods, or different sources of income, or different descriptions of person. [*TMA 1970, s 8; FA 1990, s 90(1)*]. Similar provisions apply in relation to returns by trustees. [*TMA 1970, s 8A; FA 1990, s 90(1)*].

In practice, soon after the commencement of each tax year forms are served on persons considered liable to tax and these must be completed within the time stipulated (30 days) although in practice further time is allowed. However tax returns are now often not issued every year to taxpayers whose only income is from an employment taxed under PAYE and it is accordingly especially important for such taxpayers to claim, by separate notice to their local inspector, any additional allowances to which they may become entitled.

67.2 Returns

All items comprising Total Income (see 1.6 ALLOWANCES AND TAX RATES) for the tax year must be included in the appropriate sections of the form and also computations of any chargeable gains. But where an individual's chargeable gains do not exceed the exempt amount for the year (i.e. £7,200 for 2000/01) on a total amount of related disposals not exceeding twice that exempt amount, a statement to that effect is sufficient entry on a return unless the inspector requires otherwise. [*TMA 1970, ss 12(1), 113(2); FA 1990, s 90(2); TCGA 1992, s 3*].

See 68.6, 68.19 SCHEDULE A, 71.28 SCHEDULE D, CASES I AND II for simplified accounts acceptable for smaller businesses, and the latter for rounding of profit computations.

Income subject to DEDUCTION OF TAX AT SOURCE (23) must be shown at the gross amounts and dividends must be shown with related tax credits. They are income of the tax year by reference to which the rate of tax deducted or of the tax credit is determined, irrespective of the period of accrual. [*ICTA 1988, s 835(6)*]. If shares or securities are sold, subsequent dividends etc. are normally income of the purchaser irrespective of the period of accrual (cf. *Wigmore v Thomas Summerson & Sons Ltd KB 1925, 9 TC 577; Oakley KB 1925, 9 TC 582*), but of the vendor if sold 'ex-dividend' (xd) through the Stock Exchange. See, however, 74.6 *et seq.* SCHEDULE D, CASE VI as regards certain income from securities treated as accruing on a day-to-day basis.

Each dividend received must be shown but only one figure need be shown for tax credit calculated on the total dividends received. Separate totals and credit figures should be given for husband and wife. (CCAB Statement 25 October 1977).

Interest and dividends on shares and deposits in Co-operative Societies must be included but not 'dividends' on purchases (but in *Pope v Beaumont KB 1921, 24 TC 78*, it was held that such a 'dividend' received by a trader on his purchases must be included in his profit computations). Building Society and bank deposit interest received net under the composite rate scheme must be included together with income from property owned and let, income from abroad, from trusts and all income not taxed by deduction.

Particulars must be given (but only where requested) of assets acquired where their disposal may give rise to capital gains tax (but excluding tangible movable property acquired for £6,000 or less). [*TMA 1970, s 12; FA 1989, s 123(1)*].

The return contains sections for claiming personal allowances and reliefs as applicable (see 1.14–1.19 ALLOWANCES AND TAX RATES) and relief for interest paid (see 43 INTEREST PAYABLE).

See 3 ANTI-AVOIDANCE for tax treatment in relation to certain types of transactions in securities etc.

Any person who is chargeable to tax for a tax year must, unless all his income and chargeable capital gains have been declared to the Revenue, in general give notice that he is so chargeable within one year after the end of that tax year, normally to the local inspector. [*TMA 1970, ss 7, 10, 11A; FA 1988, ss 120–122*]. See 58.1 PENALTIES.

Late returns. The Board have emphasised that an interest charge will be considered under *TMA 1970, s 88* (see 42.8 INTEREST AND SURCHARGES ON UNPAID TAX) where a taxpayer delays the rendering of a return (or sends an incomplete return and delays providing any details required to complete it) if, in consequence, an assessment is made after the normal time to make good the tax on income, profits or capital gains reported late. Interest will not generally be charged as above unless the relevant return has not been made by the later of 30 days after the date of issue of the return and 31 October following the end of the tax year in which the income or chargeable gain arose. It will similarly not be charged where it is not possible to lodge the return but, within that time limit, information sufficient for the raising of an adequate estimated assessment is provided. In case of substantial delay, penalties may be considered under *TMA 1970, s 93* (see 58.2 PENALTIES). (Revenue Pamphlet IR 131, SP 6/89, 31 July 1989).

Where a new source of income is assessed on the current year basis, and could not have been assessed in time for tax to become due on the normal due date (e.g. because income first arose after that date), interest under *TMA 1970, s 88* will normally be treated as running from the earliest date tax would have become payable had the return been made within 30 days of the date of issue. Similarly where the information for making a Schedule E assessment would not have been available in time to give rise to a tax liability on 1 January (the normal due date), *TMA 1970, s 88* interest will normally be treated as running from the following 1 July. (Revenue Tax Bulletin August 1992 p 27).

A return is not completed until any relevant computations are also submitted (e.g. an entry in the capital gains section as 'To be advised' does not comply with the requirements even though the return may be accompanied by an investment schedule giving particulars of changes in holdings and proceeds of sale). See *Cox v Poole General Commissioners Ch D 1987, 60 TC 445*. The fact that information is not available to enable a full return to be made is not, however, an excuse for failure to comply with the statutory obligation to make a return (*Alexander v Wallington Commrs and CIR CA 1993, 65 TC 777*). See also 68.19 SCHEDULE A and 71.28 SCHEDULE D, CASES I AND II for simplified accounts acceptable for small businesses. Schedules may be used where appropriate, provided that every relevant section of the official return form is marked 'see schedule attached' or words to that effect. Alternatively, a return will be accepted if the official return form bears the taxpayer's declaration that it is correct and complete, and that

(i) schedules are attached to the official return form,

(ii) each schedule is numbered (or lettered) consecutively,

(iii) each page of the official return form is crossed through with a diagonal line and marked 'See schedules X–Y' (X and Y being the first and last schedules),

(iv) the headings to schedules indicate the number of sheets comprised in each schedule if more than one.

Claims for personal allowances and reliefs may be dealt with in the same way. (Revenue Pamphlet IR 131, SP 5/83, 28 April 1983).

1996/97 and later years

See generally 78.4–78.7 SELF-ASSESSMENT. The following matters continue, however, to be relevant for 1996/97 and later years.

Signature of returns etc.. The Revenue will accept returns signed by an attorney acting under a general or enduring power where the taxpayer is physically unable to sign (and not merely unavailable to do so). The attorney must have full knowledge of the taxpayer's affairs, and provide the original power or a certified copy when such a return is first made. In cases of mental incapacity, the signature of an attorney appointed under an enduring power registered with the Court of Protection (or of a receiver or committee appointed by that Court) will be accepted. Similar requirements apply to the signature of claims on behalf of physically or mentally incapacitated taxpayers, and to other documents such as applications for TESSAs or PEPs (see 29.13(iii), 29.21 EXEMPT INCOME) and certificates of eligibility under the MIRAS scheme (see 23.13 DEDUCTION OF TAX AT SOURCE). (Revenue Pamphlet IR 131, A13 and Revenue Tax Bulletin February 1993 p 51).

Substitute return forms. The Revenue have issued a Statement of Practice (Revenue Pamphlet IR 131, SP 5/87, 15 June 1987) concerning the acceptability of facsimile and photocopied tax returns. Whenever such a substitute form is used, it is important to ensure that it bears the correct taxpayer's reference.

Facsimiles must satisfactorily present to the taxpayer the information which the Board have determined shall be before him when he signs the declaration that the return is correct and complete to the best of his knowledge. They should be readily recognisable as a return when received in the Revenue office, and the entries of taxpayers' details should be distinguishable from the background text. Approval must be obtained from Inland Revenue, Corporate Communications Office, Room 9/3A, 9th Floor, NW Wing, Bush House, London WC2B 4PP before a facsimile return is used, and the facsimile must bear an agreed unique imprint for identification purposes. Copies of the major 1996 income tax return forms and an information sheet on the guidelines for production of substitute forms were made available in January 1996, so that modifications could be incorporated in computer produced facsimiles in time for their submission.

Photocopies must bear the actual, not photocopied, signature of the relevant person. They are acceptable provided that they are identical (except as regards use of colour) to the official form. Where double-sided copies are not available, it is sufficient that all pages are present and attached in the correct order. Although the copying of official forms is in strictness a breach of HMSO copyright, action will be taken only where forms are copied on a large scale for commercial gain.

Persons in receipt of taxable income belonging to others. Returns may also be required from any person who, in whatever capacity, receives money or value etc. belonging to another person who is chargeable to income tax in respect thereof, or could be so chargeable if resident in UK and not an incapacitated person (although information may not be sought in relation to years of assessment ending more than three years before the date of the notice). [*TMA 1970, s 13; FA 1988, s 123(1)*]. This applies whether a person is in receipt of chargeable profits or gains of another or of gross receipts representing an element in the determination of such profits or gains (*Fawcett v Special Commrs and Lancaster Farmers' Auction Mart Co Ltd CA 1997, 69 TC 279*). In practice, returns may be restricted to receipts of the following nature:

(*a*) those from Schedule A or D sources which have not suffered deduction of tax;

(*b*) those exceeding £250 in aggregate in respect of any one person or estate;

(*c*) those which have not been included on any other return or repayment claim;

(*d*) those received by an agent acting on behalf of an individual not domiciled in, or (being a British subject) not ordinarily resident in, the UK.

(Law Society Press Release 29 May 1991).

Simon's Direct Tax Service. See **A3.105** *et seq.*.

67.3 **ELECTRONIC LODGEMENT OF TAX RETURNS, ETC.**

Certain returns required to be made to the Board or to an officer of the Board may, subject to the conditions detailed below, be lodged electronically. The provision under which the return is required must be specified for this purpose by Treasury order, which will also appoint a commencement day. For returns under *TMA 1970, ss 8, 8A* and *12AA* (see 78.5, 78.8 SELF-ASSESSMENT), the appointed day is 1 March 1997, so that returns due from 6 April 1997 under self-assessment are eligible. Any supporting documentation (including accounts, statements or reports) required to be delivered with a return may similarly be lodged electronically if the return is so lodged (or may instead be delivered by the last day for submission of the return).

The normal powers and rights applicable in relation to returns, etc. delivered by post are applied to information transmitted electronically. A properly made and authenticated hard copy (see (*c*) below) is treated in any proceedings as if it were the return or other document in question, but if no such copy is shown to have been made, a hard copy certified by an officer of the Board to be a true copy of the information transmitted is so treated instead.

There are four conditions for electronic lodgement.

(*a*) A person seeking approval must be given notice of the grant or refusal of approval, which may be granted for the transmission of information on the person's own behalf or on behalf of another person or persons. Approval may be withdrawn by notice from a given date, and any notice refusing or withdrawing approval must state the grounds. An appeal against refusal or withdrawal must be made within 30 days of such notice having been given, and lies to the Special Commissioners, who may grant approval from a specified date if they consider the refusal or withdrawal to have been unreasonable in all the circumstances.

(*b*) The transmission must comply with any requirements notified by the Board to the person making it, including in particular any relating to the hardware or software to be used.

(*c*) The transmission must signify, in an approved manner, that a hard copy was made under arrangements designed to ensure that the information contained in it is the information in fact transmitted.

(*d*) The information transmitted must be accepted under a procedure selected by the Board for this purpose, which may in particular consist of or include the use of specifically designed software.

As regards (*c*) above, the hard copy must have been authenticated by the person required to make the return:

(i) in the case of a return required by notice, by endorsement with a declaration that it is to the best of his knowledge correct and complete; or

(ii) otherwise by signature.

[*TMA 1970, s 115A, Sch 3A; FA 1995, s 153, Sch 28; SI 1997 No 57*].

Agents may pre-register for the electronic lodgement service. Copies of an information pack and registration form are available from the Agent Educator in all local tax offices. Revenue Statement of Practice SP 1/97, 16 January 1997, describes how the Revenue will operate electronic lodgement and the detailed requirements.

The above provisions are to be repealed from a date (or dates) to be appointed, but only to be replaced by similar rules, with appropriate modifications, under the provisions at 35.12 INLAND REVENUE: ADMINISTRATION. [*FA 1999, s 133(3)(4)*].

See Simon's Direct Tax Service A3.111A.

Incentives for electronic communications. Regulations may be made by statutory instrument by the Commissioners of Inland Revenue in relation to matters under their care and management (and by the Commissioners of Customs and Excise in relation to theirs) for the provision of incentives to use electronic communications. These may include discounts (or payments or repayments), or additional time for compliance or payment, or more convenient intervals for the delivery of information or the making of payments. Anything received by way of incentive is not regarded as income for tax purposes. The regulations may make provision as to the conditions of entitlement to incentives and for their withdrawal (which may be authorised to be made by direction), and may provide for penalties up to £1,000 for failure to comply with any specified provision. They may make different provision for different cases, and may make such incidental, supplemental, consequential or transitional provision as the Commissioners think fit. [*FA 2000, s 143, Sch 38*].

Internet filing discount. The Revenue has announced a number of incentives for which regulations as above will make provision. From April 2000 small businesses and individual taxpayers filing their self-assessment returns over the internet and paying any tax due electronically will receive a tax discount of £10. From April 2001 small businesses filing their VAT returns and/or their PAYE end-of-year returns via the internet and paying any tax due electronically will receive a discount of £50, or £100 for both VAT and PAYE filing, and a further £50 will be available where there are one or more working families' or disabled person's tax credit cases. The discounts will be available for one year for each service. (Revenue Press Releases 16 February 2000, 21 March 2000 (BN1D)).

67.4 BANKERS ETC. RETURNS OF INTEREST

On receipt of notice, any person (including the National Savings Bank and a building society) paying or crediting interest on money received or retained, in the UK, in the ordinary course of his business, and any bank (within *ICTA 1988, s 840A*, see 8.1 BANKS), must make a return, for any specified year of assessment (ending not more than three years previously), showing the names and addresses of the recipients and the gross amount of interest paid or credited to each and the amount (if any) of tax deducted therefrom. The payer may exclude from that return interest paid to a person who has so requested and has given written notice that the person beneficially entitled to the interest is a non-UK resident company. Similarly, where a declaration of non-ordinary residence has been given to the payer to enable interest to be paid gross (see 8.2 BANKS, 9.3 BUILDING SOCIETIES), and the person who made that declaration has so requested, the payer is not required to include interest paid, credited or received before 6 April 2001 in the return under this provision. Notices may be issued re parts or branches of a business. The Board have powers by statutory instrument to make regulations requiring further prescribed information with the return, or providing that prescribed information is *not* required, or requiring information or returns to be in prescribed form, or providing for inspection of books, documents, records, etc.. [*TMA 1970, s 17; FA 1988, s 123(2); FA 1990, s 92; F(No 2)A 1992, s 29; FA 1996, Sch 37 para 11; FA 2000, s 145; SI 1990 No 2231; SI 1992 No 2915*]. The Inland Revenue Financial Intermediaries and Claims Office may be contacted in relation to *section 17* returns on 0151–472 6123 as regards submission arrangements or 0151–472 6156 for technical advice.

Returns may similarly be required from any other person paying interest (including building society dividends) or receiving it on behalf of others [*TMA 1970, s 18; FA 1988, s 123(3); FA 1990, s 92; FA 1991, Sch 11 para 5; FA 1996, Sch 37 para 11; FA 2000, s 145*] and from persons collecting interest on securities on behalf of others who are resident in UK. [*TMA 1970, s 24; FA 1996, Sch 37 para 11*].

Simon's Direct Tax Service. See **A3.120**.

67.5 EMPLOYERS

Employers (including deemed employers of agency workers) must on application furnish particulars, for employees (i.e. any person whose emoluments are assessable under Schedule E) and periods specified (but not earlier than six years before year of assessment in which application made), of remuneration including payments (*a*) for 'expenses', (*b*) on employees' behalf, (*c*) for services whether rendered in course of employment or not, and stating details of any apportionments made. Also, particulars of any assessable benefits provided to an employee, whether by the employer or another person (who must furnish information on application). [*TMA 1970, ss 15, 16A*]. See also 55 PAY AS YOU EARN and, for directors and employees with emoluments at the rate of £8,500 per annum or more, 75.11 *et seq.* SCHEDULE E. See 78.37 SELF-ASSESSMENT for the position for 1996/97 and later years.

Person in UK treated as employer. Where a person performs duties for a continuous period of not less than 30 days in the UK for a non-resident employer but for the benefit of a person resident or carrying on a trade etc. in the UK, then the latter person must include him in any returns of employees and the employee may be required to include any such emoluments in his tax return. [*FA 1974, s 24*].

Simon's Direct Tax Service. See **A3.117**.

67.6 FEES, COMMISSIONS, COPYRIGHTS, ETC.

Any person carrying on any trade, etc., and any body of persons carrying on any non-trading activity (including Crown departments, public or local authorities and any other public bodies), may, by notice, be required to give particulars of all payments made (including commissions or expenses), or valuable consideration given, for services rendered by persons not employed by him, including, in the case of a trade, etc., services in connection with the formation, acquisition, development or disposal thereof. Applies also to periodical or lump-sum payments in respect of any copyright or public lending right or design right. But returns are limited to payments from which tax is not deductible, and those (*a*) exceeding £15 in total to any one person, or (*b*) made during the three tax years ending prior to the notice. [*TMA 1970, s 16; FA 1983, s 27; FA 1988, s 124*]. See Revenue Pamphlet 46Q re payments to entertainers etc. for total payments exceeding £250 in a year.

67.7 GRANTS, SUBSIDIES, LICENCES ETC.

Any person paying grants or subsidies directly or indirectly out of public funds (whether UK or European Union), or issuing licences or approvals or maintaining entries in a register which subsist after that date, may be required to furnish particulars to the inspector where they may be relevant to the determination of any tax liability. [*TMA 1970, s 18A; FA 1988, s 125*].

67.8 HOTELS AND BOARDING HOUSES

Returns of all lodgers and inmates resident in any dwelling house must be made by the proprietor, if required by notice from the inspector. [*TMA 1970, s 14*].

67.9 ISSUING HOUSES, STOCKBROKERS, AUCTIONEERS, ETC.

For the purposes of obtaining particulars of chargeable gains, an inspector may require a return of parties to transactions and description and consideration of assets dealt with from (i) an issuing house or any other person concerned in effecting public issues or placing of shares etc. or (ii) a member of a stock exchange (other than a market maker) or any other person acting as an agent or broker in share transactions or (iii) any person or body managing a clearing house for any terminal market in commodities or (iv) an auctioneer and any person carrying on a trade of dealing in any description of tangible movable property or acting as agent in such where the value in the hands of the recipient exceeds £6,000. Returns are limited to transactions effected within three years prior to the issue of the notice requiring the return. [*TMA 1970, s 25; FA 1978, s 45(5); FA 1982, s 81*].

The Board may make regulations by statutory instrument, effective from a day to be appointed therein, making appropriate provision in regard to recognised investment exchanges other than the Stock Exchange. [*FA 1986, s 63, Sch 18 para 8*].

See also *TMA 1970, s 21* as amended by *FA 1997, Sch 10 para 14* as regards other transactions by market makers.

Simon's Direct Tax Service. See **A3.126**.

67.10 **PARTNERSHIPS**

For 1995/96 and earlier years, any partner may be required to complete and deliver a return of the profits or gains of the partnership and the names and residences of all partners, and of such other information etc. as the inspector may require (the requirements being similar to those under *TMA 1970, s 8*, see 67.2 above). [*TMA 1970, s 9; FA 1990, s 90*].

67.11 **PAY AS YOU EARN**

See 55.9 PAY AS YOU EARN.

67.12 **TRUSTEES**

A return may be required from a trustee under *TMA 1970, ss 8A, 13*, see 67.2 above.

67.13 For forms of returns, see *TMA 1970, s 113* and 67.1, 67.2 above. For delivery and service of documents, see *TMA 1970, s 115*.

68 Schedule A—Property Income

[*ICTA 1988, s 15, ss 21–43; FA 1995, s 39, Sch 6*]

Simon's Direct Tax Service A4.

Other sources. See Tolley's Property Taxes and Revenue Pamphlet IR 150.

68.1 Schedule A applies to **property income.** Tax is charged on rents etc. (see 68.4, 68.14 below) after deducting allowable expenses (see 68.5, 68.7, 68.15, 68.16 below). Certain lease premiums etc. are also taxable (see 68.27 below). 'Chargeable period' in the context of this coverage means a year of assessment. [*ICTA 1988, s 832(1)*]. See 10.10 *et seq.* CAPITAL ALLOWANCES as regards relief available in respect of leased industrial buildings.

Headings in this chapter are as follows.

68.2 History
68.3 — commencement of Finance Act 1995 regime
68.4 Amounts chargeable
68.5 Computation of amounts chargeable
68.6 Simplified returns
68.7 Deductions — miscellaneous
68.8 Furnished lettings
68.9 — furnished holiday lettings
68.10 — example
68.11 'Rent a room' relief for lettings of rooms in private residences
68.12 — example
68.13 Losses
68.14 The Pre-Finance Act 1995 regime
68.15 — expenses deductible — specific items
68.16 — expenses and deficiencies deductible — general provisions
68.17 — example
68.18 — lost rents etc.
68.19 — accounts basis and returns
68.20 — assessments and payments of tax
68.21 — collection from lessee or agent
68.22 Transition to Finance Act 1995 regime
68.23 — example
68.24 Non-resident landlords — collection from agents or tenants
68.25 Apportionment of receipts and outgoings on sale of land
68.26 Information re leases
68.27 Premiums etc. on leases of up to 50 years — assessability on recipient
68.28 Premiums etc. on leases of up to 50 years — allowance to payer
68.29 Reverse premiums
68.30 Schedule A allowance on sale of trading premises

68.2 **HISTORY**

The legislation was introduced in *FA 1963* and assessments up to 1969/70 were made under Schedule D, Case VIII. From 1970/71 onwards, assessments have been made under Schedule A. A new regime, incorporating the concept of a 'Schedule A business' and *including furnished lettings* (previously chargeable under Schedule D, Case VI), was introduced by *FA 1995* for income tax purposes only. This regime was extended to corporation tax with effect from 1 April 1998 with the necessary amendments and modifications (see Tolley's Corporation Tax under Profit Computations). The new provisions for income tax are covered at 68.3 to 68.13 below and the old provisions at 68.14 to 68.21 below. See 68.22 below for Revenue guidelines on the transition from the old provisions to the new. The treatment of premiums and other matters common to both regimes are dealt with at 68.24 *et seq.* below.

68.3 **Commencement of Finance Act 1995 regime.** The provisions of *FA 1995* mentioned at 68.2 above have effect for income tax purposes for 1995/96 and subsequent years of assessment, subject to the transitional provisions for 1995/96 described below.

Transitional provisions. The old provisions continue to apply for 1995/96 in relation to a source which is chargeable under Schedule A or Schedule D, Case VI (furnished lettings) for 1994/95 and which ceases to be such a source (assuming the continuation of the old regime) in 1995/96, *provided that* the person to whom the income arose does not commence a Schedule A business, i.e. he neither acquires a new source nor recommences the old, in 1995/96. See also 68.22 below.

[*FA 1995, s 39(4)(5)*].

68.4 **AMOUNTS CHARGEABLE**

With effect as in 68.3 above, Schedule A applies to the annual profits arising from a business carried on for the exploitation, as a source of rents or other 'receipts', of any estate, interest or rights in or over land in the UK. To the extent that any transaction is entered into for such exploitation, it is taken to have been entered into in the course of such a business; this brings into charge, for example, one-off or casual lettings. Income tax under Schedule A is charged on the persons receiving or entitled to the chargeable income. See below for exclusions from Schedule A and 68.5 below for computation of amounts chargeable.

'*Receipts*', in relation to any land, includes

(*a*) any payment in respect of any licence to occupy or otherwise to use any land or in respect of the exercise of any other right over land; and

(*b*) rentcharges, ground annuals and feu duties and any other annual payments reserved in respect of, or charged on or issuing out of, that land.

See also the case law mentioned in 68.14 below in relation to the old regime. Income from the letting of immobile caravans or permanently moored houseboats is specifically brought within the charge to Schedule A. Income from letting caravan pitches, i.e. site rents, is assessable under Schedule A to the extent that it arises from exploitation of land, but, by concession, where the site proprietor carries on associated activities (e.g. shops) which constitute trading and account for a substantial part of the income, the letting income may be included as receipts of the trade under Schedule D, Case I. (Revenue Press Release 17 May 1984 and see Revenue Pamphlet IR 1, B29).

A '*Schedule A business*' means any business the profits or gains of which are chargeable to income tax under Schedule A, including the business in the course of which any such transaction as is mentioned above is treated as entered into. All such businesses and transactions entered into by a particular person or partnership are treated as, or as transactions entered into in the course of carrying on, *a single business.* (This is subject to a special rule for non-UK resident companies partly within the charge to income tax.)

In the case of a **furnished letting** (including that of a caravan or houseboat), any consideration receivable for the use of furniture is chargeable under Schedule A in the same way as rent (and expenditure incurred in providing furniture is treated accordingly). This does not apply to any amount taken into account in computing profits of a trade involving the making available of furniture for use in premises.

Schedule A does not include the following.

(i) Profits arising from the *occupation of land* (including, for example, commercial WOODLANDS (93)).

(ii) *Farming and market gardening.* Profits or gains charged under *ICTA 1988, s 53(1)* (Schedule D, Case I).

(iii) *Mineral rents, royalties etc.* charged to tax under Schedule D by virtue of *ICTA 1988, s 55, s 119* or *s 120(1)*, see under 23.2 and 23.14 DEDUCTION OF TAX AT SOURCE. However, from 6 April 1997, wayleave payments within *ICTA 1988, s 120* are charged under Schedule A (instead of Schedule D) where for the same period some or all of the land to which the easement relates is included in land by reference to which a Schedule A charge arises on the same person.

(iv) Receipts/expenses taken into account as trading receipts/expenses under *ICTA 1988, s 98* (tied premises — see 71.45 SCHEDULE D, CASES I AND II).

(Before 1998/99, yearly interest was also *specifically* excluded from Schedule A.)

[*ICTA 1988, s 15, s 21(1), s 120(1A), s 832(1); FA 1995, s 39(1)(2), Sch 6 paras 1, 28; FA 1997, s 60; FA 1998, s 38, Sch 5 paras 1, 2*].

68.5 COMPUTATION OF AMOUNTS CHARGEABLE

With effect as in 68.3 above, tax under Schedule A is to be computed on the full amount of profits arising in the year of assessment. The Revenue will no longer allow any deviation from a strict fiscal year basis (except as regards trading partnerships with ancillary Schedule A income, see below). The profit (or loss) should be arrived at by use of ordinary accounting principles and by applying the computational provisions of SCHEDULE D, CASE I (71) contained in *ICTA 1988, Pt IV, Chapter V* (*ICTA 1988, s 74 et seq.* but see also below), and the further provisions listed below, as if the Schedule A business were a trade (although Schedule A income continues to be investment income rather than trading income), i.e. on an earnings basis. By concession, a cash basis may be used where gross annual receipts do not exceed £15,000, provided that it is used consistently and gives a reasonable overall result not substantially different from that produced on the earnings basis (see Revenue Pamphlet IR 150, paras 90–92). Loan interest, to the extent that it is incurred wholly and exclusively for the purposes of the letting business, is deductible under general principles, replacing the previous special rules at 43.15 INTEREST PAYABLE. See 43.6 INTEREST PAYABLE as regards alternative concessionary relief for interest in certain cases of temporary absence from owner-occupied property, and see also below.

The following provisions relating to the computation of profits of trades and professions also apply for Schedule A purposes.

(*a*) *ICTA 1988, s 72* (method of apportioning profits) (applicable to Schedule A for 1998/99 and subsequent years) — see 71.3 SCHEDULE D, CASES I AND II.

(*b*) *ICTA 1988, s 577* (entertainment expenses) — see 71.55 SCHEDULE D, CASES I AND II.

(*c*) *ICTA 1988, s 577A* (illegal payments etc.) — see 71.63 SCHEDULE D, CASES I AND II.

(*d*) *ICTA 1988, ss 579, 580* (redundancy payments), *ICTA 1988, ss 588, 589* (training courses for employees), and *ICTA 1988, ss 589A, 589B* (counselling services for employees) — see 71.54 SCHEDULE D, CASES I AND II.

(*e*) *FA 1988, s 73(2)* (deductibility of sums paid as consideration for restrictive undertakings) (applicable to Schedule A for 1998/99 and subsequent years) — see 75.34 SCHEDULE E.

(*f*) *FA 1989, s 43* (timing of deduction for emoluments) (applicable to Schedule A for 1998/99 and subsequent years) — see 71.54 SCHEDULE D, CASES I AND II.

(*g*) *FA 1989, s 76* (expenses in connection with non-approved retirement benefits schemes) (applicable to Schedule A for 1998/99 and subsequent years) — see 66.10 RETIREMENT SCHEMES FOR EMPLOYEES.

(*h*) *FA 1989, ss 112, 113* (expenditure on security) (applicable to Schedule A for 1998/99 and subsequent years) — see 71.81 SCHEDULE D, CASES I AND II.

(*j*) *FA 1998, ss 42, 46(1)(2)* (requirement that accounts give a true and fair view etc.) — see 12.2 CASH BASIS, 46.2 LOSSES, 71.40 SCHEDULE D, CASES I AND II.

The following further provisions apply for Schedule A purposes.

(i) *ICTA 1988, ss 103–106, s 108, s 109A, s 110* — see 62 POST-CESSATION ETC. RECEIPTS AND EXPENDITURE.

(ii) *ICTA 1988, s 113* (change in the members of a partnership) — see 53.6 PARTNERSHIPS.

(iii) *ICTA 1988, s 401(1)* (relief for pre-trading expenditure) — see 71.76 SCHEDULE D, CASES I AND II.

(iv) *FA 1998, s 44, Sch 6* (change of accounting basis) — see 12.2 CASH BASIS.

The following provisions of *ICTA 1988, Pt IV, Chapter V* are excluded from applying for Schedule A purposes.

(1) *ICTA 1988, s 82* (restriction on deductibility of interest paid to non-UK residents) — see 43.2(i) INTEREST PAYABLE.

(2) *ICTA 1988, s 87* (deductibility of premiums paid) — see 71.78 SCHEDULE D, CASES I AND II.

(3) *ICTA 1988, s 96* (averaging of farming profits) — see 71.57(*a*) SCHEDULE D, CASES I AND II.

(4) *ICTA 1988, s 98* (tied premises) — see 71.45 SCHEDULE D, CASES I AND II.

ICTA 1988, s 74(1)(d) (deductibility of expenditure on repairs and renewals) applies for Schedule A purposes in a suitably modified form.

[*ICTA 1988, ss 21, 21A, 21B; FA 1995, s 39(2), Sch 6 paras 13–16, para 20, paras 22–25; FA 1998, s 38, Sch 5 para 4, Sch 27 Pt III(4)*].

Profits or losses on contracts taken out to hedge interest payments deductible in computing profits or losses of the Schedule A business (as above) will normally be taxed or relieved as receipts or deductions of that business. Such profits or losses would generally be computed on an accruals basis in accordance with normal accountancy practice. Similarly deposits paid to landlords by tenants or licensees will ordinarily be receipts of the business, to be recognised in accordance with generally accepted accountancy practice, normally by being deferred and matched with the related costs. Excess deposits which are refunded should be excluded from the business receipts. (Revenue Tax Bulletin October 1996 p 349). As regards allowable legal and professional costs, see paras 213–218 of Revenue Pamphlet IR 150 and Revenue Tax Bulletin December 1996 p 375.

A borrower who is eligible for mortgage interest relief in respect of a let property may choose each year whether to claim such relief (restricted to 15% on a maximum of £30,000) or to deduct the interest in computing the Schedule A business profits. As regards inclusion of the loan within MIRAS (mortgage interest relief by deduction at source), see 23.13 DEDUCTION OF TAX AT SOURCE. See also 43.2 INTEREST PAYABLE for concession available where part of a borrower's main residence is used for business (including a Schedule A business) purposes.

Partnerships. Ancillary Schedule A income of a trading or professional partnership is taxable on an accounts year basis (see 53.3 PARTNERSHIPS which also covers extra-statutory transitional rules for 1995/96 and 1996/97 applicable to a pre-6 April 1994 partnership). Joint ownership of property does not, of itself, create a partnership. Where the letting is not ancillary to a trade or profession, there will only be a partnership if, exceptionally, the exploitation of property constitutes the carrying on of a business (using that term without regard to the concept of a Schedule A business) jointly with a view to profit. See Revenue Tax Bulletin December 1995 pp 271, 272.

Mutual businesses. For 1998/99 and subsequent years, the normal exemption for MUTUAL TRADING (50) does not extend to Schedule A activities, the transactions and relationships involved in mutual business being instead treated as if they were between persons between whom no relationship of mutuality existed. The taxable person is the person who would be taxable if the business were not mutual business. (This does not affect the treatment of Co-operative Housing Associations — see Tolley's Corporation Tax). [*ICTA 1988, s 21C; FA 1998, s 38, Sch 5 para 5*].

68.6 SIMPLIFIED RETURNS

Landlords with a total annual gross income from property under £15,000 are required to state on their income tax returns only the gross property income, the total amount of allowable expenses and the net income or profit. There is, of course, still a need to keep accurate records to ensure the correctness of the three-line accounts. (Revenue Press Releases 7 November 1989, 1 November 1991). See generally 78.5, 78.10 SELF-ASSESSMENT.

68.7 DEDUCTIONS — MISCELLANEOUS

See also 68.5 above. The following apply with effect as in 68.3 above.

(*a*) *Capital allowances* are available under *CAA 1990, Pt II* on *machinery or plant* as if the Schedule A business were a separate trade for which the machinery or plant was provided (subject to further separation where there are furnished holiday lettings, see 68.9 below). Before 1997/98, this applied separately to each item of machinery or plant, but for 1997/98 onwards expenditure is pooled in the normal way (see 10.28 CAPITAL ALLOWANCES). Allowances are thus given as expenses, and charges treated as receipts, of the business. Machinery or plant provided for use in a dwelling-house is excluded (with a just and reasonable apportionment of expenditure where such use is partial). [*ICTA 1988, s 32; CAA 1990, s 28A; FA 1995, Sch 6 para 8; FA 1997, Sch 15 paras 1, 3, 9; FA 1998, Sch 27 Pt III(4)*].

Before 1997/98, see 10.25 CAPITAL ALLOWANCES as regards certain expenditure on industrial buildings treated as being on machinery or plant and 10.34 CAPITAL ALLOWANCES as regards entitlement to allowances for fixtures.

(*b*) *Land managed as one estate.* Where, at 5 April 1963, land was in one ownership and managed as one estate, the owner may, for years of assessment before 2001/02, elect to be treated as receiving, for any part of the estate not let (other than premises he occupies for estate management or trade) and for any part let at less than its annual value, rent at a rate equal to its annual value. The estate is thus split into two parts, the part for which rent is determined as above (Part A) and the remainder (Part B). Expenditure relating to Part A must first be set against the rents as so determined (the deemed receipts); any balance is set against Part B receipts, with any excess treated as Part A expenditure for the following chargeable period. The excess cannot be set against income from outside the estate or form part of a Schedule A loss (see 68.13 below). Expenditure relating to Part B is deductible against any balance of Part A deemed receipts (after deducting Part A expenditure, including any excess brought forward as above). Any excess Part B expenditure is treated as a Schedule A loss.

Election, applying to all subsequent years in which the estate is in the same ownership, must be made within one year after the first tax year for which the owner could have made it, and then (except in the case of the first possible election) is valid only if the previous owner had made a similar election. Except in the case of certain trusts [*ICTA 1988, s 26(5)*] property acquired after 5 April 1963 does not form part of the estate. [*ICTA 1988, s 26(4)*]. The election will not generally cease to be effective because part of the estate becomes comprised in a maintenance fund (see 81.30 SETTLEMENTS), but also see *ICTA 1988, s 27; FA 1995, Sch 6 para 6; FA 1998, s 38, Sch 5 para 8*. [*ICTA 1988, s 26; FA 1995, Sch 6 para 5; FA 1998, s 38, Sch 5 para 7, Sch 27 Pt III(4)*].

These provisions are **repealed** for 2001/02 and subsequent years of assessment. [*FA 1998, s 39*].

Annual value, see *ICTA 1988, s 837*, is the rent reasonably to be expected from a letting on terms of the tenant paying tenant's rates etc. and the landlord bearing repairs, insurance and expenses necessary to maintain the property so as to command that rent. In practice, a property's gross rateable value is taken as its annual value. (Revenue Press Release 23 July 1985). In the case of Scottish estates, 1978 gross rateable values will continue to be used for this purpose, despite the 1985 rating revaluation, 'for the time being'. (Revenue Pamphlet IR 1, B30).

(*c*) *Sea walls.* For allowances for expenditure on making sea walls, see *ICTA 1988, s 30; FA 1995, Sch 6 para 7; FA 1998, s 38, Sch 5 para 11* and *Hesketh v Bray CA 1888, 2 TC 380.*

Simon's Direct Tax Service. See **A4.330** *et seq.*.

68.8 **FURNISHED LETTINGS**

With effect as in 68.3 above, furnished lettings are taxable as, or as part of, a Schedule A business (and the computational rules at 68.5 above thus apply), having previously been within Schedule D, Case VI (subject to the right of election referred to at 68.14(i) below). See 74.4 SCHEDULE D, CASE VI for coverage of the Case VI charge on furnished lettings (including the circumstances in which such letting may amount to a trade within Case I), and 68.9, 68.11 below for furnished holiday lettings and 'rent a room' relief respectively, both of which continue to be relevant under Schedule A.

CAPITAL ALLOWANCES (10) are not due on plant let for use in a dwelling house [*CAA 1990, ss 28A(3), 61(2)*] (but see 68.9 below as regards furnished holiday lettings). Furniture and furnishing may be dealt with on the renewals basis but an alternative Revenue concession is to allow as depreciation 10% of the rents received as reduced by any council tax and water rates or material payments for services borne by landlord but normally a tenant's burden. Where the 10% deduction is allowed, no further deduction is given for the cost of renewing furniture or furnishings, nor for fixtures such as cookers, dishwashers or washing machines which, in unfurnished accommodation, the tenant would normally provide for himself. However, the cost of renewing fixtures which are an integral part of the building (e.g. baths, toilets, washbasins) may be claimed in addition, provided that they are revenue repairs to the fabric. Both bases, which applied under Case VI, are maintained under Schedule A. Any different basis in use for a particular case prior to 1975/76 will not normally be disturbed (Revenue Pamphlets IR 131, A19 and IR 1, B47 (as revised); Revenue Press Release IR28, 29 November 1994). See *Abidoye v Hennessey Ch D 1978, [1979] STC 212.*

68.9 **Furnished holiday lettings.** In so far as a Schedule A business consists in the 'commercial letting' of 'furnished holiday accommodation' in the UK, it is treated for the following purposes as a trade (separate, in relation to machinery and plant capital allowances for 1997/98 onwards (see 68.7(*a*) above), from any other trade and from the trade (if any) consisting of the remainder of the Schedule A business).

(i) Relief for losses under *ICTA 1988, ss 380–390* (see 46 LOSSES);

(ii) Capital allowances for machinery and plant (see CAPITAL ALLOWANCES (10));

(iii) Before 1996/97 (1997/98 as regards partnerships), payment of tax in two equal instalments on 1 January in the year of assessment and 1 July following;

(iv) Classification as earned income;

(v) Retirement annuity premium and personal pension contribution relief (see 60 PERSONAL PENSION SCHEMES, 65 RETIREMENT ANNUITIES).

Relief as at (i) above under *ICTA 1988, s 381* (see 46.13 LOSSES) is not available for a year of assessment if any of the accommodation concerned was first let by the same person as furnished accommodation more than three years before the beginning of the year of assessment. Loss may not be relieved both under (i) above and under any other relief provision. For 1997/98 onwards (and in practice for earlier years), *ICTA 1988, s 384(6)–(8)* (restriction on relief for capital allowances, etc. in a part-time letting trade, see 46.9(*c*) LOSSES) do not apply for these purposes.

The Revenue consider that the requirement under *section 381* that there be a reasonable expectation of profits in the period concerned or in a 'reasonable time thereafter' normally requires a reasonable and realistic expectation of profits emerging within five years from the date of commencement of furnished holiday letting activities. (Revenue Tax Bulletin October 1997 p 473).

As regards (ii) above, the 10% wear and tear allowance (see 68.8 above) is not available as an alternative to capital allowances.

All such lettings by a particular person, body of persons or partnership are treated as a single trade.

All necessary adjustment may be made where a tax charge has previously been raised for such a year on some other basis.

Any necessary apportionments, where letting of accommodation only qualifies in part under these provisions, is on a just and reasonable basis.

'*Commercial letting*' is letting (whether or not under a lease) on a commercial basis and with a view to the realisation of profits, and accommodation is let '*furnished*' if the tenant is entitled to use of the furniture. For a case in which the 'commercial letting' test was satisfied despite a significant excess of interest over letting income, see *Walls v Livesey (Sp C 4), [1995] SSCD 12*, but see also *Brown v Richardson (Sp C 129), [1997] SSCD 233* in which the opposite conclusion was reached. See Revenue Tax Bulletin October 1997 pp 472, 473 for the Revenue view of the requirements in this respect.

'*Holiday accommodation*' is accommodation which

(*a*) must be available for commercial letting to the public generally as holiday accommodation for at least 140 days in a twelve month period (see below), and

(*b*) is so let at least 70 such days.

It must, however, not normally be in the same occupation for more than 31 consecutive days at any time during a period (although not necessarily a continuous period) of seven months in that twelve month period which includes any months in which it is let as in (*b*) above (although occupation by the owner outside the lettings season does not preclude relief — see Revenue Inspector's Manual, IM 1733a). In the case of an individual or partnership, these conditions must be satisfied in the year of assessment in which the profits or gains arise, unless

(1) the accommodation was not let furnished in the preceding year of assessment but is so let in the following year of assessment, in which case they must be satisfied in the

twelve months from the date such letting commenced in the year of assessment, or

(2) the accommodation was let furnished in the preceding year of assessment but is not so let in the following year of assessment, in which case they must be satisfied in the twelve months ending with the date such letting ceased in the year of assessment.

In the case of a company, the conditions must be satisfied in the twelve months ending on the last day of the accounting period in which the profits or gains arise, with similar variations as in (1) and (2) above where the accommodation was not let furnished in the twelve months preceding or following the period in question.

In satisfying the 70 day test (as above) averaging may be applied to letting periods of any or all of the accommodation let by the same person which would be holiday accommodation if it satisfied the 70 day test. A claim for averaging must be made within, for 1996/97 and later years, twelve months after 31 January following the year of assessment to which it is to apply (for earlier years, two years after the end of that year of assessment). Only one such claim may be made in respect of accommodation in a year of assessment or accounting period.

[*ICTA 1988, ss 503, 504; CAA 1990, s 29; FA 1995, Sch 6 paras 21, 31; FA 1996, ss 134, 135, Sch 20 paras 30, 44, Sch 21 para 14; FA 1997, Sch 15 paras 2(2), 4, 9; FA 1998, s 38, Sch 5 paras 42, 51*].

Furnished holiday accommodation may include caravans. (Revenue Press Release 17 May 1984).

See 74.4 SCHEDULE D, CASE VI as to the application of these provisions to income tax under that Case prior to the new Schedule A regime. See also Tolley's Capital Gains Tax as regards relief from capital gains tax in respect of furnished holiday lettings.

Simon's Direct Tax Service. See **B7.206**.

68.10 *Example*

Mr B owns and lets out furnished holiday cottages. None is ever let to the same person for more than 31 days. Three cottages have been owned for many years but Rose Cottage was acquired on 1 June 2000 (and first let on that day) while Ivy Cottage was sold on 30 June 2000 (and last let on that day).

In 2000/01 days available for letting and days let are as follows.

	Days available	Days let
Honeysuckle Cottage	180	160
Primrose Cottage	130	100
Bluebell Cottage	150	60
Rose Cottage	150	60
Ivy Cottage	30	5

Additional information

Rose Cottage was let for 30 days between 6 April and 31 May 2001.

Ivy Cottage was let for 50 days in the period 1 July 1999 to 5 April 2000 but was available for letting for 110 days in that period.

Qualification as 'furnished holiday accommodation'

Honeysuckle Cottage qualifies as it meets both the 140-day availability test and the 70-day letting test.

Primrose Cottage does *not* qualify although it is let for more than 70 days as it fails to satisfy the 140-day test. Averaging (see below) is only possible where it is the 70-day test which is not satisfied.

Bluebell Cottage does not qualify by itself as it fails the 70-day test. However it may be included in an averaging claim.

Rose Cottage qualifies as furnished holiday accommodation. It was acquired on 1 June 2000 so qualification in 2000/01 is determined by reference to the period of twelve months beginning on the day it was first let, in which it was let for a total of 90 days.

Ivy Cottage was sold on 30 June 2000 so qualification is determined by reference to the period from 1 July 1999 to 30 June 2000 (the last day of letting). It does not qualify by itself as it was let for only 55 days in this period but it may be included in an averaging claim.

Averaging claim for 2000/01

	Days let
Honeysuckle Cottage	160
Bluebell Cottage	60
Rose Cottage	90
Ivy Cottage	55

$$\frac{160 + 60 + 90 + 55}{4} = 91.25 \text{ days} \quad \text{note } (a)$$

Note

(*a*) All four cottages included in the averaging claim qualify as furnished holiday accommodation as each is deemed to have been let for 91.25 days in the year 2000/01. If the average had been less than 70, any three of these cottages could have been included in an averaging claim leaving the other as non-qualifying. If this still did not produce the desired result, an average of any two could be tried. More than one averaging claim is possible for a year of assessment, but no cottage may be included in more than one claim.

68.11 **'Rent a room' relief for letting of rooms in private residence.** The taking in of domestic lodgers may be treated as the carrying on of a trade, where services other than accommodation are provided, or as furnished lettings. The relief described below applied for Schedule D, Case VI (as well as Case I) purposes prior to the introduction of the new Schedule A regime, and so applied for 1992/93 and subsequent years of assessment.

A special relief applies to an individual receiving sums for the use of furnished accommodation in a 'qualifying residence' or residences, or for ancillary services consisting of the provision of meals, cleaning, laundry etc., in respect of all of which the individual would otherwise be chargeable to income tax under Schedule D, Case I and/or Schedule A (previously and/or Case VI). Unless the taxpayer elects otherwise (see below), and provided that the gross sums received (i.e. without any deduction for expenses) do not exceed the individual's limit for the year (see below), the profits or gains (or losses) of the basis period for the year of assessment are treated as nil. No capital allowances or balancing charges are made to or on the individual in relation to the letting of the accommodation. If, however, the addition of such balancing charges which would otherwise be made for the year of assessment to the gross sums received would result in the individual's limit for the year being exceeded, the exemption does not apply. An election for the exemption not to apply for a year of assessment must be made, and may be withdrawn, within, for 1996/97 and later years, twelve months after 31 January following that year and, for earlier years, one year after the end of that year (or, in both cases, such longer time as the Board may allow — see Revenue Inspector's Manual, IM 1729g) by written notice, and any necessary assessment is not out of time if made within, for 1996/97 and later years, twelve months after 31 January following the tax year in which (for earlier years, one year after) the election was made (or withdrawal notice given). The exemption (and the further provisions described below) do not apply for a year of assessment for which the source(s) for income tax purposes of the gross sums concerned also include sums which are not within the reliefs.

Where the gross sums received exceed the individual's limit for the year of assessment, the individual may elect for the profits or gains of the basis period to be treated as equal to that excess. If the gross sums are treated for income tax purposes as arising from more than one source, the individual's limit is apportioned amongst those sources on the basis of the proportion of the gross sums taxable under each source. No capital allowances are made to the individual in relation to the letting of the accommodation. An election for this treatment to apply for a year of assessment must be made (and may be withdrawn) within, for 1996/97 and later years, twelve months after 31 January following that year and, for earlier years, one year after the end of that year (or, in both cases, such longer time as the Board may allow — see above) by written notice, and the election (or withdrawal) applies for all subsequent years of assessment (but, in the case of a withdrawal, without prejudicing the right to make a fresh election). Any necessary assessment is not out of time if made within, for 1996/97 and later years, twelve months after 31 January following the tax year in which (for earlier years, one year after) the election was made (or withdrawal notice given). Where an election applies to a year of assessment for which the gross sums do *not* exceed the individual's limit, the individual is deemed to have withdrawn the election for that year and subsequent years of assessment (again without prejudicing the right to make a fresh election for a subsequent year).

A '*qualifying residence*' is a 'residence' which is the individual's only or main residence at any time in the basis period for the year of assessment in relation to the source in question. The Revenue consider that the basis period does not commence until the tenancy commences, and ceases when the tenancy ceases, so that the relief cannot apply during e.g. the absence of the taxpayer abroad, even during the years of departure and return (unless, exceptionally, there is a period of overlap between the tenant's and the taxpayer's occupation of the house as a residence, e.g. where part of the house is retained for the taxpayer's use, and used, *as his main residence* at some time during a basis period). (Revenue Inspector's Manual, IM 1729l). The furnished accommodation let within the qualifying residence may be in a self-contained flat provided that the division into a self-contained unit is only temporary. (Revenue Inspector's Manual, IM 1729f).

'*Residence*' means a building (or part) occupied or intended to be occupied as a separate residence (ignoring any temporary division into separate residences of a building (or part) designed for permanent use as a single residence), or a caravan or house-boat.

The individual's limit for a year of assessment is **£4,250** (or such sum as may be specified by Treasury order) (£3,250 for 1996/97 and earlier years), but is reduced to one-half of that amount in certain cases where sums accrue to another person in respect of use of furnished accommodation in the individual's only or main residence or in respect of services ancillary (as above) to that use.

[*F(No 2)A 1992, s 59, Sch 10; FA 1995, Sch 6 para 38; FA 1996, s 135, Sch 21 para 47; SI 1996 No 2953*].

The Revenue consider that 'rent a room' relief is inapplicable to the letting of a residence (or part) as an office or for other trade or business purposes (other than the business of providing furnished living accommodation). (Revenue Tax Bulletin August 1994 p 154).

Simon's Direct Tax Service. See **B7.206A**.

68.12 *Example*

Jo and Sinisha are single persons sharing a house as their main residence. They have for some years taken in lodgers to supplement their income. Schedule D, Case VI assessments on the net rental income have been raised on a current year basis, with the 1994/95 assessments being based on the year ended 5 April 1994. As Jo pays the greater share of the mortgage interest on the house, she and Sinisha have an agreement to share the rental income in the ratio 2:1, although expenses are shared equally.

For the year ended 5 April 1996, gross rents amounted to £4,200 and allowable expenses were £600. In the year ended 5 April 1997, the couple face a heavy repair bill after uninsured damage to one of the rooms. Gross rents for that year amount to £3,600 and expenses to £3,400. For the years ended 5 April 1998 and 1999, gross rents are £6,000 and expenses £2,400, and for the year ended 5 April 2000 they are £6,000 and £2,500 respectively. For the year ended 5 April 2001 they are £8,100 and £4,500 respectively.

For 1995/96, the position is as follows

Normal Schedule A computation

	Jo	Sinisha
	£	£
Gross rents (y/e 5.4.96)	2,800	1,400
Allowable expenses	300	300
Net rents	£2,500	£1,100

Sinisha's share of *gross* rents is less than his one half share (£1,625) of the basic amount (£3,250) for 1995/96. It is assumed that he would not make the election under *Schedule 10 para 10* for the exemption under *Schedule 10 para 9* ('rent a room' relief) not to apply. His share of net rents is thus treated as nil.

Jo's share of gross rents exceeds £1,625, so the exemption in *Schedule 10 para 9* cannot apply. She can, however, elect under *Schedule 10 para 12* for *Schedule 10 para 11* to apply, the election to be made by 5 April 1997. Under *Schedule 10 para 11*, she is taxed on the excess of *gross* rents over £1,625. It is assumed that she will make the election as she will then be taxed on £1,175 rather than £2,500.

For 1996/97, the position is as follows

Normal Schedule A computation

	Jo	Sinisha
	£	£
Gross rents (y/e 5.4.97)	2,400	1,200
Allowable expenses	1,700	1,700
Net rents/(loss)	£700	£(500)

Sinisha's share of gross rents continues to be less than his one half share of the basic amount. Under *Schedule 10 para 9*, his share of net rents will be treated as nil. However, he will obtain no relief, by carry-forward or otherwise, for his loss. In order to preserve his loss, he could elect under *Schedule 10 para 10* for *Schedule 10 para 9* not to apply, the election to be made by 5 April 1998 and having effect for 1996/97 only.

Jo's share of gross rents continues to exceed her one half share of the basic amount. Therefore, her previous election under *Schedule 10 para 12* will not automatically be deemed to be withdrawn. She will be taxed under *Schedule 10 para 11* on £775 (£2,400 –

£1,625). However, this is greater than the amount taxable on a normal Schedule A computation (£700), so it is assumed she would withdraw the election with effect for 1996/97 and subsequent years. The notice of withdrawal must be made by 5 April 1998 but does not prejudice the making of a fresh election for 1997/98 or any subsequent year.

For 1997/98, the position is as follows

Normal Schedule A computation

	Jo	Sinisha
	£	£
Gross rents (y/e 5.4.98)	4,400	2,200
Allowable expenses	1,200	1,200
Net rents	£3,200	£1,000

Sinisha's share of gross rents now exceeds his share of the increased basic amount ($\frac{1}{2}$ × £4,250 = £2,125), so the exemption will not apply. He could elect for *Schedule 10 para 11* to apply, and his assessment will then be reduced to £75 (£2,200 – £2,125). This is further reduced to nil by the bringing forward of his £500 loss for 1996/97. (Although a loss cannot enter into the ascertaining of the amount assessable under *Schedule 10 para 11*, there appears to be no reason why a loss cannot be set off against the amount so ascertained.) If Sinisha did not make the election, his assessment would be on £500 with the whole of his 1996/97 loss having been utilised.

Jo can make a fresh election for *Schedule 10 para 11* to apply, with effect from 1997/98, and her 1997/98 Schedule A assessment will then be £2,275 (£4,400 – £2,125).

For 1998/99, the position is as follows.

The normal Schedule A computation is as for 1997/98. Assuming Jo and Sinisha both elected under *Schedule 10 para 11* for 1997/98, the elections will continue to apply for 1998/99, so that their respective 1998/99 Schedule A assessments are £2,275 and £75. Sinisha's assessment is further reduced to nil by the brought forward balance of £425 of the 1996/97 loss (of which the balance of £350 is carried forward to 1999/2000).

For 1999/2000, the position is as follows.

Normal Schedule A computation

	Jo	Sinisha
	£	£
Gross rents (y/e 5.4.00)	4,000	2,000
Allowable expenses	1,250	1,250
Net rents	£2,750	£750

Sinisha's share of gross rents is now below his one-half share of the basic amount, so that the election under *Schedule 10 para 11* is deemed to have been withdrawn, and under *Schedule 10 para 9* his share is treated as nil (assuming no election under *Schedule 10 para 10*). The balance of £350 of his 1996/97 loss is carried forward to 2000/01. Jo's election under *Schedule 10 para 11* will continue to apply (unless withdrawn), so that her Schedule A assessment will be £1,875 (£4,000 – £2,125).

For 2000/01, the position is as follows.

Normal Schedule A computation

	Jo	Sinisha
	£	£
Gross rents (y/e 5.4.01)	5,400	2,700
Allowable expenses	2,250	2,250
Net rents	£3,150	£450

For both Jo and Sinisha their share of gross rents now exceeds their share of the basic amount, so that the exemption will not apply, and since their share of the expenses also exceeds their share of the basic amount, the election under *Schedule 10 para 11* will be unfavourable. It is therefore assumed that Jo withdraws her election (by 31 January 2003). They are accordingly both assessed on the basis of the normal Schedule A computation, with Sinisha's £350 loss brought forward being set against his share.

68.13 LOSSES

Carry-forward. With effect as in 68.3 above, where a loss (a '*Schedule A loss*'), computed in like manner as Schedule A profits, is incurred by any person in a Schedule A business, carried on alone or in partnership, it is carried forward without time limit as a set-off against the first following profits of the business, or, if insufficient, the next, and so on. [*ICTA 1988, s 379A(1)(7); FA 1995, Sch 6 para 19(1)*].

Set-off against other income. Where a Schedule A loss is incurred in a year of assessment (the year of loss) and as regards that year,

(*a*) there is a net amount of capital allowances, (i.e. capital allowances, with the exclusion mentioned below, exceed any balancing charges), *and/or*

(*b*) the Schedule A business has been carried on in relation to land which consists of or includes an 'agricultural estate' to which 'allowable agricultural expenses' (see below) are attributable,

a claim may be made under *ICTA 1988, s 379A(3)* to set an amount of loss relief against total income for the year of loss or the following year. The amount of loss relief is restricted to the lowest of the following:

(i) the loss,

(ii) the 'relievable income' for the year to which the claim relates, and

(iii) the net capital allowances (where (*a*) above applies) or the allowable agricultural expenses (where (*b*) applies) or the sum of those two items (where *both* (*a*) and (*b*) apply).

Relief cannot normally be claimed for both years in respect of the same loss, but where relief is restricted for one year by virtue of (ii) above, the balance (i.e. the excess of the lower of (i) and (iii) above over the relief given) may be claimed for the other year. A person's '*relievable income*' is his total income after taking into account any Schedule A loss brought forward under *ICTA 1988, s 379A(1)* (see above) from a year prior to the year of loss and, where the claim relates to the year of loss, after giving effect to any *section 379A(3)* claim in respect of a loss for the preceding year. A loss carried forward under *section 379A(1)* from the year of loss is restricted or extinguished by relief given for that loss under *section 379A(3)*.

A claim under *section 379A(3)* must be made within 12 months after 31 January following *the year to which the claim relates* (where that year is 1996/97 or a later year), and must be accompanied by any necessary amendments to the claimant's SELF-ASSESSMENT (78) for that year. If the claim relates to 1995/96, the time limit is extended to two years, i.e. the claim must be made by 5 April 1998.

In computing net capital allowances (see (*a*) above) for 1995/96 or 1996/97, there must be excluded any capital allowances on machinery and plant which is let to a person who does not use it or uses it for purposes other than those of a trade (with a proportionate amount being excluded where this applies for part only of the year). An '*agricultural estate*' (see (*b*) above) means any land (including any houses or other buildings) which is managed as one estate and which consists of or includes any agricultural land, i.e. land in the UK occupied wholly or mainly for husbandry. '*Allowable agricultural expenses*' (see (*b*) above) are any deductible disbursements or expenses attributable to the agricultural estate in respect of maintenance, repairs, insurance or estate management (but excluding loan interest). For these purposes, disbursements and expenses are taken into account only to the extent that they are attributable to the parts of it used for husbandry, with those attributable to parts used partly for other purposes being proportionately reduced.

[*ICTA 1988, s 379A(2)–(10); FA 1995, Sch 6 para 19(1)(4); FA 1997, Sch 15 paras 2(1), 9*].

Transitional provisions. The following are treated as Schedule A losses carried forward to 1995/96 (and, if necessary, to subsequent years) under *ICTA 1988, s 379A(1)*.

(A) Any excess expenditure brought forward to 1995/96 which under the old Schedule A regime would have been deductible from rents received and actually brought into account in that year (see 68.16 below).

(B) Any losses which could otherwise have been brought forward to 1995/96 under *ICTA 1988, s 392* in respect of *furnished lettings* (see 74.5 SCHEDULE D, CASE VI).

(C) Any unrelieved interest which could otherwise have been brought forward to 1995/96 under *ICTA 1988, s 355(4)* provided the Schedule A business relates to property that would have satisfied the conditions of *ICTA 1988, s 355(1)(b)* for 1995/96 (letting for 26 weeks out of 52 etc.) if those provisions had been extant for that year (see 43.15 INTEREST PAYABLE).

[*FA 1995, Sch 6 para 19(2)(3)*].

Application to overseas property business. For 1998/99 and subsequent years, the provisions of *ICTA 1988, s 379A* apply equally to an overseas property business (see 73.4 SCHEDULE D, CASES IV AND V which also covers the position for unrelieved losses carried forward at 5 April 1998). [*ICTA 1988, s 379B; FA 1998, s 38, Sch 5 para 27*].

Simon's Direct Tax Service. See **A4.410**.

68.14 THE PRE-FINANCE ACT 1995 REGIME

The provisions described below and in 68.15 to 68.21 below apply for income tax purposes for 1994/95 and earlier years (see also 68.2 above) and for 1995/96 where the transitional provisions at 68.3 above have effect. They continue to apply for corporation tax purposes up to and including 31 March 1998 (see Tolley's Corporation Tax).

Rents etc.. [*ICTA 1988, s 15*]. Schedule A applies to profits or gains arising in respect of

(*a*) rents (including sums treated as such in respect of premiums, see 68.27 below) under leases (including any tenancy) of land (including buildings) in UK,

(*b*) rent-charges, ground annuals, feu duties and other annual payments reserved in respect of, or charged on or issuing out of, such land,

(*c*) any other receipts from an estate or interest in, or right over, such land or any incorporeal hereditament or incorporeal heritable subject in the UK, generally on the basis of rents or receipts arising in the chargeable period, less allowable deductions as below. Receipts from sales of turf are within (*c*) although they may alternatively be taxed as trading receipts within Schedule D, Case I (*Lowe v J W Ashmore Ltd Ch D 1970, 46 TC 597*): but from sale of colliery dross bings held to be capital (*Roberts v Lord Belhaven's Exors CS 1925, 9 TC 501*). Sums received for licence to tip soil on land held capital (*McClure v Petre Ch D 1988, 61 TC 226*).

But Schedule A does not include the following.

(i) *Rents etc. from furnished lettings.* These are assessed under SCHEDULE D, CASE VI (74) unless the landlord elects for Schedule A in respect of the payment for use of the premises within two years of the end of the chargeable period. The inclusion in this provision of payments other than rents under leases is statutory for chargeable periods beginning after 5 April 1992, but was applied in practice for earlier periods. [*ICTA 1988, s 15(1)(2); F(No 2)A 1992, s 58*]. The rent for the furnishings, etc. then remains under Case VI. See, however, 74.4 SCHEDULE D, CASE VI and 68.9, 68.11 above as to holiday lettings and the letting of furnished accommodation in private residences. See 68.4 above as regards income from letting caravan pitches.

(ii) *Woodlands.* Profits or gains arising from occupation of WOODLANDS (93) under commercial management with a view to profit.

(iii) *Yearly interest.*

(iv) *Mineral rents, royalties etc.* charged to tax under Schedule D by virtue of *ICTA 1988, s 55, s 119* or *s 120*, see under 23.2 and 23.14 DEDUCTION OF TAX AT SOURCE. [*ICTA 1988, s 15(1); FA 1988, Sch 6 para 6*].

Rents etc. from connected persons. In relation to rents etc. chargeable under Schedule A which accrue after 9 March 1992, special provisions apply where the payer and recipient are 'connected' and the rents etc. accrue in a chargeable period of the recipient before that in which they are payable. If the payer is entitled to a deduction for the rents etc. in computing profits or gains for tax purposes, the recipient is regarded as becoming entitled to the rents etc. in the chargeable period in which they accrue (rather than that in which they become payable). For these purposes, rents etc. are treated as accruing at the same times and in the same amounts as they are so treated for the purposes of calculating the deduction to which the payer is entitled in respect of them, and the payer and recipient are 'connected' if they are CONNECTED PERSONS (20) within *ICTA 1988, s 839* either when the rents etc. accrue or at any earlier time after 9 March 1992 and after the making of the lease or agreement under which they accrue.

Similar provisions apply where the recipient of rents etc. in relation to land is connected with a person, other than the payer, who is entitled to a deduction for other rents etc. payable after they accrue under a lease or agreement relating to all or part of the same land, and those other rents etc. accrued before the rents etc. in question became payable. In such a case the rents etc. are treated as accruing, and hence chargeable, at the times and in the amounts they would be so treated if paid *by* rather than *to* the recipient and relieved as a trading deduction. [*ICTA 1988, ss 33A, 33B; F(No 2)A 1992, s 57*].

68.15 **Pre-FA 1995—expenses deductible—specific items.** [*ICTA 1988, ss 25–33*]. From *rent* (including sums treated as such in respect of premiums) to which the landlord becomes entitled in any chargeable period in respect of leased premises or land there may be deducted the aggregate of payments (but not interest, *ICTA 1988, s 25(2)*, nor items recoverable under insurance or from some other person, or (except in the case of a company) paid under deduction of tax) made by him for (*a*) maintenance or repairs (arising from dilapidation during the currency of the lease and while he was landlord [*ICTA 1988, s 25(3)(b)*]), insurance or management (see below),

(*b*) other services the landlord was obliged, without separate consideration, to provide,

(*c*) rates or other charges on the occupier which the landlord was obliged to defray, and

(*d*) any rent (and see 68.28 below, re premiums), rent-charge, ground annual, feu duty or other periodical payment made by him in respect of the leased premises,

in that chargeable or any previous period, within the currency of the lease, during which he was the landlord.

In practice, relief under (*b*) above will be given for landlord's expenditure on services, amenities, etc. for tenants, even if not under an express lease covenant, but only if as under an arm's length agreement.

As regards (*c*), a deduction will normally be available for council tax (introduced on 1 April 1993) paid on let property (or for that part of any council tax paid which is attributable to the letting). (Revenue Press Release 16 March 1993). As regards the community charge, which was replaced by the council tax, a deduction is available for the standard community charge (payable in respect of premises which were not the sole or main residence of the occupier) where the property concerned was let. Similarly a deduction against rent is available for any amount of the collective community charge (payable by landlords in respect of certain houses in multiple occupation) which was not met by contributions from residents. (Revenue Press Release 10 November 1989). The deduction of business rates is unaffected by these changes.

Allowance for **maintenance and repairs** is limited to expenditure incurred by the taxpayer concerned in respect of current dilapidation [*ICTA 1988, s 25(3)*], and there is thus no allowance for remedying deterioration which occurred before he purchased the property except, by concession, where the immediately preceding owner was a deceased spouse (or trustee for the spouse). (Revenue Pamphlet IR 1, A21). As regards pre-purchase dilapidation see *Law Shipping* and *Odeon Theatres* cases under 71.79 SCHEDULE D, CASES I AND II (but *Odeon* case does not displace *section 25(3)* for Schedule A purposes).

Expenditure on improvements, additions or alterations is not allowed, nor is any outlay which has been allowed otherwise in computing income — e.g. under Schedule D, Case I [*ICTA 1988, s 31(6)*], nor expenditure balanced by the receipt of insurance moneys or recovered from, or borne by, any person other than the taxpayer (except where the receipt itself is income chargeable under Sch A). [*ICTA 1988, s 31(5)*].

But, concessionally, the estimated cost of any maintenance and repairs obviated by alterations, etc., is allowed provided the alterations are not so extensive as to amount to reconstruction, and there has been no such change in the use of the property as would have rendered the repairs, etc., unnecessary. (Revenue Pamphlet IR 1, B4).

The following are types of expenditure normally allowable in respect of the property which is let.

(i) Current repairs and redecorations, inside and out.

(ii) Where falling under (*b*) above, upkeep of gardens of flats, and remuneration of porters, cleaners, etc.

(iii) Expenditure, so far as incurred for the benefit of tenants, on keeping up private roads, drains, ditches, embankments, etc., on an estate containing property let by the landlord (but not road works payments by frontager, *Davidson v Deeks Ch D 1956, 37 TC 32*).

(iv) Maintenance of common parts of blocks of offices, etc.

(v) CAPITAL ALLOWANCES (10) under *CAA 1990, Pt II*, are given (if the taxpayer so elects in writing) on machinery or plant provided for use, or used, by a person entitled to rents or receipts falling under Sch A, for maintenance, repair, etc., of the properties concerned. See 10.25 CAPITAL ALLOWANCES as regards certain expenditure on industrial buildings treated as being on machinery or plant and 10.34 CAPITAL ALLOWANCES as regards entitlement to allowances for fixtures. An election as above, if made, has effect for the year of claim and all subsequent years, and may relate to all such machinery or, conditionally, to a specified class thereof only. Allowances or balancing charges are added to, or deducted from, total admissible outlay for the year; if a charge cannot be so dealt with it is assessed under Case VI. For corporation tax accounting periods ending after 31 March 1997, these rules are revised so that machinery and plant allowances and charges are calculated as if all the activities of the company which would constitute the Schedule A business of an individual (see 68.5 above), and which are not chargeable under Schedule D, Case VI, were a separate trade for which the machinery or plant was provided (subject to further separation where there are furnished holiday lettings, see 68.9 above). Expenditure is thus pooled in the normal way (see 10.28 CAPITAL ALLOWANCES). Allowances or charges are given or made by discharge or repayment, allowances being given primarily against Schedule A income (including any charge(s) under these provisions). Machinery or plant provided for use in a dwelling-house is excluded (with a just and reasonable apportionment of expenditure where such use is partial). From 1 April 1998, the concept of a Schedule A business is extended to corporation tax in any case (see Tolley's Corporation Tax). [*ICTA 1988, s 32; CAA 1990, ss 28A, 73(1A); FA 1997, Sch 15 paras 1, 3, 6, 9; FA 1998, s 38, Sch 5 para 57, Sch 27 Pt III(4)*]. As an alternative to the above, renewals basis may be claimed.

(vi) Insurance premiums against damage to the fabric of the property by fire, flood or tempest etc.

(vii) Valuation fees for purposes of insurance (but not for sale, probate, etc.).

(viii) Cost of rent collection. (But not rents embezzled by agent, *Pyne v Stallard-Penoyre Ch D 1964, 42 TC 183*. See also *Clapham's Trustees v Belton Ch D 1956, 37 TC 26*.)

(ix) Upkeep of estate offices.

(x) Salaries and wages of employees engaged full-time on estate management.

(xi) Pensions (not under covenant) customarily paid to retired employees or their widows so far as attributable to former services which were an allowable expense for Schedule A purposes.

(xii) Legal costs relating to the drawing up of a lease or tenancy agreement, although strictly capital, are in practice allowed, provided that:

(*a*) in the case of a first letting, the letting is for a period which does not exceed 21 years;

(*b*) on a re-letting, the re-letting is for a period which does not (and could not at the lessee's option) exceed 50 years.

(xiii) Legal and accountancy costs for preparing accounts, tax computations, etc. for the property.

(xiv) As regards agricultural property, costs of arbitration to determine rent, obtaining certificate of bad farming, or making a record of the holding. (Costs and compensation under claims for disturbance, unexhausted manures, etc., are not allowed.)

(xv) Ordinary annual subscriptions to The Country Landowners' Association, The Scottish Landowners' Federation and The National Association of Property Owners.

See generally Revenue Property Income Manual, PIM 5100-5120.

68.16 **Pre-FA 1995 — expenses and deficiencies deductible — general provisions.** See 68.13(A) above for the treatment of excess expenditure carried forward to 1995/96 where the new Schedule A regime for income tax has effect for that year.

(*a*) Expenditure on property the rent from which is assessable under Schedule A is deductible, normally on the basis of actual payments made in the chargeable period. If the income for that period is insufficient to permit of full deduction, expenditure may be allowed for the period in which the payment became due. Any unrelieved excess may be carried forward during the currency of the lease and set against rents of the next subsequent period, and so on [*ICTA 1988, ss 25, 31, 37(9)*], or, in the case of expenditure on maintenance, repair, insurance and management of agricultural property only, set against other income of the same year. [*ICTA 1988, s 33(1)*]. In the case of a property dealer, expenditure unrelieved under Schedule A in the current year may be allowed against Schedule D, Case I income. (Revenue Pamphlet IR 27, para 114, now withdrawn). There is also a limited right of offset against income from other properties in the same ownership, see below. See also 71.57(*d*) SCHEDULE D, CASES I AND II as regards maintenance expenses of non-commercial owner-occupied farms.

(*b*) Where a lease is at a *full rent* (i.e. sufficient, on average, to cover the landlord's obligations, maintenance, repairs, insurance, etc.) deductions as above include unrelieved outlay incurred during (i) the period of any previous full-rent lease of the premises by the same landlord, or (ii) any void period which either immediately follows the end of such a lease, or which commences with the acquisition of the property by the present landlord. However expenditure in these earlier periods may not be deducted if there is a period which does not fall into either (i) or (ii) between the earlier period and the period in which the deduction is claimed. A *void period* is a period during which the owner is entitled to possession of the premises but during which he is not in occupation. [*ICTA 1988, s 25(2)(5)(6)*].

(*c*) There is further relief for excess expenditure as under (*a*) or (*b*) above on properties let at a full rent (or in void periods following such lettings). Any such excess may be set against rents receivable by the same landlord from other properties, provided that those other properties are let at *full rents* and *not* on *tenant's repairing leases*. Thus in effect all rents and expenses of properties let at full rents and not on tenant's repairing leases are pooled, and against any aggregate balance of receipts may be set:

(i) excess expenditure of past years as under (*b*) above on properties in the pool; and

(ii) excess expenditure of the same year and of past years as under (*b*) above on other properties of the same landlord let at full rents on tenant's repairing leases. [*ICTA 1988, s 25(7)*].

A *tenant's repairing lease* is one under which the lessee is obliged to maintain and repair the whole, or substantially the whole, of the premises. [*ICTA 1988, s*

24(6)(c)]. A lease under which all repair and maintenance work falls on the tenant apart from one structural item, such as maintenance of the foundations, is usually regarded as a tenant's repairing lease.

Deficiencies on leases not at '*full rent*' cannot be offset against any other source of income. They can only be carried forward for relief against income from the same property under the same lease while in the same ownership. [*ICTA 1988, s 25(3)(4)*].

(*d*) For applying the above provisions to land which, at 5 April 1963, was in one ownership and *managed as one estate*, the owner may elect to be treated as receiving, for any part of the estate not let (other than premises he occupies for estate management or trade), rent at a rate equivalent to its annual value, and, for any part let at less than a full rent, rent at a rate at least equal to its annual value. He may then claim deduction of expenditure, as above, in respect of each of the properties in the estate. Any excess expenditure on such a property may not be set against rents from properties outside the estate, but excess expenditure on properties outside the estate let at full rent may be set against estate property rent, subject to the usual conditions at (*c*) above. For details of the election, meaning of 'annual value' and other matters, see 68.7(*b*) above.

(*e*) From a receipt *other than rent* (rent charges, feu duties and other non-rental income) deductions may be made for payments as under 68.15(*a*)(*d*) above, and any other non-capital expenses, constituting expenses of the transaction under which the sum arose, or which could be, but have not been, deducted from sums arising from other similar transactions in the year of assessment or any previous year. [*ICTA 1988, s 28*]. For treatment of sporting rights, and allowances for expenditure on making sea walls, see *ICTA 1988, ss 29, 30* and *Hesketh v Bray CA 1888, 2 TC 380.*

(*f*) See 68.5(*b*) above (business entertaining) and 68.5(*c*) above (expenditure involving crime) both of which apply to prohibit deductions.

Simon's Direct Tax Service. See **A4.301A** *et seq.*.

68.17 *Example*

Mr Grey lets out the following properties in 1994/95

Shop to B at full rent of £1,000 p.a., expenses £1,500 (landlord repairing lease)
Factory to C at full rent of £5,000 p.a., expenses £2,000 (landlord repairing lease)
Shop to D at full rent of £1,000 p.a., expenses £4,000 (tenant's repairing lease)
Shop to E at full rent of £6,000 p.a., expenses £500 (tenant's repairing lease)
House to F at less than full rent let at £200 p.a., expenses £500

The tax position is as follows.

	Landlord repairing leases		Tenant's repairing leases		Lease at less than full rent
	£	£	£	£	£
Rents	1,000	5,000	1,000	6,000	200
Deduct Expenses	1,500	2,000	4,000	500	500
Profit (Loss)	(500)	3,000	(3,000)	5,500	(300)
Set-off	500	(500)	—	—	—
		c/f 2,500	c/f (3,000)	c/f (5,500)	c/f (300)

	Landlord repairing leases		Tenant's repairing leases		Lease at less than full rent
	£	£	£	£	£
		b/f 2,500	b/f (3,000)	b/f (5,500)	b/f (300)
		2,500			
Set-off		(2,500)	2,500	—	—
Assessment			—	£5,500	—
Losses carried forward			£(500)	—	£(300)

68.18 **Pre-FA 1995—lost rents etc..** Where any rent or receipt to which the landlord was entitled is not in fact received (by default of the payer, despite reasonable steps for enforcement, or by waiver reasonably made, without consideration, to avoid hardship) a claim may be made to leave that sum out of account. But if any sum so ignored is subsequently recovered the Revenue must be notified (under penalty) within six months thereafter and the relevant liabilities are then readjusted (but see 68.19 below where accounts basis applies). [*ICTA 1988, s 41*]. See Simon's Direct Tax Service A4.401.

68.19 **Pre-FA 1995—accounts basis and returns.** In appropriate cases where full accounts (including balance sheets) are made up annually to the same date the Revenue will accept computations based thereon, treating the items included in the accounts as being those for the tax year in which the accounting period ends. Both receipts and expenditure must be capable of analysis as relating to (*a*) properties let at full rents (see 68.16(*b*) above); (*b*) properties let at full rents on tenants' repairing leases; (*c*) properties let at other than full rents; and (*d*) other chargeable items. But separate figures for each individual property are not necessary where it is reasonably clear that total liability will not be affected. (Revenue Pamphlet IR 27 paras 102–104, now withdrawn).

Where accounts basis applies, lost rents (as under 68.18 above) may be treated as bad debts are for Case I purposes, i.e. allowed as deductions for the year in which written off in accounts, recoveries being treated as receipts of the year in which recovered.

See 68.22 below for Revenue guidelines on the transition to the Finance Act 1995 regime.

Simplified returns. Landlords with a total annual gross income from property under £15,000 are required only to state the gross income, the total amount of allowable expenses and the net income or profit. There will, of course, still be a need to keep accurate records to ensure the correctness of the three-line accounts. (Revenue Press Releases 7 November 1989, 1 November 1991).

Simon's Direct Tax Service. See **A4.107**.

68.20 **Pre-FA 1995 — assessments and payments of tax.** Made for income tax primarily on the basis of the net income as in the preceding tax year, tax being payable accordingly, but with automatic adjustment after the year end to the basis of the income to which the recipient became entitled in the actual year of assessment, less expenditure in that actual year (subject as above). [*ICTA 1988, s 22(2); FA 1995, Sch 6 para 3*]. However, if, before 1 January (when the tax is normally due) in any year, the taxpayer shows that his actual rents and receipts (i.e. before any deductions) for that year will be less than those of the preceding year by reason of his having ceased to possess one or more sources of that income, the primary assessment, as above, will be reduced proportionately by the estimated reduction (with final adjustment after the end of the year). [*ICTA 1988, s 22(3); FA 1995, Sch 6 para 3*]. See Simon's Direct Tax Service A4.501.

68.21 **Pre-FA 1995 — collection from lessee or agent.** Income tax under Schedule A is payable by the person entitled to the rents, etc. But if he does not pay, and is not in occupation of the property concerned, any lessee of the property whose interest derives from him may be required to pay, to the extent of any rent falling due. The lessee then has a right of recoupment when paying his rent. A person receiving rents, etc., on behalf of another may, in default of payment by the latter, be required, under penalty, to pay them to the Revenue in settlement. These provisions are repealed for corporation tax purposes with effect in relation to accounting periods ending on or after 31 March 1995. [*ICTA 1988, ss 21, 23; FA 1995, s 39(4), Sch 6 para 3*]. See Simon's Direct Tax Service A4.502.

68.22 TRANSITION TO FINANCE ACT 1995 REGIME

The Revenue have, after consultation, published guidelines to its inspectors on how the transition for income tax from the old Schedule A regime or the Case VI charge on furnished lettings to the new Schedule A regime should be handled and the non-statutory adjustments that may be made so as far as possible to give a fair result, bearing in mind that the transition may involve changes in the basis of computation and/or changes of basis period (the new regime operating on a strict fiscal year basis). The adjustments will normally be made to the 1994/95 computation (but see below as regards loan interest). Where this cannot be done, because the 1994/95 assessment is already final, the adjustments should be made to the 1995/96 assessment, but not so as to affect the computation of the adjustment itself and not so as to increase the 1995/96 assessment (or reduce losses) beyond the strict statutory figure under the new regime. (Revenue Tax Bulletin December 1995 pp 268–271).

Basis of computation. The statutory basis of computation for 1994/95 and earlier for Schedule A was a receipts and payments basis, whereas that for 1995/96 onwards will be an accruals basis. By agreement between taxpayer and inspector in individual cases, (*a*) sources which first arise in 1994/95 may be dealt with as if the new regime applied for that year, thus avoiding any transition, (*b*) sources which cease soon after 1995/96 (see below) may continue to be dealt with under the old rules, and (*c*) for continuing sources a special computation may be produced for 1994/95, starting with the profit computed under the old rules and adding or deducting, as appropriate, items which would otherwise either fall into a gap between the 1994/95 and 1995/96 computations or be included in both. In some cases, by concession, an accruals basis may have operated previously, and in others (i.e. small landlords) a cash basis may continue to be acceptable under the new regime; therefore, an adjustment may not be necessary. The comments in this paragraph are not considered to be relevant for furnished lettings.

As regards (*b*) above, the old rules may continue to be used up to a date of cessation falling before 6 April 1997 provided that the taxpayer so elects and that no new Schedule A business is commenced before 5 April 1997. However, interest relief is not available under *ICTA 1988, s 355(1)(b)* for 1996/97 (see 43.15 INTEREST PAYABLE), and will also not be available as a Schedule A business expense where the old rules apply. (Revenue Tax Bulletin October 1996 p 349).

Basis periods. As mentioned at 68.19 above, an accounts basis was sometimes applied to Schedule A under the old regime. This was also the case for furnished lettings, for which a preceding year basis of assessment also often applied (see 74.3 SCHEDULE D, CASE VI). The Revenue's preferred option, in moving to a fiscal year (and current year) basis, is to invite the landlord to prepare accounts for a period starting with the end of the basis period for 1993/94 and ending with 5 April 1995 and to tax a time-based proportion of the profits. If, for example, the 1993/94 Schedule A assessment was based on accounts to 31 December 1993 under the old regime, the 1994/95 assessment will be based on $\frac{12}{15}$ of the profit for the period 1 January 1994 to 5 April 1995 under these transitional rules and 1995/96 on the year to 5 April 1996 under the new regime. For capital allowances purposes, additions and disposals for the full transitional accounting period will be taken into account but only 12 months' writing-down allowance will be given.

Loan interest. Where loan interest relief was given for 1994/95 and earlier years under the rules in 43.15 INTEREST PAYABLE on an interest paid basis, a switch to an accruals basis under the new Schedule A regime may result in some interest being unrelieved. The inspector may allow 'some further relief' by deduction in arriving at the 1995/96 Schedule A profit. The principle to be followed is that if income and expenses are taken fully into account over the lifetime of the letting business, then relief should be given for all the interest paid over that period, but if income and expenses drop out on transition, as with a change of basis period as above, it may be appropriate for the overall position taking account of interest to be considered.

Absence of agreement. Where taxpayer and inspector cannot reach agreement on adjustments, the inspector will assess income under Schedule A for 1994/95 by reference to profits of the fiscal year (calculated under the old regime) and will determine a furnished lettings basis period under *ICTA 1988, s 69* (see 74.3 SCHEDULE D, CASE VI). Apportionment of profits of different accounting periods may be necessary. 1995/96 will then be assessed on the statutory basis (under the new regime) with no intervening adjustment. Similarly, on appeal, the Commissioners can only apply the strict statutory basis for either year.

(Revenue Press Release 10 February 1995).

See the examples at 68.23 below and see also Revenue Tax Bulletin December 1995 pp 268–271 for further commentary and examples, including an example where both computational and basis period adjustments arise in the same case.

Simon's Direct Tax Service. See **A4.110.**

68.23 *Examples*

Basis periods

Brown lets a number of furnished apartments and has in the past prepared furnished lettings accounts to 31 December. For tax years up to and including 1992/93, he has been assessed under Schedule D, Case VI on a preceding year basis. Both the choice of accounting date and the application of a preceding year basis are the result of a long-established practice agreed between Brown and his tax office. To facilitate the transition to the new Schedule A basis, Brown's inspector invites him to submit accounts covering the whole of the period from the end of 1993/94 basis period to 5 April 1995. Income and allowable expenditure are as follows.

	Income (£)	Expenditure (£)
Year ended 31 December 1992	14,000	3,000
27 months to 5 April 1995	36,000	9,450
Year ended 5 April 1996	17,000	4,000

Assessments will be as follows.

		£
1993/94	Schedule D, Case VI	11,000
1994/95	Schedule D, Case VI ((36,000 – 9,450) × $\frac{12}{27}$)	11,800
1995/96	Schedule A	13,000

Basis of computation

The facts are as in the example above except that Brown also lets an unfurnished property, accounts having always been prepared to 5 April. Rent is receivable three months in advance on 6 December, 6 March, 6 June and 6 September, and was increased from £3,300 to £3,600 p.a. with effect from 6 March 1995, and to £3,720 p.a. from 6 March 1996. Gross rental income receivable as shown by the Schedule A computation to 5 April 1995, prepared on the statutory basis then prevailing, is as follows.

	£
3 × £825 (receivable 6 June, 6 September and 6 December 1994)	2,475
1 × £900 (receivable 6 March 1995)	900
	£3,375

The accounts for the year to 5 April 1996, prepared on an accruals basis in accordance with commercial accounting practice as for trades and professions, show rent receivable £3,610 calculated as follows.

	£
Rent received on the four due dates (3 × £900 + £930)	3,630
Less prepaid 6 April 1996 to 5 June 1996 (£930 × $\frac{2}{3}$)	620
	3,010
Add prepaid 6 April 1995 to 5 June 1995 (£900 × $\frac{2}{3}$)	600
	£3,610

Allowable expenses are £900 and £1,000 for the years to 5 April 1995 and 5 April 1996 respectively.

An adjustment to the 1994/95 computation may be agreed between the taxpayer and the inspector as follows.

	£
Gross rents as above	3,375
Deduct allowable expenditure	900
	2,475
Transitional adjustment	
Deduct rent for period 6 April 1995 to 5 June 1995 included in accounts to 5 April 1996	600
Schedule A taxable income	£1,875

The position for 1995/96 is as follows.

	£
Gross rents as above	3,610
Deduct allowable expenditure	1,000
	2,610
Furnished lettings (as in example above)	13,000
Profits of Schedule A business	£15,610

Note

For simplicity, the example immediately above considers only income. In practice, computational adjustments are also likely to arise as regards expenditure. See Revenue Tax Bulletin December 1995 pp 268–271 for examples.

68.24 NON-RESIDENT LANDLORDS—COLLECTION FROM AGENTS OR TENANTS

For 1996/97 and subsequent years, where a landlord is non-resident (i.e. his usual place of abode is outside the UK), tax is to be deducted at source by the agent for the property or, where there is no agent, the tenant, with a final settling up with the non-resident landlord. [*ICTA 1988, s 42A; FA 1995, s 40(1)–(3)(8); FA 1998, s 38, Sch 5 para 22, Sch 27 Pt III(4)*]. The regulations giving effect to these requirements provide broadly as follows.

(i) Letting agents who receive or have control over UK property income of a non-resident must operate the scheme.

(ii) Where there is no letting agent acting, tenants of a non-resident must operate the scheme.

(iii) Tenants who pay less than £100 per week do not have to operate the scheme unless asked to do so by the Revenue.

(iv) Letting agents and tenants who have to operate the scheme must pay tax at the basic rate each quarter on the non-resident's UK property income less certain allowable expenses and deductions, and must give the non-resident an annual certificate showing details of tax deducted.

(v) Non-residents whose property income is subject to deduction of tax may set the tax deducted against their UK tax liability through their self-assessment.

(vi) Non-residents may apply to the Revenue for approval to receive their UK property income without deduction of tax provided that:

(*a*) their UK tax affairs are up to date;

(*b*) they have never had any obligations in relation to UK tax; or

(*c*) they do not expect to be liable to UK income tax,

and that they undertake to comply with all their UK tax obligations in the future. An appeal may be made against refusal or withdrawal of approval.

The regulations also make provision for interest on unpaid tax and for payments on account under self-assessment, and set out details of the annual information requirements on those operating the scheme, and of other information to be supplied on request. Penalties apply under *TMA 1970, s 98* for non-compliance with these return and information provisions.

[*ICTA 1988, s 42A(4)–(7); FA 1995, s 40(2); SI 1995 No 2902*].

The Revenue have issued detailed guidance notes to those required to operate the scheme. See also Revenue Pamphlet IR 140 'Non-resident landlords, their agents and tenants' and Revenue Tax Bulletin December 1995 pp 261–263.

For 1995/96 and earlier years, and for corporation tax as well as income tax purposes, agents for non-UK resident landlords were assessable (including at the higher rate) on their behalf and could retain the tax paid out of money coming into their hands and be indemnified. [*TMA 1970, ss 78, 83*]. Where, however, the payment of rent etc. was made (whether in the UK or elsewhere) *directly* to a person whose usual place of abode was outside the UK, the payer had to deduct tax at the basic rate and account for it to the

Revenue as under *ICTA 1988, s 350* (see 23.3 DEDUCTION OF TAX AT SOURCE). If this resulted in an overcharge on the landlord, he could reclaim accordingly. [*ICTA 1988, s 43; FA 1995, s 40(3)*]. The tenant would not normally be held liable for tax not deducted at source if unaware of a landlord's change of abode (CCAB Memorandum TR 127, February 1974) or if he could reasonably plead ignorance of the requirement to deduct tax (Revenue Assessment Procedures Manual, AP 1268).

Simon's Direct Tax Service. See **A4.503**.

68.25 APPORTIONMENT OF RECEIPTS AND OUTGOINGS ON SALE OF LAND

Where a property is purchased or sold during the year, income or expenditure before contract, or between contract and completion, which is apportioned to the purchaser is treated as having been received or paid by him immediately after completion. Similarly, where part of a receipt or payment after completion is apportioned to the vendor that part is treated as if he had received or paid it in the period immediately before completion, and the purchaser is relieved accordingly. [*ICTA 1988, s 40; FA 1995, Sch 6 para 4(f); FA 1998, s 38, Sch 5 para 20, Sch 27 Pt III(4)*].

68.26 INFORMATION RE LEASES

Information, including consideration for their grant or assignment, etc., may be required, under penalty, from present or former lessees or occupiers, or from agents managing property or receiving rents, etc. [*TMA 1970, ss 19, 98; FA 1988, s 123(4)*].

68.27 PREMIUMS ETC. ON LEASES OF UP TO 50 YEARS — ASSESSABILITY ON RECIPIENT [*ICTA 1988, ss 34–39; FA 1995, Sch 6 paras 9–12; FA 1998, ss 38, 40, Sch 5 paras 15–18*]

Premiums. A premium receivable by the landlord (or by another person, see Note (ii) below) under a lease of land in the UK not exceeding 50 years, or otherwise under the terms subject to which a lease is granted, is treated as additional rent, receivable (from 17 March 1998, received) at the date the lease is granted (but see Notes (ii) and (v) below), equivalent to the amount of the premium less $\frac{1}{50}$th for each full year (minus one) in the lease's duration (e.g. if the lease is for 10 years, $\frac{41}{50}$ths of any premium will be chargeable). An amount so treated is taken into account in full in computing Schedule A profits for the tax year in which it is treated as received (but see Note (iii) below). [*ICTA 1988, s 34(1)(7A); FA 1998, Sch 5 para 15(5)*, and see Note (ii) below]. For this purpose, where under the terms of the lease the tenant is required to carry out work on the premises (other than normal repairs or maintenance) the value of the benefit accruing to the landlord is treated as a premium receivable at the commencement of the lease. Similarly, any sum payable by the tenant (*a*) for varying or waiving any of the terms of a lease (even if granted before 1963/64), or (*b*), under the terms of the lease, for surrendering it, or in lieu of the whole or part of the rent, is treated as if it were a premium (falling due (from 17 March 1998, received), under (*a*), at the date of the contract for variation or, under (*b*), when the sum is payable) on a lease for the period affected by the variation, etc. [*ICTA 1988, ss 34(2)–(5); FA 1995, Sch 6 paras 9, 40(1); FA 1998, s 40(3)–(5), Sch 5 para 15(3)*]. Note that these provisions refer to leases granted and not to leases assigned. See *Banning v Wright* under 68.28 below. Also see 3.13 ANTI-AVOIDANCE concerning *ICTA 1988, s 780*, and under 71.66 SCHEDULE D, CASES I AND II.

Example (i):

A person grants a 14-year lease of premises for a premium of £50,000. The amount chargeable on him in that year is

	£
Premium	50,000
Less $\frac{14-1}{50} \times 50{,}000$	13,000
Chargeable	£37,000

Note. Only complete years are taken into account. For allowance to payer, see 68.28 below.

But where a lease, etc., which gave rise to a liability as above (or would have done so but for relief as under Note (iii) below, or any exemption) is **subleased or sold,** any potential further liability on that latter event is compared with a fraction of the liability on the first transaction (proportionate to the period covered by the sublease, etc., as compared with that covered by the first lease, etc., with adjustment where the sub-lease relates to part only of the property) and only any *excess* is chargeable. [*ICTA 1988, s 37(1)–(3)(7); FA 1990, Sch 14 para 2; FA 1995, Sch 6 para 12; FA 1998, Sch 5 para 18, Sch 27 Pt III(4)*].

Example (ii):

If, after 4 years, the payer of the premium in (*i*) above grants a sub-lease of 10 years for which he receives a premium of £60,000, the amount chargeable on him is

	£
Premium	60,000
Less $\frac{10-1}{50} \times 60{,}000$	10,800
	49,200
Less 'appropriate fraction' of amount chargeable on superior landlord (see (*i*) above) $\frac{10}{14}$ths of £37,000	26,428
Chargeable	£22,772

For these purposes, the amount chargeable on the superior landlord is calculated ignoring any obligation on the tenant to carry out work on the premises in respect of which capital allowances have been or will be granted.

See also 68.28 below as regards relief where the 'appropriate fraction' of the amount chargeable on the superior landlord exceeds the amount of the premium chargeable on the intermediate landlord.

Anti-avoidance provisions. Where a lease granted at less than market value is assigned for a consideration exceeding any premium for which it was granted (or the consideration on any previous assignment) the excess, up to the limit of the amount of any premium, or additional premium, which the grantor forwent when granting the lease, is charged on the assignor to the same extent that an additional premium would have been charged on the grantor. The amount chargeable is treated as received when the consideration becomes payable and is taken into account in computing Schedule A profits for the tax year in which that time falls. Under the pre-Finance Act 1995 regime (see 68.14 above), the charge is under Schedule D, Case VI. [*ICTA 1988, s 35; FA 1995, Sch 6 para 10; FA 1998, Sch 5 para 16*].

Similarly, where an interest in land is sold on terms requiring it to be subsequently reconveyed (or leased, later than one month after the sale) to the vendor, or a person connected with him, and the price at which the interest is sold exceeds that at which it is to be reconveyed (or, in the case of a lease-back, the value of the reversionary interest plus any premium for the lease), the excess less $\frac{1}{50}$th for each full year (minus one) between the sale and the date (if at least two years after the sale) of the earliest possible reconveyance (or lease-back) is treated, at the time of sale (as defined), as a receipt of a Schedule A business carried on by the vendor, or, under the pre-Finance Act 1995 regime (see 68.14 above) is assessed on the vendor under Schedule D, Case VI. [*ICTA 1988, s 36; FA 1995, Sch 6 para 11; FA 1998, Sch 5 para 17*]. For the so-called 'Treasury Arrangement' to avoid a charge under *ICTA 1988, s 36* where there is a genuine commercial reason for the restricted sale, see Revenue Assessment Procedures Manual, AP 1560. See also 3.13 ANTI-AVOIDANCE.

Notes on above.

(i) For the above purposes the duration of a lease is governed by *ICTA 1988, s 38, Sch 30 paras 2–4*, and the tenant's rights of extension, or entitlement to a further lease, may be taken into account.

(ii) Where a premium, payment in lieu of rent or for surrender, is payable to a person other than the landlord, or where a payment for variation is due not to the landlord but to some person connected with him, then, under the pre-Finance Act 1995 regime (see 68.14 above), the recipient is not treated as receiving rent as above but is assessed on the whole receipt as profits or gains under Schedule D, Case VI. Under the new regime (see 68.2 above), the receipt is treated as a receipt of a Schedule A business (see 68.4 above) carried on by the recipient. [*ICTA 1988, s 34(6)(7); FA 1995, Sch 6 para 9; FA 1998, Sch 5 para 15(4)*].

(iii) Where any premium etc., is receivable by instalments the recipient may, at his option, pay the tax by instalments over a period not exceeding eight years (or the period during which the premium instalments are receivable if less). For 1997/98 and earlier years, he had to satisfy the Board that to pay otherwise than by instalments would cause him undue hardship. [*ICTA 1988, s 34(8); FA 1998, Sch 5 para 15(6)*].

(iv) Adjustment may be claimed under the pre-Finance Act 1995 regime to leave out of account any premium, etc., chargeable as above which is not received. (Terms as under 'Lost Rents', see 68.18 above.) [*ICTA 1988, s 41*]. (Under the new regime, bad debt relief would be available.)

(v) *No loss relief under* SCHEDULE D, CASE VI (74) may be claimed on a loss sustained on any transactions as above. [*ICTA 1988, s 392(4)*].

(vi) See Tolley's Capital Gains Tax for the treatment of chargeable gains arising from disposal by way of a lease. Note that the part of the premium chargeable to income tax is left out of the computation of chargeable gain.

Simon's Direct Tax Service. See **A4.201** *et seq.*.

68.28 **PREMIUMS ETC. ON LEASES OF UP TO 50 YEARS — ALLOWANCE TO PAYER** [*ICTA 1988, ss 37, 87; FA 1995, Sch 6 paras 12, 14; FA 1998, s 38, Sch 5 paras 18, 34*]

See generally Revenue Inspector's Manual, IM 930–939.

Where a premium paid on the grant of a lease etc. falls to be included in computing Schedule A profits of the recipient (see 68.27 above), or would have done so but for exemption, etc., the person for the time being entitled to that lease, etc., is treated as paying additional rent at a rate equivalent to the amount of that charge spread over the period to which it relates. See example below. In *Banning v Wright HL 1972, 48 TC 421* an agreed payment for waiving termination for sub-letting in breach of covenant was held to be a premium deductible from rents received. Adjustments arise in respect of sub-leases of the whole or part of the property.

The 'additional rent' so ascertained is allowable against property income, e.g. on a sub-letting [*ICTA 1988, s 37; FA 1995, Sch 6 para 12; FA 1998, s 38, Sch 5 para 18*] or against profits if the property is used in connection with a trade, profession or vocation. [*ICTA 1988, s 87; FA 1995, Sch 6 para 14; FA 1998, s 38, Sch 5 para 34*].

Example: For a premium paid as in example (i) in 68.27 above, the 'additional rent' is $\frac{1}{14}$th of £37,000 which is £2,643 per annum (allocated on a daily basis). If, however, a sub-lease is granted for a premium (as in example (ii) in 68.27 above) the 'additional rent' is restricted to the 'appropriate fraction' not used to reduce the charge on that later premium. In the example, the 'appropriate fraction' is entirely used and no 'additional rent' is available.

Anti-avoidance provision. Relief under *ICTA 1988, s37* or *s 87* will not be allowed in respect of any amount which has become chargeable under *ICTA 1988, s 36* (see 68.27 above). [*ICTA 1988, s 37(1)(a), s 87(1)(a); FA 1995, Sch 6 paras 12, 14; FA 1998, s 38, Sch 5 paras 18, 34*].

Simon's Direct Tax Service. See **A4.221** *et seq.*.

68.29 **REVERSE PREMIUMS**

Legislation (*FA 1999, s 54, Sch 6*) has been introduced to ensure that reverse premiums are taxable as revenue receipts. It applies in relation to any 'reverse premium' (as defined but broadly a payment made or benefit provided by a landlord to a prospective tenant as an inducement to enter into a lease) due and received on or after 9 March 1999. Other than in cases where the transaction is entered into for purposes of the recipient's trade etc. (or prospective trade etc.), a reverse premium is to be treated as a receipt of a Schedule A business, or (as the case may be) an overseas property business (see 73.4 SCHEDULE D, CASES IV AND V), carried on by the recipient. Subject to a specific anti-avoidance rule, it is understood that accountancy principles require the receipt to be brought into account by spreading over the period of the lease or, if shorter, to the first rent review. See 71.78 SCHEDULE D, CASES I AND II for the full provisions, and also the Revenue's views on the treatment of reverse premiums due before 9 March 1999.

68.30 **RENT FACTORING**

ICTA 1988, ss 43A–43G, introduced by *FA 2000, s 110*, apply from 21 March 2000 to companies participating in rent factoring schemes. They provide for amounts received for giving up the right to future rental income from UK land, whether by transferring the rights to receive rents or by granting a lease at a premium, to be charged to tax as income of a Schedule A business. They do not apply to genuine property investment or to capital allowance based finance leasing. For details of the legislation, see Tolley's Corporation Tax under Profit Computations.

68.31 **SCHEDULE A ALLOWANCE ON SALE OF TRADING PREMISES**

Where a trader occupied property before 6 April 1963 for the purpose of his trade, and subsequently sells that property, or otherwise ceases to occupy it, he will normally be entitled (unless he permanently ceases to carry on the trade) to a special deduction from his profits amounting to the net annual value deductions for the years 1963/64 and 1964/65 to which he would have been entitled but for the Schedule A charge in *FA 1963* less the amounts mentioned under *ICTA 1988, Sch 30 para 5*. 'Trade' includes a profession or vocation. See Revenue Pamphlet IR 27 para 105, now withdrawn. See Simon's Direct Tax Service B3.1342.

69 Schedule B—Woodlands

Simon's Direct Tax Service A5.

69.1 **Schedule B** applied to the 'occupation of woodlands in the UK managed on a commercial basis and with a view to the realisation of profit'. [*ICTA 1970, s 91*]. **It was abolished after 5 April 1988.** Where a company accounting period straddled that date, the Schedule B income was apportioned, and the part relating to the period commencing on 6 April 1988 was excluded from taxable income. [*FA 1988, s 65, Sch 6 para 2*]. Profits or gains from such occupation were not chargeable under SCHEDULE A (68).

See now 93 WOODLANDS.

70 Schedule C—Paying and Collecting Agents

[*ICTA 1988, ss 17, 44–52, Sch 3; FA 1996, s 79, Sch 7*]

Simon's Direct Tax Service A6.

70.1 For **1995/96 and earlier years** (and for company accounting periods ending before 1 April 1996), **Schedule C** applies to paying agents (bankers and others) who are entrusted with the payment in the UK of 'interest, public annuities, dividends or shares of annuities' out of the public revenue of any government and the revenue of any public authority or institution outside UK. [*ICTA 1988, s 17(1) para 1, s 45*]. 'Interest' in this context means interest on securities, and does not include interest on damages due from the Crown (*Esso Petroleum Co Ltd v Ministry of Defence Ch D 1989, 62 TC 253*). (Since the decision in the *Esso* case, payments of interest other than on securities by Government departments have been made without deduction of tax, but the Treasury announced that no steps would be taken to seek out, nor make further payments to, the recipients of earlier payments of such interest (see Revenue Press Release 2 February 1994).) The agents must deduct tax and pay the net amount to the persons entitled to the interest etc. Tax is to be deducted at the basic rate, except that the lower rate applies in the case of a foreign dividend which is neither interest nor any other annual payment made otherwise than by way of dividend. For payments after 5 April 1996 and before 29 April 1996, deduction at the lower rate applies in all cases. Tax so accounted for is applied in the discharge of the tax liability of the person entitled to the related dividends or coupon proceeds. [*ICTA 1988, s 44, Sch 3; FA 1993, Sch 6 para 17; FA 1996, Sch 6 para 25*]. This does not apply to dividends payable out of any non-UK public revenue in respect of securities held in a 'recognised clearing system' (see 23.3(ii) DEDUCTION OF TAX AT SOURCE). [*ICTA 1988, s 48(4)*]. The foregoing procedure also applies to amounts payable in Eire on UK government securities in the register of the Bank of Ireland [*ICTA 1988, s 17(1) para 2*] and to certain overseas coupons, including those held in a recognised clearing system. [*ICTA 1988, s 17(1) paras 3, 4; FA 1988, s 76(1)(2)*]. The paying agent must account for the tax deducted within 14 days after the end of the month in which the dividend etc. was paid, and deliver a return of payments within 30 days of the end of each calendar quarter. The Board may raise assessments where they consider tax which should have been accounted for has not been paid, and the tax is then due within 14 days after the date of issue of the notice of assessment. Interest runs on tax, whether assessed or not, from 14 days after the end of the month in which the dividend etc. was paid. [*ICTA 1988, Sch 3 Pt III; F(No 2)A 1992, Sch 11 para 2; SI 1992 Nos 2073, 2075*].

Exemptions apply regarding (*a*) certain UK government stocks etc. (see under 33 GOVERNMENT STOCKS), (*b*) non-residents receiving payments in UK from foreign state securities [*ICTA 1988, s 48*], (*c*) non-resident central banks as specified [*ICTA 1988, s 516*], and (*d*) charities. [*ICTA 1988, Sch 3 para 4*]. See also under 43 INTEREST PAYABLE.

Schedule C is abolished for 1996/97 and subsequent years of assessment and for company accounting periods ending after 31 March 1996, the charge being transferred to Schedule D, Case III, IV or V as appropriate. [*ICTA 1988, s 18(3B)–(3E); FA 1996, s 79, Sch 7, Sch 14 para 5*]. The obligations under Schedule C were, however, in effect preserved until 29 April 1996 by *FA 1996, Sch 7 paras 33–35* (and see above as regards deductions during this period). For the provisions for paying and collecting agents effective from that date until 31 March 2001, see *ICTA 1988, ss 118A–118K* and regulations thereunder (see *SI 1996 No 1780*, *SI 1997 No 2705*, *SI 1999 No 823*). For an article explaining the scope of these rules, see Revenue Tax Bulletin August 1996 p 329. The paying and collecting arrangements are abolished from 1 April 2001. [*FA 2000, s 111(1)(6)*]. See now 23.3(ii), 23.12 DEDUCTION OF TAX AT SOURCE.

71 Schedule D, Cases I and II—Profits of Trades, Professions etc.

Cross-references. See subjects dealt with separately under 3 ANTI-AVOIDANCE; 10 CAPITAL ALLOWANCES; 12 CASH BASIS; 25 DOUBLE TAX RELIEF; 34 HERD BASIS; 43 INTEREST PAYABLE; 44 INTEREST RECEIVABLE; 46 LOSSES; 51 NON-RESIDENTS AND OTHER OVERSEAS MATTERS; 53 PARTNERSHIPS; 56 PAYMENT OF TAX; 61 PERSONAL SERVICE COMPANIES ETC.; 62 POST-CESSATION ETC. RECEIPTS AND EXPENDITURE; 78 SELF-ASSESSMENT and 93 WOODLANDS.

For 'Whether a Trade Carried On', see 71.29 to 71.39 below and for 'Assessable Profits, Allowable Deductions Etc.' see 71.40 to 71.95 below. There is a sub-index preceding each of these divisions.

The headings in this chapter are as follows.

71.1 Charge to tax
71.2 Companies
71.3 Individuals, partnerships, etc. — bases of assessment — pre-Finance Act 1994
71.4 — opening years
71.5 — example
71.6 — intermediate years
71.7 — change of accounting date
71.8 — example
71.9 — closing years
71.10 — example
71.11 Individuals, partnerships etc. — bases of assessment — post-Finance Act 1994
71.12 — opening years
71.13 — example
71.14 — intermediate years
71.15 — change of accounting date
71.16 — examples
71.17 — closing year
71.18 — example
71.19 — overlap relief
71.20 — transitional relief for businesses commenced before 6 April 1994 — basis period for 1996/97
71.21 — examples
71.22 — transitional relief for businesses commenced before 6 April 1994 — overlap profit for 1997/98
71.23 — example
71.24 — transitional rules for businesses commenced before 6 April 1994 — cessation in 1996/97 to 1998/99
71.25 Whether or not there has been a commencement or discontinuance
71.26 — case law
71.27 — change of residence
71.28 Accounts
71.29 to 71.39 Whether a trade carried on (see separate index before 71.29)
71.40 to 71.95 Assessable profits, allowable deductions etc. (see separate index before 71.40)
71.96 General example

71.1 **CHARGE TO TAX**

Tax is charged under **Schedule D, Case I and II** on the profits or gains of trades (Case I) and professions or vocations (Case II) carried on wholly or partly in the UK by UK residents or exercised within the UK by non-residents. [*ICTA 1988, s 18*]. Businesses carried on wholly abroad are 'possessions' within SCHEDULE D, CASES IV AND V (73) but a business controlled from the UK is within Cases I and II even though the day-to-day trading activities are carried on wholly abroad. For this see 51.12 NON-RESIDENTS AND OTHER OVERSEAS MATTERS and for trades exercised within the UK by non-residents see 51.4 NON-RESIDENTS AND OTHER OVERSEAS MATTERS.

Trade 'includes every trade, manufacture, adventure or concern in the nature of trade' [*ICTA 1988, s 832(1)*]. For what is a trade, see generally 71.29–71.39 below and in particular, in relation to isolated or speculative transactions, 71.35 below. There is no statutory definition of 'profession or vocation'. There are certain provisions applicable only to trades and others applicable only to professions or vocations but the distinction between the two is of limited practical importance. There is no reported case in which it was necessary to decide between the two for income tax purposes, but in a Hong Kong case it was held that stockbrokers were carrying on a trade, not a profession or business (*Kowloon Stock Exchange Ltd v Commr of Inland Revenue PC, [1984] STC 602*). There are a number of cases turning on whether a business was an exempt profession as specially defined for the purposes of excess profits duty and similar taxes. For these see Tolley's Tax Cases. For professions or vocations (e.g. actor) which necessarily involve carrying out numerous engagements see 71.43 below.

In the rest of this section 'trade' includes 'profession or vocation' unless the context indicates otherwise and similarly Case I includes Case II.

For whether the liability is under Schedule D or Schedule E see 75.24 SCHEDULE E. See also 71.31 below for special treatment of certain divers and diving supervisors.

The Schedules are mutually exclusive, see 5.2 ASSESSMENTS. The general principle is that rents and other income derived from the exploitation of proprietary interests in land are within Schedule A and not income derived from a trade. The leading case is *Salisbury House Estate Ltd v Fry HL 1930, 15 TC 266*. For illustrations see *Sywell Aerodrome Ltd v Croft CA 1941, 24 TC 126; Webb v Conelee Properties Ltd Ch D 1982, 56 TC 149*. However, profits arising out of land are charged under Case I in the case of mines, quarries, gravel pits, sand pits, brickfields, ironworks, gas works, canals, railways, rights of markets, fairs and tolls and like concerns. [*ICTA 1988, s 55*]. Farming and market gardening within the UK is treated as trading. [*ICTA 1988, s 53(1)*]. All the farming carried on by a particular person, partnership or body of persons is treated as one trade [*ICTA 1988, s 53(2)*] (*Bispham v Eardiston Farming Co Ch D 1962, 40 TC 322*) but this does not apply to farming outside the UK (*Sargent v Eayrs Ch D 1972, 48 TC 573*). See 93 WOODLANDS for the exemption of woodlands managed on a commercial basis.

71.2 COMPANIES

Companies (and other bodies corporate, unincorporated associations and authorised unit trusts — but not partnerships, local authorities or local authority associations [*ICTA 1988, s 832(1)(2)*]) are assessable to corporation tax on their trading income as computed under the law and practice applying to Schedule D, Case I or II. [*ICTA 1988, s 9*]. The provisions below, from 71.29 onwards (relating to Assessable Profits, Allowable Deductions and other Schedule D, Case I and II matters) apply generally to companies etc. (but by reference to actual income arising in the accounting period concerned as corporation tax is assessable on an actual basis [*ICTA 1988, s 12(1)*]). Items 71.3 to 71.9 below referring to the preceding year basis and the opening and closing year provisions do not apply to companies etc.. See 71.25 below for 'notional' commencements or cessations by companies. See Tolley's Corporation Tax.

71.3 INDIVIDUALS, PARTNERSHIPS ETC. — BASES OF ASSESSMENT — PRE-FINANCE ACT 1994

The basis period rules set out in detail in 71.4 to 71.9 below (the **preceding year basis of assessment**) apply **for 1995/96 and earlier years as regards businesses commenced before 6 April 1994. They are of no application to businesses commenced after 5 April 1994.** See 71.11 to 71.19 below for new rules introduced by *Finance Act 1994*.

In summary the basis periods are generally as follows.

Opening years (see 71.4 below)

Year 1	Actual	
Year 2	First 12 months	Taxpayer may elect for both to be based on actual profits (but not either alone).
Year 3	Preceding year basis	

Intermediate years (see 71.6 below)
Preceding year basis

Closing years (see 71.9 below)

Last year but 2	Preceding year basis but actual profits if actual profits in aggregate exceed profits on preceding year basis.
Last year but 1	
Last year	Actual profits

Preceding year basis normally means that the assessment is based on the profits shown by the annual accounts ended within the preceding tax year.

Power is given to apportion profits or losses, on a time basis in proportion to the number of days (before 1 May 1995, months, or fractions of months) in the respective periods, if necessary (but only where necessary, see *Marshall Hus & Partners Ltd v Bolton Ch D 1980, 55 TC 539*) for purpose of assessments under Cases I and II. [*ICTA 1988, s 72; FA 1995, s 121*].

Simon's Direct Tax Service. See **E1.204–E1.212**.

71.4 **Opening years.** On the **commencement of a business** carried on by an individual or partnership (but not companies — see 71.2 above) the following rules apply. [*ICTA 1988, s 61*]. For what is a commencement, etc. see 71.25 below. See also 53.6 PARTNERSHIPS as regards special basis of assessment on certain partnership changes.

First tax year. The assessment will be on the profits (as adjusted for tax purposes) from the start to the following 5 April with any necessary apportionment if a trading account overlaps that date (see *Manson v Perrys (Ealing) Ltd KB 1931, 16 TC 60*).

Second tax year. The assessment will be on the profits of the first twelve months of the business with any necessary apportionment if a trading account overlaps the end of that period. (Thus, if the first account was for ten months to 31 May, followed by an account for twelve months, the assessment will be on the profits of the ten months, plus $\frac{2}{12}$ths of the following year's profits.)

Third tax year. If the only account ending in the second tax year is for twelve months commencing either at the date the business started or at the end of the basis period for that year, the assessment will be on the profits of that account. Failing that, the basis period will be fixed by the Commissioners under *ICTA 1988, s 60(4)*. It will normally be taken as the twelve months to the date in the second year which will be the future accounting date or, if this is not possible, the first twelve months of trading.

Fourth tax year. If the only account ending in the third tax year is for twelve months commencing at the end of the basis period for that year, the assessment will be on the profits of that account. Failing that, the basis period will be fixed by the Commissioners under *ICTA 1988, s 60(4)*. It will normally be taken as the twelve months to the date in the third year which will be the future accounting date.

Where a loss enters into the apportionments for the opening years, see 46.12(*e*) LOSSES.

Relief in second and third year of assessment.

(*a*) Taxpayer may apply in writing within seven years of end of second year of assessment for assessments for both second and third years of assessment (but not for one year only) to be based on the actual profits of each of those years (apportioned to 5 April on a time basis). [*ICTA 1988, s 62(2)*].

(*b*) He may give notice in writing revoking such previous notice, within six years of the end of third year of assessment. (His assessments for both years will then revert to the normal basis as explained above.) [*ICTA 1988, s 62(3)*].

(*c*) Where, during the second and third years of assessment, there is a *change of partners*, or a sole trader enters into partnership, all notices given as above (after a change in respect of which notice has been given under *ICTA 1988, s 113(2)*, see 53.6 PARTNERSHIPS), must (where the notice is given within twelve months after the end of the second year) be signed by all persons engaged in the business at any time from the beginning of the second year to the date of signing; and all notices given after the end of the third year by all such persons so engaged at any time during the second and third years. (Personal representatives in case of deceased persons.) [*ICTA 1988, s 62(6)–(8)*]. For note re Double Succession see 53.9 PARTNERSHIPS.

71.5 *Example*

Roy commenced business on 1 January 1994. His Schedule D, Case I adjusted profits (before capital allowances) are

	£
16 months to 30.4.95	16,000
Year to 30.4.96	36,000
Year to 30.4.97	30,000

Capital allowances for the year to 30.4.97 are £3,000.

His first five years' assessments will be either of (i) or (ii) below

(i) No election under section 62(2) for actual basis in second and third year

			£	£
	Basis period			
1993/94	1.1.94 – 5.4.94	£16,000 × $\frac{3}{16}$		3,000
1994/95	1.1.94 – 31.12.94	£16,000 × $\frac{12}{16}$		12,000
1995/96	1.1.94 – 31.12.94	£16,000 × $\frac{12}{16}$		12,000
	Transitional period			
1996/97	1.1.95 – 30.4.96 (16 months):			
	1.1.95 – 30.4.95	£16,000 × $\frac{4}{16}$	4,000	
	1.5.95 – 30.4.96		36,000	
			£40,000	
	£40,000 × $\frac{12}{16}$			30,000
	Basis period			
1997/98	Y/e 30.4.97 (net of capital allowances)			27,000*
Total assessments for first five years**				£84,000

* Transitional overlap relief accrued (see 71.22 below):
(1.5.96 – 5.4.97) £30,000 × $\frac{11}{12}$ £27,500

** Subject to capital allowances for 1993/94 to 1996/97 inclusive

(ii) With election under section 62(2) for actual basis in second and third year

			£	£
	Basis period			
1993/94	1.1.94 – 5.4.94	£16,000 × $\frac{3}{16}$		3,000
1994/95	6.4.94 – 5.4.95	£16,000 × $\frac{12}{16}$		12,000
1995/96	6.4.95 – 5.4.96:			
	6.4.95 – 30.4.95	£16,000 × $\frac{1}{16}$	1,000	
	1.5.95 – 5.4.96	£36,000 × $\frac{11}{12}$	33,000	
				34,000
	Transitional period			
1996/97	6.4.96 – 5.4.97:			
	6.4.96 – 30.4.96	£36,000 × $\frac{1}{12}$	3,000	
	1.5.96 – 5.4.97	£30,000 × $\frac{11}{12}$	27,500	
				30,500
	Basis period			
1997/98	Y/e 30.4.97 (net of capital allowances)			27,000*
Total assessments for first five years**				£106,500

* Transitional overlap relief accrued (see 71.22 below):
(1.5.96 – 5.4.97) £30,000 × $\frac{11}{12}$ — £27,500

** Subject to capital allowances for 1993/94 to 1996/97 inclusive

Notes

(*a*) Roy would not make the election under *ICTA 1988, s 62(2)* (actual basis for second and third years) as taxable profits would thereby be greater. Note that where a business commenced in 1993/94, such an election affects not only 1994/95 and 1995/96 but also 1996/97 (the transitional year on the changeover to the current year basis of assessment — see 71.20 below and also note (*b*) below): therefore, one needs to compare the position for all three of those years.

(*b*) Where 1995/96 is taxed on an actual basis, the transitional year 1996/97 is also taxed on an actual basis (with no averaging of profits) (see 71.20 below).

71.6 **Intermediate years** (i.e. tax years for which the special rules for opening years, as in 71.4 above, or for closing years, as in 71.9 below, do not apply).

Assessment on individuals and partnerships (but not companies etc., see 71.2 above) is on the preceding year basis, i.e. the profits (as adjusted for tax purposes) of the trading account ending in the preceding tax year if that account (i) is the only one ending in that year and (ii) is for twelve months commencing from the end of the basis period for that year. [*ICTA 1988, s 60(1)–(3)*]. If there is no account satisfying these requirements see 71.7 below.

71.7 **Change of accounting date.** Where the accounts made up do not satisfy the requirements of the preceding year basis (see 71.6 above), the following applies.

(i) The Commissioners of Inland Revenue will decide 'what period of twelve months ending on a date within the year preceding the year of assessment shall be deemed to be the year the profits or gains of which are to be taken to be' the profits of that preceding year. [*ICTA 1988, s 60(4)*].

(ii) They may also adjust the preceding year's assessment to correspond with any altered accounting date, and may make any necessary assessment or repayment, subject to a right of appeal to the General or Special Commissioners who may grant just relief and from them to the Courts. [*ICTA 1988, s 60(5)–(7)*].

There is no right of appeal against (i). See Revenue Pamphlet IR 26 as to the Revenue practice with examples. See also *CIR v Helical Bar Ltd HL 1972, 48 TC 221.*

In determining a basis period for 1995/96 (or an earlier year), these rules are applied as if the transitional rules for 1996/97 basis periods (see 71.20 below) did not apply, although any figure or basis period for 1996/97 is subsequently ignored. The transitional basis period for 1996/97 then commences immediately after the basis period determined for 1995/96. (Revenue Tax Bulletin August 1995 p 243, December 1995 p 271). This will normally apply only where accounts are prepared for a long period to a new accounting date falling within 1995/96, with no accounting date falling within 1994/95.

Simon's Direct Tax Service. See **E1.218**.

71.8 *Example*

Geoff, who has been trading for some years, has the following Schedule D, Case I adjusted profits

	£
Year to 30.9.92	24,000
Year to 30.9.93	15,000
15 months to 31.12.94	32,000

The assessable profit for 1995/96 is determined under *section 60(4)* and that for 1994/95 is considered for revision under *section 60(5)*.

The assessments are calculated as follows.

1995/96

Section 60(4) determination

The 1995/96 assessment is based on 12 months to 31.12.94

i.e. $\frac{12}{15}$ of £32,000	£25,600

1994/95

The accounting periods to be considered are those entering in whole or in part in to the *section 60(4)* basis period(s) or the 'corresponding period' under *section 60(5)*; viz

		Year of assessment
12 months to 30.9.93	15,000	1994/95
15 months to 31.12.94	32,000	1995/96
27 months	£47,000	24 months

Section 60(5) consideration

The following tests are undertaken to see if the 1994/95 assessment should be amended.

(i) Aggregate profit			
$\frac{24}{27} \times 47{,}000$			£41,777
(ii) Sum of assessments for relevant years without revision for 1994/95			
1994/95		15,000	
1995/96		25,600	
			£40,600
(iii) Sum of assessments for relevant years with revision for 1994/95			
1994/95 (revised to year to 31.12.93)			
$\frac{9}{12} \times 15{,}000$	11,250		
$\frac{3}{15} \times 32{,}000$	6,400	17,650	
1995/96		25,600	
Sum of assessments			£43,250

As the figure at (i) £41,777 is intermediate between (ii) £40,600 and (iii) £43,250 the revised assessment is

Figure at (i)	41,777	
Assessed 1995/96	25,600	
Revised assessment 1994/95		£16,177

Notes

(*a*) If the difference between the figures at (i) and (ii) above was less than 10% of the average of the 1995/96 assessment and the unrevised 1994/95 assessment (i.e. £25,600 and £15,000) and, in addition, the difference was under £1,000, the 1994/95 assessment would not have been amended i.e. it would remain at £15,000.

(*b*) If the figure at (i) was not intermediate between the figures at (ii) and (iii) above, the Inland Revenue would decide what revised assessments, if any, were necessary. This would also be the case if any year showed a loss.

(*c*) In this example, assuming that Geoff continues to prepare accounts to 31 December, the transitional basis period on the changeover to the current year basis of assessment (see 71.20 below) will be the two years to 31 December 1996. For changes of accounting date within the transitional period, see 71.21 below.

71.9 **Closing years.** If there is a **discontinuance of a business** carried on by an individual or partnership (but not companies, see 71.2 above) the following rules apply. [*ICTA 1988, ss 63, 113(1); FA 1988, Sch 3 para 3*]. For what is a discontinuance, etc. see 71.25 below.

(i) **Last year.** Assessment to be adjusted to actual profits from 6 April to date of discontinuance.

(ii) **Years preceding the last year.** If the aggregate of actual profits for the two years ending 5 April preceding the tax year in which the discontinuance occurs, arrived at by apportionment of the profits of the accounts as adjusted for tax purposes (*Manson v Wesley HL 1932, 16 TC 654*), exceeds the aggregate assessments for those years, assessments and adjustments may be made by Inland Revenue to bring into tax that excess, except where the trade is discontinued in consequence of the nationalisation of its trading assets (see *ICTA 1988, s 63(4)* and *CIR v Daniel Beattie CS 1955, 36 TC 379*). The inspector has no general discretion as to whether or not to make such assessments (*Baylis v Roberts Ch D 1989, 62 TC 384*). (*N.B.* No similar option to taxpayer if the assessments exceed the profits.) In the case of a deceased person any additional tax will be a debt payable out of his estate.

See *Townsend v Electrical Yarns KB 1952, 33 TC 166*, re effect of balancing charges under *CAA 1968, ss 33, 41* and cf. *CIR v Lloyds Bank (Scott's Exors) Ch D 1963, 41 TC 294.*

See 46.15 LOSSES for terminal losses and 46.12(*c*) LOSSES for the carry forward of certain losses where a private business is converted into a company.

Death, retirement, etc.. By concession, the above rules are not applied, unless claimed, to widow(er) continuing deceased spouse's business, but in any event no unrelieved losses, or unexhausted capital allowances applicable to the deceased can be carried forward. Capital allowances are, however, calculated as if assets had passed from the trader to the surviving spouse at open market value (the figure adopted for probate purposes being accepted for this purpose). (Revenue Capital Allowances Manual, CA 512). The concession, suitably adapted, is also extended to the survivor continuing a business previously carried on by husband and wife in partnership where no continuation election is made under *ICTA 1988, s 113(2)* (see 53.6 PARTNERSHIPS), and in such a case the losses and capital allowances which may be carried forward are restricted to the share appropriate to the surviving partner. (Revenue Pamphlet IR 1, A7). The concession is withdrawn following the introduction of the current year basis of assessment (see 71.11 *et seq.* below), from 6 April 1995 in respect of businesses commenced after 5 April 1994, and from a date to be announced (not earlier than 6 April 1997) for businesses already in existence on that date. (Revenue Press Release 4 April 1995). See also 72.4(*d*) SCHEDULE D, CASE III.

71.10 *Example*

Chris ceased business on 30 June 1996. His adjusted Schedule D, Case I profits were

			£	
Year to 30.4.93			24,000	
30.4.94			48,000	
30.4.95			96,000	
30.4.96			36,000	
2 months to 30.6.96			5,000	
His assessments will be				
	Basis periods			
1996/97	6.4.96 – 30.4.96	$\frac{1}{12}$ × 36,000	3,000	
	1.5.96 – 30.6.96		5,000	
				£8,000
Then, either				
1995/96	Year to 30.4.94			48,000
1994/95	Year to 30.4.93			24,000
				£72,000

Or				
1995/96	6.4.95 – 30.4.95	$\frac{1}{12}$ × 96,000	8,000	
	1.5.95 – 5.4.96	$\frac{11}{12}$ × 36,000	33,000	
				41,000
1994/95	6.4.94 – 30.4.94	$\frac{1}{12}$ × 48,000	4,000	
	1.5.94 – 5.4.95	$\frac{11}{12}$ × 96,000	88,000	
				92,000
				£133,000

Note

(*a*) The Inland Revenue would assess Chris on profits of £41,000 for 1995/96 and on £92,000 for 1994/95 as these figures are greater in total than the profits originally assessed for these years.

71.11 INDIVIDUALS, PARTNERSHIPS ETC. — BASES OF ASSESSMENT — POST-FINANCE ACT 1994

The basis period rules set out in detail in 71.11 to 71.19 below (the **current year basis of assessment**) apply **for 1996/97 and subsequent years as regards businesses commenced before 6 April 1994** (see 71.20 to 71.24 below for transitional provisions on the changeover from the preceding year basis of assessment). **They apply for 1994/95 and subsequent years as regards businesses commenced after 5 April 1994.** [*FA 1994, s 218(1)(2)(5)*]. See 53.3 PARTNERSHIPS as regards partnerships ceasing to be chargeable to income tax as a separate entity; the current year basis of assessment has no specific application to a partnership itself (although it applies as regards individual partners), except for 1996/97 as regards partnership businesses commenced before 6 April 1994.

A detailed Revenue booklet SAT 1(1995) 'The new current year basis of assessment — A guide for Inland Revenue officers and tax practitioners' should have been sent by tax offices to all tax practices with which they deal in August/September 1995. Further copies are available (price £7.50) from Inland Revenue Library, New Wing, Somerset House, Strand, London WC2R 1LB. Also, a series of explanatory articles on self-assessment have appeared in the Revenue Tax Bulletin from August 1993 onwards, many of which illustrate different aspects of the current year basis.

In summary the basis periods are generally as follows (subject to any change of accounting date — see 71.15 below).

Opening years (see 71.12 below)

Year 1 Actual

Year 2 12 months ending with the accounting date in the year or, if the period from commencement to the accounting date in the year is less than 12 months, the first 12 months or, if there is no accounting date in the first or second year, actual

Year 3 Normally current year basis (see 71.12 below for exception)

See 71.19 below for relief (overlap relief) where the above rules have the effect of the same profits being taxed in each of two successive years of assessment.

Intermediate years (see 71.14 below)

Current year basis.

Closing year (see 71.17 below)

Period from the end of the basis period in the penultimate year to the date of cessation in the year (which may exceed 12 months).

General. Current year basis normally means that the assessment is based on the profits shown by the annual accounts ended within the current tax year.

Power to apportion profits or losses applies as in 71.3 above. In practice, the Revenue will accept any reasonable time-based apportionment that is applied consistently. If the taxpayer wishes, they will treat an accounting date of 31 March as being equivalent to one of 5 April. (Revenue booklet SAT 1(1995), paras 1.17, 1.98, 1.99).

Simon's Direct Tax Service. See **E1.203, E1.205–E1.212**.

71.12 **Opening years.** On the **commencement of a business** by an individual (which includes his commencing to carry on an existing business in partnership), the following rules apply. For what is a commencement, etc. see 71.25 below.

First tax year. The assessment will be on the profits (as adjusted for tax purposes) from the commencement date to the following 5 April. [*ICTA 1988, s 61(1); FA 1994, s 201*].

Second tax year. If there is an accounting date (i.e. a date to which accounts are made up) in the year, the assessment is based on the twelve months to that date. If the period from commencement to the accounting date in the second year is less than twelve months, the assessment is based on the profits for the first twelve months of the business. If there is no accounting date in the first or second year, the second year's assessment will be on the actual profits for the year, i.e. 6 April to 5 April. Where there is more than one accounting date in the year, reference to the accounting date in the year is to the latest of such dates (see also the rules for changes of accounting date in 71.15 below). [*ICTA 1988, s 60(1(2)(3)(a)(5), s 61(2)(a); FA 1994, ss 200, 201*].

Third tax year. If the year is the first year in which there is an accounting date falling not less than twelve months after the date of commencement, the assessment is based on the twelve months ending with the accounting date. Otherwise, the rule for intermediate years (see 71.14 below) apply as regards the third year. [*ICTA 1988, s 60(1)–(3); FA 1994, s 200*].

See 71.19 below for relief (overlap relief) where the above rules have the effect of the same profits being taxed in each of two successive years of assessment.

71.13 *Example*

Simon commences trade on 1 September 1998 and prepares accounts to 30 April, starting with an eight-month period of account to 30 April 1999. His profits (as adjusted for tax purposes and *after* capital allowances) for the first three accounting periods are as follows.

	£
Eight months to 30 April 1999	24,000
Year to 30 April 2000	39,000
Year to 30 April 2001	40,000

His taxable profits for the first four tax years are as follows.

	Basis period		£	£
1998/99	1.9.98 – 5.4.99	£24,000 × $\frac{7}{8}$		21,000
1999/2000	1.9.98 – 31.8.99:			
	1.9.98 – 30.4.99		24,000	
	1.5.99 – 31.8.99	£39,000 × $\frac{4}{12}$	13,000	
				37,000
2000/01	Y/e 30.4.00			39,000
2001/02	Y/e 30.4.01			40,000

Overlap relief accrued:	
1.9.98 – 5.4.99 — 7 months	21,000
1.5.99 – 31.8.99 — 4 months	13,000
Total overlap relief accrued (see 71.19 below)	£34,000

71.14 **Intermediate years** (i.e. tax years for which the special rules for Opening Years, as in 71.12 above, or for the Closing Year, see 71.17 below, do not apply).

Assessment on individuals (including those trading in partnership) is on the current year basis, i.e. the profits (as adjusted for tax purposes) of the trading account ending in the current tax year (subject to changes of accounting date, see 71.15 below). [*ICTA 1988, s 60(1)(2)(3)(b); FA 1994, s 200*].

71.15 **Change of accounting date.** Where a change (an accounting change) from one accounting date (the old date) to another (the new date) is made in a year of assessment, the conditions below must be satisfied if the change of accounting date is to result in a change of basis period. (This does not apply if the year is the second or third year of assessment of the business.) An accounting change is made in a year of assessment if accounts are not made up to the old date in that year or are made up to the new date in that year. The conditions, *all of which must be satisfied*, are as follows.

(1) The first accounting period (i.e. period for which accounts are made up) ending with the new date does not exceed 18 months.

(2) Notice of the change is given to an officer of the Board in a personal (or, where appropriate, a partnership) tax return on or before the day on which that return is required to be delivered (see 78.5, 78.8 SELF-ASSESSMENT).

(3) Either

(i) no accounting change resulting in a change of basis period has been made in any of the previous five years of assessment;

or

(ii) the notice in (2) above sets out the reasons for the change and the Revenue do not, within 60 days of receiving the notice, give notice to the trader that they are not satisfied that the change is made for *bona fide* commercial reasons (which does not include the obtaining of a tax advantage). (An appeal may be made against such a Revenue notice, within 30 days beginning with the date of issue, and the Commissioners may either confirm the notice or set it aside.)

Where all the conditions are satisfied, or the accounting change is made in the second or third tax year of the business, the basis period for the year of assessment is as follows.

(*a*) If the year is the second year of assessment of the business, the basis period is the twelve months ending with the new date in the year (unless the period from commencement of the business to the new date in the second year is less than twelve months, in which case the basis period is the first twelve months of the business).

(*b*) If the 'relevant period' is a period of less than twelve months, the basis period is the twelve months ending with the new date in the year.

(*c*) If the 'relevant period' is a period of more than twelve months, the basis period consists of the relevant period.

The '*relevant period*' is the period beginning immediately after the end of the basis period for the preceding year and ending with the new date in the year.

It will be seen that a basis period can be of more than twelve months' duration but cannot be less than twelve months. If not all of the above conditions are satisfied (and the year is not the second or third tax year of the business), the basis period for the year is the twelve months beginning immediately after the end of the basis period for the preceding year. However, the accounting change is then treated as made in the following year of assessment and can thus result in a change of basis period for that following year if all the above conditions are satisfied as regards that year. An accounting change can continue to be 'carried forward' in this way until such time, if any, as a change of basis period results or the old accounting date is reverted to.

[*ICTA 1988, s 60(3)(b), s 61(2)(b), s 62, s 62A; FA 1994, ss 200–203; FA 1996, s 135, Sch 21 para 1*].

See 71.19 below for relief (overlap relief) where the above rules in (*a*) or (*b*) above have the effect of the same profits being taxed in each of two successive years of assessment, and for the use of overlap relief brought forward in computing profits in a situation within (*c*) above.

For partnership trades, notice in (2) above and an appeal within (3)(ii) above may be given or brought by such one of the partners as may be nominated by them for the purpose (any resulting change of basis period affecting the deemed trades of individual partners — see 53.3 PARTNERSHIPS). [*ICTA 1988, s 111(6); FA 1994, s 215(1); FA 1995, s 117*].

Simon's Direct Tax Service. See E1.218.

71.16 *Examples*

(i) Change to a date earlier in the tax year

Miranda commenced trade on 1 September 1996, preparing accounts to 31 August. In 1999, she changes her accounting date to 31 May, preparing accounts for the nine months to 31 May 1999. The conditions of *ICTA 1988, s 62A* are satisfied in relation to the change. Her profits (as adjusted for tax purposes and *after* capital allowances) are as follows.

	£
Year ended 31 August 1997	18,000
Year ended 31 August 1998	21,500
Nine months to 31 May 1999	17,000
Year ended 31 May 2000	23,000

Taxable profits for the first five tax years are as follows.

	Basis period		£	£
1996/97	1.9.96 – 5.4.97	£18,000 × $\frac{7}{12}$		10,500
1997/98	Y/e 31.8.97			18,000
1998/99	Y/e 31.8.98			21,500
1999/2000	1.6.98 – 31.5.99:			
	1.6.98 – 31.8.98	£21,500 × $\frac{3}{12}$	5,375	
	1.9.98 – 31.5.99		17,000	
				22,375
2000/01	Y/e 31.5.00			23,000

Overlap relief accrued (see 71.19 below)

1.9.96 – 5.4.97 — 7 months	10,500
1.6.98 – 31.8.98 — 3 months	5,375
Total overlap relief accrued	£15,875

Note

(*a*) In this example, the 'relevant period' is that from 1 September 1998 (the day following the end of the basis period for 1998/99) to 31 May 1999 (the new accounting date in the year 1999/2000 — the year of change). As the relevant period is less than 12 months, the basis period for 1999/2000 is the 12 months ending on the new accounting date.

(ii) Change to a date later in the tax year

Dennis starts a business on 1 July 1996, preparing accounts to 30 June. In 1999, he changes his accounting date to 31 December, preparing accounts for the six months to 31 December 1999. The conditions of *ICTA 1988, s 62A* are satisfied in relation to the change. His profits (as adjusted for tax purposes and after capital allowances) are as follows.

	£
Year ended 30 June 1997	18,000
Year ended 30 June 1998	21,500
Year ended 30 June 1999	23,000
Six months to 31 December 1999	12,000
Year ended 31 December 2000	27,000

Taxable profits for the first five years are as follows.

	Basis period		£	£
1996/97	1.7.96 – 5.4.97	£18,000 × $\frac{9}{12}$		13,500
1997/98	Y/e 30.6.97			18,000
1998/99	Y/e 30.6.98			21,500
1999/2000	1.7.98 – 31.12.99:			
	1.7.98 – 30.6.99		23,000	
	1.7.99 – 31.12.99		12,000	
			35,000	
	Deduct Overlap relief		9,000	
				26,000
2000/01	Y/e 31.12.00			27,000

Overlap relief accrued:

1.7.96 – 5.4.97 — 9 months	13,500
Less utilised in 1999/2000	9,000
Carried forward	£4,500

Utilisation of overlap relief in 1999/2000

Apply the formula: $A \times \frac{B - C}{D}$ (see 71.19 below)

where

A = aggregate overlap relief accrued (£13,500);

B = length of basis period for 1999/2000 (18 months);

C = 12 months; and

D = the length of the overlap period(s) by reference to which the aggregate overlap profits accrued (9 months).

Thus, the deduction to be given in computing profits for 1999/2000 is

$$£13{,}500 \times \frac{18 - 12}{9} = £9{,}000$$

Notes

(*a*) In this example, the 'relevant period' is that from 1 July 1998 (the day following the end of the basis period for 1998/99) to 31 December 1999 (the new accounting date in the year 1999/2000 — the year of change). As the relevant period is more than 12 months, the basis period for 1999/2000 is equal to the relevant period. Note that a basis period of 18 months results in this case, even though accounts were prepared for a period of only 6 months to the new date.

(*b*) The overlap relief accrued (by reference to an overlap period of 9 months) is given on cessation or, as in this example, on a change of accounting date resulting in a basis period exceeding 12 months (the relief given depending on the extent of the excess). The balance of overlap relief (£4,500) is carried forward for future relief on the happening of such an event. See 71.19 below. If Dennis had changed his accounting date to 31 March or 5 April (instead of 31 December), the use of the formula in *ICTA 1988, s 63A(2)* would have resulted in overlap relief of £13,500 being given in full in 1999/2000.

71.17 **Closing year.** If there is a **discontinuance of a business** carried on by an individual (which includes his ceasing to carry on an existing business in partnership), the following rule applies. For what is a discontinuance, etc. see 71.25 below.

The basis period for the **final year of assessment**, i.e. that in which cessation occurs, is the period beginning immediately after the end of the basis period for the penultimate year and ending with the date of cessation. [*ICTA 1988, s 63; FA 1994, s 204*]. The basis period may thus exceed twelve months, but see 71.19 below as regards the use of overlap relief brought forward in computing profits for the final year. Unlike the cessation rules under the preceding year basis of assessment (see 71.9 above), there are no special rules for the penultimate and ante-penultimate years of assessment (but see 71.24 below for transitional provisions where a business commenced before 6 April 1994 ceases in 1996/97, 1997/98 or 1998/99).

See 46.15 LOSSES for terminal losses and 46.12(*c*) LOSSES for the carry-forward of certain losses where a private business is converted into a company. See also the concession (A7) at 71.9 above where widow(er) continues deceased spouse's business (although this no longer has any practical application to partnerships).

71.18 *Example*

Robin commenced to trade on 1 May 1996, preparing accounts to 30 April. He permanently ceases to trade on 30 June 2000, preparing accounts for the two months to that date. His profits (as adjusted for tax purposes and *after* capital allowances) are as follows.

	£
Year ended 30 April 1997	24,000
Year ended 30 April 1998	48,000
Year ended 30 April 1999	96,000
Year ended 30 April 2000	36,000
Two months ended 30 June 2000	5,000
	£209,000

Taxable profits for the five tax years of trading are as follows.

	Basis period		£	£
1996/97	1.5.96 – 5.4.97	£24,000 × $\frac{11}{12}$		22,000
1997/98	Y/e 30.4.97			24,000
1998/99	Y/e 30.4.98			48,000
1999/2000	Y/e 30.4.99			96,000
2000/01	1.5.99 – 30.6.00:			
	1.5.99 – 30.4.00		36,000	
	1.5.00 – 30.6.00		5,000	
			41,000	
	Deduct Overlap relief		22,000	
				19,000
				£209,000

Overlap relief accrued (see 71.19 below):

1.5.96 – 5.4.97 — 11 months	22,000
Utilised in 2000/01	(22,000)

71.19 **Overlap relief.** An **'overlap profit'** is an amount of profits which, by virtue of the basis period rules above, is included in the computations for two successive years of assessment. It may arise as a result of the opening year rules in 71.12 above or on a change of basis period within 71.15(*a*) or (*b*) above. An **'overlap period'** in relation to an overlap profit is the number of days in the period for which the overlap profit arose. For example (working in terms of months for simplicity), if a business commences on 1 May 2000 and prepares its first accounts for the year to 30 April 2001 showing tax-adjusted profits of £24,000, the 2000/01 assessment is based on the period 1 May 2000 to 5 April 2001 (£24,000 × $\frac{11}{12}$ = £22,000) and the 2001/02 assessment is based on the year ended 30 April 2001 (£24,000). The overlap profit is £22,000 by reference to an overlap period of 11 months.

Relief for an overlap profit is given, by way of a deduction in computing profits, on a change of accounting date resulting in a basis period of more than twelve months (see 71.15(*c*) above) and/or in the final year of assessment of the business (see 71.17 above). On the first such change of accounting date, if any, the deduction is

$$A \times \frac{B - C}{D}$$

where

A = the aggregate of any overlap profits;

B = the number of days in the basis period (i.e. more than 365 or 366);

C = the number of days in the year of assessment (365 or 366); and

D = the aggregate of the overlap periods by reference to which the overlap profits in A are calculated.

For example (working in terms of months for simplicity), if the overlap profit brought forward is £22,000 by reference to an overlap period of 11 months, and the basis period for a year of assessment is 15 months, the overlap relief deductible in computing profits for that year is £22,000 × $\frac{3}{11}$ = £6,000, leaving an overlap profit of £16,000, by reference to an overlap period of eight months, to be carried forward. On subsequent applications of this formula, A and D are reduced by, respectively, the overlap profit previously relieved and the number of days referable to the previous relief.

On cessation, the deduction in computing profits for the final year of assessment is equal to the total overlap profits previously unrelieved.

Relief for an overlap profit is not restricted to the amount of profits available, and may convert a taxable trading profit into an allowable trading loss, or increase an allowable trading loss, which may be relieved in the same way as any other trading loss (see 46 LOSSES). Where it creates or augments a terminal loss claim (see 46.15 LOSSES), the full amount of the overlap profit is included, without any apportionment.

[*ICTA 1988, s 63A(1)–(3)(5); FA 1994, s 205*].

The Revenue will accept a calculation of overlap relief by reference otherwise than to days, e.g. using months or fractions of months, providing the same method is used consistently so that, over the lifetime of the business, the total profits assessed exactly equal the profits made. (Revenue booklet SAT 1(1995), para 1.86).

See 71.22 below for overlap profits arising under the transitional rules for businesses commenced before 6 April 1994.

Overlap losses. Where an amount of loss would otherwise fall to be included in the computations for two successive years of assessment, that amount (the **'overlap loss'**) is not to be so included for the second of those years. [*ICTA 1988, s 63A(4); FA 1994, s 205*].

71.20 **Transitional rules for businesses commenced before 6 April 1994 — Basis period for 1996/97.** A business commenced before 6 April 1994 is within the basis period rules in 71.3 to 71.9 above for all years up to and including 1995/96. In order to bridge what would otherwise be a gap between the basis periods for 1995/96 and 1996/97, the basis period for 1996/97 is determined as follows (subject to 71.24 below for businesses ceasing before 6 April 1999).

The standard basis period for 1996/97 is normally the twelve months ending with the accounting date (or latest accounting date) in that year. If there is no accounting date in that year (by virtue of a change of accounting date), the standard basis period is the twelve months ending on 5 April 1997 (and the change of accounting date is treated for the purposes of 71.15 above as made in the tax year in which accounts are made up to the new date).

The standard basis period as above is then extended by the period beginning immediately after the end of the basis period for 1995/96 and ending immediately before the beginning of the standard basis period (and taxpayers may, if they wish, draw up accounts to cover the whole of the extended basis period, although where there are losses this may be disadvantageous). **Tax is charged for 1996/97 on the 'appropriate percentage' of the profits of the extended basis period** (the 'transitional period'). The '*appropriate percentage*' is found by dividing 365 by the number of days in the transitional period, and expressing the result as a percentage. In a straightforward case with no change of accounting date, the transitional period will be a period of twenty-four months and 50% of the profits for that period will thus be charged to tax for 1996/97, the remaining 50% escaping tax completely. Exceptionally, if the assessment for 1995/96 is on an actual basis (6 April 1995 to 5 April 1996), e.g. because it commenced in 1993/94 and the taxpayer elected for the special rule in 71.4(*a*) above, there will be no gap and the 1996/97 assessment will also be on an actual basis (with no reduction in the profits charged).

[*FA 1994, Sch 20 paras 1, 2(1)–(3)(5)*].

Anti-avoidance measures have been introduced to deter and penalise attempts to exploit the transitional rules by moving profits into the transitional period so that they would not otherwise be fully charged to tax. Where any amount which is included in the aggregate profits of the transitional period (before applying the appropriate percentage) would not have been so included if any 'relevant change' made or any 'relevant transaction' entered into by the trader had not been made or entered into, the 1996/97 assessment is increased by 1.25 times the 'complementary percentage' (i.e. the difference between 100% and the appropriate percentage) of each amount so included. There are *de minimis* thresholds in that the said increase does not apply where the aggregate of the amounts so included in profits is less than an amount prescribed by regulations, or where the appropriate percentage of turnover (i.e. amounts derived from ordinary activities, excluding VAT and after deducting trade discounts) for the transitional period is less than an amount so prescribed. In the case of individual traders, the amounts prescribed are £10,000 aggregate profits and £50,000 average annual turnover. In the case of partnerships, the aggregate profits threshold is £7,500 per partner up to 20 partners plus £1,000 per partner in excess of 20, and the average annual turnover threshold is £50,000 per partner (in each case taking the maximum number of partners in the relevant period). [*FA 1995, s 133, Sch 22 paras 1, 21(1); SI 1997 No 1158*]. There is no provision for the penalty to be mitigated or for any corresponding reduction to the assessment for any other year. Where voluntary disclosure is made in the tax return for 1996/97 (other than by amendment to the return), the adjustment is reduced by one-quarter of the complementary percentage of each amount so disclosed. [*FA 1995, Sch 22 para 13*]. See Revenue Tax Bulletin June 1997 pp 434–436 for an article on these anti-avoidance provisions with particular reference to the *de minimis* thresholds and with worked examples.

Any 'accounting change' or 'change of business practice' is a '*relevant change*' for the above purposes *unless* it is made exclusively for *bona fide* commercial reasons or the obtaining of a tax advantage is not the main benefit that could reasonably be expected to arise therefrom. An '*accounting change*' means any modification of an accounting policy or substitution of one such policy for another. This includes a change of accounting date *except* any such change which brings the end of the basis period for 1996/97 closer to 5 April 1997. A '*change of business practice*' means any change in an *established* business practice as to the *timing* of either supplies, invoicing, debt collection/settlement, the obtaining of goods or services or the incurring of business expenses or as to the obtaining or making of payments in advance or on account. [*FA 1995, Sch 22 para 14*]. For further guidance as to their interpretation of these terms, see Revenue booklet SAT 1(1995), chapter 10.

A '*relevant transaction*' means any 'self-cancelling transaction' or any transaction with a 'connected person' *unless*, in either case, it is entered into exclusively for *bona fide* commercial reasons or the obtaining of a tax advantage is not the main benefit that could reasonably be expected to arise therefrom. An agreement by which a trader agrees to sell or transfer trading stock or work in progress is a '*self-cancelling transaction*' if by the same or any collateral agreement he either agrees to buy back or re-acquire the stock or work in progress or acquires or grants an option to do so which is subsequently exercised. '*Trading stock*' and '*work in progress*' are as defined, with necessary modifications in the latter case, by *ICTA 1988, s 100* and *s 101* respectively (see 71.83 below) and reference above to the sale or transfer of work in progress includes reference to the sale etc. of any benefits or rights accruing from the carrying out of the work. *ICTA 1988, s 839* (see 20 CONNECTED PERSONS) applies to determine whether persons are '*connected persons*' for these purposes, but disregarding the exception in 20.4 (commercial transactions in partnership assets). In addition, persons trading in partnership are connected with (i) an individual, if he controls the partnership, or (ii) a company, if the company controls the partnership or the same person controls both company and partnership, or (iii) members of another partnership, if the same person controls both partnerships. As regards a company, '*control*' is as defined by *ICTA 1988, s 416* (see Tolley's Corporation Tax, under Close Companies) and as regards a partnership it means the right to a share of more than half the partnership assets or income (see *ICTA 1988, s 840*). A person controls a company or partnership if he does so either alone or with one or more persons connected with him. [*FA 1995, Sch 22 paras 15–17*].

The obtaining of a tax advantage is not a *bona fide* commercial reason for the above purposes. [*FA 1995, Sch 22 para 21(2)*].

If necessary, an assessment may be made, or a partnership statement amended, under the discovery provisions of *TMA 1970, s 29* or *s 30B* (see 78.15, 78.16 SELF-ASSESSMENT) to give effect to the above provisions. The normal exceptions at 78.15(1)(2) do not apply to prevent such an assessment/amendment until such time as a self-assessment or partnership statement has been made for 1997/98 and is not still capable of being amended (see 78 SELF-ASSESSMENT generally). [*FA 1995, Sch 22 para 11*].

See 43.22 INTEREST PAYABLE for anti-avoidance provisions aimed at the replacement of partnership borrowings by partners' personal borrowings during the transitional period.

Simon's Direct Tax Service. See **E1.215, E1.216**.

71.21 *Examples*

Mandy has been in practice as a physiotherapist since the 1980s, preparing accounts to 30 September. In 1997, she changes her accounting date to 31 March, preparing accounts for the 18 months to 31 March 1997. It is accepted that there is no change of business practice and no transaction which would bring her within the anti-avoidance rules in 71.20 above. She ceases practice on 17 April 2000, preparing accounts for the 12 months and 17 days ending on that date. Her profits (as adjusted for tax purposes) for the six periods of account up to cessation are as follows.

	£
Year to 30 September 1994	26,000
Year to 30 September 1995	27,500
18 months to 31 March 1997	48,500
Year to 31 March 1998	31,000
Year to 31 March 1999	23,500
Period to 17 April 2000	16,500

The figures for the year to 31 March 1998 and subsequent periods are quoted net of capital allowances. Capital allowances for 1995/96 and 1996/97 are as follows.

	£
1995/96	1,800
1996/97	1,500

Mandy's taxable profits for the six tax years 1995/96 to 2000/01 are as follows.

		£	£
1995/96	(PY basis — y/e 30.9.94)	26,000	
	Deduct Capital allowances	1,800	
			24,200
1996/97	(transitional year)		
	Y/e 30.9.95	27,500	
	18 mths to 31.3.97	48,500	
	Profits for 30 months	£76,000	
	Average: £76,000 × $\frac{12}{30}$ (40%)	30,400	
	Deduct Capital allowances	1,500	
			28,900
1997/98	(CY basis — y/e 31.3.98)		31,000
1998/99	(Y/e 31.3.99)		23,500
1999/2000	(1.4.99 – 31.3.2000) £16,500 × $\frac{12}{12.5}$		15,840
2000/01	(1.4.2000 – 17.4.2000) £16,500 × $\frac{0.5}{12.5}$		660
			£124,100

Notes

(*a*) In this case, the basis period for 1996/97 is the 12 months to 31 March 1997. This is extended by the gap between basis periods to give a 30-month transitional period of which 12 months are taxed.

(*b*) The basis period for the year 1999/2000 (in which no period of account ends) is the 12 months beginning immediately after the end of the basis period for 1998/99 (see 71.15 above).

(*c*) The change of accounting date does not bring the anti-avoidance rules into play as it brings the end of the basis period for 1996/97 closer to 5 April 1997 (see 71.20 above).

Application of anti-avoidance rules

The facts are as above except that the inspector discovers that there has been a change of business practice resulting in a decrease of £12,000 in the profits for the year to 30 September 1994 (which would otherwise have been £38,000) and a corresponding increase in the combined profits of the 30 months to 31 March 1997 (which would otherwise have been £64,000). Mandy is unable to show that the change was made for commercial reasons or other than mainly to obtain a tax advantage and the anti-avoidance provisions are therefore applied.

The addition to the 1996/97 taxable profits is calculated as follows.

£12,000 × (1.25 × (100% – 40%)) = £9,000

Without the anti-avoidance rules, there would have been a tax saving on profits of £7,200 (£12,000 × 60%). The adjustment cancels out the saving and adds a penalty of £1,800

(25% of the amount on which the taxpayer sought to avoid tax and, in this particular case, 15% of the amount shifted).

Taxable profits for the six years to 2000/01 are now as follows.

		£	£
1995/96			24,200
1996/97	As above	30,400	
	Anti-avoidance addition	9,000	
		39,400	
	Deduct Capital allowances	1,500	
			37,900
1997/98			31,000
1998/99			23,500
1999/2000			15,840
2000/01			660
			£133,100

71.22 **Transitional rules for businesses commenced before 6 April 1994 — Overlap profit for 1997/98.** A business commenced before 6 April 1994 is treated as having a transitional overlap profit for 1997/98 (subject to 71.24 below for businesses ceasing before 6 April 1999). This is equal to the amount of profits taxable for 1997/98, but before deduction/addition of capital allowances/balancing charges (except in the case of a partnership with a corporate partner), which arises after the end of the basis period for 1996/97 and before 6 April 1997. For example, if accounts are regularly made up to 30 June and those for the year to 30 June 1997 show tax-adjusted profits of £20,000 before capital allowances, the 1997/98 assessment will be £20,000 *less* capital allowances and there will be a transitional overlap profit of £15,000 by reference to a transitional overlap period of nine months, 1 July 1996 to 5 April 1997 (working in terms of months rather than days, for simplicity). The transitional overlap profit is carried forward and relieved in the same way as other overlap profits (see 71.19 above). [*FA 1994, Sch 20 para 2(4)–(4B); FA 1995, s 122(2)(3)*]. The computation of transitional overlap profits is not affected by averaging claim(s) by farmers (see 71.57(*a*) below). (Revenue Tax Bulletin August 1998 pp 574, 575).

Anti-avoidance measures have been introduced to deter and penalise attempts to exploit the above rules by moving profits into the basis period for 1997/98, of which the transitional overlap period forms part, so as to otherwise increase the transitional overlap profit. Where any amount which is included in the transitional overlap profit would not have been so included if any 'relevant change' (see 71.20 above) made or any 'relevant transaction' (see 71.20 above) entered into by the trader had not been made or entered into, the transitional overlap profit is reduced by 1.25 times the aggregate of the amounts so included. (Any amount so included will itself be a proportion, dependent upon the accounting date, of an amount included in the 1997/98 basis period.) There are *de minimis* thresholds in that the said adjustment does not apply where the aggregate of the amounts so included is less than an amount prescribed by regulations, or where a percentage (based on the proportion which one year bears to the transitional overlap period) of the turnover (defined as for the anti-avoidance measures in 71.20 above) for the transitional overlap period is less than an amount to be so prescribed. In the case of individual traders, the amounts prescribed are £10,000 aggregate profits and £50,000 average annual turnover. In the case of partnerships, the aggregate profits threshold is £7,500 per partner up to 20 partners plus £1,000 per partner in excess of 20, and the average annual turnover threshold is £50,000 per partner (in each case taking the maximum number of partners in the relevant period). [*FA 1995, s 123, Sch 22 paras 3, 21(1); SI 1997 No 1158*]. There is no provision for the penalty to be mitigated or for any reduction in the assessment for 1997/98 or any other year, except that where voluntary disclosure is made in the tax return for 1997/98 (other than by amendment to the return), the adjustment is reduced by one-quarter of the aggregate amount so disclosed. [*FA 1995, Sch 22 para 13*]. See Revenue Tax Bulletin June 1997 pp 434–436 for an article on these anti-avoidance provisions with particular reference to the *de minimis* thresholds and with worked examples.

An officer of the Board cannot amend a self-assessment to give effect to the above anti-avoidance provisions unless he gives notice stating the aggregate of the amounts on which the adjustment is based. He may give such notice at any time until a self-assessment for 1998/99 has been made and is not still capable of being amended (see 78 SELF-ASSESSMENT generally). Such a notice is conclusive of the matters stated in it, subject to the right of the taxpayer to appeal within 30 days beginning with the date of the notice, the same procedures applying as for an appeal against an assessment, with the Commissioners able to confirm, set aside or modify the notice. [*FA 1995, Sch 22 para 12*].

Where a trade to which the above anti-avoidance provisions apply is carried on in partnership and a partner leaves the firm during the transitional overlap period, he will be personally assessed under Schedule D, Case I or II for 1996/97 on the amount by which his share of transitional overlap profit would have been reduced had he continued to be a partner. [*FA 1995, Sch 22 para 4*]. The discovery provisions of *TMA 1970, ss 29, 30B* apply with the same modifications and related time limits as in 71.20 above. [*FA 1995, Sch 22 para 11*].

See 43.22 INTEREST PAYABLE for the potential reduction or further reduction of the transitional overlap profit where partnership borrowings are replaced by partners' personal borrowings during a period which includes the transitional overlap period.

Simon's Direct Tax Service. See **E1.215, E1.216**.

71.23 *Example*

In the example at 71.5 above, Roy had profits of £27,000 (after deducting capital allowances of £3,000) for the year to 30 April 1997 (taxable in 1997/98) and had transitional overlap relief of £27,500 (£30,000 × $\frac{11}{12}$). The inspector discovers that Roy entered into a self-cancelling transaction (see 71.20 above) with the result that profits of £12,000 were shifted from the year ended 30 April 1998 to the year ended 30 April 1997 (which would otherwise have been £18,000), and that he did so neither for commercial reasons nor otherwise than mainly to obtain a tax advantage. The anti-avoidance provisions are therefore applied.

The 1997/98 and 1998/99 assessments are unchanged. The transitional overlap relief is reduced as follows.

	£
Relief originally calculated at	27,500
Reduction £12,000 × $\frac{11}{12}$ (1.5.96–5.4.97) = £11,000 × 1.25	13,750
Revised transitional overlap relief	£13,750

71.24 **Transitional rules for businesses commenced before 6 April 1994 — cessation in 1996/97 to 1998/99.** A business commenced before 6 April 1994 and ceasing in the tax year 1996/97 is not subject to the basis period rules in 71.11 to 71.19 above. The cessation will be dealt with as under 71.9 above.

In the case of a business commenced before 6 April 1994 and ceasing in the tax year 1997/98, an officer of the Board may direct that neither the basis period rules in 71.11 to

71.19 above nor the transitional rules in 71.20, 71.22 above should apply. Theoretically the cessation can be dealt with as under 71.9 above, but in practice the Revenue will make a direction only if it is to replace the preceding year basis for 1995/96 and the transitional basis for 1996/97 with an actual basis (6 April to 5 April) for both years (and will not normally amend 1997/98). (Revenue booklet SAT 1(1995), para 6.39).

In the case of a business commenced before 6 April 1994 and ceasing in the tax year 1998/99, a comparison is made between the profits assessable for 1996/97 under the transitional rules in 71.20 above (ignoring any brought-forward losses) and those arising on an actual basis (6 April 1996 to 5 April 1997). If the latter figure is the greater, an officer of the Board may direct that 1996/97 should be taxed on an actual basis. The assessments for 1997/98 and 1998/99 are unaffected.

The Revenue may make all such adjustments, whether by assessment or otherwise, to give effect to either of the above-mentioned directions.

[*FA 1994, Sch 20 para 3*].

Simon's Direct Tax Service. See **E1.215**.

71.25 **WHETHER OR NOT THERE HAS BEEN A COMMENCEMENT OR DISCONTINUANCE**

for purposes of 71.4, 71.9, 71.12 and 71.17 above.

The rules of 71.4 and 71.9 above for the opening and closing years apply (i) on the commencement of a new business or the permanent discontinuance of a business and (ii) on a change in the persons carrying on a business in which event there is a notional permanent discontinuance on the change and a notional commencement of a new business. [*ICTA 1988, s 113(1)*]. Where, however, the change is a partnership change (including where a sole trader acquires a partner and *vice versa*) there may be an election for the continuing basis to apply [*ICTA 1988, s 113(2)*], see 53.6 PARTNERSHIPS. Hence a notional discontinuance/commencement arises on partnership changes with no continuing basis election and on a transfer of the ownership of a business carried on by a sole trader, e.g. when it is sold or passes on death.

The rules of 71.12 and 71.14 above for the opening and closing years apply (i) on the commencement of a new business or the permanent discontinuance of a business and (ii) on an individual becoming or ceasing to be a member of a partnership (*but not so as to affect the continuing partners*) — see 53.3 PARTNERSHIPS.

See 53.8 PARTNERSHIPS as regards partnership mergers and demergers.

Although these rules do not apply to companies (see 71.2 above) the income of a company is to be computed on the basis of a commencement/cessation of a trade when it commences/ceases to carry on a trade whether or not there has been a permanent commencement/discontinuance. [*ICTA 1988, s 337(1)*]. This provision is necessary so that a provision operating on a notional cessation/commencement as well as a permanent one may, if required, be applied to companies as well as individuals. (For examples, see *ICTA 1988, ss 102(2), 110(2)*.)

Simon's Direct Tax Service. See **B3.248–B3.251, B3.3**.

71.26 **Case law.** Whether or not a person has commenced/ceased trading and, if so, the date, are questions of fact. Preliminary activities in setting up a business do not amount to trading (*Birmingham & District Cattle By-Products Co Ltd v CIR KB 1919, 12 TC 92*). For pre-trading expenditure, see 71.76 below. For whether the sale of a business can be effective for tax purposes before the vending agreement, see *Todd v Jones Bros Ltd KB 1930, 15 TC 396* and contrast *Angel v Hollingworth & Co Ch D 1958, 37 TC 714*. 'Permanent discontinuance' does not mean a discontinuance which is everlasting (see *Ingram v Callaghan CA 1968, 45 TC 151*) but a trade may continue notwithstanding a lengthy break in active trading (*Kirk & Randall Ltd v Dunn KB 1924, 8 TC 663* but contrast *Goff v Osborne & Co (Sheffield) Ltd Ch D 1953, 34 TC 441*). An intensification by a freelance television producer of his freelance activities could not effect a discontinuance and commencement of a new business (*Edmunds v Coleman Ch D 1997, 70 TC 322*).

The trade was held to have been continuous when the owner of a drifter continued to manage it after its war-time requisition (*Sutherland v CIR CS 1918, 12 TC 63*); when a merchant sold stock on hand after announcing retirement (*J & R O'Kane v CIR HL 1922, 12 TC 303*); when a flour miller and baker gave up a mill (*Bolands Ltd v Davis KB(IFS) 1925, 4 ATC 532*); when a barrister took silk (*Seldon v Croom-Johnson KB 1932, 16 TC 740*); when a partnership was dissolved but completed open forward contracts (*Hillerns & Fowler v Murray CA 1932, 17 TC 77*); when a building partnership transferred construction activities to a company but retained building land and continued to sell land with houses built thereon by the company (*Watts v Hart Ch D 1984, 58 TC 209*). A new trade was held to have commenced when the vendor of a business retained the benefit of outstanding hire-purchase agreements (*Parker v Batty KB 1941, 23 TC 739*) and when the vendor of a business got commission on open contracts completed by the purchaser (*Southern v Cohen's Exors KB 1940, 23 TC 566*).

It is similarly a question of fact whether a trader expanding by taking over an existing business and operating it as a branch has succeeded to the trade. See e.g. *Bell v National Provincial Bank of England Ltd CA 1903, 5 TC 1* (bank succeeded to trade of single-branch bank taken over); *Laycock v Freeman Hardy & Willis Ltd CA 1938, 22 TC 288* (shoe retailer did not succeed to trade of manufacturing subsidiaries taken over); *Briton Ferry Steel Co Ltd v Barry CA 1939, 23 TC 414* (steel manufacturer succeeded to trade of tinplate manufacturing subsidiaries taken over); and *Maidment v Kibby Ch D 1993, 66 TC 137* (fish and chip shop proprietor did not succeed to trade of existing business taken over). See also *H & G Kinemas Ltd KB 1933, 18 TC 116* (cinema company disposed of existing cinemas and opened new one, held to commence new trade).

Whether or not there has been a commencement etc. has arisen in a number of cases where the activities of a company have altered on e.g. a change of shareholdings or a group reconstruction or on its absorption of another trade or part-trade. Such decisions are now of limited importance to companies (see 71.25 above) and where the facts are such that they are unlikely to arise in relation to individuals, they are not referred to here. For such cases, see Tolley's Tax Cases.

For a short article on the distinction between succession to a trade, extension of an existing trade and commencement of a new trade, see Revenue Tax Bulletin February 1996 pp 285, 286. See generally Revenue Inspector's Manual, IM 1261 *et seq.*.

71.27 **Change of residence.** For 1995/96 and subsequent years as regards trades etc. commenced after 5 April 1994 and for 1997/98 and subsequent years as regards those commenced on or before that date, a special rule applies where a sole trader carrying on his trade wholly or partly outside the UK either becomes or ceases to be resident in the UK. The trade is deemed to have been permanently discontinued at the time of the change of residence and, in so far as the individual continues to carry on the actual trade, a new trade is deemed to have been set up immediately afterwards. This applies equally for the purposes of loss reliefs except that a loss incurred in the 'old' trade may be carried forward under *ICTA 1988, s 385* (see 46.12 LOSSES) and set against profits of the 'new' trade. [*ICTA 1988, s 110A; FA 1995, s 124*]. Previously, where a non-UK resident trader not within the charge to UK tax became UK resident, the date of commencement for UK tax purposes was taken to be the actual date that trading commenced and not the date of his becoming resident, i.e.

the preceding year 'continuing' basis normally applied to the first UK assessment (see *Fry v Burma Corporation Ltd HL 1930, 15 TC 113*).

Similar rules apply to individuals trading in partnership (see 53.15 PARTNERSHIPS).

For years before 1997/98 (or 1995/96) see Revenue Pamphlet IR 20, para 5.14 as regards whether a change of residence triggers a cessation.

71.28 ACCOUNTS

For 1996/97 and subsequent years of assessment, under self-assessment, it is not a requirement that accounts should accompany returns, although (except in cases where the annual turnover is less than £15,000) standardised accounts information has to be provided. (Where turnover is less than £15,000, only turnover, purchases and expenses totals need to be shown in the return.) There are, however, strict requirements as to maintenance and preservation of records. See 78.5, 78.10 SELF-ASSESSMENT.

See 71.69 below for allowability of accountancy expenses.

Rounding of tax computations. To reduce the compliance burden on large businesses whose statutory accounts are produced in round thousands, the Revenue are generally prepared to accept profit returns for tax purposes in figures rounded to the nearest £1,000 from single businesses or companies with an annual turnover of at least £5 million (including investment and estate income) in the accounts in question or in the preceding year, where rounding at least to that extent has been used in preparing the accounts. (Turnover of groups of companies is not aggregated for this purpose.) Such returns must be accompanied by a certificate by the person preparing the computations stating the basis of rounding, and confirming that it is unbiased, has been applied consistently and produces a fair result for tax purposes (and stating the program or software used where relevant), or, if there have been no changes from the previous year in these respects, confirming the unchanged basis. The rounding may not extend to the tax payable or other relevant figures of tax. Rounding is not acceptable where it would impede the application of the legislation, or where recourse to the underlying records would normally be necessary to do the computation. Thus it is not acceptable e.g. in computations of chargeable gains (except in relation to the incidental costs of acquisition and disposal), in accrued income scheme computations (see 74.6 SCHEDULE D, CASE VI), in computations of tax credit relief or in certain capital allowance computations. The inspector may exceptionally insist that roundings are not used in other circumstances. (Revenue Pamphlet IR 131, SP 15/93, 18 May 1993).

Enquiries into returns. For the investigative powers of inspectors under self-assessment for 1996/97 and later years, see 78.11 *et seq.* SELF-ASSESSMENT. The system of in-depth examination of accounts which applied for earlier years may continue to apply where returns for such years are subject to investigation without any self-assessment return being brought into question (e.g. following cessation).

The Revenue have published a Code of Practice (No 2, available from local tax offices) setting out their standards for the way in which investigations are conducted and the rights and responsibilities of taxpayers. Codes of Practice 8 and 9, dealing with Special Compliance Office Investigations in cases other than suspected serious fraud and cases of such fraud respectively, were published in January 1995 and are available from the Special Compliance Office, Angel Court, 199 Borough High Street, London SE1 1HZ.

See also 58.3, 58.7 PENALTIES. See generally Revenue Pamphlets IR 72 and IR 73.

Business Economic Notes relating to various trades, which are used by inspectors as background information in investigating returns, are available on the Revenue's website (see 35.1 INLAND REVENUE: ADMINISTRATION). They may alternatively be purchased from the

Inland Revenue, Room 28 New Wing, Somerset House, London WC2R 1LB (price £1.60 (£2.00 for no. 23 onwards) post free). Those currently available are:

1. Travel agents.
2. Road haulage (revised 1995).
3. The lodging industry.
4. Hairdressers.
5. Waste materials reclamation and disposals.
6. Funeral directors.
7. Dentists.
8. Florists.
9. Licensed victuallers.
10. The jewellery trade.
11. Electrical retailers.
12. Antiques and fine art dealers.
13. Fish and chip shops.
14. The pet industry.
15. Veterinary surgeons.
16. Catering — general.
17. — restaurants.
18. — fast-foods, cafes and snack-bars.
19. Farming — stock valuation for income tax purposes.
20. Insurance brokers and agents.
21. Residential rest and nursing homes.
22. Dispensing chemists.
23. Driving instructors.
24. Independent fishmongers.
25. Taxicabs and private hire vehicles.
26. Confectioners, tobacconists and newsagents.

WHETHER A TRADE CARRIED ON

See also 50 MUTUAL TRADING and 84 STATUTORY BODIES. See 71.1 above for statutory definition of 'trade'; meaning of 'profession or vocation'; application of Cases I and II to overseas business activities; and the principle that income within Schedules A and B is not derived from trading. Special types of activity are dealt with below in alphabetical order.

Simon's Direct Tax Service. See **B3.2**.

71.29 Avoidance schemes
71.30 Betting
71.31 Divers etc.
71.32 Futures and options
71.33 Horse racing etc.
71.34 Illegal trading
71.35 Isolated or speculative transactions
71.36 Liquidators etc. and personal representatives
71.37 Miscellaneous
71.38 Property transactions
71.39 Share dealing

71.29 AVOIDANCE SCHEMES

A line is drawn between transactions of a trading nature which remain trading even though entered into to secure tax advantages and transactions so remote from ordinary trading as to be explicable only as fiscal devices and hence not trading.

In *Ransom v Higgs* and *Kilmorie (Aldridge) Ltd v Dickinson, etc. HL 1974, 50 TC 1* the taxpayers entered into complex arrangements to siphon development profits into the hands of trustees. They succeeded, the Crown failing to establish that, looked at as a whole, the arrangements constituted trading. In *Johnson v Jewitt CA 1961, 40 TC 231* an elaborate and artificial device to manufacture trading losses was held not to amount to trading, but see *Ensign Tankers (Leasing) Ltd v Stokes HL 1992, 64 TC 617*, where the company's investment in two film production partnerships was entered into with a view to obtaining first-year capital allowances. See also *Black Nominees Ltd v Nicol Ch D 1975, 50 TC 229* and *Newstead v Frost HL 1980, 53 TC 525.* See generally ANTI-AVOIDANCE (3).

71.30 BETTING

Betting by professional bookmakers is assessable (*Partridge v Mallandaine QB 1886, 2 TC 179*) even if carried on in an unlawful way (*Southern v A B KB 1933, 18 TC 59*) but not private betting however habitual (*Graham v Green KB 1925, 9 TC 309*). Also exempt from CGT. [*TCGA 1992, s 51(1)*]. Receipts from newspaper articles based on betting system held assessable in *Graham v Arnott KB 1941, 24 TC 157.*

Lotteries and football pools promotion constitutes trading, but where a pool or small lottery is run by a supporters club or other society on terms that a specified part of the cost of the ticket is to be donated to a club or body within the purposes in *Lotteries and Amusements Act 1976, s 5(1)*, the donation element is not treated as a trading receipt. (Revenue Pamphlet IR 131, C1). See 15.7(iii) CHARITIES as regards charitable lotteries.

71.31 DIVERS AND DIVING SUPERVISORS

The emoluments of a person employed in the UK (including a designated area under *Continental Shelf Act 1964, s 1(7)*, see 51.13 NON-RESIDENTS AND OTHER OVERSEAS MATTERS) as a diver in operations to exploit the sea-bed, or as a supervisor in relation to such operations, are to be dealt with under Schedule D, Case I as if he were carrying on a trade and not under Schedule E. [*ICTA 1988, s 314*].

71.32 FUTURES AND OPTIONS

Any gain or loss arising in the course of dealing, other than in the course of trade, in commodity or financial futures or in traded or financial options on a recognised exchange, and not chargeable under *ICTA 1988, Sch 5AA* (see 3.22 ANTI-AVOIDANCE), is dealt with under the capital gains tax rules and is not chargeable to tax or relieved under Schedule D. [*ICTA 1988, s 128; TCGA 1992, s 143; FA 1994, s 95; FA 1997, s 80(3); SI 1988 No 744*]. See Tolley's Capital Gains Tax under Disposal.

Where dealing is in the course of a trade, any profit or loss is chargeable under Schedule D, Case I. In general, relatively infrequent transactions, and transactions to hedge specific investments, would not be regarded as trading, nor would purely speculative transactions. For the Revenue view on what constitutes trading in this context, see Revenue Pamphlet IR 131, SP 14/91, 21 November 1991.

Special rules are applied (by regulation) to the market formed by the merger of the London International Financial Futures Exchange (LIFFE) and the London Traded Options Market (LTOM), which operates outside the Stock Exchange. These relate to bond-washing and to stamp duty and stamp duty reserve tax. See *SI 1992 Nos 568, 570.* Regulations relating to stock lending and manufactured dividends (see *SI 1992 Nos 569, 572*) are revoked with effect from 1 July 1997 by *SI 1997 No 987.*

Pension schemes etc.. For the purposes of approved retirement benefit schemes (see 66.5(*b*), 66.13 RETIREMENT SCHEMES), personal pension schemes and retirement annuity trust schemes (see 60.1 PERSONAL PENSION SCHEMES, 65.8 RETIREMENT ANNUITIES), futures and options contracts are treated as investments (and thus as attracting tax exemption for income and capital gains). Any income derived from transactions relating to such a contract is regarded as arising from the contract, and a contract is not excluded from these provisions by the fact that any party is, or may be, entitled to receive and/or liable to make only a payment of a sum in full settlement of all obligations, as opposed to a transfer of assets other than money. [*ICTA 1988, s 659A; TCGA 1992, s 271(10)(11); FA 1990, s 81(2)(3)(5)(6)*].

See 90.1 UNIT TRUSTS as regards similar exemption for trustees of authorised unit trusts in relation to futures and options contracts.

71.33 HORSE RACING ETC.

'Private' horse racing and training is not normally trading (cf. *Sharkey v Wernher HL 1955, 36 TC 275*). But racing and selling the progeny of a brood mare held within Schedule D in *Dawson v Counsell CA 1938, 22 TC 149* and in *Norman v Evans Ch D 1964, 42 TC 188* share of prize monies for letting racehorses held within Case VI. Profits from stallion fees are assessable and assessments under both Case I and Case VI have been upheld (*Malcolm v Lockhart HL 1919, 7 TC 99; McLaughlin v Bailey CA (I) 1920, 7 TC 508; Jersey's Exors v Bassom KB 1926, 10 TC 357; Wernher v CIR KB 1942, 29 TC 20; Benson v Counsell KB 1942, 24 TC 178*) but wear and tear allowances (the forerunner of modern capital allowances on plant, etc.) for stallions refused in *Derby v Aylmer KB 1915, 6 TC 665*. Profits from greyhound breeding held trading in *Hawes v Gardiner Ch D 1957, 37 TC 671*.

71.34 ILLEGAL TRADING

Crime, e.g. burglary, is not trading but the profits of a commercial business are assessable notwithstanding the business may be carried on in an unlawful way, e.g. 'bootlegging' (*Canadian Minister of Finance v Smith PC 1926, 5 ATC 621* and cf. *Lindsay Woodward & Hiscox v CIR CS 1932, 18 TC 43*), operating 'fruit machines' illegal at the time (*Mann v Nash KB 1932, 16 TC 523*), street bookmaking illegal at the time (*Southern v A B KB 1933, 18 TC 59*) and prostitution (*CIR v Aken CA 1990, 63 TC 395*). But penalties for trading contrary to war-time regulations held not deductible (*CIR v E C Warnes & Co KB 1919, 12 TC 227; CIR v Alexander von Glehn & Co CA 1920, 12 TC 232*). See also 71.30 above.

See 71.63 below as regards prohibition on deduction of expenditure involving crime.

71.35 ISOLATED OR SPECULATIVE TRANSACTIONS

For futures, property transactions and share dealing see 71.32, 71.38 and 71.39 respectively.

Whether the surplus on the purchase and resale of assets, otherwise than in the course of an established commercial enterprise, is derived from an 'adventure or concern in the nature of trade' (see 71.1 above) depends on the facts. Para. 116 of the Final Report of the Royal Commission on the Taxation of Profits and Income (1955 HMSO Cmd. 9474) lists six 'badges of trade': (i) the subject matter of the realisation; (ii) length of period of ownership; (iii) frequency or number of similar transactions; (iv) supplementary work on assets sold; (v) reason for sale; (vi) motive. Other relevant factors may be the degree of organisation, whether the taxpayer is or has been associated with a recognised business dealing in similar assets and how the purchases were financed. For a recent review of the factors to be considered, see *Marson v Morton Ch D 1986, 59 TC 381*.

Although in disputed cases the Revenue may make alternative Case I and Case VI assessments, it would seem from *Pearn v Miller KB 1927, 11 TC 610* and *Leeming v Jones HL 1930, 15 TC 333* (see 71.38 below) that as regards isolated transactions the income tax liability, if any, will be under Case I. As regards commodity futures, see 71.32 above.

Case I assessments were upheld on a purchase and resale of war surplus linen (*Martin v Lowry HL 1926, 11 TC 297* — a leading case); a purchase, conversion and resale of a ship (*CIR v Livingston CS 1926, 11 TC 538*); transactions in brandy (*Cape Brandy Syndicate v CIR CA 1921, 12 TC 358*), whisky (*Lindsay Woodward* at 71.34 above), whisky in bond (*P J McCall decd v CIR KB(IFS) 1923, 4 ATC 522; CIR v Fraser CS 1942, 24 TC 498*); 'turning over' cotton mills (*Pickford v Quirke CA 1927, 13 TC 251*); purchase and resale of cotton spinning plant (*Edwards v Bairstow & Harrison HL 1955, 36 TC 207*); and purchase and resale of toilet rolls (*Rutledge v CIR CS 1929, 14 TC 490*). But in *Jenkinson v Freedland CA 1961, 39 TC 636* the Commissioners' finding that a profit on the purchase, repair and sale (to associated companies) of stills was not assessable, was upheld, and in *Kirkham v Williams CA 1991, 64 TC 253*, the Commissioners' decision that the sale of a dwelling house built on land partly acquired for storage, etc. was an adventure in the nature of trade was reversed in the CA.

Simon's Direct Tax Service. See **B3.211** *et seq.*.

71.36 **LIQUIDATORS ETC. AND PERSONAL REPRESENTATIVES**

Whether a liquidator or receiver is continuing the company's trade or merely realising its assets as best he can, is a question of fact and similarly for the personal representatives of a deceased trader. For liquidators or receivers see *Armitage v Moore QB 1900, 4 TC 199; CIR v 'Old Bushmills' Distillery KB(NI) 1927, 12 TC 1148; CIR v Thompson KB 1936, 20 TC 422; Wilson Box v Brice CA 1936, 20 TC 736; Baker v Cook KB 1937, 21 TC 337.*

Personal representatives were held to be trading while winding up the deceased's business in *Weisberg's Executrices v CIR KB 1933, 17 TC 696; Wood v Black's Exor HC 1952, 33 TC 172; Pattullo's Trustees v CIR CS 1955, 36 TC 87* but not in *Cohan's Exors v CIR CA 1924, 12 TC 602* (completion of ship under construction at death) and *CIR v Donaldson's Trustees CS 1963, 41 TC 161* (sale of pedigree herd). For property sales after death of partner in property dealing firm, see *Marshall's Exors v Joly KB 1936, 20 TC 256* and contrast *Newbarns Syndicate v Hay CA 1939, 22 TC 461.*

71.37 **MISCELLANEOUS**

Assessments under Case I were upheld on a committee operating golf links owned by a Town Council (*Carnoustie Golf Course Committee v CIR CS 1929, 14 TC 498*); trustees under a private Act managing a recreation ground (*CIR v Stonehaven Recreation Ground Trustees CS 1929, 15 TC 419*); temporary joint coal merchanting (*Gardner and Bowring Hardy & Co v CIR CS 1930, 15 TC 602*); promotion of mining companies to exploit mines (*Murphy v Australian Machinery etc. Co Ltd CA 1948, 30 TC 244* and cf. *Rhodesia Metals v Commr of Taxes PC 1940, 19 ATC 472*); purchase and resale of amusement equipment (*Crole v Lloyd HC 1950, 31 TC 338*).

A company which made loans to another company to finance a trading venture was held not to be trading itself (*Stone & Temple Ltd v Waters; Astrawall (UK) Ltd v Waters Ch D 1995, 67 TC 145*).

The activities of the British Olympic Association (which included the raising of funds through commercial sponsorship and the exploitation of its logo, but many of which were non-commercial) were held as a whole to be uncommercial and not to constitute a trade (*British Olympic Association v Winter (Sp C 28), [1995] SSCD 85*).

For the treatment of funds held for amateur *athletes* and of other non-professional sportsmen, see Revenue Inspector's Manual, IM 1820a–1829.

For whether *ostrich farming* (i.e. the ownership of ostriches which are looked after on the owner's behalf by others) amounts to trading, and for the consequences of such trading, see Revenue Tax Bulletin June 1996 pp 318, 319.

See also *Smith Barry v Cordy CA 1946, 28 TC 250* in which a taxpayer was held liable on his surplus from the sale or maturing of endowment policies he had purchased, *J Bolson & Son Ltd v Farrelly CA 1953, 34 TC 161* (deals in vessels by company operating boat services held a separate adventure) and *Torbell Investments Ltd v Williams Ch D 1986, 59 TC 357* (dormant company revived for purpose of acquiring certain loans held to have acquired them as trading stock). But a company formed to administer a holidays with pay scheme for the building etc. industry was held not trading (*Building & Civil Engineering, etc. Ltd v Clark Ch D 1960, 39 TC 12*). Assessments on profits from promoting a series of driving schools were upheld in *Leach v Pogson Ch D 1962, 40 TC 585*; in concluding that the profit from *first* sale was assessable, Commissioners were entitled to take into account the subsequent transactions.

For circumstances in which the profits of a trade may not accrue to the proprietor, see *Alongi v CIR CS 1991, 64 TC 304.*

71.38 PROPERTY TRANSACTIONS

This paragraph relates to transactions in land and buildings otherwise than in the course of an established business of property development, building etc. For the Revenue view, see Revenue Inspector's Manual, IM 2601–2634. For other sales of property see 71.77 below.

A line is drawn between realisations of property held as an investment or as a residence and transactions amounting to an adventure or concern in the nature of trade. The principles at 71.35 above apply suitably adapted.

In *Leeming v Jones HL 1930, 15 TC 333* an assessment on the acquisitions and disposal of options over rubber estates was confirmed by Commissioners. The Crown had defended the assessment under both Case I and Case VI. In a Supplementary Case the Commissioners found there had been no concern in the nature of the trade. The Court held there was no liability. Per Lawrence LJ 'in the case of an isolated transaction . . . there is really no middle course open. It is either an adventure in the nature of trade, or else it is simply a case of sale and resale of property.' See also *Pearn v Miller KB 1927, 11 TC 610* and *Williams v Davies* below.

Property transactions by companies held to be trading in *Californian Copper Syndicate v Harris CES 1904, 5 TC 159* (purchase of copper bearing land shortly afterwards resold); *Thew v South West Africa Co CA 1924, 9 TC 141* (numerous sales of land acquired by concession for exploitation); *Cayzer, Irvine & Co v CIR CS 1942, 24 TC 491* (exploitation of landed estate acquired by shipping company); *Emro Investments v Aller* and *Lance Webb Estates v Aller Ch D 1954, 35 TC 305* (profits carried to capital reserve on numerous purchases and sales); *Orchard Parks v Pogson Ch D 1964, 42 TC 442* (land compulsorily purchased after development plan dropped); *Parkstone Estates v Blair Ch D 1966, 43 TC 246* (industrial estate developed—land disposed of by sub-leases for premiums); *Eames v Stepnell Properties Ltd CA 1966, 43 TC 678* (sale of land acquired from associated company while resale being negotiated). See also *Bath & West Counties Property Trust Ltd v Thomas Ch D 1977, 52 TC 20.* Realisations were held to be capital in *Hudson's Bay v Stevens CA 1909, 5 TC 424* (numerous sales of land acquired under Royal Charter — contrast *South West Africa Co* above); *Tebrau (Johore) Rubber Syndicate v Farmer CES 1910, 5 TC 658* (purchase and resale of rubber estates — contrast *Californian Copper* above).

In *Rand v Alberni Land Co Ltd KB 1920, 7 TC 629* sales of land held in trust were held not trading but contrast *Alabama Coal Iron Land v Mylam KB 1926, 11 TC 232; Balgownie Land Trust v CIR CS 1929, 14 TC 684; St Aubyn Estates v Strick KB 1932, 17 TC 412; Tempest Estates v Walmsley Ch D 1975, 51 TC 305.* Sales of property after a period of letting held realisations of investments or not trading in *CIR v Hyndland Investment Co Ltd CS 1929, 14 TC 694; Glasgow Heritable Trust v CIR CS 1954, 35 TC 196; Lucy & Sunderland Ltd v Hunt Ch D 1961, 40 TC 132* but held trading in *Rellim Ltd v Vise CA 1951, 32 TC 254* (notwithstanding that company previously admitted as investment company); *CIR v Toll Property Co CS 1952, 34 TC 13; Forest Side Properties (Chingford) v Pearce CA 1961, 39 TC 665.* But sales by liquidator of property owned by companies following abandonment of plan for their public flotation held not trading in *Simmons v CIR HL 1980, 53 TC 461* (reversing Commissioners' decision).

Property transactions by individuals and partnerships. Profits held assessable in *Reynold's Exors v Bennett KB 1943, 25 TC 401; Broadbridge v Beattie KB 1944, 26 TC 63; Gray & Gillitt v Tiley KB 1944, 26 TC 80; Laver v Wilkinson KB 1944, 26 TC 105; Foulds v Clayton Ch D 1953, 34 TC 382* and *Kirkby v Hughes Ch D 1992, 65 TC 352*; in all of which the taxpayers were or had been associated with building or estate development, and contrast *Williams v Davies KB 1945, 26 TC 371* in which the taxpayers were closely associated with land development but a profit on transactions in undeveloped land in the names of their wives held not assessable. The acquisition and resale of land for which planning permission had been or was obtained held trading in *Cooke v Haddock Ch D 1960, 39 TC 64; Turner v Last Ch D 1965, 42 TC 517* and *Pilkington v Randall CA 1966, 42 TC 662* (and cf. *Iswera v Ceylon Commr PC 1965, 44 ATC 157*), but contrast *Taylor v Good CA 1974, 49 TC 277* in which a house bought as a residence was found unsuitable and resold to a developer after obtaining planning permission and held not an adventure. In *Burrell v Davis Ch D 1948, 38 TC 307; Johnston v Heath Ch D 1970, 46 TC 463; Reeves v Evans, Boyce & Northcott Ch D 1971, 48 TC 495* and *Clark v Follett Ch D 1973, 48 TC 677* the short period of ownership or other evidence showed an intention to purchase for resale at a profit and not for investment, but contrast *CIR v Reinhold CS 1953, 34 TC 389, Marson v Morton Ch D 1986, 59 TC 381* and *Taylor v Good* above. For other cases in which profits held assessable see *Hudson v Wrightson KB 1934, 26 TC 55* and *MacMahon v CIR CS 1951, 32 TC 311.*

For sales after a period of letting see *Mitchell Bros v Tomlinson CA 1957, 37 TC 224* and *Cooksey & Bibby v Rednall KB 1949, 30 TC 514.*

For sale of houses built by taxpayer and used as residences see *Page v Pogson Ch D 1954, 35 TC 545* and *Kirkham v Williams CA 1991, 64 TC 253.*

For sales after death of partner in property dealing transactions, see cases at 71.36 above. See also re partnership sales *CIR v Dean Property Co CS 1939, 22 TC 706* and *Dodd and Tanfield v Haddock Ch D 1964, 42 TC 229.*

Simon's Direct Tax Service. See **B3.6**.

71.39 SHARE DEALING

Share dealing with the public is strictly controlled by the *Financial Services Act 1986*. This paragraph is concerned with share transactions entered into (generally through the Stock Exchange) by persons not authorised to deal under that Act and the question arises whether they amount to an adventure or concern in the nature of trade. The principles of 71.35 above apply suitably adapted. The prudent management of an investment portfolio may necessitate changes in the holdings but this is not normally trading. Stock Exchange speculation, particularly by individuals, may be quasi-gambling and not trading — see Pennycuick J in *Lewis Emanuel & Son Ltd v White Ch D 1965, 42 TC 369* in which, reversing the Commissioners' finding, he held that the Stock Exchange losses of a fruit etc. merchanting company were from a separate trade of share dealing but observed that gambling by the company would have been *ultra vires*. Subsequent *Companies Act* changes have, however, removed any such restriction on the activities of most companies (see Revenue Inspector' Manual, IM 129a). In *Cooper v C & J Clark Ltd Ch D 1982, 54 TC 670*, the losses of a manufacturing company on its sale of gilts, in which it had invested temporarily surplus cash, were allowed as a set-off against its general trading profits. An individual speculating in stocks and shares and commodity futures was held to be trading in *Wannell v Rothwell Ch D 1996, 68 TC 719* (although loss relief was refused on the grounds that the trading was 'uncommercial', see 46.9(*a*) LOSSES), but the opposite conclusion was reached in *Salt v Chamberlain Ch D 1979, 53 TC 143.*

For share dealing by investment companies see *Scottish Investment Trust Co v Forbes CES 1893, 3 TC 231* and *Halefield Securities Ltd v Thorpe Ch D 1967, 44 TC 154.* For trading in secured loans, see *Torbell Investments Ltd v Williams Ch D 1986, 59 TC 357.*

For share sales connected with an existing business see 71.82 below.

ASSESSABLE PROFITS, ALLOWABLE DEDUCTIONS ETC.

See also 10 CAPITAL ALLOWANCES. Headings below after 71.40 are in alphabetical order.

71.40 General
71.41 Advertising
71.42 Application of profits
71.43 Authors and artistes
71.44 Bad and doubtful debts
71.45 Breweries, distilleries, licensed premises
71.46 Commission, cashbacks and discounts
71.47 Compensation, damages etc. — payments
71.48 Compensation, damages etc. — receipts
71.49 Contingent and future liabilities
71.50 Contracts
71.51 Copyright etc.
71.52 Deduction of tax at source — amounts paid under
71.53 Embezzlement etc.
71.54 Employees (and directors)
71.55 Entertainment expenses
71.56 Exchange gains and losses
71.57 Farming and market gardening
71.58 Film etc. production
71.59 Franchising
71.60 Gifts and other non-contractual receipts and payments
71.61 Guarantees
71.62 Hire-purchase
71.63 Illegal payments etc.
71.64 Insurance
71.65 Interest and other payments for loans
71.66 Investment income
71.67 Know-how
71.68 Lease rental payments
71.69 Legal and professional expenses
71.70 Loan finance incidental costs
71.71 Mines, quarries, etc.
71.72 Miscellaneous
71.73 Patents
71.74 Personal expenses
71.75 Pooling of profits
71.76 Pre-trading expenditure
71.77 Property receipts and sales
71.78 Rents etc. for business premises
71.79 Repairs and renewals
71.80 Scientific research and research and development
71.81 Security
71.82 Share, security etc. issues, purchase, sales and exchanges
71.83 Stock in trade and work in progress
71.84 Subscriptions etc. including trade association contributions
71.85 Subsidies, grants etc.
71.86 Taxation
71.87 Telecommunications licences
71.88 Tied petrol companies etc.
71.89 Training
71.90 Travelling and subsistence expenses
71.91 Unclaimed balances
71.92 Unremittable receipts, debts etc.
71.93 Value Added Tax
71.94 Waste disposal
71.95 Woodlands

71.40 GENERAL

The provisions for computing business profits are in *ICTA 1988, ss 74–99*. The general rules for expenses are in *ICTA 1988, s 74*. These are few and simple and, in content and wording, little changed since Napoleonic times. There are no corresponding rules for receipts. Hence practice is largely based on principles evolved over the years and endorsed by the Courts. It has, however, been clarified that the words 'receipts' and 'expenses' refer generally to items brought into account as credits or debits in computing profits, and contain no implication that an amount has actually been received or expended. [*FA 1998, s 46(1)*].

Earnings basis. For periods of account (i.e. any period for which accounts of a trade, profession or vocation are drawn up) beginning **after 6 April 1999**, the profits of a trade, profession or vocation must generally be computed for tax purposes on an accounting basis giving a true and fair view, subject to any adjustment required or authorised by law. This imposes a general requirement to apply the earnings basis for tax purposes, whilst at the same time importing the accountancy concept of 'materiality', allowing a practical view to be taken of the time when immaterial amounts are recognised. The 'true and fair view' rule requires neither the auditing of accounts, nor additional disclosure, nor the preparation of a true and fair view balance sheet. Neither does it require accounts to be drawn up on any particular basis (provided the necessary adjustments are made in the tax computation). See Revenue Press Release 17 March 1998. For the Revenue view of what is meant by 'true and fair view', see Revenue Tax Bulletin December 1998 pp 606–615.

The special computational rules for Lloyd's UNDERWRITERS (89) are not affected by these changes.

Transition to 'true and fair view'. There is a transitional exemption, allowing the continued use of the cash basis for a transitional period, for barristers and advocates, and an ongoing exemption for barristers and advocates in the early years of practice. See 12.2 CASH BASIS. Generally, a period of account beginning before 7 April 1999 which is still current on 7 April 2000 is treated as having ended on 6 April 1999, and a new period of account as having begun on 7 April 1999 (to which the 'true and fair view' rule thus applies.

[*FA 1998, ss 42, 43, 45*].

See 71.49 below as regards future and contingent liabilities generally.

For the earlier application of the cash basis in practice in certain cases, see 12.1 CASH BASIS. Case law had previously established that the legal basis is the earnings basis with provision for debtors, creditors, accruals and stock and work in progress (cf. *CIR v Gardner Mountain & D'Ambrumenil Ltd HL 1947, 29 TC 69*). Hence profits and losses which have not accrued cannot be anticipated (cf. *Willingale v International Commercial Bank Ltd HL 1977, 52 TC 242*) nor can future expenses. Conversely an expense actually incurred is allowable in full even though the benefit from it will not accrue until later years (*Vallambrosa Rubber Co Ltd v Farmer CES 1910, 5 TC 529; Duple Motor Bodies Ltd v Ostime HL 1961, 39 TC 537*).

Accountancy principles. See above as regards the introduction of a 'true and fair view' requirement in the computation of taxable profits. It has always been the case that, since the starting figure in computing profits is that brought out by the accounts of the business, accountancy principles are of the greatest importance. They cannot, however, override established income tax principles (*Heather v P-E Consulting Group Ltd CA 1972, 48 TC 293; Willingale v International Commercial Bank Ltd HL 1977, 52 TC 242*; but see *Threlfall v Jones CA 1993, 66 TC 77; Johnston v Britannia Airways Ltd Ch D 1994, 67 TC 99*). See also *RTZ Oil & Gas Ltd v Elliss Ch D 1987, 61 TC 132*. A 'provision for a future operating loss', whose inclusion could not be said to have 'violated existing accounting principles', was disallowed in *Meat Traders Ltd v Cushing (Sp C 131), [1997] SSCD 245*). See *Robertson v CIR (Sp C 137), [1997] SSCD 282* as regards timing of inclusion of insurance agents' advance commission. See also *Herbert Smith v Honour Ch D, [1999] STC 173* for the timing of deductions in respect of future rents under leases of premises ceasing to be used for business purposes, and Revenue Press Release 20 July 1999 for Revenue practice following that decision.

For articles setting out the Revenue view on the relationship between accountancy and taxable profits, see Revenue Tax Bulletin December 1997 pp 485, 486, February 1999 pp 623–625, April 1999 pp 636–641 and December 1999 pp 707–709. See also ICAEW Guidance Note TAX 10/95, 10 April 1995, for Revenue responses to a number of specific questions on Revenue practice following *Threlfall v Jones* and *Johnston v Britannia Airways*

Ltd, dealing in particular with provisions, alternative accounting policies, capitalised expenditure and changes of accounting policy. For accounting standards generally, see Revenue Inspector's Manual, IM 536a *et seq.*. For the timing of deductions where an expense is charged to an asset account in the closing balance sheet rather than immediately against profits, see Revenue Inspector's Manual, IM 608 *et seq.*. For provisions, see Revenue Press Release 20 July 1999 and Revenue Tax Bulletin December 1999 pp 707–709.

Capital receipts and expenses must, unless the Acts explicitly provide otherwise, be excluded. This principle is derived, as regards expenses, from *ICTA 1988, s 74(1)(f)(g)* and generally because the charge to tax is on *income*. See also *ICTA 1988, s 817(2)*. 'No part of our law of taxation presents such almost insoluble conundrums as the decision whether a receipt or outgoing is capital or income for tax purposes' (Lord Upjohn in *Strick v Regent Oil Co Ltd HL 1965, 43 TC 1* q.v. for a comprehensive review of the law). A widely used test is the 'enduring benefit' one given by Viscount Cave in *Atherton v British Insulated & Helsby Cables Ltd HL 1925, 10 TC 155*. For a recent review of the cases, see *Lawson v Johnson Matthey plc HL 1992, 65 TC 39*. A gain or loss on the sale of a capital asset not included in trading profits is dealt with according to the provisions relating to capital gains tax. A sale of a fixed asset on which capital allowances have been claimed may result in a balancing charge or allowance, see 10 CAPITAL ALLOWANCES. The revenue or capital nature of a payment is fixed at the time of its receipt (*Tapemaze Ltd v Melluish Ch D, [2000] STC 189*, following *Morley v Tattersall CA 1938, 40 TC 671*).

For a brief note on the Revenue approach to challenging schemes or arrangements designed to turn income into capital (or capital expenditure into a revenue deduction), see Revenue Tax Bulletin June 1997 p 438.

Wholly and exclusively. Any expense to be deductible must, *inter alia*, have been incurred 'wholly and exclusively . . . for the purposes' of the trade, etc. [*ICTA 1988, s 74(1)(a)*]. This provision underlies, explicitly or implicitly, the very large number of 'expenses' cases noted in the paragraphs below. For a review of the leading cases see *Harrods (Buenos Aires) Ltd v Taylor-Gooby CA 1964, 41 TC 450* and for a frequently quoted analysis of the words see *Bentleys, Stokes & Lowless v Beeson CA 1952, 33 TC 491*. Since that case the '*dual purpose rule*' has figured prominently in Court decisions. If an expense is for a material private or non-business purpose, the whole is strictly disallowable as it is thereby not wholly and exclusively for business purposes. For examples of its application see 71.74 and 71.90 below. In practice, this rule is not always rigidly applied (and see para. 161 of Tucker Committee Report on Taxation of Trading Profits, 1951 HMSO Cmd. 8189, where the Revenue indicated to the Committee that the inspector would generally agree a fair apportionment where an expense had objects additional to those of a purely business nature). For rent etc. of premises used both for business and as residence, see 71.78 below. See *Mallalieu v Drummond* (71.74) for an important recent HL discussion of *ICTA 1988, s 74(1)(a)*, in which it was held that the purposes of the relevant expenditure involved looking into the taxpayer's mind at the time of the expenditure, later events being irrelevant except as a reflection of that state of mind. However, the taxpayer's conscious motive at the time was not conclusive; an object, not a conscious motive (in this case the human requirement for clothing), could be taken into account. A purely incidental consequence of a business expense does not, however, preclude its being wholly and exclusively for business purposes. See, e.g., *Robinson v Scott Bader Ltd*, 71.54 below and *McKnight v Sheppard HL 1999, 71 TC 419*, 71.69, 71.74 below. *Mallalieu v Drummond* was applied in *Watkis v Ashford, Sparkes and Harward Ch D 1985, 58 TC 468*, where expenditure on meals supplied at regular partners' lunchtime meetings was disallowed, overruling the Commissioner's finding that the expenditure was exclusively for business purposes. Expenditure on accommodation, food and drink at the firm's annual weekend conference was, however, allowed. For deduction of payments by partnerships to individual partners generally, see *MacKinlay v Arthur Young McClelland Moores & Co HL 1989, 62 TC 704*. Salaries paid to partners are not deductible as trading expenses (*PDC Copyprint (South) v George (Sp C 141), [1997] SSCD 326*).

See also 71.74 below as regards personal expenses.

It should be borne in mind that the trade for whose purposes the expenditure is incurred must be that in which the expense arose. For a successful appeal against a decision in favour of the Revenue on this point, see *Vodafone Cellular Ltd v Shaw CA 1997, 69 TC 376.*

Schedule E income received by a trader should in law be excluded from his Case I and II income (see 5.2 ASSESSMENTS) but in practice the legal position is modified in certain circumstances. See Revenue Schedule E Manual, SE 1226. See *Walker v Carnaby Harrower Ch D 1969, 46 TC 561* and *CIR v Brander & Cruickshank HL 1970, 46 TC 574* for the inclusion in the Case II assessment of professions of remuneration as auditor, etc. For the tax treatment of directors' fees received by partnerships and other companies and the distinction between Schedule E and Schedule D, see 75.1(1) and 75.24 SCHEDULE E. See 75.32 SCHEDULE E as regards certain payments to redundant steel workers.

For **ancillary trading income** see 71.66 below.

Private Finance Initiative ('PFI') projects. For a series of articles on the tax aspects of PFI projects (dealing with the introduction by the public sector body of surplus land, or cash derived therefrom, with stamp duty considerations and with income arising from leases of fully serviced accommodation), see Revenue Tax Bulletin April 1999 pp 642–645, October 1999 pp 694–697.

Simon's Direct Tax Service. See **B3.9, B3.12**.

71.41 ADVERTISING

Expenditure generally is allowable (but not capital outlay such as fixed signs (but see *Leeds Permanent Building Society v Proctor Ch D 1982, 56 TC 293*), nor initial costs, etc. of new business). Contribution to campaign for Sunday opening held allowable (*Rhymney Breweries Ch D 1965, 42 TC 509*). As to political campaign see *Tate & Lyle HL 1954, 35 TC 367*, contrasted with *Boarland v Kramat Pulai Ch D 1953, 35 TC 1.* See Revenue Inspector's Manual, IM 610–613.

71.42 APPLICATION OF PROFITS

A requirement that a trading surplus is to be applied in a particular way does not remove the trade from Case I (*Mersey Docks and Harbour Board v Lucas HL 1883, 2 TC 25*) and applications of the profits under the requirement are not allowable deductions (*City of Dublin Steam Packet Co v O'Brien KB(I) 1912, 6 TC 101; Hutchinson & Co v Turner HC 1950, 31 TC 495; Young v Racecourse Betting Control Board HL 1959, 38 TC 426* and cf. *Pondicherry Rly Co PC 1931, 10 ATC 365; Tata Hydro-Electric Agencies PC 1937, 16 ATC 54; India Radio & Cable Communication Co PC 1937, 16 ATC 333*).

For circumstances in which the profits of a trade may not accrue to the proprietor, see *Alongi v CIR CS 1991, 64 TC 304.*

71.43 AUTHORS AND ARTISTES

For copyright, etc. see 71.51 below.

An actress based in the UK but with engagements abroad was held to be carrying on a single profession. Hence receipts from her overseas engagements fell to be included in her Case II assessment (*Davies v Braithwaite KB 1933, 18 TC 198* and compare *Withers v Wynyard KB 1938, 21 TC 724*). A taxpayer who, after spare time writing plays not sold, wrote a successful play was held to be carrying on the vocation of dramatist (*Billam v Griffith KB 1941, 23 TC 757*). Receipts from the occasional writing of articles are normally assessable under SCHEDULE D, CASE VI (74) but Case II assessments on a regular newspaper contributor were upheld in *Graham v Arnott KB 1941, 24 TC 157*. Receipts from the sale of an author's notebooks and memorabilia were held to be taxable as part of the fruits of his profession (*Wain v Cameron Ch D 1995, 67 TC 324*).

An artiste engaged by a theatre under a standard contract was held to be within Schedule E (*Fall v Hitchen Ch D 1972, 49 TC 433*), but see now 75.24 SCHEDULE E as regards application of Schedule D to artistes generally.

A sum received by an author on cancellation of his contract as script writer was held a revenue receipt (*Household v Grimshaw Ch D 1953, 34 TC 366*). See also *John Mills Productions Ltd v Mathias Ch D 1967, 44 TC 441*. Payment to actor for entering into restrictive covenant held not assessable (*Higgs v Olivier CA 1952, 33 TC 136*). Film writer's loss under guarantee of indebtedness of film company held allowable (*Lunt v Wellesley KB 1945, 27 TC 78*). Whether a literary prize is a receipt of the author's profession depends on the precise facts, see Revenue Inspector's Manual, IM 2691a, 2691b.

See 3.10 ANTI-AVOIDANCE for the treatment as income of certain capital sums received in lieu of earnings and 51.8 NON-RESIDENTS AND OTHER OVERSEAS MATTERS as regards certain non-resident entertainers and sportsmen.

71.44 BAD AND DOUBTFUL DEBTS

See generally Revenue Inspector's Manual, IM 635–645.

Bad debts (before 1996/97, proven bad debts), and doubtful debts to the extent they are estimated to be bad, are deductible. Where the debtor is bankrupt or insolvent, the debt is deductible except to the extent that any amount may reasonably be expected to be received on it. Debts (or parts) released wholly and exclusively for trade purposes as part of a voluntary arrangement under or by virtue of *Insolvency Act 1986* or a compromise or arrangement under *Companies Act 1985, s 425* (or NI equivalent) are also deductible. [*ICTA 1988, s 74(1)(j); FA 1994, s 144(1)(2)(6); FA 1996, s 134, Sch 20 para 4*]. Otherwise, where a debt allowed in computing profits is subsequently released, the amount released is a trading receipt of the period in which it is released. [*ICTA 1988, s 94; FA 1994, s 144(3)(a)(7)*]. Where a trade is treated as notionally discontinued (see 71.25 above), the allowance extends to debts taken over by the successor, and similar treatment applies to recoveries. [*ICTA 1988, ss 89, 106(2)*]. For debt recoveries and releases after the cessation of a trade, see 62 POST-CESSATION ETC. RECEIPTS AND EXPENDITURE. Bad debt allowances are not applicable where the business is assessed on a CASH BASIS (12). For VAT on bad debts, see 71.93 below.

The provision for a bad or doubtful debt for a period of account may reflect events after the balance sheet date insofar as they furnish additional evidence of conditions that existed at the balance sheet date. See Revenue Tax Bulletin August 1994 p 154, which also outlines the evidence which inspectors may require in support of the allowance of a provision.

Where as part of a transfer of assets and liabilities between group companies creditors consent to the release of the transferor company from its obligations in return for the transferee assuming those obligations, no charge arises under *section 94*. (Revenue Tax Bulletin August 1993 p 88).

Where an asset accepted in satisfaction of a trading debt is of market value (as at the date of acceptance) less than the outstanding debt, the deficit may be allowed as a deduction, provided that, on a disposal of the asset, any excess of disposal proceeds over that value (up to the amount by which the debt exceeds that value) is brought in as a trading receipt (such receipt being excluded from any chargeable gain computation on the disposal). (Revenue Inspector's Manual, IM 642).

For the Revenue practice in relation to bad and doubtful international loans ('country-risk debts') see Revenue Pamphlet IR 131, SP 1/83, 25 January 1983. The principles apply whether the creditor is a bank or some other commercial organisation (Hansard Vol 36 Col 84, 1 February 1983). See also *ICTA 1988, ss 88A–88C* introduced by *FA 1990, s 74*. These provisions were, however, repealed by *FA 1996, Sch 41 Pt V(3)* for 1996/97 onwards and for accounting periods ending after 31 March 1996. For the replacement corporation tax provisions in *FA 1996, Sch 9 paras 8, 9*, and the associated transitional provisions in *FA 1996, Sch 15 para 17*, see Tolley's Corporation Tax under Loan Relationships.

An allowance agreed under conditions of full disclosure cannot be withdrawn because of a subsequent change in the circumstances (*Anderton & Halstead Ltd v Birrell KB 1931, 16 TC 200*) but an allowance for year 1 may be revised, upwards or downwards, in the year 2 computation by reference to the circumstances for year 2 and similarly for later years. The amount of the allowance depends on the likelihood of recovery. This is a question of fact but the fact that the debtor is still in business is not itself a reason for refusing an allowance (*Dinshaw v Bombay IT Commr PC 1934, 13 ATC 284*). See also *Lock v Jones KB 1941, 23 TC 749*.

The allowance is made in respect of a particular debt and general bad debt provisions are not allowed. However where there are a large number of comparatively small debts, making the 'valuation' of individual debts impracticable, the Revenue will normally agree to an allowance in accordance with a formula based on the bad debt experience of the business. Typical businesses are mail-order firms and firms with a large proportion of hire-purchase sales. Where hire-purchase is involved the formula may also cover the spread of the profit on hire-purchase sales. But no provision for the estimated cost of collecting future debt instalments is permissible (*Monthly Salaries Loan Co Ltd v Furlong Ch D 1962, 40 TC 313*).

For small credit traders who collect their debts by weekly instalments (sometimes called travelling drapers or Scotch drapers) a special arrangement is available. For details see Form 189 obtainable from inspectors.

Where a builder sold houses leaving part of the sale proceeds with Building Societies as collateral security for mortgages by the purchasers, held the amounts should be brought in at valuation when houses sold and if practicable and otherwise when released by Building Society (*John Cronk & Sons Ltd v Harrison HL 1936, 20 TC 612* and cf. *Chibbett v Harold Brookfield & Son Ltd CA 1952, 33 TC 467*). A similar decision was reached in *Absalom v Talbot HL 1944, 26 TC 166* where amounts were left on loan to the purchasers. See also *Lock v Jones* above. The HL judgments in *Absalom v Talbot* are an important review of the treatment of trading debts.

The normal debt considered for allowance under *ICTA 1988, s 74(1)(j)* is one for goods or services supplied or one in a business, such as banking or money-lending, which consists of advancing money (see e.g. *AB Bank v Inspector of Taxes (Sp C 237), [2000] SSCD 229*). Losses on advances by a brewery company to its customers were allowed as on the evidence it habitually acted as banker for them in the course of its brewing business (*Reid's Brewery v Male QB 1891, 3 TC 279*). But losses on advances to clients by solicitors were refused as there was no evidence that they were money-lenders (*CIR v Hagart & Burn-Murdoch HL 1929, 14 TC 433; Rutherford v CIR CS 1939, 23 TC 8*. See also *Bury & Walkers v Phillips HC 1951, 32 TC 198* and contrast *Jennings v Barfield Ch D 1962, 40 TC 365*). An allowance was refused for an irrecoverable balance due from the managing director of a company as outside the company's trade (*Curtis v J & G Oldfield Ltd KB 1925, 9 TC 319*). See also *Roebank Printing Co Ltd v CIR CS 1928, 13 TC 864*.

Advances to finance or recoup the losses of subsidiary or associated companies are capital. Allowances were refused in *English Crown Spelter v Baker KB 1908, 5 TC 327* and *Charles Marsden & Sons v CIR KB 1919, 12 TC 217* for losses on advances to facilitate the supply of materials for the trade of the lender as were losses on an advance to a company under the same control (*Baker v Mabie Todd & Co Ltd KB 1927, 13 TC 235*), amounts written off in respect of the losses of a subsidiary (*Odhams Press Ltd v Cook HL 1940, 23 TC 233*) and payments to meet the operating losses of a subsidiary (*Marshall Richards Machine Co Ltd v Jewitt Ch D 1956, 36 TC 511*). See also *CIR v Huntley & Palmers Ltd KB 1928, 12 TC 1209; Henderson v Meade-King Robinson & Co Ltd KB 1938, 22 TC 97;* and *Stone & Temple Ltd v Waters; Astrawall (UK) Ltd v Waters Ch D 1995, 67 TC 145.* (N.B. The loss of subsidiary may now be eligible for group relief — see Tolley's Corporation Tax.)

Losses relating to trade debts with a subsidiary were, however, held allowable in *Sycamore plc and Maple Ltd v Fir (Sp C 104), [1997] SSCD 1.*

Payments by the purchaser to discharge the unpaid liabilities of the vendor to preserve goodwill, etc. allowed in *Cooke v Quick Shoe Repair Service KB 1949, 30 TC 460.*

See 71.92 below for relief for certain unremittable overseas debts of trades within Schedule D, Case I.

Note.

Loans made after 11 April 1978 to a trader for the setting up or purposes of his trade and irrecoverable are in certain circumstances allowable as a loss for capital gains tax. See Tolley's Capital Gains Tax.

For losses under guarantees see 71.61 below.

Simon's Direct Tax Service. See **B3.1461** *et seq.*.

71.45 BREWERIES, DISTILLERIES, LICENSED PREMISES

Tied houses. Receipts and expenses in respect of 'tied premises' which would otherwise be brought into account under SCHEDULE A (68) are instead brought in as trading receipts or expenses. Premises outside the UK are for this purpose treated as if they were in the UK. Any necessary apportionment (e.g. where rents etc. relate only in part to the tied premises or where only part of the premises qualifies) is on a just and reasonable basis. '*Tied premises*' are premises through which goods supplied by a trader are sold or used by another person, where the trader has an estate or interest in the premises which he treats as property employed for trade purposes. Slightly different rules applied before 17 March 1998 (see *ICTA 1988, s 98* as originally enacted). Receipts or expenses taken into account under the previous rules are not taken into account again, but any which would have been allowed under the new rules before 17 March 1998 but which were not previously taken into account are brought into account on that date. [*ICTA 1988, s 98; FA 1998, s 41*]. (*Note.* These rules are of general application, although of most common application in the licensed trade.)

Case law. Repairs, rates, insurance premiums paid on behalf of tied tenants allowable (*Usher's Wiltshire Brewery v Bruce HL 1914, 6 TC 399*) but not extra expenditure incurred to keep licensed houses open while undergoing rehabilitation (*Mann Crossman & Paulin Ltd v Compton KB 1947, 28 TC 410*) or compensation to a tenant displaced on a licence transfer (*Morse v Stedeford KB 1934, 18 TC 457*). For compensation paid on the termination of tenancies of tied houses, see *Watneys (London) Ltd v Pike Ch D 1982, 57 TC 372.* Losses on advances to 'customers and connections' held allowable (*Reid's Brewery v Male QB 1891, 3 TC 279*).

The expenses of an unsuccessful application for licences were held not allowable (*Southwell v Savill Bros KB 1901, 4 TC 430* — it was conceded that expenses of successful applications are capital) nor expenses of applying for licence transfers (*Morse v Stedeford* above; *Pendleton v Mitchells & Butlers Ch D 1968, 45 TC 341*). Contributions by a brewer to a trade association to promote Sunday opening in Wales allowed in *Cooper v Rhymney Breweries Ch D 1965, 42 TC 509*. Compensation Fund levies deductible (*Smith v Lion Brewery HL 1910, 5 TC 568*) but not monopoly value payments (*Kneeshaw v Albertolli KB 1940, 23 TC 462; Henriksen v Grafton Hotels Ltd CA 1942, 24 TC 453*).

Damages paid to hotel guest injured by falling chimney held not allowable — see *Strong & Co v Woodifield* at 71.47 below. For accrued whisky storage rents see *Dailuaine-Talisker Distilleries v CIR CS 1930, 15 TC 613; CIR v Oban Distillery Co CS 1932, 18 TC 33* and *CIR v Arthur Bell & Sons CS 1932, 22 TC 315*.

Where a brewery company ceased brewing but continued to sell beer brewed for it by another company it was held to have discontinued its old trade and commenced a new one (*Gordon & Blair Ltd v CIR CS 1962, 40 TC 358*).

Simon's Direct Tax Service. See **B3.1121** *et seq.*.

71.46 COMMISSION, CASHBACKS AND DISCOUNTS

Revenue Statement of Practice SP 4/97 sets out the Revenue's views on the tax treatment of commissions, cashbacks and discounts. It replaces the earlier Statement of Practice, SP 5/95 (see 71.64 below), which dealt only with insurance and personal pension schemes, and applies to all cases open as at 27 November 1997. The types of payment with which the Statement is concerned are as follows.

Commissions. Sums paid by the providers of goods, investments or services to agents or intermediaries as reward for the introduction of business, or in some cases paid directly by the provider to the customer. Sums paid to an agent or intermediary may be passed on to the customer or to some other person.

Cashbacks. Lump sums received by a customer as an inducement for entering into a transaction for the purchase of goods, investments or services and received as a direct consequence of having entered into that transaction. The payer may be either the provider or another party with an interest in ensuring that the transaction takes place.

Discounts, i.e. where the purchaser's obligation to pay for goods, investments or services is less than the full purchase price, other than as a result of commissions or cashbacks.

The Statement also deals with commissions or cashbacks which are netted off, or invested or otherwise applied for the benefit of the purchaser, or where extra value is added to the goods, investments or services supplied (e.g. the allocation of bonus units in an investment) (although in the case of the addition of value to investments this may represent a return on the investment, which is outside the scope of the Statement).

The Statement provides detailed guidance on the circumstances in which Schedule D liability may arise under either Case I or II or Case VI, and on deductibility of the payments under those Cases. It also considers possible liabilities under Schedule E or to capital gains tax, and the effect of commissions, etc. on life insurance policies and personal pension contributions.

Generally, ordinary retail arm's length customers will not be liable to income or capital gains tax. The Statement outlines the circumstances in which receipts are treated as tax-free, or payments qualify for tax relief, and contains an element of concession for those who, in the ordinary course of their business, earn commission relating to their own transactions. It contains a warning that the principles outlined may not be followed where tax avoidance schemes are involved, or where the arrangements for the commission, etc. include an increase in the purchase price of the goods, etc. involved. The tax treatment of the payer and the recipient are in all cases considered independently of one another.

(Revenue Statement of Practice SP 4/97, 27 November 1997).

For an article explaining the differences in the Revenue's views between the publication of SP 5/95 and SP 4/97, and the legal basis of the current approach, see Revenue Tax Bulletin February 1998 pp 505–509.

71.47 COMPENSATION, DAMAGES ETC. — PAYMENTS

For compensation and redundancy payments to directors or employees see 71.54 below. An important case is *Anglo-Persian Oil Co Ltd v Dale CA 1931, 16 TC 253* in which a substantial payment by a company for the cancellation of its principal agency, with ten years to run, was held to be allowable. It was not for a capital asset nor to get rid of an onerous contract (cf. *Mallett v Staveley Coal CA 1928, 13 TC 772*) but to enable it to rationalise its working arrangements. The decision was applied in *Croydon Hotel & Leisure Co Ltd v Bowen (Sp C 101), [1996] SSCD 466*, in which a payment for the termination of a hotel management agreement was held to be allowable. See also *Vodafone Cellular Ltd v Shaw CA 1997, 69 TC 376* (payment for release from onerous agreement), in which the principle underlying the decision in *Van den Berghs Ltd v Clark* (see 71.48(*b*) below) was applied, but cf. *Tucker v Granada Motorway Services Ltd HL 1979, 53 TC 92*, where a payment to modify the method of calculating the rent was held to be capital, and *Whitehead v Tubbs (Elastics) Ltd CA 1983, 57 TC 472*, where a payment to alter the terms of a capital loan by removing borrowing restrictions on the borrower was held to be capital.

A payment by a shipping company for cancelling an order it had placed for a ship was held capital (*'Countess Warwick' SS Co Ltd v Ogg KB 1924, 8 TC 652* and contrast *Devon Mutual Steamship Insce v Ogg KB 1927, 13 TC 184*). A payment to an associated company in return for its temporarily ceasing production held allowable (*Commr of Taxes v Nchanga Consolidated Copper Mines PC 1964, 43 ATC 20*) as were statutory levies on a brewery for a Compensation Fund where a licence is not renewed (*Smith v Lion Brewery Co Ltd HL 1910, 5 TC 568*) and a payment to secure the closure of a rival concern (*Walker v The Joint Credit Card Co Ltd Ch D 1982, 55 TC 617*). Payments by a steel company to secure the closure of railway steel works were held capital (*United Steels v Cullington (No 1) CA 1939, 23 TC 71*) as were payments to safeguard against subsidence on a factory site (*Bradbury v United Glass Bottle Mfrs CA 1959, 38 TC 369*; compare *Glenboig Union Fireclay* at 71.48(*c*) below) and a payment for cancelling electricity agreement on closure of a quarry (*CIR v Wm Sharp & Son CS 1959, 38 TC 341*). For compensation paid on the termination of tied houses of breweries, see *Watneys (London) Ltd v Pike Ch D 1982, 57 TC 372.*

Where damages awarded by a Court against a solicitor were later compounded, the compounded amount (accepted as allowable) was held to be an expense of the year in which the Court award was made (*Simpson v Jones Ch D 1968, 44 TC 599*). See also *CIR v Hugh T Barrie Ltd CA(NI) 1928, 12 TC 1223.*

Damages paid by a brewery to a hotel guest injured by a falling chimney were held to have been incurred by it *qua* property owner and not *qua* trader and not deductible (*Strong & Co of Romsey Ltd v Woodifield HL 1906, 5 TC 215*). Penalties for breach of war-time regulations and defence costs not allowed (*CIR v Warnes & Co KB 1919, 12 TC 227; CIR v Alexander von Glehn & Co Ltd CA 1920, 12 TC 232*), nor fines imposed by professional regulatory body (*McKnight v Sheppard Ch D 1996, 71 TC 419*), nor damages for breach of American 'anti-trust' law (*Cattermole v Borax & Chemicals Ltd KB 1949, 31 TC 202*). See also *G Scammell & Nephew v Rowles CA 1939, 22 TC 479; Fairrie v Hall KB 1947, 28 TC 200; Golder v Great Boulder Proprietary HC 1952, 33 TC 75; Knight v Parry Ch D 1972, 48 TC 580; Hammond Engineering v CIR Ch D 1975, 50 TC 313.*

Simon's Direct Tax Service. See **B3.1509**.

71.48 **COMPENSATION, DAMAGES ETC. — RECEIPTS**

(*a*) **Capital sums** (i.e. sums not taken into account in computing income) received as compensation for damage, injury, destruction or depreciation of assets are subject to capital gains tax [*TCGA 1992, s 22(1)*] (or corporation tax in the case of a company), but this does not apply to compensation or damages to an individual for wrong or injury to his person or in his profession or vocation. [*TCGA 1992, s 51(2)*].

(*b*) **Cancellation or variation of trading contracts and arrangements.** An important case is *Van den Berghs Ltd v Clark HL 1935, 19 TC 390* in which a receipt on the termination of a profit-sharing arrangement was held to be capital. The arrangement related to the whole structure of the recipient's trade, forming the fixed framework within which its circulating capital operated. Compensation, etc. receipts were also held to be capital in *Sabine v Lookers Ltd CA 1958, 38 TC 120* (varying car distributor's agreement); *British-Borneo Petroleum v Cropper Ch D 1968, 45 TC 201* (cancelling a royalty agreement); *Barr Crombie & Co Ltd v CIR CS 1945, 26 TC 406* (terminating agreement as ship-managers); but the opposite conclusion was reached in *Consultant v Inspector of Taxes (Sp C 180), [1999] SSCD 63* (termination of profit participation agreement). A payment by the liquidator of a shipping company to its managers as authorised by the shareholders held not assessable (*Chibbett v Robinson & Sons KB 1924, 9 TC 48*).

Compensation, etc. receipts on the cancellation of contracts receipts from which, if completed, would have been trading receipts are normally themselves trading receipts, to be credited in the computations for the period in which cancelled. See *Short Bros Ltd v CIR* and *Sunderland Shipbuilding Co Ltd v CIR CA 1927, 12 TC 955* (cancellation of order for ships); *CIR v Northfleet Coal Co KB 1927, 12 TC 1102; Jesse Robinson & Sons v CIR KB 1929, 12 TC 1241* (cancellation of contracts for sale of goods, etc.); *Greyhound Racing Assn v Cooper KB 1936, 20 TC 373* (cancellation of agreement to hire greyhound track); *Shove v Dura Mfg Co Ltd KB 1941, 23 TC 779* (cancellation of commission agreement). Similarly compensation to a merchanting company on cancellation of a contract to supply goods to it was held a trading receipt (*Bush, Beach & Gent Ltd v Road KB 1939, 22 TC 519*). See also *United Steel v Cullington (No 1) CA 1939, 23 TC 71; Shadbolt v Salmon Estates KB 1943, 25 TC 52; Sommerfelds Ltd v Freeman Ch D 1966, 44 TC 43; Creed v H & M Levinson Ltd Ch D 1981, 54 TC 477.*

Compensation received on the termination of agencies is a trading receipt unless the agency, by reason of its relative size, etc., is part of the 'fixed framework' (see *Van den Berghs* above) of the agent's business. See *Kelsall Parsons CS 1938, 21 TC 608; CIR v Fleming & Co CS 1951, 33 TC 57; CIR v David MacDonald & Co CS 1955, 36 TC 388; Wiseburgh v Domville CA 1956, 36 TC 527; Fleming v Bellow Machine Co Ch D 1965, 42 TC 308; Elson v James G Johnston Ltd Ch D 1965, 42 TC 545* (in all of which the compensation, etc. was held to be a trading receipt). See also *Anglo-French Exploration Co Ltd v Clayson CA 1956, 36 TC 545.*

For payments received on termination of building society agencies, see Revenue Capital Gains Tax Manual, CG 13050 *et seq.*.

The treatment of compensation on the termination of posts held in the course of a business (particularly a profession), the yearly remuneration having been included in the business receipts (see 75.24 SCHEDULE E), has arisen in a number of cases. In *Blackburn v Close Bros Ltd Ch D 1960, 39 TC 164*, compensation on the cancellation of an agreement by a merchant banker to provide secretarial services was held to be a trading receipt but in *Ellis v Lucas Ch D 1966, 43 TC 276* compensation on the termination of an auditorship was held to be within the ambit of the Schedule E 'golden handshake' legislation [*ICTA 1988, s 148* — see 19.4 COMPENSATION FOR

LOSS OF EMPLOYMENT (AND DAMAGES)] and hence could not be included in the profits for Case II purposes (except a small part of the payment held to be compensation for the loss of general accountancy work). Similar decisions were reached in *Walker v Carnaby Harrower, Barham & Pykett Ch D 1969, 46 TC 561* (loss of auditorship by firm of accountants) and *CIR v Brander & Cruikshank HL 1970, 46 TC 574* (loss of company secretaryships by firm of Scottish advocates) and in *Carnaby Harrower* the payment was also held not to be a professional receipt because of its *ex gratia* nature. For *ex gratia* payments, see also (*e*) below. For compensation on cancellation of contracts of authors, etc. see 71.43 above.

(*c*) **Compensation, etc. relating to capital assets.** Compensation to a company making fireclay goods for refraining from working a fireclay bed under a railway line was held to be capital (*Glenboig Union Fireclay Co Ltd v CIR HL 1922, 12 TC 427* and cf. *Thomas McGhie & Sons v BTC QB 1962, 41 ATC 144* and *Bradbury v United Glass Bottle CA 1959, 38 TC 369*), but compensation to a colliery from the Government for requisition of part of its mining area was held to be a trading receipt (*Waterloo Main Colliery v CIR (No 1) KB 1947, 29 TC 235*). Compensation to a shipping company for delay in the overhaul of a ship was held to be a trading receipt (*Burmah Steam Ship Co v CIR CS 1930, 16 TC 67*) as was compensation to a jetty owner for loss of its use after damage by a ship (*London & Thames Haven v Attwooll CA 1966, 43 TC 491*) and compensation for the detention of a ship (*Ensign Shipping Co v CIR CA 1928, 12 TC 1169* but contrast *CIR v Francis West CS 1950, 31 TC 402*).

For insurance recoveries see 71.64 below.

(*d*) **Compensation on compulsory acquisition, etc.** Where compensation is paid for the acquisition of business property by an authority possessing powers of compulsory acquisition, any amounts included as compensation for temporary loss of profits or losses on trading stock or to reimburse revenue expenditure, such as removal expenses and interest, are treated as trading receipts. (See Revenue Pamphlet IR 131, SP 8/79, 18 June 1979. This Statement of Practice was originally issued as consequence of *Stoke-on-Trent City Council v Wood Mitchell & Co Ltd CA 1978, [1979] STC 197*.)

(*e*) **Other compensation, etc. receipts.** Voluntary payments to an insurance broker on the loss of an important client company (made by its parent company) were held, approving *Chibbett v Robinson* and *Carnaby Harrower* (see (*b*) above), not to be assessable (*Simpson v John Reynolds & Co CA 1975, 49 TC 693*) and similarly for voluntary payments from a brewer to a firm of caterers for the surrender of the leases of tied premises (*Murray v Goodhews CA 1977, 52 TC 86*) but *ex gratia* payments to an estate agent who had not been given an agency he expected were held, on the facts, to be additional remuneration for work already done and assessable. (*McGowan v Brown & Cousins (Stuart Edwards) Ch D 1977, 52 TC 8*). A payment to a diamond broker under informal and non-binding arbitration as damages for the loss of a prospective client was held assessable (*Rolfe v Nagel CA 1981, 55 TC 585*). Compensation for 'loss of profits' following the destruction of the premises of a business not recommenced was held to be of a revenue nature in *Lang v Rice CA (NI) 1983, 57 TC 80*. For compensation receipts relating to the terms on which business premises are tenanted, see 71.78 below.

For the treatment of compensation received by businesses as customers of e.g. utility companies for interruptions and other service deficiencies, see Revenue Tax Bulletin December 1997 pp 490, 491.

Financial loss allowances paid to e.g. jurors, members of certain local authorities and magistrates to compensate them for loss of profit in their trade or profession are assessable under Schedule D, Case I or II as trading receipts. (Revenue Tax Bulletin May 1992 p 20). Such payments are not taxable under Schedule E (see 75.7 SCHEDULE E).

Damages awarded to a theatrical company for breach of a licence it had, were held to be assessable (*Vaughan v Parnell & Zeitlin KB 1940, 23 TC 505*) as was compensation received by a development company under legislation for restricting development (*Johnson v W S Try Ltd CA 1946, 27 TC 167*). A retrospective award for a war-time requisition of trading stock was held to be a trading receipt of the year of requisition (*CIR v Newcastle Breweries Ltd HL 1927, 12 TC 927*).

71.49 CONTINGENT AND FUTURE LIABILITIES

For forward contracts see 71.50 below.

Where a company is required under overseas legislation to make leaving payments to its employees, a provision in its accounts for its prospective liability is permissible if capable of sufficiently accurate calculation (*Owen v Southern Railway of Peru HL 1956, 36 TC 602*). The allowance each year is the actual payments as adjusted for any variation between the opening and closing provisions but the deductible provision for the year in which the legislation was enacted may include an amount in respect of previous services of the employees (*CIR v Titaghur Jute Factory Ltd CS 1978, 53 TC 675*).

No deduction is permissible for future repairs or renewals (*Clayton v Newcastle-under-Lyme Corpn QB 1888, 2 TC 416; Naval Colliery Co Ltd v CIR HL 1928, 12 TC 1017; Peter Merchant Ltd v Stedeford CA 1948, 30 TC 496*) or the future cost of collecting debts (*Monthly Salaries Loan Co v Furlong Ch D 1962, 40 TC 313*) or for future payments of damages in respect of accidents to employees unless liability has been admitted or established (*James Spencer & Co v CIR CS 1950, 32 TC 111*). See also *Albion Rovers Football Club v CIR HL 1952, 33 TC 331* (wages deductible when paid). A provision for regular major overhaul work accrued due on aircraft engines was allowed in *Johnston v Britannia Airways Ltd Ch D 1994, 67 TC 99* (but see now Revenue Tax Bulletin February 1999 p 624 and further below as regards changes in accounting practice superseding this decision).

For provisions by insurance companies for unexpired risks, etc., see *Sun Insurance Office v Clark HL 1912, 6 TC 59*. For the liability of cemetery companies in receipt of lump sums for the future maintenance of graves, see *Paisley Cemetery Co v Reith CES 1898, 4 TC 1* and *London Cemetery Co v Barnes KB 1917, 7 TC 92*.

A provision by a company engaged in the exploitation of a North Sea oil field, for anticipated future expenditure on the completion of the exploitation, in dismantling installations used and (as required under its licence) in 'cleaning up' the sea bed, was disallowed as capital when incurred in *RTZ Oil & Gas Ltd v Elliss Ch D 1987, 61 TC 132*.

See generally Revenue Inspector's Manual, IM 605c–607. See also Revenue Press Release 20 July 1999, and Financial Reporting Standard FRS 12 and articles in the Revenue Tax Bulletin April 1999 pp 636–639 and December 1999 pp 707–709 commenting on its implications for the treatment of provisions in tax computations.

Simon's Direct Tax Service. See **B3.1211** *et seq.*.

71.50 CONTRACTS

For compensation, etc. on the cancellation or variation of contracts see 71.47 and 71.48 above. For work in progress under contracts see 71.83 below.

Where a taxpayer took over a coal merchanting business on the death of his father, an amount paid for the benefit of contracts between his father and suppliers was held capital (*John Smith & Son v Moore HL 1921, 12 TC 266* and see *City of London Contract Corpn v Styles CA 1887, 2 TC 239*). The completion of outstanding contracts following a partnership dissolution (*Hillerns & Fowler v Murray CA 1932, 17 TC 77*) and on a company going into liquidation (*Baker v Cook KB 1937, 21 TC 337*) held to be trading.

Where under a long-term contract goods were invoiced as delivered, the sale proceeds are receipts of the year of delivery (*J P Hall & Co Ltd v CIR CA 1921, 12 TC 382*). If contract prices are varied retrospectively the resultant further sums are assessable or deductible for the years applicable to the sums at the original prices (*Frodingham Ironstone Mines Ltd v Stewart KB 1932, 16 TC 728; New Conveyor Co Ltd v Dodd KB 1945, 27 TC 11*). Compare *English Dairies Ltd v Phillips KB 1927, 11 TC 597; Isaac Holden & Sons Ltd v CIR KB 1924, 12 TC 768* and contrast *Rownson Drew & Clydesdale Ltd v CIR KB 1931, 16 TC 595*.

Losses because of a fall in prices fixed under forward contracts, etc. cannot be anticipated (*Edward Collins & Sons Ltd v CIR CS 1924, 12 TC 773; Whimster & Co v CIR CS 1925, 12 TC 813*) and cf. *Wright Sutcliffe Ltd v CIR KB 1929, 8 ATC 168; J H Young & Co v CIR CS 1924, 12 TC 817; CIR v Hugh T Barrie Ltd CA(NI) 1928, 12 TC 1223.*

71.51 COPYRIGHT ETC.

For the assessment of authors and artistes see 71.43 above.

Where copyrights or public lending rights in literary, dramatic, musical or artistic works, taking more than twelve months to produce, are assigned for a lump sum in circumstances which would render the proceeds assessable as profits of a single year of assessment, an option is given to spread the sum retrospectively (as set out in *ICTA 1988, s 534(2)(3)*) over that and the preceding tax year and (if the work took more than 24 months to produce) the tax year before that. [*ICTA 1988, ss 534, 537*]. This treatment applies also to sale prices, etc., of paintings, sculptures or other works of art taking more than twelve months to produce [*ICTA 1988, s 538; FA 1996, s 128(10)*] and to periodical payments, including royalties, due within two years of date of first publication, etc. A claim for 1995/96 and earlier years in relation to such periodical payments must be made by 5 April following expiration of eight years from date of publication. For claims in relation to lump sum payments, the general six-year time limit at 17.8 CLAIMS applies. A claim relating to 1996/97 or a subsequent year must be made within one year after 31 January following the year of assessment (or in the case of periodical payments the latest year of assessment) into whose basis period the payments would otherwise have fallen. Where the claim relates to periodical payments, it must cover all such payments from the same work, and for 1996/97 onwards, where payments fall into more than one year of assessment, the claim is treated as if it were two or more separate claims, being one for each of the years concerned. [*ICTA 1988, s 534(4)(b)(5)–(5B); FA 1996, s 128(5)*]. See 17.2 CLAIMS for the method of giving effect to claims.

Broadly similar provisions apply in the case of design rights in a design. [*See 537A; Copyright, Designs and Patents Act 1988, Sch 7 para 36(6); FA 1996, s 128(9)*]. See also *ICTA 1988, s 537B* as regards taxation of design royalties where the owner of such rights does not have his usual place of abode in the UK.

Alternatively, where an author assigns, wholly or partially, for *two years or more* (or similarly grants by licence an interest in) the copyright or public lending right in a literary, dramatic, musical or artistic work of his (first published ten or more years previously) for a lump sum which would normally be treated as profits of a single year, he may claim to treat that sum as receivable by equal yearly instalments (up to a maximum of six) during the period covered by the assignment or licence, the first of such sums being treated as due on the date the lump sum became receivable. But if the author permanently discontinues his profession, or dies, any subsequent instalments as above are treated as having been receivable together with the last instalment due before the cessation or death unless, within two years after that event, the author (or his personal representatives) elects for recomputation as if the assignment, etc., had been for a lesser period ending with the day before the cessation or death. This election is abolished for 1996/97 and later years. A claim under these provisions relating to 1996/97 or a subsequent year must be made within one year after 31 January following the year of assessment into whose basis period the lump sum would otherwise have fallen. Previously, the six-year time limit at 17.8 CLAIMS applied. [*ICTA 1988, s 535; FA 1996, s 128(7)(8)*].

ICTA 1988, s 534 and *s 535* are mutually exclusive. [*ICTA 1988, ss 534(6), 535(9)*].

None of the above provisions apply for corporation tax, nor, as regards any receipt after 5 April 1996, can any claim be made by a partnership. [*ICTA 1988, s 534(6A); FA 1996, s 128(6)*].

Amounts held to be assessable include advance payments of gramophone royalties to a singer (*Taylor v Dawson KB 1938, 22 TC 189*); commutations of future royalties paid to an authoress (*Glasson v Rougier KB 1944, 26 TC 86*); receipts from sale of film rights in books (*Howson v Monsell HC 1950, 31 TC 529*); sales of copyright in novels written when the author was non-resident (with no deduction for his expenses then incurred — *Mackenzie v Arnold CA 1952, 33 TC 363*). But contrast *Mitchell v Rosay CA 1954, 35 TC 496. Sharkey v Wernher* (see 71.83 below) does not apply to a gift of copyright (*Mason v Innes CA 1967, 44 TC 326*). Royalties, etc. arising after an author, etc. dies or otherwise ceases to carry on his profession or vocation may be chargeable as POST-CESSATION ETC. RECEIPTS AND EXPENDITURE (62).

Copyright and design royalties or public lending right payments paid by publisher, etc. are deductible in computing their profits but royalties to non-residents must be paid less tax, the tax being accounted for to the Revenue under *ICTA 1988, s 536* or *s 537B*.

For the treatment of expenditure on producing films and certain similar assets, see 71.58 below and 10.25 CAPITAL ALLOWANCES.

Simon's Direct Tax Services. See **B3.814** *et seq.*.

71.52 DEDUCTION OF TAX AT SOURCE—AMOUNTS PAID UNDER

The combined effect of *ICTA 1988, s 74(1)(m)(p)* (and, before 6 April 1997, *ICTA 1988, s 74(1)(q)* (repealed by *FA 1997, Sch 18 Pt VI(2)*)) is to prohibit the deduction in computing profits of annuities, annual payments (other than interest), patent royalties, etc. payable under DEDUCTION OF TAX AT SOURCE (23) but see 23.13 re certain mortgage interest. For interest see 71.65 below and for copyright royalties see 71.51 above. For the treatment of such payments as 'charges on income' for companies see Tolley's Corporation Tax. See 46.17 LOSSES where payments exceed the profits.

ICTA 1988, s 74(1)(m) applies only to amounts 'payable out of the profits' (cf. similar wording in *ICTA 1988, s 348*). Payments made before the profits can be ascertained are not payable out of the profits and therefore not within the *section 74(1)(m)* prohibition. For this see *Gresham Life Assce v Styles HL 1890, 3 TC 185* and *Paterson Engineering Co Ltd v Duff KB 1943, 25 TC 43*. See also *Ogden v Medway Cinemas Ltd KB 1934, 18 TC 691* and *Moss Empires Ltd v CIR HL 1937, 21 TC 264*.

71.53 EMBEZZLEMENT ETC.

Losses allowed but not misappropriation by partner or director. See *Bamford v ATA Advertising Ch D 1972, 48 TC 359* and cf. *Curtis v J & G Oldfield Ltd KB 1925, 9 TC 319*.

Where defalcations were made good by the auditor who admitted negligence, refund held to be a trading receipt for the year in which made (*Gray v Penrhyn KB 1937, 21 TC 252*).

See 71.63 below as regards prohibition on deduction of expenditure involving crime.

71.54 **EMPLOYEES (AND DIRECTORS)**

Bona fide remuneration is deductible including bonuses, commissions, tax deducted under PAYE and the cost of board, lodging, uniforms and benefits provided. The deduction is for the remuneration etc. payable; future payments cannot be anticipated (*Albion Rovers Football Club v CIR HL 1952, 33 TC 331*). The remuneration etc. must be shown to be wholly and exclusively for the purposes of the trade. In *Stott & Ingham v Trehearne KB 1924, 9 TC 69* an increase in the rate of commission payable to the trader's sons was disallowed as not on a commercial footing. See also *Johnson Bros & Co v CIR KB 1919, 12 TC 147*, *Copeman v Wm Flood & Sons Ltd KB 1940, 24 TC 53* and *Earlspring Properties Ltd v Guest CA 1995, 67 TC 259*. Payments by a farming couple to their young children for help on the farm were disallowed in *Dollar v Lyon Ch D 1981, 54 TC 459*. For excessive payments to 'service company' see *Payne, Stone Fraser* at 71.72 below. For wife's wages see *Thompson v Bruce KB 1927, 11 TC 607; Moschi v Kelly CA 1952, 33 TC 442*. The salary etc. of an employee for service in an overseas subsidiary was allowed in computing the profits of the parent in *Robinson v Scott Bader & Co Ltd CA 1981, 54 TC 757*. The secondment was wholly and exclusively for the purposes of the parent's business, notwithstanding the benefit to the subsidiary's business.

Any excess of the market value over the par value of shares issued to employees at par is not deductible (*Lowry v Consolidated African Selection Trust Ltd HL 1940, 23 TC 259*). For payments to trustees to acquire shares for the benefit of employees, see *Heather v P-E Consulting Group CA 1972, 48 TC 293*, *Jeffs v Ringtons Ltd Ch D 1985, 58 TC 680* and *E Bott Ltd v Price Ch D 1985, 59 TC 437*, and contrast *Rutter v Charles Sharpe & Co Ltd Ch D 1979, 53 TC 163* and *Mawsley Machinery Ltd v Robinson (Sp C 170), [1998] SSCD 236*. See also 82 SHARE INCENTIVES AND OPTIONS.

'Relevant emoluments' and 'potential emoluments' which would otherwise be deductible may be deducted only if they are paid before the end of the period of nine months beginning with the end of the period of account. Emoluments paid at a later date are deductible for the period of account *in which* they are paid. The time at which emoluments are paid is to be determined in accordance with the same rules as in 75.1 SCHEDULE E as to when emoluments are to be treated as received. Computations prepared before the end of the said nine-month period must be prepared on the basis that any unpaid 'relevant emoluments' will not be paid before the expiry of that period and are therefore not deductible for that period of account. If, in fact, such emoluments *are* paid within the said nine-month period, the computation can be adjusted accordingly on a claim being made to the inspector within two years after the end of the period of account concerned.

'*Relevant emoluments*' are emoluments for a period allocated specifically or in general to offices or employments (or both). '*Potential emoluments*' are amounts or benefits reserved in the employer's accounts (or held by an intermediary) with a view to their becoming relevant emoluments, and are paid when they become relevant emoluments which are paid. [*FA 1989, s 43; FA 1993, s 181*].

Similar provisions apply in relation to investment and insurance companies. [*FA 1989, s 44*].

Council tax and community charge. An employer who pays the council tax or community charge (or Scottish community water charge) for an employee will normally be able to claim a deduction for it. If such payments are also made on behalf of members of the employee's family, they too are deductible if part of the employee's remuneration package (which would normally mean they were paid under the contract of employment). (Revenue Press Releases 10 November 1989, 16 March 1993).

Employee share ownership plans. Subject to the exceptions below, the following are allowable deductions (in computing company trading profits or as management expenses) in connection with an approved employee share ownership plan within *FA 2000, Sch 8* (see 82.11–82.25 SHARE INCENTIVES AND OPTIONS):

(*a*) the market value (at time of acquisition by the plan trustees, and see below) of free and matching shares appropriated to employees under the plan (the deduction being given *to the employer company* for the period of account in which the shares are appropriated);

(*b*) any excess of the market value ((at time of acquisition by the plan trustees, and determined as for capital gains tax purposes) of partnership shares over the amounts paid by participating employees to acquire them (the deduction being given *to the employer company* for the period of account in which the shares are acquired on participants' behalf);

(*c*) expenditure incurred by a company in establishing a plan (the deduction being given for the period of account in which the expenditure is incurred, unless the Revenue approve the plan more than nine months after the end of that period, in which case the deduction is given for the period of account in which approval is given);

(*d*) contributions by a company to the expenses of plan trustees in operating a plan, *excluding* expenses in acquiring shares (other than incidental costs such as fees, commission, stamp duty etc.) but *including* interest on money borrowed to acquire shares.

Once a deduction is made under (*a*) or (*b*) above, no other deduction (other than any within (*c*) or (*d*) above) may be made by the employer company or any associated company (as defined) in respect of the provision of the shares, and no deduction within (*a*) or (*b*) above may then be made by any other company in that respect. Once a deduction is made under (*c*) above, no other deduction may be made in respect of the costs of setting up the plan.

For the purposes of (*a*) above, market value is determined as for capital gains tax purposes, and, for the purposes of that determination (and also for those of (iii) below), shares acquired by the trustees on different days are deemed to be awarded under the plan on a first in/first out basis. In the case of a group plan (i.e. a plan established by a parent company and extending to one or more companies under its control), the total market value of the shares appropriated is apportioned between the relevant employer companies by reference to the number of shares appropriated by each company.

No deduction is allowed under (*a*) or (*b*) above:

(i) in respect of shares awarded to an individual who is not at that time a Schedule E taxpayer in respect of emoluments from the eligible employment (whether or not on the remittance basis as regards non-UK emoluments);

(ii) in respect of shares that are liable to depreciate substantially in value for reasons that do not apply generally to shares in the company;

(iii) if a deduction has been made (on whatever basis), by the company, or an associated company (as defined) in respect of providing the same shares for the plan trust or for another trust (whatever its nature or purpose); or

(iv) in respect of the subsequent award of shares previously forfeited by participants (such shares being treated as acquired by the trustees at time of forfeit for no consideration).

No deduction is allowed under (*c*) above if any employee acquires rights under the plan, or the trustees acquire any shares, before the plan receives Revenue approval. Subject to (*d*) above, no deduction is allowed for expenses in providing dividend shares.

On withdrawal of Revenue approval to a plan, the Revenue may, by notice, direct that any deductions made under (*a*) or (*b*) above be withdrawn also, in which case the aggregate deductions made are treated as a trading receipt of the company concerned for the period of account in which the Revenue notify withdrawal of approval (or, in the case of an investment company, as income chargeable under Schedule D, Case VI arising at the time of notice of withdrawal). See 82.24 SHARE INCENTIVES AND OPTIONS for right of appeal.

[*FA 2000, Sch 8 para 2(1), para 3(1), paras 105–114, 125, 126*].

Employee share ownership trusts. Payments made by a UK resident company by way of contribution to a trust which at the time of payment is a qualifying employee share ownership trust (ESOT) from which at least some of its employees (or those of a company which it controls (within *ICTA 1988, s 840*)) are eligible to benefit are allowable on a claim to that effect being made within two years after the end of the period of account in which the payment is charged as an expense. In order for the payment to qualify for relief, the sum received must be expended by the trustees within nine months (or such longer period as the Board may, by notice, allow) after the end of the said period of account (all sums received by the trustees being deemed to be expended by them on a first in/first out basis) for one or more of the following qualifying purposes:

(*a*) the acquisition of shares in the company which established the trust;

(*b*) the repayment of borrowings;

(*c*) the payment of interest on borrowings;

(*d*) the payment of sums to beneficiaries;

(*e*) the meeting of expenses (including income or capital gains tax, see Revenue Inspector's Manual, IM 680e).

[*FA 1989, s 67*].

Contributions received are deemed to be used first to meet expenditure for qualifying purposes, expenditure for non-qualifying purposes being treated as far as possible as met out of other income (e.g. dividends or interest). (Revenue Inspector's Manual, IM 680f).

See 82.41 SHARE INCENTIVES AND OPTIONS for the definition of a qualifying ESOT and for provisions enabling a charge to tax to be made, in certain circumstances, on the trustees, but recoverable also from the company, where the above relief has previously been given.

Expenditure on establishing a qualifying ESOT is deductible in computing the company's trading profits (or as a management expense). If the deed establishing the trust is executed more than nine months after the end of the period of account in which the expenditure is incurred, it is treated as incurred in the period in which the deed is executed. [*ICTA 1988, s 85A; FA 1991, s 43*].

Non-qualifying ESOTs. For the treatment of contributions to ESOTs not within the above provisions which are not capital expenditure on general principles but which are required under UITF 13 to be treated as giving rise to an asset in the employer's accounts, see Revenue Tax Bulletin February 1997 pp 399, 400. Broadly, relief for the contributions is deferred until the rights in the shares are transferred to employees, although this would not prevent a deduction for a properly calculated provision reflecting employees' accruing entitlement to such benefits.

Profit sharing and share option schemes. Expenditure on establishing an approved profit sharing or share option scheme (see 82.9, 82.38, 82.39, 82.40 SHARE INCENTIVES AND

OPTIONS) is deductible in computing the company's trading profits (or as a management expense) provided that:

(*a*) in the case of a profit sharing scheme, the trustees acquire no shares under the scheme before it is approved; or

(*b*) in the case of a share option scheme, no employee or director obtains rights under the scheme before it is approved.

If the scheme is approved more than nine months after the end of the period of account in which the expenditure is incurred, it is for these purposes treated as incurred in the period in which the approval is given. [*ICTA 1988, s 84A; FA 1991, s 42*].

In the case of an approved profit sharing scheme, a similar deduction is available for payments made to the scheme trustees which are either (i) necessary to meet their reasonable administration expenses or (ii) applied by them, within nine months after the end of the period of account in which the expense is charged (or such longer time as the Revenue may allow), in acquiring shares for appropriation to participants. As a consequence of the phasing out of approved profit sharing schemes (see 82.9 SHARE INCENTIVES AND OPTIONS), no deduction is available under (i) above for any payment made more than three years after the last appropriation made in accordance with the scheme before 1 January 2003. Similarly, no deduction is available under (ii) above for (1) any payment made after 5 April 2002 or (2) any payment made after 20 March 2000 and before 6 April 2002 unless the shares thus acquired are appropriated no later than nine months after the end of the period of account in which the payment was made and before 1 January 2003. [*ICTA 1988, s 85; FA 2000, s 50*].

Retirement and benevolent provisions for employees. See 66.5(*a*), 66.10 RETIREMENT SCHEMES for the deductibility of payments by the employer under such schemes. *Bona fide* voluntary pensions and retirement gratuities, including pensions to widows, are allowed (*Smith v Incorporated Council of Law Reporting KB 1914, 6 TC 477*). The cost of an annuity to replace a pension is allowed but not the cost of a policy to secure payment *to the employer* of an annuity equal to pensions payable by him (*Hancock v General Reversionary & Investment Co Ltd KB 1918, 7 TC 358; Morgan Crucible Co Ltd v CIR KB 1932, 17 TC 311*). For provisions for directors of 'family companies' see *Samuel Dracup & Sons Ltd v Dakin Ch D 1957, 37 TC 377.*

Payments directly or indirectly for the benefit of employees are allowable including donations to hospitals and charities (see 71.84 below) unless capital or abnormal (*Rowntree & Co v Curtis CA 1924, 8 TC 678; Bourne & Hollingsworth v Ogden KB 1929, 14 TC 349*). See also *Hutchinson & Co v Turner HC 1950, 31 TC 495*. Subscriptions to BUPA and similar group schemes for employees are allowed (see 75.37 SCHEDULE E for position regarding the employees).

Redundancy payments, or other employer's payments, under *Employment Rights Act 1996* (or NI equivalent) allowable. Rebates recoverable are trading receipts. [*ICTA 1988, ss 579, 580; FA 1998, s 38, Sch 5 para 43, Sch 27 Pt III(4)*].

Non-statutory redundancy and similar payments are normally allowable unless made on the cessation of trading (but now see following paragraphs) (*CIR v Anglo-Brewing Co Ltd KB 1925, 12 TC 803; Godden v Wilson's Stores CA 1962, 40 TC 161; Geo Peters & Co v Smith Ch D 1963, 41 TC 264*) or as part of the bargain for the sale of shares of the company carrying on the business (*Bassett Enterprise Ltd v Petty KB 1938, 21 TC 730; James Snook & Co Ltd v Blasdale CA 1952, 33 TC 244*). See also *Overy v Ashford Dunn & Co KB 1933, 17 TC 497* and contrast *CIR v Patrick Thomson Ltd CS 1956, 37 TC 145*. A payment to secure the resignation of a life-director who had fallen out with his co-directors was allowed in *Mitchell v B W Noble Ltd CA 1927, 11 TC 372*. See also *O'Keeffe v Southport Printers Ltd Ch D 1984, 58 TC 88*. For provisions for future leaving payments see 71.49 above.

Payments made to employees taken on for trade purposes, under a pre-existing contractual or statutory obligation which was a consequence of their being so taken on, are not disallowed by *ICTA 1988, s 74(1)(a)* (see 71.40 above) just because it is the cessation of the trade that crystallises the liability to pay. (Revenue Tax Bulletin February 1999 pp 630, 631).

Payments in addition to the statutory payment made on cessation of trading (including deemed cessation on a partnership change) will be allowed if they would have been allowed had there been no cessation. Allowance is up to three times the statutory payment and payment made after cessation is treated as made on last day business carried on. [*ICTA 1988, s 90*]. In practice, allowance will also be given for such payments on a partial cessation (i.e. where an identifiable part of a trade is discontinued). (Revenue Pamphlet IR 131, SP 11/81, 6 November 1981).

Relief under *ICTA 1988, s 579* or *s 90* (as above) is due for the period of account in which the payment is made (or, if paid after discontinuance, for the last day on which the business is carried on). Where instead relief is due under general principles, a provision for future payments may be allowed for a period of account provided that:

(*a*) it appears in the commercial accounts in accordance with generally accepted accounting principles;

(*b*) it was accurately calculated (normally requiring the identification of the individual employees affected) using the degree of hindsight permitted by SSAP 17;

(*c*) a definite decision to proceed with the redundancies was taken during the period; and

(*d*) payment was made within nine months of the end of the period.

(Revenue Tax Bulletin February 1995 p 195).

See generally Revenue Inspector's Manual, IM 950–961.

Counselling services. Expenditure on outplacement counselling which falls within the Schedule E exemption under *ICTA 1988, ss 589A, 589B* (see 75.42 SCHEDULE E) is deductible either in computing the profits of the employer's trade or as a management expense under *ICTA 1988, s 75*. [*ICTA 1988, s 589A(7)–(10); FA 1993, s 108*].

Key employee insurance. Premiums on policies in favour of the employer insuring against death or critical illness of key employees are generally allowable, and the proceeds of any such policies trading receipts.

National insurance contributions ('NICs'). Under *ICTA 1988, s 617(4)*, secondary Class 1 NICs (payable by an employer in respect of employees' emoluments) are deductible if they would be so but for the general prohibition in *section 617(3)*. From 26 November 1996 (and previously by concession), relief is similarly available for Class 1A NICs (payable by an employer where cars are provided to employees wholly or partly for private use). Relief is likewise available for Class 1B NICs (payable from 6 April 1999 in respect of PAYE settlement agreements, see 55.12 PAY AS YOU EARN). [*ICTA 1988, s 617(3)(4); FA 1997, s 65; FA 1999, s 61* and see Revenue Pamphlet IR 1, B48]. As regards relief for Class 4 (self-employed) NICs, see 83.7 SOCIAL SECURITY.

Training costs. Costs incurred by an employer in respect of employee training are generally allowable as a trading expense. For a Revenue view of the circumstances in which such relief may be prohibited by *ICTA 1988, s 74(1)(a)* (see 71.40 above), see Revenue Tax Bulletin February 1997 pp 400, 401 (which also indicates that it is extremely unlikely that such expenditure would be disallowed on the grounds that it was of a capital nature).

Expenditure which falls within the Schedule E exemption under *ICTA 1988, ss 588, 589* for training costs (see 75.42 SCHEDULE E) is deductible either in computing the profits of the employer's trade or as a management expense under *ICTA 1988, s 75*. The provisions relating to assessments, information and penalties in relation to the Schedule E exemption apply equally in relation to this deduction. [*ICTA 1988, s 588(3)–(5); FA 1996, Sch 18 paras 10, 17(1)(2)*]. See 71.84 below as regards contributions to training and enterprise councils, and 92 VOCATIONAL TRAINING RELIEF as regards relief for self-employed.

Employees seconded to charities or educational bodies. If an employer seconds an employee temporarily to a charity (as defined in *ICTA 1988, s 506*, see 15.1 CHARITIES), any expenditure attributable to the employment incurred by the employer is deductible in computing its profits to the extent to which it would have been deductible if the employee's services had continued to be available for its business. This relief is extended to secondments to certain educational bodies. The bodies concerned include education authorities and educational institutions maintained by such authorities, and certain other educational bodies, the descriptions of which have been updated from 1999/2000 onwards. [*ICTA 1988, s 86; FA 1999, s 58*].

Payroll deduction scheme. See 15.18 CHARITIES.

Simon's Direct Tax Service. See **B3.1424** *et seq.*, **B3.1513**.

71.55 ENTERTAINMENT EXPENSES

Entertainment expenses not allowed (and no capital allowances on cars, etc., used for entertaining) except for staff entertainment. Covers gifts unless (*a*) carrying prominent advertisement, (*b*) not food, drink, etc., and (*c*) no more than £10 worth per person p.a. [*ICTA 1988, s 577*]. Deductions allowed for items provided in the ordinary course of a trade of providing entertainment (see *Fleming v Associated Newspapers Ltd HL 1972, 48 TC 382*) or provided gratuitously for advertising to the public generally. [*ICTA 1988, s 577(10)*]. See also the VAT cases of *C & E Commissioners v Shaklee International and Another CA, [1981] STC 776* and *Celtic Football and Athletic Co Ltd v C & E Commissioners CS, [1983] STC 470.*

For an article on the scope and application of *ICTA 1988, s 577*, see Revenue Tax Bulletin August 1999 pp 679–682 as supplemented by Revenue Tax Bulletin February 2000 p 729.

See 71.84 below as regards gifts to charitable bodies.

See generally Revenue Inspector's Manual, IM 690–695.

71.56 EXCHANGE GAINS AND LOSSES

See Tolley's Corporation Tax under Exchange Gains and Losses for special provisions applying in the case of transactions by certain 'qualifying companies'.

In general, exchange differences are taken into account in computing trading profits if they relate to the circulating capital of the business but not otherwise. In *Overseas Containers (Finance) Ltd v Stoker CA 1989, 61 TC 473*, exchange losses arising on loans transferred to a finance subsidiary set up to convert the losses to trading account were held not to arise from trading transactions.

In *Davies v The Shell Co of China Ltd CA 1951, 32 TC 133*, a petrol marketing company operating in China required agents to deposit Chinese dollars with it, repayable on the ending of the agency. Exchange profits it made on repaying the deposits were held to be capital. In *Firestone Tyre & Rubber Co Ltd v Evans Ch D 1976, 51 TC 615*, a company repaid in 1965 a dollar balance due to its US parent, the greater part of which represented advances in 1922–1931 to finance the company when it started. The Commissioners' finding that 90% of the resultant large exchange loss was capital and not allowable, was upheld. A profit by an agent on advances to the principal to finance purchases by the agent on behalf of the principal, was held to be a trading receipt (*Landes Bros v Simpson KB 1934, 19 TC 62*) as was a profit by a tobacco company on dollars accumulated to finance its future purchases (*Imperial Tobacco Co v Kelly CA 1943, 25 TC 292*). See also *McKinlay v H T Jenkins & Son KB 1926, 10 TC 372; Ward v Anglo-American Oil KB 1934, 19 TC 94; Beauchamp v F W Woolworth plc HL 1989, 61 TC 542;* and contrast *Radio Pictures Ltd v CIR CA 1938, 22 TC 106*. Where a bank operated in foreign currencies and aimed at, and generally succeeded in, matching its monetary assets and liabilities in each currency, it was held that there could be no profit or loss from matched transactions where there were no relevant currency conversions (*Pattison v Marine Midland Ltd HL 1983, 57 TC 219*). In *Whittles v Uniholdings Ltd (No 3) CA 1996, 68 TC 528* it was held that a dollar loan and a simultaneous forward contract with the same bank for dollars sufficient to repay the loan had to be treated, for tax purposes, as separate transactions, each giving rise to its own tax consequences.

Following the *Marine Midland Ltd* case (above) the Revenue issued a statement setting out their views on the general treatment of exchange differences for tax purposes. Broadly these are as follows.

Where currency assets are matched by currency liabilities in a particular currency, so that a translation adjustment on one would be cancelled out by a translation adjustment on the other, no adjustment is required for tax purposes.

Where currency assets are not matched, or are incompletely matched, with currency liabilities in a particular currency, the adjustment required to the net exchange difference debited or credited in the profit and loss account is determined along the following lines:

(i) the aggregate exchange differences, positive and negative, on capital assets and liabilities in the profit and loss account figure are ascertained;

(ii) if there are no differences as at (i), no adjustment is required;

(iii) if the net exchange difference as at (i) is a loss, and the net exchange difference in the profit and loss account is also a loss, the smaller of the two losses is the amount disallowed for tax purposes as relating to capital transactions;

(iv) if the net exchange difference as at (i) is a profit, and the net exchange difference in the profit and loss account is also a profit, the smaller of the two profits is allowed as a deduction for tax purposes;

(v) if the net exchange difference as at (i) is a loss, and the net exchange difference in the profit and loss account is a profit, or vice versa, no adjustment is required for tax purposes.

Where net exchange differences are taken to reserve rather than to the profit and loss account, the nature of the assets and liabilities will need to be considered to determine whether or not a tax adjustment is required, applying the principles as above.

In considering whether a trader is matched in a particular foreign currency, *forward exchange contracts* and *currency futures* entered into for hedging purposes may be taken into account, provided the hedging is reflected in the accounts on a consistent basis from year to year and in accordance with accepted accountancy practice. *Currency swap agreements* are treated as converting the liability in the original currency into a liability in the swap currency for the duration of the swap. Hedging through *currency options* does not result in any matching.

The statement also indicates that the accounts treatment of financial assets held on the 'realisation' basis (i.e. where profits are assessable only on their disposal) will be acceptable for tax purposes where the profits or losses on realisation are in effect recognised for accounts purposes net of exchange differences.

Where an *overseas trade*, or an *overseas branch* of a trade, is carried on primarily in a non-sterling economic environment, the Revenue will accept computations based on

(*a*) local currency accounts, with the adjusted profit (before capital allowances) translated into sterling at either average or closing rate, or

(*b*) the sterling equivalent of local currency accounts, translated using the 'net investment/closing rate' method, or

(*c*) sterling accounts produced by the 'temporal' method (see SSAP 20 paras 4–12),

provided the same method is applied consistently from year to year. The principles outlined in this Statement of Practice should be applied in considering any adjustment necessary in respect of exchange differences in the foreign currency accounts.

Where *roundabout loan arrangements* are employed in unmatched or partly matched situations, the Revenue consider that, applying the *Ramsay* principle (see 3.1 ANTI-AVOIDANCE), such arrangements may fall to be treated for tax purposes by reference to their composite effect, depending on the facts of the particular case. It will generally be for the trader to justify the adoption of any basis other than that outlined above in the particular circumstances of his case.

(Revenue Pamphlet IR 131, SP 1/87, 17 February 1987).

If not taken into account in computing trading profits, a profit/loss on the sale of currency is within the ambit of CGT unless exempted by *TCGA 1992, s 269* as currency required for an individual's (or his dependant's) personal expenditure abroad (including provision or maintenance of a residence abroad).

Simon's Direct Tax Service. See **B3.17**.

71.57 FARMING AND MARKET GARDENING

(*a*) **Averaging of profits.** Where for two consecutive years of assessment the profits of an individual or partnership from a trade of farming or market gardening in the UK for one year are less than 75% of the profits for the other, a claim for relief may be made as described below. The relief does not extend to corporation tax.

'*Farming*' for this purpose includes the intensive rearing of livestock or fish on a commercial basis for the production of food for human consumption. (Revenue Pamphlet IR 1, A29).

If the profits for either year do not exceed seven-tenths of the profits of the other (or are nil), the profits for each year are adjusted to half the total of both. If either year's profits exceed seven-tenths of the other's, but are less than three-quarters, the profits are adjusted by adding to the lower and subtracting from the higher the amount obtained by multiplying the difference by three and deducting three-quarters of the higher figure. (Thus, if the profits are £21,900 and £30,000, the adjusted profits after relief would be £23,700 and £28,200.)

'*Profits*' for this purpose are those before any adjustment for losses. Previously, no adjustment was made for capital allowances or balancing charges either (save insofar as these were taken into account in the computation of profits), and, in the case of partnerships (see also below), the relevant profits were those assessed jointly on the partnership. However, neither of these rules applies where the first of the two years to which the averaging claim relates is 1995/96 or a subsequent year as regards trades commenced after 5 April 1994 or 1996/97 or a subsequent year as regards trades commenced on or before that date.

The adjustments made under the relief are effective for all income tax purposes except that they are disregarded in reviewing the years preceding a year of discontinuance (under the pre-Finance Act 1994 basis period rules — see 71.9 above) (but see below as regards the further claim for relief which may be made where the profits of those years are adjusted under the cessation provisions). Further, they do not prevent any claim for loss relief. (Thus, if there was a loss of £5,000 in the basis period for one year and a profit of £15,000 in that for the other, the profits chargeable for each year become £7,500 but the loss of £5,000 remains eligible for loss relief in the normal way.)

A claim must (except as follows) be made to the inspector in writing within two years after the end of the second year of assessment to which it relates, but once a claim has been made, no new claim is open for earlier years. Where the first of the two years to which the claim relates is 1996/97 or a subsequent year, the time limit is twelve months from 31 January following the second year. If a claim has been made for years 1 and 2, a claim may also be made for years 2 and 3, the profits for year 2 being taken as those adjusted on the first claim, and similarly for subsequent years. In the case of partnerships, where the first of the two years to which the averaging claim relates is 1995/96 or a subsequent year as regards trades commenced after 5 April 1994 or 1996/97 or a subsequent year as regards trades commenced on or before that date, an individual partner may make his own claim, based on his share of profits, regardless of whether or not other partners make claims. For earlier years, a partnership claim must be made jointly by all the partners who are individuals and if there is a change in the partners (with an election for continuance) all the individual partners engaged in the trade before and after the change must join in making the claim (including the personal representatives of any deceased). See 17.2 CLAIMS for further provisions regarding claims.

No claim is available for a year of assessment in which the trade was commenced or discontinued or treated as having been discontinued.

If, after a claim, the profits of either or both years are adjusted for some other reason, the claim lapses but a new one may then be made, in respect of the adjusted profits, within the year of assessment following the year in which the adjustment is made. Where the first of the two years to which the original claim relates is 1996/97 or a subsequent year, the deadline for the new claim is 31 January following the year immediately after that in which the adjustment is made.

Where a claim is made as above for 1995/96 or earlier, any claim for relief for the same year under any other provisions of the *Income Tax Acts* may be made, revoked or amended within the same time limits as above but not after the claim as above is determined. Under self-assessment, a claim for other relief for either of the two years affected by an averaging claim can be made, amended or revoked within the period during which the averaging claim can be revoked by amendment of a return or otherwise (which, other than in enquiry cases, will normally end twelve months after the filing date for the return in which the averaging claim is made — see 78.7 SELF-ASSESSMENT). See also 17.2 CLAIMS for the way in which claims for other relief are given effect. [*ICTA 1988, s 96; FA 1994, s 196, s 214(1)(a)(7), s 216(3)(a)(5), Sch 19 para 37, Sch 26 Pt V(24); FA 1995, Sch 6 para 15; FA 1996, s 128(3); FA 1998, Sch 27 Pt III(4)*].

For articles on the making, calculating and implementing of averaging claims under self-assessment and on the completion of the relevant tax returns, see Revenue Tax Bulletin February 1997 pp 392–394 and August 1998 p 575.

Example

A, who has been farming for several years, earns the following profits as adjusted for Schedule D, Case I and *before* capital allowances.

Year ended	Schedule D, Case I Profit/(loss)
	£
30.9.94	8,500
30.9.95	8,000
30.9.96	16,000
30.9.97	12,000
30.9.98	7,700
30.9.99	2,300
30.9.00	(2,000)

Capital allowances for 1996/97 are £2,100. The profits/(loss) for the years ended 30.9.97 onwards are arrived at after deducting capital allowances.

Averaged profits for all years would be

			No averaging claims	Averaging claims for all years
			£	£
1995/96		note (i)	8,500	10,000
1996/97	(transitional year)	notes (i)(ii)(iii)	12,000	12,300
1997/98		note (ii)	12,000	10,200
1998/99		notes (iv)(v)	7,700	5,000
1999/2000		notes (v)(vi)	2,300	2,500
2000/01		notes (vi)(vii)	Nil	2,500
			£42,500	£42,500

Notes

(i)

1995/96	8,500
1996/97	12,000
	£20,500

As £8,500 exceeds $\frac{7}{10}$ of £12,000 but does not exceed $\frac{3}{4}$, the adjustment is computed as follows.

Difference £3,500 × 3	10,500	
Deduct $\frac{3}{4}$ × £12,000	9,000	
Adjustment	1,500	(1,500)
Existing 1995/96	8,500	
Existing 1996/97		12,000
Revised averaged profits 1995/96/1996/97	£10,000	£10,500

(ii) 1996/97 (10,500 – 2,100 =) 8,400
1997/98 12,000

£20,400 ÷ 2 = £10,200

As £8,400 does not exceed $\frac{7}{10}$ of £12,000, the straight average applies. The profit figures are averaged after deduction of capital allowances, so that the revised figure for 1996/97 *before* capital allowances is £12,300 (£10,200 + £2,100).

(iii) The assessment for 1996/97 before averaging is based on $\frac{12}{24}$ of the profits for the two years to 30 September 1996 (the transitional period) (see 71.20 above).

(iv) 1997/98 10,200
1998/99 7,700

£17,900

As £7,700 exceeds $\frac{3}{4}$ of £10,200, no averaging is permitted.

(v) 1998/99 7,700
1999/2000 2,300

10,000 ÷ 2 = £5,000

As £2,300 does not exceed $\frac{7}{10}$ of £7,700, the straight average applies.

(vi) 1999/2000 5,000
2000/01 Nil

£5,000 ÷ 2 = £2,500

(vii) The loss for the year to 30 September 2000 is not taken into account for averaging, but would be available to reduce the averaged profits for 2000/01 on a claim under *section 380*.

See generally Revenue Inspector's Manual, IM 2320–2332d.

The computation of transitional overlap profits for 1997/98 (see 71.22 above) is not affected by averaging claim(s) by farmers. (Revenue Tax Bulletin August 1998 pp 574, 575).

(*b*) **Compensation for compulsory slaughter.** Where compensation is received for compulsory slaughter of animals to which the HERD BASIS (34) does not apply, any excess of the amount received over the book value or cost of those animals may, by concession, be excluded from the year of receipt and treated, by equal instalments, as profits of the next three years. (Revenue Pamphlet IR 1, B11). In practice, the profit on an animal born in the year of slaughter is deemed to be 25% of the compensation received. For examples of the arrangements for spreading of compensation, see Revenue Inspector's Manual, IM 2268a *et seq.*.

Compensation paid under the BSE Suspects Scheme and the BSE Selective Cull (where the animal was born after 14 October 1990) is for compulsory slaughter, and for these purposes includes Selective Cull 'top-up' payments. Payments under the Calf Processing Scheme, the Over Thirty Month Scheme and the BSE Selective

Cull where the animal was born before 15 October 1990 are *not* for compulsory slaughter. (Revenue Tax Bulletin February 1997 pp 396, 397).

(*c*) **Drainage.** Where land is made re-available for cultivation by the restoration of drainage or by re-draining, the net expenditure incurred (after crediting any grants receivable) will be allowed as a revenue expenditure in farm accounts provided it excludes (i) any substantial element of improvement (e.g. the substitution of tile drainage for mole drainage) and (ii) the capital element in cases in which the present owner is known to have acquired the land at a depressed price because of its swampy condition. (Revenue Pamphlet IR 131, SP 5/81, 8 September 1981).

(*d*) **Farmhouses.** The apportionment of the running costs of a farmhouse between business and private use should be based on the facts of the case for the year of account in question, and may require revision to reflect the fact that many farmhouses are now used only to a limited extent for business purposes. The long-standing practice of accepting a one-third business/two-thirds private split will in many cases no longer be appropriate. (Revenue Tax Bulletin February 1993 p 54).

Maintenance expenses of owner-occupied farms not carried on on a commercial basis. Where a loss claim against general income is precluded by *ICTA 1988, ss 384, 397* (see 46.9 LOSSES) or *s 393A(3)* (see Tolley's Corporation Tax under Losses), relief for maintenance etc. of land, houses etc. may be claimed under *ICTA 1988, s 33* (see 68.16(*a*) SCHEDULE A). (Revenue Pamphlet IR 1, B5). Despite the repeal of *section 33* for income tax purposes, the Revenue still allow relief to be claimed, by virtue of this concession, for expenditure incurred after 5 April 1995 which would have qualified under *section 33* if it was still in force. The concession is withdrawn after 5 April 2001 (31 March 2001 for corporation tax). (Revenue Inspector's Manual, IM 2336c).

(*e*) **Gangmasters.** A special unit within the Revenue monitors compliance by agricultural gangmasters, in relation to PAYE and national insurance in respect of their workers and their own returns. It is the Agricultural Compliance Unit, Sovereign House, 40 Silver Street, Sheffield S1 2EN (tel. 01142 739099). (Revenue Press Release 2 September 1988). For whether a worker also responsible for selection of other workers acts as gangmaster, see *Andrews v King Ch D 1991, 64 TC 332.*

(*f*) **Grants and subsidies.** See generally 71.85 below. As regards the time at which a receipt should be brought in for tax purposes, a distinction should be drawn between grants to meet particular costs and those subsidising the sale proceeds of a specific crop. The former should reduce the costs in question (and if those costs are included in the closing stock valuation, the net cost should be used), whereas the latter should be recognised as income of the year in which the crop is sold. (Revenue Tax Bulletin February 1993 p 53). A grant subsidising trading income generally is a trading receipt of the period when the entitlement to the grant was established, provided that it can be quantified with reasonable accuracy. As regards instalments of grant, the tax treatment should follow accounting practice, which provides that information available before accounts are completed and signed should be taken into account as regards those to which entitlement arose in the period of account. (Revenue Tax Bulletin February 1994 p 108).

As regards animal grants and subsidies, these are generally recognised either at the end of the retention period or on receipt. Either of these bases will be accepted for tax purposes provided that it is consistently applied, as will any other basis which reflects generally accepted accounting practice provided that it does not conflict with tax law. A change of basis should be made only where the need for change outweighs the requirement for accounts to be prepared on a consistent basis, and will be dealt with in accordance with Revenue Statement of Practice SP 3/90 (see 71.83 below) (and regard should be had to the anti-avoidance provisions under the current year basis transitional rules, see 78.2 SELF-ASSESSMENT). (Revenue Tax Bulletin December 1994 p 182).

The following relate to specific types of farm support payment.

(i) *Advances under British Sugar Industry (Assistance) Act 1931*, linked with sugar production and prices, were held to be assessable as trading receipts (*Smart v Lincolnshire Sugar Co Ltd HL 1937, 20 TC 643*).

(ii) *Arable area payments.* Payments under the 1992 scheme for land set aside may be treated as sales subsidies, and hence recognised when the crops are sold. Valuations based on 75% of market value (see (*j*) below) should include the same proportion of the related arable area payments. (Revenue Tax Bulletin February 1994 p 109). See (*f*)(v) below for specific comment on oilseed support payments.

(iii) *Dairy herd conversion scheme.* Grants for changing from dairying to meat production were held to be assessable as trading receipts (*White v G & M Davis Ch D 1979, 52 TC 597; CIR v Biggar CS 1982, 56 TC 254*).

(iv) *Flood rehabilitation grants* in excess of rehabilitation costs (admitted to be capital) were held to be capital receipts (*Watson v Samson Bros Ch D 1959, 38 TC 346*).

(v) *Oilseed support scheme.* Payments of aid under the 1992 scheme are a subsidy towards the selling price, and as such should be recognised as income at the time of sale. If the final amount is not known when the accounts are prepared, but it is reasonably certain that a further payment will be received, the tax computations should be kept open to admit the final figure. If a reasonable estimate is included in the accounts and the difference when the final amount is known has only a small effect on the overall tax liability, the inspector may agree to recognise the difference in arriving at profits of the following year. (Revenue Tax Bulletin February 1993 p 53).

(vi) *Ploughing subsidies* were held to be assessable as trading receipts (*Higgs v Wrightson KB 1944, 26 TC 73*).

(*g*) **Milk.** *SLOM compensation.* The Revenue view is that such compensation is on revenue account, and should be recognised for income tax purposes in one sum in the accounting period in which legal entitlement to it arises and the amount can be quantified with reasonable certainty using information available at the time of preparation of the accounts. Additions for interest to the date of payment should be dealt with under the normal Schedule D, Case III rules. (Revenue Tax Bulletin May 1994 p 127).

Superlevy. The Revenue view is that superlevy is an allowable Schedule D, Case I deduction, but that the purchase of additional quota to avoid superlevy does not give rise to a deduction for either the superlevy thus avoided or the sum which would have been paid to lease rather than purchase the additional quota. (Revenue Tax Bulletin August 1994 p 151).

Residuary Milk Marketing Board receipts. B Reserve Fund distributions and sums repaid to producers under the Rolling Fund arrangements on the flotation of Dairy Crest (in the latter case whether taken in cash or in shares) are income receipts of the trade. Any element of a B Reserve Fund payment described as interest may also be treated as a trade receipt. Post-cessation treatment (see 62.1 POST-CESSATION ETC. RECEIPTS AND EXPENDITURE) will apply where appropriate. (Revenue Tax Bulletin August 1997 p 461).

Milk Margue Ltd shares. Bonus preference shares (or loan stock) issued in October 1998 to dairy farmers supplying the company form part of the trading receipts of the farmer, the appropriate measure of the income (and of the capital gains tax base cost) being the nominal value of the shares. (Revenue Tax Bulletin August 1999 p 685).

For capital gains tax considerations generally, see Tolley's Capital Gains Tax under Assets and Rollover Relief.

(*h*) **Share farming.** The Inland Revenue consider that both parties to a share farming agreement based on the Country Landowners Association model may be considered to be carrying on a farming trade for tax purposes. In the case of the landowner, he must take an active part in the share farming venture, at least to the extent of concerning himself with details of farming policy and exercising his right to enter onto his land for some material purpose, even if only for the purposes of inspection and policy-making. (Country Landowners Association Press Release 19 December 1991). This reverses an earlier Revenue decision to deny such treatment in respect of the landowner's share of income under a share farming agreement, which was itself a change of view from that previously held by the Revenue.

(*i*) **Short rotation coppice**. With effect from 29 November 1994, the cultivation of 'short rotation coppice' (i.e. a perennial crop of tree species planted at high density, the stems of which are harvested above ground level at intervals of less than ten years) is treated for tax purposes as farming and not as forestry, so that UK land under such cultivation is farm or agricultural land and not woodlands. [*FA 1995, s 154*]. For the Revenue view of the taxation implications of short rotation coppice, see Revenue Tax Bulletin October 1995 p 252.

(*j*) **Single trade.** All farming carried on by any particular person or partnership or body of persons is treated for all tax purposes as one trade. [*ICTA 1988, s 53(2)*]. This applies, however, only to farming of land in the UK (see *ICTA 1988, s 832(1)* and *Sargent v Eayrs Ch D 1972, 48 TC 573*).

(*k*) **Stock valuations.** See generally Business Economic Notes No 19 'Farming — stock valuations for income tax purposes' (for which see 71.28 above) and, for a commentary thereon relating particularly to changes in the basis of valuation, Revenue Tax Bulletin May 1993 p 63. See also 34 HERD BASIS and, for trading stock generally, 71.83 below. In general, livestock is treated as trading stock unless the herd basis applies, and home-bred animals may be valued, if there is no adequate record of cost, at 75% for sheep and pigs (60% for cattle) of open market value. Deadstock may be taken at 75% of market value (85% before 31 March 1993).

Where an animal grant or subsidy for which application has been made has not been taken into account for a particular period but has been applied for, and that application materially affects the value of the animal, the grant or subsidy should be taken into account as a supplement to the market value when deemed cost is computed. Grants or subsidies applied for but not recognised as income in the period concerned should also be taken into account in arriving at net realisable value for stock valuation purposes. (Revenue Tax Bulletin December 1994 p 182).

Effect of BSE on stock valuations. Against the background of bovine spongiform encephalopathy (BSE), the Revenue have clarified their approach to the valuation of livestock for stock-taking. In particular, although the principles set out in the Business Economic Notes continue to apply, a special basis of arriving at market value will be accepted for normal stock-taking dates between 20 March 1996 and 31 May 1996. See Revenue Press Release 29 April 1996 for the detailed arrangements.

(*l*) **Subscriptions** to the **National Farmers Union** are allowable in full.

(*m*) **Trading profits.** Proceeds from the sale of trees (mostly willows planted by the taxpayer) were held to be farming receipts (*Elmes v Trembath KB 1934, 19 TC 72*), but no part of the cost of an orchard with nearly ripe fruit purchased by a fruit grower was an allowable deduction in computing his profits, which included receipts from the sale of the fruit (*CIR v Pilcher CA 1949, 31 TC 314*). Proceeds from sales of turf were held to be trading receipts from farming (*Lowe v J W Ashmore Ltd Ch D 1970, 46 TC 597*).

For these and other aspects of farming taxation, see Revenue Inspector's Manual, IM 2250–2350h.

Simon's Direct Tax Service. See **B3.5**.

71.58 **FILM ETC. PRODUCTION**

In the absence of special legislation, the master negative and soundtrack of a film (or the electronic equivalent) would generally be plant for tax purposes, so that the production costs would attract capital allowances (see 10.24 *et seq.* CAPITAL ALLOWANCES), although this would not apply to e.g. expenditure on the acquisition of exhibition rights in a film. Under *CAA 1990, s 68* however, expenditure on the production or acquisition of a film, tape or disc is to be regarded as revenue rather than capital expenditure, and any receipts from the disposal of any interest or right or insurance or compensation or other similar moneys derived from the film etc. are revenue receipts. See below, however, as regards election for *section 68 not* to apply to expenditure on certain 'qualifying films' etc.. References to a film, tape or disc in relation to a film are to the original master negative of the film and its soundtrack (if any), the original master film tape or original master audio tape of the film, or the original master audio disc of the film, and include references to any rights in the film (or its soundtrack) held or acquired with them.

For expenditure on the acquisition of a film, tape or disc incurred before 6 April 2000, *section 68* applies as above but with two minor differences.

(*a*) The *section* only applies to expenditure which would otherwise have constituted expenditure on machinery or plant for capital allowance purposes (see 10.25 CAPITAL ALLOWANCES).

(*b*) References to a film, a tape or a disc are to an original master negative of the film and its soundtrack if any, an original master film or audio tape, or an original master film or audio disc, and any reference to the acquisition of a film, tape or disc includes a reference to the acquisition of any description of rights therein.

These differences similarly apply in relation to expenditure on the production of a film where principal photography commences on or after 21 March 2000, or if it commenced before that date and the film is completed on or after that date and the person incurring the expenditure so (irrevocably) elects. A film is completed for this purpose when it is in a form in which it can reasonably be regarded as ready for copies to be made and distributed for public exhibition.

[*CAA 1990, s 68(1)(2)(8); FA 2000, s 113(1)(2)(5)(6)*].

Neither the provisions of *CAA 1990, s 68*, nor the relief under *F(No 2)A 1992, s 42* (see below), apply to revenue expenditure in relation to trades in which the film etc. concerned constitutes trading stock under *ICTA 1988, s 100(2)* (see 71.83 below). [*CAA 1990, s 68(7); F(No 2)A 1992, s 42(8)*].

Under *CAA 1990, s 68(3)–(6B)* as amended by *F(No 2)A 1992, s 69*, all revenue expenditure on the production etc. of films etc. is allocated to periods of account on a just and reasonable basis having regard to the expenditure unallocated at the beginning of a period, the proportion which the estimated value of the film etc. realised in the period (whether by way of income or otherwise) bears to the aggregate of the value so realised and the estimated remaining value at the end of the period, and the need to bring the whole expenditure into account over the time during which the value of the film etc. is expected to be realised. Additional expenditure (so far as not previously allocated to the period or to any earlier period) may be claimed for a period bringing the total expenditure allocated to the period up to the value of the film etc. which is realised in the period (whether by way of income or otherwise). The claim must be made (i) for income tax for 1996/97 onwards, within twelve months after 31 January following the tax year in which the period in question ends, and (ii) for income tax for earlier years and for corporation tax, within two years after the end of the period in question. [*FA 1996, s 135, Sch 21 para 32(2)(3)*]. For an explanation and examples of how these provisions are applied in practice, see Revenue Statement of Practice SP 1/98, 25 March 1998, paras 1–31. SP 1/98 replaces the earlier Statement of Practice SP 1/93 (which itself replaced SP 2/83 and SP 2/85) with effect from 25 March 1998, but for transactions entered into between 2 July 1997 and 25 March 1998, advantage may be taken of either SP 1/98 or the earlier Statements. Expenditure in respect of which a deduction has been made for a period of account under *F(No 2)A 1992, s 42* (see below) is not allocated under these provisions, and where this applies, no expenditure on the film etc. concerned is allocated to that period.

Qualifying films, tapes or discs. A person carrying on a trade or business consisting of, or including, the exploitation of films etc. may elect for the provisions of *CAA 1990, s 68* not to apply to expenditure which is incurred on the production or acquisition of a film etc. which is certified by the Secretary of State as being a 'qualifying film' etc., and the value of which is expected to be realisable over a period of not less than two years. [*CAA 1990, s 68(9)–(9B); F(No 2)A 1992, s 69; FA 1996, s 135, Sch 21 para 32(4)–(6)*]. The election, which is irrevocable, must relate to the whole of the expenditure on the film etc. concerned. The election must be made (i) for income tax for 1996/97 onwards, within twelve months after 31 January following the tax year in which ends the period of account in which the film etc. is completed, and (ii) for income tax for earlier years and for corporation tax, within two years after the end of such period. A film etc. is completed when it is first in a form in which it can reasonably be regarded as ready for copies to be made and distributed for public exhibition or, in relation to expenditure incurred on acquisition of a film etc., the time of that acquisition, if later. No election is available in respect of expenditure in relation to any of which a claim has been made under *F(No 2)A 1992, s 41* or *s 42* (see below). In relation to films completed before 10 March 1992, the exclusion of the provisions of *CAA 1990, s 68* applies in the circumstances described above without election.

A film etc. is a '*qualifying film*' if it is within the definition applied for this purpose by *Films Act 1985, s 6, Sch 1*, broadly a film meeting certain criteria as to EU and Commonwealth content, and '*qualifying tape*' and '*qualifying disc*' are similarly defined. See Leaflet FB1 'Evidence of British Nature of a Film', available from Department of National Heritage, 2nd Floor, Grey Core, 151 Buckingham Palace Road, London SW1W 9SS. Regulations relating to certification are contained in *The Films (Certification) Regulations 1985* (*SI 1985 No 994*).

In relation to qualifying films etc. completed (as above) after 9 March 1992, an alternative deduction may be claimed for a period, in respect of any expenditure of a revenue nature incurred in producing a film completed in or before the period, of up to one-third (proportionately reduced for periods of less than twelve months) of the total production expenditure (reduced by any preliminary expenditure already deducted under *F(No 2)A 1992, s 41*, see below), subject to a maximum of the total such expenditure not already deducted. Similar relief is available in respect of expenditure of a revenue nature on the acquisition of the original master negative of a film and its soundtrack (if any) or the original master film or audio tape of a film or the original master film or audio disc of a film, where the film was completed (as above) in the period to which the claim relates (or in an earlier period), and the master negative, tape or disc is a qualifying film, tape or disc. This also applies to such expenditure on the acquisition of any rights in the film (or its soundtrack) that are held or acquired with the original master negative, tape or audio disc of the film. (For acquisition expenditure incurred before 6 April 2000, the restriction to expenditure on films completed after 9 March 1992 is not specifically applied to acquisition expenditure, the extension to expenditure on ancillary rights is to 'any description of rights in' the original master negative, tape or disc of the film, and the reference to the date of completion of the film is to the date of the acquisition if later.) These provisions do not apply where an election has been made in respect of the expenditure under *CAA 1990, s 68(9)* (see above), or where a deduction has been made in respect of it under *CAA 1990, s 68(3)–(6)* (see above), and where a deduction has been allowed for a period under *section 68(3)–(6)*, no deduction is allowed under these provisions for that period in respect of any expenditure on the film concerned. A claim is irrevocable and must be made within, for 1996/97 and later years, twelve months after 31 January following the tax year in which ends the period to which the claim relates (for income tax for earlier years and for corporation tax purposes, two years after the end of the period to which it relates). [*F(No 2)A 1992, ss 42, 43; FA 1996, s 135, Sch 21 para 46; FA 2000, s 113(3)(4)(6)*].

F(No 2)A 1992, s 42 is further amended to grant enhanced allowances for expenditure incurred in the period **from 2 July 1997 to 1 July 2002 inclusive** on a film completed after 1 July 1997 with a 'total production expenditure' of £15 million or less. As regards the time expenditure is incurred, see 10.2(iii) CAPITAL ALLOWANCES. A film is completed when it is first ready for copies to be made and distributed for public exhibition. '*Total production expenditure*' includes all such expenditure, whenever incurred and whether or not incurred by the claimant, but increased to an arm's length amount in the case of certain connected person transactions. Where these conditions are met, the allowable deduction for a period is increased from one-third (as above) to the whole of the production or acquisition expenditure (net of earlier deductions). In the case of acquisition expenditure, the deduction is limited to the total production expenditure. Where only a part of expenditure on a film falls within the 100% deduction rules, the amount deductible for a period is limited to the sum of the maximum amount deductible under the 100% deduction rules and the maximum deductible under the one-third deduction rules disregarding expenditure within the 100% deduction rules (and restricted on the assumption that the maximum 100% deduction has already been given). [*F(No 2)A 1992, s 42(4); F(No 2)A 1997, s 48; FA 1999, s 62*].

Preliminary expenditure. A deduction may be claimed for a period for any expenditure payable in the period (or in an earlier period) which can reasonably be said to have been incurred in deciding whether or not to make a film (as defined in *Films Act 1985, Sch 1 para 1*), and which is not payable under a contract etc. whereby it may be repaid if the film is not made. If the decision taken is to make the film, this applies to expenditure incurred before commencement of principal photography, up to a maximum of 20% of the budgeted expenditure as at the first day of principal photography, provided that the film etc. is a qualifying film etc. or, if it has not been completed at the time the claim is made, it is reasonably likely that, if completed, it would be a qualifying film etc. If the decision taken is not to make the film, it applies only where it is reasonably likely that it would have been a qualifying film etc. had it been completed. No relief may be claimed where a deduction has previously been made for the expenditure, or an election made in respect of it under *CAA 1990, s 68(9)* (see above). A claim must be made within, for 1996/97 and later years, twelve months after 31 January following the tax year in which ends the period in which the expenditure becomes payable (for income tax for earlier years and for corporation tax purposes, two years after the end of such period). [*F(No 2)A 1992, ss 41, 43; FA 1996, s 135, Sch 21 para 45*].

See Revenue Statement of Practice SP 1/98, 25 March 1998, paras 32–62 for guidance on procedural points in relation to the enhanced reliefs for qualifying films. SP 1/98 replaces the earlier Statement of Practice SP 1/93 (which itself replaced SP 2/83 and SP 2/85) with effect from 25 March 1998, but for transactions entered into between 2 July 1997 and 25 March 1998, advantage may be taken of either SP 1/98 or the earlier Statements.

See generally Revenue Inspector's Manual, IM 3300–3342.

Leasing. See 71.68 below as regards restrictions on relief under the above provisions where finance leasing arrangements are involved. See also Revenue Statement of Practice SP 1/98, 25 March 1998, paras 63–71.

Simon's Direct Tax Service. See B3.1307.

71.59 FRANCHISING

Under a business system franchising agreement (i.e. an agreement under which the franchisor grants to the franchisee the right to distribute products or perform services using that system), there is generally an initial fee (payable in one sum or in instalments) and continuing, usually annual, fees.

The capital or revenue treatment of the initial fee depends on what it is for. To the extent that it is paid wholly or mainly for substantial rights of an enduring nature, to initiate or substantially extend a business, it is a capital payment (as are any related professional fees). (See 71.40 above for general principles.) It is immaterial that the expenditure may prove abortive, and the treatment of the payment in the hands of the franchisor is irrelevant. However, where goods or services of a revenue nature are supplied at the outset (e.g. trading stock or staff training), the Revenue will accept that an appropriate part of the initial fee is a revenue payment, provided that the sum claimed fairly represents such items, and that it is clear that the items are not separately charged for in the continuing fees. The costs of the franchisee's own initial training are not normally allowable.

The continuing fee payable by the franchisee is generally a revenue expense.

(Revenue Tax Bulletin June 1995 p 224).

See generally Revenue Inspector's Manual, IM 2400–2403b.

71.60 GIFTS AND OTHER NON-CONTRACTUAL RECEIPTS AND PAYMENTS

See also generally 71.54 above, 71.84 and 71.85 below and CHARITIES (15).

The fact that a receipt is gratuitous is not in itself a reason for its not being a trading receipt. See *Severne v Dadswell Ch D 1954, 35 TC 649* (payments under war-time arrangements held trading receipts although *ex gratia*); *CIR v Falkirk Ice Rink CS 1975, 51 TC 42* (donation to ice rink from associated curling club held taxable); *Wing v O'Connell Supreme Court (IFS) 1926, [1927] IR 84* (gift to professional jockey on winning race taxable).

In recent years the problem has arisen in relation to *ex gratia* payments on the termination of long-standing business arrangements. A distinction is drawn between parting gifts as personal testimonials (not taxable as business receipts) and payments which, on the facts, can be seen as additional rewards for services already rendered or compensation for a loss of future profits (taxable). For cases see 71.48(*e*) above and compare the position for employees, see 75.26 SCHEDULE E. For gifts and donations made, see 71.84 below.

Cremation fees ('ash cash') assigned in advance, and paid directly, to a medical charity may escape liability under Schedule D, Case VI where the doctor entitled to them is not assessed under Case II, but liability under Case II is not affected by such assignment. See Revenue Inspector's Manual, IM 2203.

Gifts to educational establishments. A relief is available for certain gifts by traders for the purposes of 'designated educational establishments'.

Where the gift is of an article manufactured by the trader, or of a type sold by him, in his trade, and would have been classified as machinery or plant for capital allowance purposes if the educational establishment had incurred expenditure on it for the purposes of a trade carried on by it, the trader is not required to bring in any amount as a trading receipt in respect of the gift.

Similarly, where the gift is of an article on which the trader has claimed machinery and plant capital allowances, he is not required to bring in any disposal value in respect of the article in his capital allowances computation.

For 1996/97 and later years, the relief must be claimed within twelve months after 31 January following the year of assessment in whose basis period the gift was made (or, for corporation tax where self-assessment applies, within two years after the end of the accounting period in which it was made). Previously, the claim had to be made within two years after the making of the gift. The claim must specify the article and educational establishment concerned. The value of any benefit received by the donor or by a person connected with him (see 20 CONNECTED PERSONS), which is in any way attributable to the making of a gift for which relief has been given, will be assessed on the donor under Case I, Case II or Case VI of Schedule D, as appropriate.

'*Designated educational establishment*' means any educational establishment designated (or of a category designated) in regulations, broadly all UK universities, public or private schools and further and higher educational institutions (see *SI 1992 No 42* as amended by *SI 1993 No 561*).

[*ICTA 1988, s 84; FA 1991, s 68; FA 1996, s 135, Sch 21 para 2*].

Gifts in kind to charities. See 15.19 CHARITIES for relief for gifts in kind (i.e. of trading stock or machinery or plant used in the trade) to charities and certain other bodies on or after 27 July 1999, and 15.21 CHARITIES for the earlier, more limited relief for gifts for third world health or education. Where such reliefs do not apply, donations of trading stock to charities are dealt with on normal Case I principles. See Revenue Tax Bulletin June 1996 p 319 for the Revenue's view of the application of those principles.

Simon's Direct Tax Service. See **B3.1441** *et seq.*, **B3.1508**.

71.61 GUARANTEES

Losses under guarantees of the indebtedness of another are analogous to bad debt losses (see 71.44 above) and similar principles apply. Losses allowed to a solicitor under the guarantee of a client's overdraft (*Jennings v Barfield Ch D 1962, 40 TC 365*) and to a film-writer under guarantee of loans to a film company with which he was associated (*Lunt v Wellesley KB 1945, 27 TC 78*) but refused to a company under a guarantee of loans to an associated company with which it had close trading connections (*Milnes v J Beam Group Ltd Ch D 1975, 50 TC 675*) and a guarantee of loans to a subsidiary (*Redkite Ltd v Inspector of Taxes [1996] SSCD 501*). See also *Bolton v Halpern & Woolf CA 1980, 53 TC 445* and *Garforth v Tankard Carpets Ltd Ch D 1980, 53 TC 342*.

A loss by an asphalt contractor under a guarantee to an exhibition (for which he hoped but, in the event, failed to work) allowed (*Morley v Lawford & Co CA 1928, 14 TC 229*). For commission paid to guarantors see *Ascot Gas Water Heaters Ltd* at 71.65 below.

Payments under guarantees made to a trader for the setting up or the purposes of his trade and irrecoverable are in certain circumstances allowable as a loss for capital gains tax if the guarantee was made after 11 April 1978. [*TCGA 1992, s 253; FA 1996, Sch 21 para 40*]. See Tolley's Capital Gains Tax.

71.62 **HIRE-PURCHASE**

Where assets are purchased under hire-purchase agreements, the charges (the excess of the hire-purchase price over the cash price, sometimes called interest but not true interest) are, appropriately spread, allowable deductions (*Darngavil Coal Co Ltd v Francis CS 1913, 7 TC 1*). See 71.44 above for the bad debt etc. provisions of hire-purchase traders. For relief on capital element, see 10.38(vi) CAPITAL ALLOWANCES.

For whether goods sold under hire-purchase are trading stock, see *Lions Ltd v Gosford Furnishing Co Ltd & CIR CS 1961, 40 TC 256* and cf. *Drages Ltd v CIR KB 1927, 46 TC 389*.

See generally Revenue Inspector's Manual, IM 450–459, IM 710–712.

Simon's Direct Tax Service. See **B3.1161** *et seq.*.

71.63 **ILLEGAL PAYMENTS ETC.**

In computing profits chargeable under Schedule D, no deduction may be made in respect of expenditure (including incidental costs) incurred in making a payment the making of which constitutes the commission of a criminal offence. A deduction is similarly denied for any payment induced by a demand constituting blackmail or extortion. Relief as a management expense is similarly denied. [*ICTA 1988, s 577A; FA 1993, s 123; FA 1994, s 141; FA 1998, Sch 27 Pt III(4)*]. For a discussion of the circumstances in which these provisions may apply, see Revenue Inspector's Manual, IM 666–667f.

71.64 **INSURANCE**

Premiums for business purposes are normally allowable including insurance of assets, insurance against accidents to employees, insurance against loss of profits and premiums under mutual insurance schemes (cf. *Thomas v Richard Evans & Co HL 1927, 11 TC 790*; for trade associations see 71.84 below). For war risk premiums see *ICTA 1988, s 586*.

Any corresponding recoveries are trading receipts (or set off against trading expenses (see *ICTA 1988, s 74(1)(l)*) or capital, according to the nature of the policy. If capital, the recovery may be taken into account, where appropriate, for the purposes of CAPITAL ALLOWANCES (10) or capital gains tax. The whole of a recovery in respect of the destruction of trading stock is a trading receipt of the year of destruction, notwithstanding that it exceeds the market value of the stock lost or not all the stock was replaced (*Green v J Gliksten & Son Ltd HL 1929, 14 TC 364; Rownson Drew & Clydesdale Ltd v CIR KB 1931, 16 TC 595*). The total recovery under a loss of profits was held a trading receipt although in excess of the loss suffered (*R v British Columbia Fir & Cedar PC 1932, 15 ATC 624*). See also *Mallandain Investments Ltd v Shadbolt KB 1940, 23 TC 367*. For recoveries under accidents to employees see *Gray & Co v Murphy KB 1940, 23 TC 225; Keir & Cawder Ltd v CIR CS 1958, 38 TC 23*. Where a shipping company insured against late delivery of ships being built for it, both premiums and recoveries held capital (*Crabb v Blue Star Line Ltd Ch D 1961, 39 TC 482*).

Premiums on policies in favour of the employer insuring against death or critical illness of key employees are generally allowable, and the proceeds of any such policies trading receipts.

For mutual insurance trading, see 50 MUTUAL TRADING.

Health insurance. By concession, compensation for loss of income from self-employment under an individual's policy covering sickness or disability was exempt from tax for the first twelve months, provided that the benefit entitlement commenced on or after 6 April 1994. Exemption did not apply where, exceptionally, the benefits are chargeable under Schedule

E or the premiums have wholly or partly qualified for relief as pension contributions. (Revenue Pamphlet IR 1, A83). See also 75.37 SCHEDULE E. In practice, tax was not collected where insurance benefits are provided in times of sickness, disability or unemployment to meet existing specified obligations such as loan repayments. (Revenue Press Release REV 6, 28 November 1995). The concession has been replaced by statutory provisions as respects annual payments falling to be made after 5 April 1996 (and in some cases earlier payments) under certain insurance policies. Where the conditions are met, the exemption applies to all such payments and not just those for the first twelve months. See 29.12 EXEMPT INCOME for the detailed provisions.

Locum and fixed practice expenses insurance. On 30 April 1996 the Revenue announced revised arrangements for the taxation of premiums for, and benefits under, such policies. Previously, they had considered that no tax relief was available for premiums paid by professional people such as doctors and dentists to meet locum and/or fixed overhead costs in the event of their illness or incapacity, and that proceeds of such policies were not trading receipts (see Revenue Inspector's Manual, IM 2207). Their revised view is that premiums for such policies are deductible, and benefits taxable, under Schedule D, Case II, whether the professional person is obliged to insure (e.g. under NHS regulations) or does so as a matter of commercial prudence. This treatment does not apply to any part of a premium relating to other, non-business risks such as the cost of medical treatment for accident or sickness. These new arrangements will apply to all periods of account beginning after 30 September 1996. Earlier periods for which profits have not been agreed (and assessments not become final) may similarly be adjusted to the revised basis, although the earlier practice may be continued if desired. Error or mistake relief claims may be made for earlier periods for which figures have become final to be adjusted to the revised basis, subject to the normal rules for such claims, in particular the six-year time limit. Where such a claim is made, the previously unallowed relief will be reduced by any previously untaxed benefits for the earliest claim period and all subsequent settled periods. (Revenue Press Release 30 April 1996). In the case of persons carrying on business in partnership, claims must take into account premiums paid and benefits received by all partners. (Revenue Tax Bulletin August 1996 p 339).

Professional indemnity insurance premiums are normally allowable on general principles, and the Revenue will not seek to disallow a premium paid prior to cessation of trading on the grounds that the cover extends to claims lodged after cessation. (Premiums paid after cessation will generally be relievable as post-cessation expenditure, see 62.4 POST-CESSATION ETC. RECEIPTS AND EXPENDITURE.) (Revenue Tax Bulletin October 1995 p 257).

Commissions. Revenue Statement of Practice SP 5/95, 31 March 1995, (now superseded, see below) sets out the Revenue view of the taxation consequences of commissions which are:

(*a*) received;

(*b*) netted-off (i.e. only a net premium is paid);

(*c*) invested (i.e. used to obtain additional benefits); or where

(*d*) a discounted premium is paid (i.e. the premium is reduced without any explicit entitlement to commission).

This applies to any insurance policies, capital redemption policies, life annuity contracts and personal pension schemes. The Statement applies both to intermediaries (e.g. brokers or professional agents) and to policy holders in respect of policies effected for their own benefit (the latter having previously been the subject of Revenue Pamphlet IR 131, SP 3/79, 19 February 1979, which is superseded).

(Revenue Pamphlet IR 131, SP 5/95, 31 March 1995).

See Revenue Tax Bulletin April 1995 pp 201–204 for background to and reasoning behind the views expressed in the Statement.

The Statement is, however, superseded from 27 November 1997 by Revenue Statement of Practice SP 4/97 (see 71.46 above), which deals more widely with commissions, cashbacks and discounts.

See also *Robertson v CIR (Sp C 137), [1997] SSCD 282* as regards timing of inclusion of insurance agents' advance commission.

71.65 INTEREST AND OTHER PAYMENTS FOR LOANS

Interest paid for business purposes if not claimed as a relief under *ICTA 1988, s 353* is deductible, subject to certain restrictions, as described at 43.2 INTEREST PAYABLE. For 'hire-purchase interest' see 71.62 above.

Premium on repayment of mortgage (*Arizona Copper Co v Smiles CES 1891, 3 TC 149*) and on repayment of loan to finance estate development (*Bridgwater v King KB 1943, 25 TC 385*) held not allowable, as were exchange losses attendant on foreign borrowings by a company to finance its purchase of a controlling interest in another company (*Ward v Anglo-American Oil Co Ltd KB 1934, 19 TC 94*). A share of profits paid as partial consideration for a loan was held to be distribution of profits and not allowed in *Walker & Co v CIR KB 1920, 12 TC 297*.

Prior to *FA 1969*, interest paid in full on capital advances was disallowed (cf. *European Investment Trust Ltd v Jackson CA 1932, 18 TC 1*). The legislation was amended by *FA 1969*. In a case under the old law, commission paid for a guarantee of a trading liability was allowed but not for guarantee of a debenture loan (*Ascot Gas Water Heaters Ltd v Duff KB 1942, 24 TC 171*).

INTEREST ON UNPAID TAX (42) is not an allowable deduction in computing profits or losses. This applies equally to interest on unpaid or under-declared value added tax, insurance premium tax, landfill tax or climate change levy. [*TMA 1970, s 90; ICTA 1988, s 827(1)(1B)(1C)(1D); FA 1994, Sch 7 para 31; FA 1996, Sch 5 para 40; FA 2000, Sch 7 para 4*].

For the treatment of the incidental costs of obtaining loan finance, see 71.70 below. See also 43.16 INTEREST PAYABLE regarding interest relief for persons living in job-related accommodation.

Companies. For the special provisions applicable for accounting periods ending after 31 March 1996 to all profits and losses in respect of company 'loan relationships', see Tolley's Corporation Tax under Loan Relationships.

71.66 INVESTMENT INCOME (DIVIDENDS, INTEREST, RENTS, ROYALTIES)

Income received under deduction of tax may not be included in a Case I or II assessment (cf. *F S Securities Ltd v CIR HL 1964, 41 TC 666; Bucks v Bowers Ch D 1969, 46 TC 267; Bank Line Ltd v CIR CS 1974, 49 TC 307*) nor, subject to the Crown option between Cases (see 5.2 ASSESSMENTS), may income received in full from sources within Cases III, IV or V (cf. *Northend v White & Leonard & Corbin Greener Ch D 1975, 50 TC 121*) and also from sources *explicitly* within Case VI. See 46 LOSSES for treatment of certain investment income as trading profits for loss relief purposes and Tolley's Corporation Tax for similar provisions for companies. Rents receivable within Schedule A may not be assessed under Schedule D (see 5.2 ASSESSMENTS) but in practice the Revenue do not generally object to the inclusion in trading profits of rents from the letting of business accommodation temporarily surplus to requirements, provided that the premises in question continue to be partly used for the business and the rental income is comparatively small (see Revenue Tax Bulletin February 1994 p 115). See also 71.78 below.

Investment income may be treated as a trading receipt where it is the fruit derived from a fund employed and risked in the business (see *Liverpool and London and Globe Insurance Co v Bennett HL 1913, 6 TC 327*). This treatment is not confined to financial trades, but the making and holding of investments at interest must be an integral part of the trade. See *Nuclear Electric plc v Bradley HL 1996, 68 TC 670*, in which (in refusing the company's claim) the crucial test was considered to be whether the investments were employed in the business (of producing electricity) in the year of assessment in question. The Court of Appeal, whose judgment was approved, considered decisive the facts that the liabilities against which the investments were provided were liabilities to third parties, not to customers, and that, in view of the long-term nature of the liabilities, the business could be carried on for a long period without maintaining any fund of investments at all. See also *Bank Line Ltd v CIR* (above).

Payments received in lieu of dividends in contango operations held trading receipts (*Multipar Syndicate Ltd v Devitt KB 1945, 26 TC 359*); also co-operative society 'dividends' on trading purchases (*Pope v Beaumont KB 1941, 24 TC 78*). For interest received by underwriters on securities deposited with Lloyd's see *Owen v Sassoon HC 1950, 32 TC 101* and for discount receivable on bills see *Willingale v International Commercial Bank Ltd HL 1978, 52 TC 242*.

For the purposes of the excess profits tax and similar taxes it was necessary to determine whether rents and royalties were 'investment income'. For cases dealing with this, not involving the Case I or II treatment of the income, see Tolley's Tax Cases.

71.67 KNOW-HOW

'Know-how' is any industrial information and techniques of assistance in (*a*) manufacturing or processing goods or materials, (*b*) working, or searching for, etc., mineral deposits, or (*c*) agricultural, forestry or fishing operations. [*ICTA 1988, s 533(7)*]. Where know-how which has been used in the vendor's trade (the trade thereafter continuing) is disposed of, the consideration received (including any consideration for a restrictive covenant connected with the disposal) is a trading receipt (if not already taxable). [*ICTA 1988, s 531(1)*]. It should, however, be noted that, in relation to know-how on which expenditure is incurred after 31 March 1986, a balancing adjustment will normally be made in these circumstances (see 10.23 CAPITAL ALLOWANCES). [*ICTA 1988, s 530(5); FA 1994, Sch 26 Pt V(24)*]. A non-trading vendor is assessable under Schedule D, Case VI, on his net gain (treated as earned income if he devised the know-how) after deducting expenditure on acquisition or disposal. [*ICTA 1988, s 531(4)–(6)*].

But the above provisions do not apply to a sale between bodies of persons (which includes partnerships) under the same control. [*ICTA 1988, s 531(7)*].

If know-how is sold together with a trade, or part trade, both the vendor and the purchaser are treated as if the consideration for the know-how were a payment for goodwill. They may, however, jointly elect (within two years of the disposal, and provided they are not bodies under common control) for allowances instead to be made to the purchaser as if the know-how had been acquired for use in a trade he previously carried on. Such treatment will in any event apply where the trade acquired was previously carried on wholly outside the UK. [*ICTA 1988, s 531(2)(3)(7)*]. If goodwill, capital gains tax may apply.

For capital allowances on purchases of know-how, see 10.23 CAPITAL ALLOWANCES.

In *Delage v Nugget Polish Co Ltd KB 1905, 21 TLR 454*, payments for the use of a secret process, payable for 40 years and based on receipts, were held to be annual payments subject to deduction of tax at source. See also *Paterson Engineering v Duff KB 1943, 25 TC 43*.

For patents, see 71.73 below.

Simon's Direct Tax Service. See **B3.861** *et seq.*.

71.68 LEASE RENTAL PAYMENTS

Statement of Practice. In relation to finance leases entered into after 11 April 1991, the Revenue practice described below applies to rentals payable by a lessee under a finance lease, i.e. a lease which transfers substantially all the risks and rewards of ownership of an asset to the lessee while maintaining the lessor's legal ownership of the asset. The treatment of such rentals depends upon whether or not SSAP 21 has been applied. This practice has no implications for the tax treatment of rentals receivable by the lessor, nor for the availability of capital allowances to the lessor. (Revenue Pamphlet IR 131, SP 3/91 and Revenue Press Release 11 April 1991).

Finance lease rentals are revenue payments for the use of the asset, and, both under normal accounting principles and for tax purposes, should be allocated to the periods of account for which the asset is leased in accordance with the accruals concept. Where there is an option for the lessee to continue to lease the asset after expiry of the primary period under the lease, regard should be had, in allocating rentals to periods of account, to the economic life of the asset and its likely period of use by the lessee, as well as to the primary period.

Under SSAP 21, the lessee is required to treat a finance lease as the acquisition of an asset subject to a loan, to be depreciated over its useful life, with rentals apportioned between a finance charge and a capital repayment element. This treatment does not, however, affect the tax treatment, which remains as described above.

Where SSAP 21 has not been applied, the lessee's accounting treatment of rental payments is normally accepted for tax purposes, provided that it is consistent with the principles described above. If not, computational adjustments are made to secure the proper spreading of the rental payments.

Where SSAP 21 has been applied, the finance charge element of the rental payments for a period of account is normally accepted as a revenue deduction for that period. In determining the appropriate proportion of the capital repayment element to be deducted for tax purposes, a properly computed commercial depreciation charge to profit and loss account will normally be accepted. Where, however, the depreciation charge is not so computed, the appropriate proportion for tax purposes will be determined in accordance with the principles described above.

For comment on the principles set out in SP 3/91, and on their application to particular arrangements, see Revenue Tax Bulletin February 1995 pp 189–193. This considers in particular: sums paid before the asset comes into use; depreciation of leased assets (and the interaction with SSAP 21); long-life assets; termination adjustments; fixtures leases; and the interaction of SP 3/91 with statutory restrictions on relief for rental payments.

See generally Revenue Inspector's Manual, IM 2670–2679.

Lease rental anti-avoidance — return in capital form. *FA 1997, Sch 12 Pt I* applies from 26 November 1996 in relation to asset leasing arrangements which, in the case of UK-incorporated companies, are dealt with by normal accountancy practice as finance leases or loans, and whose effect is that some or all of the investment return is or may be in non-rental form and would not, apart from these provisions, be wholly taxed as lease rental. The principal purposes of the provisions are to charge any person entitled to the lessor's interest to tax by reference to the income return for accounting purposes (taking into account the substance of the matter as a whole, e.g. as regards connected persons or groups of companies); and to recover reliefs, etc. for capital and other expenditure as appropriate by reference to sums received which fall within the provisions. The provisions are described below.

In relation to all the provisions of *FA 1997, Sch 12* (see further below as regards *Parts II* and *III*), a period of account straddling 26 November 1996 is treated as two separate periods of account, ending immediately before and beginning with that date. Appropriate assumptions are made concerning accounting purposes and the application of normal accountancy practice (see *FA 1997, Sch 12 paras 23, 28, 30*).

Part I applies where an asset lease (as widely defined) is or has at any time been granted in the case of which the following conditions are or have been satisfied at some time (the '*relevant time*') in a period of account of the current lessor. Where the conditions have been satisfied at a relevant time, they are treated as continuing to be satisfied unless and until the asset ceases to be leased under the lease or the lessor's interest is assigned to a person not 'connected' with the assignor or certain other prior or subsequent lessors. Persons who are CONNECTED PERSONS (20) (within *ICTA 1988, s 839*) at any time in the period from the earliest time at which any of the leasing arrangements were made to the time when the current lessor finally ceases to have an interest in the asset or any arrangements relating to it are for these purposes treated as so connected throughout that period.

[*FA 1997, Sch 12 paras 1, 2, 23, 25, 30*].

The conditions referred to above are as follows.

(*a*) At the relevant time, and under normal accountancy practice, the leasing arrangements fall to be treated as a finance lease or loan in relation to which either:

- (i) the lessor (or a connected person) is the finance lessor; or
- (ii) the lessor is a member of a group of companies for the purposes of whose consolidated accounts (within *Companies Act 1985, s 227* or NI equivalent) the finance lease or loan is treated as subsisting.

(*b*) A sum (a '*major lump sum*') is or may be payable to the lessor (or a connected person) under the leasing arrangements which is not rent but which falls to be treated, under normal accountancy practice, partly as repayment of some or all of the investment in respect of the finance lease or loan and partly as a return on that investment.

(*c*) Not all of the part of the major lump sum which is treated as a return on the investment (as in (*b*) above) would, apart from these provisions, be brought into account for tax purposes, as 'normal rent' from the lease for periods of account of the lessor, in chargeable periods of the lessor ending with the 'relevant chargeable period'. The '*relevant chargeable period*' is the chargeable or basis period (or latest such period) consisting of or including all or part of the period of account in which that sum is or may be payable under the arrangements. A '*normal rent*' for a period of account is the amount which (apart from the current provisions) the lessor would bring in for tax purposes in the period as rent arising from the lease.

(*d*) The period of account of the lessor in which the relevant time falls (or an earlier period during which he was the lessor) is one for which the 'accountancy rental earnings' in respect of the lease exceed the normal rent. The '*accountancy rental earnings*' for a period are the greatest of the '*rental earnings*' for the period in respect of the lease (i.e. the amount treated under normal accountancy practice as the gross return on investment for the period):

- (i) of the lessor;
- (ii) of any person connected with the lessor; and
- (iii) for the purposes of consolidated group accounts of a group of which the lessor is a member.

Where (ii) or (iii) applies and the lessor's period of account does not coincide with that of the connected person or the consolidated group accounts, amounts in the periods of account of the latter are apportioned as necessary by reference to the number of days in the common periods.

The normal rent for a period of account for these purposes is determined by treating rent as accruing and falling due evenly over the period to which it relates (unless a payment falls due more than twelve months after any of the rent to which it relates is so treated as accruing).

(*e*) At the relevant time, either:

(i) arrangements exist under which the lessee (or a connected person) may directly or indirectly acquire the leased asset (or an asset representing it — see *FA 1997, Sch 12 para 26*) from the lessor (or a connected person), and in connection with that acquisition the lessor (or a connected person) may directly or indirectly receive a '*qualifying lump sum*' from the lessee (or a connected person) (i.e. a non-rental sum part at least of which would, if the recipient were a UK-incorporated company, be treated under normal accountancy practice as a return on investment in respect of a finance lease or loan); or

(ii) in the absence of such arrangements, it is in any event more likely that the acquisition and receipt described in (i) above will take place than that, before any such acquisition, the leased asset (or the asset representing it) will have been acquired in an open market sale other than by the lessor or lessee (or persons connected with either of them).

[*FA 1997 Sch 12 paras 3, 4, 20–24; FA 1998, Sch 27 Pt III(4)*].

Where *Part I* applies to a lease for a period of account of the current lessor, the consequences are as follows.

Current lessor to be taxed by reference to accountancy rental earnings.

Where the accountancy rental earnings in respect of the lease for a period of account beginning on or after 26 November 1996 exceed the normal rent for that period, the accountancy rental earnings are substituted for the normal rent for tax purposes. The substituted amount is treated as having accrued evenly over the period of account (disregarding periods for which the asset was not leased).

Where the reverse applies (i.e. the normal rent exceeds the accountancy rental earnings), and there is a 'cumulative accountancy rental excess', the rent otherwise taxable for the period (the '*taxable rent*') is reduced (although not below the accountancy rental earnings) by setting it against that excess. An '*accountancy rental excess*' for a period to which these provisions apply is the excess (if any) of the accountancy rental earnings over the normal rent for the period, and the '*cumulative accountancy rental excess*' is so much of the aggregate of accountancy rental excesses of previous periods (after allowing for certain bad debts, see below) as has not been set against taxable rents for previous periods or against certain chargeable gains disposal consideration (see below). '*Normal rental excess*' and '*cumulative normal rental excess*' (see below) are correspondingly defined, except that the normal rental excess for a period for which the taxable rent is reduced as above is the excess (if any) of the normal rent (reduced by a similar amount) over the accountancy rental earnings.

If there is a cumulative normal rent excess (as above) for a period of account for which the taxable rent is increased in amount to the accountancy rental earnings, the taxable rent for the period (as so increased) is reduced (but not below the normal rent) by set-off against that excess, and the accountancy rental excess for the period (as above) is the excess (if any) of the taxable rent as so determined over the normal rent.

On an assignment of the current lessor's interest under the lease treated under *TCGA 1992, s 35(3)(d)* as at neither gain nor loss (see Tolley's Capital Gains Tax under Assets Held on 31 March 1982), a period of account of the assignor is treated as ending, and of the assignee as beginning, with the assignment. Any unused cumulative accountancy rental excess or cumulative normal rental excess at the time of the assignment is transferred to the assignee.

Where accountancy rental earnings for a period of account are substituted for normal rent for tax purposes (as above), and a bad debt deduction in excess of the accountancy rental earnings falls to be made for the period, any cumulative accountancy rental excess for the period is reduced (but not below nil) by that excess. If the accountancy rental earnings do not exceed the normal rent, any bad debt deduction acts to reduce the amount of the normal rent against which a cumulative accountancy rental excess may be set, and the cumulative accountancy rental excess is reduced (but not below nil) by any excess of the bad debt deduction over the normal rent. There is provision for such reductions in the cumulative accountancy rental excess to be reversed in the event of subsequent bad debt recoveries or reinstatements.

There are corresponding provisions relating to the effect of bad debt deductions on cumulative normal rental excesses. There were also special provisions relating to bad debts where the current lessor is chargeable to corporation tax under Schedule A (no longer relevant after 31 March 1998 — see Tolley's Corporation Tax under Profit Computations).

In determining the *chargeable gain on a disposal* by the current lessor (or a connected person) of his interest under the lease (or of the leased asset or an asset representing it), the disposal consideration is reduced (but not below nil) by setting against it any cumulative accountancy rental excess (as above) for the period of account of the disposal. This does not preclude the exclusion from the disposal consideration under *TCGA 1992, s 37* of any amount chargeable to tax on income, except to the extent (if any) that it is represented by any cumulative accountancy rental excess set off under this provision (on the current disposal or previously). On a part disposal, the cumulative accountancy rental excess is apportioned in the same manner as the associated acquisition costs, and any further apportionment is on a just and reasonable basis where there is more than one simultaneous disposal. For all purposes of *FA 1997, Sch 12*, the period of account of the current lessor is treated as ending, and a new period as beginning, immediately before such a disposal (or simultaneous such disposals).

If these provisions come to apply to a lease to which the provisions of *FA 1997, Sch 12 Pt II* (see below) already apply, the cumulative accountancy rental excess or cumulative normal rent excess are determined as if these provisions had applied throughout the period for which *Part II* in fact applied.

[*FA 1997, Sch 12 paras 5–10, 12, 14, 30; FA 1998, Sch 27 Pt III(4)*].

Capital allowances

Where an occasion occurs on or after 26 November 1996 on which a major lump sum (as in (*b*) above) falls to be paid, there are provisions for the withdrawal of earlier reliefs, etc. for expenditure incurred by the current lessor in respect of the leased asset. This applies to reliefs, etc. for capital expenditure under *CAA 1990*, *ICTA 1988, ss 91–91B* (cemeteries etc., see 10.5 CAPITAL ALLOWANCES, or waste disposal sites, see 71.94 below) or *ICTA 1988, ss 520, 521* (patent rights, see 10.50 CAPITAL ALLOWANCES). Deductions allowed under *CAA 1990, s 68(1)(3)* or *F(No 2)A 1992, s 42* (films, etc., see 71.58 above) are similarly withdrawn. The earlier reliefs, etc. are withdrawn either by the bringing in of a disposal value or by the imposition of a balancing charge or, in the case of film, cemetery or waste disposal site expenditure allowed as a deduction, by the bringing in of a countervailing receipt. These provisions apply equally to capital allowances for contributors to capital expenditure under *CAA 1990, s 154*. [*FA 1997, Sch 12 para 11*].

Existing schemes for which (a)–(e) above become satisfied after 26 November 1996

Where a lease of an asset forms part of an 'existing scheme' (as below) for which conditions (*a*)–(*e*) above only become satisfied after 26 November 1996, *FA 1997, Sch 12* applies as if a period of account of the current lessor ended and another began both immediately before and immediately after those conditions came to be satisfied, i.e. as if there was a brief separate period of account during which they became satisfied. Any cumulative accountancy rental excess which would have arisen for that period, had the conditions been satisfied at all times on or after 26 November 1996, is treated as so arising, and the current lessor is treated as if, at the end of the immediately preceding period, there had accrued an additional amount of rent equal to that excess (which rent is, however, left out of account in determining normal rent for comparison with accountancy rental earnings, as above). Similarly a cumulative normal rent excess which would have arisen on those assumptions is treated as having arisen in the period in which the conditions came to be satisfied.

A lease of an asset forms part of an '*existing scheme*' if a contract in writing for the lease was made before 26 November 1996 and either:

(i) no terms of the contract remained to be agreed on or after that date, and any conditions were satisfied before that date; or

(ii) the requirements in (i) are satisfied before the end of the period ending with the later of 31 January 1997 and the expiry of six months after the making of the contract, or within such further time as the Commissioners of Inland Revenue may allow in any particular case, and in its final form the contract does not differ materially from how it stood when originally made. [*FA 1997, Sch 12 paras 13, 27; FA 1998, Sch 27 Pt III(4)*].

Insurance companies. If the current lessor under the lease of an asset is a company carrying on life assurance business, the provisions of *FA 1997, Sch 12 Pt I* (and *Pt II* below) are modified. See *FA 1997, Sch 12 Pt III.*

For the Revenue's views on various points of interpretation regarding these provisions, see Revenue Tax Bulletin April 1997 pp 414–417.

Finance leases not within anti-avoidance provisions. *FA 1997, Sch 12 Pt II* applies from 26 November 1996 to arrangements, not within *Part I* (above), which involve the lease of an asset and are of a kind which, in the accounts of a UK-incorporated company, would be treated under normal accountancy practice as finance leases or loans. The main purpose of the provisions is to charge tax on amounts equal to the income return on investment under normal accountancy practice (taking into account the substance of the matter as a whole, e.g. as regards connected persons or groups of companies). *Part II* accordingly applies where a lease of an asset forming part of a new scheme is granted on or after 26 November 1996, and condition (*a*) above is satisfied at some time on or after that date in a period of account of the current lessor, but the anti-avoidance provisions of *Part I* described above do not apply because not all of conditions (*b*)–(*e*) above are or have been satisfied at such a time. Where condition (*a*) was satisfied at some time on or after 26 November 1996, it is treated as continuing to be satisfied until either the asset ceases to be leased under the lease or the lessor's interest is assigned to (i) a person not connected with the assignor, (ii) any other person who was the lessor before the assignment, or (iii) any person who becomes the lessor after the assignment under arrangements made by a person who was the lessor (or a person connected with the lessor) at some time before the assignment. A lease which ceases to be within *Part II* following assignment will come within the provisions again if the conditions are again satisfied. [*FA 1997, Sch 12 paras 15, 16*].

Where *Part II* applies, the provisions of *FA 1997, Sch 12 paras 5–10, 12* for the taxation of the current lessor by reference to accountancy rental earnings (see above) apply to the lease. [*FA 1997, Sch 12 para 17*].

See above as regards special provisions relating to insurance companies.

For the Revenue's views on various points of interpretation regarding these provisions, see Revenue Tax Bulletin April 1997 pp 414–417.

Finance leasing generally. See 10.28, 10.38(iii)(vi) CAPITAL ALLOWANCES for other finance lease capital allowance restrictions. It was held in *Caledonian Paper plc v CIR (Sp C 159), [1998] SSCD 129* that annual or semi-annual payments of commitment fees, guarantee fees and agency fees relating to guarantees required in relation to finance leasing arrangements were deductible in computing profits, but that a one-off management fee was not.

71.69 LEGAL AND PROFESSIONAL EXPENSES

The costs of forming a company are capital but in so far as they relate to loan capital may qualify for relief by virtue of *ICTA 1988, ss 77, 401* (see 71.70 and 71.76 below).

The expenses of a company incorporated by charter in obtaining a variation of its charter, etc. were allowed (*CIR v Carron Co HL 1968, 45 TC 18*). See also *McGarry v Limerick Gas HC(IFS) [1932] IR 125* and contrast *A & G Moore & Co v Hare CS 1914, 6 TC 572*. In general, the costs of maintaining existing trading rights and assets are revenue expenses (*Southern v Borax Consolidated KB 1940, 23 TC 597; Bihar etc. IT Commr v Maharaja of Dharbanga PC 1941, 20 ATC 337* and compare *Morgan v Tate & Lyle Ltd HL 1954, 35 TC 367*). But the incidental costs of acquiring new assets, etc. are part of their capital cost. The expenses of obtaining or renewing a lease of business premises are strictly capital but, in practice, the expenses of renewing leases under 50 years are generally allowed (although a proportionate disallowance may apply where a lease premium is involved, see Revenue Inspector's Manual, IM 803b). The cost of an unsuccessful application to vary a carrier's licence was disallowed (*Pyrah v Annis & Co CA 1956, 37 TC 163*) as was the cost of an unsuccessful application for planning permission (*ECC Quarries Ltd v Watkis Ch D 1975, 51 TC 153* but see 10.11(*b*) CAPITAL ALLOWANCES). For excise licenses, see 71.45 above.

Legal expenses in defending charges brought by a professional regulatory body were allowed on the grounds that they were incurred to prevent suspension or expulsion and thus to protect the taxpayer's business (applying *Tate & Lyle Ltd* (above)), although the fines imposed were disallowed (see 71.47 above) (*McKnight v Sheppard HL 1999, 71 TC 419*).

The cost of tax appeals even though successful is not allowable (*Allen v Farquharson Bros & Co KB 1932, 17 TC 59; Smith's Potato Estates v Bolland HL 1948, 30 TC 267; Rushden Heel Co v Keene HL 1948, 30 TC 298*). Where an accountant, etc. agrees the tax liabilities based on the accounts he prepares, normal annual fees are allowed but not fees for a special review of settled years (*Worsley Brewery Co v CIR CA 1932, 17 TC 349*) or fees for additional work on 'back duty' investigations.

Costs incurred by a partner in connection with the dissolution of the partnership were disallowed in *C Connelly & Co v Wilbey Ch D 1992, 65 TC 208*.

Additional accountancy expenses incurred as a result of an 'in-depth' examination by the Revenue of a particular year's accounts (see 71.28 above) will normally be allowed if the investigation does not result in an adjustment to the profits of any earlier year or in the imposition of interest or interest and penalties in relation to the current year. Where the investigation reveals discrepancies and additional liabilities for earlier years, or results in a settlement for the current year including interest (with or without penalties), the expenses will be disallowed. (Revenue Pamphlet IR 131, SP 16/91, 3 December 1991). In its application to self-assessment enquiries (see 78.11 SELF-ASSESSMENT), the Statement of Practice is reworded to make it clear that the prohibition on allowance of accountancy expenses applies only where the enquiry reveals negligent or fraudulent conduct (and see Revenue Tax Bulletin October 1998 p 596).

Simon's Direct Tax Service. See **B3.1515**.

71.70 **LOAN FINANCE INCIDENTAL COSTS**

Expenditure may qualify for relief under *ICTA 1988, s 77*. The relief applies to the incidental costs of obtaining finance by means of a loan or issue of loan stock (*a*) the interest on which would be deductible in computing profits (see 71.65 above and 43.2 INTEREST PAYABLE), or, as regards companies, allowable as a charge on income, and (*b*) which does not carry a right, exercisable within three years, of conversion into, or to the acquisition of, shares or other (non-qualifying) securities.

(*b*) does not apply if the right is not wholly exercised within the three-year period, and where part only of the loan, etc. is so converted, only the corresponding part of the incidental costs is disallowed. For this purpose, incidental costs incurred before the end of the three-year period are treated as incurred immediately after that period. [*ICTA 1988, s 77*].

The incidental costs deductible are those incurred wholly and exclusively for the purpose of (i) obtaining the loan finance, whether actually obtained or not, or (ii) providing security for it, or (iii) repaying it. They include fees, commissions, advertising, printing, and other incidental matters but not stamp duty nor does the relief extend to exchange losses (or sums paid for protection against them) or a premium on repayment. [*ICTA 1988, s 77(6)*]. Costs incidental to the taking out of a life insurance policy as a condition of obtaining the loan finance are deductible, but not premiums payable on such a policy. (Revenue Tax Bulletin February 1992 p 13). Costs of a flotation the proceeds of which were used to repay loan finance were held not allowable as the motive of the company in arranging for the flotation was not wholly and exclusively to repay the debt (*Focus Dynamics plc v Turner (Sp C 182), [1999] SSCD 71*).

The timing of a deduction under *section 77* is in accordance with normal principles (i.e. it follows the accounting treatment, provided that the accounts are correctly drawn up in accordance with applicable UK accounting standards). (Revenue Tax Bulletin April 1996 p 306).

Where loan finance costs are incurred on the formation of a company before it commences trading, see 71.76 below.

These provisions do not apply for corporation tax purposes for accounting periods ending after 31 March 1996. [*ICTA 1988, s 77(8); FA 1996, Sch 14 para 9*]. See now Tolley's Corporation Tax under Loan Relationships.

Simon's Direct Tax Service. See **B3.1321**.

71.71 **MINES, QUARRIES, ETC.**

See 10.39 *et seq.* CAPITAL ALLOWANCES for mining etc. expenditure so allowable. The relevant legislation which applied before 1 April 1986 originated from 1945 and may therefore affect any pre-1945 decisions below.

The cost of sinking (*Coltness Iron Co v Black HL 1881, 1 TC 287*), deepening (*Bonner v Basset Mines KB 1912, 6 TC 146*) or 'de-watering' (*United Collieries v CIR CS 1929, 12 TC 1248*) a pit is capital.

A lump sum paid at the end of a mining lease for surface damage was held capital (*Robert Addie & Sons v CIR CS 1924, 8 TC 671*) but not periodic payments during the currency of the lease based on acreage worked (*O'Grady v Bullcroft Main Collieries KB 1932, 17 TC 93*). *Bullcroft* was decided before the enactment of what is now *ICTA 1988, s 119* and rents and tonnage payments for the right to withdraw surface support are easements within *section 119* (*CIR v New Sharlston Collieries CA 1936, 21 TC 116*). For the deduction of tax under *section 119* see 23.14 DEDUCTION OF TAX AT SOURCE and also for periodic payments for rights to minerals, sand and gravel, etc. For shortworkings, see *Broughton & Plas Power v Kirkpatrick QB 1884, 2 TC 69; CIR v Cranford Ironstone KB 1942, 29 TC 113*. Provision for the future costs of abandoning an oil field and of restoring hired equipment used therein to its original state held capital (*RTZ Oil and Gas Ltd v Elliss Ch D 1987, 61 TC 132*).

In practice, actual land restoration costs (but not provisions for future restoration expenditure) in a continuing business are generally allowable. (Revenue Inspectors' Manual, IM 2795).

Purchase of unworked deposits by sand and gravel merchant held capital (*Stow Bardolph Gravel Co Ltd v Poole CA 1954, 35 TC 459*) as was purchase of land with nitrate deposits by chemical manufacturer (*Alianza Co v Bell HL 1905, 5 TC 172*) and payment by oil company for unwon oil in wells it took over (*Hughes v British Burmah Petroleum KB 1932, 17 TC 286*). See also *Golden Horse Shoe v Thurgood CA 1933, 18 TC 280* (purchase of tailings for gold extraction, allowable) and *CIR v Broomhouse Brick CS 1952, 34 TC 1* (purchase of blaes for brick manufacture, allowable).

Production wells, etc.. Intangible costs of drilling the second and subsequent production wells in an area are not allowable where they were incurred after 25 November 1996 (unless incurred before 26 November 1997 under a contract entered into before 26 November 1996 and not varied on or after that date to increase such costs). Such costs will attract mineral extraction capital allowances (see 10.39 *et seq.* CAPITAL ALLOWANCES). [*ICTA 1988, s 91C; FA 1997, s 66*].

71.72 MISCELLANEOUS EXPENSES AND RECEIPTS

Card winnings of club proprietor, trading receipts (*Burdge v Pyne Ch D 1968, 45 TC 320*). For lotteries and football pools, see 71.30 above.

Carers. Any profits arising from payments by local authorities for taking the elderly or infirm into the home as family are assessable under Schedule D, Case I or II (although the availability of 'rent-a-room' exemption (see 68.11 SCHEDULE A) will often obviate the need for further enquiry). See Revenue Inspector's Manual, IM 1812a–1812h for the Revenue approach to determination of the assessable profit (if any) in such cases.

Computer software. The Revenue's views on the treatment of expenditure on computer software are summarised as follows.

Software acquired under licence. Regular payments akin to a rental are allowable revenue expenditure, the timing of deductions being governed by correct accountancy practice (see 71.40 above). A lump sum payment is capital if the licence is of a sufficiently enduring nature to be considered a capital asset in the context of the licencee's trade (see 71.40 above), e.g. where it may be expected to function as a tool of the trade for several years. Equally the benefit may be transitory (and the expenditure revenue) even though the licence is for an indefinite period. Inspectors will in any event accept that expenditure is on revenue account where the software has a useful economic life of less than two years. Timing of the deduction in these circumstances will again depend on correct accountancy practice.

Where the licence is a capital asset, capital allowances are available (see 10.25 CAPITAL ALLOWANCES).

Expenditure on a package containing both hardware and a licence to use software must be apportioned before the above principles are applied.

Software owned outright. The treatment of expenditure on such software (including any in-house costs) follows the same principles as are described above in relation to licensed software.

(Revenue Tax Bulletin November 1993 p 99).

For the treatment of expenditure on systems modification work relating to the Year 2000 problem and to EMU conversion, see Revenue Tax Bulletin April 1998 p 531. Broadly, such work will always be a revenue matter unless it is carried out as part of a major new project instituting changes on such a scale as to be of a capital nature in relation to the business.

See Revenue Inspector's Manual, IM 663a *et seq.* for a detailed analysis of the Revenue's views generally.

Purchases/sales of assets. See *T Beynon & Co v Ogg KB 1918, 7 TC 125* (profits of colliery agent from deals in wagons held trading receipts); *Gloucester Railway Carriage v CIR HL 1925, 12 TC 720* (sale by wagon manufacturer of wagons previously let, held trading receipts); *Bonner v Frood KB 1934, 18 TC 488* (sale of rounds by credit trader, held trading receipts).

Reimbursements of capital expenditure spread over 30 years held capital as regards both payer and recipient (*Boyce v Whitwick Colliery CA 1934, 18 TC 655*). For allowances from railway in respect of traffic on sidings paid for by trader see *Westcombe v Hadnock Quarries KB 1931, 16 TC 137; Legge v Flettons Ltd KB 1939, 22 TC 455.*

Excessive payments to **service company** of professional firm held not deductible (*Stephenson v Payne, Stone Fraser & Co Ch D 1967, 44 TC 507*).

Solicitor's fees as trustee held professional receipts (*Jones v Wright KB 1927, 13 TC 221*) even though also a beneficiary (*Watson & Everitt v Blunden CA 1933, 18 TC 402*).

Sub-postmasters. Introductory fees paid by sub-postmasters were held not to be allowable (*Dhendsa v Richardson (Sp C 134), [1997] SSCD 265*).

Timber purchases and sales. For purchases and sales of standing timber by timber merchants see *Murray v CIR CS 1951, 32 TC 238*; *McLellan, Rawson & Co v Newall Ch D 1955, 36 TC 117*; *Hood Barrs v CIR (No 2) HL 1957, 37 TC 188*; *Hopwood v C N Spencer Ltd Ch D 1964, 42 TC 169*; *Russell v Hird and Mercer Ch D 1983, 57 TC 127.* For sales of trees by farmer see *Elmes v Trembath KB 1934, 19 TC 72.*

Trade marks or designs. Fees and expenses of applications for registration and extensions are allowable. [*ICTA 1988, s 83*].

Transfer fees. The accounting treatment of transfer fees paid by football or other sports clubs may be affected by either FRS 10 issued by the Accounting Standards Board on 4 September 1997 or the FRS for Smaller Entities issued by the Board on 10 December 1998. Where a transfer fee is paid under a contract entered into before the beginning of the first accounting period for which either of those standards has effect, then unless the club elects to the contrary (within two years after the end of that accounting period), the tax treatment of the payment is not affected by anything in the standard. Any necessary adjustments to give effect to this provision may be made, notwithstanding any relevant time limits. [*FA 1999, s 63*].

Video tape rental. Relief for the cost of acquiring video tapes for hire may be obtained by way of either:

(i) capital allowances (provided the useful economic life is at least two years);

(ii) valuation basis (where the useful economic life is two years or less); or

(iii) renewals basis.

See Revenue Tax Bulletin October 1995 pp 254, 255 for a discussion of each of these methods in this context. See also Revenue Inspector's Manual, IM 3230a–3230h.

General. See also *Thompson v Magnesium Elektron CA 1943, 26 TC 1* (payments based on purchases, held trading receipts); *British Commonwealth International Newsfilm v Mahany HL 1962, 40 TC 550* (payments to meet operating expenses, trading receipts); *CIR v Pattison CS 1959, 38 TC 617* (weekly instalments for business, capital).

71.73 PATENTS

Expenses (agent's charges, patent office fees, etc.) in obtaining, or extending the term of, a patent for the purposes of a trade (including rejected or abandoned applications) are allowable. [*ICTA 1988, s 83*]. For capital expenditure on the purchase of patent rights see 10.50 CAPITAL ALLOWANCES.

Sums received on the sale of patent rights may, dependent on the facts, be trading receipts (*Rees Roturbo Development v Ducker HL 1928, 13 TC 366; Brandwood v Banker KB 1928, 14 TC 44; CIR v Rustproof Metal Window CA 1947, 29 TC 243* and cf. *Harry Ferguson (Motors) v CIR CA(NI) 1951, 33 TC 15*). Other sums are taxable under *ICTA 1988, s 524*, see 54 PATENTS.

Where a company held a patent for renovating car tyres, lump sums received by it under arrangements for giving the payer a *de facto* franchise in his area, were held to be capital receipts (*Margerison v Tyresoles Ltd KB 1942, 25 TC 59*).

Patent royalties are payable less tax and not deductible — see 71.52 above. For spreading of patent royalties received less tax, see 54 PATENTS and for DTR treatment of royalties from abroad, see 25.5(*l*) DOUBLE TAX RELIEF.

For copyright, know-how and trade marks, see 71.51, 71.67 and 71.72 respectively.

Simon's Direct Tax Service. See **B3.841** *et seq.*, **B3.1406** *et seq.*.

71.74 PERSONAL EXPENSES

Expenditure for domestic and private purposes is explicitly disallowable under *ICTA 1988, s 74(1)(b)* and is, in any event, not wholly and exclusively for business purposes and disallowable under *ICTA 1988, s 74(1)(a)*. The 'dual purpose rule' (see 71.40 above) is relevant here. Hence the cost of treatment at a nursing home was disallowed even though motivated by need for room from which to conduct business (*Murgatroyd v Evans-Jackson Ch D 1966, 43 TC 581*) as was the cost of a minor finger operation to enable a professional guitarist to continue playing as, on the evidence, he also played the guitar as a hobby (*Prince v Mapp Ch D 1969, 46 TC 169*). Medical expenses where illness said to be due to working conditions were not allowed in *Norman v Golder CA 1944, 26 TC 293*. Expenditure on ordinary clothing is not normally allowable, the leading case here being *Mallalieu v Drummond HL 1983, 57 TC 330*, in which, reversing the decisions in the lower Courts, it was held that the cost of sober clothing worn by a lady barrister to comply with Bar Council guidelines was for the dual purpose of her profession and her requirements as a human being, and not allowable. See also 71.40 above and the 'clothing' cases at 75.10(*b*) SCHEDULE E. In *Watkis v Ashford, Sparkes and Harward Ch D 1985, 58 TC 468*, expenditure on meals at regular partners' lunchtime meetings was disallowed, whilst expenditure on accommodation, food and drink at the firm's annual weekend conference was allowed. In *McKnight v Sheppard HL 1999, 71 TC 419*, legal expenses in defending charges brought by a professional regulatory body were allowed despite the fact that the taxpayer's 'personal reputation was inevitably involved'. In *MacKinlay v Arthur Young McClelland Moores & Co HL 1989, 62 TC 704*, contributions towards the removal expenses of a partner moved in the interests of the firm were not allowed. For rent, etc. of premises used both as residence and for business see 71.78 below and for travelling and subsistence expenses see 71.90 below. See also *Mason v Tyson Ch D 1980, 53 TC 333* (expenses of occasional use of flat) and *McLaren v Mumford Ch D 1996, 69 TC 173* (expenses of residential accommodation required to be occupied with licensed premises).

The personal costs (e.g. accommodation, food and drink) of a UK resident individual assessable under Schedule D, Case I or Case II (and of accompanying partner) of living abroad on business are not disallowed under *ICTA 1988, s 74(1)(a)* or *(b)*. (Revenue Inspector's Manual, IM 825).

Simon's Direct Tax Service. See **B3.1345** *et seq.*.

71.75 POOLING OF PROFITS

Where traders pool profits or act together in consortia but so as not to form PARTNERSHIPS (53) or trade jointly (cf. *Gardner and Bowring Hardy v CIR CS 1930, 15 TC 602; Geo Hall & Son v Platt Ch D 1954, 35 TC 440*) each trader's share of the pooled profits will normally be treated as a receipt of his main trade and any payment under the arrangement by one trader to another will be deductible in computing his profits (*Moore v Stewarts & Lloyds Ltd CS 1905, 6 TC 501* and cf. *United Steel v Cullington (No 1) CA 1939, 23 TC 71*). In *Utol Ltd v CIR KB 1943, 25 TC 517* payments by one company to another under a profit sharing arrangement were held to be dividends payable less tax under the law in force before SCHEDULE F (76). For compensation received on the termination of a profit sharing arrangement see *Van den Berghs* at 71.48(*b*) above.

71.76 PRE-TRADING EXPENDITURE

The general rule is that trading expenditure is deductible when incurred and hence is not allowable if incurred before trading commenced (cf. *Birmingham & District Cattle By-Products Ltd v CIR KB 1919, 12 TC 92*). The rule is modified for certain pre-trading capital expenditure, including scientific research expenditure and abortive exploration expenditure by mining concerns (see 10 CAPITAL ALLOWANCES).

There is also a special relief on expenditure incurred by a person in the seven years before he commenced to carry on a trade which, had it been incurred after he commenced, would have been deductible in computing the profits. The relief does not extend to expenditure already deductible in computing profits, e.g. pre-trading purchases of stock or advance payments of rent. For income tax purposes as regards trades commenced before 6 April 1995, such expenditure may be treated as a trading loss of the year of assessment in which the trade commenced (see (46) LOSSES, including the relief for losses in the early years of trade), to be claimed separately from any other loss relief. For income tax purposes as regards trades commenced after 5 April 1995 and for corporation tax purposes, the expenditure is treated as incurred on the day the person commences the trade. Where the company carries on the trade in partnership, see 53.14 PARTNERSHIPS. [*ICTA 1988, s 401; FA 1993, s 109(1)(4); FA 1995, s 120, Sch 6 para 20; FA 1998, Sch 27 Pt III(4)*].

The relief also applies to unrelieved trade charges paid by companies before commencement. However, for accounting periods ending after 31 March 1996 this is replaced by a special relief for non-trading debits arising under the loan relationship provisions introduced in *FA 1996* (see Tolley's Corporation Tax under Loan Relationships). [*ICTA 1988, s 401(1A)–(1AC); FA 1993, s 109(2)(4); FA 1996, Sch 14 para 20*].

Simon's Direct Tax Service. See **B3.1204**.

71.77 PROPERTY SALES AND OTHER PROPERTY RECEIPTS

For property dealing see 71.38 above and for rents received see 71.66 above. For builders and property developers generally, see Revenue Inspector's Manual, IM 1940 *et seq.*.

Sales of property by builders in special circumstances have been considered in a number of cases. Profits held trading receipts in *Spiers & Son v Ogden KB 1932, 17 TC 117* (building activities extended); *Sharpless v Rees KB 1940, 23 TC 361* (sale of land acquired for hobby abandoned for health reasons); *Shadford v H Fairweather & Co Ch D 1966, 43 TC 291* (sale of site after development plan dropped); *Snell v Rosser, Thomas & Co Ch D 1967, 44 TC 343* (sale of land surplus to requirements); *Bowie v Reg Dunn (Builders) Ch D 1974, 49 TC 469* (sale of land acquired with business); *Smart v Lowndes Ch D 1978, 52 TC 436* (sale of land in wife's name). Sales of property built but let meanwhile held trading in *J & C Oliver v Farnsworth Ch D 1956, 37 TC 51; James Hobson & Sons v Newall Ch D 1957, 37 TC 609; W M Robb Ltd v Page Ch D 1971, 47 TC 465* and this notwithstanding active building given up (*Speck v Morton Ch D 1972, 48 TC 476; Granville Building Co v Oxby Ch D 1954, 35 TC 245*). But in *Harvey v Caulcott HC 1952, 33 TC 159* the sales were held realisations of investments and in *West v Phillips Ch D 1958, 38 TC 203* some houses were treated as investments and others as trading stock. See also *Andrew v Taylor CA 1965, 42 TC 557.* Sales of houses retained after business *transferred* held sales of investments in *Bradshaw v Blunden (No 1) Ch D 1956, 36 TC 397; Seaward v Varty CA 1962, 40 TC 523.* See also *Hesketh Estates v Craddock KB 1942, 25 TC 1* (profit on sale of brine baths held trading receipt of mixed business including land development).

For house sales subject to ground rents, etc., see *CIR v John Emery & Sons HL 1936, 20 TC 213; B G Utting & Co Ltd v Hughes HL 1940, 23 TC 174; McMillan v CIR CS 1942, 24 TC 417; Heather v Redfern & Sons KB 1944, 26 TC 119.* For ground rents (England) and feu duties (Scotland) there should be credited the lower of their market value and cost, the cost being taken as the proportion of the cost of the land and building in the ratio of the market value to the sum of the market value and the sale price. For ground annuals (Scotland) which are perpetual the realisable value is brought in. The right to receive the rent then becomes part of the fixed capital of the trade, whose subsequent sale is not taken into account for income tax purposes. Any premiums on the grant of leases are part of the sale proceeds.

Turf sales by a farmer were held to be farming receipts in *Lowe v J W Ashmore Ltd Ch D 1970, 46 TC 597.* For timber sales see 71.72 above and for woodlands managed on a commercial basis see 93 WOODLANDS.

Any excess of SCHEDULE A (68) deductions over rent received by a builder from property held as trading stock may be allowed as a trading expense. (Revenue Inspectors' Manual, IM 1959).

Annuities under *Agriculture Act 1967* for giving up (after attaining age of 55) uncommercial agricultural land are treated as earned income [*ICTA 1988, s 833(5)(d)*] and receipts of grants under the same *Act* for the same reason are exempt from capital gains tax. [*TCGA 1992, s 249*].

Where sales of land, etc., are capital, the profits on assets disposed of are liable to capital gains tax. See also 3.11 ANTI-AVOIDANCE for provisions affecting land or land development. [*ICTA 1988, s 776*].

For transactions not at market value see 71.83 below.

71.78 RENTS, ETC. FOR BUSINESS PREMISES

are allowable. For repairs see 71.79 below.

Where partly used privately (e.g. shop with residential accommodation above), *ICTA 1988, s 74(1)(c)* provides for the allowance of not more than two-thirds of the rent unless the circumstances justify a higher proportion. In practice, the allowance is normally two-thirds for retail businesses and, although not provided for in the legislation, rates and 'common' repairs are similarly apportioned. For this see *Wildbore v Luker HC 1951, 33 TC 46.* For allowance for use of home for business, see *Thomas v Ingram Ch D 1979, 52 TC 428*. See also *Mason v Tyson Ch D 1980, 53 TC 333* (expenses of flat used occasionally to enable professional man to work late not allowed).

For rents from letting surplus business accommodation see 71.66 above. Where premises became redundant or were closed down, continuing rents (less sub-letting receipts) were allowed (*CIR v Falkirk Iron CS 1933, 17 TC 625; Hyett v Lennard KB 1940, 23 TC 346*) but not payments to secure the cancellation of leases no longer required (*Mallett v Staveley Coal & Iron CA 1928, 13 TC 772* (the leading case here); *Cowcher v Richard Mills & Co KB 1927, 13 TC 216; Union Cold Storage v Ellerker KB 1939, 22 TC 547; Dain v Auto Speedways Ch D 1959, 38 TC 525*). See also *West African Drug Co v Lilley KB 1947, 28 TC 140*. Where the rent of a motorway service station was calculated by reference to takings, a lump sum payment for the exclusion of tobacco duty from takings was held capital (*Tucker v Granada Motorway Services HL 1979, 53 TC 92*), but, distinguishing *Granada Motorways*, an amount received by a company in respect of its agent's negligent failure to serve its landlord with counter-notice of a notice of an increase in its rent, was held to be a trading receipt in *Donald Fisher (Ealing) Ltd v Spencer CA 1989, 63 TC 168*. Rent for a building not required for occupation for business purposes but to control access to the lessee's works was held deductible (less sub-let rents) in *Allied Newspapers v Hindsley CA 1937, 21 TC 422*.

For allowance of a provision in respect of future rents under leases of premises ceasing to be used for business purposes, see *Herbert Smith v Honour Ch D, [1999] STC 173*. Following that decision, the Revenue now accept that there is no longer a tax rule which denies provisions for anticipated loses or expenses (see Revenue Press Release 20 July 1999). See the article in the Revenue Tax Bulletin December 1999 pp 707–709 summarising the Revenue's current view, in particular in relation to error or mistake relief claims (see 17.10 CLAIMS) arising from the change of view.

Additional rent liability incurred to obtain the freehold reversion to premises already rented held capital (*Littlewoods Mail Order v McGregor CA 1969, 45 TC 519* following *CIR v Land Securities HL 1969, 45 TC 495*), as were periodical payments to reimburse capital expenditure incurred by landlord (*Ainley v Edens KB 1935, 19 TC 303*) and payments based on production for grant of sisal estates (*Ralli Estates v East Africa IT Commr PC 1961, 40 ATC 9*). But payments for the use of a totalisator calculated by reference to its cost were allowed (*Racecourse Betting Control Board v Wild KB 1938, 22 TC 182*) as were rents subject to abatement dependent on profits (*Union Cold Storage v Adamson HL 1931, 16 TC 293*). For Scottish duplicands see *Dow v Merchiston Castle School CS 1921, 8 TC 149*. Rent paid by partnership to partner owning business premises allowed (*Heastie v Veitch & Co CA 1933, 18 TC 305*). For excessive payments to professional 'service company' see *Payne, Stone Fraser* at 71.72 above.

See also Simon's Direct Tax Service B3.1341 *et seq.*.

Rates, council tax and community charge. Business rates are deductible in the same way as rent, and before their replacement by the community charge and subsequently by the council tax, domestic rates were deductible to the extent that domestic premises were used for trade purposes. Council tax may similarly be deducted where it is attributable to premises (or part) used for trade purposes. No deduction is available for the personal community charge. Where, however, the standard community charge was payable in respect of premises which were not the sole or main residence of the occupier, and which were used for trade purposes, an appropriate proportion of the charge is deductible in ascertaining the profits of the trade. Similarly, where the collective community charge was payable in respect of houses in multiple occupation, and the landlord carries on a trade (e.g. of providing accommodation), he may claim as a trading deduction any part of the charge not met by contributions from residents. No deduction is available in respect of their contribution to the collective charge to any of the residents who used the premises for business purposes, as their contribution is in lieu of the personal community charge. (Revenue Press Releases 10 November 1989, 16 March 1993).

Premiums. Certain lease premiums, etc., in relation to leases not exceeding 50 years are chargeable on the landlord to an extent which varies with the length of the lease (see 68.27 SCHEDULE A). For any part of the 'relevant period' (the duration of the lease, etc. as defined in *ICTA 1988, s 87(9)*) during which the lessee occupies the premises for purposes of a trade, etc. or (with certain limitations) deals with his interest therein as property employed for trade, he is treated as paying *additional rent* for the property, allowable against profits under Schedule D, Case I or II, at a rate calculated by spreading over the relevant period the amount which falls to be included in computing the landlord's Schedule A profits (or would fall to be so included but for certain claims which he can make) proportionately reduced for any part of the premium etc. paid which gives rise to an allowance under *CAA 1990, s 105(1)(b)* (mineral depletion), or in respect of which any other CAPITAL ALLOWANCES (10) have been, or will be, made. Partial allowance is given where part only of the property is occupied for trade etc. purposes [*ICTA 1988, s 87; FA 1995, Sch 6 para 14; FA 1998, s 38, Sch 5 para 34, Sch 27 Pt III(4)*], otherwise lease premiums not allowable. Lease premiums not within the legislation are not allowable (cf. *MacTaggart v Strump CS 1925, 10 TC 17*).

Reverse premiums. In *New Zealand Commissioner of Inland Revenue v Wattie and another PC, [1998] STC 1160,* the decision in which has persuasive authority in the UK, it was held that a lump sum paid by a landlord to a prospective tenant as an inducement to enter into a lease at an above-market rental (generally known as a reverse premium) was a receipt of a capital nature. Legislation has been introduced to counter this decision, and it applies in relation to any 'reverse premium' received on or after 9 March 1999 except where, disregarding any arrangements made on or after that date, the recipient was entitled to the premium immediately before that date. For these purposes, a '*reverse premium*' is a payment or other benefit received by way of inducement in connection with a transaction (the '*relevant transaction*') entered into by the recipient or a person 'connected' with him (see below), where

(*a*) the relevant transaction is one under which the recipient or connected person becomes entitled to an estate or interest in, or a right in or over, land; and

(*b*) the payment (or other benefit) is made (or provided) by

- (i) the person (the '*grantor*') by whom that estate, interest or right is granted, or was granted at an earlier time, or
- (ii) a person 'connected' with the grantor, or
- (iii) a nominee of (or a person acting on the directions of) the grantor or a person connected with the grantor.

As regards (*b*)(i) above, the use of the word 'grantor' means that the provisions do not apply when a freehold is conveyed. The most common occasion on which the provisions will apply will be a payment by a landlord as an inducement to a tenant to take a new lease, but they may apply where an existing tenant pays a new tenant an inducement to take over the remaining term of a lease if (and only if) (*b*)(ii) or (iii) applies to the existing tenant. (Revenue Tax Bulletin December 1999 pp 711–713).

For the purposes of these provisions, persons are '*connected*' with each other if they are connected within *ICTA 1988, s 839* (see 20 CONNECTED PERSONS) at any time during the period when the 'relevant arrangements' are entered into. The '*relevant arrangements*' comprise the relevant transaction and any arrangements entered into in connection with it (whether earlier, simultaneously or later).

A reverse premium is to be regarded as a revenue receipt. Where the relevant transaction is entered into by the recipient of the reverse premium and for the purposes of a trade profession or vocation carried on (or to be carried on) by him, the reverse premium is to be taken into account in computing the trading profits under Schedule D, Case I or II. In any other case, the reverse premium is to be treated as a receipt of a SCHEDULE A (68) business, or (as the case may be) an overseas property business (see 73.4 SCHEDULE D, CASES IV AND V), carried on by the recipient.

It is understood that accountancy principles require the receipt to be brought into account by spreading over the period of the lease or, if shorter, to the first rent review. This treatment must normally be followed for tax purposes (see 71.40 above) but, as an anti-avoidance measure, is overridden where

(A) two or more parties to the relevant arrangements (see above) are connected persons (see above), and

(B) the terms of the those arrangements differ significantly from those which, at that time and under prevailing market conditions, would be regarded as reasonable and normal between persons dealing at arm's length in the open market.

In such case, the full amount or value of the reverse premium must be brought into account in the period of account in which the relevant transaction (see above) is entered into or, where applicable, the first period of account of the trade which the recipient subsequently begins to carry on.

None of these provisions apply where the recipient is an individual and the property in question is, or will be, occupied by him as his only or main residence. Nor do they apply to the extent that the payment or benefit is consideration for the first leg of a sale and leaseback arrangement within *ICTA 1988, s 779* or *s 780(1)* (see 3.12, 3.13 ANTI-AVOIDANCE) or is taken into account under *CAA 1990, s 153* (subsidies etc.) to reduce expenditure qualifying for capital allowances (see 10.2(ii) CAPITAL ALLOWANCES).

Special provisions apply where the reverse premium is received by a company carrying on life assurance.

[*FA 1999, s 54, Sch 6*].

It will be seen that a reverse premium within the above provisions is not confined to a lump sum payment and that 'other benefit' may include, for example, a contribution to the tenant's costs or an assumption of the recipient's liabilities under an existing lease. 'Other benefit' must, however, represent money or something capable of being turned into money. It does not include a sum foregone or deferred by the provider, rather than actually expended, such as a rent free period. See the article in the Revenue Tax Bulletin December 1999 pp 711–713, in particular in relation to the meeting of the tenant's costs.

As regards any reverse premium to which the recipient became entitled before 9 March 1999 (and therefore outside the scope of the above legislation), the Revenue will be guided by the decision in *Wattie* (see above). Reversing their earlier view, they accept that the linkage of a reverse premium to an increased rental does not give it the character of a revenue receipt and that the rental itself retains its character as a revenue payment. However, a reverse premium may still be a revenue receipt if, on the evidence, it is in fact a contribution to revenue expenditure, e.g. relocation costs. If, again on the evidence, the reverse premium is in fact a contribution to expenditure qualifying for capital allowances, the expenditure so qualifying may fall to be reduced by virtue of *CAA 1990, s 153* (see 10.2(ii) CAPITAL ALLOWANCES). (Revenue Tax Bulletin April 1999 p 641). See also Tolley's Capital Gains Tax under Land.

Payment of reverse premium. The payment of a reverse premium by a company to achieve the assignment of a lease which had become disadvantageous (due to the company's failure to meet its obligations under a repairing covenant) was held to be on capital account (*Southern Counties Agricultural Trading Society Ltd v Blackler (Sp C 198), [1999] SSCD*

200). The Revenue take the view that where a reverse premium is paid by a developer trading in property, it is deductible in computing his trading profits. (Revenue Press Release 9 March 1999).

General. See 3.12 ANTI-AVOIDANCE [*ICTA 1988, s 779*] regarding restrictions where there is a lease-back at a non-commercial rent and 3.13 ANTI-AVOIDANCE [*ICTA 1988, s 780*] for taxation of capital sums received on certain lease-backs after 21 June 1971.

For deductibility of rents for wayleaves paid by Radio Relay services see 23.14 DEDUCTION OF TAX AT SOURCE.

71.79 REPAIRS AND RENEWALS

(*a*) **General.** Expenditure held to be capital as described at (*b*) and (*c*) below may now qualify for CAPITAL ALLOWANCES (10). Any allowable expenditure is deductible in the period when incurred and not when the repairs, etc. accrued (*Naval Colliery Co Ltd v CIR HL 1928, 12 TC 1017*). Provisions for future repairs and renewals were held not allowable in *Clayton v Newcastle-under-Lyme Corpn QB 1888, 2 TC 416* and *Peter Merchant Ltd v Stedeford CA 1948, 30 TC 496*, but see now 71.40, 71.48 above, and Revenue Inspector's Manual, IM 605c, 990a, for the wider current acceptance of the application of normal accountancy principles in this context. Hence a provision for regular major overhaul work accrued due on aircraft engines was allowed in *Johnston v Britannia Airways Ltd Ch D 1994, 67 TC 99* (but see now Revenue Tax Bulletin February 1999 p 624 as regards changes in accounting practice superseding this decision).

(*b*) **Business premises.** The general rule is that expenditure on additions, alterations, expansions or improvements is capital but the cost of repairs, i.e. restoring a building to its original condition, is allowable. But the use of modern materials in repairing an old building does not make the expenditure capital (*Conn v Robins Bros Ltd Ch D 1966, 43 TC 266*). If the expenditure is capital, the estimated cost of 'notional repairs' obviated by the work is not allowable (see *Wm P Lawrie* and *Thomas Wilson (Keighley)* below).

As regards provisions for such expenditure, *ICTA 1988, s 74(1)(d)* prohibits any deduction 'beyond the sum actually expended' for repairs of premises, and the Revenue previously considered that this debarred any allowance for such provisions (see Revenue Inspector's Manual, IM 990b). A Revenue contention to this effect was rejected by the Special Commissioners in *Jenners Princes Street Edinburgh Ltd v CIR (Sp C 166), [1998] SSCD 196*, and the Revenue now accept that provisions properly made under Financial Reporting Standard 12 are tax deductible except where there is an express rule to the contrary (e.g. provisions for capital expenditure). (Revenue Press Release 20 July 1999). FRS 12 imposes a requirement for accounting periods ending after 22 March 1999 that for a provision to be allowable it must be a present obligation (either legal or constructive) as a result of a past event; it must be probable that a transfer of economic benefits will be required to settle the obligation; and it must be possible to make a reliable estimate of the amount of that obligation. See Revenue Tax Bulletin April 1999 pp 636–639. See also the article in the Revenue Tax Bulletin December 1999 pp 707–709 summarising the Revenue's current view, in particular in relation to error or mistake relief claims (see 17.10 CLAIMS) arising from the change of view.

A renewal of a building, i.e. a complete re-construction, is capital (*Fitzgerald v CIR Supreme Court (IFS) 1925, 5 ATC 414; Wm P Lawrie v CIR CS 1952, 34 TC 20*). The cost of rebuilding a factory chimney was held capital in *O'Grady v Bullcroft Main Collieries KB 1932, 17 TC 93* but allowed in *Samuel Jones & Co v CIR CS 1951, 32 TC 513* where the chimney was an integral part of the building. For roof replacements see *Wm P Lawrie* (above) and *Thos Wilson (Keighley) v Emmerson Ch D 1960, 39 TC 360*. The replacement of the ring in a cattle auction mart and of a stand in a football ground were held not to be repairs in *Wynne-Jones v Bedale Auction Ltd Ch D 1976, 51 TC 426* and *Brown v Burnley Football Co Ltd Ch D 1980, 53 TC 357* respectively in which the problem is reviewed.

Cost of barrier against coastal erosion held capital (*Avon Beach & Cafe v Stewart HC 1950, 31 TC 487*); also replacing a canal embankment (*Phillips v Whieldon Sanitary Potteries HC 1952, 33 TC 213*) and building new access road (*Pitt v Castle Hill Warehousing Ch D 1974, 49 TC 638*).

For a modern case (involving the insertion of plastic pipes within a dilapidated metal gas pipe network, held to be capital), see *Auckland Gas Co Ltd v CIR PC, [2000] STC 527*.

Where on taking a lease of dilapidated property the dilapidations were made good under a covenant in the lease, the cost was held disallowable as attributable to the previous use of the premises (*Jackson v Laskers Home Furnishers Ch D 1956, 37 TC 69*) but when cinemas were acquired in a state of disrepair (but still fit for public showings) because of war-time restrictions on building work, the cost of the repairs was allowed (*Odeon Associated Theatres Ltd v Jones CA 1971, 48 TC 257*). See also (*c*) below. In practice, expenditure on repairing and redecorating newly acquired premises is allowed unless abnormal (and likely to be reflected in the purchase price or rent payable).

Dilapidations of a repair nature on the termination of a lease are generally allowed.

For repairs to tied premises see 71.45 above.

See Simon's Direct Tax Service B3.1344, B3.1514.

(*c*) **Plant and other business assets, etc.** The general rules at (*b*) above apply to plant with the important modification that expenditure on the renewal of plant is allowed as an alternative to capital allowances. For this see 10.38(x) CAPITAL ALLOWANCES. Renewals of utensils and loose tools are allowable, see *ICTA 1988, s 74(1)(d)*. The cost of additional utensils and loose tools is capital but if not ranking for capital allowances (cf. *Hinton v Maden & Ireland Ltd HL 1959, 38 TC 391*) the Revenue may in suitable cases agree to spread the cost forward.

For repairs soon after the acquisition of an asset see *Law Shipping v CIR CS 1923, 12 TC 621* and *CIR v Granite City SS Co CS 1927, 13 TC 1* in which the cost of repairs to ships attributable to their use before acquisition, was held capital. But see *Odeon Associated Theatres* at (*b*) above in which *Law Shipping* was distinguished. See also *Bidwell v Gardiner Ch D 1960, 39 TC 31* in which the replacement of the furnishings of a newly acquired hotel was held capital.

Expenditure on renewal of railway tracks was allowed in *Rhodesia Railways v Bechuanaland Collector PC 1933, 12 ATC 223*, distinguishing *Highland Railway v Balderston CES 1889, 2 TC 485* in which held capital. Abnormal expenditure on dredging a channel to a shipyard was held capital in *Ounsworth v Vickers Ltd KB 1915, 6 TC 671* but the cost to a Harbour Board of removing a wreck (*Whelan v Dover Harbour Board CA 1934, 18 TC 555*) and of renewing moorings (*In re King's Lynn Harbour CES 1875, 1 TC 23*) was allowed. For shop fittings see *Eastmans Ltd v Shaw HL 1928, 14 TC 218; Hyam v CIR CS 1929, 14 TC 479*. See also *Lothian Chemical v Rogers CS 1926, 11 TC 508.*

See generally Revenue Inspector's Manual, IM 990 *et seq.*.

71.80 **SCIENTIFIC RESEARCH AND RESEARCH AND DEVELOPMENT**

Revenue expenditure incurred by a trader on (for 1999/2000 and earlier years) 'scientific research' or (for 2000/01 and subsequent years) 'research and development' (for the definitions of which see 10.52 CAPITAL ALLOWANCES) related to his trade, whether undertaken directly or on his behalf, is allowable as a deduction from profits. Expenditure incurred in the acquisition of rights in, or arising out of, the scientific research or research and development is excluded, but the allowable expenditure otherwise includes all expenditure incurred in, or providing facilities for, carrying it out. Scientific research or research and development 'related' to a trade includes any which may lead to or facilitate an extension of the trade, or which is of a medical nature and has a special relation to the welfare of workers employed in the trade. [*ICTA 1988, s 82A; CAA 1990, ss 136, 139(1)(3); FA 2000, s 68, Sch 19 para 5*].

Relief is similarly given for any sum paid to a scientific research association having as its object scientific research (as above) related (with the extended meaning referred to above) to the class of trade concerned, or to any approved university, etc. for such research. The association or university, etc. must be approved for the purpose by the Secretary of State. [*ICTA 1988, s 82B; CAA 1990, ss 136, 139(1)(3); FA 2000, Sch 19 para 5*].

It should be noted that these reliefs are given to trades and *not* to professions or vocations.

For *capital* outlay, see 10.52 CAPITAL ALLOWANCES.

For enhanced tax reliefs for research and development expenditure *by certain companies*, see Tolley's Corporation Tax under Profit Computations.

71.81 **SECURITY**

A deduction may be allowed from profits of a trade etc. carried on by an individual (or partnership of individuals) for certain expenditure incurred in connection with the provision for or use by the individual (or any of them) of an asset or service which improves personal security. The asset or service must be provided or used to meet a special threat to the individual's personal physical security arising wholly or mainly by virtue of the trade, profession or vocation, and the sole object of the provider must be the meeting of that threat. In the case of an asset, relief is available only to the extent that the provider intends the asset to be used solely to improve personal physical security (ignoring any other incidental use), and in the case of a service, the benefit to the individual must consist wholly or mainly in such an improvement. Any improvement in the personal physical security of the individual's family resulting from the asset or service provided is disregarded for these purposes.

Excluded from relief is provision of a car, ship or aircraft, or of a dwelling (or grounds appurtenant thereto); but relief may be obtained in respect of equipment or a structure (such as a wall), and it is immaterial whether or not an asset becomes affixed to land and whether or not the individual acquires the property in the asset or (in the case of a fixture) an estate or interest in the land. [*FA 1989, ss 112, 113*]. See also 10.25 CAPITAL ALLOWANCES, 75.35 SCHEDULE E.

Simon's Direct Tax Service. See **B3.1346**.

71.82 **SHARE, SECURITY ETC. ISSUES, PURCHASES, SALES AND EXCHANGES**

For whether a trade of 'share dealing' carried on see 71.39 above. For transactions not at market value see 71.83 below.

Profits and losses on realisations of investments by a bank in the course of its business enter into its Case I profits (*Punjab Co-operative Bank v Lahore IT Commr PC 1940, 19 ATC 533* and see *Frasers (Glasgow) Bank v CIR HL 1963, 40 TC 698*) and similarly for insurance companies (*Northern Assce Co v Russell CES 1889, 2 TC 551; General Reinsurance Co v Tomlinson Ch D 1970, 48 TC 81* and contrast *CIR v Scottish Automobile CS 1931, 16 TC 381*). Profits/losses held capital in *Stott v Hoddinott KB 1916, 7 TC 85* (investments acquired by architect to secure contracts); *Jacobs Young & Co v Harris KB 1926, 11 TC 221* (shares held by merchanting company in subsidiary wound up); *Alliance & Dublin Consumers' Gas Co v Davis HC(IFS) 1926, 5 ATC 717* (investments of gas company earmarked for reserve fund). A profit by a property dealing company on the sale of shares acquired in connection with a property transaction was held a trading receipt (*Associated London Properties v Henriksen CA 1944, 26 TC 46*) but contrast *Fundfarms Developments v Parsons Ch D 1969, 45 TC 707* and see now 3 ANTI-AVOIDANCE.

Shares allotted for mining concessions granted by company dealing in concessions held trading receipts at market value (*Gold Coast Selection Trust v Humphrey HL 1948, 30 TC 209*). See also *Murphy v Australian Machinery & Investment Co CA 1948, 30 TC 244* and *Scottish & Canadian Investment Co v Easson CS 1922, 8 TC 265.*

For options, see *Varty v British South Africa Co HL 1965, 42 TC 406* (no profits or loss until shares sold). See also *Walker v Cater Securities Ch D 1974, 49 TC 625.*

Conversion etc. of securities held as circulating capital. Where a new holding of securities (as defined) is issued in exchange for an original holding beneficially owned by a person carrying on a business of banking, insurance or dealing in investments, the transaction, for purposes of Schedule D, Case I, shall be treated as not involving any disposal of the original holding; the new holding being treated as the same asset. This applies to securities where a profit on their sale would normally be a trading profit and to transactions which otherwise would result in the new holding being equated with the original holding under *TCGA 1992, ss 132, 136* (capital gains rollover relief in cases of conversions etc.) and *TCGA 1992, s 134* (compensation stock) but does not apply to a transaction on or before 31 July 1998 under *ICTA 1988, s 471* (see below) whether or not a notice has been given under that *section*. Where there is consideration in addition to the new holding, apportionment will apply. [*ICTA 1988, s 473; FA 1998, Sch 27 Pt III(23)*]. By concession, this treatment may also be claimed where the capital gains tax provisions referred to would not have applied but could have been treated as applying under the concession relating to earn-outs. (Revenue Pamphlet IR 1, D 27, now obsolete). See Tolley's Capital Gains Tax under Shares and Securities for details of the earn-out concession.

Exchange of securities by share dealers in connection with conversion operations, nationalisation etc. by Government. For exchanges on or before 31 July 1998, the securities received, together with any additional consideration, will take the place of the securities given up without involving any disposal until the new securities are realised. Election may be made for these provisions not to apply. For 1996/97 and later years, it must be made within twelve months after 31 January following the year of assessment in whose basis period the exchange takes place (or, for corporation tax where self-assessment applies, within two years after the end of the accounting period in which the exchange takes place). Previously, election had to be made within two years after the end of the relevant chargeable period. These provisions are **repealed** after 31 July 1998. [*ICTA 1988, s 471; FA 1996, s 135, Sch 21 para 12; FA 1998, s 101(1)(3)*].

Gilt-edged securities: stripping and reconsolidation. Where the computation of profits from a trade, etc. requires amounts in respect of the acquisition or redemption of a gilt-edged security to be brought into account, there are special provisions dealing with the exchange of such a security for strips of the security and for reconsolidation on the exchange of strips for the security from which they derived.

On an exchange for strips, the security is treated as having been redeemed at its market value, and the strips as having been acquired at that market value apportioned *pro rata* to their market value at the time of the exchange. Similarly on a consolidation, each strip is treated as having been redeemed at its market value, and the security as having been acquired at the aggregate market value of the strips. The Treasury may make regulations for determining market value for these purposes.

ICTA 1988, s 473 (conversion etc. of securities held as circulating capital, see above) does not apply where these provisions apply.

These provisions do not apply for the purposes of corporation tax, for which see Tolley's Corporation Tax under Loan Relationships (special cases).

[*ICTA 1988, s 730C; FA 1996, Sch 40 para 7*].

Stock lending. The following provisions are repealed with effect in relation to, and to transfers under, arrangements made on or after 1 July 1997. [*FA 1997, Sch 10 paras 1, 7(1); SI 1997 Nos 987, 991*]. See Tolley's Capital Gains Tax under Shares and Securities as regards the substitute provisions of *TCGA 1992, ss 263B, 263C* (introduced by *FA 1997, Sch 10 para 5* also with effect from 1 July 1997), which broadly ensure that stock loans do not incur a capital gains charge. See also 3.7 ANTI-AVOIDANCE as regards corresponding changes to the provisions relating to manufactured payments.

Under the earlier provisions, where arrangements are made under which securities, including stocks and shares, are transferred to a person (or his nominee) to enable him to fulfil a contract for sale of securities, and in return securities of the same kind and amount are to be transferred to the lender (or his nominee), the transfers under the arrangements are disregarded in computing trading profits or losses and for the purposes of capital gains tax. By concession, this treatment is extended to arrangements under which a loan of gilt-edged securities falls due for redemption and an appropriate cash sum is paid instead of the stock being returned, or where a loan is made to replace an existing stock loan rather than to meet a sale. (Revenue Pamphlet IR 1, B35, B36). These concessions were superseded by *SI 1995 No 3219* (below), but see also now below as regards the position after 27 May 1996. The same exemptions apply where, to enable him to fulfil such arrangements, the lender himself enters into similar arrangements with a third party. For transfers made after 30 September 1993, the exemptions also apply to arrangements made as part of a chain of arrangements all having the effect of enabling the lender to make the transfer to the seller. The exemptions are statutory for transfers after 18 August 1989, and are subject to the various conditions as to Revenue approval of the arrangements and of the participants set out in *The Income Tax (Stock Lending) Regulations 1989 (SI 1989 No 1299)* as amended by *SI 1990 No 2552*, *SI 1992 No 572*, *SI 1993 No 2003, SI 1995 No 1283*, *SI 1995 No 3219* and *SI 1996 No 1228*. From 28 May 1996, they apply only to UK equities. Regulations may also provide for the exemptions to apply in cases where the arrangements under which the securities are transferred are for purposes other than enabling a contract for sale to be fulfilled. *SI 1995 No 3219* also makes provision from that date for the exemptions to apply where the arrangements terminate on redemption of the securities. [*ICTA 1988, s 129; FA 1991, s 57; TCGA 1992, s 271(9); FA 1995, s 84; FA 1997, Sch 10 para 1(1), para 7(1)*]. See above as regards **repeal** of these provisions. See also 44.5(*f*) INTEREST RECEIVABLE, 74.25, 74.26 SCHEDULE D, CASE VI.

Cash collateral arrangements. Prior to their repeal, special provisions also apply where, in relation to a stock lending arrangement within the above provisions entered into on or after 1 May 1995, the borrower of the stock pays to the lender an amount of 'cash collateral' by way of security for the performance of the obligation under the arrangement. Where the lender earns interest (paid without deduction of tax) on the whole of the cash collateral for the period he holds it, and pays to the borrower an amount of 'rebate interest' equal to the interest so earned by the lender (and identified as such separately from any other amount payable in connection with the arrangement):

(A) the interest earned by the lender is treated as income of the borrower and not of the lender;

(B) tax is not deductible from the payment of rebate interest;

(C) no relief is available to the lender in respect of the payment of rebate interest; and

(D) the rebate interest is not treated as income of the borrower.

This applies equally to a nominee acting for the borrower or lender, and, with appropriate modification, to a chain of arrangements. [*ICTA 1988, s 129A, Sch 5A; FA 1995, s 85, Sch 19; FA 1997, Sch 10 paras 1(2), 7(1)*]. See above as regards **repeal** of these provisions.

Stock lending fees. Such fees relating to investments eligible for relief under *ICTA 1988, s 592(2), s 608(2)(a), s 613(4), s 614(3), s 620(6)* or *s 643(2)* (pension scheme funds, etc., see 66.5, 66.13, 66.11 RETIREMENT SCHEMES, 59.6 PENSIONS, 65.8 RETIREMENT ANNUITIES and 60.1 PERSONAL PENSION SCHEMES) are also eligible for relief under those *sections*, where the stock lending arrangement is entered into after 1 January 1996. [*ICTA 1988, s 129B; FA 1996, s 157; FA 1997, Sch 10 para 2*].

Dealers in securities. With effect for distributions made **after 1 July 1997** (and for payments representative of such distributions), any distribution by a UK-resident company (or payment representative of such a distribution) *received by* a dealer in securities is taken into account (exclusive of any tax credit) in computing the dealer's Schedule D, Case I or II profits. Accordingly:

(*a*) income tax under SCHEDULE F (76) is not chargeable; and

(*b*) the normal exemption from corporation tax of UK company distributions under *ICTA 1988, s 208* does not apply (and non-resident companies trading through a UK branch or agency may similarly be chargeable in respect of such distributions).

Any payment *made by* a dealer which is representative of a UK company distribution is similarly brought into the Case I or II computation.

A person is for these purposes a dealer in relation to a distribution if, on a sale of the shares or stock in respect of which the distribution is made, the price would be taken into account in computing Schedule D, Case I or II profits (assuming that it would not fall to be treated as a distribution) other than insurance business profits.

See 3.23 ANTI-AVOIDANCE as regards arrangements to pass on the value of tax credits.

For distributions made **after 25 November 1996 and before 2 July 1997**, provisions similar to those described above apply to actual or deemed qualifying distributions to which *FA 1997, Sch 7* applies (see 3.21 ANTI-AVOIDANCE), and additionally:

(i) such a distribution was not treated as received as a foreign income dividend (see 1.9 ALLOWANCES AND TAX RATES);

(ii) where, as a result of any transaction, such a distribution was receivable by a dealer, the distribution was not, in relation to that transaction, treated as interest in determining whether *ICTA 1988, s 732* applies by virtue of *ICTA 1988, s 731* (see 3.6 ANTI-AVOIDANCE);

(iii) the prohibition on the deduction of manufactured dividends by non-UK resident companies from 1 July 1997 (see 3.7 ANTI-AVOIDANCE) does not apply to payments by dealers representative of such distributions; and

(iv) the exclusion of dealing in respect of insurance business profits did not apply.

The provisions also did not apply to the redemption of 'fixed-rate preference shares', or of other preference shares issued before 6 April 1982, and redeemed on terms substantially settled before that date, if the shares were issued to and continuously held by the person from whom they were redeemed. '*Fixed rate preference shares*' for this purpose are shares issued wholly for new consideration and carrying no right to conversion into, or to the acquisition of, any other shares and securities and carrying no right to dividends unless they are at a fixed amount or fixed rate and the dividends plus any redemption money represent no more than a reasonable commercial return on the consideration for which the shares were issued.

For distributions made **before 26 November 1996**, the preceding provisions applied only in relation to payments by a company for the redemption, etc. of its own shares, the definition of 'dealer' being correspondingly revised. (*b*) above had no application, but no tax credit was available in respect of any distribution element. The disapplication of interest treatment under *ICTA 1988, s 732* did not apply.

[*ICTA 1988, s 95; FA 1997, Sch 7 para 8(1)(3); F(No 2)A 1997, s 24*].

Extra return on new issues of securities. Where

(*a*) securities of a particular kind are issued (being the original issue of securities of that kind),

(*b*) new securities of the same kind are issued subsequently,

(*c*) a sum (the 'extra return') is payable by the issuer in respect of the new securities, to reflect the fact that interest is accruing on the old securities and calculated accordingly, and

(*d*) the issue price of the new securities includes an element (separately identified or not) representing payment for the extra return,

the extra return is treated for all tax purposes (except, for new issues after 31 March 1996, corporation tax) as a payment of interest, but the issuer is not entitled to tax relief, either as a deduction in computing profits or otherwise as a deduction or set-off, for the payment. [*ICTA 1988, s 587A; FA 1991, Sch 12 paras 1, 5; FA 1996, Sch 14 para 33*].

General. See also 3 ANTI-AVOIDANCE, including transactions in securities to obtain tax advantage [*ICTA 1988, s 703*], bond washing [*ICTA 1988, s 729*], dividend-stripping [*ICTA 1988, s 736*].

For share transactions entered into to secure tax advantages see 71.29 above and for transactions in dividend-stripping before the enactment of existing legislation see Tolley's Tax Cases.

71.83 STOCK IN TRADE AND WORK IN PROGRESS

See generally Revenue Inspector's Manual, IM 547–582.

Basis of valuation. The general rule is that stock is to be valued at the lower of cost and market value and this is so notwithstanding that accounts use, and accountancy principles permit, a different basis. Leading cases are *Minister of National Revenue v Anaconda American Brass Co PC 1955, 34 ATC 330* and *BSC Footwear v Ridgway HL 1971, 47 TC 495*. Market value held to be replacement price for a merchant (*Brigg Neumann & Co v CIR KB 1928, 12 TC 1191*) and retail price for a retailer in *BSC Footwear* above (Revenue prepared to take price net of any selling commission). Stock may be valued partly at cost and partly at market value where lower (*CIR v Cock Russell & Co KB 1949, 29 TC 387*). The base stock method is not permissible (*Patrick v Broadstone Mills CA 1953, 35 TC 44*) nor is 'LIFO' (*Anaconda American Brass* above). See also *Ryan v Asia Mill HL 1951, 32 TC 275*. The cost should include as a minimum the cost of materials and direct labour but the accounts treatment of overheads is normally accepted (*Duple Motor Bodies v Ostime HL 1961, 39 TC 537*).

For accepted accountancy practice see SSAP 9 (revised September 1988), issued by the Institute of Chartered Accountants in England and Wales (ICAEW), and for Revenue's view see Pamphlet IR 131, SP 3/90, 10 January 1990.

For the use of formulae in computing stock provisions and write-downs, see Revenue Tax Bulletin December 1994 p 184. Broadly, inspectors will accept formulae which reflect a realistic appraisal of future income from the particular category of stock and which result in the stock being included at a reasonable estimate of net realisable value. Where computations are accepted without enquiry, it is on the assumption that profits are arrived at in accordance with such principles. (Revenue Tax Bulletin December 1994 p 184).

For motor dealer stock valuations, see Revenue Tax Bulletin August 1994 p 156.

As regards valuation of professional work in progress, it is understood that the following principles are, in broad terms, accepted by the Revenue:

(i) nothing should be included for partners' time;

(ii) direct employment costs of fee-earners and direct overheads applicable, such as secretarial salaries, stationery, telephone costs, etc. should be included;

(iii) general production overheads for general office areas, conference rooms, etc. should be excluded, whilst those for individual office areas directly applicable should be discounted by, say, 30% for non-productive time; and

(iv) contingent fees should be included.

(Taxation Vol 141, No 3654 p 126, 30 April 1998). For further guidance on valuation of professional work in progress, see the detailed note agreed between the Revenue and the ICAEW in Revenue Tax Bulletin December 1998 pp 607-615.

Changes in basis of valuation. Where the stock was found to be grossly undervalued it was held that an assessment to rectify the closing undervaluation must be reduced by the opening undervaluation to bring out the true profits (*Bombay IT Commr v Ahmedabad New Cotton Mills Co PC 1929, 9 ATC 574*). But where a company altered its method of dealing with accrued profits on long-term contracts and the closing work in progress in the year 1 accounts on the old basis was substantially below the opening figure in the year 2 accounts on the new basis, held, distinguishing *Ahmedabad*, the difference must be included in the year 2 profits (*Pearce v Woodall-Duckham Ltd CA 1978, 51 TC 271*). See also Revenue Pamphlet IR 131, SP 3/90, 10 January 1990.

Where there is a change in the basis of valuation, the following practice is applied for tax purposes. If the bases of valuation both before and after the change are acceptable, the opening figure for the period of change must be the same as the closing figure for the preceding period. If the change is from an unacceptable basis to an acceptable one, the opening figure for the period of change must be arrived at on the same basis as the closing figure for that period, and liabilities for earlier years will be reviewed. However, if there is no question of fraudulent or negligent conduct, tax for past years will not be recovered on an amount greater than that resulting from the uplift of the opening figure for the year of change. (Revenue Pamphlet IR 131, SP 3/90, 10 January 1990). See, however, *Woodall-Duckham Ltd* (above) as regards long-term contracts.

See generally Revenue Inspector's Manual, IM 547–551.

Long-term contracts. The Revenue now accept that accurate provisions for foreseen losses on long-term contracts (e.g. in the construction industry) made in accordance with correct accounting practice are tax deductible. (Revenue Press Release 20 July 1999). Previously, their practice was to permit provision for a proportion of an overall loss, calculated either on a time basis or by reference to expenditure, provided that all contracts, profitable or otherwise, were similarly dealt with. Provisions for foreseeable further expenditure, representing obligations up to final delivery, were normally allowed where work was substantially completed (likely to require at least 90% completion — see Revenue Inspector's Manual, IM 569) and the financial outcome of the contract was reasonably certain. Reasonable provision for future expenditure under guarantees or warranties was also normally allowed. Beyond these limits, no provision was permitted for future loss apportionable to the remainder of the contract. (Revenue Pamphlet IR 131, SP 3/90, 10 January 1990). This practice did not apply to professional work in progress.

In *Symons v Weeks and Others Ch D 1982, 56 TC 630*, it was held that progress payments under the long-term contracts of a firm of architects did not fall to be brought into account for tax before the relevant contract was completed, notwithstanding that they exceeded the figure brought in for work in progress, calculated on the correct principles of commercial accounting.

See above for changes of basis.

Goods sold subject to reservation of title. Where the supplier of goods reserves the title in them until payment is made (as a protection should the buyer become insolvent) and meanwhile the goods are treated by both parties for accountancy purposes as having been sold/purchased, the Revenue will follow the accounts treatment. (Revenue Pamphlet IR 131, B6). See Note A of Financial Reporting Standard No 5 and Revenue Inspector's Manual, IM 305.

Goods on consignment stock are normally treated as stock in the hands of the supplier until disposed of by the consignee (e.g. sale or return). (Revenue Pamphlet IR 131, B6).

For forward contracts, see 71.50 above.

Insurance recoveries. See 71.64 above.

Transactions not at market value. Where trading stock is disposed of otherwise than by way of trade, the realisable value is to be credited for tax purposes. This was established by *Sharkey v Wernher HL 1955, 36 TC 275* approving *Watson Bros v Hornby KB 1942, 24 TC 506*. It applies, *inter alia*, to goods taken out of stock by a retailer for his own use (see below). It was applied in *Petrotim Securities Ltd v Ayres CA 1963, 41 TC 389* to a disposal of shares at gross under-value as part of a tax avoidance scheme, but in *Ridge Securities Ltd v CIR Ch D 1963, 44 TC 373*, dealing with the other end of the same scheme, it was held that the same principle applied to acquisitions of trading stock otherwise than by way of trade, market price being substituted for the actual purchase price. But the principle is not applicable to sales or purchases by way of trade notwithstanding not at arm's length. Hence when a share dealing company acquired shares at substantial overvalue from an associated company, the claim by the Revenue for market value failed (*Craddock v Zevo Finance Co HL 1946, 27 TC 267*), and when a property dealing company acquired property from its controlling shareholder at substantial undervalue, its claim to substitute market value failed (*Jacgilden (Weston Hall) v Castle Ch D 1969, 45 TC 685*). See also *Skinner v Berry Head Lands Ch D 1970, 46 TC 377* and *Kilmorie (Aldridge) v Dickinson HL 1974, 50 TC 1.*

Appropriations to trading stock of assets held in another capacity are generally treated as a disposal and reacquisition at market value. Where a chargeable gain or allowable loss would otherwise arise for capital gains tax purposes under *TCGA 1992, s 161(1)*, the trader may elect for the market value to be reduced for these purposes by the amount of the chargeable gain (or increased by the amount of the allowable loss), the trading profits being computed accordingly and the appropriation being disregarded for capital gains tax purposes. The election must be made within, for 1996/97 and later years, twelve months after 31 January following the tax year in which ends the period of account in which the asset is appropriated, or for corporation tax purposes where self-assessment applies, two years after the end of the accounting period in which the asset is appropriated. Previously, the general six-year time limit at 17.8 CLAIMS applied. [*TCGA 1992, s 161(3)(3A); FA 1996, s 135, Sch 21 para 36*].

Stock taken for own use or disposed of otherwise than by sale in the normal course of trade. The case of *Sharkey v Wernher HL 1955, 36 TC 275* established the principle that such a transfer should be treated as if it were a sale at market value. Inspectors have been authorised to take a reasonably broad view in applying this principle. The case is not considered to apply to

(*a*) services rendered to the trader personally or to his household the cost of which should be disallowed under *ICTA 1988, s 74(1)(b)*;

(*b*) the value of meals provided for proprietors of hotels, boarding houses, restaurants etc. and members of their families, the cost of which should be disallowed under *ICTA 1988, s 74(1)(b)*;

(*c*) expenditure incurred by a trader on the construction of an asset which is to be used as a fixed asset in the trade.

(Revenue Pamphlet IR 131, A32).

For the Revenue's view of the application of normal Schedule D, Case I principles to donations of trading stock to charities, see Revenue Tax Bulletin June 1996 p 319.

What constitutes stock. Greyhounds kept by greyhound racing company not trading stock (*Abbot v Albion Greyhounds (Salford) KB 1945, 26 TC 390*). Payments by cigarette manufacturer for cropping trees (not owned by it) for leaves used in manufacture, held to be for materials (*Mohanlal Hargovind of Jubbulpore v IT Commr PC 1949, 28 ATC 287*). For payments for unworked minerals, sand and gravel, etc., (including tailings, etc.) by mines, quarries etc. see 71.71 above. For payments for oil by oil companies, see *Hughes v British Burmah Petroleum KB 1932, 17 TC 286; New Zealand Commr v Europa Oil (NZ) PC 1970, 49 ATC 282; Europa Oil (NZ) v New Zealand Commr PC, [1976] STC 37*. For timber see 71.72 above and *Coates v Holker Estates Co Ch D 1961, 40 TC 75*.

Valuation on discontinuance of business. Under *ICTA 1988, s 100* where a trade is discontinued (or so treated for tax purposes by *ICTA 1988, s 113* or *s 337(1)*) otherwise than on the death of a sole trader—

(1) Where the stock is '*sold or transferred for valuable consideration*' to a person carrying on (or intending to carry on) a trade in the UK who can deduct the cost as an expense for tax purposes, the stock is normally to be valued at the amount realised on the sale (or the value of the consideration). However, for cessations of trade **after 28 November 1994**, where the two parties to the sale or transfer are connected persons (defined more broadly than by *ICTA 1988, s 839* — see *ICTA 1988, s 100(1F)*), arm's length value is to be taken instead. The connected persons rule does not apply in the case of certain sovereign debts, and neither rule applies to a transfer of farm animals where the anti-avoidance rules at 34.9 HERD BASIS apply. Where arm's length value exceeds both (i) actual sale price and (ii) acquisition value (broadly, the amount that would have been deductible in respect of the stock had it been sold in the course of trade immediately before cessation), connected persons may jointly elect to substitute the greater (taking all the stock sold or transferred together) of (i) and (ii), the election to be made within two years after the end of the chargeable period in which cessation occurs. The stock valuation determined under these provisions applies both to transferor and transferee.

See *Moore v Mackenzie Ch D 1971, 48 TC 196*. If both trades are within the jurisdiction of the same body of General Commissioners appeals are dealt with by them, otherwise by Special Commissioners [*ICTA 1988, s 102(1); FA 1996, Sch 22 para 11*] and see *Bradshaw v Blunden (No 2) Ch D 1960, 39 TC 73; CIR v Barr (No 2) CS 1955, 36 TC 455*.

ICTA 1988, s 100 not applicable to woodlands managed on a commercial basis (*Coates v Holker Estates* above). For application to 'hire-purchase debts' see *Lions Ltd v Gosford Furnishing Co Ltd & CIR CS 1961, 40 TC 256.*

(2) In all other cases stock is to be valued at the price it would have realised if sold in open market at date of discontinuance.

This section applies to all kinds of property real or personal sold in usual course of the trade, materials used in manufacture etc. and services etc., which would be treated as work in progress if the trade were a profession (see below).

[*ICTA 1988, s 100; FA 1995, s 141*].

If, following the death of a sole trader, the executors continue trading, or if the business passes direct to a beneficiary, the opening stock may be brought in at market value even if valued at cost on death. (Revenue Inspector's Manual, IM 571).

Similar provisions are applied, *mutatis mutandis*, to work in progress at the date when a profession or vocation is, or is treated as, discontinued. But taxpayer may elect that for computing his profits to the date of cessation w.i.p. shall be taken at cost, and that any realised excess over cost shall be treated as POST-CESSATION ETC. RECEIPTS (62) under *ICTA 1988, s 103*. For 1996/97 and later years, the election must be made within twelve months after 31 January following the year of assessment of cessation (or, for corporation tax where self-assessment applies, within two years after the end of the accounting period of cessation). Previously, the election had to be made within twelve months after the discontinuance. [*ICTA 1988, s 101; FA 1996, s 135, Sch 21 para 3*].

See ICAEW Technical Release TAX 7/95, 15 February 1995, for a guidance note on the taxation implications of various treatments of transfers of work in progress and debtors on incorporation of a professional partnership.

Simon's Direct Tax Service. See **B3.10, B3.1517**.

71.84 SUBSCRIPTIONS, ETC. INCLUDING TRADE ASSOCIATION CONTRIBUTIONS

Gifts to charitable bodies are deductible under general rules of business expenses (i.e. requiring the outlay to be wholly and exclusively for purposes of the trade etc.) notwithstanding *ICTA 1988, s 577(8)* (see 71.55 above). [*ICTA 1988, s 577(9)*]. Concessionally, other gifts are allowed provided that they are (i) wholly and exclusively for the purposes of the business, (ii) made for the benefit of a body or association established for educational, cultural, religious, recreational or benevolent purposes which is local to the donor's business activities and not restricted to persons connected with the donor and (iii) reasonably small in relation to the sale of the donor's business. (Revenue Pamphlet IR 1, B7). In *Bourne & Hollingsworth v Ogden KB 1929, 14 TC 349* an abnormally large donation was disallowed. For donations of part of cost of ticket in football pools and lotteries, see 71.30 above. See 15.17 CHARITIES for three year covenants to charities, and see 15.11, 15.18 CHARITIES as regards certain other donations by individuals. See Tolley's Corporation Tax as regards qualifying donations by companies to charities.

Trade and professional associations. Ordinary annual subscriptions to local associations, including Chambers of Commerce, are normally allowed. Subscriptions to larger associations are allowable, and receipts therefrom assessable, if the association has entered into an arrangement with the Revenue under which it is assessed on any surplus of receipts over allowable expenditure (the association should be asked). Most associations enter into the arrangement but if not the allowance is restricted to the proportion applied by the association for purposes such that it would have been allowed if so applied by the subscriber (*Lochgelly Iron & Coal Co Ltd v Crawford CS 1913, 6 TC 267*). For other cases see Tolley's

Tax Cases. Subscriptions to the Economic League are not allowed (*Joseph L Thompson & Sons Ltd v Chamberlain Ch D 1962, 40 TC 657*).

Contributions to mutual insurance associations are allowable even though used to create a reserve fund (*Thomas v Richard Evans & Co Ltd HL 1927, 11 TC 790*). See also 50 MUTUAL TRADING.

Local enterprise agencies. Expenditure incurred in making any contribution (whether in cash or kind) to an 'approved local enterprise agency' is allowable if not otherwise deductible. There is no allowance if any related benefit is receivable by the contributor, or any person connected with him (see 20 CONNECTED PERSONS), from the agency or from any other person, and any relief already given will be recovered by a charge under Schedule D, Cases I or II or VI to the extent of the benefit.

'*Approved local enterprise agency*' is any body approved by the Secretary of State who is satisfied (i) its sole objective is the promotion or encouragement of industrial and commercial activity or enterprise in a particular area of the UK and with particular reference to small businesses, or (ii) one of its principal objectives is as in (i) *and* it maintains a separate fund for that objective. The agency must be precluded from making dividends, gifts etc. to its members or managers. Approval may be conditional and may be withdrawn retrospectively. [*ICTA 1988, s 79; FA 1990, s 75; FA 1994, s 145(1); FA 2000, s 88*].

Training and enterprise councils, local enterprise companies and business link organisations. Identical provisions to those described above in relation to local enterprise agencies apply to a contribution to a training and enterprise council which has an agreement with the Secretary of State to act as such, or to a local enterprise company which has an agreement with Scottish Enterprise or Highlands and Islands Enterprise to act as such, or to a business link organisation authorised by the Secretary of State to use a service mark designated for these purposes. [*ICTA 1988, s 79A; FA 1990, s 76; FA 1994, s 145; FA 2000, s 88, Sch 40 Pt II(9)*].

71.85 SUBSIDIES, GRANTS ETC.

Enterprise allowance, paid to assist unemployed people in setting up their own businesses, is paid under *Employment and Training Act 1973, s 2(2)(d)* or *Enterprise and New Towns (Scotland) Act 1990, s 2(4)(c)* (or NI equivalent). Payments are charged to tax under Schedule D, Case VI. This treatment does not, however, prevent the payments being treated as earned income or as 'relevant earnings' for retirement annuity or personal pension scheme purposes (see 60.8 PERSONAL PENSION SCHEMES, 65.7 RETIREMENT ANNUITIES). They may also continue to give rise to liability to Class 4 national insurance contributions. [*ICTA 1988, s 127, Sch 29 para 14*]. From 1991/92, the responsibility for payment of such allowances was transferred to the Training and Enterprise Councils (in Scotland, Local Enterprise Councils). They are now more commonly known as **business start up allowances**, but provided that they retain the essential characteristics of enterprise allowances (in particular that the recipient is unemployed or working notice and that the allowance is a flat rate weekly amount), they are in practice treated in the same way for tax purposes. (Revenue Inspector's Manual, IM 392, 392a).

Farming support payments. See 71.57 above.

Fishing grants. For the tax treatment of decommissioning grants, laying-up grants, exploratory voyage grants and joint venture grants under *SI 1983 No 1883*, see Revenue Inspector's Manual, IM 2363.

Football pools promoters. Certain contributions to the Football Trust 1990 by pools promoters for football ground improvements are allowable as deductions in the pools promoter's trade, as are certain payments by them to other trustees established mainly for the support of athletic sports or games (but with power to support the arts). [*FA 1990, s 126; FA 1991, s 121*]. See also 10.2(ii) CAPITAL ALLOWANCES.

Regional development grants. Grants under *Industry Act 1972, ss 7, 8* (and similar NI legislation) and certain other NI payments, not made towards specified capital expenditure or compensation for loss of capital assets, are trading receipts. [*ICTA 1988, s 93*]. An earlier interest relief grant under the *Act* was held to be assessable in *Burman v Thorn Domestic Appliances (Electrical) Ltd Ch D 1981, 55 TC 493*, as was a similar grant undifferentiated between revenue and capital in *Ryan v Crabtree Denims Ltd Ch D 1987, 60 TC 183*, applying *Gayjon Processes Ltd* (below) and distinguishing *Seaham Harbour* (below). Grants under *Industrial Development Act 1982, Part II* to traders, etc. or investment companies are exempt from income tax. [*ICTA 1988, s 92*].

Research grant by trading company to medical practitioner held assessable (*Duff v Williamson Ch D 1973, 49 TC 1*). For research grants and fellowships generally, see Revenue Inspector's Manual, IM 3030.

Temporary employment subsidy was paid under *Employment and Training Act 1973, s 5* (as amended by *Employment Protection Act 1975, Sch 14 para 2*) as a flat-rate weekly payment or (in the textile, clothing and footwear industries) by way of reimbursement of payments made to workers on short time.

Such payments were held to be taxable as trading receipts in *Poulter v Gayjon Processes Ltd Ch D 1985, 58 TC 350*, distinguishing the grants made by the Unemployment Grants Committee in *Seaham Harbour* (below).

Unemployment grants. Subsidy to dock company (from Unemployment Grants Committee) for extension work to keep men in employment held, although grant made in terms of interest, not a 'trade receipt' for tax purposes (*Seaham Harbour v Crook HL 1931, 16 TC 333*).

See 10.2(ii) CAPITAL ALLOWANCES for effect thereon of grants and subsidies.

See 67.7 RETURNS as regards returns of certain grant and subsidy payments.

Simon's Direct Tax Service. See **B3.929**.

71.86 TAXATION

Income tax and corporation tax are not deductible in computing profits (cf. *Allen v Farquharson Bros & Co KB 1932, 17 TC 59*). Overseas taxes may be subject to DOUBLE TAX RELIEF (25) but any such tax not relieved by credit on overseas income included in the profits may be deducted [*ICTA 1988, s 811*] but not on UK income, e.g. profits of UK branches (*CIR v Dowdall O'Mahoney & Co Ltd HL 1952, 33 TC 259*).

In *Harrods (Buenos Aires) v Taylor-Gooby CA 1964, 41 TC 450* an annual capital tax imposed by the Argentine on foreign companies trading there was not a tax on the profits and was allowable.

As regards relief for national insurance contributions by employers in respect of employees, see 71.54 above. For deduction of part of Class 4 National Insurance contributions from total income, see 1.10 ALLOWANCES AND RATES.

For taxation appeals see 71.69 above. For VAT see 71.93 below.

Simon's Direct Tax Service. See **B3.1451** *et seq.*, **B3.1516**.

71.87 TELECOMMUNICATIONS LICENCES

Special rules apply in relation to licences granted under *Wireless Telegraphy Act 1949, s 1* as a result of bidding for such licences under *Wireless Telegraphy Act 1998, s 3* regulations, and to rights derived directly or indirectly therefrom. They also apply to indefeasible rights to use a telecommunications cable system ('IRUs') acquired after 20 March 2000 other than from an 'associate' (within *ICTA 1988, s 417(3)(4)*) or an 'associated company' (within *ICTA 1988, s 416(1)* or, in relation to an individual, being a company of which that individual has control under *ICTA 1988, s 416(2)–(6)*) which acquired them on or before that date, and to derived rights.

Acquisition costs and disposal proceeds in respect of such rights which, in accordance with normal UK company accounting practice, may be taken into account in determining accounting profit or loss, and which are so taken into account in any relevant statutory accounts required under *Companies Act 1985, s 226* (or NI or foreign equivalent), are treated as being of a revenue nature in computing profits chargeable to income tax or corporation tax. This applies equally to costs of extension of attached rights or of cancellation or restriction of rights attached to derivative rights, and to receipts from cancellation or restriction of attached rights or from granting derivative rights or extensions of rights attached to derivative rights.

Similar treatment applies to amounts in respect of the revaluation of such rights provided that, in accordance with normal UK company accounting practice, they fall to be taken into account for accounting purposes, whether or not they may be so taken into account in determining profit or loss or are so taken into account in any relevant statutory accounts. The period of account for which such an amount is taken into account for tax purposes is that in which it is recognised for accounting purposes in accordance with normal UK company accounting practice.

Where the taxpayer company is a member of a group of companies (within *Companies Act 1985, s 262(1)* or NI or foreign equivalent) which is required to produce consolidated group accounts (within *Companies Act 1985, s 227* or NI or foreign equivalent), the company's accounting policies, and method of applying those policies, in respect of rights within these provisions must not be more cautious than that adopted in the group accounts. This applies in relation to each group of which the company is a member, if there is more than one.

[*FA 2000, s 87, Sch 23*].

71.88 TIED PETROL STATIONS, ETC.

For tied licensed premises see 71.45 above.

'Exclusivity payments' by petrol company to retailers undertaking to sell only its goods were allowed in computing its profits in *Bolam v Regent Oil Co Ltd Ch D 1956, 37 TC 56* (payments for repairs carried out by retailer), *BP Australia Ltd PC 1965, 44 ATC 312* (lump sums paid for sales promotion) and *Mobil Oil Australia Ltd PC 1965, 44 ATC 323*, but held capital in *Strick v Regent Oil HL 1965, 43 TC 1* where the payment took the form of a premium to the retailer for a lease of his premises (immediately sub-let to him).

In the hands of the retailer exclusivity payments were held capital when for capital expenditure incurred by him (*CIR v Coia CS 1959, 38 TC 334; McLaren v Needham Ch D 1960, 39 TC 37; Walter W Saunders Ltd v Dixon Ch D 1962, 40 TC 329*) but revenue when for repairs, etc. (*McLaren v Needham above*) or sales promotion (*Evans v Wheatley Ch D 1958, 38 TC 216*) or where petrol sales were a relatively small part (some 30%) of the company's turnover (*Tanfield Ltd v Carr (Sp C 200), [1999] SSCD 213*).

For a summary of the Revenue view of such arrangements, see Revenue Tax Bulletin August 1993 p 88.

71.89 TRAINING

Costs incurred by an employer in respect of employee training are generally allowable as a trade expense. See 71.54 above for this and as regards certain other allowable employee training costs, and 71.84 above as regards contributions to training and enterprise councils. See also 92 VOCATIONAL TRAINING RELIEF.

In general, the expenses of a training course undertaken by a self-employed person are allowed as a trade deduction under general principles only where the training is undertaken for the purposes of the trade and relates to the updating of existing expertise rather than the acquisition of new skills. See Revenue Inspector's Manual, IM 1165.

71.90 **TRAVELLING AND SUBSISTENCE EXPENSES**

The cost of travelling in the course of the business activities is allowable but not that of travelling between home and the place at or from which the business is conducted. For this see *Newsom v Robertson CA 1952, 33 TC 452* in which the expenses of a barrister between his home and his chambers were refused and contrast *Horton v Young CA 1971, 47 TC 60* in which a 'self-employed' bricklayer was allowed his expenses between his home and the sites at which he worked as, on the evidence, his business was conducted from his home. Compare the position for employees — see 75.43 SCHEDULE E. Any expenses of an employment ancillary to a profession not allowable in the Schedule E assessment may not be deducted in computing the profits of the profession (*Mitchell & Edon v Ross HL 1961, 40 TC 11*).

The 'dual purpose rule' (see 71.40 above) entails the disallowance of *all* travelling expenses with a material private purpose, i.e. the part attributable to business purposes is not allowable. Thus the expenses of a solicitor in travelling abroad partly for a holiday and partly to attend professional conferences were disallowed in *Bowden v Russell & Russell Ch D 1965, 42 TC 301* (but the expenses of an accountant to attend a professional conference abroad were allowed in *Edwards v Warmsley, Henshall & Co Ch D 1967, 44 TC 431*). Similarly the expenses of a dentist in travelling between his home and surgery were disallowed even though he collected dentures from a laboratory on the way (*Sargent v Barnes Ch D 1978, 52 TC 335*). The expenses of a farmer in visiting Australia with a view to farming there were held inadmissible (*Sargent v Eayrs Ch D 1972, 48 TC 573*). In practice, the Revenue normally allow a fair proportion of overseas trips partly for holidays if there was a genuine business purpose. (In *Bowden v Russell* above, the Revenue considered the business purpose too remote to justify apportionment.) Car expenses are also apportioned if used partly for private purposes. Parking and other motoring fines are normally disallowed in their entirety either under the 'dual purpose rule' (see 71.40 above) or under the general principles applicable to allowable trading deductions (see *CIR v Alexander von Glehn & Co Ltd CA 1920, 12 TC 232*, in which penalties for breach of wartime regulations were disallowed), although reimbursement of employee normally allowable (but see 75.7 SCHEDULE E as regards employee's liability).

Similar principles apply to hotel, etc. expenses incurred when travelling for business purposes. The reasonable cost of overnight stays is allowed but not the cost of lunches (*Caillebotte v Quinn Ch D 1975, 50 TC 222*). In practice, reasonable costs of evening meals and breakfast taken in conjunction with overnight accommodation are similarly allowed, and this treatment is extended to such costs incurred by long distance lorry drivers who sleep in their cabs. (Revenue Tax Bulletin August 1993 p 88). Normally there is no restriction for 'home saving' (cf. 75.43 SCHEDULE E). Nor will there be any disallowance of personal living expenses (i.e. accommodation, food and drink of self but not family or other dependants) incurred on longer business trips abroad. (Revenue Pamphlet IR 131, A16).

Motoring expenses. Inspectors will not object to taxpayers with low turnover using a fixed mileage rate per business mile in their accounts, provided that the rate does not exceed the appropriate Fixed Profit Car Scheme rate (see 75.43 SCHEDULE E). The turnover limit is for convenience set at the same amount as the VAT registration threshold (currently £52,000) at the time the vehicle is acquired. No other motoring expenses or related capital allowances may be claimed (except interest on a loan to purchase the vehicle), and any change to another basis of claim must be made only when one vehicle is replaced by another. Following the introduction of self-assessment, inspectors will expect taxpayers, on the next change of vehicle, either to adopt the above basis (where applicable) or to claim actual expenses. (Revenue Tax Bulletin April 1996 p 303).

See 51.12 NON-RESIDENTS AND OTHER OVERSEAS MATTERS for extended relief for travelling expenses in overseas trade.

Simon's Direct Tax Service. See **B3.1437**.

71.91 UNCLAIMED BALANCES

Unclaimed balances for which a firm was liable to account were held not assessable despite their being distributed to partners (*Morley v Tattersall CA 1938, 22 TC 51*). Such balances held by a pawnbroker are, however, assessable when claimants' rights expire (*Jay's, the Jewellers v CIR KB 1947, 29 TC 274*), and deposits on garments not collected were held trade receipts assessable when received (*Elson v Prices Tailors Ch D 1962, 40 TC 671*). The fact that trading receipts were subsequently, and correctly, treated for accountancy purposes as an element in a sale of fixed assets did not alter their nature for tax purposes (*Tapemaze Ltd v Melluish Ch D, [2000] STC 189*). See 71.44 above for releases of debts owing.

71.92 UNREMITTABLE RECEIPTS, DEBTS ETC.

Where a trade is carried on partly in the UK and partly overseas, so that liability to tax arises on all trade profits, the following amounts will be included in profits, with no relief being available under *ICTA 1988, s 584* (unremittable overseas income, see 51.14 NON-RESIDENTS AND OTHER OVERSEAS MATTERS) or *ICTA 1988, s 74(1)(j)* (bad and doubtful debts, see 71.44 above):

(*a*) amounts received overseas but not remittable to the UK;

(*b*) amounts owed to the trader overseas which temporarily cannot be paid; and

(*c*) amounts owed to the trader overseas which, even when paid, will not be remittable to the UK.

By concession, where any of (*a*)–(*c*) above applies solely as a result of local foreign exchange control restrictions, and continues to apply twelve months after the end of the accounting period in which the amount concerned was received or the debt arose, relief may be claimed, provided that:

(i) the assessment in question is not final and conclusive;

(ii) all reasonable endeavours have been made to secure payment and remittance to the UK of funds;

(iii) receipts or debts have not been used to finance expenditure or investment outside the UK;

(iv) (in the case of debts) the debt cannot be discharged in the UK; and

(v) the taxpayer agrees to the withdrawal of relief by an addition to profits for the period in which the concessional relief ceases to be available (see below).

As regards (iii) above, debts are regarded as having been used to finance expenditure outside the UK where they are used, or might have been used, to meet expenditure or guarantee a liability incurred in the same territory by the trader or by a person with whom the trader has a special relationship, or where they remain unpaid by reason of such a relationship.

Relief for debts is available only to the extent that they are not insured. Relief is given by a deduction from trading profits for the accounting period in which the receipt or debt is recognised as unremittable. Any excess may be carried forward against trading profits of subsequent periods.

Relief is withdrawn where (*a*)–(*c*) or (iii) above cease to apply, or the receipt or debt is otherwise applied outside the UK or exchanged for or discharged in a remittable currency.

This concession also applies to unremittable bank interest in appropriate circumstances.

(Revenue Pamphlet IR 1, B38).

71.93 **VALUE ADDED TAX**

For treatment in computing business profits see Revenue Pamphlet IR 131, B1.

In general, if the trader is not a 'taxable person' for VAT his expenditure *inclusive* of any VAT on it, is treated in the ordinary way.

If he is a taxable person, the receipts and expenses (including capital items) to be taken into account will generally be exclusive of VAT but if he suffers VAT on any expenditure which does not rank as 'input tax' (e.g. entertaining expenses and certain expenditure relating to motor cars) that expenditure inclusive of VAT will be taken into account for income tax, etc. purposes (although any such inclusive sum in respect of entertaining expenses may also be disallowed for income tax purposes). Any allowance for bad debts (see 71.44 above) is inclusive of any VAT not recovered but accounted for to HM Customs and Excise. (*VATA 1994, s 36* and regulations made thereunder now provide for VAT on bad debts to be refunded in certain cases.)

VAT interest, penalties and surcharge are not allowed as a deduction for income tax purposes, and repayment supplement is disregarded for income tax purposes. [*ICTA 1988, s 827*].

VAT refunds. See Revenue Tax Bulletin October 1995 pp 255, 256 for the timing of the recognition, for the purposes of computing trading profits, of certain VAT refunds (specifically, of refunds to opticians following acceptance by Customs and Excise that they had incorrectly required VAT to be charged on certain outputs).

See Revenue Inspector's Manual, IM 1172–1196i and, generally, Tolley's Value Added Tax.

71.94 **WASTE DISPOSAL**

Expenditure on purchase and reclamation of tipping sites by a company carrying on a waste disposal business was held to be capital in *Rolfe v Wimpey Waste Management Ltd CA 1989, 62 TC 399*, as were instalment payments for the right to deposit waste material in *CIR v Adam CS 1928, 14 TC 34*. See also *McClure v Petre Ch D 1988, 61 TC 226*, where the receipt of sum for licence to tip soil was also held to be capital.

Site preparation and restoration expenditure. A person making a 'site restoration payment', in the course of carrying on a trade, may deduct the payment in computing profits for the period of account (i.e. a period for which an account is made up) in which the payment is made. A payment will not qualify for relief to the extent that it represents either expenditure allowed as a trading deduction for prior periods or capital expenditure qualifying for capital allowances.

A '*site restoration payment*' is a payment made

(*a*) in connection with the restoration of a site (or part thereof), and

(*b*) in order to comply with any condition of a 'relevant licence', or any condition imposed on the grant of planning permission to use the site for the carrying out of 'waste disposal activities', or any term of a 'relevant agreement'.

For restoration expenditure generally (including provisions for such expenditure), see Revenue Tax Bulletin April 1998 p 534.

'*Waste disposal activities*' are the collection, treatment, conversion and final depositing of waste materials, or any of those activities.

A '*relevant licence*' is a disposal licence under the *Control of Pollution Act 1974, Pt I* (or NI equivalent), a waste management licence under the *Environmental Protection Act 1990, Pt II* (or NI equivalent) or (for trades commenced after 31 March 1993) an authorisation for the disposal of radioactive waste or a nuclear site licence.

A '*relevant agreement*' is an agreement under *Town and Country Planning Act 1971, s 52, Town and Country Planning (Scotland) Act 1972, s 50* or *Town and Country Planning Act 1990, s 106* (or NI equivalent) regulating the development or use of land.

[*ICTA 1988, s 91A; FA 1990, s 78; FA 1993, s 110(1)(3)*].

A deduction is available of the 'allowable amount' where a person incurs, in the course of a trade, 'site preparation expenditure' in relation to a 'waste disposal site', and, at the time when he first deposits waste materials on the site in question, he holds a relevant licence (as above) which is in force. It is not available where the person incurring the expenditure recharges it to another person who holds the licence when first depositing waste (see Revenue Tax Bulletin April 1998 p 533). A claim for the relief to apply will have to be made in the prescribed manner and the Board may also require plans and other documents to verify it. Expenditure incurred for trade purposes by a person about to carry on the trade is for this purpose treated as incurred on the first day of trading.

A '*waste disposal site*' is a site used (or to be used) for the disposal of waste materials by their deposit on the site, and in relation to such a site, '*site preparation expenditure*' is expenditure on preparing the site for the deposit of waste materials (and may include expenditure on earthworks). This includes expenditure incurred before the relevant licence is granted, and in particular expenses associated with obtaining the licence itself. (Revenue Tax Bulletin November 1992 p 45). For preparation expenditure generally, see Revenue Tax Bulletin April 1998 p 533.

In relation to the period of account in question, the '*allowable amount*' of the expenditure is

$$(A - B) \times \frac{C}{C + D}$$

where

> 'A' is the site preparation expenditure incurred by the person at any time before the beginning of, or during, the period in question in relation to the site in question and in the course of carrying on the trade. It does not include any expenditure which either has been allowed as a trading deduction for a prior period or is capital expenditure qualifying for capital allowances. In addition, where any expenditure which would otherwise be included in 'A' was incurred before 6 April 1989, 'A' is reduced by an amount determined by
>
> $$E \times \frac{F}{F + G}$$
>
> where
>
> > 'E' is so much of the initial expenditure (that is, the expenditure which would otherwise be included in 'A') as was incurred before 6 April 1989,

'F' is the volume of waste materials deposited on the site in question before 6 April 1989,

'G' is the capacity (expressed in volume) of the site in question not used up for the deposit of waste materials immediately before 6 April 1989;

'B' is the amount (or aggregate of amounts) allowed as a trading deduction under this provision in prior periods and as regards expenditure incurred in relation to the site in question;

'C' is the volume of waste materials deposited on the site in question during the period in question, excluding any deposited before 6 April 1989;

'D' is the capacity of the site in question not used up for the deposit of waste materials as at the end of the period in question.

Where, after 20 March 2000, a person (the 'predecessor') who has incurred site preparation expenditure as above in the course of a trade ceases to carry on the trade, or to carry it on so far as it relates to that site, and another person (the 'successor') begins to carry it on, or to carry on in the course of a trade the activities formerly carried on by the predecessor in relation to that site, then provided that

(i) the whole of the site is transferred to the successor (although not necessarily the same estate or interest in the site), and

(ii) the successor holds a relevant licence in relation to the site which is in force when he first deposits waste material on the site,

the successor's trade is treated for these purposes as the same as that carried on by the predecessor, and the successor stands in the predecessor's shoes as regards allowances in relation to the site.

[*ICTA 1988, ss 91B, 91BA; FA 1990, s 78; FA 1993, s 110(2)(3); FA 2000, s 89*].

See generally Revenue Inspector's Manual, IM 3245–3259.

Leasing. See 71.68 above as regards restrictions on relief under the above provisions where finance leasing arrangements are involved.

See Simon's Direct Tax Service B3.1345.

Landfill tax. Landfill tax comes into effect on 1 October 1996. The Revenue's views on the deductibility of the tax under Schedule D, Case I or II are as follows.

Site operators. Treatment of landfill tax charged on to customers will follow the generally accepted accounting practice. As regards self-generated waste, landfill tax (net of any credit following a contribution to an environmental trust) will be allowed as a deduction so long as the other costs incurred in disposing of the waste are deductible.

Customers of site operators. The landfill tax element of the global charge does not need to be separately invoiced, and deductibility of the landfill tax element will follow that of the non-landfill tax element of the charge.

Environmental trust contributions. Site operators may obtain relief from landfill tax by making such contributions, the deductibility of which is to be determined in the circumstances of each particular case under the normal test of whether the expenditure is incurred wholly and exclusively for trade purposes. In the case of an unconnected trust engaged in projects of possible use to the operator, the payment would *prima facie* be deductible. If the operator has some degree of control over the trust, or the income of the trust is ultimately received by a person connected with the operator, it might be less clear that the payment was for the purposes of the operator's own trade. Similarly if the trust's objects were insufficiently related to the operator's trade, it might be considered that contributions were for a general philanthropic, and hence non-trade, purpose.

(Revenue Tax Bulletin June 1996 pp 317, 318).

71.95 WOODLANDS

See 93.2, 93.3 WOODLANDS as regards the election for Schedule D treatment of profits arising from the commercial occupation of woodlands, and for the transitional provisions following its abolition after 14 March 1988.

With effect from 29 November 1994, short rotation coppice cultivation is treated for tax purposes as farming and not as forestry, so that UK land under such cultivation is not woodlands. [*FA 1995, s 154*]. See 71.57 above.

See generally Revenue Inspector's Manual, IM 3260–3299.

71.96 GENERAL EXAMPLE

A UK trader commences trading on 1 October 1999. His profit and loss account for the year to 30 September 2000 is

	£	£
Sales		110,000
Deduct Purchases	75,000	
Less Stock and work in progress at 30.9.00	15,000	
		60,000
Gross profit		50,000
Deduct		
Salaries (all paid by 30.6.01)	15,600	
Rent and rates	2,400	
Telephone	500	
Heat and light	650	
Depreciation	1,000	
Motor expenses	2,700	
Entertainment	600	
Bank interest	900	
Hire-purchase interest	250	
Repairs and renewals	1,000	
Accountant's fee	500	
Bad debts	200	
Sundries	700	
		27,000
Net profit		23,000
Gain on sale of fixed asset		300
Rent received		500
Bank interest received (net)		150
Profit		£23,950

Further Information

(i) Rent and rates. £200 of the rates bill relates to the period from 1.6.99 to 30.9.99.

(ii) Telephone. Telephone bills for the trader's private telephone amount to £150. It is estimated that 40% of these calls are for business purposes.

(iii) Motor expenses. All the motor expenses are in respect of the proprietor's car. 40% of the annual mileage relates to private use and home to business use.

		£
(iv) Entertainment	Staff	100
	UK customers	450
	Overseas customers	50
		£600

(v) Hire-purchase interest. This is in respect of the owner's car.

(vi) Repairs and renewals. There is an improvement element of 20% included.

(vii) Bad debts. This is a specific write-off.

(viii) Sundries. Included is £250 being the cost of obtaining a bank loan to finance business expenditure, £200 for agent's fees in obtaining a patent for trading purposes and a £50 inducement to a local official.

(ix) Other. The proprietor obtained goods for his own use from the business costing £400 (retail value £500) without payment.

(x) Capital allowances for the year to 30 September 1999 amount to £1,520.

Schedule D, Case I Computation — Year to 30.9.00

		£	£
Profit per the accounts			23,950
Add			
Repairs — improvement element			200
Hire-purchase interest (40% private)			100
Entertainment	note (*e*)		500
Motor expenses (40% private)			1,080
Depreciation			1,000
Telephone (60% × £150)			90
Goods for own use			500
Illegal payment	note (*f*)		50
			27,470
Deduct			
Bank interest received — Taxed income		150	
Rent received — Schedule A		500	
Gain on sale of fixed asset		300	
			950
			26,520
Less Capital allowances			1,520
Schedule D, Case I profit			£25,000

Notes

(*a*) Costs of obtaining loan finance are specifically allowable (see 71.70 above).

(*b*) From 1997/98, capital allowances are in all cases deductible as a trading expense (see 10.1 CAPITAL ALLOWANCES).

(*c*) The adjusted profit of £25,000 would be subject to the commencement provisions for assessment purposes (see 71.12 above).

(*d*) Pre-trading expenses are treated as incurred on the day on which trade is commenced if they are incurred within seven years of the commencement and would have been allowable if incurred after commencement. Different rules applied for trades commenced before 6 April 1995. See 71.76 above.

(*e*) All entertainment expenses, other than staff entertaining, are non-deductible (see 71.55 above).

(*f*) Expenditure incurred in making a payment which itself constitutes the commission of a criminal offence is specifically disallowed. This includes payments which are contrary to the Prevention of Corruption Acts. See 71.63 above.

72 Schedule D, Case III—Interest Receivable etc.

[*ICTA 1988, ss 18, 64, 66, 67*]

Cross-references. See generally under 23 DEDUCTION OF TAX AT SOURCE; 33 GOVERNMENT STOCKS; 44 INTEREST RECEIVABLE; 71.51 SCHEDULE D, CASES I AND II re copyrights and royalties.

Simon's Direct Tax Service B5.

72.1 Case III of Schedule D is principally concerned with the taxation of interest and annual payments. There are, however, significant changes following the abolition of SCHEDULE C (70), and the introduction of a new corporation tax regime for the taxation of most profits and gains from securities (by reference to 'loan relationships', for which see Tolley's Corporation Tax under Loan Relationships). Both of these changes take effect for 1996/97 and subsequent years and for accounting periods ending after 31 March 1996, and the charges under Cases III to V of Schedule D are accordingly now defined separately for income tax and for corporation tax purposes.

For corporation tax, Case III now includes all profits and gains from loan relationships, any annuity or other annual payment (not chargeable under Schedule A) payable in or out of the UK, and at whatever intervals, in respect of anything other than a loan relationship and any discount arising other than in respect of a loan relationship. Thus, for corporation tax purposes, Case IV is subsumed into Case III, and Case V is redefined to exclude profits or gains from loan relationships.

For income tax purposes, the abolition of Schedule C has led to the inclusion under Case III of income from the UK (and NI) public revenue previously dealt with under that Schedule. Case IV is similarly extended to include all income from securities out of the UK (including foreign public revenue income previously within Schedule C), and Cases IV and V now include income realised by disposal of coupons on overseas holdings (again previously within Schedule C). Thus, for **1996/97 and subsequent years**, income tax is charged under Schedule D, Case III in respect of:

(i) any interest of money, and any annuity or other annual payment (not chargeable under SCHEDULE A (68)) either as a charge on or reservation out of property of the payer or as a personal contractual debt or obligation, whether payable in or out of the UK and at whatever intervals received and payable;

(ii) all discounts; and

(iii) income from securities payable out of UK (or NI) public revenue.

Previously, (iii) comprised all income from securities bearing interest payable out of the public revenue unless within Schedule C.

[*ICTA 1988, s 18(3)–(3E); FA 1996, Sch 7 para 4(2)(3), Sch 14 para 5*].

The following items are additionally brought within the charge under Case III.

(*a*) Profits and losses from discounts on securities. [*FA 1996, Sch 13*]. See 72.2 below. (These provisions apply for 1996/97 and subsequent years. Previously, there was a Case III (or Case IV) charge on disposal of 'deep discount', 'deep gain' or 'qualifying convertible' securities (see 44.5–44.8 INTEREST RECEIVABLE).)

(*b*) Share or loan interest paid by a registered industrial and provident society. [*ICTA 1988, s 486(4)*].

(*c*) Borrowings against life policies in certain circumstances. [*ICTA 1988, s 554*]. See 45.4(*h*) LIFE ASSURANCE POLICIES.

(*d*) Mining rents and royalties payable in produce and, before 6 April 1997, electric line wayleave payments made without deduction of tax. [*ICTA 1988, ss 119(2), 120(3); FA 1997, s 60*]. See 23.14 DEDUCTION OF TAX AT SOURCE.

For general exemptions from charge to tax, see EXEMPT INCOME (29). The following items are additionally excluded from Case III.

(1) Distributions within SCHEDULE F (76). [*ICTA 1988, s 20(2)*].

(2) Certain annual payments by individuals. [*ICTA 1988, s 347A*]. See 1.8(i) ALLOWANCES AND TAX RATES.

(3) The capital portion of purchased life annuity payments. [*ICTA 1988, s 656*]. See 23.11(*c*) DEDUCTION OF TAX AT SOURCE.

(4) Certain payments to redundant steel workers, see 75.32 SCHEDULE E.

(5) Certain payments to theatrical angels, see 74.2 SCHEDULE D, CASE VI.

Various of the above items are payable after deduction of tax by the payer under *ICTA 1988, ss 348, 349*. See under 23 DEDUCTION OF TAX AT SOURCE for the provisions relating to such deductions and for annuities and annual payments etc. See also under 43 INTEREST PAYABLE.

For 1996/97 and subsequent years, most types of Case III income, including interest and discounts, are chargeable to income tax at the lower rate (to the extent that they do not fall within an individual's higher rate band). See 1.9 ALLOWANCES AND TAX RATES for the full provisions.

Chargeability under Case III depends upon there being a UK source. The Revenue regard the most important factors supporting the existence of a UK source of interest to be (i) the debtor's residence (i.e. the place in which the debt will be enforced), (ii) the source from which interest is paid, (iii) where the interest is paid, and (iv) the nature and location of the security for the debt. If all of these are located in the UK, it is likely that the interest will have a UK source. (Revenue Tax Bulletin November 1993 p 100).

Income from overseas securities and possessions is assessable under SCHEDULE D, CASES IV AND V (73).

For whether solicitors' client account interest is within Case III, see 44.2 INTEREST RECEIVABLE.

72.2 DISCOUNTS ON SECURITIES

Charge to and relief from tax for profits and losses realised on discounts on securities. For any year of assessment **1996/97 onwards** in which a person transfers a 'relevant discounted security', or becomes entitled, as holder, to any payment on its redemption, and where the amount payable on the transfer or redemption exceeds the amount he paid for its acquisition, he is chargeable under Schedule D, Case III (or Case IV as appropriate) on the amount of the excess net of any 'relevant costs'. A loss arising disregarding relevant costs (together with any such costs) may be relieved against income of the year of assessment of the transfer or redemption. Relief must be claimed by 31 January next but one following the end of that year. '*Relevant costs*' are those incurred by that person in connection with the acquisition and the transfer or redemption of the security.

'Transfer' for these purposes means transfer by way of sale, exchange, gift or otherwise. A transfer or acquisition under an agreement is treated as taking place when the agreement is made if entitlement to the security passes at that time. A conditional agreement is treated as made when the condition is satisfied. Where the holder dies, he is treated as having transferred the security at market value immediately before his death, and his personal representative as acquiring it at that value on his death. Except in relation to certain gilt strips (see below), 'redemption' includes the extinguishment of a security (under rights conferred by the security) by conversion into shares in a company or into any other securities, the amount payable on that deemed redemption being the market value of the replacement shares or securities.

Where a conversion of relevant discounted securities from the currency of a State which has adopted the euro into euros (a '*euroconversion*', see *SI 1998 No 3177, reg 3*) is effected solely by means of an exchange or conversion of those securities, the conversion is not treated as constituting either a transfer within *FA 1996, Sch 13 para 4* or a conversion within *FA 1996, Sch 13 para 5*. Provision is made for an adjustment to the acquisition cost in respect of any cash payment received as a result of the conversion.

A '*relevant discounted security*' is, except as below, any security such that the amount payable on redemption (excluding interest) is or might be an amount involving a '*deep gain*', i.e. the issue price is less than the amount payable on redemption by 15% of that amount or, if less, by $\frac{1}{2}$% per annum of that amount (counting months and part months as $\frac{1}{12}$th of a year) to the earliest possible redemption date. This comparison is made as at the time of issue of the security and assuming redemption in accordance with the terms of issue. 'Redemption' for these purposes referred originally to redemption on maturity or, if the holder of the security could opt for earlier redemption, the earliest occasion on which the holder might require redemption. In relation to any transfer of a security after 14 February 1999 or any occasion after that date on which a holder of a security becomes entitled to payment on redemption, the definition is widened so that one must consider, in addition to redemption on maturity, possible earlier occasions on which a security might be redeemed. The security will be a relevant discounted security if it would be such by reference to at least one such occasion. One need not take into account any occasion on which there may be a redemption other than at the option of the holder *unless* issuer and holder are connected or the obtaining of a tax advantage (as defined) is a main benefit that might be expected to accrue from the redemption provision. Additionally, where the holder has an option entitling him to redeem only on the occurrence of an 'event adversely affecting the holder' (as defined) or of a person's default *and* such entitlement is unlikely, judged at time of issue, to arise, the potential redemption is disregarded.

The following are not relevant discounted securities:

(*a*) shares in a company;

(*b*) gilt-edged securities (other than strips, see below);

(*c*) 'excluded indexed securities';

(*d*) LIFE ASSURANCE POLICIES (45);

(*e*) capital redemption policies (see 45.13(C) LIFE ASSURANCE POLICIES); and

(*f*) securities issued under the same prospectus as other securities issued previously but not themselves relevant discounted securities.

Also after 14 February 1999, however, securities within (*c*) and (*f*) above may be treated as relevant discounted securities in certain circumstances involving their being held by a person connected with the issuer. *ICTA 1988, s 839* (see 20 CONNECTED PERSONS) applies to determine whether persons are connected for these purposes, but without taking any account of the security under review or any security issued under the same prospectus.

Gilt strips (see 33.3 GOVERNMENT STOCKS) are always relevant discounted securities, without regard to their issue terms. As regards (*f*) above, if none of the securities originally issued under a prospectus would otherwise be a relevant discounted security, and some of those subsequently issued under the prospectus would be but for (*f*) above, and the aggregate nominal value of the latter at any time exceeds that of all other securities issued under the prospectus, then all securities issued under that prospectus are, from that time, treated as relevant discounted securities acquired as such.

A security is an '*excluded indexed security*' within (*c*) above if, in pursuance of any provision having effect for the purposes of the security, the amount payable on redemption (as above) is determined by applying to the amount for which the security was issued a percentage change, over the 'relevant period', in the value of chargeable assets of any particular description (or in an index of the value of such assets — the retail prices index or similar foreign general prices index is not such an index). If, however, there is such a provision which is made subject to any other provision applying to the determination of the amount payable on redemption, whose only effect is to place a lower limit on the discharge payment of a specified percentage (which must not be more than 10%) of the amount for which the security is issued, then that other provision is disregarded for this purpose. An asset is for these purposes a chargeable asset if any disposal gain would be a chargeable gain (assuming the asset (not being trading stock, etc.) to belong to the person in question (and that that person does not have the benefit of exemption under *TCGA 1992, s 100* (authorised unit trusts, etc.)), and disregarding gains previously deferred under *TCGA 1992, s 116* on a capital reorganisation, etc. involving a qualifying corporate bond, see Tolley's Capital Gains Tax under Qualifying Corporate Bonds). The '*relevant period*' is the period between the time of issue and redemption, or any other period in which almost all of that period is comprised and which differs from it exclusively for valuation purposes.

These provisions do not apply for corporation tax purposes. For accounting periods ending after 31 March 1996, a separate regime is enacted for corporation tax, broadly dealing with all interest and profits or losses on securities on revenue account, either on an accruals basis or on a mark-to-market basis. See Tolley's Corporation Tax under Loan Relationships.

Treatment of losses where income exempt. A loss under the current provisions may only be relieved against income chargeable for the same year under the current provisions where a profit under these provisions on that transfer or redemption would have been an exempt profit for the year of assessment in which the loss is sustained. An 'exempt profit' for this purpose is income:

(1) which is eligible for relief under *ICTA 1988, s 505(1)* (or which would be so eligible but for *ICTA 1988, s 505(3)*) (charitable exemptions and restrictions, see 15.4–15.7, 15.10 CHARITIES); or

(2) which is eligible for relief under *ICTA 1988, s 592(2), s 608(2)(a), s 613(4), s 614(2)–(5), s 620(6)* or *s 643(2)* (pension scheme funds, etc., see 66.5, 66.13, 66.11 RETIREMENT SCHEMES, 59.6 PENSIONS, 60.1 PERSONAL PENSION SCHEMES, 65.8 RETIREMENT ANNUITIES).

As regards (2) above, where the exemption under *ICTA 1988, s 592(2)* applies, there is special provision for the interaction with the pension fund surplus provisions of *ICTA 1988, Sch 22* (see 66.8 RETIREMENT SCHEMES).

[*FA 1996, ss 102, 105(1)(b), Sch 13 paras 1–5, 7, 10, 13, 14(1), 16; FA 1999, s 65(1)–(8); SI 1998 No 3177, reg 12*].

Trustees. Amounts chargeable under these provisions on the transfer or redemption of a security by trustees are treated for the purposes of *ICTA 1988, ss 660A–682A* (see 81.13–81.19 SETTLEMENTS) as income arising under the settlement from the security, and for the purposes of *ICTA 1988, ss 686 et seq.* (see 81.5 SETTLEMENTS) as income arising to the trustees. To the extent that tax on such an amount is chargeable on the trustees, it is chargeable at the rate applicable to trusts (see 81.5 SETTLEMENTS). This does not apply to trustees of unauthorised unit trusts (see 90.2 UNIT TRUSTS) to the extent that the amount is treated as income in the scheme accounts.

Relief for losses under these provisions may, in the case of trustees, be given only against income chargeable under these provisions. Where, in any year of assessment, losses exceed amounts chargeable, the excess is carried forward and treated as a loss sustained under these provisions in the next year of assessment (although this does not apply to the extent that the loss arises in circumstances such that a profit would have been exempt, see above).

Non-resident trustees. Charges and reliefs under these provisions do not apply to securities held under a settlement the trustees of which are non-UK resident.

[*FA 1996, Sch 13 para 6(1)–(6), para 7(2)*].

Personal representatives. On the transfer of a relevant discounted security to a legatee, personal representatives are deemed to obtain market value consideration. A 'legatee' is any person taking under a testamentary disposition or on an intestacy or partial intestacy (including an appropriation in or towards satisfaction of a legacy or other interest or share in the deceased's property). [*FA 1996, Sch 13 para 6(7)(8)*].

Gilt strips. (See 33.3 GOVERNMENT STOCKS and Tolley's Corporation Tax under Income Tax in Relation to a Company as regards gilt strips generally.) Every gilt strip is a relevant discounted security within these provisions. For these purposes:

(A) on the exchange of a gilt-edged security for strips of that security, the acquisition cost of each strip is determined by apportioning the market value of the security *pro rata* to the market value of each strip;

(B) when a person consolidates strips into a gilt-edged security by exchanging them for that security, each strip is treated as being redeemed at market value;

(C) any person holding a strip on 5 April in any year of assessment, and not transferring or redeeming it on that day, is deemed to have transferred it at market value on that day and to have re-acquired it at the deemed disposal value on the following day (without incurring any relevant costs); and

(D) the Treasury has wide powers by regulation to modify these provisions in their application to gilt strips.

[*FA 1996, Sch 13 para 14*].

Market value transfers. In addition to the deemed transfer on death and in relation to personal representatives and gilt strips (see above), the following transfers of relevant discounted securities are deemed to take place at market value.

(i) Transfers between CONNECTED PERSONS (20) (within *ICTA 1988, s 839*).

(ii) Where the consideration for the transfer is not all money or money's worth.

(iii) Where the transfer is not by way of a bargain made at arm's length.

[*FA 1996, Sch 13 paras 8, 9*].

Accrued income scheme. Where the current provisions apply on the transfer of a security, *ICTA 1988, ss 710–728* (accrued income scheme, see 74.6 *et seq.* SCHEDULE D, CASE VI) do not apply. [*FA 1996, Sch 13 para 11*].

Transfer of assets abroad. For the purposes of *ICTA 1988, ss 739, 740* (transfer of assets abroad, see 3.8 ANTI-AVOIDANCE), a profit chargeable under these provisions realised by a person resident or domiciled outside the UK is taken to be income of that person.

Simon's Direct Tax Service. See A7.6.

For 1995/96 and earlier years, a number of separate provisions dealt with discounts on securities, in addition to the accrued income scheme referred to above. See in particular 44.5, 44.7, 44.8 INTEREST RECEIVABLE and 33.4 GOVERNMENT STOCKS. These applied equally for corporation tax purposes, but see above as regards the separate regime for corporation tax introduced by *FA 1996*.

72.3 SCOPE AND ASSESSMENT

(*a*) **Assessment.** Certain interest and certain annuities and annual payments are payable under deduction of tax at source. If so paid, the deduction is treated as tax paid by the recipient who is then liable, if his total income is high enough, at the excess of the higher rate(s) of tax over the basic or lower rate (whichever is applicable) on the gross amount.

If the payer omits to deduct tax an assessment may be made on either the payer or payee. See 23.8 DEDUCTION OF TAX AT SOURCE for omission to deduct tax.

All other income not taxed at source is charged by direct assessment on the recipient. Loss relief and capital allowances are not applicable.

For years before 1996/97, for purposes of assessment, income under Case III may be assessed and charged in one sum [*ICTA 1988, s 73; FA 1995, s 115(9)*] but where there are changes in particular items they will be treated separately under the rules of new source and disposals (where applicable) in 72.4 below. [*ICTA 1988, ss 66(3), 67(1)(a); FA 1994, ss 207(4), 218*]. The person receiving or entitled to the income is assessable. [*ICTA 1988, s 59(1)*]. See also *Aplin v White Ch D 1973, 49 TC 93*. A non-resident may be assessed under Case III through an agent under *TMA 1970, s 82* (*Scales v Atalanta SS Co KB 1925, 9 TC 586*) (and see also 51.5 to 51.7 NON-RESIDENTS AND OTHER OVERSEAS MATTERS).

Bank interest is generally received when credited to the account (*Dunmore v McGowan Ch D 1978, 52 TC 307; Peracha v Miley CA 1990, 63 TC 444*), but there may be no receipt or entitlement if the bank has the right to refuse payment out of the account and the interest is not in fact paid out (*Macpherson v Bond Ch D 1985, 58 TC 579*). Interest paid by cheque is received when the sum is credited to the recipient's account, not when the cheque is received. (*Parkside Leasing Ltd v Smith Ch D 1984, 58 TC 282*). Interest credited by the deposit-taker to a suspense account in advance of the payment date was held to arise only when paid (*Girvan v Orange Personal Communications Services Ltd Ch D 1998, 70 TC 602*).

See Simon's Direct Tax Service B5.102.

(*b*) **Interest and discount.** Whether an amount described as interest in a Court or arbitration award is true interest or an element entering into the calculation of the award and capital depends on the facts. See *Schulze v Bensted (No 1) CS 1915, 7 TC 30; Westminster Bank Ltd v Riches HL 1947, 28 TC 159* and *Barnato CA 1936, 20 TC 455* and contrast *Ballantine CS 1924, 8 TC 595*. A premium on the repayment of a loan was held to be interest in *Davies v Premier Investment Co Ltd KB 1945, 27 TC 27*, but a premium on the repayment of securities quoted on the Stock Exchange or issued on terms similar to those of quoted securities is normally regarded as capital and similarly as regards the discount on securities issued at a discount. A discount within Case III is a profit of an income nature received on a discounting transaction. See *National Provident Institution v Brown HL 1921, 8 TC 57* and *Ditchfield v Sharp CA 1983, 57 TC 555* and contrast *Lomax v Peter Dixon & Son Ltd CA 1943, 25 TC 453*. Where credit balances on accounts held by members of a group of companies were set against the overdrawn balance on a current account held at the same bank by another member (C) of the group, it was held that the arrangements did not provide for C to receive interest on the credit balance, but for its obligation to pay interest to be reduced (*Cooker v Foss (Sp C 165), [1998] SSCD 189*).

Payments in pursuance of a guarantee of the capital of a company were held to be interest in *Blake v Imperial Brazilian Rly Co CA 1884, 2 TC 58*. See also *Wilson v Mannooch KB 1937, 21 TC 178* and *Ruskin Investments Ltd v Copeman CA 1943, 25 TC 187*. The interest element in loan repayments after the death of a money-lender was held to be assessable on his administrator under Case III (*Bennett v Ogston KB 1930, 15 TC 374*). Accrued interest on securities sold (if not sold 'ex-dividend') is income of the purchaser (*Wigmore v Thomas Summerson & Sons Ltd KB 1925, 9 TC 577* and *Schaffer v Cattermole CA 1980, 53 TC 499*) but see 3.3 ANTI-AVOIDANCE if arrangement to repurchase. Arrears of interest are not assessable until received — see *St Lucia Usines v Colonial Treasurer PC 1924, 4 ATC 112* and the cases noted in 28.2(*d*) EXCESS LIABILITY.

See Simon's Direct Tax Service B5.201 *et seq.*.

See now the special provisions for 1996/97 and subsequent years at 72.2 above.

(*c*) **Annual payments and annuities.** For cases where deduction of tax is involved, see 23.9 and 23.10 DEDUCTION OF TAX AT SOURCE.

Case III assessments were upheld in respect of periodical payments to a newspaper company after a merger (*Morning Post Ltd v George KB 1940, 23 TC 514*), payments to an actress from the exploitation of a film (*Mitchell v Rosay CA 1954, 35 TC 496*) and annual payments to the executors of a deceased director pursuant to an agreement entered into by him relating to special services he had rendered (*Westminster Bank Ltd v Barford Ch D 1958, 38 TC 68*). Compensation payments by the USA Government to a wounded American soldier were held not to be assessable in *Laird v CIR CS 1929, 14 TC 395* but in *Forsyth v Thompson KB 1940, 23 TC 374* periodical disability payments from a mutual insurance society were held to be assessable. But see now 75.37 SCHEDULE E.

(*d*) **Deductions.** The full amount of the income is assessable without any deduction. Cf. *Lord Inverclyde's Trustees v Millar CS 1924, 9 TC 14* and *A B (Committee of) v Simpson KB 1928, 14 TC 29*.

72.4 BASIS OF ASSESSMENT

The rules at (a)–(d) below apply for 1995/96 and earlier years as regards income from a source first arising before 6 April 1994 — see (e) and (f) below for the position for later years. They have no application to income from a source first arising after 5 April 1994, for which see (e) below.

(*a*) **Preceding year basis.** Assessment is normally on actual income of preceding year without any deduction [*ICTA 1988, s 64*] but subject to changes in items as below.

If the source is still retained, assessment to income tax continues on preceding year's income even if no profits from that source in the year of assessment. [*ICTA 1988, s 71*]. This held to apply even when interest waived for year of assessment, if money still kept on deposit and not transferred to current account (*Cull v Cowcher KB 1934, 18 TC 449*). Conversely, no liability arises unless the source is held in the year of assessment. But see (*c*)(i) and (ii) below and *National Provident Instn v Brown HL 1921, 8 TC 57; Grainger v Maxwell's Exors CA 1925, 10 TC 139.*

Income received under deduction of tax is, however, income of the year of assessment by reference to the basic or lower rate of tax for which tax is deducted from the income, without regard to the period of accrual. [*ICTA 1988, s 835(6); FA 1996, Sch 6 paras 24, 28*]. See 23.1 DEDUCTION OF TAX AT SOURCE.

For corporation tax purposes, assessment is on the actual income of the accounting period.

The preceding year basis and the rules in (*b*) and (*c*) below do not apply to maintenance payments under 'existing obligations' (taxable for years before 2000/01 — see 47.10 MARRIED PERSONS). The charge under Case III is computed on the payments falling due in the year of assessment, providing they are actually made but regardless of whether or not they are made in the year for which they are due. [*FA 1988, s 38(8); FA 1999, Sch 20 Pt III(6)*].

See 72.3(*a*) above as regards when interest is received for the purposes of Case III.

(*b*) **New Source**

If any new source or an addition to any source is acquired or if loan interest previously taxable by deduction becomes receivable gross the following rules apply.

If income first arose **on** 6 April in the first year of assessment

First tax year assessed on first year's income.

Second tax year assessed on first year's income, with option to taxpayer to substitute second year's income if claimed within six years from end of year of assessment.

Third tax year assessed on second year's income.

If income first arose **after** 6 April in the first year of assessment

First tax year assessed on first year's income.

Second tax year assessed on second year's income.

Third tax year assessed on second year's income with option to taxpayer to substitute third year's income if claimed within six years from end of year of assessment.

Each item newly acquired is to be treated separately. [*ICTA 1988, s 66*].

Large addition to bank account held to be acquisition of new source (*Hart v Sangster CA 1957, 37 TC 231*) but in practice small changes are ignored and all bank accounts owned by a taxpayer may generally be treated as one source unless the taxpayer requires that they be treated as separate sources. See also *Beese v MacKinlay Ch D, [1980] STC 228.*

(*c*) **Disposals etc..** If any particular source of income or any part thereof ceases to be possessed by the taxpayer or if loan interest previously receivable gross becomes taxable by deduction the following rules apply.

Last year	— Assessment to be adjusted to actual income from 6 April to date of disposal.
Year before the last	— If the income arising within the twelve months to 5 April of that year is greater than the assessment for that year, the excess is chargeable by assessment. [*ICTA 1988, s 67(1)(b)*].

See (*b*) above as regards all bank accounts being treated as a single source.

(i) *If no income arose during the last two years of ownership,* taxpayer may claim to be treated as if he had ceased to possess the source in the year in which income last arose provided this was not more than eight years before the claim. [*ICTA 1988, s 67(1)(c)(4)*].

(ii) *If a source, having produced income, does not do so for six consecutive years of assessment thereafter*, taxpayer may claim to be treated as above as if he had ceased to possess it at the end of the those six years and immediately thereafter acquired it as a new source. [*ICTA 1988, s 67(5)*].

Time limits for claims under (i) and (ii) are two years after end of year of actual cessation, or assumed cessation under (ii). The claims are also available to personal representatives. [*ICTA 1988, s 67(1)(c)(5)(8)*].

(*d*) **Death of spouse.** Where on the death of a spouse a source of income passes in its entirety from the deceased to the surviving spouse, cessation and commencement adjustments (see (*b*) and (*c*) above) will not be made unless requested by the personal representative or by the survivor. (Revenue Pamphlet IR 1, A7). See 71.9 SCHEDULE D, CASES I AND II as regards the application of this concession to trading profits. The concession is withdrawn following the introduction of the current year basis of assessment (see (*e*) below), from 6 April 1995 in respect of sources commencing after 5 April 1994, and from a date to be announced (not earlier than 6 April 1997) for sources already in existence on that date. (Revenue Press Release 4 April 1995).

(*e*) **Current year basis.** For 1994/95 and subsequent years as regards income from a source first arising after 5 April 1994, and for 1996/97 and subsequent years as regards income from a source first arising on or before that date (see (*f*) below for transitional rules), the assessment is on actual income of the current year without any deduction. [*ICTA 1988, s 64; FA 1994, s 206*]. There are no special rules for opening and closing years as in (*b*) and (*c*) above.

(*f*) **Transitional rules on changeover to current year basis.** The following rules apply to income from a source first arising before 6 April 1994 and continuing (without interruption) beyond 5 April 1996. If the source ceases in 1996/97 or 1997/98, the rules in (*a*)–(*d*) above apply throughout. If the source continues beyond 5 April 1998, the assessment for 1996/97 is on 50% of the income arising in 1995/96 and 1996/97, the other 50% escaping tax. This does not apply if income first arose in 1993/94 and taxpayer opts for the actual basis for 1995/96 (see (*b*) above); in this case, the 1996/97 assessment is on a current year basis with no reduction. [*FA 1994, s 218, Sch 20 paras 4, 5, 14(1)*].

Anti-avoidance measures have been introduced to deter and penalise attempts to exploit the transitional rules by moving income into the transitional period, i.e. 1995/96 and 1996/97, so that it would not otherwise be fully charged to tax. Where any amount is included in *interest* arising to a person within 1995/96 and 1996/97 (otherwise than where 1996/97 is on an actual basis) and would not have been so included if any 'relevant arrangements' made between that person and another had not been made, the 1996/97 assessment is increased by 62.5% of each amount so included. There is a *de minimis* threshold in that the increase does not apply where the aggregate of the amounts so included is less than £7,500. Any arrangements under which interest arises at irregular intervals, or there are 'artificial variations' in the rate of interest applicable, during the years 1994/95 to 1997/98 are '*relevant arrangements*' for these purposes unless the obtaining of a tax advantage is not the main benefit that could reasonably be expected to arise therefrom. All variations are '*artificial variations*' unless based on variations in a variable and regularly published rate of interest. [*FA 1995, s 123, Sch 22 paras 9, 18; SI 1997 No 1158*]. Similar measures apply as regards Case III *income other than interest* except that (i) '*relevant arrangements*' means any arrangements under which income arises at irregular intervals during the years 1994/95 to 1997/98 unless they are made exclusively for *bona fide* commercial reasons or the obtaining of a tax advantage is not the main benefit that could reasonably be expected to arise, and (ii) the measures also apply where the taxpayer has entered into any 'relevant transaction' which results in an amount being included in income for 1995/96 and 1996/97 which would not otherwise have been so included. Any transaction with a connected person (within *ICTA 1988, s 839* — see 20 CONNECTED PERSONS) is a '*relevant transaction*' for these purposes unless it is entered into exclusively for *bona fide* commercial reasons or the obtaining of a tax advantage is not the main benefit that could reasonably be expected to accrue therefrom. [*FA 1995, Sch 22 paras 10, 19, 20*]. The obtaining of a tax advantage is not regarded as a *bona fide* commercial reason for the above purposes. The discovery provisions of *TMA 1970, ss 29, 30B* apply with the same modifications and related time limits as in 71.20 SCHEDULE D, CASES I AND II. [*FA 1995, Sch 22 paras 11, 21(2)*]. There is no provision for any penalty to be mitigated or for any corresponding reduction to the assessment for any other year, except that where voluntary disclosure is made in the tax return for 1996/97 (other than by amendment to the return), the adjustment is reduced to 50% of each amount so included. [*FA 1995, Sch 22 para 13*].

The Revenue have also announced their intention to counter movements between accounts after 30 March 1994, designed to increase the income qualifying for transitional relief, by strictly applying the law so as to treat such additional deposits into a pre-6 April 1994 account as new sources and thus subject to current year basis. This will apply where it appears that pre-existing sources taxed on current year basis have been depleted and sources taxed on preceding year basis correspondingly increased. (Revenue Press Release 31 March 1994).

Simon's Direct Tax Service. See E1.3.

72.5 *Example*

Roger has the following sources of untaxed interest, chargeable under Schedule D, Case III.

	Opened/acquired	*Closed*
(1) National Savings income bonds	21.6.93	—
(2) National Savings Bank ordinary account	6.8.93	29.4.98
(3) National Savings Bank investment account	8.1.94	—

His wife, Sharon, also opens a National Savings Bank ordinary account (Source (4)) on 21 June 1993, but closes it on 31 December 1997.

Interest credited/received in each of the tax years 1993/94 to 1998/99 is as follows.

	Source (1)	Source (2)	Source (3)	Source (4)
	£	£	£	£
1993/94	800	520	—	520
1994/95	700	470	600	470
1995/96	600	550	800	550
1996/97	650	350	825	350
1997/98	575	335	775	335
1998/99	550	100	725	—

There are no 'relevant arrangements' or movements between accounts so as to bring into play the anti-avoidance measures in 72.4(*f*) above.

The interest chargeable under Schedule D, Case III for each year is as follows

(NB: the first £70 of National Savings Bank ordinary account interest for each tax year is exempt (see 29.13(iv) EXEMPT INCOME).)

	Source (1)	Source (2)	Source (3)	Source (4)
1993/94 (1st year — CY)	£800	£450	—	£450
1994/95 (2nd year — CY)	700	400		400
(CY basis)			600	
	£700	£400	£600	£400
1995/96 (3rd year — election for CY basis)	600			
(3rd year — PY)		400		400
(CY basis)			800	
	£600	£400	£800	£400
1996/97 (CY basis)	650		825	
(transitional year)		380		
(PY basis)				480
	£650	£380	£825	£480
1997/98 (CY basis)	575	265	775	
(Final year — CY)				265
	£575	£265	£775	£265
1998/99 (CY basis)	£550	£30	£725	—

Notes

(*a*) *Source 1.* Income first arose in 1993/94. Because an election is made under *ICTA 1988, s 66(1)(c)* (third year — actual), the averaging rule does not apply for 1996/97, to which the current year basis therefore applies.

(*b*) *Source 2.* Transitional rules apply for 1996/97. The amount chargeable is 50% of the aggregate income arising in 1995/96 and 1996/97. (As the source is a National Savings Bank ordinary account, the first £70 of the amount otherwise chargeable is exempt.)

(*c*) *Source 3.* Income first arises after 5 April 1994. Therefore the source goes directly onto the current year basis.

(*d*) *Source 4.* Because income last arises before 6 April 1998, the current year basis and transitional provisions do not apply, the source being taxed throughout on the preceding year basis rules.

73 Schedule D, Cases IV and V—Overseas Income

[*ICTA 1988, ss 18, 65–67*]

Cross-references. See INTEREST RECEIVABLE at 44.5 for deep discount securities, 44.7 for deep gain securities and 44.8 for qualifying convertible securities; RESIDENCE, ORDINARY RESIDENCE AND DOMICILE at 64.4 for domicile, 64.5 for residence; NON-RESIDENTS AND OTHER OVERSEAS MATTERS at 51.12 for trades etc. carried on and controlled abroad, 51.14 for unremittable overseas income; 53.15 PARTNERSHIPS for partnerships abroad; 56 PAYMENT OF TAX; 59.2 PENSIONS for foreign pensions; 63 REMITTANCE BASIS for remittances; 75.6 SCHEDULE E for foreign employment.

Simon's Direct Tax Service B6.

73.1 Persons resident in the UK are assessable under Schedule D, Cases IV and V on overseas income, except from the carrying on in the UK of a trade, profession or vocation, either solely or in partnership (assessable under Schedule D, Cases I or II) or employment income (assessable under Schedule E).

Case IV applies to interest on overseas **securities,** other (for 1995/96 and earlier years) than income assessable under SCHEDULE C (70).

Case V applies to income from overseas **possessions.** [*ICTA 1988, s 18(3); FA 1996, Sch 7 para 4(2)(b)*].

See 72.1, 72.2 SCHEDULE D, CASE III for interaction with that Case, and for variations for corporation tax purposes.

73.2 **'Securities'** are debts or claims secured on some fund or property, i.e. debenture or mortgage. (Cf. *dicta* in *Williams v Singer HL 1920, 7 TC 419*).

'Possessions' include all sources of income other than securities. The distinction between the two has ceased to be of any general practical importance.

73.3 **Overseas income** within Cases IV or V includes foreign bank interest; income as partner (*Colquhoun v Brooks HL 1889, 2 TC 490; Padmore v CIR CA 1989, 62 TC 352*); alimony paid under a foreign decree (*Anderstrom CS 1927, 13 TC 482*) (and see below); annuity paid under foreign deed of separation (*Chamney v Lewis KB 1932, 17 TC 318*); interest on unpaid instalments of a debt (*Hudson's Bay Co v Thew KB 1919, 7 TC 206*). Where the aggregate face value of foreign promissory notes exceeded the consideration for them, the excess was held to be interest within Case V (*Lord Howard de Walden v Beck KB 1940, 23 TC 384*).

Alimony, maintenance payments, etc. arising outside the UK which fall due after 14 March 1988 and before 6 April 2000 and are made in pursuance of 'existing obligations' (see 1.8(i) ALLOWANCES AND TAX RATES) are within the charge to tax under Case V, but subject (for 1988/89 and subsequent years) to the deductions and limitations described at 47.10 MARRIED PERSONS. Other maintenance payments which, if they had arisen in the UK, would not have been within the charge to tax under Case III (see 47.10 MARRIED PERSONS) are similarly exempted from charge under Case V if arising abroad. [*ICTA 1988, s 347A(4); FA 1988, ss 36(1), 38(8); FA 1999, Sch 20 Pt III(6)*].

Promissory notes issued in satisfaction of arrears were held to be assessable (*Lilley v Harrison HL 1952, 33 TC 344*) and in *Westminster Bank v National Bank of Greece HL 1970, 46 TC 472* interest on foreign bonds paid, as guarantor, by the London branch of a foreign bank was held to be within Case IV. A dividend from a foreign company out of a capital profit was held to be within Case V (*Reid's Trustees HL 1949, 30 TC 431*) but see *Lazard*

Inv Co v Rae HL 1963, 41 TC 1, where different treatment by application of Maryland law. In *Lawson v Rolfe Ch D 1969, 46 TC 199*, bonus shares received, by operation of Californian law, by the UK resident life tenant under a US will trust were held not assessable under Case V. And see *Courtaulds Investments v Fleming Ch D 1969, 46 TC 111*, distribution out of the share premium reserve of an Italian company (released, under Italian law, by accumulating out of profits a corresponding reserve fund) held a return of capital. See also *Pool v Guardian Investment Trust Co Ltd KB 1921, 8 TC 167* and *Associated Insulation Products Ltd v Golder CA 1944, 26 TC 231*. Compensation paid by a foreign government, following redundancy, in substitution for a proportion of salary was held to be assessable as income (*Beveridge v Ellam (Sp C 62), [1996] SSCD 77*).

Whether **premiums and discounts** are assessable to income tax depends upon whether recipient received altogether more than commercial interest reasonable on a sound investment (*Lomax v Peter Dixon CA 1943, 25 TC 353*, compared with *Thomas Nelson & Sons Ltd CS 1938, 22 TC 175*, and *Davis v Premier Investment KB 1945, 27 TC 27*). If exempt from income tax they may be assessable to capital gains tax. See 44.5–44.7 INTEREST RECEIVABLE for the charge on disposal of a 'deep discount' or 'deep gain security'.

Simon's Direct Tax Service. See **B6.101, B6.201** *et seq.*.

Overseas lettings of property, caravans and houseboats are assessed under Case V. See 73.4 below. For foreign pensions, see 59.2 PENSIONS and cf. *Bridges v Watterson Ch D 1952, 34 TC 47*. For foreign trust income, see 81.10 SETTLEMENTS. For Crown option between Cases of Schedule D, see 5.2 ASSESSMENTS. For treatment of blocked currency cases, see 51.14 NON-RESIDENTS AND OTHER OVERSEAS MATTERS and *ICTA 1988, ss 584, 585*.

73.4 **Overseas lettings.** For 1995/96 and subsequent years of assessment (but see the transitional provisions below) and otherwise than where the REMITTANCE BASIS (63) applies (see 73.5 below), income arising from any business (other than a trade, profession or vocation) carried on for the exploitation, as a source of rents or other receipts, of any estate, interest or rights in or over land outside the UK is chargeable under Case V but is to be computed under the rules applicable to a Schedule A business (including those for capital allowances). All such businesses carried on by one person are treated as a single business (an overseas property business). The question of whether income falls within the above description is determined as for Schedule A purposes. See 68.4, 68.5 SCHEDULE A. The following do *not*, however, apply as they would under Schedule A: (i) *ICTA 1988, ss 80, 81* — travelling expenses (see 51.12 NON-RESIDENTS AND OTHER OVERSEAS MATTERS), but see below, and (ii) *ICTA 1988, ss 503, 504* and *CAA 1990, s 29* — special rules for furnished holiday lettings (see 68.9 SCHEDULE A). Where a person carries on both a Schedule A business and an overseas property business, each is treated as a separate business without regard to the other. Domestic concepts of law are to be interpreted to produce the result most closely corresponding to that under Schedule A for land in the UK. [*ICTA 1988, s 65(2A)(2B)(4), s 65A; CAA 1990, s 161(2A); FA 1995, s 41(1)–(3)(10); FA 1996, s 134, Sch 20 para 3; FA 1998, s 38, Sch 5 paras 23, 24, 61, Sch 27 Pt III(4)*]. Under general principles, relief is available for travelling expenses incurred wholly and exclusively for the purposes of the overseas letting business. Interest on a loan to purchase an overseas property is deductible as an expense to the extent that it is incurred wholly and exclusively for the purposes of the letting business, with the interest being apportioned accordingly where the owner occupies the property, or it is otherwise unavailable for letting, for part of the year or if only part of the property is used exclusively for letting. (Revenue booklet SAT 1(1995), paras 9.151–9.153). Although all overseas let properties are regarded as a single letting business, the income from each must be calculated separately for the purposes of computing DOUBLE TAX RELIEF (25) (SAT 1(1995), para 9.160).

Transitional provisions.

(1) The above rules do not apply in any case which would be within the Schedule A transitional provisions (see 68.3 SCHEDULE A) if the land were in the UK (i.e. where the source ceases in *1995/96* without a new source being acquired).

(2) For *1995/96* and *1996/97*, where a person lets more than one overseas property, the letting of each property is treated as a separate Schedule A business without regard to the other properties.

(3) If, had it not been for the introduction of the above rules, a source would have been chargeable on the preceding year basis for *1995/96* and under the transitional rules for *1996/97* (see 73.9 below), that basis and those rules are preserved for those years (see also (6) below). However, where those rules so apply to income from any property, no capital allowances or balancing charges can be made for those years in connection with that property.

(4) The relief for SCHEDULE A losses at 68.13 does *not* apply to an overseas letting business for any of the years *1995/96, 1996/97* or *1997/98* (see also below).

[*FA 1995, s 41(5)–(9)*].

(5) *Basis of computation.* In moving onto an accruals basis for 1995/96 from some other basis (for example, receipts and payments) in 1994/95, the guidelines at 68.22 SCHEDULE A should be followed.

(6) *Basis periods.* Where an accounting date other than 5 April has previously been used to assess overseas letting income, it is necessary to move to a statutory fiscal year basis under the new rules. The Revenue's preferred option is to adjust the basis period for 1996/97 (the transitional year — see 73.9 below) to run from the end of the 1995/96 basis period to 5 April 1997, with accounts being prepared to cover that period and a proportion equivalent to twelve months' profits being taxed.

(Revenue booklet SAT 1(1995), paras 9.150, 9.161–9.164).

For years before 1998/99, deficiencies of income from overseas lettings may by concession be carried forward for set-off against future income from the same property (and this will continue for corporation tax purposes). For 1998/99 onwards, the loss regime at 68.13 SCHEDULE A operates instead (by virtue of *ICTA 1988, s 379B*), but any unrelieved losses at 5 April 1998 (including any incurred after 5 April 1995 on properties where letting ceases before 1998/99) may by concession be carried forward against future profits of the single overseas letting business. (Revenue Pamphlet IR 1, B25; Revenue Booklet SAT 1(1995), paras 9.157–9.159).

Interest payable on a loan used to purchase a flat in Gibraltar for furnished letting was held not deductible in *Ockendon v Mackley Ch D 1982, 56 TC 2* (but this has no application under the new rules above).

Simon's Direct Tax Service. See **B6.204.**

73.5 **Assessment** on income chargeable under Cases IV and V is normally on **income arising** whether remitted to this country or not but the **remittance basis** (see 63 REMITTANCE BASIS) applies to

(*a*) persons not domiciled in the UK.

(*b*) Commonwealth subjects, or citizens of Republic of Ireland, not ordinarily resident in the UK.

[*ICTA 1988, s 65(1)(4)(5); FA 1994, s 207(1)(3); FA 1996, s 134, Sch 20 para 3*].

But income from whatever source in the Republic of Ireland is assessable on the amount arising in the year of assessment whether remitted to this country or not, subject to certain deductions in the case of income not remitted. [*ICTA 1988, s 68; F(No 2)A 1992, s 60; FA 1994, s 207(5)*].

In arriving at the amount assessable on the arising basis, deductions are made of 10% in respect of certain pensions (see 59.1(iv) and 59.2 PENSIONS).

For 1996/97 and subsequent years and other than where the remittance basis applies, interest, discounts etc. within Case IV or V are chargeable to income tax at the lower rate (to the extent that such income does not fall within an individual's higher rate band). See 1.9 ALLOWANCES AND TAX RATES for the full provisions.

Simon's Direct Tax Service. See **E1.3**.

73.6 **Aggregation of income.** For years before 1996/97, for purposes of assessment, income arising (including remittances) under Case IV or V may respectively be assessed in one sum. [*ICTA 1988, s 73; FA 1995, s 115(9)*].

73.7 **Deductions.** In general the assessment is on the full amount of the income with no deductions (cf. *Aikin v Macdonald Trustees CES 1894, 3 TC 306*), but where the assessment is on the arising basis (see 73.5 above) there may be deducted from income not received in the UK (*a*) the same deductions and allowances as if it had been so received, and (*b*) any annuities or other annual payments (not being interest) payable out of the income to a resident abroad. No deduction is permitted either in respect of any annuity or annual payment falling due after 14 March 1988 which would not have been chargeable under Schedule D, Case III if made to a UK resident, nor, with effect for 1989/90 and subsequent years, in respect of any payment of maintenance within *FA 1988, s 38* (see 47.10 MARRIED PERSONS). [*ICTA 1988, ss 65(1), 347A(5); FA 1988, ss 36(1), 38(9); FA 1994, s 207(1)*].

Foreign tax for which no double tax credit is allowable (see 25.2 DOUBLE TAX RELIEF) may be deducted where the arising basis applies. [*ICTA 1988, ss 811, 795(2)*]. Where the remittance basis applies, see *ICTA 1988, s 795(1)*.

Simon's Direct Tax Service. See **E1.331**.

73.8 No assessment can be made for years during which the source of income was taxed by **deduction at source.** See 5.4 ASSESSMENTS (and cf. *Bradbury v Eng. Sewing Cotton HL 1923, 8 TC 481*).

73.9 BASIS OF ASSESSMENT

Preceding year basis. For 1995/96 and earlier years, as regards income from a source first arising (or, where the remittance basis applies, see 73.5 above, income first remitted to the UK) before 6 April 1994, the basis of assessment under Schedule D, Cases IV and V, is the same as set out under 72.4 SCHEDULE D, CASE III (i.e. preceding year basis normally applies [*ICTA 1988, s 65*] with special rules for new sources [*ICTA 1988, s 66*] and disposals etc. [*ICTA 1988, s 67*]), subject to variations as follows.

(*a*) If the remittance basis applies to the recipient (see 73.5 above) — then all assessments will be made on the basis of remittances to the UK (in the preceding year etc.) instead of on income arising. [*ICTA 1988, s 65(4)(5), s 66(6), s 67(6)*]. It is understood, however, that any sums received derived from income which arose in a year of non-residence (other than a basis year for a preceding year basis assessment) are excluded from assessment.

(*b*) If income from any foreign security or possession previously taxed by deduction ceases to be so treated — new source rules apply. [*ICTA 1988, s 66(5)*].

(*c*) If income previously assessed under Cases IV and V becomes taxable by deduction — disposal etc. rules apply. [*ICTA 1988, s 67(3)*].

(*d*) Income arising in Eire is assessed on a current year basis. [*ICTA 1988, s 68*].

(*e*) See also 73.11 and 73.12 below.

Current year basis. For 1994/95 and subsequent years (1996/97 and subsequent years as regards income from a source first arising (or, where the remittance basis applies, see 73.5 above, income first remitted to the UK) before 6 April 1994), the assessment under Case IV or V is on the income arising (or, where applicable, remitted) in the year of assessment. [*ICTA 1988, s 65; FA 1994, s 207(1)(3)(4), s 218(1)(4)*]. Generally, there are no special rules for new sources or disposals. In the case of a trade, profession or vocation chargeable under Case IV or V, the basis period rules in 71.11 to 71.19 SCHEDULE D, CASES I AND II and *ICTA 1988, s 113* (see 53.6 PARTNERSHIPS) apply (for 1997/98 and subsequent years as regards trades, etc. commenced before 6 April 1994). [*ICTA 1988, s 65(3); FA 1994, s 207(2)(6)*].

Transitional rules on changeover to current year basis. The following rules apply to income from a source first arising (or, where the remittance basis applies, see 73.5 above, income first remitted to the UK) before 6 April 1994 and continuing (without interruption) beyond 5 April 1996. If the source ceases in 1996/97 or 1997/98, the rules in 72.4(*a*)–(*d*) SCHEDULE D, CASE III apply throughout. If the source continues beyond 5 April 1998, the assessment for 1996/97 is on 50% of the income arising (or, where applicable, remitted) in 1995/96 and 1996/97, the other 50% escaping tax. This does not apply if income first arose in 1993/94 and taxpayer opts for the actual basis for 1995/96 (see 72.4 SCHEDULE D, CASE III); in this case, the 1996/97 assessment is on a current year basis with no 50% reduction. In the case of a trade, profession or vocation chargeable under Case IV or V, a transitional overlap profit may arise for 1997/98 in the same way as in 71.22 SCHEDULE D, CASES I AND II. [*FA 1994, s 218, Sch 20 paras 6, 7, 14*].

Anti-avoidance measures have been introduced to deter and penalise attempts to exploit the transitional rules by moving income into the transitional period, i.e. 1995/96 and 1996/97, so that it would not otherwise be fully charged to tax. They do not apply where the remittance basis applies. For interest and other income other than trading etc. profits, the provisions are identical to those described at 72.4(*f*) SCHEDULE D, CASE III. [*FA 1995, s 123, Sch 22 paras 9, 10, 13; SI 1997 No 1158*]. For trades, professions or vocations within Case IV or V, the anti-avoidance provisions mirror those at 71.20 SCHEDULE D, CASES I AND II with the transitional period being the tax years 1996/96 and 1996/97, and there are also measures more or less identical to those at 71.22 SCHEDULE D, CASES I AND II aimed at manipulation of the transitional overlap profit. [*FA 1995, Sch 22 paras 6–8, 13*].

Simon's Direct Tax Service. See **E1.3**.

73.10 *Example*

In July 1993 S inherited shares in X, a company resident outside the UK. S is resident, ordinarily resident and domiciled in the UK and is not liable to higher rate tax. The dividends which arise and tax deducted therefrom are as follows (the dividends arising on or after 1 October 1998 have UK tax deducted by a UK paying agent).

	Gross	Foreign tax at 15%	UK tax (at lower rate less foreign tax)
	£	£	£
1993/94	120	18.00	—
1994/95	175	26.25	—
1995/96	190	28.50	—
1996/97	180	27.00	—
1997/98	240	36.00	—
Period 6.4.98 – 30.9.98	135	20.25	—
		£156.00	
Period 1.10.98 – 5.4.99	145	21.75	7.25

S's assessments are as follows.

	£	£
1993/94 (1st year — CY)	£120	
Tax thereon at 20%	24.00	
Deduct Tax credit relief	18.00	18.00
UK tax payable	£6.00	
1994/95 (2nd year — CY)	£175	
Tax thereon at 20%	35.00	
Deduct Tax credit relief	26.25	26.25
UK tax payable	£8.75	
1995/96 (3rd year — PY)	£175	
Tax thereon at 20%	35.00	
Deduct Tax credit relief	26.25	26.25
UK tax payable	£8.75	
1996/97 (transitional year)		
Income arising in 1995/96	190	
Income arising in 1996/97	180	
	£370	
£370 × 50%	£185	
Tax thereon at 20%	37.00	
Deduct Tax credit relief:		
£(28.50 + 27.00) × 50%	27.75	27.75
UK tax payable	£9.25	

	£	£
1997/98 (CY)	£240	
Tax thereon at 20%	48.00	
Deduct Tax credit relief	36.00	36.00
UK tax payable	£12.00	
1998/99 (period 6.4.98 to 30.9.98 — CY)	£135	
Tax thereon at 20%	27.00	
Deduct Tax credit relief	20.25	20.25
UK tax payable	£6.75	
Total tax credit relief		£154.50

Notes

(*a*) S would choose to have the assessment for 1995/96 assessed under the preceding year basis since the income for 1994/95 is lower than that for 1995/96. [*ICTA 1988, s 66(1)(c)*].

(*b*) The income of £145 for the period 1.10.98–5.4.99 would normally be assessed for 1998/99 as foreign dividends. However, no assessment need be raised as S is not liable to higher rate tax and the income has effectively suffered lower rate tax at source.

(*c*) For 1993/94 onwards, dividends which are assessable under Schedule D, Case V are charged at the lower rate of 20% except to the extent that the dividend income brings the recipient into the higher rate band (see 1.3 ALLOWANCES AND TAX RATES).

(*d*) *Double taxation relief.* Tax credit relief for 1996/97 (the transitional year on the changeover to the current year basis of assessment) is restricted to 50% of the aggregate foreign tax paid on income arising from the source in question in 1995/96 and 1996/97 (see 25.5(*n*)(1) DOUBLE TAX RELIEF).

The total tax credit relief given (£154.50) is less than the total foreign tax paid (£156.00). No adjustment is made for the difference. If total tax credit relief had exceeded total foreign tax paid, an amount would have become chargeable under Schedule D, Case VI. Such amount is the excess of (A) tax credit relief given more than once because of the opening years rules (£26.25 in this example) (see *ICTA 1988, s 804(1) as originally enacted*) over (B) the tax credit relief foregone because of the 50% restriction in 1996/97 (£27.75 in this example). (In this example, there is clearly no such excess.) See 25.5(*n*)(2) DOUBLE TAX RELIEF. Where a source is subject to the current year basis throughout (i.e. where income first arises after 5 April 1994), no such adjustment will be relevant.

73.11 NEW RESIDENTS

As regards a trade, profession or vocation carried on by an individual wholly or partly outside the UK, the comments and concessions below are superseded by the statutory provisions at 71.27 SCHEDULE D, CASES I AND II which apply for 1995/96 onwards as regards trades etc. commenced after 5 April 1994 and for 1997/98 onwards as regards those commenced on or before that date.

Strictly, an individual who becomes resident (see 64.5 RESIDENCE, ORDINARY RESIDENCE AND DOMICILE) in the UK during a tax year is treated as resident throughout that year. He is assessable on income arising or remitted as appropriate (see 73.5 above) on the preceding or current year basis, as appropriate, unless the commencement provisions apply (see 73.9 above and *Back v Whitlock KB 1932, 16 TC 723; Carter v Sharon KB 1936, 20 TC 229; Joffe v Thain Ch D 1955, 36 TC 199*).

For the year in which an individual whose home has previously been abroad becomes permanently resident in the UK, however, certain concessions are generally available, provided that he was not previously ordinarily resident in the UK.

(i) The individual may be treated as resident only from the date of his arrival in the UK to take up permanent residence.

(ii) No assessment is made in respect of a source ceasing before the date of arrival in the UK to take up permanent residence.

(iii) Where income is assessable on the 'arising' basis (see 73.5 above),

(*a*) if the source ceases in the period between arrival and the end of the tax year of arrival, assessment will be restricted to the amount arising in that period;

(*b*) if the source ceases in the tax year following that of arrival, assessment for the year of arrival will be on a proportion of the income for the year of arrival or, for 1995/96 and earlier years, and if greater, for the preceding year. The proportion is that which corresponds to the period of UK residence in the year of arrival. For the following year, assessment will be on the income arising during that year to the date the source ceased;

(*c*) if income from a continuing source first arose in the tax year of arrival but before arrival, or, for 1995/96 and earlier years, in the previous tax year, assessment for the year of arrival is restricted to the same proportion as in (*b*) above of the income of that year. For 1995/96 and earlier years, if it first arose in an earlier year, assessment is on the same proportion of income of the year before that of arrival.

(iv) Where income is assessable on the 'remittance' basis (see 73.5 above),

(*a*) if the source ceases in the period between arrival and the end of the tax year of arrival, assessment is restricted to the lesser of remittances in the tax year and income arising between arrival and cessation;

(*b*) if the source ceases in the tax year following that of arrival, the assessment for the year of arrival is restricted to the lesser of (A) remittances in that year (or, if the source was in existence at 5 April 1994, and if greater, in the previous year) and (B) a proportion (as in (iii)(*b*) above) of the income arising in that year (or, if the source was in existence at 5 April 1994, and if greater, in the previous year). The sum of the assessments for the year of arrival and the following year is then restricted to the sum of the amount arrived at under (B) above and income arising in the year following that of arrival up to the date the source ceased.

(v) For arrivals in 1996/97 only, (iii) and (iv) apply as regards amounts assessable for 1996/97, but not 1997/98. The only special rules for 1997/98 apply where the source of income continues after 5 April 1998, in which case:

(*a*) where the arising basis applies, the assessment is on a proportion of 50% of the income of the two years ended 5 April 1997 corresponding to the proportion of the year to 5 April 1997 falling after the date of arrival (except that where income first arose from the source after 5 April 1994, that proportion will be applied to the full amount of the income arising in the year ended 5 April 1997);

(*b*) where the remittance basis applies, the assessment is on 50% of the sum of remittances in the two years ended 5 April 1997 (except that where income was first remitted from the source after 5 April 1994, the assessment is on the lesser of the full amount of the income remitted in the year ended 5 April 1997 and an amount worked out as under (*a*) above).

These concessions do not, however, apply to income received from a source in the Republic of Ireland (see 73.5 above) and are of limited application to individuals previously resident in the Republic.

(Revenue Pamphlet IR 20, paras 1.5, 5.4, 6.17–6.24).

See also Revenue Pamphlet IR 20, para 5.14 as regards whether a change of residence brings about a cessation of a trade, etc..

73.12 INDIVIDUALS PERMANENTLY LEAVING UK

As regards a trade, profession or vocation carried on by an individual wholly or partly outside the UK, the comments and concessions below are superseded by the statutory provisions at 71.27 SCHEDULE D, CASES I AND II which apply for 1995/96 onwards as regards trades etc. commenced after 5 April 1994 and for 1997/98 onwards as regards those commenced on or before that date.

Strictly, an individual who is resident in the UK (see 64.5 RESIDENCE, ORDINARY RESIDENCE AND DOMICILE) continues to be so for the remainder of the tax year after his permanent departure from the UK. Certain concessions are, however, available, provided that he ceases to be ordinarily resident in the UK on his departure.

(i) Where income is assessable on the 'arising' basis (see 73.5 above), the assessment for the year in which permanent residence ceases is restricted to the lesser of

(*a*) income arising between 6 April in that year and the date of his departure, and

(*b*) the proportion of the income otherwise assessable for the year (whether on the current or preceding year basis, see 73.9 above) corresponding to the period of UK residence in the year.

(ii) Where income is assessable on the 'remittance' basis (see 73.5 above), concessions apply as in (i) above, substituting 'remitted' for 'arising'.

These concessions do not, however, apply to income received from a source in the Republic of Ireland (see 73.5 above), and are of limited application to persons leaving to take up residence in the Republic.

(Revenue Pamphlet IR 20, paras 1.5, 5.4, 6.15, 6.16).

74 Schedule D, Case VI—Miscellaneous Income

[*ICTA 1988, ss 18, 69*]

Simon's Direct Tax Service B7.

74.1 Tax is charged under Schedule D, Case VI in respect of any annual profits or gains not falling under any other case of Schedule D and not charged by virtue of any other Schedule. [*ICTA 1988, s 18(3)*].

Case VI is also specifically applied to other kinds of income to include: various charges under ANTI-AVOIDANCE (3); withdrawal of relief under 26.12, 26.27 ENTERPRISE INVESTMENT SCHEME (AND BES); sale of patent rights, see 54 PATENTS; CERTIFICATES OF DEPOSIT (13); easements not falling under *ICTA 1988, ss 119, 120* and certain under-deductions where tax rate changed, see 23 DEDUCTION OF TAX AT SOURCE; interest paid by issue of bonds, see 32 FUNDING BONDS; gains on certain offshore life insurance policies, see 45.17–45.19 LIFE ASSURANCE POLICIES; formerly unremittable overseas income where source has ceased, see 51.14 NON-RESIDENTS AND OTHER OVERSEAS MATTERS; offshore income gains, see 52 OFFSHORE FUNDS; recovery of tax over-repaid, see 56.8 PAYMENT OF TAX; certain POST-CESSATION ETC. RECEIPTS (62); lease premiums and assignments at under-value etc. see 68.27 SCHEDULE A; certain furnished lettings — see 74.4 below; certain settlement income, see 81.15 SETTLEMENTS; charges on trustees of employee share ownership trusts, see 82.41 SHARE INCENTIVES AND OPTIONS; recovery of various excess reliefs for double taxation [*ICTA 1988, ss 788, 790, 804*], losses [*ICTA 1988, s 383(11)*], capital allowances [*CAA 1990, s 9(6), s 15(2)* (both now superseded), s 7*3(2), s 142(3)*] etc.. See Simon's Direct Tax Service B7.102.

74.2 Following held to be income within Case VI: commission for guaranteeing overdrafts (*Ryall v Hoare KB 1925, 8 TC 521* and *Sherwin v Barnes KB 1931, 16 TC 278*); underwriting commission (*Lyons v Cowcher KB 1926, 10 TC 438*); commission for negotiating a sale of shares (*Grey v Tiley CA 1932, 16 TC 414*); commission from an insurance company (*Hugh v Rogers Ch D 1958, 38 TC 270* and see *Way v Underdown CA 1974, 49 TC 648*); shipping dues (the two *Forth Conservancy Board cases HL 1928, 14 TC 709, HL 1931, 16 TC 103*); share of prize monies for letting racehorses (*Norman v Evans Ch D 1964, 42 TC 188*).

Held to be capital were shares allotted to members of a mining finance development scheme (*Whyte v Clancy KB 1936, 20 TC 679*) and shares allotted for a guarantee of dividends (*National United Laundries v Bennet KB 1933, 17 TC 420*).

A payment to an architect for his services relating to a property deal was held income within Case VI in *Brocklesby v Merricks KB 1934, 18 TC 576*, but payments for services in deals are not income if made gratuitously in such circumstances that the recipient has no enforceable right to them. For cases in which such payments held *not* income see *Bradbury v Arnold Ch D 1957, 37 TC 665; Bloom v Kinder Ch D 1958, 38 TC 77; Dickinson v Abel Ch D 1968, 45 TC 353*. See also *Scott v Ricketts CA 1967, 44 TC 303* in which a payment to an estate agent linked with a development scheme was held not to be income even though embodied in a contract.

Receipts of the use of copyright material were held income within Case VI in *Hobbs v Hussey KB 1942, 24 TC 153* (sale of rights in life story to newspaper) and *Housden v Marshall Ch D 1958, 38 TC 233* and *Alloway v Phillips CA 1980, 53 TC 372* (receipt for material for newspaper articles by 'ghost writer') but held capital in *Earl Haig Trustees v CIR CS 1939, 22 TC 725* (payment to trustees for permission to use diaries of deceased); *Beare v Carter KB 1940, 23 TC 353* (payment for permission to re-print book); *Nethersole v Withers HL 1948, 28 TC 501* (sale of film rights in work by deceased author).

For other copyright sales see 71.43 and 71.51 SCHEDULE D, CASES I AND II. For the line between Cases I and VI as regards surpluses on the sales of assets see 71.35 SCHEDULE D, CASES I AND II.

See Simon's Direct Tax Service B7.2.

Volunteer drivers (e.g. hospital car service drivers) are taxable in the normal way under Case VI on the profit element in any mileage allowances. Arrangements to collect such tax have been made with effect from 6 October 1991, but, by concession, the profit is taxed as to one-quarter only for the period from 6 October 1991 to 5 April 1992 and for 1992/93, as to one-half only for 1993/94 and as to three-quarters only for 1994/95. Tax is payable in full on the profit element for 1995/96 and subsequent years. This concession does not apply to taxi and mini-cab drivers and similar operators who drive for the hospital car service and other volunteer organisations. (Revenue Pamphlet IR 1, A77). See also Revenue explanatory leaflet IR 122.

Theatrical angels. UK-resident backers of theatrical productions ('angels'), although strictly assessable under SCHEDULE D, CASE III (72) on any return over and above their original investment (with the capital gains tax rules applicable to any losses), may treat the profit or loss arising on any particular transaction as within Case VI, thereby being able to utilise such losses against similar (or any other) Case VI profits. Losses so utilised cannot also qualify as capital losses. The Revenue will not insist on deduction of tax being applied to payments to angels whose usual place of abode is in the UK where it is strictly required under *ICTA 1988, s 349*. (Non-resident angels may apply for authority for tax not to be deducted, see 25.6 DOUBLE TAX RELIEF.) This concessional treatment reflects a long-standing Revenue practice. (Revenue Pamphlet IR 1, A94).

74.3 ASSESSMENT

For 1994/95 and subsequent years (1996/97 and subsequent years as regards income from a source first arising before 6 April 1994), the income tax assessment under Case VI is made on the profits arising in the year of assessment. Previously, it was made either on the profits arising in the year of assessment, or on the average of such period, not being greater than one year, as Commissioners direct. [*ICTA 1988, s 69; FA 1994, ss 208, 218(1)*]. In practice, if the income is of a recurrent nature, e.g. furnished letting profits (see 74.4 below) the assessment is often on the preceding year's income and may be on Case I or Case III lines (see 71.3 SCHEDULE D, CASES I AND II, 72.4 SCHEDULE D, CASE III) for the opening and closing years. In other cases the assessment is on the current year's income. But for corporation tax the assessment is on the actual income of the accounting period.

Where a preceding year accounting period basis has been used for 1995/96 and earlier years, an averaging computation analogous to that described at 71.20 SCHEDULE D, CASES I AND II will be used to determine the assessable income for 1996/97, with the current year basis applying thereafter. (Revenue Booklet SAT 1, para 6.63). See 68.22 SCHEDULE A for Revenue guidelines on the transition from the Case VI charge on furnished lettings to a charge under Schedule A (and see also 74.4 below).

Assessments under Case VI are not earned income unless specifically provided e.g. in *ICTA 1988, s 107* (POST-CESSATION ETC. RECEIPTS (62)), in *ICTA 1988, s 491(5)* (distribution of assets of mutual companies), in *ICTA 1988, s 531(6)* (sale of know-how, see 71.67 SCHEDULE D, CASES I AND II), in *ICTA 1988, s 775(2)* (capitalisation of earnings, see 3.10 ANTI-AVOIDANCE).

74.4 FURNISHED LETTINGS

With effect for 1995/96 and subsequent years (subject to the transitional provisions at 68.3 SCHEDULE A), income from furnished lettings is within SCHEDULE A (see 68.8). Previously, such income was normally within Case VI (and see 68.22 for Revenue guidelines on the transition from Case VI to SCHEDULE A). However, dependent on the nature of the lettings including their frequency and the extent to which the landlord provides services, e.g. cleaning, laundry and meals, the letting may amount to a trade of provision of serviced accommodation within Case I. The letting of caravans may similarly be within Case I or Case VI. (Revenue Press Release 17 May 1984 and see Revenue Pamphlet IR 1, B29). Alternatively the provision of services may be a separate trade (cf. *Salisbury House Estate Ltd v Fry HL 1930, 15 TC 266*). In *Gittos v Barclay Ch D 1982, 55 TC 633*, the letting of two villas in a holiday village was held not to amount to trading. A similar decision was reached in *Griffiths v Jackson; Griffiths v Pearman Ch D 1982, 56 TC 583* in relation to the extensive letting of furnished rooms to students. Where use of furniture is charged under Case VI, the Case VI assessment also includes payments for use of the premises *unless* the landlord elects in writing within two years after end of year of assessment for Schedule A to apply to that rent (see 68.14 SCHEDULE A). [*ICTA 1988, s 15(1)(2); F(No 2)A 1992, s 58; FA 1995, s 39*].

Assessment is on rents received less rent paid, repairs, rates, commission and any other expenses relating to the letting (which may include interest on money borrowed to purchase the property). Apportionment is necessary where only part of premises is let or personally occupied or only let for part of a year.

Expenses of residence (or loss on billeting) elsewhere not allowable (*Wylie v Eccott CS 1912, 6 TC 128* and *Smith v Irvine KB 1946, 27 TC 381*).

CAPITAL ALLOWANCES (10) are not due on plant let for use in a dwelling house [*CAA 1990, ss 28A(3), 61(2)*] (but see below as regards furnished holiday lettings). Furniture and furnishing may be dealt with on the renewals basis but an alternative Revenue concession is to allow as depreciation 10% of rents received as reduced by any council tax and water rates or material payments for services borne by landlord but normally a tenant's burden. Where the 10% deduction is allowed, no change to a renewals basis is permitted, and no further deduction is given for the cost of renewing furniture or furnishings, nor for fixtures such as cookers, dishwashers or washing machines which, in unfurnished accommodation, the tenant would normally provide for himself. However, the cost of renewing fixtures which are an integral part of the building (e.g. baths, toilets, washbasins) may be claimed in addition, provided that they are revenue repairs to the fabric. Any different basis in use for a particular case prior to 1975/76 will not normally be disturbed. (Revenue Pamphlets IR 131, A19, IR 1, B47 (as revised); Revenue Press Release IR 28, 29 November 1994). See *Abidoye v Hennessey Ch D 1978, [1979] STC 212*.

Furnished holiday lettings. See 68.9 SCHEDULE A for the full provisions relating to treatment of the commercial letting of furnished holiday accommodation as a trade for certain purposes. Those provisions also applied to the income tax charge under Case VI and the said purposes also included relief for pre-trading expenditure (see 71.76 SCHEDULE D, CASES I AND II) (such relief applying in any case to a Schedule A business). Expenses are deductible according to SCHEDULE D, CASES I AND II (71) principles as if the letting were a trade. [*ICTA 1988, ss 503, 504; CAA 1990, s 29*].

Simon's Direct Tax Service. See **B7.206**.

'Rent a room' relief for letting of rooms in private residence. See 68.11 SCHEDULE A.

74.5 LOSSES

Losses on transactions which, if profitable, would have been assessable under Schedule D, Case VI (other than losses on transactions falling under *ICTA 1988, ss 34–36*, see 68.27 SCHEDULE A), can be set off against any profit or gains charged under Case VI for the same year of assessment or carried forward against the next subsequent profits chargeable under that Case. Claims relating to the amount of losses must be made within, for losses sustained in 1996/97 and later years, five years after 31 January following the tax year in which they arose. A further claim for relief for losses brought forward must be made within five years after 31 January following the tax year for which relief is claimed. For earlier years, the time limit in both cases was six years after the end of the tax year in question. [*ICTA 1988, s 392; FA 1996, s 135, Sch 21 para 11*].

Under transitional provisions, a Case VI loss in respect of furnished lettings (see 74.4 above) can be carried forward against Schedule A income of 1995/96 and subsequent years. See 68.13(B) SCHEDULE A.

Simon's Direct Tax Service. See **E1.626.**

74.6 **ACCRUED INCOME SCHEME (BONDWASHING)**

Introduction. Provisions to counteract bondwashing took effect on 28 February 1986. Bondwashing is the practice of converting income into capital gains by disposing of securities at a time when the price obtained reflects a significant element of accrued interest. Under the accrued income provisions, interest on securities is treated as accruing on a day to day basis between 'interest payment days', and on transfer of the securities a person is charged to income tax on the interest that accrues during the 'final interest period' of his ownership with appropriate adjustments to the taxable incomes of transferor and transferee. There were transitional provisions, intended to limit forestalling before the accrued income scheme came into operation, which applied between 28 February 1985 and 27 February 1986 (for which see Tolley's Income Tax 1992/93 or earlier). The above dates are varied for UNDERWRITERS (89), see 74.26 below.

For **1996/97 onwards**, the accrued income scheme provisions do not apply on a transfer to which *FA 1996, Sch 13* applies (charge to or relief from tax on the profit or loss realised from the discount on a relevant discounted security, see 72.2 SCHEDULE D, CASE III).

A Revenue Pamphlet (IR 68) is available describing in brief terms the basic rules of the scheme. See generally Revenue Inspector's Manual, IM 4230 *et seq.*.

Simon's Direct Tax Service. See **B3.745** *et seq.*.

These provisions are disapplied for the purposes of corporation tax for accounting periods ending after 31 March 1996, except as respects transfers taking place on or before that date, and subject to transitional provisions. [*ICTA 1988, s 710(1A); FA 1996, Sch 14 para 36, Sch 15 para 18*]. For the corporation tax securities regime introduced for accounting periods ending after 31 March 1996, and for the transitional provisions, see Tolley's Corporation Tax under Loan Relationships.

74.7 The **main definitions** of terms used in the accrued income legislation are in *ICTA 1988, ss 710–712.*

'*Securities*' include any loan stock or similar security of any government, or public or local authority, or any company, or other body, whether or not secured or carrying a right to interest of a fixed amount or at a fixed rate per cent and whether or not in bearer form. Not included are shares in a company (other than certain building society shares); securities on which the whole of the return is a distribution under *ICTA 1988, s 209(2)(da)* (issued by a subsidiary to its non-resident parent, see Tolley's Corporation Tax under Distributions); national and war savings certificates (including Ulster savings certificates); CERTIFICATES OF DEPOSIT (13) and certain other rights for which a certificate of deposit could be, but has not been, issued (see 13.3 CERTIFICATES OF DEPOSIT); and redeemable zero coupon securities (see 44.5, 44.7 INTEREST RECEIVABLE). [*ICTA 1988, s 710(2)(3); FA 1991, Sch 10 para 2; F(No 2) A 1992, Sch 8 para 5*].

Securities are '*of the same kind*' if so treated by a recognised stock exchange or if they would be so treated if dealt with on such an exchange. [*ICTA 1988, s 710(4)*].

'*Transfer*' in relation to securities means transfer by way of sale, exchange, gift or otherwise, but does not include their vesting in personal representatives on a death after 5 April 1996, or exchanges of gilt-edged securities for strips (or reconsolidation of strips) except as provided by *ICTA 1988, s 722A* (see 74.24 below). It does not include an exchange or conversion of securities solely as a result of actions to effect a '*euroconversion*', i.e. a change from the currency of a State which has adopted the euro into euros (see *SI 1998 No 3177, regs 3, 32*). A transfer takes effect when an agreement for transfer is made and not at any later date. Except for this, a person '*acquires*' securities when he becomes entitled to them and '*holds*' them on any day if he is entitled to them at the end of that day. Partners in Scottish partnerships are treated as being entitled to securities held by the firm and as carrying out themselves any partnership dealings. [*ICTA 1988, s 710(5)–(9)(10); FA 1996, s 158(1)(5)*].

'*Interest*' includes dividends and any other return (however described) except a return consisting of the excess of a security's redemption amount over its issue price. [*ICTA 1988, s 711(9)*].

An '*interest payment day*' is a day on which interest is payable or, where payment may be made on more than one day, the first such day. [*ICTA 1988, s 711(2)*].

An '*interest period*' is normally the period beginning with the day after one interest payment day (or the day after issue) and ending with the next (or first) such day. If, however, an interest period would otherwise exceed twelve months, it is divided into successive twelve month interest periods with any remaining months also a separate interest period. [*ICTA 1988, s 711(3)(4)*].

The '*interest applicable to securities*' for an interest period is that due at the end of the period, unless the period does not end on an interest payment day. Where the interest period is part of a long period as above, or it is an interest period only by virtue of *ICTA 1988, s 725(9)* (see 74.26 below), the interest applicable is a pro rata proportion of that due at the end of the long period of which the interest period is part. [*ICTA 1988, s 711(7)(8)*].

The '*settlement day*', where securities are transferred through a recognised market such as the Stock Exchange, is the agreed settlement day or, if the transferee may settle on more than one day, the day he settles. If the transfer is not through such a market and the consideration is money alone and there is no interest payment day between the agreement for transfer and the agreed payment day or days, that day (or the latest such day) is the settlement day. If the transfer is not through such a market and either there is no consideration, or it is treated as a transfer by virtue of special provisions in *ICTA 1988, s 710(13), s 715(3), s 717(8), s 720(4), s 721, s 722, s 722A* or *s 724(1A)* (see 74.17, 74.21, 74.19, 74.12, 74.15, 74.16, 74.24 or 74.28 below), the settlement day is the day of transfer. There are also special rules fixing the settlement day for Lloyd's underwriters, see 74.26 below. If the settlement day is not established by one of the above, it is decided by an inspector, subject to review by the General or Special Commissioners on appeal. [*ICTA 1988, s 712; FA 1990, Sch 6 paras 9, 11; FA 1996, Sch 40 para 5*].

74.8 **Determination of accrued income.** When securities are transferred, the 'interest applicable to the securities' for 'the interest period' in which the 'settlement day' falls is apportioned between the old and new owners so that the former is charged to income tax on the interest accrued up to the date of transfer while the latter is similarly charged on the interest accruing from that date. For 1996/97 onwards, a transfer to which *FA 1996, Sch 13* applies (relevant discounted securities, see 72.2 SCHEDULE D, CASE III) is treated for these purposes as not being a transfer.

The interest actually received is chargeable to tax in the normal way. It may, however, be reduced, or a further charge may arise, as below.

Subject to exceptions in 74.10 below, if the transfer is *with accrued interest* (i.e. with the right to receive the next interest due, or 'cum div'), the transferor is treated as entitled to a sum equal to the 'accrued amount' while the transferee is treated as entitled to relief of the same amount. If, on the other hand, the transfer is *without accrued interest* (i.e. 'ex div') the transferor is treated as entitled to relief equal to the 'rebate amount' while the transferee is treated as entitled to a sum of the same amount.

The '*accrued amount*' is either the gross interest accruing to the settlement day (see 74.7 above) where this is accounted for separately by the transferee (as happens with short-dated gilts), or the 'accrued proportion' of the interest applicable for that interest period (see 74.7 above) in any other case. The '*accrued proportion*' is A/B where A is the number of days in the interest period up to and including the settlement day and B is the number of days in the whole period.

Conversely, the '*rebate amount*' is either the gross interest accruing from the settlement day to the next interest payment date where the transferor accounts to the transferee for this, or the 'rebate proportion' of the interest applicable for that interest period in any other case. The '*rebate proportion*' is (B – A)/B where A and B have the same meanings as for the accrued proportion above. [*ICTA 1988, ss 711(5), 713*].

Euroconversions. Where, in any interest period, there is both a transfer of securities and a '*euroconversion*' of those securities, i.e. a change from the currency of a State which has adopted the euro into euros, the accrued or rebate amount arising on the transfer is such amount as is just and reasonable. A euroconversion does not generally of itself give rise to a transfer within these provisions (see 74.7 above), but certain capital sums received in connection with euroconversions of securities which, on a just and reasonable view, may be attributable to a reduction or deferral of interest on those securities may give rise to adjustments under these provisions. [*SI 1998 No 3177, regs 3, 34, 35*].

74.9 **Tax charge (or relief).** The various sums and reliefs to which a person is deemed to be entitled as in 74.8 above and which relate to securities of a particular kind in an interest period (see 74.7 above) are aggregated. If the overall result is a sum chargeable to tax, it is taxed under Schedule D, Case VI as if it were income received at the end of the interest period. If, on the other hand, the overall result shows entitlement to relief, the relief is given by way of a reduction in the actual interest received at the end of the interest period so that only the reduced amount is charged to tax. If this reduction is not possible because no interest is received at the end of the interest period, the relief is carried forward to be taken into account in calculating the accrued income or relief in the next interest period. Provision is also made (where relevant) to ensure that a company does not escape liability where the date on which an interest period ends does not fall within an accounting period. [*ICTA 1988, s 714; FA 1996, Sch 41 Pt V(3)*].

For 1998/99 and subsequent years, the lower rate (rather than the basic rate) of income tax is applied to charges under these provisions (subject to any higher rate liability). This does not affect the charge on trustees at the rate applicable to trusts (see 74.12 below). [*ICTA 1988, s 1A(1)(2)(aa); FA 1998, s 100*].

74.10 **Exceptions to deeming provisions.** The following are excluded from the accrued income scheme.

(*a*) Transfers by persons who account for such transfers in the computation of their trading profits or losses (e.g. financial traders).

(*b*) Transfers by individuals, personal representatives and trustees of mentally disabled persons or persons in receipt of attendance allowance, provided that the nominal value of securities held in the capacity in question does not exceed £5,000 on any day in the year of assessment in which the interest period ends or in the preceding year of assessment.

(*c*) Transfers by persons neither resident nor ordinarily resident in the UK in the chargeable period in which the transfer is made, unless trading in the UK through a branch or agency. However, where such a person does so trade in the UK, the accrued income scheme only applies to securities used, or held, or acquired for use, for the purposes of the branch or agency, if the person is a company, and only to such of those securities as are situated in the UK (within the meaning of *TCGA 1992, s 275)* in other cases.

(*d*) Transfers of FOTRA securities (see 33.2 GOVERNMENT STOCKS) where the appropriate conditions are met. (For securities treated as FOTRA securities from 6 April 1998 by virtue of *FA 1998, s 161(1)*, exemption applies in relation to amounts a person is treated as receiving on or after that date (see *FA 1998, s 161(2)(a)*).)

(*e*) For foreign securities only, transfers by individuals who would be liable to tax on the remittance basis on actual interest on the securities under Schedule D, Case IV or V (i.e. persons not domiciled in the UK, or Commonwealth subjects or citizens of the Republic of Ireland not ordinarily resident in the UK).

The exceptions apply separately by reference to the circumstances of the transferor and the transferee. [*ICTA 1988, ss 710(9), 715; FA 1996, s 154, Sch 41 Pt V(18)*].

74.11 *Example*

The following transactions take place between individuals during the year ended 5 April 2001.

Settlement day	Sale by	Purchase by	Securities
15.6.00	X (cum div)	Y	£2,000 $13\frac{1}{2}$% Treasury Loan 2004/08
8.9.00	X (ex div)	P	£4,000 $11\frac{1}{2}$% Treasury Loan 2001/04
15.3.01	S (cum div)	Y	£1,000 9% Treasury Loan 2012

Interest payment days are as follows.

$13\frac{1}{2}$% Treasury Loan 2004/08	26 March, 26 September
$11\frac{1}{2}$% Treasury Loan 2001/04	19 March, 19 September
9% Treasury Loan 2012	6 February, 6 August

Both X and Y owned chargeable securities with a nominal value in excess of £5,000 at some time in either 1999/2000 or 2000/01, and both are resident and ordinarily resident in the UK. P is not resident and not ordinarily resident in the UK throughout 2000/01. The maximum value of securities held by S at any time in 2000/01 and 2001/02 is £4,000.

15.6.00 transaction

The transaction occurs in the interest period from 27.3.00 to 26.9.00 (inclusive).

Number of days in interest period	184
Number of days in interest period to 15.6.00	81
Interest payable on 26.9.00	£135

The accrued amount is

$$£135 \times \frac{81}{184} = \underline{£59}$$

X is treated as receiving income (chargeable under Schedule D, Case VI) of £59 on 26.9.00.

Y is given credit for £59 against the interest of £135 he receives on 26.9.00. £76 remains taxable.

8.9.00 transaction

The transaction occurs in the interest period from 20.3.00 to 19.9.00 (inclusive).

Number of days in interest period	184
Number of days in interest period to 8.9.00	173
Interest payable on 19.9.00	£230

The rebate amount is

$$£230 \times \frac{184 - 173}{184} = \underline{£14}$$

X is given credit for £14 against the interest of £230 he receives on 19.9.00. £216 remains taxable.

P is not assessed on any notional income as he is neither resident nor ordinarily resident in the UK.

15.3.01 transaction

The transaction occurs in the interest period from 7.2.01 to 6.8.01 (inclusive).

Number of days in interest period	181
Number of days in interest period to 15.3.01	37
Interest payable on 6.8.01	£45

The accrued amount is

$$£45 \times \frac{37}{181} = \underline{£9}$$

S is not assessed on any notional income. He is not within the accrued income scheme provisions as his holdings do not exceed £5,000 at any time in 2000/01 or 2001/02 (the year in which the interest period ends).

Y is given credit for £9 against the interest of £45 he receives on 6.8.01. £36 remains taxable.

74.12 ACCRUED INCOME SCHEME: SPECIAL CASES

Nominees and trustees. Transfers made by or to a nominee, or by or to a trustee of a person or persons absolutely entitled as against the trustee (including persons who would be so entitled if not an infant or under a disability), are treated for accrued income scheme purposes as being made by or to the person on whose behalf the nominee or trustee acts. [*ICTA 1988, s 720(1)(2)*].

A person who becomes entitled to securities as trustee immediately after holding them in another capacity is treated as making a transfer within the new legislation. Such a transfer is 'with accrued interest' (see 74.8 above) if the person was entitled to receive any interest payable on the day of transfer or on the next interest payment day. [*ICTA 1988, ss 711(6), 720(4)*].

Trustees' accrued income (i.e. excluding that deemed to be that of a beneficiary, see above) is chargeable at the rate applicable to trusts (see 81.5 SETTLEMENTS). This tax is set against any subsequent tax charge under *ICTA 1988, s 687* (payments by trustees of discretionary trusts). The charge does not apply to certain funds in court within *ICTA 1988, s 328* (which is, however, repealed from 6 April 1999), and special rules apply to calculation of the income of such funds in receipt of interest on securities. [*ICTA 1988, s 720(5); FA 1993, Sch 6 para 13; FA 1999, Sch 20 Pt III(17)*].

Where a trustee is treated as receiving accrued income (see 74.9 above), or where he would have been treated as receiving, or receiving a greater amount of, accrued income if he had been UK resident or domiciled, the SETTLEMENTS (81) provisions apply with the effect that the accrued amount is, broadly, treated as income of the settlor where any actual income would be so treated. Similarly, any actual income received in those circumstances is reduced where the trustee is entitled to relief under the accrued income scheme (see 74.9 above). [*ICTA 1988, s 720(6)–(8); FA 1995, Sch 17 para 17*].

74.13 **Interest payable in foreign currency.** Provision is made for establishing the rate of exchange to be used in converting into sterling certain figures used in calculating the accrued income charge.

The accrued amount and the rebate amount (see 74.8 above). Where accrued interest is accounted for separately and the parties specify a sterling equivalent themselves, this figure is used. Otherwise accrued interest is converted at the rate of exchange (the London closing rate) on the settlement day.

Nominal values are converted at the London closing rate for the day in question.

[*ICTA 1988, s 710(12), s 713(7)–(9)*].

74.14 **Foreign securities: delayed remittances.** A person (or his personal representatives) may claim to postpone all or part of sums which would be chargeable under the accrued income provisions if

(*a*) he makes a claim within six years of the end of the interest period in which the transfer occurred, and

(*b*) he was unable (through no want of reasonable endeavour) to remit the proceeds of transfer(s) to the UK, either because of the laws or government action of the territory in question or because of the impossibility of obtaining foreign currency there.

The postponed sums are taken into account in the chargeable period in which (*b*) above ceases to apply. [*ICTA 1988, s 723*].

74.15 **Death,** subject to below and to special provisions for Lloyd's underwriters (see 74.26 below), is, for deaths **before 6 April 1996**, treated as the occasion of a transfer of all securities to the deceased's personal representatives. The transfer is 'with accrued interest' (see 74.8 above) if the deceased was entitled to receive any interest payable on the day of death or on the next interest payment day thereafter. Any taxable accrued income is deemed to arise on the day of death. Where the transfer to personal representatives and the latters' transfer (with accrued interest) to a legatee takes place in the same interest period, the transfer on death is regarded as being made to the legatee and the transfer by the personal representatives is disregarded. Where death occurs **after 5 April 1996**, the death is *not* treated as giving rise to a transfer to the personal representatives. Where a transfer by the personal representatives to a legatee takes place in the interest period in which the death occurs, the transfer is disregarded for the purposes of the current provisions. [*ICTA 1988, ss 711(6), 721; FA 1996, s 158*].

74.16 **Trading stock: appropriations, etc..** A transfer is deemed to be made under the new provisions where a person appropriates to trading stock securities previously held as investments, and vice versa. The transfer is 'with accrued interest' (see 74.8 above) if the person was entitled to receive any interest payable on the day of transfer or on the next interest payment day thereafter. [*ICTA 1988, ss 711(6), 722*].

74.17 **Conversions.** On a conversion of securities within *TCGA 1992, s 132*, the person entitled to them immediately before the conversion is treated as transferring them on the day of the conversion (if there is no actual transfer). The transfer is 'with accrued interest' (see 74.8 above) if the person was entitled to receive any interest payable on the day of conversion or on the next interest payment day thereafter. The 'interest period' (see 74.7 above) in which the conversion is made is treated as ending on the day on which it would have ended but for the conversion. [*ICTA 1988, ss 710(13), 711(6)*].

74.18 **Transfer of unrealised interest (bearer securities).** Provision is made to ensure that accrued interest which has already become payable before the settlement day (e.g. on bearer securities) does not escape the accrued income scheme. The transferor is treated as entitled to that interest and taxed accordingly while the transferee is not taxed when he actually receives the interest. The exceptions at 74.10 above apply to a charge so arising on the transferor and to the relief arising to the transferee. The capital gains tax calculation of the gain on the disposal by the transferor is adjusted to exclude the accrued interest from the consideration received and the transferee's base cost is similarly reduced by the amount of the relief obtained as above. Where necessary, the unrealised interest is converted into sterling at the London closing rate of exchange on the settlement day. [*ICTA 1988, s 716; TCGA 1992, s 119(4)*]. See also 74.20 below where there is a default in interest payments.

74.19 **Variable rate bonds.** Special rules apply to the transfer of securities unless either

(*a*) they carry interest from issue to redemption at one, and only one, of the following rates:

  (i) a constant fixed rate; or

  (ii) a rate fixed in relation to a standard published base rate or the retail prices index (or foreign equivalent), or

(*b*) they were deep discount securities (prior to their abolition from 6 April 1996) for which the rate of interest for each interest period did not exceed the yield to maturity (see 44.5 INTEREST RECEIVABLE).

Where an interest rate change may arise solely from provision for actions required to effect a '*euroconversion*' of a security, i.e. a change from the currency of a State which has adopted the euro into euros, this does not of itself bring the security concerned within these provisions (see *SI 1998 No 3177, regs 3, 33*).

Where securities not within (*a*) or (*b*) above are transferred at any time between issue and redemption, then:

(1) if they are transferred without accrued interest, they are treated as transferred with accrued interest;

(2) the transferor is treated as entitled to a sum equal to such amount (if any) as is just and reasonable (for 1995/96 and earlier years, such amount, if any, as an inspector (or the Commissioners on appeal) decides is just and reasonable);

(3) no relief is available to the transferee; and

(4) the person entitled to the securities immediately before their redemption is treated as transferring them with accrued interest on the day of redemption, giving rise to a charge as in (2) and (3) above.

Where there is a deemed transfer as a result of (4) above, in relation to which the settlement day falls after the end of the only or last interest period in relation to the securities the period from the day following that interest period to the settlement day (inclusive) is treated as an interest period (even if it is longer than twelve months). [*ICTA 1988, s 717; FA 1996, s 134, Sch 20 para 35; FA 1998, Sch 27 Pt III(22)*].

74.20 **Interest in default.** Where there has been a failure to pay interest on the securities, the charge under the accrued income scheme on transfer is calculated by reference to the value of the right to receive the interest on the interest payment day in question rather than the full amount of the interest payable. The provisions regarding transfers of unrealised interest (see 74.18 above) similarly apply by reference to the value of the right to receive the interest (if less than the amount of the unrealised interest). If the transferee subsequently receives the unrealised interest, the assessment on the interest is reduced by the amount of the value of the right to receive the interest at the time of purchase (i.e. the relief given to him at that time). If he transfers the securities with the unrealised interest, the charge on him under the current provisions is restricted to any increase in the value of the right to receive the interest between purchase and re-sale. Special rules apply where unrealised interest is partially repaid and where part of a holding of securities is transferred. [*ICTA 1988, ss 718, 719; TCGA 1992, s 119(5)*]. For the application of these provisions in practice, see Revenue Inspector's Manual, IM 4257.

74.21 **Charities** are excluded from the accrued income scheme if any interest actually received would be exempt under *ICTA 1988, s 505(1)(c)(d)*, but where securities cease to be subject to charitable trusts the trustees are treated for the purposes of the legislation as making a transfer at that time. Such a transfer is 'with accrued interest' (see 74.8 above) if the trustees were entitled to receive any interest payable on the day of transfer or on the next interest payment day thereafter. [*ICTA 1988, s 711(6), s 715(1)(d)(2)(3)*].

74.22 **Retirement schemes.** Transfers to or by pension funds are excluded from the accrued income scheme as regards the pension fund if any interest received would be exempt under *ICTA 1988, s 592(2)*. [*ICTA 1988, s 715(1)(k)(2)*].

74.23 **Sale and repurchase of securities.** Where, under an agreement or agreements entered into under the same arrangement, securities are sold and the transferor, or a person connected with him (within *ICTA 1988, s 839*), either buys them (or similar securities) back or acquires an option to do so which he subsequently exercises, the accrued income scheme provisions are disapplied to both transfers. Securities are 'similar' for this purpose if they entitle the holder to the same rights against the same persons as to capital and interest, and to the same enforcement remedies, and where securities are converted from the currency of a State which has adopted the euro into euros (a '*euroconversion*'), the new securities are treated as 'similar' (see *SI 1998 No 3177, regs 3, 14*). The exclusion of such transfers applies where the sale agreement is entered into **on or after 1 May 1995**, except that in relation to any description of securities for which the appointed day under the manufactured payments provisions of *ICTA 1988, s 737A* (see 3.7 ANTI-AVOIDANCE) falls after 1 May 1995, it applies instead to sale agreements entered into on or after that appointed day. [*ICTA 1988, s 727A; FA 1995, s 79*].

The Treasury has broad powers to make regulations providing for the above provisions to apply with modifications (including exceptions and omissions) in relation to cases involving any arrangement for the sale and repurchase of securities where the obligation to repurchase is not performed, or the repurchase option not exercised, or where provision is made by or under any agreement:

(*a*) for different or additional securities to be treated as, or included with, securities which, for the purposes of the repurchase, are to represent securities transferred in pursuance of the original sale; or

(*b*) for any securities to be treated as not included with securities which, for repurchase purposes, are to represent securities transferred in pursuance of the original sale; or

(*c*) for the sale or repurchase price to be determined or varied wholly or partly by reference to fluctuations, in the period from the making of the agreement for the original sale, in the value of securities transferred in pursuance of that sale, or in the value of securities treated as representing those securities, or for any person to be required, where there are such fluctuations, to make any payment in the course of that period and before the repurchase price becomes due.

Regulations may also make such modifications in relation to cases where corresponding arrangements are made by an agreement, or by related agreements, in relation to securities which are to be redeemed in the period after their sale, those arrangements being such that the vendor (or a person connected with him), instead of being required to repurchase the securities or acquiring an option to do so, is granted rights in respect of the benefits that will accrue from their redemption.

[*ICTA 1988, s 737E; FA 1995, s 83(1)*].

74.24 **Gilt strips.** Where a person exchanges a gilt-edged security for strips of that security, that person is deemed to have transferred the security with accrued interest (unless the exchange is after the balance has been struck for a dividend on the security but before the day the dividend becomes payable), without any person being treated as the transferee within *ICTA 1988, s 713(2)(b)* (see 74.8 above), and without affecting the end of the interest period in which the exchange takes place. Similarly where strips are reconstituted by any person into the security from which they derived, the security is deemed to have been transferred to that person with accrued interest (unless the reconstitution is after the balance has been struck for a dividend on the security but before the day the dividend becomes payable) without any person being treated as the transferor, and the interest period in which the reconstitution takes place is deemed to have begun on the day specified for that purpose in the security. [*ICTA 1988, s 710(13A)(13B), s 722A; FA 1996, Sch 40 paras 3, 4, 6*].

74.25 **Stock lending.** The exclusion from the accrued income scheme of transfers by financial traders, etc. (see 74.10(*a*) above) is not affected by *ICTA 1988, s 129(3)*, which (prior to its repeal from 1 July 1997) enables certain stock lending transactions to be ignored in computing profits or gains (see 71.82 SCHEDULE D, CASES I AND II). The accrued income scheme provisions are specifically disapplied in relation to stock lending transactions disregarded for chargeable gains purposes under *TCGA 1992, s 271(9)* or *s 263B(2)*. [*ICTA 1988, s 727; FA 1997, Sch 10 para 5(3), Sch 18 Pt VI(10)*].

74.26 **Underwriters.** The accrued income scheme is modified to make it workable within the framework of the special rules which apply to UNDERWRITERS (89). However, the scheme has no application to underwriters' premiums trust funds. [*ICTA 1988, s 725; FA 1993, Sch 23 Pt III(12)*]. It also has no effect for new-style special reserve funds under *FA 1993* (see 89.7(*b*) UNDERWRITERS). Special terms used below are as defined in *ICTA 1988, s 457* and

FA 1993, s 184, see 89 UNDERWRITERS below. [*ICTA 1988, s 710(14); FA 1993, s 183(4)*].

For the underwriting year 1993 and earlier years, an underwriter is treated as if he himself made the transfers made by the trustees of his premiums trust fund. For 1991/92 and earlier years of assessment, this also applied with respect to an underwriter's special reserve fund. It continues to apply with respect to an ancillary trust fund (see 89.3 UNDERWRITERS). [*ICTA 1988, s 720(3); FA 1993, s 176(1), s 183(5), Sch 23 Pt III(12)*].

For the underwriting year 1993 and earlier years, there is a deemed transfer of securities forming part of a premiums trust fund between one calendar year and the next, with accrued interest where appropriate, and with the settlement day being 31 December. This paragraph does not apply where 31 December is an interest payment day for the securities (as the normal provisions will then cater adequately for underwriters). [*ICTA 1988, s 725(1)–(6); FA 1993, Sch 23 Pt III(12)*]. For the purposes of these provisions, certain transfers within *ICTA 1988, s 129* (stock lending — see 71.82 SCHEDULE D, CASES I AND II) made by the trustees of a premiums trust fund are, effectively, to be regarded as not having taken place. [*ICTA 1988, s 725(10)(11); FA 1989, s 91; TCGA 1992, s 207(4)(5); FA 1993, Sch 23 Pt III(12)*].

Division of periods straddling year end. Where securities of a premiums trust fund are transferred in a period straddling the end of a calendar year which would otherwise be an interest period (see 74.7 above), that period is not itself an interest period but is instead divided into two interest periods, with the first ending on 31 December and the second beginning on the following 1 January (although this does not apply to other parties to such transfers unless themselves trustees of such funds). [*ICTA 1988, s 725(7)–(9); FA 1993, Sch 23 Pt III(12)*].

Death. When an underwriter dies the normal rules on death (see 74.15 above) do not apply to securities which form part of his premiums trust fund (for 1993 and earlier years), special reserve fund (for 1991/92 and earlier years) or ancillary trust fund (see 89.3 UNDERWRITERS). Instead his personal representatives are treated as carrying out the deceased's transfers in the interest period in which he died. [*ICTA 1988, s 721(5)(6); FA 1993, s 176(3)(a)(4), Sch 23 Pt III(12)*].

Special reserve fund transfers. As far as the calculation of his annual transfer to an old-style special reserve fund (see 89.7 UNDERWRITERS) is concerned, any accrued income which arises from the underwriter's premiums trust fund, special reserve fund or other required or authorised trust fund is treated as if it were actual income. [*ICTA 1988, s 452(8); FA 1993, Sch 23 Pt III(12)*].

74.27 **Interest etc. on debts between associated companies or to associates of banks.** For accounting periods ending before 1 April 1996, certain debts owed by non-UK resident companies (or certain third parties) to UK resident 'associated' companies (within *ICTA 1988, s 416*), or by any company to a UK resident company associated with a company carrying on a UK banking business, are classed as 'qualifying debts'. Where the debt on a 'security' (within 74.7 above) is a qualifying debt, it is treated as transferred for the purposes of the accrued income scheme on becoming or ceasing to be a qualifying debt, at the end of each accounting period, and on the provisions in question coming into force. [*FA 1993, ss 61–63, s 66; FA 1995, ss 88, 89; FA 1996, Sch 41 Pt V(3)*]. See Tolley's Corporation Tax under Profit Computations for the detailed provisions, and under Loan Relationships for the provisions substituted for later accounting periods.

74.28 **Insurance companies.** For accounting periods ending before 1 April 1996, there are also special provisions dealing with insurance companies. See *ICTA 1988, s 724* as amended. See now Tolley's Corporation Tax under Loan Relationships.

74.29 **New issues.** Where

(*a*) securities of a particular kind are issued (being the original issue of securities of that kind),

(*b*) new securities of the same kind are issued subsequently, and after 18 March 1991,

(*c*) a sum (the 'extra return') is payable by the issuer in respect of the new securities, to reflect the fact that interest is accruing on the old securities and calculated accordingly, and

(*d*) the issue price of the new securities includes an element (separately identified or not) representing payment for the extra return,

then, for the purposes of the accrued income scheme,

(i) the new securities are treated as having been issued on the '*relevant day*' (being the last 'interest payment day' (see 74.7 above) prior to the actual day of issue, or, if there is no such day, the day on which the original securities were issued);

(ii) they are treated as transferred *to* the person to whom they are issued, but are not treated as transferred *by* any person; and

(iii) the transfer is treated as being 'with accrued interest' (see 74.8 above) and as made on the actual day of issue of the new securities, that day being treated as the settlement day (notwithstanding *ICTA 1988, s 712* — see 74.7 above).

If *ICTA 1988, s 717* (see 74.19 above) applies to the new securities, after applying (i) above, (ii) and (iii) above do not apply.

The 'accrued amount' (see 74.8 above) in respect of the transfer in (ii) above is the 'accrued proportion' (see 74.8 above) of the interest applicable for the interest period in which the settlement day falls. If, however, the new securities are issued under an arrangement whereby the 'extra return' (see (*c*) above) is accounted for separately to the issuer by the person to whom the securities are issued, the accrued amount is equal to the extra return so accounted for (or to its sterling equivalent calculated by reference to the London closing rate of exchange on the settlement day, in cases where interest on the new securities is payable in a foreign currency).

[*ICTA 1988, s 726A; FA 1991, Sch 12 paras 2, 5*].

74.30 **INTERACTION WITH OTHER TAXES AND PROVISIONS**

Income tax. For **1996/97 onwards**, the accrued income scheme provisions do not apply on a transfer to which *FA 1996, Sch 13* applies (charge to or relief from tax on the profit or loss realised from the discount on a relevant discounted security, see 72.2 SCHEDULE D, CASE III).

Corporation tax. The accrued income scheme provisions are disapplied for the purposes of corporation tax for accounting periods ending after 31 March 1996, except as respects transfers taking place on or before that date, and subject to transitional provisions. [*ICTA 1988, s 710(1A); FA 1996, Sch 14 para 36, Sch 15 para 18*]. For the corporation tax securities regime introduced for accounting periods ending after 31 March 1996, and for the transitional provisions, see Tolley's Corporation Tax under Loan Relationships.

Capital gains tax. Adjustments are necessary to capital gains tax computations where the accrued income scheme applies. The consideration for the disposal is adjusted to exclude or add the accrued or rebate amounts as appropriate (see 74.8 above) and the sums allowed as a deduction to the transferee on a future disposal are correspondingly adjusted. [*TCGA 1992, s 119(1)–(3)*]. Where there is a CGT disposal which is not a transfer (see 74.7 above) for accrued income scheme purposes but which would be within the scheme if it were such a transfer, a transfer is deemed to be made on the day of the disposal and the capital gains tax consideration and sums deductible are adjusted accordingly as above. [*TCGA 1992, s 119(6)–(9)*]. Where there is a conversion of securities within *TCGA 1992, s 132* or an exchange not involving a disposal within *TCGA 1992, Pt IV, Ch II* (reorganisations, etc.) a capital gains tax adjustment is made to allow for the effect of the accrued income scheme. Any accrued amount which the transferor is treated as receiving (see 74.8 above) is first treated as reducing any consideration receivable on the conversion, etc., and then as consideration given for the conversion, etc., while any rebate amount is treated as consideration received for the conversion, etc. [*TCGA 1992, s 119(10)(11)*].

74.31 **Double taxation relief.** Where a person is treated as receiving accrued income taxable under Schedule D, Case VI (see 74.9 above) and any interest actually received would be liable both to UK tax under Schedule D, Case IV or V (foreign securities) and to foreign tax, he is allowed credit against UK tax on accrued income for foreign tax at the rate at which tax would be payable on interest on the securities. The credit is treated as if it were allowed under *ICTA 1988, s 790(4)*. See 25.4 DOUBLE TAX RELIEF.

Where a person is entitled to double tax relief under *ICTA 1988, ss 788, 790(4)* against UK tax on interest which is treated as reduced under the accrued income scheme (see 74.9 above), the credit is reduced to the same proportion that the interest actually taxable bears to the interest which would have been taxable without the reduction. There is a similar reduction where relief is allowed by way of deduction of foreign tax from interest received under *ICTA 1988, s 811(1)*. The proportionate reduction in the credit does not apply if the person entitled to it is an individual unless the interest arises from securities to which he became or ceased to be entitled during the interest period.

[*ICTA 1988, s 807*].

Section 807 does not apply for corporation tax purposes for accounting periods ending after 31 March 1996 [*ICTA 1988, s 807(6); FA 1996, Sch 14 para 45*], but an equivalent corporation tax relief is provided for such periods by *ICTA 1988, s 807A* introduced by *FA 1996, Sch 14 para 46*.

74.32 **Anti-avoidance.** Several anti-avoidance measures are affected by this legislation.

Transfer of assets abroad. Where a non-UK resident or non-UK domiciled person would have been treated as receiving income under the accrued income scheme (see 74.9 above) if he had been so resident or domiciled, the accrued income which he would have been treated as receiving is treated as income becoming payable to him for the purposes of *ICTA 1988, ss 739–741* (transfer of assets abroad). A corresponding reduction in interest payable for these purposes is made where it would have been made under the accrued income scheme. See 3.8 ANTI-AVOIDANCE. [*ICTA 1988, s 742(4)–(7)*].

Sale and repurchase of securities. Securities within the accrued income scheme are excluded from *ICTA 1988, s 729* (see 3.3 ANTI-AVOIDANCE). [*ICTA 1988, s 729(10)(b)*].

ICTA 1988, s 734 (see 3.6 ANTI-AVOIDANCE) similarly does not apply. [*ICTA 1988, s 731(9)*].

ICTA 1988, s 737 (prior to its repeal) and *ICTA 1988, Sch 23A* (manufactured dividends and interest, see 3.7 ANTI-AVOIDANCE) take precedence over the accrued income scheme and the latter does not apply to the extent that the transfer is covered by those provisions [*ICTA 1988, s 715(6)(7); FA 1994, s 123(1)(6); FA 1997, Sch 18 Pt VI(10)*].

74.33 POWER TO REQUIRE INFORMATION

Inspectors have power by notice in writing to require Stock Exchange members and other persons acting as UK agents or brokers to provide information about transactions in securities effected by them. Information may not be required about transactions effected more than three years before service of the inspector's notice.

Market makers are excluded from these information requirements. The Board has powers, by regulation by statutory instrument, to broaden the scope of information requirements to include other recognised investment exchanges.

Similarly, any person in whose name securities are registered can be required to state who is the beneficial owner.

The penalty provisions of *TMA 1970, s 98* (failure to comply with notices etc.) apply. See 58.4 PENALTIES.

[*ICTA 1988, s 728*].

75 Schedule E—Emoluments

[*ICTA 1988, ss 19, 131–207*]

Cross-references. See 19 COMPENSATION FOR LOSS OF EMPLOYMENT (AND DAMAGES); 25 DOUBLE TAX RELIEF; 64 RESIDENCE, ORDINARY RESIDENCE AND DOMICILE for definitions of those terms; 55 PAY AS YOU EARN; 56 PAYMENT OF TAX; 59 PENSIONS; 60 PERSONAL PENSION SCHEMES; 61 PERSONAL SERVICE COMPANIES ETC.; 63 REMITTANCE BASIS; 65 RETIREMENT ANNUITIES; 66 RETIREMENT SCHEMES; 82 SHARE INCENTIVES AND OPTIONS; 83 SOCIAL SECURITY for taxation of benefits.

Simon's Direct Tax Service E4.

Other sources. See Butterworths Schedule E Compliance Manual.

The headings in this chapter are as follows.

75.1 Basic principles — assessment
75.2 Basic principles — the three Cases
75.3 Earnings from work done abroad
75.4 — example
75.5 Work done abroad — travelling expenses etc.
75.6 Employees of non-UK domicile
75.7 to 75.46 Assessable income, allowable deductions etc. (see separate index before 75.7)

75.1 BASIC PRINCIPLES — ASSESSMENT

Tax is chargeable under Schedule E on the emoluments of offices and employments [*ICTA 1988, s 19*] including 'all salaries, fees, wages, perquisites and profits whatsoever'. [*ICTA 1988, s 131(1)*]. For what constitutes an office see *Edwards v Clinch HL 1981, 56 TC 367* and Revenue Schedule E Manual, SE 521 *et seq.*. See also 75.24 below. The charge is under three 'Cases', see 75.2 below. Where, as is normally the case, the employment is held by a person resident and ordinarily resident in the UK and the duties are wholly performed in the UK for a UK employer, the assessment is under Case I.

All the relevant legislation extends to 'offices' as well as employments held.

Receipts basis. Emoluments are assessable in the year of assessment in which they are received (or, in the case of Case III emoluments, received in the UK), regardless of whether or not the office or employment is held at the time of receipt (or receipt in the UK) and whether the emoluments relate to the year of receipt or to a different year. Emoluments received after the death of the person entitled to them may be assessed and charged on his executors or administrators, and the tax thereon is payable out of the estate. [*ICTA 1988, s 202A; FA 1989, s 37*].

For the purposes of the receipts basis, in its application to Schedule E, Cases I and II, emoluments are to be treated as received at the earliest of the following times ((*c*)–(*e*) apply only where the person concerned is a 'director' of a company at any time in the year of assessment in which the event occurs and the emoluments are from an office or employment with that company, whether or not the office or employment is that of director):

(*a*) when payment is actually made of, or on account of, emoluments;

(*b*) when a person becomes entitled to such payment;

(*c*) when sums on account of emoluments are credited in the company's accounts or records, regardless of any restrictions on the director's right to draw those sums;

(*d*) when a period of account ends and the amount of emoluments for that period has already been determined;

(*e*) when the amount of emoluments for a period of account is determined and that period has already ended.

A '*director*' is defined as being any of the following:

(i) a member of a board of directors, or similar body, which manages the company;

(ii) a single director, or similar person, who manages the company;

(iii) a member of the company, in cases where the company is managed by its members;

(iv) a person on whose advice, given other than in a professional capacity, the directors, as defined in (i)–(iii) above, are accustomed to act.

These rules for determining time of receipt do not apply to emoluments in the form of benefits not consisting of money. These are generally treated as received at the time when, or in the year or period in which, the benefit is provided. See also 19.5 COMPENSATION FOR LOSS OF EMPLOYMENT (AND DAMAGES) for the time at which terminal payments within *ICTA 1988, s 148* are treated as being received. [*ICTA 1988, s 202B; FA 1989, s 37; FA 1998, s 58, Sch 9 para 3*].

Prospective and retrospective remuneration. Without prejudice to the application of the receipts basis, where emoluments would otherwise be for a year of assessment in which a person does not hold the office or employment concerned, then

(A) if the office or employment has never been held, the emoluments are treated as emoluments of the first year of assessment in which it is so held, and

(B) if the office or employment is no longer held, the emoluments are treated as emoluments of the last year of assessment in which it was so held.

[*ICTA 1988, s 19(1); FA 1989, s 36(3)(5)*].

Exception: pensions etc. Pensions and social security benefits generally continue to be assessable by reference to the amount accruing in respect of the year of assessment, irrespective of the time of payment. [*FA 1989, s 41*].

See Revenue Press Release 28 July 1989 for guidance on operation of PAYE (55) under the receipts basis, and ICAEW Technical Release TAX 11/93, 9 July 1993 for a review of the tax implications of certain payments to directors. See generally Revenue Schedule E Manual, SE 5300 *et seq.*.

Other matters.

(1) *Directors' fees received by other companies.* Where a company has the right to appoint a director to the board of another company and the director is required to hand over to the first company any fees or emoluments received from the second company and does so, and the first company agrees to accept liability to corporation tax on the fees, the director is not charged to tax on those fees. Where the first company is not chargeable to corporation tax but to income tax (e.g. a non-resident company not trading through a branch or agency in the UK) and agrees to accept liability, tax is deducted at the basic rate from the fees. This practice is extended to the case where the first company has no formal right to appoint the director to the board but the director is required to, and does, hand over his fees, provided the first company is (*a*) chargeable to corporation tax on its income and (*b*) not a company over which the director has control. '*Control*' for this purpose has the meaning given by *ICTA 1988, s 840* (see 20.8 CONNECTED PERSONS), but in determining whether the director has control of the company the rights and powers of his spouse, his children and their spouses and his parents, will also be taken into account (Revenue Pamphlet IR 1, A37). For directors' fees received by professional partnerships, see 75.24 below.

(2) *Formal assessments* need not be made in cases where the tax collected under PAY AS YOU EARN (55) is correct, unless the taxpayer gives notice within five years after the end of the year of assessment. [*ICTA 1988, s 205*]. In other cases an assessment will be issued in the usual manner. See *SI 1993 No 744, regs 102–104* for payment by instalments in certain cases. In practice, assessments with tax liability of £75 or less will not be made on National Insurance pensioners and war widows with small tax liabilities which cannot be collected in any other way. (Revenue Pamphlet IR 131, A12).

(3) *Changes in practice.* Where income dealt with under PAYE was received more than twelve months before the beginning of the year *in* which the assessment on the income is made, that assessment, if made after the period of twelve months following the year *for* which it is made, is to accord with the practice generally prevailing at the end of that period. [*ICTA 1988, s 206; FA 1995, s 111(2)*]. *Section 206* cannot, however, displace an unqualified statutory exemption relating to the income in question (*Walters v Tickner CA 1993, 66 TC 174*).

(4) *Error or Mistake.* Subject to the above, *TMA 1970, s 33* (see 17.10 CLAIMS) applies to Schedule E.

(5) *Repayments of tax.* See 41 INTEREST ON OVERPAID TAX for attribution of deductions and repayments and 56.7 PAYMENT OF TAX for administrative practice.

(6) *Divers.* See 71.31 SCHEDULE D, CASES I AND II for treatment of certain divers etc. under Schedule D, Case I.

Simon's Direct Tax Service. See **E4.103** *et seq.*.

As regards remuneration planning generally, see Butterworths Schedule E Compliance Manual.

75.2 BASIC PRINCIPLES — THE THREE CASES

The emoluments of an employment are charged under one or more of three Cases, the Case applicable being dependent on the residence and ordinary residence of the employee and where he performs the duties and also, as regards 'foreign emoluments' (see 75.6 below), on his domicile and the residence of the employer. [*ICTA 1988, s 19(1)*].

Case I applies to employees **resident and ordinarily resident** in the UK wherever the duties are performed (but with the exclusion of those receiving 'foreign emoluments', see 75.6 below, in respect of duties performed wholly abroad). The liability is on the total emoluments subject to deductions, see 75.3 to 75.6 below, from earnings from work done abroad and from 'foreign emoluments'. [*ICTA 1988, ss 19(1), 192–195*].

Case II applies to employees **not resident (or if resident, not ordinarily resident)** in the UK. The liability is on emoluments from duties performed in the UK subject to a deduction, see 75.6 below, from 'foreign emoluments'. [*ICTA 1988, ss 19(1), 195*].

But see 25.2 DOUBLE TAX RELIEF regarding non-resident employees working in the UK for an overseas employer.

Case III applies to employees **resident** in the UK **(whether ordinarily resident or not)** so far as the emoluments do not fall within Case I or II. The liability is on emoluments received in the UK (i.e. on the REMITTANCE BASIS (63)). [*ICTA 1988, s 19(1)*]. Thus, Case III applies to

(*a*) employees not domiciled in the UK in respect of emoluments from a non-resident employer (i.e. 'foreign emoluments', see 75.6 below) — *where the duties are performed wholly abroad* and where the employee concerned is resident and ordinarily resident in the UK, and (*b*) employees (wherever domiciled) resident but not ordinarily resident in the UK — *in respect of duties performed abroad* (whether for a resident or non-resident employer), including the part abroad if the employment is carried on partly in the UK and partly abroad.

Tax is not chargeable under Case III on emoluments which, had the new legislation had effect for years before 1974/75, would have fallen under Case I or Case II. [*ICTA 1988, Sch 30 para 19*].

Remittances include any sums paid, used or enjoyed in the UK, and any 'constructive remittances', see 63.4 REMITTANCE BASIS. Capital allowances are not applicable, but expenses which would have been allowable (under *ICTA 1988, s 198(1)*, see 75.10 below), had the remuneration been assessable under Schedule E, Case I in the year it arose, may be deducted. [*ICTA 1988, s 132(5), s 198(2)(3)*].

Apportionment of emoluments. Where a person resident but not ordinarily resident in the UK performs duties of a single employment both inside and outside the UK, the emoluments will be taxable in full under Case II in respect of the UK duties, but under Case III on amounts remitted to the UK in respect of the non-UK duties. Apportionment of the emoluments between UK and non-UK duties is a question of fact, but time apportionment based on working days inside and outside the UK will normally be applied, unless clearly inappropriate. Where part of the emoluments is paid in the UK, the Revenue practice is to accept that, where a reasonable apportionment has been made between emoluments assessable under Case II and Case III, liability arises under Case III only on any excess of the aggregate of emoluments paid and benefits received in the UK and emoluments remitted to the UK over the amount assessable under Case II. Where none of the emoluments is paid in the UK, remittances are generally taken in the first instance as out of income liable under Case II. (Revenue Pamphlet IR 131, SP 5/84, 28 March 1984).

As regards *tax equalisation* payments to non-UK ordinarily resident employees, for 1997/98 and subsequent years these are treated as being chargeable wholly under Case II. For 1994/95 to 1996/97 inclusive, the Revenue will accept a compromise under which the tax payable on such payments is one-half of the difference between that payable on a wholly Case II basis and that payable on the basis of the payments being apportioned between Case II and Case III in the same way as the other emoluments of the employment. (Revenue Tax Bulletin February 1997 pp 386, 387). For self-assessment returns in cases involving tax equalisation, see Revenue Tax Bulletin October 1997 pp 467, 468 and June 1998 p 551.

Duties deemed to be performed in the UK (for the above purposes).

(i) Offices and employments under the *Crown* of a public nature remunerated out of UK public revenue [*ICTA 1988, s 132(4)(a)*] including civil servants (*Graham v White Ch D 1971, 48 TC 163* and *Caldicott v Varty Ch D 1976, 51 TC 403*) and HM Forces. See 75.27 below, 29.5 and 29.31 EXEMPT INCOME. Certain educational allowances under the Overseas Services Aid Scheme, and daily subsistence allowances paid to Detached National Experts on secondment to the European Commission, are exempt from income tax. (Revenue Pamphlet IR 1, A44, A84). No UK tax is charged in the case of locally engaged unestablished staff working abroad who are not UK resident if the maximum pay for their grade is less than that of an executive officer in UK Civil Service in Inner London. (Revenue Pamphlet IR 1, A25). See also 43.6 INTEREST PAYABLE as regards concessional mortgage interest relief.

(ii) Duties by *seafarers and members of aircraft crews* if (i) the voyage does not extend to a port outside the UK or (ii) the person concerned is resident in UK and (*a*) the voyage or flight begins or ends in the UK, or (*b*) it is a part, beginning or ending in the UK, of a voyage which does not so begin or end. [*ICTA 1988, s 132(4)(b)*]. But see 75.3 Note (C) below.

Incidental duties in the UK (for the above purposes). If the employment is substantially one where the duties for the year are due to be performed abroad, any duties incidental thereto performed in UK are treated as if performed abroad. [*ICTA 1988, s 132(2)*]. As to whether duties 'incidental' to foreign duties see *Robson v Dixon Ch D 1972, 48 TC 527* (airline pilot employed abroad but occasionally landing in UK where family home maintained, held UK duties more than incidental). But Revenue will normally disregard a single take-off and landing on *de minimis* grounds. (Revenue Pamphlet IR 131, A10). See also Revenue Pamphlet IR 20, paras 5.7, 5.8, and 75.3 Note (D) below.

Leave periods, etc.. Emoluments of periods of absence from an employment, all or part of the duties of which are ordinarily performed in the UK, are treated as emoluments for duties performed in the UK, except insofar as, but for that absence, they would have been for duties performed outside the UK. [*ICTA 1988, s 132(1); FA 1996, s 134, Sch 20 para 6*]. An airline pilot, the great majority of whose work was performed outside the UK, could not rely on this provision to treat his days of absence from work as days of absence from the UK in the same proportion as his working days (*Leonard v Blanchard CA 1993, 65 TC 589*). It is understood that the Revenue will, by concession, normally regard a university or college lecturer during a period of study leave abroad as performing his duties wholly abroad for the purposes of relief under *ICTA 1988, s 193(1)* (see 75.3 below).

Simon's Direct Tax Service. See **E4.111** *et seq.*.

75.3 EARNINGS FROM WORK DONE ABROAD

Deductions are made as below from *emoluments within Case I*.

(i) *Duties performed wholly or partly outside UK*. Where such duties are performed in the course of a 'qualifying period' of 365 days or more (which can include days outside the tax year concerned), a deduction is made of **100%** of the emoluments for those duties attributable to the period (i.e. they are completely relieved from tax). **In relation to emoluments attributable to 'qualifying periods' beginning on or after 17 March 1998, and to emoluments attributable to earlier 'qualifying periods' which are received on or after that date, this relief applies only to duties of employment as a 'seafarer'.** Employment as a '*seafarer*' for this purpose is an employment consisting of the performance of duties on a ship (disregarding incidental duties), from which are specifically excluded offshore installations under the *Mineral Workings (Offshore Installations) Act 1971* (disregarding for this purpose the limitation under that *Act* to controlled waters). The question whether emoluments are attributable to a 'qualifying period' beginning before 17 March 1998 must be determined without reference to any arrangements entered into on or after that date.

    A '*qualifying period*' consists either (*a*) entirely of consecutive days of absence from the UK or (*b*) of days of absence from the UK *plus* any earlier qualifying period *plus* the intervening period in the UK, provided that the total number of days in the UK in the intervening period and in the earlier qualifying period is not more than a specified proportion of the total number of days in the new qualifying period, and that no intervening period is of more than a specified number of days. In the case of seafarers (which, before the relief was restricted to seafarers, did not specifically exclude those working on offshore installations — although see *Clark v Perks Ch D, [2000] STC 428*, where a mobile offshore drilling unit was held not to be a ship for this purpose) the specified proportion is one-half and the specified number of days is 183. In any other case, the specified proportion is one-sixth and the specified number of days is 62. Successive intervening periods and periods of absence may continue to qualify as long as these conditions are met in relation to each new period of absence. Overseas duties merely incidental to a UK employment are treated for this purpose as performed in the UK.

The employee must have been resident and ordinarily resident in the UK for tax purposes throughout the qualifying period. It may therefore be more favourable for a taxpayer departing from or returning to the UK to be treated, in strict accordance with the statute, as UK resident throughout the year of assessment of departure or return, rather than only being so treated for the part of that year falling before the departure or after the return under Revenue Extra-statutory Concession A11 (see 64.5 RESIDENCE, ORDINARY RESIDENCE AND DOMICILE). Schedule E liabilities are normally calculated on the basis that the concession applies unless the application of the statutory basis is requested. (Revenue Tax Bulletin November 1992 p 40).

A period spent in the UK during a contract of employment but not followed by a period abroad may not be included in the qualifying period (*Robins v Durkin Ch D 1988, 60 TC 700*).

A day of absence means absent from the UK at the end of it.

Emoluments for duties attributable to a qualifying period include emoluments from that employment for a period of leave immediately following that period (and so qualify for the 100% deduction) but not so as to make emoluments for one year of assessment emoluments for another. [*ICTA 1988, ss 192A, 193(1), Sch 12 paras 3, 4, 6; FA 1988, s 67; FA 1991, s 45; FA 1998, s 63*]. See Notes below.

(ii) '*Foreign emoluments*'. See 75.6 below.

Notes to above.

(A) The 100% deduction under (i) above is applied to the emoluments as reduced by capital allowances and allowable deductions (e.g. expenses, superannuation contributions, foreign travel and accommodation expenses (see 75.5, 75.6 below) and certain 'corresponding' foreign deductions (see 75.6 below)). [*ICTA 1988, Sch 12 para 1A; F(No 2)A 1992, s 54*].

(B) *Emoluments eligible for relief.* Where the duties of the employment *or* any associated employment are not performed wholly outside the UK, then in (i) above the emoluments relievable are not to exceed a reasonable proportion of the total emoluments having regard to the nature of and the time devoted to duties performed outside and in the UK and to all other relevant considerations.

Employments are associated if the employers are under common control or one controls the other, control being as in *ICTA 1988, s 416* (for companies) and *s 840* (for individuals and partnerships, see 20.8 CONNECTED PERSONS). [*ICTA 1988, Sch 12 para 2; FA 1996, s 134, Sch 20 para 42*].

(C) Duties performed on a ship or aircraft on any part of a voyage, etc. (or the whole if there is no intervening place of call) beginning or ending in the UK and ending or beginning abroad, are to be treated as performed abroad notwithstanding they may fall to be treated as performed in the UK under *ICTA 1988, s 132(4)(b)* (see 75.2 above). [*ICTA 1988, Sch 12 para 5; FA 1998, s 63(4)(b)*].

(D) The question under (i) above as to where any duties are performed or whether a person is absent from the UK shall not be affected by *ICTA 1988, s 132(2)* (incidental duties in the UK, see 75.2 above). [*ICTA 1988, s 132(3)*].

(E) For deductions for travelling expenses etc., see 75.5, 75.6 below and for seafarers regularly travelling to the same UK port, see 55.37 PAY AS YOU EARN.

See generally Revenue Pamphlet IR 58.

Simon's Direct Tax Service. See **E4.112, E4.113**.

75.4 *Example*

F is sales director of G (UK) Ltd, a UK resident company. He is resident in the UK and made a number of business trips abroad, as follows.

Departed UK	D1	30.9.96
Returned UK	R1	23.12.96
Departed UK	D2	3.1.97
Returned UK	R2	31.5.97
Departed UK	D3	30.6.97
Returned UK	R3	18.12.97
Departed UK	D4	16.1.98
Returned UK	R4	31.3.98

F then worked in the UK for the next three months.

The following steps must be considered.

(i) The period D1–R1 consists of 84 consecutive days of absence and will therefore be a qualifying period.

(ii) The period D1–R2 must next be considered to establish if the period R1–D2 exceeds 62 days or if that period exceeds $\frac{1}{6}$ of the number of days in the period D1–R2. Period R1–D2 comprises 11 days; it is therefore not more than 62 days and not more than $\frac{1}{6}$ of 243 days and so D1–R2 becomes a qualifying period.

(iii) The period D1–R3 is then examined on the same basis as the previous period. Period R2–D3 comprises 30 days; it is therefore not more than 62 days and since R1–D2 (11 days) and R2–D3 (30 days), or 41 days in total, are not more than $\frac{1}{6}$ of D1–R3 (444 days), D1–R3 becomes a qualifying period (and is a qualifying period of at least 365 days).

(iv) The final period D1–R4 (547 days) is then examined. Period R3–D4 comprises 29 days; it is therefore not more than 62 days and since the previous 41 days (see (iii) above) and the 29 days (70 days in total) are not more than $\frac{1}{6}$ of 547 days, D1–R4 becomes a qualifying period.

The position can be summarised as follows.

		Total	*1996/97*	*1997/98*	*Days in UK*	*$\frac{1}{6}$ of total*
Abroad	D1–R1	84	84			
In UK	R1–D2	11	11		11	
Abroad	D2–R2	148	93	55		
D1–R2		243			11	40
In UK	R2–D3	30		30	30	
Abroad	D3–R3	171		171		
D1–R3		444			41	74
In UK	R3–D4	29		29	29	
Abroad	D4–R4	74		74		
D1–R4		547	188	359	70	91

Note

(*a*) D1–R3 is itself a 365-day qualifying period, so the 100% deduction becomes due at this point. However, the qualifying period can be extended by R3–R4, thus enabling further emoluments to qualify. As F then spent three months (i.e. more than 62 days) in the UK, the qualifying period D1–R4 cannot be further extended even if there are subsequent periods of working abroad. No further relief will therefore be available to F.

75.5 **WORK DONE ABROAD — TRAVELLING EXPENSES ETC.**

For travelling expenses generally, see 75.43 below. For certain expenses of MPs, see 29.16 EXEMPT INCOME.

Where the duties of an employment by an employee resident and ordinarily resident in the UK are performed abroad, the following deductions may be made from his emoluments (if not 'foreign emoluments', see 75.6 below).

(i) **Where duties performed wholly outside the UK**

(*a*) Travelling expenses incurred by the employee from any place in the UK to take up the overseas employment and to return on its termination.

(*b*) Board and lodging outside the UK provided or reimbursed by the employer (so far as included in the assessable emoluments) to enable the employee to perform the duties of the overseas employment.

[*ICTA 1988, s 193(2)–(4)*].

(ii) **More than one employment**

Where two or more employments are held and at least one of them is performed wholly or partly outside the UK, and travelling expenses are incurred by the employee in travelling from one place where duties of one employment were performed to another place to perform duties of another, and either or both places are outside the UK, the expenses are deductible from the emoluments of the second employment (if not 'foreign emoluments', see 75.6 below). [*ICTA 1988, s 193(5)(6)*].

Apportionment applies where expenses are partly for performing the duties and partly for another purpose.

(iii) **Where duties are performed partly outside the UK**

Travel facilities, provided or reimbursed by the employer (so far as included in the assessable emoluments), between any place in the UK and the place of performance of any of the duties outside the UK, either

(*a*) for the employee, provided that the duties concerned can only be performed outside the UK, and that the absence from the UK is wholly and exclusively for the purpose of performing the duties concerned, or

(*b*) where there is absence from the UK for a continuous period of 60 days or more, for the spouse and any children under 18 (at beginning of outward journey) accompanying the employee at the beginning of the period of absence or visiting him during that period, including the return journey, but with a limit of two outward and return journeys per person in any year of assessment.

For these purposes, duties performed on a ship or aircraft on a voyage or flight extending to a port outside the UK are not treated under *ICTA 1988, s 132(4)* (see

75.2(ii) above) as performed in the UK, and the requirements as to place of performance of duties are suitably modified.

[*ICTA 1988, s 194*].

For travel on leave by HM Forces, see 75.27 below.

See generally Revenue Pamphlet IR 58.

Simon's Direct Tax Service. See **E4.709**.

75.6 EMPLOYEES OF NON-UK DOMICILE

UK resident employer. A deduction may be allowed from emoluments for duties performed in the UK for the cost of certain travel facilities provided or reimbursed by the employer (so far as included in assessable emoluments) for a period of five years beginning with the date of arrival in the UK to perform the duties of the employment. This applies to facilities provided

(*a*) for any journey between the employee's usual place of abode (i.e. the country outside the UK where he normally lives) and any place in the UK in order to perform, or after performing, any duties of the employment, and

(*b*) where the employee is in the UK for the purpose of performing the duties of any such employment for a continuous period of 60 days or more (ignoring an occasional day's absence abroad on business — see Revenue Schedule E Manual, SE 4712), for any outward and return journey by his spouse or child (under 18 at the beginning of the journey to the UK) between his usual place of abode and the place where any of those duties are performed in the UK, either to accompany him at the beginning of the period or to visit him during it (but limited to two outward and return journeys by any person in a year of assessment).

No deduction is, however, available unless, on a date on which he arrives in the UK to perform the duties, either

(i) he was not resident in the UK in either of the two immediately preceding years of assessment, or

(ii) he was not in the UK for any purpose at any time in the two years ending immediately before that date.

If this condition is satisfied on more than one date in a year of assessment, relief is given by reference to the first such date only. [*ICTA 1988, s 195(1)–(12)*].

Non-UK resident employer. Emoluments of a person not domiciled in the UK from an employer not resident in the UK (other than emoluments of a UK resident from an employer resident in Eire) are '*foreign emoluments*'. [*ICTA 1988, s 192(1)*]. The existence of a branch or agency of an overseas employer does not normally of itself make the overseas employer UK resident for this purpose, even where profits of the branch or agency are liable to UK tax (Tolley's Practical Tax 1983 p 156).

Foreign emoluments are excepted from Case I but remain within Case III where the duties are performed *wholly abroad*. Where the duties are performed *wholly or partly in the UK*, the normal rules apply and they are within Case I, II or III as appropriate (see 75.2 above). [*ICTA 1988, s 192(2)*].

Certain payments made by an employee out of 'foreign emoluments' 'in circumstances corresponding to those in which the payments would have reduced his liability to income tax' may be allowed as a deduction in computing the amount of the emoluments. [*ICTA 1988, s 192(3); F(No 2)A 1992, s 60*]. See Revenue Schedule E Manual, SE 4201–4206.

Travelling expenses. The conditions for relief for travelling expenses described above in relation to employments with UK resident employers apply equally to employments with non-resident employers. [*ICTA 1988, s 195*].

Simon's Direct Tax Service. See **E4.115, E4.709**.

ASSESSABLE INCOME, ALLOWABLE DEDUCTIONS ETC.

Main headings below are in alphabetical order.

75.7 Assessable income generally
75.8 Benefits
75.9 Clergymen etc.
75.10 Deductions generally
75.11 **Directors or higher-paid employees**
75.12 — Expenses
75.13 — Benefits-in-kind generally
75.14 — example
75.15 — Cars
75.16 — Mobile telephones
75.17 — Beneficial loan arrangements
75.18 — example
75.19 — Employee shareholdings
75.20 — Scholarships
75.21 — Sporting and recreational facilities
75.22 — Dispensations
75.23 Employee liabilities and indemnity insurance
75.24 Employment or profession?
75.25 Flat rate expenses for employees
75.26 Gifts, testimonials etc. received
75.27 HM Forces
75.28 Legal
75.29 Living accommodation etc.
75.30 Luncheon vouchers
75.31 Profit-related pay
75.32 Redundancy payments
75.33 Relocation packages
75.34 Restrictive covenants
75.35 Security of employees
75.36 Shares, etc.
75.37 Sick pay and health insurance
75.38 Social security
75.39 Subscriptions
75.40 Taxation
75.41 Termination payments
75.42 Training, counselling etc.
75.43 Travelling, subsistence etc.
75.44 Vouchers and credit-tokens
75.45 Wages in lieu of notice
75.46 Workers supplied by agencies

See also cross-references immediately before 75.1 above.

For treatment of particular occupations, see Revenue Schedule E Manual, SE 7000 *et seq.*. See generally Butterworths Schedule E Compliance Manual.

75.7 ASSESSABLE INCOME GENERALLY

The income assessable as *emoluments* of an office or employment includes 'all salaries, fees, wages, perquisites and profits whatsoever'. [*ICTA 1988, s 131(1)*]. (For other income assessable under Schedule E, see 59 PENSIONS; 83 SOCIAL SECURITY; 19 COMPENSATION FOR LOSS OF EMPLOYMENT (AND DAMAGES) and 82 SHARE INCENTIVES AND OPTIONS.) See 3.10 ANTI-AVOIDANCE regarding capital sums received in lieu of earnings. [*ICTA 1988, s 775*]. The emoluments assessable are those arising from the office or employment, regardless of by whom they are provided (see e.g. *Shilton v Wilmshurst HL 1991, 64 TC 78*).

In general terms, where there is no explicit legislation to the contrary, the assessable income is what comes to the employee in respect of the employment in money or money's worth. For an early and important statement of this, see *Tennant v Smith HL 1892, 3 TC 158*. Where an employee was granted a share option, the emolument was the granting of the option (any subsequent increase in value not being an emolument) (*Abbott v Philbin HL 1960, 39 TC 82*). See, however, *Bootle v Bye; Wilson v Bye (Sp C 61), [1996] SSCD 58*, where payments under an agreement with a third party, and not the rights under the agreement, were held to be emoluments.

Whether 'money's worth' received by an employee comes to him as an emolument may be a difficult question of fact. For modern examples see *Hochstrasser v Mayes HL 1959, 38 TC 673* (compensation for loss on sale of house on transfer, held not assessable); *Wilcock v Eve Ch D 1995, 67 TC 223* (payment for loss of rights under share option scheme, held not assessable), and contrast *Hamblett v Godfrey CA 1986, 59 TC 694* (payment for loss of trade union, etc. rights, held assessable); *Laidler v Perry HL 1965, 42 TC 351; Brumby v Milner HL 1976, 51 TC 583*; *Tyrer v Smart HL 1978, 52 TC 533*. The meeting by the employer of a pecuniary liability of the employee constitutes money's worth, see e.g. *Hartland v Diggines HL 1926, 10 TC 247* (tax liability), *Nicoll v Austin KB 1935, 19 TC 531* (rates, etc. of employee's residence), and *Glynn v CIR PC 1990, 63 TC 162* (payment direct to school of child's school fees); this applies to payment of the employee's community charge (and, in Scotland, community water charge) (Revenue Press Release 10 November 1989) or council tax (Revenue Press Release 16 March 1993), and to payment of parking etc. fines of employees (although certain fixed penalties relating to company cars may be the employer's liability). (Revenue Inspector's Manual, IM 699). For specific items and legislation modifying the general rule, see 75.8 onwards below.

Hence, subject to any special legislation, board, lodging, uniforms, etc. provided by the employer and not convertible into money are not assessable, but cash allowances *in lieu* are generally assessable, e.g. a clothing allowance to a 'plain-clothes' policeman (*Fergusson v Noble CS 1919, 7 TC 176*); a meals allowance when working abnormal hours (*Sanderson v Durbridge Ch D 1955, 36 TC 239*); lodging allowances to army personnel (*Nagley v Spilsbury Ch D 1957, 37 TC 178*); an allowance to meet extra cost of living abroad (*Robinson v Corry CA 1933, 18 TC 411*). Allowances in lieu of uniform to uniformed staff are, however, not treated as emoluments (see Revenue Schedule E Manual, SE 1450). See 75.30 below for luncheon vouchers. See also 29.16 EXEMPT INCOME as regards accommodation allowances for Members of Parliament and 75.29 below as regards living accommodation generally. Where deductions were made from salary for board etc., held gross amount assessable (*Cordy v Gordon KB 1925, 9 TC 304; Machon v McLoughlin CA 1926, 11 TC 83*). Where a higher salary may be taken in lieu of the provision of free board and lodging, the value of the provision is taxable, but see Revenue Pamphlet IR, A60 as regards concessional treatment of agricultural workers. It is understood that a similar concession is applied to stable lads employed by racehorse trainers.

Where an employee used his car in the course of his duties, a lump sum and mileage allowances were held to be emoluments (*Perrons v Spackman Ch D 1981, 55 TC 403*). See 75.43 below as regards mileage allowances and travelling and subsistence allowances generally. 'Garage allowances' to salesmen with company cars were held to be assessable in *Beecham Group Ltd v Fair Ch D 1983, 57 TC 733*, but expenditure on the provision of car (or, for 1999/2000 and subsequent years, cycle or motor cycle) parking facilities for an employee at or near his place of work does not constitute an emolument. [*ICTA 1988, s 197A; FA 1999, s 49*].

Financial loss allowances, or payments for loss of earnings, to members of public bodies, or to magistrates or those on jury service, are not taxable under Schedule E (although when received by the self-employed they are taxable as business receipts, see 71.48(*e*) SCHEDULE D, CASES I AND II). (Revenue Schedule E Manual, SE 1165). For the PAYE treatment of local councillors' attendance allowances, see 55.32 PAY AS YOU EARN.

By concession, cash allowances to miners in lieu of free coal are not assessed. (Revenue Pamphlet IR 1, A6).

Employer's gift of clothing assessable on *second-hand* value (*Wilkins v Rogerson CA 1960, 39 TC 344*), but gift voucher available for use only in specified shop assessable on face value

(*Laidler v Perry HL 1965, 42 TC 351*) but see 75.44 below for legislation now applicable although the case remains an important authority on what constitutes an emolument. Also see *Heaton v Bell HL 1969, 46 TC 211* (assessment on free use of car connected with reduction in wages but see company car legislation at 75.15 below).

Interest on money loaned interest-free, subject to conditions and repayable on demand, by the employer to a trust for the benefit of an employee held to be emoluments within Schedule E (*O'Leary v McKinlay Ch D 1990, 63 TC 729*).

Endowment premiums paid by employers are assessable (*Richardson v Lyon KB 1943, 25 TC 497*). But trustees' payments out of fund set up by employers for assisting education of employees' children held not assessable on parent (*Barclays Bank v Naylor Ch D 1960, 39 TC 256*) but see now educational scholarships under 75.20 below. In *Ball v Johnson Ch D 1971, 47 TC 155*, a discretionary payment to employee for passing an examination was held not assessable (but see Revenue Schedule E Manual, SE 1160, and see also 75.13 below for treatment of such awards as benefits-in-kind). Commission applied in taking up shares held assessable (*Parker v Chapman CA 1927, 13 TC 677*). In *Clayton v Gothorp Ch D 1971, 47 TC 168*, a loan to a former employee for improving qualifications, which became non-repayable when the employee returned to employer's service after qualification, was held assessable for year in which it became non-repayable. Where wages paid in gold sovereigns, held their market value to be taken as the measure of the emoluments (*Jenkins v Horn Ch D 1979, 52 TC 591*).

Whether lump sum payments, etc. on taking up an employment are emoluments of the employment or non-taxable inducements is a question of fact. Signing-on fees to an amateur footballer on joining a Rugby League club were held to be assessable in *Riley v Coglan Ch D 1967, 44 TC 481*, distinguishing *Jarrold v Boustead CA 1964, 41 TC 701*. Before 2 January 1996, however, a fee not exceeding £8,500 paid for surrender of amateur status to a rugby player turning professional was treated as free of tax, although a fee exceeding that figure was taxable in full. (Revenue Schedule E Manual, SE 7423). In *Shilton v Wilmshurst HL 1991, 64 TC 78*, a transfer fee paid by his old club to a professional footballer was taxable as an emolument of his new employment. The value of shares allotted to an accountant on becoming managing director of a company was held not to be assessable in *Pritchard v Arundale Ch D 1971, 47 TC 680*, but an opposite conclusion was reached on the facts in *Glantre Engineering Ltd v Goodhand Ch D 1982, 56 TC 165*. See now 75.34 below. A lump sum payment for giving up rights to trade union representation was assessable (*Hamblett v Godfrey CA 1986, 59 TC 694*).

For the Revenue view of the taxation implications of guaranteed selling price (or similar) schemes for houses as part of employee relocation packages, see Revenue Tax Bulletin May 1994 p 122 and April 1995 p 211.

Simon's Direct Tax Service. See **E4.1**.

75.8 **BENEFITS**

Generally, if an employee receives money or money's worth from his employment he is chargeable to tax on that amount. However, he or his family may receive benefits by reason of his employment where special legislation is required if taxation is to apply. For benefits derived by directors and certain employees from their employment, see 75.11 *et seq.* below. For other benefits of general application, see under the appropriate heading of this chapter. A benefit provided by a third party (e.g. a car provided by a car dealer to a football player for promotional purposes) is potentially within the benefits charging provisions where it is provided by reason of the employment.

See 59.1 pensions as regards the provision of benefits to retired employees.

Certain of the exceptions listed at 75.13 below from the special charge on benefits apply also where a charge would otherwise arise under the general Schedule E provisions. See in particular 75.13(v)–(viii), (x)–(xii), (xxii).

See 55.12 PAY AS YOU EARN as regards PAYE settlement agreements whereby employer accounts for tax on minor benefits, which do not then count as employees' income.

75.9 CLERGYMEN, ETC.

By *ICTA 1988, s 332*, a clergyman is not assessable on any sums paid for or refunded to him in respect of any 'statutory amounts' payable or 'statutory deductions' made in connection with the residence made available to him by a charity or ecclesiastical corporation for carrying out his duties (except in so far as they relate to any part of the premises which he lets). This exemption applied to the meeting of the Scottish community water charge, but not to the personal community charge (Revenue Press Release 10 November 1989). In addition (unless he is in 'director's or higher-paid' employment, see 75.11 below) no account is taken of the value of any expenses relating to his own living accommodation so provided [*ICTA 1988, s 332(2)(c)*], and, by concession, no liability arises in respect of payment or reimbursement of his heating, lighting, cleaning or gardening expenses (Revenue Pamphlet IR 1, A61). Up to one-quarter of the aggregate of any expenses of maintenance, repair, insurance or management of the premises borne by him may be allowed as a deduction from his emoluments.

If he pays rent in respect of a dwelling-house any part of which is used mainly or substantially for his duties, up to one-quarter thereof may be deducted from emoluments, under *ICTA 1988, s 332(3)(b)*. Also, expenses necessarily etc., incurred in performance of duties (e.g. postage, stationery, telephone, car, etc.) may be deducted. Concessionally, regard is had to the cost of *locum tenens* for illness or holidays and (sometimes) lighting, heating, cleaning and rates of study. The expenses of a minister in visiting his congregation were allowed (*Charlton v CIR CS 1890, 27 SLR 647*) but not expenses of a curate in moving from one curacy to another (*Friedson v Glyn-Thomas KB 1922, 8 TC 302*). In *Mitchell v Child KB 1942, 24 TC 511*, cost of opposing a Bill which would have dispossessed rector of parsonage was allowed.

Gifts to a clergyman including voluntary subscriptions and collections (*In re Strong C/E/S 1878, 1 TC 207; Slaney v Starkey KB 1931, 16 TC 45*), Easter offerings (*Cooper v Blakiston HL 1908, 5 TC 347*) and grants (*Herbert v McQuade CA 1902, 4 TC 489; Poynting v Faulkner CA 1905, 5 TC 145*) are assessable but not where in recognition of past service (*Turner v Cuxson QB 1888, 2 TC 422*). The cost of maintenance of a priest living in communal presbytery held not assessable as not convertible into money (*Daly v CIR CS 1934, 18 TC 641*).

An unbeneficed clergyman was held to be within Schedule E (*Slaney v Starkey* above) as was a professed nun employed as a teacher (*Dolan v K Supreme Court (IFS), 2 ITC 280*) but not the headmaster of a school established by a congregation of secular priests (*Reade v Brearley KB 1933, 17 TC 687*).

For the treatment of contemplative religious communities, see Revenue Pamphlet IR 131, B10.

Simon's Direct Tax Service. See **E4.712**.

75.10 DEDUCTIONS GENERALLY

(*a*) **General.** For **1998/99** and subsequent years, a deduction is generally allowed from emoluments assessable under Schedule E for expenses the holder of an office or employment is obliged to incur and defray out of those emoluments which are either 'qualifying travelling expenses' or other amounts expended wholly, exclusively and necessarily in the performance of the duties of the office or employment.

'*Qualifying travelling expenses*' are amounts necessarily expended on travelling in the performance of the duties of the office or employment, or other travel expenses which

(i) are attributable to necessary attendance at any place of the holder of the office or employment in the performance of those duties, and

(ii) are not expenses of either 'ordinary commuting' or 'private travel'.

Expenses of travel between two places at which duties are performed of different offices or employments under or with companies in the same group are treated as necessarily expended in the performance of the duties to be performed at the destination. Companies are members of the same group for this purpose if one is a 51% subsidiary (by reference to ordinary share capital) of the other or both are 51% subsidiaries of a third company.

'*Ordinary commuting*' means travel between home (or a place other than a 'workplace' in relation to the office or employment) and a place which is a 'permanent workplace' in relation to the office or employment. '*Private travel*' means travel between home and a place that is not a 'workplace' in relation to the office or employment, or between two places neither of which is a 'workplace' in relation to the office or employment. Travel which for practical purposes is substantially ordinary commuting or private travel is treated as such.

A '*workplace*' is a place at which attendance is necessary in the performance of the duties of the office or employment. It is a '*permanent workplace*' if it is not a 'temporary workplace' and attendance there in the performance of those duties is regular. Except as below, it is a '*temporary workplace*' if the purpose of attendance there is to perform a task of limited duration or some other temporary purpose.

A workplace is *not* a 'temporary workplace' if attendance there is in the course of a 'period of continuous work' at that place lasting more than 24 months or comprising all (or almost all) of the period for which the office or employment is likely to be held, or if it is reasonable to assume that it will be in the course of such a period. A '*period of continuous work*' at a place is a period over which, looking at the whole period and considering all the duties of the office or employment, those duties fall to be performed to a significant extent at that place. Actual or contemplated modifications of the place at which the duties are performed which do not have any substantial effect on the journey or on the travelling expenses are disregarded.

A place regularly attended in the performance of the duties of the office or employment which forms the base from which those duties are performed, or which is the place at which the tasks to be carried out in the performance of those duties are allocated, is treated as a permanent workplace. Similarly where the duties are defined by reference to an area (whether or not requiring attendance outside the area), and attendance is required at different places in the area (none of them a permanent workplace) in the performance of the duties, then that area is treated as a permanent workplace if it would be so treated (as above) were it a place.

[*ICTA 1988, s 198(1)(1A)(1B), Sch 12A as amended and introduced by FA 1998, s 61, Sch 10*].

For three leading articles explaining the new rules, with numerous examples, see Revenue Tax Bulletin December 1997 pp 477–485, February 1998 pp 497–505 and April 1998 pp 524–527. Revenue Booklet 490 'Employee Travel: A Tax and NICs Guide for Employees' also provides comprehensive guidance, and Pamphlet IR 161 a short guide.

For **1997/98** and earlier years, the deductions allowed are expenses necessarily incurred on travelling in the performance of the duties of the office or employment and any other expenses incurred wholly, exclusively and necessarily in the performance of those duties (and certain other equine expenses). [*ICTA 1988, s 198(1) as originally enacted*].

The requirements that expenditure be incurred 'necessarily' and (other than in the case of expenses within (i) above) 'in the performance of the duties' impose additional restrictions on the allowability of items under Schedule E compared with those generally deductible under Schedule D. 'Necessarily' has been held to require that every holder of the office or employment would have to incur the expenditure, regardless of personal circumstances (see *Ricketts v Colquhoun HL 1925, 10 TC 118*). As regards 'in the performance of the duties', it follows that expenses incurred prior to entering upon duties or merely in preparation for them are not allowed. See *Nolder v Walters KB 1930, 15 TC 380*, air pilot allowed hotel expenses because incurred *in course of duty*, but not car and telephone *merely in preparation for it*, and *Bhadra v Ellam Ch D 1987, 60 TC 466* where a doctor's travelling and secretarial expenses in relation to locum posts obtained through medical agencies were not allowed, as his duties commenced only on arrival at the hospital concerned. But contrast *Pook v Owen HL 1969, 45 TC 571* where a GP with a part-time Schedule E hospital appointment was allowed his expenses of travelling to the hospital from his home (where his surgery was), not covered by his mileage allowance, because, on the facts, his home as well as the hospital was a place where he carried out the duties of his appointment. See also *Gilbert v Hemsley Ch D 1981, 55 TC 419* and 75.43 below generally.

Employees' costs of upkeep, replacement or repair of protective clothing or of uniforms (recognisable as such) are allowable where their duties require them to be worn. (Revenue Schedule E Manual, SE 4122, 4123).

Use of room at home for business purposes allowed (*Newlin v Woods CA 1966, 42 TC 649*) but not alternative room for son's homework (*Roskams v Bennett Ch D 1950, 32 TC 129*) or mortgage interest on loan to purchase property used as office (*Baird v Williams Ch D 1999, 71 TC 390*). No deduction was allowable for any part of the employee's personal community charge liability, but a deduction may be due for a proportion of the council tax payable where a room or rooms are used exclusively for work purposes. (Revenue Press Releases 10 November 1989, 16 March 1993).

Expenses of a part-time Schedule E appointment not allowable under Schedule E may not be deducted in computing the profits of an associated business within Schedule D (*Mitchell & Edon v Ross HL 1961, 40 TC 11*).

(*b*) **Expenses not allowed** include: employment agency fees (*Shortt v McIlgorm KB 1945, 26 TC 262*); meal expenses paid out of meal allowances (*Sanderson v Durbridge Ch D 1955, 36 TC 239*); living expenses paid out of living allowances when working away from home (*Elderkin v Hindmarsh Ch D 1988, 60 TC 651*); headmaster's course to improve background knowledge (*Humbles v Brooks Ch D 1962, 40 TC 500*); articled clerk's examination fees (*Lupton v Potts Ch D 1969, 45 TC 643*); cost of ordinary clothing (*Hillyer v Leeke Ch D 1976, 51 TC 90; Woodcock v CIR Ch D 1977, 51 TC 698; Ward v Dunn Ch D 1978, 52 TC 517*); rental of telephone installed at employer's behest, but not used *wholly* and *exclusively* in performance of duties (*Lucas v Cattell Ch D 1972, 48 TC 353*); telephone and other expenses of consultant anaesthetist (*Hamerton v Overy Ch D 1954, 35 TC 73*); and journalists' expenditure on newspapers and periodicals (*Fitzpatrick and Others v CIR, Smith v Shuttleworth and Others HL 1994, 66 TC 407*).

Any excess cost of living in place where required by work (*Bola v Barlow KB 1949, 31 TC 136; Collis v Hore (No 1) KB 1949, 31 TC 173; Robinson v Corry CA 1933, 18 TC 411*); cost of domestic assistance where wife employed (*Bowers v Harding QB 1891, 3 TC 22*); cost of looking after widower's children (*Halstead v Condon Ch D 1970, 46 TC 289*). Entertaining expenses are not allowed [*ICTA 1988, s 577*], but see 71.55 SCHEDULE D, CASES I AND II for exceptions. However where an employer is not allowed a deduction for expenditure on business entertainment paid by him, directly or indirectly, to a member of his staff, and that sum is also taxable as emoluments of the employee (see 75.12 below) the employee is allowed an equivalent deduction from taxable emoluments for expenses defrayed out of that sum. [*ICTA 1988, s 577(3)*].

(*c*) For travelling, subsistence and incidental overnight expenses etc., see 75.43 below, and for other specific deductions, see below at 75.25 (flat rate expenses), 75.39 (subscriptions) and 75.42 (training, etc.).

(*d*) For provision of security assets and services for employees, see 75.35 below.

(*e*) For capital allowances where plant or machinery is provided for the purposes of an employment, see 10.24 CAPITAL ALLOWANCES. See also 75.43 below.

(*f*) For expenditure by Members of Parliament on accommodation, see 75.29 below.

(*g*) For charitable donation payroll deduction scheme, see 15.18 CHARITIES.

(*h*) For deduction of agents' fees by artistes, see 75.24 below.

(*j*) For expenditure on indemnity insurance and on certain liabilities such as legal costs in relation to the employment, see 75.23 below.

Simon's Direct Tax Service. See **E4.7**.

75.11 DIRECTORS OR HIGHER-PAID EMPLOYEES

(*Note.* The term 'higher-paid employee' was replaced by a reference to employment with emoluments at the rate of £8,500 p.a. or more by *FA 1989, s 53.* No alteration to the import of the benefits legislation results from the change, and the term 'higher-paid employee' is for convenience retained in the coverage of that legislation in this section.)

The provisions of *ICTA 1988, ss 153–168* apply to

(I) every director, except if he has no material interest (i.e. broadly if his and/or his associates' interests in the company do not exceed 5%) in the company *and either* is a full-time working director *or* the company is non-profit-making (i.e. it does not carry on a trade nor is its main function the holding of investments or other property) *or* the company is a charity,

(II) any person with emoluments at the rate of £8,500 a year or more including all chargeable benefits etc. (together with certain amounts otherwise covered by the special car benefit rules, and a modified amount in respect of certain beneficial home loans) before any deduction for necessary expenses of employment etc., but after deducting any contributions to approved superannuation funds in respect of which the individual is entitled to tax relief as an expense (see 66.5(*a*) RETIREMENT SCHEMES), any exempt profit-related pay (see 75.31 below) and any contributions under an approved payroll giving scheme (see 15.18 CHARITIES). For 1995/96 onwards, where an alternative is offered to a company car such that if it had been chargeable under general Schedule E rules the taxable amount would have exceeded the car and fuel benefits computed as in 75.15(i)(iv) below, the excess is taken into account in ascertaining emoluments for this purpose. All employments with the same employer are treated as director's or higher-paid if (i) the total of emoluments from those employments is at the rate of £8,500 a year or more or (ii) one or more of those employments is director's or higher-paid. An individual, partnership or body is deemed to be the employer where he or it controls the employing partnership or body. [*ICTA 1988, ss 167, 168(8)–(12); FA 1991, Sch 6 para 2; FA 1993, Sch 6 para 1; FA 1995, s 43(3)(4)*]. Where the rate of emoluments varies during a tax year throughout which an employment continues, it is the total emoluments for the year which are considered — the Revenue will not seek to split the year into those months where the £8,500 limit is exceeded and those where it is not. (Revenue Schedule E Manual, SE 3015).

A person under (I) or (II) above will be assessable under Schedule E on payments and benefits (so far as not refunded or paid for by him) received *and not otherwise taxable*, but may claim relief under *ICTA 1988, s 198* (expenses 'wholly and necessarily incurred', see 75.10 above), *ICTA 1988, s 201* (see Subscriptions at 75.39 below), *ICTA 1988, s 201AA* (see Employee liabilities and indemnity insurance at 75.23 below) and *ICTA 1988, s 332(3)* (see Clergymen at 75.9 above).

No amount will be assessable where a payment or provision is made by an employer, being an individual, in the normal course of his domestic, family or personal relationships. [*ICTA 1988, ss 153, 154, 168(3); FA 1995, s 91(2); FA 1996, s 134, Sch 20 para 10(1)*].

See 75.22 below for dispensations.

A director excluded from (I), e.g. by working for a charity, may nevertheless be within (II), e.g. if his emoluments exceed the prescribed amount.

Detailed application of the provisions is covered in 75.12–75.22 below.

Simon's Direct Tax Service. See **E4.6**.

75.12 **Expenses.** All payments for expenses, including sums put at employee's disposal and paid away by him, are assessable. [*ICTA 1988, s 153*]. Includes use of employer's credit card. See also the exceptions at 75.13 below. See 55.12 PAY AS YOU EARN as regards PAYE settlement agreements whereby employer accounts for tax on minor payments of expenses within the agreement, which do not then count as employees' income.

75.13 **Benefits-in-kind generally.** All benefits provided (including to employee's family or household) of accommodation (other than living accommodation, for which see 75.29 below), entertainment, domestic or other services and other benefits and facilities whatsoever are assessable. See 75.15–75.20 for special charging provisions. The amount to be assessed is the cash equivalent of the benefit (see below). Included are benefits provided by reason of an employment by someone other than the employer. [*ICTA 1988, ss 154, 155(1)*]. The Treasury does, however, have powers to exempt minor benefits by order, such exemption being conditional on the benefit(s) in question being made available to the employer's employees generally on similar terms (and it is understood that welfare counselling will be exempted under such regulations). [*ICTA 1988, s 155ZB; FA 2000, s 57, Sch 10 para 3*].

In relation to the timing of a benefit, 'provided' refers to the receipt by the employee of the benefit, rather than to steps taken or costs incurred by the employer (*Templeton v Jacobs Ch D 1996, 68 TC 735*).

See 59.1 PENSIONS as regards benefits provided to retired employees.

Following the decision in *Wicks v Firth HL 1982, 56 TC 318*, payments of cash are potentially within the benefits legislation, so that for example examination awards which would otherwise not be taxable following *Ball v Johnson* (see 75.7 above) fall within the benefits charge. (ICAEW Technical Memorandum TR 786, 15 March 1990).

Legal expenses incurred by a company in defending a dangerous driving charge against a director were held to be a benefit (*Rendell v Went HL 1964, 41 TC 641*). Parking, etc. fines met by employer would generally constitute a benefit (see 75.7 above).

Exceptions.

(i) (From 6 April 2000) provision of accommodation, supplies or services used by the employee in performing the duties of the employment, provided that either:

(A) if the benefit is provided on premises occupied by the employer or other person providing it, any private use (i.e. use other than in performing those duties) by the employee (or by the employee's family or household) is not significant; or

(B) in any other case, the sole purpose of providing the benefit is to enable the employee to perform those duties, any private use (as in (A)) is not significant, and the benefit is not an 'excluded benefit'.

Subject to Treasury regulations (which may provide that a benefit is an 'excluded benefit' only if prescribed conditions are met as to the terms on which, and persons to whom, it is provided), '*excluded benefit*' consists of the provision of a motor vehicle, boat or aircraft, or of a benefit which involves the extension, conversion or alteration of any living accommodation or the construction, extension, conversion or alteration of a building or other structure on land adjacent to and enjoyed with living accommodation.

[*ICTA 1988, s 155ZA; FA 2000, s 57, Sch 10 para 2*].

Before 6 April 2000, the exemption applied only to the provision, in premises occupied by the employer or other person providing it, of accommodation, supplies or services used by the employee solely in performing duties of the employment. [*ICTA 1988, s 155(2); FA 2000, Sch 40 Pt II(2)*].

(ii) Provision of living accommodation and connected expenses in certain circumstances, see 75.29 below. [*ICTA 1988, ss 154(2), 155(3), 163*].

(iii) Provision of any pension, annuity, lump sum, gratuity or other like benefit to employee or his dependants to be given on his death or retirement. (But see under 66.1 RETIREMENT SCHEMES.) [*ICTA 1988, s 155(4)*]. This is extended by concession to include provision of death or retirement benefits to any member of the employee's family or household, e.g. including a parent or a son- or daughter-in-law. (Revenue Pamphlet IR 1, A72).

(iv) Provision of meals in any canteen in which meals are provided for staff generally. [*ICTA 1988, s 155(5)*]. Relief is extended by concession to all free or subsidised meals provided on the business premises, and to the use of any ticket or token to obtain such meals, if meals are provided on a reasonable scale and either free or subsidised meals are available on a reasonable scale to all employees, whether on the business premises or elsewhere, or free or subsidised meal vouchers are provided for staff for whom meals are not provided. The concession applies to light refreshments as it does to meals. It does not extend to provision in a hotel or catering, etc. business of staff meals in a restaurant or dining-room at a time when meals are being served to the public, unless part of it is designated for staff use only. (Revenue Pamphlet IR 1, A74; Revenue Press Release 19 November 1999).

(v) Provision of travel, accommodation and subsistence during public transport disruption caused by industrial action. (Revenue Pamphlet IR 1, A58). See also 75.43 below.

(vi) Provision of transport between home and place of employment (or training) for disabled employees. (Revenue Pamphlet IR 1, A59 as revised; Revenue Press Release 28 June 2000). See also 75.15, 75.43 below.

(vii) Provision of transport for occasional late night journeys from work to home, or following a failure of car-sharing arrangements, subject to certain conditions. (Revenue Pamphlet IR 1, A66 as revised; Revenue Press Release 9 March 1999). See also 75.43 below.

(viii) Provision of transport between mainland and offshore rig, etc., and necessary overnight accommodation on the mainland, for offshore oil and gas workers. (Revenue Pamphlet IR 1, A65).

(ix) Travelling expenses (including reasonable hotel expenses) of

(A) a director of two or more companies within a group of companies, between his main place where he acts as director and other places within the UK in the course of his duties as a director. Similarly where a person is a director of one company and an employee of another company in the same group;

(B) an unremunerated director of a company not managed with a view to dividends (e.g. a club);

(C) a director who holds the position as part of a professional practice, provided no claim is made to a deduction under Schedule D;

(D) a spouse accompanying a director on his or her duties abroad because of his or her precarious health.

(Revenue Pamphlet IR 1, A4). See also 75.43 below.

(x) Removal expenses. For the statutory relief from charge under Schedule E of certain payments and benefits received in connection with job-related residential moves, see 75.33 below. Before 6 April 1993, a concessionary relief applied in relation to removal expenses (see Revenue Schedule E Manual, SE 1230 *et seq.*).

For the Revenue view of the taxation implications of guaranteed selling price (or similar) schemes for houses as part of employee relocation packages, see Revenue Tax Bulletin May 1994 p 122 and, in relation in particular to the application of the concession at (xxi) below, April 1995 p 211.

(xi) Miners' free coal and allowances in lieu thereof. (Revenue Pamphlet IR 1, A6).

(xii) Luncheon vouchers. See 75.30 below.

(xiii) Medical insurance for treatment and medical services where the need for treatment arises while abroad in performance of duties. [*ICTA 1988, s 155(6)*].

(xiv) Car parking facilities. No benefit arises from the provision for the employee of a car (or, for 1999/2000 and subsequent years, a cycle or motor cycle) parking space at or near his place of work. [*ICTA 1988, s 155(1A); FA 1999, s 49*]. See also 75.7 above, 75.44 below.

(xv) Entertainment by third parties. No benefit arises from the provision of entertainment for the employee (or for his family or household), unless it is provided either

(*a*) in recognition or anticipation of particular services by the employee in the course of the employment, or

(*b*) directly or indirectly by the employer or by any person connected with the employer (within *ICTA 1988, s 839*, see 20 CONNECTED PERSONS).

[*ICTA 1988, s 155(7)*].

'Entertainment' covers any form of hospitality (dinners, parties, hospitality tents at sporting events, etc.) and events such as theatrical performances or sporting events where a host invites someone to accompany him as a guest. It includes associated costs, such as transport or overnight accommodation. (Revenue Schedule E Manual, SE 3271).

See also 75.44 below and, as regards concessionary relief in respect of gifts from third parties, 75.26 below.

(xvi) Christmas parties, etc. The Revenue will not seek tax on modest expenditure on an annual Christmas party or similar annual function open to the staff generally. Expenditure of up to £75 (£50 for 1994/95 and earlier years) per head per annum, including VAT and any transport or accommodation costs, will be regarded as modest, and where expenditure exceeds this amount the full amount will be taxable. The total cost is for this purpose divided by the total number of people attending the function to determine whether the limit is exceeded. For 1995/96 and subsequent years, the expenditure may be split between more than one annual event, and where the total expenditure for the year exceeds the £75 limit, a function or functions whose cost or the sum of whose costs is within the limit will not be taxed, the cost of the remaining functions being taxed in full. Casual hospitality is not regarded as constituting an annual function for these purposes. No P11D return (see 55.9 PAY AS YOU EARN) is required in respect of expenditure not exceeding the limit. (Revenue Pamphlet IR 1, A70).

(xvii) Child care facilities. No benefit arises from the provision of care for a child to the extent that

(*a*) either the employee has parental responsibility (within *Children Act 1989, s 3(1)*) for the child or the child is resident with or (being a child or step child of the employee) maintained by the employee,

(*b*) the care is provided other than on premises wholly or mainly used as a private dwelling,

(*c*) the care is provided either on premises made available by the employer alone or under arrangements made by persons who include the employer, on premises made available by one or more of them, with the employer being 'wholly or partly responsible for financing and managing the provision of the care' (for the Revenue interpretation of which expression see Revenue Tax Bulletin April 1998 pp 531-533), and

(*d*) the premises or the person providing the care are registered if so required under *Nurseries and Child-Minders Regulation Act 1948, s 1* (or NI equivalent) or *Children Act 1989, s 71*.

'Care' means any form of care or supervised activity, whether or not provided on a regular basis, other than supervised activity provided primarily for educational purposes. 'Child' means a person under 18.

[*ICTA 1988, s 155A; FA 1990, s 21*].

(xviii) Certain training and counselling expenses, see 75.42 below.

(xix) It is understood that the provision of driver training courses for employees will not be taxed as a benefit.

(xx) Medical check-ups. The provision of routine health checks or medical screening for employees does not confer a chargeable benefit, whether carried out by the employer's own medical staff or by an outside firm. (Revenue Tax Bulletin May 1993 p 74). This applies also to such provision for members of the employee's family or household. (Revenue Schedule E Manual, SE 3216).

(xxi) Asset acquisition costs. Normal purchaser's costs in relation to the sale or transfer of an asset by the employee to the employer (or to some other person by reason of the employment) are by concession disregarded in calculating any benefit arising to the employee. (Revenue Pamphlet IR 1, A85). See Revenue Tax Bulletin April 1995 p 210 as regards the application of this concession in relation to guaranteed selling price (or similar) schemes for houses as part of employee relocation packages (and see (x) above).

(xxii) Incidental overnight expenses. For 1995/96 and subsequent years, a benefit is exempt from tax where its provision is incidental to the employee's being away from home on business during a 'qualifying absence' in relation to which the authorised maximum (£5 per night spent in the UK and £10 per night spent abroad) is not exceeded, being a benefit the cost of which is not otherwise deductible from emoluments. [*ICTA 1988, s 155(1B)(1C); FA 1995, s 93(3)*]. See also 75.43 below.

(xxiii) Mobile telephones. For 1999/2000 and subsequent years, no benefit arises from the making available (without any transfer of property) of a 'mobile telephone' to an employee (or to his family or household). This exemption replaces the flat rate charge applicable for earlier years (see 75.16 below).

A '*mobile telephone*' is defined to include provision in connection with a car, van or heavier commercial vehicle, whether or not a company car etc., but to exclude cordless extensions to fixed telephones and certain short-range radio apparatus.

[*ICTA 1988, s 155AA; FA 1999, s 44*].

(xxiv) Computer equipment. For 1999/2000 and subsequent years, the making available (without any transfer of property) of certain computer equipment to an employee (or to his family or household) gives rise to a benefits charge only to the extent that the aggregate cash equivalent of the benefit exceeds £500 for a year of assessment. For example, the provision of the use of £2,000 of equipment (at 20% cash equivalent) plus £100 of related expenses, or the provision of equipment rented at an annual rental of £500, would be within the exemption. The arrangements by the employer for providing employees with computer equipment must not be limited to directors, and must not make more favourable provision in relation to any director(s).

'Computer equipment' includes printers, scanners, modems, discs and other peripheral devices designed to be used with a computer, and the provision of a right to use software together with the provision of hardware is included (but not provision of access to, or use of, any public telecommunications system (within *Telecommunications Act 1984*)).

[*ICTA 1988, s 156A; FA 1999, s 45*].

(xxv) Bus services. For 1999/2000 and subsequent years, two exemptions apply in relation to bus services for employees.

(*a*) No benefit arises from the provision for employees of a '*works bus service*', i.e. a service provided by means of a bus carrying at least 12 passengers conveying employees of one or more employers on 'qualifying journeys'. A '*qualifying journey*' for an employee is a journey between home and workplace (i.e. a place at which the employee's attendance is necessary in performance of the duties of the employment) or thereabouts (see Hansard Standing Committee B, 25 May 1999), or between workplaces, in connection with the performance of those duties. The service must be available generally to employees of the employer(s) concerned, and the main use must be for qualifying journeys by those employees. The service must also substantially be used only by those employees or their children aged under 18 (including step- and illegitimate children). Provision of a voucher for use of such a service is similarly exempt from charge under *ICTA 1988, s 141* (non-cash vouchers, see 75.44(*a*) below).

(*b*) No benefit arises in respect of financial or other support for a public passenger transport service provided by means of a road vehicle used by employees of one or more employers for 'qualifying journeys' (as under (*a*) above). The service must be available generally to employees of the employer(s) concerned on terms no more favourable than those available to other passengers.

[*ICTA 1988, ss 197AA, 197AB; FA 1999, s 48*].

(xxvi) Cycles and cyclists' safety equipment. For 1999/2000 and subsequent years, no benefit arises from the provision (without any transfer of property) for an employee of a cycle or cyclist's safety equipment, provided that

(*a*) the facility is available generally to employees of the employer concerned, and

(*b*) the employee uses the cycle or equipment mainly for 'qualifying journeys' (as under (xxv)(*a*) above). Employers are not, however, expected to monitor employees' other cycling journeys (see Hansard Standing Committee B, 25 May 1999).

Provision of a voucher for use of a cycle or safety equipment is similarly exempt from charge under *ICTA 1988, s 141* (non-cash vouchers, see 75.44(*a*) below).

See also (xiv) above, 75.7 above and 75.44(*a*)(*d*) below as regards cycle parking facilities at work places.

[*ICTA 1988, s 197AC; FA 1999, s 50(1)(3)*].

(xxvii) Following the bringing of benefits in kind within the Class 1A charge to national insurance contributions, it is proposed to exempt from tax and NICs minor benefits arising from the private use of items (such as tools) provided by the employer for use in the workplace, and from the provision for all employees of welfare counselling services. (Revenue Press Release 19 November 1999).

See 75.35 below as regards provision of security assets and services for employees.

See 55.12 PAY AS YOU EARN as regards PAYE settlement agreements whereby employer accounts for tax on minor benefits within the agreement, which do not then count as employees' income.

Cash equivalent of the benefit is the cost (including a proper proportion of any expense relating partly to the benefit and partly otherwise) less any part made good by the employee to those providing the benefit. [*ICTA 1988, s 156(1)(2)*]. VAT is included whether or not recoverable by the employer. (Revenue Pamphlet IR 131, A7). The cost of 'in-house' benefits (i.e. those consisting of services or facilities enjoyed by the employee which it is part of the employer's business to provide to members of the public) is the additional or marginal cost of their provision to the employee, rather than a proportionate part of total costs incurred in their provision both to employees and to the public. See *Pepper v Hart HL 1992, 65 TC 421*, in which only the marginal cost of providing school places for the children of masters at the school was assessable, regardless of whether or not the children occupied places which would otherwise have been provided to members of the public. (*Note.* This decision was based on consideration of statements by the Financial Secretary to the Treasury in Standing Committee debates on the enacting legislation. See 4.7 APPEALS as regards the circumstances in which this is permissible.) For how the Revenue proposed to deal with repayments etc. arising from this decision, see Revenue Press Release 21 January

1993, which also offers the Revenue's view of how the marginal cost rule should apply in practice. In particular, nil or negligible cost arises in the case of:

(i) rail or bus travel by employees (provided fare-payers are not displaced);

(ii) goods sold to employees for not less than the wholesale price; and

(iii) provision of professional services not requiring additional staffing (excluding disbursements).

It is accepted that no additional benefit arises where teachers pay 15% or more of normal school fees.

The decision also affects the calculation of the benefit of the provision of assets for part business, part private use. Fixed costs need not now be taken into account where the private use is incidental to the business use. The cash equivalent is the proper proportion of the 'annual value' of the asset (see below) together with any *additional* running expenses.

(Revenue Press Release 21 January 1993).

See 75.44(*a*) below as regards valuation of incentive awards.

Where the benefit is the *use of an asset* other than a car or (from 1993/94) a van (as to which see 75.15 below), the cash equivalent is the annual value (or if higher, the rent or hire charge paid by those providing the benefit) plus any expenses related to the asset's provision (excluding the cost of acquiring or producing it and excluding also any rent or hire charge payable for the asset by those providing the benefit). [*ICTA 1988, s 156(5)(7)*].

Where the benefit is the transfer of an asset after it has been used or depreciated since the transferor acquired it, the cost of the benefit is the market value at the time of the transfer. However, if the asset (not a car or van) was first applied for the provision of any benefit for a person or for members of his family or household by reason of his employment after 5 April 1980 and a person (whether or not the present transferee) has been chargeable to tax on its use, the cost of the benefit (unless a higher benefit is obtained by taking market value at the time of transfer) is its market value when it was first so applied less the total amounts charged to tax for its use in the years up to and including the year of transfer. [*ICTA 1988, s 156(3)(4)*].

Annual value of the use of an asset is:

for land, its annual value under *ICTA 1988, s 837*, see 68.7(*e*) SCHEDULE A;

for any other case, 20% of market value at time asset was first provided as a benefit. [*ICTA 1988, s 156(6)*].

In practice, where an asset is not available for the whole of a year of assessment, only a corresponding proportion of the annual value is brought in as the cost of the benefit (see Revenue Schedule E Manual, SE 3140).

Simon's Direct Tax Service. See **E4.611** *et seq.*.

75.14 *Example*

During 2000/01 P Ltd transferred to R a television set which it had previously leased to him for a nominal rent of £2 per month. The company also leased a suit to R under the same arrangements. R's salary is £30,000 p.a..

Television

First leased to R in April 1999 (when its market value was £560); transferred to R on 6 March 2001 for £50, the market value at that time being £175.

	£	£
R's benefits are		
1999/2000		
Cost of benefit 20% × £560		112
Deduct Rent paid by R		24
Cash equivalent of benefit		£88
2000/01		
Cost of benefit 20% × £560 × $\frac{11}{12}$		103
Deduct Rent paid by R (11 months)		22
Cash equivalent of benefit		81
Greater of		
(i) Market value at transfer	175	
Deduct Price paid by R	50	
	£125	
and		
(ii) Original market value	560	
Deduct Cost of benefits note (*b*)	215	
	345	
Deduct Price paid by R	50	
	£295	
		295
Total		£376

Suit

First leased to R on 6 November 2000 (when its market value was £340).

R's benefit for 2000/01 is	
Cost of benefit 20% × £340 × $\frac{5}{12}$	28
Deduct Rent paid by R (5 months)	10
Cash equivalent of benefit	£18

Notes

(*a*) Although there is no statutory provision for time apportionment where an asset is not available for the whole of a year of assessment (as in the case of cars made available for private use), in practice only a corresponding proportion of the annual value is brought in as the cost of the benefit (see Revenue Schedule E Manual, SE 3140).

(*b*) On the transfer of the television set, the cost of the benefits to date (£112 + 103), not the cash equivalents, is deducted from the original market value.

(*c*) It is assumed that the television set and suit have been bought by P Ltd and are not goods provided from within its own business. If the latter was the case, R would be assessed on the marginal cost to P Ltd in providing the benefit (in accordance with *Pepper v Hart* — see 75.13 above).

75.15 **Motor vehicles provided for private use.** The provision by an employer of a car or van partly or wholly for 'private use' by an employee (or a member of his family or household), without the transfer of any property in it, is the subject of a special basis of charge. '*Private use*' means any use for travel other than that for which a deduction is allowed under *ICTA 1988, s 198* (see 75.10 above), and a car or van is deemed to be available for private use unless the terms on which it is made available prohibit such use *and* there was no such use. [*ICTA 1988, s 157(1), s 159AA(1), s 168(5)(5A)(6); FA 1993, Sch 4 paras 4, 6; FA 1996, s 134, Sch 20 para 10(2); FA 1997, s 62(4)*]. See 75.43 below as regards business use where more than one place of work. See also *Gilbert v Hemsley Ch D 1981, 55 TC 419*. Where a car salesman or demonstrator has to take a car home as part of his normal duties in order to call on a prospective customer, this will not of itself make the car available for his private use. The use of test or experimental cars by engineers in the motor and components industries will be considered on the facts of each particular case. (Revenue Booklet 480). See also Revenue Schedule E Manual, SE 3470.

A car provided by a third party (e.g. by a car dealer to a football player for promotional purposes) is within these provisions where it is provided by reason of the employment. (Revenue Schedule E Manual, SE 3413).

Where such a special basis of charge applies, no other charge arises in respect of any expenses or reimbursements etc. in relation to the vehicle. It appears that this would not normally apply to the payment of fines etc. by the employer (although certain parking fines may be the liability of the employer, see 75.7 above). The provision of a driver is a separate benefit under 75.13 above (subject to an expense claim for business use). [*ICTA 1988, s 154(2), s 155(1), s 157(3), s 159AA(3); FA 1993, Sch 4 paras 2–4*]. See 75.16 below for flat rate charge on mobile telephones for 1998/99 and earlier years, and 75.13(xxiii) above for the general exemption of the provision of mobile telephones thereafter. The provision of a personalised registration number does not enter into the computation under the special basis of charge, whether under (i) or (ii) below, and is normally excluded from charge as above. (Revenue Tax Bulletin December 1994 p 177). The provision of a benefit which could equally be enjoyed by the employee when using a car of his own (e.g. a season ticket for a toll bridge) is not excluded from charge. (Revenue Schedule E Manual, SE 3404).

For 1995/96 and subsequent years, the mere fact that an employee is offered an alternative (for example, a cash alternative) to a company car does not make the benefit chargeable under the general Schedule E rules as opposed to the special company car provisions. [*ICTA 1988, s 157A; FA 1995, s 43(1)(4)*]. Previously, the benefit *was* so chargeable where use of a company car was freely exchangeable for cash (see *Heaton v Bell HL 1969, 46 TC 211*). The new rule is aimed principally at avoidance of national insurance contributions (see Revenue Press Release 21 July 1994).

A car is any mechanically propelled road vehicle *except* (i) a vehicle constructed primarily for carrying goods, (ii) a vehicle of a type unsuitable and not commonly used as a private vehicle, (iii) a motor cycle and (iv) an invalid carriage. [*ICTA 1988, s 168(5)(a)*]. A car owned by the fire brigade and equipped with a flashing light and other emergency equipment was held to be within (ii) (*Gurney v Richards Ch D 1989, 62 TC 287*).

A van is a mechanically propelled road vehicle, other than a motor cycle, of a construction primarily suited for the conveyance of goods or burden and designed (or adapted) not to exceed a laden weight of 3,500 kgs. in normal use. [*ICTA 1988, s 168(5A)(a)(e); FA 1993, Sch 4 para 6*].

Excluded from charge, by concession, is any specially adapted vehicle provided for a disabled employee provided that private use is prohibited and no such use is made other than for the employee's travel from home to work (and, if the vehicle is available for private use, such travel is treated as business use). (Revenue Pamphlet IR 1, A59 (revised by Revenue Press Release 28 June 2000) and Booklet 480). See also 75.13(vi) above, 75.43 below. This concession also exempts a severely and permanently disabled employee from the fuel scale charge (see (iv) below) if the only private fuel supplied by the employer relates to home-to-work mileage (regardless of whether the conditions for the car scale charge exemption are met). (Revenue Schedule E Manual, SE 3465).

The provision of parking facilities for an employee at or near his place of work (including such provision in relation to a privately-owned vehicle) constitutes neither an emolument nor a benefit. [*ICTA 1988, s 155(1A); FA 1988, s 46*].

Where two members of the same family are each supplied with a car for their private use by the same employer, and each is in director's or higher-paid employment, each will be charged separately according to his/her own usage but, by concession, will not be charged in respect of the car supplied to the other. Similarly, if one of them is not in such employment, but is supplied with the car in his/her own right either in equivalent circumstances to other employees in similar employment or in accordance with normal commercial practice for a job of that kind, the other will not be charged in respect of the car supplied to the lower-paid employee. Where two or more persons are chargeable in respect of their shared use of the same car, a single charge will be apportioned between them. (Revenue Pamphlet IR 1, A71).

Compensation to an employee from whom a company car was withdrawn following a change of policy by the employer was held to be an assessable emolument in *Bird v Martland; Bird v Allen Ch D 1982, 56 TC 89.*

Where the special basis of charge applies to provision of a car, a separate charge also arises in respect of provision of any fuel for private use (see (iv) below). In the case of provision of a van, no separate charge arises on provision of fuel.

Simon's Direct Tax Service. See **E4.614**.

(i) *Cars for private use: 1994/95 to 2001/02.* For 1994/95 to 2001/02 inclusive, the cash equivalent of the benefit of provision of a company car for private use is **35%** of the 'price of the car as regards a year'. Where the employee is required by the nature of his employment to use, and does use, the car for at least 18,000 miles of business travel in a year, this is reduced to **15%** for 1999/2000 and subsequent years (for 1998/99 and earlier years, by two-thirds, i.e. to $11\frac{2}{3}$%). Where such use amounts to at least 2,500 but less than 18,000 business miles, the reduction is to **25%** for 1999/2000 and subsequent years (for 1998/99 and earlier years, by one-third, i.e. to $23\frac{1}{3}$%). Where an employee is taxable in respect of the benefit of the provision of two or more cars available concurrently, for all such cars other than the one used to the greatest extent for business travel in the period of concurrent availability the reduction for 18,000 or more business miles is to **25%** instead of 15% for 1999/2000 and subsequent years (by one-third to $23\frac{1}{3}$% instead of by two-thirds to $11\frac{2}{3}$% for 1998/99 and earlier years), and no reduction is made where business miles are less than 18,000. The figures of 2,500 and 18,000 are reduced *pro rata* where the car is 'unavailable' for part of the year. Where there is a change in the vehicle provided during a year of assessment, they are similarly reduced *pro rata* and applied to the period for which each vehicle was provided (*Henwood v Clarke Ch D 1997, 69 TC 611*).

The cash equivalent is reduced, or further reduced, by one-quarter (one-third for 1998/99 and earlier years) where the car is four or more years old at the end of the year of assessment in question. It is similarly reduced *pro rata* where the car is 'unavailable' for part of the year.

Where the employee is required, as a condition of the car being available for private use, to pay for that use, the cash equivalent determined as above for a year is reduced (or extinguished) by the amount so paid in respect of the year. No reduction was allowed for a payment made to the employer to obtain a better car (*Brown v Ware (Sp C 29) [1995] SSCD 155*) or for a payment made for the insurance of the car for both private and business use (*CIR v Quigley CS, [1995] STC 931*).

A car is '*unavailable*' on a day falling before the first day on which it is made available to the employee (or a member of his family or household) or after the last day on which it is made so available, or on a day falling within a period of 30 or more consecutive days throughout which it is not so available. See below as regards regulations modifying these provisions in cases where a replacement car is provided during a period in which the car normally available to an employee is not so available for a period of less than 30 days.

The '*price of a car as regards a year*' is its 'list price' (or its 'notional price' if it has no list price) on the '*relevant day*', i.e. the day immediately before the date on which the car was first registered under the *Vehicle Excise and Registration Act 1994* or corresponding legislation, plus the price of certain accessories and net of certain capital contributions, and the age of a car commences with the date of its first registration. For 1998/99 and subsequent years, in the case of a car manufactured so as to be capable of running on 'road fuel gas' (as defined), e.g. LPG, the price as so determined is reduced by so much of it as is reasonably attributable to the car's being manufactured to be so capable rather than only being capable of running on petrol.

The '*list price*' of a car is the price published by the manufacturer, importer or distributor (as the case may be) as the inclusive price (including delivery charges and taxes, but not vehicle excise duty) appropriate for a car of that kind (including any standard accessories) sold in the UK singly in an open market retail sale, plus the price so published (including any fitting charges) of any optional accessories with the car when it was first made available to the employee (or to a member of his family or household). The price advertised by a car dealer cannot be used instead of that published by the manufacturer, etc. (see Revenue Tax Bulletin December 1994 p 177). If no such price is available for an optional accessory, no adjustment is made to the list price in respect of the accessory (which may, however, be the subject of a separate addition, see below). The accessories taken into account for these purposes are those attached to the car (whether or not permanently) for use with the car (without any transfer of the property) and not necessarily provided for use in the performance of the employee's duties. The following are excluded from being taken into account as accessories for this purpose:

(*a*) mobile telephones (see 75.13(xxiii) above and 75.16 below);

(*b*) (for 1995/96 onwards) equipment either designed solely for use by a chronically sick or disabled person or made available to enable an employee holding, at the time the car is first made available to him, a disabled person's badge (an 'orange badge') to use the car in spite of the disability which entitles him to hold that badge at that time; and

(*c*) (for 1998/99 onwards) equipment by means of which the car is capable of running on 'road fuel gas' (as defined), e.g. LPG (and see above as regards cars manufactured with that capability).

The charge is based on the list price of an individual car at the time it is first registered, not on average prices. However, where there are very frequent changes of car, inspectors may agree to arrangements under which average prices are used (see Revenue Schedule E Manual, SE 3471 *et seq.*).

The '*notional price*' of a car is that which might reasonably be expected to have been its list price (as above) (including accessories) had such a price been published.

There is, however, an overall limit of **£80,000** (or such greater sum as the Treasury may specify by order) on the price, whether list or notional, after taking account of accessories (as below), to be taken into account under these provisions.

Optional accessories not having a list price and hence not taken into account as above, are the subject of a separate addition to the price of the car equal to their price delivered and fitted (list or notional, as above, as appropriate). A separate addition is similarly made where such accessories are fitted after the car is first made available to the employee (or to a member of his family or household), but ignoring for this purpose any accessory whose price is less than £100 (or such greater sum as the Treasury may specify by order). Again, mobile telephones, accessories designed solely for use by the disabled and road fuel gas conversions (see (*a*)–(*c*) above) are excluded.

The Treasury may make regulations (which may make different provision for different cases) as regards the fitting of replacement accessories, to provide either that the price of the car will remain the same as if the accessory replaced had continued in use, or that the above provisions are to be modified in some other way to take account of the replacement.

Where the employee makes a capital contribution to the cost of the car or accessories taken into account as above, the price of the car for the purposes of the charge on the employee for the year in which the contribution is made and subsequent years is reduced by the lesser of the amount of the contribution (or the sum of such contributions) and £5,000 (or such greater sum as may be specified by Treasury order). An agreement for the employee to receive a proportionate return of his capital contribution on disposal of the car will not prejudice relief in respect of the contribution, and will not give rise to any Schedule E charge on the amount repaid. An agreement to refund the contribution in full will result in the contribution being disregarded. (Revenue Tax Bulletin December 1994 p 177).

[*ICTA 1988, s 157(2), ss 168A–168E, s 168G, Sch 6; FA 1993, Sch 3 paras 1–5, 7; FA 1995, s 44; FA 1996, s 134, Sch 20 para 40; FA 1998, s 60; FA 1999, s 44(4), s 47*].

Classic cars. There are special provisions substituting market value for the price determined as above where the market value is at least £15,000 (or such greater sum as the Treasury may specify by order) and exceeds that price, and the car is 15 years or more old at the end of the year concerned. Capital contributions are taken into account on a similar basis to that described above, and the £80,000 overall limit similarly applies. [*ICTA 1988, ss 168F, 168G; FA 1993, Sch 3 para 4*].

Replacement cars and accessories. Regulations provide for the situation where a double charge would otherwise arise where a temporary replacement car is provided while the normal car is unavailable for use for less than 30 days. The replacement car is ignored, and mileage in it treated as mileage in the normal car, provided that either it is of a similar quality to the normal car or it is not provided as part of an arrangement to supply a better car. Similarly, where an accessory is fitted which replaces another, regulations provide that the 'price' of the car will not be affected where the replacement is of the same kind and does not cost more than the price of the old accessory (or, if greater, the current price of an equivalent to the old accessory). The addition to the 'price' in respect of a more costly replacement accessory is restricted to the excess cost over the amount (if any) included in the 'price' in respect of the old accessory. [*SI 1994 Nos 777, 778*].

Administration. See generally Revenue Pamphlet IR 172. See also 55.16 PAY AS YOU EARN.

See Simon's Direct Tax Service E4.614B.

Example

A, B and C are employees of D Ltd. Each earns at least £8,500 per annum and each is provided with a company car throughout 2000/01. The company also bears at least part of the cost of petrol for private motoring (see (iv) below).

A is provided with a 1,800 cc car first registered in October 1997 with a list price (including VAT, car tax (but not road tax), delivery charges and standard accessories) of £19,000. The car was made available to A in April 1998. An immobilisor was fitted in September 1998 at a cost of £200. A's business mileage is 20,000 for 2000/01. He is required to pay the company £250 per year as a condition of using the car for private motoring, and duly pays this amount.

B is provided with a 1,400 cc car first registered in March 1996 with a list price of £9,000. B drives 8,000 business miles in 2000/01. He was required to make a capital contribution of £1,000 on provision of the car in January 1999.

C is provided with a luxury car first registered in February 1999 with a list price of £85,000 (which includes optional accessories). He made a capital contribution of £3,000 in 1998/99. C's business mileage was 2,000 in 2000/01.

Car and fuel benefits for 2000/01 are as follows.

	A	B	C
	£	£	£
List price	19,000	9,000	85,000
Later optional accessories	200	—	—
	19,200		
Capital contributions	—	(1,000)	(3,000)
			£82,000
Price cap for expensive cars			80,000
Price of car	£19,200	£8,000	£80,000
Cash equivalent — 35% of price of car			28,000
— 15%	2,880		
— 25%		2,000	
Reduction for older cars ($\frac{1}{4}$)	—	(500)	—
Contribution for private use	(250)	—	—
Car benefit	2,630	1,500	28,000
Fuel benefit (see (iv) below)	2,170	1,700	3,200
Total car and fuel benefits	£4,800	£3,200	£31,200

(ii) *Cars for private use: 2002/03 and subsequent years.* For 2002/03 and subsequent years, the basis of charge for 2001/02 and earlier years (see (i) above) continues, but instead of the fixed charge of 35% of list price subject to reduction in respect of business travel and age of the car, the cash equivalent of the benefit is a percentage of the list price dependent on carbon dioxide emissions and certain related factors. Thus the detailed provisions described at (i) above, apart from the first two paragraphs, continue to apply (except in relation to certain bi-fuel cars, see (*c*) below), and the pro-rata reduction for periods of unavailability continues to apply with a minor revision to take account of leap years.

The percentage of list price which determines the cash equivalent of the benefit (the '*appropriate percentage*') varies (except as further detailed below) from 15% to 35% depending on the 'applicable carbon dioxide emissions figure' for the car, expressed in grams per kilometre (g/km). If it does not exceed the '*lower threshold*' for the year (165 g/km for 2002/03, 155 g/km for 2003/04, 145 g/km for 2004/05 and subsequent years, subject (after 5 April 2005) to a different figure being substituted by the Treasury by order), the 15% figure applies. For each 5 g/km by which it exceeds the lower threshold (rounding the emissions figure down to the nearest multiple of 5), the 15% figure is increased by 1%, up to a maximum of 35%.

The 'applicable carbon dioxide emissions figure' is determined as follows.

(*a*) If the car was first registered after 31 December 1997 but before 1 October 1999 and conformed to a vehicle type with an 'EC type-approval certificate' (as defined), or had a 'UK approval certificate' (as defined), specifying a carbon dioxide emissions figure in terms of g/km driven, it is that figure.

(*b*) If the car is first registered after 30 September 1999 on the basis of an 'EC certificate of conformity' (as defined) or UK approval certificate specifying a carbon dioxide emissions figure in terms of g/km driven, it is that figure or, if more than one figure is quoted, the carbon dioxide emissions (combined) figure.

(*c*) If a bi-fuel car is first registered after 31 December 1999 on the basis of an EC certificate of conformity or UK approval certificate specifying separate carbon dioxide emissions figures in terms of g/km driven for the different fuels, it is the lowest figure specified or, if more than one figure is specified in relation to each fuel, the lowest carbon dioxide emissions (combined) figure. (In the case of such bi-fuel cars, the specific list price provisions applicable for 2001/02 and earlier years to cars capable of running on 'road fuel gas' are disapplied.)

The official carbon dioxide emissions figures referred to in (*a*)–(*c*) above are recorded on the vehicle registration document from November 2000. For earlier registrations, an online carbon dioxide emissions enquiry service has been set up by the Society of Motor Manufacturers and Traders under an agreement with the Revenue.

Cars with no carbon dioxide emissions figure. If the car is first registered after 31 December 1997 but (*a*)–(*c*) above do not apply, then if the car has an internal combustion engine with reciprocating piston(s), the appropriate percentage is 15% if the cylinder capacity is 1,400cc or less, 25% if it is 1,401–2,000cc inclusive, 35% if it is more than 2,000cc. If the car is an '*electrically propelled vehicle*' (i.e. if it is propelled solely by electrical power derived from an external source or from a battery not connected to any source of power when the vehicle is in motion), it is 15%. In any other case it is 35%.

Automatic cars made available to disabled drivers. Where an employee holding a disabled person's badge (an 'orange badge') can only drive a car with automatic transmission, and an automatic car to which (*a*) or (*b*) above applies is made available to him or her (and not merely deemed to be made available to him or her because it is made available to a member of his or her family or household), then if the applicable carbon dioxide emissions figure for the car is higher than that for the 'equivalent manual car', the manual figure is substituted. The '*equivalent manual car*' is the closest non-automatic variant available of the same make and model of car first registered at or about the same time. A car has automatic transmission for these purposes if the gear ratio cannot be varied by the driver independently of the accelerator and brakes, or if the driver can independently vary the gear ratio but not by means of a manually-operated clutch pedal or lever.

Diesel car supplement. Where a car propelled solely by diesel is first registered after 31 December 1997, the appropriate percentage, determined as above, is increased by 3%, subject to a maximum of 35%.

Discounts. The Treasury may make regulations providing for a reduction in any of the appropriate percentage figures as above in such circumstances, and subject to such conditions, as may be prescribed. It is intended that this will enable the diesel supplement to be waived for very low emission diesels and discounts (possibly to below 15%) provided for cars using particularly environmentally friendly fuels and technologies.

Cars registered before 1 January 1998. If the car has an internal combustion engine with reciprocating piston(s), the appropriate percentage is 15% if the cylinder capacity is 1,400cc or less, 22% if it is 1,401–2,000cc inclusive, 32% if it is more than 2,000cc. If the car is an electrically propelled vehicle, it is 15%. In any other case it is 32%.

[*ICTA 1988, ss 157, 157A, 168(5)(6), 168A–168G, Sch 6; FA 1995, s 44; FA 1998, s 60; FA 1999, s 44(4); FA 2000, s 59, Schs 11, 40 Pt II(3); SI 1994 Nos 777, 778*].

(iii) *Vans for private use.* Where a van is available for an employee's private use, the employee is to be taxed on the benefit in accordance with a standard scale.

Unless the van is a 'shared van' (see below) for all or part of the year, the scale benefit is **£500**, reduced to **£350** for a van aged four years or more at the end of the year. The scale benefit is reduced pro-rata if for any part of the year it is either 'unavailable' or is a shared van. A van is '*unavailable*' on a day falling before the first day on which it is made available to the employee (or a member of his family or household) or after the last day on which it is made so available, or on a day falling within a period of 30 or more consecutive days throughout which it is not so available. The scale benefit is reduced (or extinguished) by any monetary contribution which the employee is required to make, and does make, as a condition for private use. The age of a van commences with the date of its first registration.

A van is a '*shared van*' for any period throughout which it is available concurrently or otherwise to two or more employees of the same employer, and in which there is no period exceeding 30 consecutive days during which it is exclusively available to one employee. A van shared for part of a day is treated as shared throughout that day. Each employee to whom one or more shared vans are available for private use while they are shared vans and who makes private use of the van (or at least one of them) while it is a shared van is a '*participating employee*'.

Scale benefits of £500 or £350 (depending on the van's age) are allocated to each shared van, these amounts being reduced pro-rata where for any part of the year the van is not a shared van or where the van is incapable of use for 30 or more consecutive days. The aggregate scale benefit for all shared vans is then divided equally among the participating employees, and the result is the amount on which each such employee is taxed for the year, except that if that amount is more than £500 it is reduced to £500.

A participating employee may claim an alternative method of calculation (such a claim being counted as a claim for relief for the purposes of penalties under *TMA 1970, s 95*, see 58.3 PENALTIES), as follows.

(*a*) For each van involved, take the number of days in the year of assessment during which the employee (or a member of his family or household) makes private use of a van while it is a shared van.

(*b*) Aggregate the numbers arrived at under (*a*) (where more than one van is involved).

(*c*) Multiply the number in (*a*) or, where applicable, the number in (*b*) by £5.

The result is the amount on which the employee is taxed.

The amount on which the employee would otherwise be taxed, whether calculated under the standard or the alternative method, is reduced, or extinguished, by any monetary contribution which the employee is required to make, and does make, as a condition for private use of a shared van while it is a shared van. Where more than one van is involved, the aggregate of such contributions is taken.

Where, in respect of the same van, an employee has a taxable benefit for a year under both the non-shared van and the shared van provisions as above, the benefits are aggregated to arrive at his total taxable benefit for the year.

There is an overall limit of £500 on the charge under these provisions on an employee for a year at no one time during which more than one van was available for the private use of the employee or a member of his family or household.

[*ICTA 1988, s 159AA(1)(2), s 168(5A), Sch 6A; FA 1993, Sch 4 paras 4, 6–8*].

There is no separate charge for fuel provided for private motoring in a van.

Revenue Pamphlet IR 136 provides an employees' and employers' guide to the taxation of company vans.

See Simon's Direct Tax Service E4.615A.

Example

L is an employee of N Ltd, earning £18,000 per annum. From 1 October 2000 to 5 April 2001, L is provided by his employer with exclusive use of a one-year old company van (Van A) on terms which do not prohibit private use and which provide for a deduction of £4 per month to be made from his net salary at the end of each month in consideration for private use. For the period 6 April 2000 to 30 September 2000 inclusive, L had shared the van with another employee, M. Either L or a member of his family or household had made private use of the shared van for 42 days during that period, and M also made private use of the van. No payment for private use was required.

In addition to the van mentioned above, four other company vans are shared between five employees of N Ltd (excluding L and M) throughout the year ended 5 April 2001, three of which vans are aged less than four years at the end of that year. All the employees make some private use of one or more of the vans. One of the vans is off the road and incapable of use for three weeks in March 2001.

All vans mentioned have a normal laden weight not exceeding 3,500 kilograms.

The taxable benefit to L for 2000/01 of company vans is calculated as follows.

Non-shared van

	£
Cash equivalent of benefit before adjustment	500
Exclude Period for which van is a shared van:	
$£500 \times \frac{178}{365}$ (6.4.00 – 30.9.00)	244
	256
Deduct Payment for private use (6 × £4 per month)	24
Cash equivalent of benefit	£232

Shared van

	£	£
Basic values:		
Van A	500	
Exclude Period for which van is not a shared van:		
$£500 \times \frac{187}{365}$ (1.10.00 – 5.4.01)	256	244
Other vans ((3 × £500) + (1 × £350))		1,850
Sum of basic values		£2,094
Divide £2,094 equally between seven participating employees		£299
Cash equivalent of benefit to L (maximum £500)		£299

Total benefits to L

	£
Non-shared van	232
Shared van	299
Total cash equivalent of benefit	£531
But restricted by *Sch 6A para 11* to	£500

L will thus be taxed on a van benefit of £500 for 2000/01.

In relation to the shared van, L then makes a claim for the alternative calculation under Schedule 6A para 8.

Number of relevant days for Van A	42
Number of relevant days for other shared vans	Nil
Aggregate number of relevant days	42
Cash equivalent of benefit to L (42 × £5 per day)	£210

Total benefits to L (revised)

	£
Non-shared van	232
Shared van	210
Total cash equivalent of benefit	£442

L will thus be taxed on a van benefit of £442 for 2000/01.

(iv) *Fuel for private use.* A scale charge applies to free fuel provided for private motoring in 'company' cars, i.e. a vehicle which attracts, or could attract, a charge within (i) or (ii) above. The charge varies with the cylinder capacity of the car. Separate scales apply for petrol and diesel cars. The scale charge does not apply to fuel provided for vans (see (iii) above).

The scale charges are as follows.

Table for 2000/01

	Petrol (£)	Diesel (£)
(*a*) with cylinder capacity of		
Up to 1,400 cc	1,700	2,170
1,401 cc to 2,000 cc	2,170	2,170
2,001 cc or more	3,200	3,200
(*b*) without a cylinder capacity	£3,200	

[*SI 2000 No 810*]

Table for 1999/2000

	Petrol (£)	Diesel (£)
(*a*) with cylinder capacity of		
Up to 1,400 cc	1,210	1,540
1,401 cc to 2,000 cc	1,540	1,540
2,001 cc or more	2,270	2,270
(*b*) without a cylinder capacity	£2,270	

[*SI 1999 No 684*]

Table for 1998/99

	Petrol (£)	Diesel (£)
(*a*) with cylinder capacity of		
Up to 1,400 cc	1,010	1,280
1,401 cc to 2,000 cc	1,280	1,280
2,001 cc or more	1,890	1,890
(*b*) without a cylinder capacity	£1,890	

[*FA 1998, s 59*]

Table for 1997/98

	Petrol (£)	Diesel (£)
(*a*) with cylinder capacity of		
Up to 1,400 cc	800	740
1,401 cc to 2,000 cc	1,010	740
2,001 cc or more	1,490	940
(*b*) without a cylinder capacity	£1,490	

[*SI 1996 No 2954*]

Table for 1996/97

	Petrol (£)	Diesel (£)
(*a*) with cylinder capacity of		
Up to 1,400 cc	710	640
1,401 cc to 2,000 cc	890	640
2,001 cc or more	1,320	820
(*b*) without a cylinder capacity	£1,320	

[*SI 1995 No 3035*]

Table for 1995/96

	Petrol (£)	Diesel (£)
(*a*) with cylinder capacity of		
Up to 1,400 cc	670	605
1,401 cc to 2,000 cc	850	605
2,001 cc or more	1,260	780
(*b*) without a cylinder capacity	£1,260	

[*SI 1994 No 3010*]

Table for 1994/95

	Petrol (£)	Diesel (£)
(*a*) with cylinder capacity of		
Up to 1,400 cc	640	580
1,401 cc to 2,000 cc	810	580
2,001 cc or more	1,200	750
(*b*) without a cylinder capacity	£1,200	

[*FA 1994, s 87*]

Where the charge for private use of a car is reduced by reason of its being unavailable for part of the year (see (i) and (ii) above), the scale rate for private fuel is similarly reduced. There are no special rules for second cars, cars with low business mileage or older cars. If the employee is required to make good to his employer the cost of *all* company fuel used for private purposes (including travel between home and work), and in fact does so during the year in question (or without unreasonable delay thereafter), the scale charge is cancelled, but there is no reduction where fuel is provided for part only of a year. Fuel provided only for home-to-work travel of severely and permanently disabled employees is ignored for this purpose (see Revenue Booklet 480). Where the scale charge applies, there is no charge under other provisions (e.g. on expense allowances or use of credit cards or vouchers which enable the employee to obtain private fuel) and, accordingly, the *method* by which private fuel is obtained does not affect the employee's tax liability. The rates do not apply to fuel provided for use in individuals' own cars, hire cars etc. where the existing rules continue to apply (i.e. the employer will notify the Revenue on form P11D of the actual cost of fuel provided by him). The Treasury may alter the Table by statutory instrument.

[*ICTA 1988, s 158; F(No 2)A 1992, s 53; FA 1993, s 71(2)(3), Sch 3 paras 6, 7; FA 1995, s 43(2)*].

See Simon's Direct Tax Service E4.615.

(v) *Pooled vehicles.* Cars or vans provided as *pooled cars* or *pooled vans* will not be treated as being available for private use by any employee.

Conditions are

(*a*) the vehicle must have been included for the year in a car or van pool for use of employees of one or more employers and actually used by more than one of those employees by reason of their employment and not ordinarily used by one of them to the exclusion of the others, and

(*b*) any private use of the vehicle in the year by an employee was merely incidental to his other use of it, and

(*c*) the vehicle was not normally kept overnight at or near any of the residences of the employees concerned (except on the employer's premises).

As regards (*b*) above, the Revenue interpret the requirement that private use is 'merely incidental to' other use as a qualitative test requiring consideration, in the case of each employee using the vehicle during the year, of whether the private use is independent of the employee's business use (so that it is not 'merely incidental' to it) or follows from the business use (so that it is). Thus if a business journey requiring an early start cannot reasonably be undertaken starting from the normal place of work, the journey from work to home the previous day (although private) is merely incidental to the business use. Similarly minor private use (e.g. to visit a restaurant) while away from home on a business trip is merely incidental to the business use. On the other hand use for an annual holiday would not be merely incidental to business use, no matter how small in comparison to business travel in the year. As regards cars with drivers, carrying and working on confidential papers, whilst a factor in determining whether a journey is business or private (and if private whether merely incidental to business use), is not determinative of the issue. The need to deliver papers to a client, or to have them available for a meeting at the employee's home, may be additional relevant factors. (Before 1996/97, it was accepted that all such journeys could be merely incidental to business use, without regard to their frequency or length or to other use of the car.) Where a chauffeur is obliged to take the car home for the night, in order to collect or deliver passengers, this does not disqualify the car from treatment as a pooled vehicle. (Revenue Pamphlet IR 131, SP 2/96, 29 March 1996).

For 1995/96 and earlier years, claims may be made to the inspector by any employee concerned or by employer on behalf of all and any determination arising from an appeal is binding on all for that car or van in that year. For 1996/97 onwards, claims are unnecessary. [*ICTA 1988, ss 159, 159AB; FA 1993, Sch 4 para 4; FA 1996, s 134, Sch 20 para 8*].

The Revenue accept that condition (*c*) above is satisfied if the occasions on which the vehicle is taken home by employees do not amount to more than 60% of the year. However, where a vehicle is garaged at employees' homes on a large number of occasions (although less than 60% of the year), they consider it 'unlikely' that all home-to-work journeys would satisfy the 'merely incidental' test in (*b*) above. Such use by a chauffeur employed to drive a car does not prevent its being a pooled car. (Revenue Booklet 480).

See Simon's Direct Tax Service E4.616.

(vi) *Heavier commercial vehicles.* Where a 'heavier commercial vehicle' is made available to an employee in such circumstances that had it been a van it would have been chargeable under the provisions described at (iii) above, no charge will arise in respect of its provision unless the vehicle is wholly or mainly used for private purposes. A benefit will, however, arise on the provision of any driver for the vehicle. A '*heavier commercial vehicle*' is defined in the same terms as a van under (iii) above, but with a design laden weight limit exceeding 3,500 kgs. in normal use. [*ICTA 1988, s 159AC; FA 1993, s 74*]. See Simon's Direct Tax Service E4.615A.

75.16 **Mobile telephones. For 1998/99 and earlier years**, where a 'mobile telephone' is made available to a director or employee (or to a member of his family or household) by the employer, and is available for private use, an amount of **£200** (which may be increased by Treasury order) is treated as an emolument of the employment (unless the benefit is otherwise chargeable to tax as income). If in any year there is no private use, or the employee is required to, and does, make good the full cost of private use, the charge is reduced to nil. The full cost of private use for this purpose is the cost of private calls, plus a proportionate share of the higher of the equipment rental and 20% of the market value of the equipment when first used to provide a benefit (plus, unless the purpose of the provision of the telephone was to make it available for business use, a proportionate share of any other expenses incurred, e.g. line rental, in connection with its provision) (see Revenue Tax Bulletin August 1994, p 158). Only outgoing private calls (and incoming reversed charge private calls) are taken into account for this purpose. A call is private unless made wholly, exclusively and necessarily in the performance of the duties of the employment. Although the requirement to reimburse must be imposed in advance, where the telephone is provided for business use only but a non-business call is made entirely due to an exceptional and genuine emergency, reimbursement for that call by the employee will be regarded as satisfying the condition. (Revenue Tax Bulletin May 1992 p 20).

The charge is reduced *pro rata* for days on which the telephone is unavailable, either before or after it is provided at all or during a period of 30 consecutive days on which it is incapable of being used at all. A further charge applies for each additional mobile telephone made available, but the fact that different apparatus may be supplied on different days is disregarded.

'*Mobile telephone*' is defined to include provision in connection with a car or a van or heavier commercial vehicle, whether or not a company car etc., but to exclude cordless extensions to fixed telephones and certain short-range radio apparatus.

These provisions are repealed for 1999/2000 and subsequent years. See now 75.13(xxiii) as regards exclusion of mobile telephones from benefits charge.

[*ICTA 1988, s 159A; FA 1991, s 30; FA 1993, s 74(2), Sch 4 para 5; FA 1999, s 44(2)(6)*].

Simon's Direct Tax Service. See **E4.617**.

75.17 **Beneficial loan arrangements.** Where a director or employee within 75.11 above and in employment the emoluments from which are assessable under Schedule E (or a 'relative' of the employee) obtains a loan (which includes any form of credit) from the employer (or prospective employer), and the loan (or any part) is outstanding at any time during a year of assessment, the employee is chargeable to tax on the difference between the interest (if any) he pays and interest calculated by reference to an official rate prescribed by the Treasury by statutory instrument (see below). The charge applies to a loan made by a company controlling, or under the control of, the employer company or where a person controls both companies, and similarly for a partnership, and, if any of those companies is a close company, where the loan is by a person having a material interest in any of those companies. It also applies to arranging, guaranteeing or in any way facilitating the continuation of an existing loan as it does to the making of a loan. A loan made to replace a beneficial loan used to be treated in the same way as the original loan, but this no longer generally applies for 1995/96 onwards (although there are now more specifically targeted rules on replacement loans).

Revenue Pamphlet IR 145 provides a guide for employees on the taxation of such loans.

It is not necessary for the application of these provisions that there be any benefit from the loan in terms of something of an advantage to the employee (*Williams v Todd Ch D 1988,*

60 TC 727). A loan secured by a charge on a house purchased by a relocated employee, with an agreement that when the charge was called in the employing company would receive the same proportion of the sale price or valuation as the loan bore to the purchase price, was within these provisions (*Harvey v Williams (Sp C 49), [1995] SSCD 329; (Sp C 168), [1998] SSCD 215*). The payment of the expenses of an estate agency by a service company of which one of the partners in the agency was a director was within the provisions from the time the services were provided for so long as the payments were not reimbursed (with agreed mark-up) to the company (*Grant v Watton and cross-appeal Ch D 1999, 71 TC 333*).

Before 2000/01, the prescribed rate was adjusted with changes in typical mortgage rates. With effect for 2000/01 and subsequent years, it is set in advance for the whole year, although it may be decreased (but will *not* be increased) during the year should there be a sharp fall in typical mortgage rates during a future tax year. (Revenue Press Release 25 January 2000). Subject to this *caveat* as regards the rate set for 2000/01, the prescribed rate from 1 January 1993 is as follows.

9%	p.a. from 1 January 1993 to 5 January 1993
8.25%	p.a. from 6 January 1993 to 5 March 1993
7.75%	p.a. from 6 March 1993 to 5 January 1994
7.5%	p.a. from 6 January 1994 to 5 November 1994
8%	p.a. from 6 November 1994 to 5 October 1995
7.75%	p.a. from 6 October 1995 to 5 February 1996
7.25%	p.a. from 6 February 1996 to 5 June 1996
7%	p.a. from 6 June 1996 to 5 November 1996
6.75%	p.a. from 6 November 1996 to 5 August 1997
7.25%	p.a. from 6 August 1997 to 5 March 1999
6.25%	**p.a. from 6 March 1999 5 April 2001**

[*SI 1978 No 28; SI 1980 No 439; SI 1982 No 1273; SI 1987 Nos 512, 886, 1493, 1989; SI 1988 Nos 757, 1279, 1622, 2186; SI 1989 No 1001; SI 1991 Nos 889, 1120, 1377, 1695, 2070; SI 1992 Nos 265, 1338, 2075, 2451, 2818, 3167; SI 1993 Nos 222, 3171; SI 1994 No 2657; SI 1995 No 2436; SI 1996 Nos 54, 1321, 2644; SI 1997 No 1681; SI 1999 No 419*].

The average rate for 1998/99 was thus 7.16% (1997/98 7.08%, 1996/97 6.93%, 1995/96 7.79%, 1994/95 7.70%, 1993/94 7.688%).

Regulations may provide for a different official rate of interest in relation to a loan in the currency of a country or territory outside the UK, the benefit of which is obtained by reason of the employment of a person who normally lives in that country or territory and who has lived there at some time in the year in question or the preceding five years. In this context, 'lives' and 'has lived' are considered to connote a degree of continuance if not permanence, i.e. more than a return for a short holiday. (Revenue Tax Bulletin October 1994 p 162). The following different rates are applicable.

Japan	3.9% p.a. from 6 June 1994 onwards.
Switzerland	5.7% p.a. from 6 June 1994 to 5 July 1994.
	5.5% p.a. from 6 July 1994 onwards.

[*SI 1994 Nos 1307, 1567*]. The average rates for 1994/95 are thus 4.50% (Japan) and 5.85% (Switzerland). For the circumstances in which loans taken out prior to an employee coming to work in the UK are within the beneficial loan provisions, see Revenue Tax Bulletin October 1994 p 161.

The amount chargeable in respect of the loan for a year of assessment is treated as an emolument chargeable under Schedule E. The employee is treated as having paid interest on the loan in that year of that amount. It is not treated as 'relevant loan interest' (i.e. it is not within MIRAS, see 23.13 DEDUCTION OF TAX AT SOURCE), nor is it treated as income of the lender, but it is treated as accruing during, and paid at the end of, the year (or, if different, the period during the year when the employee was in the employment and the loan was outstanding). For 1995/96 and earlier years, all loans in the same currency outstanding at any time in a year between the same employer and employee had to be treated as a single loan, but excluding

(*a*) loans for interest on which relief is available under *ICTA 1988, s 353* (or would be so available but for being relevant loan interest or for exceeding the qualifying maximum under *ICTA 1988, s 357(1)(b)*) (see 43.5, 43.10 INTEREST PAYABLE), and

(*b*) loans interest on which is deductible under Schedule D, Case I or II,

or on which such relief would be available if interest were payable. For 1996/97 and subsequent years, as regards all loans whenever made, such aggregation of loans no longer applies, except that, where the lender is a close company (see Tolley's Corporation Tax under Close Companies) and the borrower a director, the lender may elect, on or before 6 July following the tax year, to treat as a single loan all loans with that borrower which are in the same currency, are not within (*a*) or (*b*) above ((*b*) above being extended, for 2000/01 onwards, to include loans interest on which is deductible in a Schedule A business), were obtained by reason of employment, and the rate of interest on which has been below the official rate throughout the year.

A claim may be made for late payments of interest to be related to the year to which they apply, and for assessments to be adjusted accordingly.

The above provisions do not apply as regards a loan to a 'relative' if the employee derived no benefit from the loan, or if the loan was made by an individual in the normal course of domestic, family or personal relationships. They also do not apply where a loan made for a fixed and unvariable period and at a fixed and unvariable rate of interest (originally not less than the official rate) becomes a beneficial loan only by reason of an increase in the official rate, or on similar unvariable loans made before 6 April 1978 where the rate of interest is not less than could have been expected to apply between persons not connected with each other.

[*ICTA 1988, ss 160, 161(2)–(4), 161A, Sch 7 paras 1–3; FA 1995, s 45(2); FA 1996, ss 107(1)(4), 134, Sch 20 paras 9, 41; FA 2000, Sch 10 para 4*].

Interest qualifying for relief. For 2000/01 and subsequent years, the above provisions do not apply to a loan in any year of assessment in which, if interest were paid on the loan (whether or not it is in fact so paid), the whole of the interest paid on it would either be eligible for relief under *ICTA 1988, s 353* (or would be so but for being relevant loan interest, see 23.13 DEDUCTION OF TAX AT SOURCE) or would be an allowable deduction to the payer under Schedule D, Case I or II or in a Schedule A business (see 71.65 SCHEDULE D, CASES I AND II, 68.5 SCHEDULE A). [*ICTA 1988, s 161A; FA 2000, s 57, Sch 10 para 4*]. Previously, such loans were within *section 160*, the amount chargeable being treated as interest paid and therefore attracting relief as appropriate in the normal way, and this continues to apply to loans interest on which only partly qualifies for relief. [*ICTA 1988, s 160(1); FA 1994, s 88(1)(6)*].

Ordinary commercial loans. For 2000/01 and subsequent years, the above provisions do not apply to a loan on '*ordinary commercial terms*', i.e. a loan made in the ordinary course of business by a lender whose business includes either the lending of money or the supply of goods or services on credit, and in relation to which the following conditions are satisfied.

(*a*) When the loan was made, loans for the same or similar purposes and on the same terms and conditions were available to all those who might be expected to avail themselves of the services provided by the lender in the course of business, and a substantial proportion (broadly 50% or more, see Revenue Schedule E Manual, SE 3529) of such loans (including the loan in question) made at or about that time were made to members of the public (i.e. those with whom the lender deals at arm's length). All such loans so made to members of the public at or about that time must be held on the same terms as the loan in question, and any change in those terms since that time must have been imposed in the ordinary course of the lender's business. As regards loans made before 1 June 1994, terms and conditions are considered for this purpose disregarding any fees, commission or other incidental expenses incurred by the borrower to obtain the loan.

(*b*) If the loan was varied before 6 April 2000, further conditions apply in relation to the loan in question, to any existing loans varied at or about the same time so as to be held on the same post-variation terms and to any new loans made by the same lender at or about the time of the variation. A substantial proportion (as in (*a*) above) of all such loans (including the loan in question) must have been made to members of the public. All such loans so made to members of the public at or about the time of the variation must be held on the same terms as the loan in question, and any change in those terms since that time must have been imposed in the ordinary course of the lender's business. Terms are considered for this purpose disregarding any fees, commission or other incidental expenses incurred by the borrower to obtain the loan and any penalties, interest or similar amounts incurred by the borrower as a result of varying the loan.

(*c*) If the loan is varied on or after 6 April 2000, further conditions apply. A substantial proportion (as in (*a*) above) of the loan in question, of any existing loans varied at or about the same time so as to be held on the same post-variation terms and of any new loans made by the same lender at or about the time of the variation must have been made to members of the public. At the time of the variation, members of the public who had loans from the lender for similar purposes must have had a right to vary their loans on the same terms and conditions as applied in relation to the variation of the loan in question, and the post-variation terms on which any existing loans so varied and the loan in question are held must be the same. Any change in those terms since that time must have been imposed in the ordinary course of the lender's business. Terms and conditions are considered for these purposes disregarding any fees, commission or other incidental expenses incurred by the borrower to obtain the loan and any penalties, interest or similar amounts incurred by the borrower as a result of varying the loan.

[*ICTA 1988, s 161B, Sch 7A; FA 2000, s 57, Sch 10 para 5*].

For 1999/2000 and earlier years, a similar exclusion applies in relation to loans made in the ordinary course of a business which includes the lending of money and which is carried on by the lender, if

(A) at the time the loan was made, loans made for the same or similar purposes, and on the same terms and conditions, were available to all the lender's usual customers,

(B) of all such loans (including the loan in question) made at or about the same time by the lender, a substantial proportion (broadly 50% or more, see Revenue Schedule E Manual, SE 3529) was made at arm's length to members of the public,

(C) the loan in question and all arm's length loans referred to in (B) are held on the same terms, and

(D) if the terms on which the loan in question is held are altered, such alteration was imposed in the ordinary course of business.

As regards (A) above, a loan not within the exception at the time it was made, but the terms of which were subsequently varied so as to fall within (A)–(D) above, did not come within the exception (*West v Crossland; West v O'Neill Ch D 1999, 71 TC 314*).

As regards (A), (C) and (D) above, for loans made before 1 June 1994, differences in fees, commission or other incidental expenses incurred by the borrower for the purpose of obtaining the loan are disregarded in determining whether the same terms and conditions apply to that and other loans.

For loans made on or after 1 June 1994, the terms and conditions must be exactly the same, so that the exemption would *not* apply where e.g. the lending criteria were relaxed in favour of employees or any normal application or loan fees or charges were waived or reduced in their favour. For this and generally, see Revenue Tax Bulletin August 1994 p 157.

[*ICTA 1988, s 161(1)–(1B); FA 1994, s 88; FA 2000, s 57, Sch 10 para 5(4)*].

De minimis exemption. No amount is treated as emoluments (or as interest paid) in respect of a loan under the above provisions if the loan (or aggregate loans) at no time in the year exceed £5,000. Similarly if a loan (or the aggregate loans) not falling within (*a*) or (*b*) above does not exceed £5,000, the above provisions do not apply to that loan or those loans. The Revenue have confirmed that, in consequence of the general abolition of mortgage interest tax relief for 2000/01 onwards (see 43.3 INTEREST PAYABLE), affected loans must be aggregated with other non-qualifying loans in applying the £5,000 exemption, possibly resulting in the latter becoming chargeable benefits for the first time. (Revenue Tax Bulletin December 1999 p 706).

[*ICTA 1988, s 161(1); FA 1994, s 88(3)(6)*].

'*Relative*' for these purposes means spouse of the employee, or parent, ancestor, lineal descendant, brother or sister (or those persons' spouses), of the employee or spouse. [*ICTA 1988, s 160(6)*].

Bridging loans. By concession, reimbursement by an employer of the net interest on a bridging loan is not charged to tax, nor is the benefit of a bridging loan advanced by an employer in excess of the relief limit. See 75.13(*b*)(x) above.

Relief is also given from a charge under *ICTA 1988, s 160* on another loan which is chargeable only because of the existence of the bridging loan. (Revenue Pamphlet IR 1, A5(*b*)).

Expense advances. There is also no charge, in practice, on advances for employee's expenses necessarily incurred in employment provided (*a*) the maximum amount at any one time does not exceed £1,000; (*b*) the advances are spent within six months; and (*c*) the employee accounts to his employer at regular intervals for the expenditure of the sum advanced. Where there are good reasons for exceeding the limits, they will not, in practice, be charged. Where the conditions are met, no entry is required on form P11D for beneficial loans but details of expense payments are still necessary. (Revenue Pamphlet IR 131, SP 7/79, 11 April 1979).

Calculation of interest at the official rate. The normal method for any year of assessment ('the relevant year') is (*a*) to take the average of the amounts of the loan outstanding at the commencement and end of the relevant year (or at the date the loan was made or discharged if falling within that year), (*b*) multiply that figure by the number of whole months (a month begins on sixth day of each calendar month) during which the loan was outstanding in that year and divide by twelve, (*c*) multiply the result by the official rate of interest in force, or if the rate changed, the average rate. [*ICTA 1988, Sch 7 para 4(1)*]. For 1995/96 and subsequent years, a replacement loan (whenever made) is treated for averaging purposes as being the same loan as the original if it is a 'further employment-related loan' which replaces (i) the original loan or (ii) a non-employment related loan which itself replaced the original, the second replacement occurring in the same tax year, or within 40 days thereafter, as the first. A '*further employment-related loan*' is a loan the benefit of which is obtained by reason of the same employment or other employment with the same employer or a person connected with him (within *ICTA 1988, s 839* — see 20 CONNECTED PERSONS). [*ICTA 1988, Sch 7 para 4(2)–(4); FA 1995, s 45(4)(5)*].

An alternative method may be required by the inspector or elected by the employee. For 1996/97 and subsequent years, as regards all loans whenever made, notice of requirement or election must be given within twelve months after 31 January following the relevant year of assessment (previously, the inspector had to give notice of requirement when raising or amending an assessment and the employee had to elect within thirty days of an assessment, or longer if the inspector agreed, or if no assessment made, within six years after end of the relevant year). The alternative method is to calculate the figures by reference to the daily amounts of the loan and official rates of interest (leap years being ignored in determining the effective daily rate of interest). [*ICTA 1988, Sch 7 para 5; FA 1996, s 107(2)–(4)*].

For 2000/01 and subsequent years, where two or more employees are chargeable under the above provisions in respect of the same loan, the cash equivalent is apportioned between them in a fair and reasonable manner, the portion allocated to each being treated as the cash equivalent as far as that employee is concerned. Any election for the alternative method of calculation in such a case must be made by all the employees concerned. [*ICTA 1988, Sch 7 para 5A; FA 2000, s 57, Sch 10 para 6*].

General. See ICAEW Technical Release TAX 11/93, 9 July 1993 as regards loans to directors.

Interest on money loaned interest-free, subject to conditions and repayable on demand, by the employer to a trust for the benefit of an employee held to be emoluments within Schedule E (*O'Leary v McKinlay Ch D 1990, 63 TC 729*).

Loans written off. Any amount released from, or written off, a loan (whenever made and including any form of credit) obtained by reason of employment will be charged as an emolument, unless otherwise taxable as income. Where however it would be taxable under *ICTA 1988, s 148* (see 19.5 COMPENSATION FOR LOSS OF EMPLOYMENT (AND DAMAGES)) it will instead be taxable under *ICTA 1988, s 160(2)* and where the loan is one which is a capital sum within *ICTA 1988, s 677* (see 81.19 SETTLEMENTS) the charge will be on the excess of the amount released over sums previously treated as the employee's income under *section 677*. These provisions continue to apply after termination of employment, and to a loan replacing the original loan, but they cease on death of the employee. They apply if the loan is to a relative (see above) unless the employee shows he derived no benefit himself. They do not apply to arrangements to protect a person from a fall in value of shares acquired before 6 April 1976. [*ICTA 1988, s 160(2)–(7), s 161(4)–(7); FA 1995, s 45(3)*].

Where the lender is a company in which the employee is also a participator and a charge arises under *ICTA 1988, s 160(2)*, the Revenue would not seek to treat the amount written off as a distribution. Similarly, where the lending company is close and a charge arises under *ICTA 1988, s 421* (see 28.3 EXCESS LIABILITY), the Revenue would not seek to treat the amount written off as a distribution or to raise an assessment under *ICTA 1988, s 160(2)*. (Tolley's Practical Tax 1993 p 144).

Simon's Direct Tax Service. See **E4.631** *et seq.*.

75.18 *Examples*

(i)

D, who is an employee of A Ltd earning £25,000 per annum, obtained a loan of £10,000 from the company on 10 October 1998 for the purpose of buying a car. Interest at a nominal rate is charged on the outstanding balance while the principal is repayable by instalments of £1,000 on 31 December and 30 June commencing 31 December 1998. The interest paid by D in 1998/99 amounted to £50 and, in 1999/2000 to £250. The official rates of interest were as listed below.

From 6.8.97 to 5.3.99	7.25% p.a.
From 6.3.99	6.25% p.a.

D will be assessed for 1998/99 as follows.

Normal method (averaging)

	£
Average balance for period $\dfrac{£10{,}000 + £9{,}000}{2}$	£9,500
£9,500 × $\frac{5}{12}$	£3,958
£3,958 × 7.25% × $\frac{147}{178}$	237
£3,958 × 6.25% × $\frac{31}{178}$	43
	280
Deduct Interest paid in year	50
Cash equivalent of loan benefit	£230

Alternative method

Period	Balance of loan in period	Interest at official rate on balance	
	£		£
10.10.98 – 31.12.98	10,000	£10,000 × 7.25% × $\frac{83}{365}$	165
1.1.99 – 5.3.99	9,000	£9,000 × 7.25% × $\frac{64}{365}$	114
6.3.99 – 5.4.99	9,000	£9,000 × 6.25% × $\frac{31}{365}$	48
			327
Deduct Interest paid in year			50
Cash equivalent of loan benefit			£277
Amount chargeable to tax note (*b*)			£277

D will be assessed for 1999/2000 as follows.

Normal method (averaging)

	£
Average balance for year $\dfrac{£9{,}000 + £7{,}000}{2}$	£8,000
£8,000 × 6.25%	500
Deduct Interest paid in year	250
Cash equivalent of loan benefit	£250

Alternative method

Period	Balance of loan in period	Interest at official rate on balance	
	£		£
6.4.99 – 30.6.99	9,000	£9,000 × 6.25% × $\frac{86}{365}$	133
1.7.99 – 31.12.99	8,000	£8,000 × 6.25% × $\frac{184}{365}$	252
1.1.00 – 5.4.00	7,000	£7,000 × 6.25% × $\frac{95}{365}$	114
			499
Deduct Interest paid in year			250
Cash equivalent of loan benefit			£249
Amount chargeable to tax note (*b*)			£250

Notes

(*a*) The period 10 October 1998 to 5 April 1999 is, for the purpose of calculating the average balance, five complete months (months begin on the sixth day of each calendar month). However, in applying the interest rate change, the actual number of days during which the loan was outstanding is taken into account.

(*b*) The inspector will probably require the alternative method to be applied for 1998/99. It is assumed that the employee will not elect for the alternative method in 1999/2000 as the difference is negligible.

(ii)

B, another employee of A Ltd, earns £33,000 per annum and obtained a loan from the company of £50,000 in January 1999 for house purchase (B's principal private residence). At 5 April 1999, no capital had been repaid but on 1 August 1999 B repays £10,000 of the loan. The rate of interest on the loan is 2.5% per annum on the daily outstanding balance and interest paid in 1999/2000 is £1,080. The official rates of interest are as in *Example* (i) above. B has no other source of taxable income for 1999/2000. He is a single man.

A Ltd also gives B a season ticket loan of £2,400, interest-free and repayable in equal monthly instalments, on 10 January 2000.

The cash equivalent of the loan benefit for 1999/2000 is computed as follows.

(i) Normal method (averaging)

	£
Average balance for year $\dfrac{£50{,}000 + £40{,}000}{2}$	45,000
£45,000 × 6.25%	2,812
Deduct Interest paid in year	1,080
Cash equivalent of loan benefit	£1,732

(ii) Alternative method

Period	Balance of loan in period	Interest at official rate on balance	
	£		£
6.4.99 – 1.8.99	50,000	£50,000 × 6.25% × $\frac{118}{365}$	1,010
2.8.99 – 5.4.00	40,000	£40,000 × 6.25% × $\frac{247}{365}$	1,692
			2,702
Deduct Interest paid in year			1,080
Cash equivalent of loan benefit			£1,622

Amount chargeable to tax (on assumption that B elects for the alternative method) £1,622

B is also treated as having paid notional interest on the loan of an amount equal to that chargeable to tax. Interest eligible for tax relief is as follows.

(i) Interest actually paid

Interest paid		Interest eligible for relief	
	£		£
6.4.99 – 1.8.99 (118 days)			
£50,000 × 2.5% × $\frac{118}{365}$	404	£404 × $\frac{30,000}{50,000}$	243
2.8.99 – 5.4.00 (247 days)			
£40,000 × 2.5% × $\frac{247}{365}$	676	£676 × $\frac{30,000}{40,000}$	507
	£1,080		£750

(ii) Notional interest paid

Interest paid		Interest eligible for relief	
	£		£
6.4.99 – 1.8.99	1,010	£1,010 × $\frac{30,000}{50,000}$	606
2.8.99 – 5.4.00	1,692	£1,692 × $\frac{30,000}{40,000}$	1,269
	2,702		1,875
Deduct actual interest	1,080		750
	£1,622		£1,125

B's tax liability for 1999/2000 is computed as follows.

	£	£
Salary		33,000
Benefit (home loan)		1,622
Schedule E income		34,622
Other income		—
Total income		34,622
Deduct Personal allowance		4,335
Taxable income		£30,287
Tax payable:		
1,500 @ 10%		150.00
26,500 @ 23%		6,095.00
2,287 @ 40%		914.80
		7,159.80
Deduct Interest relief:		
Actual interest	750	
Notional interest	1,125	
	£1,875	
£1,875 @ 10%		187.50
Tax liability		£6,972.30

Notes

(*a*) The season ticket loan does not give rise to a taxable benefit as it is not a qualifying loan and at no time in the tax year does the amount outstanding exceed £5,000.

(*b*) Mortgage interest is abolished for 2000/01 and subsequent years.

75.19 **Employee shareholdings.** Where an employee or person connected with him (see 20 CONNECTED PERSONS) acquires shares in any company at an under-value in pursuance of a right or opportunity available by reason of the employment, then he will be treated as if he had the benefit of an interest-free notional loan, with the effect that

(i) termination of that loan under (*b*) or (*c*) below may give rise to a charge under *ICTA 1988, s 160(2)* (see 75.17 above) (such a charge being deductible for capital gains), and

(ii) a charge may arise on notional interest under *ICTA 1988, s 160(1)* (see 75.17 above).

No charge can arise, however, where a corresponding amount representing the same benefit is otherwise included in emoluments.

A right, etc. is 'available' to the taxpayer although he may himself have stipulated its being granted (*CIR v Herd CS 1992, 66 TC 77*).

The initial amount of the notional loan is so much of the market value of fully paid-up shares of that class (less any payments then made) as is not otherwise chargeable as an emolument. The loan may be reduced by later payments or terminated by (*a*) payments to clear the loan,

(*b*) if shares not fully paid up at acquisition, the release etc. of any outstanding or contingent obligation to pay for them,

(*c*) disposal of the shares,

(*d*) death of employee.

Where shares are acquired as above, *but whether or not at an under-value*, and disposed of at more than market value, the excess is treated as emoluments of the employment for the year of disposal.

These provisions continue to apply up to the death of the employee notwithstanding any prior termination of employment. Where there is less than full beneficial ownership of the shares, the provisions apply proportionately. [*ICTA 1988, s 162; TCGA 1992, s 120(3)*].

As regards the circumstances in which a charge under *section 162* may arise on exercise of an option to acquire shares, see Revenue Schedule E Manual, SE 3619.

See also 75.36 below and 82.7, 82.8 SHARE INCENTIVES AND OPTIONS.

Simon's Direct Tax Service. See E4.621.

75.20 **Scholarships.** Where payments are made under scholarship awards *ICTA 1988, s 331* is not to be construed as conferring exemption from tax on any person other than the holder of the scholarship. If a scholarship (including an exhibition, bursary or other similar educational endowment) is provided to a member of the family or household of a director or higher-paid employee by reason of the latter's employment the payments are assessable on such director etc. as a benefit under *ICTA 1988, s 154*. A scholarship is to be taken to have been provided by reason of a person's employment if provided, directly or indirectly, under arrangements entered into by, or by a person connected with, his employer.

However *section 154* will not bring into charge as a benefit a payment under a scholarship awarded out of a trust fund, or under a scheme, to a person receiving full-time instruction at an educational establishment, where 25% or less of the payments made out of the fund, etc. in any year of assessment are scholarship payments provided, or treated as provided, by reason of a person's employment (regardless of whether or not the employment is director's or higher-paid or in the UK).

Payments which are *in fact* provided by reason of a person's employment are taxable even if the fund meets the 25% test.

[*ICTA 1988, s 165*].

For administrative procedures in relation to educational trust scholarships, see Revenue Schedule E Manual, SE 3706–3708.

See also 29.26 EXEMPT INCOME for payments to employees to attend sandwich courses.

Simon's Direct Tax Service. See **E4.618.**

75.21 **Sporting and recreational facilities.** The provision to an employee (or to a member of his family or household) of

(*a*) any benefit consisting in, or in a right or opportunity to make use of, any sporting or other recreational facilities made available generally to, or for use by, the employees of the employer in question, or

(*b*) any non-cash voucher (see 75.44 below) capable of being exchanged only for such a benefit is exempted from any charge to tax under Schedule E.

Excluded from the relief (unless prescribed by regulation) is any benefit consisting in

(i) an interest in, or the use of, any mechanically propelled vehicle (including ships, boats, aircraft and hovercraft),

(ii) an interest in, or the use of, any holiday or other overnight accommodation or associated facilities,

(iii) a facility provided on domestic premises (i.e. premises used wholly or mainly as a private dwelling, or belonging to or enjoyed with such premises),

(iv) a facility available to, or for use by, the general public,

(v) a facility not used wholly or mainly by persons whose right or opportunity to use it derives from employment, or

(vi) a right or opportunity to make use of any facility within (i)–(v) above.

As regards (iv) above, where employers group together to provide facilities for members of all their staffs, this does not of itself mean that they are available to members of the general public. In practice, the opening of facilities to a restricted section of the public (e.g. those living in the immediate vicinity) as well as to employees will similarly not result in loss of the relief. (Revenue Schedule E Manual, SE 3385, 3386).

As regards (v) above, a right or opportunity derives from employment only if it derives from the person's being (or having been) an employee of a particular employer (or a member of such a person's family or household) and the facility is available generally to employees of that employer.

The Treasury may by regulation prescribe exceptions from, and conditional inclusions in, this relief.

[*ICTA 1988, s 197G; FA 1993, s 75*].

Simon's Direct Tax Service. See **E4.612**.

75.22 **Dispensations** (notices of nil liability). If an employer supplies the inspector with a statement of the cases and circumstances in which particular types of expense payments and benefits are made or provided by him for any employees (whether his own or those of anyone else) and the inspector is satisfied that such benefits etc. give rise to no tax liability, he shall issue a notice of nil liability, but this can be revoked later. [*ICTA 1988, s 166*]. Dispensations are frequently given for e.g. travelling and subsistence expenses on an approved scale for business journeys in the UK, but not generally for 'round sum' expense allowances. Scale rate payments merely reimbursing average expenditure are not regarded as round sum allowances (see Revenue Schedule E Manual, SE 1302). The effect is to exclude such items from the PAYE scheme, returns, etc. They are not given, however, where the effect would be to remove the employee from liability under the benefits legislation (see 75.11 above). See Revenue Pamphlets IR 69 for conditions and 480 generally. See also Revenue Schedule E Manual, SE 3800 *et seq.*.

Provided that the circumstances under which a dispensation was issued have not changed, it will also be accepted as evidence that the expenses covered are not earnings for national insurance contributions purposes. (Revenue Tax Bulletin August 1995 p 245).

Simon's Direct Tax Service. See **E4.651**.

75.23 EMPLOYEE LIABILITIES AND INDEMNITY INSURANCE

For 1995/96 and subsequent years of assessment, there may be deducted from Schedule E emoluments out of which they are paid (*a*) any amount paid in or towards the discharge of a 'qualifying liability' of the employee;

(*b*) costs or expenses incurred in connection with any claim that the employee is subject to a 'qualifying liability' or with any related proceedings; and

(*c*) so much of any premium (or similar payment) paid under a 'qualifying contract' of insurance as relates to the indemnification of the employee against a 'qualifying liability' or to the payment of such costs and expenses as in (*b*) above.

Where any amount in (*a*)–(*c*) above is met by the employer or a third party, there may be made a deduction to offset a resultant taxable benefit (see 75.11 above). However, no deduction may be made for any such liability, costs or expenses if it would have been unlawful for the employer to insure against them (for example, costs arising from criminal convictions, and see Revenue Tax Bulletin October 1995 p 258).

A liability is a '*qualifying liability*' of the employee if it is imposed either

(i) in respect of any acts or omissions of the employee in his capacity as such or in any other capacity in which he acts in the performance of his duties, or

(ii) in connection with any proceedings relating to or arising from claims in respect of such acts or omissions.

A '*qualifying contract*' of insurance is one

(A) which, as regards the risks insured against, relates exclusively to one or more of the following

  (i) indemnification of any employee against any qualifying liability,

  (ii) indemnification of any person against any vicarious liability in respect of acts or omissions giving rise to a qualifying liability of another,

  (iii) payment of costs and expenses in connection with any claim that a person is subject to a liability to which the insurance relates or with related proceedings, and

  (iv) indemnification of any employer against any loss from the payment by him to an employee of his of any amount in respect of either a qualifying liability or costs and expenses as in (iii) above;

(B) which is not 'connected' with any other contract (see below);

(C) a significant part of the premium for which does not relate to rights to payments or benefits other than cover for the risks insured against and any right of renewal; and

(D) the period of insurance under which is not more than two years (disregarding renewals) and which the insured is not required to renew.

Two contracts are '*connected*' (see (B) above) if either was entered into by reference to the other or to enable the other to be, or to facilitate the other being, entered into on particular terms *and* the terms of either contract would have been significantly different if it had not been for the other. Connected contracts, each of which satisfy (A), (C) and (D), are qualifying contracts despite (B) above, where the only significant difference in terms consists in certain premium reductions.

Where applicable, for the purposes of these provisions, an insurance premium may be reasonably apportioned as between the different risks, persons or employments to which the contract relates.

[*ICTA 1988, s 201AA; FA 1995, s 91*].

For clarification of certain points on operation of the relief, see Revenue Tax Bulletin October 1995 pp 257, 258.

See Simon's Direct Tax Service E4.718A.

Post-employment deductions. Relief against total income (and capital gains, see below) may be claimed for payments made by a former employee which are made after the employment ceases and no later than six years after the end of the year of assessment in which it ceased and which would have been deductible under *ICTA 1988, s 201AA* (see above) if the employment had continued and if the payment had been made out of the emoluments. Relief is given for the year in which the payment is made and unused relief cannot be carried forward. In determining whether the payment would have been deductible under *section 201AA*, only acts or omissions relating to the actual period of employment are taken into account.

Relief is not available for any payment the cost of which is ultimately borne by the former employer, by a successor to the former employer's business or to his liabilities, by a person connected with either of those (see (20) CONNECTED PERSONS) or out of related insurance proceeds. However, where such a payment falls to be treated as a taxable emolument of the former employee or as a taxable benefit provided under an unapproved retirement benefit scheme (see 66.9 RETIREMENT SCHEMES), he is treated as having paid an equivalent amount out of that emolument or benefit, so as to effectively cancel the tax charge (providing the payment qualifies for relief under these provisions). No tax is charged under *ICTA 1988, s 148* (see 19.5 COMPENSATION FOR LOSS OF EMPLOYMENT (AND DAMAGES)) in respect of any amount paid, or benefit provided, to reimburse the former employee for a payment, which, had he not been reimbursed, would have attracted relief under these provisions; the same applies as regards amounts paid etc. to the former employee's executors or administrators.

Relief against capital gains. Where a claim is made as above and the claimant's income for the year is insufficient to fully utilise the relief, he may make a claim to have the excess relief treated as an allowable loss for that year for capital gains tax purposes. The allowable loss may not exceed the amount of the claimant's gains for the year *before* deducting any losses brought forward, the capital gains tax annual exemption, any relief available under *FA 1991, s 72* for trading losses (see 46.5 LOSSES) or any relief available to a former trader etc. for post-cessation expenditure (see 62.4 POST-CESSATION ETC. RECEIPTS AND EXPENDITURE); any excess over that amount is *not* available to carry forward against gains of a later year.

[*FA 1995, s 92; FA 1998, s 58, Sch 9 para 5*].

See Simon's Direct Tax Service E4.718B.

75.24 EMPLOYMENT OR PROFESSION?

Whether a person holds an office or employment or carries on a profession or vocation depends on the facts including the relevant contract(s). A distinction is drawn between a contract *of service* (Schedule E) and a contract *for services* (Schedule D). A vision mixer engaged under a series of short-term contracts was within Schedule D (*Hall v Lorimer CA 1993, 66 TC 349*), as was an artiste who entered into a series of engagements (*Davies v Braithwaite KB 1933, 18 TC 198*), but contrast *Fall v Hitchen Ch D 1972, 49 TC 433* in which a ballet dancer engaged by a theatrical management under a standard form of contract, but able to work elsewhere when not required by the management, was held to be within Schedule E. See now below as regards artistes. A barristers' clerk was not the holder of an office (*McMenamin v Diggles Ch D 1991, 64 TC 286*), but in *Horner v Hasted Ch D, [1995] STC 766* an unqualified accountant contributing capital to, and sharing profits of, a firm of accountants was held not to be a partner. The provision of catering services under contract at a golf club was held to be within Schedule D, Case I (*McManus v Griffiths Ch*

D 1997, 70 TC 218). See *Andrews v King Ch D 1991, 64 TC 332* as regards agricultural gangmasters.

See also *Barnett v Brabyn Ch D 1996, 69 TC 133* for a case in which the taxpayer unsuccessfully appealed against Schedule D, Case I additional assessments on the grounds that he was employed, where the original assessments had been agreed on the basis of his contention that he was self-employed.

Problems may arise in relation to part-time activities. A part-time medical appointment of a doctor in private practice assessable under Schedule D was held to be within Schedule E (*Mitchell & Edon v Ross HL 1961, 40 TC 11*) as were the lecture fees of a full-time consultant within Schedule E (*Lindsay v CIR CS 1964, 41 TC 661*) and a non-practising barrister (*Sidey v Phillips Ch D 1986, 59 TC 458*), the evening class fees of a teacher (*Fuge v McClelland Ch D 1956, 36 TC 571*) and the remuneration as lecturer of a professional singer (*Walls v Sinnett Ch D 1986, 60 TC 150*), but *ad hoc* Crown appointments were held to be within Schedule D (*Edwards v Clinch HL 1981, 56 TC 367*). Salaries of sub-postmasters carrying on a retail trade from the same premises as the sub-post office are in practice treated as part of their Schedule D income. Where a company operates sub-post offices in its shops with its directors as nominee sub-postmasters, and the directors are required to, and do, hand over their salaries as sub-postmasters to the company, the salaries will similarly be brought into the company's Schedule D, Case I computation and not assessed on the directors under Schedule E. (Revenue Schedule E Manual, SE 7781). As regards sub-postmasters generally, see *Dhendsa v Richardson (Sp C 134), [1997] SSCD 265*.

Certain appointments, such as auditorships and registrarships, are strictly offices within Schedule E but if held by practising accountants or solicitors the annual remuneration therefrom is, in practice, usually included in the Schedule D assessment on the profession. Fees from directorships of professional partnerships may be included in Schedule D assessment provided that the directorship is a normal incident of the profession and the practice concerned, and that the fees are only a small part of total profits and are pooled for division among the partners under partnership agreement. A written undertaking must be given that the full fees received will be included in gross income of the basis period whether or not the directorship is still held in the year of assessment or the partner concerned is still a partner. (Revenue Pamphlet IR 1 (1992) A37). For directors' fees received by other companies see 75.1(1) above. However any compensation etc. payments on the termination of such appointments are dealt with under *ICTA 1988, s 148*, see 19.4 COMPENSATION FOR LOSS OF EMPLOYMENT (AND DAMAGES) and *Brander & Cruickshank HL 1970, 46 TC 574* and the cases referred to therein.

See generally Revenue Schedule E Manual, SE 541 *et seq.* and, for the questions likely to be raised in any interview in relation to the question of employment or self-employment, SE 900. See also Revenue Pamphlet IR 56.

See also 61.4, 61.18 PERSONAL SERVICE COMPANIES ETC. which are concerned with the question of whether an individual providing his services through an intermediary would be an employee if engaged directly by a client, but which are also of wider application.

Artistes (i.e. actors, singers, musicians, dancers and theatrical artists). It is understood that the Revenue accept that the earnings of most artistes should be assessed under Schedule D, Case I. Circumstances in which Schedule E and PAYE should be applied would e.g. be where the artiste is engaged for a regular salary to perform in a series of different productions at the direction of the engager, and with a period of notice stipulated before termination of the contract. This might apply e.g. to permanent members of an opera, ballet or theatre company or an orchestra. (*Taxation* 8 September 1994, p 553). See Revenue Inspector's Manual, IM 1810 for a general discussion of this distinction.

See generally Revenue Schedule E Manual, SE 7332 *et seq.*.

A **dentist** employed by a Panamanian company, which contracted with a UK practice to supply his services in return for a proportion of the NHS fees and a management charge, was held to be within Schedule E, although the legality of the arrangements was in question (*Cooke v Blacklaws Ch D 1984, 58 TC 255*).

Divers etc. employed in UK area of the Continental Shelf are assessed under Schedule D, Case I, see 71.31 SCHEDULE D, CASES I AND II.

Film, etc. technicians. From 6 April 1983, the Revenue reclassified certain grades of such technicians as employed persons liable under Schedule E, subject to the usual rights of appeal. (Revenue Press Release 30 March 1983). A vision mixer was, however, held to be self-employed in *Hall v Lorimer CA 1993, 66 TC 349*. See Revenue Schedule E Manual, SE 7321 *et seq.*.

Simon's Direct Tax Service. See E4.2.

75.25 **FLAT RATE EXPENSES FOR EMPLOYEES**

Deductions are allowed for tools, special clothing etc. necessarily provided by an employee without reimbursement, and which the employer does not make available. If tools or protective clothing are supplied, but not both, or if some of the tools are provided, the rate of allowance may be reduced accordingly. These are mostly agreed with trade unions, but the agreed rates do not preclude further claims, if justified, under *ICTA 1988, s 198(1)*. See Revenue Pamphlet IR 1, A1 Appendix and *Ward v Dunn Ch D 1978, 52 TC 517*.

Industry Code	*Industry Group*	*Occupation*	*Allowances from 6 April 1995 (1991)* £
10	Agriculture	All Workers	70 (60)
20	Forestry	All Workers	70 (60)
30	Seamen	a. Carpenters Passenger Liners (Seamen)	135 (140)
		b. Carpenters Cargo Vessels, (Seamen) Tankers, Coasters and Ferries	130 (110)
50	Iron Mining	a. Fillers, Miners and Underground Workers	100 (85)
		b. All Other Workers	75 (65)
60	Quarrying	All Workers	70 (60)
70	Iron and Steel	a. Day Labourers, General Labourers, Stockmen, Timekeepers, Warehouse Staff and Weighmen	60 (50)
		b. Apprentices	45 (40)
		c. All Other Workers	120 (105)
90	Brass and copper	All Workers	100 (85)
100	Aluminium	a. Continual Casting Operators, Process Operators, De-Dimplers, Driers, Drill Punchers, Dross Unloaders, Firemen, Furnace Operators and their helpers, Leaders, Mouldmen, Pourers, Remelt Department Labourers, Roll Flatteners	130 (110)

Industry Code	*Industry Group*	*Occupation*	*Allowances from 6 April 1995 (1991)* £
		b. Cable Hands, Case Makers, Labourers, Mates, Truck Drivers and Measurers, Storekeepers	60 (50)
		c. Apprentices	45 (40)
		d. All Other Workers	100 (85)
110	Engineering	a. Pattern Makers	120 (105)
		b. Labourers, Supervisory and Unskilled Workers	60 (50)
		c. Apprentices and Storekeepers	45 (40)
		d. Motor Mechanics in Garage Repair Shops	100 (85)
		e. All Other Workers	100 (85)
120	Shipyards	a. Blacksmiths and their Strikers, Boilermakers, Burners, Carpenters, Caulkers, Drillers, Furnacemen (Platers), Holders Up, Fitters, Platers, Plumbers, Riveters, Sheet Iron Workers, Shipwrights, Tubers and Welders	115 (95)
		b. Labourers	60 (50)
		c. Apprentices and Storekeepers	45 (40)
		d. All Other Workers	75 (65)
130	Vehicles	a. Builders, Railway Wagon etc. Repairers, and Railway Wagon Lifters	105 (90)
		b. Railway Vehicle Painters and Letterers, Railway Wagon etc. Builders' and Repairers' Assistants	60 (50)
		c. All Other Workers	40(30)
140	Particular Engineering	a. Pattern Makers	120 (105)
		b. All Chainmakers-Cleaners, Galvanisers, Tinners and Wire Drawers in the Wire Drawing Industry-Toolmakers in the Lockmaking Industry	100 (85)
		c. Apprentices and Storekeepers	45 (40)
		d. All Other Workers	60 (50)
150	Constructional Engineering	a. Blacksmiths and their Strikers, Burners, Caulkers, Chippers, Drillers, Erectors, Fitters, Holders Up, Markers Off, Platers, Riggers, Riveters, Rivet Heaters, Scaffolders, Sheeters, Template Workers, Turners and Welders	115 (95)
		b. Banksmen Labourers, Shophelpers, Slewers and Straightenders	60 (50)
		c. Apprentices and Storekeepers	45 (40)
		d. All Other Workers	75 (65)

Industry Code	Industry Group	Occupation	Allowances from 6 April 1995 (1991) £
160	Precious Metals	All Workers	70 (60)
170	Electrical and Electricity Supply	a. Those workers incurring laundry costs only (generally CEGB employees)	25 (20)
		b. All Other Workers	90 (75)
180	Textiles	a. Carders, Carding Engineers, Overlookers (all), and Technicians in Spinning Mills	85 (70)
		b. All Other Workers	60 (50)
190	Clothing	a. Lacemakers, Hosiery Bleachers, Dyers, Scourers and Knitters, and Knitwear Bleachers and Dyers	45 (40)
		b. All Other Workers	30 (25)
200	Textile Prints	All Workers	60 (50)
210	Leather	a. Curriers (Wet Workers), Fellmongering Workers and Tanning Operatives (Wet)	55 (45)
		b. All Other Workers	40 (30)
220	Food	All Workers	40 (30)
230	Printing	a. The following occupations in the Letterpress Section Electrical Engineers (Rotary Presses), Electro-typers, Ink and Roller Makers, Machine Minders (Rotary), Maintenance Engineers (Rotary Presses) and Stereotypers	105 (90)
		b. Bench Hands (P&B), Compositors (Lp), Readers (Lp), T&E Section Wireroom Operators, Warehousemen (PprBox)	30 (25)
		c. All Other Workers	70 (60)
240	Glass	All Workers	60 (50)
250	Building Materials	a. Stone Masons	85 (70)
		b. Tile Makers and Labourers	40 (30)
		c. All Other Workers	55 (45)
260	Wood and Furniture	a. Carpenters, Cabinet Makers, Joiners, Wood Carvers and Woodcutting Machinists	115 (95)
		b. Artificial Limb Makers (other than in wood), Organ Builders and Packaging Case Makers	90 (75)
		c. Coopers not providing own tools, Labourers, Polishers and Upholsterers	45 (40)
		d. All Other Workers	75 (65)

Industry Code	*Industry Group*	*Occupation*	*Allowances from 6 April 1995 (1991)* £
270	Building	a. Joiners and Carpenters	105 (95)
		b. Cement Works, Roofing Felt and Asphalt Labourers	55 (45)
		c. Labourers and Navvies	40 (30)
		d. All Other Workers	85 (70)
280	Heating	a. Pipe Fitters and Plumbers	100 (90)
		b. Coverers, Laggers, Domestic Glaziers, Heating Engineers and their Mates	90 (75)
		c. All Gas Workers and All Other Workers	70 (60)
290	Railways	All Workers except Craftsmen (For craftsmen see the appropriate industry code lists e.g. engineering)	70 (60)
300	Public Service	i. Dock and Inland Waterways	
		a. Dockers, Dredger Drivers and Hopper Steerers	55 (45)
		b. All Other Workers	40 (30)
		ii. Public Transport	
		a. Garage Hands (including Cleaners)	55 (45)
		b. Conductors and Drivers	40 (30)
320	Prisons	Uniformed Prison Officers	55 (45)
330	Banks	Uniformed Bank Employees	40 (30)
355	Police Force	Uniformed Police Officers (ranks up to and including Chief Inspector)	55 (45)
—	Fire Service	Uniformed Fire Fighters and Fire Officers	60*
—	Healthcare	*a.* Ambulance Staff on Active Service (i.e. excluding staff who take telephone calls or provide clerical support)	110**
		b. Nurses and Midwives, Chiropodists, Dental Nurses, Occupational, Speech and other Therapists, Orthoptists, Phlebotomists, Physiotherapists, Radiographers	70**
		c. Plaster Room Orderlies, Hospital Porters, Ward Clerks, Sterile Supply workers, Hospital domestics, Hospital catering staff	60**
		d. Laboratory staff, Pharmacists, Pharmacy Assistants	45**

* Agreed with fire service unions in 1994. ** Introduced for 1998/99 onwards. Employees may claim allowances for up to six years previously, i.e. from 1992/93 onwards. (Revenue Press Release 5 March 1999).

It is understood that an allowance of £18 p.a. is available to nurses to cover the cost of shoes and tights. (Tolley's Practical Tax 1993 p 72).

Notes.

1. Industry Code is an industry identification term used for Inland Revenue computer purposes.
2. The expressions 'all workers' and 'all other workers' refer only to manual workers, or certain other workers who have to bear the cost of upkeep of tools or special clothing. They do not extend to other employees such as office staff.
3. 'Cost of upkeep' means the cost of replacement, repair or cleaning, but not the initial cost of providing the tools or special clothing.
4. 'Special clothing' means overalls or other protective clothing or uniform, but does not include ordinary clothing of the sort which is also worn off duty.

75.26 **GIFTS, AWARDS ETC. RECEIVED**

Gifts etc. are taxable when they arise out of the employment but not if they are given to the recipient in a personal capacity. The line between the two may be fine. Although emoluments may be voluntary and irregular, they are assessable. Also all commissions, Xmas presents, 'cost of living', cash and other bonuses. For 'tax-free' payments and awards, see 75.40 below. For payments to clergymen, see 75.9 above.

Bonus to a director described as a gift held assessable (*Radcliffe v Holt KB 1927, 11 TC 621*). Proceeds of a *public benefit match* for a cricketer held to be a gift and not chargeable (*Reed v Seymour HL 1927, 11 TC 625*), but see *Moorhouse v Dooland CA 1954, 36 TC 1* re collections. In *Davis v Harrison KB 1927, 11 TC 707, Corbett v Duff and other cases KB 1941, 23 TC 763*, payments to professional football players *in lieu of benefit* or on *transference to another club*, held assessable. World Cup bonus to professional footballer not assessable (*Moore v Griffiths Ch D 1972, 48 TC 338*). Present to *successful jockey* by owner of racehorse assessable (*Wing v O'Connell Supreme Court (Ireland) 1926, 1 ITC 170*) also *taxi-driver's tips* (*Calvert v Wainwright KB 1947, 27 TC 475*) and gifts to Hunt servant (*Wright v Boyce CA 1958, 38 TC 160*). Betting winnings on own games by professional golfer not assessable (*Down v Compston KB 1937, 21 TC 60*).

Gift to employee by company to which his services were lent by employer held not assessable, *Morris CS 1967, 44 TC 685*. But amount to company secretary, agreed by directors for negotiating sale of works and paid by liquidator, held assessable (*Shipway v Skidmore KB 1932, 16 TC 748*) as were payments to a director for negotiating sale of a branch (*Mudd v Collins KB 1925, 9 TC 297*) and to a director for special services abroad (*Barson v Airey CA 1925, 10 TC 609*). Commission for work outside ordinary duties assessable (*Mudd v Collins KB 1925, 9 TC 297*). Sums paid as compensation for loss of benefit under an abandoned salvage scheme held assessable (*Holland v Geoghegan Ch D 1972, 48 TC 482*), also assets distributed to employees on termination of profit-sharing trust fund before termination of employment (*Brumby v Milner HL 1976, 51 TC 583*). See, however, *Bray v Best HL 1989, 61 TC 705* as regards such a distribution after termination of employment.

See 75.36 below regarding gifts of shares.

Pensions (voluntary or otherwise) to retired employees are assessable (see 59.1(v) PENSIONS) as are certain payments in consideration of, in consequence of, or in connection with the termination, or change, of employment (see 19 COMPENSATION FOR LOSS OF EMPLOYMENT (AND DAMAGES)).

Suggestion scheme awards are, by concession, not taxed under Schedule E provided that there is a formally constituted scheme open to all employees on equal terms, and that the suggestion concerned is outside the scope of the employee's normal duties. Suggestions put forward at meetings held for that purpose are excluded. Awards under the scheme must either be 'encouragement' awards of £25 or less for meritorious suggestions not implemented, or must follow a decision to implement the suggestion. In the latter case, the decision to make the award must relate to the benefit expected to flow from implementation, and the amount of the award must not exceed 50% of the first year's expected net benefit, or 10% of the expected benefit over a period of up to five years, with an overriding maximum of £5,000. Any excess over £5,000 is not covered by the concession. Where a suggestion is put forward by more than one employee, the award must be divided on a reasonable basis. (Revenue Pamphlet IR 1, A57 as revised).

Long service awards, of tangible articles or of shares in the employing company (or in another group company), to employees, including directors, for service of 20 years or more, will not be taxed to the extent that cost to employer does not exceed £20 for each year of service and provided that no similar award has been made to recipient within previous 10 years. (Revenue Pamphlet IR 1, A22). Cash awards are assessable (*Weston v Hearn KB 1943, 25 TC 425*).

Gifts from third parties. Gifts (other than cash) costing not more than £150 (inclusive of VAT) in any tax year (£100 for 1994/95 and earlier years) received from a person other than the employer are, by concession, exempt from tax, subject to similar conditions as apply to the provision of entertainment by third parties (see 75.13(xv) above) and provided that they are not made under any sort of reciprocal arrangement. (Revenue Pamphlet IR 1, A70).

Simon's Direct Tax Service. See **E4.461** *et seq.*.

75.27 HM FORCES

Mess and ration allowances and certain bounties and gratuities are exempt. [*ICTA 1988, s 316*]. No tax allowance may be claimed for lodging expenses paid out of assessable lodging allowance (*Evans v Richardson, Nagley v Spilsbury Ch D 1957, 37 TC 178*), nor for mess expenses (*Lomax v Newton Ch D 1953, 34 TC 558*).

Territorial Army pay assessable but not annual bounty and training expenses. [*ICTA 1988, s 316(4)*]. Certain payments and other benefits (including commutation of annual sums) are exempt from any charge under *ICTA 1988, s 148* (see 19 COMPENSATION FOR LOSS OF EMPLOYMENT (AND DAMAGES)). [*ICTA 1988, s 188(1)(e), Sch 11 para 3; FA 1998, Sch 9 Pt I, Sch 27 Pt III(9)*]. See also 29.5 and 29.31 EXEMPT INCOME and 59.4 PENSIONS. Travel facilities (including allowances, vouchers and warrants) for going on, or returning from, leave are exempt from tax. [*ICTA 1988, s 197*].

Uniform allowances. Serving officers generally receive an annual tax-free allowance which, taking one year with another, covers the costs they are obliged to incur in maintaining their uniforms. The allowance is automatically included in their emoluments, with a corresponding deduction being made. [*ICTA 1988, s 199*]. No further action is thus generally required. The allowances for **1998/99 onwards** are as follows.

Army	£
Officers serving at full mounted duty	1,012.88
Male dismounted Officers, Colonels and above	749.78
Female Officers, Colonels and above (except QARANC (below))	499.84
Dismounted Officers (Household Division) below Colonel	673.19
Male dismounted Officers below Colonel (except Household Division)	589.29
Female Officers below Colonel (except QARANC (below))	488.30
QARANC: Female Nursing Officers, Colonels and above	671.48

	£
Female Nursing Officers below Colonel	652.87
Male SSLC and SSVC Officers	186.55
Female SSLC and SSVC Officers	201.20
Royal Air Force	£
Male RAF Officers (including PMRAFNS)	
Air Officers	422.76
Group Captains	402.72
Wing Commander and below	361.10
Female officers of PMRAFNS	
Air Officers	589.16
Group Captains	586.00
Wing Commander and below	579.70
Female RAF Officers	
Air Officers	477.98
Group Captains	460.74
Wing Commander and below	421.69
Royal Navy and Royal Marines	£
Officers Flag and equivalent ranks	1,071.00
Officers below Flag rank	792.12
WRNS Officers: seagoing only	853.80
non-seagoing	680.52
Women Medical and Dental Officers: seagoing	792.60
non-seagoing	567.48
QARNNS Officers (female)	
Matron and above	544.68
Below Matron	828.00
QARNNS Officers (male)	
Chief Nursing Officer and above	489.36
Below Chief Nursing Officer	456.48

75.28 LEGAL

In *Eagles v Levy KB 1934, 19 TC 23* held (*a*) costs of action to recover remuneration not an allowable deduction, and (*b*) lump sum amount in settlement of action for balance remuneration assessable in full.

Where company had special need of director's services and paid more than necessary in legal costs of defence on motoring charge, no apportionment between benefits to company and employee and all assessable (*Rendell v Went HL 1964, 41 TC 641*).

Simon's Direct Tax Service. See **E4.718**.

75.29 LIVING ACCOMMODATION ETC.

Provision of living accommodation etc., for an employee may be taxable emoluments under general principles (see 75.7 above), but see below as regards 1996/97 onwards. In *Nicoll v Austin KB 1935, 19 TC 531*, a company maintained a large house owned and occupied by its managing director and controlling shareholder, paying the rates, fuel bills and other outgoings. The expenditure was held to be assessable on him as emoluments of his office.

There may also be liability under special legislation as described below. For 1996/97 and subsequent years, the charge under this legislation takes priority over any charge under general principles, the latter applying only if, and to the extent that, the charge would exceed that under *ICTA 1988, s 145* and *s 146* below. [*ICTA 1988, s 146A; FA 1996, s 106(2)(3)*]. This is an anti-avoidance measure aimed at salary sacrifices.

'Living accommodation' for these purposes includes all kinds of residential accommodation – e.g. mansions, houses, flats, houseboats, holiday homes or apartments – but not overnight or hotel accommodation or board and lodging. Whether such accommodation is provided for an employee is a question of fact — if it is habitable and available for his occupation, it will normally be regarded as available for him, whether or not, for particular reasons, he actually occupies it. Where accommodation is provided for a number of employees but remains unoccupied at times, the charge will be apportioned between them according to the facts of the case. (Revenue Schedule E Manual, SE 2210, 2211).

Basic charge

For any employee, any living accommodation provided to him, or to members of his family or household, by his employer (and, before 1996/97, not otherwise taxable), is treated as an emolument equal to the value of the accommodation to him for the period, less any sum made good by the employee to those providing the accommodation, *unless* it is provided in the normal course of domestic, family and personal relationships, or by a local authority under its usual terms for non-employees.

A charge may also arise where the accommodation is provided by someone other than the employer but 'by reason of' the employment, i.e. where the accommodation would not have been provided but for the employment. In practice the Revenue normally assume that a benefit which is provided by someone other than the employer but which is plainly connected with the employment has been provided by reason of the employment. (Revenue Schedule E Manual, SE 2212, 3042).

The value of the accommodation for a period is normally rent for the period equivalent to an annual rent equal to the annual value ascertained under *ICTA 1988, s 837* (which is equivalent to the gross rateable value, see 68.7(*e*)(*d*) SCHEDULE A), or any actual rent, if greater, paid by those providing the benefit, reduced by any amount which would be deductible as an expense under *ICTA 1988, s 198* (see 75.10 above) or *ICTA 1988, s 332(3)* (see 75.9 above, Clergymen) if the employee had paid for the accommodation himself. [*ICTA 1988, s 145(1)–(3)(6); FA 1996, s 106(1)(3)*]. In Scotland, where the 1985 rating revaluation produced annual values out of line with those in the rest of the UK, a figure lower than the gross rateable value is, by concession, used as annual value. The 1985 valuation figure is scaled back by the average increase in Scottish rateable values between 1978 and 1985 (170%), e.g. a 1985 value of £270 becomes £100 for this purpose. (Revenue Pamphlet IR 1, A56). For new properties which do not appear on the domestic rating lists, and for those where there has been a material change since the lists ceased to be maintained, estimates will be agreed of what the gross annual value would have been had domestic rates been continued. In the case of Scotland these will then be scaled back to 1978 values. (Revenue Press Releases 10 November 1989, 19 April 1990). For determination of the annual value (under *ICTA 1988, s 837*) of property situated outside the UK, see Revenue Schedule E Manual, SE 2244.

Where a property is provided as living accommodation to more than one employee or director in the same period, the total amounts charged under *ICTA 1988, s 145* and *s 146* (see below) will, by concession, not exceed the amount which would have been chargeable if the property had been provided to a single employee in that period. (Revenue Pamphlet IR 1, A91).

Exemptions to the above charge are

(*a*) where it is necessary for the proper performance of his duties for the employee to reside in the accommodation;

(*b*) where the employment is such that it is customary for employees to be provided with accommodation for the better performance of their duties;

(*c*) where there is a special threat to the employee's security, and he resides in the accommodation as part of special security arrangements in force;

(*d*) where the employer is an individual and the provision of accommodation is made in the normal course of his domestic, family or personal relationships;

(*e*) where the employer is a local authority and the accommodation provided is on no better terms than those for similar accommodation to non-employees.

[*ICTA 1988, s 145(4)(7); FA 1996, s 134, Sch 20 para 7*].

See *Vertigan v Brady Ch D 1988, 60 TC 624* as regards the scope of (*a*) and (*b*) above.

Notes to above.

(A) *Rates, etc.* Where (*a*), (*b*) or (*c*) applies, there is also no liability if the rates or council tax are paid or reimbursed by the employer (otherwise there could be liability under general principles, see above). [*ICTA 1988, s 145(4)*]. The exemption does not apply to payments of the community charge (and, in Scotland, the community water charge), which are the employee's (or his family's) personal liability. (Revenue Press Release 10 November 1989).

(B) *Directors.* Neither (*a*) nor (*b*) above applies to accommodation provided by a company, or associated company, to its director unless for each such directorship he has no material interest in the company (i.e. broadly if his and/or his associates' interests in the company do not exceed 5%) *and either* he is a full-time working director *or* the company is non-profit-making (i.e. it does not carry on a trade nor is its main function the holding of investments or other property) *or* the company is a charity. [*ICTA 1988, s 145(5)(8)*].

(C) As regards (*b*) above, it is accepted that the following employees are within the exemption: police officers; MOD police; prison governors, officers and chaplains; clergymen and ministers of religion (unless engaged on purely administrative duties); members of HM forces; members of the Diplomatic Service; managers of newsagent shops with paper rounds; managers of off-licence shops with opening hours broadly equivalent to those of public houses; head teachers and teachers with 24-hour pastoral duties provided with accommodation on or adjacent to the school premises. Veterinary surgeons assisting in veterinary practices and managers of camping and caravan sites living on or adjacent to the site will be accepted as meeting the test that provision of accommodation is 'customary', but must individually satisfy the test that the provision is for the 'better performance' of their duties. (Revenue Schedule E Manual, SE 2256).

Simon's Direct Tax Service. See **E4.412**.

Additional charge in respect of certain properties

For all employees, if there is a liability to tax on living accommodation under *section 145* (as above), or there would be a liability if the employee's contributions towards the cost were disregarded, and the cost of providing the accommodation exceeds £75,000, the employee will, in addition to any charge under *section 145*, be assessed under Schedule E on the 'additional value' to him of the accommodation. Where, however, the charge under *section 145* is based on the full open market rent the property might fetch, the Revenue will, by concession, not seek to impose an additional charge under *section 146*. (Revenue Press Release (REV 35) 28 November 1995). Any rent paid by the employee which exceeds the value of the accommodation as determined under *section 145* is deducted from the additional value. The '*additional value*' is the rent which would have been payable for the period if the annual rent was the 'appropriate percentage' of the amount by which the cost of providing the accommodation exceeds £75,000. The '*appropriate percentage*' is the 'official rate' in force for the purposes of the beneficial loan arrangements of *ICTA 1988, s 160* (see 75.17 above) at the beginning of the year of assessment (i.e. 6.25% for 2000/01).

The cost of providing the accommodation is the aggregate of expenditure incurred by any 'relevant person' in acquiring the property together with any improvement expenditure incurred before the year of assessment in question *less* any payments by the employee to any relevant person as reimbursement of such expenditure or as consideration for the grant of a tenancy, or subtenancy, to him. Where the employee first occupies the property on a date after 30 March 1983 and any estate or interest in the property was held by any relevant person throughout the period of six years ending with that date (i.e. the date of first occupation), then the cost of providing the accommodation, for the purposes of calculating the additional value, is the aggregate of the market value of the property at that date, together with any improvement expenditure incurred after that date and before the year of assessment, less any employee contributions as above. A '*relevant person*' is the person providing the accommodation, or, if different, the employee's employer, and any person, other than the employee, connected with such persons under *ICTA 1988, s 839* (see 20 CONNECTED PERSONS). '*Market value*' is open market value assuming vacant possession and disregarding any options on the property held by the employee, a person connected with him or any relevant person as defined above.

Where an employee is provided with more than one property, the £75,000 limit is applied separately to each property. (Revenue Press Release 22 November 1990). Where a property is provided as living accommodation to more than one employee or director in the same period, the total amounts charged under *section 145* (see above) and *section 146* will, by concession, not exceed the amount which would have been chargeable if the property had been provided to a single employee in that period. (Revenue Press Release (REV 35) 28 November 1995).

It is understood that the Revenue would not normally seek to revise the cost of providing the accommodation for these purposes where the property in question happens to be transferred for administrative reasons within a group, although continuing to be provided for the same employee. (Tolley's Practical Tax 1985 p 120).

Any surplus of amounts deductible as necessary expenses from assessable emoluments under *section 145* may be deducted from any assessment on the additional value of the accommodation.

[*ICTA 1988, s 146*].

Example

S, the founder and managing director of S Ltd, a successful transport company, has since April 1996 occupied a mansion house owned by S Ltd. The house was acquired by S Ltd in August 1990 for £150,000 and, since acquisition, but before 6 April 1999, £80,000 has been spent by S Ltd on alterations and improvements to the house. The gross annual value of the house for rating purposes before 1 April 1990 (when the community charge replaced general rates) was £1,663. S pays annual rental of £2,000 to the company in respect of 2000/01 only. He pays all expenses relating to the property.

S will have assessable benefits in respect of his occupation of the house for 1999/2000 and 2000/01 as follows.

	£	£
1999/2000		
Gross annual value		1,663
Additional charge		
Acquisition cost of house	150,000	
Cost of improvements	80,000	
	230,000	
Deduct	75,000	
Additional value	£155,000	
Additional value at 6.25%		9,687
		£11,350
2000/01		
Gross annual value		Nil*
Additional charge		
Acquisition cost of house	150,000	
Cost of improvements	80,000	
	230,000	
Deduct	75,000	
Additional value	£155,000	
Additional value at 6.25%		9,687
		9,687
Rental payable by S	2,000	
Deduct Gross annual value	1,663	
		337*
		£9,350

* No taxable gross annual value arises in 2000/01 because the rental of £2,000 payable by S exceeds the gross annual value of £1,663. The excess is deductible from the amount of the benefit arising under the additional charge.

Simon's Direct Tax Service. See **E4.413.**

Directors and certain employees

For 'directors or higher-paid employees' the provision of living accommodation is excluded as a benefit under the special legislation applying to them (see 75.11 above) but they are chargeable under the provisions above.

Expenses connected with living accommodation discharged or borne on behalf of the employee may be benefits-in-kind (see 75.13 above), but

(i) *Alterations and repairs* to accommodation provided for directors and higher-paid employees will not be treated as benefits if

(A) the alterations or additions are of a structural nature, or

(B) the repairs would be the obligation of the lessor if the premises were leased and *Landlord and Tenant Act 1985, s 11* applied. [*ICTA 1988, s 155(3)*].

(ii) *Other expenses.* Where one of the exemptions in (*a*), (*b*) or (*c*) above applies, any amount to be treated as emoluments in respect of expenditure on heating, lighting, cleaning, repairs, maintenance, decoration, provision of furniture etc. normal for domestic occupation is limited to 10% of the net emoluments of the employment for the period concerned less any sum made good by the employee. *Emoluments* include any from an associated company (i.e. where one company has control of the other or both are under control of the same person). *Net emoluments* are (ignoring the benefit in question) after deducting capital allowances, allowable expenses, superannuation, retirement annuities and approved retirement benefits scheme payments. [*ICTA 1988, s 163*]. The emoluments concerned are those for the year under review, regardless of the year in which they are assessed (i.e. the year of receipt, see 75.1 above). (Revenue Schedule E Manual, SE 3192).

Simon's Direct Tax Service. See E4.620.

Example

N is employed by the G Property Co Ltd, earning £12,000 p.a. He occupies, rent-free, the basement flat of a block of flats for which he is employed as caretaker/security officer. The annual value of the flat is determined at £250. In 2000/01, G Ltd incurred the following expenditure on the flat.

	£
Heat and light	700
Decoration	330
Repairs	210
Cleaning	160
Conversion of large bedroom into two smaller bedrooms	3,000

In addition, the company pays N's council tax which amounts to £500.

As the company does not have a pension scheme, N pays a personal pension premium of £200 (net) on 31 October 2000, but apart from his personal allowance, he has no other reliefs.

N's taxable income for 2000/01 is

	£
Salary	12,000
Annual value of flat	—
Heat and light, decoration, repairs, cleaning £1,400 restricted to	1,200
	13,200
Deduct	
Personal allowance	4,385
Taxable	£8,815

Notes

(*a*) N is not assessed on the annual value of the flat as long as he can show that it is necessary for the proper performance of his duties for him to reside in the accommodation.

(*b*) The structural alterations costing £3,000 will not be regarded as a benefit.

(*c*) The emoluments treated as having arisen in respect of the heat and light, decoration, repairs and cleaning costs will be restricted to the lesser of

(i) the expenses incurred £1,400

(ii) 10% × £12,000 (net emoluments) £1,200

The personal pension contribution is not deductible in arriving at net emoluments for this purpose, although retirement annuity premiums and occupational pension scheme contributions are so deductible. (The contribution is not shown above as a deduction from taxable income as basic rate relief has been given at source and higher rate relief is not applicable.)

(*d*) Where the benefit of living accommodation is exempt under *ICTA 1988, s 145(4)*, the payment by the employer of the employee's council tax is also exempt. (Revenue Press Release 16 March 1993).

Case law

The following cases, decided under earlier legislation, may be relevant to a charge under *ICTA 1988, s 154* in respect of expenses related to living accommodation. *Butter v Bennett CA 1962, 40 TC 402* ('representative occupier' held to be assessable on provisions for fuel and gardening); *Doyle v Davison QB(NI) 1961, 40 TC 140* (repairs paid for by employer held to be benefits); *McKie v Warner Ch D 1961, 40 TC 65* (flat provided at reduced rent held to be benefit); *Luke HL 1963, 40 TC 630* (certain expenses held not to be benefits — house owned by employer); *Westcott v Bryan CA 1969, 45 TC 476* (apportionment approved where company house provided to accommodate company guests).

Other matters relating to living accommodation etc.

(A) **Compulsory transfers.** *Guarantee payments* making good loss on sale of employee's house when compulsorily transferred were held not assessable in *Hochstrasser v Mayes, Jennings v Kinder HL 1959, 38 TC 673.*

(B) **Members of Parliaments and Assemblies.** Members of the House of Commons, the Scottish Parliament or the Wales or Northern Ireland Assemblies are not allowed a deduction for expenditure incurred on residential or overnight accommodation to enable duties to be performed where the body of which they are a member sits or in the area which they represent. [*ICTA 1988, s 198(4); FA 1999, Sch 5 para 2(2)*]. See 29.16 EXEMPT INCOME as regards exempt accommodation allowances. See Simon's Direct Tax Service E4.334.

As regards board and lodging allowances, see 75.7 above and for subsistence allowances, see 75.43 below. For deductibility of the cost of living accommodation etc., see 75.10(*b*) above.

75.30 LUNCHEON VOUCHERS

No assessment on employee if vouchers are (i) non-transferable, (ii) used for meals only, (iii) limited to 15 pence per working day, (iv) if limited in issue, available to lower-paid staff.

The value of any voucher or part voucher not satisfying these conditions is assessable. (Revenue Pamphlet IR 1, A2). See 75.13(iv) above for canteen meals.

75.31 PROFIT-RELATED PAY [*ICTA 1988, ss 169–184, Sch 8; FA 1989, s 61, Sch 4; FA 1991, s 37; FA 1994, ss 98, 99; FA 1995, ss 136, 137(1)(6); FA 1997, s 61, Sch 18 Pt VI(3); FA 1999, s 46*]

Profit-related pay is charged in accordance with the receipts basis (see 75.1 above) subject to the exemption (until phased out — see below) from tax of so much of the profit-related pay as does not exceed the lower of:

(*a*) one-fifth of the aggregate, for the employment to which the scheme relates, of non-profit-related pay (within PAYE but excluding benefits) in the '*profit period*' (i.e. the accounting period by reference to which the profit-related pay is calculated), or in the part of that period by reference to which eligibility for profit-related pay arises, and the profit-related pay itself, and

(*b*) £4,000 (proportionately reduced where the profit period is less than twelve months or the employee is entitled to profit-related pay by reference to part only of that period).

The £4,000 limit in (*b*) above is reduced to £2,000 for profit periods beginning on or after 1 January 1998 and before 1 January 1999, and to £1,000 for profit periods beginning on or after 1 January 1999 and before 1 January 2000. The relief is **abolished** altogether for profit periods beginning **on or after 1 January 2000**. Registration of schemes (see below) is accordingly restricted. *FA 1998, s 62, Sch 11* prevent exploitation of the phasing-out provisions, by preventing employees in a registered scheme from obtaining a higher relief limit for a longer period by joining another scheme on or after 17 March 1998. This applies where the scheme employers of the two schemes are the same person or are CONNECTED PERSONS (20). The cancellation by the Revenue of a new scheme designed to obtain such an advantage, before enactment of these provisions, was upheld on the general anti-avoidance principles laid down in *Furniss v Dawson* (see 3.1 ANTI-AVOIDANCE) (*Colours Ltd (formerly Spectrum Ltd) v CIR (Sp C 156), [1998] SSCD 93*).

The profit-related pay must be paid under a registered scheme (see below) under which a part of the emoluments in the 'employment unit' to which the scheme relates is determined by reference to the profits in a profit period of that 'employment unit'. '*Employment unit*' means the undertaking (or part) to which a scheme relates.

[*ICTA 1988, ss 169–171; FA 1989, s 42(4), Sch 4 para 2, Sch 17 Pt IV; FA 1991, s 37*].

Example

E is employed by C Ltd and receives, on 1 May 2000, profit-related pay of £4,200 for the year to 31 March 2000 (the profit period). His earnings received in the year to 31 March 2000, excluding profit-related pay, amounted to £16,600 and he was also provided with a company car on which both car and fuel benefits arise.

The amount of profit-related pay to be included in E's taxable emoluments for 2000/01 is as follows.

	£	£
Amount received		4,200
Deduct tax-free amount, being the *lower* of		
(i) 20% of £20,800	4,160	
(ii) Overriding maximum	1,000	
		1,000
Taxable profit-related pay		£3,200

Relief is denied where either

(i) the profit-related pay relates to a period when the employee had another employment in respect of which he receives profit-related pay which is exempt under these provisions, or

(ii) no Class 1 National Insurance contributions are payable by the employer in respect of the profit-related pay (unless they are not payable only because the employee's earnings are below the earnings threshold (before 6 April 1999, the lower earnings limit) — see 83.7 SOCIAL SECURITY). [*ICTA 1988, s 172; Social Security Act 1998, Sch 7 para 16*].

Excluded employments. Crown and local authority employments (as widely defined) cannot be covered by a scheme seeking registration (see below). [*ICTA 1988, s 174*].

Conditions for registration. To qualify for registration, a scheme must satisfy the following conditions.

(A) Its terms must be set out in writing.

(B) It must identify

(i) the 'scheme employer' and any other person by whom emoluments of scheme employees are paid, and

(ii) the undertaking (or distinct part) to which the scheme relates (which must be carried on with a view to profit).

(C) It must enable employees to whom it relates to be identified.

(D) It must exclude employees (or their associates, as defined) with a 'material interest' (broadly, a 25% interest) in the company throughout a profit period.

(E) It must ensure that payments are not made under the scheme by reference to any profit period at the beginning of which less than 80% of the employees in the employment unit are covered by the scheme (ignoring employees excluded under (D) above and certain short service and (in relation to schemes registered before 1 May 1995) part-time employees who are excluded from the scheme).

(F) It must identify the accounting period(s) by reference to which profit-related pay is to be calculated. Any such period must be of twelve months' duration unless either the scheme is cancelled with effect from a date after the start of the period, or the scheme is a 'replacement scheme' in which case it may only provide for two periods, the first of which may be less than twelve months. Some leeway is allowed where an employer makes up his financial accounts to slightly varying dates; the twelve month period may be increased or reduced by up to seven days. (Revenue Press Release 22 December 1987).

(G) It must provide for a method for calculating the '*distributable pool*' (i.e. the amount which may be paid to scheme employees in respect of a profit period). Except in the case of a 'replacement scheme', one of two methods must be specified. These are set out as 'Method A' and 'Method B' in *ICTA 1988, Sch 8 paras 13–14A*, which broadly allow the distributable pool to be equal *either* to a fixed percentage of the profits of the employment unit in the profit period *or* to a percentage of the distributable pool for the previous profit period (with a notional pool being specified for the first profit period). In either case, there is a formula for ensuring that, where profits remain unchanged, the pool is at least 5% of the annual equivalent of scheme employees' pay (within PAYE but excluding benefits) at the beginning of the first profit period (as reasonably estimated at the time of application for registration). Equally, either method may provide for profit increases in excess of 60% (or a specified higher figure) to be disregarded in arriving at the pool, and for there to be no pool when profits are below a specified level (which must be below that giving rise to the 5% minimum referred to above). Where there is accordingly no pool for a profit period and the following year's pool is to be a set percentage of the earlier year's pool, the percentage is applied to the pool that would have arisen but for the special provision for there to be no pool.

The requirement for a 5% minimum is abolished in relation to schemes registered after 2 February 1989. (Revenue Press Release 3 February 1989). In consequence, the requirement to be met for there to be no distributable pool is replaced by a requirement that the profits limit below which there is to be no pool must not exceed profits representing a zero increase. Any of the rules included in a scheme which moderate the effect of profit changes on the distributable pool may take effect either from the first profit period or from any later profit period determined in accordance with the scheme.

For schemes registered after 2 August 1992, the requirement that the scheme specify a fixed percentage (Method A) or the amount of a notional pool (Method B) will *not* be met where a formula is specified rather than an actual figure, unless the factors used in the formula are ascertained at the time the scheme is written, so that the actual figure derived from the formula may be fully and finally identified at that time. (Revenue Pamphlet IR 131, SP 7/92, 3 August 1992).

Schemes registered after 30 November 1993 which include a 60% (or higher) limit on profit increases to be taken into account in arriving at the pool must also include a provision for that upper limit to be increased where there is a fall in the taxable pay (ignoring PRP) by comparison with the previous profit period (or the base year) (or, in the case of Method B, the previous twelve months). The percentage decrease must be applied as an increase in the amount of the 160% (or higher) limit. Also, where a scheme registered after 30 November 1993 includes provision for either a 60% (or higher) upper profits limit or a lower profits level below which there is no pool, profit-related pay and secondary Class 1 national insurance contributions must be accorded the same accountancy treatment in arriving at the profits for both the current and the previous profit period (or the base year) (or, in the case of Method B, the previous twelve months).

A 'replacement scheme' must provide for the distributable pool to be a specified percentage of the profits of the profit period.

(H) It must provide for the whole of the distributable pool to be paid to employees in the employment unit, and for the timing of such payments.

(J) Its provisions must ensure that employees participate on similar terms, although payments may vary according to objective factors such as length of service or level of remuneration.

(K) It must provide for the preparation of a profit and loss account giving a true and fair view of the profit or loss of the employment unit to which the scheme relates in respect of each profit period (and any other necessary period). *Companies Act 1985, Sch 4* (or NI equivalent) applies, with appropriate modification, to such accounts which must not, however, include a deduction for the remuneration (as widely defined) of any person excluded from the scheme as having a material interest (see above). Certain other restrictions apply as to what the scheme may require to be included in or excluded from the accounts notwithstanding *Companies Act* requirements, and as to what changes in accounting policy between periods may be permitted (see *ICTA 1988, Sch 8 paras 19–20 as amended* and Revenue Pamphlet IR 1, B44). The permitted adjustments include PRP itself (and see Revenue Tax Bulletin August 1997 pp 457, 458 as regards dealing with differences between PRP charged in the accounts and the full amount of PRP for a period). See also Revenue Tax Bulletin June 2000 pp 759, 760 for Revenue practice as regards the impact of the revised FRS11 in preparing PRP accounts.

(L) In relation to schemes registered after 26 July 1989, where the employment unit is part of an undertaking, and the scheme requires the profits to be taken as equivalent to those of the whole (identified) undertaking, the provisions of *ICTA 1988, Sch 8* apply as if those profits were the profits of the employment unit. The scheme must, however, contain provisions ensuring that no payments are made under it by reference to a profit period unless, at the beginning of the period, the number of scheme employees does not exceed 33% of the total number of employees in other registered schemes relating to employees of the same undertaking (disregarding other schemes whose rules require the profits for scheme purposes to be taken as equivalent to those of the whole undertaking, or under which no payments could be made for the profit period concerned by virtue of the rules required by (E) above). Where two or more schemes relating to employment units which are parts of the same undertaking both have rules requiring their profits for scheme purposes to be taken as equivalent to those of the whole undertaking, an employee to whom another scheme relates cannot be included for the purposes of the above 33% test in connection with more than one of those schemes.

For schemes registered after 30 November 1993, there is a further condition that the scheme must ensure that its fixed percentage (in the case of schemes employing Method A) or notional or distributable pool (in the case of schemes employing Method B) (see (G) above) does not exceed a limit calculated by reference to the ratio of PRP to total pay in the other scheme or schemes registered for the business. The ratio is calculated by reference to the figures for pay and PRP paid for a specified earlier period.

The '*scheme employer*' is the person by whom the emoluments of all employees to whom the scheme relates are paid or, if there is no one such person, the parent company of the group of companies (i.e. consisting of the parent company and its 51% subsidiaries) where all the persons paying such emoluments are members of the group. Changes in the members of a partnership which is a scheme employer are ignored for these purposes.

A scheme is a '*replacement scheme*' if it relates to employees to not less than one-half of whom another registered scheme (or schemes) applied, and the registration of the previous scheme was cancelled because of changes in the employment unit or in the circumstances relating to the scheme which occurred within the three months before the start of the first profit period of the new scheme. The Board must also be satisfied as to certain other matters.

[*ICTA 1988, ss 169, 173, 183, Sch 8; FA 1989, Sch 4 paras 9–15; FA 1994, ss 98, 99; FA 1995, s 136*].

Registration. Application for registration of a profit-related pay scheme must be in such form, and supported by such information, as the Board may require, and must specify the profit period(s) to which it relates. It must be made to the Board by the scheme employer, and must contain a declaration that the scheme complies with the conditions referred to above. It previously had to contain an undertaking that any requirements under minimum wage legislation would be met without taking profit-related pay into account, but this requirement is abolished with effect from 28 July 1998. The application must also be accompanied by a report by an 'independent accountant', in a form prescribed by the Board, to the effect that, in his opinion, the scheme complies with the conditions referred to above, and the books and records are adequate for preparation of the annual return required (see below). If it is made more than three months before the beginning of the period (or first period) to which the scheme relates, it is guaranteed that the scheme will, if approved, be registered from the beginning of that period. There is provision for further information in support of the application to be sought by the Board. If the Board are not satisfied that the application meets the various requirements, the application will be refused (subject to appeal, see below). Later applications may, if the Board are satisfied, lead to registration before the beginning of the first period to which they relate, but will otherwise be regarded as having been refused (again, subject to appeal). Notice of registration or refusal must be in writing.

An '*independent accountant*' is a qualified auditor who does not employ scheme employees and who is not (and is not an employee of) a partner, officer, employee or partner of an employee of a person who employs scheme employees or whose subsidiary or holding company or fellow subsidiary employs scheme employees. A report may be signed in the name of a firm of accountants, provided that all partners meet these qualifications. (Revenue Press Release 22 December 1987).

[*ICTA 1988, ss 173, 175, 176, 184; FA 1989, Sch 4 para 10(2); SI 1991 No 1997; FA 1999, s 46(1)*].

Change of employer. Where there is a change in the scheme employer, and the successor would be eligible to apply for registration, and there is no other material change in the employment unit to which the scheme relates or in the circumstances affecting the scheme, the predecessor and successor may, within one month of the change, jointly elect for the scheme registration to be amended by substitution of the successor for the predecessor. Provided that there are not other grounds for cancellation of the scheme, it will continue to operate under the amended registration as if the successor had been the original applicant. [*ICTA 1988, s 177*]. After 26 July 1989, a scheme registration may be amended following the death of the scheme employer to substitute his personal representatives, on written application within one month of the grant of probate, etc., provided that there would be no grounds apart from the death for cancellation of the registration. The provisions then apply as if the personal representatives had been the scheme employer throughout. The scheme registration may be cancelled with effect from the date of death if the personal representatives so request within the same period. [*ICTA 1988, ss 177A, 178(5A); FA 1989, Sch 4 paras 3, 4(4)*].

Alteration of scheme terms. After 26 July 1989, where the terms of a registered scheme are altered, the Board may cancel the registration with effect from the beginning of the profit period during which the alteration took place or any later profit period, although such alteration does not of itself invalidate the registration. The scheme employer may, however, apply to the Board, in a prescribed form and within one month of the alteration, for registration of the alteration, which precludes cancellation of the registration by virtue of the alteration. Provided that the alteration meets one of the conditions listed below, and the scheme employer declares (and a report in a prescribed form by an independent accountant confirms) that it does so and that the scheme as altered complies with *ICTA 1988, Sch 8* (as at the date the scheme was registered subject to any specified subsequent amendments to that *Schedule*), the Board will register such an alteration. The Board's decision on the application must in any event be given within three months of receipt and notified to the scheme employer. If it subsequently appears to the Board that the application did not meet the above requirements or that the declaration by the scheme employer was false, the registration may be cancelled with effect as if the alteration had not been registered.

The conditions referred to above are that the alteration either:

(*a*) relates to a term not relevant to the scheme's complying with the requirements of *ICTA 1988, Sch 8*; or

(*b*) relates to a term identifying any person (other than the scheme employer) who pays scheme employees' emoluments; or

(*c*) consists of the addition of a term providing for an abbreviated profit period following cancellation of registration; or

(*d*) amends the provisions identifying scheme employees for subsequent profit periods; or

(*e*) relates to a scheme provision dealing with the computation under Method A or Method B (see (G) above) for subsequent profit periods; or (*f*) amends the provisions as to when payments are made to employees for subsequent profit periods; or

(*g*) is made to bring the scheme into compliance with the requirements of *ICTA 1988, Sch 8* (as it had effect either at the time of registration or at the date of application for registration of the alteration) if it did not so comply at the time of registration, provided that

(i) it is made for the purposes of all profit periods to which the scheme relates,

(ii) it is made within two years of the beginning of the first profit period, and

(iii) it does not wholly or partly invalidate any payment of profit-related pay already made under the scheme.

[*ICTA 1988, ss 177B, 178(3A)(3B); FA 1989, Sch 4 paras 3, 4(3)*].

Cancellation of registration. The Board may (subject to appeal, see below) cancel registration of a scheme, by notice in writing, where certain conditions have not been complied with or where losses have arisen, or if the scheme employer so requests in writing. The cancellation generally applies from the beginning of the profit period in which the change giving rise to the cancellation takes place. Any shortfall in tax deducted from profit-related pay as a result of cancellation of registration is payable by the scheme employer (or by his personal representatives or by the UK payer if the scheme employer is non-UK resident) to the Board, and PAYE regulations provide for collection and recovery and interest on unpaid amounts. [*ICTA 1988, ss 178, 179; FA 1989, Sch 4 paras 4, 5, 10(2); FA 1999, s 46(2)(3); SI 1995 No 917*]. With effect from 14 July 1995, interest is charged on tax recovered from employers in respect of payments incorrectly made tax-free under PRP schemes for 1994/95 and subsequent years. Penalties will be sought where there has been fraud or negligence in making late or incorrect returns for such years. (Revenue Press Release 14 July 1995).

See also the preceding paragraphs as regards death of the scheme employer and scheme alterations.

Appeals. An appeal against refusal or cancellation of registration, or against refusal to register an alteration or amend a registration on the death of the scheme employer, must be made within 30 days of notification of the refusal, etc., and lies to the Special Commissioners. [*ICTA 1988, s 182; FA 1989, Sch 4 para 8*].

Returns and other information. An annual return and a report by an independent accountant (including confirmation that the scheme terms have been complied with in the period) are required, as laid down by the Board (see Revenue Press Release 1 February 1988), within ten months of the end of each scheme accounting period (seven months in the case of public companies). The time limit may be extended by three months in certain cases where a company has overseas interests.

There is a general requirement to provide relevant information requested by the Board, and for the scheme employer to notify the Board of anything of which he becomes aware which may be a ground for cancellation of that registration. The personal representatives of a deceased scheme employer must inform the Board of his death within one month of the grant of probate, etc. [*ICTA 1988, ss 180, 181; FA 1989, Sch 4 paras 6, 7*].

Penalties apply for failure to furnish information as above. [*TMA 1970, s 98*].

Guidance notes and **model rules** on profit-related pay schemes are available from Profit Related Pay Office, Inland Revenue, St Mungo's Road, Cumbernauld, Glasgow G67 1YZ.

Simon's Direct Tax Service. See **E4.301** *et seq.*.

75.32 **REDUNDANCY PAYMENTS**

Amounts received under *Employment Rights Act 1996*, or NI equivalent, may be taken into account for purposes of *ICTA 1988, s 148*, see 19.5 COMPENSATION FOR LOSS OF EMPLOYMENT (AND DAMAGES), but are otherwise exempt under Schedule E. [*ICTA 1988, ss 579, 580*]. Other redundancy payments may be assessable emoluments, see 19.5 *et seq.* COMPENSATION FOR LOSS OF EMPLOYMENT (AND DAMAGES). See Simon's Direct Tax Service E4.327.

75.33 **RELOCATION PACKAGES**

Certain payments and benefits received in connection with job-related residential moves are exempted from charge under Schedule E. This applies in relation to changes in employment after 5 April 1993, and replaces the reliefs previously provided by concession.

The statutory exemption applies to

(*a*) any sums paid to the employee, or to another person on behalf of the employee, in respect of 'qualifying removal expenses', and

(*b*) any 'qualifying removal benefit' provided for the employee or to members of his family or household (including sons- and daughters-in-law, servants, dependants and guests),

to the extent that they do not exceed a 'qualifying limit'.

'*Qualifying removal expenses*' are 'eligible removal expenses' reasonably incurred by the employee, and '*qualifying removal benefits*' are 'eligible removal benefits' reasonably provided, on or before the 'relevant day' on a change of the employee's sole or main residence 'in connection with the employment'. The change of residence does not require the disposal of the former residence, but the new residence must, on the facts of the particular case, become the main residence of the employee. (Revenue Press Release 14 April 1993).

For a change of residence to be 'in connection with the employment', it must result from the employee commencing employment with the employer, or from an alteration of his duties in the employment, or from an alteration of the place where those duties are normally to be performed. The change must be made wholly or mainly to bring the employee's residence within a reasonable daily travelling distance of the place he normally performs, or is to perform, those duties. What is a 'reasonable daily travelling distance' is not defined, but is a matter for common sense, taking account of local conditions. It may depend on either or both travelling time or distance. (Revenue Tax Bulletin November 1993 p 94).

The '*relevant day*' is the last day of the year of assessment following that in which the commencement or change of duties etc. took place, unless the Board grants an extension in a particular case to the end of a later year of assessment.

'*Eligible removal expenses*' fall into seven different categories.

(i) Expenses of disposal, i.e. legal expenses, loan redemption penalties, estate agents' or auctioneers' fees, advertising costs, disconnection charges, and rent and maintenance etc. costs during an unoccupied period, relating to the disposal of his interest (or of the interest of a member of his family or household) in the employee's former residence. Expenses of a sale which falls through are eligible provided that the residence is in fact still changed.

(ii) Expenses of acquisition, i.e. legal expenses, procurement fees, insurance costs, survey fees, Registry fees, stamp duty and connection charges, relating to the acquisition by the employee (or by a member of his family or household) of an interest in his new residence.

(iii) Expenses of abortive acquisition, i.e. expenses which would have been within (ii) above but for the interest not being acquired, for reasons beyond the control of the person seeking to acquire it or because that person reasonably declined to proceed with it.

(iv) Expenses of transporting belongings, i.e. expenses, including insurance, temporary storage and disconnection and reconnection of appliances, connected with transporting domestic belongings of the employee and of members of his family or household from the former to the new residence.

(v) Travelling and subsistence expenses (subsistence meaning food, drink and temporary accommodation). These are restricted to:

(*a*) such costs of the employee and members of his family or household on temporary visits to the new area in connection with the change;

(*b*) the employee's travel costs between his former residence and new place of work;

(*c*) (other than in the case of a new employment) the employee's travel costs, before the change in the employment, between his new residence and old place of work;

(*d*) the employee's subsistence costs (not within (*a*));

(*e*) the employee's travel costs between his old residence and any temporary living accommodation;

(*f*) (other than in the case of a new employment) the employee's travel costs, before the change in the employment, between his new residence and any temporary living accommodation;

(*g*) the travel costs of the employee and members of his family or household between the former and new residences;

(*h*) certain costs incurred to secure continuity of education for a member of the employee's family or household who is under 19 at the beginning of the year of assessment in which the commencement or change of duties etc. takes place.

Expenses for which a deduction is allowable under *ICTA 1988, ss 193–195* (certain foreign travel expenses, see 75.5, 75.6 above) are excluded.

(vi) Bridging loan expenses, i.e. interest payable by the employee (or by a member of his family or household) on a loan raised at least partly because there is a gap between the incurring of expenditure in acquiring the new residence and the receipt of the proceeds of disposal of the former residence. Interest on so much of the loan as either

(*a*) exceeds the market value of his interest (or the interest of a member of his family or household) in the former residence (at the time the new residence is acquired), or

(*b*) is not used for the purpose of either redeeming a loan raised by the employee (or by a member of his family or household) on his former residence or acquiring his interest (or the interest of a member of his family or household) in the new residence

is excluded.

(vii) Duplicate expenses, i.e. net expenses incurred as a result of the change on the replacement of domestic goods used at the former residence but unsuitable for use at the new residence.

The Treasury may by regulation amend these categories so as to add any expenses from a day to be specified in the regulations, with effect for commencements or changes of duties etc. taking place on or after that day.

'*Eligible removal benefits*' fall into six different categories, consisting of the benefit of services corresponding, as applicable, to the expenses specified under (i)–(v) and (vii) above in relation to eligible removal expenses (but, under (v), excluding the provision of a company car or van also available for general private use). They may include administration fees of a relocation management company charged to the employer. The Treasury has similar powers to those applicable in the case of eligible removal expenses.

The '*qualifying limit*' as regards any change of residence applies to the aggregate of qualifying removal expenses paid and the value of qualifying removal benefits received in respect of the change. The value attributed to such benefits is their cash equivalent under the general benefits legislation (75.13 above) or, as appropriate, the amount of the living accommodation charge under *ICTA 1988, s 145* and, where applicable, *ICTA 1988, s 146* (net of any attributable contribution by the employee and of any amount which would have been deductible under *ICTA 1988, s 198* or *s 332(3)* (see 75.10, 75.9 respectively)) (see 75.29 above).

The amount of the '*qualifying limit*' is **£8,000**. This may be varied upwards by Treasury order from a day to be specified in the order, with effect for commencements or changes of duties etc. taking place on or after that day.

Bridging loan finance obtained before the relevant day (as above) by reason of the employment within *ICTA 1988, s 160* (see 75.17 above) on a move meeting the above conditions may attract a measure of relief where the expenses and benefits for which relief is obtained in respect of the move are in total less than the £8,000 (or increased) limit. Relief is obtained by delaying the implementation of *section 160* for a number of days after the making of the loan such that the interest (at the official rate at the time the loan was made, see 75.17 above) on the maximum sum borrowed for those days would equate to the amount by which the £8,000 (or increased) limit exceeds the amount of expenses and benefits otherwise relieved. If the loan is discharged before those days have expired, no charge arises under *section 160*. An assessment made under *section 160* for a year of assessment ending before the relevant day on the assumption that the maximum relief would be utilised by the payment of qualifying removal expenses and benefits may be adjusted as necessary if that turns out not to be the case.

Commencement. These provisions apply to changes of residence resulting from commencements, changes of duties etc. taking place after 5 April 1993 (but see above as regards transitional arrangements in certain cases where a new job commenced before 3 August 1993).

[*ICTA 1988, ss 191A, 191B, Sch 11A; FA 1993, s 76, Sch 5*].

PAYE should not be applied to payments made under a relocation package, even if the qualifying limit is exceeded. Flat rate allowances may be paid gross, provided that the inspector is satisfied that they do no more than reimburse employees' eligible expenses. Any taxable payments are to be included in the annual return of benefits. See *SI 1993 No 2276* and Revenue Press Release 14 April 1993.

For the application of these provisions to relocation company management fees, and in particular to guaranteed sale price schemes, see Revenue Schedule E Manual, SE 1246a–1246c. See generally SE 1241 *et seq.*.

Simon's Direct Tax Service. See E4.635–E4.646.

75.34 **RESTRICTIVE COVENANTS**

Where, after 8 June 1988, the present, past or future holder of an office or employment, the emoluments of which are within Cases I or II of Schedule E, gives, in connection therewith, an undertaking (whether qualified or legally valid or not) restricting his conduct or activities, any sum paid to any person in respect of the giving or fulfilment (in whole or part) of the undertaking is, if it would not otherwise be so, treated as an emolument of the office or employment for the year of assessment of payment. If such a payment is made after the death of the individual concerned, it is treated as having been paid immediately before his death. Where valuable consideration rather than money is given, a sum equal to the value of that consideration is treated as having been paid. Sums to which this section applies may be deducted as an expense in computing the profits of the trade, profession or vocation of the payer, or treated as a management expense if paid by an investment company.

For such sums paid in respect of undertakings given before 9 June 1988, the grossed-up equivalent of the sum paid is treated as part of the individual's total income received after deduction of basic rate tax. No assessment is raised in respect of basic rate tax, no repayment may be made thereof, and the gross amount may not be used to cover charges under *ICTA 1988, ss 348, 349* (see 23.2, 23.3 DEDUCTION OF TAX AT SOURCE). The payer of such a sum must give particulars to the inspector within one month of the end of the year of assessment of the payment, subject to penalties under *TMA 1970, s 98*. [*ICTA 1988, s 313; FA 1988, s 73*].

Termination settlements. Financial settlements relating to the termination of an employment may require the employee to undertake that the agreement is in 'full and final settlement' of his claims relating to the employment, and/or not to commence, or to discontinue, legal proceedings in respect of those claims. They may also reaffirm undertakings about the employee's conduct or activity after termination which formed part of the employment terms. The Revenue accept that such undertakings do not give rise to a charge under *ICTA 1988, s 313*, without prejudice to the treatment of other restrictive undertakings, whether or not contained in the settlement. (Revenue Pamphlet IR 131, SP 3/96, 4 April 1996).

75.35 **SECURITY OF EMPLOYEES**

Where an asset or service which improves personal security is provided for an employee by reason of his employment, or is used by the employee, and the expenditure was (wholly or partly) borne by (or for) a person other than the employee, then a Schedule E deduction is allowed to the extent that the provision gives rise to emoluments chargeable under Schedule E on the employee. The asset or service must be provided or used to meet a special threat to the employee's personal physical security arising wholly or mainly by virtue of the employment, and the sole object of the provider must be the meeting of that threat. In the case of an asset, relief is available only to the extent that the provider intends the asset to be used solely to improve personal physical security (ignoring any other incidental use), and in the case of a service, the benefit to the employee must consist wholly or mainly in such an improvement. Any improvement in the personal physical security of the employee's family resulting from the asset or service provided is disregarded for these purposes.

Excluded from relief is provision of a car, ship or aircraft, or of a dwelling (or grounds appurtenant thereto) or living accommodation; but relief may be obtained in respect of equipment or a structure (such as a wall), and it is immaterial whether or not an asset becomes affixed to land and whether or not the employee acquires the property in the asset or (in the case of a fixture) an estate or interest in the land.

Similar relief applies where the employee incurs the expenditure out of his emoluments and is reimbursed by some other person, and to office holders. [*FA 1989, ss 50–52*].

See also 10.25 CAPITAL ALLOWANCES, 71.81 SCHEDULE D, CASES I AND II.

Simon's Direct Tax Service. See E4.622.

75.36 SHARES ETC.

The value of a gift or transfer of shares to a director or employee, if regarded as a reward for services or part of his emoluments, is assessable on him. Held, liability did not arise in *Bridges v Bearsley CA 1957, 37 TC 289* (because gift of shares in default of legacy held to be testimonial not remuneration). Where shares were issued to employees at par value which was less than market value, the difference was held assessable (*Weight v Salmon HL 1935, 19 TC 174; Ede v Wilson KB 1945, 26 TC 381; Patrick v Burrows Ch D 1954, 35 TC 138; Bentley v Evans Ch D 1959, 39 TC 132; Tyrer v Smart HL 1978, 52 TC 533*). See also 75.19 above.

A payment received from the parent company of a group after the employing company left the group, in consideration of loss of rights under the parent company's savings-related share option scheme (see 82.38 SHARE INCENTIVES AND OPTIONS), was not assessable (*Wilcock v Eve Ch D 1995, 67 TC 223*).

For capital gains tax, such gifts are treated as an acquisition for nil consideration where there is no corresponding disposal of the shares, i.e. where the shares are issued by the company concerned. [*TCGA 1992, s 17*].

For the circumstances in which the Revenue will accept that shares or share options were acquired by a director or employee in a different capacity and not by reason of the office or employment, see Revenue Inspector's Manual, IM 5329.

Priority allocations for employees, etc.. Where a director or employee (or future or past director or employee) is entitled, as such, to priority allocation of shares in a *bona fide* public offer at fixed price or by tender made after 22 September 1987, there is no charge to tax under Schedule E on any benefit arising thereby provided that

(*a*) the shares reserved for such priority allocation do not exceed

- (i) 10% of the total shares subject to the offer, or
- (ii) in relation to an offer made after 10 October 1988 which is part of arrangements under which shares of the same class are offered to the public under more than one offer, either 40% of the total shares subject to the offer or 10% of all the shares of that class subject to any such offers,

(*b*) all persons entitled to priority allocation are so entitled on similar terms (which may, however, vary according to level of remuneration, length of service or similar factors), and

(*c*) the persons entitled to priority allocation are not restricted to directors or to those whose remuneration exceeds a particular level.

As regards offers made on or after 26 July 1990, (*b*) above is still satisfied where allocations to directors and employees of the company are greater than those to other persons, provided that

(A) the aggregate value of priority allocations made under the offer and under other public offers made at the same time in respect of the shares of other companies to those persons, and

(B) the aggregate value of the shares allocated to comparable directors and employees of the company

are, as nearly as practicable, the same.

In relation to offers made after 10 October 1988, the benefit of a discount on the fixed price or lowest price successfully tendered is not covered by this exemption. Previously, no exemption at all was available where such a discount applied. After 15 January 1991, any 'registrant discount' is disregarded for this purpose. Broadly, the '*registrant discount*' is any discount which, subject to any conditions imposed, may be available in respect of all or some part of the shares allocated to any person, whether a member of the public or an employee or director applying for shares as such. For this to apply, at least 40% of the shares allocated to members of the public (other than employees or directors of the company) must be allocated to individuals entitled either to the discount or to some benefit of similar value.

In relation to offers made after 15 January 1991, relief is extended to cases where there is a *bona fide* offer to the public of a combination of shares in two or more companies at a fixed price or by tender, and at the same time there is such an offer of shares in any one or more, but not all, of those companies to directors and employees (with or without others) of any company, any of whom is entitled, by reason of his office or employment, to priority in the allocation of shares over members of the public subscribing as such. The limits in (*a*) above must be satisfied in relation to each of the companies whose shares are included in the combination. The extension of relief is achieved by treating both the public offer and the employee offer as being a single offer of shares to the public. Where the extended relief applies, the denial of exemption on any employee discount on the offer price (see above) is imposed by reference to an '*appropriate notional price*' for shares in each company concerned, i.e. the fixed price at which the shares might have been expected to be offered in a separate offer to the public, proportionately varied where the sum of the notional prices for all the companies concerned would otherwise differ from the combined offer price to the public.

For capital gains tax purposes, the market value rules do not apply to shares so acquired, which are thus treated as acquired for the actual consideration paid. [*FA 1988, s 68; FA 1989, s 66; FA 1990, s 79; FA 1991, s 44*].

See Simon's Direct Tax Service E4.515. See also 82 SHARE INCENTIVES AND OPTIONS.

75.37 SICK PAY AND HEALTH INSURANCE

Continuing pay from an employer during sickness or other absence from work is taxable under the general Schedule E provisions. Any payments of statutory sick pay under *Social Security Contributions and Benefits Act 1992, s 15* are similarly taxable. [*ICTA 1988, s 150(c)*].

Any employed person assessable under Schedule E is chargeable to tax under that Schedule on any sum not otherwise chargeable paid to him (or to his spouse, to a son or daughter or spouse of a son or daughter, or to a parent or dependant) as a result of any arrangements entered into by the employer, in respect of his absence from work by reason of sickness or disability. There is no charge under *ICTA 1988, s 154* (benefits, see 75.13 above) on the right to receive such sums, and these provisions do not apply to the extent that the contributions are paid by the employee. [*ICTA 1988, ss 149, 154(2)*]. See further below as regards treatment of self-funded arrangements.

A lump sum received under a life, accident or sickness or insurance policy is not normally taxable.

By concession (and see now the statutory provisions mentioned below), benefits under an individual's permanent health or other insurance policy providing benefits which compensate for loss of income from employment or self-employment during ill-health or disability are exempt from income tax for the first twelve months (unless, exceptionally, the benefits are chargeable under Schedule E or the policy premiums have wholly or partly qualified for relief as pension contributions). The concession does not apply to benefits payable to the employer, nor where the premiums are paid by the employer. Tax will not be deducted from payments covered by the concession. The concession applies where a policy holder first becomes entitled to benefit on or after 6 April 1994, and replaces an earlier concession. The previous concession will continue to apply to benefits to which a policy holder first became entitled before 6 April 1994, and also where entitlement first arises on or after that date but in relation to a period of absence extending before that date and for which benefit entitlement had arisen under one or more policies before that date. (Revenue Pamphlet IR 1, A83).

In practice, tax has not been collected where insurance benefits are provided in times of sickness, disability or unemployment to meet existing specified obligations such as loan repayments. (Revenue Press Release REV 6, 28 November 1995).

The above-mentioned concessions are effectively superseded by statutory provisions applicable to annual payments falling to be made after 5 April 1996 under certain insurance policies. Where the conditions are satisfied, all such payments are exempt and not just those for the first twelve months. Subject to further conditions, the provisions also apply to payments falling due on or before that date, thereby giving statutory effect to the practice mentioned immediately above. See 29.12 EXEMPT INCOME for the detailed provisions.

See generally Revenue Schedule E Manual, SE 1210, 1340 *et seq.*.

See also 71.64 SCHEDULE D, CASES I AND II.

75.38 SOCIAL SECURITY BENEFITS

See 83 SOCIAL SECURITY.

75.39 SUBSCRIPTIONS

Professional subscriptions etc.. [*ICTA 1988, s 201*]. There may be deducted from Schedule E assessments on emoluments out of which they are paid

(*a*) provided the registration, retention etc. is a condition of the performance of the duties, statutory fees payable for the retention of name on the Register of Architects, or registers of dentists, ancillary dental workers, ophthalmic opticians, dispensing opticians or pharmaceutical chemists; annual fees payable by registered patent agents, registered veterinary surgeons or persons on the Supplementary Veterinary Register; fee (and contribution to the Compensation Fund or Guarantee Fund) payable on issue of solicitor's practising certificate;

(*b*) annual subscription, or part thereof, to bodies approved by the Board as being conducted, otherwise than for profit, for advancing or spreading knowledge, maintaining or improving professional conduct and competence, or indemnifying or protecting professional persons against claims incurred in exercising their profession, provided the activities of the body concerned are relevant to the office or employment and the body is not of a mainly local character.

As to approval of bodies by the Board, withdrawal of approval, apportionment of subscription and appeals generally see *ICTA 1988, s 201(3)(4)(6)(7)*. Applications for approval should be made in writing to Inland Revenue, Personal Tax Division 5, Sapphire House, 550 Streetsbrook Road, Solihull, West Midlands B91 1QU. A list of bodies approved by the Board for this purpose is available, price £5.00, from Inland Revenue Library, Room 28, New Wing, Strand, London WC2R 1LB.

Other subscriptions. Bank manager's club subscriptions reimbursed by bank not allowed, *Brown v Bullock CA 1961, 40 TC 1*, but subscriptions to clubs to obtain cheaper accommodation on visits to London were allowed, *Elwood v Utitz CA (NI) 1965, 42 TC 482*.

75.40 **'TAX-FREE PAYMENTS'**

If an employer pays an employee without deducting tax under PAY AS YOU EARN (55), the employee's gross emoluments will be that gross figure which includes tax paid, or deemed to be paid, on his behalf. The employer should account for PAYE tax on that gross amount so that the employee effectively 'pays tax on tax'. (*Income Tax (Employments) Regulations 1993, SI 1993 No 744, reg 22* and see *North British Rly v Scott HL 1922, 8 TC 332; Hartland v Diggines HL 1926, 10 TC 247; Jaworski v Institution of Polish Engineers CA 1950, 29 ATC 385*). See also Revenue Pamphlet P7 (Employer's Guide to PAYE).

Special forms and tax tables are available to assist employers who pay employees on a 'net of tax' basis to calculate how much tax is due. (Revenue Press Release 2 March 1984).

Where an employer paying emoluments of a director fails, in whole or in part, to deduct and account for PAYE tax at the proper time, and that tax is subsequently accounted for by someone other than the director, such tax paid, less so much as is made good by the director, will be treated as an emolument chargeable under Schedule E unless the director has no material interest in the company and either he is a full-time working director or the company is non-profit-making.

Any amounts accounted for after cessation of employment are treated as having arisen in the year of assessment in which the employment ended but no amounts accounted for after the death of the director will be chargeable. [*ICTA 1988, s 164*].

An agreement to reimburse tax as 'expenses' was held not to be enforceable as the contract was illegal (*Miller v Karlinski CA 1945, 24 ATC 483*, and see also *Napier v National Business Agency CA 1951, 30 ATC 180*).

Interim payments of tax under self-assessment made by an employer on an employee's behalf, as part of *tax equalisation* arrangements where full in-year gross up is used, should not figure in the employment pages of the employee's self-assessment tax return (see Revenue Tax Bulletin June 1998 p 551).

See Simon's Direct Tax Service E4.451.

Taxed award schemes. Employers may, if they wish, enter into arrangements with the Revenue to meet the liability of employees on the grossed-up value of non-cash incentive prizes and awards. The arrangements involve a legally binding contract for payment of the related tax together with simplified reporting arrangements. The arrangements may involve payment of tax at the basic rate or at the higher rate or both, although separate contracts are required in relation to basic rate and higher rate schemes. Previously only basic rate schemes were permitted. Where only basic rate liabilities are met, higher rate liabilities continue to be collected from employees in the usual way. Valuation of an award will depend on details of the scheme and whether or not the recipient is in director's or higher-paid employment (see 75.11 above). Details of the arrangements may be obtained from Inland Revenue, Incentive Award Unit, Manchester Blackfriars TDO, Trinity Bridge House, 2 Dearmans Place, Salford M3 5BH (tel. 0161–261 3269), which also deals with national insurance aspects. (Revenue Press Releases 2 November 1984, 18 January 1990; Revenue Tax Bulletin April 2000 p 747).

See generally Revenue Schedule E Manual, SE 2070–2073.

For the valuation of incentive awards generally, see 75.44 below and Revenue Pamphlet IR 131, SP 6/85, 29 July 1985.

75.41 TERMINATION PAYMENTS

See 19.3 COMPENSATION FOR LOSS OF EMPLOYMENT (AND DAMAGES) for the assessment of such payments under general Schedule E principles (see 75.7 above). See also 75.32 above for statutory redundancy payments and 75.45 below for wages in lieu of notice.

Certain payments to persons ceasing to be members of the House of Commons, the European Parliament, the Scottish Parliament, the Assembly for Wales or the Northern Ireland Assembly, or to persons ceasing to hold a ministerial (or equivalent) office, are exempted from the general Schedule E charge. They are, however, liable in the normal way under *ICTA 1988, s 148* (see 19 COMPENSATION FOR LOSS OF EMPLOYMENT (AND DAMAGES)). [*ICTA 1988, s 190; FA 1998, s 58, Sch 9 para 2; FA 1999, Sch 5 para 1*].

75.42 TRAINING, COUNSELLING ETC.

Employer training costs. Expenditure incurred by the employer in paying or reimbursing 'relevant expenses', incurred in connection with a 'qualifying course of training' undertaken by a past or present employee, does not give rise to any emoluments forming part of the employee's income for any purpose of Schedule E. The course must be undertaken '*with a view to retraining*' the employee, which requires that the employee begins the course during, or within one year of leaving, the employment, and has left that employment by two years after the end of the course, and that he is not re-employed by the employer within two years of leaving. If, after the relief has been given, any of these conditions fail to be met, an assessment may be raised to withdraw the relief within six years of the end of the year of assessment in which the failure occurred. The employer must notify such failure to the inspector within 60 days of coming to know of it, and the inspector may require information from the employer in relation to any such failure where he has reason to believe that the employer has failed to give such notice. Penalties apply under *TMA 1970, s 98* for failure to give such notice or furnish such information.

A '*qualifying course of training*' must

(*a*) be designed to impart or improve skills or knowledge relevant to, and intended to be used in the course of, gainful employment (or self-employment) of any description, and

(*b*) be devoted entirely to the teaching and/or practical application within the UK of such skills or knowledge, and

(*c*) not last more than one year, and

(*d*) be available on similar terms to all, or to a particular class or classes of, past or present employees,

and the employee must

(i) attend the course on a full-time or substantially full-time basis, and

(ii) be employed full-time by the employer throughout the two years prior to starting the course (or prior to his earlier leaving that employment — see above).

'*Relevant expenses*' are

(A) course attendance and examination fees, and

(B) costs of essential course books, and

(C) travelling expenses which would be deductible as a Schedule E expense if attendance at the course was a duty of the employment, and if the employee was in that employment when the expenses were incurred.

[*ICTA 1988, ss 588, 589; FA 1996, Sch 18 paras 10, 17(1)(2)*].

For relief to the employer, see 71.54 SCHEDULE D, CASES I AND II.

Work-related training. For 1997/98 and subsequent years, and subject to the exceptions below, where an employer pays or reimburses the cost of providing 'work-related training' to employees, no charge under Schedule E arises in respect of such expenditure or of any benefit. Similar relief applies to any incidental costs incurred wholly and exclusively as a result of the employee's undertaking the training, any expenses in connection with an assessment of what the employee has gained from the training, and the costs of obtaining for the employee any consequent qualification, registration or award.

'*Work-related training*' means any training course or other activity designed to impart, instil, improve or reinforce any knowledge, skills or personal qualities likely to prove useful to the employee in performing the duties of any 'relevant employment', or which will qualify (or better qualify) the employee to undertake any such employment or to participate in any charitable or voluntary activities available to be undertaken in association with any such employment. A '*relevant employment*' is any office or employment held under the employer or to be held under the employer or a person connected with the employer (within *ICTA 1988, s 839*), or to which the employee has a serious opportunity (or can in due course reasonably expect to have a serious opportunity) of being appointed with the employer or a connected person.

Exceptions. The above exemption does not apply to the payment or reimbursement of costs to the extent that facilities or other benefits are provided or made available for any of the following purposes:

(*a*) to enable the employee to enjoy them for entertainment or recreational purposes, or in the course of any leisure activity, unconnected with the promotion of knowledge, skills or personal qualities (as above);

(*b*) to reward the employee for the performance of the duties of his employment or for the manner of their performance;

(*c*) to provide the employee with an inducement, unconnected with the promotion of knowledge, skills or personal qualities (as above), to remain in or accept an employment with the employer or a connected person.

The cost of provision of any asset, or of the use of any asset, to the employee is excluded except where:

(i) the asset is not for use other than in the course of the training or in the performance of the duties of the employment;

(ii) it consists of training materials, e.g. stationery, books, tapes, disks, etc.; or

(iii) it consists in something made by the employee during the training, or incorporated into something so made.

Expenditure exempted under *ICTA 1988, s 588* (qualifying course of training, see above) or *FA 1991, s 32* (vocational training, see 92 VOCATIONAL TRAINING RELIEF) is excluded.

Travelling and subsistence expenses are not excluded provided that they would have been deductible under *ICTA 1988, s 198* (see 75.10 above) if the training had been undertaken in the performance of the duties of the employment and the expenses incurred out of the emoluments therefrom.

Third party expenditure. Benefits consisting in, or provided in connection with, work-related training as above but at the expense of a person other than the employer are exempt to the same extent that they would have been had they been provided at the employer's expense.

[*ICTA 1988, ss 200B–200D; FA 1997, s 63(1)(3)*].

These provisions largely replace two concessions which apply generally for 1996/97 and earlier years. Under the first of these, relief from any charge to tax on the employee is available where the costs (and certain associated expenses) of external training courses in the UK, e.g. day release courses, attended by an employee are borne by the employer, provided that the course either

(*a*) is a course of general education for young employees (i.e. under 21 at commencement) of a type commonly undertaken at school, or

(*b*) leads to the acquisition of job-related knowledge or skills.

The course need not lead to any qualification.

A similar concession applies where an employee bears the costs of attending an external training course relating to his employment, but is not reimbursed by the employer. In this case, however, the course must be full-time and the course (or each block) must last four weeks or more. Provided that he continues to receive full salary and attends the course during normal working hours, the costs incurred may be allowed as a deduction from his emoluments. Expenses relating to 're-sit' courses are excluded.

In the case of both concessions, additional costs of travelling and subsistence may be included where the course requires the employee temporarily to be absent from his normal place of work, and fees for which tax relief is due under *FA 1991, s 32* (see 92 VOCATIONAL TRAINING RELIEF) are excluded. An employee can only be regarded as temporarily away from his normal place of work if the period away will not exceed twelve months, after which he will return to the normal place of work.

(Revenue Pamphlet IR 1, A63, A64).

The residual elements of concession A64 are withdrawn from 1 September 2000, in tandem with the abolition of VOCATIONAL TRAINING RELIEF (92). (Revenue Press Release 25 July 2000).

Education and training funded by employers. For 2000/01 and subsequent years, and subject to the exceptions below, where an employer makes a payment to the provider in respect of the costs of providing 'qualifying education or training' for a 'fundable employee' of the employer, no charge under Schedule E arises in respect of such expenditure or of any benefit. Similar relief applies in respect of the payment or reimbursement of any incidental costs incurred wholly and exclusively as a result of the employee's undertaking the education or training, any expenses in connection with an assessment of what the employee has gained from the education or training, and the costs of obtaining for the employee any consequent qualification, registration or award.

For the exemption to apply the expenditure must be incurred in giving effect to 'fair opportunity arrangements' in place when the employer agreed to incur the expenditure. This requires that, at that time, arrangements are in place which provide for such employer contributions to be generally available, on similar terms, to all current office-holders or employees of the employer. Special provisions apply in relation to Crown servants.

'*Qualifying education or training*' is education or training of a kind which qualifies for grants authorised by regulations under *Learning and Skills Act 2000, s 108* or *s 109* or by corresponding provision in Scotland. A '*fundable employee*' of an employer is a person who holds or has held an office or employment under that employer and who holds an account qualifying under *Learning and Skills Act 2000, s 104*, or who is a party to arrangements which qualify under *Learning and Skills Act 2000, s 105* or *s 106* or Scottish equivalent.

Exceptions. The above exemptions do not apply to expenditure to the extent that facilities or other benefits are thereby provided or made available to the employee:

(*a*) for entertainment or recreation (including in the course of any leisure activity); or

(*b*) to reward the employee for the performance of the duties of his office or employment or for the manner of their performance.

Travelling and subsistence expenses are excluded unless they would have been deductible under *ICTA 1988, s 198* (see 75.10 above) if the education or training had been undertaken in the performance of the duties of the office or employment (or last office or employment under the employer) and the expenses incurred out of the emoluments therefrom.

The cost of provision of any asset, or of the use of any asset, to the employee is excluded except where:

(i) the asset is for use only in the course of the education or training; or

(ii) it is for use in the course of the education or training and in the performance of the duties of the office or employment and not to any significant extent for any other use; or

(iii) it consists of training materials, e.g. stationery, books, tapes, disks, etc., provided in the course of the education or training; or

(iv) it consists in something made by the employee during the education or training, or incorporated into something so made.

Expenditure exempted under *ICTA 1988, s 200B* (work-related training, see above) or *ICTA 1988, s 588* (qualifying course of training, see above) is excluded.

Third party expenditure. Benefits consisting in, or provided in connection with, education or training as above but at the expense of a person other than the employer are exempt to the same extent that they would have been had they been provided at the employer's expense.

[*ICTA 1988, ss 200E–200J; FA 2000, s 58*].

Youth training scheme. A trainee allowance (and any 'topping-up' payments) paid to a non-employee under the YTS is tax-free. Travel and accommodation payments to trainees in receipt of such allowances are also tax-free. (Revenue Schedule E Manual, SE 7503).

See also 29.26 EXEMPT INCOME as regards sandwich courses.

Counselling services provided by employers. Exemption is provided from Schedule E tax in respect of 'qualifying counselling services' and necessary related travelling expenses provided for, or paid or reimbursed on behalf of, an employer in connection with the termination of his employment. This applies whether or not the services or expenses are provided or paid by the employer.

'*Qualifying counselling services*' are services provided in the UK consisting wholly of giving advice and guidance, imparting or improving skills, and providing or making available the use of office equipment or similar facilities to enable an employee to adjust to his job loss and/or find other employment. The employee must have been employed by the employer full-time throughout the period of two years to the date the services are provided or, if earlier, the time he ceases to be employed. The opportunity to receive the services must be generally available to employees or a particular class of employees. Where services are provided partly outside the UK, a just and reasonable apportionment can be made.

[*ICTA 1988, ss 589A, 589B; FA 1993, s 108*].

For relief to the employer, see 71.54 SCHEDULE D, CASES I AND II.

See Simon's Direct Tax Service B4.1432, E4.327.

Employee training costs. See 92 VOCATIONAL TRAINING RELIEF.

75.43 TRAVELLING, SUBSISTENCE ETC.

See generally Revenue Booklet 490 'Employee Travel — A Tax and NICs Guide for Employers'.

Travelling expenses deductible are those necessarily incurred in the performance of the duties (see 75.10(*a*) above) and hence exclude those of travelling to the place of employment from home or from a place at which a business or another employment is carried on. From 1998/99 onwards, there is additionally relief for expenses of travel to work *other than* 'ordinary commuting' (i.e. so-called 'triangular travel'), net of savings on commuting costs, (see again 75.10(*a*) above), which supersedes and codifies certain of the practices and decisions described below.

A leading case here is *Ricketts v Colquhoun HL 1925, 10 TC 118* in which a barrister practising in London was refused his expenses of travelling to Portsmouth where he was employed as Recorder. See also *Cook v Knott QB 1887, 2 TC 246; Revell v Directors of Elworthy Bros & Co Ltd QB 1890, 3 TC 12; Nolder v Walters KB 1930, 15 TC 380; Burton v Rednall Ch D 1954, 35 TC 435; Bhadra v Ellam Ch D 1987, [1988] STC 239* (see 75.10(*a*) above); *Parikh v Sleeman CA 1990, 63 TC 75; Smith v Fox Ch D 1989, 63 TC 304; Miners v Atkinson Ch D 1995, 68 TC 629* and contrast *Pook v Owen* (see below and 75.10(*a*) above) and *Taylor v Provan HL 1974, 49 TC 579* in both of which *Ricketts v Colquhoun* was distinguished. The deduction is refused notwithstanding that the taxpayer is unable to live nearer his place of employment (*Andrews v Astley KB 1924, 8 TC 589; Phillips v Keane HC(IFS), 1 ITC 69*). No allowance to an assistant required to attend classes (*Blackwell v Mills KB 1945, 26 TC 468*). For extra-statutory concession for directors and employees of two or more group companies, see 75.13(ix) above.

If an employee with a normal place of work travels directly from home to another place at which he is required to perform duties of the employment, or *vice versa*, the allowable travel and subsistence expenditure (including business mileage) is the lesser of that actually incurred and that which would have been incurred if the journey (by the same mode of transport) had started or finished at the normal place of work. In general, business travel by a route other than the shortest possible is acceptable, provided that the longer route was selected for good business reasons. (Revenue Booklet 480; Revenue Tax Bulletin December 1994 p 185).

If an emergency call-out requires an employee to travel from home to the normal place of employment, reimbursed travel expenses will be chargeable emoluments unless the conditions underlying the decision in *Pook v Owen HL 1969, 45 TC 571* (for which see also 75.10(*a*) above) are met, i.e. (i) advice on handling the emergency is given on receipt of the telephone call; (ii) responsibility for those aspects appropriate to the employee's duties is accepted at that time; and (iii) the employee has a continuing responsibility for the emergency whilst travelling to the normal place of employment. A claim for a deduction for expenses not reimbursed will be allowed on the same basis. Where an emergency call-out requires travel from home to a place other than the normal place of employment, reimbursed expenses are not chargeable emoluments, and a claim for expenses not reimbursed should be allowed. (Revenue Schedule E Manual, SE 1410, 1411).

By concession, reasonable reimbursement of expenses of home to work travel is not taxed where the expenses are incurred either (*a*) as a result of public transport disruption owing to industrial action, or (*b*) by disabled employees unable to use public transport. (Revenue Pamphlet IR 1, A58, A59; Revenue Press Release 28 June 2000). See also 75.13(v)(vi) above.

By concession, the provision by an employer of private transport, e.g. taxis, hired cars, etc., for the journey home of employees required to work late will not result in a charge to tax on the employee, providing (*a*) the employee is occasionally required to work late, i.e. until 9 p.m. or later, but those occasions are not regular, i.e. they do not follow a predictable pattern, and (*b*) either public transport between the employee's place of work and his home has ceased for the day or it would not be reasonable to expect him to use it, for example if the journey would take much longer than usual due to low availability or reliability of services at that hour. From 6 April 1999, this concession is extended to cover the payment for or provision of transport home by the employer where regular home to work car-sharing arrangements with other employees fail on a particular occasion due to unforeseen or exceptional circumstances. This includes circumstances where travel home is at the normal time but, for reasons beyond the employee's control, he cannot travel in the shared car at that time, and where he expects to travel in the shared car at the normal time (and the car travels at that time) but in the event he needs to travel home at a different time. They do not include circumstances where, on any occasion, inability to travel home in the shared car might reasonably have been anticipated. The concession applies to a maximum of 60 journeys in a tax year, and from 6 April 1999 this applies to the aggregate of journeys under both legs of the concession (i.e. late night journeys and car-share breakdowns). (Revenue Pamphlet IR 1, A66 (as revised); Revenue Press Release 9 March 1999).

Travel and subsistence expenditure is allowed, and reimbursement thereof not taxed, when working temporarily away from home and normal place of employment. This is intended to cover the extra cost of travelling and subsistence incurred because of being away on duty — but not the cost of travelling from home to normal place of work or usual expenses on food or meals taken when at normal place of work. (Revenue Pamphlet IR 131, SP 16/80, 20 November 1980). It also covers any reimbursement of the standard (*not* personal) community charge on temporary accommodation occupied near the temporary place of work. (ICAEW Guidance Note TR 795, 14 June 1990). An absence is regarded as temporary where it is not expected to, and does not, exceed twelve months, and the employee returns to the normal place of work at the end of it. Where it becomes clear during such a period that the absence will extend beyond twelve months, the exemption will apply only to amounts paid up to the date the change of circumstances became known. (Revenue Tax Bulletin May 1994 p 130). As regards what is meant by the 'normal place of employment', the Revenue normally accept that it is the place where an employee spends more than 50% of his working time, and a lower proportion may be acceptable depending on the circumstances of each business and the employee's pattern of work. Employers should be able to agree with their local inspector to divide employees into groups for these purposes. (ICAEW Technical Memorandum TR 760, 6 September 1989). A claim for a deduction corresponding to living allowances paid while working away from home was refused where an engineer without a permanent work base was required to undertake assignments necessitating his living away from home for long periods (*Elderkin v Hindmarsh Ch D 1988, 60 TC 651*).

In addition, reasonable reimbursement of expenditure on subsistence, etc. is, by concession, not taxed where (*a*) an employee occupies overnight accommodation near his normal place of work as a result of public transport disruption owing to industrial action, or (*b*) it is necessary for an offshore oil or gas worker to take overnight accommodation near the point of his departure from the mainland for the offshore rig, etc. (Revenue Pamphlet IR 1, A58, A65). See also 75.13(v)(vi) above.

See 75.13(x) as regards certain removal expenses.

Private transport used for office or employment. A proportion of the costs of running privately-owned transport used partly in the performance of the duties of an office or employment is allowable as a deduction from emoluments where the normal requirements of *ICTA 1988, s 198* are met (see 75.10 above). Similar proportionate relief is available by way of capital allowances (under *CAA 1990, s 27*, see 10.24 CAPITAL ALLOWANCES), for expenditure incurred on provision of a car (or, for 1999/2000 and subsequent years, a cycle), and interest relief (under *ICTA 1988, s 359*, see 43.18 INTEREST PAYABLE), for interest on a loan for its purchase.

In considering capital allowances and interest relief, there is no requirement that the car (or cycle) be 'necessarily' provided for use in the office or employment (i.e. that the duties of the office or employment could not be carried out without its provision, see 75.10(*a*) above). Any balancing allowance (see 10.30 CAPITAL ALLOWANCES) on the car (or cycle) being disposed of, or starting to be used wholly for purposes other than those of the office or employment, is reduced to the proportion that the number of years of assessment for which capital allowances have been claimed for use of the car (or cycle) in the office or employment bears to the number of years of assessment for which allowances were available for such use. [*ICTA 1988, s 359(3); CAA 1990, s 27; FA 1990, s 87; FA 1999, s 50(2)(3)*].

As an alternative to keeping detailed records of costs, employees may, for 1996/97 and subsequent years, apply the 'tax-free' rates under the Fixed Profit Car Scheme (see below) to their business mileage to support a tax deduction for allowable motoring expenses (after allowing for any mileage allowances received). (Revenue Press Release (REV 32) 28 November 1995). See below as regards similar schemes for cyclists and motor cyclists.

Mileage allowances. As a general rule, the excess of such allowances paid to an employee (or office-holder) over the costs necessarily incurred in travelling in the performance of the duties of the employment is taxable on the employee, but the treatment of a particular payment will depend on the facts of the case. In *Pook v Owen HL 1969, 45 TC 571* (see 75.10(*a*) above) the mileage allowance paid to a doctor was held not to be part of his emoluments, and this decision was applied in *Donnelly v Williamson Ch D 1981, 54 TC 636* (mileage allowance paid to a schoolteacher for use of her car when attending parents' meetings) but distinguished in *Perrons v Spackman Ch D 1981, 55 TC 403* (lump sum and mileage allowances to a county council employee treated as part of his emoluments, but he was allowed to deduct his actual car expenses on official duties, including a proportion of his repairs and standing expenses). Deductions for car expenses in excess of the employer's allowance were refused to a Regional Hospital Board employee (*Hamerton v Overy Ch D 1954, 35 TC 73*) and a civil servant (*Marsden v CIR Ch D 1965, 42 TC 326*).

Strictly, the employer should return the full amount of such allowances paid, and the employee submit a detailed claim for relief based on actual expenses and business/private mileage. The Revenue, however, operate with some employers a simplified administrative arrangement known as the Fixed Profit Car Scheme (FPCS) under which an employee's taxable business mileage profit is determined by reference to engine size and the excess of the mileage allowance paid over the FPCS 'tax-free' rates, which are as follows (*a*) for the first 4,000 miles in the year and (*b*) for mileage in excess of 4,000.

Capacity	Up to 1,000cc		1,001–1,500cc		1,501–2,000cc		Over 2,000cc	
	(*a*)	(*b*)	(*a*)	(*b*)	(*a*)	(*b*)	(*a*)	(*b*)
	28p	17p	35p	20p	45p	25p	63p	36p

The rates for years before 1997/98 were as follows.

1996/97	27p	16p	34p	19p	43p	23p	61p	33p
1995/96	27p	15p	34p	19p	43p	23p	60p	32p
1994/95	27p	15p	33p	19p	41p	23p	56p	31p
1993/94	26p	15p	32p	18p	40p	22p	54p	30p

Banded payments by employers are matched as closely as possible to the FPCS bands, and where uniform allowances are paid, the average of the two middle FPCS bands is used. Relief for interest on a loan for purchase of the car (see 43.18 INTEREST PAYABLE) is not included in the FPCS rates, and needs to be claimed separately. (Revenue Press Release 14 December 1999).

Where the employer has not entered into the FPCS, employees may, for 1996/97 and subsequent years, nevertheless use the FPCS rates to calculate any taxable profit on mileage allowances received. (Revenue Press Release (REV 32) 28 November 1995).

For cars provided by the employer ('company cars'), see 75.15 above. Expenditure on the provision of car (or, from 6 April 1999, cycle or motor cycle) parking facilities for an employee at or near his place of work (whether the car etc. is company-owned or private) does not constitute an emolument. [*ICTA 1988, s 155(1A); FA 1999, s 49*].

Volunteer drivers (e.g. hospital car service drivers). See 74.2 SCHEDULE D, CASE VI.

See generally Revenue Pamphlet IR 125.

Cyclists. A similar scheme for cyclists permits the payment from 5 April 1999 of a tax-free allowance of up to 12p per mile. See Revenue Press Release (IR 5) 9 March 1999 and Revenue Press Release 14 December 1999.

Motor cyclists. A similar scheme for motor cyclists permits the payment from 5 April 2000 of a tax-free allowance of up to 24p per mile. See Revenue Press Release 14 December 1999.

Incidental overnight expenses. For 1995/96 and subsequent years, payments made to or on behalf of an employee in respect of his overnight personal incidental expenses (e.g. laundry, newspapers, telephone calls home) while away from home on business are exempt from tax up to certain limits. Payments above the limits are taxable in full. The exemption covers expenses incidental to the employee's being away from home during a 'qualifying absence' other than one in relation to which the 'authorised maximum' is exceeded, being expenses which would not otherwise be deductible. A '*qualifying absence*' is a continuous period throughout which the employee is obliged to stay away from home and which includes at least one overnight stay but does not include any such stay at a place the expenses of travelling to which would not be either deductible under normal rules or, for 1997/98 onwards, exempt under *ICTA 1988, s 200B* (work-related training costs, see 75.42 above) or, for 2000/01 onwards, exempt under *ICTA 1988, s 200E* (education and training, see 75.42 above). The '*authorised maximum*', in relation to a qualifying absence, is £5 for each night spent in the UK and £10 for each night any part of which is spent outside the UK (such amounts being subject to increase by Treasury Order from a date specified therein). In determining whether the authorised maximum is exceeded, payments by non-cash voucher or credit token and the providing of benefits are taken into account as well as cash payments. [*ICTA 1988, s 200A; FA 1995, s 93(4)(5); FA 1997, s 63(2)(3); FA 2000, s 58(2)(3)*]. Inland Revenue guidance notes for employers on the practical application of these provisions (see Revenue Booklet 480 and the Employer's Guide to PAYE (P7)) are available (see Revenue Press Release 16 May 1995).

Working Rule Agreements. Where Working Rule Agreements are drawn up between employers and trade unions and include payments of allowances for daily travel and subsistence, the Revenue have agreed that certain of these payments (or part) should not be taxed because of the high degree of mobility required in the industries concerned. Consistent treatment is accorded to site-based staff who work alongside operatives who are covered by a Working Rule Agreement and who have broadly the same working circumstances. Employers must obtain authority from their local tax district before making any such tax-free payments. (Revenue Press Release 13 February 1981).

Lodging allowances may generally be paid tax-free to an employee engaged under the terms of a Working Rule Agreement, provided that he is married, or has dependants living with him, and incurs extra expense while working away from home in addition to the cost of maintaining a permanent home. This treatment is extended to single men without dependants who maintain a permanent home. (ICAEW Memorandum TR 713, August 1988).

Travelling appointments. Excess expenditure on meals away from home may be claimed by employees holding full-time travelling appointments (e.g. lorry drivers) not restricted to a limited area. Bills, receipts etc. must be produced as evidence. Estimated figures will not be accepted. Relief is not restricted by amount saved by not having meals at home or a fixed place of work. (Revenue Pamphlet IR 131, SP 16/80, 20 November 1980). The Revenue has agreed a tax-free overnight subsistence allowance of £22.55 (from 1 January 1998 — £21.75 for calendar year 1997, £21.15 for 1996, £20.50 for 1995, £19.90 for 1994, £19.50 for 1993, £19.00 for 1992) (reduced by 25% where a sleeper cab is available) under certain industry agreements. (Revenue Schedule E Manual, SE 7620–7629).

Employment abroad. Tax will not be charged on the reimbursement to an employee, whose duties are carried on wholly abroad and who retains an abode in the UK, of expenses, including reasonable hotel expenses necessarily incurred, in travelling (whether alone or with his wife and family) to the country where his duties are performed and returning to the UK. Similar concession for persons receiving 'foreign emoluments' and travelling between UK and abode in home country. See 75.5 and 75.6 above. For allowances for travelling etc. expenses to members of the European Parliament, see *Lord Bruce of Donington v Aspden CJEC, [1981] STC 761.*

For overseas trips see *Newlin v Woods CA 1966, 42 TC 649* (cost of journey for health reasons disallowed); *Maclean v Trembath Ch D 1956, 36 TC 653* (business trip accompanied by wife; expenses attributable to wife disallowed); *Thomson v White Ch D 1966, 43 TC 256* (expenses of farmers and wives on organised trip partly for sightseeing and partly to see farms overseas disallowed); *Owen v Burden CA 1971, 47 TC 476* (expenses of county surveyor voluntarily to attend overseas road conference disallowed). Expenses of spouse of director or higher-paid employee who accompanies director on business journey abroad because his or her health is too precarious for travel alone are not assessable on employee. (Revenue Pamphlet IR 1, A4). See 29.16 EXEMPT INCOME as regards certain overseas travel costs of MPs.

Simon's Direct Tax Service. See **E4.708.**

75.44 VOUCHERS AND CREDIT-TOKENS

The following, when provided for an employee (or his spouse, parent, child or spouse of his child or any dependant of the employee), are taxable as emoluments of his employment. For the application of PAYE, see 55.2 PAY AS YOU EARN. Dispensations (see 75.22 above) may apply where appropriate.

(*a*) **Non-cash vouchers** (i.e. vouchers, stamps or similar documents or tokens capable of being exchanged, either singly or together, immediately or later, for money, goods or services or any combination of these but excluding cash vouchers, see below). The tax charge is on the expense incurred by the person at whose cost the voucher, and the money, goods or services for which it is capable of being exchanged, are provided, and in or in connection with that provision, with 'just and reasonable' apportionment in the case of schemes relating to groups of employees, and less any amounts made good by the employee. The charge is reduced to the extent that relief would have been claimable by the employee under *ICTA 1988, s 198* (necessary expenses etc., see 75.10(*a*) above), *ICTA 1988, s 201* (professional subscriptions, see 75.39 above), *ICTA 1988, s 201AA* (employee liabilities and indemnity insurance, see 75.23 above) or *ICTA 1988, s 332(3)* (re clergymen, see 75.9 above) if he had incurred the cost himself. The year of assessment is the year in which the expense is incurred by the employer or, if different and later, the year in which the voucher is received by, or appropriated to, the employee but, for cheque vouchers, it is the year in which the voucher is handed over in exchange for money, goods or services (time of posting is treated as time of handing over). [*ICTA 1988, s 141(1)–(5)(7), s 144(3); FA 1994, s 89(1)(2); FA 1995, s 91(2)*]. This provision does not affect the treatment of luncheon vouchers as in 75.30 above.

Expense incurred by the employer in providing vouchers or any other incentive awards includes expenses beyond the direct cost of buying the goods or services provided where the expenses contribute more or less directly to the advantage enjoyed by the employee, e.g. costs of selecting and testing goods or services, or of after-sales service, or of storage and distribution. More remote expenses, e.g. costs of planning or administering a scheme or of promotional literature, etc., are excluded. See Revenue Pamphlet IR 131, SP 6/85, 29 July 1985.

Transport vouchers are specifically included in the above provisions but *not included* is a voucher provided for an employee of a passenger transport undertaking under arrangements in operation on 25 March 1982 to enable that employee (including spouse or family, as above) to obtain passenger transport services from his employer or his employer's subsidiary or parent company or another passenger transport undertaking. 'Transport voucher' means any ticket, pass or other document or token intended to enable a person to obtain passenger transport services (whether or not in exchange for it). [*ICTA 1988, s 141(6)(7)*]. See also 75.13(xxv)(xxvi) above.

Cheque vouchers are also included in the above provisions. '*Cheque voucher*' means a cheque provided for an employee and intended for his use wholly or mainly for payment for particular goods or services or for goods or services of one or more particular classes. [*ICTA 1988, s 141(7)*].

A voucher used by an employee to obtain the use of a *car parking space* (or, for 1999/2000 and subsequent years, a cycle or motor cycle parking space) at or near his place of work is excluded from these provisions [*ICTA 1988, s 141(6A); FA 1999, s 49*], and a voucher provided neither by the employer nor by a person connected with the employer (within *ICTA 1988, s 839*, see 20 CONNECTED PERSONS) and used to obtain *entertainment* for the employee (or a relation) is similarly excluded, subject to the same conditions as are specified in 75.13(xv) above. [*ICTA 1988, s 141(6B); FA 1994, s 89(3)*]. See also 75.21 above for the exclusion of vouchers relating to certain sports and recreational facilities.

Incidental overnight expenses. For 1995/96 and subsequent years, there is excluded from these provisions a voucher used to obtain goods or services (or to obtain money to buy goods or services) incidental to the employee's being away from home on business during a 'qualifying absence' in relation to which the authorised maximum (£5 per night spent in the UK and £10 per night spent abroad) is not exceeded, where the cost of such goods or services is not otherwise deductible from emoluments. [*ICTA 1988, s 141(6C)(6D); FA 1995, s 93(1)*]. See also 75.43 above.

General. The above provisions do not apply if a person supplies the inspector with a statement of the cases and circumstances in which vouchers are provided to any employee (whether his own or not) and the inspector is satisfied that no additional tax is payable under these provisions and notifies that person accordingly. Such notification may be revoked retrospectively. [*ICTA 1988, s 144(1)(2)*].

See Simon's Direct Tax Service E4.432.

(*b*) **Cash vouchers** (as defined below). Where, as in some holiday pay schemes, a cash voucher is provided for an employee (including spouse or family as for non-cash vouchers, see (*a*) above) for redemption for cash which will be an emolument, tax is to be charged on the redemption amount when the voucher is received by, or appropriated to, the employee, with 'just and reasonable' apportionment in the case of schemes relating to groups of employees, *unless* the voucher is issued under a scheme which is approved by the Board as being practicable for PAYE to be applied at the time the vouchers are exchanged for cash.

'*Cash voucher*' means any voucher, stamp or similar document capable of being exchanged, either singly or together, immediately or later, for a sum of money not substantially less than the cost to the person at whose cost it is provided, but excluding any document for a sum which would not have been chargeable under Schedule E if paid to the employee directly and excluding any savings certificate on which accumulated interest is exempt from tax. Where the sum of money is substantially less than the cost, any part of the difference representing benefits in connection with sickness, personal injury or death will be disregarded in deciding if the voucher is a cash voucher.

The above provisions do not apply if a person supplies the inspector with a statement of the cases and circumstances in which cash vouchers are provided to any employee (whether his own or not) and the inspector is satisfied that no additional tax is payable under these provisions and notifies that person accordingly. Such notification may be revoked retrospectively. [*ICTA 1988, ss 143, 144(1)–(3); FA 1994, s 89(8)–(14)*].

See Simon's Direct Tax Service E4.431.

(*c*) **Luncheon Vouchers.** See 75.30 above.

(*d*) **Credit-tokens** (as defined below). Tax is charged, when the employee uses a credit token to obtain money, goods or services, on the expense incurred by the person at whose cost the money, goods or services are provided (before 3 May 1994, by the person providing the credit token), in or in connection with that provision, with 'just and reasonable' apportionment in the case of schemes relating to groups of employees. See (*a*) above as regards valuation of expenses incurred. The money, goods or services obtained by the employee are disregarded (to avoid a double charge). The charge is reduced by any amounts made good by the employee and by any amounts for which relief would have been claimable under *ICTA 1988, s 198, s 201, s 201AA* or *s 332(3)* (see (*a*) above) if he had purchased the goods etc. himself. *ICTA 1988, s 142* does not apply if a person supplies the inspector with a statement of the cases and circumstances in which credit-tokens are provided to any employee (whether his own or not) and the inspector is satisfied that no additional tax is payable under *section 142* and notifies that person accordingly. Such notification may be revoked retrospectively. [*ICTA 1988, s 142(1)–(3), s 144(1)(2); FA 1994, s 89(5)(6); FA 1995, s 91(2)*].

A token used by an employee to obtain the use of a *car parking space* (or, for 1999/2000 and subsequent years, a cycle or motor cycle parking space) at or near his place of work is excluded from these provisions [*ICTA 1988, s 142(3A); FA 1999, s 49*], and a token provided neither by the employer nor by a person connected with the employer (within *ICTA 1988, s 839*, see 20 CONNECTED PERSONS) and used to obtain *entertainment* for the employee (or a relation) is similarly excluded, subject to the same conditions as are specified in 75.13(xv) above. [*ICTA 1988, s 142(3B); FA 1994, s 89(7)*].

Incidental overnight expenses. For 1995/96 and subsequent years, there is excluded from these provisions a token used to obtain goods or services (or to obtain money to buy goods or services) incidental to the employee's being away from home on business during a 'qualifying absence' in relation to which the authorised maximum (£5 per night spent in the UK and £10 per night spent abroad) is not exceeded, where the cost of such goods or services is not otherwise deductible from emoluments. [*ICTA 1988, s 142(3C)(3D); FA 1995, s 93(2)*]. See also 75.43 above.

'*Credit-token*' means a card, token or other thing given to a person by another person who undertakes that (*a*) on the production of it (whether or not some other action is also required) he will supply money, goods or services on credit or (*b*) on similar production to a third party, he will pay that third party for the money etc. supplied (whether or not taking any discount or commission). '*Production*' includes the use of an object provided to operate a machine. Not included is a cash voucher and a non-cash voucher already chargeable in (*b*) or (*c*) above. [*ICTA 1988, s 142(4)(5)*].

See Simon's Direct Tax Service E4.433.

75.45 **WAGES IN LIEU OF NOTICE**

The taxation treatment of payments in lieu of notice ('PILONs') is governed by the general principles applying to payments on cessation of employment, for which see 19.3 *et seq.* COMPENSATION FOR LOSS OF EMPLOYMENT (AND DAMAGES). Where the payment is not within the general Schedule E charge, it will generally fall within *ICTA 1988, s 148*, subject to the exemptions from charge under that *section*.

The Revenue have set out their approach to the application of general Schedule E principles to PILONs, as follows.

(*a*) Where contractual arrangements provide for a PILON, the contract is terminated in accordance with its terms on a summary dismissal. The compensation is a contractual entitlement rather than liquidated damages and is chargeable as an emolument under general Schedule E principles.

(*b*) Where the employer and employee agree at the time of termination that the employment is to be terminated without proper notice but on the making of a PILON, and there was no existing understanding in this respect which could be construed as a contractual provision or amendment, the source of the payment lies only in the agreement to terminate the employment. The payment is therefore not an emolument from the employment.

(*c*) In establishing whether contractual arrangements provide for a PILON, all relevant factors, e.g. rules in staff handbooks or wage agreements, or oral agreements, have to be considered. Even in the absence of any direct contractual arrangements, there may be an implied contractual term of service where an employer has established a practice of making PILONs instead of giving due notice.

(*d*) Where neither (*a*) nor (*b*) above applies, failure to give due notice is a breach of contract, and a payment made for such a breach represents liquidated damages and is not an emolument from the employment.

(*e*) The existence of a reserved right or discretion of the employer to make a PILON where due notice is not given is not a determining factor where the right or discretion is not exercised. Where it is exercised, (*a*) above applies.

The Revenue reject the view that a contractual PILON is properly analysed as a payment of damages for breach of contract (in particular by analysis of the true effect of (what is now) *Employment Rights Act 1996, s 86*). They also reject the view that a PILON is a redundancy payment.

Payments for a period where notice is given but not in fact worked ('gardening leave') are emoluments from the employment.

(Revenue Tax Bulletin August 1996 pp 325–327).

In *EMI Group Electronics Ltd v Coldicott CA 1999, 71 TC 455*, it was held that payments following exercise by the employer of a reserved right as under (*e*) above were emoluments chargeable under Schedule E.

Simon's Direct Tax Service. See **E4.805**.

75.46 **WORKERS SUPPLIED BY AGENCIES**

Where an individual worker (including a partner in a firm and a member of an unincorporated body) has a contract or arrangement with another person (e.g. with an agency, which term includes an unincorporated body of which the worker is a member) under which he is obliged to render personal services to the client which are subject to supervision, direction or control as to the manner in which the services are rendered, he will be chargeable under Schedule E (if not already so chargeable) on the remuneration received for those services. '*Remuneration*' includes every form of payment, perquisites, benefits etc. but not anything which would not otherwise be chargeable under Schedule E if receivable from an office or employment. [*ICTA 1988, s 134*]. For the existence of a contract, see *Brady v Hart Ch D 1985, 58 TC 518*.

See also *Bhadra v Ellam Ch D 1987, 60 TC 466*, where a doctor obtaining locum posts through medical agencies was held to be within *section 134*.

The above provisions do not apply (*a*) to entertainers or fashion etc. models, or (*b*) if the services are wholly rendered in the worker's own home or at other premises which are neither under the control or management of the client nor at which the services are required by their nature to be rendered, or (*c*) as regards payments made in respect of services rendered (or to be rendered) after 5 April 1998, if the worker is a sub-contractor within the CONSTRUCTION INDUSTRY TAX SCHEME (21) (and see below). [*ICTA 1988, s 134(5); FA 1998, s 55(1)(3), Sch 27 III(7)*].

The person paying the remuneration (i.e. the agency or the client) must include the worker in his return of employees under *TMA 1970, s 15*, see 67.5 RETURNS. Where a worker is engaged through a foreign agency which does not have a branch or permanent agency operating PAYE, the client is deemed to be the employer and is responsible for operating PAYE and National Insurance arrangements.

See 55.3 PAY AS YOU EARN as regards application of PAYE generally.

As regards the scope of the legislation on agency workers, see Revenue Schedule E Manual, SE 713. These provisions are independent of, and are not affected by, the rules at 61 PERSONAL SERVICE COMPANIES ETC..

Transitional provisions for sub-contractors. Where a trade

(i) consists of or includes the rendering of services under contracts relating to construction operations (as defined in 21.2 CONSTRUCTION INDUSTRY TAX SCHEME),

(ii) was being carried on at the end of 1997/98,

(iii) included receipts which would have been chargeable under Schedule E for 1997/98 had it not been for the exemption at (*c*) above (now removed),

then *unless the trader elects to the contrary* (see below), the trade is treated as permanently discontinued at 5 April 1998 and, to the extent that the trade includes activities in addition to agency engagements chargeable under Schedule E, a new trade is deemed to commence on 6 April 1998. Losses may nevertheless be carried forward under *ICTA 1988, s 385* (see 46.12 LOSSES) from the old trade to the new (and this also applies where there is no deemed recommencement of the old trade as above but an actual new construction trade is commenced during 1998/99). The deemed cessation at 5 April 1998 cannot give rise to a Revenue direction revising the basis of assessment for 1995/96 and 1996/97 in the case of a business commenced before 6 April 1994 (see 71.24 SCHEDULE D, CASES I AND II). An election to disapply these provisions must be made in a self-assessment tax return or, as the case may be, a partnership return. It is a further condition that the return be submitted on or before the statutory filing date. See 78.5, 78.8 SELF-ASSESSMENT. [*FA 1998, s 56*].

Simon's Direct Tax Service. See **E4.204**.

76 Schedule F—Dividends etc.

Simon's Direct Tax Service D1.

76.1 Schedule F commenced on 6 April 1966 and applies to dividends and other distributions of UK companies. [*ICTA 1988, s 20; FA 1993, s 183(1)*].

76.2 Up to 5 April 1973, the company was required to account (to the Revenue) for the standard rate of income tax on the dividends etc.

76.3 Until 5 April 1999, the company pays (to the Revenue) advance corporation tax (at a prescribed rate) on paying the dividend etc. and the recipient gets an equivalent 'tax credit' (subject to special provisions for 1993/94) except (until 5 April 1999) in the case of certain 'foreign income dividends'—see 1.9 ALLOWANCES AND TAX RATES. From 6 April 1999, following the abolition of advance corporation tax, the tax credit is set at one-ninth of the amount of the dividend etc.. [*ICTA 1988, ss 231, 246C; FA 1993, s 78(3); FA 1994, Sch 16 para 1; F(No 2)A 1997, s 30, Sch 6 para 3; FA 1998, s 31*].

From 6 April 1999, following the change referred to above in the rate of tax credit, special rates of tax apply to Schedule F income and 'equivalent foreign income' (see 1.9 ALLOWANCES AND TAX RATES). Where the income falls within the basic rate limit (treating it as the top slice of total income), the rate is the 'Schedule F ordinary rate', initially set at 10%, so that the liability is met by the tax credit. To the extent that the income exceeds the basic rate limit, the rate is the 'Schedule F upper rate', initially set at 32.5% (equivalent to a further liability of 25% of the amount of the dividend etc., which is the same as that applicable before 6 April 1999). [*ICTA 1988, ss 1A, 1B; F(No 2)A 1997, s 31*]. See 1.9 ALLOWANCES AND TAX RATES as regards dividend taxation generally and in particular the treatment of tax credits.

See also Tolley's Corporation Tax under Advance Corporation Tax and Distributions.

77 Scientific Research Associations

Simon's Direct Tax Service C4.535.

77.1 Scientific research associations are, on a claim, granted the same exemptions from tax as CHARITIES (15), including exemptions from tax on capital gains, if

(*a*) object is scientific research which may lead to extension of any class(es) of trade, and association is approved for this purpose by the Secretary of State, and

(*b*) the Association is prohibited by Memorandum or similar instrument from distribution of income or property, in any form, to its members (other than reasonable payments for supplies, labour, power, services, interest and rent). [*ICTA 1988, s 508; TCGA, s 271(6)(b)*].

The Department of Trade and Industry (which is primarily responsible for determining whether a body is a scientific research association) issued new guidance on 4 September 1998 on the criteria they will apply, with effect from that date, in making such determinations. By concession, tax exemptions will continue to be granted on the previous basis for accounting periods beginning before 1 September 1999, provided that exemption would have continued to apply under the previous practice and the association continues to satisfy (*b*) above. This applies also to bodies established before 4 September 1998 which would have obtained approval under the previous practice. (Revenue Pamphlet IR 1, C31).

See also 71.80 SCHEDULE D, CASES I AND II as regards relief for contributions to scientific research associations.

78 Self-Assessment

Cross-reference. See also 79 SELF-ASSESSMENT—KEY DATES.

Simon's Direct Tax Service E1.8.

(See also Revenue Pamphlet IR 142.)

The headings in this chapter are as follows.

78.1 Introduction
78.2 — changes to facilitate self-assessment
78.3 Interpretation of references to assessments, etc.
78.4 Notice of chargeability
78.5 Annual returns of income and chargeable gains
78.6 Self-assessments
78.7 — amendments of self-assessments other than where enquiries made
78.8 Partnership returns
78.9 Partnership statements
78.10 Records
78.11 Enquiries into returns
78.12 — power to call for documents
78.13 — amendment of self-assessment or partnership statement where enquiries made
78.14 Determination of tax where no return delivered
78.15 Discovery assessments
78.16 — amendment of partnership statement where loss of tax discovered
78.17 Interim payments of tax on account
78.18 — example
78.19 Final payment (repayment) of tax
78.20 — due date: further provisions
78.21 Surcharge on unpaid tax
78.22 Interest on unpaid tax
78.23 Interest on overpaid tax
78.24 Date of payment by cheque
78.25 Penalties
78.26 — failure to make timeous return for income tax and capital gains tax
78.27 — failure to make partnership return
78.28 — fraud or negligence
78.29 — failure to produce documents
78.30 Assessments: procedure and time limit
78.31 Appeals
78.32 Claims, etc.
78.33 Jurisdiction of Commissioners
78.34 Over-repayments of tax
78.35 Collection and recovery
78.36 Liability of relevant trustees
78.37 Employers' obligations and returns
78.38 Taxation of non-residents

78.1 INTRODUCTION

Self-assessment will have effect generally for 1996/97 and subsequent years of assessment, although certain aspects of the system come into effect in earlier or later years. The term 'self-assessment' refers to the system whereby the annual tax returns filed by individuals and trustees should include a self-assessment of the taxpayer's liability for income tax and capital gains tax. Payment of tax will then be due automatically, based on the self-assessment. The main body of legislation is contained in *Finance Act 1994*, although there have been further provisions in subsequent Finance Acts.

Two detailed Revenue booklets, SAT 1 'The new current year basis of assessment' and SAT 2 'Self Assessment: the legal framework', both guides for Inland Revenue officers and tax practitioners, should have been sent by tax offices to all practices with which they deal in August/September 1995. Further copies are available (price £7.50 and £5.00 respectively) from Inland Revenue Reference Library, New Wing, Somerset House, Strand, London,

WC2R 1LB. A booklet SAT 3 'Self Assessment: what it will mean for employers' should also have been sent to employers as part of an information pack in July 1995. Further copies are available free from tax offices, as are the following explanatory pamphlets:

SA/BK3 Self Assessment: a guide to keeping records for the self-employed
SA/BK4 Self Assessment: a general guide to keeping records
SA/BK6 Self Assessment: penalties for late tax returns
SA/BK7 Self Assessment: surcharges for late payment of tax
SA/BK8 Self Assessment: your guide

A series of articles has been published in the Revenue Tax Bulletin from August 1993 onwards on various aspects of self-assessment. See 79 SELF-ASSESSMENT—KEY DATES for a calendar of key dates and events.

Information pack including final draft returns. In September 1996, the Revenue issued to professional tax advisors an information pack containing *inter alia* the final drafts of the self-assessment tax returns for individuals and partnerships together with draft guidance notes and helpsheets. These are also available for inspection at Tax Enquiry Centres. (Revenue Press Release 3 September 1996). The return for individuals consists of a basic eight pages to which will be attached any supplementary pages relevant to the individual concerned, forming a single 'customised' tax return. The supplementary pages are colour-coded and cover employment, share schemes, self-employment, partnership income, land and property, foreign income, trust income, capital gains and non-residence etc. Each individual will also receive a tax return guide containing explanatory notes relevant to his circumstances. It is the individual's responsibility to obtain any supplementary pages he needs but has not received, which he may do by telephoning a Revenue Orderline, by which means he may also obtain the relevant explanatory notes and/or 'helpsheets' on specific topics. Each return sent out will be accompanied by a tax calculation guide designed to assist the individual in calculating his tax liability if he chooses to do so. Partnership returns follow a similar pattern.

Returns. The first returns to be affected will be those covering the tax year 1996/97, normally sent out by the Revenue in April 1997. Such returns must normally be filed by 31 January following the year of assessment (see 78.5 below). Taxpayers who would prefer not to compute their own liabilities will not have to do so providing they file their return early, normally by 30 September following the year of assessment (see 78.6 below). Penalties will be imposed for late submission of returns, subject to appeal on the grounds of reasonable excuse (see 78.26 below). There are provisions for making amendments to self-assessments (see 78.7 below). The Revenue are given broadly one year from the filing date to give notice of their intention to enquire into the return (see 78.11 below). A formal procedure is laid down for such enquiries (see 78.11 to 78.13 below). If they do not give such notice, the return becomes final and conclusive, subject to any 'error or mistake' claim by the taxpayer (see 17.10 CLAIMS) or 'discovery' assessment by the Revenue (see 78.15 below). In the event of non-submission of a return, the Revenue will be able to make a determination of the tax liability; there will be no right of appeal but the determination may be superseded upon submission of the return (see 78.14 below). Capital losses must be quantified if they are to be allowable losses (see Tolley's Capital Gains Tax).

A new style of return will have to be filed by partnerships. This must include a statement of the allocation of partnership income between the partners. See 78.8, 78.9 below.

An electronic version of the tax return (SA/BK5) is available from tax offices.

Payment of tax. Income tax (on all sources of taxable income) for a year of assessment will be payable by means of two interim payments of equal amounts, based normally on the liability for the previous year and due on 31 January in the year of assessment and the following 31 July, and a final balancing payment due on the following 31 January (on which date any capital gains tax liability will also be due for payment). Taxpayers will have the right to reduce their interim payments if they believe their liability will be less than that for the previous year or to dispense with interim payments if they believe they will have no liability. Interim payments will not in any case be required where substantially all of a taxpayer's liability is covered by deduction of tax at source, including PAYE, or where the amounts otherwise due are below *de minimis* limits to be prescribed by regulations. See 78.17 to 78.20 below.

Interest on overdue payments will run from the due date to the date of payment (see 78.22 below). There will also be a 5% surcharge on any tax unpaid by 28 February following the year of assessment and a further 5% surcharge on any tax unpaid by the following 31 July, such surcharges being subject to appeal on the grounds of reasonable excuse (see 78.21 below). Interest on tax overpaid will run from the due date (or date of payment if later) to the date of repayment (see 78.23 below); the rate of interest will be lower than that on overdue tax.

Internet filing. From April 2000 small businesses and individual taxpayers filing their self-assessment returns over the internet and paying any tax due electronically will receive a tax discount of £10 for one year. (Revenue Press Release 16 February 2000). See 67.3 RETURNS as regards other electronic filing discounts. For the operation of the Revenue's internet filing and payment service generally, see Revenue Tax Bulletin June 2000 pp 757, 758.

Miscellaneous. Numerous consequential amendments are made to taxes management provisions and time limits. There is a new statutory requirement for taxpayers to keep records for the purpose of making returns and to preserve such records for specified periods (see 78.10 below).

The above changes are covered in this chapter, except for changes to time limits and other consequential amendments which are dealt with in the appropriate chapters.

78.2 **Changes to facilitate self-assessment.** Fundamental changes are made by *Finance Act 1994* to the system of computing tax liabilities under Schedule D. The principal change involves a move from a preceding year basis of assessment to a current year basis, but they also involve amendments to the provisions on, for example, trading loss reliefs, capital allowances and to the means by which members of partnerships are charged to tax. The provisions are summarised below and covered in detail in the appropriate chapters.

As regards businesses commenced, and other sources of income first arising, after 5 April 1994, the new provisions have effect for 1994/95 and subsequent years of assessment. As regards businesses commenced, and other sources of income first arising, before 6 April 1994, they generally come into effect for 1996/97 and subsequent years. For such businesses, etc., there are transitional provisions to facilitate the changeover from the old system to the new. Some of the provisions affecting partnerships do not have effect until 1997/98.

Current year basis. Subject to special rules for opening years (see 71.12 SCHEDULE D, CASES I AND II) and the closing year (see 71.17 SCHEDULE D, CASES I AND II), individuals carrying on a trade, profession or vocation will be taxed for a year of assessment on the profits made in the period of account ending in that year (see 71.14 SCHEDULE D, CASES I AND II). There are statutory rules for determining the basis period in the event of a change of accounting date; these can produce a basis period of more than 12 months but not one of less than 12 months (see 71.15 SCHEDULE D, CASES I AND II).

The broad intention is that over the lifetime of a business the profits taxed should equate to the profits earned (as adjusted for tax purposes). Profits will, in fact, sometimes be taxed twice (as a result of the opening year rules or certain changes of accounting date). However, the amount taxed twice can be deducted (known as overlap relief) in computing profits for the year of cessation or for a year of assessment the basis period for which is longer than

12 months, i.e. as a result of a change of accounting date. See 71.19 and 71.22 SCHEDULE D, CASES I AND II.

Income chargeable under Schedule D, Cases III to VI will be taxed for a year of assessment on the basis of the income arising in that year. See 72.4(*e*) SCHEDULE D, CASE III, 73.9 SCHEDULE D, CASES IV AND V and 74.3 SCHEDULE D, CASE VI.

Transitional provisions. For businesses commenced before 6 April 1994, 1996/97 will be a transitional year. The basis period will run from the end of the basis period for 1995/96 (on a preceding year basis) to the end of the basis period for 1996/97 (applying the current year basis). Assuming no change of accounting date, this will be a two-year period and the taxable profit will be one half of the profits for that period, the other half escaping tax. Where this transitional period is more or less than two years, the profits will be apportioned so that twelve months' profits are taxed and the balance escapes tax. A trading loss for any part of the transitional period will qualify for relief in full, with no apportionment. See 71.20 SCHEDULE D, CASES I AND II.

For businesses commenced before 6 April 1994, the current year basis and the transitional rules above will not apply if the business ceases before 6 April 1997. Special rules, based on the closing year rules under the preceding year basis, may be applied as regards 1995/96 and 1996/97 where such a business ceases in 1997/98 and as regards 1996/97 only for a cessation in 1998/99. See 71.24 SCHEDULE D, CASES I AND II.

Similar rules will apply to other sources of Schedule D income on the changeover to a current year basis. See 72.4(*f*) SCHEDULE D, CASE III and 73.9 SCHEDULE D, CASES IV AND V.

There are anti-avoidance provisions designed to deter and penalise attempts to exploit the transitional rules by shifting income either into the transitional basis period so that it will not be fully charged to tax (see 71.20 SCHEDULE D, CASES I AND II, 72.4(*f*) SCHEDULE D, CASE III and 73.9 SCHEDULE D, CASES IV AND V) or (for trading etc. profits only) into the transitional overlap period (see 71.22 SCHEDULE D, CASES I AND II and 73.9 SCHEDULE D, CASES IV AND V). There are various triggers which automatically bring these measures into play, subject to statutory let-outs based on motive and benefit and to *de minimis* limits. The counteraction is to increase the assessment for the transitional year 1996/97 or reduce the transitional overlap profit (see 71.22) by 1.25 times the amount on which the taxpayer sought to avoid tax (reduced by 0.25 times that amount to the extent that disclosure is made voluntarily in the tax return). There are also provisions aimed at the refinancing of partnership borrowings for the transitional basis period or transitional overlap period by means of loans taken out by individual partners after 31 March 1994 (see 43.22 INTEREST PAYABLE).

Losses. Under the current year basis, trading losses will always be computed for tax purposes on an accounts basis (as was usually the case in practice under the preceding year basis of assessment) rather than a fiscal year basis. Loss relief under *ICTA 1988, s 380* (against other income) will be available against income of the tax year in which the loss is incurred and/or the previous year. See 46.3 LOSSES. This also applies, for 1994/95 onwards, to income tax relief for losses on unquoted shares (see 46.18 LOSSES). Other consequential changes are made to loss relief provisions (see 46 LOSSES generally).

Capital allowances. Capital allowances are to be treated as trading expenses (and balancing charges as trading receipts) in the same way as has long since applied for corporation tax purposes (see 10.1 CAPITAL ALLOWANCES). The chargeable period for capital allowances purposes will be the period of account rather than the year of assessment (see 10.2(vi) CAPITAL ALLOWANCES). For businesses commenced before 6 April 1994, these changes apply for 1997/98 and later years. Other consequential changes are made to capital allowances provisions (see 10 CAPITAL ALLOWANCES generally).

Partnerships. A partnership will no longer be taxed as a separate entity. Instead, each individual partner's share of profits, after all partnership expenses and capital allowances, will fall to be included in his or her self-assessment. Profits will be allocated between partners by reference to the sharing ratios for the period of account (rather than those for the year of assessment). A change in the members of a partnership will no longer be regarded as a cessation for tax purposes (provided there is at least one continuing partner), and continuation elections under *ICTA 1988, s 113(2)* will thus be defunct. The commencement and cessation provisions will instead apply to partners individually. For partnership businesses commenced before 6 April 1994, these changes apply for 1997/98 and later years. A deemed cessation and recommencement after 5 April 1994 will bring the new rules into effect immediately as regards the new partnership. See 53 PARTNERSHIPS.

Double taxation relief. Special rules are introduced to ensure that all relief available for foreign tax on business profits is given over the lifetime of a business. See 25.5 (*j*)(*n*) DOUBLE TAX RELIEF.

78.3 INTERPRETATION OF REFERENCES TO ASSESSMENTS, ETC.

Following the introduction of self-assessment, references to an individual (or trustee) being assessed to tax, or being charged to tax by an assessment, are to be construed as including a reference to his being so assessed, or being so charged, by a self-assessment under *TMA 1970, s 9* (see 78.6 below) or by a determination under *TMA 1970, s 28C* (see 78.14 below) which has not been superseded by a self-assessment. [*FA 1994, s 197*].

78.4 NOTICE OF CHARGEABILITY

For *1995/96 and subsequent years*, a person chargeable to income tax or capital gains tax for a year of assessment who has not been required by a notice under *TMA 1970, s 8* (see 67.2 RETURNS for 1995/96 and 78.5 below for later years) to deliver a return for that year must, within six months after the end of that year, notify an officer of the Board that he is so chargeable. The maximum penalty for non-compliance is the amount of tax in which the person is assessed for that year which is not paid on or before 31 January following that year. A person is not required to give notice under these provisions if his total income for the year consists of income from the sources below and he has no chargeable gains. The said sources are those in respect of which

(*a*) all payments, etc. are dealt with under PAYE, or

(*b*) all income has been or will be taken into account either in determining the chargeable person's liability to tax or under PAYE, or

(*c*) the income is chargeable under Schedule F or is other income from which income tax has been, or is treated as having been, deducted, provided that the chargeable person is not liable for that year at the higher rate or (from 6 April 1999) the Schedule F upper rate, or

(*d*) all income for that year is income on which the chargeable person could not become liable to tax under a self-assessment under *TMA 1970, s 9* (see 78.6 below) in respect of that year (or, as regards 1995/96 only, under assessments made more than six months after the end of that year).

These provisions also apply with the appropriate modifications to 'relevant trustees' (as defined in 78.36 below) of settlements.

[*TMA 1970, s 7; FA 1994, s 196, Sch 19 para 1; FA 1995, s 103(1)(2), s 115(1), Sch 21 para 1; F(No 2)A 1997, Sch 4 para 1; FA 1999, s 22(11)*].

As regards items within (*b*) above, the Revenue will normally accept that employees in receipt of copy form P11D (or equivalent particulars) from their employer (see 78.37 below) can assume that any items on it not already taken into account for PAYE will be so taken into account, so there is no need to notify chargeability in respect of such items. Notice of chargeability is, however, necessary to the extent that the P11D is incorrect or incomplete or if the employee knows that the actual form has not been submitted to the Revenue. Employees are not relieved of any obligation to notify chargeability if they have not received a copy P11D or in respect of non-P11D items which ought to have been reported by the employer to the Revenue on other returns. For 1995/96, as there is no statutory obligation on the employer to provide employees with particulars of P11D items, the Revenue will take the absence of such information into account as a mitigating factor in determining penalties for failure to notify such items. (Revenue Pamphlet IR 131, SP 1/96, 1 February 1996).

Pension schemes. Tax returns for 1997/98 were sent to the trustees of some 20% of approved occupational self-administered pension schemes in August/September 1998, and these are required to be completed and sent back within the normal time limits (even if there is no tax to pay or repayment due). Schemes which did not receive a return, but which have income or capital gains on which tax is due, should have informed their tax office by 5 October 1998, and are then similarly subject to the normal time limits for making their return. It is proposed to issue tax returns to trustees of all such schemes for 1998/99. (Revenue Press Release 4 August 1998, and see Pension Schemes Office Update No 49, 24 August 1998). For the detailed administrative arrangements, see Revenue Tax Bulletin February 1999 pp 628, 629.

78.5 ANNUAL RETURNS OF INCOME AND CHARGEABLE GAINS

For the purposes of establishing a person's income, chargeable gains and net income tax liability for 1996/97 or a subsequent year of assessment, an officer of the Board may by notice require that person to deliver a return on or before 31 January following the year or, if later, within three months beginning with the date of the notice (and see also 78.26 below). The return must contain such information and be accompanied by such accounts, statements and documents as may reasonably be required. The return must include a declaration that, to the best of the knowledge of the person making it, it is complete and correct. The information, accounts and statements required by the notice may differ in relation to different periods, or different sources of income, or different descriptions of person. [*TMA 1970, s 8; FA 1990, s 90(1); FA 1994, s 178(1), s 199(2)(a); FA 1995, s 104(1)(3); FA 1996, s 121(1)–(3)*]. Similar provisions apply in relation to returns by trustees, by reference to any 'relevant trustee' (see 78.36 below). [*TMA 1970, s 8A; FA 1990, s 90(1); FA 1994, s 178(2), s 199(2)(a); FA 1995, s 103(3), s 104(1); FA 1996, s 121(1)–(3)*].

Before making their return, taxpayers may ask their Tax Office (on Form CG34) to check their valuation for capital gains tax purposes of an asset they have disposed of. (Revenue Press Release 4 February 1997).

A return containing a provisional figure will be accepted provided that the figure is reasonable, taking account of all available information, and is clearly identified as such and that an acceptable explanation is given as to why the final figure is not available, all reasonable steps having been taken to obtain it, and when it is expected to be available (at which time it should be notified without unreasonable delay). Pressures of work and complexity of tax affairs are not regarded as acceptable explanations. If the final figure is not provided by the expected date the Revenue will take appropriate action to obtain it, which may mean opening an enquiry (see 78.11 below). See Revenue Tax Return Guide and Revenue Tax Bulletins October 1998 pp 593–596 and December 1999 p 705. Note that a provisional figure is different to an estimate that will not be superseded by a more accurate figure. A return omitting a figure or stating 'to be agreed' will be treated as an incomplete return. (Revenue booklet SAT 2 (1995), para 2.53). See 78.26 below as regards incomplete returns generally.

As regards the use of pence in returns, see Revenue Tax Bulletin October 1997 pp 470, 471. Broadly, income (or aggregate income) figures may be rounded down and tax credits and deductions (or aggregate figures) rounded up.

Business accounts are not required with the return except in the case of partnerships with an annual turnover exceeding £15 million. Instead, the return will include a section in which standard accounts information (SAI) *must* be completed as well as space for additional information. See 78.15 below re the option of submitting accounts (in addition to completing SAI) to possibly reduce the risk of a discovery assessment. Accounts should otherwise be retained in case of enquiry (see 78.11 below). (Revenue Press Release 31 May 1996, Tax Bulletins June 1996 pp 313–315, June 1997 p 436 and booklet SAT 2(1995), para 2.22). For the transitional year 1996/97, a single set of SAI may, if the taxpayer wishes, be provided covering two or more sets of accounts drawn up for the transitional period, unless a loss was incurred in one or more of the account periods, in which case separate SAI is required for each set of accounts. (Revenue Tax Bulletin December 1996 p 371).

In the case of a person carrying on a profession, trade or business in partnership, a return under *TMA 1970, s 8* must include each amount, which according to any 'relevant statement' is his share of any income, loss, tax, credit or charge for the period covered by the statement. A '*relevant statement*' is a statement falling to be made, as respects the partnership, under *TMA 1970, s 12AB* (see 78.9 below) for a period which includes, or includes any part of, the year of assessment or its basis period. [*TMA 1970, s 8(1B)(1C); FA 1994, s 178(1); FA 1995, s 104(2)*].

For details of special instructions on practical measures to make the completion of the Employment Pages of returns more straightforward for foreign nationals working in the UK who have made *tax equalisation* arrangements with their employer, see Revenue Tax Bulletin October 1997 pp 467–469 and June 1998 p 551. (See also Help Sheet IR212 issued with the Employment Pages of the return, which will, from April 1999, fully reflect these instructions.) Interim tax payments (see 78.17 below) made by an employer on any employee's behalf, as part of tax equalisation arrangements where full in-year gross up is used, should not figure in the employment pages of the employee's self-assessment tax return (see Revenue Tax Bulletin June 1998 p 551).

The Revenue will, on request, issue a return before the end of the tax year

(*a*) in which the taxpayer dies (or administration of the estate is completed), to the personal representatives of the deceased, or

(*b*) in which a trust is wound up, to the trustees.

(Revenue Press Release 4 April 1996). See also 78.11 below as regards enquiries into such returns.

See 3.2(vii) ANTI-AVOIDANCE as regards the exclusion from self-assessment of possible charges under *ICTA 1988, s 703 et seq.*.

See 78.26 below as regards penalties for non-compliance.

See 67.2 RETURNS as regards signature of returns and use of substitute return forms.

78.6 SELF-ASSESSMENTS

For 1996/97 and subsequent years, every return under *TMA 1970, s 8* or *s 8A* (see 78.5 above) must include, subject to the exception below, an assessment (a self-assessment) of the amounts in which, based on the information in the return and taking into account any reliefs and allowances claimed therein, the person making the return is chargeable to income tax and capital gains tax for the year of assessment and of his net income tax liability for the year, taking into account tax deducted at source and tax credits on dividends. In the event of non-compliance, an officer of the Board *may* make the assessment on his behalf, based on the information in the return, and send the person a copy.

The tax to be self-assessed does not include any chargeable on the administrator of an approved retirement benefits or personal pension scheme under *ICTA 1988, s 658A* (see 60.1 PERSONAL PENSION SCHEMES, 66.4 RETIREMENT SCHEMES).

A person need not comply with this requirement if he makes and delivers his return on or before 30 September following the year of assessment or, if later, within two months beginning with the date of the notice to deliver the return. For returns submitted outside these time limits, the Revenue will still, if the taxpayer so requests, carry out the computations based on the return, but will not guarantee that the relevant filing date will be met. In the event of a person making no self-assessment under this option, an officer of the Board *must* make the assessment on his behalf, based on the information in the return, and send the person a copy. If, by reason only of Revenue delay, the assessment is made less than 30 days before the due date for payment of the tax, the date from which any interest or surcharge is triggered (see 78.21, 78.22 below) is 30 days after the issue of the assessment. (ICAEW Technical Release TAX 9/94, 7 June 1994).

Assessments made as above by an officer of the Board are treated as self-assessments by the person making the return.

A self-assessment must not show as repayable any notional tax treated as deducted from certain income deemed to have been received after deduction of tax, for example STOCK DIVIDENDS (85).

[*TMA 1970, s 9(1)–(3); FA 1994, ss 179, 199(2)(a); FA 1995, s 104(4), s 115(2); FA 1996, s 121(4), s 122(1); FA 1998, s 98(2)(3)*].

The Revenue need not give notice to deliver a return under 78.5 above, and thus a self-assessment will not be required, in cases where tax deducted under PAY AS YOU EARN (55) equates to the total tax liability for the year. The taxpayer may, however, give notice requiring a return to be issued so that he can make a self-assessment, such notice to be given within the five years after 31 October following the year of assessment. [*ICTA 1988, s 205; FA 1995, s 111(1)*].

SCHEDULE E (75) taxpayers who wish to have a liability of less than £1,000 coded out through PAYE (55) are advised to comply with the earlier date of 30 September whether or not they choose to complete their own self-assessment. (Revenue booklet SAT 2(1995), para 2.37; Revenue Tax Bulletin June 1996 p 315). Coding out of an underpayment will reduce the payments on account (see 78.17 below) due for the next tax year.

An error in the 1996/97 tax calculation guide could result in an overpayment of tax by a member of a pre-6 April 1994 partnership which pays annual charges. Another error could give the wrong amount of top-slicing relief for life assurance policy gains in unusual cases where gains consistently average over the basic rate threshold and there are allowances and deductions which cannot be set against other income. Although the Revenue are aware of these problems, agents should draw the Inspector's attention to cases where they may arise. (Revenue Tax Bulletin August 1997 pp 452, 453, December 1997 p 487).

78.7 Amendments of self-assessments other than where enquiries made

At any time within nine months beginning with the delivery of a person's return, an officer of the Board may by notice to that person amend his self-assessment to correct ('repair') obvious errors (whether of principle, arithmetical or otherwise).

At any time within twelve months beginning with the filing date (i.e. the date by which the return must be delivered, as in 78.5 above), that person may by notice to an officer of the Board amend his self-assessment to give effect to any amendments to his return which he has notified to such an officer. It should, however, be noted that amendment of a self-assessment by the taxpayer does not preclude penalty action by the Revenue where there is evidence that the taxpayer has acted fraudulently or negligently (see Revenue Tax Bulletin October 1998 p 597).

However, no such amendment of a self-assessment may be made (by the taxpayer or the Revenue) after an officer of the Board has given notice of intention to enquire into the return (see 78.11 below) and before his enquiries are completed.

[*TMA 1970, s 9(4)–(6); FA 1994, s 179*].

See 78.13 below for amendments to self-assessments where the Revenue make enquiries into the return.

78.8 **PARTNERSHIP RETURNS**

The following provisions apply for 1996/97 and subsequent years or, as regards corporate partners, for accounting periods ending on or after 1 July 1999.

Any partner may be required by notice to complete and deliver a return of the partnership profits together with accounts, statements, documents, etc. (see also 78.9 below). The return must include information as to taxable partnership income, reliefs and allowances claimed, tax at source and tax credits plus the names, residences and tax references of all persons (including companies) who were partners during the period specified in the notice and such other information as may reasonably be required by the notice, which may include information relating to disposals and acquisitions of partnership property. The general requirements are similar to those for personal returns under *TMA 1970, s 8* (see 78.5 above). The notice will specify the period (the relevant period) to be covered by the return and the date by which the return should be delivered (the filing date). For a partnership including at least one individual, the filing date will be no earlier than 31 January following the year of assessment concerned (normally that in which the relevant period ends). For a partnership including at least one company, the filing date will be no earlier than the first anniversary of the end of the relevant period. In both cases, the filing date will be deferred until, at the earliest, the last day of the three-month period beginning with the date of the notice, if this is a later date than that given above.

Where the partner responsible for dealing with the return ceases to be available, a successor may be nominated for this purpose by a majority of the persons (or their personal representatives) who were partners at any time in the period covered by the return. A nomination (or revocation of a nomination) does not have effect until notified to the Revenue. Failing a nomination, a successor will be determined according to rules on the return form or will be nominated by the Revenue.

[*TMA 1970, s 12AA; FA 1994, ss 184, 199; FA 1995, s 104(6), s 115(4); FA 1996, s 121(6)(7), s 123(1)–(4); FA 1998, Sch 19 para 3*].

See 78.27 below as regards penalties for non-compliance.

It will not be possible for individual partners to make, in their personal tax returns, supplementary claims for expenses incurred on the partnership's behalf or capital allowances on personal assets used in the partnership. If not included in the accounts, adjustments for such expenditure etc. must be included in the tax computation forming part of the partnership return. (Revenue booklet SAT 1(1995), para 5.17 and see Revenue Tax Bulletin August 1997 p 453).

See Revenue Tax Bulletin April 1996 pp 293–298 for an article explaining the relationship between the 1996/97 partnership assessment and the self-assessment returns issued for that year to partnerships and partners. See Revenue Tax Bulletin August 1997 pp 450–456 for an article answering a number of questions on self-assessment and on the transition to current year basis of assessment as it impacts on partnerships and partners. Points covered include the allocation of personal allowances etc., reliefs carried back from 1997/98 to 1996/97, an error in the Revenue tax calculation guide, returning details of partners' personal expenses, returning accounts information where a sole trader becomes a partnership and *vice versa*, a change of partners on 5 April 1997 with a continuation election, revision to 1996/97 assessment where business ceases before 5 April 1999, returning details of a continuing source of untaxed interest in the event of a pre-6 April 1997 change of partners, overlap relief on untaxed interest, returning details of taxed income, and capital allowances in partnerships involving both individuals and companies.

78.9 PARTNERSHIP STATEMENTS

Every partnership return under 78.8 above must include a statement (a partnership statement) showing, in respect of the period covered by the return and each period of account ending within that period,

(*a*) the partnership income or loss from each source, after taking into account any relief or allowance due to the partnership and for which a claim is made under any of the provisions in *TMA 1970, s 42(7)* (see 17.1 CLAIMS),

(*b*) the amount of consideration for each disposal of partnership property,

(*c*) the amounts of any tax deducted at source from or tax credits on partnership income, and

(*d*) the amount of each charge on partnership income,

and each partner's share of that income, loss, consideration, tax, credit or charge. Provisions similar to those in 78.7 above apply as regards amendments to partnership statements. Where a partnership statement is so amended, the partners' self-assessments will be amended by the Revenue accordingly, by notice to each partner concerned. [*TMA 1970, s 12AB; FA 1994, s 185; FA 1995, s 104(7)(8); FA 1996, s 123(5)(6); FA 1998, Sch 19 para 4*].

78.10 RECORDS

Any person who may be required to make and deliver a return under 78.5 above (personal and trustee's returns) or 78.8 (partnership returns) for a year of assessment or other period will be statutorily required to keep all necessary records and to preserve them until the end of the 'relevant day'. The '*relevant day*' is normally

(*a*) in the case of a person carrying on a trade (including, for these purposes, any letting of property), profession or business alone or in partnership or a company, the fifth anniversary of 31 January following the year of assessment or, for partnership or company returns, the sixth anniversary of the end of the period covered by the return; and

(*b*) in any other case, the first anniversary of 31 January following the year of assessment.

Where notice to deliver the return is given before the day in whichever is the applicable of (*a*) or (*b*) above, the '*relevant day*' is the *later* of that day and whichever of the following applies:

(i) where Revenue enquiries are made into the return (or into an amendment of the return), the day on which the enquiries are statutorily treated as completed (see 78.13 below);

(ii) where no such enquiries are made, the day on which the Revenue no longer have power to enquire (see 78.11 below).

Where notice to deliver the return is given *after* the day in whichever is the applicable of (*a*) and (*b*) above, (i) and (ii) above still apply to determine the relevant day but only in relation to such records as the taxpayer has in his possession at the time the notice is given.

In the case of a person within (*a*) above, the records in question include records concerning business receipts and expenditure and, in the case of a trade involving dealing in goods, all sales and purchases of goods. All supporting documents (including accounts, books, deeds, contracts, vouchers and receipts) relating to such items must also be preserved. Generally, copies of documents may be preserved instead of the originals and are admissible in evidence in proceedings before the Commissioners. (See Revenue Tax Bulletin February 1996 p 283 as regards the use of optical imaging to preserve records.) Exceptions to this are vouchers, certificates etc. which show tax credits or deductions at source of UK or foreign tax, e.g. dividend vouchers, interest vouchers (including those issued by banks and building societies) and evidence of tax deducted from payments to sub-contractors under the CONSTRUCTION INDUSTRY TAX SCHEME (21), which, with effect on or after 29 April 1996, must be preserved in their original form.

The maximum penalty for non-compliance in relation to any year of assessment or accounting period is £3,000. This penalty does not apply where the failure relates to records which might have been requisite only for the purposes of claims, elections or notices which are *not* included in the return (but see 17.3 CLAIMS for the requirement as regards records relating to such claims etc. and the penalty for non-compliance), or to vouchers, certificates etc. showing UK tax credits or deductions at source (e.g. dividend vouchers and interest certificates) where the inspector is satisfied that other documentary evidence supplied to him proves any facts he reasonably requires to be proved and which the voucher etc. would have proved.

[*TMA 1970, s 12B; FA 1994, s 196, Sch 19 para 3; FA 1995, s 105; FA 1996, s 124(2)–(5)(9)*].

The Revenue have published guidance notes as to the type of records to be kept. The above-mentioned penalty will not be charged for any failure to keep records in accordance with those notes which occurred before 6 April 1996. (Revenue Pamphlet SA/BK3).

Simon's Direct Tax Service. See **E1.809**.

78.11 **ENQUIRIES INTO RETURNS**

Power to enquire. An officer of the Board may enquire into a return (or amendment of a return) on the basis of which a person's self-assessment under *TMA 1970, s 9* (see 78.6 above) has been made (or amended by that person), or into any claim or election included in a return (by amendment or otherwise). The officer must give notice in writing of his intention to so enquire, such notice to be given,

(*a*) in the case of a return delivered or amendment made on or before the filing date (i.e. the date on or before which the return must be delivered — see 78.5 above), within twelve months beginning with that date; and

(*b*) otherwise on or before the quarter day (meaning 31 January, 30 April, etc.) next following the first anniversary of the day of delivery or amendment.

As regards (*a*), it was held by a Special Commissioner that service of a notice is treated as effected at the time at which the letter would be delivered in the ordinary course of post, i.e. on the second working day after posting for first class mail or on the fourth working day after posting for second class mail (*Wing Hung Lai v Bale (Sp C 203), [1999] SSCD 238*). See also *Holly v Inspector of Taxes (Sp C 225), [2000] SSCD 50*. The Revenue now accept that it is the time of receipt of the notice, rather than that of its issue, by reference to which the time limit applies. See Revenue Tax Bulletin Special Edition April 2000 p 8 for this and for the appropriate action which may be taken by taxpayers or their agents in respect of 1996/97 notices issued shortly before 30 January 1999 but received after that date. As regards (*b*), where a 1998/99 return is treated as filed on 1 February 2000, but with no late filing penalty (see 78.26 below), no enquiry will be opened in the three months to 30 April 2001. (Revenue Tax Bulletin Special Edition April 2000 p 8).

A return or amendment cannot be enquired into more than once. [*TMA 1970, s 9A; FA 1994, s 180; FA 1996, Sch 19 para 2*].

In the case of a return by the personal representatives of a deceased taxpayer (for the year of death or of completion of administration of the estate), the Revenue will give early written confirmation if they do not intend to enquire into the return (although, in exceptional circumstances, an enquiry at a later date would not thereby be precluded if the return was discovered to be incomplete or incorrect). Such early confirmation will also be given to trustees in relation to the return for the year in which the trust is wound up. (Revenue Press Release 4 April 1996). See also 78.5 above as regards early issue of returns in such cases.

Similar provisions apply as regards a partnership return on the basis of which a partnership statement (see 78.9 above) was made and to claims or elections included therein. The notice of intention to enquire may be given to a successor (see 78.8 above) of the person who made the return or amendment. The giving of such notice is deemed to include the giving of notice under *TMA 1970, s 9A* (see above) (or, where applicable, the equivalent corporation tax provision) to each partner affected. [*TMA 1970, s 12AC; FA 1994, s 186; FA 1996, s 123(7), Sch 19 para 2; FA 1998, Sch 19 para 5*].

Conduct of enquiry. A Code of Practice (COP 11, see 35.7 INLAND REVENUE: ADMINISTRATION, or, in certain simple cases, a short, single-page version) will be issued at the start of every such enquiry. This sets out the rules under which enquiries are made into income tax returns and explains how taxpayers can expect the Revenue to conduct enquiries. It describes what the Revenue will do when they receive a return and how they will select cases for enquiry, how they will open and carry out enquiries, and what happens if they find something wrong.

Where an enquiry remains open after the time by which notice to enquire into the return had to be given solely because of an unagreed capital gains tax valuation, the Revenue will not raise further enquiries into matters unrelated to that capital gains tax computation unless, had the enquiry already been completed, a discovery under *TMA 1970, s 29* (see 78.15 below) could have been made. (Revenue Pamphlet IR 131, SP 1/99, 28 January 1999).

The Revenue have also published an Enquiry Handbook as part of their series of internal guidance manuals (see 35.10 INLAND REVENUE: ADMINISTRATION) and, as an extended introduction to the material on operational aspects of the enquiry regime covered in the manual, a special edition of their Tax Bulletin (Special Edition 2, August 1997). The following points are selected from the Bulletin.

(i) Early submission of a tax return will not increase the likelihood of selection for enquiry.

(ii) The Revenue do not have to give reasons for opening an enquiry — and they *will not do so.*

(iii) Enquiries may be full enquiries or 'aspect enquiries'. An aspect enquiry will fall short of an in-depth examination of the return (though it may develop into one), but will instead concentrate on one or more aspects of it.

(iv) Greater emphasis than before will be placed on examination of underlying records. The Revenue will make an informal request for information before, if necessary, using their powers under *TMA 1970, s 19A* (see 78.12 below).

(v) Where penalties are being sought, the Revenue will aim to conclude the enquiry by means of a contract settlement (as was the case with pre-self-assessment investigations — see 6.11 BACK DUTY) rather than by the issue of a completion notice under *TMA 1970, s 28A* (see 78.13 below).

It is intended to reduce the time taken to complete full enquiries into business returns. A Supplement to Special Edition 2 (published with the October 1997 Tax Bulletin) contains an 'enquiry model' setting out what a 'faster working' enquiry might look like. Faster working is available (at the taxpayer's option) from April 1998. (Revenue Press Release 31 March 1998). See also Revenue pamphlet IR 162.

Where income is received from co-owned property where the letting activity does not amount to a partnership (see 68.5 SCHEDULE A), and the name and address of the managing co-owner is provided in co-owners' returns, the Revenue will confine initial enquiries relating to that income to the managing co-owner's return. (Revenue Tax Bulletin October 1996 p 350).

For the allowability of additional accountancy expenses incurred in connection with self-assessment enquiries, see 71.69 SCHEDULE D, CASES I AND II and Revenue Tax Bulletin October 1998 p 596.

See ICAEW Technical Release TAX 23/98, 30 September 1998, paras 3–40 and Appendix for Revenue comment on various procedural matters in relation to self-assessment enquiries.

78.12 **Power to call for documents.** At the same time as giving notice under 78.11 above to any person, or subsequently, an officer of the Board may by notice in writing require that person, within a specified period of at least 30 days (from the date of receipt of the notice — see *Self-assessed v Inspector of Taxes (Sp C 207), [1999] SSCD 253* and Revenue Tax Bulletin Special Edition April 2000 p 8), to produce to the officer such documents (as are in the person's possession or power) and such accounts or particulars as the officer may reasonably require to check the validity of the return or amendment. Copies of documents may be produced but the officer has power to call for originals, and may himself take copies of, or make extracts from, any document produced. A person is not obliged under these provisions to produce documents, etc. relating to the conduct of any pending appeal by him. There is provision for a person to appeal, within 30 days beginning with the date of the notice, against any requirement imposed by a notice as above. In restricted cases, an officer may, alternatively or in addition, require documents, accounts etc. to enable him to exercise the 'Crown Option' (see 78.13 below). [*TMA 1970, s 19A; FA 1994, s 187; FA 1996, Sch 19 para 3, Sch 22 para 2*]. For a case on the scope of such a notice, see *Mother v Inspector of Taxes (Sp C 211), [1999] SSCD 279*. See 78.29 below as regards penalties for non-compliance. See ICAEW Technical Release TAX 23/98, 30 September 1998, paras 3–15 for the Revenue approach to the obtaining and retention of records in relation to self-assessment enquiries.

78.13 **Amendment of self-assessment or partnership statement where enquiries made.** Where notice has been given by an officer of the Board under 78.11 above of intention to enquire into the taxpayer's return, amendment, claim or election, the officer's enquiries are treated as completed at such time as he, by notice, informs the taxpayer that he has completed his enquiries and states his conclusions as to the amount of tax which should be contained in the taxpayer's self-assessment and as to any claims or elections into which he has enquired. The taxpayer may before that time apply to the Commissioners for a direction that the officer shall give such notice within a period specified in the direction, such application to be heard and determined in the same way as an appeal against an amendment of a self-assessment and the Commissioners to give such a direction unless they are satisfied that the officer has reasonable grounds for not giving such notice.

The taxpayer is given 30 days beginning with the date of completion of the officer's enquiries to amend his self-assessment in accordance with the officer's conclusions. Where the enquiry was into a return rather than an amendment, and the return was made before the expiry of twelve months beginning with the due date for delivery (see 78.5 above), the taxpayer also has this 30-day period to amend his self-assessment in accordance with any amendments to the return which he has notified to the officer. The officer then has a further 30 days in which to amend the self-assessment himself.

If, in the officer's opinion, there is otherwise likely to be a loss of tax to the Crown, the officer may by notice amend the self-assessment before his enquiries are completed.

Similar provisions allow firstly the taxpayer and then the officer to amend or omit, within the same time limits, claims and elections included in the return which do not directly affect the self-assessment, for example a claim to carry forward trading losses, but which the officer thinks should be wholly or partly disallowed, and this is notwithstanding any statutory provision under which the claim or election would otherwise be unamendable or irrevocable.

Where the enquiry is into an amendment by the taxpayer to the return, rather than into the return itself, any amendment by the officer of the self-assessment, whether before or after completion of the enquiry, must be restricted to any deficiency or excess of tax as is attributable to the taxpayer's amendment.

[*TMA 1970, s 28A; FA 1994, s 188; FA 1996, Sch 19 paras 2, 4(1)(2), Sch 22 para 3*].

Similar provisions apply in the case of an enquiry into a partnership return etc., taking references above to the self-assessment as references to the partnership statement (see 78.9 above) based on the return. However, there is no provision for the officer to amend the partnership statement before completion of his enquiries. Where a partnership statement is amended under these provisions, the officer will, by notice, make any necessary consequential amendments to the self-assessments of the partners (including company partners).

[*TMA 1970, s 28B; FA 1994, s 189; FA 1996, Sch 19 paras 2, 5(1); FA 1998, Sch 19 para 10*].

See 78.31 below for right of appeal against an amendment by the Revenue to a self-assessment or partnership statement.

There are provisions concerning enquiries into a personal or partnership return which includes amounts which may be taxed using more than one method, with the Revenue having the right to choose which method is to be used (the 'Crown Option'). These are restricted to cases where amounts may be taxed either under Case I or II or under any of Cases III to V of Schedule D (applicable normally to dividends and interest forming part of a financial trader's profits). [*TMA 1970, s 28A(7A)–(7C), s 28B(6A)(6B); FA 1994, ss 188, 189; FA 1996, Sch 19 para 4(3), para 5(2)*].

78.14 DETERMINATION OF TAX WHERE NO RETURN DELIVERED

Where a notice has been given under *TMA 1970, ss 8, 8A* (notice requiring an individual or trustee to deliver a return — see 78.5 above) and the return is not delivered by the due date (the filing date), an officer of the Board may make a determination of the amounts of taxable income, capital gains and income tax payable which, to the best of his information and belief, he estimates for the year of assessment. The officer must serve notice of the determination on the person concerned. Tax is payable as if the determination were a self-assessment, with no right of appeal. No determination may be made after the expiry of five years beginning with the filing date.

A determination is automatically superseded by any self-assessment made (whether by the taxpayer or the Revenue), based on information contained in a return. Such self-assessment must be made within the five years beginning with the filing date or, if later, within twelve months beginning with the date of the determination. Any tax payable or repayable as a result of the supersession is deemed to have fallen due for payment or repayment on the normal due date, usually 31 January following the year of assessment (see 78.19 below).

Any recovery proceedings commenced before the making of such a self-assessment may be continued in respect of so much of the tax charged by the self-assessment as is due and payable and has not been paid.

[*TMA 1970, ss 28C, 59B(5A); FA 1994, s 190; FA 1996, s 125*].

Simon's Direct Tax Service. See **E1.814**.

78.15 DISCOVERY ASSESSMENTS

If, as regards 1996/97 and subsequent years, an officer of the Board or the Board 'discover', as regards any person (the taxpayer) and a chargeable period (i.e. for income tax and capital gains tax purposes, a year of assessment), that

(*a*) any income or chargeable gains which ought to have been assessed to tax (see 78.3 above) have not been assessed, or

(*b*) an assessment is or has become insufficient, or

(*c*) any relief given is or has become excessive,

then with the exceptions below, an assessment (a discovery assessment) may be made to make good to the Crown the apparent loss of tax.

No discovery assessment may be made in respect of a chargeable period, where a return under *TMA 1970, s 8* or *s 8A* (see 78.5 above) has been delivered,

(1) if it would be attributable to an error or mistake in the return as to the basis on which the liability ought to have been computed and the return was, in fact, made on the basis, or in accordance with the practice, generally prevailing at the time when it was made; or

(2) unless either

 (*a*) the loss of tax is attributable to fraudulent or negligent conduct by the taxpayer or a person acting on his behalf (for an example of which see *Hancock v CIR (Sp C 213), [1999] SSCD 287*), or

 (*b*) at the time when an officer of the Board either ceased to be entitled to enquire (see 78.11 above) into the return or informed the taxpayer of the completion of his enquiries, he could not have been reasonably expected, on the basis of the information so far made available to him (see below), to be aware of the loss of tax.

For the purposes of (2)(*b*) above, information is regarded as having been made available to the officer if it has been included in

(i) the return (or accompanying accounts, statements or documents) for the chargeable period concerned or for either of the two immediately preceding it, or

(ii) a partnership return (see 78.8 above), where applicable, in respect of the chargeable period concerned or either of the two immediately preceding it, or

(iii) any claim for the chargeable period concerned, or

(iv) documents, etc. produced for the purposes of any enquiries into such a return or claim,

or is information the existence and relevance of which could reasonably be expected to be inferred from the above-mentioned information or are notified in writing to the Revenue. See also below.

An objection to a discovery assessment on the grounds that neither (*a*) nor (*b*) in (2) above applies can be made only on an appeal against the assessment. (See 78.31 below for right of appeal.)

[*TMA 1970, s 29; FA 1994, s 191(1), s 199(2)(a)*].

See 78.20 below as regards due date of payment. The above provisions supersede the earlier discovery assessment provisions of *TMA 1970, s 29(3)(4)* (see 5.3 ASSESSMENTS). As regards partnership businesses commenced (or deemed to commence) before 6 April 1994, the existing provisions continue to apply for all years of assessment before 1997/98. [*FA 1994, s 191(2)*].

A change of Revenue opinion on information previously made available to them is not grounds for a discovery assessment.

Particularly in large or complex cases, the standard accounts information details and other information included in the tax return (see 78.5 above) may not provide a means of disclosure adequate to avoid falling within (2)(*b*) above. The submission of further information, including perhaps accounts, may be considered appropriate but will not necessarily provide protection against a discovery assessment beyond that arising from submission of the return alone. The reasonable expectation test (see (2)(*b*) above) must be satisfied. Where voluminous information beyond the accounts and computations is sent with the return, the Revenue recommend that there should be a brief indication of the relevance of the material. The Revenue will accept that for *TMA 1970, s 29* purposes documents submitted within a month of the return 'accompany' it (see (i) above) provided the return indicates that such documents have been or will be submitted. They will consider sympathetically a request that this condition be treated as satisfied where the time lag is longer than a month. (Revenue Press Release 31 May 1996 and Tax Bulletin June 1996 pp 313–315).

See generally Revenue Assessment Procedures Manual, AP 2144–2160.

Simon's Direct Tax Service. See **E1.815.**

78.16 **Amendment of partnership statement where loss of tax discovered.** Provisions broadly similar to those described in 78.15 above apply, for 1996/97 and subsequent years, as regards an understatement of profits or excessive claim for relief or allowance in a partnership statement (see 78.9 above), although the Revenue's remedy in this case is to amend the partnership statement, with consequent amendment of partners' self- assessments. [*TMA 1970, s 30B; FA 1994, ss 196, 199(2)(a), Sch 19 para 6; FA 1995, s 115(5); FA 1998, Sch 19 para 14*]. See 78.31 below for right of appeal.

78.17 INTERIM PAYMENTS OF TAX ON ACCOUNT

For 1997/98 and subsequent years (see below as regards 1996/97), where, as regards the year immediately preceding the year of assessment in question,

(*a*) a person is assessed to income tax under *TMA 1970, s 9* (self-assessment — see 78.6 above), (*b*) the assessed amount exceeds any income tax deducted at source (including tax deducted under PAYE, taking in any deduction in respect of that year but to be made in a subsequent year but subtracting any amount paid in that year but in respect of a previous year, tax treated as deducted from, or as paid on, any income, and tax credits on dividends), and

(*c*) the said excess (the 'relevant amount') and the proportion which the relevant amount bears to the assessed amount are not less than, respectively, £500 and 20%,

the person must make two interim payments on account of his income tax liability for the year of assessment in question, each payment being equal to 50% of the relevant amount (see (*c*) above) and the payments being due on or before, respectively, 31 January in the year of assessment and the following 31 July. If the preceding year's self-assessment is made late or is amended, the relevant amount is determined as if the liability as finally agreed had been shown in a timeous self-assessment, with further payments on account then being required where appropriate. If a discovery assessment (see 78.15 above) is made for the preceding year, each payment on account due is deemed always to have been 50% of the relevant amount plus 50% of the tax charged by the discovery assessment as finally determined.

At any time before 31 January following the year of assessment, the taxpayer may make a claim stating his belief that he will have no liability for the year or that his liability will be fully covered by tax deducted at source and his grounds for that belief, in which case each of the interim payments is not, and is deemed never to have been, required to be made. Within the same time limit, the taxpayer may make a claim stating his belief that his liability for the year after allowing for tax deducted at source will be a stated amount which is less than the relevant amount, and stating his grounds for that belief, in which case each of the interim payments required will be, and deemed always to have been, equal to 50% of the stated amount. Either claim should be made on form SA 303. The maximum penalty for an incorrect statement made fraudulently or negligently in connection with either claim is the amount or additional amount he would have paid on account if he had made a correct statement. Interim payments of tax are subject to the same recovery provisions as any other payments of tax.

An officer of the Board may direct, at any time before 31 January following a year of assessment, that a person is not required to make payments on account for that year, such adjustments being made as necessary to give effect to the direction.

[*TMA 1970, s 59A; FA 1994, s 192; FA 1995, s 108; FA 1996, s 126(1), Sch 18 paras 2, 17(1); SI 1996 No 1654; SI 1997 No 2491*].

For an article on payments on account (including the special arrangements for 1996/97 — see below), see Revenue Tax Bulletin October 1996 pp 353–356. For an article on Revenue practice on repayment, and allocations and reallocations of overpayments, see Revenue Tax Bulletin June 1999 pp 673, 674.

Interim payments made by an employer on an employee's behalf, as part of *tax equalisation* arrangements where full in-year gross up is used, should not figure in the employment pages of the employee's self-assessment tax return (see Revenue Tax Bulletin June 1998 p 551).

Special provisions apply to determine the amount of interim payments in respect of 1996/97. Broadly, such payments are based on the excess of income tax assessed (as finally determined) for 1995/96, disregarding any excess of higher rate tax over basic rate tax on taxed investment income, over tax deducted at source for that year. That excess is then reduced by any amount by which any Schedule E liability exceeds tax deducted under PAYE or otherwise collected during 1995/96, to give the '*relevant amount*'. The first interim payment due, on 31 January 1997, is equal to such part of the relevant amount as consists of tax under Schedule A or any of Cases III to VI of Schedule D plus 50% of the balance of the relevant amount. The amount due on 31 July 1997 is equal to the remaining 50% of the balance of the relevant amount. Claims may be made as above to eliminate interim payments or make reduced payments. [*FA 1995, s 116(1), Sch 21 para 2*]. The effect is that payment on account of tax under Schedule A and Schedule D, Cases III to VI is made in one instalment on 31 January 1997 and payment on account of tax under Schedule D, Case I or II (and Class 4 national insurance — see below) is made in two equal instalments on 31 January and 31 July 1997, no payment on account being required in respect of Schedule E tax or higher rate tax on taxed income (see the example at 78.18 below). Tax on furnished holiday lettings (see 68.9 SCHEDULE A) is payable in two instalments (i.e. on 31 January and 31 July 1997) if it was payable in two instalments in 1995/96. (Revenue Tax Bulletin October 1996 p 356).

Of the two *de minimis* limits at (*c*) above, only the monetary limit (i.e. £500) applies for 1996/97.

A personal pension payment (or retirement annuity contribution) made in 1996/97 but related back to 1995/96 (see 60.5 PERSONAL PENSION SCHEMES, 65.4 RETIREMENT ANNUITIES) is taken into account in determining the interim payment required for 1996/97. (Revenue Press Release 21 March 1996; Revenue Tax Bulletin April 1996 p 299).

Payments due on account for 1998/99 should have been notified by the Revenue in statements of account sent out in late December 1998/January 1999 (and see below re notification to agents). See 78.22 below for remission of interest on late payment in certain circumstances where the statement of account was issued late.

These provisions (and those described at 78.19–78.21 below) apply equally to Class 4 national insurance contributions. [*Social Security Contributions and Benefits Act 1992, s 16(1)(b); FA 1994, Sch 19 para 45*].

See Revenue Tax Bulletin February 1997 pp 387–392 for 1996/97 payments on account generally.

For **1997/98 only**, an error in the 1996/97 return tax calculation working sheet may produce the wrong payment on account figure in a small number of cases. This applies to taxpayers who have most of their tax deducted at source and who also are treated as having paid certain notional tax and/or made payments under charitable covenants, annuities or Gift Aid. See Revenue Tax Bulletin October 1997 p 470.

As part of an experiment, self-assessment taxpayers sent a statement of account (see below) in December 1999 are given the opportunity to pay their tax by debit card over the telephone. (Revenue Tax Bulletin December 1999 p 704).

Agents for whom the Revenue holds the taxpayer's authority on form 64–8, for information to be copied, are automatically provided in January and April/early May each year with details (on form SA327) of their clients' taxpayer statements of account, i.e. advisory statements (on form SA300) issued to taxpayers notifying them of payments due and outstanding. A customised payslip is attached to the agent statement. A taxpayer may also elect, again using form 64-8, for his statement of account to be sent to his agent instead of to him. Agents registered for electronic lodgement (see 67.3 RETURNS), and authorised to receive copy information, automatically receive electronic copies of statements of account. (Revenue Press Release 12 December 1997 and Revenue Tax Bulletin December 1998 pp 618–620 and December 1999 pp 703–705).

Simon's Direct Tax Service. See **E1.821**.

78.18 *Example*

Calculation of interim payments for 2000/01

For 1999/2000, Kylie's self-assessment shows the following.

	£
Gross income tax liability	8,664
Gross capital gains tax liability	2,122
Gross Class 4 NIC liability	198
PAYE tax deducted (all relating to 1999/2000)	3,740
Tax credits on dividends received	200
Tax deducted from interest received	300

The payments on account for 2000/01 (unless Kylie claims to pay different amounts) are based on relevant amounts as follows.

	£
Income tax (£8,664 – £3,740 – £200 – £300 =)	4,424
Class 4 NIC	198

Half of the relevant amounts is due on each of 31 January 2000 and 31 July 2000. No payment on account is made in respect of capital gains tax liability.

78.19 **FINAL PAYMENT (REPAYMENT) OF TAX**

For 1996/97 and subsequent years, a final payment is due for a year of assessment if a person's combined income tax and capital gains tax liabilities contained in his self-assessment (see 78.6 above) exceed the aggregate of any payments on account (whether under *TMA 1970, s 59A*, see 78.17 above, or otherwise) and any income tax deducted at source. If the second total exceeds the first, a repayment will be made. Tax deducted at source has the same meaning as in 78.17(*b*) above (but see below as regards partnership tax for 1996/97).

The due date for payment (or repayment) is 31 January following the year of assessment. The one exception is where the person gave notice of chargeability under *TMA 1970, s 7* (see 78.4 above) within six months after the end of the year of assessment, but was not given notice under *TMA 1970, s 8* or *s 8A* (see 78.5 above) until after 31 October following the year of assessment; in such case, the due date is the last day of the three months beginning with the date of the said notice.

[*TMA 1970, s 59B(1)–(4)(7)(8); FA 1994, ss 193, 199(2)(a); FA 1996, s 122(2), s 126(2)*].

As regards partnership businesses commenced (or deemed to commence) before 6 April 1994, each partner's share of income tax assessed on the partnership for 1996/97 is treated for the purposes of determining that partner's final payment or repayment for that year as if it were tax deducted at source. [*FA 1995, s 116(1), Sch 21 para 3*]. See Revenue Tax Bulletin April 1996 pp 296–298.

See 78.18 above as regards notifications to agents.

78.20 **Due date: further provisions.** Where a person's self-assessment is amended under the relevant provisions in 78.7, 78.13 or 78.16 above, the due date for the final payment (or repayment) is normally as in 78.19 above but is deferred, as regards any tax payable (or repayable) by virtue of the amendment and subject to the appeal and postponement provisions in 78.31 below, until, if later, 30 days after the date of notice of the amendment (but note that this does not defer the date from which interest accrues on unpaid tax — see 78.22 below).

Where an officer of the Board enquires into the return (see 78.11 above) and a repayment is otherwise due, the repayment is not required to be made until the enquiry is completed (see 78.13 above) although the officer may make a provisional repayment at his discretion. This does not affect the due date of repayment for interest purposes (see 78.23 below).

Unless otherwise provided, the due date for payment of tax charged by any assessment other than a self-assessment, e.g. a discovery assessment under *TMA 1970, s 29* (see 78.15 above), is 30 days after the date of the assessment (but see 78.22 below as regards interest on unpaid tax).

[*TMA 1970, s 59B(4A)(5)(6); FA 1994, ss 193, 199(2)(a); FA 1995, s 115(6); FA 1996, s 127*].

78.21 **SURCHARGE ON UNPAID TAX**

For 1996/97 and subsequent years, where income tax or capital gains tax has become payable in accordance with *TMA 1970, s 59B* (see 78.19 and 78.20 above) or *s 55* (payment and postponement of tax pending appeal — see 78.31 below) and any of the tax remains unpaid more than 28 days after the due date, the taxpayer will be liable to a surcharge of 5% of the unpaid tax. A further 5% surcharge will be levied on any tax still unpaid more than six months after the due date. Interest (at the INTEREST AND SURCHARGES ON UNPAID TAX (42) rate) will accrue on an unpaid surcharge with effect from the expiry of 30 days beginning with the date of the notice imposing the surcharge.

An appeal may be made, within that same 30-day period, against the imposition of a surcharge as if it were an assessment to tax. The Commissioners may, on appeal, set aside the surcharge if it appears to them that, throughout the period from the due date until payment, the taxpayer had a reasonable excuse for not paying the tax. Inability to pay the tax is not a reasonable excuse. For the Revenue's general approach to what constitutes a 'reasonable excuse' for late payment, see Revenue Tax Bulletin April 1998 pp 527–529. Common examples which the Revenue might regard as reasonable are where a cheque is lost in the post or by the Revenue (although evidence may be required to show that every effort was made to pay by the due date); where a cheque is dishonoured solely through bank error (and payment made immediately after the taxpayer learned of the bank's action); serious illness of the taxpayer or a close relative or domestic partner which began shortly before the due date; or the death of a close relative or domestic partner at or around the due date. Examples of excuses *not* considered reasonable by the Revenue are the fact that the return had not been submitted; pressure of work; failure by a tax agent; not knowing how much to pay; or the absence of a reminder that the tax is due. It is, however, stressed that these are the Revenue's views, and that it is for the Commissioners to adjudicate where the taxpayer takes a different view. Although, as stated above, the 'reasonable excuse' must strictly continue throughout the period of default in payment, in practice the Revenue normally allow a further 14 days for payment to be made after the excuse has ceased (for which see also Revenue booklet SA/BK7).

See also *Steeden v Carver (Sp C 212), [1999] SSCD 283*, in which reliance on the Revenue's advice as to the practical extension of a deadline, unequivocally given, was held to be 'as reasonable an excuse as could be found'.

There are provisions to prevent a double charge where tax has been taken into account in determining certain tax-geared penalties; such tax will not be subject to a surcharge. The Board have discretion to mitigate, or to stay or compound proceedings for recovery of, a surcharge and may also, after judgment, entirely remit the surcharge.

These surcharge provisions also apply to an assessment for 1995/96 or an earlier year which is made on or after 6 April 1998.

[*TMA 1970, s 59C; FA 1994, ss 194, 199(2)(a); FA 1995, s 109; SI 1998 Nos 310, 311*].

No surcharge will be imposed where a taxpayer has entered into a 'Time to Pay' arrangement (see 56.3 PAYMENT OF TAX), provided that the payment proposals are received by the Revenue before the relevant surcharge date, they lead to an acceptable agreement to settle the full liability for the self-assessment year, and the terms of the arrangement are adhered to, such that it is not cancelled. (Revenue Self-Assessment Manual — Payments section — para 7.2.48).

See generally Revenue booklet SA/BK7.

78.22 **INTEREST ON UNPAID TAX**

For 1996/97 and subsequent years (1997/98 and subsequent years as regards partnerships whose business commenced before 6 April 1994), interest is chargeable as follows on interim payments (see 78.17 above) and final payments (see 78.19 and 78.20 above) of income tax and capital gains tax which are made late, on tax chargeable on any assessment other than a self-assessment and on tax becoming payable under *TMA 1970, s 55* (payment and postponement of tax pending appeal — see 78.31 below). Interest accrues from the 'relevant date' (even if a non-business day) to the date of payment. For the two interim payments under 78.17 above, the '*relevant dates*' are the due dates, i.e. 31 January in the year of assessment and the following 31 July respectively. In any other case, the '*relevant date*' is 31 January following the year of assessment (with the one exception that where the due date of a final payment is deferred until three months after notice is given to deliver a return – see 78.19 above – the relevant date is identically deferred).

In practice, however, where no statement of account (see 78.17 above) was issued by the Revenue before the end of December 1996, even though the taxpayer had provided all relevant information at the appropriate time, interest on interim tax paid after its due date of 31 January 1997 will run only from 30 days after the date of notification to the taxpayer of the amount due. Confirmation should be sought from the tax office if there is any doubt as to whether the reason for a statement of account not being received in time falls within this practice. (Revenue Press Release 27 January 1997). For subsequent years, where a self-assessment return is submitted by 30 September for calculation by the Revenue of the tax due (see 78.6 above), the relevant date, where it would otherwise have been the following 31 January, is deferred until 30 days after notification of the liability to the taxpayer if this occurs later than 31 December following the tax year (Revenue Self-Assessment Manual — Interest, penalties and surcharge section — para 1.2.1).

There are provisions to remit interest charged on interim payments to the extent that an income tax repayment is found to be due for the year. There are also provisions covering the situation where a taxpayer makes a claim to dispense with or reduce his interim payments (see 78.17 above) and the total income tax liability for the year is found to be such that interim payments should have been made or should have been greater. Interest is chargeable as if each interim payment due had been equal to half the current year's liability or half the previous year's liability, whichever is less.

Interest is also chargeable under these provisions in respect of an income tax or capital gains tax assessment **for 1995/96 or an earlier year which is made on or after 6 April 1998**, the '*relevant date*' being 31 January following the year of assessment.

[*TMA 1970, s 86; FA 1995, s 110; FA 1996, s 131, Sch 18 paras 3, 17(1)(2)*].

Interest is also chargeable on late payment of surcharges (see 78.21 above) and penalties (see 78.25 below).

The rate of interest charged on unpaid tax is in line with the average rate for borrowing. The rate paid on overpaid tax (see 78.23 below) is in line with the average return on profits.

(Revenue booklet SAT 2(1995), para 3.114). See 42.1 INTEREST AND SURCHARGES ON UNPAID TAX for details of rates.

Where the above provisions of *TMA 1970, s 86* have effect, *TMA 1970, s 88* (interest on tax recovered to make good loss of tax due to taxpayer's fault — see 6.6 BACK DUTY) no longer has effect. [*FA 1996, Sch 18 paras 4, 17(3)(4)*].

Transitional cessation adjustments. Where a business which commenced before 6 April 1994 ceases trading in 1997/98 or 1998/99, the inspector may direct that the 1995/96 and 1996/97 assessments (in the case of a cessation in 1998/99, only the 1996/97 assessment) be revised to the actual profits arising in the year(s) of assessment (see 71.24 SCHEDULE D, CASES I AND II). By concession, where an interest charge under *TMA 1970, s 86* would otherwise arise as a result of the adjustments required following such a direction, including increased payments on account required for 1996/97 and/or 1997/98, such interest will not normally be sought. The concession does not apply to interest arising in relation to any of those years for any other reason. (Revenue Press Release 9 February 1998).

Simon's Direct Tax Service. See **E1.825**.

78.23 **INTEREST ON OVERPAID TAX**

The provisions of *ICTA 1988, s 824* are amended for 1996/97 and subsequent years (1997/98 as regards partnership businesses commenced (or deemed to commence) before 6 April 1994). A repayment of income tax (including an amount paid on account as in 78.17 above), or of a surcharge under *TMA 1970, s 59C* (see 78.21 above) or of a penalty incurred by an individual under any provision of *TMA 1970* will be increased by an amount (a repayment supplement) equal to interest on the amount repaid for the period (if any) between the 'relevant time' and the date of repayment. The '*relevant time*' is,

(*a*) as regards interim payments (see 78.17 above) and payments of income tax not deducted at source, the date of the payment,

(*b*) as regards income tax deducted at source, 31 January next following the year of assessment for which the tax is deducted, and

(*c*) as regards a penalty or surcharge, the date on which the penalty or surcharge was paid.

Income tax is deducted at source for a year of assessment for these purposes if it is so deducted (or treated as deducted) from any income, or treated as paid on any income, in respect of that year, or if it is a tax credit in respect of that year (but excluding tax deducted under PAYE (55) in respect of previous years). Repayments in respect of income tax for a year of assessment are attributed first to the final payment (see 78.19 above) in respect of income tax for that year, secondly in two equal parts to the interim payments for that year, and finally to income tax deducted at source for that year. Where a payment was made in instalments, any repayment is attributed to later instalments before earlier ones.

Other amendments consequential to the introduction of self-assessment are made to *section 824*. See 41.1 INTEREST ON OVERPAID TAX.

[*ICTA 1988, s 824; FA 1994, ss 196, 199(2)(a), Sch 19 para 41; FA 1997, s 92*].

The rate of interest paid on overpaid tax is in line with the average return on profits. The rate charged on unpaid tax (see 78.22 above) is in line with the average rate for borrowing. (Revenue booklet SAT 2(1995), para 3.114). See 41.1 INTEREST ON OVERPAID TAX for details of rates.

78.24 DATE OF PAYMENT BY CHEQUE

For the purposes of *TMA 1970* and *ICTA 1988, s 824* (see 78.23 above), *s 825* and *s 826*, where any payment to an officer of the Board or the Board is received by cheque after 5 April 1996 and the cheque is paid on its first presentation to the bank on which it is drawn, the payment is treated as made on the date of receipt of the cheque by the officer or the Board. [*TMA 1970, s 70A; FA 1994, s 196, Sch 19 para 22*]. See also 56.1 PAYMENT OF TAX.

78.25 PENALTIES

The penalty provisions described at 78.26 to 78.30 below apply for 1996/97 and subsequent years. See also 78.4 above for the penalty for failing to give notice of chargeability to tax and see 78.10 above and 17.3 CLAIMS for penalties for failing to keep and preserve records. Penalties for special returns (see 58.4 PENALTIES) continue to apply as before, as do the statutory provisions on mitigation and limitation of penalties described at 58.7 PENALTIES.

For 1996/97 and subsequent years, a penalty under 78.4 above (notice of chargeability), 78.10 above (records), 78.17 above (payments on account), 17.3 CLAIMS (records relating to claims) or any penalty under *TMA 1970, ss 93–107* carries interest, calculated from the due date to the date of payment, at the INTEREST AND SURCHARGES ON UNPAID TAX (42) rate. [*TMA 1970, s 103A; FA 1994, Sch 19 para 33; FA 1995, s 115(8); SI 1998 Nos 310, 311*].

Consequential amendments are made to *TMA 1970, s 100B* (appeals against penalty determinations — see 58.6 PENALTIES). [*TMA 1970, s 100B; FA 1994, ss 196, 199(2)(a), Sch 19 para 31; FA 1995, s 115(7)*]. See 53.19 PARTNERSHIPS as regards penalties under *TMA 1970, s 98B* in relation to European Economic Interest Groupings.

78.26 **Failure to make timeous return for income tax and capital gains tax.** A person (the taxpayer) who fails to deliver a return when required to do so by notice under *TMA 1970, s 8* or *s 8A* (see 78.5 above) is liable to a penalty of £100. For continuing failure, a further penalty of up to £60 per day may be imposed by the Commissioners (but not at any time after the failure has been remedied) on application by an officer of the Board, such daily penalty to start from the day after the taxpayer is notified of the Commissioners' direction (but not for any day for which such a daily penalty has already been imposed). Although the Revenue is responsible for setting the amount of any daily penalty, it is understood that the Commissioners should not in practice impose a daily penalty of an unspecified amount. If the failure continues for more than six months beginning with the filing date (i.e. the due date for delivery of the return — see 78.5 above), and no application for a daily penalty was made within those six months, the taxpayer is liable to a further £100 penalty. If failure continues after the anniversary of the filing date, and there would have been a liability under *TMA 1970, s 59B* (see 78.19 above), based on a proper return promptly delivered, the taxpayer is liable to a further penalty of an amount not exceeding that liability. See 78.36 below as regards trustees.

If the taxpayer proves that his liability under *TMA 1970, s 59B*, based on a proper return promptly delivered, would not have exceeded a particular amount, his liability to penalties other than the daily and tax-geared penalties is reduced to that amount. Thus a payment on account, made under *TMA 1970, s 59A* or otherwise, which reduces the liability outstanding at 31 January to less than £100 will similarly reduce any automatic penalty otherwise chargeable (see Revenue Enquiry Handbook, EH 640).

On an appeal against either of the £100 penalties (reduced where appropriate), the Commissioners may either confirm the penalty or, if it appears to them that throughout the period of failure the taxpayer had a reasonable excuse for not delivering the return, set it aside.

[*TMA 1970, s 93; FA 1994, ss 196, 199(2)(a), Sch 19 para 25*].

For the Revenue's approach to 'reasonable excuse' for failure to deliver a return, see Revenue Tax Bulletin April 1998 pp 527-529. Common examples which the Revenue might regard as reasonable are where they are satisfied that the taxpayer did not receive the return; where the return was posted in good time but held up by an unforeseen disruption to the postal service; where the taxpayer's records were lost through fire, flood or theft and could not be replaced in time to meet the deadline; where serious illness immediately before the filing date made timeous submission impossible; or the death of a close relative or domestic partner shortly before the deadline (provided that all necessary steps to meet the deadline had been taken). Examples of excuses *not* considered reasonable by the Revenue are claims that the return is too difficult to complete; pressure of work on the taxpayer or agent; failure by an agent; unavailability of information needed to complete the return; or the absence of a reminder that the return was overdue. It is, however, stressed that these are the Revenue's views, and that it is for the Commissioners to adjudicate where the taxpayer takes a different view. Although, as stated above, the 'reasonable excuse' must strictly continue throughout the period of default, in practice the Revenue normally allow a further 14 days for submission of the return after the excuse has ceased.

See also *Steeden v Carver (Sp C 212), [1999] SSCD 283*, in which reliance on the Revenue's advice as to the practical extension of a deadline, unequivocally given, was held to be 'as reasonable an excuse as could be found'. Following the decision in this case, the Revenue announced that 1998/99 returns delivered before 7.30am on 2 February 2000 would not incur a late delivery penalty. (Revenue Tax Bulletin December 1999 pp 705, 706). As regards 1998/99 returns due before the end of 31 January 2001, there will similarly be no late delivery penalty where returns are delivered before 7.30am on 2 February 2001. (Revenue Tax Bulletin Special Edition April 2000 p 8).

The Revenue's general intention is to use the sanction of the daily penalty where the tax at risk is substantial and they believe the fixed penalties to be an insufficient deterrent. (Revenue booklet SAT 2(1995), para 2.74).

See generally Revenue booklet SA/BK6.

Incomplete returns. Where a 1997/98 return delivered to the Revenue **on or before 31 January 1999** is found to be incomplete and is returned to the taxpayer (or agent) on or after 18 January 1999, the taxpayer will be given 14 days in which to complete the return and deliver it back to the Revenue. A completed return delivered within this 14 day period will be treated as having met the filing deadline. This will apply only where the return is incomplete as a result of a genuine oversight, and not in a deliberate attempt to take advantage of the concession (e.g. where it is deliberately sent in without a relevant set of pages or unsigned, to buy a little more time to complete them or to obtain the signature). (Revenue Tax Bulletin October 1998 pp 593, 594). A similar concession applied for 1996/97 returns (see Revenue Press Release 3 February 1998). See 78.5 above for the circumstances in which a return is likely to be accepted even though it contains a provisional figure.

78.27 **Failure to make partnership return.** The same fixed penalties (including the daily penalty) as in *TMA 1970, s 93* (see 78.26 above) apply in the case of failure to submit a partnership return as required by a notice under *TMA 1970, s 12AA* (see 78.8 above). However, there is no tax-geared penalty and no provision for reducing the £100 penalties. Each person who was a partner at any time during the period in respect of which the return was required is separately liable to each penalty. The penalties apply by reference to failure by the representative partner, i.e. the partner required by the notice under *TMA 1970, s 12AA* to deliver the return, or his successor (see 78.8 above). Where penalties are imposed on two or more partners, an appeal cannot be made otherwise than by way of composite appeal by the representative partner (or successor). The same reasonable excuse provisions apply as under *TMA 1970, s 93* but by reference to the representative partner (or successor). [*TMA 1970, s 93A; FA 1994, ss 196, 199(2)(a), Sch 19 para 26; FA 1996, s 123(8)–(11)*].

78.28 **Fraud or negligence.** The provisions of *TMA 1970, s 95* (tax-geared penalty for fraudulently or negligently delivering an incorrect return, accounts, etc. — see 58.3 PENALTIES) continue to apply, with consequential amendments, under self-assessment. [*TMA 1970, s 95; FA 1994, ss 196, 199(2)(a), Sch 19 para 27*].

Similar provisions will apply as regards partnerships. They apply where a partner (the representative partner) delivers an incorrect partnership return (see 78.8 above), or, in connection with such a return, makes an incorrect statement or declaration or submits incorrect accounts, and either he does so fraudulently or negligently or his doing so is attributable to fraudulent or negligent conduct on the part of a 'relevant partner' (i.e. any person who was a partner at any time in the period covered by the return). Each relevant partner is liable to a penalty not exceeding the income tax (or corporation tax) underpaid by him as a result of the incorrectness. Where penalties are imposed on two or more partners, an appeal cannot be made otherwise than by way of composite appeal by the representative partner, or his successor (see 78.8 above). [*TMA 1970, s 95A; FA 1994, ss 196, 199(2)(a), Sch 19 para 28; FA 1996, s 123(12)(13)*].

78.29 **Failure to produce documents.** A penalty applies where a person fails to comply with a notice or requirement under *TMA 1970, s 19A* or *TMA 1970, Sch 1A para 6(2)(3A)(b)* (notice requiring production of documents, etc. for purpose of Revenue enquiry into a return — see 78.12 above). He is liable to a fixed penalty of £50 and, for continuing failure after the fixed penalty is imposed, a daily penalty not exceeding the 'relevant amount'. No penalty may be imposed after the failure has been remedied. An officer of the Board may determine the daily penalty under *TMA 1970, s 100* (see 58.6 PENALTIES), in which case the '*relevant amount*' is £30, or may commence proceedings under *TMA 1970, s 100C* (see 58.6 PENALTIES) for determination of the penalty by the Commissioners, in which case the '*relevant amount*' is £150. [*TMA 1970, s 97AA; FA 1994, ss 196, 199(2)(a), Sch 19 para 29; FA 1996, Sch 19 para 3(4); FA 1998, Sch 19 para 36*]. See Revenue Tax Bulletin Special Edition April 2000 p 8 as regards discharge of penalties raised after 14 December 1998 for non-compliance with notices subsequently determined to be invalid because they did not allow 30 days *from receipt* for compliance (see 78.12 above).

78.30 ASSESSMENTS: PROCEDURE AND TIME LIMIT

The procedure for the raising of assessments other than self-assessments is set out in *TMA 1970, s 30A*. All income tax falling to be charged by such an assessment may, even if chargeable under more than one Schedule, be included in one assessment. [*TMA 1970, s 30A; FA 1994, ss 196, 199(2)(a), Sch 19 para 5*].

The normal time limit for the making of an assessment to income tax and capital gains tax for 1996/97 or a subsequent year is five years after 31 January following the year of assessment. [*TMA 1970, s 34(1); FA 1994, ss 196, 199(2)(a), Sch 19 para 10*]. The extended time limit in cases of fraudulent or negligent conduct is twenty years after 31 January following the year of assessment. [*TMA 1970, s 36(1); FA 1994, ss 196, 199(2)(a), Sch 19 para 11(1)*]. The latest time for assessing the personal representatives of a deceased person is three years after 31 January following the year of assessment in which death occurred. [*TMA 1970, s 40(1)(2); FA 1994, ss 196, 199(2)(a), Sch 19 para 12*]. (For time limits applying before 1996/97, see 5.7 ASSESSMENTS and 6.4, 6.5 BACK DUTY.)

78.31 APPEALS

For 1996/97 and subsequent years, a right of appeal is conferred by *TMA 1970, s 31* against

(*a*) any assessment other than a self-assessment,

(*b*) an amendment by an officer of the Board of a self-assessment or partnership statement on enquiry into the return on which it is based (see 78.13 above),

(*c*) an amendment of a partnership statement where loss of tax is 'discovered' (see 78.16 above), and

(*d*) a disallowance, in whole or in part, of a claim or election included (by amendment or otherwise) in a return.

Written notice of appeal must be given within 30 days after the issue of the notice of assessment, amendment or disallowance. An appeal within (*b*) above against an amendment to a self-assessment cannot be heard and determined before the officer gives notice that he has completed his enquiries, if he has not already done so (see 78.13 above). An appeal within (*b*) to (*d*) above cannot question the exercise by the Revenue of the 'Crown Option' (see 78.13 above).

[*TMA 1970, s 31(1)–(3); FA 1994, ss 196, 199(2)(a), Sch 19 para 7; FA 1996, Sch 19 para 6, Sch 22 para 4*].

Consequential amendments are made to *TMA 1970, s 50* (procedure on appeals heard by Commissioners — see 4.6 APPEALS). The Commissioners are given the power to vary the extent to which a claim or election included in a return is disallowed. [*TMA 1970, s 50(6)–(9); FA 1994, ss 196, 199(2)(a), Sch 19 para 17; FA 1996, Sch 19 para 7*]. Otherwise, the provisions in 4 APPEALS generally continue to apply.

Payment of tax pending appeal. The provisions of *TMA 1970, s 55* (payment and postponement of tax pending appeal — see 56.2 PAYMENT OF TAX) continue to apply in respect of

(i) an assessment other than a self-assessment, and

(ii) an amendment by an officer of the Board of a self-assessment on enquiry into the return on which it is based (see 78.13 above).

[*TMA 1970, s 55; FA 1994, ss 196, 199(2)(a), Sch 19 para 18; FA 1996, Sch 18 paras 1, 17(1)(2)*]. See 78.22 above as to the date from which interest on unpaid tax will accrue.

78.32 CLAIMS, ETC.

For full details as to the making of, and the ramifications of, claims and elections under self-assessment, see 17.1–17.4 CLAIMS.

78.33 JURISDICTION OF COMMISSIONERS

As regards any proceedings relating to 1996/97 or a subsequent year (or for corporation tax any accounting period to which self-assessment applies), certain questions which may be in dispute on appeal (but not necessarily the entire appeal) must be determined by the Special Commissioners.

The questions concerned mirror those previously contained in *TMA 1970, s 31(3)* (see 4.3 APPEALS) and *s 47* and involve the application of provisions on SETTLEMENTS (81), DECEASED ESTATES (22), liability on transfers of assets abroad (see 3.8 ANTI-AVOIDANCE) and in respect of controlled foreign companies (see Tolley's Corporation Tax under Controlled Foreign Companies), and liability in relation to territorial sea and designated areas (see

51.13 NON-RESIDENTS AND OTHER OVERSEAS MATTERS). They also include any question as to the value for the purposes of capital gains tax or corporation tax on chargeable gains of any unquoted shares or securities in a UK resident company (any question for those purposes as to the value of any land or lease of land being determined by the relevant Lands Tribunal).

The above applies as regards appeals against a Revenue amendment, following enquiry, of a self-assessment, partnership statement (including an amendment on discovery — see 78.16 above), claim or election or a complete or partial disallowance of a claim or election (see 78.13 above and, as regards claims etc. not in returns, 17.3 CLAIMS) and appeals against assessments other than self-assessments.

[*TMA 1970, ss 46B, 46D; FA 1996, Sch 22 para 7*].

An appeal against an assessment made by the Board or under *ICTA 1988, s 350* (assessment to collect tax deducted from payments made — see 23.3 DEDUCTION OF TAX AT SOURCE) *must*, as previously, be to the Special Commissioners. [*TMA 1970, s 31(3); FA 1996, Sch 22 para 4*]

Where, on an appeal against an amendment of a self-assessment or partnership statement, the question in dispute concerns a claim made to the Board or made under any one or more specified provisions, the question must be determined by the Special Commissioners. This effectively continues the rules previously in *TMA 1970, Sch 2 paras 2, 3.* The specified provisions cover double taxation relief, management expenses of the owner of mineral rights, exemptions for certain friendly societies, trade unions and employers' associations, and reliefs in respect of royalties, copyright payments etc. [*TMA 1970, s 46C; FA 1996, Sch 22 para 7*].

Rules for assigning procedures to General Commissioners. Where the General Commissioners have jurisdiction, the rules for prescribing the appropriate division are adapted for self-assessment (see 4.3 APPEALS as regards previous rules and general practice). For proceedings relating to income tax or capital gains tax (except those concerning PAYE or partnerships or where the Board otherwise direct, see below), either the taxpayer or an officer of the Board (whichever commences the proceedings) may elect by notice to the other in writing for the proceedings to be heard in the division in which is situated either the taxpayer's place of residence, his place of business (as defined) or his place of employment (as defined and regardless of whether the proceedings are in connection with the employment). An officer may make the election if the taxpayer fails to exercise his right to do so when giving notice of appeal or otherwise commencing proceedings or at such later time as the Board allow. The taxpayer's election is irrevocable. The division for PAY AS YOU EARN (55) appeals is governed by the *Income Tax (Employments) Regulations 1993 (SI 1993 No 744)* except to the extent that the appellant elects as above. Proceedings relating to a partnership to which a partner is a party are brought before the division in the place where the partnership business is, or is mainly, carried on. For proceedings relating to corporation tax (or income tax where a UK resident company is a party), there are rules similar, but suitably modified, to those above for income tax and capital gains tax.

Notwithstanding the above, the Board may direct that specified proceedings be brought before the General Commissioners for a specified division. An officer of the Board must serve on the taxpayer written notice stating the effect of the direction, and the taxpayer may object in writing within 30 days of the notice being served, in which case the direction has no effect. The Board may also give directions for determining the appropriate division, other than in PAYE appeals, where there is no place of residence, business or employment (or corporation tax equivalents) as described above, or where that place would otherwise be outside the UK; procedure is as above except that the taxpayer has no right of objection.

The parties to proceedings may supersede the above rules by coming to an agreement that the proceedings be brought before the General Commissioners for a division specified therein. The rules are also subject to specified provisions in relation to which two or more parties other than the Revenue are involved (which have their own rules), to regulations under *TMA 1970, s 46A* (see 4.3, 4.6 APPEALS) and to regulations for capital gains tax appeals (see Tolley's Capital Gains Tax under Appeals).

[*TMA 1970, s 44(1)(2), Sch 3; FA 1988, s 133(2); FA 1996, Sch 22 para 10; Sch 41 Pt V(12)*].

78.34 OVER-REPAYMENTS OF TAX

TMA 1970, s 30 (assessments to recover tax over-repaid — see 56.8 PAYMENT OF TAX) continues to apply but subject, for 1996/97 and subsequent years, to the same exceptions (modified as appropriate) as in 78.15 above (discovery assessments). The normal time limit for such an assessment is extended, if necessary, to the later of the end of the chargeable period following that in which the repayment was made and, where relevant, the day on which an officer of the Board's enquiries into a return (or amendment of a return) delivered by the person concerned are treated as completed (see 78.13 above). [*TMA 1970, s 30(1B)(5); FA 1994, ss 196, 199(2)(a), Sch 19 para 4*].

78.35 COLLECTION AND RECOVERY

For 1996/97 and subsequent years, miscellaneous amendments are made to provisions covering the collection and recovery by the Revenue of tax, interest on tax, surcharges and penalties. The limit of £1,000 referred to in 56.3 PAYMENT OF TAX is raised to £2,000. [*TMA 1970, ss 65, 69, 70; FA 1994, ss 196, 199(2)(a), Sch 19 paras 19–21*].

78.36 LIABILITY OF RELEVANT TRUSTEES

In relation to income and chargeable gains, the '*relevant trustees*' of a settlement are the persons who are the trustees when the income arises or in the year of assessment in which the chargeable gain or life assurance policy gain accrues or arises and, in both cases, any persons who subsequently become trustees. Where the relevant trustees are liable to a penalty under the self-assessment regime, to interest on a penalty, to a surcharge and/or interest thereon, to make interim and final payments of income tax and payments on an assessment to recover tax over-repaid, or to interest on unpaid tax, the penalty etc. may be recovered (but only once) from any one or more of them. As regards penalties and surcharges (and interest on either), the liability of any relevant trustee is, however, restricted to those incurred after the day that he became a relevant trustee (a daily penalty being regarded as incurred on a daily basis). The 'reasonable excuse' provisions in 78.21 and 78.26 above have effect by reference to each of the relevant trustees. [*TMA 1970, ss 7(9), 107A; FA 1995, s 103; FA 1998, Sch 14 para 5*].

Trustees of 'bare' (or 'simple') trusts treated as such for tax purposes are not required to complete self-assessment returns or make payments on account, the beneficiaries under such trusts being liable to give details of the income and gains in their own tax returns. The trustees may, if they and the beneficiaries so wish, make returns of income (but *not* of capital gains or capital losses), accounting for tax at the basic or lower rate (or, from 6 April 1999, the Schedule F ordinary rate), as appropriate to the class of income, provided that they so notify the trust district and follow this course consistently from year to year. This does not, however, affect the liability of the beneficiaries to make the appropriate self-assessment returns of income and gains. (Revenue Tax Bulletin February 1997 p 395, December 1997 pp 486, 487).

78.37 EMPLOYERS' OBLIGATIONS AND RETURNS

With effect for 1996/97 and later years, amendments are made to *The Income Tax (Employments) Regulations 1993 (SI 1993 No 744)*, i.e. the PAYE (55) Regulations, to ensure that sufficient information is given to employees, and in good time, to enable them to complete their self-assessments. The Revenue have undertaken to provide an education and assistance programme for employers, which includes a booklet SAT 3 'Self Assessment: what it will mean for employers' sent out to employers as part of an information pack in July 1995 and available free from tax offices. The amendments are as follows.

(*a*) A time limit is introduced for providing an employee with form P60 (certificate of pay and tax deducted — see 55.10 PAYE). It must be provided no later than 31 May following the tax year to which it relates, commencing with 31 May 1997. [*SI 1993 No 744, reg 39; SI 1995 No 1284, reg 3*].

(*b*) The deadline for submitting to the Revenue forms P9D and P11D (returns of benefits and expenses payments — see 55.9 PAYE and (*c*) below) is extended to no later than 6 July (previously 6 June) following the tax year, commencing with 6 July 1997. Within the same time limit, there is a new requirement for the employer to provide each employee for whom such a form is relevant with particulars of the information stated therein. Where an employer operates the Fixed Profit Car Scheme (FPCS) (see 75.43 SCHEDULE E), he must provide each scheme employee with either his taxable business mileage profit figure or the figures for allowances paid and mileage covered. An employer is not obliged to provide any of the above particulars to an employee who left during the tax year in question unless requested to do so within three years after the end of that tax year, the information to be provided within 30 days of receipt of the request if later than the normal 6 July deadline. [*SI 1993 No 744, regs 46(1), 46AA; SI 1995 No 1284, reg 4*].

(*c*) In addition to the information specified at 55.9 PAYE, forms P11D and P9D must contain the following information:

(i) whether emoluments relating to business entertainment (see 71.55 SCHEDULE D, CASES I AND II) have been or will be disallowed as a deduction in the employer's business tax computations (see also 75.10(*b*) SCHEDULE E);

(ii) the cash equivalent of benefits provided, i.e. the amount chargeable to tax under the relevant legislation disregarding certain deductions which may be claimed by the employee in his own return, e.g. expenses 'wholly and necessarily incurred' and allowable professional subscriptions; and

(iii) particulars, including cash equivalents as in (ii) above, of payments made and benefits provided by third parties *by arrangement with the employer*. 'Arranging' includes guaranteeing or facilitating the payment or provision of the benefit — see Revenue booklet SAT 3(1995), paras 2.10 to 2.21. See also (*d*) below.

[*SI 1993 No 744, reg 46; SI 1995 No 1284, reg 4*].

(*d*) Where a third party makes payments or provides benefits which if done by arrangement with the employer would have fallen to be included on forms P11D and P9D (see (*c*)(iii) above), he must provide particulars, including cash equivalents, to the *employee* by 6 July following the tax year. The third party is not obliged to provide such particulars to the Revenue unless required to do so by notice under *TMA 1970, s 15* (see below). [*SI 1993 No 744, reg 46AB; SI 1995 No 1284, reg 4*].

There are also changes to form P45 (for employees changing jobs — see 55.22 to 55.24 PAYE) from 6 April 1996. The form will contain an additional part for retention by the employee.

Penalties under *TMA 1970, s 98* for failure to provide information to the Revenue (see 58.4 PENALTIES) apply equally to failure to comply with the above requirements for providing particulars to employees.

The following amendments are made to the provisions of *TMA 1970, s 15* (employers' returns of employees' emoluments etc. — see 67.5 RETURNS) as respects payments made or benefits provided on or after 6 April 1996.

(i) An employer will not have to include in his return information relating to any year of assessment if notice to deliver the return is given more than five years after 31 January following that year (replacing the six year rule previously in force).

(ii) The return must include particulars of payments made/benefits provided to employees by third parties by arrangement with the employer, plus the name and business address of the third party; also, the name and business address of any person who, to the employer's knowledge, has made payments/provided benefits to an employee in respect of the employment other than by such arrangement.

(iii) When providing particulars of benefits, cash equivalents must be given as at (*c*)(ii) above.

(iv) The Revenue's power to require returns by third parties is extended.

[*TMA 1970, s 15; FA 1995, s 106*].

78.38 TAXATION OF NON-RESIDENTS

Non-UK residents are taxed on the shoreline principle, i.e. on income arising in or connected with the UK. New rules were introduced by *Finance Act 1995* to simplify the procedures for taxing non-residents and align them with self-assessment. See 51.5 to 51.7 NON-RESIDENTS AND OTHER OVERSEAS MATTERS for rules under *FA 1995, ss 126, 127, Sch 23* which apply where a non-resident carries on a trade in the UK through a branch or agency and for the obligations and liabilities of his UK representative. See 68.24 SCHEDULE A for provisions of *FA 1995, s 40* on income from UK property. See 51.1 NON-RESIDENTS AND OTHER OVERSEAS MATTERS for provisions of *FA 1995, s 128* which limit the income tax chargeable on a non-resident's total UK income, and Tolley's Corporation Tax under Residence for corresponding provisions applicable to non-resident companies. See Revenue Tax Bulletin August 1995 p 237 for a summary of the rules for taxing various types of income of non-residents under self-assessment.

Individuals who regard themselves as not resident, not ordinarily resident or not domiciled in the UK are required to self-certify their status in the self-assessment tax return. See 64.5 RESIDENCE, ORDINARY RESIDENCE AND DOMICILE under *Administrative procedures.*

79 Self-Assessment—Key Dates

Cross-references. See also 78 SELF-ASSESSMENT.

79.1 The Table below sets out key dates and events in the operation of the self-assessment regime.

Date	*Event*
31 January 2000	1998/99 tax return to be filed on or before this date (see 78.5 SELF-ASSESSMENT).
31 January 2000	Balancing payment of income tax and payment of capital gains tax due for 1998/99 (see 78.19 SELF-ASSESSMENT).
31 January 2000	First interim payment on account due for 1999/2000 (see 78.17 SELF-ASSESSMENT).
February 2000	Revenue begin to issue fixed penalty notices, and in some cases take daily penalty action, for non-filing of 1998/99 tax returns (see 78.26 SELF-ASSESSMENT).
February 2000	Revenue may issue determinations of tax due for 1998/99 where no tax return filed (see 78.14 SELF-ASSESSMENT).
28 February 2000	Initial surcharge due of 5% of any 1998/99 income tax and capital gains tax due on 31 January 2000 and remaining unpaid on this date (see 78.21 SELF-ASSESSMENT).
April 2000	Revenue issue majority of 1999/2000 self-assessment tax returns (see 78.5 SELF-ASSESSMENT).
April/May 2000	Revenue provide taxpayer agents (where authority held on form 64–8) with details of their clients' taxpayer statements of account (see 78.17 SELF-ASSESSMENT).
31 May 2000	Deadline for employers to provide employees with Form P60 for 1999/2000 (see 78.37(*a*) SELF-ASSESSMENT).
6 July 2000	Deadline for employers to provide both the Revenue and employees with P11D/P9D information etc. for 1999/2000 (see 55.9 PAY AS YOU EARN and 78.37(*b*) SELF-ASSESSMENT).
31 July 2000	Second interim payment on account due for 1999/2000 (see 78.17 SELF-ASSESSMENT).
31 July 2000	Further surcharge due of 5% of any 1998/99 income tax and capital gains tax due on 31 January 2000 and remaining unpaid on this date (see 78.21 SELF-ASSESSMENT).
1 August 2000	Further £100 penalty due where 1998/99 tax return due to be filed on 31 January 2000 not filed before this date (see 78.26 SELF-ASSESSMENT).
1 August 2000	If 1999/2000 tax return issued after this date, normal 30 September deadline for filing return if Revenue to calculate tax is deferred until two months from date of issue (see 78.6 SELF-ASSESSMENT).

30 September 2000	1999/2000 tax return to be filed on or before this date if *either* (*a*) taxpayer wishes Revenue to calculate tax *or* (*b*) taxpayer wishes 1999/2000 tax underpayment of less than £1,000 to be collected by adjustment to 2001/02 PAYE code (see 78.6 SELF-ASSESSMENT).
5 October 2000	Chargeability to tax for 1999/2000 to be notified to Revenue on or before this date if no tax return received (see 78.4 SELF-ASSESSMENT).
1 November 2000	If 1999/2000 tax return issued on or after this date, normal 31 January deadline for filing return if taxpayer to calculate tax liability is deferred until three months from date of issue (see 78.5 SELF-ASSESSMENT) as is due date of balancing payment and payment of capital gains tax provided notice of chargeability given timeously (see above, and see 78.19 SELF-ASSESSMENT).
January 2001	Revenue provide taxpayer agents (where authority held on form 64-8) with details of their clients' taxpayer statements of account (see 78.17 SELF-ASSESSMENT).
31 January 2001	1999/2000 tax return to be filed on or before this date (see 78.5 SELF-ASSESSMENT).
31 January 2001	Balancing payment of income tax and payment of capital gains tax due for 1999/2000 (see 78.19 SELF-ASSESSMENT).
31 January 2001	First interim payment on account due for 2000/01 (see 78.17 SELF-ASSESSMENT).
February 2001	Revenue begin to issue fixed penalty notices, and in some cases take daily penalty action, for non-filing of 1999/2000 tax returns (see 78.26 SELF-ASSESSMENT).
February 2001	Revenue may issue determinations of tax due for 1999/2000 where no tax return filed (see 78.14 SELF-ASSESSMENT).
28 February 2001	Initial surcharge due of 5% of any 1999/2000 income tax and capital gains tax due on 31 January 2001 and remaining unpaid on this date (see 78.21 SELF-ASSESSMENT).
April 2001	Revenue issue majority of 2000/01 self-assessment tax returns (see 78.5 SELF-ASSESSMENT).
April/May 2001	Revenue provide taxpayer agents (where authority held on form 64-8) with details of their clients' taxpayer statements of account (see 78.17 SELF-ASSESSMENT).
31 May 2001	Deadline for employers to provide employees with Form P60 for 2000/01 (see 78.37(*a*) SELF-ASSESSMENT).
6 July 2001	Deadline for employers to provide both the Revenue and employees with P11D/P9D information etc. for 2000/01 (see 55.9 PAY AS YOU EARN and 78.37(*b*) SELF-ASSESSMENT).
31 July 2001	Second interim payment on account due for 2000/01 (see 78.17 SELF-ASSESSMENT).
31 July 2001	Further surcharge due of 5% of any 1999/2000 income tax and capital gains tax due on 31 January 2001 and remaining unpaid on this date (see 78.21 SELF-ASSESSMENT).

79.1 Self-Assessment—Key Dates

1 August 2001	Further £100 penalty due where 1999/2000 tax return due to be filed on 31 January 2001 not filed before this date (see 78.26 SELF-ASSESSMENT).
1 August 2001	If 2000/01 tax return issued after this date, normal 30 September deadline for filing return if Revenue to calculate tax is deferred until two months from date of issue (see 78.6 SELF-ASSESSMENT).
30 September 2001	2000/01 tax return to be filed on or before this date if *either* (*a*) taxpayer wishes Revenue to calculate tax *or* (*b*) taxpayer wishes 2000/01 tax underpayment of less than £1,000 to be collected by adjustment to 2002/03 PAYE code (see 78.6 SELF-ASSESSMENT).

80 Self-Employed Persons

80.1 The individual in business, whether full-time or part-time, on his own or in partnership with others, is subject to particular tax legislation and practices. Such legislation etc. is included in this book under various subject headings and the following paragraphs indicate where the detailed provisions are to be found.

See also 37 INLAND REVENUE EXPLANATORY PAMPHLETS for the pamphlets which are obtained free from Inspectors of Taxes, etc. (including Pamphlets IR 28 'Starting in Business' and IR 57 'Thinking of Working for Yourself?').

See 75.24 SCHEDULE E—EMOLUMENTS as regards the distinction between employment and self-employment.

See 61 PERSONAL SERVICE COMPANIES ETC. as regards individuals providing their services through an intermediary in circumstances such that they would fall to be categorised as employees if engaged directly.

80.2 ASSESSMENTS, ETC.

Profits and income are assessed under SCHEDULE D, CASES I AND II (71). Special provisions relate to the opening and closing years of a business. Particular items of expenditure or receipt may, or may not, be included in the computation of taxable profits. Where a business is discontinued, see also 62 POST-CESSATION ETC. RECEIPTS AND EXPENDITURE. Partnership matters are dealt with under 53 PARTNERSHIPS. Farmers may elect for the HERD BASIS (34) to apply to their animals. Special provisions apply to UNDERWRITERS (89).

Where the accounts of a business do not include accruals and unbilled work, assessment may be on the CASH BASIS (12). Some transactions may result in an assessment because they contravene legislation on ANTI-AVOIDANCE (3).

For general assessment procedure, see SELF-ASSESSMENT (78). See also 5 ASSESSMENTS and 4 APPEALS.

Property. For 1995/96 and subsequent years, property income is assessed under SCHEDULE A (68). Previously, income from furnished letting was generally assessed under SCHEDULE D, CASE VI (74) but other property income was under Schedule A.

Assets. The acquisition or ownership of business assets may give rise to CAPITAL ALLOWANCES (10) as the tax substitute for the disallowable depreciation charge (if any) in the accounts. The disposal of assets may result in balancing adjustments, and also to an assessment to capital gains tax unless certain exemptions and reliefs apply.

Overseas. Income from trades etc. carried on wholly abroad is assessed under SCHEDULE D, CASES IV AND V (73). See 51.4 NON-RESIDENTS AND OTHER OVERSEAS MATTERS for non-residents trading in the UK.

Losses. If trading losses are incurred, relief may be obtained by various alternatives, see under 46 LOSSES.

80.3 EMPLOYEES

If staff are employed, then the regulations under the PAY AS YOU EARN (55) system must be complied with.

80.4 **PAYMENT OF TAX**

For times of payment, see under SELF-ASSESSMENT (78). See also 56 PAYMENT OF TAX and 42 INTEREST AND SURCHARGES ON UNPAID TAX. Special provisions relate to the construction industry, see CONSTRUCTION INDUSTRY TAX SCHEME (21).

See 14 CERTIFICATES OF TAX DEPOSIT for a method of payment.

80.5 **PROVISION FOR RETIREMENT**

Special legislation allows tax relief for payments made for PERSONAL PENSION SCHEMES (60) and RETIREMENT ANNUITIES (65).

80.6 **SOCIAL SECURITY**

Class 4 contributions will be levied and included with certain assessments of business profits, see 83 SOCIAL SECURITY. For partial deduction from total income, see 1.10 ALLOWANCES AND TAX RATES.

80.7 **VALUE ADDED TAX**

The detailed provisions of VAT are outside the scope of this book but registration is generally required when the 'taxable turnover' of the business will exceed £52,000 (£51,000 before 1 April 2000) in a year. For detailed information, see Tolley's Value Added Tax.

81 Settlements

Cross-references. See 3.8 ANTI-AVOIDANCE for transfer of assets abroad; 23 DEDUCTION OF TAX AT SOURCE generally and at 23.10 for annuities etc. and 23.17 for tax-free annuities under wills etc.; 64.5 RESIDENCE, ORDINARY RESIDENCE AND DOMICILE for residence of trustees; 78.4, 78.5, 78.36 for management provisions relating to trustees under SELF-ASSESSMENT. See also Revenue Pamphlet IR 152.

Simon's Direct Tax Service C4.

81.1 Legislation providing specially for the tax treatment of settlements is dealt with at 81.13 to 81.30 below. The general tax treatment of trust income and trustees is in 81.2 to 81.12 below and, where appropriate, is applicable to trusts created by a will. For the income of estates of deceased persons in course of administration, see 22 DECEASED ESTATES.

The headings in this chapter are as follows.

81.2 General points on trust taxation
81.3 Assessments on trust income
81.4 — examples
81.5 Discretionary and accumulation trusts
81.6 — examples
81.7 Personal position of trustee
81.8 Income of beneficiaries
81.9 Annuities and other annual payments
81.10 Foreign trust income
81.11 Claims by trustees and beneficiaries
81.12 Claims for personal allowances etc. on income up to 1968/69
81.13 Liability of settlor
81.14 — exclusion for income given to charity
81.15 — the charge to tax
81.16 — definitions etc.
81.17 Settlor retaining an interest
81.18 Children's settlements
81.19 Capital sums, loans and repayments of loans to settlor from settlement or connected body corporate
81.20 — example
81.21 Liability of settlor — 1994/95 and earlier years
81.22 — disposition which cannot exceed six (or three) years
81.23 — settlement by parent in favour of own child
81.24 — revocable (or diminishable) settlements
81.25 — where settlor retains an interest
81.26 — discretionary trusts that could possibly benefit settlor or spouse
81.27 — income settlements
81.28 — income payments by settlor to trustees
81.29 — settlements (e.g. covenants) of income only (i.e. capital not divested)
81.30 Maintenance funds for historic buildings — tax exemption for settlors etc.

81.2 GENERAL POINTS ON TRUST TAXATION

(*a*) **Trustees** of settlements are taxed in their representative capacities under the Schedule appropriate to the income received (see 81.3 below). They are charged to income tax at the basic rate or the lower rate or, from 6 April 1999 the Schedule F ordinary rate (see 1.9 ALLOWANCES AND TAX RATES) as appropriate to the class of income, except in the case of discretionary and accumulation trusts (see 81.5 below). The latter are generally charged at the 'rate applicable to trusts' (currently 34%) or, in respect of dividends and other similar income from 6 April 1999, the 'Schedule F trust rate' (see 81.5 below for detailed provisions).

Trustees of 'bare' (or 'simple') trusts treated as such for tax purposes are not required to deduct tax from payments to beneficiaries or to complete self-assessment returns or make payments on account. The beneficiaries under such trusts are liable to give details of the income and gains in their own tax returns. The trustees may, if they and the beneficiaries so wish, make returns of income (but *not* of capital gains or capital losses), accounting for tax at the basic or lower rate or, from 6 April 1999, the Schedule F ordinary rate, as appropriate to the class of income, provided that they so notify the trust district and follow this course consistently from year to year. This does not, however, affect the liability of the beneficiaries to make the appropriate self-assessment returns of income and gains. (Revenue Tax Bulletin February 1997 p 395, December 1997 pp 486, 487).

(*b*) **Beneficiaries** receive income from settlements which is treated as net of the tax accounted for by the trustees. The grossed-up amount of the income is treated as part of the total income of the beneficiary for tax purposes. If the total income of a beneficiary is high enough, he will suffer income tax at the excess of the higher rate or, from 6 April 1999, the Schedule F upper rate over the tax accounted for by the trustees on the grossed-up income from the trust. He may alternatively be entitled to a repayment of some or all of the tax suffered by the trustees where it exceeds his own liability (although this does not extend to non-repayable tax or non-payable tax credits of the trustees). See also 81.5 below for tax repayments to non-residents.

In determining the income of beneficiaries, trustees' expenses, so far as properly chargeable to income (or so chargeable but for any express provisions of the trust) are to be treated as set against, broadly, income chargeable at the lower rate in priority to other income and, from 6 April 1999, against dividends and similar income before other savings income (see 1.9 ALLOWANCES AND TAX RATES). [*ICTA 1988, s 689B; FA 1993, s 79(3); FA 1996, Sch 6 paras 16, 28, Sch 41 Pt V(1); F(No 2)A 1997, Sch 4 para 16, Sch 6 para 11*]. See also 81.3, 81.5 below for rules on trustees' expenses.

(*c*) **Scottish trusts.** Provided that the trustees are UK resident, the rights of a beneficiary of a Scottish trust are deemed to include an equitable right in possession to any trust income to which such a right would have arisen if the trust had effect under the law of England and Wales. [*FA 1993, s 118*]. This enables such beneficiaries to obtain the benefit of the application of the lower rate of tax to dividend income.

(*d*) **Demergers.** For the income and capital gains tax treatment of shares received by trustees as a result of exempt demergers under *ICTA 1988, s 213* (for which see Tolley's Corporation Tax under Groups of Companies), see Revenue Tax Bulletin October 1994 pp 162–165 and Revenue Capital Gains Tax Manual, CG 33900 *et seq.*.

(*e*) Trustees are also liable to capital gains tax.

81.3 ASSESSMENTS ON TRUST INCOME

General. Income may be assessed and charged on and in the name of any one or more of the trustees to whom settlement income arises, or (from 6 April 1998) in the year of assessment in which life assurance policy gains arise, and any subsequent trustees of the settlement. [*FA 1989, s 151; FA 1998, Sch 14 paras 6, 7*]. See also 78 SELF-ASSESSMENT as regards 1996/97 and later years.

The untaxed income of a trust within Schedules A or D may be assessed on the trustee as the person receiving it [*ICTA 1988, ss 21(1), 59(1)* and cf. *Reid's Trustees v CIR CS 1929, 14 TC 512*] but if, under his authority, it is paid direct to the beneficiary and he returns it under *TMA 1970, s 13*, he will not be assessable. [*TMA 1970, s 76*]. See also

Williams v Singer HL 1920, 7 TC 387 (trustees not assessable where overseas income paid direct to non-resident beneficiary) and compare *Kelly v Rogers CA 1935, 19 TC 692* (UK trustee of foreign trust held assessable in respect of overseas income as there was no ascertainable non-resident beneficiary entitled to the income) and *Dawson v CIR HL 1989, 62 TC 301* (sole UK resident trustee of foreign trust with three trustees held not assessable in respect of income not remitted). See, however, 64.5 RESIDENCE, ORDINARY RESIDENCE AND DOMICILE as regards special residence provisions. Held in *Pakenham HL 1928, 13 TC 573* that settlement trustees not assessable in respect of beneficiary's super-tax liability; presumably this will apply to excess liability.

Expenses of administering the trust are not deductible in the assessments on the trustee (*Aikin v Macdonald Trustees CES 1894, 3 TC 306; Inverclyde's Trustees v Millar CS 1924, 9 TC 14*) even though deductible in arriving at the beneficiaries' income as at 81.8 below.

In computing the amount of a beneficiary's taxable income from a trust, for 1996/97 and subsequent years, and subject to *ICTA 1988, s 689A* (see below), trust expenses, in so far as they are properly chargeable to income (or would be so chargeable but for any express provisions of the trust) are to be set firstly against certain specified types of income (for example, foreign income dividends, stock dividends) which carry a notional and non-repayable tax credit, secondly against other 'savings income' chargeable at the lower rate (see 1.9 ALLOWANCES AND TAX RATES) and finally against other income. From 6 April 1999, dividends and similar income (see 1.9 ALLOWANCES AND TAX RATES) are included in the income against which expenses are first set, and they are then set against foreign income equivalent to dividends, etc. before other savings income. [*ICTA 1988, s 689B; FA 1996, Sch 6 paras 16, 28; F(No 2)A 1997, Sch 4 para 16, Sch 6 para 11*]. For 1993/94 to 1995/96 inclusive, expenses were set against dividend income chargeable at the lower rate (see 1.9 ALLOWANCES AND TAX RATES) in priority to other income. [*FA 1993, s 79(3); FA 1996, Sch 41 Pt V(1)*]. See the examples at 81.4 below.

For 1996/97 and subsequent years, where a beneficiary is not liable to income tax on part of his share of the trust income, by virtue wholly or partly of his being non-UK resident or being deemed under a double tax agreement to be resident in a territory outside the UK, the management expenses otherwise deductible in computing his income are reduced in the same proportion as that which such non-taxable income bears to his full share of income (using in each case the income net of UK and foreign tax). Where the beneficiary's income tax liability is limited under the provisions at 51.1 NON-RESIDENTS AND OTHER OVERSEAS MATTERS, excluded income (see 51.1), other than that which is subject to deduction of tax at source, must be included in non-taxable income for the purposes of this apportionment. [*ICTA 1988, s 689A; FA 1996, Sch 6 paras 16, 28*].

A trustee may be required to make a return under *TMA 1970, s 8A* (as inserted by *FA 1990, s 90(1)*) of the income chargeable on him or on the settlor or beneficiaries. In practice, trustees normally make an annual statement of all the trust income, expenses, etc. from which is ascertained any tax payable by the trustees and each beneficiary's share of the net trust income. For 1996/97 and subsequent years, trustees are within the self-assessment regime (see 78.5, 78.6, 78.36 SELF-ASSESSMENT).

See 81.5 below for trustees' liability where trust income is accumulated.

81.4 *Examples*

A is sole life-tenant of a settlement which has income and expenses in the year 2000/01 of

	£	£
Property income		500
Taxed investment income (tax deducted at source £300)		1,500
Dividends	900	
Add Tax credits	100	
	—	1,000
		£3,000
Expenses chargeable to revenue		£400

The tax assessable on the trustees will be £110 (£500 at 22%). The expenses are not deductible in arriving at the tax payable by the trustees. The 10% starting rate band applies only to individual taxpayers and not to trustees, although the 10% Schedule F ordinary rate and the 20% rate on, respectively, dividend and interest income (see 1.9 ALLOWANCES AND TAX RATES) do apply to trustees.

A is sole life-tenant of the above settlement and as such is absolutely entitled to receive the whole settlement income.

A's income for 2000/01 will include the following.

	£	£	£
Trust dividend income (gross)	1,000		
Trust interest income		1,500	
Other trust income			500
Deduct: Schedule F ordinary rate tax (10%)	(100)		
Lower rate tax (20%)		(300)	
Basic rate tax (22%)			(110)
	900	1,200	390
Deduct Expenses (note (*b*))	400		
Net income entitlement	500	£1,200	£390
Grossed-up amounts: £500 × $\frac{100}{90}$	£556		
£1,200 × $\frac{100}{80}$		£1,500	
£390 × $\frac{100}{78}$			£500

Notes

(*a*) This income falls to be included in A's return even if it is not actually paid to him, as he is absolutely entitled to it. He will receive a tax certificate (form R185E) from the trust agents, showing three figures for gross income (£556, £1,500 and £500), tax deducted (£56, £300 and £110) and net income (£500, £1,200 and £390).

(*b*) The trust expenses are deducted from income falling within *ICTA 1988, s 1A* (savings income) in priority to other income, firstly against dividend and similar income and then against other savings income (see 81.3 above).

(*c*) That part of A's trust income which is represented by dividend and other savings income (£500 and £1,200 net) is treated in A's hands as if it were such income received directly by A. It is thus chargeable at the Schedule F ordinary rate and lower rate only, the liability being satisfied by the 10% and 20% tax credit respectively, except to the extent, if any, that it exceeds his basic rate limit.

81.5 DISCRETIONARY AND ACCUMULATION TRUSTS

Income received by a trust which is to be accumulated, or payable at the discretion of the trustees or some other person, is, for 1998/99 and earlier years, taxed at the 'rate applicable to trusts' rather than at the basic or (where otherwise applicable, see 1.9 ALLOWANCES AND RATES) lower rate. The '*rate applicable to trusts*' is **34%**, or such other rate as Parliament may determine. For 1996/97 it was similarly 34% (previously 35%), being defined for those years as the sum of the basic and additional rates for the year. From 6 April 1999, the rate applicable to trusts (which remains at 34%) continues to apply generally, but a special 'Schedule F trust rate' (initially set at 25%) applies to '*Schedule F type income*', i.e. income falling within any of the following categories.

(i) UK company dividends and other distributions chargeable under Schedule F, and 'equivalent foreign income' (see 1.9 ALLOWANCES AND TAX RATES).

(ii) Qualifying distributions arising to non-UK resident trustees (who are thus not entitled to any tax credit).

(iii) Distributions which are not qualifying distributions.

(iv) Certain stock dividends and loans or advances written off or released which, by virtue of *ICTA 1988, s 249(6)(b)* or *s 421(1)(a)* respectively, are treated as giving rise to income of the trustees.

(v) Distributions within *ICTA 1988, s 686A* (see below) consisting of the purchase etc. by a company of its own shares.

See Revenue Tax Bulletin February 1999 pp 629, 630 for an illustrative Revenue interpretation of the application of the Schedule F trust rate.

The special charge does not apply where (*a*) the trust is exempt as a charity (see 15 CHARITIES), (*b*) the income arises from property held for the purposes of certain retirement benefit or personal pension schemes, or (*c*) the income is income of any person other than the trustees or treated as income of a settlor (see 81.13 to 81.30 below). As regards (*c*), for 1995/96 onwards, the position is considered *before* the income is distributed, so that income paid to the settlor's unmarried minor children does not fall within the exemption. See also 44.5, 44.7 INTEREST RECEIVABLE as regards a similar charge in respect of deep discount and deep gain securities. The trustees may offset management expenses against trust income for the purpose of determining income chargeable at the rate applicable to trusts or the Schedule F trust rate, although income so relieved remains subject to basic rate, lower rate or Schedule F ordinary rate tax, as the case may be. They must, however, be expenses properly chargeable to income (or which would be so chargeable but for any express provisions of the trust) (see *Carver v Duncan; Bosanquet v Allen HL 1985, 59 TC 125*). The order of set-off, subject to the apportionment of expenses in the circumstances described below, is determined by *ICTA 1988, s 689B* (broadly first against dividend income, then against other savings income, and finally against other income) or, before 1996/97, by *FA 1993, s 79(3)* (see 81.3 above), disregarding for this purpose the fact that all income is in fact chargeable at the rate applicable to trusts or the Schedule F trust rate (the tax saving being the difference between whichever of those rates applies and the basic, lower or Schedule F ordinary rate, as appropriate to the class of income — see the examples at 81.6 below). Where the trust has income not chargeable to income tax, by virtue wholly or partly of the trustees being non-UK resident or being deemed under a double tax agreement to be resident in a territory outside the UK, the management expenses otherwise available for offset are reduced in the same proportion as that which such non-taxable income bears to the total trust income for the year. For 1996/97 and later years, where the trustees' income tax liability is limited under the provisions at 51.1 NON-RESIDENTS AND OTHER OVERSEAS MATTERS, excluded income (see 51.1), other than that which is subject to deduction of tax at source, must be included in non-taxable income for the purposes of this apportionment. 'Income' of the trustees for the purposes of these provisions includes income receipts by trustees (which will be treated as net of tax at the applicable rate) from personal representatives during administration of estate. [*ICTA 1988, ss 686, 832(1); FA 1988, ss 24(4), 55(3); FA 1989, Sch 17 Pt V; FA 1990, Sch 5 para 13; FA 1993, Sch 6 para 8; FA 1995, Sch 17 para 13; FA 1996, Sch 6 paras 13, 15, 28; FA 1997, s 54(3)(4), Sch 7 para 12, Sch 18 Pt VI(1); F(No 2)A 1997, s 32*].

Certain payments made on the redemption, repayment or purchase by a company of its own shares, or on the purchase of rights to acquire its own shares, are treated as income to which *section 686* applies from, broadly, 5 December 1996 (see 3.21 ANTI-AVOIDANCE). With effect from 6 April 1999, following the repeal of those provisions, *ICTA 1988, s 686A* (introduced by *F(No 2)A 1997, s 32(9)(11)*) applies to similar effect (and see (v) above as regards applicable tax rate from that date).

For certain capital proceeds of mineral lease rents and timber cropping previously considered to be accumulations within *section 686*, see Revenue Tax Bulletin December 1996 p 374.

Where the income of the trustees includes a distribution other than a qualifying distribution, liability is restricted to the difference between the Schedule F trust rate (before 6 April 1999, the rate applicable to trusts) and the Schedule F ordinary rate (before 6 April 1999 the lower rate) on so much of the distribution as otherwise falls to be assessed at the Schedule F trust rate (or the rate applicable to trusts). [*ICTA 1988, s 233(1B); FA 1993, Sch 6 para 2; F(No 2)A 1997, Sch 4 para 6*]. Where the income of non-resident trustees includes a qualifying distribution which is grossed up at the Schedule F ordinary rate (see 1.9 ALLOWANCES AND RATES) or, before 6 April 1999, the lower rate, a credit is allowed for the Schedule F ordinary or lower rate tax (which may not, however, be repaid). [*ICTA 1988, s 233(1)(1A); FA 1993, Sch 6 para 2; FA 1996, s 122(3)(4); F(No 2)A 1997, Sch 4 para 6*]. See *ICTA 1988, s 246D(4)* (introduced by *FA 1994, Sch 16 para 1*) as regards receipt of foreign income dividends within *ICTA 1988, Pt VI, Ch VA* prior to their abolition from 6 April 1999.

Discretionary payments by trustees, if treated for tax purposes as income of the payee, are treated as net after tax at the rate applicable to trusts. For 1995/96 and later years, this also applies to payments to the settlor's unmarried minor children which are treated under *ICTA 1988, s 660B* as the settlor's income (see 81.18 below). [*ICTA 1988, s 687(1)(2)(a); FA 1995, Sch 17 para 14*]. For whether a payment is received as income, see *Stevenson v Wishart and Others (Levy's Trustees) CA 1987, 59 TC 740.*

The tax treated as deducted from the payments is assessable on the trustees but the amount will be reduced by

(*a*) tax already suffered by them at the Schedule F trust rate or, before 6 April 1999, the rate applicable to trusts or, in certain cases, at the excess of the Schedule F trust rate over the Schedule F ordinary rate (before 6 April 1999, at the excess of the rate applicable to trusts over the lower rate of tax), and

(*b*) tax suffered up to 5 April 1973, which for this purpose is deemed to be two-thirds of net amount of income available for distribution at 5 April 1973.

Amounts of tax within (*a*) and (*b*) above are known collectively as the 'Section 687(3) tax pool'. After 5 April 1999, in contrast to the position previously, tax credits on UK dividends do not form part of this pool. See Revenue Tax Bulletin February 1999 p 630.

[*ICTA 1988, s 687(2)(b)(3); FA 1989, s 96(2); FA 1990, Sch 5 para 14; FA 1993, s 79(2), Sch 6 para 9; FA 1994, Sch 16 para 15; FA 1996, Sch 14 para 35; F(No 2)A 1997, Sch 4 para 15, Sch 6 para 10*].

By concession, tax paid by trustees of a non-resident trust may, subject to conditions, similarly be set against any liability of the settlor under *section 660B*. (Revenue Pamphlet IR 1, A93; Revenue Press Release 1 April 1999).

Employee trusts which are discretionary trusts are, by concession, and subject to conditions as regards returns and evidence, able to reclaim from the Revenue tax at the rate applicable to trusts on payments to employee beneficiaries made in any year which are taxed under Schedule E as emoluments in the hands of the employees without credit being available for the tax deducted from the payments (but limited to the total tax which the trustees would have available to set against their liability in respect of payments to beneficiaries in the year). (Revenue Pamphlet IR 1, A68).

Taxed overseas income included in payments by trustees may be certified as such by them and recipient may claim appropriate double tax relief within six years of the end of the tax year in which the income arose to the trustees. [*ICTA 1988, s 809*].

Where *section 687* applies (as above) to a payment made after 1 July 1997 to a company within the charge to corporation tax other than a charity (within *ICTA 1988, s 506(1)*, see 15.1 CHARITIES) or a body treated as a charity under *ICTA 1988, ss 507, 508* (see 30.3, 30.9, 30.14, 30.20 EXEMPT ORGANISATIONS, 77.1 SCIENTIFIC RESEARCH ASSOCIATIONS), the payment is disregarded for corporation tax purposes, and no credit is given, or repayment made, of the tax deducted. In the case of non-UK resident companies, this applies to so much (if any) of the payment as is comprised in the company's profits for corporation tax purposes. [*F(No 2)A 1997, s 27*].

Payments to beneficiaries — concessionary reliefs. A non-resident beneficiary of a UK resident discretionary trust who receives income treated as net of tax may claim relief in respect of the tax exemption on 'FOTRA' securities (see 33.2 GOVERNMENT STOCKS) or under the terms of a double taxation agreement, where such relief would have been available had the beneficiary received the income directly instead of through the trustees. Repayment may similarly be claimed where the beneficiary would not have been chargeable to UK tax in those circumstances. Relief is granted provided that the payment is out of income which arose to the trustees not earlier than six years before the end of the year of assessment in which the payment was made to the beneficiary. The trustees must have submitted trust returns supported by tax certificates and relevant information. For 1999/2000 and subsequent years, the trustees must also have paid all tax, interest, surcharge and penalties and keep available for inspection any relevant tax certificates, and the beneficiary must claim the relief or exemption within five years and ten months after the end of the year of assessment in which the payment was received from the trustees.

A similar concession applies where a beneficiary receives a payment from discretionary trustees which is not within *ICTA 1988, s 687(2)* (see above) (e.g. from a non-resident trust). A non-resident beneficiary who, had he received the income out of which the payment was made, would have been liable to UK tax thereon may claim relief under *ICTA 1988, s 278* (personal reliefs, see 51.11 NON-RESIDENTS AND OTHER OVERSEAS MATTERS) and may be treated as if he received the payment from a UK resident trust, but credit may be claimed only for UK tax actually paid by the trustees on the income out of which the payment was made. For 1999/2000 and later years, exemption may also be claimed in respect of income arising from 'FOTRA' securities (as above). A UK resident beneficiary of a non-UK resident trust may similarly claim credit for tax actually paid by the trustees on the income out of which the payment was made as if the payment were from a UK resident trust. In all cases, the trustees must have submitted trust returns supported by tax certificates and relevant information, and have paid tax under *section 686* (see above) at the applicable rate on the UK income of the trust. For 1999/2000 and subsequent years, the trustees must have paid *all* tax due and any interest, surcharge and penalties, and keep available for inspection any relevant tax certificates, and the beneficiary must claim the relief or exemption within five years and ten months after the end of the year of assessment in which the payment was received from the trustees. No credit is given for tax treated as paid on income received by the trustees which would not be available for set-off under *section 687(2)* (see above) if that section applied, and that tax is not repayable and is not taken into account in calculating the beneficiary's gross income.

(Revenue Pamphlet IR 1, B18; Revenue Press Release 1 April 1999).

However, where the beneficiary is resident in a country with which the UK has a double taxation agreement, and the 'Other Income' Article in that agreement gives sole taxing rights in respect of such income to that country, the above concession does not apply, and the tax paid by the trustees will be repaid in full to the beneficiary, subject to the conditions in the Article being met. (Revenue Pamphlet IR 131, SP 3/86, 2 April 1986).

Simon's Direct Tax Service. See C4.203.

81.6 *Examples*

An accumulation and maintenance settlement set up by W for his grandchildren in 1979 now comprises quoted investments and an industrial property. The property is let to an engineering company. Charges for rates, electricity etc. are paid by the trust and recharged yearly in arrears to the tenant. As a result of the delay in recovering the service costs, the settlement incurs overdraft interest.

The relevant figures for the year ended 5 April 2001 are as follows.

	£
Property rents (Schedule A)	40,000
UK dividends (including tax credits of £500)	5,000
Taxed interest (tax deducted at source £700)	3,500
	£48,500
Trust administration expenses — proportion chargeable to revenue	1,350
Overdraft interest	1,050
	£2,400

The tax liability of the trust for 2000/01 is as follows

	£	£
Schedule A £40,000 at 34%		13,600
Gross interest at 14% (34 – 20)		490
Net dividends	4,500	
Deduct Expenses	(2,400)	
	£2,100	
£2,100 grossed at $\frac{100}{90}$ = £2,333 @ 15% (25 – 10)		350
Tax payable by assessment		c/f 14,440

	£
	b/f 14,440
Add: Tax deducted at source	700
Tax credits	500
Total tax borne	£15,640

Notes

(*a*) Expenses (including in this example the overdraft interest) are set firstly against the Schedule F income and then against the other savings income falling within *ICTA 1988, s 1A* before other income (*ICTA 1988, s 689B*). The effect is that the expenses, grossed-up at 10%, save tax at 15% (the difference between the 10% rate applicable to dividend income and the Schedule F trust rate of 25%).

(*b*) The net revenue available for distribution to the beneficiaries, at the trustees' discretion, will be £30,460 (£48,500 – £15,640 – £2,400), but see note (*c*) below.

(*c*) Of the tax borne, only £15,140 goes into the Section 687(3) tax pool. For 1999/2000 onwards, tax credits on dividends cannot enter the pool. Unless there is sufficient balance brought forward from earlier years, the effect is that if the whole of the distributable income is in fact distributed, there will be insufficient tax in the pool to frank the distribution (£30,460 × 34/66 = £15,691), and the trustees will have a further liability which they may not have the funds to settle.

M, the 17-year old grandson of W, is one of the beneficiaries to whom the trustees can pay the settlement income. The trustees make a payment of £3,000 to M on 31 January 2001. He has no other income in the year 2000/01.

M's income from the trust is

	£
Net income	3,000.00
Tax at $\frac{34}{66}$	1,545.45
Gross income	£4,545.45

He can claim a tax repayment for 2000/01 of

	£
Total income	4,545
Deduct Personal allowance	4,385
	£160
Tax thereon at 10% (within starting rate band)	16.00
Tax accounted for by trustees	1,545.45
Repayment due	£1,529.45

Note

(*a*) Unlike the position with interest in possession trusts (see 81.4 above), no distinction is made between dividend and interest income and other income in the beneficiary's hands, the full amount of the payment to him having suffered tax at a single rate of 34% in the hands of the trustees.

81.7 **PERSONAL POSITION OF TRUSTEE**

Annual remuneration paid to a trustee under a will or settlement is an annual payment within Case III of Schedule D from which tax is deductible at source, and is not chargeable on him under any other case or schedule (*Baxendale v Murphy KB 1924, 9 TC 76; Hearn v Morgan KB 1945, 26 TC 478* and cf. *Clapham's Trustees v Belton Ch D 1956, 37 TC 26*). Where a trustee is empowered to, and does, charge for his professional services, his fees are part of his receipts for Schedule D, Case II purposes (*Jones v Wright KB 1927, 13 TC 221*) even where he is also a beneficiary (*Watson & Everitt v Blunden CA 1933, 18 TC 402*).

81.8 **INCOME OF BENEFICIARIES**

In the case of life-tenants and those with similar interests in trust income, the beneficiary's income for tax purposes (see 81.2(*b*) above) is the grossed-up amount of the net income after deducting any trust outgoings payable out of the income (*Lord Hamilton of Dalzell CS 1926, 10 TC 406; Murray v CIR CS 1926, 11 TC 133; MacFarlane v CIR CS 1929, 14 TC 532*) — see 81.3 above re trust expenses generally. In other cases, the tax treatment of payments under a trust depends on the circumstances. Payments to a parent for the maintenance of children were held to be income of the children assessable on the parent in *Drummond v Collins HL 1915, 6 TC 525* (remittances to mother as guardian of minors, all resident in UK, of income of American trust) and *Johnstone v Chamberlain KB 1933, 17 TC 706*. Payments for the rates etc. and the super-tax of a beneficiary and payments for the maintenance of beneficiaries were held to be income in their hands in *Lord Tollemache v CIR KB 1926, 11 TC 277; Shanks v CIR CA 1928, 14 TC 249; Waley Cohen v CIR KB 1945, 26 TC 471*. In a number of cases, the outgoings of a residence provided for the beneficiary, grossed-up, have been held to be income of the beneficiary (*Donaldson's Exors v CIR CS 1927, 13 TC 461; Sutton v CIR CA 1929, 14 TC 662; Lady Miller v CIR HL 1930, 15 TC 25*). Income applied in reducing charges on the trust fund was held not to be income of the life-tenant (*Wemyss CS 1924, 8 TC 551*). Shares allotted to trustees in consideration of arrears of dividends were held to be income and not capital of the trust fund (*In re MacIver's Settlement Ch D 1935, 14 ATC 571*).

Interest on money loaned interest-free, subject to conditions and repayable on demand, by the employer to a trust for the benefit of an employee held to be emoluments within Schedule E (*O'Leary v McKinlay Ch D 1990, 63 TC 729*).

The tax treatment of income accumulated (e.g. during the minority of a beneficiary) has arisen in a number of cases. The test is whether the beneficiary's interest under the trust is vested or contingent. If vested, the accumulated income is his income as it arises. (N.B. If the accumulated income is the beneficiary's, 81.5 above does not apply. If the interest was contingent, see 81.12 below). Decision involves the general law of trusts, outside the scope of this book. For tax cases in which the accumulated income has been treated as income of the beneficiary, see *Gascoigne v CIR KB 1926, 13 TC 573; Stern v CIR HL 1930, 15 TC 148*, and *Brotherton v CIR CA 1978, 52 TC 137*; for cases where the income was held not to be the beneficiary's, see *Stanley v CIR CA 1944, 26 TC 12* (where the position under the *Trustee Act 1925, s 31* was considered); *Cornwell v Barry Ch D 1955, 36 TC 268*, and *Kidston CS 1936, 20 TC 603*. For the release of accumulated income on the termination of a trust, see *Hamilton-Russell's Exors v CIR CA 1943, 25 TC 200*, and on termination of legally permissible period of accumulation, see *Duncan v CIR CS 1931, 17 TC 1*.

See also 22 DECEASED ESTATES.

Simon's Direct Tax Service. See **C4.220** *et seq.*.

81.9 **ANNUITIES AND OTHER ANNUAL PAYMENTS**

Annuities and other annual payments under settlements or wills are subject to the normal rules for DEDUCTION OF TAX AT SOURCE (23). Annual remuneration to a trustee is an annual payment for this purpose (see 81.7 above). Where the annuity etc. is paid out of the capital of the trust fund, the tax deducted is assessed on the trustees under *ICTA 1988, s 350*. (Where tax is not deducted, the beneficiary may be assessed under Case III.) Payments out of capital may be directed or authorised by the settlor or testator, as where he directs a stipulated annual amount to be paid out of capital (*Jackson's Trustees v CIR KB 1942, 25 TC 13; Milne's Exors v CIR Ch D 1956, 37 TC 10*) or authorises the beneficiary's income to be augmented to a stipulated amount out of capital (*Brodie's Trustees v CIR KB 1933, 17 TC 432; Morant Settlement Trustees v CIR CA 1948, 30 TC 147*), or direct payments out of capital for the maintenance etc. of the recipient (*Lindus & Hortin v CIR KB 1933, 17 TC 442; Esdaile v CIR CS 1936, 20 TC 700*) even though discretionary (*Cunard's Trustees v CIR CA 1945, 27 TC 122*). For position if annuity exceeds income of fund on which charged, see *Lady Castlemaine KB 1943, 25 TC 408*. Annuities directed to be paid out of capital but paid out of accumulated income forming part of the capital were held to have been paid out of income (*Postlethwaite v CIR Ch D 1963, 41 TC 244*).

For 'free of tax' annuities, see 23.17 DEDUCTION OF TAX AT SOURCE.

81.10 FOREIGN TRUST INCOME

There are no special provisions for the income tax treatment of foreign trust income. For the liability of trustees within the jurisdiction as regards foreign trust income, see the case of *Williams v Singer, Dawson v CIR* and *Kelly v Rogers* at 81.3 above.

The income of a life-tenant of a foreign trust fund depends first on the nature of his interest under the relevant foreign law. See for this the cases of *Archer-Shee v Baker HL 1927, 11 TC 749* and *Garland v Archer-Shee HL 1930, 15 TC 693*, dealing with the same life-tenancy. In the first, with no evidence as to the foreign law, the life-tenant was held to be assessable on the basis that the investments forming part of the fund were separate foreign possessions or securities. In the second case, relating to later years, it was held that having regard to evidence given as to the foreign law, she was assessable on the basis that the income was from a single foreign possession. (N.B. The decisions have lost some of their practical importance because of subsequent changes in the basis rules of Schedule D, Cases IV and V, but the principles established remain important.) See also *Nelson v Adamson KB 1941, 24 TC 36* and *Inchyra v Jennings Ch D 1965, 42 TC 388*. Stock dividends received by trustees of an American trust fund were part of the trust income under the relevant American law but held not to be income of a UK life-tenant, as not of an income nature under UK principles (*Lawson v Rolfe Ch D 1969, 46 TC 199*).

Discretionary remittances from foreign trustees are assessable and become income when the discretion is exercised (*Drummond v Collins HL 1915, 6 TC 525*) but cf. *Lawson v Rolfe*, see 73.3 SCHEDULE D, CASES IV AND V.

See 51.14 NON-RESIDENTS AND OTHER OVERSEAS MATTERS for unremittable foreign income and 73 SCHEDULE D, CASES IV AND V for assessments on overseas income generally.

81.11 CLAIMS BY TRUSTEES AND BENEFICIARIES

Only such claims as relate to the Trust can be made by the trustee — except as regards incapacitated persons for whom he is assessable, e.g., under *TMA 1970, s 72*. [*TMA 1970, s 42(6)*]. Beneficiaries other than these must claim in their own (or husband's) name. See 81.2(*b*) and 81.5 above. Beneficiaries claiming refund on their share of trust income must each make a separate claim showing their total income from all sources and tax paid on it.

In claim by non-resident life-tenants of residue subject to annuity, held that (where no 'appropriation') latter not to be treated as paid out of UK taxed income but rateably out of all investments. (*Crawshay CA 1935, 19 TC 715*).

81.12 **CLAIMS FOR PERSONAL ALLOWANCES ETC. ON INCOME UP TO 1968/69 — from specified 'Contingent Interests' on obtaining a specified age or marrying**

Under *ITA 1952, s 228*, where an individual has an interest under a will or settlement that is contingent on his or her attaining a specified age or marrying, and income is directed to be accumulated meantime, claims by that individual for personal allowances etc. may be made within six years after the end of the tax year in which the contingency happens, in respect of all income so compulsorily accumulated prior to 6 April 1969. [*ICTA 1970, Sch 14 para 1*]. Such claims cannot be made in respect of income which is deemed to be the income of the settlor as below. See 41 INTEREST ON OVERPAID TAX.

Where income is legally vested in beneficiaries, relief as above is refused; it is important, therefore, to ascertain whether income legally vested or contingent (*Roberts v Hanks KB 1926, 10 TC 351; Jones v Down KB 1936, 20 TC 279*), and when the 'contingency' happens (*Stonely v Ambrose KB 1925, 9 TC 389*, and *Lynch v Davies Ch D 1962, 40 TC 511*).

The section applies only when the contingency is the claimant's attainment of a specified age or marriage (*Bone CS 1927, 13 TC 20* and *White v Whitcher KB 1927, 13 TC 202*). Claimant's right must depend solely on happening of one of these contingencies *and on nothing else*, and no claim can be made if right to receive income is wholly at trustee's discretion (*Dain v Miller KB 1934, 18 TC 478*, and see *Maude-Roxby CS 1950, 31 TC 388*). See also *Cusden v Eden KB 1939, 22 TC 435* as to accumulations.

Tax on income accumulated but directed to be capitalised on happening of contingency may nevertheless be claimed under this section (*Dale v Mitcalfe CA 1927, 13 TC 41*).

The amount recovered belongs to the beneficiary (*Fulford v Hyslop Ch D 1929, 8 ATC 588*). In *Chamberlain v Haig Thomas KB 1933, 17 TC 595* where accumulations directed (from 1913 onwards) for infant children subject to power of appointment (which not in fact exercised until 1922), section held to apply to income of intervening period.

81.13 **LIABILITY OF SETTLOR**

In 81.17, 81.18 below, there are set out the provisions of *ICTA 1988, ss 660A, 660B*, introduced by *FA 1995, s 74, Sch 17*, which treat the income of settlements as the income of the settlor in certain circumstances. **These provisions apply for 1995/96 and subsequent years to all settlements, whenever made.** [*FA 1995, s 74(2)*]. They are intended as a simplification of those in *ICTA 1988, ss 660–676, ss 679–681* and *ss 683–685* which applied for 1994/95 and earlier years and which they replaced (the earlier rules being covered at 81.21, 81.29 below). The rules in *ICTA 1988, ss 677, 678* dealing with loans etc. to the settlor continue to apply and are covered at 81.19 below. The Finance Act 1995 provisions are divided into two areas:

(*a*) income under settlements where settlor retains an interest [*ICTA 1988, s 660A*] (see 81.17 below); and

(*b*) payments out of, or, in certain cases, income accumulated in, a settlement to or for an unmarried minor child of the settlor [*ICTA 1988, s 660B*] (see 81.18 below).

Settlors have an obligation to notify their tax office of any liability under the new provisions even if they do not normally receive a tax return. (Revenue Press Release 4 January 1995).

Simon's Direct Tax Service. See **C4.301** *et seq.*.

81.14 **Exclusion for income given to charity.** *ICTA 1988, ss 660A, 660B* do not apply to 'qualifying income' which arises to a 'UK trust' after 5 April 2000 and which either

(*a*) is given by the trustees to a 'charity' in the tax year in which it arises, or (*b*) is income to which a 'charity' is entitled under the terms of the trust.

For these purposes, a '*UK trust*' is a trust the trustees of which are UK-resident, for which see the appropriate rules at 64.5 RESIDENCE, ORDINARY RESIDENCE AND DOMICILE. '*Charity*' has the meaning in 15.1 CHARITIES but also includes the bodies listed in *ICTA 1988, s 507* (see 30.3, 30.9, 30.14, 30.20 EXEMPT ORGANISATIONS). '*Qualifying income*' is widely defined to cover the income of accumulation, discretionary and interest in possession trusts.

Where the qualifying income arises from different sources (e.g. interest, dividends etc.) and *part* of that income for any tax year is excluded as above, the remainder is rateably apportioned for tax purposes between the different sources. However, this rule is overridden by any requirement in the terms of the trust that the whole or part of a *particular* source of income be given to charity. Any trust management expenses are rateably apportioned between income excluded as above, with the effect that relief is to that extent available for such expenses, and any remainder.

Where there is more than one settlor, *ICTA 1988, s 660E* (see 81.16(*c*) below) is applied *before* taking account of the above provisions.

[*FA 2000, s 44*].

81.15 **The charge to tax** under *ICTA 1988, ss 660A, 660B* is under Schedule D, Case VI (except for dividends and other distributions (and certain similar types of income), which are chargeable as for dividend income generally (see 1.9 ALLOWANCES AND TAX RATES)). Income treated under these provisions as income of the settlor is deemed to be the top slice of his income, but before taking into account income chargeable under *ICTA 1988, s 148* (payments on loss of office, see 19.5 COMPENSATION FOR LOSS OF EMPLOYMENT (AND DAMAGES)) or *ICTA 1988, s 547(1)(a)* (life assurance gains, see 45.13 LIFE ASSURANCE POLICIES). The same deductions and reliefs are allowed as if the income had actually been received by the settlor. [*ICTA 1988, s 660C; FA 1995, Sch 17 para 1; F(No 2)A 1997, Sch 4 para 14*]. The settlor is entitled to recover the tax paid from any trustee or any person to whom the income is payable under the settlement, and to that end can obtain from the Revenue a certificate specifying the amount of income charged on him and the tax paid. If the settlor receives a tax repayment by virtue of setting an allowance or relief against income chargeable on him under these provisions, he must pay it over to the trustee or any person(s) to whom the income is payable under the settlement, with the General Commissioners having the final decision on any question as to the amount payable or how it should be apportioned. Nothing in these provisions precludes tax being charged on the trustees as persons by whom any income is received. [*ICTA 1988, s 660D; FA 1995, Sch 17 para 1*].

Revenue information powers. An officer of the Board can, by notice, require from any party to a settlement such particulars as he thinks necessary (subject to penalty under *TMA 1970, s 98* for non-compliance). [*ICTA 1988, s 660F; FA 1995, Sch 17 paras 1, 23*]. See *Cutner v CIR QB 1974, 49 TC 429* and *Wilover Nominees v CIR CA 1974, 49 TC 559* in connection with similar information powers under the pre-Finance Act 1995 provisions.

81.16 **Definitions etc.**. The following apply for the purposes of *ICTA 1988, ss 660A, 660B*, covered in 81.17, 81.18 below.

(*a*) '*Settlement*' includes any disposition, trust, covenant, agreement, arrangement or transfer of assets. [*ICTA 1988, s 660G(1); FA 1995, Sch 17 para 1*]. The latter includes a gift of shares (*Hood Barrs v CIR CA 1946, 27 TC 385*) or of National Savings Bank deposit (*Thomas v Marshall HL 1953, 34 TC 178*). For shares in new company issued at par, see *Butler v Wildin Ch D 1988, [1989] STC 22*. See also *Yates v Starkey CA 1951, 32 TC 38* re Court Orders and *Harvey v Sivyer Ch D 1985, 58*

TC 569 re provision for children whether under compulsion or not. The creation of a new class of preference shares in a company, and their allotment to the wives of the directors, who had previously also been the sole shareholders, was held to be a settlement by the directors (*Young v Pearce; Young v Scrutton Ch D 1996, 70 TC 331*).

Parent's release of expectant life interest is a settlement (*Buchanan CA 1957, 37 TC 365*) and see *D'Abreu v CIR Ch D 1978, 52 TC 352.*

A distinction can be made between arrangements which amount to a settlement and bona fide commercial transactions without any element of bounty which do not (*Copeman v Coleman KB 1939, 22 TC 594; Bulmer v CIR Ch D 1966, 44 TC 1*) and this notwithstanding that tax avoidance was a motive for the transactions (*CIR v Plummer HL 1979, 54 TC 1*). See also *CIR v Levy Ch D 1982, 56 TC 67.* For whether 'arrangements' are a settlement, see also *Prince-Smith KB 1943, 25 TC 84; Pay Ch D 1955, 36 TC 109; Crossland v Hawkins CA 1961, 39 TC 493; Leiner Ch D 1964, 41 TC 589; Wachtel Ch D 1970, 46 TC 543; Mills v CIR HL 1974, 49 TC 367; Chinn v Collins HL 1980, 54 TC 311; Butler v Wildin Ch D 1988, 61 TC 666.*

For 'property comprised in a settlement', see *Vestey v CIR HL 1949, 31 TC 1.* Where the settlement is of shares in a company controlled by the settlor, the assets of the company are not comprised in the settlement (*Chamberlain v CIR HL 1943, 25 TC 317; Langrange Trust v CIR HL 1947, 28 TC 55*).

Where the trust is imperfect, income not disposed of reverts to the settlor (*Hannay's Exors v CIR CS 1956, 37 TC 217*).

A foreign settlement of UK income by a non-resident was held to be within the ambit of the pre-Finance Act 1995 settlements legislation (*Kenmare HL 1957, 37 TC 383*).

A settlement does not include any arrangement consisting of a loan of money by an individual to a charity (as defined in 81.14 above) either for no consideration or for a consideration consisting only of interest. This exclusion has effect in relation to income arising after 5 April 2000 on any such loans, whenever made. [*FA 2000, s 45*]. Previously, an interest-free or low interest loan to a charity constituted a settlement, with the result that any income received by the charity on investment of the loan monies could be treated as the lender's income; it is understood that the Revenue did not always apply this in practice. (Treasury Explanatory Notes to Finance Bill 2000).

(*b*) '*Settlor*', in relation to a settlement, means any person by whom the settlement was made. A person is deemed to have made a settlement if he has made or entered into it directly or indirectly and/or has provided or undertaken to provide funds directly or indirectly for the purpose of the settlement or has made reciprocal arrangements for another person to make or enter into the settlement. [*ICTA 1988, s 660G(1)(2); FA 1995, Sch 17 para 1*]. See *Crossland v Hawkins CA 1961, 39 TC 493, Leiner Ch D 1964, 41 TC 589* and *Mills HL 1974, 49 TC 367.*

(*c*) If there is *more than one settlor.* Each is to be treated as the sole settlor, but only in respect of income or property he has himself provided, directly or indirectly. [*ICTA 1988, s 660E; FA 1995, Sch 17 para 1; FA 1999, s 64(7)*].

(*d*) '*Income arising under a settlement*' includes any income chargeable to income tax, by deduction or otherwise, or which would have been so chargeable if received in the UK by a person domiciled, resident and ordinarily resident in the UK, but not income on which the settlor, if he were himself entitled to it, would not have been chargeable by reason of non-domicile, non-residence etc. (but such income *is* treated as arising under the settlement in a year of assessment in which it is subsequently remitted to the UK if, were the settlor entitled to the income when remitted, he would be chargeable to income tax by reason of his UK residence). [*ICTA 1988, s 660G(3)(4); FA 1995, Sch 17 para 1*].

(*e*) *Payment of inheritance tax by trustees on assets put into settlement by settlor.* Where the trustees have power to pay, or do in fact pay, inheritance tax on assets which the settlor puts into the settlement, the Revenue will not argue that such a power renders that income the settlor's income for income tax purposes. This is because both the settlor and the trustees are liable for such inheritance tax. (Revenue Pamphlet IR 131, SP 1/82, 6 April 1982).

81.17 **SETTLOR RETAINING AN INTEREST** [*ICTA 1988, s 660A; FA 1995, Sch 17 para 1; FA 2000, Sch 13 para 26*]

See also 81.13, 81.14, 81.16 above.

Income arising under a settlement during the life of the settlor is treated for all income tax purposes as the income of the settlor (and not of any other person), *unless* the income arises from property in which the settlor has no interest (see below).

For the purposes of these provisions, a settlement does not include:

(*a*) an outright gift between spouses of property from which income arises (but a gift which does not carry a right to the whole of that income is not excluded, nor is a gift of a right to income); or

(*b*) (for 2000/01 and earlier years) an irrevocable allocation of pension rights between spouses under a relevant statutory scheme (see 66.1 RETIREMENT SCHEMES) (and see (iv) below as regards wider exclusion in later years).

As regards (*a*) above, a gift is not an outright gift if it is conditional or if the property or any 'derived property' could in any circumstances become payable to the donor or be applied for his benefit.

The following income is excluded from these provisions:

(i) income arising under a marriage settlement made between spouses after separation, divorce or annulment, being income payable to or for the benefit of the spouse being provided for;

(ii) annual payments by an individual for *bona fide* commercial reasons in connection with his trade, profession or vocation;

(iii) qualifying donations within 15.13 CHARITIES made after 5 April 2000, and both qualifying donations and covenanted payments to charity made before 6 April 2000 (see 15.16, 15.17 CHARITIES); and

(iv) (for 2001/02 and subsequent years) benefits under 'approved pension arrangements' (as widely defined).

A settlor has an *interest in property* if that property or any 'derived property' could in any circumstances become payable to the settlor or his spouse or be applied for the benefit of either. For this purpose, a spouse does not include a possible future spouse, a separated spouse or a widow/widower of the settlor. A settlor does *not* have an interest in property if it could become so payable or be so applied only in the event of

(A) the bankruptcy of a current or potential beneficiary,

(B) an assignment of, or charge on, the property or 'derived property' being made or given by a current or potential beneficiary,

(C) in the case of a marriage settlement, the death of both spouses and all or any of their children, or

(D) the death of a child of the settlor who has become beneficially entitled to the property etc. at an age not exceeding 25,

or if (and so long as) there is a beneficiary alive under the age of 25 during whose life the property etc. cannot become so payable etc. except in the event of the beneficiary becoming bankrupt or assigning or charging his interest.

'*Derived property*', in relation to any property, means income from that property or any other property directly or indirectly representing proceeds of, or of income from, that property or income therefrom.

Simon's Direct Tax Service. See **C4.310–C4.312**.

81.18 **CHILDREN'S SETTLEMENTS** [*ICTA 1988, s 660B; FA 1995, Sch 17 para 1; FA 1999, s 64*]

See also 81.13, 81.14, 81.16 above.

Income arising under a settlement which during the life of the settlor is paid to or for the benefit of an unmarried minor child (i.e. a child under 18, including a stepchild or illegitimate child) of the settlor in any year of assessment is treated for all income tax purposes as income of the settlor (and not of any other person) for that year. However, this does *not* apply for any tax year if the aggregate amount that would otherwise be treated as the settlor's income for that year in relation to any particular child does not exceed £100. Nor does it apply if the income falls to be treated under 81.17 above as that of the settlor.

As regards income arising under a settlement made on or after 9 March 1999, and income arising directly or indirectly from funds added on or after that date to a pre-existing settlement (any necessary apportionment being made on a just and reasonable basis), the provisions are extended to apply the same treatment as above to undistributed income which would otherwise be treated as income of an unmarried minor child of the settlor in any year of assessment. This is intended to catch income accumulated in a bare trust. The above-mentioned £100 limit applies, per parent per child, by reference to the aggregate of income paid out or accumulated.

Retained or accumulated income. Any payment made on or after 9 March 1999 under the settlement to or for the child is taken into account as above to the extent that there is available retained or accumulated income, i.e. aggregate income arising since the settlement was entered into exceeds the aggregate amount of such income which has been:

(*a*) treated as income of the settlor; or

(*b*) paid (as income or capital) to or for the benefit of, or otherwise treated as the income of, a beneficiary other than an unmarried minor child of the settlor; or

(*c*) treated as the income of an unmarried minor child of the settlor, and 'subject to tax', in any of the years 1995/96, 1996/97 or 1997/98; or

(*d*) used to pay expenses of the trustees which were properly chargeable to income (or would have been so chargeable but for express provisions of the trust).

For the purposes of (*c*) above, the income so treated is '*subject to tax*' to the extent that it does not exceed the child's taxable income (i.e. total income, inclusive of the settlement income, after allowances and deductions). For payments made before 9 March 1999, similar rules applied as above, the main difference being that any income treated as the income of an unmarried minor child, whether charged to tax or not, was deductible in arriving at available retained or accumulated income.

Any provision by a parent for his child may create a settlement, whether made under compulsion or merely under parental obligation (*Harvey v Sivyer Ch D 1985, 58 TC 569*), although in practice the Revenue do not treat payments made under a Court Order as being under a settlement for this purpose. '*Stepchild*' includes a child of the wife by a previous marriage (*CIR v Russell CS 1955, 36 TC 83*).

Simon's Direct Tax Service. See C4.315, C4.316.

81.19 CAPITAL SUMS, LOANS AND REPAYMENTS OF LOANS TO SETTLOR FROM SETTLEMENT OR CONNECTED BODY CORPORATE —

treated as income of settlor to extent that settlement has undistributed income. [*ICTA 1988, ss 677, 678*]

Where in any year of assessment the trustees of a settlement pay any 'capital sum' to the settlor or spouse (or to the settlor jointly with another person), such an amount (grossed up at the rate applicable to trusts) is treated as income of the settlor to the extent that it falls within the amount of 'income available in the settlement' up to the end of that year of assessment or, to the extent that it does not fall within that amount, to the end of the next and subsequent years of assessment up to a maximum of eleven years after the year of payment. [*ICTA 1988, s 677(1)(6)(9); FA 1993, Sch 6 para 7*]. There is a corresponding deduction for any amount included in the settlor's income under *ICTA 1988, s 421* (see 28.3(*a*) EXCESS LIABILITY) in respect of a loan. [*ICTA 1988, s 677(3)*]. See also 81.30 below.

Any 'capital sum' paid before 6 April 1981 and not treated as income under these provisions before that date is for these purposes treated as having been paid on that date. [*FA 1982, s 63(4)*].

'*Income available in the settlement*' up to the end of any tax year is the aggregate amount of income arising under the settlement (see 81.16 above), for that and any previous year, which has not been distributed (see 81.21 below), less

(*a*) any amount of that income which has already been 'matched' against a capital payment for assessment on the settlor (see above), and

(*b*) any income taken into account under these provisions in relation to capital sums previously paid to the settlor, and

(*c*) sums treated as income of the settlor under *ICTA 1988, ss 671–674A, s 683* (see 81.24–81.27, 81.29 below) or *ss 660A, 660B* (see 81.13–81.18 above), and

(*d*) sums not allowed as an income deduction to the settlor under *ICTA 1988, s 676* (see 81.28 below), and

(*e*) sums from an accumulation settlement for children treated as income of the settlor under *ICTA 1988, s 664(2)(b)* (see 81.23(iv) below), and

(*f*) the tax at the rate applicable to trusts on the accumulated undistributed income less the amounts in (*c*) to (*e*) above. [*ICTA 1988, s 677(2); FA 1993, Sch 6 para 7; FA 1995, Sch 17 para 9*].

'*Capital sum*' includes a loan or loan repayment and any other sum (other than income) paid otherwise than for full consideration (but excluding sums which could not have become payable to the settlor except in one of the events mentioned in 81.25 above or, in the case of sums paid after 5 April 1995, in 81.17(A)–(D) above (or on the death under the age of 25 of the person referred to in the paragraph following 81.17(A)–(D) above). [*ICTA 1988, s 677(9); FA 1995, Sch 17 para 9*]. As regards loans and repayment of loans, see *Potts' Exors v CIR HL 1950, 32 TC 211; De Vigier HL 1964, 42 TC 24; Bates v CIR HL 1966, 44 TC 225; McCrone v CIR CS 1967, 44 TC 142; Wachtel Ch D 1970, 46 TC 543* and *Piratin v CIR Ch D 1981, 54 TC 730.*

There is also treated as a capital sum paid to the settlor any sum paid to a third party at the settlor's direction or by assignment of his right to receive it (where the direction or assignment is after 5 April 1981) and any other sum otherwise paid or applied for the settlor's benefit. [*ICTA 1988, s 677(10)*].

Loan to settlor. Where the capital sum represents a loan to the settlor, there will be no tax charge on him for any tax year after the year in which the loan is repaid. If previous loans have been made and wholly repaid, any new loan will only be charged on its excess, if any, over so much of the earlier loans as have been treated as his income. [*ICTA 1988, s 677(4)*].

Repayment to settlor of loan. Where the capital sum is repayment of a loan by a settlor, a charge arises on him but will not apply for any year after the year in which he makes a further loan at least equal in amount to the loan repaid. [*ICTA 1988, s 677(5)*].

The tax charge under Schedule D, Case VI on the settlor is at the rate or rates in excess of the rate applicable to trusts (i.e. he will receive credit for the grossing up at that rate). Such deductions and reliefs are allowed as would have been given if the sum treated as income had actually been received as income. [*ICTA 1988, s 677(7)(8); FA 1993, Sch 6 para 7*].

ICTA 1988, ss 660E (more than one settlor — see 81.16 above), *660F* (Revenue information powers — see 81.15 above) and *660G* (definitions — see 81.16 above) apply for the purposes of these provisions as they apply for those of *ICTA 1988, ss 660A, 660B*. [*ICTA 1988, s 682A; FA 1995, Sch 17 para 11*].

Payment of IHT by trustees, see 81.16 above.

Connected companies. A capital sum (as above) paid to a settlor by a company connected with the settlement (see 20.8 CONNECTED PERSONS) is treated as paid to him by the trustees of the settlement irrespective of whether or not the funds originated from that settlement if there has been an 'associated payment' (made directly or indirectly) to the company (or to another company associated with that company under *ICTA 1988, s 416* at that time) from the settlement (which, before 6 April 1995, was assumed to be the case unless the settlor showed otherwise). Such company payments to the settlor in a tax year will be 'matched' with associated payments from the trustees to the company up to the end of that year (less any amounts already 'matched') in order to determine the amount deemed paid to the settlor by the trustees in the year, any 'unmatched' balance being 'matched' with associated payments in subsequent years. Such amounts are then 'matched' with the 'income available in the settlement' as above. [*ICTA 1988, s 678(1)(2)(4)(5)(7); FA 1995, Sch 17 para 10*].

'*Associated payment*' is any capital sum paid, or any other sum paid or asset transferred for less than full consideration, to the company by the trustees within five years before or after the capital sum paid to the settlor by the company. [*ICTA 1988, s 678(3)*].

Loans. The above provisions do not apply to any payment to the settlor by way of loan or repayment of a loan if (i) the whole of the loan is repaid within twelve months and (ii) the total period during which loans are outstanding in any period of five years does not exceed twelve months. [*ICTA 1988, s 678(6)*].

Simon's Direct Tax Service. See C4.320–C4.324.

81.20 *Example*

The trustees of a settlement with undistributed income of £1,375 at 5 April 1998 made a loan of £15,000 to B, the settlor, on 30 September 1998.

B repays the loan on 31 December 2000. Undistributed income of £3,500 arose in 1998/99, £6,500 in 1999/2000 and £5,500 in 2000/01. B has taxable income of £40,000 in each year (excluding savings income).

B will be treated as receiving the following income.

	£
1998/99 £4,875 × $\frac{100}{66}$	7,386
1999/2000 £6,500 × $\frac{100}{66}$	9,848
2000/01 £3,625 × $\frac{100}{66}$ note (*a*)	5,492

B will pay additional tax of

	£
1998/99 £7,386 at 6% (40% – 34%)	443
1999/2000 £9,848 at 6% (40% – 34%)	591
2000/01 £5,492 at 6% (40% – 34%)	329
	£1,363

Note

(*a*) The amount treated as income in 2000/01 is limited to the amount of the loan less amounts previously treated as income (£15,000 – (£4,875 + £6,500)).

81.21 LIABILITY OF SETTLOR — 1994/95 AND EARLIER YEARS

The provisions in *ICTA 1988, ss 660–685* are not mutually exclusive, and if a disposition etc. falls under any one (or more) of them it is invalid for tax purposes to the extent provided by each section (*Gillies v CIR CS 1928, 14 TC 329*). However, to prevent double assessment, there are provisions whereby an assessment under a particular provision below is reduced by any assessments on the same amounts made under preceding provisions. The Revenue may require information from any party to a settlement [*ICTA 1988, ss 669, 680*] and see the cases mentioned at 81.15 above.

(*a*) '*Settlement*' includes any disposition, trust, covenant, agreement or arrangement, and also, as regards settlor's own children, any transfer of assets. [*ICTA 1988, ss 660(3), 670, 681(4)*]. See also the cases mentioned at 81.16(*a*) above.

A foreign settlement of UK income by a non-resident was held to be within the ambit of the settlements legislation (*Kenmare HL 1957, 37 TC 383*).

(*b*) '*Settlor*' includes a person by whom the settlement was made, or who has directly or indirectly provided the funds, or who has made reciprocal arrangements. [*ICTA 1988, ss 670, 681(4)*]. See also the cases mentioned at 81.16(*b*) above.

(*c*) If there is *more than one settlor*. Each to be treated as a sole settlor, but only in respect of income or property he has himself provided, directly or indirectly. [*ICTA 1988, ss 662, 668, 679*].

(*d*) '*Wife of settlor*' in legislation now in *ICTA 1988, ss 672, 673* does not include his widow (*Vestey v CIR HL 1949, 31 TC 1*).

(*e*) '*Income arising under a settlement*' (under 81.24–81.29 below) includes any income chargeable to income tax, whether by deduction or otherwise, or which would have been so chargeable if received in UK by a person domiciled, resident and ordinarily resident, but not income on which the settlor, if he were himself entitled to it, would not have been chargeable by reason of non-domicile, non-residence, etc.

In calculating '*undistributed*' income, deductions are made for (i) sums other than interest paid to beneficiaries, etc., as income for tax purposes, (ii) trustees' expenses properly chargeable to income, and (iii) exempt income of charitable trusts. Interest may not be included in (ii) if otherwise eligible for tax relief (see 43 INTEREST

PAYABLE) or payable to the settlor or spouse. A proportion of other interest may be allowable corresponding to the proportion of total income (after expenses including interest) represented by payments within (i) other than to settlor or spouse. [*ICTA 1988, s 682*].

(*f*) *Recovery by Settlor from Trustees.* Additional income tax paid by the settlor by reason of income attributed to him under 81.22–81.27 below may be recovered by him from the trustees, and for this purpose he may require the inspector to supply him with a certificate. On the other hand, an additional repayment must be handed over to the trustees. [*ICTA 1988, ss 661, 667, 675(3), Sch 30 para 10(6)*].

(*g*) *Payment of inheritance tax by trustees on assets put into settlement by settlor.* See 81.16(*e*) above.

Simon's Direct Tax Service. See **C4.345** *et seq.*.

81.22 **Pre-1995/96 — disposition which cannot exceed six (or three) years — income is treated as that of settlor.** [*ICTA 1988, ss 660–662*]. Where under a disposition (including trust, deed of covenant, agreement or arrangement) income is payable to, or for the benefit of, any person for a period which cannot exceed six years (or three years, see below), that income is treated for all tax purposes as income of the disponor if living (and of no other person) unless the disposition was made for valuable and sufficient consideration. [*ICTA 1988, s 660*]. In *Becker v Wright Ch D 1965, 42 TC 591* held that *section 660* applies only to income which could be deemed income of a UK resident settlor, and does not displace income received by a UK beneficiary from a short-term settlement made by a non-resident. See *Racal Group Services Ltd v Ashmore CA 1995, 68 TC 86* for an unsuccessful attempt retrospectively to amend a deed to achieve the intended effect for tax purposes.

For 'valuable and sufficient consideration', see *CIR v Plummer HL 1979, 54 TC 1* (but substantive decision has been superseded by *ICTA 1988, s 125*, see 3.19 ANTI-AVOIDANCE). See also 15.17 CHARITIES.

Deeds of covenant executed after 14 March 1988 (other than those providing for payments either to charity or for *bona fide* commercial reasons in connection with the payer's trade, profession or vocation) are ineffective for tax purposes, payments thereunder being ineligible for tax relief and not forming part of the taxable income of any person. [*ICTA 1988, s 347A; FA 1988, s 36*].

Six years. Notwithstanding that a deed may be for seven years, yet if the last payment under it is due less than six years from the date of the deed, it is void for tax purposes under *ICTA 1988, s 660 (Hostel of St Luke CA 1930, 15 TC 682)*. But see *Verdon-Roe CA 1962, 40 TC 541.* The restriction must also be considered where some of the provisions in a deed are in force for a period of less than seven years, although the others cover a longer period. See also *Nicolson and Bartlett Ch D 1953, 34 TC 354* dealing with supplemental deeds extending seven year period; and *D'Ambrumenil v CIR KB 1940, 23 TC 440*, where held that there 'must be some constant element in yearly payment', but that the same fractional part of income might be sufficient. But cf. *Black CA 1940, 23 TC 715*, when also held immaterial that period which could have exceeded six years did not, in fact, do so. If payments are to continue after settlor's death, they are legally payable out of capital unless contrary direction in Will (see 81.9 above).

Three years. For covenanted payments to charity, the period of six years stated above is reduced to three years. A '*covenanted payment to charity*' means a payment under a covenant in favour of a body of persons or trust established for charitable purposes only and under which the annual payments become payable for a period which can exceed three years. The covenant must not be for a consideration in money or money's worth and can only be terminable within the three year period with the consent of the charity. [*ICTA 1988, s 660*].

See also 81.29(vii) *et seq.* below regarding restrictions on higher-rate relief for covenantor.

81.23 **Pre-1995/96 — settlement by parent in favour of own child — income is treated as that of parent while child is unmarried and under 18** (but note exceptions below). [*ICTA 1988, ss 663–670*]. Where under a settlement (see definition in 81.22(*a*) above) income is, or may become, payable to, or for the benefit of, a child of the settlor, that income is treated for all tax purposes as the income of the parent if living (and not of the child). This rule only applies if at the time of payment the child is unmarried and also under 18. [*ICTA 1988, ss 663(1), 664(1)*].

Exceptions to the above rule are as follows.

(i) Irrevocable settlements made before 22 April 1936. [*ICTA 1988, s 663(3), Sch 30 para 10*]. For meaning of 'irrevocable', see *ICTA 1988, s 665*. See also cases in 81.24 below.

(ii) If the aggregate amount in any tax year for one child does not exceed £100 (£5 for 1990/91 and earlier years). [*ICTA 1988, s 663(4); FA 1990, s 82*].

(iii) If the parent is not taxable as a UK resident. [*ICTA 1988, s 663(5)*].

(iv) 'Accumulation settlements' which are irrevocable as defined in *ICTA 1988, s 665*. The rule above (i.e. income treated as that of parent) only applies to such settlements to the extent that (*a*) settlement income consists of or represents sums (e.g. annual payments) allowable as deductions from settlor's total income, or (*b*) income (or capital in lieu) is paid to, or for the benefit of, the child, so assessment on the parent can generally be avoided by accumulating all the capital and income of the settlement. [*ICTA 1988, s 664*].

'Child' includes stepchild, adopted child and illegitimate child. [*ICTA 1988, s 670(1)*]. *'Stepchild'* includes a child of the wife by a previous marriage (*CIR v Russell CS 1955, 36 TC 83*). Any provision by a parent for his child may create a settlement, whether made under compulsion or merely under parental obligation (*Harvey v Sivyer Ch D 1985, 58 TC 569*), although in practice the Revenue do not treat payments made under a Court Order as being under a settlement for this purpose.

If the trustees pay any interest (other than to the settlor or his spouse) on which they are not entitled to tax relief (see 43 INTEREST PAYABLE), payments to, or for, an unmarried infant child (as above) of the settlor, are deemed to be increased by an amount equal to the part of that interest bearing the same proportion to the total interest paid as payments to or for such children bear to the total income of the settlement (net of trustees' expenses properly chargeable to income) for that year of assessment. [*ICTA 1988, s 666*].

81.24 **Pre-1995/96 — revocable (or diminishable) settlements — income is treated as that of settlor.** [*ICTA 1988, ss 671, 672*]. So long as an *income settlement* is subject to a power of revocation (or of diminution of payments under the settlement) which, if exercised, would enable the settlor (or spouse) to cease to make (or reduce) annual payments due under the settlement, those payments (or the part corresponding to the potential diminution) are treated as income of the settlor (and of no other person). [*ICTA 1988, s 671*]. Similarly, if a *capital settlement* is subject to a power of revocation (or of diminution of the settlement property or of payments under the settlement) which, if exercised, would, or might, entitle the settlor (or spouse) to the whole or part of the income or capital of the settled property, the whole (or a corresponding part) of the settlement income is treated as income of the settlor (and of no other person). [*ICTA 1988, s 672*].

But where the power of revocation, etc., cannot be exercised within six years (three years in the case of a 'covenanted payment to charity') from the date of the first annual payment (such payments being continuous), or from the date of the first transfer of property to the settlement, the above does not apply so long as the power remains unexercisable (in the case of a 'covenanted payment to charity' under a covenant made on or after 7 May 1992 or where the revocation power cannot be exercised before that day, unexercised rather than unexercisable). [*ICTA 1988, ss 671(2), 672(2); F(No 2)A 1992, s 27*]. Cf. *Nicolson and Bartlett Ch D 1953, 34 TC 354*. As regards a 'covenanted payment to charity', see 81.22 above for definition. [*ICTA 1988, s 671(2)(a)*].

For certain settlements made before 16 April 1958, see *ICTA 1988, Sch 30 para 11*. For certain payments of IHT by trustees, see 81.21(*g*) above.

Power to revoke or determine. A power of appointment is a power of determination (*Jamieson v CIR HL 1963, 41 TC 43*). See also *Warden CS 1938, 22 TC 416; Delamere KB 1939, 22 TC 525; Payne CA 1940, 23 TC 610; Morton CS 1941, 24 TC 259; Rainsford-Hannay CS 1941, 24 TC 273; Dalgety v CIR KB 1941, 24 TC 280; Prince-Smith KB 1943, 25 TC 84; Eastwood CA 1943, 25 TC 100; Vestey HL 1949, 31 TC 1; Wolfson HL 1949, 31 TC 141* and *Cookson CA 1977, 50 TC 705*.

81.25 **Pre-1995/96 — where settlor retains an interest — income is treated as that of settlor.** [*ICTA 1988, s 673*]. So long as the settlor has an interest in the income or property of a settlement (i.e. if any income or capital may *in any circumstances* be paid or applied for the benefit of the settlor or spouse) the income under the settlement, or a part proportionate to the interest retained, is to be treated as that of the settlor (and not of any other person) to the extent that it remains undistributed (and so long as the settlor is alive).

Exceptions to the above rule are as follows.

(*a*) Where settlor's interest can arise only on

- (i) bankruptcy of beneficiary, or charge or assignment by him, or
- (ii) in a marriage settlement, death of both parties and all or any of the children, or
- (iii) in a contingent trust, beneficiary's death before vesting age (25 or less).

(*b*) If and so long as some person is alive and under 25 during whose life (unless bankrupt etc.) settlor cannot benefit. [*ICTA 1988, s 673(3)*].

See *Glyn KB 1948, 30 TC 321; Tennant KB 1942, 24 TC 215; Barr's Trustees v CIR CS 1943, 25 TC 72; Jenkins CA 1944, 26 TC 265; Vestey HL 1949, 31 TC 1; Vandervell HL 1966, 43 TC 519*. Cf. *Muir CA 1965, 43 TC 367; Wachtel Ch D 1970, 46 TC 543*.

As to power of advancement see *CIR v Bernstein CA 1960, 39 TC 391*. For certain payments of IHT by trustees, see 81.21(*g*) above.

See also 81.26 and 81.30 below.

81.26 **Pre-1995/96 — discretionary trusts that could possibly benefit settlor or spouse — income treated as that of settlor.** [*ICTA 1988, s 674*]. Income arising under a settlement (wherever made) is treated as that of the settlor, and not of any other person, to the extent that it, or property comprised in the settlement, is capable, by exercise of a discretionary power, of being paid or applied for the benefit of the settlor (or the wife or husband of the settlor), except where the conditions in 81.25(*a*) or (*b*) above apply. Where the discretionary power cannot be exercised within six years from the time income first arose to, or property became comprised in, the settlement, the above does not apply to that income, or the income from that property, so long as the power remains unexercisable. [*ICTA 1988, s 674*]. See *Blausten v CIR CA 1971, 47 TC 542*, regarding trustees' power to add to class after wife excluded by Deed of Appointment. See *ICTA 1988, Sch 30 para 12* as regards certain settlements made before 9 July 1958.

Under the Revenue interpretation of the decision in *CIR v Tennant KB 1942, 24 TC 215*, both *ICTA 1988, s 673* (see 81.25 above) and *s 674* apply if (*a*) the settlor being presently unmarried, benefit could arise to any person whom he might marry in the future, or (*b*) whether settlor presently married or not, if the terms of the settlement indicate a specific intention to benefit a future wife (or husband). (Revenue Pamphlet IR 131, A30).

81.27 **Pre-1995/96 — income settlements — income treated as that of settlor.** [*ICTA 1988, s 674A; FA 1989, s 109*]. Income arising under a settlement (other than income consisting of annual payments under 'existing obligations' within *FA 1988, s 36(3)* (see 1.8(i) ALLOWANCES AND TAX RATES)) payable to a person other than the settlor is treated as income of the settlor. The conditions and exemptions are identical to those applicable for the purposes of higher rate liability (see 81.29 below), except that the exemption for covenanted payments to charity in 81.29(vii) applies without the restriction where *ICTA 1988, s 505(3)* applies.

81.28 **Pre-1995/96 — income payments by settlor to trustees — are not allowed as a deduction from the income of the settlor to the extent that there is undistributed income in the settlement at the end of a tax year.** [*ICTA 1988, s 676*]. Where the settlor (or spouse) makes payments (e.g. under covenant) to the trustees of a settlement that would otherwise be eligible for deduction from his income for tax purposes, such payments are not so deductible to the extent that there is undistributed income in the settlement at the end of a tax year. [*ICTA 1988, s 676(1)*].

Sums paid by the settlor to a body corporate which is connected with the settlement (see 20.8 CONNECTED PERSONS for meaning) are treated as if paid to the trustees. [*ICTA 1988, s 676(2)*].

See *Pay Ch D 1955, 36 TC 109* re mortgage interest paid to trustees by the settlor. See also 81.30 below.

Trust income equivalent to the amounts disallowed is not available for tax relief. [*ICTA 1988, s 676(3)*]. *Section 676* applies for all income tax purposes. However, it does not apply to settlements made before 27 April 1938 except for certain revocable settlements varied on or after that date. [*ICTA 1988, s 676(4)*].

81.29 **Pre-1995/96 — settlements (e.g. covenants) of income only (i.e. capital not divested) are generally ineffective for purposes of excess liability (i.e. excess of higher rates of income tax over basic and lower rates, and (for 1983/84 and earlier) investment income surcharge).** [*ICTA 1988, ss 683–685*]. The definition of 'settlement' in 81.21(*a*) above is, for the purposes of *ICTA 1988, s 683*, modified in two respects for 1990/91 onwards.

(*a*) It does not include an unconditional outright gift between spouses of property from which income arises unless either the gift does not carry the right to the whole of the income, or the property given is wholly or substantially a right to income, or the donor retains any actual or potential benefit.

(*b*) It does not include the irrevocable allocation between spouses of pension rights under a relevant statutory scheme (see 66.1 RETIREMENT SCHEMES). [*FA 1989, s 108*].

As regards (*a*) above, preference shares created in a company, and given to the wives of the directors, were held to be property consisting wholly or substantially of a right to income (*Young v Pearce; Young v Scrutton Ch D 1996, 70 TC 331*).

'Divestment of capital'. In order to fall outside the scope of *section 683*, the settlor must divest himself completely of the property from which the income arises, so that in no circumstances can benefit come to himself or spouse [*ICTA 1988, s 683(1)(d), s 685(1)*] subject to exceptions in 81.25(*a*) above. [*ICTA 1988, s 685(2)*]. See *Watson v Holland Ch D, [1984] STC 372.*

Otherwise, the income is treated for excess liability purposes as that of the settlor (and not of any other person) unless one of the following exceptions applies (and see also 81.22 above for deeds of covenant non-effective for tax purposes).

(i) The settlement was made before **7 April 1965** [*ICTA 1988, s 683(1)*] but certain restrictions apply to settlements made between 10 April 1946 and 6 April 1965 (the main restriction being that covenants etc. in favour of charities are not effective for surtax or excess liability purposes). [*ICTA 1988, s 684*].

(ii) The income consists of *annual payments* made for full consideration **under a partnership agreement** to a **former partner** or, if he is dead, to his widow (or, after 5 April 1990, widower) or dependants, or to a person who receives a right to the payments on the former partner's death (but limited in this case to a period of ten years since the partner ceased to be a member of the partnership). [*ICTA 1988, s 683(1)(a)(8); FA 1988, Sch 3 para 20(1)(2)*].

(iii) The income consists of *annual payments* made for full consideration by an individual in connection with the **acquisition of a business, or part, from a partnership** to

(*a*) a former partner (or widow, etc. as in (ii) above) of that or any 'preceding partnership', or

(*b*) an individual (or, on the individual's death, to widow, etc.) whose business, or part, was acquired by that or any 'preceding partnership',

but only if such annual payments are in substitution for, or matched by reductions in, payments which would themselves be eligible for relief under (ii) above in the case of (*a*) and (iv) below in the case of (*b*).

A '*preceding partnership*' is one that transfers its business, or part, to another if one or more partners are members of both. [*ICTA 1988, s 683(6)(b)(7)(8)(10)(b); FA 1988, Sch 3 para 20(4)*].

(iv) The income consists of *annual payments* made by an individual for full consideration, **in connection with the acquisition of a business,** to, or for the benefit of, the individual from whom the business was acquired, or the widow, etc. as in (ii) above if the individual is dead. [*ICTA 1988, s 683(6)(a); FA 1988, Sch 3 para 20(3)*].

(v) *Where (ii), (iii) or (iv) above applies* to an annual payment to a former partner or, if dead, to the widow, etc. as in (ii) above and the payment falls short of the limit for the year under *ICTA 1988, s 628* (amount of partnership retirement annuity treated as earned income, see 53.16 PARTNERSHIPS), any additional annual payment up to that limit will be similarly treated notwithstanding that it is not given for full consideration. [*ICTA 1988, s 683(9); FA 1988, Sch 3 para 20(5)*].

(vi) The income is under a **marriage settlement** made by one party to a marriage as provision for the other after separation etc. or dissolution or annulment of marriage. [*ICTA 1988, s 683(1)(c)*]. (But see 47.10 MARRIED PERSONS for the tax treatment of maintenance payments generally.)

(vii) The income consists of **'covenanted payments to charity'** (see definition in 81.22 above). There is no restriction on the overall amount of the covenanted payments made, but where £1,000 or more of such payments in the year is, in the hands of the charity or charities receiving them, denied relief by *ICTA 1988, s 505(3)* (see 15.10 CHARITIES), the amount on which relief is so denied is similarly denied excess liability relief under these provisions. [*ICTA 1988, s 683(3)–(5)*]. See also 15.16 CHARITIES as regards donations treated as covenanted payments.

A covenanted payment within *section 683* remains as a deduction in computing the settlor's income for basic or lower rate tax purposes but it must then be added back for the purpose of establishing liability at the higher and additional rates. Any amount so added back under *section 683* is income arising under a settlement and thus investment income, despite the fact that the actual payment may have been made out of earned income. (*Ang v Parrish Ch D 1980, 53 TC 304*).

For the deductibility of annual payments for which the consideration is a capital amount, see *ICTA 1988, s 125* (3.19 ANTI-AVOIDANCE) and for the position before that legislation, see *CIR v Plummer HL 1979, 54 TC 1*.

81.30 **MAINTENANCE FUNDS FOR HISTORIC BUILDINGS — tax exemption for settlors etc..** [*ICTA 1988, s 691*]

Where the Treasury has directed under *IHTA 1984, Sch 4 para 1* that funds put into a settlement for the maintenance, repair or preservation of qualifying property are exempt for inheritance tax purposes, the trustees may elect in writing for any year of assessment that (*a*) any income arising shall not be treated as income of the settlor (see 81.13 to 81.29 above) and (*b*) any sum applied for the purposes (as above) of the settlement shall not be treated as income of any person by virtue of his interest in, or occupation of, the building or land or by virtue of *ICTA 1988, s 677* (see 81.19 above). The election must be made within, for 1996/97 and later years, twelve months after 31 January following the year of assessment to which it relates (for earlier years, two years after the end of that year of assessment). If no election made, then (*b*) still applies to any sums so applied in excess of the income for that tax year. Under certain circumstances, an election (as above) may be made separately for different parts of a year of assessment. [*ICTA 1988, ss 690, 691; FA 1996, s 135, Sch 21 para 19*].

An income tax charge will arise when any property (whether capital or income) of a fund is applied for purposes other than within a Treasury direction as above (i.e. (i) the maintenance of, or public access to, the property, or (ii) for the benefit of specified national bodies, or (iii) for charities whose sole or main object is the preservation for public benefit of buildings, land etc. of historic, national etc. interest) or when any settlement property devolves on any body or charity other than mentioned in (ii) or (iii). The charge will also apply if property devolves on a body or charity mentioned in (ii) and (iii) *and* at or before that time an interest under the settlement is or has been acquired for money or money's worth by that or another such body or charity (but any acquisition from another such body or charity will be disregarded). The charge is on all income which has arisen from the property since the last charge under this provision or, otherwise, since the creation of the settlement, and has not been applied as in (i), (ii) or (iii) above. The charge will not apply to income which is treated as income of the settlor under *ICTA 1988, ss 660–689* (see 81.13 *et seq.* above) and sums applied otherwise than in (i) to (iii) above will be treated as paid first out of such income treated as the settlor's and only the excess charged in this way. There is no charge where the whole of the settlement property is transferred to another exempt settlement within 30 days of any charge otherwise arising as above or where immediately before and after the transfer the property is subject to a Treasury direction as above. The charge is assessed on the trustees and is in addition to tax charged under any other provision. The rate of charge is the higher rate of income tax *less* the rate applicable to trusts, i.e. (from 1996/97) 6%. [*ICTA 1988, s 694; FA 1993, Sch 6 para 10; FA 1995, Sch 17 para 16; FA 1997, s 54(3)*].

Reimbursement of settlor. Where a settlor incurs expenditure on the maintenance of an historic building which the Treasury has approved for the purposes of capital transfer or inheritance tax (under *IHTA 1984, Sch 4 para 1*, see above) and the settlor is carrying on a trade of showing the property to the public or, for 1995/96 onwards, a SCHEDULE A (68) business, and that expenditure is reimbursed to the settlor by the trustees of the settlement, then the reimbursement will not reduce the expenditure deductible in computing the profits of the trade or business and will only be taxed as income of the settlor under *ICTA 1988, ss 660–685* (see 81.13 to 81.29 above). [*ICTA 1988, s 692; FA 1995, Sch 6 para 26*].

Simon's Direct Tax Service. See C4.340–C4.342.

82 Share Incentives and Options

(See Revenue Pamphlets IR 16, 17 and 95 to 98, 101 and 102 and the Revenue's dedicated website at www.inlandrevenue.gov.uk/shareschemes).

Simon's Direct Tax Service E4.5.

82.1 For general tax liability in respect of shares given to directors or employees as part of their emoluments, see 75.19 and 75.36 SCHEDULE E.

82.2 Legislation applies where there are arrangements to allow employees to acquire shares in their employing companies, as follows.

(*a*) Share options under *ICTA 1988, s 135*, see 82.3 below.

(*b*) Share incentives under *ICTA 1988, s 138* or *FA 1988, Pt III, Ch II*, see 82.4, 82.5 below.

(*c*) Conditional acquisitions of shares under *ICTA 1988, s 140A*, see 82.7 below.

(*d*) Convertible shares acquired by directors and employees under *ICTA 1988, s 140D*, see 82.8 below.

(*e*) (Before 6 April 2002) profit sharing schemes under *ICTA 1988, s 186*, see 82.9 below.

(*f*) Employee share ownership plans under *FA 2000, Sch 8*, see 82.11 below.

(*g*) Enterprise management incentives under *FA 2000, Sch 14*, see 82.26 below.

(*h*) Savings-related share options under *ICTA 1988, s 185(1)(a)*, see 82.38 below.

(*j*) Executive share option schemes under *ICTA 1988, s 185(1)(b)*, see 82.39 below. Now superseded by (*k*) below.

(*k*) Company share option plans under *ICTA 1988, s 185(1)(b)* and *FA 1996*, see 82.40 below.

(*l*) Employee share ownership trusts under *FA 1989, ss 67–74, Sch 5*, see 71.54 SCHEDULE D, CASES I AND II and 82.41 below.

'*Shares*' in (*a*), (*b*), (*e*) and (*g*)–(*l*) above includes stocks [*ICTA 1988, s 136(5)(d), s 139(11), s 187(2); FA 1988, s 87(1); FA 2000, Sch 14 para 71(1)*] and, for (*b*) and (*c*) above, also includes securities. [*ICTA 1988, s 139(11), s 140A(9); FA 1988, s 87(1)*].

A *jointly owned company* (or subsidiary of such a company) cannot strictly participate in an approved scheme under (*e*), (*h*), (*j*) or (*k*) which is a group scheme established by either of its joint owners, because it will not be controlled by the company which established the scheme as the legislation requires. By concession, a group scheme expressed to extend to a jointly owned company will normally be approved upon application by the company establishing the scheme, provided that:

(i) the jointly owned company is not controlled (under *ICTA 1988, s 840*) by any single person;

(ii) it is controlled between them by two persons, one of whom established the scheme; and

(iii) in relation to each of (*e*), (*h*), (*j*) and (*k*) it only participates in a scheme established by one of the companies controlling it.

A similar concession applies in relation to subsidiaries of a jointly owned company which satisfies (i) and (ii) above, provided that (iii) above would also be satisfied if it related both to the jointly owned company and to its subsidiaries.

Such concessionary approval is conditional upon the scheme ceasing to apply to the jointly owned company or its subsidiaries where (i) or (ii) above ceases to be satisfied (unless the companies thereby pass into the control of the company which established the scheme). It must similarly cease to apply to a company which ceases to be a subsidiary of the jointly owned company (again, unless it thereby passes into the control of the company which established the scheme). The company establishing the scheme for which the concession is sought must undertake to notify the Revenue of any change of control of any of the companies concerned.

(Revenue Pamphlet IR 1, B27).

As regards (*f*) above, see 82.12 below.

For *capital gains tax* purposes, when shares acquired under the above arrangements are disposed of, any sum assessed to income tax under (*a*), (*b*), (*c*), (*d*), (*g*), (*j*) or (*k*) above is treated as a cost of acquiring the shares but for (*e*) and (*f*) above capital gains tax is charged without deduction for any amount charged to income tax. [*TCGA 1992, s 120(1)(4)–(6), s 238(2); FA 1993, s 105; FA 1998, s 54*]. For (*h*) above, the consideration given will be the cost of acquisition. [*ICTA 1988, s 185(3)(b)*]. See also Tolley's Capital Gains Tax under Employee Share Schemes.

Self-assessment implications. See Revenue Tax Bulletin October 1996 pp 351–353 for an article on the self-assessment implications (i.e. reporting requirements for employees, arrangements for payment of tax due and interim payments on account) of income tax liability arising for 1996/97 onwards from shares or share options received by reason of employment.

For a summary of *employer reporting deadlines*, see Revenue Tax Bulletin April 2000 p 739.

82.3 SHARE OPTIONS — CHARGE TO TAX

(*a*) Where a person realises a gain by exercising, assigning or releasing an option to acquire shares in a company which he obtained at any time as a present, past or prospective director or employee, within Case I of Schedule E, of that, or of any other, company, he is assessable under Schedule E on the difference between

(i) the then open-market value of those shares (or, in the case of an assignment or release, the consideration received for the assignment or release) and

(ii) the consideration (apart from services in his office or employment) which he gave for the option (if any) plus that for the acquisition of the shares.

For the circumstances in which the Revenue will accept that shares or share options were acquired by a director or employee in a different capacity and not by reason of the office or employment, see Revenue Inspector's Manual, IM 5329.

The charge is independent of any charge on grant of the option, and depends solely on the above conditions being satisfied (*Ball v Phillips Ch D 1990, 63 TC 529*).

A person is treated as assigning or releasing a right for this purpose if he receives money or money's worth in connection with omitting, or undertaking to omit, to exercise the right, or granting, or undertaking to grant, to another a right to acquire the shares or an interest therein. Further application of these provisions is not prevented, but any consideration given for the original grant of the right may be taken into account only once for this purpose.

Provisions prevent avoidance by having the option granted, or assigned, to a third party, or by assigning the option, in whole or in part, for another option, or by entering into joint arrangements with another person or persons having chargeable options. There are reporting requirements relating to any of the events which may give rise to a charge under these provisions (see *ICTA 1988, s 136(6)–(8); FA 2000, s 56(3)(4)*). Information should be sent to Inland Revenue, Employee Share Schemes Unit, Savings and Investment Division, First Floor, SW Wing, Bush House, Strand, London WC2B 4RD. (Revenue Tax Bulletin February 1994 p 110).

Where, under a voluntary agreement or a joint election under *Social Security Contributions and Benefits Act 1992, Sch 1 para 3A* or *para 3B* (or NI equivalent), whenever made, a liability to secondary Class 1 national insurance contributions (i.e. employer contributions) on a share option gain chargeable to tax under these provisions is borne by the employee who realised the gain, the amount so borne is deductible in arriving at the amount on which the employee is chargeable to tax. In the case of a voluntary agreement, or an election to which Revenue approval is withdrawn, no such amount is deductible to the extent that it is borne by the employee later than 60 days after the end of the tax year in which occurs the event giving rise to the charge to tax. Any such deduction is disregarded in determining the allowable cost of the shares for capital gains tax purposes as in 82.2 above.

For the requirement to operate PAYE on payments made on the exercise, assignment or release of share options, see 55.2(*e*)(*f*) PAY AS YOU EARN.

(*b*) If a right, as under (*a*) above, can be exercised more than ten years after being obtained (seven years in relation to rights obtained before 6 April 1998), tax liability can arise at the time the right is obtained, as well as on exercise of the right. Any tax so charged is deducted from the charge under (*a*) above. Otherwise no liability arises on receipt of a right as under (*a*) above.

(*c*) No charge arises under these provisions where an option is exercised after the death of the grantee by his personal representative or legatee. When shares so acquired are disposed of, a capital gains tax charge arises by reference to a base cost of the market value of the option at the date of death plus the price paid for the shares on its exercise. (Revenue Pamphlet IR 16, para 2.10).

[*ICTA 1988, ss 135, 136, 140(1)(a), 187A; FA 1998, s 49; FA 2000, s 56(1)(3)(4)*].

Example

An employee is granted an option exercisable within five years to buy 1,000 shares at £5 each. The option costs 50p per share. He exercises the option in 2000/01 when the shares are worth £7.50. The option is not granted under an approved scheme.

He is chargeable to income tax under Schedule E in 2000/01 as follows

	£	£
Open market value of shares 1,000 × £7.50		7,500
Price paid 1,000 × £5 — shares	5,000	
1,000 × 50p — option	500	
		5,500
Assessable		£2,000

Notes

(*a*) The result would be the same if, instead of exercising the option, the employee transferred his option to a third party for £2,500.

(*b*) The capital gains tax base cost of the shares will be £7,500. [*TCGA 1992, s 120(4)*]. See Tolley's Capital Gains Tax.

As regards obtaining from the Revenue Shares Valuation Division valuations of unquoted company shares (where either an option which may be exercised after more than ten (or seven) years is granted under an unapproved scheme, or income tax liability arises on exercise of an option under *section 135*), see Revenue Tax Bulletin December 1996 pp 374, 375.

Payment of tax. Tax on a charge under *section 135*, on a gain realised by the exercise of a right to acquire shares obtained before 6 April 1984, may be paid by instalments if (i) the acquisition of the shares was for a consideration not less than the market value (determined as for capital gains tax) of shares of that class when the right was granted (or, if granted before 6 April 1982, 90% of that market value) and (ii) the tax payable exceeds £250 and (iii) an election to pay by instalments is made in writing to the inspector within 60 days after the end of the year of assessment in which the right was exercised. In such cases the tax is payable in equal instalments: for options exercised before 6 April 1983, by three instalments, the first 14 days after the tax is demanded under PAYE regulations, the third on the last day of the third year after the end of the year in which the right was exercised and the second on the date midway between the first and third instalments; for options exercised after 5 April 1983, by five instalments, the first as before, the fifth on the last day of the fifth year after the end of the year in which the right was exercised, the intermediate instalments at regular intervals between. If the first instalment is not due until after the final instalment is due, then all instalments become due on the later date. All tax may be paid early and will become due immediately if the taxpayer becomes bankrupt. The gain is to be treated as being the highest part of the taxpayer's income of the year of assessment in which the right was exercised, subject to any other provisions for determining the highest part of his income. If the consideration is less than required in (i) above only because the shares are diminished in market value solely because the share capital of the issuing company was varied after the right to acquire the shares was granted, the consideration is treated as being not less than that required under (i). [*ICTA 1988, s 137*]. Where the tax charged under the Schedule E assessment for the year in which the gain arises is less than that attributable to the gain (because e.g. of offset losses), the instalment arrangements apply only to the tax payable under the assessment (i.e. it is not possible to claim instalment payment of the full amount of the tax attributable to the gain and a refund of tax deducted under PAYE) (*Hunt v Murphy Ch D 1991, 64 TC 427*).

Simon's Direct Tax Service. See **E4.521** *et seq.*.

82.4 'SHARE INCENTIVES' — CHARGE TO TAX

Shares acquired before 26 October 1987. The provisions in *ICTA 1988, ss 138–140* **do not apply to shares acquired after 25 October 1987,** for which see the provisions of *FA 1988, Pt III, Ch II* described below. In relation to shares acquired before 26 October 1987, the following continues to apply, but see the transitional provisions under the *FA 1988* scheme.

Where (unless exempted as below) the holder of an office or employment, the emoluments from which are chargeable to tax under Case I of Schedule E, acquires shares (or an interest in shares) in a company under a right or opportunity given him by reason of that office or employment, he is chargeable to income tax under Schedule E, as earned income, (*a*) on the value of any benefit, not applicable to the majority of the ordinary shareholders, which he receives in respect of such shares acquired after 5 April 1972 and before 26 October 1987, and

(*b*) at the end of seven years from the acquisition (or, if earlier, when he parts with the shares or they cease to be subject to specified restrictions (see *ICTA 1988, s 138(6)(9)(c)*) on any excess of their market value then over their value when acquired. [*ICTA 1988, s 138(1)(9)(12), s 140(1)(a)*].

A right, etc. is 'offered' to the taxpayer although he may himself have stipulated its being granted (*CIR v Herd CS, [1992] STC 264*).

For the circumstances in which the Revenue will accept that shares or share options were acquired by a director or employee in a different capacity and not by reason of the office or employment, see Revenue Inspector's Manual, IM 5329.

Neither (*a*) nor (*b*) above applies if the shares are acquired:

(i) in pursuance of an offer to the public [*ICTA 1988, s 138(1)*]; or

(ii) under an arrangement whereby a company gives its employees, as part of their emoluments, shares as a predetermined participation in profits, and for new schemes (or existing schemes modified) after 22 March 1973 if (A) equal participation is allowed to all full-time employees taxable under Case I of Schedule E over 25 years of age and with five years continuous service, (B) shares are in a company which is either quoted on a recognised stock exchange or not controlled by another company, (C) shares have no restrictions which may result in subsequent increase in value and (D) shares cannot be exchanged or converted into shares subject to such restrictions [*ICTA 1988, s 138(2)(4)*],

and (*b*) above does not apply:

(1) where immediately after the shares were acquired (A) the shares were not subject to specified restrictions (see *section 138(6)*), nor exchangeable into such shares, and the majority of available shares (exclusive of associated company shareholdings) of the same class were acquired otherwise than as under *section 138(1)* (see above), or (B) the shares were not subject to specified restrictions (see *section 138(6)(a)(b)*), nor exchangeable into such shares, and the majority of the available shares of the same class (as above) were acquired by present or past employees or directors (of the company or a subsidiary) who together had control of the company [*ICTA 1988, s 138(3)(a)*]; or

(2) for acquisitions after 5 April 1984 of shares in authorised unit trusts (see 90.1 UNIT TRUSTS) approved by the Board for this purpose, provided that shares in the employer company (or in any associated company) do not make up more than 10% of the value of the trust investments for a continuous period of one month or more throughout which a director or employee of the employer company has such a right as is dealt with under these provisions to acquire unit trust shares, or retains an interest in shares so acquired. [*ICTA 1988, s 138(3)(b), (7)*].

Before 19 March 1986, the ending of the restrictions specified in *FA 1972, s 79(2A)* (the predecessor to *section 138(6)*) triggered the charge under (*b*) above, but where such restrictions cease after 18 March 1986, the charge is triggered only if, had the shares been acquired immediately after the restrictions were lifted, they would have been excluded from the operation of (*b*) above by virtue of (1) above. [*ICTA 1988, s 138(9)(c)*].

Additional shares (or an interest therein), acquired after 18 March 1986 by virtue of a holding of (or of an interest in) shares which are not excluded from (*b*) above, are for the purposes of (*b*) above treated with the original holding as one holding acquired at the same time and in the same circumstances as the original holding, the market value of the original holding being attributed proportionately over all shares in the new holding. Any consideration given for the additional shares is treated as an increase in the consideration for the original holding and thus as reducing any charge arising under (*b*) above. [*ICTA 1988, s 138(10)(11)*].

The Board has information and penalty powers as regards approval of authorised unit trusts under (2) above. [*ICTA 1988, s 139(6); TMA 1970, s 98*].

As regards (i) above, shares (or an interest in shares) acquired by a director or employee are treated as acquired in pursuance of an offer to the public where

(A) they were acquired at a discount under an offer (the 'discount offer') to directors or employees in their capacity as such;

(B) the discount offer was made in conjunction with an offer to the public on the same terms but without the discount;

(C) the director or employee is chargeable under Schedule E on an amount equal to the discount on shares acquired by him; and

(D) at least 75% of the shares acquired under the discount offer and the offer to the public together were acquired under the offer to the public.

[*ICTA 1988, s 139(1)(2)*].

The amount of the charge under (*b*) is reduced where, under acquisition terms, any increased consideration is subsequently payable or the shares are disposed of at less than market value. [*See 138(8)*].

A profit on the sale of shares was held to be assessable under the legislation, notwithstanding that the employee had purchased the shares through the Stock Exchange (*Cheatle v CIR Ch D 1982, 56 TC 111*).

Company reconstructions, etc. Where shares are disposed of after 18 March 1986 in circumstances such that a 'new holding' of shares is acquired which is treated as the same asset as the original holding under *TCGA 1992, ss 127–130*, the new holding is similarly treated for the purposes of *section 138*. Any consideration given for the new holding is treated as an increase in the consideration for the original holding, and thus as reducing any charge under (*b*) above. Any consideration received for the original holding, other than the new holding, is treated as proportionately increasing the market value of the shares comprised in the new holding at any subsequent time. [*ICTA 1988, s 139(13)*].

See Simon's Direct Tax Service E4.541 *et seq.*.

82.5 **Shares acquired after 25 October 1987.** The provisions at 82.4 above cease to apply in respect of shares acquired after 25 October 1987, and, subject to *ICTA 1988, s 140A* (conditional acquisition of shares — see 82.7 below), are replaced by the following.

Where a person acquires shares, or an interest in shares, in a company in pursuance of a right conferred on him, or opportunity offered him, by reason of his being a director or employee, past, present or future, within Case 1 of Schedule E, of that or any other company, a charge to tax may arise on him (as below) unless the acquisition is made in pursuance of an offer to the public. Where such a right is assigned to a person, and the right was conferred on some other person by reason of the assignee's office or employment, the assignee is treated as having acquired the shares in pursuance of a right conferred on him by reason of that office or employment. [*FA 1988, ss 77, 87(4); FA 1998, s 50(2)*]. An option to acquire shares does not constitute an interest in the shares for this purpose. (ICAEW Memorandum TR 739, para 32, 13 February 1989). A right, etc. is 'offered' to the taxpayer although he may himself have stipulated its being granted (*CIR v Herd CS 1992, 66 TC 77*).

The Revenue consider that all share acquisitions by employees potentially fall within these provisions, regardless of any investment element in the acquisition (e.g. in a management buy-out). (Revenue Schedule E Manual, SE 2908). For the circumstances in which the Revenue will accept that shares or share options were acquired by a director or employee in a different capacity and not by reason of the office or employment, see Revenue Inspector's Manual, IM 5329.

Where combinations of shares in two or more companies are offered to the public, and at the same time shares in one or more but not all of those companies are offered to directors or employees, and the offers are treated for the purposes of *FA 1988, s 68* as a single offer to the public (see 75.36 SCHEDULE E), they are similarly treated for these purposes. [*FA 1991, s 44(9)*].

A charge under Schedule E will arise in the following situations.

(*a*) *Removal of restrictions, etc.* If a 'chargeable event' occurs while he still has a beneficial interest in the shares, and the shares are in a company which was not a 'dependent subsidiary' at the time either of this acquisition or of the 'chargeable event', the charge will be made for the year in which the 'chargeable event' occurs on the amount by which that event increases the value of the interest (or would do so but for some other event).

A '*chargeable event*' is the removal or variation of a restriction, or the creation or variation of a right, relating to the shares, or the imposition or variation of a restriction, or removal or variation of a right, relating to other shares in the company, which increases (or would do so but for another event) the value of the shares. This does not normally apply on the triggering of certain kinds of performance-related rights or restrictions attached at the outset to the shares acquired (known as 'equity ratchets') which are commonly found in management buy-outs. Under these, the managers' share of the company's equity is increased on some predetermined basis by reference to the company's performance. (Revenue Press Release 14 April 1988). It is understood that this applies equally to such arrangements in situations other than management buy-outs. (Tolley's Practical Tax 1995 p 15).

An event is *not* a '*chargeable event*' unless, at any time within the previous seven years, the person acquiring the shares was a director or employee of the company, or of the company as director or employee of which he acquired the shares, or of an 'associated company' of either. Nor is it a '*chargeable event*' if, in relation to all shares of the same class, it is a removal, etc. as above and, at the time of the event, either

(i) the majority of shares of that class are held otherwise than by, or for the benefit of, directors or employees of the company or an 'associated company', or the 'associated company' itself, or

(ii) the company is 'employee-controlled' by virtue of holdings of shares of that class, or

(iii) the company is a subsidiary other than a 'dependent subsidiary', and its shares are of a single class.

[*FA 1988, s 78*].

(*b*) *Shares in dependent subsidiaries.* If the shares are in a company which

(i) was a 'dependent subsidiary' at the time of the acquisition, or

(ii) became one before the person acquiring the shares ceased to have a beneficial interest in them,

and there is a 'chargeable increase' in the value of the shares, the charge is made, for the year in which ends the period for which the 'chargeable increase' is determined, on the amount of the increase (or appropriate part where the interest in the shares is less than full beneficial ownership). If, under the terms of the acquisition, the consideration is subsequently increased, the amount taxable is correspondingly reduced. If, under those terms, the person acquiring the shares subsequently ceases to have any beneficial interest in them by a disposal for consideration less than the value of the shares at the time of the disposal, the amount taxable is reduced by the excess of that value over that consideration.

Where (*b*)(i) above applies, there is a '*chargeable increase*' if the value of the shares, at the earlier of seven years from acquisition and the time when the person acquiring the shares ceases to have any beneficial interest in them, exceeds their value at the time of acquisition.

Where (*b*)(ii) above applies, there is a '*chargeable increase*' if the value of the shares, at the earliest of

(A) seven years from the time of the company becoming a 'dependent subsidiary',

(B) the time when the person acquiring the shares ceases to have any beneficial interest in them, and

(C) the time when the company ceases to be a dependent subsidiary,

exceeds their value at the time when the company became a 'dependent subsidiary', but only if, at some time during the seven years before the company became a 'dependent subsidiary', that person was a director or employee of the company, or of the company as a director or employee of which he acquired the shares, or of an 'associated company' of either of them.

If, before the time by reference to which the chargeable increase is determined, a charge arises under either *ICTA 1988, s 140A(4)* (employee's interest in shares ceasing to be conditional, see 82.7 below) or *ICTA 1988, s 140D(3)* (charge on conversion of convertible shares, see 82.8 below) on any amount in respect of the shares, that amount is deducted from the amount on which tax is chargeable under these provisions.

[*FA 1988, s 79; FA 1998, ss 50(3), 51(2)*].

(*c*) *Special benefits.* If the person acquiring the shares receives a 'special benefit' through his ownership of them, and was at some time during the previous seven years a director or employee as mentioned under (*b*) above, then unless the benefit is taxable under another provision of the *Taxes Acts*, the charge is made for the year in which the benefit is received on the value thereof.

A benefit received when the company is a 'dependent subsidiary' whose shares are of a single class is a '*special benefit*'. In any other case, a benefit is a '*special benefit*' *unless*, when it becomes available, it is available to at least 90% of holders of shares of the same class and, when it is received, either

(i) the majority of shares in respect of which the benefit is received are held otherwise than by, or for the benefit of, directors or employees of the company or an 'associated company', or the 'associated company' itself, or

(ii) the company is 'employee-controlled' by virtue of holdings of shares of the class, or

(iii) the company is a subsidiary which is not a 'dependent subsidiary', and the majority of its shares in respect of which the benefit is received are held otherwise than by, or for the benefit of, directors or employees of the company or of an 'associated company', or by, or for the benefit of, an 'associated company' other than a company of which it is a subsidiary.

[*FA 1988, s 80; F(No 2)A 1992, s 37*].

Any increase or reduction in a person's interest in shares is for these purposes treated as a proportionate acquisition or disposal of a separate interest. [*FA 1988, s 81*].

A company is '*employee-controlled*' for these purposes by virtue of shares of a class if the majority of shares of that class (other than those held by or for an 'associated company') are held by or for employees or directors of the company or a company which it controls, and those employees and directors as holders of the shares are together able to control the company. Control is defined by *ICTA 1988, s 840*. [*FA 1988, s 87(2)(3)*]. '*Associated company*' is as defined by *ICTA 1988, s 416*.

A subsidiary is a '*dependent subsidiary*' throughout a period of account unless

(i) the whole (or substantially the whole) of its business during that period is carried on with persons who are not members of the same group (i.e. the principal company, which is not itself a subsidiary, and all its subsidiaries), and

(ii) during that period, any increase in the value of the company from intra-group transactions not on arm's length terms (other than group relief payments) does not exceed 5% of the company's value at the beginning of the period (or pro rata for periods other than twelve months), and

(iii) the directors of the principal company give the inspector, within two years of the end of the period, a certificate that in their opinion (i) and (ii) are satisfied for that period, and attached to that certificate is a report from the subsidiary's auditors that, after enquiry, they are not aware of anything to indicate that the directors' opinion is unreasonable. [*FA 1988, s 86(1)*].

As regards (i) above, business carried on by a company with a subsidiary is treated as carried on with a non-member of the group unless all (or substantially all) of the business of that or any other subsidiary during the period of account is carried on with members of the group other than the company and its subsidiaries. [*FA 1988, s 86(2)*]. Also as regards (i) above, the Revenue consider that, to meet this condition, at least 90% of the company's business must be carried on outside the group, although a higher percentage may be required in any particular case. (Revenue Schedule E Manual, SE 2923).

Connected persons. Shares acquired by a person connected with a director or employee (within *ICTA 1988, s 839*, see 20 CONNECTED PERSONS) are deemed to be acquired by the director or employee for these purposes, as is any benefit received by such a connected person. A disposal, other than by an arm's length bargain with a non-connected person, is disregarded for these purposes until there is an onward disposal by such a bargain (except that this does not apply if the disposal is to the company concerned under the terms on which the shares were acquired), and any benefit received during such deemed ownership is deemed to be received by the person who originally acquired the shares. [*FA 1988, s 83*].

Company reorganisations. Any additional shares acquired by virtue of a holding within these provisions is treated as having been acquired at the same time, and in like manner, as the originally-acquired shares (whether or not consideration was given for the additional shares). As regards (*b*) above, all the shares are treated as one holding, their value being determined accordingly and the acquisition value allocated proportionately, and any consideration given for the additional shares is treated as additional consideration for the originally-acquired shares under the terms of the original acquisition.

If the shares originally acquired are converted into a new holding (within *TCGA 1992, ss 127–130*), the original and new holdings are equated for the purposes of these provisions, any new consideration *given* is treated as additional consideration under the terms of the original acquisition, and any consideration *received* is apportioned among the shares in the new holding, whose value is increased accordingly. [*FA 1988, s 82*].

Capital gains tax. Any amount charged under these provisions is treated as allowable expenditure for capital gains tax purposes on the first disposal (subject to the CONNECTED PERSONS (20) rules, see above). [*TCGA 1992, s 120(1)*].

Information. The company whose shares are acquired (and, if different, the company as a director or employee of which they were acquired) must, under penalty, notify the inspector of the acquisition and of any chargeable event or special benefit (see (*a*), (*c*) above) in relation to those shares. [*FA 1988, s 85*]. Information should be sent to Inland Revenue, Employee Share Schemes Unit, Savings and Investment Division, First Floor, SW Wing, Bush House, Strand, London WC2B 4RD. (Revenue Tax Bulletin February 1994 p 110).

Transitional provisions. If tax is chargeable under the earlier provisions applying to shares acquired before 26 October 1987 (see 82.4 above) by reference to the market value after that date of shares in a company which is not a dependent subsidiary (see above) on that date, and that market value is greater than the market value on that date, the latter is substituted.

Except as regards (*b*) and (*c*) above, the new provisions apply to shares acquired before 26 October 1987, unless the company was a dependent subsidiary on that date. However, the removal of a restriction on such shares is not a chargeable event (see (*a*) above) if it would have been excluded from being a chargeable event before that date by *FA 1973, Sch 8 para 7*. [*FA 1988, s 88*].

See Simon's Direct Tax Service E4.531 *et seq.*.

82.6 *Example*

E, an employee of Perks Ltd, exercised, on 1 June 1987, an option, conferred on him by reason of his employment, to acquire 3,000 shares in that company, their open market value at that time being £12,000. He was duly charged to tax under Schedule E under the rules in 82.3 above. The shares were subject to one of the restrictions in *section 138(6)*. Market value per share at 26 October 1987 and at 1 June 1994 was £4.50 and £4.75 respectively. On 1 November 2000, a chargeable event under *FA 1988, s 78(2)* occurs by virtue of the restriction being removed. Removal of the restriction increases the value per share from £5.00 to £7.50. E has remained in the company's employment throughout the period and at no time has the company been a 'dependent subsidiary'.

E will be charged to income tax under Schedule E as follows.

		£	£
(i) Charge under ICTA 1988, s 138(1)(a) in 1994/95			
Market value at 26.10.87	note (*a*)	13,500	
Less market value at 1.6.87		12,000	
			£1,500
(ii) *Charge under FA 1988, s 78(3) in 2000/01*			
Increase in market value resulting from chargeable event (3,000 × £2.50)	note (*b*)		£7,500

Notes

(*a*) A charge arises on the seventh anniversary of acquisition (1 June 1994), but under the transitional provisions of *FA 1988, s 88(2)* it is calculated by reference to market value at 26 October 1987 as this is less than market value at 1 June 1994.

(*b*) The charge under *FA 1988, s 78(3)* is on the increase in value as a result of the chargeable event. Note that the increase between 26 October 1987 and 31 October 2000 escapes any charge to income tax. If the value had decreased, no relief would have been available for the decrease.

(*c*) On a sale of the shares, the capital gains tax base cost would include the amounts chargeable under (i) and (ii) above, such amounts being regarded as consideration given for the acquisition of the shares under *TCGA 1992, s 120(5)* and *s 120(1)* respectively (see Tolley's Capital Gains Tax).

82.7 CONDITIONAL ACQUISITION OF SHARES

Where a conditional beneficial interest in company shares is acquired **on or after 17 March 1998** by any person (the 'employee') as a director (as widely defined) or employee of that or any other company, there is no charge to tax in respect of that acquisition (other than under *ICTA 1988, s 135* or *s 162*, see 82.3 above, 75.19 SCHEDULE E) provided the interest will cease to be conditional within five years or less. As regards shares acquired before 27 July 1999 on terms such that the interest could continue to be conditional for more than five years, there was a specific Schedule E charge under *ICTA 1988, s 140A(2)* on the basis that the interest was emoluments of the employment. As regards shares acquired on or after that date on such terms, there is no such specific charge, but a charge to tax may nevertheless arise under the normal rules at 75.36 SCHEDULE E.

Shares for these purposes includes securities. See below as regards whether shares are acquired by an employee as a director or employee of a company.

Whether or not the conditionality may or will continue for more than five years, if and when it ceases without the employee's beneficial interest ceasing, or the employee (without previously having become chargeable under this provision) disposes of any beneficial interest in the shares, a charge arises under Schedule E. The charge is on the amount (if any) by which the open market value of the original interest immediately after the event in question exceeds the sum of

(*a*) any consideration given for the original interest,

(*b*) any amount brought into charge under Schedule E in respect of acquisition of that interest, and

(*c*) any amount brought into charge under *FA 1988, s 78* or *s 79* (see 82.5 above) in respect of the shares on an earlier or simultaneous event.

(*a*) above includes consideration given by the employee or by any other person whose acquisition of the shares is within these provisions (see below). The amount of consideration taken into account includes any given for a right to acquire the shares or by virtue of which the interest in the shares ceases to be conditional (with apportionment of sums partly in respect of other matters on a just and reasonable basis). The performance by the director or employee of any duties of or in connection with the office or employment by reference to which the interest was acquired is not consideration for this purpose. There is provision to prevent the double counting of any consideration. *ICTA 1988, s 136(1)–(3)* (see 82.3(*a*) above) apply for determining the consideration where rights are exchanged.

Treatment of interest in shares as conditional. A beneficial interest in shares is treated as conditional for these purposes for so long as the terms (however imposed) on which the employee is entitled to the interest:

(i) provide that if certain circumstances arise, or do not arise, there will be a transfer, reversion or forfeiture as a result of which the employee will cease to be entitled to any beneficial interest in the shares; and

(ii) are not such that the employee will thereon be entitled to receive an amount equal to or more than the open market value of the interest at that time (disregarding the provision for transfer, reversion or forfeiture).

The 'circumstances' under (i) above may include the expiration of a period specified in or determined under the terms, or the death of any person, and the exercise by any person of any power conferred on the person by or under the terms.

The employee's interest in a company's shares is *not* treated as conditional by reason only that:

(A) where there is no restriction on the meeting of calls by the employee, the shares are unpaid or partly paid and may be forfeited for non-payment of calls; or

(B) the articles of association of the company require the employee to offer the shares for sale, or transfer them, on ceasing to be an officer or employee of the company or of any one or more companies in the same 51% group; or

(C) the employee may be required to offer the shares for sale, or transfer them, on ceasing, by reason of misconduct, to be an officer or employee of the company or of any one or more companies in the same 51% group; or

(D) in the case of securities, the securities may be redeemed on payment of any amount.

The term 'articles of association' in (B) above does not include foreign company equivalents. For this and other points concerning (A)–(D) above, see Revenue Tax Bulletin April 2000 pp 731–733, 736.

Shares acquired as director or employee. For the above purposes a person acquires shares as a director or employee of a company

(I) if he acquires them in pursuance of a right or opportunity available to him by reason of his holding or having held the office or employment, or

(II) if the shares are assigned to him after being acquired by some other person by reason of the assignee's holding or having held the office or employment, or

(III) if a right or opportunity in pursuance of which he acquires them is assigned to him after being made available to some other person by reason of the assignee's holding or having held the office or employment.

Only offices or employments within Case I of Schedule E (see 75.2 SCHEDULE E) are considered for these purposes (and this applies to the last chargeable period in which the office or employment was held in the case of a past holder).

Where

(*aa*) a person has (or is treated as having) acquired a conditional interest in any shares as a director or employee of a company, and

(*bb*) as a result of any two or more transactions he ceases to be entitled to that interest and he or a connected person (see 20 CONNECTED PERSONS) becomes entitled to any conditional interest in any shares,

that person is treated as if the interest to which he becomes entitled were also acquired by him as a director or employee of the company in question.

For these purposes references to shares or securities include references to interests in shares or securities.

Death of the employee. Where the employee dies holding the original interest, the above provisions apply as if he had disposed of that interest immediately before his death, and as if the open market value at that time were to be determined on the basis that it is known that the disposal is being made immediately before the employee's death and that any restriction on disposal subject to which the shares were held is to be disregarded in so far as it is a restriction terminating on death.

Information powers. Where any person provides an individual with a conditional interest in shares in circumstances such that a charge may arise under these provisions, each 'relevant person' must deliver to the Revenue written particulars of the interest and its provision. Similarly where an employee has a conditional interest in shares and a charge arises as above on the conditionality ceasing, or on the shares being disposed of or the employee dying, each 'relevant person' must deliver to the Revenue written particulars of the shares and the event giving rise to the charge. The '*relevant persons*' are the person who provided the shares in question and the person under or with whom the office or employment in question was held. In each case the particulars must be delivered within 30 days after the end of the year of assessment in which the interest is provided or the event occurs. Penalties apply for failure to comply.

[*ICTA 1988, ss 140A–140C, s 140G, s 140H; FA 1998, ss 50, 52, 53; FA 1999, ss 42, 43*].

For the requirement to operate PAYE on amounts chargeable by virtue of the conditionality ceasing or any disposal of the employee's beneficial interest, see 55.2(*e*) PAY AS YOU EARN.

For notes on the interaction between the above provisions and both *ICTA 1988, s 162* (see 75.19 SCHEDULE E) and *FA 1988, ss 78, 79* (see 82.5 above), see Revenue Tax Bulletin April 2000 pp 733, 734.

For *capital gains tax* purposes, an acquisition within the above provisions is not treated under *TCGA 1992, s 17* as an acquisition at market value. Instead, the consideration for the acquisition is taken as the actual amount of the consideration (determined as above), subject to any addition in respect of any amount brought into charge under the above provisions (see 82.2 above). This does not affect the calculation of the consideration received by the person from whom the acquisition is made. [*TCGA 1992, s 149B; FA 1998, s 54(5)*].

As regards shares acquired **before 17 March 1998** and subject to risk of forfeiture, it was originally the Revenue's view that an income tax charge arose when that risk was lifted and by reference to the value of the shares at that time. Following legal advice received on 26 May 1995, they now take the view that a charge arises at the time of acquisition and by reference to the then value of the shares taking into account the risk of forfeiture, with no charge arising on the risk being lifted. Where the relevant tax return was made before 27 March 1995 on the basis of the original Revenue view, the position will not be reconsidered. In the case of later returns made on that basis, and subject to an error or mistake claim (see 17.10 CLAIMS) where a tax liability has otherwise become final, the Revenue will charge tax according to their revised view but will postpone collection of tax thereby due for the tax year of acquisition (and also the date from which interest on unpaid tax accrues) until after risk of forfeiture is lifted. Such tax will not be charged, or will be written off, if the shares are forfeited. The capital gains tax acquisition cost of the shares will follow the income tax treatment. See Revenue Tax Bulletin June 1998 pp 545–548.

82.8 CONVERTIBLE SHARES PROVIDED TO DIRECTORS AND EMPLOYEES

A special Schedule E charge may arise where, **on or after 17 March 1998**, a person (the 'employee') acquires 'convertible' shares in a company as a director (as widely defined) or employee of that or any other company. Shares are '*convertible*' for this purpose if they confer on the holder an immediate or conditional entitlement to convert them into shares of a different class, or are held on terms (however imposed) which authorise or require the grant of such an entitlement to the holder if certain circumstances arise or do not arise. Such 'circumstances' may include the expiration of a period specified in or determined under the terms, or the death of any person, and the exercise by any person of any power conferred on the person by or under the terms.

See below as regards whether shares are acquired by an employee as a director or employee of a company.

Subject to the exceptions referred to below, the charge arises if, at a time when the employee has a beneficial interest in the shares, they are converted into shares of a different class in pursuance of such a conversion entitlement, and is made for the year of assessment in which the conversion occurs.

The charge is on the amount (if any) by which the open market value at the time of the conversion of the shares into which the convertible shares are converted exceeds the sum of

(*a*) any consideration given for the convertible shares or for the conversion,

(*b*) any amount brought into charge under Schedule E in respect of the acquisition of the shares,

(*c*) any amount brought into charge under *FA 1988, s 78* or *s 79* (see 82.5 above) in respect of the shares on an earlier or simultaneous event, and

(*d*) if the convertible shares were acquired through a series of conversions within these provisions, the amount of the gain from each such conversion (so far as not within (*b*) above).

(*a*) above includes consideration given for acquisition of the shares by the employee or by any other person whose acquisition of the shares is within these provisions (see below). The amount of consideration taken into account includes any given for a right to acquire the shares, and sums partly in respect of one thing and partly in respect of another are apportioned on a just and reasonable basis. The performance by the director or employee of any duties of or in connection with the office or employment by reference to which the shares were acquired is not consideration for this purpose. There is provision to prevent the double counting of any consideration. *ICTA 1988, s 136(1)–(3)* (see 82.3(*a*) above) apply for determining the consideration where rights are exchanged.

These provisions apply in relation to an interest in shares as they apply in relation to shares.

Exceptions. No charge arises under these provisions if the conversion is of all the shares of one class only into shares of one other class only, and immediately before the conversion the majority of the company's shares of the original class are either:

(i) held otherwise than by or for the benefit of

  (*a*) directors (as widely defined) or employees of the company or of an associated company (within *ICTA 1988, s 416*), or

  (*b*) an associated company; or

(ii) (disregarding any held by or for the benefit of an associated company) held by or for the benefit of directors or employees of the company, or of another company having control (within *ICTA 1988, s 840*) of the company, who are together able as holders of those shares to control the company.

There is similarly no charge under these provisions where the employee's interest in the shares into which the convertible shares are converted is a conditional interest within *ICTA 1988, s 140A* (see 82.7 above).

Shares acquired as director or employee. For the above purposes a person acquires shares as a director or employee of a company

(I) if he acquires them in pursuance of a right or opportunity available to him by reason of his holding or having held the office or employment, or

(II) if the shares are assigned to him after being acquired by some other person by reason of the assignee's holding or having held the office or employment, or

(III) if a right or opportunity in pursuance of which he acquires them is assigned to him after being made available to some other person by reason of the assignee's holding or having held the office or employment.

Only offices or employments within Case I of Schedule E (see 75.2 SCHEDULE E) are considered for these purposes (and this applies to the last chargeable period in which the office or employment was held in the case of a past holder).

Rights and opportunities for this purpose include any arising from the fact that any shares acquired (or treated as acquired) as a director or employee are convertible. Without prejudice to this, where

(*aa*) a person has (or is treated as having) acquired any convertible shares as a director or employee of a company, and

(*bb*) as a result of any two or more transactions he ceases to be entitled to those shares and he or a connected person (see 20 CONNECTED PERSONS) becomes entitled to any convertible shares,

that person is treated as if the shares to which he becomes entitled were also acquired by him as a director or employee of the company in question.

For these purposes references to shares include references to interests in shares.

Death of the employee. Where shares in which a person has an interest at the time of his death are, wholly or partly as a consequence of his death, converted into shares of a different class on or within twelve months after the death, these provisions apply as if the conversion had taken place immediately before the death in pursuance of a conversion entitlement conferred on the deceased.

Information powers. Where any person provides an individual with convertible shares, which are subsequently converted into shares of a different class in circumstances such that a charge may arise under these provisions, each 'relevant person' must deliver to the Revenue written particulars of the shares and their conversion. The '*relevant persons*' are the person who provided the shares in question and the person under or with whom the office or employment in question was held. In each case the particulars must be delivered within 30 days after the end of the year of assessment in which the conversion takes place. Penalties apply for failure to comply.

[*ICTA 1988, ss 140D–140H; FA 1998, ss 51–53*].

For the requirement to operate PAYE on amounts chargeable under the above provisions, see 55.2(*e*) PAY AS YOU EARN.

82.9 PROFIT SHARING SCHEMES — APPROVAL

The provisions of *ICTA 1988, ss 186, 187, Sch 9* allow directors and employees of companies to receive shares free of income tax under certain conditions.

Approved profit sharing schemes are being **phased out** following the introduction of employee share ownership plans (see 82.11 below). A scheme will not be approved by the Board unless the application for approval, accompanied by necessary particulars, is received by them before 6 April 2001. No appropriations of shares to employees may be made after 31 December 2002 under approved schemes. [*ICTA 1988, s 186(1); FA 2000, s 49*]. In the meantime, approval will be withdrawn if shares are appropriated to a participant who has already had *free shares* appropriated to him in the same tax year under an approved employee share ownership plan established by the same company (or by a 'connected company', as defined) (or to a participant who would have had such shares appropriated to him but for his failure to meet set performance targets). [*ICTA 1988, Sch 9 para 3(2)(4)–(6); FA 2000, s 51*].

Otherwise, under a scheme approved by the Board a company provides funds to UK resident trustees who purchase certain defined shares (see below) and appropriate such shares to eligible employees (see below). The limit on the market value of shares which may be appropriated to any one individual in any year of assessment is the greater of £3,000 and 10% of his salary (net of pension contributions — CCAB Memorandum TR 511, 26 August 1983) for PAYE purposes (less any benefits taxable, see 75.11 *et seq.*, 75.29 SCHEDULE E) for that year (or for the preceding year if greater), subject to a ceiling of £8,000. An employee to whom the trustees have appropriated shares ('a participant') contracts (i) not to assign or dispose of his beneficial interest in the shares within a 'period of retention' (see below); (ii) to permit the trustees to retain his shares for that period; (iii) to pay to the trustees a sum equal to income tax at the basic rate on the 'appropriate percentage' of the 'locked-in value' (see 82.10 below) should he direct them to transfer the shares to him before the 'release date', and (iv) not to direct them to dispose of his shares before the release date other than by sale for the best consideration obtainable or, if the shares are redeemable shares in a 'workers' co-operative', by redemption. The participant may, however, at any time direct the trustees to accept, in respect of his shares, certain share exchanges or other offers (including, in certain cases, qualifying corporate bonds) made to all holders of the same class of shares. Any contravention of (i) above renders him ineligible for the tax relief (and he is charged to tax as at the time the shares were appropriated to him). With effect after 20 March 2000, the Board must be satisfied both that the arrangements (as widely defined) of the scheme do not provide, directly or otherwise, for loans to be made to any of the employees of the company or of a participating company in a group scheme and that the operation of the scheme is in no way associated with such loans. Alterations to the scheme must be approved. Approval of a scheme may be withdrawn if Board ceases to be satisfied with conditions. Appeal is available to the Special Commissioners within thirty days of notification of the Board's decision to refuse approval of a scheme or of an alteration in a scheme or in the trust deed.

[*ICTA 1988, s 186(1), s 187(2)(5), Sch 9 para 2(2)–(2B), para 3(2), paras 4–6, Sch 10 para 1, para 6(1)(2); FA 1989, s 63; FA 1991, s 41; FA 1994, s 101; FA 2000, s 53*]. See *CIR v Burton Group plc Ch D 1990, 63 TC 191*, where an appeal against Revenue refusal of approval of a share option scheme under identical statutory provisions was upheld.

'*Period of retention*' begins on the date the shares are appropriated to the participant and ends two years later or, if earlier, at cessation of employment due to injury, disability, redundancy or death, or on reaching the 'relevant age' or, if the shares are redeemable shares in a 'workers' co-operative', on his ceasing to be employed by, or by a subsidiary of, the co-operative. [*ICTA 1988, Sch 10 para 2; FA 1991, s 38(3)*].

The '*relevant age*' must be specified in the scheme rules, must be the same for men and women, and must not be less than 60 or more than 75. In relation to schemes approved before 25 July 1991, it is the normal state pensionable age (although in practice the Revenue have permitted the alteration of scheme rules to make the relevant age 60 for both men and women for this purpose). [*ICTA 1988, Sch 9 para 8A; FA 1991, s 38(5)*].

The '*release date*' is the third anniversary of the date of appropriation of the shares to the participant if that anniversary occurs on or after 29 April 1996. Previously, it was the fifth anniversary of the date of appropriation, except that 29 April 1996 is itself the release date if it falls after the third anniversary but before the fifth anniversary. [*ICTA 1988, s 187(2); FA 1996, s 116*].

A '*workers' co-operative*' is a registered industrial and provident society within *ICTA 1988, s 486* (see Tolley's Corporation Tax under Industrial and Provident Societies) which is a co-operative society whose rules restrict membership to employees of the society, or of a subsidiary of the society, and trustees of its profit-sharing scheme, all of whom must be entitled to membership subject to any qualifications as regards age, length of service or other factors. Where the rules of the society include provisions to enable it to set up such a scheme, these provisions are disregarded in determining whether the society is a *bona fide* co-operative society within the *Industrial and Provident Societies Act 1965* (or NI equivalent). [*ICTA 1988, s 187(10); FA 1986, s 24*].

A specimen set of scheme documents is included in the explanatory notes for employers, Revenue Pamphlet IR 96, available free of charge from Inland Revenue Information Centre, Ground Floor, SW Wing, Bush House, Strand, London WC2B 4RD (tel. 020–7438 6420/6425/7772). A non-technical explanatory booklet (IR 95) aimed at employees is also available from local tax offices and tax enquiry centres.

The shares must be (*a*) quoted on a recognised stock exchange or (*b*) in a company not controlled by another company or (*c*) in a company controlled by a quoted company (other than a company which is, or would be if resident in the UK, a close company); and they must be ordinary shares of the company concerned, its controlling company or a company (or its controlling company) which is a member of a consortium owning the company concerned (or its controlling company). The shares must be fully paid up, not redeemable (unless they are shares in a workers' co-operative) and (except as below) not subject to any restrictions differing from those attaching to other shares of the same class. Certain restrictions connected with cessation of employment may apply to scheme shares without applying to all shares of the same class. The articles of association may impose a restriction requiring all shares held by directors or employees to be disposed of on cessation of the employment, and all shares acquired by persons who are not directors or employees, but which were acquired in pursuance of rights or interests obtained by directors or employees, to be disposed of immediately they are so acquired. The required disposal must be by sale for money on specified terms, and the articles must also provide that any person disposing of shares of the same class (however acquired) may be required to sell them on the same terms. The restriction must not, however, require a disposal before the release date of shares the ownership of which has not been transferred to the participant, unless the shares are redeemable shares in a workers' co-operative. After 20 March 2000, but not so as to affect shares acquired by the scheme trustees on or before that date, scheme shares must not carry any restrictions affecting the rights attaching to them as regards dividends or assets on a winding-up, unless those restrictions apply to all other ordinary shares in the company.

Where there is more than one class of shares, the majority of the class of shares appropriated under the scheme must either (i) be held by persons other than directors or employees who received special rights of acquisition, or trustees for such persons or where shares are within (*c*) above and not within (*a*) above, companies which control the company whose shares are in question or of which that company is an associated company (as defined), or (ii) be '*employee-control shares*', i.e. shares held by persons who are or have been directors or employees, and who are together able to control the company by virtue of their holdings.

After 20 March 2000, but not so as to affect shares acquired by the scheme trustees on or before that date, the shares must not be shares in companies ('*employer companies*') whose business is substantially the provision of the services of its employees either to businesses, including partnerships, who control the company or to associated companies. The prohibition extends to shares in certain companies which have control of employer companies.

[*ICTA 1988, Sch 9 paras 10–12, 14; FA 1989, s 64; FA 2000, s 52*].

Persons eligible must include all employees (for schemes approved before 1 May 1995, all full-time employees) and full-time directors subject to tax under Case I of Schedule E (and may include any person who was such during the eighteen months preceding appropriation of shares to him, part-timers, and those chargeable under Case II or Case III of Schedule E) and employed for a maximum qualifying period of five years by the company or group concerned and all those who do participate must do so on similar terms (although variations by reference to salary, length of service, etc. do not prevent this condition being met). The terms must not in effect either discourage any description of eligible participant, or confer benefits wholly or mainly on directors or the highest-paid employees in a group scheme. A person is not eligible if, in the same year of assessment, shares have been appropriated to him under another approved scheme by the company or group concerned, or if within the preceding twelve months he and/or certain associates of his had a material (broadly more than 25% of ordinary share capital) interest in such a company which was a close company or would be if it were resident in the UK or if its shares were not publicly quoted. [*ICTA 1988, s 187(3), Sch 9 para 2(3)(4), para 8, paras 35–40; FA 1989, s 65; FA 1995, s 137(4)(7)*].

See 71.54 SCHEDULE D, CASES I AND II as regards deduction available to company for expenses in setting up the scheme and in meeting expenses of trustees in administering the scheme and acquiring shares under the scheme.

Personal equity plans. See 29.21 EXEMPT INCOME for the transfer of shares emerging from profit-sharing schemes into personal equity plans.

Simon's Direct Tax Service. See **E4.561–E4.571**.

82.10 PROFIT SHARING SCHEMES — CHARGE TO TAX

Note that profit sharing schemes are being **phased out** and that no appropriations of shares to employees may be made after 31 December 2002 under approved schemes (see 82.9 above).

There is no charge to income tax on an eligible employee when the shares are appropriated to him. [*ICTA 1988, s 186(2)*]. On disposal or other chargeable event before the 'release date', tax is chargeable under Schedule E for the year of assessment in which the disposal or event takes place on a percentage of the 'locked-in' value (see below) as follows.

Disposals etc. on or after 29 April 1996:	
Before third anniversary of appropriation	100%
Disposals etc. before 29 April 1996:	
Before fourth anniversary of appropriation	100%
On or after fourth anniversary and before fifth anniversary	75%
On or after fifth anniversary	No charge

The '*release date*' is the third anniversary of the date of appropriation of the shares to the participant if that anniversary occurs on or after 29 April 1996. Previously, it was the fifth anniversary of the date of appropriation, except that 29 April 1996 is itself the release date if it falls after the third anniversary but before the fifth anniversary.

If the participant ceases employment with the company because of injury, disability, redundancy or reaching the 'relevant age' before the disposal and before the third anniversary (for disposals before 29 April 1996, before the fifth anniversary), the appropriate percentage is 50%. The '*relevant age*' in relation to schemes approved on or after 25 July 1991 must be specified in the scheme rules, must be the same for men and women, and must not be less than 60 or more than 75. For schemes approved before that date, it is generally the normal state pensionable age. However, in practice, such older schemes have been permitted to alter their rules to make 60 the relevant age for men as well as women for the purposes of the period of retention rules (see 82.9 above), and where this has been the case, for events occurring after 29 November 1993 (and after the scheme rules were altered), the relevant age for men for the purposes of determining the appropriate percentage is also 60.

[*ICTA 1988, s 186(4), s 187(2), Sch 10 para 3; FA 1991, s 38; FA 1994, s 100; FA 1996, ss 116, 117*].

Locked-in value of shares is their initial market value when appropriated to the employee (or any earlier dates as agreed in writing between the Board and the trustees) as reduced by any capital receipt charged to income tax under these provisions (see below), or the disposal proceeds, if less.

Proceeds are reduced by any payment to the trustees previously made for a rights issue but payments received from a disposal of rights are disregarded. Disposals are allocated to appropriations on a first in, first out basis. [*ICTA 1988, s 186(5)–(10), s 187(8), Sch 9 para 30(4); FA 1996, s 117(2), s 134, Sch 20 para 11*].

Any **excess or unauthorised shares** (i.e. in excess of the limit (see 82.9 above) or appropriated to a person not eligible (see 82.9 above)) are chargeable to tax on the market value at whichever is the earlier: date of disposal; release date; or death. The charge on anniversary of appropriation is applied by reference to authorised shares before excess or unauthorised shares. [*ICTA 1988, Sch 10 para 6*].

Capital receipts are charged on the appropriate percentage (as above) and after any appropriate allowance (see below) for the year in which the trustees or the participant become entitled to them but do not include (*a*) taxable income in hands of recipient or (*b*) disposal proceeds on any of the chargeable events referred to above or (*c*) new shares issued in a company reconstruction under *TCGA 1992, ss 132, 136* (except redeemable shares not issued for new consideration or bonus issues following repayment of share capital and stock dividends) or (*d*) proceeds of rights used to exercise other rights. Capital receipts are charged only on the excess over the 'appropriate allowance', which, for any tax year, is £20 multiplied by one plus the number of years which fall within the three years (before 1997/98, five years) immediately preceding the year in question and in which the shares were appropriated to the participant, up to a maximum of £60 (before 1997/98, £100). If more than one capital receipt arises to the trustees or the participant in any year (before the release date), the receipts are set against the appropriate allowance in the order received. [*ICTA 1988, s 186(3)(12), Sch 10 paras 4, 5; FA 1978, s 56(6); FA 1980, s 46(6); FA 1982, s 42(1)(2); FA 1985, s 45(4); FA 1996, s 118*].

PAYE applies to disposals as above. The trustees shall pay to the company out of the disposal proceeds, the sum of money on which tax is chargeable and the company must deduct tax under PAYE and pay the balance to the participant. The company is the employing company or, if more than one, whichever company the Board directs. If there is no appropriate company, the Board may direct the trustees to apply PAYE as if the participant were a former employee of theirs. [*ICTA 1988, Sch 10 para 7*].

Capital gains tax is chargeable on disposal of the shares by the participants, without deduction for any amount determined for purposes of charging income tax under the above provisions. For this purpose, a participant is absolutely entitled to his shares as against the trustees. The allowable cost is the initial market value of the shares. No CGT arises to the trustees if they appropriate shares to participants within eighteen months of acquisition. [*TCGA 1992, s 238(1)(2)*].

Dividends received on shares by the trustees are not liable to the additional rate if the shares are appropriated within eighteen months of acquisition. [*ICTA 1988, s 186(11)*].

Simon's Direct Tax Service. See **E4.572** *et seq.*.

82.11 **EMPLOYEE SHARE OWNERSHIP PLANS**

Introduction. An employee share ownership plan (ESOP) is a plan established by a company, and approved **on or after 28 July 2000** by the Revenue (see 82.24 below), providing for shares to be appropriated without payment to employees (*'free shares'* — see 82.13 below) and/or for shares to be acquired on employees' behalf from sums deducted from their salary (*'partnership shares'* — see 82.14 below). A plan providing for partnership shares may also provide for shares to be appropriated without payment to employees (*'matching shares'* — see 82.15 below) in proportion to the partnership shares acquired by them. See 82.17, 82.18 below for tax consequences in each case. See 82.16 below as to reinvestment of dividends on plan shares. Where a plan provides for more than one of the above kinds of shares, it may leave it to the company to decide when each such provision is to have effect. A plan established by a company which controls (within *ICTA 1988, s 840*) other companies (a *'parent company'*) may extend to one or more of those other companies, whereupon it is known as a *'group plan'*. Companies that for the time being are party to a group plan are known as *'participating companies'*. [*FA 2000, s 47, Sch 8 paras 1, 2, 129(1)*].

The remainder of this coverage is set out under the following headings.

82.12	General requirements etc.	82.20	Performance allowances
82.13	Free shares	82.21	Requirements as to type of share used
82.14	Partnership shares	82.22	Company reconstructions/ Rights issues
82.15	Matching shares	82.23	The plan trustees
82.16	Dividend shares	82.24	Revenue approval and information powers
82.17	Income tax consequences for participants	82.25	Termination of plan
82.18	Capital gains tax		
82.19	Eligibility of employees		

See 71.54 SCHEDULE D, CASES I AND II as regards deductions which the employer company may make for corporation tax purposes.

Guidance, including model plan rules, trust deed and share agreements, is provided by the Revenue on a dedicated website at www.inlandrevenue.gov.uk/shareschemes/esp_faqs.htm

82.12 **General requirements.** The purpose of the plan must be to provide benefits to employees by way of shares which give them a continuing stake in a company. A plan must contain no features which are neither essential nor reasonably incidental to that purpose. It *must* provide that every employee who is eligible (as in 82.19 below) in relation to an award of shares under the plan, and whose related employment is within Case I of SCHEDULE E (75), may participate in the award and be invited to do so, and it should not contain any features (other than those required or authorised under these provisions) to discourage participation. It *may* provide for an eligible employee to be invited to participate in an award even though his related employment is *not* within Case I of Schedule E. An individual who *must* be invited, or who under terms as above *may* be invited, to participate in an award is a *'qualifying employee'* in relation to that award.

All employees invited to participate in an award must be invited to participate on the same terms, and those who do participate must actually do so on the same terms. Free shares may be awarded by reference to remuneration, length of service or hours worked, or (within confines) more than one of these factors, but not by reference to other factors. Free shares may, however, be allocated, in accordance with 82.20 below, by reference to performance. Subject to the above, no feature of the plan must have the likely effect of conferring benefits wholly or mainly on directors or employees receiving higher levels of remuneration. In the case of a group, the identity of the company, or of the participating companies in a group plan, must not be such as to have similar likely effect. No conditions may be imposed on an employee's participation in an award, except as required or permitted under these provisions. The arrangements (as broadly defined) for the plan must not provide for loans to employees of the company (or of participating companies in a group plan), and neither those arrangements nor the operation of the plan must in any way be associated with any such loans.

[*FA 2000, Sch 8 paras 6–12*].

Awards of shares. Shares are '*awarded*' under a plan on each occasion when, in accordance with the plan, free or matching shares are appropriated to employees or partnership shares are acquired on behalf of employees. Shares are awarded to a particular employee (a '*participant*') when free or matching shares are appropriated to him, or partnership shares are acquired on his behalf, as part of the global award. [*FA 2000, Sch 8 para 3*].

Shares leaving the plan. Shares '*cease to be subject to the plan*' when

(*a*) they are 'withdrawn from the plan'; or

(*b*) the participant ceases to be in '*relevant employment*' (which term comprises employment by the company and employment by any 'associated' company), in which case his shares cease to be subject to the plan on the date of leaving (but see below for exception); or

(*c*) the plan trustees dispose of the shares in order to meet PAYE obligations (see 82.17 below).

For the purpose of determining any charge to income tax, shares cease to be subject to the plan in the order in which they were awarded to the participant. Shares awarded on the same day cease to be so subject in the order which results in the lowest income tax charge.

Shares are '*withdrawn from the plan*' (see (*a*) above) when, on the direction of the participant (or, after his death, of his personal representatives), the plan trustees either transfer them (whether to the participant etc. or to another person) or dispose of them and similarly account for the proceeds, or when the participant etc. assigns, charges or otherwise disposes of his beneficial interest in them.

For the purposes of (*b*) above and of these provisions generally (except where otherwise stated), two companies are '*associated*' if one controls the other or they are under common control, 'control' being interpreted in accordance with *ICTA 1988, s 416(2)–(6)*.

Where an individual ceases to be in relevant employment during the 'acquisition period' relating to an award of partnership shares, he is treated for the purposes of (*b*) above as ceasing to be in such employment immediately after the shares are awarded to him. The '*acquisition period*' begins with the deduction from salary and ends with the 'acquisition date' or, where relevant, begins with the end of the 'accumulation period' and ends immediately before the 'acquisition date' (see 82.14 below for meaning of terms used here).

[*FA 2000, Sch 8 paras 122, 123, 126*].

Jointly owned companies. To enable a jointly owned company to participate in a group plan (though it cannot thereby participate in more than one), such a company, and any company under its control (within *ICTA 1988, s 840*), is treated as being under the control of each of its two joint owners (though not for the purposes of 82.21(ii) below). [*FA 2000, Sch 8 paras 127, 129(1)*].

In the case of a company registered outside the UK, **shares** include fractions of shares for the purposes of these provisions, where such fractions are recognised under local law. [*FA 2000, Sch 8 para 129(3)*].

82.13 **Free shares.** The 'initial market value' of free shares awarded (see 82.12 above) to a participant in any tax year under a plan providing for free shares (see 82.11 above) must not exceed **£3,000**. The '*initial market value*' of shares is their market value (determined as for capital gains tax purposes) on the date of the award. Where the market value of shares on any date falls to be determined, the Revenue and the plan trustees may agree that it be determined by reference to a different date or a number of specified dates. In arriving at the market value of shares subject to restrictions or to risk of forfeiture (such that the interest that may be acquired is only conditional — see 82.7 above), such restrictions or risk are disregarded. [*FA 2000, Sch 8 paras 23, 24, 125*].

As regards each award of free shares, the plan must require the company to specify a period (the holding period) during which a participant is bound by contract, for so long as he remains in relevant employment (see 82.12 above), to permit his shares to remain in the hands of the trustees and not to assign, charge or otherwise dispose of his beneficial interest. The holding period must not be less than three years, nor more than five, beginning with the date the shares are awarded to the participant, and must be the same for all shares in the same award. See 82.17 below for income tax consequences of free shares leaving the plan. The plan *may* enable different holding periods to be specified from time to time, though not so as to increase the holding period for free shares already awarded. Notwithstanding the foregoing, the participant may direct the trustees to accept or agree to

(*a*) an offer resulting in a new holding being equated with his original free shares for capital gains tax purposes (see Tolley's Capital Gains Tax under Shares and Securities); or

(*b*) an offer of cash and/or a qualifying corporate bond (see Tolley's Capital Gains Tax), with or without other assets, which is part of a general offer designed to give the person making it control of the company; or

(*c*) a transaction pursuant to a compromise, arrangement or scheme affecting all the shares or all the shares of the particular class concerned or all those held by a class of shareholders (identified otherwise than by reference to employment or participation in the plan).

[*FA 2000, Sch 8 paras 31, 32*].

The holding period requirement is subject to the provisions for termination of plans (see 82.25 below) and those requiring the trustees to be enabled to meet certain PAYE obligations (see 82.17 below).

82.14 **Partnership shares.** A plan providing for partnership shares (see 82.11 above) must provide for qualifying employees (see 82.12 below) to enter into agreements ('*partnership share agreements*') with the company whereby the employee authorises the company to make deductions from his salary for the purchase of partnership shares to be awarded to him under the plan. It must specify the amount or percentage to be deducted from salary and the intervals at which deductions are to be made, although the company and employee may agree to vary both of these. It must also contain a notice in prescribed form giving prescribed information as to the possible effect of deductions on an employee's entitlement to social security benefits, statutory sick pay and statutory maternity pay.

The amount deducted from salary must not exceed **£125** in any month (or proportionate amount in the case of non-monthly pay intervals). Furthermore, it must not exceed 10% of the employee's salary, i.e. if the plan provides for an accumulation period (see below), 10% of the salary payments over that period, or, if it does not, 10% of the salary payment from which the deduction is made. The plan may authorise the setting of maximum limits which are lower than the aforementioned; different limits may be set for different awards. Any amount deducted from salary in excess of the applicable limits must be returned to the employee. The plan may also set a minimum deduction limit, which operates by reference to a month (regardless of actual pay intervals) and which cannot exceed £10.

For these purposes an employee's salary means his emoluments otherwise subject to PAYE, excluding any taxable benefits and expenses within 75.11–75.20 SCHEDULE E. See 82.17 below as regards tax relief for amounts deducted.

[*FA 2000, Sch 8 paras 33–38, 48*].

Amounts deducted from salary are to be paid over to the trustees and held by them (in a bank, building society etc.) on the employee's behalf until applied in acquiring partnership shares on his behalf (which includes their appropriating to him shares already held by them). If such monies are held in an interest-bearing account, the plan must require the trustees to account to the employee for the interest.

If the plan does not provide for an accumulation period (see below), it must provide for deductions from salary to be applied as above on the '*acquisition date*', which for *this* purpose is a date which is set by the trustees and is within 30 days after the date of the last salary deduction in relation to the partnership share award in question. Subject to any restriction imposed in accordance with the plan (see below), the number of shares awarded (see 82.12 above) to each employee is to be determined by reference to market value at the acquisition date.

A plan may provide for accumulation periods not exceeding 12 months. If it does so, the partnership share agreement must specify when each such period begins (which in the case of the first period must be no later than the date of the first salary deduction) and ends. The accumulation period for each award of shares must be same for all eligible individuals. Subject to this, the agreement may specify that an accumulation period shall end on the occurrence of a specified event, and may additionally provide that salary deductions be in such cases returned to participants. The plan may provide for continuity in the event of certain share exchanges. The plan must provide for deductions from salary to be applied by the trustees in acquiring, on the employee's behalf, partnership shares on the '*acquisition date*', which for *this* purpose is a date which is set by the trustees and is within 30 days after the end of the accumulation period applicable to the partnership share award in question. Subject to any restriction imposed in accordance with the plan (see below), the number of shares awarded to each employee is to be determined by reference to the lower of market value at the beginning of the accumulation period and market value at the acquisition date. If an employee ceases to be in relevant employment (see 82.12 above) during an accumulation period, salary deductions made must be paid over to him.

Any surplus monies held after acquiring shares as above may, with the employee's agreement, be carried forward to the next deduction or, where applicable, carried forward to the next accumulation period; otherwise they must be paid over to the employee.

The plan *may* authorise the company to restrict the number of shares to be included in a particular partnership share award to a specified maximum, subject to its giving employees advance notification. Where necessary, in such case, the number of shares in each individual award is to be scaled down.

[*FA 2000, Sch 8 paras 39–43*].

An employee may, by written notice to the company, stop salary deductions in pursuance of a partnership share agreement. He may similarly re-start deductions (though the plan *may* impose a limit of one re-start per accumulation period, where applicable) but is not permitted to make up deductions missed. The company must give effect to a notice to stop or re-start within 30 days of receiving it, unless the employee specifies a later date in the notice. An employee may also, again by written notice to the company, withdraw from a partnership share agreement, such notice to take effect within 30 days unless a later date is specified therein. Any monies deducted and still held on his behalf must then be paid over to him. On withdrawal of Revenue approval to a plan (see 82.24 below) or on the issue of a plan termination notice (see 82.25 below), any monies deducted and still held on an employee's behalf must be paid over to him as soon as practicable. [*FA 2000, Sch 8 paras 44–46*].

Access to partnership shares. An employee may at any time withdraw from the plan any or all of the partnership shares awarded to him. See 82.17 below for income tax consequences of withdrawal. [*FA 2000, Sch 8 para 47*].

82.15 **Matching shares.** In a plan providing for matching shares (see 82.11 above), the partnership share agreement (see 82.14 above) must specify the ratio of matching shares to partnership shares for the time being offered by the company and the circumstances and manner in which the ratio may be changed. The ratio must apply by reference to the *number* of shares and must not be greater than **two matching shares to each partnership share**. If the ratio changes before shares are awarded under the agreement, employees must be notified accordingly. Matching shares must be of the same class and carry the same rights as the partnership shares to which they relate. They must be awarded (see 82.12 above) on the day the related partnership shares are awarded and must be awarded to all participants on exactly the same basis. See 82.21 below as to permitted provision for forfeiture. The provisions of *FA 2000, Sch 8 paras 31, 32* (holding period and related matters — see 82.13 above) apply to matching shares as they apply to free shares. [*FA 2000, Sch 8 paras 49–52*].

82.16 **Dividend shares.** The plan *may* provide that, where the company so directs and subject to the limit below, all cash dividends on plan shares are to be reinvested in further shares ('*dividend shares*') on participants' behalf. Participants may be allowed to choose whether or not to reinvest. The company may revoke a direction. Where cash dividends are not required to be reinvested, they must be paid over to the participants.

The maximum dividend reinvestment per participant per tax year is **£1,500**. This is a global limit embracing all approved ESOPs established by the company and its associated companies (within *FA 2000, Sch 8 para 126*). Any cash dividends in excess of the limit must be paid over to the participant.

Dividend shares must be of the same class and carry the same rights as the shares on which the dividend is paid and must not be subject to any provision for forfeiture. The trustees must acquire dividend shares on participants' behalf (which includes their appropriating to participants shares already held by them) on the '*acquisition date*', which for this purpose is a date which is set by the trustees and is within 30 days after they receive the dividend. The number of shares acquired on behalf of each participant is to be determined by reference to market value at the acquisition date. There are provisions for carrying forward for future reinvestment, as a separately identifiable amount, any remaining balance, and for such amounts to be paid over to the participant in certain circumstances.

The holding period, during which dividend shares must not leave the plan (other than on cessation of employment), must be three years. In other respects, the provisions of *FA 2000, Sch 8 paras 31, 32* (holding period and related matters — see 82.13 above) apply to dividend shares as they apply to free shares.

[*FA 2000, Sch 8 paras 53–58*].

82.17 **Income tax consequences for participants.** *General.* An award of shares (see 82.12 above) to an employee, or an acquisition of dividend shares (see 82.16 above) on his behalf, under an approved ESOP does not attract an income tax charge. In addition, the following charging provisions are disapplied:

(i) the notional loan provisions of *ICTA 1988, s 162* (see 75.19 SCHEDULE E) in respect of shares acquired at an undervalue (but not the separate charge under that *section* where shares are disposed of at more than market value);

(ii) (as regards the removal or variation of a permitted provision for forfeiture — see 82.21 below) *ICTA 1988, s 140A* (conditional acquisition — see 82.7 above) and *FA 1988, s 78* (removal of restrictions — see 82.5(*a*) above);

(iii) (if the chargeable event under that provision is the end of the holding period for free, matching or dividend shares) *FA 1988, s 78* (as above); and

(iv) (as regards any shares of the participant that are subject to the plan at the end of the period for which the chargeable increase is determined) *FA 1988, s 79* (charge on increase in value of shares in dependent subsidiaries — see 82.5(*b*) above).

Neither the above exemptions nor the income tax consequences below apply to an individual if, at the time of the award in question, he is not chargeable under Schedule E in respect of the employment by reference to which he meets the employment requirement at 82.19 below.

[*FA 2000, Sch 8 paras 77, 78, 80*].

Capital receipts. Where a 'capital receipt' is received by a participant in respect of, or by reference to, free, matching or partnership shares awarded to him fewer than five years previously or dividend shares acquired on his behalf fewer than three years previously, he is chargeable under Schedule E for the tax year of receipt on the amount or value of the receipt (see below as regards PAYE). For these purposes, a '*capital receipt*' means any money or money's worth except to the extent that

(A) it constitutes taxable income of the recipient (or would do so but for the exemptions conferred by these provisions);

(B) it consists of the disposal proceeds of the shares;

(C) it consists of the proceeds of a part disposal by the trustees (at the direction of the participant) of rights under a rights issue in respect of the shares where those proceeds are used to take up other such rights;

(D) it consists of 'new shares' following a company reconstruction (see 82.22 below); or

(E) it is received by the participant's personal representatives after his death.

[*FA 2000, Sch 8 para 79*].

Free or matching shares leaving plan. If free shares (see 82.13 above) or matching shares (see 82.15 above) cease to be subject to the plan (see 82.12 above) within less than five years of their being awarded to him, the participant is chargeable under Schedule E (subject to the exceptions at (*a*)–(*c*) below). If the shares leave the plan in less than three years, the charge is on their market value (determined as in 82.13 above) when they leave the plan. If they leave the plan after three years or more but less than five years, the charge is on the lower of their market value when they leave the plan and their market value at the date they were awarded. If the latter, the tax is reduced by any tax paid on 'capital receipts' (see above) in respect of the shares.

If, within the holding period (see 82.13, 82.15 above) specified for the award of free or matching shares, the participant, in breach of his obligations under the plan, assigns, charges or otherwise disposes of his beneficial interest, the above does not apply but he is chargeable under Schedule E on the market value of the shares on their leaving the plan. The tax is reduced by any tax paid on 'capital receipts' (see above) in respect of the shares.

There is no charge on free or matching shares leaving the plan after five years or more, nor is there any charge on the forfeiture of such shares.

[*FA 2000, Sch 8 paras 81, 82*].

There is no income tax charge on shares ceasing to be subject to the plan within five years by reason of the participant's ceasing to be in relevant employment (see 82.12 above) due to

(*a*) injury, disability, redundancy (as defined), his employer company losing its 'associated company' status (see 82.12 above), or a transfer within the *Transfer of Undertakings (Protection of Employment) Regulations 1981 (SI 1981 No 1794)*; or

(*b*) his retirement on or after reaching a retirement age specified in the plan, which must be not less than 50 and the same for men and women; or

(*c*) his death.

[*FA 2000, Sch 8 para 87*].

Partnership shares generally. Deductions from an employee's salary in accordance with a partnership share agreement (see 82.14 above) are allowable deductions for income tax purposes. Such deductions are, however, disregarded for the purposes of ascertaining the employee's remuneration for the purposes of RETIREMENT SCHEMES (66) or his relevant earnings for the purposes of PERSONAL PENSION SCHEMES (60) and RETIREMENT ANNUITIES (65). [*FA 2000, Sch 8 para 83*].

An individual is chargeable under Schedule E on any amount deducted from salary and subsequently paid back to him within the provisions of 82.14 above. The charge arises at the time the money is paid back to him. He is similarly chargeable on any money or money's worth received by him in respect of the cancellation of a partnership share agreement entered into by him. [*FA 2000, Sch 8 paras 84, 85*].

Partnership shares leaving plan. If partnership shares (see 82.14 above) cease to be subject to the plan (see 82.12 above) within less than five years of the 'acquisition date', the participant is chargeable under Schedule E (subject to the same exceptions as for free and matching shares — see (*a*)–(*c*) above). (The '*acquisition date*' depends on whether or not there is an accumulation period, and is separately defined in 82.14 above for each such possibility.) If the shares leave the plan in less than three years, the charge is on their market value (determined as in 82.13 above) when they leave the plan. If they leave the plan after three years or more but less than five years, the charge is on the lower of their market value when they leave the plan and the amount of salary deductions used to acquire them. If the latter, the tax is reduced by any tax paid on 'capital receipts' (see above) in respect of the shares. There is no charge on partnership shares leaving the plan after five years or more. [*FA 2000, Sch 8 para 86*].

Dividend shares generally. The amount applied by the trustees in acquiring dividend shares (see 82.16 above) on behalf of a participant is not treated as his income for any tax purposes. He is not entitled to a dividend tax credit in respect of amounts so applied. Any balance carried forward as in 82.16 above is treated in the same way, but any amount eventually paid over to the participant is chargeable to income tax under Schedule F or Schedule D, Case V, whichever is appropriate, as if it were a dividend received by him (with accompanying tax credit) in the tax year in which it is paid over (see 1.9 ALLOWANCES AND TAX RATES for taxation of dividends generally). [*FA 2000, Sch 8 paras 89–92*].

Dividend shares leaving the plan. If dividend shares (see 82.16 above) cease to be subject to the plan (see 82.12 above) within less than three years of their acquisition on the participant's behalf, the participant is chargeable to income tax on a notional dividend (subject to the same exceptions as for free and matching shares — see (*a*)–(*c*) above). The notional dividend is equal to the amount of cash dividend applied to acquire the shares, and is chargeable to income tax under Schedule F or Schedule D, Case V, whichever is appropriate, as if it were a dividend received by the participant (with accompanying tax credit) in the tax year in which the shares cease to be subject to the plan (see 1.9 ALLOWANCES AND TAX RATES for taxation of dividends generally). The tax due (after deduction of tax credits) is reduced by any tax paid on 'capital receipts' (see above) in respect of the shares. There is no charge on dividend shares leaving the plan after three years or more. [*FA 2000, Sch 8 para 93*].

PAYE. Where a tax charge arises as above on shares leaving the plan and those shares are 'readily convertible assets', PAYE must be applied by the 'employer company'. A '*readily convertible asset*' is as defined in *ICTA 1988, s 203F* (see 55.2 PAY AS YOU EARN) except that, in determining for these purposes whether or not shares fall within that definition, there is disregarded any market for the shares which is created by virtue of the trustees acquiring shares for the plan and exists solely for the purposes of the plan. The '*employer company*' is a company of which the participant is an employee when the shares leave the plan and which is within the PAYE regulations. The plan may require the participant to pay to the employer company a sum sufficient to meet the PAYE liability. Otherwise, the trustees must make such payment to the employer company (see 82.23 below as regards the raising of the necessary funds). The company must account for PAYE and return any unused balance to the participant. If there is no employer company, or if the Revenue consider that it is impracticable for the employer company to make a PAYE deduction and so direct, the obligation to make the deduction falls on the trustees instead. *ICTA 1988, s 203C* (non-UK employers — see 55.2 PAY AS YOU EARN) is then disapplied. [*FA 2000, Sch 8 paras 94, 95, 128*].

Where the trustees receive a sum of money by way of a capital receipt chargeable under Schedule E on receipt by the participant (see above), the trustees must pay to the 'employer company' (defined as above but by reference to the time of receipt by the trustees) the amount on which such tax is chargeable. The employer company must make a PAYE deduction and account to the participant for the net amount. The obligation to deduct PAYE may be transferred to the trustees in similar circumstances to those described above. [*FA 2000, Sch 8 para 96*].

Plan trustees. For the tax position of the trustees in respect of dividends on unappropriated shares, see 82.23 below.

82.18 **Capital gains tax.** A participant is treated for capital gains tax purposes as absolutely entitled as against the plan trustees to any shares awarded to him under an approved ESOP. Shares ceasing to be subject to the plan (see 82.12 above) at any time are deemed to have been disposed of and immediately reacquired by the participant at their then market value, but no chargeable gain or allowable loss arises on the deemed disposal. If any of a participant's shares are forfeited (see 82.21 below as regards provision for forfeiture), they are deemed to have been disposed of by the participant and acquired by the plan trustees at their market value at the date of forfeiture, but again no chargeable gain or allowable loss arises. [*FA 2000, Sch 8 paras 99, 101, 102*]. A form of rollover relief is available for shares transferred (other than by a company) to the trustees of an approved ESOP. [*TCGA 1992, s 236A, Sch 7C; FA 2000, s 48, Sch 9*].

For details, see Tolley's Capital Gains Tax under Employee Share Schemes.

82.19 **Eligibility of employees.** An approved ESOP must provide that only an individual who is eligible may participate in an award of shares (see 82.12 above), such eligibility to be judged, in the case of free shares, at the time the award is made and, in the case of partnership shares (and related matching shares), at the time of the salary deduction relating to the award or, if there is an accumulation period (see 82.14 above), the first such salary deduction. An individual is eligible only if the requirements (as detailed below) as to employment, no material interest and non-participation in other share schemes are met. An individual whose related employment is not within Case I of Schedule E must satisfy any further eligibility requirements set out in the plan. [*FA 2000, Sch 8 para 13*].

Employment. The individual must be an employee of the company which established the plan or, in the case of a group plan, of a participating company (see 82.11 above). The plan *may* provide for a qualifying period, in which case the individual is required to have been at all times during that period an employee of the company or of a company that is a participating company at the end of that period. The qualifying period, if any, must be

(i) (in the case of free shares) a period of not more than 18 months ending with the date of the award; and

(ii) (in the case of partnership shares and related matching shares) a period of not more than 18 months ending with the salary deduction related to the award, or, where relevant, a period of not more than six months ending with the start of the accumulation period (see 82.14 above) related to the award.

In relation to an award, the same qualifying period must apply in relation to all employees of the company or, where applicable, of the participating companies. The plan may authorise the company to specify different qualifying periods in respect of different awards.

[*FA 2000, Sch 8 para 14*].

No material interest. An individual is not eligible to participate in an award if he has, or has had within the preceding 12 months, a 'material interest' in

(*a*) a close company whose shares may be awarded under the plan; or

(*b*) a company which has control (within *ICTA 1988, s 840*) of such a company or is a member of a consortium which owns such a company. (For this purpose, a company is a member of a consortium owning another company if it is one of a number of companies which between them beneficially own at least 75% of, and each of which beneficially owns at least 5% of, the other company's ordinary share capital.)

For these purposes, an individual has a '*material interest*' in a company if he, and/or certain associates of his (within *FA 2000, Sch 8 paras 20–22*),

(1) beneficially owns or controls (directly or indirectly) more than 25% of ordinary share capital; or

(2) (where the company is a close company, or would be but for being a non-UK resident company or a quoted company) possesses or is entitled to acquire rights to more than 25% of the assets available for distribution among the participators (within *ICTA 1988, s 417(1)*) in a winding-up or in any other circumstances.

Rights to acquire shares must be taken into account (in accordance with *FA 2000, Sch 8 para 18*). Shares or rights held by trustees of an approved profit sharing scheme (see 82.9 above) or an approved ESOP and *not* appropriated to, or acquired on behalf of, any individual are disregarded.

[*FA 2000, Sch 8 paras 15, 17–19, 129(1)(4)*].

Non-participation in other share schemes. An individual is not eligible to participate in an award of *free* shares in a tax year if in that year

(A) shares have been (or are at the same time to be) appropriated to him under an approved profit sharing scheme (see 82.9 above) established by the same company or by a 'connected company'; or

(B) he has participated (or is at the same time to participate) in another approved ESOP established by the same company or by a 'connected company'.

An individual is not eligible to participate in an award of *partnership* or *matching* shares in a tax year if, in that year, he participates (or is at the same time to participate) in an award of shares under another approved ESOP established by the same company or by a 'connected company'. For the purposes of these requirements, an individual is treated as having participated in an award of free shares under an ESOP if he would have done so but for his failure to obtain a performance allowance (see 82.20 below).

For this purpose, a '*connected company*' is

(I) a company which controls (within *ICTA 1988, s 840*) the first company, or which is controlled by the first company, or which is controlled by a company which also controls the first company; or

(II) a company which is a member of a consortium (as in (*b*) above) owning the first company or which is owned in part by the first company as a member of a consortium.

[*FA 2000, Sch 8 paras 16, 129(1)*].

82.20 **Performance allowances.** If the plan provides for performance allowances, i.e. for the award of free shares, or the number or value of free shares awarded, to be conditional on performance targets being met, the company must use one of the two methods described below.

Under *Method 1*, in relation to a particular award of shares (see 82.12 above),

(*a*) at least 20% of the shares must be awarded other than by reference to performance; and

(*b*) the highest performance-related award (in terms of the number of shares) made to any individual may not exceed four times the highest non-performance-related award so made.

If different classes of share are awarded, the above applies separately in relation to each class. The overall requirement (at 82.12 above) to award free shares on similar terms to all participating employees is disapplied as regards the performance-related shares.

Under *Method 2*, in relation to a particular award of shares, some or all of the shares must be awarded by reference to performance, and the overall requirement to award free shares on similar terms to all participating employees is applied separately as regards each performance unit.

Whichever method is used, performance allowances in relation to an award must be available to each qualifying employee. Performance measures must be based on business results or other objective criteria and be fair and objective measures of the performance of the applicable units, and performance targets must be set for performance units comprising one or more employees. An employee cannot belong to more than one performance unit for the purposes of a particular award of shares. The plan must require

(i) performance targets and measures to be notified to participants, and

(ii) (in general terms and subject to reasonable considerations as to commercial confidentiality) performance measures to be notified to all qualifying employees (see 82.12 above) of the company (or of all participating companies under a group plan),

such notifications to be given as soon as reasonably practicable.

[*FA 2000, Sch 8 paras 25–30*].

82.21 **Requirements as to type of share used.** The requirements below must all be met with respect to any shares ('*eligible shares*') that may be awarded under an approved ESOP.

Eligible shares must form part of:

(*a*) the company which established the plan;

(*b*) a company which has control (within *ICTA 1988, s 840*) of the company in (*a*) above;

(*c*) a company which is a member of a consortium (as in 82.19(*b*) above) owning either the company in (*a*) above or a company within (*b*) above; or

(*d*) a company which has control of a company within (*c*) above.

Eligible shares must be

(i) shares of a class listed on a recognised stock exchange ;

(ii) shares in a company not under the control (within *ICTA 1988, s 840*) of another company; or

(iii) shares in a company under the control of a company (other than a close company) whose shares are listed on a recognised stock exchange. Reference here to a close company includes a company which would be a close company if it were UK-resident.

Eligible shares must be fully paid up and, except in relation to shares in a co-operative (as defined), not redeemable (or capable of becoming redeemable). Shares are not fully paid up for this purpose if there is any undertaking to pay cash to the company at a future date.

Eligible shares must not be subject to any restrictions (as to their disposal or the exercise of rights conferred etc. — see *FA 2000, Sch 8 para 63(2)–(4)* for full definition and disregards) other than

(A) those involved in there being a holding period (i.e. for free, matching and dividend shares — see respectively 82.13, 82.15, 82.16 above);

(B) those affecting all ordinary shares in the company; or

(C) permitted restrictions as to voting rights, provision for forfeiture or pre-emption conditions (see below in each case).

Eligible shares must not be shares in an '*employer company*', i.e. a company whose business is substantially the provision of the services of its employees either to businesses, including partnerships, who control the company or to associated companies (as specially defined for this purpose). The prohibition extends to shares in certain companies which have control of employer companies. '*Control*' for these purposes is determined in accordance with *ICTA 1988, s 416(2)–(6)*.

[*FA 2000, Sch 8 para 1(4), paras 59–63, 67, 129(1)*].

Voting rights. Eligible shares may be shares carrying no voting rights or limited voting rights.

Provision for forfeiture (i.e. provision to the effect that a participant shall cease to be beneficially entitled to the plan shares on the occurrence of certain events). As regards free or matching shares (see 82.13, 82.15 above), provision may be made for forfeiture where the participant

(1) ceases to be in relevant employment (see 82.12 above), or

(2) withdraws the shares from the plan (see 82.12 above),

within the '*forfeiture period*', i.e. a period not exceeding three years as specified in the plan and beginning with the date on which the shares were awarded (see 82.12 above) to the participant. However, shares cannot be made subject to provision for forfeiture in the event of shares ceasing to be subject to the plan for any of the reasons at 82.17(*a*)–(*c*) above. As regards matching shares only, provision may be made for forfeiture if the participant withdraws from the plan, within the said forfeiture period, the partnership shares in respect of which the matching shares were awarded to him. Forfeiture cannot be linked to performance, and the same provision for forfeiture, if any, must apply to all free or matching shares included in the same award.

Pre-emption conditions. Eligible shares may be made subject to provision requiring shares awarded to an employee and held by him (or by a permitted transferee under the company's articles) to be offered for sale on his ceasing to be in relevant employment (see 82.12 above). Such provision can be made only if, under the company's articles, the same provision applies to all employees, the shares must be offered for sale at a specified price, and anyone disposing of shares of the class in question (whether or not as an employee) is required to offer them for sale on no better terms.

[*FA 2000, Sch 8 paras 64–66*].

82.22 **Company reconstructions.** For the purposes of the ESOP provisions (and subject to the rules below for rights issues),

(a) a company reconstruction (see below) is treated as not involving a disposal of shares comprised in the original holding;

(*b*) new shares (see below) are deemed to have been awarded to (or acquired on behalf of) a participant on the date the corresponding original shares were awarded or so acquired;

(*c*) the requirements at 82.21 above are treated as fulfilled with respect to new shares if they were fulfilled (or treated as fulfilled) with respect to the original shares;

(*d*) references throughout the provisions to a participant's plan shares are to be construed as including any new shares; and

(*e*) the tax provisions at 82.17, 82.18 above apply to new shares as they would have applied to the original shares.

If, as part of a company reconstruction, the trustees become entitled to a capital receipt, their entitlement is deemed to arise before the new holding comes into being.

For the above purposes, a '*company reconstruction*' is a transaction in relation to any of a participant's plan shares

(i) which results in a new holding being equated with the original holding for capital gains tax purposes (see Tolley's Capital Gains Tax under Shares and Securities), or

(ii) which would do so but for the new holding consisting of or including a qualifying corporate bond (see Tolley's Capital Gains Tax under Qualifying Corporate Bonds);

and '*new shares*' means shares, securities and rights comprised in the new holding. Certain share issues treated as distributions chargeable to income tax are treated for the purposes of these provisions as *not* forming part of the new holding.

[*FA 2000, Sch 8 para 115*].

Rights issues. Subject to the exceptions below, where the trustees take up rights under a rights issue in respect of a participant's plan shares, the resulting new shares or securities or rights are treated as synonymous with the original shares. This does not apply where

(A) the funds used to acquire the new shares etc. are provided other than by the part disposal of rights in order to take up other rights under the issue; or

(B) the rights are not conferred in respect of all ordinary shares in the company.

Where the rule is disapplied, the new shares etc. are not plan shares and do not fall to be equated with the original shares for capital gains tax purposes.

[*FA 2000, Sch 8 para 116*].

82.23 **The plan trustees.** An ESOP must provide for the establishment of a trust, constituted under UK law and with UK-resident trustees, the principal duties of the trustees being to acquire shares and appropriate them as free or matching shares to employees, and to acquire partnership and dividend shares on behalf of employees, in accordance with the plan. The trustees' other duties must include:

(*a*) giving an employee notice of shares awarded to him and of dividend shares acquired on his behalf, such notice to include specified information;

(*b*) maintaining such records as may be necessary for the purposes of their own, and the employer's, plan-related PAYE obligations (see 82.17 above);

(*c*) (where relevant) giving a participant notice of any foreign tax deducted at source from plan share dividends from a non-UK resident company; and

(*d*) informing a participant of the facts relevant to determining any income tax liability which he incurs under these provisions.

The trust instrument must require the trustees to act only at the direction of a participant as regards disposing of his plan shares and dealing with rights issues, but, except in the case of partnership shares, must also prohibit them from disposing of shares (to the participant or otherwise), except in certain specified circumstances, within the holding period for those shares (see 82.13, 82.15, 82.16 above), unless the participant has ceased to be in relevant employment (see 82.12 above). The plan may provide for participants' directions to be given in general terms. Subject to the above, the trustees may partly dispose of rights under a rights issue in order to raise funds to take up other rights under the issue. With certain exceptions, the trust instrument must require the trustees to account to participants for any money or money's worth received by them in respect of or by reference to plan shares.

The plan must provide for the trustees to raise funds to meet PAYE obligations on shares leaving the plan (see 82.17 above), either by disposing of a participant's plan shares (including a disposal to themselves as trustees) or by obtaining the necessary amount from the participant.

If authorised by the trust instrument, the trustees may borrow to acquire shares and for other specified purposes.

The trust instrument

(i) must provide that shares acquired by the trustees by way of qualifying transfer of relevant shares from an employee share ownership trust (see 82.41 below) are not awarded under the plan as partnership shares but are otherwise awarded in priority to other available shares; and

(ii) must not contain any terms which are neither essential nor reasonably incidental to complying with the statutory requirements.

A disposal of the participant's beneficial interest in any of his shares is treated as a disposal of those shares by the trustees for like consideration (or, in the case of a transaction not at arm's length, for their market value). For these purposes, the vesting of an interest on the insolvency of the participant (or Scottish law equivalent) or otherwise by operation of law does not constitute a disposal of that interest.

[*FA 2000, Sch 8 paras 68–76, 129(1)*].

Tax exemption for dividends on unappropriated shares. Tax is not chargeable at the Schedule F trust rate (see 81.5 SETTLEMENTS) in respect of dividends or other distributions on shares held by the trustees on their own account, provided that the shares satisfy the requirements at 82.21 above as to the type of share that may be used in the plan and are awarded (see 82.12 above) (or acquired as dividend shares) within a statutory period. The period within which shares must be awarded depends on whether or not any of the shares in the company in question are 'readily convertible assets' (see 82.17 above under PAYE) at the time of the acquisition of shares by the trustees. If they are, the period is the two years from acquisition. Otherwise, it is five years from acquisition, but if within those five years the shares acquired become readily convertible assets the period ends no later than two years after the date on which they did so. For these purposes,

(A) shares of a particular class are deemed to be awarded by the trustees on a first in/first out basis; and

(B) shares subject to provision for forfeiture (see 82.21 above) are deemed to be acquired by the trustees if and when forfeiture occurs.

[*FA 2000, Sch 8 para 88*].

For *capital gains tax* matters relevant to the trustees, see Tolley's Capital Gains Tax under Employee Share Schemes.

82.24 **Revenue approval.** On application by the company, the Revenue will approve an ESOP if they are satisfied that it meets the statutory requirements. Applications must contain such information and be supported by such information as the Revenue may require. The company may appeal within 30 days against refusal of Revenue approval; the appeal lies to the Special Commissioners. On a successful appeal, the Special Commissioners may direct the Revenue to approve the plan from a specified date no earlier than the original date of application. [*FA 2000, Sch 8 paras 4, 5*].

Withdrawal of approval. If any disqualifying event occurs, the Revenue may by notice withdraw their approval of the plan with effect from, at the earliest, the time of the disqualifying event. The withdrawal does not affect the treatment of shares awarded to participants (see 82.12 above) before the effective time of withdrawal. Any of the following is a disqualifying event:

(*a*) a contravention, in relation to the operation of the plan, of any of the statutory requirements, the plan itself or the plan trust;

(*b*) an alteration made in a 'key feature' of the plan or in the terms of the plan trust without Revenue approval (see further below);

(*c*) the setting under *Method 2* (see 82.20 above) of performance targets that are not comparable in terms of the likelihood of their being met by the performance units to which they apply;

(*d*) an alteration in the share capital of the company whose shares are the subject of the plan, or in the rights attaching to any of its shares, that materially affects the value of plan shares;

(*e*) plan shares of a particular class receiving different treatment from the other shares of that class, particularly in respect of dividends (other than in limited circumstances as specified), repayment, restrictions, or any offer of substituted or additional shares, securities or rights of any kind in respect of the shares (see further below);

(*f*) the trustees, the company, or, in the case of a group plan, any company which is or has been a participating company failing to furnish any information called for under the Revenue's information powers below.

As regards (*b*) above, an alteration is to a '*key feature*' if it relates to a provision which is necessary in order to meet the statutory requirements. The Revenue are not to withhold approval to the alteration unless it appears to them that the plan, as altered, would not receive approval on an initial application. As regards (*e*) above, there is no disqualifying event where the difference in treatment arises from a 'key feature' or from any participants' shares being subject to provision for forfeiture (see 82.21 above).

The company may appeal, within 30 days, against a withdrawal of approval, an associated withdrawal of corporation tax relief (see 71.54 SCHEDULE D, CASES I AND II), or a refusal to approve an alteration as in (*b*) above; the appeal lies in each case to the Special Commissioners.

[*FA 2000, Sch 8 paras 118, 119*].

Revenue information powers. The Revenue have wide-ranging powers to require any person to furnish them with such information as they reasonably require and as that person possesses or can reasonably obtain. The information must be supplied within a period specified in the notice, which must not be less than three months. Penalties under *TMA 1970, s 98* are exigible for non-compliance. [*FA 2000, Sch 8 para 117*].

82.25 **Termination of plan.** An ESOP may provide for the company to terminate the plan in such circumstances as the plan may specify. This is accomplished by the issue of a plan termination notice, a copy of which must be given without delay to the Revenue, the plan trustees and each individual who has plan shares or has entered into a current partnership share agreement. Any money held on an individual's behalf by the plan trustees must be paid over to him as soon as practicable after the plan termination notice is issued. Plan shares must be removed from the plan as soon as practicable after the end of three months following the issue of the plan termination notice or, if later, after the first date on which they may be removed without giving rise to an income tax charge (see 82.17 above). Shares may be removed earlier with the participant's consent. The trustees can remove shares from the plan either by transferring them to, or at the direction of, the participant (or, after his death, his personal representatives) or by disposing of them and similarly accounting for the proceeds.

[*FA 2000, Sch 8 paras 120, 121*].

82.26 ENTERPRISE MANAGEMENT INCENTIVES

Introduction. With effect **on and after 28 July 2000**, 'small higher risk' trading companies are able to grant options over shares worth up to £100,000 (at time of grant) to each of up to 15 eligible employees without income tax consequences (except to the extent that the option is to acquire shares at less than their market value at time of grant). Any gain on sale of the shares by such an employee is chargeable to capital gains tax on the difference between net proceeds and the combined cost of the option and the shares (together with any amount charged to income tax). For the purposes of taper relief, the period of ownership starts on the date the option is granted and not the date it is exercised.

The company may be quoted or unquoted but must be an independent company trading or preparing to trade wholly or mainly in the UK and whose gross assets do not exceed £15 million. A company carrying on certain specified activities deemed to be lower risk activities does not qualify, such exclusions being similar to those at 26.7(*a*)–(*c*)(*e*)–(*m*) ENTERPRISE INVESTMENT SCHEME (AND BES). Broadly, an employee is eligible if he is employed by the company for at least 25 hours per week or, if less, at least 75% of his total working time, and he controls no more than 30% of the company's ordinary share capital. Companies are not required to obtain Revenue approval to schemes but must give notification to the Revenue within 30 days after an option is granted.

[*FA 2000, s 62, Sch 14*].

The coverage below is set out under the following headings.

82.27 Qualifying options
82.28 Tax consequences of qualifying option
82.29 Qualifying companies
82.30 Qualifying trades
82.31 Eligible employees
82.32 Requirements as to terms of option etc.
82.33 Replacement options
82.34 Notice of grant of option
82.35 Returns
82.36 Revenue information powers
82.37 Compliance with time limits

82.27 **Qualifying options.** A qualifying option is an option (i.e. a right to acquire shares) in relation to which the general requirements below and the further requirements at 82.29–82.32 below are met at the time it is granted, and of which notice is given to the Revenue as in 82.34 below. [*FA 2000, Sch 14 paras 1, 71(1)*].

The option must be granted for commercial reasons in order to recruit or retain a key employee in a company, and not as part of a tax avoidance scheme or arrangement. It must be granted to the employee by reason of his employment with the '*relevant company*' (i.e. the company whose shares are the subject of the option) or, if the relevant company is a parent company, his employment with that company or another group company. See 82.29 below as to qualifying companies and 82.31 below as to eligible employees. See 82.32 below for requirements as to the terms of the option, including the type of share that may be acquired.

No more than **15** employees may hold qualifying options in respect of shares in the relevant company at the same time.

Maximum entitlement. An employee cannot at any time hold unexercised qualifying options in respect of shares with a value (see below) of more than **£100,000**. If the limit is already exceeded at the time an option is granted, that option is not a qualifying option. If the grant of an option causes the limit to be exceeded, that option is not a qualifying option so far as it relates to the excess. Where an employee has been granted qualifying options in respect of shares with a total value of £100,000, then, whether or not those options remain unexercised (and disregarding any release of options), no further *qualifying* option may be granted to him within three years after the date of grant of the last qualifying option. If, at the time an option is granted under these provisions, the employee holds unexercised options under an approved company share option plan (as in 82.40 below), those options count towards the limit as if they were qualifying options.

The £100,000 limit is a global limit covering options granted by reason of employment with one company or with any number of companies in the same group. The legislation is framed to prevent the above provisions being circumvented if options are granted to an individual by reference to his employment with different companies within a group.

For the above purposes, the value of shares is their market value (determined as for capital gains tax purposes), *at the time the option is granted*, of shares of the same class, and an option is treated as granted in respect of the maximum number of shares that may be acquired under it. Where the market value of shares on any date falls to be determined for any purpose of these provisions, the Revenue and the employer company may agree that it be determined by reference to a different date or a number of specified dates. If market value is not agreed between the Revenue and the employer company, the Revenue have power to determine it. The employer company may appeal within 30 days against a notice of determination (see also 82.37 below as regards compliance with time limits). Alternatively, the company may, by notice to the Revenue before a notice of determination is given, refer the question of market value to the Commissioners, who must then determine it in like manner as on appeal. The appeal or referral lies to the General Commissioners, unless the company elects under *TMA 1970, s 46(1)* (see 4.3 APPEALS) for the Special Commissioners. In arriving at the market value of shares subject to restrictions or to risk of forfeiture (such that the interest that may be acquired is only conditional — see 82.7 above), such restrictions or risk are disregarded.

The £100,000 limit may be amended in the future by Treasury Order.

[*FA 2000, Sch 14 para 1(2)(d), paras 8–11, 66, 67, 69*].

See 82.34 below re possibility and consequences of Revenue enquiry into an option.

82.28 **Income tax consequences of qualifying option.** No income tax is chargeable on the *grant* of a qualifying option. The *exercise* of a qualifying option attracts the following special treatment (but only if it occurs within ten years after the time of the grant). Subject to any disqualifying event (see below), no income tax charge arises under *ICTA 1988, s 135* (see 82.3 above) on the exercise of a qualifying option to acquire shares at not less than their market value at the time of the grant. On the exercise of a qualifying option to acquire shares at nil cost or otherwise at less than their market value at the time of the grant, the amount chargeable under *section 135* is limited (if it would otherwise be greater) to the lower of

(*a*) the excess of the market value of the shares at the time of the grant over the amount (if any) for which the shares are acquired; and

(*b*) the excess of the market value of the shares at the time the option is exercised over the amount (if any) for which the shares are acquired; if there is no such excess, no charge arises.

In the case of a replacement option (see 82.33 below), all references above to the time of the grant are to the time of grant of the original option.

[*FA 2000, Sch 14 paras 42–46, 53(3)*].

The notional loan provisions of *ICTA 1988, s 162* (see 75.19 SCHEDULE E) in respect of shares acquired at an undervalue do not apply in relation to shares acquired on the exercise of a qualifying option (whether or not at a discount). However, the separate charge under *section 162* (also at 75.19 SCHEDULE E) where shares are disposed of at more than market value is not prevented from applying. [*FA 2000, Sch 14 para 54*]. There is no income tax exemption in respect of the *release* of a qualifying option, which is thus chargeable as in 82.3 above. Similarly, the provisions of *FA 1988, s 78* (removal of restrictions) and *FA 1988, s 80* (special benefits) (see, in both cases, 82.5 above) apply to shares acquired under a qualifying option. So do those of *ICTA 1988, s 140A* on an employee's interest in shares ceasing to be conditional (see 82.7 above) and *ICTA 1988, s 140D* on the conversion of convertible shares (see 82.8 above); however, the amounts deductible in arriving at the charge under either of these provisions include the amount (or additional amount) that would have been chargeable under *ICTA 1988, s 135* if the shares had not been acquired under a qualifying option. [*FA 2000, Sch 14 para 55*].

Disqualifying events. Where a 'disqualifying event' occurs in relation to a qualifying option before it is exercised, and the option is not exercised within 40 days after that event, the amount chargeable under *ICTA 1988, s 135* on the exercise of the option is (or, in a case where there is already a charge, is increased by) the amount (if any) by which the market value of the shares on exercise exceeds their market value immediately before the disqualifying event (but not so as to increase the amount chargeable if these provisions were disregarded).

Any of the following is a '*disqualifying event*' in relation to a qualifying option.

(i) The 'relevant company' (see 82.27 above) becomes a 51% subsidiary of another company or otherwise comes under the control of another company (with or without the aid of CONNECTED PERSONS (20)). In a case where a replacement option has been granted (see 82.33 below), such an event is not a disqualifying event in relation to the original option if it occurred during the period beginning at the same time as the period within which the replacement had to be granted and ending with the release of rights under the old option.

(ii) The relevant company ceases to meet the trading activities requirement (see 82.29 below).

(iii) The relevant company was a qualifying company by virtue only of its *preparing to carry on* a qualifying trade (see 82.29, 82.30 below), and either the preparations cease or two years elapse from the date of grant without the relevant company or any company in its group commencing that trade.

(iv) The employee ceases to be an eligible employee in relation to the relevant company by reason of his ceasing to satisfy the requirements at 82.31(*a*) or (*b*) below (and see also below as to actual 'relevant working time').

(v) A variation is made of the terms of the option, the effect of which is to increase the market value of the option shares or that the statutory requirements would no longer be met in relation to the option.

(vi) An alteration of a specified kind (see *FA 2000, Sch 14 para 49(1)*) is made to the share capital of the relevant company without prior Revenue approval. Approval will not be withheld unless, in the Revenue's view, the effect of the alteration would be to increase the market value of the option shares or that the statutory requirements would no longer be met in relation to the option. Refusal of approval is subject to notice of appeal being given to the Revenue within 30 days by the employer company. The appeal lies to the General Commissioners, unless the company elects under *TMA 1970, s 46(1)* (see 4.3 APPEALS) for the Special Commissioners.

(vii) Any of the shares to which the option relates are converted to shares of a different class. There is an exception similar to that in 82.8 above, and subject to similar conditions, where all the shares of one class only are converted into shares of one other class only.

(viii) The employee is granted a CSOP option (i.e. an option under an approved company share option plan — see 82.40 below) by reason of his employment with the same company or by a company in the same group as that company, *and* immediately afterwards holds unexercised 'employee options' in respect of shares with a total value of over £100,000. For this purpose, '*employee options*' include the qualifying option in question and any other qualifying option or CSOP option granted by reason of employment with the same company or group.

A disqualifying event is also treated as occurring if in any tax year the employee's 'relevant working time' is less than 25 hours per week or, if less, 75% of his 'working time' (see 82.31 below). An employee's '*relevant working time*' is the time he, in fact, spends as an employee in 'relevant employment' (see 82.31 below) on the business either of the relevant company or, if it is a parent company, of the group. The cumulative position must be examined as at the end of each calendar month. If the working time requirement is not then satisfied by reference to the tax year to date, the disqualifying event is deemed to have occurred at the end of the previous calendar month (or, if the review is being carried out as at the end of April, at the end of the previous tax year). If the employee begins or ceases to be in 'relevant employment' during the tax year, only the appropriate part of the tax year is taken into account for these purposes. If under these rules a disqualifying event would otherwise be treated as occurring before the grant of an option, the option is treated as if it had never been a qualifying option.

[*FA 2000, Sch 14 para 1(3), paras 47–53, 71(2)*].

The comments in 82.27 above regarding the market value of shares apply equally for the above purposes.

Capital gains tax consequences of qualifying option. See 82.26 above, and for the detailed provisions see Tolley's Capital Gains Tax under Employee Share Schemes.

82.29 **Qualifying companies.** The company whose shares are the subject of the option must be a qualifying company. [*FA 2000, Sch 14 para 1(2)(b)*]. To be a qualifying company, it must meet the requirements detailed below as to independence, qualifying subsidiaries, gross assets and trading activities. [*FA 2000, Sch 14 para 12*]. The company may be quoted or unquoted, and there is no requirement that it be UK-resident (though see 82.30(i) below as regards qualifying trades).

Independence. The company must not be a 51% subsidiary of another company or otherwise under the control (within *ICTA 1988, s 840*) of another company, or of another company and persons connected with it (within *ICTA 1988, s 839* — see 20 CONNECTED PERSONS). No arrangements must exist whereby the company could become such a subsidiary or fall under such control. 'Arrangements' is very broadly defined, but for this purpose any arrangements with a view to a 'qualifying exchange of shares' (see 82.33 below) are disregarded. [*FA 2000, Sch 14 paras 13, 71(1)(2)*].

Qualifying subsidiaries. If the company has subsidiaries, each 'subsidiary' must be a 'qualifying subsidiary'. A '*subsidiary*' is a company which the company controls (within *ICTA 1988, s 416(2)–(6)*), with or without the aid of CONNECTED PERSONS (20). A subsidiary is a '*qualifying subsidiary*' of a company if the following conditions are met:

(A) the company, or another of its subsidiaries, possesses at least 75% of both the issued share capital and the voting power, and is beneficially entitled to at least 75% of the assets available for distribution to shareholders on a winding-up etc. and of the profits available for distribution to shareholders;

(B) no other person has control (within *ICTA 1988, s 840*) of the subsidiary; and

(C) no arrangements exist whereby (A) or (B) would cease to be satisfied (though see also below).

The fact that a subsidiary or another company is being wound up does not prevent the subsidiary from continuing to be a qualifying subsidiary, provided that the above conditions would otherwise be met and the winding-up is for commercial reasons and not part of a tax avoidance scheme or arrangement. Similarly, the fact that arrangements may exist for the disposal of the entire interest held in the subsidiary does not prevent the subsidiary from continuing to be a qualifying subsidiary if the disposal is to be for commercial reasons and is not part of a tax avoidance scheme or arrangement. Otherwise, 'arrangements' is very broadly defined.

[*FA 2000, Sch 14 paras 14, 15, 71(1)(2)*].

Gross assets. The value of the company's gross assets must not exceed £15 million. If the company is the parent company of a group, that limit applies by reference to the aggregate value of the gross assets of the group (disregarding certain assets held by any member of the group which correspond to liabilities of another member). The limit may be amended in the future by Treasury Order. [*FA 2000, Sch 14 paras 16, 69*].

See Revenue Pamphlet IR 131, SP 5/98 (at 26.5 ENTERPRISE INVESTMENT SCHEME (AND BES)) for the Revenue's approach to the gross assets requirement (in relation, at present, to other legislation but expected to be extended to cover enterprise management incentives).

Trading activities. If the company is a single company (i.e. not the parent company of a group), it must exist wholly for the purpose of carrying on one or more qualifying trades (see 82.30 below) and must actually be carrying on such a trade or preparing to do so. Purposes having no significant effect (other than in relation to incidental matters) on the extent of the company's activities are disregarded.

If the company is a parent company, the business of the group (treating the activities of the group companies, taken together, as a single business) must not consist wholly or as to a substantial part in the carrying on of 'non-qualifying activities', and at least one group company must satisfy the above trading activities requirement for a single company. '*Non-qualifying activities*' means 'excluded activities' (as in 82.30 below) and non-trading activities.

Purposes for which a company exists are disregarded to the extent that they consist of

(i) (as regards a single company) the holding and managing of property used by the company for one or more qualifying trades carried on by it; or

(ii) (as regards a group company) any activities within (*a*)–(*c*) below.

For the purposes of determining the business of a group, activities of a group company are disregarded to the extent that they consist of

(*a*) holding shares in or securities of, or making loans to, another group company;

(*b*) holding and managing property used by a group company for the purposes of one or more qualifying trades carried on by a group company; or

(*c*) incidental activities of a company which meets the above trading activities requirement for a single company.

Amendments to the trading activities requirement (including the provisions at 82.30 below) may be made in the future by Treasury Order.

[*FA 2000, Sch 14 paras 17, 69*].

82.30 **Qualifying trades.** A trade is a qualifying trade (see the trading activities requirement at 82.29 above) if

(i) it is carried on wholly or mainly in the UK;

(ii) it is conducted on a commercial basis and with a view to profit;

(iii) it does not consist wholly or as to a 'substantial' part in the carrying on of 'excluded activities' (see below).

See Revenue Pamphlet IR 131, SP 7/98 (at 26.6 ENTERPRISE INVESTMENT SCHEME (AND BES)) for the Revenue's approach to the requirement at (i) above (in relation, at present, to other legislation but expected to be extended to cover enterprise management incentives). '*Substantial*' is not defined, but in its application to similar legislation is taken by the Revenue to mean 20% or more of total activities (see 26.7 ENTERPRISE INVESTMENT SCHEME (AND BES)).

Activities of research and development (within *ICTA 1988, s 837A*, see 10.52 CAPITAL ALLOWANCES) from which it is intended that a 'connected qualifying trade' will be derived or will benefit are treated as a notional qualifying trade, but preparing to carry on such activities is not treated as preparing to carry on a qualifying trade. A '*connected qualifying trade*' is a qualifying trade carried on either by the company carrying out the research and development or, where applicable, by another member of the group.

'*Excluded activities*' are as follows:

(*a*) dealing in land, commodities or futures, or in shares, securities or other financial instruments;

(*b*) dealing in goods otherwise than in an ordinary trade of wholesale or retail distribution (see further below);

(*c*) banking, insurance, money-lending, debt-factoring, hire purchase financing or other financial activities;

(*d*) leasing or receiving royalties or licence fees (see further below);

(*e*) providing legal or accountancy services;

(*f*) property development (see further below);

(*g*) farming or market gardening;

(*h*) holding, managing or occupying woodlands, any other forestry activities or timber production;

(*j*) operating or managing hotels or comparable establishments (including guest houses, hostels and other establishments whose main purpose is to offer overnight accommodation with or without catering) or property used as such (see further below);

(*k*) operating or managing nursing homes or residential care homes (both as defined) or property used as such (see further below);

(*l*) providing services or facilities for any business consisting to a substantial extent of activities within (*a*)–(*k*) above and carried on by another person, where a person (other than a parent of the provider company) has a controlling interest (see below) in both that business and the business of the provider company.

As regards (*b*) and (*f*) above, see the comments at 26.7 ENTERPRISE INVESTMENT SCHEME (AND BES), which apply equally here. The exclusions at (*j*) and (*k*) above apply only if the person carrying on the activity has an estate or interest (e.g. a lease) in the property concerned or occupies that property.

The term 'leasing' in (*d*) above includes the letting of ships on charter or other assets on hire. As regards ships (other than oil rigs or pleasure craft — both as defined), see the exception at 26.7 ENTERPRISE INVESTMENT SCHEME (AND BES), which applies equally to these provisions.

A trade is not excluded from being a qualifying trade solely because it consists to a substantial extent in the receiving of royalties or licence fees (see (*d*) above) substantially attributable (in terms of value) to the exploitation of intangible assets, such as intellectual property, which have been created by the company carrying on the trade or by a fellow group company — for more details, see the similar let-out at 26.7 ENTERPRISE INVESTMENT SCHEME (AND BES).

As regards (*l*) above, see the comparable exclusion at 26.7 ENTERPRISE INVESTMENT SCHEME (AND BES) as regards the meaning of 'controlling interest'.

[*FA 2000, Sch 14 paras 18–26, 71(1)*].

82.31 **Eligible employees.** The individual to whom the option is granted must be an eligible employee in relation to the 'relevant company' (see 82.27 above). An individual is an eligible employee in relation to the relevant company if he satisfies the following three requirements.

(*a*) *Employment.* He must be an employee of that company or, if it is a parent company, of that company or a qualifying subsidiary (see 82.29 above).

(*b*) *Commitment of working time.* His 'committed time' must amount to at least 25 hours per week or, if less, 75% of his 'working time'. (See 82.30 above for disqualifying event where it transpires that *actual* working time falls below these limits.) His '*committed time*' is the time he is required, as an employee in 'relevant employment', to spend on the business of the relevant company or, where applicable, its group (and also includes certain permissible periods of absence, for example through ill-health, maternity leave, reasonable holiday entitlement, gardening leave etc.) His '*working time*' is the total time he spends on 'remunerative work' as an employee or self-employed person (including the same permissible periods of absence). '*Remunerative work*' means work undertaken to produce income taxable under Schedule E or Schedule D, Case I or II (or which would be so taxable if the employee were UK-resident and ordinarily resident). An employee is in '*relevant employment*' if he is employed by the relevant company or, where applicable, by any company in its group.

(*c*) *Material interest test.* He must not have a 'material interest' in the company or, where applicable, in any of its subsidiaries. For these purposes, an individual has a '*material interest*' in a company if he, and/or certain 'associates' of his (within *FA 2000, Sch 14 paras 34–36*),

(i) beneficially owns or controls (directly or indirectly) more than 30% of ordinary share capital (as defined by *ICTA 1988, s 832(1)*), or,

(ii) (where the company is a close company, or would be but for its being non-UK resident or having a stock exchange quotation) possesses or is entitled to acquire rights to more than 30% of the assets available for distribution among the participators (within *ICTA 1988, s 417(1)*) in a winding-up or in any other circumstances.

Rights to acquire shares must be taken into account (in accordance with *FA 2000, Sch 14 para 32*, though see below as regards qualifying options). Shares or rights held by trustees of an approved profit sharing scheme (see 82.9 above) or approved employee share ownership plan (see 82.11 above) and *not* appropriated to, or acquired on behalf of, any individual are disregarded.

In applying the material interest test, no account is taken of shares that the individual may acquire under a qualifying option, although account *is* taken of shares already so acquired.

[*FA 2000, Sch 14 para 1(2)(c), paras 27–36, 71(1)*].

82.32 **Requirements as to terms of option etc.** An option is not a qualifying option unless all the requirements set out below are met. [*FA 2000, Sch 14 para 37*].

The *shares that can be acquired* under the option must be fully paid up shares forming part of the 'ordinary share capital' (within *ICTA 1988, s 832(1)*) of the 'relevant company' (see 82.27 above), and must be neither redeemable nor capable of becoming redeemable. Shares are not fully paid up for this purpose if there is any undertaking to pay cash to the company at a future date. [*FA 2000, Sch 14 paras 38, 71(1)*].

The option must be *capable of being exercised within ten years* beginning with the date of grant. If the exercise of the option is dependent on conditions being fulfilled, it is treated as so capable if the conditions may be fulfilled within those ten years. [*FA 2000, Sch 14 para 39*].

The option must take the form of a *written agreement* between the person granting the option and the employee, which states

(*a*) the date on which the option is granted;

(*b*) that it is granted under *FA 2000, Sch 14*;

(*c*) the number, or maximum number, of shares that may be acquired;

(*d*) the price (if any) for which the shares may be acquired, or the method by which that price is to be determined;

(*e*) when and how the option may be exercised;

(*f*) any conditions, e.g. performance conditions, affecting the employee's entitlement;

(*g*) details of any restrictions attaching to the shares; and

(*h*) where the interest that may be acquired is only conditional (within 82.7 above) details of those conditions.

[*FA 2000, Sch 14 para 40*].

Non-assignability of rights. The terms on which the option is granted must prohibit the grantee from transferring any of his rights under it. The terms *may* permit the option to be exercised within up to one year after the grantee's death. [*FA 2000, Sch 14 para 41*].

82.33 **Replacement options.** A company (the acquiring company) which obtains control (within *ICTA 1988, s 840*) of a company whose shares are subject to an as yet unexercised qualifying option (as a result of a general offer to acquire the whole of its issued ordinary share capital or all the shares of the same class as those to which the option relates) may grant to the holder of a qualifying option (by agreement with him, and in consideration of his releasing his rights under the option) equivalent rights (a '*replacement option*') relating to shares in the acquiring company. The replacement option must be granted within six months after the acquiring company obtains control and any condition subject to which the offer is made is satisfied. The replacement is a qualifying option only if the requirements listed below are met.

The same applies where the acquiring company obtains such control in pursuance of a compromise or arrangement with creditors and members which is sanctioned by the court under *Companies Act 1985, s 425* (or NI equivalent) (in which case the replacement option must be granted within six months after the acquiring company obtains control) or becomes bound or entitled to acquire shares (of the same class as those to which the option relates) under *Companies Act 1985, ss 428–430* (or NI equivalent) (in which case the replacement option must be granted within the period during which the acquiring company remains so bound or entitled).

The above also applies where the acquiring company obtains all the shares of the company (the old company) whose shares are subject to such an option as a result of a 'qualifying exchange of shares' (in which case the replacement option must be granted within six months after the acquiring company obtains control). A '*qualifying exchange of shares*' means arrangements whereby the old company becomes a wholly-owned subsidiary of a new holding company (the new company) by means of an exchange of shares. All the following conditions must be met (and for these purposes, references to 'shares', other than to 'subscriber shares', include references to securities).

(1) The consideration for the shares in the old company (the old shares) must consist wholly of the issue of shares (new shares) in the new company.

(2) The new shares must be issued only at times when the new company has no issued shares other than subscriber shares (and any new shares already issued in consideration of old shares).

(3) The consideration for new shares of each description must consist wholly of old shares of the corresponding description (i.e. shares of equivalent class and carrying equivalent rights).

(4) New shares of each description must be issued to holders of old shares of the corresponding description in respect of, and in proportion to, their holdings.

(5) The exchange of shares must not fall to be treated as a disposal and acquisition for capital gains tax purposes.

Requirements for replacement option to be a qualifying option. The replacement option is itself a qualifying option if it is granted to the holder of the old option by reason of his employment with the acquiring company or with a member of a group of which it is the parent company, and

(*a*) at the time of the release of rights under the old option,

- (i) the replacement option is granted for the reasons given in 82.27 above,
- (ii) the limit of 15 on the number of employees holding qualifying options (see 82.27 above) is met in relation to the replacement option,
- (iii) the requirements in 82.29 above as to independence and trading activities are met in relation to the acquiring company,
- (iv) the individual to whom the replacement option is granted is an eligible employee (see 82.31 above) in relation to the acquiring company, and
- (v) the requirements at 82.32 above (terms of option etc.) are met in relation to the replacement option;

(*b*) the total market value, immediately before the release, of shares which were subject to the old option is equal to the total market value, immediately after the grant of the replacement option, of the shares in respect of which it is granted; and

(*c*) the total amount payable by the employee for shares under the option remains the same.

General. For the purposes of the enterprise management incentives provisions, a replacement option which is a qualifying option is treated as if granted on the date the original option was granted. Such a replacement option may be replaced by a further replacement option if one of the above circumstances and the above qualifying requirements are again satisfied.

[*FA 2000, Sch 14 paras 59–63*].

82.34 **Notice of grant of option.** Notice (in prescribed form) of an option must be given to the Revenue by the employer company within 30 days after the option is granted, failing which the option is not a qualifying option (see 82.27 above). The notice must incorporate such information as the Revenue may require, and must contain

- (i) a declaration by a director or the company secretary (of the employer company) that, in his opinion, the statutory requirements are met in relation to the option and that the information provided is to the best of his knowledge correct and complete; and
- (ii) a declaration by the employee that he meets the requirement at 82.31(*b*) above as to commitment of working time.

The notice should be sent to Inland Revenue, Employee Share Schemes Unit, Room 76, New Wing, Somerset House, Strand, London WC2R 1LF.

The Revenue may correct obvious errors or omissions in the notice. They must give notice of such correction to the employer company within nine months after the notice of grant is given, and the company may give notice rejecting the correction within three months from the date of issue of the notice of correction.

Revenue enquiry. Where notice of grant of an option is given as above, the Revenue may

(*a*) enquire into the option, by giving the employer company notice of enquiry; and/or (*b*) enquire into the employee's commitment of working time, in which case notice of enquiry must be given to the employee, with a copy to the employer company.

In either case, notice of enquiry must normally be given within 12 months after the end of the 30-day period within which notice of the grant of the option must be given (see above), but it may be given at any time if the Revenue *discover* that any of the information provided was false or misleading in a material particular. In the absence of such discovery, no more than one enquiry can be made under either of (*a*) or (*b*) above.

While an enquiry under (*a*) above remains open, the employer company may apply to the Commissioners for a direction that it be closed within a specified period, such application to be heard and determined in the same way as an appeal. The Commissioners must give such a direction unless satisfied that the Revenue have reasonable grounds for keeping the enquiry open. On completion of the enquiry, the Revenue must issue a 'closure notice' informing the company that the enquiry is complete and stating their decision as to whether the statutory requirements are met in relation to the option. If that decision is negative, the Revenue must also notify the employee. The employer company may appeal, within 30 days after a closure notice is given, against a Revenue decision that the statutory requirements have not been met or that notice of grant was not properly given. Both an application for closure and an appeal lie to the General Commissioners, unless, in either or both cases, the company elects under *TMA 1970, s 46(1)* (see 4.3 APPEALS) for the Special Commissioners. These provisions also apply, with appropriate modifications, to an enquiry under (*b*) above.

In the absence of an enquiry, the option can be taken to be a qualifying option. In the event of an enquiry, the Revenue's decision, as stated in the closure notice, is conclusive, subject to any appeal and, where the option has been found to be a qualifying option, to any further enquiry as a result of a Revenue discovery (see above).

[*FA 2000, Sch 14 paras 2–7*].

See also 82.37 below as regards compliance with time limits.

82.35 **Returns.** A company whose shares are the subject of a qualifying option at any time in a tax year is required to make a return, containing such information as the Revenue may require, within three months after the end of that tax year. Penalties are exigible under *TMA 1970, s 98* for non-compliance. [*FA 2000, Sch 14 para 65*]. See also 82.37 below as regards compliance with time limits.

82.36 **Revenue information powers.** The Revenue have wide-ranging powers to require any person to furnish them with information within such time (not being less than three months) as they may direct. Penalties are exigible under *TMA 1970, s 98* for non-compliance. [*FA 2000, Sch 14 para 64*]. See also 82.37 below as regards compliance with time limits.

82.37 **Compliance with time limits.** For the purposes of 82.34–82.36 above and for determining market value as in 82.27 above, a person is not taken to have failed to do anything within a time limit if he had a reasonable excuse and, if the excuse ceased, did it without unreasonable delay thereafter. In such circumstances, any further time limit expressed by reference to the original time limit operates by reference to the actual time of performance of the original task. [*FA 2000, Sch 14 para 70*].

82.38 **SAVINGS-RELATED SHARE OPTION SCHEMES**

Savings-related schemes were introduced by *FA 1980, s 47, Sch 10* and are now contained in *ICTA 1988, s 185, Sch 9*. A company may establish a scheme for its directors and employees to obtain options to acquire shares in itself or another company without any charge to income tax on the receipt of the options and on any increase in value of the shares between the date of the option being granted and the date on which it is exercised (see 82.4, 82.5 above) and, for capital gains tax purposes, the market value of the shares will not be substituted for the consideration given. Reliefs are withdrawn where option is exercised within three years of being obtained in the circumstances described at (*j*) or (*l*) below, except that for options acquired after 31 December 1991, the exemption from charge on receipt of the option continues to apply in those circumstances.

The scheme must be linked to an approved savings scheme (see 29.13(vi) EXEMPT INCOME), on which interest and bonuses are exempt from tax, to provide the funds for the acquisition of the shares when the option is exercised. Three- or five-year contracts are available, and five-year contracts may offer the option of repayment on the seventh anniversary. Monthly contributions to all such schemes must not be permitted to exceed £250, and the minimum monthly contribution set for any scheme must not exceed £10 (although monthly contributions as low as £5 are permitted). The limits may be altered by the Treasury, as may the interest and bonuses on the associated savings scheme, but not so as to affect existing contracts. The requirements for approval of the share option scheme and its participants etc. are stated below. [*ICTA 1988, s 185(1)(a)(2)–(4), Sch 9 para 24; FA 1991, s 39(3)(4)(8), s 40; SI 1991 No 1741*].

See 71.54 SCHEDULE D, CASES I AND II as regards deduction available to company for expenses in setting up the scheme.

Approval of scheme is by the Board (on application in writing by the company which has established the scheme, 'the company concerned') if the following conditions are included.

(*a*) The directors and employees may obtain rights to acquire 'scheme shares', see below.

(*b*) The scheme shares are to be paid for out of savings (and interest) with a certified contractual savings scheme (SAYE) (under *ICTA 1988, s 326*) which is approved by the Board for this purpose.

(*c*) Rights under the scheme must not (save as permitted under (*d*) to (*m*) below) be exercisable before the 'bonus date' i.e. the date on which the SAYE repayments fall due. For this purpose, the repayments may be taken as including, or as not including, a bonus, and the decision on this must be taken when options under the scheme are acquired. Where repayments are taken as including the maximum bonus, the time when the repayments fall due is the earliest date on which the maximum bonus is payable and in any other case, the earliest date on which a bonus is payable.

(*d*) If a participant dies before the bonus date, the rights must be exercised, if at all, within twelve months after his death and if he dies within six months after the bonus date, the rights may be exercised within twelve months after the bonus date.

(*e*) If a participant ceases to hold the office or employment which makes him eligible for the scheme because of injury, disability, redundancy or retiring on reaching a 'specified age', his rights must be exercised, if at all, within six months of his so ceasing, and if he so ceases for any other reason within three years of obtaining the rights, they cannot be exercised at all (except as under (*l*) below). If he so ceases for any other reason more than three years after obtaining the rights, the scheme must provide for forfeiture of the rights or their exercise within six months of so ceasing.

(*f*) A participant continuing in employment after reaching a 'specified age' may exercise his rights under the scheme within six months.

(*g*) Rights under the scheme must not be transferable or capable of being exercised later than six months after the bonus date (except as under (*d*) above).

(*h*) The participant's contribution under the SAYE contract must secure, as nearly as may be, repayment equal to the amount required for purchase of the shares in the option acquired. See (*c*) above for determining the repayments.

(*i*) The price at which scheme shares may be acquired under the option must be stated when the option is obtained and not be manifestly less than 80% of the market value of shares of the same class at that time or, if Board and company agree in writing, at some earlier time. The scheme may provide for such variation of the stated price as may be necessary to take account of any variation in the share capital of which the scheme shares form part.

As regards (*e*) and (*f*) above, the '*specified age*' must be specified in the scheme rules, must be the same for men and women, and must not be less than 60 or more than 75. In relation to approvals before 25 July 1991, it was the normal state pensionable age.

The scheme *may* also include the following provisions.

(*j*) If a person obtains control of the company whose shares are scheme shares as a result of making a general offer to acquire the whole of its issued share capital or of all the shares of the same class as the scheme shares, rights under the scheme to acquire shares may be exercised within six months of that person obtaining control. Rights under the scheme may also be exercised at any time when a person becomes bound or entitled to acquire shares in the company under the *Companies Act 1985, s 428* (or NI equivalent) (power to acquire shares of dissenting shareholders). Where the court sanctions a compromise or arrangement with creditors and members under the *Companies Act 1985, s 425* (or NI equivalent) or if the company passes a resolution for voluntary winding-up, rights under the scheme to acquire shares may be exercised within six months of the sanction or the resolution. If these rights are exercised within three years of their being obtained, then the exemption from income tax as above will not apply.

(*k*) If any other company (the 'acquiring company') obtains control of the company whose shares are scheme shares, or is bound or entitled to acquire shares in the company, in the circumstances described in (*j*) above, the scheme may provide for the rights to acquire scheme shares to be exchanged for rights to acquire shares in the acquiring company, or in another company falling within (i) below in relation to the acquiring company, which are equivalent, as regards value and conditions, to the rights under the existing scheme. The new rights are then treated as having been granted at the time the original rights were granted, and the exchange is not treated itself as the acquisition of a right. The exchange must take place within six months of the company taking unconditional control, or of the court sanctioning the compromise or arrangement, or within the period during which the acquiring company remains bound or entitled to acquire the shares. Where a scheme approved before 1 August 1987 was altered before 1 August 1989 to include such a provision, the alteration may apply to rights obtained before the date on which the alteration took effect, and may permit an exchange where the event on which it depends occurs after 16 March 1987 but before the date on which the alteration took effect. An exchange may be permitted in a case where, following the event in question, the rights would otherwise have ceased to be exercisable. The approval of the Board is required in the normal way for an alteration to a scheme permitting such exchanges.

(*l*) Where the office or employment giving rise to eligibility under the scheme is in a subsidiary of which the company which established the scheme ceases to have control, or if it relates to a business (or part) which is transferred to a person other than a subsidiary or associated company, the rights under the scheme may be exercised within six months of the change.

(*m*) The scheme may extend to other companies of which the company concerned has control and is then a 'group scheme' with 'participating companies' (for which see *CIR v Reed International plc and cross-appeal CA 1995, 67 TC 552*).

(*n*) If at the bonus date, rights under a scheme are held by a person who is then employed by a company which is not a participating company (see (*m*) above) but which is an associated company of or under the control of the company which established the scheme, the rights may be exercised within six months of that date. This applies to options granted on or after 29 April 1996 but, if the scheme is altered accordingly (subject to the Board's approval) before 5 May 1998, it may also be applied to options granted before the alteration and before 29 April 1996 (whether or not the bonus date falls before that date). Such alteration is not regarded as giving rise to the acquisition of new rights by an option holder.

The Board need not approve a scheme if it appears to them that there are features which are neither essential nor reasonably incidental to its purpose, or which are designed to discourage an eligible person from participating. Where the company establishing the scheme is a member of a group of companies, the scheme must not in effect be restricted wholly or mainly to directors or the more highly-paid employees in the group. If, after approval, any of the above conditions cease to be satisfied or any unapproved alteration is made to the scheme or information is not provided, approval is withdrawn but existing right to tax-free exercise of option remains. There is a right of appeal to the Special Commissioners within thirty days of notification of the Board's decision to withhold or withdraw approval of a scheme or of an alteration to a scheme. [*ICTA 1988, Sch 9 paras 1–6, 9, 15–25; FA 1989, s 62(3); FA 1991, s 38; FA 1996, s 113*]. See *CIR v Burton Group plc Ch D 1990, 63 TC 191* where an appeal against a Revenue refusal to approve an alteration imposing performance conditions was upheld. In *CIR v Reed International plc and cross-appeal CA 1995, 67 TC 552*, a similar decision was reached where the amendment removed a contingency on which options would be exercisable and would be required to be exercised within a specified period. This did not amount to the acquisition of a new and different right to acquire scheme shares. See also *CIR v Eurocopy plc Ch D 1991, 64 TC 370.*

A specimen set of scheme documents is contained in the explanatory notes for employers, Revenue Pamphlet IR 98, available free of charge from Inland Revenue Information Centre, Ground Floor, SW Wing, Bush House, Strand, London WC2B 4RD (tel. 020–7438 6420/6425/7772). A non-technical explanatory booklet (IR 97) aimed at employees is also available from local tax offices and tax enquiry centres.

'Scheme shares' must

(i) form part of the ordinary share capital of the company concerned; or a company which has control of the company concerned; or a company which either is, or has control of, a company which is a member of a consortium owning either the company concerned or a company controlling that company;

(ii) be (*a*) quoted on a recognised stock exchange or (*b*) shares in a company not under the control of another company or (*c*) be shares in a company under the control of a quoted company (other than a company which is, or would be if resident in the UK, a close company);

(iii) be fully paid and not redeemable and not subject to any restrictions (as defined but excluding any provisions similar to the Stock Exchange Model Code for Securities Transactions by Directors of Listed Companies (November 1984)) other than restrictions which attach to all shares of the same class. Certain restrictions connected with cessation of employment may apply to scheme shares without applying to all shares of the same class. The articles of association may impose a restriction requiring all shares held by directors or employees to be disposed of on cessation of the employment, and all shares acquired by persons who are not directors or employees, but which were acquired in pursuance of rights or interests obtained by directors or employees, to be disposed of immediately they are so acquired. The required disposal must be by sale for money on specified terms, and the articles must also provide that any person disposing of shares of the same class (however acquired) may be required to sell them on the same terms;

(iv) except where the scheme shares are in a company whose ordinary share capital is all one class, the majority of shares of the same class must either (1) be held by persons other than (*a*) shareholders who acquired their shares as directors or employees of that or any other company and not in pursuance of an offer to the public and (*b*) trustees for such shareholders and (*c*) where shares are within (ii)(*c*) above and not within (ii)(*a*) above, companies which control the company whose shares are in question or of which that company is an associated company; or (2) be '*employee-control shares*', i.e. shares held by persons who are or have been directors or employees, and who are together able to control the company by virtue of their holdings. [*ICTA 1988, Sch 9 paras 10–14; FA 1989, s 64*].

Persons eligible to participate must include every person who

(A) is an employee (for schemes approved before 1 May 1995, a full-time employee) or a full-time director of the company concerned or, in the case of a group scheme, a participating company, and

(B) has been such an employee or director at all times during a qualifying period, not exceeding five years, and

(C) is chargeable to tax in respect of his office or employment under Case I of Schedule E.

It may include part-time directors or employees and those whose emoluments are not chargeable under Case I of Schedule E.

The above persons must be able to obtain and exercise rights on similar terms, and those who do participate must actually do so on similar terms, but there may be variation of rights between participants according to their remuneration, length of service or similar factors. A person must not be eligible if he, and/or certain associates of his, has, or at any time within the preceding twelve months has had, a material interest (broadly more than 25% of ordinary share capital) in a close company (within meaning of *ICTA 1988, s 414*) which is a company whose shares may be obtained under the scheme or that company's holding company or a member of a consortium owning such a company. For this purpose 'close company' includes a non-resident company which would otherwise be close and a company which would be close except for its stock exchange quotation. [*ICTA 1988, s 187(3), Sch 9 paras 8, 26, 37–40; FA 1989, s 65; FA 1995, s 137(2)(7); FA 1996, s 113(3)*].

Transitional arrangements. A person who already had a SAYE contract before 15 November 1980 and has obtained rights under an existing scheme (see below) to acquire shares in a company of which he is an employee or director (or a company of which such a company has control) using repayments made under that contract, may come under the scheme described above and tax relief will be restricted to the proceeds which would have been available if the terms of that contract had corresponded to those of a scheme approved as above. [*ICTA 1988, Sch 9 para 16(2)(3)*].

Information. The Board may by notice in writing require any person to provide (in not less than thirty days) such information as the Board think necessary, and as the person to whom the notice is addressed has or can reasonably provide, for the performance of their functions under these provisions. [*ICTA 1988, Sch 9 para 6*].

'Associated company'. For the above purposes, a company is an 'associated company' of another at a given time, if at that time (or, except in (*e*) or (*l*) above, at any time in the previous twelve months), one of the two has control of the other, or both are under the control of the same person or persons. [*ICTA 1988, s 187(2)*].

Personal equity plans. See 29.21 EXEMPT INCOME for the transfer of shares emerging from SAYE share option schemes into personal equity plans.

Simon's Direct Tax Service. See **E4.581** *et seq.*.

82.39 EXECUTIVE SHARE OPTION SCHEMES

(**Note.** Reliefs under the type of scheme described below are **withdrawn** by *FA 1996* for options granted **on or after 17 July 1995**, unless they were granted within 30 days of a written offer or invitation to apply for them made before that date. Relief is, however, available under a type of scheme introduced by *FA 1996* (Company Share Option Plans) which is more restrictive than, but which retains many of the features of, the type of scheme described below. See 82.40 below for details of the *FA 1996* scheme and of the transition from the old type of scheme to the new.)

FA 1984, s 38, Sch 10 introduced a more flexible type of share option scheme, now contained in *ICTA 1988, s 185, Sch 9.* Where an individual obtains, as a director or employee of a company, the right to acquire shares in that or any other company, under a scheme approved under *Schedule 9* (see below), a liability will arise under Schedule E (as earned income) on any excess of the market value at that time of a similar quantity of the shares in question over the aggregate of the consideration given for the right and the price at which the shares may be acquired under the right. (See, however, (vi) below as regards certain options acquired after 31 December 1991.) Otherwise no tax is chargeable in respect of receipt of the right. Similarly, no tax is chargeable on exercise of the right, and for capital gains tax purposes the shares are treated as acquired for the actual consideration given plus the amount of any charge on receipt of the right (as above), provided that:

(*a*) it is not exercised less than three or more than ten years after it was obtained by the individual; and

(*b*) it is not exercised by the individual within three years of his exercise of a right under the same or any other scheme approved under these provisions attracting relief from income tax treatment (although other rights exercised on the same day may be disregarded for this purpose).

In the case of rights exercised by a personal representative not more than ten years after they were obtained by the deceased individual, (*a*) and (*b*) above do not have to be satisfied.

Where a charge arises on receipt of the right (as above), and a charge subsequently arises under *ICTA 1988, s 135* (see 82.3 above) or *s 162* (see 75.19 SCHEDULE E) (e.g. because the scheme has ceased to be approved under *Schedule 9* (below)), relief is given for the charge previously borne. [*ICTA 1988, s 185(1)–(3)(5)–(8), Sch 9 para 27(3)*].

The conditions for approval by the Board of a company share option scheme under *Schedule 9* are as follows.

(i) The scheme must provide for directors and employees to obtain rights to acquire shares (see (iv) below). [*ICTA 1988, Sch 9 para 9(1)*].

(ii) Only full-time directors and 'qualifying employees' of participating companies (see (vii) below) may participate, although a scheme may permit exercise of rights by persons who have ceased to be full-time directors or qualifying employees, and by personal representatives of deceased participants (not more than one year after the date of death). 'Full-time' generally means working 25 or more hours per week excluding meal breaks (see *Explanatory notes* referred to below), and an employee is a '*qualifying employee*' if he is not a director of the company or of any other participating company in a group scheme (see (vii) below) (and, for schemes approved before 1 May 1995, if he is required under his terms of employment to work for the company for at least 20 hours per week (again excluding meal breaks)). Schemes approved before 1 May 1995 may be altered after that date to admit part-time employees. A person must not be eligible to participate (i.e. to obtain or exercise rights) if he, and/or certain associates of his, has, or at any time in the preceding twelve months has had, a 'material interest' (broadly more than 10% of ordinary share capital) in a close company which is a company whose shares may be obtained under the scheme or that company's holding company or a member of a consortium owning such a company. For this purpose, 'close company' includes a non-resident company which would otherwise be close and a company which would be close except for its stock exchange quotation. [*ICTA 1988, s 187(3), Sch 9 paras 8, 27, 37–40; FA 1989, s 65; FA 1995, s 137(3)(7)*]. Shares which the participant may acquire under an option are included when considering the 'material interest' test, i.e. the total holding including such shares must, if appropriate, be brought down to the 10% level or below twelve months before the exercise of the option (see *Explanatory notes* referred to below).

(iii) The value (at the time of grant of the right) of shares over which an individual may hold unexercised rights must not exceed the greater of £100,000 and four times his emoluments (within PAYE but excluding benefits-in-kind and after deducting employee's superannuation contributions to which net pay arrangement applies) of the current or preceding year. Where there were no such emoluments in the preceding year, the alternative limit is four times such emoluments for the twelve months from the first day in the current year for which there were such emoluments. [*ICTA 1988, Sch 9 para 28*].

(iv) The shares over which options are granted must meet identical conditions to those relating to scheme shares under 82.38 above [*ICTA 1988, Sch 9 paras 10–14; FA 1989, s 64*], except that the restrictions referred to in 82.38(iii) above do not include any terms for repayment of, or security for, a loan. [*FA 1988, s 69*].

(v) Rights must be non-transferable (but see (ii) above as regards personal representatives of deceased participants and (viii) below as regards certain changes of control). [*ICTA 1988, Sch 9 para 27(2)*].

(vi) Except as detailed below for options granted after 31 December 1991, the price to be paid must be fixed at the time of grant of the right, and must not be manifestly less than the market value of the shares at that time (or at any earlier time if the Board and company so agree). The scheme may provide for such variation of the stated price as may be necessary to take account of any variation in the share capital of which the shares subject to the option form part. The market value will normally be fixed at a date not more than 30 days prior to grant of the option. If the market value is, or should have been, known at the date of grant of the option to exceed the aggregate of any consideration for the option and the option price, then no option can be granted on such terms in accordance with an approved scheme. Only where an accidental error occurs in valuing the shares (within the normal tolerances for such valuations) can that aggregate be less than market value without being 'manifestly' so. The involvement of Shares Valuation Division should prevent such errors in practice. See above as regards the income tax liability on grant of an option at less than market value. No such charge will, however, arise solely because of an increase in market value between an agreed valuation date and the date of grant of the option. (See *Explanatory notes* referred to below.)

After **31 December 1991**, shares may in certain circumstances be acquired at a price not manifestly less than 85% of the market value at the time the option is granted (or such earlier time as is agreed with the Board, as above). This applies where:

(*a*) the company has established, or (at the time the option is granted) is a participating company in relation to, an approved savings-related share option scheme (see 82.38 above) or an approved profit sharing scheme (see 82.9 above) (a '*qualifying scheme*') (although there is no requirement for the scheme to have been put into operation); and

(*b*) either

(i) where there is only one qualifying scheme, every employee eligible to participate in that scheme at the time the option under the approved share option scheme is granted has, in the preceding twelve months, been informed of the existence of the qualifying scheme by either the employing company, the company establishing the scheme or (in the case of a group scheme) any participating company, or

(ii) where there is more than one qualifying scheme, the condition in (i) above is satisfied in relation to each of them.

As regards (*a*) above, withdrawal of approval of a qualifying scheme after the date of grant of the option is disregarded even if it applies retrospectively from a time before that date. As regards (*b*) above, the annual return for the scheme will be required to set out how the notification requirement has been fulfilled. (Revenue Tax Bulletin November 1991 p 2). Both (*a*) and (*b*) above must be satisfied, where the approved share option scheme is a group scheme (see (vii) below) at the time the option is granted, as respects each company to which the scheme is expressed to extend at that time; otherwise they must be satisfied as respects the company establishing the scheme. The provision for an income tax charge, in the exceptional case where the aggregate of any consideration for the option and the option price is less than the market value of the shares (see above), is correspondingly amended in cases where options are granted at 85% of market value. [*ICTA 1988, s 185(6B), Sch 9 para 29; FA 1991, s 39*].

(vii) The scheme may extend to other companies of which the company setting up the scheme has control, and all companies in such a 'group scheme' are 'participating companies'. [*ICTA 1988, Sch 9 para 1(3)(4)*]. See also *Explanatory notes* referred to below.

(viii) The scheme may also include a provision for exchange of options following a change of control, etc., subject to the same conditions as apply in relation to *FA 1980* schemes (see 82.38(*k*) above). [*ICTA 1988, Sch 9 para 15*].

The Board need not approve a scheme if it appears to them that there are features which are neither essential nor reasonably incidental to its purpose. If, after approval, any of the above conditions cease to be satisfied, or any unapproved alteration is made to the scheme, or information required by the Board (see below) is not provided, approval may be withdrawn. There is a right of appeal to the Special Commissioners within thirty days of notification of the Board's decision to withhold or withdraw approval of a scheme or of an alteration to a scheme. [*ICTA 1988, Sch 9 paras 2(1), 3(1), 4, 5*]. The Board's refusal to accept an amendment to the rules of an approved scheme, allowing for the imposition or variation, after the date of grant of options, of 'key task' conditions on whose fulfilment the number of shares to which an employee was entitled under the scheme depended, was reversed on appeal in *CIR v Burton Group plc Ch D 1990, 63 TC 191*. A similar conclusion was reached in *CIR v Reed International plc and cross-appeal CA 1995, 67 TC 552*, where the amendment removed a contingency on which options would be exercisable and would be required to be exercised within a specified period. This did not amount to the acquisition of a new and different right to acquire scheme shares. In *CIR v Eurocopy plc Ch D 1991, 64 TC 370*, however, the Board's refusal to accept (in relation to existing options) an amendment to a scheme, bringing forward the earliest date on which options could be exercised, was upheld. A different right would be acquired as a result of the amendment, so that the option price set at the time of the original grant would be 'manifestly less' (see (vi) above) than the market value of the shares at the time the new right was acquired.

The existence of a 'phantom' scheme alongside an approved scheme, designed to provide the employee with the cash needed to subscribe for shares under the approved scheme, does not affect either the approval of the option scheme or the tax relief on exercise of the option. (Revenue Tax Bulletin May 1992 p 19).

The Board may, by notice in writing, require any person to provide (in not less than thirty days) such information as the Board consider necessary, and as the person to whom the notice is addressed has or can reasonably provide, for the performance of the Board's functions under these provisions. [*ICTA 1988, Sch 9 para 6*].

See 71.54 SCHEDULE D, CASES I AND II as regards deduction available to company for expenses in setting up the scheme.

Simon's Direct Tax Service. See **E4.591** *et seq.*.

82.40 COMPANY SHARE OPTION PLANS

Company share option plans are discretionary share option schemes approved under *ICTA 1988, Sch 9* and subject to the provisions of *ICTA 1988, s 185, Sch 9* (see 82.39 above) as amended by *FA 1996*. They are designed to replace executive share option schemes (see 82.39 above). They retain most of the rules and features of such schemes but are more restrictive, being aimed particularly at employees in the middle and lower income ranges. The provisions described below apply to rights granted on or after 29 April 1996 but see also the transitional provisions below as regards existing executive schemes.

The provisions relating to company share option plans differ from those relating to executive schemes and described in 82.39 above in the following respects.

(*a*) It is a condition of approval of a scheme by the Board (replacing the condition at 82.39(iii) above) that the aggregate market value (at the time of the grant of the right) of shares over which an individual may hold unexercised rights under the scheme (or any other approved share option scheme, other than a savings-related scheme, established by the company or an associated company) must not exceed £30,000.

(*b*) It is a further condition of approval that the price to be paid must be fixed at the time of the grant and must not be manifestly less than the market value of the shares at that time (or at any earlier time if the Board and company so agree). Whilst this duplicates the principal condition at 82.39(vi) above, the further possibility therein mentioned of granting options at a discount of up to 15% in specified circumstances is not permitted under the company share option plan provisions. The possibility of the scheme providing for necessary variations in the stated price is retained. See 82.39(vi) above as regards meaning of 'manifestly less' and further comment.

(*c*) Amendments purely consequential to the removal of the right to grant options at a discount are made to *ICTA 1988, s 185* and *TCGA 1992, s 120*.

[*ICTA 1988, s 185(6), Sch 9 paras 28, 29; TCGA 1992, s 120(6); FA 1996, s 114, Sch 41 Pt V(5)*].

Transitional provisions. As regards rights granted on or after 29 April 1996, executive share option schemes (see 82.39 above) approved before that date (existing schemes) are deemed to have incorporated into their rules the conditions at (*a*) and (*b*) above, notwithstanding anything included in the scheme to the contrary. Such deemed alterations to schemes are treated as having been approved by the Board before 29 April 1996. If, however, a company does not wish to adopt both conditions into its scheme, it may give notice to that effect to the Board before 1 January 1997. The scheme will then cease to be an approved scheme as from the date of the notice. [*FA 1996, s 114(9), Sch 16*].

As regards rights obtained by a person on or after 17 July 1995 and before 29 April 1996 under an existing scheme, the conditions at (*a*) and (*b*) above must be satisfied as if they applied in respect of rights granted during that period and as if the scheme had adopted them accordingly. In the event of the conditions not being met, the rights in question are treated as having been obtained otherwise than under an approved scheme. In considering whether or not the £30,000 limit at (*a*) above is breached, the value of unexercised options granted before 17 July 1995 must be taken into account. [*FA 1996, s 115(1)–(3)(5)*].

In the case of an executive scheme approved before 17 July 1995, rights obtained on or after that date but within 30 days of a written offer or invitation to apply for them made before that date are regarded as having been obtained before that date (so that the above provision does not apply and the options fall within 82.39 above). [*FA 1996, s 115(4)*].

Explanatory notes on the setting up of a scheme under these provisions, including a specimen set of scheme rules, are in Revenue Pamphlet IR 102, available free of charge from Inland Revenue Information Centre, Ground Floor, SW Wing, Bush House, Strand, London WC2B 4RD (tel. 020–7438 6420/6425/7772). A non-technical explanatory booklet (IR 101) aimed at employees is also available from local tax offices and tax enquiry centres.

Simon's Direct Tax Service. See **E4.591** *et seq.*.

82.41 EMPLOYEE SHARE OWNERSHIP TRUSTS

Under provisions introduced by *FA 1989, ss 67–74, Sch 5*, companies may claim an allowable deduction, for corporation tax, for payments to qualifying employee share ownership trusts (ESOTs), being, broadly, trusts set up to acquire shares in the employer company and distribute them to employees. A deduction is also available for the costs of setting up such a trust. See 71.54 SCHEDULE D, CASES I AND II for details of these deductions. Investment companies may also obtain the deduction by treating payments as management expenses. Neither the ESOT nor its beneficiaries qualify for any special income tax or capital gains tax reliefs, although such a trust may be used in conjunction with an approved profit sharing scheme (see 82.9 above) or, for trusts established on or after 29 April 1996, an approved savings-related share option scheme (see 82.38 above), thus enabling beneficiaries to receive shares free of income tax. In certain circumstances (see below), where the above-mentioned deduction has been made, the tax relief given to the company may, effectively, be clawed back by means of a charge under Schedule D, Case VI on the trustees, with powers to recover the tax so charged from the company.

Definition. A trust is an ESOT at any time (the relevant time) if it was a 'qualifying ESOT' at the time it was established, regardless of whether or not it is a qualifying ESOT at the relevant time. A '*qualifying ESOT*' is a trust established, by means of a trust deed, by a UK resident company (the 'founding company') which is not controlled by another company, and which, at the time of establishment, satisfies the conditions in *FA 1989, Sch 5 paras 3–11* as summarised below. A trust is established when the deed under which it is established is executed. [*FA 1989, Sch 5 paras 1, 2, 13, 17; FA 1994, Sch 13 para 8*].

The trust deed must deal with the appointment, retirement, removal and replacement of **trustees**. The trustees must number at least three, must all be UK resident and must include a trust corporation or a solicitor (or member of such other professional body as the

Board may allow). Most of the trustees must be employees, either of the founding company or of a UK resident company controlled by it, who have never had a material interest (broadly more than 5% of ordinary share capital) in any such company, and those trustees must be selected by a majority of employees or by the employees' elected representatives. Most of the trustees must never have been directors of either the founding company or a UK resident company controlled by it.

For ESOTs set up after 3 May 1994, two other possible trust structures are permitted: a 'paritarian' trust structure; or a UK resident corporate trustee controlled by the founding company and with directors composed in the same way as the trustees in a 'paritarian' trust structure. The 'paritarian' trust structure requires three or more UK resident trustees, of whom at least one must be, and at least two must not be, 'professional' trustees. A '*professional*' trustee is a trust corporation or a solicitor (or member of such other professional body as the Board may allow), other than an employee or director of the founding company (or of a UK resident company controlled by it), selected by the non-professional trustees. Also, at least half of the non-professional trustees must be employees of the founding company (or of a UK resident company controlled by it) who have never had a material interest (as above) in any such company and who are selected either by election (with all such employees being able to stand for election or to vote) or by selection by elected representatives of those employees.

A trust is not a qualifying ESOT at any time when the requirements as to trustees are not satisfied.

[*FA 1989, Sch 5 paras 3–3C, 12, 12A; FA 1994, s 102, Sch 13 paras 2–5*].

The terms of the trust deed must be such that a person is a **beneficiary** at a particular time if

(*a*) he is then an employee or director of the founding company or a UK resident company then under its control, and

(*b*) he has been an employee or director of such a company throughout a period specified in the trust deed, which must not be more than five years (and which, for trusts established before 29 April 1996, had to be at least one year), ending at that time, working for at least twenty hours a week (ignoring holidays and sickness). (For trusts established under deeds executed on or after 1 May 1995, the minimum hours restriction applies only to directors.)

The trust deed *may* provide that where a person has been an employee or director as required under (*a*) above throughout a period of the length specified in the trust deed as under (*b*) above and ending when the employment/directorship ceased or the company ceased to be controlled by the founding company, that person may continue to be a beneficiary for 18 months thereafter. For trusts established on or after 29 April 1996, the deed *may* also provide for a person to be a beneficiary at a given time if at that time he is eligible to participate in an approved savings-related share option scheme (see 82.38 above) established by a member of the founding company's group; the deed must then provide that the only powers and duties the trustees may exercise in relation to such beneficiaries (if they would not otherwise be beneficiaries) are those exercisable under such a scheme. A trust deed *may* also provide for a charity to be a beneficiary if the trust is being wound up in consequence of there being no qualifying beneficiaries under the deed. All persons not satisfying these conditions at a particular time must be excluded from being beneficiaries at that time. Notwithstanding the fact that a person satisfies these conditions, he cannot be a beneficiary at a particular time if he then has, or has had at any time in the previous twelve months, a material interest (broadly more than 5% of ordinary share capital) in the founding company (but this restriction does not apply to persons who qualify as beneficiaries only by virtue of their being eligible to participate in a savings-related scheme).

[*FA 1989, Sch 5 para 4; FA 1995, s 137(5)(9); FA 1996, ss 119, 120(1)(5)–(7)(12)*].

The **general functions of trustees** must be to receive sums and to acquire, retain and manage and eventually to transfer sums or securities (i.e. shares and debentures) to beneficiaries or transfer securities at not less than market value to trustees of approved profit sharing schemes (see 82.9 above) or, for trusts established on or after 29 April 1996, grant rights to acquire shares (i.e. under approved savings-related share option schemes — see 82.38 above) to beneficiaries. Any sum received, whether from the founding company or by way of loan or otherwise, must be expended, within the 'relevant period', for a qualifying purpose (see 71.54 SCHEDULE D, CASES I AND II), being retained in cash or in a bank or building society account in the meantime. The '*relevant period*' is the period of nine months after the end of the period of account, of the company making the payment to the trust, for which the payment is charged as an expense, or, in the case of sums received other than from the founding company or a company under its control, nine months from the date of receipt of the sum in question.

Sums received are to be treated as being expended on a first in/first out basis, and all sums paid to different beneficiaries at the same time must be paid on similar terms (although variations according to remuneration, length of service or similar factors are permitted). The trust deed must not contain features which are not essential or reasonably incidental to the purposes herein described as being the general functions of the trustees. [*FA 1989, Sch 5 paras 5, 6, 10; FA 1996, s 120(8)(11)(12)*].

The **securities** to be acquired by the trust must be fully paid up, non-redeemable ordinary shares in the founding company which are free of restrictions other than those attaching to all shares of the same class or certain restrictions imposed by the company's articles of association. The deed must preclude the trustees from acquiring shares either at greater than open market value or at a time when the founding company is under the control of another company. It *may* allow for the trustees to acquire securities other than shares in the founding company if they are acquired as a result of a company reorganisation or reconstruction within *TCGA 1992, s 126* or *s 135* and the shares originally held were shares in the founding company. The trustees must transfer securities to beneficiaries within seven years (twenty years in the case of trusts established under deeds executed after 3 May 1994) of their acquisition (securities acquired being deemed to be transferred on a first in/first out basis) and on 'qualifying terms'. A transfer is made on '*qualifying terms*' if

(i) all securities transferred at the same time (other than to savings-related share option scheme participants — see below) are transferred on similar terms (allowing, if desired, for differences in levels of remuneration, length of service or similar factors),

(ii) securities have been offered to all existing beneficiaries (disregarding those who would be not be beneficiaries but for their being participants in a savings-related scheme) at the time of transfer, and

(iii) securities are transferred to all such persons who have accepted.

As regards trusts established on or after 29 April 1996, a transfer of securities is also made on '*qualifying terms*' if made to a person exercising a right to acquire shares under an approved savings-related share option scheme (see 82.38 above) established by the founding company or a company under its control, where the consideration for the transfer is payable to the trustees.

The trust deed must contain specified provisions determining the time at which the trustees are deemed to acquire and transfer securities and when they are considered to retain securities.

[*FA 1989, Sch 5 paras 7, 8, 9, 11; FA 1994, Sch 13 para 7; FA 1996, s 120(9)(10)(12)*].

See *FA 1989, Sch 5 paras 14–16* as regards interpretation of the provisions of *Schedule 5*.

Clearance. Requests for clearance that a trust is a qualifying ESOT, supported by copies of the trust deed or draft deed and any other relevant information, should be sent to Inland Revenue, Business Profits Division (Employee Share Schemes), Room 111A, New Wing, Somerset House, Strand, London WC2R 1LB.

Tax charge on trustees. Where a 'chargeable event' occurs in relation to the trustees of an ESOT, they will be charged tax under Schedule D, Case VI, for the year of assessment in which the event occurs, on the 'chargeable amount' at the rate applicable to trusts (see 81.5 SETTLEMENTS) for that year. If they fail to pay the tax in full within six months of the assessment's becoming final and conclusive, a notice of liability for the unpaid tax may be served either on the founding company or on any company which has previously made a payment to the trust and obtained tax relief thereon. The company is also liable for any interest, accruing before or after the date of the notice, on the unpaid tax. If any tax and/or interest still remains unpaid three months after the date of notice, it may be recovered from the trustees without prejudice to the right to recover it instead from the company.

A '*chargeable event*' occurs whenever the trustees of an ESOT do any of the following:

(A) make a transfer, other than a 'qualifying transfer', of securities;

(B) make a transfer of securities, other than on 'qualifying terms' (see above), to beneficiaries;

(C) retain securities for more than seven years (for ESOTs established under deeds executed after 3 May 1994, more than twenty years);

(D) make a payment other than for a 'qualifying purpose' (see 71.54 SCHEDULE D, CASES I AND II);

(E) make a 'qualifying transfer' to the trustees of an approved employee share ownership plan (see below) for a consideration, and fail to apply the whole of that consideration (or an equivalent amount) for 'qualifying purposes' (see 71.54 SCHEDULE D, CASES I AND II) within the period beginning with the transfer and ending nine months after the end of the period of account (of the company which established the ESOT) in which the transfer took place; the chargeable event is the expiry of that permitted period.

A '*qualifying transfer*' is a transfer made either to a beneficiary, or at not less than open market value to the trustees of an approved profit sharing scheme (see 82.9 above), or (after 31 December 1991) by way of exchange of shares within *TCGA 1992, s 135(1)*. A transfer is also a '*qualifying transfer*' if it is a transfer of 'relevant shares' to the trustees of an employee share ownership plan (see 82.11 above), approved at the time of transfer, for a consideration (if any) not exceeding market value. '*Relevant shares*' are shares held by the trustees of the ESOT at midnight on 20 March 2000 or purchased with funds held (in a bank or building society account) at that time. For these purposes, all payments of any kind made by the trustees after 20 March 2000 are deemed to be made as far as possible out of such funds, and any disposal or transfer of shares of a particular class by the trustees after that date is treated as far as possible as a transfer or disposal of relevant shares.

The '*chargeable amount*' is determined as follows:

(I) if the event falls within (A), (B) or (C) above, the chargeable amount, if the event constitutes a disposal for capital gains tax purposes, is the amount of allowable expenditure under *TCGA 1992, s 38(1)(a)(b)*, or, if the event does not constitute such a disposal, is the amount that would have been so allowable if it did so;

(II) if the event falls within (D) above, the chargeable amount is the amount of the payment made;

(III) if the event falls within (E) above, the chargeable amount is the amount of consideration not so applied within the permitted period;

but see below for limitation on the chargeable amount.

Once a chargeable event as defined above has occurred, then if at that time there was outstanding any principal of any borrowings by the trustees and if the chargeable amount was limited as described below, a further chargeable event will occur at the end of any year of assessment in which any part of such principal is repaid by the trustees. Amounts borrowed earlier are for these purposes taken to be repaid before amounts borrowed later. The chargeable amount in this case is the amount repaid (but subject to limitation, see below) and is chargeable and recoverable in the same way as on other chargeable events. There are provisions to prevent a double charge in respect of the same borrowings where two or more chargeable events, of the kind first described above, occur at different times.

The chargeable amount, however arising, is limited to the total amount of payments received by the trustees before the chargeable event in question which have either qualified for corporation tax relief or would so qualify if a claim to that effect were made immediately before the occurrence of the event. For the purpose of determining whether or not the limit has been exceeded, any previous chargeable amounts must be aggregated with the chargeable amount in question. There is also a limitation on the chargeable amount in respect of repaid borrowings by reference to earlier chargeable amounts.

[*FA 1989, ss 68–72; F(No 2)A 1992, s 36; FA 1993, Sch 6 para 20; FA 1994, Sch 13 para 6; FA 1996, s 120(3)(4)(12); FA 2000, s 55*].

Capital gains relief on introduction of shares. A form of capital gains rollover relief may be available on the transfer of shares into a qualifying ESOT before 6 April 2001. See Tolley's Capital Gains Tax under Employee Share Schemes for details.

Information. Where any payments to an ESOT have been allowed for tax purposes, the inspector must notify the trustees, stating the amount involved. He may, by written notice to the trustees, require the submission by them, with penalties for failure to comply, of a return containing such further information as is specified in the notice. This may include information about sums received, sums borrowed, expenditure incurred, assets acquired, transfers of assets made, etc. [*FA 1989, s 73*]. Similar provisions apply in relation to claims for capital gains tax relief on the introduction of shares. [*TCGA 1992, s 235*].

Simon's Direct Tax Service. See **D2.221** *et seq.*.

83 Social Security

83.1 The *Social Security Acts of 1973* and *1975* were designed to assimilate earlier national insurance and industrial injuries legislation. Subsequent *Acts* have introduced many detailed changes and extended the scope of the social security system. The legislation was consolidated in 1992. For details of individual benefits, see Tolley's Social Security and State Benefits.

83.2 **Contributions** by an employee are not allowable for tax purposes. An employer is allowed his contributions for employees as an expense or deduction. [*ICTA 1988, s 617(3)(4); FA 1997, s 65; FA 1999, s 61*]. See 71.54 SCHEDULE D, CASES I AND II. See also 1.10 ALLOWANCES AND TAX RATES as regards Class 4 contributions.

83.3 **Benefits taxable** (as earned income under Schedule E) are

Incapacity benefit (1995/96 onwards) (see below)
Income support when paid to unemployed and strikers (see below)
Industrial death benefit (if paid as pension)
Invalid care allowance
Invalidity allowance when paid with retirement pension
Jobseeker's allowance (up to 'taxable maximum')
Job release allowance
Old persons' pension
Retirement pension
Statutory maternity pay
Statutory sick pay
Unemployment benefit (pre-6/10/96)
Widowed mother's allowance
Widow's pension

[*ICTA 1988, ss 151A, 617(1)(2)(6); FA 1994, s 139*]. See 29.32 EXEMPT INCOME for certain exemptions on war widow's pension and 29.28 for other exemptions. See inside back cover for **rates** of main taxable benefits.

To reduce the administration of receiving returns before assessing retirement pensions and widow's pensions, the Revenue are generally notified by the DSS of the amounts each year. (Revenue Press Release 26 July 1979).

Incapacity benefit (which replaces invalidity benefit from 6 April 1995) is taxable under Schedule E (and may be within PAYE) *except for* short-term benefit payable otherwise than at the higher rate, i.e. benefit payable for the first 28 weeks of incapacity (and except for any child addition). There is also an exclusion for certain payments where invalidity benefit was previously payable in respect of the same period of incapacity. [*FA 1994, s 139; FA 1995, s 141*]. For the application of PAYE to taxable payments of incapacity benefit, see *SI 1995 No 853*.

Income support is taxable under Schedule E only if the entitlement to it is subject to the condition specified in the *Social Security Act 1986, s 20(3)* (or NI equivalent) as regards availability for employment, or if the claimant is one of a couple (whether or not married) and *Social Security Act 1986, s 23* (or NI equivalent) (trade disputes) applies to the claimant but not to the other person (i.e. broadly if the claimant is unemployed or on strike). There is a maximum amount in any period which is taxable, and this maximum applies to the sum of income support and unemployment benefit where both are in payment. There is provision for notification of, and objection to, determination of the taxable amount by the benefit officer. [*ICTA 1988, ss 151, 152*]. See Revenue Pamphlets IR41 (Income Tax and Job Seekers), IR42 (Income Tax: Lay-offs and Short-time Work) and IR43 (Income Tax and Strikes).

See also 55.43 PAY AS YOU EARN regarding the withholding of tax refunds from the unemployed and strikers.

Statutory sick pay and **statutory maternity pay** paid by employers is taxable. See 75.37 SCHEDULE E.

Simon's Direct Tax Service. See **E4.129**.

83.4 **Benefits not taxable are**

Means-tested benefits

Council tax benefit
Disabled person's tax credit (see 83.6 below)
Educational maintenance allowance
Hospital patients' travelling expenses
Housing benefit
Income support (if not taxable as in 83.3 above)
Social fund payments
Student grants
Uniform and clothing grants
Working families' tax credit (see 83.6 below)

Industrial injury benefits

Industrial death benefit child allowance
Disablement benefit, including
Constant attendance allowance
Exceptionally severe disablement allowance
Reduced earnings allowance
Retirement allowance
Unemployability supplement

Short-term benefits

Incapacity benefit (not at the higher rate, see 83.3 above)
Maternity allowance
Sickness benefit

War disablement benefits

Disablement pension, including
Age allowance
Allowance for lowered standard of occupation
Clothing allowance
Comforts allowance
Constant attendance allowance
Dependant allowance
Education allowance
Exceptionally severe disablement allowance
Invalidity allowance
Medical treatment allowance
Severe disablement occupational allowance
Unemployability allowance

Other benefits

Attendance allowance
Back to work bonus (paid by way of jobseeker's allowance or income support)
Bereavement payment
Child benefit
Child dependency additions *paid with* widowed mother's allowance, retirement pension, invalid care allowance or unemployment benefit
Child's special allowance
Christmas bonus for pensioners
Disability living allowance
Employment rehabilitation allowance
Employment training allowance
Fares to school

Guardian's allowance
Home improvement, repair and insulation grants
Invalidity allowance when paid with invalidity pension
Invalidity pension
Jobfinder's grant
Jobmatch payments and training vouchers
Jobseeker's allowance (in excess of 'taxable maximum')
Job search allowances
Mobility allowance
One parent benefit
Severe disablement allowance
War orphan's pension
War widow's pension
Widow's payment
Youth training scheme allowance (unless trainee has employee status)

[*ICTA 1988, s 315, s 614(1), s 617(1)(2); FA 1996, s 152; Tax Credits Act 1999, Sch 1 para 6(c)*]. See also 83.3 above.

Foster care allowances. Foster parents may receive many different types of allowances and grants. The National Foster Care Association at 87 Blackfriars Road, London SE1 8HA has published guidelines agreed with the Revenue on the taxation treatment of these allowances etc. In general, to the extent that local authority payments made to a foster carer do no more than meet the actual costs of caring, the payments are not taxable. (Hansard 26 October 1994, Vol 248, Col 628).

New Deal Employment Option. Payments made during 1997/98 and 1998/99 to employees whose employer received a subsidy in respect of their employment under the Department of Education and Employment's New Deal programme are taxable only to the extent that they exceeded that weekly subsidy (which ranged from £40 to £75 per week). A refund may be claimed from the local tax office in appropriate cases. (Revenue Press Release 28 May 1999).

New Deal 50plus programme. Employment credits and in-work training grants under the New Deal 50plus programme are disregarded for income tax purposes (and consequently exempt from Class 4 NICs). [*FA 2000, s 84*]. Exemption from Class 1 NICs applies under *SI 1999 No 2736*.

Employment Zones programme. Payments to a person as a participant in an Employment Zones programme are disregarded for income tax purposes (and consequently exempt from Class 4 NICs). [*FA 2000, s 85*]. Exemption from Class 1 NICs applies under *SI 2000 No 723*.

Payments by foreign governments to UK residents which correspond to UK child benefit or to benefits exempt under *section 617(1)* will also be exempt from tax (with special rules in relation to incapacity benefit, see 83.3 above). (Revenue Pamphlet IR 1, A24).

83.5 **Benefits under Government pilot schemes.** For 1996/97 and later years, the question as to whether or not, or to what extent, any benefit under a Government pilot scheme is to be within the charge to income tax is to be determined by Treasury Order. The Treasury may also by order provide for any such benefit to be wholly or partly left out of account in determining whether expenditure otherwise qualifying for capital allowances has been subsidised by the Crown etc. (see 10.2(ii) CAPITAL ALLOWANCES). For these purposes, a Government pilot scheme means, broadly, any arrangements made for a trial period by the Government which provide for new social security benefits or benefits under work incentive schemes. [*FA 1996, s 151*]. The first such Order exempts payments made under the scheme known as Earnings Top-up. [*SI 1996 No 2396*].

83.6 **Working families' tax credit** ('WFTC') and **disabled person's tax credit** ('DPTC') are payable to eligible claimants from 5 October 1999, replacing family credit and disability working allowance respectively (although awards already in payment at 5 October 1999 are allowed to run their course before the change to WFTC or DPTC comes into effect). Both tax credits are non-taxable and are not related to the amount of a claimant's tax liability. Awards are normally fixed for a period of 26 weeks. Both credits are administered by the Revenue through their Tax Credit Office. For 1999/2000 and continuing thereafter as regards the self-employed and those not in employment, the tax credits are payable by the Revenue direct to recipients. On and after 6 April 2000 as regards employees, they are payable by employers via the PAYE system, such payment being funded by the Revenue (see further below). The main provisions are in *Tax Credits Act 1999*, with much of the detail provided by regulations made by statutory instrument. See in particular *SI 1999 Nos 2487, 2570 (as amended), 2571, 2572, 3110, 3219* (and NI equivalents).

WFTC is payable to UK resident single parents and couples, married or otherwise, who are responsible for children and who work (or one of whom works) at least 16 hours per week (being entitled to work in the UK), and with savings not exceeding £8,000. It consists of a basic adult credit (one per family), a child credit in respect of each child (varying according to age), a 30-hour credit if the claimant or at least one partner works at least 30 hours per week, and, subject to further qualifying conditions, a childcare credit reimbursing up to 70% of eligible childcare costs up to maximum costs of £100 per week for one child or £150 per week for two or more children. From October 2000, a further component, a disabled child's credit, will be added where relevant. The total credit is reduced by 55 pence for each £1 of the single parent's or couple's income (net of tax and national insurance contributions) over £90 per week (£91.45 for 2000/01). Couples eligible for WFTC may choose which partner applies for and receives the credit.

Eligibility for DPTC is based on illness or disability affecting a claimant's capacity to work. DPTC is payable to UK resident claimants, with or without children, who work at least 16 hours per week (being entitled to work in the UK), qualify for certain disability benefits (or have done so within a stipulated time prior to the claim) and have savings not exceeding £16,000. It consists of the same components as the WFTC with the addition of a higher adult credit for couples and including from the outset a disabled child's credit where applicable. The total credit is reduced by 55 pence for each £1 of net income over £70 per week for single persons without children and £90 per week for single parents and couples (for 2000/01, £71.10 and £91.45 per week respectively). For claims made on or after 1 October 2000, entitlement to DPTC will extend to certain people who become long-term sick or disabled while in work.

Payment by employers. For 2000/01 onwards, payments of WFTC and DPTC (other than initial payments) are to be made by employers to their employees through the payroll at their normal pay intervals. The Revenue will give an employer advance notice of credits due to any of his employees. The employer obtains reimbursement by deducting the total amount of credits paid from his monthly (or quarterly) PAYE, NIC and student loan remittances. If, for any month (or quarter) the employer expects to incur a shortfall (i.e. total credits exceed the total otherwise due to the Revenue), he may apply to the Revenue for advance funding. Entries relating to tax credits are required on End of Year Returns P14 and P35 and, where relevant, employees' P60s (see 55.9, 55.10 PAY AS YOU EARN, the former also as regards an initial £50 discount where returns are filed over the internet and payments made electronically). *TMA 1970, s 20* (Revenue's power to call for documents etc.) and *s 20B* (restrictions on such powers) (see 6.8 BACK DUTY) are applied with appropriate modifications to employer's obligations with regard to tax credits. See *SI 1999 No 3219* for detailed provisions. See also below re penalties.

Penalties and recovery. Where a person fraudulently or negligently makes any incorrect statement or declaration in connection with a claim for WFTC or DPTC, he is liable to a penalty not exceeding the amount overclaimed. Employers are liable to penalties similar to those of *TMA 1970, s 98* (see 58.4 PENALTIES) in relation to their obligations regarding delivery and accuracy of returns and other documents, and also face a maximum penalty of £3,000 (per employee affected) for refusal or repeated failure to make payment of tax credits as required (such that the Revenue have to take over the payment obligation) or for making or receiving inaccurate payments. Company directors may be held personally liable for fraudulent or negligent misuse of funds provided by the Revenue to pay tax credits.

There are provisions to recover an overpayment of tax credit as if it were tax charged by an assessment. Where the claimant is liable to a penalty as above, interest will also be charged on the overpayment. Interest is also chargeable on penalties themselves. In relation to penalties, procedural rules mirror those of *TMA 1970, ss 100–100D*, the Board's power to mitigate mirrors that of *TMA 1970, s 102*, and there are time limits similar to those of *TMA 1970, s 103* (see 58.6–58.8 PENALTIES).

See also Revenue leaflet 'Working Families Tax Credit and Disabled Person's Tax Credit' (November 1999), Revenue Tax Bulletin October 1999 pp 691–693 (as regards employers' obligations), and Revenue Press Release 9 November 1999 (as regards levels of credit components). See generally Tolley's Social Security and State Benefits for further coverage.

83.7 **National Insurance contributions** for **2000/01** (and for 1999/2000 in brackets where different) are as follows.

Class 1 (earnings-related)

Not contracted out

The employee contribution is **10%** of earnings between **£76** (£66) p.w. and **£535** (£500) p.w..

The employer contribution is **12.2%** of all earnings in excess of the first **£84** (£83) p.w..

Contracted out

The 'not contracted out' rates for employees are reduced on the band of earnings from **£76** (£66) p.w. to **£535** (£500) p.w. by **1.6%**. For employers, they are reduced on the band of earnings from **£84** (£83) p.w. to **£535** (£500) p.w. by **3.0%** for employees in salary-related schemes or **0.6%** for employees in money purchase schemes. In addition, there is an employee rebate of **1.6%** on earnings from **£67** p.w. up to **£76** p.w. (there having been no comparable rebate for 1999/2000) and an employer rebate of **3.0%** or **0.6%**, as appropriate, on earnings from **£67** (£66) p.w. up to **£84** (£83) p.w..

Married women

The reduced employee rate for certain married women and widows with a certificate of election is **3.85%**.

Class 1A (cars and car fuel and other benefits)

Employer contributions at **12.2%** are required on a scale charge value of cars and fuel made available to employees for private use and (from 6 April 2000) on most other benefits.

Class 1B (PAYE settlement agreements)

Employer contributions at **12.2%** are required on the value of all items included in a PAYE settlement agreement and the tax paid under the agreement (see 55.12 PAY AS YOU EARN).

Class 2 (self-employed, flat rate)

The flat weekly rate of contribution is **£2.00** (£6.55). The annual limit of net earnings for exception from Class 2 liability is **£3,825** (£3,770).

Class 3 (voluntary contributions)

The flat weekly rate of contribution is **£6.55** (£6.45).

Class 4 (self-employed, profit-related) (see Revenue Pamphlet IR 24)

The 2000/01 contribution rate is **7%** on the band of profits between **£4,385** and **£27,820.** See below for earlier years' figures. Class 4 contributions are levied, generally, on profits assessed under Schedule D, Cases I and II (plus any enterprise allowance, see 71.85 SCHEDULE D, CASES I AND II) and are shown separately on the notice of assessment for payment at the same time as the tax. Profits for this purpose are after capital allowances and certain interest and annual payments for trade purposes. [*Social Security Contributions and Benefits Act 1992, Sch 2 paras 2, 3(5)*]. Trading losses set against other income may, *for Class 4 purposes,* be carried forward and set against the first available profits. [*SSCBA 1992, Sch 2 para 3(4)*]. Contributions to personal pension schemes and retirement annuity premiums are not deductible in arriving at profits for Class 4 purposes by virtue of *Social Security Contributions and Benefits Act 1992, Sch 2 para 3(2)(f)(g)*. For 1995/96 and earlier years, 50% of Class 4 contributions is deductible in arriving at total income. There are various exceptions from Class 4 liability, including persons over State pensionable age, divers etc. assessed under Schedule D (see 71.31 SCHEDULE D, CASES I AND II) and, on application, those under 16 at the beginning of the year of assessment. [*SI 1979 No 591, regs 58–60*]. Non-UK residents and sleeping partners are not within the scope of Class 4.

Interest is chargeable on overdue Class 4 contributions under *TMA 1970, s 86* and *s 88* as it is for income tax purposes (see 42 INTEREST AND SURCHARGES ON UNPAID TAX), and repayment supplement (see 41 INTEREST ON OVERPAID TAX) is similarly available. [*SSCBA 1992, Sch 2 para 6; SI 1993 No 1025*].

The Class 4 rates and bands for earlier years are as follows.

	Rate	Band
1999/2000	6%	£7,530 – £26,000
1998/99	6%	£7,310 – £25,220
1997/98	6%	£7,010 – £24,180
1996/97	6%	£6,860 – £23,660
1995/96	7.3%	£6,640 – £22,880
1994/95	7.3%	£6,490 – £22,360

83.8 See Tolley's Social Security and State Benefits and Tolley's National Insurance Contributions for full details of this subject.

84 Statutory Bodies

84.1 *Marketing Boards.* Payments by Marketing Boards into certain compulsory reserve funds for maintaining guaranteed prices etc., allowed (on conditions) as deductions, and withdrawals (generally) treated as trading receipts. [*ICTA 1988, s 509*].

84.2 *Atomic Energy Authority and National Radiological Protection Board* are entitled to certain exceptions. [*ICTA 1988, s 512; TCGA 1992, s 271(7)*].

84.3 *Harbour reorganisation schemes* are subject to special tax treatment. [*ICTA 1988, s 518; TCGA 1992, s 221*].

84.4 *Local authorities, local authority associations and health service bodies* are exempt from tax. [*ICTA 1988, ss 519, 519A, 842A as amended; TCGA 1992, s 271(3)*].

84.5 Subject to the special provisions above and, where appropriate, to the Crown exemption (see 30.6 EXEMPT ORGANISATIONS), statutory bodies are liable in the ordinary way to corporation tax on their income and capital gains. Whether their activities amount to trading depends on the facts. See *Mersey Docks and Harbour Board v Lucas HL 1883, 1 TC 385, 2 TC 25* (held to be chargeable under legislation now in *ICTA 1988, s 55*) and *Port of London Authority v CIR CA 1920, 12 TC 122* and contrast the *Forth Conservancy Board* cases, *14 TC 709, 16 TC 103* (liable under Case VI on surplus from shipping dues) and *British Broadcasting Corporation v Johns CA 1964, 41 TC 471* (liable under Case I on profits from publications etc. but not on rest of surplus; not entitled to Crown exemption). See also *Sowrey v King's Lynn Harbour Mooring Commrs QB 1887, 2 TC 201; Humber Conservancy Board v Bater KB 1914, 6 TC 555.*

84.6 *Statutory corporation borrowing in foreign currency.* Interest on securities issued by, or on a loan to, a statutory corporation (as defined) in foreign currency (for securities issued before 6 April 1982, in a currency outside the scheduled territories) shall, if the Treasury directs, be paid without deduction of income tax and be exempt from income tax (but not corporation tax) in the hands of a non-resident beneficial owner of such securities or, in the case of a loan, in the hands of the person for the time being entitled to repayment or eventual repayment of the loan. [*ICTA 1988, s 581*].

85 Stock Dividends

Simon's Direct Tax Service D1.202.

85.1 Shares issued by a UK company in lieu of a cash dividend are chargeable on the individual beneficial shareholder on an amount equal to the cash they replace grossed up at, from 6 April 1999, the Schedule F ordinary rate (previously the lower rate) of tax, as if it was dividend income (see 1.9 ALLOWANCES AND TAX RATES). No charge to, or repayment of, the Schedule F ordinary (or lower) rate tax is made, and the gross amount is not available to cover charges. Where there is no cash equivalent or this equivalent is substantially above or below (i.e. more than one or two percentage points outside 15% either way: Revenue Pamphlet IR 131, A8) the market value of shares issued, the market value is used. Similarly chargeable are bonus shares issued in respect of shares held under terms which carry the right to the bonus. The shareholder is treated as receiving the shares on the due date of issue i.e. the earliest date the company was required to issue the shares. Where more than one person is entitled to the shares issued, apportionment is made according to their respective interests. [*ICTA 1988, s 249(1)–(4), s 251; F(No 2)A 1992, s 19(4); FA 1993, s 77(3); FA 1996, s 122(5), Sch 6 paras 6, 28, Sch 41 Pt V(1); F(No 2)A 1997, Sch 4 para 10*].

85.2 **Capital gains tax.** With effect from 6 April 1998, the issue of shares treated as income as in 85.1 above (or 85.4, 85.5 below) does not constitute a reorganisation of share capital within *TCGA 1992, ss 126–128*. The person acquiring the shares is treated for capital gains tax purposes as having acquired them for whichever of the cash equivalent or market value was used in determining the amount treated as income under 85.1 above. [*TCGA 1992, s 142; FA 1998, s 126*]. Previously, the shares were treated as acquired for that consideration as part of the new holding following the reorganisation of share capital, except that where the shares were issued to a bare or nominee trustee, the position is as applies generally after 5 April 1998 (as above). [*TCGA 1992, ss 141, 142 as originally enacted*].

85.3 **Companies.** For provisions affecting companies issuing and receiving stock dividends, see Tolley's Corporation Tax.

85.4 **Deceased estates.** Stock dividends issued to personal representatives during the administration period are grossed as in 85.1 above and deemed part of the aggregate income of the estate, see 22 DECEASED ESTATES. [*ICTA 1988, s 249(5)*].

85.5 **Discretionary and accumulation trusts.** The provisions in 85.1 above apply to trustees as they do to individuals, with any necessary modifications. See 81.5 SETTLEMENTS as regards the application of *ICTA 1988, s 686.*. [*ICTA 1988, s 249(6); F(No 2)A 1997, Sch 4 para 10*].

85.6 **Enhanced stock dividends received by trustees of interest in possession trusts.** Where the trustees of an interest in possession trust have concluded that either

(*a*) an enhanced stock dividend belongs to the income beneficiary, or

(*b*) it forms part of the trust's capital, or

(*c*) while adding the enhanced stock dividend to capital, the trustees should compensate the income beneficiary for the loss of the cash dividend he would otherwise have received, and the view they have taken of the trust law position is supportable on the facts, the Revenue will not seek to challenge what the trustees have done. The income tax consequences of each view are as follows.

(*a*) Since the beneficiary is beneficially entitled to the shares comprised in the dividend, the provisions described at 85.1 above apply.

(*b*) Since the stock dividend is regarded as capital, there is no income tax liability.

(*c*) The payment to the beneficiary is an annual payment from which basic rate tax must be deducted.

For full details of this treatment and of the capital gains tax consequences, and for differences under Scottish law, see Revenue Pamphlet IR 131, SP 4/94, 17 May 1994.

86 Time Limits—Fixed Dates

Note. This chapter lists fixed date time limits falling in the year to 30 September 2001. See also 87 TIME LIMITS—MISCELLANEOUS.

Simon's Direct Tax Service A3.620 *et seq.*.

86.1 TIME LIMITS OF ONE YEAR OR LESS

(*a*) **5 October 2000** for action in respect of 1999/2000.

Notification of chargeability. Any person who is chargeable to tax for a year of assessment must give notice to the Revenue that he is so chargeable within six months after the end of that year, unless his income comes solely from certain sources (e.g. income dealt with under PAYE or Schedule F) and he has no chargeable gains. [*TMA 1970, s 7 as amended*]. See 78.4 SELF-ASSESSMENT.

(*b*) **31 January 2001** for action in respect of 1999/2000.

(i) *Returns under self-assessment* when required by notice before 2 November 1999. See 78.5 SELF-ASSESSMENT.

(ii) *Personal pension contributions (and retirement annuity contract payments).* (*a*) Claim for contributions paid in 1999/2000 to be relieved as if paid in 1998/99. See 60.5 PERSONAL PENSION SCHEMES, 65.4 RETIREMENT ANNUITIES. (*b*) Claim for relief for contributions paid in 2000/01 (and before 31 January 2001) and carried back to 1999/2000 to be set against balancing liability for 1999/2000. See 17.2 CLAIMS.

(iii) *Cash basis withdrawal.* Election for increased adjustment charge to be made for a year of assessment under the transitional provisions. See 12.2 CASH BASIS.

(*c*) **5 April 2001** — advance time limit for action in respect of 2001/02.

Transfer of married couple's (where available) and blind person's allowances. Election by wife to receive one-half of the married couple's allowance, or by spouses jointly for wife to receive the whole of the allowance, or by husband to receive one-half where a joint election has been made for wife to receive the whole of the allowance, must be made before the start of the first year of assessment to which the election is to apply (subject to a 30 day extension where notice of intention to elect was given to the inspector before the start of that year). Withdrawals of such elections similarly do not have effect until the year of assessment after that in which notice of withdrawal was given. Similar rules apply to transfers inter-spouse of blind person's allowance. See 47.2 MARRIED PERSONS.

(*d*) **5 April 2001** for action in respect of 1999/2000.

(i) *Claims following late assessments.* A claim (including a supplementary claim) which could not have been allowed but for the making of an assessment to income tax or capital gains tax after the year of assessment to which it relates may be made before the end of the year of assessment following that in which the assessment was made. [*TMA 1970, s 43(2)*].

(ii) *Land managed as one estate at 5 April 1963.* Election to include notional rents and deduct certain expenses. See 68.7(*b*) SCHEDULE A.

(*e*) **5 May 2001** for action in respect of 2000/01.

Employee conditional and convertible shares. Information relating to such shares must be supplied within 30 days after the end of the year of assessment in which certain events take place. See 82.7, 82.8 SHARE INCENTIVES AND OPTIONS.

(*f*) **4 June 2001** for action in respect of 2000/01.

Exercise of option to acquire shares. Election to pay tax by instalments. See 82.3 SHARE INCENTIVES AND OPTIONS.

(*g*) **6 July 2001** for action in respect of 2000/01.

Election for treatment as a single loan of beneficial loans to director by close company lender must be made within three months of the end of the tax year. [*ICTA 1988, s 160(1B); FA 1996, s 107(1)*]. See 75.17 SCHEDULE E.

86.2 **TIME LIMITS ONE TO TWO YEARS**

(*a*) **31 January 2001** for action in respect of 1998/99.

(i) *Capital allowances.* The following time limits apply.

(A) *Agricultural buildings and works.* Election for balancing adjustments to apply on a disposal, etc.. See 10.3 CAPITAL ALLOWANCES.

(B) *Machinery and plant.* Notification of expenditure qualifying for allowances to the Revenue. See 10.25 CAPITAL ALLOWANCES.

(C) *Machinery and plant.* Claim to offset allowances against income other than that against which they are primarily to be given. See 10.32 CAPITAL ALLOWANCES.

(D) *Ships.* Notice requiring the postponement or reduction of first-year allowances, see 10.27 CAPITAL ALLOWANCES. Also notice requiring postponement of writing-down allowances, and that the 'single ship trade' provisions are not to apply, see 10.28(B) CAPITAL ALLOWANCES. Also claim for deferment of balancing charge, see 10.30 CAPITAL ALLOWANCES.

(E) *Short-life assets.* Election for certain expenditure to be treated as on short-life assets, and for certain transfers between connected persons to be treated as at tax written-down value. See 10.28(F) CAPITAL ALLOWANCES.

(F) *Equipment leasing.* Election for fixtures to be treated as belonging to the lessor and not the lessee. See 10.34(*b*) CAPITAL ALLOWANCES.

(ii) *Herd basis.* Election where 1998/99 was either the first year of assessment (after that in which trading commenced) during the basis period for which a herd was kept, or the first year of assessment in the basis period for which compensation was received for compulsory slaughter. See 34.4, 34.8 HERD BASIS.

(iii) *Qualifying interest.* Election for residence basis to apply. See 43.10 INTEREST PAYABLE.

(iv) *Qualifying interest: married couples.* Election (or withdrawal) for apportionment of interest payments and/or sharer's limits between spouses. See 43.12 INTEREST PAYABLE.

(v) *Claim for loss in trade etc.* to be set off against general income (see 46.3 LOSSES) or carried back (see 46.13 LOSSES).

(vi) *Claim for losses on shares* in unlisted companies. See 46.18 LOSSES.

(vii) *Maintenance payments.* Election for such payments to be treated as *not* made under 'existing obligations'. See 47.10 MARRIED PERSONS.

(viii) *Unremittable overseas income.* Claim for relief. See 51.14 NON-RESIDENTS AND OTHER OVERSEAS MATTERS.

(ix) *Patent rights* election where capital sum received. See 54.5 PATENTS.

(x) *Post-cessation receipts.* Election for such receipts to be treated as received on date of discontinuance. See 62.1 POST-CESSATION ETC. RECEIPTS AND EXPENDITURE.

(xi) *Post-cessation expenditure.* Claim for relief against total income. See 62.4 POST-CESSATION ETC. RECEIPTS AND EXPENDITURE.

(xii) *Furnished holiday lettings.* Election for averaging treatment. See 68.9 SCHEDULE A.

(xiii) *Rent-a-room relief.* Election (or withdrawal) for relief not to apply, or for profits or gains to be treated as equal to excess of gross rents over relief limit. See 68.11 SCHEDULE A.

(xiv) *Schedule A losses.* Claim for relief against 1998/99 total income. See 68.13 SCHEDULE A.

(xv) *Copyright etc.* Claim for spreading back or (in certain cases) forward of lump sum receipts. See 71.51 SCHEDULE D, CASES I AND II.

(xva) *Farming.* Claim to average profits of 1997/98 and 1998/99, see 71.57(*a*) SCHEDULE D, CASES I AND II.

(xvi) *Films.* Certain expenditure on production or acquisition may be reallocated to other periods. See 71.58 SCHEDULE D, CASES I AND II.

(xvii) *Gifts to educational establishments.* Claim for gifts of certain articles to be excluded from trading accounts. See 71.60 SCHEDULE D, CASES I AND II.

(xviii) *Share dealers.* Election for rollover relief not to apply on exchange of securities by government in connection with conversion operations, nationalisation etc.. See 71.82 SCHEDULE D, CASES I AND II.

(xix) *Appropriations to and from trading stock.* Election for market value to be adjusted in certain cases where a chargeable gain or allowable loss would otherwise arise. See 71.83 SCHEDULE D, CASES I AND II.

(xx) *Work in progress on cessation.* Election for work in progress to be taken at cost on cessation in 1998/99. See 71.83 SCHEDULE D, CASES I AND II.

(xxi) *Discounts on securities.* Claim for relief for losses on transfer or redemption. See 72.2 SCHEDULE D, CASE III.

(xxii) *Beneficial loan arrangements.* Election (or requirement by inspector) for alternative method of calculating benefit. See 75.17 SCHEDULE E.

(xxiii) *Settlements for maintenance of historic buildings.* Election for tax exemption on income. See 81.30 SETTLEMENTS.

(*b*) **5 April 2001** for action in respect of 1998/99.

(i) *Valuation of trading stock on discontinuance.* Election for transfers between CONNECTED PERSONS (20) to be reduced below market value in certain cases. See 71.83 SCHEDULE D, CASES I AND II.

86.3 **TIME LIMITS TWO TO THREE YEARS**

31 January 2001 for action in respect of 1997/98.

Deceased estates. Claim for adjustment of assessments where administration was completed in 1996/97. See 22.3 DECEASED ESTATES.

86.4 **FOUR-YEAR TIME LIMITS**

There are no four-year time limits, so 1996/97 need not be considered in the present context.

86.5 **FIVE-YEAR TIME LIMITS**

Schedule E formal assessment request in respect of 1995/96, see 75.1(2) SCHEDULE E.

86.6 **SIX-YEAR TIME LIMITS**

Except where other time limits are prescribed, claims must be made within six years of the end of the year of assessment to which they relate. Such claims, as listed below, for 1994/95 must accordingly be made by 5 April 2001. For 1996/97 and subsequent years, such claims must be made by 31 January following the end of the fifth year of assessment after that to which the claim relates. [*TMA 1970, s 43(1); FA 1994, Sch 19 para 14*].

(*a*) *Error or mistake claims.* See 17.10 CLAIMS.

(*b*) *Claim for additional personal allowances etc.* omitted from the taxpayer's tax return.

(*c*) *Claim against double assessment* where the same person has been assessed 'for the same cause' in the same year. [*TMA 1970, s 32*].

(*d*) DOUBLE TAX RELIEF (25).

(*e*) INTEREST PAYABLE (43).

(*f*) LOSSES (46) except where shorter time limits apply.

(*g*) MINERAL ROYALTIES (49).

(*h*) NON-RESIDENTS AND OTHER OVERSEAS MATTERS at 51.14. Delayed remittances of overseas income or gains.

(*i*) PERSONAL PENSION SCHEMES (60) and RETIREMENT ANNUITIES (65). Unused relief may be claimed.

(*j*) SCHEDULE D CASES I AND II at 71.4. Claim for actual basis for the second and third years of assessment must be made within six years of the end of the third year of assessment (i.e. where a business commenced in 1992/93 claims may be made up to 5 April 2001).

(*k*) SCHEDULE D, CASES I AND II at 71.51. Spreading of certain lump sums received for copyrights. See also 86.2 (xv) above.

(*l*) SCHEDULE D, CASE III (72) and SCHEDULE D, CASES IV AND V (73). Claim for actual basis to apply for the first year of assessment to which the preceding year basis would otherwise apply. Claim for cessation basis may be made if there is no income from a source for six years or if no income arose in the last three years of ownership (see *ICTA 1988, s 67(4)(5)* for full details).

(*m*) SETTLEMENTS at 81.12. Claims for personal allowances etc. up to 1968/69 in respect of specified contingent interests must be made by 5 April 2001 if the contingency occurred in 1994/95.

(*n*) Any other matter not specified in 86.1–86.6 above for which relief from income tax is claimed.

86.7 COMPANIES

Claims and elections in respect of companies, where applicable, usually have the same time limits as shown above except that the expiry date is by reference to the end of the company's accounting period instead of the end of the year of assessment.

87 Time Limits—Miscellaneous

See also 86 TIME LIMITS—FIXED DATES above. Time limits other than to fixed dates are set out below. In some (but not all) cases, the periods can be extended at the discretion of the Inland Revenue.

Simon's Direct Tax Service A3.620 *et seq.*.

87.1 TIME LIMITS OF ONE YEAR OR LESS

(*a*) **30 days**

(i) Returns of income for 1995/96 and earlier years, following notice. See 67.2 RETURNS.

(ii) Enquiries into returns. Amendment by taxpayer of self-assessment following completion of enquiries. See 78.13 SELF-ASSESSMENT.

(iii) Appeals against assessments, amendments to self-assessments or partnership statements and disallowances of claims or elections in returns. Lodging of notice of appeal. See 4 APPEALS, 78.31 SELF-ASSESSMENT.

(iv) Appeals to High Court. Request for Stated Case following determination of appeal. See 4.7 APPEALS.

(v) Payment of tax following issue of notice of assessment (if due and payable date not later) (although see now 78.17–78.20 SELF-ASSESSMENT). See 56.1 PAYMENT OF TAX.

(vi) Patent rights election after death, winding-up or partnership change. See 54.6 PATENTS.

(vii) There are many instances in which Revenue information powers and clearance procedures require a response within 30 days, see e.g. 3.2 ANTI-AVOIDANCE.

(*b*) **60 days**

There are a number of circumstances in which information is required to be provided within 60 days, see e.g. 26.17, 26.31 ENTERPRISE INVESTMENT SCHEME (AND BES).

(*c*) **Three months**

(i) Returns of income, partnership statements etc. for 1996/97 onwards, following notice requiring delivery (if not before 31 January following year for which return required). See 78.5, 78.8, 78.9 SELF-ASSESSMENT.

(ii) Appeals relating to questions of (i) personal reliefs for non-residents, (ii) residence, ordinary residence or domicile, (iii) pension funds for service abroad. [*TMA 1970, s 42(3) (as originally enacted), Sch 1A para 9; ICTA 1988, s 207*].

(iii) Application for judicial review must be made within three months of the date when the grounds for application arose. See 4.8 APPEALS.

(*d*) **Six months**

Payment of retirement annuity and personal pension payments by an individual (if not made during the tax year) may be made within six months of the agreed assessment for that year, together with an election, in certain circumstances. See 65.5 RETIREMENT ANNUITIES, 60.6 PERSONAL PENSION SCHEMES.

(*e*) **Twelve months**

(i) *Enterprise investment scheme* relief must be claimed within twelve months after the authorisation by the inspector of the issue of Form EIS 3 by the company. See 26.11 ENTERPRISE INVESTMENT SCHEME (AND BES).

(ii) *Double tax relief.* Notice must be given to the Revenue within one year of a foreign tax credit becoming excessive. See 25.5(*e*) DOUBLE TAX RELIEF.

87.2 **TWO-YEAR TIME LIMITS**

(*a*) *Industrial buildings.* Election for allowances to apply to holder of long lease out of relevant interest within two years of lease taking effect. See 10.14 CAPITAL ALLOWANCES.

(*b*) *Sales without change of control.* Election for transfer of assets at tax written-down value. See 10.22(i) CAPITAL ALLOWANCES.

(*c*) *Equipment leasing.* Election for certain fixtures on which expenditure incurred by incoming lessee to be treated as belonging to lessee within two years of date of lease taking effect. See 10.34(*d*) CAPITAL ALLOWANCES.

(*d*) *Successions.* Election for transfers between 'connected persons' to be at tax written-down value. See 10.38(xi) CAPITAL ALLOWANCES.

(*e*) *Know-how payment.* Election within two years of disposal for it not to be treated as a payment for goodwill. See 71.67 SCHEDULE D, CASES I AND II.

88 Trade Unions

88.1 Trade Unions are entitled to the tax exemptions below providing they are registered (which means listed under the *Trade Union and Labour Relations Act 1974* or NI equivalent) and providing they are precluded from assuring more than £4,000 by way of gross sum or £825 by way of annuity (excluding retirement annuities approved under *ICTA 1988, s 620(9)*) in respect of any one person. The limits may be increased by the Treasury by order. [*ICTA 1988, s 467; ICTA 1970, s 338; FA 1987, s 31; FA 1991, s 74*].

Exemption is then granted on income which is not trading income and is applicable and applied to *provident benefits* (as defined in *ICTA 1988, s 467(2)* as amended by *FA 1988, Sch 3 para 17*) which include legal expenses incurred in representing members at Industrial Tribunal hearings of cases alleging unfair dismissal, or in connection with a member's claim in respect of accident or injury suffered, and general administrative expenses of providing such benefits. (Revenue Pamphlet IR 131, SP 1/84, 17 February 1984). See also *R v Special Commrs* (*ex p NUR*) *QB 1966, 43 TC 445*. Similar exemption is granted on capital gains so applied. [*ICTA 1988, s 467(1)(b)*].

Similar provisions apply to employers' associations registered as trade unions [*ICTA 1988, s 467(4)(b)*] and to the Police Federations for England and Wales, Scotland and Northern Ireland and other police organisations with similar functions. [*ICTA 1988, s 467(4)(c)*].

89 Underwriters

Simon's Direct Tax Service E5.6.

Other sources. For a detailed treatment of this subject, see Tolley's Taxation of Lloyd's Underwriters. See also Revenue Inspector's Manual, IM 2710–2715.

89.1 Special tax provisions for Lloyd's underwriters were contained in *ICTA 1988, ss 450–457* and *Sch 19A*. With effect generally for 1992/93 and subsequent years, but with some changes taking effect later than 1992/93, these provisions are repealed and replaced with a new tax regime for underwriters contained in *FA 1993, ss 171–184, Schs 19, 20* (as amended). The new regime partly mirrors the old but also includes substantive changes. Further changes in *FA 1994, s 228, Sch 21* facilitate the introduction of self-assessment by revising the relationship between the underwriting year and the year of assessment. Various further provisions are contained in *SI 1974 Nos 896, 1330* (amending), *SI 1990 No 2524* (amending) and in annual regulations as noted in 89.5 below. See also 74.26 SCHEDULE D, CASE VI for the application of the accrued income and forestalling charges ('bondwashing') to underwriters for underwriting years before 1994.

Following the admission of corporate members to Lloyd's from 1 January 1994, special provisions are contained in *FA 1994* for the application of corporation tax to such members. Broadly, the effect of these is as follows.

(*a*) Corporation tax will continue to be chargeable, and Pay and File to apply, in the normal way.

(*b*) Schedule D, Case I rules apply in determining the income from the Lloyd's underwriting trade, and in addition profits and gains from syndicate participation, premium trust funds, ancillary funds, etc. are included.

(*c*) Profits and gains from syndicate participation are treated as accruing uniformly over the underwriting year in which they are declared and apportioned to the concurrent accounting periods.

(*d*) Non-syndicate income and gains are taxable as income (as for corporate insurers generally).

(*e*) There are special rules for items such as stop-loss insurance, reinsurance to close, premiums trust fund assets and cessation.

(*f*) There is no provision for a special reserve fund.

See *FA 1994, ss 219–227, 229, 230, 248* (as amended).

As regards Scottish limited partnerships, see *SI 1997 No 2681*.

89.2 **Self-assessment.** To enable the self-assessment rules to be applied for 1997/98 and subsequent years, a revised basis of assessment applies to profits or losses from syndicate membership, including syndicate investment income, and arising from assets forming part of the premiums trust fund. The profits or losses in a year of assessment are those declared in the underwriting year ending in the year of assessment, i.e. profits of underwriting year 1994 are generally declared in 1997 and assessed for 1997/98. Profits of 1993 continue to be assessed for 1993/94, and there will be no assessments for 1994/95, 1995/96 or 1996/97. [*FA 1993, s 172(1); FA 1994, Sch 21 para 2*]. The transitional administrative arrangements up to and including 1997/98 operate as follows.

(i) Tax in respect of the 1992 underwriting year, assessable 1992/93, was due on 1 January 1996 (basic rate, as previously) and 31 January 1997 (higher rate, previously

1 July 1996). The dates for underwriting year 1993, assessable 1993/94, are 1 January 1997 and 31 January 1998 respectively. For underwriting year 1994, assessable 1997/98, tax is due under the normal self-assessment rules on 31 January 1998, 31 July 1988 and 31 January 1999, and so on for subsequent years.

(ii) For 1994/95, 1995/96 and 1996/97, for which no underwriting profits, etc. fall to be assessed, tax in respect of personal receipts (such as ancillary fund income) is due on 31 January 1998.

(iii) Information relating to underwriting years 1992 and 1993 is required with the income tax returns issued in April 1996 and April 1997 respectively, one year later than under current rules. Information relating to 1994/95, 1995/96 and 1996/97 is also sought with the latter return, although for convenience it may be noted on earlier returns as it becomes available. If it is clear that a loss has arisen in any of those years, relief will be allowed on submission of a claim as soon as the figures are available, and early relief may similarly be allowed where the results for 1992/93 and 1993/94 show a loss, provided that all the information that would have been required in the tax return is given.

[*SI 1995 No 352*].

For these purposes, an individual commencing underwriting business at Lloyd's during underwriting year 1994 is treated as having commenced business on 6 April 1994. [*FA 1994, s 218(3)*].

See Revenue Tax Bulletin October 1998 pp 599, 600 as regards the appropriate figures for self-assessment returns for 1997/98 (1994 underwriting account).

89.3 UNDERWRITING PROFITS

The aggregate of a member's **underwriting profits** is chargeable under Schedule D, Case I. Underwriting profits include income from premiums trust fund assets and income arising after 5 April 1993 from 'ancillary trust fund' assets. An '*ancillary trust fund*' does not include a premiums trust fund or special reserve fund but otherwise means any trust fund required or authorised by Lloyd's rules or required by an underwriter's member's agent or (before 1994/95) the managing agent of a syndicate of which he is a member. [*ICTA 1988, s 450(2); FA 1988, s 58(1); FA 1993, s 171(1)(2)(4), s 184(2)(b); FA 1994, Sch 21 para 8(1)*].

Foreign income dividends within *ICTA 1988, Pt VI, Ch VA* are included in premiums trust fund income for 1992/93 until their abolition after 5 April 1999 at the actual amount received. [*FA 1993, s 171(2A); FA 1994, Sch 21 para 1(1)(3)(a); F(No 2)A 1997, Sch 6 para 20*]. Distributions made after 1 July 1997 in respect of any asset of a premiums trust fund do not carry any entitlement to a tax credit (and see the provisions against arrangements to pass on the value of tax credits at 3.23 ANTI-AVOIDANCE). [*F(No 2)A 1997, s 22(1)(7)*].

After 31 December 1993, annual appreciation in value of and profits on disposal of premiums trust fund assets are included in underwriting profits for income tax purposes and annual depreciation in value and losses on disposal are deducted in arriving at such profits. For the purposes of computing appreciation and depreciation in value of premiums trust fund assets, certain transfers within *ICTA 1988, s 129* prior to its repeal (stock lending — see 71.82 SCHEDULE D, CASES I AND II) are, effectively, regarded as not having taken place, and there is an exemption similar to that in 74.10(*d*) SCHEDULE D, CASE VI (FOTRA securities). [*FA 1993, ss 174, 184(2); FA 1994, Sch 21 para 3; FA 1996, s 154, Sch 41 Pt V(18); FA 1997, Sch 18 Pt VI(10)*]. Before 1 January 1994, such appreciation, profits etc. constitute gains and losses for capital gains tax purposes. [*ICTA 1988, s 450(6); TCGA 1992, ss 206–209; FA 1993, Sch 23 Pt III(12)*]. Under Lloyd's rules, gains and losses on disposals and deemed disposals for the underwriting year 1994 are apportioned between the 1992, 1993 and 1994 underwriting accounts and those for 1995 to the 1993, 1994 and 1995 accounts. Thus, a proportion of total gains and losses allocated to 1992 and 1993 will qualify for income tax treatment. There are transitional provisions affecting the calculation of syndicate profits for income tax purposes for those two years. [*FA 1993, Sch 19 para 10(2)(b)(c)(3)(c)(d)(4)*]. Gains and losses on ancillary trust fund assets remain within the capital gains tax regime. [*FA 1993, s 176(2)*].

For 1993/94 and subsequent years, underwriting profits are treated as derived from the carrying on of a business and thus as **earned income**. [*FA 1993, s 180*]. For earlier years, underwriting profits are treated as earned income only where the underwriter is a 'working name', i.e. is actively engaged in the business of underwriting and is employed full-time (i.e. at least 75% of a full working week) in the Room at Lloyd's or in the office of an underwriting agent or broker. Where this was not the case, such profits are not 'relevant earnings' for the purposes of contributions to PERSONAL PENSION SCHEMES (60) and RETIREMENT ANNUITIES (65) (*Koenigsberger v Mellor CA 1995, 67 TC 280*).

Stop-loss insurance premiums are allowable as an expense in computing underwriting profits, and insurance money received in respect of a loss is a trading receipt of the year of assessment corresponding to the underwriting year in which the loss arose or, in relation to underwriting year 1997 onwards, was declared. This treatment is extended to payments into and receipts out of the High Level Stop Loss Fund, i.e. the fund of that name established under Lloyd's rules for the underwriting year 1993 and subsequent years. For 1992/93 and subsequent years, a repayment of insurance money received etc. is likewise allowed as an expense, as is any amount payable under a quota share contract, i.e. a contract made in accordance with Lloyd's rules and practice between the underwriter and another person which provides for that other person to take over any rights and liabilities of the underwriter under any of his syndicates. Also for 1992/93 onwards, the treatment of insurance receipts etc. is modified where the inspector is not notified of the receipt in time to raise the necessary assessment for the year corresponding to that in which the loss arose; in such a case, the trading receipt is treated as arising in the year of assessment corresponding to the underwriting year in which the payment of insurance money etc. was made to the underwriter. [*ICTA 1988, s 450(4); FA 1988, s 59; FA 1993, ss 178, 184(1); FA 1994, Sch 21 para 5*].

Reinsurance premiums. A restriction is placed on relief for such premiums payable in respect of liabilities outstanding at the end of an underwriting year for the purpose of closing the accounts for the underwriting year, where the member by whom the premium is payable is also a member of the syndicate as a member of which the reinsurer is entitled to receive it. Relief is restricted to an amount which must not exceed an assessment, arrived at with a view to producing neither profit nor loss to the member to whom it is payable, of the value of the liabilities in respect of which it is payable, and a corresponding reduction is made in his profits or gains as a member of the reinsurer syndicate. [*ICTA 1988, s 450(5)(5A); FA 1988, s 60; FA 1993, s 177; FA 1994, Sch 21 para 4*].

See Revenue Tax Bulletin October 1998 p 599 as regards the proportion of such premiums generally allowable for tax purposes, in particular in relation to the 1994 underwriting account.

Bank guarantee fees paid initially to secure membership as a Lloyd's underwriter are not deductible, but annual payments for the maintenance of such facilities are deductible.

General insurance reserves. For periods of account beginning after 1 January 2000, there are provisions for bringing in as a trading receipt or expense an amount representing interest on any allowance in respect of technical provisions to the extent that it subsequently becomes apparent that it was excessive or insufficient. [*FA 2000, s 107*].

Association of Lloyd's members. It is understood that subscriptions to the Association are allowable, as is the cost of League Tables and Syndicate Results. Two-thirds of the cost of prospective names seminars, and one-half of the cost of most other conferences and meetings, is also allowable, with proportionate allowance of travelling expenses other than to or from London (the place of business).

For the 1993 Account and thereafter, **personal accountancy fees** are allowed on the usual 'wholly and exclusively' basis applicable to traders generally, by reference to the amount paid in the year of account. For 1993 only, a Name may instead either claim the amount paid in the period 6 April to 31 December 1993 against the 1993/94 Schedule D, Case I assessment, or opt for a scale fee equal to two-thirds of the 1992 scale fee (as below). For the 1992 Account and earlier, personal accountancy fees are in most cases given automatically on a non-statutory Revenue scale according to the number of syndicates of which the individual is a member. Formal claims must be submitted for any higher allowance. For the 1991 and 1992 Accounts, the scale allowance is £300 for the first syndicate, £90 for each of the next five and £37.50 for each of the next twenty-one.

Compensation payments from managing or members' agents are likely to be treated as trading receipts of the underwriting year in which the entitlement to compensation arises, and thus as not being chargeable to capital gains tax. Any legal fees incurred, together with any payments out of the compensation to stop-loss insurers, are deductible for tax purposes. (Revenue Tax Bulletin May 1992 p 17). For confirmation that such compensation payments are taxable, see *Deeny and others v Gooda Walker Ltd HL 1996, 68 TC 458*.

Members' agent pooling arrangements ('MAPAs'). For the tax treatment from 6 April 1999 of individuals' shares of the various syndicate membership rights held through each MAPA, see Tolley's Capital Gains Tax under Underwriters. [*FA 1999, ss 82–84*].

Simon's Direct Tax Service. See **E5.611** *et seq.*.

89.4 ASSESSMENT AND COLLECTION

For 1993/94 and earlier years, underwriting profits are assessed on a current year basis by reference to the underwriting year corresponding with the year of assessment (i.e. underwriting year 1993, the year to 31 December, is assessed for 1993/94). However, an underwriting year is generally kept open for two years before it is closed and the profit ascertained. Assessments are, under administrative arrangements (see 89.5 below), delayed until the account is closed. For 1997/98 and subsequent years, underwriting profits are assessed by reference to the underwriting year whose profits are declared in the year of assessment (i.e. underwriting year 1994, whose profits are declared in 1997, is assessed for 1997/98), and, subject to transitional provisions (see 89.2 above), the normal self-assessment payment dates apply. No underwriting profits are, accordingly, assessed for 1994/95, 1995/96 or 1996/97. [*ICTA 1988, ss 450(1), 457(2); FA 1993, ss 172, 184(2)(a); FA 1994, Sch 21 para 2*].

For double tax relief arrangements, see *SI 1997 No 405*.

On cessation (on death or otherwise), the final year of assessment is that which corresponds to the underwriting year in which the underwriter's Lloyd's deposit is paid over to him or his personal representatives or assigns, except that if the underwriter dies before 6 April 1994 and before the end of that underwriting year, his final year of assessment is that in which he dies. Any underwriting profits or losses which do not fall to be taken as profits or losses of an earlier year of assessment are taken to be profits or losses of the final year of assessment. These provisions do not apply where the payment of the Lloyd's deposit to the underwriter etc. was made before 1 January 1993. [*FA 1993, s 179; FA 1994, Sch 21 para 6(1)(2)*]. Where a member dies after 5 April 1994 (*a*) he is treated for these purposes as having died on 5 April in the underwriting year in which he actually died, and

(*b*) the business is treated as continuing until the member's deposit is paid over to his personal representatives, whose carrying on of the business is not treated as a change in the persons so engaged. [*FA 1993, s 179A; FA 1994, Sch 21 para 6(2)(3)*].

If underwriting commenced before 2 January 1971 and a cessation occurs, a claim may be made for assessments (*a*) for the final year of assessment for which underwriting profits or losses fall to be included (being profits or losses declared in the underwriting year following the closing year) to be based on the actual profits from 6 April to 31 December in that underwriting year, and (*b*) for the preceding year to be reduced by the lesser of (i) the whole of the profits of that year and (ii) the underwriting profits for the underwriting year 1972. [*SI 1995 No 351, reg 13*].

For 1996/97 and earlier years, *retirement annuity premiums and personal pension contributions* may be related back to the third previous year of assessment, see 65.4 RETIREMENT ANNUITIES, 60.5 PERSONAL PENSION SCHEMES for special provisions.

Simon's Direct Tax Service. See E5.619A.

89.5 The general administrative arrangements for assessment and collection of tax (see below) are contained in *FA 1993, Sch 19* (before 1992/93, *ICTA 1988, Sch 19A*). Annual arrangements for 1986/87 are contained in *SI 1989 No 421*, those for 1987/88 in *SI 1990 No 627*, those for 1988/89 in *SI 1991 No 851*, those for 1989/90 in *SI 1992 No 511*, those for 1990/91 in *SI 1993 No 415*, those for 1991/92 in *SI 1994 No 728*, those for 1992/93 to 1996/97 inclusive in *SI 1995 Nos 351, 352* (as amended by *SI 1996 Nos 781, 782*) and those for 1997/98 onwards in *SI 1995 No 351*.

These arrangements broadly enable the inspector to require a return of syndicate profits at any time after the beginning of a year of assessment (before 1997/98, after the end of the closing year (i.e. the year of assessment next but one following the year of assessment concerned)), and a payment on account of basic rate tax. Penalties apply for failure to comply with a notice requiring such a return.

The return must be submitted by 1 September in the year of assessment (before 1997/98, by 1 September following the end of the closing year) or three months after service of the notice requiring the return if later. The inspector may determine the syndicate profit or loss either in accordance with the return or, subject to the usual appeal procedures, to the best of his judgement if he is not satisfied with the return, and the determination is conclusive as regards the tax liability of each member. A return may be required apportioning the profits so determined between syndicate members, again subject to penalty for failure to comply.

The return of syndicate profit or loss is to be made by the managing agent, who may also, within six years from 1 March next following the end of the closing year (i.e. the underwriting year next but one following the underwriting year concerned), claim repayment of tax suffered by deduction on syndicate investment income and, from 6 April 1992 to 1 July 1997, tax credits in respect of qualifying distributions forming part of such income (and for this purpose, a non-resident member is treated as entitled to tax credits as if he were UK resident, and for all individual members the tax credit will be treated as income from premiums trust fund assets (see 89.3 above)). Any such repayment must be apportioned and, where there is a syndicate profit available for distribution, paid to the members' agents within 90 days of receipt. No repayment supplement is available.

For 1993/94 and earlier years of assessment, the member's agent may also (and subject to similar conditions) be required to make a return of the member's profit in respect of those syndicates in relation to which he is the agent of the member, including a statement of tax at the basic rate for the year of assessment on such profit. Certain additions and deductions in arriving at the profit so returned are specified, and the return is to be made by 1 October in the year of assessment following the closing year (or three months after service of notice requiring the return, if later). The payment on account (i.e. the basic rate liability, if any, stated in the return) must be made by the members' agent on or before 1 January following the end of the closing year for the year of assessment concerned, and may be the subject of assessment and interest by reference to that date if not made in accordance with the above provisions. Any discrepancy between the payment on account and the amount deducted by the members' agent in accounting to the member is adjusted between them.

For 1992/93 onwards, there are special provisions relating to stop-loss insurance, to reasonable excuse for certain failures to deliver returns, to determinations and to cessations. For 1992/93 and 1993/94, there are also provisions relating to members' agents, to error or mistake relief claims, to extended time limit assessments and to payment of tax. The extended time limit provisions apply also for 1994/95, and the payment provisions for 1994/95 to 1996/97 inclusive. For underwriting years 1994 and 1995 there are special provisions for running-off syndicates.

For 1988/89, 1989/90 and 1990/91, there are special provisions for the date of payment of assessed tax, for reasonable excuse for certain failures by the managing agent or members' agent, for error or mistake relief, and for the amendment of various provisions of the *Taxes Acts* in their application to underwriters.

Member's liability. The amount of basic rate tax apportioned to a member as above is regarded as a payment on account of the member's liability in respect of his share of the profits, any additional liability or repayment being dealt with directly between the member and the Revenue. Tax is due in respect of profits from all a member's syndicates under the normal SELF-ASSESSMENT (78) rules, with credit being given for the basic rate tax accounted for as above by the member's agents.

For the purposes of assessment in cases involving fraudulent or negligent conduct, anything done or omitted to be done by the managing agent is treated as having been done or omitted by each syndicate member. [*ICTA 1988, Sch 19A; FA 1988, s 58(4), Sch 5; FA 1989, ss 149(6), 170(5); SI 1990 No 2524; FA 1993, ss 173, 184(1), Sch 19; FA 1994, Sch 21 paras 9–11; F(No 2)A 1997, Sch 8 Pt II (5)*].

89.6 LOSSES

An underwriting loss can be **carried forward** for relief against underwriting profits in subsequent tax years (under the normal provisions for carry-forward of losses under *ICTA 1988, s 385(1)*).

An underwriting loss for a tax year can also be **offset against other income** of the underwriter of the same tax year under the normal tax provisions of *ICTA 1988, s 380(1)*. Note that, for 1989/90 and earlier years, if the underwriter is not a working name, a loss will be set off first against unearned income. For 1996/97 and earlier years, the loss can also be offset against other income of the immediately preceding tax year providing he was an underwriter during that preceding tax year, so far as relief cannot be given against income of the tax year in which the loss was sustained and can be given after any relief for a loss in that preceding tax year. However, similarly for 1996/97 and earlier years, an underwriting loss cannot be carried forward for use against other income of the underwriter in the succeeding tax year under *ICTA 1988, s 380(2)*. [*ICTA 1988, s 450(3); FA 1993, s 171(3)*].

An underwriting loss in the early years of the business may be carried back and offset against other income under *ICTA 1988, s 381*.

A claim to relief under *section 380* or *section 381* must normally be made within two years of the end of the year of assessment in which the loss is incurred, but prior to the introduction of a revised basis of assessment for 1997/98 onwards (see 89.2 above), this was generally extended for Lloyd's underwriters, by annual regulations, to four years.

See 46 LOSSES.

Simon's Direct Tax Service. See E5.621 *et seq.*.

89.7 **SPECIAL RESERVE FUND**

An underwriter may set up a Special Reserve Fund into which he may make payments (eligible for tax relief — see below) for the purpose of meeting future losses.

(*a*) **1991/92 and earlier years**

The arrangements must satisfy the requirements of *ICTA 1988, ss 452 et seq.*, be approved by the Revenue and certified by the Board of Trade. [*ICTA 1988, s 452(1)*]. The funds must be vested in trustees, who may invest them and income from these investments must be held on trust for the underwriter. An underwriter carrying on business personally and also through an agent, or through more than one agent, may have more than one special reserve fund. [*ICTA 1988, s 452(2)(3)(4)(a)*].

Payments into the fund. The underwriter may pay into the fund(s) annually amounts limited, in aggregate, to (when grossed-up at the basic rate) the lesser of £7,000 or 50% of his underwriting profit (inclusive of investment income on all trust and reserve funds). [*ICTA 1988, s 452(5)(7)(8); FA 1988, s 61(1)(d); FA 1989, s 96(1)(4)*]. Such payments are treated as 'annual payments', from which tax has been deducted at the basic rate, in the year of assessment in which the underwriting year ends, deductible from underwriting income (and from underwriting investment income last). [*ICTA 1988, ss 454, 457(2)*]. Thus the underwriter receives relief (where relevant) for income tax at the higher rates in excess of the basic rate and at the additional rate.

No election is necessary for making payments into a special reserve fund but the amount of any such payment must be notified to the inspector within twelve months after the deemed date of closing the accounts of an underwriting year. The payment must be made not more than 30 days after the inspector has notified his agreement, or 30 days after the expiration of the aforesaid twelve months, if later. [*ICTA 1988, s 452(6)*].

Payments out of the fund. There will be made out of the capital of the special reserve fund (into the underwriter's 'premiums trust fund') payments which, when grossed-up at the basic rate equal underwriting losses (as certified by the inspector, with right of appeal — *ICTA 1988, s 453(4)*). These payments may be made on a provisional basis pending final adjustment of the loss, whereafter adjustment will be made. [*ICTA 1988, s 453*]. Such payments (other than provisional amounts) are treated as 'annual payments' receivable by the underwriter from which tax has been deducted at the basic rate, in the year of assessment in which the underwriting year ends [*ICTA 1988, s 454(3)*] and relief for a loss is given as far as possible against the income represented by the payment (for which see *Peterson v De Brunner (Sp C 64), [1996] SSCD 91*). [*ICTA 1988, s 454(4)*].

On the underwriter ceasing to carry on business, the capital of his special reserve fund (so far as not required for a loss as above) shall be paid over to him, or his personal representatives or assigns. [*ICTA 1988, s 452(4)(b)*]. Tax consequences are as follows.

(i) *If he ceases to carry on business before his death* — payment out is treated as an 'annual payment' to him, from which tax has been deducted at the basic rate, on the last day on which he carried on business. [*ICTA 1988, s 454(5)*].

(ii) *If he dies while carrying on business* — there is to be ascertained that part of the fund which represents the excess in the fund (after withdrawals for losses) over what would be in the fund if payments in had been limited to amounts which, when grossed-up, had not in any year exceeded £5,000 or 35% of the profit, whichever was the less. This excess, grossed-up at the rates of tax applicable to the relevant years, is treated as an annual payment to him in the relevant year of assessment in which each part of the excess was deemed to be paid in. [*ICTA 1988, s 455(1)(2)*].

Any withdrawal for a loss made at any time is, for the above purpose, treated as having been met (*a*) out of payments made into the fund for years before that loss was incurred, and before withdrawal for any later loss, (*b*) primarily out of payments made for any underwriting year up to limits of £5,000 or 35%, and (*c*) out of excess payments over £5,000 or 35%, but taking those of later years before earlier years. [*ICTA 1988, s 455(1)(3)*]. In cases where the income of an underwriter falls to be treated as investment income, transfers out of the fund shall be treated as investment income to the extent of any transfer not offset by reliefs. [*ICTA 1988, s 456(1)*].

See Simon's Direct Tax Service E5.641 *et seq.*.

(*b*) **1992/93 and subsequent years**

Special reserve funds within (*a*) above cease to apply with effect for 1992/93 and subsequent years and must be closed (see (*c*) below). For those years, a new-style special reserve fund may be set up in relation to each underwriter under arrangements complying with the requirements of *FA 1993, Sch 20 Pt I* and approved by the Revenue (who may consent to any variation of the arrangements). The fund must be vested in trustees who have control over it, and there must be appointed a fund manager, authorised under Lloyd's rules and who may be the trustees or one or more of them, to invest the capital and vary the investments. Payments into and out of the fund (which, unless a contrary intention appears in the legislation, must be in money) must be allowed only where required or permitted (expressly or by necessary implication) by the provisions of *Schedule 20*. Otherwise, the income arising from the fund must be added to capital and retained in the fund. The underwriter is absolutely entitled as against the trustees to the fund assets, but subject to the rules of cessation (see below) and (for 1994/95 onwards) without affecting the operation of capital gains tax on a disposal of an asset by the underwriter to the trustees. The fund manager must value the fund in a manner to be prescribed by regulations (see *SI 1995 No 353*) as at the end of each underwriting year, commencing with the underwriting year 1994, and must report the value (and such other matters as may be prescribed by regulations) to the underwriter. [*FA 1993, s 175(1)(2), Sch 20 paras 1(1), 2, 6(1), 8; FA 1994, Sch 21 paras 12(1), 13; FA 1995, s 143; SI 1999 No 3308, reg 4*].

Payments into and out of the special reserve fund are, respectively, deductions and additions in arriving at the underwriter's profit (to be included, for 1992/93 and 1993/94, in the member's agent's return, see 89.5 above). [*FA 1993, Sch 19 para 10(2)(a)(3)(a), Sch 20 para 10*]. This does not apply for 1994/95, 1995/96 or 1996/97, for which no underwriting profits fall to be assessed (see 89.2 above). [*FA 1994, Sch 21 para 14(3)*]. See also below.

Tax exemption. Profits arising from special reserve fund assets are exempt from both income tax and capital gains tax, and losses are not allowable. The fund manager may, at any time after the end of an underwriting year, claim repayment of income tax deducted from such profits for that year and (before 6 April 1999) of tax credits in respect of qualifying distributions forming part of the fund income for that year. [*FA 1993, Sch 20 para 9; F(No 2)A 1997, Sch 4 para 30*].

For the purposes of the provisions described below, an underwriter's '*syndicate profit*' for an underwriting year is the excess of his aggregate profits over his aggregate losses, profits or losses being those shown in syndicate accounts as arising to him and disregarding payments into or out of the special reserve fund. Profits of a run-off underwriting year are attributable to the last underwriting year but one preceding the run-off year. An underwriter's '*syndicate loss*' is to be construed accordingly. [*FA 1993, Sch 20 para 1; SI 1995 No 353; F(No 2)A 1997, Sch 4 para 30*].

Payments into the fund out of syndicate profits. If an underwriter has made a syndicate profit for an underwriting year, he may pay into his special reserve fund, before the end of a period to be prescribed by regulations (see *SI 1995 No 353*), the lesser of

(i) 50% of that profit, and

(ii) the excess, if any, of an amount equal to 50% of the underwriter's 'overall premium limit' for the closing year (i.e. the year next but one following the underwriting year) over the value of the fund at the end of that year.

An underwriter's '*overall premium limit*' for an underwriting year means the maximum amount which, under Lloyd's rules, he may accept by way of premiums in that year. If the underwriter did not accept premiums in the closing year, the reference in (ii) above to the closing year is to be taken as a reference to the latest underwriting year in which he did so. The above provisions are not to apply, in the case of any underwriter, to any year of assessment after a year of assessment in which the Revenue cancel their approval of the arrangements referred to above, having first given notice to Lloyd's of their intention to do so.

The payment into the fund in respect of an underwriting year is deductible as an expense in arriving at underwriting profits. For 1992/93 and 1993/94, it is made for the year of assessment to which the underwriting year corresponds (i.e. 1992 and 1993 respectively). From 1997/98 onwards, it is made for the year of assessment next but two after that year (i.e. a payment made in underwriting year 1994 is deducted in 1997/98). [*FA 1993, s 175(3), Sch 20 paras 1(1), 3, 10(1); FA 1994, Sch 14*].

Payments out of the fund. Payments *must* be made out of the fund in the following circumstances.

(1) To cover 'cash calls'. A '*cash call*' means a request for funds made to the underwriter by an agent of a syndicate of which he is a member, being made in pursuance of a contract made in accordance with Lloyd's rules and practices. If a cash call is made in respect of an underwriting year, there must be paid out of the underwriter's special reserve fund into a premiums trust fund of his an amount equal to the amount of the call (or, if less, the amount of the special reserve fund). There are provisions for a payment to be made back into the special reserve fund if a stop-loss payment (i.e. a payment of insurance money under a stop-loss insurance or a payment out of the High Level Stop Loss Fund — see 89.3 above) is made to the underwriter, and for a further payment out of the fund if a stop-loss payment is wholly or partly repaid. [*FA 1993, Sch 20 para 4; SI 1995 No 353*].

(2) To cover syndicate losses. If an underwriter sustains a syndicate loss for an underwriting year, there must be paid out of his special reserve fund into a premiums trust fund of his an amount equal to the 'net amount of the loss' (or, if less, the amount of the special reserve fund). The '*net amount of the loss*'

is the amount of the syndicate loss as reduced by any payment made out of the special reserve fund for the year to cover a cash call (see (1) above). As in (1) above, there are provisions for payments into and out of the special reserve fund in the event of stop-loss payments and repayments of stop-loss payments. If a stop-loss payment is made in respect of the loss before any payment out of the special reserve fund in respect of the loss, no payment is required into the fund but the said payment out of the fund is determined as if the net amount of the loss were reduced by the amount of the stop-loss payment. [*FA 1993, Sch 20 para 5*].

(3) To eliminate excess amounts. If on the valuation (see above) of the special reserve fund at the end of the underwriting year, it is found that the value of the fund exceeds 50% of the higher of the underwriter's overall premium limit (see above) for that year and the corresponding figure for the previous year (or 50% of his overall premium limit for the last year in which he accepted premiums), the excess must be paid to the underwriter (or to his personal representatives or assigns). Before 31 December 1999, the overall premium limit for the preceding year was not taken into account. [*FA 1993, Sch 20 para 6(2); SI 1999 No 3308, reg 3*].

(4) On cessation. On a person ceasing to be an underwriter (on death or otherwise), the amount of his special reserve fund (net of any amount required to be paid out to cover cash calls or syndicate losses) must be paid over to the underwriter (or to his personal representatives or assigns), the payment to be in money or in assets forming part of the fund, as the recipient may direct. [*FA 1993, Sch 20 para 7; FA 1994, Sch 21 para 12(2)*].

Any payments required to be made out of or into the fund under (1)–(3) above must be made before the end of a period to be prescribed in each case by regulations (see *SI 1995 No 353*). [*FA 1993, Sch 20 paras 4(8), 5(10), 6(3)*].

In computing underwriting profits for a year of assessment, payments into the special reserve fund under (1) and (2) above in respect of the corresponding (for 1997/98 onwards, the 'relevant') underwriting year are deductible as expenses, and the following are treated as trading receipts:

(A) payments out of the fund in respect of the corresponding or 'relevant' underwriting year to cover cash calls and losses;

(B) payments out of the fund as a result of the repayment of stop-loss payments (see (1) and (2) above) in the corresponding or 'relevant' underwriting year; and

(C) any payment out of the fund under (3) above in respect of the corresponding or 'relevant' underwriting year's closing year (i.e. the underwriting year next but one following the corresponding or 'relevant' underwriting year).

The '*relevant*' underwriting year for this purpose (which applies for 1997/98 onwards) is the underwriting year next but two before the corresponding underwriting year, i.e. for 1997/98, for which the corresponding underwriting year is 1997, the relevant underwriting year is 1994.

[*FA 1993, Sch 20 para 10(2)–(4); FA 1994, Sch 21 para 14*].

Cessation. The aggregate of any payments made out of the special reserve fund under (4) above is treated, in computing underwriting profits for the 'relevant year of assessment', as made immediately after the end of the 'relevant underwriting year' and as being a trading receipt. Where cessation occurs by reason of death, such payments are treated for the purposes of INTEREST AND SURCHARGES ON UNPAID TAX

(42) as if made immediately after the beginning of the member's final year of assessment. The amount of the said trading receipt is the value of the fund at the end of the 'penultimate underwriting year' as reduced by subsequent payments out (other than under (3) or (4) above) and as increased by:

(I) subsequent payments in (excluding payments made before 1 January 2000 out of syndicate profits);

(II) subsequent repayments of tax (and, in respect of 1998/99 and earlier years, tax credits) in respect of fund income;

(III) (for 2000/01 and subsequent years) the amount of any subsequent profits, net of any losses, arising to the trustees from assets (any net deficit being deducted), leaving aside any gain or loss on an asset transferred to the member etc. and treated as an acquisition by him for capital gains tax purposes (see below); and

(IV) any payments made before the end of the penultimate underwriting year (and after 31 December 1999) by the trustees to the member etc., whether under (4) above or otherwise than out of the special reserve fund, including the market value of any asset transferred by way of such payment.

On the transfer of an asset by the trustees to the member, his personal representatives or assigns, whether under (4) above or otherwise, there are rules to determine for capital gains tax purposes both the date and cost of acquisition by the member etc., for which see the corresponding chapter of Tolley's Capital Gains Tax.

For 1994/95 and subsequent years, the '*relevant year of assessment*' is the final year of assessment except that, where a member dies before the occurrence of certain events, it is the year of assessment at the end of which he is treated as having died (see 89.4 above). The events in question are where the member's deposit is paid over to any person (or a substituted arrangement ceases) or the last open year of account of any syndicate of which he was a member is closed or is regarded as having closed. The '*relevant underwriting year*' is the underwriting year corresponding to the year of assessment immediately preceding the final year of assessment except that, where the member dies before the occurrence of certain events (as above), it is the underwriting year immediately preceding that corresponding to the relevant year of assessment (as above). The '*penultimate underwriting year*' is the underwriting year corresponding to the year of assessment immediately preceding the final year of assessment. Before 1994/95, the '*relevant year of assessment*' was the final year of assessment in all cases, and the '*relevant underwriting year*' and the '*penultimate underwriting year*' were in all cases the underwriting year immediately preceding that in which the member's deposit was paid over to him or his personal representatives or assigns. [*FA 1993, Sch 20 para 11; FA 1994, Sch 21 para 15; SI 1995 No 353, reg 8; SI 1995 No 1185, reg 5; F(No 2)A 1997, Sch 4 para 30; SI 1999 No 3308, reg 6*].

Death. Where a member dies after 5 April 1994 and his personal representatives carry on his underwriting business after his death, the above provisions are modified to apply to the personal representatives. [*SI 1995 No 353, regs 7, 7A; SI 1995 No 1185, reg 4*].

See Simon's Direct Tax Service E5.645.

(*c*) **Winding-up of old-style funds**

The following provisions have effect as respects the winding-up of any special reserve fund set up under the arrangements in (*a*) above (an '*old-style fund*') and which belongs to an underwriter for whom a special reserve fund may be set up under the arrangements in (*b*) above (a '*new-style fund*').

An underwriter may, at any time before the end of the 'relevant period', direct that so much of the capital of any old-style fund of his as represents sums paid into it under *section 452* (see (*a*) above) be transferred at the end of that period into his new-style fund, such transfer to be made in money or in assets forming part of the fund or both, as he may direct (the transfer of an asset being treated as a disposal at market value by the underwriter for capital gains tax purposes). Where such a transfer is made, the Revenue will make a payment to the new-style fund representing basic rate tax on the gross equivalent of the amount transferred (i.e. an amount equal to one-third of the amount transferred).

If an underwriter does not direct that a transfer be made, so much of the capital of any old-style fund of his as represents sums paid into it under *section 452* must be paid over to the underwriter at the end of the 'relevant period'. In computing for income tax purposes the underwriter's profits for 1992/93, the amount paid is to be grossed up by reference to the basic rate of tax (25%) and the gross amount treated as a trading receipt.

Whether or not the transfer is made, any remaining capital of the old-style fund is to be paid over to the underwriter at the end of the 'relevant period'.

For the above purposes, any withdrawals made from the old-style fund under *section 453* (see (*a*) above) are treated as having been made primarily out of payments into the fund under *section 452*.

The '*relevant period*' is the period of three months beginning with the 'closing date'. The '*closing date*' is the earliest date on which each of the following has occurred as respects 1991/92 and earlier years of assessment:

(i) the time for making payments into the fund under *section 452* has expired, or the underwriter has given notice to the inspector that he will not be making any (or any further) payments; and

(ii) any withdrawals from the fund under *section 453* have been made.

References above to items being paid over to the underwriter include references to their being paid over to his personal representatives or assigns. [*FA 1993, s 175(4), Sch 20 paras 12–14; FA 1994, Sch 21 para 16*].

90 Unit Trusts

Cross-references. For corporation tax provisions applicable to authorised unit trusts, see Tolley's Corporation Tax under Unit and Investment Trusts. See 52 OFFSHORE FUNDS for unit trusts which are offshore funds.

Simon's Direct Tax Service D4.413 *et seq.*.

90.1 AUTHORISED UNIT TRUSTS

An '*authorised unit trust*' is a 'unit trust scheme' which is the subject of an order under *Financial Services Act 1986, s 78* for the whole or part of an accounting period. A '*unit trust scheme*' is as defined under *Financial Services Act 1986*, but subject to certain exclusions by Treasury order (see *SI 1988 No 267, SI 1992 Nos 571, 3133, SI 1994 No 1479*). [*ICTA 1988, ss 468(6), 469(7); TCGA 1992, s 99(2)*]. The *Tax Acts* have effect as if the trustees were a company resident in the UK, and the rights of unit holders were shares in the company (but without prejudice to the making of 'interest distributions' (see below)). Expenses of management (including managers' remuneration) are allowed as if the company were an investment company. [*ICTA 1988, s 468(1)(4); FA 1994, Sch 14 para 3*]. For capital gains purposes, any unit trust scheme is treated as if the scheme were a company and the rights of the unit holders shares in the company, and, in the case of an authorised unit trust, as if the company were UK resident and ordinarily resident. [*TCGA 1992, s 99(1)*].

A special rate of corporation tax applies to the trustees of an authorised unit trust. For financial year 1996 and subsequent years, the rate is equivalent to the lower rate of income tax (currently 20%) for the year of assessment beginning in the financial year concerned. [*ICTA 1988, s 468(1A); FA 1996, Sch 6 para 10(1)(2); FA 1999, s 28(3)*]. Previously, the rate was equivalent to the basic rate of income tax for the year of assessment beginning in the financial year concerned, except that in certain cases (see below) it was the lower rate of income tax that applied. Relief for interest as a charge on income was denied in respect of certain borrowings breaching duties imposed under *Financial Services Act 1986, s 81* (or such borrowings as might be specified in substitution by Treasury regulation). [*ICTA 1988, s 468E; FA 1994, s 111; FA 1996, Sch 6 para 10(3)*]. For the special corporation tax loan relationship provisions, see Tolley's Corporation Tax under Loan Relationships (special cases).

For financial years 1994 and 1995, the corporation tax rate was equivalent to the lower rather than the basic rate of income tax (as above) where, on a claim for an accounting period all or part of which fell in the financial year concerned, the inspector was satisfied that, throughout the accounting period, no more than 60% of the market value of the investments subject to the trusts (disregarding cash awaiting investment) was represented by 'qualifying investments'. The claim had to be made within twelve months of the end of the accounting period. '*Qualifying investments*' are defined as

(*a*) money placed at interest,

(*b*) building society shares,

(*c*) securities (other than company shares) of any Government, public or local authority or company, whether secured or unsecured, and including any loan stock or similar security, and

(*d*) an entitlement to a share in the investments of another authorised unit trust unless, throughout the accounting period in question, no more than 60% of the market value of that other unit trust's investments is represented by investments falling within (*a*)–(*c*) above, but the Treasury may, by order, extend or restrict the meaning of 'qualifying investments', including any necessary or expedient transitional provisions. [*ICTA 1988, s 468EE; FA 1994, s 111(2); FA 1996, Sch 6 para 10(3)*].

'*Umbrella schemes*' (i.e. schemes which provide separate pools of contributions between which participants may switch) which are authorised unit trusts may treat each of the separate pools as an authorised unit trust. This applies from 1 April 1994, subject to transitional arrangements for schemes which were umbrella schemes immediately before that date. [*ICTA 1988, s 468(7)–(9); FA 1994, s 113*].

Futures and options. Income derived from transactions relating to futures or options contracts is exempt from tax under Schedule D, Case I in the hands of the trustees. A contract is not excluded from this exemption by the fact that any party is, or may be, entitled to receive and/or liable to make only a payment of a sum (rather than a transfer of assets other than money) in full settlement of all obligations. [*ICTA 1988, s 468AA; FA 1990, s 81(1); FA 1999, Sch 20 Pt III(17)*].

For **distribution periods beginning after 31 March 1994**, the total amount available for distribution to unit holders is to be shown in the distribution accounts as available for distribution either as dividends which are not foreign income dividends within *ICTA 1988, Ch VI, Pt VA* (a 'dividend distribution'), or as foreign income dividends (a 'foreign income distribution'), or as yearly interest (which may not include any amount deriving from Schedule A income) (an 'interest distribution') or as divided between the first two categories (in which case no discrimination between unit holders is permitted). For distribution periods ending after 25 November 1996, amounts deriving from distributions to which *FA 1997, Sch 7* applies (see 3.21 ANTI-AVOIDANCE) must be shown as available for distribution as foreign income dividends, as must other amounts which would fall to be treated as distributions to which *FA 1997, Sch 7* applies if they were shown as available for distribution as dividends. Foreign income dividends are abolished from 6 April 1999 (and *FA 1997, Sch 7* is repealed from that date), and these requirements are correspondingly modified from that date. These provisions do not apply to an authorised unit trust which is an approved personal pension scheme (see 60.1 PERSONAL PENSION SCHEMES). [*ICTA 1988, ss 468H(6), 468I; FA 1994, Sch 14 paras 2, 7; F(No 2)A 1997, Sch 6 para 8*].

For these purposes, the making of a distribution includes the investment of an amount on behalf of the unit holder in respect of his accumulation units. [*ICTA 1988, s 468H(2); FA 1994, Sch 14 para 2; FA 1997, Sch 7 para 11*]. See, however, Revenue Pamphlet IR 1, C30 as regards concessional relief from such treatment in the case of certain *de minimis* distribution (or accumulation) waivers.

As regards dividend distributions, they are treated as dividends on shares paid on the '*distribution date*' (i.e. the date specified under the trust or, if there is no such date, the last day of the distribution period), in respect of which no foreign income dividend election may be made (pending the abolition of foreign income dividends after 5 April 1999). See 1.9 ALLOWANCES AND TAX RATES as regards taxation of dividends. [*ICTA 1988, s 468J; FA 1994, Sch 14 para 2; F(No 2)A 1997, Sch 6 para 8*]. Special provisions apply to dividend distributions to unit holders within the charge to corporation tax (see *ICTA 1988, s 468Q* introduced by *FA 1994, Sch 14 para 2*).

As regards foreign income distributions (prior to the abolition of foreign income dividends after 5 April 1999), they are treated as foreign income dividends on shares paid on the '*distribution date*' (as above) to which *ICTA 1988, ss 246A, 246B* (elections for foreign income dividend treatment), *ss 246K–246M* (subsidiaries) and *ss 246S–246W* (international headquarters companies) do not apply (and for which provisions see Tolley's Corporation Tax under Foreign Income Dividends). [*ICTA 1988, s 468K; FA 1994, Sch 14 para 2; F(No 2)A 1997, Sch 6 paras 3, 8*]. Special provisions apply where, on the distribution date, the unit holder is within the charge to corporation tax (see *ICTA 1988, s 468R* introduced by *FA 1994, Sch 14 para 2*).

As regards interest distributions, they are treated as payments of yearly interest made on the '*distribution date*' (as above). They are not charges on income within *ICTA 1988, s 338(1)*, but if paid under deduction of tax (see below) they are deductible from total profits (see *ICTA 1988, s 468L(5)–(7)* (as amended), introduced by *FA 1994, Sch 14 para 2*). Lower rate tax (for 1995/96 and earlier years, basic rate tax) is deductible under *ICTA 1988, s 349(2)* except in certain cases where the unit holder to whom the payment is made satisfies the residence condition of *ICTA 1988, ss 468O, 468P* (introduced by *FA 1994, Sch 14 para 2*) on the distribution date, broadly that a valid declaration is made in prescribed form that either he is non-UK ordinarily resident or, if he holds the units as personal representative of a deceased unit holder, at the time of his death the unit holder was non-UK ordinarily resident. In relation to company unit holders, the declaration must be that the company is not UK resident. In the case of distributions made to or received under a trust, under regulations effective from 27 September 1994 (see *SI 1994 No 2318*), the requirement is for a valid declaration from the trustees both that they are non-UK resident and that each beneficiary known to them satisfies the individual or company residence conditions as appropriate (except that where the whole of the distribution is, or is treated as, income of a person other than the trustees, the residence conditions apply only to that person). If the gross income in the distribution accounts derives entirely from 'eligible income', payments to unit holders satisfying the appropriate residence condition may be made without deduction of tax. There is a formula for determining the amount which may be paid without deduction of tax where the gross income does not derive entirely from 'eligible income' (see *ICTA 1988, s 468N(4)–(6)* introduced by *FA 1994, Sch 14 para 2*). *SI 1994 No 2318* also provides the Revenue with the appropriate powers to determine whether interest distributions have properly been paid gross. '*Eligible income*' is defined in *ICTA 1988, s 468M(4)(5)* (introduced by *FA 1994, Sch 14 para 2*) as amended, and is broadly income which would not be subject to deduction if received directly by a non-resident.

Interest distributions made after 5 April 1996 are subject to tax deductions at source at the lower rate, under the general principle at 1.9 ALLOWANCES AND TAX RATES (previously the basic rate). For *distribution periods ending after 31 March 1996*, an interest distribution may be made only if the authorised unit trust satisfies the qualifying investments test throughout the distribution period, which it does if, at all times in that period, the market value of 'qualifying investments' exceeds 60% of the market value of all the investments of the trust (disregarding cash awaiting investment). The definition of '*qualifying investments*' is equivalent to that given above (i.e. for determining the corporation tax rate for financial years 1994 and 1995) but (from 25 February 1997) including qualifying shares in open-ended investment companies, and subject to further extension or restriction by Treasury Order.

[*ICTA 1988, ss 468L, 468M, 468N; FA 1994, Sch 14 para 2; FA 1996, Sch 6 para 11, Sch 7 para 17, Sch 14 para 26; SI 1997 No 212*].

Simon's Direct Tax Service. See D4.413–D4.418.

90.2 UNIT TRUSTS NOT TREATED AS AUTHORISED UNIT TRUSTS

Special provisions apply to the income of a unit trust scheme not within 90.1 above unless the trustees are non-UK resident. Such a trust is outside the scope of *ICTA 1988, s 468* (see 90.1 above). Income arising to the trustees is treated as income of the trustees (rather than the unit holders), and is subject to basic rate tax. Capital allowances are available to the trustees (but, since the trustees are not treated as a company, there is no relief for management expenses). The unit holders are treated as receiving annual payments, under deduction of basic rate tax, equal to their respective entitlements to the grossed-up income available for distribution or investment. The date the payment is treated as having been made is the latest (or only) date for distribution under the terms of the trust or (if there is no such date or it is more than twelve months after the end of the distribution period) the last day of the distribution period. For the definition of 'distribution period', see *ICTA 1988, s 469(6)* as amended by *FA 1994, Sch 14 para 5*.

For 1996/97 and later years, the income of the trustees, and thus of the unit holders, continues to be chargeable at the basic rate, as opposed to the lower rate (or, from 6 April 1999, the Schedule F ordinary rate), even if the nature of the income is such that the lower (or Schedule F ordinary) rate would otherwise apply (see 1.9 ALLOWANCES AND TAX RATES).

UK company qualifying distributions (see 1.9 ALLOWANCES AND TAX RATES) made after 1 July 1997 but before 6 April 1999 which are income of the trustees are treated as foreign income dividends (see 1.9 ALLOWANCES AND TAX RATES) if they would not otherwise be so treated. This does not, however, apply to common investment funds under *Administration of Justice Act 1982, s 42* (but see 90.3 below from 6 April 1999) or if, were it not treated as income of the trustees, the whole of a distribution would be income either of a charity (within *ICTA 1988, s 506(1)*, see 15.1 CHARITIES) or of a body treated as a charity under *ICTA 1988, ss 507, 508* (see 30.3, 30.9, 30.14, 30.20 EXEMPT ORGANISATIONS, 77.1 SCIENTIFIC RESEARCH ASSOCIATIONS). With effect from 6 April 1999, no tax credit is attached to any qualifying distributions received by the trustees, who are not treated as having paid income tax thereon (and the latter applies also to distributions other than qualifying distributions received by the trustees). See also 3.23 ANTI-AVOIDANCE as regards arrangements to pass on the value of a tax credit.

The liability of the trustees to account for tax deducted from annual payments treated as made by them, so far as not covered by tax deducted from income received, is reduced where there is a cumulative uncredited surplus of income on which they are chargeable to tax over such annual payments.

[*ICTA 1988, s 469; FA 1988, s 71; FA 1994, Sch 14 para 5; FA 1996, Sch 6 paras 12, 28, Sch 41 Pt V(1); FA 1997, s 80(5); F(No 2)A 1997, s 29, Sch 4 paras 4, 12*].

Pension fund pooling. Regulations which came into force on 11 July 1996 make special provision to ensure that certain international pooled pension funds (registered as 'pension fund pooling vehicles') are transparent for UK tax purposes, by disapplying the tax rules for unauthorised unit trusts (as above). Participants in such schemes must be approved by the Revenue, and are treated for income tax, capital allowances and capital gains tax purposes as though they themselves owned directly a share of each of the trust assets. There is also relief from stamp duty (or stamp duty reserve tax) on transfers of assets (other than land or buildings) by participants into the scheme. Participation in pension fund pooling vehicles is restricted to exempt approved pension schemes, UK-based superannuation funds used primarily by companies employing British expatriates working overseas, and pension funds established outside the UK broadly equivalent to UK exempt approved pension schemes. [*SI 1996 Nos 1583, 1584, 1585*]. See generally Revenue Inspector's Manual, IM 4227–4227h. The position in the country in which any overseas participator is based will of course be crucial to the operation of such schemes.

Simon's Direct Tax Service. See **D4.420**.

90.3 COURT COMMON INVESTMENT FUNDS

Court common investment funds (CCIFs) are a form of unit trust set up by the Lord Chancellor under *Administration of Justice Act 1982, s 42(1)*. They are available only for individuals whose money is under control of certain Courts, e.g. road accident victims and the mentally incapacitated. The Public Trustee as Accountant General of the Supreme

Court holds all units in the fund on the investors' behalf. As regards any income arising to a CCIF after 5 April 1999 and any distribution made for a distribution period beginning after that date, CCIFs are treated for tax purposes as authorised unit trusts within 90.1 above. The investment manager is treated as the trustee, and the persons whose interests entitle them, as against the Accountant General (or other authorised person), to share in the fund's investments are treated as the unit holders. Previously, CCIFs fell to be treated as unauthorised unit trusts within 90.2 above. For these purposes, a distribution period of a CCIF in existence on 5 April 1999 is deemed to have ended on that date, and its first accounting period and distribution period under the authorised unit trust regime are deemed to begin on 6 April 1999. [*ICTA 1988, s 469A; FA 1999, s 68*].

91 Venture Capital Trusts

Simon's Direct Tax Service E3.6.

91.1 From 6 April 1995, the venture capital trust scheme described at 91.2 *et seq.* below is introduced to encourage individuals to invest in unquoted trading companies through such trusts. The provisions dealing with the approval of companies as venture capital trusts, and with the reliefs for investors, are introduced in *FA 1995, ss 70–72, Schs 14–16*. The Treasury has wide powers to make regulations governing all aspects of the reliefs applicable to venture capital trust investments, and for the requirements as regards returns, records and provision of information by the trust. [*FA 1995, s 73; FA 1996, Sch 18 paras 16, 17(1)(3)*]. See now *SI 1995 No 1979; SI 1999 No 819.*

91.2 **CONDITIONS FOR APPROVAL** [*ICTA 1988, s 842AA; FA 1995, s 70; FA 1997, s 75; FA 1998, s 73(1)(6), Sch 27 Pt III(13); FA 1999, s 69(4)(5)*]

A '*venture capital trust*' ('VCT') is a company approved for this purpose by the Board, close companies being excluded. The time from which an approval takes effect is specified in the approval, and may not be earlier than the time the application for approval was made or, for approvals given in 1995/96, 6 April 1995.

Except as detailed further below, approval may not be given unless the Board are satisfied that the following conditions are met.

(*a*) The company's income in its most recent complete accounting period has been derived wholly or mainly from shares or securities, and not more than 15% of its income from shares and securities has been retained.

(*b*) Throughout that period at least 70% by value of the company's investments has been represented by shares or securities in 'qualifying holdings' (see 91.3 below), at least 30% of which (by value) has been represented by holdings of '*eligible shares*', i.e. ordinary shares carrying no present or future preferential right to dividends or to assets on a winding up and no present or future right (before 6 April 1998, present or future preferential right) to redemption.

(*c*) The company's ordinary shares (or each class thereof) have been listed in the Official List of the Stock Exchange throughout that period.

(*d*) No holding in any company other than a VCT (or a company which could be a VCT but for (*c*) above) has at any time in that period represented more than 15% of the value of the company's investments.

'Securities' for these purposes are deemed to include liabilities in respect of certain loans not repayable within five years, and any stocks or securities relating to which are not re-purchasable or redeemable within five years of issue. Provided that the loan is made on normal commercial terms, the Revenue will not regard a standard event of default clause in the loan agreement as disqualifying a loan from being a security for this purpose. If, however, the clause entitled the lender (or a third party) to exercise any action which would cause the borrower to default, the clause would not be regarded as 'standard'. (Revenue Pamphlet IR 131, SP 8/95, 14 September 1995).

As regards the 15% limits in (*a*) and (*d*) above, the provisions which apply to the similar restrictions on investment trusts (see Tolley's Corporation Tax under Unit and Investment Trusts) apply modified as appropriate.

Where (*a*)–(*d*) above are met, the Board must also be satisfied that they will be met in the accounting period current at the time of application for approval. Where any of (*a*)–(*d*) above are not met, approval may nevertheless be given where the Board are satisfied as to the meeting of those conditions (and in certain cases other conditions imposed by regulations) in future accounting periods.

On a second and subsequent issues by an approved VCT, the requirements of condition (*b*) above similarly do not have to be met, in relation to the money raised by the further issue, in the accounting period of the further issue or any later accounting period ending no more than three years after the making of the further issue.

Where the 70% limit in (*b*) is breached inadvertently, and the position corrected without delay after discovery, approval will in practice not be withdrawn on this account. Full details of any such inadvertent breach should be disclosed to the Revenue as soon as it is discovered. (Revenue Press Release 14 September 1995).

The value of any investment for the purposes of (*b*) and (*d*) above is the value when the investment was acquired, except that where it is added to by a further holding of an investment of the same description, or a payment is made in discharge of any obligation attached to it which increases its value, it is the value immediately after the most recent such addition or payment.

Share exchanges and conversions. With effect from 16 June 1999, certain transactions in shares held by a VCT are in effect disregarded in considering the value of holdings for the purposes of the 70%, 30% and 15% tests in (*b*) and (*d*) above. The transactions concerned are as follows.

(i) Where, as part of a restructuring, shares or securities in a company are exchanged for corresponding shares and securities in a new holding company. Certain deemed securities (see above) which are not thus acquired by the new company may be disregarded where these provisions would otherwise be prevented from applying.

(ii) Where a VCT exercises conversion rights in respect of certain convertible shares and securities.

In these circumstances, and subject to detailed conditions (see *ICTA 1988, Sch 28B paras 10C, 10D* introduced by *FA 1999, s 69*), the value of the new shares is taken to be the same as the value of the old shares when they were last valued for these purposes.

Approval may be **withdrawn** where there are reasonable grounds for believing that either:

(A) the conditions for approval were not satisfied at the time the approval was given; or

(B) a condition that the Board were satisfied (as above) would be met has not been or will not be met; or

(C) in either the most recent complete accounting period or the current one, one of conditions (*a*)–(*d*) above has failed or will fail to be met (unless the failure was allowed for as above); or

(D) where, in relation to a second or further issue by an approved VCT, (*b*) above does not have to be met in the period of issue or certain following accounting periods (see above), one of conditions (*a*)–(*d*) above will fail to be met in the first period for which (*b*) above must be met; or

(E) any other conditions prescribed by regulations have not been met in relation to, or to part of, an accounting period for which (*b*) above does not have to be met.

The withdrawal is effective from the time the company is notified of it, except that:

(1) where approval is given on the Board's being satisfied as to the meeting of the relevant conditions in future accounting periods, and is withdrawn before all the

conditions (*a*)–(*d*) above have been satisfied in relation to either a complete twelve-month accounting period or successive complete accounting periods constituting a continuous period of twelve months or more, the approval is deemed never to have been given; and

(2) for the purposes of relief for capital gains accruing to a VCT under *TCGA 1992, s 100* (see 91.11 below), withdrawal may be effective from an earlier date, but not before the start of the accounting period in which the failure occurred (or is expected to occur).

An assessment consequent on the withdrawal of approval may, where otherwise out of time, be made within three years from the time notice of the withdrawal was given.

For the detailed requirements as regards granting, refusal and withdrawal of approval, and appeals procedures, see *SI 1995 No 1979, Pt II.*

91.3 **Qualifying holdings.** Shares or securities in a company are comprised in a VCT's '*qualifying holdings*' at any time if they were first issued to the VCT, and have been held by it ever since, and the following conditions are satisfied at that time.

(*a*) The company is an '*unquoted company*' (whether or not UK resident), i.e. none of its shares, stocks, debentures or other securities is

(i) listed on a recognised stock exchange, or a designated exchange outside the UK, or

(ii) dealt in on the Unlisted Securities Market, or outside the UK by such means as may be designated for the purpose by order.

Securities on the Alternative Investment Market ('AIM') are treated as unquoted for these purposes. (Revenue Press Release 20 February 1995).

If the company ceases to be an unquoted company at a time when its shares are comprised in the qualifying holdings of the VCT, this condition is treated as continuing to be met, in relation to shares or securities acquired before that time, for the following five years.

(*b*) Either

(i) the company must exist wholly for the purpose of carrying on one or more 'qualifying trades' (disregarding any purpose having no significant effect on the extent of its activities as a whole), or

(ii) (after 26 November 1996) it must be the 'parent company of a trading group' (previously, its business had to consist entirely in holding shares in or securities of, or making loans to, one or more 'qualifying subsidiaries' (for which see *ICTA 1988, Sch 28B para 10*, as originally introduced by *FA 1995, Sch 14 para 10*), with or without the carrying on of one or more 'qualifying trades').

In addition, the company, or a 'relevant qualifying subsidiary', must, when the shares were issued to the VCT and ever since, have been carrying on a 'qualifying trade' wholly or mainly in the UK, or preparing to carry on such a trade intended to be carried on wholly or mainly in the UK. In the latter case, there is a time limit of two years from the issue of the shares for the trade to be commenced as intended. A '*relevant qualifying subsidiary*' is, broadly, a company which is 90% owned by the company (or by a subsidiary of the company) and which otherwise satisfies the conditions of *ICTA 1988, Sch 28B para 10* (as amended).

A trade is a '*qualifying trade*' if it meets the same conditions as apply in relation to the Enterprise Investment Scheme (EIS) (see 26.7 ENTERPRISE INVESTMENT SCHEME

(AND BES)), but without the exclusion of oil extraction activities, and taking references to the 'relevant period' in relation to that scheme as references to the period since issue of the shares to the VCT. The exclusions that apply in relation to EIS shares issued after 16 March 1998 have effect for the purpose of determining whether any shares or securities are, as at any time after that date, to be regarded as comprised in the qualifying holdings of a VCT. However, those exclusions do not apply in relation to shares and securities acquired by the VCT by means of the investment of:

(1) money raised by the issue before 17 March 1998 of shares in or securities of the VCT; or

(2) money derived from the investment by the VCT of money so raised.

The changes in the rules concerning receipt of royalties and licence fees which apply in relation to EIS shares issued after 5 April 2000 also have effect for the purpose of determining whether shares or securities issued after that date are to be regarded as comprised in a VCT's qualifying holdings.

The definition of 'controlling interest' in relation to the above-mentioned conditions is also revised to permit holdings of non-voting fixed-rate preference shares, and rights as a loan creditor, to be disregarded. 'Research and development' from which it is intended that there will be derived a qualifying trade carried on wholly or mainly in the UK is treated as the carrying on of a qualifying trade. For the purpose of determining whether shares or securities issued after 5 April 2000 are to be regarded as comprised in a VCT's qualifying holdings, '*research and development*' has the meaning given by *ICTA 1988, s 837A* (see 10.52 CAPITAL ALLOWANCES). Previously, it meant any activity intended to result in a patentable invention (within *Patents Act 1977*) or in a computer program.

In considering whether a trade is carried on 'wholly or mainly in the UK', the totality of the trade activities is taken into account. Regard will be had, for example, to where capital assets are held, where any purchasing, processing, manufacturing and selling is done, and where the employees customarily carry out their duties. No one of these factors is itself likely to be decisive in any particular case. Accordingly a company may carry on some such activities outside the UK and yet satisfy the requirement, provided that the major part of them, that is over one-half of the aggregate of these activities, takes place within the UK. Thus relief is not excluded solely because a company's products or services are exported, or because its raw materials are imported, or because its raw materials or products are stored abroad, or because its marketing facilities are supplied from abroad. Similar principles apply in considering the trade(s) carried on by a company and its qualifying subsidiaries.

In the particular case of a ship chartering trade, the test is satisfied if all charters are entered into in the UK and the provision of crews and management of the ships while under charter take place mainly in the UK. If these conditions are not met, the test may still be satisfied depending on all the relevant facts and circumstances.

(Revenue Pamphlet IR 131, SP 7/98, 30 November 1998, replacing SP 2/94, 9 May 1994 as revised).

A company is the '*parent company of a trading group*' if it has one or more subsidiaries, each of which is a 'qualifying subsidiary' (within *ICTA 1988, Sch 28B para 10* as amended by *FA 1997, Sch 9 para 5* and by *FA 1998, s 73(2)*), and if, taking all the activities of the company and its subsidiaries as one business, neither that business nor a substantial part of it consists in either or both of:

(*aa*) activities within 26.7(*a*)–(*c*)(*e*)–(*m*) ENTERPRISE INVESTMENT SCHEME (AND BES) (other than those within 26.7(*e*) which do not result in a trade being excluded from being a qualifying trade); and

(*bb*) non-trading activities.

To the extent that the activities in (*aa*) above apply for EIS purposes in relation to shares issued after 16 March 1998 (see 26.7), they have effect for VCT purposes as described above under the definition of 'qualifying trade'.

Activities are for these purposes disregarded to the extent that they consist in:

(AA) holding shares in or securities of, or making loans to, one or more of the company's subsidiaries; or

(BB) holding and managing property used by the company or any of its subsidiaries for the purposes of either

(i) 'research and development' (see above) from which it is intended that a qualifying trade to be carried on by the company or any of its subsidiaries will be derived, or

(ii) one or more qualifying trades so carried on.

Activities of a subsidiary are similarly disregarded to the extent that they consist in the making of loans to the company or, where the subsidiary exists wholly for the purpose of carrying on one or more qualifying trades (apart from '*insignificant purposes*', i.e. purposes capable of having no significant effect, other than in relation to incidental matters, on the extent of the subsidiary's activities), of activities carried on in pursuance of those insignificant purposes.

(*c*) The money raised by the issue of shares to the VCT must have been employed wholly for the purposes of, or of preparing for the carrying on of, the qualifying trade (disregarding insignificant amounts used for other purposes), or be intended to be so employed. In the latter case, the money must actually be so employed within twelve months of the later of the issue of the shares to the VCT and the date the qualifying trade was commenced.

After 26 November 1996, where the company is a 'parent company of a trading group' within (*b*)(ii) above, the '*trader company*' (i.e. the company carrying on (or preparing to carry on) the required qualifying trade) must either:

(i) satisfy the requirements in (*b*)(i) above; or

(ii) be a company in relation to which those requirements would be satisfied if activities within (*b*)(AA) or (*b*)(BB) above, or consisting of a subsidiary making loans to its parent, were disregarded; or

(iii) be a 'relevant qualifying subsidiary' which either

(1) exists wholly for the purpose of carrying on activities within (*b*)(BB) above (disregarding purposes capable of having no significant effect (other than in relation to incidental matters) on the extent of its activities), or

(2) has no corporation tax profits and no part of its business consists in the making of investments.

A '*relevant qualifying subsidiary*' is, broadly, a company which is 90% owned by the investee company (or by a subsidiary of that company) and which otherwise satisfies the conditions of *ICTA 1988, Sch 28B para 10* (as amended).

Money whose retention can reasonably be regarded as necessary or advisable for financing current trade requirements is regarded as employed for trade purposes, but by the end of the twelve months funds should no longer be held which are clearly surplus to day-to-day needs. (Revenue Inspector's Manual, IM 7209).

(*d*) The aggregate of money raised from shares issued by the company to the VCT must not have exceeded the 'maximum qualifying investment' of £1 million in the period from six months before the issue in question (or, if earlier, the beginning of the year of assessment of the issue) to the time of the issue in question. Disposals are treated as far as possible as eliminating any such excess. The £1 million limit is proportionately reduced where, at the time of the issue, the qualifying trade is carried on, or to be carried on, in partnership or as a joint venture, and one or more of the other parties is a company.

(*e*) The value of the company's 'relevant assets' did not exceed £15 million immediately before the issue or £16 million immediately thereafter. As regards shares and securities issued by investee companies before 6 April 1998, these limits were £10 million and £11 million respectively. '*Relevant assets*' are the gross assets of the company and, at any time when it has one or more qualifying subsidiaries, of all such subsidiaries. In the latter case, assets consisting in rights against, or shares in or securities of, another member of the group consisting of the company and its qualifying subsidiaries are disregarded.

The general approach of the Revenue is that the value of a company's gross assets is the sum of the value of all the balance sheet assets. Where accounts are actually drawn up to a date immediately before or after the issue, the balance sheet values are taken provided that they reflect usual accounting standards and the company's normal accounting practice, consistently applied. Where accounts are not drawn up to such a date, such values will be taken from the most recent balance sheet, updated as precisely as practicable on the basis of all the relevant information available to the company. Values so arrived at may need to be reviewed in the light of information contained in the accounts for the period in which the issue was made, and, if they were not available at the time of the issue, those for the preceding period, when they become available. The company's assets immediately before the issue do not include any advance payment received in respect of the issue. Where shares are issued partly paid, the right to the balance is an asset, and, notwithstanding the above, will be taken into account in valuing the assets immediately after the issue regardless of whether it is stated in the balance sheet. (Revenue Pamphlet IR 131, SP 5/98, 30 November 1998, replacing SP 7/95, 14 September 1995).

(*f*) The company must not 'control' (with or without 'connected persons') any company other than a qualifying subsidiary, nor must another company (or another company and a person connected with it) control it. Neither must arrangements be in existence by virtue of which such control could arise. For these purposes, '*control*' is as under *ICTA 1988, s 416*, except that possession of, or entitlement to acquire, fixed-rate preference shares (as defined) of the company which do not, for the time being, carry voting rights is disregarded, as is possession of, or entitlement to acquire, rights as a loan creditor of the company. '*Connected persons*' are as under *ICTA 1988, s 839* (see 20 CONNECTED PERSONS) except that the definition of 'control' therein is similarly modified. For the application of the 'control' test to co-investors in a company, and in particular the question of whether co-investors are connected by virtue of their 'acting together to secure or exercise control' of the company, see Revenue Tax Bulletin October 1997 pp 471, 472.

(*g*) Where the company is being wound up, none of conditions (*a*)–(*f*) above are regarded on that account as not being satisfied provided that those conditions would be met apart from the winding up, and that the winding up is for *bona fide* commercial reasons and not part of a scheme or arrangement a main purpose of which is the avoidance of tax. After 20 March 2000, the company does not cease to meet condition (*b*) above by reason of anything done as a consequence of its being in administration or receivership (both as defined), provided everything so done and the making of the relevant order are for *bona fide* commercial (and not tax avoidance) reasons.

(*h*) The holding in question must not include any securities (as defined in 91.2 above) relating to a guaranteed loan. A security relates to a guaranteed loan if there are arrangements entitling the VCT to receive anything (directly or indirectly) from a 'third party' in the event of a failure by any person to comply with the terms of the security or the loan to which it relates. It is immaterial whether or not the arrangements apply in all such cases. '*Third party*' includes any person other than the investee company itself and, if it is a parent company of a trading group (see (*b*) above), its subsidiaries. This condition applies for accounting periods (of the VCT) ending after 1 July 1997, but does not apply in the case of shares or securities acquired by the VCT by means of investing money raised by the issue by it before 2 July 1997 of shares or securities (or money derived from the investment of any such money raised).

(*j*) At least 10% (by value) of the VCT's *total* holding of shares in and securities of the company must consist of 'eligible shares' (as defined in 91.2(*b*) above — broadly, ordinary, non-preferential, shares). For this purpose, the value of shares etc. at any time is taken to be their value immediately after the most recent of the events listed below, except that it cannot thereby be taken to be less than the amount of consideration given by the VCT for the shares etc. The said events are as follows.

(i) The acquisition of the shares etc. by the VCT.

(ii) The acquisition by the VCT (other than by way of bonus issue for no consideration) of any other shares etc. in the same company which are of the same description as those already held.

(iii) The making of any payment in discharge (or part discharge) of any obligation attached to the shares etc. in a case where such discharge increases the value of the shares etc.

This condition applies for accounting periods (of the VCT) ending after 1 July 1997, but, if necessary in order to satisfy the condition, one may disregard shares and securities acquired by the VCT by means of investing money raised by the issue by it before 2 July 1997 of shares or securities (or money derived from the investment of any such money raised).

As regards (*c*) and (*d*) above, where either condition would be met as to only part of the money raised by the issue, and the holding is not otherwise capable of being treated as separate holdings, it is treated as two separate holdings, one from which that part of the money was raised, the other from which the rest was raised, with the value being apportioned accordingly to each holding. In the case of (*c*), this does not require an insignificant amount applied for non-trade purposes to be treated as a separate holding.

As regards (*c*) above, in relation to buy-outs (and in particular management buy-outs), the Revenue will usually accept that where a company is formed to acquire a trade, and the funds raised from the VCT are applied to that purchase, the requirement that the funds be employed for the purposes of the trade is satisfied. Where the company is formed to acquire another company and its trade, or a holding company and its trading subsidiaries, this represents an investment rather than employment for the purposes of the trade. However, the Revenue will usually accept that the requirement is satisfied if the trade of the company, or all the activities of the holding company and its subsidiaries, are hived up to the acquiring company as soon as possible after the acquisition. In the case of a holding company and its subsidiaries, to the extent that the trades are not hived up, the holding cannot be a qualifying holding. (Revenue Tax Bulletin August 1995 pp 243, 244).

As regards (*b*)–(*f*) and (*j*) above, with effect from 16 June 1999, certain transactions in shares held by a VCT are in effect disregarded in considering whether the relevant condition is satisfied. The transactions concerned are as follows.

(A) Where, as part of a restructuring, shares or securities in a company are exchanged for corresponding shares and securities in a new holding company. Certain deemed securities (see 91.2 above) which are not thus acquired by the new company may be disregarded where these provisions would otherwise be prevented from applying.

(B) Where a VCT exercises conversion rights in respect of certain convertible shares and securities.

In these circumstances, and subject to detailed conditions (see *ICTA 1988, Sch 28B paras 10C, 10D* introduced by *FA 1999, s 69*), to the extent that the condition was satisfied in relation to the old shares, it will generally be taken to be satisfied in relation to the new shares.

Where, after 20 March 2000 under a company reorganisation etc.,

(i) a VCT exchanges a qualifying holding for other shares or securities, and

(ii) the exchange is for *bona fide* commercial reasons and not part of a tax avoidance scheme or arrangements,

then under regulations to be made by the Treasury, the new shares or securities may be treated as being qualifying holdings even if some or all of the above requirements are not otherwise satisfied. The regulations may specify the circumstances in which, and conditions subject to which, they apply, which requirements are to be treated as met, and the period for which those requirements are to be so treated; and they may make the necessary administrative provisions. They may also provide for the value of the new holding and of any original shares retained to be taken to be of such amount as to continue to satisfy the requirements at 91.2(*b*) and (*d*) above.

The Treasury have power by order to modify the requirements under (*b*) above as they consider expedient, and to alter the cash limits referred to in (*d*) and (*e*) above.

[*ICTA 1988, s 842AA(5AD)(5AE)(13), Sch 28B; FA 1995, Sch 14; FA 1996, s 161; F(No 2)A 1997, s 25; FA 1998, s 70(1)(3), s 72, s 73(2)–(6), Sch 12 paras 3, 4, 5(2)(3); FA 1999, s 69(2)(3)(5); FA 2000, Sch 18 paras 4–8*].

91.4 **INCOME TAX RELIEFS** [*ICTA 1988, s 332A, Sch 15B; FA 1995, s 71, Sch 15*]

Relief from income tax is granted for 1995/96 and subsequent years in respect of both investments in VCTs and distributions from such trusts.

91.5 **Relief in respect of investments.** Subject to the conditions described below, an individual may claim relief for a year of assessment for the amount (or aggregate amounts) subscribed by him on his own behalf for 'eligible shares' issued to him in a year of assessment by a VCT (or VCTs) for raising money. There is a limit of **£100,000** on the relief which may be claimed for any year of assessment.

'*Eligible shares*' means new ordinary shares in a VCT which, throughout the three years following issue (five years for shares issued before 6 April 2000), carry no present or future preferential right to dividends or to assets on a winding up and no present or future right (before 6 April 1998, present or future preferential right) to redemption.

Relief is given by a reduction in what would otherwise be the individual's income tax liability for the year of assessment by the lesser of

(i) tax at the lower rate (currently 20%) on the amount(s) subscribed, and

(ii) an amount sufficient to reduce that liability to nil.

In determining what would otherwise be the individual's income tax liability for the year of assessment for this purpose, no account is taken of:

(A) any income tax reduction in respect of enterprise investment scheme investments (see 26.8 ENTERPRISE INVESTMENT SCHEME (AND BES)), personal reliefs (see 1.15, 1.16, 1.17 ALLOWANCES AND TAX RATES), qualifying maintenance payments (see 47.10 MARRIED PERSONS), interest relief (see 43.5 INTEREST PAYABLE) or medical insurance (see 48.1 MEDICAL INSURANCE);

(B) any reduction of liability to tax by way of DOUBLE TAX RELIEF (25);

(C) any basic rate tax on income the tax on which the individual is entitled to charge against any other person or to deduct, retain or satisfy out of any payment; or

(D) any basic rate tax deemed to have been deducted at source from a charitable donation made after 5 April 2000 under the Gift Aid scheme (see 15.12 CHARITIES).

Where relief is given by repayment of tax more than twelve months after the end of the year of assessment in which the shares were issued, interest under *ICTA 1988, s 824* (see 41.2 INTEREST ON OVERPAID TAX) is payable.

An individual is **not** entitled to relief where:

(*a*) he was under 18 years of age at the time of issue of the shares;

(*b*) circumstances have arisen which, had the relief already been given, would have resulted in the withdrawal or reduction of the relief (see 91.7 below);

(*c*) the shares were issued or subscribed for other than for *bona fide* commercial purposes or as part of a scheme or arrangement a main purpose of which was the avoidance of tax; or

(*d*) a loan is made to the individual (or to an 'associate' within *ICTA 1988, s 417*, but excluding a brother or sister) by any person at any time in the period beginning with the incorporation of the VCT (or, if later, two years before the date of issue of the shares) and ending three years after the date of issue of the shares (five years for shares issued before 6 April 2000), and the loan would not have been made, or would not have been made on the same terms, if he had not subscribed, or had not been proposing to subscribe, for the shares. The granting of credit to, or the assignment of a debt due from, the individual or associate is counted as a loan for these purposes.

[*ICTA 1988, Sch 15B paras 1, 2, 6; FA 1990, s 25(6)(b)(7); FA 1995, Sch 15 paras 1, 2, 6; FA 1998, s 73(1)(6), Sch 27 Pt III(13); FA 2000, s 39(6)(10), Sch 18 paras 1(2)(4), 3*].

As regards (*d*) above, for this restriction to apply, the test is whether the lender makes the loan on terms which are connected with the fact that the borrower (or an associate) is subscribing for eligible shares. The prime concern is why the lender made the loan rather than why the borrower applied for it. Relief would not be disallowed, for example, in the case of a bank loan if the bank would have made a loan on the same terms to a similar borrower for a different purpose. But if, for example, a loan is made specifically on a security consisting of or including the eligible shares (other than as part of a broad range of assets to which the lender has recourse), relief would be denied. Relevant features of the loan terms would be the qualifying conditions to be satisfied by the borrower, any incentives or benefits offered to the borrower, the time allowed for repayment, the amount of repayments and interest charged, the timing of interest payments, and the nature of the security. (Revenue Pamphlet IR 131, SP 6/98, 30 November 1998, replacing SP 3/94, 9 May 1994, as revised).

An individual subscribing for eligible shares may obtain from the VCT a certificate giving details of the subscription and certifying that certain conditions for relief are satisfied. [*SI 1995 No 1979, reg 9*].

91.6 *Example*

On 1 May 2000, Miss K, who is 66 and whose pension is £19,955 p.a., subscribes for 40,000 eligible £1 shares issued at par to raise money by VCT plc, an approved venture capital trust. On 1 September 2000 she purchases a further 90,000 £1 shares in VCT plc for £70,000 on the open market. The trust makes no distribution in 2000/01. Miss K's other income for 2000/01 consists of dividends of £16,200. PAYE tax deducted is £3,163.

Miss K's tax computation for 2000/01 is as follows.

	£	£
Pension		19,955
Dividends	16,200	
Add Tax credit	1,800	18,000
Total income		37,955
Deduct Personal allowance		4,385
Taxable income		£33,570
Tax payable:		
1,520 @ 10% (starting rate)		152
14,050 @ 22%		
12,830 @ 10% (Schedule F ordinary rate)		
5,170 @ 32.5% (Schedule F upper rate)		
		3,091
		1,283
		1,680
		6,206
Deduct Relief for investment in VCT plc, 20% of £40,000 subscribed, but restricted to		6,206
Net tax payable		—

PAYE tax of £3,163 is repayable. Dividend tax credits are not repayable for 1999/2000 onwards.

91.7 **Withdrawal of relief on investment.** *Disposal of investment.* Where an individual disposes of eligible shares, in respect of which relief has been claimed as under 91.5 above, within thre years of their issue (five years for shares issued before 6 April 2000) and other than to a spouse when they are living together (see below), then:

(*a*) if the disposal is otherwise than at arm's length, relief given by reference to those shares is withdrawn;

(*b*) if the disposal is at arm's length, the relief given by reference to those shares is reduced by an amount equivalent to tax at the lower rate (for the year for which relief was given) on the consideration received for the disposal (or withdrawn if the relief exceeds that amount).

Relief is **not** withdrawn where the disposal is by one spouse to the other at a time when they are living together. However, on any subsequent disposal the spouse to whom the shares were transferred is treated as if he or she were the person who subscribed for the shares, as if the shares had been issued to him or her at the time they were issued to the transferor spouse, and as if his or her liability to income tax had been reduced by reference to those shares by the same amount, and for the same year of assessment, as applied on the subscription by the transferor spouse. Any assessment for reducing or withdrawing relief is made on the transferee spouse.

Identification of shares. For the above purposes, disposals of eligible shares in a VCT are identified with those acquired earlier rather than later. As between eligible shares acquired on the same day, shares by reference to which relief has been given are treated as disposed of after any other eligible shares.

Withdrawal of approval. Where approval of a company as a VCT is withdrawn (but not treated as never having been given) (see 91.2 above), relief given by reference to eligible shares in the VCT is withdrawn as if on a non-arm's length disposal immediately before the withdrawal of approval.

Assessments withdrawing or reducing relief, whether because relief is subsequently found not to have been due or under the above provisions, are made under SCHEDULE D, CASE VI (74) for the year of assessment for which the relief was given. No such assessment is, however, to be made by reason of an event occurring after the death of the person to whom the shares were issued.

Information. Particulars of all events leading to the reduction or withdrawal of relief must be notified to the inspector by the person to whom the relief was given within 60 days of his coming to know of the event. Where the inspector has reason to believe that a notice so required has not been given, he may require that person to furnish him, within a specified time not being less than 60 days, with such information relating to the event as he may reasonably require. The requirements of secrecy do not prevent the inspector disclosing to a VCT that relief has been given or claimed by reference to a particular number or proportion of its shares. Penalties under *TMA 1970, s 98* apply for failure to comply with these requirements.

[*ICTA 1988, Sch 15B paras 3–5; FA 1995, s 71(3), Sch 15 paras 3–5; FA 2000, Sch 18 paras 1(3), 3*].

91.8 *Example*

On 1 May 2002, Miss K in the *Example* at 91.6 above, who has since 2000/01 neither acquired nor disposed of any shares in VCT plc, gives 25,000 shares to her son. On 1 January 2003, she disposes of the remaining 105,000 shares for £85,000. The relief given as in 91.6 above is withdrawn as follows.

Disposal on 1 May 2002

The shares disposed of are identified with 25,000 of those subscribed for, and, since the disposal was not at arm's length, the relief given on those shares is withdrawn.

	£
Relief withdrawn $\frac{25,000}{40,000} \times 6,206 =$	3,879
Disposal on 1 January 2003 The balance of £2,327 of the relief originally given was in respect of 15,000 of the shares disposed of. The disposal consideration for those 15,000 shares is $85,000 \times \frac{15,000}{105,000} = £12,143$ The relief withdrawn is the lesser of the relief originally given and 20% of the consideration received, i.e. 20% of £12,143 = £2,429	
Relief withdrawn is therefore	2,327
The 2000/01 Schedule D, Case VI assessment is therefore	£6,206

91.9 **Relief on distributions.** A 'relevant distribution' of a VCT to which a 'qualifying investor' is beneficially entitled is not treated as income for income tax purposes, provided that certain conditions are fulfilled as regards the obtaining of an 'enduring declaration' from the investor, and that the VCT claims the related tax credit, which it is required to pass on to the investor.

A '*qualifying investor*' is an individual aged 18 or over who is beneficially entitled to the distribution either as the holder of the shares or through a nominee (including the trustees of a bare trust).

A '*relevant distribution*' is a dividend (including a capital dividend) in respect of ordinary shares in a company which is a VCT which were acquired at a time when it was a VCT by the recipient of the dividend, and which were not shares acquired in excess of the 'permitted maximum' for the year. Shares acquired after 8 March 1999 must also have been acquired for *bona fide* commercial purposes and not as part of a tax avoidance scheme or arrangements. A relevant distribution does not include any dividend paid in respect of profits or gains of any accounting period ending when the company was not a VCT.

Shares are acquired in excess of the '*permitted maximum*' for a year where the aggregate value of ordinary shares acquired in VCTs by the individual or his nominee(s) in that year exceeds **£100,000**, disregarding shares acquired other than for *bona fide* commercial reasons or as part of a scheme or arrangement a main purpose of which is the avoidance of tax. Shares acquired later in the year are identified as representing the excess before those acquired earlier, and in relation to same-day acquisition of different shares, a proportionate part of each description of share is treated as representing any excess arising on that day. Shares acquired at a time when a company was not a VCT are for these purposes treated as disposed of before other shares in the VCT. Otherwise, disposals are identified with earlier acquisitions before later ones, except that as between shares acquired on the same day, shares acquired in excess of the permitted maximum are treated as disposed of before any other shares. There are provisions for effectively disregarding acquisitions arising out of share exchanges where, for capital gains purposes, the new shares are treated as the same assets as the old.

[*ICTA 1988, Sch 15B paras 7–9; FA 1995, Sch 15 paras 7–9; FA 1999, s 70; SI 1995 No 1979, reg 10*].

For the detailed requirements as regards obtaining relief for distributions before 6 April 1999, including the obtaining of the 'enduring declaration' and the claiming of tax credits, see *SI 1995 No 1979, regs 10–21*. For distributions on or after that date, entitlement to tax credits on qualifying distributions is limited to individuals chargeable to tax on the distributions (see 1.9 ALLOWANCES AND TAX RATES), and those *regulations* are revoked.

91.10 *Example*

In 2001/02, Miss K in the *Example* at 91.6 above, whose circumstances are otherwise unchanged, receives a distribution from VCT plc of 9p per share.

The shares in VCT plc were acquired in 2000/01 for £110,000, so that distributions in respect of shares representing the £10,000 excess over the permitted maximum of £100,000 are not exempt. The 40,000 shares first acquired for £40,000 are first identified, so that the shares representing the excess are one-seventh of the 90,000 shares subsequently acquired for £70,000, i.e. 12,857 of those shares.

Miss K's tax computation for 2001/02 is as follows (assuming for the purposes of this example that the quantum of tax rates and allowances remains unchanged from 2000/01).

	£	£
Pension		19,955
Dividends (other than VCT plc)	16,200	
Add Tax credit	1,800	18,000
VCT plc distribution in respect of 12,857 shares	1,157	
Add Tax credit ($\frac{1}{9}$)	128	1,285
Total income		39,240
Deduct Personal allowance		4,385
Taxable income		£34,855
Tax payable:		£
1,520 @ 10% (starting rate)		152
14,050 @ 22%		3,091
12,830 @ 10% (Schedule F ordinary rate)		1,283
6,455 @ 32.5% (Schedule F upper rate)		2,098
Tax payable		6,624
Deduct Tax credits		1,928
Net tax liability (subject to PAYE)		£4,696

91.11 **CAPITAL GAINS TAX RELIEFS** [*TCGA 1992, ss 151A, 151B, Sch 5C; FA 1995, s 72, Sch 16*]

From 6 April 1995, the capital gains of a VCT are not chargeable gains. [*TCGA 1992, s 100(1); FA 1995, s 72(2)*]. In addition, for 1995/96 and subsequent years, individual investors in VCTs are entitled to two reliefs:

(*a*) on disposal of VCT shares (see 91.12 below); and

(*b*) by deferral of chargeable gains on re-investment in VCT share issues (see 91.14 below).

Various provisions of *TCGA 1992* which are superseded for these purposes by specific provisions (as below) are disapplied or applied separately to parts of holdings which do not fall within the reliefs.

Withdrawal of approval. Where approval of a company as a VCT is withdrawn (but not treated as never having been given) (see 91.2 above), shares which (apart from the withdrawal) would be eligible for the relief on disposal (see 91.12 below) are treated as disposed of at their market value at the time of the withdrawal. For the purposes of the relief on disposal, the disposal is treated as taking place while the company is still a VCT, but the re-acquisition is treated as taking place immediately after it ceases to be so.

91.12 **Relief on disposal.** A gain or loss accruing to an individual on a 'qualifying disposal' of ordinary shares in a company which was a VCT throughout his period of ownership is not a chargeable gain or an allowable loss. A disposal is a '*qualifying disposal*' if:

(*a*) the individual is 18 years of age or more at the time of the disposal;

(*b*) the shares were not acquired in excess of the 'permitted maximum' for any year of assessment; and

(*c*) the shares were acquired for *bona fide* commercial purposes and not as part of a scheme or arrangement a main purpose of which was the avoidance of tax.

The identification of those shares which were acquired in excess of the '*permitted maximum*' is as under 91.9 above (in relation to income tax relief on distributions — broadly those in excess of an annual limit of £100,000), and the identification of disposals with acquisitions for this purpose is similarly as under 91.9 above.

[*TCGA 1992, ss 151A, 151B; FA 1995, s 72(3)*].

See 91.11 above as regards relief on withdrawal of approval of the VCT.

91.13 *Example*

On the disposals in the *Example* at 91.8 above, a chargeable gain or allowable loss arises only on the disposal of the shares acquired in excess of the permitted maximum for 2000/01. As in the *Example* at 91.10 above, these are 12,857 of the shares acquired for £70,000 on 1 September 2000. The disposal identified with those shares is a corresponding proportion of the 105,000 shares disposed of for a consideration of £85,000 on 1 January 2003.

Miss K's capital gains tax computation for 2002/03 is therefore as follows.

Disposal consideration for 12,857 shares —

	£
$85{,}000 \times \dfrac{12{,}857}{105{,}000} =$	10,408
Deduct Cost —	
$70{,}000 \times \dfrac{12{,}857}{90{,}000} =$	10,000
Chargeable gain (subject to taper relief)	£408

91.14 **Deferred charge on re-investment.** *TCGA 1992, Sch 5C* (introduced as *FA 1995, Sch 16* by *FA 1995, s 72(4)*) applies where:

(*a*) a chargeable gain accrues to an individual after 5 April 1995 on the disposal of any asset (or on the occurrence of certain events in relation to enterprise investment scheme investments, see *TCGA 1992, Sch 5B paras 4, 5* introduced as *FA 1995, Sch 13 para 4(3)*, or under the current provisions, see below);

(*b*) the individual makes a 'qualifying investment'; and

(*c*) the individual is UK resident or ordinarily resident both when the chargeable gain accrues to him and when he makes the 'qualifying investment', and is not, at the latter time, regarded as resident outside the UK for the purposes of any double taxation arrangements the effect of which would be that he would not be liable to tax on a gain arising on a disposal, immediately after their acquisition, of the shares comprising the 'qualifying investment', disregarding the exemption under *TCGA 1992, s 151A(1)* (see 91.12 above).

A '*qualifying investment*' is a subscription for shares in a company which is a VCT, by reference to which relief is obtained under 91.5 above, within twelve months (extendible by the Board) before or after the time of the accrual of the chargeable gain in question, and, if before, provided that the shares are still held at that time.

Broadly, the provisions allow a claim for the chargeable gain to be rolled over into the VCT shares, and for the gain to become chargeable on certain events in relation to those shares (including, in particular, on their disposal). For the detailed provisions, see *TCGA 1992, Sch 5C paras 2–6*, introduced as *FA 1995, Sch 16 paras 2–6*, and see Tolley's Capital Gains Tax under Venture Capital Trusts.

92 Vocational Training Relief

92.1 Where, **before 1 September 2000**, a UK-resident individual (or a Crown employee whose duties are for tax purposes treated as performed in the UK, see 75.2(i) SCHEDULE E) pays fees in connection with his own training under a 'qualifying course of vocational training', he is entitled to income tax relief on the amount so paid, provided that

(*a*) at the time of the payment, he has not received, and is not entitled to receive, public financial assistance (as defined by Treasury order, see *SI 1992 No 734; SI 1993 No 1074; SI 1995 No 3274; SI 1996 No 3049; SI 1997 No 635*) in relation to the course, and

(*b*) he is not otherwise entitled to tax relief in respect of the payment,

(*c*) at the time of the payment, the individual is aged 16 or over, and, if under 19, he is not being provided with full-time education at a school (including any institution at which such education is provided to persons at least some of whom are under 16), and

(*d*) he undertakes the course neither wholly nor mainly for recreational purposes or as a leisure activity.

Qualifying payments made before 6 April 1999 are treated as deductions from income of the tax year of payment and thus attract relief at the individual's marginal tax rate. Payments made after 5 April 1999 are not so treated and attract relief at the basic rate only. Subject to conditions specified by the Board in regulations (see *SI 1992 No 746; SI 1993 Nos 1082, 3118; SI 1996 No 1185; SI 1997 No 661*), basic rate relief may be obtained by deduction of basic rate tax from the payment, with the recipient recovering the amount deducted from the Board on a claim. The Board consider that where a payment *may* be made under deduction of basic rate tax, basic rate relief can *only* be obtained by deduction. The tax deducted from payments is not clawed back where the individual is liable only at the lower or starting rate of income tax or has no income tax liability.

Where relief may not be obtained by deduction (e.g. where fees are paid to a non-UK provider), and for higher rate purposes before 1999/2000, relief must be claimed by the individual. For 1999/2000 onwards, the basic rate relief is given by way of an income tax reduction, and this is restricted as necessary to such amount as reduces the individual's liability to nil. The reduction is, however, given in priority to any income tax reductions due in respect of personal reliefs (see 1.15–1.17 ALLOWANCES AND TAX RATES), qualifying maintenance payments (see 47.10 MARRIED PERSONS) or loan interest (see 43.5 INTEREST PAYABLE), any reduction of tax liability by way of DOUBLE TAX RELIEF (25), or any basic rate tax on income the tax on which the individual is entitled to charge against any other person or to deduct, retain or satisfy out of any payment.

The Treasury may make regulations for the withdrawal of relief in whole or in part in prescribed circumstances, and requiring either the individual or the recipient of the fees (as the regulations may prescribe) to account for the tax from which relief was given. The first such regulations (*SI 1992 No 734 amended by SI 1996 No 3049*) deal with payments refunded to the trainee by the training provider, and with awards by the training provider to the trainee by virtue merely of the course being undertaken, completed or completed successfully.

A '*qualifying course of vocational training*' is any programme of activity capable of counting towards a qualification accredited as a National or Scottish Vocational Qualification by the appropriate Council.

In relation to payments made **after 5 May 1996** by individuals *aged 30 or over* at the time the payment is made, a '*qualifying course of vocational training*' also includes any course of training, whether or not leading towards a qualification as above, which

(i) is designed to impart or improve skills or knowledge relevant to, and intended to be used in the course of, gainful employment (including self-employment) of any description,

(ii) is devoted entirely to the teaching and/or practical application within the UK of such skills or knowledge (treating time devoted to study in connection with the course as such practical application),

(iii) requires participation on a full-time, or substantially full-time, basis, and

(iv) extends for a period consisting of or including four *consecutive* weeks but does not last more than one year.

The Revenue have appropriate regulatory powers. Penalties under *TMA 1970, s 98* apply for failure to furnish information etc. required under such regulations, and various assessment, interest and penalty provisions apply in relation to invalid claims by the recipients of fees for repayment of tax deducted therefrom.

[*FA 1991, ss 32, 33; FA 1994, s 84; FA 1996, ss 129, 144, Sch 18 paras 14, 17(1)–(4)(8); FA 1999, s 59, Sch 20 Pt III(15)*].

A Training Pack is available from Inland Revenue, FICO (Savings and Investment) (Vocational Training Unit), St John's House, Merton Road, Bootle, Merseyside L69 9BB, containing details of the scheme and the appropriate Forms for registration of the training provider (VTR 21), for a declaration of entitlement by the trainee (VTR 1), and for annual and interim claims by the provider for repayment of tax deducted from fees (VTR 14, VTR 10).

The Revenue have published a Code of Practice (No 4, available from tax offices) setting out their standards for the carrying out of inspections of tax relief at source schemes operated by financial intermediaries.

The Inland Revenue Financial Intermediaries and Claims Office may be contacted in relation to vocational training relief on 0151–472 6109 as regards repayments or 0151–472 6159 for technical advice.

See also 71.89 SCHEDULE D, CASES I AND II and 75.42 SCHEDULE E.

See generally Simon's Direct Tax Service E2.13 and Revenue Leaflet IR 119.

These provisions are abolished after 31 August 2000.

93 Woodlands

93.1 **Introduction.** Before 6 April 1988, SCHEDULE B (69) applied to the 'occupation of woodlands in the UK managed on a commercial basis and with a view to the realisation of profit'. [*ICTA 1970, s 91*]. It was abolished after 5 April 1988, and where a company accounting period straddled that date, the Schedule B income was apportioned, and the part relating to the period commencing on 6 April 1988 was excluded from taxable income. [*FA 1988, s 65; FA 1988, Sch 6 para 2*].

Profits or gains from the commercial occupation of woodlands are not chargeable under SCHEDULE A (68). [*ICTA 1988, s 15(1)*].

Subject to the transitional provisions described at 93.3 below, the commercial occupation of land which comprises woodlands or is being prepared for use for forestry purposes is thus now not within the charge to income tax [*ICTA 1988, s 54(4); FA 1988, Sch 6 para 6(7)*], as their non-commercial occupation has always been. In *Jaggers (trading as Shide Trees) v Ellis Ch D 1997, 71 TC 164*, land on which trees were planted and cultivated in a manner normally associated with Christmas tree production was held not to be woodland. Short rotation coppice cultivation is (from 29 November 1994) treated for tax purposes as farming and not forestry, so that UK land under such cultivation is not woodlands. [*FA 1995, s 154*].

93.2 **ELECTION FOR SCHEDULE D ASSESSMENT**

Before 15 March 1988, an occupier of woodlands could elect, within two years after the end of the year of assessment (or company accounting period), to be assessed under Schedule D, rather than Schedule B. Such an election had to extend to all woodlands so occupied on the same estate, but woodlands planted or replanted within the previous ten years could be treated as a separate estate. The election remained in force for all subsequent years in which the woodlands continued to be occupied by the person making the election. [*ICTA 1970, s 111*]. CAPITAL ALLOWANCES (10) were available. [*CAA 1990, ss 27(1), 140(8)*]. An election for Schedule D treatment did not allow a claim under *ICTA 1988, s 381* (previously *FA 1978, s 30,* losses in early years of trade, see 46.13 LOSSES) to be made.

This election was abolished after 14 March 1988, subject to transitional provisions (see 93.3 below). Accordingly, profits or losses arising after that date from the occupation of commercial woodlands are, subject to the transitional provisions, not chargeable under Schedule D. Again subject to the transitional provisions, interest paid after that date by any person on a loan to buy an interest in a close company, an employee-controlled company or a partnership carrying on a business consisting of the occupation of commercial woodlands is not eligible for income tax relief (see 43.19, 43.21, 43.22 INTEREST PAYABLE), a just and reasonable apportionment being made where part only of the business so consists. A company's charges on income are similarly restricted where the company (or group) carries on such a business. [*FA 1988, s 65, Sch 6 para 3*].

The management of woodlands in respect of which an election for Schedule D assessment has been given does not necessarily constitute the carrying on of a trade, and standing timber is not stock for the purposes of *ICTA 1988, s 100* (*Coates v Holker Estates Ch D 1961, 40 TC 75*). See also *ICTA 1988, s 99(1)* as to purchase and sales of woodlands by dealers in land, and *CGTA 1979, s 113* for exclusion from capital gains tax of trees, standing or felled, on woodlands managed on a commercial basis. See also 71.83 SCHEDULE D, CASES I AND II (valuation of stock). As to profits from sawmills on an estate see *Christie v Davies KB 1945, 26 TC 398,* and *Williamson Bros CS 1950, 31 TC 370.* Felled timber processed in sawmill at some remove held covered by Schedule B assessment down to planking stage (*Collins v Fraser Ch D 1969, 46 TC 143*).

93.3 TRANSITIONAL PROVISIONS

Assessment under Schedule D and tax allowances for interest paid (see 93.2 above) continued to be available until 5 April 1993 where an election under *ICTA 1970, s 111* was made before 15 March 1988. An election subject to similar conditions and to the same effect could be made under *FA 1988, Sch 6 para 4(1)* after 14 March 1988 and before 6 April 1993 where, in relation to a person's occupation of woodlands, either

(*a*) he had entered into a contract for occupation of the woodlands, or made arrangements evidenced by an instrument or document for such occupation, before 15 March 1988, or

(*b*) he was occupying them on that date, or

(*c*) he occupies them after that date and had before that date entered into a contract or made arrangements for the afforestation (including the replanting) of the land, or

(*d*) he occupies them after that date and a grant application by him under *Forestry Act 1979, s 1* (or NI equivalent) had been received by the Forestry Commissioners (or Department of Agriculture) before that date.

In the event of the death of the occupier, the election may be made by any other person occupying the woodlands by virtue of any disposition of property comprised in his estate immediately before his death.

A pre-15 March 1988 election is treated as if made under *FA 1988, Sch 6 para 4(1)*. Where an election applies, profits or gains and losses are calculated disregarding any '*relevant grant*', (i.e. any grant under *Forestry Act 1979, s 1* (or NI equivalent) made on terms and conditions first published after 15 March 1988 and not supplementary to a grant made on terms and conditions first published before that date), and expenditure the subject of such a grant is not deductible. An election ceases to have effect for any chargeable period if, before the beginning of the period, a relevant grant has been made with respect to any woodlands on the same estate. For this purpose (and for the purposes of an election under *FA 1988, Sch 6 para 4(1)*) woodlands may be treated as being on a separate estate by election within two years of their being planted or replanted.

For CAPITAL ALLOWANCES (10) purposes, any gap between the end of the basis period for the final year of assessment for which an election has effect and the beginning of the next year of assessment is treated as forming part of that basis period. If, however, a loss is incurred in that final year of assessment, so that the capital allowances in the basis period for the next following year of assessment may augment that loss, then it is that basis period which is extended to the end of the final year of assessment. [*FA 1988, s 65, Sch 6 paras 4, 5*].

94 Finance Act 2000 — Summary of Provisions

(Royal Assent 28 July 2000)

INCOME TAX PROVISIONS

s 31 **Charge and rates for 2000/01.** The starting, basic and higher rates of income tax for 2000/01 are 10%, 22% and 40% respectively. See 1.3 ALLOWANCES AND TAX RATES.

s 32 **Extension of starting rate to savings income of individuals.** See 1.3, 1.9 ALLOWANCES AND TAX RATES.

s 33 **Deduction of income tax from foreign dividends.** The rate of deduction under the paying and collecting agents scheme is set retrospectively. See 23.12 DEDUCTION OF TAX AT SOURCE.

s 34 **Children's tax credit.** The initial rate of credit for 2001/02 is increased to £4,420. See 1.18 ALLOWANCES AND TAX RATES.

s 38 **Giving to charity: payroll deduction scheme.** The annual limit is removed, a temporary 10% supplement provided and a number of consequential amendments made. See 15.18 CHARITIES.

s 39 **Giving to charity: gift aid payments by individuals.** The lower limit on donations is removed and the scope of the scheme extended. See 15.11–15.15 CHARITIES.

s 41 **Giving to charity: covenanted payments to charities.** Amendments are made consequential on such payments being brought within the Gift Aid scheme. See 15.12, 15.17 CHARITIES.

s 42 **Giving to charity: millennium gift aid.** Minor amendments are made to the scheme following the extension of Gift Aid (see *section 39* above). See 15.21 CHARITIES.

s 43 **Giving to charity: gifts of shares and securities to charities etc..** A deduction from total income is introduced for such gifts. See 15.20 CHARITIES.

s 44 **Giving to charity: gifts to charity from certain trusts.** Certain charitable gifts out of settlements are excluded from being treated as income of the settlor. See 81.14 SETTLEMENTS.

s 45 **Giving to charity: loans to charities.** Such loans are generally excluded from being treated as settlements. See 81.16(*a*) SETTLEMENTS

s 46 **Giving to charity: exemption for small trades etc..** The existing concessionary reliefs are extended.

s 47, Sch 8 **Employee share ownership plans.** A new share scheme is introduced. See 82.11–82.25 SHARE INCENTIVES AND OPTIONS.

s 48, Sch 9 **Relief for transfers to employee share ownership plans.** Capital gains tax rollover relief is available for certain transfers of shares to the new plans (see *section 47* above). See 82.18 SHARE INCENTIVES AND OPTIONS.

s 49 **Phasing out of approved profit sharing schemes.** See 82.8, 82.9 SHARE INCENTIVES AND OPTIONS.

s 50 **Phasing out of relief for payments to trustees of profit sharing schemes.** See 71.54 SCHEDULE D, CASES I AND II.

s 51 **Approved profit sharing scheme: other awards of shares.** The obtaining of relief under both profit sharing schemes and the new employee share ownership plans (see *section 47* above) is prevented. See 82.8 SHARE INCENTIVES AND OPTIONS.

s 52 **Approved profit sharing schemes: restriction on type of shares.** An anti-avoidance measure is introduced preventing the use of shares in certain service companies. See 82.8 SHARE INCENTIVES AND OPTIONS.

s 53 **Approved profit sharing schemes: loan arrangements.** An anti-avoidance measure is introduced preventing the granting of certain employee loans under scheme arrangements. See 82.8 SHARE INCENTIVES AND OPTIONS.

s 54 **Employee share ownership trusts.** Capital gains tax rollover relief on transfers of shares to such trusts is withdrawn. See 82.41 SHARE INCENTIVES AND OPTIONS.

s 55 **Shares transferred from employee share ownership trust.** Provision is made for transfers of shares by the trustees of such trusts to employee share ownership plans (see *section 47* above). See 82.41 SHARE INCENTIVES AND OPTIONS.

s 56 **Further provisions about share options.** Employer national insurance contributions borne by an employee are deductible in computing the employee's share option gain for income tax purposes. Certain amendments are made to employer reporting requirements. See 82.3 SHARE INCENTIVES AND OPTIONS.

s 57, Sch 10 **Benefits in kind: deregulatory amendments.** A number of relaxations of conditions and of reporting requirements are introduced. See 75.13, 75.17 SCHEDULE E.

s 58 **Education and training.** Relief is introduced for employer contributions to education and training costs of employees with individual learning accounts. See 75.42 SCHEDULE E.

s 59, Sch 11 **Cars available for private use.** A new company car scheme is introduced from 6 April 2002. See 75.15(ii) SCHEDULE E.

s 60, Sch 12 **Provision of services through intermediary.** Provisions are introduced aimed at removing the tax advantages of personal service companies and other intermediaries. See 61 PERSONAL SERVICE COMPANIES ETC..

s 61, Sch 13 **Occupational and personal pension schemes.** Changes are made to facilitate the inclusion under the personal pension scheme provisions of stakeholder pension arrangements. See 60 PERSONAL PENSION SCHEMES (INCLUDING STAKEHOLDER PENSIONS).

s 62, Sch 14 **Enterprise management incentives.** A new share incentive scheme is introduced. See 82.26–82.37 SHARE INCENTIVES AND OPTIONS.

s 63, Schs 15, 16 **Corporate venturing scheme.** New reliefs are introduced for investments by companies in certain small, higher-risk trading companies. See 26.12 ENTERPRISE INVESTMENT SCHEME (AND BES) and 46.18 LOSSES, and Tolley's Corporation Tax under Corporate Venturing Scheme.

s 64, Sch 17 **Enterprise investment scheme: amendments.** Certain relief restrictions are relaxed. See 26 ENTERPRISE INVESTMENT SCHEME (AND BES)

s 65, Sch 18 **Venture capital trusts: amendments.** Certain relief restrictions are relaxed. See 91.3, 91.5, 91.7 VENTURE CAPITAL TRUSTS.

s 68, Sch 19 **Meaning of "research and development".** A revised definition is adopted for both capital and revenue expenditure reliefs. See 71.80 SCHEDULE D, CASES I AND II, 10.52 CAPITAL ALLOWANCES.

s 70 **Capital allowances: first year allowances for small or medium-sized enterprises.** The temporary 40% allowances are made permanent. See 10.27 CAPITAL ALLOWANCES.

s 71 **Capital allowances: first year allowances for information and communications technology expenditure by small enterprises.** 100% allowances are introduced for such expenditure. See 10.27 CAPITAL ALLOWANCES.

s 72 **Capital allowances: expenditure of a small enterprise.** 'Small enterprise' in *section 71* is defined. See 10.27 CAPITAL ALLOWANCES.

s 73 **Capital allowances: repeal of notification requirements.** The requirement to notify expenditure on machinery and plant is removed. See 10.27 CAPITAL ALLOWANCES.

s 74 **Capital allowances: pool for certain leased assets and inexpensive cars.** The separate pool is abolished. See 10.35(*a*) CAPITAL ALLOWANCES.

s 75 **Capital allowances: machinery and plant allowances for non-residents etc..** The basis of relief for non-residents is clarified, and new rules relating to changes in use introduced. See 10.24, 10.28(C), 10.34(*b*), 10.38(ix) CAPITAL ALLOWANCES.

s 76 **Capital allowances: production animals.** The herd basis rules are extended to shared animals (as previously applied by concession), and the exclusion of capital allowances for farm animals confirmed. See 10.25 CAPITAL ALLOWANCES, 34.2 HERD BASIS.

s 77 **Capital allowances: sale and leaseback.** An anomalous result of the existing provisions is corrected. See 10.38(iii) CAPITAL ALLOWANCES.

s 78 **Capital allowances: meaning of "fixture".** The existing practice as regards space or water heating system equipment is made statutory. See 10.34 CAPITAL ALLOWANCES.

s 79 **Capital allowances: leased assets under the Affordable Warmth Programme.** Allowances are granted on certain equipment installed under the programme. See 10.34(*b*) CAPITAL ALLOWANCES.

s 80 **Capital allowances: fixtures and machinery and plant on hire-purchase etc..** It is confirmed that the special fixtures provisions take precedence over the hire-purchase provisions of *CAA 1990, s 60*. See 10.38(i)(vi) CAPITAL ALLOWANCES.

s 81 **Capital allowances: production sharing contracts.** The availability of capital allowances where oil production assets pass into foreign government ownership is clarified. See 10.27 CAPITAL ALLOWANCES.

s 83 **Relief for interest on loans to buy annuities.** The relief limit and rate are fixed at £30,000 and 23% respectively. See 43.3, 43.24 INTEREST PAYABLE.

s 84 **Exemption of payment under New Deal 50plus.** See 83.4 SOCIAL SECURITY.

s 85 **Exemption of payments under Employment Zones programme.** See 83.4 SOCIAL SECURITY.

s 87, Sch 23 **Tax treatment of acquisition, disposal or revaluation of certain rights.** Relief is introduced for acquisition costs of certain telecommunications licences. See 71.87 SCHEDULE D, CASES I AND II.

s 88 **Contribution to local enterprise agencies, etc..** Relief for such contribution is made permanent. See 71.84 SCHEDULE D, CASES I AND II.

s 89	**Waste disposal: entitlement of successor to allowances.** See 71.94 SCHEDULE D, CASES I AND II.
s 103, Sch 30	**Double taxation relief.** A number of significant changes are made to the scope of double tax reliefs. See 25.2, 25.4, 25.5 DOUBLE TAX RELIEF.
s 107	**General insurance reserves.** Provision is made for the clawback of excess provisions. See 89.3 UNDERWRITERS and Tolley's Corporation Tax under Life Insurance Companies.
s 111	**Payments under deduction of tax.** The paying and collecting agents scheme is abolished, and consequential changes made to the rules for deduction of tax in certain cases. See 23.3(ii), 23.12 DEDUCTION OF TAX AT SOURCE, 33.1 GOVERNMENT STOCKS, 70.1 SCHEDULE C.
s 112	**UK public revenue dividends: deduction of tax.** A new tax deduction scheme is introduced. See 23.3(ii) DEDUCTION OF TAX AT SOURCE, 33.3 GOVERNMENT STOCKS
s 113	**Tax treatment of expenditure on production or acquisition of films.** Minor technical revisions and clarifications are made to the reliefs available. See 71.58 SCHEDULE D, CASES I AND II.
s 143, Sch 38	**Power to provide incentives to use electronic communications.** The Revenue are given powers to offer incentives to taxpayers using electronic communications. See 35.12 INLAND REVENUE: ADMINISTRATION, 67.3 RETURNS.
s 144	**Offence of fraudulent evasion of income tax.** A new offence is introduced. See 6.12 BACK DUTY, 58.10 PENALTIES.
s 145	**Information about interest etc. paid, credited or received.** Changes are made to third party information requirements. See 67.4 RETURNS.
s 146	**International exchange of information: general.** Provision is made for international exchange of tax-related information. See 35.13 INLAND REVENUE: ADMINISTRATION, 36.2(*c*) INLAND REVENUE: CONFIDENTIALITY OF INFORMATION.
s 148	**Use of minimum wage information.** See 36.2(*r*) INLAND REVENUE: CONFIDENTIALITY OF INFORMATION.
s 149, Sch 39	**Orders for the delivery of documents.** New powers are provided, subject to judicial approval. See 6.8 BACK DUTY.
s 150	**Search warrants: miscellaneous amendments.** See 6.9, 6.10 BACK DUTY.
s 155	**Interpretation.**
s 156, Sch 40	**Repeals.**
s 157	**Short title.**

OTHER PROVISIONS

ss 1–29, Schs 1–5	**Customs and Excise.**
s 30, Schs 6, 7	**Climate change levy.**
s 35	**Corporation tax: charge and main rate for financial year 2001.** The full rate is set at 30%. See Tolley's Corporation Tax under Introduction and Rates of Tax.
s 36	**Corporation tax: small companies' rate for financial year 2000.** The small companies' rate is set at 20%, and the marginal relief fraction at one fortieth. See Tolley's Corporation Tax under Small Companies—Reduced Rates.

s 37	**Capital gains tax: application of starting rate to capital gains tax.** See 11.3 CAPITAL GAINS TAX.
s 40	**Giving to charity: gift aid payments by companies.** The lower limit and certain other restrictions are removed, and other scheme conditions revised. See Tolley's Corporation Tax under Charities.
s 66	**Capital gains tax: taper relief: taper for business assets.** The maximum taper is to be achieved after holding the asset for four years rather than ten as before. The bonus year addition for assets held at 17 March 1998 is withdrawn for such disposals. See Tolley's Capital Gains Tax under Taper Relief.
s 67	**Capital gains tax: taper relief: assets qualifying as business assets.** The definition of a business asset is widened to include all shareholdings in unquoted companies, quoted shares in the taxpayer's employer company and quoted shares held by an outside investor able to exercise at least 5% of the voting rights. See Tolley's Capital Gains Tax under Taper Relief.
s 69, Schs 20, 21	**Tax relief for expenditure on research and development.** Enhanced reliefs are available for research and development expenditure by small and medium-sized companies. See Tolley's Corporation Tax under Profit Computations.
s 82, Sch 22	**Tonnage tax.** A new tonnage-based corporation tax regime is introduced for shipping companies. See Tolley's Corporation tax under Profit Computations.
s 86	**Loan where return bears inverse relationship to results.** Subject to conditions, interest on such loans is not treated as a distribution. See Tolley's Corporation Tax under Distributions.
s 90	**Capital gains tax: restriction of gifts relief.** Business asset hold-over relief is no longer available on a transfer of shares or securities to a company. See Tolley's Capital Gains Tax under Hold-Over Reliefs.
s 91, Sch 24	**Capital gains tax: disposal of interest in settled property: deemed disposal of underlying assets.** A disposal, for consideration, of an interest in a UK settlement in which the settlor has an interest sparks a deemed disposal and reacquisition at market value. See Tolley's Capital Gains Tax under Settlements.
s 92, Schs 25, 26	**Capital gains tax: transfers of value by trustees linked with trust borrowing.** Certain transfers of funds by trustees, where any outstanding trustee borrowings have not been used for 'normal trust purposes', are treated as giving rise to a disposal and reacquistion by the trustees at market value of settlement assets. See Tolley's Capital Gains Tax under Settlements and Offshore Settlements.
s 93	**Capital gains tax: restriction on set-off of trust losses.** Where assets have been transferred into a UK settlement, using gifts hold-over relief, by a person who acquired an interest in the settlement for consideration, trust losses cannot be offset against a gain accruing on a disposal of those assets. See Tolley's Capital Gains Tax under Settlements.
s 94	**Capital gains tax: attribution to trustees of gains of non-resident companies.** Where any part of a gain accruing to an offshore company falls to be attributed under *TCGA 1992, s 13* to trustees of a UK settlement, nothing in any double tax agreement is to be taken as averting the tax charge otherwise arising. See Tolley's Capital Gains Tax under Settlements.
s 95	**Capital gains tax: disposal of interest in non-resident settlement.** On the emigration of a UK settlement, the normal uplift in the acquisition cost of a beneficiary's interest is disapplied if the settlement has gains which were realised during an earlier period of non-UK residence and do not fall to be attributed to UK beneficiaries. See Tolley's Capital Gains Tax under Offshore Settlements.

s 96 **Capital gains tax: payments by trustees to non-resident companies.** A change is made to the rules for attributing to beneficiaries capital payments made by an offshore trust to an offshore company controlled by the beneficiaries. The rules can no longer be circumvented by including non-residents within the group of persons who control the offshore company. See Tolley's Capital Gains Tax under Offshore Settlements.

s 97, Sch 27 **Groups and group relief: group relief for non-resident companies etc..** The reliefs are extended to UK branches or agencies of non-resident companies. See Tolley's Corporation Tax under Groups of Companies for the principal changes.

s 98, Sch 28 **Groups and group relief: recovery of tax payable by non-resident company.** Provision is made for the recovery from third party companies of tax unpaid by non-resident companies. See Tolley's Corporation Tax under Groups of Companies.

s 99 **Groups and group relief: joint arrangements for claims.** Minor change to the authority required under the simplified arrangements for group claims. See Tolley's Corporation Tax under Groups of Companies.

s 100 **Groups and group relief: limit on amount of group relief in case of consortium claim.** A minor technical defect is corrected. See Tolley's Corporation Tax under Groups of Companies.

s 101 **Groups and group relief: notional transfers within groups of companies.** Two group companies may elect that a disposal by one of them to a person outside the group be deemed to have been made by the other and to have been preceded by an intra-group transfer of the asset at no gain/no loss. See Tolley's Capital Gains Tax under Companies.

s 102, Sch 29 **Groups and group relief: chargeable gains: non-resident companies and groups etc..** The condition that members of a CGT group of companies be UK-resident is removed. Various specific provisions instead now focus on whether assets are within the charge to UK corporation tax. There are numerous consequential changes. See Tolley's Capital Gains Tax under Companies for the principal changes.

s 104, Sch 31 **Controlled foreign companies.** A number of new anti-avoidance measures are added to the controlled foreign companies provisions. See Tolley's Corporation Tax under Controlled Foreign Companies.

s 105 **Corporation tax: use of currencies other than sterling.** New rules are provided for the calculation of company profits in currencies other than sterling. See Tolley's Corporation Tax under Exchange Gains and Losses.

s 106 **Foreign exchange gains and losses: use of local currency.** A number of changes are made to the exchange gains and losses rules, mainly in consequence of the changes introduced by *section 105*. See Tolley's Corporation Tax under Exchange Gains and Losses.

s 108 **Overseas life assurance business.** The definition of such business is made more flexible by the use of secondary legislation. See Tolley's Corporation Tax under Life Insurance Companies.

s 109 **Insurance business: apportionment rules.** Changes are made to the rules for apportionment of income and gains between different classes of business. See Tolley's Corporation Tax under Life Insurance Companies.

s 110 **Rent factoring.** Anti-avoidance provisions are introduced relating to sales of rights to future rental income by companies. See 68.30 SCHEDULE A and Tolley's Corporation Tax under Profit Computations.

ss 114–134, Schs 32–34	**Stamp duty and stamp duty reserve tax.**
ss 135–137, Schs 35, 36	**Value added tax.**
s 138	**Inheritance tax.**
s 139	**Petroleum revenue tax.**
ss 140–142, Sch 37	**Landfill tax.**
s 147	**International exchange of information: inheritance tax.** Provision is made for international exchange of IHT-related information. See 6.8 BACK DUTY.
ss 151–154	**Government borrowings etc..**

95 Table of Leading Cases

This Table lists those of the approximately 2,000 cases referred to in this book which are considered to be of most general application and interest. For fuller details of these cases, and of all other tax cases relevant to current or recent legislation, see Tolley's Tax Cases.

A

AB, Southern *v* 71.30; 71.34
KB 1933, 18 TC 59; [1933] 1 KB 713.
Abbott *v* Philbin 75.7
HL 1960, 39 TC 82; [1961] AC 352; [1960] 2 All ER 763.
Absalom *v* Talbot 71.44
HL 1944, 26 TC 166; [1944] AC 204; [1944] 1 All ER 642.
Alexander von Glehn & Co Ltd, CIR *v* 71.34; 71.47; 71.90
CA 1920, 12 TC 232; [1920] 2 KB 553.
Allan, ex p. (R *v* CIR) 4.8
QB 1999, [1999] STC 531.
Allen, Bosanquet *v* 81.5
HL 1985, 59 TC 125; [1985] STC 356; [1985] 2 WLR 1010; [1985] 2 All ER 645.
Allen *v* Farquharson Bros & Co 4.9
KB 1932, 17 TC 59.
Anderton & Halstead Ltd *v* Birrell 71.44
KB 1931, 16 TC 200; [1932] 1 KB 271.
Andrews, Rignell *v* 1.21
Ch D 1990, 63 TC 312; [1990] STC 410.
Ang *v* Parrish 81.28
Ch D 1980, 53 TC 304; [1980] STC 341; [1980] 1 WLR 940; [1980] 2 All ER 790.
Anglo Brewing Co Ltd, CIR *v* 66.10; 71.54
KB 1925, 12 TC 803.
Anglo-Persian Oil Co Ltd *v* Dale 71.47
CA 1931, 16 TC 253; [1932] 1 KB 124.
Archer-Shee, Garland *v* 81.10
HL 1930, 15 TC 693; [1931] AC 212.
Archer-Shee *v* Baker 81.10
HL 1927, 11 TC 749; [1927] AC 844.
Arthur Young McClelland Moores & Co, MacKinlay *v* 53.3; 71.40; 71.74
HL 1989, 62 TC 704; [1989] STC 898; [1989] 3 WLR 1245; [1990] 1 All ER 45.
Atherton *v* British Insulated & Helsby Cables Ltd 66.10; 71.40
HL 1925, 10 TC 155; [1926] AC 205.
Attorney-General *v* Metropolitan Water Board 23.3(i)
CA 1927, 13 TC 294.
Attwooll, London & Thames Haven Oil Wharves Ltd *v* 71.48(*c*)
CA 1966, 43 TC 491; [1967] Ch 772; [1967] 2 All ER 124.

B

BSC Footwear Ltd *v* Ridgway 71.83
HL 1971, 47 TC 495; [1972] AC 544; [1971] 2 All ER 534.
Bairstow & Harrison, Edwards *v* 4.7; 71.35
HL 1955, 36 TC 207; [1956] AC 14; [1955] 3 All ER 48.
Baker, Archer-Shee *v* 81.10
HL 1927, 11 TC 749; [1927] AC 844.

95 Table of Leading Cases

Banin *v* Mackinlay 4.6(*a*)
CA 1984, 58 TC 398; [1985] STC 144; [1985] 1 All ER 842.
Banning *v* Wright 68.28
HL 1972, 48 TC 421; [1972] 1 WLR 972; [1972] 2 All ER 987.
Barnet London Borough Council (ex p. Nilish Shah), R *v* 64.6
HL 1982, [1983] 2 WLR 16; [1983] 1 All ER 226.
Baylis *v* Gregory 4.4; 5.1
HL 1988, 62 TC 1; [1988] STC 476; [1988] 3 WLR 423; [1988] 3 All ER 495.
Beauchamp *v* F W Woolworth plc 71.56
HL 1989, 61 TC 542; [1989] STC 510; [1989] 3 WLR 1.
Beeson, Bentleys Stokes & Lowless *v* 71.40
CA 1952, 33 TC 491; [1952] 2 All ER 82.
Bell, Heaton *v* 75.7; 75.15
HL 1969, 46 TC 211; [1970] AC 728; [1969] 2 All ER 70.
Bennett, Liverpool & London & Globe Insurance Co *v* 5.2; 71.66
HL 1913, 6 TC 327; [1913] AC 610.
Bentleys Stokes & Lowless *v* Beeson 71.40
CA 1952, 33 TC 491; [1952] WN 280; [1952] 2 All ER 82.
Best, Bray *v* 75.26
HL 1989, 61 TC 705; [1989] STC 159; [1989] 1 WLR 167; [1989] 1 All ER 969.
Bestway (Holdings) Ltd *v* Luff 10.11
Ch D 1998, 70 TC 512; [1998] STC 357.
Bird & others *v* CIR and related appeals 3.2
HL 1988, 61 TC 238; [1988] STC 312; [1988] 2 WLR 1237; [1988] 2 All ER 670.
Birmingham & District Cattle By-Products Ltd *v* CIR 71.26; 71.76
KB 1919, 12 TC 92.
Birrell, Anderton & Halstead Ltd *v* 71.44
KB 1931, 16 TC 200; [1932] 1 KB 271.
Bishopp, ex p. (R *v* CIR) 4.8
QB 1999, [1999] STC 531.
Black, Coltness Iron Co *v* 71.71
HL 1881, 1 TC 287; (1881) 6 App Cas 315.
Blackpool Marton Rotary Club *v* Martin 5.1; 18.1; 53.2
CA 1989, 62 TC 686; [1990] STC 1.
BMI (No 3) Ltd, Melluish *v* 10.27; 10.34
HL 1995, 68 TC 1; [1995] STC 964; [1995] 3 WLR 630; [1995] 4 All ER 453.
Bolland, Smith's Potato Estates Ltd *v* 4.9; 71.69
HL 1948, 30 TC 267; [1948] AC 508; [1948] 2 All ER 367.
Borax Consolidated Ltd, Southern *v* 71.69
KB 1940, 23 TC 597; [1941] 1 KB 111; [1940] 4 All ER 412.
Bosanquet *v* Allen 81.5
HL 1985, 59 TC 125; [1985] STC 356; [1985] 2 WLR 1010; [1985] 2 All ER 645.
Botnar, CIR *v* 3.8
CA 1999, [1999] STC 711.
Bowden *v* Russell & Russell 71.90
Ch D 1965, 42 TC 301; [1965] 1 WLR 711; [1965] 2 All ER 258.
Bradley, Nuclear Electric plc *v* 71.66
HL 1996, 68 TC 670; [1996] STC 405; [1996] 1 WLR 529.
Brady *v* Group Lotus Car Companies plc and Another 4.6(*a*); 4.7
CA 1987, 60 TC 359; [1987] STC 635; [1987] 3 All ER 1050.
Braithwaite, Davies *v* 71.43; 75.24
KB 1933, 18 TC 198.
Brander & Cruickshank, CIR *v* 71.40; 71.48(*b*); 75.24
HL 1970, 46 TC 574; [1971] 1 WLR 212: [1971] 1 All ER 36.

Bray *v* Best 75.26
HL 1989, 61 TC 705; [1989] STC 159; [1989] 1 WLR 167; [1989] 1 All ER 969.
Brebner, CIR *v* 3.2
HL 1967, 43 TC 705; [1967] 1 All ER 779.
Britannia Airways Ltd, Johnston *v* 71.40; 71.49; 71.79(*a*)
Ch D 1994, 67 TC 99; [1994] STC 763.
British Commonwealth International Newsfilm Agency Ltd *v* Mahany 23.10; 71.72
HL 1962, 40 TC 550; [1963] 1 WLR 69; [1963] 1 All ER 88.
British Insulated & Helsby Cables Ltd, Atherton *v* 66.10; 71.40
HL 1925, 10 TC 155; [1926] AC 205.
British Salmson Aero Engines Ltd, CIR *v* 23.15(*b*)
CA 1938, 22 TC 29; [1938] 2 KB 482; [1937] 3 All ER 464.
British Telecom Pension Fund Trustees, Clarke *v* 66.5
CA 2000, [2000] STC 222.
British Transport Commission *v* Gourley 19.7
HL 1955, 34 ATC 305; [1956] AC 185; [1955] 3 All ER 796.
Brixton Commrs, R *v* 4.6(*a*)
KB 1912, 6 TC 195.
Broadstone Mills Ltd, Patrick *v* 71.83
CA 1953, 35 TC 44; [1954] 1 WLR 158; [1954] 1 All ER 163.
Brodie's Trustees *v* CIR 5.3
KB 1933, 17 TC 432.
Brooks, Colquhoun *v* 51.12; 73.3
HL 1889, 2 TC 490; 14 App Cas 493.
Brown *v* Bullock 75.39
CA 1961, 40 TC 1; [1961] 1 WLR 1095; [1961] 3 All ER 129.
Bruce, Thompson *v* 1.22
KB 1927, 11 TC 607.
Bruce, Usher's Wiltshire Brewery Ltd *v* 71.45
HL 1914, 6 TC 399; [1915] AC 433.
Buckingham *v* Securitas Properties Ltd 10.11
Ch D 1979, 53 TC 292; [1980] STC 166; [1980] 1 WLR 380.
Bullcroft Main Collieries Ltd, O'Grady *v* 71.71; 71.79(*b*)
KB 1932, 17 TC 93.
Bullock, Brown *v* 75.39
CA 1961, 40 TC 1; [1961] 1 WLR 1095; [1961] 3 All ER 129.
Burma Corporation Ltd, Fry *v* 71.27
HL 1930, 15 TC 113; [1930] AC 321.
Burmah Steam Ship Co Ltd *v* CIR 71.48(*c*)
CS 1930, 16 TC 67.
Butt *v* Haxby 46.2
Ch D 1982, 56 TC 547; [1983] STC 239.

C

Californian Copper Syndicate Ltd *v* Harris 71.38
Ex (S) 1904, 5 TC 159.
Campbell & Another *v* CIR 15.17(*b*)
HL 1968, 45 TC 427; [1970] AC 77; [1968] 3 All ER 588.
Carver *v* Duncan 81.5
HL 1985, 59 TC 125; [1985] STC 356; [1985] 2 WLR 1010; [1985] 2 All ER 645.
Cenlon Finance Co Ltd *v* Ellwood 5.3
HL 1962, 40 TC 176; [1962] AC 782; [1962] 1 All ER 854.

Chamberlain, Salt *v* 71.39
Ch D 1979, 53 TC 143; [1979] STC 750.
Chambers (GH) (Northiam Farms) Ltd *v* Watmough 10.28(C)
Ch D 1956, 36 TC 711; [1956] 1 WLR 1483; [1956] 3 All ER 485.
Church Commissioners for England, CIR *v* 23.10; 23.11(*a*); 28.2(*g*)
HL 1976, 50 TC 516; [1976] STC 339; [1977] AC 329; [1976] 2 All ER 1037.
Clark, Reed *v* 64.5
Ch D 1985, 58 TC 528; [1985] STC 323; [1985] 3 WLR 142; [1986] Ch 1.
Clark, Van den Berghs Ltd *v* 71.47; 71.48(*b*); 71.75
HL 1935, 19 TC 390; [1935] AC 431.
Clark *v* Oceanic Contractors Incorporated 55.34
HL 1982, 56 TC 183; [1983] STC 35; [1983] 2 WLR 94; [1983] 1 All ER 133.
Clarke *v* British Telecom Pension Fund Trustees 66.5
CA 2000, [2000] STC 222.
Clarke, Girobank plc *v* 10.11
CA 1997, 70 TC 387; [1998] STC 182; [1998] 1 WLR 942; [1998] 4 All ER 312.
Clayton *v* Lavender 19.3
Ch D 1965, 42 TC 607; [1965] TR 461.
Cleary, CIR *v* 3.2
HL 1967, 44 TC 399; [1968] AC 766; [1967] 2 All ER 48.
Clinch, Edwards *v* 75.1; 75.24
HL 1981, 56 TC 367; [1981] STC 617; [1981] 3 WLR 707; [1981] 3 All ER 543.
Clixby *v* Pountney 6.2; 58.3
Ch D 1967, 44 TC 515; [1968] Ch 719; [1968] 1 All ER 802.
Clore and Others, Official Solicitor *v*, Re Clore (dec'd.) (No 2) 64.4
Ch D 1984, [1984] STC 609.
Coldicott, EMI Group Electronics Ltd *v* 75.45
CA 1999, 71 TC 445; [1999] STC 803.
Cole Bros Ltd *v* Phillips 10.25
HL 1982, 55 TC 188; [1982] STC 307; [1982] 1 WLR 1450; [1982] 2 All ER 247.
Collins, Drummond *v* 81.8; 81.10
HL 1915, 6 TC 525; [1915] 2 AC 1011.
Colquhoun, Ricketts *v* 75.43
HL 1925, 10 TC 118; [1926] AC 1.
Colquhoun *v* Brooks 51.12; 73.3
HL 1889, 2 TC 490; 14 App Cas 493.
Coltness Iron Co *v* Black 71.71
HL 1881, 1 TC 287; (1881) 6 App Cas 315.
Commerzbank AG, ex p. (R *v* CIR) 25.2; 41.2
CJEC 1993, 68 TC 252; [1993] STC 605; [1994] 2 WLR 128; [1993] 4 All ER 37.
Congreve & Congreve *v* CIR 3.8
HL 1948, 30 TC 163; [1948] 1 All ER 948.
Conservators of Epping Forest (Corporation of London as), CIR *v* 23.10
HL 1953, 34 TC 293; [1953] 1 WLR 625; [1953] 1 All ER 747.
Consolidated African Selection Trust Ltd, Lowry *v* 71.54
HL 1940, 23 TC 259; [1940] AC 648; [1940] 2 All ER 545.
Consolidated Goldfields plc; Gold Fields Mining and Industrial Ltd *v* CIR 4.7
Ch D 1990, 63 TC 333; [1990] STC 357; [1990] 2 All ER 398.
Cook, George Humphries & Co *v* 53.8
KB 1934, 19 TC 121.
Cook, Odhams Press Ltd *v* 71.44
HL 1940, 23 TC 233; [1940] 3 All ER 15.
Copol Clothing Ltd *v* Hindmarch 10.11
CA 1983, 57 TC 575; [1984] STC 33; [1984] 1 WLR 411.

Cordy, Smith Barry *v* 71.37
CA 1946, 28 TC 250; [1946] 2 All ER 396.
Corporation of London (as Conservators of Epping Forest), CIR *v* 23.10
HL 1953, 34 TC 293; [1953] 1 WLR 625; [1953] 1 All ER 747.
Costain Property Investments Ltd, Stokes *v* 10.27
CA 1984, 57 TC 688; [1984] STC 204; [1984] 1 WLR 763; [1984] 1 All ER 849.
Craven *v* White 3.1
HL 1988, 62 TC 1; [1988] STC 476; [1988] 3 WLR 423; [1988] 3 All ER 495.
Crawford, Lochgelly Iron & Coal Co Ltd *v* 71.84
CS 1913, 6 TC 267.
Crawley and Others, CIR *v* 15.17(*g*); 23.1; 23.2
Ch D 1986, 59 TC 728; [1987] STC 147.
Crook, Seaham Harbour Dock Co *v* 71.85
HL 1931, 16 TC 333.
Curtis *v* Oldfield (J & G) Ltd 71.44; 71.53
KB 1925, 9 TC 319.

D

DTE Financial Services Ltd *v* Wilson 55.2
Ch D 1999, [1999] STC 1061.
Dale, Anglo-Persian Oil Co Ltd *v* 71.47
CA 1931, 16 TC 253; [1932] 1 KB 124.
Dale *v* de Soissons 19.3
CA 1950, 32 TC 118; [1950] 2 All ER 460.
Daphne *v* Shaw 10.25
KB 1926, 11 TC 256.
Davies *v* Braithwaite 71.43; 75.24
KB 1933, 18 TC 198; [1931] 2 KB 628.
Davis, Floor *v* 20.7
HL 1979, 52 TC 609; [1979] STC 379; [1979] 2 WLR 830; [1979] 2 All ER 677.
Dawson, Furniss *v* 3.1
HL 1984, 55 TC 324; [1984] STC 153; [1984] 2 WLR 226; [1984] 1 All ER 530.
De Soissons, Dale *v* 19.3
CA 1950, 32 TC 118; [1950] 2 All ER 460.
Delbourgo *v* Field 4.4
CA 1978, 52 TC 225; [1978] STC 234; [1978] 2 All ER 193.
Dewhurst, Hunter *v* 19.3
HL 1932, 16 TC 605.
Dixon *v* Fitch's Garage Ltd 10.25
Ch D 1975, 50 TC 509; [1975] STC 480; [1976] 1 WLR 215; [1975] 3 All ER 455.
Dixon (Peter) & Son Ltd, Lomax *v* 72.3(*b*); 73.3
CA 1943, 25 TC 353; [1943] 2 All ER 255.
Drummond, Mallalieu *v* 71.40; 71.74
HL 1983, 57 TC 330; [1983] STC 665; [1983] 3 WLR 409; [1983] 2 All ER 1095.
Drummond *v* Collins 81.8; 81.10
HL 1915, 6 TC 525; [1915] 2 AC 1011.
Duke of Westminster *v* CIR 3.1
HL 1935, 19 TC 490.
Duncan, Carver *v* 81.5
HL 1985, 59 TC 125; [1985] STC 356; [1985] 2 WLR 1010; [1985] 2 All ER 645.
Dunn, Kirk & Randall Ltd *v* 71.26
KB 1924, 8 TC 663.

Duple Motor Bodies Ltd *v* Ostime 71.83
HL 1961, 39 TC 537; [1961] 1 WLR 739; [1961] 2 All ER 167.

E

EMI Group Electronics Ltd *v* Coldicott 75.45
CA 1999, 71 TC 455; [1999] STC 803.
EVC International NV (formerly European Vinyls Corp (Holdings) BV), Steele *v* 20.7
CA 1996, 69 TC 88; [1996] STC 785.
Earl Howe *v* CIR 23.10; 28.4(*a*)
CA 1919, 7 TC 289; [1919] 2 KB 336.
Edon, Mitchell &, *v* Ross 5.2; 71.90; 75.10(*a*); 75.24
HL 1961, 40 TC 11; [1961] 3 All ER 49.
Edwards *v* Bairstow & Harrison 4.7; 71.35
HL 1955, 36 TC 207; [1956] AC 14; [1955] 3 All ER 48.
Edwards *v* Clinch 75.1; 75.24
HL 1981, 56 TC 367; [1981] STC 617; [1981] 3 WLR 707; [1981] 3 All ER 543.
Ellam, Essex County Council *v* 23.10
CA 1989, 61 TC 615; [1989] STC 317; [1989] 2 All ER 494.
Elliss, Gaspet Ltd *v* 10.52
CA 1987, 60 TC 91; [1987] STC 362; [1987] 1 WLR 769.
Ellwood, Cenlon Finance Co Ltd *v* 5.3
HL 1962, 40 TC 176; [1962] AC 782; [1962] 1 All ER 854.
Emery *v* CIR 3.2
Ch D 1980, 54 TC 607; [1981] STC 150.
Emanuel (Lewis) & Son Ltd *v* White 71.39
Ch D 1965, 42 TC 369; [1965] TR 99.
Ensign Tankers (Leasing) Ltd *v* Stokes 10.25; 10.27; 71.29
HL 1992, 64 TC 617; [1992] STC 226; [1992] 2 WLR 469; [1992] 2 All ER 275.
Epping Forest, Conservators of (Corporation of London as), CIR *v* 23.10
HL 1953, 34 TC 293; [1953] 1 WLR 625; [1953] 1 All ER 747.
Essex County Council *v* Ellam 23.10
CA 1989, 61 TC 615; [1989] STC 317; 2 All ER 494.
European Investment Trust Co Ltd *v* Jackson 71.65
CA 1932, 18 TC 1.
European Vinyls Corp (Holdings) BV (now EVC International NV), Steele *v* 20.7
CA 1996, 69 TC 88; [1996] STC 785.

F

Fall *v* Hitchen 75.24
Ch D 1972, 49 TC 433; [1973] STC 66; [1973] 1 WLR 286; [1973] 1 All ER 368.
Farquharson Bros & Co, Allen *v* 4.9
KB 1932, 17 TC 59.
Ferguson, CIR *v* 23.16; 23.17(*a*)
HL 1969, 46 TC 1; [1970] AC 442; [1969] 1 All ER 1025.
Field, Delbourgo *v* 4.4
CA 1978, 52 TC 225; [1978] STC 234; [1978] 2 All ER 193.
Firth, Wicks *v* 75.13
HL 1982, 56 TC 318; [1983] STC 25; [1983] 2 WLR 34; [1983] 1 All ER 151.
Fitch's Garage Ltd, Dixon *v* 10.25
Ch D 1975, 50 TC 509; [1975] STC 480; [1976] 1 WLR 215; [1975] 3 All ER 455.
Fletcher, Yuill *v* 3.11
CA 1984, 58 TC 145; [1984] STC 401.

Floor *v* Davis 20.7
HL 1979, 52 TC 609; [1979] STC 379; [1979] 2 WLR 830; [1979] 2 All ER 677.
Foster, Henry *v* 19.3
CA 1932, 16 TC 605.
Fry, Salisbury House Estate Ltd *v* 5.2; 71.1; 74.4
HL 1930, 15 TC 266; [1930] AC 432.
Fry *v* Burma Corporation Ltd 71.27
HL 1930, 15 TC 113; [1930] AC 321.
Fulford-Dobson, ex p., R *v* HMIT 35.4
QB 1987, 60 TC 168; [1987] STC 344; [1987] 3 WLR 277.
Furlong, Munby *v* 10.25
CA 1977, 50 TC 491; [1977] STC 232; [1976] 1 WLR 410; [1976] 1 All ER 753.
Furniss *v* Dawson 3.1
HL 1984, 55 TC 324; [1984] STC 153; [1984] 2 WLR 226; [1984] 1 All ER 530.

G

Gallagher *v* Jones 71.40
CA 1993, 66 TC 77; [1993] STC 537; [1994] 2 WLR 160.
Gardner Mountain & D'Ambrumenil Ltd, CIR *v* 71.40
HL 1947, 29 TC 69; [1947] 1 All ER 650.
Garland *v* Archer-Shee 81.10
HL 1930, 15 TC 693; [1931] AC 212.
Garvin, CIR *v* 3.2
HL 1981, 55 TC 24; [1981] STC 344; [1981] 1 WLR 793.
Gaspet Ltd *v* Elliss 10.52
CA 1987, 60 TC 91; [1987] STC 362; [1987] 1 WLR 769.
Gayjon Processes Ltd, Poulter *v* 71.85
Ch D 1985, 58 TC 350; [1985] STC 174.
General Reversionary & Investment Co Ltd, Hancock *v* 66.10; 71.54
KB 1918, 7 TC 358; [1919] 1 KB 25.
Girobank plc *v* Clarke 10.11
CA 1997, 70 TC 387; [1998] STC 182; [1998] 1 WLR 942; [1998] 4 All ER 312.
Girvan *v* Orange Personal Communication Services Ltd 72.3(*a*)
Ch D 1998, 70 TC 602; [1998] STC 567.
Glaxo Group Ltd *v* CIR 3.9; 4.6(*a*); 4.7
CA 1995, 68 TC 166; [1996] STC 191.
Glenboig Union Fireclay Co Ltd *v* CIR 71.47; 71.48(*c*)
HL 1922, 12 TC 427.
Gliksten (J) & Son Ltd, Green *v* 71.64
HL 1929, 14 TC 364; [1929] AC 381.
Gloucester Railway Carriage & Wagon Co Ltd *v* CIR 71.72
HL 1925, 12 TC 720; [1925] AC 469.
Goff *v* Osborne & Co (Sheffield) Ltd 71.26
Ch D 1953, 34 TC 441; [1953] TR 265.
Golder, Spofforth & Prince *v* 4.9
KB 1945, 26 TC 310; [1945] 1 All ER 363.
Good, Taylor *v* 71.38
CA 1974, 49 TC 277; [1974] STC 148; [1974] 1 WLR 556; [1974] 1 All ER 1137.
Good (John) & Sons Ltd, Jarrold *v* 10.25
CA 1962, 40 TC 681; [1963] 1 WLR 214; [1963] 1 All ER 141.
Goodhews, Murray *v* 71.48(*e*)
CA 1977, 52 TC 86; [1978] STC 207; [1978] 1 WLR 499; [1978] 2 All ER 40.

Gourley, British Transport Commission *v* 19.7
HL 1955, [1956] AC 185; [1955] 3 All ER 796.
Granada Motorway Services Ltd, Tucker *v* 71.47; 71.78
HL 1979, 53 TC 92; [1979] STC 393; [1979] 1 WLR 683; [1979] 2 All ER 801.
Green *v* Gliksten (J) & Son Ltd 71.64
HL 1929, 14 TC 364; [1929] AC 381.
Gregory, Baylis *v* 4.4; 5.1
HL 1988, 62 TC 1; [1988] STC 476; [1988] 3 WLR 423; [1988] 3 All ER 495.
Group Lotus Car Companies plc and Another, Brady *v* 4.6(*a*); 4.7
CA 1987, 60 TC 359; [1987] STC 635; [1987] 3 All ER 1050.

H

Hagart & Burn-Murdoch, CIR *v* 71.44
HL 1929, 14 TC 433; [1929] AC 286.
Hancock *v* General Reversionary & Investment Co Ltd 66.10; 71.54
KB 1918, 7 TC 358; [1919] 1 KB 25.
Harris, Californian Copper Syndicate Ltd *v* 71.38
Ex (S) 1904, 5 TC 159.
Harrison, Bairstow & Edwards *v* 4.7; 71.35
HL 1955, 36 TC 207; [1955] 3 All ER 48.
Harrods (Buenos Aires) Ltd *v* Taylor-Gooby 71.40; 71.86
CA 1964, 41 TC 450.
Hart, Pepper *v* 4.7; 75.13; 75.14
HL 1992, 65 TC 421; [1992] STC 898; [1992] 3 WLR 1032; [1993] 1 All ER 42.
Hart, Westward Television Ltd *v* 46.12(*e*)
CA 1968, 45 TC 1; [1969] Ch 201; [1968] 3 All ER 91.
Haughey, Mairs *v* 19.3
HL 1993, 66 TC 273; [1993] STC 569; [1993] 3 WLR 393; [1993] 3 All ER 801.
Haxby, Butt *v* 46.2
Ch D 1982, 56 TC 547; [1983] STC 239.
Hay, Newbarns Syndicate *v* 71.36
CA 1939, 22 TC 461.
Heather *v* P-E Consulting Group Ltd 71.54
CA 1972, 48 TC 293; [1973] Ch 189; [1973] 1 All ER 8.
Heaton *v* Bell 75.7; 75.15
HL 1969, 46 TC 211; [1970] AC 728; [1969] 2 All ER 70.
Helen Slater Charitable Trust Ltd, CIR *v* 15.1
CA 1981, 55 TC 230; [1981] STC 471; [1981] 3 WLR 377; [1981] 3 All ER 98.
Henry *v* Foster 19.3
CA 1932, 16 TC 605.
Herbert Smith *v* Honour 71.40; 71.77
Ch D 1999, [1999] STC 173.
Higgs, Ransom *v* 71.29
HL 1974, 50 TC 1; [1974] STC 539; [1974] 1 WLR 1594; [1974] 3 All ER 949.
Hillerns & Fowler *v* Murray 53.2; 71.26; 71.50
CA 1932, 17 TC 77.
Hindmarch, Copol Clothing Ltd *v* 10.11
CA 1983, 57 TC 575; [1984] STC 33; [1984] 1 WLR 411.
Hinton *v* Maden & Ireland Ltd 10.25; 10.38(x); 71.79(*c*)
HL 1959, 38 TC 391; [1959] 1 WLR 875; [1959] 3 All ER 356.
Hitchen, Fall *v* 75.24
Ch D 1972, 49 TC 433; [1973] STC 66; [1973] 1 WLR 286; [1973] 1 All ER 368.

Hoare, Ryall *v* 74.2
KB 1925, 8 TC 521; [1923] 2 KB 447.
Hochstrasser *v* Mayes 75.7; 75.29(A)
HL 1959, 38 TC 673; [1959] 3 All ER 817.
Holmes *v* Mitchell 1.22; 47.7
Ch D 1990, 63 TC 718; [1991] STC 25.
Honour, Herbert Smith *v* 71.40; 71.77
Ch D 1999, [1999] STC 173.
Hood Barrs *v* CIR (No 3) 4.7; 5.3
CA 1960, 39 TC 209; [1960] TR 113.
Howe (Earl) *v* CIR 23.10; 28.4(*a*)
CA 1919, 7 TC 289; [1919] 2 KB 336.
Humphries (George) & Co *v* Cook 53.8
KB 1934, 19 TC 121.
Hunter *v* Dewhurst 19.3
HL 1932, 16 TC 605.
Hurren, Re 58.9
Ch D 1982, 56 TC 494; [1982] STC 850; [1983] 1 WLR 183; [1982] 3 All ER 982.

I

Innes, Mason *v* 71.51
CA 1967, 44 TC 326; [1967] Ch 1079; [1967] 2 All ER 926.
Inspector of Taxes, R *v* (ex p. Fulford-Dobson) 35.4
QB 1987, 60 TC 168; [1987] STC 344; [1987] 3 WLR 277.
Inspector of Taxes and Others, R *v* (ex p. Lansing Bagnall Ltd) 4.8; 35.4
CA 1986, 61 TC 112; [1986] STC 453.
International Commercial Bank Ltd, Willingale *v* 71.40; 71.66
HL 1977, 52 TC 242; [1978] STC 75; [1978] 2 WLR 452; [1978] 1 All ER 754.
Irving *v* Tesco Stores (Holdings) Ltd 3.9
Ch D 1982, 58 TC 1; [1982] STC 881.

J

Jackson, European Investment Trust Co Ltd *v* 71.65
CA 1932, 18 TC 1.
Jarrold *v* John Good & Sons Ltd 10.25
CA 1962, 40 TC 681; [1963] 1 WLR 214; [1963] 1 All ER 141.
John Good & Sons Ltd, Jarrold *v* 10.25
CA 1962, 40 TC 681; [1963] 1 WLR 214; [1963] 1 All ER 141.
John Reynolds & Co (Insurances) Ltd, Simpson *v* 71.48(*e*)
CA 1975, 49 TC 693; [1975] STC 271; [1975] 1 WLR 617; [1975] 2 All ER 88.
Johnson Matthey plc, Lawson *v* 71.40
HL 1992, 65 TC 39; [1992] STC 466; [1992] 2 WLR 826; [1992] 2 All ER 647.
Johnston *v* Britannia Airways Ltd 71.40; 71.49; 71.79(*a*)
Ch D 1994, 67 TC 99; [1994] STC 763.
Joiner, CIR *v* 3.2
HL 1975, 50 TC 449; [1975] STC 657; [1975] 1 WLR 1701; [1975] 3 All ER 1050.
Jones, Gallagher *v* 71.40
CA 1993, 66 TC 77; [1993] STC 537; [1994] 2 WLR 160.
Jones, Leeming *v* 71.35; 71.38
HL 1930, 15 TC 333; [1930] AC 415.
Jones, Morley-Clarke *v* 15.17(*c*); 47.10
CA 1985, 59 TC 567; [1985] STC 660; [1985] 3 WLR 749; [1985] 3 All ER 193.

Jones, Odeon Associated Theatres Ltd *v* 68.15; 71.79(*b*)(*c*)
CA 1971, 48 TC 257; [1973] Ch 288; [1972] 1 All ER 681.
Jones, Simpson *v* 71.47
Ch D 1968, 44 TC 599; [1968] 1 WLR 1066; [1968] 2 All ER 929.
Jones, Threlfall *v* 71.40
CA 1993, 66 TC 77; [1993] STC 537; [1994] 2 WLR 160.

K

Keiner *v* Keiner 23.4; 28.4(*a*)
QB 1952, 34 TC 346; [1952] WN 139; [1952] 1 All ER 643.
Kelsall Parsons & Co *v* CIR 71.48(*b*)
CS 1938, 21 TC 608.
Kilmarnock Equitable Co-operative Society Ltd *v* CIR 10.11
CS 1966, 42 TC 675; [1966] TR 185.
Kingston Smith, ex p., R *v* CIR 6.9
QB 1996, 70 TC 264; [1996] STC 1210.
Kirk & Randall Ltd *v* Dunn 71.26
KB 1924, 8 TC 663.

L

Lansing Bagnall Ltd (ex parte), R *v* HMIT and Others 4.8; 35.4
CA 1986, 61 TC 112; [1986] STC 453.
Lavender, Clayton *v* 19.3
Ch D 1965, 42 TC 607.
Law Shipping Co Ltd *v* CIR 68.15; 71.79(*c*)
CS 1923, 12 TC 621.
Lawford & Co, Morley *v* 71.61
CA 1928, 14 TC 229.
Lawrie (William P) *v* CIR 71.79(*b*)
CS 1952, 34 TC 20; [1952] TR 305.
Lawson *v* Johnson Matthey plc 71.40
HL 1992, 65 TC 39; [1992] STC 466; [1992] 2 WLR 826; [1992] 2 All ER 647.
Le Fevre *v* Pettit 23.17(*c*)
Ch D 1922, 38 TLR 787.
Leeming *v* Jones 71.35; 71.38
HL 1930, 15 TC 333; [1930] AC 415.
Levene *v* CIR 64.6
HL 1928, 13 TC 486; [1928] AC 217.
Levy's Trustees, Stevenson *v* 81.5
CA 1987, 59 TC 740; [1987] STC 266; [1987] 1 WLR 1204; [1987] 2 All ER 428.
Lewis Emanuel & Son Ltd *v* White 71.39
Ch D 1965, 42 TC 369.
Liverpool & London & Globe Insurance Co *v* Bennett 5.2; 71.66
HL 1913, 6 TC 327; [1913] AC 610.
Liverpool Corn Trade Assn Ltd *v* Monks 50.1
KB 1926, 10 TC 442; [1926] 2 KB 110.
Lochgelly Iron & Coal Co Ltd *v* Crawford 71.84
CS 1913, 6 TC 267.
Lomax *v* Peter Dixon & Son Ltd 72.3(*b*); 73.3
CA 1943, 25 TC 353; [1943] 1 KB 671; [1943] 2 All ER 255.
London & Thames Haven Oil Wharves Ltd *v* Attwooll 71.48(*c*)
CA 1966, 43 TC 491; [1967] Ch 772; [1967] 2 All ER 124.

Lookers Ltd, Sabine *v* 71.48(*b*)
CA 1958, 38 TC 120.
Lowry, Martin *v* 71.35
HL 1926, 11 TC 297; [1927] AC 312.
Lowry *v* Consolidated African Selection Trust Ltd 71.54
HL 1940, 23 TC 259; [1940] AC 648; [1940] 2 All ER 545.
Lowther and Another, Page *v* 3.11
CA 1983, 57 TC 199; [1983] STC 799.
Lucas, Mersey Docks and Harbour Board *v* 71.42; 84.5
HL 1883, 1 TC 385; 2 TC 25; [1883] 8 App Cas 891.
Luff, Bestway (Holdings) Ltd *v* 10.11
Ch D 1998, 70 TC 512; [1998] STC 357.
Luipaard's Vlei Estate & Gold Mining Co Ltd *v* CIR 23.3(i)
CA 1930, 15 TC 573; [1930] 1 KB 593.
Lysaght *v* CIR 64.5
HL 1928, 13 TC 511; [1928] AC 234.

M

McGuckian, CIR *v* 3.1
HL 1997, 69 TC 1; [1997] STC 908; [1997] 1 WLR 901; [1997] 3 All ER 817.
MacKinlay, Banin *v* 4.6(*a*)
CA 1984, 58 TC 398; [1985] STC 144; [1985] 1 All ER 842.
MacKinlay *v* Arthur Young McClelland Moores & Co 53.3; 71.40; 71.74
HL 1989, 62 TC 704; [1989] STC 898; [1989] 3 WLR 1245; [1990] 1 All ER 45.
McKnight *v* Sheppard 71.40; 71.47; 71.69; 71.74
HL 1999, 71 TC 419; [1999] STC 669; [1999] 1 WLR 1133; [1999] 3 All ER 491.
Maden & Ireland Ltd, Hinton *v* 10.25; 10.38(x); 71.79(*c*)
HL 1959, 38 TC 391; [1959] 1 WLR 875; [1959] 3 All ER 356.
Mahany, British Commonwealth International Newsfilm Agency Ltd *v* 23.10; 71.72
HL 1962, 40 TC 550; [1963] 1 WLR 69; [1963] 1 All ER 88.
Mairs *v* Haughey 19.3
HL 1993, 66 TC 273; [1993] STC 569; [1993] 3 WLR 393; [1993] 3 All ER 801.
Male, Reid's Brewery Co Ltd *v* 71.44; 71.45
QB 1891, 3 TC 279; [1891] 2 QB 1.
Mallalieu *v* Drummond 71.40; 71.74
HL 1983, 57 TC 330; [1983] STC 665; [1983] 3 WLR 409; [1983] 2 All ER 1095.
Mallett *v* Staveley Coal & Iron Co Ltd 71.47; 71.78
CA 1928, 13 TC 772; [1928] 2 KB 405.
Marine Midland Ltd, Pattison *v* 71.56
HL 1983, 57 TC 219; [1984] STC 10; [1984] 2 WLR 11.
Marson *v* Morton and related appeals 71.35; 71.38
Ch D 1986, 59 TC 381; [1986] STC 463; [1986] 1 WLR 1343.
Martin, Blackpool Marton Rotary Club *v* 5.1; 18.1; 53.2
CA 1989, 62 TC 686; [1990] STC 1.
Martin *v* Lowry 71.35
HL 1926, 11 TC 297; [1927] AC 312.
Mason *v* Innes 71.51
CA 1967, 44 TC 326; [1967] Ch 1079; [1967] 2 All ER 926.
Matrix-Securities Ltd, ex p. (R *v* CIR) 4.8; 35.6
HL 1994, 66 TC 587; [1994] STC 272; [1994] 1 WLR 334; [1994] 1 All ER 769.
Mayes, Hochstrasser *v* 75.7; 75.29(A)
HL 1959, 38 TC 673; [1959] 3 All ER 817.

Melluish *v* BMI (No 3) Ltd — 10.27; 10.34
HL 1995, 68 TC 1; [1995] STC 964; [1995] 3 WLR 630; [1995] 4 All ER 453.
Memec plc *v* CIR — 25.2
CA 1998, 71 TC 77; [1998] STC 754.
Mersey Docks and Harbour Board *v* Lucas — 71.42; 84.5
HL 1883, 1 TC 385; 2 TC 25; [1883] 8 App Cas 891.
Metropolitan Water Board, A-G *v* — 23.3(i)
CA 1927, 13 TC 294; [1928] 1 KB 833.
Mitchell, BW Noble Ltd *v* — 71.54
CA 1927, 11 TC 372; [1927] 1 KB 719.
Mitchell, Holmes *v* — 1.21; 47.7
Ch D 1990, 63 TC 718; [1991] STC 25.
Mitchell & Edon *v* Ross — 5.2; 71.90; 75.10(*a*); 75.24
HL 1961, 40 TC 11; [1962] AC 814; [1961] 3 All ER 49.
Monks, Liverpool Corn Trade Association Ltd *v* — 50.1
KB 1926, 10 TC 442; [1926] 2 KB 110.
Moodie *v* CIR & Sinnett — 3.1; 3.19
HL 1993, 65 TC 610; [1993] STC 188; [1993] 1 WLR 266; [1993] 2 All ER 49.
Morgan *v* Tate & Lyle Ltd — 71.41; 71.69
HL 1954, 35 TC 367; [1955] AC 21; [1954] 2 All ER 413.
Morley *v* Lawford & Co — 71.61
CA 1928, 14 TC 229.
Morley *v* Tattersall — 71.91
CA 1938, 22 TC 51; [1938] 3 All ER 296.
Morley-Clarke *v* Jones — 15.17(*c*); 47.10
CA 1985, 59 TC 567; [1985] STC 660; [1985] 3 WLR 749; [1985] 3 All E R 193.
Morrison, CIR *v* — 12.1
CS 1932, 17 TC 325.
Morton, Marson *v* — 71.35; 71.38
Ch D 1986, 59 TC 381; [1986] STC 463; [1986] 1 WLR 1343.
Munby *v* Furlong — 10.25
CA 1977, 50 TC 491; [1976] 1 WLR 410; [1976] 1 All ER 753.
Murray, Hillerns & Fowler *v* — 53.2; 71.26; 71.50
CA 1932, 17 TC 77.
Murray *v* Goodhews — 71.48(*e*)
CA 1977, 52 TC 86; [1978] STC 207; [1978] 1 WLR 499; [1978] 2 All ER 40.

N

National Bank of Greece SA, Westminster Bank Exor & Trustee Co (Channel Islands) Ltd *v* — 23.4; 73.3
HL 1970, 46 TC 472; [1971] AC 945; [1971] 1 All ER 233.
National Federation of Self-Employed and Small Businesses Ltd, ex p., R *v* CIR — 4.8; 6.1; 35.4; 58.7
HL 1981, 55 TC 133; [1981] STC 260; [1981] 2 WLR 722; [1981] 2 All ER 93.
New York Life Insurance Co, Styles *v* — 50.1
HL 1889, 2 TC 460; (1889) 14 App. Cas. 381.
Newbarns Syndicate *v* Hay — 71.36
CA 1939, 22 TC 461.
Newsom *v* Robertson — 71.90
CA 1952, 33 TC 452; [1953] Ch 7; [1952] 2 All ER 728.
Nilish Shah, ex p., R *v* Barnet London Borough Council — 64.6
HL 1982, [1983] 2 WLR 16; [1983] 1 All ER 226.

Noble (BW) Ltd *v* Mitchell 71.54
CA 1927, 11 TC 372; [1927] 1 KB 719.
Northern Bank Ltd, ex p., R *v* O'Kane and Clarke 6.8
QB 1996, 69 TC 187; [1996] STC 1249.
Nuclear Electric plc *v* Bradley 71.66
HL 1996, 68 TC 670; [1996] STC 405; [1996] 1 WLR 529.

O

Oceanic Contractors Incorporated, Clark *v* 55.34
HL 1982, 56 TC 183; [1983] STC 35; [1983] 2 WLR 94; [1983] 1 All ER 133.
Odeon Associated Theatres Ltd *v* Jones 68.15; 71.79(*b*)(*c*)
CA 1971, 48 TC 257; [1973] Ch 288; [1972] 1 All ER 681.
Odhams Press Ltd *v* Cook 71.44
HL 1940, 23 TC 233; [1940] 3 All ER 15.
Official Solicitor *v* Clore & Others (re Clore deceased) 64.4
Ch D 1984, [1984] STC 609.
O'Grady *v* Bullcroft Main Collieries Ltd 71.71; 71.79(*b*)
KB 1932, 17 TC 93.
O'Kane and Clarke, R *v* (ex p. Northern Bank Ltd) 6.8
QB 1996, 69 TC 187; [1996] STC 1249.
Oldfield (J & G) Ltd, Curtis *v* 71.44; 71.53
KB 1925, 9 TC 319.
Olin Energy Systems Ltd *v* Scorer 5.3
HL 1985, 58 TC 592; [1985] STC 218; [1985] 2 All ER 375.
Orange Personal Communication Services Ltd, Girvan *v* 72.3(*a*)
Ch D 1998, 70 TC 602; [1998] STC 567.
Osborne & Co (Sheffield) Ltd, Goff *v* 71.26
Ch D 1953, 34 TC 441.
Ostime, Duple Motor Bodies Ltd *v* 71.83
HL 1961, 39 TC 537; [1961] 1 WLR 739; [1961] 2 All ER 167.
Overseas Containers (Finance) Ltd *v* Stoker 71.56
CA 1989, 61 TC 473; [1989] STC 364; [1989] 1 WLR 606.
Owen, Pook *v* 75.10(*a*); 75.43
HL 1969, 45 TC 571; [1970] AC 244; [1969] 2 All ER 1.
Owen *v* Southern Railway of Peru Ltd 71.49
HL 1956, 36 TC 602; [1957] AC 334; [1956] 2 All ER 728.

P

P-E Consulting Group Ltd, Heather *v* 71.54
CA 1972, 48 TC 293; [1973] Ch 189; [1973] 1 All ER 8.
Page *v* Lowther and Another 3.11
CA 1983, 57 TC 199; [1983] STC 799.
Parkside Leasing Ltd *v* Smith 72.3(*a*)
Ch D 1984, 58 TC 282; [1985] STC 63; [1985] 1 WLR 310.
Parrish, Ang *v* 81.29
Ch D 1980, 53 TC 304; [1980] STC 341; [1980] 1 WLR 940; [1980] 2 All ER 790.
Patrick *v* Broadstone Mills Ltd 71.83
CA 1953, 35 TC 44; [1954] 1 WLR 158; [1954] 1 All ER 163.
Pattison *v* Marine Midland Ltd 71.56
HL 1983, 57 TC 219; [1984] STC 10; [1984] 2 WLR 11.
Pemsel, Special Commissioners of Income Tax *v* 15.1
HL 1891, 3 TC 53; [1891] AC 531.

Pepper *v* Hart & Others 4.7; 75.13; 75.14
HL 1992, 65 TC 421; [1992] STC 898; [1992] 3 WLR 1032; [1993] 1 All ER 42.
Peter Dixon & Son Ltd, Lomax *v* 72.3(*b*); 73.3
CA 1943, 25 TC 353; [1943] 1 KB 671; [1943] 2 All ER 255.
Pettit, in re, Le Fevre *v* Pettit 23.17(*c*)
Ch D 1922, 38 TLR 787; [1922] 2 Ch 765.
Philbin, Abbott *v* 75.7
HL 1960, 39 TC 82; [1961] AC 352; [1960] 2 All ER 763.
Phillips, Cole Bros Ltd *v* 10.25
HL 1982, 55 TC 188; [1982] STC 307; [1982] 1 WLR 1450; [1982] 2 All ER 247.
Pigott *v* Staines Investments Co Ltd 3.1
Ch D 1995, 68 TC 342; [1995] STC 114.
Pilcher, CIR *v* 71.57(*m*)
CA 1949, 31 TC 314; [1949] 2 All ER 1097.
Plummer, CIR *v* 3.19; 23.3(i); 28.4(*b*); 81.16(*a*); 81.22; 81.29
HL 1979, 54 TC 1; [1979] STC 793; [1979] 3 WLR 689; [1979] 3 All ER 775.
Plummer *v* CIR 64.4
Ch D 1987, 60 TC 452; [1987] STC 698; [1988] 1 WLR 292; [1988] 1 All ER 97.
Pook *v* Owen 75.10(*a*); 75.43
HL 1969, 45 TC 571; [1970] AC 244; [1969] 2 All ER 1.
Poulter *v* Gayjon Processes Ltd 71.85
Ch D 1985, 58 TC 350; [1985] STC 174.
Pountney, Clixby *v* 6.2; 58.3
Ch D 1967, 47 TC 515; [1968] Ch 719; [1968] 1 All ER 802.
Pratt, CIR *v* 3.8
Ch D 1982, 57 TC 1; [1982] STC 756.
Preston, ex p. R *v* CIR 3.2; 35.4
HL 1985, 59 TC 1; [1985] STC 282; [1985] 2 WLR 836; [1985] 2 All ER 327.
Provan, Taylor *v* 75.43
HL 1974, 49 TC 579; [1974] STC 168; [1975] AC 194; [1974] 1 All ER 1201.

R

R *v* Barnet London Borough Council (ex p. Nilish Shah) (and other appeals) 64.6
HL 1982, [1983] 2 WLR 16; [1983] 1 All ER 226.
R *v* Brixton Commrs 4.6(*a*)
KB 1912, 6 TC 195.
R *v* CIR (ex p. Allan) 4.8
QB 1999, [1999] STC 531.
R *v* CIR (ex p. Bishopp) 4.8
QB 1999, [1999] STC 531.
R *v* CIR (ex p. Commerzbank AG) 25.2; 41.2
CJEC 1993, 68 TC 252; [1993] STC 605; [1994] 2 WLR 128; [1993] 4 All ER 37.
R *v* CIR (ex p. Kingston Smith) 6.9
QB 1996, 70 TC 264; [1996] STC 1210.
R *v* CIR (ex p. Matrix-Securities Ltd) 4.8; 35.6
HL 1994, 66 TC 587; [1994] STC 272; [1994] 1 WLR 334; [1994] 1 All ER 769.
R *v* CIR (ex p. J Rothschild Holdings plc) and cross-appeal 4.8; 35.4
CA 1987, 61 TC 178; [1987] STC 163.
R *v* CIR (ex p. Preston) 3.2; 35.4
HL 1985, 59 TC 1; [1985] STC 282; [1985] 2 WLR 836; [1985] 2 All ER 327.
R *v* CIR (ex p. Rossminster Ltd) 6.9
HL 1979, 52 TC 160; [1979] STC 688; [1979] 3 All ER 385.

R *v* CIR (ex p. Ulster Bank Ltd) 4.8; 6.8
CA 1997, 69 TC 211; [1997] STC 837.
R *v* CIR (ex p. Unilever plc) 4.8
CA 1996, 68 TC 205; [1996] STC 681.
R *v* CIR (ex p. Woolwich Equitable Building Soc) 41.3
HL 1990, 63 TC 589; [1990] STC 682; [1990] 1 WLR 1400; [1991] 4 All ER 92.
R *v* HMIT (ex p. Fulford-Dobson) 35.4
QB 1987, 60 TC 168; [1987] STC 344; [1987] 3 WLR 277.
R *v* HMIT (ex p. Lansing Bagnall Ltd) 4.8; 35.4
CA 1986, 61 TC 112; [1986] STC 453.
R *v* O'Kane and Clarke (ex p. Northern Bank Ltd) 6.8
QB 1996, 69 TC 187; [1996] STC 1249.
R *v* W and Another 6.11
CA 1998, [1998] STC 50.
Ramsay, CIR *v* 23.10; 28.4(*a*)
CA 1935, 20 TC 79.
Ramsay (W T) Ltd *v* CIR 3.1
HL 1981, 54 TC 101; [1981] STC 174; [1981] 2 WLR 449; [1981] 1 All ER 865.
Ransom *v* Higgs (and associated appeals) 71.29
HL 1974, 50 TC 1; [1974] STC 539; [1974] 1 WLR 1594; [1974] 3 All ER 949.
Reed *v* Clark 64.5
Ch D 1985, 58 TC 528; [1985] STC 323; [1985] 3 WLR 142; [1986] Ch 1.
Reed *v* Seymour 75.26
HL 1927, 11 TC 625; [1927] AC 554.
Reed *v* Young 53.10
HL 1986, 59 TC 196; [1986] STC 285; [1986] 1 WLR 649.
Reed International plc *v* CIR 82.38; 82.39
CA 1995, 67 TC 552; [1995] STC 889.
Regent Oil Co Ltd, Strick *v* 71.40; 71.88
HL 1965, 43 TC 1; [1966] AC 295; [1965] 3 All ER 174.
Reid's Brewery Co Ltd *v* Male 71.44; 71.45
QB 1891, 3 TC 279; [1891] 2 QB 1.
Reid's Trustees *v* CIR 22.2; 73.3; 81.3
CS 1929, 14 TC 512.
Rendell *v* Went 75.13; 75.28
HL 1964, 41 TC 641; [1964] 1 WLR 650; [1964] 2 All ER 464.
Reynolds (John) (Insurances) Ltd, Simpson *v* 71.48(*e*)
CA 1975, 49 TC 693; [1975] STC 271; [1975] 1 WLR 617; [1975] 2 All ER 88.
Richardson & Bottoms Ltd, Slater *v* 4.6(*a*)
Ch D 1979, 53 TC 155; [1979] STC 630; [1980] 1 WLR 563; [1979] 3 All ER 439.
Riches, Westminster Bank Ltd *v* 72.3(*b*)
HL 1947, 28 TC 159; [1947] AC 390; [1947] 1 All ER 469.
Ricketts *v* Colquhoun 75.43
HL 1925, 10 TC 118; [1926] AC 1.
Ridgway, B S C Footwear Ltd *v* 71.83
HL 1971, 47 TC 495; [1972] AC 544; [1971] 2 All ER 534.
Rignell *v* Andrews 1.22
Ch D 1990, 63 TC 312; [1990] STC 410.
Robertson, Newsom *v* 71.90
CA 1952, 33 TC 452; [1953] 1 Ch 7; [1952] 2 All ER 728.
Robinson *v* Scott Bader & Co Ltd 71.40; 71.54
CA 1981, 54 TC 757; [1981] STC 436; [1981] 1 WLR 1135; [1981] 2 All ER 1116.
Rogerson, Wilkins *v* 75.7
CA 1960, 39 TC 344.

Ross, Mitchell & Edon *v* 5.2; 71.90; 75.10(*a*); 75.24
HL 1961, 40 TC 11; [1962] AC 813; [1961] 3 All ER 49.
Rossminster Ltd, ex p., R *v* CIR 6.9
HL 1979, 52 TC 160; [1980] STC 42; [1980] 2 WLR 1; [1979] 3 All ER 385.
Rothschild (J) Holdings plc, ex p., R *v* CIR 4.8; 35.4
CA 1987, 61 TC 178; [1987] STC 163.
Russell & Russell, Bowden *v* 71.90
Ch D 1965, 42 TC 301; [1965] 1 WLR 711; [1965] 2 All ER 258.
Ryall *v* Hoare 74.2
KB 1925, 8 TC 521; [1923] 2 KB 447.

S

Sabine *v* Lookers Ltd 71.48(*b*)
CA 1958, 38 TC 120; [1958] TR 213.
Salisbury House Estate Ltd *v* Fry 5.2; 71.1; 74.4
HL 1930, 15 TC 266; [1930] AC 432.
Salmon, Weight *v* 75.36
HL 1935, 19 TC 174.
Salt *v* Chamberlain 71.39
Ch D 1979, 53 TC 143; [1979] STC 750.
Saxone Lilley & Skinner (Holdings) Ltd *v* CIR 10.11
HL 1967, 44 TC 122.
Scorer *v* Olin Energy Systems Ltd 5.3
HL 1985, 58 TC 592; [1985] STC 218; [1985] AC 645; [1985] 2 All ER 375.
Scott Bader & Co Ltd, Robinson *v* 71.40; 71.54
CA 1981, 54 TC 757; [1981] STC 436; [1981] 1 WLR 1135; [1981] 2 All ER 1116.
Scottish & Newcastle Breweries Ltd, CIR *v* 10.25
HL 1982, 55 TC 252; [1982] STC 296; [1982] 1 WLR 322; [1982] 2 All ER 230.
Seaham Harbour Dock Co *v* Crook 71.85
HL 1931, 16 TC 333.
Securitas Properties Ltd, Buckingham *v* 10.11
Ch D 1979, 53 TC 292; [1980] STC 166; [1980] 1 WLR 380.
Seymour, Reed *v* 75.26
HL 1927, 11 TC 625; [1927] AC 554.
Sharkey *v* Wernher 50.1; 71.33; 71.51; 71.83
HL 1955, 36 TC 275; [1956] AC 58; [1955] 3 All ER 493.
Shaw, Daphne *v* 10.25
KB 1926, 11 TC 256.
Shaw, Vodafone Cellular Ltd *v* 71.40; 71.47
CA 1997, 69 TC 376; [1997] STC 734.
Sheppard, McKnight *v* 71.40; 71.47; 71.69; 71.74
HL 1999, 71 TC 419; [1999] STC 669; [1999] 1 WLR 1133; [1999] 3 All ER 491.
Sherdley *v* Sherdley 47.10
HL 1987, [1987] STC 217; [1987] 2 WLR 1071; [1987] 2 All ER 54.
Shilton *v* Wilmshurst 19.3; 75.7
HL 1991, 64 TC 78; [1991] STC 88; [1991] 2 WLR 530; [1991] 3 All ER 148.
Short Bros Ltd *v* CIR 71.48(*b*)
CA 1927, 12 TC 955.
Simpson *v* John Reynolds & Co (Insurances) Ltd 71.48(*e*)
CA 1975, 49 TC 693; [1975] STC 271; [1975] 1 WLR 617; [1975] 2 All ER 88.
Simpson *v* Jones 71.47
Ch D 1968, 44 TC 599; [1968] 1 WLR 1066; [1968] 2 All ER 929.

Singer and Others, Williams *v* 81.3; 81.10
HL 1920, 7 TC 387; [1921] 1 AC 65.
Sinnett, CIR and, Moodie *v* 3.1; 3.19
HL 1993, 65 TC 610; [1993] STC 188; [1993] 1 WLR 266; [1993] 2 All ER 49.
Slater (Helen) Charitable Trust, CIR *v* 15.1
CA 1981, 55 TC 230; [1981] STC 471; [1981] 3 WLR 377; [1981] 3 All ER 98.
Slater *v* Richardson & Bottoms Ltd 4.6(*a*)
Ch D 1979, 53 TC 155; [1979] STC 630; [1980] 1 WLR 563; [1979] 3 All ER 439.
Smart, Tyrer *v* 75.36
HL 1978, 52 TC 533; [1979] STC 34; [1979] 1 WLR 113; [1979] 1 All ER 321.
Smith, Parkside Leasing Ltd *v* 72.3(*a*)
Ch D 1984, 58 TC 282; [1985] STC 63; [1985] 1 WLR 310.
Smith, Tennant *v* 75.7
HL 1892, 3 TC 158; [1892] AC 150.
Smith Barry *v* Cordy 71.37
CA 1946, 28 TC 250; [1946] 2 All ER 396.
Smith's Potato Estates Ltd *v* Bolland 4.9; 71.69
HL 1948, 30 TC 267; [1948] AC 508; [1948] 2 All ER 367.
Southern *v* AB 71.30; 71.34
KB 1933, 18 TC 59; [1933] 1 KB 713.
Southern *v* Borax Consolidated Ltd 71.69
KB 1940, 23 TC 597; [1941] 1 KB 111; [1940] 4 All ER 412.
Southern Railway of Peru Ltd, Owen *v* 71.49
HL 1956, 36 TC 602; [1957] AC 334; [1956] 2 All ER 728.
Special Commrs *v* Pemsel 15.1
HL 1891, 3 TC 53.
Spofforth & Prince *v* Golder 4.9
KB 1945, 26 TC 310; [1945] 1 All ER 363.
Staines Investments Co Ltd, Pigott *v* 3.1
Ch D 1995, 68 TC 342; [1995] STC 114.
Staveley Coal & Iron Co Ltd, Mallett *v* 71.47; 71.78
CA 1928, 13 TC 772; [1928] 2 KB 405.
Steele *v* EVC International NV (formerly European Vinyls Corp (Holdings) BV) 20.7
CA 1996, 69 TC 88; [1996] STC 785.
Stevens *v* Tirard 47.10
CA 1939, 23 TC 321; [1939] 4 All ER 186; [1940] 1 KB 204.
Stevenson *v* Wishart and Others (Levy's Trustees) 81.5
CA 1987, 59 TC 740; [1987] STC 266; [1987] 1 WLR 1204; [1987] 2 All ER 428.
Stoke-on-Trent City Council *v* Wood Mitchell & Co Ltd 19.7; 71.48(*d*)
CA 1978, [1979] STC 197; [1980] 1 WLR 254; [1979] 2 All ER 65.
Stoker, Overseas Containers (Finance) Ltd *v* 71.56
CA 1989, 61 TC 473; [1989] STC 364; [1989] 1 WLR 606.
Stokes, Ensign Tankers (Leasing) Ltd *v* 10.25; 10.27; 71.29
HL 1992, 64 TC 617; [1992] STC 226; [1992] 2 WLR 469; [1992] 2 All ER 275.
Stokes *v* Costain Property Investments Ltd 10.27
CA 1984, 57 TC 688; [1984] STC 204; [1984] 1 WLR 763; [1984] 1 All ER 849.
Strick *v* Regent Oil Co Ltd 71.40; 71.88
HL 1965, 43 TC 1; [1966] AC 295; [1965] 3 All ER 174.
Strong & Co of Romsey Ltd *v* Woodifield 71.45; 71.47
HL 1906, 5 TC 215; [1906] AC 448.
Styles *v* New York Life Insurance Co 50.1
HL 1889, 2 TC 460; (1889) 14 App Cas 381.
Summerson (Thomas) & Sons Ltd, Wigmore *v* 28.2(*d*); 67.2; 72.3(*b*)
KB 1925, 9 TC 577.

Symons *v* Weeks and Others 71.83
Ch D 1982, 56 TC 630; [1983] STC 195.

T

Talbot, Absalom *v* 71.44
HL 1944, 26 TC 166; [1944] AC 204; [1944] 1 All ER 642.
Tate & Lyle Ltd, Morgan *v* 71.41; 71.69
HL 1954, 35 TC 367; [1955] AC 21; [1954] 2 All ER 413.
Tattersall, Morley *v* 71.91
CA 1938, 22 TC 51; [1938] 3 All ER 296.
Taylor *v* Good 71.38
CA 1974, 49 TC 277; [1974] STC 148; [1974] 1 WLR 556; [1974] 1 All ER 1137.
Taylor *v* Provan 75.43
HL 1974, 49 TC 579; [1974] STC 168; [1975] AC 194; [1974] 1 All ER 1201.
Taylor-Gooby, Harrods (Buenos Aires) Ltd *v* 71.40; 71.86
CA 1964, 41 TC 450.
Tennant *v* Smith 75.7
HL 1892, 3 TC 158; [1892] AC 150.
Tesco Stores (Holdings) Ltd, Irving *v* 3.9
Ch D 1982, 58 TC 1; [1982] STC 881.
Thompson *v* Bruce 1.23
KB 1927, 11 TC 607.
Threlfall *v* Jones 71.40
CA 1993, 66 TC 77; [1993] STC 537; [1994] 2 WLR 160.
Tilley, Wales *v* 19.3
HL 1943, 25 TC 136; [1943] AC 386; [1943] 1 All ER 280.
Tirard, Stevens *v* 47.10
CA 1939, 23 TC 321; [1939] 4 All ER 186; [1940] 1 KB 204.
Tucker *v* Granada Motorway Services Ltd 71.47; 71.78
HL 1979, 53 TC 92; [1979] STC 393; [1979] 1 WLR 683; [1979] 2 All ER 801.
Tyrer *v* Smart 75.36
HL 1978, 52 TC 533; [1979] STC 34; [1979] 1 WLR 113; [1979] 1 All ER 321.

U

Ulster Bank Ltd, ex p., R *v* CIR 4.8; 6.8
CA 1997, 69 TC 211; [1997] STC 837.
Uniholdings Ltd (No 3), Whittles *v* 71.56
CA 1996, 68 TC 528; [1996] STC 914.
Unilever plc, ex p., R *v* CIR 4.8
CA 1996, 68 TC 205; [1996] STC 681.
Universities Superannuation Scheme Ltd, CIR *v* 3.2
Ch D 1996, 70 TC 193; [1997] STC 1.
Usher's Wiltshire Brewery Ltd *v* Bruce 71.45
HL 1914, 6 TC 399; [1915] AC 433.

V

Van den Berghs Ltd *v* Clark 71.47; 71.48(*b*); 71.75
HL 1935, 19 TC 390; [1935] AC 431.
Vestey *v* CIR (No 1) (and associated appeals) 3.8; 35.4
HL 1979, 54 TC 503; [1980] STC 10; [1979] 3 WLR 915; [1979] 3 All ER 976.

Vestey's (Lord) Exors & Vestey *v* CIR — 81.16(*a*); 81.21(*d*); 81.24; 81.25
HL 1949, 31 TC 1; [1949] 1 All ER 1108.
Vodafone Cellular Ltd *v* Shaw — 71.40; 71.47
CA 1997, 69 TC 376; [1997] STC 734.

W

W and Another, R *v* — 6.11
CA 1998, [1998] STC 50.
Wales *v* Tilley — 19.3
HL 1943, 25 TC 136; [1943] AC 386; [1943] 1 All ER 280.
Watmough, G H Chambers (Northiam Farms) Ltd *v* — 10.28(C)
Ch D 1956, 36 TC 711; [1956] 1 WLR 1483; [1956] 3 All ER 485.
Weeks and Others, Symons *v* — 71.83
Ch D 1982, 56 TC 630; [1983] STC 195.
Weight *v* Salmon — 75.36
HL 1935, 19 TC 174.
Went, Rendell *v* — 75.13; 75.28
HL 1964, 41 TC 641; [1964] 1 WLR 650; [1964] 2 All ER 464.
Wernher, Sharkey *v* — 50.1; 71.33; 71.51; 71.83
HL 1955, 36 TC 275; [1956] AC 58; [1955] 3 All ER 493.
Westminster (Duke of) *v* CIR — 3.1
HL 1935, 19 TC 490.
Westminster Bank Exor & Trustee Co (Channel Islands) Ltd *v* National Bank of Greece SA — 23.4; 73.3
HL 1970, 46 TC 472; [1971] AC 945; [1971] 1 All ER 233.
Westminster Bank Ltd *v* Riches — 72.3(*b*)
HL 1947, 28 TC 159; [1947] AC 390; [1947] 1 All ER 469.
Westward Television Ltd *v* Hart — 46.12(*e*)
CA 1968, 45 TC 1; [1969] Ch 201; [1968] 3 All ER 91.
White, Craven *v* — 3.1
HL 1988, 62 TC 1; [1988] STC 476; [1988] 3 WLR 423; [1988] 3 All ER 495.
White, Lewis Emanuel & Son Ltd *v* — 71.39
Ch D 1965, 42 TC 369.
Whittles *v* Uniholdings Ltd (No 3) — 71.56
CA 1996, 68 TC 528; [1996] STC 914.
Wicks *v* Firth — 75.13
HL 1982, 56 TC 318; [1983] STC 25; [1983] 2 WLR 34; [1983] 1 All ER 151.
Wigmore *v* Summerson (Thomas) & Sons Ltd — 28.2(*d*); 67.2; 72.3(*b*)
KB 1925, 9 TC 577.
Wilkins *v* Rogerson — 75.7
CA 1960, 39 TC 344; [1961] Ch 133; [1961] 1 All ER 358.
Williams *v* Singer and Others — 81.3; 81.10
HL 1920, 7 TC 387; [1921] 1 AC 65.
Willingale *v* International Commercial Bank Ltd — 71.40; 71.66
HL 1978, 52 TC 242; [1978] STC 75; [1978] AC 834; [1978] 1 All ER 754.
Willoughby, CIR *v* — 3.8
HL 1997, 70 TC 57; [1997] STC 995; [1997] 1 WLR 1071; [1997] 4 All ER 65.
Wilmshurst, Shilton *v* — 19.3; 75.7
HL 1991, 64 TC 78; [1991] STC 88; [1991] 2 WLR 530; [1991] 3 All ER 148.
Wilson, DTE Financial Services Ltd *v* — 55.2
Ch D 1999, [1999] STC 1061.
Wilson, Yuill *v* — 3.11
HL 1980, 52 TC 674; [1980] STC 460; [1980] 1 WLR 910; [1980] 3 All ER 7.

Wishart and Others (Levy's Trustees), Stevenson *v* 81.5
CA 1987, 59 TC 740; [1987] STC 266; [1987] 1 WLR 1204; [1987] 2 All ER 428.
Withers *v* Wynyard 64.5; 71.43
KB 1938, 21 TC 724.
Wood Mitchell & Co Ltd, Stoke-on-Trent City Council *v* 19.7; 71.48(*d*)
CA 1978, [1979] STC 197; [1980] 1 WLR 254; [1979] 2 All ER 65.
Woodifield, Strong & Co of Romsey Ltd *v* 71.45; 71.47
HL 1906, 5 TC 215; [1906] AC 448.
Woolwich Equitable Building Society, ex p., R *v* CIR 41.3
HL 1990, 63 TC 589; [1990] STC 682; [1990] 1 WLR 1400; [1991] 4 All ER 92.
Woolwich Equitable Building Society *v* CIR 41.3
HL 1992, 65 TC 265; [1992] STC 657; [1992] 3 WLR 366; [1992] 3 All ER 737.
Woolworth (F W) plc, Beauchamp *v* 71.56
HL 1989, 61 TC 542; [1989] STC 510; [1989] 3 WLR 1.
Wright, Banning *v* 68.28
HL 1972, 48 TC 421; [1972] 1 WLR 972; [1972] 2 All ER 987.
Wynyard, Withers *v* 64.5; 71.43
KB 1938, 21 TC 724.

Y

Young, Reed *v* 53.10
HL 1986, 59 TC 196; [1986] STC 285; [1986] 1 WLR 649.
Yuill *v* Fletcher 3.11
CA 1984, 58 TC 145; [1984] STC 401.
Yuill *v* Wilson 3.11
HL 1980, 52 TC 674; [1980] STC 460; [1980] 1 WLR 910; [1980] 3 All ER 7.

96 Table of Statutes

1890 Partnership Act
s 4(2) 53.1
1907 Limited Partnership Act 53.2; 53.10
1911 Perjury Act
s 5 58.10
1925 Land Registration Act
s 129 36.2(*i*)
1934 Petroleum (Production) Act 51.13
1948 Nurseries and Child-Minders Regulation Act
s 1 75.13(xvii)
1948 National Assistance Act
s 29 1.19
1949 Wireless Telegraphy Act
ss 1, 3 71.87
1952 Income Tax Act
s 228 41.1; 41.2; 81.12
1955 Pensions (India, Pakistan and Burma) Act 59.4(iv)
1958 Overseas Service Act 59.4(v)
1958 Recreational Charities Act
s 1 15.1
1960 Caravan Sites and Control of Development Act
s 29(1) 10.26
1960 Charities Act 15.1
ss 22, 22A 15.10
1961 Trustee Investments Act
Sch 1 Pts I–III 15.10(A)
1964 Continental Shelf Act
s 1(7) 51.13; 71.31
1965 Industrial and Provident Societies Act 82.8
1967 Agriculture Act 71.77
1967 Land Commission Act
Pt III 49.1
1967 Parliamentary Commissioner Act
s 8 36.2(*k*)
1968 Capital Allowances Act
s 1(1) 10.13
(1A) 10.13
(4) 10.17
(5) 10.13
(6) 10.13; 10.18
s 2 10.14
s 3 10.15
s 5(1) 10.13
ss 18–22 10.37(*c*)
s 23 10.37(*c*); 10.49
ss 24–32 10.37(*c*)
s 33 10.37(*d*); 71.9
ss 34–36 10.37(*d*)
s 40 10.32; 10.37(*d*)
s 41 10.37(*d*); 71.9
s 42 10.37(*c*)
s 43 10.37(*c*)
s 44 10.37(*d*)
ss 51–55 10.39; 10.49
ss 56, 57 10.39; 10.47; 10.49
ss 58, 59 10.39; 10.49
ss 60, 61 10.39; 10.47; 10.49
s 62 10.39; 10.49
ss 63–66 10.39
s 67(1), (7) 10.7
ss 68, 69 10.3
s 71 10.3
s 78 10.37(*d*); 10.49
s 86 10.37(*d*)
Sch 1 10.7
para 1 10.37(*c*); 10.49(A)
Sch 2 10.37(*c*)
Sch 4 10.37(*c*)
Schs 5, 6 10.39; 10.49
Sch 7 paras 1, 4 10.49
1968 Finance Act
Pt IV 41.1
1968 Provisional Collection of Taxes Act
s 2 23.6(*c*)
1969 Administration of Justice Act
s 12 4.7
1969 Finance Act 71.65
s 58 36.2(*b*)
1970 Income and Corporation Taxes Act
s 8(1) 1.21; 1.22; 1.24
(1A), (1B) 1.24
(2) 1.23
s 15 1.22
s 19(4) 45.10(ii)
s 52(1) 23.8(*a*)
s 91 69.1; 93.1
s 99(1) 93.2
s 100 93.2
s 111 46.13(*e*); 93.2; 93.3
s 196 10.37(*d*)
s 199 55.26
s 208 55.14; 66.3; 66.13
s 220 19.6(ii); 66.3; 66.12
s 221 66.3

1970 Income and Corporation Taxes Act
s 221(1), (2) 19.6(iii)
ss 222–225 66.3
s 338 88.1
Sch 1 para 3 31.3
Sch 12 Pt III 51.12
Sch 14 para 1 81.12
1970 Taxes Management Act
s 1(1) 35.1
s 2 35.3(*a*)
s 4 35.3(*b*)
s 6 36.1
s 7 42.4; 58.1; 67.2; 78.4; 78.19; 86.1(*a*)
(9) 78.36
s 8 35.12; 58.1; 58.2; 67.2; 67.3; 67.10; 78.4–78.6; 78.8; 78.14; 78.15; 78.19; 78.26
(8) 28.4(*a*)
s 8A 67.2; 67.3; 67.12; 78.5; 78.6; 78.14; 78.15; 78.19; 78.26; 81.3
s 9 35.12; 58.2; 67.10; 78.3; 78.4; 78.11; 78.17
(1) 78.6
(1A) 60.1; 66.4; 78.6
(2), (3) 78.6
(4)–(6) 78.7
s 9A 35.12; 78.11
s 10 67.2
s 11 78.15
s 11A 58.1; 67.2
s 12 58.2; 67.2
(1) 67.2
s 12A 53.19
s 12AA 67.3; 78.8; 78.27
s 12AB 78.5; 78.9
s 12AC 78.11
s 12B 78.10
s 13 67.2; 67.12; 81.3
s 14 67.8
s 15 67.5; 75.46; 78.37
s 16 51.10; 67.6
s 16A 67.5
s 17 9.2; 67.4
s 18 67.4
s 18A 67.7
s 19 68.26
s 19A 78.11; 78.12; 78.29
s 20 4.8; 6.8; 35.13; 83.6
(3), (8A) 4.6
s 20A 6.8
s 20B 6.8; 83.6
s 20B(3), (8) 6.10
(9)–(13) 4.6
s 20BA 6.8–6.10
s 20BB 6.8
s 20C 6.8; 6.9
(4) 6.10
s 20CC 6.8; 6.9
s 20D 6.8; 6.9
s 21 67.9
s 24 67.4
s 25 67.9
s 28A 78.11; 78.13
s 28B 78.13
s 28C 78.3; 78.14
s 29 5.1; 17.11; 35.3; 43.22; 56.8; 71.20; 71.22; 72.4(*f*); 78.11; 78.15; 78.20
(3) 5.3
(4) 5.3
(6) 5.5
s 30 56.8
(1B), (5) 78.34
s 30A 78.30
s 30B 43.22; 71.20; 71.22; 72.4(*f*); 78.16
s 31 4.1; 5.1; 78.31
(1) 4.2
(3) 3.8; 4.3; 23.3; 78.33
(5) 4.2
(5A)–(5E) 4.3
s 32 5.4; 86.6(*c*)
s 33 5.3; 17.10; 75.1(4)
s 33A 17.9
s 34 5.7; 6.4
(1) 78.30
s 35 5.7
s 36 5.7; 6.4; 53.19
(1) 78.30
s 37 5.7; 6.4; 58.8
s 37A 5.7; 6.4
s 38 5.7; 6.4
s 39 5.7; 58.8
s 40 5.7; 53.19
(1) 5.7; 6.5; 78.30
(2) 6.4; 6.5; 58.8; 78.30
s 41 5.7
(1) 6.4
s 42 4.1; 4.3; 17.1; 51.8
(3) 51.11; 64.8; 87.1(*c*)
(6) 81.11
(7) 78.9
(11) 17.3
(11A) 17.2
s 43 1.11; 46.12(*g*)

1970 Taxes Management Act
s 43(1) 17.4; 17.8; 86.6
(2) 86.1(*d*)
ss 43A, 43B 17.11
s 44 4.3
(1), (2) 78.33
s 46(1) 4.3; 82.27; 82.28; 82.34
(2) 4.6(*a*)
s 46A 4.3; 78.33
s 46B 4.6(*a*); 78.33
ss 46C, 46D 78.33
s 47 4.3
s 47B 26.5; 26.21
s 49 4.2
s 50 78.31
(6)–(8) 4.6(*a*); 6.6; 58.6
s 51 4.6
s 53 4.6(*a*); 58.5
s 54 4.4; 5.3
s 55 42.3; 56.2; 78.21; 78.22; 78.31
s 56 4.7
(6) 5.1
(9) 42.3; 56.2
s 56A 4.7
ss 56B–56D 4.6
s 58 4.7
s 59(6) 42.3; 56.2
s 59A 78.17; 78.19
s 59B 42.4; 78.21; 78.26
(1)–(4) 78.19
(4A), (5) 78.20
(5A) 78.14; 78.20
(6) 78.20
(7), (8) 78.19
s 59C 41.1; 42.4; 78.21; 78.23
(6) 42.1
s 60 35.2
ss 61–64 35.2; 56.3
s 65 35.2; 56.3; 78.35
ss 66–68 35.2; 56.3
s 69 35.2; 42.1; 42.2; 78.35
s 70 35.2; 78.35
(3) 6.6
s 70A 78.24
s 72 16.3; 81.11
s 73 16.3
s 74 22.1
s 76 81.3
s 78 38; 40; 51.4(*b*); 51.5; 68.24
s 79 51.4(*b*); 51.5
ss 80, 81 51.4(*a*); 51.5
s 82 51.4(*b*); 51.5; 72.3(*a*)
s 83 51.4(*b*); 51.5; 68.24
s 84 51.4(*b*); 51.5
s 85 51.4(*c*); 51.5
s 86 6.6; 23.13; 42.1; 42.2; 42.3; 42.7; 78.22; 83.7
s 88 4.5; 6.6; 23.13; 40; 42.1; 42.7; 67.2; 78.22; 83.7
s 88A 6.6
s 89 6.6
s 90 6.6; 42.1; 42.2; 71.65
s 91 42.1; 42.2
s 92 42.6
s 93 67.2; 78.26; 78.27
(1) 58.2; 58.6
(2)–(4) 58.2
(5) 42.4; 58.2
(6), (7) 58.2
s 93A 78.27
s 94(1) 58.6; 67.1
(6) 58.6
s 95 42.4; 58.3; 75.15(iii); 78.28
s 95A 42.4; 58.3; 78.28
ss 96, 97 58.3
s 97A 58.7
s 97AA 78.29
s 98 10.30; 15.7; 26.17; 26.31; 45.11; 51.8; 55.11; 58.4; 58.5; 60.1; 66.8; 68.24; 68.26; 74.33; 75.31; 75.34; 78.37; 81.15; 82.4; 82.24; 82.35; 82.36; 83.6; 91.7; 92.1
(1) 58.6
s 98A 21.7; 55.11; 58.4
(2) 58.6
s 98B 53.19, 58.4; 78.25
(2) 58.6
s 99 6.8(*d*); 58.3; 58.8
s 99A 8.2; 9.3
s 100 58.6; 78.29; 83.6
s 100A 58.6; 83.6
s 100B 58.6; 78.25; 83.6
s 100C 4.6; 58.6; 78.29; 83.6
s 100D 58.6; 83.6
s 102 58.7; 83.6
s 103 58.8; 83.6
s 103A 42.1; 78.25
s 105 58.6
s 106 23.8(*e*)
(2) 23.16
s 107 58.10
s 107A 78.36
s 108 4.6(*a*)
s 113 67.13
(1A), (1B) 5.1

1970 Taxes Management Act
s 113(2) 67.2
s 114(1) 5.1
s 115 67.13
s 115A 67.3
s 118 6.3; 16.3
(1) 51.5
(2) 6.6; 67.1
(4) 6.4
Sch 1 36.1
Sch 1AA 6.8
Sch 1A 17.3; 51.11; 64.8; 78.29; 87.1(*c*)
Sch 1B 17.2; 17.5
Sch 2 4.3; 17.9
para 2 78.33
para 3 51.11; 64.8; 78.33
Sch 3 4.3; 78.33
Sch 3A 67.3

1971 Finance Act
s 32 1.4
s 33 1.4
s 34 1.4
(4) 28.2(*a*)
ss 35–39 1.4
s 40(2), (3) 10.37(*a*)
s 41(1), (3) 10.27
s 42 10.27
s 43 10.27(i)
s 44 10.28
s 48 10.32
s 50(4) 10.27
s 52 10.49(A)
Sch 3 66.3
Schs 6, 7 1.4
Sch 8 para 1 10.27(iv)
para 3 10.27(iii)
para 4 10.27(iii); 10.28
para 5 10.27
para 7 10.38(ix)
para 8 10.27
para 13 10.27(ii)
para 14 10.28
para 15 10.27(ii)
para 17 10.32; 10.37(*d*)
Sch 14 Pt I 45.10(ii)
Pt II 23.8(*a*)

1971 Fire Precautions Act
ss 5(4), 10 10.25(i)

1971 Town and Country Planning Act
s 52 71.94

1972 European Communities Act
s 2 27.2

1972 Finance Act
s 31(1) 5.1
ss 65, 66 1.4
s 67 10.27
s 68 10.27(iii)
(1) 10.37(*a*)
s 79(2A) 82.4
s 127 36.2(*d*)

1972 Industry Act
ss 7, 8 71.85

1972 Town and Country Planning (Scotland) Act
s 50 71.94

1973 Domicile and Matrimonial Proceedings Act
ss 1, 3, 4, 17(5) 64.4

1973 Employment and Training Act
ss 2, 5 71.85

1973 Finance Act
s 38 40; 51.13
Sch 8 para 7 82.5
Sch 15 51.13

1973 Overseas Pensions Act
s 1 59.2

1973 Social Security Act 83.1
s 89(2) 36.2(*e*)

1974 Control of Pollution Act
Pt I 71.94

1974 Finance Act
s 22(2) 59.2
s 24 67.5
Sch 8 para 7 82.4

1974 Friendly Societies Act
Sch 1 para 1 31.3

1974 Trade Union and Labour Relations Act 88.1

1975 Employment Protection Act
Sch 14 para 2 71.85

1975 Finance Act
s 57 35.3(*a*)

1975 Finance (No 2) Act
s 44(5) 5.1
s 45 56.2
s 67(1) 4.2; 5.1
s 70(9), (10) 58.4

1975 OECD Support Fund Act
s 4 29.18

1975 Social Security Act 83.1

1975 Social Security Pensions Act
ss 42, 45 66.8(*d*)
s 58B 66.5(*a*)

1976 Finance Act
s 39 10.37(*b*)

1976 Finance Act
s 58 56.3
s 70 55.26
Sch 15 10.37(*b*)
1976 Industrial Common Ownership Act
s 2 43.20
1976 Lotteries and Amusements Act
ss 3, 5 15.7(iii)
s 5(1) 71.30
1977 National Health Service Act
Sch 2 para 2 29.28
1978 Finance Act
s 14 1.4
s 30 93.2
s 38 10.18; 40
s 39 10.3
s 45(5) 67.9
s 56(6) 82.10
s 77 36.2(*c*)
Sch 6 10.18
1979 Banking Act 65.5
1979 Capital Gains Tax Act
s 19(3) 46.18
s 78 52.1(*b*)
s 113 93.2
1979 Finance (No 2) Act
s 14 10.27(i)
1979 Forestry Act
s 1 93.3
1980 Finance Act
s 18(2) 1.4
s 46(6) 82.10
s 47 82.38
s 70(3) 10.32
s 71 10.25(iv)
s 72(4), (5) 10.35
s 75 10.21
(5) 10.13
s 76 10.17
s 79 52.10(*c*)
Sch 10 82.38
Sch 12 Pt I 10.27; 10.35
Pt II 10.35
para 1 10.27
Sch 13 10.21
1980 Housing Act
ss 56, 56B 10.9
1980 Tenants Rights (Scotland) Act
s 1 36.2(*n*)
1981 British Nationality Act
Sch 3 59.1(iv); 59.4(iv)
1981 Finance Act
s 73(2), (3) 10.13
s 74 10.14
1981 Supreme Court Act
s 31 4.8
s 35A 41.3
1982 Administration of Justice Act
s 42 90.2; 90.3
1982 Finance Act
s 26 36.2(*j*)
s 42(1), (2) 82.10
s 63(4) 81.19
s 68 56.2
s 70(10), (12) 10.35
s 73 10.21
s 74 10.13
s 77 10.35
s 81 67.9
s 86(5) 52.10
s 149 56.8
Sch 7 para 12 36.2(*j*)
Sch 12 para 1 10.9
Sch 13 52.10
1982 Insurance Companies Act 45.15(*h*)
Sch 2 Pt I 48.4
1983 Finance Act
s 27 67.6
s 31 10.21
s 33 10.35
1983 Finance (No 2) Act
s 3 43.24
s 6(2) 10.9
1983 National Audit Act
s 8 36.2(*l*)
1984 Data Protection Act
s 17 36.2(*m*)
1984 Finance Act
s 22 43.24
s 38 82.39
s 57 56.3
s 58 10.9; 10.27
s 59 10.27
s 61 10.27(i)
s 92(1) 52.1
s 95(8) 52.4
s 127 4.3; 35.3(*b*)
Sch 7 para 1 1.4
Sch 10 82.39
Sch 12 para 1 10.13
para 2 10.27
para 3 10.9
Sch 22 para 1 35.3(*b*)
paras 3, 5 4.3
1984 Inheritance Tax Act
s 158(5) 36.2(*c*)
s 220A 35.13; 36.2(*c*)

1984 Inheritance Tax Act
s 233(3) 29.13(vii)
s 235(2) 29.13(vii)
Sch 4 para 1 81.30
1984 Police and Criminal Evidence Act
ss 12, 13 6.8
1985 Companies Act
s 117 26.12; 26.27
ss 226, 227 71.87
s 247 10.27
s 262 71.87
s 425 71.44; 82.33; 82.38
s 428 82.33; 82.38
ss 429, 430 82.33
s 744 8.2
Sch 4 75.31
1985 Films Act
s 6 71.58
Sch 1 71.58
1985 Finance Act
s 37 43.24
s 45(4) 82.10
s 50 51.4(*b*)
s 55(2) 10.27(v); 10.28
s 58(1) 10.27
s 59(7) 10.27
s 61 10.7
s 63(7) 10.52
s 66 10.18
Sch 14 para 2 10.27
paras 3, 5 10.28
para 8 10.38(ix)
para 15 10.25(iv)
1985 Housing Act
ss 508, 604 26.19
1985 Housing Associations Act 10.9(*b*)
s 62 36.2(*j*)
s 79 23.13
s 89 21.2
1985 Landlord and Tenant Act
s 11 75.29
1985 Representation of the People Act
ss 1, 3 64.4
1986 Finance Act
s 20 43.24
s 24 82.9
s 55(3), (4) 10.39
s 63 67.9
Sch 11 51.8
Sch 14 10.47
Sch 18 para 8 67.9
1986 Financial Services Act 71.39
s 62 29.3
s 75(8) 9.3(*m*); 29.21
ss 78, 81 91.1
Sch 1 para 15 29.3
1986 Insolvency Act 71.44
s 386 55.18; 56.5
Sch 6 55.18; 56.5
1986 Social Security Act
ss 20(3), 23 83.3
1987 Banking Act 65.5
1987 Finance Act
s 25 43.24
s 30(8) 31.4
s 31 88.1
1987 Finance (No 2) Act
s 62(2) 53.15
s 69 36.2(*b*)
s 72(2) 10.9
s 83 58.6
s 94 67.1
Sch 6 para 7 51.4(*c*)
1988 Copyright, Designs and Patents Act
Sch 7 para 36 71.51
1988 Income and Corporation Taxes Act
s 1(2) 1.3; 1.5; 28.2(*a*)
(2A), (3) 1.3
(4)–(6) 1.13
(6A) 1.3
s 1A 1.3; 1.9; 22.3; 22.4; 74.9; 76.3; 81.4; 81.6
s 1B 1.9; 76.3
s 3 15.12; 23.8(*a*); 28.4(*a*)
s 4 23.2; 23.3; 23.5
(1A) 1.9
s 5(1)–(3) 56.1
(4) 28.1; 56.1
s 9 71.2
s 11 23.3(ii)
s 12(1) 71.2
(8) 4.8
s 13A(2) 43.19
s 14(2) 3.2
(3) 1.9
s 15 68.4; 68.14
(1) 74.4; 93.1
(2) 74.4
s 17(1) 70.1
s 18 71.1
(1) 51.4(*a*); 51.12; 64.3
(3) 51.12; 72.1; 73.1; 74.1
(3A) 72.1

1988 Income and Corporation Taxes Act
s 18(3B) 3.4; 70.1; 72.1
(3C)–(3E) 70.1; 72.1
s 19 75.1
(1) 19.5; 59.1; 64.3; 66.9; 75.1; 75.2
s 20 76.1
(2) 72.1(1)
s 21 68.5; 68.21
(1) 5.1; 68.4; 81.3
(3) 43.2
ss 21A–21C 68.5
s 22(2), (3) 68.20
s 23 68.21
s 24(6) 68.16(*c*)
s 25 68.15; 68.16
ss 26, 27 68.7; 68.15
ss 28, 29 68.15; 68.16(*e*)
s 30 68.7; 68.15; 68.16(*e*)
s 31 68.15; 68.16
s 32 68.7; 68.15
(1B) 10.25(ii); 10.32
(1C) 10.25(ii)
s 33 38; 68.15; 71.57(*d*)
(1) 68.16(*a*)
ss 33A, 33B 68.14
s 34 10.22(i); 68.27; 74.5
s 35 68.27; 74.5
s 36 68.27; 68.28; 74.5
s 37 68.27; 68.28
(9) 68.16(*a*)
ss 38, 39 68.27
s 40 68.25
s 41 68.18; 68.27(iv)
s 42A 23.3(iii); 68.24
s 43 23.3(iii); 68.24
ss 43A–43G 68.30
s 44 23.3(iv); 70.1
s 46 33.6(ii)
s 47 33.2
s 48 24.1; 70.1
s 49(2) 30.6
s 50 33.3
ss 51A–51B 33.3
s 53 46.12; 68.4
(1) 71.1
(2) 71.1; 71.57(*j*)
s 54(4) 93.1
s 55 68.4; 68.14(iv); 71.1
(2) 23.14
s 56 13; 51.1
(5) 13.1; 15.10
s 56A 13.3
s 57 44.5
s 58 66.9
(1) 59.2(i)
(2) 1.7(iii); 59.2(ii)
s 59 51.4(*b*)
(1) 5.1; 72.3(*a*); 81.3
s 60 71.12
(1), (2) 71.6; 71.14
(3) 71.6; 71.14; 71.15
(4) 22.1; 71.4; 71.7; 71.8
(5) 71.7; 71.8
(6), (7) 71.7
(8) 22.1
s 61 71.4
(1) 71.12
(2) 71.12; 71.15
(4) 53.6
s 62 46.10(*a*); 71.4; 71.15
(2) 34.8; 71.5
(4), (5) 53.6
(9) 22.1
(10) 5.5
s 62A 10.33; 71.15; 71.16
s 63 10.8; 53.9; 71.9; 71.17
(3) 22.1
(4) 71.9(ii)
s 63A(1) 71.19
(2) 71.16; 71.19
(3)–(5) 71.19
s 64 72.4(*a*)(*e*)
s 65 59.2; 73.9
(1) 45.4(*h*); 73.5; 73.7
(2A), (2B) 73.4
(3) 51.12
(4) 51.12; 63.1(A); 73.4; 73.5
(5) 1.9; 63.1(A); 73.5
(6)–(9) 3.8; 63.4
s 65A 73.4
s 66 72.4(*b*); 73.9
(1) 72.5; 73.10
(3) 72.3(*a*)
s 67 72.4(*c*); 73.9
(1) 72.3(*a*)
(4), (5) 86.6(*l*)
s 68 25.3; 51.12; 63.1(A); 73.5; 73.9
s 69 68.22; 74.3
s 71 72.4(*a*)
s 72 68.5; 71.3
s 73 72.3(*a*); 73.6
s 74 68.5; 71.40
(1)(*a*) 56.12; 60.8; 65.7; 71.54; 71.74
(*b*) 71.74; 71.83
(*c*) 71.78

Statute	Paragraph
1988 Income and Corporation Taxes Act	
s 74(1)(*d*)	10.38(ix); 71.79(*c*)
(*f*)	43.2
(*j*)	71.44; 71.92
(*l*)	71.64
(*m*)	43.2; 60.8; 65.7; 71.52
(*n*)	43.2
(*o*)	23.13
(*p*)(*q*)	60.8; 65.7; 71.52
s 75	3.12; 3.14; 52.6; 66.10; 71.54
s 76	3.12; 3.14
s 77	71.69; 71.70
ss 79, 79A	71.84
ss 80, 81	51.12; 73.4
s 82	43.2; 68.5
ss 82A, 82B	71.80
s 83	71.72; 71.73
s 83A	15.19
s 84	71.60
s 84A	71.54
ss 85, 85A	71.54
s 86	71.54
s 86A	15.18
s 87	10.41; 68.5; 68.28; 71.78
ss 88A–88C	71.44
s 89	62.1; 71.44
s 90	40; 71.54
s 91	10.5
(9)	10.2(ii)
ss 91A–91BA	71.94
s 91C	71.71
ss 92, 93	71.85
s 94	10.28(A); 71.44
s 95	71.82
s 96	17.2; 68.5; 71.57(*a*); 78.33
s 97	34.1
s 98	68.4; 68.5; 71.45
s 99(1)	93.2
(2), (3)	3.11
s 100	62.1; 71.20; 71.83; 93.2
(2)	71.58
s 101	62.1; 71.20; 71.83
s 102(1)	71.83(1)
(2)	71.25
s 103	1.7(ii); 62.1; 62.2; 68.5; 71.83
s 104	1.7(ii); 62.2; 68.5
(4)	12.2
s 105	10.17; 62.1; 62.4; 62.5; 68.5
s 106	68.5
(2)	62.1; 71.44
s 107	1.7(ii); 62.3; 74.3
s 108	17.2; 62.1; 68.5; 78.33
s 109	62.2
s 109A	1.10(vi); 62.4; 62.5; 68.5
s 110	62.4; 68.5
(2)	62.1; 71.25
(3)	62.1
s 110A	71.27
s 111	53.3; 53.12; 53.15
(2)	53.14(i)
(3)	53.5
(6)	71.15
s 112	53.15; 53.19
s 113	10.7; 46.15(*c*); 51.12; 53.6; 53.8; 53.11(*b*); 62.1; 68.5; 71.83; 73.9
(1)	12.2; 53.14(iii); 71.9; 71.25
(2)	10.35(*b*)(*c*)(*d*)(*g*); 46.10(*a*); 53.14(iii); 71.4(*c*); 71.9; 71.25; 78.2
(3)	53.9
s 114	53.14(i)
(1)	10.35(*b*)(*c*)(*d*)(*g*)
(3)	46.15(*c*); 53.14(iii)
s 115(1)–(3)	53.14(i)
(4), (5)	53.15
s 116	46.1; 53.14(iv)
s 117	53.10
ss 118A–118E	23.3(ii); 23.12; 33.1; 33.3; 70.1
s 118F	23.3(ii); 23.12; 33.1; 33.3; 56.1; 70.1
ss 118G–118K	23.3(ii); 23.12; 33.1; 33.3; 70.1
s 119	1.9; 23.2; 23.6; 23.14; 68.4; 68.14(iv); 71.71; 74.1
(2)	72.1(*d*)
s 120	1.9; 23.2; 23.6; 23.14; 68.4; 68.14(iv); 72.1(*d*); 74.1
(1)	82.5
(3)	72.1(*d*)
(4)	46.17(*a*)
s 121	49.1
s 122	23.14; 49
s 123	44.5; 44.7(2)
(3)	3.4
(4)	24.1
s 124	9.3; 23.3(ii); 40
s 125	1.10(i); 3.19; 28.4(*b*); 53.16; 81.22; 81.29
s 126	29.29; 33.4
s 127	71.85
s 127A	3.22
s 128	71.32
s 129	3.7; 38; 71.82; 74.26; 89.3
(3)	44.5; 74.25
ss 129A, 129B	71.82

1988 Income and Corporation Taxes Act

s 131(1) 75.1; 75.7
s 132 75.2
(2) 75.3(D)
(3) 75.3(D)
(4) 15.13; 26.20; 43.6; 48.1; 60.1; 75.3(C); 75.5
(5) 63.4
s 133 1.7(iii); 59.1(v)
s 134 21.2; 55.3; 61.1; 75.46
s 135 55.2; 82.2(*a*); 82.3; 82.7; 82.28; 82.39
s 136 82.3
(1)–(3) 82.7; 82.8
(5) 82.2
s 137 82.3
s 138 1.7(xi); 82.2(*b*); 82.4
(1), (6) 82.6
s 139 82.4
(11) 82.2
s 140 82.4
(1) 82.3
(3) 82.2
s 140A 55.2(*e*); 82.2(*c*); 82.5; 82.7; 82.8; 82.17; 82.28
ss 140B, 140C 82.7
s 140D 55.2(*e*); 82.2(*d*); 82.5; 82.8; 82.28
ss 140E, 140F 82.8
ss 140G, 140H 82.7; 82.8
s 141 75.13(xxv) (xxvi); 75.44(*a*)
s 142 75.44(*d*)
s 143 75.44(*b*)
s 144(1), (2) 75.44(*a*) (*b*) (*d*)
(3) 75.44(*a*)(*b*)
s 144A 55.4
s 145 38; 39; 75.29; 75.33
s 146 38; 39; 75.29; 75.33
s 146A 75.29
s 148 1.9; 10.28; 19.2; 19.3; 19.5; 19.6; 38; 40; 55.9; 59.4(i)(vi); 60.8; 66.4; 66.9; 66.12; 71.48(*b*); 75.1; 75.17; 75.23; 75.27; 75.32; 75.41; 75.45; 81.15
s 149 39; 75.37
s 150 1.7(iv); 55.33
(*b*) 1.23
(*c*) 75.37
s 151 1.7(iv); 83.3
s 151A 83.3
s 152 83.3
s 153 75.11; 75.12
s 154 75.11; 75.13; 75.20; 75.37
(2) 75.13; 75.15; 75.29
s 155(1) 75.13; 75.15
(1A) 75.13(xiv); 75.15; 75.43
(1B), (1C) 75.13(xxii)
(2) 75.13(i)
(3) 75.29
(4)–(7) 75.13
s 155ZA 75.13(i)
s 155A 75.13(xvii)
s 155AA 75.13(xxiii)
s 156(1)–(7) 75.13
s 156A 75.13 (xxiv)
s 157 75.15
s 157A 75.15
s 158 75.15(iv)
s 159 75.15(v)
s 159A 75.16
s 159AA(1)–(3) 75.15
s 159AB 75.15(v)
s 159AC 75.15(vi)
s 160 75.17; 75.33
(1) 75.19
(1B) 86.1(*g*)
(2) 75.19
ss 161–161B 75.17
s 162 75.19; 82.7; 82.17; 82.28; 82.39
s 163 75.29
s 164 75.40
s 165 75.20(ii)
s 166 55.26; 75.11; 75.22
s 167 75.11(II)
(5) 55.9(*b*)
s 168(3) 75.11
(4) 61.6
(5)–(6) 75.15
(8)–(12) 75.11(II)
ss 168A–168G 75.15
ss 169–184 75.31
s 185 1.7(xi); 82.2(*f*)–(*h*); 82.38; 82.39; 82.40
(3) 82.2
s 186 82.2(*e*); 82.9
(2)–(12) 82.10
s 187 82.9
(2) 82.2; 82.10; 82.38
(3) 82.38; 82.39(ii)
(8) 82.10
s 187A 82.3
s 188(1) 19.6; 40; 75.27
(2) 19.6
(3) 19.6
(4), (5), (7) 19.5

1988 Income and Corporation Taxes Act
s 189 66.12
s 190 75.41
s 191A 75.33
s 191B 75.33
s 192 75.2
(1)–(3) 75.6
s 192A 75.3
s 193 75.2; 75.33
(1) 75.3(i)
(2)–(6) 75.5
s 194 75.2; 75.5; 75.33
s 195 75.2; 75.6; 75.33
s 196 59.1(iv)
s 197 75.27
s 197A 75.7
ss 197AA, 197AB 75.13(xxv)
s 197AC 75.13(xxvi)
s 197G 75.21
s 198 60.8; 61.11; 75.11; 75.15; 75.29; 75.33; 75.42; 75.43; 75.44(*a*)(*d*)
(1) 3.12; 75.2; 75.10(*a*)
(1A)(1B) 75.10(*a*)
(2), (3) 75.2
s 200 29.16
s 200ZA 29.16
s 200AA 29.16
s 200A 75.43
s 200B 75.42; 75.43
ss 200C, 200D 75.42
s 200E 75.42; 75.43
ss 200F–200J 75.42
s 201 37; 60.8; 75.11; 75.39; 75.44(*a*)(*d*)
s 201AA 75.11; 75.23; 75.44(*a*)(*d*)
s 202 15.18
s 202A 75.1
s 202B 75.1
s 203 55.3; 56.1(*b*)
(2), (9) 55.8
(10) 55.1
s 203A 55.3; 55.19
s 203B 55.3; 55.4
s 203C 55.3; 55.4; 82.17
s 203D 55.2; 55.3
s 203E 55.3
s 203F 55.2; 55.3; 55.4; 82.17
ss 203G–203J 55.2; 55.3; 55.4
ss 203K, 203L 55.2; 55.3
s 204 55.40
s 205 55.2; 75.1(2); 78.6
s 206 4.7; 75.1(3); 75.3(A)
s 206A 55.12
s 207 64.8; 87.1(*c*)
s 207A 1.3; 1.9
s 208 71.82
s 209(2) 3.5; 44.5; 44.8; 74.7
(3) 3.18
ss 210, 211 3.18
s 213 81.2(*d*)
s 215 3.2
s 219 1.9
s 225 3.2
s 231 1.9; 56.1(*d*); 76.3
(1) 15.6
s 231A 1.9; 25.2
ss 231AA, 231AB 3.7
s 232 1.9
s 233(1) 1.9; 15.12; 22.3; 81.5
(1A) 1.9; 81.5
(1B), (2) 81.5
s 235 3.17; 15.6
s 236 3.17; 15.6
s 237 3.18; 15.6; 46.1
ss 242, 243 3.2
s 246A 3.21; 90.1
s 246B 90.1
s 246C 1.9; 76.3
s 246D 1.9
(1)–(3A) 22.3
(4) 81.5
ss 246K–246M 90.1
ss 246S–246W 90.1
s 247 3.21
s 249(1)–(3) 85.1
(4) 15.12; 85.1
(5) 85.4
(6) 81.5; 85.5
s 251 85.1
(2) 40
s 252 1.9; 15.6
s 256 1.15; 1.16; 1.17; 28.2(*a*)
(3) 1.11; 23.8(*a*)
s 257 1.14; 47.2
(1) 1.21; 1.22
(2)–(5) 1.24
(6) 1.23; 1.24
(7) 1.23
(8) 1.22
s 257A 1.15; 47.2
s 257AA 1.18
s 257BA 47.2
s 257BB 47.2
(2) 47.3
s 257C 1.13
s 257D 47.5(*a*); 51.11
s 257E 47.5(*b*)

Statute	Paragraph
1988 Income and Corporation Taxes Act	
s 257F	47.5(*c*)
s 259	1.17; 1.22; 47.11
s 260	1.17
s 261	1.15; 1.17; 1.22
s 261A	1.17
s 262	1.16
s 265	1.19; 47.2
s 266	23.11(*c*)(ii)
(1)	45.3(i)
(2)	45.3(i); 45.4(*c*)
(3)	45.1; 45.3(i); 45.4(*b*); 45.6; 45.13
(4)	45.1; 45.4(*d*)
(5)	45.1
(6), (7)	45.3(ii)
(8), (9)	45.4(*d*)
(10)	45.10(i)(iii)
(11)	45.4
(13)	45.3(ii); 45.4(*c*)
s 268	38; 45.5(i)(ii)
s 269	38; 45.5(ii)
s 270	45.5(iii)
s 272	45.5(iv)
s 273	23.11(*c*)(ii); 45.3(iii)
s 274	45.2
s 276	1.10(i); 1.11
(1), (1A)	23.8(*a*)
s 277	53.5
s 278	45.4(*d*); 51.11; 81.5
s 279	47.1
s 282	47.7
(1)(2)	47.10
ss 282A, 282B	47.4
s 284(4)	58.2
s 289(1)	26.2; 26.19
(2)	26.6; 26.19
(3)	26.2; 26.19
(4)	26.6; 26.22
(5)	26.6; 26.24
(6)	26.2; 26.12; 26.24
(7)	26.4; 26.24
(8)	26.6; 26.19
(9)	26.2
(10)	26.27
(11)	26.31
(12)	26.20; 26.21; 26.23
(13)	26.19
(14), (15)	26.24
s 289A	26.2
(1)–(5)	26.8
(6)–(8A)	26.11
(9)	26.8
s 289B	26.2; 26.8
ss 290, 290A	26.10; 26.25
s 291	26.3; 26.20
ss 291A, 291B	26.3
s 292	26.3
ss 293–296	26.5; 26.21
s 297	26.7; 26.23
(9)	26.19
s 298	26.7; 26.23
(1), (2)	26.21
(2A)	26.5
(4)	26.5
s 299	26.12; 26.17; 26.27
s 299A	26.12; 26.27
s 299B	26.12
ss 300–303	26.12; 26.27
s 303A	26.12
s 304	26.15; 26.29
s 304A	26.12; 26.16; 26.30
s 305	26.8; 26.31
s 305A	26.8; 46.18
s 306	26.11; 26.26
s 307	26.12; 26.27
s 308	26.6(*a*); 26.14; 26.19; 26.28
s 309	26.28
(4)	26.27
(5)	26.20
(8)	26.27
s 310	26.12; 26.17; 26.31
(2)	26.11; 26.26
s 311(1)–(2B)	26.2; 26.19
(3)	26.10; 26.19; 26.25
(4)–(6)	26.11
s 312(1)	26.2–26.6; 26.12; 26.14; 26.19; 26.21
(1A)	26.3; 26.5; 26.6
(1B)–(1E)	26.5
(2)	26.21
(2A)	26.2; 26.5
(4)	26.12
(4B)	26.12
s 313	19.6(iv); 28.3(*a*); 75.34
s 314	71.31
s 315	29.33; 59.4(ii); 83.4
s 316	29.31; 75.27
s 317	29.6
s 318	29.32
s 319	29.5
s 320	24.1; 38
ss 321, 322	24.1
s 323	30.21
s 324	29.18
s 325	29.13(iv)
s 326	29.13(vi); 82.38
ss 326A–326D	29.13(iii)

1988 Income and Corporation Taxes Act
s 327 29.28
s 328 74.12
s 329 29.13(i)
ss 329A–329C 29.4
s 330 29.7
s 331 29.27; 75.20
s 331A 29.13(x)
s 332(2) 75.9
(3) 60.8; 75.9; 75.11; 75.29; 75.33; 75.44(*a*)(*d*)
s 332A 90.4
ss 333, 333A 29.21
s 335 64.5
s 336 64.5; 64.6
s 337(1) 12.2; 62.1; 71.25; 71.83
s 338 3.5; 51.9(ii)
(1) 90.1
(4) 25.6
(5) 53.16
s 339 23.7
s 343 21.2
(2) 10.35(*b*)(*g*)
s 344(1)–(3) 26.3; 26.12; 26.20; 26.27
s 347A 1.8(i); 22.3; 28.4(*b*); 72.1(2); 81.22
(1), (2) 1.10(i)
(4) 73.3
(5) 73.7
(7), (8) 15.17
s 347B 47.10
s 348 3.2; 3.17; 3.18; 8.2; 15.12; 15.16; 23.1; 23.2; 23.5; 23.7–23.9; 23.11; 23.14; 25.6; 38; 44.5; 44.7(2); 46.15(*a*); 47.10; 71.52; 72.1; 75.34
(1) 1.10(i); 29.4
(2) 1.10(i); 23.15(*b*)
(3) 15.17
s 349 8.2; 9.3; 15.12; 23.2–23.7; 23.14; 25.6; 43.2(i); 44.1; 44.5; 44.7(2); 72.1; 74.2; 75.34
(1) 1.10; 3.2; 3.17; 3.18; 8.2; 15.17; 23.9–23.11; 23.15(*a*)(*b*); 29.4; 54.5(*b*); 59.6
(2) 1.9; 23.3(ii); 23.12; 46.17(*a*); 53.14(ii)
(3) 1.9; 23.3(ii)
(3AA)–(3AB) 23.3(ii)
s 350 4.3; 15.12; 23.3; 38; 44.5; 44.7(2); 46.10(*b*); 46.15(*a*); 46.17; 53.3(iii); 68.24; 78.33; 81.9
(1) 1.10(i); 3.7
(1A) 1.10(i)
s 350A 23.3(ii)
s 352 23.7
s 353 3.17; 3.18; 23.13(*b*); 38; 43.2; 43.3; 43.5; 43.25; 46.17(*b*); 53.10; 71.65; 75.17
s 354 43.17
(1) 23.13(*a*); 43.5; 43.6; 43.8
s 355 23.13(*a*)
(1) 43.3(ii); 43.6; 43.8; 43.9; 43.15; 68.13; 68.22
(1A), (1B) 43.7
(2) 43.6
(2A)–(2C) 43.8
(3) 43.6
(4) 43.15; 68.13
(5) 43.17
s 356 23.13(*a*); 43.16
s 365A(1)–(8) 43.10
s 356B 43.12
s 356C 43.10
s 356D 43.10
s 357 43.10
(1) 43.24; 75.17
ss 357A–357C 43.13
s 358 43.6
s 359 43.18; 75.43
s 360 43.19
s 360A(1)–(7) 43.19
s 361(1), (2) 43.20
(3)–(8) 43.21
s 362 43.22
s 363 43.19–43.22
s 364 43.23
s 365 23.13(*a*); 43.24; 45.15(*f*)
s 366 43.5
s 367(1) 43.12; 43.17
(2) 43.5; 43.17; 43.19
(3), (4) 43.5; 43.17
(5) 43.10
s 368 43.25
s 369 23.13
(1) 23.3(ii)
s 370 23.13
ss 372–374 23.13
s 375 23.13
(8) 41.1; 41.2
ss 376, 377 23.13

1988 Income and Corporation Taxes Act

s 379A 68.13
s 379B 68.13; 73.5
s 380 1.10(iv); 3.6(*c*); 3.20; 34.4; 34.8; 38; 46.3–46.5; 46.7–46.10; 46.12–46.14; 46.16; 46.18; 51.12; 53.10; 53.11; 71.95; 89.6
(1) 46.6; 46.11; 71.57(*a*)
(2) 46.11
s 381 1.10(iv); 3.6(*c*); 3.20; 46.4; 46.10(*a*)(*c*); 46.13; 46.14; 46.18; 51.8; 51.12; 53.10; 68.9; 69.2; 89.6
s 382 51.12
(3) 46.2; 46.3; 46.12(*e*); 46.13
(4) 46.3; 46.12(*e*); 46.13
s 383 46.7; 46.9(*b*)(*c*); 51.12
(1) 53.10
(11) 74.1
s 384 46.9(*a*); 51.12; 71.57(*d*)
(6)–(8) 46.9(*c*); 68.9
s 385 9.4; 23.3(i); 46.4; 46.10(*d*); 46.12; 46.14; 46.17(*a*); 51.8; 51.12; 53.10; 53.11; 53.15; 61.17; 71.26; 75.46
(1) 89.6
(5) 53.11(*b*)
s 386 46.12(*c*); 46.17(*a*); 51.12; 53.10; 53.11(*b*)
(4) 53.11(*b*)
s 387 23.3(i); 46.15(*a*); 46.17(*a*)
(3) 46.17(*b*)
s 388 9.4; 46.7; 46.10(*a*); 46.15; 46.16; 46.17(*a*)(*b*); 51.8; 51.12; 53.10
s 389(1) 46.17(*a*)
(2)–(7) 46.15
s 390 9.4; 43.2; 46.17(*b*)
s 391 51.12
s 392 3.22; 68.13; 74.5
(4) 68.27(v)
s 393(2) 3.20; 34.4; 46.9(*b*)
s 393A(1) 34.4; 46.9
(3) 71.57(*d*)
s 396 3.22
s 397 46.9(*b*); 71.57(*d*)
s 398 13.2
s 399 3.20
s 401 71.69; 71.76
(1) 68.5
s 402 3.2
s 404 10.38(xi)
s 412(3) 17.7
s 414 82.38
s 416 20.8; 26.3; 26.5; 26.7; 26.12; 26.20; 26.21; 44.7(8); 52.3; 61.5; 66.4; 71.20; 71.87; 75.3(B); 81.19; 82.5; 82.8; 82.12; 82.21; 82.29; 91.3
s 417 91.5
(1) 61.5; 82.19; 82.31
(3), (4) 26.3; 26.7; 26.20(iii); 26.27; 61.6; 71.87
(5) 60.8; 66.4
s 421 28.3(*a*); 75.17; 81.19
(1) 15.12; 81.5
s 431 3.9(*dd*)
s 431B 45.15(*h*)
s 432A 3.22
s 436 52.10(*d*)
s 437(2) 52.12
s 441 52.10(*d*)
s 445 45.17
s 450(1) 44.5(*f*); 89.4
(2) 89.3
(3) 89.6
(4)–(6) 89.3
s 452 89.7(*a*)(*c*)
(8) 74.26
s 453 89.7(*a*)(*c*)
s 454 89.7(*a*)
ss 455(1)–(3) 89.7(*a*)
s 456(1) 89.7(*a*)
s 457 44.5(*f*); 74.26
(2) 89.4; 89.7(*a*)
s 458(2) 46.12(*b*)
s 458A 45.17
s 459 31.1
s 460(1)–(6) 31.1
s 461(2), (3) 31.5
ss 461A–461C 31.1
s 462 31.3
s 462A 31.3
s 464 31.2
s 465A 31.1
s 466(2) 31.3
s 467 88.1
s 468 3.22; 15.20; 90.1; 90.2
s 468AA 90.1
s 468E 90.1
ss 468H–468R 90.1
s 469 3.21; 20.8; 90.1; 90.2
(7) 52.1(*b*); 52.3
s 469A 90.3
s 470 20.8
ss 471, 473 71.82

1988 Income and Corporation Taxes Act
s 474(1) 51.9(i)
s 475 51.9(ii)
s 476 9.1
s 477A 9.1; 9.3; 23.7
s 480A 8.2; 23.7
ss 480B, 480C 8.2
ss 481–482 8.2
s 482A 9.3
s 486 82.9
(4) 72.1(*b*)
(12) 46.18
s 487 29.13(ix)
s 488 10.9(*b*); 30.10
s 489 30.10
s 491(5) 1.7(vii); 74.3
s 492(1) 3.9
s 503 1.7(x); 39; 68.9; 73.4; 74.4
s 504 68.9; 73.4; 74.4
(2) 46.9(*a*)
s 505 15.10
(1) 9.3(*d*); 15.4; 15.5; 15.7; 72.2; 74.21
(3) 72.2; 81.27; 81.29(vii)
s 506 15.10; 15.19; 71.54
(1) 15.1; 81.5; 90.2
s 507 15.3; 15.6; 15.11; 15.17; 15.18; 15.20; 30.3; 30.9; 30.14; 81.5; 81.14; 90.2
(1) 15.19; 30.20
s 508 77.1; 81.5; 90.2
s 509 84.1
s 510 30.1
s 510A 53.19
s 512 84.2
s 515 30.11
s 516 30.2; 70.1
s 517 30.2
s 518 84.3
s 519 30.12; 84.4
s 519A 9.3(*m*); 30.12; 84.4
ss 520, 521 10.50; 71.68
ss 522, 523 10.50
s 524 23.3(iii); 46.17(*a*); 54.5; 54.6; 71.73
s 525 54.6
s 526 54.2
s 527 54.4
s 528 10.50
s 529 1.7(vi); 54.3; 60.8; 65.7
s 530 10.23
(5) 71.67
s 531(1)–(5) 71.67
(6) 1.7(ix); 71.67; 74.3
s 531(7) 71.67
(8) 10.23
s 532 10.2(ii); 10.50
s 533(1) 54.1
(5), (6) 54.5
(7) 10.23; 71.67
s 534 17.2; 71.51
s 535 71.51
ss 536, 537 23.3(iii); 23.15(*a*); 46.17(*a*); 51.10; 71.51
s 537A 17.2; 46.17(*a*); 71.51
s 537B 23.3(iii); 23.15(*a*); 46.17(*a*); 51.10; 71.51
s 538 17.2; 71.51
s 539 45.13; 45.19
(4) 45.15
s 540 31.4; 45.13; 45.15
s 541 45.13; 45.15; 45.16
s 542 23.11(*c*); 31.4; 45.13; 45.15
s 543 23.11(*c*); 45.13; 45.15
s 544 45.13
s 545 45.13; 45.15
s 546 45.15
s 547 1.9; 45.13; 81.15
(5) 15.12
s 547A 45.13
s 548(3) 45.15(*f*)
s 549 45.15(*b*)
s 550 31.4; 45.13; 45.19
ss 551–552B 45.13
s 553 45.19
ss 553A, 553B 45.17
s 553C 45.13
s 554 45.4(*h*); 72.1(*c*)
s 555 61.7
(2) 51.8
s 558(4) 36.2(*h*)
s 559 21.2
(4) 21.7
(4A)–(5A) 21.7
s 560 21.2
s 561 21.4
(1) 21.2
(6) 21.4
(8), (9) 21.7
(10), (11) 21.7; 58.4
(12), (13) 58.4
s 562 21.4
s 564 21.4
(2A)–(2C) 21.5
s 565 21.4
(2A)–(2D) 21.5
s 566 21.7
(2A) 21.3; 21.5

1988 Income and Corporation Taxes Act

s 566(2B) 21.2; 21.5; 21.7
(2C)–(2F) 21.7
s 567 21.2
s 574 26.8; 26.13; 46.18; 46.19
s 575 46.18
(1), (3) 26.8
s 576 26.8; 46.18
s 577 68.5; 71.55; 75.10(*b*)
(1) 10.24
(8) 71.84
(9) 71.84
s 577A 68.5; 71.63
s 578 29.9
s 579 19.3; 29.23; 68.5; 71.54; 75.32
s 580 68.5; 71.54; 75.32
(3) 19.5
ss 580A, 580B 29.12
s 581 23.12; 84.6
s 582 32.1
s 582A 24.1
s 583 29.18
s 584 51.14; 71.92; 73.3
s 585 51.14; 73.3
s 587A 71.82
s 587B 15.20
s 588 68.5; 71.54; 75.42
ss 589–589B 68.5; 71.54; 75.42
s 590 45.10(iii); 66.4
s 591 23.11(v); 66.4
ss 591A, 591B 66.4
s 591C 66.4
s 591D 66.4
(6) 66.9
s 592(1) 9.3(*e*); 66.4
(2) 66.5; 71.82; 72.2; 74.22
(3)–(8) 66.5
s 593 66.5(*a*)
s 594 66.11
s 595 19.6(ii); 66.12
(1) 66.1; 66.2; 66.9; 66.10
(5) 66.1
s 596(1) 19.6(iii); 23.11(vii); 66.1; 66.12
(2)–(4) 66.1
s 596A 19.6(i); 66.1; 66.9; 66.12
s 596B 19.5; 66.9
s 596C 66.9
s 597 59.1(vi); 66.5(*d*)
ss 598, 599 66.5(*c*); 66.8
s 599A 66.6; 66.8
s 600 66.5(*c*); 66.8; 66.12
ss 601, 602 66.8
ss 605–606A 66.4
s 607 66.11
s 608 55.14; 66.4; 66.13
(2) 71.82; 72.2
s 611 66.1
(3) 60.2
s 611A 66.1
s 611AA 66.4
s 612(1) 65.12; 66.1; 66.4
s 613(1) 66.11
(3) 59.1(vii); 66.11
(4) 66.11; 71.82; 72.2
s 614(1) 83.4
(2) 72.2
(3) 59.6; 71.82; 72.2
(4) 72.2
(5) 59.6; 72.2
s 615 59.4(iv)
(1), (2) 59.4(v)
(3) 59.6
(6) 59.4(vi); 59.6; 66.10
s 616(1) 38
(3) 59.2; 59.3
(4) 59.3
s 617 1.7(iv); 59.1(i)
(1), (2) 38; 83.3; 83.4
(3) 59.5; 71.54; 83.2
(4) 59.5; 71.54; 83.2
(5) 1.10(viii)
(6) 83.3
s 618 65.8
(1) 65.1
(2), (4) 65.2
s 619 23.11(vii)
(1) 65.1
(2), (3) 65.3
(4) 65.4
s 620 65.1; 65.2
(2) 65.6
(5) 65.8
(6) 65.8; 71.82; 72.2
(9) 88.1
s 621 45.13; 65.1; 65.3
(1)–(4) 65.2
(5) 65.8
s 623 65.7
s 624 23.11(*c*)(iv); 45.10(ii)
(1)–(3) 65.7
s 625 65.5
s 626 65.3
s 627 65.4
s 628 1.7(iii); 53.16; 81.29(v)
s 630 60.2; 60.3
s 631 60.2; 66.12

1988 Income and Corporation Taxes Act

ss 631A, 632 60.2
ss 632A, 632B 60.1
ss 633–638A 60.2
s 639 60.1
(1) 60.3
ss 640, 640A 60.3
s 641, 641A 60.5
s 642 60.6
s 643 60.1
(2) 71.82; 72.2
ss 644–646D 60.8
s 647 60.1; 60.2
ss 648–648B 60.1
ss 650–651 60.2
ss 651A–653 60.1
s 653A 60.1; 60.2
s 654 60.1
s 655(1) 60.3; 65.3; 65.5
(4), (5) 60.2
s 656 23.11(*c*); 72.1(3)
s 657 23.11(*c*)(v)
s 658A 60.1; 66.4; 78.6
s 659A 71.32
ss 659B, 659C 60.2
s 659D 23.11
s 660 81.22
(3) 81.21(*a*)
s 660A 1.8(i); 1.10(i); 72.2; 81.13–81.17; 81.19
s 660B 1.8(i); 1.10(i); 52.12; 81.5; 81.13–81.16; 81.18; 81.19
ss 660C, 660D 81.15
s 660E 81.14; 81.16(*c*); 81.19
s 660F 81.15; 81.19
s 660G 81.19
(1) 20.8; 81.16(*a*)(*b*)
(2) 20.8; 81.16(*b*)
(3), (4) 81.16(*d*)
s 661 81.21(*f*); 81.22
s 662 81.21(*c*); 81.22
s 663 81.23
(2) 52.12
s 664 81.23
(2) 81.19(*e*)
ss 665, 666 81.23
s 667 81.21(*f*); 81.23
s 668 81.21(*c*); 81.23
s 669 81.21; 81.23
s 670 81.21(*a*)(*b*); 81.23
s 671 81.19(*c*); 81.24
s 672 81.19(*c*); 81.21(*d*); 81.24
s 673 81.19(*c*); 81.21(*d*); 81.25; 81.26
s 674 81.19(*c*); 81.26
s 674A 81.19(*c*); 81.27
(1) 3.19
s 675(3) 81.21(*f*)
s 676 81.19(*d*); 81.28
s 677 75.17; 81.19; 81.30
s 678 81.19
s 679 81.21(*c*)
s 680 81.21
s 681(1) 81.19(*f*)
(4) 20.8; 81.21(*a*)(*b*)
(5) 20.8
s 682A 81.19
(2) 20.8
s 683 47.10; 81.19(*c*); 81.29
(1), (6) 3.19
ss 684, 685 81.29
s 686 3.21; 3.22; 8.2; 9.3(*q*); 72.2; 81.5; 85.5
s 686A 81.5
s 687 23.7; 74.12
(1) 81.5
(2), (3) 52.12; 81.5
s 689A 81.3
s 689B 81.2(*b*); 81.3; 81.5; 81.6
ss 690–692 81.30
s 694 81.30
ss 695–698A 22.3
s 699 22.3; 28.6
ss 699A–702 22.3
s 703 3.2; 3.21; 15.6; 71.82; 78.5
ss 704–708 3.2
s 709 3.2; 3.23
(1) 44.8
s 710 72.2; 74.7
(1A) 74.6; 74.30
(9) 74.10
(12) 74.13
(13) 74.17
(13A), (13B) 74.24
(14) 74.26
s 711 74.7
(5) 74.8
(6) 74.12; 74.15–74.17; 74.21
s 712 74.7; 74.29
s 713 74.8
(2) 74.24
(7)–(9) 74.13
s 714 74.9
s 715 74.10
(1), (2) 74.21; 74.22
(3) 74.1; 74.21
(6), (7) 74.32
s 716 74.18

1988 Income and Corporation Taxes Act

s 717	74.19; 74.29
(8)	74.7
ss 718, 719	74.20
s 720	74.12
(3)	74.26
(4)	74.7
s 721	74.7; 74.15
(5), (6)	74.26
s 722	74.7; 74.16
s 722A	74.7; 74.24
s 723	74.14
s 724	74.28
(1A)	74.7
s 725	74.26
(9)	74.7
s 726A	74.29
s 727	74.25
s 727A	74.23
s 728	74.33
s 729	3.3; 3.6(*a*); 71.82; 74.32
s 730	3.4
s 730A	3.5
(2)	9.3(*p*)
s 730B	3.5; 3.6
s 730C	71.82
s 731	3.6; 71.82
(9)	74.32
s 732	3.6; 71.82
s 733	3.6
s 734	3.6; 74.32
s 735	3.6
s 736	71.82
ss 736A, 736B	3.7
s 737	3.5; 3.7; 46.17(*a*); 74.32
s 737A	3.3; 3.5–3.7; 3.16; 74.23
(5)	3.6
s 737B	3.7
s 737C	3.5; 3.7
s 737D	3.7
s 737E	3.5; 3.7; 74.23
s 738	3.7
(1)	3.6
s 739	3.8; 3.22; 52.12; 72.2; 74.32
s 740	3.8; 3.22; 52.12; 72.2; 74.32
s 741	3.8; 74.32
s 742	3.8
(4)–(7)	74.32
ss 743–746	3.8
s 757	52.1
(2), (3)	52.2
s 758	52.2
s 759	52.3
s 760	52.4
s 761	52.8
ss 762–764	52.12
ss 768, 769	46.1; 46.12(*h*)
s 770	3.9; 51.4(*a*)
ss 770A–773	3.9
s 775	3.10; 3.11; 19.3; 23.10; 75.7
(2)	1.7(viii); 74.3
s 776	3.10; 3.11; 23.10; 71.77
s 777	3.10; 3.11
(9)	23.10
s 778	3.10; 3.11
s 779	3.12; 3.13; 3.14; 71.78
s 780	3.13; 3.15; 68.27; 71.78
s 781	3.14
s 782	3.14; 3.15
s 783	3.14
(10)	3.12
s 784	3.14
s 786	3.16
s 787	43.2(ii); 43.3
s 788	25.1; 25.2; 74.1; 74.31
(2)	36.2(*c*)
(5)	25.5(*i*)
(6)	25.5(*e*)
s 789	25.2
s 790	25.1; 25.2; 25.4; 74.1
(4)	25.5(*g*); 74.31
(6)	25.5(*b*)
s 793	25.2; 25.5(*g*)
s 793A	25.4
(1)	25.5(*ka*)
s 794	25.2; 25.4
s 795	25.5(*b*)
(1)	73.7
(2)	25.2; 73.7
s 795A	25.5(*g*)
s 796	25.5(*g*)
s 804	25.5(*j*)(*n*); 74.1
(1)	73.10
(7)	25.5(*e*)
s 805	25.2; 25.5(*b*)
s 806	25.5(*b*)(*e*)
s 806K	25.5(*da*)
s 807	74.31
s 807A	74.31
s 808	51.9(iii)
ss 808A, 808B	25.2
s 809	81.5
s 811	25.2; 25.5(*b*)(*n*); 71.86; 73.7
(1)	3.9; 74.31
s 815AA	25.2
s 815B	3.9; 25.5(*m*)

1988 Income and Corporation Taxes Act
s 815C 35.13; 36.2(*c*)
s 816 36.2(*c*)
(2ZA) 36.2(*c*)
(2A) 3.9; 36.2(*o*)
s 817(1) 43.2
(2) 71.40
s 818(2) 23.16
ss 821, 822 23.6
s 824 41; 78.23; 78.24; 91.5
(8) 29.24
ss 825, 826 78.24
s 827 71.65; 71.93
(1) 42.10; 58.11
(1A) 58.11
(1B), (1C), (1D) 42.10; 58.12
(2) 29.24
s 829 30.6
s 830 51.13
s 832(1) 9.1; 68.1; 68.4; 71.1; 71.2; 71.57(*j*); 81.5; 82.31; 82.32
(2) 71.2
(5) 16.5
s 833(4) 1.7(i)(ii)(iii); 12.2
(5) 1.7(iii)(iv)(v); 1.23; 71.77
s 835 1.6
(1), (3) 28.2(*a*)
(4) 1.10; 1.14; 1.19; 28.2(*a*)
(5) 28.2(*a*)
(6) 23.1; 28.2(*d*); 28.4(*c*); 72.4(*a*)
(7) 28.2(*c*)
s 837 68.7; 75.13
s 837A 10.52; 26.6; 82.30; 91.3
s 837B 10.52
s 838 29.20; 43.19
s 839 3.7; 3.11; 10.27(iii); 10.28(F); 10.37(*a*); 10.38(xi); 20; 26.5; 26.7(A)(B); 26.12; 26.21; 44.7; 51.6(3); 52.12; 53.3; 66.4; 68.14; 71.20; 71.78; 71.83; 72.2; 72.4(*f*); 74.23; 75.17; 75.29; 75.44(*d*); 82.5; 82.29; 91.3
s 840 3.9; 3.12; 10.38(xi); 20.8; 21.7; 26.3(*c*); 26.5; 26.14(*b*); 26.20(v); 26.28; 60.8; 66.4; 71.20; 71.54; 75.1(1); 75.3(ii); 82.2(i); 82.5; 82.8; 82.11; 82.12; 82.19; 82.21; 82.29; 82.33
s 840A 3.8; 8.1; 15.10; 23.3(ii); 67.4
s 841 15.10; 15.20
s 841A 23.3(ii)
s 842A 9.3(*k*); 30.12; 84.4
s 842AA 91.2; 91.3
Sch 3 23.3(iv); 70.1
Sch 4 44.5; 44.6
para 21 44.8
Sch 5 paras 1–10 34
Sch 5A 71.82
Sch 5AA 3.20; 3.22; 71.32
Sch 6 75.15
Sch 6A 75.15(iii)
Schs 7, 7A 75.17
Sch 8 75.31
Sch 9 82.9; 82.38–82.40
para 30 82.10
para 39 43.19
Sch 10 82.9; 82.10
paras 3–7 82.8
paras 9–12 68.12
Sch 11 19.5; 19.6
para 3 40; 75.27
Sch 11A 75.33
Sch 12 75.3
Sch 12A 75.10(*a*)
Sch 13B 1.18
Sch 14 para 1 45.4(*j*)
paras 2, 3 45.4(*g*)
paras 4, 5 45.2
para 6 38; 45.2; 45.4(*d*)
para 7 45.1
para 8 45.1; 45.12
Sch 15 45.6
para 1 45.7; 45.9; 45.12(*a*)
para 2 45.8
paras 3, 4 31.3
para 6 31.2
paras 7–9 45.12(*b*)
para 10 45.7
para 14 45.11
paras 17, 18 38; 45.12(*d*); 45.18
para 19 45.12(*d*)(*f*); 45.18
para 20 45.12(*d*); 45.18
para 22 45.12(*e*)
para 24 45.17
paras 25, 26 45.18
para 27 45.17
Sch 15A 29.13(vi)
Sch 15B 91.4; 91.5
paras 3–5 91.7
paras 7–9 91.9
Sch 16 3.7; 8.2; 23.3

1988 Income and Corporation Taxes Act
Sch 18 para 1 26.3(*b*); 26.14(*b*); 26.20(iv); 26.28; 44.6
para 3 26.3(*b*); 26.14(*b*); 26.20(iv); 26.28
Sch 19A 89.1; 89.5
Sch 20 15.10
Sch 22 66.8; 72.2
Sch 23 66.6; 66.7
Sch 23ZA 60.2; 60.8; 66.4
Sch 23A 3.7; 3.21; 74.32
Sch 27 para 1 52.5
paras 2, 3 52.6
para 4 52.4; 52.6
para 5 52.5
para 6 52.4; 52.6
para 7 52.4
para 8 52.6
para 9 52.4; 52.6
para 10 52.4
para 11 52.4; 52.6
paras 12–14 52.4
paras 15–20 52.7
Sch 28 paras 1–5 52.10
paras 6–8 52.11
Sch 28AA 3.9
Sch 28B 91.3
Sch 29 para 14 71.85
Sch 30 paras 2–4 68.27(i)
para 5 68.31
para 10 81.21(*f*); 81.23(i)
para 11 81.24
para 12 81.26
para 19 75.2
1988 Finance Act
s 24(4) 81.5
s 25(1) 1.21–1.24
s 29 45.1
s 30 1.17
s 31 51.11
s 32 47.1
s 33 1.13; 1.14; 1.15; 1.21–1.24; 47.2; 47.5
s 34 47.4
s 35 1.17
s 36 1.8(i); 28.4(*b*); 47.10; 81.22
(1) 1.10(i); 22.3; 73.3; 73.7
(3) 1.10(i); 81.27
s 37 1.8(i); 47.10
s 38 1.8(i); 47.10; 73.7
(3A) 47.10
(7) 23.9
(8) 72.4(*a*); 73.3
s 39 47.10
s 40 1.8(i); 47.10
s 41 43.10; 43.24
s 42 43.10
(3) 23.13
s 43(1) 43.8
(2) 43.16
(3) 23.13
s 44 23.13; 43.9
(4) 43.6
s 46 75.15
s 50 26.19
s 51 26.25
(1) 26.10
s 52 26.5; 26.21
s 53 26.2; 26.10; 26.19
s 54 60.2; 65.1; 65.2; 65.8
s 55(2) 60.2
(3) 81.5
(4) 60.2
s 56 66.7
s 57 66.12
s 58(1) 89.3
(4) 89.5
ss 59, 60 89.3
s 61(1) 89.7(*a*)
s 65 69.1; 93.1; 93.2; 93.3
s 67 75.3(i)
s 68 75.36; 82.5
s 69 82.39(iv)
s 71 90.2
s 73 75.34
(2) 68.5
s 75 3.13
s 76(1), (2) 70.1
s 77 82.5
s 78 39; 82.5; 82.7; 82.8; 82.17; 82.28
(2), (3) 82.6
s 79 82.5; 82.7; 82.8; 82.17
s 80 82.5; 82.28
ss 81–83 82.5
s 85 82.5
s 86(1), (2) 82.5
s 87(2)–(4) 82.5
s 88 82.5
(2) 82.6
s 94 10.25(iv)
s 119 5.1
s 120 58.1; 67.2
s 121 67.2
s 122 58.1; 67.2
s 123(1) 67.2
(2), (3) 67.4

1988 Finance Act	
s 123(4)	68.26
s 124	67.6
s 125	67.7
s 127	6.8; 55.35; 58.4
s 128(1), (2)	55.8
s 129	58.7
s 133(1)	4.3
(2)	4.3; 78.33
(3)	4.3
s 134(1)	35.3
s 145	9.6
Sch 3 para 3	71.9
para 4	55.3
para 5	1.13; 1.17
para 6	1.15; 1.17
para 7	1.16
para 8	1.19; 47.2
para 9	45.4(*d*)
para 10	45.3(iii)
para 11	47.7
para 12	26.29
para 13	47.10
para 14	43.12
para 15	43.21
para 17	88.1
para 18	66.4
para 19	53.16
para 20	81.29(ii)–(v)
para 21	1.7(iii)
para 25	47.1
para 28	58.2
para 30	6.4
paras 32, 33	1.8(i)
Sch 4	26.19
para 2	26.21
para 3	26.25
paras 4, 5	26.20
paras 6, 7	26.21
para 9	26.27
para 10	26.26
paras 11, 12	26.28
para 13	26.19
Sch 5	89.5
Sch 6 para 2	69.1; 93.1
para 3	93.2
para 4	46.13(*e*); 93.3
para 5	93.3
para 6	68.14(iv); 93.1
Sch 11 para 4	44.8
Sch 12	9.6
Sch 13 para 7	41
para 12	52.6(*c*)
Sch 14 Pt VIII	46.18
1988 Housing Act	10.9
Sch 17 para 115	23.13
1989 Children Act	
ss 3(1), 71	75.13(xvii)
1989 Finance Act	
s 31	1.24
s 33(10)	47.2; 47.5(*a*)
s 36(3), (5)	75.1
ss 37, 41	75.1
s 42(4)	75.31
s 43	68.5; 71.54
s 44	71.54
s 45	55.3; 55.19
s 46	43.10; 43.24
ss 47, 48	43.19
ss 50–52	75.35
s 53	75.11
s 54	48.1
s 55	48.2–48.5
s 56	48.2
s 57	48.7
s 59	15.6(*b*)
s 60	30.3
s 61	75.31
s 62(3)	82.38
s 63	82.9
ss 64, 65	82.9; 82.38; 82.39
s 66	75.36
s 67	71.54; 82.2(*j*); 82.41
ss 68–74	82.2(*j*); 82.41
s 76	66.10; 68.5
(6A)–(6C)	38
s 81	52.2
s 83	3.22
s 86	3.9(*dd*)
ss 88, 88A	3.9(*dd*)
s 90	45.13
s 91	74.26
s 95	29.29; 33.4
s 96(1)	89.7(*a*)
(2)	44.5(*f*); 81.5(*b*)
(4)	89.7(*a*)
s 105	43.19
s 108	81.29(*b*)
s 109	81.27
(2)	3.19
s 110	64.5
(5)	41
s 111	64.5
(8)	3.8
ss 112, 113	68.5; 71.81
s 114	71.76
(4)	41
s 116	23.3(ii)

Statute	Paragraph
1989 Finance Act	
s 123(1)	67.2
ss 142–145	6.8
s 146	6.8; 6.9
(4)	6.10
s 147	6.8; 6.9
s 148	6.8
s 149	5.7; 6.4
(3)	56.8
(4)	6.5; 26.12; 26.27
(6)	89.5
s 150	17.11
s 151	22.1; 81.3
ss 152–155	56.3
s 156(1)	42.3
(2)	42.3; 56.2
s 158(2)	41
s 159	6.6
s 160(1)–(3)	6.6
s 161	6.6
s 162	58.2
s 163	58.3
ss 164, 165	58.4
s 166	58.3
s 167	58.6
s 168(2)	6.8
(4)	58.7
(5)	58.6
s 169	58.8
s 170	26.26
(4)	60.1
(5)	89.5
ss 178, 179	41; 42.2
s 182	36.4
(5)	8.2
s 182A	3.9; 36.4
Sch 4	75.31
Sch 5	82.2(j); 82.41
Sch 6	66.4
para 5	66.5
para 6	66.11
para 8	66.1
para 9	66.9
para 10	66.5
para 12	66.8
para 15	66.1
para 17	66.7
paras 19, 20	66.6
para 21	66.5
paras 22–30	66.6
paras 32–34	66.6
Sch 7	60.2; 60.8
paras 3, 4	60.3
Sch 9	45.13
Sch 10	44.5
Sch 11	29.21; 44.7
para 22	44.8
Sch 12 para 12	43.19
para 14	46.18
para 15	65.7
para 16	60.8
para 17	3.8
Sch 13 para 15	10.27
para 27	10.50
para 28	38
Sch 17 Pt IV	75.31
Pt V	81.5
1990 Capital Allowances Act	
s 1	10.12; 10.19
(1)	10.13; 10.17
(5), (6), (10)	10.13
s 2	10.12
s 2A	10.12; 10.13; 10.18
s 3	10.12; 10.14
s 4	10.9; 10.12; 10.15; 10.18; 10.19(iv)
(1)	10.14
s 4A	10.19
s 5	10.12; 10.22(i)
s 6	10.12; 10.19
(5)	10.13
s 7	10.12; 10.18
s 8	10.12; 10.14
(12)	10.15
s 9	10.17
(6)	74.1
s 10	10.9; 10.12; 10.19
(1)	10.11
(2)	10.11
(4), (5)	10.14; 38
ss 10A, 10B	10.12; 10.19
s 10C	10.12
(11)	10.19
s 10D	10.12
s 11	10.12; 10.14; 10.19(iv)
ss 12, 13	10.12
s 14	10.11
s 15	10.11
(2)	10.17; 74.1
(2A)(3)	10.17
s 15ZA	10.17
(3)	40
s 15A	10.17; 38
s 17(1)	46.15(*d*)
s 17A	10.19
s 18	10.11; 10.26
(8)	10.12; 38
s 19	10.18; 10.19
(6)	10.13

Provision	Paragraph
1990 Capital Allowances Act	
s 20	10.14
s 21(1)	10.12
(3)	10.12; 10.20
(4), (5)	10.19
(5A)	10.17
(5AA)	10.11
(6), (7)	10.22(i)
s 22	10.27; 10.35
(1)	10.24
(4)	10.19(iii)
ss 22AA–22C	10.27
s 23	10.27; 10.35
s 24(1)	10.24; 10.28
(1A)	10.28
(2)	10.28; 10.30
(3), (4)	10.28
(5)	10.30; 10.32
(6)	10.28
(6A)	10.25
(7), (8)	10.28
s 25	10.28
s 26	10.28; 10.43
(1), (2AA)	10.25
(3), (4)	10.38(iii)
s 27	10.24; 61.8; 75.43
(1)	93.2
s 28A	10.25(ii); 10.32; 68.7(*a*); 68.15(v)
(3)	68.8; 74.5
s 29	68.9; 73.4; 74.4
s 30	10.27
s 31	10.28(B)(G)
ss 32, 33	10.28(B)
ss 33A–33F	10.30
s 34	10.28(A)
s 35	10.28(A)
(2), (2A)	38
s 36	10.27(i); 10.28(A)
ss 37, 38	10.28(F); 40
ss 38A–38F	10.28(G)
s 38G	10.38(G); 10.38(xi)
s 38H	10.27; 10.28(G)
ss 39, 40	10.24; 10.35
s 41	10.24; 10.35; 10.38(xi)
(1)	10.28(A)
s 42	10.24; 10.35; 10.36
s 43	10.24; 10.28(F); 10.35
ss 44–50	10.24; 10.35
s 51	10.26; 10.34; 10.38(i)(vi)
ss 52–59C	10.34
s 60	10.38(i)(vi)
s 60A	10.38(i)(vi)
s 61	10.28(E)(G)
s 61(1)	10.24
(2)	68.8; 74.4
(4)	10.38(vii)
s 62	10.25; 10.28
s 63	10.46
s 64A	10.24; 10.27
s 65	10.38(viii); 43.18(*a*)
s 66	10.25; 10.34(*h*)
s 67	10.19; 10.25(ii); 10.26
s 67A	10.25; 10.26
s 68	10.26; 71.58
(1), (3)	71.68
s 69	10.25(i); 10.26
s 70	10.25(iii); 10.26
s 71	10.25; 10.26
s 72	10.25
s 73	10.32
(1A)	68.15(v)
(2)	74.1
s 74	10.24
s 75	10.24; 10.27(iii); 10.28(F); 10.35(*a*); 10.38(iii)(ix)
ss 76, 76A	10.24; 10.38(iii)(ix)
s 76B	10.38(iii)
s 77	10.24; 10.27(ii); 10.35; 10.38(xi)
s 78	10.24; 10.27(ii); 10.38(viii)(xi)
s 79	10.27; 10.28(C)(G)
(5)	10.30
s 79A	10.28(C)
s 80	10.28(D)(G); 10.38(xii)
s 81	10.38(v)(ix)
s 82(1)	10.37(*b*)
(2)	10.25
s 82A	10.35(iii)
s 83(2)	10.27
(2A)	10.24
s 84	10.9
s 85	10.9; 26.19
ss 86–90	10.9
ss 91–91B	10.9; 71.67
ss 92–97	10.9
s 98	10.42
s 99	10.43
ss 100–103	10.44
s 104	10.45
s 105	10.40
(1)	71.78
(4)	10.46
s 106	10.40; 10.46
ss 107–109	10.40
s 110	10.41
s 111	10.41
s 112	10.43
ss 113–118	10.41

1990 Capital Allowances Act
s 119(2)–(5) 10.47
s 120(1), (2) 10.40
s 121(1) 10.39; 10.40
(2) 10.39
ss 122–133 10.3
s 134 10.7
(8) 10.2(ii)
s 135 10.7
s 136 71.80
ss 137–138B 10.52
s 139 10.52
(1), (3) 71.80
s 140 10.1; 10.2(vi); 10.3; 10.7; 10.9; 10.17; 10.32
(1), (2) 10.52
(5) 10.52
(8) 93.2
s 141 10.9; 10.17; 10.32; 53.10
s 142 10.9; 46.9(*c*)
(1), (2) 46.9(*d*)
(3) 46.9(*d*); 74.1
(4) 46.9(*d*)
s 143 10.9
s 144 10.1; 10.9
s 145 10.9
s 145A 10.32
s 146 10.7
s 147 10.2(iv)
ss 150, 151 10.2(i)
s 152(1), (2) 10.22(iv)
(3) 10.22(iii)
s 153 10.2(ii); 71.78
s 154 10.2(ii); 10.25(i) 10.28(G); 10.34(*h*); 71.68
s 155 10.2(ii)
s 157 10.3; 10.7; 10.9; 10.22(i); 10.50; 10.52
s 158 10.9; 10.22(i); 10.41; 10.50; 10.52
(5) 10.3
s 159(1), (1A) 10.25
(2)–(8) 10.2(iii)
s 159A 10.2(v)
s 160 10.2(vi); 10.17; 10.32; 46.7
(2) 10.33
(5) 10.14
s 161(2) 10.2(vi); 10.17
(2A) 73.4
Sch A1 10.32
Sch AA1 10.26

1990 Courts and Legal Services Act
Sch 10 para 30 35.3(*b*)

1990 Enterprise and New Towns (Scotland) Act
s 2(4) 71.85

1990 Environmental Protection Act
Pt II 71.94

1990 Finance Act
s 21 75.13(xvii)
s 25 15.11–15.16; 15.21
(6) 1.10(iii); 25.5(*g*); 26.8; 91.5
(7) 26.8; 91.5
s 28 29.13(iii)
s 29 29.13(vi)
s 30 9.1
s 49(1), (2) 31.1
(3), (4) 31.2
s 53 3.6
s 56 44.8
ss 57, 58 44.7
s 59 44.5
s 66 3.8
s 69 53.19
s 71 43.10; 43.24
s 73 26.19
s 74 71.44
ss 75, 76 71.84
s 78 71.94
s 79 75.36
s 81(1) 90.1
(2)–(8) 71.32
s 82 81.23(ii)
s 87 75.43
s 90 67.10
(1) 67.2; 78.5; 81.3
(2) 67.2
s 92 9.2; 67.4
s 93 6.8
s 102 10.32
s 104(2), (4) 56.2
s 105 56.8
s 125(1), (2) 6.8
(5) 36.2(*c*)
(6) 6.8; 36.2(*c*)
s 126 71.85
Sch 5 9.1
para 4 9.3
paras 7–9 8.2
para 10 8.2; 9.3
para 11 8.2; 23.7
para 12 8.2
paras 13, 14 81.5
Sch 6 para 6 52.12
paras 9, 11 74.7
Sch 7 para 7 52.10
Sch 10 44.8

1990 Finance Act
Sch 10 para 26 44.5
para 27 44.7
Sch 11 53.19
Sch 13 para 1 10.18; 10.19
para 3 10.38(xi)
Sch 14 para 2 68.27
para 4 24.1; 30.21
para 5 29.13(vi)
para 10 52.1
para 11 52.8
paras 17, 19 26.31
Sch 16 10.32
Sch 17 para 2 10.13; 10.19
para 3 10.27
paras 5, 6 10.28
para 7 10.27
para 8 10.28(B)
para 9 10.35(*a*)
paras 10, 11 10.35(*g*)
para 12 10.35(*h*)
para 14 10.28(C)
para 15 10.38(xii)

1990 Town and Country Planning Act
s 106 71.94

1991 Child Support Act
s 7 47.10

1991 Finance Act
s 22 1.15
s 26 43.10; 43.24
s 27(1) 43.5
(2) 23.13
s 30 75.16
s 32 75.42; 92.1
(2) 1.10(v)
s 33 92.1
(4) 47.2
ss 34–36 66.4
s 37 75.31
s 38 82.10; 82.38
(3), (5) 82.9
s 39 82.38; 82.39
s 40 82.38
s 41 82.9
ss 42, 43 71.54
s 44 75.36
(9) 82.5
s 45 75.3(i)
s 52 9.3
ss 55, 56 3.6
s 57 71.82
s 58 3.7
s 59 10.2(v)
s 60(3) 10.14
(4) 10.11
(5) 10.14
(6), (8) 10.17
(10) 10.11
s 61 10.28(A)
s 68 71.60
s 70 29.21
s 71(5), (6) 15.16
s 72 46.5; 46.6; 62.4; 75.23
s 74 88.1
s 75 8.2; 9.3
s 76 23.11(*c*)
s 81 51.4(*b*)
s 82 8.2; 9.3
s 118 24.1
s 121 71.85
Sch 6 para 2 75.11(II)
Sch 7 para 10 52.10
Sch 9 para 1 31.1
para 2 31.3
para 3 31.2
para 4 31.3
Sch 10 para 2 74.7
Sch 11 9.3
para 1 23.3(ii)
para 5 67.4
Sch 12 para 1 71.82
para 2 74.29
para 3 44.5(*g*)
para 4 44.7(6)
para 5 44.5(*g*); 44.7(6); 71.82; 74.29
Sch 13 3.7
Sch 14 10.2(v)
para 1 10.19
para 2 10.13
para 3 10.14
para 4 10.15
para 5 10.14
para 6 10.27
para 7 10.28
para 8 10.28; 10.38(iii)
para 9 10.28(F)
para 10 10.34(*c*)
para 11 10.38(iii)
paras 12, 13 10.52
para 14 10.2(iii)
Sch 15 para 3 53.14(iii)

1992 Charities Act
Sch 6 para 17 15.10

1992 Finance Act
s 9(8) 1.3
s 10(3) 1.15

1992 Finance Act
s 10(4) 43.10; 43.24
Sch 9 31.1

1992 Finance (No 2) Act
s 19(1) 58.1
(2) 45.13; 66.8
(3) 23.13; 43.5
(4) 1.9; 85.1
(5) 23.13
s 23 11.3
s 27 81.24
s 28 15.3
s 29 9.2; 67.4
s 36 82.41
s 37 82.5
s 38 26.19
s 39 26.28
s 40 26.19
s 41 71.58
s 42 71.58; 71.68
s 43 71.58
s 51 3.9; 25.5(*m*)
(2) 36.2(*o*)
(3) 36.4
s 52 25.2
s 53 75.15(iv)
s 54 75.3(A)
s 57 68.14
s 58 68.14(i); 74.4
s 59 68.11
s 60 73.5; 75.6
s 61 47.10
s 62(1) 47.10
(2) 1.8(i)
(3) 47.10
s 68 10.25
(7) 10.28(F)
s 69 71.58
s 71 10.28(A)
s 75 35.3
Sch 5 para 2 47.2
para 3 47.5(*a*)
para 4 47.5(*c*)
paras 5, 6 1.17
para 7 1.16
para 8 47.2
para 9 6.4; 17.11
Sch 6 para 7 51.4(*c*)
Sch 7 44.7
Sch 8 para 1 13.3
paras 2, 3 9.3
para 4 8.2
para 5 74.7
Sch 9 para 2 45.3(ii); 45.4(*c*)
Sch 9 para 3 23.13
paras 4, 5 31.1
para 11 31.2
para 14 31.3
para 17 60.2
para 18 45.4(*g*)
Sch 10 68.11
Sch 11 para 2 70.1
Sch 13 10.19
Sch 16 para 3 4.3
para 4 4.6

1992 Museums and Galleries Act
Sch 8 para 1 30.3

1992 Social Security Administration Act
s 106 47.10
s 121E 36.2(*f*)
s 121F 35.4
s 122 36.2(*f*)
s 122AA 36.2(*q*)

1992 Social Security (Consequential Provisions) Act
Sch 4 6.6

1992 Social Security Contributions and Benefits Act
s 15 75.37
s 16(1) 78.17
Sch 1 82.3
Sch 2 6.6; 83.7
para 3 60.1; 65.1

1992 Taxation of Chargeable Gains Act
s 2 52.8
s 3 67.2
ss 4–6 11.3
s 7 56.1(*e*)
s 10 51.5; 52.8
s 11 24.1
s 12 52.8
(2) 63.4
s 13 52.12
s 17 75.36; 82.7
(2) 46.18
s 22(1) 71.48(*a*)
s 24 46.18
s 30 46.18
s 35(3) 71.68
s 37 11.2; 71.68
(1) 52.10(*d*)
s 38(1) 82.41
s 39(3) 26.31
s 42(2) 52.12
s 45 34.1
s 51(2) 71.48(*a*)

1992 Taxation of Chargeable Gains Act
s 56(2) 52.10(*a*)
s 58 44.7
s 59 53.3
s 67 52.10(*c*)
ss 80–98 15.8; 52.12
s 99(1), (2) 90.1
s 100 72.2; 91.2
(1) 30.19; 91.11
s 108 44.5(*d*); 44.7(4)
s 116 72.2
s 118 44.5; 44.6
s 119(1)–(3) 74.30
(4) 74.18
(5) 74.20
(6)–(11) 74.30
s 120 82.40
(1) 82.2; 82.5; 82.6
(3) 75.19
(4) 82.2; 82.3
(5) 82.2; 82.6
(6) 82.2
s 126 26.29; 82.41; 85.2
(2) 26.8
s 127 26.27; 26.31; 46.18; 52.2; 52.4; 52.6(*a*); 82.4; 82.5; 85.2
s 128 26.31; 82.4; 82.5; 85.2
s 129, 130 26.31; 82.4; 82.5
s 132 13.3; 44.5; 44.6; 52.2; 71.82; 74.17; 82.10
s 134 71.82
s 135 26.31; 38; 52.1; 52.2; 52.6(*a*); 52.13; 82.41
(3) 44.5; 44.6
s 136 26.31; 52.1; 71.82; 82.10
(1) 44.6
s 137 46.18
s 138(2) 26.16
ss 141, 142 85.2
s 143 3.22; 71.32
s 144 3.22
(8) 3.6
s 144A 3.22
s 149B 82.7
s 150 26.31
ss 150A–150C 26.17
s 151 29.21
s 151A 91.11; 91.12
(1) 91.14
s 151B 91.11; 91.12
s 161 3.11; 71.83
s 162 52.10(*b*); 52.12
s 164MA 26.17
ss 201–203 49
s 206 89.3
s 207 89.3
(4), (5) 74.26
ss 208, 209 89.3
ss 216, 217 9.6
ss 217A–217C 31.1
s 221 84.3
s 222 3.11(i)
s 224(3) 3.11(i)
s 235 82.41
s 236A 82.18
s 238(1) 82.10
(2) 82.2; 82.10
s 239B 60.2
s 249 71.77
s 253 71.61
s 256 15.10
(1), (2) 15.8
s 263A 3.5
s 263B 71.82; 74.25
s 263C 71.82
s 269 71.56
s 271(1) 59.6; 60.1; 65.8; 66.5(*b*)
(2) 66.13
(3) 30.12; 84.4
(4) 29.13(iii)
(5) 30.11
(6) 30.3; 77.1
(7) 30.9; 30.14; 84.2
(8) 30.2
(9) 71.82; 74.25
(10), (11) 71.32
s 272(5) 52.3
s 275 74.10(*c*)
s 276 51.13
s 277 25.2; 25.5(*d*)
(4) 36.2(*c*)
Sch 5B 26.17
paras 4, 5 91.14
Sch 5C 91.11; 91.14
Sch 7C 82.18
Sch 8 26.19
Sch 10 para 14 3.8

1993 Charities Act
s 10 15.1; 36.2(*g*)
ss 24, 25 15.10

1993 Finance Act
s 52 1.14; 1.15
s 55 43.10; 43.24
s 56 43.13
s 57 38; 43.7
(3) 43.24
(5) 43.24

1993 Finance Act
s 58 23.13
s 59 8.2; 23.3(ii)
ss 61, 62 44.5(*h*); 44.7(8); 74.27
s 63 74.27
s 64 44.5(*h*)
s 65 44.7(8)
s 66 44.5(*h*); 74.27
s 67(2), (4) 15.16
s 68 15.18
s 69 15.18
s 70 75.15(ii)
s 71(1)–(3) 75.15(iv)
s 74 75.15(vi)
(2) 75.16
s 75 75.21
s 76 75.33
s 77 1.3; 1.9
(3) 85.1
(4) 28.3(*a*)
s 78(1) 1.9; 15.6
(3) 1.9; 15.6; 76.3
(6) 3.17
s 79(2) 81.5(*b*)
(3) 81.2(*b*); 81.3; 81.5
s 80 15.6
s 85 29.21
s 105 82.2
s 106 66.4
s 107 1.13; 66.4
s 108 71.54; 75.42
s 109 71.76
s 110(1)–(3) 71.94
s 111 26.27
(1) 26.12
(2) 26.17; 26.31
(3) 26.12
s 112 66.5(*a*)
s 113(1) 10.13
(3) 10.12
(4) 10.12; 10.19(i)
(6) 10.11
s 115(1), (2) 10.27
(3) 10.35
s 116(1) 10.35(*c*)
(2)–(4) 10.35
s 117 10.22(i)
(3)–(5) 10.52
s 118 81.2(*c*)
s 122 30.6
s 123 71.63
s 124 29.16
ss 125–133 52.5
ss 136, 136A 3.9
s 171 89.1; 89.3
(3) 89.6
s 172 89.1; 89.3; 89.4
(1) 89.2
s 173 89.1; 89.5
s 174 89.1; 89.3
s 175 89.1
(1)–(3) 89.7(*b*)
(4) 89.7(*c*)
s 176 89.1
(1) 74.26
(2) 89.3
(3) 44.5(*f*); 44.7(5); 44.8(2); 74.26
(4) 74.26
ss 177, 178 89.1; 89.3
s 179 89.1; 89.4
s 179A 89.1; 89.4
s 180 1.7(ii); 89.1; 89.3
s 181 71.54; 89.1
s 182 89.1
s 183 89.1
(1) 76.1
(2) 8.2
(3) 60.5; 65.4
(4) 74.26
(5) 44.5(*f*); 44.7(5); 44.8(2); 74.26
(6) 44.5(*f*); 44.7(5); 44.8(2)
s 184 74.26; 89.1
(1) 44.5(*f*); 89.3; 89.5
(2) 89.3; 89.4
s 208(1), (4) 64.5
Sch 3 paras 1–5 75.15(i)
para 6 75.15(iv)
para 7 75.15(i)(iv)
Sch 4 paras 2–4 75.15
para 5 75.16
paras 6–8 75.15
Sch 5 75.33
Sch 6 para 1 23.13; 43.5; 75.11(II)
para 2 1.9; 81.5
para 3 3.17; 3.18
para 6 28.6
para 7 81.19
paras 8, 9 81.5
para 10 81.30
para 11 22.3
para 12 3.2
para 13 52.12; 74.12
para 14 3.7
para 17 70.1
para 18 44.5(*e*)

Statute	Paragraph
1993 Finance Act	
Sch 6 para 19	3.7
para 20	44.7; 82.41
para 21	44.8(1)
para 22	11.3
Sch 12	10.3
Sch 13 para 3	10.27
para 4	10.28(F)
para 5	10.35(*d*)
para 6	10.35(*b*)
paras 7, 8	10.35(*f*)
para 9	10.35(*g*)
para 10	10.35(*h*)
para 11	10.35
para 12	10.38(v)(ix)
para 13	10.2(iv)
Sch 14 para 2	17.11
Sch 19	89.1; 89.5
para 10	89.3; 89.7(*b*)
Sch 20	89.1; 89.7(*b*)
paras 12–14	89.7(*c*)
Sch 23 Pt III(12)	44.5(*f*); 44.7(5); 44.8(2); 74.26; 89.3
1993 Pension Schemes Act	
s 144	66.5(*a*)
1994 Finance Act	78.1; 78.2
ss 8–11	58.11
s 18(7)	58.11
s 75	1.5
s 76	1.14
s 77	1.15; 1.16; 1.17; 47.2
(1)	1.11; 23.8(*a*); 28.2(*a*)
s 78	1.15
s 79	47.10
(2)	1.8(i)
s 80	43.10; 43.24
s 81	23.13
(1), (2)	43.3
(3)	23.3(ii)
s 82	1.19
s 84	92.1
s 87	75.15(iv)
s 88	75.17
s 89(1)–(3)	75.44(*a*)
(5)–(7)	75.44(*d*)
(8)–(14)	75.44(*b*)
s 93	46.18
s 95	71.32
ss 98, 99	75.31
s 100	82.10
s 101	82.9
s 102	82.41
s 103(1), (2)	66.4
ss 104–107	66.4
s 108(1)–(6)	66.9
(7), (8)	19.6(ii); 66.12
s 109	60.1
s 110	66.5(*d*)
s 111	90.1
s 113	90.1
s 117	10.26
s 118	10.25
(6)	10.28
s 119(1)	10.22(i); 10.52
s 120	10.19(iv)
s 121	10.19(ii)
s 122	3.7
s 123	3.7
(1), (6)	74.32
s 124	3.7
s 125	55.3
s 126	55.2; 55.3
ss 127–130	55.2
s 131	55.2–55.4
s 132	55.4
s 133	55.3
(3)	55.2
s 137	26.1; 46.18
s 139	83.3
s 141	71.63
s 142	23.13
s 144	71.44
(3)	62.1
s 145	71.84
ss 159, 160	52.5
s 176(2)	52.5
s 178(1), (2)	78.5
s 179	78.6; 78.7
s 180	78.11
s 184	78.8
s 185	78.9
s 186	78.11
s 187	78.12
ss 188, 189	78.13
s 190	78.14
s 191(1), (2)	78.15
s 192	78.17
s 193	78.19; 78.20
s 194	78.21
s 196	1.11; 17.1; 17.3; 17.4; 17.10; 17.11; 34.4; 34.8; 41; 42.3; 42.4; 46.12(*g*); 53.19; 55.8; 58.8; 71.57(*a*); 78.4; 78.10; 78.16; 78.23–78.31; 78.34; 78.35
s 197	78.3

1994 Finance Act
s 199 17.11; 42.3; 53.19; 55.8; 58.8; 78.8
(2) 1.11; 17.1; 17.3; 17.4; 17.10; 34.4; 34.8; 41; 42.4; 46.12(*g*); 78.5; 78.6; 78.15; 78.16; 78.19–78.21; 78.23; 78.25–78.31; 78.34; 78.35
s 200 22.1; 71.12; 71.14; 71.15
s 201 71.12; 71.15
ss 202, 203 71.15
s 204 71.17
s 205 71.19
s 206 72.4(*e*)
s 207 51.12; 73.5; 73.9
(1) 73.7
(3) 63.1(A)
(4) 72.3(*a*)
(5) 25.3; 63.1(A)
s 208 74.3
s 209(1) 46.3
(2) 46.13
(3) 46.3; 46.13
(4), (5) 46.12
(6) 46.15
(7) 46.3; 46.13; 46.15
(8) 46.3; 46.12; 46.13
(9) 46.3; 46.13
s 210 46.18
s 211 10.1; 10.2(vi); 10.17; 10.32; 10.52
(2) 10.7
s 212(1) 10.2(vi); 10.14
(2) 10.2(vi)
s 213(1) 10.2(vi)
(2), (3) 10.14
(4) 10.28
(5), (6) 10.28(A)
(7) 10.9
(8) 10.42
(9) 10.7
(10) 10.52
s 214(1) 46.7; 46.9(*a*); 46.15; 71.57(*a*)
(2) 46.9(*c*)
(3) 46.9(*b*)
(4) 10.50
(5) 10.2(vi)
(6) 10.23
s 215 53.14
(1) 53.3; 53.5; 71.15
(1A) 62.1
(4), (5) 53.5; 53.6
s 216(1), (2) 53.6
s 216(3) 46.9(*a*); 46.12; 46.13; 46.15(*c*); 71.57(*a*)
(4) 46.15(*c*)
(5) 71.57(*a*)
s 217 25.5(*j*)
s 218 51.12; 71.11; 72.3(*a*); 72.4(*f*); 73.9
(1) 74.3
(3) 89.2
ss 219–227 89.1
s 228 89.1
(2), (4) 60.5; 65.4
ss 229, 230 89.1
s 248 89.1
s 254 4.6
s 255 6.8
Sch 7 para 31 42.9; 58.12; 71.65
Sch 8 para 1 1.15
paras 2, 3 47.2
para 4 47.5(*a*)
para 5 47.5(*c*)
paras 6–8 1.17
para 9 1.16
para 10 47.2
para 11 1.10(i); 1.11; 23.8(*a*)
para 12 25.5(*g*)
para 13 6.4
Sch 9 para 1 23.13
para 2 3.18
para 3 43.5
para 4 43.15
para 5 43.16
para 6 43.10
para 7 43.10; 43.13
para 9 43.25
paras 10, 11 23.13
para 12 43.7
Sch 10 para 2 48.1
para 3 47.2; 47.5(*a*)
para 4 48.1
para 5 48.2; 48.5
para 6 48.2
Sch 12 46.18
para 1 10.13
Sch 13 82.41
Sch 14 90.1
para 5 90.2
Sch 15 26.1; 26.18
para 2 26.2; 26.4; 26.6; 26.8; 26.11
para 3 26.10; 26.25
para 4 26.10
paras 5, 6 26.3

1994 Finance Act
Sch 15 paras 7–9 26.5
paras 10, 11 26.7
paras 12–17 26.12
para 18 26.15
para 19 26.8
para 20 26.8; 46.18
para 21 26.11
para 22 26.12
paras 23, 24 26.14
para 25 26.17
para 26 26.2
para 27 26.12
paras 28–34 26.17
Sch 16 para 1 1.9; 22.3; 76.3; 81.5
para 15 81.5(*b*)
para 17 3.6
para 18 3.7
Sch 18 para 1 52.5
Sch 19 para 1 78.4
para 2 53.19
para 3 78.10
para 4 78.34
para 5 78.30
para 6 78.16
para 7 78.31
paras 8, 9 17.10
para 10 78.30
paras 11, 12 78.30
para 13 17.1; 17.3
para 14 1.11; 17.4; 46.12(*g*); 86.6
para 15 17.11
para 17 78.31
para 18 42.3; 78.31
paras 19–21 78.35
para 22 78.24
para 25 78.26
para 26 78.27
paras 27, 28 78.28
para 29 78.29
para 30 53.19
para 31 78.25
para 32 58.8
para 33 78.25
para 35 17.3
para 37 71.57(*a*)
para 38 55.8
para 41 41; 78.23
para 43 34.4; 34.8
para 45 78.17
Sch 20 para 1 71.20
para 2 71.20; 71.22
Sch 20 para 3 46.10(*a*); 71.24
paras 4, 5 72.4(*f*)
paras 6, 7 73.9
para 8 46.3; 46.18
para 9 10.2(vii)
paras 10–13 25.5(*n*)
para 14 25.5(*n*); 72.4(*f*); 73.9
Sch 21 89.1
para 1 89.3
para 2 89.2; 89.4
paras 3–5 89.3
para 6 89.4
para 8 89.3
paras 9–11 89.5
paras 12–15 89.7(*b*)
para 16 89.7(*c*)
Sch 26 Pt V 11.3; 47.2; 47.5(*a*)
(1) 1.8(i)
(23) 28.1; 56.1(*a*)(*c*)(*d*)
(24) 10.2(iii)(v)(vi); 10.3; 10.7; 10.9; 10.14; 10.15; 10.17; 10.18; 10.23; 10.25; 10.27; 10.28; 10.30; 10.32; 10.35(*g*)(*h*); 10.43; 10.44; 10.50; 10.52; 46.5; 71.57(*a*); 71.67
1994 Value Added Tax Act
s 36 71.93
ss 79, 80 29.24
1995 Finance Act
s 35 1.5
s 36 1.14
s 39 43.2; 68; 74.4
(1) 68.4
(2) 68.4; 68.5
(4) 68.3; 68.21
(5) 68.3
s 40 78.38
(1), (2) 68.24
(3) 23.3(iii); 68.24
(8) 68.24
s 41 73.4
s 42(1) 43.15
(2) 43.3; 43.12; 43.13; 43.16
(3)–(5) 43.15
s 43(1) 75.15
(2) 75.15(iv)
(3) 75.11(II)
(4) 75.11(II); 75.15
s 44 75.15
s 45(2)–(5) 75.17
s 55(1)–(3) 45.6
(4) 45.12(*e*)

1995 Finance Act

Provision	Paragraph
s 55(5)	45.17
(6)	45.18
(7)	45.17
(8)	45.19
s 56(1)	45.13
(2)	45.19
s 59(2)	66.4
(4), (5)	60.2
s 60	60.2
(1)	66.4
s 61	66.4
(1)	66.9
ss 62, 63	29.13(iii)
s 64	29.21
s 65	29.13(vi)
s 66(2)	26.3
(3)	26.5
(4)	26.8
s 67	26.17
s 68(2)	26.21
(3)	26.31
s 69	26.31
s 70	91.1
s 71	91.1; 91.4
(3)	91.7
s 72	91.1; 91.11
(2)	30.19
(3)	91.12
(4)	91.14
s 73	91.1
s 74	15.16; 81.13
s 76(1), (4)	22.3
s 77	33.3
s 78	33.3
(6)	62.1
s 79	74.23
s 80(1), (4), (5)	3.5
s 81	3.6
s 82	3.7
s 83(1)	3.5; 3.7; 74.23
s 84	71.82
s 85	71.82
s 86	8.2
ss 88, 89	44.5(*h*); 44.7(8); 74.27
s 90	1.10(vi); 62; 62.4
(4)	62.5
s 91	75.23
(2)	75.11; 75.44(*a*)(*d*)
s 92	75.23
(1)	1.10(vii)
s 93(1)	75.44(*a*)
(2)	75.44(*d*)
(3)	75.13(xxii)
s 93(4), (5)	75.43
ss 94–98	10.30
s 99(2)	10.14
(3), (4)	10.15
(5)	10.11
(6)	10.14
(7)	10.11
(8)	10.17
s 100	10.12
s 101	10.11
s 103	78.36
(1), (2)	78.4
(3)	78.5
s 104(1)–(3)	78.5
(4)	78.6
(6)	78.8
(7), (8)	78.9
s 105	78.10
s 106	78.37
s 107	17.1
(10), (11)	17.3
s 108	78.17
s 109	42.4; 78.21
s 110	42.1; 78.22
s 111(1)	78.6
(2)	75.1(3)
s 112	23.13
s 115(1)	78.4
(2)	78.6
(3)	58.1
(4)	78.8
(5)	78.16
(6)	78.20
(7), (8)	78.25
(9)	72.3(*a*); 73.6
(10)	23.3(iii); 23.15(*a*); 51.10
s 116(1)	78.17; 78.19
s 117	53.3; 53.5; 53.14(i); 71.15
(1), (3)	62.1
s 118	46.3; 46.12; 46.13; 46.15
s 119	46.18
s 120	71.76
s 121	71.3
s 122(2), (3)	71.22
(4), (5)	25.5(*n*)
s 123	43.22; 71.22; 72.4(*f*); 73.9
s 124	71.27
s 125	53.15
(4)	53.14(i)
s 126	51.5; 78.38
s 127	51.6; 78.38
s 128	38; 51.1; 51.2; 78.38

1995 Finance Act
s 133 71.20
s 134 52.3
(4), (9) 52.5
s 136 75.31
s 137(1) 75.31
(2) 82.38
(3) 82.39
(4) 82.9
(5) 82.41
(6) 75.31
(7) 82.9; 82.38; 82.39
(9) 82.41
s 138 15.7(iii)
s 139 21.2
(1) 21.7
s 141 71.83; 83.3
s 142 29.4
s 143 89.7(*b*)
s 145 23.2(*b*)
s 153 67.3
s 154 71.57(*i*); 71.95; 93.1
s 156 56.3
Sch 6 68
para 1 68.4
para 2 51.12
para 3 68.20; 68.21
para 4 68.25
paras 5–7 68.7
para 8 10.25(ii); 10.32; 68.7
paras 9–11 68.27
para 12 68.27; 68.28
para 13 43.2(i); 68.5
para 14 68.5; 68.28; 71.78
para 15 68.5; 71.57(*a*)
para 16 68.5
para 17 43.25
para 18 23.13
para 19 68.13
para 20 68.5; 71.76
para 21 68.9
paras 22–25 68.5
para 26 81.30
para 27 3.12
para 28 68.4
para 29 10.17
para 31 68.9
para 32 10.25(ii)
para 33 10.32
para 34 10.9
para 35 10.3
para 38 68.11
para 40 68.27
Sch 8 para 25 51.9(i)(ii)
Sch 10 para 1 31.1
para 2 31.2
Sch 11 paras 1–9 60.2
para 10 60.3
paras 11, 12 60.1
Sch 12 29.13(vi)
Sch 13 paras 1–3 26.17
para 4 26.17; 92.14
Sch 14 91.1; 91.3
Sch 15 91.1; 91.4; 91.5
paras 3–5 91.7
paras 7–9 91.9
Sch 16 91.1; 91.11; 91.14
Sch 17 81.13
para 1 20.8; 52.12; 81.15–81.18
para 2 3.19
para 4 1.8(i); 1.10(i); 15.17; 28.4(*b*)
para 7 15.10
paras 9, 10 81.19
para 11 20.8; 81.19
paras 13, 14 81.5
para 16 81.30
para 17 74.12
para 18 3.8
para 19 3.12
para 20 20.8
para 23 81.15
para 26 15.16
Sch 18 22.3
Sch 19 71.82
Sch 20 17.3
Sch 21 para 1 78.4
para 2 78.17
para 3 78.19
Sch 22 para 1 71.20
para 2 43.22
paras 3, 4 71.22
para 5 43.22
paras 6–8 73.9
paras 9, 10 72.4(*f*); 73.9
para 11 43.22; 71.20; 71.22; 72.4(*f*)
para 12 43.22; 71.22
para 13 71.20; 71.22; 72.4(*f*); 73.9
paras 14–17 71.20
paras 18–20 72.4(*f*)
para 21 43.22; 71.20; 71.22; 72.4(*f*)
Sch 23 51.7; 78.38
Sch 27 paras 1, 2 21.2
para 3 21.4; 21.7

1995 Finance Act
Sch 27 para 4 — 21.4; 21.5
para 5 — 21.4
paras 6, 7 — 21.4; 21.5
para 9 — 21.7
Sch 28 — 67.3
Sch 29 Pt VIII(1) — 43.17
(2) — 23.13; 43.3; 43.10; 43.15; 43.17
(8) — 3.19; 11.3
(14) — 56.1(*e*)
(15) — 53.14(iii)
(16) — 36.4; 53.3; 53.19
(22) — 23.3(i); 28.4(*a*)

1995 Civil Evidence Act
Sch 1 para 6 — 6.8

1995 Criminal Injuries Compensation Act
s 8 — 29.4

1995 Jobseekers Act
s 23 — 47.10
Sch 2 para 15 — 47.10

1996 Employment Rights Act — 29.23; 71.54; 75.32
s 86 — 75.45
s 139 — 19.3

1996 Finance Act
s 72 — 1.5
s 73 — 1.3; 1.9
(2)–(4) — 23.2; 23.3(i)(ii); 23.5
s 74 — 1.14
s 75 — 1.19
s 76 — 43.10; 43.24
s 79 — 70; 70.1
ss 80–96 — 33.1
s 97 — 3.7; 33.1
ss 98–101 — 33.1
s 102 — 33.1; 72.2
ss 103, 104 — 33.1
s 105 — 33.1
(1) — 72.2
s 106(1)–(3) — 75.29
s 107(1) — 75.17; 86.1(*g*)
(2)–(4) — 75.17
s 108 — 29.16
s 109 — 15.18
s 110 — 55.12
s 113 — 82.38
s 114 — 82.40
s 115(1)–(5) — 82.40
s 116 — 82.9; 82.10
ss 117, 118 — 82.10
ss 119, 120 — 82.41
s 121(1)–(3) — 78.5
(4) — 78.6
(6), (7) — 78.8
s 122(1) — 78.6
(2) — 78.19
(3), (4) — 1.9; 81.5
(5) — 1.9; 85.1
(6) — 28.3(*a*)
(7) — 66.8
s 123(1)–(4) — 78.8
(5), (6) — 78.9
(7) — 78.11
(8)–(11) — 78.27
(12), (13) — 78.28
s 124 — 78.10
(4) — 17.3
s 125 — 78.14
s 126(1) — 78.17
(2) — 78.19
s 127 — 78.20
s 128(1) — 17.1
(2) — 17.2
(3) — 71.57(*a*)
(4) — 62.1
(5)–(10) — 71.51
s 129 — 48.1; 48.7; 92.1
s 130 — 17.1
(6)–(8) — 17.3
s 131 — 42.1; 78.22
s 134 — 1.14; 1.15; 1.17; 1.19; 26.11; 26.31; 32.1; 45.2; 46.9(*a*)(*b*); 46.13; 47.2; 47.5(*b*)(*c*); 51.11; 51.12; 51.14; 62.4; 63.1(A); 66.5(*b*); 66.13; 68.9; 71.44; 73.4; 73.5; 74.19; 75.2; 75.3(B); 75.11; 75.15; 75.17; 75.29; 82.10
s 135 — 3.14; 10.3; 10.25; 10.27; 10.28; 10.32; 10.34(*b*); 19.6; 22.3; 25.5(*e*)(*j*); 26.11; 43.10; 43.12; 46.13; 47.2; 47.5(*a*); 47.10; 51.14; 54.5; 60.5; 65.4; 68.9; 68.11; 71.15; 71.58; 71.60; 71.82; 71.83; 74.5; 81.30
s 143 — 29.12
s 144 — 92.1
s 145 — 51.11
s 146 — 15.4; 15.5; 15.7; 38
s 147 — 1.10(viii)
s 148 — 29.3

Provision	Paragraph
1996 Finance Act	
s 149	1.8(i)
s 150	29.4
s 151	83.5
s 152	83.4
s 154	33.2; 74.10; 89.3
s 155	33.3
s 156	33.3
s 157	71.82
s 158	74.15
(1), (5)	74.7
s 159(1)	3.3; 3.7; 3.16
(2)–(9)	3.7
s 161	91.3
s 162(1)	45.6; 45.12(*e*)
s 167(1)	45.12(*b*)
(5), (6)	45.1
(7)	45.7(*c*); 45.8
(8)	45.12(*b*)
s 168(5)	45.19
s 171(3), (4)	45.3(ii)
s 172	60.2
s 175	3.2
s 178	21.3; 21.7
(1)	21.2
s 200	64.4
Sch 5 para 40	42.9; 58.12; 71.65
Sch 6 para 2	23.2; 23.3(i)(ii); 23.5
para 3	28.1; 56.1(*d*)
para 4	33.3; 73.1
para 5	1.9; 22.3
para 6	85.1
para 7	29.13(iii)
para 8	1.10(i)
para 9	28.3(*a*)
paras 10, 11	90.1
para 12	90.2
para 13	28.6; 81.5
para 14	32.1
para 15	81.5
para 16	81.2(*b*); 81.3
para 17	22.3
paras 18, 19	3.7
para 20	3.8
para 22	23.6(*a*)
para 23	23.6(*d*)
para 24	23.1; 28.2(*d*); 72.4(*a*)
para 25	70.1
para 27	11.3
para 28	1.9; 1.10(i); 3.7; 3.8; 11.3; 23.1; 23.2; 23.3(i)(ii); 23.5; 23.6(*a*)(*d*);
Sch 6 para 28	228.1; 28.2(*d*); 28.3(*a*); 28.6; 56.1(*d*); 72.4(*a*); 81.2(*b*); 81.3; 81.5; 85.1; 90.2
Sch 7	70; 70.1
para 4	72.1
para 7	23.3(iv)
para 15	24.1
para 17	90.1
para 18	51.9(i)
para 19	15.5
para 22	24.1
para 23	3.4
para 26	23.3(ii)
para 27	23.3(iv)
paras 33–35	70.1
Sch 8	33.1
Sch 9	33.1
paras 8, 9	71.44
Sch 10	33.1
para 3	52.5
Sch 11	33.1
Sch 12	33.1
Sch 13	33.1; 44.5; 44.7; 44.9; 72.1(*a*); 72.2; 74.6; 74.8; 74.30
para 12	3.8
Sch 14	33.1
para 5	70.1; 72.1
para 6	13.4
para 9	71.70
para 18	23.3(ii)
para 20	71.76
para 26	90.1
para 27	51.9(ii)
para 31	29.13(ix)
para 33	71.82
para 35	81.5
para 36	74.6; 74.30
para 37	3.5
para 38	3.7
paras 45, 46	74.31
para 50	44.5
para 52	3.7
para 57	44.7
para 58	44.8
Sch 15	33.1
para 17	71.44
para 18	74.6; 74.30
para 19	44.5
para 20	44.7
para 21	44.8
paras 27–29	44.7
Sch 16	82.40
Sch 17	17.2

1996 Finance Act

Sch 18	para 1	78.31
	para 2	78.17
	para 3	42.1; 78.22
	para 4	6.6; 42.1; 78.22
	para 5	26.12; 26.27
	paras 6–8	23.13
	para 10	71.54; 75.42
	para 11	45.1; 45.2; 45.4(*d*)
	para 12	48.7
	para 14	92.1
	para 16	91.1
	para 17	6.6; 23.13; 26.12; 26.27; 42.1; 45.1; 45.2; 45.4(*d*); 48.7; 71.54; 75.42; 78.17; 78.22; 78.31; 91.1; 92.1
Sch 19	para 2	78.11; 78.13
	para 3	78.12; 78.29
	paras 4, 5	78.13
	paras 6, 7	78.31
	paras 8–10	17.3
Sch 20	para 3	51.12; 63.1(A); 73.4; 73.5
	para 4	71.44
	para 5	62.4
	para 6	75.2
	para 7	75.29
	para 8	75.15(v)
	para 9	75.17
	para 10	75.11; 75.15
	para 11	82.10
	para 13	1.14
	para 14	1.15; 47.2
	para 15	47.5(*b*)
	para 16	47.5(*c*)
	paras 17, 18	1.17
	para 19	1.19
	para 20	45.2
	para 21	51.11
	paras 22, 23	26.11
	para 24	46.13
	para 25	46.9(*a*)
	para 27	46.9(*b*)
	para 30	68.9
	para 32	32.1
	paras 33, 34	51.14
	para 35	74.19
	para 36	3.6
	para 40	75.15(i)
	para 41	75.17
	para 42	75.3(B)
	para 44	68.9
	para 54	26.31
Sch 20	para 63	66.5(*b*); 66.13
Sch 21	para 1	71.15
	para 2	71.60
	para 3	71.83
	para 4	47.2
	para 5	47.5(*a*)
	para 6	47.2
	para 7	26.11
	para 8	43.12
	para 9	43.10
	para 10	46.13
	para 11	74.5
	para 12	71.82
	para 14	68.9
	para 15	54.5
	para 16	51.14
	para 17	65.4
	para 18	60.5
	para 19	81.30
	para 20	22.3
	para 21	3.14
	para 22	25.5(*e*)(*j*)
	para 23	25.5(*e*)
	para 24	19.6
	para 25	47.10
	para 26	10.28
	para 27	10.27
	paras 28, 29	10.28(B)
	para 30	10.28(F)
	para 31	10.34(*b*)
	para 32	71.58
	para 33	10.3
	para 34	10.32
	para 36	71.83
	para 40	71.61
	paras 45, 46	71.58
	para 47	68.11
	para 48	10.25
Sch 22	para 2	78.12
	para 3	78.13
	para 4	78.31; 78.33
	para 5	17.10
	para 6	17.9
	para 7	78.33
	para 9	17.3
	para 10	78.33
	para 11	71.83
Sch 26		29.4
Sch 27	para 2	1.9
Sch 28		33.2
	para 3	51.9(ii)
Sch 29		33.3
	para 1	56.1
	para 4	23.3(ii)

1996 Finance Act
Sch 29 para 6 24.1
Sch 35 10.30
Sch 37 23.3(ii)
para 1 8.1
para 2 3.8; 15.10
paras 5, 10 15.10
para 11 67.4
Sch 38 para 6 15.10; 23.3(ii); 46.18
para 9 3.6
Sch 39 para 1 10.17; 10.28(A)
para 2 66.10
Sch 40 paras 3, 4 74.24
para 5 74.7
para 6 74.24
para 7 71.82
Sch 41 Pt V(1) 1.3; 1.9; 81.2(*b*); 81.3; 85.1; 90.2
(3) 23.3(ii); 29.29; 33.4; 44.5; 44.7; 44.8; 71.44; 74.9; 74.27
(5) 82.40
(12) 17.9; 78.33
(18) 74.10; 89.3
(19) 23.3(ii)
(21) 3.6; 3.7

1997 Finance Act
s 54 1.5; 81.5; 81.30
s 55 1.14
s 56 1.13; 1.19
s 57 43.10; 43.24
s 60 23.14; 68.4; 72.1(*d*)
s 61 75.31
s 63 75.42; 75.43
s 65 59.5; 71.54; 83.2
s 66 10.41; 71.71
s 69 3.21
s 70 3.17
s 73 3.2
s 75 91.2
s 77 3.6
s 78 23.3(ii)
s 79 45.15
s 80 3.22
(3) 71.32
(4) 3.20
(5) 90.2
s 81 3.8
s 89 38
s 92 41; 78.23
s 110 35.4
Sch 7 3.7; 3.21; 71.82; 81.5; 90.1
Sch 8 26.2; 26.5; 26.7; 26.10; 26.14
Sch 9 91.3(*b*)
Sch 10 3.7; 67.9; 71.82; 74.25
Sch 11 3.22
Sch 12 71.68
Sch 14 10.28(F)(G); 10.35(*a*)(*f*)(*g*)(*h*); 10.38(xi)
Sch 15 10.2(iii); 10.25; 10.32; 68.7(*a*); 68.9; 68.13; 68.15(v)
Sch 16 10.2(iv); 10.34
Sch 18 Pt VI(1) 81.5
(2) 1.9; 23.2; 23.3(i); 23.6; 28.4(*a*); 46.17(*a*); 71.52
(3) 75.31
(10) 3.7; 46.17; 74.25; 74.32; 89.3
(11) 10.17; 10.25(ii); 10.32
(12) 10.34

1997 Finance (No 2) Act
s 15 23.13; 43.3
s 16 43.10; 43.24
s 17 48.1
s 19 25.2
s 21 22.3
s 22 89.3
s 24 3.7; 3.21; 71.82
s 25 3.21; 91.3
s 26 3.6
s 27 81.5
s 28 3.23
s 29 90.2
s 30 1.9; 15.6; 25.2; 29.10; 76.3
s 31 1.9; 76.3
s 32 81.5
s 33 22.3
s 35 15.6
s 36 3.21
s 37 33.3
s 42 10.27; 10.35
s 43 10.27
s 44 10.28
s 45 10.38(vi)
ss 46, 47 10.38(iii)
s 48 71.58
Sch 4 para 1 78.4
para 4 90.2
para 6 1.9; 81.5
para 7 3.17; 3.18
para 10 85.1; 85.5
para 11 28.3(*a*)
para 12 90.2
para 14 81.15

1997 Finance (No 2) Act
Sch 4 para 15 — 81.5
para 16 — 81.2(*b*); 81.3
para 17 — 28.6
para 19 — 3.2
para 20 — 3.8
paras 24, 25 — 11.3
para 30 — 89.7(*b*)
Sch 5 — 15.6
Sch 6 para 3 — 1.9; 22.3; 76.3; 90.1
para 8 — 90.1
para 10 — 81.5
para 11 — 81.2(*b*); 81.3
para 12 — 22.3
para 14 — 3.6
para 17 — 3.7
para 20 — 89.3
para 21 — 3.21
Sch 8 Pt II (4) — 3.2
(5) — 89.5
(8) — 3.21
(9) — 3.21; 25.2
(11), (12) — 3.21

1997 Social Security (Administration) Fraud Act
s 1 — 36.2(*f*)

1998 Finance Act
s 25 — 1.5
s 26 — 1.17
s 27 — 1.13; 1.15; 1.16; 1.17; 47.10
s 31 — 76.3
s 37 — 33.3
s 38 — 10.3; 10.9; 10.25; 10.27; 10.28(E); 10.32; 10.34; 68.4; 68.5; 68.7(*b*); 68.9; 68.13; 68.15; 68.24; 68.25; 68.27; 68.28; 71.54; 71.78; 73.4
s 39 — 68.7(*b*)
s 40 — 68.27
s 41 — 71.45
s 42 — 12.2; 68.5; 71.40
s 43 — 12.2; 71.40
s 44 — 12.2; 68.5
s 45 — 12.2; 71.40
s 46 — 46.2; 71.40
(1), (2) — 68.5
ss 47, 48 — 15.21
s 49 — 82.3
s 50 — 82.5; 82.7
s 51 — 82.5; 82.8
ss 52, 53 — 82.7; 82.8
s 54 — 82.2
s 54(5) — 82.7
s 55 — 21.2; 75.46
s 56 — 75.46
s 58 — 19.5; 66.12; 75.1; 75.23; 75.41
s 59 — 75.15(iv)
s 60 — 75.15
s 61 — 75.10(*a*)
s 62 — 75.31
s 63 — 75.3
ss 64–68 — 55.2
s 69 — 55.2–55.4
s 70 — 26.5; 91.3
s 71(1), (2) — 26.12
(3), (4) — 26.17
(5) — 26.12; 26.17
s 72 — 91.3
s 73(1) — 91.2; 91.5
(2)–(5) — 91.3
(6) — 91.2; 91.3; 91.5
s 74 — 26.2–26.5; 26.8; 26.10–26.12; 26.14; 26.17
s 75 — 29.10
s 76 — 29.10; 29.21
s 77 — 29.10
s 78 — 29.13(iii)
s 79 — 43.19
s 80 — 46.18; 46.19
s 83 — 10.27
s 84 — 10.27; 10.35
s 85 — 10.27
(1), (4) — 10.35
(5) — 10.35(*g*)(*h*)
(7) — 10.35(*f*)
(8), (9) — 10.38(iii)
s 87 — 45.13
s 88 — 45.17
s 89 — 45.13
s 90 — 31.1
s 91 — 66.9
ss 94, 95 — 60.2
s 96 — 60.1
s 97 — 60.1; 60.2
s 98 — 60.1; 66.4; 78.6
s 99 — 3.22
s 100 — 1.10; 74.9
s 101 — 71.82
s 102 — 3.7
s 107 — 25.5(*e*)
s 108 — 3.9
ss 110, 111 — 3.9
s 118 — 17.5
s 119 — 55.1
s 120 — 11.3

1998 Finance Act
s 126 85.2
s 161 33.2; 74.10
Sch 3 paras 32–34 3.2
Sch 5 paras 1, 2 68.4
paras 4, 5 68.5
paras 7, 8 68.7(*b*)
para 11 68.7(*b*)
paras 15–17 68.27
para 18 68.27; 68.28
para 20 68.25
para 22 68.24
paras 23, 24 73.4
para 27 68.13
para 34 68.28; 71.78
para 42 68.9
para 43 71.54
paras 47–50 10.17
para 51 68.9
para 52 10.28(B)
para 53 10.34(*a*)
para 54 10.34(*b*)
para 55 10.28(E)
para 56 10.25(ii)
para 57 10.32; 68.15
para 58 10.9
para 59 10.3
para 60 10.25
para 61 73.4
Sch 6 12.2; 68.5
Sch 8 para 2 21.2; 21.7
paras 3–5 21.5
para 6 21.7
Sch 9 19.6
Pt I 19.5; 75.27
para 1 66.12
para 2 75.41
para 3 75.1
para 5 75.23
Sch 10 75.10(*a*)
Sch 11 75.31
Sch 12 paras 1, 2 26.7
paras 3, 4 91.3
para 5 26.7; 91.3
Sch 13 para 1 26.2; 26.4
paras 2, 3 26.8
paras 4, 5 26.10
paras 6, 7 26.3
para 8 26.3; 38
para 9 26.5
paras 10, 11 26.7
paras 12–15 26.12
para 16 26.15
para 17 26.16
Sch 13 para 18 26.8; 46.18
para 19 26.11
para 20 26.12
para 21 26.14
para 22 26.17
para 23 26.3; 26.5; 26.12
paras 24–36 26.17
para 38 26.21
para 39 26.27
para 40 26.29
para 41 26.30
para 42 26.31
Sch 14 45.13
para 4 45.19
para 5 78.36
para 6 22.1; 81.3
para 7 22.1; 45.19; 81.3
Sch 15 66.4
Sch 16 3.9
Sch 18 para 18 58.6
Sch 19 para 3 78.8
para 4 78.9
para 5 78.11
para 10 78.13
para 14 78.16
para 36 78.29
para 38 58.6
para 42 17.3
Sch 27 Pt III(1) 47.10
(4) 10.17; 10.25; 10.28(E); 10.32; 10.34(*b*); 17.1; 43.2; 68.5; 68.7; 68.15; 68.24; 68.25; 68.27; 71.54; 71.57; 71.63; 71.68; 71.76; 71.78; 73.4
(6) 62.1; 62.2
(7) 75.46
(9) 5.7; 19.6; 75.27
(13) 91.2; 91.5
(14) 26.3–26.5; 26.10–26.12; 26.17; 26.31
(16) 46.18
(21) 60.1
(22) 74.19
(23) 71.82
(29) 11.3
1998 Government of Wales Act
Sch 12 36.4
Sch 16 21.2; 23.13
1998 Late Payment of Commercial Debts (Interest) Act 23.3(ii)

1998 National Minimum Wage Act
ss 13, 16 — 36.2(*r*)
1998 Petroleum Act — 51.13
1998 Scotland Act
Pt IV — 1.3
1998 Social Security Act
Sch 7 para 16 — 75.31
1999 Finance Act
s 22 — 1.3
(1) — 1.5
(4) — 1.13
(7) — 1.9
(8) — 45.13
(9) — 28.6
(11) — 78.4
s 23 — 1.5
s 24 — 1.14
s 25 — 1.13
s 26 — 11.3
s 28(3) — 90.1
s 30 — 1.18
(3) — 1.13
s 31 — 1.15; 47.2
s 32 — 1.15; 47.2
(2), (4) — 47.5
s 33 — 1.15; 1.17
s 34 — 1.16
s 35 — 1.15; 1.16; 1.18
s 36 — 47.10
(7), (8) — 1.8(i)
s 37 — 43.10; 43.24
s 38 — 23.13; 43.3
s 39 — 23.13; 43.24
s 40 — 43.24
s 41 — 23.13; 41
ss 42, 43 — 82.7
s 44 — 75.13(xxiii)
(2) — 75.16
(4) — 75.15
(5) — 29.16
(6) — 29.16; 75.16
s 45 — 75.13(xxiv)
s 46 — 75.31
s 47 — 75.15(i)
s 48 — 75.13(xxv)
s 49 — 75.7; 75.13(xiv); 75.43; 75.44(*a*)(*d*)
s 50(1) — 75.13(xxvi)
(2) — 75.43
(3) — 75.13(xxvi); 75.43
s 51 — 29.16
s 53 — 21.5
s 54 — 68.29; 71.78
s 55 — 15.19
s 55(2), (3) — 15.21
ss 56, 57 — 15.21
s 58 — 71.54
s 59 — 1.10(v); 92.1
s 60 — 29.13(x)
s 61 — 59.5; 71.54; 83.2
s 62 — 71.58
s 63 — 71.72
s 64 — 81.18
(7) — 81.16(*c*)
s 65 — 72.2
s 68 — 90.3
s 69 — 91.2; 91.3
s 70 — 91.9
s 71 — 26.2
s 73 — 26.17
ss 77, 78 — 10.27
s 80 — 23.11
ss 82–84 — 89.3
ss 85–87 — 3.9
s 132 — 35.12
s 133 — 35.12
(3), (4) — 67.3
Sch 3 — 1.18
Sch 4 para 1 — 43.3
para 2 — 43.5–43.10; 43.12; 43.13; 43.16; 43.17
paras 4–13 — 23.13
para 16 — 45.15(*f*)
para 18(3) — 45.15(*f*)
Sch 5 para 1 — 75.41
para 2 — 10.24; 29.16; 75.29(B)
para 3 — 29.16
para 4 — 66.11
para 6 — 60.1
Sch 6 — 68.29; 71.78
Sch 8 — 26.17
Sch 10 paras 2, 3 — 66.4
paras 4, 5 — 66.1
para 6 — 66.9
paras 9, 10 — 66.1
para 11 — 59.6
paras 12–14 — 60.2
para 15 — 60.8
paras 16, 17 — 23.11
para 18 — 66.4
Sch 11 para 6 — 10.34
Sch 20 Pt III(1) — 11.3
(3) — 51.11
(6) — 1.8(i); 1.10(i); 28.4(*b*); 47.10; 72.4; 73.3
(7) — 23.13

1999 Finance Act
Sch 20 Pt III(15) 47.2; 92.1
(17) 74.12; 90.1
1999 Social Security Contributions (Transfer of Functions, etc.) Act
s 7 36.1
Sch 6 para 1 35.4; 36.2(*f*)
para 2 36.2(*f*)
para 9 36.4
1999 Tax Credits Act 83.6
s 6 55.20; 55.46
s 12 36.4
Sch 1 para 6 83.4
Sch 5 para 1 36.3
para 2 36.2(*f*)
para 3 36.2(*g*)
paras 4, 5 36.2(*p*)
para 7 35.4
1999 Welfare Reform and Pensions Act
s 24(1) 23.11(vii); 60.2; 60.8; 66.1; 66.4
2000 Finance Act
s 31 1.3
s 32 1.3; 1.9
s 33 23.12
s 34 1.18
s 37 11.3
s 38 15.18
s 39 15.13; 15.14
(6) 25.5(*g*); 26.8; 15.12; 91.5
(8) 47.2
(9) 1.18
(10) 15.12; 25.5(*g*); 26.8; 47.2; 91.5
s 41 15.17
(2) 1.8; 1.10(i)
(5) 15.10
(8) 15.12
(9) 1.8; 1.10(i); 15.10
s 42 15.21
s 43 15.20
s 44 81.14
s 45 81.16(*a*)
s 46 15.7(i)
s 47 82.11–82.25
s 48 82.18
s 49 82.9; 82.10
s 50 71.54
ss 51–53 82.9
ss 54, 55 82.41
s 56 55.2; 82.3
s 57 75.13; 75.17
s 58 75.42
(2)(3) 75.43
s 59 75.15(ii)
s 60 61
s 62 82.26
s 63 46.18
s 68 10.52; 71.80
s 70 10.27
s 71 10.27; 10.35
s 72 10.27
s 73 10.25; 10.28
s 74 10.28(A); 10.35(*a*)
s 75 10.24; 10.28(C); 10.34; 10.38(ix)
s 76 10.25; 38
(2), (3) 34.2
s 77 10.38(iii)
s 78 10.34
s 79 10.34(*b*)
s 80 10.38(i)(vi)
s 81 10.27
s 83 23.13; 43.3; 43.24
s 84 83.4
s 85 83.4
s 87 71.87
s 88 71.84
s 89 71.94
s 107 89.3
s 110 68.30
s 111 8.2; 9.3; 23.3(ii); 23.12; 33.1; 56.1; 70.1
s 112 23.3(ii)
(1) 33.3
s 113 71.58
s 143 35.12; 67.3
s 144 6.12; 58.10
s 145 67.4
(10) (11) 9.3
s 146 35.13
(2) 36.2(*c*)
(3), (4) 6.8
s 147 35.13
(1) 36.2(*c*)
s 148 36.2(*r*)
s 149 6.8
s 150 6.9
(4) 6.10
Sch 7 para 4 42.10; 58.12; 71.65
Sch 8 82.2
para 1 82.11
(4) 82.21
para 2 82.11
(1) 71.54
para 3 82.12
(1) 71.54

2000 Finance Act

Sch 8 paras 4, 5 82.24
paras 6–12 82.12
paras 13–22 82.19
paras 23, 24 82.13
paras 25–30 82.20
paras 31, 32 82.13; 82.15; 82.16
paras 33–47 82.14
para 48 82.14
paras 49–52 82.15
paras 53–58 82.16
paras 59–67 82.21
paras 68–76 82.23
paras 77–87 82.17
para 88 82.23
paras 89–96 82.17
para 99 82.18
paras 101, 102 82.18
paras 105–114 71.54
paras 115, 116 82.21
paras 117–119 82.24
paras 120, 121 82.25
paras 122, 123 82.12
para 125 71.54; 82.13
para 126 71.54; 82.12; 82.16
para 127 82.12
para 128 82.17
para 129(1) 82.11; 82.12; 82.19; 82.21; 82.23
(3) 82.12
(4) 82.19

Sch 9 82.18

Sch 10 paras 2, 3 75.13
paras 4–6 75.17

Sch 11 75.15(ii)

Sch 12 61
para 1 61.3
(4) 61.4
para 2 61.7
paras 3–5 61.5
para 6 61.7
paras 7, 8 61.8
paras 9, 10 61.9
para 11 61.11
para 12 61.15
para 13 61.14
paras 14–16 61.16
paras 17, 18 61.13
para 19 61.5; 61.6
para 21 61.3; 61.5; 61.6; 61.8
para 22 61.2
para 23 61.17

Sch 12 para 24 61.1

Sch 13 para 3 66.4
para 4 60.2; 66.1
paras 5–7 60.2
para 8 60.1
paras 9–14 60.2
para 15 60.1
para 16 60.3
paras 17, 18 60.5
para 19 60.6
paras 20–23 60.8
para 24 60.2
para 25 60.3
para 26 81.17
para 27 60.2
para 28 60; 60.1–60.3; 60.8
para 29 60.8
para 30 60

Sch 14 82.1; 82.26–82.37
para 1 82.27
(2) 82.29; 82.31
(3) 82.28
paras 2–7 82.34
paras 8–11 82.27
paras 12–17 82.29
paras 18–26 82.30
paras 27–36 82.31
paras 37–41 82.32
paras 42–55 82.28
paras 59–63 82.33
para 64 82.36
para 65 82.35
paras 66, 67 82.27
paras 69 82.27; 82.29
para 70 82.37
para 71(1) 82.27; 82.29–82.32
(2) 82.28; 82.29

Sch 16 para 2 26.12
para 3 46.18

Sch 17 para 1 26.4
paras 2, 3 26.3
paras 4, 5 26.12
paras 6 26.3; 26.4; 26.6
para 7 26.17
para 8 26.3; 26.4; 26.12
para 9 26.2; 26.5; 26.11
paras 10, 11 26.5
para 12 26.2; 26.5; 26.11
para 13 26.7
para 14 26.5; 26.12; 26.14
para 15 26.2; 26.5; 26.6

Sch 18 paras 1, 3 91.5; 91.7
paras 4–8 91.3

2000 Finance Act

Sch 19	10.52
para 5	71.80
para 8	10.15; 10.34(*h*)
Sch 23	71.87
Sch 26 para 6	3.8
Sch 30 para 4	25.4(*d*)
para 5	25.4; 25.5(*ka*)
para 6	25.5(*g*)
para 20	25.5(*e*)
para 22	25.5(*da*)
para 25	25.2
Sch 30 para 27	25.5(*b*)
para 28	25.2
Sch 38	35.12; 67.3
Sch 39	6.8
Sch 40 Pt II(2)	75.13(i)
(3)	75.15(ii)
(5)	26.12
(9)	71.84
(17)	3.7; 23.3(ii)

2000 Learning and Skills Act

ss 104–109	75.42

97 Index

This index is referenced to the chapter and paragraph number.
The entries printed in bold capitals are main subject headings in the text.

A

Abroad, *see* Non-residents and other Overseas Matters
Accommodation, 75.29
allowances (MPs etc.), 29.16
available, 64.5, 64.7
expenses (MPs etc.), 75.29
job-related, 43.16
Accountancy expenses, 71.69
underwriters, 89.3
Accountants,
Revenue power to call for tax papers, 6.8
Accounting basis, 12, 71.40
change of, 12.2
Accounting date,
change, 71.7
Accounting periods,
bases of assessment, 5.9
— companies, 71.2
cash basis, 12
change, 71.7
Accounts, 71.28
basis, Sch A, 68.19
in-depth examination, 71.28
negligent, 58.3
re-opening of, 71.28
self-assessment, 78.5
Accrued income and accumulations,
dividends after death, 22.2
interest, 72.3(*b*)
minor's interest in settlement, 81.23
scheme, 74.6 *et seq.*
securities, on, 3.3, 3.6, 74.6 *et seq.*
unit trusts, 90.1
Accrued income scheme, 74.6 et seq.
anti-avoidance provisions, interaction with, 74.32
associated companies, interest on debts between, 74.27
banks, associates of, interest to, 74.27
bearer securities, 74.18
capital gains tax interaction, 74.30
charities, 74.21
conversions, 74.17
corporation tax interaction, 74.6, 74.30
death, 74.15
determination of accrued income, 74.8
discounts on securities, 72.2, 74.30
double taxation relief, 74.31
euroconversions, 74.7, 74.8, 74.19, 74.23
exceptions to deeming provisions, 74.10
foreign currency, 74.13
foreign securities, delayed remittances, 74.14
gilt strips, 74.24
information powers, 74.33
insurance companies, 74.28
interest in default, 74.20
new issues, 74.29
nominees, 74.12
retirement schemes, 74.22
securities, sale and repurchase of, 74.23, 74.32
stock lending, 74.25
trading stock, appropriations, 74.16
transfer of unrealised interest, 74.18
trustees, 74.12
underwriters, 74.26
unrealised interest, transfer of, 74.18
variable rate bonds, 74.19
Accumulation trusts, 81.5
Actors, 75.24
Additional assessments, 5.3, 17.11
Additional personal allowance, 1.17
Additional rate, 81.5
Additional voluntary contributions, 66.4–66.7
mis-sold schemes, compensation for, 29.3
Addresses, Inland Revenue, etc., 35.1
Adjudicator, 35.9
Agricultural Compliance Unit, 71.57(*e*)
Bank of England, 33.2
Board of Inland Revenue, 35.1
Capital and Valuation Division, 3.2
Charity Commissioners, 15.1
Claims Branch, 15.3, 51.11
Clerk to the Special Commissioners, 4.6(*b*)
Commissioners of Inland Revenue, 35.1
Company Tax Division, 26.2
— Business Expansion Scheme, 26.19
Corporate Communications Office, 67.2
Employee Share Schemes Unit, 82.3

97 Index

Addresses Inland Revenue, etc
Finance Division, 39
Financial Intermediaries and Claims Office, 15.1
— International, 25.6, 41.2
— Savings and Investments, 23.13
— Scotland, 15.3
Incentive Award Unit, 75.40
Information Centre, 39
International Division, 25.2
Internet site, 35.1
Library, 37
Oil Taxation Office, 3.9
Pension Schemes Office, 66
Profit-Related Pay Office, 75.31
Section 703 Compliance Unit, 3.2
Special Compliance Office, 35.7
Special Investigations, 3.2
Technical Division,
— Business Expansion Scheme, 26.19
— Offshore Funds, 52.7
Administration, *see* Inland Revenue
Administration of estates, 22.3
Adopted children, 1.17
adoption allowances, 29.1
settlements on, 81.23
Advance pricing agreements, 3.9
Adventure in nature of trade, 71.35
Advertising, 71.41, 71.55
Affordable Warmth programme,
capital allowances, 10.34
Age allowances, 1.14, 1.15, 1.24, 47.5
Agency,
cancellation of agreements, 71.47, 71.48
charity, 15.18
non-residents trading in UK, 51.4(*b*)
Schedule A, 68.21
workers supplied by, 55.3, 75.46
Agent,
agreement by, taxpayer bound, 4.4
assessment on non-resident, 51.4(*b*)
diplomatic, exemption for, 24.1
fraud by, 6.2
notices of assessment to, 5.1
refusal to be sworn, right of, 58.5
self-assessment, under, 78.17
taxation in name of (Schedule A), 68.21
trading in UK through, 51.4–51.7
Agents-General, 24
Aggregation of income,
Sch D, Cases IV and V, 73.6
Agreements with Revenue, 4.4
Agricultural buildings,
capital allowances, 10.3
Agricultural gangmasters, 71.57(e)
Agricultural land, 10.3
Agricultural societies, 30.1
Agricultural workers, board and lodging, 75.7
Aircraft personnel,
duties deemed in UK, 75.2
Airline pilots, resident overseas, 75.2
Alimony, 47.10
deduction of tax, 23.4, 23.9
from abroad, 25.5(*a*), 73.3
tax-free, 23.17(*d*)
Allowable deductions,
bad debts, 62.1
lease premiums, 68.28
post-cessation receipts, allowance against, 62.1
Schedule A, 68.15, 68.16
Schedule D Cases I and II, 71.40–71.95
Schedule E, 75.10 *et seq.*
ALLOWANCES AND TAX RATES, 1
additional personal allowance, 1.17
age allowance, 1.14, 1.15, 1.24, 47.5
children's tax credit, 1.15, 1.18
common law wife, allowance not due, 1.22
examples, 2
life assurance relief, 45.1
maintenance payments, 47.10
married couple's allowance, 1.15, 47.2, 47.5
married persons, 47.2–47.5
mortgage interest, 43.6
national insurance contributions, 1.9(viii)
non-residents, 51.11
personal allowance, 1.14
proportionate, to non-residents, 51.11
twelve-year summary, *inside front cover*
widow's bereavement allowance, 1.16
wife's earned income relief, 1.23
Almshouses, 15.2(*a*)
Alternative Investment Market (AIM), 26.5, 29.21(i), 46.18, 91.3
Amalgamations,
partnership, 53.8
Amateur status, loss of, 75.7
Amnesties, 35.4
Angels, 74.2
Annual charges, *see* Charges on income
Annual interest,
deduction of tax from, 43.1, 43.2
mortgage, 23.13
Annual payments, 1.8(i), 1.10(i), 23.10
agricultural land, for, 71.77
capital, out of, 81.9

Annual payments
carry-forward, 23.3(i), 46.17(*a*), 53.10
charges on income, 1.10
charities, to, 15.12, 15.16, 15.17, 28.4(*b*), 81.22, 81.24, 81.29(vii)
covenant, by, 81.21–81.29
deductibility, 1.8(i), 1.10(i), 22.3, 28.4(*b*), 81.22
deduction of tax, 1.8(i), 3.19, 23.10
— certificates, 23.7
— underdeductions, 23.6
excess liability, 23.17(*b*), 28.2(*d*)
exempt gallantry awards, 29.6
existing obligations (pre-15.3.1988), 1.8(i), 81.22
insurance policies, under, 29.12
loan transactions, 3.16
losses, treated as, 46.17
maintenance payments, 23.17(*d*), 47.10
non-residents, 51.10
non-taxable consideration, 1.10(i), 3.19, 28.4(*b*)
PAYE, 55.13, 55.14
Schedule D Case III, 72.3(*c*)
settlements, 81.9
surtax, 23.17(*b*)
theatrical angels, 74.2
trustees remuneration, 81.7
untaxed income, from, 23.3(i)
Annual returns, 67.2
Annual value,
Sch A, 68.16(*b*)
Sch E, 75.13
Annual voluntary settlements, 55.12
Annuities,
agricultural land, for, 71.77
capital element in, 23.11
capital, out of, 81.9
charges on income, 1.10
covenant, by, 81.21–81.29
death, 22.2
deduction for, 1.8(i), 1.10(i)
deduction of tax, 23.11
excess liability, 23.17(*b*), 28.2(*d*)
exempt gallantry awards, 29.6
exempt German annuities, 29.7
income, 1.8(i)
life,
— gains on, 45.13, 45.15
— loans to buy, 23.13(*a*), 43.24
— purchased, capital element, 23.11
loan transactions, 3.16
maintenance payments, 1.8(i), 47.10
non-residents, to, 51.10
non-taxable consideration, for, 3.19
partnership retirement, 53.16
PAYE, 55.14
personal injury compensation, 29.4
purchased, 1.9, 23.11(*c*), 43.24
— interest on loans for, 43.24
repayment of tax to annuitant, 23.17(*c*)
retirement, 60, 65
sale of rights to annuities, 3.4
Sch D, Case III, 72.3(*c*)
settlements, 81.9
surtax, 23.17(*b*)
tax-free annuities, 23.16, 23.17
— overseas taxes under, 23.17(*e*)
total income, 1.8(i)
trustees remuneration, 81.7
untaxed income, from, 23.3(i)
widow or widower, payments by, 45.3(iii)
ANTI-AVOIDANCE, 3
accrued income scheme, 74.6 *et seq*
annuities, sale of right to, 3.4
associated persons, transactions between, 3.9
capital allowances, 10.9, 10.22, 10.28, 10.38(iii)(vi), 10.50, 10.52, 71.68
capital sums received in lieu of earnings, 3.10
commodity futures, dealings in, 3.20
company purchase of own shares, 3.21
connected persons, 20
Courts, approach of, 3.1
current year basis, change to, 43.22, 71.20, 71.22, 72.4(*f*), 73.9, 78.2
derivatives, use of, 3.22
finance leasing, 10.28, 10.38(iii)(vi), 71.68
futures and options, 3.22
general principles, 3.1
income from personal activities, sale of, 3.10
land,
— leaseback transactions, 3.12, 3.13
— transactions in, 3.11
leaseback transactions, 3.12, 3.13, 10.38(iii)
leases, assets other than land, 3.14, 3.15
loan transactions, 3.16
manufactured dividends, 3.7, 3.21
non-taxable consideration, 3.19
offshore funds, *see* Offshore Funds
options, futures and, 3.22
overvalue, transactions at, 3.9
— double tax relief, 25.5(*m*)
own share purchase, 3.21
persons exempt from tax, 3.17, 3.18

97 Index

Anti-avoidance
pre-sale distributions, 3.21
sale and leaseback, 3.12, 3.13
securities,
— held for one month or less, 3.6
— sale and repurchase, 3.3, 3.5, 3.7, 33.3
— transactions in, 3.2
— transfers of income arising from, 3.4
special dividends, 3.21, 81.5
tax credits, 3.17, 3.18, 3.23
transfers of assets abroad, 3.8
— discounts on securities, 72.2
undervalue, transactions at, 3.9
— double tax relief, 25.5(*m*)
Anticipated losses and expenses, 71.49
APPEALS, 4
agreement, 4.4, 5.3
assessments, against, 4.1
Case Stated, 4.7
Commissioners, 4.6
— jurisdiction of, 4.3, 78.33
— numbers, 35.3
— power to obtain information, 58.5
construction industry tax scheme, 21.7
costs, 4.9
Court of Appeal, to, 4.7
Court of Session, to, 4.7
courts, to, 4.7
determination of, 4.6
dissatisfaction on point of law, 4.7
domicile and residence, 64.8
evidence, 4.6
General Commissioners, 4.3
— hearing by, 4.6
grounds of, 4.2
handling of, 4.5
Hansard, reference to, 4.7
hearing before Commissioners, 4.6
High Court, to, 4.7
House of Lords, to, 4.7
judicial review, 4.8
jurisdiction of Commissioners, 4.3, 78.33
Lands Tribunal, 4.3
late appeal, 4.2
mandamus and certiorari, 4.8
Northern Ireland, 4.7
number of appeals, 35.3
offshore funds, 52.7
Parliamentary debates, reference to, 4.7
payment of tax pending, 56.2
penalties, against, 58.6, 58.7
postponement applications, 56.2
power of Commissioners to obtain information, 4.6, 58.5
precepts, 4.6, 58.5
prerogative orders, 4.8
procedure, 4.5, 4.6
proceedings brought out of time, 4.2
residence, etc., 64.8
right of appeal, 4.1
self-assessment, 17.3, 78.31
settlement by agreement, 4.4, 5.3
Special Commissioners, 4.3
— hearing by, 4.6
Stated Case, 4.7
statutory construction, 4.7
time limits, 4.2
withdrawal of, 4.1
witnesses, 4.6
Apportionments,
emoluments, 75.2
losses, 46.10(*a*)
partnerships, 53.5
profits, 71.3
Approved profit-sharing schemes, 82.9, 82.10
Approved share option schemes, 82.38, 82.39, 82.40
Armed forces, 75.27
allowances, bounties and gratuities, 29.31, 75.27
bravery awards, annuities, 29.6
exempt income, 29.6, 29.31–29.33
gallantry awards, 29.6
leave travel facilities, 75.27
PAYE, 55.28
Schedule E, 75.2(i), 75.27
terminal grants etc., 19.6(vii)
uniform allowances, 75.27
visiting, 30.21
war gratuities, pensions, etc., 29.31–29.33
war service death pensions, 29.32
wound and disability pensions, 29.33, 59.4(ii), 83.4
Arrears,
deduction of tax in, 23.8
due to official error, 38.A19, 56.6
tax, 56.3
— interest on, 42
Artificial transactions, 3.1
Artist(e)s, 75.24
capital sum in lieu of earnings, 3.10
copyright receipts, 71.51
employment or profession, 75.24
trading receipts, 71.43
Arts associations, 15.2(b)
'Ash cash', 71.60

Assemblies (Northern Ireland and Wales), Members of,
accommodation,
— allowances, 29.16
— expenses, 75.29(B)
capital allowances, 10.24
ministers, etc.,
— transport and subsistence, 29.16
overnight expenses, 29.16
reimbursed expenses, 29.16
retirement schemes, 66.11
termination payments, 75.41
travel expenses, 29.16
Assessable profits, 71.40
ASSESSMENTS, 5
additional, power to make, 5.3
agreement of, 4.4, 5.3
alternative, 5.4
appeal against, 4.2
back duty, 6.4
basis of,
— Schedule A, 68.20
— Schedule B, 69.2
— Schedule C, 70
— Schedule D Cases I and II, 71.3–71.24
— Schedule D Case III, 72.3, 72.4
— Schedule D Cases IV and V, 73.5, 73.9
— Schedule D Case VI, 74.3
— Schedule E, 75.1
— Schedule F, 76
capital allowances exceeding, 10.3, 10.7, 10.9, 10.17, 10.32, 10.49, 10.50, 10.52
choice of, by Revenue, 5.2
Commonwealth citizens, 64.5
construction industry sub-contractors, 21.7
current year basis, 5.1, 78.2
— capital allowances, 10.1, 10.2(vi)(vii), 10.17, 10.32, 10.52
— double tax relief, 25.5(*j*)(*n*)
— farming, 71.57(*a*)
— losses, 46.3, 46.7, 46.12, 46.15, 46.18
— overlap profits, 25.5(*j*), 71.19, 71.22
— partnerships, 53.1, 53.3, 53.6, 53.11, 53.14(i)
— Schedule D, Cases I and II, 71.11–71.24
— Schedule D, Case III, 72.4(*e*)(*f*)
— Schedule D, Cases IV and V, 73.9
— Schedule D, Case VI, 74.3
date of, 5.7
deceased persons, on, 6.5
discovery, 5.3, 78.15
double, 5.4
employments, 75.1
error or mistake, 17.10
exclusiveness of Schedules, 5.2
extended time limits, 6.4
final and conclusive, 5.5
fraud, wilful default or negligence, 6.2, 6.3
fraudulent or negligent conduct, 6.4
further assessments, 5.3, 17.11
husband and wife, 47.1
individuals and partnerships, 5.9
Lloyd's underwriters, 89.4
minors, 16.3
mistake in, 5.1
non-resident trading in UK, 51.4–51.9
notice of, 5.1
offshore funds, 52.7, 52.8
partnerships, 53.3
pensions, 59.1, 59.2
personal representatives, 22.1
procedure, 5.1, 78.30
recovery of over-repaid tax, 56.8
remittances, 63.3
Sch A, 68.20
B, 69.2
C, 70
D, Cases I and II, 71.1, 71.3-71.24
III, 72.3, 72.4
IV & V, 73.5, 73.9
VI, 74.3
E, 75.1, 75.7
F, 76
self, 78, *and see* Self-assessment
time limits, 5.7, 78.30
— back duty, 6.4
tolerance limit, 5.8
trades, on, 71.1, 71.3–71.24
trust income, 81.3
underwriters, 89.4
whether to best of assessor's judgment, 5.1
Assets,
capital allowances, 10
lease of, capital sum received, 3.14
settlements, transferred to, 81.16(*e*)
transferred abroad, 3.8, 74.32
Associated companies, interest on debts between, accrued income scheme, 74.27
Associated persons, transactions between, 3.9

97 Index

Assured tenancy housing,
business expansion scheme, 26.19
capital allowances, 10.9
Athletes, 71.37
Atomic Energy Authority, 84.2
Auctioneers,
returns by, 67.9
Authors, *see* Artist(e)s
Averaging of profits, 17.2, 71.57(a)
Avoidance, 3
associated persons, transactions between, 3.9
capital sums received in lieu of earnings, 3.10
commodity futures, dealings in, 3.20
connected persons, 20
Courts, approach of, 3.1
general principles, 3.1
income from personal activities, sale of, 3.10
interest payments, restriction of relief, 43.2(ii), 43.3
land,
— leaseback transactions, 3.12, 3.13
— transactions in, 3.11
leaseback transactions, 3.12, 3.13
leases, assets other than land, 3.14, 3.15
loan transactions, 3.16
manufactured dividends, 3.7
non-taxable consideration, 3.19
sale and leaseback, 3.12, 3.13
schemes, not trading, 71.29
securities,
— held for one month or less, 3.6
— sale of with right to repurchase, 3.3, 3.5, 3.7, 33.3
— transactions in, 3.2
— transfers of income arising from, 3.4
transfer of assets abroad, 3.8
Award schemes, 75.7, 75.40, 75.44(a)

B

BACK DUTY, 6
accountants' working papers, 6.8
advocates, 6.10
agent, fraud or wilful default by, 6.2
assessments, 6.4
barristers, 6.10
certificate of disclosure, 6.7
claims, 6.1
criminal proceedings, 6.11, 58.10
deceased persons, 6.5
discovery, 5.3
documents, powers to obtain, 6.8
extended time limits, 6.4
fraud, 6.2
independent taxation, 6.7
interest on contract settlements, 6.11
interest on underpaid tax, 6.6
international information exchange, 35.13, 36.2(*c*)
investigatory powers, 6.8
judicial review, 4.8
monetary settlements, 6.11, 58.7
neglect, 6.3
offers, 6.11
penalties, 58
prerogative orders, application for, 4.8
production of documents, 6.8
proof, onus of, 6.2
retirement annuity relief, 6.11
returns, failure to make, 6.3, 67.1
search and seizure, 6.9
settlements, 6.11
solicitors, 6.10
time limits, 6.4, 6.5
understated profits, 6.7
unpaid tax, interest on, 42
wife's income, omission of, 6.2
wilful default, 6.2
Bad debts, 71.44
received after discontinuance, 62.1
Balancing allowances and charges,
agricultural land and buildings, 10.3
cessation of trade, 10.28
dredging, 10.7
dwelling-houses, 10.9
excess liability, 28.2(*g*)
industrial buildings, 10.15
know-how, 10.23
machinery and plant, 10.30, 10.32, 10.37
mines, etc., 10.44, 10.49
patents, 10.50
scientific research, adjustments, 10.52
ships, 10.30
BANKRUPTCY, 7
payment of tax, 56.5
penalties after, 58.9
BANKS, 8
associates of, interest paid to, 74.27
deposits with, 8.2
interest,
— deduction of tax, 8.2
— received by charities, 15.5
non-resident, 51.9
— exempt income, 30.2
returns of interest by, 67.4

Barristers,
basis of assessment, 12
law books, 10.25
production of documents, 6.10
Basic rate, 1.3, 1.5
income tax, payment, 56, 57
Scottish variation, 1.3
Basis of assessment, 5.9
current year, *see* Current year basis of assessment
remittances, 63
Sch A, 68.20
B, 69.2
C, 70
D, Cases I & II, 71.3-71.24
III, 72.3, 72.4
IV & V, 73.5, 73.9
VI, 74.3
E, 75.1
F, 76
Basis periods,
capital allowances, 10.17, 10.32, 10.52
trading profits, 71.3–71.9
Beneficial loans, 75.17
'Beneficial occupation', 75.29
Beneficiaries, 81.2(b)
claims by, 81.11
income of, 81.8
settlements, 81
sums paid to, 22.3
Benefits,
asset transfer costs, 75.13(xxi)
award schemes, 75.40, 75.44(*a*)
bus services, 75.13(xxv)
cars, 75.15
cash equivalent, 75.13
cash vouchers, 75.44
cheque voucher, 75.44
child care facilities, 75.13(xvii)
Christmas parties, 75.13(xvi)
compensation for loss of employment, on, 19.5
computer equipment, 75.13(xxiv)
counselling, 75.13(xxvii)
credit tokens, 75.44
cycles etc., 75.13(xxvi)
directors or higher-paid employees, 75.11
disability, 29.12, 71.64, 75.37
education, 75.42
examination awards, 75.13
expenses, 75.12
— advances for, 75.17
general charge, 75.13
gifts from third parties, 75.13(xvi), 75.26
incentive awards, 75.40, 75.44(*a*)
light refreshments, 75.13(iv)
living accommodation, 75.29
loans, 75.17
loss of employment, on, 19.5
meal vouchers, 75.30
meals, 75.13(iv)
medical check-ups, 75.13(xx)
medical expense insurance, 75.37
Members of Parliament, 29.16
miners' coal, 29.17
mobile telephones, 75.13(xxiii), 75.15, 75.16
moves to higher-cost housing areas, 75.29
non-cash vouchers, 75.44
notice of nil liability, 75.22
nurseries, 75.13(xvii)
parking facilities, 75.13(xiv)
PAYE, 55.15
petrol, 75.15
pooled cars, 75.15
private use of assets, 75.13(xxvii)
— cars, 75.15
removal expenses, 75.13(x)
returns of, 55.9, 67.5, 78.37
Schedule E, 75.8, 75.11
scholarships, 75.20
security assets and services, 75.35
shareholdings, 75.19, 82
sickness, 29.12, 71.64, 75.37
Social Security, 83.3–83.5
tax-free payments, 75.40
tea, coffee, etc., 75.13(iv)
telephones, mobile, 75.15, 75.16
third party, provision by, 75.13(xv)
training courses, 75.42
travel, etc. expenses, 75.13(v)–(ix)
VAT on, 55.9, 75.13
value-shifting, from, 3.19
welfare counselling, 75.13(xxvii)
works bus service, 75.13(xxv)
Benevolent funds, 15.2(c)
Betterment levy,
mineral royalties, 49.1
Betting, 71.30, 71.33
Bicycles, *see* Cycles
Blackmail, 71.63
Blind persons relief, 1.19, 47.2
Board & lodging, 75.7, 75.43
Board of Inland Revenue, 35.1
amnesty, powers of, 35.4
care and management, powers of, 35.4
codes of practice, 35.7
concessions, extra-statutory, 38

Board of Inland Revenue
confidentiality of information held by, 36
explanatory pamphlets issued by, 37
penalties,
— mitigation of, by, 58.7
— proceedings for, by, 58.6
press releases issued by, 39
statements of practice issued by, 40
Taxpayers' Charter, 35.7
Boarding house keepers,
returns by, 67.8
Bond washing, 3.3, 74.6 *et seq.*
Bonus issues,
disallowance of reliefs, 3.18
exempt persons, restrictions, 3.18
stock dividend not treated as, 85.1
Bonuses,
deduction from profits, 71.54
loss of office, 19.3, 19.4
salary, 75.1
Bookmakers, 71.30
Branch or agency in UK, 51.4(b)
self-assessment, 51.5–51.8
Brewers,
receipts of, 71.45
Bridging loans, 75.17
British Museum, 30.3
British subjects abroad,
claims for non-residence, 64.7
ordinarily resident, 64.6
personal reliefs, 51.11
residence, 64.5(*b*)
working abroad, 75.3, 75.5
Builders,
property, assessability of receipts, 71.77
BUILDING SOCIETIES, 9
administration fees, 43.6
certificates of non-liability to income tax, 8.2
company, transfer of business to, 9.6
deduction of tax, 9.1, 9.3
interest and dividends, 9.3
— deduction of tax, 9.3
— excess liability on, 28.3(*a*)
— payable to, 9.4, 43.6–43.14
losses on shares in, 46.18
marketable securities, 9.3, 23.3(ii)
permanent interest bearing shares, 9.3, 23.3(ii)
transfer of business to company, 9.6
Building sub-contractors, 21
Buildings,
agricultural, 10.3
enterprise zones, in, 10.19
industrial, 10.10
Sch A, 68
Bus services,
benefits in mind, 75.13(xxv)
Business,
assets, replacement of, 71.79(*c*)
economic notes, Revenue, 71.28
enterprise investment scheme, 26
entertainment, 71.55
expansion scheme, 26.18 *et seq.*
franchising, 71.59
interest payable, 43.2
link organisations, 71.84
medium-sized, 10.27
new, 71.4, 71.11
passing to spouse, 71.9
premises, expense of, 71.78, 71.79
profits, double tax relief, 25.5(*c*)
small, 10.27
start up allowance, 71.85
stock-in-trade, 71.83
work-in-progress, 71.83
Business expansion scheme, 26.18 et seq.
anti-avoidance, 26.31
appeals relating to land, 26.21
approved investment funds, 26.19
assured tenancy housing, 26.19
CGT considerations, 26.31
carry-back of relief, 26.24
claims under, 26.26
conditions for relief, 26.19
date of issue of shares, 26.19, 26.27
disposal of shares, 26.19
'eligible shares', 26.22
enterprise investment scheme, interaction with, 26.25
holding companies, 26.30
housing, 26.19
information powers, 26.31
joint holdings, 26.19
land and buildings, 26.21
limits on relief, 26.25
loan-linked investments, 26.27
married persons, 26.29
nominees and bare trustees, 26.19
oil exploration, 26.19, 26.23
parallel trades, 26.20, 26.21
private rented housing, 26.19
'qualifying company', 26.21
'qualifying individual', 26.20
'qualifying trade', 26.23
relief under, 26.24
— claims, 26.26

Business expansion scheme
— limits, 26.25
— restriction of, 26.27
— withdrawal of, 26.27
reorganisation of share capital, 26.31
replacement capital, 26.27
research and development, 26.19
subscriber shares, 26.20
subscriptions, limits, 26.25
subsidiaries, 26.28
value received from company, 26.27
withdrawal of relief, 26.27
Business link organisations, 71.84
Business start up allowances, 71.85

C

Cable television,
capital allowances, 10.25
Canteens, 75.13(iv)
CAPITAL ALLOWANCES, 10
abortive expenditure, 10.12, 10.38(i)
Affordable Warmth programme, 10.34
agricultural buildings and works, 10.3
anti-avoidance, 10.9, 10.22(i), 10.38(iii), 10.50, 10.52
apportionments, procedure on, 10.2(i)
assured tenancy schemes, 10.9
balancing adjustments on cessation, 10.28
basis of assessment, 10.1, 10.2 (vi)(vii), 78.2
— industrial buildings, 10.17
— machinery or plant, 10.32
— scientific research, 10.52
cable television, 10.25
cars, 10.27(i), 10.28(A), 10.35(*a*), 10.37(*c*), 10.38(ii), 75.43
cemeteries and crematoria, 10.5
chargeable periods, 10.2(vi)
commercial buildings, 10.19
composite sales, 10.2(i)
computer software, 10.25
connected persons, 10.3, 10.7, 10.9, 10.22(i), 10.38(iii), 10.50, 10.52
contributions to capital expenditure, 10.2(ii), 10.25(i)
control of buyer by seller or vice versa, 10.3, 10.7, 10.9, 10.22(i), 10.52
double allowances, 10.2(iv), 10.3, 10.9, 10.17, 10.22(ii), 10.38(iv), 10.52
dredging, 10.7
dwelling-houses, 10.9
educational establishments, gifts to, 71.60
employment, in, 10.24, 75.43
enterprise zones, 10.19
entitlement to, 10.34
exceeding profits, 10.3, 10.7, 10.9, 10.17, 10.32, 10.49, 10.50, 10.52
farm animals, 10.25
farmhouse, 10.3
film production, 10.25, 71.58
finance leasing, 10.28, 10.38(iii)(vi), 71.68
fire safety, 10.25(i)
first-year allowances, 10.27, 10.35
forestry, 10.3, 93.3
gifts to educational establishments, 71.60
glasshouses, 10.25, 10.28(G)
grants and subsidies, 10.2(ii)
heat insulation, 10.25(ii)
highway undertakings, 10.11, 10.14–10.17
hire purchase, 10.38(vi)
hotels, 10.18, 10.25(v)
industrial buildings, 10.10 *et seq.*
— appropriation from trading stock, 10.12
— balancing allowances and charges, 10.15
— enterprise zones, 10.19
— hotels, 10.18
— initial allowances, 10.13
— let properties sold by developers, 10.14
— making of allowances and charges, 10.17
— private roads, 10.12
— qualifying buildings, 10.11
— qualifying expenditure, 10.12
— small workshops, 10.21
— writing-down allowances, 10.14
information and communications technology, 10.27
know-how, 10.23
lease rentals, 71.68
leasehold interests,
— apportionment of consideration, 10.2(i)
— exchanges and surrenders, 10.2(i)
— grant treated as sale, 10.14
— industrial buildings, 10.14, 10.15
leasing, machinery and plant, 10.28(E), 10.34, 10.35
— accounting practice, 10.24
— cars, 10.28(A), 10.38(ii)
— joint lessees, 10.35(*f*)
long-life assets, 10.28(G)
losses, increased by, 46.7
— unused on cessation, 46.7

Capital allowances
machinery and plant generally, 10.24 *et seq.*
— amendment of claim, 10.27, 10.28
— balancing allowances and charges, 10.30
— connected persons, 10.38(iii)
— eligible expenditure, 10.25
— entitlement to allowances (fixtures), 10.34
— farm animals, exclusion of, 10.25
— first-year allowances, 10.27, 10.35
— fixtures, entitlement to allowances for, 10.34
— information and communications technology, 10.27
— leasing, 10.35
— making of allowances and charges, 10.32
— medium-sized businesses, 10.27
— motor cars, 10.27(i), 10.28(A), 10.35(*a*), 10.37(*c*), 10.38(ii), 75.43
— notification of expenditure, 10.25
— old scheme (before 27 October 1970), 10.37
— renewals basis, change from, 10.38(x)
— restrictions on eligible expenditure, 10.26
— short-life assets, 10.28(F)
— small businesses, 10.27
— writing-down allowances, 10.28, 10.35
mines, oil wells, etc., 10.39–10.49
— balancing allowances and charges, 10.44
— disposal receipts, 10.43
— limitations on qualifying expenditure, 10.41
— machinery and plant allowances, 10.46
— making of allowances and charges, 10.45
— old scheme (before 1 April 1986), 10.49
— qualifying expenditure, 10.40
— transitional provisions, 10.47
— writing-down allowances, 10.42
motor cars, 10.27(i), 10.28(A), 10.35(*a*), 10.37(*c*), 10.38(ii), 75.43
partnership changes, effect on, 53.11
patent rights, 10.50
periods of account, 10.2(vi)
pooling basis, 10.37(*b*)
— exclusion, 10.37(*b*)
quarantine premises, 10.25(iv)
renewals, 10.38(x)
restaurants, 10.25(v)
roads, private, 10.12
Schedule A, 10.32, 68.7(*a*), 68.8, 68.15(v)
Sch E purposes, 10.24, 75.3(A)
scientific research, 10.52
security assets, 10.25
ships, 10.27, 10.28(B), 10.30, 10.37(*b*)
short life assets, 10.28(F)
small workshops, 10.21
sports pavilions, 10.11
sports stadiums, 10.25(iii)
subsidies, 10.2(ii)
successions to trades, 10.38(xi)
thermal insulation, 10.25(ii)
time limits, 86.2(*a*)(i)
time of expenditure, 10.2(iii)
toll roads, 10.11, 10.14–10.17
value added tax, and, 10.2(v), 10.13–10.15, 10.19, 10.27, 10.28, 10.34, 10.38(iii), 10.52
video tape rental, 71.72
wear and tear, 10.38(xii)
workshops, 10.21
writing-down allowances, 10.3, 10.7, 10.9, 10.14, 10.28, 10.35, 10.42, 10.50

CAPITAL GAINS TAX, 11
accrued income scheme, interaction with, 74.30
business expansion scheme, 26.31
charities, 15.8
compensation, 71.48(*a*)
damages, exemption, 71.48(*a*)
double tax relief, 25.5(*d*)
employee share ownership plans, 82.18
ESOTs, shares transferred to, 82.41
enterprise investment scheme, 26.17
enterprise management incentive schemes, 82.26
land, transactions in, 3.11
losses set against, 46.5
offshore income gains, effect of, 52.12
personal equity plans, shares transferred to, 29.21
post-cessation expenditure set against, 62.4
post-employment deductions set against, 75.23
rate, 11.3
remittance basis, 63.1(A)(i)
share option and incentive schemes, 82.2
trading losses set against, 46.5
trading stock, appropriation of, 71.83
venture capital trusts, 91.11–91.14
see also Tolley's Capital Gains Tax

Capital goods scheme (VAT)
capital allowances and, 10.2(v)
Capital profits, 71.40, 71.48
Capital redemption policies, 45.13(C)
Caravans,
furnished letting of, 74.4
mortgage interest, 23.13, 43.17
overseas letting of, 73.3
sites, treatment of income from, 68.4
Care for children, 75.13(xvii)
Carers, 71.72
Cars,
benefits, 75.15
capital allowances, 10.27(i), 10.28(A), 10.37(*c*)
— leasing, 10.28(A), 10.35(*a*), 10.38(ii)
— part private use, 10.28(C), 75.43
Class 1A national insurance contributions, 83.7
company, 75.15
disabled, for, 29.28, 75.15
employer, provided by, 75.15
fines, 71.90, 75.7, 75.13
fuel, 75.15
garage allowances, 75.7
hiring, 10.28(A)
mileage allowances, 71.90, 75.43
parking facilities, 75.7, 75.13(xiv), 75.43, 75.44(*a*)(*d*)
pooled, 75.15(v)
Schedule E expenses, 75.43
sharing arrangements, 75.13(vii), 75.43
telephones, 75.15, 75.16
use by employees, 75.15
Case Stated, 4.7
CASH BASIS, 12
post-cessation receipts, 62.2
withdrawal, 12.2
Cash equivalent, 75.13
Cash vouchers, 75.44
Cashbacks, 71.46
Cemeteries and crematoria, 10.5
Central African Pension Fund, 59.4(v)
Central banks, non-resident, 51.9
exempt organisations, 30.2
Certificate of disclosure, 6.7
Certificate of tax deducted, 23.7
CERTIFICATES OF DEPOSIT, 13
building society, issued by, 9.3
paperless, 8.2, 9.3, 13.3
CERTIFICATES OF TAX DEPOSIT, 14
Certiorari, 4.8
Cessation of trade, 71.9, 71.17, 71.25, 71.26
balancing adjustment, 10.28
balancing charge on sale of building after, 10.17
capital allowances unused on, 46.7
receipts after, 62
redundancy payments, additional, 71.54
successions on, 71.25, 71.26
Channel Islands, 51.13
double tax relief, 25.4(*b*)
Charges on income, 1.10
accounting for tax deducted, 23.1
deduction of tax from partnership, 53.3(iii)
excess liability, 28.4
CHARITIES, 15
accrued income scheme, 74.21
agency, 15.18
almshouses, 15.2(*a*)
arts, organisations for promotion of, 15.2(*b*)
benevolent funds, etc., 15.2(*c*)
capital gains, 15.8
claims by, 15.3
covenanted payment to, 15.17, 28.4(*b*), 81.22, 81.24, 81.29(vii)
displaced persons relief, 15.21
education, 15.2(*d*)
— advancement of, overseas, 15.21
— land held for, 15.1
employees seconded to, 71.54
exemptions from tax, specific, 15.3–15.9
fund-raising events, 15.7(ii)
gift aid, 15.10–15.16
gifts by traders, 15.19, 15.21, 71.84
gifts in kind, 15.9–15.21
hospitals, 15.2(*e*)
income from settlements, 81.14, 81.27
inspection of records of, 15.3
investment income, 15.5, 15.6
land, 15.4
— educational purposes, for, 15.1
lotteries, 15.7(iii)
medical, overseas, 15.21
overseas relief, 15.21
payroll deduction scheme, 15.18
political organisations not charitable, 15.2(*f*)
poorest countries, gifts for relief in, 15.21
poverty relief, overseas, 15.21
professional associations, etc., 15.2(*g*)
public schools, 15.2(*h*)
qualifying donations, 1.10(iii), 15.10–15.16, 15.21
qualifying expenditure, 15.10

Charities
qualifying investments, 15.10
qualifying loans, 15.10
refugee relief, 15.21
religious organisations, 15.2(*i*)
rents, 15.4
repayments to, 15.17
restrictions on relief, 15.10, 28.4(*b*), 81.29(vii)
Schedule F transitional relief, 15.6
securities, accrued income scheme, 74.21
shares and securities, gifts of, 15.20
tax credits, 15.6
trading activities, 15.7
trading stock donated to, 15.19, 15.21, 71.60
underwriting commissions, 15.7(iv)
unit trust schemes, 15.9
Charity Commissioners, 15.1
Cheque voucher, 75.44
Child care facilities, 75.13(xvii)
CHILDREN, 16
additional relief for, 1.17
adopted, 1.17, 16.5, 29.1, 81.23
adult, covenants to, 81.29
assessability of, 16.2, 16.3
care for, 75.13(xvii)
child care facilities, 75.13(xvii)
contingent and vested interests of, 81.12
court orders, 47.10
covenants to, 81.18, 81.23
domicile, 64.4
education policies for,
— deduction of tax from, 23.11(*f*)
illegitimate, 1.17, 81.18, 81.23
maintenance payments for, 1.8(i), 47.10
nurseries, 75.13(xvii)
returns and claims by, 16.3
settlements, 81.18, 81.23
— claim for personal allowances, 81.12
tax credit for, 1.15, 1.18
Civil servants,
pensions, 59.1(ii)
CLAIMS, 17
additional allowances, 17.6
additional assessments, 17.11
appeals, 17.9, 78.31, 78.33
back duty, 6.1
beneficiaries, by, 81.11
charities, 15.17(*e*)
double tax relief, 25.5(*e*)
electronic, 17.5
error or mistake, 17.1, 17.10
form of, 17.6
further assessments, 17.11
incapacitated person, for, 17.5, 81.11
partnership, 17.1
personal allowances, 1.11
— on income of contingent interest, 81.12
procedure for making, 17.5
repayment, 17.6
self-assessment, 17.1–17.4
telephone, 17.5
time limits for, 17.4, 17.8
trustees, by, 81.11
Class 4 national insurance contributions, 1.10(viii), 83.7
interest on, 42.2
personal pension schemes and, 60.1, 83.7
repayment supplement, 41.2
retirement annuities and, 65.1, 83.7
self-assessment, 78.17
Clearance,
employee trusts, 82.41
Inland Revenue rulings, 35.6
redundancy payments, 19.3
transactions,
— land, 3.11
— securities, 3.2
Clergymen, 75.9
Climate change levy,
interest on, 42.10
penalties, 58.12
Close companies,
loans for purchase of interest in, 43.19
loans to participators, 28.3(*a*)(ii)
Closing years of trade, assessment, 71.9, 71.17
Clothing allowances, 71.74, 75.7
CLUBS AND SOCIETIES, 18
transfer fees, 71.72
Coal, free, for miners, 29.17
Codes of Practice, 35.7
open Government, 35.10
Collecting agents, *see* Paying and collecting agents
Collection of tax, 56.3
held over, interest on unpaid tax, 42.3
occupier or agent, from, 68.21
PAYE, 55.1
Sch A, tax, from occupier, etc. 68.21
self-assessment, 78.35
service abroad, 51.3
wife, income tax from, 47.1
Collective investment schemes, 90.1
Collectors of taxes, 35.2
payment to under PAYE, 55.8
powers of, 56.3

Collectors of taxes
unauthorised demands by, 41.3
Commencement of trade, 71.4, 71.11, 71.25, 71.26
successions, 71.25, 71.26
Commission, 71.46
agreements, cancellation of, 71.47, 71.48
insurance, 71.64
underwriting, 15.7(iv)
Commissioners,
appeals to, 4.3 *et seq.*
General, 4.3, 35.3
hearings by, 4.6
Inland Revenue, of, 35.1
jurisdiction, 4.3, 78.33
Special, 4.3, 35.3
Commodity futures, 3.20, 71.32
Commonwealth citizens,
accrued income scheme, 74.10(*e*)
deep gain securities of, 44.7(3)
personal allowances, 51.11
remittance basis, 51.12, 73.5(*b*)
residence of, 64.5
Community charge, 68.15, 71.54, 71.78, 75.7, 75.9, 75.10, 75.29, 75.43
standard, 75.13(x), 75.43
Commutation of annual payments,
compensation, 71.47, 71.48
royalties, 71.51
Commuting, 75.10(a)
Companies,
business transferred to, losses, 46.12(*c*)
capital allowances, 10.1
cars, *see* Motor cars
commencement of trade, 71.25, 71.26
connected persons, 20.5–20.8
deduction of tax from interest, by, 23.3
discontinuance of trade, 71.25, 71.26
discretionary trust payments to, 81.5
distributions, 1.9, 3.21, 28.2(*d*), 76
double tax relief, 25.7
interest on unpaid tax, 42.5
interest paid by, 43.1
interest paid to, 9.5(*d*)
investment in, 26, 46.18
partnership, 53.14
payment of tax, 56.4
personal service, 61
purchase of own shares, 1.9, 3.21
residence, 51.4(*c*)
Schedule D, Case I, 71.2
securities held for one month, 3.6(*d*)
securities issued by, 44.5–44.9
settlements, connected with, 81.19
share dealing, dividend stripping, 3.7
share schemes, 82
trading income, assessability, 71.2
transactions in securities, 3.2
Compensation received,
additional voluntary contribution schemes, mis-sold, for, 29.3
amateur status, loss of, 75.7
damages, reduction for tax, 19.7
death, injury, disability, 19.6(i)
employment, loss of, 19
— £30,000 exemption, 19.5
— exceptions from charge, 19.6
— PAYE return, 55.9
farm animals, 34.7, 34.8, 71.57
gifts, testimonials, etc., 71.48(*e*), 75.26
Gourley principle, 19.7
Holocaust victims, 29.7, 29.13(xi)
legal costs, 19.6(viii)
milk quotas, 71.57(*g*)
mis-sold pensions products, for, 29.3
Nazi victims, exemptions, 29.7, 29.13(xi)
PAYE return, 55.9
payable, Sch D, 71.47
— to employees, 71.54
payments in lieu of notice, 19.3, 75.45
personal injury, for, 29.4, 29.13(i)
personal pensions, mis-sold, for, 29.3
premature retirement, 19.6(i)
receipts, assessability, Sch D, 71.48
— capital assets, 71.48(*c*)
— capital sums, 71.48(*a*)
— compulsory acquisition, 71.48(*d*)
receipts, assessability, Sch E, 19.3, 19.5
redundancy payments, 19.5, 75.32
slaughter of animals, 34.8, 71.57
terminal payments, 19.5
transfer fee, 19.3, 75.7
wages in lieu of notice, 19.3, 75.45
Competent authority, 25.2
Computer equipment,
benefits in kind, 75.13(xiv)
Computer software, 10.25, 71.72
Codes of practice, 35.7
CONNECTED PERSONS, 20
anti-avoidance provisions, 3.5, 3.7, 3.9, 3.11, 3.12, 3.16
beneficial loans, 75.17
benefits in kind,
— employee shareholdings, 75.19
— entertainment, 75.13(xv)
— living accommodation, 75.29
— loans, 75.17
— scholarships, 75.20

Connected persons
business expansion scheme, 26.21, 26.23, 26.27, 26.28, 26.31
capital allowances,
— agricultural buildings allowances, 10.3
— assured tenancy housing, 10.9
— contributors, 10.2(ii)
— dredging, 10.7
— fixtures, 10.34
— industrial buildings, 10.14, 10.15, 10.22(i)
— leasing, 10.35
— mines, etc., 10.49(C)
— patent rights, 10.50
— plant and machinery, 10.27, 10.28(F), 10.30, 10.31, 10.34, 10.35, 10.37, 10.38(ii)(iii)(xi)
— scientific research allowances, 10.52
— successions, 10.7, 10.38(xi)
charitable donations, 15.8(i), 71.60
companies, 20.5–20.8
credit tokens, 75.44(*d*)
current year basis transitional rules, 71.20, 72.4(*f*)
deep gain securities, 44.7
discounts on securities, 72.2(i)
educational establishments, gifts to, 71.60
employee share ownership trusts, 82.41
employee shareholdings, 75.19, 82.4, 82.5
enterprise investment scheme, 26.3, 26.5, 26.7, 26.12, 26.14, 26.16, 26.19(iii)
gifts to educational establishments, 71.60
herd basis, 34.9
individuals, 20.2
interest payable, 43.17
investment managers, 51.5(3)
lease premiums, 68.27
local enterprise agencies, contributions to, 71.84
losses, 46.9
non-resident entertainers and sportsmen, 51.8
offshore funds, 52.12(*c*)
partners, 20.4
PAYE, 55.3
pension schemes, 66.4
post-employment deductions, 75.23
qualifying convertible securities, 44.8
qualifying donations, 15.13, 15.14
rents, 68.14
securities,
— deep gain, 44.7
— discount on, 72.2(i)
— qualifying convertible, 44.8
— sale and repurchase, 74.23
settlements, 81.19, 81.28
share incentives, 75.19, 81.4, 81.11
stock valuation, 71.83
trade associations, contributions to, 71.84
trustees, 20.3
venture capital trusts, 90.3(*f*)
vouchers, 75.44(*a*)
CONSTRUCTION INDUSTRY TAX SCHEME, 21
administration, 21.7
carpet fitting, 21.2
construction operations, definition, 21.2
contractor, definition, 21.2
deduction of tax from payments, 21.2, 21.7
failure to make deductions, 21.7
old scheme, 21.8
penalties, 21.7, 58.4
registration cards, 21.3
small payments, exclusion of, 21.2
sub-contractor's tax certificate, 21.4
— misuse of, 21.7
— renewal application, 21.6
transitional arrangements, 21.1
turnover threshold, 21.5
Construction workers, *see* Construction Industry Tax Scheme
agency workers, 75.46
travel and subsistence allowances, 75.43
Constructive remittances, 63.4
Consul & consular employees, 24
Contemplative religious communities, 38.B10
Contingent interests, 81.12
Contingent liabilities, 71.49
Contracts,
profits from, 71.48, 71.50
Contractual savings schemes,
interest and bonuses, 29.13(vi)
savings-related share option schemes, 82.38
share option and incentive schemes, 82
Controlled sales, 3.9
Conventional basis, 12.1, 62.2
Convertible securities, 44.8
Co-operatives,
loans to purchase interest in, 43.20
mutual trading, 50.1
profit-sharing schemes in workers' co-operatives, 83.6

Copyright and design and public lending rights,
assignment by executor, exemption, 62.1(ii)
author, receipts, 71.51
owner abroad, taxation of royalties, 23.3(iii), 23.15, 51.10
public lending right payments, 23.3(iii), 23.15, 51.10
receipts, spreading of, 17.2, 71.51
returns, 67.6
royalties, 17.2, 71.51
— annual sums to non-residents, 51.10
— deduction of tax, 23.15(*a*)
— double tax relief, 25.5(*l*)
— non-residents, deduction of tax, 51.10
— treated as losses, 46.17(*a*)
sale after ten years or more, 71.51
self-assessment, 17.2
Corporation tax, *see* Companies *and Tolley's Corporation Tax*
Costs, award of, 4.9
Councillors, 55.32, 71.48(*e*), 75.7
Counselling, 75.42
benefits-in-kind exemption, 75.13(xxvii)
Country-risk debts, 71.44
County Court,
Northern Ireland, appeals, 4.3
recovery of tax in, 56.3
Coupon-stripping, 44.6
Court,
Appeal, of, 4.7
avoidance transactions, approach to, 3.1
common investment funds, 90.2, 90.3
county,
— Northern Ireland, 4.3
— recovery of tax in, 56.3
decisions, of, 4.7
High, appeals to, 4.7
Orders, 47.10
Session, of, 4.7
Covenants,
charitable, 15.17
children, to, 81.23
— adult, 81.29
covenanted payment to charity, 15.17, 28.4(*b*), 81.22, 81.24, 81.29(vii)
escape clauses, 15.17(*d*)
excess liability, 81.29
requirements, 81.22
restrictive, 28.3(*a*)(iii), 75.34
retrospective validation of, 15.17(*c*)
revocable, 81.24
settlement, 81.21(*a*)
six-year rule, 81.22
subscriptions, 15.17(*b*)
three-year rule, 81.22
Credit tokens, 75.44
Credit traders, 71.44
Credit Unions, 29.13(ix)
Cremation fees, 71.60
Crematoria, 10.5
Criminal payment, 71.63
Criminal penalties, 58.10
Crown,
exempt, 30.6
pensions, 59.1(ii)
priority, 56.5
— PAYE, 55.18
servants, overseas, 43.6, 75.2(i), 92.1
Currency,
gains and losses, 71.56
unremittable income, 51.14
unremittable trade receipts, 71.92
Current year basis of assessment, 5.1, 78.2
anti-avoidance, 43.22, 71.20, 71.22, 72.4(*f*), 73.9, 78.2
capital allowances, 10.1, 10.2(vi)(vii)
— industrial buildings, 10.17
— machinery or plant, 10.32
— scientific research, 10.52
double tax relief, 25.5(*j*) (*n*)
farming, 71.57(*a*)
losses, 46.3, 46.7, 46.10(*a*), 46.12, 46.15, 46.18
overlap profits, 71.19, 71.22
— double tax relief, 25.5(*j*)
— farming, 71.57(*a*)
partnerships, 43.22, 53.1, 53.3, 53.6, 53.11, 53.14(i)
Schedule D, Cases I and II, 71.11-71.24
Schedule D, Case III, 72.4(*e*)(*f*)
Schedule D, Cases IV and V, 73.9
Schedule D, Case VI, 74.3
Cycles,
mileage allowances, 75.43
parking facilities, 75.7, 75.13(xiv), 75.43, 75.44(*a*)(*d*)
provision by employer,
— benefits in kind, 75.13(xxvi)
safety equipment,
— benefits in kind, 75.13(xxvi)

D

Dairy herds, 34
Damages, *see also* Compensation received
reduction for tax, 19.7
Dates,
cessation, 71.9, 71.17, 71.25, 71.26
change of ownership, 71.25, 71.26
commencement of business, 71.4, 71.11, 71.25, 71.26
due, interest on unpaid tax, 42
due, interest on overpaid tax, 41
payment of tax, 56.1, 57
Dealers in securities, 71.82
non-resident, 51.9
securities held for one month or less, 3.6(*a*)
Death,
administration of estates, 22.3
back-duty, 6.5
before tax paid, 42.9
deceased estates, 22
discontinuance of business on, 71.9
employee, of, 55.23
excess liability on, 28.6
executor's claims and liability, 22.2
married person, 1.15, 1.16, 47.9
partners, 53.6(*c*)
payments for loss of office on, 19.6(i)
securities, deemed transfer on, 74.15
Ulster savings certificates, 33.6
Debts,
bad and doubtful, 71.44
losses on transactions in, 13.2
overseas governments etc., 71.44
PAYE, 55.2
received after discontinuance, 62.1
unclaimed, 71.91
unremittable trade, 71.92
DECEASED ESTATES, 22
Deceased persons,
back duty, 6.4, 6.5
Decorations,
annuities exempt, 29.6
DEDUCTION OF TAX AT SOURCE, 23
advance corporation tax, 76.3
annual payments, 1.8(i), 23.10
annuities, 23.11, 60.1, 65.1
change of tax rate, 23.6
charitable donations, 15.16, 15.17
construction sub-contractors, 21.2
dividends, 76.2
entertainers, non-resident, 36.2(*h*), 51.8
Eurobonds, 23.3(ii)
foreign agreements, under, 23.4
foreign dividends, 23.12
Government stocks, 33.3
interest, 1.9, 8.2, 9.3, 43.1, 43.2, 53.14(ii)
international organisations, by, 24.1
local authorities, 23.12
loss relief, 23.3(i)
medical insurance, 48
mortgage interest, 23.13
non-resident, by, 23.4
omission to deduct, 23.8, 47.10
PAYE, 55
pension premiums, 60.1, 66.5(*a*)
public revenue dividends, 23.3(ii)
rate change, 23.6
rents, 68.24
retrospective, 23.8(*b*)
Sch D, Case I or II, 71.51
III, 72.3(*a*)
Sch F, 76.2
sportsmen, non-resident, 36.2(*h*), 51.8
UK public revenue dividends, 23.3(ii)
vocational training costs, 71.89, 75.42
Deductions working sheets, 55.6
Deeds of covenant, 15.17
Deep discount securities, 29.29, 44.5, 44.8, 44.9
coupon-stripping, 44.6
Deep gain securities, 29.29, 44.7
Default,
back duty assessment, 6.2, 6.4
interest on unpaid tax, 42.8
Deferred delay appeals, 4.5
Delayed remittances, 51.14
Demolition,
costs, capital allowances, 10.15
Dependent relatives,
property occupied by, interest relief, 43.9
Deposits,
assessability, Schedule D Case I, 71.91
certificates of, 13
Deposit-takers, 8.2
Depreciation, *see also* Capital Allowances
charged in accounts, 10.1
Derivatives, use of, 3.22
Design rights, *see* Copyright and design and public lending rights
Dilapidations, 71.79(b)
DIPLOMATIC IMMUNITY, 24
Directors,
benefits, 75.11
compensation for loss of office, 19
emoluments, 75.1, 75.11

Directors
expenses, 75.12
fees of professional partnerships, 75.24
fees received by other companies, 75.1(1)
living accommodation, 75.29
loans on property for company use, 43.3(ii)
personal pension schemes, 60
— relevant earnings, 60.8
remuneration, 75.1
— credit to account, 55.19
retirement annuities, 65
— relevant earnings, 65.7
retrospective remuneration, 75.1
Sch E, 75.11
— receipts basis, 75.1
share schemes, 82
shares transferred to, 75.36
tax-free payments, 75.40
travelling expenses, 75.13(ix)
Disability,
benefits, 29.12, 71.64
— paid during absence from work, 75.37
— retirement annuities, 65.7
— travel from home to work, 75.13(vi), 75.15, 75.43
car provided for disabled person, 75.15
cessation of employment caused by, 19.6(i)
disabled person's tax credit, 83.4, 83.6
— information, 36.3
— PAYE, 55.20
employee benefits, 75.15, 75.43
insurance, 29.12, 71.64, 75.37
loss of office, payment for, 19.6(i)
payments, 59.1
pensions, 59.4(iii)
vehicle maintenance grant, 29.28
Disclosure of information,
Inland Revenue, by, 36.2
Discontinuance,
partnership, 53.6
trade, 71.9, 71.17, 71.25, 71.26
valuation of stock on, 71.83
Discounts, 71.45
Discounts on securities, 44.5, 44.8, 44.9, 72.2
accrued income scheme, 74.30
Sch D, Case III, 72.2, 72.3(*b*)
Treasury securities, 33.4
Discovery, 5.3
documents of, 4.8, 35.4
self-assessment, 78.15
Discretionary trusts, 81.5
Disincorporation,
capital allowances, 10.38(xi)
succession to trade, 71.25
Dispensations, 75.22
Dispositions,
three and six year rules, 81.22
Distilleries,
receipts of, 71.45
Distraint, 56.3
Divers, 71.31
Dividends and distributions, 1.9
abnormal amount, 3.2
building society shares, 9.6
deduction of tax, Sch F, 76.2
double taxation, 25.6
due after death, 22.2
equivalent foreign income, 1.9
excess liability, 28.2(*d*)
foreign, 23.12, 38.C1
— securities, 73.3
foreign income, 1.9, 3.6, 3.7, 3.21, 22.3, 76.3, 81.3, 81.5, 89.3, 90.1
manufactured, 3.7, 3.21, 74.32
non-residents, to, 25.6
offshore funds, from, 52.5, 52.6
own share purchase, 1.9, 3.21
personal service companies, paid by, 61.14
pre-sale, 3.21
sale of right to, 3.4
savings income, 1.9
Sch F, 76
special, 3.21, 81.5
stock dividends, 85
total income, 1.8(ii)
transactions in securities, 3.2
Divorce, 47.9, 47.10 *and see* Alimony
pension-sharing, 23.11(*c*)(vii), 60.2, 60.8, 66.1, 66.4
Doctors and dentists,
retirement schemes, 66.11
superannuation contributions, 66.11
Documents,
production of, 4.6(*a*), 6.8
Domestic workers, 55.21
Domicile, 64.1, 64.4 *and see* Residence, Ordinary Residence and Domicile
remittance basis, 63.1(A)
Double assessment, 5.4
DOUBLE TAX RELIEF, 25
see also Overseas Matters
accrued income scheme, interaction with, 74.31
agency profits, 51.4(*b*)

Double tax relief
agreements, 25.2
air transport agreements, 25.2
alimony, 25.5(*a*)
arising basis, 25.5(*b*)(ii)
capital gains, 25.3, 25.5(*d*)
carry back or forward, 25.5(*da*)
claims, 25.5(*e*)
companies, 25.7
competent authority, 25.2
credit, limits on, 25.5(*g*)
current year basis of assessment, 25.5(*n*)
— overlap profits, 25.5(*j*)
disclosure of information, 3.9, 36.2(*o*)
discretionary trusts, 81.5
double relief prevention, 25.5(*ka*)
Eire, 25.3
foreign entities, 25.2
foreign tax, 25.5(*b*)
— adjustments, 25.5(*e*)
— unilateral relief, 25.4
interest on overpaid tax, 25.2, 41.2
international information exchange, 35.13, 36.2(*c*)
know-how payments, 25.5(*l*)
limit on relief, 25.5(*g*)
Lloyd's underwriters, 25.5(*e*)(*h*)
mutual agreement procedure, 25.2
non-resident,
— interest paid to, 25.6
— participator, 25.2, 25.6
notional tax, 25.5(*i*)
opening and closing years, 25.5(*j*)
partnerships, 25.5(*k*), 53.15
payments abroad by UK residents, 25.6
permanent establishment, 25.2, 25.3
provisional treaty relief, 25.6
remittance basis, 25.5(*b*)
royalties and know-how, 25.2, 25.5(*l*)
shipping profits agreements, 25.2
special relationships, 25.2
tax credits, 25.2, 25.6
tax-exempt interest and dividends, 51.9(iii)
transfer pricing, 25.5(*m*)
unilateral relief, 25.4
unused relief, utilisation of, 25.5(*da*)
Doubtful debts, 71.44
Dredging, 10.7
Drilling rigs, leasing by non-residents, 51.13
Dwelling-houses let on assured tenancies, 10.9

E

Earned income, 1.7
Civil list pensions, 1.7(iii)
patents, 1.7(vi), 54.3
personal pensions, 60.1
retirement annuities, 65.1
Sch E, assessment, 75.1
Earned income relief,
wife's, 1.23
Earnings,
from working abroad,
— Sch E, 75.3
sale for capital sum, 3.10
Earnings basis, 12.2, 62.1, 71.40
Easements, 23.14
Easter offerings, 75.9
Education,
charity, 15.2(*d*)
employees, of, 71.54, 75.42
gifts to schools etc., 71.60
resident for, 64.6
sandwich courses, 29.26
scholarships, 29.27, 75.20
Educational bodies,
employees seconded to, 71.54
gifts to, 71.60
— overseas, 15.21
Eire,
double tax relief, 25.3
subjects becoming resident in UK, 73.11
subjects working in UK, 75.6
see also Tolley's Taxation in the Republic of Ireland
Elderly persons,
allowances, 1.14, 1.15, 1.24, 47.5
Elections, *see* Claims
Electronic,
communications, 35.12
returns, 67.3, 78.1
Embezzlement, 71.53
Emoluments,
abroad, 64.2
apportionment of, 75.2
cash vouchers, 75.44
charge under Schedule E, 75.1
compensation for loss of office, 19.3–19.6
deductibility under Schedule D, 71.54
deductions from, 75.10
earned income, 1.7
foreign, 75.6
— remittance basis, 63.1(A)(ii), 63.1(B)
insurance companies, paid by, 71.54
investment companies, paid by, 71.54

Emoluments
- maternity pay, 55.33
- PAYE, 55.2
- profit-related, 75.31
- receipts basis, 75.1
- received in UK, 75.2
- Schedule E, 75
- sick pay, 75.37
- tax paid on director's behalf, 75.40
- travel expenses of non-domiciled employees, 75.6

Employee-controlled companies,
- interest on loan to purchase shares in, 43.21

Employee share schemes, 82.3–82.41
- allowable deductions, 71.54
- conditional acquisitions, 82.7
- convertible shares, 82.8
- costs, 71.54
- enterprise management incentive schemes, 82.26–82.37
- profit-sharing schemes,
- — approval, 82.9
- — charge to tax, 82.10
- savings-related share option schemes, 82.38
- share incentives, 82.4, 82.5
- share options, 82.3, 82.38–82.40
- share ownership plans, 82.11–82.25
- share ownership trusts, 82.41
- unapproved, 82.4, 82.5

Employee trusts, 71.54, 81.5, 82.41

Employees,
- actors, 75.24
- amateur status, loss of, 75.7
- approved share option and incentive schemes, 82.9–82.40
- artistes, 75.24
- basis of assessment, 75.1
- benefits in kind, 75.8
- capital allowances, 10.24, 75.43
- cars, 75.15, 75.43
- cash equivalent, 75.13
- charities, seconded to, 71.53
- compensation, 19, 71.54
- construction industry, 21.7
- deductions for, Sch D, Cases I and II, 71.54
- disabled, 75.15, 75.43
- — benefits, 29.12, 75.37
- education, 71.54, 75.42
- emoluments, return of, 55.9, 67.5, 75.46
- entertainment of, 75.13, 75.44(*a*)(*d*)
- enterprise management incentive schemes, 82.26–82.37
- expenses, 75.5, 75.6, 75.9, 75.10, 75.12, 75.25 *et seq.*
- gifts to, 75.26
- higher-paid, 75.11
- indemnity insurance, 75.23
- liabilities of, 75.23
- living accommodation, 75.29
- loans to, 75.17
- long-service awards, 75.26
- loss of employment, 19
- mileage allowances, 75.43
- national insurance, 83.7
- non-UK domiciled, 75.2, 75.6
- overnight expenses, 75.13(xxii), 75.43, 75.44(*a*)
- overseas, 75.3–75.6
- part-time,
- — share schemes for, 75.31, 82.9, 82.38–82.41
- PAYE regulations, 55
- payments to, 71.54
- payroll deduction scheme, 15.18
- personal service companies etc., 61
- persons treated as, returns of, 67.5
- post-employment deductions, 75.23
- priority share allocations, 75.36
- profit-related pay, 75.31
- profit sharing schemes, 71.54, 82.9
- redundancy, 75.32
- relocation expenses, 75.13(x)
- restrictive covenants, 75.34
- retirement schemes, 66.1
- returns, 55.9, 67.5, 75.46, 78.37
- savings-related schemes, 82.38
- seconded to charities, 71.54
- seconded to education bodies, 71.54
- security of, 10.25, 75.35
- self-assessment returns, 78.37
- shareholdings, 75.19, 75.36, 82
- share ownership plans, 71.54, 82.11–82.25
- share ownership trusts, 71.54, 82.41
- share schemes, 82
- sickness benefits, 29.12, 75.37
- subsistence, etc. allowances, 75.13(xxii), 75.43
- suggestion scheme awards, 75.26
- training costs, 71.54, 71.89, 75.42, 92
- transfer fees, 19.3, 75.7
- travelling, etc., 75.43
- trusts for, 71.54, 81.5, 82.41
- vocational training, 92
- working abroad, 75.3–75.5

Employers,
associations, exempt, 30.18
helpline, 35.11
national insurance, 83.7
PAYE operated by, 55
quarterly payments, 55.8
returns by, 55.9, 67.5, 75.46, 78.37
self-assessment obligations, 78.37
Employment Zones programme, 83.4
Employments, 75
abroad, 75.3–75.5
compensation for loss of office, 19
directors and 'higher-paid', 75.11
loss of, 19
lump sums on taking up, 75.7
new deal option, 83.4
PAYE, 55
personal service companies, etc., 61
place of performance, 75.2
redundancy payment, 75.32
schedule of taxation, 21.7, 75.24
temporary in UK, 64.5
Endowment policies,
life assurance relief, 45.8
Enterprise, small or medium-sized,
capital allowances, 10.27
Enterprise allowance, 71.85
ENTERPRISE INVESTMENT SCHEME, 26
anti-avoidance, 26.2, 26.12
approval, provisional, 26.5
approved fund, 26.2
business expansion scheme, interaction with, 26.10
capital gains tax, 26.17
conditions for relief, 26.2
corporate venturing scheme, interaction with, 26.12
disposal of shares, 26.12
eligible shares, 26.4
excluded trades, 26.7
films, etc., 26.7
fund investment, 26.2
gross assets test, 26.5
holding companies, 26.16
husband and wife, 26.15
information, 26.17
interest on overpaid tax, 26.8
interest on unpaid tax, 26.11, 26.12
joint investors, 26.2
land and buildings, 26.5
loan linked investments, 26.12
losses, 26.8, 46.18
married persons, 26.15
nominees, 26.2
parallel trades, 26.3
pre-arranged exits, 26.12
property development, 26.7
qualifying business activity, 26.6
qualifying company, 26.5
qualifying individual, 26.3
qualifying trade, 26.7
relief,
— attribution of, 26.8
— claims, 26.11
— conditions, 26.2
— form of, 26.8
— limits, 26.10
— restrictions, 26.12
— withdrawal of, 26.12
replacement capital, 26.12
research and development, 26.2, 26.6
shares,
— date of issue, 26.2
— disposal of, 26.12
— eligible, 26.4
ship charters, 26.7
subsidiaries, 26.2(iii), 26.3, 26.14, 26.16
unquoted company, 26.5
value received, 26.12
withdrawal of relief, 26.12
Enterprise management incentive schemes, 82.26–82.37
Enterprise zones, 10.19
Entertainers, 75.24
non-resident, 36.2(*h*), 51.8
Entertaining expenses, 71.55
Equitable liability, 56.9
Error or mistake, 17.10
self-assessment, 17.1
ESOTs, 71.54, 82.41
Estate duty,
loan to pay, interest on, 43.23
Estate management, 68.7(*b*), 68.16(d)
expenses, 68.15
machinery and plant for use in, 10.24
Estates of deceased persons, 22
Estoppel, 5.3
Euro,
conversion to, 3.5, 3.7, 72.2, 74.7, 74.8, 74.19, 74.23
Eurobonds, 3.3, 3.6(*a*), 3.7(*c*), 9.3, 23.3(ii)
EUROPEAN COMMUNITY LEGISLATION, 27
European Economic Interest Groupings, 53.19
Evasion, 6
income tax fraud, 58.10

Evidence, 4.6
Examination awards, 75.7, 75.13
EXCESS LIABILITY, 28
Exchange control,
restrictions, interest on unpaid tax, 42.6
unremittable income, 51.14
unremittable trade receipts, 71.92
Exchange gains and losses, 71.56
Exchange rate,
effect on double tax relief, 25.5(*f*)
Exclusivity payments, 71.88
Executors,
assessments on, 22.1
interest on unpaid tax, 42.9
settlements, 81
trading by, 71.36
EXEMPT INCOME, 29
additional voluntary contribution scheme compensation, 29.3
adoption allowances, 29.1
annuities, personal injury, for, 29.4
compensation,
— loss of employment, for, 19
— mis-sold personal pensions, for, 29.3
— personal injury, for, 29.4, 29.13(i)
disability benefits, 29.12
foreign service allowance, 29.5
gallantry awards, 29.6
German and Austrian annuities, 29.7
Holocaust victims, 29.13(xi)
Hong Kong officials, 38.A39
housing grants, 29.9
individual savings accounts, 29.10, 29.13(iii), 29.21
interest, 29.10, 29.13
international organisations, income from, 24
long-service awards, 75.26
luncheon vouchers, 75.30
Members of Parliament, 29.16, 75.29
miners' free coal, 29.17
mortgage protection, 29.12
non-residents, 29.18
— partnerships, 53.15
notice, payments in lieu of, 19.3, 75.45
overseas income, 29.19
overseas pension funds, 59.4(vi), 59.6
pensions, 59.4
— products, mis-sold, compensation for, 29.3
personal equity plans, 29.21
personal injury compensation, 29.4, 29.13(i)
personal pensions compensation, 29.3
post-cessation receipts, 62.1
profit-related pay, 75.31
redundancy payments, 29.23, 75.32
repayment supplement, 29.24
retirement funds, 66.5(*b*)
sandwich courses, 29.26
Schedule C, 70
scholarship income, 29.27
sickness benefits, 29.12
social security benefits, 29.28
Treasury securities, discounts on, 29.29
wages in lieu of notice, 19.3, 75.45
war gratuities, 29.31
war widows, etc., 29.32
wound and disability pensions, 59.4(ii)
EXEMPT ORGANISATIONS, 30
agricultural societies, 30.1
banks, non-resident, 30.2
British Museum, 30.3
charities, 15
clubs and societies, 18
Crown, 30.6
diplomatic immunity, 24
friendly societies, 31
Historic Buildings and Monuments Commission for England, 30.9
Housing Associations, 30.10
International Maritime and Satellite Organisation, 30.11
local authorities, 30.12
mutual trading, 50
National Heritage Memorial Fund, 30.14
scientific research associations, 77
statutory bodies, 84
superannuation funds, 30.17
trade unions, 88
unit trusts for exempt unit-holders, 30.19
UK Ecolabelling Board, 30.20
venture capital trusts, 91
visiting forces, 30.21
Exempt persons,
bonus issues, 3.18
distribution relating to pre-acquisition profits, 3.17
Expenses,
agents' fees, 75.24
allowance for, 38.A5
deductible, 71.40 *et seq.*
employment, 75.5, 75.9, 75.10, 75.12, 75.25 *et seq.*
entertaining, 71.55
law costs of appeals, 71.69
legal and professional, 71.69
mining and quarrying, 71.71

Expenses
patents etc., 71.73
payments, 55.25, 75.12
— PAYE, 55.26
personal, 71.74
property, 71.77
rates, lighting, repairs, etc., 71.89, 75.29
removal, 75.13(x)
Sch A, 68.15, 68.16
Sch D, 71.40 *et seq.*
Sch E, 75.5, 75.9, 75.10, 75.12, 75.25 *et seq.*
travelling, 51.11, 75.5, 75.6, 75.43
Extortion, 41.3, 71.63
Extra-statutory concessions, 35.4, 38

F

False statements, 58
Farm drainage, 71.57
Farmhouses, 10.3
Farming,
agricultural buildings allowances, 10.3
agricultural gangmasters, 71.57(*c*)
agricultural societies, exemption, 30.1
animals, herd basis, 34
— capital allowances, excluded from, 10.25
— slaughter, 34.8, 71.57(*b*)
averaging of profits, 17.2, 71.57(*a*)
buildings, 10.3
business expansion scheme, 26.23(*h*)
computation of profits, Schedule D Case I, 71.57
current year basis, 71.57(*a*)
deficiency payments, 38.B6
drainage, 71.57(*b*)
EEC grant, 71.85
fluctuating profits, 17.2, 71.57(*a*)
grants, 71.57(*f*)
herd basis, 34
losses, 46.9(*b*)
maintenance expenses, 38.B5
milk receipts, 71.57(*g*)
NFU subscriptions, 71.57(*k*)
overlap profits, 71.57(*a*)
overseas, 71.1
Schedule A exemption, 68.4(iii)
Schedule D charge, 71.1
self-assessment, 17.2, 34.4, 34.8, 71.57(*c*)
share, 71.57(*d*)
short rotation coppice, 71.57(*i*)
stock-in-trade, etc., 71.57(*j*)
subsidies, 71.57(*f*)
trading profits, 71.57(*l*)
Fees and subscriptions, to professional bodies, 75.33
Feu duty, 71.77
Film, etc. technicians, 75.24
Film production, 10.25, 26.7, 71.58
video tape rental, 71.72
FINANCE ACT 2000,
summary of provisions, 94
Finance leasing, 10.28, 10.38(iii)(vi), 71.68
Financial futures, 3.22, 30.17, 66.5(b), 71.32
Financial loss allowances, 71.48, 75.7
Fines, 71.90, 75.7, 75.13
Fire safety, 10.25(i)
First-year allowances, 10.27
exclusions, 10.35
restriction of use, 10.35, 46.9(*c*)(*d*)
Fiscal year, 1.2
Fishing grants, 71.85
Fixed Profit Car Scheme, 75.43
Flat rate expenses, 75.25
Football,
ground improvements, 10.2(ii), 71.85
pools promoters, 10.2(ii), 71.30, 71.85
Foreign agreements,
deduction of tax under, 23.4
Foreign currency,
gains and losses, 71.56
securities, issued by local authorities, 23.12
— statutory bodies, 84.6
unremittable income, 51.14
Foreign dividends, 23.12, 64.3
Foreign emoluments, 75.6
Foreign forces visiting, 30.21
Foreign income, 73.1, 73.3
Foreign income dividends, 1.9, 22.3, 76.3, 81.3, 81.5, 89.3, 90.1
— anti-avoidance provisions, 3.6, 3.7, 3.21
Foreign invalidity benefits, 83.4
Foreign possessions,
Sch D, Case V, 73.1, 73.2
Foreign securities, accrued income scheme, 74.14
Foreign service allowance, 29.5
Foreign tax, 25
Forestry land, 10.3, 69.1, 93
Foster care allowances, 83.4
FOTRA securities, 33.2
Franchising, 71.59

Fraud, 6.2
back duty assessments, 6.2, 6.4
income tax, 6.12, 58.10
interest, 6.6, 42.8
losses due to, 71.53
penalties, 58
Fraudulent or negligent conduct, 6.1
assessments, 6.4
interest, 6.6, 42.8
penalties, 58.3, 58.4
Free of tax annuities, 23.17
FRIENDLY SOCIETIES, 31
taxable policy gains, 45.13
FUNDING BONDS, 32
Furnished holiday lettings, 68.9, 74.4
Furnished lettings, 68.2, 68.4, 68.8, 68.14, 74.4
Further assessments, 5.3, 17.11
Future liabilities, 71.49
Futures, 3.20, 3.22, 30.17, 52.6(c), 71.32

G

Gallantry awards, 29.6
Gambling, 71.30, 71.33
Garage allowances, 75.7
Gas rig workers, transport to mainland, 75.13(viii), 75.43
General Commissioners, 35.3
appeals to, 4.3, 4.6
duties of, 4.6
German annuities, 29.7
Gift Aid, 15.10–15.16
Gifts,
charities, to, 15.10–15.21
covenant, by, 15.17
educational establishments, to, 71.60
educational purposes, for, 15.21
kind, in, 15.19–15.21
life assurance policies, with, 45.6
medical purposes, for, 15.21
overseas relief, for, 15.21
poorest countries, for relief in, 15.21
promotional, 71.55
retirement, on, 66.1, 75.26
trading stock, of, 15.19, 15.21
Sch D, 71.60
Sch E, 75.26
Gilt strips, 71.82, 72.2, 74.24
Gilt-edged securities, *see* Government Stocks
Glasshouses, capital allowances, 10.25
Golden handshakes, 19
GOVERNMENT STOCKS, 33
accrued income scheme, 74.10(*d*)
capital gains tax, 33.1
charities, held by, 33.3
corporation tax regime, 33.1
deduction of tax at source, 33.3
discounts, 33.1, 33.4, 72.2
FOTRA securities, 33.2
gross payment, 33.3
individual savings accounts, 29.10
non-residents, held by, 33.2
premium bonds, 33.5
'repos', 3.5, 33.3
sale and repurchase, 3.5, 33.3
savings certificates, 33.6
Schedule C, 70
strips, 71.82, 72.2, 74.24
Grants, 71.85
farming, 71.57(*f*)
housing, 29.9
Members of Parliament, etc., to, 19.5, 75.41
returns of, 67.7
Ground rents, 68.14, 71.77
Guaranteed income bonds, 45.15(h)
Guarantees,
losses under, 71.61
underwriters, 89.3
Guardians, 16.3

H

Hansard, consideration in appeals, 4.7
Harbour reorganisation schemes, 84.3
Health insurance, *see* Medical insurance
Health service bodies, 30.12, 84.4
HERD BASIS, 34
High Court,
appeals to, 4.7
penalty proceedings before, 58.6
recovery of tax in, 56.3
Higher rates, 1.3, 1.5, 28
income tax, payment dates, 57
Highway undertakings, 10.11, 10.14–10.17
Hire purchase, 71.62
capital allowances, 10.38(vi)
— motor cars, 10.28(A)
no interest relief, 43.3
Historic Buildings and Monuments Commission for England, 30.9
HM Forces, *see* Armed forces
Holiday clubs, etc., 18.2
Holiday lettings, 68.9, 68.14, 74.4
Holiday pay, 55.29

Holocaust victims, 29.7
exempt interest, 29.13(xi)
Home improvements, 43.8
Hong Kong,
— double tax treaty, 25.2
— officials, 38.A39
— status of residents, 51.11
Horses,
racing and sale of, 71.33
Hotels etc.,
capital allowances, 10.18
fire safety, 10.25(i)
owners, returns by, 67.8
House, *see* Private Residence
House of Commons,
debates considered in appeals, 4.7
Members of,
— accommodation allowances, 29.16
— accommodation expenses, 75.29(B)
— capital allowances, 10.24
— ministers, etc., transport and subsistence, 29.16
— overnight expenses, 29.16
— pension fund, 59.1(vii), 66.11
— personal pension schemes, 60.1
— reimbursed expenses, 29.16
— retirement schemes, 66.11
— termination payments, 75.41
— travel expenses, 29.16
House of Lords, 4.7
Houseboat,
lettings, 68.4
overseas letting of, 73.3
Housing accommodation, Sch E, 75.29
Housing associations, 30.10
MIRAS scheme, 23.13
Housing grants, 29.9
Husband and wife, 47
age allowances, 1.14, 1.15, 1.24. 47.5
alimony, 47.10
assessment, 47.1
back duty, 6.4, 6.7
blind person's allowance, 47.2
business expansion scheme, 26.29
death, 1.15, 1.16, 47.9
decree of nullity, 47.8
domicile, 64.4
end of marriage, 47.9
enterprise investment scheme, 26.15
independent taxation, 47.1
interest paid by, 43.12
investigation cases, 6.4, 6.7
jointly held property, 47.4
life assurance, 45.4(*j*)
living together, 47.7
maintenance, 1.8(i), 47.10
married couple's allowance, 1.15–1.17, 47.2, 47.10
mortgage interest relief, 43.12
partnership, in, 53.13
personal reliefs, 1.14, 1.15, 1.22, 1.23
— transfer of, 47.2
— transitional, 47.5
residence, 47.7
Schedule A, deferred repairs, 68.15
separate taxation, 47.1
separation, 1.17, 47.5, 47.7, 47.9, 47.10
settlement on future spouse, 81.26
transfer of allowances, 47.2
widow's bereavement allowance, 1.16
wife's earned income relief, 1.23
wife's income, 47.1
year of marriage, 1.15, 43.12
— life assurance, 45.4(*j*)
Husbandry, 10.3

I

Illegal trading, 71.34
Illegitimate children, 1.17, 81.23
Improvements, 43.8
Incapacitated persons,
assessments on trustee, guardian, etc., 16.3
claims on behalf of, 17.5, 81.11
trustees, etc., assessability, 81.11
vehicle maintenance grant, 29.28
Incapacity benefit, 55.30, 83.3
Incentive awards, 75.40, 75.44(a)
share schemes, 82
Income, definition, 1.6–1.8
earned, 1.7
investment, 1.8
total, 1.6, 1.10
Income support, 83.3, 83.4
Income tax,
assessments, 5
basic rate, 1.3, 1.5
charges on income, 1.10
collection, 56.3
Crown priority, 56.5
dates for payment, 57
deduction at source, 23
deduction from profits, 71.86
fraudulent evasion, 6.12, 58.10
higher rates, 1.3, 1.5
instalments of, 57
interest on overpaid, 41

Income tax
interest on unpaid, 42
lower rate, 1.3, 1.5
notice of liability to, 58.1
payment, 56
rates, 1.3, 1.5
returns, 67
starting rate, 1.3, 1.9
Schedule F rates, 1.9, 76.3, 81.2(*a*), 81.5
Incorporation,
capital allowances, 10.38(xi)
losses on, 46.12(*c*)
partnerships, of, 53.16
succession to trade, 71.25
Independent taxation of married persons, 47.1
back duty, 6.4, 6.7
Indexation,
partnership annuities, 53.16
personal reliefs, 1.13
securities, of, 44.7, 44.8
tax thresholds, 1.13
India, Reserve Bank of, 30.2
Indian, Pakistan and colonial pensions, 59.4(iv)
Individual savings accounts, 29.10, 29.13(iii), 29.21
Individuals,
connected persons, 20.2
payment of tax, 56.1, 57
savings accounts, 29.10, 29.13(iii), 29.21
set-off of losses, 46.2, 46.3, 46.5
trades, professions, etc., assessment, 71.3
Industrial buildings, 10.10 *et seq.*
appropriation from trading stock, 10.12
balancing allowances and charges, 10.15
enterprise zones, 10.19
heat insulation, 10.25(ii)
hotels, 10.18
initial allowances, 10.13
making of allowances and charges, 10.17
qualifying buildings, 10.11
qualifying expenditure, 10.12
small workshops, 10.21
writing-down allowances, 10.14
Information and communications technology,
capital allowances, 10.27
Information exchange, international, 35.12, 36.2(*c*)
Inheritance tax,
excess liability, overlap with, 28.6
interest on overpaid, 29.13(vii)
loan to pay, interest on, 43.23
payment by trustees, 81.16(*e*)
Initial allowances,
agricultural buildings, 10.3
dredging, 10.7
industrial buildings, 10.13
machinery and plant, 10.37(*c*)
mines, oil wells, etc., 10.49(A)
Injury,
damages for, awarded by foreign court, 29.13(i)
loss of office, 19.6(i)
Inland Revenue addresses, 35.1
Adjudicator, 35.9
Agricultural Compliance Unit, 71.57(*e*)
Capital and Valuation Division, 3.2
Central Accounting Office, 39
Claims Branch, 15.3, 51.11
Clerk to Special Commissioners, 4.6(*b*)
Company Tax Division, 26.2, 26.19
Corporate Communications Office, 67.2
Employee Share Schemes Unit, 82.3
Financial Intermediaries and Claims Office, 15.1
— International, 25.6, 41.2
— Savings and Investments, 23.13
— Scotland, 15.3
Incentive Award Unit, 75.40
Information Centre, 39
International Division, 25.2
Internet site, 35.1
Library, 37
Oil Taxation Office, 3.9
Pension Schemes Office, 66
Profit-Related Pay Office, 75.31
Section 703 Compliance Unit, 3.2
Special Compliance Office, 35.7
Special Investigations, 3.2
Technical Division,
— Business Expansion Scheme, 26.19
— Offshore Funds, 52.7
INLAND REVENUE ADMINISTRATION, 35
advance pricing agreements, 3.9
amnesty, power of, 35.4
annual voluntary settlements, 55.12
business economic notes, 71.28
care and management, powers of, 35.4
codes of practice, 35.7
Collectors of Taxes, 35.2
Commissioners of Inland Revenue, 35.1
construction industry, 21.7
electronic communications, 35.12
employers' helpline, 35.11
Enquiry Handbook, 78.11

Inland Revenue administration
equitable liability, 56.9
estoppel, 5.3
General Commissioners, 35.3
guidance manuals, 35.10
Inspectors of Taxes, 35.1
internet site, 35.1
open Government, 35.10
PAYE settlement agreements, 55.12
provisional treaty relief scheme, 25.6
Revenue Adjudicator, 35.9
Revenue error, 35.8
— interest on overpaid tax, 41.4
— interest on unpaid tax, 42.7
rulings, 35.6
Special Commissioners, 35.3
Taxpayers' Charter, 35.7
telephone claims, 17.5
INLAND REVENUE:
CONFIDENTIALITY OF INFORMATION, 36
EXPLANATORY PAMPHLETS ETC., 37
EXTRA-STATUTORY CONCESSIONS, 38
PRESS RELEASES, 39
STATEMENTS OF PRACTICE, 40
Inland Revenue manuals, 35.10, 78.11
Inland Revenue rulings, 35.6
Insolvency, 7, 56.5
Inspectors of taxes, 35.1
claims to, 17.5
Instalments,
income tax, of, 57
share option gains, 82.3
Insurance,
annual payments, 29.12
commissions, 71.46, 71.64
disability, 29.12, 71.64, 75.37
employee, for, 71.64, 75.23
health, 29.12, 71.64, 75.37
key employee, 71.54
life, relief, 45.1
locum, 71.64
medical, 48, 75.13(xiii)
mortgage protection, 29.12
mutual, 50
premiums allowable, 71.64
professional indemnity, 71.64
qualifying policies, 45.6
Insurance companies,
accrued income scheme, 74.28
non-resident, 51.9
offshore income gains, 52.12
Insurance premium tax,
interest on, 42.10
penalties, 58.12
Inter-American Development Bank, 29.18
Interest,
accrued income scheme, 74.6 *et seq.*
administration fees, 43.6
annual, 43.3(*a*), 53.14(ii)
— deductible, 43.3(*a*)
anti-avoidance, 43.2(ii)
assessment of, Sch D, Case III, 72.3(*b*), 72.4
bank, 8.2, 43.3(*b*)
beneficial loans, on, 75.17, 75.19
bondwashing, 3.3, 74.6 *et seq.*
bridging loans, 75.17
building society, 9
business, 43.2, 43.3
certificates of tax deposit, on, 14
charge on income, 1.10(ii)
close company, loans to purchase interest in, 43.19
companies, paid by, 43.1
co-operatives, loans to purchase interest in, 43.20
credit cards, 75.44(*d*)
damages, on, exempt, 29.13(i)
deduction of tax, 1.9, 8.2, 9.3, 23, 33.3, 43.1, 43.2, 53.14(ii)
deep discount securities, 44.5, 44.6, 44.8
delayed tax repayments, on, 41.2
discount house, to, 43.3(*d*)
discount treated as, 44.5, 44.8, 44.9, 72.2
double relief, exclusion of, 43.25
employee-controlled companies, loans for, 43.21
estate duty, loans for, 43.23
Eurobond, 23.3(ii)
executors, on unpaid tax, 42.9
exempt, 29.10, 29.13
foreign currency, payable in, accrued income scheme, 74.13
Government stocks, 33.2, 33.3
home improvement loans, 43.8
indexed stock, on, 44.9
industrial or provident society, paid by, 72.1(*b*)
inheritance tax, loans for, 43.23
— overpaid, 29.13(vii)
land, loans for, 43.6
life annuity, loans for, 43.24
limits on relief, 43.10
losses, treated as, 46.17

Interest
lower rate of tax, 1.9
machinery or plant, loans for, 43.18
married persons, paid by, 43.12
mortgage, 9.4, 23.13, 43.5, 43.6
National Savings Certificates, 29.13(v)
non-resident,
— paid to, 25.6, 43.2(i), 51.3
official rate, 75.17
omission to deduct tax, 23.8
overdrafts, 43.17
overdue tax, on, 42, 78.22
overpaid tax, on, 41, 78.23
paid, returns of, 67.4
partnership, loans for, 43.22
payable, 43, 71.65
receivable, 44
relevant loan, 23.13
relief, restriction, 43.3, 43.5, 71.65
residences, loans for, 43.5, 43.6
returns, 67.4
sale of right to, 3.4
SAYE savings schemes, 29.13(vi)
savings bank, exempt, 29.13(iv)
savings income, 1.9
Sch D, Case I, 71.65
Sch D, Case III, 72
Sch D, Case VI deduction, 43.2
securities, on, 74.6 *et seq.*
shares, new issues of, on, 71.82
short, 43.3(*a*)
Stock Exchange member to, 43.3(*c*)
student loans, on, 29.13(x)
tax-free arrangements, 23.16
tax repayments, on, 41
total income, 1.8(ii)
unpaid tax, on, 42, 78.22
Interest on overdue tax, 42
INTEREST ON OVERPAID TAX, 41
double tax relief, 25.2
enterprise investment scheme, 26.8
over-repayments, 41.5
PAYE, 55.8
rates, 41.2
Revenue error, 41.4
self-assessment, 41.1, 78.23
unauthorised demands, 41.3
INTEREST AND SURCHARGES ON UNPAID TAX, 42, 71.65
appeal, pending, 42.3
back duty, 6.6
climate change levy, 42.10
companies, 42.5
enterprise investment scheme, 26.11, 26.12
exchange restrictions, 42.6
executors, 42.9
fraud, wilful default or neglect, 6.6
insurance premium tax, 42.10
landfill tax, 42.10
PAYE, 55.8
postponed tax, 42.3
rates, 42.2
reckonable date, 42.3
Revenue error, 42.7
self-assessment, 42.1, 42.4, 78.21, 78.22
tax lost through fault of taxpayer, 42.8
value added tax, 42.10
INTEREST PAYABLE, 43
apportionment, 43.3
beneficial loans, 75.17
business interest, 43.2
cessation of residence, temporary relief after, 43.7
close company, loans to purchase interest in, 43.19
companies, by, 43.1
co-operative, loans to purchase interest in, 43.20
deduction of tax, 8.2, 9.3, 23, 43.1, 43.2, 53.14(ii)
dependent relatives, property occupied by, 43.9
double relief, exclusion of, 43.25
employee-controlled company, loans to purchase interest in, 43.21
higher rate relief, restriction of, 43.5
home improvement loans, 43.8
inheritance tax, loans to pay, 43.23
job-related living accommodation, borrower resident in, 43.16
life annuity, loans to purchase, 43.24
married couples, 43.12
machinery and plant, loans to purchase, 43.18
MIRAS, 23.13
partnership, loans to purchase interest in, 43.22
property let at commercial rent, 43.15
property, loans to purchase, 43.6–43.17
rate of relief, 43.5
relief, 43.5
Schedule A businesses, 23.13, 43.2, 43.15
substitution of security, 43.13

INTEREST RECEIVABLE, 44
companies, by, 9.3
damages for personal injuries, awarded by foreign court, 29.13(i)
deep discount securities, 44.5
deep gain securities, 44.7
Eurobonds, 23.3(ii), 51.3
non-resident, 51.3
qualifying convertible securities, 44.8
savings income, 1.9
Intermediaries, *see* Personal Service Companies Etc.
International information exchange, 35.12, 36.2(*c*)
International loans, 71.45
International Maritime Satellite Organisation, 30.11
International organisations,
immunity from tax, 24, 30.11
securities of, 29.18
Internet,
filing discount, 55.9, 67.3, 78.1
incentives for use, 67.3
Revenue website, 35.1
Investigations in-depth, 71.28
Investigatory powers, 6.8
Investment grants, 10.27(iv)
Investment in corporate trades, 26
Investment income, *see also* Savings income
lower rate of tax, 1.9
meaning of, for investment income surcharge, 1.8
remittance basis, 63.1(A)(iii), 63.1(C)
savings income, 1.9
Schedule D, 71.66
'total income', 1.8
Investment income surcharge, 1.4, 28
investment income, meaning of, 1.8
Investment reliefs,
business expansion scheme, 26.18 *et seq.*
enterprise investment scheme, 26
losses on unquoted shares, 46.18
venture capital trusts, 91
Ireland,
Northern, 51.13
— appeals, 4.3
Republic of, double tax relief, 25.3
— subjects becoming or ceasing to be resident in UK, 73.11, 73.12
— subjects working in UK, 75.6
see also Tolley's Taxation in the Republic of Ireland
Issuing houses,
returns by, 67.9

J

Job-related accommodation, 43.16
Jobseekers allowance, 47.10, 55.31, 83.3, 83.4
Jointly held property, 47.4
Journalists' expenses, 75.10
Judicial review, 4.8
Jurors, 71.48(*e*), 75.7

K

Key employee insurance, 71.54
Know-how, 71.67
capital allowances, 10.23
double tax relief, 25.5(*l*)
sale of, 71.67

L

Land,
annual value, Sch A, 68.7(*b*)
business expansion scheme, 26.21
charitable use, 15.1, 15.4
commercial occupation of, 69.1, 93
dealers in, 3.11
educational purposes, for, 15.1
election for Sch D, assessment, 93.2
enterprise investment scheme, 26.5
lease-back, 3.12, 3.13
— capital sum received, 3.11
loans for purchase of interest in, 43.6
lost rents, 68.18
premiums on leases, allowability, 68.28
premiums on leases, assessability, 68.27
Private Finance Initiative projects, in, 71.40
reconveyance, sale with right of, 68.27
rent charges, 68.15(*d*)
rent factoring, 68.30
reverse premiums, 68.29, 71.78
sale and lease-back, 3.12, 3.13
Schedule A, 68
transactions in, 3.11
waste disposal, use of for, 71.94
woodlands, 69.1, 93
Landfill tax, 71.94
interest on, 42.10
penalties, 58.12
Lands Tribunal, 4.3

Leases,
assets, capital sums for, 3.14
— rentals restrictions, 3.15
assignments, 68.27
duration of, 68.27
information concerning, 68.26
premiums for, 68.27, 68.28, 71.78
— Sch D, expenditure, 71.78
rent, allowable expenses, 71.78, 71.79
rental payments, 71.68
sale and lease-back, land, 3.12, 3.13
Leasing,
cars, 10.28(A), 10.35(*a*), 10.38(ii)
finance, 10.28, 10.38(iii)(vi), 71.68
international, 10.35
machinery and plant, 10.35
non-resident lessor, 51.13
rentals, 71.68
short-term, 10.35(*e*)
television sets, 10.35
viewdata sets, 10.35
Legacies,
settlements, 81
tax-free annuities under wills, 23.17
Legal expenses,
allowable, 71.69
compensation for loss of employment, 19.6(viii)
Sch A, 68.15(xii)(xiii)
Sch E, 75.28
tax appeals, 4.9, 71.69
Lettings, 68
furnished, 68.2, 68.4, 68.8, 68.14, 74.4
holiday, 68.9, 74.4
overseas, 73.4
Licensed premises (and *see* Tied houses),
receipts, of, 71.45
Licences,
returns of, 67.7
telecommunications, 71.87
Life annuities,
see also Life Assurance Policies
purchased, 23.11(*c*)
— interest on loans for, 43.24
Life assurance,
borrowings against, 72.1(*c*)
relief, 45.1
retirement benefit scheme unapproved, 66.2
LIFE ASSURANCE POLICIES, 45
admissible premiums, 45.3
— limits, 45.2
assignment of, 45.13
association staff, house purchase loans to, 45.15(*f*)
borrowings treated as income, 45.4(*h*)
certificates, 45.12(*e*)
cessation of premium collection, 45.13
chargeable events, 45.13, 45.19
children's policies, 45.4(*g*)
commission, 71.64
disqualification of, 45.11
early conversion or surrender, 45.5
endowment policies, 45.8
free gifts, 45.6
gains on, 45.13, 45.19
guaranteed income bonds, 45.15(*h*)
individual savings accounts, 29.10
loans to policyholders, 45.15(*f*)
married persons, 45.4(*j*)
minor infringements, 45.12(*h*)
mortgage protection policies, 45.12(*b*)
non-qualifying policies, 45.13
non-residents, 45.4(*c*), 45.13
non-resident policies, 45.17, 45.18, 45.19
offshore policies, 45.17, 45.18, 45.19
overseas life office, UK branch of, 45.4(*c*)
partial surrenders, 45.15
pension schemes, 45.10
personal portfolio bonds, 45.13
premium relief, 45.1
qualifying policies, 45.6
relief, 45.1
retirement schemes, 66.2
short-term assurances, 45.7
surrender, etc. after four years, 45.5
variation, 45.12(*c*)
whole life assurances, 45.9
widows' annuities, 45.3(iii)
withdrawal of relief, 45.5
Lifeboatmen, 55.45
Light refreshments,
benefits-in-kind exemption, 75.13(iv)
Limited partnerships, 53.10
Liquidator,
trading by, 71.36
Literary prize, 71.43
Living accommodation, 75.29
job-related, 43.16
Living expenses,
agricultural workers, 75.7
clergymen, 75.9
construction industry workers, 75.43
lorry drivers, 75.43
'Living together', married couples, 47.7

Lloyd's underwriters, 89
accrued income, 74.26
corporate, 89.1
deep discount/gain securities, 44.5, 44.7, 44.8
interest paid gross to, 9.3
members' agent pooling arrangements, 89.3
personal pension schemes, 60.5
retirement annuities, 65.4
self-assessment, 89.2
Loan and money societies, 18.3
Loan finance, incidental costs of obtaining, 71.70
Loan interest relief, 43
close company, purchase of interest in, 43.19
co-operative, purchase of interest in, 43.20
dependent relative, purchase of residence, 43.9
double relief, exclusion of, 43.25
employee-controlled company, purchase of interest in, 43.21
home improvement loans, 43.8
inheritance tax, loan to pay, 43.23
life annuity, loan to purchase, 43.24
loss relief, 43.2
machinery or plant, purchase of, 43.18
main residence, purchase of, 43.6
— borrower resident in job-related accommodation, 43.16
married couples, 43.12
partnership, purchase of interest in, 43.22
restricted categories of loan, 43.5
Loans,
close company, by, excess liability, 28.3(*a*)(ii)
close company, purchase of interest in, 43.19
employees, to, 75.17
house purchase, life insurance association staff, 45.15(*f*)
inherited property subject to, 43.6
payments for, 71.65
settlor, to, 81.19
transactions, anti-avoidance, 3.16
Local authorities,
associations, 30.12
attendance allowances, 55.32, 71.48(*e*), 75.7
deduction of tax from interest paid, 23.12
exemption, 30.12
interest paid gross to, 9.3
securities issued in foreign currency, 23.12
Local enterprise agencies, 71.84
Local enterprise companies, 71.84
Locum insurance, 71.64
Lodgers, 68.11
Lodging allowances, 75.7, 75.43
London International Financial Futures Exchange, 3.6, 71.32
London Traded Options Market, 3.6, 71.32
Long-life assets, 10.28(G)
Long service award,
Sch E, 75.26
Loss of employment or office,
compensation for, 19
redundancy payments, 75.32
wages in lieu of notice, 75.45
LOSSES, 46
abroad, trade carried on, 51.12
annual payments, treated as, 46.17
anticipated, 71.49
apportionment of, 46.10(*a*)
balancing charge after cessation of trade, 10.17, 46.12(*i*)
capital allowances, 46.7
capital gains, set against, 46.5
carry-back of terminal losses, 46.2, 46.15
carry-forward, 46.2, 46.12
certificates of deposit, on, 13.2
claim for set-off, 46.2, 46.3, 46.5
— late, 46.10(*c*)
— restrictions, 46.9
— self-assessment, 17.1, 17.2
commodity futures, dealing in, 3.20
computation of, 46.5, 46.13(*b*)
current year basis of assessment, 46.3, 46.7, 46.12, 46.15, 46.18, 78.2
early years of trade, in, 46.13
enterprise investment scheme shares, 26.8, 46.18
farming and market gardening, 46.9(*b*)
first-year allowances, 46.9
general income, set-off against, 1.10(iv), 46.3
interest payments as, 46.17
limited partnerships, 53.10
partnership,
— apportionment, 53.10
— changes, 53.11
— limited, 53.10
pre-trading expenditure, 71.76

Losses
rents, 68.18
residence, change of, on, 46.12(*j*)
restriction of relief, 46.9, 53.14(iv)
Schedule A, 68.13, 68.16, 68.18
Sch D, Case V, 73.4
Sch D, Case VI, 74.5
self-assessment, 17.1, 17.2
set-off, 46.2, 46.3, 46.5
shares in unquoted trading companies, 46.18
terminal, 46.2, 46.15
— mineral royalties, 49
theatrical angels, 74.2
time limit for claims, 46.3, 46.12(*g*), 46.13, 46.18
trading, 46.2
underwriters, 89.6
unlisted shares, 26.8, 46.18
woodlands, 46.13
Lotteries, 71.30
charitable, 15.7(iii)
Lower rate, 1.3, 1.5, 11.3
dividends, 1.9
savings income, 1.9
Lump sums,
see also Compensation, Damages, etc.
commutation of pension, 66.4(*f*), 66.12
compensation, capital assets, 71.48
copyright sale, 71.51
employment, on taking up, 75.7
pension fund, initial contribution, 66.10
retirement, on, 60.2, 65.2, 66.4, 66.6, 66.7, 66.9, 66.12
Luncheon vouchers, 29.15, 75.30

M

Machinery and plant,
abortive expenditure, 10.38(i)
balancing allowances and charges, 10.30, 10.37(*d*)
capital allowances, etc., 10.24 *et seq.*
capital expenditure on,
— to 26.10.70, 10.37
— from 27.10.70, 10.24 *et seq.*
cars, 10.27(i), 10.28(A), 10.35(*a*), 10.37(*c*), 10.38(ii), 75.43
connected persons, sales between, 10.38(iii)
demolition costs, 10.25, 10.28, 10.37(*d*)
double allowance, exclusion of, 10.2(iv)
eligible expenditure, 10.25
films, 10.25, 71.58
first-year allowances, 10.27
fixtures, 10.34
foreign leasing, 10.35
hire purchase,
— to 26.10.70, 10.37(*c*)
— from 27.10.70, 10.38(vi)
installation of, building alterations for, 10.25
lease of, 10.28(E), 10.35
lessee's expenditure, 10.38(vii)
lessors, allowances to, 10.35
loans to purchase interest in, 43.18
medium-sized businesses, 10.27
method of making allowances, 10.32
mines, oil wells, etc., 10.46
motor cars, 10.27(i), 10.28(A), 10.35(*a*), 10.37(*c*), 10.38(ii), 75.43
not brought into use, 10.27(v)
notification of expenditure, 10.25
partial business use, 10.28(C)
partnership, 10.38(viii)
— changes, 53.11
— company, 53.14(i)
private use, 10.28(C)
restrictions on eligible expenditure, 10.26
sale and leaseback, 10.27(iii)
ships, 10.27, 10.28(B)
short-life assets, 10.28(F)
small businesses, 10.27
successions to trades, 10.38(xi)
televisions, 10.35
writing down allowances, 10.28
Magistrates, 71.48(*e*), 75.7
Magistrates' Courts, recovery of tax in, 56.3
Maintenance assessments, 1.8(i), 47.10
Maintenance funds for historic buildings,
tax exemption for settlors, 81.30
Maintenance payments,
concessionary relief, 23.8, 47.10
failure to deduct tax, 23.8, 47.10
farms, 71.57(*d*)
foreign, 73.3
funds for historic buildings, 81.30
investment income, 1.8(i)
retrospective dating, 47.10
Sch A, 68.15, 68.16(*a*)
school fees, 47.10
under UK Court Order, 47.10
unearned income, 1.8(i)
Management expenses,
estate, 68.15
mineral rights, and royalties, 49.1

Mandamus, 4.8
Manufactured dividends, 3.7, 3.21, 74.32
Market gardening,
agricultural buildings allowances, 10.3
fluctuating profits, 17.2, 71.57
losses, 46.9(*b*)
Market price,
trading transactions at other than, 3.9
Marketing boards, 84.1
Married couple's allowance, 1.15, 1.16, 1.17, 47.2, 47.10
MARRIED PERSONS, 47
age allowances, 1.14, 1.15, 1.24, 47.5
alimony, 47.10
allowance, 1.22
assessment, 47.1
back duty, 6.4, 6.7
blind person's allowance, 47.2
business expansion scheme, 26.29
death, 1.15, 1.16, 47.9
decree of nullity, 47.8
divorce, 47.9, 47.10
— pension-sharing, 23.11(*c*)(vii), 60.2, 60.8, 66.1, 66.4
domicile, 64.4
end of marriage, 47.9
enterprise investment scheme, 26.15
independent taxation, 47.1
interest paid by, 43.12
investigation cases, 6.4, 6.7
jointly held property, 47.4
life assurance, 45.4(*j*)
living together, 47.7
maintenance, 1.8(i), 47.10
married couple's allowance, 1.15, 1.16, 1.17, 47.2, 47.10
mortgage interest relief, 43.12
partnership, in, 53.13
personal reliefs, 1.14, 1.15, 1.22, 1.23
— transfer of, 47.2
— transitional, 47.5
residence, 47.7
Sch A, deferred repairs, 68.15
separate taxation, 47.1
separation, 1.17, 47.5, 47.7, 47.9, 47.10
settlement on future spouse, 81.26
transfer of allowances, 47.2
widow's bereavement allowance, 1.16
wife's earned income relief, 1.23
wife's income, 47.1
year of marriage, 1.15, 43.12
— life assurance, 45.4(*j*)
Maternity pay, 55.33
Meal vouchers, 29.15, 75.30
Medals, 29.6
MEDICAL INSURANCE, 48
services abroad, 75.13(xiii), 75.43
sickness benefits, 29.12, 71.64, 75.37
Members of Parliament, *see* House of Commons and Scottish Parliament
Members' clubs, 18.1, 18.5
Mileage allowances, 71.90, 75.43
Milk receipts, 71.57(*g*)
Mineral extraction, 10.39–10.49, 71.71
Mineral lease, 49
MINERAL ROYALTIES, 49
tax deducted from, 23.14, 72.1(*d*)
Miners' free coal etc., 29.17
Mines, oil wells, etc.,
balancing allowances and charges, 10.44
capital allowances, etc., 10.39–10.49
demolition costs, 10.44, 10.49(C)
disposal receipts, 10.43
expenses not deductible, 71.71
exploration or exploitation activities, 51.13
land outside UK, 10.40, 10.49(*d*), (*e*)
losses, 46.15(*d*)
machinery and plant for use in, 10.46
making of allowances and charges, 10.45
mineral royalties, 49
oil licences, 10.41
old scheme (before 1 April 1986), 10.49
pre-trading expenditure, 10.40
qualifying expenditure, 10.40, 10.41
restoration expenditure, 10.40
Schedule D charge, 71.1
time expenditure incurred, 10.40
transitional provisions, 10.47
writing-down allowances, 10.42
Ministers of religion, 75.9
Minors, 16
interest in settlement, 81.18, 81.23
MIRAS, 23.13
Miscellaneous income and expenses (Schedule D), 71.72
Mobile telephones, 75.13(xxiii), 75.15, 75.16
Mobility allowance, 83.4
Mortgage interest, 9.4, 43.5, 43.6
relief at source, 23.13
Mortgage protection insurance, 29.12
Mortgages *see* Building Societies
Motor cars, *see* Cars

Motor cycles,
mileage allowances, 75.43
parking facilities, 75.7, 75.13(xiv), 75.43, 75.44(*a*)(*d*)
Motoring fines, 71.90, 75.7, 75.13
MUTUAL TRADING, 50
Schedule A business, 68.5

N

Nannies, 55.21
National Assembly for Wales, *see* Assemblies
National Farmers Union subscriptions, 71.57(l)
National Heritage Memorial Fund, 30.14
National insurance contributions, 1.10(viii), 55.39, 71.54, 83.7
dispensations, 75.22
share schemes, 82.3
National Radiological Protection Board, 84.2
National Savings Bank interest, 29.13(iv)
National Savings Certificates, 29.13(v), 33.6
National Savings Stock Register, 33.3(ii)
National Socialist persecution, compensation for, 29.7, 29.13(xi)
Natural History Museum, 30.3
Neglect,
back duty assessment, 6.3, 6.4
interest on tax unpaid, 42.8
penalties, 58
Negligence, 6.3, 6.4
interest on tax, 42.8
penalties, 58.3
Net relevant earnings, 60.8, 65.7
New businesses, 71.4, 71.12
New deal employment programmes, 83.4
New employments, 55.22
New residents,
Sch D, Cases IV and V, 73.11
Non-cash vouchers, 75.44(a)
Non-domiciled employees, 75.6
Non-notification of chargeability, 58.1
NON-RESIDENTS AND OTHER OVERSEAS MATTERS, 51, 64.3, 78.43 *and see also* Overseas income and Overseas pensions
absence abroad,
— in employment, 75.3
agents for, 51.4(*b*), 68.21
annual sums to, 51.10
appeals, 64.8
banks, etc., 51.9
charge on percentage of turnover, 51.4(*a*)
chargeable income, limit on, 51.1
collection of tax, 51.3
dealers in securities, 51.9
deduction of tax by, 23.4
dividends to, 25.6
double tax relief, 25, 64.3
earnings abroad, 75.3
employment, 75.2
entertainers, 36.2(*h*), 51.8
European Economic Interest Groupings, 53.19
excess liability, 28.7
exempt income, 29.18
foreign entities, 25.2
FOTRA securities, 33.2
government stocks, 33.2
income from property, 68.24
interest to, 25.6, 43.2(i), 51.3
lettings, 73.4
life assurance, 45.13
— policies, 45.17–45.19
limit on income chargeable on, 51.1
method of charging, 51.4(*b*)
offshore income gains of, 52.12
participators, 25.2, 25.6
partnerships, 53.15
personal allowances, 51.11
personal equity plans, 29.20
profits in UK, 51.4(*a*), 51.5
remittances to UK, 63
rent, 68.24
self-assessment, 51.5–51.7, 78.38
social security benefits, foreign, 29.28, 83.4
sportsmen, 36.2(*h*), 51.8
tax credit repayable to, 25.2, 25.6
territorial seabed, 51.13
trades, etc. carried on and controlled abroad, 51.12
trading, becoming resident, 71.27
trading in UK, 51.4–51.9
transfer of assets abroad, 3.8, 52.12
— discounts on securities, 72.2
travelling expenses, 51.12, 75.5, 75.43
trusts, 81.10
UK government securities held by, 33.2
unremittable foreign income, 51.14
unremittable trade receipts, 71.92
Northern Ireland, 51.13
appeals, 4.3, 4.7
Assembly, *see* Assemblies

Northern Ireland
capital allowances, 10.27
Notice, wages in lieu, 75.45

O

Occupational pension schemes, 66
OECD Support Fund, 29.18
Official error, remission of tax, 56.6
OFFSHORE FUNDS, 52
account period, 52.4
— apportionments between, 52.5
accrued income, 52.2, 52.6
capital gains tax, 52.12
certification, 52.4, 52.7
commodity dealing, 52.6
computation of gain, 52.9
disposal of material interest, 52.1
distribution test, 52.2, 52.4–52.6
— non-UK legal restrictions, 52.5
equalisation,
— accrued income, 52.2, 52.6
— arrangements, 52.2
— commodity dealing fund, 52.6
— element, 52.11
— funds operating arrangements, 52.2, 52.6, 52.11, 52.12
income tax charge, 52.8–52.11
material interest,
— disposal of, 52.1
— meaning of, 52.3
non-qualifying,
— disposal of material interest in, 52.1
— meaning of, 52.4
offshore income gain,
— charge to income tax, 52.8–52.11
— computation of, 52.10, 52.11
— insurance companies, of, 52.12
— non-UK residents, of, 52.12
— trustees, of, 52.12
subsidiary companies, 52.4(C)
— commodity dealing, 52.6
— dealing and management, 52.4(D)
trading companies, investments in, 52.4
UK equivalent profits, 52.5
Offshore life assurance policies, 45.17, 45.18, 45.19
Oil rig workers, transport to mainland, 75.13(viii), 75.43
Oil wells, 10.39–10.49, 71.71
balancing allowances and charges, 10.44
disposal receipts, 10.43
limitations on qualifying expenditure, 10.41
machinery and plant allowances, 10.46
making of allowances and charges, 10.45
old scheme (before 1 April 1986), 10.49
qualifying expenditure, 10.40, 10.41
transitional provisions, 10.47
Old age allowance, 1.14, 1.15, 1.24, 47.5
Open Government, 35.10
Open-ended investment companies,
personal equity plans, in, 29.21
Opening years,
of trade, assessment, 71.4, 71.12
Options,
financial, 71.32
futures and, 3.22
gains and losses, 71.32
repurchase of shares, 3.3, 3.5, 3.6, 3.7
share scheme, 82.3, 82.38, 82.39, 82.40
traded, 30.17, 71.32
Ordinarily resident, 64.6 *and see* Residence, Ordinary Residence and Domicile
remittance basis, 63.1(B), (C)
Organisations, exempt, 30
Ostrich farming, 71.37
Overdue tax, interest on, 42
Overnight expenses, 75.13(xxii), 75.43, 75.44(*a*)
Overpaid tax, interest on, 41
self-assessment, 78.23
Overpayment of tax, 56.7
Over-repayments, 56.8
interest, 41.5
self-assessment, 78.34
Overseas income,
assessment, 73
dividends, 23.12
double tax relief, 25
emoluments, 75.3
exempt, 29.19
lettings, 73.3
remittances, 63
Sch D, Cases IV and V, 73
Sch E, 75.3
trusts, 81.10
unremittable, 51.14
Overseas matters, *see* Non-residents and other Overseas Matters
Overseas pensions,
assessable, 59.2
funds, 59.4(vi), 59.6
relief for, 59.3, 59.4(iv), (v)
remittance, 63.1(A)(iv), 63.1(C)
Overseas property business, 68.13, 73.4

Overseas residents, 64.3
agents for, 51.4(*b*), 68.21
annual sums paid to, 51.10
banks, etc., 51.9
charge on percentage of turnover, 51.4(*a*)
chargeable income, limit on, 51.1
dealers in securities, 51.9
deduction of tax by, 23.4
double tax agreements, 25.2, 64.3
employment, 75.2
entertainers, 36.2(*h*), 51.8
exempt income, 29.18
FOTRA securities, 33.2
government stocks, 33.2
income from property, 68.24
interest to, 43.2(i), 51.3
life assurance, 45.13
— policies, 45.17, 45.18, 45.19
limit on chargeable income, 51.1
method of charging, 51.4(*b*)
offshore income gains of, 52.12
partnerships, 53.15
personal allowances, 51.11
profits in UK, 51.4(*a*), 51.5
remittances to UK, 63
rent, 68.24
self-assessment, 51.5–51.7, 78.38
sportsmen, 36.2(*h*), 51.8
tax credit repayable to, 25.6
trading, becoming resident, 71.27
trading in UK, 51.4–51.9
travelling expenses, 51.12, 75.5, 75.43
trusts, 81.10
UK Government securities held by, 33.2
Overseas Service Pension Fund, 59.4(v)

P

Pakistan, India and, pensions, 59.4(iv)
Pamphlets, Revenue, 37
Parking,
facilities, *see* Cars, Cycles and Motor cycles
fines, 71.90, 75.7, 75.13
Parliament, *see* House of Commons and Scottish Parliament
Part-time employees,
share schemes for, 82.9, 82.38, 82.39, 82.40
Participators,
loans to, from close company, 28.3(*a*)(ii)
non-resident, 25.2, 25.6
PARTNERSHIPS, 53, *see also* Personal Service Companies Etc.
abroad, 53.15
accounting adjustments, 53.3
amalgamation into, 53.8
annual payments to retired partner, 53.16
apportionment of assessment, 53.5
— losses, 53.10
assessments, 53.3
assets, CGT, 53.3
basis of assessment, 53.3, 53.14(i), 71.3–71.24
capital gains tax, 53.3
changes, 53.6, 53.14(iii)
— capital allowances on successions, 10.38(viii)
— effect on losses and capital allowances, 46.15(*c*)
claims, 17.1, 17.10
companies, 53.14
computation of profits, 53.3
connected persons, 20.4
continuation elections, 53.6
controlled abroad, 53.15
current year basis of assessment, 43.22, 53.1, 53.3, 53.6, 53.11, 53.14(i), 78.2
death of partner, 53.6
demergers, 53.8
director's fees, 75.24
double successions, 53.9
double tax relief, 25.5(*k*), 53.15
European Economic Interest Groupings, 53.19
excess liability, 28.2(*e*), 53.12
exempt profits, 53.15
foreign control, 53.15
fraudulent or negligent conduct by, 6.4
incorporation of, 53.16
intermediaries, *see* Personal Service Companies Etc.
limited, 53.10
loans, interest on, 43.3(*i*), 43.22
losses, 46.9(*d*), 46.12(*d*), 53.10
— restrictions on, 53.14(iv)
machinery or plant used in, 10.38(viii)
mergers, 53.8
nature of, 53.1, 53.2
non-resident, 53.15
non-trading income, 53.3
opening year rules, 71.4, 71.12
payment of tax, 56.1
personal allowances, 53.5
residence of partner, change of, 53.15
retirement annuities, 53.16
returns, 67.10, 78.8
— failure to deliver, 78.27
self-assessment, 78.8, 78.9, 78.16, 78.27

Partnerships
statements, 78.9, 78.16
succession, 53.6, 53.9
wife as partner, 53.13
PATENTS, 54
capital allowances, 10.50
expenses, 54.2, 71.73
income, 54.3
receipts, spreading of, 54.4
rights, capital allowances, 10.50
royalties,
— assessability, 54.4
— deduction of tax, 23.15(*b*)
— double tax relief, 25.5(*l*)
sales, 54.5
PAY AS YOU EARN, 55
agency workers, 55.3, 75.46
annual payments, 55.13
annual returns, 55.9
annual voluntary settlements, 55.12
— national insurance contributions, 71.54, 83.7
annuities, 55.14
assessments, 55.2
attendance allowances, 55.32
benefits in kind, 55.15
cash vouchers taxable under, 75.44(*b*)
certificate to employee, 55.10
charitable donations, 55.17
codes, 55.4
— claims adjustments, 17.3
commodities, etc., 55.2
councillors' allowances, 55.32
credit tokens, 55.2
Crown priority, 55.18
death of employee, 55.23
deductions working sheets, 55.6
directors' remuneration, 55.19
disabled person's tax credit, 55.20
domestic workers, 55.21
employee arriving, 55.22
employee dying, 55.23
employee leaving, 55.24
employee, recovery from, 55.7
employee share ownership plans, 82.17
exemption, 55.25
expense payments, etc., 55.26
free-of-tax payments, 55.27
HM Forces, 55.28
holiday pay, 55.29
incapacity benefit, 55.30
intermediaries, payment by, 55.3, 61.12
internet filing discount, 55.9
'K' codes, 55.4
local councillors, 55.32
maternity pay, 55.33
nannies, 55.21
notional payments, 55.2–55.4
overseas matters, 55.34
payment,
— definition, 55.3
— kind, in, 55.2
— to Collector, 55.8
penalties, 58.4
pensions, 66.5(*d*)
personal pensions, 60.1
personal service companies etc., 61.12
readily convertible assets, 55.2
records, 55.35
recovery from employee, 55.7
religious centres, 55.36
repayments, 55.40
returns, end of year, 55.9
seamen, 55.37
settlement agreements, 55.12
— national insurance contributions, 71.54, 83.7
share options, 55.2
superannuation contributions, 55.39
tax refunds, 55.40
tax tables, 55.5
termination payments, 55.9
tradeable assets, 55.2
trade debts, 55.2
tronc arrangements, 55.42
unemployed, 55.43
VAT, 55.44
voluntary lifeboatmen, 55.45
vouchers, 55.2
working families' tax credit, 55.46
Paying and collecting agents, 23.12, 33.3, 56.1, 70
PAYMENT OF TAX, 56
appeal, pending, 56.2
certificate of tax deposit, by, 14.1
collection, 56.3
companies, 56.4
Court proceedings, 56.3
Crown priority, 56.5
date of, 56.1
determination of appeal, 56.2
due dates, 57
effective date of payment, 56.1
equitable liability, 56.9
interest on tax unpaid, 42
internet filing discount, 55.9, 67.3, 78.1
official error, arrears arising through, 56.6

Payment of tax
overpayment of tax, 56.7
over-repayment of tax, 56.8
pay as you earn, 55
paying and collecting agents, 23.12, 33.3, 56.1, 70
pending appeal, 56.2
postponement, 56.2
provisional repayment, 56.7
remission for official error, 56.6
repayment supplement, 29.24, 41
self-assessment, 56, 78.1, 78.17–78.20
— interest, 78.22, 78.23
— surcharge, 78.21
unauthorised demands for, 41.3
underwriters, 89.5
PILONs, 75.45
Payroll deduction scheme, 15.18
PENALTIES, 58
agent, negligence by, 58.3
appeals, 58.6
bankrupts, 58.9
chargeability, failure to notify, 58.1
climate change levy, 58.12
Commissioners' precepts, 58.5
construction industry tax scheme, 21.7
criminal liability, 58.10
destroying documents, 6.8
determination by Revenue officer, 58.6
disabled person's tax credit, 83.6
failure to notify chargeability, 58.1
failure to render return, 58.2
falsification of documents, 6.8
fraud, 58.3
incorrect returns, 58.3
insurance premium tax, 58.12
late returns, 58.2
mitigation or limitation of, 58.7
negligence, 58.3
negotiated settlements, 6.11
notification of chargeability, 58.1
payable, Schedule D deduction not allowed, 71.47
personal pension schemes, false information, 60.1
precepts, 58.5
procedure, 58.6
returns, failure to make, 58.2
Scotland, summary proceedings, 58.10
self-assessment, 78.10, 78.25–78.29
— surcharge on unpaid tax, 78.21
time limits, 58.8
two or more in respect of same tax, 58.7
variation of, 58.7
VAT, 58.11
working families' tax credit, 83.6
Pension-sharing,
annuities, purchased, 23.11(*c*)(vii)
personal pension schemes, 60.2, 60.8
purchased annuities, 23.11(*c*)(vii)
retirement benefit schemes, 66.1, 66.4
Pensioners, *see also* Pensions
assessment tolerance, 5.8
social security, 83
PENSIONS, 59 *see also* Overseas pensions
basis of assessment, 75.1
contributions to secure, 59.5, 60.1, 65.1
disability, 59.4(iii)
divorce, in, 23.11(*c*)(vii), 60.2, 60.8, 66.1, 66.4
earned income, 1.7(iii)
exemptions, 59.4, 59.6, 75.1(2)
ex gratia, 66.12
foreign, arrears of, 59.2
funds, 66
House of Commons, 59.1(vii), 66.11
mis-sold products, compensation for, 29.3
overseas
— funds, 59.4(vi), 59.6
— relief in respect of, 59.3
personal, 60
— mis-sold, 29.3
retirement annuities, 65
retirement schemes, 66
— surpluses, 66.8
Schedule D Case V, 59.2
Schedule E, 59.1
stakeholder, *see* Personal Pension Schemes
superannuation funds, 59.5
— exempt income, 30.17
voluntary, 59.1(v), 59.2(ii), 59.4(i)
war widows, 29.32
wound and disability, 59.4(ii)
Period of retention, 82.9
Permanent establishment, 25.2, 25.3
Permanent interest bearing shares, 9.3, 23.3(ii)
Personal allowances,
age allowance, 1.24
additional personal allowance, 1.17
blind person's allowance, 1.19
children's tax credit, 1.15, 1.18
married couple's allowance, 1.15
married man's allowance, 1.22
personal allowance, 1.14
single person's allowance, 1.21
widow's bereavement allowance, 1.16

Personal allowances
wife's earned income allowance, 1.23
Personal equity plans, 29.10, 29.21
Personal expenses,
not deductible, Sch D, Cases I and II, 71.74
Personal injuries, 29.4, 29.13(i)
PERSONAL PENSION SCHEMES (AND STAKEHOLDER PENSIONS), 60
administrators 60.1
approval, 60.2
Class 4 NICs and, 60.1, 83.6
compensation, 29.3
contract requirements, 60.2
conversion of schemes, 60.2
earned income, treatment of annuity as, 60.1
income withdrawals, 60.1, 60.2
information, 60.1
investigation settlements, 6.11
limits of relief, 60.3
Lloyd's underwriters, 60.5
members of parliaments, 60.1
mis-sold, compensation for, 29.3
PAYE, application of, 60.1
premiums related back, 60.5
relevant earnings, 60.8
retirement benefits schemes conversions, 60.2
small lump sum schemes, and, 60.8
trivial funds, 60.2
unapproved arrangements, employer's contributions, 60.1
unauthorised payments, 60.1
unused relief carried forward, 60.6
Personal portfolio bonds, 45.13
Personal reliefs, 1
age allowance, 1.24
additional personal allowance, 1.17
blind person's allowance, 1.19
British subjects resident abroad, 51.11
children, additional relief in respect of, 1.17
claims, 1.11
— settlement income to 1968/69, 81.12
deceased persons, 22
indexation, 1.13
married couple's allowance, 1.15
married man's allowance, 1.22
married persons, 47.2, 47.5
medical insurance, 48
non-residents, 1.12, 51.11
partners, 53.5
personal allowance, 1.14
twelve-year summary, *inside front cover*
widow's bereavement allowance, 1.16
wife's earned income allowance, 1.23
Personal representatives, 22.1
assessments on, 6.5, 22.1
discounts on securities, 72.2
interest,
— on unpaid tax, 42.9
— paid by, 43.6
residence of, 64.5
trading by, 71.36
Personal security, *see* Security assets and services
PERSONAL SERVICE COMPANIES ETC., 61
deemed Schedule E payment, 61.7–61.9
— date of, 61.15
— tax treatment, 61.11
dividends paid by, 61.14
employment, 61.4, 61.18
intermediaries, 61.3, 61.5
— computation of profits, 61.13
— dividends paid by, 61.14
— multiple, 61.16
partnerships, 61.5, 61.13, 61.15
PAYE, 61.12
transitional provisions, 61.17
Petrol companies, 71.88
Petrol, private, assessable benefit, 75.15
PILONs, 75.45
Pilots' benefit fund, 66.11
Plant,
capital allowances, 10.24 *et seq.*
— amendment of claim, 10.27, 10.28
— balancing allowances and charges, 10.30, 10.37(*d*)
— connected persons, 10.38(iii)
— eligible expenditure, 10.25
— entitlement to allowances for fixtures, 10.34
— first-year allowances, 10.27
— fixtures, entitlement to allowances for, 10.34
— leasing, 10.35
— long-life assets, 10.28(G)
— making of allowances and charges, 10.32
— old scheme (before 27 October 1970), 10.37
— renewals basis, change from, 10.38(x)
— short-life assets, 10.28(F)
leases, lease-backs, 3.14, 3.15
repair and renewal, 71.79(*c*)

Poind, 56.3
Police Federations, 88
Political organisations, 15.2(f)
Poll tax, *see* Community charge
Pooling profits, 71.75
Possessions,
overseas, Sch D, Case V, 73.2
Post-cessation receipts,
allowable deductions, 62.1
claims, 17.2
conventional basis, 62.2
earned income, treated as, 62.3
earnings basis, 62.1
election for carry-back, 62.1
individuals born before 1917, 62.2
self-assessment, 17.2
transfer of rights to receive, 62.1
Post-cessation expenditure, 1.10(vi), 62.4
Post-employment deductions, 1.10(vii), 75.23
Postponement of tax, 56.2
Powers of inspection, exempt bodies, 15.3
Precepts, 4.6, 58.5
Premium savings bonds, 33.5
Premiums,
leases, on,
— allowance to payer, 68.28
— assessability of recipient, 68.27
— reverse, 68.29, 71.78
— Sch D, allowances, 71.78
life insurance, 45.1 *et seq.*
personal pension scheme, 60.2–60.6
retirement annuity, 65.2–65.5
reverse, 68.29, 71.78
trust fund, 89.3
Prerogative orders, 4.8
Pre-sale distributions, 3.21
Press releases, Revenue, 39
Pre-trading expenditure, 68.5(iii), 71.76
Priority employee share issues, 75.36
Private Finance Initiative projects, 71.40
Private medical insurance, 48, 75.37
Private residence,
interest on loans for, 43.6
Privatisation employee share issues, 75.36
Professional associations, 15.2(g)
Professional indemnity insurance, 71.64
Professional privilege, 6.10
Professional subscriptions, 37, 75.39
Professions, (*see* Trades)
basis of assessment, 71.3 *et seq.*
— cash basis, 12.1
capital allowances, 10.1
closing years, 71.9, 71.17
deductions allowable, 71.40 *et seq.*
discontinuance, 71.25
individuals, assessment, 71.3
opening years, 71.4, 71.12
post-cessation receipts, 62
Sch D, Case II, 71
subscriptions, 75.39
whether employment, 75.24
Profit-related pay, 75.31
Profits,
See also Trade
capital, 71.40, 71.48
pooling, 71.75
understated, back duty, 6.7
underwriting, 89.3
Profit-sharing schemes, 82.9, 82.10
administration costs, 71.54
employee share ownership trusts, 71.54, 82.41
personal equity plans, shares transferred to, 29.21
setting up costs, 71.54
share acquisition costs, 71.54
Property,
dealing, 71.38
let at commercial rent, interest on, 43.15
loans to purchase, interest on, 43.6–43.17
overseas, 68.13, 73.4
sales, 71.77
Sch A, 68
Prostitution, 71.34
Provisional treaty relief scheme, 25.6
Public Departments, 30.6
Public lending rights, *see* Copyright and design and public lending rights
Public revenue dividends, 23.3(ii)
Public schools, 15.2(h)
Purchase by a company of its own shares, 1.9, 3.21, 81.5
Purchased life annuities, 23.11(c)
loans for, interest on, 43.24
savings income, 1.9
Purchase of property, relief for interest paid, 43.6

Q

Qualifying convertible securities, 44.8
Qualifying deposit rights, 9.3
Qualifying donations, 1.10(iii), 15.10–15.16, 15.21
Quarantine premises, 10.25(iv)

Quarries, 71.1
rent payable in connection with, 23.14

R

Rates, 71.78
capital gains tax, 11.3
income tax, 1.3, 1.5
Sch A, 68.15
Sch D, 71.78
Receipts basis (Schedule E), 71.54, 75.1
Reckonable date, 42.3
Records,
PAYE, 55.35
maintenance of, 78.10
production of, 4.6, 6.8
Recovery of tax,
Court proceedings, 56.3
distraint, 56.3
lessee, from, 68.21
poinding, 56.3
repayment claims, 17.6
third parties, from, 68.21
Redundancy payments,
deduction for additional payments, 71.54
exempt, 19.5, 29.23, 75.32
non-statutory, 19.5
paid, 71.54
received, Sch E, 75.32
Refugee relief, 15.21
Registration cards, 21.3
Relevant earnings, 60.8, 65.7
Religious centres,
PAYE, 55.36
Religious communities, 38.B10
Religious societies, 15.2(i)
Relocation packages, 75.33
Remission for official error, 56.6
REMITTANCE BASIS, 63
application, 63.1
basis of assessment, 63.2
constructive remittances, 63.4
double tax relief, 25.5(*b*)
general, 63.3
Remittances,
basis, 63
constructive, 63.4
double tax relief, 25.5(*b*)
new residents, by, 73.11
unremittable overseas income, 51.14
unremittable trade receipts, 71.92
Removal expenses, 75.13(x)
Remuneration, 71.54, 75
Renewals, 71.79
capital allowances, 10.38(x)
Rent-a-room relief, 68.11, 74.4
Rents,
business premises, 71.78
connected persons, from, 68.14
deductions from, 68.5, 68.15, 68.16
deductions of tax from, 23.14, 68.24
electric line wayleaves, 23.2, 23.14
factoring, 68.30
furnished lettings, 68.2, 68.4, 68.8, 68.14, 74.4
land managed as one estate, 68.7(*e*), 68.16(*d*)
lost, 68.18
mines and quarries, 23.2, 23.14
non-residents, payments to, 68.24
premiums, 68.27, 68.28
Sch A, 68
Sch D, 71.78
tied premises, 71.45
Repairs, 71.79
Sch A, 68.15
Repayment,
annuitants, to, 23.17(*c*)
charities, to, 15.17
claims, 17.6
construction industry tax scheme, 21.7
example, 2.2
interest on, 41
self-assessment, 78.23
official error, cases of, 56.6
PAYE, 55.40
provisional, 56.7
supplement, 29.24, 41
tax overpaid, 41, 56.7
Repos, 3.5, 3.6, 33.3
Research and development,
capital allowances, 10.52
enterprise investment scheme, 26.2, 26.6
revenue expenditure, 71.80
venture capital trusts, 91.3
RESIDENCE, ORDINARY RESIDENCE AND DOMICILE, 64
administrative procedures, 64.5
appeals, 64.8
change of residence,
— losses on, 46.12(*j*)
— partnerships, 53.15
— traders, 71.27
domicile, 64.4
double tax relief, 25, 64.3
house, *see* Private residence
husband and wife, 47.7

Residence, ordinary residence and domicile
ordinarily resident, 64.6
residence, 64.2, 64.5
— part of year, 64.5, 73.11, 73.12
— temporary, 64.5
— working abroad, 64.5, 75.2, 75.3
Scottish taxpayer, 1.3
self-assessment, 64.5, 78.38
visits abroad, 64.7
Residuary income, 22.3
Residuary legatees, 22.3
Restrictive covenants, 75.34
excess liability, 28.3(*a*)(iii)
Retirement,
lump sum on, 19.3–19.6, 66.12
partnership annuities, 53.16
RETIREMENT ANNUITIES, 65
back-duty relief, 6.11
cancellation of contract, 65.6
carry-back of premiums, 65.4
carry-forward, 65.5
Class 4 NICs and, 65.1, 83.6
compensation, 29.3
contracts, 65.2
death and disability benefits, 65.7
dentists, 66.11
dependant, for, 65.2
doctors, 66.11
earned income, treated as, 65.1
investigation settlements, 6.11
limits of relief, 65.3
Lloyd's underwriters, 65.4
lump sum on death, contract for, 65.2, 65.3
older annuitants (aged over 50), 65.3
partnership, 53.16
premiums related back, 65.4
qualifying premiums, 65.2
relevant earnings, 65.7
small lump sum schemes, and, 65.7
spouse, for, 65.2
trust schemes, 65.8
unused relief carried forward, 65.5
RETIREMENT SCHEMES, 66
additional voluntary contributions, 66.4–66.7
— mis-sold schemes, compensation for, 29.3
administrator, 66.4
annuities, 66.5(*d*)
approval, 66.3–66.5
— cessation of, 66.4
— discretionary, 66.4
benefits received, charge to tax, 66.1, 66.12
cessation of approval, 66.4
commutation of pension, charge to tax, 66.5(*c*)
conditions for approval, 66.3, 66.4
conversion to personal pension schemes, 60.2
deductibility by employer, 66.10
definition, 66.1
doctors and dentists, 66.11
effects of approval, 66.5
employees, payments to, 66.8
employers,
— payments by, 66.1
— payments to, 66.8
ex gratia benefits, 66.12
exempt approved scheme, 66.4
funds approved before 6 April 1980, 66.13
life assurance relief, 66.2
lump sums on retirement, 66.12
Members of Parliament, 66.11
money purchase schemes, 66.4
payment out of surplus funds, charge to tax, 66.8
pensions, charge to tax, 66.5(*d*)
personal pension schemes, 60
— conversion to, 60.2
pilots' benefit funds, 66.11
pooling, 90.2
regulations, 66.4
relevant statutory scheme, 66.1
relief by deductions from contributions, 66.5(*a*)
repayment of employees' contributions, 66.5(*c*), 66.8
retirement annuities, 65
schemes approved before 27 July 1989, 66.6
schemes approved before 23 July 1987, 66.7
small lump sum schemes, 60.8, 65.7
surpluses, 66.8
unapproved, 66.9, 66.10
unauthorised payments, 66.5(*c*), 66.8
whether payments assessable, 66.1
RETURNS, 67
agency workers, 67.5
auctioneers, 67.9
banks, by, 67.4
commissions, 67.6
electronic lodgement, 67.3, 78.1
emoluments, 67.5

Returns
employers, 67.5, 78.37
error or mistake in, 17.1, 17.10
failure to make, 58.2, 58.4
false statement in, 58.3
fees, commissions, copyrights, etc., 67.6
form of, 67.1, 67.2
fraud, 58.3
grants, subsidies, licences, etc., 67.7
herd basis, 34.10
hotels and boarding houses, 67.8
incomplete, 67.2
interest, of, 67.4
internet filing discount, 55.9, 67.3, 78.1
issuing houses, stockbrokers, auctioneers, etc., 67.9
late, 67.2
licences, 67.7
lodgers, 67.8
negligent or fraudulent, 58.3, 58.4
notice of liability, 58.1
partnerships, 67.10
PAYE, 55.9
penalties for failure to submit, 58.2, 58.4
public funds, payments out of, 67.7
Schedule A, 68.6, 68.19, 68.26
self-assessment, 78.1, 78.4, 78.5–78.9
— enquiries into, 78.11–78.13
signature of attorney, 67.2
simplified, 68.19, 71.28
stockbrokers, 67.9
substitute, 17.5, 67.2
taxable income belonging to others, 67.2
trustees, 67.2, 67.12, 78.4
underwriters, 89.5
Reverse premiums, 68.29, 71.78
Revocable settlements, 81.17, 81.24
Rotary club, 53.2
Royalties,
copyright, 17.2, 71.51
— annual sums to non-residents, 51.10
— deduction of tax, 23.15(*a*)
— double tax relief, 25.5(*l*)
— losses, treated as, 46.17(*a*)
— non-residents, to, deduction of tax, 51.10
— owner abroad, taxation of, 23.3(iii), 23.15, 51.10
deduction of tax from, 23.15
double tax relief, 25.2, 25.5(*l*)
mineral, 49
— tax deducted from, 23.14, 72.1(*d*)
patent,
— assessability, 54.4
— deduction of tax, 23.15(*b*)
— double tax relief, 25.5(*l*)
— expenses, 71.73
Sch D, 71.51, 71.73
spreading of receipts, 17.2, 71.51
Rubbish disposal sites, 71.94

S

Safety, *see also* Security Assets and Services
capital allowances, 10.25(i)(iii)
deduction of expenditure, 71.81
employee benefits, 75.35
Salaries, 75.1
Sale and leaseback of land, 3.12, 3.13
Sale of income, 3.10
Sales not at market price, 3.9
Sandwich courses, 29.26
Save as you earn schemes, 29.13(vi), 82.38
Savings accounts, tax-exempt, 29.10, 29.13(iii)
Savings bank interest, 29.13(iv)
Savings certificates, 33.6
Savings income, 1.9
lower rate, 1.3, 1.5
Savings-related share schemes, 82.38
SCHEDULE A, 68
amounts chargeable, 68.4, 68.5, 68.14
annual value, 68.7(*b*)
apportionment of receipts, etc. on sale, etc., 68.25
assessments and payment of tax, 56.1(*c*), 68.4, 68.20
businesses, 68.2–68.13
— amounts chargeable, 68.4, 68.5
— capital allowances, 10.32, 68.7(*a*), 68.8
— deductions, 68.7
— interest relief, 23.13, 43.2, 43.15
— losses, 68.13
— partnerships, 68.5
— returns, 68.6
capital allowances, 10.32, 68.7(*a*), 68.8, 68.15(*v*)
caravan sites, 68.4, 74.4
collection from agent, etc., 68.21, 68.24
deduction of tax, 68.24
entertaining, 68.5(*b*), 68.16(*f*)
expenses deductible, 68.4, 68.15, 68.16
extorted payments, 68.5(*c*), 68.16(*f*)
full rent, lease at, 68.16(*b*)
furnished lettings, 68.2, 68.4, 68.8, 68.14, 74.4
— election, 74.4

Schedule A
— holiday, 68.9, 74.4
— renewals, 68.8
illegal payments, 68.5(*c*), 68.16(*f*)
information concerning leases, 68.26
land managed as one estate, 68.7(*b*), 68.15, 68.16(*d*)
lodgers, 68.11
losses, 68.13, 68.16, 68.18
maintenance and repairs obviated by alterations, 68.15
mutual business, 68.5
non-resident landlords, 68.24
partnerships, 68.5
person chargeable, 68.21
pre-trading expenditure, 68.5(iii)
premiums, etc.,
— allowance to payer, 68.28
— assessability on recipient, 68.27
— reverse, 68.29, 71.78
rent factoring, 68.30
rent-a-room relief, 68.11
rents, etc., 68.4, 68.14
— full, 68.16(*b*)
— unpaid, 68.18
returns, 68.6, 68.19, 68.26
reverse premiums, 68.29, 71.78
scope and exceptions, 68.4, 68.14
sea walls, 68.7(*c*), 68.16(*e*)
sporting rights, 68.16(*e*)
spouse, deceased, 68.15
tenant's repairing leases, 68.16(*c*)
trading premises, allowance on sale of, 68.31
transitional provisions, 68.3, 68.13, 68.22
SCHEDULE B, 69
SCHEDULE C, 70
SCHEDULE D CASES I AND II, 71
accountancy expenses, 71.69
accounting basis, 12, 71.40
accounting date, change of, 71.7, 71.15
accounts, 71.28
accruals basis, 71.40
allowable deductions, 71.40–71.95
assessable profits, 71.40–71.95
basis of assessment, 71.3 *et seq.*
— change of accounting date, 71.7, 71.15
— closing years, 71.9, 71.17
— current year basis, 71.11–71.24
— double tax relief, 25.5(*j*)
— intermediate years, 71.6, 71.14
— opening years, 71.4, 71.12
— preceding year basis, 71.6
caravan sites, 68.4, 74.4
carers, 71.72
cash basis, 12
cessation, 71.9, 71.17, 71.25
change of accounting date, 71.7, 71.15
charities, gifts by traders to, 15.21, 71.60, 71.84
closing years of assessment, 71.9, 71.17
commencement, 71.4, 71.12, 71.25
companies, 71.2
compulsory acquisition, compensation for, 71.48(*d*)
computation of profits, 71.40–71.95
— accounting basis, 12, 71.40
— advertising, 71.41
— application of profits, 71.42
— 'ash cash', 71.60
— athletes, 71.37
— authors and artistes, 71.43
— bad and doubtful debts, 71.44
— breweries, distilleries, licensed premises, 71.45
— cashbacks, 71.46
— commission, 71.46, 71.64
— compensation, damages, etc. payments, 71.47
— compensation, damages, etc. receipts, 71.48
— computer software, 71.72
— contingent and future liabilities, 71.49
— contracts, 71.50
— copyright, etc., 71.51
— cremation fees, 71.60
— damages, 71.47, 71.48
— deduction of tax at source, amounts paid under, 71.52
— deposits, 71.91
— discounts, 71.46
— distilleries, 71.45
— embezzlement, etc., 71.53
— employees and directors, 71.54
— entertainment expenses, 71.55
— exchange gains and losses, 71.56
— exclusivity agreements, 71.88
— extorted payments, 71.63
— farming and market gardening, 71.57
— film, etc. production, 71.58
— finance lease rentals, 71.68
— franchising, 71.59
— gifts and other non-contractual receipts and payments, 71.60
— grants, subsidies, etc., 71.85
— guarantees, 71.61
— health insurance, 71.64
— hire-purchase, 71.62

Schedule D Cases I and II
— illegal payments, 71.63
— insurance, 71.46, 71.54, 71.64
— interest and other payments for loans, 71.65
— interest on unpaid tax, 71.65
— investment income, 71.66
— key employee insurance, 71.54
— know-how, 71.67
— lease premiums, 71.78
— lease rental payments, 71.68
— legal and professional expenses, 71.69, 71.72
— licensed premises, 71.45
— loan finance incidental costs, 71.70
— locum insurance, 71.64
— market gardening, 71.57
— mines, quarries, etc., 71.71
— miscellaneous, 71.72
— ostrich farming, 71.37
— patents, 71.73
— personal expenses, 71.74
— pooling of profits, 71.75
— pre-trading expenditure, 71.76
— professional indemnity insurance, 71.64
— property receipts and sales, 71.77
— provisions, 71.49
— redundancy payments, 71.54
— rents, etc. for business premises, 71.78
— repairs and renewals, 71.79
— reverse premiums, 68.29, 71.78
— scientific research, 71.80
— security, 71.81
— service companies, 71.72
— share etc. issues, purchase and sales, 71.82
— share schemes, 71.54
— stock in trade and work in progress, 71.83
— subscriptions (including trade association contributions), 71.84
— subsidies, grants, etc., 71.85
— subsistence, 71.90
— taxation, 71.86
— telecommunications licences, 71.87
— tied houses, 71.45
— tied petrol companies, etc., 71.88
— timber, 71.72
— trade marks, 71.72
— training, 71.89
— transfer fees, 71.78
— travelling and subsistence expenses, 71.90
— 'true and fair view', 71.40
— unclaimed balances, 71.91
— unremittable receipts, debts, etc., 71.92
— value added tax, 71.93
— video tape rental, 71.72
— waste disposal, 71.94
— woodlands, 71.95
death of trader, business passing to spouse, 71.9
deductible expenses, 71.40–71.95
discontinuance, 71.9, 71.17, 71.25
divers and diving supervisors, 71.31
due date for payment of tax, 56.1
earnings basis, 71.40
employment, 71.54
farming, 71.57
film, etc. production, 71.58
franchising, 71.59
gifts, etc., 15.19–15.21, 71.60, 71.84
goods for personal consumption, 71.83
insurance commission, 71.46, 71.64
landfill tax, 71.94
living expenses abroad, 71.90
mines, etc., 71.1
national insurance contributions, 71.54
opening years of assessment, 71.4, 71.12
overlap profits, 71.19, 71.22
— double tax relief, 25.5(*j*)
payroll deduction scheme costs, 15.18
Private Finance Initiative projects, 71.40
residence, change of, 53.15, 71.27
securities, borrowing and lending, 71.82
share schemes, 71.54
sub-postmasters, 71.72
successions, 71.25
telecommunications licences, 71.87
underwriting profits, 89.3
waste disposal, 71.94
whether a trade carried on, 71.29–71.39
— avoidance schemes, 71.29
— betting, 71.30
— divers, etc., 71.31
— futures and options, 71.32
— horse racing, etc., 71.33
— illegal trading, 71.34
— isolated or speculative transactions, 71.35
— liquidators, etc. and personal representatives, 71.36
— miscellaneous, 71.37
— property transactions, 71.38
— share dealing, 71.39
woodlands, 71.95

Schedule D Cases I and II
video tape rental, 71.72
SCHEDULE D CASE III, 72
annual payments and annuities, 72.3(*c*)
basis of assessment,
— current year, 72.4(*e*)(*f*)
— disposals, 72.4(*c*)
— new source, 72.4(*b*)
— preceding year basis, 72.4(*a*)
deductions not permitted, 72.3(*d*)
discount, 72.2, 72.3(*b*)
interest, 72.1, 72.3(*b*)
lower rate of tax, 1.9
savings income, 1.9
spouse, death of, 72.4(*d*)
SCHEDULE D CASES IV AND V, 73
aggregation of income, 73.6
basis of assessment, 73.9
deductions, 73.7
delayed remittances, 51.14
Eire, income from, 73.5
foreign pensions, 59.2
individuals permanently leaving UK, 73.12
lower rate of tax, 1.9
new residents, 73.11
overseas income, 73.3
overseas property business, 68.13, 73.4
possessions, 73.2
savings income, 1.9
securities, 73.2
unremittable overseas income, 51.14
SCHEDULE D CASE VI, 74
accrued income scheme, 74.6–74.33 *and see* Accrued income scheme
basis of assessment, 74.3
certificates of deposit, 13.2
enterprise allowance, 71.85
furnished lettings, 74.4
leases, assignments of, 68.27
losses, 74.5
offshore funds, 52.8–52.12
patent rights, 54.5
post-cessation receipts, 62
premiums, etc., 68.27
scope of, 74.1
theatrical angels, 74.2
volunteer drivers, 74.2
SCHEDULE E, 75
agencies, workers supplied by, 55.3, 75.46
assessable income, 75.7
basic principles of assessment, 75.1
beneficial loan arrangements, 75.17
benefits, 75.8, 75.13
bus services, 75.13(xxv)
cars, 75.15
Cases I, II and III, 75.2
clergymen, etc., 75.9
commuting, 75.10(*a*)
compensation for loss of employment, 19
counselling, 75.13(xxvii), 75.42
cycles etc., provision of, 75.13(xxvi)
deductions, 75.10
delayed remittances, 51.14
directors or 'higher-paid' employees, 75.11
dispensations, 75.22
divers and diving supervisors, 71.31
earnings from work done abroad, 75.3
education, 75.42
emoluments, definition, 75.7
employee liabilities and indemnity insurance, 75.23
employee shareholdings, 75.19
employment or profession, 21.7, 75.24
expenses, 75.12
flat-rate expenses, 75.25
gifts, testimonials, etc., 75.26
health insurance, 75.13(xiii), 75.37
HM Forces, 75.27
income support, 83.3
indemnity insurance, 75.23
legal costs, 75.28
living accommodation, etc., 75.29
loan arrangements, 75.17
loss of employment, 19
luncheon vouchers, 75.30
medical insurance, 75.13(xiii), 75.37
ministers of religion, 75.9
mobile telephones, 75.13(xxiii), 75.15, 75.16
non-domiciled employees, 75.6
overnight expenses, 75.13(xxii), 75.43, 75.44(*a*)
pay as you earn, 55
payments in lieu of notice, 75.45
pensions, 59.1
personal pension schemes, 60.1
personal service companies etc., 61.7–61.9
post-employment deductions, 1.10(vii), 75.23
profit-related pay, 75.31
public offices, 43.6, 75.2(i), 92.1
receipts basis, 75.1
redundancy payments, 19, 75.32
relocation packages, 75.33
restrictive covenants, 75.34

Schedule E
retirement annuities, 60.1
retirement benefit schemes, 66.1
scholarships, 29.27, 75.20
scope of charge, 75.1
security of employees, 75.35
shares, etc., 75.36
sick pay and health insurance, 29.12, 75.37
social security, 75.38
sporting and recreational facilities, 75.21
subscriptions, 75.39
subsistence, 75.13(xxii), 75.43
taxation, 75.40
termination payments, 19, 75.41
training, counselling, etc., 75.42
travelling and subsistence expenses, 75.10(*a*), 75.13, 75.43
— work done abroad, 75.5
VAT, 55.9, 55.44
vouchers and credit tokens, 75.44
wages in lieu of notice, 75.45
work-related training, 75.42
workers supplied by agencies, 55.3, 75.46
works bus service, 75.13(xxv)
SCHEDULE F, 76
ordinary rate, 1.9, 76.3
trust rate, 81.2(*a*), 81.5
upper rate, 1.9, 76.3
Scholarships, 29.27, 75.20
School fees,
benefit, 75.13
under Court order, 47.10
Scientific research,
associations, 77
capital allowances, 10.52
revenue expenditure, 71.80
SCIENTIFIC RESEARCH ASSOCIATIONS, 77
Scotland, *see also* Scottish Parliament
appeals, 4.7
basic rate variation, 1.3
curator bonis, 29.13(iii), 29.21
living accommodation, benefit of, 75.29
maintenance orders, 47.10
partnership, 53.1
poinding, 56.3
property sales, 71.77
recovery of tax, 56.3
Scottish Parliament,
Members of,
— accommodation allowances, 29.16
— accommodation expenses, 75.29(B)
— capital allowances, 10.24
— ministers, etc., transport and subsistence, 29.16
— overnight expenses, 29.16
— personal pension schemes, 60.1
— reimbursed expenses, 29.16
— retirement schemes, 66.11
— termination payments, 75.41
— travel expenses, 29.16
tax-varying power, 1.3
Sea walls, 68.7(c), 68.16(e)
Seamen,
duties deemed in UK, 75.2
duties outside UK, 75.3
lifeboatmen, 55.45
PAYE, 55.37, 55.45
Search and seizure, 6.9
Securities, *see also* Shares
accrued income schemes, 74.6 *et seq. and see* Accrued income scheme
bondwashing, 74.6 *et seq.*
borrowing and lending, 71.82
building society, 9.3, 23.3(ii)
cancellation of tax advantages, 3.2
convertible, 44.8
deep gain, 29.29, 44.7
discounts on, 29.29, 44.5, 44.8, 44.9, 72.2
euro, conversion to, 3.5, 3.7, 72.2, 74.7, 74.8, 74.19, 74.23
Eurobonds, 23.3(ii)
FOTRA, 33.2
gifts of, 15.20
gilt-edged, 33
— strips, 71.82, 72.2, 74.24
government, 33
income received on, held for 1 month, 3.6, 74.32
indexed, 44.8, 44.9
interest payable gross, 33.3
manufactured dividends, 3.7
new issues, 44.5(*g*), 44.7(6), 71.82, 74.29
overseas, Sch D, Case IV, 73.2
qualifying convertible, 44.8
sale and repurchase, 3.3, 3.5, 3.7, 9.3(*h*), 33.3, 74.23, 74.32
stock lending, 71.82, 74.25
strips, 71.82, 72.2, 74.24
Treasury securities, discounts on, 29.29
Security, substitution of, 43.13
Security assets and services,
benefit-in-kind, 75.35
capital allowances, 10.25
deduction of expenditure, 71.81
employees, 75.35

SELF-ASSESSMENT, 78
accounts, 78.5
agents, 78.17
anti-avoidance, 78.2
appeals, 17.3, 78.31
— jurisdiction of Commissioners, 78.33
branches or agencies, 51.5–51.7
chargeability, notice of, 78.4
claims, 17.1–17.4
Class 4 national insurance contributions, 78.17
collection and recovery, 78.35
copyright receipts, 17.2
'Crown option', 78.12, 78.13
determinations, 78.14
discovery, 78.15
domicile, 64.5, 78.38
due date, 78.19, 78.20
elections, 17.1–17.3
employers' obligations and returns, 78.37
enquiries, 78.11–78.13
equitable liability, 56.9
error or mistake relief, 17.1, 17.10
estimates, 78.6
farming, 17.2, 34.4, 34.8, 71.57(*a*)
fraud or negligence, 78.28
herd basis elections, 34.4, 34.8
interest on overpaid tax, 41.1, 78.23
interest on unpaid tax, 42.1, 78.22
internet filing discount, 78.1
investigations, 78.11–78.13
key dates, 79
Lloyd's underwriters, 89.2
losses,
— capital, 78.1
— claims, 17.1, 17.2
market gardening, 17.2, 71.57(*a*)
non-residents, 51.5–51.7, 78.38
notice of chargeability, 78.4
ordinary residence, 64.5, 78.38
over-repayments, 78.34
partnerships, 78.8, 78.9, 78.16, 78.27
payment of tax, 78.1, 78.17–78.20
penalties, 78.4, 78.10, 78.17, 78.21, 78.25–78.29, 78.37
post-cessation receipts, 17.2
records, 78.10
relevant trustees, 78.36
representatives, 51.5–51.7
residence, 64.5, 78.38
returns, 78.1, 78.4, 78.5–78.9
— electronic, 78.1
— employers', 78.37
— enquiries, 78.11–78.13
— failure to deliver, 78.14, 78.26, 78.27
— incomplete, 78.26
— trustees, 78.4
share schemes, 82.2
surcharge, 42.4, 78.21
transactions in securities, 3.2(vii)
transfer pricing, 3.9
trustees, liability of, 78.4, 78.36
UK representatives, 51.5–51.7
SELF-ASSESSMENT—KEY DATES, 79
Self-build societies, 30.10
MIRAS scheme, 23.13
SELF-EMPLOYED PERSONS, 80
job-related accommodation, 43.16
personal pensions, 60
personal service companies etc., 61
retirement annuities, 65
Separation allowances, 47.10
SETTLEMENTS, 81
accumulated income, 81.8
accumulation, 81.5
— deposit interest, 8.2(A), 9.3(*i*)
additional rate, 81.5
administration expenses, 81.3, 81.5
annuities, 81.9
assessment on trust income, 81.3
assets put into, 81.16(*e*)
beneficiaries,
— income of, 81.8
— payments to, 81.5
— relief from UK tax, 81.5
capital sums, etc. to settlor, 81.19
children, on, 81.18, 81.23
corporate body connected with, 81.19
covenants, 81.22
definitions, 81.16, 81.21
demergers, shares received in, 81.2(*d*)
discretionary powers, 81.17, 81.26
discretionary trusts, 81.5
— deposit interest, 8.2(A), 9.3(*i*)
— savings income, 1.9
dispositions which cannot exceed six (or three) years, 81.22
distributions to, 3.21
employee trusts, 71.54, 81.5, 82.41
expenses, 81.3, 81.5
foreign trust income, 81.10
future spouse, benefit to, 81.17, 81.26
historic buildings, maintenance funds, 81.30
income given to charity, 81.14
income only, 81.27, 81.29
inheritance tax paid by trustees, 81.16(*e*)
loans and repayments to settlor, 81.19

Settlements
management expenses, 81.3, 81.5
parent's settlement in favour of child, 81.18, 81.23
personal allowances, 81.12
protective, 81.17, 81.25
revocable, 81.17, 81.24
savings income, 1.9
Schedule F trust rate, 81.2(*a*), 81.5
Scottish, 81.2(*c*)
settlor, 81.16(*b*), 81.21(*b*)
— benefit to, 81.17, 81.26
— income of, 81.15–81.27, 81.29
— liability of, 81.13, 81.14, 81.21
— loans to, 81.19
— payments to trustees, 81.28
— recovery from trustees, 81.21(*f*)
— retaining interest, 81.17, 81.25
six- (or three-) year rule, 81.22
trustees,
— claims by, 81.11
— personal position, 81.7
unit trusts, income from, 90.1
Settlements on children,
parent's, 16.4, 81.18, 81.23
Settlor, 81.16(b), 81.21(b)
Share dealer,
securities held for short period, 3.6
Share farming, 71.57(h)
SHARE INCENTIVES AND OPTIONS, 82
approved schemes, 82.9–82.40
company share option plans, 82.40
conditional acquisitions, 82.7
convertible shares, 82.8
employee share ownership plans, 82.11–82.25
employee share ownership trusts, 82.41
enterprise management incentive schemes, 82.26–82.37
executive share option schemes, 82.39
incentives, 82.4, 82.5
national insurance contributions, 82.3
options, 82.3, 82.38–82.40
payment of tax by instalments, 82.3
personal equity plans, 29.21
profit-sharing schemes,
— approval, 82.9
— charge to tax, 82.10
running costs, 71.54
savings-related share option schemes, 82.38
setting up costs, 71.54
Shares, *see also* Securities and Share Incentives and Options
accrued income scheme, 74.6–74.33 *and see* Accrued income scheme
acquisition by employees, 75.19, 75.36, 82
bonus issues, restrictions, 3.18
company purchasing own, 1.9, 3.21
conditional acquisitions, 82.7
convertible, 82.8
date of issue, 26.2, 26.19, 26.27
dealing, whether trading, 71.39
definition, 82.2
employees, held by, 75.19, 75.36, 82
enterprise investment scheme, 26
gifts of, 15.20
individual savings accounts, 29.10
issue, date of, 26.2, 26.19, 26.27
locked-in value, 82.10
losses on unlisted, 46.18
new issues, 71.82
personal equity plans, 29.21
profits of dealers in, 71.39, 71.82
purchases of, 71.82
realisations of, 71.82
self-assessment, 82.2
stock dividends, 85
stock lending, 71.82, 74.25
transactions in, cancellation of tax advantage, 3.2
unlisted shares, losses on, 46.18
venture capital trusts, 91
Sharkey v Wernher, 71.83
Ships,
expenditure on, 10.27, 10.28(B), 10.30, 10.37(*b*)
Short-life assets, 10.28(F)
Short rotation coppice, 71.57(i)
Sick pay, 75.37
Sickness benefits, 29.12, 71.64, 75.37
Signing-on fees, 75.7
Single currency,
conversion to, 3.5, 3.7, 72.2, 74.7, 74.8, 74.19, 74.23
Single person,
allowance, 1.14, 1.21
Small workshops, 10.21
SOCIAL SECURITY, 83
Affordable Warmth programme,
— capital allowances, 10.34
benefits, basis of assessment of, 75.1, 75.38
unemployment benefit, 55.43
Societies and clubs, 18

Special Commissioners, 35.3
appeals before, 4.3, 4.6
costs awarded by, 4.6
decisions, publication of, 4.6
election for appeal to be heard by, 4.3
leave for extended time limit assessments, 6.4
penalty proceedings before, 58.6
precepts, 58.5
Special dividends, 3.21, 81.5
Special reserve fund, 89.7
Speculative transactions,
whether trading, 71.35
Sport,
benefit matches etc., 75.26
betting, 71.30, 71.33
clubs, VAT and, 18.5
employees, facilities for, 75.21
football ground improvements, 10.2(ii), 10.25(iii), 71.85
golf clubs, 50
greyhounds, 71.33, 71.83
members' clubs, 18.1, 18.5
non-resident sportsmen, 36.2(*h*), 51.8
pools promoters, 10.2(ii), 71.30, 71.85
sporting rights, 68.16(*e*)
stadiums, 10.25(iii)
transfer fees, 19.3, 71.72, 75.7
Sports grounds, safety expenditure, 10.25(iii)
Stakeholder pensions, *see* Personal Pension Schemes
Starting rate, 1.3, 1.9, 11.3
State Bank of Pakistan, 30.2
Stated Case, 4.7
Statements of practice, Revenue, 40
STATUTES, TABLE OF, 96
STATUTORY BODIES, 84
Statutory construction,
Hansard, consideration of, 4.7
Statutory maternity pay, 83.3
Statutory retirement benefit scheme, 66.11
Statutory sick pay, 75.37, 83.3
Stock, 71.83
charitable donation, 15.19, 15.21, 71.60
deep discounted, 44.5, 44.6, 44.8, 44.9
farming, valuation for, 71.57(*k*)
government, 33
indexed, 44.8, 44.9
lending, 71.82, 74.25
STOCK DIVIDENDS, 85
enhanced, 85.6
Stock exchange member,
returns by, 67.9
Stock lending, 71.82, 74.25
Stockbrokers, returns by, 67.9
Strikers' benefits, 55.43
Strips, 71.82, 72.2, 74.24
Student loans,
exempt interest on, 29.13(x)
Sub-contractors in construction industry, *see* Construction industry tax scheme
agency workers, 75.46
travelling and subsistence allowances, 75.43
Sub-postmasters, 71.72, 75.24
Subscriptions, 71.84
Sch E, 75.39
Subsidies, 71.85
effects on capital allowances, 10.2(ii)
returns of, 67.7
Subsistence allowance, 75.43
incidental overnight expenses, 75.13(xxii), 75.43, 75.44(*a*)
Successions, 71.25, 71.26
capital allowances, 10.38(xi)
double, partnership, 53.9
Suggestion scheme awards, 75.26
Superannuation contributions, 55.39
police, 45.3(ii)
Superannuation funds,
contributions to, 59.5
exempt income and gains, 30.17
Surcharges,
self-assessment, 42.4, 78.21

T

Tax accountant, 6.8(c)
Tax avoidance, 3
accrued income scheme, 74.6 *et seq.*
annuities, sale of right to, 3.4
associated persons, transactions between, 3.9
capital allowances, 10.9, 10.22, 10.38(iii), 10.50, 10.52
capital sums received in lieu of earnings, 3.10
commodity futures, dealings in, 3.20
connected persons, 20
Courts, approach of, 3.1
current year basis, change to, 43.22, 71.20, 71.22, 72.4(*f*), 73.9, 78.2
general principles, 3.1
income from personal activities, sale of, 3.10

Tax avoidance
land,
— leaseback transactions, 3.12, 3.13
— transactions in, 3.11
leaseback transactions, 3.12, 3.13
leases, assets other than land, 3.14, 3.15
loan transactions, 3.16
manufactured dividends, 3.7
non-taxable consideration, 3.19
offshore funds, *see* Offshore Funds
overvalue, transactions at, 3.9
— double tax relief, 25.5(*m*)
personal service companies etc., 61
persons exempt from tax, 3.17, 3.18
sale and leaseback, 3.12, 3.13
securities,
— held for one month or less, 3.6
— sale and repurchase, 3.3, 3.5, 3.7, 33.3
— transactions in, 3.2
— transfers of income arising from, 3.4
transfer of assets abroad, 3.8
— discounts on securities, 72.2
undervalue, transactions at, 3.9
— double tax relief, 25.5(*m*)
Tax credit, 1.9, 56.1(*d*)
arrangements to pass on value, 3.23
charities, 15.6
children, for, 1.15, 1.18
disabled person's, 83.4, 83.7
— information, 36.3
— PAYE, 55.20
fraction, 1.9
non-residents, 25.2
repayment claim, 1.11
working families', 83.4, 83.7
— information, 36.3
— PAYE, 55.46
Tax-exempt special savings accounts, 29.13(iii)
Tax-free,
annuities, 23.17
arrangements, 23.16
payments, 75.40
savings accounts, 29.13
Tax year, 1.2
Taxation,
Schedule D Cases I or II, 71.86
Schedule E, 75.40
Taxed payments,
deduction of tax at source, 23
losses, treated as, 46.17
Taxpayers' Charter, 35.7
open Government, 35.10
Technical education, 71.54
Telecommunications licences, 71.87
Telephone,
claims, 17.5
mobile, 75.13(xxiii), 75.15, 75.16
Temporary Employment Subsidy, 71.85
Terminal loss, 46.15
mineral royalties, 49
Termination payments, 75.41
compensation etc., 19.3–19.6
wages in lieu of notice, 75.45
Territorial sea, 51.13
TESSAs, 29.10, 29.13(iii)
Testimonials, etc.
Sch D, 71.48
Sch E, 75.26
Theatrical angels, 74.2
Theatrical entertainers, 75.24
Third world charities, 15.21
Thrift funds, 18.2
Tied garages, 71.88
Tied houses, 71.45
Timber, 69.2, 71.72
TIME LIMITS—FIXED DATES, 86
beneficial loans, 86.1(*g*), 86.2(*a*)(xxii)
blind persons' allowance, 86.1(*c*)
capital allowances, 86.2(*a*)(i)
cash basis withdrawal, 86.1(*b*)(iii)
chargeability to tax, 86.1(*a*)
claims for allowances, 86.6(*b*)
copyright receipts, 86.6(*k*)
deceased estates, 86.3
discounts on securities, 86.2(*a*)(xxi)
double assessment, 86.6(*c*)
double tax relief, 86.6(*d*)
employee shares, 86.1(*e*)
error or mistake claims, 86.6(*a*)
farming, 86.2(*a*)(ii)(xva)
films, 86.2(*a*)(xvi)
furnished holiday lettings, 86.2(*a*)(xii)
gifts to educational establishments, 86.2(*a*)(xvii)
herd basis, 86.2(*a*)(ii)
historic buildings, maintenance settlements, 86.2(*a*)(xxiii)
interest payable, 86.2(*a*)(iii)(iv), 86.6(*e*)
land managed as one estate, 86.1(*d*)(ii)
late assessments, 86.1(*d*)(i)
loss incurred in trade, 86.2(*a*)(v)
loss on unlisted shares, 86.2(*a*)(vi)
losses, general, 86.6(*f*)
maintenance payments, 86.2(*a*)(vii)
married couple's allowance transfer, 86.1(*c*)
mineral royalties, 86.6(*g*)

Time Limits—fixed dates
non-residents and other overseas matters, 86.6(*h*)
patent rights, 86.2(*a*)(ix)
personal pensions, 86.1(*b*)(ii), 86.6(*i*)
post-cessation expenditure, 86.2(*a*)(xi)
post-cessation receipts, spreading back, 86.2(*a*)(x)
rent-a-room relief, 86.2(*a*)(xiii)
residence basis election, 86.2(*a*)(iii)
retirement annuities, 86.1(*b*)(ii), 86.6(*i*)
returns, 86.1(*b*)(i)
Schedule A losses, 86.2(*a*)(xiv)
Schedule D Cases I and II claims, 86.6(*j*)(*k*)
Schedule D Case III claims, 86.6(*l*)
Schedule D Cases IV and V claims, 86.6(*l*)
self-assessment returns, 86.1(*b*)(i)
settlements, 86.6(*m*)
share dealers, 86.2(*a*)(xviii)
share options, 86.1(*f*)
stock valuations, 86.2(*a*)(xix)(xx), 86.2(*b*)(i)
trading loss, 86.2(*a*)(v)
unremittable overseas income, 86.2(*a*)(viii)
work in progress valuation, 86.2(*a*)(xx)
TIME LIMITS—MISCELLANEOUS, 87
appeals, for, 4.2
assessments, for, 5.7
back duty, 6.4
claims, 17.4, 17.8
deceased persons, 6.5
penalties, 58.8
Tipping sites, 71.94
Tips,
troncs, 55.42
Toll roads, 10.11, 10.14–10.17
Tools allowance, 75.25
Top-slicing,
life assurance policies, 45.13
premiums etc. on leases, 68.27
Total income, 1.6
deductions in computing, 1.10
Trade,
adventure in the nature of, 71.35
basis of assessment, 71.3 *et seq.*
— cash basis, 12.1
capital allowances, 10.1
carried on etc. abroad, 51.12, 63.1(A)(v), (C)
closing years, 71.9, 71.17
— double tax relief, 25.5(*j*)
companies, 71.2
debts, unclaimed, 71.91
deductions allowable, 71.40 *et seq.*
discontinued, 71.9, 71.17
entertainers, treated as carrying on, 51.8
individuals, assessment, 71.3 *et seq.*
losses, 46.2
nature of, 71.29–71.39
opening years, 71.4, 71.12
— double tax relief, 25.5(*j*)
partnerships, assessment, 53.3, 71.3 *et seq.*
post-cessation receipts, 62
premises, sale of, 68.31
Sch D, Case I, 71
sportsmen, treated as carrying on, 51.8
stock in, valuation, 71.83
successions to, 71.25, 71.26
unremittable receipts, 71.92
work-in-progress, 71.83
Trade associations, 50, 71.84
TRADE UNIONS, 88
Traded options, 30.17, 71.32
Trademarks, 71.72
Tradepoint, 3.6, 3.7
Trading,
charities, by, 15.7
company, 46.18
illegal, 71.34
liquidator, by, 71.36
mutual, 50
non-resident, in UK, 51.4–51.9
personal representatives, by, 71.36
pre-trading expenditure, 71.76
stock, 71.83
— farming, valuation for, 71.57(*k*)
— gifts of, 15.19, 15.21
— herd basis, 34
transfer pricing, 3.9
unremittable receipts, 71.92
whether, 71.29–71.39
— avoidance schemes, 71.29
— betting, 71.30
— divers, etc., 71.31
— futures and options, 71.32
— horse racing, etc., 71.33
— illegal trading, 71.34
— isolated or speculative transactions, 71.35
— liquidators, etc. and personal representatives, 71.36
— miscellaneous, 71.37
— property transactions, 71.38
— share dealing, 71.39

Trading losses, 46.2
Trading profits, 71.40–71.95
Training and enterprise councils, 71.84
Training costs, 1.10(vi), 71.54, 71.89, 75.42, 92
Transactions,
in securities, cancellation of tax advantage, 3.2
isolated, trading, 71.35
Transfer fees, 19.3, 71.72, 75.7
Transfer of assets abroad, 3.8, 74.32
discounts on securities, 72.2
Transfer pricing, 3.9, 25.5(m)
Transport vouchers, 75.44(a)
Travelling expenses, 71.90
commuting, 75.10(*a*), 75.13
cycle, 75.43
disabled employees, 75.13(vi), 75.15, 75.43
foreign emoluments, 75.6
incidental overnight expenses, 75.13(xxii), 75.43, 75.44(*a*)
late night journeys, 75.13(vii), 75.43
MPs, of, 29.16
motoring, 71.90, 75.43
offshore rig workers, 75.13(viii), 75.43
overseas trades, 51.12
public transport disruption, 75.13(v), 75.43
Sch E, 75.5, 75.6, 75.43
Treasury,
discount on securities, 29.29, 33.4
Troncs, 55.42
'True and fair view', 12.2, 71.40
Trustees, 81
assessability, 81.2, 81.3
claims by, 81.11
connected persons, 20.3
deceased estates, 22
deep discount/gain securities, 44.5, 44.7, 44.8
demergers, shares received in, 81.2(*d*)
discounts on securities, 72.2
expenses, 81.3
incapacitated persons, 81.11
non-resident, 81.10
offshore income gains of, 52.12
payment of inheritance tax, 81.16(*e*)
payments by settlor to, 81.28
personal position, 81.7
recovery by settlor, 81.21(*f*)
residence of, 64.5
returns by, 67.2
schemes, retirement annuities, 65.8
self-assessment, 78.4, 36
stock dividends received by, 85.6
Trusts, 81
see Settlements

U

Unclaimed balances, 71.91
UNDERWRITERS, 89
accrued income, 74.26
assessment and collection, 89.4–89.6
corporate, 89.1
deep discount/gain securities, 44.5, 44.7, 44.8
double tax relief, 25.5(*e*)(*h*)
losses, 89.7
members' agent pooling arrangements, 89.3
personal pension schemes, 60.5
profits, 89.3
retirement annuities, 65.4
self-assessment, 89.2
Special Reserve Fund, 89.8
Unearned income, 1.8
Unemployment benefits, 55.43, 83.3
Unified tax, 1.4
Uniform allowances, 75.27
Unilateral relief, 25.4
UNIT TRUSTS, 90
authorised, 90.1
charitable, 15.9
court common investment funds, 90.2, 90.3
exempt, 30.19
futures and options, 90.1
individual savings accounts, 29.10
interest paid gross to, 9.3
offshore funds, 52
pension fund pooling, 90.2
personal equity plans, in, 29.21
savings income, 1.9
share option schemes, 82.4
unauthorised, 90.2
United Kingdom, 51.13
UK Ecolabelling Board, 30.20
UK public revenue dividends, 23.3(ii)
UK tax representatives, 51.5–51.7
Unlisted shares, losses on, 46.18
Unpaid tax,
back duty, 6
interest on, 42
— self-assessment, 78.22
surcharges, 42.4, 78.21

Unremittable foreign income, 51.14
remittance basis, 63
Unremittable trade receipts, etc., 71.92

V

Valuation of stock and work in progress, 71.83
Value added tax,
benefits in kind, 55.9, 75.13
business profits, 71.93
capital allowances and, 10.2(v), 10.13–10.15, 10.19, 10.27, 10.28, 10.34, 10.38(iii), 10.52
emoluments, for PAYE, 55.44
interest on tax overdue, 42.10
PAYE, 55.9, 55.44
penalties, 58.11
repayment supplement, 29.24
Schedule E, 55.9, 55.44
self-employed, registration, 80.7
sports clubs, 18.5
Vehicle maintenance grants, 29.28
VENTURE CAPITAL TRUSTS, 91
approval, 91.2
— withdrawal of, 91.2, 91.7, 91.11
capital gains tax reliefs, 91.11
— disposal, on, 91.12
— re-investment, on, 91.14
distributions from, 91.9
income tax reliefs, 91.4
— distributions, on, 91.9
— eligible shares, 91.5
— investment, on, 91.5
— withdrawal of, 91.7
investment in, 91.5
— withdrawal of relief, 91.7
re-investment relief (CGT), 91.14
relevant distributions, 91.9
research and development, 91.3
qualifying holdings, 91.3
Video tape rental, 71.72
Viewdata receivers, 10.35
Visiting forces, 30.21
Visitors, 64.5
VOCATIONAL TRAINING RELIEF, 1.10(v), 92
Vocations, *see* Professions, Trades
Voluntary allowances, 23.18
Voluntary associations, 18
Voluntary pensions, 59.1(v), 59.2(ii)
exempt, 59.4(i)
Vouchers, 75.44

W

Wages,
in lieu of notice, 75.45
in sovereigns, 75.7
Wales, *see* Assemblies
War gratuities, 29.31
War widows, 29.32
Warehouses, whether industrial buildings, 10.11
Warrants, applications by Revenue for, 6.9
Waste disposal sites, 71.94
Wayleaves (electricity), 23.14, 72.1(d)
Wear and tear allowances, 10.38(xii)
Welfare expenditure,
counselling, 75.13(xxvii), 75.42
industrial building allowance, 10.11
Sch D, Cases I and II, 71.54
Wholly, exclusively, etc.,
Sch D, Cases I and II, 71.40
Sch E, 75.10
Widow(er)s,
children, additional relief, 1.17
Widow's bereavement allowance, 1.16
Wife,
alimony, 47.10
assessability, 47.1
collection from, 47.1
partnership with, 53.13
separate taxation, 47.1
separated, 47.5, 47.7, 47.9, 47.10
small maintenance payments, 47.10
Wilful default,
back duty assessments, 6.2, 6.4
interest on tax unpaid, 42.8
WOODLANDS, 93
capital allowances, 10.3, 93.3
Schedule A exclusion, 68.4(i), 68.14(ii)
Schedule B, 69
Schedule D Case I, 71.95
transitional provisions, 93.3
Work-in-progress, 71.83
post-cessation receipts, 62.2
Work-related training, 75.42
Workers supplied by agencies, 55.3, 75.46
Workers' co-operatives, 82.9
Working families' tax credit, 83.4, 83.6
information, 36.3
PAYE, 55.46
Working Rule Agreements, 75.43
Works bus services, 75.13(xxv)
Workshops, 10.21

Wound and disability pensions, 59.4(ii)
Writing-down allowances,
agricultural buildings, 10.3
dredging, 10.7
dwelling-houses, 10.9
industrial buildings, 10.14
know-how, 10.23
machinery and plant, 10.28, 10.35, 10.37
mines, oil-wells, etc., 10.42, 10.49(B)
motor cars, 10.28(A)
patents, 10.50

Y

Year of assessment, 1.2
Year of marriage, 1.15, 43.12
YTS trainee allowance, 75.42